Hoover's Handbook of

Emerging Companies

2017

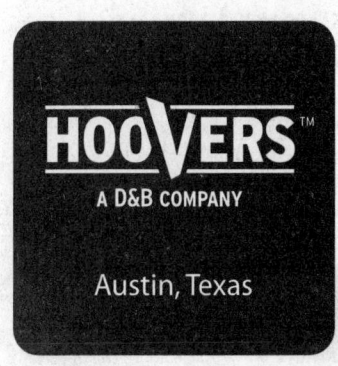

HOOVERS™
A D&B COMPANY

Austin, Texas

Hoover's Handbook of Emerging Companies 2017 is intended to provide readers with accurate and authoritative information about the enterprises covered in it. Hoover's researched all companies and organizations profiled, and in many cases contacted them directly so that companies represented could provide information. The information contained herein is as accurate as we could reasonably make it. In many cases we have relied on third-party material that we believe to be trustworthy, but were unable to independently verify. We do not warrant that the book is absolutely accurate or without error. Readers should not rely on any information contained herein in instances where such reliance might cause financial loss. The publisher, the editors, and their data suppliers specifically disclaim all warranties, including the implied warranties of merchantability and fitness for a specific purpose. This book is sold with the understanding that neither the publisher, the editors, nor any content contributors are engaged in providing investment, financial, accounting, legal, or other professional advice.

The financial data (Historical Financials sections) in this book are from a variety of sources. Mergent Inc., provided selected data for the Historical Financials sections of publicly traded companies. For private companies and for historical information on public companies prior to their becoming public, we obtained information directly from the companies or from trade sources deemed to be reliable. Hoover's, Inc., is solely responsible for the presentation of all data.

Many of the names of products and services mentioned in this book are the trademarks or service marks of the companies manufacturing or selling them and are subject to protection under US law. Space has not permitted us to indicate which names are subject to such protection, and readers are advised to consult with the owners of such marks regarding their use. Hoover's is a trademark of Hoover's, Inc.

A D&B COMPANY

10 9 8 7 6 5 4 3 2 1

Publishers Cataloging-in-Publication Data

Hoover's Handbook of Emerging Companies 2017

    Includes indexes.

    ISBN: 978-1-68200-314-5

    ISSN 1073-6433

    1. Business enterprises — Directories. 2. Corporations — Directories.

HF3010 338.7

U.S. AND WORLD BOOK SALES

Mergent Inc.

580 Kingsley Park Drive

Fort Mill, SC 29715

Phone: 800-342-5647

e-mail: orders@mergent.com

Web: www.mergentbusinesspress.com

MERGENT

BUSINESS PRESS

Mergent Inc.

Publisher: Jonathan Worrall

Executive Managing Director: John Pedernales

Executive Vice President of Sales: Fred Jenkins

Managing Director of Print Products: Thomas Wecera

Director Print Products: Charlot Volny

Quality Assurance Editor: Wayne Arnold

Production Research Assistant: Davie Christna

Data Specialist: Jason Horvat

Mergent Customer Service

Support and Fulfillment Manager: Melanie Horvat

ABOUT MERGENT INC.

Mergent, Inc. is a leading provider of business and financial data on global publicly listed companies. Based in the U.S, the company maintains a strong global presence, with offices in New York, Charlotte, San Diego, London, Tokyo and Melbourne.

Founded in 1900, Mergent operates one of the longest continuously collected databases of: descriptive and fundamental information on domestic and international companies; pricing and terms and conditions data on fixed income and equity securities; and corporate action data. In addition, Mergent's Indxis subsidiary develops and licenses equity and fixed income investment products based on its proprietary investment methodologies. Our licensed products have over $9 billion in assets under management and are offered by major investment management firms. The Indxis calculation platform is the chosen technology for some of the world's largest index companies. Its index calculation and pricing distribution protocols are used to administer index rules and distribute real-time pricing data.

Abbreviations

AFL-CIO – American Federation of Labor and Congress of Industrial Organizations
AMA – American Medical Association
AMEX – American Stock Exchange
ARM – adjustable-rate mortgage
ASP – application services provider
ATM – asynchronous transfer mode
ATM – automated teller machine
CAD/CAM – computer-aided design/ computer-aided manufacturing
CD-ROM – compact disc – read-only memory
CD-R – CD-recordable
CEO – chief executive officer
CFO – chief financial officer
CMOS – complementary metal oxide silicon
COO – chief operating officer
DAT – digital audiotape
DOD – Department of Defense
DOE – Department of Energy
DOS – disk operating system
DOT – Department of Transportation
DRAM – dynamic random-access memory
DSL – digital subscriber line
DVD – digital versatile disc/digital video disc
DVD-R – DVD-recordable
EPA – Environmental Protection Agency
EPS – earnings per share
ESOP – employee stock ownership plan
EU – European Union
EVP – executive vice president
FCC – Federal Communications Commission
FDA – Food and Drug Administration
FDIC – Federal Deposit Insurance Corporation
FTC – Federal Trade Commission

GATT – General Agreement on Tariffs and Trade
GDP – gross domestic product
HMO – health maintenance organization
HR – human resources
HTML – hypertext markup language
ICC – Interstate Commerce Commission
IPO – initial public offering
IRS – Internal Revenue Service
ISP – Internet service provider
kWh – kilowatt-hour
LAN – local-area network
LBO – leveraged buyout
LCD – liquid crystal display
LNG – liquefied natural gas
LP – limited partnership
Ltd. – limited
mips – millions of instructions per second
MW – megawatt
NAFTA – North American Free Trade Agreement
NASA – National Aeronautics and Space Administration
NASDAQ – National Association of Securities Dealers Automated Quotations
NATO – North Atlantic Treaty Organization
NYSE – New York Stock Exchange
OCR – optical character recognition
OECD – Organization for Economic Cooperation and Development
OEM – original equipment manufacturer
OPEC – Organization of Petroleum Exporting Countries
OS – operating system
OSHA – Occupational Safety and Health Administration
OTC – over-the-counter

PBX – private branch exchange
PCMCIA – Personal Computer Memory Card International Association
P/E – price to earnings ratio
RAID – redundant array of independent disks
RAM – random-access memory
R&D – research and development
RBOC – regional Bell operating company
RISC – reduced instruction set computer
REIT – real estate investment trust
ROA – return on assets
ROE – return on equity
ROI – return on investment
ROM – read-only memory
S&L – savings and loan
SEC – Securities and Exchange Commission
SEVP – senior executive vice president
SIC – Standard Industrial Classification
SOC – system on a chip
SVP – senior vice president
USB – universal serial bus
VAR – value-added reseller
VAT – value-added tax
VC – venture capitalist
VoIP – Voice over Internet Protocol
VP – vice president
WAN – wide-area network

Contents

Companies Profiled

Companies Profiled (continued)

Companies Profiled (continued)

Companies Profiled (continued)

About Hoover's Handbook of Emerging Companies 2017

Hoover's Handbook of Emerging Companies enters its 23nd year as one of America's premier sources of business information on younger, growth-oriented enterprises. Given our current economic realities, finding value in the marketplace becomes ever more difficult, and so we are particularly pleased to present this edition of Hoover's Handbook of Emerging Companies 2016 — the result of a search of our extensive database of business information for companies with demonstrated growth and the potential for future gains.

The 600 companies in this book were chosen from the universe of public US companies with sales between $10 million and $2.5 billion. Their selection was based primarily on sales growth and profitability, although in a few cases we made some rather subjective decisions about which companies we chose to include. They all have reported at least three years of sales and have sustained annualized sales growth of at least 7% during that time. Also, they are profitable (through year-end September 2015).

In addition to the companies featured in our handbooks, comprehensive coverage of more than 40,000 business enterprises is available in electronic format on our website, Hoover's Online (www.hoovers.com). Our goal is to provide one site that offers authoritative, updated intelligence on US and global companies, industries, and the people who shape them. Hoover's has partnered with other prestigious business information and service providers to bring you all the right business information, services, and links in one place.

Hoover's Handbook of Emerging Companies is one of our four-title series of handbooks that covers, literally, the world of business. The series is available as an indexed set, and also includes Hoover's Handbook of American Business, Hoover's Handbook of World Business, and Hoover's Handbook of Private Companies. This series brings you information on the biggest, fastest-growing, and most influential enterprises in the world.

We believe that anyone who buys from, sells to, invests in, lends to, competes with, interviews with, or works for a company should know as much as possible about that enterprise. Taken together, Hoover's Handbook of Emerging Companies 2014 and the other Hoover's products represent the most complete source of basic corporate information readily available to the general public.

How to use this book

This book has four sections:

1. "Using Hoover's Handbooks" describes the contents of our profiles.

2. "A List-Lover's Compendium" contains lists of the fastest-growing and most profitable companies. The lists are based on the information in our profiles, or compiled from well-known sources.

3. The company profiles section makes up the largest and most important part of the book — 600 profiles arranged alphabetically. Each profile features an overview of the company; some larger and more visible companies have an additional History section. All companies have up to five years of financial information, product information where available, and a list of company executives and key competitors.

4. At the end of this volume are the combined indexes from our 2015 editions of all Hoover's Handbooks. The information is organized into three separate sections. The first sorts companies by industry groups, the second by headquarters location. The third index is a list of all the executives found in the Executives section of each company profile. For a more thorough description of our indexing style, see page xii.

Using Hoover's Handbooks

ORGANIZATION

The profiles in this volume are presented in alphabetical order. This alphabetization is generally word by word, which means that Bridge Bancorp precedes Bridgepoint Education. You will find the commonly used name of the enterprise at the beginning of the profile; the full, legal name is found in the Locations section. If a company name starts with initials, such as BJ's Restaurants or U.S. Physical Therapy, look for it under the combined initials (in the above example, BJ or US, respectively).

Basic financial data is listed under the heading Historical Financials; also included is the exchange on which the company's stock is traded, the ticker symbol used by the stock exchange, and the company's fiscal year-end. The annual financial information contained in the profiles is current through fiscal year-ends occurring as late as January 2016. We have included certain nonfinancial developments, such as officer changes, through January 2017.

OVERVIEW

In the first section of the profile, we have tried to give a thumbnail description of the company and what it does. The description will usually include information on the company's strategy, reputation, and ownership. We recommend that you read this section first.

HISTORY

This extended section, which is available for some of the larger and more well-known companies, reflects our belief that every enterprise is the sum of its history and that you have to know where you came from in order to know where you are going. While some companies have limited historical awareness, we think the vast majority of the enterprises in this book have colorful backgrounds. We have tried to focus on the people who made the enterprises what they are today. We have found these histories to be full of twists and ironies; they make fascinating reading.

EXECUTIVES

Here we list the names of the people who run the company, insofar as space allows. In the case of public companies, we have shown the ages and pay of key officers. The published data is for the previous fiscal year, although the company may have announced promotions or retirements since year-end. The pay represents cash compensation, including bonuses, but excludes stock option programs.

Although companies are free to structure their management titles any way they please, most modern corporations follow standard practices. The ultimate power in any corporation lies with the shareholders, who elect a board of directors, usually including officers or "insiders," as well as individuals from outside the company. The chief officer, the person on whose desk the buck stops, is usually called the chief executive officer (CEO). Often, he or she is also the chairman of the board.

As corporate management has become more complex, it is common for the CEO to have a "right-hand person" who oversees the day-to-day operations of the company, allowing the CEO plenty of time to focus on strategy and long-term issues. This right-hand person is usually designated the chief operating officer (COO) and is often the president of the company. In other cases one person is both chairman and president.

A multitude of other titles exists, including chief financial officer (CFO), chief administrative officer, and vice chairman. We have always tried to include the CFO, the chief legal officer, and the chief human resources or personnel officer. Our best advice is that officers' pay levels are clear indicators of who the board of directors thinks are the most important members of the management team.

The people named in the Executives section are indexed at the back of the book.

The Executives section also includes the name of the company's auditing (accounting) firm, where available.

LOCATIONS

Here we include the company's full legal name and its headquarters, street address, telephone and fax numbers, and website, as available. The back of the book includes an index of companies by headquarters locations.

In some cases we have also included information on the geographic distribution of the company's business, including sales and profit data. Note that these profit numbers, like those in the Products/Operations section below, are usually operating or pretax profits rather than net profits. Operating profits are generally those before financing costs (interest income and payments) and before taxes, which are considered costs attributable to the whole company rather than to one division or part of the world. For this reason the net income figures (in the Historical Financials section) are usually much lower, since they are after interest and taxes. Pretax profits are after interest but before taxes.

PRODUCTS/OPERATIONS

This section lists as many of the company's products, services, brand names, divisions, subsidiaries, and joint ventures as we could fit. We have tried to include all its major lines and all familiar brand names. The nature of this section varies by company and the amount of information available. If the company publishes sales and profit information by type of business, we have included it.

COMPETITORS

In this section we have listed companies that compete with the profiled company. This feature is included as a quick way to locate similar companies and compare them. The universe of competitors includes all public companies and all private companies with sales in excess of $500 million. In a few instances we have identified smaller private companies as key competitors.

HISTORICAL FINANCIALS

Here we have tried to present as much data about each enterprise's financial performance as we could compile in the allocated space. Although the information varies somewhat from industry to industry, the following is generally present.

A five-year table, with relevant annualized compound growth rates, covers:

- Sales — fiscal year sales (year-end assets for most financial companies)
- Net income — fiscal year net income (before accounting changes)
- Net profit margin — fiscal year net income as a percent of sales (as a percent of assets for most financial firms)
- Employees — fiscal year-end or average number of employees
- Stock price — the fiscal year closing price
- P/E — high and low price/earnings ratio
- Earnings per share — fiscal year earnings per share (EPS)
- Dividends per share — fiscal year dividends per share
- Book value per share — fiscal year-end book value (common shareholders' equity per share)

The information on the number of employees is intended to aid the reader interested in knowing whether a company has a long-term trend of increasing or decreasing employment. As far as we know, we are the only company that publishes this information in print format.

The numbers on the left in each row of the Historical Financials section give the month and the year in which the company's fiscal year actually ends. Thus, a company with a September 30, 2015, year-end is shown as 9/15.

In addition, we have provided in graph form a stock price history for each company. The graphs, covering up to five years, show the range of trading between the high and the low price, as well as the closing price for each fiscal year.

Key year-end statistics in this section generally show the financial strength of the enterprise, including:

- Debt ratio (long-term debt as a percent of shareholders' equity)
- Return on equity (net income divided by the average of beginning and ending common shareholders' equity)
- Cash and cash equivalents
- Current ratio (ratio of current assets to current liabilities)
- Total long-term debt (including capital lease obligations)
- Number of shares of common stock outstanding
- Dividend yield (fiscal year dividends per share divided by the fiscal year-end closing stock price)
- Dividend payout (fiscal year dividends divided by fiscal year EPS)
- Market value at fiscal year-end (fiscal year-end closing stock price multiplied by fiscal year-end number of shares outstanding)

Per-share data has been adjusted for stock splits. The data for public companies has been provided to us by Morningstar, Inc. Other public company information was compiled by Hoover's, which takes full responsibility for the content of this section.

Hoover's Handbook of

Emerging Companies

A List-Lover's Compendium

The 300 Largest Companies by Sales in
Mergent's Database for the 2017 Hoovers Emerging Handbook

Rank	Company	Sales ($ mil.)	Rank	Company	Sales ($ mil.)	Rank	Company	Sales ($ mil.)
1	Wal–Mart Stores, Inc.	$482,130	61	Dow Chemical Co.	$48,158	121	Plains GP Holdings LP	$23,152
2	Exxon Mobil Corp	$268,882	62	Lockheed Martin Corp	$47,248	122	US Foods Holding Corp	$23,128
3	Apple Inc	$215,639	63	Coca–Cola Co (The)	$44,294	123	Amgen Inc	$22,991
4	Berkshire Hathaway Inc	$210,821	64	Energy Transfer Equity LP	$42,126	124	Arconic Inc	$22,534
5	McKesson Corp	$190,884	65	Energy Transfer Corp LP	$42,126	125	International Paper Co	$22,365
6	UnitedHealth Group Inc	$184,840	66	American Airlines Group Inc	$40,990	126	AutoNation, Inc.	$21,609
7	CVS Health Corp	$177,526	67	Centene Corp	$40,607	127	U.S. Bancorp (DE)	$21,494
8	General Motors Co.	$166,380	68	HCA Holdings Inc	$39,678	128	Burlington Northern & Santa F	$21,401
9	AT&T Inc	$163,786	69	Delta Air Lines Inc (DE)	$39,639	129	Starbucks Corp.	$21,316
10	Ford Motor Co. (DE)	$151,800	70	Best Buy Inc	$39,528	130	Eli Lilly & Co	$21,222
11	AmerisourceBergen Corp.	$146,850	71	Merck & Co Inc	$39,498	131	Staples Inc	$21,059
12	Chevron Corporation	$138,477	72	Honeywell International Inc	$39,302	132	AFLAC Inc.	$20,872
13	Amazon.com Inc.	$135,987	73	Goldman Sachs Group, Inc.	$39,208	133	Progressive Corp. (OH)	$20,854
14	Verizon Communications Inc	$131,620	74	Caterpillar Inc.	$38,537	134	Abbott Laboratories	$20,853
15	Cardinal Health, Inc.	$121,546	75	Morgan Stanley	$37,897	135	Whirlpool Corp	$20,718
16	Costco Wholesale Corp	$118,719	76	Cigna Corp	$37,876	136	Danaher Corp	$20,563
17	General Electric Co	$117,386	77	United Continental Holdings	$37,864	137	Southwest Airlines Co	$20,425
18	Walgreens Boots Alliance Inc	$117,351	78	Oracle Corp	$37,047	138	Dollar General Corp	$20,369
19	Federal Reserve System	$113,468	79	Tyson Foods, Inc.	$36,881	139	Union Pacific Corp	$19,941
20	Fannie Mae	$110,359	80	Allstate Corp.	$36,534	140	ManpowerGroup	$19,654
21	Kroger Co (The)	$109,830	81	Energy Transfer Partners LP	$34,292	141	Community Health Systems, In	$19,437
22	JPMorgan Chase & Co	$101,006	82	American Express Co.	$33,823	142	Bristol–Myers Squibb Co.	$19,427
23	Express Scripts Holding Co	$100,288	83	Gilead Sciences, Inc.	$32,639	143	Penske Automotive Group Inc	$19,285
24	Boeing Co.	$94,571	84	Publix Super Markets, Inc.	$32,619	144	Kohl's Corp.	$19,204
25	Bank of America Corp.	$93,056	85	NIKE Inc	$32,376	145	Exelon Generation Co LLC	$19,135
26	Alphabet Inc	$90,272	86	Sprint Corp (New)	$32,180	146	Fluor Corp.	$19,037
27	Wells Fargo & Co.	$90,033	87	T–Mobile US Inc	$32,053	147	Tenet Healthcare Corp.	$18,634
28	Home Depot Inc	$88,519	88	Exelon Corp	$31,360	148	Lear Corp.	$18,558
29	Citigroup Inc	$88,275	89	General Dynamics Corp.	$31,353	149	Hartford Financial Services	$18,377
30	Valero Energy Corp.	$87,804	90	TJX Companies, Inc.	$30,945	150	Jabil Circuit, Inc.	$18,353
31	Phillips 66	$85,777	91	Rite Aid Corp.	$30,737	151	Kraft Heinz Co (The)	$18,338
32	Microsoft Corporation	$85,320	92	CHS Inc	$30,347	152	Kimberly–Clark Corp.	$18,202
33	International Business Machi	$81,741	93	3M Co	$30,109	153	Xerox Corp	$18,045
34	Comcast Corp	$80,403	94	Mondelez International Inc	$29,636	154	CenturyLink, Inc.	$17,900
35	Anthem Inc	$79,157	95	Charter Communications Inc (	$29,003	155	PG&E Corp. (Holding Co.)	$17,666
36	Philip Morris International	$74,953	96	Time Warner Inc	$28,118	156	Supervalu Inc.	$17,529
37	Target Corp	$73,785	97	Facebook Inc	$27,638	157	Cummins, Inc.	$17,509
38	Marathon Petroleum Corp.	$72,258	98	Travelers Companies Inc (The	$27,625	158	Southern Co.	$17,489
39	Johnson & Johnson	$70,074	99	21st Century Fox Inc	$27,326	159	NextEra Energy Inc	$17,422
40	MetLife Inc	$69,951	100	Macy's Inc	$27,079	160	AECOM	$17,412
41	Federal Reserve Bank Of New Y	$68,534	101	Enterprise Products Partners	$27,028	161	Marriott International, Inc.	$17,072
42	Procter & Gamble Co	$65,299	102	World Fuel Services Corp.	$27,016	162	Paccar Inc.	$17,033
43	Freddie Mac	$63,491	103	Deere & Co.	$26,644	163	Thermo Fisher Scientific Inc	$16,965
44	Aetna Inc.	$63,155	104	Tech Data Corp.	$26,380	164	Sunoco LP	$16,935
45	PepsiCo Inc	$62,799	105	Avnet Inc	$26,219	165	General Mills, Inc.	$16,563
46	Archer Daniels Midland Co.	$62,346	106	AbbVie Inc	$25,638	166	American Electric Power Co.,	$16,453
47	United Parcel Service Inc	$60,906	107	Altria Group Inc	$25,434	167	Nucor Corp.	$16,439
48	Intel Corp	$59,387	108	McDonald's Corp	$25,413	168	PNC Financial Services Group	$16,270
49	Lowe's Companies Inc	$59,074	109	Sears Holdings Corp	$25,146	169	Performance Food Group Co	$16,105
50	Prudential Financial, Inc.	$58,779	110	Capital One Financial Corp	$25,038	170	Colgate–Palmolive Co.	$16,034
51	American International Group	$58,327	111	Du Pont (E.I.) de Nemours &	$24,594	171	Halliburton Company	$15,887
52	United Technologies Corp	$57,244	112	Tesoro Corporation	$24,582	172	Freeport–McMoRan Inc	$15,877
53	Disney (Walt) Co. (The)	$55,632	113	Northrop Grumman Corp	$24,508	173	Gap Inc	$15,797
54	Humana, Inc.	$54,379	114	United Services Automobile A	$24,361	174	Whole Foods Market, Inc.	$15,724
55	Sysco Corp	$50,367	115	ConocoPhillips	$24,360	175	Dollar Tree Inc	$15,498
56	FedEx Corp	$50,365	116	Raytheon Co.	$24,069	176	Bank of New York Mellon Corp	$15,494
57	Hewlett Packard Enterprise C	$50,123	117	Arrow Electronics, Inc.	$23,825	177	Omnicom Group, Inc.	$15,417
58	Cisco Systems Inc	$49,247	118	Qualcomm Inc	$23,554	178	Genuine Parts Co.	$15,280
59	Pfizer Inc	$48,851	119	Duke Energy Corp	$23,459	179	Icahn Enterprises LP	$15,272
60	HP Inc	$48,238	120	Plains All American Pipeline	$23,152	180	Goodyear Tire & Rubber Co.	$15,158

SOURCE: MERGENT INC., DATABASE, DECEMBER 2016

The 300 Largest Companies by Sales in
Mergent's Database for the 2017 Hoovers Emerging Handbook (continued)

Rank	Company	Sales ($ mil.)	Rank	Company	Sales ($ mil.)	Rank	Company	Sales ($ mil.)
181	Carmax Inc.	$15,150	222	Penney (J.C.) Co.,Inc. (Hold	$12,625	263	Core Mark Holding Co Inc	$11,069
182	Visa Inc	$15,082	223	Reynolds American Inc	$12,503	264	CSX Corp	$11,069
183	Dish Network Corp	$15,069	224	Viacom Inc	$12,488	265	Citigroup Global Markets Hol	$11,049
184	FirstEnergy Corp	$15,026	225	Becton, Dickinson & Co.	$12,483	266	Xcel Energy, Inc.	$11,024
185	AES Corp.	$14,963	226	Cognizant Technology Solutio	$12,416	267	Jacobs Engineering Group, In	$10,964
186	PPG Industries Inc	$14,751	227	Micron Technology Inc.	$12,399	268	Lennar Corp	$10,950
187	INTL FCStone Inc.	$14,727	228	Principal Financial Group, I	$12,394	269	Leucadia National Corp.	$10,886
188	NRG Energy Inc	$14,674	229	VF Corp.	$12,377	270	CBRE Group Inc	$10,856
189	Emerson Electric Co.	$14,522	230	Devon Energy Corp.	$12,197	271	PayPal Holdings Inc	$10,842
190	Office Depot, Inc.	$14,485	231	Ameriprise Financial Inc	$12,170	272	Applied Materials, Inc.	$10,825
191	Nordstrom, Inc.	$14,437	232	Horton (D.R.) Inc.	$12,157	273	Mastercard Inc	$10,776
192	Aramark	$14,416	233	L Brands, Inc	$12,154	274	Praxair Inc	$10,776
193	WellCare Health Plans Inc	$14,237	234	Bed, Bath & Beyond, Inc.	$12,104	275	Unum Group	$10,731
194	Molina Healthcare Inc	$14,178	235	Consolidated Edison Inc	$12,075	276	AutoZone, Inc.	$10,636
195	WestRock Co	$14,172	236	Ross Stores, Inc.	$11,940	277	State Street Corp.	$10,635
196	Synnex Corp	$14,062	237	Edison International	$11,869	278	Group 1 Automotive, Inc.	$10,633
197	DaVita Inc	$13,782	238	NGL Energy Partners LP	$11,742	279	DTE Energy Co	$10,630
198	Synchrony Financial	$13,620	239	Las Vegas Sands Corp	$11,688	280	Tennessee Valley Authority	$10,616
199	Waste Management, Inc. (DE)	$13,609	240	Dominion Resources Inc	$11,683	281	Herc Holdings Inc	$10,535
200	Illinois Tool Works, Inc.	$13,599	241	Automatic Data Processing In	$11,668	282	Sunoco Logistics Partners LP	$10,486
201	Lincoln National Corp.	$13,572	242	Florida Power & Light Co.	$11,651	283	Toyota Motor Credit Corp.	$10,483
202	Ecolab Inc	$13,545	243	Conagra Brands Inc	$11,643	284	Santander Holdings USA Inc.	$10,474
203	Monsanto Co	$13,502	244	United States Steel Corp.	$11,574	285	L3 Technologies Inc	$10,466
204	Robinson (C.H.) Worldwide, I	$13,476	245	Henry Schein Inc	$11,572	286	Reinsurance Group of Amer	$10,418
205	Textron Inc	$13,423	246	BB&T Corp.	$11,538	287	Public Service Enterprise Gr	$10,415
206	HollyFrontier Corp.	$13,238	247	Entergy Corp. (New)	$11,513	288	Consolidated Edison of NY	$10,328
207	CBS Corp	$13,166	248	Southern California Edison C	$11,485	289	Global Partners LP	$10,315
208	PBF Energy Inc	$13,124	249	First Data Corp (New)	$11,451	290	Huntsman Corp	$10,299
209	Yum! Brands Inc	$13,105	250	Biogen Inc	$11,449	291	Sempra Energy	$10,231
210	Loews Corp.	$13,105	251	CST Brands Inc	$11,444	292	Discover Financial Services	$10,002
211	Kinder Morgan Inc.	$13,058	252	Stanley Black & Decker Inc	$11,407	293	Liberty Interactive Corp	$9,989
212	Kellogg Co	$13,014	253	BlackRock, Inc.	$11,401	294	Grainger (W.W.), Inc.	$9,973
213	Land O' Lakes Inc	$13,008	254	Parker-Hannifin Corp	$11,361	295	Baxter International Inc.	$9,968
214	Texas Instruments, Inc.	$13,000	255	Voya Financial Inc	$11,341	296	Norfolk Southern Corp.	$9,888
215	Western Digital Corp	$12,994	256	Sherwin-Williams Co (The)	$11,339	297	Baker Hughes Inc.	$9,841
216	CDW Corp	$12,989	257	Stryker Corp.	$11,325	298	Western Refining Inc	$9,787
217	Marsh & McLennan Comp	$12,893	258	Hilton Worldwide Holdings In	$11,272	299	Advance Auto Parts Inc	$9,737
218	Chesapeake Energy Corp.	$12,764	259	Lauder (Estee) Cos., Inc. (T	$11,262	300	Owens & Minor, Inc. (New)	$9,723
219	Murphy USA Inc	$12,699	260	RR Donnelley & Sons Com	$11,257			
220	Occidental Petroleum Corp	$12,699	261	Celgene Corp.	$11,229			
221	Federal Reserve Bank of SF	$12,696	262	Alcoa Corporation	$11,199			

The 300 Largest Companies by Employees in Mergent's Database for the 2017 Hoovers Emerging Handbook

Rank	Company	Employees	Rank	Company	Employees	Rank	Company	Employees
1	Wal–Mart Stores, Inc.	2,200,000	62	Microsoft Corporation	114,000	123	Chipotle Mexican Grill Inc	64,570
2	Kelly Services, Inc.	558,100	63	Tyson Foods, Inc.	114,000	124	Autoliv Inc.	64,100
3	Yum! Brands Inc	505,000	64	Dollar General Corp	113,400	125	VF Corp.	64,000
4	United Parcel Service Inc	434,000	65	Synnex Corp	110,000	126	Raytheon Co.	63,000
5	Kroger Co (The)	431,000	66	ABM Industries, Inc.	110,000	127	Bed, Bath & Beyond, Inc.	62,000
6	McDonald's Corp	420,000	67	Intel Corp	106,000	128	Amphenol Corp.	62,000
7	Yum China Holdings Inc	400,000	68	Procter & Gamble Co	105,000	129	Fluor Corp.	61,551
8	Home Depot Inc	385,000	69	Penney (J.C.) Co.,Inc. (Hold	105,000	130	Chevron Corporation	61,500
9	International Business Machi	377,757	70	Emerson Electric Co.	103,500	131	Jones Lang LaSalle Inc	61,500
10	Walgreens Boots Alliance Inc	360,000	71	Barrett Business Services, I	103,250	132	DaVita Inc	60,400
11	Amazon.com Inc.	341,400	72	Kindred Healthcare Inc	102,000	133	Arconic Inc	60,000
12	Target Corp	341,000	73	Bloomin' Brands Inc	100,000	134	Marsh & McLennan Companies I	60,000
13	General Electric Co	333,000	74	Mondelez International Inc	99,000	135	Brinks Co (The)	59,900
14	Berkshire Hathaway Inc	331,000	75	General Dynamics Corp.	98,800	136	MGM Resorts International	59,500
15	Lowe's Companies Inc	270,000	76	Pfizer Inc	97,900	137	Computer Sciences Corp	59,000
16	AT&T Inc	268,000	77	Lockheed Martin Corp	97,000	138	Brinker International, Inc.	58,335
17	Aramark	266,500	78	Caterpillar Inc.	95,400	139	Automatic Data Processing In	57,000
18	Wells Fargo & Co.	264,700	79	Conduent Inc	93,700	140	Deere & Co.	56,800
19	PepsiCo Inc	264,000	80	Whirlpool Corp	93,000	141	American Express Co.	56,400
20	Starbucks Corp.	254,000	81	3M Co	91,584	142	Morgan Stanley	56,218
21	CVS Health Corp	250,000	82	Charter Communications Inc (	91,500	143	Dow Chemical Co.	56,000
22	JPMorgan Chase & Co	234,598	83	XPO Logistics, Inc.	89,000	144	International Paper Co	56,000
23	HCA Holdings Inc	233,000	84	Genesis Healthcare Inc	88,700	145	Cummins, Inc.	55,400
24	Half Robert International In	231,400	85	Rite Aid Corp.	88,000	146	Fidelity National Informatio	55,000
25	Citigroup Inc	231,000	86	L Brands, Inc	87,900	147	Jacobs Engineering Group, In	54,900
26	UnitedHealth Group Inc	230,000	87	AECOM	87,000	148	Sykes Enterprises, Inc.	54,550
27	Marriott International, Inc.	226,500	88	Whole Foods Market, Inc.	87,000	149	Humana, Inc.	54,200
28	General Motors Co.	225,000	89	Delta Air Lines Inc (DE)	84,000	150	Fidelity National Financial	54,091
29	Cognizant Technology Solutio	221,700	90	United Continental Holdings	84,000	151	Stanley Black & Decker Inc	54,023
30	Costco Wholesale Corp	218,000	91	AutoZone, Inc.	84,000	152	Southwest Airlines Co	53,500
31	TJX Companies, Inc.	216,000	92	GameStop Corp	82,000	153	Anthem Inc	53,000
32	Bank of America Corp.	213,000	93	Danaher Corp	81,000	154	PNC Financial Services Group	52,513
33	United Technologies Corp	201,600	94	Philip Morris International	79,500	155	RMR Group Inc (The)	52,450
34	Ford Motor Co. (DE)	201,000	95	Omnicom Group, Inc.	78,500	156	Thermo Fisher Scientific Inc	52,000
35	Disney (Walt) Co. (The)	195,000	96	Ross Stores, Inc.	77,800	157	Sysco Corp	51,900
36	Hewlett Packard Enterprise C	195,000	97	Brookdale Senior Living Inc	77,600	158	Bank of New York Mellon Corp	51,200
37	Publix Super Markets, Inc.	180,000	98	Staples Inc	75,371	159	Becton, Dickinson & Co.	50,928
38	Sears Holdings Corp	178,000	99	Abbott Laboratories	75,000	160	On Assignment, Inc.	50,920
39	Verizon Communications Inc	177,700	100	Universal Health Services, I	74,600	161	T–Mobile US Inc	50,000
40	FedEx Corp	168,000	101	Icahn Enterprises LP	73,786	162	Halliburton Company	50,000
41	Dollar Tree Inc	167,800	102	Cisco Systems Inc	73,700	163	Illinois Tool Works, Inc.	50,000
42	Hilton Worldwide Holdings In	164,000	103	Exxon Mobil Corp	73,500	164	Baxter International Inc.	50,000
43	Comcast Corp	159,000	104	Advance Auto Parts Inc	73,000	165	LabCorp	50,000
44	Macy's Inc	157,900	105	Cracker Barrel Old Country S	73,000	166	Michaels Companies Inc	50,000
45	Boeing Co.	150,500	106	Western Digital Corp	72,878	167	Interpublic Group of Compani	49,800
46	Darden Restaurants, Inc. (Un	150,000	107	Nordstrom, Inc.	72,500	168	Prudential Financial, Inc.	49,739
47	Lear Corp.	148,400	108	Alphabet Inc	72,053	169	Aetna Inc.	49,500
48	Xerox Corp	143,600	109	O'Reilly Automotive, Inc.	71,943	170	HP Inc	49,000
49	Gap Inc	141,000	110	NIKE Inc	70,700	171	Office Depot, Inc.	49,000
50	Kohl's Corp.	140,000	111	CBRE Group Inc	70,000	172	Abercrombie & Fitch Co.	49,000
51	Jabil Circuit, Inc.	138,000	112	MetLife Inc	69,000	173	Parker–Hannifin Corp	48,950
52	Community Health Systems, In	137,000	113	RR Donnelley & Sons Company	68,400	174	Texas Roadhouse Inc	47,900
53	Oracle Corp	136,000	114	McKesson Corp	68,000	175	Panera Bread Co	47,200
54	Tenet Healthcare Corp.	134,630	115	Merck & Co Inc	68,000	176	Foot Locker, Inc.	47,025
55	Honeywell International Inc	131,000	116	HanesBrands Inc	67,800	177	PPG Industries Inc	47,000
56	Convergys Corp	130,000	117	Laureate Education Inc	67,800	178	Ecolab Inc	47,000
57	Johnson & Johnson	127,100	118	Northrop Grumman Corp	67,000	179	Las Vegas Sands Corp	46,500
58	Best Buy Inc	125,000	119	American International Group	66,400	180	Du Pont (E.I.) de Nemours &	46,000
59	Coca-Cola Co (The)	123,200	120	Goodyear Tire & Rubber Co.	66,000	181	Lauder (Estee) Cos., Inc. (T	46,000
60	American Airlines Group Inc	118,500	121	Ascena Retail Group Inc	66,000	182	Marathon Petroleum Corp.	45,440
61	Apple Inc	116,000	122	U.S. Bancorp (DE)	65,433	183	Capital One Financial Corp	45,400

SOURCE: HOOVER'S, INC., DATABASE, DECEMBER 2015

The 300 Largest Companies by Employees in Mergent's Database for the 2017 Hoovers Emerging Handbook (continued)

Rank	Company	Employees	Rank	Company	Employees	Rank	Company	Employees
184	Sanmina Corp	45,397	223	Goldman Sachs Group, Inc.	36,800	262	Duke Energy Corp	29,188
185	Hyatt Hotels Corp	45,000	224	National Oilwell Varco Inc	36,627	263	Dover Corp	29,000
186	Regis Corp.	45,000	225	Quintiles IMS Holdings Inc	36,100	264	EMCOR Group, Inc.	29,000
187	Buffalo Wild Wings Inc	44,500	226	Big Lots, Inc.	35,900	265	Barnes & Noble Inc	29,000
188	Burlington Northern & Santa F	44,000	227	Textron Inc	35,000	266	Cooper-Standard Holdings, In	29,000
189	Quest Diagnostics, Inc.	44,000	228	Cintas Corp	35,000	267	Red Robin Gourmet Burgers In	28,933
190	TeleTech Holdings, Inc.	44,000	229	Casey's General Stores, Inc.	34,997	268	Ruby Tuesday, Inc.	28,900
191	Six Flags Entertainment Corp	43,900	230	Freeport-McMoRan Inc	34,500	269	Progressive Corp. (OH)	28,580
192	Allstate Corp.	43,500	231	Ryder System, Inc.	34,500	270	Avon Products, Inc.	28,300
193	CenturyLink, Inc.	43,000	232	Exelon Corp	34,396	271	Cinemark USA Inc	28,300
194	Union Pacific Corp	42,919	233	PVH Corp	34,200	272	Cinemark Holdings Inc	28,300
195	Kraft Heinz Co (The)	42,000	234	Mohawk Industries, Inc.	34,100	273	Williams Sonoma Inc	28,100
196	Kimberly-Clark Corp.	42,000	235	State Street Corp.	33,783	274	Norfolk Southern Corp.	28,044
197	Eli Lilly & Co	41,975	236	United States Steel Corp.	33,200	275	United Services Automobile A	28,000
198	Waste Management, Inc. (DE)	41,200	237	Stryker Corp.	33,000	276	ManpowerGroup	28,000
199	Jones Financial Companies LL	41,000	238	Baker Hughes Inc.	33,000	277	Genesco Inc.	27,500
200	Select Medical Holdings Corp	41,000	239	Republic Services Inc	33,000	278	HealthSouth Corp	27,110
201	Sherwin-Williams Co (The)	40,706	240	Caesars Entertainment Corp	33,000	279	CSX Corp	27,000
202	Corning Inc	40,700	241	Command Center, Inc.	32,810	280	BorgWarner Inc	27,000
203	Dillard's Inc.	40,000	242	NCR Corp.	32,600	281	Owens-Illinois, Inc.	27,000
204	LifePoint Health Inc	40,000	243	YRC Worldwide Inc	32,000	282	Vail Resorts Inc	27,000
205	Cedar Fair LP	39,700	244	Archer Daniels Midland Co.	31,800	283	BG Staffing Inc	26,840
206	Genuine Parts Co.	39,600	245	Micron Technology Inc.	31,400	284	Southern Co.	26,703
207	Cigna Corp	39,300	246	LKQ Corp	31,100	285	Praxair Inc	26,657
208	General Mills, Inc.	39,000	247	Mattel Inc	31,000	286	Ulta Beauty Inc	26,500
209	WestRock Co	39,000	248	Travelers Companies Inc (The	30,900	287	Ingles Markets Inc	26,500
210	Pilgrims Pride Corp.	38,850	249	Bob Evans Farms Inc	30,625	288	AMERCO	26,400
211	Supervalu Inc.	38,000	250	Centene Corp	30,500	289	Acadia Healthcare Company In	26,400
212	L3 Technologies Inc	38,000	251	Qualcomm Inc	30,500	290	Regal Beloit Corp	26,200
213	Colgate-Palmolive Co.	37,900	252	Energy Transfer Equity LP	30,078	291	AutoNation, Inc.	26,000
214	Wyndham Worldwide Corp	37,800	253	Energy Transfer Corp LP	30,078	292	Ralph Lauren Corp	26,000
215	American Eagle Outfitters, I	37,800	254	Sprint Corp (New)	30,000	293	Masco Corp.	26,000
216	Cheesecake Factory Inc. (The	37,600	255	AbbVie Inc	30,000	294	Harman International Industr	26,000
217	BB&T Corp.	37,500	256	Herc Holdings Inc	30,000	295	Bright Horizons Family Solut	26,000
218	Burlington Stores Inc	37,500	257	Avis Budget Group Inc	30,000	296	Civitas Solutions Inc	26,000
219	Kellogg Co	37,369	258	Tenneco Inc	30,000	297	Regal Entertainment Group	25,915
220	Cardinal Health, Inc.	37,300	259	Texas Instruments, Inc.	29,977	298	Grainger (W.W.), Inc.	25,800
221	Dick's Sporting Goods, Inc	37,200	260	Sally Beauty Holdings Inc	29,665	299	Volt Information Sciences In	25,800
222	Huntington Ingalls Industrie	37,000	261	TTM Technologies Inc	29,570	300	Express Scripts Holding Co	25,600

The 300 Largest Companies by Net Income in
Mergent's Database for the 2017 Hoovers Emerging Handbook

Rank	Company	Net Income ($ mil.)	Rank	Company	Net Income ($ mil.)	Rank	Company	Net Income ($mil.)
1	Apple Inc	$45,687	61	Prudential Financial, Inc.	$4,368	121	Kroger Co (The)	$2,039
2	JPMorgan Chase & Co	$24,442	62	Dow Chemical Co.	$4,318	122	Illinois Tool Works, Inc.	$2,035
3	Berkshire Hathaway Inc	$24,083	63	Union Pacific Corp	$4,233	123	Citigroup Global Markets Hol	$2,022
4	Wells Fargo & Co.	$22,894	64	Walgreens Boots Alliance Inc	$4,173	124	Celgene Corp.	$1,999
5	Alphabet Inc	$19,478	65	PNC Financial Services Group	$4,143	125	Molson Coors Brewing Co.	$1,976
6	Gilead Sciences, Inc.	$18,108	66	Mastercard Inc	$4,059	126	Thermo Fisher Scientific Inc	$1,975
7	Verizon Communications Inc	$17,879	67	Capital One Financial Corp	$4,050	127	Las Vegas Sands Corp	$1,966
8	Citigroup Inc	$17,242	68	Valero Energy Corp.	$3,990	128	Publix Super Markets, Inc.	$1,965
9	Microsoft Corporation	$16,798	69	Time Warner Inc	$3,833	129	Suntrust Banks, Inc.	$1,933
10	Exxon Mobil Corp	$16,150	70	NIKE Inc	$3,760	130	PPL Corp	$1,902
11	Bank of America Corp.	$15,888	71	Charter Communications Inc (	$3,745	131	Dominion Resources Inc	$1,899
12	Johnson & Johnson	$15,409	72	Biogen Inc	$3,703	132	Allstate Corp.	$1,877
13	Wal-Mart Stores, Inc.	$14,694	73	Corning Inc	$3,695	133	FedEx Corp	$1,820
14	International Business Machi	$13,190	74	Level 3 Communications, Inc.	$3,433	134	Tyson Foods, Inc.	$1,768
15	AT&T Inc	$12,976	75	United Parcel Service Inc	$3,431	135	Franklin Resources, Inc.	$1,727
16	Fannie Mae	$10,954	76	Express Scripts Holding Co	$3,404	136	Applied Materials, Inc.	$1,721
17	Cisco Systems Inc	$10,739	77	Target Corp	$3,363	137	CSX Corp	$1,714
18	Procter & Gamble Co	$10,508	78	Danaher Corp	$3,357	138	Fifth Third Bancorp (Cincinn	$1,712
19	Intel Corp	$10,316	79	BlackRock, Inc.	$3,345	139	General Mills, Inc.	$1,697
20	Facebook Inc	$10,217	80	Hewlett Packard Enterprise C	$3,161	140	Hartford Financial Services	$1,682
21	General Motors Co.	$9,427	81	Bank of New York Mellon Corp	$3,158	141	Public Service Enterprise Gr	$1,679
22	Disney (Walt) Co. (The)	$9,391	82	Travelers Companies Inc (The	$3,014	142	Norfolk Southern Corp.	$1,668
23	Oracle Corp	$8,901	83	Texas Instruments, Inc.	$2,986	143	Florida Power & Light Co.	$1,648
24	Comcast Corp	$8,695	84	General Dynamics Corp.	$2,955	144	Stryker Corp.	$1,647
25	Amgen Inc	$7,722	85	Marathon Petroleum Corp.	$2,852	145	Emerson Electric Co.	$1,635
26	American Airlines Group Inc	$7,610	86	Starbucks Corp.	$2,818	146	Cognizant Technology Solutio	$1,624
27	Coca-Cola Co (The)	$7,351	87	Duke Energy Corp	$2,816	147	Marsh & McLennan Companies I	$1,599
28	United Continental Holdings	$7,340	88	NextEra Energy Inc	$2,762	148	Ameriprise Financial Inc	$1,562
29	Mondelez International Inc	$7,267	89	21st Century Fox Inc	$2,755	149	Phillips 66	$1,555
30	eBay Inc.	$7,266	90	Eli Lilly & Co	$2,738	150	Praxair Inc	$1,547
31	UnitedHealth Group Inc	$7,017	91	Anthem Inc	$2,560	151	Deere & Co.	$1,524
32	Home Depot Inc	$7,009	92	Enterprise Products Partners	$2,558	152	Crown Castle International C	$1,521
33	Philip Morris International	$6,967	93	Priceline Group Inc. (The)	$2,551	153	Automatic Data Processing In	$1,493
34	Pfizer Inc	$6,960	94	Lowe's Companies Inc	$2,546	154	HD Supply Holdings Inc	$1,472
35	Freddie Mac	$6,376	95	AFLAC Inc.	$2,533	155	Sempra Energy	$1,448
36	PepsiCo Inc	$6,329	96	Du Pont (E.I.) de Nemours &	$2,513	156	Schwab (Charles) Corp.	$1,447
37	Morgan Stanley	$6,127	97	HP Inc	$2,496	157	Viacom Inc	$1,438
38	Goldman Sachs Group, Inc.	$6,083	98	Symantec Corp	$2,488	158	AmerisourceBergen Corp.	$1,428
39	Reynolds American Inc	$6,073	99	BB&T Corp.	$2,442	159	Cardinal Health, Inc.	$1,427
40	Visa Inc	$5,991	100	Southern Co.	$2,435	160	Intercontinental Exchange In	$1,422
41	AbbVie Inc	$5,953	101	Amazon.com Inc.	$2,371	161	PG&E Corp. (Holding Co.)	$1,407
42	Caesars Entertainment Corp	$5,920	102	Costco Wholesale Corp	$2,350	162	Hilton Worldwide Holdings In	$1,404
43	U.S. Bancorp (DE)	$5,879	103	Discover Financial Services	$2,297	163	PayPal Holdings Inc	$1,401
44	Qualcomm Inc	$5,705	104	Visteon Corp.	$2,284	164	Abbott Laboratories	$1,400
45	American Express Co.	$5,408	105	TJX Companies, Inc.	$2,278	165	Cummins, Inc.	$1,394
46	CVS Health Corp	$5,317	106	United Services Automobile A	$2,272	166	Colgate-Palmolive Co.	$1,384
47	MetLife Inc	$5,310	107	Aetna Inc.	$2,271	167	GGP Inc	$1,375
48	Lockheed Martin Corp	$5,302	108	McKesson Corp	$2,258	168	Exelon Generation Co LLC	$1,372
49	Altria Group Inc	$5,241	109	Southwest Airlines Co	$2,244	169	Energy Transfer Partners LP	$1,364
50	United Technologies Corp	$5,055	110	Synchrony Financial	$2,214	170	Ford Motor Credit Company LL	$1,363
51	3M Co	$5,050	111	Raytheon Co.	$2,211	171	Monsanto Co	$1,336
52	Burlington Northern & Santa F	$4,915	112	Northrop Grumman Corp	$2,200	172	Principal Financial Group, I	$1,317
53	Boeing Co.	$4,895	113	American International Group	$2,196	173	Public Storage	$1,311
54	Honeywell International Inc	$4,809	114	Kimberly-Clark Corp.	$2,166	174	Edison International	$1,311
55	Ford Motor Co. (DE)	$4,596	115	State Street Corp.	$2,143	175	Yum! Brands Inc	$1,293
56	Chevron Corporation	$4,587	116	Simon Property Group, Inc.	$2,139	176	Ally Financial Inc	$1,289
57	McDonald's Corp	$4,529	117	HCA Holdings Inc	$2,129	177	Archer Daniels Midland Co.	$1,279
58	Bristol-Myers Squibb Co.	$4,457	118	S&P Global Inc	$2,106	178	Georgia Power Co.	$1,277
59	Merck & Co Inc	$4,442	119	Cigna Corp	$2,094	179	Progressive Corp. (OH)	$1,268
60	Delta Air Lines Inc (DE)	$4,373	120	American Electric Power Co.,	$2,047	180	Goodyear Tire & Rubber Co.	$1,264

SOURCE: MERGENT INC., JANUARY 2017

The 300 Largest Companies by Net Income in
Mergent's Database for the 2017 Hoovers Emerging Handbook (continued)

Rank	Company	Net Income ($ mil.)	Rank	Company	Net Income ($ mil.)	Rank	Company	Net Income ($mil.)
182	L Brands, Inc	$1,253	222	Becton, Dickinson & Co.	$976	262	Eastman Chemical Co	$848
183	CME Group Inc	$1,247	223	Lear Corp.	$975	263	Alaska Air Group, Inc.	$848
184	Consolidated Edison Inc	$1,245	224	Northern Trust Corp.	$974	264	Dr Pepper Snapple Group Inc	$847
185	AutoZone, Inc.	$1,241	225	Baxter International Inc.	$968	265	TD Ameritrade Holding Corp	$842
186	Tennessee Valley Authority	$1,233	226	Stanley Black & Decker Inc	$965	266	Bed, Bath & Beyond, Inc.	$841
187	VF Corp.	$1,232	227	Sysco Corp	$950	267	Citizens Financial Group Inc	$840
188	Spectra Energy Partners LP	$1,225	228	Antero Resources Corp	$941	268	MetLife Insurance Company of	$839
189	T Rowe Price Group, Inc.	$1,215	229	Moody's Corp.	$941	269	Camden Property Trust	$838
190	Prologis Inc	$1,210	230	International Paper Co	$938	270	Jones Financial Companies LL	$838
191	Exelon Corp	$1,204	231	Toyota Motor Credit Corp.	$932	271	Western Union Co	$838
192	Discovery Communications, In	$1,194	232	O'Reilly Automotive, Inc.	$931	272	Santander Consumer USA Holdi	$827
193	Energy Transfer Equity LP	$1,189	233	Gap Inc	$920	273	Amphenol Corp.	$823
194	Energy Transfer Corp LP	$1,189	234	KeyCorp	$916	274	Zoetis Inc	$821
195	Waste Management, Inc. (DE)	$1,182	235	Lam Research Corp	$914	275	Magellan Midstream Partners	$819
196	MGIC Investment Corp. (WI)	$1,172	236	Lennar Corp	$912	276	Alabama Power Co.	$811
197	Adobe Systems Inc	$1,169	237	Equity Residential	$908	277	Boston Properties L.P.	$809
198	Dollar General Corp	$1,165	238	Vornado Realty Trust	$907	278	Parker-Hannifin Corp	$807
199	Electronic Arts	$1,156	239	ERP Operating L.P.	$904	279	Vornado Realty L.P.	$804
200	Lincoln National Corp.	$1,154	240	Plains All American Pipeline	$903	280	CA Inc	$783
201	Omnicom Group, Inc.	$1,149	241	Celanese Corp (DE)	$900	281	Marriott International, Inc.	$780
202	Lauder (Estee) Cos., Inc. (T	$1,115	242	Best Buy Inc	$897	282	Grainger (W.W.), Inc.	$769
203	Southern California Edison C	$1,111	243	Regeneron Pharmaceuticals, I	$896	283	Paychex Inc	$757
204	Virginia Electric & Power Co	$1,087	244	Popular Inc.	$895	284	Dish Network Corp	$747
205	Consolidated Edison Co. of N	$1,084	245	RiverSource Life Insurance C	$895	285	SCANA Corp	$746
206	Duke Energy Carolinas LLC	$1,081	246	Kimco Realty Corp.	$894	286	Sirius XM Holdings Inc	$746
207	M & T Bank Corp	$1,080	247	Activision Blizzard, Inc.	$892	287	AvalonBay Communities, Inc.	$742
208	Qwest Corp	$1,074	248	Hormel Foods Corp.	$890	288	HollyFrontier Corp.	$740
209	Macy's Inc	$1,072	249	Welltower Inc	$889	289	Southern Copper Corp	$736
210	Brown-Forman Corp.	$1,067	250	Whirlpool Corp	$888	290	Intuitive Surgical Inc	$736
211	Regions Financial Corp	$1,062	251	Horton (D.R.) Inc.	$886	291	Tesoro Corporation	$734
212	CIT Group, Inc.	$1,057	252	Eversource Energy	$886	292	T-Mobile US Inc	$733
213	Constellation Brands Inc	$1,055	253	Prologis LP	$881	293	Rockwell Automation, Inc.	$730
214	Sherwin-Williams Co (The)	$1,054	254	CenturyLink, Inc.	$878	294	Rockwell Collins, Inc.	$728
215	Ross Stores, Inc.	$1,021	255	PPG Industries Inc	$877	295	Fiserv Inc	$712
216	Ecolab Inc	$1,002	256	Liberty Interactive Corp	$869	296	Blackstone Group LP	$710
217	VMware Inc	$997	257	DTE Energy Co	$868	297	Quest Diagnostics, Inc.	$709
218	Navient Corp	$997	258	Unum Group	$867	298	Kinder Morgan Inc.	$708
219	Skyworks Solutions, Inc.	$995	259	Fortive Corp	$864	299	Genuine Parts Co.	$706
220	Xcel Energy, Inc.	$984	260	Analog Devices Inc	$862	300	KLA-Tencor Corp.	$704
221	Intuit Inc	$979	261	PSEG Power LLC	$856			

Hoover's Handbook of

Emerging Companies

2017

1-800 Flowers.com, Inc.

Some say it's all in the name but 1-800-FLOW-ERS.COM does more than deliver the daisies. The company sells fresh-cut flowers floral arrangements and plants through its toll-free number and websites; it also markets gifts for every occasion via catalog TV and radio ads and third-party online affiliates. Through subsidiaries 1-800-FLOW-ERS.COM offers gift baskets gourmet foods chocolates and candies cookies and popcorn. Its BloomNet service provides products and services to florists too. Inspired by the emergence of toll-free calling founder and CEO James McCann launched the flower business in 1976 and over time established a national brand that was further fueled by the evolution of the Internet.

Geographic Reach

Aside from its online business 1-800-FLOW-ERS operates a retail store in New York and eight retail shops across the Midwest. Its nearly 200 franchised floral stores operate in some of the country's top retail markets such as New York Los Angeles Chicago San Francisco San Diego and Phoenix among others.

Operations

The company's consumer floral business generated 56% of its 2014 revenue. 1-800-FLOWERS' BloomNet Wire Service (11% of revenue) and gourmet food and gift baskets (33%) brought in the rest.

Sales and Marketing

1-800-FLOWERS works to make its business synonymous with "sending smiles." To this end the retailer aims to reach customers through online and offline media direct marketing public relations and strategic Internet partnerships. In fiscal 2014 the firm's advertising expenses reached $83 million up steadily from $77.9 million in 2013 and $75.1 million in 2012.

Mergers and Acquisitions

The online flower giant expanded its menu to include gift baskets and gourmet foods with its purchase of Oregon-based Harry & David Holdings (HDH) known for its Royal Riviera Pears and Moose Munch popcorn snacks. The company offered $142.5 million in cash for HDH whose sales are approaching $400 million. The deal which includes HDH's brands and websites as well as its manufacturing and distribution facilities and orchards in Medford Oregon and 47 retail stores throughout the country among other assets closed in September 2014. The acquisition is consistent with 1-800-FLOWERS.COM's strategy of pursuing a competitive position in the gourmet food and gift basket marketplace.

Strategy

Going forward 1-800-FLOWERS.COM is adopting a strategy that focuses on controlling costs while merchandising original new products across all business categories that ring up a higher average order. (Formerly the company used promotional pricing and markdowns and free shipping to woo demand.)

The shift in strategy is likely to most impact its consumer floral sales business. During 2011 1-800-FLOWERS.COM added to the business' offerings by acquiring Fine Stationery an online retailer of personalized stationery invitation and announcements. More significant in reversing an unfavorable trend in the consumer floral business the company cites its marketing efforts led by its 2010 launch of a mobile shopping app Mobile Flower & Gift Center. Quick turnaround is further facilitated by BloomNet 1-800-FLOWERS.COM's network of independent local florists.

Financial Performance

1-800-FLOWERS rang up $756.3 million in revenue in fiscal 2014 (ended June) —representing a $20.8 million increase from 2013's $735.5 million —following several years of steady gains. Driving growth were an $9.8 million increase in its 1-800-FLOWERS consumer floral business combined with both BloomNet Wire Service revenue (a 3% gain) and Gourmet Food & Gift Baskets revenue (4% rise). The retailer's net income has fluctuated during the past five years. In 2014 1-800-FLOW-ERS posted a profit of $15.4 million a 25% increase from 2013. Increased sales in 2014 were dragged down by rising operating expenses from marketing and sales technology and development and general and administrative expenses.

HISTORY

Social worker Jim McCann bought a New York City florist shop in 1976 to supplement his income from St. John's Home for Boys. By 1986 he had expanded his Flora Plenty chain to 14 shops in the New York metropolitan area and made the floral business his full-time job.

The next year McCann paid $9 million for 1-800-FLOWERS a young struggling Dallas-based floral-delivery company that had been founded by John Davis and Jim Poage. McCann's shops had worked with 1-800-FLOWERS but he had to sell most of his Flora Plenty stores to keep the telemarketing business from wilting altogether. By 1990 however business was blossoming and 1-800-FLOWERS was profitable.

In 1992 the company began selling flowers online through Compuserve. 1-800-FLOWERS launched its own website three years later and teamed with online providers such as America Online (now Time Warner Inc.) and Microsoft Network.

1-800-FLOWERS added home and garden merchandise to its offerings —and picked up catalog expertise —when it bought an 80% stake in Plow & Hearth in 1998 (it acquired the remainder in 1999). In May 1999 the company received more than $100 million from Benchmark Capital Japanese technology firm SOFTBANK and luxury goods kingpin LVMH. 1-800-FLOWERS then added ".COM" to its name and went public in August 1999.

In late 1999 the company bought online gourmet foods retailer GreatFood.com for $18.5 million. It added jewelry to its offerings by teaming up with retailer Finlay Enterprises in 2000. It also launched its Spanish language Web site —1-800-LASFLO-RES.COM. New additions in 2001 included a partnership with Touchpoint allowing customers to create personalized cards and photos and the addition of children's gifts dolls crafts and other toys and games with the acquisition of The Children's Group.

1-800-FLOWERS.COM continued its acquisitive ways in 2002 by acquiring The Popcorn Factory (direct marketing of premium popcorn chocolates and other food gift products packaged in decorative tins and baskets). That year the firm agreed to cross-promote its goods with American Greetings; under the agreement 1-800-FLOW-ERS.COM became the exclusive provider of flowers on several American Greetings Web sites. And in 2004 it got into the wine distribution business with its purchase of The Winetasting Network which is now a subsidiary.

In March 2005 the company acquired cookie-and-baked-gifts-maker Cheryl & Co. for an undisclosed price. The company moved its corporate headquarters to Carle Place New York the next year. In mid-2006 the Internet flower company acquired candy maker Fannie May Confections Brands for $85 million.

1-800-FLOWERS.COM bought gourmet gift basket maker DesignPac Gifts in May 2008 for about $36 million. It also purchased Napco Marketing which wholesales and markets products for the floral industry for $9 million.

In March 2009 the company acquired certain assets of online wine seller Geerlings & Wade Inc. for about $2 million to complement its Winetasting Network business. It also launched 1-800-BAS-KETS.com that year.

To focus on its core floral and food units 1-800-FLOWERS.COM sold its home décor and children's gift brands to PH International a Virginia-based home décor distributor in January 2010. The deal which was worth $17 million included the brands of HearthSong Magic Cabin Plow & Hearth Problem Solvers and Wind & Weather.

EXECUTIVES

SVP Finance and Administration Treasurer and CFO, William E. Shea, age 57, $721,002 total compensation
SVP Retail and Fulfillment and COO Consumer Floral Brand, Thomas G. Hartnett, age 53
President and CEO, Christopher G. (Chris) McCann, age 55, $721,002 total compensation
President BloomNet, Mark Nance, age 66
President Gourmet Foods and Gift Baskets, David L. (Dave) Taiclet, age 53, $439,409 total compensation
CIO, Arnold P. (Arnie) Leap
Vice President of Product Development, Valerie (Val) Ghitelman
Vice President Ecommerce Product Management, Chris (Chrissy) Barca
Senior Vice President, Jerald (Jerry) Gallagher
Vice President of Marketing, Amit (Mit) Shah
Vice President Of Sales, Kevin Cochran
Vice President, Ted (Teddy) Nelson
Vice President, Julie McCann-Mulligan
Senior Vice President Information Technology and Chief Technology Officer, Harriet Harriet Wolpin Wolpin
Vice President Operations, Camilo Escobar
National Sales Manager, Earl Hurd
Vice President Operations, David (Dave) French
Senior Vice President Business Development And Strategy, Ed Slezak
Vice President Technology, Marc Grzeskowiak
Vice President, Mark Lefkin
Vice President Information Technology Operations, Angel (Ann) Rivera
Vice President Franchise, Ann (Annie) Frisbie
Vice President of Corporate Systems, Phil (Philly) Disanto
Senior Vice President Strategy and Business Development, Ian Hardman
Vice President Operational Accounting, Barbara (Barb) Noll
Vice President of Marketing, Tony (Tone) Valado
Senior Vice President and Chief Data Officer, Tim (Timmy) Mummers
Executive Chairman, James F. (Jim) McCann, age 65
Auditors: BDO USA, LLP

LOCATIONS

HQ: 1-800 Flowers.com, Inc.
One Old Country Road, Carle Place, NY 11514
Phone: 516 237-6000
Web: www.1800flowers.com

PRODUCTS/OPERATIONS

2016 sales

	$ mil.	% of total
1-800-Flowers.com consumer floral	418.5	36
Gourmet food & gift baskets	670.5	57
BloomNet Wire Service	85.5	7
Corporate	1.0	-
Adjustments	(2.5)	-
Total	**1,173.0**	**100**

2016 sales

	$ mil.	% of total
E-commerce	882.8	75
Other	290.2	25
Total	**1,173.0**	**100**

Selected Brands

The BloomNet Wire Service
  BloomNet
  BloomNet Technologies
  Napco
Consumer floral
  1-800-Flowers.com
  Celebrations
  FineStationery.com
Gourmet Food and Gift Baskets
  1-800-Baskets
  Cheryl's
  Mrs. Beasley's
  DesignPac
  Fannie May Confections Brands
  Fannie May
  Harry London
  Harry & David
  The Popcorn Factory
  Wintasting.com

Selected Products and Services

BloomNet products and services
  Advertising
  Member directories
  On-line directory
  Clearinghouse services
  Communications services
  Bloomlink
  Other services
  Point of sale
  Web hosting
  Wholesale products
  Branded and non-branded floral supplies
Flowers and plants
  Floral arrangements
  Fresh-cut flowers
  Plants
Gourmet foods and gift baskets
  Chocolate and candy
  Cookies and baked gift items
  Gourmet gift baskets
  Popcorn and specialty snack products
  Wine

Selected Domain Names

www.1800flowers.com
www.800flowers.com
www.1800baskets.com
www.ambrosiawine.com
www.celebrations.com
www.cheryls.com
www.designpac.com
www.fanniemay.com
www.finestationery.com
www.flowers.com
www.geerwade.com
www.greatfood.com
www.harrylondon.com
www.mybloomnet.net
www.napcoimports.com
www.thepopcornfactory.com
www.winetasting.com

COMPETITORS

AMES International	Hickory Farms
Dean & DeLuca	KaBloom

Edible Arrangements	Martha Stewart Living
FTD	Provide Commerce
Godiva Chocolatier	Teleflora
Hallmark	Vermont Teddy Bear

HISTORICAL FINANCIALS

Company Type: Public

Income Statement

FYE: July 3

	REVENUE ($ mil.)	NET INCOME ($ mil.)	NET PROFIT MARGIN	EMPLOYEES
07/16*	1,173.0	36.8	3.1%	4,490.0
06/15	1,121.5	20.2	1.8%	4,524.0
06/14	756.3	15.3	2.0%	2,034.0
06/13	735.5	12.3	1.7%	2,150.0
07/12	716.2	17.6	2.5%	2,200.0
Annual Growth	**13.1%**	**20.2%**		**19.5%**

*Fiscal year change

2016 Year-End Financials

Debt ratio: 23.2%	No. of shares (mil.): 65.2
Return on equity: 16.0%	Dividends
Cash ($ mil.): 27.8	Yield: —
Current ratio: 1.38	Payout: —
Long-term debt ($ mil.): 97.9	Market value ($ mil.): 587.0

	STOCK PRICE ($) FY Close	P/E High/Low	PER SHARE ($) Earnings	Dividends	Book Value
07/16*	8.99	19 11	0.55	0.00	3.72
06/15	10.38	42 16	0.30	0.00	3.21
06/14	5.74	30 19	0.23	0.00	2.86
06/13	6.19	34 15	0.19	0.00	2.65
07/12	3.49	13 8	0.27	0.00	2.51
Annual Growth	**26.7%**	**— —**	**19.5%**	**—**	**10.4%**

*Fiscal year change

1st Constitution Bancorp

In order to "secure the blessings of liberty" the founding fathers established the US Constitution. As for promoting the general welfare some banks share the same dedication to "We the people." 1st Constitution Bancorp is the parent of 1st Constitution Bank which serves consumers small businesses and not-for-profits through more than a dozen branches in Middlesex Mercer and Somerset counties in New Jersey. Services and products include demand savings and time deposits as well as loans and mortgages. Commercial mortgages business loans and construction loans make up more than half of the bank's lending portfolio.

In 2011 1st Constitution acquired three branch locations from another New Jersey company Amboy Bank. The acquisition added some $110 million in deposits and boosted the company's presence in Mercer and Somerset counties.

EXECUTIVES

Vice President Business Develoment, Joseph Barbiere
Vice President, Tom Berger
Auditors: BDO USA LLP

LOCATIONS

HQ: 1st Constitution Bancorp
  2650 Route 130, P.O. Box 634, Cranbury, NJ 08512
Phone: 609 655-4500
Web: www.1stconstitution.com

COMPETITORS

Amboy Bancorp	Provident Financial
Bank of America	Services
Brunswick Bancorp	Sovereign Bank
Hudson City Bancorp	Sun Bancorp (NJ)
OceanFirst Financial	Wells Fargo
PNC Financial	

HISTORICAL FINANCIALS

Company Type: Public

Income Statement

FYE: December 31

	ASSETS ($ mil.)	NET INCOME ($ mil.)	INCOME AS % OF ASSETS	EMPLOYEES
12/15	967.9	8.6	0.9%	183.0
12/14	956.7	4.3	0.5%	187.0
12/13	742.3	5.7	0.8%	173.0
12/12	840.9	5.0	0.6%	152.0
12/11	791.7	3.9	0.5%	150.0
Annual Growth	**5.2%**	**21.8%**	**—**	**5.1%**

2015 Year-End Financials

Return on assets: 0.9%	Dividends
Return on equity: 9.4%	Yield: —
Long-term debt ($ mil.): —	Payout: —
No. of shares (mil.): 7.5	Market value ($ mil.): 97.0
Sales ($ mil): 48.2	

	STOCK PRICE ($) FY Close	P/E High/Low	PER SHARE ($) Earnings	Dividends	Book Value
12/15	12.87	12 10	1.07	0.00	12.72
12/14	10.89	19 17	0.58	0.00	11.63
12/13	11.00	13 10	0.86	0.00	10.30
12/12	8.76	11 8	0.82	0.00	9.87
12/11	6.98	14 9	0.67	0.00	9.33
Annual Growth	**16.5%**	**— —**	**12.6%**	**—**	**8.1%**

8Point3 Energy Partners LP

Auditors: PRICEWATERHOUSECOOPERS LLP

LOCATIONS

HQ: 8Point3 Energy Partners LP
  77 Rio Robles, San Jose, CA 95134
Phone: 408 240-5500
Web: www.8point3energypartners.com

HISTORICAL FINANCIALS

Company Type: Public

Income Statement

FYE: November 30

	REVENUE ($ mil.)	NET INCOME ($ mil.)	NET PROFIT MARGIN	EMPLOYEES
11/16	61.2	27.1	44.3%	0.0
11/15*	10.6	(24.0)	—	0.0
12/14	9.2	(1.2)	—	0.0
12/13	24.4	(3.8)	—	0.0
Annual Growth	**35.7%**			

*Fiscal year change

2016 Year-End Financials

Debt ratio: 28.9%
Return on equity: 7.9%
Cash ($ mil.): 14.2
Current ratio: 1.33
Long-term debt ($ mil.): 384.4

No. of shares (mil.): 79.0
Dividends
 Yield: 7.1%
 Payout: 72.0%
Market value ($ mil.): 1,011.0

	STOCK PRICE ($) FY Close	P/E High/Low	PER SHARE ($) Earnings	Dividends	Book Value
11/16	12.78	13 10	1.27	0.91	3.43
11/15*	12.23	22 11	0.94	0.16	5.75
12/14	0.00	— —	(0.00)	0.00	(0.00)
Annual Growth	—		—	—	—

*Fiscal year change

AAC Holdings Inc

Auditors: BDO USA, LLP

LOCATIONS

HQ: AAC Holdings Inc
 200 Powell Place, Brentwood, TN 37027
Phone: 615 732-1231
Web: www.americanaddictioncenters.com

HISTORICAL FINANCIALS
Company Type: Public

Income Statement
FYE: December 31

	REVENUE ($ mil.)	NET INCOME ($ mil.)	NET PROFIT MARGIN	EMPLOYEES
12/15	212.2	11.1	5.3%	1,600.0
12/14	132.9	7.5	5.7%	880.0
12/13	115.7	0.7	0.7%	750.0
12/12	66.0	1.5	2.3%	0.0
Annual Growth	47.6%	95.1%	—	—

2015 Year-End Financials

Debt ratio: 45.9%
Return on equity: 9.0%
Cash ($ mil.): 18.7
Current ratio: 2.52
Long-term debt ($ mil.): 140.3

No. of shares (mil.): 22.8
Dividends
 Yield: —
 Payout: —
Market value ($ mil.): 435.0

	STOCK PRICE ($) FY Close	P/E High/Low	PER SHARE ($) Earnings	Dividends	Book Value
12/15	19.06	91 36	0.48	0.00	6.21
12/14	30.92	79 44	0.41	0.00	4.93
12/13	0.00	— —	0.12	0.00	6.26
Annual Growth	—		—100.0%	—	(0.4%)

Abaxis, Inc.

Abaxis makes a praxis of analyzing blood. Its two types of point-of-care blood analyzers (one for animals and one for humans) can each perform more than a dozen tests on their respective veterinary and human health patients. The analyzers are portable require little training provide on-the-

spot results and offer built-in quality control and calibration. Abaxis also sells compatible chemical reagent supplies. In the veterinary market its systems bear the VetScan name; in the human medical market Piccolo Xpress. Abaxis sells to veterinarians hospitals managed care organizations and the military.

Operations
The company's veterinary segment accounts for about three-fourths of revenues. Abaxis sells its chemistry blood analysis systems to vets and doctors and then generates additional income from the same customers by supplying consumable supplies for the systems. These supplies which account for about 80% of annual revenues primarily consist of single-use reagent disks that allow for automated testing of several conditions at once.

The company's vet division also sells a handheld testing instrument as well as hematology instruments for blood clot detection. Abaxis Veterinary Reference Laboratories (AVRL) operates a reference lab facility in Olathe Kansas that provides routine and specialty testing services to vets across the US.

Geographic Reach
Abaxis' products are sold in about 30 countries worldwide. The US accounts for 79% of revenue.

Marketing and Sales
A direct sales force markets the company's veterinary products in North America where the company conducts more than 80% of its business. Products are then delivered to end-users by third-party distributors including Animal Health International which accounts for 15% of Abaxis' annual revenues. Other distributors include Merritt Veterinary Supplies and MWI Veterinary Supply. Outside the US Abaxis' products are sold through direct sales units (including Abaxis Europe) and through independent representatives and distributors for sales.

The company's medical (human) products are distributed in the US through an exclusive contract with Abbott Labs which began in 2013.

Financial Analysis
Revenues which had been climbing steadily for years peaked in 2013 at $186 million then took a spill in 2014 dropping 8% to $182 million as Abbott Labs paid lower prices for its human analyzers and instruments and sales softened for vet products. Net income tagged along losing 48% from $27.5 million to $14.2 million. Cash from operations however has been growing since 2012 and posted a $6 million increase from 2013 to 2014.

Strategy
The company regularly introduces new and next-generation versions of its veterinary blood analyzers instruments and testing reagents to keep pace with customer demand for innovative and easy-to-use products. For instance in 2011 Abaxis introduced new VetScan rapid canine tests for heartworm Lyme disease and parvovirus and in 2012 it launched a feline rapid heartworm test and a kidney disease test for multiple species of animals. The company is also working to expand its foothold in the human diagnostics market.

In 2013 the company signed an exclusive contract for Abbott Labs to distribute its medical products in the US. The deal originally included China as well but Abaxis took back that region early on.

EXECUTIVES

Chairman President and CEO, Clinton H. (Clint) Severson, age 68, $478,116 total compensation
CTO, Kenneth P. Aron, age 63, $258,500 total compensation

Managing Director Abaxis Europe, Achim Henkel, age 58
President and COO, Donald P. (Don) Wood, age 64, $258,500 total compensation
VP Finance and CFO, Ross Taylor
VP Sales and Marketing, Craig Tockman
Executive Vice President Customer Service, Sigrid Rose
Vice President of Commercial Operations, Ilya Frumkin
Vice President Government Affairs, Vladimir E (Vlad) Ostoich
Auditors: Burr Pilger Mayer, Inc.

LOCATIONS

HQ: Abaxis, Inc.
 3240 Whipple Road, Union City, CA 94587
Phone: 510 675-6500
Web: www.abaxis.com

PRODUCTS/OPERATIONS

2016 Sales

	$ mil.	% of total
Veterinary market	177.7	81
Medical market	37.8	17
Other	3.4	2
Total	**218.9**	**100**

2016 Sales

	$ mil.	% of total
Consumables	165.0	75
Instruments	43.1	20
Other products	10.8	5
Total	**218.9**	**100**

Selected Products
Piccolo Xpress (human blood chemistry analyzer and panels)
VetScan HM5 and HM2 (blood cell counters and reagents)
VetScan i-STAT (handheld analyzer for veterinarians amd cartridges)
VetScan Rapid Test Kits
  VetScan Avian Influenza Rapid Test Kit
  VetScan Giardia Rapid Test Kit
  VetScan Canine Heartworm Rapid Test Kit
  VetScan Canine Parvovirus Rapid Test Kit
  VetScan Canine Lyme Rapid Test
  VetScan Kidney Profile Plus Rotor
VetScan VS2 (veterinary blood chemistry analyzer and profiles)
VetScan VSpro (point-of-care coagulation analyzer and cartridges)

COMPETITORS

Abbott Labs	IDEXX Labs
Alere	Immucor
Beckman Coulter	Johnson & Johnson
Becton Dickinson	Quidel
Hemagen Diagnostics	Roche Diagnostics
Heska	VCA

HISTORICAL FINANCIALS
Company Type: Public

Income Statement
FYE: March 31

	REVENUE ($ mil.)	NET INCOME ($ mil.)	NET PROFIT MARGIN	EMPLOYEES
03/16	218.9	31.6	14.4%	549.0
03/15	202.5	27.3	13.5%	582.0
03/14	171.8	14.1	8.3%	520.0
03/13	186.0	27.4	14.8%	535.0
03/12	156.6	13.0	8.4%	491.0
Annual Growth	8.7%	24.7%	—	2.8%

2016 Year-End Financials

Debt ratio: 0.1%　　　　　No. of shares (mil.): 22.4
Return on equity: 13.8%　　Dividends
Cash ($ mil.): 88.3　　　　Yield: 0.9%
Current ratio: 7.27　　　　Payout: 29.3%
Long-term debt ($ mil.): 0.3　Market value ($ mil.): 1,017.0

	STOCK PRICE ($) FY Close	P/E High/Low	PER SHARE ($) Earnings	Dividends	Book Value
03/16	45.39	46 28	1.38	0.44	10.55
03/15	64.11	55 31	1.20	0.40	9.77
03/14	38.88	80 51	0.63	0.00	8.69
03/13	47.32	38 21	1.23	1.00	7.97
03/12	29.13	53 34	0.58	0.00	7.36
Annual Growth	11.7%	—	24.2%	—	9.4%

ABIOMED, Inc.

ABIOMED gives weary hearts a rest. The medical device maker has developed a range of cardiac assist devices and is developing a self-contained artificial heart. Its Impella micro heart pumps can temporarily take over blood circulation during surgery or catheterization. Its AB5000 ventricular assist device temporarily takes over the heart's pumping function and improves circulatory flow in patients with acute heart failure thus allowing their hearts to rest and recover. ABIOMED markets its products through both a direct sales force and distributors.

Operations

ABIOMED has also developed a battery-powered implantable replacement heart system called AbioCor which can be used to extend life for dying patients who aren't eligible for a heart transplant. ABIOMED developed the AbioCor system based on technology developed at Pennsylvania State University. However due to the limited number of patients that qualify for use of the AbioCor the company places little emphasis on marketing efforts for this product line.

Geographic Reach

While many of ABIOMED's products are approved for use in other countries international sales to Canada parts of Europe Asia South America and the Middle East only make up some 10% of its revenue. The company intends to improve its international results with more sales and support teams in Europe. It manufactures its Impella products at a facility in Germany while the rest of its products are made in Massachusetts.

In addition to its locations in Massachusetts and Aachen Germany the company has a sales and marketing office in Paris and another office in Tokyo where it is preparing for a commercial launch of products.

Financial Performance

After years of steady sales growth ABIOMED made its first profit in 2012. Sales have continued to rise and in fiscal 2015 (ended March) revenue rose 25% to $230.3 million on higher sales of the Impella system. This was largely due to disposable catheter sales in the US and growing business in Europe primarily Germany.

Net income jumped more than 1000% in fiscal 2015 to $113.7 million. That sharp increase was driven both by the higher revenues and changes in income tax benefit provisions. Operating cash flow increased 84% to $43.3 million that year.

Strategy

The company's research efforts are focused on developing new products for acute heart failure patients as well as next-generation versions and support systems for its existing products. The company has shifted more of its development and sales efforts onto the Impella product line in order to expand its uses and variations while gradually discontinuing its other products.

In addition to expanding its product portfolio and approvals the company also dedicates personnel and financial resources to raising awareness of its products in the medical community. ABIOMED also continuously evaluates opportunities for strategic acquisitions. To that end it acquired a German heart catheter pump maker in 2014 expanding its product line and German sales efforts.

Mergers and Acquisitions

In 2014 as part of its plan to expand it product line and its German sales force ABIOMED purchased Berlin-based ECP Entwicklungsgesellschaft for $14 million. ECP produces heart catheter pumps that use an external drive shaft to increase circulation.

HISTORY

Company Background

David Lederman founded ABIOMED in 1981 to make products he had designed (such as artificial heart pumps and valves) as well as dental diagnostic products. ABIOMED went public in 1987. In 1988 it got about $1 million from the National Institutes of Health for heart replacement device (HRD) research and development. In 1990 it began working with Canada's World Heart on HRD technology. In 1992 ABIOMED launched BVS-5000.

In 1990 the company formed ABIODENT to consolidate its dental operations. It received FDA clearance to market the PerioTemp device in 1994. In 1996 it voluntarily recalled some of its BVS-5000 blood pumps citing component irregularities (it said no patients were affected).

To fund product development ABIOMED accepted government funding to finish testing its battery-powered HRD (1996) and to develop a laser-based tissue-welding system (1998). Biotech firm Genzyme invested about $15 million in ABIOMED that year acquiring 14% of the firm.

In 1998 ABIOMED again recalled some lots of BVS-5000 this time for electrical problems. The company attributed 1998's losses to an increase in self-funding on the HRD project as well as to red ink in its now-discontinued dental business.

ABIOMED received funding from the National Heart Lung and Blood Institutes in 2000 to support the testing of its AbioCor product an implantable heart replacement device. The following year AbioCor became the first artificial heart implanted in a patient.

The FDA approved the use of the artificial hearts in five patients in 2001 all of whom were considered too sick to receive heart transplants. The first patient died the same year but the cause of death was not attributed to AbioCor.

The fifth patient to receive the device died early in 2002. By late 2002 seven patients had been fitted with the device but only one was living. A moratorium on recruiting new patients was imposed. ABIOMED wanted patients that were healthy enough to live long past the time of implantation but only patients that were extremely ill would be considered candidates for the device.

By January of 2003 the moratorium had been lifted and three more patients had received implants by March. Because of the troubles with finding qualified recipients for its AbioCor product the company began focusing on other products to sustain revenues. It got good news on that front that same year when the FDA approved ABIOMED's AB5000 Circulatory Support System Console a device that temporarily pumps the patient's blood when the heart has failed.

EXECUTIVES

Vice President Global Product Oprs, William (Bill) Bolt
Chairman President and CEO, Michael R. Minogue, age 49, $519,663 total compensation
Chief Medical Officer, Karim Benali, age 50, $171,200 total compensation
VP Healthcare Solutions, Andrew J. Greenfield, age 44, $211,592 total compensation
CTO, Thorsten Siess
COO, David M. Weber, age 55, $341,844 total compensation
VP and General Manager Global Sales and Marketing, Michael G. Howley, age 52, $296,970 total compensation
VP and CFO, Michael Tomsicek, age 50
Vice President Human Resources, Franky Leblanc
Vice President Corporate Marketing, Raymond (Ray) Kelley
Auditors: Deloitte & Touche LLP

LOCATIONS

HQ: ABIOMED, Inc.
22 Cherry Hill Drive, Danvers, MA 01923
Phone: 978 646-1400　　**Fax:** 978 777-8411
Web: www.abiomed.com

PRODUCTS/OPERATIONS

2015 Revenues

	$ mil.	% of total
Impella products	212.7	92
Service & other revenue	13.8	6
Other products	3.5	2
Funded research & development	0.3	
Total	**230.3**	**100**

COMPETITORS

CardiacAssist	St. Jude Medical
Edwards Lifesciences	Teleflex
Getinge	Terumo
HeartWare	Thoratec Corp
Medtronic	

HISTORICAL FINANCIALS

Company Type: Public

Income Statement

FYE: March 31

	REVENUE ($ mil.)	NET INCOME ($ mil.)	NET PROFIT MARGIN	EMPLOYEES
03/16	329.5	38.1	11.6%	747.0
03/15	230.3	113.6	49.4%	589.0
03/14	183.6	7.3	4.0%	511.0
03/13	158.1	15.0	9.5%	467.0
03/12	126.3	1.5	1.2%	397.0
Annual Growth	27.1%	124.8%	—	17.1%

2016 Year-End Financials

Debt ratio: —　　　　　　No. of shares (mil.): 42.6
Return on equity: 11.5%　　Dividends
Cash ($ mil.): 48.2　　　　Yield: —
Current ratio: 6.20　　　　Payout: —
Long-term debt ($ mil.): —　Market value ($ mil.): 4,039.0

STOCK PRICE ($)		P/E		PER SHARE ($)		
	FY Close	High/Low		Earnings	Dividends	Book Value
03/16	94.81	118	66	0.85	0.00	8.66
03/15	71.58	26	7	2.65	0.00	7.05
03/14	26.04	158	86	0.18	0.00	4.22
03/13	18.67	65	32	0.37	0.00	3.55
03/12	22.19	588	252	0.04	0.00	3.22
Annual Growth	43.8%	—	—114.7%		—	28.1%

Acadia Healthcare Company Inc.

Acadia Healthcare helps people to be mentally healthy. Acadia operates nearly 600 behavioral health facilities with 17800 licensed beds in 39 US states the UK and Puerto Rico. Its mental health and addiction treatment services include adult geriatric and adolescent inpatient residential and partial hospitalization programs. The company also offers treatment options for children with autism eating disorders fetal alcohol syndrome substance abuse and traumatic brain injury as well as for sexually abused children. Acadia offers services nationwide.

Sales and Marketing
Patients are referred to Acadia's behavioral health care facilities through health care workers public programs other treatment facilities managed care organizations unions emergency departments judicial officials social workers and police departments. It also gets patient referrals via word of mouth from previously treated patients and their families and other sources.

Strategy
The company primarily grows through acquisitions. However it does make divestitures as it sees fit. In 2016 Acadia agreed to sell 22 behavioral health care facilities in the UK to BC Partners for some $390 million. That sale will help address competition concerns related to Acadia's earlier acquisition of UK behavioral health care firm Priory Group (which operates more than 300 facilities in the nation).

Mergers and Acquisitions
Acadia completed a major deal in 2015 when it acquired CRC Health Group which runs some 150 behavioral health facilities throughout the US. The following year it acquired UK-based Priory Group operator of 300 behavioral health care facilities.

In 2013 the company acquired Nashville-based Behavioral Centers of America for $145 million. The firm operates three inpatient psychiatric facilities and one psychiatric hospital in Michigan Ohio and Texas.

In 2012 Acadia acquired three acute care inpatient psychiatric hospitals from Haven Behavioral Healthcare for $91 million in cash. The purchase added about 165 beds at facilities in Tucson; Wichita Falls Texas; and Ada Oklahoma and marked the company's entrance into the Oklahoma market. The company also entered Illinois in 2012 by acquiring a 122-bed inpatient behavioral health care facility in Lemont Illinois for about $90 million. It also picked up Park Royal Hospital a 76-bed acute inpatient psychiatric hospital in Ft. Myers Florida for $33.4 million.

Company Background
Acadia was founded in 2005 by Waud Capital Partners to acquire and operate behavioral health facilities. Its first centers were purchased in 2008 and 2009 in Georgia Louisiana and Tennessee.

EXECUTIVES

Chairman and CEO, Joey A. Jacobs, age 63, $660,000 total compensation
President, Brent Turner, age 51, $435,000 total compensation
EVP and General Counsel, Christopher L. (Chris) Howard, age 50, $420,000 total compensation
COO, Ron Fincher, age 63, $450,000 total compensation
CFO, David Duckworth, $327,000 total compensation
Vice President of Risk Management, Dule Mooney
Vice President Human Resources, Kim Brady
Vice President of Marketing, Michael (Mel) Drake
Assistant Vice President Clinical Services, Anne (Annie) Kelly
Vice President Eastern Division Chief Financial Officer, Dwight Willingham
Director of Him, Hema Patel
Vice President of Government Relations, Bryan (Bry) Kaegi
Vice Chairman, Bruce A. Shear, age 62
Auditors: Ernst & Young LLP

LOCATIONS

HQ: Acadia Healthcare Company Inc.
  6100 Tower Circle, Suite 1000, Franklin, TN 37067
Phone: 615 861-6000
Web: www.acadiahealthcare.com

PRODUCTS/OPERATIONS

2015 Sales

	% of total
Medicaid	33
Commercial	23
NHS	19
Medicare	12
Self-pay	10
Other	3
Total	**100**

Selected Facilities
Arizona
  Parc-Place (residential adolescents ages 11-17)
Arkansas
  Ascent Children's Health Services (day treatment all ages)
  Millcreek of Arkansas (long-term residential ages 6-21 years with mental retardation and/or related developmental disabilities)
Delaware
  MeadowWood Hospital (in-patient and out-patient adults and seniors)
Florida
  Park Royal Hospital
The Refuge
Georgia
  Blue Ridge Mountain Recovery
Greenleaf Centers
Lakeview Behavioral Health
  RiverWoods Behavioral Health System (outpatient and partial hospitalization adults and seniors)
Illinois
Timberline Knolls (residential treatment)
Indiana
  Resolute Treatment Center (residential males ages 11-18)
  Resource Treatment Center (residential ages 8-20)
  Options Behavioral Health System (residential ages 8-18)
Louisiana
  Acadia Vermilion Hospital (inpatient and outpatient all ages)

Acadiana Addiction Center (inpatient and outpatient adults)
Michigan
  Detroit Capstone Academy (residential adjudicated adolescents)
  Harbor Oaks Hospital (inpatient all ages)
  Harbor Oaks Outpatient Clinic (outpatient all ages)
  Pioneer Counseling Centers (outpatient all ages)
  Renaissance Recovery (residential ages 12-17)
  Wellplace Michigan (local call center clinical screening and access center)
Mississippi
  Millcreek of Magee (residential 21 years and younger)
  Millcreek of Pontotoc (residential ages 6-18)
Missouri
  Lakeland Regional Hospital (residential and long term ages 4-17)
Montana
  Acadia Montana (residential ages 5-18)
Nevada
  Harmony Healthcare (outpatient all ages)
  Seven Hills Behavioral Institute (outpatient ages 12 and up)
New Mexico
  Desert Hills of New Mexico (residential ages 5-18)
Ohio
  Ohio Hospital for Psychiatry (adults and seniors)
  Shaker Clinic (adults and seniors)
  Ten Lakes Center (adults ages 55 and up)
Oklahoma
  Rolling Hills Hospital (acute inpatient psychiatric care for adults geriatrics intellectually disabled patients as well as addiction treatment)
Pennsylvania
  Southwood Hospital (various programs ages 4-18)
  Wellplace (outpatient all ages)
Tennessee
  Dealt Medical Center
  The Village (residential ages 13-17)
Texas
  Acadia Abilene (residential all ages)
Utah
  Highland Ridge Hospital (inpatient all ages)
  Wellplace (employee assistance programs and 24 hour call center)
Virginia
  Mount Regis Center (inpatient and outpatient adults)
Puerto Rico
  Hospital San Juan Capestrano Rio Piedras Puerto (treatment services for mental health conditions and addiction problems of Puerto Rico)

COMPETITORS

Betty Ford	Horizon Health
CIGNA Behavioral Health	Magellan Health
CRC Health	Mental Health Network
Comprehensive Care	Northwestern Human Services
Devereux Foundation	Universal Health Services
HCA	
Hazelden Betty Ford	

HISTORICAL FINANCIALS
Company Type: Public

Income Statement
FYE: December 31

	REVENUE ($ mil.)	NET INCOME ($ mil.)	NET PROFIT MARGIN	EMPLOYEES
12/15	1,794.4	112.5	6.3%	26,400.0
12/14	1,004.6	83.0	8.3%	15,500.0
12/13	713.4	42.5	6.0%	11,000.0
12/12	407.4	20.4	5.0%	7,200.0
12/11	221.3	(34.8)	—	5,820.0
Annual Growth	68.7%	—	—	45.9%

2015 Year-End Financials

Debt ratio: 52.3%	No. of shares (mil.): 70.7
Return on equity: 8.7%	Dividends
Cash ($ mil.): 11.2	Yield: —
Current ratio: 1.02	Payout: —
Long-term debt ($ mil.): 2,195.3	Market value ($ mil.): 4,419.0

	STOCK PRICE ($)	P/E	PER SHARE ($)		
	FY Close	High/Low	Earnings	Dividends	Book Value
12/15	62.46	50 34	1.64	0.00	23.90
12/14	61.21	42 27	1.50	0.00	14.88
12/13	47.33	57 27	0.85	0.00	9.60
12/12	23.35	46 18	0.53	0.00	8.67
12/11	9.97	— —	(1.86)	0.00	3.00
Annual Growth 58.2%		— —	—	—	68.0%

Acadia Realty Trust

Acadia Realty acquires redevelops and manages retail properties in the Northeast Mid-Atlantic and Midwest. The self-managed real estate investment trust (REIT) specializes in community shopping centers and mixed-use properties in urban areas. It owns 90 properties —mostly shopping centers anchored by a grocery store drug store or big box store —sporting more than 5.5 million sq. ft. of leasable space. The REIT's largest tenants include SUPERVALU Best Buy Stop & Shop Target and LA Fitness. Acadia Realty owns joint venture interests in another 60 similar properties with investments in self-storage units mortgage loans and other real estate investments.

Operations

Acadia Realty operates three business segments. Its Core Portfolio segment which generated 69% of the REIT's total revenue during 2015 counts its high-quality street retail and urban properties as well as suburban properties in densely-populated trade areas with high-barriers-to-entry. Acadia's Funds segment (23% of revenue) invests through joint ventures while the Structured Financing segment (8% of revenue) offers specialized loans.Geographic ReachThe Rye New York-based REIT has 90 properties in California Delaware Indiana Massachusetts Pennsylvania New York Virginia and the District of Columbia. Sales and MarketingThe company's top five largest tenants in 2015 included: Stop & Shop SUPERVALU Best Buy Target and LA Fitness. No individual tenant accounted for more than 3.1% of Acadia's rental revenue which represents a wide tenant base.

Financial Performance

Acadia Realty's annual revenues have risen 45% since 2011 as the REIT has expanded its property portfolio through acquisitions and has charged higher rental rates as the real estate market has strengthened. Its annual profits have also grown over 25% over the same period as a result.The REIT's revenue climbed 11% to $217.26 million during 2015 mostly as new Core property acquisitions in 2015 and 2014 spurred additional rental income. Despite double-digit revenue growth in 2015 Acadia Realty's net income tumbled nearly 8% to $65.71 million for the year as Core portfolio acquisition-related operating costs and associated income taxes increased. The REIT's operating cash levels jumped 38% to $113.5 million as its newly acquired Core and Fund properties increased cash-based rental revenue during the year.

Strategy

Since its founding in 1998 Acadia has focused on growing its portfolio in densely-populated high barrier-to-entry markets. Most of its properties also are anchored by discount and necessity stores (such as grocery stores and pharmacies) that rely less on discretionary consumer spending. Acadia also carefully culls low-growth and non-core properties. That strategy (along with a healthy balance sheet and access to fresh capital) helped Acadia weather the economic recession which was marked by high unemployment low consumer confidence and retailer bankruptcies.

Toward its core portfolio acquisition-growth strategy Acadia in late 2014 purchased an 88.4% interest in an 87000 square foot four-story street-retail property in Chicago for $144.3 million —an amount equal to more than half its 2015 revenues. This property located on Michigan Avenue was 100% occupied by Verizon and H&M which both maintained their long-term lease contracts.Beyond its direct investment Acadia prefers to engage in discretionary fund joint ventures through which it can conduct its acquisition redevelopment and leasing activities. One such fund carries out its New York Urban Infill Redevelopment Initiative which is dedicated to retail and mixed-use redevelopment projects in dense urban areas of the New York metropolitan region. Another fund invests in properties owned by retailers.Ownership

Investment firms FMR LLC and The Vanguard Group each own about 11% of Acadia's shares. BlackRock Inc. owns 10%.

EXECUTIVES

SVP General Counsel Chief Compliance Officer and Corporate Secretary, Robert Masters, age 71, $327,500 total compensation

President and CEO, Kenneth F. Bernstein, age 54, $582,700 total compensation

EVP and CIO, Joel Braun, age 64, $404,000 total compensation

EVP and COO, Christopher Conlon, age 56, $381,900 total compensation

CFO, John Gottfried

Executive Vice President, Jason Blacksberg

Vice President Counsel, Heather (Heath) Moore

Senior Vice President, Herb Eilberg

Vice President Chief Accounting Officer, Jon Grisham

Vice President Construction, Mark Inglis

Auditors: BDO USA, LLP

LOCATIONS

HQ: Acadia Realty Trust
411 Theodore Fremd Avenue, Suite 300, Rye, NY 10580
Phone: 914 288-8100
Web: www.acadiarealty.com

PRODUCTS/OPERATIONS

2015 Sales

	$ mil.	% of total
Rental income	158.6	73
Expense reimbursements	36.3	17
Interest income	16.6	8
Other	5.7	2
Total	**217.2**	**100**

2015 sales

	% of total
Core Portfolio	69
Funds	23
Structured Financing	8
Total	**100**

Selected Major Tenants

A&P (Waldbaum's Pathmark)
Ahold (Stop & Shop)
Barnes & Noble
Best Buy
BJ's Wholesale Club

CVS
Home Depot
JP Morgan Chase
LA Fitness
Pier 1 Imports
Restoration Hardware
Sleepy's
Stage Deli
Supervalu (Shaw's)
TJX Companies (T.J. Maxx Marshalls Homegoods)
Walgreens
Wal-Mart

COMPETITORS

Brixmor
CBL & Associates Properties
DDR
Federal Realty Investment
General Growth Properties

Kimco Realty
National Retail Properties
Pennsylvania Real Estate
Ramco-Gershenson
Realty Income

HISTORICAL FINANCIALS

Company Type: Public

Income Statement

FYE: December 31

	REVENUE ($ mil.)	NET INCOME ($ mil.)	NET PROFIT MARGIN	EMPLOYEES
12/15	217.2	65.7	30.2%	116.0
12/14	195.0	71.0	36.4%	114.0
12/13	168.2	40.1	23.8%	120.0
12/12	134.4	39.7	29.5%	126.0
12/11	150.1	51.5	34.3%	114.0
Annual Growth	**9.7%**	**6.3%**	**—**	**0.4%**

2015 Year-End Financials

Debt ratio: 44.8%	No. of shares (mil.): 70.2
Return on equity: 6.1%	Dividends
Cash ($ mil.): 72.7	Yield: 3.6%
Current ratio: 1.68	Payout: 127.0%
Long-term debt ($ mil.): 1,358.6	Market value ($ mil.): 2,329.0

	STOCK PRICE ($)	P/E	PER SHARE ($)		
	FY Close	High/Low	Earnings	Dividends	Book Value
12/15	33.15	39 30	0.94	1.22	15.66
12/14	32.03	28 21	1.18	1.23	15.50
12/13	24.83	41 32	0.72	0.86	12.66
12/12	25.08	30 23	0.85	0.72	11.87
12/11	20.14	17 14	1.26	0.72	9.02
Annual Growth 13.3%		— —	(7.1%)	14.1%	14.8%

ACI Worldwide Inc

ACI Worldwide helps money go mobile. The company develops e-payment and electronic funds transfer (EFT) software for companies around the world. Customers use its software to process transactions involving ATMs credit and debit cards on-line banking and payment processing point-of-sale terminals smart cards and wire transfers. ACI also makes network integration software and it offers services such as design implementation and facilities management. The company serves the financial services and retail industries with more than 750 customers in some 80 countries. ACI agreed to sell its community bank-oriented community financial services business to Fiserv for $200 million in early 2016.

Operations

Proving processing for retail payments is ACI's biggest revenue producer accounting for 38% of the total. The company's billers services generates 23% of revenue. The online banking and community financial services segment which ACI is selling to Fiserv has contributed 21% of revenue.

Geographic ReachACI generates some 60% of its sales from the US with the EMEA and Asia-Pacific regions contributing 24% and about 8% respectively. The company saw revenues rise across all regions in 2015 but for the Americas outside the US.

Sales and MarketingThe company distributes products primarily through its own sales force but also utilizes third-party distributors in certain regions (primarily Asia and Latin America). Among those distributors are DataOne (Thailand) Optimisa (Chile) and Syscom Computer (China).

ACI counts18 of the top 20 banks worldwide as customers as well as more than 300 of the leading retailers.

Financial AnalysisACI has reported strong revenue growth since 2009 when sales fell amid the worst of the economic recession. Since then the company has had six straight years of revenue growth and eight years of rising profit.

In 2015 revenue increase 3% to $1.05 billion from $1.02 billion in 2014. A 9% rise in EMEA sales due to license and hosting revenue paced the company followed by a 2% gain in the US. The US revenue was lifted by incremental revenue from the ReD fraud product hosting and services revenue.

Net income bumped up a robust 26% on the higher revenue and lower costs.

Cash flow from operations was $183 million in 2015 up 23% from 2014.

Strategy

The sale of the community banking business clears the way for ACI to focus on software products and SaaS-based serivces for real-time electronic and eCommerce payments. The company is targeting those services to large financial institutions and enablers retailers and billers where the company said is where high growth opportunities are. The PAY.ON acquisition is part of that strategy.

Mergers and Acquisitions>

In 2015 ACI acquired PAY.ON a Munich Germany-based provider of eCommerce payment gateway services for $200 million. PAY.ON has a white label global payment gateway product for payment services providers and acquirers. PAY.ON's solution features connectivity to more than 300 alternative payment methods and card acquirers in more than 160 countries. The company brings eCommerce payment and Card Not Present capabilities to ACI.

HISTORY

Early History

Applied Communications Inc. (ACI) was formed by computer programmer James Cody and two other men in 1975. ACI's electronic funds software for banks seemed to be so ahead of its time that Cody made one successful sales call in mismatched shoes. The company went public in 1983. Combining its software with Tandem computers also aided ACI's fortunes. ACI was acquired by Baby Bell U S WEST in 1986; it then formed ACIL a joint venture with Sema Group. In 1991 Tandem Computers (later acquired by Compaq which was itself bought by Hewlett-Packard) bought ACI and ACIL.

Management led by president and CEO William Fisher bought the units in 1993. The company changed its name to Transaction Systems Architects (TSA) in 1994 and went public again the next year.

In the mid-1990s the company went on a buying spree. It acquired Open Systems Solutions a maker of Windows NT-based payment management software in 1996. The next year TSA expanded its presence in Europe by buying the software and service division of Italian firm Banksiel. With the acquisitions of Smart Card Integrators and Media Integration which were among TSA's half-dozen 1998 purchases the company further expanded its smart card product expertise.

In 1999 TSA bought SDM International a provider of electronic payment and electronic data interchange software. That year the company acquired and restructured Insession a maker of ICE network connectivity software. In 2000 TSA filed to spin off the subsidiary renamed Insession Technologies in a public stock offering (plans which were shelved in 2001 amid a weakening economy).

In 2001 TSA acquired MessagingDirect a provider of software for the delivery and processing of electronic statements and bills. The following year the company sold its Regency Systems subsidiary a provider of software for community banks to S1 Corporation.

The company bought S2 Systems a provider of electronic payments software with operations in Europe the Middle East and the Asia/Pacific region in 2005. Later that year the company implemented a reorganization which combined three of its subsidiaries (ACI Worldwide Intranet Worldwide and Insession Technologies) into one organization operating under the ACI Worldwide name; in 2007 the company officially changed its name to ACI Worldwide.

In 2006 the company acquired P&H Solutions for $150 million. Later that year the company completed the divestiture of its e-Courier and Work-Point product lines.

Its 2007 purchase of Visual Web Solutions expanded its presence in the Asia/Pacific region (and bolstered its product offerings by adding international trade finance and Web-based cash management capabilities) while its acquisition that year of Stratasoft Sdn. Bhd. added electronic payment offerings in Malaysia.

In 2009 the company purchased UK-based Euronet Essentis Limited a division of Euronet Worldwide that provided payment products and services for card issuing and merchant acquisition. ACI also began selling its products directly in some international markets instead of relying on distributors for sales as it had in the past.

EXECUTIVES

President and CEO, Philip G. (Phil) Heasley, age 66, $700,000 total compensation

Group President Customer Management and Maintenance, Daniel J. (Dan) Frate, age 55, $400,000 total compensation

EVP and Chief Administrative Officer, Dennis P. Byrnes, age 52, $310,000 total compensation

SEVP and Chief of Technology, Tony Scotto

EVP and Chief Risk Officer, David N. Morem, age 58, $275,000 total compensation

EVP Treasurer and Corporate Development Officer, Craig A. Maki, age 49, $275,000 total compensation

SEVP and CFO, Scott W. Behrens, age 44, $340,000 total compensation

Group President ACI On Demand, Carolyn B. Homberger, $275,000 total compensation

EVP Global Markets and Strategic Products, Craig Saks

Vice President Americas Sales Operations and Planning, Cliff (Clifford) Elam

Vice President Human Resources Business Partner, Shirley (Shirl) Guidroz

Senior Vice President and Chief Human Resources Officer, Ron (Ronnie) Kitlas

Vice President Engineering, Raj Vaidyanathan

Executive Vice President Global Markets And Product, Dan (Danny) Frate

Vice President Product Management, Vivian (Viv) Jimenez

Vice President Americas Customer Management and Sales Operations, Ann (Annie) Adams

Vice President Enterprise Risk Management, Brad (Brady) Mullman

Vice President Software Engineering, Paul (Pauly) Mureev

Vice President Software Engineering, Steven (Steve) Kilby

Vice President Finance, Ashley (Ash) Crandall

Chairman, Harlan F. Seymour, age 67

Auditors: Deloitte & Touche LLP

LOCATIONS

HQ: ACI Worldwide Inc
  3520 Kraft Rd, Suite 300, Naples, FL 34105
Phone: 239 403-4600
Web: www.aciworldwide.com

PRODUCTS/OPERATIONS

2015 Sales

	$ mil.	% of total
Licensing	251.2	24
Maintenance fees	241.9	23
Services	106.8	10
Hosting	446.1	43
Total	**1,046.0**	**100**

2015 Sales by Productline

	% of total
Retail payment processing	38
Online Banking and community financial services	21
Billers	23
Wholesale baking payments	4
Payment fraud management	3
Tools and infrastructure	4
Card and merchant management	7
Total	**100**

Selected Service Areas

Online banking and cash management
Payment fraud detection
Retail
Retail banking payments
Tools and infrastructure
Wholesale banking payments

COMPETITORS

Fair Isaac	Ingenico Corp.
Fidelity National Information Services	Intuit Financial Services
First Data	Total System Services
Fiserv	VeriFone
Fundtech	

HISTORICAL FINANCIALS

Company Type: Public

Income Statement

FYE: December 31

	REVENUE ($ mil.)	NET INCOME ($ mil.)	NET PROFIT MARGIN	EMPLOYEES
12/15	1,045.9	85.4	8.2%	4,576.0
12/14	1,016.1	67.5	6.6%	4,472.0
12/13	864.9	63.8	7.4%	4,329.0
12/12	666.5	48.8	7.3%	3,530.0
12/11	465.1	45.8	9.9%	2,131.0
Annual Growth	22.5%	16.8%	—	21.1%

2015 Year-End Financials

Debt ratio: 47.1%
Return on equity: 13.8%
Cash ($ mil.): 102.2
Current ratio: 0.99
Long-term debt ($ mil.): 843.2

No. of shares (mil.): 119.0
Dividends
Yield: —
Payout: —
Market value ($ mil.): 2,547.0

	STOCK PRICE ($) FY Close	P/E High/Low	PER SHARE ($) Earnings	Dividends	Book Value
12/15	21.40	35 24	0.72	0.00	5.50
12/14	20.17	110 29	0.58	0.00	5.03
12/13	65.00	119 79	0.53	0.00	4.66
12/12	43.69	111 67	0.41	0.00	4.52
12/11	28.64	83 55	0.45	0.00	3.14
Annual Growth	(7.0%)	— —	12.7%	—	15.0%

Acorda Therapeutics Inc

Acorda Therapeutics hopes its products really get on your nerves. The company is developing prescription drugs that aim to restore neurological function for patients with central nervous system disorders. The company's marketed drugs include Ampyra which enhances conduction in nerves damaged from multiple sclerosis (MS); Zanaflex a muscle spasm controller; and Qutenza which treats post-shingles nerve pain. Acorda is working with Biogen to market Ampyra outside the US. Acorda's other drug candidates include potential new therapies for MS and other central nervous system disorders as well as cardiac conditions.

Operations

Sales of commercial products have helped Acorda increase its product revenues in recent years with Ampyra as the company's main breadwinner that the firm hopes will drive growth in future years. The drug is the first to improve the functionality of damaged nerve fibers; other MS treatments generally treat symptoms or slow its progression. Biogen holds rights to market Ampyra outside of the US and pays royalties to Acorda on the drug's sales. Biogen has gained approval for Ampyra (known internationally as Fampyra) in markets including Australia Canada Israel and the European Union.

Zanaflex on the other hand has seen dwindling sales as the capsules have generic competition. (Zanaflex tablets are still under patent protection.) Acorda markets its own authorized generic capsule version with Allergan (formerly Actavis) in order to offset losses. In addition Acorda is stepping up efforts to broaden its product offerings.

The Qutenza patch which utilizes capsaicin from chili peppers is formulated to manage post-shingles nerve pain. The company has commercialization and development rights for the drug in the Americas but it may face competition after its marketing exclusivity in the US expired in 2016. Acorda acquired Qutenza from NeurogesX in 2013.

The company doesn't have its own manufacturing operations; it instead uses Patheon and Alkermes as its third-party manufacturers.

Acorda's candidate pipeline includes treatments for Parkinson's disease seizures and post-stroke walking deficits.

Geographic Reach

Acorda has locations in New York and Massachusetts.

Sales and Marketing

Acorda markets its products in the US through a direct sales force that targets neurologists and other specialists as well as primary care physicians specialty pharmacies hospitals managed care companies and drug distribution companies. It has some 90 sales representatives in all. Additionally the firm distributes products through specialty pharmacy providers.

Zanaflex capsules are distributed through wholesale distributors and Qutenza is delivered by specialty distributors Besse Medical and ASD Specialty Healthcare.

Financial Performance

Acorda's revenue has been climbing for the past five years. In 2015 it rose 23% to $492.7 million on higher product revenues which increased 25% that year. The company also recognizes license and royalty revenues for the sale of Fampyra outside of the US; combined those totaled some $20 million in 2015.

Net income which spiked in 2012 to $155 million declined the following year and has yet to recover. In fiscal 2015 net income fell 37% to $11.1 million as research and development cost of sales and other operating expenses increased.

Strategy

The company is focused on increasing sales of Ampyra. It is also looking to add new uses for Ampyra which was first approved as a therapy to improve the ability to walk in people who suffer from MS. The firm is developing the drug for additional MS-related functional impairment indications as well as for potential use in cerebral palsy and chronic stroke treatment.

In its internal R&D programs Acorda is exploring applications for its nerve and tissue repair technologies in cardiology and neurology fields. For instance in addition to the Ampyra development programs the company has candidates for treatment of spinal cord injury stroke epilepsy and heart failure as well as a new potential treatment for MS.

Mergers and Acquisitions

In 2016 Acorda agreed to buy Biotie Therapies a Finland-based biotech firm with an advanced clinical-stage program for the treatment of Parkinson's disease. Biotie's San Francisco operations will be maintained after the acquisition; the future of its headquarters in Finland will be decided later on.

Company Background

The company was founded by CEO Ron Cohen in 1995 to develop therapies for multiple sclerosis and other neurological conditions.

EXECUTIVES

President CEO and Director, Ron Cohen, age 60, $768,750 total compensation
Chief Scientific Officer, Andrew R. Blight, age 65, $404,467 total compensation
Chief of Business Operations and Principal Accounting Officer, David Lawrence, age 58, $293,683 total compensation
President International General Counsel and Corporate Secretary, Jane Wasman, age 59, $552,408 total compensation
EVP Corporate Communications, Tierney Saccavino
EVP Human Resources, Denise J. Duca
Chief Commercial Officer, Lauren M. Sabella, age 55, $407,750 total compensation
CTO and Site Head, Richard P. (Rick) Batycky, age 48
Chief Business Development Officer and Financial Planning and Analysis and Investor Relations, Andrew A. Hindman, age 43
Vice President Business Development, Soon Lee
Vice President Trade Relations and Operations, Tara (Tar) Stevens
Assistant Treasurer, Elizabeth Keating
Auditors: Ernst & Young LLP

LOCATIONS

HQ: Acorda Therapeutics Inc
420 Saw Mill River Road, Ardsley, NY 10502
Phone: 914 347-4300   **Fax:** 914 347-4560
Web: www.acorda.com

PRODUCTS/OPERATIONS

2015 Sales

	$ mil.	% of total
Product sales	466.1	94
Royalty	17.5	4
License	9.1	2
Total	**492.7**	**100**

COMPETITORS

Allergan plc	Cephalon
Alseres Pharmaceuticals	Cytokinetics
	InVivo Therapeutics
Apotex	Meda Pharmaceuticals
Bayer HealthCare Pharmaceuticals	Mylan
	Novartis
Bayhill	Sanofi
BioMarin Pharmaceutical	Shire
	Teva
Biogen	Upsher-Smith
Catalyst Pharmaceutical	

HISTORICAL FINANCIALS

Company Type: Public

Income Statement

FYE: December 31

	REVENUE ($ mil.)	NET INCOME ($ mil.)	NET PROFIT MARGIN	EMPLOYEES
12/15	492.6	11.0	2.2%	535.0
12/14	401.4	17.6	4.4%	489.0
12/13	336.4	16.4	4.9%	421.0
12/12	305.8	154.9	50.7%	378.0
12/11	292.2	30.6	10.5%	328.0
Annual Growth	13.9%	(22.5%)	—	13.0%

2015 Year-End Financials

Debt ratio: 26.6%
Return on equity: 1.9%
Cash ($ mil.): 153.2
Current ratio: 4.98
Long-term debt ($ mil.): 296.5

No. of shares (mil.): 42.9
Dividends
Yield: —
Payout: —
Market value ($ mil.): 1,839.0

	STOCK PRICE ($) FY Close	P/E High/Low		PER SHARE ($) Earnings	Dividends	Book Value
12/15	42.78	171	99	0.25	0.00	14.03
12/14	40.87	96	65	0.42	0.00	12.90
12/13	29.20	99	61	0.39	0.00	10.77
12/12	24.86	7	6	3.84	0.00	9.70
12/11	23.84	42	24	0.76	0.00	5.22
Annual Growth	15.7%	—	—	(24.3%)	—	28.0%

Adeptus Health Inc

Auditors: KPMG LLP

LOCATIONS

HQ: Adeptus Health Inc
2941 Lake Vista Drive, Lewisville, TX 75067
Phone: 972 899-6666
Web: www.adhc.com

HISTORICAL FINANCIALS

Company Type: Public

Income Statement

FYE: December 31

	REVENUE ($ mil.)	NET INCOME ($ mil.)	NET PROFIT MARGIN	EMPLOYEES
12/15	364.6	13.2	3.6%	3,202.0
12/14	210.6	(3.3)	—	1,869.0
12/13	102.8	(2.9)	—	993.0
12/12	72.6	3.2	4.4%	0.0
Annual Growth	71.3%	60.4%	—	—

2015 Year-End Financials

Debt ratio: 24.5%
Return on equity: 18.8%
Cash ($ mil.): 16.0
Current ratio: 2.00
Long-term debt ($ mil.): 121.2
No. of shares (mil.): 20.7
Dividends
  Yield: —
  Payout: —
Market value ($ mil.): 1,132.0

	STOCK PRICE ($) FY Close	P/E High/Low		PER SHARE ($) Earnings	Dividends	Book Value
12/15	54.52	111	29	1.09	0.00	4.43
12/14	37.40	—	—	(0.34)	0.00	2.33
12/13	0.00	—	—	(0.00)	0.00	(0.00)
Annual Growth	—	—	—	—	—	—

Aerocentury Corp.

With a high-flyin' inventory AeroCentury leases used turboprop aircraft and engines to domestic and foreign regional airlines and other commercial customers. The company buys equipment from an airline and then either leases it back to the seller buys assets already under lease and assumes the obligations of the seller or makes a purchase and then immediately enters into a new lease with a third-party lessee (when it has a customer committed to a lease). Typically lessees are responsible for any maintenance costs. AeroCentury owns over 40 aircraft mainly deHavilland and Fokker models. Almost 90% of the company's lease revenues come from airlines headquartered outside the US.

In a deviation from the norm high oil prices have actually been helping AeroCentury. Turboprop aircraft are more fuel efficient than jets so demand for their use on shorter routes has increased. Still the company has felt the pangs of decreased demand. Regional carriers often lease aircraft from AeroCentury to expand routes; however air travel took a nosedive in 2008 and 2009 and the demand for leased aircraft went with it. In other cases customers chose not to renew their leases.

AeroCentury was formed by the consolidation of the aircraft equipment leasing and management partnerships JetFleet Aircraft and JetFleet Aircraft II. AeroCentury is managed by JetFleet Management which in turn is overseen by AeroCentury officers.

Chairman and president Neal Crispin and SVP Toni Perazzo each own 22% of AeroCentury. JetFleet Holding Corp. also holds about a 22% stake in the company.

EXECUTIVES

Vp Finance, Harold Lyons
Vice President Operations, Thomas (Thom) Cunningham
Vice President Corporate Devel, Brian (Bri) Ginna
Vice President, Maurice (Maury) Takahashi
Auditors: BDO USA, LLP

LOCATIONS

HQ: Aerocentury Corp.
1440 Chapin Avenue, Suite 310, Burlingame, CA 94010
Phone: 650 340-1888
Web: www.aerocentury.com

COMPETITORS

AAR Corp.	GE Capital Aviation Services
AIG	
Airbus Group	ILFC
Aviation Capital Group	Jetscape
Boeing Capital	Saab AB
Bombardier	Willis Lease

HISTORICAL FINANCIALS

Company Type: Public

Income Statement

FYE: December 31

	REVENUE ($ mil.)	NET INCOME ($ mil.)	NET PROFIT MARGIN	EMPLOYEES
12/15	38.5	6.4	16.7%	0.0
12/14	28.7	(11.2)	—	0.0
12/13	32.2	3.2	10.0%	0.0
12/12	29.3	5.1	17.7%	0.0
12/11	24.5	(1.4)	—	0.0
Annual Growth	11.9%	—	—	—

2015 Year-End Financials

Debt ratio: 59.4%
Return on equity: 16.9%
Cash ($ mil.): 2.7
Current ratio: 4.29
Long-term debt ($ mil.): 107.6
No. of shares (mil.): 1.5
Dividends
  Yield: —
  Payout: —
Market value ($ mil.): 20.0

	STOCK PRICE ($) FY Close	P/E High/Low		PER SHARE ($) Earnings	Dividends	Book Value
12/15	12.70	3	2	4.17	0.00	26.35
12/14	8.71	—	—	(7.32)	0.00	22.58
12/13	17.18	11	7	2.03	0.00	31.81
12/12	14.09	4	2	3.32	0.00	29.73
12/11	6.15	—	—	(0.94)	0.00	26.37
Annual Growth	19.9%	—	—	—	—	(0.0%)

Affiliated Managers Group Inc.

Affiliated Managers Group (AMG) is an asset management company that owns interests in more than 30 boutique investment management firms in North America Europe and Asia. Together the firm's affiliates manage nearly $630 billion in assets and offer more than 500 investment products including more than 200 mutual funds. AMG typically acquires majority stakes in its affiliates which cater to institutional investors and wealthy individuals. The structure allows affiliates to retain partial ownership of their firms and operate with relative autonomy. AMG usually allocates a percentage of revenues to affiliates for operating expenses such as compensation.

OperationsAMG operates three business segments organized by distribution channel including: the Mutual Fund segment which generated 50% of its revenue during 2015; Institutional (39% of revenue); and High Net Worth (11% of revenue).Geographic Reach

AMG's main offices are in West Palm Beach Florida and London. Its other offices are in Conshohocken Pennsylvania; Greenwich Connecticut; Chicago; Sydney Australia; Toronto; Zurich; Hong Kong; and Dubai. The firm generated about 40% of its revenue from business outside of the US during 2015.Sales and MarketingAMG's Mutual Fund segment provides advisory or sub-advisory services to active return-focused mutual funds UCITS and other retail products. The firm's Institutional segment serves large institutional investors around the world including foundations endowments sovereign wealth funds and corporate and municipal retirement plans. The firm's High Net Worth segment advises high net worth and ultra-high net worth individuals families trusts foundations endowments and retirement plans.The firm distributes its products and services through its direct sales team or through consultants from around the world.

Financial Performance

Fueled by a rising stock market and a growing investor base AMG has nearly doubled its assets under management since 2011 –from $327.5 million to $611.3 million at the end of 2015 —which has led strong fee and advisory income growth over the past few years. The firm's annual revenue has risen 45% over that period while its profit has more than tripled.AMG's revenue dipped 1% to $2.48 billion during 2015 however mostly as its assets under management tumbled 5% to $611.3 million and partly as its clients switched to investments with lower expense ratios –both factors led to lower asset-based fee income. The firm collected 4% less in fees from Institutional clients and collected 9% more in fees from High-Net-Worth clients. Mutual Fund client fees were flat for the year.Despite the small revenue decline in 2015 the firm's net income jumped 14% to $516 million mostly thanks to a sharp decline in sub-advisory and distribution expenses in the Mutual Fund distribution channel and lower acquisition-related professional fees. AMG's operating cash levels fell 13% to $1.2 billion for the year due to unfavorable working capital changes related to a decrease in payables accrued liabilities and other liabilities as it made more accrued compensation and distribution payments than in 2014.

Strategy

AMG adds to its funds and strategies offerings mainly by acquiring smaller investment firms (including traditional alternative and wealth management firms) from around the world with the goal of attracting new investors and their capital. The firm also looks to help its affiliate firms grow in value by providing a centralized source of support for strategy marketing distribution product development and operations.

Mergers and Acquisitions

In June 2014 AMG acquired Louisville Kentucky-based River Road Asset Management from Aviva Investors North America Holdings Inc. (a subsidiary of Aviva plc). In March 2014 the firm purchased a majority equity stake in SouthernSun Asset Management LLC. With some $6 billion in assets under management SouthernSun managed long-term concentrated portfolios through a fundamental research-intensive investment process.

To further expand in the Asian market AMG in April 2014 purchased a majority equity interest in Veritas Asset Management LLC. With offices in London and Hong Kong Veritas manages approximately £10 billion ($17 billion) across both funds and segregated portfolios for institutional and retail investors in the UK and around the world.Company BackgroundIn early 2014 the company rebranded its US domestic retail distribution business as AMG Funds and the alignment of Aston Asset Management (acquired in 2010) within the AMG Funds business by acquiring the remaining equity of Aston that it didn't already own. (AMG purchased a majority interest in Chicago-based Aston Asset Management by acquiring Aston's parent company Highbury Financial. Aston is the principal adviser to the Aston Funds a family of about 25 mutual funds with some $6 billion of assets.)In July 2012 AMG acquired a majority stake in Austin Texas-based Yacktman Asset Management with approximately $17 billion of assets under management.

EXECUTIVES

President and COO, Nathaniel Dalton, age 49, $500,000 total compensation
Chairman and CEO, Sean M. Healey, age 54, $750,000 total compensation
CFO, Jay C. Horgen, age 46, $500,000 total compensation
EVP and Head Global Distribution, Andrew Dyson, $403,550 total compensation
EVP and General Counsel, David M. Billings, $400,000 total compensation
Auditors: PricewaterhouseCoopers LLP

LOCATIONS

HQ: Affiliated Managers Group Inc.
777 South Flagler Drive, West Palm Beach, FL 33401
Phone: 800 345-1100
Web: www.amg.com

PRODUCTS/OPERATIONS

2015 Sales by segment

	$ mil.	% of total
Mutual funds	1,238.2	50
Institutional	979.4	39
High-net-worth clients	266.9	11
Total	**2,484.5**	**100**

Selected Affiliates

AQR Capital Management Holdings LLC
Artemis Investment Management LLP (UK)
Aston Asset Management LLC
Beutel Goodman & Company Ltd.
BlueMountain Capital Management LLC

Chicago Equity Partners LLC
Deans Knight Capital Management Ltd. (Canada)
Essex Investment Management Company LLC
First Quadrant L.P.
Foyston Gordon & Payne Inc. (Canada)
Friess Associates LLC
Frontier Capital Management Company LLC
Gannett Welsh & Kotler LLC
Genesis Asset Managers LLP (UK)
Harding Loevner LP
J.M. Hartwell L.P.
Managers Investment Group LLC
Montrusco Bolton Investments Inc. (Canada)
Pantheon (UK)
The Renaissance Group LLC
Systematic Financial Management L.P.
Third Avenue Management LLC
TimesSquare Capital Management LLC
Trilogy Global Advisors
Tweedy Browne Company LLC
ValueAct Capital Management L.P.
Welch & Forbes LLC

COMPETITORS

AllianceBernstein	Nuveen
Asset Alliance	Old Mutual (US)
BlackRock	T. Rowe Price
Conning	The Vanguard Group
FMR	U.S. Trust
Federated Investors	Virtus Investment
GAMCO Investors	Partners
Neuberger Berman	

HISTORICAL FINANCIALS

Company Type: Public

Income Statement

FYE: December 31

	REVENUE ($ mil.)	NET INCOME ($ mil.)	NET PROFIT MARGIN	EMPLOYEES
12/15	2,484.5	516.0	20.8%	3,200.0
12/14	2,510.9	452.1	18.0%	2,900.0
12/13	2,188.8	360.5	16.5%	2,500.0
12/12	1,805.5	174.0	9.6%	2,230.0
12/11	1,704.8	164.9	9.7%	2,020.0
Annual Growth	**9.9%**	**33.0%**	**—**	**12.2%**

2015 Year-End Financials

Debt ratio: 20.4%	No. of shares (mil.): 55.8
Return on equity: 18.8%	Dividends
Cash ($ mil.): 563.8	Yield: —
Current ratio: 1.79	Payout: —
Long-term debt ($ mil.): 1,589.6	Market value ($ mil.): 8,915.0

	STOCK PRICE ($) FY Close	P/E High/Low	PER SHARE ($) Earnings	Dividends	Book Value
12/15	159.76	24 15	9.28	0.00	50.84
12/14	212.24	26 22	8.01	0.00	48.11
12/13	216.88	32 19	6.55	0.00	39.60
12/12	130.15	39 29	3.28	0.00	38.67
12/11	95.95	35 23	3.11	0.00	34.62
Annual Growth	**13.6%**	**— —**	**31.4%**	**—**	**10.1%**

AG Mortgage Investment Trust Inc

AG Mortgage Investment Trust invests in acquires and manages a diverse portfolio of residential mortgage assets as well as other real estate-related securities and financial assets. Residential mortgage-backed securities backed by US government agencies including Fannie Mae Freddie Mac and Ginnie Mae known as "Agency RMBS" make up about 70% of the mortgage real estate investment trust's (REIT) portfolio. Credit assets including RMBS not issued or backed by the government account for most of the rest. Formed in 2011 by executives of investment adviser Angelo Gorden looking to profit from a recovery in the US mortgage bond market the mortgage REIT is managed by a subsidiary of Angelo Gordon.

IPO

The REIT went public in June 2011 with an offering worth $110 million far less than the $300 million it initially planned on raising.

Strategy

In the months after its IPO the REIT primarily focused on investing in Agency RMBS. However as market conditions and US monetary policy evolved the firm has focused more on credit assets of late. Indeed the REIT has gradually shifted its deployment of capital to its credit portfolio increasing its allocation as a percentage of assets from 9% to 22% to nearly 35% as of December 31 2011 2012 and 2013 respectively.

In January 2014 the mortgage REIT closed on a $10 million commercial real estate investment secured by a hotel property.

Financial Performance

AG Mortgage reported net interest income of $125.4 million in 2013 up from $81.4 million and $17.1 million in 2012 and 2011 respectively. However substantial losses on other income sources and rising expenses led to a loss of $31.6 million in 2013 versus a profit of $135 million in 2012. Cash flow from operations has risen steeply since the REIT's inception from $15.4 million in 2011 to $130.8 million in 2013.

The REIT's portfolio was valued at $3.4 billion at the end of 2013.

EXECUTIVES

CFO Principal Accounting Officer and Treasurer, Brian C. Sigman, age 38, $150,000 total compensation
Chairman and CEO, David N. Roberts, age 54
President and Chief Investment Officer, Jonathan Lieberman, age 53
General Counsel and Secretary, Raul E. Moreno, age 35, $28,493 total compensation
Auditors: PricewaterhouseCoopers LLP

LOCATIONS

HQ: AG Mortgage Investment Trust Inc
245 Park Avenue, 26th Floor, New York, NY 10167
Phone: 212 692-2000

COMPETITORS

ARMOUR Residential REIT	Galiot Capital
	Hatteras Financial
Annaly Capital Management	MFA Financial
	MFResidential
Bimini Capital Management	PIMCO REIT
CYS Investments	PennyMac Mortgage
Capstead Mortgage	Provident Mortgage Capital

Company Type: Public

Income Statement

FYE: December 31

	REVENUE ($ mil.)	NET INCOME ($ mil.)	NET PROFIT MARGIN	EMPLOYEES
12/15	141.2	13.8	9.8%	0.0
12/14	141.5	109.4	77.3%	0.0
12/13	151.0	(31.5)	—	0.0
12/12	96.3	134.9	140.0%	0.0
12/11	18.7	18.9	101.2%	0.0
Annual Growth	65.7%	(7.6%)	—	—

2015 Year-End Financials

Debt ratio: 13.4%
Return on equity: 1.9%
Cash ($ mil.): 46.2
Current ratio: 0.06
Long-term debt ($ mil.): 426.9

No. of shares (mil.): 28.2
Dividends
Yield: 17.7%
Payout: 22,750.0%
Market value ($ mil.): 363.0

	STOCK PRICE ($) FY Close	P/E High/Low		PER SHARE ($) Earnings	Dividends	Book Value
12/15	12.84	1952	1258	0.01	2.28	23.58
12/14	18.57	6	5	3.37	2.40	25.81
12/13	15.64	—	—	(1.61)	2.80	24.83
12/12	23.48	3	3	7.18	2.97	29.47
12/11	20.13	7	5	3.20	1.10	20.61
Annual Growth	(10.6%)	—	—	(76.4%)	19.9%	3.4%

Agree Realty Corp.

Shopping sprees really agree with Agree Realty. The self-managed real estate investment trust (REIT) owns develops and manages retail real estate primarily freestanding big-box properties. It owns around 280 retail properties spanning 5.5 million square feet of leasable space across 40-plus states. Most of its tenants are national retailers with its largest tenants being Wal-Mart Wawa and Walgreens. The REIT typically acquires either property portfolios or single-asset net lease retail properties (worth between $2 million and $30 million per asset) with creditworthy tenants. It was founded in 1979 by CEO Richard Agree.

OperationsThe REIT's portfolio was made up of 278 properties in 41 states at the end of 2015 which spanned 5.2 million square feet of gross leasable space. All but three of these properties were net lease properties that contributed 97.6% to the REIT's rental income. The three others were community shopping centers.Geographic Reach-While Agree Realty had properties in 41 US states during 2015 about 20% of its rental revenue came from properties in Michigan while another 20% came from properties based in Florida Ohio and Texas. All other regions each accounted for less than 6% of its revenue.Sales and MarketingThe REIT mostly leases properties to retailers such as pharmacies restaurants general merchandisers apparel retailers grocery stores warehouse clubs sporting goods stores health & fitness centers convenience stores and dollar stores among others.Agree Realty's largest tenant by revenue continues to be Walgreens which leased 32 properties and contributed 17.2% to the REIT's total rental income during 2015. Its four next largest tenants that year were Wal-Mart (5.5% of rental income) Wawa (3.4%) CVS (3.4%) and Academy

Sports (2.8%).Financial PerformanceAgree Realty's annual revenues have more than doubled since 2011 mostly as rent-boosting acquisitions have increased its gross leasable square footage by 46% while nearly tripling its property count from 87 to 278 at the end of 2015. The REIT's net income has nearly quadrupled over the period as it's managed to keep a lid on rising operating expenses.The REIT's revenue climbed 31% to almost $70 million during 2015 mostly as its 150 property acquisitions made from 2014 through 2015 boosted minimum rental revenues. Its existing property rental income increased by 13% thanks to better tenant performance and higher rental rates.Strong revenue growth combined with $12.1 million in property sale gains in 2015 caused Agree Realty's net income to more than double to $39 million for the year. The company's operating cash levels jumped 28% to $44.7 million in 2015 mostly thanks to a spike in cash-denominated earnings from higher rental income.StrategyThe REIT typically acquires either property portfolios or single-asset net lease retail properties (worth between $2 million and $30 million per asset) with creditworthy tenants to diversify its portfolio of "industry-leading" retailers. Agree Realty normally holds onto its properties for long-term investment which is why it prefers to establish long-term leases and invest in capital improvements. Indeed at the end of 2015 the REIT's property portfolio boasted a 99.5% occupancy rate and a weighted average remaining lease term of 11.4 years.

EXECUTIVES

President CEO and Director, Joey Agree, age 38, $386,250 total compensation
COO, Laith Hermiz, age 45, $244,150 total compensation
EVP CFO and Secretary, Matthew M. Partridge
Chairman, Richard Agree, age 73
Auditors: Grant Thornton LLP

LOCATIONS

HQ: Agree Realty Corp.
70 E. Long Lake Road, Bloomfield Hills, MI 48304
Phone: 248 737-4190 **Fax:** 248 737-9110
Web: www.agreerealty.com

PRODUCTS/OPERATIONS

2015 sales

	in mil.	%of total
Minimum rents	64.3	92
operating cost reimbursement	5.3	8
Percentage rents	0.2	-
other income	0.2	-
Total	**70.0**	**100**

COMPETITORS

CBL & Associates Properties	Kimco Realty
DDR	Pennsylvania Real Estate
Equity One	Ramco-Gershenson
General Growth Properties	Simon Property Group
	Taubman Centers

Company Type: Public

Income Statement

FYE: December 31

	REVENUE ($ mil.)	NET INCOME ($ mil.)	NET PROFIT MARGIN	EMPLOYEES
12/15	69.9	39.0	55.8%	20.0
12/14	53.5	18.4	34.5%	14.0
12/13	43.5	19.6	45.2%	14.0
12/12	35.7	18.0	50.4%	14.0
12/11	36.3	9.5	26.3%	13.0
Annual Growth	17.8%	42.2%	—	11.4%

2015 Year-End Financials

Debt ratio: 40.3%
Return on equity: 9.7%
Cash ($ mil.): 2.7
Current ratio: 0.52
Long-term debt ($ mil.): 319.5

No. of shares (mil.): 20.6
Dividends
Yield: 5.4%
Payout: 86.6%
Market value ($ mil.): 701.0

	STOCK PRICE ($) FY Close	P/E High/Low		PER SHARE ($) Earnings	Dividends	Book Value
12/15	33.99	16	13	2.16	1.85	21.86
12/14	31.09	26	22	1.24	1.74	20.16
12/13	29.02	22	18	1.50	1.64	19.46
12/12	26.79	16	13	1.62	1.60	17.08
12/11	24.38	26	20	0.99	1.60	16.19
Annual Growth	8.7%	—	—	21.5%	3.6%	7.8%

Air Lease Corp

Air Lease doesn't really lease air unless of course you include the air inside the cabins of its fleet of airplanes. An aircraft leasing company Air Lease buys new and used commercial aircraft from manufacturers and airlines and then leases to airline carriers in Europe the Asia-Pacific region and the Americas. It owns a fleet of almost 240 aircraft comprised of 181 single-aisle narrowbody jet aircraft 40 twin-aisle widebody jet aircraft and 19 turboprop aircraft. In addition to leasing Air Lease also offers fleet management services such as lease management and sales.

Geographic Reach

Air Lease is based in Los Angeles and has airline customers throughout the world. Europe accounted for 32% of its net sales in 2015. Other markets included China (22%); Asia excluding China (19%); Central America South America and Mexico (10%); the Middle East and Africa (8%); the US and Canada (5%); and the Pacific Australia and New Zealand (4%).

Sales and Marketing

Its customers have included Air Canada; Sunwing Airlines; WestJet; AeroMexico; Aeromar; Interjet; Volaris; Hawaiian Airlines; Southwest Airlines; Spirit Airlines; Sun Country; United Continental Holdings; Liat Airline; and Caribbean-Airlines.

Financial Performance

Air Lease has experienced explosive growth over the years with revenues reaching a record-setting $1.22 billion in 2015. Profits also remained consistent hovering around the $255 million mark for both 2014 and 2015. The static profits for 2015 was attributed to about $72 million it paid in litigation settlement expenses. The company's cash from operating activities has gradually increased the last five years climbing by 9% from 2014 to 2015.

The historic growth for 2015 was fueled by an 18% spike in the rental of flight equipment. This was aided by the delivery of 51 additional aircraft all of which were leased at the time of delivery. Air Lease also enjoyed major growth in the key markets of the Middle East and Africa (89%); the Pacific Australia and New Zealand (52%) and China (21%).

Strategy

Although the largest portion of its fleet is leased to customers in Western Europe Air Lease is setting its sights on markets in the Asia-Pacific region Eastern Europe South America and the Middle East where it predicts the travel industry will grow the fastest in coming years. It has also targeted carriers in stable but slower-growing travel markets such as North America.

One way Air Lease has achieved impressive revenue growth over the years is by adding to its fleet size. In 2015 it purchased and took delivery of 51 aircraft and sold 24 aircraft ending the year with a total of 240 owned aircraft. During 2015 it increased its managed fleet by 12 aircraft ending the year with 29 aircraft in its managed fleet portfolio. (The company typically sells aircraft that are currently operated by an airline with multiple years of lease term remaining on the contract.)

Company Background

Air Lease went public in 2011. Udvar-Házy and other Air Lease used a significant portion of the proceeds raised to acquire additional aircraft and for general corporate purposes. With sufficient capital and financing already in place Air Lease has placed orders for some 150 new aircraft to be delivered by 2017. While most of its fleet will consist of Boeing and Airbus passenger airplanes the company has ordered similar aircraft manufactured by Embraer and turboprops from Avions de Transport Régional (ATR).

Udvar-Házy had co-founded ILFC now one of the largest aircraft leasing companies in the industry in the 1970s. He stayed on after AIG bought ILFC in the 1990s and continued to head the company until 2010 when he retired in the wake of the ongoing financial trouble that hit AIG in 2008. Udvar-Házy subsequently founded Air Lease with the help of institutional investors including some that were large shareholders prior to the IPO's filing (Ares Management which held an 11% stake; Leonard Green & Partners 11%; and Commonwealth Bank of Australia 10%). Udvar-Házy maintained a 7% stake in Air Lease in 2013.

EXECUTIVES

Executive Vice President Managing Director of Asia, Jie Chen
Senior Vice President, Toby Maccary
Executive Vice President of Marketing, Kishore Korde
Assistant Vice President and Assistant Controller, Sabrina (Brina) Lemmens
Executive Vice President General Counsel, Grant Levy
Executive Vice President Marketing, Marc H Baer
Assistant Vice President, Stephanie Brimmer
Assistant Vice President, Czar Vigil
Vice President Technical Asset Management, Pierce Chang
Executive Vice President and General Counsel Corporate Secretary and Chief Compliance Officer, Carol (Care) Forsyte
Assistant Vice President Human Resources, Courtney (Court) Mckeown

Vice President and Corporate Counsel, Jenny (Jen) Van Le
Assistant Vice President, Sara Evans
Executive Vice President, Alex Khatibi
Assistant Vice President Information Technology, Pablo Chavez
Treasurer, Aj Abedin
Auditors: KPMG LLP

LOCATIONS

HQ: Air Lease Corp
2000 Avenue of the Stars, Suite 1000N, Los Angeles, CA 90067
Phone: 310 553-0555
Web: www.airleasecorp.com

PRODUCTS/OPERATIONS

2015 Sales

	$ mil.	% of total
Rental of flight equipment	1,174.5	96
Aircraft sales trading and other	48.3	4
Total	**1,222.8**	**100**

COMPETITORS

AerCap	Fly Leasing
Aircastle	GE Capital Aviation
Aviation Capital Group	Services
Boeing Capital	ICON Capital
CIT Transportation	ILFC
Finance	

HISTORICAL FINANCIALS

Company Type: Public

Income Statement

FYE: December 31

	REVENUE ($ mil.)	NET INCOME ($ mil.)	NET PROFIT MARGIN	EMPLOYEES
12/15	1,222.8	253.3	20.7%	74.0
12/14	1,050.4	256.0	24.4%	65.0
12/13	858.6	190.4	22.2%	63.0
12/12	655.7	131.9	20.1%	52.0
12/11	336.7	53.2	15.8%	47.0
Annual Growth	38.0%	47.7%	—	12.0%

2015 Year-End Financials

Debt ratio: 62.4%
Return on equity: 8.7%
Cash ($ mil.): 156.6
Current ratio: 1.16
Long-term debt ($ mil.): 7,712.4

No. of shares (mil.): 102.5
Dividends
  Yield: 0.5%
  Payout: 7.2%
Market value ($ mil.): 3,434.0

	STOCK PRICE ($) FY Close	P/E High/Low		PER SHARE ($) Earnings	Dividends	Book Value
12/15	33.48	16	12	2.34	0.17	29.44
12/14	34.31	17	12	2.38	0.13	27.07
12/13	31.08	18	11	1.80	0.11	24.78
12/12	21.50	20	14	1.28	0.00	23.04
12/11	23.71	50	30	0.59	0.00	21.61
Annual Growth	9.0%	—	—	41.1%	—	8.0%

Air Methods Corp.

It's a bird it's a plane ... it's an ambulance! With a fleet of more than 400 medically equipped aircraft mainly helicopters Air Methods is the largest provider of emergency medical air-transportation services in the US. The company operates through three divisions. A community-based operating segment which represents roughly 85% of revenues offers transportation and in-flight medical care from hubs in some two dozen states. It also provides tourism operations around the Grand Canyon and Hawaiian Islands. The smallest division United Rotorcraft designs manufactures and installs aircraft medical-transport products.

Geographic ReachThe company has more than 300 bases of operations that serve 48 states in the US. It operates eight maintenance centers throughout the country and a national communications center.

OperationsThe company mainly provides air medical transportation services throughout the US and designs manufactures and installs medical aircraft interiors and other aerospace and medical transport products. It also provides tourism operations in and around the Grand Canyon and Hawaiian Islands.

Financial Performance

Air Methods has achieved extraordinary growth over the years with 2014 revenues peaking at the $1 billion mark for the first time in its history. Profits also climbed 52% from $62 million in 2013 to to a record-setting $95 million in 2014.

The historic growth was fueled by an explosion in tourism segment revenue —this segment more than doubled its revenue from 2013 to 2014. Air Methods also generated additional sales from new revenue generated from the addition of 41 new bases throughout the year.

Strategy

Business acquisitions are part of the company's strategy to gain market share. It in 2013 acquired Helicopter Consultants of Maui LLC (doing business as Blue Hawaiian Helicopters) for a cash purchase price of $67 million. The deal enhanced Air Methods' tourism segment and helped it to post milestone revenues during 2014.

EXECUTIVES

CEO and Director, Aaron D. Todd, age 54, $765,000 total compensation
President Sundance Helicopters, James (Jim) Greiner
President Domestic Air Medical Services, Michael D. Allen, $459,000 total compensation
VP Information Technology, Doni Perry
Director Operations, Dennis McCall
EVP Business Development, David M. Doerr, $408,000 total compensation
CFO and Treasurer, Peter P. Csapo
President Tourism Division, David Doerr
Senior Vice President Patient Business Services, Mark Keene
Senior Vice President General Counsel Corp, Crystal L (Cristy) Gordon
Senior Vice President, Jonathan (Jon) Collier
Vice President Clinical Services, Tina (Tin) Giangrasso
Vice President of Corporate Development, Craig (Craigy) Yale
Senior Vice President, Dave Richardson
Vice President Internal Audit, Elizabeth Womersley
Regional Vice President Hospital Based Services, Jeffery (Jeff) See
Senior Vice President, Sally Rodriguez
Senior Vice President Business Development, Howard Ragsdale
Vice President Safety, Mark (Marky) Rambis
Chairman, C. David Kikumoto, age 66
Auditors: KPMG LLP

LOCATIONS

HQ: Air Methods Corp.
7301 South Peoria, Englewood, CO 80112
Phone: 303 792-7400
Web: www.airmethods.com

PRODUCTS/OPERATIONS

2014 Sales

	$ mil.	% of total
AMS	863.9	85
Tourism	116.0	11
United Rotorcraft	36.2	4
Corporate Activities	86.0	0
Adjustments	(11.4)	-
Total	**1,004.8**	**100**

Fleets
AS 350
EC 135
EC 130
Bell 407
EC 145
Bell 429
BK 117
A-109
SA 365
Bell 222
Bell 430
Bell 206
MD 902
King Air
PC 12
Agusta 119Kx
Services
AirCom
Complete Billing Solutions
DirectCall
TAMMA
United Rotorcraft
LifeShield Alliance

COMPETITORS

Acadian Ambulance
  Service Inc.
Bristow Group Inc

CHC Group
Evergreen Holdings
PHI Inc.

HISTORICAL FINANCIALS

Company Type: Public

Income Statement

FYE: December 31

	REVENUE ($ mil.)	NET INCOME ($ mil.)	NET PROFIT MARGIN	EMPLOYEES
12/15	1,085.6	108.6	10.0%	4,798.0
12/14	1,004.7	94.8	9.4%	4,556.0
12/13	881.6	62.3	7.1%	4,227.0
12/12	850.8	93.1	10.9%	3,961.0
12/11	660.5	46.5	7.1%	3,935.0
Annual Growth	**13.2%**	**23.6%**	**—**	**5.1%**

2015 Year-End Financials

Debt ratio: 44.9%	No. of shares (mil.): 39.0
Return on equity: 20.7%	Dividends
Cash ($ mil.): 5.8	Yield: —
Current ratio: 3.16	Payout: —
Long-term debt ($ mil.): 639.9	Market value ($ mil.): 1,635.0

	STOCK PRICE ($) FY Close	P/E High/Low	PER SHARE ($) Earnings	Dividends	Book Value
12/15	41.93	20 12	2.73	0.00	14.71
12/14	44.03	24 17	2.46	0.00	12.03
12/13	58.26	38 21	1.54	0.00	9.42
12/12	36.91	50 33	2.39	7.00	7.73
12/11	84.45	72 41	1.21	0.00	7.53
Annual Growth	**(16.1%)**	**— —**	**22.6%**	**—**	**18.2%**

Akamai Technologies Inc

For companies who provide and use cloud computing Akamai moves the data back and forth. The company's hardware software and algorithms enables corporations and government agencies to deliver digital content and applications such as ads business transaction tools streaming video and websites over the Internet. It also offers applications that supply network data feeds and website analytics to customers. With a network of more than 107000 servers in 102 countries around the world Akamai analyzes and manages Web traffic transmitting content from servers that are geographically closest to end users. In addition to its 11 US offices the company has more than 25 international locations. Customers include Apple Hitachi and SAP.

Operations

The company has five different core products – AQUA Web Solutions AURA Network Solutions KONA Security Solutions SOLA Media Solutions and TERRA Enterprise Solutions – that provide application and cloud performance services digital media and software distribution and storage website optimization and security tools.

For example AQUA WEB Solutions speeds up applications using compression connection optimization dynamic caching and routing technologies. It is tailored for such online applications as airline reservation systems course planning tools customer order processing and human resources.

KONA is a suite of services and software used to guard against data theft and other Web attacks while SOLA enables streaming live or on-demand HD video to online viewers across several technologies including Adobe Flash Microsoft Silverlight and Apple iOS.

Geographic Reach

Akamai operates from about 40 offices in 25 countries across the Americas Asia and Europe. The US however is its largest market accounting for more than 70% of sales. The company has about a dozen US locations.

Sales and Marketing

The comp any sells its products through a direct sales force as well as more than 100 channel partners such as AT&T IBM Verizon and Spain's top telco Telefonica. It does business with a large number of private and public sector customers; no one accounts for more than 10% of sales.

Customers include Apple BMW Bombay Stock Exchange IBM Qualcomm Salesforce.com Turner Sports USAA and Virgin America.

Financial Performance

Overall sales grew almost 24% in 2014 reaching a record $1.9 billion. The company saw continued strong demand for services across its operations and geographies. The acquisition of Prolexic completed in 2014 also contributed to the healthy revenue increase. Akamai notched increased sales of incremental services to existing customers and traffic in excess of committed amounts as well as one-time events for specific customers.

Net income increased 14% to $334 million in 2014 from 2013 powered by the higher revenue.

Strategy

Akamai is testing a service that could improve viewing video on mobile devices. The Predictive Video Over Cellular product forecasts cellular traffic loads and viewer preferences and analyzes content recommendation engines. It pre-slots selected HD videos on the subscriber's mobile device. The company has pumped up its research and development spending in the past three years. R&D spending was $125 million in 2014 $94 million in 2013 and $74.7 million.

In 2014 Akamai formed a partnership with China Telecom Corporation cloud division CT Cloud. The deal should strengthen Akamai's China content delivery network (CDN) offering for accelerating content from global customers to Chinese consumers.

Mergers and Acquisitions

Akamai uses acquisitions to supplement its internal product development efforts particularly in the area of optimizing Web page and data delivery to the growing number of mobile devices tapping the Internet.

In 2014 Akamai completed the acquisition of Prolexic Technologies Inc. for $392 million. Prolexic develops security products for protecting websites data centers and enterprise IP applications and strengthens Akamai's security portfolio.

Akamai acquired Xerocole a provider of recursive DNS functionality in a cash transaction in 2015. The deal should allow Akamai to expand its DNS product portfolio.

EXECUTIVES

EVP; General Counsel and Secretary, Melanie Haratunian, age 56, $399,192 total compensation
President Products and Development, Rick M. McConnell, age 50, $499,031 total compensation
CEO, Tom (Tom) Leighton, age 59
President Worldwide Operations, Robert W. (Bob) Hughes, age 49, $499,054 total compensation
SVP and General Manager Web Experience Division, Michael M. (Mike) Afergan
VP and General Manager Carrier Products Division, Mick Scully
SVP and CIO, Kumud Kalia
EVP Platform Division, Robert Blumofe
EVP and CFO, Jim Benson, $392,731 total compensation
SVP and General Manager Americas, Jim Ebzery
SVP and General Manager APJ, Sanjay Singh
SVP and General Manager Emerging Products Division, Willie Tejada
SVP and General Manager Media Products Division, Bill Wheaton
SVP and General ManagerEMEA, Doug Tilford
SVP Networks and Chief Network Architect, Noam Freedman
SVP and General Manager Security Division, Stuart Scholly
Vice President..Human Resources Operations, Susan (Sue) LaPointe
Vice President Americas Channels, Mark Rogers
Senior Vice President And GM Web Experience Business Unit, Mike (Mikey) Afergan
Senior Vice Presdient Engineering, Harald Prokop
Vice President of Network Security Engineering, Louis (Lou) Suchy
Vice President, John (Jack) Summers
Vice President..Product Management and Operations, Scott (Scotty) Brown
Vice President Solutions Engineering Media Division, Dev Gupta
Vice President Sales, Gene (Genie) Meyer
Vice Chairman, Paul L. Sagan, age 57
Chairman, George H. Conrades, age 78
Auditors: PricewaterhouseCoopers LLP

HQ: Akamai Technologies Inc
150 Broadway, Cambridge, MA 02142
Phone: 617 444-3000   **Fax:** 617 444-3001
Web: www.akamai.com

PRODUCTS/OPERATIONS

2014 Sales

	% of total
Media Delivery Solutions	47
Performance & Security Solutions	46
Service and Support Solutions	7
Total	**100**

Selected Products

Terra
  Alta
Aqua
  Aqua Ion
  Aqua Ion Mobile
  Dynamic Site Accelerator
Sola
  Sola Media Experience
  Sola Software Distribution
Kona
  Site Defender
  Web Application Firewall
Aura
  Aura Accelerated Network Partner Program
  Managed CDN
  Licensed CDN

Selected Acquisitions

COMPETITORS

Brilliant Digital Entertainment	Limelight
CDNeworks Co.	MediaMind
Digital River	Mirror Image Internet
EyeWonder	NaviSite
Internap	NeuStar
Level 3 Communications	Onstream Media

HISTORICAL FINANCIALS

Company Type: Public

Income Statement
FYE: December 31

	REVENUE ($ mil.)	NET INCOME ($ mil.)	NET PROFIT MARGIN	EMPLOYEES
12/15	2,197.4	321.4	14.6%	6,084.0
12/14	1,963.8	333.9	17.0%	5,105.0
12/13	1,577.9	293.4	18.6%	3,908.0
12/12	1,373.9	203.9	14.8%	3,074.0
12/11	1,158.5	200.9	17.3%	2,380.0
Annual Growth	**17.4%**	**12.5%**	—	**26.4%**

2015 Year-End Financials

Debt ratio: 14.9%	No. of shares (mil.): 177.2
Return on equity: 10.6%	Dividends
Cash ($ mil.): 289.4	Yield: —
Current ratio: 3.77	Payout: —
Long-term debt ($ mil.): 624.2	Market value ($ mil.): 9,327.0

	STOCK PRICE ($) FY Close	P/E High/Low		PER SHARE ($) Earnings	Dividends	Book Value
12/15	52.63	44	28	1.78	0.00	17.61
12/14	62.96	35	25	1.84	0.00	16.52
12/13	47.18	32	20	1.61	0.00	14.72
12/12	40.91	36	24	1.12	0.00	13.19
12/11	32.28	48	17	1.07	0.00	12.15
Annual Growth	**13.0%**	—	—	**13.6%**	—	**9.7%**

Akorn Inc

Akorn has its roots firmly planted in the pharmaceutical industry. The firm makes and sells branded and generic drugs in therapeutic and diagnostic categories including ophthalmology injectables and specialty therapeutics. Akorn's ophthalmic segment includes antibiotics steroids glaucoma treatments and diagnostic stains and dyes as well as prescription and OTC eye care products. The firm's injectable and hospital-administered therapeutics segment includes anti-infectives antidotes anesthesia agents pain management drugs and other specialty substances. Akorn also provides contract drug manufacturing services. Chairman John Kapoor is the company's largest shareholder owning a one-third stake in Akorn.

Geographic Reach

Akorn has manufacturing plants in the US (one in Illinois one in New York and one in New Jersey) and India and nearly all of its revenues come from sales in the US market. The company also operates a Research and Development center in Vernon Hills Illinois and a distribution warehouse in Gurnee Illinois.

Operations

The company's largest operating segment is ophthalmics which brings in about 36% of annual revenues followed by hospital drugs and injectables which together account for 57% of sales. Many of Akorn's products are generic drugs licensed from external sources though it is working to increase the number of internally developed products in both the branded and generic categories. The company manufactures a variety of pharmaceutical products for third party pharmaceutical customers based on their specifications. Contract services accounted for 7% of Akorn's revenues in 2013.Through subsidiary Advanced Vision Research the company makes and markets a line of over-the-counter (OTC) ophthalmic products for the treatment of dry eye under the TheraTears brand name as well as a portfolio of private label OTC ophthalmic products.

Sales and Marketing

Akorn's products are sold nationally to hospitals physicians optometrists group purchasing organizations pharmacies and wholesalers via direct sales representatives and independent distributors. The company's three biggest customers accounting for about two-thirds of its 2013 sales are wholesalers Cardinal Health(23%) McKesson(16%) and AmerisourceBergen(19%).

Financial Performance

The company has reported year-to-year revenue growth since 2009. Revenues rose by 24% in 2013 due to primarily from increased sales of new and revived products which accounted for $48.5 million of the increase. Its hospital drugs & injectables saw a surge in the sales of new and revived products with more than half of the increase attributable to progesterone capsules and Td vaccine. Ophthalmic segment revenues grew due to increase in OTC product sales of TheraTears branded products and private label products and sales of products acquired late in 2013 from Merck. Contract services revenue also increased due to a rise in US contract services.Akorn's net income increased by 48% in 2013 due to a bargain purchase gain and a decline in interest expense related to a debt discount and to the change in fair value of its additional consideration of $15 million payable to Lundbeck (related to its acqui-

sition of various injectable products from that company in 2011).Operating cash flow increased by $31 million in 2013 due to a decline in cash used in trade accounts receivable and inventories.

Strategy

In addition to regular growth through acquisitions Akorn is working to increase its internal product development efforts to speed up the time it takes to bring a new product to market (as well as to reduce its dependence on licensing deals and acquisitions).

Mergers and Acquisitions

In 2014 Akon acquired the US NDA rights to Zioptan (a prescription ophthalmic eye drop indicated for reducing elevated intraocular pressure in patients with open-angle glaucoma or ocular hypertension) from Merck Sharp and Dohme Corp. and the NDA rights to Betimol (a prescription ophthalmic eye drop for the reduction of eye pressure in glaucoma patients) from Japan-based Santen Pharmaceutical Co. Ltd.

In 2013 the company acquired from Merck the US rights to three branded ophthalmic products (AzaSite Cosopt and Cosopt PF) for $52.8 million. It began selling Cosopt and Cosopt PF at the end of 2013 and began selling AzaSite in early 2014. This acquisition allows Akorn to leverage its existing ophthalmic sales force and physician relationships.

Also in 2013 Akorn agreed to acquire Hi-Tech Pharmacal for some $640 million. The purchase will expand Akorn's development pipeline as well as its offerings of generic and branded OTC and prescription products. Hi-Tech Pharmacal makes a number of dosage forms including liquid semi-solid oral topical nasal spray and sterile ointments and gels.

HISTORY

Joseph Yazbeck founded Akorn in Metairie Louisiana in 1971; the name was chosen so the firm would appear near the front of alphabetical listings. Akorn initially distributed eye care products from various suppliers. In 1988 the firm went public. In 1989 Yazbeck retired (replaced by John Kapoor) and Akorn bought its first manufacturing facility from Irish drug company Norbrook Holdings; two years later after product recalls and a push from the FDA to modernize Akorn closed the facility. The company resumed manufacturing operations in 1992 with the purchase of Taylor Pharmaceuticals.

Akorn diversified in 1995 starting a surgical instrument repair unit and boosted its line of injectable drugs the next year. Akorn moved its headquarters from Louisiana to Illinois in 1997 and introduced a generic version of Merck's antiglaucoma drug Timoptic.

In 1998 Akorn increased earnings by acquiring eight new products including worldwide rights to Allergan's Fluress stain. The purchase of a manufacturing facility in New Jersey decreased dependency on outside suppliers. In 1999 Akorn partnered with CIBA Vision to market a generic form of that company's Ocupress glaucoma treatment. In 2000 the company sought permission to begin testing a treatment for age-related macular degeneration a leading cause of blindness in elderly people.

That same year the FDA issued a warning about problems at the company's manufacturing facility in Decatur Illinois. Additional inspections in 2002 2003 and 2004 revealed other "deviations" at the facility which the company has since responded to and corrected. These difficulties prevented Akorn from developing new products at Decatur for several years which had a significant impact on its business.

Arthur Przybyl resigned as CEO in 2009. The board then appointed newcomer Raj Rai as CEO in mid-2009.

Akorn decided in 2009 to exit the market for flu vaccine distribution. Biologics and vaccines previously accounted for about 40% of Akorn's sales in 2009. The company discontinued the rest of the division's operations (tetanus-diphtheria vaccines) in early 2010. The exit didn't impact Akorn's revenues as it increased sales within its other segments during 2009 and 2010.

The company centralized its R&D operations in early 2010 by opening a focused R&D center in Skokie Illinois; previously the company's internal research was performed at its two manufacturing plants.

A major boost in the ophthalmics segment came when Akorn entered the OTC eye care market through the 2011 purchase of Advanced Vision Research for some $26 million in cash. The purchase added such brands as TheraTears and MacuTrition. Akorn is already familiar with the products having been their primary contract manufacturer for several years. To round out its offerings it plans to manufacture private label eye care products and license new products.

The company's generic injectables division experienced increased demand in 2011 (due to shortages of certain products in the US market) and in response Akorn decided to ride that wave by growing the segment's operations. To expand its portfolio of proprietary branded products Akorn acquired manufacturing and marketing rights for three injectable drugs from Danish firm Lundbeck for some $50 million that year (plus potential future milestone payments). The drugs include Nembutal a controversial drug used in lethal injection executions; Cogentin for Parkinson's disease symptoms; and Diuril a diuretic and antihypertensive medicine. To focus on its most profitable growth offerings the firm sold its stake in a portfolio of injectable products marketed with Strides Arcolab to Pfizer in 2011.

To increase its production of injectables Akorn acquired a compound of contract manufacturing facilities for sterile injectables from India-based Kilitch Drugs in a deal worth some $60 million in 2012. The purchase expanded Akorn's capabilities in emerging international markets and the firm plans to apply for FDA certification of the facility to boost its US offerings as well. As portions of the India facility are still under construction the purchase also provided future capacity for additional products including new ophthalmics and expansion into cancer drugs in both the US and international markets.

EXECUTIVES

EVP Global Quality Assurance and Alliance Management, Mark M. Silverberg, age 63, $288,287 total compensation
SVP National Accounts and Trade Relations, John R. Sabat, age 66, $288,449 total compensation
CEO, Raj Rai, age 49
Chief Financial Officer, Timothy A. (Tim) Dick, age 46, $309,000 total compensation
COO, Bruce Kutinsky, age 51, $423,630 total compensation
EVP Pharmaceutical Operations, Steve Lichter, age 57
Vice President, Joseph (Jo) Bonaccorsi
Vice President Information Technology, Bill Bradford

Vice President Information Technology, Bradford Greg
Vice President Business Development, Sean Brynjelsen
Vice President Research and Development, Pati Biswajit
Executive Vice President Global Quality Compliance, Jaspreet Gill
Vice President Of Engineering, Brett Novak
Senior Vice President Operations, Michae Stehn
Vice President Information Technology, Brad Williams
Senior Vice President Chief Financial Officer Secretary and Treasurer, Bernard (Bern) Pothast
Vice President Contract Manufacturing, Jay Stern
Vice President Human Resources, Greg (Greggy) Lawless
Vice President Engineering, John (Jack) Valley
Chairman, John N. Kapoor, age 72
Auditors: BDO USA, LLP

LOCATIONS

HQ: Akorn Inc
 1925 W. Field Court, Suite 300, Lake Forest, IL 60045
Phone: 847 279-6100
Web: www.akorn.com

PRODUCTS/OPERATIONS

2015 Sales

	$ mil.	% of total
Prescription Pharmaceuticals	924.5	94
Consumer Health	60.6	6
Total	**985.1**	**100**

Selected Products

Atropine Sulfate Ophthalmic Solution
Clobetasol Propionate Ointment
Dehydrated Alcohol Injection
Ephedrine Sulfate Injection
Hydralazine Hydrochloride Injection
Lidocaine Ointment
Methylene Blue Injection
Myorisan Soft Gelatin Capsules
Nembutal Sodium Solution
Progesterone Capsules

COMPETITORS

Aerie Pharmaceuticals	Hospira
Apotex	InSite Vision
Bausch & Lomb	Novartis
Baxter International	Pfizer
CBL	Sagent Pharmaceuticals
Fresenius Kabi	Sun Pharmaceutical
Hikma	Teva

HISTORICAL FINANCIALS

Company Type: Public

Income Statement

FYE: December 31

	REVENUE ($ mil.)	NET INCOME ($ mil.)	NET PROFIT MARGIN	EMPLOYEES
12/15	985.0	150.8	15.3%	2,172.0
12/14	593.0	35.3	6.0%	1,881.0
12/13	317.7	52.3	16.5%	1,462.0
12/12	256.1	35.3	13.8%	767.0
12/11	136.9	43.0	31.4%	564.0
Annual Growth	**63.8%**	**36.8%**	**—**	**40.1%**

2015 Year-End Financials

Debt ratio: 50.8%
Return on equity: 29.9%
Cash ($ mil.): 346.2
Current ratio: 3.24
Long-term debt ($ mil.): 1,021.4
No. of shares (mil.): 119.4
Dividends
 Yield: —
 Payout: —
Market value ($ mil.): 4,456.0

	STOCK PRICE ($) FY Close	P/E High/Low		PER SHARE ($) Earnings	Dividends	Book Value
12/15	37.31	43	17	1.22	0.00	5.20
12/14	36.20	131	62	0.33	0.00	3.46
12/13	24.62	48	23	0.46	0.00	2.69
12/12	13.36	45	29	0.32	0.00	2.10
12/11	11.12	26	11	0.41	0.00	1.67
Annual Growth	**35.3%**	**—**	**—**	**31.3%**	**—**	**32.9%**

Alamo Group, Inc.

Remember the Alamo Group for tractor-mounted mowing equipment —rotary flail and sickle-bar! The company designs manufactures and distributes a slew of right-of-way maintenance and agricultural equipment. Its branded lines Alamo Industrial and Tiger hydraulically powered tractor-mounted mowers serve US government agencies. Rhino Products and M&W Gear subsidiaries sell rotary cutters and other equipment to farmers for pasture upkeep. UK McConnel and Bomford and France's S.M.A. subsidiaries market vegetation maintenance equipment such as hydraulic boom-mounted hedge and grass mowers.

Geographic Reach

The company operates almost 25 plants in North America Europe and Australia. The US generates 68% of its sales. Other major markets include France (11%) the UK (7%) Canada (6%) and Australia (2%).

Sales and Marketing Alamo sells its products primarily through a network of independent dealers and distributors to governmental end-users related independent contractors as well as to the agricultural and commercial turf markets. The primary markets for its products are North America Western Europe and Australia.

Financial Performance

Alamo has achieved unprecedented growth the last few years with revenues climbing 24% to peak at a record-setting $839 million in 2014. Profits also reached a net income milestone of $41 million in 2014. The company's operating cash flow has fluctuated over the years falling slightly in 2014 due to changes in inventories and prepaid expenses.

The historic growth for 2014 was fueled by a 46% surge in North American Industrial sales and a 14% bump in European sales. The increases were largely attributed to additional revenue from acquisitions and higher demand for mowers sweepers excavators vacuum trucks and snow equipment. Alamo also enjoyed growth in the UK and France during 2014.

Strategy

Alamo's sales are impacted by a myriad of variables including global economic conditions pricing and availability of raw materials government budgets and policies interest rates and access to credit for capital. Even more directly demand for the company's products may teeter with a drop in farm incomes droughts and floods animal disease outbreaks and pest infestations of crops worldwide general demand for farm produce and limits on agricultural imports.

Alamo has sought to counter the adverse events endemic to its industry by strategically cultivating its geographic presence and product portfolio primarily through acquisitions of businesses and branded lines that enhance dominate or promise to significantly rival competitors within their equipment markets. Since its start more than 40 years ago Alamo has invested in some two dozen companies.

Mergers and Acquisitions

Acquisitions are an important part of the company's growth strategy. It used acquisitions to fuel revenue milestones for 2014. It made three key acquisitions in 2014. It picked up Kellands Agricultural a UK-based manufacturer of self-propelled sprayers and multi-purpose load-carrying tractor vehicles. The acquisition enhanced its manufacture and distribution capabilities of agricultural machinery and opened the door to the self-propelled sprayer market.Alamo purchased Fieldquip Australia a manufacturer of rotary cutters as well as a distributor of various agricultural products. The deal broadened its presence in both the manufacturing and distribution of agricultural machinery sectors in Australia. The company also in 2014 snapped up Specialized Industries LP and its subsidiaries Super Products Wausau-Everest and Howard P. Fairfield. The transaction enhanced its market position both in vacuum trucks and snow removal equipment primarily in North America.

EXECUTIVES

VP; Managing Director Alamo Group (EUR) Ltd., Geoffrey (Geoff) Davies, age 68, $327,753 total compensation

CEO and President, Ronald A. (Ron) Robinson, age 63, $504,265 total compensation

Vice President Of Information Systems, Terry Stevens

EVP and CFO, Dan E. Malone, age 55, $253,299 total compensation

VP; Manager Agricultural Division, Richard D. Pummell, age 70, $258,825 total compensation

VP; Manager Industrial Division, Jeffery A. Leonard, $275,606 total compensation

EVP North American Agricultural Division, Richard H. (Rick) Raborn

Vice President Manager Director, Dwayne (Wayne) Engler

Vice President Technical support Director, John (Jack) Fisher

Vice President Manager Director, Rick (Ricky) Solano

Vice President of Human Resour, Janet (Jan) Pollock

Vice President Sales And Marketing, Greg Pollock

Vice President Information Technology, Keith Krichevsky

Vice President and General Counsel, Edward (Ed) Rizzuti

Executive Vice President And General, Ian Budern

Chairman, James B. Skaggs, age 78

Auditors: KPMG LLP

LOCATIONS

HQ: Alamo Group, Inc.
1627 East Walnut, Seguin, TX 78155
Phone: 830 379-1480   **Fax:** 830 372-9683
Web: www.alamo-group.com

PRODUCTS/OPERATIONS

2014 Sales

	$ mil.	% of total
North American		
Industrial	436.0	52
Agricultural	214.4	26
European	188.7	22
Total	**839.1**	**100**

Selected Products

Boom mowers/power arms
Excavators
Flail mowers
Loader/backhoes
Rotary mowers
Snow removal equipment
Street sweepers
Vacuum trucks

COMPETITORS

AGCO	R.P.M. Tech
Art's-Way	Scag Power Equipment
Deere	TYMCO
Elgin Sweeper Company	Tennant
MTD Products	Toro Company

HISTORICAL FINANCIALS

Company Type: Public

Income Statement

FYE: December 31

	REVENUE ($ mil.)	NET INCOME ($ mil.)	NET PROFIT MARGIN	EMPLOYEES
12/15	879.5	43.2	4.9%	3,030.0
12/14	839.0	41.1	4.9%	3,070.0
12/13	676.8	36.0	5.3%	2,550.0
12/12	628.4	28.9	4.6%	2,470.0
12/11	603.5	32.0	5.3%	2,500.0
Annual Growth	**9.9%**	**7.7%**	**—**	**4.9%**

2015 Year-End Financials

Debt ratio: 23.8%	No. of shares (mil.): 11.3
Return on equity: 12.3%	Dividends
Cash ($ mil.): 26.9	Yield: 0.6%
Current ratio: 4.27	Payout: 8.5%
Long-term debt ($ mil.): 144.0	Market value ($ mil.): 591.0

	STOCK PRICE ($) FY Close	P/E High/Low	PER SHARE ($) Earnings	Dividends	Book Value
12/15	52.10	17 12	3.76	0.32	31.76
12/14	48.44	17 11	3.42	0.28	29.98
12/13	60.69	20 11	2.96	0.28	29.03
12/12	32.64	14 11	2.40	0.24	25.89
12/11	26.93	11 7	2.68	0.24	23.33
Annual Growth	**17.9%**	**— —**	**8.8%**	**7.5%**	**8.0%**

Alarm.com Holdings Inc

Auditors: PricewaterhouseCoopers LLP

LOCATIONS

HQ: Alarm.com Holdings Inc
8281 Greensboro Drive, Suite 100, Tysons, VA 22102
Phone: 877 389-4033
Web: www.alarm.com

HISTORICAL FINANCIALS

Company Type: Public

Income Statement

FYE: December 31

	REVENUE ($ mil.)	NET INCOME ($ mil.)	NET PROFIT MARGIN	EMPLOYEES
12/15	208.8	11.7	5.6%	507.0
12/14	167.3	13.5	8.1%	400.0
12/13	130.2	4.5	3.5%	253.0
12/12	96.4	8.9	9.3%	165.0
Annual Growth	**29.4%**	**9.6%**	**—**	**45.4%**

2015 Year-End Financials

Debt ratio: 2.9%	No. of shares (mil.): 45.4
Return on equity: 9.3%	Dividends
Cash ($ mil.): 128.3	Yield: —
Current ratio: 5.54	Payout: —
Long-term debt ($ mil.): 6.7	Market value ($ mil.): 759.0

	STOCK PRICE ($) FY Close	P/E High/Low	PER SHARE ($) Earnings	Dividends	Book Value
12/15	16.68	— —	(0.30)	0.00	3.74
12/14	0.00	—	0.14	0.00	30.83
Annual Growth (87.9%)	**—**	**— —**	**—**	**—**	**—**

Alerus Financial Corp

National commercial banks nsk

EXECUTIVES

Senior Vice President, Mike (Mikey) Winkel
President; Chief Executive Officer Chairman Director, Randy Newman
Auditors: CliftonLarsonAllen LLP

LOCATIONS

HQ: Alerus Financial Corp
401 Demers Avenue, Grand Forks, ND 58021
Phone: 701 795-3200   **Fax:** 701 795-3378
Web: www.alerusfinancial.com

HISTORICAL FINANCIALS

Company Type: Public

Income Statement

FYE: December 31

	ASSETS ($ mil.)	NET INCOME ($ mil.)	INCOME AS % OF ASSETS	EMPLOYEES
12/15	1,744.8	16.5	0.9%	0.0
12/14	1,488.3	20.2	1.4%	0.0
12/13	1,380.7	20.2	1.5%	584.0
12/12	1,322.1	17.8	1.4%	0.0
12/11	1,156.6	10.7	0.9%	525.0
Annual Growth	**10.8%**	**11.4%**	**—**	**—**

2015 Year-End Financials

Return on assets: 1.0%	Dividends
Return on equity: 9.3%	Yield: 2.2%
Long-term debt ($ mil.): —	Payout: 28.1%
No. of shares (mil.): 13.4	Market value ($ mil.): 254.0
Sales ($ mill): 149.5	

	STOCK PRICE ($) FY Close	P/E High/Low	PER SHARE ($) Earnings	Dividends	Book Value
12/15	18.90	17 15	1.17	0.42	13.61
12/14	19.75	42 14	1.44	0.38	(0.00)
12/13	51.00	35 21	1.46	0.34	11.21
12/12	31.00	47 20	1.29	0.31	10.49
12/11	25.50	34 25	0.80	0.30	(0.00)
Annual Growth	(7.2%)	— —	9.9%	9.1%	—

Alexander & Baldwin Inc.

Alexander & Baldwin (A&B) is all about its real estate and agribusiness operations in The Aloha State. Its A&B Properties subsidiary engages in real estate development and property management for commercial properties both in Hawaii and five states on the US mainland. It owns 88000 acres of land in Hawaii primarily on the islands of Maui and Kauai. In addition the company produces sugarcane molasses and sugar products (under the Maui Brand) through its Hawaiian Commercial & Sugar Company. In mid-2012 A&B separated from its former ocean transportation subsidiary Matson which carries freight mainly between ports in Hawaii Guam China Alaska and Puerto Rico and the continental US.

Geographic Reach

Headquartered at Honolulu Hawaii A&B operates a commercial portfolio comprising 4.9 million sq. ft. of retail office and industrial space comprising nearly 60 properties located in Hawaii and in five US states through subsidiary A&B Properties. A&B Properties owns over 88000 acres of land primarily on the islands of Maui and Kauai.

Operations

The company operates in four segments: Real Estate Development and Sales (18% of net sales) Real Estate Leasing (23%) Materials and Construction (38%) and Agribusiness (21%).

Sales and Marketing

About $38 million was generated directly and indirectly from projects administered by the City and County of Honolulu. For 2015 revenue of approximately $81 million was generated directly and indirectly from the State of Hawaii. Hawaiian Commercial & Sugar Company a consolidated subsidiary included in its Agribusiness segment derived approximately $72 million of revenue from C&H Sugar Company in fiscal 2015.

Financial Performance

A&B's revenues peaked at a record-setting $571 million in 2015 while its profits plummeted by 52% to fall to almost $30 million. The historic revenue growth for 2015 was fueled by a 26% spike from its Real Estate Development and Sales segment. Its decline in profits was attributed to an increase in the costs of Agribusiness goods and services in addition to the absence of income from discontinued operations.

Strategy

A&B seeks to organically grow its commercial portfolio through active management including its re-positioning and re-development activities in order to increase occupancy secure quality tenants and reduce costs. It is focused on pursuing and investing in attractive real estate opportunities in Hawaii where it can leverage its market knowledge experience and financial strength to expand and diversify its existing portfolio and pipeline.

EXECUTIVES

Chairman and CEO, Stanley M. Kuriyama, age 63, $525,000 total compensation
President and COO, Christopher J. (Chris) Benjamin, age 53, $439,089 total compensation
SVP CFO Treasurer and Controller, Paul K. Ito, age 46, $303,375 total compensation
Vice President Acquisitions and Investments A and B Properties, Lance Parker
Vice President Human Resources, Son-Jai Paik
Vice President of Corporate Development, George Morvis
Auditors: Deloitte & Touche LLP

LOCATIONS

HQ: Alexander & Baldwin Inc.
822 Bishop Street, Honolulu, HI 96813
Phone: 808 525-6611
Web: www.alexanderbaldwin.com

PRODUCTS/OPERATIONS

2015 Sales

	$ mil.	% of total
Materials and construction	219.0	38
Real estate leasing	133.8	23
Agribusiness	117.2	21
Real estate development and sales	100.5	18
Total	**570.5**	**100**

COMPETITORS

American Crystal Sugar	Hillwood
Barnwell Industries	Sterling Sugars
Castle & Cooke	Tate & Lyle
Douglas Emmett	
Forest City Enterprises	

HISTORICAL FINANCIALS

Company Type: Public

Income Statement

FYE: December 31

	REVENUE ($ mil.)	NET INCOME ($ mil.)	NET PROFIT MARGIN	EMPLOYEES
12/15	570.5	29.6	5.2%	1,496.0
12/14	560.0	61.4	11.0%	1,502.0
12/13	365.2	36.9	10.1%	1,446.0
12/12	296.7	20.5	6.9%	946.0
12/11	268.7	23.5	8.7%	961.0
Annual Growth	20.7%	5.9%	—	11.7%

2015 Year-End Financials

Debt ratio: 26.2%
Return on equity: 2.4%
Cash ($ mil.): 1.3
Current ratio: 0.83
Long-term debt ($ mil.): 497.8

No. of shares (mil.): 48.9
Dividends
  Yield: 0.5%
  Payout: 38.8%
Market value ($ mil.): 1,727.0

	STOCK PRICE ($) FY Close	P/E High/Low	PER SHARE ($) Earnings	Dividends	Book Value
12/15	35.31	81 62	0.54	0.21	25.26
12/14	39.26	35 28	1.25	0.17	24.67
12/13	41.73	55 35	0.82	0.04	23.99
12/12	29.37	71 53	0.48	0.00	21.31
Annual Growth	6.3%	— —	4.0%	—	5.8%

Align Technology Inc

Brace-face begone! Align Technology produces and sells the Invisalign system which corrects malocclusion or crooked teeth. Instead of using metal or ceramic mounts that are cemented on the teeth and connected by wires (traditional braces) the system involves using an array of clear and removable dental Aligners to move a patient's teeth into a desired alignment. The company markets its products to orthodontists and dentists worldwide. Align also provides training for practitioners to model treatment schemes using its online ClinCheck application which simulates tooth movement and suggests the appropriate Aligner. It also makes and sells orthodontic scanning and CAD (computer-assisted design) devices.Operations

The company operates through two segments: Clear Aligner and Scanners and CAD/CAM Services ("SCCS"). Clear Aligner is the Invisalign product lines and it accounts for 94% of revenue. The Invisalign system is offered in more than 80 countries by more than 43000 doctors to teenage and adult patients.

SCCS includes the iTero intra-oral 3D scanning system for orthodontic and restorative dentistry and OrthoCAD services.Geographic ReachAlign Technology has administrative and manufacturing locations in Costa Rica Mexico Israel the Netherlands and the US; it has R&D facilities in Russia Israel and the US (California). Its products are primarily marketed in the US (accounting for about three-fourths of sales) and Europe. It also operates in areas of Latin America and the Asia/Pacific region and is working to expand sales into Middle Eastern African and smaller European countries. Invisalign is available in 80 countries worldwide.Sales and MarketingAlign Technology sells its products through a direct sales force in North America and select international markets as well as through distribution partners in other regions. The company primarily markets its products to orthodontist and dental practices who then commit to sell the products to consumers. It is targeting general practice dentists as a primary sales growth channel since general dentists have larger patient populations than orthodontists who traditionally treat malocclusion. The company also distributes its products to restorative dentists including prosthodontists periodontists and oral surgeons.Financial PerformanceAlign Technology has seen several years of increasing revenue and 2014 was no exception. The company reported a 15% increase to $751 million as all products and geographic regions saw higher sales. Clear Aligner North America net revenues increased due to both higher volumes and to a lesser extent a higher average selling price as customers opted for higher-priced products. Clear Aligner international net revenues increased that year too primarily as a result of the company's acquiring its distributor in the Asia/Pacific region in mid-2013. Price increases and a favorable impact from foreign exchange rates also contributed to the rise. Finally Scanner and Services net earnings increased due to higher volume despite lower average selling prices.The higher revenues in 2014 helped net income more than double to $146 million; the absence of impairment of goodwill also helped. Cash flow from operations grew 22% to $227 million both as a result of the higher profits and an increase in accrued and other long-term liabilities and accounts payable.StrategyTo stay ahead of potential competitors looking to enter the clear alignment market Align Technology continuously tries to expand sales of its Invisalign system by increasing the number of dentists and orthodontists that are committed to selling the products. It also increases brand awareness through consumer marketing programs. Geographically the firm is looking to expand into new markets. In 2013 it transitioned Asian markets back to a direct sales model coordinated out of its new regional headquarters in Singapore. It also launched a branding campaign across Western Europe which led to higher sales.To widen use of its products Align Technology also develops new versions and variations of the Invisalign system as well as tools that make it easier for dentists to adopt use of the Invisalign offerings. In 2013 and 2014 it launched the Invisalign G5 system which helps doctors manage treatment of patients with deep bites and rolled out the latest iterations for its ClinCheck and iTero products. It also upgraded its iTero intraoral scanner to increase practice efficiency. Some of the company's product development efforts are conducted through partnerships with other medical device firms such as Danaher. In 2014 Align Technology inked an agreement with Zimmer Dental; through the deal the iTero scanner will support connectivity with Zimmer Zfx custom abutments for implants.The company focuses its efforts on expanding its sales territory coverage in all of its direct sales areas especially in the highest-growing markets of Europe and the Asia/Pacific.

EXECUTIVES

VP Legal Affairs and General Counsel, Roger E. George, age 51, $382,368 total compensation

President and CEO, Joseph M. (Joe) Hogan, age 58, $548,077 total compensation

VP and General Manager Americas, Lynn S. Pendergrass

VP Operations, Emory M. Wright, age 47, $349,543 total compensation

VP and Managing Director North America, Christopher C. Puco, age 55

VP Research and Development, Zelko Relic, age 51, $366,231 total compensation

VP iTero Scanner and Services Chief Marketing Portfolio and Business Development Officer, Raphael S. Pascaud, age 44, $374,317 total compensation

VP and Managing Director EMEA, Simon Beard, age 49

VP and Managing Director Asia Pacific, Julie Tay, age 49

VP and Managing Director Doctor-Directed Consumer Channel, Jennifer Olson-Wilk

CFO, John F. Morici

Vice President Product Innovation, Srini Kaza

Chairman, C. Raymond Larkin, age 67

Auditors: PricewaterhouseCoopers LLP

LOCATIONS

HQ: Align Technology Inc
2560 Orchard Parkway, San Jose, CA 95131
Phone: 408 470-1000
Web: www.aligntech.com

PRODUCTS/OPERATIONS

2014 Sales

	$ mil.	% of total
Clear Aligner	712.6	94
Scanners & Services	49.1	6
Total	**761.7**	**100**

Selected Products and Services

CAD/CAM services
Invisalign Assist
Invisalign Express 5
Invisalign Express 10
Invisalign Full
Invisalign G3
Invisalign G4
Invisalign G5
Invisalign Lite
Invisalign Teen
iTero scanners
OrthoCad iOC intra-oral scanners
Vivera Retainers

COMPETITORS

3M	Nobel Biocare
Ceradyne	Patterson Companies
Dentsply Sirona	Straumann
Henry Schein	Sybron Dental
National Dentex	Young Innovations

HISTORICAL FINANCIALS

Company Type: Public

Income Statement

FYE: December 31

	REVENUE ($ mil.)	NET INCOME ($ mil.)	NET PROFIT MARGIN	EMPLOYEES
12/15	845.4	144.0	17.0%	4,375.0
12/14	761.6	145.8	19.1%	3,580.0
12/13	660.2	64.3	9.7%	3,420.0
12/12	560.0	58.6	10.5%	3,176.0
12/11	479.7	66.7	13.9%	2,593.0
Annual Growth	**15.2%**	**21.2%**	—	**14.0%**

2015 Year-End Financials

Debt ratio: —
Return on equity: 17.9%
Cash ($ mil.): 167.7
Current ratio: 2.69
Long-term debt ($ mil.): —
No. of shares (mil.): 79.5
Dividends
Yield: —
Payout: —
Market value ($ mil.): 5,235.0

	STOCK PRICE ($) FY Close	P/E High/Low		PER SHARE ($) Earnings	Dividends	Book Value
12/15	65.85	38	29	1.77	0.00	10.67
12/14	55.91	35	25	1.77	0.00	9.39
12/13	57.14	73	32	0.78	0.00	7.87
12/12	27.75	54	31	0.71	0.00	7.21
12/11	23.73	29	17	0.83	0.00	6.23
Annual Growth	**29.1%**	—	—	**20.8%**	—	**14.4%**

ALJ Regional Holdings Inc

ALJ Regional Holdings owns a steel mini-mill in Kentucky which it acquired in 2005. The mill is operated by Kentucky Electric Steel which produces bar flat products that it sells to service centers as well as makers of truck trailers steel springs and cold drawn bars. Kentucky Electric Steel produces steel in both Merchant Bar Quality and Special Bar Quality. The company also recycles steel from scrap to produce steel. Kentucky Electric Steel operates mainly in the US Canada and Mexico.

EXECUTIVES

President and CEO, John Scheel, age 61
CFO and Secretary, Rob Christ
Auditors: Mayer Hoffman McCann P.C.

LOCATIONS

HQ: ALJ Regional Holdings Inc
244 Madison Avenue, PMB #358, New York, NY 10016
Phone: 212 883-0083   **Fax:** 606 929-1261
Web: www.aljregionalholdings.com

COMPETITORS

Nucor	United States Steel
Steel Dynamics	

HISTORICAL FINANCIALS

Company Type: Public

Income Statement

FYE: September 30

	REVENUE ($ mil.)	NET INCOME ($ mil.)	NET PROFIT MARGIN	EMPLOYEES
09/16	268.3	10.9	4.1%	2.0
09/15	209.9	11.8	5.7%	0.0
09/14	149.6	15.6	10.5%	3,202.0
09/13	0.0	66.1	—	3,002.0
09/12	158.7	13.2	8.4%	152.0
Annual Growth	**14.0%**	**(4.8%)**	—	**(66.1%)**

2016 Year-End Financials

Debt ratio: 48.7%
Return on equity: 15.7%
Cash ($ mil.): 5.2
Current ratio: 1.48
Long-term debt ($ mil.): 93.7
No. of shares (mil.): 34.5
Dividends
Yield: —
Payout: —
Market value ($ mil.): 163.0

	STOCK PRICE ($) FY Close	P/E High/Low		PER SHARE ($) Earnings	Dividends	Book Value
09/16	4.70	18	12	0.30	0.00	2.14
09/15	3.95	13	8	0.35	0.00	1.83
09/14	3.50	7	2	0.48	0.00	1.53
09/13	0.82	1	0	1.47	0.00	1.04
09/12	0.41	2	2	0.22	0.00	(0.23)
Annual Growth	**84.6%**	—	—	**8.1%**	—	—

Allegiant Travel Company

Allegiant Travel pledges to serve the vacation needs of residents of more than 100 small US cities in 41 states. Through Allegiant Air the company provides nonstop service to tourist destinations such as Las Vegas Los Angeles and Orlando Florida from places such as Cedar Rapids Iowa; Fargo North Dakota; and Toledo Ohio. It maintains a fleet of about 50 MD-80 series aircraft. Besides scheduled service Allegiant Air offers charter flights for casino operators Caesars Entertainment (formerly Harrah's Entertainment) and MGM MIRAGE in addition to other customers. Sister company Allegiant Vacations works with partners to allow customers to book hotel rooms and rental cars along with their airline tickets.
Geographic Reach

The company has a route network providing service on 294 routes between 87 cities and 17 leisure destinations. It serves 41 US states.

Operations

Allegiant Travel's operating fleet consists of 51 MD-80 aircraft 26 A320 series aircraft and five Boeing 757-200 aircraft providing service on 294 routes to 104 cities. The company is also expecting that the services would expand to 322 routes and 111 cities by late 2016.

Financial Performance

Allegiant Travel has achieved extraordinary growth over the last five years with revenues surging 11% from $1.14 billion in 2014 to peak at $1.26 billion in 2015 a company milestone. Profits also more than doubled from $87 million in 2014 to reach a record-setting $220 million in 2015 mostly due to the lower price of fuel. Cash flow has also followed the same upward trend climbing by 35% in 2015.

The historic growth for 2015 was attributed to a spike in ancillary air-related revenue fueled by an increase in scheduled service passengers as well as continued revenue optimization efforts. In addition increased customer convenience fees and the effective yield management of other existing products drove an increase in its average ancillary air-related fare per passenger.

Strategy

Allegiant Travel's business strategy includes expanding its ancillary products and services and adding new destinations to its flight network. During 2015 the company added service to four leisure destinations commenced service on 69 new routes and discontinued service on under-performing routes. Based on its currently published schedule through August 2016 the company plans to increase total routes to 322 increase the number of leisure destinations served to 19 and increase the number of cities served to 92. In 2016 the company entered into forward purchase agreements for 11 Airbus A320 series aircraft. It expects delivery of seven aircraft in 2016 and the remaining four in the first half of 2017.

EXECUTIVES

President, John T. Redmond, age 58
President CEO and Director, Maurice J. (Maury) Gallagher, age 66
SVP and CIO, Scott M. Allard, age 48, $195,000 total compensation
SVP and CFO, D. Scott Sheldon, age 38, $195,000 total compensation
COO, Jude Bricker, $195,000 total compensation
VP and Principal Accounting Officer, Gregory C. Anderson, $147,500 total compensation
Vice President Application Development, Todd Cinnamon
Vice President People Services, Rebecca Henry
Auditors: KPMG, LLP

LOCATIONS

HQ: Allegiant Travel Company
1201 North Town Center Drive, Las Vegas, NV 89144
Phone: 702 851-7300
Web: www.allegiant.com

PRODUCTS/OPERATIONS

Selected Products and Services
Air-related ancillary products and services.
Fixed fee contract air transportation.
Scheduled service air transportation.
Third party ancillary products and services

2015 Sales

	$ mil.	% of total
Scheduled service	735.6	58
Ancillary revenues		
Air-related charges	434.3	34
Third party products	40.2	3
Fixed fee contract revenues	19.7	2
Other	32.4	3
Total	**1,262.2**	**100**

COMPETITORS

AirTran Airways	Horizon Air
Alaska Air	JetBlue
American Airlines Group	Southwest Airlines
	US Airways
Delta Air Lines	United Continental
Frontier Airlines	

HISTORICAL FINANCIALS

Company Type: Public

Income Statement
FYE: December 31

	REVENUE ($ mil.)	NET INCOME ($ mil.)	NET PROFIT MARGIN	EMPLOYEES
12/15	1,262.1	220.3	17.5%	3,018.0
12/14	1,137.0	86.6	7.6%	2,564.0
12/13	996.1	92.2	9.3%	2,235.0
12/12	908.7	78.6	8.6%	1,938.0
12/11	779.1	49.4	6.3%	1,719.0
Annual Growth	12.8%	45.3%	—	15.1%

2015 Year-End Financials

Debt ratio: 47.4%	No. of shares (mil.): 16.8
Return on equity: 68.5%	Dividends
Cash ($ mil.): 97.4	Yield: 1.6%
Current ratio: 1.02	Payout: 27.8%
Long-term debt ($ mil.): 567.6	Market value ($ mil.): 2,820.0

	STOCK PRICE ($) FY Close	P/E High/Low	PER SHARE ($) Earnings	Dividends	Book Value
12/15	167.83	18 11	12.94	2.75	20.83
12/14	150.33	30 18	4.86	2.50	16.82
12/13	105.44	23 15	4.82	2.25	20.26
12/12	73.41	19 12	4.06	2.00	20.71
12/11	53.34	21 15	2.57	0.00	18.42
Annual Growth	33.2%	— —	49.8%	—	3.1%

Allete Inc.

ALLETE provides light to the northern climes. Most of its business is classified within its regulated operations which include electric gas and water utilities located in northeastern Minnesota and northwestern Wisconsin. Those operations are conducted through subsidiaries Minnesota Power (about 144000 customers) and Superior Water Light and Power (37000 electric gas and water customers). ALLETE's other segment includes coal mining operations emerging technologies related to electric utilities and a real estate business (large land tracts in Florida). Subsidiary BNI Coal operates a mine in North Dakota that supplies primarily two generating co-ops Minnkota Power and Square Butte.

Geographic Reach

ALLETE has operations in Florida Illinois Michigan Minnesota North Dakota and Wisconsin.

Operations

The company's regulated operations include utilities Minnesota Power and Superior Water Light and Power as well Rainy River Energy which holds an 8% stake in American Transmission Company(ATC) a Wisconsin-based regulated utility that owns and maintains electric transmission assets in parts of Illinois Michigan Minnesota and Wisconsin.

Minnesota Power holds franchises to construct and maintain an electric distribution and transmission system in 91 cities. The remaining cities villages and towns served do not require a franchise to operate. Superior Water Light and Power serves customers with electric natural gas and/or water systems in 1 city and 16 villages or towns.

In 2014 industrial customers represented 54% of the company's total regulated utility kilowatt-hour sales.

Non-regulated assets included BNI Coal (coal mining operations in North Dakota) ALLETE Properties (10000 acres of Florida real estate investments) ALLETE Clean Energy (wind solar biomass hydro natural gas/liquids shale resources clean coal and other clean energy projects). Other activities include business development and corporate expenditures unallocated interest expense a small amount of non-rate base generation approximately 5000 acres of land in Minnesota and earnings on cash and investments.

BNI Coal owns and operates a surface lignite mine in Center North Dakota producing about 4 million tons annually.ALLETE Clean Energy operates independently of Minnesota Power to develop or acquire capital projects aimed at creating energy solutions via wind solar biomass midstream gas and oil infrastructure among other energy-related projects. It intends to market to electric utilities cooperatives municipalities independent power marketers and large end-users across North America through long-term contracts or other sale arrangements.

Sales and Marketing

Minnesota Power has 10 Large Power Customer contracts each serving requirements of 10 MW or more of customer load. The customers consist of five taconite producing facilities (two of which are owned by one company and are served under a single contract) one iron nugget plant one concentrate reclamation facility and four paper and pulp mills.

Large industrial power customers includes ArcelorMittal Blandin Paper Mill Boise White Paper Hibbing Taconite Co. NewPage Corporation United Taconite LLC and USS Corporation.

That year the company's residential and commercial customers represented 20% of total regulated utility kilowatt-hour sales.ALLETE's power marketing activities consist of purchasing energy in the wholesale market to serve its regulated service territory when energy requirements exceed generation output; and selling excess available energy and purchased power. From time to time its utility operations may have excess energy that is temporarily not required by retail and municipal customers in its regulated service territory. It actively sells any excess energy to the wholesale market to optimize the value of its generating facilities.

Financial Performance

ALLETE's revenues have consistently increased since 2010.In 2014 net sales grew by 12% due to higher revenues from regulated operations and investment and other. Operating revenues increased by 8% in 2014 primarily due to a 5% increase in kilowatt-hour sales higher cost recovery rider revenues transmission revenues gas sales and fuel adjustment clause recoveries.Revenue from Investments and Other increased by 43% primarily due to higher revenues from ALLETE Clean Energy due to the 2014 wind facility acquisitions and higher BNI Coal sales resulting from increased coal deliveries and higher expenses in 2014.ALLETE's net income has followed the similar trend to that of the company's revenues. In 2014 net income increased by 19% due to higher revenues partially offset by a growth in operating and maintenance expenses (up by 7%). (An expense was recorded to reflect a liability associated with environmental mitigation projects required as part of an EPA Consent Decree settlement. It was also higher due to a rise in transmission expense purchased gas and property taxes partially offset by lower benefit expense). The company's net cash provided by the operating activities increased by 13%.

Strategy

To meet the growing demand for electricity and comply with Minnesota's carbon emission regulations the company anticipates adding up to 500 MW of renewable energy capacity (primarily through building hydropower and wind facilities) by 2025. It also plans to increase the use of biomass as a cleaner-burning fuel at its fossil-fueled plants.

The company's current strategy for its assets is to complete and maintain key entitlements and infrastructure improvements without requiring significant additional investment sell the portfolio when opportunities arise and reinvest the proceeds in our growth initiatives. ALLETE does not intend to acquire additional Florida real estate.Minnesota Power will continue to pursue customer growth opportunities and cost recovery rider approval for environmental renewable and transmission investments as well as work with regulators to earn a fair rate of return. The company believes that ATC is poised for future growth both organically and through its partnership with Duke Energy. The company also plans to make investments in transmission opportunities that strengthen or enhance the transmission grid or take advantage of its geographical location between sources of renewable energy and end users. These include the GNTL and the CapX2020 initiative as well as investments to enhance its own transmission facilities and investments in other transmission assets (individually or in combination with others).In 2015 Minnesota Power completed latest phase of its Bison Wind Energy Center. The 205-megawatt expansion makes it the largest wind farm in North Dakota and ranks Minnesota Power as one of America's top-10 wind power-owning electric utilities.

In 2014 BNI Coal signed an agreement with Minnkota Power Cooperative to continue supplying lignite coal to the North Dakota electric generating cooperative through 2037. The agreement extends the current contract which would have ended in 2027 by 10 years.

Mergers and Acquisitions

In 2015 ALLETE acquired US Water Services consistent with ALLETE's stated strategy of investing in energy infrastructure and related services to complement its core regulated utility balance exposure to business cycles and changing demand and provide potential long-term earnings growth. ALLETE initially purchased 87% of U.S. Water for $168 million based on a total implied enterprise value of $194 million. US Water has a national footprint and serves a growing and diverse mix of over 3600 industrial customers including a significant number of Fortune 500 companies. Water and energy are intricately linked and attention to that nexus was increasing.In 2015 ALLETE Clean Energy acquired a handful of wind facilities including AES Armenia Mountain Wind

LLC a 100.5 MW wind facility in Pennsylvania and a 97.5 MW wind generation facility in Minnesota for $47.5 million from a subsidiary of EDF Renewable Energy. In 2014 ALLETE Clean Energy acquired wind energy facilities located in Lake Benton Minnesota Storm Lake Iowa and Condon Oregon for $26.9 million.

Company BackgroundIn 2013 Minnesota Power began construction on a 200-MW expansion of its Bison wind project that will deliver more economical carbon-free energy to customers while substantially meeting Minnesota's renewable energy standard of 25% renewable energy by 2025. The project will be the single largest wind addition to the company's fleet.

Growing its long-term power supply arrangements in 2012 Minnesota Power entered into a long-term deal with Minnkota Power through which Minnkota Power will by 50MW of capacity and the energy associated with that capacity from 2016 to 2020.

In 2011 the company launched ALLETE Clean Energy to leverage industry knowledge and innovation to bring clean energy to customers across North America.

Expanding its transmission capacity in 2011 American Transmission Company and Duke Energy formed the Duke-American Transmission Co. joint venture (DATC) to build own and operate a new electric transmission infrastructure in the US and Canada.

ALLETE's primary unit Minnesota Power was founded in 1906.

EXECUTIVES

SVP General Counsel and Secretary, Deborah A. (Deb) Amberg, age 50, $322,306 total compensation
SVP External Affairs, David J. McMillan, age 53, $279,539 total compensation
SVP and CFO, Steven Q. (Steve) DeVinck, age 56, $291,901 total compensation
Chairman President and CEO, Alan R. Hodnik, age 56, $585,676 total compensation
SVP Energy Centric Businesses and Chief Risk Officer, Robert J. Adams, age 53, $258,021 total compensation
President and General Manager BNI Energy, Wade W. Boeshans
President ALLETE Clean Energy, Al Rudeck
COO Minnesota Power, Bradley W. Oachs
VP ALLETE Information Technology Solutions and President SWLP, Bethany M. Owen
CEO U.S. Water Services, Allan Bly
Treasurer, Donald (Don) Stellmaker
Auditors: PRICEWATERHOUSECOOPERS LLP

LOCATIONS

HQ: Allete Inc.
30 West Superior Street, Duluth, MN 55802-2093
Phone: 218 279-5000
Web: www.allete.com

PRODUCTS/OPERATIONS

2014 Sales

	$ mil.	% of total
Regulated operations	1,003.5	88
Investments & other	133.3	12
Total	**1,136.8**	**100**

COMPETITORS

Alliant Energy	Pittsburgh Independent
Coteau Properties	Auto Auction
Dynegy	United Road Services
Florida Public Utilities	United Utilities Utilities Inc.
MGE Energy	WEC Energy
Otter Tail	Xcel Energy

HISTORICAL FINANCIALS

Company Type: Public

Income Statement
FYE: December 31

	REVENUE ($ mil.)	NET INCOME ($ mil.)	NET PROFIT MARGIN	EMPLOYEES
12/16	1,339.7	155.3	11.6%	1,963.0
12/15	1,486.4	141.1	9.5%	1,945.0
12/14	1,136.8	124.8	11.0%	1,625.0
12/13	1,018.4	104.7	10.3%	1,560.0
12/12	961.2	97.1	10.1%	1,361.0
Annual Growth	8.7%	12.5%	—	9.6%

2016 Year-End Financials

Debt ratio: 31.7%
Return on equity: 8.3%
Cash ($ mil.): 27.5
Current ratio: 0.74
Long-term debt ($ mil.): 1,370.4

No. of shares (mil.): 49.6
Dividends
Yield: 0.0%
Payout: 66.2%
Market value ($ mil.): 3,184.0

	STOCK PRICE ($) FY Close	P/E High/Low	PER SHARE ($) Earnings	Dividends	Book Value
12/16	64.19	21 15	3.14	2.08	38.17
12/15	50.83	20 16	2.92	2.02	37.07
12/14	55.14	20 15	2.90	1.96	35.06
12/13	49.88	20 16	2.63	1.90	32.44
12/12	40.98	16 15	2.58	1.84	30.50
Annual Growth	11.9%	— —	5.0%	3.1%	5.8%

Allied Motion Technologies Inc

Allied Motion Technologies has the motor to control your drive. The company makes specialized motors optical encoders and brushless drives used in mechanical motion control applications. Its products are incorporated into a number of end products including high-definition printers barcode scanners surgical tools robotic systems wheelchairs and satellite tracking systems. Allied Motion targets applications in the alternative energy automotive aerospace and defense industrial automation medical printing and imaging and semiconductor equipment markets.

Geographic Reach

The company manufactures its products in the US Canada China the Netherlands and Sweden. Products are sold through the company's direct sales force and through distributors. It has 15 direct sales offices. The US accounts for nearly 60% sales.

Operations

Allied Motion is organized around six technology units: Allied Motion Controls Emoteq Corporation Motor Products Corporation Precision Motor Technology B.V. (Premotec) Stature Electric and Östergrens Elmotor.

Financial Performance

Allied Motion enjoyed unprecedented growth for the year as revenues jumped 23% from $102 million in 2012 to a record-high of $126 million in 2013. The growth for 2013 was due to the acquisition of Globe in addition to increases in its vehicle and aerospace and defense markets.

However its profits have been falling over the last three years with earnings declining from $7 million in 2011 to $4 million in 2013. The erosion of profits was due to expenses incurred as a result of acquisitions which included a rise in business development and interest expenses.

Allied Motion's cash flow from operations steadily grew from $2.8 million in 2009 to $8.9 million in 2011. After decreasing to $4.6 million in 2012 cash flow shot up again to almost $11 million in 2013 due to changes in working capital.

Mergers and Acquisitions

The company makes acquisitions in order to add to its customer base product lines and market reach. In 2013 Allied Motion acquired Globe Motors from Safran USA for about $90 million. Globe Motors is stationed in Dayton Ohio with additional operations in Dothan Alabama; Reynosa Mexico; and Oporto Portugal. The deal expanded its global reach and fortified its sales marketing and manufacturing capabilities.

EXECUTIVES

Chairman President and CEO, Richard S. (Dick) Warzala, age 62
VP Marketing and CTO, Kenneth R. Wyman, age 74
CFO, Robert P. (Rob) Maida
CFO, Michael R. (Mike) Leach
Board Member, Richard D (Dick) Smith
Auditors: EKS&H LLP

LOCATIONS

HQ: Allied Motion Technologies Inc
495 Commerce Drive, Suite 3, Amherst, NY 14228
Phone: 716 242-8634
Web: www.alliedmotion.com

PRODUCTS/OPERATIONS

Selected Products
Brushless DC motors
Brushless drives
Encoders
Gearmotors
Permanent magnet DC motors
Servo motors
Small precision motors
Torque motors
Transaxles

COMPETITORS

ACS Motion Control	Danaher
Applied Industrial Technologies	Galil Motion Control Moog
Custom Sensors & Technologies	Newport Corp. UQM Technologies

HISTORICAL FINANCIALS

Company Type: Public

Income Statement

FYE: December 31

	REVENUE ($ mil.)	NET INCOME ($ mil.)	NET PROFIT MARGIN	EMPLOYEES
12/15	232.4	11.0	4.8%	1,046.0
12/14	249.6	13.8	5.6%	977.0
12/13	125.5	3.9	3.1%	942.0
12/12	101.9	5.4	5.3%	418.0
12/11	110.9	6.9	6.3%	476.0
Annual Growth	20.3%	12.3%	—	21.8%

2015 Year-End Financials

Debt ratio: 41.4%	No. of shares (mil.): 9.2
Return on equity: 18.3%	Dividends
Cash ($ mil.): 21.2	Yield: 0.3%
Current ratio: 2.22	Payout: 6.0%
Long-term debt ($ mil.): 58.9	Market value ($ mil.): 243.0

	STOCK PRICE ($) FY Close	P/E High/Low		PER SHARE ($) Earnings	Dividends	Book Value
12/15	26.18	34	14	1.20	0.10	6.96
12/14	23.69	16	7	1.51	0.10	6.07
12/13	12.45	28	15	0.45	0.10	5.28
12/12	6.60	13	9	0.63	0.10	4.88
12/11	5.64	11	6	0.81	0.04	4.29
Annual Growth	46.8%	—	—	10.3%	25.7%	12.9%

Almost Family Inc

Almost Family steps in when you're more than an arm's reach from family members with health needs. With its home health nursing services Almost Family offers senior citizens in 26 states (including Florida) an alternative to institutional care. Its Visiting Nurse unit provides skilled nursing care and therapy services at home under a variety of names including Apex Caretenders Community Home Health and Mederi-Caretenders. Its Personal Care Services segment operating under the Almost Family banner offers custodial care such as housekeeping meal preparation and medication management. Almost Family operates 175 Visiting Nurse agencies and about 65 Personal Care Services locations.

Operations

The company's services are carried out by nurses speech and occupational therapists medical social workers and home health aides. The services provided to a patient are determined by physician's prescribed plan of care —generally issued upon the patient's discharge from a hospital. Payments from Medicare account for 93% of revenue in the Visiting Nurse segment making Almost Family sensitive to any changes in Medicare reimbursement policies. The Personal Care segment receives 86% of its revenues from Medicare payments with the balance coming from private insurance private pay and Medicaid. This diversification of reimbursement risk is intentional but the company is also confident that its home-based services will always be lower in cost than institutional care.

Geographic Reach

As part of its business Kentucky-based Almost Family extends its reach to 16 states in the Northeast Southeast and Midwest. Florida Ohio and Tennessee are the company's three largest markets (in order of revenue significance).

Financial Performance

Almost Family posted a 4% rise in revenue in 2013 compared to 2012 to $357.8 million on a 4% increase in the Visiting Nurse segment primarily due to a pair of acquisitions (both in 2013) and an increase in service revenues. The company's Personal Care business which accounted for 23% of revenue in 2013 posted a 6% gain on incremental revenue from an acquisition as well as organic volume growth. Net income slid 52% year over year to $8.2 million in 2013 on higher expenses due to an increase in the provision for uncollectable commercial accounts and denials by

Medicare. (Medicare is the company's single largest source of revenue accounting for about 71% of revenue in 2013.)

Strategy

As the health care industry grows and consolidates Almost Family is looking to grow through acquisitions and continue to open home health care agencies in existing and new markets. Its expansion is focused on the eastern US. In late 2013 the company made the largest acquisition in its history: SunCrest.

Mergers and Acquisitions

In 2015 the company had its most acquisitive year ever. It acquired Willcare Health Care adding to its operations in New York and elsewhere; it built up its operations in Ohio with the $40 million purchase of Black Stone Operations (which operates under the brand name Home Care by Black Stone). It also bought New Jersey-based Bayonne VNA Home Health Agency and Massachusetts-based Long Term Solutions (in-home nursing assessments for the insurance industry) both for undisclosed amounts.

In early 2017 Almost Family bought an 80% stake in Community Health Systems' (CHS') home health and hospice unit for $128 million. That business includes 74 home health locations and 15 hospice centers in 22 states. After that purchase Almost Family became the third-largest Medicare home health provider in the nation. Together with CHS the company provides services to some 50000 patients daily.

HISTORY

Company Background

Almost Family was founded in 1976 as National Health Industries a Louisville Kentucky-based home health care company. After William Yarmuth became president in 1981 he expanded the company into such service areas as home infusion and home medical equipment.

The company became Caretenders Health in 1985 and in 1991 the company merged with Senior Service Corporation a small public adult day care services company. The company further expanded the range of services it offered to the elderly through its home health care operations. It established beachheads in new geographic markets by opening home health offices (or buying them) and then adding day care centers. It also bought some existing care centers.

The company grew energetically following its decision to specialize in elder care. It made three acquisitions in 1997 and surpassed that feat by closing on four acquisitions in little over a month in early 1998. The company lost one of its revenue streams that year: Two home health agencies in the Louisville area that had been managed by Caretenders were sold by their owner Columbia/HCA (now HCA). Caretenders sued Columbia/HCA for breach of contract and in 1999 won a $1.5 million settlement.

That year the company also sharpened its focus by selling its product operations (including infusion therapy respiratory and medical equipment) to Lincare Holdings but decided not to discontinue its visiting nurses services.

In 2000 the company changed its name to Almost Family to underscore its focus on adult day care. The following year it bought back the 23% stake that rehabilitation titan HEALTHSOUTH had maintained in the company.

EXECUTIVES

President and Principal Financial Officer, Steve (Steve) Guenthner, age 55, $446,000 total compensation

Chairman President and CEO, William B. Yarmuth, age 63, $677,000 total compensation

SVP and COO, Daniel J. Schwartz, age 49, $360,000 total compensation

SVP and Chief Clinical Officer, Rajneesh (Raj) Kaushal, age 55, $300,000 total compensation

SVP Administration, Patrick T. (Todd) Lyles, age 54, $325,000 total compensation

VP and CIO, Perry F. Pruett

Auditors: Ernst & Young LLP

LOCATIONS

HQ: Almost Family Inc
9510 Ormsby Station Road, Suite 300, Louisville, KY 40223
Phone: 502 891-1000
Web: www.almostfamily.com

PRODUCTS/OPERATIONS

2016 Sales

	$ mil.	% of total
Home Health		
Visiting Nurse	401.0	75
Personal Care	127.7	24
Healthcare Innovations	3.5	1
Total	**532.2**	**100**

Selected Agencies

Almost Family Medlink
Apex Home Healthcare Services
Better@Home
Cambridge Home Health Care
Caretenders
Community Home Health
Florida Home Health
Mederi Caretenders
Patient Care
Quality of Life

COMPETITORS

Amedisys	Home Instead
Apria Healthcare	Hooper Holmes
Capital Senior Living	LHC Group
Chemed	NHC
Continucare	National Home Health
Diversicare Healthcare	Odyssey HealthCare
Services	Providence Service
Gentiva	U.S. Physical Therapy
Girling Health Care	

HISTORICAL FINANCIALS

Company Type: Public

Income Statement

FYE: January 1

	REVENUE ($ mil.)	NET INCOME ($ mil.)	NET PROFIT MARGIN	EMPLOYEES
01/16*	532.2	20.0	3.8%	14,200.0
12/14	495.8	13.7	2.8%	10,900.0
12/13	357.8	8.2	2.3%	11,500.0
12/12	348.5	17.2	5.0%	8,000.0
12/11	339.8	20.8	6.1%	9,000.0
Annual Growth	**11.9%**	**(1.0%)**	**—**	**12.1%**

*Fiscal year change

2016 Year-End Financials

Debt ratio: 25.8%
Return on equity: 7.9%
Cash ($ mil.): 7.5
Current ratio: 2.00
Long-term debt ($ mil.): 120.3
No. of shares (mil.): 10.0
Dividends
  Yield: —
  Payout: —
Market value ($ mil.): 383.0

	STOCK PRICE ($) FY Close	P/E High/Low	PER SHARE ($) Earnings	Dividends	Book Value
01/16*	38.23	24 14	2.05	0.00	27.04
12/14	28.95	23 14	1.45	0.00	24.26
12/13	32.33	38 21	0.88	0.00	22.77
12/12	20.26	14 9	1.85	2.00	21.90
12/11	16.58	18 6	2.22	0.00	22.02
Annual Growth	**23.2%**	**— —**	**(2.0%)**	**—**	**5.3%**

*Fiscal year change

AMAG Pharmaceuticals, Inc.

It's rare when the illness and cure are one in the same; but in AMAG Pharmaceuticals' case iron is the problem and the solution. The biopharmaceutical company is focused on the development and commercialization of an iron compound to treat iron deficiency anemia (IDA). Its primary money maker is Makena a drug a drug to reduce the risk of pre-term births. Another product Feraheme Injection treats IDA in patients with chronic kidney disease (CKD). AMAG sells Feraheme in the US and Canada through its own sales force. AMAG's other product MuGard Mucoadhesive Oral Wound Rinse is used in the management of oral mucositis; it is also marketed in the US.

Operations

Makena which accounted for some 60% of revenues in 2015 is exclusively marketed by Lumara Health. AMAG gained Makena in late 2014 when it acquired Lumara's Maternal Health operations.

AMAG also owns Cord Blood Registry a newborn stem cell bank. Cord Blood Registry holds more than half of the US' privately stored cord units; it partners with academic institutions to evaluate the use of stem cells in treating autism cerebral palsy and other diseases and conditions.

Geographic Reach

The company's products are sold in the US and Canada.

Sales and Marketing

Makena is distributed through specialty pharmacies specialty distributors and home infusion companies; customers include health care providers hospitals government entities and health groups. The company sells Feraheme to health care providers in hospitals hematology and oncology centers and nephrology clinics.AMAG markets its product outside of North America primarily through its alliance with Takeda. It also use sales call channel to market MuGard and sells to wholesalers and specialty pharmacies.In 2015 AmerisourceBergen accounted for 25% of AMAG's revenues; Takeda 12%;and McKesson 11%.

Financial Performance

After seeing flat revenues through 2013 and a nice jump in 2014 revenue spiked more than 200% to $418 million in 2015. That growth was driven by sales of the recently acquired Makena as well as higher sales (and selling price) of Feraheme. The 2015 acquisition of Cord Blood Registry also boosted service revenue. Finally deferred revenue related to the termination of an agree-

ment with Takeda in 2015 contributed to the dramatic rise.

AMAG was losing money until 2014 when it made a profit of $136 million. However despite the spike in revenue in 2015 net income fell 76% to $33 billion that year as operating expenses (including acquisition-related costs) rose. Income tax provisions also impacted the bottom line.

Cash flow from operations roses 741% to $96 million that year due to several non-cash operating items including deferred income taxes equitybased compensation expense and inventory writedowns.

Strategy

AMAG is looking to expand its portfolio organically or through the acquisition of additional specialty pharmaceutical products or companies. It is seeking complementary products that will leverage its commercial infrastructure and focus on hematology and oncology centers hospital infusion centers or other sites of care where iron is administered intravenously.

In 2014 the company entered the maternal health market when it acquired specialty pharmaceutical Lumara Health. The following year it entered an agreement with Velo gaining the option to buy the rights to an orphan drug candidate that is being developed to treat severe preeclampsia in pregnant women.

The company pours much of its research and development funds into growing applications and markets for Feraheme since the drug has seen faces challenges in the US due to changes in the way dialysis services are reimbursed by programs such as Medicare and Medicaid. The changes make it less likely that dialysis providers would choose to use Feraheme so AMAG expects the majority of demand for Feraheme in the US to come from the non-dialysis CKD market.

To diversify its uses Feraheme is being tested to treat iron deficiency in a broad range of patients for whom oral iron treatments don't work including women with abnormal uterine bleeding patients with cancer or gastrointestinal diseases and post-partum women.

In 2015 AMAG terminated its existing development and commercialization agreement with Takeda which held the rights for Faraheme in the European Union and Switzerland. AMAG retained the worldwide development and commercialization rights for the drug.

Mergers and Acquisitions

In 2015 AMAG broadened its maternal health business with the $700 million acquisition of Cord Blood Registry a firm that collects and stores umbilical cord blood and tissue stem cell samples.

Company Background

In a move to try to diversify its product base AMAG agreed to buy Allos Therapeutics (maker of cancer drug Folotyn) in mid-2011 in a deal worth about $686 million; however the deal was terminated later that year. In the midst of its negotiations with Allos Therapeutics AMAG received a proposal from one of its minority investors MSMB Capital Management which sought to acquire AMAG for some $378 million. MSMB opposed the Allos transaction believing that the company's current strategy was not beneficial to its stockholders. AMAG's board disagreed and rejected MSMB's bid choosing instead to continue with plans to acquire Allos. Ultimately though the Allos transaction was voted down by AMAG's shareholders.

Following the failure of the Allos deal AMAG returned to its previous growth strategy which hinges upon gaining approval for additional uses of Feraheme in more countries and regions. The drug is currently approved for use as an IV iron replacement therapy in both the dialysis and non-dialysis CKD markets.

EXECUTIVES

Evp And Chief Medical Officer, Lee F Allen, age 65
EVP and COO, Frank E. Thomas, age 46
President and CEO AMAG, William K. Heiden, age 56
SVP Clinical Development and Regulatory Affairs and Chief Medical Officer, Julie Krop
SVP CFO and Treasurer, Edward (Ted) Myles
SVP Sales and Marketing, Edward Jordan
SVP Business Development and Strategy, Melissa Bradford Klug
SVP Quality and Technical Operations, Scott T. McMillan
Vice President of Marketing, Amit Verma
Senior Vice President Medical Scientific Affairs, Robert (Bob) Kaper
Senior Vice President of Human Resources, Elizabeth (Beth) Bolgiano
Vice President Commercial Analytics and Sales Operations, Jeffrey (Jeff) Hart
Vice President Legal Affairs Chief Compliance Officer, Robert (Bob) Blood
Senior Vice President General Counsel Secretary, Joseph (Jo) Vittiglio
Senior Vice President Sales Marketing for Hematology Oncology Business, Paul Williams
Vice President Sales, Mike (Mikey) Cahill
Vice President of Research and Development, Mike (Mikey) Jozwiakowski
General Manager Cord Blood Registry and Senior Vice President of Consumer Sales and Marketing, Todd (Toddy) Van Horn
Chairman, Gino Santini
Auditors: PricewaterhouseCoopers LLP

LOCATIONS

HQ: AMAG Pharmaceuticals, Inc.
1100 Winter Street, Waltham, MA 02451
Phone: 617 498-3300
Web: www.amagpharma.com

PRODUCTS/OPERATIONS

2015 Sales

	% of total
US product sales	82
Lisence fee & other collaboration revenues	12
Service revenue	6
Total	**100**

Selected Products
Approved
Feraheme (ferumoxytol iron replacement therapy)
Makena (hydroxyprogesterone caproate injection reduce risk for preterm birth)
MuGard (an oral rinse for the management of oral mucositis)

COMPETITORS

Allergan plc	Guerbet
Bayer HealthCare Pharmaceuticals	Luitpold Pharmaceuticals
Cryo-Cell	Luna Innovations
Daiichi Sankyo	Teva Pharmaceuticals
FMCNA	USA

HISTORICAL FINANCIALS

Company Type: Public

Income Statement

FYE: December 31

	REVENUE ($ mil.)	NET INCOME ($ mil.)	NET PROFIT MARGIN	EMPLOYEES
12/15	418.2	32.7	7.8%	552.0
12/14	124.3	135.8	109.2%	257.0
12/13	80.8	(9.6)	—	148.0
12/12	85.3	(16.7)	—	129.0
12/11	61.2	(77.0)	—	174.0
Annual Growth	**61.7%**	**—**	**—**	**33.5%**

2015 Year-End Financials

Debt ratio: 40.3%
Return on equity: 4.7%
Cash ($ mil.): 228.7
Current ratio: 2.47
Long-term debt ($ mil.): 985.6

No. of shares (mil.): 34.7
Dividends
  Yield: —
  Payout: —
Market value ($ mil.): 1,049.0

	STOCK PRICE ($) FY Close	P/E High/Low		PER SHARE ($) Earnings	Dividends	Book Value
12/15	30.19	74	25	0.93	0.00	26.84
12/14	42.62	7	3	5.45	0.00	17.97
12/13	24.28	—	—	(0.44)	0.00	7.92
12/12	14.71	—	—	(0.78)	0.00	8.03
12/11	18.91	—	—	(3.64)	0.00	8.48
Annual Growth	**12.4%**	—	—	**—**	**—**	**33.4%**

Ambarella, Inc.

Ambarella's technology helps capture crisp clear digital images in cameras designed for sports autos drones and security. The company designs and markets video processing semiconductors for taking high-definition video and still images. It combines its system-on-a-chip semiconductor designs with proprietary software to create both industry and consumer products. The hardware/software combo helps cameras compensate for motion as a skier swoops downhill or a drone sweeps over a mountain. In security applications Amabarella's video chips can gather high-def images in low light. The company designs its chips which are made by contractors for small form factors and to run on low power.

Operations
Ambarella's chips and software allow for greater compression of the HD video signal which translates to broadcasters being able to offer more channels in fixed bandwidths and consumer products that capture higher quality video in smaller devices.

Samsung Electronics handles most of Ambarella's contract manufacturing chores. Ambarella also works with contractors Global UniChip Corp. and Taiwan Semiconductor Manufacturing Co.

Geographic Reach
Ambarella has offices and design centers in China Hong Kong Italy Japan South Korea and Taiwan. Hong Kong accounts for 90% of sales with the remainder split between the rest of Asia the US other North American countries and Europe.

Sales and Marketing
Ambarella's chips are used by GoPro Inc. Hikvision Digital Technology Co. Robert Bosch Garmin

Ltd. Motorola Mobility Inc. and Asia Optical Co. While Ambarella has a number of end users most of its sales go through two companies. About two-thirds of sales are made via logistic services provider Wintech Microelectronics Co. and another 20% are through Chicony Electronics an original design manufacturer.

Financial Performance
A snapshot of Ambarella's financials for 2016 (ended January) shows revenue profit and cash flow headed up. The company's revenue shot up 55% in 2016 to $316 million. The increase came from strong demand for its A9 A7L S2L and A12 SoCs for the IP security drone automotive aftermarket and wearable sports camera markets. In the second half of the year however Ambarella saw a decline in wearables because of high inventory levels at GoPro a major end customer.

The revenue increase helped Ambarella post a 51% increase in net income to $77 million in 2016 despite spending more for research and development and other expenses. The company has been profitable since 2012. Cash flow from operations increased to $124 million in 2016 from $52 million in 2015 on higher net income decreased accounts receivable and decreased inventory.

Strategy
In 2011 Ambarella lost a good chunk of its business when Kodak stopped making cameras. Ambarella rebounded finding new customers in wearable sports cameras security cameras and aerial drones. But once again it ran into problems when sales stalled at one its major customers GoPro. Ambarella had to work through a load of inventory of its chips held by GoPro which held up new sales to the camera company.

But Ambarella increased its supply of chips for drones and security and added automotive applications to its arsenal with virtual reality applications on the horizon. To maintain the pipeline of new products Ambarella increased R&D spending to $83 million in 2016 from $58 million in 2015. The company has concentrated more technology on its systems-on-a-chip which has enables camera manufacturers to reduce the size of their products. A new automotive application is cameras for sideview mirrors which provide wider views for tasks such as parking.

Camera makers like Ambarella's chips for their capability of capturing high resolution video. Nikon became a first time customer using the A9AC SOC for 4K ultra-HD video in a new underwater camera. Home security customer Bosch incorporated Ambarella's HD chip into cameras that capture a 360-degree view. For virtual reality headsets Ambarella released a line of SoCs that capture HD video at high rates of speed at 360 degrees.

Mergers and Acquisitions
In 2015 Ambarella acquired VisLab a privately held company based in Italy for $30 million. VisLab is a pioneer in perception systems and autonomous vehicle research. The acquisition provides expertise for research into computer vision for the automotive IP security wearable and drone markets.

EXECUTIVES

CFO, George W. Laplante, age 64
CTO and Director, Les Kohn, age 59, $226,250 total compensation
EVP, Didier LeGall, age 61, $217,500 total compensation
Vice President Of Engineering, Chris (Chrissy) Day
Auditors: PricewaterhouseCoopers LLP

LOCATIONS

HQ: Ambarella, Inc.
 3101 Jay Street, Santa Clara, CA 95054
Phone: 408 734-8888
Web: www.ambarella.com

COMPETITORS

Canon	Panasonic Corp
Fujitsu	Samsung Electronics
Intel	Sony
NVIDIA	Texas Instruments

HISTORICAL FINANCIALS

Company Type: Public

Income Statement

FYE: January 31

	REVENUE ($ mil.)	NET INCOME ($ mil.)	NET PROFIT MARGIN	EMPLOYEES
01/16	316.3	76.5	24.2%	640.0
01/15	218.2	50.5	23.2%	524.0
01/14	157.6	25.6	16.3%	495.0
01/13	121.0	18.1	15.0%	444.0
01/12	97.2	9.8	10.1%	425.0
Annual Growth	34.3%	67.1%	—	10.8%

2016 Year-End Financials

Debt ratio: —	No. of shares (mil.): 32.3
Return on equity: 26.0%	Dividends
Cash ($ mil.): 307.8	Yield: —
Current ratio: 7.57	Payout: —
Long-term debt ($ mil.): —	Market value ($ mil.): 1,283.0

	STOCK PRICE ($) FY Close	P/E High/Low	PER SHARE ($) Earnings	Dividends	Book Value
01/16	39.68	52 15	2.27	0.00	10.81
01/15	55.31	36 13	1.57	0.00	7.69
01/14	32.03	38 10	0.85	0.00	5.44
01/13	9.96	20 9	0.60	0.00	4.16
Annual Growth	58.5%	— —	55.8%	—	37.5%

America First Multifamily Investors LP

Auditors: Deloitte & Touche LLP

LOCATIONS

HQ: America First Multifamily Investors LP
 1004 Farnam Street, Suite 400, Omaha, NE 68102
Phone: 402 444-1630
Web: www.ataxfund.com

HISTORICAL FINANCIALS

Company Type: Public

Income Statement

FYE: December 31

	ASSETS ($ mil.)	NET INCOME ($ mil.)	INCOME AS % OF ASSETS	EMPLOYEES
12/15	872.5	26.6	3.0%	0.0
12/14	744.2	15.0	2.0%	0.0
12/13	534.2	17.7	3.3%	0.0
12/12	413.1	4.4	1.1%	0.0
12/11	297.9	(2.2)	—	0.0
Annual Growth	30.8%	—	—	—

	STOCK PRICE ($) FY Close	P/E High/Low	PER SHARE ($) Earnings	Dividends	Book Value
12/15	5.06	17 15	0.34	0.50	5.20
12/14	5.26	26 21	0.25	0.50	5.14
12/13	6.29	18 16	0.40	0.50	3.98
12/12	6.67	50 36	0.14	0.50	4.25
12/11	4.94	— —	(0.04)	0.50	4.35
Annual Growth	0.6%	— —	—	(0.0%)	4.5%

American Campus Communities Inc

American Campus Communities (ACC) actually does most of its business off campus. The self-managed real estate investment trust (REIT) owns and operates student housing properties located at or near colleges and universities in more than 25 states. The company leases the ground for on-campus properties from the schools which in turn receive half of the net cash flow from these properties. ACC also works with schools to develop new properties and renovate existing housing and provides third-party leasing and management services for other student housing owners. In all the REIT manages about 206 properties (with some 133000 beds) at more than 90 schools in the US and Canada.

Operations

The company is a fully integrated self-managed and self-administered equity real estate investment trust with expertise in the design finance development construction management and operational management of student housing properties. It has four reportable segments: Wholly-Owned Properties (which generate 94% of revenue) On-Campus Participating Properties Development Services and Property Management Services.

Many of ACC's properties feature resort-style amenities making them more desirable than your typical dorm facility. The company has been successful in establishing strong relationships with school systems which pays off in earning repeat business as various campuses seek to add new housing options. Among the REIT's developments are sites in Texas and New Mexico.

ACC owns 168 student housing properties containing approximately 103200 beds. Including its owned and third-party managed properties ACC's total managed portfolio consists of 205 properties with approximately 133100 beds.

Sales and Marketing

The company has been increased spending on marketing and advertising initiatives in recent years In 2015 it spent $12 million (down from $14 million in 2014.

Financial Performance

ACC continued a decade-long run of increasing revenue with a 3% rise to $753 million in 2015. Higher occupancy rates in its properties helped ACC raise rents which raised revenue. Same-property revenue increased in 2015 from 2014.

The sale of 20 wholly-owned properties in 2015 drove ACC's net income 85% to $116 million from 2014.

Cash flow from operates rose a slim $1 million to $261 million in 2015 from 2014.

Strategy

ACC has expanded its portfolio by both buying existing properties and developing new ones. It regularly buys properties in bulk adding thousands of beds at a time. In addition to buying and developing new housing communities the REIT also sells properties when they are no longer considered core to its long-term investment strategy.

In late 2015 ACC had more than $300 million of owned development and presale development underway for delivery in 2016. The 2017 property pipeline was $443 million with properties worth $365 million under construction in late 2015.

Mergers and Acquisitions

In 2015 ACC made eight acquisitions containing 1488 units and 4061 beds for about $380 million in college towns in Texas New York Florida and Tennessee.

Company Background

In 2012 ACC acquired 15 properties with nearly 6600 beds in several states for some $627 million. The previous year the REIT acquired four properties as well as shopping center it plans to redevelop into a mixed-use community. It also completed and opened four new communities.

EXECUTIVES

EVP CFO and Treasurer, Jonathan A. Graf, age 51, $400,000 total compensation

President and CEO, William C. Bayless, age 52, $750,000 total compensation

EVP and COO, James C. Hopke, age 55, $350,000 total compensation

EVP and Chief Investment Officer, William W. Talbot, age 42, $350,000 total compensation

EVP Public and Private Transactions, James E. (Jamie) Wilhelm, age 53, $225,000 total compensation

SVP Capital Markets, Daniel B. Perry, age 43, $275,000 total compensation

EVP and CTO, Jorge de C°rdenas

EVP and Controller, Kim K. Voss

Vice President Risk Management, Jane Downing

Vice President Asset Managment and Developement Services, Heather (Heath) Laney

Vice President Facilities, Bryan (Bry) Storey

Vice President Public Private Partnerships, Mark Rogers

Senior Vice President Information Technologies, Jorge De Cardenas

Vice President Or Director of Management Information Systems Or Information Technology, Greg McCarty

Vice President, Brett Hahnel

Vice President Financial Reporting, Jason (Jase) French

Senior Vice President Management Services, Steve Crawford

Senior Vice President Construction Management, Clint Braun

Vice President Marketing, Meredith (Edith) Patton

Vice President Project Management and Construction, John (Jack) Delacruz

Senior Vice President Marketing Business Development, Jason Wills

Senior Vice President Transactions, Brian (Bri) Winger

Vice President Management Services, Dan Shoepe

Vice President Investor Relations, Ryan (Ry) Dennison

Vice President Management Services, Jimmy Henson

Vice President Project Management and Construction, William (Bill) Baker

Vice President Internal Audit, Stacey (Stace) Heller

Executive Vice President Public and Private Transactions, Jamie (James) Wilhelm
Regional Vice President, Heath Hines
Senior Vice President Management servicesv, Larry (Lar) Greenberg
Vice President Recruiting, Tim (Timmy) Bilz
Vice President Acquisitions, Kris (Krissy) Kelly
Senior Vice President, Meredith (Edith) Elliott
Chairman, Edward Lowenthal, age 72
Auditors: Ernst & Young LLP

LOCATIONS

HQ: American Campus Communities Inc
12700 Hill Country Blvd., Suite T-200, Austin, TX 78738
Phone: 512 732-1000
Web: www.americancampus.com

PRODUCTS/OPERATIONS

2015 Sales

	$ mil.	% of total
Wholly owned properties	704.9	94
On-campus participating properties	31.6	4
Third-party management services	8.8	1
Third-party development services	5.0	1
Resident services	3.1	-
Total	**753.4**	**100**

COMPETITORS

AMLI Residential	Campus Apartments
Allen & O'Hara	Education Realty
Alliance Residential	Fairfield Residential
Apartment Investment and Management	JPI
Camden Property	Place Properties

HISTORICAL FINANCIALS

Company Type: Public

Income Statement
FYE: December 31

	REVENUE ($ mil.)	NET INCOME ($ mil.)	NET PROFIT MARGIN	EMPLOYEES
12/15	753.3	115.9	15.4%	3,108.0
12/14	733.9	62.8	8.6%	3,227.0
12/13	657.4	104.6	15.9%	3,059.0
12/12	491.2	56.6	11.5%	2,913.0
12/11	390.3	56.6	14.5%	2,387.0
Annual Growth	17.9%	19.6%	—	6.8%

2015 Year-End Financials

Debt ratio: 49.2%
Return on equity: 4.3%
Cash ($ mil.): 16.6
Current ratio: 0.96
Long-term debt ($ mil.): 2,967.9
No. of shares (mil.): 112.3
Dividends
Yield: 3.8%
Payout: 154.9%
Market value ($ mil.): 4,645.0

	STOCK PRICE ($) FY Close	P/E High/Low	PER SHARE ($) Earnings	Dividends	Book Value
12/15	41.34	44 31	1.02	1.58	24.66
12/14	41.36	71 55	0.58	1.50	24.35
12/13	32.21	48 32	0.98	1.42	25.05
12/12	46.13	72 62	0.65	1.35	25.30
12/11	41.96	52 38	0.80	1.35	18.90
Annual Growth	(0.4%)	— —	6.3%	4.0%	6.9%

American Outdoor Brands Corp

Smith & Wesson has built a successful business shooting for the stars. Operating through subsidiary Smith & Wesson Corp. Smith & Wesson Holding Corporation makes and markets pistols revolvers tactical rifles and police accessories as well as gun-safety devices under the M&P Series name. The company founded in 1852 also sells handcuffs and hunting rifles and car boat and home alarm system packages. Smith & Wesson is the exclusive importer of Walther pistols with US production rights for the Walther PPK model. To diversify and add breadth to its brand the company licenses its name to makers of apparel watches sunglasses gift sets and more.Geographic Reach-Smith & Wesson sells its products globally. Besides the US the company serves Europe Asia and Latin America. It maintains production facilities for its firearms in Springfield Massachusetts and in Houlton Maine. StrategySmith & Wesson aims to diversify its products portfolio as the company evolves from being a gun maker to a top supplier of a variety of arms. As a result the company has traded sales of revolvers in favor of pistols. Smith & Wesson is also working to expand its products in the areas of tactical and long-gun lines as well as nonfirearm products.

The company supports its firearms business through deals with other companies to make Smith & Wesson-branded products. A licensing agreement with BBC Imagewear inked in 2009 provides Smith & Wesson with branded T-shirts jackets and shirts. A similar deal with Kudzu/The Game offers branded hats and caps and hats T-shirts jackets gun pads license plates decals pins patches key chains glassware and mugs with the Thompson/Center Arms logo. Its licensing agreement with TruckVault calls for Smith & Wesson-brand lockable steel handgun safes for homes vehicles and public safety agencies including police government agencies fire departments and the military.

Financial Performance

Smith & Wesson has seen its net sales rise in recent years particularly following the November 2008 US presidential election as consumers began to stockpile arms for fear of losing some rights under new leadership. In 2011 however Smith & Wesson logged slightly fewer orders across the company's firearms businesses –returning to more normal levels temporarily as compared to the strong consumer demand it has experienced for years.

In fiscal 2012 net sales increased 20% and net income rose 119% as compared to 2011. Net cash outflow during the same reporting period was $1 million vs. $20 million in 2011. Net sales increases can be attributed to a 25% rise in handgun product sales and a 94% increase in sales of modern sporting rifles thanks to the late fiscal 2011 introduction of a new sport model that was competitively priced. International sales meanwhile accounted for 4% of Smith & Wesson's sales. The company's net income boost came from rising operating income due to increased sales volumes. Its net cash outflow in 2012 was primarily related to cash used in financing activities such as repurchasing Convertible Notes.

Sales and Marketing

Smith & Wesson taps several distribution channels to get its products in the hands of customers. Customers include distributors government and military agencies businesses retailers and consumers as well as federal state and municipal law enforcement agencies and officers. The company which spent $14.7 million on advertising and promotion expenses in 2012 leverages its websites to market products and services.

The company has increased its sales in recent years by forming and maintaining its own sales force instead of relying on the representatives of independent manufacturers to sell its products including its line of polymer pistols.

Mergers and Acquisitions

In 2016 Smith & Wesson acquired laser sighting systems company Crimson Trace Corp. for $95 million. The company established its Electro-Optics Division from Crimson Trace's assets and operations.

Company BackgroundAmid a shift in government spending the company exited the perimeter security systems business in 2011. It moved to divest its perimeter security division —Tennessee-based Universal Safety Response (later renamed Smith & Wesson Security Solutions) to Detroit Michigan-based FutureNet Group in mid-2012. Smith & Wesson Security Solutions has provided barriers and installation and other services used in approximately 110 military installations and more than a dozen federal agencies and commercial facilities. The operations generated about $130 million during the past three years accounting for some 10% of Smith & Wesson's sales.

EXECUTIVES

EVP CFO and Treasurer, Jeffrey D. Buchanan, age 61, $351,370 total compensation
President and CEO, P. James Debney, age 49, $553,408 total compensation
President Manufacturing Services Division, Mark P. Smith, age 40, $270,284 total compensation
VP Chief Compliance Officer General Counsel and Secretary, Robert J. Cicero, age 49, $283,155 total compensation
President Firearms Division, Matt Buckingham
Auditors: Deloitte & Touche LLP

LOCATIONS

HQ: American Outdoor Brands Corp
2100 Roosevelt Avenue, Springfield, MA 01104
Phone: 800 331-0852
Web: www.smith-wesson.com

PRODUCTS/OPERATIONS

2016 Sales

	$ mil.	% of total
Firearms Division		
Handguns	485.4	67
Long Guns	127.6	18
Walther - -		
Other Products & Services	44.6	6
Accessories Division	65.3	9
Total	**722.9**	**100**

2016 Sales

	$ mil.	% of total
Firearms Division		
Sporting Goods Distribution Channel	579.6	80
Professional Channel	62.9	9
Other Products & Services	15.1	2
Accessories Division	65.3	9
Total	**722.9**	**100**

Selected Products

Accessories

Cases
Fiber optic sights
Gloves
Grips
Holsters
Locks
Magazines
Apparel
Firearms
Pistols
Revolvers
Rifles
Knives
Handcuffs and restraints
Personal security
Safes
Vaults

COMPETITORS

American Derringer	Marlin Firearms
Browning Arms	Mossberg
Bushmaster Firearms	Para USA
Colt Defense	Remington Arms
Colt's	Ruger
Fabbrica D'Armi Pietro	Savage Arms
Beretta	Springfield Armory
Freedom Group	Taurus International
Glock	Tyco Fire & Security
Heckler & Koch	

HISTORICAL FINANCIALS
Company Type: Public

Income Statement
FYE: April 30

	REVENUE ($ mil.)	NET INCOME ($ mil.)	NET PROFIT MARGIN	EMPLOYEES
04/16	722.9	93.9	13.0%	1,853.0
04/15	551.8	49.6	9.0%	1,749.0
04/14	626.6	89.3	14.3%	1,758.0
04/13	587.5	78.7	13.4%	1,475.0
04/12	412.0	16.1	3.9%	1,346.0
Annual Growth	15.1%	55.4%	—	8.3%

2016 Year-End Financials

Debt ratio: 27.9%
Return on equity: 37.3%
Cash ($ mil.): 191.2
Current ratio: 2.72
Long-term debt ($ mil.): 166.5

No. of shares (mil.): 56.0
Dividends
  Yield: —
  Payout: —
Market value ($ mil.): 1,222.0

	STOCK PRICE ($) FY Close	P/E High/Low		PER SHARE ($) Earnings	Dividends	Book Value
04/16	21.83	17	9	1.68	0.00	5.50
04/15	14.87	19	10	0.90	0.00	3.60
04/14	15.35	10	6	1.49	0.00	3.01
04/13	8.78	9	5	1.18	0.00	2.82
04/12	8.25	34	9	0.25	0.00	1.73
Annual Growth	27.5%	—	—	61.0%	—	33.6%

American Railcar Industries Inc

American Railcar Industries (ARI) doesn't make the little engine that could but it does make the cars that the engine pulls. A North American manufacturer of railcars and railcar components the company also provides maintenance and fleet management services to freight shippers railcar leasing companies and railroads. Its two Arkansas manufacturing facilities make several types of railcars including covered hoppers for grains cement and other dry bulk and tank cars for liquid and gas commodities. The company also serves non-rail industries with industrial products such as steel and aluminum casting machining stamping welding and fabrication.

Geographic Reach

Headquartered at Saint Charles Missouri ARI has eight manufacturing plants that fabricate and assemble raw materials including two Arkansas-based railcar manufacturing plants; seven railcar repair plants; and 13 mobile repair and mini-shop locations throughout the US (primarily concentrated in Texas and Missouri) and Canada (Ontario).

Operations

ARI divides its operations across three segments: manufacturing (80% of total sales) railcar services (12%) and railcar leasing (8%).

Sales and Marketing

The company sells and markets its products and services through marketing personnel and sales representatives directly to its customers in North America. It serves primarily leasing companies industrial companies and clients that use railcars for freight transport or shippers and Class I railroads. Its top 10 customers accounted for 75% of its total revenues in 2015.

Financial Performance

After suffering through the decline in demand for new railcars due to the economic downturn ARI has enjoyed exceptional growth over the last few years. Revenues peaked at a record-setting $889 million in 2015 mainly due to increased sales across all segments especially manufacturing. Profits also peaked at $133 million in 2015 another company milestone.

Manufacturing sales climbed by 17% due to higher Hopper railcar shipments for direct sale as a result of demand shifts towards more specialty hopper railcar types. Railcar leasing revenue also surged by 79% due to an increase in the number of railcars on lease. In addition railcar services revenues for 2015 increased by 7%.

Strategy

The company is focused on investing capital and evaluating opportunities to further expand its manufacturing flexibility and repair capacity. It completed three repair expansion projects in 2015 and one in early 2016 to tank railcar manufacturing facilities. In 2014 ARI expanded its railcar repair capabilities with a new repair facility in Brookhaven Mississippi.

EXECUTIVES

President and CEO, Jeffrey S. Hollister, age 47, $325,000 total compensation
SVP CFO and Treasurer, Luke M. Williams, age 38
CIO, Subbu Subramanian
Vice President Marketing, Jim Doty
Vice President Of Human Resources, Tim (Timmy) Lograsso
Vice President of Sales, Harold (Harry) Storz
Chairman, SungHwan Cho, age 41
Auditors: Grant Thornton LLP

LOCATIONS

HQ: American Railcar Industries Inc
100 Clark Street, St. Charles, MO 63301
Phone: 636 940-6000
Web: www.americanrailcar.com

PRODUCTS/OPERATIONS

Selected Products and Services
Industrial Products
  Aluminum Casting
  Custom Plate Burning
  Heat Treating
  Machining and Inspection
  Robotic Fabrication
  Roll Forming
  Specialty Welding
  Steel and Alloy Casting
  Structural Fabrication
Manufacturing
  Cement and Sand Railcars
  Grain Railcars
  Hopper railcars
  Ore Railcars
  Plastic Pellet Railcars
  Pressureaide Railcars
  Specialized Railcars

2015 Sales

	$ mil.	% of total
Manufacturing operations	700.0	79
Railcar leasing	116.7	13
Railcar services	72.6	8
Total	**889.3**	**100**

COMPETITORS

FreightCar America	Miner Enterprises
GE Rail Services	Trinity Industries
Greenbrier Companies	Union Tank Car
Kawasaki Rail Car	

HISTORICAL FINANCIALS
Company Type: Public

Income Statement
FYE: December 31

	REVENUE ($ mil.)	NET INCOME ($ mil.)	NET PROFIT MARGIN	EMPLOYEES
12/15	889.3	133.4	15.0%	2,407.0
12/14	733.0	99.5	13.6%	2,865.0
12/13	750.5	86.9	11.6%	2,663.0
12/12	711.7	63.8	9.0%	2,643.0
12/11	519.3	4.3	0.8%	2,413.0
Annual Growth	14.4%	135.5%	—	(0.1%)

2015 Year-End Financials

Debt ratio: 45.8%
Return on equity: 25.8%
Cash ($ mil.): 314.9
Current ratio: 2.48
Long-term debt ($ mil.): 575.8

No. of shares (mil.): 19.8
Dividends
  Yield: 3.4%
  Payout: 28.4%
Market value ($ mil.): 918.0

	STOCK PRICE ($) FY Close	P/E High/Low		PER SHARE ($) Earnings	Dividends	Book Value
12/15	46.28	9	5	6.39	1.60	27.02
12/14	51.50	18	9	4.66	1.60	23.20
12/13	45.75	12	7	4.07	1.00	20.32
12/12	31.73	12	7	2.99	0.25	17.30
12/11	23.93	142	70	0.20	0.00	14.53
Annual Growth	17.9%	—	—	137.7%	—	16.8%

American Woodmark Corp.

American Woodmark has more cabinet selections than the prime minister of Russia. A top maker of home cabinets in the US the company makes and distributes about 500 styles of low- to mid-priced kitchen cabinets and vanities. Styles vary by finish (oak cherry hickory maple as well as laminate) and door design. Brands include American Woodmark Shenandoah Cabinetry Timberlake and Waypoint. Targeting the remodeling and new home construction markets American Woodmark sells its lineup through home centers and independent dealers and distributors; it also sells directly to major builders. American Woodmark was established through a leveraged buyout of Boise Cascade's cabinet division.

Operations

Business is divided between two markets —remodeling and new home construction. Products are distributed through four assembly plants and a third-party logistics network.

Through its seven service centers nationwide American Woodmark offers complete turnkey installation services to its direct builder customers.

The company keeps in stock about 85 door designs in more than 20 colors.

Geographic Reach

Virginia-based American Woodmark operates nine manufacturing facilities in Arizona Georgia Indiana Kentucky Maryland Tennessee Virginia and West Virginia. Its coast-to-coast service centers expand its customer reach beyond the Sun Belt construction market.

Sales and Marketing

Together Lowe's and The Home Depot accounted for 45% of the company's fiscal 2015 (ended April) sales.

Through three primary channels —home centers builders and independent dealers and distributors —American Woodmark services the remodeling and new home construction markets. Its brand names include American Woodmark Timberlake (sold to major home builders) Shenandoah Cabinetry (Lowe's) Potomac (Lowe's) and Waypoint Living Spaces.

In fiscal 2015 advertising expenses totaled $34.3 million up from $30.4 million in fiscal 2014 but down from $36.5 million in fiscal 2013.

Financial Performance

American Woodmark has enjoyed rising revenue since 2009. In fiscal 2014 (ended April) the cabinet maker reported sales of $825.5 million a 14% increase versus the prior year. The double-digit growth was largely driven by increased sales in the new construction market as well as higher per-unit revenue.

After experiencing losses in 2011 and 2012 the company's profits have rebounded. Higher revenues helped net income rise 73% to $35.5 million in fiscal 2015 (although increased income tax expense partially offset those gains). Cash flow from operations also rose growing 45% to $58.7 million that year.

HISTORY

Company Background

Alvin Goldhush in 1951 started cabinet company Form Laminates which lumber giant Boise Cascade acquired two decades later. Four senior managers of Boise Cascade's cabinet division — William Brandt Jeff Holcomb Al Graber and Donald Mathias —engineered an LBO of the unit in 1980 and named it American Woodmark after a popular line of cabinets. The company started selling cabinets nationwide through distribution centers and went public in 1986.

American Woodmark spent the first half of the 1990s diversifying its product and brands. In 1990 it introduced Timberlake a cabinet line for the construction industry. Other brands including Coventry and Case Crestwood and Scots Pine were added and quintupled its product line.

President and COO Jake Gosa became CEO in 1996. The sales cupboard was rather bare that year from a downturn in the closely linked home centers industry. The market surged in 1997 causing American Woodmark's profits to nearly triple and new equipment and manufacturing techniques boosted output. In 1998 the company began offering hickory cabinets (its first new wood species in a decade) kitchen accessories and high-quality ready-to-assemble framed cabinets (Flat Pack).

In 1999 American Woodmark expanded its hickory cabinet offerings (adding the Newport and Charleston brands). The company began operations at its new assembly facility in Gas City Indiana in 2000. To both preserve and increase market share in a slow-growth economy in 2001 American Woodmark initiated plans to expand two plants and open two more in Kentucky and Oklahoma.

EXECUTIVES

SVP and General Manager New Construction, R. Perry Campbell, age 50, $240,623 total compensation
President and CEO, S. Cary Dunston, age 50, $396,218 total compensation
SVP Remodel Sales and Marketing, Bradley S. (Brad) Boyer, age 56, $267,984 total compensation
CFO, M. Scott Culbreth, age 44
Vice President Personnel, Jeff Bahr
Vice President Of Field Sales For The, Barry Rudolph
Chairman, Kent B. Guichard, age 59
Auditors: KPMG LLP

LOCATIONS

HQ: American Woodmark Corp.
3102 Shawnee Drive, Winchester, VA 22601
Phone: 540 665-9100
Web: www.americanwoodmark.com

PRODUCTS/OPERATIONS

Selected Brands
American Woodmark
Potomac
Shenandoah Cabinetry
Timberlake
Waypoint Living Spaces

COMPETITORS

Armstrong World Industries	MasterBrand Cabinets
Elkay Manufacturing	Norcraft Companies Inc.
Masco	US Home Systems

HISTORICAL FINANCIALS

Company Type: Public

Income Statement

FYE: April 30

	REVENUE ($ mil.)	NET INCOME ($ mil.)	NET PROFIT MARGIN	EMPLOYEES
04/16	947.0	58.7	6.2%	5,600.0
04/15	825.4	35.5	4.3%	5,070.0
04/14	726.5	20.4	2.8%	4,916.0
04/13	630.4	9.7	1.5%	4,537.0
04/12	515.8	(20.7)	—	3,791.0
Annual Growth	16.4%	—	—	10.2%

2016 Year-End Financials

Debt ratio: 5.1%
Return on equity: 22.9%
Cash ($ mil.): 200.2
Current ratio: 3.27
Long-term debt ($ mil.): 22.4
No. of shares (mil.): 16.2
Dividends
  Yield: —
  Payout: —
Market value ($ mil.): 1,183.0

	STOCK PRICE ($) FY Close	P/E High/Low	PER SHARE ($) Earnings	Dividends	Book Value
04/16	72.84	25 13	3.57	0.00	17.28
04/15	50.70	25 12	2.21	0.00	14.29
04/14	30.01	30 23	1.31	0.00	12.31
04/13	33.65	54 24	0.66	0.00	9.86
04/12	17.95	— —	(1.45)	0.27	9.03
Annual Growth	41.9%	— —	—	—	17.6%

Ameris Bancorp

Ameris Bancorp enjoys the financial climate of the Deep South. It is the holding company of Ameris Bank which holds roughly $3.6 billion in assets and serves retail and consumer customers through more than 75 full-service and mortgage branches in Alabama Georgia South Carolina and northern Florida. In addition to its standard banking products and services the bank also provides treasury services mortgage and refinancing solutions and investment services through an agreement with Raymond James Financial. Loans secured by commercial real estate accounted for approximately 45% of the company's loan portfolio while 1-4 family residential and construction & land development mortgages accounted for nearly a quarter and about 10% respectively.

Operations

Like most banks Ameris earns the vast majority of its recurring revenue (71.5%) from interest income from loans. Nearly 80% of these loans are made up of commercial real estate 1-4 family residential and construction & land development loans. The remaining 20% are from a mix of commercial multi-family residential and consumer loans (home improvement home equity personal lines of credit auto loans and student loans).

Traditional banking products (deposit accounts) and services along with investment products and services (which primarily earn income from fees and commissions) made up about 28% of the bank's annual sales in fiscal 2013.

Sales and Marketing

Through an acquisition-oriented growth strategy Ameris seeks to grow its brand and presence in the markets it currently serves in Georgia Alabama Florida and South Carolina as well as in neighboring communities. In addition the bank expects its community-oriented philosophy will help strengthen existing customer relations and attract new customers.

The company spent $1.62 million on advertising and public relations in Fiscal Year 2013 just under the $1.622 million it spent in 2012 and more than double the $722000 it spent in 2011. The company increased its advertising spending by $900000 during 2012 to support its revenue and growth- strategies during the year.

Financial Performance

Ameris carried $3.67 billion in total assets as of December 31 2013. Loans made up $2.5 billion (approximately 68.9% of total assets). The bank also reported carrying $3 billion in deposits.

Ameris' net revenue dipped in fiscal 2013 declining 5% to $163 million from its high of $172 million in 2012 mostly from an $11.3 million dip in non-interest revenue. But this dip in non-interest revenue is primarily because the bank recorded a large gain of $20 million from acquisitions in 2012. When excluding this acquisition gain from 2012's revenues and thanks to $6.1 million revenue increase in mortgage banking activity management reports that total non-interest income actually increased $8.7 million in 2013 compared to 2012. A decline in interest-earning loan assets from $2.47 billion in 2013 compared to $2.5 billion in 2012 also played a role in the dip in net revenues.

Thanks to aggressive acquisitions and despite revenue decreasing net income jumped a whopping 43% to $20 million in 2013 from $14 million in 2012. This is only slightly below the bank's net income high of $21 million in 2011. It's most notable acquisition of Prosperity Bank increased Ameris' total assets by $744.9 million and added $449.7 million in loans to its interest-earning loan portfolio. Adding to the extra income from new loans Ameris collected higher net interest margins on all of its loans which increased to 4.74% in 2013 from 4.60% in 2012.

Strategy

Ameris plans to continue using its community banking philosophy to lessen its risk and identify prime local lending markets. Management reports that by encouraging a personalized service experience and building deeper customer relationships the bank has already grown a "substantial" base of low-cost core deposits (which pad the bank's reserves and lessen financial risk). And between its bench of experienced decision makers and lenders operating in a "decentralized" structure (which differentiates Ameris from mega banks) and its deep familiarity with local markets management believes the bank can better identify prime growth markets (for lending and bank services) with managed risk in the years ahead.

Mergers and Acquisitions

Integral to the bank's growth strategy Ameris has aggressively acquired banks to broaden its reach into its primary southern markets. Ameris Bancorp purchased Jacksonville Bancorp and its eight branches more than doubling its branch network in Jacksonville Illinois to 14 branches.

Company Background

In addition to acquiring several troubled and failing banks with help from the FDIC Ameris merged with Prosperity Bank in 2013 which broadened its reach into Florida through Prosperity's branches in St. Augustine Jacksonville Panama City Lynn Haven Palatka and Ormand Beach.Georgia's economy was one of the hardest hit in the US during the recession and Ameris has taken advantage of the plethora of banks seized by regulators in the state. Since 2009 the company has acquired about 10 failed banks in Georgia though FDIC-assisted transactions adding some

20 branches to its network. Ameris also snagged the failed First Bank of Jacksonville in Florida which had two locations.

EXECUTIVES

Chief Banking Executive Ameris Bancorp and Ameris Bank, Andrew B. (Andy) Cheney, age 66, $400,000 total compensation
EVP and Chief Credit Officer, Jon S. Edwards, age 54, $260,000 total compensation
EVP Chief Administrative Officer and Corporate Secretary, Cindi H. Lewis, age 62, $90,333 total compensation
President and CEO, Edwin W. (Ed) Hortman, age 62, $625,000 total compensation
EVP and Chief Banking Officer Georgia and Alabama, Lawton E. Bassett
EVP CFO and COO, Dennis J. Zember, age 46, $320,000 total compensation
EVP and Chief Risk Officer, Stephen A. Melton, $275,000 total compensation
EVP and Chief Banking Officer, James A. LaHaise
Vice President, David B (Dave) Batchelor
Assistant Vice President, Ann Dunn
Assistant Vice President, Ann (Annie) Dunn
Chairman, Daniel B. Jeter, age 64
Auditors: Crowe Horwath LLP

LOCATIONS

HQ: Ameris Bancorp
310 First Street S.E., Moultrie, GA 31768
Phone: 229 890-1111
Web: www.amerisbank.com

PRODUCTS/OPERATIONS

Selected Acquisitions
American United Bank
Central Bank of Georgia
Darby Bank & Trust
First Bank of Jacksonville
High Trust Bank
Montgomery Bank & Trust
One Georgia Bank
Satilla Community Bank
Tifton Banking Company
United Security Bank

COMPETITORS

BBVA Compass Bancshares
Bank of America
Capital City Bank
Colony Bankcorp
Community Capital Bancshares
First South Bancorp (NC)
Regions Financial
Southwest Georgia Financial
SunTrust
Thomasville Bancshares

HISTORICAL FINANCIALS

Company Type: Public

Income Statement

FYE: December 31

	ASSETS ($ mil.)	NET INCOME ($ mil.)	INCOME AS % OF ASSETS	EMPLOYEES
12/15	5,588.9	40.8	0.7%	1,304.0
12/14	4,037.0	38.7	1.0%	1,027.0
12/13	3,667.6	20.0	0.5%	984.0
12/12	3,019.0	14.4	0.5%	866.0
12/11	2,994.3	21.0	0.7%	746.0
Annual Growth	**16.9%**	**18.0%**	**—**	**15.0%**

2015 Year-End Financials

Return on assets: 0.8%
Return on equity: 9.2%
Long-term debt ($ mil.): —
No. of shares (mil.): 32.2
Sales ($ mil): 275.9
Dividends
Yield: 0.5%
Payout: 15.7%
Market value ($ mil.): 1,095.0

	STOCK PRICE ($) FY Close	P/E High/Low	PER SHARE ($) Earnings	Dividends	Book Value
12/15	33.99	27 18	1.27	0.20	15.98
12/14	25.64	18 13	1.46	0.15	13.67
12/13	21.11	28 16	0.75	0.00	12.62
12/12	12.49	29 22	0.46	0.00	11.72
12/11	10.28	15 11	0.76	0.00	12.37
Annual Growth	**34.8%**	**— —**	**13.7%**	**—**	**6.6%**

Amerisafe Inc

AMERISAFE has what it takes to insure roughnecks and truckers. AMERISAFE specializes in providing workers' compensation insurance for businesses in hazardous industries including agriculture manufacturing construction logging and sawmill oil and gas maritime and trucking. Through its subsidiaries American Interstate Insurance Silver Oak Casualty and American Interstate Insurance of Texas the company writes coverage for more than 7900 employers (mainly small and midsized firms). In addition AMERISAFE offers worksite safety reviews loss prevention and claims management services. AMERISAFE sells its products in more than 30 states and the District of Columbia.

Geographic Reach

AMERISAFE's largest markets are Louisiana Georgia and Pennsylvania with each accounting for roughly 10% of its gross premiums written.

Sales and Marketing

The company sells its products through more than 3100 independent agents as well as through its Amerisafe General Agency.

Financial Performance

Like all workers' compensation providers AMERISAFE saw its revenues drop during the economic recession for the simplest reason: when employers trim their workforces they need less workers' compensation coverage.

However the company's revenue has been increasing year-over-year since 2010. It reported $356.3 million in revenue for fiscal 2013 up from $321.2 million in revenue for fiscal 2012 and $280.7 million in revenue for fiscal 2011.

AMERISAFE's net income has also been trending up across recent fiscal years. The company netted more than $43 million in fiscal 2013 after reporting a net income of about $29 million for fiscal 2012 and $24 million for fiscal 2011.

The company's cash flow remains strong. It had almost $50 million more on hand at the end of fiscal 2013 than it did at the close of fiscal 2012.

Strategy

AMERISAFE's strategy for growth is based on managing its capital and focusing on its underwriting profitability. It hopes to increase its book value and produce favorable returns by maintaining rate levels that are in balance with the risks it underwrites improving its risk selection and pricing and reducing the frequency and severity of claims through workplace safety reviews medical cost containment and rapid closing of claims. Additionally the company is looking to increase market penetration in the states where it operates as well as seek opportunities in the 12 other states and the US Virgin Islands where it licensed.

Another key element of the company's strategy is to capitalize on its information technology tools. These include its GEAUX underwriting and agency management system and ICAMS its customized operational system which together with the analytical data warehouse that ICAMS feeds improve its ability to select risk write profitable business and administer billing claims and audit functions more cost-effectively.

EXECUTIVES

Executive Vice President and CIO, Brendan Gau
President and COO, G. Janelle Frost, age 46, $370,833 total compensation
EVP and Chief Risk Officer, Vincent J. Gagliano, age 43, $202,000 total compensation
Vice President Treasurer, Angela (Angie) Lannen
Svp Claims Operations, Henry O (Hal) Lestage
Vice President Sales Northeast Region, Ed (Eddie) Ennis
Vice President, Martin (Marti) Rozboril
Senior Vice President Sales Marketing, David (Dave) Morton
Vice President Sales Midwest Region, Mark (Marky) Burger
Sales Vice President, Chris Lastoch
Executive Vice President Sales and Marketing, Craig (Craigy) Leach
Senior Vice President Safety Operations, Leon Lagneaux
Vice President Of Sales, Martha Mcleod
Chairman, Jared A. Morris, age 40
Auditors: Ernst & Young LLP

LOCATIONS

HQ: Amerisafe Inc
2301 Highway 190 West, DeRidder, LA 70634
Phone: 337 463-9052
Web: www.amerisafe.com

PRODUCTS/OPERATIONS

2015 sales

	$ mil.	% of total
Premiums earned	375.9	93
Net investment income	27.9	7
Net realized losses on investments	(2.5)	.
Loss on disposal of assets	(0.7)	.
Fee and other income	0.3	.
Total	**400.9**	**100**

COMPETITORS

ACSTAR	McM Corporation
Baldwin & Lyons	Nationwide
Bituminous Insurance Companies	SeaBright Insurance
	W. R. Berkley
Farm Family Holdings	Zenith National

HISTORICAL FINANCIALS

Company Type: Public

Income Statement

FYE: December 31

	ASSETS ($ mil.)	NET INCOME ($ mil.)	INCOME AS % OF ASSETS	EMPLOYEES
12/15	1,502.0	70.4	4.7%	451.0
12/14	1,457.2	53.6	3.7%	445.0
12/13	1,329.0	43.6	3.3%	437.0
12/12	1,220.9	29.3	2.4%	429.0
12/11	1,148.5	24.1	2.1%	428.0
Annual Growth	**6.9%**	**30.7%**	**—**	**1.3%**

2015 Year-End Financials

Return on assets: 4.7%	Dividends
Return on equity: 15.6%	Yield: 7.0%
Long-term debt ($ mil.): —	Payout: 114.6%
No. of shares (mil.): 19.1	Market value ($ mil.): 974.0
Sales ($ mil): 400.9	

	STOCK PRICE ($) FY Close	P/E High/Low	PER SHARE ($) Earnings	Dividends	Book Value
12/15	50.90	15 11	3.69	3.60	23.73
12/14	42.36	15 12	2.84	1.98	23.65
12/13	42.24	19 11	2.32	0.32	22.41
12/12	27.25	17 14	1.58	0.00	20.88
12/11	23.25	18 13	1.29	0.00	19.33
Annual Growth	**21.6%**	**— —**	**30.0%**	**—**	**5.3%**

AMN Healthcare Services Inc

Understaffed hospitals say "amen" for AMN Healthcare Services. Operating under such brands as American Mobile Healthcare Medical Express NurseChoice NursesRx Medfinders Med Travelers Staff Care and O'Grady-Peyton International the firm is one of the leading temporary health care staffing companies in the world. It places nurses technicians and therapists for 13-week stints at hospitals clinics and schools nationwide. With professionals recruited from Australia Canada South Africa the UK and the US AMN provides travel reimbursement and housing for its nurse and health care workers on assignment. The majority of temporary assignments for its clients are at acute-care hospitals in the US.

Geographic Reach

The company has offices in California Illinois North Carolina Oregon Colorado Indiana New Jersey Pennsylvania Florida Massachusetts New Mexico South Carolina Georgia Maryland New York Tennessee Hawaii Minnesota Ohio Texas Iowa Missouri Oklahoma and Virginia.

Financial Performance

AMN reported revenue of a little more than $1 billion for fiscal 2014. That was an increase of about $24 million compared to the prior fiscal period.

The company's net income was $33 million in fiscal 2014. That was a slight increase compared to fiscal 2013.

AMN's cash from operations decreased by about $32 million during fiscal 2014 compared to fiscal 2013 levels but the company still had more than

$27 million in cash on hand at the end of the fiscal year.

Strategy

AMN's growth strategy consists of increasing its network of temporary health care workers and making strategic acquisitions that complement its core offerings.

EXECUTIVES

CEO President and Director, Susan R. Salka, age 52, $695,250 total compensation
Chief Clinical Officer and SVP Operations, Marcia R. Faller
President Strategic Workforce Solutions, Robert E. (Bob) Livonius
President Healthcare Staffing, Ralph S. Henderson, age 55, $400,000 total compensation
Division President Locum Tenens, Sean Ebner
President Merritt Hawkins & Associates, Mark Smith
CFO Chief Accounting Officer and Treasurer, Brian M. Scott, age 46, $350,000 total compensation
Division President Local Staffing/Strategic Accounts, Becky Kahn
Division President Travel Nursing, Landry Seedig
CIO, Jeanette Sanchez
Division President Allied, Jeff Decker
President ShiftWise, Steve Schwartz
SVP Candidate Sourcing and Digital Marketing, Brian McCloskey
President Strategic Workforce Solutions, Dan White
Chairman, Douglas D. (Doug) Wheat, age 65
Auditors: KPMG LLP

LOCATIONS

HQ: AMN Healthcare Services Inc
12400 High Bluff Drive, Suite 100, San Diego, CA 92130
Phone: 866 871-8519
Web: www.amnhealthcare.com

PRODUCTS/OPERATIONS

2014 Sales

	$ mil.	% of total
Nurse & allied health care staffing	695.2	67
Locum tenens staffing	296.2	29
Physician permanent placement services	44.7	4
Total	**1,036.1**	**100**

COMPETITORS

ATC Healthcare	Kelly Services
CHG Healthcare	Maxim Healthcare
CompHealth	Services Inc.
Cross Country Healthcare	On Assignment
Gentiva	TeamStaff

HISTORICAL FINANCIALS

Company Type: Public

Income Statement

FYE: December 31

	REVENUE ($ mil.)	NET INCOME ($ mil.)	NET PROFIT MARGIN	EMPLOYEES
12/16	1,902.2	105.8	5.6%	2,990.0
12/15	1,463.0	81.8	5.6%	2,550.0
12/14	1,036.0	33.2	3.2%	1,800.0
12/13	1,011.8	32.9	3.3%	1,900.0
12/12	953.9	17.1	1.8%	1,700.0
Annual Growth	**18.8%**	**57.6%**	**—**	**15.2%**

2016 Year-End Financials

Debt ratio: 30.5%
Return on equity: 26.4%
Cash ($ mil.): 10.6
Current ratio: 1.64
Long-term debt ($ mil.): 359.1
No. of shares (mil.): 47.6
Dividends
  Yield: —
  Payout: —
Market value ($ mil.): 1,831.0

	STOCK PRICE ($) FY Close	P/E High/Low	PER SHARE ($) Earnings	Dividends	Book Value
12/16	38.45	20 10	2.15	0.00	9.44
12/15	31.05	22 11	1.68	0.00	7.29
12/14	19.60	28 15	0.69	0.00	5.50
12/13	14.70	22 15	0.69	0.00	4.73
12/12	11.55	31 10	0.37	0.00	3.99
Annual Growth	35.1%	— —	55.3%	—	24.1%

Amplify Snack Brands Inc

Auditors: Deloitte & Touche LLP

LOCATIONS

HQ: Amplify Snack Brands Inc
  500 West 5th Street, Suite 1350, Austin, TX 78701
Phone: 512 600-9893
Web: www.amplifysnackbrands.com

HISTORICAL FINANCIALS
Company Type: Public

Income Statement
FYE: December 31

	REVENUE ($ mil.)	NET INCOME ($ mil.)	NET PROFIT MARGIN	EMPLOYEES
12/15	183.9	9.8	5.4%	45.0
12/14*	64.0	4.7	7.4%	0.0
07/14	68.3	30.5	44.7%	0.0
12/13	55.7	24.7	44.4%	0.0
Annual Growth	48.9%	(26.4%)	—	—

*Fiscal year change

2015 Year-End Financials

Debt ratio: 55.7%
Return on equity: 14.4%
Cash ($ mil.): 18.7
Current ratio: 0.65
Long-term debt ($ mil.): 188.3
No. of shares (mil.): 74.8
Dividends
  Yield: —
  Payout: —
Market value ($ mil.): 862.0

	STOCK PRICE ($) FY Close	P/E High/Low	PER SHARE ($) Earnings	Dividends	Book Value
12/15	11.52	126 78	0.13	0.00	0.21
12/14*	0.00	— —	0.06	0.00	1.62
Annual Growth (87.2%)	—	— —	116.7%	—	—

*Fiscal year change

Angie's List Inc.

Better not get on Angie's bad side —she's got a list. Angie's List provides consumer ratings on companies in the service industry. Consumers rate local providers in more than 550 business service categories including roofing plumbing home remodeling and doctors. The company has amassed a collection of some 2.2 million reviews receiving about 40000 new reviews each month from consumers in 175 markets across the US. Revenues come from ads and subscription fees. Angie's List has more than 1 million paying members who access ratings and reviews via AngiesList.com and Angie's List Magazine. The firm was founded by Angie Hicks and Bill Oesterle in 1995. It filed to go public in 2011.

Angie's List joined the current spate of Internet public offerings which include buzzed-about companies such as LinkedIn and Groupon. It raised some $114 million in the offering which it is using to fund its advertising strategy and for general corporate purposes. The company intends to deepen its market penetration particularly in New York City and Los Angeles as well as expand into new categories. The IPO adds to prior funding efforts; so far it has raised nearly $100 million from investment firms such as Battery Ventures T. Rowe Price City Investment Group and Cardinal Ventures.

Though Angie's List is in major growth-mode the company has yet to earn a profit. In 2010 revenues were $59 million and the company reported a net loss of about $27 million. The loss is mostly due to its strategy of expansion by investing on major national advertising campaigns; such marketing costs totaled about $30 million in 2010.

While spending big on advertising its own services the company receives a majority of its revenues from other advertisers. Members grade service providers on an A to F scale and Angie's List allows businesses that average an A or B rating and at least two current reviews to advertise by providing discounts to members. Angie's List earns about 57% of revenues from the sale of advertising to service providers; the remaining 43% of revenues come from subscription fees.

Board members John Chuang and Steven Kapner own about 20% of Angie's List through their positions at venture capital firm TRI Ventures. Angie Hicks founded the company as a result of her frustrations in finding reliable contractors in suburban Columbus Ohio.

EXECUTIVES

CFO, Thomas R. Fox, age 41, $336,323 total compensation
COO, J. Mark Howell, age 51, $447,874 total compensation
EVP General Counsel and Corporate Secretary, Shannon M. Shaw, age 41, $293,461 total compensation
President CEO and Director, Scott Durschslag, $142,308 total compensation
CTO, Darin E. Brown, age 48, $275,000 total compensation
Executive Vice President Sales, Michael (Mel) Rutz
Vice President Of Marketing, Dan (Danny) Smith
National Account Manager, Charity Rupp
National Sales Manager, Matt Lubbers
Vice President Data Analytics, Anthony Palella
Vice President Investor Relations, Sherri Adams
National Account Manager, Keisha Moss
Vice President, Mike Rutz

Vice President of User Experience, Anand Tharanathan
Chairman, Thomas R. Evans, age 62
Chief Marketing Officer and Director, Angela R. Hicks Bowman, age 43
Auditors: Ernst & Young LLP

LOCATIONS

HQ: Angie's List Inc.
  1030 E. Washington Street, Indianapolis, IN 46202
Phone: 888 888-5478
Web: www.angieslist.com

PRODUCTS/OPERATIONS

2015 Sales

	$ mil.	% of total
Service provider	276.1	80
Membership	68.0	20
Total	**344.1**	**100**

Service provider
Appraisals
Bodywork
Carpet cleaning
Chrome work
Custom painting
Dentists
Dermatologists
Detailing
Elder care
Electrical
Engine modification
Handymen
Heating & A/C
Hospitals
Housecleaning
OB/GYN
Ophthalmologists
Painting
Parts locators
Pediatricians
Plastic surgeons
Plumbing
Primary care
Psychiatrists
Remodeling
Restoration
Roofing
Storage
Wheels and tires
Windows

COMPETITORS

Amazon.com	Facebook
Better Business Bureaus	Google
Buy.com	Groupon
CityGrid Media	LivingSocial
Classified Ventures	Shopping.com
Consumers Union	Yahoo!
Dex Media	Yelp
	craigslist

HISTORICAL FINANCIALS
Company Type: Public

Income Statement
FYE: December 31

	REVENUE ($ mil.)	NET INCOME ($ mil.)	NET PROFIT MARGIN	EMPLOYEES
12/15	344.1	10.2	3.0%	1,730.0
12/14	315.0	(12.0)	—	1,852.0
12/13	245.6	(32.9)	—	1,637.0
12/12	155.8	(52.8)	—	1,158.0
12/11	90.0	(49.0)	—	349.0
Annual Growth	39.8%	—	—	49.2%

2015 Year-End Financials

Debt ratio: 33.7%		No. of shares (mil.): 58.6	
Return on equity: —		Dividends	
Cash ($ mil.): 32.6		Yield: —	
Current ratio: 0.81		Payout: —	
Long-term debt ($ mil.): 57.6		Market value ($ mil.): 548.0	

	STOCK PRICE ($) FY Close	P/E High/Low	Earnings	PER SHARE ($) Dividends	Book Value
12/15	9.35	60 21	0.17	0.00	(0.04)
12/14	6.23	— —	(0.21)	0.00	(0.38)
12/13	15.15	— —	(0.57)	0.00	(0.32)
12/12	11.99	— —	(0.92)	0.00	0.09
12/11	16.10	— —	(1.60)	0.00	0.81
Annual Growth	(12.7%)	— —	—	—	—

ANI Pharmaceuticals Inc

ANI Pharmaceuticals wants to stabilize hormonal ups and downs. The firm is developing topical hormone therapy gels to deliver supplemental estrogen progestogen and testosterone. It focuses on areas including narcotics anti-cancers hormones and steroids and complex products with extended release or combination formulations. More than half of the company's earnings come from its menopause treatment Esterified Estrogen with Methyltestosterone (EEMT); other products include Hydrocortisone Enema (for ulcerative colitis) Methazolamide (for ocular conditions) and Opium Tincture (diarrhea). The firm is also developing potential cancer vaccine therapies. ANI also performs contract manufacturing.

Operations

Generic products account for nearly three-fourths of ANI's revenues while branded products bring in some 15%. Contract services and manufacturing represent the rest of the firm's earnings.

Geographic Reach

ANI Pharmaceuticals operates in the US. It has two manufacturing facilities (totaling some 173000 sq. ft.) in Baudette Minnesota.

Sales and Marketing

The company markets and distributes its products through wholesalers such as McKesson and AmerisourceBergen and through retail outfits including Walgreen and Wal-Mart. It also uses distributors such as ExpressScripts and Omnicare as well as group purchasing organizations (MedAssets etc.). Wholesalers McKesson Cardinal Health and AmerisourceBergen bring in more than 60% of ANI's net revenues.

Financial Performance

Revenues have been on the rise for the past three years. In 2015 revenue rose 36% to $76 million thanks largely to a 54% jump in generics sales. This was attributed to an increase in the sales price of EEMT as well as the recent launches of Methazolamide Etodolac Propafenone and Vancomycin. Branded product sales remained steady and contract manufacturing operations slowed down but contract services and royalty income rose that year.

Net income which had been rising significantly declined 47% to $15 million in 2015 due to higher selling general and administrative expenses. Cash flow from operations has followed net income's

suit: In 2015 it fell 22% to $17 million on the lower profits as well as changes in income taxes and accounts payable.

Strategy

ANI Pharmaceuticals is actively launching new products to grow its prescription drug sales. In 2015 it received abbreviated new drug applications (ANDAs) for more than 20 generic products. The company will buy portfolios of existing drugs to boost its portfolio. It also partners with other firms to introduce products to the US market. For example it entered a distribution agreement with IDT Australia in 2015 through which it will market a number of products.

Mergers and Acquisitions

The company acquired a portfolio of Inderal LA assets from Cranford Pharmaceuticals in 2015. It also acquired 22 generic drugs from Teva Pharmaceuticals for $25 million.

EXECUTIVES

SVP Finance CFO and Secretary, Phillip B. Donenberg, age 56, $285,552 total compensation
VP Operations, Bill Milling
President and CEO, Arthur S. Przybyl
Chairman, Louis W. Sullivan, age 81
Auditors: EisnerAmper LLP

LOCATIONS

HQ: ANI Pharmaceuticals Inc
210 Main Street West, Baudette, MN 56623
Phone: 218 634-3500
Web: www.biosantepharma.com

PRODUCTS/OPERATIONS

2015

	% of total
Generic pharmaceutical products	72
Branded pharmaceutical products	15
Contract manufacturing	6
Contract services and other income	7
Total	**100**

Selected Brands

Cortenema
Lithobid
Reglan
Vancocin

Selected Products and Candidates

Hormone therapy products and candidates
Bio-T-Gel (transdermal testosterone supplement for men with Teva)
Elestrin (transdermal estrogen supplement)
LibiGel (transdermal testosterone supplement for women)
Pill Plus (birth control with androgen)
Cancer vaccine candidates

COMPETITORS

Abbott Labs	Lumara
Agenus	Noven Pharmaceuticals
Allergan plc	Pfizer
Boehringer Ingelheim	Upsher-Smith
GlaxoSmithKline	Warner Chilcott

HISTORICAL FINANCIALS

Company Type: Public

Income Statement

FYE: December 31

	REVENUE ($ mil.)	NET INCOME ($ mil.)	NET PROFIT MARGIN	EMPLOYEES
12/15	76.3	15.3	20.1%	108.0
12/14	55.9	28.7	51.4%	92.0
12/13	30.0	0.3	1.0%	81.0
12/12	2.3	(27.7)	—	23.0
12/11	0.4	(51.6)	—	54.0
Annual Growth	263.9%	—	—	18.9%

2015 Year-End Financials

Debt ratio: 39.7%		No. of shares (mil.): 11.5	
Return on equity: 10.2%		Dividends	
Cash ($ mil.): 154.6		Yield: —	
Current ratio: 16.38		Payout: —	
Long-term debt ($ mil.): 113.4		Market value ($ mil.): 519.0	

	STOCK PRICE ($) FY Close	P/E High/Low	Earnings	PER SHARE ($) Dividends	Book Value
12/15	45.13	54 28	1.32	0.00	13.91
12/14	56.39	23 7	2.59	0.00	12.26
12/13	20.08	— —	(0.92)	0.00	4.25
12/12	1.23	— —	(7.62)	0.00	6.90
12/11	0.50	— —	(18.72)	0.00	12.37
Annual Growth	207.9%	— —	—	—	3.0%

Anika Therapeutics Inc.

Anika Therapeutics uses hyaluronic acid (HA) a natural polymer extracted from rooster combs and other sources to make more than 20 products that treat bone cartilage and soft tissue. Anika's Orthovisc treats osteoarthritis of the knee and other joints and is available in the US and overseas. (DePuy Mitek sells the product in the US.) The company also makes and sells products that maintain eye shape and protect tissue during eye surgery. Other items include surgical anti-adhesive products veterinary osteoarthritis therapies and dermatology products. The US accounts for about four-fifths of sales.

Operations Orthobiologics products make up about 85% of the company's annual revenues. In addition to Orthovisc Anika markets osteoarthritis drugs in international markets: Orthovisc mini (for treatment in small joints); Monovisc a next-generation single-injection therapy; and Cingal an HA formulation plus steroid. Anika received Canadian approval for Monovisc in 2009 and FDA approval for Monovisc in 2014. It received Canadian approval for Cingal in 2015 followed by European approval for the product in 2016. It has additional osteoarthritis and joint health treatments under development.

The company is seeking FDA approval for Cingal and Hyalofast a biodegradable support for bone marrow stem cells used in cartilage regeneration.

Geographic Reach

Headquartered in Massachusetts Anika has an international office in Italy. The US accounts for more than 80% of revenue followed by Europe which accounts for about 10% of revenue.

Sales and Marketing

The company uses a contract sales organization to market Cingal in the US but it ultimately hopes to bring those functions in-house.

While Anika markets some products on its own a number are sold through additional partnering firms and distribution representatives. DePuy Mitek is Anika's largest customer accounting for 72% of product sales.

Dermal products are sold through a network of distributors in Europe Latin America and the Middle East; surgical products are sold through a similar network in Europe the Middle East and in certain Asian markets.

Anika also has partnerships to distribute products with such firms as Medtronic Boehringer Ingelheim Vetmedica and Medline Industries.

Financial Performance Anika has seen strong revenue growth over the past several years including a 41% jump to $105.6 million in 2014. However revenue declined 12% to $93 million in 2015 in the absence of certain milestone payments (despite growth of sales that year).

Net income has also risen and like revenue dropped in 2015. It fell 20% to $31 million that year due to the lower revenue and an increase in R&D costs. Cash flow from operations slipped 2% to $39 million over the same period.

Strategy The company's growth efforts stem from adding new products adding new indications for existing products and expanding its geographic reach. Its orthobiologics products are seeing the fastest growth now accounting for some 85% of sales. Additionally Anika seeks more partnerships with others to commercialize its products. In 2016 the company gained European approval for Cingal as a medical device to treat knee pain. R&D spending is largely dedicated to developing products for tissue protection repair and regeneration. In 2015 R&D spend totaled $9 million up from $8.1 million in 2014 and $7.1 million in 2013.

Anika is taking on the manufacturing of its HYAFF (HA-based) products which have been made by an Italian third party. By doing so it can bring additional products to the markets more quickly.

EXECUTIVES

President and CEO, Charles H. Sherwood, $505,447 total compensation
Chief Scientific Officer, John W. Sheets
CFO, Sylvia Cheung
Chief Medical Officer, Stephen R. Mascioli
COO, Dana M. Alexander
Vice President of Human Resources, Steven (Steve) Cyr
Auditors: PricewaterhouseCoopers LLP

LOCATIONS

HQ: Anika Therapeutics Inc.
32 Wiggins Avenue, Bedford, MA 01730
Phone: 781 457-9000
Web: www.anikatherapeutics.com

PRODUCTS/OPERATIONS

2015 Sales

	$ mil.	% of total
Product sales		
Orthobiologics	73.2	79
Surgical	5.8	6
Dermal	2.3	2
Other	6.4	7
Licensing milestone & contract revenue	5.3	6
Total	**93.0**	**100**

Selected Products

Orthobiologics
  Hyalofast (bone marrow support)
  Hyaloglide (tenolysis)
  Hyalograft C (autograft for cartilage regeneration)
  Hyalonect (graft gauze wrap)
  Hyaloss (bone regeneration)
  Monovisc (osteoarthritis)
  OrthoVisc (osteoarthritis marketed by DePuy Mitek)
  OrthoVisc mini (osteoarthritis in small joints)
Dermal
  Elevess/Hydrelle (aesthetic dermatology products)
  Hyalograft 3D (skin regeneration)
  Hyalomatrix (burn and ulcer treatment)
Ophthalmic
  Amvisc (eye surgery product sold by Bausch & Lomb)
  Amvisc Plus (eye surgery product sold by Bausch & Lomb)
  AnikaVisc (eye surgery product)
  Optivisc (formerly ShellGel ophthalmic product)
  STAARVISC II (ophthalmic product sold by STAAR Surgical)
Surgical
  Hyalobarrier (post-operative adhesion barrier)
  Incert (post-surgical adhesion prevention product)
Veterinary
  Hyvisc (equine osteoarthritis treatment distributed by Boehringer Ingelheim)

COMPETITORS

Exactech	Pathfinder Cell
Fibrocell Science	Therapy
Genzyme Biosurgery	Pfizer
Harvard Bioscience	Quidel
ImmunoGen	RTI Surgical
Integra LifeSciences	Smith & Nephew
Lifecore Biomedical	Solta Medical
Medicis Pharmaceutical	Stryker
Merz Aesthetics	XOMA
Obagi Medical	Zimmer Biomet
OrthoLogic	

HISTORICAL FINANCIALS

Company Type: Public

Income Statement

FYE: December 31

	REVENUE ($ mil.)	NET INCOME ($ mil.)	NET PROFIT MARGIN	EMPLOYEES
12/15	93.0	30.7	33.1%	107.0
12/14	105.5	38.3	36.3%	102.0
12/13	75.0	20.5	27.4%	102.0
12/12	71.3	11.7	16.5%	106.0
12/11	64.7	8.4	13.1%	129.0
Annual Growth	9.5%	38.1%	—	(4.6%)

2015 Year-End Financials

Debt ratio: —	No. of shares (mil.): 15.0
Return on equity: 15.8%	Dividends
Cash ($ mil.): 110.7	Yield: —
Current ratio: 10.21	Payout: —
Long-term debt ($ mil.): —	Market value ($ mil.): 574.0

	STOCK PRICE ($) FY Close	P/E High/Low		PER SHARE ($) Earnings	Dividends	Book Value
12/15	38.16	22	15	2.01	0.00	14.02
12/14	40.74	19	11	2.51	0.00	11.99
12/13	38.16	26	7	1.39	0.00	9.49
12/12	9.94	20	10	0.82	0.00	7.86
12/11	9.80	17	8	0.62	0.00	6.95
Annual Growth	40.5%	—	—	34.2%	—	19.2%

Ansys Inc.

It's good to look before you leap – and even before you make. That's why ANSYS helps designers and engineers see how their ideas play out even before a prototype is built by simulating designs on a computer. The company's software analyzes the models for their response to combinations of such physical variables as stress pressure impact temperature and velocity. Ranging from small consulting firms to multinational enterprises its customers come from a broad range of industries and have included Delphi Airbus Invensys and Plexus. ANSYS generates two-thirds of its revenue from outside the US with Japan and Germany among its leading international markets.

Operations

ANSYS makes money by licensing its software to customers and by maintaining and servicing those accounts. About 60% of the company's revenue comes from licensing. Leasing accounts for 34% of total revenue and perpetual licenses for about 26%. Maintenance is the biggest chunk of revenue at 37% with services accounting for the final 3%.

Geographic Reach

ANSYS has more than 75 sales offices around the world. The US accounts for about one-third of revenue and Germany and Europe for another third.

Sales and Marketing

The company sells its products directly and through channel partners worldwide. It uses distribution partners in more than 40 countries. Indirect sales accounted for about one-fourth of ANSYS' total revenues in 2014. ANSYS also partners with hardware suppliers —including AMD Dell Cray Intel Microsoft and Hewlett-Packard among others —to ensure that its products are compatible with technology upgrades. In addition it collaborates with CAD and electronic design automation (EDA) system providers such as Autodesk and Cadence to provide links between products and support data transfer between design packages and ANSYS' simulation portfolio. These strategic alliances provide additional marketing opportunities for the company.

Financial Performance

Sales for 2014 were up 9% to $936 million on increases in both software license and maintenance revenues. New sales also contributed to the year's revenue growth. Net income for 2014 rose to an all-time high of $254.7 million a 4% increase from 2013. Cash flow from operations followed the same trajectory rising to $385 million in 2014 from $333 million in 2013.

Strategy

A key to ANSYS maintaining steady revenue and net income growth is delivering timely updates to its product line. In January 2015 the company released version 16.0 of its flagship product. A major feature of the new release is the capability to model connections to the Internet of Things the notion that devices anywhere can be connected to the Internet for communication with each other. ANSYS spends about 18% of annual revenue on research and development.

Mergers and Acquisitions

Not all of ANSYS's products are born of its in-house research so the company makes acquisitions to extend product lines and fill in product holes. The company acquired SpaceClaim Corporation a provider of 3-D modeling technology for $85 million in 2014. In 2015 ANSYS bought the assets of Newmerical Technologies International which develops software that simulate in-flight icing of aircraft. Newmerical's suite of specialized software can solve problems in aerodynamics in-flight icing heat transfer fluid-structure interaction and wind engineering.

Also in 2014 it bought Reaction Design a California company whose CHEMKIN-PRO chemistry simulation software is used by more than 400 customers around the world. Chemistry simulation software is used by transportation and energy companies to develop products without having to rely solely on experiments which could be dangerous.

EXECUTIVES

VP Finance and Administration and CFO, Maria T. Shields, age 51, $345,333 total compensation
Chief Product Officer, Walid Abu-Hadba, age 50, $347,500 total compensation
VP and CIO, Manish Sinha
President and CEO, Ajei S. Gopal
VP Marketing, Mark Hindsbo, age 44, $151,667 total compensation
Vice President and Chief Technology Officer, Dipankar Choudhury
Vice President Marketing, Joshua (Josh) Fredberg
Sales Training Vice President, John (Jack) Gilmore
Vice President and General Manager Electronics Business Unit, Shane Emswiler
Vice President Sls and Support, Robert (Bob) Kocis
Vice President Sales North America, Wade Smith
Vice President, Paolo Colombo
Vice President Customer Support at ASG Inc., Vinay Carpenter
Vice President, Eric (Ric) Bienvenu
Vice President, Michael (Mel) Engelman
GM Vice President, John (Jack) Lee
Chairman, James E. (Jim) Cashman, age 62
Treasurer, Kristi Fenner
Auditors: Deloitte & Touche LLP

LOCATIONS

HQ: Ansys Inc.
2600 ANSYS Drive, Canonsburg, PA 15317
Phone: 844 462-6797
Web: www.ansys.com

PRODUCTS/OPERATIONS

2014 Sales

	$ mil.	% of total
Software licenses	564.5	60
Maintenance & service	371.5	40
Total	**936.0**	**100**

Selected Acquisitions

FY 2015
Newmerical Technologies (simulation software for aircraft)
FY 2014
Reaction Design (California chemistry simulation software)
FY 2013
Evolutionary Engineering AG (Switzerland composite analysis)
FY 2012
Esterel Technologies (France critical systems simulation software)
FY 2011
Apache Design Solutions (semiconductor simulation software)
FY 2008
Ansoft (electronic design automation software)
FY 2006
Aavid Thermal Technologies
FY 2005
Century Dynamics

COMPETITORS

Altair Engineering	Kubotek USA
Autodesk	MSC Software
Bentley Systems	MathWorks
Cadence Design	Mentor Graphics
Dassault	PTC
Delcam	Siemens PLM Software

HISTORICAL FINANCIALS
Company Type: Public

Income Statement
FYE: December 31

	REVENUE ($ mil.)	NET INCOME ($ mil.)	NET PROFIT MARGIN	EMPLOYEES
12/15	942.7	252.5	26.8%	2,800.0
12/14	936.0	254.6	27.2%	2,700.0
12/13	861.2	245.3	28.5%	2,600.0
12/12	798.0	203.4	25.5%	2,400.0
12/11	691.4	180.6	26.1%	2,100.0
Annual Growth	**8.1%**	**8.7%**	**—**	**7.5%**

2015 Year-End Financials

Debt ratio: —	No. of shares (mil.): 88.1
Return on equity: 11.4%	Dividends
Cash ($ mil.): 784.1	Yield: —
Current ratio: 2.22	Payout: —
Long-term debt ($ mil.): —	Market value ($ mil.): 8,153.0

	STOCK PRICE ($) FY Close	P/E High/Low		PER SHARE ($) Earnings	Dividends	Book Value
12/15	92.50	35	28	2.76	0.00	24.90
12/14	82.00	31	26	2.70	0.00	24.43
12/13	87.20	34	25	2.58	0.00	23.14
12/12	67.34	34	26	2.14	0.00	20.94
12/11	57.28	32	23	1.91	0.00	18.94
Annual Growth	**12.7%**	**—**	**—**	**9.6%**	**—**	**7.1%**

Antero Midstream Partners LP

Auditors: KPMG LLP

LOCATIONS

HQ: Antero Midstream Partners LP
1615 Wynkoop Street, Denver, CO 80202
Phone: 303 357-7310
Web: www.anteromidstream.com

HISTORICAL FINANCIALS
Company Type: Public

Income Statement
FYE: December 31

	REVENUE ($ mil.)	NET INCOME ($ mil.)	NET PROFIT MARGIN	EMPLOYEES
12/15	387.3	117.6	30.4%	0.0
12/14	95.7	7.4	7.8%	0.0
12/13	22.3	(14.3)	—	0.0
12/12	0.6	(4.5)	—	0.0
12/11	0.4	(1.7)	—	0.0
Annual Growth	**444.4%**	**—**	**—**	**—**

2015 Year-End Financials

Debt ratio: 31.3%	No. of shares (mil.): 176.1
Return on equity: —	Dividends
Cash ($ mil.): 6.8	Yield: 2.9%
Current ratio: 0.76	Payout: 88.0%
Long-term debt ($ mil.): 620.0	Market value ($ mil.): 4,020.0

	STOCK PRICE ($) FY Close	P/E High/Low		PER SHARE ($) Earnings	Dividends	Book Value
12/15	22.82	39	22	0.76	0.67	6.15
12/14	27.50	580	463	0.05	0.00	8.84
Annual Growth	**(17.0%)**	**—**	**—**	**1420.0%**	**—**	**(30.5%)**

Apogee Enterprises Inc

Apogee Enterprises goes to great panes for its glass customers. The company designs and develops value-added glass products primarily for the US market. Its architectural products and services segment fabricates and installs glass that features specialized colors or coatings and aluminum framing systems for commercial and institutional buildings. Customers include architects general contractors glazing subcontractors and building owners. Its large-scale optical (LSO) technologies segment manufactures anti-reflective UV-protected glass and acrylic under the Tru Vue brand for custom picture framing. Tru Vue products are sold through independent distributors and mass merchandisers.

Operations

Apogee divides its operations across four segments with three of the segments serving the commercial construction market: architectural glass (more than 35% of total sales) architectural framing systems (roughly 30%) architectural services (almost 25%) and large-scale optical products (LSO; 10%). Its LSO segment caters to the custom picture framing market.

High-performance glass made by its architectural glass segments allows for specific light transmission levels and features solar options. High-performance glass is typically fabricated into custom insulating units or laminated units to allow for installation into window frames curtain walls storefronts or entrances. The architectural framing segments also offer thermally-enhanced aluminum framing systems as well as ones with recycled content and energy-efficient glass coatings to target architects and contractors demanding specialty glass for constructing green commercial buildings.

Geographic Reach

Within the installation services market Apogee is one of only a few companies to have a national presence with offices in seven locations serving multiple US markets. It also has an office each in Canada and Brazil but the US continues to be Apogee's main market representing about 95% of sales.

Sales and Marketing

LSO glass and acrylic products are distributed primarily in North America through mass merchandisers and independent distributors which supply national and regional chains and local picture framing shops. Apogee occasionally supplies products directly to museums and public and private galleries. It also has limited distribution in global markets through independent distributors.

Financial Performance

Apogee has enjoyed unprecedented growth over the years with revenues peaking at a record-setting

$981 million in 2016. Mostly due to the additional revenue profits also peaked at $65 million in 2016 another company milestone. In addition cash flow from operating activities soared from $69 million in 2015 to $124 million in 2016 mostly due to tax refunds and additional billings from uncompleted contracts.

The historic growth for 2016 was driven by surges in sales from its architectural glass and architectural services segments and higher demand form its architectural framing systems segment. These increases were mainly due to pricing and volume growth resulting from strong commercial construction activity in the US partially offset by declines in the Canadian and Brazilian commercial construction markets.

Strategy

Apogee has identified several opportunities for growth in the coming years. It has recorded increased interest from the non-residential and high-end multi-family building sectors in upgrading the front of buildings and improving buildings' energy efficiency.

Its strategy pertaining to its LSO segment involves continuing to convert the custom picture framing and fine art markets from clear uncoated glass and acrylic products to value-added products that protect art from UV damage and minimize reflection both within the US and international markets. Apogee has also identified new display markets that desire the value-added properties its glass and acrylic products provide.

Mergers and Acquisitions

Apogee in late 2016 acquired Sotawall a North America-based designer and fabricator of high-performance unitized curtain wall systems for commercial construction projects for $135 million. The deal extended Apogee's geographic presence and enhanced its product offerings.

EXECUTIVES

General Counsel and Secretary, Patricia A. Beithon, age 62, $327,981 total compensation
CFO, James S. (Jim) Porter, age 55, $405,385 total compensation
SVP Operations and Supply Chain Management, John A. Klein, $263,654 total compensation
CEO, Joseph F. (Joe) Puishys, $834,904 total compensation
VP and Treasurer, Gary R. Johnson, $228,090 total compensation
Vice President Building Retrofit Strategy, John (Jack) Bendt
Chairman, Bernard P. (Bernie) Aldrich, age 66
Auditors: Deloitte & Touche LLP

LOCATIONS

HQ: Apogee Enterprises Inc
4400 West 78th Street - Suite 520, Minneapolis, MN 55435
Phone: 952 835-1874
Web: www.apog.com

PRODUCTS/OPERATIONS

2016 Sales

	$ mil.	% of total
Architectural glass	377.7	37
Architectural framing systems	308.6	30
Architectural services	245.9	24
Large-scale optical technologies	88.5	9
Adjustments	(39.5)	-
Total	**981.2**	**100**

COMPETITORS

Asahi Glass	Pilkington North
Cardinal Glass	America
Guardian Glass	Saint-Gobain
Nippon Sheet Glass	Schott Corporation
PPG Industries	Vitro
Pilkington Group	

HISTORICAL FINANCIALS
Company Type: Public

Income Statement
FYE: February 27

	REVENUE ($ mil.)	NET INCOME ($ mil.)	NET PROFIT MARGIN	EMPLOYEES
02/16	981.1	65.3	6.7%	4,614.0
02/15*	933.9	50.5	5.4%	4,802.0
03/14	771.4	27.9	3.6%	4,266.0
03/13	700.2	19.1	2.7%	3,871.0
03/12	662.4	4.6	0.7%	3,636.0
Annual Growth	10.3%	93.7%	—	6.1%

*Fiscal year change

2016 Year-End Financials

Debt ratio: 3.1%
Return on equity: 16.6%
Cash ($ mil.): 60.4
Current ratio: 1.90
Long-term debt ($ mil.): 20.4

No. of shares (mil.): 28.6
Dividends
Yield: 0.0%
Payout: 20.5%
Market value ($ mil.): 1,130.0

	STOCK PRICE ($) FY Close	P/E High/Low		PER SHARE ($) Earnings	Dividends	Book Value
02/16	39.41	27	15	2.22	0.46	14.16
02/15*	45.85	27	16	1.72	0.41	13.17
03/14	34.23	38	23	0.95	0.37	12.18
03/13	26.21	39	18	0.67	0.36	11.69
03/12	12.60	87	48	0.17	0.33	11.45
Annual Growth	33.0%	—	—	90.1%	8.7%	5.5%

*Fiscal year change

Apollo Commercial Real Estate Finance Inc.

Apollo Commercial Real Estate Finance thinks the sky is the limit for commercial property loans. The New York-based mortgage real estate investment trust (REIT) originates buys and manages performing US commercial real estate loans subordinate loans commercial mortgage-backed securities (CMBS) and other commercial real estate debt investments. About 40% of its $2.6 billion investment portfolio is made up of commercial mortgage loans while another 35% is made up of subordinate loans. Formed in 2009 by Apollo Global Management the REIT is externally managed by ACREFI Management (an indirect subsidiary of Apollo Global Management).

OperationsAbout 39% of the REIT's $2.57 billion investment portfolio was made up of commercial mortgage loans at the end of 2015 while another 36% was made up of subordinate loans. The rest was made up of CMBS (19% of portfolio assets) and CMBS held-to-maturity (6%).Apollo Commercial Real Estate Finance (which is abbreviated as ARI) generates all of its revenue from interest income from its portfolio. Around 48% of its

revenue came from subordinate loan interest during 2015 while interest income from commercial mortgage loans and securities made up 29% and 23% of annual revenues respectively.Financial PerformanceARI's annual revenues and profits have quadrupled since 2011 as its interest-earning loan assets have swelled. The REIT's revenue spiked 52% to $192.16 million during 2015 as it continued to earn higher interest from acquired loans. Strong revenue growth drove ARI's net income up 25% to $103.26 million while the REIT's operating cash levels jumped 31% to $88.12 million on higher cash earnings.StrategyWhile Apollo's priority is to invest in senior performing commercial mortgage loans CMBS and commercial real estate debt and loans it's expanding into other asset types. Its 2016 acquisition of Apollo Residential Mortgage for example more than doubled its loan portfolio while also diversifying its investments into residential mortgage loans.Mergers and AcquisitionsIn February 2016 ARI would enter the residential mortgage market and double its loan portfolio after agreeing to buy Apollo Residential Mortgage Inc. along with its $3.4 billion worth of Agency and non-Agency residential mortgage backed securities (RMBS) residential mortgage loans and other investments. Company BackgroundThe REIT raised $200 million from its initial public offering in 2009.

EXECUTIVES

President and CEO, Stuart A. Rothstein, age 50
Secretary Treasurer and CFO, Jai Agarwal
Chief Investment Officer, Scott Weiner
Chairman, Jeffrey M. (Jeff) Gault, age 71
Auditors: Deloitte & Touche LLP

LOCATIONS

HQ: Apollo Commercial Real Estate Finance Inc.
c/o Apollo Global Management, LLC, 9 West 57th Street, 43rd Floor, New York, NY 10019
Phone: 212 515-3200
Web: www.apolloreit.com

PRODUCTS/OPERATIONS

2015 Sales

	$ mil.	% of total
Interest income from subordinate loans	90.8	48
Interest income from commercial mortgage loans	56.1	29
Interest income from securities	33.2	17
Interest income from securities held-to-maturity	12.1	6
Total	**192.2**	**100**

COMPETITORS

Capital Trust	Resource Capital
Petra Real Estate	iStar Financial Inc

HISTORICAL FINANCIALS
Company Type: Public

Income Statement
FYE: December 31

	REVENUE ($ mil.)	NET INCOME ($ mil.)	NET PROFIT MARGIN	EMPLOYEES
12/15	192.1	103.2	53.7%	0.0
12/14	123.3	82.7	67.1%	0.0
12/13	77.4	52.4	67.8%	0.0
12/12	57.0	40.1	70.4%	0.0
12/11	52.9	25.8	48.9%	0.0
Annual Growth	38.0%	41.3%	—	—

2015 Year-End Financials

Debt ratio: 43.1%
Return on equity: 9.2%
Cash ($ mil.): 97.5
Current ratio: 2.19
Long-term debt ($ mil.): 1,173.9

No. of shares (mil.): 67.2
Dividends
Yield: 10.3%
Payout: 115.5%
Market value ($ mil.): 1,158.0

	STOCK PRICE ($)	P/E		PER SHARE ($)		
	FY Close	High/Low	Earnings	Dividends	Book Value
12/15	17.23	12 10	1.54	1.78	20.47
12/14	16.36	10 9	1.72	1.60	18.23
12/13	16.25	15 12	1.26	1.60	18.51
12/12	16.23	11 8	1.64	1.60	19.50
12/11	13.13	13 9	1.35	1.60	16.39
Annual Growth	7.0%	— —	3.3%	2.7%	5.7%

Apollo Global Management LLC

In Greek and Roman mythology Apollo is the god of light medicine arts and archery but Apollo Global Management is even more diverse. The alternative asset manager invests in across a range of nine core industries including chemicals commodities consumer and retail and media on behalf of institutional and individual investors. Apollo has some $160 billion of assets under management spread among its private equity capital markets and real estate segments. It specializes in buying distressed businesses and debt and has had some of its biggest successes investing during economic downturns. The publicly-traded firm has offices in the US Europe and Asia and is run by billionaire Leon Black.

Operations

Apollo divides its business into three reportable segments. The largest is Credit accounting for nearly 60% of the firm's revenue in 2014. Private Equity accounted for more than 35% while Real Estate contributed the remainder of revenue. The credit segment with $109 billion in AUM invests in US performing credit structured credit opportunistic credit non-performing loans and European credit. The private equity business boasts nearly $42 billion in assets under management (AUM) and focuses on distressed buyouts and debt investments corporate carve-outs opportunistic buyouts and natural resources. The real estate arm has nearly $10 billion in AUM and invests in commercial mortgage-backed securities senior and subordinated debt and global opportunistic and value-added investments in distressed debt and equity recapitalizations.

Geographic Reach

New York-based Apollo Management has offices in Frankfurt Hong Kong Houston London Los Angeles Luxembourg Mumbai and Singapore. Substantially all of Apollo's revenue is generated in the US.

Financial Performance

Apollo's revenue tends to vary widely mostly due to the timing of distributions and fluctuation in carried interest income which is dependent on fund performance. Generally if a fund's cumulative returns exceed the preferred return distributions are made to the company's private equity investors as well as certain credit and real estate fund in-

vestors.After two years of healthy top-line growth revenue sharply reversed course in 2014 plummeting by 58% to $1.56 billion. This was mostly because the Private Equity segment collected roughly $2.28 billion less in carried interest income as it paid out significant distributions to investors from Fund VII and Apollo Investment Fund VI L.P. that caused the segment's assets under management (AUM) to decrease by $8.9 billion over the year. Advisory and transaction and management fee income increased however thanks to growth in the company's Credit division anProfit also dove by 74% to $168.23 million in 2014 mostly because of steep revenue declines but also because of higher income tax expenses as the company earned more management business income which is subject to corporate-level taxation. Cash levels also dove in 2014 with operations using $372.92 million primarily because of lower earnings.

Strategy

Apollo typically invests capital over periods of seven or more years with the intention of generating long-term results. Apollo also looks to make investments in distressed securities and build positions in companies with stressed balance sheets. Specific areas of interest are in the cable chemicals packaging and transportation industries. To this end in 2014 the company launched Alteri Investors a joint venture that will seek opportunities to provide debt and equity financing to performing stressed and distressed retail sector companies in Europe. In 2012 it bought Taminco from CVC Capital Partners after Tamimco withdrew its offer to go public due to lack of investor interest; it paid some $1.4 billion for the Belgian chemical company. Also in 2012 Apollo along with Riverstone Holdings acquired the oil an gas exploration assets of El Paso Corporation for more than $7 billion. It was one of the largest leveraged buyout deals since the end of the financial crisis.

Apollo continues to make other alternative investments as well. In early 2015 partnering with its affiliate MidCap FinCo Limited the company launched its direct origination platform designed to offer direct lending services in the senior secured credit market for a wide range of industries and asset classes. In 2014 the company diversified its holdings by purchasing North American oilfield services company Express Energy Services. That year it also purchased family dining company CEC Entertainment Inc. along with its well-known 577-store Chuck E. Cheese restaurant chain for $1.3 billion.In 2013 the firm was active in the oil patch forming strategic partnerships with Apex Energy to invest in oil and gas properties in the Appalachian Basin and Double Eagle Energy Holdings to invest in oil and gas in Oklahoma. It also partnered with NRI Management Group to invest in mining properties worldwide with a focus on coal. In 2012 Apollo also acquired indoor water park operator Great Wolf Resorts. On a tastier note in spring 2013 Apollo and C. Dean Metropoulos & Co. were the winning bidders for the majority of the Hostess Brands snack cake business. It also purchased the McGraw-Hill Education business of S&P Global.

Ownership

Apollo Global Management is managed and operated by AGM Management LCC which in turn is indirectly wholly owned and controlled by Leon Black Joshua Harris and Marc Rowan all billionaires and co-founders of the firm.

Company Background

Established in 1990 Apollo initially earned a reputation for being a vulture investor by specializing in distressed assets. The company was co-founded by Leon Black formerly the head of merg-

ers and acquisitions at Drexel Burnham Lambert and a dozen other Drexel refugees after that firm collapsed. The newly established firm invested in former Drexel clients —notably the $3 billion dollar junk bond portfolio of failed California insurer Executive Life.The firm often tackles industries that its competitors try to avoid and Apollo is not afraid to make big investments during times of economic and financial distress. During the most recent recession Apollo deployed about $28 billion in capital and focused on distressed assets and buyout investments. The company also acquired some $15 billion of distressed debt and $37 billion of leveraged senior loans at deep discounts.

EXECUTIVES

Chairman and CEO, Leon D. Black, age 65, $100,000 total compensation
Senior Managing Director; Managing Partner Apollo Management L.P., Joshua J. (Josh) Harris, age 51
Senior Managing Director; Managing Partner Apollo Management L.P., Marc J. Rowan, age 54
Managing Director Credit; CEO and Director Apollo Investment Corp., James C. Zelter, age 54, $1,200,000 total compensation
Chief Legal Officer, John Suydam, age 56, $3,000,000 total compensation
CFO, Martin Kelly, age 48, $1,000,000 total compensation
Chief Accounting Officer and Controller, Christopher Weidler, $400,000 total compensation
Co President, Tolga Uzuner
Auditors: Deloitte & Touche LLP

LOCATIONS

HQ: Apollo Global Management LLC
9 West 57th Street, 43rd Floor, New York, NY 10019
Phone: 212 515-3200
Web: www.apolloic.com

PRODUCTS/OPERATIONS

2014 Sales

	% of total
Management fees from affiliates	55
Carried interest income (loss) from affiliates	25
Advisory & transaction fees from affiliates	20
Total	**100**

2014 Sales

	$ mil.	% of total
Credit	959.5	59
Private equity	605.3	37
Real estate	58.8	4
Adjustment	(63.5)	-
Total	**1,560.1**	**100**

Selected Portfolio Companies

Brit Insurance
Core Media Group (formerly CKx)
EP Energy LLC
Great Wolf Resorts
Pinnacle-Jimmy Sanders
Sprouts Famers Markets
Talos Energy LLC
Taminco Group Holdings
Welspun

COMPETITORS

Blackstone Group	Investcorp
Clayton Dubilier & Rice	KKR
	TPG
Equity Group Investments	The Carlyle Group
	Thomas H. Lee Partners
HM Capital Partners	Wingate Partners

HISTORICAL FINANCIALS

Company Type: Public

Income Statement

FYE: December 31

	REVENUE ($ mil.)	NET INCOME ($ mil.)	NET PROFIT MARGIN	EMPLOYEES
12/15	1,041.6	134.5	12.9%	945.0
12/14	1,560.0	168.2	10.8%	845.0
12/13	3,733.5	659.3	17.7%	710.0
12/12	2,859.9	310.9	10.9%	634.0
12/11	171.6	(468.8)	—	548.0
Annual Growth	57.0%	—	—	14.6%

2015 Year-End Financials

Debt ratio: 40.0%	No. of shares (mil.): 181.0
Return on equity: 11.0%	Dividends
Cash ($ mil.): 674.1	Yield: 12.9%
Current ratio: 1.34	Payout: 311.1%
Long-term debt ($ mil.): 1,826.5	Market value ($ mil.): 2,749.0

	STOCK PRICE ($) FY Close	P/E High/Low	PER SHARE ($) Earnings	Dividends	Book Value
12/15	15.18	42 24	0.61	1.96	3.59
12/14	23.58	58 34	0.62	3.11	10.96
12/13	31.61	8 4	4.03	3.95	18.03
12/12	17.36	8 5	2.06	1.35	20.51
12/11	12.41	— —	(4.18)	0.66	5.86
Annual Growth (11.6%)	5.2%	— —	—	31.3%	

Apple Hospitality REIT Inc

Auditors: Ernst & Young LLP

LOCATIONS

HQ: Apple Hospitality REIT Inc
814 East Main Street, Richmond, VA 23219
Phone: 804 344-8121
Web: www.applehospitalityreit.com

HISTORICAL FINANCIALS

Company Type: Public

Income Statement

FYE: December 31

	REVENUE ($ mil.)	NET INCOME ($ mil.)	NET PROFIT MARGIN	EMPLOYEES
12/15	898.3	117.2	13.1%	54.0
12/14	803.9	6.8	0.9%	51.0
12/13	387.9	115.2	29.7%	52.0
12/12	365.5	75.4	20.6%	0.0
12/11	320.5	69.9	21.8%	0.0
Annual Growth	29.4%	13.8%	—	—

2015 Year-End Financials

Debt ratio: 26.8%	No. of shares (mil.): 174.3
Return on equity: 4.1%	Dividends
Cash ($ mil.): 22.6	Yield: 4.0%
Current ratio: 0.29	Payout: 89.8%
Long-term debt ($ mil.): 998.1	Market value ($ mil.): 3,482.0

	STOCK PRICE ($) FY Close	P/E High/Low	PER SHARE ($) Earnings	Dividends	Book Value
12/15	19.97	32 25	0.65	0.80	15.18
Annual Growth	—	— —	—	—	—

Applied Optoelectronics Inc

When it comes to making lasers Applied Optoelectronics stays on the beam. The company designs and makes fiber-optic networking components that go into communications equipment used by cable-TV providers broadband network providers and Internet data centers to allow for faster network connections. Applied Optoelectronics makes laser chips components subassemblies and modules using its proprietary Molecular Beam Epitaxy (MBE) fabrication process. Customers include Arris Group Aurora Networks Cisco Systems Harmonic and Motorola. Founded in 1997 the company went public in 2013 raising $36 million in its IPO.

Operations

Applied Optoelectronics serves three end-markets: data center cable television or CATV and fiber-to-the-home or FTTH.

Data centers are the company biggest 49% of sales and fastest growing a 232% increase in 2014 market. CATV is the company's most established market and accounts for 36% of revenue in 2014. Another big increase came in the market for FTTH products. It grew 211% in 2014 to account for 11% of the company's sales.

Geographic Reach

The company uses its vertically integrated manufacturing process at its three manufacturing plants in China Taiwan and the US. Its Texas plant handles research and development and manufactures laser chips sub-assemblies and components. In Taiwan it makes transceivers and optical components such as butterfly lasers which incorporate the US-made laser chips sub-assemblies and components. In China the company takes advantage of lower labor costs and makes the more labor-intensive components and optical equipment systems such as cable-TV transmitters and cable-TV outdoor equipment.

Sales and Marketing

Applied Optoelectronics sells its products to cable-television OEMs; Cisco is its largest customer accounting for a third of sales. Data center operators snapped up the company's 10 gigabits-per-second and 40 gigabits-per-second transceivers to keep connections humming. While it primarily uses a direct sales force the company also uses third-party sales representatives and distributors such as Biogenomics Corp. About 80% of sales come from customers located outside the US.

Financial Performance

The need to speed in data centers drove revenue 66% for Applied Optoelectronics in 2014 to reach $130.5 million from $78.2 million in 2013. The FTTH revenue increase was driven by demand for the company's wavelength multiplexing devices-passive optical network devices (which split one incoming signal into multiple signals).

The company generated so much revenue than some of it spilled to the bottom line despite increased spending on research and development and sales and marketing to create a profit. Applied Optoelectronics posted net income of $4.28 million in 2014 compared to a net loss of $1.4 million in 2013.

Cash flow from operations also increased in 2014 to $7.24 million in 2014 from negative cash flow of $65. million in 2013.

Strategy

Applied Optoelectronics finds itself in a good place selling critical components to a fast-growing industry that demands more speed and capabilities for data center cable and fiber-to-the-home applications. The company doubled its research and development spending to about $16 million in 2014 from 2013. The get its technology from research to customers Applied Electronics has increased capacity and performance at its factories in Sugar Land Texas and Taiwan. The new Taiwan facility more than doubles the size of its previous plant.

EXECUTIVES

Chairman President and CEO, Lin (Thompson) Chih-Hsiang, age 53, $336,533 total compensation
SVP Optical Component Business Unit, Chang (Fred) Hung-Lun, age 52, $196,788 total compensation
SVP Network Equipment Module Business Unit, Yeh (Joshua) Shu-Hua, age 50
CFO and Chief Strategy Officer, Stefan J. Murry, age 44, $218,575 total compensation
SVP and General Manager Asia, Li (Ford) Chung-Yao
Vice President Sales And Marketing, Cynthia (Cyn) Hernandez
Auditors: Grant Thornton LLP

LOCATIONS

HQ: Applied Optoelectronics Inc
13139 Jess Pirtle Blvd., Sugar Land, TX 77478
Phone: 281 295-1800
Web: www.ao-inc.com

PRODUCTS/OPERATIONS

2014 Sales by End Market

	% of total
Data center	49
Cable TV	36
Fiber-to-the-home	11
Other	4
Total	**100**

COMPETITORS

ANADIGICS	Oclaro
Broadcom	Optek Technology
EMCORE	Sumitomo Electric
Finisar	Viavi Solutions
NeoPhotonics	

HISTORICAL FINANCIALS

Company Type: Public

Income Statement

FYE: December 31

	REVENUE ($ mil.)	NET INCOME ($ mil.)	NET PROFIT MARGIN	EMPLOYEES
12/15	189.9	10.7	5.7%	2,513.0
12/14	130.4	4.2	3.3%	1,447.0
12/13	78.4	(1.4)	—	1,146.0
12/12	63.4	(0.9)	—	927.0
12/11	47.8	(5.3)	—	0.0
Annual Growth	41.2%	—	—	—

2015 Year-End Financials

Debt ratio: 23.7%
Return on equity: 7.7%
Cash ($ mil.): 28.0
Current ratio: 2.08
Long-term debt ($ mil.): 34.0

No. of shares (mil.): 16.8
Dividends
  Yield: —
  Payout: —
Market value ($ mil.): 289.0

	STOCK PRICE ($) FY Close	P/E High/Low	PER SHARE ($) Earnings	Dividends	Book Value
12/15	17.16	32 12	0.65	0.00	9.82
12/14	11.22	91 32	0.28	0.00	7.76
12/13	15.01	— —	(0.14)	0.00	4.99
Annual Growth	6.9%		—	—	40.3%

Arbor Realty Trust Inc

Money doesn't grow on trees so Arbor Realty Trust invests in real estate-related assets. The real estate investment trust (REIT) buys structured finance assets in the commercial and multifamily real estate markets. It primarily invests in bridge loans (short-term financing) and mezzanine loans (large and usually unsecured loans) but also invests in discounted mortgage notes and other assets. The REIT targets lending and investment opportunities where borrowers seek interim financing until permanent financing is attained. Arbor Realty Trust is managed by financing firm Arbor Commercial Mortgage though in early 2016 the REIT agreed to buy Arbor Commercial Mortgage for $250 million to expand into the government-sponsored multi-family real estate loan origination business.

EXECUTIVES

Secretary and Director, Walter K. Horn, age 73, $225,000 total compensation
Chairman President and CEO; Chairman and CEO Arbor Commercial Mortgage, Ivan Kaufman, age 55, $800,000 total compensation
EVP Structured Finance, Fred Weber, age 55, $500,000 total compensation
EVP Structured Securitization, Gene Kilgore, age 49, $500,000 total compensation
CFO and Treasurer; CFO Arbor Commercial Mortgage, Paul Elenio, age 48, $270,000 total compensation
Chief Credit Officer, Andrew Guziewicz
SVP Asset Management, John Felletter, $225,000 total compensation
Senior Vice President Structured Finance, Gianni Ottaviano
Secretary and Director, Walter K. Horn, age 73
Director, Archie R. Dykes, age 85

Director, C. Michael Kojaian, age 54
Director, Melvin F. (Mel) Lazar, age 77
Director, John J. Bishar Jr., age 66
Director, William Helmreich, age 70
Director, Joseph Martello, age 60
Director, Karen K. Edwards, age 59
Independent Director, William Green
Auditors: Ernst & Young LLP

LOCATIONS

HQ: Arbor Realty Trust Inc
333 Earle Ovington Boulevard, Suite 900, Uniondale, NY 11553
Phone: 516 506-4200
Web: www.arborrealtytrust.com

COMPETITORS

Annaly Capital Management	Newcastle Investment
Anworth Mortgage Asset	RAIT Financial Trust
Capital Trust	Redwood Trust
Impac Mortgage Holdings	Starwood Property
Institutional Financial Markets	iStar Financial Inc

HISTORICAL FINANCIALS

Company Type: Public

Income Statement

FYE: December 31

	REVENUE ($ mil.)	NET INCOME ($ mil.)	NET PROFIT MARGIN	EMPLOYEES
12/15	142.5	53.4	37.5%	39.0
12/14	141.0	93.0	66.0%	37.0
12/13	129.1	21.3	16.5%	37.0
12/12	111.4	21.7	19.5%	30.0
12/11	98.2	(40.1)	—	32.0
Annual Growth	9.8%	—	—	5.1%

2015 Year-End Financials

Debt ratio: 64.2%
Return on equity: 9.7%
Cash ($ mil.): 188.7
Current ratio: 1.36
Long-term debt ($ mil.): 1,036.9

No. of shares (mil.): 50.9
Dividends
  Yield: 8.1%
  Payout: 63.7%
Market value ($ mil.): 364.0

	STOCK PRICE ($) FY Close	P/E High/Low	PER SHARE ($) Earnings	Dividends	Book Value
12/15	7.15	8 7	0.90	0.58	11.09
12/14	6.77	4 4	1.70	0.52	10.61
12/13	6.66	21 15	0.39	0.50	8.91
12/12	5.99	8 4	0.79	0.29	7.34
12/11	3.52	— —	(1.61)	0.00	7.04
Annual Growth	19.4%		—	—	12.0%

ARC Logistics Partners LP

Arc Logistics Partners owns more than a dozen fuel storage terminals in 10 states that can hold almost 5 million barrels of oil ethanol and other types of petroleum products. It also owns two rail transloading facilities in Alabama that can move 23000 barrels per day and a liquefied natural gas storage facility in Mississippi. Customers include oil and gas companies refineries marketers distributors and other industrial manufacturers. Arc Lo-

gistics Partners was formed by Lightfoot Capital Partners (which is majority owned by GE). Organized as a limited partnership Arc is exempt from paying corporate income tax as long as it distributes quarterly dividends to shareholders. The partnership went public in 2013.

EXECUTIVES

Senior Vice President Chief Financial Officer and Treasurer, Brad (Brady) Oswald
Auditors: PricewaterhouseCoopers LLP

LOCATIONS

HQ: ARC Logistics Partners LP
725 Fifth Avenue, 19th Floor, New York, NY 10022
Phone: 212 993-1290
Web: www.arcxlp.com

COMPETITORS

Buckeye Partners	NuStar Energy
Enbridge Energy	Sunoco Logistics
Enterprise Products	TransMontaigne
Kinder Morgan Energy Partners	Williams Companies
	World Point

HISTORICAL FINANCIALS

Company Type: Public

Income Statement

FYE: December 31

	REVENUE ($ mil.)	NET INCOME ($ mil.)	NET PROFIT MARGIN	EMPLOYEES
12/15	81.7	10.7	13.1%	111.0
12/14	54.9	1.2	2.3%	95.0
12/13	47.8	12.8	26.8%	83.0
12/12	22.8	5.4	23.7%	80.0
12/11	21.0	5.3	25.5%	0.0
Annual Growth	40.4%	19.0%	—	—

2015 Year-End Financials

Debt ratio: 34.8%
Return on equity: —
Cash ($ mil.): 5.8
Current ratio: 1.13
Long-term debt ($ mil.): 226.0

No. of shares (mil.): 19.2
Dividends
  Yield: 12.7%
  Payout: 432.0%
Market value ($ mil.): 256.0

	STOCK PRICE ($) FY Close	P/E High/Low	PER SHARE ($) Earnings	Dividends	Book Value
12/15	13.27	52 29	0.39	1.69	20.01
12/14	17.06	524370	0.05	1.40	16.45
12/13	21.90	90 82	0.10	0.00	17.56
Annual Growth	(22.2%)		— 97.5%	—	6.7%

Ares Commercial Real Estate Corp

Auditors: Ernst & Young LLP

LOCATIONS

HQ: Ares Commercial Real Estate Corp
245 Park Avenue, 42nd Floor, New York, NY 10167
Phone: 212 750-7300
Web: www.arescre.com

HISTORICAL FINANCIALS

Company Type: Public

Income Statement

FYE: December 31

	REVENUE ($ mil.)	NET INCOME ($ mil.)	NET PROFIT MARGIN	EMPLOYEES
12/15	121.7	43.3	35.6%	870.0
12/14	98.7	24.6	24.9%	750.0
12/13	47.3	13.7	29.1%	790.0
12/12	9.2	0.8	9.3%	560.0
12/11	0.0	(0.1)	—	0.0
Annual Growth	1319.3%	—	—	—

2015 Year-End Financials

Debt ratio: 63.2%
Return on equity: 10.6%
Cash ($ mil.): 9.0
Current ratio: 4.01
Long-term debt ($ mil.): 871.6

No. of shares (mil.): 28.6
Dividends
  Yield: 8.7%
  Payout: 83.3%
Market value ($ mil.): 327.0

	STOCK PRICE ($) FY Close	P/E High/Low	PER SHARE ($) Earnings	Dividends	Book Value
12/15	11.44	11 9	1.20	1.00	14.31
12/14	11.48	16 13	0.85	1.00	14.10
12/13	13.10	24 17	0.72	1.00	14.25
12/12	16.42	600520	0.03	0.37	17.85
Annual Growth	(11.3%)	—	—242.0%	39.3%	(7.1%)

Ares Management LP

Auditors: Ernst & Young LLP

LOCATIONS

HQ: Ares Management LP
  2000 Avenue of the Stars, 12th Floor, Los Angeles, CA 90067
Phone: 310 201-4100
Web: www.aresmgmt.com

HISTORICAL FINANCIALS

Company Type: Public

Income Statement

FYE: December 31

	REVENUE ($ mil.)	NET INCOME ($ mil.)	NET PROFIT MARGIN	EMPLOYEES
12/15	814.4	19.3	2.4%	870.0
12/14	603.8	34.9	5.8%	800.0
12/13	478.6	180.4	37.7%	700.0
12/12	334.0	220.6	66.1%	0.0
12/11	206.9	97.3	47.0%	0.0
Annual Growth	40.8%	(33.2%)	—	—

2015 Year-End Financials

Debt ratio: 59.5%
Return on equity: 3.5%
Cash ($ mil.): 281.2
Current ratio: 3.53
Long-term debt ($ mil.): 2,186.0

No. of shares (mil.): 80.6
Dividends
  Yield: 6.8%
  Payout: 314.2%
Market value ($ mil.): 1,043.0

	STOCK PRICE ($) FY Close	P/E High/Low	PER SHARE ($) Earnings	Dividends	Book Value
12/15	12.93	90 54	0.23	0.88	3.35
12/14	17.14	46 36	0.43	0.42	16.67
Annual Growth	(24.6%)	—	—(46.5%)	109.5%	(79.9%)

Argan Inc

Argan makes sure its customers stay all juiced up. The holding company owns subsidiaries that provide power services and products for the government telecommunications power and personal health care industries. Its main subsidiary Gemma Power Systems designs builds and maintains power plants including traditional and alternate fuel plants. The company's Southern Maryland Cable unit provides inside-premise wiring and also performs splicing and underground and aerial telecom infrastructure construction services to carriers government entities service providers and electric utilities. Argan's power industry segment accounts for more than 95% of its total revenues.

OperationsArgan operates two main segments: Power Industry Services which generated 98% of its total revenue in fiscal 2015 (ended January 2015) and operates through Gemma Power Systems and Atlantic Projects Company; and Telecom Infrastructure Services which operates through Southern Maryland Cable. Main subsidiary Gemma Power Systems (GPS) has completed projects at more than 76 power-generating facilities (representing some 11000 megawatts of capacity). It has expertise working with combined-cycle cogeneration facilities simple-cycle peaking plants emergency peaking plants and boiler plants. The firm also completes renovation work for utilities. Subsidiary Atlantic Projects Company (acquired in mid-2015) installs turbines boilers and large rotating equipment. It also provides commissioning and outage services to original equipment manufacturers global construction firms and plant owners around the globe.Geographic ReachArgan operates in the US as well as internationally in Hong Kong and Singapore.Sales and MarketingGPS serves a variety of customers including public utilities independent power project owners municipalities public institutions and private companies. Southern Maryland Cable serves the federal government local governments telecommunications and broadband service providers and electric utilities. Atlantic Projects Company serves customers in the power generation oil & gas industrial and process industries.Argan's major customers in fiscal 2015 (ended January 2015) included: Howard County and the state of Maryland Verizon EDS and the Southern Maryland Electric Cooperative (SMECO). About 25% of SMC's revenues that year came from outside plant services provided under its contract with SMECO.Financial PerformanceArgan's annual revenues while volatile have been trending higher over the past few years as demand for energy continues to grow in the US. Its profits have been rising steadily over the past few years as well.The company's revenue spiked 68% to $383.11 million in fiscal 2015 (ended January 2015) thanks to higher construction activity on two natural gas-fired combined cycle power plant projects (the Panda Liberty and Panda Patriot power plants).Despite revenue growth in FY2015 Argan's net income fell 24% to $30 million for the year due to higher operating costs and overhead expenses all resulting from more activities going toward the Panda Liberty and Panda Patriot projects. The company's operating cash levels dipped 5% to $93 million as the company's cash earnings fell during the year.StrategyArgan's main subsidiary GPS continued in 2015 to work on high-profile power projects (usually extending up to three years) recently expanding into alternative energy generation to cover EPC contracting services for alternative energy facility owners including biomass plants wind farms and solar fields.Some of GPS's projects completed between FY2013 through FY2015 included: an 800 MW simple-cycle quick start peaking power plant in Desert Hot Springs California; wind-energy farms with 150 turbines powering 230 MW in the states of Illinois and Pennsylvania; and two large solar energy fields in Massachusetts with 40000 photovoltaic panels. Its past projects include biodiesel production plants in Texas and a natural gas-fired power plant in California.Mergers and AcquisitionsIn May 2015 Argan bought Ireland-based Atlantic Projects Company Limited a private company that provides turbine boiler and large rotating equipment installation commissioning and outage services. The deal expanded Argan's service lines and extended its operations internationally thanks to office acquisitions in Hong Kong Singapore and New York.

EXECUTIVES

SVP CFO and Secretary, Arthur F. Trudel Jr., age 63, $200,000 total compensation
Chairman President and CEO, Rainer H. Bosselmann, age 72, $200,000 total compensation
Vice Chairman and CEO Gemma Power Systems, William F. (Bill) Griffin Jr., age 59, $365,000 total compensation
President Gemma Power Systems, Daniel L. (Dan) Martin
Director, William F. Leimkuhler, age 63
Director, DeSoto S. Jordan, age 70
Director, James W. (Jim) Quinn, age 57
Director, Daniel A. (Dan) Levinson, age 54
Director, W.G. Champion (Champ) Mitchell, age 67
Director, Henry A. Crumpton, age 58
Director, Cynthia Flanders, age 60
Independent Director, Brian Sherras
Auditors: Grant Thornton LLP

LOCATIONS

HQ: Argan Inc
  One Church Street, Suite 201, Rockville, MD 20850
Phone: 301 315-0027
Web: www.arganinc.com

PRODUCTS/OPERATIONS

2015 Sales

	$ mil.	% of total
Power industry services	376.7	98
Telecommunications infrastructure services	6.4	2
Total	383.1	100

COMPETITORS

Bechtel	John Wood Group
CH2M HILL	Kiewit Power
Chicago Bridge & Iron	Constructors
EMCOR	Quanta Services
Fagen Inc.	SNC-Lavalin
Fluor	Skanska
IES Holdings	

HISTORICAL FINANCIALS

Company Type: Public

Income Statement

FYE: January 31

	REVENUE ($ mil.)	NET INCOME ($ mil.)	NET PROFIT MARGIN	EMPLOYEES
01/16	413.2	36.3	8.8%	1,188.0
01/15	383.1	30.4	7.9%	862.0
01/14	227.4	40.1	17.6%	359.0
01/13	278.6	23.2	8.3%	246.0
01/12	141.8	9.2	6.5%	239.0
Annual Growth	30.6%	40.7%	—	49.3%

2016 Year-End Financials

Debt ratio: —
Return on equity: 17.9%
Cash ($ mil.): 160.9
Current ratio: 1.87
Long-term debt ($ mil.): —

No. of shares (mil.): 14.8
Dividends
Yield: 0.0%
Payout: 28.9%
Market value ($ mil.): 447.0

	STOCK PRICE ($) FY Close	P/E High/Low	PER SHARE ($) Earnings	Dividends	Book Value
01/16	30.12	17 12	2.42	0.70	14.73
01/15	30.41	19 13	2.05	0.70	12.68
01/14	28.41	11 5	2.78	0.75	10.94
01/13	18.80	11 8	1.65	0.60	8.65
01/12	14.50	26 12	0.67	0.50	7.41
Annual Growth	20.1%	—	37.9%	8.8%	18.7%

Arista Networks Inc

Auditors: Ernst & Young LLP

LOCATIONS

HQ: Arista Networks Inc
5453 Great America Parkway, Santa Clara, CA 95054
Phone: 408 547-5500
Web: www.arista.com

HISTORICAL FINANCIALS

Company Type: Public

Income Statement

FYE: December 31

	REVENUE ($ mil.)	NET INCOME ($ mil.)	NET PROFIT MARGIN	EMPLOYEES
12/15	837.5	121.1	14.5%	1,200.0
12/14	584.1	86.8	14.9%	1,000.0
12/13	361.2	42.4	11.8%	850.0
12/12	193.4	21.3	11.0%	0.0
12/11	139.8	34.0	24.3%	0.0
Annual Growth	56.4%	37.3%	—	—

2015 Year-End Financials

Debt ratio: 3.5%
Return on equity: 18.0%
Cash ($ mil.): 687.3
Current ratio: 4.15
Long-term debt ($ mil.): 41.2

No. of shares (mil.): 68.1
Dividends
Yield: —
Payout: —
Market value ($ mil.): 5,303.0

	STOCK PRICE ($) FY Close	P/E High/Low	PER SHARE ($) Earnings	Dividends	Book Value
12/15	77.84	48 31	1.67	0.00	11.57
12/14	60.76	66 39	1.29	0.00	8.48
Annual Growth	28.1%	—	29.5%	—	36.4%

Ashford Hospitality Trust Inc

Ashford Hospitality is in with the inn crowd. A self-administered real estate investment trust (REIT) Ashford owns more than 85 luxury hotel properties representing 17200 rooms in states primarily on the East Coast West Coast and Texas. Most of its properties operate under the upscale and upper upscale Embassy Suites Hilton Marriott Hyatt Starwood and Intercontinental Hotels Group brands. In addition to making direct investments in hotels the REIT also originates loans secured by hotel properties. About 80% of Ashford's revenue comes from its Rooms while around 15% comes from its food and beverage services.

Geographic ReachThe REIT's hotel properties are in several states including Texas Virginia Nevada New York Arizona Florida Pennsylvania California and Oregon.Sales and MarketingAshford Hospitality spent $3.3 million on advertising in 2014 compared to $4.1 million and $4.0 million in 2013 and 2012 respectively. Financial PerformanceAshford's revenues have trended higher over the past several years as it has expanded its property portfolio through acquisitions and has charged higher room rates as the economy has strengthened. The REIT has been suffering from losses however mostly as high interest expenses and amortization of loan costs on its debt have persistedThe REIT's revenue fell by 16% to $795 million in 2014 however mostly due to its Ashford Prime spin-off and the sale of its Pier House Resort which led to a double-digit decline in room and food and beverage revenues. Its existing property room revenues increased for the year helping to absorb some of the top-line declines.Despite lower revenue in 2014 Ashford's losses receded to $31.4 million (compared to losses of $41.3 million in 2013) as its interest expenses on its debt hotel operating expenses and depreciation and amortization costs declined with fewer hotel properties in operation. The REIT's operating cash levels shrank to $111.3 million as it collected less income after its Ashford Prime spin-off and property dispositions during the year. Strategy

Ashford Hospitality has been actively building up its hotel portfolio as the lodging industry has strengthened with the overall economy. The REIT targets hotel property investments in full-service hotels in the up-scale and upper-upscale segments of the lodging industry that have RevPAR of less than twice the national average. Some of its 2015 acquisitions included: the 237-room W Atlanta Downtown Hotel (managed by Starwood Hotels) for $56.8 million the 229-room W Minneapolis Hotel - The Foshay and the 60-room Le Meridien Chambers Minneapolis hotel for $101 million cash; and an acquisition of a 9-hotel portfolio for $224 million ($179000 per key).The REIT selectively sells off its non-core properties to free up resources for its target investment properties. In 2015 for example Ashford planned to sell 23 of its select-service hotels that were brand-managed and expressed interest in selling its remaining select-service properties in the future (though its advisor Ashford Inc may pursue a select-service acquisition platform).

Beyond direct hotel investments Ashford in 2015 planned to grow revenues by providing mezzanine financing through origination or acquisition offering first-lien mortgage financing and participating in sale-leaseback transaction to grow its

business as the lodging industry continued to improve. Company BackgroundAshford established a joint venture with Prudential Real Estate Investors that acquired a 28-property portfolio formerly owned by Highland Hospitality in 2011. Among the assets gained in that transaction were the Churchill and Melrose hotels in Washington DC; and the Ritz-Carlton in Atlanta. Highland defaulted on the properties which the partnership acquired through a $1.3 billion consensual foreclosure. In 2014 because the Highland Hospitality property exceeded performance expectations Ashford purchased all of Prudential Real Estate's stake in the property portfolio.

EXECUTIVES

President, Douglas A. Kessler, age 56, $625,000 total compensation
COO and General Counsel, David A. Brooks, age 57, $475,000 total compensation
EVP Asset Management, Jeremy J. Welter, $425,000 total compensation
CFO, Deric S. Eubanks
Senior Vice President Of Sales, Brian R (Bri) Hughes
Vice President, Victor (Vic) Grant
Senior Vice President Of Tax, Pia Ackerman
Vice President and Controller of Corporate Communications, Tripp Foshee
Vice President of Asset Management, John (Jack) O'Sullivan
Vice President, Mitch (Mitchell) Roberts
Vice President Asset Management, Doug (Dougie) Smolinski
Vice President Of Risk Management, Phil (Philly) Flanary
Vice President Of Asset Management And Underwritin, Patrick (Paddy) Webber
Vice President Of Capital Management, Eric Batis
Vice President Of Tax, Pam Golden
Vice President Accounting, Stephanie Bily
Vice President Of Capital Management, Mark (Marky) Matz
Vice President Property Tax, Victor Grant
Vice President Human Resources, Nancy (Nance) Hafner
Chairman, Monty J. Bennett
Vice President Treasurer, Adil Eduljee
Auditors: BDO USA LLP

LOCATIONS

HQ: Ashford Hospitality Trust Inc
14185 Dallas Parkway, Suite 1100, Dallas, TX 75254
Phone: 972 490-9600   **Fax:** 972 980-2705
Web: www.ahtreit.com

PRODUCTS/OPERATIONS

2014 Sales

	$ mil.	% of total
Hotel operations		
Rooms	640.3	81
Food & beverage	112.7	14
Other	26.9	3
Advisory Services revenue	10.8	1
Others	4.1	1
Total	**794.8**	**100**

COMPETITORS

Capital Hotel Management	John Q. Hammons
Crescent Real Estate	LaSalle Hotel Properties
DiamondRock Hospitality	MHI Hospitality
FelCor	Sage Hospitality
	Strategic Hotels

Hospitality Properties Trust
Host Hotels & Resorts
Sunstone Hotel Investors

HISTORICAL FINANCIALS

Company Type: Public

Income Statement

FYE: December 31

	REVENUE ($ mil.)	NET INCOME ($ mil.)	NET PROFIT MARGIN	EMPLOYEES
12/15	1,336.9	270.9	20.3%	108.0
12/14	794.8	(31.4)	—	92.0
12/13	942.2	(41.2)	—	83.0
12/12	922.6	(53.7)	—	78.0
12/11	889.8	2.1	0.2%	75.0
Annual Growth	10.7%	236.7%	—	9.5%

2015 Year-End Financials

Debt ratio: 77.3%
Return on equity: 40.3%
Cash ($ mil.): 215.0
Current ratio: 2.71
Long-term debt ($ mil.): 3,840.6

No. of shares (mil.): 95.4
Dividends
Yield: 7.6%
Payout: 19.9%
Market value ($ mil.): 602.0

	STOCK PRICE ($) FY Close	P/E High/Low		PER SHARE ($) Earnings	Dividends	Book Value
12/15	6.31	5	3	2.35	0.48	8.50
12/14	10.48	—	—	(0.75)	0.48	5.94
12/13	8.28	—	—	(1.00)	0.48	7.67
12/12	10.51	—	—	(1.30)	0.44	12.21
12/11	8.00	—	—	(0.73)	0.40	14.31
Annual Growth	(5.8%) (12.2%)	—	—	—	4.7%	

Aspen Technology Inc

Aspen Technology (AspenTech) helps its customers scale mountains of supply chain and engineering challenges. It provides supply chain manufacturing and engineering process optimization software to some 2100 companies in the energy chemical construction and pharmaceutical industries among others. The company's software — which includes supplier collaboration inventory management production planning and collaborative engineering functions –is offered under its aspenONE subscription service. AspenTech which generates most of its sales outside the US also provides related technical and professional services such as technical support training and systems implementation and integration.

Operations

AspenTech's subscription and software segment accounts for 92% of revenue with services accounting for the rest.

Geographic Reach Europe is the company's largest geographic segment accounting for about 35% of sales. The US contributes 31% of sales. Other markets served include the Asia-Pacific region Canada Latin America and the Middle East.

Sales and Marketing AspenTech sells directly through resellers in non-core markets and by licensing to universities to encourage future demand. It continues to target global process manufacturers whose capital-intensive technologically advanced operations require more specialized software and services than are available in broader en-

terprise resource planning (ERP) applications. It counts some 2500 customers. Financial Analysis

In 2015 AspenTech's revenue increased a healthy 13% to $440 million from $391 million in 2014 based on a 16% rise in subscription and software. Service revenue slid 16% lower for the year.

Net income jumped 38% to $118 million in 2015 from about $86 million in 2014. AspenTech reduced costs n several areas to boost profit.

Cash flow generated from operations fell to $192 million in 2105 from $200 million in 2014. Strategy

The company also targets global growth especially in emerging markets. As its customers move into China India Russia Latin America and the Middle East AspenTech is establishing customer support and sales operations in Russia and the Middle East with plans for more international locations. AspenTech is also focused on the continued adoption of its aspenONE subscription model by customers. The service which was launched in mid-2009 gives customers access to all applications within the software suite they license including upgrades and future products. The company believes this allows clients more flexibility to increase their usage of the software as needs change.

Mergers and Acquisitions

In 2016 ApenTech agreed to buy KBC Advanced Technologies a provider of strategic consulting and software to the oil and gas industry for ab out $230 million.

The 2015 acquisition of BLOWDOWN a software firm in the UK provides modeling capabilities for depressurization scenarios.

The Sulsim sulfur simulation software from Sulphur Experts acquired in 2014 brings technology to optimize acid gas cleaning and sulfur recovery design and operations.

AspenTech acquired Hamburg Germany-based flowsheet simulation software developer SolidSim Engineering in 2012. The purchase augmented the company's existing solids process modeling tools contained in its core aspenONE application.

In 2013 it purchased pipeline and dock scheduling software from Refining Advantage which will enhance the supply chain services AspenTech offers its petroleum customers.

Ownership Mutual fund manager Waddell & Reed owns 17% of the company.

HISTORY

Early History

Lawrence Evans was a chemical engineering professor at MIT in 1976 when he became the principal investigator for the Energy Department's ASPEN (Advanced System for Process Engineering) project to develop synthetic fuels. He was joined by Joseph Boston and Herbert Britt (both chemical engineers) in 1977. Four years later they formed Aspen Technology to develop and market computer-aided chemical engineering software for process manufacturers.

The company launched its first product in 1982 and introduced process simulation software the following year. Boston became AspenTech's president and Evans became chairman and CEO in 1984.

The company went public in 1994. A series of acquisitions followed –including the purchases of Industrial Systems in 1995 and Dynamic Matrix Control and Setpoint in 1996 —which gave the company operation control software. In 1997 it bought consultant Special Analysis & Simulation Technologies and intelligent software expert NeuralWare.

EXECUTIVES

SVP General Counsel and Secretary, Frederic G. Hammond, age 56, $330,000 total compensation

President and CEO, Antonio J. Pietri, age 51, $500,000 total compensation

EVP and CFO, Mark P. Sullivan, age 60, $370,000 total compensation

SVP Worldwide Marketing, Suresh Sundaram

Senior Vice President Human Resources, Joana Nikka

Vice President of Product Management E, Steve Williams

Vice President, Toni (Antonio) Rudnicki

Executive Vice President, Paul Taylor

Vice President Of Technology, Chauchyun Chen

Vice President Engineering, Boz Elloy

Vice President Corporate Sales, Greg Mason Greg Mason

Vice President Enterprise Technologies, Desmond Jacas

Senior Vice President Research And Dev, Willie (Will) Chan

Vice President Sales, Jim Boozer

Vice President Worldwide Sales Operations and Business Development, Clint (Clinton) Clemans

Vice President Technology, Basil Joffe

Vice President of Technology, Ashok Subramanian

Vice President, Michael (Mel) Welch

Executive Vice President, John (Jack) Hague

Senior Vice President of Corporate Development, Glover Lawrence

Senior Vice President Marketing, Blair Wheeler

Vice President Strategy and Research, Joanna (Anna) Nikka

Vice President Research And Development, Bill (Billy) Mock

Vice President Marketing Strategy and Research, Alison (Alli) Smith

Senior Vice President Information Technology, William (Bill) Chan

Vice President Sales Northern Europe, Matthew (Matt) Holland

Vice President Product Management, John (Jack) Wylie

Vice President Tax, John (Jack) LaMountain

Vice President Strategic Alliances, Luis (Lu) Figueroa

Board Of Directors, Steve Jennings

Chairman, Robert M. Whelan, age 64

Secretary Of The Special Working Group, Gabriel (Gabe) Aurioles

Treasurer, Roger (Rog) Kuebel

Auditors: KPMG LLP

LOCATIONS

HQ: Aspen Technology Inc
20 Crosby Drive, Bedford, MA 01730
Phone: 781 221-6400
Web: www.aspentech.com

PRODUCTS/OPERATIONS

2015 Sales

	$ mil.	% of total
Subscription & software	405.6	92
Services	34.8	8
Total	**440.4**	**100**

Selected Products

Aspen Plus
Aspen HYSYS
Aspen Exchanger Design and Rating
Aspen Economic Evaluation
Aspen Basic Engineering
Aspen Info Plus.21
Aspen DMCplus
Aspen Collaborative Demand Manager

Aspen Petroleum Scheduler
Aspen PIMS
Aspen Plant Scheduler
Aspen Supply Chain Planner
Aspen Inventory Management & Operations Scheduling
Aspen Petroleum Supply Chain Planner
Aspen Fleet Optimizer

COMPETITORS

ABB	OSIsoft
Dassault	Oracle
GSE Systems	PTC
Honeywell	QAD
International	Rockwell Automation
Infor Global	SAP
JDA Software	Shell Global Solutions
KBC Advanced	Siemens AG
Technologies	Yokogawa Electric

HISTORICAL FINANCIALS

Company Type: Public

Income Statement
FYE: June 30

	REVENUE ($ mil.)	NET INCOME ($ mil.)	NET PROFIT MARGIN	EMPLOYEES
06/16	472.3	139.9	29.6%	1,396.0
06/15	440.4	118.4	26.9%	1,372.0
06/14	391.4	85.7	21.9%	1,344.0
06/13	311.3	45.2	14.5%	1,328.0
06/12	243.1	(13.8)	—	1,325.0
Annual Growth	18.1%	—	—	1.3%

2016 Year-End Financials

Debt ratio: 33.3%
Return on equity: —
Cash ($ mil.): 318.3
Current ratio: 0.84
Long-term debt ($ mil.): —

No. of shares (mil.): 80.1
Dividends
  Yield: —
  Payout: —
Market value ($ mil.): 3,226.0

	STOCK PRICE ($) FY Close	P/E High/Low	PER SHARE ($) Earnings	PER SHARE ($) Dividends	PER SHARE ($) Book Value
06/16	40.24	27 18	1.68	0.00	(0.94)
06/15	45.55	35 24	1.33	0.00	(0.57)
06/14	46.40	51 31	0.92	0.00	0.91
06/13	28.79	68 46	0.47	0.00	1.09
06/12	23.15	— —	(0.15)	0.00	1.22
Annual Growth	14.8%		—	—	—

Astronics Corp

In the glare of its own lights but without histrionics Astronics Corporation displays its talents daily to a specialized audience. Astronics makes external and internal lighting systems as well as power generation and distribution technology for commercial general aviation and military defense aircraft. Products include cabin emergency lighting systems (escape path markers and exit locators) cockpit lighting systems (avionics keyboards ambient light sensors annunciator panels and electronic dimmers) external lights and military test equipment. Astronics operates subsidiaries include Astronics Advanced Electronic Systems Corp. Ballard Luminescent Systems and DME Corporation.Geographic ReachThe company's Aerospace segment has 11 principal operating facilities located in New York Florida Illinois New Hampshire Oregon and Washington; international resides in Canada and Montierchaume France. Its Test Systems segment has facilities located in Florida and California.Operations

The company operates in two segments: Aerospace (almost 80% of net sales) and Test Systems (20%). The Aerospace segment designs and makes a range of products for the global aerospace industry. Its products include aircraft lighting airframe power avionics airfield lighting and cabin electronics. The Test Systems segment designs develops and manufactures communications and weapons test systems and training and simulation devices for military clients.

Sales and Marketing

Astronics' customers include the Department of Defense (DOD) Federal Aviation Administration and airport operators US military forces foreign military agencies and makers of military communication systems.

Financial Performance

The company has achieved explosive growth the last two years mostly due to a surge in Aerospace sales and additional revenue from acquisitions. Revenues grew 5% to peak at a record-setting $692 million in 2015. Profits also jumped 19% to reach $67 million in 2015 another company milestone.

The historic growth for 2015 was fueled by an 11% spike in Aerospace sales and a 15% rise in sales from North America. This growth was driven by a spike in electrical power and motion sales particularly in-seat power products. Its lighting and safety product line increased due to growth passenger service unit sales. Systems certification sales also received a boost from acquisitions.

Astronics' unprecedented profit total for 2015 was due to the higher net sales coupled with a decrease in interest expenses due to decreased debt levels. The company's operating cash flow has trended upwards until 2015 when it decreased by 21%.

Strategy

The company continues to invest in new technologies and aircraft programs for each of its markets even while the aerospace industry as a whole is experiencing a slowdown along with the economy in general. In particular Astronics is developing an electrical power distribution system for the Learjet 85 that shows promise of becoming a standard component of business jets. Its products and technologies are also used in the F-35 Joint Strike Fighter the Airbus A380 XWB and the Boeing 787 to name a few.

Mergers and Acquisitions

Growing its Aerospace portfolio in 2015 Astronics paid $52 million to purchase Armstrong Aerospace located in Itasca Illinois. Armstrong is a provider of engineering design and certification products and services for commercial aircraft specializing in connectivity in-flight entertainment and electrical power systems.

Company Background

Founded in 1968 Astronics was originally involved in electroluminescent products until it began to diversify into the packaging and printing industries. The company acquired MOD-PAC a maker of paperboard packaging in 1972 and Krepe-Kraft a specialized printing company in 1987.

EXECUTIVES

Vice President, Brian Price
Executive Vice President Luminescent Systems, James S. (Jim) Kramer, $242,000 total compensation
President and Chief Executive Officer, Peter J. Gundermann, age 54, $430,000 total compensation
VP and CFO, David C. Burney, age 54, $270,000 total compensation
Executive Vice President Astronics Advanced Electronic Systems, Mark Peabody, $310,000 total compensation
Chairman of the Board, Kevin T. Keane, age 83
Auditors: Ernst & Young LLP

LOCATIONS

HQ: Astronics Corp
  130 Commerce Way, East Aurora, NY 14052
Phone: 716 805-1599
Web: www.astronics.com

PRODUCTS/OPERATIONS

2015 Sales

	$ mil.	% of total
Aerospace	549.7	79
Test systems	142.5	21
Total	692.2	100

Aircraft lighting
Astronics Advanced Electronic Systems Corp
Ballard Technology Inc
DME Corporation
Luminescent Systems Canada Inc
Luminescent Systems Inc
Max-Viz Inc

COMPETITORS

AIM Aviation	Indel
B/E Aerospace	L-3/IS
C&D Zodiac	TransDigm Group
Ducommun	Ultra Electronics
Honeywell Aerospace	Zodiac Aerospace

HISTORICAL FINANCIALS

Company Type: Public

Income Statement
FYE: December 31

	REVENUE ($ mil.)	NET INCOME ($ mil.)	NET PROFIT MARGIN	EMPLOYEES
12/15	692.2	66.9	9.7%	2,300.0
12/14	661.0	56.1	8.5%	2,000.0
12/13	339.9	27.2	8.0%	1,715.0
12/12	266.4	21.8	8.2%	1,156.0
12/11	228.1	21.5	9.5%	1,081.0
Annual Growth	32.0%	32.7%	—	20.8%

2015 Year-End Financials

Debt ratio: 27.8%
Return on equity: 25.3%
Cash ($ mil.): 18.5
Current ratio: 2.40
Long-term debt ($ mil.): 167.2

No. of shares (mil.): 29.4
Dividends
  Yield: —
  Payout: —
Market value ($ mil.): 1,197.0

	STOCK PRICE ($) FY Close	P/E High/Low	PER SHARE ($) Earnings	PER SHARE ($) Dividends	PER SHARE ($) Book Value
12/15	40.71	33 15	2.22	0.00	10.21
12/14	55.31	37 22	1.88	0.00	7.87
12/13	51.00	54 23	0.94	0.00	6.05
12/12	22.88	46 25	0.76	0.00	4.54
12/11	35.81	40 21	0.88	0.00	4.37
Annual Growth	3.3%		— 26.1%	—	23.6%

Athenahealth Inc

athenahealth knows that managing physician practices can result in a splitting headache especially when patients are late paying bills or miss appointments. The company provides health care organizations with online software for cloud-based electronic health record (EHR) practice management and patient communication services. Offerings include revenue cycle management (athenaCollector) medical record automation (athenaClinicals) and patient relations and referral systems (athenaCommunicator and athenaCoordinator). Its services help health care providers streamline workflow data and billing and collection tasks. athenahealth's programs are managed through its cloud-based athenaNet network.

Operations

More than 80000 medical providers including some 55000 physicians use the company's athenaCollector services. In 2015 athenahealth's offerings were used by its clients to post nearly $19 billion in physicians' collections and to process about 60 million medical claims.

The company's cloud-based businesses services (basically all of its software) generates 96% of revenue. The other 4% comes from implementations and other services.

Geographic Reach

athenahealth serves clients throughout the US. It has operations in several US cities and in India and the Philippines.

Sales and Marketing

athenahealth primarily uses a direct sales force to promote its products though it also has third-party distribution channels in certain regions. Its sales force is divided into enterprise group hospital and small group teams while the channel partners are typically compensated for passing on sale leads.

The company serves hospitals clinics and medical professionals including family practice offices and practitioners. athenahealth employs a variety of marketing techniques to recruit new customers and increase its brand awareness including online and print advertising campaigns; trade shows; email and phone programs; and information sessions and seminars for potential clients.

athenahealth ramped up advertising in 2015 spending $28 million a healthy increase from the total of some $29 million for 2014 and 2015.

Financial Performance

athenahealth reported a 23% increase in revenues in 2015 to about $925 million which was attributed to its larger customer base and a broader array of implementation and business services provided to those customers. The company rebounded from a $3 million loss in 2014 to post a $14 million profit in 2015.

Cash flow from operations rose to $164 million in 2015 from $149 million in 2014.

Strategy

There is a huge opportunity for health care information technology services in the US as the Patient Protection and Affordable Care Act (PPACA) is driving more people to have health insurance.

athenahealth's strategy includes meeting the needs of specific clients (and thus garnering loyalty) integrating multiple programs into clients' comprehensive workflows and forming new client relationships through focused marketing efforts. It also seeks to provide products that are easy to adopt into daily practice routines while helping customers to reduce administrative costs.

athenahealth is especially focused on increasing use of its newer athenaRules offering which helps health care clients comply with the reimbursement rules of government and commercial health plans.

Mergers and Acquisitions

The company has typically acquired small but promising companies to broaden its market presence. athenahealth made a move into the lucrative hospital sector in early 2015 with its acquisition of startup RazorInsights. The acquired firm specializes in EHR services for rural critical access and community hospitals with 50 beds and under.

Also in 2015 athenahealth bought Arsenal Health which has been a third-party in some athenahealth customer deals. With the acquisition Arsenal Health's schedule optimization product will be available as a native part of athenaNet.

EXECUTIVES

President Client Organization, Stephen N. Kahane, age 58, $496,846 total compensation
President and CEO, Jonathan S. Bush, age 46, $612,692 total compensation
SVP and Chief Medical Officer, Todd Rothenhaus
SVP and CFO, Karl Stubelis
SVP and Chief Product Officer, Kyle Armbrester, $273,362 total compensation
Vice President Clinical, Laurie (Laur) Saltonstall
Senior Vice President and President Qualcomm Government Technologies, Laurie (Laur) Mullin
Vice President Sales, Craig (Craigy) Surette
Vice President Operations, Matt (Matty) Levesque
Vice President Information Technology Enterprise Business Development, Christopher (Chris) Davis
Vice President Product Strategy, Evan Grossman
Vice President Enterprise Sales at athenahealth, Mark (Marky) Gowetski
Vice President of Enterprise Solutions, Michael (Mel) Maus
Vice President Sales, Gavin Hoopes
Vice President, Pierre Valette
Vice President Government and Regulatory Affairs; Assistant General Counsel, Dan (Danny) Haley
Vice President Sales, Gavin (Vinny) Hoopes
Vice President of Enterprise Engineering, Jay (JayJay) Jungalwala
Vice President, Sheila (Sheil) Wiese
Auditors: Deloitte & Touche LLP

LOCATIONS

HQ: Athenahealth Inc
311 Arsenal Street, Watertown, MA 02472
Phone: 617 402-1000
Web: www.athenahealth.com

PRODUCTS/OPERATIONS

2015 Sales

	$ mil.	% of total
Business services	886.1	96
Implementation & other	38.7	4
Total	**924.8**	**100**

Selected Software

athenaClinicals (medical record management)
athenaCollector (claims management)
athenaCommunicator (patient communication management)
athenaCoordinator (referrals management)
athenaNet (cloud system)
athenaRules (compliance system)

COMPETITORS

Allscripts	McKesson
CBIZ	Quality Systems
Epic Systems	Sage Software
GE Healthcare	Siemens Healthcare
Greenway Medical Technologies	UnitedHealth Group
	eClinicalWorks

HISTORICAL FINANCIALS
Company Type: Public

Income Statement
FYE: December 31

	REVENUE ($ mil.)	NET INCOME ($ mil.)	NET PROFIT MARGIN	EMPLOYEES
12/16	1,082.9	21.0	1.9%	5,305.0
12/15	924.7	14.0	1.5%	4,668.0
12/14	752.6	(3.1)	—	3,676.0
12/13	595.0	2.5	0.4%	2,966.0
12/12	422.2	18.7	4.4%	2,339.0
Annual Growth	**26.5%**	**2.9%**	**—**	**22.7%**

2016 Year-End Financials

Debt ratio: 24.4%	No. of shares (mil.): 39.5
Return on equity: 3.5%	Dividends
Cash ($ mil.): 147.4	Yield: —
Current ratio: 1.73	Payout: —
Long-term debt ($ mil.): 272.8	Market value ($ mil.): 4,154.0

	STOCK PRICE ($) FY Close	P/E High/Low		Earnings	PER SHARE ($) Dividends	Book Value
12/16	105.17	312	174	0.52	0.00	16.03
12/15	160.97	466	310	0.35	0.00	13.96
12/14	145.70	—	—	(0.08)	0.00	12.46
12/13	134.50	2039	1047	0.07	0.00	10.48
12/12	73.29	186	96	0.50	0.00	8.59
Annual Growth	**9.4%**	**—**	**—**	**1.0%**	**—**	**16.9%**

Atlas Financial Holdings Inc.

EXECUTIVES

Chb, Gordon G Pratt
V Pres Operations, Leslie Dimaggio
Vice President Claims, Joe Shugrue
Auditors: BDO USA, LLP

LOCATIONS

HQ: Atlas Financial Holdings Inc.
150 Northwest Point Boulevard, Elk Grove Village, IL 60007
Phone: 847 472-6700 **Fax:** 847 228-2580
Web: www.atlas-fin.com

HISTORICAL FINANCIALS
Company Type: Public

Income Statement
FYE: December 31

	ASSETS ($ mil.)	NET INCOME ($ mil.)	INCOME AS % OF ASSETS	EMPLOYEES
12/15	411.5	14.4	3.5%	214.0
12/14	283.9	17.7	6.2%	118.0
12/13	219.2	6.1	2.8%	98.0
12/12	163.0	3.1	1.9%	78.0
12/11	172.1	(2.4)	—	89.0
Annual Growth	**24.3%**	**—**	**—**	**24.5%**

2015 Year-End Financials

Return on assets: 4.1%	Dividends
Return on equity: 12.0%	Yield: —
Long-term debt ($ mil.): —	Payout: —
No. of shares (mil.): 12.0	Market value ($ mil.): 239.0
Sales ($ mil): 156.8	

	STOCK PRICE ($) FY Close	P/E High/Low		PER SHARE ($) Earnings	Dividends	Book Value
12/15	19.90	18	13	1.13	0.00	10.79
12/14	16.32	11	7	1.56	0.00	9.29
12/13	14.72	15	6	0.74	0.00	6.76
Annual Growth 16.3%		—	—	23.6%	—	26.3%

AV Homes Inc

AV Homes (formerly Avatar Holdings) aspires to be the embodiment of stylish retirement living. The company develops active adult and primary residential communities and builds homes in Florida Arizona and North Carolina. Its Joseph Carl Homes unit builds homes for people of all ages in Florida and Phoenix. AV Homes owns some 23000 acres of developed and developable land. AV Homes also operates a title insurance agency and manages the day-to-day operations of its communities' amenities. The company gets nearly 90% of its revenue from homebuilding developments while the remainder comes from land sales.

OperationsAV Homes focuses on developing active adult communities with age restrictions targeting the age 55 and up demographic. It also builds primary residential communities to be sold to first-time and move-up buyers.As of December 2014 the company owned more than 3500 developed residential lots over 2850 partially developed residential lots nearly 9600 undeveloped residential lots and 7220 acres of mixed use commercial and industrial land.Geographic ReachArizona-based AV Homes primarily builds active adult and primary residential home communities in Florida Arizona and North Carolina. Sales and MarketingThe company markets its homes through the use of model homes newspaper and magazine advertising and via the internet through its website online and social media channels. AV Homes spent $3.1 million on advertising in 2014 compared to $2.4 million and $2.9 million in 2013 and 2012 respectively.Financial PerformanceAV Homes' revenues have more than tripled since 2010 thanks to higher prices and sales volumes with increased demand for new homes in the strengthening economy. And while the company has not been profitable since 2007 as its low operating margins have been eaten up by interest expenses on long-term debts AV Homes has been steadily climbing out of the red in recent years with higher revenues. The builder's sales nearly doubled to $285.91 million in 2014 thanks to a 98% increase in home sales volumes coupled with a 7% increase in the average sales price on homes closed. Land sales also doubled during the year mostly because of the sale of a multi-family property in Arizona as well as the sale of a land position in Florida in the third quarter of the year.

The company suffered another net loss during 2014 though losses improved significantly to $1.93 million (compared to a net loss of $9.48 million in 2013) as AV Homes posted higher revenue for the year. The builder used $81.41 million on operations or 30% more cash than in 2013 mostly as it spent nearly $112 million more toward building up its land and other inventories for future developments. StrategyWith its eye on collecting higher home prices and gross margins as well as expanding its geographic footprint AV Homes strategically acquires land and lots for development in high buyer-demand markets. In early 2015 the company announced the opening of its 900-home "Encore" 55-Plus community in the master-planned community of Eastmark in Mesa Arizona. In 2014 in continuing its expansion into new markets AV Homes purchased 80 acres in the Jacksonville market and announced a 72-home community project in Huntersville North Carolina (the second project from its Carolina's division) which would begin rolling out homes in the Vermillion master-planned community later that year. In addition to acquiring land and developing homes from scratch the company also acquires small homebuilder operations for further development or for home sales. Mergers and AcquisitionsIn 2015 the company agreed to acquire the North Carolina-based Bonterra Builders which specializes in move-up buyer homes in the Greater Charlotte market for $96 million in cash. The deal added Bonterra Builders' collection of more than 30 active communities. Also in 2015 AV Homes acquired Florida-based Royal Oak Homes along with select land positions from affiliated land development companies for a total of $65 million. Royal Oak Homes specialized in building move-up buyer homes in the Greater Orlando and Central Florida market.

EXECUTIVES

President and CEO, Roger A. Cregg, age 60, $400,000 total compensation
Executive Vice President General Counsel and Corporate Secretary, Dave M. Gomez, age 51, $240,000 total compensation
EVP; President Avatar Properties, Joseph Carl Mulac, age 55, $300,000 total compensation
President Arizona, Chris Cady
EVP and CFO, Michael S. Burnett, $63,461 total compensation
Vice President Of Purchasing, Ken Kulinowski
Vice President of Operations, Dennis (Denny) Palmer
Vice President Of Purchasing, Lucas (Luke) Morris
Vice President of Operations, Shawn Budd
Chairman, Joshua L. Nash, age 54
Auditors: Deloitte & Touche LLP

LOCATIONS

HQ: AV Homes Inc
8601 N. Scottsdale Rd., Suite 225, Scottsdale, AZ 85253
Phone: 480 214-7400
Web: www.avatarholdings.com

PRODUCTS/OPERATIONS

2014 Sales

	$ mil.	% of total
Real estate revenues		
Home building and amenity	253.3	89
Land Sales	32.6	11
Total	**285.9**	**100**

COMPETITORS

ACTS Retirement-Life Communities	PulteGroup
Bonita Bay Group	St. Joe
John Wieland Homes	Toll Brothers
Lennar	WCI Communities

HISTORICAL FINANCIALS

Company Type: Public

Income Statement

FYE: December 31

	REVENUE ($ mil.)	NET INCOME ($ mil.)	NET PROFIT MARGIN	EMPLOYEES
12/15	517.7	11.9	2.3%	308.0
12/14	285.9	(1.9)	—	214.0
12/13	143.7	(9.4)	—	133.0
12/12	107.4	(90.2)	—	112.0
12/11	88.9	(165.8)	—	100.0
Annual Growth 55.3%		—		32.5%

2015 Year-End Financials

Debt ratio: 44.0%	No. of shares (mil.): 22.4
Return on equity: 4.0%	Dividends
Cash ($ mil.): 46.9	Yield: —
Current ratio: 1.35	Payout: —
Long-term debt ($ mil.): 326.7	Market value ($ mil.): 288.0

	STOCK PRICE ($) FY Close	P/E High/Low		PER SHARE ($) Earnings	Dividends	Book Value
12/15	12.81	31	22	0.54	0.00	13.44
12/14	14.57	—	—	(0.09)	0.00	12.93
12/13	18.17	—	—	(1.34)	0.00	13.01
12/12	14.22	—	—	(7.19)	0.00	12.95
Annual Growth (3.4%)		—	—	—	—	1.2%

AvalonBay Communities, Inc.

AvalonBay Communities has it down in the apartment department. The real estate investment trust (REIT) buys develops renovates and operates multifamily properties in the US. It specializes in upscale properties in high barrier-to-entry markets such as Boston Los Angeles New York City San Francisco Seattle and Washington DC. By providing luxury living in high-demand areas where apartment-zoned land is in low supply AvalonBay can also charge premium rent. The REIT owns about 180 apartment communities with more than 53000 units. It also has more than 30 properties under construction or redevelopment and owns rights to develop more than 30 additional ones.Most of AvalonBay's properties are garden-style but the company also owns mid- and high-rise apartment buildings. Its core Avalon brand comprises upscale apartments with high-end amenities in urban and suburban markets. Its AVA brand consists of smaller apartments in urban areas near public transportation and entertainment options while Eaves by Avalon offers less expensive price points to renters in suburban settings.The REIT handles its own leasing and management operations and usually acts as its own general contractor and construction manager for the development or renovation of properties. To attract and retain residents it offers amenities such as fully equipped kitchens with modern appliances patios and decks swimming pools fully equipped kitchens with modern appliances at many of its properties.AvalonBay which is divesting most of its holdings in the Midwest sold about a dozen properties in 2011. The dispositions helped the REIT attain earnings of more than $441 million in 2011 which represented an increase of more than 150% compared to the previous year ($175.3 million). Meanwhile revenues rose from $874 million in 2010 to $968.7 million an increase of about 10%. The company benefitted from higher occupancy rates at its communities a continued decline in home ownership rates and a limited supply of new multifamily construction projects from competitors. AvalonBay often sells non-strategic properties to fund new developments or acquisitions. The company has ramped up its development activity in anticipation of a further improving economy in order to capitalize on the aforementioned trends. It also expects to accelerate its acquisition activity which it put on hold during the recession.

EXECUTIVES

Executive Vice President Human Resources, Charlene Rothkopf

Chief Investment Officer, Matthew H. (Matt) Birenbaum, age 50, $490,385 total compensation

Chief Administrative Officer, Leo S. Horey, age 53, $420,192 total compensation

EVP Development, William M. (Bill) McLaughlin, age 51, $390,000 total compensation

Chairman President and CEO, Timothy J. (Tim) Naughton, age 54, $950,000 total compensation

EVP General Counsel and Secretary, Edward M. (Ted) Schulman, age 53, $319,282 total compensation

EVP Development, Stephen W. (Steve) Wilson, age 59, $425,000 total compensation

COO, Sean J. Breslin, age 49, $490,385 total compensation

SVP Investment Management, Kevin P. O'Shea, age 50, $480,769 total compensation

Chief Construction Officer, Michael M. Feigin, age 55

Senior Vice President Development, Sean Clark

Vice President Sales and Marketing, Kurt Hesser

Senior Vice President Development, Frederick (Fred) Harris

Executive Vice President Corporate Strategy, Matthew Fry

Vice President Property Operations, Sarah Mathewson

Vice President, Steve (Stevie) Wilson

Auditors: Ernst & Young LLP

LOCATIONS

HQ: AvalonBay Communities, Inc.
Ballston Tower, 671 N. Glebe Road, Suite 800, Arlington, VA 22203
Phone: 703 329-6300   **Fax:** 703 329-9130
Web: www.avalonbay.com

PRODUCTS/OPERATIONS

2011 Sales

	$ mil.	% of total
Rental & other income	959.0	99
Management development & other fees	9.7	1
Total	**968.7**	**100**

COMPETITORS

AMLI Residential	Essex Property Trust
Apartment Investment and Management	Gables Residential Services
Camden Property	Home Properties
Equity Residential	UDR

HISTORICAL FINANCIALS

Company Type: Public

Income Statement

FYE: December 31

	REVENUE ($ mil.)	NET INCOME ($ mil.)	NET PROFIT MARGIN	EMPLOYEES
12/15	1,856.0	741.7	40.0%	2,981.0
12/14	1,685.0	683.5	40.6%	3,006.0
12/13	1,462.9	353.1	24.1%	0.0
12/12	1,038.6	423.8	40.8%	2,178.0
12/11	968.7	441.6	45.6%	2,095.0
Annual Growth	17.7%	13.8%	—	9.2%

2015 Year-End Financials

Debt ratio: 38.1%	No. of shares (mil.): 137.0
Return on equity: 7.8%	Dividends
Cash ($ mil.): 400.5	Yield: 2.7%
Current ratio: 2.02	Payout: 91.7%
Long-term debt ($ mil.): 6,456.9	Market value ($ mil.): 25,226.0

	STOCK PRICE ($) FY Close	P/E High/Low		PER SHARE ($) Earnings	Dividends	Book Value
12/15	184.13	33	29	5.51	5.00	71.83
12/14	163.39	32	23	5.21	4.64	68.51
12/13	118.23	51	42	2.78	4.28	66.42
12/12	135.59	35	29	4.32	3.88	59.76
12/11	130.60	29	22	4.87	3.57	46.18
Annual Growth	9.0%	—	—	3.1%	8.8%	11.7%

AZZ Inc

AZZ's products act as a shield for steel. The company has two business segments: galvanizing services and energy. To protect steel from environmental corrosion galvanizing services dip steel products into baths of molten zinc. The process is vital for steel fabricators who serve highway construction electrical utility transportation and water-treatment firms. Through subsidiaries AZZ makes electrical power distribution systems industrial lighting switchgear motor control centers bus duct systems and tubular goods. Industrial petrochemical and power generation and transmission companies use the company's products.

Operations

AZZ's energy segment (around 55% of total sales) is a manufacturer of specialty equipment focusing on the safe and reliable transmission of power from generation sources to end customers. Products include custom switchgear electrical enclosures medium and high voltage bus ducts explosion proof and hazardous duty lighting and tubular products.

The company is also a third party supplier of safety related equipment for the nuclear industry. The galvanizing services segment (45%) provides hot dip galvanizing to the steel fabrication industry through facilities located throughout Canada and the US.

Geographic Reach

AZZ operates 45 galvanizing plants across the US and Canada. The company earned over 80% of its revenue from the US.

Sales and Marketing

The company sells energy products through manufacturers' representatives distributors agents and its own sales force. Its galvanizing products serve fabricators or manufacturers that provide services to the electrical and telecommunications bridge and highway petrochemical and general industrial markets along with numerous original equipment manufacturers.

Financial Performance

AZZ has achieved dramatic growth over the last few years. Revenues surged 11% from $817 million in 2015 to peak at $903 million in 2016 a historic milestone for the company. In 2016 its profits jumped 18% to $77 million due to the increased revenue. Cash flow from operations followed suit in 2016 jumping from $118 million to $144 million.

The historic growth in 2016 was driven by a 9% spike in energy sales and a 12% bump in galvanizing services. Both segments generated additional revenue from strategic acquisitions made during 2015 and 2016. The growth was also attributed to greater penetration and project scope expansion in specialty welding services for petroleum refining both domestically and internationally.

In addition the introduction of new technology continued to deliver positive results and drive growth within the energy segment. For the galvanizing segment the solar and original equipment manufacturer (OEM) markets added to a spike in sales and steel processed volumes during the year.

Mergers and Acquisitions

AZZ has achieved explosive revenue growth over the years mainly through the use of acquisitions. In 2016 it picked up Maryland-based Power Electronics a manufacturer and integrator of electrical enclosure systems serving the utility and industrial markets. The acquisition expanded AZZ's electrical power enclosure portfolio manufacturing capacity and geographical reach along the East Coast of North America.

The company in mid-2015 acquired US Galvanizing a Texas-based provider of galvanizing services welding services specialty electrical equipment and highly engineered services. The deal fortified the company's network of galvanizing plants and expanded its penetration in the states of Texas Louisiana and Mississippi.

EXECUTIVES

President and CEO, Thomas E. (Tom) Ferguson, age 60, $214,205 total compensation

SVP Finance CFO and Secretary, Paul W. Fehlman, age 52, $6,771 total compensation

SVP Galvanizing Services, Tim E. Pendley, age 54, $330,000 total compensation

VP Information Technology, Matt Emery, age 48, $220,000 total compensation

VP and Chief Accounting Officer, Robert J. Steines, $64,167 total compensation

Senior Vice President And General Manager Sro Non Nuclear Services, Doug Vail

Vice President of Human Resour, Trey Quinn

Vice President Corporate Devel, Christopher (Chris) Izzo

Vice President Marketing Electrical Products And, David (Dave) Nark

Chairman, Kevern R. Joyce, age 69

Auditors: BDO USA, LLP

LOCATIONS

HQ: AZZ Inc
One Museum Place, Suite 500, 3100 West 7th Street, Fort Worth, TX 76107
Phone: 817 810-0095
Web: www.azz.com

PRODUCTS/OPERATIONS

2016 Sales

	$ mil.	% of total
Energy	500.8	55
Galvanizing Services	402.4	45
Total	**903.2**	**100**

2016 Sales

	$ mil.	% of total
US	724.6	80
Other countries	179.8	20
Eliminations -1.2 -		
Total	**903.2**	**100**

Selected Products and Services

Galvanizing Services
  Coordinated multi-plant operations
  Custom hot-dip galvanizing
  Duplex finishes
  Finished material warehousing
Electrical and Industrial Products
  Air and gas insulated bus duct
  Electrical power distribution centers
  Industrial hazardous-duty lighting
  Metal-clad outdoor switchgear
  Protective relay panels
  Tubular goods

COMPETITORS

ABB
Chamberlin
Earle M. Jorgensen
Energy Focus
Friedman Industries
GE
Gewiss
JJI Lighting
LSI Industries
Legrand
Powell Industries
Professional Luminaires North America
SPX

HISTORICAL FINANCIALS

Company Type: Public

Income Statement

FYE: February 29

	REVENUE ($ mil.)	NET INCOME ($ mil.)	NET PROFIT MARGIN	EMPLOYEES
02/16	903.1	76.7	8.5%	3,538.0
02/15	816.6	64.9	8.0%	3,244.0
02/14	751.7	59.6	7.9%	2,927.0
02/13	570.5	60.4	10.6%	2,632.0
02/12	469.1	40.7	8.7%	2,154.0
Annual Growth	17.8%	17.2%	—	13.2%

2016 Year-End Financials

Debt ratio: 33.2%
Return on equity: 16.9%
Cash ($ mil.): 40.1
Current ratio: 2.08
Long-term debt ($ mil.): 303.7

No. of shares (mil.): 25.8
Dividends
  Yield: 1.1%
  Payout: 20.1%
Market value ($ mil.): 1,307.0

	STOCK PRICE ($) FY Close	P/E High/Low		Earnings	PER SHARE ($) Dividends	Book Value
02/16	50.50	20	14	2.96	0.60	18.60
02/15	45.42	19	15	2.52	0.58	16.32
02/14	44.37	21	15	2.32	0.56	14.70
02/13	44.66	28	13	2.37	0.53	13.16
02/12	50.20	33	23	1.61	0.50	11.43
Annual Growth	0.1%	—	—	16.5%	4.7%	12.9%

B Riley Financial Inc

EXECUTIVES

Chb-ceo, Andy Gumaer
Senior Vice President And Controller, Chris (Chrissy) Mcginley
Senior Vice President General Counsel, Mark Naughton
Senior Vice President of Strategy and Corporate Development, Phil (Philly) Ahn
Vice President Financial Planning and Analysis, Dario Lucciola
Executive Vice President, David (Dave) Seiden
Board Member, Christopher Mahoney
Auditors: Marcum LLP

LOCATIONS

HQ: B Riley Financial Inc
21860 Burbank Boulevard, Suite 300, South Woodland Hills, CA 91367
Phone: 818 884-3737
Web: www.brileyfin.com

HISTORICAL FINANCIALS

Company Type: Public

Income Statement

FYE: December 31

	REVENUE ($ mil.)	NET INCOME ($ mil.)	NET PROFIT MARGIN	EMPLOYEES
12/15	112.5	11.8	10.5%	220.0
12/14	77.1	(5.8)	—	225.0
12/13	76.1	1.0	1.4%	176.0
12/12	83.9	3.5	4.2%	330.0
12/11	63.5	0.6	0.9%	305.0
Annual Growth	15.4%	110.4%	—	(7.8%)

2015 Year-End Financials

Debt ratio: 2.0%
Return on equity: 11.4%
Cash ($ mil.): 30.0
Current ratio: 3.32
Long-term debt ($ mil.): 1.1

No. of shares (mil.): 16.4
Dividends
  Yield: 3.2%
  Payout: 43.8%
Market value ($ mil.): 163.0

	STOCK PRICE ($) FY Close	P/E High/Low		Earnings	PER SHARE ($) Dividends	Book Value
12/15	9.90	19	13	0.73	0.32	6.65
12/14	9.90	—	—	(0.60)	0.03	6.08
12/13	0.28	1	0	0.80	0.00	(2.78)
12/12	0.31	0	0	2.40	0.00	(3.40)
12/11	0.12	2	0	0.40	0.00	(5.33)
Annual Growth	201.4%	—	—	16.2%		

B&G Foods Inc

Peter Piper picks more than a peck of peppers from B&G Foods. The company makes markets and distributes jalapeños beans maple syrup fruit spreads and other shelf-stable foods and household goods. B&G's products are sold under brand names many of which are regional or national best-sellers including B&G and Trappey (beans) Green Giant (frozen and canned foods) Ac'cent (meat flavoring) Spice Islands (seasonings) Ortega (Mexican condiments) Grandma's and

Brer Rabbit (molasses) and Underwood (meat spread). They're sold through B&G's subsidiaries to supermarkets mass merchants warehouse clubs and drug store chains as well as institutional and food service operators in the US Canada and Puerto Rico.Geographic ReachBased in Parsippany New Jersey B&G Foods makes sells and distributes a diverse portfolio of shelf-stable foods nationwide and in Canada and Puerto Rico.OperationsB&G Foods serves a single industry segment. The company balances its branded-product retail sales business with sales to institutions and food service customers as well as making products under private labels for others. Many of its branded items boast leading regional or national market shares.The food company operates three distribution centers located in Texas Tennessee and Pennsylvania. It has seven manufacturing and warehouse locations in Maryland Maine Wisconsin Vermont New Jersey and North Carolina. B&G Foods stores products in facilities in Quebec and Maryland and houses its major sales offices in Arkansas and Illinois.The company distributes certain brands –such as Cream of Wheat Ac'cent Underwood Polaner Static Guard Mrs. Dash New York Style and Sugar Twin –to similar food channels in Canada.Sales and MarketingB&G Foods has a unique sales strategy for each of its brands. To this end the food company allocates brand-specific promotional spending. Its regional sales managers coordinate promotions with customers. The company's marketing department partners with the sales department to coordinate special account activities and marketing support the likes of public relations media advertising and couponing. Marketing executives typically use the radio Internet social media and limited television advertising. B&G Foods spent about $5.9 million in advertising in fiscal 2012 as compared to $4.3 million in 2011.The 120-year-old company sells markets and distributes its products through a multichannel system. It serves all major US food channels selling and shipping to mass merchants supermarkets warehouse clubs food service distributors and direct accounts specialty food distributors military commissaries and non-food outlets the likes of drug store chains and dollar stores. To better serve Wal-Mart which accounts for nearly 20% of sales B&G Foods operates a sales office in Wal-Mart's hometown of Bentonville Arkansas.The company sells its products primarily through broker sales networks to supermarket chains mass merchants food service outlets warehouse clubs non-food outlets and specialty distributors. This network incidentally handles B&G Foods' sales at the retail level. Regional sales managers sell its food items nationwide through national and regional brokers with separate organizations concentrating on food service grocery chain accounts and special markets.Financial PerformanceThe company has seen its net sales rise during the past five years. Due to several recent acquisitions B&G Foods logged its highest net sales in 2012. Sales price increases and acquiring Culver Specialty Brands and the New York Style and Old London brands all contributed a 17% boost in net sales in fiscal 2012. B&G Foods' net income rose 18% for the same reporting period thanks to a jump in net sales partially offset by an increase in selling general and administrative expenses. These expenses rose mainly due to increases in consumer marketing selling and warehousing expenses.During fiscal 2012 B&G Foods logged cost increases (net of cost savings) for raw materials of less than 2% of the cost of goods sold which were more than offset by rising sales prices. B&G Foods anticipates cost decreases for raw materials in the marketplace during 2013. Through

2013 it's currently locked into supply and prices for a majority of its most significant commodities (excluding maple syrup among others) at a cost decrease of $1 million.StrategyThe company's growth strategy involves four initiatives. It's working to expand its brand portfolio by purchasing complementary branded businesses. B&G is focused on quickly developing and taking new products to market as well. It works to leverage its multiple sales channels and distribution system and continues to focus in higher-growth customers and distribution channels. To boost its ailing seasonings business B&G in 2012 partnered with Crock-Pot maker Jarden Corporation to rollout a line of Crock-Pot Seasoning Mixes. Working through unit Jarden Consumer Solutions (JCS) B&G has plans to expand the line which initially includes single-serve packets named Hearty Beef Stew Savory Pot Roast and BBQ Pulled Pork.Mergers and AcquisitionsThe food manufacturer has acquired and integrated more than 25 brands into its company since 1996. In recent years B&G Foods has focused on acquiring companies that serve the snack foods sector. Besides buying the New York Style Old London JJ Flats and Devonsheer brands the company has purchased the TrueNorth nut cluster brand from DeMet's Candy Company. Varieties include Almond Pecan Crunch Chocolate Nut Crunch and Cashew Crunch. It also acquired Robert's American Gourmet Food LLC which does business as Pirate Brands. The gourmet food company is known for its Pirate's Booty Smart Puffs and Original Tings. The company funded the acquisition –at the tune of $195 million in cash –using proceeds from a recently completed senior notes offering.In line with its growth goals in 2016 the company acquired ACH Food Companies' spice and seasonings business for $365 million in cash. Through the deal the company added Spice Islands Tone's Durkee and Weber brands to its product line up. The acquisition significantly expands the company's existing flavor enhancing products which include Ms. Dash Ac'cent and Emeril's seasonings.B&G in mid-2015 bought the Green Giant and Le Sueuer frozen and canned vegetables brands from General Mills for about $765 million. Green Giant became the company's largest product line and boost its revenue to about $1.4 billion. The deal fulfilled B&G's long-term goal of moving into the frozen foods business.

EXECUTIVES

EVP Finance and CFO, Thomas P. Crimmins, age 47, $307,692 total compensation

President and CEO, Robert C. (Bob) Cantwell, age 59, $700,000 total compensation

EVP General Counsel Secretary and Chief Compliance Officer, Scott E. Lerner, age 43, $412,000 total compensation

EVP Sales and Marketing, Vanessa E. Maskal, age 59, $400,000 total compensation

EVP Operations, William F. (Bill) Herbes, age 61, $291,500 total compensation

EVP Quality Assurance and Research and Development, William H. (Bill) Wright, age 71

EVP Human Resources and Chief Human Resources Officer, Eric H. Hart, age 49

Vice President, Steve Fortunato

Vice President Export Sales, Greg (Greggy) Price

Vice President of Trade Marketing, Anthony Pacelli

Vice President Quality Assurance Research and Development, Bill (Billy) Wright

National Account Manager, Ben (Benny) Baugh

Chairman, Stephen C. Sherrill, age 63

Auditors: KPMG LLP

LOCATIONS

HQ: B&G Foods Inc
4 Gatehall Drive, Parsippany, NJ 07054
Phone: 973 401-6500
Web: www.bgfoods.com

PRODUCTS/OPERATIONS

2015 Sales

	$ mil.	% of total
Ortega	145.9	15
Green Giant	106.2	11
Pirate Brands	81.7	9
Maple Grove Farms of Vermont	77.7	8
Mrs. Dash	63.2	7
Cream of Wheat	62.4	6
Bear Creek Country Kitchens	53.9	6
Las Palmas	36.7	4
Polaner	33.8	3
Bloch & Guggenheimer	26.2	3
New York Style	23.3	2
Spring Tree	20.9	2
All other brands	234.5	24
Total	**966.4**	**100**

Selected Products

Bagel chips
Canned meats and beans
Dry soups
Frozen and canned vegetables
Fruit spreads
Hot cereals
Hot sauces
Maple syrup
Mexican-style sauces
Molasses
Nut clusters
Peppers
Pickles
Pizza crusts
Puffed corn
Rice snacks
Salad dressings
Salsas
Seasonings
Spices
Taco shells and kits
Wine vinegar

Selected Brands

Ac'cent
B&G
B&M
Baker's Joy
Brer Rabbit
Cream of Rice
Cream of Wheat
Devonsheer
Don Pepino
Emeril's (licensed)
Grandma's Molasses
JJ Flats
Joan of Arc
Kleen Guard (sells and distributes)
Las Palmas
Maple Grove Farms of Vermont
Molly McButter
Mrs. Dash
New York Style
Old London
Ortega
Polaner
Red Devil
Regina
Sa-son
Sclafani
Static Guard (sells and distributes)
Sugar Twin
Trappey's
TrueNorth
Underwood
Vermont Maid
Wright's

COMPETITORS

ACH Food Companies	Hormel
Adams Extract & Spice	Kikkoman
Best Maid Products	La Flor
Big Heart Pet Brands	MOM Brands
Bolner's Fiesta	McCormick & Company
Products	McIlhenny
Bruce Foods	MegaMex Foods
Bush Brothers	Mondelez International
Campbell Soup	Nestl©
ConAgra	PepsiCo
Frito-Lay	Pinnacle Foods
General Mills	Ren©e's Gourmet Foods
Goya	Smucker
Heinz	Snyder's-Lance
Herdez	Spectrum Organic
Homestat Farm	Products

HISTORICAL FINANCIALS

Company Type: Public

Income Statement

FYE: January 2

	REVENUE ($ mil.)	NET INCOME ($ mil.)	NET PROFIT MARGIN	EMPLOYEES
01/16	966.3	69.0	7.1%	2,003.0
01/15*	848.0	40.9	4.8%	956.0
12/13	724.9	52.3	7.2%	984.0
12/12	633.8	59.2	9.3%	999.0
12/11	543.8	50.2	9.2%	739.0
Annual Growth	**15.5%**	**8.3%**	**—**	**28.3%**

*Fiscal year change

2016 Year-End Financials

Debt ratio: 68.4%
Return on equity: 17.4%
Cash ($ mil.): 5.2
Current ratio: 3.43
Long-term debt ($ mil.): 1,725.8
No. of shares (mil.): 57.9
Dividends
Yield: 0.0%
Payout: 113.1%
Market value ($ mil.): 2,030.0

	STOCK PRICE ($) FY Close	P/E High/Low		PER SHARE ($) Earnings	Dividends	Book Value
01/16	35.02	31	23	1.22	1.38	7.89
01/15*	29.68	46	36	0.76	1.36	6.30
12/13	33.93	38	28	0.98	1.23	7.08
12/12	27.60	27	18	1.20	1.10	6.87
12/11	24.07	23	13	1.04	0.86	4.94
Annual Growth	**9.8%**	**—**	**—**	**4.1%**	**12.5%**	**12.4%**

*Fiscal year change

Badger Meter Inc

No Badger Meter does not measure the frequency of the appearance of a certain nocturnal carnivorous mammal. Instead it provides water utilities and industrial customers with instruments that measure and control the flow of liquids. Badger is a major manufacturer of water meters and automatic meter reading (AMR) and advanced metering infrastructure (AMI) products which are mainly sold to municipalities. Its flow instrumentation business is made up of metering technologies including concrete HVAC water and wastewater chemicals and food and beverage. Established in 1905 Badger also makes handheld devices that dispense and monitor oil and other fluids for the automotive market.

Geographic Reach

The company manufactures its products at facilities located around the globe including four in the US (Arizona Oklahoma and two in Wisconsin). It also operates international facilities in the China Czech Republic Germany Mexico Singapore and Switzerland. The US accounts for 85% of its total sales.

Operations

Badger's product lines fall into two categories: sales of water meters and related technologies to municipal water utilities and sales of meters to various industries for water and other fluids and gases.

Both the company's ORION AMR and GALAXY AMI products take advantage of leading communications networks in the market and can interface with other meter reading systems that transmit a signal such as mobile power-line carrier fixed base or Wi-Fi applications. The company has also developed cost-savings products like its residential meter encasement that uses less copper.

Financial Performance

Badger has achieved unprecedented growth over the last three years. Revenues jumped 4% from $365 million in 2014 to peak at $378 million in 2015 a historic milestone. The growth for 2015 was driven by a surge in municipal water sales due to higher demand for residential and commercial meters.

Badger's profits however have fluctuated wildly the last several years. After increasing in 2015 profits fell 13% to $26 million in 2015 due to expenses related to making acquisitions.

Strategy

In addition to its organic growth the company is expanding its products portfolio and international reach through small strategic acquisitions. In 2015 Badger expanded its geographical presence in the eastern US with acquisition of United Utilities a distributor of Badger Meter products for the municipal water utility market serving customers in Georgia and Tennessee for $3.3 million.

EXECUTIVES

Senior Vice President Administ, Ronald (Ron) Dix
Chairman President and CEO, Richard A. Meeusen, age 61, $587,100 total compensation
SVP Finance CFO and Treasurer, Richard E. Johnson, age 61, $315,000 total compensation
Vice President - International Operations, Horst E. Gras, age 60, $322,781 total compensation
VP General Counsel and Secretary, William R. A. Bergum, age 51
Vice President - Sales and Marketing, Kimberly K. Stoll, age 49, $175,100 total compensation
Board of Directors Management, Pstokke Ceci
Auditors: Ernst & Young LLP

LOCATIONS

HQ: Badger Meter Inc
4545 W. Brown Deer Road, Milwaukee, WI 53223
Phone: 414 355-0400
Web: www.badgermeter.com

PRODUCTS/OPERATIONS

2015 Sales

	% of total
Municipal water	75
Flow instrumentation	25
Total	**100**

Selected Products

Industrial
Actuators
Automotive fluid management systems
Chemical dispenser systems
Concrete batch meters

Cox Flow Measurement
Electromagnetic meters
Lubrication meters (for automobiles)
Oscillating piston meters
Oval gear transmitters
Valves
Utility
Disc and compound water meters
Gas utility management system
Instrumentation systems
ORION gas module selector
Reclaimed water meters
Transmitter registers
Turbo meters

COMPETITORS

A. O. Smith Water Products
CIRCOR International
Colfax
Coperion K-Tron
Dwyer Instruments
ESCO
Elster Group SE
Flow International
Franklin Electric
Fuel Systems Solutions
Gorman-Rupp
Itron
Jordan Company
Lindsay Corporation
Liquid Controls LLC
MFRI Measurement Specialties
Mesa Laboratories
Mueller Water Products
Robbins & Myers
Roper Technologies
Siemens Water Technologies
SpiraxSarco
Teledyne Isco
Thermo Fisher Scientific
Watts Water Technologies

HISTORICAL FINANCIALS

Company Type: Public

Income Statement

FYE: December 31

	REVENUE ($ mil.)	NET INCOME ($ mil.)	NET PROFIT MARGIN	EMPLOYEES
12/15	377.7	25.9	6.9%	1,514.0
12/14	364.7	29.6	8.1%	1,431.0
12/13	334.1	24.6	7.4%	1,360.0
12/12	319.6	28.0	8.8%	1,366.0
12/11	262.9	19.1	7.3%	1,220.0
Annual Growth	**9.5%**	**7.9%**	**—**	**5.5%**

2015 Year-End Financials

Debt ratio: 20.0%
Return on equity: 11.6%
Cash ($ mil.): 8.1
Current ratio: 1.43
Long-term debt ($ mil.): —
No. of shares (mil.): 29.0
Dividends
Yield: 2.6%
Payout: 86.6%
Market value ($ mil.): 1,702.0

	STOCK PRICE ($) FY Close	P/E High/Low	PER SHARE ($) Earnings	Dividends	Book Value
12/15	58.59	73 61	0.90	0.78	8.00
12/14	59.35	58 46	1.03	0.74	7.41
12/13	54.50	65 50	0.85	0.70	6.82
12/12	47.41	49 30	0.98	0.66	5.98
12/11	29.43	71 42	0.64	0.30	5.93
Annual Growth	**18.8%**	**— —**	**9.1%**	**27.0%**	**7.8%**

Balchem Corp.

Believe Balchem when they say they have it covered. The company has developed a technology that covers or encapsulates ingredients used in food and animal health products; the encapsulation improves nutritional value and shelf life and allows for controlled time release. Balchem also provides specialty gases such as ethylene oxide (used to sterilize medical instruments) propylene oxide (used to reduce bacteria in spice treating and chemical processing) and methyl chloride (a refrigerant). It also provides SensoryEffects provide microencapsulation solutions to a variety of applications in food pharmaceutical and nutritional ingredients.

Operations

Balchem's operations are divided into four main business segments: SensoryEffects; Animal Nutrition and Health; Specialty Products; and Industrial Products.

Its ARC Specialty Products segment offers repackaging and distribution of select chemicals (including ethylene oxide and propylene oxide) to healthcare and other markets. The Animal Nutrition and Health segment makes and supplies products (including choline chloride) to several animal health markets and also certain derivative chemical products for industrial use. Balchem's SensoryEffects segment provides human-grade choline and microencapsulation products for a range of applications in human food pharmaceutical and nutrition markets.

The company's unencapsulated feed ingredients unit (BCP Ingredients) supplies the nutrient choline chloride to poultry and swine farmers. Reashure an encapsulated choline product increases milk production in dairy cows.

SensoryEffects the largest segment accounts for 50% of total sales; Animal Nutrition & Health 30%; Specialty Products 10%; and Industrial Products 10%.

Geographic Reach

Balchem operates two four subsidiaries in the US: BCP Ingredients SensoryEffects Inc. SensoryEffects Cereal Systems Inc. and Aberco. It also has two subsidiaries in Europe: Balchem BV and Balchem Italia which has a manufacturing facility in Italy that makes and distributes methylamines (a building block for choline products) and choline. The company operates repackaging facilities in South Carolina and Missouri and uses distribution points in New York California and Puerto Rico. It also has manufacturing facilities in Utah Virginia Louisiana Minnesota Wisconsin Pennsylvania Ohio and Nebraska as well as in Canada.

Sales and Marketing

The company sells its products through its own sales force independent distributors and sales agents.

Financial Performance

Balchem has recorded rising net revenues over the last five years. In 2015 it had net revenue of $552.5 million up 2% on 2014 due to an increase in SensoryEffects results. Net sales for the SensoryEffects segment increased by 35% due to the acquired SensoryEffects business that contributed $69.8 million to the overall increase. The Powder & Flavor Systems and Cereal Systems product lines comprised $56.5 million and $10.2 million of the increase respectively. Also contributing to the higher sales was an 11.1% rise in encapsulated ingredients used for baking and food preservation primarily due to greater volume. Specialty Products segment sales were flat compared to the prior year and revenue from the Animal Nutrition & Health and Industrial Products segments decreased. Balchem's net income has also risen over the last five years. In 2015 net income was $59.7 million up 13% due to higher net sales outpacing an increase in operating expenses. Cash from operating activities was $103.8 million up 22% compared to 2014.

Strategy

The company is continuing to focus on leveraging its plant capabilities driving efficiencies from core volume growth broadening product applications of human and animal health specialty products as well as capitalizing on its varied choline production capabilities. It invested $41.3 million in capital expenditures in 2015 up from $13.2 million in 2014.

In 2015 Balchem integrated SensoryEffects and made significant investments in new production capacity and technology. Looking forward growth for this segment will be fueled by its investment in agglomeration technology Curemark and the RDI and EFSA first-ever intake recommendations for choline. The company will continue to drive strategic growth initiatives through both organic investments in new manufacturing capabilities and new product development as well as acquisitions.

In 2015 the company expanded its Verona Missouri facility by adding another ReaShure manufacturing unit.

In 2014 Taminco and Balchem built and operated a choline chloride facility in St. Gabriel Louisiana where both companies operate production facilities.

Mergers and Acquisitions

In 2016 Balchem acquired Utah-based Albion International (a privately held manufacturer of mineral amino acid chelates specialized mineral salts and mineral complexes) for $116.4 million. The acquisition of Albion continues to expand Balchem's science-based human health and wellness products and increases its product offerings in the nutritional ingredient market. Additionally the company also benefits from a broader geographic footprint and a stronger position as a technological leader in spray-drying and ingredient delivery products.

To accelerate the growth of its food and nutrition platforms with new product offerings in 2014 Balchem spent $567 million to acquire Missouri-based Performance Chemicals & Ingredients Company (aka SensoryEffects) a privately held supplier of customized food and beverage ingredient systems.

HISTORY

Company Background

Herbert Weiss Leslie Balassa three ex-officers of the Alcolac company and a group of Baltimore-based investors founded Balchem in 1967 in New York City. The company focused on the development of encapsulated specialty ingredients (the coating of individual particles that allow precise control of nutrient delivery). Initially Balchem developed food ingredients used in meat processing flavor enhancement and dough leavening as well as in nutritional supplements. In 1971 the company won its first big order: encapsulating the ingredients in pudding mix for General Foods. Balchem later applied the same technology to foaming agents for plastics aquaculture supplements and animal feeds. It also developed a line of specialty gases.

In 1994 Balchem boosted its gas business with the purchase of AlliedSignal's sterilant gas business (used to sterilize medical devices). Weiss retired as CEO in 1996 and was succeeded by EVP Raymond Reber. Reber left the company a few months later and chemical industry veteran Dino Rossi replaced him. The next year Balchem developed a rumen-protected choline chloride for the animal nutrition market.

Balchem restructured its operations in 1998 away from aquaculture and towards animal nutrition and other growth markets. After successful university and field trials the company introduced Reashure its encapsulated choline product for dairy cows.

In 2000 Balchem was granted a patent for its technology that increases milk production in dairy cows. In 2001 the company acquired the choline and encapsulated product lines of DCV Inc. and its DuCoa L.P. affiliate which contributed to the company's increase in net sales by about 30% in 2002. In 2002 sales continued to build as the encapsulated/nutritional products segment introduced several new products and product applications for the enhancement of shelf-life and fortification of products in certain markets of the food industry.

Balchem's unencapsulated feed ingredients segment also referred to as BCP Ingredients got larger in 2007 when the company acquired two choline-related businesses. The first was in Italy from Akzo Nobel and the other deal was for a company called Chinook Global Limited whose operations were integrated into Balchem's business. Those deals nearly tripled the size of BCP Ingredients making it Balchem's largest unit.

In 2010 the company's growth increased again with the acquisition of Maryland-based Aberco a marketer and distributor of propylene oxide.

In 2013 Balchem's capital expenditures were about $8.2 million out of which $3.3 million was invested in its new manufacturing facility in Covington Virginia. Balchem expanded production capacities to meet growing demand by opening the Covington plant in 2012 which doubled the output capacity for the Animal Nutrition and Health ruminant sector.

EXECUTIVES

VP Administration Treasurer and Assistant Secretary, Francis J. (Frank) Fitzpatrick, age 55, $280,000 total compensation
VP and General Manager ARC Specialty Products, David F. Ludwig, age 58, $260,000 total compensation
Chairman President and CEO, Theodore L. (Ted) Harris, age 50, $319,617 total compensation
General Counsel and Secretary, Matthew D. Houston, age 52, $222,000 total compensation
CFO, William A. Backus, $246,400 total compensation
Auditors: RSM US LLP

LOCATIONS

HQ: Balchem Corp.
52 Sunrise Park Road, New Hampton, NY 10958
Phone: 845 326-5600

PRODUCTS/OPERATIONS

2015 sales

	$ mil.	% of total
Sensory Effects	278.3	50
Animal Nutrition & Health	165.8	30
Specialty Products	54.2	10
Industrial product	54.2	10
Total	**552.5**	**100**

Selected Products

BCP Ingredients
  Choline chloride (essential nutrient for animal health)
  Choline chloride derivatives
Encapsulated/Nutritional Products
  Food Pharma & Human Nutrition Products
  Bakeshure (leavening agents dough conditioners fortifiers acidifiers and antimicrobials)
  Confecshure (acidulants for flavor)
  Flavorshure (taste and flavor masking)
  Meatshure (acidifiers antioxidants and flavors)
  Vitashure (vitamins nutraceuticals and botanicals)
  Animal Nutrition & Health Products
  Niashure
  Niacine (prevents niacin degradation)

Urea (regulates nitrogen/carbohydrates ratio in proteins)
Reashure (rumen-stable choline for dairy cows)
Specialty Products
  Ethylene oxide (sterilant gas for the health care industry)
  Methyl chloride (specialty herbicides)
  Propylene oxide (bacteria reduction in spices)

COMPETITORS

ABCO Laboratories	Coating Place
Air Products	Dow Chemical
Airgas	IGENE
BASF Corporation	Mitsubishi Chemical
BioDelivery Sciences	Praxair
International	Sigma-Aldrich
Clariant	

HISTORICAL FINANCIALS

Company Type: Public

Income Statement

FYE: December 31

	REVENUE ($ mil.)	NET INCOME ($ mil.)	NET PROFIT MARGIN	EMPLOYEES
12/15	552.4	59.7	10.8%	875.0
12/14	541.3	52.8	9.8%	845.0
12/13	337.1	44.8	13.3%	387.0
12/12	310.3	40.0	12.9%	376.0
12/11	291.8	38.7	13.3%	365.0
Annual Growth	**17.3%**	**11.4%**	**—**	**24.4%**

2015 Year-End Financials

Debt ratio: 33.7%	No. of shares (mil.): 31.5
Return on equity: 13.9%	Dividends
Cash ($ mil.): 84.8	Yield: 0.5%
Current ratio: 2.45	Payout: 17.0%
Long-term debt ($ mil.): 262.5	Market value ($ mil.): 1,917.0

	STOCK PRICE ($) FY Close	P/E High/Low	PER SHARE ($) Earnings	Dividends	Book Value
12/15	60.80	36 27	1.89	0.34	14.71
12/14	66.64	39 28	1.69	0.30	12.71
12/13	58.70	39 24	1.45	0.26	10.96
12/12	36.45	30 19	1.32	0.22	9.27
12/11	40.54	34 24	1.28	0.18	7.95
Annual Growth	**10.7%**	**— —**	**10.2%**	**17.2%**	**16.6%**

Banc of California Inc

Banc of California offers deposit and loan services at 35 branches in Southern California's Los Angeles Orange County and San Diego. Customers enjoy checking savings and money market accounts as well as mobile online and card payment services telephone banking automated bill payment safe deposit boxes direct deposit and wire transfers. Customers can also access their accounts through a nationwide network of 55000 surcharge-free ATMs. In addition to its branches the $9 billion-asset Banc of California operates around 70 mortgage loan production offices in California Arizona Oregon Indiana Idaho Nevada and Virginia.

OperationsBanc of California operates three core segments: Commercial Banking which offers commercial consumer and real estate secured loans as well as deposit accounts; Mortgage Banking which originates conforming SFR loans and sells the loans in the secondary market; and the Financial

Advisory segment which purchases sells and manages SFR mortgage loans. Unlike most retail banks Banc of California's income streams are less dependent on interest rates. The bank made 50% of its revenue from loan interest (including fees) during 2015 and another 5% from interest on investments. But it also made 29% of its revenue from its mortgage banking business while the rest came from other non-interest income sources.Geographic ReachThe Irvine California-based bank has 90-plus banking locations in California including 35 branches in San Diego Orange Santa Barbara and Los Angeles Counties (as of mid-2016). It has 68 loan production offices in California Arizona Oregon Virginia Indiana Maryland Colorado Idaho and Nevada.Sales and MarketingThe bank spent $6.2 million on advertising during 2015 or 23% more than in the prior year due to higher overall marketing costs tied to the bank's continued expansion.Financial Performance

Banc of California's revenue has risen seven-fold since 2011 as a slew of bank acquisitions and organic growth have driven its loan and deposit business as well as its mortgage banking business.

The bank's revenue jumped 46% to $486.5 million during 2015 thanks to a 34% spike in loan interest income on more loan origination and loan and lease purchase activity; and thanks to a 52% rise in mortgage banking income as the bank originated and sold nearly twice as many mortgage loans on the secondary market than in 2014.

Strong revenue growth in 2015 caused Banc of California's net income to double to $62 million despite an uptick in salary and benefits cost that stemmed from additional hiring and commercial banking and mortgage banking expansion. The bank's operations used $45.24 million during the year or less than one-tenth as much cash as in 2014 mostly after adjusting its earnings for non-cash items related to proceeds of mortgage banking loans held-for-sale and proceeds from other loans held-for-sale.

StrategyWith its eye on becoming "California's Bank" Banc of California sometimes acquires smaller banks or bank branch networks to boost its loan and deposit business while expanding its branch network (mostly around California).

From 2010 through 2015 the bank has made seven acquisitions including three bank acquisitions (Gateway Bancorp Beach Business Bank and The Private Bank of California) and three other specialty financial firm acquisitions (Palisades Group which it divested in 2016; CS Financial; and Renovation Ready.)

Mergers and AcquisitionsIn November 2014 the bank bought 20 branches in Southern California from Banco Popular North America (BPNA) along with $1.07 billion in loans and $1.08 billion in deposits for a total price of $24 million.In January 2014 Banc of California purchased service contracts and intellectual property of RenovationReady a specialized loan services provider that served financial institutions and mortgage bankers that originated agency-eligible residential renovation and construction loan products.Company BackgroundIn 2012 it paid $15.5 million for Gateway Business Bank and $37 million for Beach Business Bank. The next year it took over The Private Bank of California for $25 million and bought The Palisades Group a residential mortgage investment advisory firm and specialty finance company CS Financial. In 2014 it announced plans to buy 20 branches of Banco Popular North America to reach California's Hispanic community.

In 2013 it sold eight branches to AmericanWest Bank in order to reshape its retail branch network

to focus on servicing small – to midsized businesses and high net worth families.

EXECUTIVES

Senior Vice President Branch Operations, Rachel Carrillo
EVP Division General Counsel: Lending, John F. Madden, age 55
EVP Enterprise Risk Analytics, Gilda Youdeem
Managing Director Institutional Banking and Fiduciary Services, Steven C. (Steve) Canup
EVP and General Counsel Banking, Angelee J. Harris, age 46
Chief Investment Officer, Brian P. Kuelbs, age 53
Managing Director Community Banking, Gaylin D. Anderson
Vice Chairman and EVP, Jeffrey T. Seabold, age 49, $647,917 total compensation
Chief Risk Officer and Interim Co-CEO, Hugh F. Boyle, age 56, $404,167 total compensation
Managing Director Warehouse Lending, Zoila Price
Head Central Operations, Thedora A. Nickel, age 51
SVP Marketing, Neal Mendelsohn
Managing Director Banc Home Loans, Ted Ray
EVP and Chief Compliance Officer, Diane M. Summers
EVP Community Development, Gary S. Dunn
EVP and CIO, Ken Plummer
EVP Division General Counsel: Banking, Manisha K. Merchant
Managing Director Construction Lending, Jim Fraser
Managing Director CRE Lending, Thomas Senske
Managing Director SBA Lending, Heather Endresen
Managing Director Commercial Banking, David Park
Chief Strategy Officer and Interim CEO, J. Francisco A. Turner, age 41
Chief Credit Officer, Paul Simmons
Managing Director Portfolio Lending, Julie Duong
SVP Operations, Robert Villaneda
SVP Marketing, Samantha Haugh
Managing Director Payment Solutions, Ben Kessler
Senior Vice President, Tina Van der Zee
Executive Vice President And Chief Administrative Officer, Richard (Dick) Herrin
Group Vice President, John C (Jack) Grosvenor
Vice President Information Systems, Chris Giglio
Executive Vice President Finance, Fred (Freddy) Mahintorabi
Vice President Physical Security, Gary (Gar) Dersarkissian
Vice President Commercial Servicing Manager, Sylvia (Sylv) Jaques
Senior Vice President Controller, Fernando (Ferdinand) Pelayo
Vice President Customer Support Manager, Enrique (Rick) Mason
Assistant Vice President Secondary Marketing, Jennifer (Jen) Mcgaw
Vice President Business Development Offi, Kristin (Kristy) Koptyra
Assistant Vice President Branch Service, Heidi (Hei) Johnson
Assistant Vice President Servicing, Julian Tioseco
Vice President and Business Development Officer, Jason (Jase) Fischer
Assistant Vice President Underwriter, Erin Stuart
Vice President Loan Portfolio Manager, Edward (Ed) Massey
Assistant Vice President Branch Manager, Jason Sparks
Vice President Treasury Manager, AL Sondag
Senior Vice President Loan Group Manager Private Bank, Gary Seferian

Assistant Vice President Accounting, Courtney Smith
Executive Vice President And Chief Lending Officer, Chang Liu
Vice President Human Resources, Anjanette Valenta
Assistant Vice President Compliance Officer II, Dennis (Denny) Hughes
Assistant Vice President and Director Human Resources, Stephanie (Steph) Castro
Assistant Vice President Central Operations, Robert (Bob) Faucett
FVP TPO Operations Manager, Christy (Christ) Flanagan
Assistant Vice President Marketing Director, Patricia (Pat) Ramirez
Vice President Product Development, Tigran Karavardanyan
Vice President Portfolio Manager, Gary (Gar) Ambart
Vice President SBA Bdo, Nathan (Nate) Stalker
Assistant Vice President Credit Portfolio Manager, Aida Rodriguez
Vice President, Michael (Mel) Urtel
Assistant Vice President Information Technology Service Delivery, Brian (Bri) Spears
Assistant Vice President Marketing Director, Robin (Rin) Gray
Senior Vice President Treasury Management Sales Director, Gary (Gar) Tackoor
Chairman, Robert D. Sznewajs, age 69
Auditors: KPMG LLP

LOCATIONS

HQ: Banc of California Inc
  18500 Von Karman Ave., Suite 1100, Irvine, CA 92612
Phone: 855 361-2262
Web: www.bancofcal.com

PRODUCTS/OPERATIONS

2013 Sales

	% of total
Interest and dividend income	
Loans including fees	53
Securities and others	2
Noninterest income	
Net gain on mortgage banking activities	31
Gain on sale of branches	6
Net gain on sale of loans	4
Loan servicing income	1
Customer service fees	1
Others	2
Total	**100**

COMPETITORS

American Business Bank	East West Bancorp
Bank of America	JPMorgan Chase
Bank of the West	MUFG Americas Holdings
BofI	PacWest Bancorp
California Bank & Trust	Pacific Mercantile
	Pacific Premier
City National	Simplicity Bancorp
Comerica	U.S. Bancorp

HISTORICAL FINANCIALS
Company Type: Public

Income Statement
FYE: December 31

	ASSETS ($ mil.)	NET INCOME ($ mil.)	INCOME AS % OF ASSETS	EMPLOYEES
12/15	8,235.5	62.0	0.8%	1,710.0
12/14	5,971.5	30.3	0.5%	1,470.0
12/13	3,628.0	0.0	0.0%	1,384.0
12/12	1,682.7	6.0	0.4%	614.0
12/11	999.0	(2.7)	—	147.0
Annual Growth	69.4%	—	—	84.7%

2015 Year-End Financials

Return on assets: 0.8%
Return on equity: 10.7%
Long-term debt ($ mil.): —
No. of shares (mil.): 38.0
Sales ($ mil): 486.5

Dividends
  Yield: 3.2%
  Payout: 32.8%
  Market value ($ mil.): 556.0

	STOCK PRICE ($) FY Close	P/E High/Low		PER SHARE ($) Earnings	Dividends	Book Value
12/15	14.62	11	8	1.34	0.48	17.15
12/14	11.47	15	11	0.91	0.48	14.47
12/13	13.41	—	—	(0.14)	0.48	16.13
12/12	12.27	33	26	0.40	0.48	15.87
12/11	10.25	—	—	(0.31)	0.45	15.85
Annual Growth	9.3%	—	—	—	1.6%	2.0%

Bank of North Dakota (Bismarck, N.D.)

EXECUTIVES

Pres-ceo, Eric Hardmeyer
Auditors: Eide Bailly LLP

LOCATIONS

HQ: Bank of North Dakota (Bismarck, N.D.)
  1200 Memorial Hwy, PO Box 5509, Bismarck, ND
  58506-5509
Phone: 701 328-5600
Web: www.banknd.nd.gov

HISTORICAL FINANCIALS
Company Type: Public

Income Statement
FYE: December 31

	ASSETS ($ mil.)	NET INCOME ($ mil.)	INCOME AS % OF ASSETS	EMPLOYEES
12/15	7,407.9	130.6	1.8%	0.0
12/14	7,215.6	110.9	1.5%	0.0
12/13	6,873.4	94.2	1.4%	0.0
12/12	6,155.2	81.5	1.3%	0.0
12/11	5,375.0	70.3	1.3%	0.0
Annual Growth	8.3%	16.7%	—	—

2015 Year-End Financials

Return on assets: —
Return on equity: —
Long-term debt ($ mil.): —
No. of shares (mil.): —
Sales ($ mil): 201.9

Dividends
  Yield: —
  Payout: —
  Market value ($ mil.): —

Bank Of Princeton

LOCATIONS

HQ: Bank Of Princeton
  183 Bayard Lane, Princeton, NJ 08540
Phone: 609 921-1700

HISTORICAL FINANCIALS
Company Type: Public

Income Statement
FYE: December 31

	ASSETS ($ mil.)	NET INCOME ($ mil.)	INCOME AS % OF ASSETS	EMPLOYEES
12/15	1,013.3	11.0	1.1%	138.0
12/14	955.2	9.0	0.9%	0.0
12/11	664.8	2.8	0.4%	110.0
12/10	488.2	2.3	0.5%	0.0
Annual Growth	27.6%	66.4%	—	—

2015 Year-End Financials

Return on assets: 1.1%
Return on equity: 12.9%
Long-term debt ($ mil.): —
No. of shares (mil.): 4.6
Sales ($ mil): 45.5

Dividends
  Yield: —
  Payout: —
  Market value ($ mil.): —

	STOCK PRICE ($) FY Close	P/E High/Low		PER SHARE ($) Earnings	Dividends	Book Value
12/15	0.00	—	—	2.30	0.00	19.51
Annual Growth						

Bank of the Ozarks Inc

Bank of the Ozarks is the holding company for the bank of the same name which has about 260 branches in Alabama Arkansas California the Carolinas Florida Georgia New York and Texas. Focusing on individuals and small to midsized businesses the $12-billion bank offers traditional deposit and loan services in addition to personal and commercial trust services retirement and financial planning and investment management. Commercial real estate and construction and land development loans make up the largest portion of Bank of the Ozarks' loan portfolio followed by residential mortgage business and agricultural loans. Bank of the Ozarks grows its loan and deposit business by acquiring smaller banks and opening branches across the US.

OperationsThe bank makes three-fourths of its total revenue from interest income while the rest comes from fee-based sources. About 43% of Bank of the Ozark's total revenue came from non-purchased loan interest in 2014 while another 26% came from interest on purchased loans and a further 8% came from interest on its investment securities. The rest of its revenue came from service charges on deposit accounts (8% of revenue) mortgage lending income (1%) trust income (1%) and other non-recurring sources.Geographic Reach

Bank of the Ozarks had 174 branches in eight states at the end of 2014 with 81 of them in Alabama and another 75 branches split among Georgia North Carolina and Texas. It has two loan offices in Houston and Manhattan that serve as an extension of the bank's Dallas-based Real Estate Specialties Group.Sales and MarketingThe bank spent $3.03 million on advertising and public relations expenses in 2014 compared to $2.2 million and $4.09 million in 2013 and 2012 respectively.
  Financial Performance

Bank of the Ozarks' annual revenues and profits have doubled since 2010 mostly as its loan assets have doubled from recent bank acquisitions spawning higher interest income. The bank's revenue jumped 31% to $376 million during 2014 mostly thanks to strong purchased and non-purchased loan asset growth during the year from recent bank acquisitions. Its non-interest income grew 12% thanks to a 20% increase in deposit account service charges stemming from newly acquired deposit customers.Strong revenue growth in 2014 boosted Bank of the Ozarks' net income by 30% to $119 million for the year. Its operating cash levels jumped 22% to $61 million during the year mostly thanks to higher cash earnings.
  Strategy

Bank of the Ozarks continues its strategy of loan and deposit volume growth by acquiring smaller banks in new and existing geographic markets. It has also opened new branches and loan offices sparingly. During 2014 for example the bank opened retail branches in Bradenton Florida; Cornelius North Carolina; and Hilton Head Island South Carolina along with a new loan production office in Asheville North Carolina.
  Mergers and Acquisitions

In July 2016 Bank of the Ozarks acquired Georgia-based Community & Southern Holdings and its Community & Southern Bank subsidiary. Adding some 45 branch locations in Georgia plus another in Florida it was the company's largest acquisition to-date.

Also in July 2016 the bank purchased C1 Financial along with its 32 CI Bank branches on the west coast of Florida and in Miami-Dade and Orange Counties. The deal added $1.7 billion in total assets $1.4 billion in loans and $1.3 billion in deposits. This transaction was the bank's fifteenth acquisition in the past six years.In August 2015 the bank purchased Bank of the Carolinas Corporation (BCAR) —and its eight Bank of the Carolinas branches in North Carolina $345 million in total assets $277 million in loans and $296 million in deposits —for a total price of $65.4 million.In February 2015 Bank of the Ozarks bought Intervest Bancshares Corporation and its seven Intervest National Bank branches in (five in Clearwater Florida and two more in New York City and Pasadena Florida) for $238.5 million. The deal added $1.5 billion in assets including $1.1 billion in loans and $1.2 billion in deposits.In May 2014 it bought Arkansas-based Summit Bancorp Inc. and its 23 Summit Bank branches across Arkansas for $42.5 million though it closed more than a handful of them later in the year.In March 2014 the company acquired Houston-based Bancshares Inc. and its subsidiary Omnibank N.A. for $21.5 million adding three branches in Houston Texas and a branch each in Austin Cedar Park Lockhart and San Antonio.
  Company Background

The expansion strategy of Bank of the Ozarks - which had a mere five branches in Arkansas 20 years ago —centered on opening new locations in smaller communities in Arkansas. But with the financial crash the bank was able to expand to more states through a series of FDIC-assisted transactions to take over failed banks. It bought Chestatee State Bank First Choice Community Bank Horizon Bank Oglethorpe Bank Park Avenue Bank Unity National and Woodlands Bank.

Chairman and CEO George Gleason initially bought the bank more than three decades ago at age 25.

EXECUTIVES

Chief Credit Officer Bank of the Ozarks, Darrel Russell, age 62, $252,308 total compensation
Chairman; Chief Executive Officer of the Company and the Bank, George G. Gleason, age 62, $1,730,769 total compensation
President Leasing Division Bank of the Ozarks, Scott Hastings, age 58, $181,925 total compensation
President Mortgage Division Bank of the Ozarks, Gene Holman, age 68, $150,042 total compensation
President Trust and Wealth Management Division Bank of the Ozarks, Rex Kyle, age 59, $241,674 total compensation
President Real Estate Specialties Group Bank of the Ozarks, Dan Thomas, age 53, $1,242,308 total compensation
CFO and Chief Accounting Officer Bank of the Ozarks, Inc. and Bank of the Ozarks, Greg McKinney, age 48, $368,077 total compensation
EVP Retail Banking Bank of the Ozarks, Tyler Vance, age 41, $366,923 total compensation
President Western Division, Don Keesee
Senior Vice President Information Technology Security Officer, Chad Necessary
Vice President, Mike (Mikey) Atkins
Executive Vice President and Market Leader, Randy (Rand) Whitaker
Senior Vice President, Patrick Brown
Vice President, Jeremy (Jer) McAlister
Executive Vice President Customer Service, Shameka Hansberry
Senior Vice President Training, Lorie (Lor) Smith
Vice President Relationship Manager, Ray Dunavant
Vice President Information Technology Webloyalty, Steve (Stevie) Due
Assistant Vice President And Commercial Lending, Suzanne (Sue) Cole
Vice President Accounting, Tina Chandler
Vice President, Wes (Wesley) Anderson
Vice President, Jeffery Martin
Executive Vice President, Stewart Griggs
Senior Vice President And Regional Operations Manager, Janet (Jan) Paulette
Assistant Vice President, Corum Webb
Vice President Branch Manager, Laura (Laur) Wyne
Vice President, Kevin (Kev) Gross
Vice President Technology Services Manager, Jeff (Jeffy) Starke
Vice President Commercial Lending, Jason (Jase) Wallis
Senior Vice President Human Resources, Cherylon Reid
Assistant Vice President, Robbie Strange
Vice President Commercial Lender, Denise McKenzie
Senior Vice President Market Leader, Russell (Russ) Hewatt
Vice President And Special Assets, Dale E (Dal) Crowe
Vice President and Branch Manager, Olivia Howard
Vice President Commercial Lending, Jeff (Jeffy) Cooper
Vice President Deposit Operations, Libby (Libs) Buck
Vice President, David C (Dave) Garrett
Senior Vice President, Pat (Patty) Strack
Senior Vice President Market Leader, Torrie Sunstrom
Vice President, Brad (Brady) Webb
Assistant Vice President Special Assets Division, Nikki Kundrat

Executive Vice President, Samuel (Sam) Mchard
Vice President Market, Tammy (Tam) Whitley
Vice President Marketing, Duane Bickings
Assistant Vice President Credit Analyst, Chris (Chrissy) Henderson
Vice President Commercial Lending, Brandon (Bran) Scallion
Senior Vice President of Information Systems, Malcolm Hicks
Senior Vice President Real Estate Acquisitions And Development, Phil (Philly) Byers
Senior Vice President, Sheila Mayden
Senior Vice President, Chris (Chrissy) Bragg
Vice President, Wanda Gage
Vice President Business Development, Diane (Di) Jester
Vice President Regional Manager, Lisa (Lis) Amato
Vice President, Debbie (Deb) Townsend
Vice President Lending, Erik (Rik) Larson
Vice President, James (Jamie) Loyd
Vice President Leasing, Scott (Scotty) Harrell
Executive Vice President Originations, Greg (Greggy) Newman
Assistant Vice President Community Development Officer, Kimberly L (Kim) Marshall
Vice President Marketing, Mark (Marky) Greenhaw
Division President South Texas, Julie (Jules) Cripe
Executive Vice President Commercial Lending, Joe (Joey) Dunn
Senior Vice President Treasury Management, Steve (Stevie) Woodruff
Auditors: PricewaterhouseCoopers LLP

LOCATIONS

HQ: Bank of the Ozarks Inc
17901 Chenal Parkway, Little Rock, AR 72223
Phone: 501 978-2265   **Fax:** 501 978-2224
Web: www.bankozarks.com

PRODUCTS/OPERATIONS

2014 Sales

	$ mil.	% of total
Interest income		
Non-purchased loans and leases	162.5	43
Purchased loans	98.2	26
Investment securities	30.7	8
Non-interest income		
Service charges on deposit accounts	26.6	8
Other income from purchased loans net	14.8	4
Others	43.5	11
Total	**376.3**	**100**

Selected Services

Personal Banking
Apple PayChecking AccountsCredit CardsFree Bill PayFREE Debit CardsCustom Debit CardsEMV Chip CardsMobile BankingMortgage LoansMy Change KeeperOnline BankingOverdraft ProtectionPersonal LoansReloadable Spending CardsRetirement PlanningReorder ChecksSafe
Business Banking
Business ProductsApple Pay for BusinessDebit CardEMV Chip CardsBusiness Credit CardsChecking & Money MarketCommercial LoansExpress DepositMerchant ProcessingOnline BankingOverdraft ProtectionReorder ChecksTreasury Management Services
Online & Mobile Banking
Online BankingMobile BankingMobile DepositOnline Bill Pay
Wealth Management Services
Investment ProgramsFinancial PlanningCustomer Service

COMPETITORS

Arvest Bank	IBERIABANK
BOK Financial	JPMorgan Chase
BancorpSouth	Regions Financial
Bank of America	Simmons First

Bear State Financial   SunTrust
Cullen/Frost Bankers   Wells Fargo
Home BancShares

HISTORICAL FINANCIALS
Company Type: Public

Income Statement   FYE: December 31

	ASSETS ($ mil.)	NET INCOME ($ mil.)	INCOME AS % OF ASSETS	EMPLOYEES
12/15	9,879.4	182.3	1.8%	1,642.0
12/14	6,766.5	118.5	1.8%	1,479.0
12/13	4,787.0	87.1	1.8%	1,223.0
12/12	4,040.2	77.0	1.9%	1,120.0
12/11	3,839.9	101.3	2.6%	1,084.0
Annual Growth	26.6%	15.8%	—	10.9%

2015 Year-End Financials

Return on assets: 2.1%	Dividends
Return on equity: 15.3%	Yield: 1.1%
Long-term debt ($ mil.): —	Payout: 26.3%
No. of shares (mil.): 90.4	Market value ($ mil.): 4,475.0
Sales ($ mil): 514.7	

	STOCK PRICE ($) FY Close	P/E High/Low	PER SHARE ($) Earnings	Dividends	Book Value
12/15	49.46	26 15	2.09	0.55	16.19
12/14	37.92	46 20	1.52	0.47	11.37
12/13	56.59	48 28	1.21	0.36	8.48
12/12	33.47	31 25	1.11	0.25	7.20
12/11	29.63	36 13	1.47	0.19	6.16
Annual Growth	13.7%	— —	9.2%	31.3%	27.3%

Bankwell Financial Group Inc

Auditors: Whittlesey & Hadley, P.C.

LOCATIONS

HQ: Bankwell Financial Group Inc
220 Elm Street, New Canaan, CT 06840
Phone: 203 652-0166

HISTORICAL FINANCIALS
Company Type: Public

Income Statement   FYE: December 31

	ASSETS ($ mil.)	NET INCOME ($ mil.)	INCOME AS % OF ASSETS	EMPLOYEES
12/15	1,330.3	9.0	0.7%	125.0
12/14	1,099.5	4.5	0.4%	130.0
12/13	779.6	5.1	0.7%	0.0
12/12	0.0	1.2	—	0.0
Annual Growth	—	95.2%	—	—

2015 Year-End Financials

Return on assets: 0.7%	Dividends
Return on equity: 6.9%	Yield: 0.2%
Long-term debt ($ mil.): —	Payout: 5.3%
No. of shares (mil.): 7.5	Market value ($ mil.): 149.0
Sales ($ mil): 54.2	

	STOCK PRICE ($) FY Close	P/E High/Low	PER SHARE ($) Earnings	Dividends	Book Value
12/15	19.85	17 14	1.21	0.05	17.53
12/14	21.00	28 21	0.78	0.00	17.98
12/13	20.90	16 9	1.44	0.00	17.93
12/12	13.50	38 32	0.38	0.00	(0.00)
/0.00	—	—(0.00)	0.00	(0.00)	
Annual Growth	—	— —	—	—	—

Banner Corp.

Flagging bank accounts? See Banner Corporation. Banner is the holding company for Banner Bank which serves the Pacific Northwest through about 100 branches and 10 loan production offices in Washington Oregon and Idaho. The company also owns Islanders Bank which operates three branches in Washington's San Juan Islands. The banks offer standard products such as deposit accounts credit cards and business and consumer loans. Commercial loans including business agriculture construction and multifamily mortgage loans account for about 90% of the company's portfolio. Bank subsidiary Community Financial writes residential mortgage and construction loans.

Geographic Reach

Washington-based Banner Bank is focused on five primary markets in the Northwest: the Puget Sound region of Washington; the greater Portland Oregon market; Boise Idaho; and Spokane Washington. The fifth is the bank's historical base in the agricultural communities in the Columbia Basin region of Washington and Oregon.

Sales and Marketing

Banner Corp. reported advertising and marketing expenses of $6.9 million in 2013 versus $7.2 million in 2012. Banner Bank launched a redesigned website and new ad campaign in Boise Seattle and Portland and on social media in fall 2014.

Financial Performance

The regional bank holding company reported revenue of $223 million in 2013 an increase of 4% versus 2012. The rise in revenue was due to increased operating income as a result of gains on the sale of securities and a fee received from the termination of the bank's proposed acquisition of Home Federal Bancorp. The bank's growing customer base led to increased income from deposit fees and other service charges of $1.3 billion (5%) in 2013 versus the prior year. Net income declined 28% in 2013 versus 2012 to $46.6 million primarily due to higher provision for income tax expenses. After three consecutive years of losses (2008 thru 2010) the bank returned to profitability in 2011 and has remained profitable.

Banner Corp. has total consolidated assets of about $4.5 billion.

Strategy

Historically Banner Corp. has grown by acquisition. Since going public (in 1995) Banner has acquired about 10 commercial banks. Islanders Bank was acquired in 2007 the same year Banner acquired F&M Bank and NCW Community Bank of Wenatchee both also based in Washington. After the spate of acquisitions the company focused on opening branches. The company continues to look for acquisition opportunities with an eye on banks shut down by regulators.

In 2013 however a plan to merge with Home Federal Bancorp was terminated when that bank received a better offer from Cascade Bancorp. Also the company abandoned plans to buy Idaho Banking Company out of bankruptcy after being outbid.

Mergers and Acquisitions

In August 2014 Banner Bank acquired Siuslaw Financial Group the holding company for Siuslaw Bank the operator of 10 branches along the coast of Oregon. In June 2014 Banner Bank purchased six branches in Oregon from Sterling Savings Bank.

EXECUTIVES

EVP and CFO Banner Corporation, Lloyd W. Baker, age 67, $260,724 total compensation

EVP Retail Banking and Administration, Cynthia D. (Cindy) Purcell, age 58, $289,038 total compensation

EVP and Chief Lending Officer Banner Corporation and Banner Bank, Richard B. Barton, age 72, $264,895 total compensation

President and CEO, Mark J. Grescovich, age 51, $716,415 total compensation

EVP Real Estate Lending Operations, Douglas M. Bennett, age 63, $236,174 total compensation

EVP and CIO, Steven W. (Steve) Rust, age 68

EVP Retail Products and Services, Gary W. Wagers, age 55

EVP and Commercial Executive East Region, M. Kirk Quillin, age 53

EVP and Commercial Executive West Region, James T. (Jim) Reed, age 53

EVP and CFO Banner Bank, Peter J. Conner, age 50

EVP Human Resources, Kayleen Kohler

EVP and Mortgage Banking Director, Kenneth A. (Ken) Larsen, age 46

EVP and General Counsel Banner Bank, Craig Miller

EVP and Chief Risk Officer Banner Bank, Judy Steiner

EVP and Commercial Executive (South Region), Keith A. Western, age 60

Senior Vice President SBA Manager, Walter Mclaughlin

Assistant Vice President And Senior Underwriter, Nancy (Nance) Piestrack

Vice President And Portfolio Manager, Michael (Mel) Thomas

Assistant Vice President Branch Manager, Narinder Kumar

Assistant Vice President Training Manager, Terri (Terr) Anderson

Vice Chairman Banner Corporation and Banner Bank, Jesse G. Foster, age 78

Chairman Banner Corporation and Banner Bank, Gary L. Sirmon, age 73

Auditors: Moss Adams LLP

LOCATIONS

HQ: Banner Corp.
10 South First Avenue, Walla Walla, WA 99362
Phone: 509 527-3636
Web: www.bannerbank.com

PRODUCTS/OPERATIONS

2015 Sales

	$ mil.	% of total
Interest		
Loans receivable	237.3	75
Mortgage-backed securities	9.0	3
Securities & cash equivalents	8.1	2
Noninterest		
Deposit fees & other service charges	40.6	13
Mortgage banking	17.7	5
BOLI	2.5	1
Miscellaneous	2.8	1
Net loss on sale of securities	(0.5)	—
Net change in valuation of financial instruments carried at fair value	(0.8)	—
Total	**223.1**	**100**

Selected Solutions

Personal Solutions
Banner's Best Savings
Connected Checking
Home Equity
Home Loans
Money Market
Online and Mobile Banking
Pendleton Round-Up® TruRewards® MasterCard
Personal Line of Credit
Personal Loan
Premium Checking
Rewards Checking
Savings Account
Student Loan
TruRewards® MasterCard®
Vehicle Loan
World Rewards® MasterCard®
Business Solutions
Agriculture Loans
Banner's Best Business Savings
Business Money Market
Business Savings Account
Equipment & Term Loans
Home Builder Construction Financing
Income Property Construction Financing
Income Property Permanent Financing
Lines of Credit
Mergers & Acquisitions
Owner-Occupied Real Estate Financing
Public Financing
QuickStep® Loans
SBA Lending

Selected Subsidiaries

Banner Bank
Islanders Bank

COMPETITORS

Bank of America	Sound Financial
Cascade Bancorp	U.S. Bancorp
Columbia Banking	Umpqua Holdings
FCA	Washington Federal
Glacier Bancorp	Wells Fargo
KeyCorp	

HISTORICAL FINANCIALS

Company Type: Public

Income Statement

FYE: December 31

	ASSETS ($ mil.)	NET INCOME ($ mil.)	INCOME AS % OF ASSETS	EMPLOYEES
12/15	9,796.3	45.2	0.5%	2,143.0
12/14	4,723.9	54.1	1.1%	1,193.0
12/13	4,388.1	46.5	1.1%	1,131.0
12/12	4,265.5	64.8	1.5%	1,173.0
12/11	4,257.3	5.4	0.1%	1,111.0
Annual Growth	**23.2%**	**69.7%**	**—**	**17.8%**

2015 Year-End Financials

Return on assets: 0.6%	Dividends
Return on equity: 4.8%	Yield: 1.5%
Long-term debt ($ mil.): —	Payout: 29.1%
No. of shares (mil.): 34.2	Market value ($ mil.): 1,570.0
Sales ($ mil): 331.1	

	STOCK PRICE ($) FY Close	P/E High/Low	PER SHARE ($) Earnings	Dividends	Book Value
12/15	45.86	28 21	1.89	0.72	37.97
12/14	43.02	16 13	2.79	0.72	29.82
12/13	44.82	19 12	2.40	0.54	27.63
12/12	30.73	10 6	3.16	0.04	26.10
12/11	17.15	— —	(0.15)	0.02	30.39
Annual Growth	27.9%	— —	—	144.9%	5.7%

Barrett Business Services, Inc.

Barrett Business Services likes to put people to work. The company offers both temporary and long-term staffing to some 1750 small and mid-sized businesses. Its staffing services focus on light industrial clerical and technical businesses. Barrett also does business as a professional employment organization (PEO) providing outsourced human resource services such as payroll management benefits administration risk management recruiting and placement for more than 1500 clients. Established in 1965 Barrett operates through about 45 branch offices across 10 US states. Each year about 90% of its PEO revenue comes from customers residing in the states of California and Oregon.

Barrett depends mostly on the light-industrial sector for the majority of its staffing services revenue (the sector represented 86% of its total revenue in 20010). Its light-industrial workers operate machinery and perform manufacturing loading and unloading and construction-site cleanup tasks.

After experiencing declines in revenue and a net loss for 2009 Barrett bounced back by generating a 15.5% increase in revenue and a positive net income of $7.4 million at the end of 2010. The increase in PEO service fee revenue was mostly attributed to the signing of new customers while its staffing revenue levels rose because of increased demand for existing customers in its northwest and intermountain markets. Barrett's growth strategy involves diversifying its revenue mix by expanding (through acquisitions) outside of California and Oregon.

EXECUTIVES

VP and COO Corporate Operations, Gregory R. (Greg) Vaughn, age 60, $400,000 total compensation
President and CEO, Michael L. (Mike) Elich, age 51, $650,000 total compensation
VP and COO Field Operations, Gerald R. Blotz, age 46, $400,000 total compensation
CFO, Gary Kramer, age 36
Vice President Chief Sales Officer, Heather (Heath) Gould
Board Member, Roger (Rog) Johnson
Chairman, Anthony Meeker, age 77
Auditors: Deloitte & Touche LLP

LOCATIONS

HQ: Barrett Business Services, Inc.
8100 NE Parkway Drive, Suite 200, Vancouver, WA 98662
Phone: 360 828-0700   **Fax:** 360 828-0701
Web: www.barrettbusiness.com

PRODUCTS/OPERATIONS

2015 Sales

	$ mil.	% of total
PEO service fees	572.3	77
Staffing services	168.5	23
Total	**740.8**	**100**

Selected Services

PEO services
  Employee benefits
  Health insurance
  Human resource administration
  Drug testing
  Hiring
  Interviewing
  Placement
  Recruiting
  Regulatory compliance
  Payroll
  Workers' compensation coverage
  Workplace safety programs
Staffing services
  Contract
  Long-term
  Short-term

COMPETITORS

ADP TotalSource	ManpowerGroup
Adecco	Paychex
Insperity	TeamStaff
Kelly Services	TriNet Group

HISTORICAL FINANCIALS

Company Type: Public

Income Statement

FYE: December 31

	REVENUE ($ mil.)	NET INCOME ($ mil.)	NET PROFIT MARGIN	EMPLOYEES
12/15	740.8	25.4	3.4%	103,250.0
12/14	636.1	(27.0)	—	93,040.0
12/13	532.8	17.8	3.4%	79,315.0
12/12	402.6	13.1	3.3%	64,315.0
12/11	314.8	14.3	4.5%	49,355.0
Annual Growth	**23.9%**	**15.5%**	**—**	**20.3%**

2015 Year-End Financials

Debt ratio: 3.9%
Return on equity: 54.7%
Cash ($ mil.): 25.2
Current ratio: 0.96
Long-term debt ($ mil.): —
No. of shares (mil.): 7.2
Dividends
  Yield: 2.0%
  Payout: 25.3%
Market value ($ mil.): 314.0

	STOCK PRICE ($) FY Close	P/E High/Low	PER SHARE ($) Earnings	Dividends	Book Value
12/15	43.54	15 7	3.47	0.88	7.57
12/14	27.40	— —	(3.78)	0.76	5.42
12/13	92.74	38 15	2.42	0.57	10.13
12/12	38.09	23 10	1.67	0.46	7.68
12/11	19.96	14 9	1.41	0.38	10.30
Annual Growth	**21.5%**	**— —**	**25.3%**	**23.4%**	**(7.4%)**

Bassett Furniture Industries, Inc

Bassett Furniture Industries is busy building a better furniture business. The company founded in 1902 makes wooden and upholstered furniture for home use featuring bedroom and dining suites sofas chairs love seats and home office furniture. Bassett sells its products primarily through some 94 Bassett Furniture Direct stores (more than half of which are licensed) and Bassett Home Furnishings locations. Bassett boasts about 55 company-owned stores located mostly in the southern and northeastern US. Operating in more than 20 states nationwide Texas is Bassett's largest market by store count.

Operation
Bassett breaks its operations into wholesale and retail segments which split revenue split almost evenly. Wholesale which had 51% of sales designs makes and distributes furniture products to the Retail segment which sells them.

Geographic Reach
Based in Bassett Virginia the company's network of furniture stores reaches to more than 20 US states. Texas which accounts for 20% of its store count is its core market.

Sales and Marketing
Upholstered furniture brings in 60% of Bassett's wholesale sales with most of the rest coming from wooden pieces. Approximately 42% of its 2013 wholesale sales were generated from imported products compared to 50% in 2012.

Bassett has stepped up advertising spending in recent years reaching $15.6 million in 2014 from $14.8 million in 2013 and $13.3 million in 2012.

Financial Performance
Bassett's revenue increased 6% in 2014 from 2013 to more than $340 million. The higher revenue came from six more Bassett owned-and-operated stores and growth of wholesale shipments outside the licensee network. Bassett's net income has lurched from loss to profit in the past 10 years but the company posted a profit of $9.3 million in 2014 —an 82% increase over 2013. The increase was attributed to the higher income. The company reported that cash flow from operations increased to about $30 million in 2014 from about $20 million in 2013.

Strategy
The company continues to build its network of retail stores. It opened six stores in 2014 after opening two each in 2013 and 2012. It plans to open another six in 2015 in with two stores in Maryland and one each in Texas Connecticut New York and Massachusetts.

HISTORY

The Bassett Furniture Company was founded in 1902 by brothers John Charles and Samuel Bassett and their brother-in-law Reed Stone. Their goal: to make affordable furniture out of the oak that grew so abundantly nearby. The first bed sold for $1.50. Associate companies were spawned in the 1920s but in 1930 John brought the three Bassett furniture firms under one umbrella Bassett Furniture Industries. Eight years later the firm introduced its hallmark Waterfall design. The company made truck bodies during WWII.

Robert Spilman Sr. took charge of the company in the early 1960s. By 1971 Bassett's revenues were over $144 million. In 1972 with the acquisitions of E.B. Malone Bedding and National Furniture of Mt. Airy the company operated 31 plants across the US. Acquisitions of smaller furniture companies continued through the 1980s.

Bassett's profits began a steady decline in 1992 coinciding with a slump in home furnishing sales. The company vertically integrated in 1994 when the first licensed Bassett stores opened. Bassett made the California Public Employees' Retirement System's list of the 10 worst companies (in terms of stock performance) for 1996 and 1997. Robert Spilman Jr. was named president and COO in 1997 and outsider Paul Fulton became chairman and CEO. Also in 1997 as sales continued to fall Bassett trimmed its product lines closed or sold 14 factories and cut about 1000 jobs.

In 1999 the company sold its mattress division to LIS Corporation which agreed to produce Bassett-brand bedding under license. Bassett opened its first company-owned furniture stores in 1999 and then formed The Ladin Retail Group a joint venture (51%-owned by Bassett) combining those stores with licensed stores operated by Phillip and Ronnie Ladin.

In 2000 Spilman Jr. became CEO. Also that year Bassett announced it would consolidate some of its wood manufacturing operations and eliminate about 280 jobs; it cut 100 more jobs in March 2001. In August the company announced plans to increase levels of imported occasional tables and cribs thus negatively impacting domestic production. In 2002 Bassett purchased five stores (in California and Virginia) from LRG Furniture. In February 2003 the company shut down a wood manufacturing plant in Georgia and laid off about 300 of its employees.

In June 2003 Bassett's wholly owned subsidiary Weiman Furniture acquired certain assets of Preview Furniture. The same year Bassett acquired an additional 29% of LRG Furniture bringing its total stake in the retailer to 80%. Bassett sold Weiman in 2006. In 2004 the company acquired the final 20% of LRG that it didn't own.

By 2015 the company had 60 retail stores which provided 49% of revenue.

EXECUTIVES

Vice President Information Technology, Thomas (Thom) Prato

Senior Vice President Retail, Jason Camp

Chairman President and CEO, Robert H. (Rob) Spilman, age 60, $388,750 total compensation

SVP Global Sourcing, John E. Bassett, age 57, $189,167 total compensation

SVP Upholstery, Mark S. Jordan, age 62, $189,167 total compensation

SVP and CFO, J. Michael Daniel, age 54, $189,167 total compensation

VP Information Technology, Stephen D. Harmon

President and CEO Zenith Freight Lines LLC, Jack L. Hahn, age 62

Senior Vice President, Bruce (Brucey) Cohenour

Vice President, Stanley (Stan) Payne

Vice President Wood Division, Thomas (Thom) Brockman

Vp Corporate Retail Southeast Region, Louis Mossotti

Vice President Licensed Retail, David (Dave) Walsh

Vice President Of Domestic Manufacturi, Tom (Tommy) Brockman

Vice President and Director Purchasing, Bill (Billy) Dalton

Vice President Information Technology, Ronda Wilson

Auditors: Ernst & Young LLP

LOCATIONS

HQ: Bassett Furniture Industries, Inc
  3525 Fairystone Park Highway, Bassett, VA 24055
Phone: 276 629-6000   **Fax:** 276 629-6332
Web: www.bassettfurniture.com

PRODUCTS/OPERATIONS

2015 Sales

	$ mil.	% of total
Wholesale	252.2	44
Retail	249.4	43
Logistics	77.2	13
Eliminations	(147.9)	-
Total	**430.9**	**100**

2015 Sales

	$ mil.	% of total
Furniture and accessories	387.4	90
Logistics	43.5	10
Total	**430.9**	**100**

Selected Products

Accent pieces
Bedroom suites
Bookcases and cabinets
Chairs
Desks
Dining room suites
Love seats
Recliners
Sofas
Tables

COMPETITORS

Ashley Furniture	Hooker Furniture
Boyles Distinctive	Kimball International
Furniture	Klaussner Furniture
Bush Industries	La-Z-Boy
Chromcraft Revington	Rooms To Go
Decorize	Rowe Fine Furniture
Ethan Allen	Sauder Woodworking
Havertys	Stanley Furniture
Heritage Home Group	W.S. Badcock
Home Meridian	

HISTORICAL FINANCIALS

Company Type: Public

Income Statement

FYE: November 26

	REVENUE ($ mil.)	NET INCOME ($ mil.)	NET PROFIT MARGIN	EMPLOYEES
11/16	432.0	15.8	3.7%	2,620.0
11/15	430.9	20.4	4.7%	2,237.0
11/14	340.7	9.3	2.7%	1,568.0
11/13	321.2	5.1	1.6%	1,501.0
11/12	269.6	26.7	9.9%	1,412.0
Annual Growth	**12.5%**	**(12.3%)**	**—**	**16.7%**

2016 Year-End Financials

Debt ratio: 2.5%	No. of shares (mil.): 10.7
Return on equity: 8.8%	Dividends
Cash ($ mil.): 35.1	Yield: 0.0%
Current ratio: 1.83	Payout: 39.7%
Long-term debt ($ mil.): 3.8	Market value ($ mil.): 317.0

	STOCK PRICE ($) FY Close	P/E High/Low		PER SHARE ($) Earnings	Dividends	Book Value
11/16	29.55	23	15	1.46	0.58	16.85
11/15	31.76	20	10	1.88	0.54	16.25
11/14	19.60	22	14	0.87	0.48	14.95
11/13	15.77	36	23	0.47	0.22	14.50
11/12	11.25	5	3	2.41	1.95	14.51
Annual Growth	**27.3%**	—	—	**(11.8%)**	**(26.2%)**	**3.8%**

Bear State Financial Inc

Bear State Financial (formerly First Federal Bancshares of Arkansas) is the holding company for Bear State Bank and Metropolitan Bank which serve businesses and individuals through a total of 55 branches mostly in Arkansas but also in southeastern Oklahoma and southwestern Missouri. Founded in 1934 the thrift offers standard retail services such as checking and savings accounts money markets and CDs. More than 50% of the bank's loan portfolio is made up of one-to-four-family residential and commercial real estate mortgages while business loans make up another 15%. The bank changed its name in mid-2014 to match its holding company's brand.

OperationsThe bank makes more than 80% of its revenue from interest income. About 77% of its total revenue came from loan interest during 2015 while another 5% came from interest on investment securities. The rest of its revenue came from deposit fee income (11%) loan sale gains (4%) earnings on life insurance policies (2%) and other miscellaneous income sources.Bear State Financial had more than half of its loan portfolio split between one-to-four family residential mortgages and non-farm commercial real estate loans at the end of 2015. The remainder of its portfolio was tied to commercial loans (17% of loan assets) construction and land development mortgages (8%) farmland mortgages (6.5%) multifamily residential mortgages (5%) and consumer loans (3%). Geographic Reach

The company operates more than 40 Bear State Bank branches across Arkansas and in Southeast Oklahoma; and a dozen Metropolitan National Bank branches in Southwest Missouri.

Sales and Marketing

Loans are originated through a variety of means such as walk-ins from its own banking branches or referrals from realtors and loan officers. Bear State uses radio online and newspaper advertisements to promote its services. The bank spent $2.52 million on advertising and public relations during 2015 nearly twice as much as the $1.35 million it spent in 2014.Financial Performance-Bear State Financials' revenues have more than tripled since 2011 as its loan assets have quadrupled to $1.44 billion. The bank's annual profits have soared back from losses in 2011 as it's managed to keep a lid on overhead cost growth.The bank's revenue jumped 42% to $74.37 million during 2015 mostly thanks to its recent acquisitions of First National Security and Metropolitan Bank which drove higher interest income as its loan assets grew by 38% while boosting non-interest income by 35% on deposit fee and insurance policy growth. Despite strong revenue growth in 2015 Bear State's net income fell by more than half to $10.57 million mostly on higher salary and compensation costs tied to added personnel from the two new bank acquisitions. The bank's operating cash levels more than doubled to $13.7 million after adjusting its cash for non-cash items related to net proceeds from loan sales.

Strategy

Bear State has been acquiring other banks to expand its branch network into new markets while boosting its loan and deposit business.

Mergers and Acquisitions

In October 2015 the group acquired $442 million-asset Metropolitan National Bank along with its $340 million in loans $375 million in deposits and 12 branches across Southwest Missouri. In

June 2014 Bear State expanded into central and southwest Arkansas and southeast Oklahoma after it acquired Hot Springs-based First National Security Corporation. The deal added 23 new branches (under the First National Bank and Heritage Bank brands) and boosted Bear State's total assets by over 160%.

EXECUTIVES

SEVP CFO and Chief Accounting Officer Bear State Financial Inc. and Bear State Bank, Sherri R. Billings, age 59, $202,975 total compensation
President and CEO Bear State Financial Inc. and CEO Bear State Bank, J. Matthew (Matt) Machen, age 35, $219,615 total compensation
SEVP and COO, R. Thomas (Tom) Fritsche, age 55, $320,097 total compensation
EVP and Chief Marketing Officer, Shelly Loftin, age 34
EVP and Human Resources Director, Donna Merriweather, age 56
EVP and Director Operations, Yurik Paroubek
Chairman, Richard N. Massey
Board Member, John P (Jack) Hammerschmidt
Auditors: BKD, LLP

LOCATIONS

HQ: Bear State Financial Inc
900 South Shackleford Rd., Suite 605, Little Rock, AR 72211
Phone: 501 975-6033
Web: www.ffbh.com

PRODUCTS/OPERATIONS

2015 sales

	% of total
Interest income	
Loans receivable	77
Investment securities	5
Other	0
Non Interest income	
Net gain on sales and calls of investment securities	0
Deposit fee income	11
Earnings on life insurance policies	2
Gain on sales of loans	4
Other	1
Total	**100**

COMPETITORS

Arvest Bank	IBERIABANK
BOK Financial	Regions Financial
Bank of America	Simmons First
Bank of the Ozarks	U.S. Bancorp
Home BancShares	

HISTORICAL FINANCIALS

Company Type: Public

Income Statement

FYE: December 31

	ASSETS ($ mil.)	NET INCOME ($ mil.)	INCOME AS % OF ASSETS	EMPLOYEES
12/15	1,920.2	10.5	0.6%	586.0
12/14	1,514.6	24.3	1.6%	423.0
12/13	548.8	0.7	0.1%	190.0
12/12	530.4	0.7	0.1%	192.0
12/11	579.0	(19.0)	—	221.0
Annual Growth	**34.9%**	**—**	**—**	**27.6%**

2015 Year-End Financials

Return on assets: 0.6%	Dividends
Return on equity: 5.3%	Yield: —
Long-term debt ($ mil.): —	Payout: —
No. of shares (mil.): 37.9	Market value ($ mil.): 411.0
Sales ($ mil): 74.3	

	STOCK PRICE ($) FY Close	P/E High/Low	PER SHARE ($) Earnings	Dividends	Book Value
12/15	10.83	36 26	0.30	0.00	5.87
12/14	10.99	13 8	0.84	0.00	5.11
12/13	8.70	278211	0.03	0.00	3.20
12/12	9.75	298119	0.04	0.00	3.25
12/11	4.32	— —	(0.60)	0.00	3.22
Annual Growth	**25.8%**	**— —**	**—**	**—**	**16.3%**

Behringer Harvard Opportunity REIT II Inc

Auditors: Deloitte & Touche LLP

LOCATIONS

HQ: Behringer Harvard Opportunity REIT II Inc
15601 Dallas Parkway, Suite 600, Addison, TX 75001
Phone: 866 655-3650
Web: www.behringerinvestments.com

HISTORICAL FINANCIALS

Company Type: Public

Income Statement

FYE: December 31

	REVENUE ($ mil.)	NET INCOME ($ mil.)	NET PROFIT MARGIN	EMPLOYEES
12/15	50.2	6.9	13.9%	0.0
12/14	48.6	(0.0)	—	0.0
12/13	43.3	8.7	20.1%	0.0
12/12	32.7	1.6	5.1%	0.0
Annual Growth	**15.4%**	**61.2%**	**—**	**—**

2015 Year-End Financials

Debt ratio: —	No. of shares (mil.): 25.5
Return on equity: 5.0%	Dividends
Cash ($ mil.): 81.4	Yield: —
Current ratio: 0.39	Payout: 925.9%
Long-term debt ($ mil.): —	Market value ($ mil.): —

	STOCK PRICE ($) FY Close	P/E High/Low	PER SHARE ($) Earnings	Dividends	Book Value
12/15	0.00	— —	0.27	2.50	4.29
Annual Growth	**—**	**— —**	**—**	**—**	**—**

Bel Fuse Inc

Bel Fuse manufactures electronic components for networking telecommunications high-speed data transmission and automotive and consumer electronics. Its magnetic products include discrete components power transformers and MagJack connector modules. It also offers power conversion modules for a variety of applications. Bel Fuse's miniature micro and surface-mounted fuses create supplementary circuit protection for consumer electronics. The company also makes passive jacks plugs and cable assemblies. Top customers include Hon Hai (14% of sales) and Flextronics (10% of sales).

Geographic Reach
Bel Fuse has nearly two dozen manufacturing plants in China Czech Republic Dominican Republic Mexico the UK and the US (in Arizona Florida Minnesota New York Pennsylvania and Texas.)

The US is Bel Fuse's biggest market accounting for 50% of revenue. Asia (specifically Macao) accounts for about 30% of sales with Europre generating 13%.

Sales and Marketing
The company sells its products through one of three channels: direct strategic account managers regional sales managers working with independent sales reps or authorized distributors.

Financial Performance
Bel Fuse posted high revenue and significantly higher profit in 2015.

Revenue rose 16% in 2015 to $567 million (a company high) on stronger sales of its power solutions and protection and connectivity solutions businesses. The company also saw strong growth —a 40% increase —in the US.

Profit jumped 111% higher to $19.2 million in 2015 from $9.1 million. The company had lower material costs especially for its connectivity products which helped boost net income.

Cash flow from operations increased to about $66 million in 2015 from $22 million in 2014.

Strategy
The electronic components industry is highly competitive in good times and bad and increased competition from low-cost suppliers is one factor that drives the company to lower its average selling prices for products on a regular basis. Customers pressure Bel Fuse to cut prices and prices tend to decline rapidly over the life cycle of a product.

The company invests in R&D to reduce material costs and it has closed six facilities and consolidating operations into other facilities. It opened a new more efficient Power Solutions operation in California where researchers can work directly with manufacturing.

Bel Fuse sold the Network Power Systems division that was part of Power Solutions business it acquired from ABB. The company will use the $9 million from buyer Unipower to reduce debt.

Mergers and Acquisitions
On the competitive front Bel Fuse continues to jockey for a bigger slice of the diversified electronics OEM market expanding its product and technology lineup and customer base through acquisitions.

Most recently it bought divisions of major manufacturers Emerson ABB and TE Connectivity. In 2014 it bought the Power One Solutions business from ABB for $117 million in cash. Power One Solutions makes power conversion products from two plants in China and Slovakia. It also agreed to buy the Emerson Network Power Connectivity Solutions (ECS) business of Emerson for $98 million in cash. ECS has plants in China the UK and the US. In 2013 it bought the transpower magnetics business from TE Connectivity for $22.4 million in cash. Renamed TRP International the company makes integrated connector module (ICM) products at its plant in China.

EXECUTIVES

President and CEO, Daniel (Dan) Bernstein, age 62, $225,000 total compensation

VP Finance and Secretary, Colin Dunn, age 71, $190,000 total compensation

President Bel Power Solutions, Dennis Ackerman, age 53, $175,000 total compensation

VP Asia Operations, Raymond Cheung, age 59, $170,000 total compensation

President Bel Connectivity Solutions, Peter Bittner, age 46

Auditors: Deloitte & Touche LLP

LOCATIONS

HQ: Bel Fuse Inc
206 Van Vorst Street, Jersey City, NJ 07302
Phone: 201 432-0463
Web: www.belfuse.com

PRODUCTS/OPERATIONS

2015 Sales

	$ mil.	% of total
Power solutions and protection	241.8	38
Connectivity solutions	181.7	32
Magnetic solutions	170.6	30
Total	**567.1**	**100**

Selected Products

Magnetics
Discrete components
Integrated connector modules (MagJack)
Power transformers
Interconnect
Cable assemblies
Passive jacks
Plugs
Modules
Custom modules
Integrated analog front end modules
Power conversion modules (DC/DC converters)
Fuses (miniature micro and surface mount)

COMPETITORS

API Technologies	Littelfuse
Alcatel-Lucent	Pulse Electronics
CTS Corp.	S&C Electric
Curtis Instruments	Spang & Company
Digital Power	Standex
Espey Mfg.	TE Connectivity
Gowanda Electronics	Torotel
Hytek Microsystems	Yokogawa Electric

HISTORICAL FINANCIALS

Company Type: Public

Income Statement

FYE: December 31

	REVENUE ($ mil.)	NET INCOME ($ mil.)	NET PROFIT MARGIN	EMPLOYEES
12/15	567.0	19.2	3.4%	7,971.0
12/14	487.0	9.1	1.9%	8,210.0
12/13	349.1	15.9	4.6%	6,370.0
12/12	286.5	2.4	0.8%	4,166.0
12/11	295.1	3.7	1.3%	3,451.0
Annual Growth	**17.7%**	**50.3%**	**—**	**23.3%**

2015 Year-End Financials

Debt ratio: 31.8%
Return on equity: 8.3%
Cash ($ mil.): 85.0
Current ratio: 2.34
Long-term debt ($ mil.): 162.4

No. of shares (mil.): 11.8
Dividends
  Yield: 1.6%
  Payout: 18.7%
Market value ($ mil.): 205.0

Stock Price Table

	STOCK PRICE ($) FY Close	P/E High/Low	PER SHARE ($) Earnings	Dividends	Book Value
12/15	17.29	18 11	1.53	0.28	19.63
12/14	27.34	40 25	0.73	0.28	18.95
12/13	21.31	17 10	1.32	0.28	19.87
12/12	19.55	123 86	0.17	0.28	18.65
12/11	18.75	94 49	0.28	0.28	18.72
Annual Growth	**(2.0%)**	**—**	**52.9%**	**(0.0%)**	**1.2%**

Berkshire Hills Bancorp, Inc.

Berkshire Hills Bancorp is the holding company for Berkshire Bank which serves individuals and small businesses through some 90 branches in Massachusetts New York Connecticut and Vermont. Established in 1846 the bank provides standard deposit products such as savings checking and money market accounts CDs and IRAs in addition to credit cards investments private banking wealth management and lending services. Real estate mortgages make up nearly three-quarters of Berkshire Hills Bancorp's loan portfolio which also includes business and consumer loans. In addition to its banking activities the company also owns insurance agency Berkshire Insurance Group.

Geographic Reach

Berkshire Hills Bancorp also is eyeing further expansion into Connecticut and other parts of New England and New York by opening new branches and through acquisitions.

Financial Performance

Berkshire Hills Bancorp's revenue increased in fiscal 2013 compared to the prior year. It reported $262 million in revenue for fiscal 2013 up from $230 million in fiscal 2012. Net income also went up to $58 million in fiscal 2013 compared to the $47 million Berkshire Hills Bancorp reported for net income in fiscal 2012.

The company's cash on hand increased by more than $100 million in fiscal 2013 compared to fiscal 2012 levels.

Strategy

Berkshire Hills Bancorp which was established in 1846 believes one of its competitive advantages is the regional niche it serves which has been relatively unscathed by the recession compared to other parts of the country.

The bank's performance has been boosted by an increase in business development in the company's market area in addition to growth in its asset-based lending and private banking businesses. The bank also has grown its loans and deposits and has plans to grow its insurance and wealth management operations as well.

In 2016 the company completed the $150 million acquisition of New Jersey-based First Choice Bank. That deal which add eight bank branches and introduce Berkshire Hills to the greater Philadelphia area will bring the bank's network to more than 100 branches.

EXECUTIVES

President and CEO, Michael P. Daly, age 54, $575,000 total compensation

EVP Human Resources, Linda A. Johnston

COO Berkshire Bank, Sean A. Gray, $350,000 total compensation

EVP Commercial Banking, George F. Bacigalupo, $229,554 total compensation

President Berkshire Bank, Richard M. Marotta, $350,000 total compensation

EVP, Glenn S. Welch, age 54

SEVP and CFO Berkshire Hills Bancorp Inc. and Berkshire Bank, James M. (Jamie) Moses

Vice President Retail Banking, Tami Gunsch

Senior Vice President, Mark Foster

Vice President, Theresa Wituszynski

Vice President Od, Lauren Harvey

Vice President Risk Credit Administration and Policy, Patricia (Pat) Nebosky

Vice President Commercial Workout, Steve (Stevie) Dunham

Vice President Relationship Manager, Justin Priddle

Senior Vice President and Treasurer, Richard (Dick) Thevenet

Assistant Vice President Relationship Manager, Levante Gregg

Chairman, William J. (Bill) Ryan, age 73

Treasurer, Mike Macy

Auditors: PricewaterhouseCoopers LLP

LOCATIONS

HQ: Berkshire Hills Bancorp, Inc.
24 North Street, Pittsfield, MA 01201
Phone: 413 236-3149
Web: www.berkshirebank.com

PRODUCTS/OPERATIONS

2015 Sales

	% of total
Interest and dividend income	
Loans	70
Securities and other	12
Non-interest income	
Loan related income	3
Mortgage banking income	1
Deposit related fees	8
Insurance commissions and fees	3
Wealth management fees	3
Other	-
Gain on securities net	-
Total	**100**

COMPETITORS

Bank of America	KeyCorp
Citizens Financial Group	Pathfinder Bancorp
Hudson City Bancorp	Sovereign Bank
	TD Bank USA

HISTORICAL FINANCIALS

Company Type: Public

Income Statement

FYE: December 31

	ASSETS ($ mil.)	NET INCOME ($ mil.)	INCOME AS % OF ASSETS	EMPLOYEES
12/15	7,831.9	49.5	0.6%	1,221.0
12/14	6,502.0	33.7	0.5%	1,091.0
12/13	5,672.8	41.1	0.7%	939.0
12/12	5,296.8	33.1	0.6%	1,012.0
12/11	3,991.2	17.5	0.4%	760.0
Annual Growth	**18.4%**	**29.5%**	**—**	**12.6%**

2015 Year-End Financials

Return on assets: 0.6%
Return on equity: 6.2%
Long-term debt ($ mil.): —
No. of shares (mil.): 30.9
Sales ($ mil): 301.3

Dividends
  Yield: 2.6%
  Payout: 46.0%
Market value ($ mil.): 902.0

	STOCK PRICE ($) FY Close	P/E High/Low	PER SHARE ($) Earnings	Dividends	Book Value
12/15	29.11	17 14	1.73	0.76	28.64
12/14	26.66	20 16	1.36	0.72	28.17
12/13	27.27	18 14	1.65	0.72	27.08
12/12	23.86	16 14	1.49	0.69	26.53
12/11	22.19	24 18	0.98	0.65	26.17
Annual Growth	7.0%	— —	15.3%	4.0%	2.3%

Bio-Techne Corp

Bio-Techne (formerly TECHNE Corporation) is a biotechnology research specialist. Through subsidiaries including Research and Diagnostic Systems (R&D Systems) Boston Biochem BiosPacific and Tocris the firm makes and distributes biological research supplies used by researchers around the globe to study cellular and immune system responses. Bio-Techne's products include cytokines (purified proteins that affect cell behavior) and diagnostic reagents (including antibodies and enzymes) as well as its Quantikine assay kits that determine the amount of cytokine in a given sample. R&D Systems also makes hematology controls and calibrators for blood analysis systems and sells them to equipment makers.

Operations

The company operates through three reportable segments: Biotechnology Clinical Controls and Protein Platforms.

Bio-Techne's Biotechnology segment which makes products used by laboratories for both drug discovery research and clinical diagnostic purposes accounts for more than 70% of sales. Cytokines are a key product offering as commercial and institutional researchers are increasingly using the proteins as a swift and effective means of impacting the processes of cells and tissues. Subsidiary R&D Systems and its BiosPacific Boston Biochem and R&D Systems China as well as the R&D Systems Europe (UK) unit and its Tocris and R&D Systems (Germany) units are all included in the Biotechnology segment.

The newest segment established in 2014 is Protein Platforms (15% of sales). It develops and commercializes systems for protein analysis. The smallest Clinical Controls segment (13% of sales) develops and manufactures controls and calibrators for the global clinical market.

Altogether Bio-Techne sells more than 275000 products under such brands as Novus Biologicals Tocris Bioscience ProteinSimple R&D Systems BiosPacific CLINIQA and RNA Medical.

Geographic Reach

The US market accounts for more than half of Bio-Techne's annual revenues. Europe is the second-largest region accounting for about 30% of sales; the firm also conducts sales in Asia and other regions.

The company has operations in the US Europe and China.

Sales and Marketing

Bio-Techne sells its products through subsidiaries and third-party distributors worldwide. Its R&D Systems Europe and Tocris subsidiaries handle distribution efforts abroad and have a direct presence in France Germany and the UK. The company is growing its Asian distribution network

which includes the R&D Systems China subsidiary. Thermo Fisher Scientific distributes Bio-Techne's R&D Systems Tocris and Boston Biochem products in the US and Canada.

Customers of the Biotechnology segment include researchers employed by pharma and biotech drug companies as well as universities and government agencies.

Bio-Techne has been increasing its advertising expenditures which totaled $4.1 million in fiscal 2015 (ended June). It spent $3.4 million in fiscal 2014 and $3.2 million in fiscal 2013.

Financial Performance

Revenue which has been trending upward over the past five years increased 26% to $452.2 million in fiscal 2015 (ended June). Both the Biotechnology and Clinical Controls segment saw growth that year thanks to the recent acquisitions of Novus Biologicals and Bionostics as well as through continuing organic growth. (The newly formed Protein Platforms segment was no slouch either contributing 15% of the company's total earnings that year.)

After years of remaining relatively flat net income slipped a marginal 3% to $107.7 million in fiscal 2015. Despite the revenue growth higher operating expenses related to acquisitions as well as investments in resources and infrastructure ended up cutting into profits.

Cash flow from operations rose 2% to $139.4 million that year as cash inflows from accounts payable more than offset the decline in net income.

Strategy

Bio-Techne works to expand its product offerings through internal R&D efforts. The firm develops hundreds of new biological proteins antibodies and immunoassays each year. It also develops new hematology control technologies to keep up with changing technologies and markets as well as to provide efficient and high-quality offerings. In addition Bio-Techne grows its offerings through acquisitions partnerships and joint ventures.

The company has expanded the scope of its operations over the years by building up a collection of minority stakes in a number of drug developers and biotech companies working in complementary areas. It owns about 15% of drug developer ChemoCentryx which is researching chemokines a type of cytokine involved in immune response. Other investments have included blood filtration technology firm Hemerus Medical diagnostics developer Nephromics and biotechnology firm ACT-Gen.

In 2015 the company launched its first Simple Plex platform member Ella through its new Proteins Platform segment. It rebranded the CyPlex immunoassay platform acquired from CyVek under the name ProteinSimple.

TECHNE changed its name to Bio-Techne in 2014 bringing its various brands under one common name.

Mergers and Acquisitions

The company expanded its manufacturing and distribution operations in the field of clinical in vitro diagnostics (primarily glucose and blood gas tests) through the $104 million acquisition of Bionostics in 2013.

The following year it acquired a number of firms to boost its portfolio. It bought Chinese recombinant protein manufacturer Shanghai PrimeGene Bio-Tech gaining more than 400 new protein products; ProteinSimple a developer of systems and consumables for protein analysis (for $300 million); Novus Holdings which supplies antibodies and other reagents for life science research (for $60 million); and CyVek which developed the Cy-Plex transformative immunoassay technology (now branded ProteinSimple).

Bio-Techne continued its buying streak in 2015 with the purchase of Cliniqa Corporation which develops and manufactures clinical controls products that focus on in vitro diagnostic devices.

HISTORY

Company Background

David Mundschenk founded biological products maker Research and Diagnostics Systems in 1976. In 1983 Mundschenk made a disastrous move buying heavily indebted French hematology instrument maker Hycel. R&D System's disgruntled board named Thomas Oland (at the time a consultant) CEO.

Enter TECHNE. Founded in 1981 by George Kline and Peter Peterson to pursue profitable acquisitions it went public in 1983 and in 1985 bought R&D Systems (which became an operating subsidiary of TECHNE) a sign of their confidence in Oland. TECHNE formed a biotechnology division in 1986 to produce and market human cytokines. In 1988 Kline resigned following a failed acquisition attempt by medical test kit maker Incstar.

In 1991 TECHNE bought Amgen's research reagent and diagnostic assay kit business and began selling Quantikine cytokine diagnostic kits. In 1993 it acquired what would become the company's R&D Europe unit.

In 1995 the company debuted 10 new Quantikine immunoassay kits. TECHNE restructured its European research operation in 1997 pulling underperforming molecular biology products from the market and refocusing on TECHNE's core cytokine-related products. The next year TECHNE bought Genzyme's research products business (antibodies proteins and research kits) for about $65 million.

As drug and biotechnology research became growth markets in the late 1990s and early 21st century TECHNE expanded through purchases. In 1999 it bought the reagent business and immunoassay patents of partner Cistron. The next year the firm increased its ownership in drug developer ChemoCentryx to almost 50% (reduced in 2001 to about 25% and then again in 2004 to 20%). TECHNE also acquired research and diagnostic market rights to all products developed by the firm. A similar deal was made in 2001 with functional genomics firm Discovery Genomics; that investment was not realized to TECHNE's satisfaction so it wrote off the investment in 2004.

It didn't wait long to fill the gap when it acquired the operations of Fortron Bio Science and Biospacific in 2005. The makers of antibodies and reagents had been partners since 1992 before they were integrated into TECHNE's R&D Systems division.

In 2007 the company set up a sales and distribution subsidiary in Shanghai to capitalize on the growing Chinese market. In 2007 TECHNE acquired minority stakes in two additional companies: diagnostics developer Nephromics and biotechnology firm ACTGen.

EXECUTIVES

SVP Clinical Controls, Marcel Veronneau, age 62, $210,000 total compensation
CFO and Vice President - Finance and Treasurer, Gregory J. (Greg) Melsen, age 65, $384,375 total compensation
President and CEO, Charles R. (Chuck) Kummeth, age 56
CIO, Fernando Bazan

Senior Vice President General Counsel, Brenda (Bren) Furlow
Senior Vice President Biotechnology, Kevin (Kev) Reagan
Vice President Human Resources, Struan Robertson
Vice President of Marketing, Karen (Kare) Padgett
Vice Chairman, Roger C. Lucas, age 73
Chairman, Robert V. Baumgartner, age 60
Auditors: KPMG LLP

LOCATIONS

HQ: Bio-Techne Corp
  614 McKinley Place N.E., Minneapolis, MN 55413-2610
Phone: 612 379-8854
Web: www.bio-techne.com

PRODUCTS/OPERATIONS

2015 Sales by Segment

	$ mil.	% of total
Biotechnology	325.9	72
Protein Platforms	66.2	15
Clinical Controls	60.4	13
Adjustments	(0.3)	-
Total	**452.2**	**100**

Selected Products and Services

R&D Systems
  Activity assays and reagents
  Antibodies
  Biomarker testing service
  ELISAs
  ELISpot kits & FluoroSpot kits
  Flow cytometry and cell selection/detection
  General laboratory reagents
  Multiplex assays/arrays
  Proteins
  Stem cell and cell culture products
Tocris
  Caged compounds
  Controlled substances
  Fluorescent probes
  Ligand sets
  Peptides
  Screening libraries
  Small molecules
  Toxins
Boston Biochem
  Affinity matrices/proteins
  Antibodies
  Buffers solutions and standards
  Fractions
  Inhibitors
  Kits
  Proteasome
  Substrate Proteins
  Ubiquitin

COMPETITORS

ABCAM PLC	Merck KGaA
Abbott Labs	Ortho-Clinical
BD Biosciences	Diagnostics
Beckman Coulter	Santa Cruz
Bio-Rad Labs	Biotechnology
Enzo Biochem	Sigma-Aldrich
GE Healthcare Medical	Streck
Diagnostics	Thermo Fisher
Life Technologies	Scientific
Corporation	
Marker Gene	
Technologies	

HISTORICAL FINANCIALS
Company Type: Public

Income Statement
FYE: June 30

	REVENUE ($ mil.)	NET INCOME ($ mil.)	NET PROFIT MARGIN	EMPLOYEES
06/16	499.0	104.4	20.9%	1,560.0
06/15	452.2	107.7	23.8%	1,356.0
06/14	357.7	110.9	31.0%	1,021.0
06/13	310.5	112.5	36.2%	854.0
06/12	314.5	112.3	35.7%	847.0
Annual Growth	**12.2%**	**(1.8%)**	**—**	**16.5%**

2016 Year-End Financials

Debt ratio: 8.1%	No. of shares (mil.): 37.2
Return on equity: 12.0%	Dividends
Cash ($ mil.): 64.2	Yield: 1.1%
Current ratio: 4.69	Payout: 45.5%
Long-term debt ($ mil.): 91.5	Market value ($ mil.): 4,201.0

	STOCK PRICE ($) FY Close	P/E High/Low		PER SHARE ($) Earnings	Dividends	Book Value
06/16	112.77	41	29	2.80	1.28	23.60
06/15	98.47	35	30	2.89	1.27	22.80
06/14	92.57	32	23	3.00	1.23	21.49
06/13	69.08	25	21	3.05	1.18	20.02
06/12	74.20	28	21	3.04	1.11	18.31
Annual Growth	**11.0%**	**—**	**—**	**(2.0%)**	**3.6%**	**6.5%**

Biospecifics Technologies Corp.

BioSpecifics Technologies specifically uses collagenase (an enzyme that breaks the bonds of collagen) to treat a variety of skin-thickening diseases and conditions. Its current product named Xiaflex is an injectable collagenase that treats Dupuytren's disease (marketed) and is being tested for Peyronie's disease frozen shoulder and cellulite. The company is working with Auxilium Pharmaceuticals on these indications. On its own BioSpecifics is also testing a collagenase treatment for human and canine lipoma (benign fatty tumor). The company was formed in 1990 to make a topical collagenase for burns and skin ulcers; it sold that business in 2006 but still received payments until 2013.

Operations

The company's agreement with DFB the company that bought its topical business expired in 2013 but it may still collect royalties if the treatment is used for new indications.

BioSpecifics' other source of revenue is from its agreement with Auxilium from which it receives sublicense royalty milestone and mark-up payments. Xiaflex is approved in the US and Auxilium has the rights to sell it in Canada Australia Brazil and Mexico for Dupuytren's contracture once it's approved.

Clinical trials for using Xiaflex to treat lipoma are in the early stages.

The company and Pfizer dissolved their agreement for Pfizer to commercialize Xiaflex for Dupuytren's disease in Europe.

Financial Perfomance

BioSpecifics reported a 2% decline in revenue for 2012 due to a decline in licensing revenue though there was an increase in net sales of Xiaflex. Net income dropped 55% as R&D expenses rose as the company worked to develop Xiaflex for lipoma. Investing and financing activities took a bite out of cash flow dropping it about 30%.

Strategy

The company will continue to develop Xiaflex for Peyronie's disease frozen shoulder cellulite and lipomas while looking for additional indications where the drug would be useful. It will also continue to seek marketing and distribution partners especially in Europe.

EXECUTIVES

President, Thomas L. Wegman, age 61, $350,000 total compensation
Auditors: Tabriztchi & Co., CPA, P.C.

LOCATIONS

HQ: Biospecifics Technologies Corp.
  35 Wilbur Street, Lynbrook, NY 11563
Phone: 516 593-7000
Web: www.biospecifics.com

PRODUCTS/OPERATIONS

2015 Sales

	$ mil.	% of total
Royalties	20.8	91
Licensing	1.9	9
Total	**22.7**	**100**

COMPETITORS

Genzyme Biosurgery	Pfizer

HISTORICAL FINANCIALS
Company Type: Public

Income Statement
FYE: December 31

	REVENUE ($ mil.)	NET INCOME ($ mil.)	NET PROFIT MARGIN	EMPLOYEES
12/15	22.7	9.6	42.3%	5.0
12/14	14.0	4.6	33.0%	5.0
12/13	14.4	5.2	36.5%	5.0
12/12	11.1	2.9	26.7%	5.0
12/11	11.4	6.6	57.9%	5.0
Annual Growth	**18.9%**	**9.9%**	**—**	**0.0%**

2015 Year-End Financials

Debt ratio: —	No. of shares (mil.): 6.9
Return on equity: 25.6%	Dividends
Cash ($ mil.): 5.1	Yield: —
Current ratio: 45.76	Payout: —
Long-term debt ($ mil.): —	Market value ($ mil.): 297.0

	STOCK PRICE ($) FY Close	P/E High/Low		PER SHARE ($) Earnings	Dividends	Book Value
12/15	42.97	49	26	1.32	0.00	6.48
12/14	38.62	57	29	0.66	0.00	4.50
12/13	21.67	28	18	0.76	0.00	3.51
12/12	14.95	45	27	0.43	0.00	2.74
12/11	16.62	26	13	0.95	0.00	2.35
Annual Growth	**26.8%**	**—**	**—**	**8.6%**	**—**	**28.9%**

BioTelemetry Inc

BioTelemetry knows how to keep a beat. The company provides real-time outpatient cardiac rhythm monitoring and telemetry services for patients throughout the US. Its core product Mobile Cardiac Outpatient Telemetry (MCOT) helps physicians diagnose and monitor heart arrhythmia in patients by providing continuous heartbeat monitoring and transmitting a complete picture of the heart's functions to physicians. The system which uses real-time two-way wireless communication accommodates patient mobility and remote physician adjustment. BioTelemetry also manufactures and sells traditional cardiac event and Holter monitors that record patient heart rhythm data but cannot transmit the data in real time.

Operations

BioTelemetry's CardioNet MCOT services rely on the system's FDA-approved monitoring equipment wireless transmission network proprietary software and a 24-hour monitoring center. The MCOT system automatically detects rhythm irregularities and transmits the corresponding ECG (electrocardiogram) data to the monitoring center.

The company operates through three segments: patient services which provides diagnosis and monitoring services to physicians; product which manufactures and services its heart monitoring devices; and research services which provides consulting heart monitoring and data management services to companies conducting medical trials.

Sales and Marketing

The CardioNet System is marketed directly to doctors and patients throughout the US and has been used with more than 500000 patients. While Medicare reimbursements account for a more than a third of the company's revenues it also has contracts with more than 400 commercial payers. Part of BioTelemetry's strategy is to increase the number of (more lucrative) commercial payer contracts it has as compared to its government contracts.

Strategy

BioTelemetry has plans to use its technology to create instant telemetry beds (which allow patients to be continually monitored by technology) in rural hospitals step-down units or skilled nursing facilities to help cope with acute nursing shortages by reducing the number of nurses needed to oversee ECG monitoring and reduce capital equipment costs. The company also leverages acquisitions to expand its products services and geographic range.

Mergers and Acquisitions

Acquisitions have helped BioTelemetry with its expansion of products services and geographic range. The company intends to move beyond arrhythmia monitoring into new market areas such as disease management for congestive heart failure diabetes and other diseases that require outpatient or ambulatory monitoring and management.

To that end BioTelemetry bought VirtualScopics for $15.5 million in 2016. VirtualScopics provides clinical trial imaging solutions to speed up the development processes for drugs and medical devices. The deal expands BioTelemetry's clinical research offerings.

EXECUTIVES

President and CEO, Joseph H. (Joe) Capper, age 52
SVP Sales and Marketing, Andy Broadway
CFO, Heather C. Getz, age 41
Svp, George Hrenko, age 54
Auditors: Ernst & Young LLP

LOCATIONS

HQ: BioTelemetry Inc
1000 Cedar Hollow Road, Malvern, PA 19355
Phone: 610 729-7000

PRODUCTS/OPERATIONS

Selected Acquisitions
ECG Scanning & Medical Services (2012 $6 million patient monitoring services)
Biotel (2010 $11 million wireless monitoring technology & data management services)
PDSHeart (2007 $52 million monitoring services)

COMPETITORS

Criticare
Diagnostic Health
GE Healthcare
LifeWatch
Philips Healthcare
Philips Remote Cardiac Services

Spacelabs Healthcare
United Therapeutics
Welch Allyn
eResearchTechnology

HISTORICAL FINANCIALS
Company Type: Public

Income Statement
FYE: December 31

	REVENUE ($ mil.)	NET INCOME ($ mil.)	NET PROFIT MARGIN	EMPLOYEES
12/15	178.5	7.4	4.2%	938.0
12/14	166.5	(9.7)	—	922.0
12/13	129.5	(7.3)	—	622.0
12/12	111.4	(12.2)	—	728.0
12/11	119.0	(61.4)	—	665.0
Annual Growth	10.7%	—	—	9.0%

2015 Year-End Financials
Debt ratio: 19.0%
Return on equity: 10.6%
Cash ($ mil.): 18.9
Current ratio: 1.97
Long-term debt ($ mil.): 22.0
No. of shares (mil.): 27.2
Dividends
Yield: —
Payout: —
Market value ($ mil.): 319.0

	STOCK PRICE ($) FY Close	P/E High/Low	Earnings	Dividends	Book Value
12/15	11.68	62 30	0.26	0.00	2.78
12/14	10.03	— —	(0.37)	0.00	2.39
12/13	7.94	— —	(0.29)	0.00	2.59
12/12	2.28	— —	(0.49)	0.00	2.78
12/11	2.37	— —	(2.51)	0.00	3.18
Annual Growth	49.0%	— —	—	—	(3.3%)

BJ's Restaurants Inc

The Windy City inspires the food and drink at BJ's. BJ's Restaurants owns and operates 175 restaurants in California and almost 25 other mostly western states under the names BJ's Restaurant & Brewhouse BJ's Restaurant & Brewery and BJ's Pizza & Grill. The casual-dining eateries offer Chicago-style pizza salads sandwiches pasta and the company's own hand-crafted beers. Its Restaurant & Brewery locations which feature an onsite microbrewery help supply beer to the rest of the chain. The Brewhouse locations sell beer from company breweries and from third-parties using the company's recipes. The smaller Pizza & Grill shops have limited menus. The first BJ's opened in California in 1978.

Geographic Reach

The company restaurants are concentrated in California Texas and Florida.

Financial Performance

BJ's reported revenue of $919 million in for fiscal 2015. That was an increase of $74 million compared to the company's fiscal 2014 revenue. Its net income was $45 million in fiscal 2015 which was an increase of almost $18 million compared to BJ's net income the prior fiscal year.

The company ended fiscal 2015 with $127 million in cash on hand. That was an increase of more than $27 million compared to the BJ's cash levels at the end of fiscal 2014.

Strategy

More than 80% of its locations operate under the Brewhouse brand which is similar to its Brewery restaurants except they do not manufacture beer. However the company will continue to build additional Brewery locations in certain areas where it is more appropriate to brew its own beer. It also opens smaller-format BJ's Pizza and Grill locations (the company's legacy format) in densely-populated urban areas or in smaller cities where a larger location is not feasible or appropriate.

During 2015 BJ's opened a total of 16 new restaurants. The company plans to open around 20 new restaurants during fiscal 2016.

EXECUTIVES

Executive Vice President Oprs, Lon F Ledwith
Regional Vice President Operations, Christopher (Chris) Pinsak
President and CEO, Gregory A. (Greg) Trojan, age 56
EVP CFO and Secretary, Gregory S. (Greg) Levin, age 49, $350,000 total compensation
EVP and Chief Development Officer, Gregory S. (Greg) Lynds, age 55, $325,000 total compensation
EVP and Chief Restaurant Operations Officer, Wayne L. Jones, age 57, $325,000 total compensation
Chief Supply Chain Officer, John D. Allegretto, age 53, $218,500 total compensation
Area Vice President Operations, Mel (Melanie) Landuyt
Area Vice President Information technology, Eric (Ric) Berman
Regional Vice President Operations, Moe Robiglio
Vice President Of Operations Services, Ame Kuyper
Vice President, Cindy Taunton
Vice President of Restaurant Planning, Roger (Rog) Ortiz
Senior Vice President Of Brewing Operations, Alex Puchner
Vice President, Britannie Sellars
Executive Vice President Chief Mkt Officer, Kevin (Kev) Mayer
Vice President Construction, Steve Demetor
Senior Vice President Operations Service, Ame Hull
Vice President Marketing and Communications, Robert (Bob) Deliema
Sr V Pres-gen Counsel-asst Sec, Kendra (Dra) Miller
Auditors: Ernst & Young LLP

LOCATIONS

HQ: BJ's Restaurants Inc
7755 Center Avenue, Suite 300, Huntington Beach, CA 92647
Phone: 714 500-2400
Web: www.bjsrestaurants.com

PRODUCTS/OPERATIONS

Restaurant Brands
BJ's Restaurant & Brewery
BJ's Restaurant & Brewhouse
BJ's Pizza & Grill
BJ's Grill

Selected Menu Items
Shareable Appetizer
sBJ's Snacks & Small Bites
Lunch Specials
Sandwiches and Tacos
Handcrafted Burgers
Housemade Soups & Salads
Starter Salads
Garden Fresh Specialty Salads
Beverages
Handcrafted Beers
Cocktails and Wine
Pizza
Pasta favorites

COMPETITORS

Applebee's	Johnny Rockets
International	OSI Restaurant
Brinker	Partners
California Pizza	Pat & Oscars
Kitchen	Rock Bottom
Carlson Restaurants	Restaurants
Darden	Round Table Pizza
Gordon Biersch	Ruby Tuesday
Jerry's Famous Deli	Uno Restaurants

HISTORICAL FINANCIALS

Company Type: Public

Income Statement

FYE: December 29

	REVENUE ($ mil.)	NET INCOME ($ mil.)	NET PROFIT MARGIN	EMPLOYEES
12/15	919.6	45.3	4.9%	20,500.0
12/14	845.5	27.4	3.2%	18,700.0
12/13*	775.1	21.0	2.7%	18,695.0
01/13	708.3	31.4	4.4%	16,430.0
01/12	620.9	31.5	5.1%	14,360.0
Annual Growth	10.3%	9.5%	—	9.3%

*Fiscal year change

2015 Year-End Financials

Debt ratio: 14.7%
Return on equity: 13.6%
Cash ($ mil.): 34.6
Current ratio: 0.80
Long-term debt ($ mil.): 100.5

No. of shares (mil.): 24.6
Dividends
Yield: —
Payout: —
Market value ($ mil.): 1,105.0

	STOCK PRICE ($) FY Close	P/E High/Low		PER SHARE ($) Earnings	Dividends	Book Value
12/15	44.78	30	24	1.73	0.00	12.83
12/14	50.30	51	26	0.97	0.00	13.29
12/13*	31.06	54	34	0.73	0.00	14.19
01/13	32.90	48	29	1.09	0.00	13.25
01/12	44.03	49	29	1.08	0.00	11.98
Annual Growth	0.4%	—	—	12.5%	—	1.7%

*Fiscal year change

Blackbaud, Inc.

Blackboud wants to make it easy to give. The company provides financial fundraising and administrative software for not-for-profit organizations and educational institutions. Software offerings include The Raiser's Edge for fundraising management Blackbaud Enterprise CRM for customer relationship management The Financial Edge for accounting and The Education Edge for managing school admissions registration and billing. Blackbaud has about 35000 customers in more than 60 countries including colleges environmental groups health and human services providers churches and animal welfare groups. The company generates most of its sales in the US.

Operations

Blackbaud generates 52% of its revenue from subscriptions to its cloud-based services to which the company has transitioned over the past few years. Maintenance and services revenue account for 24% and 21% respectively. Licensing and fee revenue for its on-premise software packages generated just 3% of revenue in 2015 and that was down 23% from 2014.

Geographic Reach

The US is its largest market accounting for 89% of sales. Canada and Europe each account for 4% of sales while the Australia generates 3%. Blackbaud has roughly 10 offices spanning the US and a handful of international offices in Australia Canada the Netherlands New Zealand and the UK.

Sales and Marketing

Blackbaud sells into three markets. The General Markets Business is the biggest generating 49% of revenue. It focuses on marketing sales delivery and support to emerging and mid-sized prospects and customers in North America.

The Enterprise Customer Business unit sells to and works wit large and strategic prospects and customers in North America. It accounts for 44% of sales.

The self-explanatory International Business unit delivered 7% of sales.

Financial PerformanceBlackbaud has experienced strong revenue growth over the past decade with 2015 sales up 13% to reach $638 million. Subscriptions for its cloud-based software offerings rose 26%. The company also had double digit growth in its general markets and enterprise businesses. International sales fell 11%.

Increased spending on sales and marketing reduced profit 9% to $25.6 million in 2015 from 2014. It was the second straight year of declining profit as Blackbaud invests in sales and marketing to drive customers to its cloud products and increase market share.

Cash flow from operations rose to $114 million in 2015 from $102 million in 2014.

Strategy

Blackbaud is looking to expand its product offerings for the Internet. Online donations account for a growing percentage of charitable donations and marketing membership newsletters event management and volunteer recruitment can often be done over the Internet at a lower cost and a higher success rate. Its Sphere eMarketing Suite which facilitates online giving can be integrated into its most popular product The Raiser's Edge.

The latest product Blackbaud SKY is part of the company's cloud strategy. It combines infrastructure processes and integrated services (payments analytics email and online donations) to help customers achieve their goals.

The company's strategy also includes expanding geographically. Over the years it has established a Hong Kong office and a Mexico City office which joined other international offices in Canada the UK and Australia.

Mergers and Acquisitions

In 2015 Blackbaud completed the acquisition of Smart a provider of payment software and services for private schools and parents. With Smart Tuition the company expanded their offerings in the K-12 market. The prices was $187.8 million in cash. Smart Tuition operates as a wholly-owned subsidiary.

EXECUTIVES

EVP and President General Markets, Kevin W. Mooney, age 58, $412,274 total compensation
EVP Human Resources, John J. Mistretta, age 61
CTO, Mary Beth Westmoreland
SVP and Chief Scientist, Charles L. (Chuck) Longfield, age 59, $226,667 total compensation
EVP Finance and Administration and CFO, Anthony W. (Tony) Boor, age 53, $434,567 total compensation
President and CEO, Michael P. (Mike) Gianoni, age 55, $613,506 total compensation
President and General Manager everydayhero, Jerry Needel
EVP and President Enterprise Business, Brian E. Boruff, age 56, $272,023 total compensation
EVP Corporate and Product Strategy, Charles T. (Charlie) Cumbaa, age 63, $393,666 total compensation
SVP Business Operations, Stephen Halleck
EVP Research Delivery and Operations, Kevin McDearis
President Higher Education Solutions Group, Tim Hill
President Healthcare Solutions Group, Russ Cobb
CIO, Todd Lant
Senior Vice President Products and Marketing, Jana Eggers
Vice President Customer Support, Dorie Wallace
Vice President Data Management Services, Wendy Fox
Vice President And Corporate Controller, Chad Anderson
Vice President Sales, Kathy (Kat) Gallagher
Vice President Sales, Christopher (Chris) Todd
Executive Vice President Of Information Technology, Jessica Bobbitt
Vice President of Customer Strategy, Tiffany (Tiff) Getch
Chairman, Andrew M. Leitch, age 72
Treasurer, Mary Donnellon
Secretary, Rebecca White
Corporate Treasurer, Tom Griffin
Auditors: PRICEWATERHOUSECOOPERS LLP

LOCATIONS

HQ: Blackbaud, Inc.
2000 Daniel Island Drive, Charleston, SC 29492
Phone: 843 216-6200   **Fax:** 843 216-6100
Web: www.blackbaud.com

PRODUCTS/OPERATIONS

2015 Sales

	$ mil.	% of total
General Markets Business Unit (GMBU)	313.9	49
Enterprise Customer Business Unit (ECBU)	279.9	44
International Business Unit (IBU)	42.0	7
Other	2.1	-
Total	**637.9**	**100**

2015 Sales

	$ mil.	% of total
Subscriptions	331.8	52
Maintenance	153.8	24
Services	132.9	21
Licenses	19.4	3
Total	**637.9**	**100**

Selected Products

Accounting software
  Blackbaud Forms (wealth identification)
  The Financial Edge (not-for-profit accounting)
Analytical services
  Prospect Management (prospect management and
  research)
  Wealth & Affluence Indicators (wealth identification
  and information)
Business intelligence software
  Altru (general admissions management)
  The Patron Edge (ticketing management for
  admissions)
Customer relationship management
  Blackbaud Enterprise CRM
  eTapestry
Education administration software
  The Education Edge (admissions registrar business
  office and development office software)
  Small Colleges (suite for colleges under 300 students)
  Student Billing
  Total Campus Solution (suite for colleges under 2000
  students)
Fundraising management software
  The Raiser's Edge (fundraising management system)

COMPETITORS

Acorn Systems	Microsoft
Advanced Solutions	Oracle
Auctionpay	Sage Software
Campus Management Corp	SunGard
Intuit	salesforce.com
MicroEdge	

HISTORICAL FINANCIALS
Company Type: Public

Income Statement   FYE: December 31

	REVENUE ($ mil.)	NET INCOME ($ mil.)	NET PROFIT MARGIN	EMPLOYEES
12/15	637.9	25.6	4.0%	3,095.0
12/14	564.4	28.2	5.0%	3,033.0
12/13	503.8	30.4	6.0%	2,666.0
12/12	447.4	6.5	1.5%	2,705.0
12/11	370.8	33.2	9.0%	2,256.0
Annual Growth	14.5%	(6.3%)	—	8.2%

2015 Year-End Financials

Debt ratio: 33.3%	No. of shares (mil.): 46.9
Return on equity: 12.9%	Dividends
Cash ($ mil.): 15.3	Yield: 0.7%
Current ratio: 0.70	Payout: 92.3%
Long-term debt ($ mil.): 404.2	Market value ($ mil.): 3,093.0

	STOCK PRICE ($) FY Close	P/E High/Low	PER SHARE ($) Earnings	Dividends	Book Value
12/15	65.86	121 75	0.55	0.48	4.48
12/14	43.26	72 47	0.62	0.48	4.01
12/13	37.65	62 34	0.67	0.48	3.50
12/12	22.83	226141	0.15	0.48	3.24
12/11	27.70	40 28	0.75	0.48	3.12
Annual Growth	24.2%	— —	(7.5%)	(0.0%)	9.5%

Blackhawk Network Holdings Inc

When choosing a gift green always fits. But how about plastic? Blackhawk Network sells gift phone sports ticket prepaid debit and prepaid wireless phone cards through a network of more than 195000 retailers around the world. The cards can be found in convenience drug grocery and specialty stores including Chevron Food Lion Kroger and Safeway (Blackhawk's founder). Blackhawk offers more than 600 brands of cards from companies such as Apple Barnes & Noble iTunes Starbucks Visa and the NBA. The cards can be found online or at Gift Card Mall racks which display hundreds of cards that can be redeemed online or on-site at retail locations. Grocer Safeway took Blackhawk public in 2013.

Operations

Prepaid cards account for more than 90% of the sales. The company's Blackhawk Incentives Group (BIG) caters to corporations that provide reward cards or other types of gift cards to its employees or customers. BIG handles the delivery and activation of millions of these types of cards each month.

Geographic Reach

The US accounts for about 80% of California-based Blackhawk's business. The company is extending its international presence with new office openings staff appointments and retail partnerships. Beyond the US the company has offices in Canada Australia France Germany Japan and the UK.

Sales and Marketing

Blackhawk Network's retail distribution network includes nine of the top 10 and 90% of all grocery locations operated by the top 50 convential grocery retailers in the US. As of early 2015 the company also sold its products through 150000 active retail distribution locations outside of the US spanning 290 partners. Its two largest clients are tech-company Apple and Kroger which each contributed nearly 15% to total revenue in 2014. Meanwhile Giant Eagle and Safeway contributed another 7% and 9% to overall revenue respectively. The company spent $189.4 million on sales and marketing expenses in 2014 representing about 13% of its total operating revenue. That's up from $150.52 million spent in 2013 and $120.98 million spent in 2012.

Financial Performance

The young company has enjoyed healthy revenue and profit growth over the past several years as the popularity of prepaid cards continues to rise. Revenue in 2014 jumped 27% to a record $1.44 billion thanks to higher prepaid card sales through its retail distribution channel as its retail network expanded and as existing retailers sold more cards. Additionally the company's incentive product sales grew thanks to its recent acquisitions of InteliSpend (2013) and Parago (2014). Its online and digitial distribution channels also enjoyed growth. Despite higher revenue in 2014 profit reversed course with net income falling by 16% to $45.55 million. This was mostly because the company paid nearly $16.5 million more toward amortization expenses for intangible assets related to company's acquisitions of Parago CardLab and Incentec. Cash levels spiked to $286.3 million in 2014 mostly because of the timing of received and outgoing payments. Due to the timing of December holiday sales cash outflows to the company's content providers and inflows from retail distribution partners can vary wildly which can cause cash levels to fluctuate from year to year.

Strategy

Blackhawk Network has been pursuing partnerships to position itself for more growth overseas. In 2014 its German-based subsidiary Retailo (acquired in late 2013) partnered with Deutsche Kreditbank AG to allow customers to purchase Blackhawk prepaid cards using their online bank accounts. It also made similar deals that year with T-Mobile for the telecom company's own prepaid card and leading UK bank Barclays Bank so the bank customers could use "eGifts" for use with the bank's Pingit mobile banking service. In 2013 Blackhawk partnered with Opengate to launch new prepaid content in South Africa. The company has also pursued strategic acquisitions to fortify its incentive and engagement offerings for its clients. In 2014 for example after having recently acquired Parago Intelispend CardLab and Incentec Solutions the company was able to launch its new Blackhawk Engagement Solutions divisions to provide customized engagement incentive and rebate programs for consumers employees and sales channels. In 2013 it officially moved into the business prepaid space with its purchase of InteliSpend.Blackhawk has also been expanding its localization initiatives to deliver a customized mix of prepaid products tailored to individual markets such as local restaurants merchants and service providers.

Mergers and Acquisitions

In a move to expand its global operations the company acquired employee loyalty specialist Grass Roots Group in mid-2016.

In 2014 Blackhawk Network purchased Parago Inc a leader in global incentive and engagement solutions for $262.3 million. The deal effectively expanded the company's expertise and capabilities in the consumer and corporate incentives markets.Also in 2014 the company bought Card-Lab Inc. an online provider of customizable prepaid incentive and rewards cards along with Incentec Solutions Inc. a provider of cloud-based software platforms in the incentive and reward industry. The total cost of both acquisitions amounted to $33.7 million and enhanced Blackhawk's product and service offerings in their incentives business.In December 2013 Blackhawk Network acquired Germany's Retailo AG a privately-held third-party gift card distributor that operates in Germany Austria and Switzerland for €51.7 million ($71.2 million) thereby expanding its reach into Germany. In November 2013 Blackhawk bought InteliSpend Prepaid Solutions LLC from Maritz Holdings for $97.4 million. InteliSpend distributes prepaid products through businesses for their awards incentives and loyalty programs. Missouri-based InteliSpend operates as a business unit of Blackhawk and remains based in Missouri.

Company Background

In April 2013 with a majority stake in the company grocery giant Safeway took subsidiary Blackhawk Network public in an offering valued at $230 million. Existing shareholders including Safeway were the sellers. Post IPO Safeway maintained majority ownership of Blackhawk. However Safeway which has agreed to be acquired by Albertson's spun off the rest of Blackhawk stock as part of a special dividend to its shareholders in April 2014 making Blackhawk a 100% publicly traded company.In 2011 Blackhawk acquired San Francisco-based Cardpool which operates a gift card exchange marketplace to provide a solution to those unwanted cards lying about in desk drawers wallets and pocketbooks. Terms of the deal were not disclosed.

EXECUTIVES

Chairman and Head of International, William Y.
  Tauscher, age 66, $819,292 total compensation
CFO and Chief Administrative Officer, Jerry N.
  Ulrich, age 61, $443,269 total compensation
President, Talbott Roche, age 49, $636,538 total
  compensation
Chief Security Officer, Henry Ivey

SVP and CTO, Sachin Dhawan
Vice President Corporate Controller, Joan Lockie
Group Vice President Strategy And Innovation,
 Tim Attinger
Vice President Of Sales, Jayson Berg
Vice President Technology And Operations
 Asiapac, Scott (Scotty) Shields
Auditors: Deloitte & Touche LLP

LOCATIONS

HQ: Blackhawk Network Holdings Inc
 6220 Stoneridge Mall Road, Pleasanton, CA 94588
Phone: 925 226-9990
Web: www.blackhawknetwork.com

PRODUCTS/OPERATIONS

2014 Sales

	$ mil.	% of total
Commission and fees	1,107.8	77
Program interchange marketing and other fees	220.3	15
Product sales	116.9	8
Total	**1,445.0**	**100**

2014 Sales

	% of total
Retail	88
Incentives	5
Others	7
Total	**100**

2014 Sales

	% of total
US Retail and Incentives & Rewards	77
International Retail	23
Total	**100**

Selected Products and Services

Corporate incentive program
Gift card mall (instore displays carrying hundreds of
 premium brand gift cards)
Prepaid long-distance cards
Prepaid wireless phones
Reloadable debit cards from Visa and MasterCard
Retail gift cards
Sports cards from major leagues and teams
Ticket cards for theme parks ski resorts and more

COMPETITORS

American Express	NetSpend
Citi Prepaid Services	Outerwall
Comdata	Wal-Mart
Euronet	Western Union
Green Dot	nFinanSe
MoneyGram	
International	

HISTORICAL FINANCIALS

Company Type: Public

Income Statement

FYE: January 2

	REVENUE ($ mil.)	NET INCOME ($ mil.)	NET PROFIT MARGIN	EMPLOYEES
01/16	1,801.0	45.6	2.5%	2,331.0
01/15*	1,444.9	45.5	3.2%	1,860.0
12/13	1,138.0	54.1	4.8%	1,316.0
12/12	959.0	48.1	5.0%	725.0
12/11	751.8	36.5	4.9%	0.0
Annual Growth	**24.4%**	**5.7%**	**—**	**—**

*Fiscal year change

2016 Year-End Financials

Debt ratio: 10.4%
Return on equity: 9.0%
Cash ($ mil.): 914.5
Current ratio: 0.93
Long-term debt ($ mil.): 324.4

No. of shares (mil.): 55.7
Dividends
 Yield: —
 Payout: 0.1%
Market value ($ mil.): 2,467.0

	STOCK PRICE ($) FY Close	P/E High/Low	PER SHARE ($) Earnings	Dividends	Book Value
01/16	44.21	57 40	0.81	0.00	13.08
01/15*	37.01	47 26	0.83	0.00	5.25
12/13	25.66	26 20	1.02	0.00	4.22
Annual Growth	**31.3%**	**—**	**—(10.9%)**	**—**	**76.1%**

*Fiscal year change

Blackstone Mortgage Trust Inc

Capital Trust thinks investing in commercial mortgages is a capital idea. The self-managed real estate investment trust (REIT) originates under-writes and invests in commercial real estate assets on its own behalf and for other investors. Its portfolio includes first mortgage and bridge loans mezzanine loans and collateralized mortgage-backed securities. Subsidiary CT Investment Management which the company is selling manages five private equity funds and a separate account for third parties. Most Capital Trust's assets are related to US properties but the REIT does make occasional investments in international instruments.

In the aftermath of the subprime mortgage crisis wherein the credit markets slowed and property values fell Capital Trust cut back on its own origination and investment activities. In 2011 the REIT restructured its recourse debt obligations a move that included the transfer of a substantial portion of its assets to a newly formed subsidiary CT Legacy REIT. Investment firm Five Mile Capital Partners acquired nearly a quarter of the unit and ownership of almost another quarter was transferred to lenders; Capital Trust holds a majority. In 2012 Capital Trust agreed to sell CT Investment Management to Blackstone for $20 million; Blackstone will also purchase an 18% stake in Capital Trust.

Co-founder John Klopp retired as the company's CEO in late 2009. He was succeeded by longtime COO Stephen Plavin. Billionaire property mogul Samuel Zell has served as the company's chairman since 1997. He serves in the same capacity at several other firms as well including Equity Group Investments Equity LifeStyle Properties and Equity Residential.

W. R. Berkley a holding company involved mainly in insurance owns around 17% of Capital Trust.

EXECUTIVES

Managing Director Euromena Fund, Romen Mathieu
Vice President, Robert (Bob) Holder
Auditors: Deloitte & Touche LLP

LOCATIONS

HQ: Blackstone Mortgage Trust Inc
 345 Park Avenue, 42nd Floor, New York, NY 10154
Phone: 212 655-0220
Web: www.bxmt.com

COMPETITORS

Annaly Capital	MFA Financial
Management	Newcastle Investment
Arbor Realty Trust	RAIT Financial Trust
Institutional	Redwood Trust
Financial Markets	iStar Financial Inc

HISTORICAL FINANCIALS

Company Type: Public

Income Statement

FYE: December 31

	REVENUE ($ mil.)	NET INCOME ($ mil.)	NET PROFIT MARGIN	EMPLOYEES
12/15	410.6	196.8	47.9%	0.0
12/14	184.7	90.0	48.7%	0.0
12/13	53.1	15.0	28.3%	0.0
12/12	34.9	181.0	518.1%	0.0
12/11	132.2	258.1	195.2%	29.0
Annual Growth	**32.7%**	**(6.6%)**	**—**	**—**

2015 Year-End Financials

Debt ratio: 66.9%
Return on equity: 9.9%
Cash ($ mil.): 96.4
Current ratio: 1.54
Long-term debt ($ mil.): 6,280.1

No. of shares (mil.): 93.7
Dividends
 Yield: 8.5%
 Payout: 112.8%
Market value ($ mil.): 2,507.0

	STOCK PRICE ($) FY Close	P/E High/Low	PER SHARE ($) Earnings	Dividends	Book Value
12/15	26.76	13 11	2.41	2.28	26.60
12/14	29.14	16 14	1.86	1.98	25.15
12/13	27.13	4 0	8.10	0.72	24.33
12/12	2.10	0 0	73.10	20.00	25.09
12/11	2.25	0 0	107.80	0.00	(49.72)
Annual Growth	**85.7%**	**—**	**—(61.3%)**	**—**	**—**

Blue Buffalo Pet Products Inc

Auditors: KPMG LLP

LOCATIONS

HQ: Blue Buffalo Pet Products Inc
 11 River Road, Wilton, CT 06897
Phone: 203 762-9751
Web: www.bluebuffalo.com

HISTORICAL FINANCIALS

Company Type: Public

Income Statement

FYE: December 31

	REVENUE ($ mil.)	NET INCOME ($ mil.)	NET PROFIT MARGIN	EMPLOYEES
12/15	1,027.4	89.3	8.7%	1,900.0
12/14	917.7	101.9	11.1%	1,700.0
12/13	719.5	78.2	10.9%	0.0
12/12	523.0	65.5	12.5%	0.0
Annual Growth	**25.2%**	**10.9%**		

2015 Year-End Financials

Debt ratio: 75.6%
Return on equity: —
Cash ($ mil.): 224.2
Current ratio: 3.71
Long-term debt ($ mil.): 383.1

No. of shares (mil.): 196.2
Dividends
  Yield: —
  Payout: —
Market value ($ mil.): 3,671.0

	STOCK PRICE ($) FY Close	P/E High/Low	PER SHARE ($) Earnings	Dividends	Book Value
12/15	18.71	62 37	0.45	0.00	0.05
12/14	0.00	— —	0.52	0.00	(0.45)
Annual Growth	—	— —(13.5%)	—	—

Blue Hills Bancorp Inc

Auditors: Wolf & Company, P.C.

LOCATIONS

HQ: Blue Hills Bancorp Inc
  320 Norwood Park South, Norwood, MA 02062
Phone: 617 361-6900
Web: www.bluehillsbancorp.com

HISTORICAL FINANCIALS

Company Type: Public

Income Statement

FYE: December 31

	ASSETS ($ mil.)	NET INCOME ($ mil.)	INCOME AS % OF ASSETS	EMPLOYEES
12/15	2,114.3	7.2	0.3%	209.0
12/14	1,728.1	(0.1)	—	202.0
12/13	1,314.2	2.6	0.2%	147.0
12/12	1,228.6	7.8	0.6%	0.0
12/11	0.0	7.5	—	0.0
Annual Growth	—	(1.1%)	—	—

2015 Year-End Financials

Return on assets: 0.3%
Return on equity: 1.7%
Long-term debt ($ mil.): —
No. of shares (mil.): 28.4
Sales ($ mil): 66.9

Dividends
  Yield: 0.2%
  Payout: 14.2%
Market value ($ mil.): 436.0

	STOCK PRICE ($) FY Close	P/E High/Low	PER SHARE ($) Earnings	Dividends	Book Value
12/15	15.31	59 46	0.28	0.04	14.00
12/14	13.58	— —	(0.00)	0.00	14.46
Annual Growth	12.7%	— —	—	—	(3.2%)

BNC Bancorp

BNC Bancorp knows the ABCs of the financial world. The firm is the holding company for Bank of North Carolina which boasts more than 55 branches mostly across North and South Carolina but also in Virginia. In addition to offering traditional loan and deposit products (including checking savings and money market accounts credit cards and certificates of deposits) for local business and retail customers BNC also offers wealth management retirement planning and brokerage services and insurance products. Nearly 40% of its loans are commercial real estate loans while residential mortgages make up another 15%. Founded in 1991 the bank now has more than $5 billion in total assets.

OperationsBNC Bancorp generated 76% of its revenue from loan interest in 2014 and another 10% from interest on its tax-exempt and taxable securities. About 4% of revenue came from mortgage fees while another 4% came from service charges on accounts. The bank staffed 823 full-time employees at the end of 2014.Geographic ReachAbout 60% of Thomasville-based BNC Bancorp's 57 branches are located in North Carolina while more than 20% are in South Carolina. The rest of its branches are located in Virginia.Sales and MarketingThe bank serves individuals and small to medium-sized local businesses.Financial PerformanceBNC Bancorp's revenues and profits have been growing at a healthy clip thanks mostly to new loan business from acquisitions and declining loan loss provisions as its loan portfolio's credit quality has improved with the strengthened economy. The company's revenue jumped by 13% to a record $183.2 million in 2014 as it boosted its loan assets by one-third after its three bank acquisitions made during the year. Its non-interest income also grew by nearly double digits thanks to higher fee income on newly acquired deposit accounts. Higher revenue lower interest expense on deposits and a continued decline in loan loss provisions in 2014 drove BNC Bancorp's net income higher by 70% to $29.4 million. The company's operating cash levels fell by 75% to $40.5 million for the year after adjusting its earnings for non-cash income sources.StrategyBNC Bancorp has made a string of acquisitions in recent years to grow its loan business and branch network. Its 2014 acquisitions added nearly $770 million in new loan business (boosting BNC's total loan assets by 33% in one year) while its 2015 acquisitions of Valley Financial Corporation and seven branches of CertusBank alone added almost $840 million in new loan assets. Additionally its Valley Financial acquisition extended the bank's reach into Virginia for the first time.Mergers and AcquisitionsIn July 2015 BNC Bancorp entered Virginia for the first time after acquiring Valley Financial Corporation which added $854 million in assets $628 million in new loan business and nine branches in Roanoke and Salem Virginia. In June 2015 the company agreed to buy seven branch offices in South Carolina from CertusBank which also included $284 million in deposits and $210 million in loans. In December 2014 BNC Bancorp furthered its reach into South Carolina after purchasing Harbor National Bank including the commercial bank's four branches in the Charleston and Mt. Pleasant. The deal also added some $325 million in total assets and $281 million worth of new loan business. In June 2014 the company bought Community First Financial Group along with its $165.4 million in loan assets and three Harrington Bank branches based in the Raleigh-Durham-Chapel Hill area of North Carolina. In April 2014 BNC acquired South Street Financial and its four Home Savings Bank branches in Charlotte North Carolina. The deal added $278 million in total assets and $195 million in new loan business.In November 2012 BNC Bancorp purchased First Trust Bank and its three branches in the Charlotte area for some $35 million. Its 2012 acquisitions of Regent Bank and single-branch KeySource Financial further extended the bank's reach in the state.

Company Background
In 2010 the company acquired the failed Beach First National Bank in an FDIC-facilitated transaction expanding Bank of North Carolina's branch network into South Carolina. BNC Bancorp acquired another failed bank in 2011 with assistance from the FDIC Blue Ridge Savings Bank in North Carolina.

EXECUTIVES

President CEO and Director; President and CEO Bank of North Carolina, W. Swope Montgomery, age 67, $345,200 total compensation
EVP COO and Director; EVP and COO Bank of North Carolina, Richard D. Callicutt, age 57, $268,650 total compensation
EVP and CFO BNC and Bank of North Carolina, David B. Spencer, age 53, $251,200 total compensation
Vice President Special Assets, Danny (Dan) Broach
Vice President Special Assets, Lance Miller
Assistant Vice President Branch Manager, Lucy (Lucia) Ortiz
Vice President, Ann Walker
Vice President, Daren Fuller
Senior Vice President City Executive, John (Jack) Bencini
Senior Vice President Business Banking, Jimmie Bowman
Assistant Vice President Assistant Operations Manager, Diane (Di) Anderson
Senior Vice President, Ginny (Gin) Smith
Vice President Commercial Relationship Manager, Chase Allen
Vice President Commercial Relationship Manager, Mark (Marky) Crum
Chairman Emeritus, W. Groome Fulton, age 77
Chairman of the Board, Thomas R. Sloan, age 71
Auditors: Cherry Bekaert LLP

LOCATIONS

HQ: BNC Bancorp
  3980 Premier Drive, Suite 210, High Point, NC 27265
Phone: 336 476-9200
Web: www.bankofnc.com

PRODUCTS/OPERATIONS

2014 Sales

	$ mil.	% of total
Interest		
Loans including fees	140.0	76
Debt securities	17.6	10
Other	0.5	-
Noninterest		
Mortgage fees	7.8	4
Service charges	6.1	4
Other	11.2	6
Total	**183.2**	**100**

COMPETITORS

BB&T	NewBridge Bancorp
Bank of America	Piedmont Federal
Carolina Bank	Southern Community
CommunityOne Bancorp	Financial
First Bancorp (NC)	Wells Fargo
First Citizens BancShares	

HISTORICAL FINANCIALS

Company Type: Public

Income Statement

FYE: December 31

	ASSETS ($ mil.)	NET INCOME ($ mil.)	INCOME AS % OF ASSETS	EMPLOYEES
12/15	5,668.1	44.4	0.8%	850.0
12/14	4,072.5	29.3	0.7%	823.0
12/13	3,229.5	17.2	0.5%	620.0
12/12	3,083.7	10.4	0.3%	564.0
12/11	2,454.9	6.9	0.3%	455.0
Annual Growth	23.3%	59.1%	—	16.9%

2015 Year-End Financials

Return on assets: 0.9%
Return on equity: 9.0%
Long-term debt ($ mil.): —
No. of shares (mil.): 40.7
Sales ($ mil): 230.9

Dividends
Yield: 0.7%
Payout: 16.1%
Market value ($ mil.): 1,035.0

	STOCK PRICE ($) FY Close	P/E High/Low	PER SHARE ($) Earnings	Dividends	Book Value
12/15	25.38	21 13	1.24	0.20	14.52
12/14	17.21	19 15	1.01	0.20	11.98
12/13	17.14	28 13	0.61	0.20	9.94
12/12	8.01	18 14	0.48	0.20	11.45
12/11	7.25	20 14	0.45	0.20	18.00
Annual Growth	36.8%	— —	28.8%	(0.0%)	(5.2%)

BofI Holding, Inc.

BofI Holding owns Bank of Internet USA a savings bank that operates online in all 50 states. The bank offers checking savings and money market accounts CDs and ATM and check cards. Multifamily real estate loans account for nearly two-thirds of the company's loan portfolio although the bank only offers them in selected states; it also acquires them on the secondary market. Offered nationwide single-family residential mortgages make up nearly 30% of its loan portfolio. Bank of Internet USA also issues home equity automobile and recreational vehicle loans. Officers and directors own more than 30% of BofI Holding's stock.

EXECUTIVES

EVP and CFO BofI Holding Inc. and BofI Federal Bank, Andrew J. Micheletti, age 59, $231,000 total compensation

President and CEO BofI Holding Inc. and BofI Federal Bank, Gregory Garrabrants, age 45, $375,000 total compensation

EVP Specialty Finance and Chief Legal Officer BofI Federal Bank, Eshel Bar-Adon, age 61, $250,000 total compensation

EVP and Chief Credit Officer BofI Federal Bank, Thomas Constantine, age 54, $235,000 total compensation

EVP and Chief Lending Officer BofI Federal Bank, Brian Swanson, age 36, $235,000 total compensation

EVP Chief of Staff and Chief Performance Officer BofI Federal Bank, Jan Durrans

EVP Chief Deposit Officer and Chief Marketing Officer BofI Federal Bank, Eduardo Urdapilleta

Vice President CONTROLLER, Pete Bauer

Executive Vice President, Adriaan V Zyl

Senior Vice President, Lisa (Lis) Collett

Senior Vice President Deposit Operations, Lorena Mcwilliams

Chairman, Paul J. Grinberg, age 55

Vice Chairman, Nicholas A. Mosich

Auditors: BDO USA, LLP

LOCATIONS

HQ: BofI Holding, Inc.
4350 La Jolla Village Drive, Suite 140, San Diego, CA 92122
Phone: 858 350-6200
Web: www.bofiholding.com

PRODUCTS/OPERATIONS

2016 Sales

	$ mil.	% of total
Interest and dividend income		
Loans and leases including fees	291.1	76
Investments	26.6	7
Non-interest income		
Banking service fees and other income	36.2	9
Other	30.1	8
Total	**384.0**	**100**

COMPETITORS

Bank of America	ISN Bank
Citigroup	MUFG Americas Holdings
E*TRADE Bank	Steel Partners
First IB	Holdings

HISTORICAL FINANCIALS

Company Type: Public

Income Statement

FYE: June 30

	ASSETS ($ mil.)	NET INCOME ($ mil.)	INCOME AS % OF ASSETS	EMPLOYEES
06/16	7,601.3	119.2	1.6%	647.0
06/15	5,823.7	82.6	1.4%	467.0
06/14	4,403.0	55.9	1.3%	366.0
06/13	3,090.7	40.2	1.3%	312.0
06/12	2,386.8	29.4	1.2%	230.0
Annual Growth	33.6%	41.8%		29.5%

2016 Year-End Financials

Return on assets: 1.7%
Return on equity: 19.5%
Long-term debt ($ mil.): —
No. of shares (mil.): 63.2
Sales ($ mil): 384.0

Dividends
Yield: —
Payout: —
Market value ($ mil.): 1,120.0

	STOCK PRICE ($) FY Close	P/E High/Low	PER SHARE ($) Earnings	Dividends	Book Value
06/16	17.71	77 7	1.85	0.00	10.81
06/15	105.71	79 49	1.34	0.00	8.59
06/14	73.47	109 48	0.96	0.00	6.41
06/13	45.82	65 26	0.72	0.00	4.88
06/12	19.76	32 20	0.58	0.00	4.49
Annual Growth	(2.7%)	— —	33.5%	—	24.6%

Boot Barn Holdings Inc

Auditors: Deloitte & Touche LLP

LOCATIONS

HQ: Boot Barn Holdings Inc
15345 Barranca Pkwy., Irvine, CA 92618
Phone: 949 453-4400
Web: www.bootbarn.com

HISTORICAL FINANCIALS

Company Type: Public

Income Statement

FYE: March 26

	REVENUE ($ mil.)	NET INCOME ($ mil.)	NET PROFIT MARGIN	EMPLOYEES
03/16	569.0	9.8	1.7%	2,900.0
03/15	402.6	13.7	3.4%	1,700.0
03/14	345.8	5.3	1.6%	1,800.0
03/13	233.2	0.6	0.3%	0.0
03/12	58.2	(4.3)	—	0.0
Annual Growth	76.8%			

2016 Year-End Financials

Debt ratio: 47.2%
Return on equity: 6.5%
Cash ($ mil.): 7.2
Current ratio: 1.33
Long-term debt ($ mil.): 204.8

No. of shares (mil.): 26.3
Dividends
Yield: —
Payout: —
Market value ($ mil.): 246.0

	STOCK PRICE ($) FY Close	P/E High/Low	PER SHARE ($) Earnings	Dividends	Book Value
03/16	9.34	89 15	0.37	0.00	6.13
03/15	23.21	46 30	0.54	0.00	5.51
Annual Growth	(59.8%)	— —	(31.5%)	—	11.1%

Boston Beer Co Inc (The)

A half-pint compared to megabrewers like the world's #1 beer maker Anheuser-Bush InBev The Boston Beer Company holds a distinction all its own –it is the US's largest craft brewer. The company produces more than 50 seasonal and year-round varieties of craft beers at breweries in Boston and four other states. Annually it sells around 4.2 million barrels of lagers and ales (including its flagship Samuel Adams Boston Lager and other Sam Adams brand beers) and Twisted Tea malt beverages. it also brews beer for third parties. Founded in 1984 by its chairman James Koch The Boston Beer Company has grown along with America's increasing thirst for better beer.Geographic ReachIn addition to Boston The Boston Beer Company owns breweries in Breinigsville Cincinnati Breinigsville Pennsylvania and Los Angeles. The company distributes its brews primarily in the US but they are also sold in Canada the Caribbean Europe Israel Mexico and the Pacific Rim.OperationsBeyond beer the company makes 12 flavored malt beverages under the Twisted Tea brand name and 10 hard ciders under the Angry Orchard brand. The Boston Beer Company's A&S Brewing Collaborative (dba Alchemy & Science) subsidiary makes 40 beers under four brand names. A&S recently formed House of Shandy (since renamed Traveler Beer Co.) which brews shandy style beers (beer mixed with citrus flavored soda carbonated lemonade ginger beer or cider).In addition to production at its own breweries the company contracts some of its production to brewers among them Wisconsin-based City Brewing Company and New York-based Pleasant Valley Wine.Sales and MarketingThe Boston-based brewer distributes its products through a network of some 340 wholesale distributors who in turn sell its beverages to retailers including pubs restaurants food and liquor stores and stadiums. Boston Beer employs a sales force of approximately 420 people. The company's media campaigns include TV radio billboards and print. The brewer complements is media buying by sponsoring cultural and community events local beer festivals industry-related trade shows and promotional events at local establishments. Boston Beer reported spending on advertising and promotions of $120 million in 2015 and $100 million in 2015. Financial PerformanceBoston Beer Company achieved record-setting revenues in 2015 with sales reaching almost $960 million. Profits reached a milestone peaking at $98 million during 2015. Cash flow from operations has also trended upwards the last five years jumping 19% in 2015. The historic growth for 2015 was fueled by increased shipments and increased revenue per barrel due primarily to price spikes and changes in product and package mix due to a shift in the mix from bottles and cans. Shipment volume for core brands also climbed by 4% due primarily to increases in shipments of Coney Island Twisted Tea Angry Orchard and Traveler brand products that were partially offset by shipment declines in Samuel Adams brand products.StrategyThe domestic beer industry is dominated by two major brewers Anheuser-Busch InBev and MillerCoors which together account for more than 85% of all US domestic beer production (excluding exports). Boston Beer —along with a growing number of craft brewers —competes in the Better Beer (as opposed to mass-produced) category.However in order to growth further the beer giants have begun developing their own specialty beers and acquiring craft brewers to compete in this small growth market. To keep adventurous drinkers brand-loyal Boston Beer follows a strategy of frequently offering new beverages and discontinuing others. During 2015 the company launched specialty variety six-packs under the Samuel Adams Rebel Rider IPA Samuel Adams Grapefruit IPA and Samual Adams Rebel Raw names.

Company Background

Management consultant James Koch started The Boston Beer Company with his former secretary Rhonda Kallman in 1983. With Koch's $100000 in life savings plus $300000 raised from family and friends the company contracted with Pittsburgh Brewing to make beer using Koch's great-great-grandfather's recipe. (Louis Koch had brewed beer in Germany before opening a St. Louis brewery in 1860.)

EXECUTIVES

VP Brewing, David A. Grinnell, age 58
President CEO and Director, Martin F. Roper, age 53, $783,000 total compensation
CFO and Treasurer, Frank H. Smalla, age 50
Vice President Operations, Thomas (Thom) Lance
Vice President Information Technology, Paul (Pauly) Moss
National Account Manager, Nicole Monsen
Chairman, C. James (Jim) Koch, age 66
Auditors: Ernst & Young LLP

LOCATIONS

HQ: Boston Beer Co Inc (The)
One Design Center Place, Suite 850, Boston, MA 02210
Phone: 617 368-5000   **Fax:** 617 368-5500
Web: www.bostonbeer.com

PRODUCTS/OPERATIONS

Selected Brands and Year Introduced
Barrel Room Collection
   Samuel Adams American Kriek 2009
   Samuel Adams New World Tripel 2009
   Samuel Adams Stony Brook Red 2009
   Samuel Adams Thirteenth Hour 2011
Brewmaster's Collection
   Samuel Adams Black Lager 2005
   Samuel Adams Blackberry Witbier 2009
   Samuel Adams Boston Ale 1987
   Samuel Adams Cherry Wheat 1995
   Samuel Adams Coastal Wheat 2009
   Samuel Adams Cranberry Lambic 1990
   Samuel Adams Cream Stout 1993
   Samuel Adams Irish Red 2008
   Samuel Adams Latitude 48 IPA 2010
   Samuel Adams Pale Ale 1999
Core Focus Beers
   Samuel Adams Boston Lager 1984
   Sam Adams Light 2001
Flavored Malt Beverages
   Twisted Tea Backyard Batch Hard Iced Tea 2009
   Twisted Tea Half Hard Iced Tea & Half Hard Lemonade 2003
   Twisted Tea Hard Iced Tea 2001
   Twisted Tea Light Hard Iced Tea 2007
   Twisted Tea Peach Hard Iced Tea 2005
   Twisted Tea Raspberry Hard Iced Tea 2001
   Twisted Tea Blueberry Hard Iced Tea 2011
Hard Cider
   Angry Orchard Crisp Apple 2011
   Angry Orchard Apple Ginger 2011
   HardCore Crisp Hard Cider 1997
Imperial Series
   Samuel Adams Double Bock 1988
   Samuel Adams Imperial Stout 2009
   Samuel Adams Imperial White 2009
   Samuel Adams Wee Heavy 2011
Limited Edition Beers
   Infinium 2010
   Samuel Adams Utopias 2001
Seasonal Beers
   Samuel Adams Octoberfest 1989
   Samuel Adams Summer Ale 1996
   Samuel Adams Winter Lager 1989
   Samuel Adams Alpine Spring 2011

COMPETITORS

Anchor Brewers	Lion Brewery
Anheuser-Busch InBev	MillerCoors
Asahi Breweries	New Belgium Brewing
Bacardi	Pabst
Carlsberg	Pyramid Breweries
Craft Brew Alliance	Rogue Ales
Diageo	Shipyard Brewing
Grupo Modelo	Company
Heineken	Sprecher
Kirin Brewery of	Stoudt's Brewing
America	Victory Brewing
Lancaster Brewing Co.	Weyerbacher Brewing

HISTORICAL FINANCIALS

Company Type: Public

Income Statement
FYE: December 26

	REVENUE ($ mil.)	NET INCOME ($ mil.)	NET PROFIT MARGIN	EMPLOYEES
12/15	959.9	98.4	10.3%	1,429.0
12/14	903.0	90.7	10.0%	1,325.0
12/13	739.0	70.3	9.5%	1,120.0
12/12	580.2	59.4	10.2%	950.0
12/11	513.0	66.0	12.9%	840.0
Annual Growth	17.0%	10.5%	—	14.2%

2015 Year-End Financials

Debt ratio: 0.0%
Return on equity: 21.9%
Cash ($ mil.): 94.1
Current ratio: 2.01
Long-term debt ($ mil.): 0.4

No. of shares (mil.): 12.7
Dividends
   Yield: —
   Payout: —
Market value ($ mil.): 2,620.0

	STOCK PRICE ($) FY Close	P/E High/Low	PER SHARE ($) Earnings	Dividends	Book Value
12/15	205.40	43 26	7.25	0.00	36.16
12/14	295.74	43 29	6.69	0.00	33.37
12/13	242.10	47 24	5.18	0.00	23.70
12/12	132.98	30 21	4.39	0.00	19.13
12/11	108.56	22 14	4.81	0.00	14.41
Annual Growth	17.3%	— —	10.8%	—	25.9%

Boston Properties Inc

Boston Properties knows more than beans about real estate. The self-administered real estate investment trust (REIT) buys develops and manages mostly Class-A office buildings in large US cities with its core markets being in Boston New York San Francisco and Washington DC. As one of the nation's largest office owners and developers Boston Properties owns around 160 office and office/technical properties with 46.5 million rentable square feet. Its largest tenants include the US government Bank of America Biogen and Citibank. The REIT also owns a handful of retail hotel residential properties as well as land sites for development. The firm's chairman is media czar Mort Zuckerman (U.S. News & World Report and Daily News).

Operations

Boston Properties leased 158 office properties with 46.5 million sq. ft. of rentable space during 2015. About 95% of the REIT's total revenue comes from its 127 Class A Office properties which the REIT defines as centrally-located buildings that are professionally managed and maintained and command upper-tier rental rates. The firm also owned more than 30 office/technical properties that support office research and development laboratory and other technical uses. Beyond offices the REIT owns one hotel five retail properties and three residential buildings.

The REIT owns stakes in some rather iconic buildings. It has a 60% stake in New York's GM Building which was acquired from the ailing Macklowe Properties for $2.8 billion a record-setting price for a US office building. Boston Properties also owns Times Square Tower in New York Embarcadero Center in San Francisco and Metropolitan Square in Washington DC.

Geographic Reach

Despite its name firm's largest market is actually in New York City where its properties generate more than 40% of its total revenue. Its Boston-based properties contribute more than 30% to its revenue while its properties in Washington DC and San Francisco made up another roughly 15% and 10% of its revenue respectively.

Sales and Marketing

The REIT's tenants come from a variety of sectors including the legal services media & technology financial services retail and public sectors. The US government is the REIT's largest tenant occupying 4% of its rented space. Citibank Biogen and

Bank of America each occupy about 2% of space. Other high-profile tenants include Genentech Microsoft and Google.

Financial Performance

Boston Properties' annual revenues have risen 45% since 2011 thanks to rent-boosting property acquisitions and appreciating property valuations that have commanded higher rental rates.The REIT's revenue climbed 4% to $2.5 billion during 2015 mostly as its average revenue per square foot increased by $1.42 and because its termination income grew with 36 tenant terminations the bulk of which came from New York followed by San Francisco.Revenue growth combined with higher gains on real estate sales and lower interest expenses on debt in 2015 drove the Boston Properties' net income up 31% to $583.1 million. The REIT's operating cash levels rose 15% to $799.4 million for the year thanks to a rise in cash-based earnings.

Strategy

Boston Properties continues to focus on the Boston New York San Francisco and Washington DC. markets where it aims to be among the leading –and preferably the leading –owners and developers of office properties.Aside from acquiring new properties the REIT also develops its own. At the end of 2014 Boston Properties had 10 projects under construction including nine office properties and one residential building which combined measure approximately 3.3 million square feet. The firm estimates that the total investment to complete these projects is approximately $2.1 billion of which it had already invested about $0.9 million by the end of 2014.

HISTORY

Company BackgroundIn 1970 Mortimer Zuckerman and Edward Linde took their shares in a number of properties many on the West Coast and left Boston developer Cabot Cabot & Forbes to start Boston Properties. The new company built its first projects in San Francisco and then shifted its focus east to New York Washington DC and the Boston area.

Boston Properties' activities included an aborted development 700 yards from Walden Pond which Henry David Thoreau made famous. The company weathered the real estate downturns of the late 1980s and early 1990s by ceasing speculative construction and holding on to the buildings it had developed. Zuckerman used his real estate fortune to fund his media empire.

Noting that REIT IPOs were drawing top dollar Zuckerman and Linde took Boston Properties public in 1997; they used most of the proceeds to pay off debt. After an aggressive acquisition program in late 1997 and early 1998 the company made a second offering and further acquisitions.

After a while Boston Properties decided to add to its portfolio by building from the ground up. By 2005 the company was successfully balancing conservative purchasing practices with development deals funded with its more than $7 billion in equity.

In 1998 the REIT bought Prudential Center in Boston and a portfolio of office buildings in Princeton and East Brunswick New Jersey. Also that year the company made the winning bid for the highly sought-after Embarcadero Center in San Francisco buying it for $1.22 billion in 1999. (That same year Zuckerman sold his Atlantic Monthly; a year later he sold new-economy magazine Fast Company to German publisher Gruner + Jahr.)

The REIT inked a major tenant deal in 1999 and secured a construction site to begin moving the 48-story Times Square Tower project from the drawing board to reality. In 2001 Boston Properties acquired the Citigroup Center in New York through a partnership with rising mogul Eric Hadar's privately held real estate company. In 2002 the company purchased (for $1 billion) Citigroup's corporate headquarters at 399 Park Ave. in Manhattan.

After a while the company added to its portfolio by building from scratch. By 2005 it was successfully juggling conservative purchasing activities with lucrative development deals funded by its more than $7 billion in equity. In 2006 Boston Properties bought out partners' interests in Citigroup Center giving the REIT control of the entire property.

Boston Properties sold 280 Park Avenue for $1.2 billion in 2006 and 5 Times Square (the headquarters for Ernst & Young) for $1.3 billion in 2007. The REIT didn't sell any major assets in the weakened real estate market of 2008.

Among other tenants Lehman Brothers and General Motors both rejected their leases in bankruptcy in 2009.

In 2011 Boston Properties opened two major mixed-use developments in Boston and Washington DC.

EXECUTIVES

EVP San Francisco Region, Robert E. Pester, age 60, $248,462 total compensation
President and Director, Douglas T. (Doug) Linde, age 53, $713,462 total compensation
EVP Washington DC Region, Peter D. Johnston, age 58
SEVP, Raymond A. Ritchey, age 66, $708,462 total compensation
SVP and Regional Manager Boston, Bryan J. Koop, age 58, $388,846 total compensation
SVP Finance, Michael E. LaBelle, age 52, $488,846 total compensation
CEO and Director, Owen D. Thomas, age 53, $773,077 total compensation
EVP New York Region, John F. Powers, age 69
Senior Vice President and General Cou, Frank (Frankie) Burt
Auditors: PricewaterhouseCoopers LLP

LOCATIONS

HQ: Boston Properties Inc
Prudential Center, 800 Boylston Street, Suite 1900, Boston, MA 02199-8103
Phone: 617 236-3300
Web: www.bostonproperties.com

PRODUCTS/OPERATIONS

2015 Sales

	$ mil.	% of total
Rents		
Base rent	1,964.7	79
Recoveries from tenants	355.5	14
Parking & other	102.0	4
Hotel	46.0	2
Development & management services	22.6	1
Total	**2,490.8**	**100**

2015 Rental Revenue by Property Type

	% of total
Class A office	95
Office/technical	2
Hotel	2
Residential	1
Total	**100**

Selected Tenants

Ann Inc. (fka Ann Taylor Corp.)
Bank of America

Bingham McCutchen
Biogen
Citibank
Finnegan Henderson Farabow
Genentech
Google
Kirkland & Ellis
Manufactures Investment (ManuLife)
Mass Financial Services
Microsoft
O'Melveny & Myers
Parametric Technology
Ropes & Gray
Shearman & Sterling
State Street Bank and Trust
U.S. Government
Weil Gotshal Manges
Wellington Management
2013 Projects Under construction
Office
250 West 55th Street
535 Mission Street
601 Massachusetts Avenue
680 Folsom Street
804 Carnegie Center
Annapolis Junction Building Seven (50% ownership)
Transbay Tower
Residential
The Avant at Reston Town Center (359 units)

COMPETITORS

Beacon Capital Partners	LeFrak Organization
Bresler & Reiner	Mack-Cali
Brookfield Office Properties	Macklowe Properties
	SL Green Realty
Duke Realty	Shorenstein
Equity Commonwealth	Silverstein Properties
Equity Office	The Trump Organization
FelCor	Tishman Speyer
Forest City Enterprises	Vornado Realty
	Washington Real Estate

HISTORICAL FINANCIALS

Company Type: Public

Income Statement

FYE: December 31

	REVENUE ($ mil.)	NET INCOME ($ mil.)	NET PROFIT MARGIN	EMPLOYEES
12/15	2,490.8	583.1	23.4%	756.0
12/14	2,397.0	443.6	18.5%	750.0
12/13	2,135.5	749.8	35.1%	760.0
12/12	1,876.2	289.6	15.4%	730.0
12/11	1,759.5	272.6	15.5%	700.0
Annual Growth	9.1%	20.9%	—	1.9%

2015 Year-End Financials

Debt ratio: 50.1%
Return on equity: 10.2%
Cash ($ mil.): 723.7
Current ratio: 2.08
Long-term debt ($ mil.): 9,216.5

No. of shares (mil.): 153.5
Dividends
Yield: 3.0%
Payout: 96.9%
Market value ($ mil.): 19,588.0

	STOCK PRICE ($) FY Close	P/E High/Low		PER SHARE ($) Earnings	Dividends	Book Value
12/15	127.54	39	29	3.73	3.85	37.18
12/14	128.69	48	35	2.83	7.10	37.21
12/13	100.37	24	20	4.86	4.85	37.86
12/12	105.81	60	51	1.92	2.30	34.35
12/11	99.60	60	45	1.86	2.05	33.23
Annual Growth	6.4%	—	—	19.0%	17.1%	2.8%

Boston Properties L.P.

Auditors: PricewaterhouseCoopers LLP

LOCATIONS

HQ: Boston Properties L.P.
Prudential Center, 800 Boylston Street, Suite 1900,
Boston, MA 02199-8103
Phone: 617 236-3300
Web: www.bostonproperties.com

HISTORICAL FINANCIALS

Company Type: Public

Income Statement

FYE: December 31

	REVENUE ($ mil.)	NET INCOME ($ mil.)	NET PROFIT MARGIN	EMPLOYEES
12/15	2,490.8	809.1	32.5%	765.0
12/14	2,397.0	541.2	22.6%	750.0
12/13	2,135.5	841.5	39.4%	760.0
12/12	1,876.2	334.6	17.8%	730.0
12/11	1,759.5	317.1	18.0%	700.0
Annual Growth	9.1%	26.4%	—	2.2%

2015 Year-End Financials

Debt ratio: 51.0%
Return on equity: —
Cash ($ mil.): 723.7
Current ratio: 2.08
Long-term debt ($ mil.): 9,216.5

No. of shares (mil.): 153.5
Dividends
Yield: —
Payout: —
Market value ($ mil.): —

Bridge Bancorp, Inc. (Bridgehampton, NY)

Bridge Bancorp wants you to cross over to its subsidiary The Bridgehampton National Bank which operates about 25 branches on eastern Long Island New York. Founded in 1910 the bank offers traditional deposit services to area individuals small businesses and municipalities including checking savings and money market accounts and CDs. Deposits are invested primarily in mortgages which account for some 80% of the bank's loan portfolio. Title insurance services are available through bank subsidiary Bridge Abstract; wealth management services include financial planning estate administration and trustee services. Bridge Bancorp bought Hamptons State Bank in 2011 to fortify its presence on Long Island.

Geographic Reach

Bridgehampton New York-based Bridge Bancorp's market area is Suffolk County in eastern Long Island. The bank serves customers in the towns of East Hampton Southampton Southold and Riverhead. It also has branches in Brookhaven Babylon and Islip.

Financial Performance

The bank reported net income of $13.1 million in 2013 versus $12.8 million in 2012. Revenue increased 3% to $67.3 million on rising net interest income. Bridge Bancorp had total assets of $1.9 billion in 2013 an increase of 17% versus the prior year. Total deposits rose 9% in 2013 versus 2012 to $1.5 billion.

Mergers and Acquisitions

In February 2014 Bridge Bancorp acquired FNBNY Bancorp and its wholly-owned subsidiary the First National Bank of New York and converted its three branches to Bridgehampton National Bank (BNB) branches. The purchase expanded BNB's reach into Nassau County. Following the acquisition Bridge Bancorp's assets totaled approximately $2.1 billion with loans of approximately $1.1 billion and deposits of $1.7 billion with 26 branches throughout Long Island and one loan production office in Manhattan.

EXECUTIVES

President and CEO, Kevin M. O'Connor, age 53, $300,000 total compensation
SVP and Chief Lending Officer Bridgehampton National Bank, Kevin L. Santacroce, $180,000 total compensation
SVP and CIO, Thomas H. Simson, $175,000 total compensation
President CEO and Director, Kevin OConnor
Chief Financial Officer, Adam Hall
EVP and Chief Retail Banking Officer, James J. Manseau, $235,000 total compensation
Assistant Vice President Fin Operations, Michelle (Michie) Dosch
Vice President and Manager, Steven (Steve) Bodziner
Vice President Director Of Marketing, Claudia Pilato
Vice President, Aidan Wood
Vice Chairman, Dennis A. Suskind, age 73
Vice Chairperson Bridge Bancorp and Bridgehampton National Bank, Marcia Z. Hefter, age 72
Auditors: Crowe Horwath LLP

LOCATIONS

HQ: Bridge Bancorp, Inc. (Bridgehampton, NY)
2200 Montauk Highway, Bridgehampton, NY 11932
Phone: 631 537-1000
Web: www.bridgenb.com

COMPETITORS

Bank of America	JPMorgan Chase
Bank of New York Mellon	Suffolk Bancorp

HISTORICAL FINANCIALS

Company Type: Public

Income Statement

FYE: December 31

	ASSETS ($ mil.)	NET INCOME ($ mil.)	INCOME AS % OF ASSETS	EMPLOYEES
12/15	3,781.9	21.1	0.6%	433.0
12/14	2,288.6	13.7	0.6%	348.0
12/13	1,896.7	13.0	0.7%	271.0
12/12	1,624.7	12.7	0.8%	257.0
12/11	1,337.4	10.3	0.8%	227.0
Annual Growth	29.7%	19.5%	—	17.5%

2015 Year-End Financials

Return on assets: 0.7%
Return on equity: 8.1%
Long-term debt ($ mil.): —
No. of shares (mil.): 17.3
Sales ($ mil): 118.9

Dividends
Yield: 3.0%
Payout: 73.6%
Market value ($ mil.): 529.0

	STOCK PRICE ($) FY Close	P/E High/Low	PER SHARE ($) Earnings	Dividends	Book Value
12/15	30.43	22 17	1.43	0.92	19.62
12/14	26.75	23 20	1.18	0.92	15.03
12/13	26.00	19 14	1.36	0.92	14.10
12/12	20.34	17 13	1.48	1.15	13.32
12/11	19.90	17 11	1.54	0.69	12.82
Annual Growth	11.2%	— —	(1.8%)	7.5%	11.2%

Bright Horizons Family Solutions, Inc

EXECUTIVES

Senior Vice President of Strategic Planning, Ann (Annie) Pickens
Senior Vice President Of Business Operations, Dave Shaby
Chief Executive Officer Director; Executive Chairman, Roger H Brown
Vice President Education and Training, Linda (Lin) Whitehead
Senior Vice President Marketing and Partnership Services, Gary (Gar) O'Neil
Vice President Compliance and Internal Control, Daniel (Dan) Joyce
Division Vice President Of Operations, Leslie (Les) Spanier
Vice President Digital Media, Bill (Billy) Kerrigan
Vice President Construction And Property Management, Martin Nagle
Vice President Client Services, Jean (Jeannie) Schulte
Division Vice President of Operations, Tammy (Tam) Chuprevich
Vice President Information Security and Risk Manager, Javed Ikbal
Vice President of Design and Construction, Daniel (Dan) Lenyo
Vice President Human Resources, Ilene Smith
Vice President, Eileen (Elle) Smith
Vice President of Communications, Ilene Hoffer
Vice President Client Solutions Back up Centers, Kevin (Kev) Brown
Vice President Consulting Services, Kim Callaway
Vice President Assistant Treasurer, Jim Plocica
Senior Vice President Marketing, Gary Oniel
Auditors: Deloitte & Touche LLP

LOCATIONS

HQ: Bright Horizons Family Solutions, Inc
200 Talcott Avenue South, Watertown, MA 02472
Phone: 617 673-8000
Web: www.brighthorizons.com

HISTORICAL FINANCIALS

Company Type: Public

Income Statement

FYE: December 31

	REVENUE ($ mil.)	NET INCOME ($ mil.)	NET PROFIT MARGIN	EMPLOYEES
12/15	1,458.4	93.9	6.4%	26,000.0
12/14	1,353.0	72.0	5.3%	25,400.0
12/13	1,218.7	12.6	1.0%	25,000.0
12/12	1,070.9	8.1	0.8%	22,000.0
12/11	973.7	4.7	0.5%	22,000.0
Annual Growth	10.6%	110.8%	—	4.3%

Brixmor Property Group Inc

Brixmor Property Group hopes you swing by the grocery store more than once a week. The internally-managed real estate investment trust (REIT) owns a portfolio of about 520 strip mall-style shopping centers across 38 states. Its properties are situated in high-traffic commercial areas anchored by grocery store chains such as Ahold Kroger Publix Safeway and Wal-Mart. Besides the main grocery store tenant its shopping centers offer a mix of smaller retailers such as Dollar Tree or other big box stores such as Best Buy Kmart and TJX Cos. Altogether Brixmor Property Group owns some 87 million sq. ft. of leasable space; each shopping center averages about 166100 sq. ft. The trust went public in 2013.

IPO

Brixmor Property Group raised a whopping $825 million in its November 2013 IPO. It plans to use the proceeds to pay down debt.

Geographic Reach

New York-based Brixmor has properties in 38 states including California Florida New York and Texas. Texas and Florida are home to 68 and 59 of the REIT's properties respectively.

Operations

The REIT's property portfolio has been through several owners. Initially it was built up by Heritage Property Trust and New Plan Excel Realty Trust two retail REITs that were bought by Australia-based Centro Properties before the real estate crash of 2008. After the crash (and with fewer shoppers spending freely) Centro Properties then sold the shopping centers to private equity giant Blackstone Group for $9.4 billion in 2011. Blackstone invested $310 million into renovating and improving the shopping centers all the while grooming the properties for an IPO as a real estate investment trust.

Financial Performance

In its first year as a public company Brixmor's revenue grew 5% to $1.17 billion in 2013 versus $1.12 billion in 2012 on increasing rental income expense reimbursement and other revenue sources. Despite the rise in revenue the REIT posted a net loss of $118.9 million.

Strategy

AS the owner of the nation's largest wholly owned 70% grocery-anchored shopping center portfolio Brixmor's scale gives it tremendous access to retailers. Clients who include Wal-Mart

Stores' Neighborhood markets are attracted by the REIT's geographic diversity which allows national chains to shop for space in multiple markets. Also the REIT boasts long-term leases that mature on a fairly regular basis. The firm is focused on tenant diversification as well. Grocery giant Kroger the REIT's largest tenant accounts for only about 3% of its annual base rents.

Company Background

As a real estate investment trust (REIT) Brixmor Property Group is exempt from paying federal income tax as long as it makes quarterly distributions to shareholders.

EXECUTIVES

Executive Vice President Acquisitions Dispositions, Dean Bernstein
Legal Secretary, Lisa M (Lis) Quiroga
Vice President of Human Resour, Lisa (Lis) Tronzano
Vice President of Management Accounting, Jeong Chang
Vice President Management Accounting, Dan (Danny) Reilly
Vice President National Accounts, Christine Leising
Executive Vice President, Michael (Mel) Moss
Senior Vice President Corporate Finance and Budgeting, Yolande Clerc
Vice President, Mark (Marky) Worley
Vice President Of Property Management West Region, Tom Wellman
Vice President Corporate Finance, Praneet Talukdar
Executive Vice President GC, Steven (Steve) Siegel
Regional Vice President Leasing, Nick (Nicky) Andreadis
Vice President Regional Legal Services West, Jason (Jase) Mahoney
Auditors: Deloitte & Touche LLP

LOCATIONS

HQ: Brixmor Property Group Inc
  450 Lexington Avenue, New York, NY 10017
Phone: 212 869-3000
Web: www.brixmor.com

PRODUCTS/OPERATIONS

Shopping centers locations

Texas
Florida
Georgia
Pennsylvania
New York
California
Illinois
Ohio
North Carolina
Michigan
New Jersey
Tennessee
Connecticut
Indiana
Kentucky
Virginia
Massachusetts
Minnesota
South Carolina
Colorado
Missouri
Iowa
Maryland
NewHampshire
Wisconsin
Alabama
Louisiana
Mississippi
Nevada
Arizona
Kansas

Maine
New Mexico
West Virginia
Delaware
Oklahoma
Rhode Island
Vermont

COMPETITORS

Acadia Realty Trust
American Assets Trust
CBL & Associates
  Properties
DDR
Equity One
Federal Realty
  Investment
General Growth
  Properties
IRC Retail Centers
Kimco Realty

Macerich
National Retail
  Properties
Realty Income
Regency Centers
Retail Properties of
  America
Simon Property Group
Spirit Realty Capital
Taubman Centers
Vornado Realty
Weingarten Realty

HISTORICAL FINANCIALS
Company Type: Public

Income Statement

	REVENUE ($ mil.)	NET INCOME ($ mil.)	NET PROFIT MARGIN	EMPLOYEES
12/15	1,265.9	193.7	15.3%	447.0
12/14	1,236.6	89.0	7.2%	443.0
12/13	1,174.7	(93.5)	—	456.0
12/12	1,125.8	(122.5)	—	475.0
12/11	565.6	115.3	20.4%	0.0
Annual Growth	22.3%	13.8%		

FYE: December 31

2015 Year-End Financials

Debt ratio: 62.9%
Return on equity: 6.7%
Cash ($ mil.): 69.5
Current ratio: 0.66
Long-term debt ($ mil.): 5,974.2

No. of shares (mil.): 299.1
Dividends
  Yield: 3.4%
  Payout: 166.6%
Market value ($ mil.): 7,724.0

	STOCK PRICE ($) FY Close	P/E High/Low	PER SHARE ($) Earnings	Dividends	Book Value
12/15	25.82	42 34	0.65	0.90	9.59
12/14	24.84	70 56	0.36	0.73	9.79
12/13	20.33	— —	(0.50)	0.00	10.29
Annual Growth	12.7%	— —	—	—	(3.5%)

Brookline Bancorp Inc (DE)

Brookline Bancorp is the holding company for Brookline Bank Bank Rhode Island (BankRI) and First Ipswich Bank (formerly The First National Bank of Ipswich) which together operate more than 45 full-service branches in eastern Massachusetts and Rhode Island. Commercial and multifamily mortgages backed by real estate such as apartments condominiums and office buildings account for the largest portion of the company's loan portfolio followed by indirect auto loans commercial loans and consumer loans. Established in 1997 as Brookline Savings Bank the bank went public five years later and changed its name to Brookline

Bank in 2003. Brookline Bancorp. has expanded by acquiring other regional banks.

Geographic Reach

Boston-based Brookline Bancorp operates 47 full-service branches in greater Boston and greater Providence Rhode Island.

Operations

The holding company also provides indirect automobile loans through Brookline Bank and equipment financing through its Eastern Funding and Macrolease Corp. subsidiaries. Eastern Funding LLC a majority-owned firm with more than $1 billion in in direct loans that specializes in financing coin-operated laundry dry cleaning and convenience store equipment in the New York City metropolitan area.

Financial Performance

The multi-bank holding company has $5.3 billion in assets. In 2013 Brookline Bancorp reported net income of $35.4 million compared with $37.1 million in 2012. Net earnings from operations were $36 million in 2013 compared to $41.1 million for 2012.

Strategy

Brookline has grown from a sleepy suburban community savings bank to a publicly-traded commercial lender with loan volumes that put it among Massachusetts' top banks. As it transitions to a commercial bank Brookline has also been growing geographically through acquisitions.

Mergers and Acquisitions

In January 2012 Brookline acquired Providence-headquartered Bancorp Rhode Island for $234 million in cash and stock adding 18 BankRI branches in that state. BankRI retained its brand and operates as a subsidiary of Brookline Bancorp.

In February 2011 it acquired The First National Bank of Ipswich a six-branch bank serving Massachusetts' North Shore. The $19.7 million transaction gave First National Bank of Ipswich a much-needed boost as that bank had been struggling with loan losses during the recession. It also expanded Brookline Bancorp's market area as there was no overlap between the two banks.

Brookline Bancorp's board rejected a takeover offer by an unnamed suitor in early 2010. Two directors had voted to accept the bid however including former longtime chairman Richard Chapman. Both resigned in the aftermath of the vote.

EXECUTIVES

President and CEO, Paul A. Perrault, age 65, $715,000 total compensation

COO, James M. Cosman, age 65, $265,000 total compensation

President and CEO Bank Rhode Island, Mark J. Meiklejohn, age 52, $330,000 total compensation

Chief Risk Officer General Counsel and Secretary, Michael W. McCurdy, age 47

Chief Credit Officer, M. Robert Rose, age 64, $288,000 total compensation

President and CEO The First National Bank of Ipswich, Russell G. Cole, age 58

CFO, Carl M. Carlson, age 52, $335,000 total compensation

Vice President Project Management, Esther Pinto

Senior Vice President, Bill Mackenzie

Vice President Regional Manager, Cathy Pierce

Vice President, Tony Glazier

Vice President Of Commercial Lending, Tim Steiner

Vice President Regional Manager, Cathy (Cat) Pierce

Senior Vice President Commercial Banking, Bill (Billy) Mackenzie

Vice President Underwriting And Operations, Gretchen Annese

Senior Vice President, Jane (Ginny) Wolchonok

Vice President of Commercial Lending, Tim (Timmy) Steiner

Vice President, Jim (Jimmy) Horrigan

Assistant Vice President Information Technology Project Management Office, Brian McCarthy

Assistant Vice President, Timothy J (Tim) Steiner

Assistant Vice President Branch Manager, Lisa (Lis) Clark

Chairman, Joseph J. Slotnik, age 80

Treasurer, Reed Whitman

Auditors: KPMG LLP

LOCATIONS

HQ: Brookline Bancorp Inc (DE)
131 Clarendon Street, Boston, MA 02116
Phone: 617 425-4600
Web: www.brooklinebancorp.com

PRODUCTS/OPERATIONS

2015 sales

	$ mil.	% of total
Interest and dividend income:		
Loans and leases	212.6	86
Debt securities	11.4	5
Marketable and restricted equity securities	2.8	1
Short-term investments	0.1	-
Non-interest income:		
Deposit fees	8.7	4
Loan level derivative income net	3.4	1
Gain on sales of loans and leases held-for-sale	2.2	1
Other	5.8	2
Total	**247.0**	**100**

Selected Services

Personal
Checking
Savings
Borrowing
Investment Services
Business
Signature Business Banking
Business Checking Accounts
Business Savings
Business Lending
Business Online Banking
Cash Management
Service Center
Branch Locations
ATM Locations
Online Banking
Mobile Banking
Telephone Services
Mail Services
Order Checks
Order Foreign Currency
Overdraft Privilege Service

COMPETITORS

Bank of America	Eastern Bank
Boston Private	Sovereign Bank
Central Bancorp	TD Bank USA
Century Bancorp (MA)	
Citizens Financial Group	

HISTORICAL FINANCIALS
Company Type: Public

Income Statement
FYE: December 31

	ASSETS ($ mil.)	NET INCOME ($ mil.)	INCOME AS % OF ASSETS	EMPLOYEES
12/15	6,042.3	49.7	0.8%	718.0
12/14	5,799.8	42.7	0.7%	725.0
12/13	5,325.1	35.3	0.7%	720.0
12/12	5,147.5	37.1	0.7%	662.0
12/11	3,299.0	27.6	0.8%	358.0
Annual Growth	**16.3%**	**15.9%**	**—**	**19.0%**

2015 Year-End Financials

Return on assets: 0.8%	Dividends
Return on equity: 7.6%	Yield: 3.0%
Long-term debt ($ mil.): —	Payout: 52.9%
No. of shares (mil.): 70.8	Market value ($ mil.): 815.0
Sales ($ mil): 247.0	

	STOCK PRICE ($) FY Close	P/E High/Low		PER SHARE ($) Earnings	Dividends	Book Value
12/15	11.50	17	13	0.71	0.36	9.42
12/14	10.03	17	14	0.61	0.34	9.06
12/13	9.55	20	16	0.51	0.34	8.70
12/12	8.50	18	14	0.53	0.34	8.70
12/11	8.44	24	15	0.47	0.34	8.50
Annual Growth	**8.0%**	**—**	**—**	**10.9%**	**1.1%**	**2.6%**

Brown & Brown, Inc.

Insurance agency Brown & Brown (B&B) provides property/casualty life and health insurance and risk management services through its retail division mainly to commercial clients. Its national programs division designs customized programs for such niche clients as dentists lawyers optometrists and towing operators. Its wholesale brokerage unit distributes excess and surplus commercial insurance as well as reinsurance to retail agents. B&B's services segment provides self-insured and third-party administrator services. The company has 240 offices in about 40 states as well as offices in London the Cayman Islands and Bermuda.OperationsB&B's retail segment accounts for about half of revenue while its national programs segment accounts for about a quarter of sales. The wholesale brokerage and service segments round out the firm's earnings.Geographic ReachThe company's largest market is Florida where it operates more than 40 agency or brokerage locations. The firm also has significant operations in California Georgia Illinois Indiana Kansas Kentucky Massachusetts Michigan New Jersey New York North Carolina Oregon Pennsylvania Texas Virginia and Washington. Although B&B has expanded its operations to serve the UK market the US still accounts for nearly all of its revenues.Sales and MarketingB&B network of agency offices sell insurance policies that are underwritten by third-party carriers. B&B's retail division employs more than 3900 agents and receives commission fees on policy sales to customers including commercial businesses government agencies trade groups and individual consumers. The national programs division sells niche policies to businesses and professionals through independent agents and through B&B's retail offices. The wholesale brokerage division sells commercial policies to independent brokers and agents (as well as some B&B retail offices).Financial PerformanceRevenues have grown steadily over the past decade (with the exception of 2009 when the insurance industry experienced a downturn due to economic conditions). In 2015 revenue rose 5% to $1.7 billion as all segments saw growth —primarily from higher commissions and fees new business and new client advocacy services. Net income has also been on the rise with the exception of 2014 when B&B acquired flood insurance carrier Wright. Profits resumed their climb in 2015 growing 18% to $243 million thanks to the higher revenue plus gains from disposals. This was partially offset by higher operating expenses such as salaries and benefits.Cash flow from operations increased 7% to $412 million in 2015.StrategyB&B has a long-term growth strategy that is focused on acquisitions —it has acquired the assets or operations of more than 470 firms since 1993. Acquisitions target a range of growth areas including retail and wholesale brokerage and employee benefit plan development. In 2015 the company acquired 13 smaller firms for a combined cost of $136 million; in 2014 it completed 10 acquisitions for a combined $721.9 million.The company prefers to acquire agencies whose principal executives intend to stay after the sale and whose corporate cultures are a good fit. Following its acquisitions B&B tends to leave things in place but lifts some administrative duties off of an agency freeing up its agents to sell more.Mergers and AcquisitionsIn 2014 B&B completed a larger-than-usual acquisition when it purchased flood insurance carrier Wright Insurance Group for $609.2 million. It gained Wright National Flood Insurance through the deal; the subsidiary writes policies adhering to the National Flood Insurance Program a FEMA-administered program as well as excess flood insurance coverage.The ongoing acquisitions continued in 2015 when B&B purchased such firms as New York-based Spain Agency Washington-based Bellingham Underwriters Colorado-based Fitness Insurance and Massachusetts-based Strategic Benefit Advisors. In 2016 purchases included California-based BayRisk Insurance Brokers and Oregon-based Lumbermens Insurance and Risk Solutions.

EXECUTIVES

COO and Regional President, Linda S. Downs, age 66, $475,000 total compensation
Regional President and Chief Acquisitions Officer, J. Scott Penny, age 49, $308,844 total compensation
EVP and People Officer, Richard Freebourn, age 68
Regional EVP, Sam R. Boone, age 62
President Peachtree Special Risk Brokers, Anthony T. (Tony) Strianese, age 54, $450,000 total compensation
Retail Division President, Charles H. (Charlie) Lydecker, $450,000 total compensation
EVP CFO and Treasurer, R. Andrew Watts
Chief Information Officer, B. Carl Owen
President and CEO, J. Powell Brown, $565,000 total compensation
National Programs Division President, Chris Walker
Vice President New Business Marketing Manager, Julie Aai
Executive Vice President, Scott J Penny
Senior Vice President Sales Manager, Ty Beba
Executive Vice President, Michael (Mel) Riordan
Vice President, Nancy Scott
Vice President Benefits Operations, Ann Brandt
Executive Vice President, Aaron Phillips
Vice President, Stephen (Steve) Farmer
Regional Vice President, P Brown
Vice President and Sales Leader, Tony (Tone) Leavine
Vice President, R Freebourn
Chairman, J. Hyatt Brown, age 78
Auditors: Deloitte & Touche LLP

LOCATIONS

HQ: Brown & Brown, Inc.
220 South Ridgewood Avenue, Daytona Beach, FL 32114
Phone: 386 252-9601
Web: www.bbinsurance.com

PRODUCTS/OPERATIONS

2015 Sales

	% of total
Core commissions and fees	96
Profit-sharing contingent commissions	3
Guaranteed supplemental commissions	1
Investment income	—
Other income net	—
Total	**100**

2015 Sales

% of total	$ mil
Retail	52
National Programs	26
Wholesale Brokerage	13
Services	9
Other	—
Total	**100**

Selected Products and Services

Personal Insurance
Business Insurance
Employee Benefits
Wholesale Brokerage
Services Division
Financial Services
Trade Credit
Surety Bonds
Risk Management

COMPETITORS

Alexander Forbes	Hub International
All Risks	IMA Financial Group
Alliant	Marsh & McLennan
Aon	NIA group
Barney & Barney	Rutherfoord
Bollinger Inc.	Sedgwick Claims
Bolton & Company	Management Services
Burns & Wilcox	The Lockton Companies
CRC Insurance	USI
Campbell Group	Wells Fargo Insurance
Crawford & Company	Services
Gallagher	Willis Towers Watson

HISTORICAL FINANCIALS

Company Type: Public

Income Statement

FYE: December 31

	REVENUE ($ mil.)	NET INCOME ($ mil.)	NET PROFIT MARGIN	EMPLOYEES
12/15	1,660.5	243.3	14.7%	7,807.0
12/14	1,575.8	206.9	13.1%	7,591.0
12/13	1,363.2	217.1	15.9%	6,992.0
12/12	1,200.0	184.0	15.3%	6,438.0
12/11	1,013.5	164.0	16.2%	5,557.0
Annual Growth	**13.1%**	**10.4%**	**—**	**8.9%**

2015 Year-End Financials

Debt ratio: 23.0%
Return on equity: 11.4%
Cash ($ mil.): 443.4
Current ratio: 1.16
Long-term debt ($ mil.): 1,079.8
No. of shares (mil.): 138.9
Dividends
  Yield: 1.4%
  Payout: 30.9%
Market value ($ mil.): 4,461.0

	STOCK PRICE ($) FY Close	P/E High/Low	PER SHARE ($) Earnings	Dividends	Book Value
12/15	32.10	20 18	1.70	0.45	15.47
12/14	32.91	23 20	1.41	0.41	14.73
12/13	31.39	23 17	1.48	0.37	13.80
12/12	25.46	22 17	1.26	0.35	12.56
12/11	22.63	23 15	1.13	0.33	11.47
Annual Growth	**9.1%**	**— —**	**10.7%**	**8.6%**	**7.8%**

Bryn Mawr Bank Corp

Bryn Mawr Bank Corporation stands atop a "big hill" in Pennsylvania. Bryn Mawr (which in Welsh translates as "big hill") is the bank holding company for Bryn Mawr Trust operates some 20 offices in Pennsylvania and Delaware. The bank offers traditional services as checking and savings accounts CDs mortgages and business and consumer loans in addition to insurance products equipment leasing investment management retirement planning tax planning and preparation and trust services. Founded in 1889 Bryn Mawr boasts more than $5 billion of assets under administration and management.

OperationsBryn Mawr operates two business segments. Its Banking segment which makes up two-thirds of overall business provides commercial and retail banking services. The Wealth Management division which includes the Bryn Mawr Trust of Delaware and Lau Associates businesses makes up about one-third of the bank's overall revenue and provides a variety of custody investment management tax and brokerage services. Broadly speaking the company generated 60% of its total revenue from interest and fees on loans and leases in 2014 while another 30% of its total revenue came from fees for wealth management services. Bryn Mawr operated 19 full-service branches seven Life Care Community Offices five wealth offices and a full-service insurance agency in 2014. Geographic ReachThe bank corporation has branches and offices across Montgomery Delaware Chester and Dauphin counties in Pennsylvania and New Castle county in Delaware.Financial Performance-Bryn Mawr has enjoyed rising revenues and profits over the past several years reflecting strong growth in its loan business and wealth management business. The bank's revenue rose by 4% to a record $131.23 million in 2014 mostly thanks to higher interest income from loans as it grew its loan assets by $153.9 million during the year. The company's Wealth Management services fees also grew by 5% thanks to new business acquisitions and solid market appreciation during the year which resulted in higher assets under management.Higher revenue and a strong grip on costs in 2014 also boosted Bryn Mawr's net income by 14% to a record $27.84 million. Despite higher earnings the bank's operating cash declined by 6% to $37.68 million for the year as it made less in net proceeds from the sales of its loans held for resale.StrategyBryn Mawr Bank Corporation continued to push its acquisition strategy in 2015 designed to broaden its service offerings boost its loan and deposit business and expand its branch network. The bank looks to strategically acquire smaller insurance businesses small to mid-sized banks and community banks wealth management companies and advisory and planning services firm that complement its existing businesses. Besides acquisitions the company has been growing its wealth management business through marketing campaigns to raise brand awareness.Mergers and AcquisitionsIn April 2015 to grow its wealth management business the bank purchased Robert J. McAllister Agency which provides insurance and risk management solutions to individuals and businesses in the Philadelphia region. In January 2015 Bryn Mawr acquired the Continental Bank Holdings and its Plymouth Meeting-based flagship Continental Bank adding some $433 million in loans and $480 million in deposits along with 10 full-service branches located in key markets in Montgomery Chester and Philadelphia counties. In October 2014 Bryn Mawr bought the Rosemont Pennsylvania-based insurance agency Powers Craft Parker & Beard Inc. (PCPB) for $7 million to enhance its own insurance business among individuals and commercial clients. In 2012 as part of a strategy to build its wealth management division the company acquired Davidson Trust adding some $1 billion in assets under management. Company BackgroundIn 2011 the company bought the private wealth management business of Hershey Trust Company for more than $14.5 million; that deal brought in approximately $1 billion of assets under management. In 2010 the company purchased First Keystone Financial adding about 10 bank branches in Pennsylvania and some $2.7 billion in trust and investment assets.

EXECUTIVES

Executive Vice President Wealth Management Division, Matthew (Matt) Waschull

EVP and COO, Alison E. Gers, age 58, $250,000 total compensation

EVP and Chief Lending Officer Bryn Mawr Trust, Joseph G. (Joe) Keefer, age 57, $238,500 total compensation

President and CEO, Francis J. Leto, age 56, $310,000 total compensation

EVP Secretary and Chief Risk Officer, Geoffrey L. Halberstadt

CFO and Treasurer Bryn Mawr Bank Corporation; EVP CFO and Treasurer Bryn Mawr Bank, Michael W. (Mike) Harrington, age 53

EVP Wealth Management Division, Harry R. Madeira

Vice President Senior Investment Advisor, William A Reasner

Vice President Trust Administration, Lynne Rubin Lewitt

Vice President, Joseph (Jo) Brown

Vice President bmtc, John (Jack) Metz

Senior Vice President, Richard (Dick) Gentile

Vice President Risk Manager, David (Dave) Waltz

Vice President, John (Jack) Roman

Vice President, Anrita Mcginn

Vice President, Susan (Sue) Callahan

Senior Vice President Wealth Management, Barbara (Barb) Pettit

Senior Vice President Market Leader, Tony (Tone) Poluch

Assistant Vice President, Leslie (Les) Herrick

Assistant Vice President And Trust Advisor, Yvonne (Vonne) Lalime

Executive Vice President, Gary (Gar) Madeira

Vice President Wealth Management Division, J Keefer-Hugill

Chairman, Britton H. Murdoch

Auditors: KPMG LLP

LOCATIONS

HQ: Bryn Mawr Bank Corp
801 Lancaster Avenue, Bryn Mawr, PA 19010
Phone: 610 525-1700
Web: www.bmtc.com

PRODUCTS/OPERATIONS

2014 Sales

	$ mil.	% of total
Interest		
Interest & fees on loans & leases	78.5	60
Investment securities	4.2	3
Cash & cash equivalents	0.2	-
Noninterest		
Fees for wealth management services	36.7	30
Service charges on deposits	2.6	2
Net gain on sale of residential mortgages	1.8	1
Loan Servicing and other fees	1.8	1
Other	5.4	3
Total	**131.2**	**100**

Selected Subsidiaries

Bryn Mawr Advisors Inc.
Bryn Mawr Asset Management Inc.
Bryn Mawr Brokerage Co. Inc.
Bryn Mawr Financial Services Inc.
Bryn Mawr Trust Company of Delaware
Joseph W. Roskos Co. Inc.
Lau Associates LLC
The Bryn Mawr Trust Company
  BMT Leasing Inc.
  BMT Mortgage Services Inc.
  BMT Settlement Services Inc.
  Insurance Counsellors of Bryn Mawr Inc.

COMPETITORS

Alliance Bancorp of Pennsylvania	Royal Bancshares
	Sovereign Bank
Firstrust Savings Bank	Wells Fargo
PNC Financial	

HISTORICAL FINANCIALS

Company Type: Public

Income Statement

FYE: December 31

	ASSETS ($ mil.)	NET INCOME ($ mil.)	INCOME AS % OF ASSETS	EMPLOYEES
12/15	3,031.0	16.7	0.6%	530.0
12/14	2,246.5	27.8	1.2%	444.0
12/13	2,061.6	24.4	1.2%	432.0
12/12	2,035.8	21.1	1.0%	432.0
12/11	1,774.9	19.7	1.1%	391.0
Annual Growth	**14.3%**	**(4.0%)**	**—**	**7.9%**

2015 Year-End Financials

Return on assets: 0.6%	Dividends
Return on equity: 5.4%	Yield: 2.7%
Long-term debt ($ mil.): —	Payout: 43.3%
No. of shares (mil.): 17.0	Market value ($ mil.): 490.0
Sales ($ mil): 164.5	

	STOCK PRICE ($) FY Close	P/E High/Low		PER SHARE ($) Earnings	Dividends	Book Value
12/15	28.72	33	29	0.94	0.78	21.42
12/14	31.30	15	13	2.01	0.74	17.83
12/13	30.18	17	12	1.80	0.69	16.84
12/12	22.27	14	12	1.60	0.64	15.18
12/11	19.49	14	10	1.54	0.60	14.09
Annual Growth	**10.2%**	**—**	**—**	**(11.6%)**	**6.8%**	**11.0%**

BSB Bancorp Inc. (MD)

BSB Bancorp is the holding company for Belmont Savings Bank a community back with about half a dozen branches in southeastern Middlesex County in the suburbs of Boston. Serving local businesses and individuals the $2 billion-asset bank offers checking savings money market retirement accounts and a variety of lending products. Almost 50% of its loan portfolio is made up of one-to-four family residential mortgages while commercial real estate loans make up another 30%. While Belmont Savings Bank traces its roots back to 1885 BSB Bancorp was formed in 2011 to take the company public.

OperationsBSB Bancorp mostly originates one-to-four family residential mortgages and commercial real estate loans for office buildings owner-occupied commercial buildings industrial buildings and strip mall centers. About 46% of its loan portfolio was made up of one-to-four family residential mortgages at the end of 2015 while another 29% was made up of commercial real estate loans. The rest of the portfolio was made up of home equity loans (10% of loan assets) construction (4%) business loans (3.5%) auto loans (6%) and other consumer loans (less than 1%).The bank also makes more than 90% of its revenue from interest income. About 87% of its total revenue came from loan interest (including fees) during 2015 while another 7% came from interest on investment securities. The remainder of its revenue came from non-interest income sources including customer service fees.Geographic Reach

While its primary market area is in the greater Boston area the company serves southeastern Massachusetts in the Essex Middlesex Norfolk and Suffolk Counties from branches in Belmont Watertown Waltham Newton and Cambridge.Sales and MarketingBSB Bancorp has been cutting back on its marketing in recent years. It spent $926000 on marketing in 2015 down from $975000 and $999000 in 2014 and 2013 respectively.

Financial Performance

BSB Bancorp's annual revenues have doubled since 2011 as its loan assets have more than tripled to $1.53 billion as a result new branch openings and organic growth with the strengthening economy around Boston. The bank's net income has skyrocketed more than five-fold over the time period as it's kept a lid on rising operating costs and benefited from the low-interest environment.The bank's revenue jumped 23% to $51.57 million during 2015 mostly as a 30% increase in loan assets spurred higher interest income.Strong revenue growth in 2015 drove BSB Bancorp's net income higher by 61% to $6.91 million. The bank's operating cash levels fell 14% to $18.1 million for the year mostly after adjusting its earnings for non-cash items related to its net proceeds from loan sales.

Strategy

BSB Bancorp reiterated in 2016 that it planned to continue focusing on growing its one-to-four family residential mortgage commercial real estate and home equity lending business which made up more than 85% of its loan assets in 2015. With its eye on being the "Bank of Choice" for small businesses and municipalities in its core Boston market area it plans to organically grow its deposit and lending business in the parts of Eastern Massachusetts that weren't as affected by the most recent recession. In 2013 BSB Bancorp expanded its reach by 50% after opening two branches inside Shaw's Supermarkets in Cambridge and Newton (its first supermarket branch was opened in Waltham in 2012).

EXECUTIVES

President and CEO, Robert M. (Bob) Mahoney, age 67

EVP and COO, Hal R. Tovin, age 60

Executive Vice President for Consumer Lending, Christopher Y. (Chris) Downs, age 65

SVP CFO and Secretary BSB Bancorp Inc. and Belmont Savings Bank, John A. Citrano, age 52

President Bob Mahoney, Belmont Bank

Auditors: Baker Newman & Noyes

LOCATIONS

HQ: BSB Bancorp Inc. (MD)
2 Leonard Street, Belmont, MA 02478
Phone: 617 484-6700
Web: www.belmontsavings.com

COMPETITORS

Bank of America	Hingham Institution
Boston Private	for Savings
Brookline Bancorp	Independent Bank (MA)
Century Bancorp (MA)	Meridian Bancorp
Citizens Financial	Middlesex Savings
Group	Peoples Federal
DCU	Bancshares Inc.
Eastern Bank	Sovereign Bank
Enterprise Bancorp	TD Bank USA

HISTORICAL FINANCIALS

Company Type: Public

Income Statement

FYE: December 31

	ASSETS ($ mil.)	NET INCOME ($ mil.)	INCOME AS % OF ASSETS	EMPLOYEES
12/15	1,812.9	6.9	0.4%	132.0
12/14	1,425.5	4.2	0.3%	128.0
12/13	1,054.6	1.9	0.2%	127.0
12/12	838.0	1.4	0.2%	119.0
12/11	669.0	0.3	0.0%	101.0
Annual Growth	**28.3%**	**119.3%**	**—**	**6.9%**

2015 Year-End Financials

Return on assets: 0.4%	Dividends
Return on equity: 4.8%	Yield: —
Long-term debt ($ mil.): —	Payout: —
No. of shares (mil.): 9.0	Market value ($ mil.): 213.0
Sales ($ mil): 51.5	

	STOCK PRICE ($) FY Close	P/E High/Low	PER SHARE ($) Earnings	Dividends	Book Value
12/15	23.39	30 23	0.78	0.00	16.09
12/14	18.63	38 30	0.49	0.00	15.11
12/13	15.09	69 56	0.22	0.00	14.40
12/12	12.23	84 66	0.16	0.00	13.98
12/11	10.54	— —	(0.00)	0.00	14.34
Annual Growth	**22.1%**	**— —**	**—**	**—**	**2.9%**

Buffalo Wild Wings Inc

Hot sauce fuels the flight of this restaurateur. Buffalo Wild Wings (BWW) operates a chain of more than 1120 Buffalo Wild Wings Grill & Bar quick-casual dining spots that specialize in serving Buffalo-style chicken wings. The eateries found throughout North America the Philippines and the UAE offer more than a dozen unique dipping sauces to go with the spicy wings as well as a complement of other items such as chicken tenders and legs. BWW's menu also features appetizers burgers tacos salads and desserts along with beer wine and other beverages. The company owns and operates about 515 of the restaurants while the rest are operated by franchisees.

Geographic Reach

The majority of the company's restaurants are located in California Illinois Indiana Michigan Ohio and Texas. Many BWW locations are found in suburban areas typically near established retail and entertainment developments.

Operations

Typical in the casual dining industry the BWW chain comprises a mix of corporate-run and franchised locations. Its large estate of owned and operated eateries accounts for the greatest share of the company's sales (about 94% in fiscal 2014) and allows it to maintain control over the Buffalo Wild Wings dining experience while its franchising efforts help expand the chain with fewer construction and operating costs.

Food and nonalcoholic beverages accounted for about 79% of restaurant sales in fiscal 2014. The remaining 21% of restaurant sales was from alcoholic beverages.

Sales and Marketing

The BWW concept is designed to appeal to a broad mix of customers but the chain promotes itself as a place for groups and families to gather and watch sporting events. (Some locations have as many as 50 TV screens to give everyone a good view of the big game.)

BWW competes broadly against other casual dining chains such as Applebee's and T.G.I. Friday's (owned by Carlson Restaurants Worldwide) but within its target audience the chain faces competition from Dave & Buster's the Fox & Hound chain of sports bars and of course Hooters.

The company's advertising expenses for fiscal 2014 were $1.8 million compared to $1 million in 2013. BWW's primary media vehicles include national television national and local radio and digital media outlets.

Financial Performance

The company's revenue was $1.5 billion in fiscal 2014. That was an increase of about $250 million (or 20%) compared to the previous fiscal period. The revenue spike was driven by increased sales at company-owned restaurants and increased franchise royalties.

BWW reported net income of $94 million in fiscal 2014 which was an increase of $22.5 million (or 32%) compared to its fiscal 2013 net income. BWW's net income went up even though the company's labor cost increased by $83.9 million (or 23%) in fiscal 2014 compared to the prior fiscal year.

The company's cash flow from operations remains strong. BWW ended fiscal 2014 with more than $217 million in cash on hand which was an increase of $38.5 million compared to fiscal 2013 levels.

Strategy

The company is working toward the goal of eventually reaching about 1700 locations in the US and Canada with plans calling for corporate-owned restaurants to make up about 40% of the chain. BWW's current growth strategy is to continue to open both company-owned restaurants and franchised restaurants. The company expects to open approximately 50 company-owned and 50 franchised Buffalo Wild Wings restaurants in 2015.

Company Background

Jim Disbrow and Scott Lowery opened the first Buffalo Wild Wings restaurant on the campus of Ohio State University in Columbus in 1982. (Legend has it that they started the eatery because they craved the style of chicken wings they had eaten in Buffalo New York.) Originally called Buffalo Wild Wings & Weck (a reference to the Kimmelweck brand rolls used for sandwiches) the chain became known as BW3 for short. Rapid expansion and financial mismanagement pushed Buffalo Wild Wings to the brink of bankruptcy by the mid-1990s. Sally Smith became CEO in 1996 and helped retool the chain's branding strategy to appeal more to families and non-students.

EXECUTIVES

President CEO and Director, Sally J. Smith, age 59, $841,346 total compensation

EVP and President North America Buffalo Wild Wings, Judith A. (Judy) Shoulak, age 57, $409,817 total compensation

EVP and CFO, Alexander H. (Alex) Ware, age 54

COO, James M. Schmidt, age 57, $511,837 total compensation

CIO, Santiago Abraham

Senior Vice President Information Systems, Lee Patterson

Vice President of Marketing Communications, Bob (Bo) Ruhland

Executive Vice President Global Operations and Human Resources, Carol (Care) Meyer

Vice President Talent Management Services, Julie (Jules) Letner

Senior Vice President Corporate Controller, Jeff (Jeffy) Sorum

Director, James M. Damian, age 65

Auditors: KPMG LLP

LOCATIONS

HQ: Buffalo Wild Wings Inc
5500 Wayzata Boulevard, Suite 1600, Minneapolis, MN 55416
Phone: 952 593-9943
Web: www.buffalowildwings.com

PRODUCTS/OPERATIONS

2014 Sales

	$ mil.	% of total
Restaurant sales	1,423.0	94
Franchise royalties and fees	93.2	6
Total	**1,516.2**	**100**

2015 Locations

	No.
Franchised	603
Company-owned	517
Total	**1,120**

COMPETITORS

Applebee's	Houlihan's
International	Johnny Rockets
Brinker	OSI Restaurant
Carlson Restaurants	Partners
Damon's	Rock Bottom
Darden	Restaurants
Dave & Buster's	Ruby Tuesday
Famous Dave's	Wingstop
Hooters	

HISTORICAL FINANCIALS

Company Type: Public

Income Statement

FYE: December 27

	REVENUE ($ mil.)	NET INCOME ($ mil.)	NET PROFIT MARGIN	EMPLOYEES
12/15	1,812.7	95.0	5.2%	44,500.0
12/14	1,516.2	94.0	6.2%	37,200.0
12/13	1,266.7	71.5	5.6%	31,700.0
12/12	1,040.5	57.2	5.5%	25,500.0
12/11	784.4	50.4	6.4%	21,000.0
Annual Growth	**23.3%**	**17.2%**	**—**	**20.7%**

2015 Year-End Financials

Debt ratio: 6.8%	No. of shares (mil.): 18.9
Return on equity: 15.5%	Dividends
Cash ($ mil.): 120.3	Yield: —
Current ratio: 0.75	Payout: —
Long-term debt ($ mil.): 70.9	Market value ($ mil.): 3,070.0

Cadence Design Systems Inc

Cadence Design Systems helps engineers pick up the development tempo. A leader in the market for electronic design automation (EDA) software Cadence sells and leases software and hardware products used to design integrated circuits (ICs) printed circuit boards (PCBs) and other electronic systems. Semiconductor and electronics systems manufacturers use its products to build components for wireless devices networking equipment and other applications. The company also provides maintenance and support and offers design and methodology consulting services. Customers have included Pegatron Silicon Labs and Texas Instruments. Cadence gets more than half of its sales from customers outside the US.

Operations

Cadence's products and maintenance account for 94% of its revenue with services bringing in the other 6%.

Geographic Reach

With its main headquarters in the US Cadence Design has regional headquarters near customers in China India and Japan. It has about 56 other sales offices design centers and research and development facilities most outside the US.

The US is its largest single market accounting for almost 45% of sales. Customers in Asia (where most of the world's electronics are made) account for 34% of sales and Europe makes up rest.

Sales and Marketing

Cadence Design Systems primarily uses a direct sales force but certain products such as its OrCAD or Incisive series are sold by resellers. Due to the complex nature of EDA products and the electronic design process the company's sales cycle is generally long averaging three to six months or more.

Customers include Fujitsu Polycom Cavium STM Ricoh VIA Telecom and Faraday Technology.

Financial Performance

Since two sub-billion years (2010 and 2011) Cadence has been rebuilding its revenue. It rose 8% to $1.6 billion in 2014 from $1.46 billion in 2013. Increased levels of business and incremental contributions from acquisition fueled the growth. Net income however dropped about 5% to $159 million in 2014 from 2013. Cadence increased research and development spending 13% in 2014 and posted other higher operating costs related to acquisitions made in 2013 and 2014. Cash flow from operations was $316.7 million in 2014 a decrease from $367.6 million in 2013.

Strategy

The company's product strategy is focused around design activities that include functional verification digital IC design custom IC design and system interconnect. Cadence products include Incisive (functional verification) Encounter (digital IC design) Virtuoso (custom design) and Allegro (system interconnect platforms).

Mergers and Acquisitions

Cadence acquired Jasper Design Automation Inc. a privately held provider of formal analysis software for $139 million in 2014. Jasper's technology complements Cadence's system design and verification platforms. The company made two other deals for Forte Design Systems and the assets of TransSwitch in 2014 for a total of $27.5 million.

In 2013 the company made three acquisitions. It bought India-based Cosmic Circuits a provider of analog and mixed signal IP cores the IP business of Polish firm Evatronix and California-based Tensilica a provider of intellectual property cores for dataplane processing for $380 million.

HISTORY

Cadence Design Systems arose from the 1988 merger of software firms ECAD (formed in 1982) and SDA Systems (founded 1983). The stock market crash of 1987 helped propel SDA Systems an EDA company that gave up its planned IPO in the wake of the crash into its merger with ECAD which was publicly held to form Cadence Design. Private venture capital investor and SDA chairman Donald Lucas became chairman of Cadence. Joe Costello the young charismatic and tall (6-foot-7) president and COO of SDA was named president and CEO of Cadence. It became the world's leading electronic design automation (EDA) software supplier by enlarging and improving the range of software it developed in-house and via such acquisitions as Tangent Systems (1989) and Valid Logic Systems (1991).

The company grew through a series of acquisitions. Cadence concluded long-running litigation with Avant! (after Avant! was acquired by Synopsys) with a $265 million payment to Cadence.

EXECUTIVES

Corporate Vice President, Daniel (Dan) Salisbury
Senior Vice President General Manager Verification Acceleration Group, Christopher (Chris) Tice
Vice President Product Marketing, Charlie (Charles) Giorgetti
Corporate Vice President Strategic Planning, Craig (Craigy) Johnson
Senior Vice President Human resources, Tina (Tin) Jones
SVP and CFO, Geoffrey G. (Geoff) Ribar, age 58, $400,000 total compensation
President and CEO, Lip-Bu Tan, age 56, $650,000 total compensation
SVP Marketing and Business Development, Nimish H. Modi, age 54, $289,080 total compensation
SVP and General Manager Custom IC and PCB Group, Thomas P. (Tom) Beckley, $375,000 total compensation
SVP Research and Development, Anirudh Devgan, $375,000 total compensation
SVP Worldwide Field Operations, Neil Zaman, $322,129 total compensation
Vice President Finance, James (Jamie) Haddad
Vice President Research and Development, Moshe Rubin
Admin for Ananthan Thandri Vice President of Applications, Elvira Cuenca

Senior Vice President, Henry Salvia
Vice President Software Engineering Architect, Limin He
05 Vice President Engineering Director Engineering, Michael (Mel) Bershteyn
Vice President, Erik Panu
Executive Vice President And General Manager Products And Solutions Business, Lavi Lev
Vice President of Sales, Mike (Mikey) Yeager
Vice President Design Methodology Engineering, Joe Mastroianni
Vice President Customer Driven Research And Development Ic Digital Solutions Group, David Jarmon
Vice President Sales Global Accounts, Veronica Watson
Vice President, Lou (Lewis) Holt
Vice President of Operations, Peter (Pete) Connor
Vice President System Design Spectrum Services Group, Steve Manser
Corporate Vice President Research and Development, Donald (Don) Friedberg
Vice President Corporate Tax, Dean Ozawa
Senior Vice President Marketing, Victor Berman
Vice President Technology, Matt Bromley
Vice President Research And Development, Saugat Sen
Corporate Vice President Sales, Vikas Kumar
Vice President, Jim (Jimmy) Cowie
Senior Vice President and Chief Marketing Officer, Johnathan (John) Bruggeman
Vice President and Associate General Counsel, Yoonie Chang
Senior Vice President of Worldwide Field Operations, Aneel Zaman
Chairman, John B. Shoven, age 68
Board Member, Ron (Ronnie) Vogelsong
Auditors: KPMG LLP

LOCATIONS

HQ: Cadence Design Systems Inc
2655 Seely Avenue, Building 5, San Jose, CA 95134
Phone: 408 943-1234
Web: www.cadence.com

PRODUCTS/OPERATIONS

Selected Software
Analog simulators (Spectre)
Cycle-based simulators (SpeedSim)
Deep submicron design (Envisia)
Digital IC design (Encounter platform including First Encounter SoC Encounter and Nano Encounter)
Digital simulators (NC-simulator NC-Verilog NC-VHDL)
Editing and synthesis compaction device-level editing (Virtuoso family)
Equivalence checking (Affirma)
Hardware emulators (CoBALT Mercury)
Model checking (Affirma Formalcheck)
Place and routing (Envisia Silicon Ensemble)
Printed circuit board design and packaging (Allegro SPECCTRA)
Synthesis (Envisia Ambit BuildGates)
Verification (Assura line including Diva and Dracula; Incisive platform; Palladium)

Selected Services
Education
IC design services (Cadence Design Foundry)
IC implementation
Intellectual property (IP Gallery)
Methodology
Wireless design

2014 Sales

	$ mil.	% of total
Product and Maintenance	1479.2	94
Services	101.7	6
Total	**1580.9**	**100**

2014 Sales

	% of total
Functional verification & design IP	22
Digital IC design and Signoff	29
Custom IC design	27
System interconnect and Analysis	11
IP	11
Total	**100**

COMPETITORS

ANSYS	Mentor Graphics
Agilent EEsof	PDF Solutions
Altium	Synopsys
Intrinsix	Zuken

HISTORICAL FINANCIALS

Company Type: Public

Income Statement

FYE: January 2

	REVENUE ($ mil.)	NET INCOME ($ mil.)	NET PROFIT MARGIN	EMPLOYEES
01/16	1,702.0	252.4	14.8%	6,700.0
01/15*	1,580.9	158.9	10.1%	6,100.0
12/13	1,460.1	164.2	11.2%	5,700.0
12/12	1,326.4	439.9	33.2%	5,200.0
12/11	1,149.8	72.2	6.3%	4,700.0
Annual Growth	**10.3%**	**36.7%**	**—**	**9.3%**

*Fiscal year change

2016 Year-End Financials

Debt ratio: 14.8%	No. of shares (mil.): 309.3
Return on equity: 18.6%	Dividends
Cash ($ mil.): 616.6	Yield: —
Current ratio: 1.80	Payout: —
Long-term debt ($ mil.): 348.7	Market value ($ mil.): 6,438.0

	STOCK PRICE ($) FY Close	P/E High/Low		Earnings	PER SHARE ($) Dividends	Book Value
01/16	20.81	26	19	0.81	0.00	4.45
01/15*	18.83	34	25	0.52	0.00	4.57
12/13	13.93	27	21	0.56	0.00	4.01
12/12	13.44	8	6	1.57	0.00	3.26
12/11	10.40	43	30	0.27	0.00	1.51
Annual Growth	**18.9%**	**—**	**—**	**31.6%**	**—**	**31.1%**

*Fiscal year change

CAI International Inc

Is it bigger than a breadbox? CAI International can pack it. The company leases large steel boxes to ship freight by plane train or truck around the world. More than 65% of its container fleet is owned by CAI and the balance owned by container investors is managed by CAI. The leasing segment offers 280-plus shipping companies short-term and long-term leases with some leases giving the lessees the option to purchase the container. The container management segment provides container investors with the ability to lease re-lease and dispose of their container portfolio; services also include container repair relocation and storage.

Geographic Reach

CAI caters to 280 customers from 16 offices spanning 13 countries. CAI purchases the majority of its containers in China and operates from of-

fices in Belgium Hong Kong Japan Korea Singapore Taiwan the UK and the US among others.

Sales and Marketing

The top ten largest lessees account for about 60% of its total leasing segment sales (approximately 55% of total sales). Its largest customer CMA CGM generates 11% of sales.

Financial Performance

CAI has enjoyed four straight years of unprecedented growth. Revenues climbed 7% from $212 million in 2013 to reach a historic high of $228 million in 2014. Profits however fell 6% from $64 million in 2013 to $60 million in 2014 due to increased storage handling and other expenses.

The growth for 2014 was driven by a 8% spike in rental revenue due to an increase in the average number of owned containers on lease. The company was also helped by a 11% bump in finance lease sales. This growth was offset by a 17% decrease in management fee revenue.

Company Background

Founded by Hiromitsu Ogawa in 1989 CAI has evolved from solely an intermodal leasing concern to a more ambitious manager of containers owned by investors.

EXECUTIVES

President and CEO, Victor M. Garcia, age 48, $323,833 total compensation

VP Operations, Camille G. Cutino, age 57, $164,800 total compensation

CFO, Timothy Page

Vice President Finance and Corporate Controller, David B (Dave) Morris

Senior Vice President Global Marketing, Daniel Hallahan

Vice President Rail Services, James Magee

Auditors: KPMG LLP

LOCATIONS

HQ: CAI International Inc
Steuart Tower, 1 Market Plaza, Suite 900, San Francisco, CA 94105
Phone: 415 788-0100
Web: www.capps.com

PRODUCTS/OPERATIONS

2014 Sales

	% of total
Rental revenue	93
Management fee revenue	3
Finance lease income	4
Gain on sale of container portfolios	0
Total	**100**

Selected Operations

Container leasing
  Container owned by CAI
  Full benefits of ownership
  Placed on long- and short-term leases to shipping lines
Container management
  Container sold to investors
  Generate cash flow through management fee revenue and trading income
  Managed by CAI over expected life of asset

COMPETITORS

COSCO Group	Seaco
SeaCube Container	Touax
Seacastle	XTRA Corp.

HISTORICAL FINANCIALS

Company Type: Public

Income Statement

FYE: December 31

	REVENUE ($ mil.)	NET INCOME ($ mil.)	NET PROFIT MARGIN	EMPLOYEES
12/15	249.6	26.8	10.7%	128.0
12/14	227.5	60.2	26.5%	101.0
12/13	212.4	63.9	30.1%	85.0
12/12	173.9	63.4	36.5%	91.0
12/11	125.7	50.1	39.9%	83.0
Annual Growth	**18.7%**	**(14.5%)**	**—**	**11.4%**

2015 Year-End Financials

Debt ratio: 72.0%	No. of shares (mil.): 20.1
Return on equity: 5.9%	Dividends
Cash ($ mil.): 52.5	Yield: —
Current ratio: 0.66	Payout: —
Long-term debt ($ mil.): 1,259.2	Market value ($ mil.): 203.0

	STOCK PRICE ($) FY Close	P/E High/Low		Earnings	PER SHARE ($) Dividends	Book Value
12/15	10.08	20	7	1.28	0.00	22.87
12/14	23.20	9	6	2.85	0.00	21.27
12/13	23.57	10	7	2.82	0.00	18.64
12/12	21.95	7	5	3.18	0.00	15.73
12/11	15.46	10	4	2.55	0.00	11.92
Annual Growth	**(10.1%)**	**—**	**—**	**(15.8%)**	**—**	**17.7%**

Cal-Maine Foods Inc

Cal-Maine Foods' more than 26 million laying hens are some of its top performers. The nation's largest shell egg producer and marketer the company sells more than 880 million dozen eggs a year. It is also one of the top suppliers of specialty shell eggs (which are Omega-3 enhanced organic and cage free) that are marketed under the Egg-Land's Best Farmhouse and 4Grain brands. Cal-Maine's operations span all phases of shell egg production: hatching chicks making feed housing hens and distributing eggs. Customers include US grocery stores (such as Publix) superstores the likes of Wal-Mart and warehouse clubs (Sam's Club) as well as foodservice distributors and makers of egg products dotting 29 states.

Geographic Reach

The company's operations extend nationwide across nearly 30 states.

Mergers and Acquisitions

Cal-Maine continues to grow its share of the shell-egg market through acquisitions of existing production and processing operations. It has made nearly 20 acquisitions since 1989. Each added between 600000 to 7.5 million laying hens (called layers) and related facilities as well as expanded the company's portfolio of name brands. Such investments and acquisitions have boosted Cal-Maine's flock of layers pullets and breeders. The flock is likely the largest in the US.

The company acquired certain egg operations from Pilgrim's Pride in 2012. Cal-Maine gained two production facilities in Texas with capacity for some 1.4 million laying hens and stepped up its presence in the Southwest market as a result. Adding to its Texas holdings Cal-Maine in late 2012 acquired Maxim Production Co. The purchases complement its 2009 acquisition of Florida's Tampa Farms' 4Grain brand of specialty shell eggs.

Strategy

Cal-Maine also looks to shore up operations through construction of new more efficient egg production and processing plants paired with a pullet growing facility. It also regularly disposes of older less efficient facilities.

On several separate occasions the company was hit by a nationwide food recall. The 2011 and 2010 recalls were attributable to possible salmonella contamination from eggs produced by Hillandale Farms of Iowa as well as from other outside contractors. In addition Cal-Maine is under pressure from animal welfare advocates who argue for better treatment of its flock of hens including larger cages fewer beak trimmings and decreased forced molting practices (which put chickens under stress to lay more eggs). The Humane Society of the United States and the United Egg Producers agreed in 2011 to press toward new federal legislation which if passed will increase the production costs of housing and feeding hens.

Financial Performance

Net sales rose 18% in fiscal 2012 as compared to 2011 due in part to an 8% increase in total dozens of eggs sold and a boost in the average selling price of shell eggs. Cal-Maine's 48% increase in net income during the same reporting period is primarily attributable to the increase in net sales partially offset by the increase in cost of sales. Contributing to the cost of sales bump were the increase in dozens produced dozens purchased from outside shell egg producers and cost of feed ingredients.

Sales and Marketing

Cal-Maine markets its shell eggs through a distribution network serving a diverse group of customers. It caters to national and regional grocery store chains club stores foodservice distributors and egg product makers. Together Wal-Mart and Sam's Club account for 31% of sales and Publix Super Markets generates 10%.

The company's advertising costs totaled $4245 $5768 and $2098 in fiscal 2012 2011 and 2010 respectively.

Company Ownership

Cal-Maine also faces significant control by a small party. Founder and chairman emeritus Fred Adams Jr. owns about 53% of the company's voting power. The son-in-law of Adams Adolphus "Dolph" Baker is president and CEO and holds a 14% stake.

HISTORY

One can side with the chicken or the egg in the which-came-first argument but it was Fred Adams Jr. who came first at Cal-Maine. A former salesman with pet food giant Ralston Purina (now Nestlé Purina PetCare) Adams founded a poultry and egg business in Mendenhall Mississippi in 1957. He focused exclusively on egg sales in 1960 and merged his company in 1969 with Maine Egg Farms and Dairy Fresh Foods in California to form Cal-Maine Foods.

Cal-Maine cracked new markets through internal growth and the acquisition of rival egg firms. The company acquired Egg City (Arkansas 1989) Sunny Fresh Foods (Arkansas 1990) Sunnyside Eggs (North Carolina 1991) Wayne Detling Farms (Ohio 1994) A&G Farms (Kentucky 1995) and Sunbest Farms (Arkansas 1996). After going public in 1996 Cal-Maine bought two Georgia firms: Southern Empire Egg Farm (1997) and J&S Farms (1998).

In 1998 the company sold off its egg products division which provided food makers with egg

whites and yolks and accounted for 4% of total sales.

In 1999 Cal-Maine bought two egg producers and processors: Kentucky-based Hudson Brothers and Texas-based Smith Farms. Declining supplies in the cyclical egg market and increasing demand in late 2000 raised the company out of the loss column for the first time in 18 months. In late 2001 Cal-Maine's board of directors voted to explore the possibility of the company becoming privately held but abandoned the idea because of a sagging egg market. Industry-wide overproduction helped to drive down egg prices pecking away at the company's profits in 2002.

In 2003 Cal-Maine's board of directors voted to take the company private. However as demand for eggs shot up so did Cal-Maine stock prices and shareholders were unconvinced such a move would benefit them. Faced with shareholder lawsuits in November of that year the board voted to terminate the proposal to take the company private.

After years of oversupply and weak prices starting in 2003 the entire egg industry enjoyed a boost from the popular protein-heavy Atkins diet. Cal-Maine's sales jumped as people chose hard-boiled eggs as snacks. However by 2004 its popularity had peaked leaving the market (and Cal-Maine) with an egg glut and plunging sales. In 2005 the company acquired egg supplier Hillandale Farms.

In 2006 the company formed a 50-50 joint venture (Green Forest Foods) with Pier 44 Properties to lease and operate Green Forest Egg's production assets which included about 1 million laying hens at facilities located in Arkansas. Cal-Maine's bought of Pier 44's interest in Green Forest in 2007 and purchased the shell-egg division of George's Inc. for which it paid $11 million in cash.

Fred Adams Jr. founder and chairman handed over the title of CEO to former COO Dolph Baker in late 2010.

EXECUTIVES

VP CFO Secretary Treasurer and Director, Timothy A. Dawson, age 62, $264,738 total compensation
Chairman President and CEO, Adolphus B. (Dolph) Baker, age 59, $361,106 total compensation
VP Feed Mill Division, Joe M. Wyatt, age 77, $134,553 total compensation
VP Operations, Sherman L. Miller, age 41, $173,461 total compensation
VP Egg Products, James (Jim) Hull
VP and General Counsel, Robert L. (Rob) Holladay, age 40, $179,231 total compensation
Vice President Sales, Kyle Morris
Vice President Egg Sales, Matt (Matty) Arrowsmith
Vice President Finance, Charles (Charlie) Collins
Vice President, Rob (Robbie) Holladay
Auditors: Frost, PLLC

LOCATIONS

HQ: Cal-Maine Foods Inc
3320 W. Woodrow Wilson Avenue, Jackson, MS 39209-3409
Phone: 601 948-6813   **Fax:** 601 969-0905
Web: www.calmainefoods.com

PRODUCTS/OPERATIONS

2015 Sales

	% of total
Shell eggs	
Non-specialty shell eggs	65
Specialty shell eggs	28
Co-pack specialty shell eggs	2
Egg products	4
other sales	1
Total	**100**

Selected Brands
4Grain
Cal-Maine
Egg-Land's Best (licensed from Egg-Land's Best Inc.)
Farmhouse
Rio Grande
Sunny Meadow
Sunups

COMPETITORS

Cargill Kitchen Solutions	Ise America
Chino Valley Ranchers	Luberski
ConAgra	Michael Foods
Cooper Farms	Moark
Egg Innovations	National Food
Hickman's Family Farms	Rose Acre Farms
	Wilson Farms

HISTORICAL FINANCIALS
Company Type: Public

Income Statement

FYE: May 28

	REVENUE ($ mil.)	NET INCOME ($ mil.)	NET PROFIT MARGIN	EMPLOYEES
05/16	1,908.6	316.0	16.6%	3,277.0
05/15	1,576.1	161.2	10.2%	2,872.0
05/14*	1,440.9	109.2	7.6%	2,645.0
06/13	1,288.1	50.4	3.9%	2,479.0
06/12	1,113.1	89.7	8.1%	2,175.0
Annual Growth	**14.4%**	**37.0%**	**—**	**10.8%**

*Fiscal year change

2016 Year-End Financials

Debt ratio: 2.3%
Return on equity: 39.1%
Cash ($ mil.): 29.0
Current ratio: 7.50
Long-term debt ($ mil.): 9.2

No. of shares (mil.): 48.5
Dividends
  Yield: 0.0%
  Payout: 38.1%
Market value ($ mil.): 2,220.0

	STOCK PRICE ($) FY Close	P/E High/Low		PER SHARE ($) Earnings	Dividends	Book Value
05/16	45.74	10	7	6.53	2.49	18.86
05/15	56.69	29	10	3.33	1.20	14.51
05/14*	69.76	31	20	2.26	0.51	12.28
06/13	44.74	44	33	1.05	0.64	10.74
06/12	34.84	22	15	1.88	0.42	10.01
Annual Growth	**7.0%**			**— —**	**36.6% 56.3%**	**17.1%**

*Fiscal year change

CalAmp Corp

When machines talk CalAmp helps you listen. The former military supplier makes hardware and software to track trucks planes and industrial equipment and to keep them communicating. It provides asset tracking devices mobile telemetry units fixed and mobile wireless gateways and wireless router transmission for machine resource management (MRM) and machine-to-machine (M2M) communication. CalAmp keeps track of it all through cloud-based telematics and applications offered through as-a-service models. The company's customers are in the energy government heavy equipment transportation and automotive markets. CalAmp discontinued its satellite business when EchoStar its only customer consolidated suppliers.

Operations

CalAmp's operations have been segmented into Wireless Datacom and Satellite units.

Some 86% of CalAmp's 2016 (ended February) revenue came from the Wireless Datacom line with the rest generated by Satellite services.

Most of the company's manufacturing and assembly is handled by contractors.

Geographic Reach

Based in Oxnard California the company also operates wireless datacom locations in Virginia and Minnesota in the US and in Quebec Canada and Auckland New Zealand.

About 83% of sales are to customers in the US with international customers supplying the other 17%.

Sales and Marketing

CalAmp offers its wireless datacom through direct and indirect sales force in US and through sales personnel in Latin America Israel and the UK.

Its Satellite segment has sold its products primarily to EchoStar an affiliate of DISH Network which has accounted for a diminishing portion of revenue. It was 14% in 2016 (ended January) 15% in 2015 and 21% in 2014.

Financial Performance

In 2016 (ended January) CalAmp reported revenue growth of 12% to about $281 million driven by higher wireless datacom revenues (up 13%) due to increased sales of MRM products into the fleet management and non-vehicle asset tracking markets. The company also had a boost from an order from a heavy equipment manufacturer.

Net income increased 2.6% in 2016 to about $17 million from 2015. Higher sales combined with a tax benefit to produce a profit.

Cash provided by operations strengthened to $47 million in 2016 from $28.6 million in 2015.

Strategy

CalAmp is not looking back wistfully at its satellite business. With the loss of EchoStar as a customer CalAmp discontinued that part of its operations in its 2017 fiscal year ended February. It is moving deeper into wireless data communications and expects no negative impact from cutting its Satellite business.

A major way CalAmp is expanding its wireless operations is through acquisitions that add technology for MRM and M2M products and services to its lineup.

Mergers and Acquisitions

In 2016 CalAmp spent about $131 million to buy LoJack Corp. a provider of vehicle theft recovery systems and advanced fleet management technologies. The acquisition should accelerate CalAmp's progress into the automotive telematics business.

In 2015 CalAmp Corp. made a similar acquisition with privately held Crashboxx an early stage company focused on insurance telematics applications. The price was $1.5 million.

CalAmp invested in another telematics startup SmartDriverClub Ltd. which develops connected car services and applications aimed at consumers and auto dealers in the UK.

EXECUTIVES

SVP and General Manager Satellite Products, Robert Hannah, $215,000 total compensation

EVP CFO and Secretary, Richard K. (Rick) Vitelle, age 62, $330,000 total compensation

President and CEO, Michael J. Burdiek, age 56, $440,000 total compensation

SVP Operations, John J. Warwick

SVP and General Manager Wireless Networks, Michael P. (Mike) Zachan, age 67

SVP Marketing and Business Development, Justin Schmid

SVP and General Manager MRM/M2M, Greg Gower

Vice President Sales and Marketing, Gallin Chen

Vice President Information Technology, Mark (Marky) Beckner

Senior Vice President, Richard (Dick) Rose

Vice President of Advanced Technologies, Mark (Marky) Anderson

Vice President Software Engineering, Anand Rau

Vice President and Legal Counsel, Steve (Stevie) Moran

Chairman, A.J. (Bert) Moyer

Auditors: BDO USA, LLP

LOCATIONS

HQ: CalAmp Corp
15635 Alton Parkway,, Suite 250, Irvine, CA 92618
Phone: 949 600-5600
Web: www.calamp.com

PRODUCTS/OPERATIONS

2016 Sales

	$ mil.	% of total
Wireless DataCom	241.4	86
Satellite	39.3	14
Total	**280.7**	**100**

2016 Sales

	$ mil
% of total	
Products	85
Application subscriptions and other services	15
Total	**100**

Selected Products

Satellite components
  Amplifiers
  Downconverters
  Feedhorns
Wireless access equipment
  Antennas
  Broadband analog scrambling/decoding systems (MultiCipher)
  Transceivers (passive planar stand-alone)

COMPETITORS

AML Communications
Broadcast Microwave Services
COM DEV
Cohu
Enfora
Filtronic
Kratos Defense & Security Solutions
Motorola Solutions
Novatel Wireless
STC Microwave Systems
Sharp Corp.
Sierra Wireless
Trimble Navigation
WebTech
Wistron NeWeb

HISTORICAL FINANCIALS

Company Type: Public

Income Statement

FYE: February 28

	REVENUE ($ mil.)	NET INCOME ($ mil.)	NET PROFIT MARGIN	EMPLOYEES
02/16	280.7	16.9	6.0%	490.0
02/15	250.6	16.5	6.6%	530.0
02/14	235.9	11.8	5.0%	490.0
02/13	180.5	44.6	24.7%	380.0
02/12	138.7	5.2	3.8%	370.0
Annual Growth	**19.3%**	**34.2%**	**—**	**7.3%**

Calavo Growers, Inc.

Calavo (a combination of "California" and "avocado") began as a growers' marketing cooperative founded in 1924 in order to transform the exotic hobby crop avocados into a culinary staple. Mission accomplished. Since the avocado has become if not a staple a regular in US supermarket shopping carts. Calavo procures and processes avocados papaya pineapple tomatoes and other fresh fruits grown mainly in California but the company also uses fruit from Chile Peru and Mexico. The products are then distributed to retail food outlets food service operators and produce wholesalers throughout the world.

Operations

Calavo operates its business through three segments: Fresh Products (59% of sales in 2015) Calavo Foods (7%) and Renaissance Food Group (RFG 34%).

Some 1900 growers deliver their crops to Calavo for processing. In addition to whole avocados the company manufactures avocado pulp and frozen peeled avocado halves through its Fresh business unit. Meanwhile its Calavo Foods business unit sells guacamole and the Salsa Lisa line of fresh salsas hummus and tortilla chips. RFG produces markets and distributes healthy high-quality products (fresh-cut fruit and vegetables grab-and-go salads snacks and sandwiches) for consumers nationwide through retailers.

FreshRealm is the company's technology firm that's focused on building a platform for those who are in the fresh food business.

Geographic Reach

Calavo operates a number of facilities throughout the US including packaging houses in California and operating and distribution centers in California Arizona Florida Hawaii Minnesota New Jersey and Texas. It also has facilities in Michoacán and Jalisco Mexico.

Sales and Marketing

The company distributes its goods to food service industry and retail customers. It develops various store packaging and displays to entice buyers particularly impulse buyers in the produce section.

The Fresh Products segment's five largest customers accounted for a combined 18% of its consolidated revenues; RFG's top five customers accounted for 23% of its consolidated revenues.

Calavo logged $200000 in advertising expenses in fiscal 2015 and 2014 up from $100000 in 2013.

Financial Performance

Revenues have been on a steady rise for the past five years. In fiscal 2015 revenue increased 9% to $856.8 million largely due to growth in the RFG segment (although the Fresh Products and Calavo Foods segments also saw sales increases). RFG's growth was attributed to a rise in sales of cut fruits and vegetables and deli products.

After taking a net loss of $97000 in 2014 the company returned to the black in 2015 when net income jumped to $27.2 million. That turnaround was partly due to higher sales but also due to the absence of contingent considerations related to the 2011 acquisition of RFG. Cash flow from operations rose 52% to $37.2 million that year.

Strategy

The Calavo Foods and RFG segments represent the company's move beyond fresh avocados and commodity produce into the market for fresh refrigerated packaged foods. It has expanded such holdings through acquisitions.

In the Fresh Products segment Calavo still seeks to expand its presence in the avocado market but also considers the distribution of other promising crops. In order to grow its business the company pursues partnerships with major food services companies.

In 2015 Calavo added a second packinghouse in Mexico in the prime growing region of Jalisco.

EXECUTIVES

Vice President of Fresh Operations, Mike Browne
Chairman President and CEO, Lecil E. (Lee) Cole, age 77, $584,855 total compensation
VP Sales and Fresh Marketing, Robert J. (Rob) Wedin, age 67, $259,900 total compensation
VP Processed Product Sales and Production, Alan C. (Al) Ahmer, age 68, $249,904 total compensation
Director Operations Calavo de Mexico, Dionisio Ortiz
VP Fresh Operations, Michael A. (Mike) Browne, age 58, $259,900 total compensation
CFO and Secretary, B. John Lindeman, $75,000 total compensation
VP Foods Division Sales and Operations, Ron Araiza
Vice President, Alex Ramirez
Auditors: Deloitte & Touche LLP

LOCATIONS

HQ: Calavo Growers, Inc.
1141-A Cummings Road, Santa Paula, CA 93060
Phone: 805 525-1245   **Fax:** 805 921-3223
Web: www.calavo.com

PRODUCTS/OPERATIONS

2015 Sales

	$ mil.	% of total
Fresh Products	500.7	59
RFG (Renaissance Food Group)	293.9	34
Calavo Foods	62.2	7
Total	**856.8**	**100**

Selected Products

Fresh
  Whole avocado
  Avocado halves
  Avocado pulp
  Papaya
  Pineapple
  Tomato
Calavo Foods
  Guacamole
  Salsa Lisa
  Tortilla chips

Selected Services

Growing
Ripening
Packing
Sales
Warehousing
Shipping & distribution

COMPETITORS

Azteca Foods	Gentile Bros.
BC Hot House Foods	Giumarra Companies
Brooks Tropicals	Goya
Caribe Food	Gruma Corporation
Chiquita Brands	Grupo Bimbo
Coast Citrus	H. J. Heinz Limited
Distributors	Hain Celestial
ConAgra	Index Fresh
Dole Food	Interfresh
Don Miguel Mexican	JR Simplot
Foods	La Tortilla Factory
Eastern Fresh Growers	Oceanside Produce
Inc.	Pacific Tomato Growers
Fresh Del Monte	Pinos Produce
Produce	Rancho Mission Viejo
FreshPoint	Shamrock Foods

HISTORICAL FINANCIALS

Company Type: Public

Income Statement

FYE: October 31

	REVENUE ($ mil.)	NET INCOME ($ mil.)	NET PROFIT MARGIN	EMPLOYEES
10/16	935.6	38.0	4.1%	2,096.0
10/15	856.8	27.2	3.2%	2,064.0
10/14	782.5	0.1	0.0%	1,987.0
10/13	691.4	17.3	2.5%	1,848.0
10/12	551.1	17.0	3.1%	1,531.0
Annual Growth	**14.1%**	**22.2%**	**—**	**8.2%**

2016 Year-End Financials

Debt ratio: 5.9%	No. of shares (mil.): 17.4
Return on equity: 19.0%	Dividends
Cash ($ mil.): 13.8	Yield: 0.0%
Current ratio: 1.23	Payout: 36.7%
Long-term debt ($ mil.): 0.4	Market value ($ mil.): 1,032.0

	STOCK PRICE ($) FY Close	P/E High/Low		Earnings	PER SHARE ($) Dividends	Book Value
10/16	59.15	32	22	2.18	0.80	12.28
10/15	51.41	39	25	1.57	0.75	10.64
10/14	48.54	4863	2830	0.01	0.70	10.37
10/13	29.69	28	19	1.17	0.65	8.17
10/12	23.61	26	19	1.15	0.55	7.42
Annual Growth	**25.8%**	**—**	**—**	**17.3%**	**9.8%**	**13.4%**

Cambrex Corp

Cambrex focuses on health. Providing products services and technologies which help to accelerate the development and commercialization of small molecule therapeutics the company develops products for the human health care market that include active pharmaceutical ingredients (APIs) and intermediates for over-the-counter and prescription branded and generic pharmaceuticals. It also makes intermediates used in cosmetics and food additives. Cambrex focuses on developing drug delivery technologies and the manufacture of high-potency compounds and controlled substances.

Geographic Reach

Cambrex has facilities in Estonia Germany India Italy Sweden and the US. R&D and specialty manufacturing facilities are located in Europe India and the US. In 2012 Europe accounted for 54% of sales North America 38%.

Sales and Marketing

The company sells its products through a combination of direct sales and independent agents. In 2012 Gyma Laboratories of America accounted for 13% of the company's sales. One active pharmaceutical ingredient (API) sold to multiple customers accounted for 12% of Cambrex's 2012 total revenues.

Financial Performance

Cambrex's revenues grew by 8% in 2012 despite foreign currency exchange rate that unfavorably impacted sales by 3.4%. Excluding foreign currency sales volumes increased in most of the company's product lines including controlled substances generic APIs custom development and products using Cambrex's drug delivery technology. It also experienced a modest increase in its custom manufacturing product sales including APIs and pharmaceutical intermediates sold to innovative drug companies. Higher demand for certain APIs was partially offset by a newly approved product in which the customer built up inventory in 2011. In 2012 custom development and manufacturing product contributed 45% of Cambrex's total revenues; generic APIs 36%.

However net income spiked by 468% in 2012 thanks to higher revenues increased income from continuing operations the increased absorption of R&D expenses into inventory and the lower cost of goods sold as a result of increased revenue generating custom development activity.

StrategyCambrex's stated strategy is to grow its portfolio of customer development projects –primarily those in the latter stages of the clinical trial process –and secure long-term supply agreements to make APIs and intermediates for recently approved drug products. It also seeks to expand sales based on its technologies and to partner with generic drug manufacturers to expand the company's portfolio of APIs. It also drives growth in strategic business segments through the selective acquisition of businesses products product lines technologies and capabilities.In 2013 Cambrex and Dow Chemical signed a deal for Cambrex to contract make Dow Hydroxypropyl Methylcellulose Acetate Succinate for Drug Solubility Enhancement. Dow's polymer science and application expertise coupled with Cambrex's capabilities positions Dow for rapid entry into the market using the AFFINISOL™ product platform.In 2012 Cambrex also agreed to supply an active pharmaceutical ingredient for a customer's Phase 3 program during 2013 and 2014.Mergers and Acquisition

In 2016 the company acquired PharmaCore a privately-owned company located in High Point North Carolina specializing in developing manufacturing and scaling up small molecule APIs for clinical phase projects.

The company acquired a 51% stake in Zenara Pharma in 2010 giving Cambrex a platform within India's growing pharmaceutical market and making it a global player in the nicotine replacement therapy market. Cambrex has an option to obtain the remaining 49% in 2016.OwnershipFund advisor BlackRock owns nearly 10% of Cambrex.

EXECUTIVES

Vice President Operations, Joe Nettleton
President CEO and Director, Steven M. (Steve) Klosk, age 59, $533,333 total compensation
Marketing Manager Cambrex Profarmaco Milano, Aldo Magnini, $338,666 total compensation
EVP Corporate Development and Strategy, Gregory P. (Greg) Sargen, age 50, $400,000 total compensation
EVP and COO, Shawn P. Cavanagh, $412,500 total compensation
Vice President, JAMES (Jamie) FARRELL
EVP and CFO, Tom Vadaketh
Tax Director Vice President, Andrew (Andy) Spada
Vice President Finance, Greg Sargen
Vice President Finance, Robert Congiusti
Vice President Finance, Greg (Greggy) Sargen
Auditors: BDO USA, LLP

LOCATIONS

HQ: Cambrex Corp
One Meadowlands Plaza, East Rutherford, NJ 07073
Phone: 201 804-3000 **Fax:** 201 804-9852
Web: www.cambrex.com

PRODUCTS/OPERATIONS

Selected Mergers and Acquisitions
2010
Zenara Pharma (51%; India; nicotine replacement therapy)

COMPETITORS

Aceto
Albany Molecular Research
Boehringer Ingelheim
Sigma-Aldrich

Valeant Pharmaceuticals
West Pharmaceutical Services

HISTORICAL FINANCIALS

Company Type: Public

Income Statement

FYE: December 31

	REVENUE ($ mil.)	NET INCOME ($ mil.)	NET PROFIT MARGIN	EMPLOYEES
12/16	490.6	81.6	16.6%	1,295.0
12/15	433.3	57.2	13.2%	1,228.0
12/14	374.6	57.3	15.3%	1,117.0
12/13	318.1	25.9	8.1%	936.0
12/12	276.5	62.3	22.5%	891.0
Annual Growth 15.4%		7.0%		9.8%

2016 Year-End Financials

Debt ratio: —
Return on equity: 22.7%
Cash ($ mil.): 74.1
Current ratio: 3.38
Long-term debt ($ mil.): —

No. of shares (mil.): 32.3
Dividends
Yield: —
Payout: —
Market value ($ mil.): 1,745.0

	STOCK PRICE ($) FY Close	P/E High/Low		PER SHARE ($) Earnings	Dividends	Book Value
12/16	53.95	23	12	2.48	0.00	12.53
12/15	47.09	30	12	1.76	0.00	9.77
12/14	21.62	13	9	1.81	0.00	8.08
12/13	17.83	23	13	0.84	0.00	6.90
12/12	11.38	7	3	2.06	0.00	5.46
Annual Growth 47.6%		—		—	4.7%	— 23.1%

Cantel Medical Corp

Just ask Cantel Medical —cleanliness is second to nothing when it comes to medical and scientific equipment. Through its subsidiaries the firm sells infection prevention and control products to hospitals dentists drug makers researchers and others in the US and abroad in the field of health care. Its diverse offerings include medical device reprocessing systems and disinfectants for dialyzers and endoscopes water purification equipment masks and bibs used in dental offices and therapeutic filtration systems. Fast-growing Cantel Medical employs an active acquisition strategy.

OperationsCantel Medical's major subsidiaries include: Mar Con Purification (water filtration and purification); Medivators (disposables disinfection sterilization); Crosstex (infection control and prevention); and Saf-T-Pak (packaging medical shipping systems). International units include Cantel Medical (UK) Cantel Medical Asia/Pacific Cantel Medical Devices (China) Biolab Equipment Medivators and Cantel Medical (Italy).The company operates through four segments: Endoscopy Water Purification and Filtration Healthcare Disposables and Dialysis.Endoscopy products include medical device reprocessing systems disinfectants detergents and other supplies for disinfection. The segment also provides technical maintenance services. Endoscopy is Cantel Medical's largest segment accounting for more than half of its total revenue.Water Purification and Filtration offerings include filtration and separation products disinfectants and sterilization and decontamination products for the medical biotech pharmaceutical beverage and commercial industrial industries. That segment accounts for about a quarter of total sales.Meanwhile Healthcare Disposable offers single-use products such as face masks sterilization pouches towels and bibs tray covers saliva ejectors wipes and disinfectants as well as products for maintaining safe dental unit waterlines. Healthcare Disposables contributes about 15% of Cantel's total sales.The smallest segment Dialysis (about 5% of sales) provides medical device reprocessing systems sterilants and disinfectants dialysate concentrates and other supplies used in renal dialysis.Geographic ReachCantel Medical rings up about 80% of its sales in the US. Foreign markets include Canada Europe Africa the Middle East South America and the Asia/Pacific region.Sales and MarketingCantel's customers include diagnostic clinical and university laboratories; pharma and biotech companies; US and Canadian government agencies; hospitals; and medical research facilities.In the US the company uses its own sales force to market its products; in international markets it employs independent distribution companiesIn fiscal 2016 (ended July) Cantel Medical spent $3.3 million on advertising in line with what it spent in 2015 and up from the $2.7 million it spent in 2014.Financial PerformanceCantel Medical's revenues and net income have been steadily rising for the past five years. In fiscal 2016 (ended July) revenue rose 18% to $664.8 million as organic product sales and service income increased. Growing demand in the endoscopy market was a primary driver of the higher sales; additionally in the health care disposables business the company's profits increased as Cantel sold more higher margin product and demand for its products grew in response to the Ebola virus. Overall net income rose 25% to $60 million thanks to the higher revenue but partially offset by higher cost of sales and operating expenses (including growth initiatives).
Strategy

Cantel Medical intends to double its sales and profits within the next five years. It has seen strong growth in its endoscopy and healthcare disposables businesses thanks partly to acquisitions of other firms that have added to its product portfolio.

The company has grown and diversified by employing an active acquisition strategy. It targets companies in the infection prevention and control market health care disposable products and water purification and filtration markets among others. More recently Cantel has focused on endoscopy its largest segment. It supplements acquisitions with occasional product launches such as the recently introduced SECURE FIT earloop face mask.

In 2015 the company sold its specialty packaging business a non-core operation.
Mergers and Acquisitions

Cantel Medical's biggest purchase of late was the 2015 purchase of Medical Innovations Group for $79.5 million. That acquisition expanded Cantel's endoscopy infection prevention product line.

In early 2016 Cantel bought the Sterility Assurance Monitoring Products division of North American Science Associates for $13.5 million. That unit makes biological and chemical indicators to monitor sterilization effectiveness for the industrial market and the deal gave Cantel entry into a new end-market for its health care disposables business.

Also that year the company bought certain assets of Vantage to expand distribution and sales of its Medivators endoscopy products in Canada one of its largest non-US markets. It then acquired Accutron a private manufacturer of nitrous oxide conscious sedation equipment and single-use nasal masks for use in dental procedures. That $52.5 million deal further broadened the health care disposables portfolio and created opportunities for cross-selling existing products.

EXECUTIVES

Senior Vice President Cao, Steven C (Steve) Anaya
Senior Vice President Marketing, Joanna (Anna) Albrecht
President Asia Pacific and Emerging Markets, David Rosen
EVP General Counsel and Secretary, Eric W. Nodiff, age 59, $361,875 total compensation
CEO, Jorgen B. Hansen, age 50, $453,529 total compensation
EVP and CFO, Peter G. Clifford, age 47, $128,077 total compensation
President Medivators Division, David C. Hemink
President Americas Sales and Global Service, Michael G. Spicer
Vice President Market Development, Matt (Matty) Conlon
Vice President Business Systems and Procurement, Lawrence Conway
Vice Chairman, George L. Fotiades, age 63
Chairman, Charles M. Diker, age 81
Auditors: Ernst & Young LLP

LOCATIONS

HQ: Cantel Medical Corp
150 Clove Road, Little Falls, NJ 07424
Phone: 973 890-7220 **Fax:** 973 890-7270
Web: www.cantelmedical.com

PRODUCTS/OPERATIONS

2016 Sales

	$ mil.	% of total
Endoscopy	341.7	51
Water purification & filtration	177.6	27
Healthcare Disposables	112.6	17
Dialysis	32.8	5
Total	**664.7**	**100**

Selected Acquisitions

FY2014
  PuriCore International Limited ($27 million; Somerset UK; endoscope products)
FY2013
  Jet Prep Ltd ($5 million; Herzliya Israel; developer of JET PREP Flushing device)
FY2012
  Byrne Medical Inc. ($100 million; Houston TX; infection control products)
FY2011
  ConFirm Monitoring Systems Inc. ($7.5 million; Denver Colorado; sterilization monitoring products)
  Gambro Medical Water Systems ($23.7 million; Colorado; production of medical grade water)

Selected Subsidiaries

Biolab Equipment Ltd.
Carsen Group Inc. (Canada)
Crosstex International Inc.
Medivators Inc.
Medivators Japan K.K.
Saf-T-Pak Inc. (Canada)
Strong Dental Products Inc.

COMPETITORS

3M Health Care	Getinge
CONMED Corporation	Johnson & Johnson
Danaher	Kimberly-Clark Health
Dentsply Sirona	Olympus
Ecolab	STERIS
Fresenius	Siemens AG
GE Water and Process Technologies	TIDI Products

HISTORICAL FINANCIALS

Company Type: Public

Income Statement

FYE: July 31

	REVENUE ($ mil.)	NET INCOME ($ mil.)	NET PROFIT MARGIN	EMPLOYEES
07/16	664.7	59.9	9.0%	2,000.0
07/15	565.0	47.9	8.5%	1,680.0
07/14	488.7	43.2	8.9%	1,534.0
07/13	425.0	39.2	9.2%	1,292.0
07/12	386.4	31.3	8.1%	1,198.0
Annual Growth	**14.5%**	**17.6%**	**—**	**13.7%**

2016 Year-End Financials

Debt ratio: 16.7%
Return on equity: 13.8%
Cash ($ mil.): 28.3
Current ratio: 2.31
Long-term debt ($ mil.): 116.0

No. of shares (mil.): 41.7
Dividends
  Yield: 0.0%
  Payout: 8.3%
Market value ($ mil.): 2,792.0

	STOCK PRICE ($) FY Close	P/E High/Low	Earnings	PER SHARE ($) Dividends	Book Value
07/16	66.95	51 34	1.44	0.12	10.89
07/15	54.88	48 29	1.15	0.10	9.77
07/14	33.53	36 25	1.04	0.09	8.81
07/13	26.54	39 26	0.95	0.07	7.81
07/12	26.12	42 25	0.77	0.06	6.79
Annual Growth	**26.5%**	**—**	**17.1%**	**17.8%**	**12.6%**

Cardinal Financial Corp

Cardinal Financial can help you keep out of the red. The holding company owns Cardinal Bank which operates some 30 branches in northern Virginia and the Washington DC metropolitan area. Serving commercial and retail customers it offers such deposit options as checking savings and money market accounts; IRAs; and CDs as well as trust services. Commercial real estate loans make up more than 40% of Cardinal Financial's loan portfolio; residential mortgages construction loans business loans and home equity and consumer loans round out the bank's lending activities. West Virginia-based United Bankshares is buying Cardinal Financial for $912 million.

Change in Company Type

In mid-2016 Cardinal agreed to be acquired by United Bankshares which has been rapidly expanding in the District of Columbia region. Cardinal Bank will merge into United subsidiary United Bank.

Operations

Subsidiary Cardinal Wealth Services provides brokerage and investment services through an alliance with Raymond James Financial.

Other units include money manager Wilson/Bennett Capital Management which focuses on value-oriented investing and large-cap stocks and George Mason Mortgage which originates residential mortgages for sale into the secondary market through about 15 branches in Cardinal Bank's market area.

Financial Performance

The company's revenue has been up and down in recent fiscal years. Its revenue decreased in fiscal 2013 compared to the prior year. The company reported revenue of $144 million for fiscal 2013 down from $178.4 million in fiscal 2012 but up from the $137.2 million it reported for revenue in fiscal 2011.

More concerning than the dip in total annual revenue during fiscal 2013 was the drop in net income compared to fiscal 2012. Cardinal Financial reported net income of $25 million in fiscal 2013 down from $45 million in fiscal 2012.

However despite the decreased annual revenue and net income the company's cash flow recovered from negative levels in fiscal 2012 to positive territory by the close of fiscal 2013.

EXECUTIVES

EVP Retail Banking Human Resources and Marketing Cardinal Bank, Eleanor D. Schmidt, age 52
Acting President and CEO, Christopher W. Bergstrom, age 56, $346,667 total compensation
Regional President Cardinal Bank, F. Kevin Reynolds, age 56, $263,000 total compensation
EVP and COO, Alice P. Frazier, age 50, $346,667 total compensation
EVP and Chief Lending Officer, Dennis M. Griffith, age 67, $154,985 total compensation
EVP and CFO Cardinal Financial Corporation and Cardinal Bank, Mark A. Wendel, age 57, $223,667 total compensation
President and CEO George Mason Mortgage LLC, Bob Brower
Executive Vice President, Carl Dodson
Vice President Retail Lending, John (Jack) Madeira
Chairman Cardinal Financial Corporation and Cardinal Bank, Bernard H. Clineburg, age 67
Auditors: Yount, Hyde & Barbour, P.C.

LOCATIONS

HQ: Cardinal Financial Corp
  8270 Greensboro Drive, Suite 500, McLean, VA 22102
Phone: 703 584-3400
Web: www.cardinalbank.com

PRODUCTS/OPERATIONS

2015 Sales

	% of total
Interest income	
Loans receivable	60
Loans held for sale	7
Investment securities	6
Other	-
Non-interest income	
Realized and unrealized gains on mortgage banking activities	22
Litigation settlement	2
Service charges on deposit accounts	1
Loan fees	1
Others	1
Total	**100**

COMPETITORS

Access National	PNC Financial
BB&T	SunTrust
Bank of America	United Bankshares
Burke & Herbert Bank	Virginia Commerce
Capital One	Bancorp
Millennium Bankshares	

HISTORICAL FINANCIALS

Company Type: Public

Income Statement

FYE: December 31

	ASSETS ($ mil.)	NET INCOME ($ mil.)	INCOME AS % OF ASSETS	EMPLOYEES
12/15	4,029.9	47.3	1.2%	851.0
12/14	3,399.1	32.6	1.0%	733.0
12/13	2,894.2	25.5	0.9%	809.0
12/12	3,039.1	45.3	1.5%	706.0
12/11	2,602.7	28.0	1.1%	510.0
Annual Growth	**11.5%**	**14.0%**	**—**	**13.7%**

2015 Year-End Financials

Return on assets: 1.2%
Return on equity: 11.9%
Long-term debt ($ mil.): —
No. of shares (mil.): 32.3
Sales ($ mil): 193.1

Dividends
  Yield: 1.9%
  Payout: 29.7%
Market value ($ mil.): 736.0

	STOCK PRICE ($) FY Close	P/E High/Low	Earnings	PER SHARE ($) Dividends	Book Value
12/15	22.75	17 12	1.43	0.44	12.76
12/14	19.83	20 16	1.00	0.34	11.76
12/13	17.99	22 18	0.82	0.28	10.57
12/12	16.30	11 7	1.51	0.20	10.19
12/11	10.74	13 9	0.94	0.12	8.83
Annual Growth	**20.6%**	**—**	**11.1%**	**38.4%**	**9.6%**

Cardtronics Plc

Cardtronics is the largest non-bank owner and operator of automated teller machines (ATMs) and related financial services equipment in the world. It maintains more than 112600 cash machines in Europe and North America including 92000 locations in the US many of which are branded by banks such as Chase PNC and Citibank. The company also leases and sells machines to airports convenience stores supermarkets malls and drug stores including Walgreens and CVS stores. Most clients pay the company to handle some or all of the maintenance services or operational services of their ATMs. Cardtronics also operates Allpoint which is the largest surcharge-free ATM network in the US with 55000 machines.

Operations

Cardtronics operates two main operating segments: North America which made up 69% of the company's total revenue during 2015 and includes its operations in the US Canada Mexico and Puerto Rico; and Europe (31% of revenue) which includes its business in the UK Germany and Poland. In the UK the company operates its own armored courier operation Green Team Services with secure cash deposit facilities in London and Manchester England.ATM operating revenues accounted for 94% of Cardtronics' total revenue during 2015 while the rest came from ATM product sales. In addition to dispensing cash and responding to balance inquiries some Cardtronics ATMs take bill payments cash checks and transfer money. The firm's Allpoint surcharge-free ATM model allows financial institutions to pay Cardtronics for participation instead of users paying transaction fees.

Geographic Reach

Houston-based Cardtronics operates in the US (including all 50 states and the territories of Puerto Rico and the Virgin Islands) Mexico Canada the UK Germany and Poland. Nearly 70% of the company's revenue came from its business in North America during 2015 while the rest came from Europe (the UK Germany and Poland). With its pending purchase of DirectCash Payments the company plans to expand into the Asia/Pacific region.Sales and MarketingThe company has sales teams in each of its international markets. The teams market and sell its products and services to financial institutions stored-value debit card issuers and retailers. Cardtronic's top five clients in 2015 included 7-Eleven CVS Co-Op Food Walgreens and Speedway. Others included Target Safeway Santander Citi Scotiabank and PNC.Cardtronics spent $5.4 million on advertising during 2015 compared to $5.4 million and $4.4 million in 2014 and 2013 respectively.

Financial Performance

Cardtronics' annual revenues have nearly doubled since 2011 as its ATM network (including ATM operations and the ATMs for which it provides managed services and processing) has more than tripled from 52886 to nearly 190000 today.The company's revenue jumped 14% to $1.2 billion during 2015 mostly thanks to ATM operating revenue growth stemming from its acquisition of Welch and Columbus Data Services which more than tripled the amount of service-contract ATMs in its network to 112622 (from 31989 in 2014).Strong revenue growth in 2015 coupled with $14 million worth of profitable sales of its non-core UK businesses drove Cardtronic's net income up 87% to $65.98 million for the year. The company's operating cash levels rose 36% to $256.55 million thanks to a rise in cash-based earnings.

Strategy

Cardtronics continues to expand its ATM network globally by acquiring similar companies or partnering with new clients in new geographic markets. In March 2015 for example the company entered Poland after partnering with and providing 50 ATMs through Shell Poland stations across the country while also adding 50 more ATMs at

multiple convenience and groceries stores there. In August 2013 the fast-growing company entered the highly-fragmented ATM market in Germany with the purchase of UK-based Cardpoint Limited. The purchase more than doubled Cardtronics' ATM portfolio in the UK and expanded its footprint to Germany.

Other growth initiatives include expanding its ATM service offerings to build business with existing and new merchant customers and expanding the company's Allpoint surcharge-free network in the US as well as in newer international markets. In recent years Cardtronics also has attracted new customers who use prepaid debit cards to make cash withdrawals. These unbanked or underbanked customers previously could not use ATMs. However increased use of prepaid cards have allowed those users access to Cardtronics' kiosks.

Mergers and Acquisitions

In October 2016 the company agreed to buy DirectCash Payments which operates some 25000 ATMs in Australia New Zealand and across North America. This deal will provide Cardtronics with entry into Australia and New Zealand; the company further expects to use its presence in Australia as an anchor for expansion in the Asia/Pacific region.

In July 2015 Cardtronics bought Columbus Data Services (CDS) an independent transaction processor for ATM deployers and payment card issuers for nearly $81 million. The deal added more than 90000 new ATMs to Cardtronic's service-contract network nearly tripling its current service-contract ATM count (which was around 31000 at the time).In October 2014 the company acquired Welch ATM adding 26350 US ATMs and growing Cardtronics' domestic portfolio to 93350 ATMs. The $160 million purchase created a combined Walgreens portfolio of 5100 ATMs giving Cardtronics a significant portion of the drugstore chain's national footprint. It also added 3100 ATMs in Ride-Aid stores. In February 2014 the firm acquired Arizona-based Automated Financial LLC adding 2100 merchant ATM contracts and a sales and service office in Arizona. (Previous acquisitions added regional hubs in New Jersey Minnesota Oregon and California.)

In June 2013 Cardtronics bought the Merrimak ATM Group an independent ATM deployer based in California. Merrimak provides ATM managed services to a nationwide network of some 4800 ATMS. In May 2013 the company acquired Portland Oregon-based Aptus Financial a leader in ATM sales ATM leasing and management services. In March its UK subsidiary bought i-design group plc a Scottish firm that provides technology and services that print ads on ATM screens and receipts for third-party advertisers.Company BackgroundCardtronics entered Canada with the 2011 purchase of Mr. Cash ATM Network (renamed Cardtronics Canada). The deal added some 600 machines throughout the country. In late 2012 Cardtronics Canada acquired privately-held Can-Do-Cash Ltd. an ATM services company headquartered in Ottawa.In 2010 Allpoint entered Australia's market through a partnership with that country's largest ATM operator Customers Limited. In 2011 Allpoint entered Mexico by adding more than 2500 ATMs across the country.

EXECUTIVES

President U.S. Business Group, Rick Updyke, age 57, $309,679 total compensation
COO and CFO, Edward H. (Ed) West
EVP of Network and Financial Services, Ben Psillas

President Global Services, Michael H. (Mike) Clinard, age 49, $400,582 total compensation
CEO, Steven A. (Steve) Rathgaber, age 63, $569,384 total compensation
President Enterprise Growth Group, David Dove
EVP and Division Executive ATM Services, Carleton K. (Tres) Thompson, age 47, $200,170 total compensation
EVP of Audit and Risk Management, Randy Rice
EVP of U.S, Tony Muscarello
EVP of Product Management, Bill Knoll
General Manager Mexico, Scott Abogado
EVP Corporate Development, Phillip Chin
SEVP Sales and Relationship Management, Todd Clark, age 49, $335,000 total compensation
EVP Global Operations, Jeffrey B. Keith
Chief Information Officer, Mike McCarthy
EVP of Global Operations, Jeffery B. Keith
EVP of Human Resources, Debra Bronder
EVP - Global Procurement, Ric Davis
Chief Commercial Officer, Jonathan Simpson-Dent
Senior Vice President Planning and Treasurer, Todd (Toddy) Ruden
Vice President National Sales, Ralph Depp
Vice President Tax, Christine (Chrissy) Nguyen
Vice President Information Technology, Ernie Arbour
Vice President Financial Services, John Dyer
Senior Vice President, Jorge Fernandez
Senior Vice President Eft and Revenue Accounting, Tracy (Trace) Israel
Vice President Retail Sales, Ken Gaston
Vice President Global Procurement, Jeff Ude
Vice President Relationship Management, Joseph Biener
Vice President, Diana (Ana) Hayes
Vice President Business Planning and Analysis, Bennett Robinson
Vice President of Sales and Business Development, Lloyd Nobles
Vice President Process Improvement, Melissa (Mel) Justice
Vice President Client Executive, Mike Sears
Vice President of Financial Services, Christy (Christ) Nusz
Vice President Tax, Christine Nguyen
Vice President Marketing, Joel Antonini
Vice President Of Retail Sales, Lucia Crater
Senior Vice President of Operations, Kurt Duhn
Executive Vice President, Jorge Fern??ndez
Senior Vice President FI Sales, Adam (Ad) Hobelmann
Chairman, Dennis F. Lynch, age 67
Secretary, Brad (Brady) Conrad
Auditors: KPMG LLP

LOCATIONS

HQ: Cardtronics Plc
3250 Briarpark Drive, Suite 400, Houston, TX 77042
Phone: 832 308-4000
Web: www.cardtronics.com

PRODUCTS/OPERATIONS

2015 Sales

	$ mil.	% of total
ATM operating revenues	1,134.0	94
ATM product sales & other	66.3	6
Total	**1,200.3**	**100**

Selected Mergers & Acquisitions

COMPETITORS

BBVA Bancomer	Lloyds Banking Group
Banamex	NYCE Payments Network

Bank of America
Barclays Bank
DirectCash
Electronic Cash
Systems
Fifth Third
First Data
HSBC Fianzas

PNC Financial
PayPoint
Payment Alliance
Payzone
Royal Bank of Scotland
U.S. Bancorp
WRG Services

HISTORICAL FINANCIALS
Company Type: Public

Income Statement
FYE: December 31

	REVENUE ($ mil.)	NET INCOME ($ mil.)	NET PROFIT MARGIN	EMPLOYEES
12/15	1,200.3	65.9	5.5%	1,739.0
12/14	1,054.8	35.1	3.3%	2,683.0
12/13	876.4	23.8	2.7%	1,070.0
12/12	780.4	43.2	5.5%	740.0
12/11	624.5	70.1	11.2%	643.0
Annual Growth	17.7%	(1.5%)	—	28.2%

2015 Year-End Financials
Debt ratio: 43.3%
Return on equity: 20.0%
Cash ($ mil.): 26.3
Current ratio: 0.77
Long-term debt ($ mil.): 575.4

No. of shares (mil.): 44.9
Dividends
  Yield: —
  Payout: —
Market value ($ mil.): 1,513.0

	STOCK PRICE ($) FY Close	P/E High/Low	PER SHARE ($) Earnings	Dividends	Book Value
12/15	33.65	27 21	1.48	0.00	8.23
12/14	38.58	53 34	0.82	0.00	6.51
12/13	43.45	85 45	0.52	0.00	5.61
12/12	23.74	32 23	0.96	0.00	3.30
12/11	27.06	18 10	1.58	0.00	2.54
Annual Growth	5.6%	— —	(1.6%)	—	34.2%

CareTrust REIT Inc

Auditors: Ernst & Young LLP

LOCATIONS
HQ: CareTrust REIT Inc
  905 Calle Amanecer, Suite 300, San Clemente, CA 92673
Phone: 949 542-3130
Web: www.caretrustreit.com

HISTORICAL FINANCIALS
Company Type: Public

Income Statement
FYE: December 31

	REVENUE ($ mil.)	NET INCOME ($ mil.)	NET PROFIT MARGIN	EMPLOYEES
12/16	104.6	29.3	28.0%	50.0
12/15	74.9	10.0	13.4%	46.0
12/14	58.9	(8.1)	—	43.0
12/13	48.8	(0.4)	—	0.0
12/12	42.0	0.1	0.3%	0.0
Annual Growth	25.6%	304.2%	—	—

2016 Year-End Financials
Debt ratio: 48.6%
Return on equity: 8.1%
Cash ($ mil.): 7.5
Current ratio: 0.58
Long-term debt ($ mil.): 449.7

No. of shares (mil.): 64.8
Dividends
  Yield: 0.0%
  Payout: 130.7%
Market value ($ mil.): 993.0

	STOCK PRICE ($) FY Close	P/E High/Low	PER SHARE ($) Earnings	Dividends	Book Value
12/16	15.32	30 19	0.52	0.68	6.98
12/15	10.95	57 40	0.26	0.64	5.50
12/14	12.33	— —	(0.36)	6.01	3.63
Annual Growth	11.5%	— —	—	(66.4%)	38.7%

Carter Validus Mission Critical REIT Inc

Auditors: KPMG LLP

LOCATIONS
HQ: Carter Validus Mission Critical REIT Inc
  4890 West Kennedy Blvd., Suite 650, Tampa, FL 33609
Phone: 813 287-0101
Web: www.cvmissioncriticalreit.com

HISTORICAL FINANCIALS
Company Type: Public

Income Statement
FYE: December 31

	REVENUE ($ mil.)	NET INCOME ($ mil.)	NET PROFIT MARGIN	EMPLOYEES
12/15	214.8	68.3	31.8%	0.0
12/14	154.2	37.6	24.4%	0.0
12/13	68.3	14.6	21.5%	0.0
12/12	28.4	(5.6)	—	0.0
Annual Growth	96.2%	—	—	—

2015 Year-End Financials
Debt ratio: 35.0%
Return on equity: 4.7%
Cash ($ mil.): 28.5
Current ratio: 1.28
Long-term debt ($ mil.): 836.3

No. of shares (mil.): 181.2
Dividends
  Yield: —
  Payout: 196.9%
Market value ($ mil.): —

	STOCK PRICE ($) FY Close	P/E High/Low	PER SHARE ($) Earnings	Dividends	Book Value
12/15	0.00	— —	0.36	0.00	7.88
Annual Growth	—	— —	—	—	—

Cavco Industries Inc (DE)

Cavco's constructions keep customers covered whether they're at home work or vacation. Cavco

Industries designs makes and sells manufactured homes (retail prices range from $26000 to more than $190000) under brands including Cavco Palm Harbor and Fleetwood. Its products include full-sized homes (about 500 sq. ft. to 3300 sq. ft.); park model homes (less than 400 sq. ft.) for use as recreational and retirement units; camping cabins; and commercial structures for use as portable classrooms showrooms and offices. Cavco operates about 15 factories in the West and Midwest; its homes are sold by more than 1000 independent retailers and company-owned outlets in the US Canada Mexico and Japan.

Operations

Cavco operates two business segments: factory-built housing accounting for more than 90% of sales; and a finance and insurance arm which represents the rest. Cavco's mortgage subsidiary CountryPlace Mortgage is an approved Fannie Mae and Ginnie Mae seller and servicer offering mortgages to buyers of the company's homes. Its insurances subsidiary Standard Casualty provides property and casualty insurance to owners of manufactured homes. Cavco owns 51% of Fleetwood Homes (acquired in 2009).

Financial Analysis

Cavco's fiscal 2012 (ends March) sales increased 158% vs. the prior year while net income rose 438% over the same period. The triple-digit increase in sales was driven by an 137% increase in sales of its factory-built homes and revenue growth from its financial services segment. The acquisition of the assets of bankrupt Palm Harbor Homes in 2011 increased sales and profits in fiscal 2012. Indeed Cavco sold 7860 homes in fiscal 2012 vs. 4786 in the previous year. Sales by company-owned stores increased dramatically although independent retailers sell more than three times as many Cavco homes.

Strategy

Cavco is the second-largest manufacturer of manufactured homes in the US. It markets a variety of brands styles floor plans and price ranges to appeal to a wide customer base. Cavco primarily targets the manufactured housing industry's mainstream market —high-value homes for entry-level and move-up buyers. It also targets specialty markets such as vacation homebuyers and developers of residential subdivisions and senior living communities. Cavco is one of the nation's largest producers of HUD-code manufactured homes which account for some 80% of the manufacturer's homes.

The company has been successful at capitalizing on the woes of its competitors especially during the recent deep recession which led to consolidation of the industry. By acquiring assets of its former rivals Cavco has added production capacity especially for niche market opportunities. In 2009 acquired nine plants from failed competitor Fleetwood for $22 billion. The deal included mothballed facilities in California and Texas as well as operations in new states for Cavco: Idaho Georgia Oregon Tennessee and Virginia. Two years later Cavco went shopping for another ailing competitor. It formed a new subsidiary Fleetwood Homes which bought the assets of bankrupt Palm Harbor for more than $83 million. The deal included Palm Harbor's construction retail and finance units.

Ownership

Wells Fargo & Co. and Third Avenue Management each own about 13% of Cavco's shares. Columbia Wanger Asset Management owns 11% while T. Rowe Price Associates owns more than 10%.

HISTORY

Alfred Ghelfi and partner Bob Curtis began a part-time business in 1965 making pickup truck camper shells. The business Roadrunner Manufacturing became Cavalier Manufacturing in 1966 incorporated in 1968 and went public in 1969. The Cavalier name was already in use so in 1974 the company's name was changed to Cavco. After the 1970s oil crisis nearly wiped out the firm Ghelfi bought out Curtis' share and began making mobile homes. In time Cavco began leasing movable storage buildings but the only successful part of that business was the security container segment (the rest was sold in 1994). A mid-1980s housing market crash in Arizona spurred Cavco to enter a totally new field —health care utilization management —in 1987.

In 1995 Cavco partnered with Japan's Auto Berg Enterprises to begin selling modular housing in Japan. The next year Cavco teamed up with Arizona Public Service to develop solar-powered manufactured housing and it also sold its health care business. Centex acquired nearly 80% of Cavco for $75 million in 1997. The next year Cavco moved into Texas (one of the biggest markets for factory-built homes) acquiring Texas retailer Boerne Homes.

With demand shrinking and surplus inventory building up the company closed its Belen New Mexico factory in 2000 and moved its production to plants in Phoenix and Seguin Texas. That fall Centex tapped manufactured housing veteran Joseph Stegmayer as chairman of its manufactured housing segment.

In 2001 the company launched Factory Liquidators a new retail concept focusing on repossessed homes.

Centex's board of directors approved the tax-free distribution to its shareholders of all of Cavco's outstanding common stock in 2003. The spin-off was completed in June of that year. Continued weakness within the industry forced Cavco to close eight of its company-owned retail outlets in fiscal 2004 and seven more in 2005.

EXECUTIVES

National Vice President of Park Models and Cabins, Tim (Timmy) Gage
Chairman President and CEO, Joseph H. (Joe) Stegmayer, age 65, $520,000 total compensation
VP CFO and Treasurer, Daniel L. Urness, age 48, $245,000 total compensation
President Fleetwood Homes; Inc, Charles E. Lott, age 68, $235,000 total compensation
SVP, Steven K. Like, $130,000 total compensation
Vice President Operations, Dave (Davie) Blank
Auditors: RSM US LLP

LOCATIONS

HQ: Cavco Industries Inc (DE)
  1001 North Central Avenue, Suite 800, Phoenix, AZ 85004
Phone: 602 256-6263
Web: www.cavco.com

PRODUCTS/OPERATIONS

2016 Sales

	$ mil.	% of total
Factory-built housing	655.1	92
Financial Services	57.2	8
Total	**712.3**	**100**

Selected Operations
Camping cabins

Commercial structures
Manufactured homes
Model homes and vacation homes
Park model homes

Selected Trademarks
AAA Homes
Catalina
Cavco
Cavco Cabins
Cavco Gold Key Guarantee
Cavco Home Center
Cavco Homes
Cedar Court
Desert Rose
Elite
Litchfield Limited
Nationwide Homes
Palm Harbor Homes
Saguaro
SmartBuilt
Sun Villa
Sunbuilt
Sunburst
Vantage
Villager
Westcourt
Winrock

COMPETITORS

All American Group	Fairmont Homes
American Homestar	Liberty Homes
Cavalier Homes	PulteGroup
Champion Home Builders	Skyline
Clayton Homes	Sunshine Homes

HISTORICAL FINANCIALS
Company Type: Public

Income Statement
FYE: April 2

	REVENUE ($ mil.)	NET INCOME ($ mil.)	NET PROFIT MARGIN	EMPLOYEES
04/16*	712.3	28.5	4.0%	3,750.0
03/15	566.6	23.8	4.2%	3,700.0
03/14	533.3	16.2	3.0%	3,000.0
03/13	452.3	4.9	1.1%	2,600.0
03/12	443.0	15.2	3.4%	2,600.0
Annual Growth	**12.6%**	**17.0%**	**—**	**9.6%**

*Fiscal year change

2016 Year-End Financials
Debt ratio: 11.0%
Return on equity: 8.3%
Cash ($ mil.): 107.9
Current ratio: 2.39
Long-term debt ($ mil.): 54.9
No. of shares (mil.): 8.9
Dividends
  Yield: —
  Payout: —
Market value ($ mil.): 832.0

	STOCK PRICE ($) FY Close	P/E High/Low	Earnings	Dividends	Book Value
04/16*	93.20	31 20	3.15	0.00	39.56
03/15	75.03	32 24	2.64	0.00	36.14
03/14	78.64	42 21	1.94	0.00	32.84
03/13	47.57	74 59	0.71	0.00	25.39
03/12	46.58	24 13	2.19	0.00	24.43
Annual Growth	**18.9%**	**— —**	**9.5%**	**—**	**12.8%**

*Fiscal year change

CB Financial Services Inc

Business services nec nsk
Auditors: Baker Tilly Virchow Krause, LLP

LOCATIONS

HQ: CB Financial Services Inc
  100 N. Market Street, Carmichaels, PA 15320
Phone: 724 966-5041
Web: www.communitybank.tv

HISTORICAL FINANCIALS
Company Type: Public

Income Statement
FYE: December 31

	ASSETS ($ mil.)	NET INCOME ($ mil.)	INCOME AS % OF ASSETS	EMPLOYEES
12/15	830.6	8.4	1.0%	198.0
12/14	846.3	4.2	0.5%	193.0
12/13	546.4	4.2	0.8%	0.0
12/12	0.0	4.2	—	0.0
12/07	378.1	3.9	1.0%	0.0
Annual Growth	**21.7%**	**21.1%**	**—**	**—**

2015 Year-End Financials
Return on assets: 1.0%
Return on equity: 9.9%
Long-term debt ($ mil.): —
No. of shares (mil.): 4.0
Sales ($ mil): 39.5
Dividends
  Yield: 3.7%
  Payout: 39.1%
Market value ($ mil.): 94.0

	STOCK PRICE ($) FY Close	P/E High/Low	Earnings	Dividends	Book Value
12/15	22.92	11 9	2.07	0.85	21.29
12/14	19.90	13 12	1.63	0.84	20.12
12/13	19.75	13 11	1.72	0.84	18.24
12/12	19.00	12 10	1.70	0.84	(0.00)
12/07	17.95	11 9	1.60	0.64	13.88
Annual Growth	**6.3%**	**— —**	**6.7%**	**7.4%**	**11.3%**

CEB Inc

Don't fear the competition; learn from it. So says CEB a provider of business research and analysis services to more than 10000 companies worldwide. Its program areas cover "best practices" in such topics as finance human resources information technology operations and sales and marketing. Unlike consulting firms which engage with one client at a time CEB operates on a membership-based business model. Members subscribe to one or more of the company's programs and participate in the research and analysis thus sharing expertise with others. Besides reports on best practices CEB offers seminars customized research briefs and decision-support tools.

Geographic Reach

CED has offices in almost 20 locations through the US and almost 15 in Europe. The US accounts for 62% of its net sales; Europe generates 20% and other countries account for the remainder.

OperationsThe company operates through two segments: CEB (79% of net sales) and CEB Talent Assessment (21%). The CEB segment provides data analysis research and advisory services that align to executive leadership roles and key recurring decisions and enable members to focus efforts to address emerging and recurring business challenges. CEB Talent Assessment segment includes its SHL product and services of cloud-based products for talent assessment development strategy analytics decision support and professional services.

Financial Performance

CEB achieved unprecedented growth in 2015 with revenues peaking at a record-setting $928 million in 2015. The historic growth was fueled by a 4% bump in CEB segment sales and a 4% increase in the US. CEB was also helped by an increase in 2014 sales bookings and the positive impact of acquisitions.

Profits also skyrocketed by 80% to reach $93 million in 2015 another company milestone primarily due to the absence of an impairment loss which it incurred the previous year. After years of posting steadily increasing cash flow CEB saw its operating cash flow decrease by $34 million from 2014 to 2015 primarily due to unfavorable changes in deferred revenue and other liabilities.

Mergers and Acquisitions

One of the ways in which CEB posted milestone revenue growth for 2015 was through the use of acquisitions. In 2016 CEB agreed to acquire Evanta Ventures for $275 million. Portland Oregon-based Evanta offers best practices data for information technology human resources and finance executives through nearly 200 annual events online and offline learning platforms and subscription information offerings. In 2015 CEB picked up Wanted Technologies Corporation a provider of real-time market intelligence and analytics for staffing and talent sourcing professionals. The same year CEB acquired Australia-based CEO Forum Group a provider of membership–based peer group briefing services serving senior executives of foreign-owned multinational organizations doing business in Australia.

EXECUTIVES

Chief Administrative Officer, Melody L. Jones, age 56, $507,500 total compensation
Chairman and CEO, Thomas L. (Tom) Monahan, age 49, $915,000 total compensation
Group President, Haniel Lynn, age 46, $466,900 total compensation
General Manager EMEA and ANZ Markets, Anthony Parslow
Group President, Warren Thune, age 48
CIO, Price Jett
Head Corporate Strategy and Development, Jesse Levin
Chief Financial Officer, Kim Patmore
Associate Vice President L Investments, Laura Wilson
Vice President Global Oem Sales, Laura McKenna
Vice President Global Engine Oem Sales, Priscilla Destefano
Vice President, Miriam Imoberstag
Vice President of Technology, David (Dave) Braun
Vice President Solutions Management, Sarah A (Sar) Woronoff
Vice President of Information Technology, Mathew (Matt) Heck
Auditors: Ernst & Young LLP

LOCATIONS

HQ: CEB Inc
1919 North Lynn Street, Arlington, VA 22209
Phone: 571 303-3000
Web: www.cebglobal.com

PRODUCTS/OPERATIONS

2015 Sales

	% of total
CEB	79
CEB Talent Assessment	21
Total	**100**

Selected Practice Areas

Communications
Financial services
General management
Human resources
Information technology
Legal and compliance
Operations and procurement
Sales and marketing
Strategy and research and development

COMPETITORS

A.T. Kearney	Conference Board
Accenture	Kantar Group
Booz Allen	McKinsey & Company
Boston Consulting	PA Consulting
Computer Sciences Corp.	

HISTORICAL FINANCIALS

Company Type: Public

Income Statement

FYE: December 31

	REVENUE ($ mil.)	NET INCOME ($ mil.)	NET PROFIT MARGIN	EMPLOYEES
12/15	928.4	92.5	10.0%	4,600.0
12/14	908.9	51.1	5.6%	4,300.0
12/13	820.0	31.9	3.9%	3,900.0
12/12	622.6	37.0	6.0%	3,400.0
12/11	484.6	52.6	10.9%	2,093.0
Annual Growth	**17.6%**	**15.1%**	**—**	**21.8%**

2015 Year-End Financials

Debt ratio: 41.9%
Return on equity: 142.5%
Cash ($ mil.): 113.3
Current ratio: 0.75
Long-term debt ($ mil.): 556.4

No. of shares (mil.): 32.9
Dividends
 Yield: 2.4%
 Payout: 49.3%
Market value ($ mil.): 2,020.0

	STOCK PRICE ($) FY Close	P/E High/Low	PER SHARE ($) Earnings	Dividends	Book Value
12/15	61.39	33 21	2.75	1.50	1.33
12/14	72.53	53 38	1.50	1.05	2.58
12/13	77.43	82 50	0.94	0.90	4.16
12/12	47.46	49 31	1.10	0.70	3.46
12/11	38.10	29 18	1.53	0.60	2.39
Annual Growth (13.7%)	**12.7%**	**— —**	**15.8%**	**25.7%**	

Celadon Group, Inc.

Celadon Group provides long-haul dry van truckload service throughout North America via subsidiaries Celadon Trucking Services Celadon

Canada and Mexico-based Jaguar. The group maintains a fleet of about 3300 tractors and 8700 trailers. Celadon also offers dedicated contract carriage in which drivers and equipment are assigned to a customer long-term as well as freight brokerage and warehousing services. Its clients have included large shippers with strict time-delivery requirements such as Arconic Procter & Gamble Philip Morris and Wal-Mart. An e-commerce unit TruckersB2B serves as a purchasing cooperative for smaller trucking fleets and provides discounts on fuel tires and satellite systems.

Geographic Reach

Celadon operates a network of 36 terminal locations including facilities in Laredo and El Paso Texas. The company serves 2500 customers across Canada (11% of total sales) Mexico (5%) and the US (84%).

Operations

Celadon's operations are divided across two segments: asset-based (dry van carrier and rail services) and asset-light (warehousing brokerage and less-than-load operations).

Financial Performance

As the economy bounces back Celadon has enjoyed unprecedented growth over the last several years. Revenues for 2015 peaked at the $900 million mark for the first time in the company's history. Profits also topped $37 million another company milestone due to the higher revenue coupled with gains on the selling of equipment.

The historic growth for 2015 was fueled by a spike in freight revenue as a result of freight rates due to the increasing demand for freight services and reduced capacity as well as an increase in loaded miles.

Celadon's operating cash flow however declined sharply during 2014 and 2015. It decreased by $37% to $45 million in 2015 primarily due to changes in working capital as a result of large increases in equipment held for resale and changes in income tax receivable and payable.

Strategy

Celadon has benefited from the manufacturing boom in Mexico fueled by the North American Free Trade Agreement (NAFTA) and from trade between the US and Canada —more than 40% of the company's shipments cross the US border. Celadon plans to continue to expand its transborder operations while still striving to attract domestic business in the US. The company views its abilities to handle Mexico-US transports as a major competitive edge over its peers. Celadon is versed in the language culture as well as border crossing requirements.

Mergers and Acquisitions

Celadon augments its list of services and extends its geographic reach through the use of acquisitions. In 2014 the company acquired A&S Services Group a regional for-hire and dedicated truckload carrier based in New Freedom Pennsylvania. A&S's fleet operations provide dry van transportation services to the Mid-Atlantic and Northeast regions. The deal enhanced Celadon's leadership position in the transportation and logistics industry and accelerated growth in both those regions.

In 2013 it purchased Rock Leasing (based in Warren Indiana) and Kelly Logistics (Wadley Alabama); both deals expanded Celadon's temperature control transportation capabilities and increased its warehousing space. Also that year the company increased its penetration in the Canadian market through the purchase of Hyndman Transport based in Ontario.

Company Background

Stephen Russell and Leonard Bennett started Celadon in 1986. They named the company for a type of ancient light-green pottery from China in hopes of conjuring universal appeal. An early customer was Chrysler which needed to ship components to a Mexican assembly plant.

EXECUTIVES

Chairman and CEO, Paul A. Will, age 50, $500,000 total compensation

VP Risk Management and Secretary, Kenneth Core, age 66, $152,884 total compensation

President Celadon Logistics, Jonathan (Jon) Russell, age 45, $335,000 total compensation

EVP CFO and Treasurer, Bobby Peavler

VP Mexico, George Chasteen

President Specialized Business, Chad Hoffman

President Truckload Operations, Lauren Howard

President Eagle Logistics Services, Nathan Roberts

VP and CIO, Michael (Mike) Gabbei, $161,731 compensation

President Chief Operating Officer, Eric Meek

Executive Vice President Technology, Nick Then

Vice President Operations, John (Jack) Slamin

Regional Vice President, Jenyce Houg

Vice President Of Operations, Matt Douglass

Vice President Of Safety Compliance, Bill Osborn

Vice President Of Sales, Derek (Der) Doddridge

Executive Vice President, JON (Jonny) RUSSELL

Auditors: BKD, LLP

LOCATIONS

HQ: Celadon Group, Inc.
9503 East 33rd Street, One Celadon Drive, Indianapolis, IN 46235-4207
Phone: 317 972-7000
Web: www.celadontrucking.com

PRODUCTS/OPERATIONS

2015 Sales

	$ mil.	% of total
Freight revenue	769.9	85
Fuel surcharge revenue	130.8	15
Total	**900.7**	**100**

2015 Sales

	$ mil.	% of total
Asset based	810.2	90
Asset light	90.5	10
Total	**900.7**	**100**

Selected Services

Brokerage service (eStat) (Carrier Hub)
Environmental initiatives
Expedited Truck-Rail
LTL consolidation
Real-time tracking and reporting
Supply chain solutions
Transportation management
Transport in and between NAFTA countries
Warehousing

COMPETITORS

AmeriQuest Business Services	P.A.M. Transportation
Con-way Truckload	Schneider National
Covenant Transportation	Swift Transportation
Crete Carrier	U.S. Xpress
J.B. Hunt	UPS Supply Chain Solutions
Landstar System	USA Truck
	Werner Enterprises

HISTORICAL FINANCIALS

Company Type: Public

Income Statement

FYE: June 30

	REVENUE ($ mil.)	NET INCOME ($ mil.)	NET PROFIT MARGIN	EMPLOYEES
06/16	1,065.3	24.8	2.3%	7,286.0
06/15	900.7	37.2	4.1%	7,606.0
06/14	759.3	30.6	4.0%	4,876.0
06/13	613.6	27.2	4.4%	4,351.0
06/12	598.9	25.5	4.3%	3,982.0
Annual Growth	**15.5%**	**(0.7%)**	**—**	**16.3%**

2016 Year-End Financials

Debt ratio: 40.8%	No. of shares (mil.): 28.2
Return on equity: 6.6%	Dividends
Cash ($ mil.): 9.0	Yield: 0.9%
Current ratio: 1.33	Payout: 6.1%
Long-term debt ($ mil.): 399.4	Market value ($ mil.): 231.0

	STOCK PRICE ($) FY Close	P/E High/Low		PER SHARE ($) Earnings	Dividends	Book Value
06/16	8.17	25	8	0.88	0.08	13.50
06/15	20.68	18	12	1.52	0.08	13.16
06/14	21.32	18	13	1.29	0.08	10.99
06/13	18.25	18	11	1.17	0.08	9.73
06/12	16.38	15	7	1.12	0.06	8.53
Annual Growth	**(16.0%)**	**—**	**—**	**(5.9%)**	**7.5%**	**12.2%**

Century Casinos Inc.

In the 19th century people rushed to Cripple Creek Colorado seeking their fortune in gold. Today thanks to Century Casinos they can do basically the same thing (but via midsized regional casinos rather than through prospecting). The company's Womacks Casino & Hotel in Cripple Creek offers some 440 slot machines and video devices as well as a handful of gaming tables. It also owns the Century Casino & Hotel in Central City Colorado and another Century Casino & Hotel in Edmonton Canada. In addition it operate four cruise ship casinos and is the casino concessionaire for cruise lines run by TUI Cruises a joint venture between German travel operator TUI and #2 cruise ship operator Royal Caribbean.

Strategy

After a period of major expansion Century Casinos has been focused on upgrading its properties and making targeted acquisitions. In early 2010 the company acquired the Silver Dollar casino in Alberta Canada from struggling Evergreen Gaming for some $9.5 million. It spent nearly $2 million to renovate the gaming floor and dining area at Womacks during 2008.

Geographic Reach

Outside of North America Century Casinos continues to own a controlling stake in Casinos Poland Ltd. (CPL) owner and operator of eight casinos in Poland. Century Casinos owns 33% of CPL and in 2012 the company agreed to up its stake to 66.6%.

After a experiencing decreased gaming revenue at all of its properties during the global recession the company disposed of its properties in the Czech Republic and South Africa. It sold the Caledon Hotel Spa & Casino near Cape Town South Africa to Tsogo Sun Gaming in 2009. The deal included a 60% stake in Century Casino Newcastle.

Also that year it sold its Century Casino Millennium in the Marriott hotel in Prague to Viva Casino Group.

EXECUTIVES

SVP Principal Financial Officer Secretary and Treasurer; COO North America, Larry J. Hannappel, age 62, $160,000 total compensation

Vice Chairman President and Co-CEO, Peter Hoetzinger, age 52, $462,342 total compensation

Chairman and Co-CEO, Erwin Haitzmann, age 61, $462,342 total compensation

Strategic Compliance Corporate Governance and Broad Based Black Economic Empowerment South African Operations, Rossouw Lubbe

Investor Relations and Communications Manager, Ulrike Pichler

General Manager Century Casino Central City Colorado, Mickey Rosenbaum

General Manager Century Casino Alberta Canada, Geoff Smith

General Manager Century Casino Millennium Prague Czech Republic, Michael Grill

Director Operations Cruise Ship Operations, Nick Rowland

General Manager Century Casino Newcastle South Africa, John McGregor

Managing Director Century Casinos Africa, Paul Campbell

Manager SEC and Reporting, Michael Snider

Managing Director Century Casinos Europe GmbH and Century Casinos Poland Sp. z o.o. Compliance Officer Vienna Stock Exchange, Nikolaus Strohriegel

CIO and VP Cruise Ships and Caribbean Operations; Managing Director Century Casinos Europe GmbH, Andreas Terler

Manager Corporate Communications, Sandra Grinschgl

General Manager Womacks Casino and Hotel, Robert P. (Bob) Jeffries

General Manager Century Casino Calgary, Al Wilson

Vice Chairman President and Co-CEO, Peter Hoetzinger, age 52

Director, Gottfried Schellman, age 61

Director, Robert S. Eichberg, age 68

Director, Dinah Corbaci, age 60

Independent Director, Gottfried Schellmann

Auditors: Deloitte & Touche LLP

LOCATIONS

HQ: Century Casinos Inc.
455 E. Pikes Peak Ave., Suite 210, Colorado Springs, CO 80903
Phone: 719 527-8300
Web: www.cnty.com

PRODUCTS/OPERATIONS

Selected Properties

North America
Century Casino & Hotel (Century City Colorado)
Century Casino & Hotel (Edmonton Alberta Canada)
Womacks Casino & Hotel (Cripple Creek Colorado)
Poland
Casinos Poland Ltd. (33% 7 full casinos and one slot casino)

COMPETITORS

Global Casinos	Riviera Holdings
Herbst Gaming	Sun International
Isle of Capri Casinos	Limited
Majestic Star	Trans World
Nevada Gold & Casinos	Corporation

HISTORICAL FINANCIALS

Company Type: Public

Income Statement

FYE: December 31

	REVENUE ($ mil.)	NET INCOME ($ mil.)	NET PROFIT MARGIN	EMPLOYEES
12/15	134.4	11.9	8.9%	1,638.0
12/14	120.0	1.2	1.0%	1,620.0
12/13	104.5	6.1	5.9%	1,600.0
12/12	71.8	4.0	5.7%	1,000.0
12/11	70.8	3.0	4.3%	1,000.0
Annual Growth	17.4%	40.9%	—	13.1%

2015 Year-End Financials

Debt ratio: 19.5%	No. of shares (mil.): 24.4
Return on equity: 9.8%	Dividends
Cash ($ mil.): 29.3	Yield: —
Current ratio: 1.48	Payout: —
Long-term debt ($ mil.): 32.4	Market value ($ mil.): 190.0

	STOCK PRICE ($) FY Close	P/E High/Low	PER SHARE ($) Earnings	Dividends	Book Value
12/15	7.78	16 10	0.49	0.00	5.01
12/14	5.05	161 98	0.05	0.00	4.86
12/13	5.21	24 11	0.26	0.00	5.00
12/12	2.84	19 15	0.17	0.00	4.90
12/11	2.53	26 16	0.13	0.00	4.71
Annual Growth	32.4%	—	39.3%	—	1.6%

Charles River Laboratories International Inc.

Chickens and rats have an important part to play in Charles River Laboratories International's specialty portfolio of medical products. The company produces lab rats and mice bred specifically for use in medical testing through its Research Models and Services (RMS) segment. It also provides contract drug discovery and development services including toxicology and pathology through its RMS Discovery and Safety Assessment and Manufacturing Support segments. To a smaller degree the company also supplies pathogen-free fertilized chicken eggs used in vaccine production. Charles River Laboratories which traces its roots back to 1947 has operations in 17 countries around the world.

Operations

In 2014 the company realigned its reportable segments after acquiring Argenta and BioFocus. Its three operating segments are now Research Models and Services Discovery and Safety Assessment (DSA) and Manufacturing Support.

The RMS segment accounts for 40% of total revenue and includes the research models and research model services businesses. They offer commercial production and sale of small research models and supply large research models. The Genetically Engineered Model Services unit performs contract breeding and related services while the Research Animal Diagnostic Services unit provides health monitoring and diagnostics services related

to research models. IS provides colony management of clients' research operations including recruitment training staffing and management services.

The DSA segment which accounted for 41% of revenue in 2014 includes services required to take a drug through early development including discovery services.

Meanwhile Manufacturing Support (19% of revenue in 2014) includes Endotoxin and Microbial Detection (EMD) including non-animal lot-release testing products and microbial detection and species identification services. It also includes Biologics Testing Services which provides testing of biologics and devices; and Avian Vaccine Services which supplies specific-pathogen-free fertile chicken eggs and chickens. The Accugenix subsidiary provides cGMP-compliant contract microbial identification and genetic sequence testing.

Geographic Reach

The company has approximately 60 locations in 17 countries. While sales in the US account for about half of its annual revenues the company is also growing its operations in other key markets including Canada Europe and Japan.

Charles River Laboratories has laboratories in the US Germany Scotland and Ireland. It owns large (over 50000 sq. ft. of space) facilities for the DSA segment in Canada Ireland Scotland and the US; it leases large facilities in the US and the UK. For the RMS segment it owns large facilities in Canada China France Germany Japan the UK and the US. The company also owns large Manufacturing Support facilities in the US and China.

Sales and Marketing

Charles River Laboratories provides its products and services directly to customers around the globe. Customers include small and midsized pharmaceutical companies biotechnology firms contract research organizations (CROs) agricultural and chemical companies life science companies and veterinary medicine firms as well as educational health care and government institutions.

The company primarily sells its products and services through a direct sales force and account management teams in North America Europe and the Asia/Pacific region. Its promotional activities include organizing scientific symposia publishing scientific papers and newsletters webinars and presentations at conferences and trade shows in North America Europe and Asia. It also participates in online marketing and direct mail. In some markets the group's direct sales force is assisted by international distributors and agents.

In fiscal 2014 the company spent $1.3 million on advertising up from $1.1 million in 2013 and $0.9 million in 2012.

Financial Performance

Revenues were flat between 2010 and 2013 but in 2014 revenue rose 11% to $1.3 billion primarily due to growth in the DSA segment. That segment benefited from the 2014 acquisitions of Argenta and BioFocus which contributed a combined $71.4 million in revenue growth. The Safety Assessment business also saw higher earnings.

Net income which more than doubled in 2011 due to a decline in expenses rose 23% to $127 million in 2014 on higher revenue and lower interest expenses. Cash flow from operations also increased rising 21% to $252 million.

Strategy

Charles River Laboratories' strategy is based on leveraging its deep scientific knowledge and strong client support to deliver a comprehensive and integrated portfolio of quality early-stage products and services. This allows its clients to maintain the flexible infrastructure they need in order to bring

new therapies to market faster and more cost effectively.

In 2014 the firm introduced a rapid bacterial contamination test the PTS-Micro. The test for bacterial contamination is an improvement over current technologies because of its working speed.

Its acquisition strategy takes into account geographic factors as well as expansion of existing core services. The company is partnering with a number of venture capital firms that invest in life sciences health care and technology companies.

Charles River Laboratories has aligned its sales force to improve its ability to support clients to focus on three particular customer segments: global biopharmaceutical companies mid-tier biopharmaceuticals and academic and government institutions.

Mergers and Acquisitions

Charles River Laboratories has been on a buying spree as of late spending more than $1 billion on acquisitions since 2014. In April of that year the company spent $179 million to buy UK-based Argenta and BioFocus as well as certain related Dutch assets to form the core of its Early Discovery business. Later that year it bought VivoPath a discovery service company; and ChanTest Corporation a provider of ion channel testing services. In 2015 Charles River acquired Celsis International boosting its EMD business for $212 million. It then acquired Germany-based CRO Oncotest which specializes in discovery and validation services for preclinical oncology research for $36 million.

Charles River Laboratories started off 2016 with a major acquisition this time buying WIL Research for some $585 million. WIL Research provides safety assessment and contract development and manufacturing services to biopharmaceuticals and chemical companies worldwide; the purchase expands Charles Rivers' presence in Europe as well as its portfolio of service offerings.

Later in 2016 the company acquired Massachusetts-based Agilux a specialist in molecule bioanalytical drug metabolism pharmacology and pharmacokinetic services for $64 million.

EXECUTIVES

Corporate EVP Human Resources Chief Administrative Officer General Counsel and Secretary, David P. Johst, age 54, $567,496 total compensation

Senior Financial Advisor, Thomas F. Ackerman, age 62, $512,245 total compensation

Chairman President and CEO, James C. Foster, age 65, $1,069,089 total compensation

Corporate SVP; President European Preclinical Services, Brian Bathgate, age 56

Corporate EVP and Chief Scientific Officer, Nancy A. Gillett, age 60, $500,523 total compensation

Corporate EVP Global Productivity and Efficiency, J¶g M. Geller, age 61, $400,520 total compensation

Corporate EVP and President Global Research Models & Services and Preclinical Services Operations, Davide Molho, $450,853 total compensation

Corporate SVP Global Sales and Marketing, William D. Barbo

SVP Information Technology and CIO, Arthur C. Hubbs

Corporate SVP and General Manager Research Models & Services Europe and Asia, Colin Dunn

EVP and CFO, David R. Smith

Senior Vice President Information Security, Caroline (Carol) Dunnell

Senior Vice President of Human Resources, Andre (Andy) Merza

National Sales Manager, Ian Jester

Auditors: PRICEWATERHOUSECOOPERS LLP

LOCATIONS

HQ: Charles River Laboratories International Inc.
251 Ballardvale Street, Wilmington, MA 01887
Phone: 781 222-6000
Web: www.criver.com

PRODUCTS/OPERATIONS

2014 Sales

	$ mil.	% of total
Discovery and safety assessment	538.2	41
Research Models & Services	507.4	40
Manufacturing support	252.1	19
Total	**1,297.7**	**100**

Selected Services

Agrochemical & veterinary services
Antibody production services
Avian products & services
Biopharmaceutical services
Clinical trial services
Consulting & staffing services
Discovery & imaging services
Endotoxin & microbial detection
Equipment & instrumentation
Facilities design & management services
Genetic testing services
Genetically engineered models & services
In Vitro services
Pathology associates
Preclinical services
Program management
Regulatory navigator services
Research animal diagnostic services
Research animal models
Surgical model services

COMPETITORS

Albany Molecular	Nordion
Research	PAREXEL
BioReliance	PRA Health Sciences
Bioanalytical Systems	PharmaNet Development
Covance	Group
Deltagen	Quintiles
Harlan Laboratories	Transnational
ICON	Taconic Farms
Jackson Laboratory	WuXi PharmaTech
MPI Research	

HISTORICAL FINANCIALS

Company Type: Public

Income Statement

FYE: December 31

	REVENUE ($ mil.)	NET INCOME ($ mil.)	NET PROFIT MARGIN	EMPLOYEES
12/16	1,681.4	154.7	9.2%	11,000.0
12/15	1,363.3	149.3	11.0%	8,600.0
12/14	1,297.6	126.7	9.8%	7,900.0
12/13	1,165.5	102.8	8.8%	7,700.0
12/12	1,129.5	97.3	8.6%	7,200.0
Annual Growth	**10.5%**	**12.3%**	**—**	**11.2%**

2016 Year-End Financials

Debt ratio: 45.5%
Return on equity: 19.4%
Cash ($ mil.): 117.6
Current ratio: 1.53
Long-term debt ($ mil.): 1,207.7
No. of shares (mil.): 47.3
Dividends
  Yield: —
  Payout: —
Market value ($ mil.): 3,609.0

	STOCK PRICE ($) FY Close	P/E High/Low		PER SHARE ($) Earnings	Dividends	Book Value
12/16	76.19	27	20	3.23	0.00	17.67
12/15	80.08	26	19	3.13	0.00	15.70
12/14	64.29	24	19	2.66	0.00	14.20
12/13	53.33	25	17	2.12	0.00	13.48
12/12	36.88	20	13	2.01	0.00	12.46
Annual Growth	**19.9%**	**—**	**—**	**12.6%**	**—**	**9.1%**

Chase Corp.

Duct tape is great but when the job calls for higher-tech stuff Chase has it. The company has made and sold Chase & Sons branded protective tape and coatings including conducting and insulating products for cable and wire makers for more than 50 years. Chase processes almost any flexible material produced on a roll —films to fabrics. It makes laminates sealants and coatings for pipeline construction electronics as well as printing markets. Chase pipe coating tapes Tapecoat and Royston are sold to oil companies and gas utilities. The company also offers expansion/control joint systems and asphalt additives for roads bridges and stadiums. US customers represent about 84% of revenues.

Operations

Chase operates through two segments Industrial Materials and Construction Materials. Industrial Materials almost 75% of revenue provides products that are added to another company's products. The company's stalwart Chase & Sons trademark is included in this segment. Major product families in the segment include insulating and conducting materials moisture protective coatings laminated durable papers and flexible composites and laminates.

Construction Materials (25%) are sold in final form for use in the transportation and architectural as well as construction markets. This segment's products include protective pipe coating tapes a polymer additive for waterproofing waterproofing sealants and expansion joints.

Financial Performance

Chase's revenues reached a milestone total of $238 million in 2015. Its profits remained consistent hovering around the $26 million mark during 2014 and 2015.

Strategy

Acquisitions are included in Chase's strategy for growth. In 2014 Chase acquired the remaining 50% it didn't already own in NEPTCO which supplies engineered materials for producing copper cable and electronic packaging products. The acquisition broadened the menu of products offered by Chase and created synergies between the markets targeted by Chase and Neptco.

Company Background

Brothers Edward and Francis Chase founded Chase & Sons in 1946 to make rubberized power cable tape fabric. Under Francis' long tenure as president and CEO the company expanded into related markets. Purchases included Columbia Technical Corporation (electrical insulating varnish and laminates 1971) and Royston Laboratories (corrosion-resistant pipeline coating 1972). The company which by 1973 was called Columbia Chase (shortened to Chase in 1988) won a contract in 1975 to protect seams on the Alaska pipeline. Chase stumbled financially in the late 1980s after diversifying into non-petroleum energy markets. In 1988 Francis retired.

EXECUTIVES

Vice President Program Management, Cherie (Cher) Phillips
Application Development Lead (Vice President), Amandeep Ghuman
Vice President Senior Marketing Manager Marketing Strategy, Nicole Jacks
Auditors: PricewaterhouseCoopers LLP

LOCATIONS

HQ: Chase Corp.
295 University Avenue, Westwood, MA 02090
Phone: 718 332-0700
Web: www.chasecorp.com

PRODUCTS/OPERATIONS

2014 Sales

	$ mil.	% of total
Industrial Materials	169.7	76
Construction Materials	54.3	24
Total	**224.0**	**100**

2014 Sales

	$ mil.	% of total
Sales	221.0	99
Royalties & commissions	3.0	1
Total	**224.0**	**100**

Selected Products and Services

Electrical cable insulation tapes
Electrical splicing & terminating & repair tapes
Flexible composites & laminates for wire & cable aerospace & industrial laminate markets
Flexible packaging for industrial & retail use
Fluid applied coating & lining systems for the water & wastewater industry
Insulating & conducting materials for wire and cable manufacturers
Laminated durable papers
Moisture-protective coatings for electronics and printing services
Protectants for highway bridge deck metal supported surfaces
Protective conformal coatings
Protective pipe coating tapes
Slit film for the building wire market & telecommunication cable
Specialty tapes & related products for the electronic and telecommunications industries
Tapecoat® for anti-corrosion applications in the gas & oil & marine pipeline markets
Tapes & membranes for roofing & other construction applications
Waterproofing sealants expansion joints & accessories

COMPETITORS

3M	Iracore
American Biltrite	PPG Industries
Benchmark Electronics	Praxair
Dow Corning	Saint-Gobain
ELANTAS PDG	W. R. Grace
Flextronics	

HISTORICAL FINANCIALS

Company Type: Public

Income Statement

FYE: August 31

	REVENUE ($ mil.)	NET INCOME ($ mil.)	NET PROFIT MARGIN	EMPLOYEES
08/16	238.0	32.8	13.8%	677.0
08/15	238.0	26.3	11.1%	671.0
08/14	224.0	26.6	11.9%	667.0
08/13	216.0	17.2	8.0%	666.0
08/12	148.9	9.3	6.3%	719.0
Annual Growth	12.4%	36.9%	—	(1.5%)

2016 Year-End Financials

Debt ratio: 16.5%
Return on equity: 19.9%
Cash ($ mil.): 73.4
Current ratio: 2.03
Long-term debt ($ mil.): —

No. of shares (mil.): 9.2
Dividends
 Yield: 1.0%
 Payout: 20.2%
Market value ($ mil.): 597.0

	STOCK PRICE ($) FY Close	P/E High/Low	PER SHARE ($) Earnings	Dividends	Book Value
08/16	64.37	18 11	3.50	0.65	18.76
08/15	39.50	15 10	2.82	0.60	16.79
08/14	35.50	13 9	2.86	0.45	15.00
08/13	29.72	16 8	1.87	0.40	12.44
08/12	16.27	17 10	1.03	0.35	10.90
Annual Growth	41.0%	— —	35.8%	16.7%	14.5%

Chatham Lodging Trust

Self-advised real estate investment trust (REIT) Chatham Lodging acquires upscale extended-stay hotels including Residence Inn by Marriott Homewood Suites by Hilton and Hyatt House locations To a lesser extent the firm will also buy select-service and full-service hotels such as Courtyard by Marriott Hampton Inn and Hilton Garden Inn. Chatham Lodging owns nearly 40 hotels with almost 5700 rooms across 15 US states. Through two joint ventures it also has minority interests in 95 other hotels with 12500 rooms/suites. When assembling its portfolio the REIT seeks properties being sold at a discount particularly in large US metropolitan markets including Dallas Denver and Pittsburgh.

Operations

Chatham Lodging operates mainly select service or limited service hotels and as such does not book significant revenue from food and beverages or group conference facilities. Indeed room revenue accounted for 94% of the REIT's total revenue during 2014.

Geographic Reach

Palm Beach-based Chatham Lodging has properties in 16 states: California Colorado Connecticut Florida Georgia Kentucky Maine Massachusetts Minnesota New Hampshire New York Pennsylvania Tennessee Texas Virginia Washington and Washington DC.Sales and MarketingThe REIT has been boosting its advertising spend in recent years to support sales growth. It spent $3.7 million on advertising during 2014 up from $2.8 million and $2.3 million in 2013 and 2012 respectively.

Financial Performance

Chatham Lodging's revenue has grown more than eight-fold since 2010 as it has expanded its property portfolio through acquisitions and has charged higher rental rates as the real estate market has strengthened. It's also been climbing back from years of losses as it's kept a lid on operating costs and interest expenses on its long-term debt.The REIT's revenue spiked 56% to $197.22 million during 2014 mostly thanks to added room revenue stemming from six hotel acquisitions in 2013 and nine hotel acquisitions in 2014. Strong revenue growth in 2014 drove Chatham Lodging's net income sharply up to $67.1 million (compared to $3 million in 2013). The REIT's operating cash levels jumped 56% to $49.3 million for the year as cash earnings rose.

Strategy

Chatham reiterated in 2016 that it looked to acquire upscale extended-stay hotels and premium branded select-service hotel properties in the 25 largest metro areas in the US that are priced below replacement costs in their markets. Indeed through acquisitions made between 2010 and 2014 the REIT has more than quintupled its hotel property investments from $208 million to nearly $1.1 billion. While Chatham also takes minority interests in other hotels through joint ventures it also sells off properties that could yield big profits. In 2014 for example the REIT reached an agreement to sell the hotels owned by its joint venture with Cerberus Capital Management (acquired in 2011) to Northstar Realty Finance with Chatham netting a gain of $80 million on the $1.3 billion sale.

EXECUTIVES

Chairman President and CEO, Jeffrey H. Fisher, age 61, $209,589 total compensation
EVP and COO, Dennis M. Craven, age 44, $88,233 total compensation
EVP and Chief Investment Officer, Peter M. Willis, age 49, $199,110 total compensation
CFO, Jeremy Wegner
Vice President and General Counsel, Eric (Ric) Kentoff
Auditors: PricewaterhouseCoopers LLP

LOCATIONS

HQ: Chatham Lodging Trust
 222 Lakeview Avenue, Suite 200, West Palm Beach, FL 33401
Phone: 561 802-4477
Web: www.chathamlodgingtrust.com

PRODUCTS/OPERATIONS

2014 sales

	% of total
Room	94
Food and Beverage	1
Cost reimbursements	1
Others	4
Total	**100**

COMPETITORS

Ashford Hospitality Trust
Chesapeake Lodging
DiamondRock Hospitality
FelCor

Hersha Hospitality
Host Hotels & Resorts
Innkeepers USA
Sunstone Hotel Investors

HISTORICAL FINANCIALS

Company Type: Public

Income Statement

FYE: December 31

	REVENUE ($ mil.)	NET INCOME ($ mil.)	NET PROFIT MARGIN	EMPLOYEES
12/15	276.9	32.9	11.9%	47.0
12/14	197.2	66.8	33.9%	45.0
12/13	126.2	2.9	2.4%	27.0
12/12	100.4	(1.4)	—	25.0
12/11	73.1	(9.1)	—	6.0
Annual Growth	39.5%	—	—	67.3%

2015 Year-End Financials

Debt ratio: 45.3%
Return on equity: 5.1%
Cash ($ mil.): 21.0
Current ratio: 1.28
Long-term debt ($ mil.): 607.8

No. of shares (mil.): 38.3
Dividends
 Yield: 5.8%
 Payout: 324.3%
Market value ($ mil.): 785.0

	STOCK PRICE ($) FY Close	P/E High/Low	PER SHARE ($) Earnings	Dividends	Book Value
12/15	20.48	36 23	0.86	1.20	18.09
12/14	28.97	13 9	2.30	0.93	17.22
12/13	20.45	163 112	0.13	0.84	14.58
12/12	15.38	— —	(0.12)	0.78	14.74
12/11	10.78	— —	(0.69)	0.70	15.64
Annual Growth	17.4%	— —	—	14.4%	3.7%

Chefs' Warehouse Inc (The)

Before a gourmet chef can say "bon appétit" he must first procure his ingredients. A distributor of specialty food products Chefs' Warehouse sells such gourmet food items as artisan charcuterie specialty cheeses hormone-free protein truffles caviar and chocolates as well as basic food ingredients like cooking oils flour butter milk and eggs. The company's core customers include chefs from independent restaurants fine dining establishments culinary schools hotels and country clubs. It is a leading gourmet ingredient distributor in culinary centers like New York City San Francisco Los Angeles and Washington DC. Tracing its roots back to 1985 Chefs' Warehouse went public in 2011.

IPO

Shares climbed following the company's market debut. The supplier for restaurants caterers and other foodservice businesses raised $135 million; the proceeds from the IPO were about $63.1 million after expenses which went to repay debt and fund general corporate activity. Company CEO Christopher Pappas Christopher's brother John Pappas and brother-in-law Dean Facatselis collectively retain control of Chefs' Warehouse.

Geographic Reach

Based in Connecticut Chefs' Warehouse operates in one segment —food product distribution — along the East and West coasts. It serves some of the nation's culinary hot spots including New York California Nevada and Washington as well as in Ohio Maryland Florida and Oregon.

Financial Performance

Except for revenue slump in 2009 due to the global economic recession Chefs' Warehouse has seen an upward trend in revenue from 2008 to 2012. The company has logged rising net income in all fiscal years from 2008-2012 due to increased net sales and decreased operating expenses. Chefs' Warehouse revenue jumped 20% in fiscal 2012 as compared to 2011 thanks to net sales increases resulting from organic sales growth and the acquisitions of Michael's and Praml in 2012 and Provvista in late 2011. The company's net sales growth was negatively impacted by Hurricane Sandy however during the fourth quarter of 2012 and the prior year impact of an extra week in 2011. Chefs' Warehouse reports $14.51 million in 2012 net income —an 88% increase —due to increased net sales in 2012 and reduced interest expenses.

Mergers and Acquisitions

Going forward Chefs' Warehouse's growth strategy continues to include acquisitions of small food distributors that beef up its entree offerings. In 2013 the company purchased Qzina Specialty Foods North America a Florida-based supplier of gourmet chocolate dessert and pastry products that serves pastry chefs in a deal worth some $32.7 million. In 2012 it bought out Michael's Finer Meats a Midwest distributor of meat and seafood for approximately $54.3 million. The deal was one of several; earlier in the year Chefs' Warehouse purchased Praml International a specialty foods importer and foodservice distributor founded in 1987. The acquisition extended the company's reach to some 500 locations in Las Vegas and Reno. Chefs' Warehouse expanded its operations into south Florida after acquiring Monique & Me Inc. (dba Culinaire Specialty Foods) for $3.7 million in 2010. The previous year it bought the San Francisco division of European Imports for $3.8 million. The transaction bolstered its California operations.

Strategy

Besides acquiring other companies Chefs' Warehouse is expanding its customer base in existing markets and bolstering its product offerings to its existing customers. It is also taking steps to control costs by improving its logistics and inventory management systems. In recent years Chefs' Warehouse has experienced significant financial growth due in large part to a rise in revenue generated by sales to both new and existing customers.

Sales and Marketing

Chefs' Warehouse works to cover a number of popular markets including Philadelphia Boston Napa Valley and Seattle. As part of its business the company serves chefs working in country clubs independent restaurants fine dining establishments culinary schools and hotels.

The company distributes its specialty food products to more than 12500 distinct customer locations from distribution centers located in New York San Francisco Los Angeles Las Vegas Miami Portland Columbus Cincinnati and Washington DC. Its products are sourced from more than 2700 different suppliers.

Company Ownership

Chefs' Warehouse is 17% owned by Christopher Pappas; John Pappas retains another 15% stake.

Company Background

The Pappas family originally founded the company in 1985 as Dairyland USA a specialty dairy product distributor that served chefs in the New York metropolitan area. The company later expanded into other large US markets through acquisitions of small specialty food products distributors.

EXECUTIVES

Chief Information Officer, Frank ODowd
CFO, John D. Austin
Executive Vice President Supply Chain, John (Jack) Scott
Regional Vice President, Bruce (Brucey) Luong
Vice Chairman, John Pappas, age 52
Auditors: BDO USA, LLP

LOCATIONS

HQ: Chefs' Warehouse Inc (The)
100 East Ridge Road, Ridgefield, CT 06877
Phone: 203 894-1345
Web: www.chefswarehouse.com

PRODUCTS/OPERATIONS

2015 Products sales

	% of total
Center of plate	46
Dry Goods	18
Pastries and other bakery products	14
Cheeses	8
Dairy Products	6
Oils and Vinegars	6
Kitchen supplies	2
Total	**100**

Selected Products

Baking
Beverages
Caviar
Cheese & dairy
Chocolate
Coffee & tea
Condiments
Dry goods
Foie gras & pate
Fruits & nuts
Gluten-free
Molecular gastronomy
Oil & vinegar
Organic
Pasta
Specialty meats
Specialty seafood
Spices
Regional

COMPETITORS

American Milk Products	European Imports
DPI Specialty Foods	World Finer Foods
Dole & Bailey Inc.	atalanta
Economy Foods	

HISTORICAL FINANCIALS

Company Type: Public

Income Statement

FYE: December 25

	REVENUE ($ mil.)	NET INCOME ($ mil.)	NET PROFIT MARGIN	EMPLOYEES
12/15	1,059.0	16.2	1.5%	1,693.0
12/14	836.6	14.2	1.7%	1,281.0
12/13	673.5	16.9	2.5%	1,160.0
12/12	480.2	14.5	3.0%	780.0
12/11	400.6	7.7	1.9%	600.0
Annual Growth	**27.5%**	**20.5%**	**—**	**29.6%**

2015 Year-End Financials

Debt ratio: 46.8%
Return on equity: 9.7%
Cash ($ mil.): 2.4
Current ratio: 2.27
Long-term debt ($ mil.): 268.5

No. of shares (mil.): 26.2
Dividends
  Yield: —
  Payout: —
Market value ($ mil.): 457.0

	STOCK PRICE ($) FY Close	P/E High/Low	PER SHARE ($) Earnings	Dividends	Book Value
12/15	17.37	37 21	0.63	0.00	7.15
12/14	22.03	51 27	0.57	0.00	5.86
12/13	29.14	37 19	0.77	0.00	5.28
12/12	15.40	36 18	0.69	0.00	1.87
12/11	17.86	42 27	0.43	0.00	1.13
Annual Growth	**(0.7%)**	**— —**	**10.0%**	**—**	**58.6%**

Chemical Financial Corp

Chemical Financial has banking down to a science. It's the holding company for Chemical Bank which provides standard services such as checking and savings accounts CDs and IRAs credit and debit cards and loans and mortgages to individuals and businesses through nearly 190 branches in the lower peninsula of Michigan. The majority of the bank's loan portfolio is made up of commercial loans while consumer loans make up the remainder. Boasting assets of $9 billion Chemical is the second largest bank in Michigan. The company also offers trust investment management brokerage and title insurance services through subsidiaries.

OperationsIts Wealth Management division which has some $4 billion in assets under custody offers trust services estate planning investment management and employee benefit programs. Chemical Financial Advisors offers mutual funds and marketable securities while CFC Title Services issues title insurance for mortgage properties. CFC Capital manages the company's municipal investment securities portfolio.About 72% of Chemical Financial's total revenue came from loan interest (including fees) in 2014 while another 6% came from interest on its investment securities. The rest of its revenue came from deposit account service charges and fees (8%) wealth management revenue (6%) mortgage banking income (2%) and other miscellaneous sources of income. Sales and MarketingChemical Financial spent $3.45 million on advertising in 2014 up from $2.97 million and $3.11 million in 2013 and 2012 respectively.Financial PerformanceChemical Financial's revenues and profits have been rising over the past few years thanks growing loan and deposit business from acquisitions lower interest expenses on deposits and declining loan loss provisions as its loan portfolio's credit quality has improved with higher property valuations in the strengthened economy. The bank's revenue rose by 6% to $290.4 million in 2014 as the bank as its acquisition of Northwestern Bancorp boosted its loan business during the year. Higher revenue lower interest expenses and a continued decline in loan loss provisions drove the bank's net income up by 9% to a record $62.1 million. The bank's operating cash levels inched higher to $89.9 million on higher cash earnings.StrategyThe bank follows an aggressive acquisition strategy to boost its loan and deposit business while expanding its branch network into key parts of Michigan. Indeed its acquisitions in 2015 and 2014 boosted the bank's presence in northwestern Michigan and along the Michigan-Indiana border. By the end of 2014 the bank had acquired some 21 community banks and 36 branch bank offices. Mergers and AcquisitionsIn June 2015 it acquired Lake Michigan Financial Corporation along with its The Bank of Holland and The Bank of Northern Michigan subsidiaries and branches for some $187.4 million. The acquisition added $1.2 billion in assets $959 million in loans and $956 million in deposits to Chemical's books.In April 2015 Chemical Financial purchased Monarch Community Bancorp and its Monarch Community Bank subsidiary for $27.2 million which grew the company's presence and market share along the Michigan-Indiana border. The deal also added $174 million in assets $130 million in new loan assets and $142 million in new deposits. In October 2014 Chemical Financial bought Northwestern Bancorp and its Northwestern Bank subsidiary for $121 million representing its largest expansion into northwestern Michigan to date.

The company now plans to buy Talmer Bancorp holding company of Talmer Bank and Trust in a $1.4 billion transaction.

Company BackgroundIn late 2012 the company acquired 21 branches in northeastern Michigan and Battle Creek from Independent Bank. That more than $8-million transaction further expands Chemical Bank's presence geographically. Additional acquisitions including FDIC-assisted takeovers of failed banks are possible.

EXECUTIVES

First Vice President Corporate Human Resources, Joseph (Jo) Torrence
Chairman President and CEO, David B. Ramaker, age 60, $569,042 total compensation
EVP CFO and Treasurer, Lori A. Gwizdala, age 58, $297,924 total compensation
EVP; President East Region, Kenneth W. Johnson, age 54, $265,534 total compensation
President South Region, Richard J. DeVries, age 60
EVP and COO Business Operations, Leonardo Amat
EVP and Chief Risk Management Officer, Lynn Kerber
EVP General Counsel and Secretary, William Collins, age 63
Regional President - West Region Chemical Bank, Joel Rahn
EVP and COO Customer Experience, Robert S. Rathbun
SVP and Senior Investment Officer, Pavel Konecny
SVP and CIO, Greg Meidt
Vice President of Information Technology Operations, Tad Sumner
Vice President, Robert O (Bob) Burgess
Assistant Vice President Product Development, Jim (Jimmy) Hubinger
Vice President and Partner, JoAnna L (Anna) Kolbiaz
Vice President Of Information Technology Operations, Ted Sumner
Vice President of Human Resour, Kim (Kimmy) Butcher
Vice President Commercial Loan Officer, Jeff Hyde
Executive Vice President Chief Operating Officer, James (Jamie) Milroy
Vice President, Carl Ahearn
Vice President And Trust Officer, David (Dave) Farkas
Senior Vice President and Trust Officer, Jude Patnaude
Vice President Information Technology, Gary Richard
Vice President Senior Financial Advisor East Region Sales Manager, Brenda Rajewski

Senior Vice President Loans, Gary (Gar) Dolezan
Mortgage Officer Assistant Vice President, Sue (Susie) Moody
Vice President and Community Reinvestment Act Officer, Robert (Bob) BurgessJr
Vice President, Jenna (Jen) Draisma
Vice President, Katie (Kat) Abbate
Vice President, Cristina (Chris) Blanchette
Vice President, Regina (Gina) Payne
Vice President, Ann (Annie) Weiss
Vice President Investments Financial Advisor, Mike (Mikey) Kelly
Vice Chairman, Thomas W. Kohn, age 62
Auditors: KPMG LLP

LOCATIONS

HQ: Chemical Financial Corp
235 E. Main Street, Midland, MI 48640
Phone: 989 839-5350
Web: www.chemicalbankmi.com

PRODUCTS/OPERATIONS

2014 Sales

	$ mil.	% of total
Interest		
Loans including fees	209.4	72
Investment securities	17.4	6
Other	0.4	-
Non-interest		
Service charges on deposit accounts	22.3	8
Wealth management revenue	16.0	6
Other customer service charges & fees	18.6	6
Other	6.1	2
Total	**290.4**	**100**

COMPETITORS

1st Source Corporation	Flagstar Bancorp
Bank of America	Huntington Bancshares
Comerica	Independent Bank (MI)
Fifth Third	Mercantile Bank
Firstbank	

HISTORICAL FINANCIALS

Company Type: Public

Income Statement

FYE: December 31

	ASSETS ($ mil.)	NET INCOME ($ mil.)	INCOME AS % OF ASSETS	EMPLOYEES
12/15	9,188.8	86.8	0.9%	2,100.0
12/14	7,322.1	62.1	0.8%	2,000.0
12/13	6,184.7	56.8	0.9%	1,700.0
12/12	5,917.2	51.0	0.9%	1,859.0
12/11	5,339.4	43.0	0.8%	1,700.0
Annual Growth	14.5%	19.2%	—	5.4%

2015 Year-End Financials

Return on assets: 1.0%	Dividends
Return on equity: 9.5%	Yield: 2.9%
Long-term debt ($ mil.): —	Payout: 41.8%
No. of shares (mil.): 38.1	Market value ($ mil.): 1,308.0
Sales ($ mil): 372.0	

	STOCK PRICE ($) FY Close	P/E High/Low	PER SHARE ($) Earnings	Dividends	Book Value
12/15	34.27	15 12	2.39	1.00	26.62
12/14	30.64	17 13	1.97	0.94	24.32
12/13	31.67	16 12	2.00	0.87	23.38
12/12	23.76	13 10	1.85	0.82	21.69
12/11	21.32	15 9	1.57	0.80	20.82
Annual Growth	12.6%	— —	11.1%	5.7%	6.3%

Chesapeake Lodging Trust

As a real estate investment trust (REIT) focused on the hospitality industry Chesapeake Lodging Trust targets upper-upscale hotels located in major US business centers and popular convention markets. The company owns 22 hotels with a total of nearly 6700 rooms in nine US states and Washington DC. Southern California is a major market for the company. Chesapeake Lodging's properties operate under several major brands including Hyatt Marriott and W Hotels. In evaluating properties for purchase the company considers rebranding and renovation options. Formed in mid-2009 Chesapeake Lodging Trust went public in 2010.

OperationsChesapeake Lodging Trust generated about 76% of its total revenue from Room revenue in 2014 while another 20% came from its Food and Beverage services.Geographic ReachNearly 50% of the REIT's hotel properties are in California (in Los Angeles San Francisco San Diego and Santa Barbara). Its other hotels are in Massachussetes (Boston and Newton); Seattle; Chicago; Washington DC; Denver; Minneapolis; New York City; and New Orleans.Financial PerformanceThe REIT's revenues and profits have been growing at a healthy clip over the past several years as it has quadrupled the amount of rent-generating hotel properties and expanded its room number to nearly 6700 from 1638 in 2010.Chesapeake's revenue jumped 14% to a record $478 million in 2014 mostly thanks to new hotel acquisitions. About one-quarter of the growth came from comparable hotel growth resulting from increased demand from corporate and leisure for rooms located in San Francisco Boston Seattle and San Diego as well as from higher demand from group customers at its hotels in Boston San Francisco and Denver driven by favorable convention calendars for their respective markets during the year.Higher revenue and a $7 million gain from the sale of its Courtyard Anaheim hotel property in 2014 drove the REIT's net income higher by 35% to a record $60.95 million while Chesapeake's operating cash levels grew by 20% to $120 million on higher cash earnings.StrategyChesapeake Lodging Trust targets investments in upper-upscale hotels in major business and convention markets and selectively acquires select-services hotels in urban areas or unique locations in the US.Some of its major acquisitions in 2015 included its $103 million purchase of the historic Ace Hotel Downtown and The Theater at Ace Hotel in Los Angeles which would continue to be managed by Ace Hotel Group; and the $278 million acquisition of The Royal Palm hotel in Miami Beach Florida to be managed by HEI Hotels & Resorts and franchised to Starwood Hotels & Resorts. In 2014 Chesapeake bought the JW Marriott San Francisco Union Square for $147.2 million under the continued management of Marriott International.The REIT also selectively sells off under-performing properties for a profit and uses the proceeds for investments in new properties in its target markets. In 2014 it sold its 153-room Courtyard Anaheim at Disneyland Resort in California for $32.5 million netting a gain on the sale of $7 million.

EXECUTIVES

EVP and CFO, Douglas W. Vicari, age 57, $475,000 total compensation

President and CEO, James L. Francis, age 54, $700,000 total compensation

SVP Chief Accounting Officer and Secretary, Graham J. Wootten, age 42, $252,000 total compensation

EVP and COO, D. Rick Adams, $400,000 total compensation

Vice President Treas, Nishil Patel

Chairman, Thomas A. Natelli

Auditors: Ernst & Young LLP

LOCATIONS

HQ: Chesapeake Lodging Trust
1997 Annapolis Exchange Parkway, Suite 410, Annapolis, MD 21401
Phone: 410 972-4140
Web: www.chesapeakelodgingtrust.com

COMPETITORS

Ashford Hospitality Trust
DiamondRock Hospitality
FelCor
Hospitality Properties Trust
Host Hotels & Resorts
LaSalle Hotel Properties
Pebblebrook
RLJ Lodging
Ryman
Strategic Hotels
Sunstone Hotel Investors

HISTORICAL FINANCIALS

Company Type: Public

Income Statement

FYE: December 31

	REVENUE ($ mil.)	NET INCOME ($ mil.)	NET PROFIT MARGIN	EMPLOYEES
12/15	582.6	67.5	11.6%	12.0
12/14	477.9	60.9	12.8%	13.0
12/13	420.1	45.3	10.8%	13.0
12/12	278.2	27.1	9.8%	10.0
12/11	172.1	9.0	5.2%	9.0
Annual Growth	35.6%	65.3%	—	7.5%

2015 Year-End Financials

Debt ratio: 37.0%
Return on equity: 5.8%
Cash ($ mil.): 50.5
Current ratio: 1.70
Long-term debt ($ mil.): 776.2
No. of shares (mil.): 59.6
Dividends
Yield: 5.9%
Payout: 172.4%
Market value ($ mil.): 1,501.0

	STOCK PRICE ($) FY Close	P/E High/Low		PER SHARE ($) Earnings	Dividends	Book Value
12/15	25.16	39	25	0.99	1.50	20.27
12/14	37.21	38	23	1.00	1.20	19.74
12/13	25.29	34	27	0.75	1.00	19.09
12/12	20.88	32	24	0.66	0.88	19.28
12/11	15.46	64	38	0.30	0.80	16.17
Annual Growth	12.9%		—	34.8%	17.0%	5.8%

Chimera Investment Corp

This Chimera has the body of a mortgage real estate investment trust (REIT) but its head is that of its external manager FIDAC (Fixed Income Discount Advisory Company) a fixed-income investment management firm wholly-owned by Annaly Capital Management. Formed in 2007 Chimera invests in residential mortgage loans; residential mortgage-backed securities (RMBS) such as those guaranteed by government agencies Fannie Mae and Freddie Mac; real estate-related securities; and other assets including collateralized debt obligations or CDOs. The REIT went public in 2007 shortly after it was formed.

Institutional investors hold approximately 40% of Chimera Investment's stock led by Wellington Management's 11% stake. Annaly owns about 9% of the company.

EXECUTIVES

CFO and Secretary, A. Alexandra Denahan, age 45
Managing Director; Head - Business Development, Matthew Lambiase, age 49
Head of Investments, Christian J. Woschenko, age 55
Head of Underwriting, William B. Dyer, age 69
Chairman, Paul Donlin, age 54
Director, Jeremy Diamond, age 52
Director, Mark Abrams, age 67
Director, Gerard (Gerry) Creagh, age 57
Managing Director; Head - Business Development, Matthew Lambiase, age 49
Director, Paul A. Keenan, age 49
Director, Dennis Mahoney
Independent Director, John Reilly
Auditors: Ernst & Young LLP

LOCATIONS

HQ: Chimera Investment Corp
520 Madison Avenue, 32nd Floor, New York, NY 10022
Phone: 212 626-2300
Web: www.chimerareit.com

COMPETITORS

Annaly Capital Management
Capstead Mortgage
Impac Mortgage Holdings
MFA Financial
Walter Investment Management

HISTORICAL FINANCIALS

Company Type: Public

Income Statement

FYE: December 31

	REVENUE ($ mil.)	NET INCOME ($ mil.)	NET PROFIT MARGIN	EMPLOYEES
12/15	603.1	250.3	41.5%	32.0
12/14	768.3	589.2	76.7%	0.0
12/13	498.7	362.6	72.7%	0.0
12/12	513.4	327.7	63.8%	0.0
12/11	337.3	137.3	40.7%	0.0
Annual Growth	15.6%	16.2%	—	—

2015 Year-End Financials

Debt ratio: —
Return on equity: 7.6%
Cash ($ mil.): 114.0
Current ratio: 0.02
Long-term debt ($ mil.): —
No. of shares (mil.): 187.7
Dividends
Yield: 10.5%
Payout: 218.1%
Market value ($ mil.): 2,560.0

	STOCK PRICE ($) FY Close	P/E High/Low		PER SHARE ($) Earnings	Dividends	Book Value
12/15	13.64	13	2	1.25	1.44	15.70
12/14	3.18	1	1	2.85	1.80	17.55
12/13	3.10	2	1	1.75	2.80	16.21
12/12	2.61	2	1	1.60	1.90	17.24
12/11	2.51	7	4	0.65	2.55	14.83
Annual Growth	52.7%		—	17.8%	(13.3%)	1.4%

Churchill Downs, Inc.

You might say this company has put its money on the sport of champions to win. Churchill Downs is a leading operator of horse racing tracks in the US with four major race courses including its namesake track that hosts the world-famous Kentucky Derby. Other tracks include Arlington Park (Illinois) Calder Race Course (Florida) and Fair Grounds Race Course (Louisiana). In addition to horse racing Churchill Downs has gaming assets. It operates a number of simulcast networks and off-track betting facilities as well as a TwinSpires wagering deposit service that allows punters to place bets online. Richard Duchossois who controls diversified holding company Duchossois Group owns about 20% of Churchill Downs.

Geographic ReachChurchill Downs operates the racetracks in Florida Illinois Kentucky and Louisiana. The company's off-track betting facilities widen its reach.Financial PerformanceWhile still grounded in live horse racing Churchill Downs has been actively investing in new ventures —both gaming and non-gaming —to diversify its revenue stream. The company has enjoyed an upward trend in revenues during recent fiscal years. It reported $779.3 million in fiscal 2013 after bringing in $732.4 million in fiscal 2012 and $696.9 million in fiscal 2011.StrategyIn addition to its emphasis on new technology Churchill Downs is focused on investing in its traditional horseracing and gaming sphere. In 2012 Churchill Downs entered into a 50% joint venture with Delaware North Companies Gaming & Entertainment to develop a new harness racetrack and video lottery terminal gaming facility in Lebanon Ohio. The project will involve the relocation of the current operations of Lebanon Raceway to a new location along the Interstate 75 corridor between Cincinnati and Dayton.

HISTORY

Inspired by a tour of European horse racing meets Colonel Lewis Clark founded the Louisville Jockey Club in 1874. The next year the first Kentucky Derby debuted at a site that by 1883 was called Churchill Downs (after Clark's uncles the Churchills who leased him the land). The track suffered financially until 1903 when it showed its first profit. Over the next 25 years the Jockey Club added four more tracks but when the Great Depression hit the company began selling and closing its tracks. Churchill Downs incorporated in

1937 and by 1952 the Kentucky Derby was televised. The company had never really prospered since the Depression and company executives thwarted a takeover bid by National Industries in 1969; two other takeovers were attempted in 1984.

Thomas Meeker who once had served as the company's lawyer took over as president and CEO of Churchill Downs in 1984. He sought to turn the track around and pitched a five-year $25 million renovation of the company's facilities. The investment to revitalize Churchill Downs drove earnings up for the company in the late 1980s.

During the 1990s Churchill Downs diversified into different states and media. Its first simulcast wagering facility opened in 1992 and in 1994 the company gained a majority interest in Hoosier Park (sold 2007). The company acquired a third racetrack Ellis Park in 1998. The following year it launched the Kentucky Derby Auction site on the Web which features the buying and trading of memorabilia related to the race. The firm moved into the technical side of gambling when it formed a joint venture (Charlson Broadcast Technologies LLC) with Charlson Industries to provide simulcast graphic software and video services to its racing and off-track betting sites. Also in 1999 Churchill Downs expanded its geographical base with the $86 million purchase of Calder Race Course in Miami and the Hollywood Park Race Track and adjacent card casino in Southern California.

The company bought Arlington International Racecourse near Chicago as well as five related off-track betting and pari-mutuel operations in Illinois from Duchossois Industries (later The Duchossois Group) in 2000. The next year it joined the New York Racing Association in its bid to buy New York City Off-Track Betting but the group failed to snag the OTB operation which was won by a consortium led by Magna Entertainment. Also in 2001 Churchill Downs sold a 15% stake in Hoosier Park to Centaur Racing for $4.5 million (the company still owned 62% of Hoosier Park with Centaur owning the rest). In 2002 Churchill Downs sold its 35% interest in EquiSource a procurer of equine industry supplies and services.

In 2004 Churchill Downs acquired the Fair Grounds Race Course in New Orleans from Fair Grounds Corporation for $47 million. It also acquired Video Services Inc. (VSI) that year. VSI runs the Louisiana poker business. A year later Churchill Downs sold its Hollywood Park track to Bay Meadows Land Company.

The company's Louisiana Fair Grounds and nearby betting facilities were closed in 2005 in the wake of Hurricane Katrina. Horse races scheduled for the Fair Grounds were moved to Bossier City's Louisiana Downs (operated by Harrah's (now Caesars Entertainment). The following year Robert Evans replaced longtime CEO Meeker. In 2007 Churchill Downs sold its stake in Hoosier Park to Centaur.

The company acquired interactive-betting technology company Youbet.com in 2010 in order to expand its online wagering capabilities; it combined the site with its Twinspires wagering deposit service. Later that year Churchill Downs acquired Harlow's Casino Resort & Hotel in Greenville Mississippi for about $138 million

EXECUTIVES

EVP and CFO, Marcia A. Dall, age 53
CEO, William C. (Bill) Carstanjen, age 48, $511,539 total compensation
SVP and President Churchill Downs Racetrack, T. Kevin Flanery, age 51

President Churchill Downs Interactive, James E. (Ted) Gay, $344,363 total compensation
President and COO, William E. (Bill) Mudd, age 44, $462,500 total compensation
President Big Fish Games, Paul Thelen
SVP and President Fair Grounds Race Course and Slots, Timothy W. (Tim) Bryant
SVP and CTO, Ben Murr
EVP and General Counsel, Alan K. Tse, age 44, $345,000 total compensation
General Manager Arlington Park, Tony Petrillo
Senior Vice President, Kevin (Kev) Flanery
Vice President Finance and Treasurer, Mike (Mikey) Anderson
Vice President Corporate Tax, Erik Furlan
Vice President Sales and Operations Cdsn, Patrick (Paddy) Troutman
Vice President, Tom (Tommy) Jenkins
Chairman, G. Watts Humphrey, age 71
Assistant Treasurer, Karen Cecil
Auditors: PricewaterhouseCoopers LLP

LOCATIONS

HQ: Churchill Downs, Inc.
600 North Hurstbourne Parkway, Suite 400, Louisville, KY 40222
Phone: 502 636-4400
Web: www.churchilldownsincorporated.com

PRODUCTS/OPERATIONS

2015 Sales

	$ mil.	% of total
Big Fish Games	413.7	34
Casinos	332.3	27
Racing	262.8	21
TwinSpires	201.2	16
Other Investments	20.2	2
Corporate	0.9	-
Eliminations	(18.8)	-
Total	**1,212.3**	**100**

Selected Operations

Racetracks
  Arlington Park (Arlington Heights IL)
  Calder Race Course (Miami)
  Churchill Downs (Louisville KY)
  Fair Grounds Race Course and Slots (New Orleans)
Gaming
  Calder Casino (slot machines Florida)
  Harlow's Casino Resort & Hotel (casino Mississippi)
  Video Services (video poker machines Louisiana)
  Fair Ground Slots (slot machines Louisiana)
Online
  Bloodstock Research Information Services (equine industry information)
  Horse Racing TV (HRTV minority stake)
  TwinSpires (deposit wagering service)
Other operations
  Churchill Downs Simulcast Productions
  United Tote Company (pari-mutuel wagering systems)

COMPETITORS

Boyd Gaming
Caesars Entertainment
Daily Racing Form
Dover Downs Gaming
Equibase
Granite REIT
Jacksonville Greyhound Racing

MTR Gaming
Penn National Gaming
Pinnacle Entertainment
Seminole Tribe of Florida

HISTORICAL FINANCIALS

Company Type: Public

Income Statement

FYE: December 31

	REVENUE ($ mil.)	NET INCOME ($ mil.)	NET PROFIT MARGIN	EMPLOYEES
12/15	1,212.3	65.2	5.4%	4,530.0
12/14	812.9	46.3	5.7%	4,825.0
12/13	779.3	54.9	7.0%	2,600.0
12/12	732.3	58.2	8.0%	2,300.0
12/11	696.8	64.3	9.2%	2,000.0
Annual Growth	**14.8%**	**0.3%**	**—**	**22.7%**

2015 Year-End Financials

Debt ratio: 34.3%
Return on equity: 9.9%
Cash ($ mil.): 74.5
Current ratio: 0.35
Long-term debt ($ mil.): 765.5

No. of shares (mil.): 16.6
Dividends
  Yield: 0.8%
  Payout: 46.1%
Market value ($ mil.): 2,349.0

	STOCK PRICE ($) FY Close	P/E High/Low	PER SHARE ($) Earnings	Dividends	Book Value
12/15	141.49	40 24	3.71	1.15	37.18
12/14	95.30	39 32	2.64	1.00	40.06
12/13	89.65	29 21	3.06	0.87	39.27
12/12	66.45	19 15	3.34	1.32	36.93
12/11	52.13	14 10	3.76	0.60	34.00
Annual Growth	**28.4%**	**— —**	**(0.3%)**	**17.7%**	**2.3%**

Chuy's Holdings Inc

Where can Tex-Mex connoisseurs and Elvis fans dine under one roof? Chuy's Holdings operates the Chuy's Tex-Mex casual dining restaurant chain which serves up a menu of enchiladas fajitas tacos and "big as yo' face" burritos as well as signature drinks like fresh-squeezed lime margaritas and Texas Martinis. Each of its nearly 70 restaurants offer patrons a funky vibrant and eclectic atmosphere decked out with Mexican folk art vintage hubcap-coated ceilings and a shrine to the "King of Rock and Roll" himself. Originally founded in Austin Texas in 1982 the company went public in mid-2012.

Geographic Reach
Outside of its home state of Texas Chuy's now has locations in Alabama Arkansas Florida Georgia Indiana Kentucky Missouri Ohio Oklahoma North Carolina South Carolina Tennessee and Virginia.

Operations
Unlike some chains Chuy's owns and operates all of its restaurants and does not offer franchises.

Sales and Marketing
Chuy's markets its restaurants through local advertising e-marketing and social media channels. Its marketing costs include local restaurant marketing programs community service and sponsorship activities.

Financial Performance
Chuy's has enjoyed revenue growth and net income growth during the past several fiscal years. The company's revenue increased to about $287 million in fiscal 2015 up 17% from the $245 million it reported in fiscal 2014. The growth in revenue has come largely from opening new restaurants.

Chuy's net income was $12.89 million in fiscal 2015. That was a 12% increase compared to the prior fiscal period. The company ended fiscal 2015 with more than $45 million in cash on hand which was a 56% increase compared to its cash levels at the conclusion of fiscal 2014.

Strategy

Chuy's has focused on opening restaurants in major cities in Texas and in states in the southeastern US; going forward it plans to open additional locations in new and existing markets. During 2016 Chuy's expects to open at least eleven new restaurants. The company plans to expand at around that same rate of 10-15 new locations per year for the next several years.

EXECUTIVES

CFO, Jon W. Howie, age 48, $250,480 total compensation
President CEO and Director, Steve Hislop, age 56, $392,316 total compensation
VP Operations Southeast Region, Frank Biller, $169,343 total compensation
VP Real Estate and Development, Michael Hatcher, $159,006 total compensation
VP Operations, Ted Zapp, age 64, $178,805 total compensation
Chairman and Treasurer, Jose (Joe) Ferreira, age 60
Auditors: RSM US LLP

LOCATIONS

HQ: Chuy's Holdings Inc
1623 Toomey Road, Austin, TX 78704
Phone: 512 473-2783
Web: www.chuys.com

PRODUCTS/OPERATIONS

SELECTED MENU
TORTILLAS
NEVER FROZEN
GREEN CHILES
SAUCES
CHICKEN
LIME JUICE

COMPETITORS

Acapulco/El Torito Restaurants	Chipotle
Applebee's International	Darden
Brinker	OSI Restaurant Partners
Carlson Restaurants	Texas Roadhouse

HISTORICAL FINANCIALS

Company Type: Public

Income Statement
FYE: December 27

	REVENUE ($ mil.)	NET INCOME ($ mil.)	NET PROFIT MARGIN	EMPLOYEES
12/15	287.0	12.9	4.5%	7,295.0
12/14	245.1	11.4	4.7%	6,567.0
12/13	204.3	11.0	5.4%	5,712.0
12/12	172.6	5.4	3.2%	4,770.0
12/11	130.5	3.4	2.7%	3,954.0
Annual Growth	21.8%	38.9%	—	16.5%

2015 Year-End Financials

Debt ratio: —
Return on equity: 10.2%
Cash ($ mil.): 8.5
Current ratio: 0.68
Long-term debt ($ mil.): —
No. of shares (mil.): 16.4
Dividends
  Yield: —
  Payout: —
Market value ($ mil.): 514.0

	STOCK PRICE ($) FY Close	P/E High/Low	Earnings	PER SHARE ($) Dividends	Book Value
12/15	31.14	44 25	0.77	0.00	8.07
12/14	19.49	62 27	0.69	0.00	7.19
12/13	36.63	64 33	0.66	0.00	6.38
12/12	22.43	59 31	0.37	0.00	5.49
Annual Growth	11.6%	— —	27.7%	—	13.7%

CIM Commercial Trust Corp

PMC Commercial Trust likes lending to little businesses. The real estate investment trust (REIT) makes small business loans primarily to limited-service hotel franchisees. The loans ranging from $100000 to $4 million are secured by first liens on real estate and written for hotel owner/operators of national franchises such as Comfort Inn and Holiday Inn Express. PMC Commercial Trust also lends to owners of convenience stores restaurants and other small businesses. About 20% of its loan portfolio is concentrated in Texas. Subsidiaries are active in Small Business Administration (SBA) lending and in investing (as small business investment companies or SBICs). The company was founded in 1993.PMC Commercial Trust has ramped up its SBA lending activities.In 2006 the company sold its portfolio of about a dozen hotel properties to concentrate on its lending business. The hotels had previously been leased to Arlington Hospitality which filed for Chapter 11 bankruptcy protection in 2005. After regaining possession of the properties PMC Commercial Trust put them on the market.

Siblings Andrew Rosemore (chairman) Lance Rosemore (CEO) and Martha Greenberg (director) together own more than 10% of PMC Commercial Trust.

EXECUTIVES

EVP COO Chief Investment Officer and Treasurer, Jan F. Salit, age 62, $282,329 total compensation
EVP and CFO, Barry N. Berlin, age 52, $282,329 total compensation
President CEO and Secretary, Lance B. Rosemore, age 64, $418,903 total compensation
Independent Trustee, Nathan G. Cohen, age 70
Independent Trustee, Irving Munn, age 67
Independent Trustee, Barry A. Imber, age 69
Trustee, Martha Morrow
Auditors: BDO USA, LLP

LOCATIONS

HQ: CIM Commercial Trust Corp
17950 Preston Road, Suite 600, Dallas, TX 75252
Phone: 972 349-3200
Web: www.cimcommercial.com

PRODUCTS/OPERATIONS

829691195

COMPETITORS

Amerisource Funding	JER Investors Trust
Archon Group	Jameson Inns
Ashford Hospitality Trust	Janus Hotels
Capital Trust	Texas Capital Bancshares
Cullen/Frost Bankers	Vestin
FirstCity Financial	

HISTORICAL FINANCIALS

Company Type: Public

Income Statement
FYE: December 31

	ASSETS ($ mil.)	NET INCOME ($ mil.)	INCOME AS % OF ASSETS	EMPLOYEES
12/15	2,098.1	24.3	1.2%	10.0
12/14	2,094.6	24.3	1.2%	33.0
12/13	253.4	19.5	7.7%	32.0
12/12	247.7	(2.1)	—	32.0
12/11	251.2	3.6	1.5%	33.0
Annual Growth	70.0%	60.8%	—	(25.8%)

2015 Year-End Financials

Return on assets: 1.1%
Return on equity: 1.8%
Long-term debt ($ mil.): —
No. of shares (mil.): 97.5
Sales ($ mil): 268.4
Dividends
  Yield: 5.6%
  Payout: 673.0%
Market value ($ mil.): 1,517.0

	STOCK PRICE ($) FY Close	P/E High/Low	Earnings	PER SHARE ($) Dividends	Book Value
12/15	15.54	84 58	0.25	0.88	13.28
12/14	15.01	93 18	0.25	0.66	13.93
12/13	8.60	10 7	1.00	2.50	63.77
12/12	7.10	— —	(1.05)	3.00	65.31
12/11	7.00	6 4	1.70	3.20	69.43
Annual Growth	22.1%	— —	(38.1%)	(27.7%)	(33.9%)

Cirrus Logic, Inc.

Cirrus Logic takes a sound approach to computing. The fabless semiconductor company long a leader in audio chips of all kinds develops integrated circuits (ICs) for specialized applications in consumer electronics energy and industrial equipment. Its more than 700 products include audio encoder/decoders (codecs) digital amplifiers digital audio converters and energy management devices. Cirrus Logic's audio chips are used in smartphones tablet and laptop computers Blu-ray Disc players gaming devices and digital TVs. Energy management products include LED driver ICs ADCs and DACs used to make LEDs digital utility meters and power supplies. The company gets most of its sales from customers in China.

HISTORY

Suhas Patil a professor who had developed a chip-level software system for controlling disk drives while at MIT founded Patil Systems in 1981. When his firm failed to find buyers for its advanced products Patil sought advice from semiconductor executive Michael Hackworth. Impressed with the products' possibilities Hackworth joined Patil Systems as CEO. In 1984 the company was renamed Cirrus Logic after the high-flying clouds.

The company initially focused on chips for computer peripherals but during the 1980s it also began making chips for PCs. It debuted the first controller chips small enough to be built directly into a disk drive unit an advance that prompted the PC industry's shift to smaller-profile disk drives. When IBM introduced its Video Graphics Array (VGA) graphics display standard in 1987 Cirrus Logic quickly followed with the market's first VGA controller chip.

Cirrus Logic went public in 1989. Its 1991 acquisitions of Crystal Semiconductor and Pixel Semiconductor provided it with access to audio and video technology for the multimedia and fax/modem markets. It bought PC graphics chip maker Acumos in 1992 and Pacific Communication Sciences (products for cellular communications) in 1993. The next year it bought PicoPower Technology a maker of system controller chips.

In 1996 Cirrus Logic sold its wireless infrastructure equipment unit to ADC Telecommunications. That year the company formed wafer fabrication joint venture Cirent with Lucent's microelectronics unit (which became Agere Systems later acquired by LSI Corp.).

An industry downturn led Cirrus Logic to cut its workforce by 13% in 1996 and by another 15% in 1997. That year Patil stepped away from the company's day-to-day operations (he continued to serve as chairman emeritus and a director) and Hackworth became chairman.

In 1998 continuing to expand its offerings Cirrus Logic debuted products for DVDs. In response to a prolonged slump in the semiconductor industry it eliminated its PC graphics and video accelerator product lines and sold voice compression technology subsidiary Nuera Communications to management. Also that year Cirrus Logic spun off its PC modem business as Ambient Technologies. Analog Devices VP/GM David French was named president and COO in 1998.

In 1999 about 500 more employees were laid off. In an effort to phase out more of its wafer fabrication operations the company that year handed over control of its MiCRUS joint venture (founded in 1994) to partner IBM and transferred its ownership of Cirent to Lucent (now Alcatel-Lucent). Also that year French became CEO; Hackworth remained chairman.

In 2000 Cirrus Logic moved its headquarters from Fremont California to Austin Texas. The next year the company announced that it would focus growth efforts on semiconductors used in consumer entertainment devices. Despite historically dismal conditions in the chip industry Cirrus Logic took steps to pursue this strategy in 2001 when it acquired private chip makers Peak Audio (digital audio hardware and software) LuxSonor ($65 million DVD video processors) ShareWave ($92 million wireless home networking chips and software) and Stream Machine ($110 million digital video encoding chips).

Later in 2001 the company announced that it would lay off about 300 workers –30% of its staff –in the face of continued poor conditions in the global chip market. The next year Cirrus exited the magnetic storage chip business in order to focus on products for the consumer entertainment market. In 2003 the company announced more job cuts and discontinued the wireless product line acquired as part of the ShareWave acquisition. It also sold its chip testing facilities to ChipPAC (now

part of STATS ChipPAC) which in turn supplied Cirrus Logic with assembly test and packaging services.

As conditions in the worldwide semiconductor market turned choppy again in 2004 Cirrus Logic had a 7% reduction in force more than 50 workers mostly affecting employees in California and Texas.

In 2005 the company received $25 million from a legal settlement with Amkor Technology Fujitsu and Sumitomo Bakelite. The litigation was over faulty semiconductors sold by Cirrus to Fujitsu. Cirrus and Fujitsu first sued each other in 2001; Amkor and Sumitomo were added as parties to the litigation (which shifted from federal court to state court) in 2003. The insurance carriers for the four vendors reached a settlement through arbitration in 2005.

That same year Cirrus Logic sold its digital video IC product line to Magnum Semiconductor an entity formed by investors led by Investcorp and August Capital Management. The company received a minority equity stake in Magnum Semi for the assets of the digital video line.

In 2006 Cirrus acquired Shanghai-based Caretta Integrated Circuits for about $10 million in cash. Caretta designed power management ICs for the large single-cell lithium-ion battery market.

David French resigned as president and CEO in 2007 after a special committee of the board investigated the company's past practices in granting stock options and found that French was significantly involved in backdating certain option grants. Chairman Michael Hackworth stepped in as acting president and CEO. VP/GM Jason Rhode a Cirrus Logic employee since 1995 was named to succeed French as president and CEO.

In 2007 the SEC's Division of Enforcement informed Cirrus Logic that its informal investigation of the company's historical stock option practices initiated a year earlier was elevated to a formal inquiry. The SEC later notified the company that the inquiry was concluded and the commission's staff was not recommending any enforcement action against the company.

Cirrus acquired Apex Microtechnology for $42 million in cash in 2007. Apex Micro developed precision high-power analog amplifiers for aerospace and industrial applications used in motors piezoelectrics programmable power supplies and other devices. Founded in 1980 the company (also known as Apex Precision Products) had some 1200 customers with about $20 million in annual sales and employed around 90 people.

In 2008 the company decided that things weren't working out with Caretta Integrated Circuits in terms of its long-term strategic plan. It shut down the subsidiary and laid off about 30 employees in China as a result.

The global financial crisis of 2008 which restricted the worldwide availability of credit destabilized the general economy and triggered a significant slowdown in orders for Cirrus Logic.

EXECUTIVES

Vice President General Counsel and Corporate Secretary, Gregory S (Greg) Thomas
VP and Chief Culture Officer, Jo-Dee M. Benson, age 56
President CEO and Director, Jason P. Rhode, age 46, $658,500 total compensation
SVP; General Manager Mixed-Signal Audio Division, Scott A. Anderson, age 62, $322,319 total compensation
Acting CFO, Thurman K. Case, $323,171 total compensation

VP Supply Chain Management, Randy Carlson
VP and General Manager MEMS Division, Brad Fluke
Vice President of Product Marketing, Carl Alberty
Vice President Billing, Isa V Card
Division Vp & General Manager, Eric (Ric) Smith
Vice President Engineering, Thomas Schoen
Vice President Of Marketing Communications, Stan Victor
Vice President Chief Culture Officer, Dee M Benson
Vice President Chief Culture Officer, JoDee Benson
Vice President Sales Major Accounts, Bruce Tull
Vice President Strategic Account, Nate Yeakel
Vice President. Corporate Communications and Human Resources, Jo (Joseph) Benson
Vice President WW Channel Sales and Sales Operations, Dave (Davie) Airel
Vice President Video Products Marketing, Jack (Jackie) Guedj
Chairman, Alan R. Schuele
Auditors: Ernst & Young LLP

LOCATIONS

HQ: Cirrus Logic, Inc.
  800 W. 6th Street, Austin, TX 78701
Phone: 512 851-4000
Web: www.cirrus.com

PRODUCTS/OPERATIONS

2016 Sales

	$ mil.	% of total
Portable Audio Products	989.1	85
Non-Portable Audio and Other Products	180.2	15
Total	**1,169.3**	**100**

Selected Products

Amplifier integrated circuits
Analog-to-digital converters
Digital amplifiers
Digital interface integrated circuits
Digital-to-analog converters
Linear amplifiers
Volume controls

COMPETITORS

AMD	Macronix International
Actions Semiconductor	Marvell Technology
Analog Devices	Maxim Integrated
Analogic	Products
Asahi Kasei	NXP Semiconductors
Atmel	O2Micro
Conexant Systems	ON Semiconductor
Creative Technology	Power Integrations
Dialog Semiconductor	STMicroelectronics
Fairchild	Samsung Electronics
Semiconductor	Sigma Designs
Infineon Technologies	Sunplus
Integrated Device	Texas Instruments
Technology	VIA Technologies
Intel	Yamaha
Linear Technology	ams AG

HISTORICAL FINANCIALS
Company Type: Public

Income Statement
FYE: March 26

	REVENUE ($ mil.)	NET INCOME ($ mil.)	NET PROFIT MARGIN	EMPLOYEES
03/16	1,169.2	123.6	10.6%	1,291.0
03/15	916.5	55.1	6.0%	1,104.0
03/14	714.3	108.1	15.1%	751.0
03/13	809.7	136.6	16.9%	652.0
03/12	426.8	87.9	20.6%	676.0
Annual Growth	28.7%	8.9%	—	17.6%

2016 Year-End Financials
Debt ratio: 13.5%	No. of shares (mil.): 62.6
Return on equity: 15.3%	Dividends
Cash ($ mil.): 168.7	Yield: —
Current ratio: 3.95	Payout: —
Long-term debt ($ mil.): 160.4	Market value ($ mil.): 2,159.0

	STOCK PRICE ($) FY Close	P/E High/Low	Earnings	PER SHARE ($) Dividends	Book Value
03/16	34.47	19 13	1.87	0.00	13.72
03/15	33.29	39 19	0.85	0.00	12.00
03/14	19.52	15 10	1.65	0.00	10.29
03/13	22.75	21 10	2.00	0.00	8.66
03/12	23.80	18 9	1.29	0.00	7.23
Annual Growth	9.7%	— —	9.7%	—	17.4%

Clearfield Inc

Broadband providers can get all the fiber they need from Clearfield Inc. The company provides fiber optic cable and related optical networking equipment. Products include fiber distribution panels and cable management systems optical components (couplers multiplexers and splitters) and copper and fiber optic cable assemblies. Broadband companies can assemble a network from source to premise with Clearfield products which include optical cable connectors and microduct or areas where installing fiber has been cost prohibitive. More than 90% of Clearfield's revenue comes from customers in the US.

Operations

Most of Clearfield's final production is handled at its plants in Brooklyn Park Minnesota and Mexico. It has manufacturing support from partners in the US and overseas. The company can produce products for scheduled delivery or for a quick-turn and scheduled delivery basis. It makes some sales directly customers and other sales go through two-tier distribution partners. The company also sells to original equipment manufacturers who stick their labels on the products. In 2015 one customer accounted for a quarter of sales.

Financial Performance

Clearfield recorded about $60 million in revenue in 2015 a 4% increase from 2014. Net income dipped 14% to $4.6 million in 2015 from 2014. It had higher expenses in 2105 for increased compensation and expansion of facilities. Cash flow from operations fell to $6.8 million down 14% in 2015 on changes in inventory and accounts receivable.

Strategy

Clearfield expanded its manufacturing footprint in Tijuana Mexico in 2014 with the completion of another facility. It bases at least 20% of its North American production in Mexico with the expansion. The company also expanded its sales staff in Mexico as well as for its large accounts such as Verizon Communications.

EXECUTIVES
President CEO and Director, Cheri P. Beranek, age 54, $218,696 total compensation
COO, John P. (Johnny) Hill, age 50, $167,231 total compensation
VP and Interim CFO, Dan Herzog
Chairman, Ronald G. (Ron) Roth, age 71
Board of Directors, Jason (Jase) Luftman
Auditors: Baker Tilly Virchow Krause, LLP

LOCATIONS
HQ: Clearfield Inc
   7050 Winnetka Avenue North, Suite 100, Brooklyn Park, MN 55428
Phone: 763 476-6866
Web: www.clearfieldconnection.com

PRODUCTS/OPERATIONS

Selected products
Accessories
Boxes
Cabinets
Cassettes
Copper Assemblies
Fiber Assemblies
Frames
Optical Components
Panels
Patch Cords
Pedestal Inserts
Pedestals
Pushable Fiber and Microduct
Splice-On Connectors
Terminals
Test Access Points
Vaults
Wall Boxes

COMPETITORS
Alcatel-Lucent	TE Connectivity
American Furukawa	Telect
Corning Cable Systems	

HISTORICAL FINANCIALS
Company Type: Public

Income Statement
FYE: September 30

	REVENUE ($ mil.)	NET INCOME ($ mil.)	NET PROFIT MARGIN	EMPLOYEES
09/16	75.2	8.0	10.6%	222.0
09/15	60.3	4.6	7.8%	182.0
09/14	58.0	5.4	9.4%	185.0
09/13	53.3	4.7	8.9%	179.0
09/12	37.4	7.7	20.6%	159.0
Annual Growth	19.1%	1.0%	—	8.7%

2016 Year-End Financials
Debt ratio: —	No. of shares (mil.): 14.1
Return on equity: 14.0%	Dividends
Cash ($ mil.): 28.0	Yield: —
Current ratio: 6.96	Payout: —
Long-term debt ($ mil.): —	Market value ($ mil.): 266.0

	STOCK PRICE ($) FY Close	P/E High/Low	Earnings	PER SHARE ($) Dividends	Book Value
09/16	18.80	33 20	0.59	0.00	4.43
09/15	13.43	56 32	0.34	0.00	3.74
09/14	12.73	62 29	0.40	0.00	3.40
09/13	13.43	39 11	0.36	0.00	3.09
09/12	5.11	12 6	0.60	0.00	2.70
Annual Growth	38.5%	— —	(0.4%)	—	13.1%

CNL Growth Properties Inc

Auditors: PricewaterhouseCoopers LLP

LOCATIONS
HQ: CNL Growth Properties Inc
   CNL Center at City Commons, 450 South Orange Avenue, Orlando, FL 32801
Phone: 407 650-1000
Web: www.cnlgrowthproperties.com

HISTORICAL FINANCIALS
Company Type: Public

Income Statement
FYE: December 31

	REVENUE ($ mil.)	NET INCOME ($ mil.)	NET PROFIT MARGIN	EMPLOYEES
12/15	32.9	82.2	249.7%	0.0
12/14	15.3	(3.0)	—	0.0
12/13	3.5	(3.9)	—	0.0
12/12	0.0	(3.1)	—	0.0
Annual Growth	1720.6%	—	—	—

2015 Year-End Financials
Debt ratio: 60.8%	No. of shares (mil.): 22.5
Return on equity: 58.4%	Dividends
Cash ($ mil.): 19.0	Yield: —
Current ratio: 0.82	Payout: —
Long-term debt ($ mil.): 269.2	Market value ($ mil.): —

	STOCK PRICE ($) FY Close	P/E High/Low	Earnings	PER SHARE ($) Dividends	Book Value
12/15	0.00	— —	1.37	0.00	5.43
Annual Growth	—	— —	—	—	—

Coastal Banking Co Inc

Hoping to provide traditional small-town banking amid rapid growth in the Southeast a group of area banking veterans formed Coastal Banking Company in 2000. The holding company owns CBC National Bank which does business as Lowcountry National Bank from around five branches in southern South Carolina and First National Bank of Nassau County which operates loan offices in Atlanta and Savannah Georgia and Jacksonville

Florida in addition to one bank branch in Meigs Georgia under The Georgia Bank name. The banks offer standard products and services including business and consumer loans checking and savings accounts and CDs.

Coastal Banking acquired a bank branch in Georgia from Ameris Bancorp in 2006. The location in Meigs Georgia is now part of First National Bank.

More than 90% of Coastal Banking's loan portfolio is devoted to real estate mortgage and construction loans.

Directors and executive officers of Coastal Banking Company collectively own around 20% of the firm.

EXECUTIVES

President CEO and Director; President and CEO CBC National Bank, Michael G. Sanchez, age 67, $201,000 total compensation

Chairman Coastal Banking and and CBC National Bank, Suellen R. Garner, age 60

Vice Chairman Coastal Banking and and CBC National Bank, Ladson F. Howell, age 73

South Carolina Market President CBC National Bank, William G. (Gary) Horn, age 67, $145,350 total compensation

Executive Vice President Chief Financial Office, Paul R. Garrigues, age 61, $154,500 total compensation

Executive Vice President - Mortgage Division of CBC National Bank, Charles Wagner

President CEO and Director; President and CEO CBC National Bank, Michael G. Sanchez, age 67

Vice Chairman Coastal Banking and and CBC National Bank, Ladson F. Howell, age 73

Independent Director, Mark B. Heles, age 66

Auditors: Mauldin & Jenkins, LLC

LOCATIONS

HQ: Coastal Banking Co Inc
1891 South 14th Street, Fernandina Beach, FL 32034
Phone: 904 321-0400
Web: www.coastalbanking.com

COMPETITORS

Ameris	First Citizens
BB&T	Bancorporation
Bank of America	Regions Financial
Bank of South Carolina	South State

HISTORICAL FINANCIALS

Company Type: Public

Income Statement

FYE: December 31

	ASSETS ($ mil.)	NET INCOME ($ mil.)	INCOME AS % OF ASSETS	EMPLOYEES
12/15	464.6	5.8	1.3%	0.0
12/14	421.9	3.1	0.7%	349.0
12/13	375.6	1.5	0.4%	333.0
12/12	475.0	1.8	0.4%	362.0
12/11	477.6	0.3	0.1%	356.0
Annual Growth	(0.7%)	101.0%	—	—

2015 Year-End Financials

Return on assets: 1.3%	Dividends
Return on equity: 16.4%	Yield: —
Long-term debt ($ mil.): —	Payout: —
No. of shares (mil.): 2.6	Market value ($ mil.): 32.0
Sales ($ mil): 78.2	

	STOCK PRICE ($) FY Close	P/E High/Low		PER SHARE ($) Earnings	Dividends	Book Value
12/15	12.00	6	5	1.85	0.00	12.39
12/14	9.25	11	0	0.86	0.00	14.27
12/13	0.09	22	0	0.40	0.00	13.33
12/12	5.00	12	3	0.51	0.00	13.24
12/11	2.25	—	—	(0.08)	0.00	12.78
Annual Growth	52.0%	—	—	—	—	(0.8%)

Coca-Cola Bottling Co. Consolidated

Southerners like their drinks sweet and for Coca-Cola Bottling Co. Consolidated (CCBCC) there's nothing sweeter than a Coke. CCBCC produces bottles and distributes beverages principally the products of The Coca-Cola Company. Its distribution territory is mainly in the southeastern US. The company is the largest independent coke bottler in the US serving areas in 11 states –home to about 20 million prospective and hopefully thirsty consumers. Coca-Cola products account for about 88% of CCBCC's sales. The company does however handle other manufacturers' beverages and actually owns some brands including the flavored and vitamin-enhanced Tum-E Yummies drink and Country Breeze bottled tea.

Geographic Reach

The North Carolina-based company holds the bottling rights from Coca-Cola for the majority of North Carolina South Carolina and West Virginia as well as parts of Alabama Mississippi Tennessee Kentucky Virginia Pennsylvania Georgia and Florida.

Operations

CCBCC operates five production centers and 47 distribution centers in nine southeastern states. The regional bottler produces roughly 150 million cases of soft drinks annually. Sparkling beverages account for about two-thirds of CCBCC's total sales with still beverages (including water teas juices and sports drinks) accounting for the rest. The company has agreements to produce distribute and market Dr. Pepper in some regions and distributes and markets various other beverages including Monster Energy drinks and Sundrop.

Sales and Marketing

CCBCC's beverages are sold and distributed directly to retail stores and other customers including food markets institutional accounts and vending machine operators. Retail giant Wal-Mart Stores and the regional supermarket operator Food Lion are CCBCC's largest customers accounting for 15% and 6% of total net sales respectively.

Financial Performance

The company's sales increased 3% in 2012 versus 2011 to about $1.6 billion. The increase was primarily due to a 2% increase in bottle/can sales price per unit for sparkling beverages (excluding energy drinks) and a 1% increase in bottle/can volume to retail customers primarily due to increased sales of still beverages. CCBCC sold more of its company-owned products as well as data analysis and supply chain and logistics consulting services in 2012 versus 2011.

Still beverage sales increased 6.5% year over year versus a 2% gain in sales of sparkling beverages as consumers increasingly shun soda for water juice and other healthier drinks.

Despite the uptick in sales net income fell 5% to $27.2 million. Net income has been trending downward since 2009 while sale have increased in each of the past three years.

Strategy

CCBCC has boasted that its territories have some of the highest per capita Coca-Cola consumption in the world. The company attributes this success in part to anticipating consumer needs and investing in multi-pack packaging such as its 15-packs of 20-ounce bottles and 20-packs of 12-ounce cans.

Recognizing the continuing decline in demand for sugar-sweetened carbonated beverages the company concentrates on adding to its roster of diet sports-drink bottled-water and energy-beverage products including Coke's FUZE and Energy Brands' vitaminwater smartwater and vitaminenergy beverages. It has a 20-year agreement (entered into in 2008) with Monster Beverage Corporation (formerly Hansen Natural) to distribute Monster brand energy drinks. It is also the sole licensee of Cinnabon Premium Coffee Lattes and produces and markets Dr Pepper in some of its regions. Brands owned by CCBCC include regular and diet Country Breeze tea and Tum-E Yummies a flavored and vitamin-C-enhanced drink.

Ownership

Chairman and CEO Frank Harrison and his family control approximately 85% of CCBCC's voting stock; combined The Coca-Cola Company owns nearly 35% of its outstanding common stock.

HISTORY

North Carolina entrepreneurs J. B. Harrison J. Luther Snyder and J. P. Gibbons started the Greensboro Coca-Cola Bottling Company in 1902. They bottled Coca-Cola by hand using refillable bottles and sold it from horse-drawn carriages. With a loyal customer base the company survived the Great Depression and the sugar rationing of two World Wars. It went public in 1972 and in 1980 changed its name from Coca-Cola Bottling Company of Mid-Carolina to Coca-Cola Bottling Co. Consolidated (CCBCC).

In the 1980s CCBCC began expanding its territory with a string of acquisitions. In 1993 it formed Piedmont Coca-Cola Bottling Partnership (Piedmont CCBP) a 50-50 joint venture with The Coca-Cola Company to distribute and market soft drinks in the Carolinas. The next year the bottler struck a 10-year deal to manage South Atlantic Canners a manufacturing cooperative based in South Carolina. J. Frank Harrison III great-grandson of a company founder was named CEO in 1994 and chairman in 1996.

CCBCC bought Coca-Cola Southeast (Alabama) and St. Paul Coca-Cola (Virginia) in 1998. It added Carolina Coca-Cola Bottling Co. (South Carolina) and Lynchberg Coca-Cola Bottling (Virginia) in 1999. Also in 1999 CCBCC revealed that 4% of its stock had been acquired by #1 US Coke bottler Coca-Cola Enterprises (CCE) a company known for its aggressive growth. Harrison stated that CCBCC is not for sale. CCE upped its stake in CCBCC to almost 9% in 2000.

In an effort to streamline its operations CCBCC in 2000 sold its Ohio and Kentucky sales territories to CCE and initiated a restructuring that included layoffs and a $3 million write-down.

In 2002 CCBCC raised its stake in Piedmont CCBP to nearly 55%; as a result operations of

Piedmont were consolidated with those of CCBCC. The next year it bought 50% of Coca-Cola's remaining ownership of Piedmont raising its stake to more than 77%.

EXECUTIVES

President BYB Brands, Norman C. George, age 60, $299,157 total compensation
SVP and CFO, Clifford M. Deal, age 54
Chairman and CEO, J. Frank Harrison, age 61, $921,790 total compensation
EVP Business Transformation, James E. (Jamie) Harris, age 53, $493,772 total compensation
President and COO, Henry W. Flint, age 61, $659,750 total compensation
EVP Human Resources and Product Supply, David M. Katz
EVP Franchise Strategy and Operations, Robert G. Chambless, age 50, $425,375 total compensation
Senior Vice President Of Sales, Ray C Mayhall
Vice Chairman, William B. (Bill) Elmore, age 60
Auditors: PricewaterhouseCoopers LLP

LOCATIONS

HQ: Coca-Cola Bottling Co. Consolidated
4100 Coca-Cola Plaza, Charlotte, NC 28211
Phone: 704 557-4400
Web: www.cokeconsolidated.com

PRODUCTS/OPERATIONS

2015 Sales

	$ mil.	% of total
Nonalcoholic Beverages	2,245.8	91
All Other	160.2	7
Eliminations	(99.5)	-
Total	**2,306.5**	**100**

2015 Sales

	$ mil.	% of total
Bottle/can sales		
Sparkling beverages	1,503.7	65
Still beverages	397.9	17
Other sales		
Sales to other Coca-Cola bottlers	178.8	8
Post-mix and other	226.1	10
Total	**2,306.5**	**100**

Selected Brands

Sparkling beverages
  Barqs Root Beer
  Coca-Cola Zero
  Coke Cherry
  Coke Zero Cherry
  Diet Coke
  Diet Coke Plus
  Diet Coke Splenda
  Diet Dr Pepper (licensed)
  Dr Pepper (licensed)
  Fanta Flavors
  Fresca
  Full Throttle
  Mello Yello
  Monster Energy (licensed)
  NOS
  Pibb Xtra
  Sprite
  Sprite Zero
  Tab
  Vault
Still beverages
  Country Breeze Tea (company-owned)
  Dasani
  Dasani Flavors
  Dasani Plus
  Diet Country Breeze Tea (company-owned)
  FUZE
  Gold Peak tea
  Minute Maid Adult Refreshments
  Minute Maid Juices To Go

Nestea (licensed)
POWERade
POWERade Zero
smartwater
Tum-E Yummies (company-owned)
V8 juice (licensed)
vitaminenergy
vitaminwater

COMPETITORS

Aquaterra Corporation	Jones Soda
Big Red	Monarch Beverage (GA)
Buffalo Rock	Mountain Valley
Carolina Beverage	Naked Juice
Clearly Canadian	National Beverage
Coke United	Nestl© Waters
Cott	Odwalla
Crystal Rock Holdings	Pepsi Amercias
DS Services	Beverages
Danone Water	Pepsi Bottling
Dr Pepper Snapple	Ventures
Group	Polar Beverages
Eldorado Artesian	Red Bull
Springs	Reed's
Faygo	Sunny Delight
Georgia Crown	Suntory Holdings
Hain Celestial	Sweet Leaf Tea
Hawaiian Springs	True Drinks
Hornell Brewing	Welch's
IZZE	Wet Planet Beverages
Impulse Energy USA	

HISTORICAL FINANCIALS

Company Type: Public

Income Statement

FYE: January 3

	REVENUE ($ mil.)	NET INCOME ($ mil.)	NET PROFIT MARGIN	EMPLOYEES
01/16*	2,306.4	59.0	2.6%	9,500.0
12/14	1,746.3	31.3	1.8%	7,300.0
12/13	1,641.3	27.6	1.7%	6,700.0
12/12	1,614.4	27.2	1.7%	6,500.0
01/12	1,561.2	28.6	1.8%	6,100.0
Annual Growth	**10.2%**	**19.8%**	**—**	**11.7%**

*Fiscal year change

2016 Year-End Financials

Debt ratio: 36.7%
Return on equity: 27.2%
Cash ($ mil.): 55.5
Current ratio: 1.34
Long-term debt ($ mil.): 672.6

No. of shares (mil.): 9.2
Dividends
  Yield: 0.0%
  Payout: 15.8%
Market value ($ mil.): 1,696.0

	STOCK PRICE ($) FY Close	P/E High/Low	PER SHARE ($) Earnings	Dividends	Book Value
01/16*	182.51	34 14	6.33	1.00	26.16
12/14	88.55	28 20	3.37	1.00	19.80
12/13	72.98	24 19	2.98	1.00	20.68
12/12	65.58	24 19	2.94	1.00	14.65
01/12	58.55	24 17	3.09	1.00	14.26
Annual Growth	**32.9%**	**— —**	**19.6%**	**(0.0%)**	**16.4%**

*Fiscal year change

Cognex Corp.

Machines might not possess big picture vision but Cognex machines have excellent vision when it comes to detail. The company is one of the world's largest producers of systems that linked to a video camera serve as eyes where human vision is insufficient. Semiconductor consumer goods health care and automotive companies among others use the company's machine vision and industrial identification systems to position and identify products gauge sizes and locate defects. Cognex serves three primary markets: factory automation semiconductor and electronics capital equipment and surface inspection. It also offers consulting and educational services as well as tech support for its products. Sales to customers based outside the US account for about two-thirds of sales.

Operations

Cognex operates two business segments. The largest is its Modular Vision Systems Division (MVSD) which accounts for about 88% of its sales. MVSD develops manufactures and markets modular vision systems and ID products that are used to automate the manufacturing and tracking of discrete items by locating identifying inspecting and measuring them during the manufacturing or distribution process. The smaller Surface Inspection Systems Division (SISD) develops makes and markets surface inspection vision systems that are used to inspect surfaces of materials processed in a continuous fashion such as metals papers plastics and glass to ensure that there are no defects on the surfaces. Parsed another way Cognex products brings in 93% of revenue and services 7%.

Geographic Reach

Customers in Europe accounted for 42% of Cognex's $486 million in sales in 2014. It took in 30% from US customers 9% from Japanese customers with the rest of the world US rounding almost a fifth of sales. Internationally Cognex has been expanding its sales force in China India Brazil and Eastern Europe. The company's products are assembled by a contract manufacturer in Indonesia. Testing and shipping is done from its Natick Massachusetts facility for US customers and from its Ireland facility for customers outside the US.

Sales and Marketing

Cognex sells its MVSD products through a worldwide direct sales force and via a global network of integration and distribution partners. SISD which is the smaller of the two businesses and has fewer customers in a concentrated group of industries sells its products primarily through a worldwide direct sales force. Direct and indirect sales to Apple were 14% of Cognex revenue in 2014.

Financial Performance

it doesn't take a Cognex product to recognize the company's sales growth. It reported sales of $486 million in 2014 a 37% increase from 2013 sales of $354 million. Sales rose in each of the three segments with factory automation recording a 41% gain over 2014. Sales to surface inspection customers were 29% higher and up 14% for customers in semiconductor and electronics. The higher revenue flowed to the company's bottom line which stood at $121.5 million for 2014 a 65% improvement over 2013. A gain in foreign currency also contributed to the profit rise.

Strategy

Cognex's successful expansion into the factory automation market has significantly widened its customer base. The company maintains its focus on factory automation as its best bet for continued growth. To that end it's investing in new product development and functionality to make its machine vision products easier to use and more affordable. Cognex has opened sales offices in emerging markets such as China India and Brazil where it sees ample opportunity for the adoption of its factory automation products. Cognex's business strategy includes selective expansion into new machines vision applications through the acquisition of businesses and technologies.

In 2014 the company released several new products designed to expand its portfolio to more customers. Three new models the DS1050 DS1101 and DS1300 combined higher resolution video and easier-to-use software to increase accessibility to a wider range of users. An update to its Data-Man 8600 series of handheld bar code readers should enable reliable readings of challenging direct part bar codes.

HISTORY

Robert Shillman and two MIT colleagues Marilyn Matz and William Silver started Cognex (short for "cognition experts") in 1981 to create vision replacement machines for factories. Competition and inadequate technology forced the firm to reevaluate its distribution strategy in 1986. Cognex began supplying machine vision technology to original equipment manufacturers. The company introduced the first custom vision chip in 1988 and went public the next year.

Cognex found success where human vision fails –in the high-speed detailed repetitive processes required in making semiconductors. The company expanded by purchasing Acumen a developer of machine vision systems for semiconductor wafer identification (1995); Isys Controls a maker of quality control systems (1996); and Mayan Automation a maker of surface inspection systems (1997).

Low demand for semiconductor and printed circuit board manufacturing equipment in Asia hurt sales in 1998. Nonetheless the company boosted R&D by 10% and acquired some of Rockwell Automation's machine vision operations also becoming the preferred global supplier to Rockwell's plants. Orders picked up in early 1999 and Cognex invested $1 million in upstart Avalon Imaging (machine vision for the plastics industry) its first investment in such a company.

A series of acquisitions and in-house innovations enabled Cognex to expand into factory automation inspection which accounts for more than 90% of its business.

EXECUTIVES

VP Finance and CFO, Richard A. Morin, age 66, $276,058 total compensation

President CEO and Director, Robert Willett, age 48, $351,346 total compensation

VP and Business Unit Manager ID Products, Carl Gerst

Vice President Sales and Marketing, Sean Lett

Vice President MVSD Sales and Service Europe, Dirk Rathsack

Vice President Marketing, Scott (Scotty) Audette

Manufacturing Vice President, Jim (Jimmy) Quinlivan

Vice President Global Operations, Rocco Volpe

Vice President Operations, Herb Lade

Vice President Marketing, Dinh Tran

Vice President Marketing, John (Jack) Nelson

Vice President and Chief Legal Officer, Jim (Jimmy) Peck

Vice President Sales and Service Asia, Patrice (Pat) Denizard

Senior Vice President Of Research and Development, John E (Jack) Mcgarry

Executive Vice President, RICHARD A (Dick) MARRION

Chairman President and CEO, Robert J. (Bob) Shillman, age 69

Auditors: Grant Thornton LLP

LOCATIONS

HQ: Cognex Corp.
One Vision Drive, Natick, MA 01760-2059
Phone: 508 650-3000
Web: www.cognex.com

PRODUCTS/OPERATIONS

2014 Sales

	$ mil.	% of total
Product	451.1	93
Service	35.2	7
Total	**486.3**	**100**

2014 Sales by Segment

	$ mil.	% of total
Modular Vision Systems	426.5	88
Surface Inspection Systems	59.8	12
Total	**486.3**	**100**

Selected Products

DataMan 100 and 200 Series (image-based ID readers)
DisplayInspect (LCD inspection software)
In-Sight 5000 (machine vision system)
SmartAdvisor (web monitoring technology)
SmartView Paper (paper web inspection system)
SmartView Metals (flat-rolled metals surface inspection system)

COMPETITORS

Adept Technology	Integral Vision
Camtek	KLA-Tencor
Clemex	National Instruments
CyberOptics	Orbotech
Data Translation	PPT VISION
Elbit Vision	Perceptron
Electro Scientific	RoboGroup T.E.K.
Industries	Scanner Technologies
Image Sensing Systems	

HISTORICAL FINANCIALS

Company Type: Public

Income Statement

FYE: December 31

	REVENUE ($ mil.)	NET INCOME ($ mil.)	NET PROFIT MARGIN	EMPLOYEES
12/15	450.5	187.0	41.5%	1,305.0
12/14	486.2	121.4	25.0%	1,322.0
12/13	353.8	73.5	20.8%	1,077.0
12/12	324.2	68.1	21.0%	984.0
12/11	321.9	69.8	21.7%	919.0
Annual Growth	**8.8%**	**27.9%**	**—**	**9.2%**

2015 Year-End Financials

Debt ratio: —
Return on equity: 23.9%
Cash ($ mil.): 51.9
Current ratio: 8.36
Long-term debt ($ mil.): —

No. of shares (mil.): 84.8
Dividends
  Yield: 0.6%
  Payout: 9.8%
Market value ($ mil.): 2,866.0

	STOCK PRICE ($) FY Close	P/E High/Low		PER SHARE ($) Earnings	Dividends	Book Value
12/15	33.77	24	15	2.13	0.21	9.73
12/14	41.33	31	23	1.36	0.00	8.51
12/13	38.18	76	35	0.83	0.00	7.42
12/12	36.79	56	38	0.78	0.77	6.65
12/11	35.79	44	30	0.82	0.18	6.55
Annual Growth	**(1.4%)**	**—**	**—**	**27.1%**	**3.9%**	**10.4%**

Cohen & Steers Inc

One of the nation's largest managers of real estate funds Cohen & Steers administers about two dozen mutual funds closed-end funds and exchange-traded funds that are invested in real estate securities global infrastructure utilities and large-cap value stocks. It also manages about 95 separate account portfolios for institutional investors and offers alternative investments such as hedged real estate securities portfolios. The company's real estate investment banking practice Cohen & Steers Capital Advisors (now CSCA Capital Advisors) was sold off in 2009 to former managing directors of the unit. Cohen & Steers has nearly $46 billion of assets under management.Geographic ReachNew York-based Cohen & Steers boasts offices in London Hong Kong Tokyo and Seattle. The US is its largest market contributing 80% of annual revenue. Japan accounts for 14%.OperationsCohen & Steers manages three account types: institutional accounts (numbering some 95 total) open-end mutual funds (about 15) and closed-end mutual funds (about 10).About 57% of Cohen & Steers' managed assets in 2013 were concentrated in US real estate securities. Another 13% was concentrated in non-US real estate securities.Financial Performance-Sales and profits have risen in relative lockstep in recent years due to market appreciation and growth in assets under management. In 2013 the firm reported revenue of $297.7 million an increase of 9% versus 2012 on higher investment advisory and administration fees as assets under management rose partially offset by lower portfolio consulting and other revenue. Investment advisory and administration fees increased 11% year over year. Net income rose 3% over the same period to $68.1 million buoyed by higher revenue and a gain on the sale of trading securities. Thanks to a net income increase and change in working capital Cohen & Steers posted $75.9 million in cash flow from operations in 2013 vs. 2012.StrategyFrom its focus on the REIT market Cohen & Steers has diversified to include products and services outside the US real estate securities area such as commodities and natural resources. To this end in 2014 the firm launched the Cohen & Steers Active Commodities Strategy Fund an open-end mutual fund that invests in commodities futures. The launch of the fund was the next step in the firm's long-term goal to become a preeminent provider of investment vehicles to institutional and individual investors in liquid real assets including real estate infrastructure and commodities.Company BackgroundMartin Cohen and Robert Steers founded the firm in 1986 and continue to share top billing as co-chairmen and co-CEOs; together the two own a majority of Cohen & Steers' common shares.

EXECUTIVES

Senior Vice President, Luke (Lucas) Sullivan

EVP and CFO, Matthew S. (Matt) Stadler, age 61, $325,000 total compensation

CEO and Director, Robert H. Steers, age 63, $750,000 total compensation

President and Chief Investment Officer, Joseph M. Harvey, age 52, $600,000 total compensation

EVP and COO, Adam M. Derechin, age 51, $325,000 total compensation

EVP, Douglas R. Bond, age 56

EVP and Director Fixed Income and Portfolio
  Manager Preferred Securities Portfolios, William
  F. Scapell
EVP and General Counsel, Francis C. Poli, age 53,
  $325,000 total compensation
EVP, Jon Y. Cheigh
EVP, Thomas N. Bohjalian
EVP and Director of Global Marketing and
  Product Solutions, Todd Glickson, age 48
Senior Vice President And National Sales
  Manager, Kevin (Kev) Crook
Vice President And Assistant Portfolio Manager
  Strategy, Dev Subhash
Vice President Regional Sales Manager, Ron Pucillo
Senior Vice President, Robert (Bob) Becker
Vice President, Andy Humble
Senior Vice President and Chief Accounting
  Officer, Elena (Lena) Dulik
Senior Vice President, James (Jamie) McAdams
Vice President, Christopher (Chris) Rhine
Senior Vice President, James M (Jamie) Giallanza
Vice President, William (Bill) Cheng
Vice President, Frank McNamara
Senior Vice President And Associate General
  Counsel, Adam (Ad) Johnson
Vice President, Joanna Kennedy
Vice President, Kim Spellman
Senior Vice President and Director Consultant
  Relations, Ed (Eddie) Rieger
Executive Vice President And Director, William
  (Bill) Frischling
Vice President, Pascal Van Garderen
Vice President, Mike Loftus
Vice President, Matthew Karcic
Vice President, Lorraine (Irene) Tutovic
Vice President, Jamelah Leddy
Vice President, Neil Bloom
Vice President, Austin Fagan
Vice President, Luis Polit
Senior Vice President, Veronika Jhirad
Vice President, James (Jamie) Macpherson
Vice President and Associate General Counsel,
  Tina (Tin) Payne
Senior Vice President, Chris Henderson
Senior Vice President National Sales Manager, Joe
  (Joey) Williams
Vice President, Jason (Jase) Williams
Vice President, Emily (Em) Conte
Vice President, Raquel (Rae) McLean
Vice President of Facilities, Betsy Shaar-Krudener
Co-Chairman and Co-CEO, Martin Cohen, age 67
Board Member Managing Director, Richard (Dick)
  Norman
Auditors: Deloitte & Touche LLP

LOCATIONS

HQ: Cohen & Steers Inc
  280 Park Avenue, New York, NY 10017
Phone: 212 832-3232   Fax: 212 832-3622
Web: www.cohenandsteers.com

PRODUCTS/OPERATIONS

2015 Sales

	$ mil.	% of total
Investment advisory & administration fees	303.8	92
Distribution & service fees	16.0	5
Portfolio consulting & other	8.9	3
Total	328.7	100

COMPETITORS

AllianceBernstein
BlackRock
CBRE Group
Eaton Vance
FMR

Janus Capital
Legg Mason
MFS
Morgan Stanley Investment Management
Nuveen
PIMCO
State Street
The Vanguard Group
Waddell & Reed

HISTORICAL FINANCIALS
Company Type: Public

Income Statement   FYE: December 31

	REVENUE ($ mil.)	NET INCOME ($ mil.)	NET PROFIT MARGIN	EMPLOYEES
12/15	328.6	64.5	19.6%	275.0
12/14	313.9	75.5	24.1%	263.0
12/13	297.7	68.1	22.9%	247.0
12/12	273.5	66.1	24.2%	240.0
12/11	237.2	54.3	22.9%	239.0
Annual Growth	8.5%	4.4%	—	3.6%

2015 Year-End Financials

Debt ratio: —
Return on equity: 28.0%
Cash ($ mil.): 142.7
Current ratio: 5.53
Long-term debt ($ mil.): —

No. of shares (mil.): 45.4
Dividends
  Yield: 4.9%
  Payout: 93.1%
Market value ($ mil.): 1,385.0

	STOCK PRICE ($) FY Close	P/E High/Low	PER SHARE ($) Earnings	Dividends	Book Value
12/15	30.48	33 19	1.41	1.50	5.10
12/14	42.08	26 21	1.65	1.88	5.09
12/13	40.06	28 19	1.51	1.80	5.05
12/12	30.47	25 18	1.49	2.22	4.95
12/11	28.90	32 19	1.23	1.60	5.34
Annual Growth	1.3%	— —	3.5%	(1.6%)	(1.1%)

Cole Credit Property Trust IV Inc

Auditors: Deloitte & Touche LLP

LOCATIONS

HQ: Cole Credit Property Trust IV Inc
  2325 East Camelback Road, Suite 1100, Phoenix, AZ
  85016
Phone: 602 778-8700
Web: www.colecapital.com

HISTORICAL FINANCIALS
Company Type: Public

Income Statement   FYE: December 31

	REVENUE ($ mil.)	NET INCOME ($ mil.)	NET PROFIT MARGIN	EMPLOYEES
12/15	367.7	64.7	17.6%	0.0
12/14	256.2	11.1	4.4%	0.0
12/13	102.5	(32.8)	—	0.0
12/12	7.8	(13.7)	—	0.0
Annual Growth	260.7%	—	—	—

2015 Year-End Financials

Debt ratio: 45.1%
Return on equity: 2.6%
Cash ($ mil.): 34.5
Current ratio: 0.87
Long-term debt ($ mil.): 2,066.5

No. of shares (mil.): 312.0
Dividends
  Yield: —
  Payout: —
Market value ($ mil.): 2,793.0

	STOCK PRICE ($) FY Close	P/E High/Low	PER SHARE ($) Earnings	Dividends	Book Value
12/15	8.95	43 43	0.21	0.00	7.65
12/14	8.95	224 224	0.04	0.00	8.03
12/13	0.00	— —	(0.36)	0.00	8.38
Annual Growth	—	— —	—	—	(4.5%)

Colony NorthStar Inc

Auditors: Grant Thornton LLP

LOCATIONS

HQ: Colony NorthStar Inc
  399 Park Avenue, 18th Floor, New York, NY 10022
Phone: 212 547-2600
Web: www.nsamgroup.com

HISTORICAL FINANCIALS
Company Type: Public

Income Statement   FYE: December 31

	REVENUE ($ mil.)	NET INCOME ($ mil.)	NET PROFIT MARGIN	EMPLOYEES
12/15	435.8	119.7	27.5%	383.0
12/14	259.1	19.1	7.4%	202.0
12/13	89.9	(2.0)	—	162.0
12/12	50.7	(17.3)	—	0.0
12/11	13.0	(25.6)	—	0.0
Annual Growth	140.4%	—	—	—

2015 Year-End Financials

Debt ratio: 26.6%
Return on equity: 63.5%
Cash ($ mil.): 84.7
Current ratio: 1.12
Long-term debt ($ mil.): —

No. of shares (mil.): 189.9
Dividends
  Yield: 0.0%
  Payout: 66.6%
Market value ($ mil.): 2,305.0

	STOCK PRICE ($) FY Close	P/E High/Low	PER SHARE ($) Earnings	Dividends	Book Value
12/15	12.14	41 17	0.60	0.40	0.92
12/14	22.57	227 165	0.10	0.10	1.03
Annual Growth	(46.2%)	—	— 500.0%	300.0%	(10.1%)

Columbia Banking System Inc

Columbia Banking System (CBS) is the $8.5 billion-asset holding company for Columbia State Bank (also known as Columbia Bank). The regional community bank has about 150 branches in Washington from Puget Sound to the timber country in the southwestern part of the state as well as in northern Oregon and Idaho. Targeting retail and small and medium-sized business customers the bank offers standard retail services such as checking and savings accounts CDs IRAs credit cards loans and mortgages. Commercial and multifamily real estate loans make up more than 40% of the company's loan portfolio while business loans make up another 40%. CBS is expanding in the Pacific Northwest through acquisitions of other community banks.

Operations

The bank's Columbia Private Banking division offers customized financial services for businesses and affluent families. Subsidiary CB Financial Services provides investment products through a pact with third-party provider PrimeVest.Like other retail banks Columbia makes most of its money from interest income. About 68% of its total revenue came from loan interest during 2015 while another 10% came from interest on taxable and tax-exempt securities. The rest of its revenue came from service charges and other fees (15% of revenue) merchant service fees (2%) and other non-interest income sources.

Geographic Reach

Tacoma-based Columbia Banking System has 149 bank branches (as of mid-2016) with about half in the state of Washington 60 across Oregon and 16 in Idaho.Sales and MarketingThe bank spent $4.7 million on advertising and promotion in 2015 up from $3.9 million and $4.1 million in 2014 and 2013 respectively.

Financial Performance

Columbia Bank's annual revenues have nearly doubled since 2011 as its loan assets have more than doubled to $5.8 billion (at the end of 2015). Its profits have also doubled over the time period as it's kept a handle on costs.The bank's revenue jumped 14% to $420.36 million during 2015 on higher interest income as it increased its loan business and interest-earning security assets. The company also earned more in service charges and other non-interest income thanks to its organically growing customer base and its Intermountain acquisition.Revenue growth in 2015 drove the bank's net income up 21% to $98.83 million. Columbia Bank's operating cash levels dipped 2% to $134.76 million for the year mostly due to unfavorable working capital changes related to other liabilities.

Strategy

Columbia reiterated in 2016 that it would focus on expanding its branches into new markets (either on its own or through acquisitions) while focusing on high-quality loan growth. One of its most recent acquisitions –the purchase of Intermountain Community Bancorp –expanded its presence in Idaho for the first time.

Mergers and Acquisitions

In November 2014 the bank expanded its presence into Idaho after purchasing $960 million-asset Intermountain Community Bancorp and its Panhandle State Bank branches in the state.In April 2013 Columbia acquired West Coast Bancorp –the parent company of West Coast Bank which operated nearly 60 bank branches in Oregon and Washington. The purchase boosted Columbia's total assets to more than $7 billion and furthered Columbia's goal of becoming the leading regional community bank in the Pacific Northwest. Company BackgroundColumbia Banking System took advantage of the rash of bank failures in past years to increase its presence in the Pacific Northwest region. It added more than 30 branches

in 2010 when it acquired most of the deposits and assets of failed banks Columbia River Bank and American Marine Bank a week apart. In similar transactions in 2011 it acquired most of the operations of the failed institutions Summit Bank First Heritage Bank and Bank of Whitman. Those deals added more than a dozen branches in Washington.

EXECUTIVES

President and CEO; President and CEO Columbia Bank, Melanie J. Dressel, age 63, $452,283 total compensation
EVP and Chief Banking Officer Columbia Bank, Mark W. Nelson, age 64, $253,073 total compensation
EVP and Chief Credit Officer, Andrew L. (Andy) McDonald, age 56, $209,998 total compensation
EVP and CFO, Clint E. Stein, $174,667 total compensation
EVP and COO, Hadley Robbins, age 55
Senior Vice President Senior Financial Advisor, Rhonda Arnett
Vice President, Michelle (Mitch) Claeys
Vice President, Thomas (Thom) Poole
Senior Vice President and Banking Solutions Manager, Bruce (Brucey) Morehead
Chairman, William T. Weyerhaeuser, age 72
Auditors: Deloitte & Touche LLP

LOCATIONS

HQ: Columbia Banking System Inc
1301 " A" Street, Tacoma, WA 98402-2156
Phone: 253 305-1900
Web: www.columbiabank.com

PRODUCTS/OPERATIONS

2015 Sales

	$ mil.	% of total
Interest Income:		
Loans	286.2	68
Taxable securities	30.8	7
Tax-exempt securities	11.8	3
Deposits in banks	0.1	-
Non-interest Income:		
Service charges and other fees	61.9	15
Merchant services fees	9.0	2
Other	24.6	5
FDIC loss-sharing asset	(4.0)	-
Total	**420.4**	**100**

COMPETITORS

BECU	JPMorgan Chase
Bank of America	KeyCorp
Banner Corp	U.S. Bancorp
Heritage Financial	Washington Federal
HomeStreet	Wells Fargo

HISTORICAL FINANCIALS

Company Type: Public

Income Statement

FYE: December 31

	ASSETS ($ mil.)	NET INCOME ($ mil.)	INCOME AS % OF ASSETS	EMPLOYEES
12/15	8,951.7	98.8	1.1%	1,868.0
12/14	8,578.8	81.5	1.0%	1,844.0
12/13	7,161.5	60.0	0.8%	1,695.0
12/12	4,906.3	46.1	0.9%	1,198.0
12/11	4,785.9	48.0	1.0%	1,256.0
Annual Growth	**16.9%**	**19.8%**	**—**	**10.4%**

2015 Year-End Financials

Return on assets: 1.1%
Return on equity: 8.0%
Long-term debt ($ mil.): —
No. of shares (mil.): 57.7
Sales ($ mil): 420.3
Dividends
Yield: 4.1%
Payout: 84.2%
Market value ($ mil.): 1,877.0

	STOCK PRICE ($) FY Close	P/E High/Low	PER SHARE ($)		
			Earnings	Dividends	Book Value
12/15	32.51	21 15	1.71	1.34	21.52
12/14	27.61	19 16	1.52	0.94	21.38
12/13	27.49	23 14	1.21	0.41	20.55
12/12	17.94	20 14	1.16	0.98	19.25
12/11	19.27	18 11	1.21	0.27	19.22
Annual Growth	**14.0%**	**— —**	**9.0%**	**49.3%**	**2.9%**

Columbia Sportswear Co.

Gertrude Boyle is called chairman and occasionally one tough mother. The nonagenarian and face of Columbia Sportswear's "tough mother" and "tested tough" ads heads one of the global powerhouses in the development marketing and distribution of active outerwear. Columbia's trademark Bugaboo parka with weatherproof shell put the company on the map in upscale outdoor wear. Columbia offers performance apparel for a variety of activities as well as sportswear accessories boots and rugged footwear sold under the Columbia Mountain Hardwear Sorel prAna and Montrail brands. Founded as a hat company in 1938 Columbia Sportswear is controlled by the Boyle family and run by president and CEO Tim Boyle son of Gert.

Operations

Columbia Sportswear's operations are divided between two product categories: The largest category apparel accessories and equipment generated 78% of the company's total sales during 2015. Footwear including Sorel brand boots accounted for the rest. In the US the sportswear maker operated 109 outlet stores 24 branded retail stores two employee stores and five brand-specific e-commerce sites. The company had 241 concession-based branded outlet and shop-in-shop locations in Japan and 169 additional such stores in Korea. It had a handful of retail stores in Canada and 10 outlet retail stores in the EMEA region. Geographic Reach

Columbia Sportswear's products are sold in North America and 100 more countries worldwide. The company generated 63% of its sales in the US during 2015 while another 7% came from Canada. Latin America and the Asia-Pacific region (LAAP) –which includes stores in Japan and Korea –is the company's second-largest market behind North America accounting for 20% of sales. Other markets include Europe the Middle East and Africa.

Sales and Marketing

Columbia's products are primarily sold through 8000-plus wholesale distributors to specialty outdoor and sporting goods stores and major retail chains. The company also sells directly to consumers through domestic and international banner retail outlets and stores (Columbia-operated and dealer-operated) as well as online. In countries where it does not trade the Columbia sells to about two dozen independent distributors. Almost all of Columbia's items are made in Asia by independent manufacturers.

The company uses a variety of media to market its products including online advertising and social media sites TV and print. It also sponsors events and operates branded and outlet retail stores in high-profile locations. Columbia has been boosting its advertising spend in recent years. It spent $120.8 million on advertising in 2015 up from $110.1 million and $78.1 million in 2014 and 2013 respectively.

Financial Performance

Columbia Sportswear's sales and profits have been trending higher in recent years thanks to the success of its direct-to-consumer channel which sells through company-operated retail stores and e-commerce sites.The sportswear maker's revenue jumped 11% to $2.33 billion during 2015 mostly thanks to a 21% jump in its US sales led by the wholesale business as retail customers ordered more fall season product (especially the Columbia Sorel and prAna brands) in advance. US direct-to-consumer sales were also up thanks to 16 net new retail store openings and stronger e-commerce sales. Sales in Canada were up 11% on better wholesale and direct-to-consumer sales but were down by 5% and 10% in the LAAP and EMEA regions respectively entirely due to unfavorable foreign currency exchange rates (sales were essentially unchanged in the two regions after excluding FX).Double-digit revenue growth in 2015 drove Columbia Sportswear's net income up 27% to $174.3 million. The company's operating cash levels fell by nearly half to $95.1 million for the year mostly as the company built up its inventories but also because of unfavorable working capital changes related to its accounts receivable and income taxes payables.Strategy

Columbia Sportswear has strategically expanded its geographic presence and product offerings through acquisitions alliances and licensing deals. The company typically acquires or partners with brands that move it into new and complementary consumer categories especially ones that reduce its dependence on cold-weather products. In December 2015 for example Columbia expanded into new clothing territory after forming an exclusive licensing agreement with Delta Galil Industries which would begin developing producing and distributing performance-based underwear under the Columbia Sportswear brand.

To expand the Columbia and Mountain Hardwear brands in China Columbia in 2014 launched its 60-40 joint venture with Swire Resources a subsidiary of trading conglomerate Swire Pacific. Swire operates some 70 Columbia banner retail stores and has exclusively sold both brands through a network of wholesale dealers since 2004. Swire has also distributed the brands in Hong Kong and Macau since 2002. Mergers and AcquisitionsIn May 2014 Columbia Sportswear diversified its brand portfolio after buying prAna Living LLC and its prAna Lifestyle Apparel brand from owner Steelpoint Capital Partners for $188.5 million cash. The deal included seven company-owned retail stores an e-commerce site and direct-mail catalogue.

HISTORY

Paul Lanfrom acquired a small hat distributor in 1938 which he renamed Columbia Hat Co. His daughter Gertrude married Neal Boyle in the late 1940s and Neal took control of the firm when Lan-from died in 1963. Building on a fishing vest designed by Gertrude Columbia Sportswear moved into hunting and fishing apparel. When Neal died suddenly in 1970 Gertrude assumed control of the floundering company.

Columbia struggled as Gertrude and her son Tim learned to run the business; but in the 1980s the company introduced its breakthrough product: the Bugaboo jacket with a shell and lining that can be worn separately or zipped together for added warmth.

Columbia launched its rugged footwear and Tough Mother denim lines in 1993. It opened its flagship Portland Oregon retail outlet in 1996 then launched its Asian retail operations with a Seoul Korea store in 1997. Columbia Sportswear went public in March of the following year.

To consolidate the company shuttered its only owned manufacturing facility in 1999 cutting nearly 15% of its workforce. Columbia Sportswear also launched a program that year licensing its name for socks and other items. In early 2000 it cut licensing deals with leather goods manufacturer Humphreys for belts and other leather accessories and with Cerf Brothers for travel bags. Also in 2000 Columbia acquired Sorel a well-known but bankrupt boot maker.

To further advance its outdoor brand the company signed a licensing agreement with L'Amy Group for the design manufacture and marketing of a line of men's and women's sunglasses and ski goggles (which hit stores in 2003). Also in 2003 Columbia increased distribution of its apparel and footwear in Europe by beginning operations at its distribution center in France. It also acquired climbing gear and apparel company Mountain Hardware.

In 2004 Columbia signed a licensing agreement with Granger's International for shoe and apparel care products including repellents cleaners and conditioners.

Columbia purchased outdoor footwear maker Montrail for $15 million in 2006. The Montrail brand is known for its IntegraFit technology for running walking and hiking. And at auction the company was the winning bidder for outerwear and sportswear brand Pacific Trail which was sold by the bankrupt London Fog Industries in 2006 for $20 million.

Trying something new Columbia in 2007 began to license its name for pet products made by RC Pet Products. Items include dog coats and pet accessories.

EXECUTIVES

CEO and Director, Timothy P. (Tim) Boyle, age 66, $928,846 total compensation
President and COO, Bryan L. Timm, age 52, $729,394 total compensation
EVP Chief Administrative Officer General Counsel and Secretary, Peter J. Bragdon, age 54, $470,193 total compensation
President SOREL Brand, Mark Nenow, age 59
EVP CFO and Treasurer, Thomas B. Cusick, age 49, $560,539 total compensation
SVP and General Manager - EMEA Region, Franco Fogliato, age 46, $462,622 total compensation
VP Design and Innovation Columbia Brand, Michael W. (Woody) Blackford, age 47
SVP Columbia Brand Merchandising and Design, Joseph P. (Joe) Boyle, age 35
SVP North America and EMEA Retail, D. Shawn Cox, age 52
VP E-Commerce, Patricia E. Higgins, age 48
SVP and Chief Marketing Officer, Stuart B. Redsun, age 50
VP and CIO, Michael Hirt
CEO prAna Brand, Scott W. Kerslake, age 51
SVP Global Sourcing and Manufacturing, Stephen P. (Steve) Woodside, age 51
Vice President of Operations, Daniel (Dan) Dougherty
Vice President Client Services, Sanders Davis
Vice President Apparelsales, Joe (Joey) Craig
Vice President, Brittany (Brit) Frazier
Vice President, Francois Boulot
Vice President Global Innovation, Woody Blackford
Executive Assistant to Steve Woodside Senior Vice President Global Sourcing and Manufacturing, Elena (Lena) Stocks
Chairman, Gertrude (Gert) Boyle, age 91
Auditors: Deloitte & Touche LLP

LOCATIONS

HQ: Columbia Sportswear Co.
14375 Northwest Science Park Drive, Portland, OR 97229
Phone: 503 985-4000
Web: www.columbia.com

PRODUCTS/OPERATIONS

2015 Sales

	$ mil.	% of total
Apparel accessories & equipment	1,821.2	78
Footwear	505.0	22
Total	**2,326.2**	**100**

2015 Sales by Brand

	$ mil.	% of total
Columbia	1,864.7	80
Sorel	209.2	9
Mountain Hardwear	116.3	5
prAna	125.3	6
Other	10.7	
Total	**2,326.2**	**100**

Selected Brands

Bugaboo
Columbia
Convert
Mountain Hardwear
Montrail
OutDry
Pacific Trail
prAna
Sorel

COMPETITORS

Amerex	Levi Strauss
American Eagle	NIKE
Outfitters	Nautica Apparel
American Recreation	North Face
Products	PVH
Benetton	Patagonia Inc.
Berghaus	Quiksilver
Burton	Ralph Lauren
Carhartt	Skechers U.S.A.
Crocs	Spyder
Deckers Outdoor	The Gap
Fila USA	Williamson-Dickie
Hanesbrands	Manufacturing
Kellwood	Wolverine World Wide
L.L. Bean	Woolrich Inc.
Lafuma	adidas
Lands' End	

HISTORICAL FINANCIALS
Company Type: Public

Income Statement
FYE: December 31

	REVENUE ($ mil.)	NET INCOME ($ mil.)	NET PROFIT MARGIN	EMPLOYEES
12/15	2,326.1	174.3	7.5%	5,978.0
12/14	2,100.5	137.1	6.5%	5,326.0
12/13	1,685.0	94.3	5.6%	4,320.0
12/12	1,669.5	99.8	6.0%	4,166.0
12/11	1,693.9	103.4	6.1%	4,161.0
Annual Growth	8.3%	13.9%	—	9.5%

2015 Year-End Financials

Debt ratio: 0.1%
Return on equity: 12.7%
Cash ($ mil.): 369.7
Current ratio: 3.41
Long-term debt ($ mil.): —

No. of shares (mil.): 69.2
Dividends
Yield: 1.2%
Payout: 25.3%
Market value ($ mil.): 3,378.0

	STOCK PRICE ($) FY Close	P/E High/Low		PER SHARE ($) Earnings	Dividends	Book Value
12/15	48.76	29	17	2.45	0.62	20.21
12/14	44.54	44	18	1.94	0.57	19.24
12/13	78.75	58	36	1.36	0.46	18.00
12/12	53.36	39	30	1.47	0.44	17.11
12/11	46.55	46	28	1.52	0.43	15.97
Annual Growth	1.2%	—	—	12.8%	9.6%	6.1%

Concert Pharmaceuticals Inc

Concert Pharmaceuticals wants to use deuterium chemistry to conduct a symphony of drugs. The company's process lets it substitute deuterium (also called heavy hydrogen) for hydrogen in a chemical compound thereby making the compound more stable without changing its other properties. It also believes this process will lead to shorter time from discovery to trial for certain drugs. Concert has a handful of clinical-stage candidates in various stages of the approval process including treatments for spasticity kidney disease and neurologic disorders. It collaborates with Avanir Celgene and Jazz Pharmaceuticals on development. Concert began its song in 2006 and took the show public in 2014.

IPO

The company raised $84 million in its IPO. It plans to use the funds to continue trials development and R&D to expand its pipeline of candidates.

Sales and Marketing

Concert plans to pursue strategic development and marketing partnerships while retaining full rights to and control over certain drugs. It intends to build out its production and marketing capability in the US.

Financial Performance

Since Concert doesn't have a product on the market yet its revenues from licensing and R&D payments has been minimal. It shows net losses for every year since its founding and an accumulated deficit of $108 million. The company expects this trend to continue for years to come.

Strategy

The company plans to continue pushing its pipeline candidates through FDA approval acquiring rights to additional candidates and seeking collaborative partners to help it develop and commercialize its products.

EXECUTIVES

SVP and Chief Development Officer, James V. (Jim) Cassella, age 61, $353,684 total compensation
COO, Nancy Stuart, age 57, $300,054 total compensation
President and CEO, Roger D. Tung, age 56, $435,537 total compensation
CFO, Ryan Daws, age 41
SVP and General Counsel, Ian Robert (Robert) Silverman, $325,337 total compensation
Chairman, Richard H. Aldrich, age 62
Auditors: Ernst & Young LLP

LOCATIONS

HQ: Concert Pharmaceuticals Inc
99 Hayden Avenue, Suite 500, Lexington, MA 02421
Phone: 781 860-0045
Web: www.concertpharma.com

PRODUCTS/OPERATIONS

2015 Sales

	$ mil.	% of total
License & research and development	6.5	10
Milestone	10.0	15
Other	50.2	75
Total	**66.7**	**100**

COMPETITORS

AbbVie	Merck
AstraZeneca	Novartis
Auspex	Pfizer
Bayer AG	Roche Holding
GW Pharmaceuticals	Sanofi
GlaxoSmithKline	

HISTORICAL FINANCIALS
Company Type: Public

Income Statement
FYE: December 31

	REVENUE ($ mil.)	NET INCOME ($ mil.)	NET PROFIT MARGIN	EMPLOYEES
12/15	66.7	24.1	36.2%	59.0
12/14	8.5	(31.7)	—	55.0
12/13	25.4	(6.0)	—	45.0
12/12	12.8	(20.4)	—	43.0
12/11	19.4	(11.3)	—	0.0
Annual Growth	36.1%	—	—	—

2015 Year-End Financials

Debt ratio: —
Return on equity: 26.0%
Cash ($ mil.): 92.5
Current ratio: 21.75
Long-term debt ($ mil.): —

No. of shares (mil.): 22.1
Dividends
Yield: —
Payout: —
Market value ($ mil.): 420.0

	STOCK PRICE ($) FY Close	P/E High/Low		PER SHARE ($) Earnings	Dividends	Book Value
12/15	18.97	22	11	1.09	0.00	5.89
12/14	13.32	—	—	(2.00)	0.00	3.01
Annual Growth	42.4%	—	—	—	—	96.0%

CONE Midstream Partners LP

Auditors: Ernst & Young LLP

LOCATIONS

HQ: CONE Midstream Partners LP
1000 CONSOL Energy Drive, Canonsburg, PA 15317-6506
Phone: 724 485-4000
Web: www.conemidstream.com

HISTORICAL FINANCIALS
Company Type: Public

Income Statement
FYE: December 31

	REVENUE ($ mil.)	NET INCOME ($ mil.)	NET PROFIT MARGIN	EMPLOYEES
12/15	203.4	71.2	35.0%	95.0
12/14	130.1	56.9	43.8%	90.0
12/13	65.6	28.1	42.9%	70.0
12/12	42.6	19.9	46.8%	0.0
Annual Growth	68.4%	52.9%	—	—

2015 Year-End Financials

Debt ratio: 7.9%
Return on equity: —
Cash ($ mil.): 0.2
Current ratio: 1.21
Long-term debt ($ mil.): 73.5

No. of shares (mil.): 58.3
Dividends
Yield: 8.8%
Payout: 72.9%
Market value ($ mil.): 575.0

	STOCK PRICE ($) FY Close	P/E High/Low		PER SHARE ($) Earnings	Dividends	Book Value
12/15	9.85	21	7	1.20	0.88	5.37
12/14	24.12	—	—	(0.00)	0.00	5.03
12/13	0.00	—	—	(0.00)	0.00	(0.00)
Annual Growth	—	—	—	—	—	—

Connecticut Water Service, Inc.

The operations of Connecticut Water Service (CWS) consist of managing a lot of water in its namesake state and more recently in Maine as well. CWS's regulated subsidiaries —Connecticut Water Company Maine Water and Biddeford & Saco Water —provide water supply and services to 120000 customers in 76 municipalities in Connecticut and Maine. The non-operating holding company's subsidiaries gather water from yield from its 235 active wells and 25 surface water supplies and produce 72 million gallons daily. Other subsidiaries offer fire protection other water-related services and real estate services.

Geographic Reach

CWS operates in Connecticut and Maine.

Operations

Of the company's six key operating subsidiaries its regulated subsidiaries are the Connecticut Water the Maine Water and Biddeford & Saco

Water. These businesses own and operate 30 water filtration facilities (a combined treatment capacity of 52 million gallons per day). Their transmission and distribution systems consists of 2100 miles of main and a reservoir storage capacity of 8.5 billion gallons. Connecticut Water CWS' largest subsidiary supplies water to about 300000 people in 56 towns in Connecticut. Unregulated companies include Chester Realty (real estate in Connecticut) and New England Water Utility Services (contract water and sewer operations and other water related services).

Financial Performance

CWS' revenues increased by 21% in 2012 due to added revenues associated with the acquisitions of Maine Water and Biddeford and Saco Water (which contributed about 87% of increased revenues). In addition rate increases and higher late payment fees lifted revenues by 4%.The company's net income increased by 21% in 2012 due to the acquisitions as well as increased non-water sales earnings and a higher gain on real estate transactions. That year the unregulated companies together with real estate transactions within Connecticut Water contributed about 17% of the CWS' net income through real estate transactions (and services and rentals).

Strategy

In recent years the company has grown primarily through acquisitions.

In 2013 CWS' Connecticut Water unit signed an agreement with state authorities to voluntarily return the benefit of an IRS tax law change to customers through a rate reduction over a 2 year period starting from April 2014 and to delay the filing of its next general rate case. The arrangement provides a rate reduction for customers while allowing for continued investment in the infrastructure.

Mergers and Acquisitions

In 2012 the company acquired Aqua America's Maine operations for $54 million.

The acquisition of Aqua Maine allowed the company to expand into New England. The regional company now known as The Maine Water Company and Connecticut Water received $33.7 million more in additional rates and increased its customer base by 16000. The transaction also made Connecticut Water the largest publicly traded water utility company in New England with 106000 customers in Connecticut and Maine.

That year it also acquired Biddeford and Saco Water (15500 customers in the Maine communities of Biddeford Saco Old Orchard Beach and Scarborough) for $12 million.

In 2011 the company acquired Green Springs Water Company (Madison Connecticut) which serves about 12000 people.

EXECUTIVES

VP Finance CFO and Treasurer Connecticut Water Service and Connecticut Water Company, David C. Benoit, age 59, $304,330 total compensation
Chairman President and CEO, Eric W. Thornburg, age 56, $458,898 total compensation
President The Maine Water Company, Judy E. Wallingford, age 59, $216,457 total compensation
VP Service Delivery, Craig J. Patla
President The Maine Water Company, Richard Knowlton
Auditors: Baker Tilly Virchow Krause, LLP

LOCATIONS

HQ: Connecticut Water Service, Inc.
93 West Main Street, Clinton, CT 06413
Phone: 860 669-8636
Web: www.ctwater.com

PRODUCTS/OPERATIONS

2015 Sales

	$ mil.	% of total
Residential	58.4	61
Fire protection	18.0	19
Commercial	11.8	12
Industrial	3.2	4
Public authority	3.2	3
Other	1.4	1
Total	**96.0**	**100**

2015 Sales

Water	97.4	95
Services & rentals	5.6	5
Total	**96.0**	**100**

COMPETITORS

American Water	United Water Inc.
Aquarion	Veolia Water North
Pennichuck	America

HISTORICAL FINANCIALS

Company Type: Public

Income Statement

FYE: December 31

	REVENUE ($ mil.)	NET INCOME ($ mil.)	NET PROFIT MARGIN	EMPLOYEES
12/15	96.0	22.7	23.7%	266.0
12/14	94.0	21.3	22.7%	265.0
12/13	91.4	18.2	20.0%	259.0
12/12	83.8	13.6	16.3%	259.0
12/11	69.4	11.3	16.3%	198.0
Annual Growth	**8.5%**	**19.1%**	**—**	**7.7%**

2015 Year-End Financials

Debt ratio: 27.4%
Return on equity: 10.4%
Cash ($ mil.): 0.7
Current ratio: 0.73
Long-term debt ($ mil.): 177.6

No. of shares (mil.): 11.1
Dividends
Yield: 2.7%
Payout: 51.4%
Market value ($ mil.): 425.0

	STOCK PRICE ($) FY Close	P/E High/Low	PER SHARE ($) Earnings	Dividends	Book Value
12/15	38.01	19 16	2.04	1.05	20.08
12/14	36.29	19 16	1.92	1.01	18.90
12/13	35.51	21 17	1.66	0.98	17.99
12/12	29.78	21 17	1.53	0.96	17.01
12/11	27.13	22 18	1.29	0.94	13.59
Annual Growth	**8.8%**	**— —**	**12.1%**	**2.8%**	**10.3%**

ConnectOne Bancorp Inc (New)

ConnectOne Bancorp (formerly Center Bancorp) is the holding company for ConnectOne Bank which operates some two dozen branches across New Jersey. Serving individuals and local businesses the bank offers such deposit products as checking savings and money market accounts; CDs; and IRAs. It also performs trust services. Commercial loans account for about 60% of the bank's loan portfolio; residential mortgages account for most of the remainder. It also has a subsidiary that sells annuities and property/casualty life and health coverage. The former Center Bancorp acquired rival community bank ConnectOne Bancorp in 2014 and took that name.

Geographic Reach

ConnectOne has 24 branches in Bergen Essex Hudson Manhattan Mercer Monmouth Morris and Union Counties in New Jersey.

Mergers and Acquisitions

In 2014 Center Bancorp acquired ConnectOne Bancorp in an all-stock deal valued at approximately $243 million. The merged bank with nearly $4 billion in assets now does business under the ConnectOne brand name.

EXECUTIVES

Executive Vice President Chief Compliance Officer, Laura (Laur) Criscione
Svp And Chief Relationship Officer, Laurel Merse
Auditors: Crowe Horwath LLP

LOCATIONS

HQ: ConnectOne Bancorp Inc (New)
301 Sylvan Avenue, Englewood Cliffs, NJ 07632
Phone: 201 816-8900
Web: www.centerbancorp.com

COMPETITORS

BCB Bancorp	New York Community
Bank of America	Bancorp
Citizens Financial Corp.	Oritani Financial
	PNC Financial
Fulton Financial	Provident Financial
Hudson City Bancorp	Services
Investors Bancorp	Sovereign Bank
JPMorgan Chase	Valley National
Kearny Financial	Bancorp
Lakeland Bancorp	Westamerica

HISTORICAL FINANCIALS

Company Type: Public

Income Statement

FYE: December 31

	ASSETS ($ mil.)	NET INCOME ($ mil.)	INCOME AS % OF ASSETS	EMPLOYEES
12/15	4,016.7	41.3	1.0%	0.0
12/14	3,448.5	18.5	0.5%	0.0
12/13	1,673.0	19.9	1.2%	166.0
12/12	1,629.7	17.5	1.1%	178.0
12/11	1,432.7	13.9	1.0%	163.0
Annual Growth	**29.4%**	**31.2%**	**—**	**—**

2015 Year-End Financials

Return on assets: 1.1%
Return on equity: 8.9%
Long-term debt ($ mil.): —
No. of shares (mil.): 30.0
Sales ($ mil): 152.1

Dividends
Yield: 1.6%
Payout: 22.0%
Market value ($ mil.): 562.0

	STOCK PRICE ($) FY Close	P/E High/Low	PER SHARE ($) Earnings	Dividends	Book Value
12/15	18.69	16 13	1.36	0.30	15.87
12/14	19.00	25 21	0.79	0.30	15.03
12/13	18.76	16 10	1.21	0.26	10.30
12/12	11.58	11 9	1.05	0.17	9.83
12/11	9.77	14 10	0.80	0.12	8.32
Annual Growth	**17.6%**	**— —**	**14.2%**	**25.7%**	**17.5%**

Conns Inc

Conn's has managed to outlive human life expectancy. Begun as a plumbing and heating business the regional retailer has more than 120 years under its belt. It sells primarily consumer electronics and appliances through about 80 mostly leased stores located in Arizona Colorado New Mexico Tennessee Texas Oklahoma and Louisiana as well as via its website. Conn's markets about 2300 brand-name products such as refrigerators freezers washers dryers air conditioners vacuums TVs and home theater systems. The retailer which offers customers financing also sells lawn mowers furniture bedding and track items including DVD players digital cameras video game equipment camcorders and speakers.

Geographic Reach

Conn's headquartered in the Houston suburb of The Woodlands serves customers nationwide online and through brick-and-mortar stores in more than half a dozen US states. The company continues to extend its retail reach each fiscal year.

Operations

Conn's operates a chain of specialty stores in Texas Arizona Colorado Louisiana New Mexico Tennessee and Oklahoma. It generates 83% of its revenue selling products such as name-brand appliances TVs lawn mowers furniture bedding and video game equipment. Commissions on repair service agreements service revenues and finance changes account for the balance of Conn's revenue. About three-fourths of its product sales in fiscal 2014 were from the sale of home appliances furniture mattresses and consumer electronics.

Retail stores which range in size from 20000 sq. ft. to 50000 sq. ft. are located in densely populated areas and typically serve as anchor stores in strip malls. Its about 2300 products come from 200 manufacturers and distributors such as Dell Microsoft Samsung Nikon Eureka and General Electric.

The retailer also offers its customers several financing options. Extending credit accounts for 17% of its revenue. Its financing options include an in-house credit program third-party financing program and third-party rent-to-own payment program. Many of its credit customers which in 2013 had an average 602 credit score use Conn's in-house credit program. Indeed in fiscal 2014 Conn's financed 77% of its retail sales. This included down payments.

Sales and Marketing

Conn's designs its own marketing and advertising programs which are focused on boosting brand recognition educating consumers about its products and services and generating more foot traffic at its stores to increase sales. Advertising programs include direct mail TV ads newspaper and radio ads telephone campaigns and the company's website. Conn's looks to engage customers through a variety of promotional programs such as discounts product bundling rebates and no-interest financing plans.

In recent years Conn's has dug deeper into its pockets to fund spending on advertising. These expenses came in at $50.7 million in fiscal 2014 up from 2013's $34.7 million and $29.7 million in 2012.

Strategy

Stung by the most recent recession and its accompanying tightened credit markets Conn's is now hitting its stride and pushing its profits in a positive direction.

The company's primary vehicle for growth today is aggressively expanding its network of stores with new locations. It's planning to bump up its store count by up to 60 new stores through fiscal 2017. (Conn's added 19 new stores in fiscal years 2013 and 2014 and plans to open another 15-20 stores in fiscal 2015.) It added Colorado to its list of operating states in 2014.

In 2011 the retailer also rolled out a new Conn's HomePlus store format which ranges in size from 30000 sq. ft. to 45000 sq. ft. The format dedicates more floor space to furniture and mattresses two of its key categories. Besides adding new stores Conn's is remodeling existing stores. Like other retailers Conn's regularly shutters a handful of stores each year that do not meet its sales expectations for mature stores. (The concentration of its stores in Texas where the economy fared better than the rest of the nation has generally helped to insulate the regional retailer from the global economic downturn.)Conspiring against the company's growth trajectory has been the revolving door on its executive suite. Former chairman and CEO Thomas Frank Sr. stepped down in 2009 as the recession took root and handed the job to son Timothy Frank who had served as president and COO. The younger Frank eventually left in early 2011 looking "to pursue entrepreneurial opportunities with earlier growth stage businesses." Conn's chairman Theodore Wright was appointed interim president and CEO. He was made permanent in November 2011. Wright brings experience as president and CFO of Sonic Automotive.Financial PerformanceAfter several years of nearly flat revenue growth (since fiscal 2010) Conn's logged noteworthy growth in fiscal 2014 (ended January) with $1.19 billion in revenue an increase of $328.7 million. As compared to fiscal 2013 revenue in 2014 rose about 38%. Indeed both the Retail and Credit segments reported double-digit growth. A 27% increase in same-store sales helped to boost retail revenues by 39%. Credit revenue jumped 34% during the reporting period driven for the most part by 30% year-over-year growth in the average balance of the customer receivable portfolio and increased origination volumes.Net income for the specialty retailer reached $93 million in 2014 up $40.8 million the previous year. After posting a loss in both fiscal 2011 and 2012 Conn's posted growing profits in fiscal 2013 and 2014 thanks to rising revenue. Profits in 2014 increased by 78% vs. 2013.

EXECUTIVES

EVP and COO, Michael J. Poppe, age 48, $460,000 total compensation
VP and CIO, Todd Renaud, $300,000 total compensation
Chairman President and CEO, Norman L. (Norm) Miller, age 55, $351,325 total compensation
CFO, Lee Wright
President and COO Retail, Coleman R. (CR) Gaines
Vice President and Treasurer, Melissa (Lissa) Allen
Vice President Store Operations, Tate Malpass
Senior Vice President Information Technology, Clint Harwood
Assistant Vice President, Muthu Muthuswamy
Vice President of Purchasing, Jung Lee
Executive Assistant to Senior Vice President of Logistics and Vice President of Service, Chantae Whitaker
Auditors: Ernst & Young LLP

LOCATIONS

HQ: Conns Inc
4055 Technology Forest Blvd, Suite 210, The Woodlands, TX 77381
Phone: 936 230-5899
Web: www.conns.com

PRODUCTS/OPERATIONS

2016 Sales

	$ mil.	% of total
Product sales	1,199.1	74
Repair service agreement commissions	109.8	7
Service revenues	13.7	1
Finance charges & other	290.6	18
Total	**1,613.2**	**100**

2016 Stores

	$ mil.	% of total
Retail	1,324.2	82
Credit	289.0	18
Total	**1,613.2**	**100**

Primary Markets Served
Dallas/Fort Worth
Houston
Oklahoma
San Antonio/Austin
South Texas
Southeast Texas
Southern Louisiana

Selected Brands

Appliances
  Dyson
  Eureka
  Frigidaire
  Haier
  Hoover
  Kitchen Aid
  LG
  Samsung
Consumer electronics
  Bose
  Canon
  Compaq
  Garmin
  Hewlett Packard
  JVC
  LG
  Microsoft
  Mitsubishi
  Nintendo
  Panasonic
  Samsung
  Sony
Furniture
  Ashley
  Better Homes & Gardens
  Broyhill
  Jackson Furniture
  Lane
Lawn & garden
  Husqvarna
  Toro
  MTD
  Poulan
  Weedeater
Mattresses
  Serta

COMPETITORS

Amazon.com	Office Depot
Bed Bath & Beyond	Rooms To Go
Best Buy	Sears
Costco Wholesale	Staples
Home Depot	Target Corporation
Lowe's	Wal-Mart

HISTORICAL FINANCIALS

Company Type: Public

Income Statement

FYE: January 31

	REVENUE ($ mil.)	NET INCOME ($ mil.)	NET PROFIT MARGIN	EMPLOYEES
01/16	1,613.1	30.8	1.9%	4,600.0
01/15	1,485.2	58.5	3.9%	4,300.0
01/14	1,193.7	93.4	7.8%	3,600.0
01/13	865.0	52.6	6.1%	2,700.0
01/12	792.3	(3.7)	—	2,550.0
Annual Growth	19.5%	—	—	15.9%

2016 Year-End Financials

Debt ratio: 61.7%
Return on equity: 5.1%
Cash ($ mil.): 12.2
Current ratio: 7.96
Long-term debt ($ mil.): 1,248.8

No. of shares (mil.): 30.6
Dividends
  Yield: —
  Payout: —
Market value ($ mil.): 377.0

	STOCK PRICE ($) FY Close	P/E High/Low		PER SHARE ($) Earnings	Dividends	Book Value
01/16	12.32	49	14	0.87	0.00	17.57
01/15	15.74	38	9	1.59	0.00	17.98
01/14	60.71	30	11	2.54	0.00	16.31
01/13	28.44	19	7	1.56	0.00	13.48
01/12	11.60	—	—	(0.12)	0.00	10.99
Annual Growth	1.5%	—	—	—	—	12.4%

Consolidated-Tomoka Land Co.

From golf courses and retail centers to timber and hay farms land developer Consolidated-Tomoka owns a chunk of the Southeast. The company focuses on Florida but also has holdings in other neighboring states. Its portfolio includes retail properties (tenants include Bank of America CVS Walgreens a couple of golf courses (including the national headquarters of the LPGA) and some 10000 acres of agricultural land that the company is converting into other income properties. Through its subsidiaries it also holds subsurface oil gas and mineral interests on land throughout Florida and properties in North Carolina and Georgia. Consolidated-Tomoka was founded in 1902.

Operations

The company divides its operations across four segments: real estate operations income property golf and investment in a commercial mortgage loan collateralized by a hotel property in Atlanta.

Its income properties are the biggest money-maker accounting for about half of overall sales. It owns 35 single-tenant income properties in seven states that are triple or double net leases and ground leases where the tenant pays for all real estate taxes insurance utilities maintenance and capital expenditures.

Geographic Reach

Consolidated-Tomoka is headquartered in Florida. The majority of its real estate is located there but other properties are in Arizona California Colorado Georgia Illinois and North Carolina.

Financial Performance

Overall sales grew almost 50% in 2013 to $25 million after the company recognized rents from nine properties bought in 2013 and a full year of results for six properties bought in late 2012. In addition Consolidated-Tomoka bought a mortgage loan in 2013 and began adding the accrued interest to its revenue mix. Profits grew 514% from $600000 in 2013 to $3 million in 2013.

Mergers and Acquisitions

As part of its strategy of investing in income-producing properties in 2013 Consolidated-Tomoka bought nine income properties for a combined $39 million including four buildings leased to Bank of America in Southern California and two office complexes leased to Hilton in Florida. At the same time it sold five properties for $18.6 million.

EXECUTIVES

SVP General Counsel and Corporate Secretary, Daniel E. Smith, $185,000 total compensation
President and CEO, John P. Albright, $500,000 total compensation
SVP and CFO, Mark E. Patten, $220,500 total compensation
SVP Investments, Steven R. Greathouse
Vice Chairman, A. Chester Skinner
Chairman, Thomas P. Warlow
Auditors: Grant Thornton LLP

LOCATIONS

HQ: Consolidated-Tomoka Land Co.
1530 Cornerstone Boulevard, Suite 100, Daytona Beach, FL 32117
Phone: 386 274-2202   **Fax:** 386 274-1223
Web: www.ctlc.com

PRODUCTS/OPERATIONS

2015 Sales

	% of total
Income Properties	44
Real Estate Operations	37
Golf Operations	12
Interest Income from Commercial Loan Investments	7
Agriculture and Other income	-
Total	**100**

COMPETITORS

AV Homes	Rayonier
Alico Inc.	St. Joe
Anthony Forest Products	Stiles
	Stratus Properties
Echelon Development	Tejon Ranch
Forestar	Turnberry Associates

HISTORICAL FINANCIALS

Company Type: Public

Income Statement

FYE: December 31

	REVENUE ($ mil.)	NET INCOME ($ mil.)	NET PROFIT MARGIN	EMPLOYEES
12/15	43.0	8.3	19.4%	14.0
12/14	35.5	6.3	18.0%	14.0
12/13	25.8	3.6	14.3%	13.0
12/12	17.3	0.6	3.5%	13.0
12/11	14.7	(4.7)	—	18.0
Annual Growth	30.8%	—	—	(6.1%)

2015 Year-End Financials

Debt ratio: 41.4%
Return on equity: 6.3%
Cash ($ mil.): 4.0
Current ratio: 0.44
Long-term debt ($ mil.): 168.4

No. of shares (mil.): 5.9
Dividends
  Yield: 0.1%
  Payout: 14.0%
Market value ($ mil.): 311.0

	STOCK PRICE ($) FY Close	P/E High/Low		PER SHARE ($) Earnings	Dividends	Book Value
12/15	52.71	44	34	1.43	0.08	22.81
12/14	55.80	54	30	1.10	0.07	21.83
12/13	36.29	66	48	0.64	0.06	20.53
12/12	31.01	331	255	0.10	0.04	19.58
12/11	27.07	—	—	(0.82)	0.04	19.41
Annual Growth	18.1%	—	—	—	18.9%	4.1%

Consumer Portfolio Service, Inc.

Consumer Portfolio Services (CPS) buys sells and services auto loans made to consumers who probably don't have portfolios. The company finances vehicles for subprime borrowers who can't get traditional financing due to poor or limited credit; these loans typically carry a higher interest rate than prime loans. CPS purchases contracts from both new car and independent used car dealers in more than 45 states; the company then securitizes (bundles and sells) them on the secondary market. Its total managed portfolio comprises some $900 million in contracts. The bulk of the contracts CPS acquires finance used vehicles. The company has servicing operations in California Florida Illinois and Virginia.

Geographic Reach

Headquartered in California CPS has three servicing branches in Florida Illinois and Virginia.

Sales and Marketing

CPS directs its marketing efforts to automotive dealers not consumers. It works with about 12000 dealers about 75% of which are franchised dealers that sell both new and used vehicles; the remainder are independent used car dealers.

Financial Performance

The financial crisis took a serious toll on CPS as the credit markets inhibited funding for the company. Skittish investors have also increasingly avoided the asset-backed securities that were formerly CPS' bread and butter. As a result the company lost money from 2008 to 2011.

However CPS was back in the black by 2012. That year overall revenues grew 30% to $187 million (half of what it earned in 2008.) CPS makes its money on interest income and that year it took in another $47.5 million in interest income alone which was offset by a decrease in loan servicing fees. In addition the company enjoyed record profits of almost $70 million.

Mergers and Acquisitions

CPS has returned to growing its portfolio of contracts in the aftermath of the recession to boost its interest earnings. In September 2011 it acquired a portfolio of some $218 million of finance receivables from Fireside Bank in California. That figure alone was nearly double the amount of contracts acquired in all of 2010.

EXECUTIVES

Senior Vice President Originations, Teri Clements
Auditors: Crowe Horwath LLP

LOCATIONS

HQ: Consumer Portfolio Service, Inc.
3800 Howard Hughes Parkway, Suite 1400, Las Vegas, NV 89169
Phone: 949 753-6800 **Fax:** 949 753-6805
Web: www.consumerportfolio.com

PRODUCTS/OPERATIONS

2012 Sales

	$ mil.	% of total
Interest		
Finance receivables	174.0	93
Residual interest	0.5	-
Other	0.8	1
Servicing fees	2.3	1
Other	9.6	5
Total	**187.2**	**100**

COMPETITORS

American Honda Finance	Ford Motor Credit
Automotive Finance Corporation	GM Financial
Credit Acceptance	Nicholas Financial
DriveTime Automotive	United PanAm Financial
First Investors Financial Services	

HISTORICAL FINANCIALS

Company Type: Public

Income Statement

FYE: December 31

	REVENUE ($ mil.)	NET INCOME ($ mil.)	NET PROFIT MARGIN	EMPLOYEES
12/15	363.6	34.6	9.5%	935.0
12/14	300.2	29.5	9.8%	869.0
12/13	255.7	21.0	8.2%	705.0
12/12	187.2	69.4	37.1%	574.0
12/11	143.1	(14.4)	—	530.0
Annual Growth	26.3%	—	—	15.2%

2015 Year-End Financials

Debt ratio: 91.1%
Return on equity: 24.0%
Cash ($ mil.): 19.3
Current ratio: 70.03
Long-term debt ($ mil.): 1,952.2
No. of shares (mil.): 25.6
Dividends
Yield: —
Payout: —
Market value ($ mil.): 133.0

	STOCK PRICE ($) FY Close	P/E High/Low		Earnings	PER SHARE ($) Dividends	Book Value
12/15	5.19	6	3	1.10	0.00	6.29
12/14	7.36	8	5	0.92	0.00	4.98
12/13	9.39	13	5	0.67	0.00	3.94
12/12	5.36	2	0	2.72	0.00	3.09
12/11	0.89	—	—	(0.76)	0.00	(0.73)
Annual Growth	55.4%	—	—	—	—	—

Cooper Companies, Inc. (The)

The Cooper Companies specializes in eye care and lady care. The global company makes specialty medical devices in two niche markets: vision care and gynecology. Its CooperVision subsidiary makes specialty contact lenses including toric lenses for astigmatism multifocal lenses for presbyopia and cosmetic lenses. The company also offers spherical lenses for more common vision problems such as nearsightedness and farsightedness. Subsidiary CooperSurgical specializes in women's health care; its wide range of products includes bone densitometers (for diagnosing osteoporosis) contraceptive devices surgery instruments and fetal monitors. Cooper's products are sold in more than 100 countries.

Operations

The Cooper Companies operates through two business units: CooperVision the larger of the two (around 80% of annual sales) is one of the largest contact lens manufacturers in the world; meanwhile CooperSurgical provides diagnostic and therapeutic products used by obstetricians and gynecologists.

Spherical lenses account for more than half of CooperVision's net sales while toric lenses accounts for about 30%. The unit also sells contact lenses using its PC Technology which attracts water and keeps lenses hydrated.

CooperSurgical has been a consolidator in the fragmented women's medical device market acquiring more than 30 niche companies since its inception in 1990. Trends that it is taking advantage of include the increase in laparoscopic procedures and a shifting of procedures done in doctor's offices rather than in hospital settings. Products used in office and surgical procedures account for about two-thirds of the unit's net sales; fertility products account for the rest.

Geographic Reach

California-based Cooper rings up nearly half of its sales in the US and about 30% in Europe. The company has manufacturing and distribution facilities for optical products in the US (New York and Puerto Rico) the UK Australia and Japan. Its medical device and surgical instrument products are manufactured and distributed from facilities in Germany and the US (California Connecticut and Texas).

Sales and Marketing

Cooper markets its products through its own sales representatives in North America and through a mix of direct sales and distributors elsewhere. It markets its products in professional journals and via e-commerce telemarketing and social media.

Financial Performance

Cooper has enjoyed rising net revenue over the past five years. In fiscal 2015 (ended October) revenue increased 5% to $1.8 billion primarily due to higher sales of contact lenses. However Cooper-Surgical saw declines in sales of medical equipment and fertility products the latter of which was largely due to the negative impact of the weakening of foreign currencies.

Net income which had been on the rise declined in 2014 and 2015. In 2015 it dropped 25% to $203.5 million on higher expenses related to the 2014 acquisition of European manufacturer Sauflon's and the 2015 acquisition of genetics laboratory Reprogenetics. An increase in inventory and the decline in profits led to a 14% drop in operating cash flow which fell to $391 million.

Strategy

CooperVision is working to expand internationally by increasing operations in various high-growth geographic markets. It is building a plant in Costa Rica. The lens maker is attempting to expand its market share by launching new products. Its R&D team is working on several new products using its PC moisturizing technology. It is also developing new products using silicone hydrogel a more breathable lens material that is healthier and more comfortable for the eye including single-use (throwaway) toric and multifocal lenses. The company is also expanding through acquisitions. For example it acquired Sauflon a European manufacturer and distributor of soft contact lenses in 2014.

CooperSurgical is also growing by acquiring complementary technologies products and businesses. Additionally it seeks to launch products utilizing advanced technologies.

Mergers and Acquisitions

CooperSurgical paid some $44 million in late 2014 for EndoSee Corporation developer of an office-based disposable hysterectomy system. The following year the unit acquired Reprogenetics a genetics laboratory specializing in preimplantation genetic screening and diagnosis used in the in-vitro fertilization process. It also bought UK-based Research Instruments which makes in-vitro fertilization medical devices and systems for some $51 million. In 2016 CooperSurgical acquired the commercial assets of genetic testing firm Recombine for some $85 million; Recombine specializes in carrier screening which can predict genetic disorders in offspring.

CooperVision bought European firm Sauflon which makes and distributes soft contact lenses and aftercare solutions for $1.1 billion in 2014. Among other items that purchase added Sauflon's clariti 1day brand of single-use lenses.

HISTORY

Company Background

Cooper Labs (medical devices founded in 1958 and dissolved 1985) created CooperVision as a subsidiary in 1980. CooperVision diversified into diagnostic equipment and drugs; by 1987 (when it was renamed The Cooper Companies) debt had increased sixfold and creditors came knocking.

Two scandal-tainted families (the Sturmans and the Singers –fraud/organized crime and Medicaid fraud respectively) then bought their way onto the board. Proxy fights cronyism nepotism indictments and lawsuits ensued. Meanwhile cash-strapped Cooper sold most of its international and part of its US contact lens business as well as its ophthalmic surgical products and medical diagnostics businesses. Co-chairman Gary Singer took a leave of absence after being indicted in 1992.

Cooper bought Hospital Group of America and its hospitals that year. Singer resigned shortly before being convicted on 21 counts including racketeering mail and wire fraud and money laundering in 1994. Pharmaceutical industry veteran Thomas Bender joined the board that year and was named CEO in 1995. He was elected chairman in 2002.

Cooper rebuilt its contact business and turned to the women's health field in the early 1990s. In 1996 it bought a line of disposable gynecological products and worked to boost lens-making capacity. The next year it bought a line of colored contact lenses a minimally invasive gynecological surgical and disposable products company and a UK lens maker.

In 1998 The Cooper Companies discontinued its Hospital Group of America operations. It sold the group's hospitals treatment centers and clinics to Universal Health Services in 1999. In 2000 the company made three acquisitions including two makers of gynecological instruments. In 2002 The Cooper Companies bought Biocompatibles Eye Care one of the world's largest contact lens manufacturers.

The company's acquisitions in 2003 included Avalon Medical Corporation (distributor of female sterilization system) and Prism Enterprises (manufacturer of medical devices for the women's health care markets). The Cooper Companies bought gynecology products manufacturer Milex Products in 2004.

It nearly doubled its revenue with the 2005 acquisition of leading contact lens maker Ocular Sciences. The purchase strengthened its presence in the spheric (non-specialty) lens market; it also opened up new geographic markets particularly Germany and Japan. It also purchased NeoSurg Technologies and Inlet Medical in 2005 both of which made devices used in laparoscopic surgeries.

In 2006 it purchased Lone Star Medical Products adding a line of gynecological surgical products. The following year it added medical instrument maker Wallach Surgical Devices.

EXECUTIVES

EVP Secretary Chief Administrative Officer and Chief Governance Officer, Carol R. Kaufman, age 66, $454,000 total compensation
President and CEO, Robert S. Weiss, age 69, $875,000 total compensation
VP Finance and COO CooperSurgical, Paul L. Remmell, age 58, $295,000 total compensation
EVP CFO and Chief Strategy Officer, Albert G. White, age 46, $425,000 total compensation
EVP and COO; President CooperVision, Daniel G. (Dan) McBride, age 51, $495,000 total compensation
Vice Chairman, Allan E. Rubenstein, age 71
Chairman, A. Thomas Bender, age 77
Secretary, Beverly (Bev) Nicholl
Auditors: KPMG LLP

LOCATIONS

HQ: Cooper Companies, Inc. (The)
6140 Stoneridge Mall Road, Suite 590, Pleasanton, CA 94588
Phone: 925 460-3600   **Fax:** 925 460-3648
Web: www.coopercos.com

PRODUCTS/OPERATIONS

2015 Sales

	% of total
CooperVision	
Toric lens	24
Multifocal lens	9
Single-use sphere lens	20
Non-Single-use sphere and other products	30
CooperSurgical	
Office and surgical procedures	11
Fertility	6
Total	**100**

COMPETITORS

Abbott Medical Optics	Gyrus ACMI
Alcon	Hoya Corp.
Bausch & Lomb	Irvine Scientific
Boston Scientific	Johnson & Johnson
Carl Zeiss	Luxottica
Cook Incorporated	Marchon Eyewear
Essilor International	Orthometrix
Femcare	Shamir Optical

HISTORICAL FINANCIALS

Company Type: Public

Income Statement

FYE: October 31

	REVENUE ($ mil.)	NET INCOME ($ mil.)	NET PROFIT MARGIN	EMPLOYEES
10/16	1,966.8	273.9	13.9%	10,600.0
10/15	1,797.0	203.5	11.3%	10,200.0
10/14	1,717.7	269.8	15.7%	9,460.0
10/13	1,587.7	296.1	18.7%	8,000.0
10/12	1,445.1	248.3	17.2%	7,800.0
Annual Growth	**8.0%**	**2.5%**	**—**	**8.0%**

2016 Year-End Financials

Debt ratio: 29.8%
Return on equity: 10.1%
Cash ($ mil.): 100.8
Current ratio: 1.74
Long-term debt ($ mil.): 1,107.4
No. of shares (mil.): 48.7
Dividends
Yield: 0.0%
Payout: 1.4%
Market value ($ mil.): 8,588.0

	STOCK PRICE ($) FY Close	P/E High/Low		Earnings	PER SHARE ($) Dividends	Book Value
10/16	176.04	34	21	5.59	0.06	55.34
10/15	152.36	45	33	4.14	0.06	55.26
10/14	163.90	29	21	5.51	0.06	53.38
10/13	129.21	22	15	5.96	0.06	50.10
10/12	95.98	19	11	5.05	0.06	45.27
Annual Growth	**16.4%**	**—**	**—**	**2.6%**	**(0.0%)**	**5.2%**

Copart, Inc.

What happens after cars are totaled in wrecks or natural disasters? How about stolen cars recovered after the insurance settlement? Perhaps Copart happens; it takes junked cars and auctions them for insurers auto dealers and car rental agencies. The buyers are mostly rebuilders licensed dismantlers and used-car dealers and exporters. It's replaced live auctions with Internet auctions using a platform known as Virtual Bidding Third Generation (VB3 for short). Copart also provides services such as towing and storage to buyers and other salvage companies as well as an online database and search engine for used parts. Copart serves customers throughout North America Europe the Middle East and Brazil.

OperationsThe majority of the vehicles Copart processes are auctioned under an incentive program in which Copart gets a percentage of the proceeds; the rest are auctioned under a fixed-fee consignment basis (generally $50 to $175). Copart's other services include Copart Dealer Services which sells trade-ins for franchises and independent dealerships using VB3 and CoPartfinder which enables customers to bid on a vehicle search for parts from Keystone Automotive Industries and receive e-mail notifications when cars matching their criteria come up for sale.About 86% of Copart's revenue came from its service offerings in fiscal 2015 (ended July 2015) while the remainder came from vehicle sales. Geographic Reach

North America is by far Copart's largest market accounting for 80% of sales in fiscal 2015 (ended July 2015). The UK generated another 18% of the company's sales that year. Copart also serves customers in the United Arab Emirates (UAE) Oman Bahrain India and Brazil and provides vehicle remarketing services in Germany and Spain.

Sales and Marketing
Copart's customer base of vehicle sellers mostly consists of insurance companies (which make up more than 80% of the vehicles Copart processes each year) though it also includes banks and financial institutions charities car dealerships fleet operators and vehicle rental companies. Copart sells its vehicles mostly to licensed vehicle dismantlers rebuilders repair licensees used vehicle dealers and exporters and to the general public in select locations.Overall the company spent $4.9 million on advertising in fiscal 2015 (ended July 2015) compared to $5 million per year in both FY2014 and FY2013.

Financial Performance
Copart's annual revenues and profits have been trending higher over the past several years.The company's sales dipped by less than 2% to $1.15 billion in fiscal 2015 (ended July 31 2015) mostly because vehicle sales fell 22% as volumes from insurance sellers declined and as auction selling prices dipped as well. Service revenue (the company's main revenue driver) grew thanks to higher volume as the company boosted its market share and enjoyed a marginal increase in revenue per car serviced. By geography revenue grew by 1% in North America (its largest market) and declined by 10% or more in the UK and other countries. Despite modest revenue declines in FY2015 Copart's net income spiked 23% to a record $219.8 million for the year mostly because in FY2014 it incurred asset impairment charges after terminating its contract with KPIT (formerly known as Sparta Consulting); KPIT would have designed and implemented an SAP-based replacement for Copart's business operating software that would have addressed Coparts international expansion needs among other things. Copart's operating cash levels inched up 1% to $265 million for the year on higher cash earnings.

Strategy
With its market in the US maturing Copart continues to expand into more foreign markets and online through acquisitions and new facility openings. During 2015 the company opened new facilities in Manama Bahrain; Muscat Oman; and Moncton Canada. In 2014 it opened new facilities in Seaford Delaware; Itaquaquecetuba Brazil; and India while also acquiring online rights to hundreds of potentially valuable web domains to boost its online presence.

Copart also planned in 2015 to pursue more national and regional vehicle supply agreements expand its online auctions and vehicle remarketing service offerings to more sellers and members and extend the application of its latest Virtual Bidding platform (VB3) into new markets and to new sellers across the vehicle market.

Mergers and Acquisitions
During fiscal 2014 (ended July 31 2014) Copart purchased a facility in Montreal Canada; a salvage vehicle auction business in Brazil; and the assets of an online marketing company and rights to hundreds of web domains including www.cashforcars.com and www.cash4cars.com. The total purchase price of these assets amounted to $14.5 million.

Ownership
Founder and former-CEO Willis Johnson owns about 11% of Copart's shares.

HISTORY

Company BackgroundCopart was co-founded in 1982 by Willis Johnson who had owned and operated an auto dismantling business for more than 10 years. After buying out his partner in 1986 he became CEO and used his own money to expand the company into a network of four California salvage yards by 1991. In the next two years Copart nearly tripled the number of salvage operations it owned by acquiring companies throughout the US. HPB Associates a private investor group came on board in 1993 buying 26% of the firm for $10 million and the company went public the next year.

Copart doubled its total facilities in 1995 with the acquisition of NER Auction Systems the largest privately held salvage auction company in the US. The firm acquired or opened more than 30 facilities between 1995 and 1997. In 1998 the company started an online auction site; expanded through acquisitions into Alabama Iowa Michigan and South Carolina; and opened new locations in California and Minnesota. The next year rival Insurance Auto Auctions spurned its merger overtures.

In 2000 Copart opened three new salvage vehicle auction facilities and acquired eight more. That year the company also signed an agreement to sell Keystone Automotive Industries' parts through its Web site. In 2001 and 2002 the company acquired or opened 13 new locations. Continuing its acquisition strategy the company opened or acquired five more facilities in 2004.

In 2005 the company made two acquisitions for about $4.5 million: Kentucky Auto Salvage Pool a 25-acre salvage facility in Lexington Kentucky; and Insurance Auctions of Missouri. In November Copart acquired the salvage pool assets of Central Penn Sales a vehicle salvage disposal company with four sites in Pennsylvania and Maryland totaling 255 acres. In December the company opened a second salvage facility in Michigan.

In June 2007 Copart acquired Universal Salvage the operator of about 10 salvage yards in the UK and a vehicle remarketer to the insurance and automotive industries for about $120 million. Adding to its UK holdings in August Copart purchased Century Salvage Sales Limited which has three salvage yards and AG Watson which has four salvage yards in England and Scotland.

During 2008 the company launched CopartDirect. The service allows Copart to sell cars to the general public using its VB2 application so that individuals can avoid the inconvenience of selling a vehicle themselves.

In February 2010 Willis Johnson relinquished the CEO's title to A. Jayson Adair who formerly served as president of Copart. Johnson continued as chairman of the company.In 2011 Copart acquired the Indiana-based auto auction firm Barodge Auto Pool expanding its presence in Indiana and surrounding states. The company also broadened its existing range of farming equipment in the UK when it acquired Hewitt International an auctioneer of agricultural vehicles and equipment based in central England in 2011. In 2012 the company made several acquisitions in international markets including Brazil Canada Germany and Dubai UAE. That year Copart expanded into Germany (the world's fourth largest auto market) with the purchase of WOM Wreck Online Marketing a leading European salvage vehicle auction platform there. Earlier in the year it bought Canada's Diamond Auto Bids and Disposals a privately-held automotive auction that gives Copart a foothold in Western Canada specifically Calgary and Edmonton. It also extended the reach of its business into South America through its purchase of Central de Leiloes LTDA based in Sao Paulo Brazil.

EXECUTIVES

CEO, A. Jayson Adair, age 46
EVP, William E. Franklin, age 60, $363,423 total compensation
President, Vincent W. Mitz, age 53, $265,000 total compensation
SVP and CFO, Jeffrey Liaw, age 40
Vice President Of Global Business Processes, Diane (Di) Yassa
Senior Vice President and Chief Technology Officer, Rama Prasad
Vice President Strategic Consulting, Jerry (Jerr) Sullivan
Executive Vice President Strategic Initiatives, Vikrant Bhatia
National Sales Manager, Jim (Jimmy) Miller
Vice President, Brett Adair
National Account Manager, Richard (Dick) Giaramita
Vice President Corporate Sponsorships, Don (Donnie) Wolak
National Account Manager, Daniel (Dan) Smith
Copart Direct VPA, Marlon Ford
Copart Direct VPA, Elijah Fleming
Auditors: Ernst & Young LLP

LOCATIONS

HQ: Copart, Inc.
  14185 Dallas Parkway, Suite 300, Dallas, TX 75254
Phone: 972 391-5000
Web: www.copart.com

PRODUCTS/OPERATIONS

2015 Sales

	$ mil.	% of total
Services	985.4	86
Vehicles	160.7	14
Total	**1,146.1**	**100**

Selected Services

Copart Access (online vehicle information retrieval)
Copart Dealer Services (online trade-in vehicle sales)
Copart Direct (online used car sales)
CoPartfinder (online used-parts search engine)
DMV processing (title document processing)
Monthly reporting (summary of all vehicles processed by company for suppliers)
Online bidding (online auctions)
Salvage brokerage network (coordination of vehicle disposal outside areas of current operation)
Salvage Lynk (software providing online information on vehicles being processed)
Transportation services (fleet of transport trucks)
Vehicle inspection stations (central locations for insurance companies to inspect vehicles)
Vehicle preparation and merchandising (cleaning and weather protection direct mailings to buyers)

COMPETITORS

Advance Auto Parts	KAR Auction Services
Columbus Fair Auto Auction	LKQ
Cox Automotive	Pittsburgh Independent Auto Auction
Cox Enterprises	

HISTORICAL FINANCIALS

Company Type: Public

Income Statement

FYE: July 31

	REVENUE ($ mil.)	NET INCOME ($ mil.)	NET PROFIT MARGIN	EMPLOYEES
07/16	1,268.4	270.3	21.3%	4,844.0
07/15	1,146.0	219.7	19.2%	4,267.0
07/14	1,163.4	178.6	15.4%	4,179.0
07/13	1,046.3	180.0	17.2%	3,875.0
07/12	924.1	182.1	19.7%	2,981.0
Annual Growth	**8.2%**	**10.4%**	**—**	**12.9%**

2016 Year-End Financials

Debt ratio: 38.8%
Return on equity: 31.0%
Cash ($ mil.): 155.8
Current ratio: 1.79
Long-term debt ($ mil.): 564.3

No. of shares (mil.): 110.1
Dividends
  Yield: —
  Payout: —
Market value ($ mil.): 5,555.0

	STOCK PRICE ($) FY Close	P/E High/Low		PER SHARE ($)		
				Earnings	Dividends	Book Value
07/16	50.44	22	14	2.21	0.00	7.03
07/15	36.03	22	17	1.67	0.00	8.03
07/14	33.38	26	22	1.36	0.00	7.96
07/13	32.51	26	16	1.39	0.00	6.08
07/12	23.76	38	16	1.39	0.00	4.51
Annual Growth	**20.7%**	**—**	**—**	**12.3%**	**—**	**11.7%**

Core Molding Technologies Inc

The core business of Core Molding Technologies is fiberglass reinforced plastic and sheet molding composite materials. Through compression molding sprayup hand layup and vacuum-assisted resin infusion molding the company makes truck components (air deflectors fenders hoods) and personal watercraft parts (decks hulls and engine hatches). It divides its operations into two segments: Products and Tooling. Navistar International accounts for one-third sales and other major customers include heavy-duty truck manufacturers Volvo and PACCAR. The company's sales are confined to North America.

Geographic Reach

Core Molding operates plants in Columbus and Cincinnati Ohio; Gaffney South Carolina; and Matamoros Mexico.Sales and MarketingWith Navistar and PACCAR collectively representing 68% of sales and the medium and heavy-duty truck market accounting for more than 80% it's an understatement to say that Core Molding Technologies has a limited number of customers.Financial Performance

After posting $162 million in 2012 (a company milestone) Core Molding saw its revenues decline 11% to $144 million in 2013. Profits also slipped 16% from $8.2 million in 2012 to $6.9 million in 2013 due to a spike in selling general and administrative expenses.The revenue decline for 2013 was driven by lower demand for its products from customers in the medium and heavy-duty truck market. In particular Core Molding experienced an overall decline in demand from Navistar. After expeeriencing two straight years of growth Core Molding saw its operating cash flow decrease by $8 million in 2013.Company Background

Core Molding evolved in 1996 from the Columbus Plastics unit of International Truck & Engine (now Navistar Inc.).

EXECUTIVES

Vice President Sales, Terry (Terr) Donovan
Auditors: Crowe Horwath LLP

LOCATIONS

HQ: Core Molding Technologies Inc
  800 Manor Park Drive, Columbus, OH 43228-0183
Phone: 614 870-5000
Web: www.coremt.com

PRODUCTS/OPERATIONS

Selected Services
Assembly Machining and Paint Products
Closed molding
Compression Molding
Glass Mat Thermoplastic Compound
Open Molded Products
Post Molding
Product Development
Reaction Injection Molding
Resin Transfer Molding
Sheet Molding Compound

COMPETITORS

Clarion Technologies
Crane Composites
Flex-N-Gate
Industrial Molding
  Corp.
Lacks Enterprises
Magna International
Molded Fiber Glass
Primex Plastics
Sigma Industries
Toledo Molding and Die

HISTORICAL FINANCIALS

Company Type: Public

Income Statement

FYE: December 31

	REVENUE ($ mil.)	NET INCOME ($ mil.)	NET PROFIT MARGIN	EMPLOYEES
12/15	199.0	12.0	6.1%	1,525.0
12/14	175.2	9.6	5.5%	1,490.0
12/13	144.1	6.8	4.8%	1,458.0
12/12	162.4	8.1	5.0%	1,373.0
12/11	143.4	10.5	7.3%	1,596.0
Annual Growth	8.5%	3.4%	—	(1.1%)

2015 Year-End Financials

Debt ratio: 9.6%
Return on equity: 14.6%
Cash ($ mil.): 8.9
Current ratio: 2.01
Long-term debt ($ mil.): 9.7

No. of shares (mil.): 7.6
Dividends
  Yield: —
  Payout: —
Market value ($ mil.): 97.0

	STOCK PRICE ($) FY Close	P/E High/Low		PER SHARE ($) Earnings	Dividends	Book Value
12/15	12.83	18	7	1.58	0.00	11.68
12/14	14.00	12	9	1.28	0.00	10.07
12/13	13.70	15	7	0.92	0.00	9.22
12/12	6.62	9	6	1.11	0.00	8.13
12/11	8.09	6	4	1.44	0.00	7.11
Annual Growth	12.2%	—	—	2.3%	—	13.2%

CorEnergy Infrastructure Trust Inc

A closed-end investment management firm CorEnergy Infrastructure Trust (formerly Tortoise Capital Resources) invests in privately held and public micro-cap energy companies including midstream and downstream oil and gas companies and coal companies. The firm typically makes equity or debt investments in low-risk established energy companies that will generate steadily increasing returns on its investments over the long term. CorEnergy which has more than $90 million in assets under management is managed by Tortoise Capital Advisors a fund manager with five other publicly traded funds under management.

EXECUTIVES

President CEO and Director, David J. Schulte, age 55
Chief Accounting Officer Treasurer and Secretary, Rebecca Sandring
Chairman, Richard C. Green, age 62
Auditors: Ernst & Young LLP

LOCATIONS

HQ: CorEnergy Infrastructure Trust Inc
  1100 Walnut, Suite 3350, Kansas City, MO 64106
Phone: 816 875-3705
Web: www.corenergy.corridortrust.com

PRODUCTS/OPERATIONS

2015 Sales

	% of total
Lease	68
Transportation	20
Sales	10
Financing	2
Total	100

COMPETITORS

Adams Express
FMR
First Reserve
OHA Investment
Petroleum & Resources
  Corporation
Prospect Capital
The Vanguard Group

HISTORICAL FINANCIALS

Company Type: Public

Income Statement

FYE: December 31

	REVENUE ($ mil.)	NET INCOME ($ mil.)	NET PROFIT MARGIN	EMPLOYEES
12/15	71.2	12.3	17.3%	22.0
12/14	40.3	7.0	17.4%	21.0
12/13	31.2	4.5	14.4%	0.0
12/12*	1.7	(1.5)	—	0.0
11/12	10.5	12.3	116.8%	0.0
Annual Growth	61.1%	(0.1%)		

*Fiscal year change

2015 Year-End Financials

Debt ratio: 32.0%
Return on equity: 3.3%
Cash ($ mil.): 14.6
Current ratio: 0.38
Long-term debt ($ mil.): 151.2

No. of shares (mil.): 11.9
Dividends
  Yield: 0.4%
  Payout: 348.1%
Market value ($ mil.): 177.0

	STOCK PRICE ($) FY Close	P/E High/Low		PER SHARE ($) Earnings	Dividends	Book Value
12/15	14.84	30	5	0.79	2.75	35.01
12/14	6.48	8	6	1.05	2.57	33.31
12/13	7.12	8	6	0.95	1.88	36.68
12/12*	6.03	—	—	(0.50)	0.00	37.46
11/12	8.46	1	1	6.70	2.20	53.78
Annual Growth (10.2%)	15.1%	—	—	(41.4%)	5.7%	

*Fiscal year change

CoreSite Realty Corp.

CoreSite Realty leases data center space to those with data center needs. The real estate investment trust (REIT) owns develops and operates these specialized facilities which require enough power security and network interconnection to handle often complex IT operations. Its property portfolio includes more than 15 operating data center facilities with additional space under development. These properties comprise around 3 million rentable sq. ft. and are located in major US tech hubs including Silicon Valley. Tenants include enterprise organizations communications service providers media and content companies government agencies and schools. The REIT has grown along with demand for data center space.

OperationsUnlike most REITs which earn virtually all of their revenue from lease income CoreSite also makes money from the power and cross connections it supplies to its tenants. About 56% of its total revenue came from rental income during 2015 while about 27% came from power revenue and 13% came from interconnection revenue.Geographic Reach

Denver-based CoreSite Realty operates 17 data center campuses in nine North American markets. Almost 75% of the REIT's rental income came from its properties in Los Angeles San Francisco Bay and Northern Virginia during 2015 while another nearly 25% came from its properties in Chicago Boston and New York. The rest came from its Miami- and Denver-based properties.

Sales and Marketing

The REIT boasts a global customer base of more than 900 tenants (as of early 2016) including ISPs (Internet Service Providers) and telecommunications carriers (including AT&T Verizon Comcast Time Warner China Mobile and Tata Communications) content and media entertainment providers (such as Facebook Google Microsoft and DreamWorks Animation) cloud providers (Amazon Computer Science Corp. Hewlett-Packard) as well as enterprise financial educational institutions and government agencies. CoreSite's 10 largest tenants made up 35.6% of its annualized rent during 2015 reflecting a diversified tenant base.

Financial Performance

CoreSite Realty's annual revenues have nearly doubled since 2011 as new property acquisitions and demand for data center space has driven higher rental income. The REIT's profits have skyrocketed as it has managed to keep a lid on the growth of operating costs.The REIT's revenue jumped 22% to a record $333.29 million during 2015 as new and expansion leases increased its occupied space by 20% to 1.49 million net rental square feet (NRSF) boosting rental and power income sources. Interconnection revenue also rose 25% as new and existing customers added 2226 new cross connections.Strong revenue growth in 2015 drove CoreSite's net income up 52% to a record $34.71 million. The company's operating cash levels spiked 43% to $142.6 million for the year as its cash-based rental power and interconnection revenues increased.

Strategy

The properties in CoreSite's portfolio are strategically located in major metropolitan cities known for being high-tech hotbeds such as Boston Chicago Los Angeles New York City and the San Francisco Bay and Northern Virginia areas. Data centers especially outsourced ones (which are cheaper than in-house ones) are growing in these cities and others because they meet specific technology needs with specialized infrastructures that supply multiple network connectivity uninterruptible power backup generators cooling equipment fire suppression systems and physical security.

The company hopes to capitalize on demand that is outpacing supply for outsourced data centers in these markets. Supply of new data center facilities has been hampered in part by industry consolidation and lack of capital to develop additional space. CoreSite intends to market its existing portfolio —coupled with its development capabilities and the network interconnection services it offers —to attract more quality tenants.Company Background

The company's first data center was purchased in 2000. Acquisitions of these properties throughout its history have been funded and held through real estate funds affiliated with global private equity firm The Carlyle Group.

CoreSite Realty Corp. started in 2001 as CRG West a portfolio company of The Carlyle Group. CoreSite Realty went public in September 2010 with an offering worth $270.4 million. CoreSite used the proceeds of its IPO to develop and redevelop additional data centers and to retire debt.

EXECUTIVES

President and CEO, Paul E. Szurek, age 56

CFO, Jeffrey S. (Jeff) Finnin, age 52, $382,308 total compensation

SVP Field Operations and Network Engineering, Dominic M. Tobin, age 62, $203,750 total compensation

SVP General Counsel and Secretary, Derek S. McCandless, age 45, $291,635 total compensation

SVP Product and Marketing, Brian P. Warren, age 46, $225,961 total compensation

SVP Sales and Sales Operations, Steven J. Smith, age 51, $310,961 total compensation

Vice President Controller, Mark (Marky) Jones

Senior Management (Senior Vice President General Manager Director), Matt (Matty) Gleason

Vice President Finance, Jeff Dorr

Vice President Enterprise Architecture, Chuck (Chucky) Fredrick

Vice President Design and Construction, Kevin (Kev) Beck

Vice President, Yvonne (Vonne) Deir

Vice President of Sales, Maile Kaiser

Vice President, Gerry Fassig

Senior Vice President Sales and Sales Engineering, Chris (Chrissy) Ancell

Vice President Sales, Adam (Ad) Siegel

Auditors: KPMG LLP

LOCATIONS

HQ: CoreSite Realty Corp.
1001 17th Street, Suite 500, Denver, CO 80202
Phone: 866 777-2673
Web: www.coresite.com

PRODUCTS/OPERATIONS

2015 Sales

	$ mil.	% of total
Data Center:		
Rental	183.3	56
Power	89.4	27
Interconnection	44.2	13
Tenant reimbursement &other	8.3	2
Office light-industrial & other	8.0	2
Total	**333.2**	**100**

COMPETITORS

AT&T	Internap
CenturyLink	QTS Realty Trust Inc.
CyrusOne	SAVVIS
Digital Realty	Telx Group
DuPont Fabros	Terremark Worldwide
Equinix	Zayo Group

HISTORICAL FINANCIALS

Company Type: Public

Income Statement

FYE: December 31

	REVENUE ($ mil.)	NET INCOME ($ mil.)	NET PROFIT MARGIN	EMPLOYEES
12/16	400.3	58.7	14.7%	422.0
12/15	333.2	34.7	10.4%	391.0
12/14	272.4	22.7	8.4%	354.0
12/13	234.8	18.8	8.0%	363.0
12/12	206.9	5.0	2.4%	316.0
Annual Growth	17.9%	84.7%	—	7.5%

2016 Year-End Financials

Debt ratio: 47.5%	No. of shares (mil.): 33.9
Return on equity: 13.7%	Dividends
Cash ($ mil.): 4.4	Yield: 0.0%
Current ratio: 0.24	Payout: 155.1%
Long-term debt ($ mil.): 690.4	Market value ($ mil.): 2,690.0

	STOCK PRICE ($) FY Close	P/E High/Low	PER SHARE ($) Earnings	Dividends	Book Value
12/16	79.37	59 35	1.54	2.39	12.85
12/15	56.72	57 37	1.03	1.79	13.58
12/14	39.05	58 44	0.66	1.47	14.83
12/13	32.19	77 55	0.49	1.16	15.54
12/12	27.66	126 83	0.22	0.81	15.95
Annual Growth	30.2%	— —	62.7%	31.1%	(5.3%)

Cousins Properties Inc

Cousins Properties only wants the best office properties in the Deep South. The real estate investment trust (REIT) buys develops and manages Class-A office properties mainly in high-growth markets in the Sunbelt region of the US. Its portfolio includes around 41 office properties with almost 20 million sq. ft. of space in Atlanta Austin Houston and Charlotte. While the REIT also owns a handful of retail centers and apartment complexes in Atlanta it's been winding those down to focus on prime office properties. Cousins Properties also provides property and construction management services and develops properties for third parties.

OperationsCousins Properties' highest-grossing office rental properties include the Greenway Plaza (which made up 33% of its net operating income in 2015) and the Post Oak Central (12%) properties in Houston; and the Northpark Town Center property in Atlanta (10%).Geographic Reach The Atlanta-based REIT owns properties in its Atlanta; Austin Texas; Houston and Charlotte. About 40% of the company's net operating income came from its office properties in Houston during 2015 while another 39% came from its office properties in Atlanta. The rest came from its properties in Austin (8% of net operating income) and Charlotte (6%). Sales and MarketingReflecting a broad tenant base the REIT's top 20 tenants made up 41% of its annualized base rental income during 2015 with no single tenant accounting for more than 8% of its rental income. More than 20% of its rental base comes from tenants in the energy sector. Some of the REIT's tenants include the American Cancer Society and Fifth Third Bank. Past tenants have included Bank of America and Dimensional Fund Advisors.Financial PerformanceThe REIT's annual revenues have more than tripled since 2011 as property acquisitions in new markets have spurred additional rental income. Its profits have also skyrocketed over the same period thanks to property sale gains and tight operating cost controls.Cousins Properties' revenue climbed 6% to $381.6 million during 2015 mostly thanks to added rental income stemming from its newly-operational Colorado Tower property and its 2014 property acquisitions. Its same-property rental revenue increased by 0.2%.Revenue growth in 2015 combined with higher property sale gains from its North Point Center East The Points at Waterview and 2100 Ross dispositions more than doubled the REIT's net income to $125.5 million. Cousins Properties' operating cash levels rose 7% to $151.6 million for the year thanks to a rise in cash-based earnings. Strategy Cousins Properties acquires develops and manages Class-A office properties in high-growth Sunbelt markets though it also may buy mixed-use commercial buildings if the right opportunity arises. To diversify its revenue streams it continues to to acquire properties outside of Atlanta moving into the Houston and Austin markets in Texas and also into Charlotte North Carolina in recent years.Some of its more recent acquisitions include the proposed $1.95 billion acquisition of Parkway Properties and its 41 properties in the Southeast in 2016; the $27 million-purchase of 4.2 acres of land in Atlanta to build NCR's corporate headquarters in 2015 and the the $348 million-acquisition of the 1.5 million sq. ft. Northpark Town Center in Atlanta in 2014; and the 2014 purchase of the almost 700000 sq. ft. Fifth Third Center in Charlotte for $215 million.Mergers and AcquisitionsIn October 2016 Cousins Properties acquired Orlando-based Parkway Properties for $1.95 billion in stock. The deal expanded Cousins' presence to 41 properties in the Southeast.

The combined group immediately spun off its Houston-based assets creating a new public REIT named Parkway.

Company BackgroundCousins Properties experienced challenges from the depressed economy and the downturn in the real estate markets following the financial crisis. The REIT responded by restructuring reducing headcount selling non-core assets and curtailing new development projects. It sold all of its industrial properties to focus on Class-A office properties. It also continues to wind down its multifamily residential portfolio. Institutional investors own about a third of Cousins Properties' stock. Morgan Stanley holds the largest stake at more than 11% followed by BlackRock Inc. and The Vanguard Group. Chairman Emeritus Thomas G. Cousins owns about 11% of the firm's shares.

EXECUTIVES

Vice President and Controller Retail Division, Wendy C Fitchjarrell

Vice President Information Systems, Dennis Granger

EVP and CFO, Gregg D. Adzema, age 51, $390,000 total compensation

Chairman and CEO The Cousins Foundation Inc., Lillian C. Giornelli, age 55

EVP, John S. McColl, age 54, $341,453 total compensation

President and CEO, Lawrence L. Gellerstedt, age 60, $600,000 total compensation

SVP, J. Thad Ellis, $294,175 total compensation

EVP and COO, M. Colin Connolly, age 40, $250,000 total compensation

Executive Vice President And Chief Information Off, David (Dave) Shope

Vice President Human Resources, Marva Lewis

Senior Vice President and Director of Leasing, Darryl Bonner

Executive Vice President And Director Of Development Retail Division, William Bassett

Chairman, S. Taylor Glover, age 64

Auditors: Deloitte & Touche LLP

LOCATIONS

HQ: Cousins Properties Inc
191 Peachtree Street, Suite 500, Atlanta, GA 30303-1740
Phone: 404 407-1000
Web: www.cousinsproperties.com

PRODUCTS/OPERATIONS

2011 Sales

	$ mil.	% of total
Rental property	135.6	76
Third-party management &leasing	19.4	11
Fee income	13.8	8
Multifamily residential unit sales	4.7	3
Residential & outparcel	3.0	2
Other	2.0	-
Total	**178.5**	**100**

COMPETITORS

American Realty Investors	Highwoods Properties
Chelsea Property	Macerich
DDR	Poag & McEwen Lifestyle Centers
Duke Realty	Simon Property Group
Equity Office	Trammell Crow Residential
General Growth Properties	

HISTORICAL FINANCIALS

Company Type: Public

Income Statement

FYE: December 31

	REVENUE ($ mil.)	NET INCOME ($ mil.)	NET PROFIT MARGIN	EMPLOYEES
12/15	381.6	125.5	32.9%	257.0
12/14	361.3	52.0	14.4%	257.0
12/13	210.7	121.7	57.8%	237.0
12/12	148.2	45.7	30.8%	159.0
12/11	178.4	(128.4)	—	320.0
Annual Growth	**20.9%**	**—**	**—**	**(5.3%)**

2015 Year-End Financials

Debt ratio: 27.7%	No. of shares (mil.): 211.5
Return on equity: 7.4%	Dividends
Cash ($ mil.): 2.0	Yield: 4.8%
Current ratio: 0.83	Payout: 78.2%
Long-term debt ($ mil.): 721.2	Market value ($ mil.): 1,995.0

	STOCK PRICE ($) FY Close	P/E High/Low		Earnings	PER SHARE ($) Dividends	Book Value
12/15	9.43	20	15	0.58	0.32	7.96
12/14	11.42	60	46	0.22	0.30	7.73
12/13	10.30	15	11	0.76	0.18	7.68
12/12	8.35	26	20	0.32	0.18	5.96
12/11	6.41	—	—	(1.36)	0.18	5.85
Annual Growth	**10.1%**	**—**	**—**	**—**	**15.5%**	**8.0%**

Cowen Group Inc

The Cowen Group aims to herd its clients' investments in the right direction. The firm along with its subsidiaries offers alternative investment management research investment banking and sales and trading services. Its Ramius arm with some $12.5 billion of assets under management handles alternative investments while another subsidiary Cowen and Company represents the firm's investment banking and brokerage practice which mainly entails strategic advisory and corporate finance services for small to midsized companies. Cowen Group offers expanded trading operations through LaBranche & Co. a market maker for options exchange-traded funds and futures.

OperationsCowen operates two main business segments: Broker-Dealer and Alternative Investment. The firm's broker-dealer business Cowen and Company provides investment banking services to growth-oriented companies. Its services include advisory global capital markets origination and research services as well as a sales and trading platform for institutional investors. Its research team covers nearly 800 companies mostly across the health care technology energy capital goods and industrial basic materials consumer and real estate sectors. The smaller alternative investment segment includes hedge funds mutual funds managed futures funds fund of funds real estate and healthcare royalty funds among other types of strategies.Cowen Group generated roughly 40% of its total revenue from its investment banking services in 2014 with an additional 33% of revenues coming from its brokerage services. Management fees made up another 9% of total revenues while interest and dividends on the company's investments made up another 11%.Geographic Reach

Based in New York Cowen Group operates globally through US offices in New York Georgia Massachusetts Illinois Ohio and California as well as through international offices in Hong Kong London and Luxembourg. It serves China through Cowen and Company (Asia) Limited and Europe through UK broker-dealer Cowen International Limited (CIL).

Sales and Marketing

Cowen Group's institutional investors include pension funds insurance companies banks foundations and endowments wealth management organizations and family offices.Its broker-dealer businesses include research brokerage and investment banking services to companies and institutional investor clients primarily in the healthcare technology media and telecommunications consumer aerospace and defense industrials REITs and clean technology sectors. Its research and brokerage businesses serve more than 1000 domestic and international clients.

Financial Performance

As the financial markets have been strongly appreciating over the last few years so have Cowen Group's revenues and profits. The firm's revenue jumped by 31% to $427.78 million in 2014 which was mostly driven by 62% growth in its investment banking revenue on higher underwriting transaction and strategic advisory transactions. Cowen's brokerage income also rose by 22% thanks to higher commission revenue on higher customer trading volumes in cash equities options and electronic trades. The company's management fees also increased by 9% thanks to higher fee income from healthcare funds. The firm's net income skyrocketed to $167.22 million in 2014 mostly thanks to higher revenues combined with a $125 million income tax benefit as the company in a prior year deferred more in federal and state taxes than was required. Cowen's cash levels declined in 2014 with operations using $66.72 million (compared to operations providing $150.58 in 2013) after adjusting its earnings for non-cash items mostly relating to its sales proceeds on its securities.

Strategy

Cowen Group has been selectively expanding its alternative management business Ramius in recent years cutting its underperforming investment strategy teams while partnering with other firms to expand its better performing strategies. In 2014 for example its Ramius subsidiary sold its interests in its global long/short credit investment strategy manager Orchard Square Partners. Meanwhile that year it partnered with Quadratic Capital to launch its options-based global macro strategy complete with low volatility and defined risk. The deal expanded Ramius' unique product offerings essential to attracting investor capital while also allowing Quadratic to take advantage of Ramius' brand strength to make it a more competitive emerging fund.After assessing the most efficient uses of its capital Cowen Group in 2014 decided to wind down its securities lending business.Mergers & Acquisitions

Cowen Group has focused on acquisitions that expand its business in multiple sectors.

Its 2013 purchase of Dahlman Rose & Company a privately-held investment bank specializing in the energy metals and mining transportation chemicals and agriculture sectors. The deal gave Cowen Group additional sectors such as energy transportation metals and mining chemicals and agriculture.

In November 2012 the company completed the acquisition of KDC Securities LP (KDC) a securities lending business. KDC was the broker-dealer subsidiary of Kellner Capital LLC an alternative investment manager. KDC was renamed Cowen Equity Finance LP (Cowen Equity Finance) following the acquisition. Also in 2012 Cowen bought multi-asset class trading business Algorithmic Trading Management.

Company Ownership

RCG Holding an entity affiliated with CEO Peter Cohen Jeffrey M. Solomon and Thomas Strauss who all came to Cowen Group from Ramius owns more than 15% of the company's stock.

EXECUTIVES

Chairman and CEO, Peter A. Cohen, age 70, $950,000 total compensation
CFO, Stephen A. Lasota, $450,000 total compensation
President; CEO Cowen and Company, Jeffrey M. Solomon, $950,000 total compensation
Vice Chairman; Chairman Ramius, Thomas W. Strauss
Chief Administrative Officer, John Holmes, $450,000 total compensation
CEO Ramius, Michael Singer
General Counsel, Owen Littman, $450,000 total compensation
Executive Vice President, Karen Cowen
Vice Chairman, Fred S. Fraenkel
Auditors: PricewaterhouseCoopers LLP

LOCATIONS

HQ: Cowen Group Inc
    599 Lexington Avenue, New York, NY 10022
Phone: 646 562-1000
Web: www.cowen.com

PRODUCTS/OPERATIONS

2014 Sales

	$ mil.	% of total
Investment Banking	170.5	40
Brokerage	140.1	33
Interest and dividend income	48.9	11
Management fees	40.6	9
Reimbursement from affiliates	12.5	3
Incentive income	2.8	1
Other revenues	9.5	2
Consolidated Funds revenues	2.9	1
Total	**427.8**	**100**

Selected Subsidiaries

Cowen Alternative Investments LLC
Cowen Asia Limited (Hong Kong)
Cowen Capital LLC
Cowen Capital Partners II LLC
Cowen and Company LLC
Cowen and Company (Asia) Limited (Hong Kong)
Cowen Financial Technology LLC
Cowen Healthcare Royalty Management LLC
Cowen Holdings Inc.
Cowen International Limited (UK)
Cowen International Trading Limited (UK)
Cowen Latitude Capital Group LLC
Cowen Latitude China Holdings Limited
Cowen Latitude Investment Consulting Co. Ltd. (China)
Cowen Overseas Investment LP
Cowen Services Company LLC
Cowen Structured Holdings Inc.
Cowen Structured Holdings LLC (Hong Kong)
Cowen Structured Products Specialists LLC
October LLC
Ramius Advisors LLC
Ramius Alternative Solutions LLC
Ramius Asia LLC
Raimus Enterprise Master Fund Ltd (Cayman Islands)
Ramius Japan Ltd.
Ramius LLC
Ramius Optimum Investments LLC
Ramius Securities LLC
Ramius Structured Credit Group LLC

COMPETITORS

Citadel
Citigroup Global Markets
Credit Suisse (USA)
D. E. Shaw
Deutsche Bank
Fortress Investment Group
Goldman Sachs
Jefferies Group
Macquarie Group
Merrill Lynch
Morgan Stanley
Robert W. Baird & Co.

HISTORICAL FINANCIALS

Company Type: Public

Income Statement

FYE: December 31

	REVENUE ($ mil.)	NET INCOME ($ mil.)	NET PROFIT MARGIN	EMPLOYEES
12/15	464.5	43.7	9.4%	769.0
12/14	427.7	167.2	39.1%	664.0
12/13	327.2	4.6	1.4%	633.0
12/12	240.4	(23.8)	—	571.0
12/11	235.2	(108.0)	—	589.0
Annual Growth	**18.5%**	**—**	**—**	**6.9%**

2015 Year-End Financials

Debt ratio: 10.9%
Return on equity: 5.9%
Cash ($ mil.): 172.4
Current ratio: 0.53
Long-term debt ($ mil.): 124.7

No. of shares (mil.): 26.4
Dividends
    Yield: —
    Payout: —
Market value ($ mil.): 101.0

	STOCK PRICE ($) FY Close	P/E High/Low		PER SHARE ($) Earnings	Dividends	Book Value
12/15	3.83	5	3	1.36	0.00	29.92
12/14	4.80	1	1	5.60	0.00	24.27
12/13	3.91	26	15	0.16	0.00	17.66
12/12	2.45	—	—	(0.84)	0.00	17.61
12/11	2.59	—	—	(4.52)	0.00	17.83
Annual Growth	**10.3%**	**—**	**—**	**—**	**—**	**13.8%**

CPI Card Group Inc

Auditors: KPMG LLP

LOCATIONS

HQ: CPI Card Group Inc
    10368 West Centennial Road, Littleton, CO 80127
Phone: 303 973-9311
Web: www.cpicardgroup.com

HISTORICAL FINANCIALS

Company Type: Public

Income Statement

FYE: December 31

	REVENUE ($ mil.)	NET INCOME ($ mil.)	NET PROFIT MARGIN	EMPLOYEES
12/15	374.1	30.8	8.2%	1,386.0
12/14	261.0	13.3	5.1%	1,255.0
12/13	196.3	8.5	4.4%	0.0
12/12	183.7	4.9	2.7%	0.0
Annual Growth	**26.7%**	**84.3%**	**—**	**—**

2015 Year-End Financials

Debt ratio: 110.2%
Return on equity: —
Cash ($ mil.): 13.6
Current ratio: 2.40
Long-term debt ($ mil.): 300.0

No. of shares (mil.): 56.5
Dividends
    Yield: —
    Payout: —
Market value ($ mil.): 603.0

	STOCK PRICE ($) FY Close	P/E High/Low		PER SHARE ($) Earnings	Dividends	Book Value
12/15	10.66	—	—	(0.04)	0.00	(1.53)
12/14	0.00	—	—	(0.76)	0.00	0.88
Annual Growth	**—**	**—**	**—**	**—**	**—**	**—**

Cray Inc

Cray makes computers that aren't just good — they're super. Its massively parallel and vector supercomputers provide the firepower behind research ranging from weather forecasting and scientific research to design engineering and classified government projects. The company also provides maintenance and support services and it sells its own and third-party data storage products primarily from NetApp and DataDirect Networks. Cray's largest customer is the US government which accounts for about two-thirds of sales. Cray also targets academic institutions and industrial companies. Around 58% of sales come from customers in the US.

Operations

All of its engineering and manufacturing facilities are in the US (in California and Wisconsin) though the company uses subcontractors to produce the majority of its components. All of its high-performance computers are built to order.

Cray has supercomputers installed at more than 100 sites worldwide. Its supercomputers run on the company's Cray Linux Environment (CLE) operating system. Cray is one of the only companies left that exclusively makes supercomputers. Competitors such as IBM also custom-design high-performance models for customers.

By segment the company's supercomputing unit accounts for 71% of revenue. The unit for storage and data management and the unit for maintenance and support each generated 13% of revenue with 3% of revenue coming from engineering services.

Sales and Marketing

Cray has a direct sales force that operates from sales and service facilities in Australia Canada China France Germany Hong Kong India Italy Japan South Korea Spain Switzerland Taiwan the UK and the US. International sales were 42% of Cray's sales in 2014 an increase of 42% from 2013.

Users of Cray computers include the US Department of Defense the University of Hawaii the US National Nuclear Security Administration and the Indian Institute of Science.

Financial Performance

With supercomputer price tags often at $10 million and up (but you can get one for about $500000) the company's annual results can fluctuate. In 2014 sales rose about 7% to $561 million from the $525 million in 2013. International sales which grew at a 42% clip made up for a 9% decline in US sales.

Cray's net income charged 93% higher on the higher revenue and lower operating costs. Cash flow from operations slipped to $58 million in 2014 from 2013 driven by a rise in inventory for systems that it expected to deliver in 2015.

Strategy

Cray released systems for the high-end of its line in 2014 aimed at power-hungry research and design projects. In 2015 Petroleum Geo-Services (PGS) a global oil-and-gas company bought an XC40 supercomputer and one of the company's Sonexion 2000 storage systems. The system for PGS runs at five petaflop and is one of the largest systems Cray has delivered to a commercial customer and among the largest supercomputers deployed in the commercial sector. Cray in 2014 opened a manufacturing center in Chippewa Falls Wisconsin.

Company Background

Formerly Tera Computer the company bought Cray Research from Silicon Graphics and changed its name to Cray in 2000. In 2004 Cray acquired Canadian supercomputer developer OctigaBay Systems which became Cray Canada. The company's name comes from the late Seymour R. Cray the "father of supercomputing" although Mr. Cray never worked for Cray Inc.

EXECUTIVES

EVP and CFO, Brian C. Henry, age 59, $352,500 total compensation
President and CEO, Peter J. Ungaro, age 47, $475,000 total compensation
SVP and CTO, Steven L. (Steve) Scott, age 50, $323,077 total compensation
VP Field Operations, Charles A. (Chuck) Morreale, age 54
VP Asia-Pacific, Andrew Wyatt
President Cray Japan, Mamoru Nakano
VP Americas Sales, Larry Hoelzeman
SVP Cluster Products and Corporate Strategy and Planning, Daniel G.B. Kim
Director EMEA Operations, Dominik Ulmer
Senior Vice President of High Performance Computing Systems, Margaret (Peg) Williams
Vice President Of Worldwide Sales, John (Jack) Josephakis
Vice President of Sales, Nick (Nicky) Gorga
Vice President Storage, John (Jack) Howarth
Chairman, Stephen C. Kiely, age 70
Auditors: Peterson Sullivan LLP

LOCATIONS

HQ: Cray Inc
901 Fifth Avenue, Suite 1000, Seattle, WA 98164
Phone: 206 701-2000
Web: www.cray.com

PRODUCTS/OPERATIONS

2014 Sales

	% of total
Supercomputing	71
Storage & data management	13
Maintenance and Support	13
Engineering services & other	3
Total	**100**

2014 Sales

	% of total
Products	82
Services	18
Total	**100**

COMPETITORS

Bull	Lockheed Martin
California Digital	NEC
Corp.	NetApp
Cirrascale	Northrop Grumman
Dell	Oracle
EMC	Panasas
Fujitsu	Penguin Computing
General Dynamics	SRC Computers
HP	Silicon Graphics
Hitachi	International
IBM	Teradata
LexisNexis	

HISTORICAL FINANCIALS

Company Type: Public

Income Statement

FYE: December 31

	REVENUE ($ mil.)	NET INCOME ($ mil.)	NET PROFIT MARGIN	EMPLOYEES
12/15	724.6	27.5	3.8%	1,282.0
12/14	561.6	62.3	11.1%	1,138.0
12/13	525.7	32.2	6.1%	1,042.0
12/12	421.0	161.2	38.3%	929.0
12/11	236.0	14.3	6.1%	860.0
Annual Growth	**32.4%**	**17.7%**	**—**	**10.5%**

2015 Year-End Financials

Debt ratio: —	No. of shares (mil.): 40.6
Return on equity: 5.8%	Dividends
Cash ($ mil.): 266.6	Yield: —
Current ratio: 3.50	Payout: —
Long-term debt ($ mil.): —	Market value ($ mil.): 1,321.0

	STOCK PRICE ($) FY Close	P/E High/Low		PER SHARE ($) Earnings	Dividends	Book Value
12/15	32.45	51	28	0.68	0.00	12.10
12/14	34.48	26	15	1.54	0.00	11.12
12/13	27.46	33	19	0.81	0.00	9.28
12/12	15.95	4	1	4.27	0.00	8.64
12/11	6.47	20	12	0.40	0.00	4.54
Annual Growth	**49.7%**	**—**	**—**	**14.2%**	**—**	**27.8%**

Credit Acceptance Corp (MI)

In the world of Credit Acceptance Corporation (CAC) to purchase a car is not an impossible dream for problem borrowers. CAC makes the effort a reality. Working with more than 55000 independent and franchised automobile dealers in the US CAC provides capital for auto loans to people with substandard credit. The company also provides other services to dealers including payment servicing receivables management marketing and service contracts. CAC which concentrates its operations in a handful of US states typically funds about 1.5 million auto loans per year.

Geographic Reach

Michigan-based CAC serves consumers nationwide. Its largest markets include New York Texas Ohio and Pennsylvania.

Sales and Marketing

CAC caters to and partners with some 56000 independent and franchised automobile dealers throughout the US.

Operations

CAC steps in to help finance auto purchases for those whose credit histories aren't ideal. Auto dealers in turn benefit from the vehicle sales and from repeat and referral sales generated by these customers.

Strategy

The company funds loans in two ways: It advances money to its dealer-partners in exchange for the servicing rights to the underlying loan or it purchases loans directly from dealers. CAC earns most of its revenues from finance charges servicing fees and monthly program fees it charges its dealer partners. Indeed finance charges in 2013 accounted for 87% of revenue.

Financial Performance

The company's revenue has been growing for several years. In fiscal 2013 CAC posted 12% increases in revenue to $682.1 million as compared to 2012's $609.2 million. CAC points to a 10% boost in finance charges due to an increase in the average net loans receivable balance for the 2013 gains. These were offset however by a drop in the average yield on loan portfolio. Thanks to a new profit-sharing arrangement CAC entered in 2012 with third party providers (TPPs) other income jumped some 68% during the reporting period. Helping other income was an increase in GPS-SID fee income due to rising fee earned per unit purchased primarily resulting from new the new profit-sharing agreement. CAC's net income has been on the same trajectory. In 2013 net income rose some 15% to $253.1 million vs. 2012's $219.7 million bolstered by the company's higher revenue offset in part by an increased provision for income tax. Cash flow from operations also rose in 2013 — from $308.6 million in 2012 to $325.7 million in 2013 —attributable to higher net income a decrease in the provision for credit losses and a change in working capital.

HISTORY

Donald Foss was a used-car dealer in Detroit where to make sales he sometimes financed cars out of his own pocket. As Foss' chain of dealerships grew so did his financing business. In 1972 he established it as a separate company and 20 years later took it public.

For most of its history CAC stood alone in the field of subprime auto lending but stagnating salaries made it a competitive growth business in the early 1990s. At mid-decade the company entered Canada and the UK to tap similar markets there. In 1996 CAC acquired Montana Investment Group a credit reporting service.

Even as rising consumer debt and bad credit continued to pump buyers into CAC's loan pipeline the economic boom of the mid-1990s paradoxically made used cars less desirable. The soft used-car market squeezed several of CAC's competitors out of business; a staggering default rate —nearing 40% –also pressured CAC whose auditors insisted it increase reserves to cover losses. The subsequent earnings dive spurred a shareholder lawsuit accusing CAC of hiding its poor fiscal health. Although bad loans had damaged its bottom line the company adopted more stringent lending policies to reduce risk. Consumers filed class-action suits alleging unethical practices in 1998 but many claims were dismissed.

To pay off debt acquired through bad loans CAC sold Montana Investment Group in 1999. In 2000 it launched CAC Leasing to further offset losses from a decrease in subprime lending but in 2002 the company exited that line deciding the lending field was more profitable. CAC stopped originating new loans in the UK and Canada in 2003.

In 2005 the SEC investigated CAC's accounting methods specifically related to its loan portfolio and the company restated portions of its past financial results.

The company found itself in hot water again in 2008 when it agreed to pay some 15000 Missouri customers to settle a class action lawsuit. The lawsuit filed more than a decade prior alleged that CAC overcharged customers for fees and interest on their loans. As part of the settlement CAC said it would write off $39 million in outstanding accounts and distribute another $13 million to customers.

EXECUTIVES

Senior Vice President, Douglas (Doug) Busk
CEO, Brett A. Roberts, age 49, $1,025,000 total compensation
President, Steven M. Jones, age 52, $625,000 total compensation
CFO, Kenneth S. Booth, age 48, $414,792 total compensation
CIO, John S. Soave, age 51
Sales Vice President, Patrick (Paddy) Norris
Senior Vice President Dpsc, Jonathan (John) Lum
Vice President Of Sales, Jeffrey Brock
Vice President special Projects, Keri Libbe
Vice President Of Sales, Patrick Norris
Vice President, Wayne Mancini
Legal Secretary, Myrna Soave
Chairman, Donald A. Foss, age 71
Auditors: Grant Thornton LLP

LOCATIONS

HQ: Credit Acceptance Corp (MI)
25505 West Twelve Mile Road, Southfield, MI 48034-8339
Phone: 248 353-2700

PRODUCTS/OPERATIONS

2015 Sales

	$ mil.	% of total
Finance charges	730.5	88
Premiums earned	48.2	6
Other	46.6	6
Total	**825.3**	**100**

Selected Subsidiaries

Arlington Investment Company
Auto Funding America Inc.
Auto Lease Services LLC
AutoNet Finance Company.com Inc.
Buyers Vehicle Protection Plan Inc.
CAC Leasing Inc.
CAC Reinsurance Ltd.
CAC Warehouse Funding Corp. II III IV
Credit Acceptance Motors Inc.
Credit Acceptance Wholesale Buyers Club Inc.
Vehicle Remarketing Services Inc.
VSC Re Company

COMPETITORS

Ally Financial
American Honda Finance
Bank of America
Capital One Auto Finance
First Investors Financial Services
Ford Motor Credit
GM Financial
Mercedes-Benz Credit
Mercedes-Benz Financial Services USA
Toyota Motor Credit
Volkswagen Financial Services
Volvo Car Finance

HISTORICAL FINANCIALS

Company Type: Public

Income Statement

FYE: December 31

	REVENUE ($ mil.)	NET INCOME ($ mil.)	NET PROFIT MARGIN	EMPLOYEES
12/15	825.3	299.7	36.3%	1,425.0
12/14	723.5	266.2	36.8%	1,303.0
12/13	682.1	253.1	37.1%	1,317.0
12/12	609.2	219.7	36.1%	1,264.0
12/11	525.1	188.0	35.8%	1,037.0
Annual Growth	12.0%	12.4%	—	8.3%

2015 Year-End Financials

Debt ratio: 61.5%
Return on equity: 36.7%
Cash ($ mil.): 6.3
Current ratio: 1.82
Long-term debt ($ mil.): 2,084.6
No. of shares (mil.): 20.1
Dividends
  Yield: —
  Payout: —
Market value ($ mil.): 4,309.0

	STOCK PRICE ($) FY Close	P/E High/Low		PER SHARE ($) Earnings	Dividends	Book Value
12/15	214.02	19	9	14.28	0.00	46.10
12/14	136.41	14	9	11.92	0.00	34.09
12/13	129.99	12	9	10.54	0.00	32.69
12/12	101.68	12	9	8.58	0.00	25.79
12/11	82.28	13	8	7.07	0.00	21.07
Annual Growth	27.0%	—	—	19.2%	—	21.6%

Croghan Bancshares, Inc.

Croghan Bancshares is helping to share the wealth in the Buckeye state. The firm is the holding company for Croghan Colonial Bank which has about 10 branches in northern Ohio. Founded in 1888 the bank provides standard products and services including checking and savings accounts money market accounts certificates of deposit and credit cards Its lending activities primarily consist of residential and commercial mortgages and to a lesser extent agricultural business construction and consumer loans. In addition the bank offers wealth management investments estate planning private banking and trust services.

EXECUTIVES

Vice President, Daniel N (Dan) Schloemer
Auditors: Plante & Moran, PLLC

LOCATIONS

HQ: Croghan Bancshares, Inc.
323 Croghan Street, Fremont, OH 43420
Phone: 419 332-7301
Web: www.croghan.com

COMPETITORS

Commercial Bancshares
Fifth Third
First Citizens Banc Corp
KeyCorp
United Community Financial

HISTORICAL FINANCIALS

Company Type: Public

Income Statement

FYE: December 31

	ASSETS ($ mil.)	NET INCOME ($ mil.)	INCOME AS % OF ASSETS	EMPLOYEES
12/15	797.4	8.4	1.1%	205.0
12/14	779.4	8.6	1.1%	203.0
12/13	817.8	4.4	0.5%	209.0
12/12	630.9	4.8	0.8%	167.0
12/11	629.6	4.7	0.8%	161.0
Annual Growth	6.1%	15.3%	—	6.2%

2015 Year-End Financials

Return on assets: 1.0%
Return on equity: 8.7%
Long-term debt ($ mil.): —
No. of shares (mil.): 2.2
Sales ($ mil): 36.5
Dividends
  Yield: 0.0%
  Payout: 37.0%
Market value ($ mil.): 81.0

	STOCK PRICE ($) FY Close	P/E High/Low		PER SHARE ($) Earnings	Dividends	Book Value
12/15	35.50	10	9	3.67	1.36	43.22
12/14	35.18	9	9	3.78	1.29	41.01
12/13	34.25	14	12	2.57	1.28	37.45
12/12	30.27	13	10	2.88	1.60	40.01
12/11	29.00	10	8	2.84	1.28	37.58
Annual Growth	5.2%	—	—	6.6%	1.5%	3.6%

CrossAmerica Partners LP

CrossAmerica Partners (formerly Lehigh Gas Partners) won't leave motorists running on empty as they drive across America. The company distributes gasoline and diesel fuel to 1174 gas stations in 16 US states mostly along the East Coast. CrossAmerica owns or leases about 660 gas stations franchised under various brands including BP ExxonMobil Shell and Valero; it also distributes branded motor fuel to Gulf and Sunoco gas stations. About 95% of the more than 906.2 million gallons of motor fuels distributed yearly by CrossAmerica is branded (including the Chevron Sunoco Valero Gulf and CITGO brands).

Change in Company Type

In 2014 independent fuel retailer CST Brands acquired the membership interests of Lehigh Gas GP LLC the general partner of Lehigh Gas Partners LP for $85 million. Lehigh Gas Partners then changed its name to CrossAmerica Partners.

Geographic Reach

CrossAmerica owns or leases about 660 sites in 16 states: Pennsylvania New Jersey Ohio Florida Illinois Indiana New York Massachusetts Kentucky New Hampshire Maine Tennessee Maryland Delaware West Virginia and Virginia.

The company counts Pennsylvania and New Jersey as its largest markets with 20% and 16% respectively of its owned and leased sites. Virginia accounts for 13%; Ohio 12%; and Massachusetts 14%. Tennessee accounts for 8%.

Operations

CrossAmerica has long-standing relationships with many of the world's largest suppliers of branded motor fuel. In 2013 it purchased some 43% of its motor fuel from Exxon Mobil more than 25% from BP 15% from Shell's Motiva and about 5% from Valero.

All of its gas stations truck stops and toll road plazas are located in high-traffic developed urban areas that don't offer much open space for competitors to build new sites. As a dealer the company doesn't own its own fleet of trucks but has contracts with transportation carriers to transport fuel from refineries to the gas pump.

The company wholesales motor fuel sales under contracts that must be periodically renegotiated or replaced. They purchase branded and unbranded fuel from major integrated oil companies refiners and unbranded fuel suppliers and distribute to lessee dealers independent dealers CST LGO and sub-wholesalers. It accounted for 82% of CrossAmerica's total revenues in 2014. Commencing with the Petroleum Marketers (PMI) acquisition in 2014 CrossAmerica also operates 87 convenience stores in Virginia and West Virginia (18% of 2014 sales).

Sales and Marketing

CrossAmerica wholesales motor fuel to lessee dealers independent dealers affiliate Lehigh Gas - Ohio LLC and sub-wholesalers.

Financial Performance

In 2014 the company reported a 38% revenue increase in fuel sales related to an increase in volume of gallons fuel distributed offset by a lower selling price. In addition revenues increased due to acquisitions partially offset by decreases in gallons related to marketplace competition the sale of wholesale fuel supply contracts to PMI the closure of sites and the termination of dealer supply contracts.

It incurred a net loss of $6.1 million in 2014 (compared to a gain in the previous year) due to an increase in all cost components except for cost of revenues from fuel sales to related parties thanks to costs related to the PMI purchase that negatively impacted merchandise sales by 25%. The decrease in net cash provided by operating activities in 2014 resulted from a drop in net income of $24.2 million partially offset by an increase in net non-cash charges of $21.2 million. Net non-cash charges were higher due to increased depreciation and amortization equity-based compensation expense and a lower deferred income tax benefit. These were partially offset by a higher gain on the sales of assets.

Strategy

The company has been able to build up its portfolio of gas stations by buying properties from major oil companies that have been divesting their motor fuel distribution operations in order to focus on core production or refining activities. As such the retail gasoline market has become more fragmented and many stations are owned and operated as small businesses. Since its 2012 IPO CrossAmerica has made 11 major acquisitions (including 337 fee and leasehold sites) for a total of $448.3 million.

It moved into Tennessee in 2013 through a handful of different acquisitions.

Diversifying its offerings in 2013 CrossAmerica teamed up with Clean Energy Fuels to develop compressed natural gas fueling stations at 20 CrossAmerica facilities across US.

Mergers and Acquisitions

As a part of its growth strategy in 2015 CrossAmericay purchased 22 convenience stores from Landmark Industries. The stores operate under the Timewise brand and provide Shell branded fuel in the San Antonio area. That year it also bought Erickson Oil Products (64 convenience stores located in Minnesota Michigan Wisconsin and South Dakota).

In 2014 CrossAmerica entered into an asset purchase agreement with affiliates of Atlas Oil to buy 55 wholesale supply contracts 11 fee or leasehold sites 2 commission marketing contracts and certain other assets for $39 million. In addition it bought other short term financing assets located in the metro Chicago area associated with the acquired wholesale supply and commission marketing contracts for $12 million. That year the company acquired Virginia-based PMI for $61 million. PMI operates two primary lines of business: convenience stores (85 convenience stores and 9 co-located branded quick service restaurants) and petroleum products distribution. PMI's convenience store businesses operate primarily along the Interstate 81 corridor in Virginia with a concentration in the Roanoke Virginia area.

In 2013 CrossAmerica entered into an asset purchase agreement with Rocky Top Markets LLC and Rocky Top Properties LLC to purchase 30 motor fuel stations assume or enter into leases for four motor fuel stations assume seven third party supply contracts and purchase certain equipment and other assets at the sites for $37 million. In 2013 it also acquired the leases of 17 motor fuel stations the acquisition of the "Zoomerz" trademark and the purchase of certain other assets and equipment for $21 million from Rogers Petroleum Inc. and affiliates. That year it also purchased 44 independent dealer supply contracts five sub-wholesale supply contracts two leasehold motor fuel stations and certain other assets and equipment in Virginia for $11 million.

Company Background

The company conducted an IPO in 2012 and received net proceeds of $112 million which it used to to pay down debt and fund expansion activities.

To strengthen its presence in the highly-traveled corridor of northeastern Pennsylvania in 2012 CrossAmerica acquired 24 sites in the metro area of Scranton and Wilkes-Barre Pennsylvania from Dunmore Oil Company Inc. and JoJo Oil Company Inc. for $29 million cash. Twenty-three of the sites are fee simple interests and one is a leasehold interest. To gain a foothold in a highly-trafficked metro market in 2012 CrossAmerica acquired Express Lane Inc. of Lynn Haven Florida including Express Lane's 47 motor fuel sites in the Florida panhandle for $45 million.

The company in 2012 added more gas stations to its network via a master lease agreement for 120 sites from an affiliate of Getty Realty. About 90 are operated under the BP brand. (Lehigh Gas got the properties after Getty Realty's operator Getty Petroleum Marketing filed for bankruptcy in 2011).

CrossAmerica was founded in 1992 as Lehigh Gas.

Auditors: Grant Thornton LLP

LOCATIONS

HQ: CrossAmerica Partners LP
515 Hamilton Street, Suite 200, Allentown, PA 18101
Phone: 610 625-8000
Web: www.crossamericapartners.com

PRODUCTS/OPERATIONS

2013 Sales

	$ mil.	% of total
Wholesale	2,347.7	82
Retail	525.9	18
Unallocated	(204.3)	-
Total	**2,669.3**	**100**

COMPETITORS

7-Eleven	Marathon Petroleum
Couche-Tard	Mirabito Fuel
Cumberland Farms	Motiva Enterprises
Global Partners	Phillips 66
Hess Corporation	Wawa Inc.

HISTORICAL FINANCIALS
Company Type: Public

Income Statement
FYE: December 31

	REVENUE ($ mil.)	NET INCOME ($ mil.)	NET PROFIT MARGIN	EMPLOYEES
12/15	2,214.8	11.4	0.5%	1,052.0
12/14	2,669.3	(6.1)	—	0.0
12/13	1,934.3	18.0	0.9%	0.0
12/12	311.6	(1.3)	—	0.0
Annual Growth	**92.3%**	**—**	**—**	**—**

2015 Year-End Financials

Debt ratio: 51.4%
Return on equity: —
Cash ($ mil.): 1.1
Current ratio: 0.74
Long-term debt ($ mil.): 430.6
No. of shares (mil.): 33.1
Dividends
  Yield: 8.6%
  Payout: 637.1%
Market value ($ mil.): 858.0

	STOCK PRICE ($) FY Close	P/E High/Low		PER SHARE ($) Earnings	Dividends	Book Value
12/15	25.92	115	60	0.35	2.23	8.12
12/14	40.29	—	—	(0.32)	2.08	8.30
12/13	28.60	25	16	1.18	1.73	5.08
12/12	18.58	—	—	(0.09)	0.00	0.97
/0.00	—	—	—	(0.00)	0.00	(0.00)
Annual Growth						

CSW Industrials Inc

Auditors: Grant Thornton LLP

LOCATIONS

HQ: CSW Industrials Inc
5420 Lyndon B. Johnson Freeway, Suite 500, Dallas, TX 75240
Phone: 214 884-3777
Web: www.cswindustrials.com

HISTORICAL FINANCIALS
Company Type: Public

Income Statement
FYE: March 31

	REVENUE ($ mil.)	NET INCOME ($ mil.)	NET PROFIT MARGIN	EMPLOYEES
03/16	319.8	25.4	8.0%	725.0
03/15	261.8	29.7	11.3%	732.0
03/14	231.7	24.7	10.7%	0.0
03/13	199.0	21.7	10.9%	0.0
Annual Growth	**17.1%**	**5.5%**	**—**	**—**

2016 Year-End Financials

Debt ratio: 22.8%
Return on equity: —
Cash ($ mil.): 25.9
Current ratio: 4.93
Long-term debt ($ mil.): 89.1
No. of shares (mil.): 15.6
Dividends
  Yield: —
  Payout: —
Market value ($ mil.): 493.0

STOCK PRICE ($)		P/E		PER SHARE ($)		
	FY Close	High/Low		Earnings	Dividends	Book Value
03/16	31.50	24 17		1.62	0.00	16.48
03/15	0.00	— —		(0.00)	0.00	(0.00)
Annual Growth	—	— —		—	—	—

CU Bancorp (CA)

National commercial banks nsk
Auditors: RSM US LLP

LOCATIONS

HQ: CU Bancorp (CA)
818 West 7th Street, Suite 220, Los Angeles, CA 90017
Phone: 213 430-7000
Web: www.cubancorp.com

HISTORICAL FINANCIALS

Company Type: Public

Income Statement
FYE: December 31

	ASSETS ($ mil.)	NET INCOME ($ mil.)	INCOME AS % OF ASSETS	EMPLOYEES
12/15	2,634.6	21.2	0.8%	265.0
12/14	2,265.1	8.9	0.4%	250.0
12/13	1,407.8	9.7	0.7%	175.0
12/12	1,249.6	1.7	0.1%	167.0
12/11	800.2	1.4	0.2%	113.0
Annual Growth	34.7%	95.1%	—	23.7%

2015 Year-End Financials

Return on assets: 0.8%
Return on equity: 7.2%
Long-term debt ($ mil.): —
No. of shares (mil.): 17.1
Sales ($ mil): 101.8

Dividends
 Yield: —
 Payout: —
Market value ($ mil.): 436.0

STOCK PRICE ($)		P/E		PER SHARE ($)		
	FY Close	High/Low		Earnings	Dividends	Book Value
12/15	25.36	22 17		1.18	0.00	17.86
12/14	21.69	29 22		0.75	0.00	16.73
12/13	17.48	21 13		0.90	0.00	12.45
12/12	11.71	61 46		0.21	0.00	11.68
12/11	10.05	58 43		0.22	0.00	11.63
Annual Growth	26.0%	— —		52.2%	—	11.3%

CubeSmart

CubeSmart (formerly U-Store-It Trust) is a real estate investment trust (REIT) that owns more than 420 self-storage facilities with nearly 30 million sq. ft. of rentable space in about 25 states and Washington DC. The company also manages manages more than 100 self-storage facilities for third parties. Amenities at its properties include security systems and wider aisles for larger vehicles as well as climate-controlled units and outdoor storage for vehicles and boats at selected sites. The REIT also sells storage-related items such as packing supplies and locks to tenants who typically rent units on a month-to-month basis.

OperationsOperating through partnership CubeSmart L.P the company generates just under 90% of its revenue from rental income from leasing out its storage units. About 10% of revenue comes from other property-related income including administrative charges late fees tenant insurance commissions and sales of storage supplies. The rest of CubeSmart's revenue comes from property management fee income (primarily from its third-party management business).Geographic ReachCubeSmart owns or manages facilities in more than 20 states across the US with facilities in New York Florida Texas and California producing over 50% of total revenues. Another 15% of the company's revenue comes from New Jersey Illinois and Connecticut. Cubesmart also owns or manages facilities in Puerto Rico.Sales and MarketingThe company spent $7.7 million on advertising and marketing in 2014 compared to $7.6 million and $8.1 million in 2013 and 2012 respectively.Financial PerformanceCubeSmart's revenues and profits have trended sharply higher over the past several years as the REIT has enjoyed more rental income from acquisitions and rental rate increases buoyed by the strengthened US economy.The REIT's revenue jumped by 18% to $377 million in 2014 mostly thanks to higher rental income from 2014 and 2013 property acquisitions but also thanks to higher net rental rates and higher average occupancy rates on existing properties. CubeSmart's property management fee income also rose by 26% for the year as its third-party management business grew which further helped the REIT's top line.Despite higher revenue in 2014 CubeSmart's net income dove 36% to $26.4 million mostly as the REIT made $27.4 million in property sale gains in 2013 compared to no comparable gains during 2014. CubeSmart's operating cash levels grew by 16% to $166 million however mostly as it generated more cash income from new property acquisitions. StrategyCubeSmart's strategy is to grow through acquisitions mainly in high-growth areas such as the Northeastern and Middle Atlantic regions in the US along with Georgia Florida Texas Illinois and California. The company hopes to gradually increase rental income by selectively acquiring properties in markets with high barriers to entry strong demographic fundamentals and high demand. In addition more locations offer higher economies of scale and greater operating efficiencies for higher operating margins. Indeed from 2011 through late 2014 management had announced more than 100 facility acquisitions totaling roughly $1.3 billion. During 2014 alone CubeSmart acquired 53 self-storage facilities for a total price of $568.2 million including a $223 million purchase of 26 facilities across six states from Harrison Street Real Estate Capital in late 2014. The company also plans to continue selling facilities in slower growing low barrier-to-entry locations and using proceeds to purchase new facilities in target markets. In 2013 for example it sold 35 locations mostly in California Indiana Tennessee and Texas for approximately $126.4 million. In 2012 it sold 26 locations (including 14 from New Mexico and Ohio) for $60 million. Besides expansion CubeSmart plans to maximize rental revenues from existing facilities by raising rent increasing occupancy levels (which are around 90% up from 80% in 2011) controlling operating expenses and expanding and enhancing the facilities themselves. As a final step for growth CubeSmart will utilize relationships with third-party owners to help source future acquisitions and expand through these existing relationships.Company BackgroundAs part of a rebranding initiative CubeSmart changed its name from U-Store-It in 2011.

EXECUTIVES

CEO, Christopher P. (Chris) Marr, age 51, $410,000 total compensation
CFO, Timothy M. (Tim) Martin, age 45, $315,000 total compensation
SVP and CIO, Ajai Nair
SVP Operations, Joel Keaton
VP Third-Party Management, Guy Middlebrooks
Vice President, Ben (Benny) Carr
Chairman, William M. Diefenderfer, age 71
Auditors: KPMG LLP

LOCATIONS

HQ: CubeSmart
5 Old Lancaster Road, Malvern, PA 19355
Phone: 610 535-5000
Web: www.cubesmart.com

PRODUCTS/OPERATIONS

2011 Sales

	$ mil.	% of total
Rental income	212.1	89
Property management fees	3.8	2
Other property-related income	21.7	9
Total	**237.6**	**100**

COMPETITORS

AMERCO	Mobile Mini
Extra Space	PODS Enterprises
Life Storage	Public Storage

HISTORICAL FINANCIALS

Company Type: Public

Income Statement
FYE: December 31

	REVENUE ($ mil.)	NET INCOME ($ mil.)	NET PROFIT MARGIN	EMPLOYEES
12/15	444.5	77.7	17.5%	1,837.0
12/14	376.9	26.3	7.0%	1,640.0
12/13	318.4	41.4	13.0%	1,442.0
12/12	283.0	1.8	0.6%	1,409.0
12/11	237.6	(0.4)	—	1,276.0
Annual Growth	17.0%	—	—	9.5%

2015 Year-End Financials

Debt ratio: 40.5%
Return on equity: 5.0%
Cash ($ mil.): 62.8
Current ratio: 0.78
Long-term debt ($ mil.): 1,262.2

No. of shares (mil.): 174.6
Dividends
 Yield: 2.2%
 Payout: 287.5%
Market value ($ mil.): 5,348.0

STOCK PRICE ($)		P/E		PER SHARE ($)		
	FY Close	High/Low		Earnings	Dividends	Book Value
12/15	30.62	73 51		0.42	0.69	9.41
12/14	22.07	164 112		0.14	0.55	8.83
12/13	15.94	75 55		0.26	0.46	7.84
12/12	14.57	— —		(0.03)	0.35	7.51
12/11	10.64	— —		(0.02)	0.28	7.83
Annual Growth	30.2%	— —		—	25.3%	4.7%

Customers Bancorp Inc

Customers Bancorp makes it pretty clear who they want to serve. Boasting some $8.5 billion in assets the bank holding company operates about 15 branches mostly in southeastern Pennsylvania but also in New York and New Jersey. It offers personal and business checking savings and money market accounts as well as loans certificates of deposit credit cards and concierge or appointment banking (they come to you seven days a week). Around 95% of the bank's loan portfolio is made up of commercial loans while the rest consists of consumer loans. It was formed in 2010 as a holding company for Customers Bank which was created in 1994 as New Century Bank.

OperationsCustomers Bancorp operates two main business lines: Commercial Lending and Consumer Lending. Its Commercial Lending business provides commercial and industrial loans small and middle-market business banking and small business administration (SBA) loans multi-family and commercial real estate loans and commercial loans to mortgage originators. Its Consumer Lending division mostly makes local market mortgage loans and home equity loans. More than 95% of the bank's loan portfolio was made up of commercial loans at the end of 2015 while the rest consisted of consumer loans.Broadly speaking the bank makes roughly 90% of its revenue from interest income. About 66% of its revenue came from loan interest during 2015 while another 19% came from interest loans held for sale and 4% came from interest on investment securities. The remainder of its revenue came from mortgage warehouse transactional fees (4%) and other miscellaneous and non-recurring sources.Geographic ReachThe bank had 14 branches at the end of 2015 including nine in Philadelphia and Southeastern Pennsylvania; four in Berks County Pennsylvania; one in Westchester County New York; and one in Mercer County New Jersey. It also had a handful of additional offices in Boston; New York City; Portsmouth New Hampshire; Providence Rhode Island; and Suffolk County New York.Sales and MarketingCustomers Bancorp's customers include private businesses business customers nonprofits and consumers. Its commercial lending division typically makes loans to companies with revenues between $1 million to $50 million needing between $0.5 million to $10 million in credit.The bank has been ramping up its advertising spend in recent years. It spent $1.48 million on advertising in 2015 up from $1.33 million and $1.27 million in 2014 and 2013 respectively.Financial PerformanceThe bank's annual revenues have nearly quadrupled since 2011 as its loan assets have more than tripled (its loan assets reached $5.45 billion by of the end of 2015). Meanwhile growing revenues strong cost controls and low interest rates have pushed the bank's annual profits up almost 15-fold over the same period.Customers Bancorp's revenue jumped 29% to $277.5 million during 2015 mostly as its average balance of interest-earning loan and securities assets rose by 31% to $6.7 billion for the year. Revenue growth in 2015 drove the bank's net income up 36% to $58.5 million. Customer Bancorp's operating cash levels declined sharply to $356.6 million for the year as the bank originated more loans held for sale than it actually sold.StrategyWith its eye on becoming the leading regional bank holding company Customers Bancorp continued in 2016 to focus on expanding its market share with its high-touch personalized Concierge Banking services and its "high-tech" BankMobile offerings which include remote account opening remote deposit capture and mobile banking. The BankMobile and online banking channels allow Customers Bancorp to slow expensive branch-expansion plans and cut operating costs significantly while giving customers faster access to banking services. But even with digital banking the bank occasionally opens new branches (and selectively acquire others) to grow its loan and deposit business. In January 2016 it opened and replaced an existing branch in Hamilton New Jersey onto Route 33 in the same city. In June 2015 Customers opened a new Long Island location in Mellville New York to expand its private and commercial banking services to local clients there. Mergers and AcquisitionsIn December 2015 Customers Bank expanded its deposit business and added 2 million new student customers after buying the One Account Student Checking and Refund Management Disbursement Services business from higher education refund disbursement provider Higher One Inc for $42 million.

Company BackgroundIn late 2011 Customers purchased Berkshire Bancorp and picked up five branches in Berks County Pennsylvania for about $11.3 million.

EXECUTIVES

Chairman and CEO, Jay S. Sidhu, age 64, $300,000 total compensation
President and COO, Richard A. Ehst, age 70, $225,000 total compensation
Executive Vice President President of Community Banking, Warren Taylor, age 58, $190,000 total compensation
EVP and Chief Credit Officer, Thomas Jastrem
EVP and Chief Administrative Officer, Jim Collins
EVP and Chief Lending Officer, Timothy D. Romig
EVP and President Special Assets Group, Robert A. White
EVP and and Director Enterprise Risk Management, James D. Hogan
EVP and Director Multi-Family and Investment CRE Lending, Kenneth A. Keiser
Executive Vice President Market Chief Lending Officer, George Maroulis
Vice President of Operations, Richard (Dick) Kirk
Auditors: BDO USA, LLP

LOCATIONS

HQ: Customers Bancorp Inc
1015 Penn Avenue, Suite 103, Wyomissing, PA 19610
Phone: 610 933-2000
Web: www.customersbank.com

PRODUCTS/OPERATIONS

2015

	% of total
Interest income	
Loans receivable including fees	66
Loans held for sale	19
Investment securities	4
Other	2
Non interest income	
Mortgage warehouse transnational fees	4
Bank-owned life insurance	3
Gains on sales of loans	1
Deposit fees	0
Mortgage loan and banking income	0
Gain (loss) on sale of investment securities)	0
Other	1
Total	**100**

Products include
Equipment Loans

Mortgage Warehouse Loans
Multi-Family And Commercial Real Estate Loans
Residential Mortgage Loans
Small Business Loans

COMPETITORS

Bank of America	Huntington Bancshares
Capital One	JPMorgan Chase
Citigroup	KeyCorp
Comerica	PNC Financial
Fifth Third	U.S. Bancorp
HSBC	Wells Fargo

HISTORICAL FINANCIALS

Company Type: Public

Income Statement

FYE: December 31

	ASSETS ($ mil.)	NET INCOME ($ mil.)	INCOME AS % OF ASSETS	EMPLOYEES
12/15	8,401.3	58.5	0.7%	517.0
12/14	6,825.3	43.2	0.6%	426.0
12/13	4,153.1	32.6	0.8%	388.0
12/12	3,201.2	23.8	0.7%	255.0
12/11	2,077.5	4.0	0.2%	0.0
Annual Growth	**41.8%**	**95.2%**	—	—

2015 Year-End Financials

Return on assets: 0.7%
Return on equity: 11.7%
Long-term debt ($ mil.): —
No. of shares (mil.): 26.9
Sales ($ mil): 277.5
Dividends
Yield: —
Payout: —
Market value ($ mil.): 732.0

	STOCK PRICE ($) FY Close	P/E High/Low		PER SHARE ($) Earnings	Dividends	Book Value
12/15	27.22	15	9	1.96	0.00	20.59
12/14	19.46	14	11	1.55	0.00	16.57
12/13	20.46	15	11	1.30	0.00	14.51
12/12	14.50	11	6	1.57	0.00	13.27
Annual Growth	**23.4%**	—	—	**7.6%**	—	**15.8%**

Cynosure Inc

HologicIf beauty is only skin deep then Cynosure can surely enhance it. The company develops makes and markets aesthetic laser and pulsed light systems used by dermatologists and doctors to remove hair reduce pigmentation rejuvenate the skin and treat vascular lesions. For patients who want to go deeper its Smartlipo workstation allows cosmetic surgeons to perform a less-invasive procedure than conventional liposuction to target and reduce fat. Cynosure's laser systems consist of a control console and one or more hand pieces. The company's direct sales force and international distributors market and sell its products worldwide under such names as Accolade Affirm Cynergy Elite and PicoSure. Hologic is buying Cynosure for $1.7 billion.

Change in Company Type

In early 2017 women's health firm Hologic agreed to buy Cynosure in a deal which will allow it to enter the medical aesthetics space. Through the deal Cynosure will gain access to a wider customer base.

Operations

In order to serve the broadest base of physician customers and patient skin types Cynosure keeps its technology and product portfolio diverse. Its products incorporate various lasers and other light-based energy sources from Alexandrite pulse dye and diode to Nd:Yag and intense pulsed light for a range of aesthetic applications. The company offers its products at various price points with many of its newer models capable of being upgraded to systems with greater functionality as customers' practices expand.

Although aesthetic treatment procedures that use lasers and light-based equipment are traditionally performed by dermatologists and plastic surgeons Cynosure also targets a non-traditional customer base by marketing to primary care physicians and OB/GYNs. It sees opportunity here as more physicians opt to open medical spas sometimes adjacent to their existing medical practices. Additionally the company partnered with Unilever to develop a laser treatment system for home use; the device received FDA approval for treating facial wrinkles in 2012 and launched in 2013.

Another key product for commercial distribution is the company's Cellulaze Cellulite Laser Workstation. Cellulaze is the only minimally invasive medical device approved for cellulite reduction. Outside the US the company markets Cellulaze in Canada the EU Australia and South Korea and is seeking regulatory approvals in other international markets.

Geographic Reach

Outside of North America Cynosure conducts sales and service operations through its wholly-owned subsidiaries in France Spain the UK Germany Australia South Korea China Japan and Mexico. The company also sells through distributors in almost 120 other countries where it doesn't maintain a direct sales presence. In those markets its distributors sell install and service Cynosure's products.

The US accounted for about half of the company's 2013 sales.

Sales and Marketing

Cynosure sells its products globally through a direct sales force to dermatologists and plastic surgeons as well as physicians obstetricians and gynecologists offering extended "medical spa" services.

Financial Performance

Revenue has risen steadily over the past few years at Cynosure keeps introducing new products. In 2013 it reported a 47% increase from $153 million to $226 million as domestic and foreign sales volume and pricing improved along with service revenue. In spite of those gains net income took a hit for the first time in years as the company incurred litigation- and acquisition-related costs. Net income went from a peak of $11 million to a net loss of $2 million. Cash used in operations has followed a similar trajectory rising to $14.6 million in 2012 but falling more than $11 million to $3.4 million in 2013 due to the drop in net income and deferred income tax.

Strategy

To fulfill its goal of becoming the world's leading provider of non-invasive and minimally invasive aesthetic treatment systems Cynosure's strategy includes offering a full range of tailored aesthetic solutions developing new and innovative solutions and products that target unmet needs in significant aesthetic treatment markets and developing applications of its technology for home use. It also relies on business from its existing customers to generate additional revenue and ongoing comprehensive customer service to retain its customers.

The company also relies on acquisitions to fuel growth and product expansion. To that end in 2014 it purchased an aesthetic laser maker. The previous year it had launched two new products in China and received approval for PicoSure to treat acne scars and remove tattoos from the US FDA.

Mergers and Acquisitions

In 2014 Cynosure purchased Kentucky-based Ellman a maker of aesthetic lasers for $13.2 million. The move added Ellman's radio frequency technology and its just-approved cellulite reduction laser to Cynosure's product line.

Cynosure acquired Palomar Medical Technologies in 2013 for some $294 million. The merger widened Cynosure's product offerings and strengthen its global distribution network; it also created cross-sales opportunities for both companies.

EXECUTIVES

Senior Vice President Of Regulatory Compliance, George Cho

COO and CFO, Timothy W. Baker, age 55, $575,000 total compensation

Chairman President and CEO, Michael R. Davin, age 58, $850,000 total compensation

EVP Sales, Douglas J. Delaney, age 49, $400,000 total compensation

CTO, Rafael Sierra, age 66

SVP International, William T. (Bill) Kelley

Vice President, Jim Palastra

Senior Vice President Of New Product Development, James (Jamie) Boll

Vice President Of Sales, Marina Kamenakis

Senior Vice President of Electrical Engineering and Application Development, Shaun Welches

Vice President Of Luminary Develpoment, Paul Wiener

Vice President Asia Pacific Sales, Bruce (Brucey) Byers

Area Vice President Sales, Bill (Billy) Hough

Auditors: Ernst & Young LLP

LOCATIONS

HQ: Cynosure Inc
5 Carlisle Road, Westford, MA 01886
Phone: 978 256-4200
Web: www.cynosure.com

PRODUCTS/OPERATIONS

2015 Sales

	$ mil.	% of total
Products	276.1	81
Parts accessories & services	63.4	19
Total	**339.5**	**100**

Selected Products

Acclaim (hair and spider vein removal)
Accolade (pigmented lesion and tattoo removal)
Affinity QS (pigmented lesion and tattoo removal)
Affirm (age spot scar and wrinkle reduction; tissue coagulation)
Apogee (hair and spider vein removal)
Cellulaze (cellulite reduction)
Cynergy (vascular and pigment lesion treatment)
Elite (laser hair removal)
Elite MPX (laser hair removal treatment of pigmentation and facial and leg veins wrinkles)
Smartlipo (localized fat treatment and laser body sculpting)
SmartSkin (skin rejuvenation)
SmoothShapes XV (cellulite reduction)
TriActive (cellulite reduction)

Selected Subsidiaries

Cynosure France
Cynosure GmbH (Germany)
Cynosure K.K.
Cynosure Korea Limited
Cynosure Mexico
Cynosure Securities Corporation
Cynosure Spain S.L.
Cynosure UK Ltd.
Suzhou Cynosure Medical Devices Company Ltd. (China)

COMPETITORS

Alma Lasers	Palomar Medical
Cutera	PhotoMedex
Dynatronics	Solta Medical
Galderma Laboratories	Sound Surgical
IRIDEX	Technologies
Lumenis	Syneron
Obagi Medical	TRIA Beauty
Osyris Medical	

HISTORICAL FINANCIALS
Company Type: Public

Income Statement
FYE: December 31

	REVENUE ($ mil.)	NET INCOME ($ mil.)	NET PROFIT MARGIN	EMPLOYEES
12/15	339.4	15.8	4.7%	857.0
12/14	292.3	31.3	10.7%	755.0
12/13	226.0	(1.6)	—	576.0
12/12	153.4	10.9	7.1%	378.0
12/11	110.6	(2.9)	—	346.0
Annual Growth	**32.4%**	**—**		**25.5%**

2015 Year-End Financials

Debt ratio: 3.3%	No. of shares (mil.): 22.7
Return on equity: 4.1%	Dividends
Cash ($ mil.): 108.5	Yield: —
Current ratio: 2.73	Payout: —
Long-term debt ($ mil.): 17.3	Market value ($ mil.): 1,014.0

	STOCK PRICE ($) FY Close	P/E High/Low	Earnings	Dividends	Book Value
12/15	44.67	63 39	0.70	0.00	17.82
12/14	27.42	22 13	1.41	0.00	16.56
12/13	26.64	— —	(0.09)	0.00	15.10
12/12	24.11	34 14	0.79	0.00	12.22
12/11	11.76	— —	(0.23)	0.00	9.52
Annual Growth	**39.6%**	**— —**	**—**	**—**	**17.0%**

Dave & Busters Entertainment Inc

Fun and games collide with food and drink at these nightspots. Dave & Buster's Entertainment owns and operates more than 85 entertainment complexes that offer casual dining full bar service and a cavernous game room. The adult fun centers feature the latest in video games and motion simulators as well as games of skill played for prizes. For dining Dave & Buster's offers a menu that features traditional American fare such as burgers seafood and steak. Partners David Corriveau and James "Buster" Corley opened the first Dave & Buster's in 1982. It went public in late 2014.

Operations

Slightly less than 50% of sales come from food and beverages while the remaining sales come from amusements such as air hockey skee-ball and video games.

Geographic Reach

Dave & Buster's owns and operates locations in 33 states and Canada. About 27 of the company's 87 entertainment complexes are concentrated within the three states of California New York and Texas.

Sales and Marketing

Dave & Buster's is concentrating on increased sales and marketing efforts to reinvigorate its brand and grow the special events portion of its business. The chain helped pioneer a new segment in casual dining but few adult fun arcade chains have followed and flourished. One notable exception is Champps a chain of suburban nightspots popular for live music games and karaoke. Dave & Buster's also faces stiff competition in the general food and drink category from such franchises as Applebee's Buffalo Wild Wings and Hooters.

Financial Performance

The company reported revenue of $866.98 million for fiscal 2016 which was an increase of $120.23 million (or 16%) compared to its fiscal 2015 revenue. The primary reason for the spike was increased revenues from comparable store sales driven by a continued focus on sports viewing new game launches and new menu offerings.

Dave & Buster's net income was $59.61 million in fiscal 2016 which was an increase of $51.98 million compared to its fiscal 2015 net income.

The company ended fiscal 2016 with $186.98 million in cash flow from operations. That was an increase of a little more than $100 million compared to Dave & Buster's cash on hand at the end of fiscal 2015.

Strategy

The chain's recent expansion efforts have slanted towards opening new units that are a smaller format store the company developed out of the need to reduce construction and operating costs. The company is focused on its growth through geographic expansion.

HISTORY

Company Background

Late in the 1970s David Corriveau and James "Buster" Corley were running two businesses located next to each other in Little Rock Arkansas. Corriveau operated a billiards and game parlor called Slick Willie's and Corley ran Buster's a restaurant that Corriveau helped finance. The two noticed a large amount of traffic between the two locales and the idea of Dave & Buster's was formed. The first site opened in a converted Dallas warehouse in 1982; the second opened six years later. Eager for expansion Corriveau and Corley sold an 80% stake in the business to Dallas retailer Edison Brothers in 1990. Edison grew weary of the cash drain however and divested its stake in 1995. The company went public that year.

The company picked up its expansion pace in 1996 opening three more locations. The next year the first West Coast Dave & Buster's opened in Ontario California and brewer Bass (later Six Continents) opened the first international site in the UK. (A second UK location opened the following year.) In 1998 Dave & Buster's signed a franchise agreement with TaiMall Development to open seven locations across the Pacific Rim (the first of which opened that year in Taiwan) and an agree-

ment with SVAG Development to open several stores in Germany Switzerland and Austria.

New stores opened in Texas and Florida the following year. Dave & Buster's also inked an agreement with Funtime Hospitality to open 10 locations in Canada. (The company opened a single location in Toronto in 2000; it acquired Funtime's assets and terminated its development rights in 2003.) Results during 1999 were disappointing however causing the company to slow its expansion plans in 2000. That year Bass terminated its license agreement and closed the UK locations. SVAG cancelled its development deal the next year. Also in 2001 the company signed an agreement to develop five locations in South Korea.

A group led by management and backed by Investcorp agreed to buy the company and take it private for $255 million in 2002. Unable to get financing however the deal was called off late that year prompting public complaints from investors. With the founders at the helm for years Dave & Buster's separated the offices of chairman and CEO in 2003. Former co-chairs and co-CEOs Corriveau and Corley gained new titles (president and CEO respectively) and director Peter Edison was named non-executive chairman.

The company opened no new stores in 2003 and only one in 2004. However in 2004 the company purchased nine Jillian's locations and the Jillian's trade name for $47 million $20 million more than the original proposal. Most of the entertainment night spots were converted to Dave & Buster's locations.

Wellspring Capital Management took Dave & Buster's private in 2006 for $375 million. Corley stepped down as CEO following the deal and turned the reins over to Stephen King formerly head of international operations for Carlson Restaurants (T.G.I. Friday's). Corriveau was replaced the following year by Starlette Johnson.

In 2008 Dave & Buster's announced plans to go public again through an IPO but that deal was later shelved due to the deteriorating economy. Wellspring sold the restaurant business to private-equity firm Oak Hill Capital for $570 million in 2010. Dave & Buster's eventually filed its IPO in 2011 only to cancel those plans in 2012.

EXECUTIVES

SVP and CFO, Brian A. Jenkins, age 54, $316,731 total compensation

SVP Purchasing and International Operations, J. Michael (Mike) Plunkett, age 65, $194,615 total compensation

CEO, Stephen M. King, age 58, $600,000 total compensation

President and COO, Dolf Berle, age 53

SVP Entertainment and Games Strategy, Kevin Bachus

Chairman, Alan J. Lacy

Auditors: KPMG LLP

LOCATIONS

HQ: Dave & Busters Entertainment Inc
2481 Manana Drive, Dallas, TX 75220
Phone: 214 357-9588
Web: www.daveandbusters.com

PRODUCTS/OPERATIONS

2015 Sales

	% of total
Food and beverage revenues	47
Amusement and other revenues	53
Total	**100**

COMPETITORS

AMF Bowling	Champps Entertainment
Applebee's	Damon's
International	Hooters
Brinker	Houlihan's
Brunswick Corp.	Rock Bottom
Buffalo Wild Wings	Restaurants
Carlson Restaurants	

HISTORICAL FINANCIALS

Company Type: Public

Income Statement

FYE: January 31

	REVENUE ($ mil.)	NET INCOME ($ mil.)	NET PROFIT MARGIN	EMPLOYEES
01/16*	866.9	59.6	6.9%	12,495.0
02/15	746.7	7.6	1.0%	10,930.0
02/14	635.5	2.1	0.3%	10,961.0
02/13	608.0	8.7	1.4%	0.0
01/12	541.5	(6.9)	—	0.0
Annual Growth 12.5%		—	—	—

*Fiscal year change

2016 Year-End Financials

Debt ratio: 33.6%	No. of shares (mil.): 41.6
Return on equity: 19.7%	Dividends
Cash ($ mil.): 25.5	Yield: —
Current ratio: 0.70	Payout: —
Long-term debt ($ mil.): 330.7	Market value ($ mil.): 1,510.0

	STOCK PRICE ($) FY Close	P/E High/Low		PER SHARE ($) Earnings	Dividends	Book Value
01/16*	36.27	29 19		1.39	0.00	8.32
02/15	28.74	140 78		0.21	0.00	6.47
Annual Growth 26.2%		—	—561.9%		— 28.6%	

*Fiscal year change

DCT Industrial Trust Inc

In industry DCT trusts. DCT Industrial Trust is a real estate investment trust (REIT) that owns develops and manages bulk distribution warehouses light industrial properties and service centers located in high-density high-volume markets in the US. It owns interests in or manages some 400 buildings spanning more than 73 million sq. ft. of leasable space in about 15 US states and Mexico. Bulk distribution warehouses account for a majority of the company's rentable space. Companies in the manufacturing wholesale and retail trade and transportation and warehousing sectors make up most of DCT's clients. Major tenants include Clorox Kellogg and DHL.

OperationsDCT Industrial operates three segments based on its properties' geographic locations: East (which generated 33% of 2014 revenue) Central (38%) and West (28%).The REIT owned 393 consolidated properties spanning 62 million sq. ft. with a 95.4% occupancy rate during 2014. It also operated 24 unconsolidated properties spanning 8.1 million sq. ft. with a 97.8% occupancy rate on behalf of its four institutional capital management partners. About 99% of its annual revenue came from rental income while the rest came from institutional capital management and other fees. Geographic ReachThe Colorado-based REIT has regional offices in Atlanta; Baltimore;

Chicago; Cincinnati; Dallas; Houston; Paramus New Jersey; Newport Beach California; Emeryville California; Orlando; and Seattle. Its five largest markets in 2014 were in Southern California Chicago Houston Atlanta and Northern California. Sales and MarketingDuring 2014 DCT had leases with some 900 customers none of which accounted for more than 2.2% of the REIT's rental income. Its top tenants (ranked by rental revenue contributions) included: Schenker Clorox The Glidden Company Distributions Alternatives United Stationers Supply YRC LLC Kellogg Company Bridgestone Corporation Deutsche Post World Net (DHL) and One Kings Lane.Financial PerformanceDCT revenues have been growing every year since 2010 as it has expanded its property portfolio through acquisitions and has charged higher rental rates as the real estate market has strengthened. It's also been climbing back from years of losses thanks to higher gains in property sales as valuations have improved.The REIT's revenue rose by 16% to $336.5 million in 2014 mostly thanks to higher rental revenue from 67 recently acquired properties (acquired since 2013).DCT also enjoyed a second profitable year in 2014 as higher revenue allowed the REIT's net income to more than triple to $49.2 million. Its operating cash levels also grew by 11% to $170 million for the year on higher cash earnings.StrategyDCT typically makes smaller acquisitions of individual buildings and parcels of land rather than entire portfolios of real estate and often divests non-strategic properties using the proceeds to invest in higher-growth assets. Indeed in 2014 the REIT acquired 36 buildings for $363.1 million and sold 37 operating properties to third-parties for proceeds totaling $283.2 million. After the sale of its entire Columbus property portfolio of 2014 DCT had exited 11 markets and earned 82.3% of its net operating income from its core markets compared to 62.6% five years prior.

The REIT also continues to develop new properties in "markets where rents and vacancy levels demonstrate the need for new construction." During 2014 it purchased seven land parcels spanning 103 acres stabilized four buildings with 1.5 million square feet had seven "shell-complete" buildings spanning 1.4 million sq. ft. and had 14 buildings under construction (partially leased) totaling another 3.4 million sq. ft; all expected to be completed in 2015.DCT focuses on maximizing the return on its properties by controlling costs physically maintaining its buildings and establishing good relations with tenants. As a result the REIT has a relatively consistent stream of rental revenue.Mergers and AcquisitionsIn 2015 DCT acquired the 691000 sq. ft. Airport Distribution Center a five-building industrial park in the I-70/Northeast submarket of Denver. The company said the "desireable" property was known for its strong tenant demand and easy access to major interstates and the Denver International Airport.In 2014 the REIT acquired a 750000 sq. ft. 100% leased bulk distribution building in Central Valley of Tracy California. The company said that the property occupied by a one strong-credit tenant added an "excellent" building to DCT's portfolio and a "high-quality tenant." Also that year DCT acquired a 650000 sq. ft. Class A facility located on the I-55 Corridor submarket and a 228000 sq. ft. distribution facility located in the O'Hare submarket which was 6% occupied and would be renovated for future lease.

EXECUTIVES

CEO, Philip L. Hawkins, age 60, $650,000 total compensation
CFO, Matthew T. Murphy, age 51, $340,000 total compensation
Managing Director East Region, Michael J. Ruen, age 49, $280,000 total compensation
EVP Investments and Portfolio Management, Teresa L. Corral
EVP Property Management, Charla K. Rios
EVP and General Counsel, John G. Spiegleman
Managing Director Central Region, Neil Doyle
Managing Director West Coast Region, Bud V. Pharris
Chairman, Thomas G. (Tom) Wattles, age 64
Auditors: Ernst & Young LLP

LOCATIONS

HQ: DCT Industrial Trust Inc
518 17th Street, Suite 800, Denver, CO 80202
Phone: 303 597-2400
Web: www.dctindustrial.com

PRODUCTS/OPERATIONS

2014 Sales

	$ mil.	% of total
Rental Revenue	334.8	99
Institutional capital management and other fees	1.7	1
Total	**336.5**	**100**

COMPETITORS

Brandywine Realty	Liberty Property Trust
CenterPoint Properties	Monmouth Real Estate
Duke Realty	PS Business Parks
First Industrial	Panattoni Development
Realty	Company
First Potomac Realty	Prologis
Industrial	
Developments	

HISTORICAL FINANCIALS

Company Type: Public

Income Statement
FYE: December 31

	REVENUE ($ mil.)	NET INCOME ($ mil.)	NET PROFIT MARGIN	EMPLOYEES
12/15	354.7	94.0	26.5%	143.0
12/14	336.5	49.1	14.6%	145.0
12/13	289.0	15.8	5.5%	136.0
12/12	260.7	(15.0)	—	131.0
12/11	253.4	(25.2)	—	117.0
Annual Growth	**8.8%**	**—**		**5.1%**

2015 Year-End Financials

Debt ratio: 42.8%	No. of shares (mil.): 88.3
Return on equity: 5.3%	Dividends
Cash ($ mil.): 18.4	Yield: 3.0%
Current ratio: 0.30	Payout: 118.9%
Long-term debt ($ mil.): 1,556.4	Market value ($ mil.): 3,300.0

	STOCK PRICE ($) FY Close	P/E High/Low		PER SHARE ($) Earnings	Dividends	Book Value
12/15	37.37	36	30	1.05	1.13	19.84
12/14	35.66	63	12	0.58	0.28	19.88
12/13	7.13	42	32	0.20	1.12	19.28
12/12	6.49	—	—	(0.24)	0.00	18.97
12/11	5.12	—	—	(0.44)	1.12	19.65
Annual Growth	**64.4%**			**—**	**0.2%**	**0.2%**

Del Frisco's Restaurant Group Inc

Del Frisco's Restaurant Group operates two upscale steakhouse chains Del Frisco's Double Eagle Steak House and Sullivan's with about 30 locations in more than 15 states. The group also runs two more casual Del Frisco's Grille restaurants. Del Frisco's Double Eagle Steak House has about 10 locations and offer upscale dining in a contemporary surrounding. The somewhat less pricey version of the 20-unit Sullivan's chain features an atmosphere reminiscent of a Chicago-style steakhouse. Both concepts serve premium cuts of beef along with seafood lamb and pork dishes and both offer an extensive wine list. The company controlled by Dallas-based private equity firm Lone Star Funds went public in 2012.

Geographic Reach
Most of the group's restaurants are found in chic urban locations or near affluent residential areas.

Sales and Marketing
Del Frisco's Restaurant Group has been working to bolster its marketing and advertising efforts to drive traffic to its established restaurants.

Financial Performance
The company reported $301.8 million in revenue for fiscal 2014. That was an increase of $30 million compared to its fiscal 2013 revenue. Del Frisco's Restaurant Group reported net income of $8.7 million for fiscal 2014. That was a slight decrease compared to prior fiscal period. The company's cash flow from operations remained strong in fiscal 2014 and Del Frisco's Restaurant Group ended the year with $31 million in cash on hand.

Strategy
Del Frisco's Grille with locations up and running in Dallas and New York City was launched to capitalize on market recognition of the Del Frisco's brand. The smaller size lower construction costs and more affordable menu for the company's newest concept offer greater potential for expansion.

EXECUTIVES

CFO, Thomas J. (Tom) Pennison, age 48, $296,154 total compensation
President CEO and Director, Norman J. Abdallah, age 54
VP Culinary and Corporate Executive Chef, Thomas G. Dritsas, age 44, $216,000 total compensation
Brand President Double Eagle Steak House, Ray Risley
Chief Development Officer, William S. Martens, age 44, $172,000 total compensation
Brand President Sullivan's Steakhouse, Scott C. Smith
Vice President Marketing, Lisa (Lis) Kislak
Vice President of Operations, Kim (Kimmy) Owens
Chairman, Ian R. Carter, age 54
Auditors: KPMG LLP

LOCATIONS

HQ: Del Frisco's Restaurant Group Inc
920 S. Kimball Ave., Suite 100, Southlake, TX 76092
Phone: 817 601-3421
Web: www.dfrg.com

PRODUCTS/OPERATIONS

2014 Sales

	$ mil.	% of total
Del Frisco's	151.1	50
Sullivan's	80.9	27
Grille	69.8	23
Total	**301.8**	**100**

COMPETITORS

B.R. Guest	Morton's Restaurant
Cameron Mitchell	Group
Restaurants	Myriad Restaurant
Darden	Group
Fox Restaurant	OSI Restaurant
Concepts	Partners
Grill Concepts	Palm Restaurants
HC Restaurant Group	Ruth's Hospitality
Hillstone Restaurant	Smith & Wollensky
Group	Wolfgang Puck Fine
Levy Restaurants	Dining
McCormick & Schmick's	

HISTORICAL FINANCIALS

Company Type: Public

Income Statement

FYE: December 29

	REVENUE ($ mil.)	NET INCOME ($ mil.)	NET PROFIT MARGIN	EMPLOYEES
12/15	331.6	16.0	4.8%	4,921.0
12/14	301.8	16.6	5.5%	4,745.0
12/13	271.8	12.2	4.5%	4,222.0
12/12	232.4	13.7	5.9%	3,796.0
12/11	201.6	8.9	4.5%	3,094.0
Annual Growth	**13.2%**	**15.6%**	**—**	**12.3%**

2015 Year-End Financials

Debt ratio: 1.2%
Return on equity: 7.3%
Cash ($ mil.): 5.1
Current ratio: 0.86
Long-term debt ($ mil.): 4.5

No. of shares (mil.): 23.3
Dividends
Yield: —
Payout: —
Market value ($ mil.): 377.0

	STOCK PRICE ($) FY Close	P/E High/Low	Earnings	Dividends	Book Value
12/15	16.19	36 18	0.68	0.00	9.77
12/14	23.45	41 27	0.70	0.00	9.00
12/13	23.57	46 28	0.51	0.00	8.40
12/12	15.33	24 18	0.67	0.00	7.48
Annual Growth	**1.8%**	**— —**	**0.5%**	**—**	**9.3%**

Diamond Hill Investment Group Inc.

Diamond Hill Investment Group takes a shine to investment management. Operating through flagship subsidiary Diamond Hill Capital Management the firm oversees some $11.5 billion in assets most of it invested in mutual funds. Serving institutional and individual clients the company administers several mutual funds and sells them mainly through independent investment advisers broker-dealers financial planners investment consultants and third-party marketing firms. The firm hews to a value-based investment philosophy and takes a long-term perspective to investing. Formed in 1990 Diamond Hill Investment Group also manages separate accounts and hedge funds.

Operations

Diamond Hill Investment Group operates through its subsidiaries: Diamond Hill Capital Management; and Beacon Hill Fund Services and BHIL Distributors collectively known as Beacon Hill. Beacon Hill provides fund administration and statutory underwriting services to various clients including Diamond Hill Funds.

Financial Performance

Diamond Hill Investment Group's revenue rose 4% in 2012 versus 2011 to $66.6 million. The increase was due to a 13% rise in fees from mutual fund administration while investment advisory fees rose a more modest 3%. Net income rose 18% over the same period to $16.9 million. Assets under management at the end of 2012 exceeded $9.4 billion an increase of nearly 9% over the prior year. The firm's revenue and profits have increased steadily since 2008 after taking a hit during the financial crisis as investors retreated from the market.

EXECUTIVES

Co-Chief Investment Officer, Christopher A. (Chris) Welch
COO, Lisa M. Wesolek, age 53
Managing Director Investments and Portfolio Manager, Chuck Bath
President CEO and Portfolio Manager, Christopher (Chris) Bingaman, age 51
CFO, Thomas E. (Tom) Line, age 50
Co-Chief Investment Officer and Portfolio Manager, Austin Hawley
Vice President, Karen (Kare) Colvin
Chairman, Roderick H. (Ric) Dillon, age 59
Auditors: KPMG LLP

LOCATIONS

HQ: Diamond Hill Investment Group Inc.
325 John H. McConnell Blvd., Suite 200, Columbus, OH 43215
Phone: 614 255-3333
Web: www.diamond-hill.com

PRODUCTS/OPERATIONS

2015 Sales

	$ mil.	% of total
Investment advisory	107.9	87
Mutual fund administration	16.5	13
Total	**124.4**	**100**

Selected Products

Diamond Hill Small Cap Fund
Diamond Hill Small-Mid Cap Fund
Diamond Hill Large Cap Fund
Diamond Hill Select Fund Fund
Diamond Hill Long-Short Fund
Diamond Hill Strategic Income Fund

COMPETITORS

AllianceBernstein	GAMCO Investors
American Century	Janus Capital
Calamos Asset	Legg Mason
Management	MFS
Cohen & Steers	Putnam
Columbia Management	Pzena Investment
Davis Advisers	Management
Duncan-Hurst	Raymond James
Eaton Vance	Financial
Edelman Financial	SEI Investments
Edward Jones	T. Rowe Price
Epoch	The Vanguard Group

FMR
Franklin Templeton

Waddell & Reed
Westwood Holdings

HISTORICAL FINANCIALS

Company Type: Public

Income Statement

FYE: December 31

	REVENUE ($ mil.)	NET INCOME ($ mil.)	NET PROFIT MARGIN	EMPLOYEES
12/15	124.4	37.0	29.8%	126.0
12/14	104.5	31.5	30.2%	107.0
12/13	81.4	22.1	27.2%	98.0
12/12	66.6	16.9	25.4%	79.0
12/11	63.8	14.3	22.5%	73.0
Annual Growth	**18.2%**	**26.8%**	**—**	**14.6%**

2015 Year-End Financials

Debt ratio: —
Return on equity: 41.2%
Cash ($ mil.): 57.4
Current ratio: 2.61
Long-term debt ($ mil.): —

No. of shares (mil.): 3.4
Dividends
Yield: 2.6%
Payout: 43.7%
Market value ($ mil.): 645.0

	STOCK PRICE ($) FY Close	P/E High/Low	Earnings	Dividends	Book Value
12/15	189.00	20 11	11.03	5.00	30.84
12/14	138.04	14 11	9.67	4.00	22.40
12/13	118.34	18 10	6.94	3.00	13.80
12/12	67.86	15 12	5.44	8.00	6.86
12/11	73.98	17 14	4.86	5.00	6.03
Annual Growth	**26.4%**	**— —**	**22.7%**	**(0.0%)**	**50.4%**

DiamondRock Hospitality Co.

If diamonds are a girl's best friend then DiamondRock Hospitality might be an investor's best friend. Operating as an umbrella partnership real estate investment trust (UPREIT) it owns (but does not operate) nearly 30 upper-upscale hotels with about 11000 rooms in the North America and the US Virgin Islands with an emphasis on major urban markets such as New York Los Angeles Chicago and Boston as well as destination resorts. Its hotels are operated under the banners of Hilton Worldwide Marriott International Starwood Hotels & Resorts Worldwide and Westin. DiamondRock mostly operates through its taxable REIT subsidiary Bloodstone TRS.

OperationsDiamondRock generated 72% of its total revenue from its Rooms in 2014 while its Food and Beverage services generated another 22% of total revenue. Because it owns its properties (and does not manage them) the firm had a staff of just 25 employees at the end of 2014.Geographic ReachNearly 45% of DiamondRock's rental revenue during 2014 came fairly evenly from its properties in Chicago Boston and New York City. Its four next largest markets were the US Virgin Islands (8% of revenue) Los Angeles (7%) Minneapolis (6%) and Denver (4%).Financial PerformanceDiamondRock's revenues and profits have been rising over the past few years from an uptick in business travel as the US economy has rebounded.The REIT's revenue jumped 9% to

$873 million in 2014 with revenue from the business transient segment leading most of the growth particularly at its Lexington Hotel New York property as a result of the hotel's rebranding and repositioning. Its group revenue was also higher mostly thanks to its two Boston-based hotels the Renaissance Worthington and Frenchman's Reef & Morning Star Marriott Beach Resort. Room revenue jumped 13% on continued growth in the lodging industry while its closely-tied food and beverage and other miscellaneous fee revenues grew by 1% and 2% respectively. Geographically the firm's property revenue grew fastest in New York (by 41%) while its property revenues in Los Angeles and Boston also grew by double-digits during the year.Higher revenue coupled with nearly $75 million in gains on hotel property sales and acquisitions in 2014 more than tripled DiamondRock's net income to $163.4 million during the year while the REIT's operating cash levels spiked by 25% to nearly $180 million on higher cash earnings.StrategyDiamondRock's growth strategy reiterated in 2015 is to acquire hotels in urban and destination resort markets particularly in prime markets on the West Coast and South Florida and other select destination resort markets. To boost room revenues from its existing properties DiamondRock regularly invests in brand and room improvements and adding conference areas spas and restaurants to build additional value.

With a preference toward "moderately sized investments" of $50 million to $150 million the REIT typically acquires hotels that are operated under nationally-recognized brands that have already established strong reservation and sales systems. One of its most recent acquisitions was its $58.5 million-purchase of the Shorebreak Hotel in the resort destination of Huntington Beach California in 2015. Some of its acquisitions in 2014 included: its $94-million purchase of the fee simple interest in the 184-suite Sheraton Suites Key West in Florida; and the $149-million acquisition of The Westin Beach Resort & Spa in Fort Lauderdale Florida which represented a payment of $345000 per guest room.

It also selectively sells properties that do not fit this "core" criteria to free up resources for investments in "higher quality hotels with brighter prospects." Some of its property divestitures in 2014 included: the $30 million sale of its 386-room Oak Brook Hills Resort and the sale of its 1004-room Los Angeles Airport Marriott hotel.

EXECUTIVES

President and CEO, Mark W. Brugger, age 47, $765,000 total compensation
EVP CFO and Treasurer, Sean M. Mahoney, age 45, $412,000 total compensation
EVP Asset Management and COO, Thomas Healy
EVP General Counsel and Corporate Secretary, William J. Tennis, $361,000 total compensation
EVP and Chief Investment Officer, Troy Furbay, age 49, $402,000 total compensation
Chairman, William W. (Bill) McCarten, age 68
Auditors: KPMG LLP

LOCATIONS

HQ: DiamondRock Hospitality Co.
3 Bethesda Metro Center, Suite 1500, Bethesda, MD 20814
Phone: 240 744-1150
Web: www.drhc.com

PRODUCTS/OPERATIONS

2011 Sales

	$ mil.	% of total
Rooms	441.5	69
Food & beverage	165.1	26
Other	31.6	5
Total	**638.2**	**100**

COMPETITORS

Ashford Hospitality Trust	Innkeepers USA
FelCor	LaSalle Hotel Properties
Hospitality Properties Trust	Strategic Hotels
Host Hotels & Resorts	Sunstone Hotel Investors

HISTORICAL FINANCIALS

Company Type: Public

Income Statement

FYE: December 31

	REVENUE ($ mil.)	NET INCOME ($ mil.)	NET PROFIT MARGIN	EMPLOYEES
12/15	930.9	85.6	9.2%	26.0
12/14	872.8	163.3	18.7%	22.0
12/13	799.6	49.0	6.1%	22.0
12/12	749.6	(16.5)	—	22.0
12/11	638.2	(7.6)	—	22.0
Annual Growth	**9.9%**	**—**	**—**	**4.3%**

2015 Year-End Financials

Debt ratio: 35.4%	No. of shares (mil.): 200.7
Return on equity: 4.6%	Dividends
Cash ($ mil.): 213.5	Yield: 5.1%
Current ratio: 1.24	Payout: 81.9%
Long-term debt ($ mil.): 1,177.7	Market value ($ mil.): 1,937.0

	STOCK PRICE ($) FY Close	P/E High/Low		PER SHARE ($) Earnings	Dividends	Book Value
12/15	9.65	37	23	0.43	0.50	9.09
12/14	14.87	19	14	0.83	0.41	9.15
12/13	11.55	47	35	0.25	0.34	8.60
12/12	9.00	—	—	(0.09)	0.32	8.69
12/11	9.64	—	—	(0.05)	0.32	8.97
Annual Growth	**0.0%**	**—**	**—**	**—**	**11.8%**	**0.3%**

Digital Realty Trust Inc

Technically Digital Realty Trust puts its chips in real estate. The real estate investment trust (REIT) owns and leases more than 140 technology properties with more than 25.5 million sq. ft. of rentable space in metropolitan areas in the US Europe and Asia including data communications hubs electronic storage and processing centers tech manufacturing facilities and offices of tech companies. Digital Realty Trust focuses on hot tech markets such as Atlanta Boston Chicago Dallas Los Angeles Phoenix New York northern Virginia Seattle and California's San Francisco Bay area and Silicon Valley (its largest market). Others are in Western Europe Australia and Asia.

Geographic ReachThe firm has properties in Atlanta Boston Chicago Dallas Los Angeles Phoenix New York northern Virginia Seattle and California's San Francisco Bay area and Silicon Valley (its largest market). Its overseas properties are in Eu-

rope (Amsterdam Dublin Geneva London Manchester and Paris) and the Asia Pacific (Hong Kong Japan Melbourne Sydney and Singapore). All told about 22% of the REIT's total revenue came from its non-US properties during 2015. Sales and MarketingDigital Realty Trust's occupancy rate was at 91.4% at the end of 2015. That year it had more than 1000 tenants with the top 20 tenants contributing 44% of its total annualized rent. The REIT's tenants come from a wide variety of sectors around the world including financial services cloud and IT services manufacturing gaming energy life sciences and consumer products. It's largest tenants by rental revenue in 2015 included IBM CenturyLink Equinix AT&T Facebook LinkedIn and Oracle.Financial PerformanceThanks to rent-boosting property acquisitions over the past few years Digital Realty's annual revenues have risen 70% since 2011 while its annual profits have nearly doubled.Digital Realty's revenue jumped 9% to $1.8 billion during 2015 mostly as its Telx acquisition added new properties which spurred more rental income. Revenue growth in 2015 drove the REIT's net income up 48% to $297 million. Its operating cash levels climbed 22% to $799 million for the year thanks to a rise in cash-based rental income.Strategy

The REIT's growth strategy includes real estate acquisitions and redevelopment of its existing properties. The company believes that upgrades to its properties lead to low tenant turnover and longer lease terms. From 2011 through the end of 2015 Digital Realty has expanded its portfolio from just over 100 properties to more than 140.Mergers and AcquisitionsIn October 2015 Digital Realty Trust purchased Telx Holdings a national provider of data center colocation interconnection and cloud enablement solutions for $1.89 billion. The deal doubled Digital Realty's footprint in the fast-growing colocation business while also providing a new interconnection platform.Company Background

Digital Realty Trust acquired 15 properties in 2010 (the busiest that the company had been since 2007) including some in new markets. The REIT added its first property in Asia when it bought a data center in Singapore. It entered Massachusetts and Connecticut with the acquisition of three data centers there.

Digital Realty Trust purchased more than a dozen properties in 2011 and 2012 including some in new markets such as London and Sydney. The latter deals added to the company's international presence in Dublin Melbourne Paris and Singapore.

EXECUTIVES

CEO, A. William (Bill) Stein, age 62, $750,000 total compensation
Managing Director Asia Pacific, Edward T. (Ted) Higase, age 49
Chief Investment Officer, Scott E. Peterson, age 54, $514,671 total compensation
COO, Jarrett B. Appleby, age 54, $297,822 total compensation
SVP and CIO, Michael Henry
CFO, Andrew P. Power, age 36, $283,333 total compensation
CTO, Chris Sharp
SVP Global Sales And Marketing, Daniel Papes
Vice President Investor Relations, Krupal Raval
Senior Vice President Taxation, Jennifer Xiao
Vice President Design Management, John (Jack) Kuchachik
Vice President Accounting, Keith (Keithy) Shupe
Vice President Global Customer Operations, Mike (Mikey) Davis

Vice President Tax, Brian (Bri) Keyser
Vice President Sales, Sean Mccarthy
Vice President Platforms and Integration, Steve
  (Stevie) Chaput
Vice Chairman, Laurence A. Chapman, age 66
Chairman, Dennis E. Singleton, age 71
Auditors: KPMG LLP

LOCATIONS

HQ: Digital Realty Trust Inc
  Four Embarcadero Center, Suite 3200, San Francisco,
  CA 94111
Phone: 415 738-6500   Fax: 415 738-6501
Web: www.digitalrealty.com

PRODUCTS/OPERATIONS

2015 Sales

	$ mil.	% of total
Rental	1,355.0	77
Tenant reimbursements	359.9	21
Interconnection and other	40.7	2
Fee income and other	7.7	-
Total	**1,763.3**	**100**

COMPETITORS

CenterPoint Properties	First Industrial
CoreSite	Realty
CyrusOne	Kilroy Realty
DuPont Fabros	Mack-Cali
Duke Realty	Prologis
EastGroup Properties	QTS Realty Trust Inc.
Equinix	Vornado Realty

HISTORICAL FINANCIALS

Company Type: Public

Income Statement

FYE: December 31

	REVENUE ($ mil.)	NET INCOME ($ mil.)	NET PROFIT MARGIN	EMPLOYEES
12/15	1,763.3	296.6	16.8%	1,295.0
12/14	1,616.4	200.1	12.4%	860.0
12/13	1,482.2	314.4	21.2%	784.0
12/12	1,279.0	210.3	16.4%	702.0
12/11	1,062.7	156.2	14.7%	532.0
Annual Growth	**13.5%**	**17.4%**	**—**	**24.9%**

2015 Year-End Financials

Debt ratio: 51.8%	No. of shares (mil.): 146.3
Return on equity: 7.0%	Dividends
Cash ($ mil.): 57.0	Yield: 4.5%
Current ratio: 0.34	Payout: 228.1%
Long-term debt ($ mil.): 5,934.2	Market value ($ mil.): 11,070.0

	STOCK PRICE ($) FY Close	P/E High/Low	PER SHARE ($) Earnings	Dividends	Book Value
12/15	75.62	49 39	1.56	3.40	30.74
12/14	66.30	70 49	0.99	3.32	28.60
12/13	49.12	35 21	2.12	3.12	28.11
12/12	67.89	54 40	1.48	2.92	27.72
12/11	66.67	50 38	1.32	2.72	23.79
Annual Growth	**3.2%**	**— —**	**4.3%**	**5.7%**	**6.6%**

DigitalGlobe Inc

Look up and smile. DigitalGlobe might be capturing an image of you –and the rest of the planet. From its array of satellites the company captures imagery used for a variety of applications including mapping urban planning oil exploration land management disaster assessment and humanitarian relief. DigitalGlobe's products include standard images panchromatic images multispectral images and color infrared images as well as mosaics and digital elevation models. About 60% of its revenues come from the US government; commercial customers include oil and gas exploration companies and GPS navigation system makers. DigitalGlobe's images and services are incorporated into popular mapping applications such as Google Maps and Microsoft Virtual Earth as well as into GPS systems from DeLorme and Garmin.

Operations

DigitalGlobe owns and operates four satellites — WorldView-1 WorldView-2 WorldView-3 and GeoEye-1 –that have collected more than 2.8 billion square kilometers of images. The WorldView-3 satellite launched in 2014. WorldView-4 the company's next satellite is under construction and is expected to launch in 2016.

Geographic Reach

Suffice it to say that the company has a global reach via its satellites. On Earth the company is based in Longmont Colorado and it serves its largest customer the US government from five US locations. International offices are in Abu Dhabi the Netherlands Singapore and the UK.

Sales and Marketing

The National Geospatial-Intelligence Agency (NGA) accounts for a majority of DigitalGlobe's sales. The federal agency buys images for use by agencies of the US government for defense intelligence and foreign policy applications. DigitalGlobe has a 10-year $3.5 billion contract that's expected to provide revenue through 2020.

Customers of the company's Direct Access Program (DAP) can order up and receive imagery from some of the company's satellites within local and regional geographic boundaries. The company sells those tools for downloading and processing imagery directly from the satellites. DAP customers include defense and intelligence customers and some commercial customers.

The company also works with resellers to market imagery from its satellites. In 2014 resellers accounted for about 10% of revenue.

Financial Performance

In 2014 DigitalGlobe downloaded $654.6 million in revenue a 7% increase from the previous year. The company received higher revenue with the WorldView-3 satellite becoming fully operational. New DAP customers also boosted revenue.

Net income came in at $18.5 million an improvement from the $68.3 million net loss posted in 2013. Higher revenue and net income helped cash flow from operations which doubled to about $225 million in 2014 from 2013.

Strategy

In 2014 the US Department of Commerce allowed DigitalGlobe to sell higher-resolution imagery to all of its customers extending its available products. It can provide images at up to 0.25 meter panchromatic and 1.0 meter multispectral ground sample distance which enables automated feature extraction agriculture boundaries and crop health land cover classification and seabed mapping.

Beyond images DigitalGlobe sells analytic services that document change and enable geospatial modeling and analysis that helps its customers predict where events will occur to help make resource allocation decisions and save time.

Mergers and Acquisitions

DigitalGlobe acquired Spatial Energy a source for digital imagery and related services for the energy industry in 2014. Spatial Energy's customers include 12 of the top 20 largest oil and gas companies. The acquisition bolsters DigitalGlobe's energy business.

In 2013 DigitalGlobe acquired top rival GeoEye in a cash and stock transaction valued at around $1.4 billion. Like DigitalGlobe GeoEye provides satellite imagery of the air land and sea used in applications that include mapping resource management environmental monitoring disaster response national security and the like. GeoEye brings substantial resources to the merger table including satellites and aircraft that provide aerial imagery. (DigitalGlobe has no similar aircraft instead buying the aerial images in its ImageLibrary from suppliers.) Both companies sell primarily to the US government as well as international governments and commercial customers. The combined company will continue to operate under the DigitalGlobe moniker. More importantly they will no longer be competing for the same contracts –giving each a more stable revenue base –and will share the substantial cost of developing and launching new satellites.

Company Background

DigitalGlobe was founded in 1993 as WorldView Imaging Corporation when the Commerce Department licensed it to build and operate a satellite system to gather digital images for commercial use.

EXECUTIVES

EVP and CTO, Walter S. Scott, age 58, $352,500
  total compensation
President and CEO, Jeffrey R. (Jeff) Tarr, age 53,
  $675,000 total compensation
SVP Global Product and Solutions, Hyune Hand
SVP Sales and Marketing, David B. (Bert) Turner,
  $347,500 total compensation
EVP Operations and Customer Experience,
  Timothy M. Hascall, $352,500 total compensation
SVP and General Manager Analytics, Tony Frazier
EVP and CFO, Gary W. Ferrara
Vice President Data, Jeff Culwell
Vice President Internal Financial Reporting,
  Suzanne Housman
Vice President Worldwide Channel Sales, David
  (Dave) Singer
Senior Vice President Government Relations;
  Senior Vice President Of Government Relations,
  Marcy Steinke
Chairman, Howell M. Estes, age 75
Auditors: PricewaterhouseCoopers LLP

LOCATIONS

HQ: DigitalGlobe Inc
  1300 West 120th Avenue, Westminster, CO 80234
Phone: 303 684-4000
Web: www.digitalglobe.com

PRODUCTS/OPERATIONS

2014 Sales

	$ mil.	% of total
US Government	395.3	60
Diversified Commercial	259.3	40
Total	**654.6**	**100**

Selected Products

Crisis Event Service (Web-based access to pre- and post-event images of world disasters)
ImageConnect (downloadable georeferenced aerial and satellite photos)
ImageScape (3D terrain models)
Orthorectified geospatial images
Satellite images (basic standard stereo pair 8-band multispectral)
WorldView Elevation Suite (elevation datasets over rural areas of low vegetation)

COMPETITORS

CARIS	Mapping Solutions
Earth Search Sciences	Microsoft
Getmapping	Trimble Navigation
Google	

HISTORICAL FINANCIALS

Company Type: Public

Income Statement

FYE: December 31

	REVENUE ($ mil.)	NET INCOME ($ mil.)	NET PROFIT MARGIN	EMPLOYEES
12/15	702.4	23.3	3.3%	1,189.0
12/14	654.6	18.5	2.8%	1,339.0
12/13	612.7	(68.3)	—	1,235.0
12/12	421.4	39.0	9.3%	749.0
12/11	339.5	(28.1)	—	708.0
Annual Growth	19.9%	—	—	13.8%

2015 Year-End Financials

Debt ratio: 37.9%
Return on equity: 1.7%
Cash ($ mil.): 126.1
Current ratio: 1.71
Long-term debt ($ mil.): 1,104.4
No. of shares (mil.): 67.4
Dividends
Yield: —
Payout: —
Market value ($ mil.): 1,055.0

	STOCK PRICE ($) FY Close	P/E High/Low		PER SHARE ($) Earnings	Dividends	Book Value
12/15	15.66	135	56	0.26	0.00	18.52
12/14	30.97	225	127	0.18	0.00	18.47
12/13	41.15	—	—	(1.00)	0.00	18.37
12/12	24.44	31	14	0.84	0.00	11.45
12/11	17.11	—	—	(0.61)	0.00	10.52
Annual Growth	(2.2%)	—	—	—	—	15.2%

Diligent Corp

Auditors: Deloitte & Touche LLP

LOCATIONS

HQ: Diligent Corp
1385 Broadway, 19th Floor, New York, NY 10018
Phone: 212 741-8181
Web: www.boardbooks.com

HISTORICAL FINANCIALS

Company Type: Public

Income Statement

FYE: December 31

	REVENUE ($ mil.)	NET INCOME ($ mil.)	NET PROFIT MARGIN	EMPLOYEES
12/15	99.3	8.1	8.2%	347.0
12/14	83.0	8.9	10.7%	264.0
12/13	64.7	6.2	9.7%	182.0
12/12	39.1	10.6	27.2%	0.0
12/11	15.5	(1.4)	—	0.0
Annual Growth	58.9%	—	—	—

2015 Year-End Financials

Debt ratio: 0.0%
Return on equity: 18.5%
Cash ($ mil.): 70.2
Current ratio: 1.56
Long-term debt ($ mil.): —
No. of shares (mil.): 87.4
Dividends
Yield: —
Payout: —
Market value ($ mil.): 354.0

	STOCK PRICE ($) FY Close	P/E High/Low		PER SHARE ($) Earnings	Dividends	Book Value
12/15	4.05	68	47	0.06	0.00	0.59
12/14	3.95	59	47	0.07	0.00	0.42
12/13	2.89	132	58	0.05	0.00	0.30
12/12	4.62	51	20	0.09	0.00	0.19
12/11	1.50	—	—	(0.02)	0.00	(0.00)
Annual Growth	28.2%	—	—	—	—	—

Dominion Midstream Partners LP

Auditors: Deloitte & Touche LLP

LOCATIONS

HQ: Dominion Midstream Partners LP
120 Tredegar Street, Richmond, VA 23219
Phone: 804 819-2000
Web: www.dommidstream.com

HISTORICAL FINANCIALS

Company Type: Public

Income Statement

FYE: December 31

	REVENUE ($ mil.)	NET INCOME ($ mil.)	NET PROFIT MARGIN	EMPLOYEES
12/15	369.6	196.5	53.2%	0.0
12/14	313.3	106.9	34.1%	0.0
12/13	343.5	109.4	31.8%	0.0
12/12	293.0	97.2	33.2%	0.0
Annual Growth	8.0%	26.4%	—	—

2015 Year-End Financials

Debt ratio: 7.2%
Return on equity: —
Cash ($ mil.): 35.0
Current ratio: 1.60
Long-term debt ($ mil.): 300.8
No. of shares (mil.): 77.6
Dividends
Yield: 2.2%
Payout: 64.9%
Market value ($ mil.): 2,382.0

	STOCK PRICE ($) FY Close	P/E High/Low		PER SHARE ($) Earnings	Dividends	Book Value
12/15	30.66	39	23	1.08	0.70	19.34
12/14	39.20	257	176	0.15	0.00	16.82
12/13	0.00	—	—	(0.00)	0.00	(0.00)
Annual Growth	—	—	—	—	—	—

Dorman Products Inc

Got parts? Dorman does. From its stock of more than 140000 products Dorman Products is a lead-

---

ing supplier of automotive replacement parts (including brake parts) fasteners and service line products to the automotive aftermarket. It also provides household hardware and organization items to mass merchants. About 85% of revenue comes from parts sold under Dorman's sub-brands which include AutoGrade FirstStop and OE Solutions. Dorman sells to auto aftermarket retailers and warehouse distributors (such as AutoZone CARQUEST) as well as to parts manufacturers for resale under private labels. Dorman distributes its products in the North America Asia Europe and the Middle East.

Geographic Reach

Pennsylvania-based Dorman Products has about 15 warehouse and office facilities throughout North America and overseas in China and India. Dorman purchases about 80% of its products from international suppliers primarily in China. More than 90% of the company's sale come from customers in North America.

Sales and Marketing

About half of Dorman's products are primarily sold through automotive aftermarket retails such as AutoZone Advance Auto Parts and O'Reilly Automotive. Distributors such as CARQUEST and NAPA account for more than 40% of the company's sales. International customers sales to mass merchants (including Wal-Mart Stores) and salvage yards represent the rest. In 2014 AutoZone Advance Auto Parts O'Reilly and Genuine Parts each accounted for more than 10% of sales and 60% of total sales.

Financial Performance

Dorman has experienced unprecedented growth over the years with revenues jumping 13% from $664 million in 2013 to peak at a record-setting $751 million in 2014. Profits also climbed 10% from $82 million in 2013 to $90 million in 2014 another company milestone. The historic growth for 2014 was attributed to new product roll-outs coupled with additional revenue from acquisitions.

Strategy

Introducing new products to the automotive aftermarket has been central to Dorman's strategy. The company attributes its growth over the years to its development of a wide assortment of parts and accessories many of which Dorman believes may not have been easily available otherwise and which improve upon the original parts being replaced. As such the firm has made increased investments in product development resources and marketing programs to strengthen its ties to customers.

Mergers and Acquisitions

In October 2013 Dorman acquired North Carolina-base Re-Involt Technologies an aftermarket leader in hybrid battery re-manufacturing technology. The purchase enables Dorman to refine its process for re-manufacturing hybrid drive batteries develop new hybrid products for the aftermarket and ultimately capture sales of replacement batteries for hybrid vehicles a growing segment of the vehicle market.

EXECUTIVES

President and CEO, Mathias J. Barton, age 56, $424,360 total compensation
SVP Sales and Marketing, Jeffrey L. Darby, age 48, $327,540 total compensation
SVP Product, Michael B. (Mike) Kealey, age 41, $327,540 total compensation
Vice President National Accounts, Robert (Bob) Castellani
Vice President National Accounts, Cliff (Clifford) Green

Vice President Of Direct Sales And Information Technology, Andrew Kurpiel
Vice President General Counsel Assistant Secretary, Thomas (Thom) Knoblauch
Executive Chairman, Steven L. Berman, age 57
Auditors: KPMG LLP

LOCATIONS

HQ: Dorman Products Inc
3400 East Walnut Street, Colmar, PA 18915
Phone: 215 997-1800
Web: www.dormanproducts.com

PRODUCTS/OPERATIONS

2014 Sales

	% of total
Power-train	37
Automotive body	29
Chassis	26
Hardware	8
Total	**100**

Selected Subsidiaries

Allparts Inc.
RB Distribution Inc.
RB Management Inc.
RB Vest Inc.

COMPETITORS

Canadian Tire	General Parts
Federal-Mogul	Genuine Parts
Ford Motor	Hahn Automotive
General Motors	Uni-Select

HISTORICAL FINANCIALS

Company Type: Public

Income Statement
FYE: December 26

	REVENUE ($ mil.)	NET INCOME ($ mil.)	NET PROFIT MARGIN	EMPLOYEES
12/15	802.9	92.3	11.5%	1,846.0
12/14	751.4	89.9	12.0%	1,785.0
12/13	664.4	81.9	12.3%	1,452.0
12/12	570.4	70.9	12.4%	1,321.0
12/11	529.2	53.2	10.1%	1,265.0
Annual Growth	11.0%	14.7%	—	9.9%

2015 Year-End Financials

Debt ratio: —
Return on equity: 18.8%
Cash ($ mil.): 78.6
Current ratio: 4.86
Long-term debt ($ mil.): —
No. of shares (mil.): 34.8
Dividends
Yield: —
Payout: —
Market value ($ mil.): 1,711.0

	STOCK PRICE ($) FY Close	P/E High/Low	Earnings	Dividends	Book Value
12/15	49.08	20 17	2.60	0.00	14.86
12/14	48.86	24 16	2.49	0.00	12.98
12/13	55.09	25 15	2.24	0.00	11.34
12/12	34.15	26 11	1.94	1.50	9.13
12/11	36.93	29 19	1.47	0.00	8.77
Annual Growth	7.4%		15.4%	—	14.1%

Douglas Dynamics, Inc.

Let it snow Let it snow Let it snow! It's a song made to order for Douglas Dynamics. The company makes snowplows and sand-and-salt spreading equipment for light trucks. One of the biggest manufacturers in its industry the company sells its lineup under brand names Western Fisher Snowex Turfex Sweepex and Blizzard via equipment distributors. It also supplies related parts and accessories. End customers are mainly snowplowers in the business of removing snow and ice for municipalities and commercial and private owners in the Midwest East and Northeast US as well as throughout Canada. Douglas traces its roots back to the 1970s.

Geographic Reach

Douglas has manufacturing facilities in Milwaukee; Rockland Maine; and Madison Heights Michigan. Most of its distributors are located throughout the snow belt regions in North America (primarily the Midwest East and Northeast regions of the US as well as all provinces of Canada) and also cater to many parts of Europe and China.

Sales and Marketing

The company sells its products through a distributor network primarily to professional snowplowers who are contracted to remove snow and ice from commercial municipal and residential areas. Douglas spent $4.5 million $4.3 million and $3 million for 2015 2014 and 2013 respectively on advertising expenses.

Financial Performance

Douglas experienced unprecedented growth for 2015 with revenues peaking at a record-setting $400 million and profits reaching $44 million another company milestone. In addition its cash flow from operations jumped 5% in 2015. The historic growth for 2015 was fueled by a 37% surge in equipment sales and an additional $96 million in sales from a previous acquisition.

Strategy

Douglas has cultivated sales by gradually expanding its distribution relationships and by purchasing related businesses. In 2014 it acquired Henderson Products a North American manufacturer of customized turnkey snow and ice control equipment for heavy-duty trucks focused on government departments for $95 million. The purchase strengthened its market position in snow and ice control across all truck segments and created new opportunities for growth in attractive adjacent markets. It also contributed to Douglas' milestone revenue totals for 2015.

EXECUTIVES

Chairman President and CEO, James L. Janik, $490,348 total compensation
EVP and CFO, Robert McCormick, $310,724 total compensation
SVP Sales and Marketing, Mark Adamson, age 59, $237,461 total compensation
SVP Operations, Keith Hagelin, age 56, $227,660 total compensation
Vice President Of Marketing, Richard (Dick) Burkhardt
Auditors: Deloitte & Touche LLP

LOCATIONS

HQ: Douglas Dynamics, Inc.
7777 North 73rd Street, Milwaukee, WI 53223
Phone: 414 354-2310
Web: www.douglasdynamics.com

PRODUCTS/OPERATIONS

2015 Sales

	$ mil.	% of total
Equipment	349.4	87
Parts & accessories	51.0	13
Total	**400.4**	**100**

Selected Brands

Blizzard
Fisher
Snowex
Sweepex
Turfex
Western

COMPETITORS

Dana	Visteon
Johnson Controls	ZF Friedrichshafen
Tenneco	

HISTORICAL FINANCIALS

Company Type: Public

Income Statement
FYE: December 31

	REVENUE ($ mil.)	NET INCOME ($ mil.)	NET PROFIT MARGIN	EMPLOYEES
12/15	400.4	44.1	11.0%	1,104.0
12/14	303.5	39.9	13.2%	993.0
12/13	194.3	11.6	6.0%	520.0
12/12	140.0	6.0	4.3%	465.0
12/11	208.8	19.0	9.1%	525.0
Annual Growth	17.7%	23.4%	—	20.4%

2015 Year-End Financials

Debt ratio: 36.8%
Return on equity: 23.6%
Cash ($ mil.): 36.8
Current ratio: 4.06
Long-term debt ($ mil.): 184.8
No. of shares (mil.): 22.3
Dividends
Yield: 4.2%
Payout: 45.8%
Market value ($ mil.): 472.0

	STOCK PRICE ($) FY Close	P/E High/Low	Earnings	Dividends	Book Value
12/15	21.07	12 10	1.94	0.89	8.96
12/14	21.43	14 8	1.77	0.87	7.78
12/13	16.82	33 25	0.51	0.84	6.99
12/12	14.39	58 47	0.26	0.82	6.95
12/11	14.62	19 14	0.85	1.18	7.42
Annual Growth	9.6%		22.9%	(6.7%)	4.8%

Dril-Quip Inc

Dril-Quip equips the folks who operate the expensive drills –the global deepwater oil and gas industry. The company specializes in deepwater harsh-environment and/or severe-condition equipment. Its products include drilling and production riser systems subsea and surface wellheads and production trees mudline hanger systems (which support the weight of each casing string at the mudline) and specialty connectors and pipe. Dril-Quip's offshore rig equipment includes drilling and completion riser systems wellhead connectors and diverters. The company also provides reconditioning tool rental and technical advisory services.

Geographic ReachDril-Quip's operations are organized into three geographic segments: Western

Hemisphere (including North and South America; headquartered in Houston) Eastern Hemisphere (including Europe and Africa; headquartered in Aberdeen Scotland) and Asia/Pacific (including the Pacific Rim Southeast Asia Australia India and the Middle East; headquartered in Singapore).Each of these segments sells similar products and services and the company has major manufacturing facilities in all three of its headquarter locations as well as in Macae Brazil. Dril-Quip has sales service and reconditioning facilities in Australia China Denmark Egypt Ghana the Netherlands Nigeria Norway Qatar and the US. In 2014 the company generated 63% of its total revenues outside of the US.OperationsDril-Quip's revenues are generated from two sources: products and services. Product revenues are derived from the sale of offshore drilling and production equipment. Service revenues are earned when the company provides technical advisory assistance services for installation of Dril-Quip's products reconditioning services of its customer-owned products and rental of running tools for installation and retrieval of the company's products. In 2014 Dril-Quip derived 83% of its revenues from the sale of products and 17% from services (compared to 84% and 16% in 2013).

Sales and Marketing

Dril-Quip markets its products through its offices and sales representatives in the world's major energy markets. It markets its products and services directly through its sales personnel in two US and 20 international locations. In addition in some international markets where the company does not maintain offices it sells through independent sales representatives. The company has sales representatives in Brazil China India Indonesia Malaysia Saudi Arabia and the UAE. Sales are geared at major integrated large independent and foreign national oil and gas companies. A portion of its customer base consists of offshore drilling contractors and engineering and construction companies.

Dril-Quip advertises its products and services in trade and technical publications and participates in industry conferences and trade shows to enhance industry awareness of its products.

The company is not dependent on any one customer; its top 15 customers represented 61% of total revenues in 2014.Financial Performance

In 2014 Dril-Quip's net revenues increased by 7%. Product revenues increased due to higher subsea and offshore rig equipment sales partially offset by sales decreases in surface equipment. The increase in subsea equipment revenues came from higher demand in the Gulf of Mexico. Product revenues increased in the Western Hemisphere by $10.2 million by $19.1 million in the Eastern Hemisphere and and by $12.3 million in the Asia-Pacific region. The company reported increased service revenues in the Western Hemisphere by $2.2 million $13.1 million in the Eastern Hemisphere and $1.7 million in the Asia-Pacific region.Dril-Quip's net income increased by 23% in 2014 due to higher net sales. Cash from operating activities decreased by 8% due to an increase in trade receivables and inventories.

Strategy

The company continually introduces new products and product enhancements and sees its ability to develop new products and maintain technological advantages as key to its future success. Dril-Quip has introduced multiple new products including liner hangers subsea control systems and subsea manifolds.Dril-Quip's product development work is conducted at its facilities in Houston Texas and Aberdeen Scotland. The company's applica-

tion engineering staff provides engineering services to customers in connection with the design and sales of its products. The company's global manufacturing and servicing locations allow it to have short supply lines and delivery times for its clients in far-flung oil and gas fields worldwide. It continued its work on several dry tree field development projects in 2014 and completed the manufacturing testing and delivery of dry tree systems for Brazil's first Tension Leg Production Platform. Several additional large-scale dry tree projects moved through the design engineering manufacturing assembly and test stages in preparation for delivery to major operators for installation in the Gulf of Mexico and the Asia-Pacific region. The company's Aftermarket Services department has demonstrated that it will be a vital component of the company's overall strategic plan going forward.Mergers and AcquisitionsIn 2016 the company agreed to acquire TIW Corporation (a 100-year old industry-leading manufacturer of downhole products for the global oil and gas market) for $143 million.Company BackgroundTaking advantage of its strong manufacturing presence in Brazil in 2012 Dril-Quip secured a $650 million four-year contract from PETROBRAS to supply subsea wellhead systems and associated tools to be used in the drilling of deepwater wells offshore Brazil.

Expanding its manufacturing base in 2011 Dril-Quip opened a new manufacturing plant in Singapore valued at $33.2 million.

Dril-Quip was founded in 1981.

EXECUTIVES

VP Finance and CFO, Jerry M. Brooks, age 65, $395,000 total compensation
President and CEO, Blake T. DeBerry, $680,000 total compensation
SVP and COO, James A. Gariepy, $625,000 total compensation
VP General Counsel and Secretary, James C. Webster, $355,000 total compensation
Vice President Corporate Development, Thomas (ted) (Thom) Owen
Vice President Sales and Marketing, JR Bateman
Chairman, John V. Lovoi, age 55
Auditors: PricewaterhouseCoopers LLP

LOCATIONS

HQ: Dril-Quip Inc
6401 N. Eldridge Parkway, Houston, TX 77041
Phone: 713 939-7711   **Fax:** 713 939-8063
Web: www.dril-quip.com

PRODUCTS/OPERATIONS

2014 Sales

	% of total
Product	83
Service	17
Total	**100**

Selected Products and Services

Products Group
Diverters
Drilling riser systems
Mudline hanger systems
Platform production trees
Platform wellheads
Production risers
Specialty connectors
Subsea production trees
Subsea wellheads
Surface wellheads
Wellhead connectors
Valves

Well systems
Services Group
Field installation
Reconditioning
Rental

COMPETITORS

ABB	Hornbeck Offshore
Aker Solutions	McDermott
Atwood Oceanics	Newpark Resources
Cameron International	Oceaneering
FMC Technologies	International
GE Oil	Parker Drilling
Global Power Equipment	Siem Offshore
GulfMark Offshore	Superior Energy
Helix Energy Solutions	Tesco Corporation
Hercules Offshore	

HISTORICAL FINANCIALS

Company Type: Public

Income Statement   FYE: December 31

	REVENUE ($ mil.)	NET INCOME ($ mil.)	NET PROFIT MARGIN	EMPLOYEES
12/15	844.3	192.0	22.7%	2,319.0
12/14	930.9	208.7	22.4%	2,720.0
12/13	872.3	169.8	19.5%	2,637.0
12/12	733.0	119.2	16.3%	2,451.0
12/11	601.3	95.2	15.8%	2,194.0
Annual Growth	8.9%	19.2%	—	1.4%

2015 Year-End Financials

Debt ratio: —	No. of shares (mil.): 37.9
Return on equity: 14.9%	Dividends
Cash ($ mil.): 381.3	Yield: —
Current ratio: 11.15	Payout: —
Long-term debt ($ mil.): —	Market value ($ mil.): 2,248.0

	STOCK PRICE ($) FY Close	P/E High/Low	PER SHARE ($) Earnings	Dividends	Book Value
12/15	59.23	16 11	4.98	0.00	34.90
12/14	76.73	22 13	5.19	0.00	31.98
12/13	109.93	29 17	4.16	0.00	30.54
12/12	73.05	26 20	2.94	0.00	26.35
12/11	65.82	34 21	2.36	0.00	23.03
Annual Growth	(2.6%)	— —	20.5%	—	11.0%

Eagle Bancorp Inc (MD)

For those nest eggs that need a little help hatching holding company Eagle Bancorp would recommend its community-oriented EagleBank subsidiary. The bank serves businesses and individuals through more than 20 branches in Maryland Virginia and Washington DC and its suburbs. Deposit products include checking savings and money market accounts; certificates of deposit; and IRAs. Commercial real estate loans represent more than 70% of its loan portfolio while construction loans make up another more than 20%. The bank which has significant expertise as a Small Business Administration lender also writes business consumer and home equity loans. EagleBank offers insurance products through an agreement with The Meltzer Group.

OperationsLike other retail banks Eagle Bancorp makes the bulk of its money from loan interest. About 86% of its total revenue came from loan interest (including fees) during 2015 while another 4% came from interest on investment securities. The rest of its revenue came from deposit account service charges (2% of revenue) and non-recurring income sources.The bank has two direct subsidiaries: Bethesda Leasing LLC which holds the bank's foreclosed real estate (owned and acquired); and Eagle Insurance Services LLC which provides commercial and retail insurance products through a referral arrangement with insurance broker The Meltzer Group.Geographic ReachThe Bethesda Maryland-based bank operates 21 branches in Maryland Virginia and Washington DC (as of mid-2016) including nine in Northern Virginia seven in Montgomery County and five in the District of Columbia.Sales and MarketingEagle Bancorp serves local businesses professional clients individuals sole proprietors small and medium-sized businesses non-profits and investors. Other clients are from the healthcare accountant and attorney markets.The bank spent $2.7 million on marketing and advertising during 2015 up 38% from the $2 million it spent in 2014 mostly due to higher digital and print advertising and sponsorship costs.Financial Performance

Eagle Bancorp's annual revenue has more than doubled since 2011 mostly thanks to strong loan growth with the addition of new branches. Meanwhile its net income has more than tripled as the bank has kept a lid on credit loss provisions and overhead costs.The bank's revenue jumped 33% to $279.8 million during 2015 largely thanks to a rise in interest income as its loan assets grew 16%. Strong revenue growth in 2015 coupled with an absence of merger expenses drove Eagle Bancorp's net income up 55% to $84.1 million. The bank's operating cash levels spiked 66% to $98.5 million for the year thanks to a strong rise in cash-based earnings.

Strategy

The company has been focused on growing within its existing markets. Its strategy for further growth includes continuing to seek opportunities to open or acquire new banking locations while waiting out record low interest rates. Eagle's strict loan underwriting standards –it didn't write subprime residential mortgages and didn't buy securities backed by subprime mortgages –has helped it have fewer problem loans the downfall for many banks.Beyond its core lending and deposit businesses Eagle Bancorp continues to expand its other product offerings as well. In 2015 it introduced a Full Service Equipment Leasing program which provided alternative and convenient financing for all types of business equipment for customers.Mergers and AcquisitionsIn November 2014 Eagle Bancorp significantly expanded its presence in Northern Virginia after it purchased Fairfax County-based Virginia Heritage. The deal added six Virginia Heritage Bank branches (renamed as EagleBank) in northern Virginia along with $917.4 million in assets –including $715 million in loans and $737 million in deposits.

EXECUTIVES

EVP and CFO Eagle Bancorp and EagleBank, James H. Langmead, age 67, $354,524 total compensation

EVP Eagle Bancorp and SEVP and COO EagleBank, Susan G. Riel, age 67, $456,006 total compensation

Chairman President and CEO Eagle Bancorp Chairman and CEO EagleBank and President Ronald D. Paul Companies, Ronald D. Paul, age 61, $863,565 total compensation

EVP and Chief Credit Officer EagleBank, Janice L. Williams, age 59, $340,659 total compensation

EVP and General Counsel Eagle Bancorp and EagleBank, Laurence E. Bensignor, age 60

EVP and Chief Lending Officer Commercial Real Estate EagleBank, Antonio F. Marquez, age 58, $320,049 total compensation

EVP and Chief Lending Officer Commercial and Industrial EagleBank, Lindsey S. Rheaume, age 56

EVP and CFO, Charles D. Levingston

Vice President, Joan Grant

Executive Vice President, Susan Schumacher

Senior Vice President Operations, Terry (Terr) Clarke

Vice President Of Marketing, Jane Cornett

Senior Vice President Commercial Banking Team Leader, Derek Whitwer

Vice President Commercial Real Estate Lender, Timothy Annett

Vice President and Credit Analyst Ii, Jackie (Jack) Ho

Senior Vice President, Elizabeth Ferrenz

Underwriting Manager Assistant Vice President, Cathy (Cat) Clarke

Assistant Vice President Business Relationship Manager, Pfashema Faber

Vice President, Samantha Perry

Vice President and Senior Portfolio Manager, Michael (Mel) Benedict

Assistant Vice President Branch Service Manager, Rosalind Alexander

Vice President Facilities Operations Manager, Shawn Cox

Vice President, Jacqueline Ames

Senior Vice President Commercial Banking Team Leader, Derek (Der) Whitwer

Assistant Vice President Branch Service Manager, Catalina Racu

Vice President Treasury Management, Mary (Mar) Nord

Vice President Treasurer, Scott Clark

Auditors: Dixon Hughes Goodman LLP

LOCATIONS

HQ: Eagle Bancorp Inc (MD)
7830 Old Georgetown Road, Third Floor, Bethesda, MD 20814
Phone: 301 986-1800
Web: www.eaglebankcorp.com

PRODUCTS/OPERATIONS

Selected Subsidiaries
EagleBank
  Bethesda Leasing LLC
  Eagle Insurance Services LLC
  Fidelity Mortgage Inc.
Eagle Commercial Ventures LLC

COMPETITORS

BB&T	OBA Financial Services
Bank of America	PNC Financial
Capital One	Sandy Spring Bancorp
M&T Bank	SunTrust

HISTORICAL FINANCIALS

Company Type: Public

Income Statement

FYE: December 31

	ASSETS ($ mil.)	NET INCOME ($ mil.)	INCOME AS % OF ASSETS	EMPLOYEES
12/15	6,076.6	84.1	1.4%	434.0
12/14	5,247.8	54.2	1.0%	427.0
12/13	3,771.5	47.0	1.2%	386.0
12/12	3,409.4	35.2	1.0%	393.0
12/11	2,831.2	24.5	0.9%	338.0
Annual Growth	21.0%	36.1%	—	6.4%

2015 Year-End Financials

Return on assets: 1.4%
Return on equity: 12.3%
Long-term debt ($ mil.): —
No. of shares (mil.): 33.4
Sales ($ mil): 279.8

Dividends
  Yield: —
  Payout: —
Market value ($ mil.): 1,689.0

	STOCK PRICE ($) FY Close	P/E High/Low	PER SHARE ($) Earnings	Dividends	Book Value
12/15	50.47	22 13	2.50	0.00	22.07
12/14	35.52	18 15	1.95	0.00	20.60
12/13	30.63	18 11	1.76	0.00	15.22
12/12	19.97	14 10	1.46	0.00	13.86
12/11	14.54	14 11	1.04	0.00	12.15
Annual Growth	36.5%	— —	24.6%	—	16.1%

Eagle Materials Inc

Eagle Materials is perched near the top of the building materials business. The company manufactures and distributes cement and gypsum wallboard which together account for nearly 75% of its total sales. Eagle Materials also produces ready-mix concrete aggregates and recycled paperboard. Its products are sold to residential commercial and industrial construction customers throughout the US. The company operates about 25 plants and manufacturing facilities. It also has about 100 railcars for shipping its wallboard products to customers across the country. Founded in 1963 Eagle Materials was spun off by homebuilder Centex Corporation in 2004.

Operations

Eagle Materials operates five main business segments: Cement Concrete and Aggregates Gypsum Wallboard Recycled Paperboard and Oil and Gas Proppants. Cement sales accounts for nearly 40% of Eagle's total sales while Gypsum Wallboard accounts for another 35%. Its Paperboard and Concrete and Aggregates segments each make up another roughly 10% of total sales while Oil and Gas Proppants generate around 5%. In addition to wholly-owned plants in Illinois Wyoming and Nevada Eagle owns a 50% stake in Texas Lehigh Cement Co. in Buda Texas. Eagle manufactures gypsum wallboard at five plants representing about 35% of sales. Republic Paperboard Co. the company's paperboard business is located in Oklahoma and accounts for about 20% Eagle's sales. Concrete and aggregates make up the rest.

Geographic Reach

Dallas-based Eagle Materials sells its gypsum wallboard throughout the US focusing on markets nearest its production facilities. The company sells cement in six regional markets including northern

Nevada and California the greater Chicago area the Rocky Mountain region the Central Plains region and Texas.Sales and MarketingMost of the demand for Eagle's cement products come from the infrastructure commercial construction and residential construction. About 50% of the total demand comes from public works infrastructure projects.

Financial Performance

Eagle's sales and profits have been rising at a healthy clip over the past few years thanks to increased demand for cement concrete and other aggregate materials amidst the strengthening US economy. The company's more recent Oil and Gas Proppants business has also been boosting annual sales.Eagle Materials' revenue jumped by 19% to a record $1.07 billion in fiscal 2015 (ended March) thanks to a combination of its CRS acquisition in the Oil and Proppants business higher average net selling prices across all of its materials segments and higher sales volumes across all segments except aggregates. Higher revenue in FY2015 drove the company's profits higher by 50% to $186.85 million (the highest level since 2007) while operating cash spiked by 37% to $234.12 million thanks to higher cash earnings.

Strategy

Strengthened demand for construction products as the US economy has gained steam has buoyed Eagle's prospects for 2015 and beyond. With its cement sales network spanning the entire nation and with infrastructure spending industrial construction and residential building activity expected to heat up the company anticipated that calender year 2015 would be good for cement demand across all of its regional cement markets.Besides growing on its own the company likes to acquire aggregate cement or other raw building materialproducers that complement or bolster its material product offerings. In recent years the company has been looking to acquire frac-sand producers to expand its service offerings in lucrative shale regions.Mergers and AcquisitionsIn 2014 Eagle Materials agreed to purchase CRS Proppants as well as its subsidiaries including Great Northern Sand LLC which has long supplied high-quality northern-white frac-sand to the energy industry. The company expressed that CRS Proppants' services were highly complementary to its own frac-sand operations.Eagle's Audubon Materials subsidiary agreed in late 2012 to purchase a pair of cement plants in Missouri and Oklahoma from rival Lafarge North America for about $446 million in cash. The purchase which included six distribution terminals two aggregates quarries eight ready-mix concrete plants and a fly ash business marked Eagle's return to acquisition mode. Company BackgroundPrior to the recession the firm had designs on expansion especially in its core wallboard and cement business. The company opened a fifth gypsum wallboard plant in 2007 to increase production capacity but the addition proved untimely.

EXECUTIVES

Vice President Finance, William R (Bill) Devlin
EVP Strategy Corporate Development and Communications, Robert S. (Bob) Stewart, age 62, $212,020 total compensation
EVP General Counsel and Secretary, James H. (Jim) Graass, age 58, $365,000 total compensation
EVP Cement Aggregates and Concrete, Gerald J. (Gerry) Essl, age 66, $386,000 total compensation
President and CEO, David B. (Dave) Powers, age 66, $386,000 total compensation
EVP Finance and Administration and CFO, D. Craig Kesler, age 40, $363,000 total compensation

COO, Michael Haack, $166,667 total compensation
Senior Vice President Finance And Treasurer, Arthur R Zunker, age 74
Chairman, Laurence E. (Larry) Hirsch, age 70
Auditors: Ernst & Young LLP

LOCATIONS

HQ: Eagle Materials Inc
  3811 Turtle Creek Blvd., Suite 1100, Dallas, TX 75219
Phone: 214 432-2000   **Fax:** 214 432-2100
Web: www.eaglematerials.com

PRODUCTS/OPERATIONS

2015 Sales

	$ mil.	% of total
Cement	488.6	39
Gypsum wallboard	437.5	35
Recycled paperboard	142.8	11
Concrete & aggregates	107.9	9
Oil and Gas Proppants	81.4	6
Adjustments	(191.8)	-
Total	**1,066.4**	**100**

Selected Subsidiaries

American Gypsum Company
Centex Materials
Illinois Cement Company
Mathews Readymix
Mountain Cement Company
Nevada Cement Company
Republic Paperboard Company
Texas Leigh Cement Company (50%)
Western Aggregates

COMPETITORS

Boral	Martin Marietta
CEMEX Inc.	Aggregates
Caraustar	Martin Marietta
Georgia-Pacific	Materials
Holcim (US)	New NGC
Lafarge North America	TXI
Lehigh Cement	U.S. Concrete
Lehigh Hanson	USG

HISTORICAL FINANCIALS

Company Type: Public

Income Statement

FYE: March 31

	REVENUE ($ mil.)	NET INCOME ($ mil.)	NET PROFIT MARGIN	EMPLOYEES
03/16	1,143.4	152.5	13.3%	2,000.0
03/15	1,066.3	186.8	17.5%	2,000.0
03/14	898.4	124.2	13.8%	1,800.0
03/13	642.5	57.7	9.0%	1,800.0
03/12	495.0	18.7	3.8%	1,350.0
Annual Growth	**23.3%**	**68.9%**	**—**	**10.3%**

2016 Year-End Financials

Debt ratio: 26.9%	No. of shares (mil.): 48.5
Return on equity: 14.8%	Dividends
Cash ($ mil.): 5.3	Yield: 0.5%
Current ratio: 3.15	Payout: 12.5%
Long-term debt ($ mil.): 499.7	Market value ($ mil.): 3,402.0

	STOCK PRICE ($) FY Close	P/E High/Low		PER SHARE ($) Earnings	Dividends	Book Value
03/16	70.11	28	15	3.05	0.40	21.44
03/15	83.56	28	19	3.71	0.40	20.11
03/14	88.66	36	24	2.49	0.40	16.61
03/13	66.63	58	24	1.22	0.40	14.06
03/12	34.75	85	37	0.42	0.30	10.44
Annual Growth	**19.2%**	**—**	**—**	**64.2%**	**7.5%**	**19.7%**

Ebix Inc

Ebix knows a lot about the insurance biz. The company sells insurance industry software products and professional services to property/casualty insurers brokerages and individuals in Asia Australia Europe and North America. The company's EbixExchange service acts as an online auction house where buyers and carriers can exchange bids for auto home health life and other types of insurance while paying Ebix a fee on each transaction. Ebix also provides agency management software that includes workflow and customer relationship management (CRM) capabilities as well as other back-office functions for insurance brokers and insurance carriers. The company generates most of its sales in North America.

Operations

About 80% of Ebix's revenue is generated by on-demand insurance Exchanges including life insurance annuity employee benefits and property and casualty exchanges. In addition to its insurance exchanges and software products Ebix also offers custom software development and business process outsourcing (BPO) services.

Geographic Reach

Atlanta-based Ebix's #1 market is the US accounting for nearly 70% of its sales. Australia accounts for about 17%. The firm's international operations are managed from Singapore. The company has more than 35 offices across the US Australia Singapore New Zealand Canada China Japan and India.

Financial Performance

Ebix registered a decade of growing revenue in 2014 posting $214.3 million a 5% increase from 2013. The company netted new clients during the year and sold additional products and services to existing customers. Contributions from recent acquisition also helped boost revenue.

The company's net income climbed out of two years of declines posting net income of $63.5 million. That was a 7% increase from 2013. Besides higher revenue the company benefited from a decline in non-operating expenses in comparison to 2013 which had security litigation costs.

Strategy

Ebix recently experienced a failed bid by an affiliate of Goldman Sachs to take it private. In May 2013 Goldman Sachs offered to buy Ebix for $820 million but decided to nix the deal a month later after Ebix was notified about an investigation into allegations of intentional misconduct over a pending shareholder class action lawsuit. Ebix had been transparent about the lawsuit which was filed before the proposed acquisition. In 2014 the lawsuit was settled.

Mergers and Acquisitions

Ebix is an acquisitive company that buys others to expand its product lines customer base and geographic footprint.In 2014 it snapped up five companies.

Two of the purchase were for more than $20 million each. For $27 million Ebix acquired Vertex a software company focused on life and annuity insurance. Ebix wants to include Vertex's products into a management consulting practice for insurance health care and financial services. Oakstone Publishing a provider of continuing education and certification for health care professionals was purchased for about $23 million and integrated into Ebix's ADAM Health Information Exchange Division.

Perhaps the most curious of the company's 2014 acquisition was CurePet an insurance exchange that connects pet owners referring veterinarians animal hospitals academic institutes and pet supply companies.

It also bought Healthcare Magic whose “Ask a Doctor” service allows patients to pose a question to a network of 15000 physicians and DCM Group known as i3 Software an insurance software company.

EXECUTIVES

Chairman President and CEO, Robin Raina, age 47, $1,300,000 total compensation
EVP and Corporate Officer of Mergers & Acquisitions and Special Projects, Robert F. (Bob) Kerris, age 62, $225,000 total compensation
SVP Agency Systems, Graham Prior, age 59, $154,126 total compensation
SVP Ebix Health, James (Jim) Senge, age 55, $225,000 total compensation
EVP and Managing Director Ebix Australia Group Head, Leon d'Apice, age 59, $164,250 total compensation
Managing Director Ebix New Zealand, Tony Wisniewski
Head of Enterprise Solutions EbixExchange, Ash Sawhney
CFO, Sean T. Donaghy, age 51
Vice President Of Operations, Ashley Franco
Corporate Vice President And Division Head; Information Technology Director, Rahul Raina
Vice President, Val Moeller
Vice President Information Technology, Gagan Sethi
Vice President Product Development, Valerie (Val) Troffer
Senior Vice President, Steve (Stevie) Isaac
Vice President Sales, Jose Lopez
Vice President Education, Shannon McGuire
Assistant Vice President Professional Services, Albert Golbasarians
Vice President Sales, David Greiff
Vice President Of Major Accounts, Juls Owensby
Vice President, Alex Mattelaer
Vice President Solution Architecture and Implementation, Andy Labrot
Auditors: Cherry Bekaert LLP

LOCATIONS

HQ: Ebix Inc
1 Ebix Way, Johns Creek, GA 30097
Phone: 678 281-2020
Web: www.ebix.com

PRODUCTS/OPERATIONS

2014 Sales

	$ mil.	% of total
Exchanges	169.4	79
Risk Compliance Solutions	21.8	9
Broker systems	17.9	10
Carrier systems	5.2	2
Total	**214.3**	**100**

COMPETITORS

Answer Financial	Guidewire Software
Applied Systems	InsWeb
BenefitMall	Intuit
CCC Information	Life Quotes
Computer Sciences	SunGard
Corp.	The Hartford
Cover-All	TriZetto
Crawford & Company	Vertafore
Datamonitor	

HISTORICAL FINANCIALS

Company Type: Public

Income Statement

FYE: December 31

	REVENUE ($ mil.)	NET INCOME ($ mil.)	NET PROFIT MARGIN	EMPLOYEES
12/15	265.4	79.5	30.0%	2,707.0
12/14	214.3	63.5	29.7%	2,343.0
12/13	204.7	59.2	29.0%	1,927.0
12/12	199.3	70.5	35.4%	1,903.0
12/11	168.9	71.3	42.2%	1,426.0
Annual Growth	12.0%	2.7%	—	17.4%

2015 Year-End Financials

Debt ratio: 30.6%
Return on equity: 18.9%
Cash ($ mil.): 57.1
Current ratio: 2.28
Long-term debt ($ mil.): 206.5

No. of shares (mil.): 100.2
Dividends
Yield: 0.9%
Payout: 41.6%
Market value ($ mil.): 3,287.0

	STOCK PRICE ($) FY Close	P/E High/Low	PER SHARE ($) Earnings	Dividends	Book Value
12/15	32.79	50 21	0.76	0.30	4.08
12/14	16.99	32 22	0.10	0.30	3.98
12/13	14.71	39 18	0.51	0.23	3.66
12/12	16.12	41 25	0.60	0.19	3.30
12/11	22.10	47 22	0.58	0.00	2.90
Annual Growth	10.4%	— —	6.8%	—	8.9%

Echo Global Logistics Inc

By land air or sea Echo Global Logistics can help you deliver the goods. The company provides a wide range of transportation and logistics services such as carrier management rate negotiation freight bill audit and payment routing compliance and shipment execution and tracking. In addition its Evolved Transportation Manager (ETM) software analyzes clients' transportation needs and helps reduce costs as well as manages all procedures in shipping. Established in 2005 Echo Global Logistics customer base are primarily companies in the manufacturing and consumer products industries.

Geographic Reach
Echo is stationed in Chicago and has about 30 business development locations spanning 15 US states.

Operations
About 30000 transportation providers make up Echo's carrier network which consists of small and midsized fleets trucking companies and single-truck owners. Less-than-truckload and truckload services collectively account for about 90% of its total revenue.

Sales and Marketing
The company caters to nearly 28500 clients which are divided into two types: enterprise (under multiyear contracts) and transactional (services provided on a shipment-by-shipment basis). For 2014 transactional clients represented 74% of its total revenue.

Financial Performance

Echo has experienced unprecedented growth over the last few years as it maintains a very impressive balance sheet. Revenues jumped 33% from $884 million in 2013 to reach roughly $1.2 billion in 2014 a historical milestone. Profits also spiked 18% to reach a record-high of $17 million in 2014 due to the recent surge in revenues and lower interest expenses. In addition Echo has experienced a steady increase from its operating cash flow each year.

The historic growth for 2014 was attributed to a major increase in its number of customers coupled with the uptick in shipment volumes. Revenue from enterprise clients jumped 13% in 2014 while revenue from transactional clients spiked 41%. Most of this growth was fueled by additional revenue from previous acquisitions.

Strategy
Although Echo's focus is on truckload (TL) less than truckload (LTL) and small parcel delivery; the company also offers intermodal (combination of rail and truck) air delivery. The company will continue to expand its geographic reach both through air and ocean modes of delivery; this strategy involves both the launching of new services and the purchasing of other businesses.

In early 2015 Echo acquired Xpress Solutions a transportation brokerage headquartered in Frankfort Illinois that caters to a portfolio of small and middle market shippers. In 2014 the company completed two acquisitions: Comcar Logistics a non-asset-based truckload brokerage based in Jacksonville Florida; and One Stop Logistics a transportation brokerage headquartered in Watsonville California. The Comcar acquisition strengthened the company's presence in the Southeastern US and Colorado whereas One Stop Logistics (purchased for $37 million) expanded its national coverage and and carrier network.

EXECUTIVES

COO, David B. (Dave) Menzel, age 54, $500,000 total compensation
Chairman and CEO, Douglas R. (Doug) Waggoner, age 57, $650,000 total compensation
CIO, Tim Kutz
CFO, Kyle L. Sauers, $325,000 total compensation
SVP Marketing, Christopher N. Clemmensen
Vice President Of Carrier Sales, Jay Gustafson
National Account Manager, John (Jack) Keating
National Account Manager, Matt (Matty) Szafranski
National Account Manager, Drew (Andrew) Evans
National Account Manager, Megan (Meg) Kidd
Executive Vice President, Andy Arquette
National Account Manager, Kevin Holtrup
National Account Manager, Daniel Kanter
National Account Manager, Brandon (Bran) Gardner
National Account Manager, Ben Boelter
National Account Manager, Jason Agostino
National Account Manager, Dustin Williams
National Account Manager, Natalie Benedettini
National Account Manager, Alex Fitzpatrick
National Account Manager, Bill Brown
National Account Manager, Stephanie Johnson
National Account Manager, Chris Silungan
National Account Manager, Bernard Hurley
Regional Vice President, Greg Sanossian
Senior Vice President Of Marketing, Chris Clemmensen
National Accounts Manager, Michael (Mel) Sacks
National Account Manager, Teresa (Terry) Unkovich
Auditors: Ernst & Young LLP

LOCATIONS

HQ: Echo Global Logistics Inc
600 West Chicago Avenue, Suite 725, Chicago, IL 60654
Phone: 800 354-7993
Web: www.echo.com

PRODUCTS/OPERATIONS

2014 Sales

	% of total
TL	53
LTL	37
Intermodal	6
Small Parts	3
Transportation	1
Total	**100**

Selected Services

Domestic Air and Expedited Services
Flex TMS (a fee-based "software-as-a-service" transportation management system)
Inter-Modal
International air and ocean transportation services
Less than Truckload (LTL)
Small Parcel
Truckload

COMPETITORS

ABF Freight System
C.H. Robinson Worldwide
Expeditors
FedEx
J.B. Hunt
MIQ Logistics
Ozburn-Hessey Logistics
Roadrunner Transportation Systems
Ryder System
Schneider Logistics
Total Quality Logistics
Transplace
UPS

HISTORICAL FINANCIALS

Company Type: Public

Income Statement

FYE: December 31

	REVENUE ($ mil.)	NET INCOME ($ mil.)	NET PROFIT MARGIN	EMPLOYEES
12/15	1,512.3	7.8	0.5%	2,335.0
12/14	1,173.3	16.7	1.4%	1,734.0
12/13	884.1	14.2	1.6%	1,297.0
12/12	757.6	12.3	1.6%	1,364.0
12/11	602.7	12.0	2.0%	913.0
Annual Growth	25.9%	(10.2%)	—	26.5%

2015 Year-End Financials

Debt ratio: 26.5%
Return on equity: 2.7%
Cash ($ mil.): 56.5
Current ratio: 1.90
Long-term debt ($ mil.): 198.4

No. of shares (mil.): 29.7
Dividends
Yield: —
Payout: —
Market value ($ mil.): 606.0

	STOCK PRICE ($) FY Close	P/E High/Low		PER SHARE ($) Earnings	Dividends	Book Value
12/15	20.39	118	59	0.28	0.00	13.30
12/14	29.20	41	22	0.71	0.00	7.84
12/13	21.48	36	28	0.61	0.00	6.95
12/12	17.97	35	29	0.54	0.00	6.21
12/11	16.15	33	21	0.53	0.00	5.39
Annual Growth	6.0%	—	— (14.7%)		—	25.3%

Education Realty Trust Inc

This company can give your college student a home away from home. Education Realty Trust a self-administered real estate investment trust (REIT) develops buys owns and operates residential communities for university students. It owns roughly 50 communities in more than 20 US states consisting of almost 28000 beds in nearly 10500 units. Through its Allen & O'Hara Education Services subsidiary the REIT manages another 20-plus student housing properties owned by others. Education Realty Trust communities offer private rooms as well as amenities such as Internet access fitness centers game rooms dining facilities swimming pools —and even study rooms.

OperationsThe REIT operates three business segments. Collegiate Housing Leasing which brought in 96% of its total revenue in 2014 rents by the bed on an individual basis on its campus properties and includes furnished rooms with utilities cable television and internet service within the rental price. Its Development Consulting Services segment (2% of revenue) provides development consulting services to colleges and universities seeking to modernize their on-campus housing communities. The Management Services segment (2% of revenue) provides third-party management services for other college communities. It managed more than 23 collegiate housing communities with nearly 12800 beds in almost 4080 apartment units on or near 17 university campuses across 10 states during 2014. Geographic ReachEducation Realty Trust has nearly half of its communities in the Mid-Atlantic (including New York Virginia and Connecticut) and South Central (including Texas Kentucky and Missisippi) regions of the US. Nearly one-fifth of its communities are in the Southeast US in the states of Florida Georgia and Alabama. Sales and MarketingEducation Realty Trust spent $4.7 million on advertising in 2014 up from $4.6 million and $3.2 million in 2013 and 2012 respectively.Financial PerformanceThe REIT's revenues and profits have been rising at a healthy clip in recent years as it has expanded its property portfolio through acquisitions and has charged higher rental rates as occupancy rates have risen and the economy has strengthened.Education Realty's revenue jumped by 22% to $226 million in 2014 mostly thanks to higher rental income from a combination of a 2.4% hike in rental rates and a 0.7% improvement in occupancy during the year. The REIT's development consulting services revenue more than doubled thanks to new business from Wichita State University and Clarion University. Its management services income grew by 7% thanks to stronger performance in its existing management portfolio.Higher revenue in 2014 caused the REIT's net income to skyrocket more than 10-fold to $47.1 million for the year while its operating cash levels rose by 15% to $89 million on higher cash earnings.StrategyThe REIT seeks to expand its holdings by buying developing or renovating undervalued properties in growing university markets. The company takes into consideration the reputation of the university the proximity of the properties to campus and other factors. It also seeks to build its third-party management services and development consulting services and maximize its net operating income on its properties through "proactive and goal-oriented property management strategies." Education Realty Trust selectively sells its non-core properties to free up resources for investment toward "newer state-of-the-art communities in close proximity to campus" that command higher rental prices. During 2014 for example it sold seven off-campus properties for $138.5 million (netting proceeds of $116.3 million) including its 480-bed Pointe West community (built in 2003) that was two miles away from the University of South Carolina campus and its sale of The Reserve on South College.The REIT may also raise funds through equity offerings to invest in target properties. In 2014 it raised equity proceeds to invest in a collegiate housing community near Arizona State University in Tempe a cottage community near the University of Louisville and the Storrs Center/The Oaks community within walking distance of the University of Connecticut. Company BackgroundIn 2009 it introduced its On-Campus Equity Plan in which it partners with universities to revitalize campus housing.

EXECUTIVES

Vice President, Susan B Arrison
Chairman and CEO, Randall L. (Randy) Churchey, age 56, $529,000 total compensation
VP Corporate Communications and Marketing, Dawn Ray
President, Thomas Trubiana, age 65, $355,350 total compensation
EVP and CFO, Edwin B. (Bill) Brewer, age 53, $285,000 total compensation
EVP and COO, Christine Richards, age 46, $285,000 total compensation
SVP and Chief Information Systems Officer, Randy Simpson
SVP and Chief Accounting Officer, Lindsey Mackie, age 31, $119,504 total compensation
Senior Vice President Of University Partnerships, Julie Skolnicki
Vice President And Chief Accounting Officer, Drew Koester
Vice President Corporate Communications And Marketing, Susan Jennings
Vice President Of Construction, Bob Earwood
Senior Vice President Of Western Development, Steve Schnoor
Vice President Of Real Estate Development, Mark Grambergs
Vice President Of Real Esate Development And Construction, Jeffrey Resetco
Senior Vice President Of University Partnerships, Julie (Jules) Skolnicki
Vice President Of Human Resources, Susan (Sue) Arrison
Vice President Of Client Relations, Brad (Brady) Shaw
Auditors: Deloitte & Touche LLP

LOCATIONS

HQ: Education Realty Trust Inc
999 South Shady Grove Road, Suite 600, Memphis, TN 38120
Phone: 901 259-2500
Web: www.edrtrust.com

PRODUCTS/OPERATIONS

2014 Sales

	$ mil.	% of total
Collegiate housing leasing revenue	206.3	91
Third-party development consulting services	6.8	3
Third-party management Services	4.0	2
Operating expenses reimbursement	8.7	4
Total	**225.8**	**100**

COMPETITORS

AMLI Residential	Camden Property
Alliance Residential	Campus Apartments
American Campus	Fairfield Residential
Communities	JPI
Apartment Investment	Place Properties
and Management	

HISTORICAL FINANCIALS

Company Type: Public

Income Statement
FYE: December 31

	REVENUE ($ mil.)	NET INCOME ($ mil.)	NET PROFIT MARGIN	EMPLOYEES
12/15	255.1	19.9	7.8%	1,237.0
12/14	225.7	47.0	20.8%	1,283.0
12/13	184.3	4.3	2.3%	1,288.0
12/12	144.9	8.4	5.8%	1,222.0
12/11	125.4	(11.0)	—	1,077.0
Annual Growth	19.4%	—	—	3.5%

2015 Year-End Financials

Debt ratio: 31.9%
Return on equity: 1.7%
Cash ($ mil.): 33.7
Current ratio: 0.47
Long-term debt ($ mil.): 638.7

No. of shares (mil.): 56.8
Dividends
  Yield: 3.8%
  Payout: 247.4%
Market value ($ mil.): 2,155.0

	STOCK PRICE ($) FY Close	P/E High/Low		PER SHARE ($) Earnings	Dividends	Book Value
12/15	37.88	99	70	0.40	1.46	21.74
12/14	36.59	34	8	1.09	1.38	20.60
12/13	8.82	98	70	0.12	1.26	18.97
12/12	10.64	49	41	0.24	1.02	20.11
12/11	10.23	—	—	(0.45)	0.72	18.36
Annual Growth	38.7%		—	—	19.3%	4.3%

Eldorado Resorts Inc

Auditors: Ernst & Young LLP

LOCATIONS

HQ: Eldorado Resorts Inc
  100 West Liberty Street, Suite 1150, Reno, NV 89501
Phone: 775 328-0100
Web: www.eldoradoresorts.com

HISTORICAL FINANCIALS

Company Type: Public

Income Statement
FYE: December 31

	REVENUE ($ mil.)	NET INCOME ($ mil.)	NET PROFIT MARGIN	EMPLOYEES
12/15	719.7	114.1	15.9%	7,800.0
12/14	361.8	(14.4)	—	7,100.0
12/13	247.1	18.9	7.6%	0.0
12/12	254.7	(0.9)	—	0.0
Annual Growth	41.4%	—	—	—

2015 Year-End Financials

Debt ratio: 65.3%
Return on equity: 54.0%
Cash ($ mil.): 78.2
Current ratio: 1.10
Long-term debt ($ mil.): 861.7

No. of shares (mil.): 46.8
Dividends
  Yield: —
  Payout: —
Market value ($ mil.): 515.0

	STOCK PRICE ($) FY Close	P/E High/Low		PER SHARE ($) Earnings	Dividends	Book Value
12/15	11.00	5	2	2.43	0.00	5.78
12/14	4.05	—	—	(0.48)	0.00	3.26
12/13	0.00	—	—	0.81	0.00	3.24
Annual Growth	—		—	73.2%	—	33.5%

Electronics for Imaging, Inc.

Electronics For Imaging (EFI) wants to take control of your color. The company makes hardware and software systems for commercial and enterprise digital printing and print management. EFI's Fiery line includes print servers as well as print controllers that copier and printer vendors such as Ricoh Xerox Canon Epson and Konica Minolta integrate into their equipment. EFI's Print MIS (management information systems) software provides supply chain and customer relationship management from job submission to fulfillment. Its Inkjet segment products include super-wide format (VUTEk) and industrial printers (Jetrion). It's also the world's largest manufacturer of digital UV ink.

Operations

EFI's biggest operating segment is Industrial Inkjet which generates 51% of revenue. The unit makes VUTEk and Matan super-wide and wide format printers Reggiani textile printers Jetrion label and packaging equipment and Cretaprint ceramic tile decoration industrial digital inkjet printers.

The productivity software unit 15% of revenue make a software suite for managing business and production workflows for the print and packaging industry.

The Fiery unit 34% of revenue develops digital front ends that transform digital copiers and printers into high performance networked printing devices for the office industrial and commercial printing markets.

Geographic Reach

The company has US manufacturing plants in Arizona Michigan and New Hampshire and international manufacturing operations in Israel.

It has sales and software design offices in Belgium Brazil Canada China Germany India New Zealand the Netherlands the UK and the US.

Sales and Marketing

Its industrial inkjet printers and software are primarily sold through a direct sales force. It also uses the annual EFI Connect trade show and other trade shows (such as Ceramics China Guangzhou for its Cretaprint products for the ceramic tile industry) to generate sales leads.

Its Fiery line of products are sold through printer manufacturers that act as distributors such as Canon/Oce Epson Konica Minolta Kyocera Mita OKI Data Ricoh Sharp and Toshiba.

Xerox has been a big customer accounting for 12% of EFI's revenue for the past three years. Other customers include Fedex Office Staples retail copy and print stores hotel business centers college campuses and libraries commercial photo labs large sign shops graphic screen printers and commercial printers.

Financial Performance

Sales grew 12% in 2015 to a record $882.5 million from $790 million in 2014. Profit slipped 1% to $33.5 million in 2015 with the company investing more in research and development and sales and marketing.

Strategy

Targets for development include scalable digital print controllers and software platforms. Among the company's recent product innovations is PrintMe Mobile which allows direct printing from mobile devices to any networked printer.

The company is leveraging its current products by offering an integrated VUTEK/Fiery/Productivity Software production workflow.

EFI is moving into French- and German-speaking regions of Europe and Africa and into emerging markets in China India and Latin America.

Mergers and Acquisitions

Acquisitions have been a significant part of EFI's strategy. It acquired a handful of companies in 2015 and followed with at least one more in early 2016.

The 2016 deal was for Rialco Limited a European supplier of dye powders and color products for digital print and industrial manufacturing industries. Rialco became part of EFI's industrial inkjet business.

In 2015 EFI bought Matan Digital Printing Ltd. for $29 million in cash adding to EFI's superwide-format display graphics printing products.

EFI purchased Reggiani Macchine in antoehr 2015 deal for $140 million. Reggiani brings an extensive lineup of industrial inkjet printers and will help drive EFI's growth in industrial textile.

In 2015 EFI also acquired Shuttleworth Business Systems a privately held UK print software provider and Corrugated Technologies Inc. a provider of manufacturing execution software for the corrugated packaging market.

HISTORY

Early History

Efi Arazi an MIT-trained engineer started Electronics For Imaging (EFI) in 1989. Arazi one of Israel's high-tech magnates had earlier founded Scitex Corp. a digital printer manufacturer; he later established Imedia a maker of routing systems for digital video; Imedia was acquired by cable modem provider Terayon.

Arazi acquired exclusive rights to an MIT patent that formed EFI's core technology. The company shipped its first Fiery server in 1991 and went public the next year. Its secondary strategy —selling its EfiColor and Cachet Color Editor software alone –failed so in 1993 the company scrapped Cachet making the development and marketing of the Fiery series top priority.

COO Dan Avida became CEO in 1995 replacing Arazi who remained chairman. That year EFI introduced the Fiery XJ series which doubled the speed of its predecessor and allowed easier upgrades. In 1996 EFI formed an alliance with Netherlands-based Océ and introduced a system for Océ's high-speed printers.

Boosting its software development EFI in 1997 bought Pipeline Associates a specialist in PostScript hypertext markup language (HTML) and printer control language interpreter technologies. During the next two years EFI partnered with AlphaGraphics Agfa and Fuji Xerox and nearly doubled its customer base. It struck deals to incorporate Fiery controllers in Hewlett-Packard laser printers and Fiery servers in ENCAD's ink jet printers. In 1998 EFI released 40 new products including its Fiery ZX (for wide-format printers) and X2 (for pre-press devices) platforms. That year Avida replaced Arazi as chairman.

EXECUTIVES

Vice President Corporate Marketing, Frank (Frankie) Tueckmantel
CEO, Guy Gecht, age 52, $620,000 total compensation
SVP Worldwide Sales and Marketing, Frank Mallozzi
CTO, Ghilad Dziesietnik
CFO, Marc Olin, age 52, $311,553 total compensation
VP Engineering; Managing Director India, Samir (Sam) Gulve
SVP and General Manager Fiery Division, Toby Weiss
SVP and General Manager Inkjet Solutions, Scott Schinlever
SVP and General Manager Productivity Software, Gabriel (Gaby) Matsliach
General Manager Inkjet Services Greater China, Moli Li
CIO, Sheri Rhodes
Interim Vice President Customer Advocacy, Waiman Cho
Vice President Product Quality Assurance And Customer Advocacy, Vicki (Vic) Sam
Senior Vice President and General Manager Productivity Software, Gaby Matsliach
Vice President Corporate Marketing, Frank Tuckmantel
Vice President Human Resources, Marjolijn Denhartog
Vice President Research and Development, Jack (Jackie) Dempsey
Vice President Ink Business And Jetrion, Rafael (Rafee) Ribeiro
Vice President of Asia Pacific, Tim (Timmy) Bates
Director, Gill Cogan, age 65
Auditors: Deloitte & Touche LLP

LOCATIONS

HQ: Electronics for Imaging, Inc.
6750 Dumbarton Circle, Fremont, CA 94555
Phone: 650 357-3500
Web: www.efi.com

PRODUCTS/OPERATIONS

2015 Sales

	$ mil.	% of total
Inkjet	447.7	51
Fiery	299.5	34
Productivity software	135.3	15
Total	**882.5**	**100**

Selected Products and Brands

Fiery
  Embedded controllers
  External print servers (Fiery)
  Stand-alone servers
Inkjet products
  Industrial printers for packaging and labeling (Jetrion)
  Super-wide format printers for billboards and other large displays (VUTEk)
Advanced Professional Print Software (APPS)
  Color proofing
  E-commerce
  Job tracking
  Supply chain management
  Workflow management

Selected Suppliers

Intel (CPUs chip sets)
Toshiba (Application-specific integrated circuits (“ASIC”) & inkjet print heads)
Open Silicon (ASICs)
Altera (ASICs & programmable devices)

Tundra (chip sets)
Avnet (contract manufacturing (Fiery))
Nazdar (contract manufacturing (solvent ink))
Columbia Tech (inkjet sub-assemblies)
Roberts Tool (inkjet sub-assemblies)
SEI S.p.A (inkjet sub-assemblies & laser finishing)
Shenzen Runtianzhi Tech (inkjet sub-assemblies)
Seiko (inkjet print heads)
Fuji (inkjet print heads)
Xaar (inkjet print heads)
Dimatix (inkjet print heads)
Progress Software (Monarch and Radius operating system)

COMPETITORS

Agfa	Oc©
Canon	Oki Data
Eastman Kodak	Peerless Systems
Fuji Xerox	Ricoh Company
HP	SCREEN Holdings
Heidelberger Druckmaschinen	Sharp Corp.
	Toshiba
Konica Minolta	Xerox

HISTORICAL FINANCIALS

Company Type: Public

Income Statement

FYE: December 31

	REVENUE ($ mil.)	NET INCOME ($ mil.)	NET PROFIT MARGIN	EMPLOYEES
12/15	882.5	33.5	3.8%	3,136.0
12/14	790.4	33.7	4.3%	2,672.0
12/13	727.6	109.1	15.0%	2,523.0
12/12	652.1	83.2	12.8%	2,393.0
12/11	591.5	27.4	4.6%	2,142.0
Annual Growth	10.5%	5.1%	—	10.0%

2015 Year-End Financials

Debt ratio: 21.6%	No. of shares (mil.): 47.3
Return on equity: 4.1%	Dividends
Cash ($ mil.): 164.0	Yield: —
Current ratio: 3.45	Payout: —
Long-term debt ($ mil.): 309.9	Market value ($ mil.): 2,212.0

	STOCK PRICE ($) FY Close	P/E High/Low		PER SHARE ($) Earnings	Dividends	Book Value
12/15	46.74	69	50	0.70	0.00	17.41
12/14	42.83	65	52	0.70	0.00	16.80
12/13	38.73	17	8	2.26	0.00	16.34
12/12	18.99	11	8	1.74	0.00	14.10
12/11	14.25	32	22	0.58	0.00	12.39
Annual Growth	34.6%	—	—	4.8%	—	8.9%

Ellie Mae Inc

Ellie Mae might sound like Fannie Mae's cousin but they're just in related industries not bloodlines. The company provides automation software and operates the Ellie Mae Network that facilitates the residential mortgage origination and funding process. Its Encompass software suite combines loan origination with CRM (customer relationship management) to gather review and verify data from a single database. Other programs handle regulatory compliance appraisal and title services underwriting tax transcripts and document preparation and management. More than 136000 mortgage professionals use its software and network to process more than 3 million new mortgages an estimated 20% of its addressable market.

Geographic Reach

Ellie Mae operates in the US from offices in California Missouri Nebraska (technical support) and New Jersey.

Sales and Marketing

The company's sales force is divided into four teams that handle account management new account acquisition sales development and solution engineering. Customers include American Home Bank HighTechLending Skyline Financial and Supreme Lending.

Mortgage originators that use Encompass software pay for it either as a service with monthly fees based on the number of users and mortgages funded or through licensing and recurring subscription fees. Lenders and service providers that use the Ellie Mae Network pay fees per transaction for business received from Encompass users.

Financial Performance

Sales grew some 57% in 2015 jumping from $161 million to $254 million year-over-year. The substantial increase was primarily due to Encompass users working with the on-demand Software-as-a-Service model. The company has grown its base of active Encompass SaaS users from about 109000 in 2014 to 136000 in 2014. Profits jumped from $15 million in 2014 to $22 million in 2015.

Mergers and Acquisitions

In October 2015 Ellie Mae acquired Mortgage Returns a provider of on-demand customer relationship management and marketing automation tools for mortgage lenders.

Strategy

A major part of Ellie Mae's SaaS focus is its "success-based" pricing model that allows customers to pay at the time loans are closed. Besides its objectives to add new Encompass users and cross-sell to existing ones the company plans to enhance its Ellie Mae Network with increased functionality and services and expand the use of settlement services on the system. Industry trends are also influencing strategy. The software industry has gone cloud crazy over the past few years and Ellie Mae has not been immune. A key part of its strategy is to emphasize the software-as-a-service (SaaS) incarnations of its Encompass offerings.

Company Background

Ellie Mae was founded in 1997 and launched the first version of its transaction network in 2000. The Encompass software suite came out in 2003.

EXECUTIVES

EVP Sales and Marketing, Cathleen Schreiner Gates, $272,083 total compensation
EVP and CFO, Edgar A. (Ed) Luce, age 64, $280,000 total compensation
President and CEO, Jonathan H. Corr, age 49, $375,000 total compensation
EVP Corporate Strategy, Joseph Tyrrell, $272,500 total compensation
SVP Finance, Matthew LaVay, age 47
EVP Technology and Operations, Peter Hirsch
EVP Human Resources, Melanie Simpson
SVP and CIO, John Abel
Chairman, Sig Anderman
Auditors: Grant Thornton LLP

LOCATIONS

HQ: Ellie Mae Inc
4420 Rosewood Drive, Suite 500, Pleasanton, CA
94588
Phone: 925 227-7000   **Fax:** 925 227-9030
Web: www.elliemae.com

PRODUCTS/OPERATIONS

2015 Sales

	% of total
On-demand	98
On-premise	2
Total	**100**

Selected Products and Services

Encompass Compliance Service
Encompass Product & Pricing Service
Encompass Fraud Service
Encompass Flood Service
Encompass 4506-T Service
Encompass Appraisal Service
Encompass Title & Closing Center
Implementation Packages
Implementation Education Packages
Additional Implementation Services
Customer Acquisition and Relationship Management
Processing
Risk Management and Business Reporting
Connectivity Personalization and Integration
Underwriting
Secondary Marketing and Trade Management
Closing and Funding
Credit Report
Product Eligibility and Pricing Engine
Automated Underwriting

COMPETITORS

D+H USA	Prymak
Davis + Henderson	Verisk
Dexma	Wolters Kluwer
FirstPoint Inc	WowTools
Fiserv	Xerox
ISGN	eLynx
MGIC Investment	
McCracken Financial	
Solutions	

HISTORICAL FINANCIALS
Company Type: Public

Income Statement
FYE: December 31

	REVENUE ($ mil.)	NET INCOME ($ mil.)	NET PROFIT MARGIN	EMPLOYEES
12/15	253.9	22.2	8.8%	857.0
12/14	161.5	14.8	9.2%	640.0
12/13	128.4	12.5	9.8%	407.0
12/12	101.8	19.4	19.1%	308.0
12/11	55.4	3.6	6.5%	270.0
Annual Growth	**46.3%**	**57.5%**	**—**	**33.5%**

2015 Year-End Financials

Debt ratio: 1.2%
Return on equity: 8.1%
Cash ($ mil.): 34.4
Current ratio: 1.93
Long-term debt ($ mil.): 0.6

No. of shares (mil.): 29.5
Dividends
Yield: —
Payout: —
Market value ($ mil.): 1,781.0

	STOCK PRICE ($) FY Close	P/E High/Low		PER SHARE ($) Earnings	Dividends	Book Value
12/15	60.23	109	53	0.72	0.00	9.84
12/14	40.32	80	45	0.50	0.00	8.75
12/13	26.87	70	40	0.44	0.00	7.49
12/12	27.75	35	7	0.76	0.00	6.40
12/11	5.65	32	17	0.18	0.00	3.75
Annual Growth	**80.7%**			**41.4%**	**—**	**27.3%**

Ellington Financial LLC

Mortgage-related assets are music to Ellington Financial's ears. The specialty finance company manages a portfolio of primarily non-agency residential mortgage-backed securities valued at more than $366 million. It also seeks to acquire other target assets such as residential whole mortgage loans commercial mortgage-backed securities commercial real estate debt and asset-backed securities. Riskier residential whole mortgage loans which are generally not guaranteed by the US government include subprime non-performing and sub-performing mortgage loans. Founded in 2007 Ellington Financial went public in 2010 in hopes of taking advantage of the current credit environment.

The company is using a substantial portion of the proceeds from its initial public offering to acquire more target assets. It plans to use the balance for interest-bearing short-term investments — such as money market accounts —as well as for working capital and general corporate expenses.

In its attempt to acquire target assets Ellington Financial will compete with other specialty finance companies mortgage REITs public and private funds and commercial and investment banks. Keeping its portfolio diverse may help it weather downturns among certain geographic regions or property types that are subject to higher risk of foreclosure.

Ellington Financial executive officers and directors together own about a quarter of the company's stock.

EXECUTIVES

Director, Edward (Ed) Resendez, age 59
Chairman and Co-Chief Investment Officer,
 Michael W. Vranos, age 54
President CEO and Director, Laurence E. Penn
Co-Chief Investment Officer, Mark Tecotzky
Chief Financial Officer, Lisa Mumford
Director, Ronald I. Simon, age 78
Director, Thomas F. Robards, age 69
Director, Edward (Ed) Resendez, age 59
President CEO and Director, Laurence E. Penn
Auditors: PricewaterhouseCoopers LLP

LOCATIONS

HQ: Ellington Financial LLC
 53 Forest Avenue, Old Greenwich, CT 06870
Phone: 203 698-1200
Web: www.ellingtonfinancial.com

COMPETITORS

Annaly Capital Management	MFA Financial
	MFResidential
Chimera	Sutherland
Galiot Capital	Western Asset Mortgage

HISTORICAL FINANCIALS
Company Type: Public

Income Statement
FYE: December 31

	REVENUE ($ mil.)	NET INCOME ($ mil.)	NET PROFIT MARGIN	EMPLOYEES
12/15	104.6	66.1	63.3%	160.0
12/14	93.8	58.7	62.6%	150.0
12/13	85.7	49.6	57.9%	130.0
12/12	63.8	24.1	37.9%	100.0
12/11	63.5	44.7	70.3%	100.0
Annual Growth	**13.3%**	**10.3%**	**—**	**12.5%**

2015 Year-End Financials

Debt ratio: —
Return on equity: 8.7%
Cash ($ mil.): 183.9
Current ratio: 0.47
Long-term debt ($ mil.): —

No. of shares (mil.): 33.1
Dividends
Yield: 14.6%
Payout: 111.3%
Market value ($ mil.): 556.0

	STOCK PRICE ($) FY Close	P/E High/Low		PER SHARE ($) Earnings	Dividends	Book Value
12/15	16.78	11	8	1.98	2.45	22.10
12/14	19.96	12	9	2.10	3.08	23.38
12/13	22.67	13	10	2.11	3.83	24.40
12/12	22.46	17	13	1.35	2.50	24.86
12/11	17.17	9	6	2.71	2.51	22.55
Annual Growth	**(0.6%)**		**—**	**(7.5%)**	**(0.6%)**	**(0.5%)**

HISTORICAL FINANCIALS
Company Type: Public

Income Statement
FYE: December 31

	REVENUE ($ mil.)	NET INCOME ($ mil.)	NET PROFIT MARGIN	EMPLOYEES
12/15	104.6	66.1	63.3%	160.0
12/14	93.8	58.7	62.6%	150.0
12/13	85.7	49.6	57.9%	130.0
12/12	63.8	24.1	37.9%	100.0
12/11	63.5	44.7	70.3%	100.0
Annual Growth	**13.3%**	**10.3%**	**—**	**12.5%**

2015 Year-End Financials

Debt ratio: —
Return on equity: 8.7%
Cash ($ mil.): 183.9
Current ratio: 0.47
Long-term debt ($ mil.): —

No. of shares (mil.): 33.1
Dividends
Yield: 14.6%
Payout: 111.3%
Market value ($ mil.): 556.0

	STOCK PRICE ($) FY Close	P/E High/Low		PER SHARE ($) Earnings	Dividends	Book Value
12/15	16.78	11	8	1.98	2.45	22.10
12/14	19.96	12	9	2.10	3.08	23.38
12/13	22.67	13	10	2.11	3.83	24.40
12/12	22.46	17	13	1.35	2.50	24.86
12/11	17.17	9	6	2.71	2.51	22.55
Annual Growth	**(0.6%)**		**—**	**(7.5%)**	**(0.6%)**	**(0.5%)**

ELXSI Corp

This restaurant operator comes with a side of technology. ELXSI Corporation's hospitality division operates about 15 family-style restaurants in New England while its CUES division manufactures sewer inspection equipment. The eateries operate under the Bickford's Grille brand and offer casual dining with an emphasis on breakfast items served throughout the day. Its equipment manufacturing operation makes remote-control video cameras and robotic cutting devices used by municipalities and contractors. ELXSI is controlled by chairman and CEO Alexander Milley.

Suffering from increasing competition in the family dining business the company shuttered several Bickford's Family Restaurant locations during 2007 and rebranded the remaining units under the Bickford's Grille banner. The effort is part of a strategy to increase lunch and dinner traffic.

ELXSI's CUES division meanwhile continues to expand through research and development. In 2007 it introduced its latest line of inspection equipment under the K2 brand.

HISTORY

ELXSI's current operations bear no resemblance to its roots. Gene Amdahl formed the company as Trilogy Limited in 1980 to develop a new generation of mainframe computers. Trilogy's 1983 IPO raised more than $230 million but by 1985 the company had produced only research. Hoping to regain momentum Trilogy acquired computer manufacturer ELXSI Corp. in 1985 (in 1987 it took the ELXSI name which stood for electronics X silicon). The merger failed to revive the company and in 1989 ELXSI was bought by

Milley & Co. and the Airlie Group as a vehicle for acquisitions.

ELXSI acquired 30 Bickford's and 12 Howard Johnson's restaurants (all located in New England) from Marriott in 1991. During the next six years the company sold six Howard Johnson's restaurants and converted five into Bickford's Family Restaurants. In 1992 the company acquired remote video system manufacturer Cues plus its Canadian and Dutch subsidiaries.

In 1995 ELXSI bought all 16 locations of Abdow's Family Restaurants converting nine of them into Bickford's. In 1998 ELXSI opened three Bickford's restaurants and closed one Abdow's restaurant. In 1999 the company closed its last Howard Johnson's restaurant. The following year it opened five more Bickford's and rebranded its remaining Abdow's.

In 2002 longtime Bickford's president Dan Bloodwell resigned from the company and was replaced by Sandy Milley. In 2004 the family dining chain began rebranding its locations under the Bickford's Grille name.

Auditors: RSM US LLP

LOCATIONS

HQ: ELXSI Corp
3600 Rio Vista Avenue, Suite A, Orlando, FL 32805
Phone: 407 849-1090

COMPETITORS

Bertucci's Corp.	Friendly's Ice Cream
Carlson Restaurants	Insituform
Cracker Barrel	Technologies
Denny's	Ruby Tuesday
DineEquity	

HISTORICAL FINANCIALS

Company Type: Public

Income Statement

FYE: December 31

	REVENUE ($ mil.)	NET INCOME ($ mil.)	NET PROFIT MARGIN	EMPLOYEES
12/15	83.3	26.1	31.3%	0.0
12/14	76.4	7.1	9.3%	0.0
12/13	64.4	4.4	7.0%	0.0
12/12	63.9	4.6	7.2%	0.0
12/11	60.3	3.7	6.2%	0.0
Annual Growth	8.4%	62.3%	—	—

2015 Year-End Financials

Debt ratio: 0.2%	No. of shares (mil.): 3.4
Return on equity: 56.0%	Dividends
Cash ($ mil.): 16.6	Yield: —
Current ratio: 5.30	Payout: —
Long-term debt ($ mil.): 0.1	Market value ($ mil.): 60.0

	STOCK PRICE ($) FY Close	P/E High/Low		PER SHARE ($) Earnings	Dividends	Book Value
12/15	17.50	3	2	7.39	0.00	17.59
12/14	14.28	7	4	2.08	0.00	9.86
12/13	9.15	10	8	1.17	0.00	7.39
12/12	11.40	12	2	1.15	0.00	5.68
12/11	3.13	4	1	0.94	0.00	4.57
Annual Growth	53.8%	—	—	67.4%	—	40.1%

Emergent BioSolutions Inc

Emergent BioSolutions is preparing for a bioterrorism or pandemic worst-case scenario. The company develops and produces vaccines that treat or protect against infectious diseases and bio-agents. The company supplies BioThrax (the US's only FDA-approved anthrax vaccine) primarily to the US Department of Defense (DOD) Centers for Disease Control (CDC) and the US Department of Health and Human Services (HHS). It is also developing a post-exposure treatment for anthrax. In 2016 the firm spun off its biosciences division which works on therapies for leukemia and lymphona and vaccines for such infectious diseases as influenza as the new public company Aptevo Therapeutics.

Operations

Prior to the split Emergent BioSolutions operated in two segments: Biodefense (more than 80% of revenue) and Biosciences. The Biodefense segment focuses on chemical biological radiological nuclear and explosives threats while Biosciences focused on therapeutics and vaccines in hematology cancer transplantation infectious disease and autoimmunity.

Products marketed by Biodefense include BioThrax BAT (the only FDA-approved heptavalent for the treatment of botulinum disease) Anthrasil (pending approval for the treatment of anthrax) VIGIV (the only FDA-licensed therapeutic addressing adverse effects of smallpox vaccination) and Reactive Skin Decontamination Lotion or RSDL (for the removal or neutralization of chemical agents from the skin). Its investigational candidates are anthrax vaccines NuThrax and PreviThrax and GC-072 the lead compound in the EV-035 series of broad spectrum antibiotics (acquired from Evolva in late 2014).

Meanshile the Biosciences' portfolio comprised four products acquired with Cangene Corporation in 2014 (WinRho SDF for the treatment of autoimmune platelet disorder HepaGam for the treatment of hepatitis B VARIZIG for the treatment of chicken pox and shingles and episil for pain relief) as well as investigational state candidates (IXINITY for bleeding episodes in people with hemophilia B ES414 for the treatment of prostate cancer and otlertuzumab for chronic lymphocytic leukemia). Biosciences also provided contract manufacturing services.

Emergent BioSolutions contracts with a third-party filling laboratory to measure BioThrax into dosage vials.

Geographic Reach

The company manufactures BioThrax at its production facility in Lansing Michigan. It also operates offices and laboratories in Maryland and Washington as well as in Germany. With its acquisition of Cangene Corporation in 2014 the company gained facilities in Winnipeg Manitoba in Canada.

International markets include Europe the Middle East and the Asia/Pacific region.

Sales and Marketing

The company markets its products primarily to US state and local governments and domestic non-governmental organizations. The US is the primary buyer of its Biodefense products providing funding for the development of drug candidates.

Its commercial operations team focuses on selling to hospitals hematology clinics medical oncology clinics and transplant centers. Products are distributed in the US through wholesalers including Cardinal Health McKesson and AmerisourceBergen. In Canada commercial products are distributed exclusively by Canadian Blood Services and Héma-Québec.

Financial Performance

Revenues had been growing slowly until 2014 when they rose 44% to $450.1 million on higher product sales contract manufacturing business and contracts grants and collaborations. The firm's RSDL product had increased sales that year; additionally products and contract manufacturing business gained from the Cangene acquisition provided new revenue sources. Finally contracts grants and collaborations revenues increased due to funding for the development of Anthrasil and BAT both acquired during 2014.

Net income has followed revenue trends. In 2014 it rose 18% to $37 million driven by the higher revenue but partially offset by a decrease in other income. Cash flow from operations rose 16% to $112 million due to an increase in cash provided by inventories and other factors.

Strategy

While Emergent BioSolutions dominates the anthrax vaccine niche its focus on a single niche product can leave it vulnerable to fluctuations in demand from a relatively narrow customer base. To reduce its vulnerability the company has broadened its customer base in recent years to include state and local governments (who might want their own stockpiles for first responders) as well as foreign governments. It has also built up its non-anthrax pipeline through acquisitions.

The company's overall product development strategy includes acquiring new candidates through company acquisitions and in-licensing transactions. In 2013 it bought the Healthcare Protective Products Division of Bracco Diagnostics Inc. and added the division's RSDL to its product offerings. Two years later it acquired biopharmaceutical Cangene Corporation adding BAT Anthrasil VIGIV WinRho Hepagam VARIZIG to its portfolio. In addition to its acquisitions the company has also divested its stake in a tuberculosis vaccine candidate and saw Pfizer terminate a collaboration agreement related to the development of a rheumatoid arthritis treatment and Abbott Laboratories terminate a collaboration for development of a leukemia treatment.

In 2015 the FDA approved IXINITY and AIGIV for the treatment of bleeding episodes in patients with hemophilia B and inhalational anthrax respectively.

Emergent BioSolutions entered into an agreement with MorphSys in 2014; they will co-develop and commercialize the novel oncology immunotherapeutic MOR 209/ES414 which targets prostate cancer.

In 2016 the company spun off its Biosciences division into Aptevo Therapeutics a separate standalone public company. The move allows each division to operate as pure-play companies with separate areas of focus.

Mergers and Acquisitions

In early 2014 the company acquired biopharmaceutical company Cangene Corporation for $222 million. The move substantially expanded its product portfolio and contract manufacturing capabilities.

Also that year it acquired the EV-035 series of molecules from Evolva Holding; the novel small molecules target bacterial type IIa topoisomerase.

EXECUTIVES

SVP and Chief Scientific Officer, W. James Jackson, age 56

President and CEO, Daniel J. Abdun-Nabi, age 61, $589,695 total compensation

EVP Corporate Services Division CFO and Treasurer, Robert G. (Bob) Kramer, age 59, $428,560 total compensation

EVP and President Corporate Affairs Division, Allen Shofe

EVP and President BioDefense Division, Adam R. Havey, age 45, $332,648 total compensation

EVP and General Counsel, A.B. Cruz

Vice President, Robert (Bob) Myers

Senior Vice President and Chief Medical OfficerScott, Scott (Scotty) Stromatt

Vice President Business Development, Jose Ochoa

Senior Vice President and Chief Scientific OfficerW, James (Jamie) Jackson

Vice President, Robert (Bob) Burrows

Senior Vice President Corporate Development, Yasmine Gibellini

Vice President, Chris (Chrissy) Frech

Vice President And Chief Security Officer, Jeff Hauk

Vice President Commercial Markets, Jeff Hackman

Vice President, Pamela (Pam) Duchars

Chairman, Fuad El-Hibri, age 58

Auditors: Ernst & Young LLP

LOCATIONS

HQ: Emergent BioSolutions Inc
400 Professional Drive, Suite 400, Gaithersburg, MD 20879
Phone: 240 631-3200
Web: www.emergentbiosolutions.com

PRODUCTS/OPERATIONS

2014 Sales

	$ mil.	% of total
Products	308.3	68
Contracts & grants	110.9	25
Contract manufacturing	30.9	7
Total	**450.1**	**100**

2014 Sales

% of total	$ mil
Biodefense	82
Biosciences	18
Total	**100**

Selected Acquisitions and Ventures

COMPETITORS

Amgen	Pfenex
Biogen	Pfizer
Elusys Therapeutics	PharmAthene
Genentech	Roche Holding
Human Genome Sciences	Soligenix

HISTORICAL FINANCIALS

Company Type: Public

Income Statement

	REVENUE ($ mil.)	NET INCOME ($ mil.)	NET PROFIT MARGIN	EMPLOYEES
				FYE: December 31
12/15	522.7	62.8	12.0%	1,292.0
12/14	450.1	36.7	8.2%	1,280.0
12/13	312.7	31.1	10.0%	1,353.0
12/12	281.8	23.5	8.3%	877.0
12/11	273.3	23.0	8.4%	811.0
Annual Growth	**17.6%**	**28.6%**	**—**	**12.3%**

2015 Year-End Financials

Debt ratio: 24.2%
Return on equity: 10.3%
Cash ($ mil.): 312.8
Current ratio: 5.41
Long-term debt ($ mil.): 253.0
No. of shares (mil.): 39.4
Dividends
  Yield: —
  Payout: —
Market value ($ mil.): 1,577.0

	STOCK PRICE ($) FY Close	P/E High/Low		PER SHARE ($) Earnings	Dividends	Book Value
12/15	40.01	25	16	1.41	0.00	16.75
12/14	27.23	29	20	0.88	0.00	14.67
12/13	22.99	28	15	0.85	0.00	13.37
12/12	16.04	28	20	0.65	0.00	12.30
12/11	16.84	38	23	0.64	0.00	11.51
Annual Growth	**24.2%**	**—**	**—**	**21.8%**	**—**	**9.8%**

Empire State Realty OP LP

Auditors: Ernst & Young LLP

LOCATIONS

HQ: Empire State Realty OP LP
One Grand Central Place, 60 East 42nd Street, New York, NY 10165
Phone: 212 687-8700
Web: www.empirestaterealtytrust.com

HISTORICAL FINANCIALS

Company Type: Public

Income Statement

	REVENUE ($ mil.)	NET INCOME ($ mil.)	NET PROFIT MARGIN	EMPLOYEES
				FYE: December 31
12/15	657.6	79.9	12.2%	850.0
12/14	635.3	70.2	11.1%	862.0
12/13*	127.5	193.4	151.6%	607.0
10/13	206.0	(37.2)		0.0
12/12	260.2	48.6	18.7%	0.0
Annual Growth	**26.1%**	**13.2%**	**—**	**—**

*Fiscal year change

2015 Year-End Financials

Debt ratio: 49.4%
Return on equity: —
Cash ($ mil.): 112.5
Current ratio: 0.30
Long-term debt ($ mil.): 884.7
No. of shares (mil.): 267.5
Dividends
  Yield: 1.8%
  Payout: 125.9%
Market value ($ mil.): 4,827.0

	STOCK PRICE ($) FY Close	P/E High/Low		PER SHARE ($) Earnings	Dividends	Book Value
12/15	18.04	65	54	0.29	0.34	5.13
12/14	17.49	66	48	0.27	0.34	5.17
12/13*	14.07	104	16	0.79	0.08	4.09
10/13	16.82	—	—	(0.00)	0.00	(0.00)
Annual Growth	**2.4%**	**—**	**—**	**—**	**—**	**—**

*Fiscal year change

Empire State Realty Trust Inc

If King Kong were around he'd be an executive at Empire State Realty Trust. The self-administered and self-managed real estate investment trust (REIT) formed in mid-2011 to take over a portfolio of high-profile Manhattan properties from its previous owners the Malkin family. Its flagship property is of course the 102-story Empire State Building but the trust also owns more than a dozen other buildings in the greater New York area totaling almost 7.7 million sq. ft. of office and retail space. In addition it plans to build a 340000-sq.-ft. building at the train station in Stamford Connecticut. Empire State Realty Trust went public in 2013 raising $929 million.

Operations

As a REIT Empire State Realty Trust doesn't pay federal income tax as long as it distributes 90% of its income back to stockholders in the form of dividends. Empire State Realty Trust was formed to consolidate a number of companies owned by the Malkin family including Malkin Properties a property manager and leasing agent and Malkin Construction a general contractor for its renovation projects. Since REITs can't have a shareholder owning more than 10% Empire State Realty Trust plans to use the proceeds from its IPO to pay off existing shareholders namely the Malkin family and loans the Malkin family made to the company.

The 2.8 million-sq.-ft. Empire State Building is the tallest building in Manhattan. Its top five tenants are Coty the FDIC Host Services Li & Fung and Walgreen's. Besides tenant revenue it makes money from two observatories and broadcasting facilities. Tourists pay anywhere from $20 to $50 to ride the elevators to the building's observation decks on either the 86th or 102nd floors and the company sold more than 4 million tickets in 2010. In addition to being a tourist attraction the Empire State Building also serves as an antenna site for broadcasting operations with more than a dozen licensed TV stations and about 20 licensed radio stations using the building to transmit signals. Empire State Realty Trust has spent $123 million renovating the building and estimates another $230 million is needed to finish the job by 2016.

Company Background

Chairman Emeritus Peter Malkin joined his father-in-law Lawrence Wien in the real estate business back in 1958. Wien had been the real estate partner of Harry Helmsley (who founded Helmsley Enterprises) since the 1940s. (Peter's son Anthony Malkin is now Chairman CEO and President of Empire State Realty Trust.) The Manhattan office properties that make up Empire State Realty Trust's portfolio were acquired between 1950 and 1979 (Wien first bought the Empire State Building in 1961 for $65 million). The Empire State Building has changed hands over the years and been involved in lawsuits with affiliates of the Helmsley family (including the notorious Leona Helmsley) and Donald Trump whose Trump Organization sold its stake in 2002. Malkin Properties gained day-to-day management of the Empire State Building in 2006.

EXECUTIVES

Executive Vice President and Director of Leasing and Operations, Thomas (Thom) Durels
Senior Vice President, Fred C (Freddy) Posniak
Senior Vice President, Jeffrey Newman
Assistant Vice President And Assistant Controller, Lotfollah Rezvan
Executive Vice President General Counsel and Secretary, Thomas N (Thom) Keltner
Senior Vice President Director Leasing and Marketing, Ryan (Ry) Kass
Auditors: Ernst & Young LLP

LOCATIONS

HQ: Empire State Realty Trust Inc
111 West 33rd Street, New York, NY 10120
Phone: 212 687-8700
Web: www.empirestaterealtytrust.com

COMPETITORS

Boston Properties	Silverstein Properties
Brookfield Office	The Trump Organization
Properties	Tishman Construction
Equity Office	Tishman Hotel
LeFrak Organization	Tishman Speyer
Related	Vornado Realty
SL Green Realty	

HISTORICAL FINANCIALS

Company Type: Public

Income Statement

FYE: December 31

	REVENUE ($ mil.)	NET INCOME ($ mil.)	NET PROFIT MARGIN	EMPLOYEES
12/15	657.6	79.9	12.2%	850.0
12/14	635.3	70.2	11.1%	862.0
12/13*	127.5	193.4	151.6%	607.0
10/13	206.0	(37.2)	—	0.0
12/12	260.2	48.6	18.7%	629.0
Annual Growth	26.1%	13.2%	—	7.8%

*Fiscal year change

2015 Year-End Financials

Debt ratio: 49.4%	No. of shares (mil.): 120.0
Return on equity: 16.0%	Dividends
Cash ($ mil.): 46.6	Yield: 1.8%
Current ratio: 0.70	Payout: 130.7%
Long-term debt ($ mil.): 1,632.4	Market value ($ mil.): 2,169.0

	STOCK PRICE ($) FY Close	P/E High/Low	PER SHARE ($) Earnings	Dividends	Book Value
12/15	18.07	63 53	0.29	0.34	4.44
12/14	17.58	66 53	0.27	0.34	4.45
12/13*	15.30	20 17	0.79	0.08	4.03
10/13	13.15	— —	(0.00)	0.00	(0.00)
Annual Growth	11.2%	— —	—	—	—

*Fiscal year change

Employers Holdings Inc

Because workers' compensation is nothing to gamble with small business owners can turn to Employers Holdings. The Reno-based holding company provides workers' compensation services including claims management loss prevention consulting and care management to small busi-nesses in low hazard industries including retailers and restaurants. The company provides workers' compensation through its Employer Insurance Company of Nevada (EICN) and Employers Compensation Insurance Company. Employers Holdings also operates Employers Assurance and Employers Preferred Insurance Company both of which also offer workers' compensation.

Geographic Reach

While it distributes its products in more than 30 states and the District of Columbia more than half of its premiums come from California.

Sales and Marketing

Employers Holdings uses independent agents and brokers to bring its wares to the public. It also markets its products along with ADP's payroll services in several states and with Anthem Blue Cross of California's group health insurance products in California. They each contribute about 10% of in-force premiums. Employers Holdings is forging additional distribution partners in other markets.

Financial Performance

After weathering a few rough years during the economic downturn Employers Holdings has seen multiple years of revenue growth. In 2013 revenue rose about 25% from $579.2 million to $723.6 million due to increased net premiums as the company issued more policies expanded existing policies and earned higher rates. Net income however dropped 40% from $107 million to $64 million as losses increased. Buoyed by the increased premiums cash flow increased by $32 million from $132 million to $164 million even though the company paid more for claims and in commissions.

Strategy

Employers Holdings maintains a strategy of engaging in low-to-medium hazard industries in order to try to keep its losses under control. Its top types of insureds include restaurants the clerical side of physician offices automobile service or repair centers and colleges (professional employees and clerical). The company also spreads its risk around and is not dependent upon any one customer for a significant portion of its income.

HISTORY

EICN was the successor to Nevada's public workers' compensation fund. The state-run system which was deeply in debt and on the verge of collapse was officially privatized in 2000 under the guidance of CEO Douglas Dirks. In 2004 EICN reorganized into a mutual insurance company which took the name EIG Mutual Holdings and included EICN as its subsidiary.

In 2006 EIG Mutual Holdings filed its initial public offering to convert from a mutual insurance holding company to a publicly traded corporation. When the company's members approved the conversion in early 2007 the name changed to Employers Holdings Inc. Eligible members received shares of the new company; non-eligible members took home just their share of the proceeds raised.

EXECUTIVES

President and CEO, Douglas D. Dirks, $927,569 total compensation
EVP Chief Legal Officer General Counsel and Corporate Secretary, Lenard T. Ormsby, $485,708 total compensation
EVP Corporate and Public Affairs, Ann W. Nelson, $354,501 total compensation
EVP and Chief Administrative Officer, John P. Nelson, $334,391 total compensation
EVP and COO, Stephen V. Festa, $488,299 total compensation
EVP and CIO, Tracey L. Berg
SVP and Chief Underwriting Officer, Lawrence S. (Larry) Rogers
EVP and CFO, Michael S. Paquette, age 53
Vice President Corporate Marketing, Ty Vukelich
Vice President Investor Relations, Vicki Erickson
Vice President Government and Regulatory Affairs, Jim (Jimmy) Werbeckes
Vice President Of Premium Audit, Sharon Morgan
Vice President and Chief Financial Officer, Jessica (Jess) Salazar
Vice President Sales East Region, Martha (Mar) Collins
Chairman, Michael D. (Mike) Rumbolz, age 63
Auditors: Ernst & Young LLP

LOCATIONS

HQ: Employers Holdings Inc
10375 Professional Circle, Reno, NV 89521
Phone: 888 682-6671

PRODUCTS/OPERATIONS

2015 Sales

	$ mil.	% of total
Net premiums earned	690.4	91
Net investment income	72.2	9
Realized losses on investments	(10.7)	-
Other income	0.2	-
Total	**752.1**	**100**

Selected Products & Services

Claims Management
Fraud Prevention
Loss Control
Loss Run Report
Managed Care Services
PrecisePay (Pay-As-You-Go)
Premium Audit
Return to Work Program
Safety Promotion Programs
Workers' Compensation Insurance

Selected Subsidiaries

AmSERV Inc.
EIG Services Inc.
Elite Insurance Services Inc.
Employers Assurance Company
Employers Compensation Insurance Company
Employers Group Inc.
Employers Insurance Company of Nevada
Employers Occupational Health Inc.
Employers Preferred Insurance Company
Pinnacle Benefits Inc.

COMPETITORS

AMERISAFE	Republic Indemnity
AmTrust Financial	Safety Insurance
Baldwin & Lyons	SeaBright Insurance
Berkshire Hathaway	Selective Insurance
CNA Financial	State Auto Financial
Donegal	State Compensation
EMC Insurance	Insurance Fund
Harleysville Group	The Hartford
Liberty Mutual	TowerGroup
Meadowbrook Insurance	Travelers Companies
Navigators	United Fire
ProAssurance	Zurich Insurance Group
RLI	

HISTORICAL FINANCIALS

Company Type: Public

Income Statement

FYE: December 31

	ASSETS ($ mil.)	NET INCOME ($ mil.)	INCOME AS % OF ASSETS	EMPLOYEES
12/15	3,755.8	94.4	2.5%	716.0
12/14	3,769.6	100.6	2.7%	709.0
12/13	3,643.4	63.8	1.8%	723.0
12/12	3,511.3	106.8	3.0%	667.0
12/11	3,481.7	48.3	1.4%	651.0
Annual Growth	1.9%	18.2%	—	2.4%

2015 Year-End Financials

Return on assets: 2.5%
Return on equity: 13.0%
Long-term debt ($ mil.): —
No. of shares (mil.): 32.2
Sales ($ mil): 752.1

Dividends
Yield: 0.8%
Payout: 8.0%
Market value ($ mil.): 880.0

	STOCK PRICE ($) FY Close	P/E High/Low		PER SHARE ($) Earnings	Dividends	Book Value
12/15	27.30	10	7	2.90	0.24	23.62
12/14	23.51	10	6	3.14	0.24	21.81
12/13	31.65	16	10	2.00	0.24	18.17
12/12	20.58	6	5	3.37	0.24	17.53
12/11	18.09	16	8	1.29	0.24	14.37
Annual Growth	10.8%	—	—	22.4%	(0.0%)	13.2%

Enanta Pharmaceuticals, Inc.

Enanta Pharmaceuticals is getting hip to Hep C. The biotech firm is developing treatments for viral infections including hepatitis C (HCV) a virus that can lead to chronic liver diseases such as cirrhosis organ failure and cancer. The company's first licensed product which is licensed to AbbVie is paritaprevir is a protease inhibitor for use against HCV. Enanta also has four small molecule drugs under development: glecaprevir another protease inhibitor for the treatment for HCV; the similar EDP-239 and EDP-494; and EDP-305 which is being studied for the treatment of non-alcoholic steatohepatitis (NASH) and primary biliary cholangitis (PBC). In late 2014 Enanta discontinued its biodefense antibiotic program.

Operations
Enanta Pharmaceuticals makes most of its money from royalties for its protease inhibitors. It also earns milestone payments related to those same compounds.

Financial Performance
The biotech has yet to make any revenue from product sales but rather has earned money on collaborations with other pharmaceuticals (primarily AbbVie) and from a now-closed government contract to develop antibiotics for biodefense purposes.

In fiscal 2016 (ended September) Enanta had revenue of $88.3 million a 45% decline from the previous year. This was primarily due to a significant drop in milestone payments from AbbVie as well as a drop in funding from the government (its antibiotics contract ended during 2015). Net income that year totaled $21.7 million a 73% decline

from fiscal 2015. Lower revenue and higher R&D expenses led to the drop in net income.

Strategy
Enanta Pharmaceuticals is currently focused on three disease areas: the liver disease NASH respiratory syncytial virus (RSV) and hepatitis B. It also continues to develop treatments for HCV. The company sees plenty of opportunity and hopes to introduce new treatments for unmet medical needs in these areas (NASH has no approved treatments for instance.). It uses funding from its AbbVie collaboration to advance its development pipeline; it is also open to other partnerships to finance its R&D activities.

EXECUTIVES

SVP Finance and Administration and CFO, Paul J. Mellett, age 61, $344,862 total compensation
President CEO and Director, Jay R. Luly, age 60, $520,748 total compensation
SVP and General Counsel, Nathaniel S. Gardiner, age 63
SVP New Product Strategy and Development, Timothy D. Ocain, age 59
SVP and Chief Medical Officer, Nathalie Adda
Chairman, Bruce L.A. Carter
Auditors: PRICEWATERHOUSECOOPERS LLP

LOCATIONS

HQ: Enanta Pharmaceuticals, Inc.
500 Arsenal Street, Watertown, MA 02472
Phone: 617 607-0800
Web: www.enanta.com

PRODUCTS/OPERATIONS

2016 Sales

	$ mil.	% of total
AbbVie Agreement		
Royalties	57.7	65
Milestones	30.0	34
NIAID contract	0.6	1
Total	88.3	100

COMPETITORS

Achillion	Johnson & Johnson
Boehringer Ingelheim	Merck
Bristol-Myers Squibb	PTC Therapeutics
Gilead Sciences	Vertex Pharmaceuticals

HISTORICAL FINANCIALS

Company Type: Public

Income Statement

FYE: September 30

	REVENUE ($ mil.)	NET INCOME ($ mil.)	NET PROFIT MARGIN	EMPLOYEES
09/16	88.2	21.6	24.5%	76.0
09/15	160.8	78.9	49.1%	69.0
09/14	47.7	34.4	72.1%	52.0
09/13	32.0	9.6	30.0%	44.0
09/12	41.7	21.4	51.3%	39.0
Annual Growth	20.6%	0.3%	—	18.2%

2016 Year-End Financials

Debt ratio: 0.1%
Return on equity: 8.5%
Cash ($ mil.): 16.5
Current ratio: 29.43
Long-term debt ($ mil.): 0.4

No. of shares (mil.): 19.0
Dividends
Yield: —
Payout: —
Market value ($ mil.): 507.0

	STOCK PRICE ($) FY Close	P/E High/Low		PER SHARE ($) Earnings	Dividends	Book Value
09/16	26.61	36	18	1.13	0.00	14.18
09/15	36.14	12	7	4.09	0.00	12.62
09/14	39.57	25	10	1.80	0.00	7.99
09/13	22.92	—	—	(0.67)	0.00	6.16
Annual Growth	5.1%	—	—	—	—	32.0%

Encore Capital Group Inc

Encore Capital Group hopes to collect from stubborn borrowers again and again. The firm and its Midland Credit Management subsidiary purchase discounted non-performing consumer receivables that banks credit unions consumer and auto finance companies credit card issuers telecommunications firms retailers and other lenders have given up on. The group then does its best to collect the money via phone direct mail third-party collection agencies and legal action; it employs skip-tracing to track down stubborn debtors. Subsidiary Ascension Capital Group provides bankruptcy support services to the financial services industry. Encore collects debts in the US the UK Ireland Colombia Peru New Zealand and the Philippines.

Operations
Encore Capital operated two business segments during 2015: Portfolio Purchasing and Recovery (which made up 97% of the company's total revenue) and Tax Liens (3%) through Propel Financial Services (which it sold in early 2016).

The company boasts one of the debt collection industry's largest financially distressed consumer databases. Volume is important for Encore Capital as the company pursues collections on only a fraction of accounts and generates payments from less than 1% of them. Practicing a "friendly but firm approach" its account managers evaluate customers' ability to pay then develop tailored payment programs. The company utilizes proprietary statistical and behavioral models account-level valuation methods customized software applications and purchased credit bureau information to determine its collection strategies.Some of the Encore Capital's major subsidiaries include Cabot Credit Management in the UK US-based Asset Acceptance Capital Corp Baycorp in the Australasia region Europe's Grove Capital Management and Latin America's Refinancia S.A. among others.Geographic Reach

The San Diego-headquartered collection company operates in 14 countries worldwide in the Americas Europe and the Australasia region. Its largest market is the US where it generated 64% of its revenue during 2015 while Europe (including the UK Spain and Australia) accounted for another 32%. Encore US operating centers are in San Diego; Phoenix; Houston; Dallas; San Antonio; McAllen Texas; St. Cloud Minnesota; Warren Michigan; New Freedom Pennsylvania; and Roanoke Virginia.Sales and MarketingEncore Capital markets its services through direct mail call centers and third-party collection agencies.Financial PerformanceThe debt collector's annual revenues have more than doubled since 2011 as portfolio acquisitions and higher gross collections have been rising over the years. Encore Capital's profits have also been trending higher as the firm has kept a lid on rising costs.Encore Capital's revenue climbed 8% to $1.2 billion during 2015 as its portfolio recoveries rose by 8% for the year with higher portfolio balances and better recovery rates.Despite revenue growth in 2015 the company's net income fell 56% to $45.14 million for the year mostly as it took a $49 million loss on the sale of its tax lien business subsidiary Propel Financial Services. Encore Capital's operating cash levels rose 3% to $114 million thanks to favorable working capital changes related to its accounts payable accrued liabilities and other liabilities.

Strategy

Encore Capital continues to acquire new portfolios of card telecom and consumer bankruptcy charge-offs. The firm is also expanding its international reach through portfolio acquisitions and recovery operations in Latin America Australasia and India (as of early 2016).

Mergers and Acquisitions

In September 2015 expanding its reach into the Australia and New Zealand markets Encore Capital bought a 50.25% stake in debt resolution specialist Baycorp.In June 2015 UK-subsidiary Cabot Credit Management Limited bought UK-based consumer debt acquirer and collector Hillesden Securities Ltd for £180.6 million.In August 2014 the company purchased Atlantic Credit & Finance (ACF) a collector of fresh higher-balance accounts in the US for approximately $70 million in cash.In April 2014 Encore acquired a controlling stake in Grove Capital Management a purchaser of credit portfolios specializing on UK insolvencies and Spanish assets. In February 2014 under Encore's ownership Cabot bought Marlin Financial Group an acquirer of non-performing consumer debt in the UK for £295 million ($481 million).In December 2013 it purchased Refinancia S.A. a manager of non-performing loans in Colombia and Peru. Refinancia also offered portfolio management services to banks for non-performing loans. In July 2013 Encore Capital expanded its business in the UK with the purchase of Cabot Credit Management a debt management firm that operates in England and Ireland for £115 million ($177 million). In June 2013 Encore acquired Asset Acceptance Capital Corp. a debt recovery firm in the US.Company BackgroundIn early 2016 the company sold its San Antonio Texas-based Propel Acquisition LLC subsidiary which acquired and serviced residential and commercial tax liens on property. The firm was the largest tax lien company in Texas.

EXECUTIVES

Senior Vice President Operations, Jim (Jimmy) Syran

Group Executive International and Corporate Development, Paul J. Grinberg, age 55, $435,102 total compensation

President and CEO, Kenneth A. (Ken) Vecchione, age 61, $571,154 total compensation

SVP IT and CIO, Carl Eberling

President Propel Financial Services, Jack Nelson

EVP Encore India, Manu Rikhye

EVP U.S. Operations, Ashish Masih, $286,656 total compensation

SVP and COO India Operations, Anupam Arun

SVP Legal Collections Operations, Ryan Bell

EVP CFO and Treasurer, Jonathan Clark

Senior Vice President Chief Scientific Officer, Christopher (Chris) Trepel

Vice President Consumer Marketing, Brian Enneking

Assistant Vice President Human Resources, Richa Kale

Vice President Credit Risk, John Chalekian

Senior Vice President Human RE, Barbara (Barb) Kennedy

Vice President Legal and Business Affairs per LinkedIn, Greg (Greggy) Call

Assistant Vice President Call Center Technology, Deepak Cherukuri

Vice President and Controller, Glen Freter

Chairman, T. Willem (Will) Mesdag, age 63

Auditors: BDO USA, LLP

LOCATIONS

HQ: Encore Capital Group Inc
3111 Camino Del Rio North, Suite 103, San Diego, CA 92108
Phone: 877 445-4581
Web: www.encorecapital.com

PRODUCTS/OPERATIONS

2015 Sales

	$ mil.	% of total
Portfolio purchasing and recovery	1,130.0	97
Tax lien business	31.6	3
Total	1,161.6	100

Selected Subsidiaries

Ascension Capital Group Inc.
Cabot Financial (UK Ireland)
Grove Financial (UK)
Marlin Financial Group (UK)
MCM Midland Management Costa Rica S.r.l.
Midland Credit Management Inc.
Midland Credit Management India Private Limited
Midland Funding LLC
Midland Funding NCC-2 Corporation
Midland India LLC
Midland International LLC
Midland Portfolio Services Inc.
MRC Receivables Corporation
Propel Financial Services (US)
Refinancia S.A. (Colombia Peru)

COMPETITORS

Asta Funding
Expert Global Solutions
FirstCity Financial
GC Services
Genesis Financial Solutions

Leland Scott & Associates
Nationwide Recovery Systems
PRA Group

HISTORICAL FINANCIALS

Company Type: Public

Income Statement
FYE: December 31

	REVENUE ($ mil.)	NET INCOME ($ mil.)	NET PROFIT MARGIN	EMPLOYEES
12/15	1,161.5	45.1	3.9%	6,700.0
12/14	1,072.7	103.7	9.7%	5,400.0
12/13	773.3	75.3	9.7%	5,300.0
12/12	555.8	69.4	12.5%	2,800.0
12/11	467.3	60.9	13.0%	2,200.0
Annual Growth	25.6%	(7.2%)	—	32.1%

2015 Year-End Financials

Debt ratio: 76.2%
Return on equity: 7.4%
Cash ($ mil.): 153.5
Current ratio: 1.94
Long-term debt ($ mil.): 3,216.5
No. of shares (mil.): 25.2
Dividends
  Yield: —
  Payout: —
Market value ($ mil.): 735.0

	STOCK PRICE ($) FY Close	P/E High/Low		PER SHARE ($) Earnings	Dividends	Book Value
12/15	29.08	25	16	1.69	0.00	23.59
12/14	44.40	13	10	3.77	0.00	24.15
12/13	50.26	17	9	2.87	0.00	22.47
12/12	30.62	11	8	2.80	0.00	17.50
12/11	21.26	13	8	2.37	0.00	15.15
Annual Growth	8.1%	—	—	(8.1%)	—	11.7%

Enduro Royalty Trust

Auditors: Ernst & Young LLP

LOCATIONS

HQ: Enduro Royalty Trust
919 Congress Avenue, Suite 500, Austin, TX 78701
Phone: 512 236-6555
Web: www.enduroroyaltytrust.com

HISTORICAL FINANCIALS

Company Type: Public

Income Statement
FYE: December 31

	REVENUE ($ mil.)	NET INCOME ($ mil.)	NET PROFIT MARGIN	EMPLOYEES
12/15	14.4	13.7	95.1%	0.0
12/14	29.3	28.5	97.2%	0.0
12/13	49.0	48.4	98.8%	0.0
12/12	59.1	58.0	98.2%	0.0
12/11	10.5	10.3	98.6%	0.0
Annual Growth	8.3%	7.3%	—	—

2015 Year-End Financials

Debt ratio: —
Return on equity: 4.2%
Cash ($ mil.): 0.1
Current ratio: —
Long-term debt ($ mil.): —
No. of shares (mil.): 33.0
Dividends
  Yield: 15.6%
  Payout: —
Market value ($ mil.): 80.0

	STOCK PRICE ($) FY Close	P/E High/Low		PER SHARE ($) Earnings	Dividends	Book Value
12/15	2.43	—	—	(0.00)	0.38	(0.00)
12/14	4.82	—	—	(0.00)	0.80	(0.00)
12/13	12.09	—	—	(0.00)	1.46	(0.00)
12/12	16.77	—	—	(0.00)	1.75	(0.00)
12/11	20.47	—	—	(0.00)	0.46	(0.00)
Annual Growth	(41.3%)	—	—	—	(4.8%)	—

Energy Focus Inc

The Illuminator may be coming to a theater near you but it isn't a movie—its what Energy Focus does. The company makes products such as energy-efficient fiber-optic light-emitting diode ceramic metal halide and high-intensity discharge lighting systems. Serving the commercial/industrial and pool lighting markets Energy Focus' systems illuminate cinemas shopping malls parking garages performing arts centers restaurants pools/spas and homes. Its lighting products include acrylic accent fixtures downlight fixtures spotlights and display-case lighting. The company's Stones River Companies (SRC) unit concentrates on turnkey lighting projects and solar retrofit jobs.

Energy Focus was in the right place at the right time with its energy-efficient products when the Energy Independence and Security Act (EISA) was enacted in 2007; the controversial act federally mandates that all incandescent bulbs by use 25% to 30% less energy by 2012. (EISA has come under fire as the so-called "light bulb ban" comes closer to going into effect.) This gives Energy Focus a competitive edge as many of its products already meet lighting efficiency standards set for 2020. The company claims that many of its products use 80% less energy than present-day incandescent bulbs. Also in Energy Focus's favor is its qualification for federal and state tax incentives and funding; the Energy Independence and Security Act will offer billions in government grants for energy conservation programs.

The company is transitioning to become a turnkey lighting systems provider. In 2009 to further its growth and profitability Energy Focus launched a restructuring plan that calls for the development of mainstream lighting technologies to compete with fluorescent and general illumination lamps as well as the divestiture of non-core nonstrategic business units. In December 2009 the company sold its German-based subsidiary LBM Lichtleit Fasertechnik with possible plans to divest its Fiberstars pools and United States commercial businesses.

Cost reduction initiatives brought about the relocation of manufacturing and assembly operations from the company's Ohio plant to a contract manufacturing facility in Mexico. Final assembly plants are located in Australia India Japan and Taiwan. Energy Focus is also building its energy services business. In December 2009 it acquired Stones River Companies (SRC) a Nashville-based lighting systems retrofitter for $5 million. Energy Focus will continue to be on the lookout for similar additions as it seeks a national sales and delivery conduit into the existing building market.

Following its long-term strategy plan the company is focusing on solar technology development and will continue its involvement with the US government's Very High Efficiency Solar Cell (VHESC) Consortium. The VHESC expects to develop a solar cell for US military applications that offers 40% or greater efficiency but also plans to market the product to the public.

EXECUTIVES

Vice President of Operations, Eric (Ric) Hilliard
CFO, Bradley White
Senior Vice President Business Development, Tom (Tommy) McAuliffe
Chairman, Ted Tewksbury
Auditors: Plante & Moran, PLLC

LOCATIONS

HQ: Energy Focus Inc
  32000 Aurora Road, Suite B, Solon, OH 44139
Phone: 440 715-1300
Web: www.energyfocusinc.com

PRODUCTS/OPERATIONS

Selected Products and Operations
Fiber-optic cable (stranded and large core)

Fixtures
  Accent lighting
  Decorative fixtures
  Downlighting
  LED products
  Merchandise and display lighting
  Outdoor outdoor feature and landscape lighting
  Specialty lighting
Illuminators (the source of light in a fiber-optic system)
Pool and spa lighting
Signage lighting
Solar retrofit projects

Selected Subsidiaries and/or Divisions

Crescent Lighting Limited (decorative and specialty lighting products)
Energy Focus Government Contracts and Sales (lighting technologies and products for the US military)
Energy Focus National Accounts (energy-efficient lighting products)
Fiberstars Commercial (decorative LED and fiber optic lighting products)
Fiberstars Pool and Spa (decorative lighting for swimming pools)
Stones River Companies LLC (design engineering project management of lighting and solar retrofits)

COMPETITORS

Astronics	Mitsubishi Corp.
Bridgestone	OSRAM Licht
Havells Sylvania	Orion Energy Systems
Hayward Industries	Pentair
Intermatic	Philips Lighting
Juno Lighting	Revolution Lighting
LSI Industries	Technologies
Lighting Science Group	Toray Industries

HISTORICAL FINANCIALS

Company Type: Public

Income Statement

FYE: December 31

	REVENUE ($ mil.)	NET INCOME ($ mil.)	NET PROFIT MARGIN	EMPLOYEES
12/15	64.4	8.7	13.6%	122.0
12/14	28.9	(5.8)	—	77.0
12/13	21.5	(2.3)	—	59.0
12/12	29.8	(5.7)	—	71.0
12/11	25.7	(6.0)	—	67.0
Annual Growth	25.8%	—	—	16.2%

2015 Year-End Financials

Debt ratio: —
Return on equity: 31.8%
Cash ($ mil.): 34.6
Current ratio: 5.16
Long-term debt ($ mil.): —

No. of shares (mil.): 11.6
Dividends
  Yield: —
  Payout: —
Market value ($ mil.): 160.0

	STOCK PRICE ($) FY Close	P/E High/Low		PER SHARE ($) Earnings	Dividends	Book Value
12/15	13.75	33	5	0.82	0.00	3.89
12/14	4.93	—	—	(0.75)	0.00	1.04
12/13	0.47	—	—	(0.50)	0.00	0.57
12/12	0.16	—	—	(1.40)	0.00	0.18
12/11	0.20	—	—	(2.50)	0.00	0.59
Annual Growth	188.0%	—	—	—	—	60.3%

Ensign Group Inc

The Ensign Group hangs its insignia at more than 200 senior living facilities. Most of its facilities are skilled nursing homes but it also operates a number of assisted-living and independent-living facilities as well as combination nursing assisted and independent-living centers. Some locations also offer rehabilitation hospice and physical therapy services. Ensign's facilities are either owned by the company or operated under lease agreements. The health care provider operates some 120 long-term care centers with a capacity of some 13200 beds in about a dozen states in the southwestern and western US. Ensign also operates home health and hospice agencies.

Operations

Ensign is a holding company that counts among its operations more than 140 facilities 15 hospice companies and about 20 home health businesses. The company has a decentralized operating structure with its portfolio of homes organized into five regional operating companies. Each home operates under local —and largely independent —management. As part of its business the company relies on reimbursement from government and commercial health insurance plans as well as sales to private pay customers. It generates about three-fourths of its revenues from Medicaid and Medicare programs.

Geographic Reach

California-based Ensign has facilities in California Arizona Texas Washington Utah Idaho Colorado Nevada Iowa Nebraska Oregon South Carolina and Wisconsin. California and Texas are the company's largest markets home to more than 50% of its beds.

Financial Performance

Ensign reported revenue of $904.6 million in 2013 an increase of 10% versus 2012 on rising Medicare Medicaid managed care and private revenue. (The Medicare and Medicaid programs are Ensign's biggest payors contributing 72% of revenue in 2013.) Despite the double-digit rise in revenue net income declined 41% over the same period to $24 million due to US government settlement expenses incurred and an increase in the loss from discontinued operations. Some of Ensign's subsidiaries were the subject of an investigation (launched in 2006 and eventually settled in 2013) by the Department of Justice regarding claims submitted to the Medicare program.

Strategy

The company split its health care and real estate business into two separate publicly traded companies in June 2014. Ensign continued to provide health care services through its existing operations while the underlying real estate became owned by CareTrust REIT.

The company's growth strategy —and a growing population of increasingly infirm patients —has resulted in a decade of steady and significant revenue growth. Ensign primarily expands its operations by snapping up underperforming nursing homes in existing or new territories and turning them around both in terms of operating performance and clinical quality. In addition to acquiring new facilities and establishing local leadership teams the company works to boost patient occupancy at its existing facilities especially those facing financial troubles and extremely low occupancy rates. It does this by developing quality staff and clinical processes and through facility upgrades as well as by adding services such as outpatient therapy services. It is also focused on attracting more high-acuity patients who require higher levels of medical and rehabilitative care and for whom the company is generally reimbursed at higher rates.

Ensign branched out into a new area of operations in 2012 when it formed a joint venture with a group of physicians to establish or acquire urgent care centers in select communities. The Immediate Clinic venture intended to provide walk-in medical care to fill the gap between primary care doctor's offices and hospital emergency rooms a growing area of need as health reform measures take effect in the US. Its first acquisition in 2012 was Doctors Express which boasts about 50 franchised urgent care centers nationwide. However Immediate Clinic turned around and sold the Doctors Express business to American Family Care in 2013 while retaining a number of urgent care clinics in the greater Seattle area; in late 2016 Ensign sold its remaining Immediate Clinic operations to MultiCare Health System. Ensign plans to focus more directly on its post-acute care operations.

Mergers and Acquisitions

In late 2014 Ensign purchased nine skilled nursing and assisted living facilities in the San Diego area from Shea Family Care. The closing of the Shea Family deal brought Ensign's growing portfolio to 136 healthcare facilities (nine of which will be owned) nine hospice companies 12 home health agencies two home care businesses and 14 urgent care clinics in 12 states. Also that year the company bought Sherwood Village Assisted Living and Memory Care a 135-unit assisted living facility in Tucson Arizona for $4.8 million.

In 2015 the company acquired Managed Care at Home and Apismellis Homecare adding to its home health operations; and skilled nursing facility Olympia Transitional Care and Rehabilitation in Washington. It also bought facilities in Arizona California and Wisconsin and expanded eastward with the purchase of a facility in skilled nursing facility in South Carolina. Ensign started off 2016 with the purchases of three more South Carolina skilled nursing facilities and separately 18 skilled nursing facilities in Texas.

Ensign capped off 2016 with the purchase of 15 assisted living facilities in Wisconsin.

EXECUTIVES

Executive Vice President and Secretary, Gregory K (Greg) Stapley

President CEO and Director, Christopher R. Christensen, age 48, $462,327 total compensation

COO Ensign Services Inc., Barry R. Port, age 42, $326,227 total compensation

President Bandera Healthcare, John P. Albrechtsen, age 39, $164,687 total compensation

CFO, Suzanne D. Snapper, age 42, $307,500 total compensation

VP and General Counsel, Beverly B. Wittekind, age 51, $410,612 total compensation

President Cornerstone Healthcare, Daniel H. (Danny) Walker

President Bridgestone Living, John Guerreri

President Milestone Healthcare, Jorge Rojas

EVP and Secretary, Chad A. Keetch, age 38, $280,833 total compensation

President Pennant Healthcare, Spencer Burton

President Keystone Healthcare, Kevin Reese

Director Of Nursing Services, Traishon Lockett

Director Of Nursing Services, Kay Gudgell

Director Of Nursing Services, Mark Turner

Vice President Human Resources, Ryan (Ry) Jones

Chairman, Roy E. Christensen, age 83

Auditors: Deloitte & Touche LLP

LOCATIONS

HQ: Ensign Group Inc
27101 Puerta Real, Suite 450, Mission Viejo, CA 92691
Phone: 949 487-9500
Web: www.ensigngroup.net

PRODUCTS/OPERATIONS

2015 Sales

	$ mil.	% of total
Medicaid	439.9	34
Medicare	395.5	29
Private & other	227.7	17
Managed care	206.8	15
Medicaid - skilled	71.9	5
Total	**1,341.8**	**100**

2015 Sales

	$ mil.	% of total
TSA Services	1,216.9	90
Home Health & Hospice Services	90.4	7
Other	37.8	3
Elimination	(3.3)	
Total	**1,341.8**	**100**

COMPETITORS

Amedisys	Enlivant
American Baptist Homes of the West	Five Star Quality Care
Apria Healthcare	Genesis Healthcare
Brookdale Senior Living	Golden Horizons
	HealthSouth
Covenant Care	Kindred Healthcare
Dignity Health	Life Care Centers
Diversicare Healthcare Services	RehabCare
	SavaSeniorCare
	Sunrise Senior Living

HISTORICAL FINANCIALS

Company Type: Public

Income Statement

FYE: December 31

	REVENUE ($ mil.)	NET INCOME ($ mil.)	NET PROFIT MARGIN	EMPLOYEES
12/15	1,341.8	55.4	4.1%	16,494.0
12/14	1,027.4	35.9	3.5%	13,229.0
12/13	904.5	24.0	2.7%	11,372.0
12/12	824.7	40.5	4.9%	10,371.0
12/11	758.2	47.6	6.3%	9,433.0
Annual Growth	**15.3%**	**3.8%**	**—**	**15.0%**

2015 Year-End Financials

Debt ratio: 13.3%	No. of shares (mil.): 51.3
Return on equity: 16.1%	Dividends
Cash ($ mil.): 41.5	Yield: 1.1%
Current ratio: 1.64	Payout: 26.6%
Long-term debt ($ mil.): 99.0	Market value ($ mil.): 1,163.0

	STOCK PRICE ($) FY Close	P/E High/Low	PER SHARE ($) Earnings	Dividends	Book Value
12/15	22.63	49 20	1.06	0.27	8.32
12/14	44.39	59 35	0.78	0.29	5.73
12/13	44.27	84 49	0.54	0.27	8.05
12/12	27.15	33 25	0.93	0.25	7.52
12/11	24.50	30 18	1.11	0.11	6.55
Annual Growth	**(2.0%)**	**— —**	**(1.0%)**	**23.9%**	**6.2%**

Entegris Inc

Entegris makes products integral to the manufacture of semiconductors and computer disk drives. The company makes some 20000 standard and custom products used to transport and protect semiconductor and disk drive materials during processing. Its semiconductor products include

wafer carriers storage boxes and chip trays as well as chemical delivery products such as pipes fittings and valves. Its disk drive offerings include shippers stamper cases and transport trays. Top customers include Applied Materials ASML MEMC Siltronic Tokyo Electron and Taiwan Semiconductor Manufacturing. More than 70% of Entegris' sales come from customers located outside the US primarily in the Asia/Pacific region.

Operations

Entegris identifies its products as capital-driven (dependent on capital spending to expand manufacturing capacity) and unit-driven and consumable (products that are used or consumed in the manufacturing process). Unit-driven products which make up nearly four-fifths of sales include liquid filters specialized graphite components and wafers shippers. They provide some protection against industry cycles by providing a recurring source of revenue. Capital-driven products 20% of revenue include wafer process carriers and gas microcontamination control systems. Those products give the company access to more capital when chip makers retrofit or expand production facilities.

Geographic Reach

Entegris has manufacturing and research and development facilities in France German Israel Singapore China Japan Malaysia South Korea Taiwan and the US. It also has sales and service offices throughout Asia and Europe.

The US and Taiwan each account for 23% of the company's revenue followed by South Korea with 14% and Japan with 12%. Combined customers in Asia account for more than 60% of its revenue.

Sales and Marketing

The company sells its products through a direct sales force and strategic distributors serving a range of markets including Semiconductor Flat Panel Display Manufacturing Compound Semiconductor Disk Data Storage Aerospace Solar/Clean Energy Life Sciences Emerging Technologies and Water Treatment industries.

In 2015 sales to the company's 10 biggest customers accounted for 44% of revenue. It sold products to 2400 companies.

Financial Performance

Entegris posted a 12% gain in revenue to reach $1.08 billion in 2015. The company realized $105.3 million in revenue from the ATMI acquisition. The company said the strong US dollar cost it almost $7 million in 2015.

The company's profit jumped sharply —more than 900% -to $80 million in 2015 from just about $8 million in 2014. A gain related to the sale of an equity investment and lack of ATMI merger costs as well as reduced integration expenditures boosted net income.

Entegris had about $121 million in cash flow in 2015 compared to $126.42 million in 2014. The company carried higher inventories in 2015.

Strategy

In order to counter the cycles of the semiconductor industry Entegris has expanded into adjacent and ancillary markets including applications in solar flat-panel displays and high-purity chemicals. Non-semiconductor industries include the aerospace biomedical glass container and electrical discharge machining markets. Its focus includes strategic acquisitions and partnerships and related transactions that enable it to complement its product markets and broaden its technological capabilities and product offerings. It expanded its operations in Taiwan to provide manufacturing capabilities to support important customers in the region and also established sales and service offices in China in anticipation of a growing semiconductor manufacturing base in that region and expanded its presence in Singapore to enhance its global and regional management of supply chain and manufacturing processes.

The company expanded engineering research and development operations in South Korea and Taiwan in late 2015 and early 2016. Entegris said the operations are to enhance collaboration between its engineers and its customers in designing and manufacturing products.

Mergers and Acquisitions

In an effort to position itself for larger orders Entegris bought fellow semiconductors materials supplier ATMI for some $1.15 billion in mid-2014 creating a leading supplier of products and materials for semiconductor and other advanced manufacturing products.

EXECUTIVES

President and CEO, Bertrand Loy, age 50, $625,000 total compensation
EVP and CFO, Gregory B. (Greg) Graves, age 55, $321,826 total compensation
SVP and COO, Todd Edlund, age 53, $291,577 total compensation
Vice President, William (Bill) Shaner
Executive Vice President Chief Financial Officer, Greg (Greggy) Graves
Senior Vice President General Counsel and Corporate Secretary, Peter (Pete) Walcott
Senior Vice President Human Resources and Corporate Affairs, Jean-Marc Pandraud
Vice President Of Information Technology, Gary Bowman
Vice President Bus Development, Corey (Core) Rucci
Senior Vice President of Human Resources, John (Jack) Murphy
Vice President of Marketing, Wenge Yang
Vice President Marketing, Norman (Norm) Jaillet
Vice President of Corporate Relations, Steven (Steve) Cantor
Vice President Manufacturing, Fred (Freddy) Faulkner
Vice President of Liquid Filtration BU, Ben Lee
Vice President Business Development, Stuart (Stu) Tison
Vice President, James (Jamie) Geller
Chairman, Paul L. H. Olson, age 65
Auditors: KPMG LLP

LOCATIONS

HQ: Entegris Inc
129 Concord Road, Billerica, MA 01821
Phone: 978 436-6500   **Fax:** 952 556-1880
Web: www.entegris.com

PRODUCTS/OPERATIONS

2015 Sales

	$ mil.	% of total
Critical Materials Handling	671.3	62
Electronic Materials	409.8	38
Total	**1,081.1**	**100**

COMPETITORS

3M	Pall Corporation
Air Products	Parker-Hannifin
Brooks Automation	Peak International
Donaldson Company	SAES Getters
Illinois Tool Works	Saint-Gobain
L'Air Liquide	Schweiter Technologies
MKS Instruments	Shin-Etsu Chemical
Mersen Group	Tokai Carbon
Mirae	

HISTORICAL FINANCIALS

Company Type: Public

Income Statement

FYE: December 31

	REVENUE ($ mil.)	NET INCOME ($ mil.)	NET PROFIT MARGIN	EMPLOYEES
12/15	1,081.1	80.3	7.4%	3,557.0
12/14	962.0	7.8	0.8%	3,528.0
12/13	693.4	74.5	10.7%	3,200.0
12/12	715.9	68.8	9.6%	3,050.0
12/11	749.2	123.8	16.5%	2,765.0
Annual Growth	**9.6%**	**(10.3%)**	**—**	**6.5%**

2015 Year-End Financials

Debt ratio: 40.2%
Return on equity: 10.3%
Cash ($ mil.): 349.8
Current ratio: 4.05
Long-term debt ($ mil.): 617.2

No. of shares (mil.): 140.7
Dividends
  Yield: —
  Payout: —
Market value ($ mil.): 1,867.0

	STOCK PRICE ($) FY Close	P/E High/Low	PER SHARE ($) Earnings	Dividends	Book Value
12/15	13.27	26 21	0.57	0.00	5.71
12/14	13.21	234 171	0.06	0.00	5.35
12/13	11.59	21 17	0.53	0.00	5.46
12/12	9.18	20 15	0.50	0.00	5.02
12/11	8.73	11 7	0.91	0.00	4.48
Annual Growth	**11.1%**	**— —**	**(11.0%)**	**—**	**6.2%**

Epam Systems, Inc.

EPAM provides software development and other IT services to US and European customers primarily from development centers in Russia Belarus Hungary Ukraine Kazakhstan and Poland. In addition to software product development the company offers services in such areas as e-commerce support data warehousing customer relationship management and application integration. EPAM also offers its own hosted and stand-alone enterprise software for sales force automation content management order management and other business processes. Half of sales come from North America.

Operations

EPAM generates 69% of its revenue from software development. Another 19% comes from testing applications with application maintenance accounting for 8%.

Geographic Reach

North America is EPAM's biggest market accounting for 50% of revenue. European customers provide 39%. Russia and former members of the Soviet Union account for 15% of revenue.

The company has expanded geographically by adding client management offices in locations that are close to customers –including the US UK Germany Sweden Switzerland Russia and Kazakhstan –and by adding new development centers. In certain cases (such as Russia and Kazakhstan) EPAM has both development centers and client management offices in the same country.

Financial Analysis

EPAM has posted steady growth in revenue and net income over the past several years. Revenue increased 31% in 2014 to $730 million. The company broadened its sales to existing customers and

found new ones to drive up revenue. Sales jumped 30% in North America in 2014.

Net income rose 12% in 2014 to $69.6 million. Cash flow from operations also rose in 2014 reaching $104 million compared to $58 million in 2013.

Strategy

The company is looking to extend its expertise in targeted industry verticals which include independent software vendors banking and financial services business information and media hospitality and travel and retail and consumer. To do this EPAM continues to recruit IT professionals with specific industry knowledge and to pursue acquisitions that add to its service portfolio and customer base. Another part of EPAM's growth strategy is to make acquisitions of companies that have a significant presence in China Latin America and other emerging markets.

Mergers and Acquisitions

EPAM widened the services it offers with the 2014 acquisitions of Netsoft Holdings Joint Technology Development Limited GGA Software Services and Great Fridays Ltd. The expanded capabilities are in health care financial services and digital design areas.

EXECUTIVES

President and CEO, Arkadiy Dobkin, age 56, $300,000 total compensation
President EPAM Systems Europe; EVP EPAM Systems, Karl Robb, age 54, $3,572 total compensation
Global Head Banking and Financial Services Industry Business Unit, Balazs Fejes, age 41, $190,973 total compensation
CFO, Anthony J. Conte
Global Head Media Entertainment and Publishing Business Unit, Alexey Vitashkevich
Global Head Travel and Consumer Industry Business Unit, Elaina Shekhter‎
Head Global Delivery Organization, Sergey Yezhkov
Head North American Business Unit, Victor Dvorkin
Head Commonwealth of Independent States Business Unit, Vasily Agafonov
Head Global Operations, Alex Lyashok
Vice President, Eli (Elijah) Feldman
Senior Vice President, Mark (Marky) Bisker
Vice President Application And Cloud, Kamesh Chetty
Senior Vice President Business Transformation Chief Of Sta, Alan (Al) Harlan
Auditors: Deloitte & Touche LLP

LOCATIONS

HQ: Epam Systems, Inc.
41 University Drive, Suite 202, Newtown, PA 18940
Phone: 267 759-9000
Web: www.epam.com

PRODUCTS/OPERATIONS

2014 Sales

	$ mil.	% of total
Software development	504.6	69
Application testing services	140.4	19
Application maintenance & support	58.8	8
Infrastructure services	14.2	2
Licensing	3.6	1
Reimbursable expenses & other revenues	8.4	1
Total	**730.0**	**100**

2014 Sales by Industry

	$ mil.	% of total
Banking & financial services	215.4	29
Independent software vendors & technology	157.9	22
Travel & hospitality	157.8	22
Business information & media	91.7	13
Other verticals	98.8	13
Reimbursable expenses & other revenues	8.4	1
Total	**730.0**	**100**

Selected Services

Application development
Application maintenance and support
Application testing
Business intelligence
Business process management
Content management
Customer Relationship Management (CRM)
Data warehousing and business intelligence
E-commerce
Enterprise application integration
Enterprise resource planning
Infrastructure and hosting
Knowledge management
Localization
Offshore software development
Quality assurance consulting and testing strategy
   transformation
Server and network management

COMPETITORS

Accenture	Infosys
Atos	MindTree
Camelot Information	Pactera
Capgemini	Sapient
Cognizant Tech	Symphony Technology
Solutions	Group LLC
Computer Sciences	Tata Consultancy
Corp.	VanceInfo
GlobalLogic	Wipro
HCL Technologies	iSoftStone
IBM Global Services	

HISTORICAL FINANCIALS

Company Type: Public

Income Statement

FYE: December 31

	REVENUE ($ mil.)	NET INCOME ($ mil.)	NET PROFIT MARGIN	EMPLOYEES
12/15	914.1	84.4	9.2%	18,354.0
12/14	730.0	69.6	9.5%	14,109.0
12/13	555.1	61.9	11.2%	11,056.0
12/12	433.8	54.4	12.6%	10,043.0
12/11	334.5	44.3	13.3%	8,125.0
Annual Growth	**28.6%**	**17.5%**	**—**	**22.6%**

2015 Year-End Financials

Debt ratio: 4.5%
Return on equity: 15.6%
Cash ($ mil.): 199.4
Current ratio: 4.14
Long-term debt ($ mil.): 35.0

No. of shares (mil.): 50.1
Dividends
   Yield: —
   Payout: —
Market value ($ mil.): 3,944.0

	STOCK PRICE ($) FY Close	P/E High/Low		PER SHARE ($) Earnings	Dividends	Book Value
12/15	78.62	48	26	1.62	0.00	12.22
12/14	47.75	35	20	1.40	0.00	9.61
12/13	34.94	29	13	1.28	0.00	8.07
12/12	18.10	18	11	1.17	0.00	6.44
Annual Growth	**63.2%**	—	—	**11.5%**	**—**	**23.8%**

ePlus Inc

ePlus wants to rate an A-plus from its customers by meeting their hardware and software needs. ePlus is a holding company and operates through two business segments that deal in technology sales and financing. Its ePlus Technology subsidiary resells and leases products from top IT infrastructure providers. Offerings include security storage and networking products as well as consulting and systems integration services. It also offers supply chain management software and services; its proprietary applications include procurement asset management spend analytics and document management tools. The company's Leasing and Financial Services arm offers lease financing and leases IT and medical equipment.

Operations
The technology business generates 97% of the company's revenue with its financing business accounting for the rest.

Geographic Reach
Virginia-based ePlus rings up 98% of its sales in the US. The firm which operates from 30-plus offices across the US also has operations in Canada and Iceland.

Sales and Marketing
ePlus markets its products and services to midsized and large businesses state and municipal government agencies and institutions of higher education. Government agencies and institutions accounted for 22% of revenue in 2015 (ended March) followed by technology 19% telecommunications media and entertainment 18% financial services and healthcare both 10%.

Products manufactured by Cisco Systems HP and NetApp were 49% 8% and 7% of ePlus's sales of product and services in 2015 (ended March).

Financial Performance
In 2015 (ended March) sales increased 8% to $1.14 billion from $1.06 billion in 2014. Growth came from increased technology product and services sales to the company's medium and large customers. The revenue from the much smaller financing segment dropped because of lower margins on financing receivables.

Net income for ePlus jumped 30% in 2015 to reach $38.5 million; it was $325 million in 2014. Besides rising sales professional and other fees dropped about $5 million in 2015 from 2014 when the company racked up fees in patent infringement litigation.

ePlus turned around its cash flow from operations to a positive $13.8 million in 2015 from a negative cash flow of $8.2 million in 2014.

Strategy
ePlus which focuses exclusively on middle market and larger enterprises is gaining market share by focusing on fast growing segments within its market including cloud virtualization collaboration and security. The firm in fall 2014 was named an HP Gold Cloud Builder Specialist partner for its expertise in the design implementation and maintenance of HP Cloud computing environments.

ePlus' strategy includes expanding its professional services offerings organically —through the opening of new service centers —and via acquisitions. In 2014 the firm opened a new managed services center in Raleigh North Carolina adding to its existing presence in the state. In 2013 it opened offices in Scottsdale Arizona; Providence Rhode Island; and Portland Maine. Since going public it has acquired more than 15 businesses.

Mergers and Acquisitions

To shore up its security offerings ePlus bought IGX Acquisition Global a provider of security products and services in 2015. Beyond products the IGX acquisition deepens ePlus' presence in New York and Boston and brings it to the Connecticut market.

In August 2014 the company acquired Granite Business Solutions Inc. (dba Evolve Technology Group) a provider of IT products and services in Sacramento California. The purchase expanded ePlus's presence in the Golden State.

EXECUTIVES

Vice President Finance, George Fox
SVP Business Operations, Steven J. (Steve) Mencarini, age 60, $275,000 total compensation
President and CEO, Mark P. Marron, age 54, $475,000 total compensation
President ePlus Systems and ePlus Content Services, Kenneth G. Farber
CFO, Elaine D. Marion, age 48, $400,000 total compensation
CTO, Mark C. Melvin
President ePlus Group, Chad Fredrick
EVP Technology Sales, Darren Raiguel
President ePlus Government, Andrew L. Norton
Vice President, Andy Shulman
Vice President, Jay (JayJay) Farrell
Vice President of Human Resour, Jim (Jimmy) Solomone
Vice President and Corporate Controller, Jim (Jimmy) Belger
Vice President, Herbert (Hank) Brown
Regional Vice President, Lisa Neal
Vice President Business Development, Kevin Detsch
Senior Vice President, Gary J (Gar) Miglicco
Vice President Of Sales, Mark Gonzalez
Vice President Sales, Marwan Bitar
Vice President Information Technology, Jay Zima
Executive Vice President ePlus Group Inc, Bruce (Brucey) Bowen
Vice President Operations and Strategic Alliances, Burt Gastonguay
Regional Vice President At Eplus Technol, John (Jack) Bengivenni
Vice President Software Engineering, MIKE (Mikey) BATES
Chairman, Phillip G. Norton, age 72
Auditors: Deloitte & Touche LLP

LOCATIONS

HQ: ePlus Inc
13595 Dulles Technology Drive, Herndon, VA 20171-3413
Phone: 703 984-8400
Web: www.eplus.com

PRODUCTS/OPERATIONS

2015 Sales

	$ mil.	% of total
Technology	1,108.5	97
Financing	34.8	3
Total	**1,143.3**	**100**

Services
Currently selected
Assessments
Project Management
Staging Configuration & Installation
Managed Services
On-Demand IT Services
Virtual CIO
ePlus Staffing Solutions
Executive Services Portfolio
OneSource IT - Procurement Services

HISTORICAL FINANCIALS

Company Type: Public

Income Statement

FYE: March 31

	REVENUE ($ mil.)	NET INCOME ($ mil.)	NET PROFIT MARGIN	EMPLOYEES
03/16	1,204.2	44.7	3.7%	1,074.0
03/15	1,143.2	45.8	4.0%	986.0
03/14	1,057.5	35.2	3.3%	934.0
03/13	983.1	34.8	3.5%	904.0
03/12	825.5	23.3	2.8%	833.0
Annual Growth	9.9%	17.6%	—	6.6%

2016 Year-End Financials

Debt ratio: 7.6%
Return on equity: 14.9%
Cash ($ mil.): 94.7
Current ratio: 1.75
Long-term debt ($ mil.): 19.0

No. of shares (mil.): 7.3
Dividends
  Yield: —
  Payout: —
Market value ($ mil.): 593.0

	STOCK PRICE ($) FY Close	P/E High/Low		PER SHARE ($) Earnings	Dividends	Book Value
03/16	80.51	17	11	6.09	0.00	43.30
03/15	86.93	14	8	6.19	0.00	37.79
03/14	55.76	15	9	4.37	0.00	33.15
03/13	46.21	11	7	4.32	2.50	29.23
03/12	31.97	12	8	2.84	0.00	27.45
Annual Growth	26.0%	—	—	21.0%	—	12.1%

EPR Properties

EPR Properties (formerly Entertainment Properties Trust) invests in places to play and learn. The self-administered real estate investment trust (REIT) owns around 140 movie megaplex theaters and theater-anchored entertainment retail centers around the US and Canada. The REIT buys properties from theater operators and leases them back to the original owners. Many of its theaters are leased to AMC Entertainment. EPR also owns ski resorts (for clients including Camelback Mountain Resorts) golf resorts (for operator TopGolf) waterparks (including Schlitterbahn parks) public charter schools early education centers and private schools.

Operations

The REIT owns three main types of properties: Entertainment Education and Recreation. Its Entertainment properties which generated 63% of its total revenue during 2015 in the form of rental income include multiplex theaters entertainment retail centers and family entertainment centers. Its Education properties (19% of revenue) consists of 70 public charter school properties 18 early childhood centers and three private schools. Its Recreation properties (17% of revenue) consist of ski areas waterparks and golf courses. Its Metro Daily Ski business consists of 14 ski properties located close to metropolitan areas including: Camelback Mountain Resort in Pennsylvania; Vermont's Mt. Snow; and a dozen other properties in Ohio and nine other mostly eastern states. EPR's waterpark properties are leased to Schlitterbahn. Its four Texas golf properties are operated by TopGolf.

Geographic Reach

The Kansas City Missouri-based REITs five largest markets are in Texas (13% of 2015 revenues) Ontario (10%) California (9%) Arizona (7%) and Illinois (6%).

Sales and Marketing

The REIT has more than 250 tenants and about 99% of its properties are currently leased. Its largest tenant is theater operator AMC which accounted for about 20% of its annual revenue during 2015. Other tenants include Schlitterbahn Regal Studio Movie Grill Altitude Trampoline Park TopGolf and Carolina Cinemas.

Financial Performance

EPR Properties' annual revenues have risen 40% since 2011 as new property acquisitions have spurred additional rental income. Its annual profits have grown nearly 70% over the same period as the REIT has kept a lid on rising operating and overhead costs. The REIT's revenue climbed 9% to $421 million during 2015 as property acquisitions (mostly movie theaters) and build-to-suite projects added to its rental revenue. Strong revenue growth and gains from property sales in 2015 boosted EPR's net income by 8% to $194.5 million for the year. The REIT's operating cash levels rose 11% to $278.5 million thanks to the rise in cash-denominated earnings.

Strategy

EPR Properties remains focused on its core movie theater business as Americans continue to flock to the movies even in uncertain markets. In April 2014 the company invested $118 million on 11 theater properties in seven states continuing to build its massive collection. Although megaplexes account for the majority of its holdings the company continues to look for opportunities to diversify its real estate holdings.

EXECUTIVES

President and CEO, Gregory K. (Greg) Silvers, age 52, $484,500 total compensation
SVP and Chief Investment Officer, Morgan G. (Jerry) Earnest, age 60, $392,700 total compensation
SVP CFO and Treasurer, Mark A. Peterson, age 52, $346,500 total compensation
SVP Secretary and General Counsel, Neil E. Sprague, age 60, $300,000 total compensation
Vice President Of Corporate Communications, Brian (Bri) Moriarty
Vice President Stategic Planning, Michael (Mel) Hirons
Senior Vice President and Chief Investment Officer, Jerry (Jerr) Morgan
Chairman, Robert J. Druten, age 69
Auditors: KPMG LLP

LOCATIONS

HQ: EPR Properties
909 Walnut Street, Suite 200, Kansas City, MO 64106
Phone: 816 472-1700   **Fax:** 816 472-5794
Web: www.eprkc.com

PRODUCTS/OPERATIONS

2015 Sales

	$ mil.	% of total
Rental Revenue	330.9	78
Mortgage and other financing income	70.2	17
Tenant reimbursements	16.3	4
Other income	3.6	1
Total	**421.0**	**100**

2015 Sales

	$ mil.	% of total
Entertainment	262.9	63
Education	82.1	19
Recreation	72.6	17
Corporate	3.0	1
Other	0.4	-
Total	**421.0**	**100**

COMPETITORS

Acadia Realty Trust
Cousins Properties
Lexington Realty Trust
National Retail Properties
One Liberty Properties
Reading International
Realty Income
Regal Entertainment
Simon Property Group
Tanger Factory Outlet
Taubman Centers
Vornado Realty

HISTORICAL FINANCIALS

Company Type: Public

Income Statement

FYE: December 31

	REVENUE ($ mil.)	NET INCOME ($ mil.)	NET PROFIT MARGIN	EMPLOYEES
12/15	421.0	194.5	46.2%	49.0
12/14	385.0	179.6	46.7%	40.0
12/13	343.0	180.2	52.5%	38.0
12/12	321.7	121.5	37.8%	31.0
12/11	301.6	115.2	38.2%	27.0
Annual Growth	8.7%	14.0%	—	16.1%

2015 Year-End Financials

Debt ratio: 47.0%
Return on equity: 9.7%
Cash ($ mil.): 4.2
Current ratio: 0.46
Long-term debt ($ mil.): 1,981.9

No. of shares (mil.): 60.8
Dividends
  Yield: 6.2%
  Payout: 122.2%
Market value ($ mil.): 3,555.0

STOCK PRICE ($)		P/E		PER SHARE ($)		
	FY Close	High/Low		Earnings	Dividends	Book Value
12/15	58.45	22	17	2.93	3.63	34.10
12/14	57.63	21	17	2.86	3.42	33.72
12/13	49.16	19	14	3.24	3.16	32.67
12/12	46.11	24	20	1.98	3.00	31.13
12/11	43.71	28	20	1.80	2.80	31.46
Annual Growth	7.5%	—	—	13.0%	6.7%	2.0%

EQT GP Holdings LP

Auditors: Ernst & Young LLP

LOCATIONS

HQ: EQT GP Holdings LP
625 Liberty Avenue, Suite 1700, Pittsburgh, PA 15222
Phone: 412 553-5700
Web: www.eqtmidstreampartners.com

HISTORICAL FINANCIALS

Company Type: Public

Income Statement

FYE: December 31

	REVENUE ($ mil.)	NET INCOME ($ mil.)	NET PROFIT MARGIN	EMPLOYEES
12/15	614.1	145.9	23.8%	0.0
12/14	476.5	103.5	21.7%	0.0
12/13	354.0	110.6	31.3%	0.0
12/12	236.2	89.6	38.0%	0.0
Annual Growth	37.5%	17.6%	—	—

2015 Year-End Financials

Debt ratio: 36.7%
Return on equity: —
Cash ($ mil.): 350.8
Current ratio: 1.15
Long-term debt ($ mil.): 669.0

No. of shares (mil.): 266.1
Dividends
Yield: 0.7%
Payout: 38.8%
Market value ($ mil.): 5,526.0

STOCK PRICE ($)		P/E		PER SHARE ($)		
	FY Close	High/Low		Earnings	Dividends	Book Value
12/15	20.76	89	46	0.39	0.15	5.89
12/14	0.00	—	—	(0.00)	0.00	16.34
Annual Growth	(64.0%)	—	—	—	—	—

Equity Lifestyle Properties Inc

Snow birds and empty nesters flock to communities developed and owned by Equity LifeStyle Properties. The real estate investment trust (REIT) owns and operates lifestyle-oriented residential properties aimed at retirees vacationers and second home owners. Other properties provide affordable housing for families. Equity LifeStyle Properties leases lots for factory-built homes cottages cabins and recreational vehicles. Available homes range in size and style. The REIT's portfolio includes more than 380 properties containing some 141000 lots in about 30 states and Canada. Properties are similar to site-built residential subdivisions with centralized entrances utilities gutters curbs and paved streets.Many of Equity LifeStyle's communities include club houses swimming pools game courts and other amenities. The company mainly focuses on developing properties in large metro areas near retirement and vacation spots.Subsidiary Realty Systems leases or finances homes at communities owned by Equity LifeStyle Properties. While home sales have dropped in recent years more customers are choosing to lease a home in light of uncertain economic conditions. The company has adjusted its strategy accordingly and significantly reduced its new home sales activities. Instead of selling new manufactured homes it rents them. Equity LifeStyle Properties also has bumped up rental rates in order to boost revenues. The company hopes to convert its home renters to buyers in the future as the economy recovers. Equity LifeStyle also is focused on offering smaller more energy efficient and affordable homes which are in high demand.The REIT which was founded in 1992 has significantly grown its portfolio over the years and continues to acquire properties located in high growth urban and resort areas such as Florida (which accounts for about 38% of revenues) Arizona and California. In 2011 the company acquired 74 manufactured home communities and one RV resort from Hometown America for some $1.5 billion. The deal added more than 31000 home sites in 16 states mostly in Florida and the northeastern US.The company also looks to expand existing properties to accommodate more tenants. It focuses on attracting customers and extending their stays by providing attractive amenities (cable TV laundry rooms) and common facilities (swimming pools tennis courts clubhouses) that foster a social atmosphere for tenants and keep occupancy turnover low.Equity LifeStyle Properties has been working to improve its membership business which gives members passes to certain properties within geographic zones in exchange for an annual fee. In 2008 it acquired Privileged Access an RV and vacation membership business which helped grow Equity LifeStyle Properties' client base. The deal added to Equity LifeStyle's other membership-based subsidiary Thousand Trails which has more than 130000 dues-paying members that have special access to campgrounds.Chairman Sam Zell (the so-called "Grave Dancer" of Equity Office Properties and Equity Residential fame) controls about 9% of the REIT.

EXECUTIVES

Vice President Human Resources, Barb (Barbie) Itter
Vice President, Norm Field
Auditors: Ernst & Young LLP

LOCATIONS

HQ: Equity Lifestyle Properties Inc
Two North Riverside Plaza, Suite 800, Chicago, IL 60606
Phone: 312 279-1400
Web: www.equitylifestyle.com

PRODUCTS/OPERATIONS

802089169

COMPETITORS

American Land Lease
Hometown America
International Leisure
Kampgrounds of America
Outdoor Resorts
Sun Communities
UMH Properties

HISTORICAL FINANCIALS

Company Type: Public

Income Statement

FYE: December 31

	REVENUE ($ mil.)	NET INCOME ($ mil.)	NET PROFIT MARGIN	EMPLOYEES
12/15	821.6	150.5	18.3%	4,100.0
12/14	776.8	138.4	17.8%	3,900.0
12/13	728.3	125.9	17.3%	3,700.0
12/12	709.8	74.4	10.5%	3,600.0
12/11	580.0	42.5	7.3%	3,500.0
Annual Growth	9.1%	37.2%		4.0%

2015 Year-End Financials

Debt ratio: 62.7%
Return on equity: 16.3%
Cash ($ mil.): 80.2
Current ratio: 0.52
Long-term debt ($ mil.): 2,145.7

No. of shares (mil.): 84.2
Dividends
Yield: 2.2%
Payout: 101.3%
Market value ($ mil.): 5,617.0

STOCK PRICE ($)		P/E		PER SHARE ($)		
	FY Close	High/Low		Earnings	Dividends	Book Value
12/15	66.67	43	33	1.54	1.50	10.98
12/14	51.55	37	25	1.41	1.30	10.87
12/13	36.23	66	26	1.28	1.00	10.72
12/12	67.29	110	96	0.66	1.75	10.33
12/11	66.69	225	171	0.32	0.75	11.28
Annual Growth	(0.0%)	—	—	48.1%	18.9%	(0.7%)

Essex Property Trust Inc

Essex Property Trust acquires develops redevelops and manages apartment communities focusing on the metropolitan areas of Los Angeles San Diego San Francisco and Seattle. The self-managed and self-administered real estate investment trust (REIT) owns more than 240 apartment communities —mostly in Southern California —and eight community properties under development. Essex also owns a handful of office buildings in its home state and has partial stakes in several apartment communities through joint ventures. The REIT adds to its portfolio through acquisitions and through the development and renovation of properties. Essex significantly expanded its property base after its 2014 acquisition of BRE Properties in a $4.3 billion deal.

OperationsEssex Property had interests in 246 communities (mostly garden-style but some midrise and high-rise) spanning 59160 apartment homes on the West Coast at the end of 2015. It also had stakes in four commercial buildings spanning over 319000 sq. ft. and eight active development projects with nearly 2450 apartment homes in various stages of development. Its property occupancy rates exceeded 96%.Rent from the apartment communities generated more than 99% of the company's total revenue in 2015.Geographic Reach

Palo Alto-based Essex Property's generated 44% of its revenue from properties in Southern California (in Los Angeles Orange San Diego and Ventura counties) during 2015; about 35% of its revenue from properties in Northern California (in the San Francisco Bay area); and 17% of its revenue from properties in the Seattle metro area. The REIT has offices in Woodland Hills Irvine San Jose and San Diego California; and in Bellevue Washington.

Financial Performance

Essex Property's annual revenues have more than doubled while its profits have grown nearly five-fold since 2011 thanks to rent-boosting property acquisitions and rising rental rates stemming from the strengthened economy.The REIT's revenue jumped 23% to $1.19 billion during 2015 mostly as newly acquired properties from the BRE merger and 10 other communities boosted rental revenues. Same-property revenues also increased thanks to an 8.1% rise in average rental rates (which reached $1741 per apartment home) as housing demand continued to strengthen.Strong revenue growth in 2015 allowed Essex Property's net income to nearly double to $232.12 million for the year. Its operating cash levels climbed 25% to $617.4 million on rising cash earnings.

Strategy

When making acquisitions Essex usually targets multifamily properties with more than 100 units and spends from $300 million to $500 million per transaction. It likes to be active in supply-constrained markets with populations of at least one million and drives rent growth through high occupancy rates (approximately 96% at year-end 2015). The REIT continually monitors its existing markets and isn't afraid to exit if the housing supply increases too much. The company sells off assets if they no longer fit into its strategy and often uses the money raised to buy newer communities and parcels of land.

Mergers and Acquisitions

During 2015 Essex bought interests in seven communities spanning 1722 apartment homes for $638 million which included the 8th & New Hope The Huxley The Dylan Reveal Avant Avant II and Enso community properties.In April 2014 Essex Property Trust acquired California-based BRE Properties forming a combined company in which former Essex shareholders hold about 63% of the combined company's stock and former BRE shareholders hold 37%. (The combined company retained the name Essex Property Trust.) The deal valued at about $4.3 billion greatly bolstered the REIT's presence in the multifamily market on the West Coast.

In 2013 Essex acquired ownership interests in eight communities comprising 1472 units for $462.5 million. The acquired apartment complexes are in San Francisco (2) Los Angeles Mountain View and San Diego California and in Kirkland and Seattle (2) Washington.

EXECUTIVES

Vice President Acquisitions, Bryan (Bry) Meyer
EVP Acquisitions, Craig K. Zimmerman, age 65, $325,000 total compensation
EVP Development, John D. Eudy, age 61, $325,000 total compensation

President and CEO, Michael J. (Mike) Schall, age 58, $450,000 total compensation
Executive Vice President Asset Management, John F. Burkart, $275,000 total compensation
Vice President Construction, Jeff (Jeffy) Lambert
Vice Chairman, Keith R. Guericke, age 67
Chairman, George M. Marcus, age 75
Auditors: KPMG LLLP

LOCATIONS

HQ: Essex Property Trust Inc
  1100 Park Place Suite 200, San Mateo, CA 94403
Phone: 650 655-7800
Web: www.essex.com

PRODUCTS/OPERATIONS

2015 Sales

	$ mil.	% of total
Rental & other property revenues		
Southern California	529.4	44
Northern California	416.3	35
Seattle Metro	201.4	17
Other real estate assets	38.3	3
Management & other fees from affiliates	9.0	1
Total	**1,194.4**	**100**

COMPETITORS

Apartment Investment and Management	Fairfield Residential
AvalonBay	Irvine Apartment Communities
Camden Property	UDR
Equity Residential	

HISTORICAL FINANCIALS

Company Type: Public

Income Statement

FYE: December 31

	REVENUE ($ mil.)	NET INCOME ($ mil.)	NET PROFIT MARGIN	EMPLOYEES
12/15	1,194.4	232.1	19.4%	1,806.0
12/14	969.3	122.1	12.6%	1,725.0
12/13	613.7	156.2	25.5%	1,173.0
12/12	543.4	125.2	23.1%	1,144.0
12/11	475.5	47.0	9.9%	1,099.0
Annual Growth	**25.9%**	**49.0%**	**—**	**13.2%**

2015 Year-End Financials

Debt ratio: 44.2%	No. of shares (mil.): 65.3
Return on equity: 3.7%	Dividends
Cash ($ mil.): 123.0	Yield: 2.4%
Current ratio: 1.03	Payout: 184.0%
Long-term debt ($ mil.): 5,315.4	Market value ($ mil.): 15,652.0

	STOCK PRICE ($) FY Close	P/E High/Low		PER SHARE ($)		
				Earnings	Dividends	Book Value
12/15	239.41	70	59	3.49	5.76	95.41
12/14	206.60	103	69	2.06	5.11	94.57
12/13	143.51	42	35	4.04	4.84	50.48
12/12	146.65	47	40	3.41	4.40	48.55
12/11	140.51	118	89	1.24	4.16	42.55
Annual Growth	**14.3%**	**—**	**—**	**29.5%**	**8.5%**	**22.4%**

Euronet Worldwide Inc.

Euronet Worldwide might soon have the whole world in its net —thanks to the growing electronic payments industry. The company offers money transfer and processing services and manages ATM networks and point-of-sale (POS) terminals for itself and others. It operates in three primary segments: epay (which sells prepaid mobile airtime and related products and services) EFT (electronic financial transaction processing software and ATM/POS management services); and consumer-to-consumer money transfer. Traditionally Euronet is highly acquisitive and has snatched up money transfer processing and similar companies around the world. Founded in 1994 its top markets are in the US Germany and the UK.

Operations

Euronet Worldwide operates through three business segments: epay the company's prepaid mobile airtime and prepaid card segment is the largest and brings in roughly 50% of sales. Consumer-to-consumer money transfers (under the Ria and AFEX Money Express brands) account for about 30% of sales while the EFT processing segment bringing in the rest. The EFT processing business manages nearly 21000 company- and client-owned ATMs as well as 672000 point-of-sale (POS) terminals worldwide. Most of its EFT income comes from interchange fees or fees paid per withdrawal or other ATM transaction. Geographic Reach

Kansas-based Euronet's five largest markets are the US (where it generated 26% of its 2014 revenue) Germany (23%) the UK (8%) Poland (7%) and Australia (5%). Other large markets include India Spain Italy Greece and New Zealand. The company has 30 offices across Europe a dozen in the Asia Pacific region and a handful of offices spread across the Middle East South America and Africa.

Sales and Marketing

Euronet Worldwide's clients include financial institutions retailers service providers and consumers. The company has 306000 retail locations across Europe the Middle East Asia Pacific the US and South America as well as an international network for distribution of prepaid mobile airtime (top-up). In Germany Euronet distributors are key intermediaries in mobile top-up sales.

Financial Performance

Euronet's revenues and profits have been rising over the past few years fueled by company acquisitions global network expansion and an overall strong consumer demand for digital payment mediums.The company's revenue jumped by 18% to a record $1.66 billion in 2014 mostly as its Money Transfer segment income swelled by 41% resulting from its acquisition of HiFX and the subsequent release of the new Walmart-2-Walmart money transfer service and growth in the volume of money transfers through Ria. Its EFT Processing segment grew 21% on an overall increase in the number of ATMs under management in its network and higher demand for DCC while its epay segment grew by 5% on increased demand for non-mobile products in Germany.Higher revenue in 2014 drove Euronet's net income up 16% to a record $101.6 million while its operating cash levels grew by 39% to $235 million on higher cash earnings and favorable working capital changes related to the timing of settlement processes with content providers in the epay segment and with correspondents in the Money Transfer segment.

Strategy

Euronet Worldwide has historically bolstered its three main business lines and entered new geographic markets by acquiring money transfer processing and similar companies in mature and emerging markets. Its 2014 acquisition of HiFX created the Walmart-2-Walmart money transfer service which allowed customers to transfer money to and from Walmart stores in the US; the new service coupled with global network expansion and strong organic growth from Ria's core business helped Euronet grow its money transfer network by 13% boosted operating income growth by 37% "and earned the confidence of the world's largest retailer" according to Euronet. The company has also been expanding its Independent ATM Deployment (IAD) networks to reach more customers worldwide. In 2015 for example it introduced new ATMs in the countries of Malaysia Cyprus and Portugal while also recently expanding its IAD network in Denmark France and the UK to bring its IAD presence to a total of 14 countries in Europe.Mergers and AcquisitionsIn mid-2014 Euronet Worldwide bolstered its Ria money transfer business after it purchased EIM (FX) Limited and its UK-based HiFX which expanded its offerings to include online-initiated account-to-account international payment and foreign exchange services to affluent individuals and small-to-medium sized businesses.In October 2015 the company acquired UK-based ATM operator YourCash adding some 5000 ATMs in the UK Ireland Belgium and the Netherlands. With that deal Euronet has independent ATM networks in 21 European countries.

Company Background

In late 2012 epay New Zealand acquired ezi-pay Ltd. making epay New Zealand the largest distributor of prepaid mobile and non-mobile content in the country. In late 2011 Euronet acquired German company cadooz AG from Palamon Capital Partners. cadooz provides vouchers and rewards for sales incentives customer acquisition and loyalty and employee satisfaction campaigns for the German Austrian and Polish markets across a broad range of industries. The unit joined Euronet's epay division.

Also in 2011 Euronet expanded its network in Poland with the acquisition of ATMs from Diebold. The deal added 535 ATMs to Euronet's Polish network (the largest in that country). In another 2011 deal Euronet acquired Smart PayNetwork which provides ATM outsourcing services card issuing and acquiring and merchant servicing in Romania. Previously in 2010 epay expanded into the growing South American markets with its acquisition of Brazil-based Telecom Net (which was known as Ativi but has since been renamed epay Brazil).

EXECUTIVES

Chairman President and CEO, Michael J. (Mike) Brown, age 59, $600,000 total compensation

EVP and General Counsel, Jeffrey B. (Jeff) Newman, age 62, $300,000 total compensation

EVP and CFO, Rick L. Weller, age 59, $365,000 total compensation

EVP and CEO Money Transfer Division, Juan C. Bianchi, age 45, $320,769 total compensation

EVP and CEO epay and EFT Asia Pacific Division, Kevin J. Caponecchi, age 50, $365,000 total compensation

Managing Director Greece, Nikos Fountas, $353,701 total compensation

SVP and CTO, Martin L. Br ckner

Auditors: KPMG LLP

LOCATIONS

HQ: Euronet Worldwide Inc.
3500 College Boulevard, Leawood, KS 66211
Phone: 913 327-4200　　**Fax:** 913 327-1921
Web: www.euronetservices.com

PRODUCTS/OPERATIONS

2014 Sales

	% of total
Epay	47
Money Transfer	31
EFT Processing	22
Adjustments	0
Total	**100**

Selected Subsidiaries

Bankomat 24/Euronet Sp. z o.o. (Poland)
Delta Euronet GmbH (Germany)
EFT Services Holding B.V. (Netherlands)
　Cashlink Bangladesh Ltd. (10%)
e-pay Holdings Limited (UK)
Euronet Adminisztracios Szolgaltato Kft (Hungary)
Euronet Business Holdings S.L. (Spain)
Euronet Card Services S.A. (Greece)
Euronet Services SRL (Romania)
Euronet TeleRecarga S.L. (Spain)
　Euronet MovilCarga S.L. (Spain 80%)
EWI Foreign Holdings Limited (Cyprus)
Gescoro Inc. (Canada)
RIA de Centroamérica S.A. de C.V. (El Salvador)
RIA Telecommunications of Canada Inc.
transact Elektronische Zahlungssysteme GmbH
　(Germany)

COMPETITORS

ACE Cash Express	MoneyGram
First Data	International
Fiserv	PULSE Network
Global Payments	Western Union

HISTORICAL FINANCIALS

Company Type: Public

Income Statement

FYE: December 31

	REVENUE ($ mil.)	NET INCOME ($ mil.)	NET PROFIT MARGIN	EMPLOYEES
12/15	1,772.2	98.8	5.6%	5,600.0
12/14	1,664.1	101.6	6.1%	4,600.0
12/13	1,413.1	87.9	6.2%	4,100.0
12/12	1,267.6	20.5	1.6%	3,900.0
12/11	1,161.3	36.9	3.2%	3,800.0
Annual Growth	11.1%	27.9%	—	10.2%

2015 Year-End Financials

Debt ratio: 19.3%	No. of shares (mil.): 53.0
Return on equity: 12.7%	Dividends
Cash ($ mil.): 457.5	Yield: —
Current ratio: 1.25	Payout: —
Long-term debt ($ mil.): 409.6	Market value ($ mil.): 3,841.0

	STOCK PRICE ($) FY Close	P/E High/Low		PER SHARE ($) Earnings	Dividends	Book Value
12/15	72.43	43	24	1.83	0.00	15.55
12/14	54.90	30	18	1.89	0.00	14.16
12/13	47.85	28	13	1.69	0.00	12.57
12/12	23.60	58	39	0.40	0.00	10.59
12/11	18.48	28	19	0.71	0.00	10.32
Annual Growth	40.7%	—	—	26.7%	—	10.8%

Evercore Partners Inc

Evercore Partners makes Investment Banking advisory its core business. It provides advisory services on mergers and acquisitions restructurings divestitures and financing to corporate clients. Boasting some $14 billion in assets under management the firm's investment management business principally manages and invests capital for clients including institutional investors such as corporate and public pension funds endowments insurance companies and high net-worth individuals. Evercore also makes private equity investments. Beyond the US the company operates globally through subsidiaries such as Evercore Europe in London. Evercore also has offices in Brazil Hong Kong and Singapore.

Operations

The firm's Investment Banking advisory segment is its core business accounting for 88% of its revenue in 2014. Evercore's Institutional Equities services offering equity research and securities trading for institutional clients resides under the Investment banking umbrella. Its Investment Management segment (12% of revenue) focuses on asset management for institutions wealthy individuals and private equity clients. The segment had $14 million in assets under management at the end of 2014 with $8.1 million of that attributable to Institutional Asset Management $5.7 billion attributable to Wealth Management and $0.3 billion attributable to Private Equity Clients. As part of this segment Evercore Trust provides investment management and trustee services to employee benefits plans.

Geographic Reach

While Evercore Partners operates globally the US accounted for about 65% of the firm's revenue in 2014. Latin America accounted for 7% while Europe and other countries made up 27%. Evercore's offices are in the US the UK Brazil Hong Kong and Singapore. It also has strategic alliances with leading firms in China Japan India Korea and Argentina.Sales and MarketingEvercore Partners had a staff of 1300 employees worldwide at the end of 2014.

Financial PerformanceEvercore Partner's rising revenues and profits over the last several years have been fueled by higher demand for its advisory services amidst a surge of merger and acquisition activity as the financial markets in the US and UK have become increasingly more attractive to investors. The firm's annual revenue jumped 20% to $915.8 million in 2014 mostly as its Investment Banking revenue rose from increased advisory fees from US- and UK-based businesses partially stemming from its late-2014 acquisition of ISI. The Investment Banking segment served some 418 clients during the year with 173 fees valued in excess of $1 million. The firm's investment advisory and management fees grew by 4% year-over-year as its assets under management in its Wealth Management unit continued to grow.Higher revenue and an absence of loss from discontinued operations in 2014 pushed Evercore's net income higher by 63% to $86.9 million while the firm's operating cash levels rose by 9% to $216 million on higher cash earnings.

Strategy

Evercore continues to grow by acquiring financial advisory firms that enhance its capabilities and by bolstering its Investment Banking business through expanding the number of sectors it serves. In 2014 Evercore continued to expand the scope of its core Advisory business by hiring experienced talent to bolster its proficiency in the fast-growing Technology Media and Telecommunications sector as well as the technology healthcare telecom and oil & gas sectors in the US and Europe. Its The firm also continues to move into new geographic markets that are receptive to its Investment Banking business model. In recent years Evercore has expanded into Canada and Singapore while forming advisory affiliates and alliances in Brazil Argentina Japan China South Korea and India as well as in Australia in early 2015. As an independent investment banking firm that isn't involved in commercial banking or proprietary trading Evercore has avoided the controversy swirling around competitors such as Goldman Sachs that results from the conflicts of interest that may occur at larger firms that both underwrite and invest in their clients.Mergers and AcquisitionsIn May 2015 Evercore expanded its reach into Germany and enhanced its sector expertise after buying the Frankfurt-based investment banking advisory boutique Kuna & Co. KG which specialized in real estate in Germany.In November 2014 the firm purchased ISI International Strategy & Investment bolstering its Investment Banking business' position as a scaled provider of non-proprietary capital markets advice and execution. The acquired company which was renamed Evercore ISI would start by providing macro research and fundamental coverage of more than 600 companies across 12 industries (60% of the S&P 500's market capitalization value).

Company Background

Some of Evercore's past high-profile transactions include the 2012 breakup of Kraft Foods (now Mondelez International) the recapitalizations of GM and CIT Group and the acquisition of Lubrizol by Berkshire Hathaway.

Evercore was launched in 1996 (it went public 10 years later) by Roger Altman who formerly led investment banking and merger advisory practices at Lehman Brothers and The Blackstone Group. Altman resigned as CEO in 2009 and was succeeded by Ralph Schlosstein co-founder of asset management giant BlackRock; Altman remained executive chairman.

EXECUTIVES

President and CEO, Ralph L. Schlosstein, age 65
Senior Managing Director and Co-Chairman Mexico Region, Pedro Aspe, age 65, $500,000 total compensation
CEO Evercore Wealth Management, Jeffrey S. (Jeff) Maurer
Senior Managing Director and General Counsel, Adam B. Frankel, age 48
Senior Managing Director Strategy and Business Development, Ciara A. Burnham
Senior Managing Director; Head Capital Markets Advisory, Jim Birle
Senior Managing Director; Global COO Investment Banking, Timothy G. LaLonde
Partner Chief Wealth Advisory Officer, Christopher Zander
Senior Managing Director; Head Restructuring, David Ying
CEO and Director Protego Asset Management Business, Sergio S⁻nchez
Senior Managing Director and CFO, Robert B. Walsh, age 60, $500,000 total compensation
Senior Managing Director; Vice Chairman and CEO Europe Investment Banking, Andrew Sibbald, age 49
EVP Process Equipment, William J. Miller

Chairman Evercore ISI; Head Economic Research Team, Ed Hyman
Senior Managing Director; CEO Private Funds Group, Richard Anthony
Senior Managing Director; Head Private Capital Advisory Group, Nigel Dawn
Partner and Chief Investment Officer, John Apruzzese
Senior Managing Director, Renato Klarnet
Senior Managing Director Evercore Mexico Capital Partners, Alfredo Castellanos
Managing Director; European Head Private Capital Advisory., Nicolas Lanel
Managing Director Private Funds Group Asia Pacific, Ian Bell
Senior Managing Director European Equity Capital Markets Advisory, Jim Renwick
Vice President Information Technology, Paolo Nicolosi
Vice President, Jay (JayJay) Mirostaw
Vice President, Fausto Borotto
Vice President Media Investment Banking, Jaison Thomas
Vice President, Donatella De Ieso
Vice President, Lana (Alana) Wong
Vice President, Ken (Kenny) Auspaker
Vice President and Litigation Counsel, Brogiin Keeton
Vice President, Steven (Steve) Becker
Executive Chairman, Roger C. Altman, age 71
Auditors: Deloitte & Touche LLP

LOCATIONS

HQ: Evercore Partners Inc
55 East 52nd Street, 38th floor, New York, NY 10055
Phone: 212 857-3100   **Fax:** 212 857-3101
Web: www.evercore.com

PRODUCTS/OPERATIONS

2011 Sales

	$ mil.	% of total
Investment banking	430.6	80
Investment management	99.2	18
Other	13.9	2
Total	**543.7**	**100**

COMPETITORS

Allen & Company	Greenhill
Atalanta Sosnoff	JPMorgan Chase
Bank of America	Lazard
Barclays Capital	Merrill Lynch
Blackstone Group	Moelis & Company
Citigroup Global	Morgan Stanley
Markets	Rothschild North
Credit Suisse	America
Deutsche Bank	UBS Investment Bank
Goldman Sachs	

HISTORICAL FINANCIALS

Company Type: Public

Income Statement

FYE: December 31

	REVENUE ($ mil.)	NET INCOME ($ mil.)	NET PROFIT MARGIN	EMPLOYEES
12/15	1,223.2	42.8	3.5%	1,400.0
12/14	915.8	86.8	9.5%	1,300.0
12/13	765.4	53.2	7.0%	1,000.0
12/12	642.3	28.8	4.5%	900.0
12/11	524.2	6.9	1.3%	800.0
Annual Growth	**23.6%**	**57.6%**	**—**	**15.0%**

2015 Year-End Financials

Debt ratio: 9.5%	No. of shares (mil.): 39.6
Return on equity: 8.1%	Dividends
Cash ($ mil.): 450.9	Yield: 2.1%
Current ratio: 1.84	Payout: 96.6%
Long-term debt ($ mil.): 141.8	Market value ($ mil.): 2,142.0

	STOCK PRICE ($) FY Close	P/E High/Low	Earnings	Dividends	Book Value
12/15	54.07	51 41	0.98	1.15	12.73
12/14	52.37	26 19	2.08	1.03	15.21
12/13	59.78	37 18	1.38	0.91	15.20
12/12	30.19	31 21	0.89	0.82	14.49
12/11	26.62	142 81	0.23	0.74	14.59
Annual Growth 19.4%		— —	43.7%	11.7%	(3.3%)

Evolution Petroleum Corp

Just as petroleum and natural gas evolves from old living forms Evolution Petroleum has evolved by producing these ancient hydrocarbons. The company operates oil and gas producing fields in Louisiana Oklahoma and Texas. Its strategy is to acquire already-established properties and redevelop them making the fields more profitable. One method it uses is gas flooding which uses carbon dioxide to free up trapped oil deposits. Assets include a CO_2-project in Louisiana's Delhi Field and patented artificial lift technology to extend the life and ultimate recoveries of wells with oil or associated water production. It reported 10.8 million barrels of oil equivalent proved reserves in fiscal 2016.

Operations

Evolution Petroleum is engaged in the acquisition exploitation and development of properties for the production of crude oil and natural gas. It five major projects are Delhi Field Enhanced Oil Recovery(EOR)—Northeast Louisiana (which has produced 192 million barrels of crude oil and substantial amounts of natural gas to date); Mississippi Lime—North Central Oklahoma Kay County (a limestone formation that horizontal drilling combined with multistage hydraulic fracturing has opened up to redevelopment); GARP (Gas Assisted Rod Pump artificial lift technology being commercialized through subsidiary NGS Technologies; and Giddings Field—Central Texas (2180 net developed acres); and Lopez Field—South Texas (782 net acres).

Geographic Reach

The company has operations in Northeast Louisiana Southeast Oklahoma South Texas Central Texas and North Central Oklahoma.

Sales and Marketing

The company markets its production to third parties. It sells its crude oil under the Delhi Field operator's agreement with Plains Marketing LP for the delivery and pricing.

Financial Performance

Evolution Petroleum's revenues decreased by 5.4% to $26.35 million in fiscal 2016 (June year end) due to a 55% slump in realized prices which more than offset a 45% increase in production volumes. The company's net income increased by 394% in fiscal 2016 to $24.7 million due to litigation settlement proceeds insurance proceeds and realized hedging gains offset in part by increased DD&A expenses litigation expenses and higher income tax expense. The company settled outstanding litigation with the operator of Delhi field during the year. In the settlement Evolution Petroleum received $27.5 million in cash.

In fiscal 2016 cash flows provided by operating activities of $30.7 million reflected $28.9 million provided by operations and $1.8 million provided by other working capital changes. Of the $28.9 million provided before working capital changes some $24.7 million came from net income and $4.2 million from non-cash expenses and gains.

Strategy

Evolution Petroleum acquires known underdeveloped oil and natural gas resources and exploit them through the application of capital sound engineering and modern technology to increase production ultimate recoveries or both.

It strategy is intended to generate scalable low unit cost development and re-development opportunities that minimize or eliminate exploration risks. These opportunities involve the application of modern technology its own proprietary technology and its specific expertise in overlooked areas of the United States where it may or may not choose to be the operator. The assets it exploits currently fit into three types of project opportunities: EOR Bypassed Primary Resources and Unconventional Development using its staff expertise in horizontal drilling.

Company Background

In 2013 to raise cash the company sold all of its non-GARP producing wells and drilling locations in its Giddings assets.

In 2008 in order to raise cash Evolution Petroleum sold its working interests in some oil fields in LaSalle and Winn Parishes Louisiana to a private buyer for $4.6 million.

The company was formed in 2003.

EXECUTIVES

President and CEO, Randall D. Keys, age 56, $295,500 total compensation
SVP and CFO, David Joe, age 51, $205,000 total compensation
Chairman, Robert S. Herlin, age 61
Auditors: Hein & Associates LLP

LOCATIONS

HQ: Evolution Petroleum Corp
1155 Dairy Ashford Road, Suite 425, Houston, TX 77079
Phone: 713 935-0122   **Fax:** 713 935-0199
Web: www.evolutionpetroleum.com

PRODUCTS/OPERATIONS

2016 Sales

	% of total
Crude oil	99
Artificial lift technology services	1
Total	**100**

Selected Operations

CO2-based enhanced oil recovery
Low-permeablitiy reservoir development
Technology-based redevelopment of old oil and gas fields

COMPETITORS

Abraxas Petroleum	EOG
Anadarko Petroleum	Midstates Petroleum
Callon Petroleum	Saratoga Resources
Carrizo Oil & Gas	Triangle Petroleum
Chesapeake Energy	

HISTORICAL FINANCIALS

Company Type: Public

Income Statement   FYE: June 30

	REVENUE ($ mil.)	NET INCOME ($ mil.)	NET PROFIT MARGIN	EMPLOYEES
06/16	26.3	24.6	93.6%	6.0
06/15	27.8	4.9	17.9%	10.0
06/14	17.6	3.6	20.4%	8.0
06/13	21.3	6.6	31.0%	11.0
06/12	17.9	5.1	28.6%	10.0
Annual Growth	10.1%	48.1%	—	(12.0%)

2016 Year-End Financials

Debt ratio: —	No. of shares (mil.): 32.9
Return on equity: 39.3%	Dividends
Cash ($ mil.): 34.0	Yield: 3.6%
Current ratio: 4.35	Payout: 133.3%
Long-term debt ($ mil.): —	Market value ($ mil.): 180.0

	STOCK PRICE ($) FY Close	P/E High/Low		PER SHARE ($) Earnings	Dividends	Book Value
06/16	5.47	10	5	0.73	0.20	2.32
06/15	6.59	85	44	0.13	0.30	1.48
06/14	10.95	151	118	0.09	0.30	1.59
06/13	10.91	54	36	0.19	0.00	1.92
06/12	8.34	62	38	0.14	0.00	1.67
Annual Growth	(10.0%)	—	—	51.1%	—	8.5%

ExlService Holdings Inc

Have an extra-large task you'd rather not take on? Outsource it to ExlService Holdings. The company known as EXL offers business process outsourcing (BPO) research and analytics and consulting services. EXL's BPO offerings which generate most of its sales include claims processing collections customer support and finance and accounting. Customers come mainly from the banking financial services and insurance industries as well as from the utilities and telecommunications sectors. EXL operates offices around the world including the US and countries in Eastern Europe and Asia. The company was established in 1999.

Geographic Reach

EXL operates through six offices in the US 19 offices in India as well as through a half-a-dozen locations in the Czech Republic Bulgaria Romania Malaysia and the Philippines. The company also has a sales office in the UK and networking and telecommunications centers in California New Jersey and New York.

Sales and Marketing

EXL earned revenue from more than 600 clients in 2014 with its top three clients generating 22% of its revenue.

Financial Performance

The company's revenue was $499 million in fiscal 2014. That was an increase of more than $20 million compared to the prior fiscal period. EXL's net income was $32.4 million in fiscal 2014 which was a decrease of $15.7 million compared to its fiscal 2013 net income. The company's cash flow from operations decreased by more than $16 million during fiscal 2014 compared to the prior fiscal period but the company still ended the year with $66.7 million in cash on hand.

EXECUTIVES

Vice Chairman and CEO, Rohit Kapoor, age 51, $600,000 total compensation
President and COO, Pavan Bagai, age 54, $242,590 total compensation
EVP and Business Head Insurance, Vikas Bhalla, age 44
EVP and Business Head Health Care, Rembert de Villa, age 59, $382,534 total compensation
EVP and CFO, Vishal Chhibbar, age 48, $251,341 total compensation
EVP General Counsel and Corporate Secretary, Nancy Saltzman, age 50
CTO, Mike Toma
EVP and Chief Human Resource Officer, Nalin Miglani, age 55, $400,000 total compensation
Chairman, Garen K. Staglin, age 71
Auditors: Ernst & Young LLP

LOCATIONS

HQ: ExlService Holdings Inc
280 Park Avenue, 38th Floor, New York, NY 10017
Phone: 212 277-7100
Web: www.exlservice.com

PRODUCTS/OPERATIONS

2014 Sales

	$ mil.	% of total
Operations Management	388.7	78
Analytics and Business Transformation	110.6	22
Total	**499.3**	**100**

COMPETITORS

Accenture	Infosys
Genpact	Tata Consultancy
HP Enterprise Services	WNS (Holdings)
IBM Global Services	Wipro

HISTORICAL FINANCIALS

Company Type: Public

Income Statement   FYE: December 31

	REVENUE ($ mil.)	NET INCOME ($ mil.)	NET PROFIT MARGIN	EMPLOYEES
12/15	628.4	51.5	8.2%	24,100.0
12/14	499.2	32.4	6.5%	22,800.0
12/13	478.4	48.1	10.1%	22,200.0
12/12	442.9	41.8	9.4%	21,000.0
12/11	360.5	34.7	9.6%	18,900.0
Annual Growth	14.9%	10.3%	—	6.3%

2015 Year-End Financials

Debt ratio: 10.8%	No. of shares (mil.): 33.0
Return on equity: 11.6%	Dividends
Cash ($ mil.): 219.0	Yield: —
Current ratio: 3.17	Payout: —
Long-term debt ($ mil.): 60.2	Market value ($ mil.): 1,487.0

	STOCK PRICE ($) FY Close	P/E High/Low		PER SHARE ($) Earnings	Dividends	Book Value
12/15	44.93	31	18	1.51	0.00	14.07
12/14	28.71	31	25	0.96	0.00	12.74
12/13	27.62	22	16	1.42	0.00	11.38
12/12	26.50	23	16	1.26	0.00	10.70
12/11	22.37	23	16	1.10	0.00	8.93
Annual Growth	19.0%	—	—	8.2%	—	12.0%

Extended Stay America Inc

Guests at this hotel chain need not worry about wearing out their welcome. The company owns and operates some 680 Extended Stay hotels. Extended Stay brands include Extended Stay America Extended Stay Canada and Crossland Economy Studios. A hybrid between a hotel and an apartment its lodgings offer all-suite accommodations targeting business and leisure travelers looking for a temporary place to call home. The rooms feature separate living and dining areas and fully-equipped kitchens. Extended Stay can charge lower rates than hotels by eliminating room service and daily maid services. In 2013 the company went public.

IPO

Extended Stay America raised $565 million which it will use to buy stock in its real estate investment trust the tax-free entity that owns its hotels' properties. Any remainder will be used to pay down debt and for general corporate purposes.

Geographic Reach

The company manages hotel properties in 44 US states and Canada. California is home to 85 properties Texas has about 70 and Florida has more than 50. All other states have less than 35 hotels. There are only three Extended Stay Canada properties.

Sales and Marketing

Extended Stay hotels cater mostly to business travelers; its average length of stay is 28 days while the average stay at a regular hotel is 2.5 days. As such the company's sales team focuses on building relationships with certain companies to attract repeat guests. While it does not offer a loyalty program it does use its customer database for targeted marketing and promotional campaigns.

Most of its reservations are made directly with the property less than 10% of stays are booked through third-party hotel booking websites. Extended Stay outsources its reservation system call center operations and the management of its website.

Financial Performance

Overall revenues increased 7% in 2012 to $1 billion up from $942000 in 2011. Room sales were up due to a 10% increase in the average daily rate the company charged despite occupancy being down 2%. The company also lost about $2 million in other revenue by offering free WiFi Internet access in 2012 but it justified the loss through customer satisfaction.

Strategy

In order to achieve brand consistency the company recently consolidated most of its brands under the Extended Stay America. Previously almost 300 hotels were branded as Homestead Studio Suites Studio Plus and Extended Stay Deluxe.

The company is also in the process of renovating 90% its hotels for a total cost of almost $380 million. About 300 hotels are being treated to a million-dollar renovation which includes remodeling of common areas new paint carpet signs floors and counters in bathrooms and kitchens as well as new mattresses and flat screen TVs artwork lighting bedspreads and refurbished furniture. The company is spending $150000 a pop on renovations at 300 other hotels which includes new mattresses flat screen TVs lighting bedspreads and signs.

Auditors: Deloitte & Touche LLP

LOCATIONS

HQ: Extended Stay America Inc
11525 N. Community House Road, Suite 100,
Charlotte, NC 28277
Phone: 980 345-1600
Web: www.extendedstay.com

COMPETITORS

Capital Hotel	Island Hospitality
Management	Sage Hospitality
Dow Hotel Company	Travelodge
Hostmark Hospitality	Westmont Hospitality
Interstate Hotels	Group

HISTORICAL FINANCIALS

Company Type: Public

Income Statement

FYE: December 31

	REVENUE ($ mil.)	NET INCOME ($ mil.)	NET PROFIT MARGIN	EMPLOYEES
12/15	1,284.7	283.0	22.0%	8,500.0
12/14	1,213.4	150.5	12.4%	9,100.0
12/13	1,132.8	86.2	7.6%	10,000.0
12/12	1,011.4	20.7	2.0%	10,400.0
12/11	942.7	45.5	4.8%	0.0
Annual Growth	8.0%	57.9%	—	—

2015 Year-End Financials

Debt ratio: 60.9%	No. of shares (mil.): 204.5
Return on equity: 33.9%	Dividends
Cash ($ mil.): 373.2	Yield: 5.7%
Current ratio: 1.95	Payout: 325.0%
Long-term debt ($ mil.): 2,762.3	Market value ($ mil.): 3,253.0

	STOCK PRICE ($) FY Close	P/E High/Low		PER SHARE ($) Earnings	Dividends	Book Value
12/15	15.90	39	29	0.55	0.91	4.30
12/14	19.31	140	93	0.19	0.53	3.86
12/13	26.26	53	48	0.49	0.00	3.64
Annual Growth	(22.2%)	—	—	5.9%	—	8.7%

Extra Space Storage Inc

When closets are bursting at the seams and garages are overflowing Extra Space Storage gives its customers room to breathe. One of the largest operators and managers of self-storage properties in the US the self-administered self-managed real estate investment trust (REIT) wholly-owns owns in joint-venture partnerships or operates for third parties about 1030 facilities with some 680000 units totaling nearly 76 million sq. ft. of rentable space. Active in metropolitan areas in nearly 35 states and Washington DC the company also offers business boat and RV storage and leases to nearly 600000 tenants nationwide.

Geographic Reach

Utah-based Extra Space Storage operates its business throughout the US in 35 states Puerto Rico and Washington DC.

Operations

Extra Space Storage operates through three segments: rental operations; tenant reinsurance; and property management acquisition and development.

The rental operations segment focuses on rentals of the self-storage facilities it owns. Tenant reinsurance covers the reinsurance of risks relating to the loss of goods stored by tenants in the company's self-storage facilities. Its last segment — property management acquisition and development —manages acquires develops and sells self-storage facilities.

Strategy

The REIT has relied on acquisitions in growing markets to expand its business. In 2014 Extra Space Storage acquired a self-storage portfolio of 17 assets located in Virginia for about $200 million. The deal gave the company 1.5 million sq. ft. of net rentable space across 14000 units. The company also has another five properties under contract for an approximate purchase price of $58 million. In 2012 Extra Space Storage added to its holdings with the acquisition of 21 properties in about a dozen states from a joint venture partner. It acquired a noteworthy 55 properties in 2011.

Extra Space Storage is also looking to expand Extra Space Management its third-party property management subsidiary.

Financial Performance

The storage company's revenue rose some $111.22 million in fiscal 2013 or 27% to $520.6 million continuing several years of incremental growth. It attributes the increases to a boost in property rental and tenant reinsurance revenue. Property rental revenue rose thanks to its purchase of 78 properties during 2013 and 91 properties during 2012.

Extra Space Storage logged $172.1 million in net income in fiscal 2013 representing a $54.78 million increase or a 47% jump overall. Higher revenues a gain on the sale of real estate assets and the purchase of a joint venture partners' interest all contributed to the spike.

Cash flow from operations also increased —by $55.38 million in 2013 —to $271.26 million from higher net income and the net change in working capital.

EXECUTIVES

Executive Vice President Chief Operating Officer, Karl Haas

CEO and Director, Joseph D. (Joe) Margolis, age 55, $290,000 total compensation

EVP and CFO, P. Scott Stubbs, $437,750 total compensation

SVP Marketing and Corporate Communications, James Overturf

VP Revenue Management, Samrat Sondhi

EVP and Chief Legal Officer, Gwyn McNeal

Senior Vice President Operations, Timothy Arthurs

Vice President, Alex Engel

Divisional Vice President, Tony Chung

Vice President General Counsel And Ass, David (Dave) Rasmussen

Vice President Treasury and Risk, Stephen (Steve) Blake

Vice President And Associate General Cou, Jed Burton

Vice President Acquisitions, Bret Durfee

Vice President Information Technology, Ellie Casanova

Senior Vice President of Acquisitions and Business Development, Jim (Jimmy) Stevens

Vice President Of Asset Management, Brent Hardy

Chairman, Kenneth M. Woolley, age 69

Auditors: Ernst & Young LLP

LOCATIONS

HQ: Extra Space Storage Inc
2795 East Cottonwood Parkway, Suite 400, Salt Lake City, UT 84121
Phone: 801 365-4600
Web: www.extraspace.com

PRODUCTS/OPERATIONS

2015 Sales

	$ mil.	% of total
Property rental	676.1	87
Tenant reinsurance	72.0	9
Management & franchise fees	34.2	4
Total	**782.3**	**100**

COMPETITORS

AMERCO	Mobile Mini
CubeSmart	PODS Enterprises
Life Storage	Public Storage

HISTORICAL FINANCIALS

Company Type: Public

Income Statement
FYE: December 31

	REVENUE ($ mil.)	NET INCOME ($ mil.)	NET PROFIT MARGIN	EMPLOYEES
12/15	782.2	209.5	26.8%	3,209.0
12/14	647.1	195.9	30.3%	2,643.0
12/13	520.6	185.5	35.6%	2,584.0
12/12	409.4	127.6	31.2%	2,283.0
12/11	329.8	58.4	17.7%	2,239.0
Annual Growth	24.1%	37.6%	—	9.4%

2015 Year-End Financials

Debt ratio: 58.2%	No. of shares (mil.): 124.1
Return on equity: 10.9%	Dividends
Cash ($ mil.): 75.8	Yield: 2.5%
Current ratio: 2.02	Payout: 118.5%
Long-term debt ($ mil.): 3,499.6	Market value ($ mil.): 10,949.0

	STOCK PRICE ($) FY Close	P/E High/Low	PER SHARE ($) Earnings	Dividends	Book Value
12/15	88.21	57 37	1.56	2.24	16.83
12/14	58.64	39 27	1.53	1.81	14.93
12/13	42.13	32 24	1.53	1.45	15.19
12/12	36.39	32 21	1.14	0.85	13.47
12/11	24.23	45 32	0.54	0.56	10.75
Annual Growth	38.1%	— —	30.4%	41.4%	11.9%

F5 Networks, Inc.

F5 Networks' products keep data running through data centers like a winning car in an F1 race: fast safe and securely. The company's products include application delivery controllers (ADC) and software that are used for network load balancing availability assurance and security assessment. The company also provides file virtualization WAN optimization and remote access products. F5 Networks products are based on its Traffic Management Operating System (TMOS) platform. The company also offers such services as network monitoring performance analysis and training. F5 Networks targets customers in telecommunications manufacturing and financial services. More than half of its sales come from the Americas.

Operations

F5's revenue is split about 50-50 between products and services. The company outsources manufacturing of its hardware products to Flex LTD. which handles everything from sourcing materials to warranty repairs.

Geographic Reach

The Americas accounts for nearly 60% of F5's sales with more than 50% of sales from the US alone. Overseas Europe generates about a quarter of F5's revenue and the Asia/Pacific region supplies less than a fifth.

The company's software developers are in Seattle (headquarters) San Jose California and Tel Aviv Israel. Hardware engineers are in Spokane Washington San Jose and Tel Aviv. F5 also operates a product testing and quality control facility in Warsaw Poland.Sales and MarketingThe company sells primarily through distributors systems integrators and resellers although it also maintains a direct sales force for major enterprise accounts. Distribution giants Westcon Group Avnet Technology Solutions Arrow Electronics and Ingram Micro together account for about 60% of the company's sales. A significant percentage of revenue comes from sales to US and foreign federal state and local governments end users.

F5 spends about $4 million a year on advertising.

Financial PerformanceF5's revenue bumped up 4% to about $2 billion in 2016 (ended September) buoyed by a 13% increase in service revenue. Working from a bigger installed base of products customers bought and renewed more maintenance contracts in 2016 from 2015 and contracted for more consulting services. Product revenue fell about 5% in 2016 from 2015 because of lower sales of application delivery networking (ADN) products.

The company's profits for 2016 and 2015 were virtually the same at about $365 million. Revenue rose enough to cover increased spending on sales and marketing (up 4%) and research and development (up 13%) and keep profit steady.

F5's operating cash flow increased to $710 million in 2016 from about $680 million in 2015 because of positive accounts receivable and a lower level of inventory.

Strategy

F5 Networks operates in a highly competitive market bumping up against tech powerhouses Cisco Systems EMC (part of Dell Technologies) Brocade and Citrix as well as smaller companies such as A10 Networks and Barracuda Networks.

The company's broader strategy for growing sales includes delivering products as integrated software modules; focusing product development on software as well as hardware and keeping an eye out for gaining new technologies through acquisitions; developing strategic technology partnerships with such vendors as Oracle and SAP; and using the company's online community of network architects and developers known as DevCentral for product development.

As Software Defined Networking (SDN) has become more prominent F5 has developed partnerships with Cisco Microsoft and VMware to provide applications services for their SDN offerings. It also has partnerships with Amazon's Amazon Web Services Microsoft's Azure VMware vCloud Air and other cloud computing providers for cloud-based application services.

Mergers and AcquisitionsIn 2014 the company acquired Defense.Net Inc. for an undisclosed price. Defense.Net was a privately-held provider of cloud-based security services for protecting data centers and Internet applications from distributed denial-of-service (DDoS) attacks.

EXECUTIVES

Senior Vice President And Corporate Compliance Officer, John (Jack) Rodriguez
Senior Vice President Product Development and Chief Technology Officer, Karl Triebes
President CEO and Director, John McAdam, age 64, $727,416 total compensation
EVP and COO, Edward J. Eames, age 57, $461,000 total compensation
President CEO and Director, Francois Locoh-Donou, age 44
EVP and Chief Marketing Officer, Benjamin (Ben) Gibson, age 47, $66,667 total compensation
EVP Worldwide Sales, John D. DiLullo, age 49, $361,068 total compensation
EVP and CFO, Andy Reinland, age 51, $450,000 total compensation
EVP and General Counsel, Scot Rogers, age 48
SVP Information Technology and CIO, Tony Bozzuti
EVP Product Development and CTO, Ryan Kearny, age 46
Vice President Worldwide Channel Sales, Dean Darwin
Executive Vice President Worldwide Sales, David (Dave) Feringa
Senior Vice President of Business Operations and Global Services, Julian (Jules) Eames
Senior Vice President Security and Strategic Solutions, Manuel (Mannie) Rivelo
Vice President Of Technology, Bill Baumann
Vice President Finance EMEA, Pat Brennan
Vice President Develop, Patrick (Paddy) Jenny
Vice President Technology and ISV Alliances F5 Networks, Calvin (Cal) Rowland
RVP, Peter (Pete) McNamara
Vice President Service Provider Sales, Jim Labovites
Area Vice President of Sales, Chris (Chrissy) Deardurff
Vice President Information Technology, Aaron Hooley
Vice President Internal Audit, Brian Blank
Vice President Marketing, Richard (Dick) Darnielle
RVP Sales, Paul Werner
Vice President Global Services And WW Service Channels, Jim (Jimmy) Tickner
Vice President WW Security Sales, Brent Simon
Vice President Business Development, Jim Ritchings
Senior Vice President Security and Strategic Solutions, Manny (Emanuel) Rivelo
Vice President Operations, Steve Levy
Vice President Of Finance, Renae Culala
Vice President Product Development, Michael (Mel) Corrigan
Executive Vice President and Chief Marketing Officer, Ben (Benny) Gibson
Chairman, Alan J. Higginson, age 69
Treasurer and Consolidations Manager, David (Dave) Scharler
Board Member, James (Jamie) Hockley
Member Board Of Directors, Sandra (Sandy) Bergeron
Auditors: PricewaterhouseCoopers LLP

LOCATIONS

HQ: F5 Networks, Inc.
401 Elliott Avenue West, Seattle, WA 98119
Phone: 206 272-5555
Web: www.f5.com

PRODUCTS/OPERATIONS

2016 Sales

	$ mil.	% of total
Services	1,050.6	53
Products	944.4	47
Total	**1,995.0**	**100**

Selected Products

Application delivery controllers (BIG-IP)
File virtualization (ARX)
Management console (Enterprise Manager)
SSL/VPN access appliances (FirePass)
WAN optimization (WANJet)

COMPETITORS

Array Networks	Fortinet
Barracuda Networks	Imperva
Blue Coat	Juniper Networks
Brocade Communications	NetApp
Checkpoint Systems	Nokia
Cisco Systems	Radware
Citrix Systems	Riverbed Technology
EMC	Symantec
Extreme Networks	Tekelec

HISTORICAL FINANCIALS

Company Type: Public

Income Statement

FYE: September 30

	REVENUE ($ mil.)	NET INCOME ($ mil.)	NET PROFIT MARGIN	EMPLOYEES
09/16	1,995.0	365.8	18.3%	4,395.0
09/15	1,919.8	365.0	19.0%	4,178.0
09/14	1,732.0	311.1	18.0%	3,834.0
09/13	1,481.3	277.3	18.7%	3,356.0
09/12	1,377.2	275.1	20.0%	3,029.0
Annual Growth	**9.7%**	**7.4%**	**—**	**9.8%**

2016 Year-End Financials

Debt ratio: —
Return on equity: 29.1%
Cash ($ mil.): 514.5
Current ratio: 1.53
Long-term debt ($ mil.): —

No. of shares (mil.): 65.3
Dividends
  Yield: —
  Payout: —
Market value ($ mil.): 8,141.0

	STOCK PRICE ($) FY Close	P/E High/Low	PER SHARE ($) Earnings	Dividends	Book Value
09/16	124.64	23 16	5.38	0.00	18.15
09/15	115.80	27 21	5.03	0.00	18.77
09/14	118.74	31 19	4.09	0.00	18.66
09/13	85.81	30 19	3.50	0.00	19.70
09/12	104.64	40 20	3.45	0.00	16.89
Annual Growth	**4.5%**	**— —**	**11.7%**	**—**	**1.8%**

FactSet Research Systems Inc.

Analysts portfolio managers and investment bankers know FactSet Research Systems has the facts down pat. The company offers global financial and economic information for investment analysis. FactSet also offers software for use in downloading and manipulating the data. (Its products can be fully integrated with Microsoft applications such as Excel and PowerPoint.) Among the company's applications are tools for presentations data warehousing portfolio analysis and report writing. Revenues are derived from month-to-month subscriptions to services databases and financial applications. More than 80% of revenue comes from investment managers; investment banking clients account for the rest.

Geographic Reach

About 30% of the company's revenues come from outside the US. Recent geographic growth efforts include the build out of new space in Paris and New York as well as the continued expansion of offices in India and the Philippines. It opened its 24th office located in Dubai in 2011. In addition to those locations FactSet has international offices in Australia Germany Italy Japan Hong Kong and the Netherlands.

Strategy

The company's success is in part due to its focus on growing its proprietary content collection efforts as well as investing in products and applications. Concurrent with the growth of its products and services the company has gained new clients and users both in the US and internationally.

HISTORY

Company Background

Howard Wille and Charles Snyder founded FactSet in 1978. Both had previously worked for Wall Street investment firm Faulkner Dawkins & Sullivan (acquired by Shearson Hayden Stone in 1977). The company spent the 1980s building its client base and developing software that allowed clients to manipulate data on their own PCs.

FactSet opened an office in London in 1993 and one in Tokyo the next year. In 1994 the company added Morgan Stanley Capital International and EDGAR SEC filings to its database offerings. It added World Bank subsidiary International Finance Corp. in 1995 and the Russell U.S. Equity Profile report and Toyo Keizai a Japanese company database the next year. FactSet went public in 1996. Market Guide's information on US firms and ADRs (American depositary receipts) as well as the economic and financial databases of DRI/McGraw-Hill were added in 1997.

Snyder retired in 1999 but remained vice chairman. The following year Wille retired and Philip Hadley became chairman and CEO. The company made its first acquisition in 2000 when it bought Innovative Systems Techniques (Insyte) a maker of database management and decision support systems.

The company then began acquiring several content businesses. Its 2003 purchase of Mergerstat gave the company a database of global merger and acquisition and related information. In 2004 the company purchased JCF Group a provider of broker estimates and other financial data to institutional investors and CallStreet a provider of quarterly earnings call transcripts to the investment community. The following year the company purchased TrueCourse a provider of corporate competitive intelligence.

FactSet continued its acquisition spree with the 2005 purchase of Derivative Solutions (DSI) which offers fixed income analytics portfolio management and risk management services to financial institutions and the 2006 purchase of AlphaMetrics which provides institutional clients with software for capturing measuring and ranking financial information.

FactSet in 2007 released its ExcelConnect offering which enables data and analytics to be compatible with Microsoft Excel. Also that year the company enhanced its wireless capabilities giving users access to market company and portfolio information via PDAs and other wireless devices.

In 2008 FactSet expanded with the acquisition of the Thomson Fundamentals business which includes a global financial database with coverage of more than 43000 companies. The company also purchased investment banking workflow tool Deal-Maven reflecting its strategy of developing tools to make client workflows more efficient.

The company expanded in 2010 with the purchase of Market Metrics a US-based market research firm focused on advisor-sold investments and insurance products. FactSet used the acquisition to increase its global sales leveraging its own international network to sell Market Metrics products outside the US.

In 2011 FactSet expanded its presence in the Middle East when it opened an office in Dubai.

EXECUTIVES

Vice Chairman Sales, Michael D. Frankenfield, age 51, $275,000 total compensation
Senior Vice President Director of Learning and Development, Laura Ruhe
Comptroller, Maurizio Nicolelli, age 48, $225,000 total compensation
VP and Regional Manager, Peter G. Walsh, age 51, $275,000 total compensation
EVP and COO, Mark J. Hale, age 43
President and CEO, Philip Snow, age 51, $290,000 total compensation
EVP Global Director of Sales, Scott Miller
Vice President of Sales, Kristina (Chris) Walsh
Vice President Principal Software Engineer, Jason Almeter
Vice President Content and Technology Solutions at FactSet Research Systems, Ibrahim Ghandour
Vice President Information Technology, Sharon Dipre
Vice President, Brian (Bri) Rowan
Vice President Institutional Sales, Sean Kennedy
Vice President Senior Product Manager, Mark Hedley
Vice President, Marc Boffardi
Vice President Director of Supplier Relations, Jeremy (Jer) Katz
Senior Vice President, Kieran M Kennedy
Vice President, Colin Armstrong
Vice President, Lisa Knoll
Vice President Sales, Jennifer (Jen) Vermeulen
Vice President Sales SouthEast Mid Atlatnic, John (Jack) Leffler
Senior Vice President Product Sales Specialist, Robert Robie
Vice President Institutional Sales Executive, Dennis (Denny) Travis
Assistant Vice President Key Accounts, Samuel (Sam) Lee
Assistant Vice President Key Accounts, Melissa (Lissa) Reich
Vice President Southeast Regional Manager, Jason (Jase) Baroni
Vice President, Brian Paul
Vice President Principal Software Engineer, Malay Shah
Vice President, Ken (Kenny) Zockoll
Vice President of Content, Olivier de Bellescize
Vice President Principal Software Engineer, Joseph (Jo) Adam
Assistant Vice President Key Accounts, Jordan (Jordy) Kamps
Vice President, Rick (Ricky) Barrett
Vice President Regional Consulting Manager, Mike (Mikey) Giordano

Vice President Content and Technology Solutions,
 Jeff (Jeffy) Spector
Chairman, Philip A. Hadley, age 54
Auditors: Ernst & Young LLP

LOCATIONS

HQ: FactSet Research Systems Inc.
 601 Merritt 7, Norwalk, CT 06851
Phone: 203 810-1000   **Fax:** 203 810-1001
Web: www.factset.com

PRODUCTS/OPERATIONS

2015 Sales

	% of total
US	67
Europe	25
Asia/Pacific	8
Total	**100**

Selected Applications

Company Analysis
Data Warehousing
Economic Analysis
Fixed Income Analysis
Pitchbook Building
Portfolio Analysis
Quantitative Analysis
Real-time Market Data

Selected Content Providers

Dow Jones & Company
Global Insight
Interactive Data Corporation
Merrill Lynch
Morningstar
Standard and Poor's
Thomson Reuters

Selected Product and Service Offerings:

Investment Managers
Equity Analysis
Quant and Risk Analysis
Portfolio Analysis
Markets and Economics
Fixed Income Analysis
Data Integration
Charting
Wireless Connectivity
Global Banking & Brokerage Professionals
Models and Presentations
Company and Industry Analytics
Deal Analytics
Idea Screening
People Intelligence
Accountability
Corporate Governance
Wireless Connectivity
Other Global Professionals
Hedge Funds
Private Equity and Venture Capital
Sell-Side Research
Equity Sales
Trading and Managing Market Data
Consultants and Advisors
Investor Relations and Corporate Strategy
Legal Accounting Management Consulting and Other
 Professionals
Academia - Professors and Students

COMPETITORS

Avention	LexisNexis
Bloomberg L.P.	MSCI
CME	Pearson plc
Capital IQ	Telvent DTN
Dealogic	Thomson Reuters
Hoover's Inc.	Track Data
Interactive Data	thinkorswim

HISTORICAL FINANCIALS

Company Type: Public

Income Statement

FYE: August 31

	REVENUE ($ mil.)	NET INCOME ($ mil.)	NET PROFIT MARGIN	EMPLOYEES
08/16	1,127.0	338.8	30.1%	8,375.0
08/15	1,006.7	241.0	23.9%	7,360.0
08/14	920.3	211.5	23.0%	6,639.0
08/13	858.1	198.6	23.1%	6,258.0
08/12	805.7	188.8	23.4%	5,735.0
Annual Growth	**8.8%**	**15.7%**	**—**	**9.9%**

2016 Year-End Financials

Debt ratio: 29.4%	No. of shares (mil.): 40.0
Return on equity: 64.4%	Dividends
Cash ($ mil.): 228.4	Yield: 1.0%
Current ratio: 2.33	Payout: 32.3%
Long-term debt ($ mil.): 300.0	Market value ($ mil.): 7,128.0

	STOCK PRICE ($) FY Close	P/E High/Low	PER SHARE ($) Earnings	Dividends	Book Value
08/16	178.03	22 16	8.19	1.88	12.92
08/15	157.92	30 20	5.71	1.66	12.87
08/14	127.40	26 20	4.92	1.48	12.23
08/13	102.35	25 19	4.45	1.32	12.51
08/12	92.27	26 19	4.12	1.16	12.47
Annual Growth	**17.9%**	**— —**	**18.7%**	**12.8%**	**0.9%**

FCB Financial Holdings Inc

Auditors: Grant Thornton LLP

LOCATIONS

HQ: FCB Financial Holdings Inc
 2500 Weston Road, Suite 300, Weston, FL 33331
Phone: 954 984-3313
Web: www.floridacommunitybank.com

HISTORICAL FINANCIALS

Company Type: Public

Income Statement

FYE: December 31

	ASSETS ($ mil.)	NET INCOME ($ mil.)	INCOME AS % OF ASSETS	EMPLOYEES
12/15	7,331.4	53.3	0.7%	649.0
12/14	5,957.6	22.3	0.4%	638.0
12/13	3,973.3	17.1	0.4%	640.0
12/12	3,245.0	(4.8)	—	0.0
Annual Growth	**31.2%**	**—**	**—**	**—**

2015 Year-End Financials

Return on assets: 0.8%	Dividends
Return on equity: 6.1%	Yield: —
Long-term debt ($ mil.): —	Payout: —
No. of shares (mil.): 40.8	Market value ($ mil.): 1,462.0
Sales ($ mil): 223.7	

	STOCK PRICE ($) FY Close	P/E High/Low	PER SHARE ($) Earnings	Dividends	Book Value
12/15	35.79	30 17	1.23	0.00	21.44
12/14	24.64	42 35	0.58	0.00	20.57
12/13	0.00	— —	0.46	0.00	19.95
Annual Growth	**—**	**— —**	**63.5%**	**—**	**3.7%**

Federated National Holding Co.

Trashed trailer crashed car damaged dwelling? Federated National Holding Company has a policy to cover that. Through Federated National Insurance Company and other subsidiaries it underwrites a variety of personal property/casualty insurance lines in Florida. Products include homeowners flood liability and nonstandard automobile coverage. Recently formed property insurance unit Monarch National (established in 2015) offers a complete homeowners policy special form (HO-3) multi-peril insurance product for Florida homeowners (and plans to introduce a similar product for condominiums). The firm distributes its products through independent agents and its Insure-Link agency.

Operations

Federated National underwrites homeowners commercial general liability federal flood personal auto and other lines of insurance. It is licensed as an admitted carrier for more than 300 classes of commercial general liability coverage in Alabama Georgia Louisiana and Texas. The company's affiliates are also able to market and underwrite other carriers' lines of business and process and adjust claims for third-party carriers.

The firm's independent agency Insure-Link distributes all of the company's products. Such vertical integration is unusual for small regional insurers but is part of Federated National's strategy to control all aspects of the insurance underwriting distribution and claims process.

Homeowners accounted for more than 90% of the firm's net premiums earned in fiscal 2014.

Geographic Reach

Federated National operates in the US Europe and Asia. In the US it primarily operates in the Southeast: Alabama Florida Georgia Louisiana Mississippi Missouri Nevada South Carolina and Texas.

Sales and Marketing

The company markets and distributes its and other carriers' products and services through its Insure-Link network of independent agents and through general agents.

Financial Performance

Federated National's revenues have spiked over the past couple of years on increases in homeowners' net premiums earned (thanks to more policies being sold) and higher commissions. In 2014 revenue increased 65% to $201 million; also contributing to the rise was higher investment earnings. Net income has followed revenue and in 2014 it rose 192% to $37 million.

However cash flow from operations fell 21% to $63 million as more cash was used in prepaid reinsurance premiums and for other expenses.

Strategy

Federated National is working on expanding its product offerings and underwriting additional profitable types of coverage. It also plans on introducing its wares in more states building on its Florida base. In 2015 its formed Monarch Insurance a new property/casualty insurance provider in Florida offering homeowners' policies.

EXECUTIVES

Vice President Accounting And Financial Reporting, Donald G (Don) Braun

CFO Treasurer and Director, Peter J. Prygelski, age 47, $192,946 total compensation

President CEO and Director; Interim Chairman, Michael H. Braun, age 48, $229,824 total compensation

Vice President of Risk Management, Gordan Jennings

Auditors: Ernst & Young LLP

LOCATIONS

HQ: Federated National Holding Co.
14050 N.W. 14th Street, Suite 180, Sunrise, FL 33323
Phone: 954 581-9993
Web: www.21stcenturyholding.com

PRODUCTS/OPERATIONS

2014 Premiums

	% of total
Homeowners	92
Commercial general liability	6
Automobile	2
Total	**100**

2014 Revenue

	$ mil.	% of total
Net premiums earned	170.9	86
Direct written policy fees	8.7	4
Net investment income	5.4	3
Commission income	4.5	2
Net realized investment gains	4.4	2
Finance revenue	1.5	1
Quota share profit sharing	2.8	1
Other income	2.5	1
Total	**200.7**	**100**

COMPETITORS

Allstate	Safeco
AssuranceAmerica	Safeway Insurance
Bankers Financial	State Farm
GEICO	Universal Insurance
Main Street America	Holdings
Progressive	
Corporation	

HISTORICAL FINANCIALS

Company Type: Public

Income Statement

FYE: December 31

	ASSETS ($ mil.)	NET INCOME ($ mil.)	INCOME AS % OF ASSETS	EMPLOYEES
12/15	638.3	40.8	6.4%	297.0
12/14	503.6	37.2	7.4%	219.0
12/13	316.7	12.7	4.0%	153.0
12/12	185.8	4.3	2.3%	116.0
12/11	179.9	(0.4)	—	112.0
Annual Growth	**37.2%**	**—**	**—**	**27.6%**

2015 Year-End Financials

Return on assets: 7.1%
Return on equity: 19.2%
Long-term debt ($ mil.): —
No. of shares (mil.): 13.8
Sales ($ mil): 249.8

Dividends
Yield: 0.5%
Payout: 5.7%
Market value ($ mil.): 408.0

	STOCK PRICE ($) FY Close	P/E High/Low		PER SHARE ($) Earnings	Dividends	Book Value
12/15	29.56	11	7	2.92	0.17	16.86
12/14	24.16	11	4	2.99	0.12	14.13
12/13	14.67	10	4	1.45	0.13	9.95
12/12	5.35	12	6	0.53	0.02	8.26
12/11	2.96	—	—	(0.05)	0.00	7.32
Annual Growth	**77.8%**	**—**	**—**	**—**	**—**	**23.2%**

Fidelity Southern Corp

Fidelity Southern Corp. is the holding company for Fidelity Bank which boasts over $3 billion in assets and some 45 branches in the Atlanta metro and in northern Florida markets. The bank offers traditional deposit services such as checking and savings accounts CDs and IRAs. Consumer loans primarily indirect auto loans which the company purchases from auto franchises and independent dealers throughout the Southeast make up more than 50% of its loan portfolio. Real estate construction commercial real estate business residential mortgage and other consumer loans round out Fidelity Southern's lending activities. Subsidiary LionMark Insurance Company offers consumer credit-related insurance products.

OperationsAbout 50% of Fidelity Southern's total revenue came from loan interest (including fees) in 2014 while another 2% came from interest on its investment securities. The rest of its revenue came from mortgage banking income (28%) indirect lending activities (9%) SBA Lending (3%) service charges on deposit accounts (2%) and other miscellaneous income sources. The bank had a staff of roughly 1040 employees at the end of 2014.Geographic ReachWhile the company mostly has a branch presence in Georgia and Florida it also offers mortgage loans indirect auto loans and Small Business Administration (SBA) loans in a dozen Southern states.Sales and MarketingFidelity Southern mostly serves individuals and small to medium-sized businesses. The company spent $2.34 million on advertising and promotions in 2014 up from $1.69 million and $1.13 million in 2013 and 2012 respectively.Financial PerformanceFidelity Southern's revenues and profits have risen over the past several years thanks to growing loan and deposit business from branch openings and acquisitions lower interest expenses and declining loan loss provisions as its loan portfolio's credit quality has improved with higher property valuations in the strengthened economy. The company's revenue inched higher by 1% to $197 million in 2014 mostly as its loan balances grew organically by 8% during the year with higher loan originations and market expansion.Higher revenue and lower interest expenses in 2014 boosted Fidelity Southern's net income by 9% to a record $30 million. Its cash levels plummeted during the year with operations using a net $141 million for the year after adjusting its earn-

ings for non-cash items related to its net proceeds from its loans held for sale.Strategy

Fidelity Southern has focused on building and diversifying its loan portfolio including originating more residential mortgages commercial loans and consumer installment loans. The bank has been opening new branches as part of this organic growth strategy. During 2014 it opened 12 new branches including five in Georgia and seven in Florida.It's also pursued small bank and branch acquisitions to grow its loan and deposit business while expanding its geographic reach in Florida and Georgia.Mergers and AcquisitionsIn October 2015 the Fidelity Bank agreed to purchase The Bank of Georgia including its $295 million in total assets $280 million in deposits and seven branches in Peachtree City Fayetteville Tyrone Sharpsburg Newnan and Fairburn. September 2015 Fidelity Southern purchased eight branches in Florida from First Bank including $154 million in deposits and $31.6 million in loans. The deal expanded Fidelity's presence in counties surrounding Bradenton Palmetto and Longboat Key.In September 2014 the company purchased six branches of CenterState Bank of Florida including $174.2 million in deposits. The deal expanded Fidelity's presence in counties surrounding Orlando and Jacksonville.

HISTORY

Company BackgroundWWII veteran Clark Harrison and five others founded Fidelity National Bank in 1973. The first office opened in downtown Decatur Georgia the next year. Fidelity National Bank opened its second branch and formed Fidelity Southern Corporation as a holding company in 1979; it formed Fidelity National Mortgage a year later. In 1984 the company received trust powers opened two new branches and began a major credit card marketing program.

The acquisition of two branches from the Resolution Trust Corporation in 1992 brought the number of branches to 10 and increased assets to $257 million. Fidelity National Capital Investors a retail brokerage was incorporated that year. In 1993 Fidelity National Bank began a consumer sales finance department to buy auto loans from car dealers.

The company opened an office in Jacksonville in 1995 to offer mortgage car and construction lending. Also that year the firm changed the name of its holding company to Fidelity National Corporation.

Fidelity National acquired Friendship Community Bank in Florida and bought six branches from First Union and NationsBank in 1996; rapid expansion and unexpectedly high credit card chargeoffs that year slashed earnings and prevented Fidelity National from opening three of its newly acquired branches. Under the scrutiny of federal regulators the bank discontinued its high-default card program the next year and shored up its finances raising capital through a stock offering.

In 1998 Fidelity National focused on maintaining capital levels and recovering from its losses while other banks expanded. Fidelity National Bank finally gained regulatory approval to open the three remaining branches acquired from NationsBank and First Union later that year. Regulators released the bank from capital and dividend restrictions in 1999 but Fidelity National had to restate its earnings for 1997 citing overestimation of an asset's value.

Fidelity National experienced moderate growth in 2001. Inspections by the Federal Reserve Board in 2000 and 2001 led to Fidelity National's adoption of a resolution that prohibits Fidelity National from redeeming its capital stock paying dividends on its common stock or incurring debt without prior approval of the Federal Reserve Board. In light of a softening economy in 2001 Fidelity National placed greater significance on credit risk management and building the secured portion of its consumer loan portfolio. The company sold its credit card business to Bank One in December.

In 2003 the company changed its name back to Fidelity Southern Corporation and its branches converted to the shortened Fidelity Bank; the bank also switched from a national to a state charter.

EXECUTIVES

President; Secretary and Treasurer LionMark Insurance Company, H. Palmer Proctor, age 48, $500,000 total compensation

Chairman and CEO, James B. Miller, age 76, $750,000 total compensation

VP; EVP Fidelity Bank; President LionMark Insurance Company, David Buchanan, age 58, $400,000 total compensation

CFO, Stephen H. Brolly, age 53, $250,000 total compensation

Vice President Commercial Banking, Kevin Lubitz

Vice President, Kena Powell

Vice President Construction Lending, Ron (Ronnie) Hendrix

Vice President, Mickey (Mic) Parker

Auditors: Ernst & Young LLP

LOCATIONS

HQ: Fidelity Southern Corp
3490 Piedmont Road, Suite 1550, Atlanta, GA 30305
Phone: 404 639-6500
Web: www.FidelitySouthern.com

PRODUCTS/OPERATIONS

2014 Sales

	$ mil.	% of total
Interest		
Loans including fees	96.7	50
Investment securities	4.9	2
Federal funds sold & bank deposits	0.1	-
Noninterest		
Mortgage banking activities	55.8	28
Indirect lending activities	18.5	9
SBA lending activities	5.0	3
Service charges on deposit accounts	4.4	2
Bank owned life insurance	1.7	1
Other fees & charges	4.3	2
Other	5.6	3
Total	**197.0**	**100**

COMPETITORS

BB&T	SunTrust
Bank of America	Synovus
Citizens Bancshares	Wells Fargo
Regions Financial	

HISTORICAL FINANCIALS
Company Type: Public

Income Statement
FYE: December 31

	ASSETS ($ mil.)	NET INCOME ($ mil.)	INCOME AS % OF ASSETS	EMPLOYEES
12/15	3,849.0	39.1	1.0%	1,242.0
12/14	3,085.2	30.0	1.0%	1,038.0
12/13	2,564.1	27.6	1.1%	890.0
12/12	2,477.2	25.3	1.0%	774.0
12/11	2,234.8	11.4	0.5%	174.0
Annual Growth	**14.6%**	**36.1%**	**—**	**63.5%**

2015 Year-End Financials

Return on assets: 1.1%	Dividends
Return on equity: 13.8%	Yield: 1.7%
Long-term debt ($ mil.): —	Payout: 23.0%
No. of shares (mil.): 23.1	Market value ($ mil.): 516.0
Sales ($ mil): 244.5	

	STOCK PRICE ($) FY Close	P/E High/Low		PER SHARE ($) Earnings	Dividends	Book Value
12/15	22.31	13	9	1.64	0.39	13.03
12/14	16.11	12	9	1.28	0.30	12.40
12/13	16.61	13	7	1.21	0.05	11.07
12/12	9.55	7	4	1.34	0.04	13.05
12/11	6.08	13	9	0.59	0.02	12.56
Annual Growth	**38.4%**	**—**	**—**	**29.1%**	**110.1%**	**0.9%**

Fiesta Restaurant Group, Inc

The restaurant business is a party for Fiesta Restaurant Group. The company owns operates and franchises the Taco Cabana and Pollo Tropical brands. Fiesta Restaurant Group owns or franchises a total of about 360 locations in the US the Caribbean Central America and South America; most of the restaurants are company operated. Taco Cabana locations found mostly in Texas feature Tex-Mex and traditional Mexican food in a quick service atmosphere. Pollo Tropical found mostly in South Florida and the Caribbean offer Caribbean-inspired dishes in a fast casual setting.

Geographic Reach

Fiesta Restaurant Group's restaurants are found in six US states and in 10 foreign countries. All Taco Cabanas are in the US mostly in Texas and are mostly owned and operated. Pollo Tropical restaurants' owned and operated locations are mostly in Florida as well as Georgia Tennessee and Texas. Its franchised locations are mostly in Puerto Rico but also in Venezuela Panama Trinidad and Tobago Honduras Guatemala and the Bahamas.

Operations

Fiesta Restaurant Group owns and operates more than 160 Taco Cabana locations which contributed a little less than 50% of revenue in fiscal 2016 and 155 Pollo Tropical restaurants which brought in a little more than 50% in revenue. Additionally it has 30 franchised locations of Pollo Tropical most in Puerto Rico and other Caribbean countries along with four franchised Taco Cabanas and three licensed locations.

Financial Performance

Fiesta Restaurant Group's revenue increased by 12% in fiscal 2016 compared to the prior fiscal period driven by a bump in sales and an increase in the number of company-owned restaurants. Net income also increased during fiscal 2016 by 7% to $38.5 million.

Cash from operations increased to $81 million during fiscal 2016 which was a 27% increase compared to the prior year's cash levels.

Strategy

To grow Fiesta Restaurant Group intends to open new restaurants within its existing markets as well as expand outside its current borders. The company will also look to increase its comparable restaurant sales by attracting new customers and encouraging current customers to visit more frequently.

Pollo Tropical has been Fiesta Restaurant Group's primary growth vehicle. During 2015 the company opened 34 new company-owned restaurants comprised of 32 Pollo Tropical restaurants and two Taco Cabana restaurants. During 2016 Fiesta Restaurant Group expects to open as many as 40 new company-owned Pollo Tropical restaurants and up to four new company-owned Taco Cabana restaurants in existing markets.

The company intends to separate the Pollo Tropical and Taco Cabana businesses in 2017 or 2018.

EXECUTIVES

COO Pollo Tropical, Danny K. Meisenheimer, age 57, $280,000 total compensation

President and CEO, Timothy P. (Tim) Taft, age 58, $525,000 total compensation

COO Taco Cabana, Todd A. Coerver, $280,000 total compensation

VP CFO and Treasurer, Lynn S. Schweinfurth, $320,004 total compensation

Chairman, Jack A. Smith, age 80

Auditors: Deloitte & Touche LLP

LOCATIONS

HQ: Fiesta Restaurant Group, Inc
14800 Landmark Boulevard, Suite 500, Dallas, TX 75254
Phone: 972 702-9300
Web: www.frgi.com

PRODUCTS/OPERATIONS

2015 Sales

	% of total
Taco Cabana	53
Pollo Tropical	47
Total	**100**

2015 Sales

	% of total
Restaurant Sales	100
Pollo Tropical	-
Total	**100**

COMPETITORS

A&W Revenue Royalties	Panera Bread
Boston Market	Quiznos
Burger King	Schlotzsky's
Chipotle	Sonic Corp.
Del Taco	Souper Salad
Fresh Choice	Subway
Jack in the Box	Wendy's
McDonald's	Whataburger
Panda Restaurant Group	YUM!

HISTORICAL FINANCIALS
Company Type: Public

Income Statement
FYE: January 3

	REVENUE ($ mil.)	NET INCOME ($ mil.)	NET PROFIT MARGIN	EMPLOYEES
01/16*	687.3	38.5	5.6%	11,550.0
12/14	611.1	36.1	5.9%	10,600.0
12/13	551.3	9.2	1.7%	9,175.0
12/12	509.7	8.2	1.6%	8,170.0
12/11	474.9	9.5	2.0%	7,900.0
Annual Growth	**9.7%**	**41.8%**	**—**	**10.0%**
*Fiscal year change				

2016 Year-End Financials

Debt ratio: 17.8%
Return on equity: 17.0%
Cash ($ mil.): 5.2
Current ratio: 0.67
Long-term debt ($ mil.): 74.2

No. of shares (mil.): 26.5
Dividends
  Yield: —
  Payout: —
Market value ($ mil.): 893.0

	STOCK PRICE ($) FY Close	P/E High/Low		PER SHARE ($) Earnings	Dividends	Book Value
01/16*	33.60	47	22	1.44	0.00	9.18
12/14	58.32	47	27	1.35	0.00	7.57
12/13	51.24	132	39	0.39	0.00	6.07
12/12	15.12	49	33	0.35	0.00	0.46
Annual Growth	30.5% 170.9%	—	—	60.2%	—	—

*Fiscal year change

Fifth Street Finance Corp

Fifth Street Finance works to put the companies it lends money to on easy street. A business development firm Fifth Street lends capital to and invests in small and midsized firms with annual revenues between $25 million and $250 million. The company typically invests $10 million to $100 million in the form of senior debt or equity per transaction. It favors established firms over start-ups and prefers to participate actively in its investments as advisors. Fifth Street's portfolio comprises more than 85 companies many of which operate in the health care manufacturing IT services and business services sectors. Formed in 2007 the specialty finance company boasts about $2 billion in assets under management.

Geographic Reach

Based in New York Fifth Street Finance operates in Connecticut Illinois California and Texas.

Sales and Marketing

Fifth Street Finance serves several customer types including financial advisors individual investors institutional investors and corporate finance professionals.

The firm has focused on advertising having spent $155 million in 2013 up significantly from $54 million in 2012.

Operations

Since inception Fifth Street Finance has originated $3.3 billion of funded debt and equity investments. Its portfolio which comprises $1.9 billion at fair value effective September 30 2013 consists of 99 investments 86 of which are in operating companies and 13 of which are in private equity funds. Additionally Fifth Street Finance holds equity investments consisting of common stock preferred stock or other equity interests in nearly half of its portfolio companies.

Fifth Street Finance is externally managed and advised by Fifth Street Management LLC.

Strategy

As a business development company Fifth Street Finance's overarching strategy includes infusing debt capital in businesses that show growth potential and then exiting its investments after businesses repay their debt or go through recapitalization.

As part of its own growth strategy the company intends to continue doing what has helped it grow so far: Focusing its lending activity on small and midsized companies which it believes to be underserved by many finance companies. Fifth Street Finance will also continue to originate its own loans to maintain control over the structuring of its investments and generate revenue from origination and exit fees.

Financial Performance

Fifth Street Finance has posted increases in both revenue and net income during the past five years.

Thanks to logging nearly $174 million in interest income from its portfolio investments and about $46 million in fee income Fifth Street Finance's 2013 revenue rose some 40% to nearly $222 million in fiscal 2013 as compared to $165 million in 2012. Increases in the firm's total investment income came from higher average levels of outstanding debt investments helped by a net increase of 18 debt investments and fees related to debt payoffs. Net income also increased by 28% to $102 million in 2012 vs. $79 million in 2012.

Mergers and Acquisitions

In 2013 the investment firm agreed to acquire Healthcare Finance Group planning to invest some $110 million.

EXECUTIVES

Chairman and CEO Fifth Street Asset Management, Leonard M. Tannenbaum, age 44
CEO, Patrick J. Dalton, age 48
Chairman Fifth Street Finance Corp. and Fifth Street Senior Floating Rate Corp; Co-President and Chief Compliance Officer Fifth Street Asset Management, Bernard D. Berman, age 45
Managing Director Sponsor Coverage, Sunny K. Khorana, age 44
CFO, Steven M. Noreika
Executive Director Investment Professionals, Andrew D. Ippolite
CIO and CTO, Ross A. Biddle
Managing Director Fifth Street Management, Matthew G. Bandini
Managing Director Portfolio Management, Brian D. Finkelstein
Managing Director Underwriting, Kyde S. Sharp
Managing Director First Star Aviation, Pradeep P. Hathiramani
Managing Director Origination, Glenn T. Kim
Executive Director Legal, Kerry S. Acocella
Executive Director Investor Relations, Robyn Friedman
Co President, Todd G Owens
Auditors: PricewaterhouseCoopers LLP

LOCATIONS

HQ: Fifth Street Finance Corp
777 West Putnam Avenue, 3rd Floor, Greenwich, CT 06830
Phone: 203 681-3600
Web: www.fifthstreetfinance.com

PRODUCTS/OPERATIONS

Selected Portfolio Companies
ADAPCO
Advanced Pain Management Holdings Inc.
Caregiver Services
Cenegenics
CRGT Inc.
DISA Inc.
Dominion Diagnostics LLC
Eagle Hospital Physicians
Enhanced Recovery Corporation
Epic MedStaff Services Inc.

Filet of Chicken
Fitness Edge
Flatout
HealthDrive
idX
IZI
JTC Education Holdings
Lighting by Gregory
MedKnowledge Group
Miche Bag LLC
NDS Surgical Imaging
Nicos Polymers & Ginding
O'Currance Teleservices
Pacific Production Technologies
Premier Trailer Leasing
Rail Acquisition Corp.
ReBath
Specialty Bakers LLC
Tegra
Traffic Control and Safety Corporation
Trans-Trade
Welocalize Inc.
Western Emulsions
WhatCounts

COMPETITORS

American Capital	MCG Capital
Ares Capital	MVC Capital
Gladstone Capital	Solar Capital

HISTORICAL FINANCIALS

Company Type: Public

Income Statement

FYE: September 30

	REVENUE ($ mil.)	NET INCOME ($ mil.)	NET PROFIT MARGIN	EMPLOYEES
09/16	247.8	106.7	43.1%	0.0
09/15	265.4	114.9	43.3%	0.0
09/14	293.9	142.5	48.5%	0.0
09/13	221.6	114.9	51.9%	0.0
09/12	165.1	88.0	53.3%	0.0
Annual Growth	10.7%	4.9%	—	—

2016 Year-End Financials

Debt ratio: 27.3%
Return on equity: 8.5%
Cash ($ mil.): 117.9
Current ratio: 0.31
Long-term debt ($ mil.): 642.2

No. of shares (mil.): 143.2
Dividends
  Yield: 12.3%
  Payout: 1,028.5%
Market value ($ mil.): 832.0

	STOCK PRICE ($) FY Close	P/E High/Low		PER SHARE ($) Earnings	Dividends	Book Value
09/16	5.81	9	6	0.71	0.72	7.97
09/15	6.17	12	8	0.75	0.79	9.01
09/14	9.18	10	9	0.99	1.00	9.64
09/13	10.29	11	9	1.01	1.15	9.85
09/12	10.98	10	8	1.07	1.18	9.92
Annual Growth	(14.7%) (5.3%)	—	—	(9.7%)	(11.7%)	

Financial Engines Inc

Like the little engine that could Financial Engines provides financial advice portfolio management and retirement assessment services. The company serves US retirement-plan participants sponsors and service providers across a wide range of industries that includes more than 100 FORTUNE 500 companies and several of the largest retirement plan operators. It delivers its services online as well as by telephone. Financial Engines boasts more than $88 billion in assets under management and serves some 9 million individual retirement-plan participants. The company went public in 2010 with an offering worth $127.2 million.

Geographic Reach

Based in California Financial Engines serves US investors.

Operations

Financial Engines provides independent portfolio management services investment advice and retirement services. It delivers its services to both plan sponsors and plan participants through agreements with retirement plan providers. The firm also supports plan sponsors through an alliance with Charles Schwab.

Sales and Marketing

The financial advisor primarily serves participants in employer-sponsored defined contribution plans such as 401(k) plans. Through direct marketing and promotional efforts Financial Engines works to encourage plan participants and individual investors to enroll in its professional management service.

Clients include the likes of Aon Hewitt Charles Schwab Fidelity Mercer T. Rowe Price and Xerox. It maintains sub-advisory relationships with Vanguard ING and JPMorgan Chase.

Strategy

Financial Engines generates revenue from professional management fees and subscription-based platform fees –that is fees paid for access to its online information and services. It markets itself to new employers through existing relationships with plan administrators. Financial Engines also markets its management services to passive plan participants to beef up fee revenues.

In 2013 the firm began managing Individual Retirement Accounts (IRAs) for 401(k) participants from select sponsors.

In addition to adding new clients through a marketing push Financial Engines plans to grow by adding new services. It is investing in R&D to expand its investment research capabilities.

Financial Performance

As demand for retirement planning increases as the population ages the company has seen its business expand. As such revenues have more than doubled during the past five years. In fiscal 2013 Financial Engines' earnings increased $53.14 million or 29% from the year prior to $238.9 million primarily driven by growth in the company's professional (34%) and platform revenue.

Net income rose by 61% to $29.95 million in 2013 as compared to $18.57 million in 2012 thanks to higher revenue and a boost in income from operations. Operating cash flow also increased to $59.26 million vs. 2012's $38.09 million. It attributes these gains to net income growth and changes in the company's working capital.

Company Background

Co-founder Bill Sharpe is a notable innovator in the analysis and valuation of investments and has written books on topics including portfolio theory and investment fundamentals. He received the Nobel Prize in Economics in 1990.

HISTORY

Financial Engines was founded in 1996 by Nobel laureate William (Bill) Sharpe (Sharp was the recipient of the 1990 Nobel Prize in Economic Sciences); former SEC Commissioner Joseph Grundfest; and the late Craig Johnson then chairman of the Venture Law Group.

Its initial services included providing individual investors with online advice regarding tax-deferred accounts and taxable investments. In 1998 the company began providing advice and assessment on retirement portfolios which consisted of a personalized printed retirement assessment. In 2004 it expanded to offer professional management services to retirement-plan participants

EXECUTIVES

EVP Investment Management and Chief Investment Officer, Christopher L. (Chris) Jones, age 49, $405,000 total compensation
EVP and CFO, Raymond J. (Ray) Sims, age 66, $340,000 total compensation
President and CEO, Lawrence M. (Larry) Raffone, age 53, $450,000 total compensation
EVP and President Financial Engines Advisors L.L.C., John B. Bunch, age 50
EVP Distribution and Institutional Services, Paul A. Gamble, age 47, $258,686 total compensation
EVP Business Operations and Corporate Marketing and Chief Risk Officer, Kelly S. O'Donnell, age 48
EVP Technology, Michael J. Campbell, age 48
EVP Customer Experience, Chung Meng Cheong, age 42
EVP Human Resources, Gina M. Cruse, age 51, $230,000 total compensation
EVP and General Counsel, Lee Antone
Vice President, Chung Cheong
Vice President General Counsel, Anne (Annie) Tuttle
Vice President Engineering, Matthew (Matt) Todd
Vice President, Kim Montana
Vice President, Jeffrey (Jeff) Grace
Chairman, Blake R. Grossman, age 53
Board Member, Heidi (Hei) Fields
Auditors: KPMG LLP

LOCATIONS

HQ: Financial Engines Inc
1050 Enterprise Way, 3rd Floor, Sunnyvale, CA 94089
Phone: 408 498-6000   **Fax:** 408 498-6010
Web: www.financialengines.com

PRODUCTS/OPERATIONS

Selected Services
Portfolio management services
Investment advice
Retirement income services
Professional Management Services
Online Advice Services

2015 Sales

	$ mil.	% of total
Professional management	277.1	89
Platform fees	30.8	10
Other	2.8	1
Total	**310.7**	**100**

COMPETITORS

Ameriprise	Fidelity Financial
BlackRock	Merrill Lynch
Charles Schwab	Morningstar
FMR	The Vanguard Group

HISTORICAL FINANCIALS
Company Type: Public

Income Statement

FYE: December 31

	REVENUE ($ mil.)	NET INCOME ($ mil.)	NET PROFIT MARGIN	EMPLOYEES
12/15	310.7	31.6	10.2%	527.0
12/14	281.9	36.9	13.1%	493.0
12/13	238.9	29.9	12.5%	442.0
12/12	185.8	18.5	10.0%	380.0
12/11	144.0	15.1	10.5%	355.0
Annual Growth	**21.2%**	**20.2%**	**—**	**10.4%**

2015 Year-End Financials

Debt ratio: —	No. of shares (mil.): 51.7
Return on equity: 7.9%	Dividends
Cash ($ mil.): 305.2	Yield: 0.8%
Current ratio: 7.68	Payout: 42.4%
Long-term debt ($ mil.): —	Market value ($ mil.): 1,741.0

	STOCK PRICE ($) FY Close	P/E High/Low		PER SHARE ($)		
			Earnings	Dividends	Book Value
12/15	33.67	75 47	0.60	0.28	8.03
12/14	36.55	97 44	0.69	0.24	7.32
12/13	69.48	115 45	0.57	0.20	6.33
12/12	27.74	70 45	0.37	0.00	5.50
12/11	22.33	84 47	0.31	0.00	4.80
Annual Growth	**10.8%**	**— —**	**17.9%**	**—**	**13.8%**

Finish Line, Inc. (The)

The Finish Line is engaged in a three-legged race for athletic footwear sales. The company sells performance and casual footwear and apparel through about 590 Finish Line stores in more than 45 states about 70 JackRabbit stores and 300-plus branded shops inside department stores (Macy's). Its core Finish Line stores are bigger than competitors' and offer a wider array of clothing accessories and other merchandise including jackets backpacks sunglasses and watches. Finish Line offers big brand names (such as adidas NIKE and Timberland) and also markets its own private-label line of T-shirts socks and other basics. The company also sells athletic shoes and apparel online.

Geographic Reach

The Indianapolis-based company has Finish Line stores in 47 states and the District of Columbia. Its largest markets are Texas Florida California Illinois Pennsylvania and Ohio home to about a quarter of Finish Line stores. Its 72 JackRabbit stores are located in 17 states and the District of Columbia with Texas Michigan New York and New Jersey accounting about half of all locations. The shoe retailer also has branded Finish Line shops inside department stores (including Macy's) in more than a dozen states.

Operations

The retailer's namesake stores average some 5400 sq. ft.; its JackRabbit stores average 3650 sq. ft. Footwear accounts for 88% of Finish Line's net sales. While Finish Line purchases products from some 120 suppliers NIKE products (some sold exclusively at Finish Line) generate about 70% of total sales. About 89% of the retailer's merchandise is purchased from its five largest suppliers. Apparel and accessories (also referred to as softgoods) account for about 12%.

Sales and Marketing

Nearly all of the company's merchandise is shipped directly from suppliers to its distribution center in Indianapolis Indiana where the it processes and ships the merchandise by contract and common carriers to its stores/shops or directly to customers.

Finish Line reported $44.2 million in advertising expenses in fiscal 2016 (ended February) up from $39.2 million and $41.8 million in 2015 and 2014 respectively.

Financial Performance

The company has achieved record-setting growth over the years with revenues peaking at $1.89 billion in 2016 a company milestone. Profits however nosedived by 73% from $82 million in 2015 to $22 million in 2016.

Footwear sales increased 5% in 2016 primarily driven by percentage increases in the low-single digits in men's low teens in women's and mid-single digits in kids' footwear sales. Softgoods sales were negatively impacted by the replacement of the company's warehouse and order management system in the third quarter of 2016.

The massive drop in profits for 2016 was driven by a large spike in selling general and administrative expenses related to the company's supply chain issues as a result of the replacement of its warehouse and order management system.

Strategy

As its brick-and-mortar operation is streamlined Finish Line is focusing more on its e-commerce and mobile businesses. The company is investing in its online channel with design and content upgrades mobile and tablet applications and an expanded presence on social media and platform enhancements. Indeed the company considers its online sites (finishline.com and run.com) to be its most visible stores attracting about 496000 visitors daily.

Company Background

In 1976 boyhood friends Alan Cohen (a lawyer) and David Klapper (a retailer) founded Athletic Enterprises the Indiana franchisee for The Athlete's Foot. By 1981 they had all The Athlete's Foot stores that the state's big malls could hold — about a dozen. To expand beyond those confines the pair teamed up with Dave Fagin and Larry Sablosky and formed The Finish Line.

EXECUTIVES

Evp Real Estate And Store Development, George S Sanders, age 59

EVP and CFO, Edward W. (Ed) Wilhelm, age 58, $530,000 total compensation

EVP and President Running Specialty Group, Bill Kirkendall, age 62, $355,385 total compensation

EVP and COO, Melissa Greenwell, age 49

CEO, Samuel M. (Sam) Sato, age 52, $635,000 total compensation

EVP and Chief Omnichannel Officer, Imran Jooma, age 44, $31,673 total compensation

Vice President Business Development, Donald J Gualdoni

Vice President of Operations, Jeff (Jeffy) Morrell

Executive Vice President; Chief Business Development Officer, Mark (Marky) Landau

Vice President Of Application Development, Jeff (Jeffy) Kish

Vice President General Counsel, Christopher Eck

Vice President Information Technology, Awilda Hernandez

Vice President of Human Resources, Michael (Mel) Smith

Vice President Of Human Resources And Payroll, Cindy Cook

Senior Vice President Distribution, Robert (Bob) Edwards

Vice President of Planning and Allocation, Jenni Dillon

Vice President Strategic Planning, Sally (Sal) McKelvey

Executive Vice President Chief Merchandise Officer, Sam Sato

Executive Vice President Strategic Initiatives, Steven J (Steve) Schneider

Vice President Of Sales, Teresa Harkness

Vice President Inventory Management, Todd (Toddy) Kuebel

Vice President Store Operations And Trai, Greg (Greggy) Davis

Chairman, Glenn S. Lyon, age 66

Auditors: Ernst & Young LLP

LOCATIONS

HQ: Finish Line, Inc. (The)
3308 North Mitthoeffer Road, Indianapolis, IN 46235
Phone: 317 899-1022
Web: www.finishline.com

PRODUCTS/OPERATIONS

2016 Sales

	$ mil.	% of total
Footwear	1,681.6	89
Softgoods	207.3	11
Total	**1,888.9**	**100**

2016 Sales

% of total	$ in mil
Brick and Mortar store	67
Digital	15
Shops within department store	13
Jack Rabbit sales	5
Total	**100**

Selected Brands

adidas
Asics
Brooks
Lacoste
Mizuno
New Balance
NIKE
Pastry
Puma
Reebok
Saucony
The North Face
Timberland
Under Armour

Selected Products

Accessories
  Athletic equipment
  Athletic socks
  Backpacks
  Gym bags
  Headbands and sweatbands
  Shoe care
  Shoe insoles and liners
  Shoe laces
  Sunglasses
  Watches
Fan
  High school
  MLB
  NBA
  NCAA
  NFL
  Kids
  Shoes
  Clothing
Men's
  Caps
  Hats
  Jackets
  Jerseys
  Pants
  Shoes
  Shorts
  Socks
  Sweatshirts/fleece
  Tanks
  T-shirts
  Workout clothing
Women's
  Caps
  Hats
  Jackets
  Jerseys
  Pants
  Shoes
  Shorts
  Socks
  Sweatshirts/fleece
  Tanks
  T-shirts
  Team clothing
  Workout clothing

COMPETITORS

Academy Sports	Patagonia Inc.
DSW	REI
Dick's Sporting Goods	Rack Room Shoes
Foot Locker	Sears
Genesco	Sports Authority
Hat World	Target Corporation
Hibbett Sports	Wal-Mart
J. C. Penney	Zappos.com
Kmart	shoebuy.com
Modell's	

HISTORICAL FINANCIALS

Company Type: Public

Income Statement

FYE: February 27

	REVENUE ($ mil.)	NET INCOME ($ mil.)	NET PROFIT MARGIN	EMPLOYEES
02/16	1,888.8	21.8	1.2%	14,300.0
02/15*	1,820.5	81.9	4.5%	12,300.0
03/14	1,670.4	76.9	4.6%	12,600.0
03/13	1,443.3	71.4	5.0%	11,900.0
03/12	1,369.2	84.8	6.2%	11,800.0
Annual Growth	8.4%	(28.7%)	—	4.9%

*Fiscal year change

2016 Year-End Financials

Debt ratio: —
Return on equity: 3.9%
Cash ($ mil.): 79.5
Current ratio: 2.36
Long-term debt ($ mil.): —

No. of shares (mil.): 42.3
Dividends
  Yield: 0.0%
  Payout: 77.0%
Market value ($ mil.): 777.0

	STOCK PRICE ($) FY Close	P/E High/Low		Earnings	PER SHARE ($) Dividends	Book Value
02/16	18.33	59	32	0.48	0.37	12.45
02/15*	24.48	18	13	1.70	0.33	12.80
03/14	27.02	18	11	1.56	0.29	12.10
03/13	18.26	18	12	1.40	0.25	10.89
03/12	23.62	15	11	1.59	0.21	10.31
Annual Growth	(6.1%)	—	—	(25.9%)	15.2%	4.8%

*Fiscal year change

First Bancshares Inc

Hoping to be first in the hearts of its customers The First Bancshares is the holding company for The First a community bank with some two dozen branch locations in southern Mississippi's Hattiesburg Alabama and Louisiana. The company provides such standard deposit products as checking and savings accounts NOW and money market accounts and IRAs. Real estate loans account for about 80% of the bank's lending portfolio including about equal portions of residential mortgages commercial mortgages and construction loans. The bank also writes business loans and consumer loans. The bank which has expanded beyond Mississippi through several acquisitions has approximately $970 million in assets.Mergers and AcquisitionsIn April 2013 The First Bancshares acquired First National Bank (FNB) of Baldwin Country a community bank in Alabama with five branches along the Gulf Coast. The purchase of FNB marked The First's entry into the Alabama market. In 2011 The First expanded into Louisiana and strengthened its hold on southern Mississippi with the acquisition of seven branch banks from Whitney National Bank and one branch from Hancock Bank of Louisiana for an undisclosed amount.

EXECUTIVES

Executive Vice President, David Bush
Vice President, Ken (Kenny) Kennedy
Executive Vice Presi, Canda Olmi
Auditors: T. E. Lott & Company

LOCATIONS

HQ: First Bancshares Inc
6480 U.S. Highway 98 West, Suite A, Hattiesburg, MS 39402
Phone: 601 268-8998
Web: www.thefirstbank.com

COMPETITORS

BancorpSouth	Peoples Financial
Community Bancshares	Renasant
of Mississippi	Trustmark
Hancock Holding	

HISTORICAL FINANCIALS

Company Type: Public

Income Statement

FYE: December 31

	ASSETS ($ mil.)	NET INCOME ($ mil.)	INCOME AS % OF ASSETS	EMPLOYEES
12/15	1,145.1	8.8	0.8%	305.0
12/14	1,093.7	6.6	0.6%	278.0
12/13	940.8	4.6	0.5%	266.0
12/12	721.3	4.0	0.6%	212.0
12/11	681.4	2.8	0.4%	212.0
Annual Growth	13.9%	32.3%	—	9.5%

2015 Year-End Financials

Return on assets: 0.7%	Dividends
Return on equity: 8.8%	Yield: 0.8%
Long-term debt ($ mil.): —	Payout: 9.5%
No. of shares (mil.): 5.4	Market value ($ mil.): 99.0
Sales ($ mil): 47.7	

	STOCK PRICE ($) FY Close	P/E High/Low		PER SHARE ($) Earnings	Dividends	Book Value
12/15	18.34	11	8	1.62	0.15	19.14
12/14	14.51	12	11	1.25	0.15	18.01
12/13	14.02	16	9	1.06	0.15	16.61
12/12	9.42	8	5	1.29	0.15	21.03
12/11	7.62	12	8	0.93	0.15	19.54
Annual Growth	24.6%	—	—	14.9%	(0.0%)	(0.5%)

First Business Financial Services, Inc.

Business comes first at First Business Financial Services which serves small and midsized companies entrepreneurs professionals and high-net-worth individuals through First Business Bank and First Business Bank - Milwaukee. The banks offer deposits loans cash management and trust services from a handful of offices in Wisconsin and Kansas. Over 60% of the company's loan portfolio is made up of commercial real estate loans. Subsidiary First Business Capital specializes in asset-based lending while First Business Equipment Finance provides commercial equipment financing. First Business Trust & Investments offers investment management and retirement services.

OperationsFirst Business Financial Services backs its subsidiaries with low-cost corporate services such as human resources finance IT and marketing. First Business Credit Cards provides revolving lines of credit and term loans for financial and strategic acquisitions capital expenditures working capital used to support rapid growth bank debt refinancing debt restructuring and other corporate financing needs. The company generated 80% of its total revenue from interest on loans and leases in 2014 and another 5% from interest on its securities. About 7% of revenue came from trust and investment services fee income while service charges on deposits and loan fees made up 4% and 2% of revenue respectively.Geographic ReachThe company's primary market areas are in Wisconsin Kansas and Missouri. First Business's loan production offices are in Wisconsin in Oshkosh Green Bay Appleton and Kenosha while its two Kansas offices are in Leawood and Overland Park. In Wisconsin it targets Madison Milwaukee Appleton Green Bay Oshkosh and their surrounding communities. Sales and MarketingBeyond individual customers the bank generally targets businesses with annual sales between $2 million and $75 million.Financial PerformanceThe company has struggled to consistently grow its revenues in recent years due to shrinking interest margins on loans amidst the low-interest environment. Its profits however have been rising thanks to declining loan loss provisions as its loan portfolio's credit quality has improved with higher property valuations in a strengthened economy.First Business had a breakout year in 2014 however as its revenue rose 9% to $67.8 million on higher loan interest as its commercial and industrial loans comercial real estate and other mortgage loans and direct financing leases businesses all enjoyed "favorable volume variances." The bank's non-interest income also jumped by

20% which was mostly driven by growth in trust and investment services fee income on higher assets under management.Higher revenue and lower interest expenses on deposits in 2014 pushed the company's net income up by 3% to $14.1 million. First Business' operating cash levels fell by 25% to $11.9 million due to unfavorable changes in working capital related to an increase in accrued interest payable and other liabilities. StrategyFirst Business Financial Services continued in 2015 to focus on maintaining its loan asset quality while organically growing its loan and lease portfolio in addition to growing its customer account based to increase its fee-based revenues on its variety of treasury management trust and investment services and SBA loans. It also planned to boost its investment in utilizing technology to support these initiatives while staying efficient as the business grows.The company occasionally opens new offices or strategically acquires other banks and financial companies to extend its reach into its target markets and to grow its loan and deposit business. In 2014 its FBB-Milwaukee bank subisidiary expanded more into the southeastern area of Wisconsin after opening a loan production office in Kenosha; while its acquisition of Aslin Group and Alterra Bank furthered its exposure to new markets and loan and deposit business in Kansas.Mergers and AcquisitionsIn November 2014 First Business Financial Services expanded its Midwest market and extended its reach into Kansas after its acquisition of Leawood-based Aslin Group including its Alterra Bank subsidiary. The deal added $223 million in total assets including $182 million in new loan assets and $192 million in new deposits.

EXECUTIVES

President and CEO, Corey A. Chambas, age 53, $416,000 total compensation
SVP and Chief Credit Officer, Michael J. Losenegger, age 58, $221,950 total compensation
President and CEO First Business Capital, Charles H. (Chuck) Batson, age 62, $242,927 total compensation
President and CEO First Business Bank - Madison, Mark J. Meloy, age 54, $201,800 total compensation
President First Business Trust & Investments, Joan A. Burke, age 64
President and CEO First Business Bank - Milwaukee, David J. (Dave) Vetta, age 61
CFO, Edward G. (Ed) Sloane, age 55
President Kenosha Region, Wesley Ricchio
SVP and COO First Business Capital Corp., Peter Lowney
COO and Interim President and CEO Alterra Bank, David R. Seiler
CIO, Daniel S. Ovokaitys, age 42
Vice President Business Development, Tom (Tommy) Rude
Senior Vice President and Division Manager, Gail Heldke
Vice President, Cymbre Van Fossen
Vice President Business Development Officer, Robert (Bob) Pieroni
Assistant Vice President Treasury Management, Natalie Glumm
Assistant Vice President Treasury Management, Wade Hanna
Senior Vice President, Gary Fossum
Vice President, Gay Denny
Chairman, Jerome R. (Jerry) Smith, age 65
Auditors: KPMG LLP

LOCATIONS

HQ: First Business Financial Services, Inc.
401 Charmany Drive, Madison, WI 53719
Phone: 608 238-8008
Web: www.firstbusiness.com

COMPETITORS

Associated Banc-Corp	TCF Financial
Bank Mutual	U.S. Bancorp
Harris	

HISTORICAL FINANCIALS

Company Type: Public

Income Statement

FYE: December 31

	ASSETS ($ mil.)	NET INCOME ($ mil.)	INCOME AS % OF ASSETS	EMPLOYEES
12/15	1,782.8	16.5	0.9%	258.0
12/14	1,629.3	14.1	0.9%	231.0
12/13	1,268.6	13.7	1.1%	164.0
12/12	1,226.1	8.9	0.7%	155.0
12/11	1,177.1	8.4	0.7%	143.0
Annual Growth	10.9%	18.3%	—	15.9%

2015 Year-End Financials

Return on assets: 0.9%
Return on equity: 11.4%
Long-term debt ($ mil.): —
No. of shares (mil.): 8.7
Sales ($ mil): 89.4

Dividends
Yield: 1.7%
Payout: 23.4%
Market value ($ mil.): 218.0

	STOCK PRICE ($) FY Close	P/E High/Low	PER SHARE ($) Earnings	Dividends	Book Value
12/15	25.01	25 12	1.90	0.44	17.34
12/14	47.91	28 21	1.76	0.42	15.88
12/13	37.63	22 13	1.75	0.28	13.85
12/12	22.95	15 10	1.65	0.14	12.71
12/11	16.50	11 7	1.62	0.14	12.23
Annual Growth	11.0%	— —	4.1%	33.1%	9.1%

First Connecticut Bancorp Inc. (MD)

One of the oldest states in the union also has some of the oldest banks in the union. First Connecticut Bancorp (FCB) is the holding company for Farmington Bank a Connecticut-based community bank tracing its roots back to the mid-1800s. The bank offers traditional deposit accounts and loan products to consumers businesses and government clients through about 25 branches in the suburban communities in central Connecticut and western Massachusetts. Its lending activity consists primarily of commercial and residential real estate loans. The bank also offers wealth management services.

OperationsThe lender specializes in originating residential real estate loans (for one-to-four family homes) and commercial real estate loans (for office buildings multi-family residences industrial and warehouse facilities and retail outlets). About 55% of its loan portfolio consisted of commercial loans at the end of 2015 while another 36% was tied to residential loans. Real estate loans made up 75%

of the loan portfolio.The bank made 86% of its revenue from interest income in 2015 mostly from its mortgage loans. The rest came from customer service fees (6% of revenue) gains on loan sales (3%) and other miscellaneous income sources.Geographic ReachFCB had 23 branches across central Connecticut (including ones in Hartford County and Rocky Hill) and western Massachusetts (including ones in Hampden County West Springfield and East Longmeadow) as of early 2016.Sales and MarketingThe company originates mortgages for developers licensed contractors and builders that work on commercial and residential properties. FCB serves a variety of sectors including the Insurance Health Services Finance Manufacturing Non-profit Education Government and Technology sectors.FCB spent $2.1 million on marketing during 2015 up from $1.6 million in 2014.Financial PerformanceFirst Connecticut's annual revenues have risen 50% since 2011 mostly as its loan assets have nearly doubled to $2.34 billion. The bank has also seen its profits more the triple over that time as its loan loss provisions have receded with an improvement in portfolio credit quality.The bank's revenue jumped 16% to $95.3 million during 2015 mostly thanks to a double-digit rise in organic loan growth. Its non-interest income increased by 48% on a combination of higher investment sale gains and more customer service fees with deposit account and debit card growth helping to buoy revenues further.Strong revenue growth and a continued decline in loan loss provisions in 2015 drove FCB's net income up 35% to $12.6 million for the year. The bank's operating cash levels fell nearly 80% to $9.3 million in 2015 mainly as the bank used more cash to originate loans.StrategyFirst Connecticut Bancorp has been focused on expanding its commercial lending business. It has also been opening several new branches in recent years through de novo branching. The bank introduced two new de novo branches in western Massachusetts in late 2015 and planned to open two more in Connecticut in 2016. It also opened a new loan production office in Branford Connecticut with plans to open another in Fairfield Connecticut in early 2016.In past years First Connecticut launched small business cash management and government banking divisions to draw in new customers. Company BackgroundIn 2011 FCB converted from a mutual holding structure to a public company. The conversion was a way for FCB to generate new capital and support the bank's strategy for continued growth.Also that year FCB formed an alliance with Essex Financial Services to offer wealth management services to high-net-worth individuals.

EXECUTIVES

Chairman President and CEO First Connecticut Bancorp and Farmington Bank, John J. Patrick, age 56, $409,692 total compensation
EVP CFO and Treasurer, Gregory A. White, age 51, $213,279 total compensation
EVP and Director Retail Banking, Kenneth F. Burns, age 56, $183,077 total compensation
EVP and Chief Risk Officer, Michael T. Schweighoffer, age 53, $232,673 total compensation
Auditors: Pricewaterhouse Coopers LLP

LOCATIONS

HQ: First Connecticut Bancorp Inc. (MD)
One Farm Glen Boulevard, Farmington, CT 06032
Phone: 860 676-4600
Web: www.farmingtonbankct.com

PRODUCTS/OPERATIONS

2015 Sales

	% of total
Interest income	
Interest and fees on loans	
Mortgage	65
Other	18
Interest and dividends on investments	
United States Government and agency obligations	2
Corporate stocks	1
Other	
Noninterest income	
Fees for customer services	6
Net gain on loans sold	3
Gain on sales of investments	
Bank owned life insurance income	2
Other	2
Total	**100**

Selected Services

Business Borrowing
Business Deposit Accounts
Business Financing
Business Services
Cash Management
Cash Management
Checking Accounts
Commercial Home
Government Home
Home Loans
Interest-Bearing Accounts
International Services
Investment Services
Municipal Services
Personal Loans
Savings Accounts
Security Awareness
Services and Tools
Services and Tools

COMPETITORS

Bank of America	Sovereign Bank
Citizens Financial Corp.	TD Bank USA
Liberty Bank	U.S. Bancorp
People's United Financial	Webster Financial

HISTORICAL FINANCIALS

Company Type: Public

Income Statement

FYE: December 31

	ASSETS ($ mil.)	NET INCOME ($ mil.)	INCOME AS % OF ASSETS	EMPLOYEES
12/15	2,708.5	12.5	0.5%	343.0
12/14	2,485.3	9.3	0.4%	328.0
12/13	2,110.0	3.7	0.2%	337.0
12/12	1,822.9	3.9	0.2%	326.0
12/11	1,617.6	(4.0)	—	299.0
Annual Growth	13.8%	—		3.5%

2015 Year-End Financials

Return on assets: 0.4%
Return on equity: 5.2%
Long-term debt ($ mil.): —
No. of shares (mil.): 15.8
Sales ($ mil): 95.3

Dividends
Yield: 1.2%
Payout: 24.7%
Market value ($ mil.): 277.0

	STOCK PRICE ($) FY Close	P/E High/Low	PER SHARE ($) Earnings	Dividends	Book Value
12/15	17.41	22 17	0.83	0.22	15.47
12/14	16.32	27 23	0.62	0.17	14.64
12/13	16.12	71 55	0.24	0.12	14.11
12/12	13.75	58 52	0.24	0.12	13.63
12/11	13.01	—	(0.29)	0.03	14.09
Annual Growth	7.6%	— —	—	64.6%	2.4%

First Financial Bankshares, Inc.

Texas hold 'em? Well sort of. First Financial Bankshares is the holding company for eleven banks consolidated under the First Financial brand all of which are located in small and midsized markets in Texas. Together they have about 50 locations. The company maintains a decentralized management structure with each of the subsidiary banks having their own local leadership and decision-making authority. Its First Financial Trust & Asset Management subsidiary administers retirement and employee benefit plans in addition to providing trust services. First Financial Bankshares also owns an insurance agency.Real estate mortgages account for approximately half of the company's loan portfolio while commercial financial and agricultural loans account for about another third. The banks also offer construction and consumer loans as well as deposit products like checking and savings accounts and CDs. Some locations offer brokerage services through arrangements with third parties.First Financial Bankshares has grown both organically and through acquisitions. In 2010 the company bought Huntsville Texas-based Sam Houston Financial Corporation the parent of The First State Bank. The deal worth more than $22 million expanded First Financial Bankshares' footprint in East Texas. The following year The First State Bank changed its name to First Financial Bank bringing all of the company's banks under the same banner.First Financial Bankshares continues to open new branches and seek out acquisitions of other banks in Texas with a continued focus on burgeoning smaller markets where competition is less intense than metropolitan areas. The company whose earnings have increased each year for a quarter-century has benefitted from the Texas economy which was not nearly as hard-hit by the recession as other regions and is one of the fastest-growing in the country. First Financial Bankshares has also gotten a boost by investing its capital wisely; a relatively large proportion of its revenues –more than 25% –comes from interest-earning assets such as mortgage-backed securities state and municipal bonds and government agency securities.

EXECUTIVES

Chairman President and CEO; Chairman First Financial Bank N.A., F. Scott Dueser, age 63, $626,666 total compensation

EVP and CFO, J. Bruce Hildebrand, age 61, $395,000 total compensation

EVP Operations; Chairman First Technology Services Inc., Gary L. Webb, age 59, $316,666 total compensation

EVP and Chief Administrative Officer, Ronald D. (Ron) Butler, age 55, $355,000 total compensation

EVP Lending, Marna Yeriga

EVP and CIO, Thomas S. (Stan) Limerick

EVP and Senior Lending Officer, Gary S.Gragg, $316,666 total compensation

Senior Vice President and Information Systems, Dennis (Denny) Steckly

Vice President Wires, Sandra (Sandy) Holt

Senior Vice President, Kay Berry

Senior Vice President, Dennis (Denny) Tarrant

Executive Vice President of Commercial Loans, Marelyn Shedd

Assistant Vice President Human Resources, Racheal Carter

Executive Vice President Lending, Brad (Brady) Seay

Assistant Vice President, Taylor Burroughs

Vice President Commercial And Real Estat, Alecia Bland

Vice President, Spencer (Spence) Murphy

Assistant Vice President, Mary (Mar) Hopkins

Senior Vice President, Kay (KayKay) Berry

Vice President, Russell (Russ) Phillips

Senior Vice President and Controller, Vickie (Vick) Pettit

Lending Officer Vice President, Chris (Chrissy) Cregger

Vice President Mortgage Loans, Corie Oconnor

Vice President Consumer Lending, Ryan (Ry) Sonntag

Assistant Vice President, Lori C (Lor) Davis

Assistant Vice President, Brad (Brady) Magers

Vice President, Blaine Caillier

Vice President, Kevin (Kev) Shipman

Senior Vice President, Mike (Mikey) Hopkins

Vice President, Jesse (Jess) Villarreal

Vice President, Murielle Gillet

Vice President and Branch Manager, Britt Stuart

Executive Vice President Chief Risk Officer, Randy (Rand) Roewe

Vice President, Isabel (Bell) Montoya

Vice President Credit Adminstration, Clay (Clayton) Trumble

Vice President Alternative Delivery Channels, Jeff Casey

Assistant Vice President Mortgage Department, Vanessa (Nessa) Faz

Assistant Vice President, Faye Dodson

SR.v.p., Guinn Smith

Senior Vice President Appraisal Services, Brandon (Bran) Harris

Vice President, Wade Spain

Vice President, Raquel (Rae) Garza

Vice President, Isabel Montoya

Executive Vice President, Robert (Bob) Pate

Executive Vice President Lending, Marna Yerigan

Vice President, Kathy (Kat) Bushnell

Senior Vice President, Cindi LaChance

Senior Vice President Mortgage, Stephen (Steve) Harding

Senior Vice President, Trent Tidwell

Assistant Vice President First Financial Trust Fort Worth, Ronda Haynes

Auditors: Ernst & Young LLP

LOCATIONS

HQ: First Financial Bankshares, Inc.
400 Pine Street, Abilene, TX 79601
Phone: 325 627-7155
Web: www.ffin.com

PRODUCTS/OPERATIONS

2015 sales

	$ mil.	% of total
Interest Income		
Interest and fees on loans	151.7	51
Interest on investment securities	69.7	24
Interest on federal funds sold and interest-bearing deposits in banks	0.2	
Non-Interest Income		
ATM interchange and credit card fees	21.9	7
Trust fees	19.2	6
Service charges on deposit accounts	17.2	6
Real estate mortgage operations	10.4	4
Net gain on sale of available-for-sale securities	0.5	.
Net gain on sale of foreclosed assets	0.5	.
Net loss on sale of assets	(0.8)	.
Other	4.6	2
Total	**295.1**	**100**

Products/ServicesPersonal

Learn
Online Banking
Mobile Banking
Consumer Education
FAQS
Privacy & Security Information
Resources
Testimonials
Tools
Bank
Checking
Savings
Invest
CDS & IRAS
Broker Services
Borrow
Mortgage Loans
Mortgage Lenders
Auto Loans
Recreational Loans
Home Equity Loans
Personal Line of Credit
CD Secured Loans
Banking with First Financial
Mobile Banking
Online Banking
Pay Bills
Get Cash
Make Deposit
Move Money
Keep Track
Business
Learn
Online Banking
Mobile Banking
Business Education
Starting your Business
Growing your Business
Tools
Business Banking Services
Manage Cash
Send Payments
Receive Payments
Manage Fraud and Risk
Other Services
Trust & Wealth Management
Investment Management
Trust Management
Estate Management
Oil & Gas Management
Real Estate and Property Management
Company Retirement Plans

Selected Subsidiaries

First Financial Bank National Association Abilene Texas.

First Technology Services Inc. Abilene Texas (wholly owned subsidiary of First Financial Bank National Association Abilene Texas).

First Financial Trust & Asset Management Company National Association Abilene Texas.

First Financial Insurance Agency Inc. Abilene Texas.

First Financial Investments Inc. Abilene Texas.

COMPETITORS

BBVA Compass Bancshares	JPMorgan Chase
Bank of America	Wells Fargo
Cullen/Frost Bankers	Woodforest Financial

HISTORICAL FINANCIALS

Company Type: Public

Income Statement

FYE: December 31

	ASSETS ($ mil.)	NET INCOME ($ mil.)	INCOME AS % OF ASSETS	EMPLOYEES
12/15	6,665.0	100.3	1.5%	1,270.0
12/14	5,848.2	89.5	1.5%	1,140.0
12/13	5,222.2	78.8	1.5%	1,100.0
12/12	4,502.0	74.2	1.6%	1,000.0
12/11	4,120.5	68.3	1.7%	980.0
Annual Growth	**12.8%**	**10.1%**	**—**	**6.7%**

2015 Year-End Financials

Return on assets: 1.6%
Return on equity: 13.5%
Long-term debt ($ mil.): —
No. of shares (mil.): 65.4
Sales ($ mil): 295.0

Dividends
Yield: 2.0%
Payout: 42.1%
Market value ($ mil.): 1,975.0

	STOCK PRICE ($) FY Close	P/E High/Low	PER SHARE ($) Earnings	Dividends	Book Value
12/15	30.17	23 16	1.54	0.62	12.30
12/14	29.88	47 20	1.39	0.55	10.72
12/13	66.11	54 31	1.24	1.03	9.26
12/12	39.01	35 26	1.18	0.99	8.92
12/11	33.43	51 23	1.09	0.47	8.15
Annual Growth	(2.5%)	— —	9.1%	7.0%	10.8%

First Foundation Inc

Auditors: Vavrinek, Trine, Day & Co., LLP

LOCATIONS

HQ: First Foundation Inc
18101 Von Karman Avenue, Suite 700, Irvine, CA
92612
Phone: 949 202-4160
Web: www.ff-inc.com

HISTORICAL FINANCIALS

Company Type: Public

Income Statement

FYE: December 31

	ASSETS ($ mil.)	NET INCOME ($ mil.)	INCOME AS % OF ASSETS	EMPLOYEES
12/15	2,592.5	13.3	0.5%	295.0
12/14	1,355.4	8.3	0.6%	207.5
12/13	1,037.3	7.8	0.8%	187.5
12/12	830.5	5.8	0.7%	0.0
Annual Growth	46.1%	32.1%	—	—

2015 Year-End Financials

Return on assets: 0.6%
Return on equity: 7.4%
Long-term debt ($ mil.): —
No. of shares (mil.): 31.9
Sales ($ mil): 93.2

Dividends
Yield: —
Payout: —
Market value ($ mil.): 754.0

	STOCK PRICE ($) FY Close	P/E High/Low	PER SHARE ($) Earnings	Dividends	Book Value
12/15	23.59	41 29	0.58	0.00	8.13
12/14	18.14	37 33	0.52	0.00	6.34
12/13	0.00	— —	0.51	0.00	5.61
Annual Growth	—	— —	7.2%	—	20.4%

First Internet Bancorp

First Internet Bancorp was formed in 2006 to be the holding company for First Internet Bank of Indiana (First IB). Launched in 1999 the bank was the first state-chartered FDIC-insured institution to operate solely via the Internet. It now operates two locations in Indianapolis after adding one via its 2007 purchase of Landmark Financial (the parent of Landmark Savings Bank) a deal that also brought aboard residential mortgage brokerage Landmark Mortgage. First IB offers traditional checking and savings accounts in addition to CDs IRAs credit and check cards consumer installment and residential mortgage loans and lines of credit. It serves customers in all 50 states.

EXECUTIVES

Chairman President and CEO First Internet Bank and Bancorp, David B. Becker, age 63, $448,461 total compensation
SVP and CFO, Kenneth (Ken) Lovik, age 47, $259,692 total compensation
COO First Internet Bancorp and First Internet Bank, Nicole S. Lorch, age 42, $174,385 total compensation
Vice President Of Mortgage Operations, Dave Fogarty
Vice President Deposit Operations And BSA Officer, Jan Jones
Vice President Portfolio Manager, Stephen (Steve) Ricks
Vice President, Tom (Tommy) Smith
Vice President Commercial Lender, Carl Osberg
Vice President Commercial Lending, Jim Laine
Vice President Commercial Lending, Kevin Lynch
Vice President and Corporate Controller, Lisa (Lis) Streeter
Vice President Commercial Lending, Jim (Jimmy) Laine
Vice President CRE Portfolio Manager, Jason (Jase) Fitzpatrick
Vice Chairman, David R. Lovejoy
Auditors: BKD, LLP

LOCATIONS

HQ: First Internet Bancorp
11201 USA Parkway, Fishers, IN 46037
Phone: 317 532-7900
Web: www.firstinternetbancorp.com

COMPETITORS

Bank of America	Citibank
BofI	E*TRADE Bank

HISTORICAL FINANCIALS

Company Type: Public

Income Statement

FYE: December 31

	ASSETS ($ mil.)	NET INCOME ($ mil.)	INCOME AS % OF ASSETS	EMPLOYEES
12/15	1,269.8	8.9	0.7%	152.0
12/14	970.5	4.3	0.4%	143.0
12/13	802.3	4.5	0.6%	130.0
12/12	636.3	5.6	0.9%	97.0
12/11	585.4	3.1	0.5%	0.0
Annual Growth	21.4%	29.4%	—	—

2015 Year-End Financials

Return on assets: 0.8%
Return on equity: 8.8%
Long-term debt ($ mil.): —
No. of shares (mil.): 4.4
Sales ($ mil): 51.5

Dividends
Yield: 0.8%
Payout: 13.3%
Market value ($ mil.): —

First Republic Bank (San Francisco, CA)

No not the original Roman Republic but rather a modern-day haven for the elite. Founded in 1985 First Republic Bank offers private banking wealth management trust and brokerage services for businesses and high-net-worth clients though about 70 branches. Its main geographic focus is on urban markets including San Francisco Los Angeles New York Boston Portland and San Diego. The bank's lending focuses on commercial and residential real estate and personal loans including vacation home mortgages and aircraft and yacht financing. Trust services are offered through the bank's First Republic Trust Company division. First Republic Bank has some $41.6 billion of assets under management.

Geographic Reach

The company operates 73 offices 66 of which are Preferred Banking locations in Boston; Los Angeles; New York; Newport Beach California; Palm Beach Florida; Palo Alto California; Portland Oregon; San Diego San Francisco and Santa Barbara California. In 2014 it opened an additional Preferred Banking office in downtown San Diego. The other seven locations offer lending wealth management or trust services.

Sales and Marketing

First Republic Bank advertises via digital media and newspaper and radio ads; its primary marketing goal is to attract deposits in its Preferred Banking offices. In 2013 the company spent $25.5 million on advertising and marketing slightly up from $25.1 million in 2012 (but down from $28.8 million in 2011).

Financial Performance

The bank has seen stable growth in earnings since 2010. In 2013 revenue grew 10% to $1.6 billion (compared to $1.5 billion in 2012) as both interest and noninterest income rose. Higher interest rates brought added income on both loans and investments while fees increases on investment advisory services net loan servicing deposits and foreign exchanges also contributed to the revenue growth. However a decline in gains on sales of loans slightly offset those improvements.

Net income which has also been on the rise grew 15% to $462.1 million in 2013 (versus $401.2 million in 2012) primarily as a result of the year's higher revenues. In turn the profit growth helped contribute to a rise of cash flow from operations which grew 28% to $562.2 million.

Strategy

A conservative lender First Republic has been relatively unscathed by the financial problems plaguing the banking industry. The company has a solid asset portfolio with few delinquencies. First Republic is focused on growing its business banking and wealth management business which spurs fee income. The bank is expanding its wealth management unit through hiring and cross-selling. The bank also caters to film and television companies by offering lending deposit and wealth management services.

EXECUTIVES

EVP Secretary and General Counsel, Edward J. Dobranski, age 65
President CEO and Director, James H. Herbert
EVP and Chief Credit Officer, David B. Lichtman

President First Republic Securities, David
Tateosian
SEVP and Chief Banking Officer, Michael D. (Mike)
Selfridge, age 48
Chairman First Republic Trust Company, Michael
J. Harrington
EVP and President Private Wealth Management,
Bob Thornton
EVP and Chief Marketing Officer, Dianne Snedaker
**Executive Vice President First Republic
Investment Management,** Nicolas Gentin
**SVP Chief Deposit Officer and Chief Investment
Officer,** Hafize Gaye (Gaye) Erkan
EVP and CFO, Michael J. (Mike) Roffler
EVP; Chief BSA and AML and Security Officer,
Bill Ward
EVP and CIO, Dale A. Smith
EVP and COO, Jason C. Bender
President First Republic Trust Company, Kelly
Johnston
Vice President and Investment Consultant, Dan
(Danny) Bessey
Vice President, Brent Chapman
Vice President Compliance Risk Manager, Steven
(Steve) Sears
Vice President, Thomas (Thom) Ehrhardt
Vice President, Michael Curley
Senior Vice President Finance, Ravi Mallela
Vice President, Todd Brantley
Vice President, Margaret AE (Maggie) Zywicz
Vice President and Assistant General Counsel,
Janisha Sabnani
Vice President, Karen (Kare) Conway
**Vice President First Republic Investment
Management,** Reynolds Ospina
Vice President, Monika Mugg
Executive Vice President, Brian (Bri) Riley
Senior Vice President Deputy General Counsel,
Jonathan (John) Santelli
Vice President of Retail Marketing, Gwenn Murphy
Vice President, Peter (Pete) Chang
**Vice President And Deputy Director Credit
Administration,** Sean Callum
Vice President, Paula Lazar
Vice President, DAVID (Dave) WEITGENANT
Senior Vice President, Bradley (Brad) Finn
Vice President Of Operations, Alexander (Al) Kiren
Vice President And Portfolio Manager, Jeff W
(Jeffy) Greene
Vice President Director Deposit Technology, Dave
(Davie) McLelland
Senior Vice President, Helene Jepson
Vice Chair, Katherine August-deWilde, age 65
Assistant Treasurer, Thomas (Thom) Lacher
Auditors: KPMG LLP

LOCATIONS

HQ: First Republic Bank (San Francisco, CA)
111 Pine Street, 2nd Floor, San Francisco, CA 94111
Phone: 415 392-1400
Web: www.firstrepublic.com

PRODUCTS/OPERATIONS

2013 Sales

	% of total
Interest income other	85
Noninterest income	15
Total	**100**

Selected Affiliates

First Republic Investment Management Inc.
First Republic Securities Company LLC
First Republic Trust Company

COMPETITORS

Bank of Marin	City National
Bank of New York	JPMorgan Private Bank
Mellon	MUFG Americas Holdings
Boston Private	Morgan Stanley
Citigroup Private Bank	TriState Capital

HISTORICAL FINANCIALS

Company Type: Public

Income Statement

FYE: December 31

	ASSETS ($ mil.)	NET INCOME ($ mil.)	INCOME AS % OF ASSETS	EMPLOYEES
12/15	58,981.2	522.1	0.9%	0.0
12/14	48,353.3	487.0	1.0%	2,506.0
12/13	42,112.7	462.0	1.1%	2,388.0
12/12	34,387.6	402.4	1.2%	2,110.0
12/11	27,791.8	352.0	1.3%	1,821.0
Annual Growth	**20.7%**	**10.4%**	**—**	**—**

2015 Year-End Financials

Return on assets: 0.9%
Return on equity: 9.9%
Long-term debt ($ mil.): —
No. of shares (mil.): 146.1
Sales ($ mil): 1,989.1

Dividends
Yield: 0.8%
Payout: 19.3%
Market value ($ mil.): 9,652.0

	STOCK PRICE ($) FY Close	P/E High/Low		PER SHARE ($) Earnings	Dividends	Book Value
12/15	66.06	21	15	3.18	0.59	39.05
12/14	52.12	18	14	3.07	0.54	34.56
12/13	52.35	16	10	3.10	0.46	31.33
12/12	32.78	12	10	2.76	0.30	25.89
12/11	30.61	13	8	2.65	0.00	19.46
Annual Growth	**21.2%**	**—**	**—**	**4.7%**	**—**	**19.0%**

Fitbit Inc

Auditors: PricewaterhouseCoopers LLP

LOCATIONS

HQ: Fitbit Inc
405 Howard Street, San Francisco, CA 94105
Phone: 415 513-1000
Web: www.Fitbit.com

HISTORICAL FINANCIALS

Company Type: Public

Income Statement

FYE: December 31

	REVENUE ($ mil.)	NET INCOME ($ mil.)	NET PROFIT MARGIN	EMPLOYEES
12/15	1,858.0	175.6	9.5%	1,101.0
12/14	745.4	131.7	17.7%	469.0
12/13	271.0	(51.6)	—	222.0
12/12	76.3	(4.2)	—	115.0
Annual Growth	**189.8%**	**—**		**112.3%**

2015 Year-End Financials

Debt ratio: —
Return on equity: 31.2%
Cash ($ mil.): 664.4
Current ratio: 2.67
Long-term debt ($ mil.): —

No. of shares (mil.): 214.7
Dividends
Yield: —
Payout: —
Market value ($ mil.): 6,355.0

	STOCK PRICE ($) FY Close	P/E High/Low		PER SHARE ($) Earnings	Dividends	Book Value
12/15	29.59	59	31	0.75	0.00	4.57
12/14	0.00	—	—	0.63	0.00	3.50
Annual Growth	**—**	**—**	**—**	**19.0%**	**—**	**30.5%**

Five Below Inc

Five Below may be growing as quickly as its youthful clientele. Operating a fast-growing chain of specialty retail stores Five Below sells a broad range of trend-right products all priced under $5. The retailer which targets teenage and pre-teen girls and boys operates close to 450 stores in shopping centers in 27 states. Core merchandise includes fun but inexpensive items that entice teens such as jewelry and accessories novelty t-shirts casual footwear sports gear decor and crafts and mobile phone accessories. Five Below was founded in 2002 by CEO Thomas Vellios and David Schlessinger. The retailer went public in 2012.

Operations

Five Below has three categories of youth-oriented merchandise: Leisure (51% of revenue) Fashion and home (30%) and Party and snack (19%). Working with vendors the chain switches products quickly trying to hit on the item of the moment.

Geographic Reach

From its base in the Northeast (the company is headquartered in Philadelphia) Five Below has aggressively expanded into the Southeast and Midwest. With a move into Texas the company has stores in 27 states.

Sales and Marketing

Five Below sources merchandise from about 800 vendors none of which account for more than 7% of its purchases. The company gets some two-thirds of its merchandise from domestic vendors. As its geography and store count has increased so has Five Below's advertising spending. It spent about $22 million $19 million and $16 million in 2015 2014 and 2013 respectively. The ad budget was just $6 million in 2011.

Financial Performance

Sales of items for $5 or less add up. Five Below's sales rose 22% in 2015 (ended January 2016) to compared to $832 million. New stores and higher same-store sales drove revenue higher. Same-store sales benefited from more transactions and higher average value per transaction.

Net income jumped 20% to about $58 million in 2015. Increased sales more than made up for higher costs associated with growth.

Strategy

Five Below seeks to differentiate itself from its discount and mass-merchant rivals through its unique focus the teen and pre-teen customer. Like many deep-discount retailers it's expanding its store base at a rapid clip. Indeed it added more than 70 new locations in 2015 (ended January 2016) with plans for 80 more in 2016. In Texas the company has stores in the Dallas-Fort Worth area and Austin. Ultimately the youth-focused retailer hopes to grow the chain to more than 2000 stores. To support its growing store base the company is investing in capital improvements including expanding its Delaware-based distribution center and updating its technologies.

EXECUTIVES

Chief Administrative Officer, Eric M. Specter, age 58, $500,000 total compensation

CFO Secretary and Treasurer, Kenneth R. Bull, age 53, $400,000 total compensation

President CEO and Director, Joel D. Anderson, age 51, $700,000 total compensation

EVP Merchandising, Michael F. Romanko, age 50, $450,000 total compensation

Vice President Information Technology, Chris DeMeester

Executive Vice President Real Estate, Linda Moser

Vice President of Information Technology, Robert (Bob) Millman

Senior Vice President Supply Chain, Gene Rosadino

Senior Vice President Product Development, Michael (Mel) Pannullo

Vice President Construction And Design, Walt (Walter) Harkins

Vice President, Karen (Kare) Procell

Senior Vice President Human RE, Bill (Billy) Clark

Chairman, Thomas G. (Tom) Vellios, age 61

Auditors: KPMG LLP

LOCATIONS

HQ: Five Below Inc
1818 Market Street, Suite 2000, Philadelphia, PA 19103
Phone: 215 546-7909
Web: www.fivebelow.com

PRODUCTS/OPERATIONS

2015 Sales

	% of total
Leisure	51
Fashion & home	30
Party & snack	19
Total	**100**

COMPETITORS

Big Lots	Hot Topic
CVS	Kmart
Claire's Stores	Rite Aid
Dollar General	TJX Companies
Dollar Tree	Target Corporation
Family Dollar Stores	Wal-Mart
Forever 21	Walgreen

HISTORICAL FINANCIALS

Company Type: Public

Income Statement
FYE: January 30

	REVENUE ($ mil.)	NET INCOME ($ mil.)	NET PROFIT MARGIN	EMPLOYEES
01/16	831.9	57.6	6.9%	7,600.0
01/15*	680.2	48.0	7.1%	6,700.0
02/14	535.4	32.1	6.0%	5,500.0
02/13	418.8	20.0	4.8%	3,750.0
01/12	297.1	16.0	5.4%	2,960.0
Annual Growth	**29.4%**	**37.6%**	**—**	**26.6%**

*Fiscal year change

2016 Year-End Financials

Debt ratio: —
Return on equity: 27.6%
Cash ($ mil.): 99.4
Current ratio: 2.59
Long-term debt ($ mil.): —
No. of shares (mil.): 54.5
Dividends
Yield: —
Payout: —
Market value ($ mil.): 1,923.0

	STOCK PRICE ($) FY Close	P/E High/Low	PER SHARE ($) Earnings	Dividends	Book Value
01/16	35.23	38 26	1.05	0.00	4.48
01/15*	33.32	52 37	0.88	0.00	3.20
02/14	36.65	92 60	0.59	0.00	2.16
02/13	37.10	— —	(1.28)	2.02	1.31
Annual Growth	**(1.7%)**	**— —**	**—**	**—**	**50.6%**

*Fiscal year change

Five Prime Therapeutics, Inc

Five Prime Therapeutics is counting down the ways to fight cancer. The clinical-stage company is developing drugs that use protein therapy to block the disease process in cancer and inflammatory diseases such as rheumatoid arthritis. Through a collaboration with GlaxoSmithKline it is developing a protein therapy that neutralizes fibroblast growth factors to inhibit cancerous tumors such as squamous non-small cell lung cancer. Another collaboration with UCB will develop therapies for fibrosis-related inflammatory diseases and central nervous system disorders. Founded by CEO Rusty Williams in 2001 the company went public in 2013 raising $62 million in its IPO which it will use toward funding clinical trials.

EXECUTIVES

President and CEO, Lewis T. (Rusty) Williams, age 67, $525,000 total compensation

SVP and CFO, Marc L. Belsky

COO, Aron M. Knickerbocker, age 47, $364,000 total compensation

SVP and Chief Scientific Officer, W. Michael Kavanaugh

SVP Development Sciences, Kevin P. Baker

EVP General Counsel and Secretary, Francis Sarena

Auditors: Ernst & Young LLP

LOCATIONS

HQ: Five Prime Therapeutics, Inc
Two Corporate Drive, South San Francisco, CA 94080
Phone: 415 365-5600
Web: www.fiveprime.com

COMPETITORS

AbbVie	Pfizer
Amgen	Pharmacyclics
CTI BioPharma	Roche Holding
Clovis Oncology	Sanofi
ImmunoGen	Seattle Genetics
Merck	Spectrum
Novartis	Pharmaceuticals
PDL BioPharma	

HISTORICAL FINANCIALS

Company Type: Public

Income Statement
FYE: December 31

	REVENUE ($ mil.)	NET INCOME ($ mil.)	NET PROFIT MARGIN	EMPLOYEES
12/15	379.8	249.6	65.7%	157.0
12/14	19.2	(37.4)	—	124.0
12/13	13.7	(28.8)	—	106.0
12/12	9.9	(27.6)	—	108.0
12/11	64.9	19.7	30.4%	0.0
Annual Growth	**55.5%**	**88.7%**	**—**	**—**

2015 Year-End Financials

Debt ratio: —
Return on equity: 96.3%
Cash ($ mil.): 149.9
Current ratio: 6.66
Long-term debt ($ mil.): —
No. of shares (mil.): 26.1
Dividends
Yield: —
Payout: —
Market value ($ mil.): 1,084.0

	STOCK PRICE ($) FY Close	P/E High/Low	PER SHARE ($) Earnings	Dividends	Book Value
12/15	41.50	5 2	9.23	0.00	16.59
12/14	27.00	— —	(1.79)	0.00	3.93
12/13	16.79	— —	(5.23)	0.00	3.45
Annual Growth	**57.2%**	**— —**	**—**	**—**	**—**
119.4%					

FleetCor Technologies Inc

Helping companies manage motor fleets is at the core of FleetCor's mission. The company is a leading provider of fleet cards and payment processing services aimed at commercial and government fleets. Its cards carry the names Fuelman CFN Mannatec Keyfuels CCS and Fuelcard. The fleet cards function like typical charge cards and can be used to purchase fuel and lodging. FleetCor tracks purchases to help manage employee spending. The company serves more than 500000 accounts and has millions of cards active in the US Canada Mexico Europe Africa and Asia. Major customers include oil giants BP Chevron and Shell. FleetCor is expanding rapidly at home and abroad via acquisitions.

OperationsOther products and services include telematics solutions which uses GPS and wireless technology to help fleet operators monitor their fleets; vehicle maintenance services in the UK; the distribution of prepaid fuel and food vouchers and cards for businesses and their employees in Mexico; and a similar workforce payment product in Brazil for those dealing in public transport and toll vouchers.FleetCor generated 72% of its total revenue from its card program fees and charges during 2015 while another 12% came from transactions tied to fuel-price spreads.Geographic Range

North America accounted for 72% of Georgia-based FleetCor's sales in 2015. Beyond North America the company does business in some 40 countries in Africa Europe (including Russia) Latin America Australia and New Zealand.Sales and MarketingFleetCor offers its commercial payment services to retailers commercial fleets major oil companies petroleum marketers and government entities in a variety of industries such as retail healthcare construction and hospitality. The company managed relationships with 800 such partners during 2015.

It's been ramping up its advertising spend in recent years spending $19.9 million in 2015 up from $14.4 million and $12.3 million in 2014 and 2013 respectively.

Financial Performance

Fueled by smaller fleet service and portfolio acquisitions FleetCor's annual revenues and profits have tripled and doubled since 2011 (the company went public in 2010).The company's revenue jumped 42% to $1.7 billion during 2015 mostly thanks to 84% growth in its North American business segment which was led by its Comdata acquisition and organic payment program growth which benefited from increased volumes and revenue per transaction. FleetCor's International segment revenue fell 11% due to poor macroecomic growth and unfavorable foreign exchange rates though organic payment program growth from higher volume and revenue per transaction helped offset some of the decline.Despite strong revenue growth in 2015 FleetCor's net income dipped 2% to $362 million for the year mostly due to costs associated with its Comdata acquisition. The company's operating cash levels climbed 24% to $754 million thanks to a combination of positive working capital changes and non-cash item adjustments related to amortization of intangible assets stock-based compensation and equity method investment losses.

Strategy

The rapidly expanding company plans to consolidate the industry further by targeting smaller and regional fleet service providers in markets it currently serves and in new markets overseas. It also looks to buy commercial account portfolios technologies services and products.Indeed FleetCor has been on an international acquisitions spree in recent years snapping up companies in growing markets in Europe Asia and Latin America. After entering Australian and New Zealand in 2013 via acquisitions in those two countries the company expanded more into Germany and broader Europe after acquiring portfolios from Shell (2014). It expanded in Brazil when it bough San Paulo-based electronic toll payment company STP in mid-2016.

Mergers and Acquisitions

In August 2016 FleetCor paid $1.05 billion to acquire San Paulo-based electronic toll payment company Servicos e Tecnologia de Pagamentos S.A (STP). That firm collects some $2.5 billion in toll parking and fuel payments from 4.5 million active users annually and provided cardless fuel payments at Shell sites throughout Brazil.In November 2014 FleetCor purchased B2B electronic payment solutions provider Comdata Inc. from Ceridian LLC for $3.45 billion to expand in payments. The deal allowed FleetCor to dramatically expand in North America and enter the business of virtual bank-card payments.In July 2014 the group purchased commercial fueling network provider US-based Pacific Pride Services LLC for $50 million In May 2014 the company expanded its clientele further after buying part of Shell' fuel card customer portfolio in Germany and signed a European framework agreement to expand potential coverage of Shell's fuel card portfolios in up to 12 more markets in Europe.

Company Background

In October 2013 the fuel card company purchased NexTraq a US-based provider of telematics services to small and medium-sized businesses. Atlanta-based NexTraq's Internet-based system seeks to enhance workforce productivity through real time vehicle tracking route optimization job dispatch and fuel usage monitoring.

In September 2013 FleetCor acquired VB Servicos Comercio e Administracao LTDA (VB) a provider of transportation cards and vouchers in Brazil.

In 2012 the company entered the Brazil market with its acquisition of CTF Technologies for $180 million. CTF provides fuel payment processing in Brazil.The company entered Russia and Brazil in 2012 and expanded into Australia and New Zealand in 2013.Founded in 2000 FleetCor went public in December 2010 via an initial public offering that raised about $290 million. The proceeds went to FleetCor's private equity shareholders Advent International Bain Capital and Summit Partners.

EXECUTIVES

Chairman and CEO, Ronald F. (Ron) Clarke, age 60, $1,000,000 total compensation
CFO, Eric R. Dey, age 56, $344,231 total compensation
CEO UK and Australasia, David D. Maxsimic, age 56
President International Partners, Andrew Blazye, $340,137 total compensation
President North America Fuel Cards, Todd W. House, age 44, $348,077 total compensation
President Corporate Lodging Consultants, Timothy J. Downs, age 58
EVP Corporate Strategy, Charles R. Freund
EVP Global Corporate Development, John S. Coughlin, $348,077 total compensation
CIO, John A. Reed
CEO FleetCor Brazil, Armando L. Netto, $280,048 total compensation
Senior Vice President Business Development, Scott (Scotty) Ruoff
Vice President Strategic Marketing, Krystl Black
Vice President of Strategic Relationships, John (Jack) Leitner
Vice President of Sales, Chet Panhans
Vice President Marketing, Robin (Rin) Gregg
Vice President Process Excellence and Program Management, Ed (Eddie) Thomas
Vice President Of Information Technology, Erik Hymel
Senior Vice President Sales and Marketing, Paul (Pauly) Citarella
Vice President Business Development, John (Jack) Ryan
Vice President Corporate Devel, James (Jamie) Howle
Vice President Product Management, Wes Williams
Vice President Financial Planning, Melissa Mayaudon
National Account Manager, Jamie (James) Pesch
Vice President Us Information Technology Operations, Angela (Angie) Hon
Executive Vice President Corporate Development, Paul (Pauly) Holland
Senior Vice President of Sales, Derrek Schartz
Vice President Information Security, Bruce R Evans, age 58
Vice President Product Management, John (Jack) Young
Senior Vice President, Sean Bowen
Senior Vice President Sales, Jeff (Jeffy) Lamb
Executive Vice President Business Development, John (Jack) Couglin
Vice President, Amit Singh
Senior Vice President of Financial Planning and Analysis, Chad Richardson
Vice President Merchant Services, James (Jamie) Prantl
Auditors: Ernst & Young LLP

LOCATIONS

HQ: FleetCor Technologies Inc
5445 Triangle Parkway, Norcross, GA 30092
Phone: 770 449-0479
Web: www.fleetcor.com

PRODUCTS/OPERATIONS

Selected Brands and Subsidiaries
CCS
CFN Holding Co.
CLC Group
Corporate Lodging Consultants Inc.
FleetCards
FleetNet
Fuelman
The Fuelcard Company
Fuel Vend Limited
Keyfuels
Mannatec Inc.
Transit Card

COMPETITORS

American Express	Sodexo USA
Arval	U.S. Bancorp
Edenred	WEX
Multi Service	World Fuel Services
Retail Decisions	

HISTORICAL FINANCIALS

Company Type: Public

Income Statement

FYE: December 31

	REVENUE ($ mil.)	NET INCOME ($ mil.)	NET PROFIT MARGIN	EMPLOYEES
12/15	1,702.8	362.4	21.3%	5,330.0
12/14	1,199.3	368.7	30.7%	4,780.0
12/13	895.1	284.5	31.8%	3,500.0
12/12	707.5	216.2	30.6%	2,650.0
12/11	519.5	147.3	28.4%	2,130.0
Annual Growth 34.5%		25.2%	—	25.8%

2015 Year-End Financials

Debt ratio: 29.4%	No. of shares (mil.): 92.3
Return on equity: 12.9%	Dividends
Cash ($ mil.): 447.1	Yield: —
Current ratio: 0.87	Payout: —
Long-term debt ($ mil.): 2,061.4	Market value ($ mil.): 13,203.0

	STOCK PRICE ($) FY Close	P/E High/Low	PER SHARE ($) Earnings	Dividends	Book Value
12/15	142.93	42 35	3.85	0.00	30.64
12/14	148.71	36 23	4.24	0.00	30.04
12/13	117.17	35 15	3.36	0.00	15.08
12/12	53.65	21 12	2.52	0.00	11.28
12/11	29.87	20 14	1.76	0.00	9.91
Annual Growth 47.9%		— —	21.6%	—	32.6%

Flexsteel Industries, Inc.

If you're not sitting down for this Flexsteel Industries might ask why not. It's not as if the company hasn't given you plenty of options. Flexsteel incorporated in 1929 makes wood and upholstered furniture for every room in the home as well as for the recreational vehicle and commercial markets.

Most of its upholstered products –including recliners rockers and sofas –incorporate a unique drop-in spring for which the company is named. Crafting its goods mostly in the US Flexsteel distributes to furniture retailers department stores catalog companies RV manufacturers hotels and health care facilities. The company's DMI Furniture unit produces furnishings for the home and office.

Geographic Reach

Iowa-based Flexsteel boasts operations throughout North America operating manufacturing facilities in Arkansas California Georgia Iowa Mississippi and Mexico in the city of Juarez.

Operations

Residential customers account for some 80% of Flexsteel's revenue; commercial customers generation the remaining 20%.

Sales and Marketing

Flexsteel sells its products through its own sales force and through independent representatives nationwide. The company's also spending more money on advertising –including national trade advertising programs –in recent years shelling out $6.1 million in fiscal 2014 up from 2013's $5.6 million and $4.9 million in 2012.

To leverage the company's more well-known name Flexsteel integrated the Wynwood product line into its namesake line. The firm aims to extend the reach of its marketplace by rolling out a combined Flexsteel Wynwood Collection in 2014.

Financial Performance

Flexsteel's sales have been trending upward during the past five years. In fiscal 2014 (ended June) the company logged a 14% increase in revenue to $438.5 million vs. $386.2 million in 2013. It points to $359.6 million in residential sales –representing an increase of $48.3 million from the previous reporting period –for the gains thanks to increased demand for upholstered and ready-to-assemble products and a more than 5% sales boost from its commercial business.

During the past four years the furniture maker has seen its net profits rise to $14.9 million in 2014 from $13.2 million in 2013. Additionally while the company's cash flow has been on a downward trend until 2013 Flexsteel posted a cash flow of $16.2 million representing an increase of $10.3 million due in part to $15 million in net income and litigation settlement costs during the reporting period.

Strategy

The furniture maker's production model includes integrating manufactured products from its half-dozen plants in the US and Mexico with finished products purchased from offshore suppliers in Asia. Flexsteel has been paring down its operations in recent years in response to decreased demand for furniture. To this end Flexsteel in recent years consolidated a pair of manufacturing plants and halted production at another contributing to a noteworthy 30% workforce reduction.

In 2014 however Flexsteel's in investment mode. The company is investing up to $40 million to purchase and equip a Midwest distribution center and spending another $6 million in other operating capital expenditures during fiscal 2015.

HISTORY

Frank Bertsch a German immigrant furniture maker living in Minneapolis and several partners bought the Rolph & Ball Furniture Co. in 1901 and renamed it Grau-Curtis after two of the partners. Bertsch bought out his partners in 1917. The company began using an innovative spring system designed by Swiss inventor Werner Schlaprittzi in 1927. That year it bought half of Schlaprittzi's Sanitas Spring Co.

The company renamed itself Northome Furniture Industries in 1929 and Bertsch was succeeded by his son Herbert (who had joined the company in 1919). Sanitas Spring was renamed Flexsteel Spring (the name of its patented seating spring system) in 1934 and in 1936 the company moved to Dubuque. In 1947 Herbert's son Frank joined Northome. The company bought its remaining stake in Flexsteel Spring in 1948 and in 1958 Northome became Flexsteel. It began making RV seating in the 1960s and first produced recliners in 1965. The company went public in 1969.

As its primary customers —small to medium-sized retailers –succumbed to bigger chains in the 1980s Flexsteel began to market its products more aggressively by establishing Flexsteel Galleries and Comfort Seating Showrooms (later renamed Flexsteel Comfort Galleries) in dealers' stores. The younger Frank Bertsch's cousin Jack Crahan was named CEO in 1990; Bruce Lauritsen succeeded him in 1993. Profits slumped in 1995 and 1996 as a result of sagging sales higher material costs and a costly plant upgrade. The company also began opening freestanding stores in 1996.

In 1997 Flexsteel purchased the bankrupt Dygert Seating (a maker of seats installed in light trucks and van conversions). But a sluggish van conversion market caused the company to close its Watkinsville Georgia plant and seek new markets such as wheelchairs and motorized scooters. In 1998 Flexsteel underwent a $2 million expansion project at its Dublin Georgia plant.

When one of its customers National Comfort Seating closed the doors of several Indiana furniture stores in 2000 Flexsteel took over operation reopening them as Comfort Seating —Flexsteel Home Furnishings stores. A slowing economy and lowered sales of recreational vehicles (RVs) were blamed for layoffs (about 7%) at the Dubuque Iowa plant in 2001. Bruce Boylen a retired executive from RV maker Fleetwood became chairman the same year.

In October 2003 Flexsteel completed its acquisition of DMI Furniture. The next month the company discontinued its retail operations.

Ron Klosterman took over as CEO in late 2006.

EXECUTIVES

SVP Finance CFO Treasurer and Secretary, Timothy E. Hall, age 58, $315,000 total compensation
President CEO and Director, Karel K. Czanderna, age 59, $600,000 total compensation
VP Home Styles Division, John Faig
VP Home Furnishings, Dan Kennedy
SVP Growth, Julia K. Bizzis, age 59, $295,000 total compensation
National Sales Manager Healthcare, David (Dave) Sullivan
Vice President Global Supply Chain, Steve (Stevie) Hall
Vice President and General Manager, Rick (Ricky) Stanley
Chairman, Eric S. Rangen, age 59
Auditors: Deloitte & Touche LLP

LOCATIONS

HQ: Flexsteel Industries, Inc.
385 Bell Street, Dubuque, IA 52001-0877
Phone: 563 556-7730
Web: www.flexsteel.com

PRODUCTS/OPERATIONS

2016 Sales

	$ mil.	% of total
Residential	420.9	84
Commercial	79.2	16
Total	**500.1**	**100**

Selected Products

Bedroom furniture
Chairs
Convertible bedding units
Desks
Dining tables and chairs
Love seats
Occasional tables
Reclining chairs
Rocker-reclining chairs
Sofas and sofa beds
Swivel rocking chairs

COMPETITORS

All American Group	La-Z-Boy
Allsteel	Leggett & Platt
Bassett Furniture	Patrick Industries
CFGroup	Rowe Fine Furniture
Decorator Industries	Standard Furniture
Heritage Home Group	Stanley Furniture
Herman Miller	Vaughan-Bassett
Klaussner Furniture	Furniture

HISTORICAL FINANCIALS

Company Type: Public

Income Statement

FYE: June 30

	REVENUE ($ mil.)	NET INCOME ($ mil.)	NET PROFIT MARGIN	EMPLOYEES
06/16	500.1	24.2	4.8%	1,460.0
06/15	466.9	22.3	4.8%	1,340.0
06/14	438.5	14.9	3.4%	1,350.0
06/13	386.1	13.1	3.4%	1,360.0
06/12	352.0	13.0	3.7%	1,300.0
Annual Growth	**9.2%**	**16.7%**	**—**	**2.9%**

2016 Year-End Financials

Debt ratio: —	No. of shares (mil.): 7.7
Return on equity: 12.2%	Dividends
Cash ($ mil.): 36.7	Yield: 1.8%
Current ratio: 5.29	Payout: 23.5%
Long-term debt ($ mil.): —	Market value ($ mil.): 305.0

	STOCK PRICE ($) FY Close	P/E High/Low		PER SHARE ($) Earnings	Dividends	Book Value
06/16	39.62	15	9	3.12	0.72	27.23
06/15	43.09	15	10	2.89	0.72	24.96
06/14	33.35	19	11	2.00	0.60	22.62
06/13	24.38	14	10	1.80	0.60	21.28
06/12	19.78	11	7	1.86	0.45	20.19
Annual Growth	**19.0%**	**—**	**—**	**13.8%**	**12.5%**	**7.8%**

FNB Corp

F.N.B. Corporation is the holding company for First National Bank of Pennsylvania which serves consumers and small to midsized businesses though almost 290 bank branches in Pennsylvania northeastern Ohio and Maryland. The company also has more than 70 consumer finance offices operating as Regency Finance in those states as well as Tennessee and Kentucky. In addition to community banking and consumer finance F.N.B. also has segments devoted to insurance and wealth management. It also offers leasing and merchant banking services. F.N.B. has extended its reach in its target states through acquisitions of banks including Metro Bancorp Annapolis Bancorp and PVF Capital Corp.

OperationsF.N.B operates four segments. The Community Banking segment which made up almost 90% of the company's total revenue during 2015 provides commercial and consumer banking services including corporate banking small business banking investment real estate financing asset-based lending capital markets services and lease financing as well as traditional consumer banking products. The company's Wealth Management segment (5% of revenue) offers trust and other fiduciary services while the Insurance segment (2% of revenue) offers commercial and personal insurance through major carriers. F.N.B.'s Consumer Finance segment (6% of revenue) which operates through subsidiary Regency Finance Company provides installment loans to individuals and buys installment loans from retail merchants.Like other retail banks F.N.B. makes the bulk of its money from interest income. Nearly 70% of the bank's total revenue came from loan and lease interest (including fees) during 2015 while 9% came from interest on taxable and non-taxable securities. The rest of money came from service charges (10% of revenue) trust income (3%) insurance commissions and fees (2%) securities commissions and fees (2%) mortgage banking (1%) and other non-interest income sources.Geographic ReachMost of the Pittsburgh-based company's branches are concentrated in Pennsylvania with the next largest markets being in Ohio Maryland and West Virginia. Its consumer finance offices are mostly in Pennsylvania and Tennessee with others in Kentucky and Ohio.Sales and MarketingF.N.B. boosted its advertising and promotional spend by 7% to $8.4 million during 2015 mostly because of higher expenses associated with the bank's recent acquisitions as it worked to get the name out in new territories such as in Cleveland Ohio and Baltimore. Financial PerformanceF.N.B. Corporation's annual revenues have risen nearly 40% since 2011 as its loan assets have nearly doubled with new branch openings and acquisitions. Its profits have doubled as well over the period as the company has kept a lid on growing costs.The bank's revenue climbed 6% to $709.21 million during 2015 thanks to continued loan business growth stemming from recent bank acquisitions.Revenue growth in 2015 drove F.N.B.'s net income up 11% to $159.65 million. The company's operating cash levels plunged 50% to $223.48 million for the year due to unfavorable changes in working capital related to securities classified as trading in business combination and sold.StrategyF.N.B. Corporation grows its loan and deposit business while expanding into new markets by acquiring smaller banks and select bank branches. In 2016 it agreed to buy North Carolina-based Yadkin Financial for $1.4 billion. That deal will add around 100 banking locations in the Carolinas and some $7.5 billion in assets. The combined bank will have some 400 branches across the Mid-Atlantic and Southeast US.

Mergers and AcquisitionsIn April 2016 the company bought 17 branch locations in the Pittsburgh area from Fifth Third Bank as well as $100000 in loans and over $300000 in deposits.In February 2016 F.N.B. Corporation purchased Metro Bancorp along its $3 billion in assets and more

than 30 Metro Bank branches in south-central Pennsylvania. The deal effectively merged Metro Bank into F.N.B.'s First National Bank of Pennsylvania subsidiary. In September 2015 the bank purchased five branches in southeastern Pennsylvania from Bank of America along with almost $155000 in associated deposits.In October 2013 F.N.B. moved to expand its presence in the greater Cleveland area by purchasing PVF Capital Corp. which owned Park View Federal Savings Bank with some 20 offices in Cleveland and northeastern Ohio.In April 2013 F.N.B. purchased Annapolis Bancorp the parent company of BankAnnapolis in an all-stock transaction valued at about $51 million. The deal expanded F.N.B.'s reach into Maryland. Company Background

F.N.B. which moved its headquarters from Pennsylvania to Florida in 2001 spun off First National Bankshares of Florida at the start of 2004 and returned to the Pittsburgh area. F.N.B. still operates two loan offices in Florida but these primarily manage the company's legacy loan portfolio there.

The bank is again rooted firmly in the Keystone State and bordering markets. After returning it expanded via several acquisitions prior to the Parkvale deal including bank holding companies NSD Bancorp Slippery Rock Financial North East Bancshares Omega Financial and Iron and Glass Bancorp. In 2011 F.N.B. expanded in northeastern Pennsylvania through the acquisition of Comm Bancorp. The deal valued at some $70 million brought in 15 branches.

EXECUTIVES

SVP and Corporate Controller, Timothy G. Rubritz, age 63, $215,016 total compensation
Chief Legal Officer, James G. Orie, age 57, $165,000 total compensation
CFO, Vincent J. Calabrese, age 53, $385,008 total compensation
Chief Credit Officer, Gary Guerrieri, age 55, $350,016 total compensation
President and CEO; CEO First National Bank, Vincent J. (Vince) Delie, age 51, $770,016 total compensation
President and Market Executive Pittsburgh First National Bank of Pennsylvania, John C. Williams, $385,008 total compensation
President Charlotte Region, Gregory L. (Greg) Heaton
Senior Vice President Market Manager, Doug Williamson
Vice President, Tom Miles
Senior Vice President Regional Banking Executive, Todd (Toddy) Hays
Assistant Vice President, Ed (Eddie) Enrietti
Vice President, Nick Gates
Senior Vice President, John (Jack) Waters
Senior Vice President Corporate Strategies Coordinator And Group Man, David (Dave) Yates
Executive Vice President, Louise Lowrey
Vice President, Andy Mittelstaedt
Assistant Vice President, Susan (Sue) Milewski
Vice President Treasury Management Sales Officer, Tracie Elza
Vice President Business Development Officer, Susan (Sue) Lavely
Assistant Vice President, Dusty Klavon
Senior Vice President Commercial Lender, Peter (Pete) Bower
Assistant Vice President, Gerry (Gerold) Gloekler
Vice President Business Banking, Christie (Chris) Olsavsky
Wealth Management Vice President, Mark Renzini
Vice President and Portfolio Manager, Wayne Suprano

Vice President Treasury Management, Sabrina Renfrew
Vice President, Chris (Chrissy) Ecola
Senior Vice President, Anthony (Tony) Marfisi
Senior Vice President Investment Real Estate, Greg (Greggy) Owens
Commercial Portfolio Manager III Assistant Vice President, Colleen O'Neill
Assistant Vice President Branch Manager, Jennifer (Jen) Bayer
Vice President, Gregory (Greg) Robb
Assistant Vice President Mortgage Originator, Elaine (Elle) Frampton
Vice President Commercial Banking, Christopher (Chris) Colella
Assistant Vice President, Kara Beresh
Senior Vice President, Craig (Craigy) Muthler
Vice President, Michael (Mel) Griffo
Vice President, Matt (Matty) Ottaway
Vice President Commercial Banker, Brian (Bri) Bucci
Vice President, Chris (Chrissy) Grobelny
Assistant Vice President Manager, Kevin (Kev) Hershock
Vice President, Matt (Matty) Kuchta
Senior Vice President Team Leader, Joe (Joey) Migliorino
Assistant Vice President Manager, Sue (Susie) Milewski
Vice President Commercial Banking, Tim (Timmy) Moorstein
Assistant Vice President Residential Mortgage Spe, Patricia (Pat) Farabaugh
Assistant Vice President Commercial Loan Review, Cynthia (Cyn) Jennings
Senior Vice President F.N.B. Commercial Leasing, Donna (Don) Yanuzzi
Chairman, Stephen J. (Steve) Gurgovits, age 72
Board Member, Stephen Martz
Auditors: Ernst & Young LLP

LOCATIONS

HQ: FNB Corp
One North Shore Center, 12 Federal Street, Pittsburgh, PA 15212
Phone: 800 555-5455
Web: www.fnbcorporation.com

PRODUCTS/OPERATIONS

2015 Sales by Segment

	$ mil.	% of total
Community banking	616.2	87
Consumer finance	42.8	6
Wealth management	35.2	5
Insurance	13.1	2
parent & other	1.8	-
Total	**709.1**	**100**

2015 Sales

	$ mil.	% of total
Interest		
Loans including fees	482.1	68
Securities including dividends	64.6	9
Other	0.1	-
Non-interest		
Service charges	70.7	10
Trust Services	20.8	3
Insurance commissions & fees	16.3	2
Securities commissions & fees	13.6	2
Other	40.9	6
Total	**709.1**	**100**

Selected Subsidiaries

F.N.B. Capital Corporation (merchant banking)
First National Bank of Pennsylvania
  Bank Capital Services LLC (also dba F.N.B. Commercial Leasing)
  First National Trust Company

F.N.B. Investment Advisors
First National Investment Services Company
First National Insurance Agency LLC
Regency Finance Company
Citizens Financial Services Inc.
F.N.B. Consumer Discount Company
Finance and Mortgage Acceptance Corporation

COMPETITORS

Bank of America	Huntington Bancshares
Citizens Financial	M&T Bank
Group	Northwest Bancshares
Dollar Bank	PNC Financial
Fifth Third	S&T Bancorp
First Commonwealth	Sandy Spring Bancorp
Financial	Sovereign Bank
Fulton Financial	United Community
Glen Burnie Bancorp	Financial

HISTORICAL FINANCIALS
Company Type: Public

Income Statement
FYE: December 31

	ASSETS ($ mil.)	NET INCOME ($ mil.)	INCOME AS % OF ASSETS	EMPLOYEES
12/15	17,557.6	159.6	0.9%	3,205.0
12/14	16,127.0	144.0	0.9%	3,145.0
12/13	13,563.4	117.8	0.9%	3,103.0
12/12	12,023.9	110.4	0.9%	2,975.0
12/11	9,786.4	87.0	0.9%	3,015.0
Annual Growth	15.7%	16.4%	—	1.5%

2015 Year-End Financials

Return on assets: 0.9%	Dividends
Return on equity: 7.7%	Yield: 3.6%
Long-term debt ($ mil.): —	Payout: 55.1%
No. of shares (mil.): 175.4	Market value ($ mil.): 2,340.0
Sales ($ mil): 709.2	

	STOCK PRICE ($) FY Close	P/E High/Low		PER SHARE ($) Earnings	Dividends	Book Value
12/15	13.34	17	14	0.86	0.48	11.95
12/14	13.32	17	14	0.80	0.48	11.62
12/13	12.62	16	13	0.80	0.48	11.16
12/12	10.62	16	13	0.79	0.48	10.02
12/11	11.31	16	12	0.70	0.48	9.51
Annual Growth	4.2%	—	—	5.3%	(0.0%)	5.9%

Fogo de Chao Inc

Auditors: PricewaterhouseCoopers LLP

LOCATIONS

HQ: Fogo de Chao Inc
14881 Quorum Drive, Suite 750, Dallas, TX 75254
Phone: 972 960-9533
Web: www.fogodechao.com

HISTORICAL FINANCIALS
Company Type: Public

Income Statement
FYE: January 3

	REVENUE ($ mil.)	NET INCOME ($ mil.)	NET PROFIT MARGIN	EMPLOYEES
01/16*	271.6	27.8	10.3%	2,848.0
12/14	262.2	17.5	6.7%	2,515.0
12/13	219.2	(0.9)	—	0.0
12/12	93.8	(9.0)	—	0.0
07/12	108.5	(8.8)	—	0.0
Annual Growth	25.8%	—	—	—

*Fiscal year change

2016 Year-End Financials

Debt ratio: 33.8%	No. of shares (mil.): 28.0
Return on equity: 13.5%	Dividends
Cash ($ mil.): 24.9	Yield: —
Current ratio: 1.40	Payout: —
Long-term debt ($ mil.): 165.0	Market value ($ mil.): 426.0

	STOCK PRICE ($) FY Close	P/E High/Low		PER SHARE ($) Earnings	Dividends	Book Value
01/16*	15.16	24	13	1.06	0.00	8.93
Annual Growth	—	—	—	—	—	—

*Fiscal year change

Fonar Corp.

SONAR finds objects hidden under the water using sound waves; FONAR uses magnetic resonance imaging (MRI) to find disease or injury hidden inside the body. The company was the first to market a commercial MRI scanner in 1980 and it is trying to stay at the forefront of the field. Its primary products include the Upright MRI which scans patients in sitting standing or bending positions and the FONAR 360 a room-sized MRI. Both systems do away with the claustrophobia-producing enclosed tubes of traditional machines. Additionally FONAR's Health Management Corporation of America (HMCA) subsidiary provides management services to more than 20 diagnostic imaging centers primarily in Florida and New York.

Operations

The company divides its operations between medical equipment and managing imaging centers. Though it touts its MRI machines the most center management actually brings the bulk of revenue - 70%.

Despite being first to market the company has struggled against larger competitors (such as GE Healthcare and Toshiba). The company is banking on the success of its Upright MRI and marketing the product aggressively to hospitals and private imaging centers. It is especially touting the machine's ability to image weight-bearing conditions that are not apparent when patients lie down.

Geographic Reach

FONAR has its headquarters in New York with operations in the Netherlands Germany the UK Libya Spain Puerto Rico Switzerland Canada Australia and Greece. Its MRIs are installed across the globe in North America Europe and Asia. The majority of its revenues come from the US.

Financial Performance

In 2013 FONAR's revenue increased 25% based on a bump in patient fees after it acquired MRI center manager Health Diagnostic Management in 2013. Net income also climbed by 50% due to the increase in revenue.

Strategy

The company has primarily been focused on software upgrades for its MRI scanners. It also plans to upgrade and expand the imaging centers it manages. FONAR has also been growing its practice management business.

Mergers and Acquisitions

As part of its strategy to expand its management business in 2013 FONAR purchased Health Diagnostic Management. The company includes about a dozen MRI imaging centers in New York and Florida.

Background

Dr. Raymond V. Damadian —the company's chairman president and founder —is widely acknowledged as one of the inventors of medical MRI technology.

EXECUTIVES

Chairman and President, Raymond V. Damadian, age 80, $72,285 total compensation
Director Communications, Daniel Culver
Director and Secretary, Claudette J. V. Chan, age 78
Lead Independent Director, Charles Data
Lead Independent Director, Charles OData
Director and Secretary, Claudette J. V. Chan, age 78
Director, Robert J. Janoff, age 89
Director, Charles N. O'Data, age 80
Director, Robert Djerejian, age 85
Independent Director, Ronald Lehman
Auditors: Marcum LLP

LOCATIONS

HQ: Fonar Corp.
110 Marcus Drive, Melville, NY 11747
Phone: 631 694-2929
Web: www.fonar.com

COMPETITORS

Esaote	RadNet
GE Healthcare	Siemens Healthcare
Hitachi	Toshiba
Philips Electronics	

HISTORICAL FINANCIALS
Company Type: Public

Income Statement
FYE: June 30

	REVENUE ($ mil.)	NET INCOME ($ mil.)	NET PROFIT MARGIN	EMPLOYEES
06/16	73.3	15.7	21.4%	501.0
06/15	69.0	12.9	18.7%	465.0
06/14	68.5	10.4	15.2%	430.0
06/13	49.1	8.6	17.7%	411.0
06/12	39.4	5.7	14.6%	244.0
Annual Growth	16.8%	28.4%	—	19.7%

2016 Year-End Financials

Debt ratio: 5.3%	No. of shares (mil.): 6.4
Return on equity: 34.5%	Dividends
Cash ($ mil.): 8.5	Yield: —
Current ratio: 2.21	Payout: —
Long-term debt ($ mil.): 2.0	Market value ($ mil.): 131.0

	STOCK PRICE ($) FY Close	P/E High/Low		PER SHARE ($) Earnings	Dividends	Book Value
06/16	20.36	9	4	2.38	0.00	8.14
06/15	10.58	7	5	1.95	0.00	5.97
06/14	12.20	16	3	1.58	0.00	3.94
06/13	6.56	6	2	1.34	0.00	2.22
06/12	4.10	7	2	0.91	0.00	0.79
Annual Growth	49.3%	—	—	27.2%	—	79.0%

Fortinet Inc

Fortinet secures the fortress against Internet marauders. The company makes network security appliances (sold under its FortiGate line) and software that integrate antivirus firewall content filtering intrusion prevention systems (IPS) and anti-spam functions to protect against computer viruses worms and inappropriate Web content. Its Forti-Guard subscription services offer continuous updates on all new threats to provide real-time network protection. The company also offers complementary products that include its FortiManager security management and FortiAnalyzer event analysis systems.

Operations

While service revenues –an important source of recurring income –account for 53% of sales product revenues –47% of sales –have taken an increasingly important place in Fortinet's earnings as well. Fortinet outsources the manufacturing of its appliance products to contract manufacturers and original design manufacturers (ODMs). The company's manufacturers include Flextronics International Ltd. Micro-Star International Co. Ltd. Adlink Technology Inc. Senao Networks Inc. and several Taiwan-based manufacturers.

Geographic Reach

Fortinet's largest geographic segment is the Americas which accounts for 42% of revenues. The Europe Middle East and Africa (EMEA) segment accounts for about 35% of sales while the Asia/Pacific region accounts for the remainder. The company operates sales and service offices in about 30 countries worldwide.

Sales and Marketing

Fortinet sells through channel partners to end-customers that range from from small businesses to large enterprises and industries that include government telecommunications technology government financial services education retail manufacturing and health care. In 2014 distributor Exclusive Networks Group accounted for 15% of revenue.

Financial Performance

Fortinet has posted steady revenue growth over the years and that continued in 2014 when revenue increased 25% to $770 million. Product revenue rose 30% driven by sales of its FortiGate product to enterprise and service provider customers. Services and other revenue increased 22% on the strength of FortiGuard security subscriptions and FortiCare technical support contracts.

The company recorded its second straight year of declining revenue in 2014 with a 43% decrease to $25.3 million. It had higher costs and paid more taxes in 2014.

Cash flow from operations was $196 million at the end of 2014 up from $147 million at the end

of 2013. The increased cash flow was due to changes in working capital because of deferred revenue.

Strategy

Fortinet sells its products to distributors and re-sellers who have significant purchasing power and deployment capabilities while at the same time strengthening its customer support network in high-growth regions. It also works to build a solid base of subscription and service customers.

In addition to expand its product offerings Fortinet conducts research and development efforts to create new software and hardware offerings for customers. The company employs about 600 R&D employees in Canada China and the US and spends some $112 million annually on research projects about 14% of revenue.

Fortinet's products are being incorporated into networking products from NTT Com Security according to an agreement the companies reached in 2015. In another 2015 agreement Fortinet has access to information about security threats from the federal Department of Homeland Security. With the agreement Fortinet participates in the Cyber Information and Sharing and Collaboration Program (CISCP) which entails sharing cyber threat incident and vulnerability information in near real-time drawing on data of observed threat activity submitted by CISCP participants.

Mergers and Acquisitions

Fortinet acquired Meru Networks an intelligent Wi-Fi networking developer in 2015. The acquisition expands Fortinet's capabilities in $5 billion market for enterprise Wi-Fi security.

EXECUTIVES

Chairman and CEO, Ken Xie, age 53, $406,372 total compensation
President and CTO, Michael Xie, age 47, $360,490 total compensation
SVP International Sales and Support, Patrice Perche
CFO, Andrew (Drew) Del Matto, $381,401 total compensation
VP Corporate Development and Strategic Alliances and General Counsel, John Whittle, $332,695 total compensation
Director Of Surgery, Jane (Ginny) Zhu
Vice President Marketing, Patrick (Paddy) Bedwell
Vice President Marketing, John Maddison
Vice President Marketing At Fortinet Inc, Tamir Hardof
National Account Manager, Jackie Kruger
Vice President Us Enterprise Sales, Scott Lewis
Vice President, Hemant Jain
Vice President of Enterprise Sales, Pete (Petey) Brant
Vice President of Latin America Sales, Pedro Paixao
Vice President, Chad Whalen
Vice President Finance And Operations, Linda (Lin) Liang
Vice President Support And Services, Dave (Davie) Monery
National Account Manager, Jeffrey Laniewski
Vice President Quality, Dayong Zhou
Vice President of Marketing, Claire Trimble
Vice President Market Development, Bob (Bo) Schwartz
Vice President and Head of Information Technology, Sreeni Garlapati
Vice President Mexico, Manuel (Mannie) Acosta
Auditors: Deloitte & Touche LLP

LOCATIONS

HQ: Fortinet Inc
899 Kifer Road, Sunnyvale, CA 94086
Phone: 408 235-7700   **Fax:** 408 235-7737
Web: www.fortinet.com

PRODUCTS/OPERATIONS

2014 Sales

	$ mil.	% of total
Products	360.6	53
Services and others	409.8	47
Total	**770.7**	**100**

Selected Products

Database security appliance (FortiDB)
E-mail antispam (FortiMail)
Endpoint security software (FortiClient)
Endpoint vulnerability management appliance (FortiScan)
Network event correlation and content archiving (FortiAnalyzer)
Network security appliances (FortiGate)
Secure wireless access product (FortiAP)
Security management (FortiManager)
Spam and virus control subscription (FortiGuard)
Support (FortiCare)
Web application firewall appliance (FortiWeb)

COMPETITORS

Bivio Networks	NetWolves
Blue Coat	Palo Alto Networks
CA Inc.	Proofpoint
Check Point Software	SteelCloud
Cisco Systems	Symantec
F5 Networks	Trend Micro
Fortrex	VeriSign
Infoblox	WatchGuard
Juniper Networks	Technologies
McAfee	e-DMZ Security
Microsoft	zvelo

HISTORICAL FINANCIALS

Company Type: Public

Income Statement   FYE: December 31

	REVENUE ($ mil.)	NET INCOME ($ mil.)	NET PROFIT MARGIN	EMPLOYEES
12/15	1,009.2	7.9	0.8%	4,018.0
12/14	770.3	25.3	3.3%	2,854.0
12/13	615.3	44.2	7.2%	2,308.0
12/12	533.6	66.8	12.5%	1,954.0
12/11	433.5	62.4	14.4%	1,583.0
Annual Growth	**23.5%**	**(40.2%)**	**—**	**26.2%**

2015 Year-End Financials

Debt ratio: —	No. of shares (mil.): 171.4
Return on equity: 1.1%	Dividends
Cash ($ mil.): 543.2	Yield: —
Current ratio: 1.87	Payout: —
Long-term debt ($ mil.): —	Market value ($ mil.): 5,343.0

	STOCK PRICE ($) FY Close	P/E High/Low		PER SHARE ($) Earnings	Dividends	Book Value
12/15	31.17	977	584	0.05	0.00	4.41
12/14	30.66	209	127	0.15	0.00	4.06
12/13	19.13	93	61	0.26	0.00	3.63
12/12	21.02	68	42	0.40	0.00	3.19
12/11	21.81	121	40	0.38	0.00	2.31
Annual Growth	**9.3%**	**—**	**—**	**(39.8%)**	**—**	**17.5%**

Fortress Investment Group LLC

Fortress Investment Group protects its investors' money. The global investment firm manages private equity and hedge funds for institutional investors wealthy individuals and on its own behalf. Its private equity arm buys long-term controlling stakes in undervalued or distressed companies and credit assets; it also manages real estate investors Newcastle Investment and Eurocastle Investment. The hedge fund arm invests in liquid markets. Fortress offers traditional asset management through Logan Circle Partners. Fortress earns fees performance-based incentive revenues and investment income on its own investments. The firm has more than $67 billion in assets under management.

OperationsFortress operates its management and investment business through six main segments differentiated by strategy including: Private Equity Funds Permanent Capital Vehicles Liquid Hedge Funds Credit Hedge Funds Credit Private Equity Funds and Logan Circle.The company generated nearly 35% of its total revenue from management fees (tied to assets under management) in 2014 while incentive income (based on alternative investment performance) and expense reimbursements made up another roughly 20% and 10% respectively. Fortress made 35% of its total revenue from its non-managed investments including nearly 20% from Advertising company investments 10% from Circulation companies and the small remainder of revenues from a mix of commercial printing and rental revenue.Geographic ReachThe investment firm has headquarters in New York City and roughly 15 offices in the US Europe and Asia. Specifically its offices are in San Francisco Philadelphia London Tokyo Dallas Frankfurt Portland Los Angeles Plano Tampa Summit Sydney New Canaan Atlanta Luxembourg City Singapore Rome Lake Oswego Shanghai Dubai Hong Kong and Tel Aviv.Sales and MarketingFortress serves more than 1700 institutional clients and private investors worldwide. Financial PerformanceFortress Investment Group's revenues and profits have been on the uptrend in recent years mostly as its assets under management have risen with the appreciating financial markets. The firm's revenue jumped by more than 40% to $1.81 billion in 2014 thanks to a $626.2 million revenue increase from the consolidation of its New Media and New Senior investments held in its NewCastle Investment real estate investor division. Beyond this non-recurring transaction overall revenue declined with the company's incentive income revenue falling by nearly $100 million for the year due to lower returns and performance from its hedge funds credit hedge funds and liquid hedge fund managed accounts. The firm's management fee income however rose by nearly $14 million (around 2%) as assets under management grew during the year.Fortress' net income plummeted by 50% to $99.96 million mostly because of a $621.3 million expense related to its consolidation of its New Media and New Senior holdings though investment manager expenses also swelled by $95 million due to higher compensation and benefits and increased general administrative and other expenses. Fortress' operating cash also dove by 45% to $239.87 million mostly due to a decline in cash earnings.Strategy

Fortress reiterated in 2015 that its main strategy is to grow its fee-paying assets under management with an eye toward generating strong risk-adjusted returns from its funds over the long haul. To boost its assets under management the firm plans to entice new investors to invest in its funds by regularly introducing new investment products. To this end during 2014 Fortress raised $6.4 billion in new third-party capital and launched four new funds. That year the company also attracted some $5.4 billion in net client inflows in its traditional asset management business. On the real estate management side Fortress eyes new investments in a variety of sectors including in the hospitality transportation senior living and financial services sectors. In 2015 for example the firm's Japan Opportunity Fund which specializes in real estate investments in the region agreed to purchase Rihga Royal Hotel Kyoto one of Japan's most prestigious hotels with plans to enhance the facilities and update its rooms with more modern features while keeping its classic look intact. In late 2013 Fortress acquired more than 50 senior-housing properties from Holiday Acquisition Holdings for more than $1 billion.

EXECUTIVES

Managing Director Fortress Investment Group LLC (UK), Jonathan Ashley, age 50

Managing Director Shanghai, Lilly H. Donohue

Chief Executive Officer Co-Founder Principal and Director, Randal A. Nardone, age 61, $200,000 total compensation

Principal and Director; Co-Chief Investment Officer of the Fortress Macro Fund and the Drawbridge Global Macro Fund, Michael E. Novogratz, age 52, $200,000 total compensation

President Liquid Markets; Senior Managing Director Strategy, Stuart H. (Stu) Bohart, age 49

Managing Director Private Equity Group, Joseph P. Adams, age 58

CFO, Daniel N. Bass, age 50, $200,000 total compensation

Managing Director Chief Executive Officer and Chief Investment Officer Fortress Partners Funds Fortress Investment Group LLC, Alexander M. Cook

Managing Director Co-Chief Investment Officer of the Credit Funds at Fortress Investment Group LLC, Constantine M. (Dean) Dakolias

Managing Director Private Equity and Chief Operating Officer Permanent Capital Business Group, Andrew P. Dempsey

Managing Director President and Chief Operating Officer Credit Funds at Fortress Investment Group LLC, Marc K. Furstein

Managing Director Capital Formation Group, A. Todd Ladda

Managing Director San Francisco, Andrew A. McKnight

Managing Director Tokyo Chief Investment Officer Fortress Real Estate (Asia) GK, Thomas W. Pulley

Managing Director Deputy President and Chief Risk Officer Fortress Liquid Markets, Sherif Sweillam

Managing Director Global Chief Operating Officer Liquid Markets Hedge Fund, Louis D. Thorne

Managing Director Credit Funds, Anthony B. Tufariello

Senior Vice President, Dora Dragomanova

Vice President, Dan Perkins

Vice President, Robyn Gewanter

Vice President, Rory Vandamme

Vice President, Scott Silvers

Vice President, Suvin Malik

Vice President, Josh Bonacci

Vice President, Jill (Jilly) Chanes

Vice President Vice President, Paul (Pauly) Stockamore

Vice President Senior Accountant, Maritza Munoz

Vice President, Adam Bodenstein

Vice President Credit Funds and Information Technology Program Manager, Armando (Mando) Conde

Vice President Of Tax Compliance Credit Funds, Johnery Laurimore

Senior Vice President And Controller, Scott (Scotty) Desiderio

Vice President, Christopher (Chris) Frey

Vice President, Solange Tsutsui

Senior Vice President Controller, Kristina (Chris) Samuelsen

Vice President, Michael (Mel) Mucciolo

Senior Vice President, Andrew (Andy) Miller

Vice President, Cristina (Chris) Gonzalez

Senior Vice President, Scott (Scotty) Schwarmann

Vice President, Carrie Sin

Vice President, Victoria Hartman

Vice President, Peter (Pete) Kobliska

Vice President, Leigh (Leah) Maranuk

Vice President, Jason (Jase) Okeefe

Vice President, Pankaj Jain

Vice President, Yoni Shtein

Vice President, Brittain Rogers

Vice President Senior Accountant, Sean Hessle

Senior Vice President, Neil Carter

Vice President Vice President, Brannen McElmurray

Senior Vice President Counsel, Alex Gillette

Vice President, Jennifer (Jen) Story

Vice President Tax Counsel, Dexter Samida

Vice President, Ed (Eddie) Montolio

Vice President Tax, Brian McGrath

Vice President, Ron (Ronnie) Cobb

Vice President, Steven Brogden

Vice President, Steven (Steve) Willemin

Vice President, John (Jack) Kwaak

Vice President, Stacey Griffin

Vice President, Patrick Diaz

Vice President, Jared (Jare) Kanefsky

Vice President, Ankur Patel

Vice President, Ryan Muller

Vice President, Mike (Mikey) Wou

Vice President, Phat Loc

Vice President Accounting, Tom (Tommy) Kelly

Vice President, Micah Kaplan

Vice President Capital Formations Group Investor Relations, Diana (Ana) Bellizzi

Vice President, Justin Bogan

Senior Vice President Information Technology, Eric (Ric) Madeson

Vice President Trading Counsel, David (Dave) Sims

Vice President, Walker Kidd

Vice President, Scott Werthamer

Vice President, Darren Halpern

Vice President Tax, Terry (Terr) Tsang

Vice President, Morgan McClure

Senior Vice President And Portfolio Manager, Daniel (Dan) Mcfarlane

Vice President Financial Analyst, Scott (Scotty) Min

Vice President, Sergey Dyakin

Vice President, Joseph Pontrello

Vice President, Peter Leibman

Vice President, Lance Sherer

Vice President, Joseph Hayek

Vice President Tax Director, Hiskias Siefkes

Vice President Sales And Marketing, Judy Godinho

Vice President Senior Business Analyst, Todd Mangel

Vice President, Marc Blanchette

Vice President, Misty Shores

Vice President, Brian (Bri) Nicholson

Vice President, Ana Fratila

Vice President, Patrick (Paddy) Schulz
Vice President, David Fasano
Vice President Fund Counsel, Christine (Chrissy) Putek
Vice President Compensation Controller, Paul Petrsoric
Senior Vice President Finance and Operations, Bhairav Patel
Vice President, Andrew (Andy) Armstrong
Vice President, Timothy Bailey
Vice President, Rhonda Ramparas
Vice President Vice President, Susan (Sue) Givens
Senior Vice President Senior Tax, Fran (Frances) Benoit
Senior Vice President and Counsel, Jonathan (John) Grebinar
Vice President, David (Dave) Schneider
Vice President, Neil Thompson
Senior Vice President and Managing Director, Joseph (Jo) Sciortino
Senior Vice President Human RE, Aimee (Ames) Quick
Vice President, Brian Morazzini
Vice President, Andrey Tsetlin
Vice President, Jocelyn (Lyn) Lewis
Vice President, Matt (Matty) Biczak
Vice President, Dan (Danny) Rodriguez
Vice President, Andrew (Andy) Webber
Vice President, Michael (Mel) Linn
Vice President Vice President, Yunyoung Shin
Vice President, Marc (Marcy) Fuhrmann
Vice President, Jonathan (John) Schechter
Vice President, Marla Cannon
Senior Vice President Controller, Naftalee Zomberg
Vice President, Clay (Clayton) Lagrone
Vice President, Greg (Greggy) Shoemaker
Vice President Assistant Controller, Trevor (Tre) Burner
Vice President, Michele (Michie) Moreland
Principal and Co-Chairman, Wesley R. (Wes) Edens, age 54
Principal and Co-Chairman, Peter L. Briger, age 53
Auditors: Ernst & Young LLP

LOCATIONS

HQ: Fortress Investment Group LLC
1345 Avenue of the Americas, New York, NY 10105
Phone: 212 798-6100

PRODUCTS/OPERATIONS

2014 Sales

	% of total
Investment Manager	65
Non-investment manager	
Advertising	19
Circulation	10
Commercial printing and others	4
Rental revenue resident fees and services	2
Total	**100**

COMPETITORS

American Capital	Investcorp
Apollo Investment	PineBridge Investments
Bessemer Trust	RREEF Funds
Blackstone Group	Schroders
Integrated Asset Management	Soros Fund Management

HISTORICAL FINANCIALS

Company Type: Public

Income Statement

FYE: December 31

	REVENUE ($ mil.)	NET INCOME ($ mil.)	NET PROFIT MARGIN	EMPLOYEES
12/15	1,213.8	78.4	6.5%	3,040.0
12/14	1,811.8	99.9	5.5%	2,860.0
12/13	1,264.9	200.4	15.8%	2,324.0
12/12	969.8	78.2	8.1%	1,996.0
12/11	858.6	(431.5)	—	979.0
Annual Growth	**9.0%**	**—**	**—**	**32.7%**

2015 Year-End Financials

Debt ratio: 10.1%	No. of shares (mil.): 386.3
Return on equity: 12.9%	Dividends
Cash ($ mil.): 339.8	Yield: 12.1%
Current ratio: 0.85	Payout: 144.1%
Long-term debt ($ mil.): 230.6	Market value ($ mil.): 1,966.0

	STOCK PRICE ($) FY Close	P/E High/Low		PER SHARE ($) Earnings	Dividends	Book Value
12/15	5.09	24	14	0.28	0.62	1.48
12/14	8.02	19	13	0.43	0.50	1.48
12/13	8.56	11	5	0.79	0.24	1.68
12/12	4.39	16	10	0.27	0.20	1.35
12/11	3.38	—	—	(2.36)	0.00	0.98
Annual Growth	**10.8%**	**—**	**—**	**—**	**—**	**10.7%**

Forward Air Corp

When it's time to haul freight Forward Air never looks back. The company transports deferred airfreight by truck —cargo that requires specific-time delivery but is less time-sensitive than airfreight. Forward Air typically receives freight that has been transported by plane sends it to a sorting facility then dispatches it by truck to a terminal near its destination. The company has nearly 3777 trailers and more than 570 owned and 100 leased tractors and straight trucks in its fleet. It operates from about 85 terminals at or near airports in the US and Canada including about a dozen regional hubs. It also provides services such as warehousing and local pick-up and delivery.

Geographic Reach

Forward Air operates regional hubs in Atlanta; Charlotte North Carolina; Chicago Dallas/Ft. Worth; Denver Kansas City; Los Angeles; New Orleans; Newark New Jersey; Newburgh New York; Orlando Florida; and Sacramento California. Its airport-to-airport network consists of terminals located in 87 cities.

In addition the company leases and maintains 76 additional terminals including its pool distribution terminals located in major cities throughout the US and Canada.

Operations

The company markets its services to airfreight forwarders air cargo carriers and airlines rather than directly to shippers. Although Forward Air does facilitate overnight delivery of freight the company doesn't compete in the parcel delivery market because it handles larger shipments.

Besides its expedited transportation business the company offers pool distribution services through a second business segment Forward Air Solutions. (Pool distribution involves combining goods from multiple shippers into loads headed to the same location.) Forward Air Solutions maintains about 30 terminals near airport in major cities. Because the segment's customers tend to be retailers located in malls and outlet-based chains revenues are dependent upon the health of the retail industry.

As with its competitors Forward Air uses a fuel surcharge as a way to compensate for fluctuating fuel prices. The rates are based upon the national average price of diesel per gallon and tonnage delivered.

Financial Performance

Forward Air has enjoyed several straight years of unprecedented growth. Revenues spiked 20% from $652 million in 2013 to peak at a record-shattering $781 million in 2014. Profits also jumped 12% from $54 million in 2013 to $61 million in 2014 another milestone.

The historic growth for 2014 was driven by surges across all its segments: Forward Air (22%) Forward Air Solutions (16%) and Total Quality (6%). The growth was mostly due to additional revenue from previous acquisitions.

In addition to rises in revenue and net income Forward Air's operating cash flow surged during 2013 and 2014.

Strategy

The company intents to grow by adding new services to its lineup and by acquiring other transportation services companies. In 2013 Forward Air acquired Total Quality a provider of temperature-controlled logistics services serving the life science and pharmaceutical sector for $66 million. The deal added a new service to Forward Air's logistics portfolio and widened its client base.

In 2014 Forward Air acquired Central States Trucking Co. and Central States Logistics (CST). CST provides container and intermodal drayage services primarily within the Midwest region of the US. CST also provides dedicated contract and container freight station warehouse and handling services. Forward Air made the transaction for $83 million in net cash and $11 million in assumed debt.

EXECUTIVES

Senior Vice President Sales, Craig Drum
Vice President Cao Contrl, Michael P (Mel) McLean
Chairman President and CEO, Bruce A. Campbell, age 65, $620,999 total compensation
EVP Operations, Chris C. Ruble, age 54, $414,072 total compensation
EVP Intermodal Services and Chief Strategy Officer, Matthew J. Jewell, age 50, $413,240 total compensation
SVP Chief Legal Officer and Secretary, Michael L. Hance, age 44, $334,200 total compensation
SVP CFO and Treasurer, Michael J. Morris, age 48
Vice President Of Sales West Region, Gavin (Vinny) Neilson
Executive Vice President Chief Legal, Daniel (Dan) Hamilton
Vice President Revenue Accounting, Terry Woods
Vice President Of Quality, Gerald (Jerry) Kane
Auditors: Ernst & Young LLP

LOCATIONS

HQ: Forward Air Corp
430 Airport Road, Greeneville, TN 37745
Phone: 423 636-7000
Web: www.forwardair.com

PRODUCTS/OPERATIONS

2014 Sales

	$ mil.	% of total
Forward Air	608.1	78
Forward Air Solutions	124.4	16
TQI	48.5	6
Total	**7,801.0**	**100**

Services
Expedited Linehaul Service
Forward Air Complete
Canadian Transborder Service
Airline Logistics Services
Freight Management Services
Container Freight Stations
Truckload Services

COMPETITORS

Alliance Air	Old Dominion Freight
CRST Expedited	Panther Expedited
CRST International	Services
Daylight Transport	Schneider National
FedEx Freight	Towne Air Freight
New Penn Motor Express	XPO logistics

HISTORICAL FINANCIALS

Company Type: Public

Income Statement

FYE: December 31

	REVENUE ($ mil.)	NET INCOME ($ mil.)	NET PROFIT MARGIN	EMPLOYEES
12/15	959.1	55.5	5.8%	4,536.0
12/14	780.9	61.1	7.8%	3,902.0
12/13	652.4	54.4	8.3%	3,537.0
12/12	584.4	52.6	9.0%	2,128.0
12/11	536.4	47.2	8.8%	3,136.0
Annual Growth	**15.6%**	**4.2%**	**—**	**9.7%**

2015 Year-End Financials

Debt ratio: 12.1%
Return on equity: 11.4%
Cash ($ mil.): 33.3
Current ratio: 1.59
Long-term debt ($ mil.): 28.8

No. of shares (mil.): 30.5
Dividends
Yield: 1.1%
Payout: 30.1%
Market value ($ mil.): 1,314.0

	STOCK PRICE ($) FY Close	P/E High/Low	PER SHARE ($) Earnings	Dividends	Book Value
12/15	43.01	32 23	1.78	0.48	16.70
12/14	50.37	25 21	1.96	0.48	15.32
12/13	43.91	24 19	1.77	0.40	14.28
12/12	35.01	21 16	1.78	0.34	12.05
12/11	32.05	22 15	1.60	0.28	10.05
Annual Growth	**7.6%**	**— —**	**2.7%**	**14.4%**	**13.5%**

Foundation Healthcare, Inc

Graymark Healthcare wants its businesses to help remedy the ills of small-town Americans. Through its operating subsidiaries Graymark Healthcare acquires and operates independent pharmacies and sleep diagnostic centers many of which are located in smaller US markets. Its ApothecaryRx subsidiary manages pharmacies doing business in a handful of central US states

and the company's Sleep Disorder Centers (SDC) subsidiary manages sleep diagnostics businesses in the South and Midwest. Formerly Graymark Productions (a film production firm) Graymark changed its name in 2008 following the acquisitions of ApothecaryRx and SDC. The company sold sell its ApothecaryRx stores to Walgreen in late 2010.

Drugstore giant Walgreen paid about $35 million for the assets of the 18 ApothecaryRx stores in Colorado Oklahoma Minnesota Missouri and Illinois. The divestment is in keeping with Graymark's increased focus on the sleep disorders side of its business. Indeed Graymark is looking to strengthen its position in the sleep diagnostics industry. To that end in 2009 it purchased the somniCare and somniTech sleep disorder testing and treatment centers from Australia's Avastra Sleep Centres. The companies operate diagnostics centers in Iowa Kansas Minnesota Missouri Nebraska and South Dakota. The acquisition complements Graymark's core markets of Texas and Oklahoma extending its presence to the Midwest. Strengthening its foothold in Texas Graymark in late 2011 acquired a majority interest in Village Sleep Center in a Dallas suburb. The move brought Graymark's number of sleep laboratories up to 100 (23 standalone facilities in large communities and 77 hospital provider or rural outreach sites). Graymark also made a $650000 equity investment in newly formed Oklahoma Health Partners in late 2012.

The company's business has been expanding rapidly since its name and industry change. The growth is due in large part to Graymark's aggressive acquisition strategy which resulted in the acquisitions of six pharmacies in Illinois and Oklahoma in 2008. The company also expanded its sleep centers business into the Nevada market the same year.

Graymark's other operations are located in Colorado Missouri and Minnesota; the company intends to continue expanding in other central US states through key acquisitions.

EXECUTIVES

President and Director, Joseph Harroz Jr.
Chairman and CEO; CEO SDC, Stanton Nelson, age 46
President and Director, Joseph (Joe) Harroz Jr., age 49, $114,583 total compensation
Chief Medical Officer, Kevin Lewis
CFO, Grant Christianson, age 47
Independent Chairman of the Board, Jamie Hopping
Interim Chief Financial Officer, Mark Kidd
President and Director, Joseph Harroz Jr.
President and Director, Joseph (Joe) Harroz Jr., age 49
Director, S. Edward Dakil, age 60
Director, Scott Mueller, age 45
Independent Director, Steven List
Auditors: Hein & Associates LLP

LOCATIONS

HQ: Foundation Healthcare, Inc
13900 N. Portland Avenue, Suite 200, Oklahoma City, OK 73134
Phone: 405 608-1700
Web: www.fdnh.com

PRODUCTS/OPERATIONS

Selected Pharmacies and Sleep Centers
Ken's Pharmacy

Hapeth Pharmacy
Parkway Drugs
Professional Pharmacy
Newt's Discount Pharmacy
Sleep Center of Edmond
Sleep Center of Tulsa South
Sleep Center of Lubbock
Sleep Center of Northwest Oklahoma City
Texas Center for Sleep Disorders at Southlake
Village Sleep Center of Plano Texas

COMPETITORS

CVS	Target Corporation
Doc's Drugs	Wal-Mart
Maxor	Walgreen
Rite Aid	

HISTORICAL FINANCIALS

Company Type: Public

Income Statement

FYE: December 31

	REVENUE ($ mil.)	NET INCOME ($ mil.)	NET PROFIT MARGIN	EMPLOYEES
12/15	127.5	5.9	4.6%	1,232.0
12/14	104.8	(1.3)	—	971.0
12/13	93.1	(19.4)	—	1,012.0
12/12	16.9	(22.4)	—	155.0
12/11	17.5	(5.8)	—	217.0
Annual Growth	**64.3%**	**—**	**—**	**54.4%**

2015 Year-End Financials

Debt ratio: 67.2%
Return on equity: —
Cash ($ mil.): 5.0
Current ratio: 1.26
Long-term debt ($ mil.): 71.3

No. of shares (mil.): 17.3
Dividends
Yield: —
Payout: —
Market value ($ mil.): 73.0

	STOCK PRICE ($) FY Close	P/E High/Low	PER SHARE ($) Earnings	Dividends	Book Value
12/15	4.20	17 1	0.30	0.00	(0.65)
12/14	0.32	— —	(0.12)	0.00	(1.04)
12/13	0.34	— —	(1.30)	0.00	(1.03)
12/12	0.23	— —	(14.60)	0.00	(10.01)
12/11	0.46	— —	(5.10)	0.00	3.30
Annual Growth	**73.8%**	**— —**	**—**	**—**	**—**

Fox Factory Holding Corp

Talk about shock value. Fox Factory makes suspension products —i.e. shocks —for high-performance mountain bikes and other powered vehicles that give riders a smooth ride over rough terrain. Some two-thirds of sales are for shocks for bicycles but the other third of revenue comes from shocks for ATVs motorcycles snowmobiles and off-road vehicles and trucks. Fox Factory sells its shocks to original equipment manufacturers (OEMs) such as Specialized and Trek (bikes) and Ford and Polaris (powered vehicles). It also sells branded apparel such as T-shirts sweatshirts and hats. Fox Factory went public in 2013.

Geographic Reach

Sales outside the US account for about two-thirds of revenue because Fox Factory sells directly to OEMs that have primary manufacturing operations in Asia. The majority of its own manufacturing operations are in California but Fox Factory does have a plant in Taiwan. The company is shifting all of its manufacturing to Taiwan by 2016.

Sales and Marketing

Fox Factory sells its suspension products to more than 150 OEMs and distributes its products to more than 2300 retail dealers and distributors worldwide. In 2012 80% of sales were to OEM customers and 20% were to dealers and distributors for resale in the aftermarket channel.

Financial Performance

The company has experienced steady growth over the years. Sales increased about 20% in 2012 due to increased demand from both OEMs and aftermarket customers. Fox Factory has also been consistently profitable.

Company Background

Fox Factory was founded in 1974 by Robert Fox who built a racing suspension shock in his friend's garage. The company was bought by Compass Diversified Holdings in 2008. In 2013 Fox Factory went public and Compass held onto a majority share; Compass subsequently divested shares in Fox Factory but still maintains a minority ownership stake.

EXECUTIVES

CEO, Larry L. Enterline, age 63, $702,821 total compensation
CFO, Zvi Glasman, age 52, $270,100 total compensation
President, Mario Galasso, age 50, $295,654 total compensation
SVP Global Operations, William H. (Bill) Katherman
Chairman, Elias J. Sabo, age 45
Auditors: Grant Thornton LLP

LOCATIONS

HQ: Fox Factory Holding Corp
915 Disc Drive, Scotts Valley, CA 95066
Phone: 831 274-6500
Web: www.ridefox.com

PRODUCTS/OPERATIONS

2015 Sales

	$ mil.	% of total
Bikes	211.7	58
Power vehicles	155.1	42
Total	**366.8**	**100**

COMPETITORS

Cannondale	SRAM
Giant Manufacturing	Tenneco
KAYABA INDUSTRY CO. LTD.	Truck-Lite
	ZF Group NAO

HISTORICAL FINANCIALS

Company Type: Public

Income Statement

FYE: December 31

	REVENUE ($ mil.)	NET INCOME ($ mil.)	NET PROFIT MARGIN	EMPLOYEES
12/15	366.8	24.9	6.8%	1,500.0
12/14	306.7	27.6	9.0%	1,000.0
12/13	272.7	24.1	8.8%	670.0
12/12	235.8	14.2	6.0%	545.0
12/11	197.7	13.5	6.8%	0.0
Annual Growth	**16.7%**	**16.5%**	—	—

2015 Year-End Financials

Debt ratio: 17.4%	No. of shares (mil.): 37.0
Return on equity: 17.7%	Dividends
Cash ($ mil.): 6.9	Yield: —
Current ratio: 1.78	Payout: —
Long-term debt ($ mil.): 45.8	Market value ($ mil.): 612.0

	STOCK PRICE ($) FY Close	P/E High/Low	PER SHARE ($) Earnings	Dividends	Book Value
12/15	16.53	29 22	0.66	0.00	4.11
12/14	16.23	25 18	0.73	0.00	3.47
12/13	17.62	28 23	0.68	0.00	2.54
Annual Growth	**(3.1%)**	— —	**(1.5%)**	—	**27.2%**

Francesca's Holdings Corp

Auditors: Ernst & Young LLP

LOCATIONS

HQ: Francesca's Holdings Corp
8760 Clay Road, Houston, TX 77080
Phone: 713 864-1358
Web: www.francescas.com

HISTORICAL FINANCIALS

Company Type: Public

Income Statement

FYE: January 30

	REVENUE ($ mil.)	NET INCOME ($ mil.)	NET PROFIT MARGIN	EMPLOYEES
01/16	439.3	38.1	8.7%	5,211.0
01/15*	377.5	32.1	8.5%	4,056.0
02/14	340.3	44.8	13.2%	3,217.0
02/13	296.3	47.0	15.9%	2,553.0
01/12	204.1	22.5	11.0%	1,970.0
Annual Growth	**21.1%**	**14.1%**	—	**27.5%**

*Fiscal year change

2016 Year-End Financials

Debt ratio: —	No. of shares (mil.): 41.1
Return on equity: 32.4%	Dividends
Cash ($ mil.): 56.2	Yield: —
Current ratio: 3.62	Payout: —
Long-term debt ($ mil.): —	Market value ($ mil.): 749.0

	STOCK PRICE ($) FY Close	P/E High/Low	PER SHARE ($) Earnings	Dividends	Book Value
01/16	18.23	20 11	0.91	0.00	3.08
01/15*	15.86	27 15	0.76	0.00	2.58
02/14	19.00	31 16	1.02	0.00	1.85
02/13	28.65	34 20	1.05	0.00	1.64
01/12	22.73	53 29	0.52	0.00	0.39
Annual Growth	**(5.4%)**	— —	**15.0%**	—	**67.7%**

*Fiscal year change

Franklin Street Properties Corp

Franklin Street Properties acquires finances leases and manages office properties in more than a dozen states across the US. The real estate investment trust (REIT) owns more than 35 properties located mainly in suburban areas and manages nearly 10 others. Its top markets include Atlanta Dallas Denver Houston and Minneapolis. The company's FSP Investment unit is an investment bank and brokerage that organizes REITs that invest in single properties and raises equity for them through private placements. Another subsidiary FSP Property Management manages properties for Franklin Street as well as for some of the REITs sponsored by FSP Investments.

OperationsFranklin Street Properties' property portfolio consisted of 36 owned properties spanning 6.7 million square feet at the end of 2015. The REIT operates through three wholly-owned subsidiaries: FSP Investments LLP FSP Property Management and FSP Holdings. Geographic Reach

More than 70% of Franklin Street's properties (by square footage) were located in five markets during 2015 —Atlanta Dallas Denver Houston and Minneapolis. The REIT also monitors the San Diego Silicon Valley Greater Boston and Greater Washington DC markets.

Sales and Marketing

Franklin Street serves a diverse mix of tenants with major clients including Headway Technologies The American Red Cross Booz Allen Hamilton Federal National Mortgage Association Id Software DIRECTV Somerset CPAs and Kaiser Foundation Health Plan among others.

Financial Performance

Franklin Street Properties' annual revenues have risen 75% since 2011 as it has expanded its property portfolio through acquisitions and has charged higher rental rates as the real estate market has strengthened. While more volatile its profits have been trending higher in recent years as its property valuations have improved.The REIT's revenue dipped 2% to $243.87 million during 2015 mostly as a handful of property sales made in 2014 and 2015 caused rental income to decline. Despite earning less in revenue Franklin Street's net income nearly tripled to $35 million during 2015 thanks to large gains from those property sales which were located in Plano; Eden Prairie Minnesota; Charlotte; and San Jose California. The REIT's operating cash levels dipped less than 1% due to unfavorable working capital changes.

Strategy

Franklin Street Properties looks to buy office properties in select urban infill and central business districts with a primary emphasis on its top five markets: Atlanta Dallas Denver Houston and Minneapolis. The office REIT seeks value-oriented investments with an eye toward long-term growth and appreciation as well as current income. Other markets on the firm's radar include San Diego and Silicon Valley Greater Boston and the greater Washington D.C. area.

EXECUTIVES

EVP and CFO, John G. Demeritt, age 56, $248,393 total compensation
Chairman and CEO, George J. Carter, age 68, $302,885 total compensation

SVP and General Counsel, Scott H. Carter, age 45, $215,994 total compensation
President and Chief Investment Officer, Jeffrey B. Carter, age 44, $210,389 total compensation
EVP and President FSP Property Management LLC, John F. Donahue, age 49
EVP and COO, Eriel Anchondo, age 38
Assistant VP and IT Manager, Matthew J. Buckley
Assistant Vice President Financial Reporting, Yi-Chin Huang
Auditors: Ernst & Young LLP

LOCATIONS

HQ: Franklin Street Properties Corp
401 Edgewater Place, Suite 200, Wakefield, MA 01880
Phone: 781 557-1300
Web: www.franklinstreetproperties.com

PRODUCTS/OPERATIONS

2015 Sales

	$ mil.	% of total
Rent	237.9	98
Management fees & interest income	5.9	2
Total	**243.8**	**100**

Selected Properties

Addison Circle One (Dallas TX)
Blue Lagoon Drive (Miami FL)
Centennial Technology Center (Colorado Springs CO)
Hillview Center (San Jose CA)
Legacy Tennyson Center (Dallas TX)
One and Two River Crossing (Indianapolis IN)
Park Seneca (Charlotte NC)
Satellite Place (Duluth GA)
TCF Tower and Bank Building (Minneapolis MN)

COMPETITORS

Boston Properties
Brandywine Realty
Corporate Office Properties Trust
Cousins Properties

Investors Real Estate Trust
Liberty Property Trust
Washington Real Estate

HISTORICAL FINANCIALS

Company Type: Public

Income Statement

FYE: December 31

	REVENUE ($ mil.)	NET INCOME ($ mil.)	NET PROFIT MARGIN	EMPLOYEES
12/15	243.8	35.0	14.4%	40.0
12/14	249.6	13.1	5.3%	39.0
12/13	213.6	19.8	9.3%	37.0
12/12	162.8	7.6	4.7%	35.0
12/11	139.4	43.5	31.2%	32.0
Annual Growth	15.0%	(5.3%)	—	5.7%

2015 Year-End Financials

Debt ratio: 47.3%
Return on equity: 3.6%
Cash ($ mil.): 18.1
Current ratio: 1.20
Long-term debt ($ mil.): 910.0

No. of shares (mil.): 100.1
Dividends
Yield: 7.3%
Payout: 316.6%
Market value ($ mil.): 1,037.0

	STOCK PRICE ($) FY Close	P/E High/Low		PER SHARE ($) Earnings	Dividends	Book Value
12/15	10.35	38	27	0.35	0.76	9.34
12/14	12.27	99	86	0.13	0.76	9.78
12/13	11.95	73	56	0.21	0.76	10.48
12/12	12.31	137	106	0.09	0.76	10.43
12/11	9.95	29	19	0.53	0.76	11.11
Annual Growth	1.0%	—	—	(9.9%)	(0.0%)	(4.2%)

FreightCar America Inc

Coal keeps FreightCar America in the black. The company designs and makes aluminum-bodied railroad cars that are used to transport coal. It also manufactures coil steel cars covered hopper cars boxcars flatcars intermodal cars mill gondola cars and bulk commodity cars. FreightCar America refurbishes and rebuilds railcars and supplies forged cast and fabricated parts for its railcars and ones made by other companies. Customers include leasing companies railroads and shippers. Its main customers include Norfolk Southern Railway CSX Transportation and CitiCorp Railmark. The company has been making railcars since 1901.

Geographic Reach

FreightCar America is headquartered in Chicago and has facilities in Cherokee Alabama; Danville Illinois; Grand Island Nebraska; Hastings Nebraska; Johnstown Pennsylvania; and Roanoke Virginia. FreightCar Rail Services has repair and maintenance and inspection facilities in Grand Island Nebraska; and Hastings Nebraska.

Sales and Marketing

In 2015 sales to FreightCar America's top five customers accounted for approximately 64% of total revenue. The company's primary customers are railroads shippers and financial institutions which represented 69% 17% and 15% respectively of its net sales in 2015.

Operations

In 2015 the company sold its Services segment which offered general railcar repair and maintenance inspections parts sales and railcar fleet management services.

Railcar deliveries totaled 8980 units consisting of 6280 new railcars 2600 rebuilt railcars and 100 railcars leased for 2015.

Financial Performance

FreightCar America's revenues increased by 29% from $599 million in 2014 to $773 million in 2015. The growth was fueled by increased sales from its primary Manufacturing segment attributable to increases in the number of railcars delivered a higher mix of new versus rebuilt railcars and favorable changes in its product mix of new railcars.

Its net income also skyrocketed from $6 million in 2014 to $32 million in 2015. This was attributed to a major gain on the sale of its railcar repair and maintenance services business and facilities.

Strategy

FreightCar America focuses on diversifying the range of railcars produced including covered hoppers intermodal and other non-tank car types. Its growth strategy depends in part on its continued development and sale of new railcar designs and design changes to existing railcars to penetrate new railcar markets and to expand or maintain its market share in its existing railcar markets.

In 2015 the company sold its railcar repair and maintenance services business for $20 million. Through that effort the company increased its focus on its railcar manufacturing parts and leasing business.

Company Background

FreightCar America was once owned by mighty steel producer Bethlehem Steel from 1923 to 1991. Transportation Technologies Industries (TTI) subsequently acquired it only to sell the company to an investor group which included Whalen in 1999. FreightCar America went public in 2005.

EXECUTIVES

SVP Marketing and Sales, Theodore W. (Ted) Baun, age 43, $213,125 total compensation
President and CEO, Joseph E. McNeely, age 52
CFO, Matthew S. (Matt) Kohnke, age 45
Vice President Marketing and International Sales, Mike (Mikey) MacMahon
Vice President Sourcing, Jeffrey (Jeff) Klamar
Senior Vice President Marketing and Sales, Ted (Teddy) Baun
Chairman, William D. (Bill) Gehl, age 69
Auditors: Deloitte & Touche LLP

LOCATIONS

HQ: FreightCar America Inc
Two North Riverside Plaza, Suite 1300, Chicago, IL 60606
Phone: 800 458-2235
Web: www.freightcaramerica.com

PRODUCTS/OPERATIONS

2015 Sales

	$ mil.	% of total
New railcar sales	607.1	79
Rebuild railcar sales	136.0	18
Maintenance and repair revenues	17.0	2
Parts sales	9.9	1
Leasing revenues	2.7	-
Other sales	0.2	-
Total	**772.9**	**100**

2015 Sales

	$ mil.	% of total
Manufacturing	745.7	96
Corporate and Other	27.2	4
Total	**772.9**	**100**

Selected Products

Aluminum Coal Cars
Dynastack Series
VersaFlood Series

COMPETITORS

ACF Industries
American Railcar Industries
Construcciones y Auxiliar de Ferrocarriles
Greenbrier Companies
Progress Rail Services
Trinity Industries
Union Tank Car

HISTORICAL FINANCIALS

Company Type: Public

Income Statement

FYE: December 31

	REVENUE ($ mil.)	NET INCOME ($ mil.)	NET PROFIT MARGIN	EMPLOYEES
12/15	772.8	31.8	4.1%	1,662.0
12/14	598.5	5.9	1.0%	1,381.0
12/13	290.3	(19.3)	—	819.0
12/12	677.4	19.1	2.8%	918.0
12/11	486.9	4.9	1.0%	941.0
Annual Growth	12.2%	59.3%	—	15.3%

2015 Year-End Financials

Debt ratio: —
Return on equity: 14.6%
Cash ($ mil.): 110.0
Current ratio: 3.87
Long-term debt ($ mil.): —

No. of shares (mil.): 12.3
Dividends
Yield: 1.8%
Payout: 17.7%
Market value ($ mil.): 240.0

	STOCK PRICE ($) FY Close	P/E High/Low		PER SHARE ($) Earnings	Dividends	Book Value
12/15	19.43	12	7	2.58	0.36	19.07
12/14	26.31	75	44	0.49	0.24	16.47
12/13	26.62	—	—	(1.61)	0.24	16.81
12/12	22.42	18	11	1.60	0.24	17.64
12/11	20.95	81	33	0.41	0.00	16.51
Annual Growth	(1.9%)	—		58.4%	—	3.7%

FS Bancorp Inc (Washington)

FS Bancorp is the holding company for 1st Security Bank of Washington which operates six branches in the Puget Sound region. The bank provides standard deposit products such as checking and savings accounts CDs and IRAs to area businesses and consumers. Its lending activities are focused on consumer loans (more than half of its portfolio) including home improvement boat and automobile loans. The bank also writes business and construction loans and commercial and residential mortgages. FS Bancorp went public via in initial public offering in 2012.

The company plans proceeds from its IPO to fund new loans purchase securities and scale up the bank's operations. Also as part of the offering the bank converted from a mutual to a stock form of ownership.

EXECUTIVES

Vice President Manager, Robert (Bob) Jorgenson
Vice President Of Finance and Treasurer, David (Dave) Tun
Auditors: Moss Adams LLP

LOCATIONS

HQ: FS Bancorp Inc (Washington)
6920 220th Street SW, Mountlake Terrace, WA 98043
Phone: 425 771-5299
Web: www.fsbwa.com

COMPETITORS

Bank of America
Banner Corp
Columbia Banking
Heritage Financial
KeyCorp
Washington Banking
Washington Federal
Wells Fargo

HISTORICAL FINANCIALS

Company Type: Public

Income Statement

FYE: December 31

	ASSETS ($ mil.)	NET INCOME ($ mil.)	INCOME AS % OF ASSETS	EMPLOYEES
12/15	677.5	8.8	1.3%	241.0
12/14	509.7	4.5	0.9%	210.0
12/13	419.1	3.9	0.9%	160.0
12/12	359.0	5.3	1.5%	131.0
12/11	283.7	1.5	0.5%	0.0
Annual Growth	24.3%	54.8%	—	—

2015 Year-End Financials

Return on assets: 1.5%
Return on equity: 12.5%
Long-term debt ($ mil.):
No. of shares (mil.): 3.2
Sales ($ mil): 49.3
Dividends
Yield: 1.0%
Payout: 9.6%
Market value ($ mil.): 84.0

	STOCK PRICE ($) FY Close	P/E High/Low		PER SHARE ($) Earnings	Dividends	Book Value
12/15	26.00	9	6	2.93	0.27	23.24
12/14	18.25	12	11	1.52	0.23	20.35
12/13	17.15	14	10	1.29	0.15	19.23
12/12	12.97	8	6	1.76	0.00	19.92
Annual Growth	26.1%	—		18.5%	—	5.3%

FS Energy & Power Fund

LOCATIONS

HQ: FS Energy & Power Fund
201 Rouse Boulevard, Philadelphia, PA 19112
Phone: 215 495-1150

HISTORICAL FINANCIALS

Company Type: Public

Income Statement

FYE: December 31

	REVENUE ($ mil.)	NET INCOME ($ mil.)	NET PROFIT MARGIN	EMPLOYEES
12/15	379.6	227.6	59.9%	0.0
12/14	289.9	174.8	60.3%	0.0
12/13	132.0	66.8	50.6%	0.0
12/12	29.9	10.1	33.9%	0.0
Annual Growth	133.1%	181.9%		

2015 Year-End Financials

Debt ratio: —
Return on equity: 9.1%
Cash ($ mil.): 368.8
Current ratio: 0.39
Long-term debt ($ mil.): —
No. of shares (mil.): 372.2
Dividends
Yield: —
Payout: 105.7%
Market value ($ mil.): —

	STOCK PRICE ($) FY Close	P/E High/Low		PER SHARE ($) Earnings	Dividends	Book Value
12/15	0.00	—	—	0.67	0.71	6.50
Annual Growth						

FS Investment Corp

Auditors: RSM US LLP

LOCATIONS

HQ: FS Investment Corp
201 Rouse Boulevard, Philadelphia, PA 19112
Phone: 215 495-1150

HISTORICAL FINANCIALS

Company Type: Public

Income Statement

FYE: December 31

	REVENUE ($ mil.)	NET INCOME ($ mil.)	NET PROFIT MARGIN	EMPLOYEES
12/15	474.8	265.0	55.8%	0.0
12/14	464.8	242.0	52.1%	0.0
12/13	474.5	244.9	51.6%	0.0
12/12	303.2	133.9	44.2%	0.0
12/11	115.4	71.3	61.8%	0.0
Annual Growth	42.4%	38.8%	—	—

2015 Year-End Financials

Debt ratio: 23.8%
Return on equity: 11.5%
Cash ($ mil.): 80.8
Current ratio: 0.12
Long-term debt ($ mil.): 989.7
No. of shares (mil.): 242.8
Dividends
Yield: 9.9%
Payout: 81.0%
Market value ($ mil.): 2,183.0

	STOCK PRICE ($) FY Close	P/E High/Low		PER SHARE ($) Earnings	Dividends	Book Value
12/15	8.99	10	8	1.10	0.89	9.10
12/14	9.93	11	10	0.97	1.08	9.83
Annual Growth	(9.5%)	—		13.4%	(17.8%)	(7.4%)

FS Investment Corp II

LOCATIONS

HQ: FS Investment Corp II
201 Rouse Boulevard, Philadelphia, PA 19112
Phone: 215 495-1150
Web: www.franklinsquare.com

HISTORICAL FINANCIALS

Company Type: Public

Income Statement

FYE: December 31

	REVENUE ($ mil.)	NET INCOME ($ mil.)	NET PROFIT MARGIN	EMPLOYEES
12/15	529.4	290.6	54.9%	0.0
12/14	398.7	242.6	60.9%	0.0
12/13	167.6	90.6	54.1%	0.0
12/12	9.4	2.8	29.6%	0.0
Annual Growth	282.2%	369.5%		

2015 Year-End Financials

Debt ratio: 22.7%
Return on equity: 10.3%
Cash ($ mil.): 4,761.6
Current ratio: 4.71
Long-term debt ($ mil.): 1,095.8
No. of shares (mil.): 321.5
Dividends
Yield: —
Payout: —
Market value ($ mil.): 0.0

	STOCK PRICE ($) FY Close	P/E High/Low		PER SHARE ($) Earnings	Dividends	Book Value
12/15	0.00	0	0	0.92	0.00	8.37
12/14	0.00	—	—	0.80	0.00	9.30
Annual Growth (10.0%)		—		15.0%	—	

G-III Apparel Group Ltd.

G-III Apparel Group made its name in leather. The company is best known for making leather jackets under the G-III Black Rivet Winlit Marvin Richards Andrew Marc and Marc New York but it also makes fashionable pants skirts and sportswear though brands such as Donna Karan DKNY Vilebrequin Jessica Howard and Eliza J. G-III has licensing agreements with brands such as Calvin Kline Tommy Hilfiger and Karl Lagerfeld. The company's customers include department stores such as Macy's Nordstrom Lord & Taylor and Kohl's and it also runs retail store networks.

Operations

The company operates in two segments: wholesale operations and retail operations. Wholesale operations include sales of products licensed by the company from third parties as well as sales of products under G-III's proprietary and private label brands. The wholesale segment accounts for around 80% of sales. G-III's retail segment which accounts for the remaining revenue sells of outerwear apparel footwear and accessories in the United States through the brands Wilsons Leather G.H. Bass and Calvin Klein Performance. G-III runs 199 Wilsons Leather stores 163 G.H. Bass stores and 5 Calvin Klein Performance stores.

The company makes genuine leather goods and as such its products are largely high-end. This includes its non-leather lines such as Vilebrequin a luxury swimwear brand.

Geographic Reach

Headquartered in New York the company has distribution centers in Dayton and Jamesberg New Jersey. It also has an office warehouse and distribution facility in Brooklyn Park Minnesota.

The company's 367 stores are found in 43 states plus Puerto Rico.

Sales and Marketing

The company's wholesale products are sold to approximately 2800 customers including retailers such as Macy's TJX Ross Stores Lord & Taylor Dillard's the Bon-Ton Stores Nordstrom Saks Fifth Avenue and JC Penney as well as membership clubs such as Costco and Sam's Club.

Sales to Macy's (which includes Macy's and Bloomingdale's chains) accounted for 20.8% of net sales in fiscal 2016 up 2 percentage points on fiscal 2015.

G-III's advertising expense for fiscals 2016 and 2015 was $81.9 million and $71.5 million.

Financial Performance

Revenue at G-III has been increasing gradually over the past five years and in fiscal 2016 it increased a further 11% to $2.3 billion. The Wholesale segment was boosted by strong performances in Calvin Klein licensed products (up $109.2 million) Ivanka Trump licensed products (up $29.4 million) and Eliza J. dresses (up $24.4 million) among others. The retail segment increased 3% due to higher comparable sales in G. H. Bass offset to an extent by a 7.6% decline in same store sales in Wilsons.

Net income has likewise been trending upwards and in fiscal 2016 it climbed 5% to $114.3 million. Higher net sales was offset to an extent by higher SGA costs particularly pertaining to higher personnel facility and advertising costs and expenses.

The company's cash position weakened a touch with cash from operations falling 21% to $64.2 million.

Strategy

With its strength in leather goods G-III does best in winter and so is working to diversify its product range to be relevant to all seasons. G-III acquired Donna Karan International which owns the Donna Karan and DKNY brands in mid-2016 in order to diversify its product lines.

In February 2016 the company expanded its Tommy Hilfiger licensing arrangement through a new license for womenswear which includes sportswear suit separates performancewear and denim. This is in addition the existing licenses for Tommy Hilfiger dresses men's and women's outerwear and luggage.

Furthermore in 2015 G-III acquired a 49% ownership interest brand rights to the Karl Lagerfeld trademarks for consumer products (with certain exceptions) and apparel in the United States Canada and Mexico. It also in 2015 teamed up with talkshow host Jimmy Fallon to produce a line of semi-novelty apparel High Hands that features teams' logos on the garment's underarm area that becomes visible when a fan raises their arms in celebration.

Mergers and Acquisitions

G-III acquired Donna Karan International which owns the Donna Karan and DKNY brands in mid-2016 for around $650 million from LVMH. Donna Karan made its name in women's workwear in the '80s and '90s but in recent years has struggled to turn a profit.

Ownership

Chairman and CEO Morris Goldfarb and investment firm FMR LLC each own about 15% of G-III's shares. Royce & Associates owns about 10%.

EXECUTIVES

COO, Wayne S. Miller, age 58, $750,000 total compensation
Chairman and CEO, Morris Goldfarb, age 66, $1,000,000 total compensation
CFO and Treasurer, Neal S. Nackman, age 56, $450,000 total compensation
President Wholesale-Design Merchandising and Sales Donna Karan, Barbara I. Kennedy
Vice Chairman and President, Sammy Aaron, age 56, $750,000 total compensation
Auditors: Ernst & Young LLP

LOCATIONS

HQ: G-III Apparel Group Ltd.
512 Seventh Avenue, New York, NY 10018
Phone: 212 403-0500
Web: www.g-iii.com

PRODUCTS/OPERATIONS

2016 Sales

	$ mil.	% of total
Wholesale	1,949.6	79
Retail	514.0	21
Eliminations	(119.5)	-
Total	**2,344.1**	**100**

Selected Divisions

Outerwear
  Andrew Marc
  Black Rivet
  Calvin Klein
  Cole Haan
  DKNY
  Dockers
  Donna Karan
  Ellen Tracy
  Guess
  Jones New York
  Kenneth Cole
  Levi's

Marc New York
Nine West
Sean John
Tommy Hilfiger
Ready to Wear
  Andrew Marc Dresses
  Calvin Klein Dresses
  Calvin Klein Performance Wear
  Calvin Klein Sportswear
  Calvin Klein Women Suits
  Eliza J Dresses
  Ellen Tracy Dresses
  Jessica Howard Dresses
  Jessica Simpson Dresses
  Marc New York Dresses
Sports
  G-III for Her
  G-III Sports by Carl Banks
  Major League Baseball
  National Basketball Association
  National Football League
  National Hockey League
  Officially Licensed Collegiate Products
  Touch by Alyssa Milano
Retail
  Wilsons Outlets

Selected Licenses

Men's and Women's
  Calvin Klein
  Cole Haan
  Guess?
  Jessica Simpson
  Kenneth Cole NY
  Levi's
  Vince Camuto
Sports
  Major League Baseball
  Major League Soccer
  National Basketball Association
  National Football League
  National Hockey League

COMPETITORS

Amerex	L.L. Bean
Armani	NIKE
Burberry	North Face
Burlington Coat	Phat Fashions
Factory	Roc Apparel
Columbia Sportswear	Sean John
Diesel SpA	Tandy Leather
FUBU	The Gap
J. Crew	Wal-Mart

HISTORICAL FINANCIALS

Company Type: Public

Income Statement

FYE: January 31

	REVENUE ($ mil.)	NET INCOME ($ mil.)	NET PROFIT MARGIN	EMPLOYEES
01/16	2,344.1	114.3	4.9%	7,693.0
01/15	2,116.8	110.3	5.2%	6,641.0
01/14	1,718.2	77.3	4.5%	6,631.0
01/13	1,399.7	56.8	4.1%	3,109.0
01/12	1,231.2	49.6	4.0%	2,592.0
Annual Growth	**17.5%**	**23.2%**	**—**	**31.3%**

2016 Year-End Financials

Debt ratio: —	No. of shares (mil.): 45.5
Return on equity: 13.8%	Dividends
Cash ($ mil.): 132.5	Yield: —
Current ratio: 3.69	Payout: —
Long-term debt ($ mil.): —	Market value ($ mil.): 2,248.0

	STOCK PRICE ($) FY Close	P/E High/Low	Earnings	Dividends	Book Value
01/16	49.36	47 16	2.46	0.00	19.50
01/15	97.20	40 25	2.49	0.00	16.93
01/14	69.97	39 18	1.86	0.00	12.79
01/13	35.89	27 16	1.40	0.00	10.67
01/12	22.86	36 14	1.23	0.00	9.05
Annual Growth	21.2%	— —	18.9%	—	21.2%

GAIN Capital Holdings Inc

There is plenty to lose in the foreign currency exchange market but this company would like you to focus on the potential gains. GAIN Capital Holdings provides over-the-counter foreign exchange (forex) services to retail traders (responsible for about 97% of the company's trading volume) and institutional investors and through financial intermediaries such as broker-dealers banks and futures commission merchants. The company's FOREXTrader platform provides online trading tools and educational resources to help individual investors deal in forex trading online. It has 133000 funded retail accounts.

Geographic Reach

GAIN provides services to retail and institutional customers in more than 180 countries worldwide conducting business from offices in New York; Bedminster New Jersey; Chicago; Powell Ohio; Grand Rapids Michigan; London; Tokyo; Sydney; Beijing; Hong Kong; and Singapore.

Financial Performance

GAIN achieved explosive growth in 2013 as revenues skyrocketed 76% from $152 million in 2012 to $268 million in 2013 a historic milestone for the company. The impressive growth for 2013 was attributed to a spike in commission revenue due to an additional $15 million from its GTX business as well as an increase of $14 million from its futures business. GAIN's sales trader acquisition also generated an additional $10 million in commission. Trading revenue increased due to higher volatility levels in the foreign exchange markets.

Profits significantly shot up from $3 million in 2012 to $31 million in 2013 due to the higher revenue coupled with an income tax benefit of roughly $14 million received in 2013. GAIN's operating cash flow fell dramatically from 2011 to 2012; however it increased by $18 million in 2013.

Strategy

GAIN in 2013 achieved historic revenue growth through the use of acquisitions. Continuing to adhere to this strategy in 2014 it purchased Galvan Research a UK-based Contract for Difference (CFD) advisory business. The deal gave GAIN a solid foundation on which to build a comprehensive advisory service for its clients in support of its FX & CFD offering.

In 2013 GAIN bought Global Futures & Forex LTD (GFT). The combined company boasts a deeper global footprint a robust offering of more than 12500 financial products and industry-leading trading technology. GAIN is using GFT's broad product offering tools and educational capabilities to further strengthen its competitive position while realizing significant synergies.

EXECUTIVES

President Retail, Samantha Roady, age 46, $350,000 total compensation
EVP and CFO, Nigel Rose, age 50, $281,250 total compensation
EVP General Counsel and Corporate Secretary, Diego A. Rotsztain, age 46, $375,000 total compensation
Managing Director GAIN Capital Payments, Jeffrey A. (Jeff) Scott, age 52, $350,000 total compensation
President CEO and Director, Glenn H. Stevens, age 53, $650,000 total compensation
CIO, Mike Lear
Chief Risk Officer, Tim OÂSullivan
CEO GTX SEF, Edward Brown
Senior Vice President Brand Marketing, Dina Grochowski
Vice President Strategic Operations, Nayan Patel
Chairman, Peter Quick, age 61
Auditors: KPMG LLP

LOCATIONS

HQ: GAIN Capital Holdings Inc
Bedminster One, 135 Route 202/206, Bedminster, NJ 07921
Phone: 908 731-0700
Web: www.gaincapital.com

PRODUCTS/OPERATIONS

2015 Sales

	$ mil.	% of total
Non-interest income		
Retail revenue	347.5	80
Institutional revenue	33.8	8
Futures revenue	45.4	10
Other	8.5	2
Interest income	1.2	.
Total	**436.4**	**100**

COMPETITORS

FX Solutions	INTL FCStone
FXCM Inc.	ISE
GFT	Rosenthal Collins

HISTORICAL FINANCIALS

Company Type: Public

Income Statement

FYE: December 31

	REVENUE ($ mil.)	NET INCOME ($ mil.)	NET PROFIT MARGIN	EMPLOYEES
12/15	435.3	10.2	2.4%	772.0
12/14	369.5	31.6	8.6%	479.0
12/13	266.3	31.3	11.8%	551.0
12/12	151.3	2.6	1.7%	363.0
12/11	181.4	15.7	8.7%	364.0
Annual Growth	24.5%	(10.0%)	—	20.7%

2015 Year-End Financials

Debt ratio: 8.5%
Return on equity: 3.6%
Cash ($ mil.): 1,092.5
Current ratio: 1.32
Long-term debt ($ mil.): 122.0
No. of shares (mil.): 48.7
Dividends
Yield: 2.4%
Payout: 35.7%
Market value ($ mil.): 396.0

	STOCK PRICE ($) FY Close	P/E High/Low	Earnings	Dividends	Book Value
12/15	8.11	47 32	0.22	0.20	6.28
12/14	9.02	16 8	0.71	0.20	6.17
12/13	7.51	17 5	0.79	0.20	5.95
12/12	4.09	86 49	0.07	0.20	4.69
12/11	6.70	22 11	0.40	0.05	4.81
Annual Growth	4.9%	—	(13.9%)	41.4%	6.9%

Gaming & Leisure Properties, Inc

Auditors: Deloitte & Touche LLP

LOCATIONS

HQ: Gaming & Leisure Properties, Inc
845 Berkshire Blvd., Suite 200, Wyomissing, PA 19610
Phone: 610 401-2900
Web: www.glpropinc.com

HISTORICAL FINANCIALS

Company Type: Public

Income Statement

FYE: December 31

	REVENUE ($ mil.)	NET INCOME ($ mil.)	NET PROFIT MARGIN	EMPLOYEES
12/15	575.0	128.1	22.3%	792.0
12/14	635.9	185.3	29.2%	807.0
12/13	242.1	19.8	8.2%	866.0
12/12	210.6	22.9	10.9%	900.0
12/11	231.8	26.6	11.5%	0.0
Annual Growth	25.5%	48.0%	—	—

2015 Year-End Financials

Debt ratio: 102.5%
Return on equity: —
Cash ($ mil.): 41.8
Current ratio: 1.28
Long-term debt ($ mil.): 2,510.2
No. of shares (mil.): 115.5
Dividends
Yield: 7.8%
Payout: 201.8%
Market value ($ mil.): 3,214.0

	STOCK PRICE ($) FY Close	P/E High/Low	Earnings	Dividends	Book Value
12/15	27.80	34 23	1.08	2.18	(2.19)
12/14	29.34	31 17	1.58	14.32	(1.10)
12/13	50.81	282229	0.17	0.00	1.61
Annual Growth	(26.0%)	—	(152.1%)	—	—

Gartner Inc

You might not know IT but Gartner does. The company helps clients understand the information technology (IT) industry and make informed decisions about IT products. It provides more than 10800 client organizations with competitive analysis reports industry overviews market trend data and product evaluation reports. Its Gartner Dataquest and other research services are made available through subscriptions primarily to CIOs and other IT professionals. Gartner also offers technology and management consulting services and it produces a number of conferences seminars and other events aimed at the technology sector.

Operations

Gartner operates through three primary business segments: research (73% of net sales) consulting (15%) and events (12%).

Geographic Reach

The company operates in about 90 countries. Canada and the US represent about 62% of its overall sales. The EMEA region contributes 26%

while other regions account for the remaining amount.

Sales and Marketing

The company has 60000 clients representing nearly 10800 distinct organizations worldwide. It publishes tens of thousands of pages of original research annually and its analysts answer 250000 client inquiries every year.

Financial Performance

The company reported revenue of $2.1 billion in fiscal 2015 which was an increase of $141.6 million (or 7%) compared to its 2014 revenue. The relatively small increase was mainly due to a 10% increase in Gartner's research revenues.

Gartner's net income was $175.6 million in fiscal 2015 which was a decrease of $8.1 million (or 4%) compared to its fiscal 2014 net income. The decreased net income was mainly due to an increase in selling general and administrative expenses.

The company ended fiscal 2015 with $345.6 million in cash flow from operations. That was a decrease of $1.2 million compared to the company's cash levels at the end of fiscal 2014.

Strategy

Gartner uses acquisitions to extend its geographic reach and penetrate fast-growing markets.

Mergers and Acquisitions

During 2016 the company increased its addressable market into supply chain and marketing through the acquisition of SCM World. The deal will help Gartner develop an expanded range of supply chain products and services to accelerate long-term growth globally.

In 2014 Gartner acquired Software Advice a company based in Austin Texas that offers detailed reviews comparisons and research to assist organizations in finding software products that best fit their current and future needs.

HISTORY

Company Background

Computer analyst Gideon Gartner founded Gartner Group in 1979. Two years after its 1986 IPO the company was acquired by ad agency Saatchi & Saatchi in that firm's futile bid to become a business services powerhouse. A management buyout backed by Dun & Bradstreet forced Gideon Gartner out in 1990. Gartner Group went public again in 1993 and Dun & Bradstreet's stake was transferred to its spinoff Cognizant in 1996.

EXECUTIVES

CEO and Director, Eugene A. (Gene) Hall, age 59, $875,324 total compensation
Senior Vice President, Dale (Dal) Kutnick
SVP Business Dev. and Research Operations, Robin (Rin) Kranch
Svp Gartner Research, Peter (Pete) Sondergaard
Vice President, Ian Weitzman
CIO, Michael P. Diliberto
SVP Business and IT Leaders Products and Services, Kendall B. (Ken) Davis, age 47
SVP Gartner Consulting, Per Anders Waern, age 54, $435,063 total compensation
SVP Gartner Worldwide Events and Marketing, Alwyn Dawkins, $435,063 total compensation
SVP Executive Programs, Chris Thomas
SVP and CFO, Craig Safian, $457,402 total compensation
Vice President Risk, John W Riley
Vice President, Bruce Ventriglia
Senior Vice President Global Sales, David (Dave) Godfrey
Vice President, Peter (Pete) Shores

Managing Vice President Product Management, Matt French
Research Vice President, Michele (Michie) Caminos
MVP, Edmond Murray
Research Vice President and Agenda Manager, Matthew (Matt) Brisse
Vice President Of Product Development And Education, Lisa (Lis) Lawlor
Vice President, Stewart (Stew) Buchanan
Group Vice President, Jose Ruggero
Regional Vice President Cpg, Mark Frederick
Vice President and Distinguished Analyst, Betsy Burton
VPMobile Business Strategies, Ken (Kenny) Dulaney
MVP, Laura (Laur) Wilhelm
Research Vice President, John-David Lovelock
Vice President, Steve Kleynhans
Group Vice President STG Operations, Joe (Joey) Sacchi
Research Vice President, Ian Finley
Vice President and Research Director Gartner Research, Patrick (Paddy) Meehan
Research Vice President, Tom Eid
Vice President and Research Director Emerging Trends and Technologies, David (Dave) McCoy
Research Vice President, Philip Dawson
Managing Vice President At Gartner, Mark (Marky) Deacon
Vice President Public Relations, Tom (Tommy) Mccall
Vice President, Atilla Mukan
Research Vice President, Ian Keene
Vice President and Research Group Director Gartner Research, Vincent (Vin) Oliva
Vice President Industries Research, Don (Donnie) Scheibenreif
Regional Vice President Sales, Tim (Timmy) Phillips
Vice President Sales Operations, Brian Martin
Research Vice President, Philip (Phil) Allega
Vice President, Linda (Lin) Price
Vice President, Rita Knox
Research Vice President, Paul (Pauly) Debeasi
Vice President, Lindsay (Linds) Mcrory
Managing Vice President, David (Dave) Cappuccio
Research Vice President, Monica Basso
Managing Vice President, Frank (Frankie) Fabricius
Research Vice President, Alexa Bona
Vice President of Product Strategy and Marketing, Andrew (Andy) McCauley
Vice President Business Development, Carol Quinn
Managing Vice President, Larry (Lar) Free
Vice President Distinguished Analyst, Robert (Bob) Desisto
Group Vice President Global Tax, Brent Gregoire
Vice President Research Area Director Gartner Research, Jim (Jimmy) Sinur
Vice President Distinguished Analyst, Richard (Dick) Hunter
Vice President Reasearch, Ricvhard Matlus
Vice President and Distinguished Analyst, Andrew (Andy) Butler
Managing Vice President of Semiconductor Research, Andrew (Andy) Phillips
Vice President And Director of Research At Gartner, Lars Mieritz
Managing Vice President Research, Susan (Sue) Landry
Vice President Executive Partner, Jean-marc Lejeune
Executive Vice President, Geraldine (Gerald) Crawford
Vice President, Robert (Bob) Goodwin
Group Vice President, Mike (Mikey) Harris
Group Vice President and Research Fellow, Jim (Jimmy) Popkin

Group Vice President Compensation and Benefits, Jim (Jimmy) Crane
Research Vice President, Simon Mingay
Vice President Information Technology, Lew Schwratz
Research Vice President for SMB Business Applications, Robert (Bob) Anderson
Managing Vice President, Phil (Philly) Schacter
Vice President consulting, Thomas (Thom) Mcclure
Group Vice President Human Resources Talent Development, Rob (Robbie) Phillips
Research Vice President, Jane (Ginny) Dosbrow
Research Vice President, Stephen (Steve) Kleynhans
Vice President and Distinguished Analyst, Frank (Frankie) Schlier
Managing Vice President, Lisa Pierce
Managing Vice President, Andrew (Andy) Rosenblatt
Vice President Service Delivery, Chris (Chrissy) Germann
Research Vice President, Bern Elliot
Vice President Information Technology Service Director, Michael (Mel) Disabato
Research Vice President, Jeff (Jeffy) Vining
Research Vice President, Michele Cantara
Managing Vice President, Dorothy (Doroth) Yu
Research Vice President Information Technology Operations Management, John P (Jack) Morency
Vice President Executive Partner, Irving Tyler
Research Vice President With Gartne, Ross Altman
Managing Vice President, Richard (Dick) Cho
VICE PRESIDENT, Jason (Jase) Mirwald
Managing Vice President, Dan (Danny) Holmes
Vice President Learning Development Event Sales, Ed (Eddie) Medeiros
Vice President and People Centered Strategies Community Chair, Adrianne Gershberg
Vice President Sales Information technology, Jim (Jimmy) Cummiskey
Vice President and Executive Partner, Bill (Billy) Caffery
Regional Vice President, Tim (Timmy) Robertson
Vice President, Jeff Schulman
Managing Vice President and Research Director, Eric (Ric) Paulak
Research Vice President, Noha Tohamy
Group Vice President, Nir Polonsky
Vice President of Marketing and Sales, Richard (Dick) Addotta
Research Vice President, Dianne (Ann) Morello
Gvp, Mike (Mikey) Parrish
Vice President of Sales Australia and New Zealand, Warren (Warr) Anderson
Regional Vice President Sales, Geoff (G.) Wright
Vice President, Martin Gutberlet
Managing Vice President, Steven (Steve) Lefebure
Analyst Vice President Mgc, Michael Rollings
Vice President Canada, Peter (Pete) Krasa
Vice President Research Communications, Terrie Landini
Vice President Canada Executive Programs, Robert Langlois
Research Vice President, Todd Applebaum
Regional Vice President, Peter Persico
Wireless Analyst And Vice President, Kevin Dulaney
National Sales Manager, Michael Gurevich
Vice Presidente, Alfredo Pinheiro
GVP, Ann Laffaye
Vice President Consulting, Patrick (Paddy) Sullivan
Research Vice President, Lydia Leong
Vice President, Ed (Eddie) Shapland
Regional Vice President, Julie Giefer
Area Vice President Smb, Jonathan Pione
Vice President And Director E Business Transformat, Hollis Bischoff
Vice President Disruptive Technology, Bart (Bartholomew) Mellink

Research Vice President, Joseph (Jo) Bugajski
Executive Vice President, Adam Rin
Research Vice President, Alex Winogradoff
Vice President Research, Ellen (Elle) Kitzis
Vice President, Partha Lyenga
Vice President And Research Fellow At Gartner, Mark (Marky) Raskino
AMR Executive Vice President, Nancy Gendron
Vice President, Jim (Jimmy) Carolan
Managing Vice President, Richard (Dick) Cockcroft
Group Vice President, Alissa Stayn
Assistant Vice President Cpg, Moolee Wong
Vice President, Paola Farina
Vice President, Ewan Thompson
Vice President, John Mann
Vice President Of Research, Edmund Thompson
Vice President Service Delivery, Peter Adler
Research Vice President, Hung Lehong
Vice President Consulting, Chris (Chrissy) Campbell
Group Vice President Digital Marketing Products, John (Jack) Flynn
Vice President, Kimberly (Kim) Ruggero
Vice President Consulting, Steve (Stevie) Bibee
Research Vice President, Trent Henry
Information Technology Services Vice President and Conference Chairperson, Eric (Ric) Rocco
Vice President, Jeffery (Jeff) Depasquale
Group Vice President and Managing Partner, Liz (Lizzie) Goodchild
Vice President Distinguished Analyst, Drue Reeves
Vice President Consulting, Anthony (Tony) Henderson
Vice President, Tom (Tommy) Mcclure
Vice President, Kyoko Taneda
Vice President, Ashley (Ash) Schwind
Regional Vice President, Nick (Nicky) Reddall
Vice President, Andy Gartner
Vice President and Research Area Director of Network Technology, Dave (Davie) Capuccio
Executive Vice President, Michael Schumer
Executive Vice President Business Development, Alvina Usher
Executive Vice President, Bill Swanton
Group Vice President World Wide Operations, Margie (Marge) Kappel
Research Vice President For Information Technology Sale, Tiffani Bova
Regional Vice President, Liz (Lizzie) Reynolds
Vice President and Client Director, Jon (Jonny) Danzig
Vice President And Research Analyst, Sandra Notardonato
Vice President and Research Fellow, Ken (Kenny) McGee
Senior Vice President Consulting, Per Waern
Regional Vice President Sales, Nathaniel (Nate) Swan
Regional Vice President Sales, Susan Davis
Vice President and Distinguished Analyst, Ted (Teddy) Friedman
Vice President Technology Research Services, Angela Imhoff
Vice President Consulting, Nino Moscardini
Vice President Application Development, Andre Pienczykowski
Research Vice President Security, Ramon (Ray) Krikken
Managing Vice President And Associate General Counsel, Raymond Bernstein
Regional Vice President, Andy Muench
Vice President, Michael Samsen
Vice President Capital Appreciation Plans, Jane (Ginny) Lucas
Regional Vice President Gartner Asia Pacific Sales, Derek (Der) Seow
Vice President, George (Georgey) Miller

Vice President of Sales and New Product Development, Alex (Al) Ebel
Managing Vice President, Jorge Lopez
Research Vice President, Mark Nicolett
Research Vice President, Stan Aronow
Research Vice President, Eric (Ric) Maiwald
Research Vice President, Helen Huntley
Vice President and Program Director, Jean-Louis Previdi
Vice President Information Technology, Julie Gottlieb
Vice President Research Analyst, Tim (Timmy) Mahon
Vice President Of Gartner Worldwide Events, Thomas Cheriyan
Research Vice President and Distinguished Analyst, Gene (Genie) Phifer
Group Vice President, Michael (Mel) Chalk
Vice President Business Development, Peter Shaw
Vice President Consulting, Marc (Marcy) Kindermans
Managing Vice President, Debra (Deb) Hofman
Vice President Applications Development, Kathy (Kat) Barefoot
Vice President, Nancy Shah
Managing Vice President Gartner Research, Alvin (Al) Park
Vice President and Research Fellow, Martin (Marti) Reynolds
Research Vice President, Leif-Olof Wallin
Research Vice President, Paul Proctor
Vice President User Experience, James (Jamie) Carolan
Vice President and Gartner Fellow, Diane (Di) Morello
Research Vice President, Niger Rayner
Research Vice President, Bill (Billy) Pray
Senior Vice President Human Resources, Michelle (Michie) Riess
Vice President Product Management, Atreyi Ray
Vice President of Research, Alejandro (Al) Soejarto
Vice President Americas Channel Marketing, Maria (Mary) Cute
Research Vice President, Simon Jacobson
Vice President Consulting Sourcing, Kyle Hardy
Reg Vice President Sales, Moe Ali
Research Vice President, Carsten Casper
Managing Vice President, Bob (Bo) Hafner
Managing Vice President, Raymond Laracuenta
Vice Presidents, Neal MacDonald
Vice President Corporate Business Systems, Rachel (Rach) Leinberger
Vice President, Ed (Eddie) Thompson
Research Vice President, Kenneth (Ken) Chin
Vice President Finance, Tom White
Senior Vice President, Peter (Pete) Sondengaard
Research Vice President Healthcare Supply Chain, Eric (Ric) O'Daffer
Research Vice President, Mike (Mikey) Griswold
Managing Vice President for Chief Information Officer Workforce Management Group, Diane (Di) Berry
Vice President, Mike (Mikey) Silver
Vice President Service Delivery Enterprise Leaders for Supply Chain and Information Technology, Christian Mortimore Christian (Chris) Mortimore
Vice President, Kelly (Kel) Scholz
Regional Vice President, Saul Pyatt
MVP, Kimm Franco
Vice President Operations, Ed (Eddie) Destefano
Group Vice President, Jamie (James) Popkin
Managing Vice President, Austin Merritt
Group Vice President Marketing, Steve (Stevie) Hardy
Vice President, Gary Burgess
Senior Vice President, Peranders Warn

Vice President Product Management, Hardik Shah
Group Vice President Strategic Technology, Mike Skorski
Vice President Customer Insights, Daniel (Dan) Brakewood
Vice President and Program Director, Rick (Ricky) Poppell
Vice President and Distinguished Analyst, John (Jack) Girard
Senior Industrial Analyst Vice President, Michael (Mel) Burkett
Senior Vice President and General Counsel, Dan (Danny) Peale
Group Vice President Investor Relations, Sherief Bakr
Chairman, James C. Smith, age 75
Auditors: KPMG LLP

LOCATIONS

HQ: Gartner Inc
P.O. Box 10212, 56 Top Gallant Road, Stamford, CT 06902-7700
Phone: 203 316-1111
Web: www.gartner.com

PRODUCTS/OPERATIONS

2015 Sales

	$ mil.	% of total
Research	1,583.5	73
Consulting	327.8	15
Events	251.8	12
Total	2,163.1	100

Selected Products and Services

Research
  Gartner Dataquest
  GartnerG2
  Publications
  Monthly Research Review
Consulting
  Enterprise process management
  Enterprise risk management
  Human capital management
  Information technology architecture
  Information technology strategy and management
  Market and business strategy
  Public sector consulting
  Sourcing
Events
  Best practice groups
  Conferences
  Executive programs
  Symposium/ITxpo
Other
  Assessment services
  Decision support software
  Performance management services

COMPETITORS

Aberdeen Group	Ipsos
Accenture	McKinsey & Company
Bain & Company	Millward Brown
Booz Allen	Nielsen
Boston Consulting	Penton Media
Datamonitor	SYS-CON Media
Forrester Research	TNS Custom
HP Enterprise Services	UBM TechWeb
IBM	WebMediaBrands
IDC	

Income Statement
FYE: December 31

	REVENUE ($ mil.)	NET INCOME ($ mil.)	NET PROFIT MARGIN	EMPLOYEES
12/15	2,163.0	175.6	8.1%	7,834.0
12/14	2,021.4	183.7	9.1%	6,758.0
12/13	1,784.2	182.8	10.2%	5,997.0
12/12	1,615.8	165.9	10.3%	5,468.0
12/11	1,468.5	136.9	9.3%	4,975.0
Annual Growth	10.2%	6.4%	—	12.0%

2015 Year-End Financials

Debt ratio: 37.9%	No. of shares (mil.): 82.3
Return on equity: 1,220.9%	Dividends
Cash ($ mil.): 372.9	Yield: —
Current ratio: 0.86	Payout: —
Long-term debt ($ mil.): 790.0	Market value ($ mil.): 7,468.0

	STOCK PRICE ($) FY Close	P/E High/Low		PER SHARE ($) Earnings	Dividends	Book Value
12/15	90.70	45	37	2.06	0.00	(1.61)
12/14	84.21	42	30	2.03	0.00	1.84
12/13	71.05	36	23	1.93	0.00	3.93
12/12	46.02	29	19	1.73	0.00	3.28
12/11	34.77	30	23	1.39	0.00	1.95
Annual Growth	27.1%	—	—	10.3%	—	—

Generac Holdings Inc

Perfect storms make good business for Generac Power Systems. That's because the company manufactures engine-driven standby and portable generators for homes businesses hospitals and recreational vehicles. The company also makes industrial power generation equipment automatic transfer switches switch gear and controls and remote monitoring software. Brands include Generac Magnum Ottomotores and Tower Light. Generac sells its products through retailers as well as through wholesale distributors. The US represents nearly 85% of the company sales.

Geographic Reach

The company is based in Waukesha Wisconsin and operates 11 manufacturing plants located principally in the US Mexico Italy Brazil and the UK. It sells its products in the US and Canada with an expanding presence internationally in Latin America Europe the Middle East Africa and Asia/Pacific regions. Generac generated 85% of its net sales from the US during 2015.

Operations

Generac divides its operations into two primary segments: residential power products (51% of sales); and commercial and industrial power products (42%). Other products account for the remainder of revenue.

Sales and Marketing

The company targets the residential light commercial industrial and construction markets. Products are sold into these regions through a broad network of independent dealers retailers wholesalers catalogs e-commerce merchants and equipment rental companies under the Generac Magnum Ottomotores and Tower Light brand names. Generac also sells direct to certain national and re-

gional account customers that are the end users of its products.

Financial Performance

Generac's revenues dropped by 10% from $1.46 billion in 2014 to $1.32 billion in 2015. Profits also fell 55% from $175 million to $78 million and the company's operating cash flow also dropped 25% during that same time period.

The declines for 2015 were fueled by lower sales from its two main segments: residential power products (7%) and commercial and industrial power products (16%). The latter segment was affected by a significant reduction in shipments into the oil and gas and general rental markets and reduced shipments to telecom national account customers.

The drop in profits for 2015 was attributed to additional tradename and goodwill impairment charges related to the transition and consolidation of various brands to the Generac tradename.

Strategy

The company plans to expand its presence in under-served North American regions by continuing to build its dealer network. Latin America Europe the Middle East and China represent favorable opportunities for the company and have piqued Generac's interest in seizing growth opportunities in international markets.

Boasting a North American market share of 70% for residential standby generators a broad distribution network (direct dealers catalog wholesale and retail) a comprehensive product line and specialized engineering and manufacturing capabilities Generac continues to invest in innovation and product development as well as technician training to ensure the repair and maintenance of its products.

Mergers and Acquisitions

Generac has grown through the help of acquisitions. In 2015 the company acquired Vermont-based Country Home Products (CHP) a manufacturer of high-quality professional-grade engine-powered equipment for $75 million.

The acquisition expanded the company's chore-related products line-up and provided additional scale to its residential engine-powered tools platform. In early 2016 the company obtained 65% of Siena Italy-based Pramac a manufacturer of stationary mobile and portable generators for $61 million. Pramac products are sold in over 150 countries through a broad distribution network. The deal augmented the company's global presence by adding product manufacturing and distribution capabilities that serve local markets around the world.

EXECUTIVES

EVP North America, Russell S. (Russ) Minick, $371,279 total compensation

Chairman President and CEO, Aaron Jagdfeld, age 44, $731,134 total compensation

CFO, York A. Ragen, age 45, $362,668 total compensation

EVP Global Engineering, Allen D Gillette, age 60, $180,009 total compensation

EVP Strategic Global Sourcing, Roger F. Pascavis, age 56, $227,740 total compensation

Senior Vice President Engineering, GREG (Greggy) WISCHSTADT

Senior Vice President Operations, Rob Stoppek

Vice President Retail Sales, Jason Hall

Executive Vice President, Terry Dolan

Vice President andndash; Service Operations, Paul (Pauly) Cannestra

National Sales Manager, Kevin Ryan

Vice President Global Supply Chain, Shawn Fortune

Vice President Of Information Technology, Jeff Koepke

Treasurer, Joseph (Jo) Kavalary

Auditors: Deloitte & Touche LLP

LOCATIONS

HQ: Generac Holdings Inc
S45 W29290 Hwy. 59, Waukesha, WI 53189
Phone: 262 544-4811
Web: www.generac.com

PRODUCTS/OPERATIONS

2015 Sales

	$ mil.	% of total
Residential power products	673.8	51
Commercial & Industrial products	548.4	42
Other	95.1	7
Total	**1,317.3**	**100**

Selected Products and Brands

Generators
  Commercial (QuietSource)
  Industrial (gaseous diesel bi-fuel modular power systems (MPS) Gemini)
  Portable (GP XG XP iX)
  Recreational vehicle (gasoline propane diesel)
  Residential (QuietSource Guardian)

Selected Markets

Agricultural/mining
Business office
Commercial/retail
Data center
Education
Healthcare
Manufacturing
Municipal
Research
Residential
Telecom

COMPETITORS

Aggreko	Doosan Corp
Atlas Copco USA Holdings	Honda Kohler
Briggs & Stratton Power Products	Multiquip Taylor Group
Caterpillar	Techtronic
Cummins Power Generation	Terex Westerbeke Corp.

HISTORICAL FINANCIALS
Company Type: Public

Income Statement
FYE: December 31

	REVENUE ($ mil.)	NET INCOME ($ mil.)	NET PROFIT MARGIN	EMPLOYEES
12/15	1,317.3	77.7	5.9%	3,156.0
12/14	1,460.9	174.6	12.0%	3,587.0
12/13	1,485.7	174.5	11.7%	3,380.0
12/12	1,176.3	93.2	7.9%	3,048.0
12/11	791.9	324.6	41.0%	2,223.0
Annual Growth	13.6%	(30.0%)	—	9.2%

2015 Year-End Financials

Debt ratio: 59.0%	No. of shares (mil.): 66.0
Return on equity: 16.2%	Dividends
Cash ($ mil.): 115.8	Yield: —
Current ratio: 3.10	Payout: —
Long-term debt ($ mil.): 1,050.1	Market value ($ mil.): 1,965.0

	STOCK PRICE ($)	P/E		PER SHARE ($)	
	FY Close	High/Low	Earnings	Dividends	Book Value
12/15	29.77	44 24	1.12	0.00	7.06
12/14	46.76	24 15	2.49	0.00	7.11
12/13	56.64	22 13	2.51	11.00	4.62
12/12	34.31	28 15	1.35	6.00	6.79
12/11	28.03	6 3	4.79	0.00	11.37
Annual Growth (11.2%)	1.5%	— —(30.5%)		—	

Genesee & Wyoming Inc.

Genesee & Wyoming (GWI) once relied on the salt of the earth –hauling salt on a 14-mile railroad for one customer. Now however the company owns stakes in more than 115 freight railroads including 103 short-line and regional freight railroads that operate over a total of more than 18000 miles of track including 15600 miles of track owned and leased by the company and another 3300 miles additional miles under contractual track access arrangements to more than 40 ports in North America Europe and Australia. Freight transported by GWI railroads includes coal forest products and pulp and paper.

Geographic Reach

GWI owns short line and regional freight railroads in the US Australia Canada the Netherlands and Belgium. Within the US the company has eight regions: Coastal (which includes industrial switching and port operations) Pacific Mountain West Central Southern Midwest Ohio Valley and Northeast.

Operations

GWI's rolling stock consists of some 1094 locomotives of which 932 are owned and 162 are leased. It also maintains 24141 railcars of which 5558 are owned and 18583 are leased.The company generates non-freight revenues from its railcar switching car hire and rental services demurrage and storage car repair services railroad construction and fuel sales to third-parties. Freight revenues represent more than 75% of total sales while non-freight revenues generate about 25%.

Sales and Marketing

GWI serves more than 2500 customers.

Financial Performance

The company has seen revenue growth over the last few years especially in 2013 when the revenues skyrocketed. In 2014 GWI's revenues increased by 4% thank to sales from new operations (like the Rapid City Pierre & Eastern Railroad Inc.) and from existing operations which grew due to an increase in freight revenues. The major changes in revenues came from Europe due to a rise in freight sales and an increase in railcar switching revenues from a new customer.In 2014 income decreased by 4% due to higher expenses primarily in labor and benefits (as the result of a rise in the number of employees due to insourced equipment maintenance activities in Australia and the Midwestern US and a growth in transportation employees as a result of higher traffic levels. It also saw an equipment rent expense increase from new operations.In 2014 GWI's operating cash flows increased by

19% due to increase in inflow of cash on materials and supplies followed by accounts receivable and prepaid expenses. This was offset by lower inflow from accounts payable and a decrease in net income.

Strategy

The company which has expanded over the years via acquisitions continues to grow by buying railroads not only in North America and Australia but also in European markets. It is focused on growing its rail traffic through regional marketing along with efficiently operating costs as it invests in track and rolling stock to ensure safe operationsIn 2014 GWI reorganized its Atlas Railroad Construction subsidiary as a region-based commercial and operating structure to facilitate expansion into the US Midwest Southeast and Southwest. As part of the move Atlas will relocate to Jacksonville Florida while maintaining a strong presence in the Pittsburgh area.

Mergers and Acquisitions

Growing its assets in 2015 the company acquired UK-based Freightliner Group from Arcapita and other shareholders for £490 million ($755 million). It also bought Pinsly Railroad Company's Arkansas Division (six short-line railroads) for $40 million.

In 2014 the company's Rapid City Pierre & Eastern Railroad (RCP&E) subsidiary acquired the west end of the Dakota Minnesota & Eastern rail line from Canadian Pacific for $210 million.The acquisition creates a fleet of 50 locomotives and 3000 railcars dedicated to RCP&E customers.

Company Background

Its $1.4 billion milestone deal to purchase RailAmerica in 2012 created the largest short-line railroad operator in the US with about 110 railroads and 15000 miles of track. The transaction helped to skyrocket GWI's revenues by nearly 80% from $875 million in 2012 to $1.57 billion in 2013.

In addition to that significant deal GWI expects freight business in Australia to pick up as the grain harvest in that country increased over the previous year's totals. To that end GWI purchased Australia's FreightLink rail network for about $332 million Australian dollars ($319 million). FreightLink which serves general freight and mining customers in South Australia will operate as part of Genesee & Wyoming Australia (GWA). GWA has managed FreightLink's rail services and operations and provided it with locomotives and crews since its inception.

The original 14-mile Genessee & Wyoming railroad was purchased out of bankruptcy in 1899 by Edward Fuller and his financial partners to transport salt from their mine in Western New York State.

EXECUTIVES

President and CEO, John C. (Jack) Hellmann, age 45, $849,750 total compensation

SVP Coastal Region Companies Genesee & Wyoming Railroad Services Inc., Andrew T. Chunko, age 47

EVP Global Corporate Development, Matthew O. Walsh, age 41, $500,000 total compensation

SVP Information Technology Genesee & Wyoming Railroad Services Inc., Mike Meyers

CFO, Timothy J. Gallagher, age 53, $466,796 total compensation

SVP Southern Region Railroads Genesee & Wyoming Railroad Services Inc., Bill Jasper

Managing Director Rotterdam Rail Feeding, Arnoud de Rade

SVP Pacific Region Railroads Genesee & Wyoming Railroad Services Inc., James E. Irvin

Vice President Transportation, Dewayne Swindall

COO, David A. Brown, age 57, $414,812 total compensation

SVP Northeast Region Railroads Genesee & Wyoming Railroad Services Inc., Dave Ebbrecht

SVP Canada Region Railroads and President Genesee & Wyoming Canada Inc., Louis Gravel

SVP Midwest Region Railroads Genesee & Wyoming Railroad Services Inc., Gary R. Long

SVP Mountain West Region Railroads Genesee & Wyoming Railroad Services Inc., J. Bradley Ovitt

Executive Director and Chief Commercial Officer Genesee & Wyoming Australia Pty Ltd., John McArthur

Managing Director Freightliner Ltd. UK, Adam Cunliffe

Managing Director Freightliner Maintenance Ltd., Dave Curtis

Managing Director Freightliner Poland, Konstantin Skorik

Senior Vice President Operations Support, Tony (Tone) Long

Assistant Vice President Training and Development, Kathi D Maness

Vice President Talent Management, Mary E (Mar) Russell

Assistant Vice President Regional Mechanical, John (Jack) Kincaid

Vice President Port Operations, Andy Chunko

Vice President Of Transportation, Blake Jones

Vice President, Donald (Don) Robey

Vice President Finance And Administration, Gerald Sattora

Vice President ?? Commercial Counsel, Kenneth Charron

Vice President Sales and Marketing, Larry (Lar) Gomez

Assistant Vice President Industrial Development, Russ (Russell) Smitley

Assistant Vice President Industrial Development, Kimberly (Kim) Thompson

Chairman, Mortimer B. Fuller, age 73

Secretary; Vice President, Harald B Findlay

Auditors: PricewaterhouseCoopers LLP

LOCATIONS

HQ: Genesee & Wyoming Inc.
20 West Avenue, Darien, CT 06820
Phone: 203 202-8900
Web: www.gwrr.com

PRODUCTS/OPERATIONS

2013 Sales

	$ mil.	% of total
Freight		
Agricultural products	130.6	9
Chemicals & plastics	128.9	8
Metals	127.8	8
Metallic ores	125.9	8
Pulp & paper	112.7	7
Coal & coke	110.8	7
Imtermodal	98.7	6
Minerals & stone	96.8	6
Lumber & forest products	79.1	5
Petroleum products	65.2	4
Food ot kindred products	32.0	2
Autos & auto parts	26.4	2
Waste	22.8	1
Other	19.7	1
Non-freight		
Railcar switching	161.9	11
Demurrage & storage	58.3	4
Construction revenue	41.7	3
Car hire & rental income	34.7	2
Car repair services	21.1	1
Fuel sales to third parties	0.4	-
Other	73.5	5
Total	**1,569.0**	**100**

COMPETITORS

Anacostia Rail Holdings	Iowa Interstate Railroad
Arkansas & Missouri Railroad	Kansas City Southern
Burlington Northern Santa Fe	Montana Rail Link
	Norfolk Southern
CSX	OmniTRAX
Canadian National Railway	Pan Am Railways
	Pinsly Railroad
Canadian Pacific Railway	Pioneer Railcorp
	Providence and Worcester Railroad
Dakota Minnesota & Eastern Railroad	Union Pacific
	Watco Companies

HISTORICAL FINANCIALS

Company Type: Public

Income Statement

FYE: December 31

	REVENUE ($ mil.)	NET INCOME ($ mil.)	NET PROFIT MARGIN	EMPLOYEES
12/15	2,000.4	225.0	11.2%	7,500.0
12/14	1,639.0	261.0	15.9%	5,200.0
12/13	1,569.0	272.0	17.3%	4,800.0
12/12	874.9	52.4	6.0%	4,600.0
12/11	829.1	119.4	14.4%	2,620.0
Annual Growth	24.6%	17.1%	—	30.1%

2015 Year-End Financials

Debt ratio: 33.9%	No. of shares (mil.): 57.7
Return on equity: 9.2%	Dividends
Cash ($ mil.): 35.9	Yield: —
Current ratio: 1.08	Payout: —
Long-term debt ($ mil.): 2,223.3	Market value ($ mil.): 3,100.0

	STOCK PRICE ($) FY Close	P/E High/Low		PER SHARE ($) Earnings	Dividends	Book Value
12/15	53.69	26	13	3.89	0.00	43.64
12/14	89.92	22	18	4.58	0.00	43.68
12/13	96.05	20	15	4.79	0.00	40.11
12/12	76.08	68	43	1.02	0.00	40.23
12/11	60.58	21	15	2.79	0.00	22.63
Annual Growth	(3.0%)	—	—	8.7%	—	17.8%

Gentex Corp.

Gentex would agree that competitors never look better than when they are in the rearview. The company focuses on designing making and marketing interior and exterior auto-dimming rearview mirrors and camera-based driver-assist systems for the automotive market. It serves customers worldwide but its largest base includes big carmakers such as Toyota General Motors and Volkswagen. Its products are found as standard or optional features on hundreds of vehicle models. To a lesser degree Gentex also makes dimmable aircraft windows found on commercial aircraft and fire protection products —including smoke detectors fire alarms and signaling devices —primarily for commercial buildings.

Geographic Reach Operating through five manufacturing facilities in Michigan Gentex has additional offices in the US Korea Canada France Mexico China Japan Sweden Hungary and the UK. Unsurprisingly the company's largest markets are the leading car production countries of the US

(32% of net sales) Germany (19%) and Japan (10%).

Operations

The company's fire protection products are primarily sold to domestic distributors and OEMs of fire and security systems. Within the aerospace industry Gentex has delivered dimmable aircraft windows to the production line of Boeing's new 787 Dreamliner series and to Hawker Beechcraft for its business-class Beechcraft King Air 350i airplane. Gentex's dimmable window systems are marketed by PPG Aerospace under the brand name Alteos Interactive Window Systems.

Sales and Marketing The company's top customer is Volkswagen (14% of sales). Other major clients have included BMW Ford Chrysler and Nissan. Gentex markets its products directly to OEMs as well as through Tier 1 suppliers.

Financial Performance The company has achieved unprecedented growth over the years with revenues jumping 17% from $223 million in 2013 to $289 million in 2014. Profits also surged 29% from $223 million to $289 million over that same time period. (Both 2014 totals counted as historical milestones for the company.)

The historic growth for 2014 was fueled by increased sales from automotive products and other products. Automotive net sales spiked due to its acquisition of HomeLink and an 11% increase in auto-dimming mirror shipments. Dimmable aircraft window sales also increased 54% year over year and fire protection sales surged by 4%.

Strategy To boost production capacity and support growth in its core geographic territories Gentex is busy making investments in its facilities. It constructed a new technology center adjacent to its headquarters in Zeeland Michigan and it is making a number of facility upgrades and renovations. The investments support the company's optimistic sales forecast and anticipated growing demand for high-tech camera-based automotive products such as Gentex's rear camera displays which consist of a liquid crystal display (LCD) that works with a rear-mounted video camera to provide a rear view while backing up and its SmartBeam high-beam assist system which uses a camera-on-a-chip to maximize forward lighting while eliminating the task of turning the high beams on and off manually. Both are integrated into Gentex auto-dimming mirrors.

Mergers and AcquisitionsGentex has also achieved milestone revenues due to acquisitions. In 2013 it obtained HomeLink a wireless vehicle/home communications product that enables drivers to remotely activate garage door openers entry door locks home lighting security systems entry gates and other radio frequency convenience products. Gentex integrated HomeLink into its interior auto-dimming rearview mirrors product portfolio. In 2014 Gentex acquired Helmet Integrated Systems Ltd (HISL). Headquartered in the UK HISL provides helmets communications equipment and respiratory protection for civil defense security and industrial personnel. The addition of HISL accelerated Gentex's international growth by providing it immediate access to new markets particularly within the UK.

HISTORY

At 23 Fred Bauer had already started and sold one company before founding Gentex in 1974. A maker of dual-cell photoelectric smoke detectors Gentex found its niche with products that had fewer false alarms and could detect slow smoldering fires. The company went public in 1981.

The next year Gentex entered the automotive market with the first electromechanical dimming mirror to beat the glare of nighttime driving. (Electrochromic technology uses electricity to darken a material.) The product was soon snapped up by Ford and General Motors to the tune of 200000 units a year. Five years later Gentex debuted the interior Night Vision Safety (NVS) electrochromic automatic-dimming mirror. Exterior NVS mirrors were introduced in 1991.

Gentex entered an agreement in 1992 with Japan's Ichikoh Industries to market mirrors in Asia. The following year it established a European office. Returning to its roots Gentex in 1993 introduced an AC/DC smoke detector. That year rival Donnelly paid $3.6 million in damages for infringing on Gentex's electrochromic mirror patent. Gentex formed a German subsidiary Gentex GmbH in 1994 and two years later opened an $8 million plant near its Michigan headquarters.

In 1997 Gentex developed a compass mirror a headlamp control mirror and a mirror that displays outside temperature. The next year it bought a stake in Photobit a developer of pixel sensor technology and sold more than 3.3 million NVS mirrors. In 1999 DaimlerChrysler agreed to equip all its models with Gentex mirrors.

Adding to its manufacturing capacity Gentex in 2000 completed the construction of a $12 million mirror manufacturing plant in Zeeland Michigan and made plans to build a factory in Europe. Adding more equipment to rearview mirrors paid off when GM announced that it would place the OnStar communications system in Gentex's interior mirrors in 1 million automobiles.

In 2002 Gentex announced that it would bring its new SmartBeam product to market by mid-2004. SmartBeam allowed drivers to use their bright lights more easily because the high beam self-dimmed when it detected an oncoming car. SureBeam came to market in 2004 the same year Gentex finished constructing a sales and engineering facility in Erlenbach Germany. The facility was intended to help Gentex better serve its European customers by offering greater logistics sales and engineering support.

EXECUTIVES

Chairman and CEO, Fred T. Bauer, age 74, $464,031 total compensation
SVP, Mark Newton, age 57, $257,040 total compensation
VP Operations, Paul Flynn, $153,273 total compensation
VP Europe, Brad Bosma
CFO and VP of Finance, Steve Downing
Vice President, Robert Steel
Vice President Marketing, Keiffer Sestric
Vice President Of Finance, Jenny Dykgraaf
Vice President Advanced Materials and Process Development, Bill (Billy) Tonar
Vice President Quality, Ken Horner
Vice President Operations, John (Jack) Arnold
Vice President of Marketing, Keifer Sestric
Senior Vice President International, James (Jamie) Hollrs
Treasurer, Jake (Jacob) Kemme
Treasurer, Randy Beute
Treasurer, Mike (Mikey) Hoffmann
Board Member, Eric (Ric) Domke
Auditors: Ernst & Young LLP

LOCATIONS

HQ: Gentex Corp.
600 N. Centennial Street, Zeeland, MI 49464
Phone: 616 772-1800   **Fax:** 616 772-7348
Web: www.gentex.com

PRODUCTS/OPERATIONS

Selected Products

Automotive
Auto-dimming mirrors
Curved glass mirrors
Custom sensors (for detecting velocity rain and humidity)
Interior lighting
Microphones
Mirror-based displays
Side blind zone indicators
SmartBeam (automatic high beam system integrated into auto-dimming mirror)
Telematics systems
Razor (turn signal lights)
Rear camera display (LCD display integrated into auto-dimming mirror that works with a video camera mounted at rear of vehicle)
Fire protection
Audio and visual signaling appliances
Bells and speakers
Carbon monoxide alarms
Photoelectric smoke alarms and detectors
Other
Dimmable aircraft windows

COMPETITORS

Ficosa
Guardian Industries
Ichikoh
Ingersoll-Rand Security Technologies
Magna Mirrors
Murakami Corp.
Safety Vision
SimplexGrinnell
UTC Climate Controls & Security
Universal Security Instruments
Visteon

HISTORICAL FINANCIALS

Company Type: Public

Income Statement

FYE: December 31

	REVENUE ($ mil.)	NET INCOME ($ mil.)	NET PROFIT MARGIN	EMPLOYEES
12/15	1,543.6	318.4	20.6%	4,757.0
12/14	1,375.5	288.6	21.0%	4,196.0
12/13	1,171.8	222.9	19.0%	3,801.0
12/12	1,099.5	168.5	15.3%	3,605.0
12/11	1,023.7	164.6	16.1%	3,481.0
Annual Growth	10.8%	17.9%	—	8.1%

2015 Year-End Financials

Debt ratio: 10.8%
Return on equity: 19.3%
Cash ($ mil.): 551.5
Current ratio: 7.51
Long-term debt ($ mil.): 225.6

No. of shares (mil.): 291.3
Dividends
  Yield: 2.0%
  Payout: 30.5%
Market value ($ mil.): 4,664.0

	STOCK PRICE ($) FY Close	P/E High/Low		PER SHARE ($) Earnings	Dividends	Book Value
12/15	16.01	33	14	1.08	0.33	5.91
12/14	36.13	38	27	0.98	0.30	5.32
12/13	32.98	43	24	0.78	0.28	4.56
12/12	18.85	53	25	0.59	0.26	3.92
12/11	29.59	58	38	0.57	0.24	3.56
Annual Growth	(14.2%)	—	—	17.3%	8.9%	13.5%

Gentherm Inc

Don't worry TED can keep your car seat cool ... or warm. Gentherm develops thermoelectric device (TED) technology and incorporates it into its branded climate-control seat (CCS) which allows year-round temperature control and ventilation of car and truck seats on more than 50 vehicle models available in North America Europe and Asia that are made by Ford General Motors and Nissan. Gentherm also provides heated and cooled cup holder and cable systems in addition to mattress systems. The company has locations around in 11 countries worldwide with the US representing its largest market.

Geographic Reach

Gentherm has facilities in Germany Mexico China Canada Japan England Korea Malta Hungary the Ukraine and the US. The US accounts for 45% of its total sales while Germany generates 11% and China accounts for 11%. Korea and Japan collectively account for 17% of Gentherm's total sales.

Sales and Marketing

Gentherm's largest customers include Johnson Controls (24% of total sales) Lear Corporation (21%) and Bosch Automotive (9%). Other major clients include General Motors Volkswagen Ford Hyundai Fiat and BMW.

Financial Performance

Gentherm has achieved unprecedented growth over the last few years primarily due to acquisitions it has made. In 2014 its revenues surged 23% to peak at a record-setting $881 million. The historic growth was fueled by overall increases in new program launches for its climate-control seat (CCS) technology coupled with additional revenue gained from an acquisition it made in 2014.

Gentherm's profits have also reached historic levels more than doubling from $34 million in 2013 to $70 million in 2014. Its operating cash flow climbed 34% from $60 million in 2013 to $80 million in 2014 due to the increased profits increases in accounts receivable due to product revenues and timing differences between the collection of sales in 2014.

Mergers and Acquisitions

The company has achieved historic revenue growth over the years primarily through the use of acquisitions. In mid-2014 it acquired Global Thermoelectric (GTE) a Calgary-based maker of industrial thermoelectric generator systems and remote power generation products. The acquisition gave the company additional expertise in thermoelectric generators and provided it with access to a number of new industrial and commercial markets. GTE operates as a subsidiary of the company and has been rebranded to Gentherm Global Power Technologies.

EXECUTIVES

VP CFO and Treasurer, Barry G. Steele, age 45, $350,000 total compensation
VP and General Counsel, Kenneth J. (Ken) Phillips, $370,000 total compensation
President Automotive Business Unit, Frithjof Oldorff, $404,575 total compensation
President and CEO, Daniel R. Coker, age 64, $700,000 total compensation
VP Product Development, Darren A. Schumacher, $319,300 total compensation
Vice President Product Strategy and Business Planning, John (Jack) Marx

Vice President Electronics Business Unit, Greg (Greggy) Steinl
Vice President Sales Marketing, Dan Pace
Vice President Business Development, Ryan (Ry) Gaul
Chairman, Oscar B. (Bud) Marx, age 77
Auditors: Grant Thornton LLP

LOCATIONS

HQ: Gentherm Inc
21680 Haggerty Road, Northville, MI 48167
Phone: 248 504-0500
Web: www.gentherm.com

PRODUCTS/OPERATIONS

2012 Sales

	% of total
W.E.T.	76
CCS	24
Total	**100**

Selected Services

Advancing core technology
Noise vibration and airflow management
Program management
Testing
Thermoelectric applications

COMPETITORS

Delphi Automotive Systems
Leggett & Platt
Magna International
Robert Bosch
Toyota Boshoku
Visteon

HISTORICAL FINANCIALS

Company Type: Public

Income Statement

FYE: December 31

	REVENUE ($ mil.)	NET INCOME ($ mil.)	NET PROFIT MARGIN	EMPLOYEES
12/15	856.4	95.3	11.1%	10,098.0
12/14	811.3	70.1	8.6%	8,607.0
12/13	662.0	33.8	5.1%	7,403.0
12/12	554.9	17.8	3.2%	116.0
12/11	369.5	10.3	2.8%	110.0
Annual Growth	23.4%	74.3%	—	209.5%

2015 Year-End Financials

Debt ratio: 15.1%
Return on equity: 28.1%
Cash ($ mil.): 144.4
Current ratio: 2.93
Long-term debt ($ mil.): 92.8

No. of shares (mil.): 36.3
Dividends
  Yield: —
  Payout: —
Market value ($ mil.): 1,722.0

	STOCK PRICE ($) FY Close	P/E High/Low		PER SHARE ($) Earnings	Dividends	Book Value
12/15	47.40	22	14	2.62	0.00	10.58
12/14	36.62	26	12	1.95	0.00	8.24
12/13	26.81	27	14	0.94	0.00	6.64
12/12	13.30	45	26	0.39	0.00	6.18
12/11	14.26	200	113	0.09	0.00	4.83
Annual Growth	35.0%	—	—	132.3%	—	21.6%

Gigamon Inc

An invisibility cloak won't fly at Gigamon. A Unified Visibility Fabric on the other hand will definitely fly. The company's visibility fabric is a layer of technology that steers information on networks to the appropriate destination. Gigamon's products such as the GigaVUE platform can handle video voice and data. Gigamon's products which include cloud-based software help IT managers of enterprises data centers and service providers see what's happening with their networks manage risks and maintain network performance. Gigamon has customers in finance health care higher education government technology and telecom as well as other businesses. The company went public in 2013.

Geographic ReachGigamon is based in Santa Clara California and also has offices in New York City and the Washington D.C. area. Overseas it has offices in the UK Russia Hong Kong China Japan Australia Singapore and Dubai. About 75% of Gigamon's sales are to US customers with the European region accounting for 14%.Sales and MarketingGigamon's direct sales organization is divided into the Americas; the Europe Middle East and Africa (EMEA); and Asia-Pacific. It also sells through channel partners which include resellers and distributors. About two-thirds of Gigamon's North American sales are through channel partners Global Convergence (formerly Interlink Communications Systems)47% and Arrow Enterprise Computing Solutions 16%. The company's end-user customers include two-thirds of the Fortune 100.Financial PerformanceGigamon's revenue has grown at a steady pace since 2010. It increased 12% to $157 million in 2014 from 2013 boosted by a 34% increase in service revenue. Sales of the high density H-Series products aided the product side's 4% growth. Gigamon's net loss was nearly $41 million in 2014 compared to a loss of about $9.5 million in 2013. The company ramped up spending on research and development and sales and marketing in the past two years as it tries to wrap up new customers in the fabric.StrategyGigamon has engineered its products to address markets beyond the large enterprises it has targeted. With the GigaVUE-HB1 platform the company has a Visibility Fabric product for smaller environments and mid-size enterprises. In another move the company in 2015 said it would make its GigaVUE-OS product available on third-party “white box” hardware. That would enable customers to choose new deployment options.

EXECUTIVES

SVP Engineering, Sachi Sambandan, age 51, $1,698,773 total compensation
CFO, Rex S. Jackson, age 56
CEO, Paul A. Hooper, age 53, $348,624 total compensation
SVP Corporate Development and Chief Legal Officer, Paul B. Shinn, age 46, $282,352 total compensation
CTO, Shehzad T. Merchant, age 47, $276,484 total compensation
VP Worldwide Operations, Dave Cox
VP Europe Middle East and Africa (EMEA), Gerard Allison
Senior Vice President Worldwide Sales, Helmut Wilke
Vice President of Product Management, Ananda Rajagopal

Vice President and Associate General Counsel, Jennifer (Jen) Miller
Regional Vice President Sales CALA, Carlos (Carl) Perea
Chairman, Corey M. Mulloy, age 44
Auditors: PricewaterhouseCoopers LLP

LOCATIONS

HQ: Gigamon Inc
   3300 Olcott Street, Santa Clara, CA 95054
Phone: 408 831-4000
Web: www.gigamon.com

PRODUCTS/OPERATIONS

2014 Sales

	$ mil.	% of total
Products	105.6	67
Services	51.5	33
Total	**157.1**	**100**

COMPETITORS

ADTRAN	HP
Alcatel-Lucent	Huawei Technologies
Arista Networks	IBM Internet Security
Brocade Communications	Systems
Check Point Software	Juniper Networks
Cisco Systems	MRV Communications
Citrix Systems	NSN
Ericsson	Riverbed Technology
Extreme Networks	Sycamore Networks
F5 Networks	Solutions
Fortinet	

HISTORICAL FINANCIALS

Company Type: Public

Income Statement

FYE: December 26

	REVENUE ($ mil.)	NET INCOME ($ mil.)	NET PROFIT MARGIN	EMPLOYEES
12/15	221.9	6.1	2.8%	482.0
12/14	157.1	(40.7)	—	371.0
12/13	140.3	(9.5)	—	352.0
12/12	96.7	7.5	7.8%	288.0
12/11	68.1	16.9	24.9%	0.0
Annual Growth	**34.4%**	**(22.3%)**	**—**	**—**

2015 Year-End Financials

Debt ratio: —
Return on equity: 4.5%
Cash ($ mil.): 120.2
Current ratio: 2.61
Long-term debt ($ mil.): —
No. of shares (mil.): 34.3
Dividends
   Yield: —
   Payout: —
Market value ($ mil.): 921.0

	STOCK PRICE ($) FY Close	P/E High/Low	PER SHARE ($) Earnings	Dividends	Book Value
12/15	26.82	193 85	0.17	0.00	4.53
12/14	17.47	— —	(1.27)	0.00	3.54
12/13	28.29	— —	(0.39)	0.00	3.96
Annual Growth	**(2.6%)**	**— —**	**—**	**—**	**6.9%**

Globus Medical Inc

If Globus Medical helps you stand up straight then the company's products are working. Globus Medical makes medical devices used during spinal surgery to treat a variety of spinal disorders and assist surgeons with different types of spinal procedures from screws and plates to disc replacement systems and biomaterials for bone grafts. Top sellers include the REVERE screw-and-rod system and the COALITION cervical fusion device. Altogether Globus Medical has more than 100 spinal devices on the market in the US; its products are also sold in about 25 international markets. Globus Medical went public in 2012.

Operations
The company divides its products into two categories –innovative fusion or disruptive technologies. Innovative fusion products are used in spinal fusion surgery a common and traditional procedure where two individual vertebrae are fused together. This division accounts for about 60% of sales.

The other 40% is made up of products in the disruptive technologies segment a growing category of newer generation products used in novel surgical procedures or as improvements to existing procedures as well as for minimally invasive procedures used as an alternative to surgery.

Geographic Reach
Even though international sales accounts for less than 10% of the company's overall revenues sales outside the US are growing rapidly.

Sales and Marketing
Globus Medical uses direct sales to promote its products in the US primarily to spine surgeons and hospitals. The company is rapidly adding direct sales personnel in international countries; it also uses distributor representatives to sell in some global markets. Global sales are conducted in Europe Australia India South Africa South America and the Middle East.

Strategy
Putting new products on the market is crucial in the medical device industry and Globus Medical has launched more than 110 new products since its inception. The firm introduced 14 new products in 2012 including the MARS anterior retractor and the SECURE-C cervical artificial disc. The company has also entered a new market by introducing the Algea Therapies line of pain management products. Globus Medical is pursuing R&D projects in both the innovative fusion and disruptive technology segments; in addition to new product development the firm works to improve existing products.

Other means of growth include pursuit of acquisitions or strategic alliances increasing market penetration growing the sales force and hiring and retaining personnel with market experience.

Mergers and Acquisitions
In 2016 Glovus Medical acquired the international business of medical device firm Alphatec for $80 million. The deal includes the international distribution business including units in Japan Brazil the UK and Italy.

Company Background
Globus Medical was founded in 2003 by CEO David Paul a former product development director at bone-related medical device maker Synthes. Globus Medical relied on venture capital funding prior to its 2012 IPO.

EXECUTIVES

Chairman and CEO, David C. Paul, age 49, $405,318 total compensation
President COO and Acting CFO, David M. (Dave) Demski, age 58, $337,765 total compensation
Group President Commercial Operations, A. Brett Murphy, age 52, $309,309 total compensation

SVP Operations, David D. Davidar, age 50, $234,738
total compensation
President, Anthony L. Williams, age 45
SVP and CFO, Daniel T. Scavilla, age 51
Vice President Of Operations, Steve McFee
Vice President Of Sales, Jay (JayJay) Martin
Auditors: Grant Thornton LLP

LOCATIONS

HQ: Globus Medical Inc
2560 General Armistead Avenue, Audubon, PA 19403
Phone: 610 930-1800   **Fax:** 302 636-5454
Web: www.globusmedical.com

PRODUCTS/OPERATIONS

2015 Sales

	$ mil.	% of total
Innovative fusion	288.1	53
Disruptive technologies	256.7	47
Total	**544.8**	**100**

Selected Products

Innovative Fusion Products:
  Cervical
  ASSURE (anterior cervical plate system)
  ELLIPSE (posterior occipital cervical thoracic
  stabilization system)
  PROVIDENCE (anterior cervical plate system)
  VIP (anterior cervical plate system)
  XTEND (anterior cervical plate system)
  Thoracolumbar:
  BEACON Posted Screw (posted pedicle screw system)
  REVERE Degen (comprehensive pedicle screw and rod
  system)
  SI-LOK (sacroiliac joint fixation system)
  Interbody/Corpectomy
  COALITION (anterior cervical stand-alone fusion
  device)
  COLONIAL (anterior cervical interbody fusion device)
  FORTIFY (self-locking expandable corpectomy device)
  INDEPENDENCE (anterior lumbar stand-alone fusion
  device)
  SUSTAIN (spacers for partial or complete
  vertebrectomy)
  XPAND (expandable corpectomy spacer)
  Deformity Tumor and Trauma
  REVERE Anterior (pedicle screw and rod deformity
  system)
  REVERE Deformity (comprehensive pedicle screw
  hook and rod deformity system)
  TRUSS (lateral compressible thoracolumbar plate
  system)
Minimally Invasive Surgery Products:
  CALIBER (expandable posterior lumbar interbody
  fusion device)
  CALIBER-L (expandable lateral lumbar interbody
  fusion device)
  INTERCONTINENTAL (lateral lumbar interbody fusion
  device)
  MARS 3V (three-blade retractor system)
  REVOLVE (minimally invasive pedicle screw and rod
  system)
  SIGNATURE (articulating transforaminal interbody
  fusion device)
  TRANSCONTINENTAL (lateral lumbar interbody
  fusion device)
  Motion Preservation:
  FLEXUS (minimally invasive unilateral PEEK
  interspinous process spacer)
  ORBIT-R (anterior lumbar disc replacement)
  SECURE-CR (articulating cervical disc replacement
  device)
  SP-FIX (interspinous process fusion device)
  TRANSITION (stabilization system)
  TRIUMPH (transforaminal lumbar disc replacement
  device)
  ZYFLEX (stabilization system)

COMPETITORS

Alphatec Spine	NuVasive
DePuy Spine	Orthofix

Integra LifeSciences	Stryker
Medtronic	Synthes
Medtronic Sofamor	Zimmer Biomet
Danek	

HISTORICAL FINANCIALS

Company Type: Public

Income Statement

FYE: December 31

	REVENUE ($ mil.)	NET INCOME ($ mil.)	NET PROFIT MARGIN	EMPLOYEES
12/15	544.7	112.7	20.7%	1,200.0
12/14	474.3	92.4	19.5%	900.0
12/13	434.4	68.6	15.8%	850.0
12/12	385.9	73.8	19.1%	810.0
12/11	331.4	60.7	18.3%	724.0
Annual Growth	**13.2%**	**16.7%**	**—**	**13.5%**

2015 Year-End Financials

Debt ratio: —
Return on equity: 17.3%
Cash ($ mil.): 86.2
Current ratio: 6.59
Long-term debt ($ mil.): —

No. of shares (mil.): 95.3
Dividends
  Yield: —
  Payout: —
Market value ($ mil.): 2,652.0

	STOCK PRICE ($) FY Close	P/E High/Low	PER SHARE ($) Earnings	Dividends	Book Value
12/15	27.82	24 17	1.17	0.00	7.50
12/14	23.77	28 19	0.97	0.00	6.18
12/13	20.18	27 14	0.73	0.00	5.06
12/12	10.49	23 13	0.80	0.00	4.23
Annual Growth	**38.4%**	**— —**	**13.5%**	**—**	**21.0%**

GMS Inc

LOCATIONS

HQ: GMS Inc
100 Crescent Centre Parkway, Suite 800, Tucker, GA
30084
Phone: 800 392-4619
Web: www.gms.com

HISTORICAL FINANCIALS

Company Type: Public

Income Statement

FYE: April 30

	REVENUE ($ mil.)	NET INCOME ($ mil.)	NET PROFIT MARGIN	EMPLOYEES
04/16	1,858.1	12.5	0.7%	3,900.0
04/15	1,570.0	(13.8)	—	3,700.0
04/14*	127.3	(18.9)	—	0.0
03/14	1,226.0	(200.8)	—	0.0
04/13	1,161.6	(182.6)	—	0.0
Annual Growth	**12.5%**	**—**	**—**	**—**

*Fiscal year change

2016 Year-End Financials

Debt ratio: 51.4%
Return on equity: 4.1%
Cash ($ mil.): 19.0
Current ratio: 2.19
Long-term debt ($ mil.): 609.0

No. of shares (mil.): 32.8
Dividends
  Yield: —
  Payout: —
Market value ($ mil.): —

Golden Entertainment Inc

Even though Lakes Entertainment doesn't own a casino it still keeps its eye on the slots. The company manages Indian-owned casinos including the Four Winds Casino Resort in New Buffalo Township Michigan (approximately 75 miles east of Chicago) for the Pokagon Band of Potawatomi Indians; and the Red Hawk Casino in El Dorado County California (some 30 miles east of Sacramento) for the Shingle Springs Band of Miwok Indians. Nearly all of Lakes Entertainment's revenues come from management fees. The company is also exploring other development projects through agreements with tribes for additional casinos in Michigan and California and a possible non-Indian casino project in Mississippi.

The amount of management fees Lakes Entertainment earns is dependent on how much revenue its casinos generate. Not surprisingly its managed casinos have been feeling the negative effects of a down economy. At Red Hawk the casino is hurting from an especially challenging market in California and in 2009 the property cut 250 of its 1750 full-time staff positions. Lakes Entertainment is also hurting from new competition that entered the Four Winds Casino Resort market that year.

Then in 2010 the Iowa Tribe of Oklahoma terminated its contract with the company for the management of its Cimarron Casino in Perkins Oklahoma. Cimarron houses approximately 375 slot machines and a snack bar. The end of that agreement put a dent in one of Lakes Entertainment's main revenue streams —Lakes had been receiving an annual management fee that amounted to 30% of Cimarron's total revenues in excess of $4 million.

Chairman and CEO Lyle Berman owns more than 15% of Lakes Entertainment.

EXECUTIVES

President CFO Treasurer and Director, Timothy J.
Cope, age 64, $350,000 total compensation
Chairman and CEO, Lyle Berman, age 74, $500,000
total compensation
Investor Relations, Janice Saeugling
**Assistant General Manager and CFO Red Hawk
Casino,** Terry Contreras, age 54
VP Gaming, Scott Just, $185,000 total compensation
General Manager Red Hawk Casino, Tracy Mimno
President CFO Treasurer and Director, Timothy J.
Cope, age 64
Director, Neil I. Sell, age 74
Director, Larry C. Barenbaum, age 70
Director, Richard D. White, age 62
Director, Ray M. Moberg, age 67
Auditors: Piercy Bowler Taylor & Kern, Certified
Public Accountants

LOCATIONS

HQ: Golden Entertainment Inc
6595 S. Jones Boulevard, Las Vegas, NV 89118
Phone: 702 893-7777
Web: www.lakesentertainment.com

COMPETITORS

Caesars Entertainment
Choctaw Resort Development Enterprise

Colville Tribal Enterprise Corporation
Hollywood Casino Bay St. Louis
Isle of Capri Casinos
Pinnacle Entertainment

HISTORICAL FINANCIALS
Company Type: Public

Income Statement   FYE: December 31

	REVENUE ($ mil.)	NET INCOME ($ mil.)	NET PROFIT MARGIN	EMPLOYEES
12/15	177.0	24.5	13.8%	2,563.0
12/14	55.1	(24.8)	—	504.0
12/13	38.7	18.6	48.1%	536.0
12/12*	10.9	3.2	29.4%	134.0
01/12	35.5	(1.8)	—	19.0
Annual Growth	49.4%	—	—	240.8%

*Fiscal year change

2015 Year-End Financials

Debt ratio: 39.2%
Return on equity: 15.2%
Cash ($ mil.): 69.1
Current ratio: 3.30
Long-term debt ($ mil.): 139.4

No. of shares (mil.): 21.8
Dividends
  Yield: —
  Payout: —
Market value ($ mil.): 224.0

	STOCK PRICE ($) FY Close	P/E High/Low		PER SHARE ($) Earnings	Dividends	Book Value
12/15	10.23	7	5	1.43	0.00	9.63
12/14	6.83	—	—	(1.86)	0.00	8.04
12/13	3.97	3	2	1.40	0.00	9.89
12/12*	3.06	13	8	0.24	0.00	8.49
01/12	1.85	—	—	(0.14)	0.00	8.24
Annual Growth	53.3%	—	—	—	—	4.0%

*Fiscal year change

Goldman Sachs BDC Inc

Auditors: PricewaterhouseCoopers LLP

LOCATIONS

HQ: Goldman Sachs BDC Inc
  200 West Street, New York, NY 10282
Phone: 212 902-0300
Web: www.goldmansachsbdc.com

HISTORICAL FINANCIALS
Company Type: Public

Income Statement   FYE: December 31

	REVENUE ($ mil.)	NET INCOME ($ mil.)	NET PROFIT MARGIN	EMPLOYEES
12/15	118.4	74.5	63.0%	0.0
12/14	73.2	52.7	72.0%	0.0
12/13	22.8	15.9	69.8%	0.0
12/12	0.1	(0.1)	—	0.0
Annual Growth	800.9%	—	—	—

2015 Year-End Financials

Debt ratio: 36.9%
Return on equity: —
Cash ($ mil.): 22.7
Current ratio: 1.66
Long-term debt ($ mil.): 419.0

No. of shares (mil.): 36.3
Dividends
  Yield: 9.4%
  Payout: 84.1%
Market value ($ mil.): 690.0

	STOCK PRICE ($) FY Close	P/E High/Low		PER SHARE ($) Earnings	Dividends	Book Value
12/15	19.00	12	8	2.14	1.80	18.97
12/14	0.00	—	—	1.77	1.69	2.54
Annual Growth	647.2%	—	—	20.9%	6.5%	—

GoPro, Inc.

Auditors: PricewaterhouseCoopers LLP

LOCATIONS

HQ: GoPro, Inc.
  3000 Clearview Way, San Mateo, CA 94402
Phone: 650 332-7600
Web: www.gopro.com

HISTORICAL FINANCIALS
Company Type: Public

Income Statement   FYE: December 31

	REVENUE ($ mil.)	NET INCOME ($ mil.)	NET PROFIT MARGIN	EMPLOYEES
12/15	1,619.9	36.1	2.2%	1,539.0
12/14	1,394.2	128.0	9.2%	970.0
12/13	985.7	60.5	6.1%	718.0
12/12	526.0	32.2	6.1%	347.0
12/11	234.2	24.6	10.5%	147.0
Annual Growth	62.2%	10.1%	—	79.9%

2015 Year-End Financials

Debt ratio: —
Return on equity: 5.1%
Cash ($ mil.): 474.0
Current ratio: 2.82
Long-term debt ($ mil.): —

No. of shares (mil.): 136.6
Dividends
  Yield: —
  Payout: —
Market value ($ mil.): 2,460.0

	STOCK PRICE ($) FY Close	P/E High/Low		PER SHARE ($) Earnings	Dividends	Book Value
12/15	18.01	248	63	0.25	0.00	5.65
12/14	63.22	88	29	0.92	0.00	4.97
Annual Growth	(71.5%)	—	—	(72.8%)	—	13.8%

GP Strategies Corp.

Auditors: KPMG LLP

LOCATIONS

HQ: GP Strategies Corp.
  70 Corporate Center, 11000 Broken Land Parkway,
  Suite 200, Columbia, MD 21044
Phone: 443 367-9600
Web: www.gpstrategies.com

HISTORICAL FINANCIALS
Company Type: Public

Income Statement   FYE: December 31

	REVENUE ($ mil.)	NET INCOME ($ mil.)	NET PROFIT MARGIN	EMPLOYEES
12/15	490.2	18.7	3.8%	3,250.0
12/14	501.8	27.1	5.4%	3,300.0
12/13	436.6	23.7	5.4%	3,009.0
12/12	401.5	22.6	5.6%	2,775.0
12/11	333.1	17.8	5.4%	2,523.0
Annual Growth	10.1%	1.3%	—	6.5%

2015 Year-End Financials

Debt ratio: 19.3%
Return on equity: 12.1%
Cash ($ mil.): 21.0
Current ratio: 1.32
Long-term debt ($ mil.): 11.1

No. of shares (mil.): 16.8
Dividends
  Yield: —
  Payout: —
Market value ($ mil.): 424.0

	STOCK PRICE ($) FY Close	P/E High/Low		PER SHARE ($) Earnings	Dividends	Book Value
12/15	25.11	34	20	1.09	0.00	9.38
12/14	33.93	23	16	1.43	0.00	8.85
12/13	29.79	24	16	1.23	0.00	10.09
12/12	20.65	17	11	1.18	0.00	8.78
12/11	13.48	15	10	0.94	0.00	7.63
Annual Growth	16.8%	—	—	3.8%	—	5.3%

Grand Canyon Education Inc

Grand Canyon Education (dba Grand Canyon University) spans a broad educational horizon. The regionally accredited educator offers graduate and undergraduate degrees online at its campus in Phoenix and onsite at corporate facilities. Grand Canyon University offers career-oriented degree programs focused on the core disciplines of business education health care and liberal arts. Working adults make up most of the school's student body. Grand Canyon University enrolls almost 60000 students annually; about 83% are in online programs and about 45% of those pursue advanced degrees. Most classes have a student-teacher ratio of about 20:1. The company was formed in 1949 as a not-for-profit college and in 2004.

Operations

Grand Canyon University keeps its enrollment numbers up by marketing itself to working adults (whom the company defines as 25 years and older) seeking to complete their education switch careers or earn a higher degree in the field in which they already work. Grand Canyon University attracts adult students with the flexibility and convenience of online classes and conversely adult students are attractive to Grand Canyon University because they are generally more stable able to finance their education and have higher completion rates than younger students. The school offers more than 100 degrees and concentrations.

Grand Canyon University derives about 80% of its income from tuition that is financed under Title IV programs (federal grants and loans to students awarded on the basis of their financial need). Other sources of income come from self-funding private loans other financial aid programs and employer tuition reimbursements.

Geographic Reach

Grand Canyon University has a traditional campus in Phoenix and it enrolls students from all 50 states and the District of Columbia in its online and corporate classes.

Sales and Marketing

Grand Canyon University markets the flexibility and convenience of online classes to working adults ad traditional students.

Financial Performance

After several years of rising revenue the trend continued in 2013 as the company made $598 million a 17% increase over the previous year. Most of that growth came from a 36% jump in enrollment. Net income increased 28% from $69 million to $89 million. Cash from operations however dropped about 18% due to provisions for bad debt and depreciation and amortization.

Strategy

To enhance its brand and continue to attract students Grand Canyon University invests in technology to update its infrastructure and expanding its physical campus. In 2012 it built its first parking garage. Other improvements have included constructing a basketball and entertainment arena a new dorm an activity center and an Arts and Sciences classroom building. The university also keeps tabs on industry trends and adjusts its course offerings accordingly. For example increased demand for nursing programs led the school to establish satellite locations at multiple hospitals where nursing students can complete their clinical education while also completing other course work online. It has similar onsite arrangements with certain employers such as schools and school districts through which students can pursue a profession in teaching. Also in 2012 it began transitioning from the NCAA's Division II to Division I a four-year process.

In 2015 it will open its second campus in Mesa Arizona. The Eastmark campus will house many of its science technology engineering and math programs.

Company Background

Originally founded as Grand Canyon College a private not-for-profit college in 1949 the university moved to its existing campus in Phoenix in 1951. In 2004 several of its stockholders acquired Grand Canyon University and converted it to a for-profit institution. The company then raised about $126 million through a public offering which was completed in 2008 after a four-month-long IPO drought in the US.

EXECUTIVES

CFO, Daniel E. (Dan) Bachus, age 45, $362,250 total compensation
President and CEO, Brian E. Mueller, age 62, $621,000 total compensation
COO, W. Stan Meyer, age 55, $362,250 total compensation
Provost, Hank Radda
Vice President of Budget Planning and Analysis, Richard (Dick) Volk
Vice President Content and Curriculum Services, Mark (Marky) Alexander
Chairman, Brent D. Richardson, age 54
Auditors: KPMG LLP

LOCATIONS

HQ: Grand Canyon Education Inc
 3300 W. Camelback Road, Phoenix, AZ 85017
Phone: 602 639-7500
Web: www.gcu.edu

PRODUCTS/OPERATIONS

2015 Student Enrollment by Degree Type

	% of total
Undergraduate degree	61
Graduate degree	39
Total	**100**

2015 Enrollment by Instructional Delivery Method

% of total	# of students
Online	80
Ground (Phoenix campus corporate studies)	20
Total	**100**

Selected Colleges

College of Humanities and Social Sciences
College of Theology
College of Education
College of Doctoral Studies
College of Fine Arts and Production
College of Nursing and Health Care Professions
College of Business
College of Science Engineering and Technology
Honors College

Selected Degree Programs

Athletic Training & Exercise Science
Business & Leadership
Computer Science & Information Technology
Health Care
Health Sciences & Pre-Med
Liberal Arts
MBA & EMBA
Nursing
Performing Arts & Digital Design
Psychology & Counseling
Teaching & Education Administration
Theology & Youth Ministry

COMPETITORS

American Public Education	Career Education
Apollo Education	DeVry Education Group
Arizona State University	Education Management
Azusa Pacific University	ITT Educational
Baylor University	Northern Arizona University
Bridgepoint Education	Strayer Education
Capella Education	UTI
	University of Arizona

HISTORICAL FINANCIALS

Company Type: Public

Income Statement

FYE: December 31

	REVENUE ($ mil.)	NET INCOME ($ mil.)	NET PROFIT MARGIN	EMPLOYEES
12/15	778.2	131.4	16.9%	3,650.0
12/14	691.0	111.4	16.1%	3,600.0
12/13	598.3	88.7	14.8%	3,100.0
12/12	511.2	69.4	13.6%	2,655.0
12/11	426.7	50.5	11.8%	2,550.0
Annual Growth	**16.2%**	**27.0%**	**—**	**9.4%**

2015 Year-End Financials

Debt ratio: 9.0%
Return on equity: 24.1%
Cash ($ mil.): 23.0
Current ratio: 1.17
Long-term debt ($ mil.): 74.0
No. of shares (mil.): 46.8
Dividends
 Yield: —
 Payout: —
Market value ($ mil.): 1,881.0

	STOCK PRICE ($) FY Close	P/E High/Low		PER SHARE ($) Earnings	Dividends	Book Value
12/15	40.12	16	13	2.78	0.00	13.02
12/14	46.66	21	15	2.37	0.00	10.19
12/13	43.60	24	11	1.92	0.00	7.49
12/12	23.47	16	10	1.53	0.00	5.23
12/11	15.96	18	11	1.12	0.00	3.69
Annual Growth	**25.9%**	—	—	**25.5%**	—	**37.1%**

Gray Television Inc

Gray Television has The Eye for local television markets. The company is the largest independent operator of TV stations affiliated with the CBS network with 17 stations in more than a dozen states. In total the company operates more than 35 stations in 30 midsized and smaller markets mostly in the Midwest and South. Its other stations are affiliated with ABC NBC and FOX. In addition to traditional analog signals Gray Television broadcasts an additional 40 digital channels mostly carrying programming from The CW and MyNetworkTV. Former CEO J. Mack Robinson and his family control nearly 40% of the company.

Operations

Approximately 70% of the company's revenues are generated from local advertising including political ads. The company also earns revenue from national ads retransmission consent (charging a fee to cable operators to carry its stations) and consulting as well as from a management contract with New Young Broadcasting Holding Company (formerly Young Broadcasting) to manage several of Young's stations.

Financial Performance

The company's revenue declined from $404 million in fiscal 2012 down to $346 million in fiscal 2013. Its net income and cash flow also decreased in fiscal 2013 compared to the previous period.

Strategy

Gray Television has benefited from its large portfolio of CBS affiliated stations as the Eye network has typically dominated the primetime ratings.

EXECUTIVES

EVP and CFO, James C. (Jim) Ryan, age 55, $500,000 total compensation
Vice Chairman President and CEO, Hilton H. Howell, age 53, $850,000 total compensation
EVP and Co-COO, Bob Smith, age 53
EVP and Co-COO, Nick Waller, age 62
EVP and Chief Digital and Technology Officer, Jason Effinger
EVP and Chief Legal and Development Officer, Kevin P. Latek, age 45, $550,000 total compensation
Auditors: RSM US LLP

LOCATIONS

HQ: Gray Television Inc
 4370 Peachtree Road, N.E., Atlanta, GA 30319
Phone: 404 504-9828
Web: www.gray.tv

PRODUCTS/OPERATIONS

2015 Sales

	% of total
Local	52
Retransmission consent	25
National	13
Internet	5
Political	3
Other	2
Total	**100**

Selected Television Stations

KAKE (ABC; Wichita-Hutchinson KS)
KBTX (CBS; Bryan TX)
KCRG (ABC MY ANT; Cedar Rapids IA)
KCWY (NBC; Casper WY)
KGIN (CBS; Grand Island NE)
KGWN (CBS NBC CW; Cheyenne WY)
KKCO (NBC; Grand Junction CO)
KKTV (CBS; Colorado Springs CO)
KLBY (ABC; Colby KS)
KMVT (CBS CWTwin Falls ID)
KNOE (CBS CW ABC; Monroe-El Dorado LA)
KOLN (CBS; Lincoln-Hastings-Kearney NE)
KOLO (ABC; Reno NV)
KOSA(CBS MY; Odessa - Midland TX)
KSNB (NBC MY; Lincoln - Hastings - Kearney NE)
KSTB (CBS CW; Scottsbluff NE)
KSVT (FOX MY; Twin Falls ID)
KUPK (ABC; Garden City KS)
KWTX (CBS; Waco-Temple-Bryan TX)
KXII (CBS; ShermanTX)
WAGM (FOX CBS; Presque Isle ME)
WAHU (FOX; Charlottesville VA)
WBKO (ABC; Bowling Green KY)
WCAV (CBS; Charlottesville VA)
WCTV (CBS; Tallahassee FL)
WEAU (NBC La Crosse-Eau Claire WI)
WHSV (ABC; Harrisonburg VA)
WIBW (CBS; Topeka KS)
WIFR (CBS; Rockford IL)
WILX (NBC; Lansing MI)
WITN (NBC; Greenville NC)
WJHG (NBC; Panama City FL)
WKYT (CBS; Lexington KY)
WMTV (NBC; Madison WI)
WNDU (NBC; South Bend IN)
WOWT (NBC; Omaha NE)
WRDW (CBS; Augusta GA)
WSAW (CBS; Wausau-Rhinelander WI)
WSAZ (NBC; Charleston WV)
WSWG (CBS; Albany GA)
WTAP (NBC; Parkersburg WV)
WTOK (ABC; Meridian MS)
WTVY (CBS; Dothan AL)
WVAW (CBS; Charlottesville VA)
WVLT (CBS; Knoxville TN)
WYMT (CBS; Hazard KY)

COMPETITORS

ACME Communications	Morris Multimedia
Barrington	New Young Broadcasting
Broadcasting	Nexstar Broadcasting
Evening Post	Quincy Newspapers
Hoak Media	Raycom Media
Journal Broadcast	Schurz Communications
Group	Sinclair Broadcast
Media General	Group

HISTORICAL FINANCIALS

Company Type: Public

Income Statement

FYE: December 31

	REVENUE ($ mil.)	NET INCOME ($ mil.)	NET PROFIT MARGIN	EMPLOYEES
12/15	597.3	39.3	6.6%	3,819.0
12/14	508.1	48.0	9.5%	2,937.0
12/13	346.3	18.2	5.3%	2,248.0
12/12	404.8	28.1	6.9%	2,084.0
12/11	307.1	9.0	2.9%	2,105.0
Annual Growth	**18.1%**	**44.4%**	**—**	**16.1%**

2015 Year-End Financials

Debt ratio: 57.6%
Return on equity: 12.1%
Cash ($ mil.): 97.3
Current ratio: 3.26
Long-term debt ($ mil.): 1,235.5
No. of shares (mil.): 72.3
Dividends
 Yield: —
 Payout: —
Market value ($ mil.): 1,179.0

	STOCK PRICE ($) FY Close	P/E High/Low	PER SHARE ($) Earnings	Dividends	Book Value
12/15	16.30	31 16	0.57	0.00	5.93
12/14	11.20	18 9	0.82	0.00	3.70
12/13	14.88	46 7	0.32	0.00	3.00
12/12	2.20	6 3	0.42	0.00	2.50
12/11	1.62	94 44	0.03	0.00	2.59
Annual Growth	**78.1%**	**—**	**—108.8%**	**—**	**23.1%**

Green Bancorp Inc

Auditors: Deloitte & Touche LLP

LOCATIONS

HQ: Green Bancorp Inc
 4000 Greenbriar, Houston, TX 77098
Phone: 713 275-8220
Web: www.greenbank.com

HISTORICAL FINANCIALS

Company Type: Public

Income Statement

FYE: December 31

	ASSETS ($ mil.)	NET INCOME ($ mil.)	INCOME AS % OF ASSETS	EMPLOYEES
12/15	3,786.1	15.4	0.4%	353.0
12/14	2,196.1	14.7	0.7%	272.0
12/13	1,703.1	12.6	0.7%	216.0
12/12	1,674.8	8.5	0.5%	0.0
12/11	0.0	1.0	—	0.0
Annual Growth	**—**	**97.4%**	**—**	**—**

2015 Year-End Financials

Return on assets: 0.5%
Return on equity: 4.3%
Long-term debt ($ mil.): —
No. of shares (mil.): 36.7
Sales ($ mil): 120.7
Dividends
 Yield: —
 Payout: —
Market value ($ mil.): 386.0

	STOCK PRICE ($) FY Close	P/E High/Low	PER SHARE ($) Earnings	Dividends	Book Value
12/15	10.48	29 19	0.53	0.00	11.67
12/14	12.04	28 19	0.64	0.00	11.02
Annual Growth	**(13.0%)**	**—**	**(17.2%)**	**—**	**5.9%**

Green Dot Corp

If you've got the green but not the plastic Green Dot would like to help. The company offers prepaid debit cards through more than 100000 retail locations in the US. The MasterCard- and Visa-branded reloadable cards function like credit cards for purchases and cash withdrawals. Green Dot which has about 4.5 million cards in circulation partners with Wal-Mart Kmart Walgreens Home Depot and other retailers to enable its customers to add funds to their accounts. The company's products are designed for people who aren't able or choose not to utilize traditional credit card and banking services. Green Dot makes most of its money from new card monthly maintenance and ATM fees.

OperationsAs the pioneer of the prepaid debit card industry Green Dot is the largest provider of reloadable prepaid debit cards and cash reload processing services in the US. Roughly 40% of its revenue comes from card revenues and other fees while cash transfer revenue and interchange revenue each make up around 30% of the company's total revenue.Green Dot also offers mobile banking services through its GoBank mobile checking account. Green Dot subsidiary TPG is largest processor of tax refund disbursements in the nation. The company also boasts the Green Dot Network which provides reload services to more than 120 third-party prepaid card programs including programs offered by UniRush and H&R Block. The Green Dot Network even facilitates cash reload services for members programs that are part of MasterCard's RePower Reload Network.Geographic Reach

California-based Green Dot has sales and support offices in Tampa Florida; Bentonville Arkansas; and in Pasadena Palo Alto and Westlake Village California.

Sales and Marketing

Green Dot provides its products and services to consumers through a "branchless bank" distribution network. The network spans more than 100000 U.S. retail locations thousands of local financial service center locations an online website major mobile app stores as well as through 25000 tax preparation offices and major online tax preparation providers.Green Dot has been the exclusive distributor of Walmart-branded general purpose reloadable (GPR) cards sold at Walmart stores since 2007. Indeed Wal-Mart Stores is the company's largest retail distributor representing 54% of its total operating revenue in 2014. Green Dot's cards are sold by mass merchants including Walmart and Kmart discount retailers (including dollar stores) drugstores convenience stores supermarkets and by financial service centers.The company has been increasing its sales and marketing spend in recent years which has mostly been tied to sales commission expenses. Green Dot spent $235.23 million on sales and marketing expenses in 2014 up from $218.37 million in 2013 and $209.87 million in 2012.

Financial Performance

Green Dot has enjoyed rising revenue over the past several years as consumers warm up to prepaid cards. The company's revenue in 2014 rose nearly 5% to a record $601.55 million mostly thanks to higher monthly maintenance fees as the number of active cards in its network grew and because more of these cards were Green Dot-branded products which carry higher average maintenance fees. Interchange revenue also grew by $6.2 million thanks to a 6% increase in purchase volume while cash transfer revenue declined slightly as the company offered more fee-free cash transfers during the year.Following two years of losses net income in 2014 rebounded by 25% to $42.69 million thanks to a combination of higher revenue and non-recurring net cash proceeds of $7.1 million which the company collected from the settlement of a lawsuit.Despite higher cash earnings in 2014 cash from operations dropped by 44% to 68.97 million primarily because it paid $48.7 million in amounts due to card issuing banks for overdrawn accounts. These payments were mostly related to Green Dot's liability settlement with GE Capital Retail Bank which involved overdrawn cardholder account balances.

Strategy

Green Dot has been adding new lines of financial products to diversify its revenue streams either through acquisitions or on its own. In 2014 for example it purchased Santa Barbara Tax Products Group to create a new income stream enhance margins and add a new distribution network to sell more of its products and services. In February 2014 Green Dot finished transitioning its card issuing program with GE Capital Retail Bank to Green Dot Bank. As a result all Walmart Money-Cards are now issued by Green Dot Bank. In 2013 the firm launched its GoBank mobile checking account developed for smartphones and other mobile devices.

In 2012 in a move to become more vertically integrated the company acquired certain processing and hardware assets of eCommLink for some $2.5 million. The move allowed Green Dot to bring its transaction processing in house rather than rely on outsourced parties such as TSYS. Also in 2012 to help attract and retain customers and expand its tech capabilities Greent Dot acquired mobile app start-up Loopt which provides mobile location-based services for consumers to learn about local business deals for some $43 million. Like other electronic payments companies serving the underbanked community Green Dot has also attracted fully banked consumers seeking to safely shop online using separate accounts. Using prepaid cards as a companion to their primary accounts also allows users to control spending and prevent overdrafts. As the electronics payments industry evolves and competitors continue to introduce new products such as contactless cards Green Dot is exploring its various technological options. In addition to technological innovations card companies like Green Dot are also focusing on maintaining a stable and secure technology infrastructure.

Company Background

The company's July 2010 initial public offering exceeded its own expectations raising nearly $165 million. Although the IPO of secondary shares raised a significant amount Green Dot did not keep any of the money for itself. Instead the money was distributed to existing shareholders the most prominent being Wal-Mart. Prior to the IPO the retail giant took a minority stake in Green Dot —a move that cemented the pair's partnership.

EXECUTIVES

CEO and Director, Steven W. Streit, age 55, $666,000 total compensation
SVP Corporate Strategy and Mergers and Acquisitions and Acting CFO, Mark Shifke, age 57, $450,000 total compensation
COO, Kuan Archer, age 44, $440,000 total compensation
CEO Green Dot Bank, Mary J. Dent

Vice President Public Relations and Media Communications, John (Jack) Ricci
Vice President Controller, James (Jamie) Vanvelthuyzen
Vice President Compensation and Benefits, Suzanne (Sue) Rickards
Vice President Green Dot Network, Taylor Driggs
Vice President Develop, John (Jack) Johansen
Vice President Information Technology Relationships, Kim Kelly
Vice President Product Development GM Gobank, Alok Deshpande
Vice President, Dave (Davie) Banta
Senior Vice President Information Technology Governance and Shared Services, Christopher (Chris) Strader
Vice President Banking Operations, Kathy (Kat) Clark
Vice President Customer Care, Katherine (Kate) Throop
Senior Vice President Technology and International Development Center, James (Jamie) Lo
Chairman, William I. Jacobs, age 75
Treasurer, Matt Kohler
Auditors: Ernst & Young LLP

LOCATIONS

HQ: Green Dot Corp
3465 E. Foothill Blvd., Pasadena, CA 91107
Phone: 626 765-2000
Web: www.greendot.com

PRODUCTS/OPERATIONS

2014 Sales

	$ mil.	% of total
Card revenues & other fees	253.2	40
Cash transfer revenues	179.3	30
Interchange revenues	178.0	30
Adjustments	(8.9)	-
Total	**601.6**	**100**

COMPETITORS

American Express	MoneyGram
Blackhawk Network	International
DFC Global	NetSpend
FSV Payment Systems	PreCash
First Data	U.S. Bancorp
H&R Block	Visa Inc
JPMorgan Chase	Western Union
Jackson Hewitt	nFinanSe

HISTORICAL FINANCIALS

Company Type: Public

Income Statement
FYE: December 31

	REVENUE ($ mil.)	NET INCOME ($ mil.)	NET PROFIT MARGIN	EMPLOYEES
12/15	694.7	38.4	5.5%	1,012.0
12/14	601.5	42.6	7.1%	857.0
12/13	573.6	34.0	5.9%	562.0
12/12	546.2	47.2	8.6%	596.0
12/11	467.4	52.0	11.1%	464.0
Annual Growth	**10.4%**	**(7.3%)**	**—**	**21.5%**

2015 Year-End Financials

Debt ratio: 5.9%
Return on equity: 5.9%
Cash ($ mil.): 772.1
Current ratio: 1.10
Long-term debt ($ mil.): 100.6
No. of shares (mil.): 50.5
Dividends
　Yield: —
　Payout: —
Market value ($ mil.): 829.0

	STOCK PRICE ($) FY Close	P/E High/Low	PER SHARE ($) Earnings	Dividends	Book Value
12/15	16.42	29 19	0.72	0.00	13.13
12/14	20.49	29 18	0.90	0.00	12.30
12/13	25.15	34 16	0.76	0.00	10.66
12/12	12.20	29 8	1.07	0.00	9.11
12/11	31.22	52 21	1.19	0.00	7.14
Annual Growth	**(14.8%)**	**— —**	**(11.8%)**	**—**	**16.4%**

GrubHub Inc

Auditors: Crowe Horwath LLP

LOCATIONS

HQ: GrubHub Inc
111 W. Washington Street, Suite 2100, Chicago, IL 60602
Phone: 877 585-7878
Web: www.grubhub.com

HISTORICAL FINANCIALS

Company Type: Public

Income Statement
FYE: December 31

	REVENUE ($ mil.)	NET INCOME ($ mil.)	NET PROFIT MARGIN	EMPLOYEES
12/15	361.8	38.0	10.5%	1,105.0
12/14	253.8	24.2	9.6%	1,090.0
12/13	137.1	6.7	4.9%	680.0
12/12	82.3	7.9	9.6%	0.0
12/11	60.6	15.2	25.1%	0.0
Annual Growth	**56.3%**	**25.8%**	**—**	**—**

2015 Year-End Financials

Debt ratio: —
Return on equity: 4.6%
Cash ($ mil.): 310.7
Current ratio: 3.98
Long-term debt ($ mil.): —
No. of shares (mil.): 84.9
Dividends
　Yield: —
　Payout: —
Market value ($ mil.): 2,057.0

	STOCK PRICE ($) FY Close	P/E High/Low	PER SHARE ($) Earnings	Dividends	Book Value
12/15	24.20	105 51	0.44	0.00	10.33
12/14	36.32	137 91	0.30	0.00	9.41
Annual Growth	**(33.4%)**	**— —**	**46.7%**	**—**	**9.8%**

GTT Communications, Inc

GTT Communications (formerly Global Telecom & Technology) provides network integration for wide area network (WAN) dedicated Internet access and managed data services to system integrators telecom carriers and government agencies. GTT combines multiple networks and technologies such as traditional OC-x MPLS and Ethernet and has distribution partnerships with more than 800 technology suppliers including iPass for wireless services. Past customers include Avaya Lockheed Martin and Telefónica. GTT counts customers in about 80 countries; it earns almost half of its revenues outside the US. Chairman Brian Thompson owns nearly 31% of the company's stock.

Operations

GTT has three primary services: EtherCloud a flexible Ethernet-based connectivity service; Internet Services high bandwidth Internet connectivity services; and Managed Services fully managed network services. The company sells a mix of the three services to many of its customers.

Geographic Reach

While GTT provides services in more than 100 countries its billings to three countries account for 98% of revenue. The company's US customers generate 58% of the company's revenue. followed by Italy with 27% and the UK with 13%. Outside its three major markets GTT has offices in Hong Kong and Frankfurt.

Sales and Marketing

The company works with 4000 some businesses. The first contracts with customers generally run from 1-3 years with some going as many as five years. Automatic renewal periods range from a month to a year.

Financial Performance

GTT has posted robust revenue increases for several years in a row. Revenue in 2014 was $207 million a 31% increase from $157 million in 2013. Driving much of the growth was the performance of United Network Services which GTT acquired in 2014. Acquisitions made in 2013 also contributed.

The company's net loss got a bit deeper in 2014 going to $23 million from a loss of nearly $21 million in 2013 as the company has higher operating expenses. Bracing its operations with cash flow resulted in a negative flow of $10 million in 2014 compared to positive cash flow of $2.8 million the year before.

Strategy

While acquisitions play a large role in GTT's growth it also develops partnerships with other providers and develops new services. The company formed a partnership with AT&T in 2015 to collaborate on their Internet protocol networks to provide reliable service. The company also started a new service Managed Secure Access which provides secure access to GTT's cloud resources. It allows trusted uses to make secure data connections from any device using Transport Layer Security.

Mergers and Acquisitions

GTT bought One Source Networks a provider of global data Internet Session Initiation Protocol (SIP) trunking and managed services for about $175 million in cash and stock. This acquisition made in 2015 adds to GTT's network reach and client list.

Earlier in the year GTT paid more than $150 million in cash and stock to buy MegaPath Managed Services which provides private wide-area-networking Internet access services managed services and managed security. The deal brings more than 500 new customers to GTT and expands its cloud networking services. The 2014 acquisition of UNSi a communications company providing data services to large enterprise and carrier clients complements GTT's strategy to extend connectivity and expand its portfolio of cloud networking services.

EXECUTIVES

Vice President, Chris McKee
President CEO Director, Richard D. (Rick) Calder, age 52, $275,625 total compensation
CFO, Michael Bauer
Vice President And Controller, Debbie Latter
Vice President, Jake (Jacob) Cummins
General Counsel Executive Vice President of Corporate Development, Chris (Chrissy) McKee
Vice President Engineering, Pahtkrit Sunthornvatin
Vice President Global Business Development, Rochelle (Chell) Quinney
Chairman, H. Brian Thompson, age 76
Auditors: CohnReznick LLP

LOCATIONS

HQ: GTT Communications, Inc
7900 Tysons One Place, Suite 1450, McLean, VA 22102
Phone: 703 442-5500
Web: www.gtt.net

PRODUCTS/OPERATIONS

Selected Subsidiaries

ETT Network Services Limited (UK)
European Telecommunications & Technology Inc. (US)
European Telecommunications & Technology Private Limited (India)
European Telecommunications & Technology (S) Pte Limited (Singapore)
Global Telecom & Technology Deutschland GmbH (Germany)
Global Telecom & Technology SARL (France)
GTT Global Telecom LLC (US)
GTT Global Telecom Government Services LLC (US)
TEK Channel Consulting LLC (US)
WBS Connect LLC (US)
WBS Connect Europe Ltd. (Ireland)

COMPETITORS

AT&T	Level 3 Communications
BT	NTT
COLT Group	Orange Business
Cable & Wireless	Services
Communications	Verizon Enterprise
CenturyLink	Solutions
Deutsche Telekom	XO Holdings
KPN	

HISTORICAL FINANCIALS

Company Type: Public

Income Statement

FYE: December 31

	REVENUE ($ mil.)	NET INCOME ($ mil.)	NET PROFIT MARGIN	EMPLOYEES
12/15	369.2	19.3	5.2%	572.0
12/14	207.3	(22.9)	—	294.0
12/13	157.3	(20.7)	—	189.0
12/12	107.8	(1.5)	—	97.0
12/11	91.1	0.2	0.3%	88.0
Annual Growth	41.9%	195.0%	—	59.7%

2015 Year-End Financials

Debt ratio: 65.1%	No. of shares (mil.): 36.5
Return on equity: 20.5%	Dividends
Cash ($ mil.): 14.6	Yield: —
Current ratio: 0.93	Payout: —
Long-term debt ($ mil.): 383.2	Market value ($ mil.): 623.0

	STOCK PRICE ($) FY Close	P/E High/Low	PER SHARE ($) Earnings	Dividends	Book Value
12/15	17.06	47 21	0.54	0.00	3.02
12/14	13.23	— —	(0.85)	0.00	2.29
12/13	7.30	— —	(0.95)	0.00	0.41
12/12	2.80	— —	(0.08)	0.00	0.89
12/11	1.18	140101	0.01	0.00	0.97
Annual Growth	95.0%	—	—171.1%	—	32.9%

Guidewire Software Inc

Guidewire Software develops software for the insurance industry. The company's InsuranceSuite offers applications to property and casualty insurers for underwriting policy administration (PolicyCenter) claims management (ClaimsCenter) and billing (BillingCenter). Its software is intended to replace paper-based processes and legacy systems built around outdated programming languages. Its products can run on-premise or from the cloud. Guidewire counts some 210 customers in two dozen countries. It customers include Tokio Marine Nationwide Mutual and Zurich Financial Services.

Operations

Licensing of the company's software brings in about 47% of revenue while service accounts for another 40%. Maintenance rounds out the revenue pie with a 13% slice.

Guidewire's software is generally licensed over a five-year contract and is priced according to the number of the insurance provider's written premiums. It charges customers in advance for both term license and maintenance fees.

Geographic ReachGuidewire's corporate headquarters is in Foster City California. It also leases facilities for distributed sales and international operations in Dublin Ireland; Edina Minnesota; London United Kingdom; Mississauga Ontario Canada; Munich Germany; Paris France; Sydney Australia; and Tokyo Japan.In 2015 the US accounted for 55% of Guidewire's revenues. The UK supplies 12% of revenue and Canada's share is 10%.

Sales and Marketing

The company has more than 230 employees in a sales and marketing capacity including 41 direct sales representatives organized by geographic region across Australia Canada France Germany Hong Kong Japan the UK and the US. Guidewire's 10 largest customers accounted for 31% of revenue in 2015 a bit lower than the 35% of 2014.

Financial Performance

Guidewire's revenue increased 8% to $380.5 million in 2015 (ended July) driven by continued adoption of the company's InsuranceSuite package. A growing customer based led to a 19% increase in maintenance fees. Geographically the company had strong growth in Europe and Asia-Pacific but saw reduced revenue from Canada and other countries in the Americas other than the US where sales increased 2%.

Net income decreased 33% in 2015 due to an increase in operating expenses such as an increase in research and development expenses and taxes. Profit has declined since it peaked at $35.5 million in 2011.

Strategy

The company has extensive relationships with system integration consulting and industry partners. It encourages partners to co-market pursue joint sales initiatives and drive broader adoption of their technology. Its leading system integrator partners include Capgemini Ernst & Young IBM Global Services and PricewaterhouseCoopers.

Guidewire is intent on expanding its insurance software footprint internationally. It established a Regional Development Centre in Krakow to help the company further expand its global operations. It is Guidewire's sixth global development center joining teams in California Dublin Pennsylvania Tokyo and Toronto.

The company also expanded its Ireland operations by the leasing of additional office space to handle its growing team. It anticipates hiring 60-80 new staff in 2015-2016.

Ownership

Funds affiliated with Bay Partners own 10.9% of the company.

Company Background

Guidewire was founded in 2001 by CEO Marcus Ryu Product Strategy Director Kenneth Branson and four others who are no longer with the company. Its ClaimCenter product launched in 2003 PolicyCenter in 2004 and BillingCenter in 2006.

Guidewire filed a $100 million initial public offering in September 2011 and began trading on the NYSE in 2012.

EXECUTIVES

New Managing Director Of Emea, Keith Stonell
Auditors: KPMG LLP

LOCATIONS

HQ: Guidewire Software Inc
1001 E. Hillsdale Blvd., Suite 800, Foster City, CA 94404
Phone: 650 357-9100 **Fax:** 650 357-9101
Web: www.guidewire.com

PRODUCTS/OPERATIONS

2014 Sales

	$ mil.	% of total
Licenses	179.2	47
Services	151.3	40
Maintenance	50.0	13
Total	**380.5**	**100**

COMPETITORS

Accenture	Pegasystems
Applied Systems	SAP
CCC Information	Sapiens
Computer Sciences	StoneRiver
Corp.	SunGard Financial
Cover-All	Systems
Duck Creek	Tata Consultancy
Ebix	Vertafore
Oracle	

HISTORICAL FINANCIALS

Company Type: Public

Income Statement

FYE: July 31

	REVENUE ($ mil.)	NET INCOME ($ mil.)	NET PROFIT MARGIN	EMPLOYEES
07/16	424.4	14.9	3.5%	1,536.0
07/15	380.5	9.8	2.6%	1,341.0
07/14	350.2	14.7	4.2%	1,183.0
07/13	300.6	15.3	5.1%	1,149.0
07/12	232.0	15.2	6.6%	837.0
Annual Growth	16.3%	(0.4%)	—	16.4%

2016 Year-End Financials

Debt ratio: —	No. of shares (mil.): 73.0
Return on equity: 2.0%	Dividends
Cash ($ mil.): 223.5	Yield: —
Current ratio: 5.94	Payout: —
Long-term debt ($ mil.): —	Market value ($ mil.): 4,490.0

	STOCK PRICE ($) FY Close	P/E High/Low	PER SHARE ($) Earnings	Dividends	Book Value
07/16	61.47	304 205	0.20	0.00	10.73
07/15	59.05	429 284	0.14	0.00	9.71
07/14	40.50	261 158	0.21	0.00	9.42
07/13	43.76	168 91	0.25	0.00	3.94
07/12	25.66	122 59	0.25	0.00	3.41
Annual Growth	24.4%	— —	(5.4%)	—	33.2%

H&E Equipment Services Inc

H&E Equipment Services sells and rents new and used equipment for construction earthmoving and materials handling made by lift crane and truck manufacturers such as JLG Bobcat and Komatsu. H&E Equipment also offers a full slate of services including planned maintenance fleet maintenance on-site and mobile repair parts supply crane manufacturing and operator and safety training. The company serves some 36400 customers across more than 20 states through about 70 service centers.

Geographic ReachThe company serves its customers across 22 states from more than 70 full-service facilities located throughout the West Coast Intermountain Southwest Gulf Coast Southeast and Mid-Atlantic regions of the US with a majority of about 14 offices residing in Texas.

Operations

H&E operates through five reportable segments: Equipment Rentals New Equipment Sales Used Equipment Sales Parts and Services. Equipment Rentals about a third of revenue focuses on four core types of construction and industrial equipment with a sales force that is divided to specialize in each equipment type. The segment monitors such factors as rental rate trends and rental equipment dollar utilization to manage the fleet.

The New Equipment Sales segment about 30% of sales includes heavy construction and industrial equipment in all four core equipment categories. About two-thirds of the company's new equipment and rental fleet is obtained from Manitowoc Komatsu and Terex. Parts Sales 10% of revenue uses an in-house inventory to provide new and used parts for customers and the company's own rental fleet. The segment also provides parts for equipment it does not sell or rent.

Used Equipment Sales 11% of sales is sourced from the company's rental fleet trade-ins for new equipment sales and purchases of used equipment from other dealers. The rental fleet accounts for about 82% of this segment's sales. The Services segment 6% of revenue provides maintenance and repair for H&E's fleet and for customers' equipment. Services include warranty repairs as well as preventative maintenance. Businesses that don't fall into these main segments classified in the Other

segment include transportation hauling parts freight and loss damage waiver charges.

Financial Performance

H&E has benefited from growth in the commercial construction markets in the US. Significant capital projects located in the Gulf Coast region related to major chemical energy and manufacturing helped drive sales above the $1 billion mark in 2014 for the first time in the company's history.

H&E's historic growth in 2014 was fueled by a bump in equipment rentals sales driven by an increase in rentals of aerial work platforms and earthmoving equipment. New equipment sales also grew in 2014 due to increased sales of new cranes and sales of parts climbed by 10% due to higher demand.

Net income grew 25% from $44 million in 2013 to $55 million in 2014. H&E's operating cash flow spiked by 14% to $158 million due to the increased net income and a positive impact of depreciation and amortization and deferred income taxes in addition to net gains on the sale of long-lived assets.

Strategy

The company's ongoing strategy for growth includes a one-stop cradle-through-grave approach that results in integrated services cross-selling and business opportunities aligned with each stage of an item's life cycle. This strategy requires a focus on parts and services to strengthen customer relationships and bring in new customers.

More broadly the company seeks to expand by looking for areas that are enjoying a high demand for construction and heavy equipment particularly when they are near the company's existing markets. The company also keeps an eye out for the many small businesses of the equipment sector for acquisitions.

HISTORY

Company Background

H&E Equipment was formed in 2002 through the merger of Head & Engquist (a subsidiary of Gulf Wide Industries) and ICM Equipment Company. Prior to their merger the regional integrated equipment service companies Head & Engquist (founded 1961 by Tom Engquist and Frank Head) and ICM Equipment Company (established 1971) were operating in contiguous geographic markets.

EXECUTIVES

Vice President Prdt Support, John (Jack) Jones
CEO, John M. Engquist, age 62, $769,027 total compensation
President and COO, Bradley W. Barber, age 43, $413,493 total compensation
CFO and Secretary, Leslie S. Magee, age 47, $383,519 total compensation
Vice President of Business Development, Kevin (Kev) Gretz
Vice President, Kevin (Kev) Chamberlain
Vice President of the Earthmoving Division, Bobby Slay
Vice President Cranes and Earthmoving, Bill (Billy) Fox
Vice President Services, Leonard (Len) St Germain
Chairman, Gary W. Bagley, age 69
Auditors: BDO USA, LLP

LOCATIONS

HQ: H&E Equipment Services Inc
7500 Pecue Lane, Baton Rouge, LA 70809
Phone: 225 298-5200
Web: www.he-equipment.com

PRODUCTS/OPERATIONS

2013 Sales

	$ mil.	% of total
Equipment rentals	338.9	34
New equipment sales	294.8	30
Used equipment sales	141.6	14
Parts sales	103.2	10
Services revenues	56.7	7
Other	52.6	5
Total	**987.8**	**100**

Selected Products

Aerial lifts
Backhoe loaders
Boom trucks
Compactors
Compressors
Cranes
Crushers
Dump trucks
Excavators
Forklifts
Generators
Lawn mowers
Light towers
Material handling equipment
Motor graders
Pavers
Pumps
Skid steers
Tractors

COMPETITORS

AMECO	NES Rentals
Atlas Lift Truck	Neff
Rentals	Park Corp.
Berry Companies	Penhall International
Finning International	Sunbelt Rentals
HOLT Texas	Toromont
Herc Holdings	United Rentals
ICON Capital	Wacker Neuson
J. A. Riggs Tractor	

HISTORICAL FINANCIALS

Company Type: Public

Income Statement

FYE: December 31

	REVENUE ($ mil.)	NET INCOME ($ mil.)	NET PROFIT MARGIN	EMPLOYEES
12/15	1,039.8	44.3	4.3%	2,045.0
12/14	1,090.4	55.1	5.1%	1,900.0
12/13	987.7	44.1	4.5%	1,775.0
12/12	837.3	28.8	3.4%	1,744.0
12/11	720.5	8.9	1.2%	1,646.0
Annual Growth	**9.6%**	**49.3%**	**—**	**5.6%**

2015 Year-End Financials

Debt ratio: 62.6%
Return on equity: 32.1%
Cash ($ mil.): 7.1
Current ratio: 0.68
Long-term debt ($ mil.): 630.7

No. of shares (mil.): 35.4
Dividends
Yield: 6.0%
Payout: 75.5%
Market value ($ mil.): 619.0

	STOCK PRICE ($) FY Close	P/E High/Low		PER SHARE ($) Earnings	Dividends	Book Value
12/15	17.48	22	11	1.25	1.05	4.02
12/14	28.09	27	17	1.56	0.50	3.79
12/13	29.63	24	12	1.26	0.00	2.69
12/12	15.07	25	14	0.82	7.00	1.38
12/11	13.42	77	28	0.26	0.00	7.53
Annual Growth (14.5%)	**6.8%**	**—**	**—**	**48.1%**	**—**	

Hallador Energy Co

Hallador Energy puts most of its energy into selling coal from its Carlisle Mine in Indiana to three utilities in the Midwest and one in Florida. Hallador has recoverable coal reserves of 43.5 million tons (34.2 million tons proven and 9.3 million tons probable). In addition to the Carlisle Mine it get coals from a mine in Clay County Indiana and has two inactive mines in Illinois. The company is exploring the possibility of other contracts with a number of coal purchasers. Additionally Hallador has a 45% stake in Savoy Energy L.P. an oil and gas company with operations in Michigan and a 50% interest in Sunrise Energy LLC a private oil and gas exploration and production company with assets in Indiana.

Sales and Marketing

Hallador sells coal in the Midwest to Duke Energy Hoosier Energy and Indianapolis Power & Light. It also sells coal to JEA in Florida.

Financial Performance

In 2012 the company's revenues declined by 10% due to a price decrease and unfavorable weather conditions crimping demand. Hallador's net income decreased by 34% due to lower net sales and higher operating costs.

Strategy

Expanding its geographic coverage in 2011 the company sold 300000 tons of coal to JEA its first such sale to a Florida-based customer. It sold 18500 tons to JEA in 2012.

Ownership

Some 70% of the company is held by officers directors and their affiliates. Chairman David Hardie holds a 12% stake in Hallador.

Company Background

Hallador was founded in 1949. In 1997 investment company Yorktown Energy Partners II and affiliates invested $5 million in Hallador.

Despite its Harry Potter-like name Hallador Petroleum could find no magic in oil and natural gas exploration and production –just a lot of hard and dirty work. It therefore decided to focus on its coal operations. The company acquired control of Sunrise Coal co-developer of the Carlisle Mine in 2008.

Hallador in Spanish means "finder" or "discoverer" or "one who leads the way."

EXECUTIVES

Chairman, David Hardie, age 66
Chief Executive Officer, Victor P. Stabio, age 69, $180,000 total compensation
CFO Sunrise Coal, Larry Martin, age 51, $102,000 total compensation
Chief Financial Officer; Chief Accounting Officer, William A. (Andy) Bishop, age 63
President and appointed to our board, Brent Bilsland
Director, Sheldon B. Lubar, age 87
Director, Bryan H. Lawrence, age 74
CEO and Director, Victor P. Stabio, age 68
Independent Director, John Heuvelen
Auditors: EKS&H LLLP

LOCATIONS

HQ: Hallador Energy Co
1660 Lincoln Street, Suite 2700, Denver, CO 80264-2701
Phone: 303 839-5504
Web: www.halladorenergy.com

PRODUCTS/OPERATIONS

2015 Sales

	$ mil.	% of total
Coal sales	339.5	99
Other	2.2	1
Equity loss - Savoy	(1.5)	-
Equity loss - Sunrise Energy	(0.1)	-
Total	**340.1**	**100**

COMPETITORS

Alpha Natural Resources	Noble Energy
Anadarko Petroleum	Peabody Energy
Arch Coal	Pioneer Natural Resources
CONSOL Energy	SandRidge Energy
Chesapeake Energy	

HISTORICAL FINANCIALS

Company Type: Public

Income Statement

FYE: December 31

	REVENUE ($ mil.)	NET INCOME ($ mil.)	NET PROFIT MARGIN	EMPLOYEES
12/15	340.1	20.1	5.9%	740.0
12/14	241.1	10.2	4.2%	1,027.0
12/13	153.8	23.1	15.0%	376.0
12/12	141.3	23.8	16.8%	330.0
12/11	157.3	35.8	22.8%	333.0
Annual Growth	**21.3%**	**(13.4%)**	**—**	**22.1%**

2015 Year-End Financials

Debt ratio: 45.7%
Return on equity: 10.1%
Cash ($ mil.): 15.9
Current ratio: 1.27
Long-term debt ($ mil.): 223.2

No. of shares (mil.): 29.2
Dividends
Yield: 3.5%
Payout: 23.5%
Market value ($ mil.): 133.0

	STOCK PRICE ($) FY Close	P/E High/Low		PER SHARE ($) Earnings	Dividends	Book Value
12/15	4.56	19	7	0.68	0.16	7.07
12/14	11.01	41	22	0.34	0.16	6.56
12/13	8.06	11	8	0.80	0.28	6.38
12/12	8.26	13	8	0.83	0.80	5.68
12/11	9.93	9	6	1.25	0.12	5.69
Annual Growth (17.7%)		**—**	**—**	**(14.1%)**	**7.5%**	**5.6%**

Hanmi Financial Corp.

No hand-me-down operation Hanmi Financial is headquartered in a penthouse suite along Los Angeles' Wilshire Boulevard. The company owns Hanmi Bank which serves California's Korean-American community and others in the multi-ethnic Los Angeles San Diego San Francisco Bay and Silicon Valley areas. Hanmi Bank offers retail and small business banking with an emphasis on the latter from more than 25 California branches and loan offices throughout the US. Commercial and industrial loans including SBA and international trade finance loans account for about 60% of its loan portfolio; real estate loans make up most of the rest.

Financial Performance

After five straight years of declines Hanmi's revenue grew 6% in 2013 to $153 million. The financial and housing crises particularly acute in California hurt Hanmi's customers many of whom operate small businesses and consequently the bank's finances. As loan volume begins to increase and bring higher yields on investment securities the company's interest income has slowly risen. While non-interest income such as insurance commissions is also on the rise other types of non-interest income such as service charges on deposit accounts is declining as customers demand lower-cost banking products and services.

In 2013 it earned $39.9 million in profit down from $90.4 million in 2012. The decrease was due to the absence of the reversal of the deferred tax asset valuation allowance which contributed an income tax benefit of $47.4 million in 2012.

Strategy

Hanmi and Korean bank Woori Finance called off plans to merge in mid-2011 instead forming a business alliance. Two years later Hanmi is still actively looking for a partner to merge with. It hopes to find a South Korean financial institution looking to establish a presence in the US.

In order to focus on its business banking in 2014 the bank sold its insurance subsidiaries Chun-Ha Insurance Services and All World Insurance Services to Chunha Holding Corporation. The two companies sold life and property/casualty insurance plans.

Mergers and Acquisitions

In its first foray outside of California in late 2013 Hanmi agreed to acquire Central Bancorp Inc. the parent of Texas-based United Central Bank. United Central Bank serves multi-ethnic communities in Texas Illinois Virginia California New York and New Jersey through some two dozen branches. Once the acquisition is complete Hanmi will have about 50 branches and two loan production offices serving a broad range of ethnic communities in California Texas Illinois New York New Jersey Virginia and Georgia.

EXECUTIVES

SEVP and COO, Bonita I. (Bonnie) Lee, age 53
Chief Compliance and BSA Officer, Jean Lim
EVP and CFO, Michael W. McCall
President CEO and Director, Chong Guk (C. G.) Kum
EVP and Chief Credit Officer, Randall G. Ewig
EVP and Chief Administrative Officer, Greg D. Kim
EVP and Chief Banking Officer, Peter Yang
EVP and Chief Lending Officer, Anthony Kim
Assistant Vice President and Special Assets Officer, Sue (Susie) Kim
Sevp-corporate Finance And Str, Romolo Santarosa
First Vice President And Loan Manager, Richard (Dick) Son
Vice President and Loan Officer, Yong Park
Assistant Vice President Compliance Officer, Michael (Mel) Santiago
Assistant Vice President Treasury Management, Debby (Deb) Sassoon
Vice President, Joonhyok Shin
Vice President, Maheboob Kurani
Vice President Loss Share Accounting Manager, Brian (Bri) Rogers
Assistant Vice President andamp; Credit Analyst, Daniel (Dan) Park
Assistant Vice President andamp; SBA Loan Officer, Sharon (Share) Min
First Vice President and Branch Manager, Annie (Ann) Chung
Chairman, Joseph K. Rho, age 75
Auditors: KPMG LLP

LOCATIONS

HQ: Hanmi Financial Corp.
3660 Wilshire Boulevard, Penthouse Suite A, Los Angeles, CA 90010
Phone: 213 382-2200
Web: www.hanmi.com

PRODUCTS/OPERATIONS

2013 Sales

	$ mil.	% of total
Interest income	122.3	80
Non-interest income	31.4	20
Total	**153.7**	**100**

COMPETITORS

Bank of America	Far East National Bank
Broadway Financial	Hope Bancorp
Cathay General Bancorp	JPMorgan Chase
East West Bancorp	Woori

HISTORICAL FINANCIALS

Company Type: Public

Income Statement

FYE: December 31

	ASSETS ($ mil.)	NET INCOME ($ mil.)	INCOME AS % OF ASSETS	EMPLOYEES
12/15	4,234.5	53.8	1.3%	622.0
12/14	4,232.4	49.7	1.2%	699.0
12/13	3,055.5	39.9	1.3%	499.0
12/12	2,882.5	90.3	3.1%	470.0
12/11	2,744.8	28.1	1.0%	483.0
Annual Growth	**11.4%**	**17.6%**	**—**	**6.5%**

2015 Year-End Financials

Return on assets: 1.2%	Dividends
Return on equity: 11.3%	Yield: 1.9%
Long-term debt ($ mil.): —	Payout: 27.8%
No. of shares (mil.): 31.9	Market value ($ mil.): 758.0
Sales ($ mil): 211.8	

	STOCK PRICE ($) FY Close	P/E High/Low	PER SHARE ($) Earnings	Dividends	Book Value
12/15	23.72	16 12	1.68	0.47	15.45
12/14	21.81	16 12	1.56	0.28	14.21
12/13	21.89	18 11	1.26	0.14	12.63
12/12	13.59	5 3	2.87	0.00	12.01
12/11	7.40	6 1	1.38	0.00	9.07
Annual Growth	**33.8%**	**— —**	**5.0%**	**—**	**14.2%**

Hawaiian Holdings Inc

Luaus leis and laying in the sun —Hawaiian Holdings knows how to get you there. The company's main subsidiary Hawaiian Airlines transports passengers and cargo between Honolulu and about a dozen major cities in the western US. The carrier also serves the six main Hawaiian Islands and destinations in the South Pacific such as American Samoa Australia New Zealand China South Korea and Tahiti. It operates a fleet of about 50 aircraft (most are Boeing 717s for flights between the Hawaiian Islands and Boeing 767s for transpacific flights). In addition to its scheduled passenger and cargo operations Hawaiian Airlines provides charter services.

Operations

To supplement its own inter-island offerings Hawaiian Airlines serves other destinations within Hawaii via a code-sharing deal with Island Air. In addition Hawaiian Airlines maintains code-sharing arrangements with carriers such as American Airlines Delta Air Lines and United. Code-sharing allows airlines to extend their networks by selling tickets on other carriers' flights.

Sales and Marketing

Hawaiian Airlines uses various distribution channels including its website (mostly for North America and regional island routes) and travel agencies and wholesale distributors for international flights. Partners include Orbitz Travelocity Expedia Hotwire and Priceline.

Financial Performance

Hawaiian Airlines has enjoyed unprecedented growth recently with revenues peaking at a record-setting $2.32 billion in 2015. The historic growth in 2015 was driven by a 5% rise in domestic revenue and a spike in sales of frequent flyer miles under its co-branded credit card agreement.

Its profits also skyrocketed by more than 160% to reach $183 million in 2015 another company milestone. The surge in profits was mainly due to a major decline in the average fuel price per gallon.

Strategy

Hawaiian Airlines is counting on continued growth in its transpacific and South Pacific operations through expanded service to Tahiti and Australia. It has instituted a code-sharing agreement with Korean Air Lines and now offers nonstop flights to that country. Hawaiian Airlines is currently the only airline to offer nonstop service from Honolulu to Pago Pago and American Samoa. To support its expansion plans the company has ordered 16 wide-body and extra-wide-body aircraft from Airbus for delivery between 2017 and 2020.

In April 2014 the airline launched a non-stop service between Honolulu and Beijing. The flight represented the airlines' 10 international destination and made China one of Hawaiian Airlines' most important visitor destinations. Shortly before it also signed a code-share agreement with Air China China's exclusive national flag carrier.

HISTORY

Company Background

In 1929 former Navy pilot Stanley Kennedy general manager of the Inter-Island Steam Navigation Company persuaded the Inter-Island board to fund a passenger line linking Honolulu (Oahu) with the other Hawaiian Islands. The new airline which started out with amphibian aircraft began inter-island airmail service in 1934.

The company became Hawaiian Airlines in 1941. TWA bought control in 1944 but sold out four years later after the new Trans-Pacific Airlines (later Aloha Airlines) ended Hawaiian's 17-year monopoly in Hawaii in 1946. The two competed intensely for the same routes. Investor John Magoon bought control of Hawaiian in 1964. The rival airlines agreed to merge in 1970 but negotiations failed a year later.

Airline deregulation in 1978 gave Hawaiian access to new markets. It adopted the name HAL in 1982 and by 1985 had added service to the US West Coast.

EXECUTIVES

SVP Human Resources, Barbara D. Falvey, age 57, $344,375 total compensation

President and CEO Hawaiian Holdings and Hawaiian Airlines, Mark B. Dunkerley, age 52, $695,000 total compensation
EVP Chief Legal Officer and Corporate Secretary, Aaron J. Alter
EVP and Chief Commercial Officer Hawaiian Airlines, Peter R. Ingram, age 49, $453,750 total compensation
SVP Marketing, Avi A. Mannis
EVP and CFO, Shannon L. Okinaka, age 41, $328,371 total compensation
EVP and Chief Administrative Officer Hawaiian Airlines, Ron Anderson-Lehman, age 52, $408,750 total compensation
VP Information Technology, Philip (Phil) Moore
EVP and COO, Jon Snook
Chairman, Lawrence S. Hershfield, age 59
Auditors: Ernst & Young LLP

LOCATIONS

HQ: Hawaiian Holdings Inc
3375 Koapaka Street, Suite G-350, Honolulu, HI 96819
Phone: 808 835-3700
Web: www.hawaiianairlines.com

PRODUCTS/OPERATIONS

2015 Sales

	$ mil.	% of total
Passenger	2,025.6	87
Other	291.9	13
Total	**2,317.5**	**100**

2015 Sales

	$ mil.	% of total
Domestic	1,775.4	77
Pacific	542.1	23
Total	**2,317.5**	**100**

Selected Services

In-Flight Services
Dining and Drinks
In-Flight Entertainment
Pau Hana Cart Duty
Free In-Flight Shopping
Hana HouTravel Products and Programs
Extra Comfort Seating
Preferred Seating
Hawaiian Airlines World

COMPETITORS

ANA Holdings	Hawaii Island Air
Air Canada	Japan Airlines
Alaska Air	Mesa Air
American Airlines Group	Qantas
	US Airways
Delta Air Lines	United Continental

HISTORICAL FINANCIALS

Company Type: Public

Income Statement

FYE: December 31

	REVENUE ($ mil.)	NET INCOME ($ mil.)	NET PROFIT MARGIN	EMPLOYEES
12/15	2,317.4	182.6	7.9%	5,548.0
12/14	2,314.8	68.9	3.0%	5,380.0
12/13	2,155.8	51.8	2.4%	5,249.0
12/12	1,962.3	53.2	2.7%	4,906.0
12/11	1,650.4	(2.6)	—	4,314.0
Annual Growth	**8.9%**	**—**	**—**	**6.5%**

2015 Year-End Financials

Debt ratio: 30.7%
Return on equity: 44.9%
Cash ($ mil.): 281.5
Current ratio: 0.96
Long-term debt ($ mil.): 694.6
No. of shares (mil.): 53.4
Dividends
 Yield: —
 Payout: —
Market value ($ mil.): 1,887.0

	STOCK PRICE ($) FY Close	P/E High	P/E Low	PER SHARE ($) Earnings	Dividends	Book Value
12/15	35.33	12	5	2.98	0.00	8.35
12/14	26.05	20	7	1.10	0.00	6.74
12/13	9.63	10	5	0.98	0.00	7.57
12/12	6.57	7	5	1.01	0.00	5.22
12/11	5.80	—	—	(0.05)	0.00	4.39
Annual Growth	**57.1%**			**—**	**—**	**17.4%**

HCI Group Inc

Floridian homeowners are picking HCI Group for their insurance needs —by default. The company's Homeowners Choice Property and Casualty Insurance (HCPCI) subsidiary provides homeowners' insurance and other property/casualty coverage in the state. HCPCI sells policies through a network of independent agents. Other HCI Group subsidiaries provide real estate reinsurance and information technology products and services. The firm changed its name from Homeowners Choice Inc. to HCI Group in 2013 to reflect its diversified businesses.

Operations

The main HCPCI subsidiary provides property/casualty insurance policies to home and condominium owners as well as renters. Other HCI Group companies include Southern Administration a provider of policy administration services to HCPCI; Homeowners Choice Managers which provides marketing claims settlement underwriting and accounting services to HCPCI; and Claddaugh Casualty Insurance which provides reinsurance services to HCPCI.

Other units lease or own real estate properties including marinas and restaurants. The company's Exzeo subsidiary provides software development and IT services to other insurance companies. The division has commercialized the technologies developed in-house to support the HCI Group operations.

Geographic Reach

While its operations primarily take place in Florida HCI Group also has a facility in Noida India to develop and maintain its software applications. The company operates in 10 countries in North America Europe the Middle East and Asia.

Sales and Marketing

HCI Group markets its products through agents as well as through companies that sell directly to customers.

Financial Performance

Revenues have been on the rise for the past five years. In 2014 net revenue increased 10% to $266.1 million primarily due to an increase in net realized investment gains. That increase was attributed to sales of fixed-maturity securities; other investment gains were due to a rise in available-for-sale securities (the bulk of its portfolio). Gross premium revenues rose 8% largely due to the company's assumption of policies held by the state-owned Citizens Property Insurance Corporation.

Net income which had been rising as well took a 4% dip to $62.7 million in 2014. The decrease was due to higher losses and loss adjustment expenses.

Cash flow from operations rose 60% to $88.7 million that year as unearned premiums increased and prepaid reinsurance premiums declined.

Strategy

The company continues to grow its business through the assumption of policies held by the state-owned Citizens Property Insurance Corporation. In 2009 the Florida Office of Insurance Regulation authorized HCI Group to assume 60000 policies from Citizens which have been transferred gradually.

HCI Group also expands through acquisitions as well as by positioning itself as an alternative insurance option to large national insurers.

HCI Group has also focused in international growth through acquisitions and partnerships. For example it acquired the UK-based firm High Resolution Consulting and Resourcing in 2015. In another deal it formed a joint venture with FMKT Sponsor; that venture will invest in the development of a retail center in Melbourne Florida.

Mergers and Acquisitions

To promote its global expansion HCI Group acquired UK-based consulting firm High Resolution Consulting and Resourcing in 2015. Domestically the company acquired Houston-based training consulting firm Expert Technical Advisors in early 2016.

Company Background

Founded in 2006 HCI Group began providing property/casualty insurance for Floridians just as large national insurers began exiting the hurricane-prone market to reduce exposure. The initial bulk of the company's insurance policies were assumed from Citizens. However HCI Group was selective and assumed policies based on its own underwriting criteria.

EXECUTIVES

VP General Counsel and Corporate Secretary, Andrew L. Graham, age 58, $205,000 total compensation
CFO, Richard R. Allen, age 69, $250,000 total compensation
Chairman and CEO, Paresh Patel, age 53, $500,481 total compensation
President Greenleaf Capital and Director, Anthony Saravanos, age 45, $175,000 total compensation
President TypTap Insurance Company, Ted Blanch
Auditors: Dixon Hughes Goodman LLP

LOCATIONS

HQ: HCI Group Inc
5300 West Cypress Street, Suite 100, Tampa, FL 33607
Phone: 813 849-9500
Web: www.hcigroup.com

PRODUCTS/OPERATIONS

2014 Sales

% of sales	
Gross premiums earned	96
Net investment income	1
Policy fee income	1
Net realized investment gains	1
Others	1
Total	**0.0** **100**

COMPETITORS

Allstate	Nationwide
Citizens Property	State Farm
Insurance	United Insurance
Federated National	Holdings
Holding	Universal Insurance
Liberty Mutual	Holdings

HISTORICAL FINANCIALS

Company Type: Public

Income Statement

FYE: December 31

	ASSETS ($ mil.)	NET INCOME ($ mil.)	INCOME AS % OF ASSETS	EMPLOYEES
12/15	636.9	65.8	10.3%	379.0
12/14	602.2	62.6	10.4%	350.0
12/13	526.3	65.5	12.5%	329.0
12/12	338.2	30.1	8.9%	290.0
12/11	214.8	9.9	4.6%	190.0
Annual Growth	31.2%	60.3%	—	18.8%

2015 Year-End Financials

Return on assets: 10.6%
Return on equity: 31.3%
Long-term debt ($ mil.): —
No. of shares (mil.): 10.2
Sales ($ mil): 285.9
Dividends
Yield: 3.4%
Payout: 19.5%
Market value ($ mil.): 359.0

	STOCK PRICE ($) FY Close	P/E High/Low		PER SHARE ($) Earnings	Dividends	Book Value
12/15	34.85	8	5	5.90	1.20	23.10
12/14	43.24	9	6	5.36	1.10	17.92
12/13	53.50	9	3	5.63	0.95	14.67
12/12	20.79	8	2	3.02	0.88	11.15
12/11	8.01	6	4	1.34	0.53	10.29
Annual Growth	44.4%	—	—	44.9%	23.0%	22.4%

Headwaters Inc

Headwaters is a modern-day alchemist turning stone and coal into money. Through subsidiaries it provides building materials such as coal combustion products (CCP) and synthetic gypsum and reclaims waste coal in North America. Headwaters' light building products segment —its largest — makes stone products and siding accessories under the Eldorado Stone brand. The heavy construction materials segment sells residuals from the coal combustion process (such as fly ash) which can be used as a substitute for Portland cement in building materials. Headwaters' energy technology segment licenses coal conversion and heavy oil upgrading technology. In late 2016 Headwaters agreed to be purchased by Australia-based Boral Limited.

Change in Company Type

Headwaters in late 2016 agreed to be acquired by Boral Limited an Australia-based maker of building and construction materials for $1.8 billion. The deal will double Boral's US presence and create the largest US supplier of fly ash.

Operations

The company conducts its operations through three reporting segments. Building products has expertise in the designing manufacturing and marketing of architectural stone under the Eldorado Stone brand and siding accessories used in residential repair and remodeling and new residential construction applications.

Construction materials is involved in the marketing of fly ash and synthetic gypsum. It procures fly ash from coal-fueled electric generating utilities and supplies it to customers as a partial replacement for portland cement in the production of concrete. The energy technology segment specializes in heavy oil upgrading processes through the sale of HCAT catalyst material.

Geographic Reach

Headwaters has offices in Wixom Michigan; San Marcos California; Oceanside California; Dallas Texas; and Alleyton Texas. Manufacturing facilities reside in Metamora Michigan; Elkland Pennsylvania; Greencastle Pennsylvania; Franklin Ohio; Westfield Massachusetts; Okeechobee Florida; Oceanside California; Alleyton Texas; Dallas Texas; Latta South Carolina; Chatham Ontario Canada; and Rosarito Mexico.

Sales and Marketing

Headwaters' building products segment markets its products to the new construction home improvement commercial and institutional markets. It sells its products throughout North America Europe and Asia primarily on a wholesale basis through a network of distributors including masonry and stone suppliers roofing and siding materials distributors fireplace suppliers and other contractor specialty stores.

The company also distributes some brands through national retail home centers. It has more than 1000 US wholesale distributors and generates incremental sales through big box stores.

Financial Performance

Headwaters' revenues peaked at $975 million in 2016 its highest total in about eight years. Profits however plunged 63% to $48 million in 2016 mainly due to the absence of income tax benefits it received the previous year. The company's operating cash flow increased to $120 million in 2016.

Revenue growth in 2016 was due to higher sales across all its major product groups as a result of demand-driven volume increases and acquisitions completed in 2015 and 2016. Led by its trim product the company's siding products contributed significantly to overall segment revenue growth and margin expansion.

Demand was also strong in its non-residential Texas markets in 2016 offsetting any impact from low oil prices on residential construction. Operational improvement efforts within its stone and block categories also contributed to margin improvement. In addition several of its product groups continued to benefit from lower raw material transportation and energy costs which more than offset increased costs in other areas.

Strategy

With the housing market projected to explode over the next few years Headwaters plans to increase the number of products it sells to core customers through internal development and bolt-on acquisitions. It is also focusing its sales and marketing spending to core customers and additionally plans to standardize non-customer interfacing infrastructure.

Mergers and Acquisitions

Headwaters' blueprint for growth involves the use of acquisitions. In 2016 it purchased Krestmark Industries which manufactures and sells vinyl windows for new residential construction in the south central region of the US for $240 million.

Also in 2016 the company gobbled up Kentucky-based Synthetic Materials an expert in the synthetic gypsum processing and management industry $38 million. The deal complemented Headwaters' coal combustion product management operations.

EXECUTIVES

CEO and Chairman, Kirk A. Benson, age 66, $720,000 total compensation

CFO, Donald P. Newman, age 52, $338,827 total compensation

Vice President of Operations, Stephanie (Steph) Black

Vice President Behaviora Director Scientific Integrity, David (Dave) Marshall

Auditors: BDO USA, LLP

LOCATIONS

HQ: Headwaters Inc
10701 South River Front Parkway, Suite 300, South Jordan, UT 84095
Phone: 801 984-9400
Web: www.headwaters.com

COMPETITORS

Acme Brick	Pavestone
Alliant Energy	Progress Energy
Arconic	Rentech
Black Hills	SCANA
CEMEX	Sasol
CertainTeed	Silverado Gold Mines
Featherlite	Southern Company
Lafarge North America	Syntroleum
Nalco	TECO Coal
Oldcastle Materials	Vectren

HISTORICAL FINANCIALS

Company Type: Public

Income Statement

FYE: September 30

	REVENUE ($ mil.)	NET INCOME ($ mil.)	NET PROFIT MARGIN	EMPLOYEES
09/16	974.8	48.1	4.9%	3,687.0
09/15	895.3	130.8	14.6%	2,831.0
09/14	791.4	15.2	1.9%	2,665.0
09/13	702.5	7.1	1.0%	2,355.0
09/12	632.7	(62.2)	—	2,465.0
Annual Growth	11.4%	—	—	10.6%

2016 Year-End Financials

Debt ratio: 60.9%
Return on equity: 18.1%
Cash ($ mil.): 65.3
Current ratio: 2.07
Long-term debt ($ mil.): 746.7
No. of shares (mil.): 74.0
Dividends
Yield: —
Payout: —
Market value ($ mil.): 1,253.0

	STOCK PRICE ($) FY Close	P/E High/Low		PER SHARE ($) Earnings	Dividends	Book Value
09/16	16.92	32	22	0.64	0.00	3.92
09/15	18.80	12	6	1.73	0.00	3.22
09/14	12.54	70	42	0.20	0.00	1.39
09/13	8.99	115	61	0.10	0.00	1.15
09/12	6.58	—	—	(1.02)	0.00	(0.05)
Annual Growth	26.6%	—	—	—	—	—

Healthcare Services Group, Inc.

Healthcare Services Group gets swept up in its work every day. The company provides housekeeping laundry and linen food and maintenance services to hospitals nursing homes rehabilitation centers and retirement facilities. It tidies up around 3500 long-term care facilities in Canada and almost every state in the US. Housekeeping and laundry and linen services are the company's top revenue generators. The company's dietary division prepares food for residents and monitors nutritional needs in more than 900 facilities. Healthcare Services Group was established in 1977.

Geographic Reach

The company based in Bensalem Pennsylvania operates in 48 states and Canada.

Operations

The company's operations are divided in two segments: Housekeeping and Dietary.

Housekeeping consists of the managing of the client's housekeeping department which is principally responsible for the cleaning disinfecting and sanitizing of patient rooms and common areas of a client's facility as well as the laundering and processing of the personal clothing belonging to the facility's patients. Dietary consists of managing the client's dietary department which is principally responsible for food purchasing meal preparation and providing dietitian consulting professional services which includes the development of a menu that meets the patient's dietary needs.

Dietary services represented 35% of consolidated revenues in 2014 while Housekeeping services represented about 65%.

Sales and Marketing

The company markets its services primarily through referrals and in-person solicitation of target facilities. They also utilize direct mail campaigns and participate in industry trade shows health care trade associations and healthcare support service seminars.

Financial Performance

The company's revenue and net income have steadily increased year over year for a a decade — until 2014.

While revenues increased 12.5% in 2014 net income tumbled more than 50% to $21.8 million in comparison with 2013. Cash flow increased by $57 million in 2014 from $32 million in 2013.

The increase in revenues was attributed to service agreements with new clients and expansion of the Dietary segment to new clients. Net income was affected by higher operating costs and a changed in an estimate related to self-insurance liability and income taxes.

EXECUTIVES

Executive Vice President, Joseph F McCartney, age 62

EVP, Michael E. McBryan, $102,492 total compensation

EVP, Bryan D. McCartney, $102,492 total compensation

President and CEO, Theodore Wahl, age 42, $996,255 total compensation

CFO, John Shea, $389,039 total compensation

Regional Vice President, Josh Dubler

Vice President, Jim Keeley

Divisional Vice President, Stephen Foresman

Regional Vice President, Ryan (Ry) Viets

Regional Vice President, Jim Bleming

Divisional Vice President, Jason Lecroy

Vice President Of Financial Services, Patrick Orr

Divisional Vice President, Donnie Warren

Regional Vice President, Tim (Timmy) Hubka

Vice President, James O'Toole

Vice President, John (Jack) Bullock

Chairman, Daniel P. McCartney, age 64

Auditors: Grant Thornton LLP

LOCATIONS

HQ: Healthcare Services Group, Inc.
3220 Tillman Drive, Suite 300, Bensalem, PA 19020
Phone: 215 639-4274   **Fax:** 215 639-2152
Web: www.hcsgcorp.com

PRODUCTS/OPERATIONS

2014 Sales

	% of total
Housekeeping services	65
Dietary services	35
Total	**100**

COMPETITORS

ABM Industries	Ecolab
ARAMARK	G&K Services
Alsco	Sodexo USA
Angelica Corporation	SureQuest Systems
Crothall Healthcare	

HISTORICAL FINANCIALS

Company Type: Public

Income Statement

FYE: December 31

	REVENUE ($ mil.)	NET INCOME ($ mil.)	NET PROFIT MARGIN	EMPLOYEES
12/15	1,436.8	58.0	4.0%	8,600.0
12/14	1,293.1	21.8	1.7%	8,600.0
12/13	1,149.8	47.1	4.1%	7,600.0
12/12	1,077.4	44.2	4.1%	7,000.0
12/11	889.0	38.1	4.3%	6,850.0
Annual Growth	**12.8%**	**11.0%**	**—**	**5.9%**

2015 Year-End Financials

Debt ratio: —	No. of shares (mil.): 72.0
Return on equity: 20.2%	Dividends
Cash ($ mil.): 33.1	Yield: 2.0%
Current ratio: 3.81	Payout: 78.3%
Long-term debt ($ mil.): —	Market value ($ mil.): 2,512.0

	STOCK PRICE ($) FY Close	P/E High/Low		PER SHARE ($) Earnings	Dividends	Book Value
12/15	34.87	47	37	0.80	0.71	4.12
12/14	30.93	103	83	0.31	0.69	3.88
12/13	28.37	43	32	0.67	0.67	4.07
12/12	23.23	37	27	0.65	0.65	3.37
12/11	17.69	33	22	0.56	0.63	3.26
Annual Growth	**18.5%**	**—**	**—**	**9.3%**	**3.0%**	**6.0%**

Healthcare Trust Of America Inc

EXECUTIVES

Chb-pres-ceo, Scott D Peters

Executive Vice President Acquisitions, Mark Engstrom

Executive Vice President Asset Management, Amanda Houghton

Senior Vice President Leasing, Jaime Northam

Vice President Operations, Judy Klein

RVP, Dawna Powell

Auditors: Deloitte & Touche LLP

LOCATIONS

HQ: Healthcare Trust Of America Inc
16435 N. Scottsdale Road, Suite 320, Scottsdale, AZ 85254
Phone: 480 998-3478   **Fax:** 480 991-0755
Web: www.htareit.com

HISTORICAL FINANCIALS

Company Type: Public

Income Statement

FYE: December 31

	REVENUE ($ mil.)	NET INCOME ($ mil.)	NET PROFIT MARGIN	EMPLOYEES
12/15	403.8	32.9	8.2%	181.0
12/14	371.5	45.3	12.2%	170.0
12/13	319.9	24.2	7.6%	160.0
12/12	299.6	(24.4)	—	110.0
12/11	274.4	5.5	2.0%	60.0
Annual Growth	**10.1%**	**56.1%**	**—**	**31.8%**

2015 Year-End Financials

Debt ratio: 50.1%	No. of shares (mil.): 127.0
Return on equity: 2.3%	Dividends
Cash ($ mil.): 28.9	Yield: 4.3%
Current ratio: 1.80	Payout: 344.1%
Long-term debt ($ mil.): 1,590.7	Market value ($ mil.): 3,426.0

	STOCK PRICE ($) FY Close	P/E High/Low		PER SHARE ($) Earnings	Dividends	Book Value
12/15	26.97	115	87	0.26	1.17	10.86
12/14	26.94	72	26	0.37	0.29	11.57
12/13	9.84	66	49	0.20	0.00	11.71
12/12	9.90	—	—	(0.22)	0.00	11.69
Annual Growth	**39.7%**	**—**	**—**	**—**	**—**	**(2.4%)**

HealthEquity Inc

Auditors: PricewaterhouseCoopers LLP

LOCATIONS

HQ: HealthEquity Inc
15 West Scenic Pointe Drive, Suite 100, Draper, UT 84020
Phone: 801 727-1000
Web: www.healthequity.com

HISTORICAL FINANCIALS

Company Type: Public

Income Statement

FYE: January 31

	REVENUE ($ mil.)	NET INCOME ($ mil.)	NET PROFIT MARGIN	EMPLOYEES
01/16	126.7	16.6	13.1%	636.0
01/15	87.8	10.1	11.6%	455.0
01/14	62.0	1.2	2.0%	381.0
01/13	46.0	11.1	24.2%	0.0
Annual Growth	40.1%	14.2%	—	—

2016 Year-End Financials

Debt ratio: —	No. of shares (mil.): 57.7
Return on equity: 9.5%	Dividends
Cash ($ mil.): 123.7	Yield: —
Current ratio: 11.82	Payout: —
Long-term debt ($ mil.): —	Market value ($ mil.): 1,244.0

	STOCK PRICE ($) FY Close	P/E High/Low		PER SHARE ($) Earnings	Dividends	Book Value
01/16	21.55	121	65	0.28	0.00	3.52
01/15	20.77	66	43	0.21	0.00	2.63
01/14	0.00	—	—	(1.26)	0.00	4.83
Annual Growth (14.6%)		—	—	—	—	—

Healthstream Inc

HealthStream supplies internet-based learning and research content to health care organizations throughout the US to meet their training certification and development needs. HealthStream's core learning product is HealthStream Learning Center (HLC) which offers educational and training courseware to about 4.8 million subscribers (representing some 4000 hospitals) via a software-as-a-service (SaaS) model. The company's research offerings include quality and satisfaction surveys data analysis and other research-based management tools; the Patient Insights survey generates most of the research business' revenues.

Operations

The company operates through two segments — HealthStream Workforce Development (employee training and development) and HealthStream Research/Patient Experience (surveys and other research). It generates more than 80% of sales through the Workforce Development unit.

HealthStream's Authoring Center is an application allowing health care organizations to move existing content or create new content onto an online platform and then share it with other organizations through a courseware exchange. Other tools provide for competency management and performance assessment.

About three-fourths of the company's earnings are derived from subscription-based services.

Geographic Reach

HealthStream serves customers in all US states from its corporate headquarters in Nashville and its satellite offices in Laurel Maryland; Brentwood Tennessee; Jericho New York; and Pensacola Florida.

Sales and Marketing

HealthStream generates sales from subscription fees based on the number of users and type of content provided. Clients include US health care or-

ganizations –primarily acute care hospitals such as HCA Catholic Health Initiatives Community Health Systems and LifePoint –and pharmaceutical and medical device companies. Other clients include private not-for-profit and government organizations.

HealthStream markets its products primarily through direct sales teams consultants and account relationship managers. Its marketing programs include catalogs trade shows online promotions telemarketing campaigns public relations direct mail and advertising.

Advertising expenses in 2014 totaled some $663000 up from $408000 in 2013 and $349000 in 2012.

Financial Performance

HealthStream's revenues have climbed steadily over the last decade. For instance in 2014 the company reported a 29% sales increase to some $171 million due to growth in both the learning and research segments. The learning division saw a 34% increase in sales due to its growing subscriber base and expanded courseware offerings while research revenues rose 12% from increased patient survey volumes. HealthStream's revenue growth also prompted a 23% increase in profits to some $10 million that year.

Cash flow from operations has also been rising for the past few years. In 2014 it grew 27% to $34 million as net income rose more cash was provided by accounts receivable and cash used in accounts and unbilled receivables declined.

Strategy

While many of its competitors are offering course material in a range of formats (print online instructor-led) HealthStream focuses on its Internet-based offerings. In order to remain competitive HealthStream tailors its HLC course delivery methods to provide clients with access to the specific educational resources they need. While HealthStream is focused on adding subscribers to the HLC platform it also aims to have existing subscribers order additional courses and new software applications. To take advantage of the increasing use of simulation technology to educate students and medical professionals HealthStream partners with Laerdal Medical in a joint venture called SimVentures. The venture sells patient simulation scenarios through a simulation management platform called SimCenter.

Partnerships are a key to HealthStream's growth. In 2014 the company began providing content from some 900 courses from The Institute for Professional Care Education QueTech and Mather LifeWays Institute on Aging via the HealthStream Learning Center.

HealthStream's Research division only brings in about 20% of its income but it could start seeing more demand since the government is increasingly tying reimbursements to improved patient safety and performance results. The company's research services are meant to complement its learning segment. Its HealthStream Improvement Center is an online system designed to help hospital leaders accelerate the execution of the improvement plans they come up with thanks to the research services. Plans are generally based on results from patient employee physician and community surveys.

In 2015 HealthStream launched its Recruiting Center an application to help health care human resources professionals find and hire candidates with the best fit for their organizations. It includes career sites applicant tracking and reporting and analytics.

Also that year the company launched Echo a new unit combining the operations of its Health-

Line Systems (acquired in 2015) and SyMed Development (acquired in 2012) businesses. Echo provides medical staff credentialing and related services.

Mergers and Acquisitions

In 2013 and 2014 HealthStream added Baptist Leadership Group the consulting practice of Baptist Health Care for about $8.5 million; and Health Care Compliance Strategies a compliance training firm for about $13 million. In 2015 the company acquired HealthLine Systems which specializes in health care practitioner credentialing and competence assessment software services. That $88 million purchase expands the firm's offerings for human resources departments which have to monitor the qualifications of their health care providers to maintain accreditation.

EXECUTIVES

Chairman President and CEO, Robert A. Frist, age 48, $292,315 total compensation

SVP and CFO, Gerard M. (Gerry) Hayden, age 61, $255,379 total compensation

SVP and COO, J. Edward Pearson, age 53, $276,207 total compensation

SVP and CTO, Jeffrey S. Doster, age 51, $128,077 total compensation

SVP and President Provider Solutions, Michael J. Sousa, age 47, $266,933 total compensation

Vice President Strategic Accounts, Jim Reeves

Vice President of Information Technology, Tom Dugger

Auditors: Ernst & Young LLP

LOCATIONS

HQ: Healthstream Inc
209 10th Avenue South, Suite 450, Nashville, TN 37203
Phone: 615 301-3100
Web: www.healthstream.com

PRODUCTS/OPERATIONS

2014 Sales

	$ mil.	% of total
Workforce Development	138.8	81
Research/Patient Experience	31.9	19
Total	**170.7**	**100**

Selected Solutions

ICD-10 Education
CAHPS Surveys
Nurse Orientation
Healthcare Compliance
Resuscitation Training
Post-Acute Care Solutions

COMPETITORS

AMA	Medscape llc
Cengage Learning	NRC
Cornerstone OnDemand	Press Ganey
EBSCO	RELX Group
Foresight Group	Saba Software
Gallup	SuccessFactors
Kenexa	SumTotal

HISTORICAL FINANCIALS
Company Type: Public

Income Statement
FYE: December 31

	REVENUE ($ mil.)	NET INCOME ($ mil.)	NET PROFIT MARGIN	EMPLOYEES
12/15	209.0	8.6	4.1%	972.0
12/14	170.6	10.3	6.1%	787.0
12/13	132.2	8.4	6.4%	686.0
12/12	103.7	7.6	7.4%	587.0
12/11	82.0	6.9	8.5%	504.0
Annual Growth	26.3%	5.6%	—	17.8%

2015 Year-End Financials

Debt ratio: —
Return on equity: 3.8%
Cash ($ mil.): 82.0
Current ratio: 2.35
Long-term debt ($ mil.): —

No. of shares (mil.): 31.6
Dividends
Yield: —
Payout: —
Market value ($ mil.): 696.0

	STOCK PRICE ($) FY Close	P/E High/Low	PER SHARE ($) Earnings	Dividends	Book Value
12/15	22.00	111 73	0.28	0.00	8.86
12/14	29.48	91 55	0.37	0.00	6.06
12/13	32.63	127 65	0.30	0.00	5.47
12/12	24.31	105 60	0.28	0.00	5.04
12/11	18.45	61 22	0.29	0.00	4.67
Annual Growth	4.5%	— —	(0.9%)	—	17.4%

Heartland Express, Inc.

Home is where the heart is and Heartland Express stays close to home as a short- to medium-haul truckload carrier –its average trip is just over 500 miles. With the exception of traffic from its Phoenix hub the company mainly operates east of the Rockies; it also offers service in the southwestern US. Although most of its loads go directly from origin to destination Heartland also operates from about 20 regional distribution hubs which are located near major customers. The company regional hubs focus on short-haul freight movements (less than 500 miles). Heartland transports general commodities including appliances auto parts consumer products food and paper products.Geographic ReachHeartland provides multiple transportation services across the US and parts of Canada through a nationwide network of regional operating divisions. Its operating centers reside in Columbus Ohio; Carlisle Pennsylvania; Richmond Virgina; Kingsport Tennessee; Atlanta; Jacksonville Florida; Memphis Tennessee; Dallas; Phoenix; and Iowa City Iowa.OperationsThe company's fleet of tractors is about two-years-old and the average trailer is about five-years old. Heartland keeps costs down by utilizing a uniform feet of vehicles that follow a standardized maintenance schedule. The company also employs independent contractors who own their own vehicles and are responsible for all upkeep costs.Sales and MarketingHeartland targets the retail food consumer goods manufacturing automotive and paper and plastic sectors. Customers include Georgia Pacific FedEx Unilever Eastman Chemical Unyson Logistics Winegard and Quaker/Gatorade.Financial PerformanceAfter posting record-setting revenues of $871 million in 2014 Heartland saw its revenues decline 15% to $736 million in 2015. Profits also

fell 14% from $85 million to $73 million during the same time period.The decreases for 2015 were attributed to reduced fuel surcharges primarily as a result of a decrease in average DOE (Department of Energy) diesel fuel prices. Revenue from trucking also dipped due to a decrease in loaded miles combined with a spike in the rate per loaded mile compared to 2014.StrategyTo combat the volatility of fuel costs Heartland purchases over-the-road fuel at negotiated price discounts through a network of fuel stops throughout the US. The company also has bulk fuel sites at 12 Heartland-owned facilities and service centers. Additional fuel saving procedures includes reducing tractor idle time and controlling out-of-route miles (additional/non-billable miles).In conjunction with its focus on short- to medium-haul transportation Heartland tries to attract customers who are more time-sensitive than price-sensitive and thus will pay higher rates. The company aims to grow by attracting more business within its existing service territory but it has indicated it will consider acquisitions.Company BackgroundRussell Gerdin founded Heartland Express in 1978 after taking over a company that had begun in 1955 as an appliance hauler. When the trucking industry was deregulated in 1979 Heartland like many other small nonunion irregular-route companies took off. It grew rapidly during the 1980s and in 1986 Gerdin took Heartland public.

EXECUTIVES

EVP Finance; Treasurer and CFO, John P. Cosaert, age 68, $229,327 total compensation
Chairman; President; CEO and Director, Michael J. Gerdin, age 46, $239,519 total compensation
Vice President Sls, Kent (Ken) Rigdon
Vice President; Controller; Secretary, Thomas (Thom) Hill
Auditors: KPMG LLP

LOCATIONS

HQ: Heartland Express, Inc.
901 North Kansas Avenue, North Liberty, IA 52317
Phone: 319 626-3600
Web: www.heartlandexpress.com

PRODUCTS/OPERATIONS

Selected Regional Hubs
Albany Oregon
Atlanta Georgia
Boise Idaho
Carlisle Pennsylvania
Chester Virginia
Clackamas Oregon
Columbus Ohio
Green Bay Wisconsin
Indianapolis Indiana
Jacksonville Florida
Kingsport Tennessee
Lathrop California
Medford Oregon
North Liberty Iowa
Olive Branch Mississippi
Pacific Washington
Phoenix Arizona
Pontoon Beach Illinois
Rancho Cucamonga California
Seagoville Texas

COMPETITORS

Arnold Transportation
Celadon
Con-way Truckload
Covenant

Landstar System
P.A.M. Transportation
Schneider National
Swift Transportation

Transportation
Crete Carrier
J.B. Hunt
Knight Transportation

U.S. Xpress
USA Truck
Werner Enterprises

HISTORICAL FINANCIALS
Company Type: Public

Income Statement
FYE: December 31

	REVENUE ($ mil.)	NET INCOME ($ mil.)	NET PROFIT MARGIN	EMPLOYEES
12/15	736.3	73.0	9.9%	4,200.0
12/14	871.3	84.8	9.7%	4,500.0
12/13	582.2	70.5	12.1%	5,220.0
12/12	545.7	61.5	11.3%	2,993.0
12/11	528.6	69.9	13.2%	2,862.0
Annual Growth	8.6%	1.1%	—	10.1%

2015 Year-End Financials

Debt ratio: —
Return on equity: 15.4%
Cash ($ mil.): 33.2
Current ratio: 2.06
Long-term debt ($ mil.): —

No. of shares (mil.): 84.1
Dividends
Yield: 0.4%
Payout: 9.0%
Market value ($ mil.): 1,432.0

	STOCK PRICE ($) FY Close	P/E High/Low	PER SHARE ($) Earnings	Dividends	Book Value
12/15	17.02	32 20	0.84	0.08	5.59
12/14	27.01	29 20	0.96	0.08	5.43
12/13	19.62	24 16	0.83	0.08	4.53
12/12	13.07	21 17	0.71	1.08	3.43
12/11	14.29	23 16	0.78	0.08	3.94
Annual Growth	4.5%	— —	1.9%	(0.0%)	9.1%

Heartland Financial USA, Inc. (Dubuque, IA)

Heartland Financial USA brings heart-felt community banking to nation's heartland. The $5.9 billion multi-bank holding company owns flagship subsidiary Dubuque Bank & Trust and nine other banks that together operate more than 75 branches in 55-plus communities in the Midwest and Southwest US. In addition to standard deposit loan and mortgage services the banks also offer retirement wealth management trust insurance and investment services including socially responsible investing. Heartland Financial USA also owns consumer lender Citizens Finance which has about a dozen offices in Illinois Iowa and Wisconsin.

OperationsHeartland operates two main segments: Community and Other Banking and Retail Mortgage Banking. The Community and Other Banking business generates revenue from interest earned on loans and investment securities and fees from deposit services. Its Retail Mortgage Banking collects revenue from interest from mortgage loans held for sale gains on sales of loans on the secondary market the servicing of mortgage loans for investors and loan origination fee income. Approximately 70% of Heartland Financial's loan portfolio comes from commercial loans and mortgages but in keeping with the bank's Midwestern identity it also makes agricultural residential mortgage and consumer loans.Heartland Financial USA's subsidiaries include: Dubuque Bank and Trust Company Galena State Bank & Trust Co. Illinois Bank & Trust Wisconsin Bank & Trust Morrill & Janes Bank and Trust New Mexico Bank & Trust Arizona Bank & Trust. It also owns multi-line insurance company DB&T Insurance Inc. and runs the community development company DB&T Community Development Corp.Geographic Reach-Heartland operates more than 75 branches in local communities in Arizona Colorado Illinois Iowa Kansas Montana Minnesota Missouri New Mexico and Wisconsin. It also has loan production offices in California Idaho Nevada North Dakota Oregon Washington and Wyoming. About 40% of the company's assets are based in Western markets.Sales and MarketingHeartland offers its banking services to businesses public sector and non-profit entities and individuals. In total the bank serves some 120000 business and consumer households. Heartland spent $5.52 million on advertising in 2014 about 4% more than it spent in 2013.Financial PerformanceHeartland's revenue was up for a second straight year jumping by 10% to $319.3 million in 2014. The boost was mostly driven by interest income from loan growth and additional investment security income as the company increased its earning assets by 18% during the year. The bank's non-interest income sources however lagged as the bank netted fewer gains on its loans held for sale and its investment security sales.The company's net income also rose in 2014 by 14% to $41.9 million rebounding from last year's dip thanks to higher revenue and because it paid lower interest on its deposits.Operations provided $80.4 million or 40% less cash than in 2013 mostly as the bank collected less in proceeds from the net sales of its loans-held-for-sale and because it used more cash toward its prepaid expenses.StrategyHeartland Financial's main growth strategy is to expand its presence in the West with the goal of making the region home to half of its total assets and balancing growth in those markets with the stability of the Midwest. In line with this the bank seeks to expand its subsidiaries through acquisitions and grow its customer base organically in its existing markets.

Consistent with this strategy in early 2015 Heartland purchased the Community Banc-Corp of Sheboygan Inc. (the parent company of Community Bank & Trust) which added 10 branches in Wisconsin and some $410 million worth of loan assets. In 2013 Heartland purchased Morrill Bancshares Inc. along with its Morrill & Janes Bank and Trust Company subsidiary effectively expanding its reach into Kansas and growing its loan assets and deposits by nearly $378 million and $665 million respectively. That year Heartland also bought Freedom Bank and its three branches which expanded its reach into Illinois and enriched its service offerings to business agri-business and consumer banking clients.Mergers and AcquisitionsIn January 2015 Heartland acquired the Community Banc-Corp of Sheboygan Inc. along with all 10 of its Community Bank & Trust branches along with $530.4 million worth of assets $410 million in loans and $429 million in deposits; in exchange for $52 million in an all-stock transaction. The Community Bank & Trust bank was folded into Wisconsin Bank & Trust under the deal.In 2013 the company acquired Morrill Bancshares Inc. the holding company of the Kansas-based Morrill & Janes Bank and Trust Company along with $377.7 million in total loans and $665.3 million worth of deposits. The Morrill & Janes Bank and Trust Company became one of Heartland's independent bank subsidiaries.In 2012 Heartland Financial acquired Heritage Bank N.A. a Phoenix-based com-

mercial bank in an all-cash deal valued at about $16 million consistent with its goal of expansion in the West.

EXECUTIVES

Vice President Marketing, Dawn (Dawny) Oelke
President and CEO Minnesota Bank & Trust, Catherine T. (Kate) Kelly
Chairman President and CEO Heartland Financial USA Inc.; Vice Chairman Dubuque Bank & Trust Wisconsin Bank & Trust New Mexico Bank & Trust Arizona Bank & Trust Rocky Mountain Bank Centennial Bank and Trust(1) Minnesota Bank & Trust and Premier Valley Bank, Lynn B. Fuller, age 66, $486,388 total compensation
EVP Lending, Douglas J. Horstmann, age 62, $275,156 total compensation
President and CEO New Mexico Bank & Trust, R. Greg Leyendecker
President Heartland Business Bank, Kevin S. Tenpas
President of Heartland Director Rocky Mountain Bank and President Heartland Financial USA Inc. Insurance Services, Bruce K. Lee, age 55, $383,519 total compensation
EVP Human Resources and Organizational Development, Mark G. Murtha, age 54
SVP Chief Accounting Officer, Janet M. Quick
President Centennial Bank and Trust, Steven E. Ward
EVP Wealth Management, Bruce C. Rehmke
EVP Commercial Sales, Frank E. Walter, age 69
EVP Senior General Counsel and Corporate Secretary, Michael J. Coyle, age 70
EVP Operations, Brian J. Fox, age 67, $190,000 total compensation
EVP and Chief Risk Officer, Rodney L. Sloan, age 56
EVP and CFO Heartland Financial USA Treasurer Citizens Finance Parent Co.. and Director Heartland Financial USA Inc. Insurance Services, Bryan R. McKeag, age 55, $305,625 total compensation
EVP Finance and Corporate Strategy, David L. Horstmann, age 66
President and CEO Arizona Bank & Trust, Jerry L. Schwallier
President and CEO Rocky Mountain Bank, Curtis Chrystal
President and CEO Morrill & Janes Bank and Trust Co., Kurt M. Saylor
EVP Private Client Services, Kelly J. Johnson, age 54
President and CEO Illinois Bank and Trust, Jeff Hultman
Chief Investment Officer, Nancy Tengler
EVP and Chief Credit Officer, Drew Townsend
EVP and Private Wealth Management Director, Rick O. Terry
President and CEO Heartland Mortgage, Paul Johnstun
CEO Centennial Bank and Trust, Jim Basey
President Heartland Mortgage, Jack Lloyd
Executive Vice President Marketing and Sales, John J (Jack) Berg
Vice President Administrative Services, Joseph V (Jo) Berretta
Vice President Finance, Jacquie Manternach
Vice President Loan Operations, Kate (Katie) Barth
Vice President, Jean (Jeannie) Harkey
Mortgage Servicing Vice President, Tony (Tone) Newkirk
Vice President Corporate Training Director, Bonnie (Bonbon) Bollin
Assistant Vice President Commercial Services, Lynn (Lyn) Stoffregen

Vice President Operations and Finance, Bret Tuley
Senior Vice President Director Retail Banking, Tut Fuller
Vice President, Rachel (Rach) Steiner
Executive Vice President Investment Services Director HTLF Investment Services, David (Dave) Wick
Vice President Credit Administration, Ted (Teddy) Kraft
Senior Vice President Small Business Loan Center Manager, Jeff (Jeffy) Ciochetto
Senior Vice President, Julie (Jules) Shanahan
Senior Vice President Special Assets REO, John (Jack) Hawkins
Vice President, Shelley (Shell) Phillips
Assistant Vice President Senior Research Analyst, Troy Steger
Vice President, Cheri Wheelan
Vice President, Craig (Craigy) Sciara
Vice President, Rod Sloan
Senior Vice President Credit Administration, Brian (Bri) McCarthy
Vice President General Counsel, David (Dave) Kapler
Senior Vice President Loan Operations Manager, Sherry (Sherr) Yonda
Vice President Finance, Harkey Jean
Senior Vice President Head of Loan Operations, Dan (Danny) Tabraham
Vice President, Mark (Marky) Erickson
Vice President CPS Senior Solutions Consultant, Premal Kadakia
Executive Vice President and Chief Credit Officer, Andrew E (Andy) Townsend
Assistant Vice President Information Services, Brent Wilke
Vice Chairman of the Board of Heartland Financial USA Inc.; Chairman and Director of Dubuque Bank and Trust, Mark C. Falb, age 68
Vice Chairman of the Board of Heartland Financial USA Inc.; Director and Vice Chairman of the Board of Dubuque Bank and Trust, Thomas L. Flynn, age 60
Auditors: KPMG LLP

LOCATIONS

HQ: Heartland Financial USA, Inc. (Dubuque, IA)
1398 Central Avenue, Dubuque, IA 52001
Phone: 563 589-2000   **Fax:** 563 589-2011
Web: www.htlf.com

PRODUCTS/OPERATIONS

2014 Sales

	$ mil.	% of total
Interest		
Loans & leases including fees	194.0	61
Securities & other	43.0	13
Noninterest		
Gains on sales of loans	31.3	10
Service charges and fees	20.1	7
Trust fees	13.1	4
Loan serving income	5.6	2
Brokerage & insurance commissions	4.5	1
Security gains	3.7	1
Other	4.0	1
Total	**319.3**	**100**

Selected Subsidiaries

Arizona Bank & Trust
Citizens Finance Co. (consumer lending)
Dubuque Bank and Trust (IA)
    DB&T Insurance Inc.
    DB&T Community Development Corp.
First Community Bank (IA)
Galena State Bank & Trust Co. (IL)
New Mexico Bank & Trust
Minnesota Bank & Trust (80%)
Riverside Community Bank (IL)

Rocky Mountain Bank (MT)
Summit Bank & Trust (87% CO)
Wisconsin Community Bank

COMPETITORS

Associated Banc-Corp   First Banks
BBVA Compass   U.S. Bancorp
Bancshares   Wells Fargo
Bank of America   Zions Bancorporation
Bank of the West

HISTORICAL FINANCIALS
Company Type: Public

Income Statement
FYE: December 31

	ASSETS ($ mil.)	NET INCOME ($ mil.)	INCOME AS % OF ASSETS	EMPLOYEES
12/15	7,694.7	60.0	0.8%	1,799.0
12/14	6,052.3	41.9	0.7%	1,631.0
12/13	5,923.7	36.7	0.6%	1,676.0
12/12	4,990.5	49.7	1.0%	1,498.0
12/11	4,305.0	28.0	0.7%	1,195.0
Annual Growth	15.6%	21.0%	—	10.8%

2015 Year-End Financials

Return on assets: 0.8%	Dividends
Return on equity: 10.3%	Yield: 1.4%
Long-term debt ($ mil.): —	Payout: 16.0%
No. of shares (mil.): 22.4	Market value ($ mil.): 704.0
Sales ($ mil): 376.6	

	STOCK PRICE ($) FY Close	P/E High/Low	PER SHARE ($) Earnings	Dividends	Book Value
12/15	31.36	14 9	2.83	0.45	29.56
12/14	27.10	13 10	2.19	0.40	26.81
12/13	28.79	14 11	2.04	0.50	23.88
12/12	26.15	10 5	2.77	0.50	23.88
12/11	15.34	15 10	1.23	0.40	21.24
Annual Growth	19.6%	—	23.2%	3.0%	8.6%

Heico Corp.

HEICO Corporation helps jets get airborne. Its Flight Support Group consisting of HEICO Aerospace and its subsidiaries makes FAA-approved replacement parts for jet engines that can be substituted for original parts including airfoils bearings and fuel pump gears. Flight Support also repairs overhauls and distributes jet engine parts as well as avionics and instruments for commercial air carriers. HEICO's second segment Electronic Technologies Group makes a variety of electronic equipment for the aerospace/defense electronic medical and telecommunications industries.

Operations

HEICO's business is comprised of two operating segments the Flight Support Group (FSG; about 65% of net sales) and the Electronic Technologies Group (ETG; 35%).

FSG competes with industry leading OEMs and to a lesser extent with smaller independent parts distributors. Historically the three main jet engine OEMs General Electric Pratt & Whitney and Rolls Royce have been the source of substantially all jet engine replacement parts for their own jet engines. HEICO is seeking to capture some of that market by adding new products at a rate of 300 to 500

manufacturer-approved parts (also called PMAs) per year.

Geographic Reach

HEICO has its operations and facilities in China India Singapore Canada France Korea Laos the Netherlands the UK and the US. The company markets its products and services in approximately 100 countries with the US counting for more than 65% of its net sales.

Sales and Marketing

HEICO sells its products through in-house personnel and independent manufacturers' representatives. It targets a broad customer base consisting of domestic and foreign commercial and cargo airlines repair and overhaul facilities other aftermarket suppliers of aircraft engine and airframe materials OEMs domestic and foreign military units electronic manufacturing services companies US and foreign governments manufacturers for the defense industry as well as medical telecommunications scientific and industrial companies. Net sales to its five largest customers account for around 20% of net sales each year.

Financial Performance

HEICO has achieved unprecedented growth over the years with revenues jumping 16% from $1.19 billion in 2015 to peak at a record-setting $1.38 billion in 2016. Profits also surged 17% from $134 million in 2015 to $156 million in 2016 another company milestone. In 2016 cash flow from operating activities increased due to a $37 million decrease in working capital a $23 million increase in net income from consolidated operations and a $12 million increase in depreciation and amortization expense (a non-cash item).

The historic growth for 2016 was fueled by increases in both of its segments. FSG jumped by 8% due to organic growth as well as additional net sales from a previous acquisition. The organic growth reflected new product offerings and favorable market conditions resulting in net sales within the aftermarket replacement parts and repair and overhaul services product lines.

ETG revenue soared by 31% due to additional net sales from a previous acquisition as well as organic growth of approximately 4%. The organic growth reflected an increase in demand for certain space and aerospace products.

Mergers and Acquisitions

HEICO uses acquisitions to build out a diverse product and service portfolio in order to reduce exposure to cyclical swings in any single market. Its current set of offerings have broad-range applications in aircraft missiles ships surveillance systems computer and networking devices telecom equipment surgical equipment CT scanners and X-ray systems.

In 2016 the company's ETG division acquired Arizona-based Robertson Fuel Systems for $255 million. Robertson has expertise in the design and production of mission-extending crashworthy and ballistically self-sealing auxiliary fuel systems for military rotorcraft. The acquisition will enhance the company's fuel systems product portfolio. In 2015 the company's FSG division purchased Astroseal Products Manufacturing Corp. Astroseal makes expanded foil mesh that is integrated into composite aerospace structures for lightning strike protection in fixed and rotary wing aircraft. The deal expanded the group's offerings of aerospace composite products.

HISTORY

Company Background

Founded in 1957 as Heinicke Instruments to make laboratory products the company moved into jet engine parts in 1974 with the acquisition of Jet Avion. The company changed its name to HEICO (a shortened version of its previous name) in 1985. After a faulty combustion chamber erupted in flames that year the FAA ordered all combustion chambers on US jets to be inspected and if necessary replaced. HEICO's sales skyrocketed but descended back to earth after airlines found they had overstocked.

EXECUTIVES

Vice President Corporate Development, William (Bill) Harlow
Co-President and Director; President and CEO HEICO Electronic Technologies, Victor H. Mendelson, age 48, $519,178 total compensation
EVP and Director; President and CEO HEICO Aerospace, Eric A. Mendelson, age 51, $519,178 total compensation
Senior Executive Vice President, Thomas S. Irwin, age 70, $238,299 total compensation
Chairman and CEO, Laurans A. Mendelson, age 78, $973,425 total compensation
EVP CFO and Treasurer, Carlos L. Macau, $553,014 total compensation
Vice President, Paul (Pauly) Belisle
Vice President Acquisitions, Adam Bentkover
Vice President Sales (HPG) Latin America, Mike (Mikey) Garcia
Vice President Finance Administration, Luis Morell
Vice President sales And Marketing, George (Georgey) Congionti
Cao-asst Treas, Steven (Steve) Walker
Auditors: Deloitte & Touche LLP

LOCATIONS

HQ: Heico Corp.
3000 Taft Street, Hollywood, FL 33021
Phone: 954 987-4000
Web: www.heico.com

PRODUCTS/OPERATIONS

2016 Sales

	$ mil.	% of total
Flight Support Group	875.9	63
Electronic Technologies Group	511.3	37
Intersegment sales	(10.9)	-
Total	**1,376.3**	**100**

Selected Products

Flight Support Group
  Cockpit/avionics parts
  Electro-mechanical components
  Engine parts
  Fuselage/interior parts
  Wing parts
Electronic Technologies Group
  Aircraft power supplies and batteries
  Circuit board shielding
  Electro-optical infrared simulation and test equipment
  Electro-optical laser products
  High-voltage interconnect and cable assembly devices
  Medical power supplies and power generators

COMPETITORS

AAR Corp.   Kellstrom Industries
ATI Ladish   LMI Aerospace
BBA Aviation   Pratt & Whitney
Barnes Group   Rolls-Royce
CIC International   SAFRAN
Doncasters   SIFCO
GE Aviation   TIMCO Aviation
Honeywell Aerospace   Triumph Group

HISTORICAL FINANCIALS
Company Type: Public

Income Statement
FYE: October 31

	REVENUE ($ mil.)	NET INCOME ($ mil.)	NET PROFIT MARGIN	EMPLOYEES
10/16	1,376.2	156.1	11.3%	4,700.0
10/15	1,188.6	133.3	11.2%	4,600.0
10/14	1,132.3	121.2	10.7%	3,500.0
10/13	1,008.7	102.4	10.2%	3,500.0
10/12	897.3	85.1	9.5%	3,100.0
Annual Growth	11.3%	16.4%	—	11.0%

2016 Year-End Financials

Debt ratio: 22.4%	No. of shares (mil.): 67.2
Return on equity: 17.5%	Dividends
Cash ($ mil.): 42.9	Yield: 0.2%
Current ratio: 2.72	Payout: 7.5%
Long-term debt ($ mil.): 457.8	Market value ($ mil.): 4,546.0

	STOCK PRICE ($) FY Close	P/E High/Low	Earnings	PER SHARE ($) Dividends	Book Value
10/16	67.56	32 21	2.29	0.16	14.32
10/15	50.44	31 24	1.97	0.14	12.11
10/14	54.24	35 26	1.80	0.47	10.51
10/13	53.58	45 25	1.53	2.27	9.14
10/12	38.63	47 26	1.28	0.11	9.33
Annual Growth	15.0%	— —	15.7%	10.3%	11.3%

Hemisphere Media Group, Inc

Auditors: RSM US LLP

LOCATIONS
HQ: Hemisphere Media Group, Inc
4000 Ponce de Leon Boulevard, Suite 650, Coral Gables, FL 33146
Phone: 305 421-6364
Web: www.hemispheretv.com

HISTORICAL FINANCIALS
Company Type: Public

Income Statement
FYE: December 31

	REVENUE ($ mil.)	NET INCOME ($ mil.)	NET PROFIT MARGIN	EMPLOYEES
12/15	129.7	13.7	10.6%	300.0
12/14	111.9	10.5	9.4%	293.0
12/13	86.0	(4.3)	—	282.0
12/12	71.3	11.0	15.5%	0.0
12/11	60.8	7.6	12.5%	0.0
Annual Growth	20.9%	15.9%	—	—

2015 Year-End Financials

Debt ratio: 39.9%	No. of shares (mil.): 45.3
Return on equity: 5.1%	Dividends
Cash ($ mil.): 179.5	Yield: —
Current ratio: 5.44	Payout: —
Long-term debt ($ mil.): 211.6	Market value ($ mil.): 669.0

	STOCK PRICE ($) FY Close	P/E High/Low	Earnings	PER SHARE ($) Dividends	Book Value
12/15	14.75	46 37	0.31	0.00	6.14
12/14	13.49	53 42	0.25	0.00	5.76
12/13	11.87	— —	(0.14)	0.00	5.45
Annual Growth	11.5%	— —	—	—	6.1%

Hennessy Advisors Inc

EXECUTIVES
Chb-pres-ceo; Chief Information Officer, Neil J Hennessy
Executive Vice President, Dan (Danny) Steadman
Vice President, Michael (Mel) Perrella
Board of Directors, Henry (Hal) Hansel
Auditors: Marcum LLP

LOCATIONS
HQ: Hennessy Advisors Inc
7250 Redwood Blvd., Suite 200, Novato, CA 94945
Phone: 415 899-1555   **Fax:** 415 899-1559
Web: www.hennessyadvisors.com

HISTORICAL FINANCIALS
Company Type: Public

Income Statement
FYE: September 30

	REVENUE ($ mil.)	NET INCOME ($ mil.)	NET PROFIT MARGIN	EMPLOYEES
09/16	51.4	14.3	27.9%	22.0
09/15	44.7	11.3	25.5%	21.0
09/14	34.5	7.6	22.2%	19.0
09/13	24.3	4.8	19.8%	18.0
09/12	7.0	0.9	13.7%	11.0
Annual Growth	64.2%	96.1%	—	18.9%

2016 Year-End Financials

Debt ratio: 35.8%	No. of shares (mil.): 5.1
Return on equity: 47.4%	Dividends
Cash ($ mil.): 3.5	Yield: 0.8%
Current ratio: 0.89	Payout: 12.0%
Long-term debt ($ mil.): 26.2	Market value ($ mil.): 181.0

	STOCK PRICE ($) FY Close	P/E High/Low	Earnings	PER SHARE ($) Dividends	Book Value
09/16	35.47	14 8	2.79	0.30	7.31
09/15	23.76	13 9	1.91	0.23	4.58
09/14	19.88	14 9	1.30	0.15	6.22
09/13	7.65	9 3	0.83	0.13	5.05
09/12	2.85	19 12	0.17	0.12	4.38
Annual Growth	87.8%	— —	101.3%	26.1%	13.7%

Heritage Commerce Corp.

If you know the way to San Jose you may also know the way to Heritage Commerce. It is the holding company for Heritage Bank of Commerce which operates 10 branches in the South Bay region of the San Francisco area. Serving consumers and small to midsized businesses and their owners and managers the bank offers savings and checking accounts money market and retirement accounts and CDs as well as cash management services and loans. Commercial construction land and mortgage loans make up most of the company's loan portfolio which is rounded out by home equity and consumer loans. The bank was founded in 1994.

EXECUTIVES
EVP and CFO, Lawrence D. McGovern, age 61, $260,753 total compensation
President and CEO, Walter T. (Walt) Kaczmarek, age 64, $368,509 total compensation
EVP and Director Business Development, Robert P. (Bob) Gionfriddo, age 70
EVP Banking Division, Michael E. Benito, $244,826 total compensation
COO, Keith A. Wilton, $243,025 total compensation
EVP and Chief Credit Officer, David E. Porter, $260,738 total compensation
EVP and Corporate Secretary, Deborah K. (Debbie) Reuter
EVP HOA and Deposit Services, Teresa Powell
Vice President Commercial Loan Officer, Shirlene Kaneda
Vice President, Nancy Landy
Vice President Business Development Officer, David (Dave) Beronio
Vice President, Robert (Bob) Magana
Vice President Credit Risk, Carol Long
Senior Vice President And Senior Relationship Manager, Diana (Ana) Kershaw
Vice President Cash Management Officer, Kelly (Kel) Swanson
Senior Vice President SBA Department Manager, Ruth (Ruthy) Brown
Director, Jack W. Conner, age 76
Auditors: Crowe Horwath LLP

LOCATIONS
HQ: Heritage Commerce Corp.
150 Almaden Boulevard, San Jose, CA 95113
Phone: 408 947-6900
Web: www.heritagecommercecorp.com

PRODUCTS/OPERATIONS

2015 Sales

	$ mil.	% of total
Interest		
Loans including fees	68.3	78
Taxable securities	6.7	8
Other	3.8	4
Noninterest		
Service charges & fees on deposit accounts	2.8	3
Increase in cash surrender value of life insurance	1.7	2
Servicing income	1.2	1
Gain on sales of securities	0.8	1
Other	2.4	3
Total	**0.0**	**100**

COMPETITORS

Bank of America	JPMorgan Chase
Bank of the West	MUFG Americas Holdings
Citibank	SVB Financial
Comerica	U.S. Bancorp
First Republic (CA)	Wells Fargo

HISTORICAL FINANCIALS

Company Type: Public

Income Statement

FYE: December 31

	ASSETS ($ mil.)	NET INCOME ($ mil.)	INCOME AS % OF ASSETS	EMPLOYEES
12/15	2,361.5	16.5	0.7%	260.0
12/14	1,617.1	13.4	0.8%	242.0
12/13	1,491.6	11.5	0.8%	193.0
12/12	1,693.3	9.9	0.6%	190.0
12/11	1,306.1	11.3	0.9%	189.0
Annual Growth	16.0%	9.7%	—	8.3%

2015 Year-End Financials

Return on assets: 0.8%
Return on equity: 7.6%
Long-term debt ($ mil.): —
No. of shares (mil.): 32.1
Sales ($ mil): 87.7

Dividends
Yield: 2.6%
Payout: 66.6%
Market value ($ mil.): 384.0

	STOCK PRICE ($) FY Close	P/E High/Low	PER SHARE ($) Earnings	Dividends	Book Value
12/15	11.96	26 17	0.48	0.32	7.64
12/14	8.83	21 19	0.42	0.18	6.96
12/13	8.24	23 18	0.36	0.06	6.58
12/12	6.98	26 17	0.27	0.00	6.45
12/11	4.74	19 13	0.28	0.00	7.52
Annual Growth	26.0%	— —	14.4%	—	0.4%

Heritage Financial Corp. (WA)

Heritage Financial is ready to answer the call of Pacific Northwesterners seeking to preserve their heritage. Heritage Financial is the holding company for Heritage Bank which operates more than 65 branches throughout Washington and Oregon. Boasting nearly $4 billion in assets the bank offers a range of deposit products to consumers and businesses such as CDs IRAs and checking savings NOW and money market accounts. Commercial and industrial loans account for over 50% of Heritage Financial's loan portfolio while mortgages secured by multi-family real estate comprise about 5%. The bank also originates single-family mortgages land development construction loans and consumer loans.

OperationsThe bank also does business under the Central Valley Bank name in the Yakima and Kittitas counties of Washington and under the Whidbey Island Bank name on Whidbey Island.About 79% of Heritage Financial's total revenue came from loan interest (including fees) in 2014 while another 7% came from interest on its investment securities. The rest of its revenue came from service charges and other fees (8%) Merchant Visa income (1%) and other miscellaneous fees. The company had a staff of 748 employees at the end of that year.Geographic ReachThe Olympia-based bank operates more than 65 branches across Washington and the greater Portland area. It has additional offices in eastern Washington mostly in Yakima county.Sales and MarketingHeritage targets small and medium-sized businesses along with their owners as well as individuals. Financial PerformanceFueled by loan and deposit growth from a series of bank acquisi-

tions Heritage Financial's revenues and profits have been on the rise in recent years.The company's revenue jumped 70% to a record $137.6 million in 2014 mostly thanks to new loan business stemming from its acquisition of Washington Banking Company. Deposit service charge income also increased thanks to new deposit business from the acquisition.Higher revenue in 2014 allowed Heritage Financial's net income to more than double to a record $21 million while its operating cash levels rose 66% to $51.3 million on higher cash earnings and net proceeds from the sale of its loans.StrategyThe bank reiterated in 2015 that it would continue to pursue strategic acquisitions of community banks to grow market share across the Pacific Northwest (its region of expertise) expand its business lines and grow its loan and deposit business. With its focus on business and commercial lending the bank also in 2015 emphasized the importance of seeking high asset quality loans lending to familiar markets that have a historical record of success. Recruiting and retaining "highly competent personnel" to execute its strategies was also key to its long-term agenda.Mergers and AcquisitionsIn May 2014 Heritage acquired Washington Banking Company and its Whidbey Island Bank subsidiary for $265 million which "significantly expanded and enhanced" its product offerings across its core geographic market.

In July 2013 the bank acquired Puyallup Washington-based Valley Community Bancshares and its eight Valley Bank branches for $44 million.In January 2013 the company purchased Lakewood Washington-based Northwest Commercial Bank along with its two branch locations in Washington state for $5 million.

EXECUTIVES

President CEO and Director Heritage Financial and CEO Heritage Bank, Brian L. Vance, age 61, $494,316 total compensation
EVP and CFO Heritage Financial and Heritage Bank, Donald J. Hinson, age 55, $255,084 total compensation
EVP and Chief Credit Officer Heritage Bank, David A. Spurling, age 63, $237,342 total compensation
EVP Heritage Financial and President and COO Heritage Bank, Jeffrey J. (Jeff) Deuel, $291,516 total compensation
EVP and Chief Lending Officer Heritage Bank, Bryan D. McDonald, age 44, $261,374 total compensation
Vice President And Financial Reporting Manager, Patrice Hernandez
Chairman, Brian S. Charneski, age 54
Auditors: Crowe Horwath LLP

LOCATIONS

HQ: Heritage Financial Corp. (WA)
201 Fifth Avenue SW, Olympia, WA 98501
Phone: 360 943-1500
Web: www.HF-WA.com

PRODUCTS/OPERATIONS

2014 Sales

	$ mil.	% of total
Interest income		
Interest and fees on loans	110.4	79
Investment securities	10.2	7
Others	0.5	-
Non-interest income		
Service charges and others	11.1	8
Merchant Visa income	1.1	1
Others	4.3	5
Total	137.6	100

COMPETITORS

Bank of America
Columbia Banking
FS Bancorp
KeyCorp
U.S. Bancorp
Washington Federal
Wells Fargo

HISTORICAL FINANCIALS

Company Type: Public

Income Statement

FYE: December 31

	ASSETS ($ mil.)	NET INCOME ($ mil.)	INCOME AS % OF ASSETS	EMPLOYEES
12/15	3,650.7	37.4	1.0%	717.0
12/14	3,457.7	21.0	0.6%	748.0
12/13	1,659.0	9.5	0.6%	373.0
12/12	1,345.5	13.2	1.0%	363.0
12/11	1,368.9	6.5	0.5%	354.0
Annual Growth	27.8%	54.9%	—	19.3%

2015 Year-End Financials

Return on assets: 1.0%
Return on equity: 8.1%
Long-term debt ($ mil.): —
No. of shares (mil.): 29.9
Sales ($ mil): 168.0

Dividends
Yield: 3.6%
Payout: 58.4%
Market value ($ mil.): 565.0

	STOCK PRICE ($) FY Close	P/E High/Low	PER SHARE ($) Earnings	Dividends	Book Value
12/15	18.84	16 12	1.25	0.69	15.68
12/14	17.55	23 19	0.82	0.50	15.02
12/13	17.10	29 22	0.61	0.42	13.31
12/12	14.69	18 14	0.87	0.80	13.16
12/11	12.56	36 25	0.42	0.38	13.10
Annual Growth	10.7%	— —	31.3%	16.1%	4.6%

Heritage Insurance Holdings Inc

Auditors: Grant Thornton LLP

LOCATIONS

HQ: Heritage Insurance Holdings Inc
2600 McCormick Drive, Suite 300, Clearwater, FL 33759
Phone: 727 362-7200
Web: www.heritagepci.com

HISTORICAL FINANCIALS

Company Type: Public

Income Statement

FYE: December 31

	ASSETS ($ mil.)	NET INCOME ($ mil.)	INCOME AS % OF ASSETS	EMPLOYEES
12/15	837.4	92.5	11.0%	247.0
12/14	615.0	47.1	7.7%	133.0
12/13	281.9	34.2	12.1%	90.0
12/12	81.8	(5.4)	—	0.0
Annual Growth	117.1%	—	—	—

2015 Year-End Financials

Return on assets: 12.7%
Return on equity: 30.2%
Long-term debt ($ mil.): —
No. of shares (mil.): 30.4
Sales ($ mil): 394.7

Dividends
Yield: 0.2%
Payout: 1.6%
Market value ($ mil.): 664.0

	STOCK PRICE ($) FY Close	P/E High/Low		PER SHARE ($) Earnings	Dividends	Book Value
12/15	21.82	9	6	3.05	0.05	11.71
12/14	19.43	10	6	1.82	0.00	8.56
12/13	0.00	—	—	2.36	0.00	7.20
Annual Growth	—	—	—	13.7%	—	27.5%

Hersha Hospitality Trust

Hersha Hospitality Trust's fortune is in hotels not chocolate. The self-advised real estate investment trust (REIT) invests in hotel properties primarily midscale upscale and extended stay properties in metropolitan markets across the US. It owns or co-owns more than 50 hotels containing nearly 8000 rooms most of them in Boston New York and Washington DC as well as in Miami and Los Angeles. The properties are operated under such brand names as Marriott International Hilton Hotels Starwood Hotels and Hyatt. Hersha Hospitality Trust owns a minority stake in Hersha Hospitality Management which manages the REIT's properties. Starwood Capital Group owns the remainder of Hersha Hospitality Management.

OperationsHersha Hospitality Trust's property portfolio consisted of 46 wholly-owned limited and full-service hotel properties with nearly 6600 rooms in 2014. Through joint ventures it held five limited and full-service properties with nearly 1370 rooms. The hotels mostly operated under brands owned by Marriott International Hilton Worldwide Intercontinental Hotels Group Hyatt Corporation and Starwood Hotels and Resorts Worldwide.Geographic ReachMore than 45% of Hersha's rental income came from its properties in New York City in 2014. Its other hotel properties were in mostly major urban areas in nearly a dozen states including Arizona California Connecticut Delaware Washington DC Florida Maryland Massachusetts New York Pennsylvania and Virginia. Financial PerformanceHersha Hospitality's revenues and profits have been growing over the past few years as it has expanded its property portfolio through acquisitions and has charged higher rental rates as its property valuations have improved.The company's revenue rose 23% to $417.2 million in 2014 mostly thanks to property acquisitions from 2014 and 2013. Hersha's same-store revenues also improved during the year. Higher revenue and larger gains on its hotel property sales in 2014 drove the REIT's net income up 37% to $68.3 million for the year. Its operating cash levels jumped 25% to $112.9 million on higher cash earnings.Strategy Hersha Hospitality focuses on investing in high-quality upscale mid-scale and extended-stay hotels in urban high-barrier gateway markets. In recent years the company has targeted such properties in New York Washington DC Boston Philadelphia South Florida and select markets on the West Coast. During 2014 Hersha purchased 107 hotels including its $42-million purchase of Hotel Milo in Santa Barbara and four strategic hotels in California South Florida and Manhattan. The company that year expressed particular interest in the Santa Barbara hotel market which it said carried some of the highest revPAR rates in the country with minimal new supply.

In addition to acquisitions in urban areas the REIT is focused on property renovations designed to boost occupancy rates and enhance hotel value –which allow the company to raise room rates. In 2014 Hersha completed renovations on properties in Philadelphia (at its luxury-urban resort The Rittenhouse Spa Club Salon and Pool) as well as in Boston Los Angeles Washington DC and South Florida.

EXECUTIVES

Director Development and Acquisitions, Neil H. Shah, age 42, $400,000 total compensation
President and COO, Jay H. Shah, age 47, $425,000 total compensation
VP Finance, Bennett Thomas
Vice President of Asset Management, Charles (Charlie) Paloux
Vice President Acquisitions And Development, Lily Yu
Vice President Of Purchasing, Bhavesh Vekaria
Vice President Of Human Resources, Keith Black
Vice President Of Financial Services, Jay Linsey
Executive Vice President of Operations, Greg (Greggy) Ade
Chief Accounting Officer Controller Assistant Secretary, Michael (Mel) Gillespie
Chairman, Hasu P. Shah, age 71
Auditors: KPMG LLP

LOCATIONS

HQ: Hersha Hospitality Trust
44 Hersha Drive, Harrisburg, PA 17102
Phone: 717 236-4400   **Fax:** 717 774-7383
Web: www.hersha.com

PRODUCTS/OPERATIONS

2014 Sales

	$ mil.	% of total
Hotel operating revenues	417.2	100
Interest from development loans - -		
Other	0.2	-
Total	**417.4**	**100**

2014 Property Management

Hotels		Rooms
Hersha Hospitality Management	45.0	6,439
Waterford HOtel Group Inc	3.0	1,087
South Bay Boston Management Inc	2.0	282
Northwood Management LLC	1.0	148
Total	**51.0**	**7,956**

COMPETITORS

Ashford Hospitality Trust
Condor Hospitality
DiamondRock Hospitality
FelCor
Hospitality Properties Trust
Host Hotels & Resorts
Innkeepers USA
LaSalle Hotel Properties
Shaner Hotel Group
Strategic Hotels
Sunstone Hotel Investors

HISTORICAL FINANCIALS

Company Type: Public

Income Statement

FYE: December 31

	REVENUE ($ mil.)	NET INCOME ($ mil.)	NET PROFIT MARGIN	EMPLOYEES
12/15	470.3	42.2	9.0%	51.0
12/14	417.4	68.2	16.4%	48.0
12/13	338.4	49.9	14.8%	49.0
12/12	358.2	22.2	6.2%	46.0
12/11	286.4	(26.9)	—	36.0
Annual Growth	**13.2%**	—	—	**9.1%**

2015 Year-End Financials

Debt ratio: 59.7%
Return on equity: 5.6%
Cash ($ mil.): 27.9
Current ratio: 0.61
Long-term debt ($ mil.): 1,177.0

No. of shares (mil.): 44.4
Dividends
Yield: 3.8%
Payout: 77.7%
Market value ($ mil.): 967.0

	STOCK PRICE ($) FY Close	P/E High/Low		PER SHARE ($) Earnings	Dividends	Book Value
12/15	21.76	51	11	0.56	0.84	15.25
12/14	7.03	7	5	1.04	1.04	16.68
12/13	5.57	10	8	0.64	0.96	16.53
12/12	5.00	36	27	0.16	0.96	16.71
12/11	4.88	—	—	(0.84)	0.92	17.20
Annual Growth	**45.3%**	—	—	(2.2%)	(3.0%)

HFF Inc

Don't huff and puff –HFF will help you finance that high-rise. The company's Holliday Fenoglio Fowler subsidiary is a large commercial real estate capital intermediary. The firm provides capital markets services including structured financing commercial loan servicing investment sales loan sales and debt placement. Real estate investment banking subsidiary HFF Securities provides advisory services seeks private and joint venture equity capital places private listings and provides institutional marketing for property investments. Unlike most commercial property brokerage firms HFF does not provide leasing or property management services. The company operates about 20 offices throughout the US.Geographic ReachThe company operates more than 20 offices throughout the US. HFF offers capital markets services throughout Canada Mexico Puerto Rico and the US.Financial PerformanceThe company has seen its revenues rebound after they plummeted during the global financial downturn when frozen credit markets reduced liquidity and severely impacted commercial real estate activity. From 2011 to 2012 the firm's revenues jumped 12% from $255 million to $285 million. This was driven by an 11% surge in capital markets services revenue as a result of production volumes and related revenues in a majority of its capital markets services platforms. The company also enjoyed an 85% increase in interest on mortgage notes due to a higher average loan value and a higher number of loans originated.StrategyThe company continues to seek to improve its market share by penetrating national and regional markets. The company's biggest capital services market is Texas accounting for about 20% of total revenues. Other key markets include Florida Massachusetts and the DC area. HFF hopes to grow by opening additional offices in key US markets and it is also looking at expanding in foreign markets.

EXECUTIVES

Executive Managing Director Dallas Office, Mark D. Gibson, age 57, $500,000 total compensation
CFO, Gregory R. Conley, age 55, $375,000 total compensation
Executive Managing Director, Gerard Sansosti
Executive Managing Director, Manny De Zarraga, $250,000 total compensation
Executive Managing Director, Scott Galloway
Executive Managing Director, Matthew D. Lawton, $250,000 total compensation
Vice Chairman President and Executive Managing Director, Joe B. (Jody) Thornton, $500,000 total compensation
Auditors: Ernst & Young LLP

LOCATIONS

HQ: HFF Inc
One Oxford Centre, 301 Grant Street, Suite 1100, Pittsburgh, PA 15219
Phone: 412 281-8714
Web: www.hfflp.com

PRODUCTS/OPERATIONS

2015 Sales

	$ mil.	% of total
Capital markets services	487.9	97
Interest on mortgage notes receivable	11.2	2
Other	2.9	1
Total	**502.0**	**100**

Selected Services

Advisory Services
Case Studies
Debt Placement
Equity Placement
Foreign Capital
Investment Sales
Loan Sales
Loan Servicing
Special Assets

COMPETITORS

Arbor Commercial	Cushman & Wakefield
BGC Partners	Eastdil Secured
Boston Capital	Jones Lang LaSalle
CBRE Group	NorthMarq Capital
Capmark	Trammell Crow Company

HISTORICAL FINANCIALS

Company Type: Public

Income Statement

FYE: December 31

	REVENUE ($ mil.)	NET INCOME ($ mil.)	NET PROFIT MARGIN	EMPLOYEES
12/15	501.9	83.9	16.7%	810.0
12/14	425.9	61.2	14.4%	721.0
12/13	355.6	51.4	14.5%	637.0
12/12	284.9	43.8	15.4%	574.0
12/11	254.6	40.0	15.7%	498.0
Annual Growth	**18.5%**	**20.4%**	**—**	**12.9%**

2015 Year-End Financials

Debt ratio: 43.0%
Return on equity: 41.8%
Cash ($ mil.): 233.9
Current ratio: 1.39
Long-term debt ($ mil.): 0.5
No. of shares (mil.): 37.8
Dividends
 Yield: 5.7%
 Payout: 90.0%
Market value ($ mil.): 1,176.0

	STOCK PRICE ($) FY Close	P/E High/Low		PER SHARE ($) Earnings	Dividends	Book Value
12/15	31.07	21	14	2.18	1.80	5.67
12/14	35.92	24	16	1.61	1.83	4.95
12/13	26.85	20	11	1.36	0.00	4.71
12/12	14.90	14	9	1.18	1.52	3.27
12/11	10.33	15	7	1.11	0.00	3.52
Annual Growth	**31.7%**	**—**	**—**	**18.4%**	**—**	**12.6%**

Hi-Crush Partners LP

Auditors: PricewaterhouseCoopers LLP

LOCATIONS

HQ: Hi-Crush Partners LP
Three Riverway, Suite 1350, Houston, TX 77056
Phone: 713 980-6200   **Fax:** 713 963-0088
Web: www.hicrushpartners.com

HISTORICAL FINANCIALS

Company Type: Public

Income Statement

FYE: December 31

	REVENUE ($ mil.)	NET INCOME ($ mil.)	NET PROFIT MARGIN	EMPLOYEES
12/15	339.6	28.2	8.3%	0.0
12/14	386.5	123.0	31.8%	0.0
12/13	141.7	58.5	41.3%	0.0
12/12	28.8	18.5	64.1%	95.0
12/11	20.3	9.2	45.6%	0.0
Annual Growth	**102.1%**	**32.1%**	**—**	**—**

2015 Year-End Financials

Debt ratio: 60.6%
Return on equity: —
Cash ($ mil.): 10.4
Current ratio: 3.84
Long-term debt ($ mil.): 251.1
No. of shares (mil.): 36.9
Dividends
 Yield: 30.8%
 Payout: 143.7%
Market value ($ mil.): 219.0

	STOCK PRICE ($) FY Close	P/E High/Low		PER SHARE ($) Earnings	Dividends	Book Value
12/15	5.92	54	7	0.73	1.83	3.70
12/14	31.03	22	10	3.00	2.24	4.76
12/13	37.98	17	7	2.08	1.92	4.51
12/12	15.09	33	21	0.68	0.24	3.49
Annual Growth	**(26.8%)**	**—**	**—**	**2.4%**	**97.3%**	**2.0%**

Hill International Inc

Hill International a leader in the construction advice business is far from over the hill. The company offers project management and construction claims consulting services worldwide. It manages all aspects of the construction process from pre-design through completion —even troubled project turnaround. Construction claims services include expert witness testimony and litigation support. The company has provided services for such clients as the Arizona Diamondbacks Consolidated Edison Kimpton Hotel & Restaurant Group and Walt Disney. It also counts US government agencies and international governments among its clients. Hill International operates out of around 100 offices in more than 35 countries.

Geographic Reach
New Jersey-based Hill International has operations in the US Canada the Asia-Pacific region Europe the Middle East and North Africa. About 70% of the firm's revenue is generated outside of North America with the Middle East contributing more than 35%.

Operations
Hill International provides program management project management construction management construction claims and other consulting services primarily to the buildings transportation environmental energy and industrial markets. Project management generates more than two-thirds of the firm's revenue. The company serves private public and government clients in diverse industries including construction environmental hightech oil and gas power telecommunications and transportation.

Hill has provided construction management services for projects such as the Comcast Center in Philadelphia and New York New York Hotel & Casino in Las Vegas. It also took on one of the world's largest and most ambitious retail outlet projects the City of Arabia Mall development in Dubai.

Financial Performance
Hill's revenue climbed 20% in 2013 versus 2012 to $576.7 million and the firm swung from a loss in 2012 to a profit of $1.6 million over the same period. Cash flow from operations also rebounded sharply. Driving the double-digit rise in revenue was an increase in consulting fee revenue (CFR) primarily due to increased work in the Middle East. Project Management CFR consisted of a $76 million increase in foreign projects and an increase of $4.3 million in domestic projects. Revenue growth from projects in Oman Qatar Saudi Arabia Iraq and Afghanistan offset decreased CFR in Spain.

Strategy
Global diversification and an active acquisition program —both at home and abroad —are key elements of Hill's growth strategy. Indeed the firm has completed 22 acquisitions since 1998 and has expanded to markets in the Middle East and Latin America. The firm also pursues organic growth through the opening of new offices and by recruiting well-connected employees who can generate new business. Another avenue for growth is joint ventures. The firm's global reach served (and continues to serve) it well when the buildings market in the US was soft.

Among the many contracts the company won in 2013 was one from the US Department of State to support its efforts to build and renovate diplomatic facilities abroad by providing program management engineering support and quality control services. The contract has a maximum value of $100 million it all option years are exercised. Hill in 2013 also signed new contracts for work in Southern California Iraq and Saudi Arabia.

Mergers and Acquisitions
In January 2014 Hill paid about $2.5 million in its own stock to acquire Boston-based Collaborative Partners a provider of project management strategic planning and regulatory services for health care life sciences educational commercial and residential construction projects throughout New England. CP has offices in Boston and Providence Rhode Island.

In May 2013 a subsidiary of the firm purchased Cape Town South Africa-based Binnington Copeland & Associates (Pty.) Ltd. (BCA). The purchase of BCA gave Hill's claims business access to Africa's large infrastructure and mining projects and allowed for expansion into the rest of sub-Saharan Africa. In February 2013 Hill Spain acquired a 60% stake in Engineering S.A. a large project management firm in Brazil.

Ownership

The family of founder chairman and CEO Irvin Richter and his son president and COO David Richter owns 38% of Hill International's stock.

EXECUTIVES

President Construction Claims Group, Frederic Z. (Fred) Samelian, age 69, $750,000 total compensation

EVP and General Counsel, William H. (Bill) Dengler, age 50

SVP Marketing and Corporate Communications, John P. Paolin

CEO, David L. Richter, age 49, $1,500,000 total compensation

President and COO, Raouf S. Ghali, age 55, $1,100,000 total compensation

SVP and CIO, Michael J. Petrisko, age 50

EVP and CFO, John Fanelli, age 62, $450,000 total compensation

SVP; Managing Director (Asia/Pacific), Abdo E. Kardous

Regional President Project Management Group (Middle East), Mohammed Al Rais, age 62, $684,294 total compensation

Svp And Southern Regional Manager, Robert A Ferguson

Svp And Managing Director Middle East And Africa Construction Claims Group, David Merritt

Senior Vice President And Director Federal Transit Group, Vincent D Gallagher

Senior Vice President, Sid Scott

Vice President, Simon Mortimer

Construction Expert Senior Vice President, Ken Baker

Senior Vice President Construction Cla, Maurice Masucci

Vice President, Ken Olup

Regional President Project Management Group (Middle East), Mohammed Rais

Chairman, Craig L. Martin, age 67

Auditors: EisnerAmper LLP

LOCATIONS

HQ: Hill International Inc
One Commerce Square, 2005 Market Street, 17th Floor, Philadelphia, PA 19103
Phone: 215 309-7700

PRODUCTS/OPERATIONS

2015 Sales

	$ mil.	% of total
Consulting fees	630.9	88
Reimbursable expenses	89.7	12
Total	**720.6**	**100**

Selected Services

Construction claims services
  Analysis and review
  Claims preparation
  Contract review and assessment
  Cost and damages assessment
  Delay and disruption analysis
  Expert witness testimony
  Litigation support
  Strategic advisory services
Project management services
  Construction management

Estimating and cost management
Management consulting
Program management
Project labor agreements
Project management
Project management oversight
Staff augmentation
Troubled project turnaround

COMPETITORS

AECOM	Hunt Construction
ARCADIS	Jacobs Engineering
Balfour Beatty	Navigant Consulting
Bechtel	Parsons Brinckerhoff
Exponent	Parsons Corporation
Fluor	Skanska
GREYHAWK	Turner Corporation
Gilbane	

HISTORICAL FINANCIALS

Company Type: Public

Income Statement

FYE: December 31

	REVENUE ($ mil.)	NET INCOME ($ mil.)	NET PROFIT MARGIN	EMPLOYEES
12/15	720.6	6.9	1.0%	4,759.0
12/14	640.2	(10.8)	—	4,558.0
12/13	576.6	1.6	0.3%	4,111.0
12/12	480.7	(28.2)	—	3,663.0
12/11	501.4	(6.0)	—	3,168.0
Annual Growth	**9.5%**	**—**	**—**	**10.7%**

2015 Year-End Financials

Debt ratio: 32.7%
Return on equity: 5.1%
Cash ($ mil.): 24.0
Current ratio: 2.04
Long-term debt ($ mil.): 140.6

No. of shares (mil.): 51.5
Dividends
  Yield: —
  Payout: —
Market value ($ mil.): 200.0

	STOCK PRICE ($) FY Close	P/E High/Low	PER SHARE ($) Earnings	Dividends	Book Value
12/15	3.88	39 23	0.14	0.00	2.21
12/14	3.84	— —	(0.25)	0.00	3.06
12/13	3.95	101 63	0.04	0.00	3.27
12/12	3.66	— —	(0.73)	0.00	3.30
12/11	5.14	— —	(0.16)	0.00	4.00
Annual Growth	**(6.8%)**	**— —**	**(13.8%)**	**—**	**—**

Hillenbrand Inc

Hillenbrand knows a thing or two about life and death. Through its largest subsidiary BatesvilleHillenbrand is a top supplier to the death care industry providing nearly half the caskets used in the US. Batesville makes a variety of caskets in materials ranging from wood to stainless steel. Increasingly it also produces urns and other cremation products to satisfy increasing demand for lower-cost cremation. The company's Process Equipment Group (PEG) designs and makes equipment and systems used by industrial manufacturers. The PEG includes subsidiaries K-Tron Rotex and Coperion and was formed by a trio of acquisitions made in the past several years. Hillenbrand was spun off from Hillenbrand Industries.

Geographic Reach

Historically a US-centric business Hillenbrand has worked to lessen its reliance on US customers by extending its reach abroad. To this end the company has concentrated on developing its presence in Switzerland and Canada. In fiscal 2012 (ended September) the US accounted for 83% of Hillenbrand's sales (versus 93% in 2009) while Switzerland and Canada accounted for 8% and 5% respectively. Batesville makes most of its caskets in the US but also operates production facilities in Mexico.

Operations

Hillenbrand has two primary businesses. The largest Batesville accounting for about 60% of Hillenbrand's sales is an established company founded in 1884 that sells its burial products through a direct sales force to more than 12000 licensed funeral homes in the US Puerto Rico Canada Mexico the UK and Australia. Batesville manufactures both metal and solid and veneer hardwood caskets cremation urns and burial vaults. It also makes caskets suitable for "green" burials.

The company's Process Equipment Group (PEG) was formed by the purchases of Coperion Rotex and K-Tron. It accounts for about 40% of sales. New Jersey-based K-Tron produces feeders crushers conveying systems and other equipment used in the industrial manufacturing processes. Under the Rotex brand the PEG designs makes sells and services dry material separation machines that sort particles based on their size. Rotex brand equipment is used in a variety of industries including frac sand potash urea phosphates plastics and food processing.

Sales and Marketing

Batesville branded burial and cremation caskets and other funeral supplies are marketed by a direct sales force to licensed funeral professionals. The PEG also sells its material handling equipment through independent sales representatives.

Financial Performance

Hillenbrand's sales topped $983 million in fiscal 2012 (ended September) an increase of 11% versus the prior year. Net income declined by 1% over the same period. Driving the double-digit increase was the PEG which posted a 53% increase in annual sales due primarily to the Rotex acquisition in 2011. Batesville's sales declined 5% over the same period. 2012 marked the third year of increasing sales for the company. The small decline in net income was attributed to increased operating expenses and the amortization expense related to the Rotex purchase.

Strategy

Hillenbrand has moved to diversify its revenue stream in recent years as consumer preferences are shifting and as the total number of deaths in North America where most of Batesville's products are sold has been flat. More consumers are choosing cremation and other alternatives to traditional burials. Cremations as a percentage of total deaths now represent more than one-third in the US and more than one-half in Canada.

Mergers and Acquisitions

Aiming to build a "family of companies" revolving around manufacturing distribution and customer service Hillenbrand acquired Stuttgart Germany-based Coperion Capital GmbH for $545 million in December 2012. The purchase expanded the company's global footprint bolstered its PEG and leveraged replacement parts and service capabilities. It's anticipated that the group with Coperion under its umbrella will generate more than $1 billion in revenue and represent two-thirds of Hillenbrand's overall sales in fiscal 2013.

Previously the firm expanded its manufacturing equipment division through the purchase of ROTEX Global from Windjammer Capital Investors for $240 million in cash in September 2011. ROTEX makes machines (along with replacement parts and accessories) that separate dry materials for various industrial applications a complementary addition to Hillenbrand's existing equipment line. Although its products are sold throughout the US and abroad ROTEX boasts a significant customer base in Europe and Asia — two regions in which Hillenbrand has been looking to strengthen its presence.

In 2010 the company acquired New Jersey-based K-Tron International which produces feeders crushers conveying systems and other equipment used in the industrial manufacturing processes. The $435-million purchase gave Hillenbrand access to a much more diverse customer base that comprises chemical food pharmaceutical and plastics companies.

EXECUTIVES

President Coperion K-Tron, Kevin C. Bowen, age 65
President Chief Executive Officer and Director, Joseph A. (Joe) Raver, age 51, $450,697 total compensation
Vice President Enterprise Information Systems, Darryl M. Maslar
SVP and CFO, Cynthia L. (Cindy) Lucchese, age 56, $348,205 total compensation
President Rotex, Anthony S. Casablanca
Senior Vice President President Batesville, Kimberly K. Ryan
President Coperion, Thomas Kehl
President TerraSource Global, Mark L. Kohler
Chairperson, F. Joseph (Joe) Loughrey, age 66
Auditors: PRICEWATERHOUSECOOPERS LLP

LOCATIONS

HQ: Hillenbrand Inc
  One Batesville Boulevard, Batesville, IN 47006
Phone: 812 934-7500
Web: www.hillenbrand.com

PRODUCTS/OPERATIONS

2016 sales

	% of total
Process equipment	63
Batesville	37
Total	**100**

Selected Subsidiaries

Batesville (Batesville Indiana)
Coperion (Germany)
K-Tron International (Pitman New Jersey)
Rotex Global (Cincinnati Ohio)

COMPETITORS

Aurora Casket	Key Technology
Badger Meter	Matthews International
Costco Wholesale	Wal-Mart
Goliath Casket	Wilbert
Heat and Control	

HISTORICAL FINANCIALS

Company Type: Public

Income Statement

FYE: September 30

	REVENUE ($ mil.)	NET INCOME ($ mil.)	NET PROFIT MARGIN	EMPLOYEES
09/16	1,538.4	112.8	7.3%	6,100.0
09/15	1,596.8	111.4	7.0%	6,000.0
09/14	1,667.2	109.7	6.6%	5,900.0
09/13	1,553.4	63.4	4.1%	6,000.0
09/12	983.2	104.8	10.7%	3,900.0
Annual Growth	**11.8%**	**1.9%**	**—**	**11.8%**

2016 Year-End Financials

Debt ratio: 31.1%
Return on equity: 18.3%
Cash ($ mil.): 52.0
Current ratio: 1.38
Long-term debt ($ mil.): 596.3
No. of shares (mil.): 63.0
Dividends
  Yield: 2.5%
  Payout: 53.2%
Market value ($ mil.): 1,993.0

	STOCK PRICE ($) FY Close	P/E High/Low		PER SHARE ($) Earnings	Dividends	Book Value
09/16	31.64	19	14	1.77	0.81	10.04
09/15	26.01	20	14	1.74	0.80	9.45
09/14	30.89	19	15	1.72	0.79	9.27
09/13	27.37	28	18	1.01	0.78	9.03
09/12	18.19	14	10	1.68	0.77	8.09
Annual Growth	**14.8%**	**—**	**—**	**1.3%**	**1.3%**	**5.5%**

Hilltop Holdings, Inc.

Hilltop Holdings sits on top of a mound of money-related businesses. The company's PlainsCapital subsidiary operates more than 80 branches in Texas and an offshore branch in the Caymans offers residential mortgages through 200 PrimeLending offices in 40-plus and provides securities brokerage and investment banking through HilltopSecurities. Subsidiary National Lloyds Corporation (NLC) offers fire and homeowners' coverage for low-value and manufactured homes and insurance through independent agents in Texas and more than 25 other (mostly) southern states. NLC operates as National Lloyds Insurance and American Summit Insurance. Hilltop has more than $12 billion in assets under management.OperationsThe purchase of PlainsCapital in a transaction valued at about $700 million moved Hilltop from insurance as its primary revenue generator to banking. It now operates in banking mortgage origination insurance and financial advisory services.The PlainsCapital entities serve niche markets such as midsized businesses investors and high-net worth individuals. NLC's operating subsidiaries primarily write the kind of lower-cost homeowners' policies that only pay out cash value instead of replacement costs and most of its policies exclude coverage for water or mold damage. Texas accounts for over 70% of the company's premiums. While personal lines account for more than 90% of its premiums the company does write a small amount of commercial insurance covering builders' risk sports liability and transportation insurance which is known as "inland marine" policies.Geographic ReachPlainsCapital's banking operations are in Texas and its mortgages are secured by property in Texas mostly in or around major cities. NLC is licensed in 42 states and sells in 27 but primarily does business in Texas Oklahoma Arizona Tennessee Georgia and Louisiana with Texas accounting for more than 60% of sales. PrimeLending concentrates on nine states and does most of its business in Texas California and North Carolina.Financial PerformanceThe PlainsCapital acquisition did what it was meant to do - gave the company a shot in the arm. For 2013 revenue rose nearly 350% to $1.3 billion. Net loss in 2012 became a net income of $125 million and cash from operations grew 71%.StrategyAfter the 2012 purchase of PlainsCapital Hilltop began to focus on being a Texas-based bank and financial services company. It plans to continue expanding its empire through organic growth and acquisitions. To that end in 2013 PlainsCapital purchased First National Bank a Texas-based company and its 51 branches. The same year Hilltop subsidiary NLASCO changed its name to National Lloyds Corporation or NLC as part of an overall re-branding effort.Mergers and AcquisitionsIn 2013 the company purchased Texas-based First National Bank with about 50 branches mostly in South Texas. It followed that up in early 2015 with the acquisition of Dallas-based securities brokerage SWS Group. In 2016 Hilltop merged its broker-dealer subsidiaries First Southwest Company and Hilltop Securities (formerly Southwest Securities) to create HilltopSecurities. (HilltopSecurities division FirstSouthwest will continue to offer municipal advisory services.)Company BackgroundThe company began life as Affordable Residential Communities (ARC) and spent its early days as a real estate investment trust (REIT). It went public in 2004 dropped its REIT status in 2006 and built up its collection of manufactured housing communities through acquisitions.After several years of losses in the housing business the company chose to transition into another industry. It acquired NLASCO a niche provider of fire and homeowners insurance for manufactured homes and other low-value properties at the start of 2007. The company then renamed itself Hilltop Holdings.

EXECUTIVES

President CEO and Director, Jeremy B. Ford, age 41, $662,500 total compensation
Vice Chairman and Chairman and CEO PlainsCapital Corporation, Alan B. White, age 67, $1,350,000 total compensation
President and COO PlainsCapital Corporation, James R. Huffines, age 65, $690,000 total compensation
Chairman and CEO Hilltop Securities, Hill A. Feinberg, age 69
President and CEO PlainsCapital Bank, Jerry L. Schaffner, age 58
CFO, William B. Furr, age 38
CEO PrimeLending, Todd L. Salmans, age 67, $750,000 total compensation
Chairman, Gerald J. Ford, age 72
Auditors: PricewaterhouseCoopers LLP

LOCATIONS

HQ: Hilltop Holdings, Inc.
  200 Crescent Court, Suite 1330, Dallas, TX 75201
Phone: 214 855-2177
Web: www.hilltop-holdings.com

PRODUCTS/OPERATIONS

2015 Sales

	% of total
Interest income	
Loans including fees	23

Securities borrowed		2
Taxable Securities		2
Tax-exempt securities		1
Other		
Noninterest income		
Net gains from sale of loans and other mortgage production income		31
Net insurance premiums earned		9
Securities commissions and fees		9
Investment and securities advisory fees and commissions		7
Mortgage loan origination fees		5
Bargain purchase gain		5
Other		6
Total		**100**

Selected Services

Financial Advisory
Clearing
Retail Brokerage
Investment Banking Services
Internet Banking
Business Check Cards

Selected Subsidiaries

PlainsCapital Bank
PrimeLending
HilltopSecurities
National Lloyds Corporation

COMPETITORS

American Modern Insurance	International Bancshares
BBVA Compass Bancshares	JPMorgan Chase Morgan Keegan
Bank of America	Raymond James
Comerica	Financial
Costco Wholesale	Republic Group
Cullen/Frost Bankers	Texas Capital
Fannie Mae	Bancshares
Foremost Insurance	Travelers Companies
Freddie Mac	Wells Fargo
ING	

HISTORICAL FINANCIALS

Company Type: Public

Income Statement

FYE: December 31

	REVENUE ($ mil.)	NET INCOME ($ mil.)	NET PROFIT MARGIN	EMPLOYEES
12/15	1,697.4	210.9	12.4%	5,300.0
12/14	1,188.0	111.6	9.4%	4,400.0
12/13	1,179.1	125.3	10.6%	4,550.0
12/12	263.2	(5.5)	—	3,950.0
12/11	152.1	(6.5)	—	135.0
Annual Growth	**82.7%**	**—**	**—**	**150.3%**

2015 Year-End Financials

Debt ratio: 9.3%
Return on equity: 13.2%
Cash ($ mil.): 775.1
Current ratio: 0.25
Long-term debt ($ mil.): 305.7
No. of shares (mil.): 98.9
Dividends
  Yield: —
  Payout: —
Market value ($ mil.): 1,901.0

	STOCK PRICE ($) FY Close	P/E High/Low		PER SHARE ($) Earnings	Dividends	Book Value
12/15	19.22	12	8	2.09	0.00	17.56
12/14	19.95	22	16	1.17	0.00	16.19
12/13	23.13	17	9	1.40	0.00	14.54
12/12	13.54	—	—	(0.10)	0.00	13.71
12/11	8.45	—	—	(0.12)	0.00	11.60
Annual Growth	**22.8%**	**—**	**—**	**—**	**—**	**10.9%**

Holly Energy Partners LP

Holly Energy Partners pipes petroleum products and crude oil from refineries. It operates petroleum product and crude gathering pipelines (in New Mexico Oklahoma Texas and Utah) distribution terminals (in Arizona Idaho New Mexico Oklahoma Texas Utah and Washington) and refinery tankage in New Mexico and Utah. It operates 1330 miles of refined petroleum pipelines (340 miles leased) 960 miles of crude oil trunk lines 10 refined product terminals one jet fuel terminal and two truck-loading facilities. It also has three 65-mile pipelines that ship feedstocks and crude oil. HollyFrontier holds a 41% stake in Holly Energy Partners.

Holly Energy Partners' strategy is to make acquisitions that complement its existing portfolio both in tandem with HollyFrontier and independently.

Holly Energy Partners is integral to HollyFrontier's business growth by developing and extending that company's assets. In 2009 it picked up the Roadrunner pipeline a 65-mile pipeline connecting HollyFrontier's refining facilities in Lovington New Mexico to the terminus of a Centurion pipeline linking West Texas and Cushing Oklahoma. In 2010 it acquired petroleum storage tanks at HollyFrontier's Tulsa refinery (2 million barrels of capacity) and other assets from HollyFrontier for $93 million.

Building the largest refinery complex in the area in 2009 HollyFrontier acquired refineries and related assets in Tulsa from Sunoco and Sinclair. In 2011 HollyFrontier's acquisition of Frontier Oil (with refineries in Kansas and Wyoming) boosted its total refining capacity to 443.000 barrels per day.

Building its portfolio in 2011 Holly Energy Partners acquired pipeline tankage loading rack and crude receiving assets from HollyFrontier's El Dorado and Cheyenne refineries for $340 million. In 2012 it also acquired HollyFrontier's 75% stake in UNEV Pipeline for $315 million. The UNEV refined products pipeline runs from Woods Cross Utah to Las Vegas Nevada.

Increased pipeline shipments and higher operating margins (thanks to the 2011 asset expansion and higher oil prices) helped to lift Holly Energy Partners' revenues and net income in 2011 by 17% and 32 % respectively.

EXECUTIVES

Vice President Engineering, Bruce (Brucey) Shaw
Vice President Treasurer, Stephen (Steve) Wise
Assistant Secretary, Walt Zimmerman
Assistant Secretary, Becca Lickteig
Board Member, Charles (Charlie) Darling
Auditors: Ernst & Young LLP

LOCATIONS

HQ: Holly Energy Partners LP
  2828 N. Harwood, Suite 1300, Dallas, TX 75201
Phone: 214 871-3555
Web: www.hollyenergy.com

COMPETITORS

ExxonMobil Pipeline	Shell Pipeline
Magellan Midstream	Wolverine Pipe Line
NuStar Energy	Company

HISTORICAL FINANCIALS

Company Type: Public

Income Statement

FYE: December 31

	REVENUE ($ mil.)	NET INCOME ($ mil.)	NET PROFIT MARGIN	EMPLOYEES
12/15	358.8	148.3	41.3%	245.0
12/14	332.5	113.8	34.2%	273.0
12/13	305.1	86.0	28.2%	257.0
12/12	292.5	91.1	31.1%	232.0
12/11	213.5	78.0	36.5%	216.0
Annual Growth	**13.9%**	**17.4%**	**—**	**3.2%**

2015 Year-End Financials

Debt ratio: 65.7%
Return on equity: —
Cash ($ mil.): 15.0
Current ratio: 1.25
Long-term debt ($ mil.): 1,008.7
No. of shares (mil.): 58.6
Dividends
  Yield: 6.9%
  Payout: 150.5%
Market value ($ mil.): 1,827.0

	STOCK PRICE ($) FY Close	P/E High/Low		PER SHARE ($) Earnings	Dividends	Book Value
12/15	31.14	23	17	1.60	2.17	4.92
12/14	29.91	31	24	1.20	2.05	5.46
12/13	32.33	82	34	0.88	1.93	6.30
12/12	65.78	57	41	1.29	1.81	6.21
12/11	53.78	45	35	1.34	1.72	6.02
Annual Growth	**(12.8%)**	**—**	**—**	**4.6%**	**6.0%**	**(4.9%)**

Home Bancorp Inc

Making its home in Cajun Country Home Bancorp is the holding company for Home Bank a community bank which offers deposit and loan services to consumers and small to midsized businesses in southern Louisiana. Through about two dozen branches the bank offers standard savings and checking accounts as well as lending services such as mortgages consumer loans and credit cards. Its loan portfolio includes commercial real estate commercial and industrial loans as well as construction and land loans. Home Bancorp also operates about half a dozen bank branches in west Mississippi which were formerly part of Britton & Koontz Bank.

Geographic Reach
Home Bancorp serves the Louisiana areas of Greater Lafayette Baton Rouge Greater New Orleans and Northshore (of Lake Pontchartrain). Its markets in Mississippi include Vicksburg and Natchez.

Financial Performance
Although the company saw assets and loans grow in 2013 net income fell 20% that year to $7.3 million on lower operating income.

Mergers and Acquisitions
In early 2014 Home Bancorp spent about $35 million on Britton & Koontz Capital Corporation the holding company of Britton & Koontz Bank; the deal added five branches in west Mississippi to Home Bancorp's operations.

EXECUTIVES

Executive Vice President, Darren (Darr) Guidry
Auditors: Porter Keadle Moore, LLC

LOCATIONS

HQ: Home Bancorp Inc
503 Kaliste Saloom Road, Lafayette, LA 70508
Phone: 337 237-1960 **Fax:** 337 264-9280
Web: www.home24bank.com

COMPETITORS

Capital One	MidSouth Bancorp
IBERIABANK	Regions Financial
JPMorgan Chase	Teche Holding
Louisiana Bancorp	

HISTORICAL FINANCIALS

Company Type: Public

Income Statement   FYE: December 31

	ASSETS ($ mil.)	NET INCOME ($ mil.)	INCOME AS % OF ASSETS	EMPLOYEES
12/15	1,551.9	12.5	0.8%	0.0
12/14	1,221.4	9.8	0.8%	0.0
12/13	984.2	7.2	0.7%	0.0
12/12	962.9	9.1	1.0%	0.0
12/11	963.7	5.1	0.5%	0.0
Annual Growth	12.6%	25.1%		

2015 Year-End Financials

Return on assets: 0.9%	Dividends
Return on equity: 7.8%	Yield: 1.4%
Long-term debt ($ mil.): —	Payout: 22.7%
No. of shares (mil.): 7.2	Market value ($ mil.): 188.0
Sales ($ mil.): 67.1	

	STOCK PRICE ($) FY Close	P/E High/Low	PER SHARE ($) Earnings	Dividends	Book Value
12/15	25.98	14 11	1.79	0.37	22.80
12/14	22.94	15 12	1.42	0.07	21.64
12/13	18.85	17 15	1.06	0.00	19.99
12/12	18.25	14 12	1.28	0.00	19.03
12/11	15.50	22 18	0.71	0.00	17.30
Annual Growth	13.8%	— —	26.0%	—	7.1%

Home BancShares Inc

At this Home you don't have to stash your cash under the mattress. Home BancShares is the holding company for Centennial Bank which operates about 150 branches in Arkansas Alabama and Florida. The bank offers traditional services such as checking savings and money market accounts; IRAs; and CDs. It focuses on commercial real estate lending including construction land development and agricultural loans which make up more than 55% of its lending portfolio. The bank also writes residential mortgage business and consumer loans. Nonbank subsidiaries offer trust and insurance services. Investments are available to customers through an agreement with third-party provider LPL Financial.

Geographic Reach

The Arkansas-based bank holding company's Centennial Bank operates 149 branches in Arkansas the Florida Keys southwestern Florida Central Florida the Florida Panhandle and south Alabama.

Financial Performance

Home BancShares reported $257.5 million in revenue in 2013 up 14% versus 2012. The rise in revenue was due primarily to increased interest in-

come from a higher level of earning assets combined with higher yields on their covered loans.

Net income rose 6% over the same period to $66.5 million. The increase was primarily due to additional net income and other non-interest income resulting from acquisitions completed in 2012.

Strategy

The acquisitive bank holding company is expanding in its core Florida and Arkansas markets through the purchase of local managed community banks. Home continues to look for additional acquisitions including institutions seized by regulators in and contiguous to its geographical markets.

Mergers and Acquisitions

In July 2014 Home BancShares completed the acquisition of Florida Traditions Bank (FTB) in a $43 million deal. FTB operated eight branches in central Florida. Post purchase Home had approximately $7 billion in total assets $5.5 billion in depositions $4.7 billion in loans and 149 branches.

In October 2013 the firm acquired the $2.8 billion holding company Liberty Bancshares Inc. parent company of 46-branch Liberty Bank of Arkansas. The Liberty purchase significantly increased Home's deposit market share in Arkansas making it the second largest bank holding company headquartered in Arkansas.Home BancShares entered another new market with the 2012 acquisition of Vision Bank from Park National. The deal included 17 branches along the Florida panhandle and Gulf Coast and gave Home BancShares its first locations in Alabama. Also in 2012 it bought Florida-based Premier Bank from Premier Bank Holding Company and Heritage Bank of Florida with offices in Tampa Lutz and Wesley Chapel.

EXECUTIVES

CFO and Treasurer and Director, Randy E. Mayor, age 51, $300,000 total compensation
President and CEO, C. Randall (Randy) Sims, age 61, $390,000 total compensation
Regional President Centennial Bank, Robert F. Birch, age 66, $290,000 total compensation
President and CEO Centennial Bank, Tracy M. French, age 54, $290,000 total compensation
Chief Lending Officer, Kevin D. Hester, age 52
COO Home BancShares Inc. and Centennial Bank, John (Stephen) Tipton
Vice President Security, Jenni Holbrook
Vice President, Brian Jackson
Senior Vice President Director Of Loan Review, Tish Cartwright
Chairman, John W. Allison, age 69
Vice Chairman, Robert H. Adcock, age 67
Auditors: BKD, LLP

LOCATIONS

HQ: Home BancShares Inc
719 Harkrider, Suite 100, Conway, AR 72032
Phone: 501 339-2929
Web: www.homebancshares.com

PRODUCTS/OPERATIONS

2015 Sales

	$ mil.	% of total
Interest		
Loans	344.3	76
Investment securities	33.1	7
Non-interest		
Other service charges & fees	26.2	6
Service charges on deposit accounts	24.3	5
Other	15.0	6
Total	**442.9**	**100**

Selected Services

Personal Banking
Business Banking
ebanking
Investment & insurance
Trust Services

COMPETITORS

Arvest Bank	Bear State Financial
BB&T	Regions Financial
BBX Capital	Simmons First
Bank of America	Woodforest Financial
Bank of the Ozarks	

HISTORICAL FINANCIALS

Company Type: Public

Income Statement   FYE: December 31

	ASSETS ($ mil.)	NET INCOME ($ mil.)	INCOME AS % OF ASSETS	EMPLOYEES
12/15	9,289.1	138.2	1.5%	1,424.0
12/14	7,403.2	113.0	1.5%	1,376.0
12/13	6,811.8	66.5	1.0%	1,497.0
12/12	4,242.1	63.0	1.5%	926.0
12/11	3,604.1	54.7	1.5%	774.0
Annual Growth	26.7%	26.1%		16.5%

2015 Year-End Financials

Return on assets: 1.6%	Dividends
Return on equity: 12.4%	Yield: 2.7%
Long-term debt ($ mil.): —	Payout: 54.4%
No. of shares (mil.): 140.2	Market value ($ mil.): 5,683.0
Sales ($ mil): 442.9	

	STOCK PRICE ($) FY Close	P/E High/Low	PER SHARE ($) Earnings	Dividends	Book Value
12/15	40.52	46 28	1.01	0.55	8.55
12/14	32.16	44 33	0.85	0.35	7.51
12/13	37.35	75 36	0.57	0.36	6.46
12/12	33.02	63 44	0.56	0.29	4.58
12/11	25.91	57 43	0.46	0.07	4.19
Annual Growth	11.8%	— —	21.6%	69.3%	19.5%

Homefed Corp.

HomeFed won't provide you with room and board but it can help you get a home. The company earns its keep by investing in and developing residential real estate. Through subsidiaries Home-Fed is developing a master-planned community in San Diego County called San Elijo Hills which contains approximately 3500 residences as well as commercial space and a town center. In 2014 Leucadia Financial increased its ownership in Home-Fed from 31% to 65%. It also enhanced Home-Fed's geographic presence by adding land and commercial real estate assets in New York Florida Maine and South Carolina.

Like many real estate developers in California HomeFed has been affected by the battered housing market. San Elijo Hills is more than 80% sold but the company completed only one residential lot sale between 2006 and 2009. HomeFed also owns a portion of another community under development Otay Ranch in addition to some 1500 acres of a grape vineyard in California that is not zoned for residential or commercial use. It did not any real estate at Otay Ranch from 2007 to 2009.

Leucadia from which the company acquired the San Elijo Hills and Otay Ranch projects controls more than 30% of HomeFed's stock. Jospeh Steinberg president of Leucadia and chairman of Home-Fed owns almost 10%. Ian Cumming who is chairman of Leucadia and a director of HomeFed holds more than 7%.

EXECUTIVES

Vice President And Senior Development Manager, Kent Aden
Auditors: PRICEWATERHOUSECOOPERS LLP

LOCATIONS

HQ: Homefed Corp.
   1903 Wright Place, Suite 220, Carlsbad, CA 92008
Phone: 760 918-8200
Web: www.homefedcorporation.com

PRODUCTS/OPERATIONS

199754961

COMPETITORS

Brookfield Homes	Newhall Land
Corky McMillin	Tejon Ranch
Irvine Company	

HISTORICAL FINANCIALS

Company Type: Public

Income Statement
FYE: December 31

	REVENUE ($ mil.)	NET INCOME ($ mil.)	NET PROFIT MARGIN	EMPLOYEES
12/15	69.5	5.8	8.4%	31.0
12/14	59.5	3.8	6.5%	27.0
12/13	56.6	11.2	19.9%	16.0
12/12	35.6	6.0	16.9%	14.0
12/11	34.1	4.4	13.2%	13.0
Annual Growth	19.5%	6.8%	—	24.3%

2015 Year-End Financials

Debt ratio: 20.8%
Return on equity: 1.4%
Cash ($ mil.): 66.6
Current ratio: 8.22
Long-term debt ($ mil.): 116.0

No. of shares (mil.): 15.4
Dividends
   Yield: —
   Payout: —
Market value ($ mil.): 525.0

	STOCK PRICE ($) FY Close	P/E High/Low	PER SHARE ($) Earnings	Dividends	Book Value
12/15	34.05	132 89	0.38	0.00	26.38
12/14	45.00	207 124	0.29	0.00	25.99
12/13	36.60	27 19	1.43	0.00	22.82
12/12	26.50	38 24	0.76	0.00	21.37
12/11	19.40	53 32	0.57	0.00	20.01
Annual Growth	15.1%	— —	(9.6%)	—	7.1%

HomeStreet Inc

HomeStreet aims to offer home and business mortgages to all in the Pacific Northwest and Hawaii. Its subsidiary HomeStreet Bank offers tra-ditional consumer banking accounts as well as commercial and private banking investment and insurance products and services through 45 branches and 65 loan offices in the Pacific Northwest California and Hawaii. Specializing in residential and commercial mortgages the bank and fellow subsidiary Homestreet Capital Corp originate home loans both directly and through a joint venture Windermere Real Estate which operates about 40 offices in Washington and Oregon. HomeStreet also provides specialty financing for income-producing properties.

Operations

HomeStreet operates two lines of business: Commercial and Consumer Banking and Mortgage Banking which originates residential mortgage loans for wale in the secondary markets to be securitized by GSAs. Its primary subsidiaries are HomeStreet Bank and HomeStreet Capital Corp. (HCC). HCC sells and services multifamily mortgage loans in conjunction with HomeStreet Bank.HomeStreet gets most of its business from mortgage originations and sales. About 53% of the company's revenue came from its mortgage banking business (origination and sales) during 2015 while another 6% came from mortgage servicing income. Another 34% of its revenue came from loan interest.

Geographic Reach

Seattle-based HomeStreet operates bank branches in Arizona California Colorado Hawaii Idaho Oregon Utah and Washington.Sales and MarketingHomeStreet provides financial services for small- and middle-market businesses as well as consumers.

Financial Performance

HomeStreet's annual revenues and profits have more than doubled since 2011 thanks to strong mortgage banking and loan business growth driven by a strengthening housing market.The company's revenue spiked 50% to $446.35 million during 2015 mostly thanks to a 64% increase in gains on mortgage loan origination sales resulting from a rise in single family mortgage interest rate lock commitments.Strong revenue growth in 2015 caused HomeStreet's net income to nearly double to $41.32 million. The company's operating cash levels spiked to $8.31 million for the year (operations had used $348.6 million in 2014) mostly because it collected more in cash-denominated proceeds from its mortgage loan sales than it did in 2014.Strategy

HomeStreet has been moving more toward commercial mortgage and SBA originations in recent years launching its HomeStreet commercial capital business in Orange County California in 2015. It also continues to acquire other small community banks in its region to grow its loan and deposit business and expand into new geographic markets. Additionally it's been expanding its retail operations its own opening two new branches in San Diego's Mission Gorge and Kearny Mesa markets in March 2016. To boost profitability HomeStreet looked in 2016 to enhance productivity and cut costs by streamlining operations.

Merger and Acquisitions

The company plans to buy two Southern California banks from Boston Private Bank & Trust. Through that acquisition HomeStreet will gain some $110 million in deposit accounts. It will then have a dozen retail branches in Southern California.

In February 2016 the company purchased Orange County Business Bank for $55 million extending its reach into "one of the premier commercial and consumer banking markets in the country" according to HomeStreet CEO and chairman Mark Mason.In March 2015 HomeStreet expanded into Southern California's retail banking market after acquiring Simplicity Bancorp and its seven Simply Bank retail deposit branches in the greater Los Angeles area. Beyond geographic expansion the deal added valuable retail deposit and loan assets.In November 2013 HomeStreet acquired Fortune Bank a community bank with two branches in Seattle and Bellevue for about $27 million. Concurrently it purchased YNB Financial Services Corp. the parent company of Yakima National Bank which operates four branches in Yakima Selah Sunnyside and Kennewick for about $10.3 million. The twin purchases along with the acquisition of two branches from AmericanWest Bank increased the number of retail deposit branches operates by HomeStreet to 29.Company BackgroundHomeStreet went public in February 2012 with an offering worth $55 million. The company sold 1.6 million shares priced at $44 each. HomeStreet had postponed two previous attempts to go public in 2011 that had planned to sell many more shares. Proceeds from the 2012 IPO were used to meet capital-ratio requirements required by regulators in the wake of allegations that the bank engaged in unsafe practices.HomeStreet was hit hard by the economic downturn and slowdown in the housing market. Trouble in its core mortgage lending business led to losses in 2009 and 2010 and the bank entered into agreements with regulators to improve its capital position earnings and management. It brought in a new management team and launched a turnaround plan to stabilize the business which included tightening its lending standards restructuring troubled loans when necessary and the sale of real estate backed by non-performing loans. The measures helped HomeStreet return to profitability in 2011 and remain in the black for several years thereafter.

EXECUTIVES

Chairman President and CEO HomeStreet Inc. and HomeStreet Bank, Mark K. Mason, age 56, $500,000 total compensation

EVP Chief Administrative Officer General Counsel and Corporate Secretary Homestreet Inc. and Homestreet Bank, Godfrey B. Evans, age 62, $247,200 total compensation

EVP Commercial Banking HomeStreet Bank, David H. Straus, age 69

EVP HomeStreet Inc. and EVP and Residential Lending Director HomeStreet Bank, Richard W. H. (Rich) Bennion, age 66, $203,000 total compensation

EVP and Chief Credit Officer HomeStreet Inc. and Homestreet Bank, Jay C. Iseman, age 56, $200,000 total compensation

EVP Chief Investment Officer and Treasurer HomeStreet Inc. and HomeStreet Bank, Darrell van Amen, age 50, $206,359 total compensation

EVP and Commercial Real Estate Lending Director HomeStreet Bank, Randy Daniels, age 54

EVP and Chief Accounting Officer HomeStreet Inc. and HomeStreet Bank, Cory D. Stewart, age 44

EVP and Mortgage Lending Director Homestreet Bank, Rose Marie David, age 52, $200,000 total compensation

EVP and Eastern Region President HomeStreet Bank, Jeffrey K. Newgard, age 44

EVP and Mortgage Lending Director, Rose David

Vice President Income Property Loan Officer, Katie (Kat) Plett

Vice President Commercial Lending Manager, George Brace

Vice President Loan Officer, Carmen Esteban

Assistant Vice President Senior Marketing Manager Analytics And Digital, Katharine Czechowski
Vice President Application Development, Ken (Kenny) Clay
Vice President Audit and Compliance, Annette (Anne) Mumford
Vice President and Relationship Manager, Todd (Toddy) Burchett
Vice President and Relationship Manager, Kris (Krissy) Hollingshead
Assistant Vice President Senior Marketing Specialist, Colleen Fehler
Auditors: Deloitte & Touche LLP

LOCATIONS

HQ: HomeStreet Inc
  601 Union Street, Suite 2000, Seattle, WA 98101
Phone: 206 623-3050
Web: www.homestreet.com

PRODUCTS/OPERATIONS

2015 Sales

	$ mil.	% of total
Interest		
Loans	152.6	34
Investment securities available for sale	11.6	3
Other	0.9	
Non-interest		
Net gains on mortgage origination & sales activities	236.4	53
Mortgage servicing	24.4	6
Depositor & other retail banking fees	5.9	1
Gain on sale of investment securities available for sale	2.4	1
Bargain purchase gain	7.7	2
Insurance agency commission Income from WMS Series LLC and other	4.4	
Total	**446.3**	**100**

Selected Services

Personal Banking
Home LoansInvestmentInsurancePrivate Bank
Commercial Banking
Builder Financing/Residential ConstructionCommercial LendingCommercial Real EstatePartnership Programs

COMPETITORS

American Savings Bank	KeyCorp
Bank of America	Sound Financial
Bank of Hawaii	U.S. Bancorp
Banner Corp	Umpqua Holdings
First Hawaiian	Washington Federal
JPMorgan Chase	Wells Fargo

HISTORICAL FINANCIALS

Company Type: Public

Income Statement

FYE: December 31

	ASSETS ($ mil.)	NET INCOME ($ mil.)	INCOME AS % OF ASSETS	EMPLOYEES
12/15	4,894.5	41.3	0.8%	2,139.0
12/14	3,535.0	22.2	0.6%	1,611.0
12/13	3,066.0	23.8	0.8%	1,502.0
12/12	2,631.2	82.1	3.1%	1,099.0
12/11	2,264.9	16.1	0.7%	613.0
Annual Growth	**21.2%**	**26.5%**	**—**	**36.7%**

2015 Year-End Financials

Return on assets: 0.9%	Dividends
Return on equity: 10.7%	Yield: —
Long-term debt ($ mil.): —	Payout: —
No. of shares (mil.): 22.0	Market value ($ mil.): 479.0
Sales ($ mil): 446.3	

STOCK PRICE ($) / P/E / PER SHARE ($)

	STOCK PRICE ($) FY Close	P/E High/Low		PER SHARE ($) Earnings	Dividends	Book Value
12/15	21.71	12	9	1.96	0.00	21.08
12/14	17.41	14	11	1.49	0.44	20.34
12/13	20.00	17	11	1.61	0.33	17.97
12/12	25.55	9	3	5.98	0.00	18.34
Annual Growth	**(5.3%)**	**—**	**—**	**(31.1%)**	**—**	**4.7%**

Hope Bancorp Inc

Hope Bancorp (formerly BBCN Bancorp) is the holding company for Bank of Hope (formerly BBCN Bank) the largest Korean-American bank in the US. Bank of Hope caters to individuals and small business owners from 85 branches in California Alabama Georgia Illinois New Jersey New York Texas Virginia and Washington. Some 80% of its loan portfolio consists of commercial real estate loans though it also offers auto loans credit cards commercial and construction loans SBA loans and international banking services. The bank has expanded its footprint through bank acquisitions in recent years; it acquired top rival Wilshire Bancorp for $1 billion in mid-2016.

OperationsHope Bancorp makes nearly 90% of its revenue from interest income. About 82% of its total revenue came from loan interest (including fees) during 2015 while another 6% came from interest on securities and other investments. The rest of its revenue came from gains on SBA loan sales (4% of revenue) deposit account service fees (3%) international service fees (1%) loan servicing fees (1%) and wire transfer fees (1%).About 78% of its loan portfolio consisted of commercial real estate loans at the end of 2015 while 16% of loan assets were tied to commercial business loans. The rest of the portfolio consisted of construction mortgages (2% of loan assets) trade finance loans (2%) and consumer and other loans (2%).Geographic ReachBBCN Bank boasted 50 branches in six states at the end of 2015 including 28 in California (Los Angeles Orange County Oakland and Silicon Valley areas); eight branches in New York City metro area and New Jersey; eight branches in the Chicago metro area; four branches in the Seattle metro area; and two branches in Virginia. The merger with Wilshire Bancorp added some 35 branches including locations in Alabama Georgia Illinois and Washington.It also had eight loan production offices in Seattle Denver Dallas Atlanta Northern California Portland and Annandale Virginia. Wilshire brought an SBA loan office in Fremont California.

Internationally Hope has a representative office in Seoul Korea that serves international businesses with US subsidiaries.Sales and MarketingThe bank spent $5.1 million on advertising and marketing during 2015 down slightly from $5.4 million and $5.2 million in 2014 and 2013 respectively.Financial PerformanceThe company's annual revenues have doubled since 2011 as its loan assets have swelled by nearly 70% to $6.25 billion. Meanwhile the bank's net income has more than quadrupled thanks to declining loan loss provisions as its loan portfolio's credit quality has improved with the strengthened economy. The bank's revenue climbed 3% to $357.3 million during 2015 mostly thanks to higher interest income stemming from

12% organic loan asset growth. Non-interest income slid 1% as the bank collected less in deposit account service charges and earned less in gains on SBA loan sales.Revenue growth and a continued decline in loan loss provisions in 2015 drove BBCN's net income up 4% to $92.2 million. The company's operating cash levels fell 9% to $122.89 million for the year mostly due to unfavorable working capital changes mostly related to changes in other assets.StrategyThe nation's largest Korean-American bank differentiates itself by honing in on its target customer base being sure to be present in areas with high concentrations of Korean Americans (such as in California). Bank of Hope has been acquiring smaller banks in recent years to expand its footprint into such markets while growing its deposit and loan business. Its mid-2016 acquisition of top Korean-American rival Wilshire Bancorp solidified its position ahead of its closest rival Hamni Financial.

Mergers and Acquisitions

In December 2015 BBCN Bancorp agreed to buy Wilshire Bancorp (the second-largest US Korean-American bank) for $1 billion in an all-stock offer. Completed in mid-2016 the combined banks control more than $13 billion in assets effectively creating the seventh-largest bank in California and the largest Korean-American bank (and only super-regional Korean-American bank) in the US ahead of rival Hamni Financial. In 2013 it bought Pacific International Bancorp which came with four branches in Seattle and Foster Bankshares which had nine branches —eight in Illinois and one in Virginia.Company BackgroundBBCN Bancorp formed in 2011 from the merger of Center Bank and Nara Bank two rivals headquartered a few blocks away from each other in the Koreatown neighborhood of Los Angeles. (Its name stood for Business Bank of Center and Nara.)

EXECUTIVES

Evp And Chief Lending Officer Bbcn Bank, Jason K Kim, age 50
Executive Vice President Chief Operations Administrator, Sook Goo
Senior Vice President and Senior Credit Administrator, Ryan (Ry) Kim
Vice President And Systems Support Manager, Joshua Chu
Vice President Compliance Officer, Robin West
Assistant Vice President and Senior Human Resources Analyst, Soon Bae
Senior Vice President and Chief Credit Officer, Peter (Pete) Koh
Auditors: KPMG LLP

LOCATIONS

HQ: Hope Bancorp Inc
  3200 Wilshire Boulevard, Suite 1400, Los Angeles, CA 90010
Phone: 213 387-3200   **Fax:** 213 235-3033
Web: www.bbcnbank.com

PRODUCTS/OPERATIONS

2015 Sales

	$ mil.	% of total
Interest income	313.7	88
Non-interest income	43.7	12
Total	**357.4**	**100**

COMPETITORS

Bank of America	Grandpoint
Broadway Financial	Hanmi Financial

Cathay General Bancorp   U.S. Bancorp
East West Bancorp   Wells Fargo
Far East National Bank   Woori

HISTORICAL FINANCIALS
Company Type: Public

Income Statement   FYE: December 31

	ASSETS ($ mil.)	NET INCOME ($ mil.)	INCOME AS % OF ASSETS	EMPLOYEES
12/15	7,912.6	92.2	1.2%	938.0
12/14	7,140.3	88.6	1.2%	915.0
12/13	6,475.2	81.7	1.3%	835.0
12/12	5,640.6	83.2	1.5%	704.0
12/11	5,166.6	27.1	0.5%	678.0
Annual Growth	11.2%	35.8%	—	8.5%

2015 Year-End Financials

Return on assets: 1.2%
Return on equity: 10.1%
Long-term debt ($ mil.): —
No. of shares (mil.): 79.5
Sales ($ mil): 357.3

Dividends
   Yield: 2.4%
   Payout: 36.2%
Market value ($ mil.): 1,370.0

	STOCK PRICE ($) FY Close	P/E High/Low	PER SHARE ($) Earnings	Dividends	Book Value
12/15	17.22	17 11	1.16	0.42	11.79
12/14	14.38	16 12	1.11	0.35	11.10
12/13	16.59	16 11	1.03	0.25	10.19
12/12	11.57	13 10	0.99	0.05	9.62
12/11	9.45	20 11	0.53	0.00	10.21
Annual Growth	16.2%	— —	21.6%	—	3.7%

Horizon Bancorp (Michigan City, IN)

For those in Indiana and Michigan Horizon Bancorp stretches as far as the eye can see. The company is the holding company for Horizon Bank (and its Heartland Community Bank division) which provides checking and savings accounts IRAs CDs and credit cards to customers through more than 50 branches in north and central Indiana and southwest and central Michigan. Commercial financial and agricultural loans make up the largest segment of its loan portfolio which also includes mortgage warehouse loans (loans earmarked for sale into the secondary market) consumer loans and residential mortgages. Through subsidiaries the bank offers trust and investment management services; life health and property/casualty insurance; and annuities.

OperationsHorizon boasted more than $2.08 billion in total assets and $1.48 billion in deposits in 2014. Commercial loans made up 49% of the bank's total loan portfolio. The bank employed nearly 450 full and part time employees that year.Horizon's subsidiaries include: Horizon Investments which manages the bank's investment portfolio; Horizon Properties which manages the real estate investment trust; Horizon Insurance Services which sells through the company's Wealth Management; and Horizon Grantor Trust which holds title to certain company-owned life insurance policies. The bank generated 61% of its

revenue from interest income on loans in 2014 while another 13% came from interest on its taxable and tax-exempt investments. About 8% of revenues came from gains on its mortgage sales while the remainder of revenues were mostly generated by a mix of service charges on deposit accounts interchange fees and fiduciary activities fees.Geographic ReachThe bank's more than 30 branches serve customers in north and central Indiana and southwest and central Michigan. Its mortgage-banking services are offered across the Midwest. Financial PerformanceHorizon Bancorp's revenues and profits have been trending higher over the past few years mostly as it's continued to grow its loan business and deposit customer base through acquisitions.The bank's revenue rose by 2% to $102.5 million in 2014 mostly as the bank increased its interest-earning assets during the year. Its non-interest income also increased thanks to higher service charges on deposits and interchange fee income resulting from the growth in transactional deposit accounts and volume. Despite higher revenue in 2014 the company's net income fell by 9% to $18.1 million for the year on higher provisions for loan losses due to loan growth and a write-off of a commercial account coupled with an increase in transaction costs related to its Summit acquisition and an increase in salaries and employee benefits due to growth. Horizon's operating cash levels fell by 62% to $17.7 million after adjusting its earnings for non-cash items related to its net proceeds on the sale of its held-for-sale loans.StrategyHorizon Bancorp continues to expand its geographic reach and loan business through acquisitions though it also opens new branches from time to time. It last opened a branch in Carmel Indiana in 2015. Mergers and AcquisitionsIn 2016 Horizon Bancorp bought LaPorte Bancorp for $98.9 million boosting its total assets by 20% to more than $3.24 billion while expanding its branch reach into the LaPorte area of Indiana. It also agreed to buy CNB Bancorp which operates Central National Bank & Trust in Attica Indiana.In 2015 Horizon Bancorp agreed to buy Peoples Bancorp and subsidiary Peoples Federal Savings Bank of DeKalb County.In April 2014 the company purchased SCP Bancorp including subsidiary Summit Community Bank and its two branches.In 2012 Horizon bought Heartland Bancshares holding company of central Indiana's Heartland Community Bank adding a half-dozen locations to Horizon's branch network.

EXECUTIVES

President CEO Chief Administrative Officer and Director; Chairman and CEO Horizon Bank, Craig M. Dwight, age 59, $300,000 total compensation

EVP; President and COO Horizon Bank, Thomas H. Edwards, age 63, $187,000 total compensation

CFO, Mark E. Secor, age 50, $131,921 total compensation

President LaPorte County Indiana Horizon Bank, Steven C. Kring

President Southwest Michigan Horizon Bank, Donald E. (Don) Radde, age 63, $166,000 total compensation

President Porter County Indiana Horizon Bank, David G. Rose

Vice President, David (Dave) Bly

Vice President Mortgage Operations, Becki Doperalski

Vice President, Mark (Marky) Ritzi

Chairman, Robert C. Dabagia, age 77

Auditors: BKD, LLP

LOCATIONS

HQ: Horizon Bancorp (Michigan City, IN)
   515 Franklin Square, Michigan City, IN 46360
Phone: 219 879-0211
Web: www.accesshorizon.com

PRODUCTS/OPERATIONS

Selected Subsidiaries
Horizon Bank National Association
   Horizon Insurance Services Inc.
   Horizon Investments Inc.
   Horizon Trust & Investment Management N.A.

COMPETITORS

1st Source Corporation   Farmers Mutual of NE
American United Mutual   Fifth Third
Bank of America   First Merchants
Brotherhood Mutual   Indiana Farmers Mutual

HISTORICAL FINANCIALS
Company Type: Public

Income Statement   FYE: December 31

	ASSETS ($ mil.)	NET INCOME ($ mil.)	INCOME AS % OF ASSETS	EMPLOYEES
12/15	2,652.4	20.5	0.8%	558.0
12/14	2,076.9	18.1	0.9%	448.0
12/13	1,758.2	19.8	1.1%	421.0
12/12	1,848.2	19.5	1.1%	419.0
12/11	1,547.1	12.8	0.8%	323.0
Annual Growth	14.4%	12.6%	—	14.6%

2015 Year-End Financials

Return on assets: 0.8%
Return on equity: 8.9%
Long-term debt ($ mil.): —
No. of shares (mil.): 17.9
Sales ($ mil): 118.9

Dividends
   Yield: 3.0%
   Payout: 45.2%
Market value ($ mil.): 501.0

	STOCK PRICE ($) FY Close	P/E High/Low	PER SHARE ($) Earnings	Dividends	Book Value
12/15	27.96	22 17	1.26	0.57	14.90
12/14	26.14	20 15	1.27	0.51	14.07
12/13	25.33	17 13	1.45	0.42	12.71
12/12	19.65	18 10	1.53	0.37	12.30
12/11	17.33	28 17	1.01	0.15	10.87
Annual Growth	12.7%	— —	5.7%	40.6%	8.2%

Hospitality Properties Trust

Hospitality Properties Trust (HPT) rolls out the welcome mat for the road-weary. The real estate investment trust (REIT) owns nearly 300 hotels throughout the US and in Canada and Puerto Rico as well as 185 full-service truck stops operating as TravelCenters of America and Petro Stopping Centers. Unlike some hospitality REITs HPT is not affiliated with any one hotel company. Its properties target different markets from upscale (Crowne Plaza Hotels & Resorts) to business and family travelers on long-term trips (Residence Inn by Marriott). HPT maintains a geographically diverse portfolio with hotels or travel centers (usually both) in nearly 45 states as well as Canada and Puerto Rico.

OperationsHPT operates two business segments: Hotel Real Estate Investments which makes up around 85% of its overall revenue and includes the hotel operating revenues from its more than 290 hotel properties spanning almost 45000 rooms; and Travel Center Real Estate Investments which make up the remainder of revenue and include its lease income from its 185 travel center properties leased to TravelCenters of America LLC (or subsidiaries). About 80% of its travel centers operate under the TravelCenters of America or TA brand while the remainder operate under the Petro Stopping Centers or Petro brand name. Geographic ReachWhile the REIT's properties are in nearly 45 states about 35% of its 2014 revenue came from properties in Texas California Georgia Illinois and Florida.Sales and MarketingAbout 27% of its revenue came from its 122 hotel properties operating under the Marriott brand in 2014 while about 20% and 10% came from its InterContinental- and Sonesta-branded hotels respectively. About 33% of its revenue came from operations under its Travel Centers of America or TA branded properties. The REIT employed 400 full-time employees as of February 2015.Financial PerformanceHPT's revenues and profits have been trending higher over the past few years mostly from added revenues from new hotel property acquisitions.The REIT's revenue jumped 11% to a record $1.74 billion in 2014 as its hotel property income grew by double digits mostly due to increases in average daily rates (ADR) but also partly thanks to new hotel acquisitions since January 2013. HPT's travel center rental income rose by 3% thanks to higher minimum rents from TA stemming from improvements HPT purchased at some of its travel centers since 2013.Higher revenue and strong cost controls in 2014 boosted HPT's net income by 48% to $197.8 million while the REIT's operating cash levels jumped by 18% to $461.7 million thanks to an increase in cash-based minimum returns and rents.StrategyWhile HPT is relatively less aggressive with the number of acquisitions it makes (it acquired just eight net new properties during 2014) it prefers to purchase new hotels in bulk from owners and operators that wish to divest their properties in order to raise capital but want to stay in the hospitality business. It also focuses its investments on hotels located in urban or high density suburban locations near major urban centers in locations convenient for business travelers.As part of its internal growth strategy HPT in 2015 planned to apply asset management strategies to improve hotel operator performance with the goal of sharing the benefits of boosting property values and correspondingly rising rental rates.Mergers and AcquisitionsIn June 2015 Hospitality Properties Trust agreed to acquire and leaseback 30 of travel centers for a total purchase price of $397 million. The REIT expected its annual net cash rental income to increase by $30.2 million per year plus a percentage of rent in the future. It also expected to acquire an additional five TA-developed sites for $118 million —an amount equal to TA's development costs.

Company Background
HPT made a bold move beyond hotels when it acquired truck stop chain TravelCenters of America (TA) in 2007 for almost $2 billion signifying the REIT's first foray into the travel convenience industry. While the hotel industry is cyclical HPT wanted to capitalize on the fact that travel centers which are located along most major US interstate highways perform well even in recession. TA was spun

off not long after the acquisition and now operates as a separate company leasing all travel center properties from owner HPT.

HISTORY

Company BackgroundLawyer Barry Portnoy founded Health and Retirement Properties Trust (now HRPT Properties Trust) in 1986 to finance New MediCo a chain of nursing homes and head injury centers owned by one of his law clients and the client's cousin Gerard Martin. When New MediCo ran into financial trouble in 1992 HRPT privately restructured the debt and took over eight of the facilities.

In 1995 HRPT established and spun off Hospitality Properties Trust (HPT) as a separate public company with an initial portfolio of 21 Marriott International mid-market hotels. Over the next several years HPT bought hundreds of hotel properties often in large blocks; an example was its 1997 acquisition of 45 Marriott-branded hotels.

The company continued to add properties as REIT stock prices soared in the 1990s. But in 1999 REITs (particularly hospitality REITs) fell out of favor because of a perceived oversupply of rooms. Nevertheless the company succeeded in raising capital in 1999 to continue enlarging its portfolio. In early 2005 it acquired a portfolio of about a dozen properties from hotel management company InterContinental Hotels Group. The package included one hotel in San Juan Puerto Rico and two in Toronto that represent HPT's first non-US properties.

EXECUTIVES

Vice President Investor Relations, Timothy (Tim) Bonang
President and COO, John G. Murray, age 55
CFO and Treasurer, Mark L. Kleifges, age 55
Senior Vice President, Ethan Bornstein
Auditors: Ernst & Young LLP

LOCATIONS

HQ: Hospitality Properties Trust
Two Newton Place, 255 Washington Street, Suite 300, Newton, MA 02458-1634
Phone: 617 964-8389
Web: www.hptreit.com

PRODUCTS/OPERATIONS

2011 Sales

	$ mil.	% of total
Hotel operating revenues	889.1	74
Rental income	304.6	25
FF&E reserve income	16.6	1
Total	**1,210.3**	**100**

Selected Hotel Tenants
Candlewood Suites
Crowne Plaza Hotels & Resorts
Country Inns & Suites by Carlson
Courtyard by Marriott
Holiday Inn Hotels & Resorts
Hyatt Place
InterContinental Hotels & Resorts
Marriott Hotels and Resorts
Park Plaza Hotels & Resorts
Radisson Hotels & Resorts
Residence Inn by Marriott
SpringHill Suites by Marriott
Staybridge Suites
TownePlace Suites by Marriott

COMPETITORS

Ashford Hospitality Trust
FelCor
Hersha Hospitality
Host Hotels & Resorts
Innkeepers USA
LaSalle Hotel Properties
Love's Country Stores
Pebblebrook
Pilot Flying J
Shaner Hotel Group
Starwood Hotels & Resorts
Strategic Hotels
Sunstone Hotel Investors

HISTORICAL FINANCIALS

Company Type: Public

Income Statement

FYE: December 31

	REVENUE ($ mil.)	NET INCOME ($ mil.)	NET PROFIT MARGIN	EMPLOYEES
12/15	1,921.9	166.4	8.7%	0.0
12/14	1,736.3	197.1	11.4%	0.0
12/13	1,563.8	133.1	8.5%	0.0
12/12	1,296.9	151.9	11.7%	0.0
12/11	1,210.3	190.4	15.7%	0.0
Annual Growth	**12.3%**	**(3.3%)**	**—**	**—**

2015 Year-End Financials

Debt ratio: 51.3%	No. of shares (mil.): 151.5
Return on equity: 5.7%	Dividends
Cash ($ mil.): 13.6	Yield: 7.6%
Current ratio: 0.21	Payout: 205.1%
Long-term debt ($ mil.): 3,287.4	Market value ($ mil.): 3,963.0

	STOCK PRICE ($) FY Close	P/E High/Low		PER SHARE ($) Earnings	Dividends	Book Value
12/15	26.15	35 26		0.97	1.99	18.56
12/14	31.00	27 21		1.18	1.95	19.94
12/13	27.03	44 32		0.73	1.89	20.63
12/12	23.42	33 26		0.84	1.82	22.11
12/11	22.98	20 15		1.30	1.80	22.66
Annual Growth	**3.3%**			**(7.1%)**	**2.5%**	**(4.9%)**

Howard Hughes Corp

The Howard Hughes Corporation (THHC) is involved in neither planes movies or medical research but one of the 20th century entrepreneur's later interests real estate. The company arose from the bankruptcy restructuring of shopping mall developer General Growth Properties (GGP) to oversee much of GGP's non-retail assets. THHC owns GGP's former portfolio of four master planned communities outside Columbia Maryland; Houston Texas; and Summerlin Nevada; as well as about two dozen other as-yet undeveloped sites and commercial properties in 16 states from New York to Hawaii including GGP's own headquarters building in downtown Chicago. Unlike GGP THHC does not operate as a REIT.

Geographic Reach
Dallas-based THHC has offices at select properties and in New York City and Los Angeles. The firm operates master planned communities in Houston and The Woodlands Texas; Howard and Price George's counties in Maryland; and in Las Vegas.

Operations
THHC owns manages and develops commercial residential and mixed-use real estate throughout

the US. It organizes its business into three segments: master planned communities; operating assets; and strategic developments. THHC's holdings include eight mixed-use and retail properties nine office properties an apartment building a resort and conference center a 36-hole golf course and country club three equity investments and four other revenue-generating assets.

The firm's 22500-acre flagship property outside Las Vegas Summerlin is home to about 100000 people and has another 7000 acres for sale and redevelopment. Its other three communities in Texas and Maryland have a combined 7000 acres for sale and redevelopment. Beyond that other holdings include nine mixed-use development projects four mall developments and seven distressed mall properties slated for redevelopment.

Financial Performance

THHC has logged substantial revenue growth in recent years. Indeed in 2013 the firm reported $474.6 million in revenue a 26% increase versus 2012. Driving the double-digit gain was growth in master planned communities due to higher demand for its residential superpad sites in Summerlin (Las Vegas) and finished lots in The Woodlands and $33 million in revenue generated from the sale of condominium rights in Hawaii to a 50:50 joint venture. Despite the revenue gain THHC posted a loss of nearly $73.8 million in 2013 versus a deeper loss in 2012. Indeed the firm has posted losses in four of the last five years.

Strategy

After taking a pounding at the hands of Superstorm Sandy in 2013 which resulted in damage and lost revenue THHC is doubling down on its investment in the South Street Seaport District in lower Manhattan with the proposed acquisition of 80 South Street. The firm is rebuilding pier 17 and is working with the community on a proposal for a mixed-use project that increased a hotel and residential units a new marina restoration of the Tin Building an extension of the East River Esplanade a food market and a plan to ensure the long-term future of the financially troubled Seaport Museum. Its plans for a 50-story hotel/condo tower on the site of the former historic Fulton Fish Market is meeting resistance from the community.

Mergers and Acquisitions

In 2011 THHC acquired the remainder of The Woodlands master planned community in Houston that it already didn't own from Morgan Stanley Real Estate Investing. The $117.5 million deal gave the company complete control over the The Woodlands brand. In addition to its residential properties Howard Hughes plans to focus on developing commercial properties within The Woodlands.

Company Background

The Summerlin name is also the company's tie to Howard Hughes. In the 1950s Mr. Hughes bought 25000 acres outside Las Vegas and named it Summerlin his maternal grandmother's maiden name. Three years before he died in 1973 Mr. Hughes created Summa Corporation which became Summerlin's new owner. Hughes' heirs sold Summa to The Rouse Company in 1996 for about $500 million. GGP bought The Rouse Company in 2004. During the bankruptcy GGP paid Hughes' heirs $230 million to settle Summerlin and in return named the new company after him.

EXECUTIVES

Senior Vice President, David (Dave) Striph
Board Member, David R (Dave) Weinreb
Auditors: Ernst & Young LLP

LOCATIONS

HQ: Howard Hughes Corp
13355 Noel Road, 22nd Floor, Dallas, TX 75240
Phone: 214 741-7744   **Fax:** 214 741-3021
Web: www.howardhughes.com

PRODUCTS/OPERATIONS

Selected Propeties

American City Building (office building in Columbia MD)
Bridgeland (master-planned community in Houston)
Century Plaza (future development in Birmingham AL)
Columbia (master-planned community in Maryland)
Kendall Town Center (future mixed-use development near Miami FL)
Landmark Mall (mall in Alexandria VA)
Ridgley Building (office building in Columbia MD)
Riverwalk Marketplace (mall in New Orleans LA)
South Street Seaport (retail site in Manhattan NY)
Summerlin (master-planned community near Las Vegas)
The Woodlands (master-planned community in Houston)

COMPETITORS

Bresler & Reiner	Macerich
CBL & Associates Properties	Newhall Land Related
Deltona	Taubman Centers
Hillwood	Washington Real Estate
Hines	Weingarten Realty

HISTORICAL FINANCIALS

Company Type: Public

Income Statement

FYE: December 31

	REVENUE ($ mil.)	NET INCOME ($ mil.)	NET PROFIT MARGIN	EMPLOYEES
12/15	797.0	126.7	15.9%	1,000.0
12/14	634.5	(23.5)	—	1,100.0
12/13	474.6	(73.7)	—	1,000.0
12/12	376.8	(127.5)	—	842.0
12/11	275.6	148.4	53.9%	835.0
Annual Growth	**30.4%**	**(3.9%)**		**4.6%**

2015 Year-End Financials

Debt ratio: 42.7%	No. of shares (mil.): 39.7
Return on equity: 5.5%	Dividends
Cash ($ mil.): 445.3	Yield: —
Current ratio: 0.68	Payout: —
Long-term debt ($ mil.): 2,443.9	Market value ($ mil.): 4,494.0

	STOCK PRICE ($) FY Close	P/E High/Low	PER SHARE ($) Earnings	Dividends	Book Value
12/15	113.16	50 34	1.60	0.00	59.43
12/14	130.42	— —	(0.60)	0.00	56.10
12/13	120.10	— —	(1.87)	0.00	56.56
12/12	73.02	— —	(3.36)	0.00	58.36
12/11	44.17	20 10	1.17	0.00	61.26
Annual Growth	**26.5%**	**— —**	**8.1%**	**—**	**(0.8%)**

Huttig Building Products, Inc.

Hut one! Hut two! Huttig Building Products works to make buying building supplies a snap. Huttig is one of the US's largest distributors of millwork building materials and wood products for new housing construction and remodeling and repair. Huttig sells doors windows moldings trusses wall panels lumber and other supplies through more than 25 distribution centers in some 40 states covering a substantial portion of the US housing market. The centers primarily sell to building materials dealers (such as 84 Lumber and BMC Stock) buying groups home centers and industrial users. Huttig's products typically end up in the hands of professional builders and contractors.

Sales and Marketing

Huttig Building Products conducts business using a two-step distribution model: it resells the products it purchases from manufacturers to its customers who then sell the products to the final end users typically professional builders and independent contractors engaged in residential construction and remodeling projects. Huttig serves more than 4400 customers. Its largest Lumbermen's Merchandising Corp. accounted for 11% of the company's 2011 sales. Building materials pro dealers are the company's single largest customer group. Huttig's top 10 customers accounted for approximately 38% of its sales in 2011.

Financial Performance

After four dismal years during which Huttig's sales plummeted from a high point of $1.1 billion in 2005 to $455 million in 2009 the company has posted back-to-back years of modest sales gains. In 2011 sales increased by about 2% vs. 2010 after posting a 3% gain in the previous annual comparison. Still the nearly $479 million Huttig rang up in 2011 is well below its 2005 high. Despite the uptick in sales the company continues to lose money –about $13.2 million in 2011 –marking its sixth consecutive year in the red. However its losses are narrowing as the company continues to control costs amid a weak sales environment.

Huttig credited its 2011 sales gain to improvement in its roofing business which was partially storm driven as well as a modest increase in housing starts. (Indeed while housing starts increased modestly in 2011 they were still below historical levels.) The firm which is highly dependent on new home construction is looking for housing starts to accelerate to return to profitability.

Strategy

In the meantime Huttig has reduced its operating expenses by cutting jobs. (It had about 1000 fewer employees in 2011 than in 2006.) Other measures taken to reduce its cost structure included selling or shuttering some 20 distribution centers. Still the firm believes that it can weather one of the most severe housing downturns in US history because of its purchasing power wide geographic presence and the infrastructure to accommodate customers in about 40 states.

Ownership

Mexico's CEMEX owns about 23% of Huttig's shares through the UK-based Rugby Group Ltd.

Company Background

Formed in 1885 by Charles Huttig Huttig Building Products was later acquired by diversified manufacturer Crane Co. In 1999 Huttig was spun off by Crane and combined with the US building products unit of UK-based The Rugby Group.

EXECUTIVES

President CEO and Director, Jon P. Vrabely, age 51, $389,231 total compensation
Vice President - Product Management and Marketing, Gregory W. (Greg) Gurley, age 62, $218,942 total compensation
Vice President; Chief Information Officer, Brian D. Robinson, age 55, $199,500 total compensation
President and COO, John Docherty
CFO, Photios Michalargias
Auditors: KPMG LLP

LOCATIONS

HQ: Huttig Building Products, Inc.
555 Maryville University Drive, Suite 400, St. Louis, MO 63141
Phone: 314 216-2600
Web: www.huttig.com

PRODUCTS/OPERATIONS

Selected Brands

CertainTeed
Fiberon
HB&G
Huttig Windows
Huttigrip Fasteners
L.J. Smith
Louisiana Pacific
Masonite
Owens Corning
Simpson Strong-Tie
Therma-Tru
Timbertech
Typar
Windsor
Woodgrain

COMPETITORS

ABC Supply
Beacon Roofing
BlueLinx
Georgia-Pacific
Guardian Building Products Distribution
MI Windows and Doors
Pacific Coast Building Products
PrimeSource Building
Universal Forest Products
Weyerhaeuser

HISTORICAL FINANCIALS

Company Type: Public

Income Statement

FYE: December 31

	REVENUE ($ mil.)	NET INCOME ($ mil.)	NET PROFIT MARGIN	EMPLOYEES
12/15	659.6	26.0	3.9%	1,000.0
12/14	623.7	2.2	0.4%	1,000.0
12/13	561.5	3.2	0.6%	1,000.0
12/12	520.5	(0.5)	—	900.0
12/11	478.7	(13.2)	—	900.0
Annual Growth	8.3%	—	—	2.7%

2015 Year-End Financials

Debt ratio: 27.4%	No. of shares (mil.): 24.9
Return on equity: 66.1%	Dividends
Cash ($ mil.): 0.3	Yield: —
Current ratio: 1.86	Payout: —
Long-term debt ($ mil.): 47.4	Market value ($ mil.): 95.0

	STOCK PRICE ($) FY Close	P/E High/Low	PER SHARE ($) Earnings	Dividends	Book Value
12/15	3.80	4 3	1.04	0.00	2.12
12/14	3.35	61 30	0.09	0.00	1.05
12/13	3.86	30 12	0.13	0.00	0.94
12/12	1.60	— —	(0.02)	0.00	0.80
12/11	0.52	— —	(0.60)	0.00	0.83
Annual Growth	64.4%	— —	—	—	26.4%

IBERIABANK Corp

IBERIABANK Corp. serves up financial services with a Cajun flare. Through its flagship bank subsidiary also called IBERIABANK the holding company operates some 267 branches in Louisiana and five other southern states. It also has about 21 title insurance offices in Louisiana and Arkansas in addition to some 61 mortgage loan offices in a dozen states. Offering deposit products such as checking and savings accounts CDs and IRAs the bank uses funds gathered mainly to make loans. Commercial real estate and business loans make up nearly three-quarters of the company's loan portfolio which also includes consumer loans and residential mortgages. IBERIABANK Corp. has $13.4 billion in assets.

Geographic Reach

The company operates 267 combined offices including 172 bank branch offices and four loan production offices in Louisiana Arkansas Florida Alabama Tennessee Georgia and Texas 21 title insurance offices in Arkansas and Louisiana and mortgage representatives in 61 locations in 12 US states.

Operations

IBERIABANK Corp. has eight wholly-owned nonbank subsidiaries including brokerage unit Iberia Financial Services IBERIABANK Insurance Services Acadiana Holdings IBERIABANK Mortgage Company Little Rock Arkansas-based Lenders Title Company and several investment funds.

IB Aircraft Holdings LLC owns a fractional share of an aircraft used by management of the company and its subsidiaries. IAM provides wealth management and trust services for commercial and private banking clients. CDE is engaged in the purchase of tax credits.

Financial Performance

After enjoying two straight years of revenue increase in 2013 IBERIABANK Corp.'s revenues decreased by 2% due to lower interest and noninterest income. Noninterest income decreased as a result of a drop in the valuation of the company's mortgage-related derivatives and a lower margin on the sales of mortgage loans both of which negatively impacted mortgage income. However IBERIABANK Corp. had a $2.9 million increase in broker commissions as well as a growth of $2 million in service charges that partially offset the mortgage income decrease. After experiencing a huge net income increase in 2012 due to a decrease in the provision for loan loss and interest expenses in 2013 the company's net income declined by 15% to $65.1 million due to increased noninterest expenses as a result of a higher impairment of FDIC loss share receivables and other long-lived assets. This was partially offset by a decline in the

provision for loan losses and interest expenses.In 2013 IBERIABANK Corp.'s operating cash inflow increased to $309.8 million (compared to cash out flow of $12.2 million in 2012) primarily due to a huge decline in the provision for loan losses and change in the assets and liabilities.

Strategy

Acquisitions have been a big part of IBERIABANK Corp.'s growth strategy since 2003. All of the acquisition activity has expanded the company's assets and branch network helped it enter new markets such as Florida and Texas and strengthen its presence in existing ones.

As part of IBERIABANK's growth through acquisition strategy in late 2014 it purchased Georgia Commerce Bank as part of a merger deal for $195 million which expanded IBERIABANK's reach into the Atlanta Georgia market for the first time. Earlier that same year the bank also acquired First Private Holdings Inc. the holding company of First Private Bank of Texas a Dallas Texas-based bank with two branch locations; Florida Bank Group; and certain assets of the Memphis Tennessee operations of Trust One Bank a division of Synovus Bank.

Company Background

In 2012 IBERIABANK Corp. struck an agreement to buy Florida Gulf Bank. In 2011 the bank completed three acquisitions: OMNI Bank with 14 offices in New Orleans and Baton Rouge Louisiana; Cameron State Bank with 22 offices in Lake Charles Louisiana; and the assets of Florida Trust Company a subsidiary of the failed Bank of Florida Corporation. (Between 2003 and 2010 the bank completed 13 acquisitions with combined total assets of more than $6 billion.)

The company was founded in 1887.

EXECUTIVES

Executive Vice President, George (Georgey) Becker
President and CEO, Daryl G. Byrd, age 61, $1,015,000 total compensation
Vice President, Barry (Barr) Berthelot
SEVP Mergers and Acquisitions Finance and Investor Relations; Director Financial Strategy and Mortgage, John R. Davis, age 55, $456,154 total compensation
Vice Chairman and Managing Director of Brokerage Trust and Wealth Management, Jefferson G. (Jeff) Parker, age 63, $480,192 total compensation
SEVP and Director Communications Facilities and Human Resources, Elizabeth A. (Beth) Ardoin, age 47
SEVP and CFO, Anthony J. Restel, age 46, $480,385 total compensation
Vice Chairman; SEVP and COO, Michael J. (Mike) Brown, age 52, $598,269 total compensation
President and CEO IberiaBank Mortgage, Bill Edwards
EVP and Director Retail Small Business and Mortgage, Robert M. (Bob) Kottler, age 57
EVP and Executive Credit Officer, H. Spurgeon Mackie, age 65
EVP and Chief Risk Officer, J. Randolph Bryan, age 48
EVP Corporate Secretary and General Counsel, Robert B. Worley, age 56
President and CEO Lender's Title Company, David B. Erb
Vice President Mortgage Executive, Ted (Teddy) Nusenow
Vice President, Bill (Billy) Neal
Vice President Commercial Relationship Manager, Chuck Kramer
Vice President, Brock Fletcher

Assistant Vice President, Dolores (Lori) Hernandez
Vice President Of Communications, Rhonda Shea
Vice President, Tom Chelewski
Vice President Bcs Ore Officer, Neel Stacy
Vice President, Mike Barnes Mike (Mikey) Barnes
Vice President Human Resources Manager, Kevin Robinson
Vice President, Bruce (Brucey) Reid
Senior Vice President Director Of Facility Services, Michael (Mel) Pou
Vice President Support Services, Jerry (Jerr) Prejean
Vice President And Senior Business Relationship Manager, Ty (Tyler) Powell
Assistant Vice President, Misty Labat
Vice President Business Credit Services Retail Officer, Mary Rice
Vice President, Jack (Jackie) Avery
Assistant Vice President, Ennio Alonso
Vice President, Debbie (Deb) Nolan
Vice President, Nancy Dost
Senior Vice President, John (Jack) Troyan
Senior Vice President Bank Owned Assets, Mark (Marky) Collier
Senior Vice President, Missy S Krantz
Vice President, Craig Peak
Vice President, Greg (Greggy) Mendez
Senior Vice President Of The Commercial Banking GR, John (Jack) Everett
Vice President Community Banking, Randall (Randy) Rojas
Vice President Of Product Management, Paula Allred
Vice President and Treasurer, Eric (Ric) Movassaghi
Vice President Business Banking, Angela Velardi
Vice President, Steve (Stevie) Barnes
Vice President Business Credit Services, Brian Buczko
Vice President Manager of Financial Analytics, Stephanie Verret
Vice President, Nancy H (Nance) Wooten
Senior Vice President Corporate Banking, C Mizelle
Vice President, Michael Hallmark
Senior Vice President, David Warlick
Assistant Vice President, Andy Gaines
Assistant Vice President, Keaton Smith
Vice President Market Executive and Branch Manager, Mary (Mar) Chase
Assistant Vice President and Human Resources General, Ashley (Ash) Townley
Vice President Retail Administration, Robin Bordelon
Vice President Branch Manager Business Development Officer, Pedro Diaz
Vice President Public Relations Director, Judi (Jude) Lejeune
Vice President Business Credit Services, Timothy Wilson
Executive Vice President Director of Organizational Deve, Donna Domick
Senior Vice President and Senior Commercial Real Estate Relationship Manager, Martin Brown Martin (Marti) Brown
Senior Vice President, Joe (Joey) Woodson
Vice President, Janet (Jan) Patton
Vice President Human Resources, Jayne Socotch
Vice President Senior Network Engineer, Jon (Jonny) Luckett
Vice President, Pauline Sampson
Assistant Vice President Bcs Portfolio Manager, Rhonda Prosser
Senior Vice President Project Management, Gina Stritzinger
Senior Vice President and Associate General Counsel, Beth (Betty) Trotter
Vice President, Kelly M (Kel) Casey

Senior Vice President, Steve Kelly
Vice President and Chatham County Market Executive, Michael (Mel) Carper
Executive Vice President and Director of Organizational Development, Barry (Barr) Rocky
Executive Vice President Retail Segment Leader, Don (Donnie) Ledet
Senior Vice President, Pat (Patty) Yates
Vice President Business Credit Services, David (Dave) Krage
Senior Vice President, Mary Guidry
Vice President Applications Programmera, Carole (Carrie) Peck
Executive Vice President And Director Enterprise Risk Ma, Elise (Elisabeth) Latimer
Senior Vice President And Commercial Rel, Jamey Vaught
Assistant Vice President And Senior Relationship Banker, Darlene (Darl) Nicks
Executive Vice President, Barry (Barr) Mulroy
Executive Vice President, Beth (Betty) Ardoin
Executive Vice President IBERIA Corporate Services Capital Markets Manager, David (Dave) Shutley
Senior Vice President, Jill Merkl
Vice President, Jason (Jase) Perrin
Vice President Commercial Lending, Jamie (James) Vaught
Vice President, Clay (Clayton) Peterson
Vice President Business Banking, William (Bill) Biossat
Assistant Vice President Human Resources Generalist, Lesley (Les) Mahoney
Senior Vice President, Cameron D (Cammie) Jones
Vice President and Coml Rel Manager Ii, Elizabeth (Beth) Bodin
Vice President, Pete (Petey) Yuan
Senior Vice President And Business And Retail Market Manger, Maurice (Maury) Butler
Vice President eBanking Business Analyst, Lisa (Lis) Hayes
Assistant Vice President And Senior Datacenter Architect, Chuck (Chucky) Cosby
Vice President Business Banking Relationship Mana, Douglas (Doug) Machado
Vice President, Randall (Randy) Rinaudo
Senior Vice President and Manager of Financial Analytics, Shawn Jordan
Chairman, William H. Fenstermaker, age 67
Vice Chairman, E. Stewart Shea, age 64
Board Member, Melanie Savell
Auditors: Ernst & Young LLP

LOCATIONS

HQ: IBERIABANK Corp
200 West Congress Street, Lafayette, LA 70501
Phone: 337 521-4003
Web: www.iberiabank.com

PRODUCTS/OPERATIONS

2015 Sales

	$ mil.	% of total
Interest		
Loans including fees	607.0	68
Securities	53.2	6
Other	10.2	1
Adjustments	(23.5)	-
Noninterest		
Mortgage income	81.1	9
Service charges on deposit accounts	42.2	5
Title revenue	22.8	3
Brokerage Commissions	17.6	2
ATM/debit card fees	14.0	2
Income from bank owned life insurance	4.3	-
Others	38.3	4
Total	**867.3**	**100**

COMPETITORS

Bank of America	Investar
Bank of the Ozarks	JPMorgan Chase
Capital One	Louisiana Bancorp
First NBC Bank	MidSouth Bancorp
Hancock Holding	Regions Financial
Home Banc	Teche Holding

HISTORICAL FINANCIALS

Company Type: Public

Income Statement

FYE: December 31

	ASSETS ($ mil.)	NET INCOME ($ mil.)	INCOME AS % OF ASSETS	EMPLOYEES
12/15	19,504.0	142.8	0.7%	3,216.0
12/14	15,758.6	105.4	0.7%	2,825.0
12/13	13,365.5	65.1	0.5%	2,638.0
12/12	13,129.6	76.4	0.6%	2,758.0
12/11	11,757.9	53.5	0.5%	2,645.0
Annual Growth	**13.5%**	**27.8%**	**—**	**5.0%**

2015 Year-End Financials

Return on assets: 0.8%	Dividends
Return on equity: 6.5%	Yield: 2.4%
Long-term debt ($ mil.): —	Payout: 37.5%
No. of shares (mil.): 41.1	Market value ($ mil.): 2,266.0
Sales ($ mil): 867.2	

	STOCK PRICE ($) FY Close	P/E High/Low		PER SHARE ($) Earnings	Dividends	Book Value
12/15	55.07	19	15	3.68	1.36	60.74
12/14	64.85	22	18	3.30	1.36	55.39
12/13	62.85	29	20	2.20	1.36	51.40
12/12	49.12	21	17	2.59	1.36	51.88
12/11	49.30	32	23	1.87	1.36	50.48
Annual Growth	**2.8%**	**—**	**—**	**18.4%**	**(0.0%)**	**4.7%**

Idexx Laboratories, Inc.

IDEXX can identify what's wrong with Fluffy Fido Flossie or Flicka. A leading animal health care company IDEXX makes diagnostic testing kits and machines for cats and dogs as well as cows and horses. Veterinarians use the company's VetTest analyzers for blood and urine chemistry and its SNAP in-office test kits to detect heartworms feline leukemia and other diseases. The company also provides lab testing services and practice management software. In addition IDEXX makes diagnostic products to detect livestock and poultry diseases and to test for contaminants in water and milk. The company sells its products worldwide.

Operations

Products and services for companion animals (aka: pets) account for more than 80% of IDEXX's sales. Most of that revenue comes from diagnostic products and services including chemistry analyzers rapid test kits and laboratory services. The company operates a network of laboratories to which vets can send patient samples for analysis.

After companion animals livestock and poultry (horses cows pigs and chickens) are the company's second-largest market. IDEXX's Livestock and Poultry Diagnostics business includes products to test for Bovine Spongiform Encephalopathy (BSE or "mad cow" disease) as well as porcine illnesses and poultry diseases. Equine products make up a smaller portion of the company's sales.

IDEXX's water testing segment produces tests to detect E. coli enterococci and Cryptosporidia. Water utilities and government laboratories are the primary customers for these products –half of sales are outside of the US. The company's dairy testing unit produces a SNAP test to measure antibiotic residues in milk which are highly regulated in markets outside of the US. The company also sells OPTI Medical Systems which measure human electrolyte blood gases and glucose levels. The systems and consumables are sold to hospitals and clinics.

Geographic Reach

More than half of the company's sales are made in the US but it also maintains sales offices in 15 countries in Asia Europe and the Pacific. While many of its products and materials are manufactured by third parties it also maintains manufacturing and assembly facilities in Georgia and Maine and in Bern Switzerland and Montpellier France.

Sales and Marketing

IDEXX distributes its products through its own marketing and sales force and through independent distributors and resellers.

Financial Performance

Although IDEXX's revenue growth had been slowed by the economic recession the company reported modest revenue increases in the last two years. It also saw net income increases by about 15% and 10% respectively in 2011 and 2012. While the Livestock and Poultry Diagnostics business grew more than 15% as a result of a jump in sales of bovine tests to government agencies in Germany in 2011 that same segment began to soften in 2012 as government testing changed.

Strategy

IDEXX continues to grow by focusing on launching new products and consumables for its instruments and test kits. It has also expanded into software by introducing web-based practice management tools for veterinarians.

Mergers and Acquisition

In 2012 the company purchased the assets of Sneakers Software which had been selling its practice management software.

HISTORY

David Shaw founded IDEXX in 1984 as AgriTech Systems. An MBA who had specialized in agribusiness consulting Shaw wanted to cut the costs and time involved in lab testing for diseases by producing kits that could be used on-site; an initial line of poultry disease tests proved successful. The company changed its name to IDEXX in 1988 and went public in 1991.

In 1994 IDEXX acquired AMIS International a leading Japanese test lab for veterinarians. The next year the company opened offices in Spain and the Netherlands and introduced the SNAP test which detects allergies in dogs.

In 1997 IDEXX acquired two software companies Advanced Veterinary Systems and Professionals Software and merged them to create IDEXX Informatics. That year the firm also bought Acumedia Manufacturers a producer of more than 300 varieties of dehydrated culture media. Looking to expand into animal drug development the company bought animal health firm Blue Ridge Pharmaceuticals in 1998. In 2000 IDEXX sold Acumedia as well as its food microbiology operations. It also launched VetConnect.com which provides veterinary information and support and product sales.

In 2008 the company sold its veterinary pharmaceutical operations which were miniscule to focus on its core test kit and consumable business.

EXECUTIVES

Vice President Of Purchasing, Rick Cotta
Chairman President and CEO, Jonathan W. (Jon) Ayers, age 59, $800,000 total compensation
Corporate Vice President rapid Assay And Digital, James (Jamie) Polewaczyk
EVP CFO and Treasurer, Brian P. McKeon, age 54, $496,153 total compensation
EVP, Johnny D. Powers, age 54, $416,923 total compensation
EVP, Michael J. Williams, age 48, $416,923 total compensation
EVP, Jay Mazelsky, $416,923 total compensation
Vice President General Manager, Scott Hamilton
Vice President Of Maintenance, Michael (Mel) Flaherty
Vice President, George (Georgey) Fennell
Vice President Research And Development, Bob Dodge
Vice President Worldwide Regulatory Affairs, Marianne (Ann) Murray
Vice President Worldwide Operations, Dan Meyaard
Corporate Vice President Human Resources, Giovani Twigge
Vice President, Daniel (Dan) Meyaard
Vice President, Steve (Stevie) Capps
DIV Vice President Worldwide Pathology and Interna, Roberta (Berta) Relford
Corporate Vice President Sales Marketing and Business Development, Tj Dupree
Vice President and Global Chief Commercial Counsel, Matthew (Matt) Forsyth
Vice President, Roy Pollock
Treasurer, Rick (Ricky) Holt
Auditors: PricewaterhouseCoopers LLP

LOCATIONS

HQ: Idexx Laboratories, Inc.
One IDEXX Drive, Westbrook, ME 04092
Phone: 207 556-0300   Fax: 207 856-0346
Web: www.idexx.com

PRODUCTS/OPERATIONS

2015 Sales

	% of total
Companion Animal Group	85
Livestock Poultry and Dairy	8
Water	6
Other	1
Total	**100**

2015 Sales

	% of total
Product	61
Service	39
Total	**100**

Selected Products

Companion animals
  Catalyst Dx chemistry analyzer
  PetChek diagnostics
  LaserCyte hematology system
  ProCyte Dx hematology system
  SNAP 3Dx (Lyme disease heartworm and Ehrlichia canis test)
  SNAP Feline Triple (FeLV heartworm FIV)
  VetLab Station (hardware platform)
  VetLyte electrolyte analyzer
  VetStat analyzer
Production animals
  Bovine spongiform encephalopathy diagnostic
  Bovine viral diarrhea diagnostic
  Swine influenza virus (H1N1 and H3N2)
  Porcine reproductive and respiratory disease syndrome diagnostic
  Swine pseudorabies diagnostic
Water quality
  Colilert (E. coli detection)
  Colisure (E. coli detection)
  Enterolert (enterococci detection)
  Filta-Max (Cryptosporidium and Giardia detection)
  Pseudalert (Pseudomonas detection)
Other
  OPTI human point-of-care analyzers
  SNAP beta-lactam test (detection of antibiotics in milk)

COMPETITORS

Abaxis	Neogen
Abbott Labs	Roche Diagnostics
Hemagen Diagnostics	Sdix
Heska	VCA
Instrumentation	
Laboratory Company	

HISTORICAL FINANCIALS

Company Type: Public

Income Statement

FYE: December 31

	REVENUE ($ mil.)	NET INCOME ($ mil.)	NET PROFIT MARGIN	EMPLOYEES
12/16	1,775.4	222.0	12.5%	7,365.0
12/15	1,601.8	192.0	12.0%	6,800.0
12/14	1,485.8	181.9	12.2%	6,400.0
12/13	1,377.0	187.8	13.6%	5,700.0
12/12	1,293.3	178.2	13.8%	5,400.0
Annual Growth	**8.2%**	**5.6%**	—	**8.1%**

2016 Year-End Financials

Debt ratio: 78.6%
Return on equity: —
Cash ($ mil.): 154.9
Current ratio: 0.90
Long-term debt ($ mil.): 593.1
No. of shares (mil.): 87.9
Dividends
  Yield: —
  Payout: —
Market value ($ mil.): 10,317.0

	STOCK PRICE ($) FY Close	P/E High/Low		PER SHARE ($) Earnings	Dividends	Book Value
12/16	117.27	49	26	2.44	0.00	(1.23)
12/15	72.92	81	30	2.05	0.00	(0.93)
12/14	148.27	84	58	1.79	0.00	1.24
12/13	106.37	62	47	1.74	0.00	5.03
12/12	92.80	62	49	1.59	0.00	5.84
Annual Growth	**6.0%**	—	—	**11.4%**	—	—

IES Holdings Inc

Lights! Camera! Action! Integrated Electrical Services (IES) has a hand in all three. It installs and maintains electrical and communications systems for residential commercial and industrial customers. Work on commercial buildings and homes includes custom design testing and maintenance on low-voltage systems such as lighting fire alarm audio/video and Internet cabling. On the industrial side IES performs high- and medium-voltage systems installation and construction on power stations oil and gas pipelines and processing plants. It has a network of more than 60 locations serving the continental US. Banking investor Jeffrey Gendell through Tontine Capital Partners owns about 57% of IES.OperationsThe company operates its business through four segments –Communications Residential Commercial & Industrial and

Infrastructure Solutions —that are organized by product and service. The residential segment serves single-family housing and multi-family apartment complexes as a regional provider of electrical installation services. Its communications segment provides infrastructure such a data centers for large corporations nationwide as well as design/build service and maintenance of data network systems for audio/visual telephone fire and alarm systems. IES's commercial and industrial segment provides electrical design construction and maintenance services on a regional and national basis. It has expertise in projects focused on power plants data centers chemical plants wind farms solar facilities and high-rise residential and office buildings among other markets. The newest segment infrastructure solutions (established through the 2013 acquisition of MISCOR Group) provides maintenance and repair services for the steel rail marine petrochemical pulp and paper energy mining and automotive industries in the US and abroad.Geographic ReachIES maintains 62 locations that serve 48 states. Besides its corporate headquarters in Houston the company boasts 26 locations (in Texas and the Sunbelt Western and Mid-Atlantic regions) that house its residential business activities 19 locations for its commercial and industrial unit (in Texas Nebraska Colorado Oregon and the Mid-Atlantic region) 11 locations focused on communications and nine locations for its infrastructure operations.Financial AnalysisAfter emerging from bankruptcy in 2006 only to be hit by the effects of the economic recession IES struggled for a few years financially. However the company has seen stable growth in revenue since 2009 as the economy has also recovered. In fiscal 2014 IES's revenue grew 4% to $512.4 million versus $494.6 million in 2013 primarily due to the inclusion of results from its new infrastructure solutions segment (which delivered $47.6 million). The residential segment also grew that year as housing demand increased but communications and commercial & industrial operations fell. Higher revenues and income from operations helped drive the company back into profitability in 2014 when IES netted $5.3 million (versus a $3.6 million loss in 2013).Cash flow from operations increased more than fivefold to $12.6 million in 2014 largely due to the increase in net income and a change in working capital.StrategyLooking to serve the growing green energy sector in new construction and existing residences IES's residential segment has been busy expanding its services for the installation of residential solar power smart meters electric car charging stations and stand-by generators. In 2013 the company established a partnership with solar company Sunrun to design engineer and manage residential solar systems. Also that year IES bought certain assets of solar energy integrator Acro Energy.IES's customer base includes corporations general contractors property developers and managers municipalities government agencies and homeowners. The company typically prefers to take on design/build construction projects that require specific market expertise such as hospitals data centers and power generation facilities. The company also benefits from providing maintenance work repair and other service-related work since those projects tend to be recurring and are less sensitive to economic downturns. IES works at both the national and regional levels with the Sunbelt states producing much of its revenue.Mergers and AcquisitionsIES acquired MISCOR Group a provider of electrical and mechanical services in 2013. It then established its infrastructure solutions segment around MISCOR's operations.

PRODUCTS/OPERATIONS

2016 Sales

	$ mil.	% of total
Residential	225.9	33
Commercial & Industrial	222.5	32
Communications	189.6	27
Infrastructure Solutions	58.0	8
Total	**696.0**	**100**

Selected Services

Alarm & safety systems
Construction services
Design/build
Engineering services
Home standby generators
Solar installation
Structured cabling
Support services
Training resources

COMPETITORS

Bergelectric	Kelso-Burnett
Comfort Systems USA	MDU Construction
Cupertino Electric	Services
Dycom	MYR Group
EMCOR	Mass Electric
Enterprise Electric	Pike Corporation
Forest Electric	Quanta Services
Industrial Specialty	Rosendin Electric
Contractors	SASCO

HISTORICAL FINANCIALS

Company Type: Public

Income Statement

FYE: September 30

	REVENUE ($ mil.)	NET INCOME ($ mil.)	NET PROFIT MARGIN	EMPLOYEES
09/16	695.9	120.7	17.4%	4,063.0
09/15	573.8	16.5	2.9%	3,106.0
09/14	512.4	5.3	1.0%	2,779.0
09/13	494.5	(3.5)	—	2,740.0
09/12	456.1	(11.8)	—	2,583.0
Annual Growth	**11.1%**	**—**	**—**	**12.0%**

2016 Year-End Financials

Debt ratio: 7.4%	No. of shares (mil.): 21.4
Return on equity: 74.1%	Dividends
Cash ($ mil.): 32.9	Yield: —
Current ratio: 1.58	Payout: —
Long-term debt ($ mil.): 29.2	Market value ($ mil.): 382.0

	STOCK PRICE ($) FY Close	P/E High/Low		PER SHARE ($) Earnings	Dividends	Book Value
09/16	17.79	3	1	5.62	0.00	10.41
09/15	7.72	12	8	0.77	0.00	4.72
09/14	8.25	29	14	0.29	0.00	4.04
09/13	4.06	—	—	(0.24)	0.00	3.48
09/12	4.55	—	—	(0.81)	0.00	3.55
Annual Growth	**40.6%**	—	—	—	—	**30.9%**

II-VI Inc

II-VI could play a mean game of laser tag but it's more interested in making things. The company (its name is pronounced "two-six") makes lenses mirrors prisms and other optical components and materials. II-VI's clients —drawn from the aerospace health care industrial military and telecom equipment sectors —use these components in lasers and other systems used in precision manufacturing communications networks military targeting and navigation systems and other applications. The company has manufacturing operations throughout the US as well as in Asia and Germany. Customers have included Caterpillar Volkswagen Raytheon and the US government.
  Operations
  II-VI's biggest source of revenue is its Laser Solutions unit which accounts for 39% of sales. It is followed by Photonics 35% of revenue and Performance Products 26%.
  Geographic Reach
  The US is II-VI's largest market accounting for 32% of its sales. China is next representing more than 19% of annual sales while Hong Kong represents about 15% and Germany 10%. The company has production facilities in 10 US states including its home state of Pennsylvania and half a dozen foreign countries such as China and Vietnam.
  Financial Performance
  II-VI's sales have increased each of past six years. The company set another revenue record for itself in 2015 (ended June) posting $742 million in sale —a 9% increase from 2014. Its photonics segment paced sales for the year with a 20% increase based on customer demand for optical filters optical components and assemblies pump lasers and fiber amplifier modules. Sales in the Performance Products unit however fell 9%.
  Net income shot up 71% in 2015 as II-VI began to realize contributions from acquisitions that resulted in bigger market share higher revenue and operating efficiencies. Net income was $66 million in 2015 compared to $38 million the year before. Net earnings also benefited from a one-time settlement related to obligations from previous acquisitions of $7.1 million (after-tax).
  II-VI had $1299 million cash flow from operations in 2015 compared to $95 million in 2014.
  Strategy
  II-VI continued a restructuring program in its Photonics and Performance Products segments to

adjust costs. It recorded after-tax restructuring charges of $4.1 million in 2015 compared to $3.4 million in f2014.

Research and development is vital to the company's success. Indeed II-VI aims to invest between 5% and 7% of its revenues each year in R&D (the figure was 6.9% in 2015). Its recent focus has been in silicon carbide substrates chemical vapor deposition (CVD) synthetic diamond materials photonics and thermoelectric materials and devices. II-VI uses a mix of internal and external funding for most areas but devotes only internal funds to CVD diamond and photonics.

II-VI's Pacific Rare Specialty Metals & Chemicals (PRM) subsidiary in 2013 discontinued its tellurium line and downsized its selenium production line to focus on providing selenium metal to the company's Infrared Optics business while distancing the business from volatile metal index price fluctuations. The company uses acquisitions to build its business around core strengths in engineered materials and components.

Mergers and Acquisitions

In early 2016 II-VI agreed to buy two businesses to expand its technology platforms and production capacity for semiconductor lasers for $110 million. The acquisitions of EpiWorks and ANADIGICS position II-VI for the fast-growing markets for Vertical Cavity Surface Emitting Lasers (VCSELs). The lasers are used in consumer electronics data centers sensing medical and industrial markets.

In September 2013 the company acquired the Switzerland-based semiconductor laser business of Oclaro Inc. for $115 million. II-VI will operate the newly acquired business as II-VI Laser Enterprise GmbH.

In 2012 it bought Connecticut-based M Cubed Technologies for about $71 million and California-based LightWorks Optics for about half that amount. M Cubed manufactures advanced ceramic materials and precision motion control products and LightWorks supplies advanced optical systems used in defense aerospace and commercial operations. The prior year brought the acquisition of Massachusetts-based Aegis Lightwave for $52 million. Aegis' tunable optical devices are used to expand bandwidth in high speed optical networks and will contribute to II-VI's near-infrared optics business.

Ownership

Columbia Wanger Asset Management owns about 12% of II-VI's shares.

HISTORY

Early History

Electrical engineer Carl Johnson who had worked at Bell Labs (now part of Alcatel-Lucent) among other companies founded II-VI in 1971 to produce infrared optical materials for the emerging laser market. These materials —including cadmium zinc telluride zinc selenide and zinc sulfide —gave the company its name; they are from the "two-six" family of materials. (Cadmium and zinc are from column two on the periodic table; tellurium and selenium are from column six.)

By the 1980s II-VI was the leading maker of optical components for carbon dioxide lasers. The company went public in 1987 and the next year added a factory in Singapore.

EXECUTIVES

VP Military and Materials Businesses, James Martinelli, age 58, $309,375 total compensation
Chairman and CEO, Francis J. Kramer, age 67, $628,000 total compensation
President and COO, Vincent D. (Chuck) Mattera, age 60, $380,000 total compensation
CFO and Treasurer, Mary Jane Raymond, age 56
Vice President and General Manager, Chuck (Chucky) Mattera
Vice President, Bob Leonard
Board Of Directors, Thomas (Thom) Mistler
Auditors: Ernst & Young LLP

LOCATIONS

HQ: II-VI Inc
375 Saxonburg Boulevard, Saxonburg, PA 16056
Phone: 724 352-4455
Web: www.ii-vi.com

PRODUCTS/OPERATIONS

2015 Sales Chart

	% of total
II-VI Laser Solutions	39
II-VI Photonics	35
II-VI Performance Products	26
Total	**100**

Selected Business Segments

dvanced Materials Development Center (AMDC)
AOFR
Aegis Lightwave
HIGHYAG Lasertechnologie
LightWorks Optical Systems
M Cubed
Marlow Industries
Max Levy Autograph
Photop Technologies
Pacific Rare Specialty Metals & Chemicals (PRM)
Wide Bandgap Materials Group

Selected Products

Beam expanders
Beam splitters
Detectors
Etalons
Infrared and near-infrared optics
Laser crystals
 Clear yttrium aluminum garnet (YAG) laser crystals
 Custom crystals and fluorides
 Machined and polished laser rods
 Monolithic crystal assemblies (MCA)
 Neodymium doped YAG
 Non-linear crystals
 Oxide laser crystal products
 Ruby laser crystals
Laser gain materials
Lenses
Military infrared optics
Mirrors
Modulators
One micron laser
Optical assemblies
Optical coatings
Output windows
Partial reflectors
Phase retarders
Polarization devices
Prisms
Rhombs
Selenium metal (material processing and refinement)
Silicon carbide substrates (SiC)
Solid-state laser optics and optical cavities
Substrates
Tellurium metal (material processing and refinement)
Thermo-electric coolers
Wave plates

COMPETITORS

AXSUN Technologies
Coherent Inc.
CoorsTek
Cree
Cymer
DRS Technologies

Dow Corning
Dynasil
Ferrotec
Jenoptik
Komatsu
Laird Technologies
LightPath
Newport Corp.
Nippon Steel & Sumitomo Metal Corporation
Northrop Grumman
Oplink Communications
Orbotech
Raytheon
Saint-Gobain
Spectra-Physics
Sumitomo Electric
Umicore
Zygo

HISTORICAL FINANCIALS

Company Type: Public

Income Statement

FYE: June 30

	REVENUE ($ mil.)	NET INCOME ($ mil.)	NET PROFIT MARGIN	EMPLOYEES
06/16	827.2	65.4	7.9%	8,927.0
06/15	741.9	65.9	8.9%	8,490.0
06/14	683.2	38.4	5.6%	6,796.0
06/13	558.4	50.8	9.1%	6,185.0
06/12	534.6	60.3	11.3%	6,030.0
Annual Growth	**11.5%**	**2.1%**	**—**	**10.3%**

2016 Year-End Financials

Debt ratio: 19.4%
Return on equity: 8.6%
Cash ($ mil.): 218.4
Current ratio: 3.40
Long-term debt ($ mil.): 215.9
No. of shares (mil.): 61.8
Dividends
 Yield: —
 Payout: —
Market value ($ mil.): 1,161.0

	STOCK PRICE ($) FY Close	P/E High/Low	PER SHARE ($) Earnings	Dividends	Book Value
06/16	18.76	22 14	1.04	0.00	12.64
06/15	18.98	18 10	1.05	0.00	11.91
06/14	14.46	33 21	0.60	0.00	10.98
06/13	16.26	25 18	0.80	0.00	10.22
06/12	16.67	29 17	0.94	0.00	9.39
Annual Growth	**3.0%**	**— —**	**2.6%**	**—**	**7.7%**

ILG Inc

Your vacation time is worth something to ILG (formerly Interval Leisure Group). The timeshare exchange broker offers services to some 2 million member-property owners. Its primary Interval Network is an exchange program that lets owners trade their timeshare intervals for accommodations at more than 2900 resorts in approximately 80 countries. In addition the company provides exchange services to owners at timeshare properties managed by vacation services subsidiary Trading Places International (TPI) while its Preferred Residences is a luxury branded membership program with Preferred Hotel Group. The company also provides resort management services.

Operations

ILG operates through two business segments: Exchange and Rental and Vacation Ownership.

The Exchange and Rental operating segment consists of Interval International (referred to as Interval) the Hyatt Residence Club the Trading Places International (known as TPI) operated exchange business Aston Hotels & Resorts Inc. (referred to as Aston) and Aqua Hospitality LLC (referred to as Aqua). The Exchange and Rental segment contributed 79% of the company's total revenue in fiscal 2014.

The company's Vacation Ownership segment engages in the management of vacation ownership resorts; sales marketing and financing of vacation ownership interests; and related services to owners and associations. The Vacation Ownership segment contributed 21% of the company's total revenue in fiscal 2014.

Sales and Marketing

ILG spent about $15.6 million on advertising and promotional expenses during fiscal 2014.

Financial Performance

The company reported revenue of $614 million in fiscal 2014. That was an increase of 23% compared to the prior fiscal period. Its net income in fiscal 2014 was $78.9 million which was a 3% decrease compared to fiscal 2013.

Strategy

ILG hopes to grow its business and expand its presence within nontraditional lodging. The company plans to invest in and grow its brand through enhanced marketing efforts. It will also continue to make strategic investments to grow in international markets.

Company Background

The firm was founded in 1976 and was acquired by IAC/InterActiveCorp (IAC) in 2002. IAC in 2008 divided into five companies in order to streamline operations with Interval becoming one of the five. Today Liberty Media Corporation owns nearly 30% of ILG. (Liberty Media is a media-related holding company. Liberty Interactive Group one of three tracking stocks that comprise Liberty Media owns a stake in IAC.)

EXECUTIVES

Senior Vice President, Victoria J Kincke
Chairman President and CEO, Craig M. Nash, age 62, $750,000 total compensation
President Interval International, David C. (Dave) Gilbert
EVP and COO, Jeanette E. Marbert, age 59, $400,000 total compensation
CFO, William L. (Bill) Harvey, age 60, $343,750 total compensation
Executive Vice President, Annie (Ann) Welsh
Auditors: Ernst & Young LLP

LOCATIONS

HQ: ILG Inc
6262 Sunset Drive, Miami, FL 33143
Phone: 305 666-1861
Web: www.iilg.com

PRODUCTS/OPERATIONS

Selected Offerings 2014 Sales

	% of total
Exchange and rental	79
Vacation Ownership	21
Total	**10**
Membership services	
Concierge services	
Golf spa and cruise exchanges	
Hotel and dining discounts	
Property management	
Timeshare exchanges	
Vacation rental	

Selected Marketing Websites

AstonHotels.com
ResortQuestHawaii.com
TradingPlaces.com
Mauicondo.com

COMPETITORS

Central Florida Investments Inc.	ResortQuest International
Hilton Grand Vacations	Starwood Vacation Ownership
HomeAway	
Marriott Vacations	Wyndham Vacation
RCI	

HISTORICAL FINANCIALS

Company Type: Public

Income Statement

FYE: December 31

	REVENUE ($ mil.)	NET INCOME ($ mil.)	NET PROFIT MARGIN	EMPLOYEES
12/15	697.4	73.3	10.5%	5,600.0
12/14	614.3	78.9	12.8%	6,100.0
12/13	501.2	81.2	16.2%	5,000.0
12/12	473.3	40.7	8.6%	3,800.0
12/11	428.7	41.1	9.6%	3,000.0
Annual Growth	**12.9%**	**15.5%**	**—**	**16.9%**

2015 Year-End Financials

Debt ratio: 32.5%	No. of shares (mil.): 57.4
Return on equity: 17.9%	Dividends
Cash ($ mil.): 109.7	Yield: 3.0%
Current ratio: 1.21	Payout: 38.1%
Long-term debt ($ mil.): 415.7	Market value ($ mil.): 897.0

	STOCK PRICE ($) FY Close	P/E High/Low	PER SHARE ($) Earnings	Dividends	Book Value
12/15	15.61	21 11	1.26	0.48	7.51
12/14	20.89	22 14	1.36	0.44	6.73
12/13	30.91	22 13	1.40	0.33	5.99
12/12	19.39	28 18	0.71	0.50	4.79
12/11	13.61	24 14	0.71	0.00	4.44
Annual Growth	**3.5%**	**— —**	**15.4%**	**—**	**14.1%**

Illumina Inc

Illumina elucidates the human genome. The firm makes tools used by life sciences and drug researchers to isolate and analyze genes. Its systems include the machinery and the software used to sequence pieces of DNA and RNA and the means to put them through large-scale testing of genetic variation and biological function. Its proprietary BeadArray technology uses microscopic glass beads which can carry samples through the genotyping process. The tests allow medical researchers to determine what genetic combinations are associated with various diseases enabling faster diagnosis better drugs and individualized treatment. Customers include pharma and biotech companies research centers and academic institutions.

Operations

Illumina's technologies also provide reproductive health solutions including preimplantation genetic screening and diagnosis noninvasive prenatal testing and neonatal health testing.

For customers who choose not to buy its systems and consumables Illumina offers outsourced

life science research services such as genome sequencing and genotyping array services. Customers for such services include schools agricultural and energy biotech research firms and drug development companies. In addition the company has a consumer genomics unit to meet the growing demand for personal genome sequencing through physician intermediaries. And while most of the company's revenues come from providing life sciences equipment and services Illumina has also established a small business in the field of molecular diagnostics which uses genetic biomarkers to diagnose clinical health conditions.

Geographic Reach

Illumina gets about half of its annual revenues from sales in the US market. Other key regions include Europe (25% of sales) and the Asia/Pacific region (18%) as well as Latin America and Canada. The company has increased revenues across all geographic markets in recent years.

Sales and Marketing

The company's customers include genomic research centers universities government labs hospitals reference laboratories and private sector clients including pharmaceuticals biotech firms agrigenomics (livestock genetics testing) firms commercial molecular diagnostic companies and consumer genomics firms. It sells through life-science distributors in certain markets in Europe Latin America the Middle East the Asia/Pacific region and South Africa.

In 2014 Illumina spent $16.4 million on advertising up from $14.5 million in 2013 and $10.5 million in 2012.

Financial Performance

Illumina has steadily augmented its life sciences product lines and has experienced rapidly climbing revenues in recent years as a result. The company reported a 31% increase in sales in 2014 to some $1.8 billion due to increased instrument sales (due to new product launches HiSeq X Ten and NextSeq) and consumable sales (driven by a higher base of installed equipment) as well as a rise in its sequencing services segment as its installed base continues to grow.

Net increased more than doubled in 2014 rising 182% to $353 million versus $125 million in 2013. The increase was led by the rise in revenue as well as a gain from legal contingencies related to an intellectual property settlement with pharmaceutical firm Syntrix.

However profits dropped by more than 15% to some $125 million that year due to increased operating expenses from sales and marketing efforts and R&D programs as Illumina continues to invest in the growth of the business. Cash flow from operations grew 30% to $501 million that year as a result of higher profits and an increase in cash provided by accrued liabilities.

Strategy

Illumina makes significant investments in research and development to make its systems faster more advanced and more affordable. (R&D expenses in 2014 were $388.1 million up from $276.7 million in 2013.) In early 2014 it upgraded its HiSeq X Ten and NextSeq 500 platforms with improved technology. In 2013 the company introduced a simpler gene sequencing panel and a new genome sequencing technology to help doctors identify genetic causes for rare or undiagnosed diseases among other products.

In 2015 the company launched TruSight HLA an end-to-end sequencing panel that sequences 11 human leikocyte antigen genes for accurate typing. It also launched the NeoPrep Library Prep Sytem to help sequencing-ready libraries prepare for next-generation sequencing.

Illumina is also focused on expanding use of its genomics products into reproductive health oncology and other clinical and research markets. It has several products in the pipeline to address these markets.

As part of its strategy to develop and identify new products and services the company also seeks suitable products technologies and companies as candidates for acquisition. It also strikes up partnerships to expand its offerings. In 2015 for example it formed a collaboration with Merck Serono (Merck's biopharmaceutical arm) to develop a next-generation sequencing-based oncology diagnostic. Also that year it formed an alliance with Lockheed Martin to develop affordable genomics solutions to provide personalized health care for national populations. In 2014 entered separate agreements with bioMérieux Biomnis Genoma and the Center for Human Genetics and Laboratory Diagnostics Martinsried.

Expanding into Russia and the Commonwealth of Independent States Illumina established a relationship with Moscow-based life science distributor Albiogen in 2014.

Mergers and Acquisitions

Acquisitions that have enhanced Illumina's offerings include the 2014 purchase of Myraqa (invitro diagnostics particularly companion diagnostics) and the 2013 purchases of NextBio (clinical and genomic informatics) Advanced Liquid Logic (digital microfluidics and liquid handling) and Varinata Health (which markets the verifi prenatal test for high-risk pregnancies).

EXECUTIVES

SVP and General Manager Reproductive and Genetic Health, Tristan B. Orpin, age 50, $379,403 total compensation

SVP and Chief Medical Officer, Richard D. Klausner, $403,692 total compensation

SVP and Chief Commercial Officer, Christian O. Henry, age 48, $467,497 total compensation

SVP and General Manager Life Sciences, Kirk D. Malloy

SVP and CTO, Mostafa Ronaghi, age 47, $337,800 total compensation

President and CEO, Francis deSouza, age 45, $689,231 total compensation

SVP Corporate and Venture Development, Nicholas J. (Nick) Naclerio

SVP and General Manager Enterprise Informatics, Sanjay Chikarmane

SVP and CFO, Sam Samad

Vice President Diagnostic Development, Karen Gutekunst

Vice President EMEA Commercial Operations, Tim (Timmy) Orpin

Vice President Of Talent Acquisition, Kerry Wright

Vice President, Keith Ryland

Vice President, Richard Rava

Vice President Of Finance, Mike Bouchard

Vice President Of Customer Solutions, John Liebig

Vice President of Regulatory Affairs, Mya Thomae

Senior Vice President and Chief Information Officer, Norm Fjeldheim

Executive Chairman, Jay T. Flatley, age 64

Auditors: Ernst & Young LLP

LOCATIONS

HQ: Illumina Inc
5200 Illumina Way, San Diego, CA 92122
Phone: 858 202-4500
Web: www.illumina.com

PRODUCTS/OPERATIONS

2014 Sales

	% of total
Product revenue	87
Services & other revenue	13
Total	**100**

Selected Systems

BaseSpace
HiScan
HiSeq 2500
HiSeq X Ten
iScan
MiSeq
NextSeq 500
Software

Selected Applications

Agrigenomics
Cancer Genomics
Cytogenomics
Forensic Genomics
Gene Expression Analysis
Gene Regulation & Epigenetic Analysis
Genetic Disease
Genotyping
Microbial Genomics
Sequencing
SNP Genotyping & CNV Analysis

COMPETITORS

Affymetrix	Life Technologies
Agilent Technologies	Corporation
Beckman Coulter	Luminex
Complete Genomics	Pacific Biosciences
Fluidigm	QIAGEN
GE Healthcare Medical	Roche Diagnostics
Diagnostics	Sequenom

HISTORICAL FINANCIALS

Company Type: Public

Income Statement

FYE: January 1

	REVENUE ($ mil.)	NET INCOME ($ mil.)	NET PROFIT MARGIN	EMPLOYEES
01/17	2,398.3	462.6	19.3%	5,500.0
01/16*	2,219.7	461.5	20.8%	4,600.0
12/14	1,861.3	353.3	19.0%	3,700.0
12/13	1,421.1	125.3	8.8%	3,000.0
12/12	1,148.5	151.2	13.2%	2,400.0
Annual Growth	**20.2%**	**32.2%**	**—**	**23.0%**

*Fiscal year change

2017 Year-End Financials

Debt ratio: 24.5%	No. of shares (mil.): 146.2
Return on equity: 22.9%	Dividends
Cash ($ mil.): 734.5	Yield: —
Current ratio: 3.29	Payout: —
Long-term debt ($ mil.): 1,047.8	Market value ($ mil.): 18,719.0

	STOCK PRICE ($) FY Close	P/E High/Low		PER SHARE ($) Earnings	Dividends	Book Value
01/17	128.04	60	39	3.07	0.00	15.03
01/16*	191.95	75	44	3.10	0.00	12.61
12/14	188.20	74	42	2.37	0.00	10.18
12/13	110.38	110	48	0.90	0.00	12.00
12/12	54.75	46	25	1.13	0.00	10.64
Annual Growth	**23.7%**	**—**	**—**	**28.4%**	**—**	**9.0%**

*Fiscal year change

Impax Laboratories Inc

Impax Laboratories is betting that its pharmaceuticals will make a positive impact on the world's health. The company makes specialty generic pharmaceuticals which it markets through its Global Pharmaceuticals division and through marketing alliances with other pharmaceutical firms. It concentrates on controlled-release versions of various generic versions of branded and niche pharmaceuticals that require difficult-to-obtain raw materials or specialized expertise. Additionally the company's branded pharmaceuticals business (Impax Pharmaceuticals) is developing and improving upon previously approved drugs that target Parkinson's disease multiple sclerosis and other central nervous system disorders.

Operations

Impax earns the majority (more than 75%) of its revenue through its Global division which produces dosage variations of about 40 generic compounds including fenofibrate (generic Lofibra for high cholesterol) midodrine HCl (generic ProAmatine) and generic Adderall XR (for attention-deficit hyperactivity disorder or ADHD). Several of those compounds are sold through licensing or collaboration partnerships with companies including Teva Shire and Tolmar. Revenues for the unit fluctuate from year to year due to competitive conditions (how many additional generic versions of a product are on the market) and shifts in consumer demand for certain medications.

Its smaller Impax Pharmaceuticals division invests heavily in R&D costs and has historically brought in few earnings though the unit produces some revenues through development partnership income. However in 2012 the division grew rapidly to account for more than 20% of sales as it launched its first commercial branded product orally disintegrating and nasal spray versions of migraine drug Zomig (licensed from AstraZeneca).

Sales and Marketing

Impax's Global Pharmaceuticals division sells its generic products to wholesalers chain drug stores and mail order pharmacies. Impax also works through strategic alliances that include co-promotion licensing third-party marketing or manufacturing and supply agreements with other generic and branded pharmaceutical manufacturers.

Strategy

To expand the operations of its main Global Pharmaceuticals division Impax works to develop new generic versions of drugs that have lost (or are about to lose) patent protection with a focus on controlled-release and specialty products. It also develops medicines that come in alternative-dosage forms such as nasal sprays inhalers ointments injectables and patches. The company's generic development programs are conducted both independently and through research or licensing partnerships with other drugmakers. Impax seeks to gain first-to-file and first-to market status with its new products and in some cases Impax enters agreements with branded pharmaceutical firms to make authorized generic versions of off-patent drugs.

The Impax Pharmaceuticals division has products in clinical stages of development including treatments for multiple sclerosis and Parkinson's disease. The division also focuses its development efforts on other central nervous system disorders such as Alzheimer's disease depression epilepsy and migraines. The company hopes to build its portfolio of branded products through internal development acquisitions and licensing agreements with the ultimate goal of selling some products commercially.

Mergers and Acquisitions

In 2016 Impax agreed to buy a portfolio of generic drugs from Teva and Allergan for $586 million. The deal includes about 20 marketed pending and development products as well as the commercial rights to the generic equivalent to Concerta. Teva and Allergan are unloading some of their products as mandated by the FTC ahead of their planned merger.

EXECUTIVES

President and CEO, G. Frederick (Fred) Wilkinson, age 56
President Impax Pharmaceuticals, Michael J. Nestor, age 63, $471,563 total compensation
President - Global Pharmaceuticals Division, Carole S. Ben-Maimon, age 57, $142,808 total compensation
President Generics Division, Douglas S. Boothe, age 52
Director, Robert L. (Bob) Burr, age 65
Auditors: KPMG LLP

LOCATIONS

HQ: Impax Laboratories Inc
30831 Huntwood Avenue, Hayward, CA 94544
Phone: 510 240-6000
Web: www.impaxlabs.com

PRODUCTS/OPERATIONS

2015 Sales

	$ mil.	% of total
Impax Generics	711.0	83
Impax Specialty Pharma	149.5	17
Total	**860.5**	**100**

COMPETITORS

Allergan plc	SkyePharma
Lumara	Teva
Mylan	URL Pharma
Par Pharmaceutical	Valeant
Companies	Pharmaceuticals
Sandoz International	
GmbH	

HISTORICAL FINANCIALS

Company Type: Public

Income Statement

FYE: December 31

	REVENUE ($ mil.)	NET INCOME ($ mil.)	NET PROFIT MARGIN	EMPLOYEES
12/15	860.4	39.0	4.5%	1,290.0
12/14	596.0	57.3	9.6%	1,061.0
12/13	511.5	101.2	19.8%	973.0
12/12	581.6	55.8	9.6%	1,125.0
12/11	512.9	65.5	12.8%	1,002.0
Annual Growth	**13.8%**	**(12.2%)**	**—**	**6.5%**

2015 Year-End Financials

Debt ratio: 22.0%
Return on equity: 4.0%
Cash ($ mil.): 340.3
Current ratio: 2.52
Long-term debt ($ mil.): 424.6
No. of shares (mil.): 72.6
Dividends
  Yield: —
  Payout: —
Market value ($ mil.): 3,108.0

	STOCK PRICE ($) FY Close	P/E High/Low		Earnings	PER SHARE ($) Dividends	Book Value
12/15	42.76	92	54	0.54	0.00	14.62
12/14	31.68	39	26	0.81	0.00	12.47
12/13	25.14	17	10	1.47	0.00	11.63
12/12	20.49	32	22	0.82	0.00	10.12
12/11	20.17	28	15	0.97	0.00	9.07
Annual Growth	**20.7%**	**—**	**—**	**(13.6%)**	**—**	**12.7%**

INC Research Holdings Inc

Auditors: Deloitte & Touche LLP

LOCATIONS

HQ: INC Research Holdings Inc
3201 Beechleaf Court, Suite 600, Raleigh, NC 27604-1547
Phone: 919 876-9300
Web: www.incresearch.com

HISTORICAL FINANCIALS

Company Type: Public

Income Statement

FYE: December 31

	REVENUE ($ mil.)	NET INCOME ($ mil.)	NET PROFIT MARGIN	EMPLOYEES
12/15	1,399.2	117.0	8.4%	6,400.0
12/14	1,178.8	(23.4)	—	5,600.0
12/13	995.0	(41.5)	—	5,500.0
12/12	868.6	(59.1)	—	4,850.0
12/11	655.9	(59.5)	—	0.0
Annual Growth	**20.9%**	**—**	**—**	**—**

2015 Year-End Financials

Debt ratio: 41.4%
Return on equity: 38.4%
Cash ($ mil.): 85.4
Current ratio: 0.89
Long-term debt ($ mil.): 472.0
No. of shares (mil.): 53.8
Dividends
  Yield: —
  Payout: —
Market value ($ mil.): 2,613.0

	STOCK PRICE ($) FY Close	P/E High/Low		Earnings	PER SHARE ($) Dividends	Book Value
12/15	48.51	25	11	1.95	0.00	4.04
12/14	25.69	—	—	(0.51)	0.00	6.41
Annual Growth	**88.8%**	**—**	**—**	**—**	**—**	**(37.0%)**

Incyte Corporation

Incyte hopes its success with inhibitors is uninhibited. The biotechnology company is focused on discovering and developing drugs that inhibit specific enzymes associated with cancer diabetes blood disorders and inflammatory diseases. The company's lead program is its JAK (Janus associated kinase) inhibitor program which covers treatments for inflammatory diseases and cancers. Its first commercial product JAKAFI is approved for treatment of myelofibrosis (a rare blood cancer). Incyte's other JAK product candidates are in various stages of research and clinical trials partially through partnerships with other drugmakers for conditions including rheumatoid arthritis psoriasis solid tumors and breast cancer.

Geographic Reach

JAKAFI is available in the US and about 30 international countries.

Operations

Incyte gained FDA approval to market JAKAFI for several types of myelofibrosis in the US market in November 2011 and the company launched the drug shortly after. The drug also gained approval for myelofibrosis treatment in the European Union in 2012 (through a partnership with Novartis). Novartis has also gained approval for the drug in additional international markets. JAKAFI is under development for similar blood cancers including polycythemia and thrombocythemia and pancreatic cancer in the US.

The company also has a partnership with Eli Lilly to develop a candidate for inflammatory disorders including rheumatoid arthritis and psoriasis. In addition Incyte has several candidates under development for solid tumor cancers one of which is being co-developed with Novartis.

Outside of the JAK development programs Incyte receives licensing fees by granting drug rights to other developers. For instance Pfizer holds rights for its CCR2 receptor antagonist program including treatments for rheumatoid arthritis and insulin-resistant obese patients.

Sales and Marketing

JAKAFI is marketed by Incyte's direct sales force to oncologists and hematologists and is distributed through third-party specialty pharmacies throughout the US. While Incyte retains all marketing rights to JAKAFI in the US market Novartis holds all international development and marketing rights for the drug.

Financial Performance

Collaboration and licensing fees are the lifeblood of pharmaceutical research and development companies helping them to sustain operations as R&D costs skyrocket. In addition dependence on partnership income causes revenues to fluctuate rapidly from year to year as the company receives milestone payments based on a candidate's progress through development and commercialization stages.

Despite having launched its first commercial product in 2011 more than half of Incyte's earnings in 2012 came from collaboration and milestone contracts. Revenues jumped 215% in fiscal 2012 to some $297 million as the company reported a healthy increase in contract revenue (from milestone payments and fees from both Novartis and Lilly) and a large jump in product income from sales of JAKAFI.

The firm has reported a net income loss each year since its formation as R&D expenses outweigh earnings and it does not expect to achieve profitability until it has more substantial commercial operations.

Strategy

In recent years Incyte has been focused on building up its commercialization infrastructure to support sales of JAKAFI in the US. It also continues to put extensive resource into its internal drug research and development programs. In addition Incyte is pursuing new commercialization partnerships for other pipeline drugs.

Ownership

T. Rowe Price owns a 17% stake in the company while Capital World Investors hold a 12% interest.

HISTORY

British entrepreneur Roy Whitfield and researcher Randal Scott met in 1989 while working for Invitron a biotech company that soon went under. They founded Incyte Pharmaceuticals in 1991 to design develop and market genomic database products software tools and related services.

The company went public in 1993 and in 1994 Pfizer became its first gene expression database subscriber. Two years later Incyte bought gene-mapping firms Genome Systems and Combion. The firm opened an office in Cambridge UK and formed joint venture diaDexus with SmithKline Beecham (now GlaxoSmithKline) to create and market diagnostic tests that use genetic data to develop effective drug reagents and services.

In 1998 the firm bought microarray maker Synteni. It made its own attempt to map the human genome using LifeSeq buying British firm Hexagen for the mapping unit. Two years later diaDexus filed an IPO and the company changed its name to Incyte Genomics to reflect its focus. The name change however seemed shortsighted when in 2001 the firm announced plans to become a drug developer. It even teamed with one-time rival Agilent to share DNA microarray technologies.

In 2003 the company made another name change –this time simply to "Incyte Corporation" — to represent its growing focus on drug development. As part of that focus that year Incyte acquired the rights to Reverset in 2003 through a licensing agreement with Pharmasset.In 2004 the company transitioned away from its former business —providing access to its genomic database and set of patents. In that year Incyte closed its Palo Alto California research facilities and headquarters. It also terminated further development of its information products including LifeSeq —a library of information and expressed sequences that links biological information analysis with proprietary genetic information to aid drug discovery. In addition to closing the Palo Alto office the company reduced its workforce by more than 50%.Following the transition a leading product candidate for the company was dexelvucitabine (also known as Reverset) to treat patients with HIV but clinical trials were discontinued in 2006. In 2008 it also halted development on a CCR5 antagonist designed to prevent the entry of HIV into target cells.

EXECUTIVES

EVP and CFO, David W. (Dave) Gryska, age 60
EVP Human Resources, Paula J. Swain, $354,029 total compensation
EVP Chief Drug Development, Richard S. Levy, $373,423 total compensation
EVP and General Counsel, Eric H. Siegel
EVP and Chief Scientific Officer, Reid M. Huber
EVP Discovery Medicinal and Process Chemistry, Wenqing Yao
EVP and Chief Commercial Officer, James M. (Jim) Daly, $506,635 total compensation
EVP Business Development and Strategic Planning, Barry P. Flannelly
SVP and Chief Medical Officer, Steven H. Stein
President, David C. Hoak
CEO, Don Larsen
CIO, Steven Lerner
President and CEO and Director, Herve Hoppenot
Vice President Exploratory Development, William (Bill) Williams

Vice President, Jayant Shukla
Group Vice President of clinic Development, Victor (Vic) Sandor
Executive Vice President General Counsel, Patricia (Pat) Schreck
Vice President, Swamy Yeleswaram
Vice President Of Sales, Eric Vogel
Vice President Investor Relations And Corporate Communications, Pamela M (Pam) Muiphy
Vice President of Development Operations, Michele (Michie) Sample
Vice President Clinical Development, Matthew (Matt) Spear
Vice President Business Development, Erin Hugger
Vice President And Controller, Paul (Pauly) Trower
Chairman, Richard U. De Schutter
Auditors: Ernst & Young LLP

LOCATIONS

HQ: Incyte Corporation
1801 Augustine Cut-Off, Wilmington, DE 19803
Phone: 302 498-6700
Web: www.incyte.com

PRODUCTS/OPERATIONS

2012 Sales

	$ mil.	% of total
Contract revenue	156.9	53
Product sales	136.0	46
Royalty revenues	3.7	1
Other	0.5	-
Total	**297.1**	**100**

COMPETITORS

Abbott Labs	Human Genome Sciences
Amgen	Janssen Biotech
Array BioPharma	Lexicon
Biogen	Pharmaceuticals
Bristol-Myers Squibb	Myriad Genetics
CTI BioPharma	PDL BioPharma
Celgene	Roche Holding
CuraGen	TargeGen
GlaxoSmithKline	Xencor

HISTORICAL FINANCIALS
Company Type: Public

Income Statement
FYE: December 31

	REVENUE ($ mil.)	NET INCOME ($ mil.)	NET PROFIT MARGIN	EMPLOYEES
12/15	753.7	6.5	0.9%	692.0
12/14	511.5	(48.4)	—	588.0
12/13	354.9	(83.1)	—	481.0
12/12	297.0	(44.3)	—	413.0
12/11	94.4	(186.5)	—	368.0
Annual Growth	**68.1%**	**—**	**—**	**17.1%**

2015 Year-End Financials

Debt ratio: 61.5%	No. of shares (mil.): 186.6
Return on equity: 14.5%	Dividends
Cash ($ mil.): 521.4	Yield: —
Current ratio: 5.01	Payout: —
Long-term debt ($ mil.): 619.8	Market value ($ mil.): 20,242.0

	STOCK PRICE ($) FY Close	P/E High/Low		PER SHARE ($) Earnings	Dividends	Book Value
12/15	108.45	3287	1787	0.03	0.00	0.92
12/14	73.11	—	—	(0.29)	0.00	(0.48)
12/13	50.63	—	—	(0.56)	0.00	(1.18)
12/12	16.61	—	—	(0.34)	0.00	(1.31)
12/11	15.01	—	—	(1.49)	0.00	(1.80)
Annual Growth	**64.0%**			**—**	**—**	**—**

Independence Realty Trust Inc

Auditors: KPMG LLP

LOCATIONS

HQ: Independence Realty Trust Inc
Two Logan Square, 100 N. 18th St., 23rd Floor,
Philadelphia, PA 19103
Phone: 215 207-2100

HISTORICAL FINANCIALS
Company Type: Public

Income Statement
FYE: December 31

	REVENUE ($ mil.)	NET INCOME ($ mil.)	NET PROFIT MARGIN	EMPLOYEES
12/15	109.5	30.1	27.5%	0.0
12/14	49.2	2.9	6.0%	0.0
12/13	19.9	1.2	6.4%	0.0
12/12	16.6	0.4	2.6%	0.0
12/11	8.6	(0.3)	—	0.0
Annual Growth	**88.6%**	**—**	**—**	**—**

2015 Year-End Financials

Debt ratio: 70.0%	No. of shares (mil.): 47.0
Return on equity: 9.8%	Dividends
Cash ($ mil.): 38.3	Yield: 9.5%
Current ratio: 2.00	Payout: 101.4%
Long-term debt ($ mil.): 975.8	Market value ($ mil.): 354.0

	STOCK PRICE ($) FY Close	P/E High/Low		PER SHARE ($) Earnings	Dividends	Book Value
12/15	7.51	13	9	0.78	0.72	7.74
12/14	9.31	76	59	0.14	0.72	7.90
12/13	8.34	73	66	0.12	0.27	7.76
Annual Growth	**(5.1%)**		**—**	**—155.0%**	**64.3%**	**(0.2%)**

Independent Bank Group Inc.

It makes sense that a company that calls itself Independent Bank Group (IBG) would do business in a state that was once its own country. The bank holding company does business through subsidiary Independent Bank which operates about 30 branches in Texas. The banks offer standard personal and business accounts and services including some focused on small business owners. IBG has total assets of nearly $2 billion and loans of about $1.4 billion. Most of its branches are in the Dallas-Fort Worth area with a few locations in Central Texas (Waco Austin San Antonio). The company traces its roots back 100 years but took its current shape in 2002; it went public in 2013.

IPO

IBG plans to use its $87million to grow both organically and through acquisitions (no specific acquisitions are in the works). It also intends to pay down part of its debt.

Operations

In addition to its banking activities IBG also owns IBG Adriatica a mixed use development in the Dallas-Fort Worth area. The company does not intend to move into real estate but purchased the development where one of its branches is located to help maintain business in the area. It had also made commercial loans to several tenants of the development and saw the purchase as a way to protect its investments rather than have the entire property go into foreclosure.

Financial Analysis

IBG has shown increasing net income for several years (26% from 2011 to 2012 5% the prior year) along with corresponding improving cash flow except for a dip in 2011 related to the Adriatica acquisition.

Strategy

The company's future strategy is all about growth. It plans to increase customer loans and deposits and to grow in current markets while expanding into new ones. Historically IBG has grown through strategic acquisitions of midsize banks and bank franchises making two such purchases in 2010 and 2012. It plans to continue looking for similar opportunities and cites the 500 Texas banks with total assets of less than $1 billion as proof of opportunity.

Mergers and Acquisitions

The company has agreed to acquire Carlile Bancshares and its subsidiary Northstar Bank for around $434 million.

EXECUTIVES

Chairman President and CEO, David R. Brooks, age 58, $650,000 total compensation

EVP and COO, James C. (Jim) White, age 51

Vice Chairman and Chief Lending Officer and President Independent Bank Central Texas, Brian E. Hobart, age 51, $350,000 total compensation

Executive Vice President and Chief Financial Officer, Michelle S. Hickox, age 49, $265,000 total compensation

EVP and Secretary and EVP and Senior Operations Officer Independent Bank, Jan C. Webb, age 58

Vice President Lending, Louann Stroup

Senior Vice President, Robert Camp

Senior Vice President Controller, Amy Feagin

Vice President Commercial Lending, Matthew McGuire

Senior Vice President Technology Services, Hector Salazar

Executive Vice President, Patrick Blossom

Senior Vice President, Randy Masters

Vice President Commercial Lending, Chris Bielss

Assistant Vice President, Angela Sheffield

Executive Vice President And Credit Officer, Mike (Mikey) Phillips

Executive Vice President, Tim Baker

Vice President of Commercial Lending, Kurt Kuehn

Vice President Commercial Banking, Ethan Everett

Vice President Commercial Lending, Richard (Dick) Berman

Vice President Market Manager, Tisha Reyes

Vice Chairman and Chief Risk Officer, Daniel W. Brooks, age 56

Auditors: RSM US LLP

LOCATIONS

HQ: Independent Bank Group Inc.
1600 Redbud Boulevard, Suite 400, McKinney, TX 75069-3257
Phone: 972 562-9004
Web: www.ibtx.com

PRODUCTS/OPERATIONS

2012 Loan Portfolio

	% of total
Real estate	
Commercial	47
Residential	23
Construction land & land development	7
Single-family interim construction	5
Commercial	12
Agricultural	3
Consumer	3
Total	**100**

Selected Acquisition

Town Center Bank (2010 North Texas)
Farmersville Bancshares Inc. (2010 North Texas)
I Bank Holding Company Inc. (2012 Austin/Central Texas)
The Community Group Inc. (2012 Dallas/North Texas)

COMPETITORS

BBVA Compass Bancshares	HSBC International Bancshares
Bank of America	Bancshares
Broadway Bancshares	JPMorgan Chase
Capital One	Lone Star Bank
Citigroup	PlainsCapital
Comerica	Prosperity Bancshares
Cullen/Frost Bankers	Texas Capital
Extraco	Bancshares
First Financial	Wells Fargo
Bankshares	Woodforest Financial

HISTORICAL FINANCIALS

Company Type: Public

Income Statement

FYE: December 31

	ASSETS ($ mil.)	NET INCOME ($ mil.)	INCOME AS % OF ASSETS	EMPLOYEES
12/15	5,055.0	38.7	0.8%	587.0
12/14	4,132.6	28.9	0.7%	511.0
12/13	2,163.9	19.8	0.9%	340.0
12/12	1,740.0	17.3	1.0%	335.0
12/11	1,254.3	13.7	1.1%	0.0
Annual Growth	**41.7%**	**29.7%**	**—**	**—**

2015 Year-End Financials

Return on assets: 0.8%	Dividends
Return on equity: 6.6%	Yield: 1.0%
Long-term debt ($ mil.): —	Payout: 14.3%
No. of shares (mil.): 18.4	Market value ($ mil.): 589.0
Sales ($ mil): 190.1	

	STOCK PRICE ($) FY Close	P/E High/Low		PER SHARE ($) Earnings	Dividends	Book Value
12/15	32.00	21	13	2.21	0.32	34.09
12/14	39.06	33	21	1.85	0.24	31.75
12/13	49.66	28	16	1.77	0.12	18.96
Annual Growth	**(19.7%)**	**—**	**—**	**11.7%**	**63.3%**	**34.1%**

Infinera Corp

To Infinera and beyond! The buzz on this company is that it designs photonic integrated circuits (PICs) intended to replace much larger components within optical networks. (Optical networks are used to provide high-speed Internet access 3G/4G mobile broadband business Ethernet services cloud-based services and wholesale bandwidth services.) Infinera also offers networking equipment built around these chips which are made from indium phosphide –a specialized compound semiconductor material that offers light-years faster performance than standard silicon. Customers include service providers cloud operators governments and enterprises. They include CenturyLink Facebook Zayo Group and Colt.

Operations

Manufacturing of Infinera chips is handled by four contract manufacturers in China Malaysia Mexico Sweden and Thailand. The company has the capability to move manufacturing to the US-qualified factories of two of its electronic manufacturing services partners.

The company gets 87% of its revenue from its products while services account for the rest.

Geographic Reach

Infinera gets 68% of sales in the US 20% from Europe and 5% from Asia. The company operates from three US offices and international locations in Canada China Hong Kong India Japan Singapore and the UK. It runs research and development facilities in the US China Canada and Sweden and it has a software development facility in India.

Sales and Marketing

Infinera makes most of its sales directly with a small portion sold through resellers. Altogether it counts about 110 customers.

Financial Performance

In 2015 Infinera's revenue spiked 33% higher to $887 million from $668 million in 2014. The increase was from continued sales momentum of the Infinera DTN-X platform in projects building new networks and those adding capacity. The Cloud Xpress platform also contributed to sales as did products acquired in the Transmode deal of 2015.

Net income leaped 276% in 2015 rising to $51 million from $13.6 million. Contributing were higher revenue and gains from foreign currency exchange rate changes and foreign currency forward contracts.

Cash flow from operations was $133 million in 2015 up from $36 million in 2014.

Strategy

Infinera is looking to diversify and expand its customer base. While it counts Tier 1 telcos as customers it would like to add more Internet content providers long-haul network operators regional and metro network operators bandwidth wholesalers subsea network operators and cable multiple systems operators. Specifically it would like to upgrade existing customers and land new customers for the Infinera DTN-X platform. Currently the company depends on a small number of customers for a large portion of sales and it doesn't have any long-term customer contracts.

In 2015 Infinera expanded its Cloud Xpress offering to include 10 gigabit Ethernet (GbE) 40 GbE and 100 GbE client interfaces to meet customer specific requirements.

Mergers and Acquisitions

In 2015 Infinera acquired Transmode a metro packet-optical networking company in Sweden. With the deal Infinera can offer a comprehensive portfolio for the metro aggregation market including metro core metro edge and metro access.

EXECUTIVES

Chief Strategy Officer, David F. Welch, age 55, $350,000 total compensation

SVP Optical Integrated Circuit Group, Frederick A. (Fred) Kish

CEO and Director, Thomas J. (Tom) Fallon, age 55,
$300,000 total compensation
SVP Systems Manufacturing and Global Supply Chain, Minoo Mortazavi
VP Systems Engineering, Dirk Corsus
CFO, Brad Feller
VP Subsea Business Group, Scott Jackson
SVP Cloud Network Strategy and Technology, Stuart Elby
Vice President, Michael Jung
Vice President, Matthew (Matt) Mitchell
Vice President Strategic Sales, Scott Chandler
Vice President Systems Manufacturing, Stan Peterson
Senior Vice President Worldwide Sales, Bob Jandro
Vice President Information Services, Todd Tuomala
Vice President Of Engineering, Prasad Paranjape
Vice President Engineering, Jeff (Jeffy) Bennett
Vice President Worldwide Customer Service and Technical Support, Lonny Orona
Vice President of Global Professional Services, Todd Hanson
Vice President Product Planning, Antti Kankkunen
Chairman, Kambiz Y. Hooshmand, age 54
Auditors: Ernst & Young LLP

LOCATIONS

HQ: Infinera Corp
140 Caspian Court, Sunnyvale, CA 94089
Phone: 408 572-5200
Web: www.infinera.com

PRODUCTS/OPERATIONS

Selected Products and ServicesProducts:Infinera ATN (CWDM and DWDM platform)Infinera DTN (switched wavelength division multiplexing system)Infinera DTN-X (multi-terabit packet optical network platform)Infinera DTN PlatformInfinera FlexILS Line SystemInfi

	% of total
Product	87
Services	13
Total	**100**

2015 Sales

	$ in mil.
% of total	
Direct	93
Indirect	7
Total	**100**

COMPETITORS

Calient Networks	Huawei Technologies
Ciena	NEC
Cisco Systems	NSN
CyOptics	Tellabs
Ericsson	ZTE
Fujitsu	

HISTORICAL FINANCIALS

Company Type: Public

Income Statement

FYE: December 26

	REVENUE ($ mil.)	NET INCOME ($ mil.)	NET PROFIT MARGIN	EMPLOYEES
12/15	886.7	51.4	5.8%	2,056.0
12/14	668.0	13.6	2.0%	1,495.0
12/13	544.1	(32.1)	—	1,318.0
12/12	438.4	(85.3)	—	1,242.0
12/11	404.8	(81.7)	—	1,181.0
Annual Growth	**21.7%**	**—**	**—**	**14.9%**

2015 Year-End Financials

Debt ratio: 10.2%		No. of shares (mil.): 140.2		
Return on equity: 8.2%		Dividends		
Cash ($ mil.): 149.1		Yield: —		
Current ratio: 2.81		Payout: —		
Long-term debt ($ mil.): 125.4		Market value ($ mil.): 2,595.0		

	STOCK PRICE ($) FY Close	P/E High/Low	Earnings	PER SHARE ($) Dividends	Book Value
12/15	18.51	63 34	0.36	0.00	5.44
12/14	14.91	141 64	0.11	0.00	3.82
12/13	9.79	— —	(0.27)	0.00	3.49
12/12	5.80	— —	(0.77)	0.00	3.17
12/11	6.28	— —	(0.78)	0.00	3.63
Annual Growth	**31.0%**	**— —**	**—**	**—**	**10.7%**

Infinity Property & Casualty Corp

Infinity Property and Casualty specializes in providing insurance coverage to high-risk drivers. The insurer primarily provides personal non-standard auto policies and is a leading writer of policies for high-risk drivers in the US. The company also offers standard and preferred personal auto commercial small fleet and classic collector auto insurance. Licensed in all 50 states the company currently focuses its business on targeted urban areas of a handful of states. Personal non-standard auto insurance accounts for more than 90% of its premiums; California accounts for about half of that business. Infinity distributes its products through more than 11800 independent agents.OperationsPersonal automobile (liability and property damage) coverage is Infinity's bread and butter but the company also offers commercial vehicle coverage which accounts for nearly 10% of total gross written premiums. Classic collector protection brings in about 1% of written premiums.Geographic ReachThe company's primary markets (or "Focus States" as it calls them) are Arizona California Florida and Texas. Other markets in which it operates include Georgia Nevada and Pennsylvania. Additionally Infinity is running down operations in other states.Sales and MarketingInfinity sells its products through independent agencies and brokers in more than 15000 locations. It also sells directly to customers from company-owned sales centers and via the Internet. Targeted customers are urban and Hispanic drivers. Its largest market is California followed by Florida.

The company has increased advertising spending and agency incentives including commissions to stimulate growth. Advertising costs totaled $9.1 million in 2015 up from $8.7 million in 2014 and $8.4 million in 2013.

Financial Performance

Net sales have been growing for the past few years and in 2015 they rose 2% to $1.4 billion. This was largely due to growth in California-based personal auto lines and commercial vehicle coverage throughout its operating markets. However net income (which has been up and down as of late) declined 11% to $51.4 million as Infinity had increased losses and increased loss adjustment expenses.

Cash flow from activities fell 46% to $72.5 million in 2015 largely due to changes in assets and liabilities.

StrategyBy targeting a narrow group of potential customers (urban and Hispanic drivers in Focus States) the company is able to specialize concentrating its resources toward a very specific demographic. It does so by offering lower prices to traditionally underserved markets. It depends on meeting customers' lifestyle and budget needs by providing flexible product offerings and pricing options. The company is also committed to building relations with its agents and brokers by investing in agency productivity lead generation and training.

Company BackgroundBefore going public in 2003 Infinity was owned by property/casualty giant American Financial Group (AFG). AFG transferred the personal insurance business of its property/casualty subsidiary Great American Financial Resources to Infinity but that business is now in runoff with no new policies being written.

EXECUTIVES

Vice President Investor Relations, Amy Jordan
Chairman President and CEO, James R. Gober, age 64, $571,885 total compensation
EVP and CFO, Roger Smith, age 55, $312,000 total compensation
EVP and General Counsel, Samuel J. Simon, age 59, $417,385 total compensation
SVP Product Management, Scott C. Pitrone, age 53, $262,500 total compensation
SVP Business Development, Glen N. Godwin, age 58, $278,077 total compensation
Senior Vice President and CIO, Ralph (Ralphy) Gravelle
Assistant Vice President Benefits, Robin Adams
Assistant Vice President Corporate Litigation, Larry Levine
Assistant Vice President Product Management, Jason Blalock
Executive Vice President, John (Jack) Finney
Auditors: Ernst & Young LLP

LOCATIONS

HQ: Infinity Property & Casualty Corp
2201 4th Avenue North, Birmingham, AL 35203
Phone: 205 870-4000
Web: www.infinityauto.com

PRODUCTS/OPERATIONS

2015 Gross Written Premiums

	% of total
Personal automobile	90
Commercial vehicle	9
Classic collector	1
Total	**100**
Vehicle Insurance	
Auto	
Motorcycle	
ATV	
RV	
Boat	
Classic Car	
Business Insurance	
Commercial Auto	
General Liability	
Property Insurance	
Home	
Renters	
Mobile Home	
Flood	
Condo	
Other Products	
Life Insurance	
Umbrella Insurance	

Infinity DriverClub®

2015 Sales

Earned premium	1,346.6	91
Installment and other fee income	96.7	7
Net investment income	36.8	2
Net realized gains on investments	2.8	-
Other income	1.1	-
Total	**1,484.0**	**100**

COMPETITORS

Affirmative Insurance	National General
Direct General	Holdings
First Acceptance	Permanent General
Corporation	Progressive
Hagerty Insurance	Corporation
Kingsway America	Safe Auto

HISTORICAL FINANCIALS

Company Type: Public

Income Statement

FYE: December 31

	ASSETS ($ mil.)	NET INCOME ($ mil.)	INCOME AS % OF ASSETS	EMPLOYEES
12/15	2,386.7	51.4	2.2%	2,300.0
12/14	2,384.8	57.2	2.4%	2,200.0
12/13	2,317.2	32.6	1.4%	2,400.0
12/12	2,303.5	24.3	1.1%	2,200.0
12/11	1,936.7	42.0	2.2%	2,100.0
Annual Growth	5.4%	5.2%	—	2.3%

2015 Year-End Financials

Return on assets: 2.1%
Return on equity: 7.4%
Long-term debt ($ mil.): —
No. of shares (mil.): 11.1
Sales ($ mil): 1,484.0

Dividends
Yield: 2.0%
Payout: 31.9%
Market value ($ mil.): 917.0

	STOCK PRICE ($) FY Close	P/E High/Low		Earnings	PER SHARE ($) Dividends	Book Value
12/15	82.23	19	15	4.51	1.72	61.66
12/14	77.26	16	13	4.95	1.44	60.75
12/13	71.75	25	19	2.80	1.20	57.09
12/12	58.24	30	24	2.04	0.90	56.55
12/11	56.74	18	13	3.39	0.72	56.59
Annual Growth	9.7%	—	—	7.4%	24.3%	2.2%

InfraREIT Inc

Auditors: Ernst & Young LLP

LOCATIONS

HQ: InfraREIT Inc
1807 Ross Avenue, 4th Floor, Dallas, TX 75201
Phone: 214 855-6700
Web: www.infrareitinc.com

HISTORICAL FINANCIALS

Company Type: Public

Income Statement

FYE: December 31

	REVENUE ($ mil.)	NET INCOME ($ mil.)	NET PROFIT MARGIN	EMPLOYEES
12/15	151.2	13.2	8.8%	0.0
12/14	1.6	(86.3)	—	0.0
12/13	73.1	32.1	43.9%	0.0
12/12	42.7	12.4	29.0%	0.0
Annual Growth	52.3%	2.2%	—	—

2015 Year-End Financials

Debt ratio: 40.8%
Return on equity: —
Cash ($ mil.): 11.1
Current ratio: 0.49
Long-term debt ($ mil.): 617.4

No. of shares (mil.): 43.5
Dividends
Yield: 4.4%
Payout: 262.9%
Market value ($ mil.): 806.0

	STOCK PRICE ($) FY Close	P/E High/Low		Earnings	PER SHARE ($) Dividends	Book Value
12/15	18.50	109	58	0.31	0.82	15.57
12/14	0.00 (50,625.00)	—	—	(86.35)	0.00	
Annual Growth	—	—	—	—	—	

Inogen, Inc

Combine innovation with oxygen and you've got Inogen. The company makes portable oxygen-concentrators that provide supplemental oxygen by people with chronic respiratory conditions. Oxygen concentrators pull nitrogen from ambient air to supply an oxygen-rich mix through a breathing tube. Its 4.8- and 7-pound models are meant to replace both large in-home concentrators as well as portable tank systems which also eliminates the need for home delivery of oxygen tanks. Unlike most suppliers in the market Inogen sells and rents directly to patients. International customers account for about a third of revenue. Inogen was formed in 2001 and went public in early 2014.

IPO
The company plans to use its $70.6 million in IPO proceeds to increase its rental-unit capacity to improve and expand its manufacturing facilities to expand its sales and marketing force and for R&D.

Operations
The majority of Inogen's revenue comes from consumer-direct supplies but it does operate though oxygen supply companies as well mostly in international markets. A growing portion of its revenues come from equipment rental which it prefers doing to the predictable and recurring nature of rental income. The company develops and manufactures its products.

Geographic Reach
Inogen sells to more than 40 countries mostly in Europe and believes its product is poised to do well internationally for several reasons. Some countries including the UK and France have insurance or other payors that reimburse better for portable oxygen concentrators than the US while other countries have infrastructure (or a lack thereof) that makes a self-sustaining portable option best. And in some countries including Australia insurance doesn't pay for portable oxygen at all making light-weight mobility and low-cost key factors for customers who have to foot the bill themselves.

Sales and Marketing
In the US about 70% of sales Inogen primarily markets directly to consumers while it uses mostly large oxygen supply distributors and gas companies overseas.

The company believes its system gives it an advantage in the marketplace since traditional systems require a delivery network for regular replacement of oxygen tanks making supply in rural areas difficult and costly. It markets directly to consumers to avoid the traditional model which is geared toward delivering oxygen tanks or supplying large home concentrators.

Financial Performance
Inogen recognizes revenue from sales rentals Medicare reimbursements sales of used equipment and from warranties service contracts and shipping markups (categorized as 'other'). In 2012 the company reported a 59% increase in total revenue as it sold and rented more units for higher prices. Accordingly it went from a net loss of about 2 million to a modest gain of .6 million and cash flow improved about 5% as operating and financing activities both improved.

Strategy
Going forward Inogen plans to leverage its direct relationship with costumers to improve existing products and develop new ones. It also intends to expand its sales and marketing efforts and sign contracts with private insurance and Medicaid.

EXECUTIVES

President and CEO, Raymond Huggenberger, age 56, $480,308 total compensation
EVP Sales and Marketing and Director, Scott Wilkinson, age 50, $278,000 total compensation
EVP Finance and CFO, Alison Bauerlein, age 34, $293,461 total compensation
EVP Operations, Matt Scribner, age 48
Founder and EVP Engineering, Brenton Taylor, age 34
VP Marketing, Byron Myers, age 36
Chairman, Heath Lukatch, age 48
Auditors: Deloitte & Touche LLP

LOCATIONS

HQ: Inogen, Inc
326 Bollay Drive, Goleta, CA 93117
Phone: 805 562-0500
Web: www.inogen.com

PRODUCTS/OPERATIONS

2014 Sales

	$ mil.	% of total
Sales	73.1	65
Rentals	39.4	35
Total	**112.5**	**100**

Selected Products

G2 Systems & Accessories
G3 Systems & Accessories
Inogen At Home Oxygen Concentrator
Inogen Freedom Bundle
Inogen Oxygen Accessories
Inogen Oxygen Concentrators for Sale

COMPETITORS

American HomePatient	Lincare Holdings
Apria Healthcare	Philips Electronics
Chart Industries	Praxair
DeVilbiss	Rotech Healthcare
Invacare	

HISTORICAL FINANCIALS

Company Type: Public

Income Statement

FYE: December 31

	REVENUE ($ mil.)	NET INCOME ($ mil.)	NET PROFIT MARGIN	EMPLOYEES
12/15	159.0	11.5	7.3%	547.0
12/14	112.5	6.8	6.1%	411.0
12/13	75.4	25.4	33.7%	354.0
12/12	48.5	0.5	1.2%	354.0
12/11	30.6	(2.0)	—	0.0
Annual Growth	50.9%	—	—	—

2015 Year-End Financials

Debt ratio: 0.2%
Return on equity: 9.1%
Cash ($ mil.): 82.9
Current ratio: 5.22
Long-term debt ($ mil.): —

No. of shares (mil.): 19.7
Dividends
  Yield: —
  Payout: —
Market value ($ mil.): 793.0

	STOCK PRICE ($) FY Close	P/E High/Low		PER SHARE ($) Earnings	Dividends	Book Value
12/15	40.09	91	50	0.56	0.00	6.77
12/14	31.37	95	42	0.30	0.00	6.20
Annual Growth	27.8%	—	—	86.7%	—	9.3%

Inovalon Holdings Inc

Auditors: Deloitte & Touche LLP

LOCATIONS

HQ: Inovalon Holdings Inc
4321 Collington Road, Bowie, MD 20716
Phone: 301 809-4000
Web: www.inovalon.com

HISTORICAL FINANCIALS

Company Type: Public

Income Statement

FYE: December 31

	REVENUE ($ mil.)	NET INCOME ($ mil.)	NET PROFIT MARGIN	EMPLOYEES
12/15	437.2	66.0	15.1%	3,323.0
12/14	361.5	65.3	18.1%	2,474.0
12/13	295.8	32.7	11.1%	2,474.0
12/12	300.2	55.1	18.4%	0.0
12/11	239.6	24.9	10.4%	0.0
Annual Growth	16.2%	27.6%	—	—

2015 Year-End Financials

Debt ratio: 25.3%
Return on equity: 18.0%
Cash ($ mil.): 114.0
Current ratio: 12.50
Long-term debt ($ mil.): 266.5

No. of shares (mil.): 151.7
Dividends
  Yield: —
  Payout: —
Market value ($ mil.): 2,579.0

	STOCK PRICE ($) FY Close	P/E High/Low		PER SHARE ($) Earnings	Dividends	Book Value
12/15	17.00	71	37	0.45	0.00	4.87
Annual Growth	—	—	—	—	—	—

Installed Building Products Inc

Installed Building Products (IBP) wants to insulate its customers from the elements. The company is a leading new residential insulation installer with more than 100 branches in about 45 states. IBP manages all aspects of the installation process for its customers including direct purchases of materials from national manufacturers to delivery and installation. In addition to insulation IBP installs garage doors rain gutters shower doors shelving fireplaces locksets and hardware and mirrors. The company's primary market is residential new home construction (about three-quarters of sales). Seeking to capitalize on the recovery in new home building IBP went public in 2014.

IPO

Installed Building Products (IBP) went public in February 2014 with an offering valued at $82 million (or $11 per share) well below the company's forecast of $14 to $16 per share. It also sold fewer shares than anticipated. The company plans to use the proceeds to repay debt and for general corporate purposes.

Geographic Reach

Ohio-based IBP has branches in 44 states including California Florida Indiana New York Ohio and Texas.

Financial Performance

The residential insulation installer's revenue increased 26% in 2012 versus 2011 to $301.3 million. It narrowed its loss from $9 million in 2011 to $1.9 million in 2012. (For the nine months ended September 2013 the firm turned a profit of nearly $3.7 million.)

Strategy

Founded in 1977 IBP has built its national presence through an aggressive acquisition strategy including more than 90 purchases since 1999. Indeed in 2012 the firm completed seven acquisitions. The firm has grown its share of the US residential new construction insulation installation market from about 5% in 2005 to approximately 16% in 2013.

Mergers and Acquisitions

In October 2016 IBP acquired East Coast Insulators expanding its presence in the mid-Atlantic region. It was the seventh acquisition made that year and the company continues to pursue additional buying opportunities.

EXECUTIVES

Chairman President and CEO, Jeffrey w. Edwards, age 52, $83,077 total compensation
EVP CFO and Director, Michael T. Miller, age 51, $194,900 total compensation
COO, Jay P. Elliott, age 54, $194,900 total compensation
President External Affairs, W. Jeffrey Hire, age 64
Regional President, R. Scott Jenkins, age 60
Regional President, Matthew J. Momper, age 55
Regional President, Warren W. Pearce, age 57
Regional President, Randall S. Williamson, age 53
Auditors: Deloitte & Touche LLP

LOCATIONS

HQ: Installed Building Products Inc
495 South High Street, Suite 50, Columbus, OH 43215
Phone: 614 221-3399
Web: www.installedbuildingproducts.com

PRODUCTS/OPERATIONS

2013 Sales

	% of total
Insulation	74
Garage doors	8
Rain gutters	6
Shower doors shelving & mirrors	6
Other	6
Total	**100**

2013 Sales

	% of total
New single-family homes	73
Commercial	11
Repair & remodel	10
New multifamily homes	6
Total	**100**

COMPETITORS

ABC Supply   HD Supply

HISTORICAL FINANCIALS

Company Type: Public

Income Statement

FYE: December 31

	REVENUE ($ mil.)	NET INCOME ($ mil.)	NET PROFIT MARGIN	EMPLOYEES
12/15	662.7	26.5	4.0%	4,510.0
12/14	518.0	13.9	2.7%	3,600.0
12/13	431.9	6.0	1.4%	3,200.0
12/12	301.2	(1.9)	—	3,100.0
12/11	238.4	(8.9)	—	0.0
Annual Growth	29.1%	—	—	—

2015 Year-End Financials

Debt ratio: 38.5%
Return on equity: 25.7%
Cash ($ mil.): 6.8
Current ratio: 1.54
Long-term debt ($ mil.): 125.7

No. of shares (mil.): 31.3
Dividends
  Yield: —
  Payout: —
Market value ($ mil.): 779.0

	STOCK PRICE ($) FY Close	P/E High/Low		PER SHARE ($) Earnings	Dividends	Book Value
12/15	24.83	35	20	0.85	0.00	3.65
12/14	17.82	—	—	(0.20)	0.00	2.91
Annual Growth	39.3%	—	—	—	—	25.3%

Interdigital Inc (PA)

InterDigital is more than just interested in wireless digital telecommunications. The company develops and licenses circuitry designs software and other technology using CDMA (code-division multiple access) and other wireless communications standards. Altogether it holds a patent portfolio of about 2200 US patents and 10900 foreign patents. InterDigital licenses its technology patents to companies that make smartphones tablets notebook computers and wireless personal digital assistants as well as wireless infrastructure equipment such as base stations and components dongles and modules for wireless devices. Top customers include Sony Samsung HTC and other makers of chips software and telecom equipment.

Geographic Reach

InterDigital operates from six research and development offices in the US one in Canada one in the UK and one in South Korea.

Taiwan is its biggest market generating about half of revenue. South Korea the US and Japan account for 16% 15% and 12% of revenue respectively.

Sales and Marketing

Historically the company generates most of its revenues from Asia where the world's electronics are manufactured. The US accounts for one-third of sales. It also relies on a small number of customers – in 2015 Pegatron Samsung and Sony Corporation of America combined accounted for 60% of sales.

Financial Performance

InterDigital's revenue rose 6% in 2015 to $441 million from $415 million in 2014. The company had higher per-unit royalties in 2015 driven by more shipments to Pegatron. It also saw a rise in fixed-fee revenue.

Net income increased 14% hitting $119 million in 2015 compared to $104 million in 2014. The company had lower administration and licensing expenses in 2015. Litigation expenses decreased to $31 million in 2015 from $52 million and $75 million in 2014 and 2013 respectively.

Cash flow from operations was $114 million in 2015 down from $242 million the previous year.

Strategy

As a patent licensing firm InterDigital must continually expand its pool of licensing customers to continue its growth and the company has a limited number of licensees contributing most of its revenues. InterDigital must also spend money on developing patentable technologies and it has had to litigate to defend the patents it holds for years at a time in some cases. In mid-2014 it settled with Samsung over mobile technology royalties for Samsung's 3G and 4G products. Over the next five years InterDigital will receive millions from Samsung.

InterDigital is developing technologies for 5G wireless networks and the Internet of Things. In 2015 it launched the MPOWER platform which enables interoperability and scalability across verticals networks and devices. It renewed a joint venture with Sony and Convida Wireless for development in 5G and the Internet of Things.

InterDigital's R&D spending was $73 million in 2015 $75 million in 2014 and $65 million in 2013.

HISTORY

Early History

InterDigital was founded in 1972 as International Mobile Machines Corporation by Sherwin Seligsohn who was its chairman until 1990. It began to develop technologies that held the potential to revolutionize radiotelephone communications but as a small company unable to usher in the digital age on its own the company patented its inventions. It went public in 1981 which allowed it to expand into product development.

The company expanded its technology portfolio by acquiring the assets of Tantivy Communications a designer of CDMA-based and other wireless gear in 2003 for $11.5 million.

Interdigital worked with Nokia at the turn of the century to develop Internet access technology for

mobile phones. A legal dispute between the two companies over the amount of royalties Nokia owed was resolved in InterDigital's favor in 2005 when a US District Court judge upheld an international tribunal's verdict ordering Nokia to pay additional royalties to InterDigital. In 2006 Nokia agreed to pay $253 million in one lump sum to InterDigital and the companies agreed to end their litigation against each other. Nokia and InterDigital immediately terminated their original license agreement and began negotiating a new pact.

Those talks apparently came to naught as InterDigital in 2007 filed a complaint against Nokia with the US International Trade Commission (ITC) alleging that Nokia's handsets infringe on patents held by InterDigital. The company sought to ban sales in the US of the Nokia N75 model and any other handsets that infringe on InterDigital patents. InterDigital separately filed a patent infringement lawsuit against Nokia in US District Court in Delaware. Nokia said it would vigorously defend against both actions.

EXECUTIVES

President and CEO, William J. Merritt, age 57, $575,000 total compensation
EVP Intellectual Property and Chief Intellectual Property Counsel; President InterDigital Patent Holding Subsidiaries, Lawrence F. Shay, age 57, $410,000 total compensation
SEVP Innovation, Scott A. McQuilkin, age 61, $375,000 total compensation
VP Systems Engineering, James J. (Jim) Nolan, age 56, $325,000 total compensation
CFO, Richard J. Brezski, age 45, $285,000 total compensation
EVP General Counsel and Secretary, Jannie K. Lau
EVP InterDigital Labs and CTO, Byung K. Yi
Chairman, Steven T. (Terry) Clontz, age 65
Auditors: PricewaterhouseCoopers LLP

LOCATIONS

HQ: Interdigital Inc (PA)
200 Bellevue Parkway, Suite 300, Wilmington, DE 19809-3727
Phone: 302 281-3600
Web: www.interdigital.com

PRODUCTS/OPERATIONS

2015 Sales

	$ mil.	% of total
Per-unit royalty	234.8	53
Fixed-fee amortized royalty	131.8	30
Past patent royalties	65.8	15
Current technology solutions	6.1	1
Past technology solutions	2.9	1
Total	**441.4**	**100**

2015 Sales

	$ mil.	% of total
Patent licensing royalties	432.5	98
Technology solutions	8.9	2
Total	**441.4**	**100**

COMPETITORS

Alcatel-Lucent	QUALCOMM
Conexant Systems	Sonics
IBM Microelectronics	Texas Instruments
Infineon Technologies	Unwired Planet
Intel	VirnetX
Marvell Technology	Xora
Nokia	

HISTORICAL FINANCIALS

Company Type: Public

Income Statement

FYE: December 31

	REVENUE ($ mil.)	NET INCOME ($ mil.)	NET PROFIT MARGIN	EMPLOYEES
12/15	441.4	119.2	27.0%	330.0
12/14	415.8	104.3	25.1%	320.0
12/13	325.3	38.1	11.7%	290.0
12/12	663.0	271.8	41.0%	290.0
12/11	301.7	89.4	29.7%	330.0
Annual Growth	**10.0%**	**7.4%**	**—**	**0.0%**

2015 Year-End Financials

Debt ratio: 33.0%
Return on equity: 24.3%
Cash ($ mil.): 510.2
Current ratio: 2.53
Long-term debt ($ mil.): 259.6
No. of shares (mil.): 35.4
Dividends
  Yield: 1.6%
  Payout: 29.2%
Market value ($ mil.): 1,737.0

	STOCK PRICE ($) FY Close	P/E High/Low		PER SHARE ($)		
				Earnings	Dividends	Book Value
12/15	49.04	18	14	3.27	0.80	14.42
12/14	52.90	21	10	2.62	0.60	12.68
12/13	29.49	52	31	0.92	1.90	13.12
12/12	41.09	7	4	6.26	1.90	12.64
12/11	43.57	38	18	1.94	0.50	10.36
Annual Growth	**3.0%**	—	—	**13.9%**	**12.5%**	**8.6%**

Investar Holding Corp

Auditors: Postlethwaite & Netterville APAC

LOCATIONS

HQ: Investar Holding Corp
7244 Perkins Road, Baton Rouge, LA 70808
Phone: 225 227-2222

HISTORICAL FINANCIALS

Company Type: Public

Income Statement

FYE: December 31

	ASSETS ($ mil.)	NET INCOME ($ mil.)	INCOME AS % OF ASSETS	EMPLOYEES
12/15	1,031.5	7.0	0.7%	168.0
12/14	879.3	5.4	0.6%	179.0
12/13	634.9	3.1	0.5%	171.0
12/12	375.4	2.3	0.6%	0.0
12/11	0.0	1.0	—	0.0
Annual Growth	**—**	**63.1%**	**—**	**—**

2015 Year-End Financials

Return on assets: 0.7%
Return on equity: 6.6%
Long-term debt ($ mil.): —
No. of shares (mil.): 7.2
Sales ($ mil): 45.6
Dividends
  Yield: 0.1%
  Payout: 3.0%
Market value ($ mil.): 128.0

	STOCK PRICE ($) FY Close	P/E High/Low		PER SHARE ($)		
				Earnings	Dividends	Book Value
12/15	17.60	18	14	0.97	0.03	15.05
12/14	13.85	15	13	0.93	0.01	14.24
Annual Growth	**27.1%**	—	—	**4.3%**	**131.9%**	**5.7%**

Investors Bancorp Inc (New)

Investors Bancorp is the holding company for Investors Savings Bank which serves New Jersey and New York from more than 130 branch offices. Founded in 1926 the bank offers such standard deposit products as savings and checking accounts CDs money market accounts and IRAs. Nearly 40% of the bank's loan portfolio is made up of residential mortgages while multi-family loans and commercial real estate loans make up more than 50% combined. The bank also originates business industrial and consumer loans. Founded in 1926 Investors Bancorp's assets now exceed $20 billion.

OperationsAbout 86% of Investors Bancorp's revenue came from interest income from loans and loans held-for-sale in 2014 while another 8% came from interest income on the bank's mortgage-backed securities municipal bonds and other debt. The remainder of its revenue came from fees and service charges (3%) and other miscellaneous income sources. Investors Bancorp boasted a staff of more than 1700 at the end of 2014.Geographic ReachBased in Short Hills New Jersey Investors Bancorp has more than 130 branches across New Jersey and New York. It also has lending offices in New York City Short Hills Spring Lake Newark Astoria and Brooklyn. Its operation center is in Iselin New Jersey.Sales and MarketingThe company offers retail and commercial banking services to individuals professional service firms municipalities small and middle-market companies commercial and industrial firms and other businesses.Financial PerformanceInvestors Bancorp's revenues and profits have been rising thanks to strong loan growth from bank acquisitions falling interest expenses on deposits and declining loan loss provisions as its loan portfolio's credit quality has improved with higher property valuations in the strengthened economy.The bank's revenue jumped by 21% to a record $702.7 million in 2014 mostly thanks to loan asset growth stemming from the bank's 2014 acquisition of Gateway Community Financial. Higher revenue and a continued decline in loan loss provisions in 2014 drove the bank's net income higher by 18% to a record $131.7 million. Investor Bancorp's operating cash levels spiked by 58% to $277.4 million for the year on higher cash earnings and favorable changes in its working capital.StrategyInvestors Bancorp continues to expand its geographic reach in its core New Jersey and New York markets and boost its loan and deposit business mainly through select bank and branch acquisitions. Indeed the bank noted in 2015 that it had made eight bank or branch acquisitions since 2008 adding that they have counted for "a significant portion" of the bank's historic growth.The company's 2014 and 2013 bank acquisitions bolstered its expansion in New Jersey into the suburbs of Philadelphia the boroughs of New York City the Nassau and Suffolk Counties on Long Island and historic markets throughout New Jersey.Mergers and AcquisitionsIn May 2016 Investors Bancorp agreed to purchase the $1 billion-asset The Bank of Princeton along with its 13 branches in the greater Princeton New Jersey and Philadelphia Pennsylvania areas. The added locations would grow Investors Bancorp's branch network by almost 10% to 156 branches in the Philadelphia to New York City corridor.In January 2014 Investors Bancorp purchased Gateway Community Financial Corp along with its four branches in Gloucester County New Jersey. The deal added nearly $255 million in customer deposits and $195 million in new loan business to its books.In December 2013 the company bought Roma Financial Corporation and its 26 branches in Burlington Ocean Mercer Camden and Middlesex counties in New Jersey. The deal added $1.34 billion in deposits and $991 million in loan assets while expanding the company's reach into the Philadelphia suburbs of New Jersey.Company BackgroundIn late 2012 the company acquired Marathon Banking Corporation (a subsidiary of Greece-based Piraeus Bank) for $135 million adding 13 branches in the New York metro area and more than doubling its branches in New York. The deal also would mark Investors Bancorp's entry into Manhattan and Staten Island.

EXECUTIVES

SEVP and COO, Domenick A. Cama, age 60, $621,000 total compensation
President and CEO, Kevin Cummings, age 61, $935,000 total compensation
EVP and Chief Lending Officer, Richard S. Spengler, age 54, $400,000 total compensation
EVP and Chief Retail Banking Officer, Paul Kalamaras, $375,000 total compensation
SVP and CFO, Sean Burke
Vice President Payroll Manager, Mary Ward
Vice President, Patricia (Pat) Brown
Senior Vice President, William (Bill) Cosgrove
Senior Vice President Information Technology, Sergio Alonso
Senior Vice President, Jawad Chaudhry
Senior Vice President Loan Operations Manager, Trent Gregory
Vice President Information Security Officer Director of Information Security, David (Dave) Van
Chairman, Robert M. Cashill, age 73
Auditors: KPMG LLP

LOCATIONS

HQ: Investors Bancorp Inc (New)
101 JFK Parkway, Short Hills, NJ 07078
Phone: 973 924-5100
Web: www.myinvestorsbank.com

PRODUCTS/OPERATIONS

2014 Sales

	$ mil.	% of total
Interest		
Loans receivable and held-for-sale	603.4	86
Mortgage-backed securities	44.2	6
Federal Home Loan Bank stock	6.9	1
Municipal bonds & other debt	5.7	1
Other	0.7	-
Non-interest		
Fees & service charges	19.3	3
Gain on loan transaction	5.3	2
Others	17.2	1
Total	**702.7**	**100**

COMPETITORS

Bank of America	M&T Bank
Bank of New York	New York Community
Mellon	Bancorp
Citigroup	OceanFirst Financial
ConnectOne Bancorp	PNC Financial
Fulton Financial	

HISTORICAL FINANCIALS

Company Type: Public

Income Statement

FYE: December 31

	ASSETS ($ mil.)	NET INCOME ($ mil.)	INCOME AS % OF ASSETS	EMPLOYEES
12/15	20,888.6	181.5	0.9%	1,768.0
12/14	18,773.6	131.7	0.7%	1,708.0
12/13	15,623.0	112.0	0.7%	1,597.0
12/12	12,722.5	88.7	0.7%	1,219.0
12/11	10,701.5	78.8	0.7%	982.0
Annual Growth	18.2%	23.2%	—	15.8%

2015 Year-End Financials

Return on assets: 0.9%
Return on equity: 5.2%
Long-term debt ($ mil.): —
No. of shares (mil.): 334.8
Sales ($ mil): 771.8

Dividends
Yield: 2.0%
Payout: 46.3%
Market value ($ mil.): 4,166.0

	STOCK PRICE ($) FY Close	P/E High/Low	PER SHARE ($) Earnings	Dividends	Book Value
12/15	12.44	24 19	0.55	0.25	9.89
12/14	11.23	74 26	0.38	0.08	9.99
12/13	25.58	64 44	0.40	0.00	3.78
12/12	17.78	58 42	0.32	0.00	3.74
12/11	13.48	53 42	0.29	0.00	3.42
Annual Growth	(2.0%)	— —	17.7%	—	30.4%

Investors Title Co.

Investors Title insures you in case your land is well not completely yours. It's the holding company for Investors Title Insurance and Northeast Investors Title Insurance which underwrite land title insurance and sell reinsurance to other title companies. (Title insurance protects those who invest in real property against loss resulting from defective titles.) Investors Title Insurance serves customers from about 30 offices in North Carolina South Carolina Michigan and Nebraska and through branches or agents in 20 additional states. Northeast Investors Title operates through an agency office in New York. Founder and CEO J. Allen Fine and his family own more than 20% of Investors Title.

While the company does business throughout the eastern and midwestern US North Carolina accounts for 50% of its title insurance premiums.

Investors Title also provides tax-deferred exchange services through its Investors Title Exchange and Investors Title Accommodation subsidiaries. Its Investors Capital Management Company subsidiary offers investment advisory and management services.

EXECUTIVES

Executive Vice President National Markets, George A Snead
Vice President Sales and Marketing, Kim (Kimmy) Dean
Assistant Vice President, Lee Brown
Assistant Vice President Nc Operations, Ruth Smith
Vice President Human Resources Executive, Mitchell (Mitch) Warren

LOCATIONS

HQ: Investors Title Co.
121 North Columbia Street, Chapel Hill, NC 27514
Phone: 919 968-2200
Web: www.invtitle.com

PRODUCTS/OPERATIONS

Selected Subsidiaries

Investors Title Accommodation Corporation
Investors Title Exchange Corporation
Investors Title Insurance Company
Investors Title Management Services Inc.
Northeast Investors Title Insurance Company

COMPETITORS

Fidelity National	Ticor Title Co.
Financial	Title Resource Group
First American	United General Title
Old Republic	Insurance
Stewart Information	
Services	

HISTORICAL FINANCIALS

Company Type: Public

Income Statement

FYE: December 31

	ASSETS ($ mil.)	NET INCOME ($ mil.)	INCOME AS % OF ASSETS	EMPLOYEES
12/15	211.5	12.5	5.9%	265.0
12/14	198.0	9.6	4.9%	263.0
12/13	188.3	14.7	7.8%	233.0
12/12	171.9	11.1	6.5%	212.0
12/11	157.9	6.9	4.4%	199.0
Annual Growth	7.6%	16.0%	—	7.4%

2015 Year-End Financials

Return on assets: 6.1%	Dividends
Return on equity: 8.9%	Yield: 0.4%
Long-term debt ($ mil.): —	Payout: 6.3%
No. of shares (mil.): 1.9	Market value ($ mil.): 195.0
Sales ($ mil): 127.2	

	STOCK PRICE ($) FY Close	P/E High/Low		PER SHARE ($) Earnings	Dividends	Book Value
12/15	100.00	16	11	6.30	0.40	73.17
12/14	72.90	67	13	4.74	0.32	67.99
12/13	80.98	12	8	7.08	0.32	62.86
12/12	60.00	13	7	5.24	0.29	56.10
12/11	35.77	13	9	3.20	0.28	50.54
Annual Growth	29.3%	—	—	18.5%	9.3%	9.7%

IPG Photonics Corp

IPG Photonics has a laser focus on spreading the use of lasers. The company makes fiber lasers and amplifiers and diode lasers which are primarily used in materials processing applications (nearly 90% of sales) such as welding cutting marking and engraving. Its fiber lasers are used in 3D printing and telecommunications. IPG Photonics is moving into automotive manufacturing applications and the developing market for medical uses. The company's customers have included BAE SYSTEMS Mitsubishi Heavy Industries and Nippon Steel. Deriving about 85% of its sales outside North America IPG Photonics operates sales offices in more than a dozen countries in Asia and Europe.

Operations

The vertically integrated manufacturer designs and makes most of the components used in its finished products (which can cost hundreds of thousands of dollars) from semiconductor diodes to optical fiber preforms finished fiber lasers and amplifiers. It also manufactures other products used in its lasers including optical delivery cables fiber couplers beam switches optical heads and chillers. By not outsourcing its manufacturing to third-party companies IPG Photonics is able to better control its proprietary processes and technologies as well as the supply of its materials.

The company's biggest market is in materials processing which accounts for 94% of revenue.

Geographic Reach

The company conducts R&D in the same city as its headquarters as well as in New Hampshire and overseas in the German city of Burbach (near Frankfurt) and in Fryazino Russia (outside Moscow).

It has four manufacturing facilities for lasers amplifiers and components one in each of its R&D cities and the fourth one in Cerro Maggiore Italy outside Milan. Manufacturing facilities for optical components are in India and China.

In terms of geographic markets China is the company's biggest accounting for 35% of revenue. The next biggest single country is the US generating 15% followed by Germany with 10% and Japan with 8%.

Sales and Marketing

IPG Photonics primarily uses a direct sales force. It has a diverse customer base – its five-largest customers only account for about 25% of sales. Its biggest customer is in China and accounts for 13% of sales. In 2015 the company shipped nearly 33000 units to moire than 3000 customers worldwide.

It has sales offices at each of its manufacturing facilities as well as in Michigan and California in the US. International sales offices are located in China Czech Republic France India Italy South Korea Spain Singapore Turkey and the UK.

Financial Performance

IPG Photonics is beaming after a 17% revenue increase in 2015. The company's sales reach $901 million for the year from $770 million in 2014. Materials processing of course provided most of the increase rising 16% with higher sales of quasi-continuous wave (QCW) pulsed lasers for welding and cutting. The company's smaller segments also grew in 2015 with the medical segment rising 100% for the year.

The rising sales at IPG Photonics drove profit 21% higher in 2015 to $242 million. Cash from operating activities also rose in 2015 from 2014.

Strategy

IPG remains focused on fiber lasers as an alternative to conventional lasers such as gas or crystal. Its strategy is to exploit the advantages that fiber lasers offer such as superiority in electrical efficiency beam quality and control maintenance costs longevity flexibility and usability. Traditional laser technologies have advantages that make them more suitable for some applications but fiber lasers continue to gain ground. Crystal lasers generate higher peak power pulses fiber lasers don't achieve the deep ultraviolet light needed for some semiconductor applications and carbon dioxide lasers are better for non-metallic applications such has plastics. Fiber lasers however have made improvements in power output that has opened them up to new markets and IPG believes the technology can reach additional nascent applications such as natural resource extraction.

IPG released a threebeam fiber laser system for brazing zinc-coated steel a process used in the automobile industry. The company is positioning fiber laser products for the auto industry and the trend toward the lighter weight metals such as high strength steel and aluminum. We are also encouraged by the potential for increased volumes of our laser seam stepper that welds auto bodies.

In 2015 some makers of consumer electronics adopted the company's QCW lasers for making their products and multi-hundred volume orders.

IPG formed a separate company IPG Medical in 2015 to focus on medical applications. The company is developing its Thulium fiber laser to break up kidney stones faster and and more simply than current technologies.

Mergers and Acquisitions

Increasing demand has led IPG to pursue operational expansion in Russia Germany and the US. In 2012 the company paid $55.4 million to acquire the 22.5% of Russia-based subsidiary NTO IRE-Polus that it did not already own to extend its control over R&D sales and manufacturing infrastructure in the country.

Also in 2012 IPG bought privately held J.P. Sercel Associates (JPSA) a New Hampshire-based supplier of UV excimer and diode-pumped solid-state industrial laser micromachining systems used in high-volume biomedical industrial automation LED microelectromechanical systems (MEMS) microfluidics thin-film solar panel and semiconductor manufacturing applications. The purchase expands IPG's custom laser system offerings to include fine processing precision cutting drilling and micromachining of ceramics glass and semiconductors. The company further enhanced its UV laser development with the purchase the following year of California-based Mobius Photonics.

HISTORY

IPG Photonics raised about $100 million in private equity funding with its investors including Apax Partners Merrill Lynch TA Associates and Winston Partners. The company filed for an IPO in 2000 and withdrew the registration statement six months later. It filed for another IPO in 2006 and completed the offering by the end of the year.

The company used proceeds of its public offering to repurchase warrants pay off debts and for general corporate purposes including working capital expansion of manufacturing facilities purchases of equipment and expansion of applications development and services.

In 2007 IPG Photonics acquired its Chinese distributor HM Laser and established a subsidiary IPG China with an office in Beijing. China is one of IPG's principal markets along with Germany Japan Russia and the US.

The company stepped forward with its purchase of laser material manufacturer Photonics Innovations (PII) in January 2010. The acquisition expanded IPG's products and services portfolio for optical and laser materials fabrication tunable laser design and optical and sensing systems. Transaction details were not divulged.

EXECUTIVES

Vice President, Paolo Paolo Sinni Sinni
Vice President Communications Products, George Buabbud
CEO and Chairman, Valentin P. Gapontsev, age 78, $687,981 total compensation
COO, Eugene Scherbakov, age 68, $450,449 total compensation
SVP and CFO, Timothy P. V. Mammen, age 47, $440,067 total compensation
CTO Deputy General Manager NTO IRE-Polus and Director, Igor Samartsev, age 54
SVP Components, Alexander (Alex) Ovtchinnikov, age 55, $400,579 total compensation
SVP U.S. Operations, Felix Stukalin, age 54
Upper Management Vice President, Laura (Laur) Richards
Vice President of Human Resources Worldwide, John (Jack) Weaver
Vice President Strategic Marketing, Yuri Erokhin
Auditors: Deloitte & Touche LLP

LOCATIONS

HQ: IPG Photonics Corp
50 Old Webster Road, Oxford, MA 01540
Phone: 508 373-1100
Web: www.ipgphotonics.com

PRODUCTS/OPERATIONS

2015 Sales by Market

	$ mil.	% of total
Materials processing	849.3	94
Advanced applications	28.9	3
Communications	14.4	2
Medical	8.6	1
Total	**901.2**	**100**

Selected Products

Broadband light sources
Continuous wave lasers
Diode laser systems
Diode-pumped solid-state laser systems
Erbium lasers
Fiber amplifiers
Fiber lasers
Fiber-coupled direct diode laser systems
Pulsed fiber lasers
Raman pump lasers
Thulium lasers
UV excimer laser systems
Ytterbium lasers

COMPETITORS

Cisco Systems	Newport Corp.
Coherent Inc.	Novanta
EMCORE	Oclaro
FANUC	Presstek
Furukawa Electric	Swatch
Huawei Technologies	TRUMPF
Mitsubishi Materials	Viavi Solutions

HISTORICAL FINANCIALS

Company Type: Public

Income Statement

FYE: December 31

	REVENUE ($ mil.)	NET INCOME ($ mil.)	NET PROFIT MARGIN	EMPLOYEES
12/15	901.2	242.1	26.9%	4,020.0
12/14	769.8	200.4	26.0%	3,370.0
12/13	648.0	155.7	24.0%	2,800.0
12/12	562.5	145.0	25.8%	2,400.0
12/11	474.4	117.7	24.8%	2,137.0
Annual Growth	**17.4%**	**19.7%**	**—**	**17.1%**

2015 Year-End Financials

Debt ratio: 1.3%
Return on equity: 21.0%
Cash ($ mil.): 582.5
Current ratio: 7.75
Long-term debt ($ mil.): 17.6

No. of shares (mil.): 52.8
Dividends
  Yield: —
  Payout: —
Market value ($ mil.): 4,715.0

	STOCK PRICE ($) FY Close	P/E High/Low	PER SHARE ($) Earnings	Dividends	Book Value
12/15	89.16	22 15	4.53	0.00	23.82
12/14	74.92	20 16	3.79	0.00	19.98
12/13	77.61	26 18	2.97	0.00	17.87
12/12	66.65	23 12	2.81	0.65	14.47
12/11	33.87	31 12	2.41	0.00	9.31
Annual Growth	**27.4%**	**—**	**17.1%**	**—**	**26.5%**

iRadimed Corp

Auditors: RSM US LLP

LOCATIONS

HQ: iRadimed Corp
1025 Willa Springs Drive, Winter Springs, FL 32708
Phone: 407 677-8022   **Fax:** 407 677-5037
Web: www.iradimed.com

HISTORICAL FINANCIALS

Company Type: Public

Income Statement

FYE: December 31

	REVENUE ($ mil.)	NET INCOME ($ mil.)	NET PROFIT MARGIN	EMPLOYEES
12/15	31.5	7.5	23.8%	68.0
12/14	15.6	2.0	13.1%	54.0
12/13	11.3	1.9	17.1%	46.0
12/12	7.6	0.9	12.6%	0.0
Annual Growth	**60.2%**	**98.3%**	**—**	**—**

2015 Year-End Financials

Debt ratio: —
Return on equity: 28.5%
Cash ($ mil.): 19.3
Current ratio: 11.73
Long-term debt ($ mil.): —

No. of shares (mil.): 11.1
Dividends
  Yield: —
  Payout: —
Market value ($ mil.): 313.0

	STOCK PRICE ($) FY Close	P/E High/Low	PER SHARE ($) Earnings	Dividends	Book Value
12/15	28.03	48 19	0.60	0.00	2.86
12/14	12.90	56 29	0.20	0.00	1.93
12/13	0.00	— —	0.22	0.00	0.77
Annual Growth	**—**	**—**	**65.1%**	**—**	**92.1%**

Ixia

Ixia nixes network glitches. The company designs network validation testing hardware and software that provides visibility into traffic performance and also addresses the network applications. Hardware consists of optical and electrical interface cards and the chassis to hold them. Its software tests the functionality of video voice conformance and security across ethernet wi-fi and 3G/LTE equipment and networks. Ixia primarily serves network equipment manufacturers (Cisco) service providers (AT&T) corporate customers (Bloomberg) the federal government (US Army) and its contractors (General Dynamics). Geographically sales are about evenly divided between the US and international customers.

Operations

Ixia's products generate 70% of its revenue with the rest coming from its services business.

Geographic Reach

Headquartered in the US Ixia has international offices in Australia Brazil Canada China Finland France Germany India Ireland Japan Russia Spain Singapore South Korea Sweden the UAE and the UK.

It outsources the manufacturing of its hardware to third-party contract and assembly companies in Malaysia.

Sales and Marketing

For the most part Ixia uses a direct sales force except in certain foreign markets where it relies on distributors partners and other resellers. Juniper Networks and Alcatel-Lucent are among Ixia's customers.

Financial Performance

In 2015 Ixia's revenue rose increased 11% to $517 million from $464 the year before on higher sales in products and services. The company shipped a higher volume of high-speed Ethernet interface cards in 2015.

Net income rose to about $6 million in 2015 following a loss of $41 million in 2014. The profit turned on higher revenue settlement proceeds for costs previously charged to a restructuring line item and a favorable lease buyout.

Strategy

Ixia's goal of being a leader in network test and visibility capabilities involves expanding its product base through acquisitions and internal research and development. R&D is a big focus; the company spends about 25% of annual revenue on it and also operates Ixia Labs a technology development incubator.

Mergers and Acquisitions

Ixia frequently adds to its product portfolio through acquisitions. In late 2013 it bought Net Optics a provider of network visibility hardware and software for $190 million in cash. The year before it network optimization systems provider Anue Systems for $145 million to strengthen its capabilities in validating wirelessly-delivered next-generation networks and applications. Later that year it bought network security testing company BreakingPoint Systems for $160 million rounding out its network test and visibility product offerings. In 2011 Ixia paid more than $15 million for Veri-Wave a performance testing company for wireless LAN and Wi-Fi enabled smart devices.

HISTORY

History

Chairman Errol Ginsberg founded Ixia in 1997 "in rather humble digs above a Mexican restaurant" in Calabasas California about an hour north of Los Angeles. The company went public in 2000 in a $57.5 million IPO but sales failed to top $100 million for three more years.

In 2003 Ixia acquired G3 Nova Technology a developer of VoIP test tools for enterprise call centers communications networks and network devices for about $12 million in cash and stock. Two years later it bought Communication Machinery Corp. (CMC) a developer of Wi-Fi network testing tools for $4 million in cash.

In 2006 Ixia acquired the video telephony test products of Dilithium Networks for around $5 million in cash. With the acquisition the company introduced a product based on the Dilithium Network Analyzer (DNA). The IxMobile Video Telephony test tools are focused on mobile wireless conformance interoperability capacity and performance testing.

Atul Bhatnagar who came from Nortel succeeded Ginsberg as CEO in 2007.

The company made two acquisitions in 2009 that helped it reach record revenues in 2010. Ixia purchased the assets of Agilent Technologies' N2X Data Networks product line for about $44 million in cash. The purchase brought an intuitive and powerful user interface as well as a customer base to open further markets in the Middle East and Asia/Pacific regions. Earlier in 2009 Ixia bought Catapult Communications for about $105 million in cash. The company sees Catapult's 3G and 4G wireless networking test products as complementary to its Internet protocol performance test systems and service verification platforms.

EXECUTIVES

SVP Corporate Affairs and General Counsel, Ronald W. (Ron) Buckly, age 64, $350,000 total compensation
President and CEO, Bethany J. Mayer, age 55
SVP Operations, Raymond de Graaf, age 50, $304,808 total compensation
Chief Product Officer, Dennis Cox
COO, Alex Pepe
CFO, Brent Novak
Vice President Human Resources, Tim Jones
Vice President Market Development, Kevin (Kev) Formby
Vice President and General Man, Raymond (Ray) Graaf
Vice President Human Resources, Christopher (Chris) Willia
Vice President Operations, Nitesh Jha
Vice President, Deepesh Arora
Chairman and Chief Innovation Officer, Errol Ginsberg, age 61
Auditors: Deloitte & Touche LLP

LOCATIONS

HQ: Ixia
26601 West Agoura Road, Calabasas, CA 91302
Phone: 818 871-1800   **Fax:** 818 871-1805
Web: www.ixiacom.com

PRODUCTS/OPERATIONS

2015 Sales

	$ mil.	% of total
Products	361.9	70
Services	155.0	30
Total	**516.9**	**100**

COMPETITORS

Agilent Technologies	Rohde & Schwarz
Anritsu	Spirent
Azimuth Systems	Sunrise Telecom
Digital Lightwave	Tektronix
EXFO	Tollgrade
Emrise	Communications
Fluke Networks	Viavi Solutions
RADCOM	

HISTORICAL FINANCIALS

Company Type: Public

Income Statement

FYE: December 31

	REVENUE ($ mil.)	NET INCOME ($ mil.)	NET PROFIT MARGIN	EMPLOYEES
12/15	516.9	5.9	1.2%	1,727.0
12/14	464.4	(41.5)	—	1,755.0
12/13	467.2	11.8	2.5%	1,846.0
12/12	413.4	45.4	11.0%	1,710.0
12/11	308.3	23.7	7.7%	1,300.0
Annual Growth	**13.8%**	**(29.3%)**	**—**	**7.4%**

2015 Year-End Financials

Debt ratio: 4.8%
Return on equity: 1.1%
Cash ($ mil.): 52.4
Current ratio: 1.35
Long-term debt ($ mil.): 34.4
No. of shares (mil.): 80.8
Dividends
  Yield: —
  Payout: —
Market value ($ mil.): 1,004.0

	STOCK PRICE ($) FY Close	P/E High/Low	PER SHARE ($) Earnings	Dividends	Book Value
12/15	12.43	225 144	0.07	0.00	6.42
12/14	11.25	— —	(0.54)	0.00	6.12
12/13	13.31	139 75	0.15	0.00	6.49
12/12	16.98	27 16	0.59	0.00	6.04
12/11	10.51	56 21	0.33	0.00	4.90
Annual Growth	**4.3%**	**— —**	**(32.1%)**	**—**	**7.0%**

---

j2 Global Inc (New)

EXECUTIVES

VP Engineering, Vincent P. (Vince) Niedzielski
VP Human Resources, Patty Brunton
EVP Corporate Strategy, Zohar Loshitzer, age 58
CEO, Nehemia (Hemi) Zucker, age 59, $459,000 total compensation
Chairman, Richard S. Ressler, age 58, $144,000 total compensation
CFO, Kathleen M. (Kathy) Griggs, age 62, $270,000 total compensation
President, R. Scott Turicchi, age 53, $375,000 total compensation
VP Products, Michael W. Harris, age 53
VP General Counsel and Secretary, Jeffrey D. (Jeff) Adelman, age 49, $270,000 total compensation
Vice President Marketing, Mike Pugh
VP Corporate Development, Ken Truesdale
VP Network Operations, Alan Alters
Vice President International, Tim McLean
VP and General Manager Europe, Paul Kinsella
Manager of Operations, Warner Bros
Vice President General Counsel Secretary, Jeff Adelman
Vice President Engineering, Vince Niedzielski

Chief Accounting Officer, Steve Dunn
Director, William B. (Brian) Kretzmer, age 61
Director, Douglas Y. Bech, age 71
Director, Robert J. Cresci, age 72
Director, John F. Rieley, age 73
Director, Michael P. Schulhof, age 74
Director, Stephen Ross, age 67
Auditors: BDO USA, LLP

LOCATIONS

HQ: j2 Global Inc (New)
6922 Hollywood Boulevard, Suite 500, Los Angeles, CA 90028
Phone: 323 860-9200
Web: www.j2global.com

COMPETITORS

CommTouch Software	Notify Technology
Deltathree	Open Text
EasyLink	Satellink
FuzeBox	

HISTORICAL FINANCIALS

Company Type: Public

Income Statement

FYE: December 31

	REVENUE ($ mil.)	NET INCOME ($ mil.)	NET PROFIT MARGIN	EMPLOYEES
12/15	720.8	133.6	18.5%	1,608.0
12/14	599.0	125.3	20.9%	1,410.0
12/13	520.8	107.5	20.6%	1,130.0
12/12	371.4	121.5	32.7%	680.0
12/11	330.1	114.7	34.8%	600.0
Annual Growth	**21.6%**	**3.9%**	**—**	**27.9%**

2015 Year-End Financials

Debt ratio: 33.5%
Return on equity: 15.6%
Cash ($ mil.): 255.5
Current ratio: 2.46
Long-term debt ($ mil.): 601.3
No. of shares (mil.): 47.9
Dividends
  Yield: 1.4%
  Payout: 45.5%
Market value ($ mil.): 3,947.0

	STOCK PRICE ($) FY Close	P/E High/Low	PER SHARE ($) Earnings	Dividends	Book Value
12/15	82.32	30 21	2.73	1.22	18.57
12/14	62.00	24 17	2.58	0.56	17.30
12/13	50.01	24 13	2.28	0.98	15.32
12/12	30.60	13 9	2.61	0.87	13.19
12/11	28.14	13 10	2.43	0.41	11.87
Annual Growth	**30.8%**	**— —**	**3.0%**	**31.2%**	**11.8%**

KBS Strategic Opportunity REIT Inc

LOCATIONS

HQ: KBS Strategic Opportunity REIT Inc
800 Newport Center Drive, Suite 700, Newport Beach, CA 92660
Phone: 949 417-6500
Web: www.kbsstrategicopportunityreit.com

HISTORICAL FINANCIALS

Company Type: Public

Income Statement
FYE: December 31

	REVENUE ($ mil.)	NET INCOME ($ mil.)	NET PROFIT MARGIN	EMPLOYEES
12/15	112.1	7.1	6.4%	0.0
12/14	106.1	(23.7)	—	0.0
12/13	68.5	11.5	16.9%	0.0
12/12	18.8	(10.1)	—	0.0
Annual Growth	**81.1%**	—	—	—

2015 Year-End Financials

Debt ratio: 54.5%	No. of shares (mil.): 58.7
Return on equity: 1.6%	Dividends
Cash ($ mil.): 23.0	Yield: —
Current ratio: 2.70	Payout: 911.6%
Long-term debt ($ mil.): 547.3	Market value ($ mil.): —

	STOCK PRICE ($) FY Close	P/E High/Low	PER SHARE ($) Earnings	Dividends	Book Value
12/15	0.00	— —	0.04	0.00	6.87
Annual Growth	—	—	—	—	—

Kearny Financial Corp (MD)

LOCATIONS

HQ: Kearny Financial Corp (MD)
120 Passaic Avenue, Fairfield, NJ 07004
Phone: 973 244-4500
Web: www.kearnybank.com

HISTORICAL FINANCIALS

Company Type: Public

Income Statement
FYE: June 30

	ASSETS ($ mil.)	NET INCOME ($ mil.)	INCOME AS % OF ASSETS	EMPLOYEES
06/16	4,500.0	15.8	0.4%	459.0
06/15	4,237.1	5.6	0.1%	491.0
06/14	3,510.0	10.1	0.3%	474.0
06/13	0.0	6.5	—	0.0
Annual Growth	—	**34.5%**	—	—

2016 Year-End Financials

Return on assets: 0.3%	Dividends
Return on equity: 1.3%	Yield: 0.6%
Long-term debt ($ mil.): —	Payout: 100.0%
No. of shares (mil.): 91.8	Market value ($ mil.): 1,155.0
Sales ($ mil): 137.6	

	STOCK PRICE ($) FY Close	P/E High/Low	PER SHARE ($) Earnings	Dividends	Book Value
06/16	12.58	74 62	0.18	0.08	12.50
06/15	11.16	191 179	0.06	0.00	12.48
06/14	0.00	— —	0.11	0.00	5.33
Annual Growth	—	— —	27.9%	—	53.2%

Kennedy-Wilson Holdings Inc

Kennedy-Wilson doesn't run for office it invests in them. The international real estate company invests in and leases mostly commercial properties and some multi-family properties while also offering a slew of real estate services in the US UK Ireland Spain and Japan. In addition to office space the company's KW Investments unit acquires and manages portfolios of multifamily loans retail space hotels condos and land. Its KW Services division provides property and asset management auction and residential sales and brokerage services. Kennedy-Wilson which has nearly $20 billion in assets under management manages more than 40 million sq. ft. of property.

OperationsKennedy-Wilson operates two segments: KW Investments which made up 89% of its revenue (mostly in the form of rental income) during 2015 and invests in real estate properties (mostly commercial with some multifamily and student housing properties) and real estate-secured loans on its own or through its investment management platform; and KW Services (11% of revenue) which generates commissions by providing investment management property services research brokerage and auction and conventional sales services.The firm makes most of its revenue from rental income. About 67% of Kennedy-Wilson's total revenue came from rental income during 2015 while another 18% came from hotel property room and operating revenue. The rest came from its real estate services (11% of revenue) and loan purchase and origination fees (3%).

Geographic Reach

The Beverly Hills-based company has 25 offices in the US (mostly in major real estate markets) and one office each in Dublin London Madrid and Tokyo. Its largest market is in Europe (including the UK Ireland and Spain) where it generated 60% of its revenue during 2015. Its next largest markets are in the Western US (38% of revenue) and Japan (2%).

Financial Performance

Kennedy-Wilson's annual revenues have risen nearly 10-fold since 2011 mostly as new property acquisitions have spurred additional rental income. The firm's profits have come back strong from losses in 2011-2013 caused by financing and acquisition costs used to its support growth.The firm's revenue jumped 52% to $603.7 million during 2015 mostly as new property acquisitions continued to boost its rental income. Its same-store rental revenue climbed 10% for its 5296 existing multifamily units and 4% for its 2.2 million existing square feet on its commercial properties. Kennedy-Wilson also collected 68% more in hotel revenue thanks to added rooms from three hotels it acquired in mid-2014 in Europe. The company's service revenue slipped 16% as it sold some of its service-oriented properties mostly in Dublin Ireland.Despite strong revenue and operating income growth in 2015 Kennedy-Wilson's net income tumbled 35% to $59 million as mostly on doubling interest expenses as it used more financing to acquire properties during the year. The company's operating cash levels climbed 82% to $178.2 million for the year thanks to strong cash-denominated revenue growth.

Strategy

Unlike real estate investment trusts which strictly focus on investments Kennedy-Wilson's unique advantage over competitors is that it can offer a full array of real estate services to the properties and tenants that it manages. As is the case with many real estate companies Kennedy-Wilson relies on bargain-priced property acquisitions to boost its rental revenue over time. During 2015 the firm used a significantly larger portion of its $3.2 billion acquisition budget to buy properties in the more promising Western US region especially in fast-growing real estate markets such as Seattle. In 2014 Kennedy-Wilson purchased an office building in Pasadena California for around $40 million. In the first half of 2014 as the market lagged a bit in Europe the company invested nearly $800 million in the UK and Ireland after spending close to $400 million there the year before. In 2013 it bought eight UK shopping centers out of bankruptcy a Hollywood office complex and an apartment complex in Salt Lake City for a total of close to $600 million.

Company Background

While many real estate companies struggled during the recession Kennedy-Wilson took advantage of the slumping US real estate market by acquiring assets at discounted prices.Kennedy-Wilson was founded in 1977 as a real estate auction firm.

EXECUTIVES

Chief Administrative Officer, Barry S. Schlesinger, $600,000 total compensation
Chairman and CEO, William J. McMorrow, $950,000 total compensation
President and CEO Kennedy Wilson Europe, Mary L. Ricks, $750,000 total compensation
EVP and President Capital Markets Group, Donald J. Herrema
President Properties Group, James A. (Jim) Rosten
President Auction Group, Richard Rhett Winchell
President Commercial Investment Group, John C. Prabhu
President Residential Investment Group, Stuart Cramer
EVP, Matt Windisch, $340,000 total compensation
CFO, Justin Enbody, $277,000 total compensation
President of Commercial Investments and Fund Management, Nicholas Colonna
Vice President, Louis (Lou) Gauthier
Auditors: KPMG LLP

LOCATIONS

HQ: Kennedy-Wilson Holdings Inc
151 S El Camino Drive, Beverly Hills, CA 90212
Phone: 310 887-6400
Web: www.kennedywilson.com

PRODUCTS/OPERATIONS

2015 Sales

	% of total
Investments	89
Services	11
Total	**100**

2015 Sales

% of total	$ in mil.
Rental	67
Hotel	18
Sale of real estate	1
Investment management property service and research fee	11
Loan purchases origination and others	3
Total	**100**

HISTORICAL FINANCIALS

Company Type: Public

Income Statement

FYE: December 31

	REVENUE ($ mil.)	NET INCOME ($ mil.)	NET PROFIT MARGIN	EMPLOYEES
12/15	603.7	59.0	9.8%	495.0
12/14	398.6	90.1	22.6%	450.0
12/13	121.2	(6.4)	—	400.0
12/12	64.0	4.2	6.6%	340.0
12/11	62.6	6.3	10.1%	300.0
Annual Growth	76.2%	74.6%	—	13.3%

2015 Year-End Financials

Debt ratio: 57.0%	No. of shares (mil.): 114.5
Return on equity: 5.8%	Dividends
Cash ($ mil.): 731.6	Yield: 1.9%
Current ratio: 1.90	Payout: 2,400.0%
Long-term debt ($ mil.): 4,360.8	Market value ($ mil.): 2,758.0

	STOCK PRICE ($) FY Close	P/E High/Low	PER SHARE ($) Earnings	Dividends	Book Value
12/15	24.08	43 34	0.66	0.48	9.90
12/14	25.30	199 149	0.14	0.36	9.38
12/13	22.25	— —	(0.21)	0.28	9.30
12/12	13.98	— —	(0.07)	0.20	7.99
12/11	10.58	— —	(0.05)	0.12	7.92
Annual Growth	22.8%	— —	—	41.4%	5.7%

Key Tronic Corp.

Contract electronics manufacturing is key for Key Tronic. The company which does business as KeyTronicEMS to highlight its focus on electronics manufacturing services provides printed circuit board assembly tooling and prototyping box build (completely built) systems and plastic injection molding. In addition Key Tronic offers such services as product design engineering materials management and in-house testing. The company also makes customized and standard keyboards for PCs terminals and workstations.

Geographic Reach

Though the company maintains facilities in the US most of its manufacturing takes place in Mexico and China. Customers located in the US account for two-thirds of Key Tronic's sales.

Sales and Marketing

A majority of Key Tronic's sales are to the communications consumer device and printer industries; its top five customers account for nearly 60% of sales.

Financial Performance

After posting milestone revenues of $361 million in 2013 Key Tronic saw its revenues fall 15% to $305 million in 2014. The declines for 2014 were driven by decreased demand from its current customer programs and a $5 million decrease in revenues related to program losses.

Key Tronic's profits fell 40% from $13 million in 2013 to $8 million in 2014. This was fueled by a dip in US sales and spike in research development and engineering expenses. The company's operating cash flow has fluctuated over the years peaking at $29 million in 2013 but dropping to nearly $1.5 million.

Strategy

To move beyond its single-product emphasis — keyboards once accounted for almost all of sales — and overcome years of spotty profitability Key Tronic rapidly expanded its contract manufacturing service offerings. As price erosion in the keyboard market made that segment less profitable the company continued its manufacturing push increasing the range of electronic products it can manufacture.

Mergers and Acquisitions

In 2014 Key Tronic paid $47 million to acquire CDR Manufacturing a provider of printed circuit board assembly and other EMS services. CDR caters to a diversified customer base including a number of large multi-national companies. In 2013 the company purchased Texas-based Sabre Assembly & Manufacturing a sheet metal fabrication company with facilities located in Juarez Mexico offering metal fabrication plastic molding PCB assembly complete product assembly design engineering and testing engineering services.

HISTORY

Lewis Zirkle who had worked for more than 20 years at General Electric in various engineering and manufacturing positions founded Key Tronic in 1969. In 1975 Key Tronic became the first independent supplier to develop and market keyboards for heavy-duty office use. By 1981 the company was a leader in manufacturing ergonomic keyboards. It went public two years later. In 1987 Key Tronic developed a membrane switch technology that integrated switching points into a custom-designed structure.

Hard times hit in 1991 and 1992 as overseas competition and a failed attempt to produce a computer notebook contributed to losses. Turnaround artist Stanley Hiller stepped in as CEO in 1992. Key Tronic acquired Honeywell's keyboard operations in 1993 and the following year it moved much of its production to Honeywell's former plant in Mexico to reduce expenses.

In 1995 more efficient operations and new products pushed Key Tronic's sales above the $200 million mark for the first time; net income also hit a 10-year high. Former Honeywell manager Jack Oehlke replaced Hiller as CEO in 1997 the year Key Tronic launched a fingerprint scanning line that let a user's fingerprints function as a password. In 1998 the company intensified a push into contract manufacturing. To reduce costs Key Tronic cut about 200 jobs at its Washington plant and moved those operations to its facility in Mexico. It also closed its manufacturing plant in Taiwan. After a profitable fiscal 1997 a decline in keyboard sales caused a loss for fiscal 1998.

In 2000 Key Tronic agreed to manufacture circuits for glucose-monitoring devices made by Cygnus and make point-of-sale printers for Ax-iohm Transaction Solutions (now TPG IPB). During the first half of 2001 the company began doing business as KeyTronicEMS as part of a company-wide transition to firmly plant itself in the electronics manufacturing services (EMS) industry. Later that year the company was ordered to pay $16.5 million in damages when a jury found that it had misappropriated trade secrets and breached a confidentiality agreement with F&G Scrolling Mouse in 1993.

Key Tronic returned to profitability in fiscal 2003 although profits were typical of the razor-thin margins in the EMS industry. Lewis Zirkle who retired from Key Tronic in 1993 died in 2005 at the age of 90.

Keyboards continued to dwindle as a business in the early 21st century from one-quarter of sales in 2001 to about 4% in fiscal 2006 and around 3% in fiscal 2007 and fiscal 2008.

After closing its Las Cruces New Mexico plant in 2005 Key Tronic sold the facility in 2007 to Adevco Corp. for about $4 million including nearly $3 million in cash. Jack Oehlke retired as president and CEO in 2009. EVP/GM Craig Gates succeeded him.

EXECUTIVES

EVP Worldwide Operations, Douglas G. (Doug) Burkhardt, age 57, $269,600 total compensation

EVP Administration and CFO, Ronald F. (Ron) Klawitter, age 64, $306,000 total compensation

President and CEO, Craig D. Gates, age 57, $504,637 total compensation

EVP Administration CFO and Treasurer, Brett R. Larsen, age 43, $190,996 total compensation

VP Supply Chain, Frank Crispigna, age 54

EVP Business Development, Philip S. Hochberg, age 54, $263,977 total compensation

EVP Eastern Division, W. Brian Porter

EVP and Eastern Division, Brian Porter

Senior Vice President Business Development Eastern Division, Craig Green

Executive Vice President Materials, Robert Alford

Vice President Engineering and Quality, Lawrence Bostwick

Chairman, Patrick Sweeney, age 81

Auditors: BDO USA, LLP

LOCATIONS

HQ: Key Tronic Corp.
N. 4424 Sullivan Road, Spokane Valley, WA 99216
Phone: 509 928-8000
Web: www.keytronicems.com

PRODUCTS/OPERATIONS

2014 Sales by Industry

	% of total
Consumer	30
Communication	23
Industrial and Commercial printer	17
Gaming	15
Transaction printer	11
Computer & peripheral	4
Total	**100**

2016 Sales by Industry

	% of total
Industrial	39
Consumer	31
Communication	13
Gaming	7
Printers	6
Transportation	3
Computer and Peripheral	1
Total	**100**

Services

Circuit board assembly
Contract design and manufacturing
Custom molding and tooling
Engineering services
Logistics
Materials management
Product design
Prototyping
Products
Computer keyboards

COMPETITORS

APEM	Jabil
Am-Mex	Mitsumi Electric
Applied Technical	Plexus
Services	Sanmina
Celestica	Sparton
Flextronics	ZF Electronic Systems
Hon Hai	

HISTORICAL FINANCIALS

Company Type: Public

Income Statement
FYE: July 2

	REVENUE ($ mil.)	NET INCOME ($ mil.)	NET PROFIT MARGIN	EMPLOYEES
07/16*	484.9	6.5	1.3%	4,947.0
06/15	434.0	4.3	1.0%	4,866.0
06/14	305.3	7.6	2.5%	3,343.0
06/13	361.0	12.5	3.5%	2,584.0
06/12	346.4	11.6	3.4%	2,700.0
Annual Growth	8.8%	(13.4%)	—	16.3%

*Fiscal year change

2016 Year-End Financials

Debt ratio: 18.7%	No. of shares (mil.): 10.7
Return on equity: 6.2%	Dividends
Cash ($ mil.): 1.0	Yield: —
Current ratio: 2.16	Payout: —
Long-term debt ($ mil.): 39.3	Market value ($ mil.): 79.0

	STOCK PRICE ($) FY Close	P/E High/Low	PER SHARE ($) Earnings	Dividends	Book Value
07/16*	7.39	18 11	0.58	0.00	9.84
06/15	10.66	29 19	0.38	0.00	9.41
06/14	10.73	16 13	0.67	0.00	9.83
06/13	10.35	10 6	1.15	0.00	8.97
06/12	8.24	12 3	1.10	0.00	7.50
Annual Growth	(2.7%)	— —	(14.8%)	—	7.0%

*Fiscal year change

Kilroy Realty Corp

Kilroy is still here especially if you're referring to the West Coast. A self-administered real estate investment trust (REIT) Kilroy Realty owns manages and develops Class A office space mostly in suburban Southern California's Orange County San Diego and Los Angeles but it has since expanded to the San Francisco Bay and greater Seattle area to woo technology companies as tenants. Its portfolio includes about 115 office properties encompassing more than 13 million square feet of leasable space. A majority of Kilroy Realty's 500-plus tenants are involved in technology media financial services and real estate.

Geographic Reach

Besides 10 office buildings in Washington all of the REIT's property is located in California.

Sales and Marketing

Its 15 largest tenants accounted for 34% of the REIT's base rental revenue in 2012; these include DIRECTV Intuit and Bridgepoint Education. Its properties are 92% occupied.

Financial Performance

Overall sales grew 10% to $405 million in 2012. Profits jumped more than 300% to $270 million after the trust recorded gains on properties it sold.

As a REIT Kilroy Realty is exempt from paying federal income tax as long as it distributes quarterly dividends to shareholders.

Strategy

Kilroy Realty has moved away from owning industrial properties in order to focus on office buildings which generally earn more in rental income. In late 2012 it sold its entire portfolio of 44 industrial properties in California to two unnamed buyers for $355 million. The industrial properties totaled almost 4 million-sq.-ft. of space.

At the same time the trust boosted its portfolio of office buildings in San Francisco and Seattle home to many of the nation's wealthy tech companies. In 2012 it paid $330 million for three properties totaling 837000 square feet in Seattle $162 million for a 374000-sq.-ft. office park in Silicon Valley and it paid $52 million for a building in downtown San Francisco that it will spend another $200 million redeveloping into a 27-story glass office tower for new tenant salesforce.com. In addition the trust is spending $315 million to develop a 587000-sq.-ft. office complex for LinkedIn in Sunnyvale California.

Not missing a beat in 2013 the trust boosted its Bay Area construction pipeline to more than 1.8 million square feet with new developments in Redwood City and downtown San Francisco (most of the space is pre-leased).

In addition Kilroy Realty has approximately 110 acres of undeveloped land in San Diego with the capacity for more than 2 million sq. ft. of rentable office space.

EXECUTIVES

EVP and CFO, Tyler H. Rose, age 56, $500,000 total compensation
EVP and COO, Jeffrey C. Hawken, age 58, $675,000 total compensation
Chairman President and CEO, John B. Kilroy, age 68, $1,225,000 total compensation
SVP Asset Management, John T. Fucci
EVP Development and Construction Services, Justin W. Smart, $500,000 total compensation
EVP Chief Accounting Officer and Controller, Heidi R. Roth
EVP Southern California, David Simon
EVP Leasing and Business Development, A. Robert Paratte
EVP Northern California, Mike L. Sanford
Executive Vice President, Eli Khouri
Vice President, Mike Shields
Vice President of Commercial Development, Robert (Bob) Little
Vice President Finance, Walter Baynes
Vice President, Jamas Gwilliam
Vice President Construction, Richard Mount
Executive Vice President Chief Financial Officer, Richard (Dick) Moran
Vice President Legal Administration, Nadine (Dina) Kirk
Vice President Coporate Finance And Corporate Counsel, Joseph Magri
Vice President, Randy Jackson
Vice President Information Technology, Stan Low

Vice President Asset Management, Brian Galligan
Treasurer, Michelle Ngo
Auditors: Deloitte & Touche LLP

LOCATIONS

HQ: Kilroy Realty Corp
12200 W. Olympic Boulevard, Suite 200, Los Angeles, CA 90064
Phone: 310 481-8400
Web: www.kilroyrealty.com

PRODUCTS/OPERATIONS

2015 Sales

	% of total
Rental income	91
Tenant reimbursements	9
Other property income	-
Total	**100**

COMPETITORS

BioMed Realty	Irvine Company
Brandywine Realty	Majestic Realty
Digital Realty	PS Business Parks
Douglas Emmett	Prologis
Equity Commonwealth	Shorenstein
Equity Office	The Koll Company
Hudson Pacific	Trammell Crow Company

HISTORICAL FINANCIALS

Company Type: Public

Income Statement
FYE: December 31

	REVENUE ($ mil.)	NET INCOME ($ mil.)	NET PROFIT MARGIN	EMPLOYEES
12/16	642.5	293.7	45.7%	245.0
12/15	581.2	234.0	40.3%	232.0
12/14	521.7	183.5	35.2%	226.0
12/13	465.1	43.8	9.4%	219.0
12/12	404.9	270.9	66.9%	201.0
Annual Growth	12.2%	2.0%	—	5.1%

2016 Year-End Financials

Debt ratio: 34.5%	No. of shares (mil.): 93.2
Return on equity: 8.7%	Dividends
Cash ($ mil.): 193.4	Yield: 0.0%
Current ratio: 1.17	Payout: 113.6%
Long-term debt ($ mil.): 2,320.1	Market value ($ mil.): 6,826.0

	STOCK PRICE ($) FY Close	P/E High/Low	PER SHARE ($) Earnings	Dividends	Book Value
12/16	73.22	26 16	2.97	3.38	38.01
12/15	63.28	32 26	2.42	1.40	34.37
12/14	69.07	36 25	1.95	1.40	30.91
12/13	50.18	161 128	0.36	1.40	29.96
12/12	47.37	14 11	2.56	1.40	29.22
Annual Growth	11.5%	— —	3.8%	24.6%	6.8%

Kilroy Realty L.P.

Auditors: Deloitte & Touche LLP

LOCATIONS

HQ: Kilroy Realty L.P.
12200 W. Olympic Boulevard, Suite 200, Los Angeles, CA 90064
Phone: 310 481-8400
Web: www.kilroyrealty.com

HISTORICAL FINANCIALS

Company Type: Public

Income Statement

FYE: December 31

	REVENUE ($ mil.)	NET INCOME ($ mil.)	NET PROFIT MARGIN	EMPLOYEES
12/15	581.2	238.1	41.0%	232.0
12/14	521.7	183.5	35.2%	226.0
12/13	465.1	44.3	9.5%	219.0
12/12	381.0	276.4	72.6%	0.0
12/11	310.4	66.9	21.6%	0.0
Annual Growth	17.0%	37.3%	—	—

2015 Year-End Financials

Debt ratio: 37.6%
Return on equity: —
Cash ($ mil.): 56.5
Current ratio: 0.25
Long-term debt ($ mil.): 2,238.5

No. of shares (mil.): 94.0
Dividends
Yield: —
Payout: 57.8%
Market value ($ mil.): —

Kimball Electronics Inc

Auditors: Deloitte & Touche LLP

LOCATIONS

HQ: Kimball Electronics Inc
1205 Kimball Boulevard, Jasper, IN 47546
Phone: 812 634-4000
Web: www.kimballelectronics.com

HISTORICAL FINANCIALS

Company Type: Public

Income Statement

FYE: June 30

	REVENUE ($ mil.)	NET INCOME ($ mil.)	NET PROFIT MARGIN	EMPLOYEES
06/16	842.0	22.2	2.6%	4,500.0
06/15	819.3	26.2	3.2%	4,300.0
06/14	741.5	24.6	3.3%	3,800.0
06/13	703.1	21.5	3.1%	0.0
06/12	616.7	23.9	3.9%	0.0
Annual Growth	8.1%	(1.7%)	—	—

2016 Year-End Financials

Debt ratio: 1.7%
Return on equity: 6.9%
Cash ($ mil.): 54.7
Current ratio: 2.07
Long-term debt ($ mil.): —

No. of shares (mil.): 28.2
Dividends
Yield: —
Payout: —
Market value ($ mil.): 351.0

	STOCK PRICE ($) FY Close	P/E High/Low		PER SHARE ($) Earnings	Dividends	Book Value
06/16	12.45	19	12	0.76	0.00	11.49
06/15	14.59	18	8	0.89	0.00	10.71
Annual Growth	(14.7%)	—	—	(14.6%)	—	7.3%

Kingstone Companies Inc

Kingstone Companies (formerly DCAP Group) keeps things covered. While the company has transformed itself from a broker into an underwriter its main business is still insurance. Its Kingstone Insurance Company (formerly Commercial Mutual Insurance Company) provides property/casualty insurance policies for individuals and businesses in New York State. Its products including auto business and homeowners' policies are sold through independent agents. The company has divested its former insurance brokerage business which offered life and property/casualty policies through owned and franchised retail locations in New York and eastern Pennsylvania.

In mid-2009 the company completed the divestiture of its more than 70 owned or franchised retail locations in New York and eastern Pennsylvania which operated under the brand names DCAP Barry Scott and Atlantic Insurance. The retail locations offered insurance policies underwritten by third parties and some of the group's locations offered income tax preparation services.

Around the same time the company acquired Commercial Mutual Insurance Company a mutual insurance underwriting firm. Commercial Mutual was converted into a stock company and was renamed Kingstone Insurance. Parent company DCAP Group changed its name to Kingstone Companies following the transaction.

CEO Barry Goldstein owns 25% of Kingstone Companies and director Michael Feinsod owns about 16% through Infinity Capital Partners.

EXECUTIVES

Cfo-treas, Victor (Vic) Brodsky
Auditors: Marcum LLP

LOCATIONS

HQ: Kingstone Companies Inc
15 Joys Lane, Kingston, NY 12401
Phone: 845 802-7900
Web: www.kingstonecompanies.com

COMPETITORS

AIG	New York Life
Allstate	Progressive
GEICO	Corporation
GNY Mutual Insurance	The Hartford
NYCM	

HISTORICAL FINANCIALS

Company Type: Public

Income Statement

FYE: December 31

	REVENUE ($ mil.)	NET INCOME ($ mil.)	NET PROFIT MARGIN	EMPLOYEES
12/15	64.1	6.9	10.8%	69.0
12/14	50.0	5.3	10.6%	66.0
12/13	36.5	2.0	5.5%	59.0
12/12	29.0	0.7	2.6%	54.0
12/11	27.6	2.5	9.0%	49.0
Annual Growth	23.4%	29.1%	—	8.9%

2015 Year-End Financials

Debt ratio: —
Return on equity: 16.2%
Cash ($ mil.): 13.5
Current ratio: 6.95
Long-term debt ($ mil.): —

No. of shares (mil.): 7.3
Dividends
Yield: 2.3%
Payout: 22.8%
Market value ($ mil.): 66.0

	STOCK PRICE ($) FY Close	P/E High/Low		PER SHARE ($) Earnings	Dividends	Book Value
12/15	9.00	11	7	0.94	0.21	6.18
12/14	8.15	12	8	0.72	0.18	5.54
12/13	7.27	14	9	0.50	0.16	4.91
12/12	4.87	33	16	0.20	0.14	4.24
12/11	3.59	6	4	0.64	0.06	4.07
Annual Growth	25.8%	—	—	10.1%	37.2%	11.0%

Kite Realty Group Trust

A real estate investment trust (REIT) Kite Realty Group Trust acquires develops and operates retail properties. It owns more than 70 strip malls and anchored shopping centers with some 12.4 million sq. ft. of leasable space in about a dozen states with about a third in Indiana. The REIT also has interests in three commercial properties a parking garage several retail sites under development and nearly 100 acres of land held for possible future development. Kite Realty also provides third-party management development and construction services. Its largest tenants include Florida grocer Publix and TJX Cos. though no single tenant accounts for more than 5% of the company's rental income.

Geographic Reach

Indianapolis-based Kite Realty Group has properties in 13 states with holdings concentrated in just three: Indiana Florida and Texas. Indeed Indiana Florida and Texas account for 30% 24% and 18% of the REIT's owned square footage respectively.

Sales and Marketing

Kite's tenants include some of the nation's best known and most high-flying retailers. Indeed the REIT's largest tenants in 2013 were Publix Super Markets TJX Cos. Bed Bath & Beyond Dick's Sporting Goods and PetSmart representing 5% 3% 2% 2% and 2% of annualized base rent respectively.

Financial Performance

Property acquisitions have led to strong growth in rental income for the REIT. In 2013 Kite Realty Group (KRG) reported $129.5 million in revenue a 28% increase versus 2012 on higher rental income and other property-related revenue. Higher rents and occupancy levels at its shopping centers helped boost results.

KRG's profitability continued on its roller coaster course posting a loss of $2.85 million in 2013 compared with a loss of $4.3 million in 2012.

Strategy

Kite's growth strategy includes the operation development and redevelopment as well as the acquisition of properties in well-located community and neighborhood shopping centers. The REIT uses debt and equity capital to acquire new retail properties redevelop or renovate its existing properties and develop shopping centers on land that it owns. The firm purchased 13 properties in its core markets and completed three development and redevelopment projects in 2013 with four more to come in 2014.

Mergers and Acquisitions

In November 2013 the REIT acquired a group of nine retail operating properties in Florida Georgia Texas and Alabama for $304 million with about 2 million square feet of leasable area that's 93% occupied. Most of the newly-acquired shopping centers are anchored by a grocery store. Other real estate purchases in 2013 included a 60000 square foot shopping center in Charlotte North Carolina for $15.9 million; a 278000 square foot shopping center in Indianapolis for $39 million; and a 285000 square foot shopping center in Nashville for $37.6 million.

EXECUTIVES

Chairman and CEO, John A. Kite, age 50, $700,000 total compensation
President and COO, Thomas K. McGowan, age 51, $450,000 total compensation
EVP and CFO, Daniel R. Sink, age 48, $400,000 total compensation
EVP General Counsel and Corporate Secretary, Scott E. Murray, $320,000 total compensation
Senior Vice President, Gregg Poetz
Executive Vice President of Leasing, W Moll
Senior Vice President, Gregg (Greggory) Poetz
Auditors: Ernst & Young LLP

LOCATIONS

HQ: Kite Realty Group Trust
30 S. Meridian Street, Suite 1100, Indianapolis, IN 46204
Phone: 317 577-5600
Web: www.kiterealty.com

PRODUCTS/OPERATIONS

2015 Sales

	$ mil.	% of total
Minimum rent	263.8	76
Tenant reimbursements	70.2	20
Other property-related revenue	13.0	4
Total	**347.0**	**100**

2015 stores

Tenant	No
TJX Companies	21
Publix	18
Bed Bath & Beyond	18
Petsmart	18
Ross Stores	17
Target	16
Wal-Mart	14
Lowe's Home Improvement	14
Kohls	9
Dick's Sporting Goods	9
Total	**154**

COMPETITORS

Acadia Realty Trust
Cedar Realty Trust
DDR
Equity One
General Growth Properties
Kimco Realty
Lauth
Regency Centers
Regency Commercial Associates
Simon Property Group
Weingarten Realty

HISTORICAL FINANCIALS

Company Type: Public

Income Statement

FYE: December 31

	REVENUE ($ mil.)	NET INCOME ($ mil.)	NET PROFIT MARGIN	EMPLOYEES
12/15	347.0	27.1	7.8%	145.0
12/14	259.5	(5.7)	—	141.0
12/13	129.4	(2.8)	—	95.0
12/12	101.0	(4.3)	—	84.0
12/11	101.9	4.9	4.9%	77.0
Annual Growth	**35.8%**	**52.7%**	**—**	**17.1%**

2015 Year-End Financials

Debt ratio: 46.0%
Return on equity: 1.5%
Cash ($ mil.): 33.8
Current ratio: 1.04
Long-term debt ($ mil.): 1,734.0
No. of shares (mil.): 83.3
Dividends
 Yield: 4.1%
 Payout: 598.6%
Market value ($ mil.): 2,161.0

	STOCK PRICE ($) FY Close	P/E High/Low		PER SHARE ($) Earnings	Dividends	Book Value
12/15	25.93	165	121	0.18	1.08	20.71
12/14	28.74	—	—	(0.24)	0.26	22.74
12/13	6.57	—	—	(0.48)	0.96	23.04
12/12	5.59	—	—	(0.72)	0.96	24.35
12/11	4.51	—	—	(0.04)	0.96	25.74
Annual Growth	**54.8%**	**—**	**—**	**—**	**2.9%**	**(5.3%)**

KKR & Co LP (DE)

Auditors: Deloitte & Touche LLP

LOCATIONS

HQ: KKR & Co LP (DE)
9 West 57th Street, Suite 4200, New York, NY 10019
Phone: 212 750-8300
Web: www.kkr.com

HISTORICAL FINANCIALS

Company Type: Public

Income Statement

FYE: December 31

	REVENUE ($ mil.)	NET INCOME ($ mil.)	NET PROFIT MARGIN	EMPLOYEES
12/15	1,043.7	488.4	46.8%	1,196.0
12/14	1,110.0	477.6	43.0%	1,209.0
12/13	762.5	691.2	90.6%	1,084.0
12/12	568.4	560.8	98.7%	1,014.0
12/11	723.6	1.9	0.3%	916.0
Annual Growth	**9.6%**	**299.3%**	**—**	**6.9%**

2015 Year-End Financials

Debt ratio: 26.3%
Return on equity: —
Cash ($ mil.): 2,519.8
Current ratio: 1.39
Long-term debt ($ mil.): 18,730.0
No. of shares (mil.): 457.8
Dividends
 Yield: 10.1%
 Payout: 179.5%
Market value ($ mil.): 7,138.0

	STOCK PRICE ($) FY Close	P/E High/Low		PER SHARE ($) Earnings	Dividends	Book Value
12/15	15.59	23	13	1.01	1.58	12.12
12/14	23.21	21	16	1.16	2.03	12.46
12/13	24.34	10	6	2.30	1.62	9.45
12/12	15.23	7	5	2.21	0.84	7.91
12/11	12.83	1896992		0.01	0.71	5.85
Annual Growth	**5.0%**	**—**		**—217.0%**	**22.1%**	**20.0%**

Knight Transportation Inc.

Knight Transportation drivers don't drive long hours into the night. The truckload carrier instead focuses on short- to medium-haul trips averaging about 500 miles. From some 35 regional operations centers mainly in the southern midwestern and western US Knight carries such cargo as consumer goods food and beverages and paper products. It has a fleet of more than 4100 tractors and 9700 trailers including nearly 900 refrigerated trailers. Besides for-hire hauling Knight provides dedicated contract carriage in which drivers and equipment are assigned to a customer long-term. It also offers freight brokerage services.

Geographic Reach

Knight is stationed in Phoenix and operates through nearly 30 locations in the US in about 25 states. Other operations reside in Canada and Mexico.

Operations

Knight has one reportable segment comprised of five operating segments including three asset-based operating segments (dry van truckload temperature-controlled truckload and port services) and two non-asset-based operating segments (brokerage and intermodal services). Its asset-based and non-asset-based operations provide transportation and arrange for the transportation of general commodities for customers throughout the US and parts of Canada and Mexico.

Sales and Marketing

Knight has a nationwide network of service centers through 450 independent contractors third-party carriers and its rail providers. In 2014 its top 10 customers represented approximately 25% of revenue; its top 5 customers represented approximately 17% of revenue.

Financial Performance

Knight has enjoyed four straight years of unprecedented growth. Revenues jumped 14% from $969 million in 2013 to peak at $1.1 billion a historical milestone. Profits also spiked 48% from $69 million to peak at a record-setting $103 million due to the higher revenue and a decrease in operating expenses.

The growth for 2014 was driven by a 42% surge in logistics and a 9% spike in trucking. In addition its tractor productivity as measured by average annual revenue increased in 2014 due to increased demand for its capacity and improvements in its freight mix and contract pricing.

Strategy

With 18 wheels of optimism the company is pushing ahead to expand into new geographic regions by opening new service centers. These regional service centers are linked to Knight's corporate computer system which provides detailed information regarding equipment shipment status and customer requirements. The company believes its regional structure helps the company control costs and not be as susceptible to regional economic downturns. The regional system also serves as an aid in recruiting drivers because it gives them more time at home.

Mergers and Acquisitions

Knight also uses acquisitions as a means for growth. In late 2014 the company acquired Barr-Nunn Transportation a provider of dry van truckload transportation services headquartered in Des Moines Iowa. Barr-Nunn has additional facilities in Ohio Pennsylvania and North Carolina and the deal improved Knight's expedited logistics operations.

Company Background

Four Knight cousins —Kevin Gary Keith and Randy —started the company in 1990.

EXECUTIVES

President and CEO, David A. (Dave) Jackson, age 40, $446,923 total compensation

EVP and COO, Kevin Quast, age 50, $244,231 total compensation

EVP Sales and Marketing, James E. Updike, age 43, $244,231 total compensation

CFO Secretary and Treasurer, Adam W. Miller, age 35, $249,538 total compensation

Vice Chairman, Gary J. Knight, age 64

Chairman, Kevin P. Knight, age 59

Auditors: Grant Thornton LLP

LOCATIONS

HQ: Knight Transportation Inc.
20002 North 19th Avenue, Phoenix, AZ 85027
Phone: 602 269-2000
Web: www.knighttrans.com

PRODUCTS/OPERATIONS

2014 Sales

	$ mil.	% of total
Revenues	926.0	84
Fuel surcharges	176.3	16
Total	**1,102.3**	**100**

2014 Sales

	$ mil.	% of total
Trucking segment	892.1	81
Logistics segment	214.4	19
Total	**1,102.3**	**100**

Selected Services

Brokerage
Dedicated truckload service
Driver training
Dry van truckload
Refrigerated truckload
Sales

COMPETITORS

C.H. Robinson Worldwide	J.B. Hunt
C.R. England	Landstar System
Celadon	Prime Inc.
Covenant Transportation	Schneider National
	Swift Transportation
Frozen Food Express	U.S. Xpress
Heartland Express	USA Truck
	Werner Enterprises

HISTORICAL FINANCIALS

Company Type: Public

Income Statement

FYE: December 31

	REVENUE ($ mil.)	NET INCOME ($ mil.)	NET PROFIT MARGIN	EMPLOYEES
12/15	1,182.9	116.7	9.9%	6,196.0
12/14	1,102.3	102.8	9.3%	5,485.0
12/13	969.2	69.2	7.1%	5,177.0
12/12	936.0	64.1	6.8%	5,176.0
12/11	866.2	60.2	7.0%	4,682.0
Annual Growth	**8.1%**	**18.0%**	**—**	**7.3%**

2015 Year-End Financials

Debt ratio: 10.0%
Return on equity: 16.4%
Cash ($ mil.): 8.6
Current ratio: 3.05
Long-term debt ($ mil.): 112.0

No. of shares (mil.): 80.9
Dividends
Yield: 0.9%
Payout: 16.5%
Market value ($ mil.): 1,962.0

	STOCK PRICE ($) FY Close	P/E High/Low		Earnings	PER SHARE ($) Dividends	Book Value
12/15	24.23	24	16	1.42	0.24	9.12
12/14	33.66	27	14	1.25	0.30	8.28
12/13	18.34	21	17	0.86	0.24	6.88
12/12	14.63	23	18	0.80	0.74	6.15
12/11	15.64	27	17	0.74	0.24	6.00
Annual Growth	**11.6%**	**—**	**—**	**17.7%**	**(0.0%)**	**11.0%**

Korn/Ferry International (DE)

High-level executives can jump ship via Korn/Ferry International. The world's largest executive recruitment firm Korn/Ferry has almost 75 offices in more than 35 countries. The company's more than 600 consultants help prominent public and private companies as well as government and not-for-profit organizations find qualified job applicants for openings in a variety of executive level positions (including CEOs CFOs and other senior-level jobs). Through Futurestep job seekers use the Internet and videotaped job interviews to find mid-level management positions. In addition the company provides management assessment as well as coaching and executive development services. Korn/Ferry was founded in 1969.

After an unprofitable 2009 Korn/Ferry seems to have bounced back on the heels of the recession. In addition to its net income skyrocketing from $5.3 million in 2010 to almost $59 million in 2011 the company saw its revenue levels increase almost 30% from $600 million to $776 million during that same time period.

The company works with more than 4700 global clients including about 47% of the Fortune 500. Throughout 2011 placements within the industrial consumer and financial services sectors collectively accounted for almost 64% of its total assignments. It relies heavily on customer loyalty with almost 75% of work coming from previous clients each year. Korn/Ferry is also focused on broadening its product and service offerings especially its mid-level recruitment operations. These

operations accounted for 26% of its overall revenue in 2011.

Over the years the company has relied on acquisitions to expand its domestic and international footprints and beef up its executive search and coaching services operations. In 2013 Korn/Ferry acquired the Minneapolis-based management consulting firm PDI Ninth House for about $80 million plus up to $15 million more based on future results. Previously in early 2010 Korn/Ferry enhanced its position in a new market when it acquired Sensa Solutions a management consulting company providing executive coaching training and strategic planning services to the federal government.

In mid-2009 Korn/Ferry expanded its core business in Europe with the acquisition of rival executive search firm Whitehead Mann for undisclosed terms. UK-based Whitehead Mann also brought strengths in the Middle East Asia Africa Australia and North America.

HISTORY

Korn/Ferry was founded in 1969 by Lester Korn and Richard Ferry. A year later the firm debuted its first specialty division a unit serving the national real estate industry. Its specialization approach was a unique (and successful) slant on the practice of headhunting and the company soon added more specialties. Korn/Ferry went public in 1972; it also expanded overseas with offices in Brussels and London that year and in Tokyo a year later. Volatile stock prices became a distraction to the two founders so in 1974 they took the company private by repurchasing all its stock. Korn/Ferry moved into Latin America in 1977 by acquiring 49% of Hazzard & Associates.

By 1980 steady growth had made Korn/Ferry one of the top headhunting firms in the country. A decade later the firm established a foothold in central Europe by opening an office in Budapest Hungary; it further strengthened its old-country presence by acquiring European search firm Carre/Orban (at the time it was the largest merger in search firm history). Traditionally a search firm for high-level executives Korn/Ferry pushed into the middle management arena in 1998 with its Internet-based Futurestep service. Also that year former COO Windle Priem took over the company from Michael Boxberger who left after 19 months.

Korn/Ferry went public again in 1999. The following year it acquired online college recruitment service JobDirect. In 2001 Priem stepped down as president and CEO and was replaced by Paul Reilly former CEO of KPMG International. Also that year in an effort to strengthen its Web offerings the company cobranded its Futurestep site with online giant Yahoo! Later in 2001 Korn/Ferry cut 500 jobs or 20% of its workforce and reduced salaries. It also reorganized management and closed JobDirect. In 2002 and 2003 the company continued reducing its workforce and streamlining its operations.

Over the next few years Korn/Ferry expanded beyond its traditional executive recruitment services (by beefing up its management assessment business among others). In 2006 Korn/Ferry primarily focusing on its information technology products portfolio launched its K/F One software platform. The product aggregates Microsoft Outlook the Internet and proprietary Korn/Ferry software. Keeping this focus on technology the company acquired Lominger Limited a provider of leadership development software for $24 million later in the year.

Gary Burnison the company's former COO and CFO took over the reins as CEO in mid-2007 while Reilly remained chairman.

To further boost its leadership and talent consulting business Korn/Ferry in late 2008 acquired Lore International a provider of leadership development executive education and coaching services that has offices in the US and Europe.

EXECUTIVES

President Global Productized Services, Andrew Huddart, age 48
President Asia Pacific Executive Search, Charles Tseng
President Global Industrial Market Executive Search, Yannick Binvel
EVP CFO and Chief Corporate Officer, Robert P. Rozek, age 55, $516,667 total compensation
President CEO and Director, Gary D. Burnison, age 55, $910,000 total compensation
President Financial Executive Search, Michael Franzino, age 66
CEO Futurestep, Byrne K. Mulrooney, age 55, $450,000 total compensation
SVP Chief Marketing Officer and President Korn Ferry Institute, Michael Distefano
President Asia Pacific Futurestep, Chong Ng
President Life Sciences Executive Search, Jay Kizer
CEO Korn Ferry Hay Group, Stephen Kaye, $187,500 total compensation
Managing Director Zurich and Senior Client Partner Consumer, Dominique Virchaux
President Technology Executive Search, Werner Penk
EVP Global Human Resources, Linda Hyman
President Europe Middle East and Africa (EMEA) and Chair Global Industrial and Consumer Markets Executive Search, Bernard S. Zen-Ruffinen
President Americas Executive Search, Doug Charles
SVP and CIO, Bryan Ackermann
Vice President Finance, Masao Sasaki
Vice President of Sales Information Technology, Mike (Mikey) Carlin
Vice President Finance And Assistant Controller, Erika Joseph
Senior Vice President of Finance and Corporate Controller, Mark (Marky) Neal
Senior Vice President Solution Management and Marketing, Sean Klunder
Vice President, Roy Dar
Vice President Internal Audit, Tom (Tommy) Saletta
Vice President Global Compensation And Benefits, Marat Fookson
Global Vice President Service Offering and Business Development, David (Dave) Grant
Vice President Software Development, Sanitourian Armen
Dish Networks Vice President Product Management, Cody Spencer
Senior Vice President Corporate Development, Brian Suh
Senior Vice President, Harry Brull
Senior Vice President LTC Global Client Services, Karin (Ren) Lucas
Senior Vice President Finance Treasury Tax Investor Relations, Gregg (Greggory) Kvochak
Chairman, George T. Shaheen, age 71
Vice Chairman and Senior Client Partner, Melanie (Mel) Kusin
Auditors: Ernst & Young LLP

LOCATIONS

HQ: Korn/Ferry International (DE)
1900 Avenue of the Stars, Suite 2600, Los Angeles, CA 90067
Phone: 310 552-1834
Web: www.kornferry.com

PRODUCTS/OPERATIONS

2016 Sales

	$ mil.	% of total
Executive Search		
North America	371.3	28
EMEA	144.3	11
Asia Pacific	80.5	6
Latin America	26.7	2
Hay Group	471.2	35
Futurestep	198.1	15
Reimbursed out-of-pocket engagement expense	54.6	3
Total	**1,346.7**	**100**

Solutions
Assessment & Succession
Board & CEO Services
Employer Branding
Executive Search
Leadership Development
Professional Search
Recruitment Process Outsourcing
Rewards & Benefits
Strategy Execution & Organization Design
Talent Strategy & Organizational Alignment
Workforce performance Inclusion & Diversity

COMPETITORS

A.T. Kearney	Handler & Associates
CCL	Heidrick & Struggles
CTPartners	J.C. Wilson Associates
Development Dimensions International	PageGroup
Diversified Search	Russell Reynolds
Egon Zehnder	Solomon Page
Gap International	Spencer Stuart

HISTORICAL FINANCIALS

Company Type: Public

Income Statement
FYE: April 30

	REVENUE ($ mil.)	NET INCOME ($ mil.)	NET PROFIT MARGIN	EMPLOYEES
04/16	1,346.7	30.9	2.3%	6,947.0
04/15	1,066.0	88.3	8.3%	3,687.0
04/14	995.5	72.6	7.3%	3,396.0
04/13	849.7	33.2	3.9%	3,272.0
04/12	826.7	54.3	6.6%	2,654.0
Annual Growth	**13.0%**	**(13.1%)**	**—**	**27.2%**

2016 Year-End Financials

Debt ratio: 7.3%
Return on equity: 3.3%
Cash ($ mil.): 273.2
Current ratio: 1.39
Long-term debt ($ mil.): 110.0

No. of shares (mil.): 57.2
Dividends
Yield: 0.0%
Payout: 68.9%
Market value ($ mil.): 1,554.0

	STOCK PRICE ($) FY Close	P/E High/Low	PER SHARE ($) Earnings	Dividends	Book Value
04/16	27.14	66 44	0.58	0.40	18.25
04/15	31.53	19 14	1.76	0.10	16.12
04/14	29.05	20 10	1.48	0.00	15.17
04/13	16.55	27 18	0.70	0.00	13.63
04/12	16.15	20 10	1.15	0.00	13.14
Annual Growth	**13.9%**	**— —**	**(15.7%)**	**—**	**8.6%**

La Quinta Holdings Inc

Auditors: Deloitte & Touche LLP

LOCATIONS

HQ: La Quinta Holdings Inc
909 Hidden Ridge, Suite 600, Irving, TX 75038
Phone: 214 492-6600
Web: www.LQ.com

HISTORICAL FINANCIALS

Company Type: Public

Income Statement
FYE: December 31

	REVENUE ($ mil.)	NET INCOME ($ mil.)	NET PROFIT MARGIN	EMPLOYEES
12/15	1,029.9	26.3	2.6%	7,426.0
12/14	976.9	(337.3)	—	7,719.0
12/13	873.8	3.9	0.5%	7,621.0
12/12	818.0	(30.9)	—	0.0
12/11	751.5	63.5	8.5%	0.0
Annual Growth	**8.2%**	**(19.7%)**	**—**	**—**

2015 Year-End Financials

Debt ratio: 57.3%
Return on equity: 3.4%
Cash ($ mil.): 86.7
Current ratio: 1.07
Long-term debt ($ mil.): 1,694.5

No. of shares (mil.): 124.3
Dividends
Yield: —
Payout: —
Market value ($ mil.): 1,692.0

	STOCK PRICE ($) FY Close	P/E High/Low	PER SHARE ($) Earnings	Dividends	Book Value
12/15	13.61	119 65	0.20	0.00	5.98
12/14	22.06	— —	(2.67)	0.00	6.16
Annual Growth	**(38.3%)**	**— —**	**—**	**—**	**(2.9%)**

Landmark Bancorp Inc

Landmark Bancorp is a tourist attraction for Kansas money. It is the holding company for Landmark National Bank which has about 15 branches in communities in central eastern and southwestern Kansas. The bank provides standard commercial banking products including checking savings and money market accounts as well as CDs and credit and debit cards. It primarily uses funds from deposits to write residential and commercial mortgages and business loans. Landmark National Bank offers non-deposit investment services through its affiliation with Investment Planners.

The company has been expanding in its region for several years through acquisitions. It now covers more than a dozen Kansas counties.

President and CEO Patrick Alexander owns more than 5% of Landmark Bancorp. Chairman Larry Schugart owns another 5%.

EXECUTIVES

Vice President, Marsha Kemper
Auditors: Crowe Chizek LLP

LOCATIONS

HQ: Landmark Bancorp Inc
701 Poyntz Avenue, Manhattan, KS 66502
Phone: 785 565-2000
Web: www.landmarkbancorpinc.com

COMPETITORS

Bank of America	First Independence
Blue Valley Ban Corp.	INTRUST
Capitol Federal	U.S. Bancorp
Financial	UMB Financial
Commerce Bancshares	

HISTORICAL FINANCIALS

Company Type: Public

Income Statement

FYE: December 31

	ASSETS ($ mil.)	NET INCOME ($ mil.)	INCOME AS % OF ASSETS	EMPLOYEES
12/15	878.3	10.5	1.2%	291.0
12/14	863.4	8.0	0.9%	277.0
12/13	828.7	4.6	0.6%	292.0
12/12	614.0	6.3	1.0%	215.0
12/11	598.2	4.4	0.7%	216.0
Annual Growth	10.1%	23.7%	—	7.7%

2015 Year-End Financials

Return on assets: 1.2%	Dividends
Return on equity: 13.8%	Yield: 2.7%
Long-term debt ($ mil.): —	Payout: 24.8%
No. of shares (mil.): 3.7	Market value ($ mil.): 97.0
Sales ($ mil): 46.1	

	STOCK PRICE ($) FY Close	P/E High/Low		PER SHARE ($) Earnings	Dividends	Book Value
12/15	26.27	10	7	2.77	0.69	21.73
12/14	21.18	11	9	2.16	0.66	19.50
12/13	19.60	17	14	1.29	0.63	17.24
12/12	19.89	12	10	1.78	0.60	17.83
12/11	18.70	17	12	1.26	0.57	16.65
Annual Growth	8.9%	—	—	21.7%	5.0%	6.9%

Lannett Co., Inc.

Lannett banks on the designation of "bioequivalent" for its products. The firm develops manufactures packages markets and distributes generic prescription drugs in the US including thyroid treatment levothyroxine digoxin for congestive heart failure migraine drug butalbital and ursodiol for gallstones. Such medicines are pharmaceutical equivalents or bioequivalents of branded medicines made by other drug companies. While Lannett maintains two plants it also relies on manufacturer Jerome Stevens Pharmaceuticals for a significant portion of its inventories. The company produces medicines in oral solid (tablets liquids and capsules) and topical dosages forms.

Operations

Two of Lannett's product lines levothyroxine sodium and digoxin collectively accounted for 50% of the company's net sales in fiscal year 2015 (ended June). Both of the top products are primarily manufactured by Jerome Stevens Pharmaceuticals.

Pain management products include Cocaine Topical Solution which is primarily used during ear nose or throat surgery; Morphine Sulfate oral Solution for pain in adults; and Oxycodone HCl Oral Solution for moderate to moderately severe pain. Through the 2015 acquisition of Silarx Pharmaceuticals Lannett added several more pain management products.

Sales and Marketing

Lannett's customers include the big wholesale US pharmaceutical distributors as well as group purchasing organizations chain drug stores and other pharmaceutical companies. Top customers include AmerisourceBergen (30% of net sales in fiscal 2015) McKesson (11%) and Cardinal Health (7%).

Lannett employs a direct sales force; it also promotes products through trade shows and publications.

Financial Performance

Revenues rose modestly in fiscal 2012 and 2013 and dramatically in 2014 and 2015. In fiscal 2015 (ended June) revenue increased 49% to $407 million largely due to tremendous growth in gallstone treatments. This in turn was driven by price increases for Ursodiol. Other treatment areas that saw growth that year included migraine glaucoma and thyroid deficiency; a new muscle relaxant product also helped revenue.

Net income which has also been on the rise rose 162% to $150 million in fiscal 2015. Higher revenue led to that growth but was partially offset by higher operating expenses and reduced gains on investments.

Following suit cash flow from operations increased 185% to $128 million in 2015.

Strategy

Like any drug developer Lannett maintains a steady stream of potential drugs in its pipeline. New product introductions are key to keeping ahead of its competitors and as such the firm focuses on developing products with few or no generic competitors. The company maintains its own R&D staff partners with third-party developers and sometimes simply purchases new products from other generic makers or buys other pharmaceutical companies outright.

In 2015 the company's newly acquired subsidiary Silarx Pharmaceuticals received FDA approval for its generic version of antidepressant Abilify. This followed the 2014 approval of Lannett's generic versions of Novartis' Femara Tablets (for treatment of breast cancer) and Lehigh Valley Technology's Oxycodone Hydrochloride Oral Solution.One of the company's focus areas of development is the market of narcotics and controlled substances as Lannett believes the demand for pain medicine will continue to increase as the Baby Boomer generation ages. Lannett is also looking to grow in new specialty fields of medicine as well as new dosage formulations (such as ophthalmic or nasal products) through strategic relationships or acquisitions.Lannett signed an agreement with Symplmed in mid-2014 through which Symplmed became the exclusive US distributor of Lannett's generic version of ACEON a treatment for high blood pressure.In early 2016 Lannett made a number of changes to cut costs including cutting 10% of its total staff (with plans to ultimately cut 20% over the next three years). It also closed the Princeton New Jersey corporate offices of the recently acquired Kremers Urban Pharmaceuticals. The restructuring efforts which aim to streamline and consolidate operations are expected to generate some $40 million in savings within 12 months.Mergers and AcquisitionsIn 2015 Lannett bought Kremers Urban Pharmaceuticals for $1.23

billion. Formerly the US generics business of Belgian firm UCB Kremers makes treatments for such ailments as ADHD and gastroesophageal reflux. The deal is one of several that have been announced or completed in the generics arena which is growing in importance as more drugs lose patent protection.Also that year the company acquired New York-based Silarx Pharmaceuticals for $42.5 million. Silarx makes and markets liquid pharmaceutical products including generic and over-the-counter products.Company BackgroundFormed in 1942 Lannett is one of the oldest generics manufacturers in the US.

EXECUTIVES

CEO, Arthur P. Bedrosian, age 71, $555,170 total compensation
VP Sales and Marketing, Kevin R. Smith, age 57, $286,340 total compensation
VP Logistics and CIO, Robert Ehlinger, age 60, $170,000 total compensation
VP Finance CFO and Treasurer, Martin P. Galvan, age 65, $326,510 total compensation
Vice President Quality, John (Jack) Abt
Chairman, William Farber, age 85
Vice Chairman, Jeffrey K. Farber, age 57
Auditors: Grant Thornton, LLP

LOCATIONS

HQ: Lannett Co., Inc.
9000 State Road, Philadelphia, PA 19136
Phone: 215 333-9000
Web: www.lannett.com

PRODUCTS/OPERATIONS

2015 Sales

	$ mil.	% of total
Wholesalers	297.7	73
Retail chains	65.1	16
Mail-order pharmacy	44.0	11
Total	**406.8**	**100**

2015 Sales

	$ mil % of total
Thyroid Deficiency	38
Gallstone	16
Cardiovascular	14
Migraine	6
Pain management	6
Glaucoma	5
Antibiotic	3
Gout	2
Muscle Relaxant	2
Obesity	1
Other	7
Total	**100**

Selected Products

Amantadine (generic Symmetrel Parkinson's Disease)
Butalbital (generic Fiorinal migraine)
Clindamycin (generic Cleocin antibiotic)
C-Topical solution (anesthetic)
Danazol (generic Danocrine endometriosis)
Dicyclomine (generic Bentyl irritable bowel syndrome)
Diethylpropion (generic Tenuate obesity)
Digoxin (generic Lanoxin congestive heart failure)
Doxycycline (generic Adoxa antibiotic)
Fluphenazine (generic Proxlixin antipsychotic)
Hydromorphone (generic Dilaudid pain management)
Levothyroxine (generic Levoxyl thyroid deficiency)
Loxapine (generic Loxitane antipsychotic)
Morphine sulfate (pain)
Oxycodone (generic Roxicodone pain management)
Phentermine (generic Adipex obesity)
Pilocarpine (generic Salagen dry mouth)
Primidone (generic Mysoline epilepsy)
Probenecid (generic Benemid gout)

Rifampin (generic Rifadin antibiotic for meningitis)
Terbutaline (generic Brethine bronchospasms)
Triamterene with hydrochlorothiazide (generic Byazide hypertension)
Unithroid (thyroid deficiency)
Ursodiol (generic Actigall gallstone)

COMPETITORS

Abbott Labs	Mylan
Akorn	Obagi Medical
Allergan plc	Par Pharmaceutical
Chiesi USA	Companies
Cumberland	Pfizer
Pharmaceuticals	Purdue Pharma
Derma Sciences	Roxane Laboratories
GlaxoSmithKline	Salix Pharmaceuticals
Hi-Tech Pharmacal	Sandoz International
IMPAX Laboratories	GmbH
Jazz Pharmaceuticals	SciClone
Momenta	Teva
Pharmaceuticals	

HISTORICAL FINANCIALS

Company Type: Public

Income Statement   FYE: June 30

	REVENUE ($ mil.)	NET INCOME ($ mil.)	NET PROFIT MARGIN	EMPLOYEES
06/16	542.4	44.7	8.3%	1,149.0
06/15	406.8	149.9	36.8%	502.0
06/14	273.7	57.1	20.9%	399.0
06/13	151.0	13.3	8.8%	356.0
06/12	122.9	3.9	3.2%	324.0
Annual Growth	44.9%	83.5%	—	37.2%

2016 Year-End Financials

Debt ratio: 60.1%	No. of shares (mil.): 36.6
Return on equity: 8.7%	Dividends
Cash ($ mil.): 224.7	Yield: —
Current ratio: 2.00	Payout: —
Long-term debt ($ mil.): 883.6	Market value ($ mil.): 871.0

	STOCK PRICE ($) FY Close	P/E High/Low	PER SHARE ($) Earnings	Dividends	Book Value
06/16	23.79	51 14	1.20	0.00	15.14
06/15	59.44	17 8	4.04	0.00	12.78
06/14	49.62	29 7	1.62	0.00	8.28
06/13	11.91	27 9	0.46	0.00	4.46
06/12	4.24	37 25	0.14	0.00	3.93
Annual Growth	53.9%	— —	71.1%	—	40.1%

LaSalle Hotel Properties

LaSalle Hotel Properties is a self-administered and self-managed real estate investment trust (REIT) that invests in renovates and leases full-service luxury hotels in the US. It owns more than 45 properties in 10 states and the District of Columbia. LaSalle Hotel Properties' holdings which altogether boast more than 12000 rooms are typically located in major urban markets near convention centers business districts and resorts. The properties are managed by outside hotel companies that operate under such names as Marriott Sheraton Hilton and Hyatt. LaSalle Hotel Proper-ties became self-managing in 2001 after three years under the wing of Jones Lang LaSalle.

Operations

LaSalle Hotel Properties owned 47 hotels spanning 12000-plus guest rooms across 10 states and the District of Columbia at the end of 2015. The REIT generated 70% of its total revenue from its rooms during 2015 while another 22% came from its food and beverage revenue.

Geographic Reach

Headquartered in Maryland LaSalle Hotel Properties owns and leases luxury hotels and resorts in 10 states. Nine of its 47 hotel properties were located in Washington DC at the end of 2015 while another seven were located in San Francisco. Its other top hotel markets were in Los Angeles (six hotels) San Diego (five) Boston (four) and New York City (four).

Sales and Marketing The REIT partners with premier lodging companies through strategic relationships to grow its business. These partners include the likes of Westin Hilton Hotels Hyatt Hotels Benchmark Hospitality Commune Hotels and Resorts and Viceroy Hotel Group among others. Financial PerformanceLaSalle Hotel Properties' annual revenues have risen 70% since 2011 as property acquisitions have spurred more room income over the years. The REIT's net income has tripled over the same period as the REIT has kept its operating costs under control.LaSalle's revenue jumped 10% to $1.22 billion during 2015 almost entirely thanks to added room income stemming from 2015 and 2014 hotel acquisitions which included the Hotel Vitale The Heathman Hotel Park Central San Francisco and The Marker Waterfront Resort. The REIT's existing properties enjoyed a 3% increase in RevPAR across the portfolio thanks to a stronger US economy.Despite revenue and operating income growth in 2015 the REIT's net income fell 36% to $135.55 million for the year as in 2014 it had collected a $93.2 million gain from property sales. LaSalle's operating cash levels climbed 19% to $337.5 million during 2015 mostly thanks to higher cash-denominate earnings as well as positive working capital changes related to its accounts payable and accrued expenses and advance deposits. Strategy

LaSalle Hotel Properties works to own redevelop and reposition upscale full-service hotels that are located in urban resort and convention markets. It specifically targets hotel investments in the metropolitan markets of Boston Chicago Los Angeles New York City San Diego San Francisco Seattle and Washington DC. One of LaSalle's most recent property acquisitions include the early 2015 $350 million purchase of The Westin Market Street hotel in San Francisco which marked its seventh property in the city. Others include the $64 million acquisition of The Heathman Hotel in Portland Oregon (December 2014) and the $130 million purchase of Hotel Vitale in San Francisco (April 2014).

Company Background

In 2013 the company purchased three properties in San Francisco: the Harbor Court Hotel and Hotel Triton (both for $47.8 million) as well as the Serrano Hotel ($71.5 million). In Key West Florida LaSalle Hotel Properties acquired the 260-room Southernmost Hotel Collection for $184.5 million.

In 2012 through a joint venture (in which the company holds a 99.99% controlling interest) LaSalle Hotel Properties acquired a majority ownership interest in The Liberty Hotel for $170 million. Located in Boston the full-service luxury hotel had 298 rooms.

EXECUTIVES

President and CEO, Michael D. (Mike) Barnello, age 50, $815,000 total compensation
EVP and COO, Alfred L. Young, age 47, $510,167 total compensation
EVP CFO Secretary and Treasurer, Kenneth G. Fuller
Chairman, Stuart L. Scott, age 78
Auditors: KPMG LLP

LOCATIONS

HQ: LaSalle Hotel Properties
7550 Wisconsin Avenue, 10th Floor, Bethesda, MD 20814
Phone: 301 941-1500   Fax: 301 941-1553
Web: www.lasallehotels.com

PRODUCTS/OPERATIONS

2015 Sales

	% of total
Hotel operating revenues	
Room	70
Food & beverage	22
Other operating department	7
Other income	1
Total	100

Selected Portfolio Property Types

Convention hotels
Resorts
Urban hotels

COMPETITORS

Ashford Hospitality	Host Hotels & Resorts
Trust	Innkeepers USA
FelCor	Starwood Hotels &
Hersha Hospitality	Resorts
Hospitality Properties	Sunstone Hotel
Trust	Investors

HISTORICAL FINANCIALS

Company Type: Public

Income Statement   FYE: December 31

	REVENUE ($ mil.)	NET INCOME ($ mil.)	NET PROFIT MARGIN	EMPLOYEES
12/15	1,216.5	135.5	11.1%	35.0
12/14	1,109.7	212.8	19.2%	35.0
12/13	977.2	89.9	9.2%	36.0
12/12	867.0	71.3	8.2%	33.0
12/11	719.0	43.6	6.1%	31.0
Annual Growth	14.1%	32.8%	—	3.1%

2015 Year-End Financials

Debt ratio: 35.0%	No. of shares (mil.): 112.9
Return on equity: 5.6%	Dividends
Cash ($ mil.): 5.7	Yield: 6.8%
Current ratio: 0.27	Payout: 158.2%
Long-term debt ($ mil.): 1,429.7	Market value ($ mil.): 2,842.0

	STOCK PRICE ($) FY Close	P/E High/Low	PER SHARE ($) Earnings	Dividends	Book Value
12/15	25.16	40 23	1.09	1.73	21.02
12/14	40.47	22 15	1.88	1.41	21.64
12/13	30.86	44 32	0.73	0.96	20.23
12/12	25.39	58 43	0.52	0.71	19.42
12/11	24.21	184 98	0.16	0.44	21.07
Annual Growth	1.0%	— —	61.6%	40.7%	(0.1%)

LCI Industries

LCI Industries (formerly Drew Industries) makes wanderlust —in comfort and style —a possibility. The company manufactures aluminum and vinyl windows and doors and other products (furniture and slide-out walls) for travel trailers and fifth-wheel recreational vehicles (RVs) (some 85% of sales) and manufactured housing (MH). LCI does business via two subsidiaries: Kinro produces windows doors and screens and Lippert Components churns out axles ramps and chassis parts as well as specialty trailers for hauling boats and snowmobiles. Brands include Equa-Flex Happijac RV Lock Solera Ground Control and Level Up.

Geographic Reach

LCI operates about 45 facilities throughout the US. About half of its manufacturing plants are concentrated in Indiana.

Operations

LCI operates through two segments: RV products and manufactured housing products (MH). About 90% of its RV segment's net sales in 2015 were of products for manufacturers of travel trailer and fifth-wheel RVs. The MH segment makes fabricating welding thermoforming painting and assembling components into finished products and operates through 13 manufacturing and warehouse facilities throughout the US.

Sales and Marketing

RV products are sold primarily to major manufacturers of RVs such as Thor Industries Forest River Jayco and other OEMs. LCI's MH products are sold primarily to major producers of manufactured homes such as Clayton Homes Cavco Industries and other OEMs. The company also sells both segments' products to distributors and retail dealers of aftermarket products.

Financial Performance

With the painful effects of the recession firmly behind it LCI has enjoyed unprecedented growth over the last five years. Revenues jumped 18% to peak at $1.4 billion in 2015. Profits also surged 19% to reach $74 million in 2015. (Both these totals represented historic milestones for the company.)

The historic growth for 2015 was driven by a 20% rise in RV sales thanks to an increase in industry-wide wholesale shipments of travel trailer and fifth-wheel RVs the company's primary RV market. LCI also experienced a bump in MH revenue as industrywide wholesale shipments of manufactured homes increased as well as sales of components for new manufactured homes.

Mergers and Acquisitions

The company has made its mark in the RV and manufactured housing industries primarily by growing through acquisitions. As a result of the economic downturn certain distressed manufacturers have placed their assets and intellectual property rights on the sales block and LCI's subsidiaries have taken advantage of those opportunities.

In 2015 the company purchased Signature Seating an Indiana-based manufacturer of furniture products and services for freshwater boat manufacturers. It also purchased Spectal Industries a Canada-based manufacturer of windows and doors.Later in 2015 it picked up EA Technologies an Indiana-based manufacturer of custom steel and aluminum parts. EA is also a provider of electro-deposition and powder coating services for RV bus medium-duty truck automotive recreational marine specialty and utility trailer and military applications.

In 2014 LCI obtained Innovative Design Solutions (IDS) located in Troy Michigan for $36 million. IDS is a designer developer and manufacturer of electronic systems encompassing a wide variety of RV applications. The acquisition provided LCI with further access to cutting-edge electronic products for the RV industry as well as adjacent industries.

EXECUTIVES

CEO, Jason D. Lippert, age 44, $840,000 total compensation
President and COO, Scott T. Mereness, age 44, $577,500 total compensation
Interim CFO, Brian M. Hall, age 41
Chairman, James F. Gero, age 72
Auditors: KPMG LLP

LOCATIONS

HQ: LCI Industries
  3501 County Road 6 East, Elkhart, IN 46514
Phone: 574 535-1125
Web: www.drewindustries.com

PRODUCTS/OPERATIONS

2013 Sales

	$ mil.	% of total
Recreational vehicles	893.7	88
Manufactured housing	121.9	12
Total	**1,015.6**	**100**

Selected Products

Manufactured housing (MH) products
  Aluminum and vinyl patio doors
  Axles
  Entry doors
  Steel and fiberglass entry doors
  Steel chassis
  Steel chassis parts
  Replacement windows doors thermoformed bath products
  Thermoformed bath and kitchen products
  Vinyl and aluminum windows and screens
Recreational vehicle (RV) products (travel trailers and fifth-wheel RVs)
  Aluminum windows and screens
  Chassis components
  Entry and baggage doors
  Entry steps
  Furniture and mattresses
  Manual electric and hydraulic stabilizer and lifting systems
  Patio doors
  Slide-out mechanisms
  Specialty trailers for hauling boats personal watercraft snowmobiles and equipment
  Thermoformed bath kitchen and other products
  Towable axles and suspensions
  Towable steel chassis
  Toy hauler ramp doors

COMPETITORS

Atwood Mobile	Meritor
Coast Distribution	Patrick Industries
Elixir Industries	Quality Trailer
Euramax	Products
Featherlite	Tuthill
LaSalle Bristol	Wozniak Industries

HISTORICAL FINANCIALS

Company Type: Public

Income Statement

FYE: December 31

	REVENUE ($ mil.)	NET INCOME ($ mil.)	NET PROFIT MARGIN	EMPLOYEES
12/15	1,403.0	74.3	5.3%	6,576.0
12/14	1,190.7	62.2	5.2%	5,845.0
12/13	1,015.5	50.1	4.9%	5,109.0
12/12	901.1	37.3	4.1%	5,179.0
12/11	681.1	30.0	4.4%	4,130.0
Annual Growth	**19.8%**	**25.4%**	**—**	**12.3%**

2015 Year-End Financials

Debt ratio: 8.0%	No. of shares (mil.): 24.3
Return on equity: 17.8%	Dividends
Cash ($ mil.): 12.3	Yield: 3.2%
Current ratio: 2.72	Payout: 66.2%
Long-term debt ($ mil.): 50.0	Market value ($ mil.): 1,483.0

	STOCK PRICE ($) FY Close	P/E High/Low		PER SHARE ($) Earnings	Dividends	Book Value
12/15	60.89	21	16	3.02	2.00	18.01
12/14	51.07	21	16	2.56	0.00	16.56
12/13	51.20	25	15	2.11	2.00	13.42
12/12	32.25	20	15	1.64	2.00	12.53
12/11	24.53	20	13	1.34	0.00	12.52
Annual Growth	**25.5%**	**—**	**—**	**22.5%**	**—**	**9.5%**

LegacyTexas Financial Group Inc

With its eye on the Lone Star State LegacyTexas Financial (formerly ViewPoint Financial) provides retail and commercial banking through its LegacyTexas Bank subsidiary which operates about 50 branches located mostly in the Dallas/Fort Worth area. LegacyTexas offers standard deposit products such as checking and savings accounts and CDs and uses deposit funds to originate primarily real estate loans: Commercial Real Estate loans account for nearly 50% of its lending portfolio while consumer real estate loans make up another nearly 20%. Non-real estate commercial loans make up almost 30% of its loan portfolio.

OperationsOutside of banking services the LegacyTexas offers brokerage services to buy and sell investments and insurance products through a third-party brokerage arrangement.About 82% of the company's total revenue came from loan interest (including fees) in 2014 and another 6% came from interest on its taxable and non-taxable securities. Most of LegacyTexas' remaining revenue came from service charges and fees on deposit accounts.Geographic ReachThe Plano-based company boasts 51 Texas branches with 48 of them located in the Dallas-Fort Worth Metroplex. Its two First National Bank of Jacksboro branches are in Jack in Wise counties in Texas. Sales and MarketingLegacyTexas' serves a diverse market of management professional and sales personnel office employees manufacturing and transportation workers service industry workers government employees and self-employed individuals. It spent

$1.54 million on advertising in 2014 compared to $2.69 million and $1.75 million in 2013 and 2012 respectively.Financial PerformanceThe company has struggled to consistently grow its revenues and profits in recent years despite growing loan business mostly stemming from lost revenues from the sale of its mortgage-banking subsidiary in 2012.LegacyTexas' revenue rebounded by 7% to $31.3 million in 2014 primarily thanks to double-digit growth in its loan interest income driven by higher commercial loan volume. Despite higher revenue in 2014 the company's net income dipped by 1% to $31.3 million mostly due to higher loan loss provisions as commercial loan production picked up. LegacyTexas' operating cash levels fell by 21% to $52 million mostly from unfavorable changes in working capital related to its assets and liabilities. StrategyThe company formerly known as ViewPoint Financial significantly boosted its loan and deposit business and the size of its branch network through its early 2015 acquisition LegacyTexas Group. The deal made its branch network swell to 48 offices from just 31 before while adding some $1.63 billion in deposits and $1.4 billion in new loan business.The new LegacyTexas Group planned in 2015 to organically grow its loan portfolio focusing especially on making commercial real estate commercial and industrial and energy loans tied to high-quality assets. To cheaply raise funding for loans the bank plans to promote its non-interest-bearing demand deposit accounts especially in the commercial sector and using its treasury management services to provide a "catalyst for deposit growth."Mergers and Acquisitions

In January 2015 the former ViewPoint Financial acquired LegacyTexas Group in a $300 million deal to create one of the largest independent banks in Texas with assets of nearly $6 billion. The parent company then changed its name to LegacyTexas Financial and the bank changed its name to LegacyTexas Bank.Company BackgroundLegacyTexas Financial converted from a mutual holding company to a stock holding company in 2010. It sold its mortgage subsidiary VPM which operated a dozen loan production offices in Texas and Oklahoma in late 2012.

EXECUTIVES

EVP Chief Lending Officer, Thomas S. Swiley, age 66, $277,300 total compensation

EVP COO Chief Risk Officer and General Counsel, Scott A. Almy, age 49, $277,300 total compensation

President CEO and Director, Kevin J. Hanigan, age 59, $549,450 total compensation

EVP Community Banking, Charles D. Eikenberg, age 61, $277,300 total compensation

EVP and CFO, J. Mays Davenport, age 48

Vice President, Jamie (James) Richardson

Chairman, Anthony J. LeVecchio, age 69

Vice Chairman, George Fisk

Auditors: Ernst & Young LLP

LOCATIONS

HQ: LegacyTexas Financial Group Inc
5851 Legacy Circle, Plano, TX 75024
Phone: 972 578-5000
Web: www.viewpointfinancialgroup.com

PRODUCTS/OPERATIONS

2014 Sales

	% of total
Interest and dividend income	88
Non interest income	12
Total	**100**

COMPETITORS

Amegy	PlainsCapital
BBVA Compass	SP Bancorp
Bancshares	Texas Capital
Bank of America	Bancshares
Cullen/Frost Bankers	Wells Fargo
North Dallas Bank	

HISTORICAL FINANCIALS

Company Type: Public

Income Statement

FYE: December 31

	ASSETS ($ mil.)	NET INCOME ($ mil.)	INCOME AS % OF ASSETS	EMPLOYEES
12/15	7,691.9	70.9	0.9%	856.0
12/14	4,164.1	31.2	0.8%	530.0
12/13	3,525.2	31.6	0.9%	576.0
12/12	3,663.0	35.2	1.0%	572.0
12/11	3,180.5	26.3	0.8%	598.0
Annual Growth	**24.7%**	**28.1%**	**—**	**9.4%**

2015 Year-End Financials

Return on assets: 1.2%	Dividends
Return on equity: 10.3%	Yield: 2.1%
Long-term debt ($ mil.): —	Payout: 41.2%
No. of shares (mil.): 47.6	Market value ($ mil.): 1,192.0
Sales ($ mil): 307.5	

	STOCK PRICE ($) FY Close	P/E High/Low	PER SHARE ($) Earnings	Dividends	Book Value
12/15	25.02	21 13	1.53	0.54	16.88
12/14	23.85	36 26	0.81	0.48	14.20
12/13	27.45	33 22	0.83	0.42	13.63
12/12	20.94	22 13	0.98	0.40	13.15
12/11	13.01	17 13	0.81	0.20	12.06
Annual Growth	**17.8%**	**— —**	**17.2%**	**28.2%**	**8.8%**

LendingTree Inc (New)

LendingTree (formerly Tree.com) helps consumers cut through a forest of options in financing education insurance home services and more. The company allows users to comparison shop for home loans through its most prominent branch LendingTree which helps match home buyers with lenders. Its lending network includes over 350 banks and other lenders. Other subsidiaries help consumers choose between colleges and home service providers. LendingTree also markets auto loans and credit cards. Services are free to consumers as the firm collects fees from the companies to which it refers business.

OperationsLendingTree operates four main business segments: Lending for consumers seeking home mortgage loans lines of credit reverse mortgages and personal loans; Auto which includes its auto refinance and purchase loan products; Education which includes a student enrollment product and student loan products; and Home Services which helps consumers research and find home improvement professional services through its marketplace of local and national contractors. Overall 80% of the company's total revenue in 2014 came from mortgage products while nonmortgage lending products (such as personal loans home equity reverse mortgages and credit cards) made up another 12%.Sales and Market-

ingThe online company has been ramping up its advertising in recent years. It spent $102.2 million on advertising in 2014 up from $80.7 million and $40.8 million in 2013 and 2012 respectively.Financial PerformanceLendingTree's revenues have more than tripled since 2011 thanks to a strengthened housing market which has driven more demand for its mortgage loan marketplace services. Its profits have also trended higher with business growth. (Note: The company's profit spiked in 2012 thanks to significant gains from the $56 million sale of its LendingTree Loans business to Discover.)The firm's revenue jumped 20% to $167.4 million in 2014 mostly thanks to strong growth in its nonmortgage lending products stemming from its 2013 introduction of its reverse mortgage credit card and personal loan products. Mortgage lending product revenue also rose by 9% on notable increases in its purchase product supported by growth of its rate table offering launched in early 2013. The number of consumers matched on its lending marketplace spiked by 64% during the year though its average revenue earned from marketplace lenders per matched customer fell by 26% as more users went for lower-margin non-mortgage lending products.Higher revenue in 2014 allowed the company's net income to more than double to $9.4 million. LendingTree's operating cash levels fell by 11% to $9.1 million due to unfavorable changes in working capital related mostly to its accounts payable accrued expenses and other current liabilities balances.StrategyLendingTree regularly introduces new products across new markets to keep consumers interested. In mid-2015 expanding beyond its mortgage-related wheelhouse LendingTree launched its new personal loan rates product which allowed consumers to shop among multiple lenders for personal loans. In 2014 the company introduced its new Small Business Loan marketplace (which included peer-to-peer lenders) and an online marketplace for car shoppers (via autos.lendingtree.com) to shop more than 2.5 million new and used cars and find auto financing through its marketplace services.

The company also releases new tools to keep visitors coming back to its website. In 2014 the company relaunched its My LendingTree platform that offered personalized loan comparison shopping free credit scores credit score analysis and an in-depth review of a consumer's credit profile.Company Background

The company's roots formed with LendingTree which was founded by CEO Doug Lebda in 1996 and acquired by IAC/InterActiveCorp (IAC) in 2003. Five years later IAC spun off LendingTree and three other subsidiaries: ILG Ticketmaster and HSN. As part of the spinoff Tree.com was formed to operate LendingTree along with its other lending and real estate businesses as a separate publicly traded company.

EXECUTIVES

Chairman and CEO, Douglas R. (Doug) Lebda, age 46, $423,077 total compensation

General Manager and COO, Greg Hanson, age 46, $200,000 total compensation

President LendingTree Loans, David Norris, age 50, $400,000 total compensation

CFO, Alexander Mandel

Auditors: PricewaterhouseCoopers LLP

LOCATIONS

HQ: LendingTree Inc (New)
11115 Rushmore Drive, Charlotte, NC 28277
Phone: 704 541-5351
Web: www.tree.com

PRODUCTS/OPERATIONS

2014 Sales

	$ mil.	% of total
Lending		
Mortgage Products	134.2	80
Non-mortgage Products	20.4	12
Others	12.8	8
Total	**167.4**	**100**

Selected Brands

DegreeTree.com
DoneRight.com
GetSmart.com
HealthTree.com
InsuranceTree.com
LendingTreeAutos.com
LendingTree.com
ServiceTree.com

COMPETITORS

Bankrate	XO Group
Internet Brands	ditech

HISTORICAL FINANCIALS

Company Type: Public

Income Statement

FYE: December 31

	REVENUE ($ mil.)	NET INCOME ($ mil.)	NET PROFIT MARGIN	EMPLOYEES
12/15	254.2	48.0	18.9%	312.0
12/14	167.3	9.3	5.6%	218.0
12/13	139.2	3.9	2.8%	192.0
12/12	77.4	46.6	60.2%	174.0
12/11	54.6	(59.5)	—	135.0
Annual Growth	**46.9%**	**—**	**—**	**23.3%**

2015 Year-End Financials

Debt ratio: —
Return on equity: 28.4%
Cash ($ mil.): 206.9
Current ratio: 4.55
Long-term debt ($ mil.): —

No. of shares (mil.): 12.3
Dividends
Yield: —
Payout: —
Market value ($ mil.): 1,106.0

	STOCK PRICE ($) FY Close	P/E High/Low		PER SHARE ($) Earnings	Dividends	Book Value
12/15	89.28	33	10	3.83	0.00	19.46
12/14	48.34	57	28	0.84	0.00	8.46
12/13	32.84	91	45	0.36	0.00	7.73
12/12	18.03	4	1	4.12	1.00	7.25
12/11	5.59	—	—	(5.41)	0.00	4.12
Annual Growth	**99.9%**	**—**	**—**	**—**	**—**	**47.5%**

LGI Homes, Inc.

LGI Homes wants everyone to stop wasting money on rent. Targeting first-time homebuyers the residential builder develops homes that appeal to renters looking to buy an affordable home in Texas Florida the Southwest the Southeast or the Northwest. During 2015 its homes were priced between $110000 and $475000 and ranged from 1100 to 4000 sq. ft. with each home selling for an average price of $185100. The builder's higher-quality Terrata Homes started at $350000 for a 2500 sq. ft. home. LGI Homes has sold more than 12000 homes since its founding in 2003. It went public in 2013.

OperationsThe builder operates five segments organized by region: Texas Florida the Southwest (Arizona Colorado New Mexico) the Southeast (Florida Georgia North Carolina South Carolina) the Northwest (Washington).Geographic ReachThe Woodlands Texas-based LGI Homes builds in 20 states with its largest state market being in Texas (particularly around the major cities) where it made 56% of its total sales during 2015. Its next largest market was Florida (especially in Tampa and Orlando) which accounted for 12% of sales. The rest of its sales came from states in the Southwest (17% of sales) Southeast (15%) and the Northwest (less than 1%).Sales and MarketingThe homebuilder targets mostly home and apartment renters and markets products through print and digital advertising including direct mail newspaper ads social media and interactive online media as well as via directional signage and billboards.It's been ramping up its advertising and direct mail spend in recent years to support sales growth. The builder spent $9.3 million on advertising and direct mail during 2015 up from $8.6 million and $3.3 million in 2014 and 2013 respectively.Financial PerformanceLGI's annual sales and profits have swelled more than ten-fold since 2011 as it's expanded into more states and as the housing market has heated up with higher home prices and more demand.The homebuilder's sales spiked 64% to a record $630.24 million during 2015 mostly thanks to a 45% rise in home closings (which totaled 3404 home deliveries for the year) but also because its average home sale prices increased by 13.8% to $185146 per home thanks to product mix changes higher price points in new markets and a more favorable environment for growing home prices. Its Oakmont acquisition which led to 269 more home closing during the year also helped boost total sales.Strong revenue growth in 2015 drove LGI Homes' net income up 87% to a record $53 million. While the homebuilder's operations used $89 million in cash for the year toward building its land inventory to support future home sales it spent about half as much cash as in 2014 as it eased up on inventory purchases. StrategyLGI Homes continued in 2016 to focus on acquiring land lots and building in its core markets which include Houston San Antonio Dallas/Fort Worth Austin Phoenix Tucson Tampa Orlando Atlanta Albuquerque Charlotte and Denver. The homebuilder hopes record-high rental rates especially in these markets will entice more potential first-time homebuyers to look at its homes.Mergers and AcquisitionsIn October 2014 LGI entered the Charlotte North Carolina market after acquiring Oakmont Home Builders as well as its 150 homes under construction and 1000 owned and controlled lots for a total price of $17.3 million. Company BackgroundLGI Homes went public in 2013 raising $99 million which it used to buy back stock from investment firm GTIS Partners as well as to buy land develop lots and build more homes.

EXECUTIVES

Chairman and CEO, Eric Lipar, age 46
President and COO, Michael Snider, age 45
CFO, Charles Merdian, age 47
EVP Acquisitions, Jack Lipar, age 48
EVP and Chief Marketing Officer, Rachel Eaton, age 35
Auditors: Ernst and Young LLP

LOCATIONS

HQ: LGI Homes, Inc.
1450 Lake Robbins Drive, Suite 430, The Woodlands, TX 77380
Phone: 281 362-8998
Web: www.lgihomes.com

COMPETITORS

AV Homes	M.D.C.
Beazer Homes	M/I Homes
CalAtlantic	Meritage Homes
D.R. Horton	NVR
Drees Homes	PulteGroup
KB Home	Taylor Morrison
Lennar	Toll Brothers

HISTORICAL FINANCIALS

Company Type: Public

Income Statement

FYE: December 31

	REVENUE ($ mil.)	NET INCOME ($ mil.)	NET PROFIT MARGIN	EMPLOYEES
12/15	630.2	52.8	8.4%	489.0
12/14	383.2	28.2	7.4%	390.0
12/13	162.8	22.3	13.7%	253.0
12/12	76.2	9.7	12.7%	191.0
12/11	50.4	3.3	6.6%	0.0
Annual Growth	**88.0%**	**99.3%**	**—**	**—**

2015 Year-End Financials

Debt ratio: 49.5%
Return on equity: 24.5%
Cash ($ mil.): 37.5
Current ratio: 8.89
Long-term debt ($ mil.): 308.1

No. of shares (mil.): 20.2
Dividends
Yield: —
Payout: —
Market value ($ mil.): 493.0

	STOCK PRICE ($) FY Close	P/E High/Low		PER SHARE ($) Earnings	Dividends	Book Value
12/15	24.33	13	5	2.44	0.00	12.20
12/14	14.92	15	10	1.33	0.00	9.19
12/13	17.79	54	37	0.34	0.00	7.92
Annual Growth	**16.9%**	**—**	**—167.9%**	**—**	**24.2%**

Liberty Tax Inc

Liberty Tax (formerly JTH Holding) wants to free you from those tax preparation shackles. It is the third-largest income tax preparation chain (behind H&R Block and Jackson Hewitt). Liberty Tax provides computerized tax preparation services through about 4200 offices throughout the US and in Canada. More than 98% of the offices are operated by franchises and are easily recognized by the costumed Uncle Sams or Lady Libertys waving out front. The company's eSmart Tax product allows customers to file their taxes online. Liberty Tax also offers tax-preparation courses refund loans audit assistance and related programs and services. CEO John Hewitt founded the company in 1997.

IPO

In September 2011 the company filed to go public. Although Liberty Tax later decided to postpone its IPO in June 2012 it declared effective its SEC registration statement and its shares of Class A common stock became available for trading on the ORC Bulletin Board. The firm later listed its Class A stock on NASDAQ.

Operations

Subsidiary JTH Financial offers loan-based financial products including refund transfer products (known as electronic refund checks or ERCs) through Republic Bank to the company's tax customers. ERCs allow customers to get their tax refunds more quickly.

Geographic Reach

Liberty Tax provides tax preparation services through some 4200 offices throughout North America. The firm operates as Liberty Tax Canada in Canada.

Financial Performance

Liberty Tax's fiscal 2012 (ends April) sales increased 14% vs. the prior year while net income grew 10% over the same period. Sales were buoyed by double-digit increases in financial products revenue tax preparation fees and to a lesser extent increases in royalties and advertising fees. The increase in financial products revenue which accounted for 21% of fiscal 2012 sales was driven by the continuing growth of JTH Financial. The increase in net income was due to the increase in revenue partially offset by higher operating expenses and a decrease in other income. Fiscal 2012 marked the third consecutive year of increasing sales and profits as the company adds tax preparation offices and financial products.

Strategy

With serious growth aspirations the company added nearly 1500 locations over the past four years and prepared more than 2 million tax returns in 2012. Indeed Liberty Tax has outpaced rivals H&R Block and Jackson Hewitt in growth for several years. The company plans to use the proceeds from its initial public offering for general corporate purposes and presumably to expand even further.

Company Background

Founder and CEO John Hewitt was previously a regional director for archrival H&R Block and the founder of Jackson Hewitt. Rather cheekily when H&R Block suffered turmoil in the boardroom in 2007 Hewitt offered himself as CEO if it would merge with Liberty. That didn't transpire but two years later he grabbed a 9% stake in Jackson Hewitt through Liberty Tax with an eye towards an outright merger of the two companies.

EXECUTIVES

CFO, Kathleen E. (Kathy) Donovan, age 57, $335,000 total compensation
Chairman President and CEO, John T. Hewitt, age 67, $1 total compensation
Vice President Affordable Care, Charles Lovelace
Vice President Human Resources, Kelly (Kel) McKinney
Vice President Of Financial Products, Mike (Mikey) Piper
Vice President Marketing, Martha (Mar) O'Gorman
Executive Vice President, Krystal Cheatham
Vice President, Tom (Tommy) Stoner
Vice President of Information Technology, Mark (Marky) Jackson
Auditors: KPMG LLP

LOCATIONS

HQ: Liberty Tax Inc
1716 Corporate Landing Parkway, Virginia Beach, VA 23454
Phone: 757 493-8855
Web: www.libertytax.com

PRODUCTS/OPERATIONS

2016 sales

	$ mil.	% of total
Royalties & advertising fees	80.3	46
Financial products	45.3	26
Interest income	13.6	8
Tax preparation fees net of discounts	19.3	11
Franchise Fee	5.0	3
AD fees	6.0	4
Other	3.9	2
Total	**173.4**	**100**

COMPETITORS

ADP	H&R Block
ATX	Intuit
CBIZ	Jackson Hewitt
ExacTax	Universal Tax
Gilman Ciocia	

HISTORICAL FINANCIALS

Company Type: Public

Income Statement

FYE: April 30

	REVENUE ($ mil.)	NET INCOME ($ mil.)	NET PROFIT MARGIN	EMPLOYEES
04/16	173.4	19.4	11.2%	1,332.0
04/15	162.1	8.6	5.4%	1,206.0
04/14	159.7	21.9	13.8%	645.0
04/13	147.6	17.6	11.9%	950.0
04/12	109.1	17.4	16.0%	788.0
Annual Growth	**12.3%**	**2.8%**	**—**	**14.0%**

2016 Year-End Financials

Debt ratio: 12.1%
Return on equity: 18.4%
Cash ($ mil.): 9.9
Current ratio: 1.98
Long-term debt ($ mil.): 17.6

No. of shares (mil.): 12.8
Dividends
Yield: 0.0%
Payout: 46.3%
Market value ($ mil.): 154.0

	STOCK PRICE ($) FY Close	P/E High/Low	PER SHARE ($) Earnings	Dividends	Book Value
04/16	11.95	20 8	1.38	0.64	8.65
04/15	27.70	62 42	0.61	0.16	7.72
04/14	27.20	18 10	1.51	0.00	8.28
04/13	17.25	14 7	1.25	0.00	6.36
Annual Growth	**(11.5%)**	**— —**	**3.4%**	**—**	**10.8%**

Life Storage Inc

A self-administered real estate investment trust (REIT) Life Storage (formerly Sovran Self Storage) operates some 650 facilities with more than 45 million sq. ft. of storage space. Its properties usually offer features such as humidity-controlled spaces; outdoor storage for cars boats and RVs; and the use of a free truck to help clients haul their stuff. Serving both individual and business customers the company owns properties in about 30 states. In mid-2016 it effected its corporate name change and began transitioning the name of its facilities from Uncle Bob's Self Storage to Life Storage.Geographic ReachThe REIT owns self-storage properties in 29 states. Florida and Texas are its largest markets.Sales and MarketingLife Storage uses internet marketing and its fleet of trucks to create brand awareness. Financial PerformanceOverall sales grew 12% in 2012 to $236 million. While occupancy rates grew the average price per square foot of storage space fell 1%. Still the trust's number of storage units grew in 2012 which contributed to its top line. Profits grew a whopping 80% to $55 million.In addition to income from rent Life Storage generates less than 10% of revenues by selling storage-related products and services such as boxes locks tarps truck rentals and renters' insurance as well as by leasing space to billboards and cell tower operators.StrategyThe company pursues growth by purchasing self-storage facilities in a largely fragmented industry dominated by independent operators. The REIT concentrates its acquisition efforts in metropolitan areas of the South and Southeast; occasionally it acquires multiple facilities in new markets.In 2016 the company bought LifeStorage which operates 84 self-storage facilities for $1.3 billion. The transaction provided it with an entry into the markets of Sacramento California and Las Vegas.The REIT now plans to rebrand its facilities under the Life Storage name.

EXECUTIVES

CEO, David L. Rogers, age 60, $484,000 total compensation
President and Director, Kenneth F. Myszka, age 67, $484,000 total compensation
CFO, Andrew J. Gregoire, $250,000 total compensation
COO, Edward F. Killeen, $250,000 total compensation
Regional VP, Jeffrey Myszka
EVP Real Estate, Paul T. Powell, $250,000 total compensation
Regional VP, Randy Hillman
Regional VP, Christopher Runckel
Regional VP, Jim Kwitchoff
Director Information Technologies, Jeffrey O'Donnell
Regional VP, Philip Wilfong
Vice President, DARREN (Darr) LARATONDA
Vice President Construction Management, Eric (Ric) Sweet
Chairman, Robert J. Attea, age 74
Auditors: Ernst & Young LLP

LOCATIONS

HQ: Life Storage Inc
6467 Main Street, Williamsville, NY 14221
Phone: 716 633-1850   **Fax:** 716 633-1860
Web: www.unclebobs.com

PRODUCTS/OPERATIONS

2015 Sales

	$ mil.	% of total
Rental income	338.4	92
Other	28.2	8
Total	**366.6**	**100**

Selected Services

Storage
Truck Rental
Moving Boxes
Vehicle Storage
Commercial Storage

COMPETITORS

AMERCO	PODS Enterprises
CubeSmart	Public Storage
Extra Space	Smart Move
Mobile Mini	

HISTORICAL FINANCIALS

Company Type: Public

Income Statement

FYE: December 31

	REVENUE ($ mil.)	NET INCOME ($ mil.)	NET PROFIT MARGIN	EMPLOYEES
12/15	366.6	112.5	30.7%	1,429.0
12/14	326.0	88.5	27.2%	1,378.0
12/13	273.5	74.1	27.1%	1,268.0
12/12	236.0	55.1	23.4%	1,228.0
12/11	211.1	30.5	14.5%	1,164.0
Annual Growth	14.8%	38.5%	—	5.3%

2015 Year-End Financials

Debt ratio: 39.1%
Return on equity: 10.3%
Cash ($ mil.): 7.0
Current ratio: 0.37
Long-term debt ($ mil.): 830.9

No. of shares (mil.): 36.7
Dividends
Yield: 2.9%
Payout: 101.2%
Market value ($ mil.): 3,939.0

	STOCK PRICE ($) FY Close	P/E High/Low		PER SHARE ($) Earnings	Dividends	Book Value
12/15	107.31	35	27	3.16	3.20	32.75
12/14	87.22	33	24	2.67	2.72	28.61
12/13	65.17	33	26	2.36	2.02	26.76
12/12	62.10	33	23	1.87	1.80	23.93
12/11	42.67	40	31	1.10	1.80	22.64
Annual Growth	25.9%	—	—	30.2%	15.5%	9.7%

Lifevantage Corp

EXECUTIVES

Pres-ceo, Douglas C Robinson
Vice President of Finance, John (Jack) Doyle
Auditors: WSRP, LLC

LOCATIONS

HQ: Lifevantage Corp
9785 S.Monroe, Ste 300, Sandy, UT 84070
Phone: 801 432-9000   **Fax:** 801 880-0699
Web: www.lifevantage.com

HISTORICAL FINANCIALS

Company Type: Public

Income Statement

FYE: June 30

	REVENUE ($ mil.)	NET INCOME ($ mil.)	NET PROFIT MARGIN	EMPLOYEES
06/16	206.5	6.0	2.9%	208.0
06/15	190.3	6.9	3.7%	166.0
06/14	213.9	11.3	5.3%	201.0
06/13	208.1	7.6	3.7%	238.0
06/12	126.1	12.4	9.9%	139.0
Annual Growth	13.1%	(16.6%)	—	10.6%

2016 Year-End Financials

Debt ratio: 18.7%
Return on equity: 77.6%
Cash ($ mil.): 7.8
Current ratio: 1.49
Long-term debt ($ mil.): 7.4

No. of shares (mil.): 14.0
Dividends
Yield: —
Payout: —
Market value ($ mil.): 191.0

	STOCK PRICE ($) FY Close	P/E High/Low		PER SHARE ($) Earnings	Dividends	Book Value
06/16	13.60	33	1	0.41	0.00	0.86
06/15	0.53	3	1	0.49	0.00	0.24
06/14	1.44	3	2	0.70	0.00	0.27
06/13	2.32	7	4	0.42	0.00	2.03
06/12	2.83	5	2	0.77	0.00	1.80
Annual Growth	48.1% (16.7%)	—	—	(14.6%)	—	

Ligand Pharmaceuticals Inc

Biopharmaceutical firm Ligand Pharmaceuticals seeks to discover disease-curing molecules. The drug development company works with gene transcription technology to address assorted illnesses. Its research and development projects include treatments for thrombocytopenia (low blood platelet count) osteoporosis Alzheimer's disease hepatitis C muscular conditions asthma and diabetes. Ligand conducts many of its programs through partnerships with other drugmakers including CyDex Pharmaceuticals GlaxoSmithKline (GSK) Pfizer and Lilly. The company is focused on expanding its development pipeline through additional partnerships and technology licensing agreements as well as via acquisitions.

Operations

Ligand has two reportable segments: The development and commercialization of drugs using Captisol technology by CyDex Pharmaceuticals; the development and/or acquisition of other royalty revenue-generating biopharmaceutical assets.

Captisol is a formulation technology that has led to six FDA approved products including Onyx's Kyprolis and Baxter International's Nexterone. It is also being developed through a number of clinical-stage partner programs.

The company's pipeline products included Hep-Direct Oral Human Granulocyte Colony Stimulating Factor and IRAK-4 in preclinical stage and Glucagon Receptor Antagonist Selective Androgen Receptor Modulator and Captisol-Enabled Clopidogrel in other phases.

Financial Performance

As a development-stage company Ligand's revenues and net income figures fluctuate from year to year depending on its income from partnerships and licensing agreements. Ligand brings in operational and R&D funding through its development partnerships either by entering new agreements or by reaching set milestones within existing agreements. It also earns some revenues from royalty payments on drug candidates licensed to third parties that have reached commercialization stages and also through Captisol material sales.

The company reported revenue growth of 56% in 2013 thanks to a more than 100% increase in Captisol sales and a more than doubling of its royalties revenues (primarily due to an increase in Promacta and Kyprolis royalties). This was offset by a decline in Collaborative Research and Development and Other Revenues due to the timing of achievement of certain regulatory milestones and licensing payments.

Ligand reported net income of $11 million in 2013 over a net loss in 2012 due to an increase in revenues and a decline in research and development costs (primarily due to the timing of costs associated with internal programs) partially offset by higher general and administrative expenses and an increase in contingent liabilities.

Strategy

Ligand's growth strategy is focused around increasing licensing milestone and royalty fees from its partners. The company's research portfolio contains more than 60 drug candidates most of which are being developed through partnerships with other drugmakers. Some of the company's targeted areas of collaboration include osteoporosis (with Pfizer) and thrombocytopenia (with GSK).

In 2014 the company entered into a licensing agreement and research collaboration with Omthera Pharmaceuticals Inc. a wholly-owned subsidiary of AstraZeneca for the development of products to treat dyslipidemia including hypertriglyceridemia.

That year partner Pfizer received approval from the FDA for DUAVEETM (conjugated estrogens/bazedoxifene) for the treatment of moderate-to-severe vasomotor symptoms associated with menopause and the prevention of postmenopausal osteoporosis and partner GSK received FDA Priority Review designation for Promacta/Revolade (eltrombopag) for the treatment of cytopenias in patients with severe aplastic anemia.

In 2013 the FDA granted orphan-drug designation for Ligand's proprietary Captisol-enabled Topiramate Injection for the treatment of partial onset or primary generalized tonic-clonic seizures in hospitalized epilepsy patients who are unable to take oral topiramate.

In 2013 the company entered into a license agreement with Spectrum Pharmaceuticals to enable Spectrum to develop and commercialize Captisol-enabled propylene glycol-free melphalan. It made other partnership and licensing deals in 2013 with Selexis SA Azure Biotech CURx Pharmaceuticals and Sage Therapeutics. Expanding geographically in 2013 the company signed a license agreement with Ethicor Pharma for the manufacture and distribution of the oral formulation of lasofoxifene in the EU Switzerland and the Indian Subcontinent.

HISTORY

Kleiner Perkins Caufield & Byers partner Brook Byers created Ligand Pharmaceuticals in 1987 to research cancer diagnostic technologies. Byers recruited Howard Birndorf a serial entrepreneur with whom he had worked on such startups as Hybritech and Idec. In 1989 the company shifted to intracellular receptors after licensing technology from the Salk Institute and became Ligand Pharmaceuticals named after chemical components that form a coordinated complex around a central atom or ion.

Birndorf left in 1991 to help found Neurocrine Biosciences. Ligand went public the next year.

In 1994 the company joined with Allergan to form Allergan Ligand Retinoid Therapeutics (ALRT) to focus on retinoid (vitamin A) research. Ligand bought out ALRT in 1997 and got custody of what became Panretin. The firm also formed partnerships with American Home Products' Wyeth-Ayerst Laboratories and Abbott Laboratories. In 1995 it bought carbohydrate researcher Glycomed.

In the late 1990s the firm began building a sales force and beefed up its pipeline by buying the rights to Elan's Morphelon morphine formulation in exchange for 8% of Ligand's stock; Ontak developer Seragen; and Marathon Biopharmeceuticals. The FDA approved Ontak and Panretin in 1999 and Targretin in 2000. That year Ligand sold Marathon's manufacturing operations opting to focus on R&D sales and marketing. The move paid off: Opioid Avinza won FDA approval in 2002. The next year Elan sold all of its shares of the company.

Ligand acquired a minority stake in Exelixis after that company bought Ligand's minority stake in drug developer X-Ceptor Therapeutics in 2004; however Ligand sold its shares in Exelixis over the course of 2005 and 2006.

Ligand sold its oncology product line to Eisai in 2006. The oncology line included four drugs — Ontak Targretin gel Targretin capsules and Panretin.

To cash in on its earlier hard work Ligand sold its pain medication Avinza to King Pharmaceuticals in 2007. Avinza was co-developed with Elan and had been Ligand's biggest seller. The divestiture coupled with the previous sale of its cancer drugs represented the sale of all of Ligand's commercial operations. As part of its refocusing the company laid off about 75% of its workforce early in 2007 consolidated its operations into one building and shut down its UK subsidiary.

One of the company's GlaxoSmithKline-partnered thrombocytopenia treatments Promacta was approved by the FDA in 2008 and added another source of royalty income for Ligand.

Moving on to new horizons it expanded its pipeline when it purchased development firm Pharmacopeia in 2008 adding therapies for hypertension renal disease muscle wasting and psoriasis as well as licensing or development agreements with companies including Bristol-Myers Squibb Schering-Plough (later Merck) and Celgene. Ligand did the same with developer Neurogen in 2009 paying about $11 million of stock to acquire the financially strapped drug developer adding Neurogen's pipeline of neurological compounds. In early 2010 the company picked up struggling biotech Metabasis Therapeutics for $3 million adding drug development candidates in areas including hepatitis C (through a partnership with Merck) diabetes and cholesterol.

In 2011 the company's revenues increased by 28% to some $30 million due to increased income from partnerships including royalties on sales of GSK's thrombocytopenia drug Promacta. Ligand also placed a dab of black ink on its balance sheet (reporting profits of $10 million) due to reduced R&D expenses as a result of a research agreement with Merck that was terminated during the year.

To expand internationally in 2011 Ligand formed a strategic relationship with Chiva Pharmaceuticals to develop certain products for the Chinese market. In addition to partnerships the company keeps up a steady stream of annual acquisitions to broaden its R&D activities.

Ligand stepped up its M&A game at the start of 2011 with its $36 million acquisition of Cydex. CyDex brought along its Captisol drug enhancement technology a handful of Captisol-enabled drugs in development and several lucrative licensing agreements with other drug makers who add Captisol to their drugs. Since the acquisition Ligand has entered a number of new Captisol licensing agreements.

EXECUTIVES

President and CEO, John L. Higgins, $500,331 total compensation

Vice President; General Counsel; Secretary, Charles S. Berkman, age 47, $283,351 total compensation

VP Biology, Keith Marschke

VP Chemistry and Pharmaceutical Sciences, Lin Zhi

President and COO, Matthew W. Foehr, $368,101 total compensation

CFO and Vice President Finance and Strategy, Nishan Silva

Chairman, John W. Kozarich

Auditors: Ernst & Young LLP

LOCATIONS

HQ: Ligand Pharmaceuticals Inc
3911 Sorrento Valley Boulevard,, Suite 110, San Diego, CA 92121
Phone: 858 550-7500
Web: www.ligand.com

PRODUCTS/OPERATIONS

2015 Sales

	$ mil.	% of total
Royalties	38.2	53
Material sales (Captisol)	27.7	39
Collaborative R&D & other	6.0	8
Total	**71.9**	**100**

COMPETITORS

Abbott Labs	GTx
Adherex Technologies	Merck
Amgen	NPS Pharmaceuticals
AstraZeneca	Novartis Corporation
Bayer HealthCare Pharmaceuticals	Protalex
	Roche Holding
Biogen	Sanofi
Chugai	Sunovion
Cytokinetics	Valeant
Eli Lilly	Vertex Pharmaceuticals
Evotec	Xencor

HISTORICAL FINANCIALS
Company Type: Public

Income Statement
FYE: December 31

	REVENUE ($ mil.)	NET INCOME ($ mil.)	NET PROFIT MARGIN	EMPLOYEES
12/15	71.9	257.3	357.8%	21.0
12/14	64.5	12.0	18.6%	19.0
12/13	48.9	11.4	23.3%	20.0
12/12	31.3	(0.5)	—	21.0
12/11	30.0	10.1	33.9%	21.0
Annual Growth	24.4%	124.2%	—	0.0%

2015 Year-End Financials

Debt ratio: 38.4%	No. of shares (mil.): 19.9
Return on equity: 155.6%	Dividends
Cash ($ mil.): 97.4	Yield: —
Current ratio: 10.35	Payout: —
Long-term debt ($ mil.): 205.3	Market value ($ mil.): 2,163.0

	STOCK PRICE ($) FY Close	P/E High/Low		PER SHARE ($) Earnings	Dividends	Book Value
12/15	108.42	9	4	12.12	0.00	15.26
12/14	53.21	135	72	0.56	0.00	1.34
12/13	52.60	103	34	0.55	0.00	2.42
12/12	20.74	—	—	(0.03)	0.00	1.31
12/11	11.87	31	17	0.52	0.00	0.87
Annual Growth	73.8%	—	—	—119.7%	—	104%

Limoneira Co

When life gives you lemons you name your company Limoneira. The agriculture and real estate development business grows you guessed it lemons in three counties in California's fertile San Joaquin Valley. It also grows avocados oranges and other crops on a total of about 11000 acres. The company one of the state's oldest citrus growers is a leading producer of both lemons and avocados. Limoneira packs its own lemons and those of other growers; its products are marketed through agreements with Sunkist (oranges) and Calavo (avocados). Real estate holdings include residential commercial and agricultural rental properties and land holdings in California and Arizona. Limoneira traces its roots to 1893.

Operations

Citrus is Limoneira's main squeeze accounting for more than 90% of total sales. The company grows and packs lemons avocados oranges and other fruits. Real estate rental and development accounts for the rest. The rental operation includes some 250 housing units in Ventura and Tulare counties. as well as several commercial office buildings and a combination convenience store/gas station. The firm also leases about 600 acres of land to agricultural tenants who grow other crops besides citrus. Also Limoneira with the help of a tenant runs an organic recycling operation in Oxnard California.

Geographic Reach

The company owns some 10000 acres in California's Ventura Tulare San Bernardino and San Luis Obispo counties as well as Arizona's Yuma County where citrus avocados and other crops are grown. Limoneira operates packinghouses in Santa Paula California and Yuma Arizona where it processes and packs its lemons and those grown by others.

Sales and Marketing

Limoneira markets its lemons directly to the foodservice industry as well as retail and wholesale customers in the US Canada and the Asia/Pacific region. Some of its citrus is sold under the Sunkist brand.

In fiscal 2015 advertising expenses totaled $0.4 million up from $0.3 million in fiscal years ending 2014 and 2013.

Financial Performance

After years of revenue growth the lemon grower reported sales of $100.3 million in fiscal 2015 (ended October) a decrease of 3% versus the prior year. Sales of all crops especially navel and Valencia oranges dropped that year and lower prices also impacted earnings. However net income grew 1% that year to $7 million thanks to gains on sales of Calavo stock and the 52-acre Wilson Ranch (which it sold to help pay for 157 acres of citrus orchards in San Joaquin valley).

Cash flow from operations declined 52% to $8 million due to changes in inventory and other factors.

Strategy

Controlling as many factors that could affect its business as possible the company owns 90% of the land it farms owns the water rights on most of its land uses solar panels to power its packing and warehouse facilities and pump its water participates in recycling programs that earn it money and provide mulch material and leases housing to many of its employees. Sunkist handles some of Limoneira's oranges and specialty citrus. Limoneira maintains its real estate operations because it believes the holdings and rentals help it retain workers and protect its revenue stream from the volatility of agricultural markets.

Going forward the company intends to grow both its agriculture business and its real estate holdings. To that end it's increasing its acreage by leasing and acquiring citrus orchards in the San Joaquin Valley and upgrading its packing capabilities to increase lemon exports. In real estate Limoneira will acquire develop and continue to lease out land to farmers; acquire and develop residential real estate holdings; and expand its industrial land holdings.

In 2015 the company completed a project to double its lemon-packing capabilities. It continues to seek third-party lemon growers especially those that will expand its international business in Mexico Chile and Argentina.

Mergers and Acquisitions

Limoneira acquired 757 acres of citrus orchards in California's San Joaquin Valley for $15.1 million in 2015; it acquired a separate 157 acres of citrus orchards nearby for another $3.4 million.

EXECUTIVES

President CEO and Director, Harold S. Edwards, age 51, $475,000 total compensation
SVP Agribusiness, Alex M. Teague, age 53, $324,039 total compensation
CFO Treasurer and Corporate Secretary, Joseph Rumley, age 57, $274,040 total compensation
Vice Chairman, John W. Blanchard, age 73
Chairman, Gordon E. Kimball, age 63
Vice Chairman, Robert M. Sawyer, age 67
Auditors: Ernst & Young LLP

LOCATIONS

HQ: Limoneira Co
1141 Cummings Road, Santa Paula, CA 93060
Phone: 805 525-5541   **Fax:** 805 525-8211
Web: www.limoneira.com

PRODUCTS/OPERATIONS

2015 Sales

	$ mil.	% of total
Agribusiness	95.1	95
Rental operations	5.1	5
Real estate development	0.1	-
Total	**100.3**	**100**

2015 Agribusiness Sales

	$ mil.	% of total
Lemons	79.0	83
Avocados	7.1	7
Navel and Valenciaoranges	5.6	6
Specialty citrus & other	3.4	4
Total	**95.1**	**100**

Selected Products Brands and Varieties

Avocados
  Hass
  Zutano
Lemons
  Bridal Veil
  Fountain
  Golden Bowl
  Level
  Paula
  Santa
Oranges
  Navel
  Valencia
Specialty citrus & other
  Cara cara oranges
  Cherries
  Minneola tangelos
  Moro blood oranges

Olives
Peaches
Pistachios
Plums
Pummelos
Satsuma mandarin oranges
Star Ruby grapefruit

COMPETITORS

American Realty Investors	Gables Residential Services
Apartment Investment and Management	Hardie's Fruit & Vegetable Company
Berkshire Property	Silver Springs
Brothers Produce	Southern Gardens Citrus
Camden Property	Stratus Properties
Chiquita Brands	Sunkist
Dole Food	Trammell Crow Residential
Edinburg Citrus	
Fresh Del Monte Produce	

HISTORICAL FINANCIALS
Company Type: Public

Income Statement
FYE: October 31

	REVENUE ($ mil.)	NET INCOME ($ mil.)	NET PROFIT MARGIN	EMPLOYEES
10/16	111.7	8.0	7.2%	276.0
10/15	100.3	7.0	7.1%	333.0
10/14	103.4	6.9	6.8%	331.0
10/13	84.8	4.9	5.8%	254.0
10/12	65.8	3.1	4.8%	226.0
Annual Growth	**14.2%**	**26.5%**	**—**	**5.1%**

2016 Year-End Financials

Debt ratio: 29.6%	No. of shares (mil.): 14.1
Return on equity: 5.9%	Dividends
Cash ($ mil.): 0.0	Yield: 1.0%
Current ratio: 0.78	Payout: 105.2%
Long-term debt ($ mil.): 88.1	Market value ($ mil.): 279.0

	STOCK PRICE ($) FY Close	P/E High/Low		PER SHARE ($) Earnings	Dividends	Book Value
10/16	19.69	38	22	0.52	0.20	9.78
10/15	15.86	56	34	0.46	0.18	9.45
10/14	25.66	60	45	0.46	0.17	9.28
10/13	26.34	75	49	0.36	0.15	7.89
10/12	22.47	90	55	0.26	0.13	4.70
Annual Growth	**(3.2%)**	**—**	**—**	**18.9%**	**11.1%**	**20.1%**

Live Oak Bancshares Inc

Auditors: Dixon Hughes Goodman LLP

LOCATIONS

HQ: Live Oak Bancshares Inc
1741 Tiburon Drive, Wilmington, NC 28403
Phone: 910 790-5867
Web: www.liveoakbank.com

HISTORICAL FINANCIALS
Company Type: Public

Income Statement
FYE: December 31

	ASSETS ($ mil.)	NET INCOME ($ mil.)	INCOME AS % OF ASSETS	EMPLOYEES
12/15	1,052.6	20.6	2.0%	366.0
12/14	673.3	10.0	1.5%	263.0
12/13	430.3	28.0	6.5%	0.0
12/12	342.4	16.1	4.7%	0.0
Annual Growth	**45.4%**	**8.6%**	**—**	**—**

2015 Year-End Financials

Return on assets: 2.3%	Dividends
Return on equity: 14.1%	Yield: 0.1%
Long-term debt ($ mil.): —	Payout: 3.5%
No. of shares (mil.): 34.1	Market value ($ mil.): 485.0
Sales ($ mil): 118.7	

	STOCK PRICE ($) FY Close	P/E High/Low		PER SHARE ($) Earnings	Dividends	Book Value
12/15	14.20	31	20	0.65	0.02	5.84
12/14	0.00	—	—	0.41	0.00	3.21
Annual Growth	**—**	**—**	**—**	**58.5%**	**—**	**81.9%**

Live Ventures Inc

LiveDeal (formerly YP Corp.) is an Internet yellow pages and local online classifieds provider. The company offers goods and services listed for sale through its online classified marketplace at classifieds.livedeal.com; LiveDeal also publishes about 17 million business listings via its business directory at yellowpages.livedeal.com. Sources of revenue include advertising sales a pay-per-lead program with major auto dealers and optional listing upgrade and e-commerce/fraud prevention fees. The company changed its name from YP Corp. after its 2007 purchase of online local classifieds marketplace LiveDeal.

The company has been focused on shifting away from its traditional listing business in order to focus on Internet services including customer acquisition. It sold approximately 14000 customers from its directory business for more than $3 million in 2009. With losses mounting however LiveDeal is exploring alternatives including selling the business.

Richard Sommer resigned as CEO in early 2010 after less than a year on the job. The company appointed Kevin Hall to lead the business as interim COO. The executive shake up was the latest in several changes at LiveDeal in recent years. Sommer had replaced Mike Edelhart who was appointed CEO in 2008.

EXECUTIVES

CFO, Virland A. Johnson
President and CEO, Jon Isaac
Vice President Mergers and Acquisitions, Jayson Martin
Auditors: Anton & Chia, LLP

HQ: Live Ventures Inc
325 E. Warm Springs Road, Suite 102, Las Vegas, NV
89119
Phone: 702 939-0231
Web: www.live-ventures.com

COMPETITORS

Amazon.com	The Berry Company
Blucora	YPM
Buy.com	Yahoo!
Dex Media	Yellowbook
Google	craigslist
Infogroup	eBay
Overstock.com	

HISTORICAL FINANCIALS

Company Type: Public

Income Statement

FYE: September 30

	REVENUE ($ mil.)	NET INCOME ($ mil.)	NET PROFIT MARGIN	EMPLOYEES
09/16	78.9	17.8	22.6%	277.0
09/15	33.3	(14.6)	—	302.0
09/14	7.2	(4.6)	—	112.0
09/13	2.3	(5.7)	—	22.0
09/12	3.0	(1.5)	—	38.0
Annual Growth	125.2%	—	—	64.3%

2016 Year-End Financials

Debt ratio: 32.6%
Return on equity: 116.5%
Cash ($ mil.): 0.7
Current ratio: 1.86
Long-term debt ($ mil.): 15.6

No. of shares (mil.): 2.7
Dividends
  Yield: —
  Payout: —
Market value ($ mil.): 5.0

	STOCK PRICE ($) FY Close	P/E High/Low		PER SHARE ($) Earnings	Dividends	Book Value
09/16	1.91	0	0	5.40	0.00	8.67
09/15	1.68	—	—	(5.58)	0.00	2.24
09/14	2.98	—	—	(2.10)	0.00	5.50
09/13	3.44	—	—	(3.68)	0.00	1.68
09/12	5.17	—	—	(1.52)	0.00	2.16
Annual Growth	(22.0%)	—	—	—	—	41.6%

LogMeIn Inc

LogMeIn wants to help you stay productive even on the go. The company provides Web-based remote access software and services to consumers small and midsized businesses and IT service providers. Its user access and remote collaboration offerings serve consumers and business users while businesses and IT service providers use LogMeIn's technology to provide remote management and support. LogMeIn offers both free and subscription-based services. Its paid services add advanced features such as file transfer remote printing and drive mapping. Corporate customers include 3M AMD and IBM. Although LogMeIn's services are sold around the world about two-thirds of sales come from US clients.

Operations

Other advanced features of LogMeIn's paid services include high-definition remote control and content streaming remote sound and file sharing and syncing.

Services used by internal IT departments and customer care teams include device management disaster recovery and software update automation.

Geographic Reach

The company's services are available in 12 languages and are used in more than 240 countries. It has international sales offices in Australia Europe (Dublin and London) and India as well as two off-shore IT offices in Hungary.

Sales and Marketing

LogMeIn uses free trials of its services to woo users and turn them into paying customers. Some of its funded marketing efforts include both online and offline advertising such as trade magazines newspapers and radio as well as tradeshows and events. With its extensive global presence and most sales still coming from the US the company plans to increase its spending on international sales and marketing. It also invests in expanding its range of connectivity services whether through internal development or strategic acquisitions. The company increased its advertising in 2014 spending $36.8 million up from $27.8 million in 2013.

Financial Performance

LogMeIn continued to generate revenue growth in 2014 raising its top line 34% to about $222 million. Much of that came from new customers as the number of subscribers to its premium join.me pro collaboration service grew. The company discontinued LogMeIn Free a free remote access service to focus on faster growing free services including join.me. The company reversed a $7 loss in 2013 (due in part to a legal settlement) to post a $7 million profit in 2014.

Strategy

LogMeIn is aiming to leverage its capabilities of connecting remote devices to become a player in the Internet of Things (the networking of sensors and other devices). Its Xively platform helps customers managed their connected devices and analyze the information collected by the devices. The 2014 acquisition of Ionia Corporation is part of LogMeIn's Internet of Things push.

Mergers & Acquisitions

LogMeIn acquired BBA Inc. known as Meldium for $10.6 million. Meldium provides single sign-on password management software and it expands LogMeIn's popular portfolio.

In an effort to capitalize on opportunities provided by the Internet of Things (allowing common objects to be connected to the network to send and receive data) LogMeIn purchased Ionia Corporation in 2014; Ionia is a systems integrator focused on connected solutions.

EXECUTIVES

Senior Vice President Sales, Kevin Harrison
Vice President; Vice President Sales and Marketing; Vice President Sales and Marketing, Jamieson Wright
SVP and Chief Marketing Officer, W. Sean Ford, age 47, $299,653 total compensation
President and CEO, William R. Wagner, age 49, $410,000 total compensation
CFO, Edward K. (Ed) Herdiech, age 49, $228,000 total compensation
CTO, Sandor Palfy
Vice President of Corporate Communications, Craig (Craigy) VerColen
Vice President Creative Director, Paul Schauder
Vice President Data Management Products, Andras Lang
Vice President Develop, Tibor Biczo
Vice President Marketing Communication, Laura (Laur) Pasquale
Vice President Network Operations, Joel Peterson

Vice President And Product Marketing, Matt (Matty) Duffy
Vice President Develop, Kevin (Kev) Bardos
Vice President of Construction Estimating, George (Georgey) Stansfield
Vice President Marketing, Michael (Mel) Parker
Vice President Sales NA, Larry (Lar) D'Angelo
Senior Vice President Strategy, Rob Lawrence
Vice President, Chris Alphen
Senior Vice President Products, Andrew Burton
Vice President Business Development, Deepak Puri
Senior Vice President Chief Marketing Officer, W Ford
Vice President Financial Planning and Analysis, Chris (Chrissy) Finn
Chairman, Michael K. Simon, age 51
Auditors: Deloitte & Touche LLP

LOCATIONS

HQ: LogMeIn Inc
320 Summer Street, Suite 100, Boston, MA 02210
Phone: 781 638-9050   **Fax:** 781 437-1803
Web: www.LogMeIn.com

PRODUCTS/OPERATIONS

Selected Products

AppGuru
BoldChat
Cubby
join.me
LogMeIn Backup
LogMeIn Central
LogMeIn Hamachi
LogMeIn Pro
LogMeIn Rescue
Meldium
RemotelyAnywhere
Xively

COMPETITORS

Adobe Systems	LivePerson
Apple Inc.	Microsoft
Box Inc.	NetSuite
Cisco Systems	Oracle
Citrix Systems	Symantec
Google	

HISTORICAL FINANCIALS

Company Type: Public

Income Statement

FYE: December 31

	REVENUE ($ mil.)	NET INCOME ($ mil.)	NET PROFIT MARGIN	EMPLOYEES
12/15	271.6	14.5	5.4%	1,006.0
12/14	221.9	7.9	3.6%	804.0
12/13	166.2	(7.6)	—	613.0
12/12	138.8	3.5	2.6%	575.0
12/11	119.4	5.7	4.8%	482.0
Annual Growth	22.8%	26.1%	—	20.2%

2015 Year-End Financials

Debt ratio: 13.1%
Return on equity: 7.6%
Cash ($ mil.): 123.1
Current ratio: 1.34
Long-term debt ($ mil.): 60.0

No. of shares (mil.): 25.1
Dividends
  Yield: —
  Payout: —
Market value ($ mil.): 1,686.0

STOCK PRICE ($)		P/E		PER SHARE ($)		
	FY Close	High/Low	Earnings	Dividends	Book Value
12/15	67.10	125 78	0.56	0.00	8.27
12/14	49.34	160 95	0.31	0.00	7.12
12/13	33.55	— —	(0.32)	0.00	6.94
12/12	22.41	304135	0.14	0.00	7.44
12/11	38.55	197115	0.23	0.00	6.35
Annual Growth	14.9%	— —	24.9%		6.8%

LTC Properties, Inc.

Specializing in TLC LTC Properties sees long-term care real estate as a healthy investment. The self-administered real estate investment trust (REIT) mostly invests in health care and long-term care facilities. Its portfolio includes more than 220 assisted living skilled-nursing and other healthcare properties with nearly 15000 living units across 30 states with its largest markets being in Texas Florida Colorado and Arizona. Its top tenant operators include Brookdale Senior Living Prestige Healthcare Senior Care Centers and Senior Lifestyle Corporation which in aggregate contribute around 45% to its total rental income. The REIT also invests in mortgage loans tied to long-term care properties.

Operations

The REIT's portfolio consisted of 224 properties at the end of 2015 including 104 assisted living centers (homes for elderly residents not requiring constant supervision) 100 skilled nursing facilities (which provide rehabilitative and restorative nursing care) seven other health care properties (such as independent living behavioral or memory care) a school and 11 land parcels. The assisted living and skilled nursing properties made up more than 90% of the REIT's rental income.As with most leasing REITs LTC Properties makes most of its revenue from rental income from tenants/operators. About 83% of its total revenue came from rental income during 2015 while interest income from mortgage loans made up another 16%.Sales and MarketingLTC Property's top tenant operators in 2015 included: Prestige Healthcare (which contributed 15% to the REIT's rental income) Brookdale Senior Living (11%) Senior Care Centers (9%) and Senior Lifestyle Corporation (9%) which in aggregate contributed around 45% to its total rental income.

Geographic Reach

LTC's properties are located in 30 states. Texas Florida Colorado and Arizona are its largest markets.

Financial Performance

The REIT's annual revenues have risen more than 60% since 2011 thanks to regular rental rate increases and some rent-boosting property acquisitions. Its net income has nearly doubled over the same period on property sale gains and as it's managed to keep its operating and overhead costs in check.LTC Property's revenue jumped 14% to $136.2 million during 2015 mostly thanks to rental rate increases associated with renewals though a two new skilled-nursing property acquisitions also helped increase its rental income. The REIT's interest income from its mortgage loans grew 34% as the company acquired more interest-earning loan assets.Despite strong revenue growth in 2015

the REIT's net income dipped less than 1% to $73.08 million mostly as it didn't earn as much from property sale gains. Its operating cash levels climbed 7% to $102.34 million as it collected more in cash-denominated earnings.StrategyLTC Properties mostly invests in assisted living and skilled nursing facilities though it also invests in related healthcare facilities and even mortgages tied to such properties. To diversify its portfolio the REIT likes to buy properties in new geographic locations with new tenant operators.

EXECUTIVES

Vice Chairman and CFO, Wendy L. Simpson, age 66, $610,500 total compensation
EVP CFO and Secretary, Pamela J. (Pam) Shelley-Kessler, age 50, $365,833 total compensation
EVP and Chief Investment Officer, Clint B. Malin, age 44, $365,833 total compensation
SVP Controller and Treasurer, Caroline L. (Cece) Chikhale, age 39, $163,327 total compensation
SVP Investment and Portfolio Management, Brent P. Chappell, age 51, $245,833 total compensation
Senior Vice President of Business Development, Douglas (Doug) Korey
Auditors: Ernst & Young LLP

LOCATIONS

HQ: LTC Properties, Inc.
2829 Townsgate Road, Suite 350, Westlake Village, CA 91361
Phone: 805 981-8655
Web: www.LTCProperties.com

PRODUCTS/OPERATIONS

2015 Sales

	$ mil.	% of total
Rental income	113.1	83
Interest income from mortgage loans	22.1	16
Interest & other income	1.0	1
Total	**136.2**	**100**

COMPETITORS

Chartwell Seniors Housing	Omega Healthcare Investors
HCP	Sabra Health Care
Healthcare Realty Trust	Senior Housing Properties
Legacy Healthcare	Tiptree
NHC	Ventas
National Health Investors	Welltower
NorthStar Healthcare Investors	

HISTORICAL FINANCIALS

Company Type: Public

Income Statement

FYE: December 31

	REVENUE ($ mil.)	NET INCOME ($ mil.)	NET PROFIT MARGIN	EMPLOYEES
12/15	136.2	73.0	53.7%	22.0
12/14	118.9	73.4	61.7%	19.0
12/13	104.9	57.8	55.1%	18.0
12/12	94.0	51.2	54.5%	18.0
12/11	85.1	49.2	57.8%	17.0
Annual Growth	**12.5%**	**10.4%**	**—**	**6.7%**

2015 Year-End Financials

Debt ratio: 44.8%
Return on equity: 11.0%
Cash ($ mil.): 12.9
Current ratio: 0.48
Long-term debt ($ mil.): 451.3

No. of shares (mil.): 37.5
Dividends
  Yield: 4.8%
  Payout: 101.4%
Market value ($ mil.): 1,620.0

STOCK PRICE ($)		P/E		PER SHARE ($)		
	FY Close	High/Low	Earnings	Dividends	Book Value
12/15	43.14	25 20	1.94	2.07	17.56
12/14	43.17	22 18	1.99	2.04	18.61
12/13	35.39	29 21	1.63	1.91	18.20
12/12	35.19	24 19	1.57	1.79	15.16
12/11	30.86	23 16	1.36	1.68	15.38
Annual Growth	8.7%	— —	9.3%	5.4%	3.4%

Lydall, Inc.

Lydall's products help to beat the heat nix the noise and filter the rest. The company makes thermal and acoustical barriers automotive heat shields and insulation products that offer protection in extreme temperatures. Lydall's thermal and acoustical products are used by the appliance and automotive industries and in industrial kilns and furnaces. The company rounds out its offerings with industrial and commercial air and liquid filtration products in addition to energy storage close-out panels and felt manufacturing services and products. Export sales represent about 35% of the company's annual net sales.

Geographic Reach

The company has operations in Europe Asia and the US which accounted for about 70% of its revenue in 2015.

Operations

Lydall's segments include Thermal/Acoustical Metals and Fibers (nearly 60% of sales) which produces noise and heat abatement products for automotive applications and Performance Materials (12%) which encompasses its filtration and industrial thermal insulation businesses. Its Industrial Filtration segment offers industrial non-woven felt media and filter bags.

Sales and Marketing

Lydall's products are primarily sold directly to customers through an internal sales force and external sales representatives and distributed via common carrier. The majority of products are sold to original equipment manufacturers and tier-one suppliers. Sales to Ford Motor Company accounted for almost 20% of net sales in 2015.

Financial Performance

After revenues peaked at a record-setting $536 million in 2014 Lydall saw its revenues fall 2% to $525 million in 2015. The company's profits however more than doubled from $22 million in 2014 to $46 million in 2015 mainly due to a gain on sale of its Life Sciences Vital Fluids business and a decrease in selling product development and administrative expenses.

The revenue dip for 2015 was fueled by lower sales from its Performance Materials segment and due to the divestiture of its Life Sciences Vital Fluids business. Performance Materials segment sales also decreased due to lower demand for air filtration products and thermal insulation products particularly in Asia and North America. It also experienced lower demand for its water purification and life protection application products and for cryogenic insulation products serving the liquid natural gas market.

Strategy

For its growth strategy Lydall focuses on new product development geographic expansion into Asia and Europe acquisitions and the application of Lean Six Sigma initiatives. A major focus for the company in 2014 is the integration of its acquired companies and the introduction of Lean Six Sigma principles to the acquired businesses.In early 2014 the company acquired the industrial filtration business from Andrew Industries Limited for $83 million. The acquisition enhanced Lydall's already strong position in the filtration and engineered materials markets.

EXECUTIVES

EVP and CFO, Scott M. Deakin, age 50
President and CEO, Dale G. Barnhart, age 63, $522,600 total compensation
President Lydall Performance Materials, Paul Marold, age 55
CIO, Joseph M. (Joe) Tait
SVP General Counsel and Chief Administration Officer, Chad A. McDaniel, $238,135 total compensation
Vice President Business Development, David Glenn
Chairman, W. Leslie Duffy, age 76
Auditors: PricewaterhouseCoopers LLP

LOCATIONS

HQ: Lydall, Inc.
One Colonial Road, Manchester, CT 06042
Phone: 860 646-1233   **Fax:** 860 646-4917
Web: www.lydall.com

PRODUCTS/OPERATIONS

2015 Sales

	$ mil.	% of total
Performance Materials Segment		
Filtration	62.7	11
Thermal Insulation	28.3	5
Life Sciences Filtration	10.5	2
Industrial Filtration Segment		
Industrial Filtration	139.1	26
Thermal/Acoustical Metals Segment		
Metal parts	141.1	26
Tooling	19.8	4
Thermal/Acoustical Fibers Segment		
Fiber parts	135.6	25
Tooling	3.2	1
Other Products and Services		
Life Sciences Vital Fluids	1.7	-
Eliminations and Other	(17.5)	-
Total	**524.5**	**100**

Selected Products

Performance Materials
Air Filtration
Liquid Filtration
High Temp. Insulation
Low Temp. Insulation
Energy Storage
Arioso for Gas Turbine
Solupor Venting Grade
HD ASHRAE
Industrial Filtration
Checkstatic
Felt Design & Specifying
Felt ManufacturingMate

COMPETITORS

CTA Acoustics	Pall Corporation
Dana	Specialty Products &
Donaldson Company	Insulation
Johns Manville	Tower International

Kaydon
Magna International
Morgan Advanced Materials
Unifrax

HISTORICAL FINANCIALS
Company Type: Public

Income Statement
FYE: December 31

	REVENUE ($ mil.)	NET INCOME ($ mil.)	NET PROFIT MARGIN	EMPLOYEES
12/15	524.5	46.2	8.8%	2,100.0
12/14	535.8	21.8	4.1%	2,100.0
12/13	397.9	19.1	4.8%	1,600.0
12/12	378.9	16.8	4.4%	1,600.0
12/11	383.5	13.7	3.6%	1,600.0
Annual Growth	**8.1%**	**35.4%**	**—**	**7.0%**

2015 Year-End Financials

Debt ratio: 5.7%
Return on equity: 20.2%
Cash ($ mil.): 75.9
Current ratio: 3.60
Long-term debt ($ mil.): 20.1

No. of shares (mil.): 17.1
Dividends
  Yield: —
  Payout: —
Market value ($ mil.): 608.0

	STOCK PRICE ($) FY Close	P/E High/Low		PER SHARE ($) Earnings	Dividends	Book Value
12/15	35.48	14	9	2.71	0.00	14.31
12/14	32.82	25	13	1.28	0.00	12.28
12/13	17.62	17	12	1.14	0.00	11.90
12/12	14.34	14	9	0.99	0.00	10.29
12/11	9.49	15	9	0.82	0.00	9.38
Annual Growth	**39.1%**	**—**	**—**	**34.8%**	**—**	**11.1%**

Lyon (William) Homes

William Lyon's is one of the largest homebuilders in the West. That's where the homebuilder and its joint venture partners design and build single-family detached and attached houses. Indeed more than 70% of William Lyon Homes are sold in the states of California Washington and Oregon though homes are also sold in Nevada Colorado and Arizona. The builder targets entry-level and move-up buyers; its homes range from $110000 to $900000 and sold at an average price of $466300 each during 2015. William Lyon owns an additional 13500 development lots and with options to buy almost 4000 additional lots. Beyond building it assists with financing through William Lyon Mortgage. The builder went public in 2013.

OperationsThe builder organizes its operations by region tied to its six largest markets: California (Orange Los Angeles Riverside Bernardino Alameda Contra Costa San Joaquin and Santa Clara counties); Oregon (Portland Metro); Washington (Seattle Metro); Nevada (Las Vegas Metro); Colorado (Denver Metro); and Arizona (Phoenix Metro).Geographic ReachWilliam Lyon's largest state market is in California where it generated 37% of its sales during 2015. Its next largest were Oregon (19% of sales) Washington (16%) Nevada (12%) Colorado (10%) and Arizona (6%).Sales and MarketingThe builder advertises online as well as through social media brochures and on billboards in strategic locations. Online it markets its products through email lists and interest lists as

well as through its website and via sales force. The company spent $61.54 million on sales and marketing to support growing sales during 2015 up from $45.9 million and $26.1 million in 2014 and 2013 respectively. Financial PerformanceWilliam Lyon's sales have more than tripled since 2012 thanks to the strengthening US housing market. The builder has struggled to consistently grow its profits however as thin operating margins have been met with costly restructuring costs.The builder's revenue jumped 23% to $1.11 billion during 2015 as its sales volumes rose 32% to 2314 home closings for the year despite its average home sale prices falling 5% to $466300 each. The bulk of the sales growth was driven by more closings in Washington and Oregon which stemmed from its acquisition of PNW Homes. Sales in Arizona and Colorado also rose by 17% and 7% during the year respectively while home sales in California fell by 25% offsetting much of the builder's top-line growth.Strong revenue growth in 2015 drove William Lyon's net income up 28% to $57.34 million for the year. The builder's operations used 8% more cash than in 2014 or $172.91 million due to a decrease in accrued expenses and an increase in accounts payable both caused by the timing of payments.StrategyWith entry-level first-time move-up and second-time move-up homebuyers in mind William Lyons continued in 2016 to build its wide range of housing types in the six core markets of Orange County Los Angeles the Inland Empire the San Francisco Bay area Phoenix Las Vegas Denver Seattle and Portland. The company hopes that these fast-growing and populous markets combined with the hot real estate market and plenty of land plot reserves (it held or had options to buy more than 17000 lots as of early 2016) will keep sales humming in the years ahead.The builder also may acquire smaller homebuilders to move into new geographic markets. Mergers and AcquisitionsIn August 2014 William Lyon expanded into the fast-growing Seattle and Portland home markets after purchasing Polygon Northwest Homes and its subsidiaries for $520 million. The acquisition formed the Washington and Oregon segments of William Lyon's operations.Company BackgroundIn 2011 the company filed for Chapter 11 bankruptcy but emerged the following year. The filing which listed some $600 million in liabilities included a pre-approved restructuring plan to raise some $85 million and reduce its debt by 37%. The Lyon family invested $25 million as part of the recapitalization plan in exchange for additional equity.

Like other homebuilders William Lyon suffered from declining sales in the economic downturn. Because of decreased home orders and high cancellation rates in all but its California market the company in 2008 slashed its workforce by about 25% and sold properties in 10 communities for about $90 million to raise cash. The company fared a bit better in 2009 as cancellations decreased and new home orders began picking up. William Lyon also cut the base prices of its homes and offered new incentives to keep sales up.

In 2010 sales continued to slump and new home orders slacked off at the end of the year after a federal tax credit for new homebuyers expired. Lyon Homes temporarily suspended development sales and marketing on certain projects. The company shifted its acquisitions on finished lots in stable markets.

EXECUTIVES

President Nevada Division, Mary J. Connelly, age 65, $225,000 total compensation

VP Development and Operations, Matthew R. Zaist, age 41
SVP and CFO, Colin T. Severn, age 45
Regional President California, Brian W. Doyle
President Colorado Division, Giles Patterson
VP Information Technology, Tom Bui
President Southern California Division, Jon W. Robertson
President Northern California Division, Carl S. Morabito
President Arizona Division, Julie E. Collins
President Oregon Division, Fred Gast
President Washington Division, Derek Straight
Vice President, Bryan (Bry) Cazier
Chairman, William H. (Bill) Lyon, age 43
Auditors: KPMG LLP

LOCATIONS

HQ: Lyon (William) Homes
4695 MacArthur Court, 8th Floor, Newport Beach, CA 92660
Phone: 949 833-3600   **Fax:** 949 476-2178
Web: www.lyonhomes.com

PRODUCTS/OPERATIONS

2015 Sales

	$ mil.	% of total
Home Sales	1079.0	98
Construction services	25.1	2
Lots land and other sales	2.5	-
Total	**1,106.6**	**100**

COMPETITORS

Beazer Homes	KB Home
CalAtlantic	Lennar
Capital Pacific	M.D.C.
Corky McMillin	Meritage Homes
D.R. Horton	Toll Brothers

HISTORICAL FINANCIALS

Company Type: Public

Income Statement

FYE: December 31

	REVENUE ($ mil.)	NET INCOME ($ mil.)	NET PROFIT MARGIN	EMPLOYEES
12/15	1,106.5	57.3	5.2%	586.0
12/14	896.6	44.6	5.0%	585.0
12/13	572.5	129.1	22.6%	350.0
12/12*	372.7	(8.8)	—	259.0
02/12	25.5	228.3	893.2%	0.0
Annual Growth	**156.5%**	**(29.2%)**	**—**	**—**

*Fiscal year change

2015 Year-End Financials

Debt ratio: 57.4%
Return on equity: 9.5%
Cash ($ mil.): 50.2
Current ratio: 11.93
Long-term debt ($ mil.): 1,105.7

No. of shares (mil.): 31.4
Dividends
 Yield: —
 Payout: —
Market value ($ mil.): 519.0

	STOCK PRICE ($) FY Close	P/E High/Low		PER SHARE ($) Earnings	Dividends	Book Value
12/15	16.50	17	9	1.48	0.00	20.08
12/14	20.27	22	13	1.34	0.00	18.21
12/13	22.14	5	0	4.95	0.00	13.80
Annual Growth	**(13.7%)**	**—**	**—**	**(45.3%)**	**—**	**20.6%**

M.D.C. Holdings, Inc.

Being king of the mountain isn't enough for M.D.C. Holdings (MDC). Operating through its Richmond American Homes subsidiary and several other units the company is one of the largest homebuilders in Colorado and is active in about a dozen other states in the West and East. The homebuilder targets first-time and move-up buyers and annually builds about 4700 single-family detached homes that sell for an average price of $345000. The company also constructs a limited number of luxury homes. Subsidiary HomeAmerican Mortgage provides loans to buyers of MDC's homes. MDC also has subsidiaries that offer homeowners and title insurance.
Geographic Reach
MDC's largest market is the West (Arizona California Nevada Washington) which contributes more than 40% of its total home sales. The Mountain states of Colorado and Utah contribute about a third while three eastern states (Maryland Virginia and Florida) represent the balance.
Operations
The company is engaged in home and land sales and to a much lesser extent financial services. Its Richmond American Homes subsidiary builds and sells primarily single-family detached homes. MDC is the general contractor for its projects and hires subcontractors for land development and home construction. It targets first-time and first-time move-up home buyers. Its HomeAmerican Mortgage arm is a full-service mortgage lender and the principal originator of mortgage loans for its home buyers.
Financial Performance
MDC's 2013 sales increased 41% versus 2012 to more than $1.6 billion. Net income was up 401% over the same period to $314.4 million. 2013 marked the second year of steeply increasing sales and profits for the homebuilder after a decline in 2011. Driving the double-digit increase in 2013 sales was an 26% jump (from 3740 in 2012 to 4710 in 2013) in the number of homes delivered and a 12% increase in average selling price year over year. However the temporary spike in mortgage interest rates from historically low levels significant year-over-year home price increases and the economic uncertainty created by the government shutdown debt ceiling debates and the discussion surrounding tapering of federal stimulus slowed housing demand during the second half of 2013.
The company's West and Mountain segments outperformed the East.
Strategy
The company focuses its homebuilding efforts on high-growth areas including metropolitcan Denver Colorado Springs Salt Lake City Las Vegas Phoenix Tucson Riverside-San Bernardino Los Angeles San Francisco Bay Area Washington D.C. Baltimore Philadelphia Jacksonville Orlando South Florida and Seattle. Buoyed by an improving housing market MDC is acquiring land on which to build more homes. The company made several land buys in Florida in early 2014.

EXECUTIVES

Vice President of Human Resources, Karen (Kare) Gard
President and COO, David D. Mandarich, age 68, $830,000 total compensation

Chairman and CEO, Larry A. Mizel, age 74, $1,000,000 total compensation
Director Corporate Finance and Investor Relations, Robert N. (Bob) Martin, $341,923 total compensation
Division President, Darin Rowe
Vice President of Information Technology, Kelly (Kel) Taga
Auditors: Ernst & Young LLP

LOCATIONS

HQ: M.D.C. Holdings, Inc.
4350 South Monaco Street, Suite 500, Denver, CO 80237
Phone: 303 773-1100
Web: www.richmondamerican.com

PRODUCTS/OPERATIONS

2015 Sales

	$ mil.	% of total
Home-building:		
West	915.3	47
Mountain	609.0	32
East	336.0	18
Financial Services:		
Mortgage operations	30.2	2
Other	18.5	1
Total	**1,909.0**	**100**

Selected Subsidiaries

Allegiant Insurance Company Inc. A Risk Retention Group
American Home Insurance Agency Inc.
American Home Title and Escrow Company
HomeAmerican Mortgage Corporation
Richmond American Construction Inc.
Richmond American Homes Corporation
StarAmerican Insurance Ltd.

COMPETITORS

Beazer Homes	M/I Homes
CalAtlantic	Meritage Homes
D.R. Horton	NVR
Hovnanian Enterprises	PulteGroup
J.F. Shea	Ryan Building
KB Home	Toll Brothers
Lennar	

HISTORICAL FINANCIALS

Company Type: Public

Income Statement

FYE: December 31

	REVENUE ($ mil.)	NET INCOME ($ mil.)	NET PROFIT MARGIN	EMPLOYEES
12/16	2,326.8	103.2	4.4%	1,318.0
12/15	1,909.0	65.7	3.4%	1,225.0
12/14	1,694.5	63.1	3.7%	1,140.0
12/13	1,680.4	314.3	18.7%	1,111.0
12/12	1,203.0	62.7	5.2%	920.0
Annual Growth	**17.9%**	**13.3%**	**—**	**9.4%**

2016 Year-End Financials

Debt ratio: 5.1%
Return on equity: 7.9%
Cash ($ mil.): 282.9
Current ratio: 1.82
Long-term debt ($ mil.): —

No. of shares (mil.): 51.4
Dividends
 Yield: 0.0%
 Payout: 47.6%
Market value ($ mil.): 1,321.0

	STOCK PRICE ($)	P/E		PER SHARE ($)		
	FY Close	High/Low	Earnings	Dividends	Book Value	
12/16	25.66	14 10	2.00	0.95	25.64	
12/15	25.53	24 19	1.28	1.00	24.47	
12/14	26.47	26 19	1.23	1.00	23.96	
12/13	32.24	7 4	6.04	0.00	23.68	
12/12	36.76	33 14	1.22	2.00	17.23	
Annual Growth	(8.6%)	—	13.2%	(16.9%)	10.5%	

M/I Homes Inc

M/I Homes sells single-family detached homes to first-time move-up empty-nest and luxury buyers under the M/I Homes Showcase Homes and TriStone Homes names. It delivers more than 2200 homes a year at prices ranging from about $140000 to $1.2 million (averaging $346000) and sizes ranging from 1400 to 5500 sq. ft. M/I Homes also builds attached townhomes and condominiums in select markets. It caters to 14 markets throughout the Midwest Mid-Atlantic and South. Its M/I Financial mortgage banking subsidiary provides title and mortgage services. M/I Homes was founded in 1976 by Melvin and Irving Schottenstein.

Operations

Complementing its homebuilding activities (97% of sales) the company provides financing through its wholly-owned subsidiary M/I Financial Corp.

Geographic Reach

The company is based in Columbus Ohio and operates in Columbus and Cincinnati Ohio; Indianapolis Indiana; Chicago; Minneapolis/St. Paul Minnesota; Tampa and Orlando Florida; Austin Dallas/Fort Worth Houston and San Antonio Texas; Charlotte and Raleigh North Carolina; and the Virginia and Maryland suburbs of Washington DC.

M/I Homes' biggest market is the Midwest (35% of sales) followed by the Mid-Atlantic region (26%). The South including Texas accounts for 36% of sales.

Financial Performance

M/I Homes has achieved extraordinary growth over the years with revenues peaking at a record-setting $1.4 billion in 2015. Its profits also jumped 2% from 2014 to 2015. The company however has experienced five straight years of negative cash flow as consistently burns up cash for its operating activities.

The historic growth was fueled by increases across all its segments: Southern homebuilding (22%) Midwest homebuilding (18%) Mid-Atlantic homebuilding (8%) and financial services (19%). Most of these segments were helped by a spike in the average sales price of homes delivered an increase in the number of homes delivered (115 units) and a bump in land sales revenue.

Strategy

As the housing market gradually bounces back M/I has made a few changes to the new homes it builds. The company is designing the homes and the communities to reap higher profit margins. Its homes are all eco-friendly slightly smaller and in line with consumer demands.

The company focuses on investing in attractive land and new market opportunities and growth in current markets particularly newer Texas and Min-

neapolis/St. Paul markets. It also grows through acquisitions.

Mergers and AcquisitionsIn 2015 M/I completed the acquisition of the residential homebuilding operations of Hans Hagen Homes a premier homebuilder in the Minneapolis/St. Paul market. The deal further cemented M/I Homes' geographic position in a healthy and dynamic housing market.

EXECUTIVES

EVP and CFO, Phillip G. Creek, age 63, $600,000 total compensation
Chairman President and CEO, Robert H. Schottenstein, age 63, $900,000 total compensation
EVP Chief Legal Officer and Secretary, J. Thomas (Tom) Mason, age 58, $450,000 total compensation
Region President Charlotte Cincinnati Columbus Orlando Raleigh Tampa and Washington D.C. Divisions, Fred J. Sikorski, age 61
Region President Austin Dallas Houston and San Antonio Divisions, Thomas W. Jacobs, age 50
Region President Chicago Indianapolis and Minneapolis/St. Paul Divisions, Ronald H. Martin, age 47
Vice President Purchasing, Mark (Marky) Nelson
Vice President of Sales and Marketing, Greg (Greggy) Jones
Vice President Of Sales and Marketing, David (Dave) Balcerzak
Division Vice President Controller, Audrey Cangialosi
Region Manager Vice President Mifc, Todd Miller
Vice President Of Land Acquisition, George Young
Vice President Sibcy Cline Mortgage Services, Valerie (Val) Fee
Senior Vice President General Counsel, Thomas (Thom) Mason
Division Vice President, Brad (Brady) Nelson
Vice President Of Product Development, Daniel Omalley
Vice President Of Purchasing, Kelly Cunningham
Vice President Finance, Angie Alexander
Vice President Branch Manager Mifc, Rick (Ricky) Rieman
Vice President of Purchasing, Kevin D (Kev) Stewart
Vice President of Operations, Gary (Gar) Rae
Vice President Sales and Marketing, Desiree (Dee) Davis
Vice President Operations, David Gipe
Vice President of Information Technology and Supply Chain, Peter (Pete) Batchelder
Vice President Of Land Acquisition, Mark Connor
Vice President Of Operations, Gary Rae
Executive Vice President Chief Legal Officer and Secretary, J T Mason
Vice President Purchasing, Kevin Markham
Vice President of Purchasing, Rick Muravski
Area President, Elliot Jones
Vice President Treasurer, Kevin Hake
Auditors: Deloitte & Touche LLP

LOCATIONS

HQ: M/I Homes Inc
3 Easton Oval, Suite 500, Columbus, OH 43219
Phone: 614 418-8000   **Fax:** 614 418-8080
Web: www.mihomes.com

PRODUCTS/OPERATIONS

2015 Sales

	$ mil.	% of total
Southern Homebuilding	514.7	36
Midwest homebuilding	500.9	35
Mid-Atlantic homebuilding	366.8	26
Financial services	36.0	3
Total	**1,418.4**	**100**

Selected Markets

Charlotte NC
Chicago IL
Cincinnati OH
Columbus OH
Dayton OH
Houston TX
Indianapolis IN
Maryland
Orlando FL
Raleigh NC
San Antonio TX
Tampa FL
Virginia

COMPETITORS

Beazer Homes	Lennar
CalAtlantic	M.D.C.
Comstock Holding	NVR
D.R. Horton	Orleans Homebuilders
David Weekley Homes	PulteGroup
Dominion Homes	Rottlund
Drees Homes	Toll Brothers
Hovnanian Enterprises	WCI Communities
John Wieland Homes	Woodbridge Holdings
KB Home	

HISTORICAL FINANCIALS

Company Type: Public

Income Statement

FYE: December 31

	REVENUE ($ mil.)	NET INCOME ($ mil.)	NET PROFIT MARGIN	EMPLOYEES
12/15	1,418.4	51.7	3.6%	1,008.0
12/14	1,215.1	50.7	4.2%	905.0
12/13	1,036.7	151.4	14.6%	827.0
12/12	761.9	13.3	1.8%	651.0
12/11	566.4	(33.8)	—	583.0
Annual Growth	25.8%	—	—	14.7%

2015 Year-End Financials

Debt ratio: 43.2%
Return on equity: 9.0%
Cash ($ mil.): 10.2
Current ratio: 10.57
Long-term debt ($ mil.): 611.8
No. of shares (mil.): 24.6
Dividends
 Yield: —
 Payout: —
Market value ($ mil.): 540.0

	STOCK PRICE ($)	P/E		PER SHARE ($)		
	FY Close	High/Low	Earnings	Dividends	Book Value	
12/15	21.92	14 10	1.68	0.00	24.20	
12/14	22.96	14 10	1.65	0.00	22.22	
12/13	25.45	5 3	5.24	0.00	20.23	
12/12	26.50	38 14	0.67	0.00	15.47	
12/11	9.60	— —	(1.81)	0.00	14.59	
Annual Growth	22.9%	— —	—	—	13.5%	

Macerich Co. (The)

Mallrats nationwide can get their fix thanks to Macerich. The self-administered real estate investment trust (REIT) acquires develops leases and manages shopping and strip malls. Its portfolio consists of about 50 regional shopping centers and seven community shopping centers totaling more than 55 million sq. ft. of leasable space. The properties are located in 26 states with top markets being in Arizona California and the New York metropolitan area. Macerich's tenants include some of the country's leading retailers including L Brands Forever 21 The Gap Dick's Sporting Goods Sears and Best Buy to name a few.

Geographic Reach

The California-based REIT's properties are concentrated in Arizona California Texas Virginia Chicago and the Greater New York Metro area (New York New Jersey and Connecticut).

Sales and Marketing

Mall staple L Brands (the owner of Victoria's Secret and Bath & Body Works stores) and fast-growing apparel chain Forever 21 are the REIT's two largest tenants as a percentage of total rents.

Financial Performance

Macerich's revenue and profits have more than doubled since 2011 with a stronger US economy and healthier retail climate in the US boosting demand for rental properties. The REIT's revenue climbed 17% to $1.29 billion during 2015 thanks to higher minimum rental income from an increase in joint venture centers redevelopment properties and same-store rental growth. Despite strong revenue and operating income growth in 2015 Macerich's net income plunged 67% to $487.56 million as in 2014 the REIT had collected $1.4 billion more in non-recurring gains on reameasurement of assets related to its PPR Queens Portfolio acquisition that year. The REIT's operating cash levels jumped 35% to $540.4 million during 2015 thanks to favorable working capital changes in assets and liabilities.

Strategy

Macerich specializes in acquiring leasing and managing and redeveloping Regional Shopping Center properties. About 75% of the REIT's rents are from mall stores and freestanding stores under 10000 square feet (as of mid-2016). Big-box stores including Best Buy and anchor tenants (Sears Macy's) account for the rest.

Company Background

In 2011 the company acquired its first outlet mall in New York and broke ground on another in the Chicago suburbs near O'Hare International Airport. Macerich also had a mixed-use project with more than 2 million sq. ft. of space –its largest to date –under development in Tysons Corner in Northern Virginia.

The commercial and retail real estate industry was hit hard by the global economic crisis that began in 2008 as property tenants increasingly renegotiated rents defaulted on payments consolidated operations or simply went out of business. To weather the storm Macerich implemented an aggressive deleveraging strategy. The company primarily raised capital by forming new joint ventures refinancing properties and selling some of its non-core assets. In 2009 it sold five community centers for some $83 million in order to help pay off debt. Despite the turmoil the retail REIT remained profitable throughout the recession and is watching its profits grow amid the recovery.In another sign of the times Macerich owned a portfolio of 45 freestanding Mervyn's stores which closed after the retailer declared bankruptcy in 2008. Macerich has sold most of the properties and began seeking new tenants to fill the remaining spaces. Founded in 1964 Macerich got its name by combining the first names of its founders Mace Siegel and Richard Cohen.

EXECUTIVES

EVP and Director, Edward C. Coppola, age 61, $800,000 total compensation
SEVP; CFO and Treasurer, Thomas E. (Tom) O'Hern, age 60, $550,000 total compensation
President CEO and Director, Arthur M. (Art) Coppola, age 64, $1,000,000 total compensation
SEVP and COO, Robert D. Perlmutter, age 54, $500,000 total compensation
EVP Real Estate, Randy L. Brant, age 63, $448,846 total compensation
EVP, Eric V. Salo
SVP Asset Management, David M. Short
SEVP; Chief Legal Officer and Secretary, Thomas J. (Tom) Leanse, $500,000 total compensation
SVP Outlet Division, Jamie Bourbeau
SVP Design and Construction, Don Foster
SVP and CIO, J.P. Jones
SVP Property Management, Christopher J. Fracas
SVP Property Management, Olivia Bartel Leigh
SVP Acquisitions, Tom Pendergrast
SVP National Leasing Services and Retailer Relations, Tom Unis
SVP Information Technology, Michael Slavin
Assistant Vice President Procurement, Carol Velasquez
Vice President Leasing, Jerry Anderson
Vice President Group Controller, Jeanne (Jeannie) Phares
Senior Vice President Property Management, Olivia Leigh
Vice President Construction, Bob (Bo) Jones
Vice Chairman, Dana K. Anderson, age 81
Auditors: KPMG LLP

LOCATIONS

HQ: Macerich Co. (The)
401 Wilshire Boulevard, Suite 700, Santa Monica, CA 90401
Phone: 310 394-6000
Web: www.macerich.com

PRODUCTS/OPERATIONS

2015 Sales

	$ mil.	% of total
Minimum rent	759.6	59
Tenant recoveries	415.1	32
Management Companies	26.3	2
Percentage rents	25.6	2
Others	61.5	5
Total	**1,288.1**	**100**

Selected Tenants

Abercrombie & Fitch Co.
Best Buy Co. Inc.
Dick's Sporting Goods Inc.
Foot Locker Inc.
Forever 21 Inc.
Gap Inc. The
L Brands Inc.
Luxottica Group S.P.A.
Nordstrom Inc.
Sears Holdings Corporation

COMPETITORS

Belz
CBL & Associates Properties
Cousins Properties
General Growth Properties
Horizon Group Properties
Kimco Realty
Pennsylvania Real Estate
Poag & McEwen Lifestyle Centers
Regency Centers
Simon Property Group
Tanger Factory Outlet
Taubman Centers
Weingarten Realty
Westfield Corporation

HISTORICAL FINANCIALS

Company Type: Public

Income Statement

FYE: December 31

	REVENUE ($ mil.)	NET INCOME ($ mil.)	NET PROFIT MARGIN	EMPLOYEES
12/15	1,288.1	487.5	37.8%	997.0
12/14	1,105.2	1,499.0	135.6%	1,117.0
12/13	1,029.4	420.0	40.8%	1,143.0
12/12	881.3	337.4	38.3%	1,368.0
12/11	791.2	156.8	19.8%	1,377.0
Annual Growth	13.0%	32.8%	—	(7.8%)

2015 Year-End Financials

Debt ratio: 46.9%	No. of shares (mil.): 154.4
Return on equity: 9.4%	Dividends
Cash ($ mil.): 86.5	Yield: 8.2%
Current ratio: 0.32	Payout: 63.4%
Long-term debt ($ mil.): 5,283.7	Market value ($ mil.): 12,459.0

	STOCK PRICE ($) FY Close	P/E High/Low		PER SHARE ($) Earnings	Dividends	Book Value
12/15	80.69	31	24	3.08	6.63	30.54
12/14	83.41	8	5	10.45	2.51	35.65
12/13	58.89	24	18	3.00	2.36	23.87
12/12	58.30	25	20	2.51	2.23	22.38
12/11	50.60	48	34	1.18	2.05	21.29
Annual Growth	12.4%	—		27.1%	34.1%	9.4%

Madden (Steven) Ltd.

Steven Madden elevates chunky heels to new heights. It operates through five business segments: wholesale footwear wholesale accessories retail first cost and licensing. Its wholesale business boasts seven divisions such as Madden Girl Steven Steve Madden Men's and Stevies as well as its Daisy Fuentes Betsey Johnson and Olsenboye accessories business through licenses. Its retail operations include about 120 Steve Madden Steven and Report stores along with several websites. Its First Cost segment designs and sources private-label footwear such as Candie's for mass merchants. Steven Madden shoes are sold in the US and Canada through its own shops and such stores as Nordstrom and Dillard's.

Geographic Reach

New York-based Steven Madden rings up 92% of its sales in the US. The company's shoes and accessories are also sold in Asia Europe the Middle East Mexico Australia South Africa South America and India through special distribution arrangements. More than 120 Steven Madden-owned stores are located across the US with noteworthy penetration in New York California and Florida.

Operations

The company's wholesale operation accounts for 85% of its revenue with footwear contributing 65% of that. Subsidiary Steven Madden Retail owns and operates about 120 stores including about 90 Steve Madden full price stores a dozen Steve Madden outlet stores a pair of Steven stores a single Report shop and Superga store and thee e-commerce sites. The retail business accounted for 15% of sales in 2012. The company's First Cost business earns commissions as a buying agent for footwear products under private labels and licensed brands such as Candies for many large mass merchants shoe chains and other retailers.

Sales and Marketing

Steven Madden looks to department stores specialty stores and independent boutiques for the majority of its revenue. The company's sells its footwear and accessories through 15 department store chains throughout North America. Major accounts include Macy's Nordstrom Bloomingdale's Dillard's and Lord & Taylor. Major specialty store accounts include DSW Famous Footwear and Journeys.

To promote itself as a leading designer of fashion footwear for style-conscious young women and men the company's marketing activities include placements in lifestyle and fashion magazines personal appearances by founder and design chief Steve Madden and in-store promotions. The company's website and social media forums including Facebook and Twitter are other sales and marketing tools.

Financial Performance

Steven Madden's sales jumped 24% in 2012 versus 2011 to $.123 billion after rising more than 50% in the previous annual comparison. Indeed 2012 marked the fourth consecutive year of rapidly rising sales and profits for the firm with growth accelerating in 2011 and 2012. The strong sales performance in 2012 was broadly supported by double-digit growth across all of the company's business segments. Gains by the wholesale business have been the primary sales driver in recent years. Net income increased 23% in 2012 versus 2011 to nearly $120 million driven by rising sales.

Strategy

Steven Madden's recent success is a result of its focus on its wholesale operation. The company is also gaining a foothold in areas beyond shoes and it continues to invest in its accessories business. (The footwear maker's accessories business has eclipsed its men's business.) While small compared to the wholesale business retail is an important avenue for growth at Steve Madden. The company has added more than 30 stores over the past two years and is looking to enter new markets.

Mergers and Acquisitions

In August 2014 Steve Madden acquired Dolce Vita Holdings a designer and wholesaler of branded and private-label footwear for $60.3 million.

In February 2012 the company acquired its licensee Steve Madden Canada (SMC) for about $29 million. Privately-held SMC markets Steven Madden products in Canada on a wholesale basis and well as in Steve Madden-branded retail stores.

Looking to increase its private-label footprint Steven Madden bought Topline Corp. for $55 million in May 2011. Topline which rang up sales of about $189 million in 2010 sells private-label and branded footwear (Report Report Signature R2 by Report) primarily to specialty retailers and department stores. Also in May Steven Madden acquired the Cejon group of design and marketing companies for about $30 million. The purchase included Cejon Inc. Cejon Accessories and New East Designs. The companies design scarves wraps winter accessories and other items and expanded Steven Madden's accessories business beyond handbags and belts.

EXECUTIVES

COO, Awadhesh K. Sinha, age 70, $600,000 total compensation

Chief Financial Officer; Secretary, Arvind Dharia, age 66, $554,719 total compensation

Brand Director, Robert (Rob) Schmertz, age 52, $725,000 total compensation

President, Amelia Newton Varela, age 44, $500,000 total compensation

Chairman and CEO, Edward R. (Ed) Rosenfeld, age 41, $607,754 total compensation

Chief Merchandising Officer, Karla Frieders

Senior Vice President Global Sourcing and Operations, Jeff (Jeffy) Goldstein

Vice President of Finance and Operations, Dante Gioia

Vice President Sales and Operations for Retail Division, Mike (Mikey) Willhite

Senior Vice President Logistics, Sanjeev Sahni

Vice President, Alan Novich

Senior Vice President Sales, Amelia Newton

Vice President Key Accounts Steve Madden, Wendy Steinberg

Senior Vice President Planning And Retail Operations, Stuart (Stu) Fishman

Vice President Wholesale E Commerce, Jorge Yannuzzi

Vice President Of Sales, Antonella Paradiso

Vice President, Cynthia (Cyn) Mora

Vice President Internal Audit, Peter (Pete) Chang

Executive Vice President Direct To Consumer, Michele (Michie) Bergerac

Senior Vice President Sales And Merchandising, Jaime (James) Levy

Vice President of Product Development, Claudio Bruxel

Vice President Production, Kevin (Kev) Houser

Executive Vice President Wholesale and Retail E Commerce, Richard (Dick) Zech

Auditors: EisnerAmper LLP

LOCATIONS

HQ: Madden (Steven) Ltd.
52-16 Barnett Avenue, Long Island City, NY 11104
Phone: 718 446-1800
Web: www.stevemadden.com

PRODUCTS/OPERATIONS

2015 Sales

	$ mil.	% of total
Wholesale		
Footwear	905.8	65
Accessories	259.1	18
Retail	240.3	17
Total	**1,405.2**	**100**

Selected Segments

Wholesale Footwear
Betsey Johnson shoes
Big Buddha Shoes
Elizabeth and James (licensed)
l.e.i. (licensed)
Madden
Madden Girl
Olsenboye (licensed)
Report
Steve Madden Men's
Steve Madden Women's
Steven
Stevies
Superga (licensed)
Wholesale Accessories
Betsey Johnson
Betseyville
Big Buddha
Cejon
Daisy Fuentes (licensed)
Olsenboye (licensed)
Steve Madden
Steven by Steve Madden
Steven Madden Retail
Steve Madden retail stores
Steven retail stores
www.stevemadden.com

First Cost
Buying agent for footwear products under private labels
Licensing
Betsey Johnson trademark
Betseyville trademark
Steve Madden trademark
Steven by Steve Madden trademark
Licensed Products
Belts
Hair accessories
Handbags
Hosiery
Jewelry
Outerwear
Socks
Sportswear
Sunglasses

COMPETITORS

Caleres	Kenneth Cole
Diesel SpA	NIKE
Donna Karan	R. Griggs
Guess?	Reebok
Iconix Brand Group	Skechers U.S.A.
Jimlar	

HISTORICAL FINANCIALS

Company Type: Public

Income Statement

FYE: December 31

	REVENUE ($ mil.)	NET INCOME ($ mil.)	NET PROFIT MARGIN	EMPLOYEES
12/15	1,405.2	112.9	8.0%	3,578.0
12/14	1,334.9	111.8	8.4%	3,256.0
12/13	1,314.2	132.0	10.0%	2,864.0
12/12	1,227.0	119.6	9.7%	2,650.0
12/11	968.5	97.3	10.0%	2,370.0
Annual Growth	**9.8%**	**3.8%**	**—**	**10.8%**

2015 Year-End Financials

Debt ratio: —
Return on equity: 16.7%
Cash ($ mil.): 72.4
Current ratio: 2.62
Long-term debt ($ mil.): —

No. of shares (mil.): 61.6
Dividends
Yield: —
Payout: —
Market value ($ mil.): 1,864.0

	STOCK PRICE ($) FY Close	P/E High/Low	PER SHARE ($) Earnings	Dividends	Book Value
12/15	30.22	23 16	1.85	0.00	11.00
12/14	31.83	21 16	1.76	0.00	10.52
12/13	36.59	27 17	1.98	0.00	10.08
12/12	42.27	24 17	1.81	0.00	9.06
12/11	34.50	37 18	1.50	0.00	7.36
Annual Growth	**(3.3%)**	**— —**	**5.4%**	**—**	**10.6%**

Main Street Capital Corp

Main Street Capital doesn't care if its investments are on Main St. Manufacturing Blvd or Professional Services Pkwy. just as long as they are not too big and are (preferably) located in the southwestern US. As an investment firm Main Street provides long-term debt and equity capital to lower middle-market companies with annual revenues between $10 million and $100 million. Its portfolio includes more than 40 active investments in traditional and niche companies in the manufacturing technology restaurant business services and other sectors. Main Street tends to partner with business owners and management and provides capital to support buyouts recapitalizations growth financings and acquisitions.

The firm typically offers debt capital in the form of single tranche debt and mezzanine loans; it often makes its equity investments in connection to its debt investments. Single tranche debt is a type of hybrid asset-backed security that combines low-risk secured debt and higher-risk subordinated debt into a single instrument. Main Street believes this type of debt capital is ideal for investments in lower middle-market companies primarily because it lessens the risk associated with such companies generates a somewhat predictable return on its investments and is structured in way that reduces complexity and benefits creditors.

While 75% of the firm's investments are located in the western and southwestern US Main Street does maintain some investments in the southeastern and central US.

Auditors: Grant Thornton LLP

LOCATIONS

HQ: Main Street Capital Corp
1300 Post Oak Boulevard, 8th floor, Houston, TX 77056
Phone: 713 350-6000
Web: www.mainstcapital.com

COMPETITORS

American Capital	MCG Capital
Apollo Investment	Sentinel Capital
Ares Capital	Partners
Capital Southwest	WestView Capital
Castle Harlan	Partners

HISTORICAL FINANCIALS

Company Type: Public

Income Statement

FYE: December 31

	REVENUE ($ mil.)	NET INCOME ($ mil.)	NET PROFIT MARGIN	EMPLOYEES
12/15	164.5	107.0	65.1%	50.0
12/14	140.7	95.5	67.9%	38.0
12/13	116.5	75.4	64.7%	37.0
12/12	90.5	59.3	65.5%	30.0
12/11	66.2	39.2	59.3%	22.0
Annual Growth	25.6%	28.5%	—	22.8%

2015 Year-End Financials

Debt ratio: 41.5%
Return on equity: 10.6%
Cash ($ mil.): 20.3
Current ratio: 1.23
Long-term debt ($ mil.): 780.4

No. of shares (mil.): 50.4
Dividends
Yield: 8.5%
Payout: 112.6%
Market value ($ mil.): 1,466.0

	STOCK PRICE ($) FY Close	P/E High/Low		PER SHARE ($) Earnings	Dividends	Book Value
12/15	29.08	15	12	2.18	2.49	21.24
12/14	29.24	16	12	2.20	2.39	20.85
12/13	32.69	17	13	2.06	2.18	19.89
12/12	30.51	15	11	2.01	1.73	18.59
12/11	21.24	13	9	1.69	1.70	15.19
Annual Growth	8.2%	—	—	6.6%	10.1%	8.8%

Malibu Boats Inc

Auditors: KPMG LLP

LOCATIONS

HQ: Malibu Boats Inc
5075 Kimberly Way, Loudon, TN 37774
Phone: 865 458-5478
Web: www.malibuboats.com

HISTORICAL FINANCIALS

Company Type: Public

Income Statement

FYE: June 30

	REVENUE ($ mil.)	NET INCOME ($ mil.)	NET PROFIT MARGIN	EMPLOYEES
06/16	252.9	18.0	7.1%	540.0
06/15	228.6	14.6	6.4%	509.0
06/14	190.9	(4.6)	—	411.0
06/13	167.0	17.9	10.8%	408.0
06/12	140.8	11.1	7.9%	0.0
Annual Growth	15.8%	12.9%	—	—

2016 Year-End Financials

Debt ratio: 32.2%
Return on equity: —
Cash ($ mil.): 25.9
Current ratio: 1.35
Long-term debt ($ mil.): 63.0

No. of shares (mil.): 17.6
Dividends
Yield: —
Payout: —
Market value ($ mil.): 214.0

	STOCK PRICE ($) FY Close	P/E High/Low		PER SHARE ($) Earnings	Dividends	Book Value
06/16	12.08	21	11	1.00	0.00	0.77
06/15	20.09	26	18	0.93	0.00	(1.50)
06/14	20.10	—	—	(0.42)	0.00	1.74
Annual Growth	(22.5%)	—	—	—	—	(33.7%)

Manhattan Associates, Inc.

Whether you're in New York or Kansas or points between or beyond Manhattan Associates keeps things moving with its supply chain management software and systems. The Atlanta-based company provides customers in retail distribution transportation and manufacturing with supply chain management software and related services. Its line of supply chain execution software includes warehouse transportation trading partner distributed order and reverse logistics management applications. Manhattan also offers performance management and radio-frequency identification tools designed to enhance the functionality of its other products and sells third-party hardware such as bar code scanners.

Operations

Manhattan sells its products and service in three segments: services software licensing and hardware. Services bring in about three-quarters of the company's revenue with software licensing ac-

counting for 15% and the rest coming from the company's small hardware operation.

Geographic ReachIn addition to the US the company has offices in Australia China France India Japan the Netherlands Singapore and the UK. It has reseller agreements or third-party representatives in a host of other markets throughout Latin America Eastern Europe the Middle East South Africa and Asia.Manhattan generates about 82% of sales from customers in North and Latin America; Europe the Middle East and Africa (EMEA) and the Asia/Pacific region contribute about 12% and 6% respectively. The company saw growth across all regions in 2014.

Sales and MarketingManhattan primarily sells through its direct sales force but it has made efforts to broaden its approach through programs such as Manhattan Value Partner and Manhattan GeoPartner that enable joint sales and marketing with organizations such as Accenture Deloitte IBM and Microsoft. A sizable portion of the company's sales comes from apparel and consumer products manufacturers and retailers including Abercrombie & Fitch PETCO American Eagle RH and The Container Store.

Financial PerformanceThe company has grown robustly since it posted a recession-based sales decline in 2009. In 2014 Manhattan reported revenue of $492 million up 19% from the prior year. Net income was also up that year jumping 22% to nearly $82 million. Revenue from services rose as customers upgraded their packages and licensing increased. The company's profit margins have also strengthened in the past few years.

Strategy

Looking ahead Manhattan's growth strategy includes international expansion and it plans to target the overseas operations of its existing client base. It is also pursuing partnerships with international systems integrators as international sales have been steadily growing as a percent of overall revenue in recent years.

In 2014 Manhattan reached agreements with clients and partners to extend its reach in Europe and more specifically France and Romania.

Mergers and Acquisitions

Manhattan expanded its inventory and order management services with the 2014 acquisition of Global Bay Mobile Technologies. The $2.8 million deal adds Global Bay's point-of-sale and clientele applications to Manhattan's omni-channel sales and fulfillment platform.

EXECUTIVES

President CEO and Director, Eddie Capel, age 54, $575,000 total compensation
SVP Americas, Robert G. (Bob) Howell, age 43, $289,000 total compensation
Interim CFO, Linda C. Pinne, age 42
SVP and CTO, Sanjeev Siotia
SVP Europe Middle East and Africa (EMEA), Henri Seroux
SVP and General Manager India, Usha Tirumala
Senior Vice President, Bruce (Brucey) Richards
Vice President Finance, Gary (Gar) Luoma
Senior Vice President and Director of Professional Services, Joshua (Josh) Whitmire
Vice President, Chris Hine
Vice President, Linda Mercadal
Vice President, Marvin Lee
Vice President, Marvin (Marve) Lee
Chairman, John J. Huntz, age 65
Auditors: Ernst & Young LLP

LOCATIONS

HQ: Manhattan Associates, Inc.
2300 Windy Ridge Parkway, Tenth Floor, Atlanta, GA 30339
Phone: 770 955-7070   **Fax:** 770 995-0302
Web: www.manh.com

PRODUCTS/OPERATIONS

2014 Sales

	$ mil.	% of total
Services	376.0	76
Licenses	71.6	15
Hardware & other	44.5	9
Total	**492.1**	**100**

Selected Services

Carrier Management
Distribution Management
Inventory Optimization
Mobile Supply Chain
Order Lifecycle Management
Planning and Forecasting
Supply Chain Event Management
Supply Chain Intelligence
Supply Chain Visibility
Total Cost to Serve
Transportation Lifecycle Management

COMPETITORS

CDC Supply Chain	JDA Software
Epicor Software	Oracle
HighJump	SAP
IBM	SAS Institute
Infor Global	Transentric

HISTORICAL FINANCIALS

Company Type: Public

Income Statement

FYE: December 31

	REVENUE ($ mil.)	NET INCOME ($ mil.)	NET PROFIT MARGIN	EMPLOYEES
12/16	604.5	124.2	20.5%	3,020.0
12/15	556.3	103.4	18.6%	2,930.0
12/14	492.1	82.0	16.7%	2,770.0
12/13	414.5	67.3	16.2%	2,530.0
12/12	376.2	51.8	13.8%	2,400.0
Annual Growth	**12.6%**	**24.4%**	**—**	**5.9%**

2016 Year-End Financials

Debt ratio: —
Return on equity: 67.9%
Cash ($ mil.): 95.6
Current ratio: 1.76
Long-term debt ($ mil.): —
No. of shares (mil.): 70.2
Dividends
  Yield: —
  Payout: —
Market value ($ mil.): 3,725.0

	STOCK PRICE ($) FY Close	P/E High/Low	PER SHARE ($) Earnings	Dividends	Book Value
12/16	53.03	39 26	1.72	0.00	2.41
12/15	66.17	55 27	1.40	0.00	2.69
12/14	40.72	114 26	1.08	0.00	2.46
12/13	117.48	139 69	0.86	0.00	2.38
12/12	60.34	95 60	0.64	0.00	2.06
Annual Growth	**(3.2%)**	**— —**	**28.0%**	**—**	**4.0%**

Marcus & Millichap Inc

If you've got several million burning a hole in your pocket or you're looking to unload that old skyscraper Marcus & Millichap can help. One of the largest commercial real estate brokers in the US (with about 75 offices) the firm focuses on investment brokerage and provides financing research and advisory services to both buyers and sellers. The company is organized into groups by property type including shopping centers apartments office and industrial buildings and distressed properties. Marcus & Millichap was one of the earliest brokerages to maintain a centralized database to link potential buyers and sellers. In 2013 the company went public raising $72 million which it will use for general corporate purposes.

IPOMarcus & Millichap went public in October 2013 with an offering 6 million shares priced at $12 each. The firm intends to use the $42.3 million in net proceeds for general corporate purposes including capital expenditures and working capital to expand its services and potential acquisitions of real estate businesses or companies. It did not receive any proceeds from the sale of shares by the selling stockholders.

Operations

Marcus & Millichap specializes in commercial real estate investment sales with more than 1300 brokers in 76 markets throughout the US and Canada. The firm also offers property financing research and advisory services.

Financial Services

The firm closed more than 6600 transactions with a value of approximately $24 billion in 2013. Revenue increased 13% versus 2012 to $435.9 million. The rise in revenue was primarily due to increasing real estate brokerage commissions. Despite the double-digit increase in revenue net income declined 71% in 2013 versus 2012 to $8.2 million on rising operating expenses as a result of stock-based compensation charges in connection with the firm's 2013 IPO. Cash flow from operations has tracked the rise in revenue over the past three years rising steeply in 2013 to $96.9 million from $35.4 million in 2012.

Strategy

The brokerage firm focuses on private clients who account for more than 80% of US commercial property sales transactions annually. Its growth plan includes increasing its market share of the private clients segment in such areas as apartment retail office hospitality and senior housing. M&M is expending its presence in Canada with the opening of three offices there in 2014.

EXECUTIVES

Managing Director, Steven Rock
Vice President Investments, Philip Saglimbeni
Associate Vice President Capital Markets, Farhan Kabani
Vice President Investments, Cliff (Clifford) David
Vice President National Director Retail, Bill (Billy) Rose
Vice President Capital Markets, Danny (Dan) Abergel
Auditors: Ernst & Young LLP

LOCATIONS

HQ: Marcus & Millichap Inc
23975 Park Sorrento, Suite 400, Calabasas, CA 91302
Phone: 818 212-2250
Web: www.marcusmillichap.com

PRODUCTS/OPERATIONS

2015 Sales

	$ mil.	% of total
Real estate brokerage commissions	632.6	92
Financing fees	42.6	6
Other	13.9	2
Total	**689.1**	**100**

Selected Specializations

Health care
Hospitality and golf
Land
Manufactured housing
Multi-family
Net-leased
Office and industrial
Retail
Self-storage
Seniors housing
Student housing
Special assets

COMPETITORS

Baird & Warner	Inland Group
CBRE Group	Johnson Capital
Cassidy Turley	Jones Lang LaSalle
Coldwell Banker	Lee & Associates
Colliers International	NorthMarq Capital
Corky McMillin	ONCOR
Cushman & Wakefield	Sperry Van Ness
Grandbridge	Trammell Crow Company
HFF	

HISTORICAL FINANCIALS

Company Type: Public

Income Statement

FYE: December 31

	REVENUE ($ mil.)	NET INCOME ($ mil.)	NET PROFIT MARGIN	EMPLOYEES
12/15	689.0	66.3	9.6%	2,243.0
12/14	572.1	49.5	8.7%	2,105.0
12/13	435.9	9.2	2.1%	1,841.0
12/12	385.7	27.9	7.2%	513.0
12/11	274.7	13.4	4.9%	0.0
Annual Growth	**25.8%**	**49.0%**	**—**	**—**

2015 Year-End Financials

Debt ratio: 3.3%
Return on equity: 43.3%
Cash ($ mil.): 96.1
Current ratio: 2.61
Long-term debt ($ mil.): 9.6
No. of shares (mil.): 37.4
Dividends
  Yield: —
  Payout: —
Market value ($ mil.): 1,090.0

	STOCK PRICE ($) FY Close	P/E High/Low	PER SHARE ($) Earnings	Dividends	Book Value
12/15	29.14	31 17	1.69	0.00	5.05
12/14	33.25	27 11	1.27	0.00	3.16
12/13	14.90	63 55	0.24	0.00	1.71
Annual Growth	**39.8%**	**— —**	**165.4%**	**—**	**72.0%**

Marine Products Corp

A day on the water for you is a day at the office for Marine Products. The company builds recreational powerboats mainly though its Chaparral subsidiary. Its lineup includes fiberglass sterndrive and inboard deckboats cruisers and sport yachts ranging from 18 feet to 42 feet. Marine Products also makes a line of freshwater/saltwater sport fishing boats known for their "unsinkable hull" through subsidiary Robalo. Boats are sold to a network of about 230 independent dealers who then sell the lines to retail customers. The US generates the majority of the company's sales.

Geographic Reach

Headquartered at Atlanta the company sells its products to clients in Europe South America Asia Russia the Middle East and the US. Sales outside of the US accounted for 11% of its sales in 2015.

Sales and Marketing

Marine Products leverages a network of roughly 60 Chaparral dealers 25 Robalo dealers and 64 dealers selling both brands throughout the US. Oversees its boats are sold through some 85 international dealers.

Financial Performance

As the economy has gradually recovered Marine Products has achieved explosive growth over the years. Its total sales increased 21% from $171 million in 2014 to $207 million in 2015. Profits also surged 60% from $9 million in 2014 to $14 million in 2015. (Both these totals represented its highest amounts in at least eight years.)

The growth for 2015 was primarily due to a 23% increase in the number of boats sold. Unit sales increased due to higher sales of its Robalo outboard sport fishing boats as well as increased unit sales of its Chaparral Vortex jet boats and Suncoast outboards.

In addition to its trending revenue and net income Marine Products' operating cash flow surged by 51% from 2014 to 2015.

Strategy

With a health level of cash from operations and increasing production the company anticipates replenishing dealer inventories now normalizing from their historic low levels. Simultaneously it aims to enhance dealer offerings and spur retail purchases by manufacturing more models with standard features and fewer options.

Marine Products has recently launched new Chaparral and Robalo models: the Chaparral H2O Sport and Fish & Ski Boats and the Robalo R180 and R200. The new models are more affordable with a small number of standard features. They adhere to the company's strategy to produce lower-priced entry level models appealing to a value-conscious consumer.

EXECUTIVES

President CEO and Director, Richard A. Hubbell, age 72, $350,000 total compensation
EVP and President Chaparral Boats, James A. Lane, age 73, $250,000 total compensation
VP CFO and Treasurer, Ben M. Palmer, age 55, $175,000 total compensation
Chairman, R. Randall Rollins, age 85
Vice President Secretary and Director, Linda H (Lin) Graham
Auditors: Grant Thornton LLP

LOCATIONS

HQ: Marine Products Corp
2801 Buford Highway, Suite 520, Atlanta, GA 30329
Phone: 404 321-7910
Web: www.marineproductscorp.com

PRODUCTS/OPERATIONS

Selected Products
Chaparral (family recreational cruiser and sport yachts)
Premiere sport yachts (fiberglass sport yachts)

Signature cruisers (fiberglass cruisers)
SSi sportboats (fiberglass closed deck runabouts)
SSX sportdecks (fiberglass bowrider crossover sportboats)
Sunesta Xtreme tow boats (fiberglass pleasure boats)
Robalo (outboard sport fishing boats)

COMPETITORS

Bombardier	Sea Fox Boats
Brunswick Corp.	Sea Ray Boats
B©n©teau	Sunseeker
Cigarette Racing Team	Taylor Made Group
Correct Craft	Viking Yacht
Duckworth Boat Works	Yamaha Motor
Fountain Powerboat	

HISTORICAL FINANCIALS

Company Type: Public

Income Statement

FYE: December 31

	REVENUE ($ mil.)	NET INCOME ($ mil.)	NET PROFIT MARGIN	EMPLOYEES
12/15	207.0	14.3	6.9%	767.0
12/14	171.0	8.9	5.2%	605.0
12/13	168.2	7.5	4.5%	651.0
12/12	148.9	6.9	4.7%	587.0
12/11	106.4	6.7	6.3%	450.0
Annual Growth	18.1%	20.7%	—	14.3%

2015 Year-End Financials

Debt ratio: —
Return on equity: 16.4%
Cash ($ mil.): 7.9
Current ratio: 3.82
Long-term debt ($ mil.): —
No. of shares (mil.): 38.1
Dividends
Yield: 3.3%
Payout: 64.5%
Market value ($ mil.): 230.0

	STOCK PRICE ($) FY Close	P/E High/Low	PER SHARE ($) Earnings	Dividends	Book Value
12/15	6.04	23 14	0.39	0.20	2.37
12/14	8.44	42 25	0.24	0.16	2.19
12/13	10.05	51 29	0.20	0.15	2.14
12/12	5.72	35 26	0.19	0.63	2.06
12/11	4.96	42 18	0.18	0.00	2.50
Annual Growth	5.0%		— — 21.3%		— (1.4%)

MarineMax Inc

MarineMax aims to float your boat. The nation's largest recreational boat dealer has about 54 locations in around 19 states. Dealerships sell new and used pleasure boats fishing boats motor yachts ski boats and high-performance boats. Sales of new boats made by Brunswick including Sea Ray and Boston Whaler boats account for around 48% of revenue. The company also sells boat engines trailers parts and accessories; arranges for financing and insurance; provides repair and maintenance; and offers boat brokerage and storage services. MarineMax is the exclusive dealer of Sea Ray in almost all of the areas where it operates. Since its founding in 1998 MarineMax has acquired about 20 boat dealers. The average selling price of one of MarineMax's premium boats was about $126000 in fiscal 2011 which was a decrease of approximately 13% from $145000 in fiscal 2010. The company had to decrease prices due to the weakened US economy but in fiscal 2011 the company

saw same-store sales (the best indicator of a retailer's performance) increase by 8% compared to a decrease of 17% in fiscal 2010. Overall company sales increased to $480.9 million in fiscal 2011 compared to $450.3 million in fiscal 2010. As the US recession wanes and the economy slowly recovers it seems that MarineMax is showing signs of improvement. Although Florida's housing crisis will be of major importance on MarineMax's future performance. The company in early 2011 acquired and added to its portfolio of cruising and fishing boats Panama City-based Treasure Island Marina's retail sales and brokerage operations. Panama City sells cruising and fishing boats under the brands Boston Whaler Grady White and Sea Ray; Panama City also has the largest boat storage facility in the Panama City region.

EXECUTIVES

EVP CFO and Secretary, Michael H. (Mike) McLamb, age 51, $315,000 total compensation
Chairman President and CEO, William H. McGill, age 73, $550,000 total compensation
EVP Chief Legal Officer and Assistant Secretary, Paulee C. Day, age 47, $260,000 total compensation
VP East Operations, Charles A. (Chuck) Cashman, age 53, $200,000 total compensation
VP West Operations, William Brett McGill, age 47, $200,000 total compensation
Vp Marketing, Thomas (Thom) Wolden
Vice President Of Products And Logistics, Bret Skonicki
Auditors: KPMG LLP

LOCATIONS

HQ: MarineMax Inc
2600 McCormick Drive, Suite 200, Clearwater, FL 33759
Phone: 727 531-1700
Web: www.MarineMax.com

PRODUCTS/OPERATIONS

2016 Sales

	$ mil.	% of total
New boat sales	645.3	69
Used boat sales	165.5	18
Maintenance repair & storage services	51.5	5
Marine Engines Related Marine Equipment and Boating Parts and Accessories	32.6	3
F&I Products	23.3	2
Brokerage Sales	18.7	2
Yacht Charter	5.1	1
Total	942.0	100

Selected Products & Trade Names

Motor Yachts
  Azimut
  Hatteras Motor Yachts
Convertibles
  Cabo
  Hatteras Convertibles
Pleasure Boats
  Meridian
  Sea Ray
Fishing Boats
  Boston Whaler
  Grady White
Ski Boats
  Axis
  Malibu

COMPETITORS

Coast Distribution	Wal-Mart
Defender Industries	West Marine
Sports Authority	

HISTORICAL FINANCIALS
Company Type: Public

Income Statement
FYE: September 30

	REVENUE ($ mil.)	NET INCOME ($ mil.)	NET PROFIT MARGIN	EMPLOYEES
09/16	942.0	22.5	2.4%	1,422.0
09/15	751.3	48.2	6.4%	1,289.0
09/14	624.6	11.2	1.8%	1,228.0
09/13	584.5	15.0	2.6%	1,227.0
09/12	524.4	1.1	0.2%	1,170.0
Annual Growth	15.8%	112.9%	—	5.0%

2016 Year-End Financials

Debt ratio: 30.4%
Return on equity: 7.5%
Cash ($ mil.): 38.5
Current ratio: 1.69
Long-term debt ($ mil.): —

No. of shares (mil.): 24.2
Dividends
 Yield: —
 Payout: —
Market value ($ mil.): 509.0

	STOCK PRICE ($) FY Close	P/E High/Low	PER SHARE ($) Earnings	Dividends	Book Value
09/16	20.95	23 15	0.91	0.00	12.87
09/15	14.13	14 7	1.92	0.00	11.72
09/14	16.85	41 26	0.46	0.00	9.88
09/13	12.20	21 11	0.63	0.00	9.42
09/12	8.29	222110	0.05	0.00	8.77
Annual Growth	26.1%	— —106.5%	— 10.1%

MarketAxess Holdings Inc.

A little creative spelling never got in the way of a good bond trade. MarketAxess offers an electronic multi-dealer platform for institutional traders buying and selling US corporate high-yield and emerging market bonds as well as Eurobonds. Participating broker-dealers include some of the world's largest such as BNP Paribas Citigroup Deutsche Bank Goldman Sachs and Merrill Lynch. In all MarketAxess serves more than 1000 investment firms mutual funds insurance companies pension funds and other institutional investors. The company also provides real-time corporate bond price information through its Corporate BondTicker service.

Operations

Nearly 85% of the company's revenue comes from monthly distribution fees and commissions for transactions executed on its platform between institutional investor and broker-dealer clients. About 10% of its revenue comes from its information and post-trade services from its Trax division (the trading name under Xtrakter Ltd.) which provides trade matching regulatory transaction reporting and market and reference data across a range of fixed income products. Less than 5% of its revenue comes from its technology products and services. MarketAxess had a staff of 303 employees at the end of 2014 with 187 of them based in teh US and the others mostly in the UK.

Geographic Reach

MarketAxess generates 85% of its revenue from the US while nearly all of the remainder comes from the UK. The company has office locations in the US UK Brazil and Singapore.Sales and MarketingTo boost awareness of its brand and electronic trading platform MarketAxess uses advertising direct marketing promotional mailings and participates in industry conferences and media engagement. As an example it worked with The Wall Street Journal to make its Corporate BondTicker service the source of WSJ's information for its daily corporate bond and high-yield tables.In the US high-grade corporate bond market more than 600 active institutional investors and 68 broker-dealers used MarketAxess' platform in 2014 including all of the top 20 broker-dealers as ranked by 2014 US corporate bond new-issue underwriting volume. The company's broker-dealer clients made up 96% of all underwriting activity for newly-issued corporate bonds in 2014.Overall the firm spent $5.8 million on advertising in 2014 up 25% from $4.6 million spent in 2013.

Financial Performance

MarketAxess' revenues and profits have risen at a healthy clip over the past several years largely as the bond market has become more attractive to investors which has led to growth in both MarketAxess' commission income and information and post-trade services income.The firm's revenue rose by 10% to $262.8 million in 2014 mostly thanks to commission income growth as trading activity in the bond market remained strong. Its revenue from its information and post-trade services also grew thanks to its 2013 acquisition of Xtrackter while favorable foreign currency exchange rates also added to the company's top-line growth.Despite generating higher revenue in 2014 MarketAxess' net income dipped by 2% to $74.8 million for the year mostly because in 2013 it had enjoyed a $7.6 million (non-recurring) gain from its since-discontinued Greenline subsidiary. MarketAxess' operating cash levels jumped 21% to nearly $110 million in 2014 mostly as it generated higher cash earnings compared to the prior year.

Strategy

MarketAxess focuses on technology investments to expand its connectivity offerings for electronic transactions. Its main objective reiterated in 2015 is to "provide the leading global electronic trading platform for fixed-income securities connecting broker-dealers and institutional investors more easily and efficiently while offering a broad array of information trading and technology services to market participants across the trading cycle."The strategy's key elements include: innovating and introducing new product offerings to the MarketAxess platform; leverage its existing client network to increase the number of potential counterparties and boost liquidity; continue to build on its existing service offerings to ensure that its platform is more full integrated into the workflow of its client base; and add new content and analytical capabilities to its Corporate BondTicker service.The firm also fosters growth by entering strategic alliances or acquiring smaller marketplace firms to expand its service capabilities extend its market reach or bolsters its existing service expertise.

Mergers and Acquisitions

In February 2013 MarketAxess expanded its capacity when it acquired Xtrakter Limited a leading provider of regulatory transaction reporting financial market data and trade matching services to the European securities markets. The acquired company became MarketAxess' Trax division.

EXECUTIVES

Chairman President and CEO, Richard M. (Rick) McVey, age 57, $400,000 total compensation
CFO, Antonio L. (Tony) DeLise, age 54, $200,000 total compensation
CIO, Nicholas Themelis, age 53, $250,000 total compensation
Chief Credit and Risk Officer, James N.B. (Jim) Rucker, $200,000 total compensation
Head of Marketing and Communications, Florencia Panizza
Head of US Sales, Kevin McPherson
Head Europe and Asia, Robert H. Urtheil
Vice President, Bill (Billy) Barnett
Vice President Information Technology Systems, Douglas Marzano
Auditors: PricewaterhouseCoopers LLP

LOCATIONS

HQ: MarketAxess Holdings Inc.
 299 Park Avenue, 10th Floor, New York, NY 10171
Phone: 212 813-6000   **Fax:** 212 813-6390
Web: www.marketaxess.com

PRODUCTS/OPERATIONS

2014 Sales

	$ mil.	% of total
Commissions	221.1	84
Information and post-trade services	31.5	12
Technology products and services	6.9	3
Investment income	0.5	-
Others	2.8	1
Total	**262.8**	**100**

Selected Mergers and Acquisitions

FY2012
Xtrakter Limited (undisclosed price; London UK; provider of regulatory transaction reporting)

COMPETITORS

BGC Partners	NEX
BondsOnline	TRADEBOOK
Cantor Fitzgerald	Tradeweb
GFI Group	Weeden
Interactive Brokers	
Intercontinental Exchange	

HISTORICAL FINANCIALS
Company Type: Public

Income Statement
FYE: December 31

	REVENUE ($ mil.)	NET INCOME ($ mil.)	NET PROFIT MARGIN	EMPLOYEES
12/15	303.1	96.0	31.7%	342.0
12/14	262.7	74.8	28.5%	303.0
12/13	238.7	76.0	31.8%	293.0
12/12	198.2	60.0	30.3%	240.0
12/11	181.1	47.7	26.3%	232.0
Annual Growth	13.7%	19.1%	—	10.2%

2015 Year-End Financials

Debt ratio: —
Return on equity: 26.5%
Cash ($ mil.): 199.7
Current ratio: 4.97
Long-term debt ($ mil.): —

No. of shares (mil.): 37.4
Dividends
 Yield: 0.7%
 Payout: 31.7%
Market value ($ mil.): 4,175.0

	STOCK PRICE ($) FY Close	P/E High/Low	PER SHARE ($) Earnings	Dividends	Book Value
12/15	111.59	44 26	2.55	0.80	10.44
12/14	71.71	36 23	2.03	0.64	8.96
12/13	66.93	34 17	2.01	1.82	8.23
12/12	35.30	23 16	1.59	1.74	6.49
12/11	30.11	24 15	1.20	0.36	8.06
Annual Growth	38.7%	— —	20.7%	22.1%	6.7%

Marlin Business Services Corp

Marlin is hooked on equipment leasing. Marlin Business Services leases more than 100 categories of commercial equipment to about 68000 small and mid-sized businesses —and it provides the financing for the deals in part through its Marlin Business Bank subsidiary. The market is known in the equipment leasing field as the "small-ticket" segment. Copiers makes up about 30% of Marlin's lease portfolio but its customers also can get products as diverse as computer hardware and software security systems telecom equipment dental implant systems water filtration systems and restaurant equipment. The company primarily operates through its main subsidiary Marlin Leasing.

Operations

The "small-ticket" segment covers the leasing of equipment up to $250000 although Marlin's average equipment lease is about $14000 and runs 50 months (leases usually range from 36 to 60 months). Customers can opt to buy equipment at the end of the initial contracts. More than 95% of the company's transactions originate through almost 12000 independent commercial equipment dealers; Marlin also uses direct communications with customers and lease brokers. Financing is increasingly offered through Marlin Business Bank; in addition it has a close relationship with Wells Fargo's Capital Finance.

About three quarters of Marlin's revenue comes from interest it charges on equipment financing. Fee income accounts for 17% of revenue with insurance at 7%.

Geographic Reach

Although Marlin Leasing has customers in across the US its business follows population trends with California and Texas as its largest markets each accounting for between 9% and 13% of lease payments.

In addition it has offices in Colorado Georgia New Jersey New Hampshire Pennsylvania and Utah.

Sales and Marketing

Marlin uses both telephone direct sales and for strategic larger accounts a team of about 140 outside sales executives.

Financial Performance

Marlin's revenue ticked 1% higher to about $90 million in 2015 from 2014. In the low interest environment the company's interst income was flat while fee and insurance income revenues were higher.

The company's net income of about $16 million in 2015 was 17% lower than 2014's figure. The company had higher expenses to deal with the exits of the chief executive and financial officers while also paying for additional workers overall.

Cash flow from operations in 2015 slipped to about $27 million a 19% drop from 2014.

Strategy

In 2015 Marlin opened several new business channels added sales people and offered a working capital loan product. It also initiated a product called Funding Stream a flexible loan program of Marlin Business Bank.

Marlin prides itself on having a diverse portfolio while working to effectively manage credit risk. It has a centralized collections department that assigns more experienced collectors to late-stage delinquent accounts and specialist collectors who focus on late fees property taxes bankruptcies and large balance accounts. While Marlin Business Bank is its primary funding source the company does have access to multiple funding sources.

EXECUTIVES

COO, Edward J. (Ed) Siciliano, age 54, $313,500 total compensation
SVP and CFO, W. Taylor Kamp, age 55, $111,919 total compensation
SVP Administration General Counsel and Secretary, Edward R. Dietz, age 41, $275,000 total compensation
CEO, Jeffrey A. Hilzinger
National Sales Manager, Gary (Gar) Crawford
Vice President Portfolio Management, Greg (Greggy) Sting
National Sales Manager Healthcare, Paul Cheslock
Assistant Vice President, Bob Fischer
Vice President Risk Management, Dan (Danny) Castellini
Vice President Of Sales, Richard (Dick) Henderson
Assistant Vice President Direct Sales, Ken (Kenny) Weaver
Assistant Vice President Strategic Accounts, Brian (Bri) Mcmahon
Assistant Vice President Of Asset Management, Bob (Bo) Basile
Vice President Of Credit, Ronald (Ron) Queen
Assistant Vice President Major Accounts, Greg (Greggy) Dietrich
Chairman, Lawrence J. (Larry) DeAngelo, age 49
Auditors: Deloitte & Touche LLP

LOCATIONS

HQ: Marlin Business Services Corp
300 Fellowship Road, Mount Laurel, NJ 08054
Phone: 888 479-9111
Web: www.marlincorp.com

PRODUCTS/OPERATIONS

2015 sales

	$ mil.	% of total
Interest	66.7	74
Fees	15.3	17
Insurance	5.9	7
Other	1.9	2
Total	**89.8**	**100**

COMPETITORS

American Express	JPMorgan Chase
CalFirst	KeyCorp
Citibank	National Funding Inc
Comerica	Presidio Technology
Deutsche Bank	Capital
GE Capital	Rabobank Group
HP Financial Services	Ricoh USA
IBM Global Financing	Wells Fargo

HISTORICAL FINANCIALS

Company Type: Public

Income Statement

FYE: December 31

	REVENUE ($ mil.)	NET INCOME ($ mil.)	NET PROFIT MARGIN	EMPLOYEES
12/15	89.7	15.9	17.8%	314.0
12/14	88.7	19.3	21.8%	285.0
12/13	83.6	16.2	19.4%	285.0
12/12	70.9	11.7	16.5%	265.0
12/11	62.1	6.1	9.9%	242.0
Annual Growth	**9.6%**	**26.8%**	**—**	**6.7%**

2015 Year-End Financials

Debt ratio: —	No. of shares (mil.): 12.4
Return on equity: 9.8%	Dividends
Cash ($ mil.): 60.1	Yield: 15.7%
Current ratio: 0.14	Payout: 183.3%
Long-term debt ($ mil.): —	Market value ($ mil.): 199.0

	STOCK PRICE ($) FY Close	P/E High/Low		Earnings	PER SHARE ($) Dividends	Book Value
12/15	16.06	17	10	1.25	2.53	12.10
12/14	20.53	19	11	1.49	0.47	13.55
12/13	25.20	22	15	1.25	2.42	12.55
12/12	20.06	25	14	0.91	0.28	13.64
12/11	12.70	28	20	0.48	0.06	12.86
Annual Growth	**6.0%**	**—**	**—**	**27.0%**	**154.8%**	**(1.5%)**

Masimo Corp.

As important as the blood running through your veins is the oxygen it carries. Masimo knows that and makes tools that monitor arterial blood-oxygen saturation levels and pulse rates in patients. The company's product range which is based on Signal Extraction Technology (SET) offers pulse oximeters in both handheld and stand-alone (bedside) form. Product benefits include the provision of real-time information and elimination of signal interference such as patient movements. In addition to general product sales Masimo licenses SET-based products to dozens of medical equipment manufacturers including CareFusion Covidien Medtronic and Welch Allyn.

Geographic Reach

While the Americas account for about three-fourths of its product sales Masimo is working to grow its operations in Africa Asia Australia Europe and the Middle East. It has operations in about 25 countries.

Sales and Marketing

The company markets its products globally through direct sales representatives and distributors. Customers include hospitals alternative care entities OEMs and wholesalers. Two distributors Owens & Minor and Cardinal Health each account for more than 10% of annual sales.

Advertising costs for fiscal 2012 was about $9.5 million compared to $5.6 million in 2011. Masimo is expanding marketing programs to build consumer brand awareness through means including print and digital advertising trade show participation and direct mail campaigns. It also distributes publications and sponsors seminars to educate medical professionals about its products.

In 2012 the company entered partnerships with several group purchasing organizations (GPOs) to facilitate increased direct sales of pulse oximetry products to hospitals.

Financial Performance

Masimo increased revenues in 2012 by 12% to $493 million due to higher product sales especially of consumable items (related to its rising number of installed equipment locations) and increased sales of new Rainbow SET products. It also experienced growth from acquisitions increased marketing efforts and through partnerships with OEMs and GPOs. Increased product sales were offset by lower royalties (caused by a decrease in the royalty rate of its partnership with Covidien).

Net income decreased 2% to $62 million in 2012 due to higher costs for goods sold and increased operating expenses (related to increased staffing levels in the administrative and research divisions) and non-operating expenses (from currency exchange recognitions).

Masimo has reported steadily rising revenues over the last five years from organic growth measures. However net income has declined over the past three years due to the increased costs of a growing business.

Strategy

Expansion is key to Masimo's strategy for growth. Its research and development efforts (with expenses of around $40 to $50 million per year) focus on novel products as well as improvements to existing products. Product enhancements have included a new monitoring capability that can detect methemoglobin (a form of hemoglobin that can cause a lack of oxygen in the blood) and the addition of total hemoglobin (oxygen in red blood cells) measurement. It is expanding the applications of its Rainbow SET products which measure multiple blood components at once; it is also adding products that reduce the invasiveness of testing and that provide remote monitoring and alarm capabilities.

To branch out beyond its traditionally targeted emergency and critical care setting markets Masimo is promoting existing products (and adding new products) to meet the general treatment needs of hospitals and non-hospital environments. For example the company is promoting its SET technology as ideal for use by home care agencies post-acute care hospitals and sleep diagnostic centers. It is also introducing new handheld products that allow for fast and simple measurement of perimeters in a variety of care settings. The company expects moves such as these to greatly expand its presence in non-critical care markets.

Masimo also expands by entering new OEM licensing agreements (such as a long-term agreement for the use of its Rainbow SET products in GE Healthcare's patient monitors in 2012); by widening agreements with wholesale distributors; and by making occasional acquisitions.

Mergers and Acquisitions

To bring manufacturing of some key components in-house Masimo acquired Spire Semiconductor for $7 million in early 2012. Masimo had been one of Spire's largest customers and having the LED manufacturer under its wing promises to speed development of new products.

Also in 2012 Masimo acquired Phasein AB which manufactures and sells ultra-compact capnography and gas analyzers for some $30 million. The added products complement the company's existing portfolio of OEM solutions.

Ownership

Chairman and CEO Joe Kiani who founded Masimo in 1989 holds roughly 10% of the company's stock. The company went public in 2007 and used proceeds from the IPO towards capital and equipment expenses and product development efforts.

EXECUTIVES

Chairman and CEO, Joe E. Kiani, age 52, $883,518 total compensation

EVP and CIO, Yongsam Lee, age 52, $340,704 total compensation

President Worldwide OEM Business and Blood Management, Rick Fishel, age 58, $357,574 total compensation

EVP Business Development, Paul R. Jansen, age 45

COO, Anand Sampath, age 50, $369,277 total compensation

EVP Finance and CFO, Mark P. de Raad, age 56, $363,034 total compensation

EVP General Counsel and Corporate Secretary, Tom McClenahan, age 43

President Masimo Worldwide Sales Professional Services and Medical Affairs, Jon Coleman, age 52, $354,103 total compensation

Vice President Of Finance Controller, Gerry Hammarth, age 57

Vice President Finance, Andy Wilsack

Vice President Information Systems, Mark Brinton

Vice President, Jerry Fronzaglio

Vice President, Mathew (Matt) Jimenez

Vice President Corporate Sales, Jim (Jimmy) Beyer

Vice President Sales Northeast, Fred (Freddy) Kelly

Vice President, Daniel (Dan) Rice

Vice President Technology Development, Lisa Hershelman

Vice President, Dennis Wynn

Global Vice President Of Sales, Brad Snow

Vice President OEM Business, Angela (Ang) Wrolstad

Senior Vice President, Dan Brothman

Vice President, Ryan Cooksey

Vice President of Sales and Marketing, Carmen (Carm) How

Vice President OEM, Steve (Stevie) Jensen

Executive Vice President, Raul Bennis

Vice President Business Development, Eli Kammerman

Senior Vice President OEM Business, Bob Kenney

Vice President Of Finance Controller, Gerry (Gerold) Hammarth

Vice President, Teresa (Terry) Howe

Board Member, Julie Bradley

Auditors: Grant Thornton LLP

LOCATIONS

HQ: Masimo Corp.
52 Discovery, Irvine, CA 92618
Phone: 949 297-7000
Web: www.masimo.com

PRODUCTS/OPERATIONS

2016 Sales

	$ mil.	% of total
Product	599.3	95
Royalty	30.8	5
Total	**630.1**	**100**

Selected Products

Capnography and Multigas Monitoring
Patient SafetyNet Remote Monitoring
Rainbow Acoustic Monitoring
Rainbow Pulse CO-Oximetry
SedLine Brain Function Monitoring
Signal Extraction Pulse Oximetry

Selected OEM Customers

3F Medical Co. Ltd (China)
Atom Medical Corporation
Biolight Meditech Co. Ltd. (China)
Bitmos GmbH (Germany)
BMEYE (The Netherlands)
CareFusion
CAS Medical Systems Inc.
Comen Medical Instruments Co. Ltd. (China)
Corpuls
Digicare
Dräger Medical AG & Co. KG (Germany)
Excel-Tech Ltd (XLTEK a Canadian division of Natus Medical Incorporated)
Fritz Stephan GmbH (Germany)
Fukuda Denshi Co. LTD. (Japan)
GE Healthcare

GETEMED Medizin- und Informationstechnik AG (Germany)
Imagenes y Medicina S.A. de C.V. (Mexico)
Impact Instrumentation Inc.
International Biomedical
IRadimed Corporation
Ivy Biomedical Systems Inc.
Medtronic Inc.
Mennen Medical Corp. (Israel)
Mindray
Newtech Inc. (China)
Nihon Kohden
Norwood Scientific
Oridion Capnography Inc.
Osypka Medical Inc.
Philips Healthcare/Respironics Inc. (The Netherlands and US)
Phoenix Medical Systems Pvt. Ltd. (India)
Physio-Control
Pooyandegan Rah Saadat Co. Ltd. (Iran)
Radiometer Medical ApS (Denmark)
RDECON
Schiller AG (Switzerland)
ShenZhen HeXin ZONDAN Medical Equipment CO. LTD (China)
Spacelabs Healthcare
Toitu Co. Ltd. (Japan)
Welch Allyn Inc.
ZOLL Medical Corporation

Selected Acquisitions

COMPETITORS

Bio-logic	Mindray
CAS Medical	Philips Healthcare
Criticare	Siemens Healthcare
GE Healthcare Instrumentation Laboratory Company	Thoratec Corp

HISTORICAL FINANCIALS

Company Type: Public

Income Statement

FYE: January 2

	REVENUE ($ mil.)	NET INCOME ($ mil.)	NET PROFIT MARGIN	EMPLOYEES
01/16	630.1	83.3	13.2%	3,700.0
01/15*	586.6	72.5	12.4%	3,600.0
12/13	547.2	58.3	10.7%	3,139.0
12/12	493.2	62.2	12.6%	2,866.0
12/11	438.9	63.7	14.5%	2,548.0
Annual Growth	**9.5%**	**6.9%**	**—**	**9.8%**

*Fiscal year change

2016 Year-End Financials

Debt ratio: 30.7%	No. of shares (mil.): 49.8
Return on equity: 28.7%	Dividends
Cash ($ mil.): 132.3	Yield: —
Current ratio: 2.26	Payout: —
Long-term debt ($ mil.): 185.0	Market value ($ mil.): 2,071.0

	STOCK PRICE ($) FY Close	P/E High/Low		PER SHARE ($) Earnings	Dividends	Book Value
01/16	41.51	27	16	1.55	0.00	5.52
01/15*	25.88	24	16	1.30	0.00	5.82
12/13	28.86	29	18	1.02	0.00	5.77
12/12	20.58	23	17	1.07	1.00	4.77
12/11	18.69	33	17	1.05	0.00	4.75
Annual Growth	**22.1%**	**—**	**—**	**10.2%**	**—**	**3.8%**

*Fiscal year change

Match Group Inc

Auditors: Ernst & Young LLP

LOCATIONS

HQ: Match Group Inc
8300 Douglas Avenue, Dallas, TX 75225
Phone: 214 576-9352
Web: www.matchgroupinc.com

HISTORICAL FINANCIALS

Company Type: Public

Income Statement

FYE: December 31

	REVENUE ($ mil.)	NET INCOME ($ mil.)	NET PROFIT MARGIN	EMPLOYEES
12/15	1,020.4	120.3	11.8%	4,800.0
12/14	888.2	147.7	16.6%	4,800.0
12/13	803.0	125.0	15.6%	0.0
12/12	713.4	85.6	12.0%	0.0
Annual Growth	12.7%	12.0%	—	—

2015 Year-End Financials

Debt ratio: 64.0%	No. of shares (mil.): 248.2
Return on equity: 22.3%	Dividends
Cash ($ mil.): 99.8	Yield: —
Current ratio: 0.58	Payout: —
Long-term debt ($ mil.): 1,193.4	Market value ($ mil.): 3,364.0

	STOCK PRICE ($) FY Close	P/E High/Low	PER SHARE ($) Earnings	Dividends	Book Value
12/15	13.55	22 19	0.65	0.00	1.12
12/14	0.00	— —	0.88	0.00	(0.00)
Annual Growth	—	—	(26.1%)	—	—

Matrix Service Co.

Matrix Service Company makes sure that oil and water don't mix. The company provides a variety of construction repair and maintenance services mainly to the petroleum and power industries in North America. Its Storage Solutions business which accounts for about 35% of sales specializes in above-ground storage tanks to hold oil gas and specialty materials. It also designs and builds plants refineries and other installations. Through its Oil Gas & Chemical segment Matrix provides preventive routine and emergency repair services focusing on turnarounds outages and shutdowns when time is of the essence. Founded in 1984 the firm has around a dozen locations in the US and Canada.

Operations

Matrix Service Company operates four business segments including: Storage Solutions (which generated 37% of the company's total revenue in FY2015); Oil Gas & Chemical (23% of revenue); Industrial (21% of revenue) which provides services for the mining and minerals sector as well as other industrial and manufacturing markets; and Electrical Infrastructure (19% of revenue) which builds and repairs substations and power generation facilities. The company's subsidiaries include:

Matrix Service Matrix NAC Matrix PDM Engineering and Matrix Applied Technologies.

Geographic Reach

Tulsa Oklahoma-based Matrix Service Company generated 90% of its revenue in the US in FY2015 while the rest came from Canada. The firm is licensed to operates in all 50 US states and four Canadian provinces. Its subsidiaries also have offices in Sydney Australia and Seoul South Korea.

Sales and Marketing

The specialty contractor serviced about 575 customers across the oil gas power petrochemical industrial mining iron and steel and minerals sectors in fiscal 2015 (ended June). These include petroleum companies refiners pipeline operators and oil and gas marketing firms. Enbridge is its single largest client accounting for about 12% of sales in FY2015.Matrix markets its products and services mostly through its marketing and business development personnel senior professional staff and its operating management.

Financial Performance

Matrix Service Company's annual revenues and profits doubled between fiscal years 2011 and 2014 (ended June 30 2014) thanks to strong growth in the energy and power sectors in North America.The company's revenue jumped 6% to $1.34 billion during FY2015 mostly thanks to added revenue stemming from its 2014 acquisition of Kvaerner North American Construction (now Matrix MAC). All of its business segments grew by more than 25% each except for Storage Solutions (its largest segment) which declined 18% during the year due to a project delay for a large customer in Canada.Despite revenue growth in FY2015 Matrix's profit fell for the first time in years with net income dropping more than 50% to $17.16 million as the company acquired a $53.4 million- EPC joint venture project charge which also increased its effective tax rate by 86%. The company's operating cash levels dove nearly 70% to $24.44 million mostly because of the drop in earnings but also because of unfavorable working capital changes related to its costs and estimated earnings in excess of billings on uncompleted contracts.

Strategy

Matrix Service Company reiterated in late 2015 that it looked to expand into the upstream energy markets through acquisitions. Longer-term the company hopes that environmental regulations will lead customers to seek out Matrix's services to help them meet compliance standards. As one of the largest above-ground storage tank builders in North America Matrix also expects that business to grow over the long term as infrastructure ages and demand for storage capacity increases.

In an effort to diversify Matrix has been focused on expanding its customer base and geographic presence. The company is making inroads in the alternative energy sector by adding products and services related to wind farms geothermal projects and solar panel installation.

Mergers and Acquisitions

In February 2016 Matrix bought global storage tank peripherals designer and manufacturer Baillie Tank Equipment (BTE) to expand its line of above-ground storage tank product offerings. The company would be renamed Matrix Applied Technologies.In August 2014 Matrix and its Matrix Service Inc subsidiary bought HDB Ltd a provider of construction fabrication and turnaround services to energy companies across the Central Valley of California. The $10 million-acquisition was part of Matrix's expansion into the upstream and midstream markets and expanded its reach into a prime oil producing market in California.In December 2013 Matrix acquired Kvaerner North

American Construction a provider of capital construction and maintenance services to power generation integrated iron and steel and industrial process facilities in North America for about $80.3 million in cash. Post sale the business was renamed Matrix North American Construction. In January 2013 the company acquired Pelichem Industrial Cleaning Services LLC a privately-owned industrial cleaning business based in Louisiana. The Pelichem purchase expanded Matrix's industrial cleaning business and extended its geographic reach along the Gulf Coast.

HISTORY

Company BackgroundDoyl West and William Lee both former officers with Tank Service founded Matrix in 1984 in Oklahoma. After buying Petrotank Equipment in 1989 they reincorporated as Matrix Environmental Co. which became Matrix Service Co. in 1990. Matrix grew rapidly through acquisitions including Midwest Industrial Contractors (1990) San Luis Tank Piping Construction (1991) and Brown Steel Contractors (1994). Its innovations included a "tank jacking" process to elevate and support water tanks during renovation and a safety nozzle that revolutionized the cleaning and desludging of crude oil tanks.

In 1993 Matrix's sales dropped from increased competition but rebounded in late 1994 as US petroleum companies rescheduled work they had postponed while the EPA finalized rules for the Clean Air Act.

To broaden its reach Matrix acquired General Service Corp. in 1997. That year ITEQ which provides liquid and gas storage systems and services agreed to buy Matrix but the deal was called off in early 1998 amid perceived integration problems. Founders West (who had served as CEO) and Lee (who had been CFO) retired in 1998. Longtime executive Martin Rinehart took over as CEO that year but left in 1999 during the company's second year of losses. Bradley Vetal (formerly COO of Matrix's industrial services unit) succeeded him.

Matrix recovered after disposing of its troubled municipal water services subsidiaries: It sold one Brown Steel Contractors to Caldwell Tanks in 1999 and closed the other San Luis Tank Piping in 2000. Once it disposed of its municipal water services Matrix was able to focus on aboveground storage tank (AST) operations and grow its construction services operations in 2001.

The next year Matrix experienced a healthy hike in sales with the growth in new tank construction (many of the industry's tanks were 20 years old or older) and an increase in the company's services to power plants.

To strengthen its presence in the mid-Atlantic region the company in 2003 acquired Pennsylvania-based Hake Group an industrial contractor for the power generation petroleum chemical and manufacturing industries.

Vetal resigned as CEO in 2005; director Michael Hall stepped in as interim CEO (Michael Bradley ultimately took over the position) and director Ed Hendrix was elected chairman. That year two employees who worked at subsidiary Matrix Service Industrial Contractors lost their lives after being exposed to nitrogen fumes while working at a Valero Energy Corporation refinery in Delaware City Delaware.

The company also expanded its capabilities when it purchased oilfield construction equipment and cryogenic tank technology use from Chicago Bridge & Iron Co. in 2008. The deal which helped grow the company's liquefied natural gas business also included $20 million in contract work.

In 2009 Matrix enhanced its electrical and instrumentation capabilities with the acquisition of S.M. Electric Company in New Jersey. The addition helps Matrix grow its business in the Mid-Atlantic and southern New England.

Michael Bradley resigned as CEO and president in 2010 along with CFO and VP Thomas Long. Both men left the firm to join the same midstream petroleum business that they had worked for before Matrix. The following year John Hewitt of Aker Solutions was named CEO of Matrix Service Company.

EXECUTIVES

President Matrix Service Inc., James P. (Jim) Ryan, age 62, $309,074 total compensation
President and CEO, John R. Hewitt, $527,307 total compensation
CFO, Kevin S. Cavanah, age 52, $249,823 total compensation
President Matrix SME, Matthew J. Petrizzo, age 54, $295,705 total compensation
COO, Joseph F. Montalbano, age 67, $381,570 total compensation
Vice President Matrix Sme, James J (Jamie) Collins
Vice President Environmental Health, Jack (Jackie) Frost
Vice President of Operations, Brad (Brady) Rinehart
Chairman, Michael J. Hall, age 72
Auditors: Deloitte & Touche LLP

LOCATIONS

HQ: Matrix Service Co.
5100 East Skelly Drive, Suite 500, Tulsa, OK 74135
Phone: 918 838-8822
Web: www.matrixservicecompany.com

PRODUCTS/OPERATIONS

2015 Sales By Segment

	$ mil.	% of total
Storage solutions	503.1	37
Oil gas & chemical	305.4	23
Industrial	276.7	21
Electrical infrastructure	257.9	19
Total	**1,343.1**	**100**

COMPETITORS

Arizona Instrument
Brown and Caldwell
Chart Industries
Chicago Bridge & Iron
Denali
ENGlobal
Halliburton
OP-TECH Environmental
Veolia Environmental Services North America
ZCL Composites

HISTORICAL FINANCIALS

Company Type: Public

Income Statement

FYE: June 30

	REVENUE ($ mil.)	NET INCOME ($ mil.)	NET PROFIT MARGIN	EMPLOYEES
06/16	1,311.9	28.8	2.2%	3,560.0
06/15	1,343.1	17.1	1.3%	4,826.0
06/14	1,263.0	35.8	2.8%	4,491.0
06/13	892.5	24.0	2.7%	3,587.0
06/12	739.0	17.1	2.3%	2,692.0
Annual Growth	**15.4%**	**13.8%**	**—**	**7.2%**

2016 Year-End Financials

Debt ratio: —   No. of shares (mil.): 26.3
Return on equity: 9.4%   Dividends
Cash ($ mil.): 71.6   Yield: —
Current ratio: 1.53   Payout: —
Long-term debt ($ mil.): —   Market value ($ mil.): 434.0

	STOCK PRICE ($) FY Close	P/E High/Low	PER SHARE ($) Earnings	Dividends	Book Value
06/16	16.49	24 13	1.07	0.00	12.04
06/15	18.28	51 26	0.63	0.00	11.09
06/14	32.79	27 11	1.33	0.00	10.61
06/13	15.58	19 11	0.91	0.00	9.12
06/12	11.33	23 12	0.65	0.00	8.20
Annual Growth	**9.8%**	**— —**	**13.3%**	**—**	**10.1%**

Matthews International Corp

Matthews International might not bury its competition but it can supply the casket and bronze marker. One of the nation's leading makers of cremation equipment and urns bronze memorials (including Elvis Presley's Graceland marker) metal and wood caskets and commemorative products (Baseball Hall of Fame plaques) Matthews also builds mausoleums. In addition it provides graphic imaging products and services for the consumer packaging and retail industries as well as merchandising services and marking and fulfillment systems. Matthews has operations in Asia Australia Canada and Europe but the US accounts for more than 60% of its sales.

Operations

Within its two major divisions —Memorialization and Brand Solutions —Matthews breaks its offerings down into six areas: cemetery products funeral home products cremation graphics imaging merchandising solutions and marking and fulfillment systems. Graphics imaging contributes the most to overall revenue some 35% with cemetery products and funeral home products each accounting for about 20%.

Geographic Reach

The US and Europe represent Matthews' largest markets accounting for more than 60% and about 35% of sales respectively. Other markets include Asia Australia and Canada. It has facilities in the US as well as in Austria Australia Belgium Canada China Germany Hong Kong Hungary Italy Malaysia Mexico the Netherlands Poland Singapore Sweden Turkey and the UK.

Sales and Marketing

The company's memorialization products are sold primarily to cemeteries memorial parks and funeral homes as well as corporations hospitals schools and other organizations. Brand solutions product and services are marketed to customers in the consumer packaged goods and retail industries.

Financial Performance

Matthews has seen sales rise in recent years. The company attributes the gains to higher sales volume within its Brand Solutions business and timely boosts from acquisitions. In 2014 revenue crossed the billion dollar mark up 12% to $1.1 billion. Although memorialization sales were down 2% as the number of casketed in-ground burials declines brand solutions sales powered by the mid-2014 acquisition of Schawk (which it renamed SGK LLC) were up a healthy 28%.

Net income and cash flow from operations however were both down as selling and administrative expenses rose significantly boosted by acquisition activity.

Strategy

Much of the company's recent growth has been an expansion of its brand solutions business which has grown from 45% of sales in 2012 to 54% in 2014. Matthews plans to extend those services globally (both organically and through acquisitions) so it can cater to multinational clients.

Mergers and Acquisitions

In 2014 Matthews made its largest acquisition to date with the purchase of Schawk (SGK). The deal valued at more than $570 million combines Matthews' brand solutions expertise in Europe with Schawk's experience in the US and Asia.

In mid-2015 the company purchased former rival casket and urn maker Aurora Casket Company for $214 million.

HISTORY

John Matthews began making stencils signs and steel stamps in 1850. Two of his sons joined his company in 1861; they renamed it Jas. H. Matthews Co. in 1894 after the youngest. The company developed the first vulcanized rubber printing plate in 1912 and began marking corrugated shipping containers. In 1927 it applied its plaque-making ability which it had been using for plaques to adorn buildings to make America's first flush bronze memorial plaque mounted in a Florida cemetery.

The company changed its name to Matthews International in 1976 to reflect its presence in other countries. Five years later it purchased the Sunland Memorial Park and Mortuary in Arizona to learn more about customers' needs. Matthews went public in 1994; sales continued to climb steadily.

In 1995 David Kelly joined the company as president and COO; he became CEO six months later and was elected chairman in 1996. That year Matthews sold its cemetery (3% of total revenues) and started expanding its product offerings and geographic markets through acquisitions beginning with its purchase of Industrial Equipment and Engineering Company in 1996. Acquisitions in 1997 and 1998 (such as Gibraltar Mausoleum Construction) expanded its graphics and memorial businesses. In 1999 the company acquired Europe's leading supplier of bronze memorialization products Caggiati SpA.

Matthews acquired The York Group the second-largest US casket maker in December 2001. A Federal Trade Commission inquiry regarding that acquisition was closed in late 2002 with no action taken.

Matthews boosted its marking products capabilities in July 2004 when it acquired Holjeron Corporation an Oregon-based industrial controls manufacturer. The same month Matthews acquired merchandising solutions provider Cloverleaf Group (formerly iDL and Big Red Rooster) to expand its presence in that market. In late 2004 the company purchased The InTouch Group a European reprographics firm. The next year Matthews expanded its Casket Division picking up Milso Industries to work alongside York.

In 2005 Matthews appointed group president David DeCarlo to the newly-created role of vice chairman and EVP Joseph Bartolacci as president and COO. In July the firm completed the acquisition of Milso Industries now a wholly-owned subsidiary of Matthews belonging to its casket division.

David Kelly remained as chairman and CEO. The next year Bartolacci replaced Kelly as CEO.

In May 2008 Matthews acquired a 78% stake in Saueressig GmbH & Co. a leading European provider of prepress and gravure printing forms based in Vreden Germany. Saueressig has manufacturing operations in Germany Poland and England. Saueressig operates as a subsidiary of the firm's Graphics Imaging Group. In December Matthews purchased a small European cremation equipment manufacturer.

In December 2009 the firm bought California-based United Memorial Products a leading supplier of granite memorial products burial vaults and caskets in the western US.

In April 2010 Matthews acquired Reynoldsville Casket Co. The Pennsylvania-based company makes and distributes caskets primarily in the Northeast.

EXECUTIVES

CFO Secretary and Treasurer, Steven F. Nicola, $399,231 total compensation

Group President Brand Solutions, Brian J. Dunn, $305,231 total compensation

President and CEO, Joseph C. Bartolacci, $669,231 total compensation

President Cremation Division, Paul F. Rahill, $188,350 total compensation

Group President Memorialization, Steven D. Gackenbach, $293,077 total compensation

V Pres Hr, Marcy Campbell

Vice President Finance and Administration, ED (Eddie) Wolford

Vice President Marketing, Mark Beauregard

Vice President, Patricia (Pat) Puc

Vice President Contrl, David F (Dave) Beck

Vice President and General Manager, Michael (Mel) Baklarz

Chairman, John D. Turner

Treasurer, Robert (Bob) Marsh

Auditors: Ernst & Young LLP

LOCATIONS

HQ: Matthews International Corp
Two Northshore Center, Pittsburgh, PA 15212-5851
Phone: 412 442-8200
Web: www.matw.com

PRODUCTS/OPERATIONS

2014 Sales

	$ mil.	% of total
Memorialization		
Funeral home	234.6	21
Cremetery	222.0	20
Cremation	51.8	5
Brand Solutions		
Graphic Imaging	398.2	36
Marking and Fullfilment Systems	100.9	9
Merchandising Solutions	99.1	9
Total	**1,106.6**	**100**

Selected Products

Bronze
  Commemorative and identification plaques
  Crypt letters and plates
  Flower vases
  Flush bronze memorials
  Granite benches
  Mausoleums
  Statuary
Caskets
  Corrugated
  Metal

Particle board
Wood
Cremation
  Cremation gardens
  Cremation memorials and urns
  Cremation niche systems
  Crematories
Graphic Systems
  Imaging systems
  Prepress services
  Printing plates (bar codes logos identification)
  Rotary and flat cutting dies
Marking Products
  Cleaners
  Hand stamps
  Ink-jet printing systems
  Inks
  Laser-marking equipment
  Solvents
Merchandising Solutions
  Brand concept shops
  Custom packaging
  Custom store fixtures
  Graphic design
  Interactive kiosks
  Model development
  Permanent displays
  Promotional signage
  Prototyping
  Temporary displays

COMPETITORS

Batesville Casket
Cold Spring Granite
DIC Corporation
Eastman Kodak
International Imaging Materials
Rock of Ages
Service Corporation International
Wilbert

HISTORICAL FINANCIALS

Company Type: Public

Income Statement

FYE: September 30

	REVENUE ($ mil.)	NET INCOME ($ mil.)	NET PROFIT MARGIN	EMPLOYEES
09/16	1,480.4	66.7	4.5%	10,300.0
09/15	1,426.0	63.4	4.4%	10,300.0
09/14	1,106.6	43.6	3.9%	9,400.0
09/13	985.3	54.8	5.6%	5,800.0
09/12	900.3	55.8	6.2%	5,400.0
Annual Growth	**13.2%**	**4.6%**	**—**	**17.5%**

2016 Year-End Financials

Debt ratio: 41.7%	No. of shares (mil.): 32.1
Return on equity: 9.2%	Dividends
Cash ($ mil.): 55.7	Yield: 0.9%
Current ratio: 2.21	Payout: 33.7%
Long-term debt ($ mil.): 844.8	Market value ($ mil.): 1,953.0

	STOCK PRICE ($) FY Close	P/E High/Low		PER SHARE ($) Earnings	Dividends	Book Value
09/16	60.76	31	23	2.03	0.60	22.05
09/15	48.97	29	21	1.91	0.52	22.23
09/14	43.89	31	25	1.53	0.44	23.69
09/13	38.08	20	14	1.98	0.40	20.16
09/12	29.82	19	14	1.98	0.36	17.30
Annual Growth	**19.5%**	**—**	**—**	**0.6%**	**13.6%**	**6.3%**

Maui Land & Pineapple Co., Inc.

Aloha! Maui Land & Pineapple (ML&P) invites you to live and play on its Hawaiian island —Maui. Through its Kapalua Land Company subsidiary the company operates the 1650-acre Kapalua Resort on Maui's northwest coast. The resort includes a minority-owned Ritz-Carlton hotel as well as tennis and spa facilities residential homes and condos and shops and restaurants. ML&P also develops residential and commercial property on its 23000 acres surrounding the resort. Its Kapalua Realty Company is a general brokerage real estate firm located within the resort. The company additionally owns forest and nature preserves on the island. Formerly one of Hawaii's largest pineapple producers the company exited that business in 2009.

Revenues declined slightly in 2010 compared to 2009 because the company ceased to own The Kapalua Villas (vacation rental) and Kapalua Adventures (zip lines ropes course and other activities) choosing instead to lease those businesses to third party operators. However its net income soared to nearly $25 million up from a loss of more than $123 million. In 2010 ML&P gained on the sale of its Kapalua Plantation Golf Course as well as the termination of post-retirement plans for employees of discontinued operations. In addition due to the real estate crash and the subsequent decline in tourism the company lost considerable profits from its 51%-owned Bay Holdings in 2009. (Bay Holdings owns the Residences at Kapalua Bay condos.) In order to cut costs ML&P eliminated more than 600 jobs in 2010 and 2009.

After David Cole resigned from his five-year stint as chairman and CEO at the end of 2008 the company split the functions appointing Warren Haruki (former president of GTE Hawaiian Tel and Verizon Hawaii) as chairman and Robert Webber as CEO. Months later Webber resigned. Haruki serves as chairman and interim CEO a position he has held since 2009.

Because of soaring oil and transportation costs ML&P exited the pineapple business in 2009 saying it could no longer sustain financial losses that threatened to destroy the company. It had grown pineapples on Maui for almost 100 years.

ML&P board member and AOL co-founder Steve Case owns more than 60% of the company. Through his Revolution LLC Case has a majority interest in Exclusive Resorts which has a 15% stake in Bay Holdings. Marriott International owns the remaining 34% of the condo project.

EXECUTIVES

Chairman and Interim CEO, Warren H. Haruki, age 63

President and COO, Ryan L. Churchill, $200,000 total compensation

CFO, Tim T. Esaki

Director, Walter A. Dods Jr., age 73

Director, Kent T. Lucien, age 62

Director, Stephen M. (Steve) Case

Director, Miles R. Gilburne, age 64

Director, David A. Heenan, age 75

Director, Fred E. Trotter III, age 84

Director, John H. Agee, age 66

Director, David C. Cole, age 62

Director, Duncan MacNaughton, age 72

Independent Director, Arthur Tokin

Auditors: Accuity LLP

LOCATIONS

HQ: Maui Land & Pineapple Co., Inc.
200 Village Road, Lahaina, Maui, HI 96761
Phone: 808 877-3351
Web: www.mauiland.com

COMPETITORS

Alexander & Baldwin	HTH Corporation
Barnwell Industries	Hilton Worldwide
Benchmark Hospitality	Outrigger Enterprises
Exclusive Resorts LLC	Sheraton Hotels
Four Seasons Hotels	

HISTORICAL FINANCIALS

Company Type: Public

Income Statement

FYE: December 31

	REVENUE ($ mil.)	NET INCOME ($ mil.)	NET PROFIT MARGIN	EMPLOYEES
12/15	22.7	6.8	29.9%	17.0
12/14	33.0	17.6	53.4%	17.0
12/13	15.2	(1.1)	—	19.0
12/12	16.1	(4.6)	—	17.0
12/11	14.5	5.0	34.9%	29.0
Annual Growth	11.9%	7.6%	—	(12.5%)

2015 Year-End Financials

Debt ratio: 87.0%	No. of shares (mil.): 18.8
Return on equity: —	Dividends
Cash ($ mil.): 1.0	Yield: —
Current ratio: 0.07	Payout: —
Long-term debt ($ mil.): —	Market value ($ mil.): 103.0

	STOCK PRICE ($) FY Close	P/E High/Low		PER SHARE ($) Earnings	Dividends	Book Value
12/15	5.46	21	14	0.36	0.00	(0.58)
12/14	6.05	10	6	0.94	0.00	(0.81)
12/13	6.09	—	—	(0.06)	0.00	(1.45)
12/12	4.15	—	—	(0.25)	0.00	(1.84)
12/11	4.17	27	14	0.27	0.00	(1.41)
Annual Growth	7.0%	—	—	7.5%	—	—

MAXIMUS Inc.

Efforts by government agencies to maximize efficiency mean money for MAXIMUS. The company brings in more than half its sales from its health services segment which offers outsourced program management and administrative services mainly to government agencies responsible for health and human services programs. Its human services segment provides administrative and consulting support to welfare-to-work programs child support enforcement and higher education and K-12 special education schools. MAXIMUS conducts consulting and programs management services for government-sponsored programs such as Medicaid Medicare the Children's Health Insurance Program (CHIP) and Welfare-to-Work.

Operations

The company operates three segments: Health Services U.S. Federal Services and Human Services. Health Services accounts for over 50% of total sales while the latter two account for 24% and 23% respectively.

Health Services and Human Services. The Health Services Segment generates around 65% of total revenue while the Human Services segment accounts for the other 35%.

Geographic Reach

Headquartered in Virginia and operating through more than 400 offices MAXIMUS rings up more than 70% of its revenue from the US where the company has drawn clients from all 50 states. It also has won contracts in Australia Canada New Zealand Saudi Arabia and the UK.

Sales and Marketing

MAXIMUS's primary customers are government agencies mostly in the US (state and federal agencies and local municipalities) but also abroad. It typically contracts with government clients under four primary pricing arrangements namely performance-based cost-plus fixed-price and time-and-materials.

Financial Performance

In fiscal 2016 revenue grew strongly up 14% to $2.4 billion amid strong increases in the Health Services and U.S. Federal Services segments. Net income ticked up 13% to $180.1 million while cash from operating activities came in at an almost identical value ($180.0 million) albeit down 13% from prior year. Cost of sales increased by 16% bringing down margin by one percentage point to 23.4%.

Strategy

MAXIMUS pursues long-term/recurring revenue opportunities believing than an incumbent has a better chance of re-winning contracts. It also makes acquisitions to expand its services offering.

Mergers and Acquisitions

In 2016 MAXIMUS acquired Ascend a provider of health assessment and data management tools to US government agencies. In 2015 it acquired Acentia LLC a provider of services to the US government and 70% of Remploy which works with the UK government.

HISTORY

David Mastran who worked for the Department of Health Education and Welfare during the Nixon administration founded MAXIMUS in 1975. The company's name comes from its goal of maximizing US government efficiency.

Most of MAXIMUS' growth has come in the past decade. In 1989 it won a contract to help California welfare recipients get job training and education and in 1995 it helped Nebraska find $50 million in federal funds. However it has not been easy sailing. In 1994 Mississippi froze a child-support collection contract with MAXIMUS when costs nearly doubled the state's expectations. MAXIMUS was disqualified from bidding on a West Virginia contract in 1995 after a state employee was convicted of bribery (MAXIMUS was not charged).

In 1996 California chose MAXIMUS to create a benefits information program for Medi-Cal applicants and beneficiaries. But late that year the federal government eliminated a Social Security Administration program that had been a major income source for MAXIMUS (55% in 1996).

MAXIMUS went public in 1997. Also that year the company added some 2500 new clients to its roster with four acquisitions which included government services providers David M. Griffith & Associates and Spectrum Consulting.

In 1999 MAXIMUS moved to bolster its human services and fleet management software capabilities respectively with acquisitions of Public Systems and Control Software. The company also landed large contracts to manage Medicaid enrollment for the state of Massachusetts child support enforce-

ment for Maryland and Wisconsin's nationally recognized welfare-to-work program.

In 2000 MAXIMUS made acquisitions across the board in such areas as Web-enabled information systems child support collection services and infrastructure management systems. MAXIMUS only made one acquisition in 2001 preferring to integrate its previous purchases into a new business structure.

The company branched out internationally in 2004 when it signed a 10-year agreement with the Ministry of Health Services in British Columbia Canada.

Mastran retired in 2004 and company veteran Lynn Davenport replaced him as CEO. Davenport was dismissed in April 2006 however because of "conduct towards a female MAXIMUS employee" the company said. Richard Montoni a former EVP and CFO of the company was named president and CEO.

To concentrate on its core operations MAXIMUS discontinued its student loan collections business and sold its corrections services business in 2006. The next year MAXIMUS engaged advisers to help evaluate a wide range of options –including a sale of the company –in an effort to improve shareholder value. After the review the company's board decided in November 2007 to sharpen its focus on its core health and human services-related operations and to buy back up to $150 million worth of stock.

EXECUTIVES

CEO, Richard A. (Rich) Montoni, age 65, $725,000 total compensation
Senior Vice President, David (Dave) Richardson
Chief of Human Capital, Mark S. Andrekovich, age 55, $395,000 total compensation
CFO and Treasurer, Richard J. Nadeau, $425,000 total compensation
President; General Manager Global Health Services, Bruce L. Caswell, age 50, $487,500 total compensation
General Manager Human Services, Akbar Piloti, age 59, $410,000 total compensation
CIO, Kelly L. Clark
Vice President Technology Solutions, Duane Stites
Vice President Real Estate, Susan (Sue) Boren
Senior Vice President and Chief Architect, Rajesh (Raj) Zade
Vice President, Jana Jones
Vice President, Viann Hardy
Vice President, Kinte Maximus
Program Executive And Vice President, Helene Fisher
Vice President, Kelly Blaschke
Vice President, Nelson Clugston
Vice President Operations, Sharon (Share) Ware
Vice President Of Systems and Data Processing, John (Jack) Donohue
Vice President, Anna Sever
Vice President, Walt Carper
Vice President Information Technology Application Integration and Operations, Lou (Lewis) Shields
Vice President Health Services Division, Peg Moster
Vice President, Rachel Zietlow
Vice President, Al Wong
Vice President, Lisa (Lis) Veith
Vice President Information Technology, Kevan McCallum
Senior Vice President and Chief Information Security Officer, Edward (Ed) Pagett
Vice President, Tom (Tommy) Naughton

Vice President Operations Services, Dan (Danny) Miller

Vice President Business Development, Joe (Joey) Murphy

Vice President of Human Capital, Catalina Murillo

Chairman, Peter B. Pond, age 71

Auditors: Ernst & Young LLP

LOCATIONS

HQ: MAXIMUS Inc.
1891 Metro Center Drive, Reston, VA 20190
Phone: 703 251-8500
Web: www.maximus.com

PRODUCTS/OPERATIONS

2016 Sales

	% of total
Health Services	53
U.S. Federal Services	24
Human Services	23
Total	**100**

COMPETITORS

Accenture	Goodwill Industries
Bain & Company	HP Enterprise Services
Booz Allen	IBM
Boston Consulting	McKinsey & Company
CACI International	Oracle
Catholic Charities USA	SAP
Computer Sciences	Unisys
Corp.	United Way
Deloitte Consulting	Xerox

HISTORICAL FINANCIALS

Company Type: Public

Income Statement

FYE: September 30

	REVENUE ($ mil.)	NET INCOME ($ mil.)	NET PROFIT MARGIN	EMPLOYEES
09/16	2,403.3	178.3	7.4%	18,800.0
09/15	2,099.8	157.7	7.5%	17,000.0
09/14	1,700.9	145.4	8.6%	13,000.0
09/13	1,331.2	116.7	8.8%	12,000.0
09/12	1,050.1	76.1	7.2%	8,657.0
Annual Growth	**23.0%**	**23.7%**	**—**	**21.4%**

2016 Year-End Financials

Debt ratio: 12.2%
Return on equity: 26.1%
Cash ($ mil.): 66.2
Current ratio: 1.82
Long-term debt ($ mil.): 165.3

No. of shares (mil.): 65.2
Dividends
  Yield: 0.3%
  Payout: 7.8%
Market value ($ mil.): 3,689.0

	STOCK PRICE ($) FY Close	P/E High/Low	PER SHARE ($) Earnings	Dividends	Book Value
09/16	56.56	26 17	2.69	0.18	11.48
09/15	59.56	29 16	2.35	0.18	9.36
09/14	40.13	23 18	2.11	0.18	8.35
09/13	45.04	47 21	1.67	0.18	7.73
09/12	59.72	53 30	1.10	0.18	6.64
Annual Growth	**(1.3%)**	**— —**	**25.2%**	**(0.0%)**	**14.7%**

MaxLinear Inc

MaxLinear provides integrated radio-frequency (RF) and mixed-signal semiconductor receivers used to receive and translate analog or digital radio television and other broadband signals into visual images. Its products which are used in cable TV set-top boxes digital TVs and mobile phones are sold to module makers OEMs and original design manufacturers (ODMs) such as ARRIS Cisco and Toshiba. Nearly all sales are to Asian customers. In 2015 MaxLinear bought Entropic Communications another chip design company for $287 million.

Operations

MaxLinear outsources its manufacturing and testing activities to a handful of third-party companies in Asia including United Microelectronics Advanced Semiconductor Engineering and Siliconware Precision Industries. It generally receives customers' purchase orders about six to 12 weeks prior to the scheduled delivery date.

Geographic Reach

MaxLinear has US offices in California where it's headquartered and Georgia and in China France India Japan South Korea and Taiwan.

Substantially all of its revenue is generated from products made in China (71% of sales) Japan (7%) and Taiwan (6%). The end products are then sold outside Asia.

Sales and Marketing

The company uses a direct sales force in the US and certain markets in Asia and Europe. In other areas it uses third-party sales representatives and a network of distributors. Distributors account for 28% of sales.

Altogether it counts 157 customers with its top 10 customers accounting for about 70% of sales. In 2013 ARRIS was its largest customer accounting for almost 31% of sales. Other top customers include LG Pace and Technicolor.

Financial Performance

MaxLinear has produced steady revenue growth over the years. Overall sales increased 11% to $133 million in 2014 due to higher sales for DOCSIS 3.0 cable modems and hybrid TV tuner applications. Still with high cost of sales and operating expenses the company has been in the red for the past four years. In 2014 it recorded a narrower net loss of about $7 million compared to a $12.7 million loss in 2013. Its cash flow decreased 5% from about $13 million in 2013 to about $12.2 million in 2014.

Strategy

MaxLinear intends to bolster its global presence particularly in the US Asia and Europe by capitalizing on the fast-growing and evolving digital television and mobile devices markets. The company hopes that its expansion efforts will broaden its customer base.

With its acquisition of Entropic Communications MaxLinear broadened its product base and increased its scale which should wring better deals from manufacturers. The $287 million purchase also nets Entropic's 1500 patents bolstering MaxLinear's intellectual property portfolio. Entropic makes multimedia over coaxial cable (MoCa) chips which expand the capabilities of the coax cable that enters the house from a cable provider.

Previously MaxLinear teamed up with Peregrine Semiconductor to produce a dual-RF-input digital TV (DTV) front-end reference design that would support both digital terrestrial TV and cable TV reception.

Mergers and Acquisitions

MaxLinear in 2014 bought Physpeed Co. a privately held developer of high-speed physical layer interconnect products for $11 million. The acquisition accelerates MaxLinear's expansion efforts into infrastructure for data center as well as metro and long-haul telecommunications operators.

EXECUTIVES

Chairman and CEO, Kishore Seendripu, age 47, $366,923 total compensation

CTO, Curtis Ling, age 51, $242,731 total compensation

CFO, Adam C. Spice, $277,596 total compensation

VP Operations, Michael J. LaChance

Vice President and Corporate Controller, Justin Scarpulla

Vice President Information Technology, Raja Pullela

Vice President Of Engineering, Joel Baker

Auditors: GRANT THORNTON LLP

LOCATIONS

HQ: MaxLinear Inc
5966 La Place Court, Suite 100, Carlsbad, CA 92008
Phone: 760 692-0711
Web: www.maxlinear.com

PRODUCTS/OPERATIONS

2014 Sales by Product

	$ mil.	% of total
Cable	86.2	65
Terrestrial	46.9	35
Total	**133.1**	**100**

COMPETITORS

Analog Devices	RDA Microelectronics
Maxim Integrated	Silicon Labs
Products	Telegent
NXP Semiconductors	

HISTORICAL FINANCIALS

Company Type: Public

Income Statement

FYE: December 31

	REVENUE ($ mil.)	NET INCOME ($ mil.)	NET PROFIT MARGIN	EMPLOYEES
12/16	387.8	61.2	15.8%	553.0
12/15	300.3	(42.3)	—	500.0
12/14	133.1	(7.0)	—	378.0
12/13	119.6	(12.7)	—	336.0
12/12	97.7	(13.2)	—	274.0
Annual Growth	**41.1%**	**—**		**19.2%**

2016 Year-End Financials

Debt ratio: —
Return on equity: 19.8%
Cash ($ mil.): 82.9
Current ratio: 3.92
Long-term debt ($ mil.): —

No. of shares (mil.): 65.0
Dividends
  Yield: —
  Payout: —
Market value ($ mil.): 1,418.0

	STOCK PRICE ($) FY Close	P/E High/Low	PER SHARE ($) Earnings	Dividends	Book Value
12/16	21.80	24 14	0.91	0.00	5.42
12/15	14.73	— —	(0.79)	0.00	4.21
12/14	7.41	— —	(0.19)	0.00	2.61
12/13	10.43	— —	(0.37)	0.00	2.45
12/12	5.02	— —	(0.40)	0.00	2.44
Annual Growth	**44.4%**	**— —**			**22.1%**

Maxus Realty Trust Inc

Maxus Realty Trust believes in the value of maximizing housing space. The real estate investment trust (REIT) invests in income-producing properties primarily multifamily residential properties. It owns a portfolio of approximately 10 apartment communities in the Midwest US. Maxus Realty Trust was originally established to invest in office and light industrial facilities but switched gears and began focusing on residential real estate in 2000. The REIT de-registered with the SEC and stopped trading on the NASDAQ in 2008.

LOCATIONS

HQ: Maxus Realty Trust Inc
104 Armour Road, P.O. Box 34279, North Kansas City, MO 64116
Phone: 816 303-4500   **Fax:** 816 221-1829
Web: www.mrti.com

COMPETITORS

AMLI Residential	Equity Office
Apartment Investment	Equity Residential
and Management	Investors Real Estate
Camden Property	Trust
CenterPoint Properties	Paragon Real Estate
Duke Realty	Trust

HISTORICAL FINANCIALS

Company Type: Public

Income Statement   FYE: December 31

	REVENUE ($ mil.)	NET INCOME ($ mil.)	NET PROFIT MARGIN	EMPLOYEES
12/15	60.5	6.6	10.9%	0.0
12/14	55.5	16.3	29.4%	0.0
12/13	41.2	1.3	3.1%	0.0
12/07	11.6	(1.5)	—	0.0
12/06	8.2	2.1	26.1%	0.0
Annual Growth	64.8%	32.7%	—	—

2015 Year-End Financials

Debt ratio: 82.7%	No. of shares (mil.): 1.1
Return on equity: 29.4%	Dividends
Cash ($ mil.): 14.1	Yield: 3.0%
Current ratio: 0.44	Payout: 45.0%
Long-term debt ($ mil.): 369.1	Market value ($ mil.): 55.0

	STOCK PRICE ($) FY Close	P/E High/Low		PER SHARE ($) Earnings	Dividends	Book Value
12/15	49.00	15	7	3.33	1.50	20.83
12/14	32.00	3	2	10.26	0.00	18.70
12/13	30.00	81	33	0.38	0.00	7.02
12/07	10.49	—	—	(1.08)	0.80	6.75
12/06	13.25	9	8	1.53	0.20	8.89
Annual Growth	38.7%	—	—	21.5%	65.5%	23.7%

MB Financial Inc

The "MB" in MB Financial doesn't stand for "Midsized Businesses" though that's its target market. The $16 billion-asset holding company owns MB Financial Bank which has about 80 branches in the Chicago area and one in Philadelphia. Commercial-related credits including mortgages operating loans lease financing and construction loans make up 85% of the bank's loan portfolio. In addition to serving small and middle-market businesses MB Financial provides retail banking and lending to consumers. The company also offers wealth management and trust services through its Cedar Hill Associates subsidiary and brokerage through Vision Investment Services. LaSalle Systems leases technology-related equipment to corporations.

OperationsMB Financial operates three main business segments: Banking which counts its deposit and lending activities; Leasing which originates leases and related services through subsidiaries LaSalle Systems Leasing Celtic Leasing Corp and MB Equipment Finance; and Mortgage Banking which originates and services residential mortgage loans to hold in its portfolio or list for sale to investors via retail or third party channels. Broadly speaking about 54% of the bank's total revenue came from loan interest during 2015 while another 10% came from interest on its investment securities. The rest of its revenue came from mortgage banking revenue (13% of revenue) lease financing (9%) commercial deposits and treasury management fees (6%) trust and asset management fees (3%) card fees (2%) capital markets and international banking fees (1%) and other miscellaneous fee sources.Geographic ReachBeyond its 80 branches in Chicago and one branch in Philadelphia MB Financial boasts 39 mortgage retail offices in 18 states.Sales and Marketing

MB Financial mostly targets small and middle market businesses and individuals. The bank spent $10.07 million on advertising during 2015 up 14% from the $8.85 million it spent in 2014.

Financial Performance

The bank's annual revenues have risen more than 65% since 2011 thanks to a combination of mortgage banking revenue growth and steady loan business growth driven by bank acquisitions. Its profits have quintupled over the same time period as a result.MB Financial's revenue jumped 37% to $816 million during 2015 mostly driven by strong loan business and mortgage banking revenue growth both stemming from the full-year results of its 2014 acquisition of Taylor Capital.Double-digit revenue growth in 2015 drove the bank's net income up 85% to $159 million for the year. MB Financial's operating cash levels climbed 23% to $205 million as cash earnings rose in 2015.

StrategyMB Financial mainly pursues growth by acquiring banks and other financial companies to expand its branch network across its target geographies and boost its loan and deposit business. Other strategies for growth include expanding its private banking and asset managements operations as well as its fee-based business services including treasury management and leasing.

Mergers and Acquisitions

In mid-2016 MB Financial bought American Chartered Bancorp —along with its 15 American Chartered Bank branches in the Chicago-area $2.8 billion in assets and $2.2 billion in deposits —in a deal valued at $449 million.

In December 2015 the company expanded its investment management and trust business after buying MSA along with its MainStreet and Cambium subsidiaries. MainStreet which boated $2.9 billion in assets under management (AUM) provided investment management services to the bank trust and independent trust markets while Cambium ($109 million in AUM) was a registered investment advisor that served affluent individuals and institutions. In August 2014 MB Financial completed its $649-million acquisition of Rosemont Illinois-based Taylor Capital Group the holding company for Cole Taylor Bank (CTB). With $5.7 billion in assets and some 10 branches in the Chicago metro area CTB was merged with MB Financial Bank. Like its acquirer CTB is a commercial bank focused on the middle market.

Company Background

Taking advantage of the dozens of bank failures in 2009 MB Financial acquired Heritage Community Bank InBank Corus Bank and Benchmark Bank in separate FDIC-assisted transactions. In 2010 it acquired failed Chicago-area institutions Broadway Bank and New Century Bank in similar deals. Gains on these acquisitions helped the company's revenues (and profits) grow in 2010. Although the company didn't have the benefit of gains on acquisitions in 2011 (and revenues fell 20% to $493.7 million) profits continued to climb that year growing 89% to $38.7 million largely due to a lowered provision for loan losses. Also that year the bank got millions of dollars of non-performing loans off of its books via a sale to Colony Capital.

EXECUTIVES

President and CEO, Mitchell S. Feiger, age 57, $895,308 total compensation
Chairman MB Financial Bank, Ronald D. Santo, age 73, $321,741 total compensation
EVP Commercial Banking, Mark A. Heckler, age 52, $293,077 total compensation
EVP Commercial Banking Specialty, Edward F. Milefchik, age 51
EVP MB Financial Bank; President MB Business Capital, Michael D. Sharkey, age 62, $456,923 total compensation
EVP and Chief Credit Officer, Michael J. Morton, age 53
President and CEO MB Financial Bank, Mark A. Hoppe, age 62, $726,923 total compensation
EVP Wealth Management Card Services Leasing and Indirect Lending, Jill E. York, age 52, $489,461 total compensation
VP MB Financial Inc. and EVP Administration MB Financial Bank, Rosemarie Bouman, age 59, $287,846 total compensation
EVP Commercial Banking, Lawrence G. Ryan, age 57
VP and CFO MB Financial Inc. and EVP COO and CFO MB Financial Bank N.A., Randall T. Conte, age 55, $451,731 total compensation
EVP Consumer Banking and Risk Management and Chief Risk Officer MB Financial Bank N.A., Brian J. Wildman, age 53, $292,846 total compensation
Vice President, Michael Scarsella
Vice President Trust Operations Manager, Abimbola Okubanjo
First Vice President, Mike (Mikey) Markovitz
Assistant Vice President Compliance Officer, Nora Reyes
Senior Vice President Of Commercial Banking, Timothy Broccolo
Vice President, Kathy Grele
Vice President Merchant Risk Operations Manager, Jennifer (Jen) Gallus
Assistant Vice President Lease Banking, Brian (Bri) Weadock
Executive Vice President, Matthew (Matt) Robertson
First Vice President, Michael (Mel) Lynch
Assistant Vice President International Banking Division, Guillermo (Gill) Villagrana
Assistant Vice President Banking Center Manager, Nataliya Dovha
Vice President, Michael Nylen

Assistant Vice President Regi, Mauricio Ibarra
Vice President Business Intelligence, George (Georgey) Ostendorf
First Vice President, Carolyn (Carol) Gergits
Senior Vice President Product Management, Judy (Jude) Hill
Senior Vice President of Commerical Banking, Carl Anfenson
Vice President, Virginia Buschman
Vice President of Compliance, Kevin (Kev) Osborn
Senior Vice President, Bernard (Bern) Bartilad
Vice President Commercial Real Estate, Pam (Pamela) Farrell
First Vice President Business Developmnt, Jerry (Jerr) Kallio
Vice President, Rick J (Ricky) Chang
Assistant Vice President Employee Relations Office, Katie Drinan (Kat) Allberry
Vice President Collateral Manager, Lisette Alamo
Vice President, Anthony (Tony) Gattuso
Vice President, Erika Berumen
Vice President Commercial Banking, Jessica (Jess) Redman
Senior Vice President, Jennifer Brogan
Vice President Business Banking, Robert Baitler
Vice President Business Banking, Jim Marshall
Senior Vice President, Greg Urban
Vice President Treasury Management Sales, Eloy Hodges
First Vice President, Sandra Biske
Assistant Vice President Compensation, Cindy Katsikas
Assistant Vice President Banking Center Manager, Galina Veksler
Senior Vice President and Division Head, Christina (Tina) Bavery
Vice President, Stephanie (Steph) Taverna
Vice President, Cindy (Cin) Voda
Vice President, Dion Haintz
First Vice President Chief Appraiser, Mitchell Zaveduk
Assistant Vice President Bsa Aml Loss Prevention Management, Michelle Mercer
First Vice President Retail Divisional Manager, Seth Heape
Senior Vice President Bsa Aml Officer, Carole Micheletto
Assistant Vice President Compensation And Benefits, Catherine Nacpil
Assistant Vice President Marketing And Crm Administrator, Cari Dam
Senior Vice President Division Head, Thomas (Thom) Moran
Senior Vice President Lease Banking, Dennis (Denny) Roesslein
First Vice President Regional Division M, Deborah (Deb) Wheeler
Senior Vice President Lease Banking, Stewart Kapnick
Vice President Senior Product Manager, Joseph (Jo) Vitale
Senior Vice President, Melissa (Lissa) Bleiweis
Vice President Commercial Banking, Dawn (Dawny) Lauderdale
Senior Vice President, Mitch (Mitchell) Morgenstern
Assistant Vice President Networking, Armando (Mando) Cabral
First Vice President, Thomas (Thom) Carmody
Vice President, Jim (Jimmy) Marshall
Vice President Commercial Banking, Michelle (Michie) Christens
Assistant Vice President Banking Center Manager, Majde Muhdi
Senior Vice President of Sales, Thomas (Thom) Prendergast
Senior Vice President Operations, Pete (Petey) Steger

Vice President Senior Treasury Analyst Alm, Dale (Dal) Saari
Senior Vice President Corporate Controller, David (Dave) Emerson
Vice President Senior Field Credit Officer, Brian Monson
Vice President Treasury Management Solutions Group, Isela Calabrese
Senior Vice President CRA Fair Lending Program Manager, Mary (Mar) Boetel
Assistant Vice President Banking Center Manager, Lesya Schrader
Vice President Commercial Banking, Kenneth (Ken) Holub
Assistant Vice President Treasury Managment Advisor, Luke (Lucas) Chesick
Assistant Vice President Prepaid Product Manager, Kelly (Kel) Mathews
Assistant Vice President Operations, Jackie (Jack) Schmitz
Assistant Vice President Customer Solutions Specialist, Lori (Lor) Rottmuller
Senior Vice President Commercial Banking, Matt (Matty) Stefani
Senior Vice President, Mark (Marky) Staunton
Senior Vice President, David (Dave) Enghauser
Senior Vice President, Jack (Jackie) Gracheck
Senior Vice President, Angela (Ang) Nuss
Senior Vice President, Donald (Don) Tomlinson
Assistant Vice President Commercial Banking, Andrea (Ann) Bukacek
Senior Vice President, Timothy (Tim) Carstens
Senior Vice President, Harold (Harry) Chmiel
Senior Vice President documentation for MB Equipment Finance, Jeannie (Jane) McManus
Mortgage Senior Vice President Lead Counsel, Mark (Marky) Reid
First Vice President, Dustin J (Dusty) Ackman
Chairman, Thomas H. Harvey, age 55
Board Member, Christina Aguinaga
Executive Board Member, Matt Weberling
Vice Chairman, Bruce Taylor
Auditors: RSM US LLP

LOCATIONS

HQ: MB Financial Inc
800 West Madison Street, Chicago, IL 60607
Phone: 888 422-6562
Web: www.mbfinancial.com

PRODUCTS/OPERATIONS

2015 Sales

	$ mil.	% of total
Interest		
Loans	413.6	51
Investment securities	80.3	10
Other	0.3	-
Noninterest		
Mortgage banking	117.4	13
Lease financing net	76.6	9
Commercial deposit and treasury management fees	45.3	6
Trust and Asset management	23.5	3
Card fees	15.3	2
Consumer and other deposit service fees	13.3	2
Loan service fees	6.2	1
Others	24.5	3
Total	**816.3**	**100**

Selected Services
Business Banking
Commercial Banking
Personal Banking
Wealth Management

Selected Subsidiaries
MB Financial Bank N.A.
 Ashland Management Agency Inc.
 Cedar Hill Associates LLC (80%)

LaSalle Systems Leasing Inc.
LaSalle Business Solutions LLC
Melrose Equipment Company LLC
MB Deferred Exchange Corporation
MB Financial Center LLC
MB Financial Center Land Owner LLC
MB Financial Community Development Corporation
Vision Investment Services Inc.
Vision Insurance Services Inc.7

COMPETITORS

Bank of America	Northern Trust
Citigroup	PNC Financial
Fifth Third	PrivateBancorp
Harris	U.S. Bancorp
JPMorgan Chase	Wintrust Financial

HISTORICAL FINANCIALS
Company Type: Public

Income Statement
FYE: December 31

	ASSETS ($ mil.)	NET INCOME ($ mil.)	INCOME AS % OF ASSETS	EMPLOYEES
12/15	15,585.0	158.9	1.0%	2,980.0
12/14	14,602.1	86.1	0.6%	2,839.0
12/13	9,641.4	98.4	1.0%	1,775.0
12/12	9,571.8	90.3	0.9%	1,758.0
12/11	9,833.0	38.7	0.4%	1,684.0
Annual Growth	**12.2%**	**42.3%**	**—**	**15.3%**

2015 Year-End Financials

Return on assets: 1.0%	Dividends
Return on equity: 7.7%	Yield: 2.0%
Long-term debt ($ mil.): —	Payout: 33.3%
No. of shares (mil.): 73.6	Market value ($ mil.): 2,385.0
Sales ($ mil): 816.3	

	STOCK PRICE ($) FY Close	P/E High/Low	PER SHARE ($) Earnings	Dividends	Book Value
12/15	32.37	18 14	2.02	0.65	28.31
12/14	32.86	25 20	1.31	0.52	27.11
12/13	32.06	18 11	1.79	0.44	24.11
12/12	19.75	14 11	1.60	0.13	23.26
12/11	17.10	42 27	0.52	0.04	25.44
Annual Growth	**17.3%**		**— —**	**40.4%100.8%**	**2.7%**

MCBC Holdings Inc
Auditors: BDO USA, LLP

LOCATIONS

HQ: MCBC Holdings Inc
100 Cherokee Cove Drive, Vonore, TN 37885
Phone: 423 884-2221
Web: www.mastercraft.com

HISTORICAL FINANCIALS
Company Type: Public

Income Statement
FYE: June 30

	REVENUE ($ mil.)	NET INCOME ($ mil.)	NET PROFIT MARGIN	EMPLOYEES
06/16	221.6	10.2	4.6%	510.0
06/15	214.3	5.5	2.6%	470.0
06/14	177.5	19.9	11.2%	475.0
06/13	162.0	2.8	1.7%	0.0
Annual Growth	**11.0%**	**53.6%**	**—**	**—**

2016 Year-End Financials

Debt ratio: 63.2%	No. of shares (mil.): 18.5
Return on equity: —	Dividends
Cash ($ mil.): 0.0	Yield: 38.9%
Current ratio: 0.41	Payout: 877.5%
Long-term debt ($ mil.): 44.3	Market value ($ mil.): 205.0

	STOCK PRICE ($) FY Close	P/E High/Low	PER SHARE ($) Earnings	Dividends	Book Value
06/16	11.05	28 18	0.56	4.30	(0.45)
06/15	0.00	— —	0.47	0.00	(3.79)
Annual Growth	—		19.1%	—	—

Medical Properties Trust Inc

Hospitals trust Medical Properties to provide the leases under which their facilities operate. The self-advised real estate investment trust (REIT) invests in and owns more than 110 health care facilities including acute care hospitals inpatient rehabilitation hospitals and wellness centers in 25 US states and Germany. California and Texas combined account for nearly 50% of the REIT's annual revenue. It leases the facilities to more than 25 hospital operating companies under long-term triple-net leases where the tenant bears most of the operating costs. Prime Healthcare Services and Ernest Health are among the REIT's largest clients. Medical Properties Trust entered the European health care market in 2013.

Geographic Reach

Alabama-based Medical Properties Trust (MPT) has properties in 25 US states and Germany. The REIT has 32 properties in Texas and 14 in California representing about 24% and 26% of its revenue respectively. New Jersey is another important market for the firm accounting for about 7% of annual revenue.

Financial Performance

MPT reported $242.5 million in revenue in 2013 an increase of 20% versus 2012. Net income increased by 8% over the same period to $97 million. The REIT has experienced rapid revenue and profit growth in recent years as it portfolio of properties has grown and rents and other income increased. Annual escalation provisions in its leases have contributed to the growth of rental revenue. Cash flow increased by $73 million in 2013 over 2013 due to an increase in cash from financing activities. MPT has more than $3 billion in assets.

Strategy

The REIT is focused on expanding and diversifying its tenant roster both in terms of the types of hospitals it owns and location. To that end Medical Properties Trust entered the European market in late 2013 with the purchase of 11 rehabilitation facilities in Germany from RHM Klinik-und Altenheimbetriebe GmbH & Co. for €184 million ($254.3 million) The REIT which is looking to expand in other markets beyond the US was attracted by Germany's strong economic position and the health care environment. Back home in the US the REIT has been investing heavily in acquisitions and other related investments in 2013 and 2012 amounting to about $655 million and $621.5 million respectively. Purchases included three gen-

eral acute-care hospitals from IASIS Healthcare LLC as well as two acute-care hospitals in Kansas.

The firm owns a variety of health care related properties including acute care hospitals inpatient rehabilitation hospitals long-term acute care hospitals wellness centers medical office buildings and surgical facilities.

Mergers and Acquisitions

In 2016 the company bought the real estate assets of nine hospitals operated by Steward Health Care in a $1.25 billion transaction; the deal included a $50 million investment in Steward as well a right of first refusal to buy future Steward facilities.

EXECUTIVES

EVP CFO and Director, R. Steven Hamner, age 59, $575,000 total compensation
Chairman President and CEO, Edward K. Aldag, age 52, $950,000 total compensation
EVP COO Treasurer and Secretary, Emmett E. McLean, age 60, $525,000 total compensation
Vice Chairman, William G. McKenzie, age 57
Auditors: PricewaterhouseCoopers LLP

LOCATIONS

HQ: Medical Properties Trust Inc
1000 Urban Center Drive, Suite 501, Birmingham, AL 35242
Phone: 205 969-3755 **Fax:** 205 969-3756
Web: www.medicalpropertiestrust.com

PRODUCTS/OPERATIONS

2015 Sales by Property Type

	% of total
General acute care hospitals	58
Rehabilitation hospitals	30
Long-term acute care hospitals	12
Wellness centers	-
Total	**100**

COMPETITORS

Extendicare	Omega Healthcare
HCP	Investors
Healthcare Realty	Physicians Realty
Trust	Universal Health
LTC Properties	Realty
National Health	Ventas
Investors	Welltower

HISTORICAL FINANCIALS

Company Type: Public

Income Statement

FYE: December 31

	REVENUE ($ mil.)	NET INCOME ($ mil.)	NET PROFIT MARGIN	EMPLOYEES
12/15	441.8	139.6	31.6%	50.0
12/14	312.5	50.5	16.2%	45.0
12/13	242.5	96.9	40.0%	38.0
12/12	201.4	89.9	44.6%	33.0
12/11	143.3	26.5	18.5%	29.0
Annual Growth	32.5%	51.4%	—	14.6%

2015 Year-End Financials

Debt ratio: 59.2%	No. of shares (mil.): 236.7
Return on equity: 8.0%	Dividends
Cash ($ mil.): 195.5	Yield: 7.6%
Current ratio: 1.95	Payout: 191.3%
Long-term debt ($ mil.): 3,322.5	Market value ($ mil.): 2,725.0

	STOCK PRICE ($) FY Close	P/E High/Low	PER SHARE ($) Earnings	Dividends	Book Value
12/15	11.51	24 17	0.63	0.88	8.88
12/14	13.78	49 42	0.29	0.84	8.00
12/13	12.22	27 18	0.63	0.81	8.33
12/12	11.96	18 13	0.67	0.80	7.70
12/11	9.87	54 36	0.23	0.80	7.48
Annual Growth	3.9%	— —	28.6%	2.4%	4.4%

Medidata Solutions, Inc.

Medidata Solutions has electronic remedies to help clinical trials run smoothly. Founded in 1999 the company offers cloud-based applications that help biotechnology pharmaceutical and other life sciences companies conduct clinical trials and related research. Its products include hosted software for administering and managing clinical trials electronic data capture applications study management applications and patient diaries. The company also offers a variety of professional services such as consulting implementation integration and maintenance. Medidata operates in more than 115 countries but most of its sales come from the US.

Geographic Reach

Medidata does most of its business in the US which accounted for more than 70% of the company's sales in 2014. Japan is the company's second-largest geographic market accounting for 10% of sales during the same period. Other key markets include the UK and Switzerland.

Sales and Marketing

The company markets its products primarily through a direct sales force across North America Europe and Asia; however it does leverage relationships with contract research organizations such as PAREXEL and Quintiles Transnational to make its software the foundation for outsourced services they provide. Medidata's top five customers including Johnson & Johnson Roche and AstraZeneca account for more than 25% of sales. Overall the company counts some 500 customers.

Financial Performance

Medidata continued its strong upward revenue trajectory in 2014 with sales increasing 21% year-over-year to $335 million. Current customers played a strong revenue role by renewing contracts and adding services. Net income fell 63% in 2014 to $6.1 billion because of a wire transaction loss (associated with a fraud against the company) and related investigation costs.

Strategy Expanding its customer base is a key element of Medidata's strategy. It has grown from less than 100 customers in 2008 to about 500 by the end of 2014. Among the segments the company is targeting are midsized companies non-US geographies the medical device industry and academic research centers and government organizations. Medidata is also focused on expanding its product line including through acquisitions.

The works with a range of technology providers in order to offer options to its customers. Medidata's technology partners include Oracle Microsoft and Amazon Web Services.

Mergers and Acquisitions In 2014 Medidata acquired Patient Profiles an early-stage US-based software company focused on data analytics in clinical trials. The acquisition provides Medidata a centralized statistical monitoring technology that it can use with its risk-based monitoring technology.

Ownership Investment management firm Brown Capital Management owns about 14% of Medidata.

EXECUTIVES

Vice President New Products, Richard (Dick) Piazza
Vice Chairman, Steven I. (Steve) Hirschfeld, age 54, $377,708 total compensation
EVP Human Resources, Eileen M. Schloss, age 62
Chairman and CEO, Tarek A. Sherif, age 54, $545,833 total compensation
Managing Director Asia-Pacific Region, Takeru Yamamoto
COO, Michael L. (Mike) Capone, age 49, $450,000 total compensation
President, Glen de Vries, age 43, $545,833 total compensation
EVP Product Development and CTO, Julie Iskow
CFO, Rouven Bergmann, age 43, $262,500 total compensation
EVP and General Counsel, Michael I. (Mike) Otner, age 45
EVP Sales, Michael Pray
EVP Professional Services, Daniel (Dan) Shannon
Vice President Application Strategy, Daniel (Dan) Mudgett
Vice President, Susan (Sue) Hailey
Vice President Corporate Strategy, Shih-Yin Ho
Vice President Implementation Services, Les Taylor
Vice President Technology Solutions, Ross Rothmeier
Senior Vice President and Chief Data Officer, David (Dave) Lee
Senior Vice President Professional Servi, Dan (Danny) Shannon
Vice President Of Data Science, John Savage
Vice President Deputy General Counsel And Assistant Secretary, Kathryn Schneider
Senior Vice President and Chief Accounting Officer, David (Dave) Colistra
Vice President, Glenn Cahaly
Vice President Professional Services, Keta Lakdawala
Vice President of Operations, David (Dave) McKie
Auditors: Deloitte & Touche LLP

LOCATIONS

HQ: Medidata Solutions, Inc.
350 Hudson Street, 9th Floor, New York, NY 10014
Phone: 212 918-1800
Web: www.mdsol.com

PRODUCTS/OPERATIONS

2014 Sales

	$ mil.	% of total
Subscription	280.0	84
Professional services	55.1	16
Total	**335.1**	**100**

Selected Customers

Pharmaceutical
  Abbott Laboratories
  Astellas Pharma
  AstraZeneca
  Baxter International
  Bayer HealthCare
  Daiichi Sankyo

F. Hoffmann-La Roche
Johnson & Johnson
H. Lundbeck
Orion Corporation
Pfizer
Roche Holding
Shionogi & Co.
Takeda Pharmaceutical
Biotechnology
  Amgen
  Array BioPharma
  Elan Pharmaceuticals
  Genzyme Corporation
  Gilead Sciences
  Infinity Pharmaceuticals
  Seattle Genetics
Medical Devices and Diagnostics
  bioMérieux
  Boston Scientific
  DePuy International
  Edwards Lifesciences
Contract Research Organizations
  CMIC
  EPS
  ICON Clinical Research
  INC Research
  Kendle International
  PRA International
  Quintiles Transnational
  Sumisho Computer Systems
Institutions
  Ludwig Institute for Cancer Research
  Northwestern University

COMPETITORS

Aptuit	MedNet Solutions
BioClinica	Merge Healthcare
DATATRAK International	Microsoft
DRS Data & Research	OmniComm
DrugLogic	Oracle
Liquent	Perceptive Informatics
M2S	eResearchTechnology

HISTORICAL FINANCIALS

Company Type: Public

Income Statement

FYE: December 31

	REVENUE ($ mil.)	NET INCOME ($ mil.)	NET PROFIT MARGIN	EMPLOYEES
12/15	392.5	13.1	3.4%	1,487.0
12/14	335.0	6.0	1.8%	1,077.0
12/13	276.8	16.6	6.0%	923.0
12/12	218.3	18.0	8.3%	796.0
12/11	184.4	39.4	21.4%	690.0
Annual Growth	**20.8%**	**(24.0%)**	**—**	**21.2%**

2015 Year-End Financials

Debt ratio: 36.7%
Return on equity: 4.8%
Cash ($ mil.): 269.6
Current ratio: 3.16
Long-term debt ($ mil.): 252.7
No. of shares (mil.): 56.3
Dividends
  Yield: —
  Payout: —
Market value ($ mil.): 2,776.0

	STOCK PRICE ($) FY Close	P/E High/Low	PER SHARE ($) Earnings	Dividends	Book Value
12/15	49.29	240 153	0.23	0.00	5.05
12/14	47.75	563 283	0.11	0.00	4.86
12/13	60.50	374 119	0.31	0.00	4.21
12/12	39.18	117 53	0.36	0.00	2.73
12/11	21.75	32 17	0.80	0.00	2.09
Annual Growth	**22.7%**	**—**	**(26.8%)**	**—**	**24.6%**

MeetMe Inc.

MeetMe is all about making new friends. Formerly called Quepasa Corporation the company aims to connect people through social games and apps across iPhone Android Web and mobile Internet platforms. The company took its current shape after merging Quepasa (which targeted a Latin American audience) with Insider Guides (doing business as myYearbook.com) in 2011; it rebranded as MeetMe in 2012. The new name reflects a less regional focus as MeetMe is designed for a global audience. The company earns revenue mainly through display advertising on its site as well as selling virtual currency for its games.

In 2011 the company acquired myYearbook.com a profitable social network that focuses on younger teenage users for about $87 million in cash and stock. It made the deal to gain myYearbook.com's growing user base; the two companies will reach a combined audience of some 70 million registered users. It will also gain myYearbook.com's mobile and social games advertising and virtual currency holdings.

EXECUTIVES

CFO, David D. Clark, age 51
EVP Business Affairs and General Counsel, Frederic (Fred) Beckley
EVP Communications and Public Relations, Robin Shallow
Chairman and CEO, John C. Abbott, age 45
CTO, Gavin M. Roy
COO; President Consumer Internet, Geoffrey Cook
Director, Lionel Sosa, age 75
Director, Jill A. Syverson-Stork, age 62
Director, Alonso Ancira, age 61
Director, Malcolm Jozoff, age 76
Chairman and CEO, John C. Abbott, age 44
Director, James S. (Jim) Ferris
Auditors: RSM US LLP

LOCATIONS

HQ: MeetMe Inc.
100 Union Square Drive, New Hope, PA 18938
Phone: 215 862-1162
Web: www.meetme.com

COMPETITORS

AOL	Myspace
Facebook	Spark Networks
Match Group	eHarmony.com

HISTORICAL FINANCIALS

Company Type: Public

Income Statement

FYE: December 31

	REVENUE ($ mil.)	NET INCOME ($ mil.)	NET PROFIT MARGIN	EMPLOYEES
12/15	56.9	5.9	10.5%	112.0
12/14	44.8	(3.9)	—	121.0
12/13	40.3	(10.9)	—	125.0
12/12	46.6	(10.3)	—	162.0
12/11	11.8	(12.7)	—	203.0
Annual Growth	**48.0%**	**—**	**—**	**(13.8%)**

Mercantile Bank Corp.

Mercantile Bank Corporation is the holding company for Mercantile Bank of Michigan (formerly Mercantile Bank of West Michigan) which boasts assets of nearly $3 billion and operates more than 50 branches in central and western Michigan around Grand Rapids Holland and Lansing. The bank targets local consumers and businesses offering standard deposit services such as checking and savings accounts CDs IRAs and health savings accounts. Commercial loans make up more than three-fourths of the bank's loan portfolio. Outside of banking subsidiary Mercantile Insurance Center sells insurance products.

OperationsMercantile Bank Corp. generated 82% of its total revenue from loan interest (including fees) in 2014 with securities interest contributing another 8% to total revenue. Service charges on deposit and sweep accounts and credit and debit card fees made up another 5% of Mercantile's total revenue while its mortgage banking income generated another 2%.Sales and MarketingMercantile provides its banking services to businesses individuals and government organizations. Its commercial banking services mostly cater to small- to medium-sized businesses. The company spent $1.315 million on advertising in 2014 compared to $1.113 million and $1.167 million in 2013 and 2012 respectively.Financial PerformanceMercantile Bank Corp's revenues had been declining for a number of years as its loan business withered while profits have remained mostly flat. The company had a breakout year in 2014 however after its historic acquisition of FirstBank Corp. The bank's revenue skyrocketed by 53% to $99.15 million (the highest level since 2009) mostly as the acquisition nearly doubled its loan assets and boosted its interest income on loans and securities by significant amounts. The bank's non-interest income also grew by 46% thanks to higher fee income across the board also resulting from the recent acquisition. Higher revenue and a $3.2 million reduction in loan loss provisions with a stronger credit portfolio in 2014 also pushed the company's net income up by 2% to $17.33 million for the year. Mercantile's operating cash declined by 50% to $14.41 million due to changes in accrued interest and other liabilities during the year.StrategyMercantile Bank Corporation has been growing its loan business and branch network reach through strategic acquisitions of smaller banks and bank branches. Its mid-2014 acquisition of Firstbank

Corporation was perhaps the most effective to date as the purchase doubled its assets and boosted the size of its branch network nearly seven-fold from seven branches to a whopping 53.Mergers and AcquisitionsIn June 2014 Mercantile Bank Corp. purchased Firstbank Corp of Alma Michigan for a total purchase price of $173 million adding 46 branches and $1.3 billion in assets. The deal which made Mercantile the third-largest bank based in the state also expanded the bank's service offerings diversified its loan portfolio boosted its loan origination capacity and significantly extended its geographic footprint into Michigan's lower peninsula.

EXECUTIVES

SVP CFO and Treasurer Mercantile Bank Corporation and SVP and CFO Mercantile Bank of Michigan, Charles E. (Chuck) Christmas, age 50, $263,000 total compensation
President and CEO, Robert B. Kaminski, age 54, $315,000 total compensation
EVP Corporate Finance and Strategic Planning Mercantile Bank Corporation and Mercantile Bank of Michigan, Samuel G. Stone, age 71, $159,833 total compensation
Vice President Internal Auditor, Sandy Jager
Executive Vice President Corporate Banking, Robert (Bob) Dewey
Senior Vice President Commercial Lending, Kevin Paul
Vice President and Branch Manager, Cheri Stanton
Senior Vice President, Michelle (Michie) Shangraw
Senior Vice President, Thomas (Thom) Lundquist
Assistant Vice President Human Resources Specialist, Tina Van Valkenburg
Senior Vice President Business Development Officer, Brian Talbot
Vice President Commercial Loan Officer, Jeff Hicks
Vice President, Teresa (Terry) Rupert
Vice President Treasury Sales, Kimberly Labadie
Senior Vice President Commercial Lending, David (Dave) Deboer
Vice President, Mike Siminski
Senior Vice President, Valicevic Joseph
Vice President, Craig Oosterhouse
Senior Vice President Corporate Banking, Matt Zimmerman
Senior Vice President Information Systems Manager, Allen (Al) Smith
Assistant Vice President and Commercial Lo, Justin Horn
Senior Vice President Operations, Richard (Dick) Rice
Vice President Corporate Banking, Bob (Bo) Klimczak
Senior Vice President Mortgage Sales Manager, Michael (Mel) Yates
Vice President, Douglas (Doug) Ouellette
Chairman, Michael H. Price, age 59
Auditors: BDO USA, LLP

LOCATIONS

HQ: Mercantile Bank Corp.
310 Leonard Street N.W., Grand Rapids, MI 49504
Phone: 616 406-3000
Web: www.mercbank.com

PRODUCTS/OPERATIONS

2014 Sales

	$ mil.	% of total
Interest income		
Loans and leases including fees	80.8	82
Securities taxable	6.4	6
Securities tax-exempt	1.6	2
Other	0.2	-
Noninterest income		
Service charges on accounts	2.6	3
Credit and debit card fees	2.5	2
Mortgage banking activities	1.7	2
Other	3.3	3
Total	99.1	100

COMPETITORS

Chemical Financial
ChoiceOne Financial Services
Comerica
Fifth Third
Flagstar Bancorp
Huntington Bancshares
Independent Bank (MI)
Macatawa Bank

HISTORICAL FINANCIALS

Company Type: Public

Meridian Bancorp Inc

Meridian Bancorp is the holding company of East Boston Savings Bank which provides standard deposit and lending services to individuals and businesses in the greater Boston area. The bank writes single-family commercial and multi-family mortgages as well as construction and business loans and consumer loans. East Boston Savings operates about 30 branches in eastern Massachusetts. Mutual holding company Meridian Financial Services owns 59% of Meridian Bancorp.

Geographic Reach

Meridian Bancorp operates across the greater Boston metropolitan area in Essex Middlesex and Suffolk counties.

Operations

The bank has about $2.7 billion in assets; commercial real estate loans comprise 45% of its loan portfolio.

Meridian owns a 40% stake in Hampshire First Bank a New Hampshire-chartered bank established in 2006.

Sales and Marketing

Meridian has devoted more dollars to advertising in recent years. It spent $2.95 million in fiscal 2013 on advertising up from $2.54 million in 2012 and $2.45 million in 2011.

Financial Performance

Like many small banks that survived the Great Recession Meridian has grown steadily the last few years. In 2013 it reported an 8% increase in revenue from $106 million to $115 million due to increased loan payments as interest rates recovered. Net income grew 24% from $12 million to $15 million on the strength of higher revenue and changes in the company's bookkeeping. Cash from operations jumped to $28 million after the company sold some of its loans.

Strategy

As part of its growth strategy the bank has bolstered its commercial real estate and business loans as well as its construction loans. Previously residential mortgages represent the company's largest loan segment.

The bank also intends to grow through the opening of new branches and pursuing branch acquisitions. It has opened 14 new branches in upscale Boston neighborhoods in the last two years and acquired another six.

To further enable growth Meridian in 2014 announced that it will convert from a mutual company to a public corporation.

EXECUTIVES

CFO and Treasurer, Mark L. Abbate, age 61
SVP Consumer and Business Banking, Keith D. Armstrong
Chairman President and CEO Meridian Interstate Bancorp and East Boston Savings Bank, Richard J. Gavegnano, age 68, $311,400 total compensation
EVP Corporate Banking, Frank Romano
EVP Lending, John Migliozzi
EVP and COO, John A. Carroll
SVP Electronic Banking, Mary Hagen
SVP Retail Banking, James Morgan
SVP Residential Lending, Joseph Nash
Auditors: Wolf & Company, P.C.

LOCATIONS

HQ: Meridian Bancorp Inc
67 Prospect Street, Peabody, MA 01960
Phone: 617 567-1500

PRODUCTS/OPERATIONS

2015 Sales

	$ mil.	% of total
Interest & dividend income		
Interest & fees on loans	118.6	87
Interest on debt securities	1.8	1
Dividends on equity securities	1.6	1
Others	1.3	1
Non-interest income		
Customer service fees	8.0	6
Gain on sales of securities net	2.4	2
Income from bank-owned life insurance	1.2	1
Loan fees	1.0	1
Mortgage banking gains & other income	0.5	-
Total	**136.4**	**100**

Selected Products & Services

Personal
  Deposit Rates
  Investments
  Personal Checking
  Personal Lending
  Personal Online Banking
  Retirement Services
  Savings & CDs

Business
  Business Checking
  Business Lending
  Business Online Banking
  Business Retirement Services
  Business Savings
  Deposit Rates
  Institutional Banking
  Merchant Services
Commercial
  Cash Management
  Commercial Lending
  Corporate Banking
  Deposit Rates

COMPETITORS

Bank of America	Middlesex Savings
Cambridge Financial	Peoples Federal
Citizens Financial Group	Bancshares Inc.
Eastern Bank	Sovereign Bank
	TD Bank USA

HISTORICAL FINANCIALS

Company Type: Public

Income Statement

FYE: December 31

	ASSETS ($ mil.)	NET INCOME ($ mil.)	INCOME AS % OF ASSETS	EMPLOYEES
12/15	3,524.5	24.6	0.7%	488.0
12/14	3,278.5	22.3	0.7%	466.0
12/13	2,682.1	15.4	0.6%	455.0
12/12	2,278.7	12.4	0.5%	433.0
12/11	1,974.3	11.9	0.6%	392.0
Annual Growth	**15.6%**	**19.7%**	**—**	**5.6%**

2015 Year-End Financials

Return on assets: 0.7%
Return on equity: 4.2%
Long-term debt ($ mil.): —
No. of shares (mil.): 54.8
Sales ($ mil): 136.3

Dividends
  Yield: 0.4%
  Payout: 13.0%
Market value ($ mil.): 774.0

	STOCK PRICE ($) FY Close	P/E High/Low	PER SHARE ($) Earnings	Dividends	Book Value
12/15	14.10	31 24	0.46	0.06	10.72
12/14	11.22	27 24	0.42	0.00	10.56
Annual Growth	**25.7%**	**— —**	**9.5%**	**—**	**1.5%**

Merit Medical Systems, Inc.

When it comes to medical devices this company believes its merits speak for themselves. Merit Medical Systems makes disposable medical products used during interventional and diagnostic cardiology radiology gastroenterology and pulmonary procedures. The company's products include catheters guide wires needles and tubing used in heart stent procedures pacemaker placement and angioplasties as well as products for endoscopy dialysis and other procedures. Merit Medical sells its products as stand-alone items or in custom-made kits to hospitals and other health care providers as well as to custom packagers and equipment makers worldwide.

Operations

The company's largest operating segment —accounting for more than 95% of sales —is its cardiovascular division which makes cardiology and radiology devices for the diagnosis of arterial and vascular disease among other conditions. Offerings include stand-alone devices custom procedure trays and kits inflation devices and catheters. It also includes embolotherapy products which use bio-engineered microspheres to create targeted vascular occlusion (the blockage of blood vessels) and drug delivery.

Merit Medical's much smaller endoscopy segment makes devices for gastroenterology and pulmonary treatments including minimally-invasive treatment of throat and biliary constriction from malignant tumors. The endoscopy operations are conducted through Merit Medical's Endotek subsidiary.

The company also conducts selected manufacturing of custom medical kits and components for third parties through its OEM division.

Geographic Reach

Though the US accounts for more than 60% of sales the company is focused on growth in overseas markets. It experienced a 37% increase in international sales during 2012.

Headquartered in South Jordan Utah Merit Medical has a major manufacturing and distribution center in Ireland. It also has manufacturing centers in Texas and Virginia in the US as well as in the Netherlands and France.

Sales and Marketing

Marketing and sales efforts in the US and abroad are conducted through a direct sales force of about 200 representatives as well as through independent distributors and manufacturers. Products are marketed to hospital and clinic-based medical professionals in fields including cardiology radiology gastroenterology pulmonary medicine vascular surgery pain management and thoracic surgery.

Financial Performance

Continuing on its growth trajectory over the last five years Merit Medical's revenues grew by 10% in 2012 thanks to increased sales from its cardiovascular and endoscopy segments. The increase in sales of guidewires hemostasis valves catheters and custom kits and trays attributed to growth in the Cardiovascular segment and a rise in sales of the EndoMAXX esophageal stent helped to grow revenue in the Endoscopy segment.

Net income has fluctuated however as Merit Medical has worked to balance costs with earnings. The company's net income decreased by 14% due to higher operating expenses primarily from the expansion of its sales and marketing force as well as higher R&D costs. In 2011 jumped by 85% in 2011 due to increased sales volumes higher gross margins and a lower effective income tax rates.

Strategy

Though a sizable part of Merit Medical's strategy is growth by acquisition the company also invests about 5% of its annual income in research and development efforts. In 2012 the company got FDA clearance to market the Merit Laureate hydrophilic guide wire as well as its 30-60um QuadraSphere Microspheres and its ONE Snare endovascular system. Also in 2012 the company made several investments to expand its international sales and distribution network especially in emerging markets such as Brazil India and Russia.

Mergers and Acquisitions

In early 2016 Merit Medical acquired the HeRO Graft product line for end-stage renal disease from CryoLife for $18.5 million. The HeRO Graft is a hemodialysis access graft used in patients who have catheter-dependent because of vein blockage. As part of the deal Merit Medical gained worldwide marketing rights customers equipment and inventory.

Ownership

Investors in Merit Medical include Edgepoint Investment Group and Blackrock each of which hold a 10% stake.

EXECUTIVES

Chairman President and CEO, Fred P. Lampropoulos, age 67, $1,108,654 total compensation
VP Human Resources, Darla R. Gill
President Merit Technology Group, Joseph (Joe) Wright
EVP Sales and Marketing, Justin Lampropoulos
CIO, Joseph Pierce
CFO, Bernard Birkett
COO, Ronald A. Frost, age 54, $317,500 total compensation
Vice President Personnel, Brent Bowen
Vice President Regulatory Affairs, Glenn Norton
Vice President Materials and Operations, Ron (Ronnie) Frost
Auditors: Deloitte & Touche LLP

LOCATIONS

HQ: Merit Medical Systems, Inc.
1600 West Merit Parkway, South Jordan, UT 84095
Phone: 801 253-1600
Web: www.merit.com

PRODUCTS/OPERATIONS

2015 Sales

	$ mil.	% of total
Cardiovascular	520.9	96
Endoscopy	21.2	4
Total	**542.1**	**100**

Selected Products

Backstop (waste handling system)
BasixCOMPAK (inflation devices)
Blue Diamond (inflation devices)
Captiva Blood Containment Device (safety and waste management)
DialEase (sheath introducers)
En Snare (retrieval device)
Fountain (thrombolytic infusion catheters)
Inqwire (diagnostic guide wire)
Intellisystem (inflation devices)
Majestik (angiography needles)
Medallion (specialty syringes)
Merit Disposal Depot (waste handling system)
Meritrans (disposable blood pressure transducer)
Monarch (inflation devices)
Prelude (sheath introducers)
ProGuide (chronic dialysis catheter)
Smart Tip (coronary control syringes)

COMPETITORS

Abbott Labs	ICU Medical
AngioDynamics	Johnson & Johnson
B. Braun Medical	Medtronic
Bard	St. Jude Medical
Baxter International	Teleflex
Boston Scientific	Terumo
Cook Incorporated	Vascular Solutions
Cordis	

HISTORICAL FINANCIALS
Company Type: Public

Income Statement
FYE: December 31

	REVENUE ($ mil.)	NET INCOME ($ mil.)	NET PROFIT MARGIN	EMPLOYEES
12/15	542.1	23.8	4.4%	3,754.0
12/14	509.6	22.9	4.5%	3,105.0
12/13	449.0	16.5	3.7%	2,888.0
12/12	394.2	19.7	5.0%	2,760.0
12/11	359.4	23.0	6.4%	2,400.0
Annual Growth	**10.8%**	**0.8%**	**—**	**11.8%**

2015 Year-End Financials

Debt ratio: 26.6%	No. of shares (mil.): 44.2
Return on equity: 5.2%	Dividends
Cash ($ mil.): 4.1	Yield: —
Current ratio: 2.32	Payout: —
Long-term debt ($ mil.): 197.5	Market value ($ mil.): 823.0

	STOCK PRICE ($) FY Close	P/E High/Low	Earnings	PER SHARE ($) Dividends	Book Value
12/15	18.59	47 28	0.53	0.00	10.53
12/14	17.33	33 22	0.53	0.00	9.98
12/13	15.74	42 25	0.39	0.00	9.47
12/12	13.90	32 25	0.46	0.00	8.98
12/11	13.38	41 21	0.58	0.00	8.50
Annual Growth	**8.6%**	**— —**	**(2.2%)**	**—**	**5.5%**

Meritage Hospitality Group Inc

This company is really big on the beef in Michigan. Meritage Hospitality Group is a leading franchisee of Wendy's fast food hamburger restaurants with about 70 locations operating mostly in western and southern Michigan. The units franchised from Wendy's/Arby's Group offer a menu of burgers and other sandwiches fries and other items. In addition to its quick-service operations Meritage runs four franchised O'Charley's casual dining restaurants in Michigan near Grand Rapids and Detroit. The company was founded in 1986 as Thomas Edison Inns. The family of chairman Robert Schermer Sr. including CEO Robert Schermer Jr. controls Meritage.

Meritage expanded its restaurant estate in 2009 when the company acquired 20 Wendy's locations from Wendy's/Arby's in the Jacksonville Florida area. The deal also diversified Meritage's operations away from the Michigan market which was hit hard by the recession and credit collapse late in 2008.

The Schermer's led a group to take Meritage private in 2007 through a reverse stock split. The buyout was a cost-cutting move in response to increased reporting equipments enacted by the US Securities and Exchange Commission (SEC). Meritage had been a public company since 1986.

Thomas Edison Inns had previously operated a small number of Michigan resort inns. Schermer and partner Don Reynolds took control of the company in 1996; the business was renamed later that year.

EXECUTIVES

Vice President Facility Maintenance, Robert (Bob) Potts
Auditors: Plante & Moran, PLLC

LOCATIONS

HQ: Meritage Hospitality Group Inc
45 Ottawa Avenue S.W., Suite 600, Grand Rapids, MI 49503
Phone: 616 776-2600 **Fax:** 616 776-2776
Web: www.meritagehospitality.com

COMPETITORS

American Dairy Queen	McDonald's
B.R. Associates	Quality Dining
Burger King	Subway
Carrols	Tubby's
Hardee's	YUM!
Interfoods	

HISTORICAL FINANCIALS
Company Type: Public

Income Statement
FYE: January 3

	REVENUE ($ mil.)	NET INCOME ($ mil.)	NET PROFIT MARGIN	EMPLOYEES
01/16*	210.0	7.0	3.3%	5,100.0
12/14	160.2	2.7	1.7%	4,000.0
12/13	137.7	3.0	2.2%	3,300.0
12/12	98.9	2.9	2.9%	3,500.0
01/12	91.9	2.3	2.5%	2,500.0
Annual Growth	**22.9%**	**32.0%**		**19.5%**

*Fiscal year change

2016 Year-End Financials

Debt ratio: 49.8%	No. of shares (mil.): 5.6
Return on equity: 41.1%	Dividends
Cash ($ mil.): 6.5	Yield: 0.0%
Current ratio: 0.33	Payout: —
Long-term debt ($ mil.): 41.2	Market value ($ mil.): 64.0

	STOCK PRICE ($) FY Close	P/E High/Low	Earnings	PER SHARE ($) Dividends	Book Value
01/16*	11.25	— —	(0.00)	0.06	3.63
12/14	4.97	— —	(0.00)	0.03	2.32
12/13	4.30	— —	(0.00)	0.02	1.94
12/12	2.63	— —	(0.00)	0.01	1.52
01/12	1.71	— —	(0.00)	0.00	0.63
Annual Growth	**60.2%**	**— —**	**—**	**—**	**54.8%**

*Fiscal year change

Mesa Laboratories, Inc.

Mesa Laboratories measures its progress by the sales of its measurement devices. And so far it hasn't plateaued. The company makes niche-market electronic measurement testing and recording instruments for medical food processing electronics and aerospace applications. Mesa's products include sensors that record temperature humidity and pressure levels; flow meters for water treatment polymerization and chemical processing applications; and sonic concentration analyzers. The company also makes kidney dialysis treatment products including metering equipment and machines that clean dialyzers (or filters) for reuse. It also provides repair recalibration and certification services.

Operations

The company is organized into four segments – instruments 42% of revenue; biological indicators 40% of revenue; continuous monitoring 13% of revenue and cold chain 5%.

The instruments division includes the DataTrace (data loggers) Bios Torqo (bottle cap test systems) DialyGuard DryCal SureTorque BGI and Nusonics (ultrasonic fluid measurement systems) brands. Biological indicators sold under the Mesa PCD and Apex brands are used by dental offices hospitals and manufacturers of medical devices and pharmaceuticals for quality control testing in sterilization processes.

Continuous monitoring created in 2013 through acquisitions provides temperature control to laboratories that require stable environments such as hospitals blood banks pharmacies and medical device manufacturers. Brands include CheckPoint and AmegaView. The cold chain segment is Mesa's newest also formed through acquisitions. It provides parameter (primarily temperature) monitoring of products consulting services such as compliance monitoring packaging development and validation or mapping of transport and storage containers and thermal packaging products such as coolers boxes insulation materials and phase-change products to control temperature during transport.

Geographic Reach

Mesa Laboratories has manufacturing plants in Lakewood Colorado; Butler New Jersey; Bozeman Montana; and Omaha Nebraska. The new continuous monitoring division operates from Marlton New Jersey; and Emeryville California. The company's sales are split about two-thirds and one-third between the US and international markets.

Sales and Marketing

The company uses a direct sales force as well as distributors in the US. Overseas the company relies on about 270 distributors to gets its products to customers.

Financial Performance

Overall sales grew 19% in 2016 (ended March) to $84 million. Revenue from biological indicators jumped 23% with the help of a series of acquisitions and 2% rise in organic growth from new customers new markets and price increases. Instruments revenue rose 8% as a 55% increase in service revenue more than balanced a 3% drop in product sales. The BGI acquisition also aided revenue growth. Continuous monitoring revenue was off 1%. The cold chain segment reported $4.5 million revenue in its first year.

Mesa posted a 17% increase in profit to just more than $11 million in 2016 compared to the year before. Expenses were about a $1 million higher in 2016 than 2015. The company also paid about $1.7 million in a legal settlement but benefited by $860000 by adopting a different standard for stock compensation. Cash flow from operations increased to $17 million in 2016 from about $11 million in 2015. The company had gains in depreciation and amortization stock-based compensation and accrued liabilities and payments.

Strategy

Mesa's strategy is to provide products that serve niche markets and carry high margins. The lure of niche markets is that they are too small for big competitors leaving the field for Mesa to exploit. The company accomplishes some of it goals through develop its own products –organic growth is a healthy 6% a year. But it revs up its growth rate through acquisitions that complement and add to its portfolio. The company is building a product range that serves the supply chain in certain medical testing and control markets.

Mergers and Acquisitions

Mesa has stepped up its pace of acquisitions to build its offerings. In fiscal 2016 (ended March) the company made 10 deals and added several others in the 2016 calendar year. Deals made the year before totaled six.

The company jumped in to the cold chain business with its July 2015 acquisition of Infitrak Inc. a provider of monitoring instruments packaging products and consulting services to the cold chain markets in Canada and the US. Mesa followed up with the purchase of another cold chain business FreshLoc Technologies Inc. in November 2015. The new business segment added about $4.5 million to Mesa's sales –5% of the total –in 2016.

Other acquisitions focused on Mesa's dental business and included a deal for North Bay Bioscience. North Bay provides sterilizer testing services for dental offices in Canada. The acquisition marks Mesa's entry into mail-in testing services. Mesa built on that with the purchase of mail-in rights from Mydent International Corp. Mydent's mail-in business involves the testing of small table-top sterilizers in the US.

HISTORY

In 2009 president John Sullivan took the reins as CEO replacing Luke Schmieder who had been CEO since founding the company in 1982. Still chairman of the board Schmieder owns about 9% of Mesa Laboratories.

EXECUTIVES

President and CEO, John J. Sullivan, age 64, $316,488 total compensation
VP and Chief Sales and Marketing Officer, Glenn E. Adriance, age 62, $212,664 total compensation
CFO, John V. Sakys, age 47, $214,335 total compensation
SVP Operations, Bryan T. Leo, $160,000 total compensation
SVP Operations, Garrett Krushefski, $160,000 total compensation
Chairman, H. Stuart Campbell, age 87
Auditors: EKS&H LLLP

LOCATIONS

HQ: Mesa Laboratories, Inc.
   12100 West Sixth Avenue, Lakewood, CO 80228
Phone: 303 987-8000
Web: www.mesalabs.com

PRODUCTS/OPERATIONS

2016 Sales

	$ mil.	% of total
Product	66,085.0	78
Services	18,574.0	22
Total	**84,659.0**	**100**

2016 Sales

	$ mil.	% of total
Instruments	35,692.0	42
Biological indicators	33,649.0	40
Continuous Monitoring	10,792.0	13
Cold Chain	4,526.0	5
Total	**84,659.0**	**100**

Selected Products

Biological and chemical indicators (Raven Biological Laboratories)
Electronic thermal sensors DATATRACE

DATATRACE Micropack Tracers
ELOGG
Flatpack Tracers
FRB Tracers
Hemodialysis products (Automata)
   Database management software (Reuse Data Management System)
   Dialyzer reprocessors (ECHO MM-1000)
   Meters (Western Meters)
Sonic fluid measurement products (NuSonics)
   Sonic concentration analyzers
   Sonic flowmeters

COMPETITORS

3M Health Care	Rockwell Medical
Badger Meter	STERIS
Cantel Medical	Siemens Corp.
Coperion K-Tron	Siemens Water
Danaher	Technologies
Emerson Electric	Teledyne Isco
Euro Tech	Thermo Fisher
GE	Scientific
Gambro AB	Velocys
MEDIVATORS	

HISTORICAL FINANCIALS

Company Type: Public

Income Statement

FYE: March 31

	REVENUE ($ mil.)	NET INCOME ($ mil.)	NET PROFIT MARGIN	EMPLOYEES
03/16	84.6	11.1	13.2%	367.0
03/15	71.3	9.5	13.4%	276.0
03/14	52.7	9.0	17.1%	273.0
03/13	46.4	8.4	18.2%	215.0
03/12	39.6	7.9	20.0%	186.0
Annual Growth	20.9%	9.0%	—	18.5%

2016 Year-End Financials

Debt ratio: 28.1%	No. of shares (mil.): 3.6
Return on equity: 14.0%	Dividends
Cash ($ mil.): 5.7	Yield: 0.6%
Current ratio: 1.55	Payout: 27.2%
Long-term debt ($ mil.): 42.2	Market value ($ mil.): 350.0

	STOCK PRICE ($) FY Close	P/E High/Low		PER SHARE ($) Earnings	Dividends	Book Value
03/16	96.35	39	22	2.97	0.64	23.28
03/15	72.20	33	20	2.63	0.62	20.63
03/14	90.25	36	18	2.49	0.58	18.43
03/13	52.78	22	17	2.35	0.54	15.57
03/12	49.32	24	12	2.29	0.50	13.22
Annual Growth	18.2%	—	—	6.7%	6.4%	15.2%

Meta Financial Group Inc

Don't worry the money is real. Meta Financial Group is the holding company for MetaBank a thrift with about a dozen branches in Iowa and South Dakota. MetaBank offers standard deposit products and services including checking and savings accounts. Its lending and investment activities are weighted towards real estate and real estate-related assets; commercial and multifamily residential mortgages comprise more than half of the bank's loan portfolio. It also writes single-family residential mortgages and business loans. Meta Financial's bread and butter however is the bank's Meta Payment Systems (MPS) division which provides prepaid cards consumer credit and ATM sponsorship services nationwide.

Strategy

The company has invested in MPS' growth by marketing new products and programs such as prepaid debit cards for tax refunds eco-friendly recycled or recyclable cards and lines of credit on prepaid cards.

In 2016 Meta Financial agreed to buy most of the assets of EPS Financial for some $42.5 million. EPS Financial provides tax-related financial transaction services including refund settlement products and merchant services.

EXECUTIVES

Chairman and CEO Meta Financial Group and MetaBank, J. Tyler Haahr, age 53, $550,000 total compensation

EVP Sales and Operations MetaBank and Director Meta Financial Group (MFG) and MetaBank, Troy Moore, age 48, $252,350 total compensation

EVP Secretary Treasurer and CFO, David W. Leedom, age 62, $215,000 total compensation

President Meta Financial Group Inc. (MFG) and MetaBank and Division President Meta Payment System, Bradley C. (Brad) Hanson, age 52, $550,000 total compensation

EVP Meta Payment Systems, Scott Galit, age 46, $235,000 total compensation

EVP and COO, Cynthia M. (Cindy) Smith, age 57

EVP and CFO Meta Financial Group (MFG) and MetaBank, Glen W. Herrick, age 53, $255,000 total compensation

Vice Chairman Meta Financial Group (MFG) and MetaBank, Frederick V. (Fred) Moore, age 60

Auditors: KPMG LLP

LOCATIONS

HQ: Meta Financial Group Inc
5501 South Broadband Lane, Sioux Falls, SD 57108
Phone: 605 782-1767
Web: www.metabank.com

COMPETITORS

Bank of America	Green Dot
Blackhawk Network	HF Financial
Citi Prepaid Services	U.S. Bancorp
First National of	West Bancorporation
Nebraska	nFinanSe
Great Western Bancorp	

HISTORICAL FINANCIALS

Company Type: Public

Income Statement

FYE: September 30

	ASSETS ($ mil.)	NET INCOME ($ mil.)	INCOME AS % OF ASSETS	EMPLOYEES
09/16	4,006.4	33.2	0.8%	672.0
09/15	2,529.7	18.0	0.7%	638.0
09/14	2,054.0	15.7	0.8%	453.0
09/13	1,691.9	13.4	0.8%	432.0
09/12	1,648.9	17.1	1.0%	410.0
Annual Growth	24.9%	18.0%	—	13.1%

2016 Year-End Financials

Return on assets: 1.0%
Return on equity: 10.9%
Long-term debt ($ mil.): —
No. of shares (mil.): 8.5
Sales ($ mil): 182.1

Dividends
Yield: 0.8%
Payout: 15.0%
Market value ($ mil.): 517.0

	STOCK PRICE ($) FY Close	P/E High/Low		PER SHARE ($) Earnings	Dividends	Book Value
09/16	60.61	16	9	3.92	0.52	39.30
09/15	41.77	20	12	2.66	0.52	33.24
09/14	35.26	18	14	2.53	0.52	28.33
09/13	38.00	16	9	2.38	0.52	23.55
09/12	24.25	5	3	4.92	0.52	26.79
Annual Growth	25.7%	—	—	(5.5%)	(0.0%)	10.1%

Methode Electronics, Inc.

When it comes to making gear for manufacturers there's no madness in Methode Electronics' methods. Methode produces a wide variety of components especially electronic connectors and controls that are used by automotive manufacturers (products made for Ford and GM together account for more than half of sales) and in computers communications equipment industrial systems aircraft and spacecraft and consumer electronics. It also makes electrical bus systems and radio remote controls among other products.

Operations

Methode Electronics divides its business into three segments: automotive (76% of sales) interface (17% of sales) and power products (7% of sales).

Automotive devices include control switches for electrical power and signals connectors for electrical devices integrated control components and switches and sensors that monitor components or systems.

The interface segment provides copper and fiber-optic interconnect and interface products such as connectors custom cable assemblies industrial safety radio remote controls and optical and copper transceivers.

The power products segment manufactures braided flexible cables current-carrying laminated bus devices custom power-product assemblies high-current low voltage flexible power cabling systems and powder coated bus bars.

The company makes its products in factories in China Egypt Malta and Mexico.

Geographic Reach

About 61% of Methode's revenue comes from the US home to its two biggest customers. Malta generates 21% and China 15%.

Sales and Marketing

Methode Electronics uses a direct sales force that works with customers to design custom-engineered and application-specific products. For certain automotive products the company distributes products to suppliers of automotive OEMs. As noted Methode's two biggest customers either directly or through suppliers account for about 50% and 11% of revenue.

Financial Performance

Methode's revenue slid 8% to $809 million in 2016 (ended in April) from 2014. Automotive sales dropped as the Ford Center Console program substantially completed production by the end 2016. But the biggest decrease was Power Products for which sales dropped 38% wiping out $32 million revenue. The segments North American sales were

---

hurt by fewer sales of PowerRail products and in Europe by lower sales of a bypass switch.

Profit which had risen for several years in a row suffered with a 16% drop to $84.6 million in 2016.

Cash from operating activities fell 10% to $110.7 million in 2016 from 2015.

Strategy

Methode sold its Trace Laboratories unit which offered electrical environmental and other industrial testing services to NTS for $11.7 million in 2015 to better focus on its core businesses.

HISTORY

William McGinley started Methode in 1947 to produce vacuum tube sockets for portable radios. Methode began making printed circuits for radios in 1952. During the early 1960s it supplied circuits for color TVs made by RCA. The rising dominance of Asian electronics manufacturers during the 1970s inspired Methode to turn to the nascent computer market for customers; it made electronic connectors for mainframe and midrange computers. During the 1980s the company began developing network products and fiber-optic connectors.

In 1993 Methode sold its automotive test equipment subsidiary to focus on interconnect products. That year the company began a prolonged acquisition drive when it bought Mikon Ltd. a UK-based supplier of fiber-optic cable assemblies and components. In 1994 Methode acquired Rogers Corp.'s power distribution business. The next year it bought Duel Systems a maker of sonic-welded PC memory cards and two cable manufacturing operations from ETOS Fujikura.

The company's 1997 acquisitions included Merit Elektrik a Malta-based maker of automotive switches and Magnetoelastic Devices a research company with a passive transducer patent. In 1998 Methode bought Stratos Ltd. a UK-based maker of fiber-optic connectors for harsh environments.

Methode sold its printed circuit board operations in 1999. The company acquired network component maker Polycore Technologies and the optoelectronics division of Spire Corporation that year. In 2000 Methode spun off most of its optical components business as Stratos Lightwave retaining an 84% stake. (Stratos Lightwave later became Stratos International and was acquired in 2007 by Emerson Electric.)

After more than 50 years at the helm of his company William McGinley died in 2001 at the age of 77. William Jensen a 45-year veteran of the company was named chairman while EVP Donald Duda became president. Also that year the company distributed its remaining stake in Stratos to shareholders.

With a stagnant economy in the early 21st century putting pressure on revenue growth Methode consolidated some of its manufacturing facilities to control costs and increase margins. In 2003 Methode acquired its longtime automotive products distributor Kill & Bolton Associates.

In 2004 Duda was named CEO. Later the same year Jensen retired as chairman and director Warren Batts (retired chairman and CEO of Tupperware Brands) was tapped to replace him. Also that year Methode acquired and then retired about two-thirds of the Class B shares owned by the estate and survivors of company founder William McGinley and agreed to buy the rest. Despite efforts by Dura Automotive Systems to purchase the remaining Class B shares in a hostile bid for control of Methode the merger of Class A and Class B shares was approved by Methode shareholders.

The company acquired Cableco Technologies a manufacturer of high-current flexible cabling systems for electronic and electrical power applications in 2005.

In 2007 Methode acquired TouchSensor Technologies from Gemtron Corporation for $65 million. TouchSensor supplied solid-state field-effect switches used in automobiles beverage dispensers and home appliances among other applications. The acquisition helped the company diversify into a variety of consumer products.

In 2008 the company acquired the assets of radio remote control manufacturer Hetronic. The deal worth nearly $54 million in cash included operations in Germany Malta the Philippines and the US. Hetronic was incorporated into Methode's Interconnect segment. The deal expanded Methode's reach in the human/machine interface market. That year Methode also restructured operations at three of its US plants.

The global automotive industry had one of its worst years on record during Methode's fiscal 2009 due to the recession and credit crisis and that dramatic downturn was reflected in the company's results. Sales were off by nearly 23% from the year before. In fiscal 2010 sales in the auto market continued to drop by 18% over 2009 as the economy continued to slump.

Sales in North America where the auto industry was particularly hard hit led the decline. Sales to Ford were lower in 2010 due to Methode's decision to relocate business from its facility in Reynosa Mexico to other suppliers. Delphi once a significant customer terminated its supply agreement with Methode in 2009. Additionally the company decided to exit the Chrysler business which was completed during 2009. That year Methode restructured by consolidating manufacturing facilities in order to cut costs. Only its torque-sensing and testing businesses were spared.

EXECUTIVES

President CEO and Director, Donald W. Duda, age 61, $664,538 total compensation
VP Europe, Joseph E. Khoury, age 51, $309,787 total compensation
VP and General Manager North American Automotive, Timothy R. Glandon, age 51, $275,192 total compensation
VP Corporate Finance and CFO, John R. Hrudicka, age 52
Chairman, Walter J. Aspatore, age 72
Auditors: Ernst & Young LLP

LOCATIONS

HQ: Methode Electronics, Inc.
7401 West Wilson Avenue, Chicago, IL 60706-4548
Phone: 708 867-6777   **Fax:** 708 867-6999
Web: www.methode.com

PRODUCTS/OPERATIONS

2016 sales

	$ mil.	% of total
Automotive	614.3	76
Interface	140.8	17
Power products	53.5	7
Other	0.3	–
corporate	0.2	–
Total	**809.1**	**100**

PRODUCTS

Active Energy Solutions
Automotive & Transportation
Biometric
Bus Bars
Cable Management
Conductive & Resistive Inks

Custom User Interface
Data Center Cabinets
Dcim Solutions
Discrete & Analog Switching
Emi receptacles
Flexible Heating Elements
Force & Load Sensors
High Voltage Switchgear
High-Speed Copper Transceivers & Modules
Level Sensors
Linear Position Sensors
Power Cabling
Power Connector & Contacts
Powerrail®
Professional Services
Radio Remote Controls
Shrinkmate™
Smartpower Stack™
Sonicrimp®
Speed & Angle Sensors
Standard User Interface
Subassembly Services
Thermal Management
Torque Sensors
White Goods

Selected Testing Services (Trace Laboratories)

Electrical
Environmental
Failure analysis
Materials
Mechanical

COMPETITORS

AVX	Molex
Amphenol	Northrop Grumman
CTS Corp.	Parlex
Delphi Automotive	QualMark
Systems	Radiall
FCI	STRATTEC
Hirose Electric	Stoneridge
ITT Corp.	TE Connectivity
Japan Aviation	Thomas & Betts
Electronics Industry	Underwriters Labs
Lear Corp	

HISTORICAL FINANCIALS

Company Type: Public

Income Statement
FYE: April 30

	REVENUE ($ mil.)	NET INCOME ($ mil.)	NET PROFIT MARGIN	EMPLOYEES
04/16*	809.1	84.6	10.5%	4,345.0
05/15	881.1	101.1	11.5%	4,295.0
05/14	772.8	96.1	12.4%	4,566.0
04/13	519.8	40.7	7.8%	3,960.0
04/12	465.1	8.3	1.8%	3,143.0
Annual Growth	**14.8%**	**78.2%**	**—**	**8.4%**

*Fiscal year change

2016 Year-End Financials

Debt ratio: 8.6%
Return on equity: 18.2%
Cash ($ mil.): 227.8
Current ratio: 4.21
Long-term debt ($ mil.): 57.0
No. of shares (mil.): 36.8
Dividends
  Yield: 0.0%
  Payout: 16.3%
Market value ($ mil.): 1,095.0

	STOCK PRICE ($) FY Close	P/E High/Low		PER SHARE ($) Earnings	Dividends	Book Value
04/16*	29.73	22	11	2.20	0.36	12.76
05/15	43.59	18	11	2.57	0.36	11.96
05/14	29.20	15	6	2.51	0.30	10.33
04/13	14.05	13	6	1.08	0.28	7.80
04/12	8.63	56	32	0.22	0.28	6.89
Annual Growth	**36.2%**	**—**	**—**	**77.8%**	**6.5%**	**16.7%**

*Fiscal year change

MGP Ingredients Inc (New)

Auditors: KPMG LLP

LOCATIONS

HQ: MGP Ingredients Inc (New)
100 Commercial Street, Atchison, KS 66002
Phone: 913 367-1480
Web: www.mgpingredients.com

HISTORICAL FINANCIALS

Company Type: Public

Income Statement
FYE: December 31

	REVENUE ($ mil.)	NET INCOME ($ mil.)	NET PROFIT MARGIN	EMPLOYEES
12/15	327.6	26.1	8.0%	293.0
12/14	313.4	23.6	7.6%	268.0
12/13	323.2	(4.9)	—	268.0
12/12	334.3	1.6	0.5%	267.0
12/11	146.4	10.6	7.3%	256.0
Annual Growth	**22.3%**	**25.3%**		**3.4%**

2015 Year-End Financials

Debt ratio: 29.3%
Return on equity: 23.7%
Cash ($ mil.): 0.7
Current ratio: 2.42
Long-term debt ($ mil.): 53.6
No. of shares (mil.): 16.6
Dividends
  Yield: 0.2%
  Payout: 3.9%
Market value ($ mil.): 433.0

	STOCK PRICE ($) FY Close	P/E High/Low		PER SHARE ($) Earnings	Dividends	Book Value
12/15	25.95	18	8	1.48	0.06	6.96
12/14	15.86	13	4	1.32	0.05	5.90
12/13	5.19	—	—	(0.29)	0.05	4.60
12/12	3.42	74	34	0.09	0.05	4.84
12/11	5.04	19	7	0.59	0.05	4.66
Annual Growth	**50.6%**	**—**	**—**	**25.8%**	**—**	**10.6%**

Microchip Technology Inc

While bigger chip makers fight over your PC and mobile phone Microchip Technology has embedded itself in your car your copier and even your wallet. The semiconductor maker offers a variety of embedded devices including eight-bit microcontrollers (it's one of the top makers of them worldwide); specialty memory products such as electrically erasable programmable read-only memories (EEPROMs); and KEELOQ brand code-hopping devices used in keyless locks garage door openers and smart cards. Its chips are used by tens of thousands of customers in the automotive consumer industrial office automation and telecommunications markets. Microchip gets about 80% of sales from customers outside the US.

Operations

Microchip Technology's product line includes microcontrollers (about 65% of sales) which offers a broad family of proprietary general purpose microcontroller products marketed under the PIC brand; Analog Interface and Mixed Signal Products (23% of sales) which consists of several families with more than 1100 power management linear mixed-signal thermal management RF Linear drivers USB ethernet and wireless products; Memory Products (about 6% of sales) consists of serial electrically erasable programmable read-only memory (referred to as Serial EEPROMs) Serial Flash memories Parallel Flash memories and Serial SRAM memories; and Technology Licensing (4% of sales) includes license fees and royalties associated with technology licenses for the use of its SuperFlash embedded flash and Smartbits one time programmable NVM technologies.

Geographic Reach

The company has three manufacturing plants in the US (two in Arizona and one in Oregon) and one in Thailand. In addition it outsources a significant portion of its wafer needs from contract manufacturers or foundries.

Sales offices are located throughout the world. Sales operations in the Americas (the US Canada and Central and South America) and Europe support much of design for products shipped for Asia.

The percentage of sales attributable to Asia has increased as more customers have moved their manufacturing operations to the region generating 59% of sales. Customers in Europe and the Americas each account about one-fifth of sales.

Sales and Marketing

Microchip Technology uses both a direct sales force and distributors to sell its products worldwide. In 2015 (year-end March) 51% of its business went through distributors and 49% was sold directly.

Financial Performance

Net sales increased 11% to a record $2.1 billion in 2015 (year-end March) driven by increase market share results from acquisitions and the general strength in the semiconductor industry. Microchip Technology is consistently profitable but profit skidded 26% lower in 2015 to $369 million. The company had higher amortization expenses for acquired intangible assets and it experienced a loss on retirement of convertible debentures in 2015. Cash flow from operations increased 7% to $721 million.

Strategy

The company's stated goal is to provide specialized semiconductor products for a wide variety of embedded control applications such as consumer automotive industrial office automation and telecommunications. Its strategic focus is on the embedded control market which includes microcontrollers high-performance analog interface and mixed-signal devices power management and thermal management devices connectivity devices interface devices Serial EEPROMs SuperFlash memory products and its patented KeeLoq security devices and Flash IP solutions. Unlike many chip makers Microchip doesn't experience significant fluctuations in average selling prices particularly in its microcontroller and analog and interface groups where a large proportion of products are considered proprietary.

Mergers and Acquisitions

Microchip started 2016 with a deal to buy microcontroller competitor Atmel for $3.6 billion. Microchip aced out Dialog whose $4.6 billion offer for Atmel declined as Atmel's shares loss value in the intervening months. The deal deepens Microchip's product portfolio and provides both companies with more resources with which to withstand the increasingly competitive semiconductor environment.

In 2015 Microchip maintained its one-acquisition-a-year pace when it purchased Micrel Inc. for about $840 million. Micrel makes semiconductor products for power management and timing and communications. Its customers are mainly in industrial automotive and communications markets.

In 2014 it paid almost $235 million for Supertex which makes mixed-signal ICs from its foundry in California. Supertex will operate as a wholly owned subsidiary of Microchip Technology. The prior year it bought EqcoLogic a Belgian fabless semiconductor company that designs equalizer and coaxial transceiver products and technologies for automotive and industrial applications.

HISTORY

Early History

Investment firm Sequoia Capital acquired a washed-up semiconductor subsidiary from General Instrument in 1989. Sequoia executive Steve Sanghi a veteran of Intel was tapped to head the operation Microchip Technology. Sanghi instituted a bare-bones operating budget and broadened the company's focus beyond low-cost memory products to include more profitable embedded microcontrollers. By 1992 Microchip turned a small profit.

In 1995 Microchip acquired the rights to KEELOQ secure data transmission products developed by South Africa's Nanoteq Ltd. The following year the company introduced its own line of secure data transmission products and its first flash memory microcontrollers. In 1997 Microchip unveiled the world's smallest erasable read-only memory to be used in devices such as keyless entries dimmers and thermostats. In 1998 Microchip settled litigation with ROHM whose Exel Microelectronics unit was an original KEELOQ licensee; ROHM surrendered its licensing rights to the technology.

Streamlining around its more cost-effective manufacturing operations Microchip in 1999 closed a wafer fabrication plant (or fab) and a test facility. In 2001 the company beefed up its analog product line by acquiring TelCom Semiconductor a maker of chips for wireless phones.

In 2002 Microchip paid $54 million in cash for privately held PowerSmart a Duracell spinoff that made embedded controllers and battery sensors. Also that year the company acquired a large wafer fab in Oregon from Fujitsu for about $180 million in cash. Microchip launched a new e-commerce Web site in 2003.

EXECUTIVES

Vice President Business Development and Investor Relations, Gordon (Gordy) Parnell
Vice President Worldwide Sales and Applications, Mitchell (Mitch) Little
Vice President Finance, Eric Bjornholt
Vice President European Sales, Gary Marsh
Chairman and CEO, Steve Sanghi, age 61, $624,897 total compensation
President and COO, Ganesh Moorthy, age 56, $302,185 total compensation
VP and CFO, J. Eric Bjornholt, age 45, $213,597 total compensation
VP Global Information Services, Robert Williams
Vice President Wireless Products Division, Stephen T Caldwell
Vice President Asia Sales, Joseph (Jo) Krawczyk
Vice President Pacific Rim Manufacturing Operations, Mathew (Matt) Bunker
Vice President Europe Finance, Nawaz Sharif
Vice President Of Marketing, Ron (Ronnie) Cates

Executive Vice President Administration, Marcella Soloway
Vice President Analog Interface Marketing, Bryan Liddiard
Vice President India Development Center, Sudarshan Iyengar
Vice President Digital Signal Controller Division, Sumit K Mitra
Vice President, Mark W (Marky) Reiten
Vice President, Ian Yue
Vice President of Advanced Microcontroller Architecture Division, Mitch Obolsky
Auditors: Ernst & Young LLP

LOCATIONS

HQ: Microchip Technology Inc
2355 West Chandler Boulevard, Chandler, AZ 85224-6199
Phone: 480 792-7200   **Fax:** 480 792-7790
Web: www.microchip.com

PRODUCTS/OPERATIONS

2015 Sales

	$ mil.	% of total
Microcontrollers	1,393.6	65
Analog & interface products	501.0	23
Memory products	132.3	6
Technology licensing	89.6	4
Other	30.5	2
Total	**2,147.0**	**100**

Selected Products

Analog and Interface Integrated Circuits (ICs)
    Interface devices
    Controllers
    Infrared codecs
    Linear devices
    Audio amplifiers
    Comparators
    Operational amplifiers
    Mixed-signal devices
    Analog-to-digital (A/D) and digital-to-analog (D/A) converters
    Digital potentiometers
    Power management devices
    DC-to-DC converters
    Linear regulators
    Power MOSFET drivers
    Switching regulators
    System supervisors
    Voltage detectors
    Voltage references
    Thermal management devices
    Brushless DC fan controllers
    Temperature sensors
KEELOQ Security Devices
    Decoders
    Encoders
    Transcoders
Memory Chips
    Serial and parallel erasable programmable read-only memories (EPROMs)
    Serial electrically erasable programmable read-only memories (EEPROMs)
Microcontrollers
    Eight-bit microcontrollers (PICmicro and rfPIC lines)
    Mixed-signal controllers
Radio-frequency identification (RFID) ICs

COMPETITORS

Altera	Mitsubishi Electric
Analog Devices	ON Semiconductor
Atmel	Oki Semiconductor
Cypress Semiconductor	ROHM
Dialog Semiconductor	RadiSys
Echelon Corporation	Ramtron International
Fairchild	Renesas Electronics
Semiconductor	STMicroelectronics
Fujitsu Semiconductor	Silicon Labs
Intel	Texas Instruments

Intersil
Linear Technology
Macronix International
Maxim Integrated
Products

Winbond Electronics
ZiLOG

HISTORICAL FINANCIALS
Company Type: Public

Income Statement
FYE: March 31

	REVENUE ($ mil.)	NET INCOME ($ mil.)	NET PROFIT MARGIN	EMPLOYEES
03/16	2,173.3	324.1	14.9%	9,766.0
03/15	2,147.0	369.0	17.2%	280.0
03/14	1,931.2	395.2	20.5%	8,604.0
03/13	1,581.6	127.3	8.1%	8,003.0
03/12	1,383.1	336.7	24.3%	6,923.0
Annual Growth	12.0%	(0.9%)	—	9.0%

2016 Year-End Financials

Debt ratio: 44.6%
Return on equity: 15.4%
Cash ($ mil.): 2,092.7
Current ratio: 8.11
Long-term debt ($ mil.): 2,483.0

No. of shares (mil.): 204.0
Dividends
Yield: 2.9%
Payout: 87.9%
Market value ($ mil.): 9,837.0

	STOCK PRICE ($) FY Close	P/E High/Low		PER SHARE ($) Earnings	Dividends	Book Value
03/16	48.20	32	25	1.49	1.43	10.54
03/15	48.90	28	21	1.65	1.43	10.12
03/14	47.76	24	17	1.82	1.42	10.68
03/13	36.77	57	45	0.62	1.41	9.84
03/12	37.20	23	17	1.65	1.39	10.31
Annual Growth	6.7%	—	—	(2.5%)	0.8%	0.6%

Mid-America Apartment Communities Inc

For Mid-America Apartment Communities the Sunbelt is where it's at. Operating as MAA the firm is a self-administered self-managed real estate investment trust (REIT) that focuses solely on buying multifamily residences. MAA owns or has interests in approximately 79500 apartment units in 15 states primarily located in the West Southeast and south-central US. Its largest markets are California Florida Tennessee and Texas. MAA which has an average property occupancy rate of 95% targets large and midsized markets. MAA bought rival Colonial Properties in 2013 in an $8.6 billion deal. It is now buying Post Properties for $3.9 billion to become the nation's largest public apartment owner by unit number.

Strategy

Rather than developing new properties MAA prefers to buy and upgrade existing complexes increasing curb appeal to attract middle-income residents. Although MAA generally considers property management and maintenance its focus and strength it does invest in new properties with joint venture partners from time to time and anticipates that that will be a growing part of its strategy.

Multifamily investors have been leading the way in the slowly recovering property markets and MAA in particular has had strongly growing sales for at least a decade.

EXECUTIVES

Senior Vice President and Controller, Rick (Ricky) Barton
Senior Vice President Director Physical Assets, Kevin (Kev) Perkins
Vice President Marketing, Melintha Ogle
Vice President Director Risk Management, Doug Clark
Senior Vice President Coastal Region Operations, Beth (Betty) Brock
Chairman President and CEO, H. Eric Bolton, age 59, $404,133 total compensation
Executive VP Chief Operating Officer, Thomas L. (Tom) Grimes, $168,928 total compensation
EVP and CFO, Albert M. (Al) Campbell, age 49, $158,223 total compensation
SVP Management Information Systems, Shelton Barron
Senior Vice President Director Finance, Tim Argo
Regional Vice President, Linda Thompson
Senior Vice President Coastal Division, Robert Donnelly
Svp East Region Operations, Jackie Melnick
Senior Vice President Information Technology, Ray Thornton
Vice President Director Of Capital Improvements, Dennis H Duke
Vice President Director Property Accounting, Peg Wahl
Senior Vice President Internal Audit, Glenn Russell
Senior Vice President Controller, Mica Holton
Senior Vice President Controller, Micah (Mic) Holton
Executive Vice President General Counsel, Robert (Bob) DelPriore
Senior Vice President East Division, Amber Fairbanks
Regional Vice President, Jon (Jonny) King
Vice President Of Property Taxes, David (Dave) Schindler
Regional Vice President, Kristine (Chris) Kee
Senior Vice President Marketing, Tilea Terry
Senior Vice President, Garret Askew
Auditors: Ernst & Young LLP

LOCATIONS

HQ: Mid-America Apartment Communities Inc
6584 Poplar Avenue, Memphis, TN 38138
Phone: 901 682-6600   **Fax:** 901 682-6667
Web: www.maac.com

PRODUCTS/OPERATIONS

2015 sales

	$ mil.	% of total
Rental	952.2	91
Other property	90.6	9
Total	**1,042.8**	**100**

COMPETITORS

AMLI Residential	Camden Property
Apartment Investment and Management	Equity Residential
Berkshire Income Realty	Milestone Management
	Southern Management
	UDR

HISTORICAL FINANCIALS
Company Type: Public

Income Statement
FYE: December 31

	REVENUE ($ mil.)	NET INCOME ($ mil.)	NET PROFIT MARGIN	EMPLOYEES
12/15	1,042.7	332.2	31.9%	1,989.0
12/14	989.3	156.2	15.8%	2,090.0
12/13	634.7	119.2	18.8%	2,241.0
12/12	497.1	105.2	21.2%	1,446.0
12/11	448.9	48.8	10.9%	1,466.0
Annual Growth	23.4%	61.5%	—	7.9%

2015 Year-End Financials

Debt ratio: 50.0%
Return on equity: 11.2%
Cash ($ mil.): 37.5
Current ratio: 3.63
Long-term debt ($ mil.): 3,427.5

No. of shares (mil.): 75.4
Dividends
Yield: 3.3%
Payout: 69.8%
Market value ($ mil.): 6,848.0

	STOCK PRICE ($) FY Close	P/E High/Low		PER SHARE ($) Earnings	Dividends	Book Value
12/15	90.81	21	16	4.41	3.08	39.79
12/14	74.68	39	31	1.97	2.92	38.48
12/13	60.74	33	26	2.25	2.78	39.45
12/12	64.75	27	23	2.56	2.64	21.71
12/11	62.55	55	42	1.31	2.51	18.54
Annual Growth	9.8%	—	—	35.5%	5.2%	21.0%

Middleby Corp

Founded in 1888 Middleby makes a slew of commercial and institutional foodservice equipment for restaurants retailers and hotels worldwide. Middleby operates through three segments: Commercial Foodservice Equipment Food Processing Equipment and Residential Kitchen Equipment. The largest Foodservice makes machines for most types of cooking and warming activities. Products are sold under some two dozen blue chip brands —Anets Blodgett Southbend and TurboChef among them. Food Processing makes cooking mixing slicing and packaging machines and Residential Kitchen makes ovens refrigerators dishwashers microwaves and other related products.

Geographic Reach

Middleby operates nearly 25 manufacturing facilities in the US and 20 internationally throughout the Americas Europe Asia and the Middle East. About 70% of its revenues come from the US and Canada. Europe and the Middle East account for 17%.

Operations

The company's mainstay Commercial Foodservice Equipment segment offers ovens ranges broilers fryers toasters coffee and tea brewers and other cooking equipment; it generates around 62% of total sales each year. Its Food Processing Equipment group (16% of sales) offers a slate of labor-saving products from batch ovens to mixing and slicing machines packaging and food safety equipment. Residential Kitchen (22%) makes everything from ovens and refrigerators to dishwashers and microwaves. The group's manufacturing facilities often neighbor major food processors.

Financial Performance

Middleby has enjoyed unprecedented growth over the last five years. Revenues rose by 12%

from $1.6 billion in 2014 to peak at a record-setting $1.8 billion in 2015. Profits also peaked at $193 million in 2014 and remained consistent in 2015.

The historic growth for 2015 was fueled by sales increases across the two segments of Commercial Foodservice (8%) and Residential Kitchen (50%). Middleby also experienced a 43% surge in sales from Europe and the Middle East. The growth was primarily attributed to additional revenue from previous acquisitions.

Strategy

Acquisitions have added to Middleby's revenue stream and strengthened its competitive position as a one-stop-shop for such giants as Cracker Barrel McDonald's Olive Garden and Panda Express. In 2015 it acquired AGA Rangemaster Group a manufacturer of residential kitchen equipment including cookers ranges ovens and refrigeration units for approximately $201 million. It also picked up Grills Inc (Lynx) a manufacturer of premium residential outdoor equipment for $84 million.

Throughout 2014 Middleby made several purchases including Processing Equipment Solutions (jet cutting equipment maker for the food processing industry) and Concordia Coffee Company (automated and self-service coffee and espresso machines) among other acquisitions.

It also in late 2014 purchased U-Line Corporation a manufacturer of residential modular ice-making refrigeration and wine preservation products for the residential sector in a transaction valued at $142 million.

EXECUTIVES

Chairman and CEO, Selim A. Bassoul, age 60, $1,000,000 total compensation
VP and CFO, Timothy J. (Tim) Fitzgerald, age 47, $575,000 total compensation
COO Commercial Foodservice, David Brewer, age 60, $400,000 total compensation
Vice President New Business Development, Todd Olds
Vice President Business Development, Brad Davis
Vice President Of Engineering, Steve Lombardo
Vice President National Accounts, Don Hawkins
Vice President Business Development Retail, James (Jamie) Baxter
Auditors: Ernst & Young LLP

LOCATIONS

HQ: Middleby Corp
   1400 Toastmaster Drive, Elgin, IL 60120
Phone: 847 741-3300
Web: www.middleby.com

PRODUCTS/OPERATIONS

2016 Sales

	$ mil.	% of total
Commercial Foodservice	1,121.1	62
Residential Kitchen	407.8	22
Food processing	297.7	16
Total	**1,826.6**	**100**

Selected Foodservice
Brands
Anets
Beech
Blodgett
Bloomfield
Britannia
Carter-Hoffmann
Celfrost
Concordia
CookTek
Desmon

Doyon
Southbend Selected Food Processing Equipment Brands
AlkarAuto-BakeArmor Inox
Baker
Cozzini
Danfotech
Drake
Maurer-Atmos Gmb
HMP Equipment
Rapid
Pak

COMPETITORS

Ali SpA	Heat and Control
Alto-Shaam	Hobart Corp.
Bally Refrigerated	Illinois Tool Works
Boxes	Ingersoll-Rand
Cleveland Range	Krack
Dover Corp.	Lincoln Foodservice
Electrolux	Manitowoc Foodservice
Franke Group	Standex
Frymaster	Vulcan-Hart
Gold Medal Products	

HISTORICAL FINANCIALS

Company Type: Public

Income Statement

FYE: January 2

	REVENUE ($ mil.)	NET INCOME ($ mil.)	NET PROFIT MARGIN	EMPLOYEES
01/16	1,826.6	191.6	10.5%	7,800.0
01/15*	1,636.5	193.3	11.8%	4,860.0
12/13	1,428.6	153.9	10.8%	4,491.0
12/12	1,038.1	120.7	11.6%	3,140.0
12/11	855.9	95.4	11.2%	2,150.0
Annual Growth	**20.9%**	**19.0%**	**—**	**38.0%**

*Fiscal year change

2016 Year-End Financials

Debt ratio: 27.7%
Return on equity: 17.6%
Cash ($ mil.): 55.5
Current ratio: 1.56
Long-term debt ($ mil.): 734.0

No. of shares (mil.): 57.3
Dividends
   Yield: —
   Payout: —
Market value ($ mil.): 6,182.0

	STOCK PRICE ($) FY Close	P/E High/Low		PER SHARE ($) Earnings	Dividends	Book Value
01/16	107.87	37	28	3.36	0.00	20.36
01/15*	99.04	88	21	3.40	0.00	17.58
12/13	242.50	89	46	2.74	0.00	14.61
12/12	125.47	60	42	2.16	0.00	11.52
12/11	94.04	55	38	1.72	0.00	9.13
Annual Growth	**3.5%**			**18.3%**	**—**	**22.2%**

*Fiscal year change

MidSouth Bancorp, Inc.

For banking in the Deep South try MidSouth. MidSouth Bancorp is the holding company for MidSouth Bank which boasts roughly $2 billion in assets and around 60 branches across Louisiana and Texas. Targeting individuals and local business customers the bank offers such standard retail services as checking and savings accounts savings bonds investment accounts and credit card services. About 55% of its loan portfolio is made up of real estate mortgages while commercial loans make up more than 35%. Consumer and construction loans round out the rest of its lending activities.

OperationsAbout 67% of MidSouth Bancorp's total revenue came from loan interest (including fees) in 2014 while another 10% came from interest on its taxable and non-taxable investment securities. The rest of its revenue came from deposit account service charges (9%) ATM and debit card income (7%) and other miscellaneous income sources. The company had a staff of nearly 550 employees at the end of 2014.Geographic ReachThe bank's branches are in Louisiana and central and east Texas along the Interstate 10 Interstate 49 Highway 90 Interstate 45 Interstate 20 and Interstate 35 corridors. Sales and MarketingThe bank offers commercial and consumer loan and deposit services to small and middle-market business their owners and employees and other individuals in its markets in Texas and Louisiana. Oil and gas is the key industry in these markets though medical technology and research companies are becoming increasingly prevalent. In addition major universities in the areas from Louisiana State University to Texas A&M contribute to a substantial number of jobs as well as a highly-educated workforce in these markets.Financial PerformanceMidSouth Bancorp's revenues and profits have been rising in recent years thanks to continued loan business growth partially stemming from the bank's late 2012 acquisition of PSB Financial and also thanks to lower interest expenses with the low-interest environment.The bank's revenue rose by 5% to $107.91 million in 2014 mostly thanks to a non-recurring $3 million-executive officer life insurance proceed and a $1.1 million gain on the sale of an ORE though its loan interest grew by 2% helping to add to the company's topline during the year.Higher revenue coupled with lower interest expenses on borrowings and a decline in salary and benefit costs in 2014 helped boost MidSouth's net income by 35% to $19.11 million during the year. Its operating cash levels grew by 15% to $29.8 million on higher cash earnings.StrategySeeking potential expansion into new market areas MidSouth Bancorp in 2015 planned to grow its loan and deposit business organically as well as through bank acquisitions. The bank would also continue its long-term strategy of focusing on commercial and small-business customers while continuing to serve its retail customers as well.Company BackgroundIn late 2012 Midsouth acquired PSB Financial which operated 16 branches in Louisiana under the Peoples State Bank banner. The deal expanded its presence into central and northwest Louisiana and east Texas.

EXECUTIVES

SEVP and CFO, James R. McLemore, age 56, $252,500 total compensation
SEVP and Chief Credit Officer MidSouth Bancorp and MidSouth Bank, Jeffery L. Blum, age 47, $225,000 total compensation
Chief Banking Officer and Director MidSouth Bancorp and President and CEO MidSouth Bank, Troy M. Cloutier, age 43, $280,000 total compensation
President and CEO, CLive R. (Rusty) Cloutier, age 69, $441,000 total compensation
Executive Vice President And Chief Credit Officer, John (Jack) Nichols
Senior Vice President, Lorraine (Irene) Miller
Vice Chairman, Joseph V. (Joe) Tortorice, age 67
Chairman, Jake Delhomme, age 41
Auditors: Porter Keadle Moore, LLC

LOCATIONS

HQ: MidSouth Bancorp, Inc.
102 Versailles Boulevard, Lafayette, LA 70501
Phone: 337 237-8343
Web: www.midsouthbank.com

PRODUCTS/OPERATIONS

2014 Sales

	$ mil.	% of total
Interest income		
Loans including fees	72.3	67
Investment securities	10.8	10
Others	0.4	-
Non-interest income		
Service charges on deposit accounts	9.9	9
ATM and debit card income	7.2	7
Others	7.3	7
Total	**107.9**	**100**

COMPETITORS

American Bancorp	Home Banc
Bank of America	IBERIABANK
Capital One	Regions Financial
Hancock Holding	Teche Holding
Henderson Citizens	
Bancshares	

HISTORICAL FINANCIALS

Company Type: Public

Income Statement
FYE: December 31

	ASSETS ($ mil.)	NET INCOME ($ mil.)	INCOME AS % OF ASSETS	EMPLOYEES
12/15	1,927.7	11.0	0.6%	536.0
12/14	1,936.7	19.1	1.0%	549.0
12/13	1,851.1	14.1	0.8%	604.0
12/12	1,851.7	9.6	0.5%	604.0
12/11	1,396.7	4.4	0.3%	444.0
Annual Growth	8.4%	25.3%	—	4.8%

2015 Year-End Financials

Return on assets: 0.5%	Dividends
Return on equity: 5.2%	Yield: 3.9%
Long-term debt ($ mil.): —	Payout: 34.2%
No. of shares (mil.): 11.3	Market value ($ mil.): 103.0
Sales ($ mil): 102.2	

	STOCK PRICE ($) FY Close	P/E High/Low	PER SHARE ($) Earnings	Dividends	Book Value
12/15	9.08	19 10	0.90	0.36	18.76
12/14	17.34	12 10	1.58	0.35	18.43
12/13	17.86	16 12	1.12	0.31	16.95
12/12	16.35	22 16	0.77	0.28	16.84
12/11	13.01	57 37	0.27	0.28	15.46
Annual Growth	(8.6%)	— —	35.1%	6.5%	4.9%

MidWestOne Financial Group, Inc.

This could be the saga of How the MidWest Was One. MidWestOne Financial Group is the holding company for MidwestOne Bank which operates about two dozen branches throughout central and east-central Iowa. The bank offers standard deposit products such as checking and savings accounts CDs and IRAs in addition to trust services credit cards insurance and brokerage and investment services. About two-thirds of MidWestOne Financial's loan portfolio consists of real estate loans including residential and commercial mortgages and farmland and construction loans. Founded in 1983 MidWestOne has total assets of $1.8 billion.

Geographic Reach

Headquartered in Iowa City MidwestOne Bank has branches and loan production offices in 15 counties in central and east-central Iowa.

Financial Performance

The company reported net income of $18.6 million in 2013 a 13% increase over 2012. Earnings have been rising steadily while the bank's revenue has been trending downward. Indeed 2013's $80.8 million in revenue was 10% below 2012. Assets declined slightly over the same period as did deposits. (The bank is facing stiff competition for deposits from aggressive credit unions offering above market deposit rates.) However loans increased 5% year over year and the growth in loans combined with stable net interest margins of about 3.5% resulted in a modest uptick in net interest income. Non-interest income got a boost from the bank's wealth management division which posted a 7% revenue gain in 2013 versus 2012.

EXECUTIVES

President and CEO, Charles N. Funk, age 62, $410,000 total compensation
EVP Chief Lending Officer and Commercial Banking, Kent L. Jehle, age 56, $250,000 total compensation
VP and Chief Risk Officer, James M. Cantrell, $205,000 total compensation
COO, Kevin Kramer
SVP and CFO, Katie A. Lorenson, age 36
Vice President Information Technology Managing Officer, Allen (Al) Schneider
Senior Vice President Loan Sales, Jason Swestka
Vice President Commercial and Ag Lending, Paul (Pauly) Jones
Vice President Senior Loan Review Officer, Jeff (Jeffy) Richards
Vice President and Program Manager, Daniel (Dan) Bailey
Chairman, Kevin W. Monson, age 64
Vice Chairman, Charles (Charlie) Howard
Auditors: RSM US LLP

LOCATIONS

HQ: MidWestOne Financial Group, Inc.
102 South Clinton Street, Iowa City, IA 52240
Phone: 319 356-5800
Web: www.midwestone.com

PRODUCTS/OPERATIONS

2015 Sales

	% of total
Interest Income	
Interest and fees on loans	71
Interest on investment securities	11
Other	1
Non-Interest Income	
Trust investment and insurance fees	5
Other service charges commissions and fees	5
Service charges and fees on deposit accounts	3
Mortgage origination and loan servicing fees	2
Other	2
Total	**100**

Selected Subsidiaries

MidWestOne Bank
MidWestOne Insurance Services Inc.
MidWestOne Statutory Trust II

COMPETITORS

Bank of the West	U.S. Bancorp
Hills Bancorporation	Wells Fargo
QCR Holdings	West Bancorporation

HISTORICAL FINANCIALS

Company Type: Public

Income Statement
FYE: December 31

	ASSETS ($ mil.)	NET INCOME ($ mil.)	INCOME AS % OF ASSETS	EMPLOYEES
12/15	2,979.9	25.1	0.8%	648.0
12/14	1,800.3	18.5	1.0%	374.0
12/13	1,755.2	18.6	1.1%	376.0
12/12	1,792.8	16.7	0.9%	390.0
12/11	1,695.2	13.3	0.8%	383.0
Annual Growth	15.1%	17.2%	—	14.0%

2015 Year-End Financials

Return on assets: 1.0%	Dividends
Return on equity: 10.2%	Yield: 1.9%
Long-term debt ($ mil.): —	Payout: 28.3%
No. of shares (mil.): 11.4	Market value ($ mil.): 347.0
Sales ($ mil): 121.8	

	STOCK PRICE ($) FY Close	P/E High/Low	PER SHARE ($) Earnings	Dividends	Book Value
12/15	30.41	14 12	2.42	0.60	25.96
12/14	28.81	13 10	2.19	0.58	23.07
12/13	27.20	13 9	2.18	0.50	20.99
12/12	20.51	12 8	1.96	0.36	20.51
12/11	14.62	11 8	1.47	0.22	18.35
Annual Growth	20.1%	— —	13.3%	28.5%	9.1%

MiMedx Group Inc

Surgical and medical instruments

EXECUTIVES

Pres-ceo-chb, Parker H Petit
Vice President Sales Marketing, Mike Carlton
Vice President, Roberta McCaw
Vice President Planning and Analysis, Al Evans
Area Vice President, Michael (Mel) Fox
Executive Vice President, Brent Miller
Vice President Information Technology, Jim (Jimmy) Dozier
Vice President Corporate Controller, John E (Jack) Cranston
Vice President Human Resources Administration, Thornton Kuntz
National Account Manager, Tammy (Tam) Holmes
Executive Vice President, Deborah (Deb) Dean
National Vice President Wound Care Sales, Detric Fox-Quinlan
Vice President Reimbursement and Health Policy MiMedx, Laura (Laur) Trivette
Auditors: Cherry Bekaert LLP

HQ: MiMedx Group Inc
1775 West Oak Commons Court, NE, Marietta, GA 30062
Phone: 770 651-9100
Web: www.mimedx.com

HISTORICAL FINANCIALS

Company Type: Public

Income Statement

FYE: December 31

	REVENUE ($ mil.)	NET INCOME ($ mil.)	NET PROFIT MARGIN	EMPLOYEES
12/15	187.3	29.4	15.7%	550.0
12/14	118.2	6.2	5.3%	386.0
12/13	59.1	(4.1)	—	222.0
12/12	27.0	(7.6)	—	166.0
12/11	7.7	(10.1)	—	52.0
Annual Growth	121.6%	—	—	80.3%

2015 Year-End Financials

Debt ratio: —	No. of shares (mil.): 107.3
Return on equity: 29.8%	Dividends
Cash ($ mil.): 31.4	Yield: —
Current ratio: 3.60	Payout: —
Long-term debt ($ mil.): —	Market value ($ mil.): 1,006.0

	STOCK PRICE ($) FY Close	P/E High/Low		PER SHARE ($) Earnings	Dividends	Book Value
12/15	9.37	46	26	0.26	0.00	1.01
12/14	11.53	198	85	0.05	0.00	0.83
12/13	8.74	—	—	(0.04)	0.00	0.70
12/12	3.84	—	—	(0.09)	0.00	0.23
12/11	1.13	—	—	(0.14)	0.00	0.16
Annual Growth	69.7%	—	—	—	—	58.3%

Minerals Technologies, Inc.

Minerals Technologies can brighten your day. Its precipitated calcium carbonate (PCC) products brighten and whiten paper polymers and teeth. Paper mills are major users of PCC —many of the company's facilities are adjacent to paper mills — along with food and pharmaceutical companies which use it for calcium and as a buffering agent in tablets. PCC products account for more than half of Minerals Technologies' sales. The company's processed mineral products also include lime (used to make PCC) limestone and talc. Minerals Technologies also sells monolithic and pre-cast refractory products which are used to coat steel cement and glass production surfaces with high-temperature-resistant material.

Geographic Reach

Minerals Technologies has operations Brazil Canada China Finland France Germany India Indonesia Japan Malaysia Mexico Poland Portugal Slovakia Thailand the US and South America.

The US accounted for 56% of the company's revenues in 2011

Operations

Minerals Technologies operates in two segments: Specialty Minerals and Refractories.

Specialty Minerals includes PCC and lime and mines processes and sells natural limestone and talc. These products are used principally by paper building materials paints and coatings glass ceramic polymers food automotive and pharmaceutical companies.

The Refractories segment includes monolithic and shaped refractory products and systems used by the steel cement and glass companies. It also makes and sells metallurgical products for the steel industry.

Sales and Marketing

The company's US marketing and sales activities are conducted from sales offices in the eastern and western US. International marketing and sales efforts are directed from Brussels Belgium; Sao Jose Dos Campos Brazil; and Shanghai China.

Major customers include International Paper Boise International Paper Domtar Georgia-Pacific and Verso Paper.

Financial Performance

Minerals Technologies' revenues decreased by 4% in 2012 due to a 7% drop in Refractories' revenues as the result of unfavorable foreign exchange lower sales to steel and other industries and lower sales of metallurgical products.

Specialty Minerals' revenues declined by 3% due to the unfavorable impact of foreign exchange rates. Sales were also affected by the closure of a PPC facility in Finland and the temporary shutdown of a precipitated calcium carbonate plant in France both of which occurred in late 2011.Minerals Technologies reported net income of $74.2 million in 2012 up from $67.5 million in 2011 due to lower operating expenses. In addition in 2012 unlike 2011 it did not report any restructuring and other costs.

Strategy

Minerals Technologies has spent the last few years going global by expanding its operations geographically particularly in the emerging economies of Brazil China and India and elsewhere in Asia. The growth has been most pronounced in its Refractories segment. It continues to see stronger sales in the recovering markets in the US and Europe. Its growth strategy is a combination of organic growth through focused spending on current operations and targeted acquisitions of technology-based materials companies primarily in the environmental energy and consumer markets.

In 2013 Minerals Technologies signed a commercial agreement with CMPC Celulose Riograndense to provide Fulfill E-325 at a paper mill in Guaiba Brazil. This marks Minerals Technologies' first such agreement in South America for the new high-filler technology.

In 2012 the company signed a deal with Henan Jianghe Paper Co. Ltd. to build a 22000-metric ton satellite PCC plant at Jianghe Paper's papermaking facility in Jiaozuo City Henan Province China. That year it also signed a joint venture agreement with Double A (1991) Public Company Ltd. to build a second satellite PCC plant in Tha Toom Thailand at a paper mill owned by Double A.

Ownership

Royce & Associates LLC owns approximately 11% of Minerals Technologies.

EXECUTIVES

SVP General Counsel Secretary and VP Human Resources, Thomas J. Meek, age 58, $478,308 total compensation
SVP and CFO, Douglas T. (Doug) Dietrich, age 47, $1,025,000 total compensation
SVP and Managing Director Paper PCC, W. Rand Mendez, age 56
SVP and Managing Director Performance Minerals and Supply Chain, Douglas W. Mayger, age 58, $356,923 total compensation
COO, D. J. Monagle, age 53, $486,921 total compensation
SVP and Managing Director Performance Materials, Gary L. Castagna, age 54, $467,789 total compensation
VP and Managing Director Minteq International Inc., Brett Argirakis
VP and Managing Director Energy Services, Andrew M. Jones, age 57
VP and Managing Director Construction Technologie, Thomas Stam
SVP Finance and Treasury and CFO, Matthew E. Garth
Vice President Finance Performance, Richard (Dick) Hasselbusch
Vice President Of Finance, Dave Browne
Senior Vice President, Dj Monagle
Vice President of Sales and Business Development, Joel Henley
Senior Vice President and Managing Director, Rand Mendez
Chairman, Duane R. Dunham, age 75
Board Member, Donald (Don) Winter
Auditors: KPMG LLP

LOCATIONS

HQ: Minerals Technologies, Inc.
622 Third Avenue, New York, NY 10017-6707
Phone: 212 878-1800
Web: www.mineralstech.com

PRODUCTS/OPERATIONS

2015 Sales

	$ mil.	% of total
Specialty minerals	624.6	35
Performance material	514.8	29
Refractories	295.9	16
Energy service segment	182.2	10
construction technologies segment	180.1	10
Total	**1,797.6**	**100**

2015 Sales

in million		% of sales
Product sales	1,615.4	90
Service revenue	182.2	10
Total	**1,797.6**	**100**

2015 Sales by Product

	% of total
Paper PC	23
Metalcasting	15
Refractory Products	13
Household Personal Care and Specialty Products	10
Energy Services	10
Building Materials and Other Products	6
Specialty PCC	4
Ground Calcium Carbonate	4
Metallurgical Products	4
Basic Minerals and Other Products	4
Environmental Products	4
Talc	3
Total	**100**

COMPETITORS

Ash Grove Cement	Saint-Gobain
BASF Catalysts	U.S. Lime & Minerals
Imerys	Vulcan Materials
Magneco/Metrel	
Martin Marietta	
Materials	

HISTORICAL FINANCIALS

Company Type: Public

Income Statement

FYE: December 31

	REVENUE ($ mil.)	NET INCOME ($ mil.)	NET PROFIT MARGIN	EMPLOYEES
12/15	1,797.6	107.9	6.0%	3,868.0
12/14	1,725.0	92.4	5.4%	4,464.0
12/13	1,018.1	80.3	7.9%	1,978.0
12/12	1,005.6	74.1	7.4%	1,992.0
12/11	1,044.8	67.5	6.5%	2,077.0
Annual Growth	14.5%	12.4%	—	16.8%

2015 Year-End Financials

Debt ratio: 42.4%
Return on equity: 12.1%
Cash ($ mil.): 229.4
Current ratio: 2.52
Long-term debt ($ mil.): 1,255.3

No. of shares (mil.): 34.7
Dividends
Yield: 0.4%
Payout: 6.2%
Market value ($ mil.): 1,595.0

	STOCK PRICE ($) FY Close	P/E High/Low	PER SHARE ($) Earnings	Dividends	Book Value
12/15	45.86	24 15	3.08	0.20	26.18
12/14	69.45	29 18	2.65	0.20	24.91
12/13	60.07	26 17	2.30	0.25	24.67
12/12	39.92	37 18	2.09	0.20	22.62
12/11	56.53	37 25	1.87	0.10	21.00
Annual Growth	(5.1%)	— —	13.4%	18.9%	5.7%

Mistras Group Inc

Mistras could be all that stands between you and a massive oil refinery explosion nuclear facility meltdown or big bridge collapse. The engineering services company conducts non-destructive testing on critical equipment and processes used by petroleum aerospace infrastructure power generation and chemical manufacturing companies worldwide. It checks plant infrastructure for defects and problems without interrupting production; inspections take place during facility design build maintenance and operation phases. Mistras works from about 75 offices in 15 nations to serve clients that include Alcan Honeywell Bechtel BP Dow Chemical Airbus and federal and state governments.

Operations

Mistras helps its customers beyond just avoiding catastrophic events. The company help clients comply with government safety standards minimize repair costs extend the useful life of assets and increase productivity.

In addition to its on-site testing services the company also offers testing equipment instruments and software through its Software and Products division. Testing services include mechanical integrity and visual testing along with digital radiography ground penetrating radar and infrared and ultrasonic sensor testing. Mistras' software offerings include databases and enterprise software to store and analyze testing data planning software and on-line monitoring systems.

Sales and Marketing

Asset heavy companies make up the bulk of Mistras' clients. Customers coming from the oil gas and chemical industries have historically comprised more than 50% of the company's international revenues stemming primarily from contracts with major oil refineries in Brazil and Russia. Smaller pieces of the revenue pie come from testing other safety-critical industrial sites infrastructure manufacturing facilities research centers and universities.

Financial Performance

The company's revenue has been growing during the past five fiscal years (2011-15). In fiscal 2015 its revenue increased by 14% to $711.25 million compared to $623.45 million in fiscal 2014 primarily due to increased revenue from the company's Services segment.

In fiscal 2015 the company's net income decreased by 29% to $16.08 million compared to $22.52 million in fiscal 2014. The drop was mainly due to increase expenses.

Mistras' operating cash inflow increased during fiscal 2015 by 37% to $50.62 million compared to $36.87 million in fiscal 2014 mainly due to changes in working capital as a result of improvement in the collections of accounts receivable.

Strategy

In the past Mistras has grown through acquisitions. More recently though the company has grown organically. The company also wants to delve into newer markets seeing opportunities in alternative energy and public infrastructure. The company hopes to expand its services into such emerging markets as India and China. Mistras also wants to expand its services to existing clients which includes providing multinational companies services in many of the countries they operate.

EXECUTIVES

SEVP CFO and Treasurer, Jonathan H. (Jon) Wolk, age 50, $335,500 total compensation
Vice President Sales, Nick Sowa
EVP General Counsel and Secretary, Michael C. Keefe, age 59, $261,174 total compensation
Chairman President and CEO, Sotirios J. Vahaviolos, age 70, $500,699 total compensation
Vice Chairman and EVP Business Development and Strategic Planning, Michael J. Lange, age 56, $314,054 total compensation
Group EVP Products and Systems, Mark F. Carlos, age 65, $130,000 total compensation
EVP Services Americas, Dennis M. Bertolotti, $289,693 total compensation
Executive Vice President Marketing and Sales, Ralph (Ralphy) Genesi
Vice President Operations, Michael (Mel) Farahani
Group Vice President Of Corporate Compliance, Chris Smith Chris Smith
National Sales Manager, Lewis (Louie) Rea
Vice President, Michael (Mel) Burch
Group Vice President, Frederick (Fred) Klorczyk
Vice President Of Services, John (Jack) Smith
Vice President and Human Resources METCO, Robert J (Bob) Silva
Auditors: KPMG LLP

LOCATIONS

HQ: Mistras Group Inc
195 Clarksville Road, Princeton Junction, NJ 08550
Phone: 609 716-4000
Web: www.mistrasgroup.com

PRODUCTS/OPERATIONS

2015 sales

	$ mil.	% of total
Services	540.2	75
International	146.9	21
Products and Systems	31.3	4
Corporate and eliminations	(7.2)	-
Total	711.2	100

2015 sales

	$ mil.	% of total
United States	491.8	69
Other Americas	68.6	10
Europe	137.1	19
Asia-Pacific	13.7	2
Total	711.2	100

COMPETITORS

GE Inspection Technologies
Lloyd's Register
SGS
Siemens AG
Team
The Carlyle Group

HISTORICAL FINANCIALS

Company Type: Public

Income Statement

FYE: May 31

	REVENUE ($ mil.)	NET INCOME ($ mil.)	NET PROFIT MARGIN	EMPLOYEES
05/16	719.1	24.6	3.4%	5,700.0
05/15	711.2	16.0	2.3%	5,700.0
05/14	623.4	22.5	3.6%	5,300.0
05/13	529.2	11.6	2.2%	4,400.0
05/12	436.8	21.3	4.9%	3,500.0
Annual Growth	13.3%	3.7%	—	13.0%

2016 Year-End Financials

Debt ratio: 21.7%
Return on equity: 9.4%
Cash ($ mil.): 21.1
Current ratio: 1.94
Long-term debt ($ mil.): 84.3

No. of shares (mil.): 28.9
Dividends
Yield: —
Payout: —
Market value ($ mil.): 718.0

	STOCK PRICE ($) FY Close	P/E High/Low	PER SHARE ($) Earnings	Dividends	Book Value
05/16	24.81	31 15	0.82	0.00	9.54
05/15	18.51	45 28	0.54	0.00	8.53
05/14	22.76	32 20	0.77	0.00	8.51
05/13	21.38	66 45	0.40	0.00	7.45
05/12	22.54	34 19	0.74	0.00	6.89
Annual Growth	2.4%	— —	2.6%	—	8.5%

Moelis & Co

Auditors: Deloitte & Touche LLP

LOCATIONS

HQ: Moelis & Co
399 Park Avenue, 5th Floor, New York, NY 10022
Phone: 212 883-3800
Web: www.moelis.com

HISTORICAL FINANCIALS

Company Type: Public

Income Statement

FYE: December 31

	REVENUE ($ mil.)	NET INCOME ($ mil.)	NET PROFIT MARGIN	EMPLOYEES
12/15	551.8	33.1	6.0%	660.0
12/14	518.7	(3.0)	—	550.0
12/13	411.3	70.2	17.1%	470.0
12/12	385.8	35.2	9.1%	0.0
12/11	268.0	(8.5)	—	0.0
Annual Growth	19.8%	—	—	—

2015 Year-End Financials

Debt ratio: —
Return on equity: 23.5%
Cash ($ mil.): 248.8
Current ratio: 1.08
Long-term debt ($ mil.): —

No. of shares (mil.): 51.5
Dividends
Yield: 3.4%
Payout: 59.1%
Market value ($ mil.): 1,503.0

	STOCK PRICE ($) FY Close	P/E High/Low	PER SHARE ($) Earnings	Dividends	Book Value
12/15	29.18	21 16	1.55	1.00	3.27
12/14	34.93	— —	(0.19)	1.40	2.21
Annual Growth	(16.5%)	— —	—	(28.6%)	48.2%

Monarch Casino & Resort, Inc.

Monarch Casino & Resort hopes high rollers will rediscover Atlantis. The company's tropical-themed Atlantis Casino Resort Spa in Reno Nevada includes nearly 825 hotel rooms a 61000-sq.-ft. casino restaurants a health club retail outlets and a family entertainment center. The company also owns and operates the Monarch Casino Black Hawk in Black Hawk Colorado. Casino operations which account for more than half of revenue include gaming tables slot and video poker machines keno and a race and sports book. The family of founder David Farahi —including John Bob and Ben Farahi —own more than half of the company.

Sales and Marketing

For its primary property the company targets Reno and Tahoe area leisure travelers convention-goers and northern Nevada residents. Monarch spent $5.2 million on advertising in fiscal 2015.

Financial Performance

The company's revenue has been increasing in the past five years (2011-15) except for a slight decrease in fiscal 2014. In fiscal 2015 the company's revenue increased by 8% to $202.25 million compared to $187.77 million in fiscal 2014.

Monarch's net income net income increased by 46% to $20.66 million in fiscal 2015 compared to $14.19 million in fiscal 2014 mainly because of decrease expenses.

The company's operating cash inflow increased by 22% to $38.24 million in fiscal 2015 compared to $31.25 million during the prior fiscal period.

Strategy

Monarch is constantly working to upgrade and improve its facilities to better serve the comprehensive needs of its guests.

EXECUTIVES

Co-Chairman and CEO, John Farahi, age 68, $750,000 total compensation
Co-Chairman and President, Bob Farahi, $150,000 total compensation
COO, David Farahi, $250,000 total compensation
CFO, Ron Rowan, $300,000 total compensation
General Manager Atlantis, Darlyne Sullivan
Auditors: Ernst & Young LLP

LOCATIONS

HQ: Monarch Casino & Resort, Inc.
3800 S. Virginia St., Reno, NV 89502
Phone: 775 335-4600
Web: www.monarchcasino.com

PRODUCTS/OPERATIONS

2015 Sales

	$ mil.	% of total
Casino	156.8	63
Food & beverage	56.5	23
Hotel	22.6	9
Other	11.2	5
Promotional allowances	(44.9)	-
Total	**202.2**	**100**

COMPETITORS

Caesars Entertainment	Station Casinos
Herbst Gaming	Tropicana
MTR Gaming	Entertainment
Pinnacle Entertainment	

HISTORICAL FINANCIALS

Company Type: Public

Income Statement

FYE: December 31

	REVENUE ($ mil.)	NET INCOME ($ mil.)	NET PROFIT MARGIN	EMPLOYEES
12/15	202.2	20.6	10.2%	2,100.0
12/14	187.7	14.1	7.6%	2,100.0
12/13	188.7	17.9	9.5%	2,100.0
12/12	170.3	8.9	5.2%	2,100.0
12/11	140.6	5.6	4.0%	1,800.0
Annual Growth	**9.5%**	**38.1%**	**—**	**3.9%**

2015 Year-End Financials

Debt ratio: 14.8%
Return on equity: 10.8%
Cash ($ mil.): 21.1
Current ratio: 0.45
Long-term debt ($ mil.): —

No. of shares (mil.): 17.2
Dividends
Yield: —
Payout: —
Market value ($ mil.): 391.0

	STOCK PRICE ($) FY Close	P/E High/Low	PER SHARE ($) Earnings	Dividends	Book Value
12/15	22.72	19 13	1.19	0.00	11.85
12/14	16.59	24 13	0.83	0.00	10.52
12/13	20.08	20 9	1.06	0.00	9.94
12/12	10.91	21 13	0.55	0.00	8.72
12/11	10.19	37 24	0.35	0.00	8.09
Annual Growth	**22.2%**	**— —**	**35.8%**	**—**	**10.0%**

Monmouth Real Estate Investment Corp

Monmouth specializes in mammoth industrial properties particularly warehouses and distribution centers. The real estate investment trust (REIT) owns about 80 industrial buildings and a single New Jersey shopping center comprising some 10.7 million sq. ft. in more than 25 states mostly in the East and Midwest. Most are net-leased (in which tenants pay insurance taxes and maintenance costs) under long-term leases. The REIT's two largest tenants FedEx and Milwaukee Electric Tool together account for half of its revenue. The firm also invests in REIT securities. Founded in 1968 Monmouth is one of the oldest public equity REITs in the nation.

Geographic Reach

New Jersey-based Monmouth's properties are located in 27 states including Arizona Connecticut Florida Illinois Michigan New Jersey New York Ohio Pennsylvania Tennessee Texas and Wisconsin.

Sales and Marketing

FedEx is the REIT's single largest customer accounting for 44% of its leasable space.

Financial Performance

The industrial REIT's revenue increased 5% in fiscal 2013 (ended September) versus the prior year to $66.3 million due to an increase in rental and reimbursement revenues generated by its larger portfolio of properties. Net income grew 15% over the same period to $21 million. The firm's revenue and profits have increased steadily over the past four years as its portfolio increased in size.

Strategy

The REIT specializes in net-leased industrial properties subject to long-term leases primarily to investment grade tenants. It derives its income primarily from real estate rental operations. Monmouth owns all of its properties with the exception of two in New Jersey in which it holds a majority interest.

In 2013 the REIT acquired five industrial properties totaling approximately 1.1 million square feet with net-leased terms ranging from 10 to 20 years of which about 237000 square feet (or 21%) is leased to FedEx Ground Package System. The REIT paid about $73.9 million for the five sites which are located in Kansas Kentucky Oklahoma Pennsylvania and Texas. The firm intends to continue increasing its real estate investments in fiscal 2014 through acquisitions and the expansion of select properties.

EXECUTIVES

CFO, Kevin S. Miller, age 46, $239,663 total compensation
President and CEO, Michael P. Landy, age 55, $525,000 total compensation
General Counsel, Allison Nagelberg, age 52, $312,656 total compensation
Chairman, Eugene W. Landy, age 83
Auditors: PKF O'Connor Davies, LLP

LOCATIONS

HQ: Monmouth Real Estate Investment Corp
3499 Route 9 North, Suite 3-D, Freehold, NJ 07728
Phone: 732 577-9996
Web: www.mreic.com

PRODUCTS/OPERATIONS

2016 Sales

	$ mil.	% of total
Rental	81.6	86
Reimbursement	13.3	14
Total	**94.9**	**100**

COMPETITORS

Brandywine Realty	Mack-Cali
CenterPoint Properties	One Liberty Properties
First Industrial	PS Business Parks
Realty	Prologis
First Potomac Realty	

Company Type: Public

Income Statement
FYE: September 30

	REVENUE ($ mil.)	NET INCOME ($ mil.)	NET PROFIT MARGIN	EMPLOYEES
09/16	94.9	32.4	34.2%	14.0
09/15	78.0	25.6	32.8%	15.0
09/14	65.8	19.8	30.1%	14.0
09/13	55.3	21.4	38.7%	14.0
09/12	53.7	18.6	34.8%	11.0
Annual Growth	15.3%	14.8%	—	6.2%

2016 Year-End Financials

Debt ratio: 45.9%
Return on equity: 6.2%
Cash ($ mil.): 95.7
Current ratio: 1.89
Long-term debt ($ mil.): 564.5

No. of shares (mil.): 68.9
Dividends
Yield: 4.4%
Payout: 130.6%
Market value ($ mil.): 984.0

	STOCK PRICE ($) FY Close	P/E High/Low	PER SHARE ($) Earnings	Dividends	Book Value
09/16	14.27	30 20	0.50	0.64	8.67
09/15	9.75	28 21	0.43	0.60	7.18
09/14	10.12	27 22	0.40	0.60	7.38
09/13	9.07	23 17	0.50	0.60	7.55
09/12	11.19	25 16	0.47	0.60	7.76
Annual Growth	6.3%	— —	1.6%	1.6%	2.8%

Monogram Residential Trust Inc

Auditors: Deloitte & Touche LLP

LOCATIONS

HQ: Monogram Residential Trust Inc
5800 Granite Parkway, Suite 1000, Plano, TX 75024
Phone: 469 250-5500
Web: www.monogramres.com

Company Type: Public

Income Statement
FYE: December 31

	REVENUE ($ mil.)	NET INCOME ($ mil.)	NET PROFIT MARGIN	EMPLOYEES
12/15	238.0	73.8	31.0%	366.0
12/14	209.0	(6.1)	—	370.0
12/13	190.6	29.7	15.6%	0.0
12/12	171.7	(12.5)	—	0.0
Annual Growth	11.5%	—	—	—

2015 Year-End Financials

Debt ratio: 46.3%
Return on equity: 6.2%
Cash ($ mil.): 83.7
Current ratio: 0.81
Long-term debt ($ mil.): 1,522.0

No. of shares (mil.): 166.6
Dividends
Yield: 3.0%
Payout: 68.1%
Market value ($ mil.): 1,626.0

	STOCK PRICE ($) FY Close	P/E High/Low	PER SHARE ($) Earnings	Dividends	Book Value
12/15	9.76	23 20	0.44	0.30	7.00
12/14	9.26	— —	(0.04)	0.08	7.21
12/13	0.00	— —	0.18	0.35	7.59
Annual Growth	—	— —	56.3%	(7.4%)	(4.0%)

Monolithic Power Systems Inc

Monolithic Power Systems (MPS) sends out mixed signals and that's a good thing. The fabless semiconductor company offers mixed-signal and analog microchips —especially DC-to-DC converters for powering flat-panel TVs wireless communications equipment notebook computers set-top boxes and other consumer electronic devices. MPS outsources production of its chips to three silicon foundries in China. The company's products are incorporated into electronic gear from tech heavyweights such as Dell Hewlett-Packard Samsung Electronics and Sony. The company was founded in 1997.

Operations

MPS has two main business segments. Its DC-to-DC products convert and control voltages in electronics from cell phones to TVs to medical equipment. The DC-to-DC chips are monolithic in that they accounted for 90% of the company's sales in 2015. MPS's lighting control products are used to backlight LCD and LED screens. The segment was 10% of sales in 2015.

Geographic Reach

MPS is headquartered in San Jose California but most of its activities are in Asia. Production assembly and packaging and testing are done at facilities in China and Malaysia. The finished products don't have far to go since 90% of sales are in Asia; China is the company's biggest market with 64% of sales. MPS has sales offices in the US Europe Singapore Taiwan China Korea and Japan.

Sales and MarketingThe company sells through distributors value-added resellers and directly to original equipment manufacturers (OEMs) original design manufacturers (ODMs) and electronic manufacturing service (EMS) companies. Sales to its largest distributor accounted for about 24% of revenue in 2015 and another distributor accounted for 10% of revenue in 2015. The MPS sales process includes working with customers in the design and use of MPS chips in their products.Financial Performance

MPS's revenue grew at a healthy rate in 2015 while net income was flat.

Sales rose 18% in the company's DC to DC segment leading to an 18% growth rate from 2014 to 2015. It combined more unit sales with higher average sale prices to reach $333 million in revenue in 2015 compared to $282 in 2014.

Net income however slipped about 1% to $35.1 million from $35.5 million. MPS increased research and development spending in 2015 and paid more taxes compared to 2014.

Cash flow from operations dipped to $69.7 million in 2015 from $74 million in 2014.

StrategyMPS is working to diversify its customers moving away from consumer-dependent products and to industrial automotive and lighting markets. It also is developing new products aimed at those markets and has signed distributor agreements. One such product is a DC-to-DC conversion technology QSMod that improves system efficiency which was introduced in 2013.MPS spends about 20% of revenue on R&D each year.

Mergers and Acquisitions

In 2014 MPS acquired Sensima Technology a developer of magnetic sensor technologies which will be combined with MPS technologies for automotive industrial and cloud computing. The purchase price includes an initial cash payment of about $12 million and a subsequent cash earn-out payment of up to $9 million based on meeting performance goals.

EXECUTIVES

Senior Vice President Design Engineering, Paul Ueunten
Chairman President and CEO, Michael R. Hsing, age 56, $448,000 total compensation
President - MPS Asia Operations, Deming Xiao, age 53, $340,000 total compensation
VP Strategic Corporate Development General Counsel and Secretary, Saria Tseng, age 45, $300,000 total compensation
SVP Worldwide Sales and Marketing, Maurice Sciammas, age 56, $300,000 total compensation
CFO, Bernie Blegen
Auditors: Deloitte & Touche LLP

LOCATIONS

HQ: Monolithic Power Systems Inc
79 Great Oaks Boulevard, San Jose, CA 95119
Phone: 408 826-0600
Web: www.monolithicpower.com

PRODUCTS/OPERATIONS

2011 Sales

	$ mil.	% of total
DC-to-DC converters	165.6	85
LCD backlight inverters	26.5	13
Audio amplifiers	4.4	2
Total	**196.5**	**100**

Selected Products
AC/DC Offline
Bridge rectifier
Controllers and regulators
Synchronous rectifiers
Audio amplifiers
Backlighting solutions
EL drivers
White LED drivers (inductors and charge pumps)
Automotive
Battery chargers
Cradle chargers
Linear chargers
Protection
Switching chargers
Full-bridge and half-bridge power drivers
Isolated and transformer-based power supplies
Lighting and illumination
Low dropout (LDO) linear regulators
Motor drivers
Brushless DC motor drivers
Stepper DC motor drivers
Photo-flash chargers and drivers
Power Over Ethernet powered device (PD) solutions
PD controllers
PD identity
Precision analog
Analog switches
High-side current sense amplifiers
Operational amplifiers

Voltage reference
Supervisory circuits and voltage supervisors
Switching power supply regulators
  DC-DC (step-down)
  Controller
  Intelli-Phase (monolithic driver + MOSFET)
  Non-synchronous switcher
  Synchronous switcher
  DC-DC (step-up)
  Controller
  Energy storage and release management
  LNB power supply
  Non-synchronous switcher
  Synchronous switcher
USB and current-limit load switches

COMPETITORS

Analog Devices	Microsemi
Fairchild	O2Micro
Semiconductor	ON Semiconductor
International	Power Integrations
Rectifier	ROHM
Intersil	Richtek Technology
Linear Technology	Corp.
Maxim Integrated	STMicroelectronics
Products	Semtech
Microchip Technology	Texas Instruments

HISTORICAL FINANCIALS

Company Type: Public

Income Statement

FYE: December 31

	REVENUE ($ mil.)	NET INCOME ($ mil.)	NET PROFIT MARGIN	EMPLOYEES
12/15	333.0	35.1	10.6%	1,260.0
12/14	282.5	35.5	12.6%	1,178.0
12/13	238.0	22.9	9.6%	1,105.0
12/12	213.8	15.7	7.4%	993.0
12/11	196.5	13.3	6.8%	922.0
Annual Growth	14.1%	27.5%	—	8.1%

2015 Year-End Financials

Debt ratio: —	No. of shares (mil.): 39.6
Return on equity: 9.8%	Dividends
Cash ($ mil.): 90.8	Yield: 1.2%
Current ratio: 7.67	Payout: 95.2%
Long-term debt ($ mil.): —	Market value ($ mil.): 2,529.0

	STOCK PRICE ($) FY Close	P/E High/Low		PER SHARE ($) Earnings	Dividends	Book Value
12/15	63.71	77	51	0.86	0.80	9.29
12/14	49.74	55	34	0.89	0.45	8.92
12/13	34.66	56	34	0.59	0.00	8.45
12/12	22.28	50	33	0.43	1.00	7.24
12/11	15.07	44	25	0.38	0.00	7.18
Annual Growth	43.4%	—	—	22.7%	—	6.6%

Monotype Imaging Holdings Inc

Monotype Imaging may be the one to thank if you're reading this whether it's on a portable electronic device or a printed page. With most sales going to device manufacturers (OEMs) the company's text imaging software is integrated into applications and embedded in electronics ranging from mobile phones to laser printers automotive displays and digital cameras as well as navigation tools set-top boxes and Internet of Things devices. Its applications manage compression scaling color and layout. Providing customers access to thousands of typefaces OEM sales are complemented by about 46% of revenue coming from licenses to creative professionals mostly commercial clients. Customers have included Apple Google Sony and Microsoft.

Operations

The US has grown as a percentage of total revenues contributing 55% of Monotype Imaging's revenues in 2015. The company does however expect international to continue to be a major percentage of total revenues. Since Asia is an underpenetrated region for Monotype Imaging it is a particularly attractive growth opportunity specifically in Chinese Japanese and Korean language markets for laser printers digital copiers and other devices.

Geographic Reach

Geographic recognition of revenue does not necessarily reflect the destination of Monotype Imaging's products as sales are attached to the subsidiary receiving the revenue. Sales by a US subsidiary to Korea-based customers for example are classified as US sales. The company's products are sold from offices in Germany Hong Kong Japan South Korea the UK and the US. Sales from Asia generally go to Asian customers while the other subsidiaries cover many different countries including the US.

The company's research and development operations are located in Woburn Massachusetts; Los Altos California; Boulder Colorado; Belfast Northern Ireland; Salford United Kingdom; Bad Homburg and Berlin Germany; Noida India; Hong Kong China; and Tokyo Japan.

Sales and Marketing

Although no customer accounts for more than 10% of sales Monotype Imaging's top ten clients account for about 40% of annual revenues. The company serves many of its target industries' leaders including e-book reader and tablet makers including Amazon and Kobo top automotive brands such as Chrysler Ford Honda and Hyundai laser printer manufacturers and phone makers. The company nearly doubled its advertising spending to $3.3 million in 2015 from $1.7 million in each of 2014 and 2013.

Financial Performance

Monotype Imaging has seen an upward trend in its revenues of the past few years. In 2015 it reported an 4% rise in revenues driven by a 14% increase in its Creative Professional revenue. OEM revenue fell 3% for the year.

Net income slipped 2% to $26 million in 2015 after several years of steady increases. The company had acquisition costs to deal with as well as higher advertising costs in 2015.

Cash flow from operations dropped to $53 million in 2015 from $61.5 million in 2014.

Strategy

At the center of Monotype Imaging's growth strategy is a focus on serving high growth consumer electronic devices such as smartphones tablets navigation devices and consumer appliances to name a few. It will however also stay focused on the slower-growth laser printer market where it holds a leadership position and sees a demand for customized driver applications such as language interpretation. The company also continues to value its creative professionals and consumer users. It has several Websites including fonts.com and linotype.com.

Monotype Imaging focuses particularly on digital marketing where it sees opportunities in HTML-5-based marketing campaigns.

In 2015 the company introduced new and remastered typefaces like Neue Haas Unica Kairos and Zapfino Arabic and the Eric Gill series. In 2014 the company expanded its Fonts.com Web Fonts inventory to include typefaces from the famous FontFont library.

Mergers and Acquisitions

Monotype Imaging in 2015 acquired Mark Boulton Design Ltd. a Web design studio based in the UK for $1.75 million. It expands Monotype Imaging's capability to provide web design and web publishing.

Another 2015 acquisition was of TextPride Inc. which operated under the name of Swyft Media for $12 million. The deal expanded monotype Imaging's services in the new and growing to branded mobile advertising.

In 2014 the company acquired Germany-based FontShop International GmbH a privately-held font distributor and its US subsidiary California-based FontShop International for $13 million. The deal supported the company's growth in international markets.

Company Background

In 2012 the company furthered its aspirations for both of its primary customer groups when it acquired major competitor Bitstream for $50 million. With that purchase Monotype Imaging gained the 62000 fonts on MyFonts.com font capabilities such as an identification service and font rendering and layout technologies fonts for embedded and mobile settings and 10 patents as well as 40 engineers and type designers at a facility in India. That year the company also acquired Design by Front Limited a privately held web strategy design and technology studio in Belfast Northern Ireland for $4.6 million.

In 2009 Monotype Imaging saw a chance to build on its strategy of expanding its offerings for OEM customers acquiring Planetweb for about $2 million. PlanetWeb provided user interface developer tools for consumer electronics manufacturers.

Monotype Imaging was formed when a group of investors including TA Associates acquired Agfa Monotype (then a subsidiary of Agfa) in 2004. The company does business as International Typeface Corporation or ITC in the US; Monotype Hong Kong and Monotype Japan in Asia; and Monotype UK and Linotype in Europe.

EXECUTIVES

Managing Director Monotype Imaging Ltd., John H. McCallum, age 60, $260,996 total compensation

VP; General Manager Creative Professional, Christopher J. (Chris) Roberts, age 50

President and CEO, Scott E. Landers, age 45, $308,550 total compensation

EVP Sales and Market Strategy, Ben Semmes

Managing Director Monotype Solutions India, Neeraj Gulati

Managing Director Monotype Imaging Hong Kong, Ricky Chun

VP; General Manager ISV and Strategic Accounts, Ira Mirochnick

SVP Engineering, Steven R. (Steve) Martin, $271,253 total compensation

VP; General Manager OEM, Joe Roberts

EVP and CFO, Anthony Callini, age 45

Vice President Corporate Development, Daniel (Dan) Gerron

Vp Corp Mkt, Lisa Landa

Vice President Global Human Resources, Jennifer (Jen) Peterson

Vice President Product Management, Tim McManus
Vice President General Counsel Sec, Janet M (Jan) Dunlap
Chairman, Robert L. (Bob) Lentz
Auditors: Ernst & Young LLP

LOCATIONS

HQ: Monotype Imaging Holdings Inc
  600 Unicorn Park Drive, Woburn, MA 01801
Phone: 781 970-6000
Web: www.monotypeimaging.com

PRODUCTS/OPERATIONS

2015 Sales

	$ mil.	% of total
OEM	104.3	54
Creative Professional	88.1	46
Total	**192.4**	**100**

Selected Customers

E-book readers
  Amazon
  Kobo
Digital TVs and set-top-boxes
  Sharp
  Toshiba
  TTE Technology
Mobile phones
  Motorola
  Nokia
  RIM
  Sony
  ZTE
Other
  Activision
  Gannett Company
  Google
  Microsoft
  Nintendo
  Ubisoft
  UBS
  TiVo
  Whirlpool

COMPETITORS

Adobe Systems	Quark
Extensis	Xara

HISTORICAL FINANCIALS

Company Type: Public

Income Statement

FYE: December 31

	REVENUE ($ mil.)	NET INCOME ($ mil.)	NET PROFIT MARGIN	EMPLOYEES
12/15	192.4	26.2	13.6%	494.0
12/14	184.5	32.5	17.6%	435.0
12/13	166.6	31.0	18.7%	354.0
12/12	149.8	28.9	19.3%	335.0
12/11	123.2	22.6	18.4%	272.0
Annual Growth	**11.8%**	**3.7%**	—	**16.1%**

2015 Year-End Financials

Debt ratio: —
Return on equity: 8.7%
Cash ($ mil.): 87.5
Current ratio: 3.09
Long-term debt ($ mil.): —
No. of shares (mil.): 40.0
Dividends
  Yield: 1.6%
  Payout: 51.9%
Market value ($ mil.): 946.0

	STOCK PRICE ($) FY Close	P/E High/Low	PER SHARE ($) Earnings	Dividends	Book Value
12/15	23.64	51 32	0.65	0.40	7.68
12/14	28.83	39 30	0.81	0.32	7.48
12/13	31.86	40 20	0.78	0.24	7.34
12/12	15.98	22 16	0.76	0.08	6.32
12/11	15.59	27 16	0.61	0.00	5.47
Annual Growth	**11.0%**	— —	**1.6%**	—	**8.8%**

Monro Muffler Brake, Inc.

If you can't stop point your car toward Monro Muffler Brake and coast on in. The company provides a full range of brake tire exhaust system suspension and steering and alignment services at more than 800 automotive repair shops. Its operations span nearly 20 states in the Northeast and Midwest and include Monro Muffler Brake & Service Mr. Tire Tread Quarters Autotire Car Care Center and Tire Warehouse. Along with under-car work the company offers air conditioning maintenance state inspections and scheduled maintenance services including fleet maintenance. Tire replacements and service account for more than 35% of sales. Monro Muffler Brake services more than 4.4 million vehicles annually.

Geographic Reach
Monro Muffler Brake operates company stores in 19 states including New York Pennsylvania Ohio Massachusetts New Jersey the Carolinas and Illinois.

Operations
Monro Muffler Brake operates about 535 service stores which specialize in repairing and replacing worn out auto parts as well as some 265 tire stores which sell install and align tires. In addition to Monro Muffler Brake's 800-plus company owned stores there are three franchised locations and 14 dealer-operated stores providing automotive under-car repair and tire services.

Sales and Marketing
Monro Muffler Brake advertises through direct mail coupon inserts and in-store promotional signage and displays. It also advertises through radio yellow pages newspapers service reminders and digital marketing. It cross markets its services promoting the Monro Muffler Brake & Service brand in its Tire Warehouse stores. During fiscal 2012 (ends March) the company launched mobile apps on the iPhone and Android platforms that allow customers to manage and maintain their vehicle maintenance records make appointments locate stores and search for promotions/coupons and tires.

Financial Performance
Monro Muffler Brake's $686.5 million in fiscal 2012 (ends March) sales was an all-time high for the fast-growing company. Indeed 2012 marked the fifth consecutive year of increasing sales and fourth year of steadily increasing profits. The company's sales climbed 8% in 2012 vs. the prior year while net income rose by 19% over the same period. Sales got a boost from the addition of new stores several acquisitions and rising comparable sales at existing shops (up 2%). Monro has

widened its margins by controlling spending on operations amid increased sales.

Strategy
The company whose roots reach back to 1957 has seen its revenues steadily climb over the years as its footprint expanded. The business continues to grow through both acquisitions and organic growth. Unlike many of its competitors Monro owns almost all of its stores believing it can better manage repair shops and train employees through more centralized control. Independent dealers operate only about 15 locations. It also operates nearly 35 full-service Monro stores onsite at BJ's Wholesale Clubs.

In recent years Monro's sales have also been helped by the economic downturn which has resulted in tightened credit markets and decreased consumer spending prompting Americans to drive and maintain their vehicles instead of trade them in for new models.

Mergers and Acquisitions
With earnings on a roll Monro in fiscal 2012 spent approximately $50 million to buy 18 retail tire and automotive repair stores in North Carolina from Colony Tire Corp. as well as 20 other tire and repair stores in Virginia from Kramer Tire Co. The Kramer purchase included two heavy-truck tire and truck repair stores two wholesale operations and a retread facility in Virginia. The acquired stores operate primarily under the Tread Quarters name. In 2011 the firm purchased Vespia Tire Centers which operated two dozen locations throughout New Jersey and Pennsylvania. During 2010 Monro acquired Import Export Tire a five-store tire chain in Pittsburgh and three Courthouse Tire auto repair and tire shops in Fredericksburg Virginia.

Ownership
T. Rowe Price owns about 12% of Monro Muffler Brakes' shares.

HISTORY

Charles August founded Monro Muffler Brake in 1957 as a franchise of Midas Muffler (later Midas Inc.). August hoped to expand his services under the Midas name but was refused so in 1966 he broke with Midas and began his own full line of undercar services. The company name was derived from Monroe County New York where it is headquartered; August decided to drop the "e" to save money on his sign. Monro Muffler Brake had 59 shops by 1984 when an investor group led by Peter Solomon and Donald Glickman purchased a controlling interest. In 1987 despite Solomon's objections August retired and was replaced by Jack Gallagher a 20-year veteran of the automotive industry. The firm went public in 1991.

Gallagher stepped down in March 1995. New CEO Lawrence Day wasted little time in expanding Monro Muffler Brake's customer base. In July 1995 the company acquired Durham North Carolina-based Muffler Xpress establishing Monro Muffler Brake in the Carolinas. The company also opened its first store in Maine that year.

In 1997 Monro Muffler Brake agreed to sell Bridgestone/Firestone tires in its stores and entered a joint venture with Q-Lube (a subsidiary of Pennzoil-Quaker State which was acquired by Royal Dutch Shell in 2002) to develop co-branded stores offering fast oil changes and undercar services. (The company abandoned the concept the following year.)

Monro Muffler Brake bought about 205 repair shops mostly in the Northeast in 1998 from Speedy Muffler King for $52 million. Store expansions hurt earnings that year and Day stepped down. Robert Gross was named president and CEO later in 1998. Monro Muffler Brake began opening shops in BJ's Wholesale Club outlets in 1999. In 2000 the company which previously had carried only Firestone tires announced it would sign with another tire supplier in order to assuage customers alarmed by the Firestone recall.

Monro Muffler Brake purchased Kimmel Automotive Inc. in 2002 and 10 Frasier Tire Service stores in 2003.

In March 2004 Monro Muffler Brake acquired more than 35 Mr. Tire locations in Maryland and Virginia from Atlantic Automotive. The next year Monro Muffler Brake added Donald B. Rice Tire and Henderson Holdings gaining a total of 15 tire and auto repair shops. The company also opened additional shops inside BJ's Wholesale Clubs.

In November 2005 Monro acquired a minority stake in Strauss Discount Auto and an option to take full ownership but the company said it would not exercise the option after Strauss filed for bankruptcy protection in August 2006. (Monro wrote-off its $2.8 million investment in Strauss in fiscal 2008.)

In 2006 the company bought key operations of bankrupt ProCare Automotive Service Solutions. The $15 million deal gave Monro an additional 75 stores in Ohio and Pennsylvania. Monro went on to acquire Valley Forge Tire & Auto Centers and Craven Tire & Auto in mid-2007 adding about 20 locations and expanding Monro's tire business to Philadelphia and Northern Virginia.

Peter Solomon stepped down as chairman in August 2007. He was succeeded by Robert Gross.

In early 2008 the firm acquired seven retail tire and automotive repair stores in Buffalo New York from the Broad Elm Group. In 2009 the company acquired privately owned Tire Warehouse Central with 40-plus locations throughout New England; Midwest Tire & Auto Repair a small chain in northwest Indiana; and Autotire Car Care Centers of St. Louis from American Tire Distributors.

EXECUTIVES

Divisional VP Southern Operations, Craig L. Hoyle, age 62, $225,000 total compensation
EVP Store Operations, Joseph Tomarchio, age 60, $242,500 total compensation
President and CEO, John W. Van Heel, age 50, $550,000 total compensation
SVP Finance and CFO, Brian J. DÂAmbrosia
Vice President Human Resources, Deb (Debbie) Palermo
Vice President Employee Relations, Ed Mullen
Vice President Controller, Brian D'Ambrosia
Executive Chairman, Robert G. Gross, age 58
Auditors: PricewaterhouseCoopers LLP

LOCATIONS

HQ: Monro Muffler Brake, Inc.
200 Holleder Parkway, Rochester, NY 14615
Phone: 585 647-6400   **Fax:** 585 647-0945
Web: www.monro.com

PRODUCTS/OPERATIONS

2016 Sales

	% of total
Tires	45
Maintenance	27
Brakes	15
Steering	10
Exhaust	3
Total	**100**

2016 Company-owned Stores

	No.
Service (including BJ's)	515
Tire	514
Total	**1,029**

COMPETITORS

AAMCO	Pep Boys
Bridgestone Retail	Precision Auto
Operations	Sears
Discount Tire	TBC
Goodyear Tire & Rubber	TCI Tire Centers
Jiffy Lube	Valvoline
Meineke	Wal-Mart
Midas	

HISTORICAL FINANCIALS

Company Type: Public

Income Statement

FYE: March 26

	REVENUE ($ mil.)	NET INCOME ($ mil.)	NET PROFIT MARGIN	EMPLOYEES
03/16	943.6	66.8	7.1%	6,725.0
03/15	894.4	61.8	6.9%	6,577.0
03/14	831.4	54.4	6.6%	6,139.0
03/13	732.0	42.5	5.8%	5,850.0
03/12	686.5	54.6	8.0%	5,113.0
Annual Growth	8.3%	5.2%	—	7.1%

2016 Year-End Financials

Debt ratio: 28.0%
Return on equity: 13.2%
Cash ($ mil.): 7.9
Current ratio: 1.01
Long-term debt ($ mil.): 269.0
No. of shares (mil.): 32.2
Dividends
  Yield: 0.0%
  Payout: 30.0%
Market value ($ mil.): 2,246.0

	STOCK PRICE ($) FY Close	P/E High/Low		PER SHARE ($) Earnings	Dividends	Book Value
03/16	69.68	37	28	2.00	0.60	16.63
03/15	64.96	35	25	1.88	0.52	14.88
03/14	56.51	36	22	1.67	0.44	13.21
03/13	39.71	31	23	1.32	0.40	11.68
03/12	41.49	27	17	1.69	0.35	10.60
Annual Growth	13.8%	—	—	4.3%	14.4%	11.9%

Multi-Color Corp.

Multi-Color Corporation's labels aren't just black and white and red all over. The company produces printed labels for product makers in markets such as home and personal care wine and spirit food and beverage and specialty consumer goods. Multi-Color serves customers in North and South America Europe the Asia/Pacific region and South Africa. The company prints and affixes heat transfer re-sealable shrink wrap pressure sensitive and other label types to glass and plastic containers. Multi-Color also offers gravure printing and injection in-mold labels. Over the years the company has counted Procter & Gamble and Miller Brewing among its biggest customers. Multi-Color traces its roots to 1916.

The company has been working to alleviate its dependency on a concentrated set of customers. Major consumer product and beverage manufacturers Procter & Gamble and Miller Lite collectively accounted for 28% of the company's total sales in

fiscal year 2011 down from 38% in 2010 45% in 2011 and 50% in 2008. Multi-Color attributes the decline to the addition of international customers and products it gained through prior acquisitions such as Collotype (a maker of pressure-sensitive labels for wine and spirits that has operations in Australia South Africa and California); Guidotti CentroStampa (a European wine spirit and olive oil label printer based in Italy); and Monroe Etiquette (a French wine label specialist based in Montagny France).

In fiscal year 2011 the company reported an increase in revenues and net income. Positive earnings were primarily due to the acquisitions of Guidotti CentroStampa and Monroe Etiquette. The remaining gains were due to growth in sales volume a favorable foreign exchange rate and the increase of operating efficiencies through cutting costs.

Multi-Color continued its international expansion strategy in 2011. That year it purchased La Cromografica an Italian wine label specialist in Florence Italy. Later that year it entered the growing Latin American wine and spirit markets when it acquired 70% of two label operations one in Santiago Chile and the other in Mendoza Argentina. It acquired rival LabelCorp Holdings doing business as York Label Group for about $356 million to expand in North America and Chile. It also entered the Chinese market establishing operations in the major southern city of Guangzhou in 2011.

EXECUTIVES

VP CFO and Chief Accounting Officer, Sharon E. Birkett, age 49, $387,500 total compensation
COO Wine and Spirit Markets, David G. Buse, age 50
COO Wine and Spirit Markets, Vadis A. Rodato, age 55, $500,000 total compensation
COO Consumer Product Goods, Floyd E. Needham, age 47, $500,000 total compensation
Chairman, Nigel A. Vinecombe, age 52
Auditors: Grant Thornton LLP

LOCATIONS

HQ: Multi-Color Corp.
4053 Clough Woods Dr., Batavia, OH 45103
Phone: 513 381-1480
Web: www.mcclabel.com

PRODUCTS/OPERATIONS

Selected Products and Services

Labels
  Heat transfer
  In-mold
  Neck bands
  Peel-away
  Pressure sensitive
  Re-sealable
  Shrink sleeve

COMPETITORS

Fort Dearborn	Outlook Group
H. S. Crocker	WS Packaging Group

HISTORICAL FINANCIALS

Company Type: Public

Income Statement

FYE: March 31

	REVENUE ($ mil.)	NET INCOME ($ mil.)	NET PROFIT MARGIN	EMPLOYEES
03/16	870.8	47.7	5.5%	5,000.0
03/15	810.7	45.7	5.6%	3,550.0
03/14	706.4	28.2	4.0%	3,250.0
03/13	659.8	30.3	4.6%	2,800.0
03/12	510.2	19.7	3.9%	2,749.0
Annual Growth	14.3%	24.8%	—	16.1%

2016 Year-End Financials

Debt ratio: 47.7%
Return on equity: 15.1%
Cash ($ mil.): 27.7
Current ratio: 1.82
Long-term debt ($ mil.): 512.7

No. of shares (mil.): 16.8
Dividends
  Yield: 0.3%
  Payout: 6.6%
Market value ($ mil.): 897.0

	STOCK PRICE ($) FY Close	P/E High/Low		PER SHARE ($) Earnings	Dividends	Book Value
03/16	53.35	28	14	2.82	0.20	20.16
03/15	69.33	26	12	2.71	0.20	17.40
03/14	35.00	22	14	1.70	0.20	18.14
03/13	25.79	14	10	1.86	0.20	17.02
03/12	22.51	21	14	1.32	0.20	15.68
Annual Growth	24.1%	—		20.9%	(0.0%)	6.5%

MVB Financial Corp

EXECUTIVES

Chief Executive Officer; President, Larry Nazza
Auditors: Dixon Hughes Goodman, LLP

LOCATIONS

HQ: MVB Financial Corp
  301 Virginia Avenue, Fairmont, WV 26554-2777
Phone: 304 363-4800
Web: www.mvbbanking.com

HISTORICAL FINANCIALS

Company Type: Public

Income Statement

FYE: December 31

	ASSETS ($ mil.)	NET INCOME ($ mil.)	INCOME AS % OF ASSETS	EMPLOYEES
12/15	1,384.4	6.8	0.5%	371.0
12/14	1,110.4	2.0	0.2%	324.0
12/13	987.0	4.0	0.4%	274.0
12/12	726.7	4.1	0.6%	221.0
12/11	533.4	2.7	0.5%	124.0
Annual Growth	26.9%	26.0%	—	31.5%

2015 Year-End Financials

Return on assets: 0.5%
Return on equity: 6.0%
Long-term debt ($ mil.): —
No. of shares (mil.): 8.0
Sales ($ mil): 83.7

Dividends
  Yield: 0.0%
  Payout: 10.5%
Market value ($ mil.): 106.0

	STOCK PRICE ($) FY Close	P/E High/Low		PER SHARE ($) Earnings	Dividends	Book Value
12/15	13.10	20	16	0.76	0.08	14.23
12/14	14.99	164	65	0.22	0.08	13.71
12/13	33.20	66	40	0.57	0.15	12.28
12/12	24.00	26	20	0.90	0.14	11.72
12/11	16.80	32	21	0.61	0.05	10.93
Annual Growth	(6.0%)	—		5.9%	12.5%	6.8%

MYR Group Inc

MYR Group's work can be electrifying. The specialty contractor builds and maintains electric delivery infrastructure systems for utilities and commercial clients. MYR Group constructs transmission and distribution lines for the oil and gas power and telecommunications industries. The company also installs and maintains electrical wiring in commercial and industrial facilities and traffic and rail systems. The group operates nationwide through subsidiaries including The L.E. Myers Co. Harlan Electric Hawkeye Construction Sturgeon Electric MYR Transmission Services and Great Southwestern Construction. MYR's transmission and distribution segment accounts for about three-fourths of the group's revenues.

Operations

The company's Transmission & Distribution customers generated 74% of MYR Group's revenue in 2014. Its Commercial & Industrial segment brought in 26% of revenue in 2014.

Completed projects include the Cross Texas Transmission 345kV Transmission Line Project Spearville to Axtell 345kV Transmission Line (also known as the KETA Project) the Meadowbrook to Loudoun 500kV Transmission Line and Carson Substation to Suffolk Substation 500kV Transmission Lines.

Sales and Marketing

Transmission & Distribution customers include electric utilities private developers cooperatives and municipalities. Its Commercial & Industrial segment provides electrical contracting services to property owners and general contractors in the Western US.

Its top 10 customers accounted for nearly 50% of revenues in fiscal 2014; no single customer accounted for more than 10% of sales.

MYR Group has logged between $400000 and $500000 each year since 2010 on selling general and administrative expenses (which include advertising expenses).

Financial Performance

With the exception of a slight dip in 2013 revenue has been on the rise for the past five years. In 2014 it increased 5% to $944 million largely on growth in the Commercial & Industrial segment. That segment's services were generally in higher demand; improving economic conditions in its core markets of Colorado and Arizona also helped boost business.

Net income has risen for the past five years and in 2014 it increased 5% to $36.6 million thanks both to MYR's higher revenue and increased interest earnings. Cash flow from operations fell 42% to $44 million that year as more cash was used for accounts payable.

Strategy

MYR Group looks to grow organically or through strategic acquisitions and joint ventures. It aims to improve its competitive position in existing markets while also expanding into new geographic markets. The company has also dog-eared funds to invest in additional properties and equipment to support its strategy.

The Transmission & Distribution segment counts some 125 cooperatives electric utilities and municipalities as customers. The business stands to benefit from a continued emphasis on improving and upgrading the country's power supply and the increasing market for alternative energy. As wind and solar farm developments grow there is an increasing demand to link the farms to large power grids. MYR Group works on numerous wind farm projects each year. The company expects increased activity in that sector.

The company's Commercial & Industrial segment has a regional focus in Colorado and Arizona.

MYR Group maintains one of the largest fleets of vehicles in the US (some 5000 units) that can be mobilized for transmission and distribution work around the country. Because of this asset MYR Group often is called to restore power in the aftermath of hurricanes floods ice storms and other natural disasters. This is a relatively small part of the company's business though.

The group's strategy to take advantage of the growing need for infrastructure work includes seeking out possible acquisition targets or joint venture partners as well as expanding into new markets. It will also add to its fleet as it deems beneficial and has been spending tens of millions of dollars on new specialty equipment and tooling.

Company Background

MYR was founded in 1891 by Lewis Edward Myers who briefly worked as a salesman with Thomas Edison.

EXECUTIVES

SVP, William H. Green, age 72, $346,000 total compensation
President and CEO, Richard S. (Rick) Swartz, age 52, $376,500 total compensation
SVP CFO and Treasurer, Betty R. Johnson, age 57
SVP East and President L.E. Myers Co., Tod Cooper
Chairman, William A. (Bill) Koertner, age 66
Auditors: Ernst & Young LLP

LOCATIONS

HQ: MYR Group Inc
  1701 Golf Road, Suite 3-1012, Rolling Meadows, IL 60008
Phone: 847 290-1891
Web: www.myrgroup.com

PRODUCTS/OPERATIONS

2014 Sales by Segment

	% of total
Transmission & Distribution	74
Commercial & Industrial	26
Total	**100**

Selected Services

Electrical
  Commercial/Industrial
  Construction
  Design-build services
  Directional boring
  Emergency storm response
  Fiber optics
  Foundations & caissons

Gas distribution
Highway lighting
Overhead distribution
PCS/Cellular towers
Preconstruction services
Substation
Telecommunications
Traffic signals
Transmission
Underground distribution
Mechanical
Boiler construction and maintenance
Erection of piping systems
General contracting
In-house fabrication
Instrumentation
Maintenance
Preconstruction services
Retrofit to existing systems

Selected Subsidiaries

ComTel Technology Inc.
Great Southwestern Construction Inc.
Harlan Electric Company
Hawkeye Construction Inc.
Meyers International Inc.
MYR Transmission Services Inc.
MYRpower Inc.
The L.E. Myers Co.
Sturgeon Electric Company Inc.

COMPETITORS

Austin Industries	MDU Resources
Cupertino Electric	MasTec
Dycom	Mass Electric
EEI	Pike Corporation
EMCOR	Quanta Services
Goldfield	Siemens AG
Henkels & McCoy	Vario Construction
IES Holdings	Company
Kelso-Burnett	

HISTORICAL FINANCIALS

Company Type: Public

Income Statement

FYE: December 31

	REVENUE ($ mil.)	NET INCOME ($ mil.)	NET PROFIT MARGIN	EMPLOYEES
12/15	1,061.6	27.3	2.6%	4,075.0
12/14	943.9	36.5	3.9%	3,650.0
12/13	902.7	34.7	3.9%	3,500.0
12/12	998.9	34.2	3.4%	3,300.0
12/11	780.3	18.3	2.3%	3,000.0
Annual Growth	8.0%	10.5%	—	8.0%

2015 Year-End Financials

Debt ratio: —	No. of shares (mil.): 19.9
Return on equity: 8.3%	Dividends
Cash ($ mil.): 39.8	Yield: —
Current ratio: 1.69	Payout: —
Long-term debt ($ mil.): —	Market value ($ mil.): 412.0

	STOCK PRICE ($) FY Close	P/E High/Low		PER SHARE ($) Earnings	Dividends	Book Value
12/15	20.61	24	14	1.30	0.00	16.52
12/14	27.40	16	13	1.69	0.00	15.51
12/13	25.08	16	12	1.61	0.00	13.95
12/12	22.25	14	9	1.60	0.00	12.28
12/11	19.14	29	17	0.87	0.00	10.57
Annual Growth	1.9%	—	—	10.6%	—	11.8%

Myriad Genetics, Inc.

Myriad Genetics is working to detect which diseases folks might develop based on their genes. The company develops and sells molecular diagnostic tests in three main areas: predictive medicine (to assess a patient's risk for developing disease) personalized medicine (to identify likelihood of drug response to therapies) and prognostic medicine (to assess risk of disease progression or recurrence). Its biggest revenue maker BRACAnalysis helps determine risk for breast or ovarian cancer. Myriad Genetics markets its products in the US through its own sales force and uses collaborations to sell them elsewhere.

OperationsThe company operates through two reporting segments –Diagnostics and Other. Diagnostics accounting for 96% of earnings provides testing that is designed to assess in individual's risk for developing diseases later in life identify a patient's likelihood of responding to drug therapy and guide dosing to ensure optimal treatment or assess a patient's risk of disease progression and disease recurrence. The Other segment (consisting of the former Research and Pharmaceutical and Clinical Services segments) provides testing products and services to research industries research and development and clinical services for patients; it also includes Myriad Genetics' corporate functions including finance legal and information technology.

Myriad Genetics' primary line of molecular diagnostic testing products includes BRACAnalysis COLARIS MELARIS and the newest addition myRisk Hereditary Cancer. (Launched in 2013 myRisk is expected to replace BRACAnalysis COLARIS BART and MELARIS with a single comprehensive test.) The company markets these to physicians engaged in preventive rather than reactive treatments. These tests are designed to assess whether a patient's genetic makeup makes the patient more likely to develop certain cancers such as breast colorectal and skin. Myriad Genetics is ramping up its sales marketing and education efforts aimed at OB/GYN doctors in the US a market that targets women.

The company's personalized medicine line of products gauges a patient's response to certain drugs and dosages which then helps physicians tailor treatments to the individual. The THERAGUIDE 5-FU product through a small blood sample shows oncologists whether a cancer patient is likely to have adverse reactions to a common chemotherapy.

A third set of tests includes prognostic medicine diagnostics that assess disease progression or recurrence rates. Its PROLARIS product helps physicians predict the aggressiveness of prostate cancer in men.

Geographic Reach

Based in the US the company serves major markets in Asia Europe and Latin America. In the US Myriad Genetics operates from offices and labs in Austin Texas; Salt Lake City; and San Francisco. In Europe it has sales offices in London; Madrid; Milan Italy; Munich Germany; and Paris; laboratory operations in Munich; and an international headquarters in Zurich. The company has additional sales offices in Canada and Australia.Sales and MarketingMyriad Genetics has sales teams in the US (including nearly 600 representatives across five sales channels) Canada Europe and Australia. Financial PerformanceThe company's revenue which had been on the rise for the past few years

declined 7% to $723 million in fiscal 2015 (ended June) as both segments saw decreased sales. BRACAnalysis sales dropped after a very strong showing the previous year and the company also lost a $12 million contract. However sales of the new VectraDA test were included for the first full fiscal year which helped offset those declines.Net income has followed revenue trends dropping 54% to $80 million in fiscal 2015. Higher cost of molecular diagnostic testing and operating expenses cut into the firm's bottom line. Likewise cash flow from operations fell 26% to $141 million.Strategy

In order to develop the next generation of molecular diagnostic products Myriad Genetics continues to develop its own proprietary technologies including bioinformatics and robotics to better understand genes and proteins and their role in human disease. It also seeks to license or acquire biomarkers or genes from third-party organizations to augment its own in-house product development programs. In 2014 and 2015 it expanded existing collaborations with AstraZeneca and AbbVie whereby its BRACAnalysis products will be used along with the other companies' diagnostic or therapeutic products.

The company is also working towards transitioning and expanding its hereditary cancer testing products from single-syndrome testing to a more accurate panel approach.

Finally Myriad Genetics is focused on international growth.

Mergers and Acquisitions

In early 2014 the company paid $270 million for autoimmune diagnostics company Crescendo Bioscience. The move gave Myriad entree into the autoimmune market and provided added product diversification. Crescendo will benefit from Myriad's superior development and sales and marketing infrastructure.

The following year Myriad Genetics acquired Privatklinik Dr. Robert Schindlbeck a private specialty clinic for internal medicine near its laboratories in Munich Germany. The $20 million purchase should help the company expand its penetration in Germany's molecular diagnostic market.

In 2016 the company bought Assurex Health a provider of genetic testing for psychotropic medicine selection for $226 million upfront plus a potential $185 million in milestone payments. Assurex's GeneSight diagnostic test will be Myriad's first commercial product in the neuroscience market.

Company Background

Myriad Genetics spun off its drug development operations in mid-2009. The spin-off of its drug development arm Myriad Pharmaceuticals into a separate publicly traded company (called Myrexis) has allowed Myriad Genetics to dedicate substantial focus on molecular diagnostics. Previously the company had used revenue from its profitable diagnostics business to fund its drug development efforts. But with the company reaching profitability overall for the first time in 2008 it revisited the dual business structure and decided to split itself into two.

EXECUTIVES

EVP General Counsel and Secretary, Richard M. Marsh, age 58, $425,811 total compensation
EVP International Operations, Gary A. King, age 60
Chief Scientific Officer, Jerry S. Lanchbury, age 57, $420,812 total compensation
President and CEO, Mark C. Capone, age 54, $501,191 total compensation
CIO, Robert G. Harrison, age 50
EVP Corporate Communications, Ronald Rogers

EVP Human Resources, Jayne B. Hart
President Myriad RBM, Ralph L. McDade
EVP CFO and Treasurer, R. Bryan Riggsbee
President Crescendo Bioscience Inc., Bernard F. Tobin
Vice President Quality and Compl, Eric (Ric) Pratts
Senior Vice President of Information Technology, Alexander (Al) Gutin
National Accounts Manager, Cristyn Lauer
Vice President Operations, Jeff Trost
Vice President Biomarker Discovery, Kirsten Timms
Vice President Business Development, Simon George
National Accounts Manager, Amisha Shah
Executive Vice President Corporate Communications, Ron (Ronnie) Rogers
Executive Vice President General Counsel And Secretary, Richard M (Dick) Arsh
Vice Chairman, Walter Gilbert
Chairman, John T. Henderson, age 72
Board Member, Lynne Daugirda
Auditors: Ernst & Young LLP

LOCATIONS

HQ: Myriad Genetics, Inc.
320 Wakara Way, Salt Lake City, UT 84108
Phone: 801 584-3600
Web: www.myriad.com

PRODUCTS/OPERATIONS

2015 Sales

	$ mil.	% of total
Molecular diagnostics testing	695.5	96
Pharmaceutical & clinical services	27.6	4
Total	**723.1**	**100**

2015 Molecular Diagnostics Sales

	$ mil.	% of total
myRisk	320.7	44
BRACAnalysis	237.6	33
VectraDA	43.7	6
Other	93.5	13
Other revenue	27.6	4
Total	**723.1**	**100**

Selected Molecular Diagnostic Tests

BRACAnalysis (breast and ovarian cancer predictive test)
COLARIS (colorectal and uterine cancer predictive test)
COLARIS AP (colon cancer predictive test)
MELARIS (melanoma predictive test)
Myraid myRisk (hereditary cancer test)
OnDose (chemotherapy dosing level personalized diagnostic test)
PREZEON (cancer drug responsivity personalized diagnostic test)
PROLARIS (prostate cancer prognostic test)
THERAGUIDE 5-FU (chemotherapy toxicity personalized diagnostic test)
Vectra DA (rheumatoid arthritis test)

Selected Companion Diagnostic Services

Multi-Analyte Profile (MAP): library contains more than 550 individual human and rodent immunoassays for use in MAP testing
Multiplexed Immunoassay Kits: enable customers to leverage Myriad's technology services with their in-house capabilities
TruCulture: a self-contained whole blood culture that can be deployed worldwide to clinical sites for acquiring cell culture data without specialized facilities or training

COMPETITORS

Abbott Labs	Hologic
Beckman Coulter	Illumina
Becton Dickinson	Innogenetics
Bio-Rad Labs	Interleukin Genetics
Celera	NeoGenomics
Clarient	Oncolab
CombiMatrix	Pathwork Diagnostics
Epigenomics	QIAGEN
EraGen Biosciences	Roche Diagnostics
Foundation Medicine	Sequenom
Genzyme	Transgenomic

HISTORICAL FINANCIALS
Company Type: Public

Income Statement
FYE: June 30

	REVENUE ($ mil.)	NET INCOME ($ mil.)	NET PROFIT MARGIN	EMPLOYEES
06/16	753.8	125.3	16.6%	2,206.0
06/15	723.1	80.2	11.1%	2,038.0
06/14	778.2	176.2	22.6%	1,649.0
06/13	613.1	147.1	24.0%	1,325.0
06/12	496.0	112.1	22.6%	1,169.0
Annual Growth	**11.0%**	**2.8%**	**—**	**17.2%**

2016 Year-End Financials

Debt ratio: —
Return on equity: 17.7%
Cash ($ mil.): 68.5
Current ratio: 4.35
Long-term debt ($ mil.): —

No. of shares (mil.): 69.1
Dividends
Yield: —
Payout: —
Market value ($ mil.): 2,114.0

	STOCK PRICE ($) FY Close	P/E High/Low		PER SHARE ($) Earnings	Dividends	Book Value
06/16	30.60	26	16	1.71	0.00	10.83
06/15	33.99	36	28	1.08	0.00	9.61
06/14	38.92	18	9	2.25	0.00	9.78
06/13	26.87	19	13	1.77	0.00	9.04
06/12	23.77	20	13	1.30	0.00	7.70
Annual Growth	**6.5%**	**—**	**—**	**7.1%**	**—**	**8.9%**

Nathan's Famous, Inc.

Patrons of this restaurateur are in the dog house. Nathan's Famous is a leading franchisor of quick-service restaurants with a chain of about 300 Nathan's outlets known for all-beef frankfurters served with a variety of toppings. The eateries located in about 25 states and a half dozen other countries also serve hamburgers crinkle-cut fries and breakfast sandwiches. More than 50 Nathan's units also feature fish and chips under the Arthur Treacher's brand. In addition to restaurants the company sells Nathan's branded products through vending machines Subway units at Wal-Mart stores and Auntie Anne's pretzel shops. Specialty Foods Group makes Nathan's hot dogs for retail sale under a licensing deal.

Geographic Reach

Nathan's has been expanding internationally in recent years. The company opened several locations in Beijing China and Nathan's first franchised location in Canada.

Operations

While its restaurant chain still forms the core identity of Nathan's the company has been focused on expanding the sale of branded products through third-party foodservice operators. It branded products segment accounts for more than 50% of sales. Meanwhile Nathan's has launched a limited-menu concept designed to allow other quick-service restaurants such as Brusters Real Ice Cream shops to offer its branded hot dogs.

Sales and Marketing

With its flagship store still operating in Coney Island New York Nathan's is the official "non-kosher" hot dog of both the New York Yankees and the New York Mets. The company also holds a competitive eating contest held at Coney Island every July Fourth.

Financial Performance

The company's revenue has increased year-over-year. It reported revenue of $82.9 million for fiscal 2014 up from $71.5 million in fiscal 2013 and $66.2 million in fiscal 2012.

Net income also went up in fiscal 2014 compared to the prior period. Nathan's reported net income of $8.3 million for fiscal 2014 up from $7.4 million in fiscal 2013. However despite the increased revenue and net income the company's cash flow decreased by more than $7 million in fiscal 2014 compared to fiscal 2013 levels.

HISTORY

Company Background

Ida Handwerker and her husband Nathan opened the first Nathan's Famous food stand in Coney Island in 1916. Ida's special blend of herbs and spices helped popularize the hot dogs and Nathan's went on to become a Coney Island institution. In 1957 the Handwerker family opened a second restaurant and by 1969 the year Nathan's went public the company operated four stores.

In 1987 investment group Equicor bought Nathan's. The next three years the company suffered through multiple changes in leadership and posted a record loss in 1990. A turnaround led by Wayne Norbitz who took over as president in 1989 helped restore the company's stability.

Nathan's went public again in 1993. Also that year Howard Lorber (who came on board as part of Equicor) was named CEO. Two years later the company opened its first outlets inside Home Depot stores. In 1996 Nathan's implemented a co-branding strategy and by the following year it participated in nearly 60 co-branded operations.

In 1998 the company introduced a new product line (chicken strips creamed spinach salads) available in grocery stores and the next year it acquired the Miami Subs sandwich shop chain (sold in 2007) and the Kenny Rogers Roasters chain of rotisserie chicken outlets (disposed of in 2008). Later in 1999 the company's traditional Fourth of July hot dog eating contest was marred by controversy when a videotape showed the winner biting into his wiener before the gun went off.

The following year Nathan's Famous became the official hotdog of the New York Yankees. The 16 new restaurants opened by the company during 2001 included locations in Israel and Egypt. Hard economic times led the company to close several stores in 2002 and Home Depot later terminated its agreements to sell Nathan's Famous in its stores. In 2003 locations in Israel and Brunei were closed and a new location in Japan was opened.

Nathan's Famous acquired the Arthur Treacher's brand and franchising system from TruFoods in 2006. The following year Eric Gatoff was named CEO; Lorber remained as chairman.

Nathan's sold Kenny Rogers Roasters to an affiliate of Malaysia's Berjaya Corporation in 2008. The company disposed of its Miami Subs sandwich chain the previous year selling the business for $3.2 million.

The company expanded into China in 2011 and plans to open locations in Canada during 2012.

EXECUTIVES

Executive Vice President; Director, Donald L. (Don) Perlyn, age 74, $210,000 total compensation

VP Development Architecture and Construction, Donald P. (Don) Schedler, age 63, $140,000 total compensation

Chief Financial Officer; Vice President - Finance; Secretary, Ronald G. DeVos, age 61, $162,750 total compensation

President; Chief Operating Officer; Director, Wayne Norbitz, age 68, $288,750 total compensation

Chairman, Howard M. Lorber, age 67, $400,000 total compensation

VP Franchise Operations, Randy K. Watts, age 60

Chief Executive Officer; Director, Eric Gatoff, age 47, $225,000 total compensation

Director, Attilio F. Petrocelli, age 72

EVP and Director, Donald L. (Don) Perlyn, age 73

President COO and Director, Wayne Norbitz, age 68

Director, Robert J. Eide, age 63

Director, Brian S. Genson, age 67

Director, Barry Leistner, age 65

Director, Charles Raich, age 73

CEO and Director, Eric Gatoff, age 47

Auditors: Grant Thornton LLP

LOCATIONS

HQ: Nathan's Famous, Inc.
One Jericho Plaza, Second Floor Wing A, Jericho, NY 11753
Phone: 516 338-8500
Web: www.nathansfamous.com

COMPETITORS

Burger King	Kahala
CKE Restaurants	McDonald's
Captain D's	Popeyes
Chick-fil-A	Potbelly Sandwich Shop
Church's Chicken	Quiznos
Dairy Queen	Sbarro
Galardi Group	Subway
Golden Krust	Wendy's
HDOS Enterprises	YUM!
Jack in the Box	

HISTORICAL FINANCIALS

Company Type: Public

Income Statement

FYE: March 27

	REVENUE ($ mil.)	NET INCOME ($ mil.)	NET PROFIT MARGIN	EMPLOYEES
03/16	100.8	6.1	6.0%	237.0
03/15	99.1	11.7	11.8%	228.0
03/14	82.9	8.3	10.0%	210.0
03/13	71.5	7.4	10.4%	161.0
03/12	66.2	6.1	9.3%	219.0
Annual Growth	11.1%	(0.3%)	—	2.0%

2016 Year-End Financials

Debt ratio: 182.0%
Return on equity: —
Cash ($ mil.): 50.2
Current ratio: 5.44
Long-term debt ($ mil.): 130.2

No. of shares (mil.): 4.1
Dividends
Yield: 0.5%
Payout: 1,824.8%
Market value ($ mil.): 176.0

	STOCK PRICE ($) FY Close	P/E High/Low		Earnings	PER SHARE ($) Dividends	Book Value
03/16	42.03	53	22	1.37	25.00	(17.32)
03/15	73.56	32	19	2.55	25.00	(13.01)
03/14	48.78	33	23	1.81	0.00	9.79
03/13	42.25	25	12	1.63	0.00	7.80
03/12	21.01	17	14	1.22	0.00	6.61
Annual Growth	18.9%	—	—	2.9%	—	—

National Commerce Corp

Auditors: Porter Keadle Moore, LLC

LOCATIONS

HQ: National Commerce Corp
813 Shades Creek Parkway, Suite 100, Birmingham, AL 35209
Phone: 205 313-8100
Web: www.nationalbankofcommerce.com

HISTORICAL FINANCIALS

Company Type: Public

Income Statement

FYE: December 31

	ASSETS ($ mil.)	NET INCOME ($ mil.)	INCOME AS % OF ASSETS	EMPLOYEES
12/15	1,763.3	9.6	0.5%	289.0
12/14	1,138.4	5.4	0.5%	235.0
12/13	791.7	4.0	0.5%	0.0
12/12	0.0	2.0	—	0.0
Annual Growth	—	67.1%	—	—

2015 Year-End Financials

Return on assets: 0.6%
Return on equity: 5.6%
Long-term debt ($ mil.): —
No. of shares (mil.): 10.8
Sales ($ mil): 63.3

Dividends
Yield: —
Payout: —
Market value ($ mil.): 271.0

	STOCK PRICE ($) FY Close	P/E High/Low		Earnings	PER SHARE ($) Dividends	Book Value
12/15	25.05	27	20	1.02	0.00	19.33
12/14	0.00	—	—	0.91	0.00	17.09
Annual Growth	—	—	—	12.1%	—	13.1%

National Health Investors, Inc.

National Health Investors has a financial investment in the nation's health. The real estate investment trust (REIT) owns or makes mortgage investments in health care properties primarily long-term care facilities. With more than 180 properties in over 30 states its holdings also include residences for people with developmental disabilities assisted-living complexes medical office buildings retirement centers and an acute care hospital. About one-third of National Health Investors' properties are leased to its largest tenant National HealthCare Corporation; half are leased to regional health care providers. A majority of the REIT's facilities are located in Florida Texas and Tennessee.

OperationsThe company owned 183 facilities in 31 states in 2014 including 106 senior housing communities 71 skilled nursing facilities four hospitals and two medical office buildings. As a REIT National Health generates nearly 95% of its business from rental income with the remainder of its revenue coming from investment income and interest income on mortgage or other notes. About 40% of the REIT's total revenue came from rental income from regional operators in 2014 while rental income from publicly-owned operators and privately-owned national chains contributed 26% and 29% to the REIT's total revenue. Smaller operators contributed the remainder.Geographic ReachTennessee-based National Health Investors has most of its properties in the states of Florida Texas and Tennessee.Sales and MarketingNational Health's three main operators (tenants) include: an affiliate of Holiday Retirement National HealthCare Corporation and Bickford Senior Living; each of which contributed more than 10% of the REIT's total revenue during 2014. Senior Living Communities began making lease payments on eight retirement communities during 2015 which would amount to more than 17% of National Health's total revenue during the year.Some of National Health's other top tenants include: Brookdale Senior Living Fundamental Health Services Management and Legend Healthcare. Financial PerformanceNational Health Investors' revenues and profits have been on the rise in recent years thanks to aggressive expansion from property acquisitions. The REIT's revenue spiked by 51% to a record $177.51 million in 2014 mostly thanks to a 57% increase in rental income stemming from nearly $749 million worth of new real estate investment properties.Despite higher revenue in 2014 National's net income dipped by 4% to $103.05 million as depreciating expenses rose with new property acquisitions and due to higher interest expenses from the company's credit borrowings during the year. The REIT's operating cash levels rose by 21% to $21.95 million after adjusting its earnings for (non-cash) depreciation and amortization expenses. StrategyNational Health Investments typically expands its property portfolio –and therefore rental income –through strategic property acquisitions of senior housing communities and assisted living properties from real estate investors mortgage loans or in operations through structures allowed by RIDEA. The REIT typically takes a purchase-leaseback approach in which it acquires properties and leases them back to their previous operators. It also may provide mortgage and construction loans to operators who agree to lease the property once built. The REIT on occasion also makes divestitures of under-performing rental properties to free up resources for further investments in higher-potential properties. In 2014 for example National Health sold three of its decades-old skilled nursing facilities in Texas which averaged 41 years in age and housed some 484 beds to an affiliate of Fundamental Long Term Care Holdings for a total of $18.49 million. Mergers and Acquisitions In 2014 NHI purchased eight senior housing communities for $476 million which would be leased to Senior Living Communities (SLC) and would continue to be managed by an SLC affiliate. Also that year it spent $42 million toward acquiring an 105-unit assisted living community in Idaho as well as three skilled nursing facilities in Oregon with plans for a sale-leaseback arrangement from Prestige Senior Living; and another $18.1 million toward the purchase of a 101-unit assisted living and memory care community in Middleton Ohio through its joint venture with Bickford Senior Living. In late 2013 the company purchased 25 independent-living properties which boasted 2841 units from Holiday Acquisition Holdings for a total of $491 million.

In April 2013 the REIT acquired a pair of skilled nursing facilities in Canton and Corinth Texas for $26.3 million. The purchase added a total of 254 beds to the REIT's portfolio.In 2012 NHI acquired a 181-unit senior living campus in Loma Linda California for $12 million from Chancellor Health Care (CHC) thereby establishing a presence in Southern California. CHC would lease and continue to operate the facility.

Ownership

Chairman and CEO Andy Adams owns about 10% of National Health Investors.

EXECUTIVES

Chief Credit Officer, Kristin S. Gaines
SVP Investments, Kevin Pascoe
Chief Accounting Officer, Roger R. Hopkins, age 55, $200,000 total compensation
President and CEO, Justin Hutchens, age 42
Chairman, W. Andrew (Andy) Adams, age 71
Auditors: BDO USA, LLP

LOCATIONS

HQ: National Health Investors, Inc.
222 Robert Rose Drive, Murfreesboro, TN 37129
Phone: 615 890-9100
Web: www.nhireit.com

PRODUCTS/OPERATIONS

2014 Sales

	$ mil.	% of total
Rental income	166.3	94
Interest income from mortgage and others	7.0	4
Investment income and other	4.2	2
Total	**177.5**	**100**

2014 Portfolio by Operations

	% of total
Regional	40
National Chain(Privately Owned)	28
Public	27
Small	5
Total	**100**

COMPETITORS

Cousins Properties	Omega Healthcare
HCP	Investors
Healthcare Realty	Senior Housing
Trust	Properties
LTC Properties	Ventas
Medical Properties	Welltower
Trust	

HISTORICAL FINANCIALS

Company Type: Public

Income Statement
FYE: December 31

	REVENUE ($ mil.)	NET INCOME ($ mil.)	NET PROFIT MARGIN	EMPLOYEES
12/15	228.9	150.3	65.6%	12.0
12/14	177.5	103.0	58.1%	12.0
12/13	117.8	107.1	91.0%	11.0
12/12	96.9	90.9	93.8%	10.0
12/11	82.7	81.1	98.1%	0.0
Annual Growth	**29.0%**	**16.7%**	**—**	**—**

2015 Year-End Financials

Debt ratio: 43.1%
Return on equity: 13.8%
Cash ($ mil.): 13.2
Current ratio: 1.38
Long-term debt ($ mil.): 926.2
No. of shares (mil.): 38.4
Dividends
  Yield: 5.5%
  Payout: 102.7%
Market value ($ mil.): 2,337.0

	STOCK PRICE ($) FY Close	P/E High/Low	PER SHARE ($) Earnings	Dividends	Book Value
12/15	60.87	19 14	3.95	3.40	29.52
12/14	69.96	23 18	3.04	3.08	27.74
12/13	56.10	19 14	3.74	2.90	23.19
12/12	56.53	18 13	3.26	2.64	16.41
12/11	43.98	17 13	2.92	2.72	15.98
Annual Growth	**8.5%**	**— —**	**7.8%**	**5.8%**	**16.6%**

National Retail Properties Inc

For National Retail Properties good things come in big boxes. The self-administered real estate investment trust (REIT) acquires develops and manages freestanding retail properties in heavily traveled commercial and residential areas. Its portfolio includes more than 2250 properties with some 25 million sq. ft. of leasable space in almost all 50 states concentrated in Texas the Southeast and the Midwest. National Retail Properties also invests in mortgages operates some of its retail properties and develops properties to sell them later for a profit. More than 30% of its rental income comes from convenience store and restaurant operators with its top clients being Sunoco Mister Car Wash LA Fitness The Pantry and Camping World.

Operations

While some retail REITs own entire strip malls or shopping malls National Retail Properties keeps it simple with freestanding retail properties. National Retail Properties typically signs triple-net leases with initial terms of 15 to 20 years in which tenants are responsible for expenses such as taxes utilities repairs and maintenance.Geographic ReachNational Retail Properties' largest markets are in Texas (20% of rental income in 2015) and Florida (9%). Other large markets include Ohio North Carolina Illinois Georgia Virginia Indiana Alabama and Tennessee which combined made up around one-third of its rental income during 2015.Sales and MarketingThe trust's retail tenants include convenience stores and gas stations full-service and limited-service restaurants and other retailers. Its five largest tenants by rental base during 2015 included Sunoco (5.9% of rental income) Mister Car Wash (4.4%) LA Fitness (3.7%) The Pantry (3.6%) and Camping World (3.6%). Other tenants include Stripes (Susser Holdings) 7-Eleven; restuarant tenants Applebee's Chili's Denny's Logan's Roadhouse Taco Bell and Wendys; and retailers Best Buy CarQuest and Pep Boys.

Financial Performance

National Retail Properties' annual revenues and profits have more than doubled since 2010 mainly as new property acquisitions have spurred higher rental income.The REIT's revenue jumped 11% to $482.91 million during 2015 mostly as its rental income increased with the acquisition of 221 new properties spanning 2.42 million square feet.Strong revenue growth in 2015 drove National Retail Properties' net income up 4% to $197.84 million. The REIT's operating cash levels climbed 15% to $341.09 million for the year as it collected more in cash-based rental income.

Strategy

Keeping a diversified tenant base in mind National Retail Properties mostly targets single-building retail real estate property located near local markets where its retail tenants trade. During 2015 it acquired 221 of such properties expanding its portfolio by more than 10% while selling just 19 properties with six more up for sale.

EXECUTIVES

EVP CFO and Treasurer, Kevin B. Habicht, age 56, $422,500 total compensation
Chairman and CEO, Craig Macnab, age 60, $750,000 total compensation
President and COO, Julian E. (Jay) Whitehurst, age 58, $510,000 total compensation
EVP and Chief Investment Officer, Paul E. Bayer, age 54, $355,000 total compensation
EVP and Chief Acquisition Officer, Stephen A. Horn, age 44
Senior Vice President Tax, Mike (Mikey) Iannone
Vice President Underwriting, Matthew (Matt) Sunderland
Vice President of Real Estate, Russell (Russ) Shelton
Chairman, Robert C. Legler, age 72
Auditors: Ernst & Young LLP

LOCATIONS

HQ: National Retail Properties Inc
450 South Orange Avenue, Suite 900, Orlando, FL 32801
Phone: 407 265-7348 **Fax:** 407 423-2894
Web: www.nnnreit.com

COMPETITORS

Acadia Realty Trust	Kimco Realty
Brixmor	One Liberty Properties
DDR	Realty Income
Federal Realty	Regency Centers
Investment	

HISTORICAL FINANCIALS

Company Type: Public

Income Statement
FYE: December 31

	REVENUE ($ mil.)	NET INCOME ($ mil.)	NET PROFIT MARGIN	EMPLOYEES
12/16	533.6	239.5	44.9%	65.0
12/15	482.9	197.8	41.0%	62.0
12/14	434.8	190.6	43.8%	64.0
12/13	392.3	160.1	40.8%	62.0
12/12	331.7	142.0	42.8%	60.0
Annual Growth	**12.6%**	**14.0%**	**—**	**2.0%**

2016 Year-End Financials

Debt ratio: 36.5%
Return on equity: 6.5%
Cash ($ mil.): 294.5
Current ratio: 16.43
Long-term debt ($ mil.): 2,311.6
No. of shares (mil.): 147.1
Dividends
  Yield: 0.0%
  Payout: 128.9%
Market value ($ mil.): 6,504.0

	STOCK PRICE ($) FY Close	P/E High/Low	PER SHARE ($) Earnings	Dividends	Book Value
12/16	44.20	38 28	1.38	1.78	26.62
12/15	40.05	37 28	1.20	1.71	23.70
12/14	39.37	33 24	1.24	1.65	23.35
12/13	30.33	38 27	1.10	1.60	22.76
12/12	31.20	29 23	1.11	1.56	20.58
Annual Growth	**9.1%**	**— —**	**5.6%**	**3.4%**	**6.6%**

National Storage Affiliates Trust

Auditors: KPMG LLP

LOCATIONS

HQ: National Storage Affiliates Trust
5200 DTC Parkway, Suite 200, Greenwood Village, CO
80111
Phone: 720 630-2600
Web: www.nationalstorageaffiliates.com

HISTORICAL FINANCIALS

Company Type: Public

Income Statement

FYE: December 31

	REVENUE ($ mil.)	NET INCOME ($ mil.)	NET PROFIT MARGIN	EMPLOYEES
12/15	133.9	12.4	9.3%	8.0
12/14	76.9	(16.3)	—	13.0
12/13*	32.8	(10.4)	—	0.0
03/13	7.3	(1.2)	—	0.0
12/12	29.2	(3.4)	—	0.0
Annual Growth 46.2%		—	—	—

*Fiscal year change

2015 Year-End Financials

Debt ratio: 51.7%	No. of shares (mil.): 23.0
Return on equity: —	Dividends
Cash ($ mil.): 6.6	Yield: 3.1%
Current ratio: 1.34	Payout: 317.6%
Long-term debt ($ mil.): 570.6	Market value ($ mil.): 394.0

	STOCK PRICE ($) FY Close	P/E High/Low	PER SHARE ($) Earnings	Dividends	Book Value
12/15	17.13	21 15	0.17	0.54	10.28
Annual Growth	—	— —	—	—	—

Nationstar Mortgage Holdings Inc

Nationstar Mortgage helps turn home ownership into more than just a wish upon a star. The company is one of the largest servicers of residential mortgage loans in the US with a servicing portfolio comprised more than 2.5 million loans that total in excess of $400 billion in unpaid principal balances. Nationstar also originates loans (primarily government- and agency-backed mortgages) which it typically sells or securitizes within one month of origination; mortgage sales make up one-third of its total revenue. The company serves consumers directly through its Texas-based call center and also offers its products through wholesalers. Its Xome subsidiary offers ancillary real estate services. Nationstar went public in 2012.

Operations

Nationstar operates three segments: Servicing which made up nearly 45% of its total revenue during 2015 and ranked as the nation's largest non-

bank servicer and fourth-largest residential mortgage servicer; Originations (35% of revenue) which makes conventional residential mortgage loans through Greenlight Financial Services and branches that are designed to be sold or securitized; and Xome (20% of revenue) which offers real estate exchange services (Xome Exchange); title valuation settlement and closing services (Xome Services); and technology-enabled data analytics and customer relationship management tools. Geographic ReachThe Copple Texas-based company services mortgage loans in all 50 US states and it is licensed as a residential mortgage loan servicer/originator and debt collector in all states that require such licensing. It also has international operations in India and the Philippines.Sales and MarketingNationstar serves residential real estate market participants such as homeowners home buyers and sellers real estate agents and investors (mostly Fannie Mae Freddie Mac and Ginnie Mae).The company spent $60.6 million on advertising during 2015 up from $41.6 million and $53.6 million in 2014 and 2013 respectively.

Financial Performance

Fueled by a steady stream of servicing portfolio acquisitions Nationstar's annual revenues have risen nearly five-fold since 2011 while annual profits have more than doubled as the company has kept a lid on growing overhead expenses.The company's revenue ticked up 1% to $1.9 billion during 2015 mostly as its Xome business grew by 40%-plus with its acquisitions of Experience 1 and Real Estate Digital and thanks to an increase in property sales and average selling prices through Homesearch.com. The Originations segment revenues climbed 15% with higher origination volumes cultivated by the low-interest environment. Servicing segment revenue declined nearly 20% as the company sold $4.6 billion in mortgage servicing rights toward its plan to become more capital light.Despite revenue growth in 2015 Nationstar's net income plunged 82% to $38.78 million as interest rate movements caused a write-down in MSR values and as add-on investments in its Xome platform led to higher personnel and operating expenses. The company's operating cash levels tumbled 61% to $417.83 million for the year mostly due to a $3 billion decrease in cash-based origination proceeds stemming from cash flow timing.

Strategy

Nationstar recently outlined its "2016 Core Initiatives" for each of its business segments. For its Servicing segment it plans to keep its margins steady on high-quality loans and put the "service" back in servicing for its customers. For the Originations segment Nationstar said it would continue focusing on generating high-quality loans increasing retention across all of its major portfolio segments and expand its origination offerings with higher-margin government lending and streamlined offerings. The company's Xome segment would look to boost the profitability of property disposition title and collateral valuations while continuing to develop new technologies designed for optimal connection between residential real estate market participants. The nation's largest non-bank residential mortgage servicer has historically seen opportunity in the weakened credit markets as it has been successful managing portfolios of higher-risk loans. Its high-touch approach an area in which the big banks tends to lack is well-suited to handling riskier loans. The firm has seen rapid growth as a result of its expanding servicing portfolio. Also by originating loans in-house Nationstar is further able to boost its servicing portfolio largely by offering borrowers refinancing options.

Mergers and Acquisitions

In June 2015 subsidiary Xome Holdings purchased digital signature and document management SaaS provider GoPaperless Solutions.In May 2015 subsidiary Xome bought real estate analytics company Quantarium LLC which specializes in automated home valuation models utilizing advanced statistical methods and proprietary algorithms.In January 2015 subsidiary Xome Holdings paid $36 million to buy Experience 1 Inc. the holding company for Title365 Xome Signing and tech subsidiaries Xome Labs and Xome Analytics a title agency and tech services provider for title insurance and escrow services.In June 2014 Nationstar purchased the mortgage origination business of Greenlight Financial Services for $75 million.In February 2013 the company acquired $97 billion in residential mortgage serving rights and certain other assets from Bank of America. Also in February 2013 it acquired Equifax Settlement Services Holding LLC (ESS) from Equifax. ESS was a leading provider of appraisal title insurance and settlement services in the US and served a broad array of blue chip clients including the largest financial institutions in the country. Nationstar combined ESS with its Solutionstar platform (now called Xome).

Company Background

Once a subsidiary of homebuilder Centex Nationstar Mortgage was acquired by Fortress Investment Group in 2006. At the time of the transaction which was valued at some $575 million Nationstar Mortgage (then named Centex Home Equity) was a subprime lender. Like many of its peers Nationstar Mortgage exited the subprime lending business in late 2007 thereby focusing on its servicing activities.

Fortress Investment Group owns about 80% of Nationstar.

HISTORY

Company BackgroundIn March 2012 the company raised $247 million through the initial public offering which coincided with the economy's modest recovery. Nationstar used the money to grow its mortgage servicing portfolio.

Shortly after its public offering it purchased the servicing assets of Aurora Loan Services a subsidiary of Aurora Bank for $268 million. The deal included $63 billion in residential mortgages. As part of the transaction affiliate Newcastle Investment paid $170 million to receive a portion of the servicing rights to the Aurora portfolio.

Once a subsidiary of homebuilder Centex Nationstar Mortgage was acquired by Fortress Investment Group in 2006. At the time of the transaction which was valued at some $575 million Nationstar Mortgage (then named Centex Home Equity) was a subprime lender. Like many of its peers Nationstar Mortgage exited the subprime lending business in late 2007 thereby focusing on its servicing activities.

EXECUTIVES

CEO, Jay Bray, age 49, $450,000 total compensation
EVP Originations, Anthony L. (Tony) Ebers, age 50, $190,385 total compensation
EVP and General Counsel, Anthony W. Villani, age 59, $375,000 total compensation
EVP and Chief Risk Officer, Ramesh Lakshminarayanan, age 53, $380,000 total compensation
EVP Servicing, Michael R. (Mike) Rawls, age 46
EVP and CFO, Robert D. Stiles, age 43, $400,000 total compensation

EVP and Chief Compliance Officer, Steve Covington

EVP and Chief Marketing Officer, Kevin Dahlstrom

EVP and Chief Customer Officer, Dana Dillard

CIO, Sridhar Sharma

EVP and Chief Human Resources Officer, Tran Taylor

Auditors: Ernst & Young LLP

LOCATIONS

HQ: Nationstar Mortgage Holdings Inc
8950 Cypress Waters Blvd., Coppell, TX 75019
Phone: 469 549-2000
Web: www.nationstarholdings.com

PRODUCTS/OPERATIONS

2015 Sales

	$ mil.	% of total
Service related	1,304.7	66
Net gain on mortgage loans held for sale	683.9	34
Total	**1,988.6**	**100**

2015 Sales

	$ mil.	% of total
Servicing	881.9	44
Originations	665.7	34
Xome	437.0	22
Corporate and Other	4.4	-
Eliminations	(0.4)	-
Total	**1,988.6**	**100**

Selected Services

MSRs - Fair Value
MSRs - LOCOM
Subservicing
Xome Exchange
Xome Services
Xome Technology and Support

COMPETITORS

Bank of America	Stonegate Mortgage
CitiMortgage	Synovus Mortgage
DHI Mortgage	UAMC
JPMorgan Chase	Wells Fargo Home
PHH Mortgage	Mortgage

HISTORICAL FINANCIALS

Company Type: Public

Income Statement
FYE: December 31

	REVENUE ($ mil.)	NET INCOME ($ mil.)	NET PROFIT MARGIN	EMPLOYEES
12/15	1,988.6	38.7	2.0%	6,740.0
12/14	1,973.0	220.7	11.2%	5,500.0
12/13	2,086.9	217.0	10.4%	6,984.0
12/12	984.3	205.2	20.9%	4,672.0
12/11	377.7	20.8	5.5%	2,599.0
Annual Growth	51.5%	16.7%	—	26.9%

2015 Year-End Financials

Debt ratio: 73.6%
Return on equity: 2.6%
Cash ($ mil.): 613.2
Current ratio: 0.20
Long-term debt ($ mil.): 8,719.2

No. of shares (mil.): 108.8
Dividends
Yield: —
Payout: —
Market value ($ mil.): 1,455.0

	STOCK PRICE ($) FY Close	P/E High/Low	PER SHARE ($) Earnings	Dividends	Book Value
12/15	13.37	83 30	0.37	0.00	16.15
12/14	28.19	15 11	2.45	0.00	13.48
12/13	36.96	24 13	2.40	0.00	10.92
12/12	30.98	15 6	2.40	0.00	8.38
Annual Growth	(24.4%)	— —	(46.4%)	—	24.5%

Natural Alternatives International, Inc.

Natural Alternatives International (NAI) is a natural alternative for nutritional supplement marketers who want to outsource manufacturing. The company provides private-label manufacturing of vitamins minerals herbs and other customized nutritional supplements. Its main customers are direct sellers such as Mannatech and NSA International for whom it makes JuicePlus+ chewables capsules and powdered products. NAI also makes some branded products for sale in the US: the Pathway to Healing brand of nutritional supplements promoted by doctor and evangelist Reginald B. Cherry.

Geographic Reach

The company has manufacturing and distribution facilities in California and in Switzerland. It also has sales support operations in Japan in order to assist clients operating in the Pacific Rim. The US accounts for 60% of NAI's sales. Outside the US NAI's primary market is Europe.

Operations

Natural Alternatives International (NAI) operates through three business segments. Private-label contract manufacturing is by far the largest representing more than 85% of sales. Its Branded Products business (just 2% of sales) markets and distributes branded nutritional supplements through direct-to-consumer marketing programs. NAI's Patent and Trademark licensing business segment is engaged in the sale and licensing of beta-alanine (an amino acid used by bodybuilders) under the CarnoSyn trade name.

NSA International and Mannatech are the company's biggest clients accounting for about 45% and 20% respectively of the company's sales. In addition to manufacturing products for its private-label clients NAI offers a range of complementary services such as regulatory assistance and packaging design.

Financial Analysis

The company's net sales grew a robust 30% in fiscal 2012 (ends June) vs. the prior year while net income fell by about 18% over the same period. Revenue from NAI's patent and trademark licensing business surged more than 350% in fiscal 2012 vs. 2011 driven by the increase in popularity of CarnoSyn as a sports nutrition supplement and expanded distribution of the product. The Private-label contract manufacturing segment saw its sales rise more than 20% due to increased sales to its two largest customers NSA International and Mannatech. Branded products was the laggard posting a 14% drop off in sales for the year which NAI blamed on soft sales of the Pathway to Healing product line.

Strategy

A key element of NAI's growth strategy is the commercialization of its beta-alanine patent through contract manufacturing royalty and licensing agreements and the protection of its proprietary rights (by legal means where necessary). Indeed the 350% surge in fiscal 2012 sales in the company's licensing business was credited to the CarnoSyn brand. To that end NAI in 2011 expanded its beta-alanine licensing programs through a supply agreement with Nestle Nutrition and a license and supply agreement with Abbott Laboratories. While the Nestle agreement expired in mid-2012 and was not renewed the agreement

granting Abbott exclusive license for the use of beta-alanine in certain medical foods and medical nutritionals continues. Also NAI is looking to growth the CarnoSyn beta-alanine business through accretive acquisitions.

The company is also focusing on developing and growing its own line of branded products primarily through direct-to-consumer sales and distribution channels. To bolster is faltering Pathway to Healing line of branded products NAI relaunched the product line and increased its marketing and advertising activities to support future sales.

Ownership

Founder chairman and CEO Mark LeDoux holds nearly 18% of the company. Edward Borg owns more than 16% of NAI's shares while Carl Terranova owns nearly 14%.

HISTORY

Marie Le Doux and her son Mark founded Natural Alternatives International (NAI) with $25000 in 1980. Mark a lawyer and former premed student had previously worked for a small California-based vitamin company and was a firm believer in the virtues of vitamins. He studied the beneficial properties of nutrients and began making vitamins for health food retailers and drugstores.

Finding the retail market too competitive for a small company the Le Doux duo refocused on specialty direct markets. Mark ramped up their production facility bringing in automated equipment from Italy. The company went public in 1986 and created private-label lines for several new customers.

Trouble struck in 1989 when NAI was forced to recall its products containing L-tryptophan (an amino acid often marketed as a sleep aid) after the FDA linked it to the potentially fatal eosinophilia-myalgia syndrome.

To help boost overseas sales NAI in 1997 bought a tablet and chewables manufacturing plant doubling its manufacturing capacity. In 1998 the firm acquired the rights to manufacture Glucotrol a fat- and cholesterol-binding diet supplement used in Japan. The next year it established subsidiary Natural Alternatives International Europe in Switzerland and began manufacturing operations there.

Faced with increased competition and decreased demand in 2000 (the company lost the business of Nu Skin Enterprises which had accounted for some 20% of its revenues) NAI cut jobs to reduce operating costs.

NAI expanded its branded products segment considerably with its 2005 Real Health Laboratories. The purchase brought in a line of products sold via mass retail outlets as well as a mail-order catalog business (As We Change) that sold proprietary and third-party nutritional and personal care products aimed at women over 40. However the lines did not meet the company's expectations and NAI first sold the catalog business to Miles Kimball Company in 2008 and then sold the remaining assets to PharmaCare in 2009.

EXECUTIVES

Chairman of the Board; Chief Executive Officer, Mark A. LeDoux, age 62, $262,831 total compensation

Chief Financial Officer; Chief Operating Officer; Treasurer; Secretary, Kenneth E. (Ken) Wolf, age 55

VP New Product Introductions and Strategic Initiatives, Marian Barker

Director of Operations, Fausto Petrini
Director of Human Resources, Jo Phillippe
Director, Joe E. Davis, age 81
Director, Lee G. Weldon, age 77
Director, Alan J. Lane, age 53
Director, Alan G. Dunn, age 61
Auditors: Haskell & White LLP

LOCATIONS

HQ: Natural Alternatives International, Inc.
1535 Faraday Ave, Carlsbad, CA 92008
Phone: 760 744-7340
Web: www.nai-online.com

COMPETITORS

Atrium Innovations	Nexgen
Botanical Laboratories	Perrigo
GNC	PureTek
Integrated BioPharma	Schiff Nutrition
NBTY	International
NNC	Soft Gel Technologies
Nature's Sunshine	USANA Health Sciences

HISTORICAL FINANCIALS

Company Type: Public

Income Statement
FYE: June 30

	REVENUE ($ mil.)	NET INCOME ($ mil.)	NET PROFIT MARGIN	EMPLOYEES
06/16	114.2	9.5	8.4%	285.0
06/15	79.5	3.3	4.2%	167.0
06/14	73.9	1.9	2.7%	181.0
06/13	62.8	1.5	2.5%	177.0
06/12	72.8	4.1	5.7%	175.0
Annual Growth	11.9%	23.1%	—	13.0%

2016 Year-End Financials

Debt ratio: —
Return on equity: 19.5%
Cash ($ mil.): 19.7
Current ratio: 2.91
Long-term debt ($ mil.): —
No. of shares (mil.): 6.8
Dividends
Yield: —
Payout: —
Market value ($ mil.): 76.0

	STOCK PRICE ($) FY Close	P/E High/Low		PER SHARE ($) Earnings	Dividends	Book Value
06/16	11.04	10	4	1.44	0.00	7.82
06/15	5.67	13	10	0.49	0.00	6.50
06/14	5.28	21	16	0.29	0.00	6.06
06/13	4.61	33	18	0.23	0.00	5.83
06/12	7.66	15	6	0.59	0.00	5.75
Annual Growth	9.6%	—	—	25.0%	—	8.0%

Natural Gas Services Group Inc

The pressure is on to enhance oil and gas well production. Natural Gas Services Group (NGS) manufactures and leases natural gas compressors used to boost oil and gas well production primarily in non-conventional plays such as coal bed methane tight gas and oil and gas shales. The company also provides flare tip burners ignition systems and components used to combust waste gases before entering the atmosphere. NGS leases compressors to third parties in Colorado Kansas Louisiana Michigan New Mexico Oklahoma Pennsylvania Texas Utah West Virginia and Wyoming. In 2012 some 1756 units of the company's rental fleet of 2279 compressors were rented out to clients.

Operations

NGS makes and sells compressors and related equipment. In additions its rental business allows it to generate revenues from oil and gas companies that do not wish to put out the capital outlay required in compressor purchases.

Sales and Marketing

The company serves a customer base of oil and natural gas exploration and production companies. In 2012 EOG Resources accounted for 32% of NGS' revenues; Devon Energy 12%.

Financial Performance

NGS' revenues grew by 44% in 2012 driven by higher equipment sales and rental income and higher natural gas prices partially offset by lower service and maintenance revenues. Equipment sales were up primarily due to the greater demand for compressor units as a result of customers' continued investment in non-conventional shale plays (which require compression to produce natural gas).

Rental revenues increased as a result of increased rental pricing and higher fleet utilization (77% in 2012).NGS' net income grew by 30% in 2012 as stronger revenues outpaced an increase in operating expenses.

Strategy

NGS has grown through a number of acquisitions. Its organic business model has fueled its growth too. The top provider of small to medium-sized horsepower compression equipment to the natural gas industry the company focuses on serving the non-conventional natural gas production market the largest and fastest-growing gas production segment in the US.

The company's growth strategy is also tied to building up its compressor rental business. It intends to increase the size of its rental fleet by fabricating compressor units to keep pace with the growth of the market. In addition to its primary rental and engineered product businesses NGS is also expanding its secondary product lines such as flares and Cylinder-in-Plane compressor products general compressor maintenance and repair services.

Company Background

The company was founded in 1998 and completed its IPO in 2002.

EXECUTIVES

Chairman President and CEO, Stephen C. Taylor, age 63, $444,798 total compensation
VP Technical Services, James R. Hazlett, age 59, $180,999 total compensation
CFO and Treasurer, G. Larry Lawrence, age 64, $152,308 total compensation
Auditors: BDO USA, LLP

LOCATIONS

HQ: Natural Gas Services Group Inc
508 W. Wall St., Suite 550, Midland, TX 79701
Phone: 432 262-2700
Web: www.ngsgi.com

PRODUCTS/OPERATIONS

2015 Sales

	$ mil.	% of total
Rental	76.4	80
Sales	18.5	19
Service & maintenance	1.0	1
Total	95.9	100

COMPETITORS

Archrock	Flotek
Baker Hughes	Miller Energy
CARBO Ceramics	Resources
Compressor Systems	Oilgear
Dresser-Rand	Weatherford
Enerflex	International

HISTORICAL FINANCIALS

Company Type: Public

Income Statement
FYE: December 31

	REVENUE ($ mil.)	NET INCOME ($ mil.)	NET PROFIT MARGIN	EMPLOYEES
12/15	95.9	10.1	10.6%	263.0
12/14	96.9	14.1	14.6%	353.0
12/13	89.2	14.3	16.1%	324.0
12/12	93.7	12.6	13.5%	285.0
12/11	65.1	9.7	15.0%	277.0
Annual Growth	10.1%	1.0%	—	(1.3%)

2015 Year-End Financials

Debt ratio: 0.1%
Return on equity: 4.6%
Cash ($ mil.): 35.5
Current ratio: 16.03
Long-term debt ($ mil.): 0.4
No. of shares (mil.): 12.6
Dividends
Yield: —
Payout: —
Market value ($ mil.): 281.0

	STOCK PRICE ($) FY Close	P/E High/Low		PER SHARE ($) Earnings	Dividends	Book Value
12/15	22.30	32	22	0.79	0.00	17.77
12/14	23.04	31	19	1.11	0.00	16.89
12/13	27.57	26	14	1.15	0.00	15.59
12/12	16.42	16	12	1.03	0.00	14.36
12/11	14.46	24	14	0.80	0.00	13.26
Annual Growth	11.4%	—	—	(0.3%)	—	7.6%

Natural Grocers By Vitamin Cottage Inc

Natural Grocers by Vitamin Cottage offers the best of both worlds –healthy food and dietary supplements. The fast-growing company operates about 75 stores in more than a dozen states that sell natural and organic food including fresh produce meat frozen food and non-perishable bulk food; vitamins and dietary supplements; personal care products; pet care products; and books. The company uses United Natural Foods as its primary distributor and it also runs a bulk food repackaging facility and distribution center in its home state of Colorado. Founded by Margaret and Philip Isely in 1958 Natural Grocers by Vitamin Cottage is run by members of the Isely family. The chain went public in 2012.

IPO

The July 2012 offering raised about $107 million. Natural Grocers by Vitamin Cottage useD the proceeds from its IPO to repay debt fund working capital and for general corporate purposes. Post IPO the founding Isely family controls more than 50% of the company's voting power.

Geographic Reach

Colorado is the company's home state and also its largest market home to more than 40% of its stores. Other major markets for the company include Texas (home to about a dozen stores) as well as Kansas Montana and New Mexico with four stores each.

Operations

The company's stores range in size from 5000 sq. ft. to 16000 sq. ft. (A typical new store averages 10000 sq. ft.) Each store offers about 20000 different natural and organic products and 6750 different dietary supplements. (None of its stores sell alcohol.) The stores don't offer paper or plastic grocery bags but customers are encouraged to bring their own reusable shopping bags. It also sells most of its non-perishable food and dietary supplements online.

Sales and Marketing

Like other grocery retailers Natural Grocers by Vitamin Cottage advertises its weekly circular by mail and in local newspapers. The company plans to attract new customers through targeted marketing efforts such as distributing health-related newsletters and sponsoring health fairs and community wellness events. The chain devotes considerable marketing resources to educating customers on the benefits of natural and organic grocery products and dietary supplements. The company also occasionally relies on TV ads that are produced locally and primarily feature members of the founding Isely family.

Natural Grocers by Vitamin Cottage reported total advertising and marketing expenses for fiscal 2013 (ended September) of $6.2 million compared with $5.1 million in the prior year.

Financial Performance

In its first full year as a public company Natural Grocers by Vitamin Cottage's sales increased by 28% in fiscal 2013 (ended September) versus the prior year to $430.7 million. Driving the double-digit increase in sales were the addition of about a dozen new stores and an 11% increase in same-store sales. Fiscal 2013 marked the fourth consecutive year of increasing sales for the fast-growing chain. Net income increased 59% year over year to about $10.5 million.

Strategy

As part of its growth strategy the company plans to continue expanding its store base. After adding 13 new stores in fiscal 2013 (ended September) another 15 are planned in fiscal 2014. The stores are slated for Colorado Idaho Kansas New Mexico Oregon Utah and Washington (a new market for the retailer). Ultimately the company believes the US can support at least 1100 Natural Grocers by Vitamin Cottage stores. It costs almost $2 million for the company to open a new store and it takes about four years for the store to become profitable. Unlike rival Whole Foods which positions stores in large markets Natural Grocers by Vitamin Cottage strategically places its stores in smaller well-heeled markets such as college towns that can support a specialty store.

To keep up with its expansion the company recently moved to a 107000-sq.-ft. bulk food repackaging facility and distribution center in Golden Colorado. In addition Natural Grocers by Vitamin Cottage uses third-party manufacturers to produce groceries and dietary supplements under private-label brands including Builders Foundation Clarion Natural Grocers and Vitamin Cottage.

EXECUTIVES

CFO, Sandra M. Buffa, age 63, $320,000 total compensation
Chairman and Co-President, Kemper Isely, age 54, $607,800 total compensation

Co-President and Director, Zephyr Isely, age 67, $576,000 total compensation
EVP Corporate Secretary and Director, Heather Isely, age 50, $528,000 total compensation
EVP and Director, Elizabeth Isely, age 61, $480,000 total compensation
Auditors: KPMG LLP

LOCATIONS

HQ: Natural Grocers By Vitamin Cottage Inc
12612 West Alameda Parkway, Lakewood, CO 80228
Phone: 303 986-4600
Web: www.naturalgrocers.com

PRODUCTS/OPERATIONS

2016 Sales

	% of total
Grocery	67
Dietary supplements	22
Body care pet care and other	11
Total	**100**

COMPETITORS

Costco Wholesale	Target Corporation
Fresh Market	Trader Joe's
GNC	Vitacost
H-E-B	Vitamin Shoppe
Kroger	Vitamin World
Safeway	Wal-Mart
Sprouts	Whole Foods

HISTORICAL FINANCIALS
Company Type: Public

Income Statement
FYE: September 30

	REVENUE ($ mil.)	NET INCOME ($ mil.)	NET PROFIT MARGIN	EMPLOYEES
09/16	705.5	11.4	1.6%	3,074.0
09/15	624.6	16.2	2.6%	2,830.0
09/14	520.6	13.4	2.6%	2,346.0
09/13	430.6	10.5	2.5%	2,003.0
09/12	336.3	6.6	2.0%	1,655.0
Annual Growth	20.3%	14.6%	—	16.7%

2016 Year-End Financials

Debt ratio: 21.0%	No. of shares (mil.): 22.4
Return on equity: 9.4%	Dividends
Cash ($ mil.): 4.0	Yield: —
Current ratio: 1.46	Payout: —
Long-term debt ($ mil.): 58.8	Market value ($ mil.): 251.0

	STOCK PRICE ($) FY Close	P/E High/Low		PER SHARE ($) Earnings	Dividends	Book Value
09/16	11.16	50	21	0.51	0.00	5.64
09/15	22.69	44	22	0.72	0.00	5.13
09/14	16.28	73	29	0.60	0.00	4.40
09/13	39.70	89	38	0.47	0.00	3.77
09/12	22.32	76	60	0.30	0.00	3.26
Annual Growth	(15.9%)	—	—	14.2%	—	14.7%

Natural Health Trends Corp.

When it comes to direct selling Natural Health Trends (NHT) was just born that way. The company through its subsidiaries sells products designed to enhance health happiness as well as beauty to a network of some 16000 independent distributors that use and/or resell the goods direct or through the Internet to consumers. Offerings are produced by third parties under the NHT Global brand (formerly Lexxus International). Core lines include skincare (trademark Skindulgence) sexual enhancement (Alura) and an energizing drink (Premium Noni Juice). NHT also sells herbal and dietary supplements for an array of complaints. Sales are generated primarily outside of North America; Hong Kong is the largest market.

Despite its reach into developing regions the company has suffered an accelerated decline in sales. Between 2005 through 2010 demand for NHT products plummeted in all markets where it has a presence except Russia. Nonetheless NHT's negative earnings have narrowed and cash from operations albeit generating a deficit are on the upswing.

The company attributes the slide in sales most significant in Hong Kong Taiwan and South Korea to a disappointing effort to recruit new members by lowering the cost of new member acquisition. In 2010 sales continued to be hurt by a decreasing number of active distributors coupled with dwindling fees from new memberships due to discounted promotions. The number of active distributors most of who are in Hong Kong has fallen more than 50% since 2008. Responding NHT has cut operating expenses as well as interest expense and focused its resources on Greater China (Hong Kong Taiwan and China) and Russia markets which are anticipated to grow.

To date although the company has failed to gain the required license for direct selling in China it has launched an e-commerce retail platform which provides an incentive for volume purchases. Hong Kong sales at risk too are largely dependent Chinese buyers who face the risk of violating their country's laws depending upon their interpretation and enforcement. Undeterred NHT has ramped up its training and public relations efforts to reinforce its position of complying with the law.

EXECUTIVES

President, Chris T. Sharng, age 52, $257,500 total compensation
Chief Financial Officer; Senior Vice President, Timothy S. Davidson, age 45, $160,000 total compensation
Chairman, Randall A. Mason, age 57
Auditors: Lane Gorman Trubitt, PLLC

LOCATIONS

HQ: Natural Health Trends Corp.
609 Deep Valley Drive, Suite 395, Rolling Hills Estates, CA 90274
Phone: 310 541-0888   **Fax:** 972 243-5428
Web: www.naturalhealthtrendscorp.com

PRODUCTS/OPERATIONS

Selected Products
Lifestyle

Alura
LaVie
Twin Slim
Valura
Skincare
24K Renaissance Skin Rejuvenation Serum
BioCell
Skindulgence 30 Minute Non-Surgical Facelift
Time Restore
Wellness and nutritional supplements
Cluster X2
EnerGin
Essential Probiotics
FibeRich
Glucosamine 2200
Premium Noni Juice
ReStore
TriFusion Max
Triotein

COMPETITORS

Amway	Merck
Bactolac	Nature's Sunshine
Pharmaceutical	Nu Skin
Burt's Bees	Pfizer
Chattem	Reliv' International
Herbalife Ltd.	USANA Health Sciences
Mannatech	ViSalus
Medicis Pharmaceutical	Walgreen

HISTORICAL FINANCIALS
Company Type: Public

Income Statement
FYE: December 31

	REVENUE ($ mil.)	NET INCOME ($ mil.)	NET PROFIT MARGIN	EMPLOYEES
12/15	264.8	47.2	17.8%	133.0
12/14	124.5	20.3	16.3%	113.0
12/13	52.5	4.0	7.8%	99.0
12/12	37.5	2.6	7.0%	98.0
12/11	31.1	2.3	7.4%	90.0
Annual Growth	70.7%	112.8%	—	10.3%

2015 Year-End Financials

Debt ratio: —
Return on equity: 113.4%
Cash ($ mil.): 104.9
Current ratio: 1.91
Long-term debt ($ mil.): —

No. of shares (mil.): 12.1
Dividends
Yield: 0.4%
Payout: 4.4%
Market value ($ mil.): 407.0

	STOCK PRICE ($) FY Close	P/E High/Low		PER SHARE ($) Earnings	Dividends	Book Value
12/15	33.53	14	3	3.82	0.14	4.68
12/14	0.35	—	—	1.61	0.03	2.11
12/13	0.35	—	—	0.36	0.00	0.54
12/12	0.35	—	—	0.23	0.00	0.17
12/11	0.35	—	—	0.21	0.00	(0.07)
Annual Growth	212.9%	—		106.5%	—	—

Natus Medical Inc.

Natus Medical designs and manufactures audiological and neurological diagnostic and screening products. While the company's focus has historically been on infants (newborn hearing screening neonatal monitoring) it has expanded its product line to include an array of screening and diagnostic systems for use with children and adults. Its systems detect such neurological conditions as epilepsy and balance and sleep disorders. Natus also manufactures newborn and infant care products to diagnose and treat brain injury and jaundice. The company sells its wares worldwide through a direct sales force and distributors.

Operations

Natus Medical technically operates in one reportable segment —health care products for the screening detection treatment and monitoring of medical ailments in newborn care hearing impairment neurological dysfunction epilepsy sleep disorders and balance and mobility disorders. Within that segment Natus sells devices which generally generate non-recurring revenue and supplies and services which generally generate recurring revenue.

Geographic Reach

The company sells its products in more than 100 countries worldwide. The US contributes about 60% of Natus' revenues.

Sales and Marketing

Natus Medical sells in the US primarily through a direct sales force though certain products are sold under private-label and distribution arrangements. Internationally the company sells some products through direct sales channels in Canada French and German speaking parts of Europe Denmark and parts of Latin America. Other products are sold in those markets and other international markets through distributors who purchase products from Natus and resell them to end users or sub-distributors. End users include hospitals clinics labs physicians nurses audiologists and government agencies.

Mergers and Acquisitions

Natus Medical has been an acquisitive company since 2003 and on average makes one to two strategic acquisitions per year. More recent acquisitions include the 2013 purchase of the Grass Technologies Product Group from Astro-Med for $18.6 million in cash which builds upon Natus' 2011 acquisition of Denver-based Embla Systems for $16.6 million in cash; both deals broaden Natus' existing diagnostic sleep analysis (polysomnography or PSG) product portfolio.

In early 2017 the company acquired GN Otometrics from GN ReSound for $145 million. Natus plans to commercialize the Otometrics digital ear scanner OTOSCAN.

EXECUTIVES

President and CEO, James B. Hawkins, age 60, $500,000 total compensation
Vice President Medical Affairs Research and Development Engineering, Christopher (Chris) Chung
VP and General Manager Newborn Care, Kenneth M. Traverso, age 55, $302,875 total compensation
VP Medical Affairs Quality and Regulatory, D. Christopher Chung, age 52, $257,000 total compensation
SVP and CFO, Jonathan A. Kennedy, age 45, $350,000 total compensation
VP and General Manager Neurology, Austin Noll, $265,000 total compensation
VP Global Engineering, Ajay A. Bhave
Vice President of Sales, Marybeth Smith
Chairman, Robert A. (Bob) Gunst, age 67
Auditors: KPMG LLP

LOCATIONS

HQ: Natus Medical Inc.
6701 Koll Center Parkway, Suite 120, Pleasanton, CA 94566
Phone: 925 223-6700
Web: www.natus.com

PRODUCTS/OPERATIONS

2015 Sales

	% of total
Neurology	
Devices & systems	45
Supplies	16
Services	2
Newborn care	
Devices & systems	20
Supplies	13
Services	4
Total	**100**

Selected Acquisitions

COMPETITORS

Astro-Med	Electrical Geodesics
Bio-logic	GE Healthcare
CAS Medical	Johnson & Johnson
CareFusion	Medela
Cleveland Medical	Starkey Laboratories
Deroyal Industries	Welch Allyn
Drägerwerk	

HISTORICAL FINANCIALS
Company Type: Public

Income Statement
FYE: December 31

	REVENUE ($ mil.)	NET INCOME ($ mil.)	NET PROFIT MARGIN	EMPLOYEES
12/15	375.8	37.9	10.1%	1,067.0
12/14	355.8	32.4	9.1%	948.0
12/13	344.1	22.8	6.6%	943.0
12/12	292.2	3.8	1.3%	1,028.0
12/11	232.6	(11.7)	—	835.0
Annual Growth	12.7%	—	—	6.3%

2015 Year-End Financials

Debt ratio: —
Return on equity: 10.2%
Cash ($ mil.): 82.4
Current ratio: 3.13
Long-term debt ($ mil.): —

No. of shares (mil.): 33.1
Dividends
Yield: —
Payout: —
Market value ($ mil.): 1,593.0

	STOCK PRICE ($) FY Close	P/E High/Low		PER SHARE ($) Earnings	Dividends	Book Value
12/15	48.05	43	29	1.14	0.00	11.78
12/14	36.04	35	22	1.00	0.00	10.80
12/13	22.50	30	15	0.74	0.00	9.75
12/12	11.16	103	76	0.13	0.00	8.93
12/11	9.43	—	—	(0.41)	0.00	8.75
Annual Growth	50.2%	—		—	—	7.7%

Nautilus Inc

Nautilus wants to pump you up. The company makes and markets cardio and strength-building fitness equipment for home use. Its products include home gyms free weights and benches treadmills exercise bikes and elliptical machines that are sold under the popular brand names Bowflex Nautilus Schwinn Fitness and Universal. Nautilus sells its fitness equipment directly to consumers through its variety of brand websites and catalogs as well as through TV commercials. The company also markets its gear through specialty retailers in the US and Canada. Nautilus exited the commercial fitness category in recent years so that it could focus entirely on providing gear that consumers can use at home.

Operations

The company operates its fitness equipment business through a pair of reportable segments. Its Direct segment (64% of revenue) sells products directly to consumers through TV advertising the Internet and catalogs. As part of its Retail segment (34%) Nautilus sells products through a network of third-party retailers that operate websites and stores located in the US and internationally.

Geographic Reach

Nautilus operates in the US and Canada with warehouse and distribution facilities located in Oregon and Ohio in the US and in Manitoba in Canada.

The US accounts for about 85% of revenue.

Sales and Marketing

Nautilus sells its products to fitness enthusiasts and to those who want to work out regularly. It sells through two sales channels: direct and retail.

In 2014 it spent about $42.6 million on advertising and expenses.

Financial Analysis

Revenue which has been on a steady upward trajectory for five years rose 25% to $274 million in 2014 on the strength of new products. But net income which has fluctuated over the years was hit by spending on selling and marketing and plummeted 61% to $18.8 million

Strategy

Mostly because it had been largely unprofitable Nautilus opted to exit its commercial fitness business to focus on its core consumer fitness segment and the direct marketing model which have been key to its growth. The deep recession in the US had urged consumers to redirect spending to mostly essential goods and pushed commercial customers to cut back on equipment purchases.

EXECUTIVES

CEO and Director, Bruce M. Cazenave, age 61, $375,000 total compensation
COO, William B. McMahon, age 51, $250,000 total compensation
CFO, Sid Nayar
Vice President General Manager Direct, Robert O. (Rob) Murdock, $180,000 total compensation
Chairman, M. Carl Johnson
Auditors: Deloitte & Touche LLP

LOCATIONS

HQ: Nautilus Inc
17750 S.E. 6th Way, Vancouver, WA 98683
Phone: 360 859-2900
Web: www.nautilusinc.com

PRODUCTS/OPERATIONS

2014 Sales

	% of total
Direct	64
Retail	34
Royalty income	2
Total	**100**

Selected Brands

Bowflex
Nautilus
Schwinn Fitness
Universal

COMPETITORS

Amer Sports	ICON Health
Beachbody	Life Fitness
Cybex International	Precor
Dorel Industries	adidas
Escalade	

HISTORICAL FINANCIALS

Company Type: Public

Income Statement

FYE: December 31

	REVENUE ($ mil.)	NET INCOME ($ mil.)	NET PROFIT MARGIN	EMPLOYEES
12/15	335.7	26.6	7.9%	470.0
12/14	274.4	18.8	6.8%	340.0
12/13	218.8	47.9	21.9%	311.0
12/12	193.9	16.8	8.7%	310.0
12/11	180.4	1.4	0.8%	320.0
Annual Growth	**16.8%**	**108.0%**	**—**	**10.1%**

2015 Year-End Financials

Debt ratio: 5.0%
Return on equity: 22.3%
Cash ($ mil.): 60.7
Current ratio: 1.73
Long-term debt ($ mil.): —
No. of shares (mil.): 31.0
Dividends
Yield: —
Payout: —
Market value ($ mil.): 518.0

	STOCK PRICE ($) FY Close	P/E High/Low		PER SHARE ($) Earnings	Dividends	Book Value
12/15	16.72	27	17	0.84	0.00	4.10
12/14	15.18	25	13	0.59	0.00	3.54
12/13	8.43	6	2	1.52	0.00	2.94
12/12	3.51	7	3	0.55	0.00	1.40
12/11	1.75	65	28	0.05	0.00	1.04
Annual Growth	**75.8%**	**—**	**—**	**102.5%**	**—**	**40.9%**

Navigators Group Inc (The)

The Navigators Group writes specialty lines of insurance and reinsurance to clients whom it hopes are good navigators themselves. The company's various subsidiaries write marine liability and other lines of business primarily in the US and the UK. Its Navigators Insurance and Navigators Underwriting Agency (NUA) units specialize in ocean marine insurance including hull energy and cargo insurance as well as property insurance for inland marine and onshore energy concerns. Navigators Specialty primarily provides excess and surplus (high risk) lines. The firm's subsidiaries are also involved in professional liability especially directors' and officers' coverage as well as general liability for contractors.

Operations In early 2015 Navigator realigned its reporting structure creating four primary segments that align with the types of coverage it writes: US Insurance International Insurance Global Reinsurance and Corporate.Navigators' global product lines are distributed through a network of retail and wholesale brokers. In addition to its specialty property/casualty insurance and reinsurance policies the company and its subsidiaries provide catastrophe risk management services.In the International Insurance segment NUA serves as a Lloyd's of London underwriting agency managing Lloyd's Syndicate 1221. The unit primarily underwrites marine and related lines of business along with off-shore energy professional liability insurance and construction coverage for onshore energy businesses.

Geographic Reach

Outside its core markets of the US and the UK Navigators has operations in several European nations such as Belgium Denmark and Sweden mainly through NUA's activity on the European Lloyd's of London insurance exchange (via Lloyd's Syndicate 1221). The firm has also established offices in emerging markets such as Brazil and China.

Financial Performance

Revenue which has largely been on the rise for the past five years rose 12% to $1 billion in 2014 on higher net written premiums and investment income. Net written premiums increased 12.6% that year due to higher retention rates in the reinsurance business as well as growth in gross written property/casualty premiums.

Net income on the other hand has been more erratic than revenue. In 2014 it grew 50% to $95 million thanks primarily to Navigator's higher revenue. Cash flow from operations has been growing every year and in 2014 it rose 63% to $222 million.

Strategy

The company is focused on strengthening and controlling costs within its existing operations. At the same time Navigators is looking for opportunities to expand into new niche coverage areas and regions aiming for underserved commercial markets with high-value assets and low-frequency loss levels.

As such in 2014 principal underwriting agency subsidiary Navigators Management Company launched NAVSecure a new cyber liability privacy and date breach coverage product. It also added to its specialty professional liability offerings with the new Allied Healthcare Errors & Omissions product.

To boost operations abroad European underwriting management subsidiary Navigators Underwriting opened new offices in Paris; Milan Italy; and Rotterdam The Netherlands in 2014.

EXECUTIVES

President CEO and Director and Chair Navigators Insurance and Navigators Management, Stanley A. (Stan) Galanski, age 57, $1,000,000 total compensation
Senior Vice President and General Counsel, Emily B (Em) Miner
SVP and Chief Underwriting Officer, H. Clay Bassett, age 50, $525,000 total compensation
President Navigators Technical Risk, Stephen R. Coward, age 62, $319,950 total compensation
President and CEO Navigators Management Company Inc., Vincent C. Tizzio, age 49, $570,833 total compensation
President International Insurance, Michael J. Casella, age 55
President Navigators Specialty, Jeff L. Saunders, $412,500 total compensation
SVP and CFO, Ciro M. DeFalco, age 60, $780,833 total compensation
SVP and Chief Marketing Officer, LoriAnn V. Lowery-Biggers, age 49
Managing Director Asia, Jon Doherty
Vice President And Corporate Treasurer, Ellen (Elle) Dion
Vice President, Rocco Malandrino
Vice President and Underwriting Officer, Chuck (Chucky) Seymour
Vice President and Group Controller, George (Georgey) Iacono

Vice President, Robert (Bob) Hatcher
East Coast Zonal Vice President Environmental Division, Paul Dastis
Senior Vice President and Chief Administrative Officer, R Eisdorfer
Vice President, Andrew (Andy) Dicob
Vice President of Application Development, Roger (Rog) Horvath
Senior Vice President, David (Dave) Stevenson
Chairman, Terence N. Deeks, age 76
Auditors: KPMG LLP

LOCATIONS

HQ: Navigators Group Inc (The)
   400 Atlantic Street, Stamford, CT 06901
Phone: 203 905-6090
Web: www.navg.com

PRODUCTS/OPERATIONS

2014 Gross Written premiums

	% of total
Insurance companies	75
Lloyd's Operations	25
Total	**100**

2014 Sales

	$ mil
% of total	
Net earned premiums	91
Net investment income	7
Net realized gains	1
Others	1
Total	**100**

Selected Subsidiaries

Millennium Underwriting Ltd. (UK)
Navigators A/S (Denmark)
Navigators Corporate Underwriters Ltd. (UK)
Navigators Holdings (UK) Ltd.
Navigators Insurance Company
Navigators Management Company Inc.
Navigators Management (UK) Limited
Navigators NV (Belgium)
Navigators Specialty Insurance Company
Navigators Underwriting Agency Ltd. (UK)
Navigators Underwriting Limited (UK)
NUAL AB (Sweden)

Selected Products and Services: Commercial Surety

Standard Transactional
Non Standard Transactional
Account
Program
Energy and Engineering
Onshore Energy
Offshore Energy
Construction
Operational Engineering
Excess Casualty
Umbrella & Excess (Wholesale Brokerage)
Umbrella & Excess (Retail Agency)
Environmental Casualty
Contractors Pollution Liability
Site Pollution Legal Liability
NP3 sm General & Environmental Liability (Mfg. & Distributors)
NP4 sm General Environmental & Professional Liability (Env'l Consultants)
Environmental Excess
Inland Marine
Commercial Output Policy
Construction
Specialty
Transportation
Management Liability
Directors & Officers Liability
Employment Practices Liability
Fiduciary Liability
Crime Liability
Nonprofit D & O Liability

Marine
Bluewater Hull
Brownwater Hull
Cargo
Specie
Transportation
Marine & Energy Liability
War
Protection & Indemnity
Primary Casualty
General Liability
NAVIGATORS RE
Accident & Health
Agriculture
Latin American & Caribbean
Professional Liability Reinsurance
Property & Casualty
Life Sciences
Global Package Solutions
Commercial Auto
Professional Liability
Lawyers Professional Liability
Accountants Professional Liability
Miscellaneous Professional Liability
Insurance Agents & Brokers E&O
Technology Media & Cyber Liability
Design Professionals Liability
Real Estate Professionals E&O

COMPETITORS

AIG
AXA Corporate Solutions
Allianz
Amica Mutual
Arch Insurance Group
Aspen Insurance
Berkshire Hathaway
CNA Financial
Global Indemnity
ProSight Specialty Insurance Group
RLI
Safeco
Specialty Underwriters' Alliance
Travelers Companies
White Mountains Insurance Group
XL Group plc
Zurich American

HISTORICAL FINANCIALS

Company Type: Public

Income Statement

FYE: December 31

	ASSETS ($ mil.)	NET INCOME ($ mil.)	INCOME AS % OF ASSETS	EMPLOYEES
12/15	4,584.0	81.0	1.8%	675.0
12/14	4,464.1	95.3	2.1%	651.0
12/13	4,169.4	63.4	1.5%	596.0
12/12	4,007.6	63.7	1.6%	567.0
12/11	3,670.0	25.6	0.7%	522.0
Annual Growth	**5.7%**	**33.4%**	**—**	**6.6%**

2015 Year-End Financials

Return on assets: 1.7%	Dividends
Return on equity: 7.6%	Yield: —
Long-term debt ($ mil.): —	Payout: —
No. of shares (mil.): 28.8	Market value ($ mil.): 2,476.0
Sales ($ mil): 1,058.9	

	STOCK PRICE ($) FY Close	P/E High/Low	Earnings	Dividends	Book Value
12/15	85.79	31 24	2.74	0.00	37.98
12/14	73.34	22 17	3.26	0.00	35.96
12/13	63.16	30 23	2.21	0.00	31.77
12/12	51.07	24 20	2.23	0.00	31.31
12/11	47.68	64 46	0.85	0.00	28.78
Annual Growth	**15.8%**	**— —**	**34.1%**	**—**	**7.2%**

NCI Building Systems, Inc.

NCI's buildings could be considered quite a "steel." NCI Building Systems also known as NCI Group engineers designs manufactures and distributes metal components (doors roofs walls and trim) and engineered building systems for nonresidential construction markets in North America. It sells its products to contractors developers and builders. The group also provides metal coil coating which is used by manufacturers of HVAC systems lighting fixtures and appliances. NCI has more than 40 manufacturing facilities in the US China and Mexico and operates distribution and sales offices in the US and Canada. Investment firm Clayton Dubilier & Rice owns NCI Group.

OperationsNCI operates three business segments. Its Metal Components segment which generated 50% of its total revenue during fiscal 2015 (ended November 1) makes and sells metal roof and wall systems as well as metal partitions trims doors and related accessories for use in industrial commercial institutional agricultural and rural markets. The Engineered Building Systems segment (37% of revenue) makes structural members and heavy-gauge plate steel panels designed to reinforce a building's framing from the stresses of the roof and walls to the external load pressures. The group's Metal Coil Coating segment (13% of revenue) cleans treats and paints different types of flat-rolled metals. It also provides metal embossing and slitting services.Geographic ReachThe Houston Texas-based group operates 42 manufacturing facilities in the US Mexico and China (as of early 2016) and has sales and distribution offices across the US and Canada. About 94% of its revenue came from sales in the US during 2015 while another 5% came from sales in Canada and less than 1% came from Mexico and other countries.Sales and MarketingThe majority of NCI's engineered building systems are made through its authorized builder networks and are mostly sold to builders general contractors developers and end users working in the commercial industrial agricultural government and community markets (non-residential markets). NCI's Metal Components business which targets the same markets sells to regional building manufacturers general contractors and subcontractors as well as to lumberyards and cooperative buying groups. The Metal Coil Coating segment sells its products mostly to original equipment manufacturer customers.The group has been ramping up its advertising spend in recent years. It spent $8.6 million on advertising in fiscal 2015 (ended November 1) up from $7.6 million and $6.6 million in 2014 and 2013 respectively.Financial PerformanceNCI's annual revenues have risen more than 60% since 2011 as the construction and commercial real estate markets have boosted demand for its products. It's also come back from losses in 2011 and 2013 as it's managed to keep its operating and overhead costs in check.The group's sales climbed 14% to $1.5 billion during fiscal 2015 (ended November 1 2015) mostly thanks to the Metal Components segment's acquisition of CENTRIA which also added increased tonnage sales volumes (specifically for single-skin products). The group's Metal Coil Coating segment sales declined 6% while Engineered Building Systems sales were down less than 1% for the year. Most of the sales growth came from the

US where sales grew 17% while the rest came from double-digit sales growth in Mexico. Sales in Canada fell by 21%.Strong revenue growth in FY2015 drove NCI's net income up 59% to $17.8 million. The group's operating cash levels more than tripled to $105 million in FY2015 mostly on strong cash earnings growth and positive working capital changes mainly related to a rise in accounts payable balances. StrategyWith its eye toward a stronger market position and increased sales and profitability NCI Group planned in 2016 to push four main initiatives including: leveraging automation and supply chain efficiencies to become "one of the lowest cost producers"; pushing its Engineered Building Systems segment to provide a "total value building solution" for customers; grow its customer base to expand on its top position in the Metal Components business; and diversify its Metal Coil Coating segment's external customer base and national footprint with plans to become a low-cost producer and grow its non-construction sales as a supply chain partner to national manufacturers. NCI also looks for opportunistic acquisitions that expand its service lines and bolster its market share.Mergers and AcquisitionsIn January 2015 NCI Building Systems strengthened its market position after purchasing Pennsylvania-based CENTRIA which made architectural insulated metal panel (IMP) wall and roof systems and provided coil coating services. The $245 million deal added CENTRIA's four manufacturing facilities in the US and another in China.

HISTORY

Company BackgroundNCI Building Systems' founder Johnie Schulte Jr. began his career in the mid-1950s when he landed a job punching and shearing metal building pieces in Houston. In 1984 he founded NCI. The enterprise made only metal building components until 1987 when it began making metal buildings. That year NCI had sales of about $2 million. The company went public in 1992 and a year later its sales had reached more than $130 million. While competitors were shuttering plants in the soft market of the early 1990s NCI was buying companies —including its 1992 purchase of A&S Building Systems a metal building maker based in Caryville Tennessee. NCI later expanded its product line to include self-storage buildings. It entered the market for roll-up steel overhead doors in 1995 when it bought Doors & Building Components (also a maker of interior steel parts) and started its own line of steel-frame homes.

The company continued to make acquisitions in 1996 picking up a metal stud plant in Texas from Alabama Metal Industries the equipment of Carlisle Engineered Metals and Mesco Metal Buildings. The next year it bought the rest of Carlisle including a manufacturing plant in Alabama and began a 51%-owned joint venture in Mexico to manufacture framing systems. NCI bought the US metal building components business of UK-based BTR in 1998 for $593 million doubling its size and adding painting and coating capabilities. The company spent 1999 integrating the large business.

NCI bought out Consolidated System's share in their DOUBLECOTE metal coil-coating joint venture for $26 million in 2000. Later that year NCI bought Midland Metals a maker of metal building components. The move strengthened NCI's presence in the Midwest.

In 2001 NCI sold its 50% interest in Midwest Metal Coatings to its joint venture partner. The company closed five manufacturing facilities during the first quarter of fiscal 2002. NCI launched

into direct selling to the public by opening a series of NCI Metal Depot retail factory stores that offer commercial and residential metal components (metal roof and wall panels light structural and tubing shapes and accessories) and a variety of small metal building packages (carports storage sheds and other metal buildings).

The company opened two retail stores in Texas in fiscal 2003. Also that year NCI entered the residential garage door market by acquiring Texas-based Able Manufacturing and Wholesale Garage Door Company for about $3.3 million. NCI shortened the company's name to Able Door Manufacturing. Able operates distribution centers in the Dallas Atlanta and Oklahoma City areas and in Ontario California.

Founder president and CEO Johnie Schulte Jr. retired as an executive in November 2003 and retired as a director the next year; he was succeeded by A. R. Ginn. The following year NCI filed a suit against Schulte alleging he had violated non-competitive agreements. Schulte filed a countersuit; an undisclosed settlement was reached in 2005.

To expand its retail and builder distribution channels for its small engineered buildings NCI bought North Little Rock Arkansas-based Heritage Building Systems and Steelbuilding.com for approximately $30 million in 2004. NCI also acquired the 49% minority stake held by its partners in its manufacturing plant in Monterrey Mexico.

The next year NCI bought the intellectual property rights of metal building and components maker STEELOX Systems of Ohio gaining the patents and trademarks copyrights common law rights names logos websites and customer lists of the established (by more than 70 years) company.

In 2006 NCI paid $370 million in cash for metal buildings maker Robertson-Ceco Corporation and its Robertson Building Systems Ceco Building Systems Star Building Systems and Steelspec divisions. Late that year Ginn stepped down as CEO with president and COO Norm Chambers becoming president and CEO. The next year Chambers assumed the chairmanship. NCI also bought Garco Building Systems in 2007.

EXECUTIVES

Vice President Of Corporate Purchasing, Mark (Marky) Golladay
Chairman and CEO, Norman C. (Norm) Chambers, age 67, $781,731 total compensation
EVP General Counsel and Corporate Secretary, Todd R. Moore, age 57, $326,923 total compensation
EVP and CIO, Eric J. Brown, age 59
EVP CFO and Treasurer, Mark E. Johnson, age 50, $387,500 total compensation
President Group Manufacturing Segment, John L. Kuzdal, age 51
EVP Strategic Initiatives, Richard W. Allen, age 41
President, Donald R. (Don) Riley
Vice President, Fred (Freddy) Schubert
Vice President Scm, Dan Ronchetto
Vice President Engineering, Stephen (Steve) Heil
Vice President Of Finance Components Div, Mark (Marky) Shearer
Vice President Finance, Chico Doughtie
Vice President Technical Services, Jerry Williams
Auditors: Ernst & Young LLP

LOCATIONS

HQ: NCI Building Systems, Inc.
10943 North Sam Houston Parkway West, Houston, TX 77064
Phone: 281 897-7788
Web: www.ncilp.com

PRODUCTS/OPERATIONS

2015 Sales by Segment

	$ mil.	% of total
Metal components	920.9	50
Engineered building systems 667.2		37
Metal coil coating	231.7	13
Adjustments	(256.1)	-
Total	**1,563.7**	**100**

Selected Brands

A&S
All American
American Building Components (ABC)
Ceco
Doors and Buildings Components (DBCI)
Garco
Heritage
IPS
MBCI
Metallic
Metal Coaters
Metal Depots
Metal Prep
Mesco
Mid-West Steel
Star
SteelBuilding.com
Steel Systems

Selected Subsidiaries

Building Systems de México S.A. de C.V.
NCI Group Inc.
Robertson Building Systems Limited (Canada)
Robertson-Ceco II Corporation
Steelbuilding.com Inc.

Selected Products and Services

Metal building components and complete buildings (carports utility buildings etc.)
Metal cladding and accessories
Mini-storage buildings
Modular offices
Roll-up doors partitions and panels

COMPETITORS

American Buildings	Gibraltar Industries
Berger Building	Horton Homes
Products	Johns Manville
Berlin Steel	Nucor
Butler Manufacturing	Overhead Door
Design Components	Varco Pruden Buildings
G-I Holdings	Williams Scotsman

HISTORICAL FINANCIALS

Company Type: Public

Income Statement

FYE: October 30

	REVENUE ($ mil.)	NET INCOME ($ mil.)	NET PROFIT MARGIN	EMPLOYEES
10/16*	1,684.9	51.0	3.0%	5,500.0
11/15	1,563.6	17.8	1.1%	5,326.0
11/14	1,371.8	11.1	0.8%	4,556.0
11/13	1,309.4	(12.8)	—	4,484.0
10/12	1,154.0	4.9	0.4%	4,293.0
Annual Growth	**9.9%**	**79.5%**	**—**	**6.4%**

*Fiscal year change

2016 Year-End Financials

Debt ratio: 38.2%	No. of shares (mil.): 70.8
Return on equity: 18.5%	Dividends
Cash ($ mil.): 65.4	Yield: —
Current ratio: 1.55	Payout: —
Long-term debt ($ mil.): 404.1	Market value ($ mil.): 1,020.0

	STOCK PRICE ($) FY Close	P/E High/Low		PER SHARE ($) Earnings	Dividends	Book Value
10/16*	14.40	25	13	0.70	0.00	3.97
11/15	10.46	83	41	0.24	0.00	3.67
11/14	19.87	141	97	0.15	0.00	3.35
11/13	14.45	—	—	(0.29)	0.00	3.38
10/12	11.24	—	—	(3.81)	0.00	12.25
Annual Growth (24.5%)	6.4%	—	—	—	—	

*Fiscal year change

Neff Corp (New)

Auditors: Deloitte & Touche LLP

LOCATIONS

HQ: Neff Corp (New)
3750 N.W. 87th Avenue, Suite 400, Miami, FL 33178
Phone: 305 513-3350
Web: www.neffrental.com

HISTORICAL FINANCIALS

Company Type: Public

Income Statement

FYE: December 31

	REVENUE ($ mil.)	NET INCOME ($ mil.)	NET PROFIT MARGIN	EMPLOYEES
12/15	383.8	15.5	4.1%	1,100.0
12/14	371.9	1.6	0.4%	1,064.0
12/13	327.2	40.4	12.4%	1,061.0
12/12	290.9	17.5	6.0%	0.0
Annual Growth	9.7%	(3.8%)	—	—

2015 Year-End Financials

Debt ratio: 111.7%
Return on equity: —
Cash ($ mil.): 0.2
Current ratio: 3.82
Long-term debt ($ mil.): 730.5

No. of shares (mil.): 25.3
Dividends
  Yield: —
  Payout: —
Market value ($ mil.): 194.0

	STOCK PRICE ($) FY Close	P/E High/Low		PER SHARE ($) Earnings	Dividends	Book Value
12/15	7.66	8	4	1.29	0.00	(3.73)
12/14	11.27	100	70	0.13	0.00	(4.34)
12/13	0.00	—	—	4.14	0.00	0.34
Annual Growth	—	—	—	(44.2%)	—	—

Neogen Corp.

Bacteriophobes have a friend in Neogen a maker of products for the food safety and animal health markets. Its food safety testing products are used by the food industry to make sure our edibles are clean unspoiled and free of toxins pathogens and allergens. In core markets in the Americas and Europe Neogen reaches end users (including dairies meat processors and animal feed producers) through a direct sales force; it uses distributors elsewhere. On the animal health front Neogen produces drugs vaccines diagnostics and instruments for the veterinary market; it also makes rat poisons and disinfectants used in animal production plants and diagnostic products for research laboratories.

OperationsSome of the company's best-selling food-safety testing products include its Reveal and Alert tests used by meat poultry and seafood processors to detect food-borne bacteria. Others include its Veratox Agre-Screen and Reveal tests which are used by grain producers to detect mycotoxins (toxins produced by fungi).When it comes to animals lead products include PanaKare a digestive aid; RenaKare a supplement for potassium deficiency in cats and dogs; and the NeogenVet brand including Vita-15 and Liver 7 which are used for the treatment and prevention of nutritional deficiencies in horses. Sales in its Animal Safety unit accounted for more than half of Neogen's revenue in 2015.Neogen also provides genomic services in Nebraska.

Geographic Reach

The firm's animal products are sold to distributors around the world as well as through farm supply retailers in North America. International sales of all of its products account for about 40% of Neogen's sales.

The company has manufacturing plants in Michigan Kentucky Wisconsin North Carolina and Iowa as well as in Scotland.Sales and Marketing-Neogen sells its products through a direct sales force in North America parts of Europe Mexico Brazil and China. Elsewhere it sells through independent distributors. The company has some 20000 customers.In 2015 advertising expenses totaled $1.4 million up from $1.3 million in 2014 and $1.1 million in 2013.Financial Performance

Neogen continued its growth trend by reporting a 14% increase in revenues from $247 million to $284 million in fiscal 2015 (ended May) due to strong product sales in both the food safety and animal safety segments. Part of the growth was from October 2014 acquisition of BioLumix which makes products to detect spoilage in supplements and cosmetics. Two animal health acquisitions (veterinary instruments firms SyrVet and Prima Tech) acquired in fiscal 2014 also contributed to the growth in revenue.

Net income has also been on the rise. In 2015 it rose 19% to $33 million thanks to the company's strong earnings. Cash flow from operations which has been in flux doubled in 2015 to $44 million.

Strategy

Though the company has primarily used acquisitions to achieve relatively rapid growth Neogen is also looking for organic growth over the longer term through new product introductions higher sales of existing products international expansion efforts (it has made strides in India and China as of late) and the formation of strategic alliances. Neogen has ongoing development projects for new diagnostic tests and other complementary products for both the food safety and animal safety markets. The company also sees its over-the-counter animal health products as being particularly ripe for growth and because of that it seeks to increase its line of rodenticides disinfectants instruments and horse care products.

In late 2014 further growing its Asia operations Neogen acquired its Chinese distribution partner Beijing Anapure BioScientific. The company believes that having a direct presence in the area will help it as it works on expansion in the region.

The following year Neogen launched an enhanced version of its AccuPoint ATP Hygiene Monitoring System which food and beverage producers use to monitor sanitation efforts.

Mergers and Acquisitions

In 2014 Neogen acquired pest control manufacturing firm Chem-Tech for $17 million. Later that year it bought the food safety and veterinary genomic operations of its Chinese distributor Beijing Anapure BioScientific for $2 million.

In order to accelerate its business growth in critical global food safety markets Neogen acquired the assets of commercial food testing lab Sterling Test House in southwest India in 2015. The lab will serve as the base for the company's new India operations. Also that year Neogen acquired Lab M Holdings in the UK. Lab M develops and manufactures microbiological culture media and diagnostic systems which will boost Neogen's Acumedia product line.

Neogen closed out 2015 with the purchase of Virbac Corporation's rodenticide assets. The deal included an active ingredient complementary to Neogen's existing portfolio of biosecurity ingredients plus more than 40 regulatory approvals for formulations in North America.

In 2016 the company acquired sister entities Preserve International and Tetradyne which provide disinfectant and related products for the livestock and food processing industries. It also bought UK-based Quat-Chem which develops and manufactures disinfectants and cleaners for dairy poultry and swine biosecurity applications. Later that year it acquired Brazilian firm Rogama which develops and manufactures rodenticides and insecticides. These three deals helped boost Neogen's growing biosecurity business.

EXECUTIVES

Chairman and CEO, James L. Herbert, age 76, $370,000 total compensation
VP and CFO, Steven J. (Steve) Quinlan, age 53, $191,000 total compensation
VP Food Safety Operations, Edward L. Bradley, age 56, $167,000 total compensation
VP Animal Safety Operations, Terri A. Morrical, age 51, $165,000 total compensation
President and COO, Richard E. (Rick) Calk
National Accounts Manager, Lisa Peterson
Vice President Plant Improvement, Dave (Davie) Melton
Auditors: BDO USA, LLP

LOCATIONS

HQ: Neogen Corp.
620 Lesher Place, Lansing, MI 48912
Phone: 517 372-9200   **Fax:** 517 372-0108
Web: www.neogen.com

PRODUCTS/OPERATIONS

2015 Sales

	$ mil.	% of total
Animal safety	151.6	54
Food safety	131.5	46
Total	283.1	100

2015 Sales

	$ mil.	% of total
Food safety		
Natural toxins allergens drug residues	60.6	21
Dehydrated culture media & other	41.1	15
Bacterial & general sanitation	29.8	11
Animal safety		
Rodenticides insecticides & disinfectants	45.9	16
Animal care & other	35.0	12
Veterinary instruments & disposables	34.3	12
DNA testing	27.7	10
Life sciences & other	8.7	3
Total	283.1	100

Selected Products

Food safety
  AccuClean (detects proteins and sugars)
  AccuPoint (rapid sanitation test)
  AgriScreen (detects mycotoxins)
  Alert (detects food-borne bacteria food allergens)
  Beta Star (detects antibiotics in milk)
  BioKits (detects allergens in food; also used for species identification)
  GeneQuence (detects food-borne bacteria)
  Reveal (detects food-borne bacteria food allergens ruminant by-products)
  Soleris (detects spoilage organisms)
  Veratox (detects mycotoxins food allergens)
Animal safety
  AgTek (Kane) products (apparel accessories etc.)
  BioSentry (chemicals)
  CyKill (rodent control)
  Di-Kill (rodent control)
  ElectroJac (automated semen collection)
  Havoc (rodenticide)
  Ideal (animal health products and instruments)
  NeogenVet (animal health products)
  Prozap (rodenticide)
  Ramik (rodenticide)
  Rodex (rodenticide)
  Squire (animal health products)

COMPETITORS

American Animal Health	Merck Animal Health
Bayer Animal Health	Merial
Celldex Therapeutics	Novartis
Ecolab	Orchid Cellmark
Eurofins Scientific	Pfizer
Hartz Mountain	Phibro Animal Health
Heska	Sdix
IDEXX Labs	Silliker
Life Technologies	Telesta
Corporation	Virbac Corporation
Merck	

HISTORICAL FINANCIALS

Company Type: Public

Income Statement

FYE: May 31

	REVENUE ($ mil.)	NET INCOME ($ mil.)	NET PROFIT MARGIN	EMPLOYEES
05/16	321.2	36.5	11.4%	1,235.0
05/15	283.0	33.5	11.8%	1,062.0
05/14	247.4	28.1	11.4%	926.0
05/13	207.5	27.1	13.1%	781.0
05/12	184.0	22.5	12.2%	746.0
Annual Growth	14.9%	12.9%	—	13.4%

2016 Year-End Financials

Debt ratio: —
Return on equity: 9.6%
Cash ($ mil.): 55.2
Current ratio: 8.74
Long-term debt ($ mil.): —

No. of shares (mil.): 37.5
Dividends
  Yield: —
  Payout: —
Market value ($ mil.): 1,855.0

	STOCK PRICE ($) FY Close	P/E High/Low	Earnings	Dividends	Book Value
05/16	49.37	62 45	0.97	0.00	10.76
05/15	46.74	57 40	0.90	0.00	9.45
05/14	37.79	93 47	0.76	0.00	8.34
05/13	54.47	75 50	0.75	0.00	7.16
05/12	38.94	75 47	0.63	0.00	6.18
Annual Growth	6.1%	— —	11.5%	—	14.9%

Neulion Inc

NeuLion is poised to pounce on Internet-delivered television. The company offers hosted services that allow customers to deliver streaming video over Internet-enabled devices. It works mostly with sports content providers (60% of revenues) such as ESPN the NFL and about 150 NCAA schools but also pay-TV networks and operators such as DISH The Independent Film Channel and Univision to distribute live and on-demand programming over the Internet viewed on personal computers laptops cell phones and televisions. NeuLion gets most of its revenues in the US and Canada but also has offices in London and Shanghai. Chairman Charles Wang and CEO Nancy Li who are married together own more than half of the company.

Although begun in 2000 as a professional IT services company NeuLion changed to its current business model in 2006 so is a relatively early-stage business. As such spending on areas such as marketing development and distribution rights acquisition remain high and profitability elusive.

The development side is particularly important since NeuLion considers its competitive edge as being a one-stop shop. While some competitors focus on certain parts of the video delivery process such as encoding digital rights management or providing the content delivery network NeuLion covers all aspects from end-to-end which includes offering advanced and custom designs in social and interactive experiences for the customer's content. Its many other services include advertising integration auction engines live video editing and tagging interactive television video player design and development app creation game highlights and alerts and customer support services among others.

Its equipment revenue includes sales rental and delivery of set-top-boxes and computer hardware. Most of this revenue (85%) comes from its non-sports (TV Everywhere) customers such as DISH.

Sales in its service revenues segment (more than 80% of total sales) increased 16% in 2011 and saw rises in its professional sports business (up 80%) and TV Everywhere (7%) while college sports sales dropped less than 2% and remaining customer sales fell off 17%.

EXECUTIVES

CFO, Tim Alavathil
Auditors: EisnerAmper LLP

LOCATIONS

HQ: Neulion Inc
  1600 Old Country Road, Plainview, NY 11803
Phone: 516 622-8300
Web: www.neulion.com

PRODUCTS/OPERATIONS

Selected Customers
Professional Sports
  Canadian Football League
  Major League Soccer
  National Basketball Association
  National Football League
  National Hockey League
  Ultimate Fighting Championship
College Sports
  Big 12 Conference
  Dartmouth College
  Duke University

Louisiana State University
Mississippi State University
North Dakota State University
Oral Roberts University
University of Oregon
University of Florida
University of Nebraska
University of North Carolina
Texas A&M University
TV Everywhere
  DISH Networks
  CBC
  Independent Film Channel
  Outdoor Channel
  Sky Angel
  Univision

COMPETITORS

Alcatel-Lucent	Minerva Networks
Avid Technology	Netflix
Cisco Systems	SeaChange
Hulu	YouTube

HISTORICAL FINANCIALS

Company Type: Public

Income Statement

FYE: December 31

	REVENUE ($ mil.)	NET INCOME ($ mil.)	NET PROFIT MARGIN	EMPLOYEES
12/15	94.0	25.9	27.6%	638.0
12/14	55.5	3.5	6.4%	767.0
12/13	47.1	(2.2)	—	453.0
12/12	38.9	(10.0)	—	395.0
12/11	39.6	(14.3)	—	369.0
Annual Growth	24.1%	—	—	14.7%

2015 Year-End Financials

Debt ratio: —
Return on equity: 40.4%
Cash ($ mil.): 53.4
Current ratio: 2.21
Long-term debt ($ mil.): —

No. of shares (mil.): 280.9
Dividends
  Yield: —
  Payout: —
Market value ($ mil.): 152.0

	STOCK PRICE ($) FY Close	P/E High/Low	Earnings	Dividends	Book Value
12/15	0.54	12 4	0.11	0.00	0.38
12/14	1.13	120 48	0.01	0.00	0.11
12/13	0.54	— —	(0.01)	0.00	0.08
12/12	0.23	— —	(0.07)	0.00	0.09
12/11	0.24	— —	(0.10)	0.00	0.13
Annual Growth	21.8%	— —	—	—	31.5%

NeuStar, Inc.

Neustar shines as a key provider of registry and clearinghouse services used in telecommunications and internet networks. The company manages the registry of North American area codes and telephone numbers and the database used by telecom carriers (Verizon AT&T) and cable companies (Comcast Cox Communications) to route phone calls. It is also a leading provider of operations support systems (OSS) clearinghouse services that provide ordering service provisioning billing and customer service functions. In addition Neustar operates an Internet registry supporting domain addresses and provides a host of other registry domain name system and IP services. In June 2016

Neustar said it would split into two public companies.

Change in Company Type

Neustar moved to split its business in two in June 2016. One company will focus on Information Services including Marketing Security and related Data Services while the other company will focus on Order Management & Numbering Services including NPAC (number portability administration center). The latter company will retain the Neustar identity.

As two separate companies each would have a sharper strategic and managerial focus and capital structures and capital allocation policies that suit them according to Neustar. The revenue generated by the information services entity was about $470 million in 2015 while the Order Management & Numbering Services business generated about $580 million.

The split is expected to be year-long process.

Operations Neustar offers such services as database services (telephone number databases domain names short-codes and fixed IP addresses) analytics platforms used for Internet security caller ID web performance monitoring services and real-time information and analytics services.

NPAC Services accounted for 48% of revenue followed by Marketing Services and Security Services 16% each and Data Services 20%.

Geographic Reach The company has more than a half-dozen locations in the US as well as presences in Australia Colombia the UK Costa Rica and India.

Sales and Marketing

In addition to major telecom and cable firms the company counts among its 12000-plus customers emerging telecom and VoIP service providers e-commerce companies information services providers media and advertising groups and domain name registrars such as Go Daddy.

Although no single customer accounts for more than 10% of sales Neustar generates some 48% of revenue under contracts with North American Portability Management an industry group representing all US telecommunications services providers.

Financial Performance The company's revenue grew 9% in 2015 hitting $1 billion as it saw growth in all segments with double-digit growth in marketing services and security services. Acquisitions such as Bombora and MarketShare also pushed revenue higher.

Profits grew 7% to $175 million on 2015's sales.

Mergers and Acquisitions

In 2015 Neustar acquired Bombora Technologies for abut $92 million. The deal expanded Neustar's registry services to include domains such as .au.

Also in 2015 Neustar bought MarketShare Partners a marketing analytics technology provider to major brands. The acquisition of MarketShare Neustar's marketing services with an organizing and planning tool for marketing. The price was about $442.4 million.

With the $173 million purchase of the caller authentication assets of Transaction Network Services Neustar accelerated its capability to provide mobile identity tools and services solutions for service providers businesses and consumers. Offerings include subscriber data storage and management caller identification and verification services.

HISTORY

In 2006 the company bought UltraDNS a Reston Virginia-based provider of Domain Name System (DNS) and directory services in a cash deal valued at $61.8 million. It additionally purchased Followap a mobile instant messaging services provider for $139 million that year.

Neustar acquired Webmetrics a provider of Web and network performance testing services in 2008 for $12.5 million in cash.

EXECUTIVES

President and CEO, Lisa A. Hook, age 57, $747,796 total compensation

SVP Data Solutions, Steven J. (Steve) Edwards, age 57, $398,434 total compensation

SVP and CFO, Paul S. Lalljie, age 43, $478,707 total compensation

SVP Product Information Services, Brian Foster

Vice President Operations and Finance, Rodney (Rod) Joffe

SVP and General Counsel, Leonard (Len) Kennedy, $430,057 total compensation

SVP Internet Of Things, Hank Skorny

Senior Vice President Operations, Alex (Al) Tulchinsky

Vice President Regulatory Affairs, Aaron Goldberger

Vice President of Strategic Technical Initiatives, Tom McGarry

Vice President Business Operat, Randy (Rand) Buffenbarger

Vice President Finance Cost Management, Duane Deason

Vice President Marketing, David Dague

Vice President Technology Strategy, John (Jack) Kelly

Vice President Marketing and Channels, Jean (Jeannie) Foster

Vice President Product Management, Andrew Onufer

Vice President Brand, Angela (Angie) Culver

Vice President Application Development, Greg Greenberg

Vice President Law And Policy, Jeff Neuman

Senior Vice President Marketing, Steve (Stevie) Johnson

Vice President Corporate Development and Managing Director, Sean Corcoran

Vice President Business Development, Greg (Greggy) Roberts

Senior Vice President External Affairs, Gerald Kovach

Vice President Platform Sales, David Pollet

Vice President, Bryan Carter

Vice President Sales, Anthony Mazzarella

Vice President finance Corporate Treasurer, Steve (Stevie) Boyce

Vice President Finance, Kevin (Kev) Welch

Vice President Product Realization, John Keaveney

Senior Vice President And Chief Technology Officer, Mark (Marky) Foster

Vice President of Marketing, Mark (Marky) Ambrose

Vice President Business Development Emea, Steve (Stevie) Sawyer

Vice President, Lori (Lor) Wardi

Vice President Total Rewards, Julie (Jules) Peterson

Vice President Legal, Charles (Chas) Divone

Vice President, John (Jack) Mcqueen

Vice President of Market Development, Tom (Tommy) McNeal

Vice President Sales, Denise (Denny) Hayman

Senior Vice President Engineering and Operations, Peter (Pete) Burke

Chairman, James G. Cullen, age 74

Head Of Investor Relations Assistant Treasurer, David (Dave) Angelicchio

Auditors: Ernst & Young LLP

LOCATIONS

HQ: NeuStar, Inc.
21575 Ridgetop Circle, Sterling, VA 20166
Phone: 571 434-5400
Web: www.neustar.biz

PRODUCTS/OPERATIONS

2015 Sales

	$ mil.	% of total
Marketing services	170.4	16
Security services	168.0	16
Data services	204.0	20
NPAC services	507.1	48
Total	**1.0**	**100**

COMPETITORS

Accenture	Infoblox
Acxiom	Infogroup
Akamai	Keynote Systems
Amdocs	NetCracker Technology
BSG Clearing Solutions	Nielsen
Billing Services Group	Nokia
CGI Group	Oracle
Computer Sciences	Register.com
Corp.	Sodalia North America
Evolving Systems	Synchronoss
F5 Networks	Syniverse
HP	TNS Custom
HP Enterprise Services	Tucows
IBM	VeriSign
ICANN	XIUS-bcgi

HISTORICAL FINANCIALS

Company Type: Public

Income Statement

FYE: December 31

	REVENUE ($ mil.)	NET INCOME ($ mil.)	NET PROFIT MARGIN	EMPLOYEES
12/15	1,049.9	175.4	16.7%	2,125.0
12/14	963.5	163.6	17.0%	1,576.0
12/13	902.0	162.7	18.0%	1,623.0
12/12	831.3	156.0	18.8%	1,543.0
12/11	620.4	160.8	25.9%	1,488.0
Annual Growth	**14.1%**	**2.2%**	**—**	**9.3%**

2015 Year-End Financials

Debt ratio: 49.7%
Return on equity: 26.1%
Cash ($ mil.): 89.1
Current ratio: 0.80
Long-term debt ($ mil.): 959.3
No. of shares (mil.): 53.5
Dividends
  Yield: —
  Payout: —
Market value ($ mil.): 1,283.0

	STOCK PRICE ($) FY Close	P/E High/Low		PER SHARE ($) Earnings	Dividends	Book Value
12/15	23.97	10	7	3.14	0.00	13.52
12/14	27.80	18	9	2.75	0.00	11.24
12/13	49.86	22	17	2.46	0.00	9.60
12/12	41.93	18	13	2.30	0.00	9.77
12/11	34.17	16	10	2.16	0.00	7.60
Annual Growth	**(8.5%)**	**—**	**—**	**9.8%**	**—**	**15.5%**

New Media Investment Group Inc

New Media Investment Group (formerly Gate-House Media) lets the local news flow freely. The company is a leading community-newspaper publisher with more than 400 publications. Its portfolio includes roughly 80 daily newspapers along with many more weeklies and shoppers that reach about 10 million readers. New Media Investment generates revenue primarily through advertising; its papers serve ads from almost 300000 business advertisers. In conjunction with its print publications the company operates more than 600 websites. New Media Investment also produces a half-dozen yellow page directories and offers commercial printing services.

Geographic Reach

New Media Investment operates newspapers and websites in about 20 states.

Operations

The company has three operating segments: advertising circulations and commercial printing. Advertising accounted for almost 70% of revenue in fiscal 2012.

Sales and Marketing

New Media Investment itself reported total advertising expenses of $3.4 million in fiscal 2012.

Financial Performance

The company's revenue decreased 6% and its net loss increased 38% in fiscal 2012 compared with the previous year. The decrease in revenue was attributed to decreases in advertising revenue and circulation revenue partially offset by an increase in commercial printing and other revenue. New Media's net loss increased primarily due to the decrease in total revenue not because of increased operating expenses.

Strategy

The downturn in the economy and the decline of the newspaper industry have forced the company to concentrate mostly on cutting costs streamlining operations and converting to a more multimedia company. The company has tried to improve the productivity of its labor force. New Media Investment also relies on the loyalty of readers interested in local news as about 85% of its newspapers have been around for more than 100 years.

Company Background

New Media Investment was formed in 1997 as Liberty Group Publishing to buy about 160 publications from newspaper giant Hollinger International (later Sun-Times Media Group). It went public in 2006 changing its name in the process.

EXECUTIVES

CFO and Chief Accounting Officer, Gregory W. (Greg) Freiberg, age 48
COO and CEO GateHouse Media, Kirk A. Davis, age 55, $494,785 total compensation
CEO and Director, Michael E. (Mike) Reed, age 50, $500,000 total compensation
CIO GateHouse Media, Paul Ameden
Chairman, Wesley R. (Wes) Edens, age 54
Auditors: Ernst & Young LLP

LOCATIONS

HQ: New Media Investment Group Inc
1345 Avenue of the Americas, New York, NY 10105
Phone: 212 479-3160
Web: www.newmediainv.com

PRODUCTS/OPERATIONS

Selected Daily Newspapers
Daily Messenger (Canandaigua NY)
The Enterprise (Brockton MA)
Evening Tribune (Hornell NY)
The Holland Sentinel (Michigan)
The Independent (Massillon OH)
Journal Star (Peoria IL)
The Leavenworth Times (Kansas)
The Leader (Corning NY)
MetroWest Daily News (Framingham MA)
The Patriot Ledger (Quincy MA)
The Repository (Canton OH)
Rockford Register Star (Illinois)
The State Journal-Register (Springfield IL)
The Times-Reporter (New Philadelphia OH)
Wellsville Daily Reporter (New York)

COMPETITORS

Advance Publications
Community Newspaper
  Holdings
Lee Enterprises
McClatchy Company
New York Times

Schurz Communications
Star Tribune
Sun-Times Media
  Holdings
TEGNA
Tribune Media

HISTORICAL FINANCIALS

Company Type: Public

Income Statement

FYE: December 27

	REVENUE ($ mil.)	NET INCOME ($ mil.)	NET PROFIT MARGIN	EMPLOYEES
12/15	1,195.8	67.6	5.7%	9,509.0
12/14	652.3	(3.2)	—	6,133.0
12/13*	103.2	7.2	7.0%	5,576.0
11/13	413.2	787.4	190.5%	0.0
12/12	488.5	(29.8)	—	4,131.0
Annual Growth 25.1%		—	—	23.2%

*Fiscal year change

2015 Year-End Financials

Debt ratio: 29.7%
Return on equity: 11.9%
Cash ($ mil.): 146.6
Current ratio: 1.89
Long-term debt ($ mil.): 353.4

No. of shares (mil.): 44.7
Dividends
  Yield: 0.0%
  Payout: 84.8%
Market value ($ mil.): 882.0

	STOCK PRICE ($) FY Close	P/E High/Low		PER SHARE ($) Earnings	Dividends	Book Value
12/15	19.73	17	9	1.52	1.29	14.47
12/14	24.09	—	—	(0.10)	0.54	12.92
Annual Growth (18.1%)		—	—	—138.9%	12.0%	

New Mountain Finance Corp

Investment firm New Mountain Finance Corporation won't make its portfolio companies climb over too many hills for a loan. The affiliate of private equity firm New Mountain Capital makes in-vestments of $10 million-$50 million in middle-market companies (those with annual revenues of less than $200 million). Its portfolio is made up of senior secured first-lien and second-lien term loans and subordinated debt. Organized as a business development company (BDC) New Mountain Finance pays little in income taxes as long as it distributes 90% of its profits back to shareholders. It is externally managed by New Mountain Finance Advisers BDC L.L.C. The company went public in 2011.

EXECUTIVES

Managing Director, James (Jamie) Stone
Board Member, Alfred (Alf) Hurley
Auditors: Deloitte & Touche LLP

LOCATIONS

HQ: New Mountain Finance Corp
787 Seventh Avenue, 48th Floor, New York, NY 10019
Phone: 212 720-0300   **Fax:** 212 582-2277
Web: www.newmountainfinance.com

COMPETITORS

Apollo Investment
Fifth Street Finance
Gladstone Capital
Golub Capital BDC
Harris & Harris
Horizon Technology
  Finance
KCAP Financial
MCG Capital

MVC Capital
Medley Capital
PennantPark
Rand Capital
Saratoga Investment
  Corp.
Solar Capital
THL Credit
Triangle Capital

HISTORICAL FINANCIALS

Company Type: Public

Income Statement

FYE: December 31

	REVENUE ($ mil.)	NET INCOME ($ mil.)	NET PROFIT MARGIN	EMPLOYEES
12/15	153.8	82.5	53.6%	0.0
12/14	135.6	80.0	59.0%	0.0
12/13	90.8	50.5	55.6%	0.0
12/12	37.5	19.7	52.8%	0.0
12/11	13.6	8.3	61.1%	0.0
Annual Growth 83.2%		77.3%	—	—

2015 Year-End Financials

Debt ratio: 46.3%
Return on equity: 10.0%
Cash ($ mil.): 30.1
Current ratio: 2.10
Long-term debt ($ mil.): 742.0

No. of shares (mil.): 64.0
Dividends
  Yield: 10.4%
  Payout: 247.2%
Market value ($ mil.): 833.0

	STOCK PRICE ($) FY Close	P/E High/Low		PER SHARE ($) Earnings	Dividends	Book Value
12/15	13.02	28	22	0.55	1.36	13.08
12/14	14.94	14	13	1.10	1.48	13.83
12/13	15.04	—	—	(0.00)	1.48	(0.00)
12/12	14.90	12	10	1.33	1.71	14.06
12/11	13.41	—	—	(0.00)	0.86	(0.00)
Annual Growth (0.7%)		—	—	—	12.1%	—

New Residential Investment Corp

EXECUTIVES

Ceo-pres, Kenneth Riis
Auditors: Ernst & Young LLP

LOCATIONS

HQ: New Residential Investment Corp
  1345 Avenue of the Americas, New York, NY 10105
Phone: 212 798-3150
Web: www.newresi.com

HISTORICAL FINANCIALS

Company Type: Public

Income Statement

	REVENUE ($ mil.)	NET INCOME ($ mil.)	NET PROFIT MARGIN	EMPLOYEES
12/15	371.0	281.8	76.0%	0.0
12/14	206.1	442.1	214.5%	0.0
12/13	72.5	265.6	366.2%	0.0
12/12	33.0	41.2	124.8%	0.0
12/11	1.2	0.7	56.7%	0.0
Annual Growth	314.3%	345.8%	—	—

FYE: December 31

2015 Year-End Financials

Debt ratio: 47.7%
Return on equity: 12.8%
Cash ($ mil.): 249.9
Current ratio: 0.36
Long-term debt ($ mil.): 7,249.5

No. of shares (mil.): 230.4
Dividends
  Yield: 14.3%
  Payout: 142.2%
Market value ($ mil.): 2,803.0

	STOCK PRICE ($) FY Close	P/E High/Low		PER SHARE ($) Earnings	Dividends	Book Value
12/15	12.16	13	8	1.32	1.75	12.13
12/14	12.77	5	2	2.53	0.38	11.28
12/13	6.68	3	3	2.06	0.99	10.00
Annual Growth	34.9%	—	—	(20.0%)	33.0%	10.1%

New York Mortgage Trust Inc

New York Mortgage Trust is a self-advised real estate investment trust (REIT) that invests in mortgage-related real estate assets and some financial assets. It mostly invests in residential mortgage loans including multi-family commercial mortgage-backed securities (CMBS) distressed residential mortgage loans and direct financing to multi-family property owners through mezzanine loans and preferred equity investments. More than 60% of its revenue comes from interest on multi-family loans held in securitization trusts though the REIT's fortunes depend heavily on security gains and losses. New York Mortgage Trust was formed in 2003 and is headquartered in New York City.

Operations

New York Mortgage Trust generated about 62% of its total revenue from interest income from multi-family loans held in securitization trusts in 2014 while another 11% came from interest on its investment securities. About 22% of its revenue came from other income sources mostly related to realized gains on investment securities and related hedges realized gains on distressed residential mortgage loans and unrealized gains on its multi-family loans and debt held in securitization trusts. The company had a staff of 7 full-time employees at the end of 2014. RiverBanc LLC; The Midway Group LP; and Headlands Asset Management LLC provide investment management services to the REIT with respect to certain of its targeted asset classes.

Financial Performance

New York Mortgage Trust's revenues and profits have been rising sharply in recent years mostly as the REIT has been generating higher interest income by acquiring more multi-family loan assets held in securitization trusts. The REIT's revenue jumped 51% to $484.1 million in 2014 mostly thanks to a combination of higher interest income stemming from the company's continued purchase of more higher-yielding credit sensitive investments and a $52.8 million realized gain on investment securities and related hedges as the REIT sold certain multi-family CMBS securities. Higher revenue in 2014 caused New York Mortgage Trust's net income to nearly double to $136.2 million. The company's operating cash levels fell by 30% to $37.6 million after adjusting its earnings for non-cash gains on its investments.

Strategy

New York Mortgage Trust's strategy for growth involves building a residential portfolio that includes elements of both interest rate and credit risk by focusing its investments on credit residential assets and leveraged residential mortgage-backed securities. Starting in 2013 and continuing throughout 2014 the REIT had been "allocating new and re-invested capital to credit sensitive higher yielding investments and allocated less capital to its Agency RMBS portfolio which is lower yielding." These moves have boosted the company's interest income —and overall financial performance —in recent years.

EXECUTIVES

Chairman President and CEO, Steven R. Mumma, age 57, $533,333 total compensation
VP and Secretary, Nathan R. Reese, age 37, $260,000 total compensation
CFO, Kristine R. Nario, age 36, $225,000 total compensation
Auditors: Grant Thornton LLP

LOCATIONS

HQ: New York Mortgage Trust Inc
  275 Madison Avenue, New York, NY 10016
Phone: 212 792-0107
Web: www.nymtrust.com

PRODUCTS/OPERATIONS

2014 Sales

	$ mil.	% of total
Interest income	378.8	78
Other income	105.2	22
Total	**484.0**	**100**

Selected Subsidiaries and Operations

Hypotheca Capital LLC
New York Mortgage Funding LLC
New York Mortgage Ownership Corporation
New York Mortgage Securities Corporation
New York Mortgage Securitization Trust 2012-1
New York Mortgage Servicing Corporation
New York Mortgage Trust 2005-1
New York Mortgage Trust 2005-2
New York Mortgage Trust 2005-3
NYM Preferred Trust I
NYM Preferred Trust II
NYMT Commercial LLC
NYMT Residential 2012-RP1 LLC
NYMT Residential Tax LLC
NYMT Residential LLC
NYMT-Midway LLC
RB Commercial Mortgage LLC
RB Commercial Trust Series 2012-RS1

COMPETITORS

Annaly Capital Management
Anworth Mortgage Asset
CIFC
Capstead Mortgage
Dynex Capital
Impac Mortgage Holdings
Institutional Financial Markets
MFA Financial
Newcastle Investment
Putnam Mortgage
Two Harbors
iStar Financial Inc

HISTORICAL FINANCIALS

Company Type: Public

Income Statement

	REVENUE ($ mil.)	NET INCOME ($ mil.)	NET PROFIT MARGIN	EMPLOYEES
12/15	384.0	78.0	20.3%	7.0
12/14	485.9	136.1	28.0%	7.0
12/13	322.0	68.9	21.4%	6.0
12/12	147.2	28.1	19.1%	4.0
12/11	22.2	4.8	21.9%	3.0
Annual Growth	103.7%	100.0%	—	23.6%

FYE: December 31

2015 Year-End Financials

Debt ratio: 87.0%
Return on equity: 9.1%
Cash ($ mil.): 61.9
Current ratio: 0.06
Long-term debt ($ mil.): 7,098.1

No. of shares (mil.): 109.4
Dividends
  Yield: 19.1%
  Payout: 99.0%
Market value ($ mil.): 583.0

	STOCK PRICE ($) FY Close	P/E High/Low		PER SHARE ($) Earnings	Dividends	Book Value
12/15	5.33	13	8	0.62	1.02	8.05
12/14	7.71	6	5	1.48	1.08	7.78
12/13	6.99	7	5	1.11	1.08	7.50
12/12	6.32	7	5	1.08	1.06	6.50
12/11	7.21	17	14	0.46	1.00	6.12
Annual Growth	(7.3%)	—	—	7.7%	0.5%	7.1%

NewStar Financial Inc

No hot air here: NewStar Financial is in the business of providing middle-market companies with the capital they need to create a spark. The commercial financier provides a variety of loans (primarily secured senior debt) for refinancing acquisitions consolidations and commercial real estate and equipment purchases to clients in the retail and consumer health care media and information and energy industries among others. Its loans typically range from $10 million to $50 million. Newstar also offers investment advisory and asset management services to institutional investors through managed credit funds that invest in its originated loans.

OperationsNewStar operates an asset management unit and three specialized lending groups including: Leveraged Finance (which generated 81% of the firm's 2014 revenue) which provides senior secured cash flow loans as well as second lien and unitranche loans; Real Estate (11% of revenue) which offers first mortgage debt mostly to finance acquisitions of commercial real estate properties; Equipment Finance (4% of revenue) which offers leases loans and lease lines to finance equipment and other capital purchases. and Business Credit (4% of revenue) which provides senior secured asset-based loans mostly to fund working capital needs of mid-sized companies; In April 2016 the company sold its Business Credit business (4% of revenue) which provided asset-based loans to mid-sized businesses needing working capital to Sterling National Bank for $112 million.Overall more than 90% of NewStar's revenue comes from interest income while less than 5% comes from fee and asset management income.Geographic ReachThe Boston-based firm has offices in Atlanta; Chicago; Dallas; Darien Connecticut; Los Angeles; New York; Portland; and San Francisco. Sales and MarketingNewStar targets its marketing and services toward private equity firms mid-sized companies corporate executives banks real estate investors and other financial intermediaries. It serves clients in industries including retail and consumer products health care media and information and energy. Its clients have included DZ Bank Wells Fargo Natixis Capital Markets TIDI Products Centerplate and Media Storm.Financial PerformanceNewStar's revenues and profits have been on the rise in recent years thanks to growing loan business and declining loan loss provisions as its loan portfolio's credit quality has improved with higher property valuations in the strengthened economy.The firm's revenue rose by 7% to $135.9 million in 2014 thanks to higher interest income from continued growth in its loan business particularly driven by its Leveraged Finance and Real Estate financing arms.Despite higher revenue in 2014 NewStar's net income dove by 57% to $10.6 million mostly as credit loss provisions nearly tripled during the year as it had to cover for more of its impaired loans. Its cash levels declined sharply with operations using $110.8 million in 2014 (compared to providing $56.8 million in 2013) after adjusting its earnings for non-cash items mostly related to net proceeds from the sale of its loans held-for-sale.StrategyNewStar Financial continues to add to its lines of specialty financing lines to grow its business. It may also partner with other financial firms to bolster its financial lending capacity.

Toward these ends in 2015 it formed its NewStar Warehouse Funding subsidiary which entered a $175 million revolving warehouse arrangement with Citibank to partially fund eligible loans originated by its Leveraged Finance Group. In late 2014 NewStar partnered with GSO Capital (the credit division of Blackstone) and Franklin Square Capital Partners (the largest manager of business development companies) to expand its lending and asset management platforms.Mergers and AcquisitionsIn October 2015 NewStar continued to add to its specialty financing lineup after purchasing private alternative asset manager Feingold O'Keeffe Capital for $19.3 million (net of acquired cash). The deal nearly added $2.3 billion in new assets under management growing NewStar's total AUM by nearly 50% to $6.4 billion.

EXECUTIVES

Managing Director and Head of Equipment Finance, Stephen J. (Steve) O'Leary
Chairman President and CEO, Timothy J. Conway, age 61, $475,000 total compensation
Managing Director and Head of Strategy and Corporate Development, Robert K. Brown
CFO, John K. Bray, age 59, $350,000 total compensation
Managing Director and Head of Commercial Real Estate, J. Daniel (Dan) Adkinson, age 60
Managing Director and Head of Treasury and Asset Management, John J. Frishkopf, age 52
Managing Director and Head of Asset-Based Lending, Michael D. Haddad
Chief Investment Officer, Daniel D. (Dan) McCready, age 59, $269,230 total compensation
Managing Director and Head of Leveraged Finance Origination, Patrick F. McAuliffe, age 58, $300,000 total compensation
Head of Leverage Financed Capital Markets, Mark R. du Four
Executive Vice President of ABL Operations, Katrina Jensen
Vice President, Kevin (Kev) Mulcahy
Assistant Vice President, Rupert Boyd
Auditors: KPMG LLP

LOCATIONS

HQ: NewStar Financial Inc
500 Boylston Street, Suite 1250, Boston, MA 02116
Phone: 617 848-2500
Web: www.newstarfin.com

PRODUCTS/OPERATIONS

2014 Lending Portfolio

	% of total
Leveraged finance	81
Real estate	11
Business credit	4
Equipment finance	4
Total	**100**

2014 Sales

	$ mil.	% of total
Interest	136.2	92
Fee income	2.5	2
Asset management income	1.0	1
Gain on derivatives & other	(0.2)	-
Other income	7.9	5
Total	**147.4**	**100**

COMPETITORS

Ally Commercial Finance	JPMorgan Chase
Bank of America	MicroFinancial
Bank of the West	ORIX USA
CIT Group	People's United Equipment Finance
Citigroup	

HISTORICAL FINANCIALS

Company Type: Public

Income Statement

FYE: December 31

	ASSETS ($ mil.)	NET INCOME ($ mil.)	INCOME AS % OF ASSETS	EMPLOYEES
12/15	4,092.1	16.8	0.4%	122.0
12/14	2,811.0	10.5	0.4%	98.0
12/13	2,606.8	24.6	0.9%	101.0
12/12	2,157.0	23.9	1.1%	104.0
12/11	1,946.3	14.1	0.7%	88.0
Annual Growth	**20.4%**	**4.5%**	**—**	**8.5%**

2015 Year-End Financials

Return on assets: 0.4%	Dividends
Return on equity: 2.6%	Yield: —
Long-term debt ($ mil.): —	Payout: —
No. of shares ($ mil.): 46.5	Market value ($ mil.): 418.0
Sales ($ mil): 220.1	

	STOCK PRICE ($) FY Close	P/E High/Low	Earnings	Dividends	Book Value
12/15	8.98	35 22	0.35	0.00	14.17
12/14	12.80	81 47	0.21	0.00	13.75
12/13	17.77	37 23	0.46	0.00	12.65
12/12	14.01	27 18	0.45	0.00	12.06
12/11	10.17	42 28	0.27	0.00	11.42
Annual Growth	**(3.1%)**	**— —**	**6.7%**	**—**	**5.5%**

Nexstar Media Group Inc

Star light star bright Nexstar Broadcasting wishes for you to tune in tonight. The company is a leading television station operator with more than 70 stations serving 40 small and midsized markets. Nexstar has duopolies (two or more stations) in many of its markets. Its portfolio includes more than a dozen affiliates each of the FOX and NBC networks as well as stations affiliated with ABC CBS The CW and MyNetworkTV. More than 15 of its TV stations are operated through local service agreements with Mission Broadcasting which owns those broadcast licenses. Private investment firm ABRY Partners owns a majority share in the company and controls 88% of the voting power.

Geographic Reach
Nexstar operates in dozens of US states. Most of the company's television stations are located in the Northeast Midwest and Southwest.

Sales and Marketing
Nexstar spend about $2 million on advertising and marketing promotions every year.

Strategy
Shared services agreements enable the Nexstar to provide sales news and other services to a second station in 66% of the markets where the company operates.

Mergers and Acquisitions
In 2016 Nexstar agreed to buy rival TV station operator Media General. Once the transaction closes (in the third or fourth quarter of 2016) Nexstar will change its name to Nexstar Media Group Inc.

EXECUTIVES

Chairman; President and CEO, Perry A. Sook, age 58, $1,191,539 total compensation
EVP and Co-COO, Timothy C. (Tim) Busch, age 53, $404,231 total compensation
EVP Co-COO, Brian Jones, age 56, $404,231 total compensation
General Manager KFDX, Julie Pruett, age 53
EVP and CFO, Thomas E. (Tom) Carter, age 58, $423,654 total compensation
EVP Digital Media and Chief Revenue Officer, Thomas (Tom) OÂBrien, age 54
SVP Regional Manager, William Sally

VP and Director Technology, Dione Rigsby
Vice President, Jon (Jonny) Skorburg
Vice President and General Manager, Albert (Al) Gutierrez
Auditors: PricewaterhouseCoopers LLP

LOCATIONS

HQ: Nexstar Media Group Inc
545 E. John Carpenter Freeway, Suite 700, Irving, TX 75062
Phone: 972 373-8800
Web: www.nexstar.tv

PRODUCTS/OPERATIONS

Selected Television Stations
KAMR (NBC; Amarillo TX)
KARD (FOX; Monroe LA)
KARK (NBC; Little Rock AR)
KBTV (NBC; Beaumont-Port Arthur TX)
KFDX (NBC; Wichita Falls TX)
KFTA (FOX; Ft. Smith-Fayetteville AR)
KLBK (CBS; Lubbock TX)
KLST (CBS; San Angelo TX)
KMID (ABC; Odessa-Midland TX)
KNWA (NBC; Ft. Smith-Fayetteville AR)
KQTV (ABC; St. Joseph MO)
KSFX (FOX; Springfield MO)
KSNF (NBC; Joplin MO)
KSVI (ABC; Billings MT)
KTAB (CBS; Abilene-Sweetwater TX)
KTAL (NBC; Shreveport LA)
WBRE (NBC; Wilkes Barre-Scranton PA)
WCFN (MyNetworkTV; Champaign-Springfield IL)
WCIA (CBS; Champaign-Springfield IL)
WDHN (ABC; Dothan AL)
WFFT (FOX; Ft. Wayne IN)
WFRV (CBS; Green Bay WI)
WFXV (FOX; Utica NY)
WHAG (NBC; Washington DC)
WJET (ABC; Erie PA)
WJMN (CBS; Marquette MI)
WLYH (CW; Harrisburg PA)
WMBD (CBS; Peoria-Bloomington IL)
WQRF (FOX; Rockford IL)
WROC (CBS; Rochester NY)
WTAJ (CBS; Johnstown-Altoona PA)
WTVW (FOX; Evansville IN)
WTWO (NBC; Terre Haute IN)

COMPETITORS

Allbritton Communications	LIN Media
Barrington Broadcasting	Local TV
	Newport Television
Granite Broadcasting	Raycom Media
Gray Television	TEGNA
Hearst Television	Tribune Media

HISTORICAL FINANCIALS

Company Type: Public

Income Statement

FYE: December 31

	REVENUE ($ mil.)	NET INCOME ($ mil.)	NET PROFIT MARGIN	EMPLOYEES
12/15	896.3	77.6	8.7%	4,422.0
12/14	631.3	64.5	10.2%	3,464.0
12/13	502.3	(1.7)	—	3,222.0
12/12	378.6	182.4	48.2%	2,411.0
12/11	306.4	(11.8)	—	2,230.0
Annual Growth	**30.8%**	**—**	**—**	**18.7%**

2015 Year-End Financials

Debt ratio: 80.4%
Return on equity: 116.6%
Cash ($ mil.): 43.4
Current ratio: 1.78
Long-term debt ($ mil.): 1,454.0
No. of shares (mil.): 30.6
Dividends
Yield: 1.2%
Payout: 31.4%
Market value ($ mil.): 1,798.0

	STOCK PRICE ($) FY Close	P/E High/Low	PER SHARE ($) Earnings	Dividends	Book Value
12/15	58.70	24 17	2.42	0.76	2.63
12/14	51.79	27 16	2.02	0.60	1.69
12/13	55.73	— —	(0.06)	0.48	(0.43)
12/12	10.59	2 1	5.94	0.00	0.10
12/11	7.84	— —	(0.42)	0.00	(6.37)
Annual Growth	**65.4%**	**—**	**—**	**—**	**—**

NextEra Energy Partners LP

Auditors: Deloitte & Touche LLP

LOCATIONS

HQ: NextEra Energy Partners LP
700 Universe Boulevard, Juno Beach, FL 33408
Phone: 561 694-4000
Web: www.nexteraenergypartners.com

HISTORICAL FINANCIALS

Company Type: Public

Income Statement

FYE: December 31

	REVENUE ($ mil.)	NET INCOME ($ mil.)	NET PROFIT MARGIN	EMPLOYEES
12/15	471.0	10.0	2.1%	0.0
12/14	301.0	3.0	1.0%	0.0
12/13	141.8	10.7	7.6%	0.0
12/12	93.4	16.0	17.1%	0.0
Annual Growth	**71.5%**	**(14.5%)**	**—**	**—**

2015 Year-End Financials

Debt ratio: 56.8%
Return on equity: —
Cash ($ mil.): 161.0
Current ratio: 1.42
Long-term debt ($ mil.): 3,352.0
No. of shares (mil.): 30.6
Dividends
Yield: 3.0%
Payout: 323.2%
Market value ($ mil.): 913.0

	STOCK PRICE ($) FY Close	P/E High/Low	PER SHARE ($) Earnings	Dividends	Book Value
12/15	29.85	104 43	0.46	0.91	30.36
12/14	33.75	236186	0.16	0.19	29.47
12/13	0.00	— —	(0.00)	0.00	(0.00)
Annual Growth					

NIC Inc.

So people can do business with government agencies NIC helps government agencies plug in to the Internet. The company is a leading provider of outsourced Web portal services for federal state and local governments. It designs implements and operates websites under contracts with more than 3500 government agencies. NIC generates much of its revenue from transaction fees for such services as online license renewals and for providing data on motor vehicle titles and business licenses to insurance companies lenders and other authorized organizations.

Geographic Reach
The company operates in about 30 states. NIC has offices in more than 40 of the top 50 major metropolitan areas in the US. It has international offices in Asia.

Sales and Marketing
The company has a national sales force and a marketing department dedicated to its outsourced portal businesses.

Strategy
To grow NIC is striving to renew its existing contracts which typically run for three- to five-year terms and to win new portal contracts. In addition the company has been developing new applications for government websites from which it can generate transaction fees especially outside the realm of motor vehicle records.

EXECUTIVES

Chairman of the Board; Chief Executive Officer, Harry H. Herington, age 56, $390,450 total compensation
Executive Vice President; Chief Administrative Officer; General Counsel; Secretary, William F. (Brad) Bradley, age 61, $267,150 total compensation
Executive Vice President Operations And Administration, Samuel (Sam) Somerhalder
CFO, Stephen M. (Steve) Kovzan, age 47, $267,150 total compensation
COO, Robert Knapp, age 47, $267,150 total compensation
Vice President of Business Development, Elizabeth (Beth) Proudfit
Vice President of Marketing, Chris (Chrissy) Neff
Vice President of Sales, Elizabeth (Beth) Riordan
Vice President Of Egovernment Innovation, Nolan Jones
Vice President, Tom Platis
Senior Vice President Sales and Marketing, Ron (Ronnie) Thornburgh
Vice President of Product Management, Mukesh Patel
Vice President of Sales, Robert (Bob) Chandler
Auditors: PricewaterhouseCoopers LLP

LOCATIONS

HQ: NIC Inc.
25501 West Valley Parkway, Suite 300, Olathe, KS 66061
Phone: 877 234-3468
Web: www.egov.com

PRODUCTS/OPERATIONS

2014 Sales

	$ mil.	% of total
Portal Revenue	255.7	94
Software & services	16.4	6
Total	**272.1**	**100**

COMPETITORS

Accenture	Manatron
Agency.com	Microsoft
CGI Group	Official Payments
Computer Sciences Corp.	Official Payments Holdings
HP Enterprise Services	Oracle
IBM Global Services	Tyler Technologies
Idea Integration	USTI
Leidos	Unisys
MAXIMUS	

HISTORICAL FINANCIALS

Company Type: Public

Income Statement

FYE: December 31

	REVENUE ($ mil.)	NET INCOME ($ mil.)	NET PROFIT MARGIN	EMPLOYEES
12/15	292.3	41.9	14.4%	859.0
12/14	272.1	39.0	14.4%	818.0
12/13	249.2	32.0	12.9%	773.0
12/12	211.1	26.3	12.5%	714.0
12/11	180.9	22.9	12.7%	653.0
Annual Growth	12.8%	16.3%	—	7.1%

2015 Year-End Financials

Debt ratio: —
Return on equity: 38.1%
Cash ($ mil.): 134.8
Current ratio: 1.88
Long-term debt ($ mil.): —

No. of shares (mil.): 65.6
Dividends
Yield: 2.7%
Payout: 88.7%
Market value ($ mil.): 1,292.0

	STOCK PRICE ($) FY Close	P/E High/Low		PER SHARE ($) Earnings	Dividends	Book Value
12/15	19.68	33	24	0.63	0.55	1.76
12/14	17.99	42	26	0.59	0.50	1.59
12/13	24.87	51	32	0.49	0.35	1.41
12/12	16.34	41	26	0.40	0.50	1.22
12/11	13.31	41	27	0.35	0.25	1.01
Annual Growth	10.3%	—	—	15.8%	21.8%	14.9%

Nicolet Bankshares Inc

EXECUTIVES

Pres-ceo, Robert Atwell
Executive Vice President, Eric Witczak
Auditors: Porter Keadle Moore LLC

LOCATIONS

HQ: Nicolet Bankshares Inc
111 North Washington Street, Green Bay, WI 54301
Phone: 920 430-1400
Web: www.nicoletbank.com

HISTORICAL FINANCIALS

Company Type: Public

Income Statement

FYE: December 31

	ASSETS ($ mil.)	NET INCOME ($ mil.)	INCOME AS % OF ASSETS	EMPLOYEES
12/15	1,214.4	11.4	0.9%	280.0
12/14	1,215.2	9.9	0.8%	280.0
12/13	1,198.8	16.1	1.3%	290.0
12/12	745.2	3.0	0.4%	175.0
12/11	678.2	1.4	0.2%	0.0
Annual Growth	15.7%	66.4%	—	—

2015 Year-End Financials

Return on assets: 0.9%
Return on equity: 10.3%
Long-term debt ($ mil.): —
No. of shares (mil.): 4.1
Sales ($ mil): 66.3

Dividends
Yield: —
Payout: —
Market value ($ mil.): 132.0

	STOCK PRICE ($) FY Close	P/E High/Low		PER SHARE ($) Earnings	Dividends	Book Value
12/15	31.79	12	9	2.57	0.00	26.36
12/14	25.00	11	7	2.25	0.00	27.35
12/13	16.54	5	4	3.80	0.00	24.73
Annual Growth	38.6%	—	—	(17.8%)	—	3.2%

Nobilis Health Corp

EXECUTIVES

Ceo, Chris Lloyd
Auditors: Crowe Horwath LLP

LOCATIONS

HQ: Nobilis Health Corp
11700 Katy Freeway, Suite 300, Houston, TX 77079
Phone: 713 355-8614   **Fax:** 713 355-8615
Web: www.northstar-healthcare.com

HISTORICAL FINANCIALS

Company Type: Public

Income Statement

FYE: December 31

	REVENUE ($ mil.)	NET INCOME ($ mil.)	NET PROFIT MARGIN	EMPLOYEES
12/15	229.2	50.8	22.2%	715.0
12/14	84.0	7.1	8.6%	452.0
12/13	31.1	1.4	4.5%	74.0
12/12	20.9	1.2	5.7%	50.0
12/11	14.3	(2.1)	—	47.0
Annual Growth	99.8%	—	—	97.5%

2015 Year-End Financials

Debt ratio: 18.4%
Return on equity: 63.3%
Cash ($ mil.): 15.6
Current ratio: 2.23
Long-term debt ($ mil.): 38.1

No. of shares (mil.): 73.6
Dividends
Yield: —
Payout: —
Market value ($ mil.): 208.0

	STOCK PRICE ($) FY Close	P/E High/Low		PER SHARE ($) Earnings	Dividends	Book Value
12/15	2.82	11	3	0.68	0.00	1.71
12/14	3.00	20	6	0.15	0.00	0.78
12/13	0.95	34	6	0.04	0.00	0.26
12/12	0.11	8	3	0.03	0.00	0.13
12/11	0.18	—	—	(0.07)	0.00	0.07
Annual Growth 120.1%	100.4%	—	—	—	—	—

Nobility Homes, Inc.

Florida's prince of prefab Nobility Homes is a leading player in the state's competitive manufactured-home market. Nobility has built and sold about 50000 homes through about 20 retail Prestige Home Centers Majestic Homes retail sales centers and on a wholesale basis to independent dealers and residential communities. Nobility offers some 100 models that range in price from about

---

$30000 to more than $100000 and in sizes from about 700 sq. ft. to 2650 sq. ft. The company also provides financing mortgage lending and brokerage and insurance services. Founder and president Terry Trexler and his family control nearly two-thirds of the company.

Nobility battled an industrywide downturn in 2008 and 2009 as the poor economic outlook for the US continued; manufactured home shipments in Florida were down 54% in 2009. The company cited a drop in consumer demand more stringent credit requirements a lack of retail and wholesale financing and increased unemployment for the downturn. High home foreclosure rates kept potential buyers out of the manufactured home market and Nobility had a growing supply of repossessed units which it successfully liquidated.

Nobility Homes has two manufacturing plants in Florida. However only the Ocala metal construction facility is in operation. Its Bellview facility was closed indefinitely in 2009 until market conditions improve. Nobility has some 15 retail sales centers across Florida.

The company provides financing through Majestic 21 a 50/50 joint venture with 21st Mortgage. It offers credit life auto and boat property/casualty and other insurance services through subsidiary Mountain Financial.

To keep its inventories down Nobility generally manufactures its homes on receipt of order. The company benefits from its ability to alter its product mix promptly in response to market changes.

In efforts to expand into affordable senior housing which the company sees as a growth area for Florida Nobility invested in two Floridian retirement communities in 2008.

HISTORY

Terry Trexler formerly a general manager at a mobile-home manufacturing plant founded his business in 1967 and named it Nobility Homes because he felt the name symbolized quality. The company which went public in 1971 focused solely on manufacturing while selling its homes through independent dealers. In the 1990s however Nobility took control of its marketing. Trexler formed TLT Inc. to develop communities that sold homes and land as packages to retirees.

For many years Nobility catered to the retirement market by offering small homes for empty nesters. Since 1991 Nobility has pursued entry-level buyers with families expanding home sizes up to five bedrooms. The Trexlers invested in Prestige Home Centers a mobile-home retailer in 1994. To keep growing Nobility began increasing the number of Prestige outlets in 1997. Also that year Nobility introduced a 30th-anniversary model a design that proved to be popular enough to be added to its permanent line.

In 1998 the company bought six retail locations in northern Florida from Lynn Haven Homes and Emerald City Homes. It also opened a new sales center increasing the company's retail locations to 22. As consumer demand in the industry crept downward Nobility closed three retail outlets in 1999. An industrywide inventory glut and tighter credit standards for qualified buyers continued to affect Nobility's bottom line in the early 2000s.

Reductions in both excess home inventories and repossessions at retail sales centers within the industry helped the company rebound in 2002 with increases in sales and profits partly due to Nobility's aggressive pursuit of sales to outside park dealers.

Trying to weather the downturn in the US economy the company has closed retail sales centers and 1 manufacturing plant in recent years. Nobility invested in two Floridian retirement communities in 2008; the company believes the affordable manufactured senior housing market is a growth opportunity.

EXECUTIVES

Secretary, Jean Etheredge, age 69
Treasurer, Lynn J. Cramer Jr., age 69
EVP CFO and Director; President Prestige Home Centers, Thomas W. Trexler, age 51, $93,500 total compensation
Chairman and President; President TLT, Terry E. Trexler, age 75, $93,500 total compensation
EVP CFO and Director; President Prestige Home Centers, Thomas W. Trexler, age 51
Director, Richard C. Barberie, age 76
Director, Robert P. Holliday, age 76
Director, Robert P. Saltsman, age 62
Auditors: WithunSmith+Brown, PC

LOCATIONS

HQ: Nobility Homes, Inc.
3741 S.W. 7th Street, Ocala, FL 34474
Phone: 352 732-5157
Web: www.nobilityhomes.com

COMPETITORS

American Homestar	Four Seasons Housing
Cavalier Homes	Giles Industries
Cavco	Liberty Homes
Champion Home Builders	Skyline
Clayton Homes	Southern Energy Homes

HISTORICAL FINANCIALS

Company Type: Public

Income Statement

	REVENUE ($ mil.)	NET INCOME ($ mil.)	NET PROFIT MARGIN	EMPLOYEES
				FYE: November 5
11/16*	34.0	5.9	17.5%	140.0
10/15	27.8	2.9	10.5%	129.0
11/14	21.1	1.2	5.9%	110.0
11/13	18.5	0.7	4.0%	97.0
11/12	15.8	0.0	0.3%	89.0
Annual Growth	21.1%	230.9%	—	12.0%

*Fiscal year change

2016 Year-End Financials

Debt ratio: —
Return on equity: 14.0%
Cash ($ mil.): 24.5
Current ratio: 7.41
Long-term debt ($ mil.): —

No. of shares (mil.): 4.0
Dividends
  Yield: —
  Payout: —
Market value ($ mil.): 62.0

	STOCK PRICE ($) FY Close	P/E High/Low		PER SHARE ($) Earnings	Dividends	Book Value
11/16*	15.50	11	8	1.48	0.00	11.16
10/15	12.85	18	13	0.72	0.00	9.70
11/14	10.25	42	26	0.31	0.00	8.99
11/13	9.25	52	25	0.18	0.00	8.67
11/12	5.40	844	442	0.01	0.00	8.45
Annual Growth	30.2%			—248.8%	—	7.2%

*Fiscal year change

Northeast Bancorp (ME)

Northeast Bancorp is the holding company for Northeast Bank which operates about a dozen branches in western and southern Maine. Founded in 1872 the bank offers standard retail services such as checking and savings accounts NOW and money market accounts CDs and trust services as well as financial planning and brokerage. Residential mortgages account for about a third of all loans; commercial mortgages and consumer loans each make up about 25%. The bank also writes business and construction loans. Newly created investment entity FHB Formation acquired a 60% stake in Northeast Bancorp in 2010. The deal brought in $16 million in capital. The 2011 sale of insurance agency Varney added another $8.4 million.

Northeast Bank Insurance has acquired about a half-dozen insurance agencies since 2006. It now has more than a dozen offices in Maine and southern New Hampshire where the company hopes to expand further by opening bank branches.

Investment firms including Sandler O'Neill Asset Management Nichols Investment Management and regional bank investor Tontine Financial Partners collectively own about a third of Northeast Bancorp.

EXECUTIVES

Vice President Commercial Lending, Tom (Tommy) Sanvick
Auditors: RSM US LLP

LOCATIONS

HQ: Northeast Bancorp (ME)
500 Canal Street, Lewiston, ME 04240
Phone: 207 786-3245
Web: www.northeastbank.com

COMPETITORS

Bar Harbor Bankshares	Norway Bancorp
Camden National	TD Bank USA
KeyCorp	The First Bancorp

HISTORICAL FINANCIALS

Company Type: Public

Income Statement

	ASSETS ($ mil.)	NET INCOME ($ mil.)	INCOME AS % OF ASSETS	EMPLOYEES
				FYE: June 30
06/16	986.1	7.6	0.8%	203.0
06/15	850.8	7.1	0.8%	191.0
06/14	761.9	2.6	0.4%	195.0
06/13	670.6	4.4	0.7%	227.0
06/12	669.2	2.1	0.3%	209.0
Annual Growth	10.2%	37.0%	—	(0.7%)

2016 Year-End Financials

Return on assets: 0.8%
Return on equity: 6.6%
Long-term debt ($ mil.): —
No. of shares (mil.): 9.3
Sales ($ mil): 55.0

Dividends
  Yield: 0.3%
  Payout: 5.0%
Market value ($ mil.): 105.0

	STOCK PRICE ($) FY Close	P/E High/Low		PER SHARE ($) Earnings	Dividends	Book Value
06/16	11.25	15	12	0.80	0.04	12.51
06/15	9.95	14	12	0.72	0.04	11.77
06/14	9.57	42	35	0.26	0.28	11.05
06/13	9.67	26	22	0.39	0.36	10.89
06/12	8.48	36	20	0.41	0.36	11.47
Annual Growth	7.3%	—	—	18.2%	(42.3%)	2.2%

Northrim BancCorp Inc

Can you get banking services at the north rim of the world? Of course! Northrim BanCorp formed in 2001 to be the holding company for Northrim Bank provides a full range of commercial and retail banking services and products through some 10 banking offices in Alaska's Anchorage Fairbanks North Star and Matanuska Susitna counties. Division offices that provide short-term capital to customers also are located in Washington and Oregon. The bank offers standard deposit products including checking savings and money market accounts; CDs; and IRAs. It uses funds from deposits to write commercial loans (40% of loan portfolio) and real estate term loans (nearly 35%) as well as construction and consumer loans.

Northrim BanCorp also owns a stake in a handful of other businesses including Residential Mortgage Holding Company which originates loans from offices throughout Alaska. The company also owns about 50% of Northrim Benefits Group an insurance brokerage company. In 2006 Northrim purchased a 24% stake in Pacific Wealth Advisors an investment advisory trust and wealth management firm in Seattle. Elliott Cove another investment advisory serivce company also is in Northrim's portfolio.

In 2007 Northrim BanCorp acquired Alaska First Bank & Trust for more than $6 million. The deal did not include Alaska First's insurance subsidiary Hagen Insurance.

EXECUTIVES

Senior Vice President and Senior Lender, Leonard F (Len) Horst
Svp Information Services, Suzanne (Sue) Whittle
Vice President, William (Bill) Staley
Vice President Commercial Cash Management, Kimberly F (Kim) Brewington
Assistant Vice President Loan Servicing Officer, Heidi (Hei) Moes
Auditors: Moss Adams LLP

LOCATIONS

HQ: Northrim BancCorp Inc
3111 C Street, Anchorage, AK 99503
Phone: 907 562-0062

PRODUCTS/OPERATIONS

2007 Sales

	$ mil.	% of total
Interest		
Loans including fees	66.5	80
Securities	4.6	6
Other	2.0	2
Noninterest		

Service charges on deposit accounts		3.1	4
Purchased receivable income		2.5	3
Other		4.2	5
Total		**82.9**	**100**

COMPETITORS

Alaska Pacific	First National Bank
Bancshares	Alaska
Alaska USA	KeyCorp

HISTORICAL FINANCIALS

Company Type: Public

Income Statement
FYE: December 31

	ASSETS ($ mil.)	NET INCOME ($ mil.)	INCOME AS % OF ASSETS	EMPLOYEES
12/15	1,499.4	17.7	1.2%	441.0
12/14	1,449.3	17.4	1.2%	426.0
12/13	1,215.0	12.3	1.0%	269.0
12/12	1,160.1	12.9	1.1%	245.0
12/11	1,085.2	11.4	1.1%	260.0
Annual Growth	**8.4%**	**11.8%**	**—**	**14.1%**

2015 Year-End Financials

Return on assets: 1.2%	Dividends
Return on equity: 10.4%	Yield: 2.7%
Long-term debt ($ mil.): —	Payout: 25.1%
No. of shares (mil.): 6.8	Market value ($ mil.): 183.0
Sales ($ mil): 104.2	

	STOCK PRICE ($) FY Close	P/E High/Low		PER SHARE ($) Earnings	Dividends	Book Value
12/15	26.60	11	8	2.56	0.74	25.74
12/14	26.24	11	9	2.54	0.70	23.97
12/13	26.24	15	11	1.87	0.64	22.05
12/12	22.65	11	9	1.97	0.56	20.93
12/11	17.51	11	10	1.74	0.50	19.39
Annual Growth	**11.0%**	**—**	**—**	**10.1%**	**10.3%**	**7.3%**

Nuvasive Inc

When a back is seriously out of whack NuVasive has some options. The company makes and markets medical devices for the surgical treatment of spinal disorders. NuVasive's products are primarily used in spinal restoration and fusion surgeries. Its minimally disruptive Maximum Access Surgery (MAS) platform enables surgeons to access the spine from the side of the body instead of from the front or back helping them to avoid hitting nerves. NuVasive also features a line of biologic bone grafting materials —both allograft and synthetic —and has a cervical disc replacement system in development. The company sells its FDA-approved products through a network of exclusive sales agents supported by an in-house sales team.

Operations

NuVasive offers more than 80 products for procedures in the lumbar thoracic and cervical regions including the mesh plates screws and biological implants used with its MAS system. Its Osteocel product is an adult stem-cell bone graft used for bone regeneration in orthopedic procedures and at one point was the only commercially available stem-cell product in the US.

NuVasive's revenues primarily come from the sale of disposable materials and implants. The full system of software and instruments are loaned to hospitals for free as long as they keep ordering disposables and implants though a small portion of the company's revenues are from the sale of instruments and systems. Revenues from its monitoring services come from hospitals and are also billed through various payers.

Geographic Reach

NuVasive maintains a facility in California where it trains doctors in the use of its products. It ships its products directly to doctors overnight from a distribution facility in Tennessee; other US facilities are located in New Jersey Ohio and Maryland. International offices are located in Australia Brazil Germany Japan the Netherlands and the UK.

The US accounts for the majority of NuVasive's sales but the company is working to establish its products in Europe and Asia. The first hurdle is obtaining regulatory approval for all of the components in its platform for each country it seeks to enter.

Sales and Marketing

NuVasive sells its products through its own direct sales force and through exclusive distributors and independent sales agents.

Financial Performance

NuVasive's revenues have steadily increased as it has grown through increased product sales new product additions and acquisitions including a 19% jump to $962.1 million in fiscal 2016. That year's growth was driven by increased spinal hardware product sales which rose 20% and higher surgical support sales which rose 14%.

Net income has fluctuated in recent years. In 2016 it fell 44% to $37.1 million —despite the higher revenue —as operating expenses such as sales and marketing and R&D costs rose.

Strategy

NuVasive's goal is to make its products and services part of the standard procedure for minimally invasive surgery up and down the entire spine. The firm is focused on expanding the reach of its MAS platform through marketing and sales force efforts to increase market penetration. It also conducts research and development efforts to improve existing offerings to make them more adaptable for surgeons and hospitals.

R&D efforts create new products as well. As cervical disc replacement technology —the holy grail for spinal device makers —is advancing rapidly NuVasive has several cervical disc replacement devices in late-stage development.

Mergers and Acquisitions

In mid-2016 NuVasive acquired Biotronic NeuroNetwork which provides intraoperative neurophysiological monitoring services for $98 million. That deal which more than doubled NuVasive's neurophysiology footprint extended the operations of the company's newly established NuVasive Clinical Services division. That unit now provides monitoring services for more than 75000 cases each year.

Also that year the company acquired Ellipse Technologies which developed magnetic growing rod implant systems for $380 million; those products which eliminate the need for repeat surgeries as pediatric patients grow are now sold by NuVasive Specialized Orthopedics. In yet another deal it purchased the LessRay software suite which enhances image quality while helping health care providers manage radiation exposure.

EXECUTIVES

Chairman and CEO, Gregory T. Lucier
President and COO, Jason M. Hannon, age 44, $400,000 total compensation
EVP Asia Pacific, Takaaki Tanaka
EVP Global Operations, Tyler P. Lipschultz
VP Accounting, Quentin Blackford
EVP International, Russell Powers
EVP Strategic Sales and Operations, Scott Durall
President U.S. Sales and Services, Matthew W. (Matt) Link, $375,000 total compensation
EVP Corporate Affairs and Human Resources, Carol Cox
CIO, Johnson Lai
Vice President Fulfillment and Operational Systems, Jeffrey (Jeff) Bertolini
Vice President Cervical, Mark (Marky) Ojeda
MVP Manager, Mike (Mikey) Inzitari
Vice President of Marketing and Development, Pat (Patty) Miles
Vice President, Jason (Jase) Hannan
Executive Vice President of Strategy and Corporate Development a, Jason (Jase) Hanson
Vice Chairman, Patrick (Pat) Miles
Auditors: Ernst & Young LLP

LOCATIONS

HQ: Nuvasive Inc
7475 Lusk Boulevard, San Diego, CA 92121
Phone: 858 909-1800   **Fax:** 858 909-2000
Web: www.nuvasive.com

PRODUCTS/OPERATIONS

Selected Acquisitions

COMPETITORS

Alphatec Spine	Natus Medical
CareFusion	Orthofix
DePuy Spine	Stryker
Globus Medical	Synthes
Integra LifeSciences	Zimmer Biomet
Interpore	
Medtronic Sofamor Danek	

HISTORICAL FINANCIALS

Company Type: Public

Income Statement
FYE: December 31

	REVENUE ($ mil.)	NET INCOME ($ mil.)	NET PROFIT MARGIN	EMPLOYEES
12/15	811.1	66.2	8.2%	1,600.0
12/14	762.4	(16.7)	—	1,500.0
12/13	685.1	7.9	1.2%	1,358.0
12/12	620.2	3.1	0.5%	1,173.0
12/11	540.5	(69.8)	—	1,093.0
Annual Growth	**10.7%**	**—**	**—**	**10.0%**

2015 Year-End Financials

Debt ratio: 29.2%	No. of shares (mil.): 52.6
Return on equity: 9.9%	Dividends
Cash ($ mil.): 192.3	Yield: —
Current ratio: 7.06	Payout: —
Long-term debt ($ mil.): 376.5	Market value ($ mil.): 2,847.0

	STOCK PRICE ($) FY Close	P/E High/Low		PER SHARE ($) Earnings	Dividends	Book Value
12/15	54.11	41	31	1.26	0.00	13.21
12/14	47.16	—	—	(0.36)	0.00	13.42
12/13	32.33	186	86	0.17	0.00	13.26
12/12	15.46	368	162	0.07	0.00	12.31
12/11	12.59	—	—	(1.73)	0.00	11.64
Annual Growth	**44.0%**	**—**	**—**	**—**	**—**	**3.2%**

NV5 Global Inc

NV5 Global wants the world to envy its engineering services. It offers infrastructure engineering support and consulting services as well as construction quality assurance and asset management. Customers include government agencies along with quasi-public and private firms in education health care and energy. NV5's enviable projects have included the international terminal at Philadelphia International Airport UC Santa Barbara's Marine Center the New Jersey Devils Arena San Diego's Manchester Grand Hyatt and a wind turbine manufacturing plant in Colorado. The company works from about 20 offices in California Colorado Florida New Jersey and Utah. It was formed in 2011 and filed to go public in 2013.

IPO

The company plans to use its anticipated $6.9 million in IPO proceeds for general corporate purposes including working capital sales and marketing and acquisitions.

Operations

NV5 divides its business into what it calls its five vertical offerings. They are- infrastructure engineering and support services; construction quality assurance; public and private consulting and outsourcing; asset management consulting; and occupational health safety and environmental consulting.

It has traditionally focused on the first two service verticals but is expanding into the others and plans to focus on those going forward.

Financial Analysis

NV5's revenues have generally been increasing while its costs have held steady except for acquisitions. The company hasn't reported 2012 numbers yet but in 2011 it nearly doubled revenue and increased net income nearly tenfold. Nolte Associates acquired during 2010 contributed all of the company's revenue for 2011.

Strategy

Going forward NV5 intends to continue to focus on public sector clients which account for about 60% of revenue while working to grow its private sector accounts. It also plans to look for strategic acquisitions and invest in attracting training and retaining personnel.

M&A Activity

In 2011 NV5 completed a reorganization to incorporate Nolte Associates acquired the previous year. In 2012 it purchased engineering firm Kaderabek (Kaco) for about $3.5 million.

EXECUTIVES

Director; EVP Strategic Growth NV5, Donald C. (Don) Alford, age 72, $240,000 total compensation
Chairman and CEO, Dickerson Wright, age 70, $400,000 total compensation
VP and CFO, Michael P. Rama, age 50, $178,077 total compensation
Executive Vice President and General Counsel, Richard Tong, age 48, $230,000 total compensation
President and COO, Alexander A. Hockman, age 59, $290,385 total compensation
Executive Vice President and Chief Administrative Officer, Mary Jo OÄBrien, age 54
Auditors: Deloitte & Touche LLP

LOCATIONS

HQ: NV5 Global Inc
200 South Park Road, Suite 350, Hollywood, FL 33021
Phone: 954 495-2112
Web: www.nv5.com

COMPETITORS

AECOM	Terracon
Amec Foster Wheeler	Tetra Tech
Bureau Veritas	The Kleinfelder Group
Cardno	Inc.
Intertek	WS Atkins
Jacobs Engineering	Willdan Group
TRC Companies	

HISTORICAL FINANCIALS
Company Type: Public

Income Statement
FYE: December 31

	REVENUE ($ mil.)	NET INCOME ($ mil.)	NET PROFIT MARGIN	EMPLOYEES
12/15	154.6	8.4	5.5%	975.0
12/14	108.3	4.8	4.5%	649.0
12/13	68.2	2.7	4.0%	436.0
12/12	60.5	1.2	2.1%	439.0
12/11	63.3	1.4	2.2%	439.0
Annual Growth	25.0%	56.4%	—	22.1%

2015 Year-End Financials

Debt ratio: 9.5%	No. of shares (mil.): 8.2
Return on equity: 14.6%	Dividends
Cash ($ mil.): 23.4	Yield: —
Current ratio: 3.32	Payout: —
Long-term debt ($ mil.): 6.3	Market value ($ mil.): 181.0

	STOCK PRICE ($) FY Close	P/E High/Low		PER SHARE ($) Earnings	Dividends	Book Value
12/15	21.98	22	8	1.18	0.00	9.83
12/14	13.00	15	8	0.87	0.00	6.19
12/13	8.14	12	9	0.70	0.00	5.23
Annual Growth	64.3%	—	—	29.8%	—	37.1%

Och-Ziff Capital Management Group LLC

In the marvelous land of OZ good investments are king. Och-Ziff Capital Management Group provides a variety of alternative asset management services for more than 600 fund investors through offices in New York and overseas in Mumbai Beijing Hong Kong and London. Och-Ziff Capital Management Group's investment strategies include private equity merger arbitrage and equity restructuring among others. With some $46.2 billion in assets under management the majority of its equity holdings are invested in Europe and Asia. The hedge fund firm which boasts about 148 investment professionals including two dozen partners began operations in 1994.

Geographic Reach

New York-headquartered Och-Ziff maintains global operations in London Hong Kong Beijing Mumbai and Dubai.

Operations

The company manages four main funds: its OZ Master Fund; OZ Europe Master Fund; OZ Asia Master Fund; and OZ Global Special Investments Master Fund. The OZ Global Special Investments fund invests in structured and distressed credit.

In 2014 the OZ Master Fund's geographic allocation was 65% in North Central and South America followed by 19% in Europe Africa and the Middle East. Asia Australia and New Zealand made up 16%.

Strategy

Och-Ziff attributes its economic resiliency to its diverse multi-strategy model which allows the firm to take advantage of a variety of opportunities in the market. Indeed the company's hedge fund industry assets under management grew some 17% in 2013 driven by performance-related appreciation and capital net inflows.

Och-Ziff is preparing for more growth spurred mostly by institutional investors. The firm is gaining new business from such investors who are attracted to its long-held policy of openness and transparency (it's the only US public hedge fund that reports fund performance and assets under management to the SEC every month). Institutional investors also are looking to hedge funds to further diversify their investments.

Company Background

Daniel Och (a former Goldman Sachs trader) and the Ziff family founded the company.

The marketplace was not kind to Och-Ziff during the global financial crisis. Overall US hedge funds lost massive amounts during the downturn. While Och-Ziff fared somewhat better than average it still saw significant losses primarily from negative investment performance and customer redemptions. Assets under management fell from $33 billion to $22 billion in 2008 and continued downward hitting $20 billion in April 2009.

EXECUTIVES

CEO, Daniel S. Och, age 55
Executive Managing Director Head US Investing and Board Member, David Windreich, age 58
Executive Managing Director and Head European Investing, Michael Cohen, age 44
Executive Managing Director and Head Asian Investing; Director Och-Ziff Consulting (Beijing), Zoltan Varga, age 42, $200,000 total compensation
Executive Managing Director and Head Global Convertible and Derivative Arbitrage, Harold Kelly, age 52
CFO, Alesia Haas
Vice President Hedge Fund Market, Frances (Fran) Orabona
Assistant Vice President, Lisa (Lis) Courtney
Vice President, Hermes Li
Vice President, Daniel (Dan) Bley
Vice President, Andres (Andre) Schumann
Auditors: Ernst & Young LLP

LOCATIONS

HQ: Och-Ziff Capital Management Group LLC
9 West 57th Street, New York, NY 10019
Phone: 212 790-0000
Web: www.ozcap.com

COMPETITORS

AXA Financial	Greenlight Capital
AllianceBernstein	Renaissance
Charles Schwab	Technologies LLC
Citigroup	UBS Financial Services
Elliott Management	

HISTORICAL FINANCIALS

Company Type: Public

Income Statement

FYE: December 31

	REVENUE ($ mil.)	NET INCOME ($ mil.)	NET PROFIT MARGIN	EMPLOYEES
12/15	1,322.9	25.7	1.9%	659.0
12/14	1,542.2	142.4	9.2%	595.0
12/13	1,895.9	261.7	13.8%	546.0
12/12	1,211.4	(315.8)	—	468.0
12/11	616.4	(418.9)	—	434.0
Annual Growth	21.0%	—	—	11.0%

2015 Year-End Financials

Debt ratio: 70.4%
Return on equity: 7.6%
Cash ($ mil.): 254.0
Current ratio: 1.10
Long-term debt ($ mil.): 7,526.5

No. of shares (mil.): 478.3
Dividends
  Yield: 13.9%
  Payout: 122.5%
Market value ($ mil.): 2,980.0

	STOCK PRICE ($) FY Close	P/E High/Low	PER SHARE ($) Earnings	Dividends	Book Value
12/15	6.23	95 38	0.14	0.87	0.87
12/14	11.68	19 13	0.80	1.72	0.53
12/13	14.80	9 5	1.62	1.42	(0.12)
12/12	9.50	— —	(2.21)	0.40	(0.58)
12/11	8.41	— —	(4.07)	1.07	(0.86)
Annual Growth	(7.2%)	— —	—	(5.0%)	—

Old Line Bancshares Inc

Old Line Bancshares is the holding company for Old Line Bank serving consumers businesses and wealthy individuals in the Old Line State and in the Washington DC area. With some 20 branch offices and total assets in excess of $1.2 billion the bank offers standard retail products including deposit accounts CDs and credit cards. Commercial and industrial and commercial real estate loans make up 75% of the bank's loan portfolio though it also offers consumer loans and luxury boat financing. The company also owns 50% of real estate firm Pointer Ridge Office Investment.

OperationsAbout 81% of its revenue came from interest income on loans in 2014 while another 7% came from interest on securities (including mortgage-backed US government agency and municipal securities). About 4% of revenue was generated from service charges on deposit accounts 4% came from fees and commissions and 2% came from gains on the sales of its loans.Geographic ReachOld Line Bank more than 20 branches mostly in suburban Maryland (which includes Washington DC and suburbs and Southern Maryland) in the counties of Anne Arundel Calvert Charles Prince George's and St. Mary's.Financial PerformanceOld Line Bancshares' revenues and profits have been trending higher over the past several years mostly driven by strong loan business growth obtained through acquisitions and organically. The bank's revenue dipped by 3% to $51.6 million in 2014 despite loan growth during the year mostly as its non-interest income shrank due to a decline in gains from the sale of its loans and investment securities compared to the prior year.Lower revenue and higher loan loss provisions from a less credit-worth loan portfolio in 2014 caused Old Line's net income to fall by 8% to $7.1 million. The company's operating cash levels declined by 35% to $10.2 million on lower cash earnings.StrategyOld Line Bancshares in 2015 laid out its short-term plans to collect on its non-accrual and past due loans and strategically selling its acquired loans and real-estate owned loans to boost its credit quality. It also expressed its strategy of extending its core banking services growing its fee income (especially in the low-interest environment) and embracing digital banking technologies such as online and mobile banking to reduce its spending on costly branch expansion plans. Management also touted success in organically growing its loan and deposit business in Montgomery Prince George's Anne Arundel counties in Maryland during 2014.The company sometimes grows its loan business and branch network by strategically acquiring banks in its primary markets. Its agreement to acquire Regal Bancorp for example would add three new banking locations to its network and $133.7 million in assets to its books –which would make it the third-largest commercial bank in Maryland by assets and the second-largest by branch network.Mergers and Acquisitions

In August 2015 the company agreed to acquire Regal Bancorp including its Regal Bank & Trust subsidiary its three branches and assets of $133.7 million. The deal was expected to close in late 2015 or early 2016.In May 2013 Old Line Bancshare closed on its $54.7-million purchase of WSB Holdings adding five Washington Savings Bank FSB branches and $310 million in assets.Previously Old Line acquired Maryland Bankcorp in 2011 in a move that doubled its branch network and asset portfolio.

EXECUTIVES

Senior Vice President, Joseph (Jo) Burnett
Senior Vice President Old Line Bank, William (Bill) Bush
Senior Vice President of Lending Management Team, Keven Zinn
Senior Vice President, David (Dave) Seyler
Executive Vice President and Chief Operating Officer, Mark (Marky) Semanie
Vice President, Rob Bowling
Senior Vice President Information Technology, Jim Thompson
Auditors: Dixon Hughes Goodman LLP

LOCATIONS

HQ: Old Line Bancshares Inc
  1525 Pointer Ridge Place, Bowie, MD 20716
Phone: 301 430-2500
Web: www.oldlinebank.com

COMPETITORS

BB&T	PNC Financial
Bank of America	Tri-County Financial
M&T Bank	

HISTORICAL FINANCIALS

Company Type: Public

Income Statement

FYE: December 31

	ASSETS ($ mil.)	NET INCOME ($ mil.)	INCOME AS % OF ASSETS	EMPLOYEES
12/15	1,510.0	10.4	0.7%	248.0
12/14	1,227.5	7.1	0.6%	228.0
12/13	1,167.2	7.8	0.7%	254.0
12/12	861.8	7.5	0.9%	182.0
12/11	811.0	5.3	0.7%	177.0
Annual Growth	16.8%	18.1%	—	8.8%

2015 Year-End Financials

Return on assets: 0.7%
Return on equity: 7.5%
Long-term debt ($ mil.): —
No. of shares (mil.): 10.8
Sales ($ mil): 58.3

Dividends
  Yield: 1.2%
  Payout: 22.3%
Market value ($ mil.): 190.0

	STOCK PRICE ($) FY Close	P/E High/Low	PER SHARE ($) Earnings	Dividends	Book Value
12/15	17.57	19 15	0.97	0.21	13.31
12/14	15.82	27 21	0.65	0.18	12.51
12/13	14.50	17 13	0.86	0.16	11.71
12/12	11.29	11 7	1.09	0.16	10.94
12/11	8.10	11 8	0.86	0.13	9.98
Annual Growth	21.4%	— —	3.1%	12.7%	7.5%

Omega Flex Inc

Like a reed in a stream Grasshopper sometimes the flexible withstand pressure better than the rigid. That's certainly a concept that Omega Flex can get behind: The company makes corrugated metal and flexible tubular and braided metal (stainless steel bronze) hoses and reinforcements for construction and industrial customers to use in liquid and gas transportation. Its products are designed to deal with high pressure motion extreme temperatures harsh liquids or gases and abrasion. Other applications include cryogenics and propane and natural gas installations. The estate of John Reed and his son chairman Stewart Reed own a majority of Omega Flex which was spun off from Mestek in 2005.

Geographic Reach

Pennsylvania-based Omega Flex has manufacturing operations in Exton Pennsylvania. Some manufacturing is performed in the UK. The company rings up about 90% of its sales in North America. International sales are mainly in the UK and elsewhere in Europe.

Omega Flex opened a new facility for stocking and sales in Houston during 2014.

Sales and Marketing

The company targets the commercial construction and general industrial sectors. Its typical customers include petrochemical plants steel mills transportation companies and pharmaceutical firms. Sales channels include independent sales representatives distributors OEMs direct sales and online sales via the company's website.

Omega Flex's brand names include OmegaFlex TracPipe AutoSnap AutoFlare and CounterStrike. Recently developed products include the DoubleTrac brand of piping used in gas stations and other underground petroleum piping applications and

SolarTrac piping for solar-heated hot water systems.

Advertising expenses advertising expenses totaled $848000 in 2014 up from $673000 in 2013.

Financial Performance

Omega Flex's revenues have been rising steadily for the past few years. The flexible metallic hose maker reported sales of $85.2 million in 2014 making it the company's best year yet. That increase was due both to higher demand for its products and a rise in prices (intended to offset higher raw material costs). Net income rose 34% over the same period to $13.5 million primarily due to the higher net sales.

Cash flow from operations also increased rising 20% to $2.4 million.

Strategy

The company's driving strategy for growth is to continue to innovate creating new products to meet new demands. For example in 2014 it introduced the AutoSnap product which is the only corrugated stainless steel tubing (CSST) fitting requiring no assembly before installation.

EXECUTIVES

President CEO and Director, Kevin R. Hoben, age 69, $381,100 total compensation
EVP COO and Director, Mark F. Albino, age 63, $305,910 total compensation
SVP Corporate Development and Facilities Management, Steven A. Treichel, age 65, $164,370 total compensation
VP Finance and CFO, Paul J. Kane, age 48
Chairman, Stewart B. Reed, age 68
Auditors: RSM US LLP

LOCATIONS

HQ: Omega Flex Inc
451 Creamery Way, Exton, PA 19341
Phone: 610 524-7272　　　**Fax:** 610 524-7282
Web: www.omegaflex.com

PRODUCTS/OPERATIONS

Selected Brands
AutoFlare
CounterStrike
OmegaFlex
TracPipe

COMPETITORS

Dixon Valve	Kelly Pipe Co. LLC
Everett J. Prescott	Redlon & Johnson
Ferguson Enterprises	Tuthill
Gates Corp.	Ward Manufacturing

HISTORICAL FINANCIALS
Company Type: Public

Income Statement
FYE: December 31

	REVENUE ($ mil.)	NET INCOME ($ mil.)	NET PROFIT MARGIN	EMPLOYEES
12/15	93.2	15.7	16.9%	132.0
12/14	85.2	13.4	15.8%	140.0
12/13	77.1	10.0	13.0%	131.0
12/12	64.0	6.8	10.7%	129.0
12/11	54.1	4.6	8.6%	116.0
Annual Growth	14.5%	35.8%	—	3.3%

2015 Year-End Financials
Debt ratio: —　　　　　　　　　No. of shares (mil.): 10.0
Return on equity: 42.2%　　　Dividends
Cash ($ mil.): 30.1　　　　　　Yield: 2.5%
Current ratio: 2.41　　　　　　Payout: 55.9%
Long-term debt ($ mil.): —　　Market value ($ mil.): 333.0

	STOCK PRICE ($) FY Close	P/E High/Low	PER SHARE ($) Earnings	Dividends	Book Value
12/15	33.01	28 16	1.56	0.85	4.05
12/14	37.81	29 13	1.33	0.49	3.35
12/13	20.46	21 12	0.99	0.43	2.53
12/12	12.36	25 15	0.68	1.00	1.95
12/11	14.13	36 23	0.46	0.00	2.26
Annual Growth	23.6%	— —	35.7%	—	15.7%

Omega Healthcare Investors, Inc.

Omega Healthcare Investors can put an end to the burdens of real-estate management. The self-administered real estate investment trust (REIT) invests in health care facilities throughout the US. It owns some 900 properties primarily long-term care facilities in more than 40 states. The REIT specializes in sales/leaseback transactions in which it purchases properties owned by health care providers and leases them back to those companies (thereby freeing the health care companies from the responsibilities of real estate management). The REIT's properties are operated by third-party health care operating companies including Genesis HealthCare System and CommuniCare Health Services.

Geographic Reach

The Maryland-based REITs largest markets are Florida Indiana and Ohio. Texas is another important market for the firm. Overall Omega Healthcare Investors has holdings in 41 states.

Sales and Marketing

The REIT's largest tenants include New Ark Investment Genesis Healthcare and CommuniCare Health Services which together represent about a third of its portfolio.

Financial Performance

Omega Healthcare Investors (OHI) reported revenue of $418.7 million in 2013 a 19% increase versus 2012. Driving the double-digit gain was rising rental income generated by investments made in 2013 and 2012. Net income grew 43% to $172.5 million on higher rental income. Both revenue and cash flow has increased steadily over the past four years and profitability has rebounded.

Strategy

The REIT is investing aggressively in the health care sector as demand for senior living facilities grows in tandem with the aging population and the real estate market makes a comeback. Indeed in 2013 the firm completed transactions totaling about $622 million in new investments. Its core portfolio consists of long-term lease and mortgage agreements. All of its leases are "triple-net" leases which require the tenants to pay all property related expenses. The REIT's mortgage revenue comes from fixed-rate loans. Omega Healthcare's geographically diverse portfolio comprises 476 skilled nursing facilities 18 assisted living locations and 11 specialty facilities such as rehabilitation hospitals. Its properties are operated by third parties.

Mergers and Acquisitions

In mid-2015 Omega acquired Aviv REIT in a deal valued at some $3 billion. The combined company is one of the largest REITs focused on skilled nursing facilities.

EXECUTIVES

CEO and Director, C. Taylor Pickett, age 54, $700,000 total compensation
COO, Daniel J. Booth, age 52, $440,000 total compensation
SVP Operations, R. Lee Crabill, age 62, $330,000 total compensation
CFO, Robert O. Stephenson, age 52, $400,000 total compensation
Chief Accounting Officer, Michael D. Ritz, age 47, $265,000 total compensation
Chairman, Bernard J. (Bernie) Korman, age 84
Auditors: Ernst & Young LLP

LOCATIONS

HQ: Omega Healthcare Investors, Inc.
200 International Circle, Suite 3500, Hunt Valley, MD 21030
Phone: 410 427-1700　　　**Fax:** 410 427-8800
Web: www.omegahealthcare.com

PRODUCTS/OPERATIONS

2015 Sales

	$ mil.	% of total
Rental income	606.0	81
Mortgage interest	68.9	9
Income from direct financing leases	59.9	8
Others	8.8	2
Total	**743.6**	**100**

COMPETITORS

G&L Realty Properties	Senior Housing
HCP	Properties
Healthcare Realty	Ventas
Trust	Welltower
LTC Properties	
National Health	
Investors	

HISTORICAL FINANCIALS
Company Type: Public

Income Statement
FYE: December 31

	REVENUE ($ mil.)	NET INCOME ($ mil.)	NET PROFIT MARGIN	EMPLOYEES
12/15	743.6	233.3	31.4%	58.0
12/14	504.7	221.3	43.9%	27.0
12/13	418.7	172.5	41.2%	25.0
12/12	350.4	120.7	34.4%	25.0
12/11	292.2	52.6	18.0%	24.0
Annual Growth	26.3%	45.1%	—	24.7%

2015 Year-End Financials
Debt ratio: 44.5%　　　　　　No. of shares (mil.): 187.4
Return on equity: 9.0%　　　 Dividends
Cash ($ mil.): 5.4　　　　　　Yield: 6.2%
Current ratio: 14.58　　　　　Payout: 154.6%
Long-term debt ($ mil.): 3,569.0　　Market value ($ mil.): 6,555.0

	STOCK PRICE ($)	P/E		PER SHARE ($)	
	FY Close	High/Low	Earnings	Dividends	Book Value
12/15	34.98	35 25	1.29	2.18	19.95
12/14	39.07	23 17	1.74	2.02	10.98
12/13	29.80	26 16	1.46	1.86	10.52
12/12	23.85	22 17	1.12	1.69	9.00
12/11	19.35	53 31	0.46	1.55	8.50
Annual Growth	16.0%	— —	29.4%	8.9%	23.8%

Omega Protein Corp.

Omega Protein is the alpha dog of the fish-meal market. With a handful of US processing plants a fleet of some 40 fishing vessels and 30-plus spotter aircraft the company is the largest US producer of fish meal and fish oil derived from menhaden (an inedible fish found in the Gulf of Mexico and along the East Coast). Animal-feed makers and livestock ranchers use Omega Protein's fish meal for protein additives in feed; the fish oil is used in Europe in margarine and for industrial ends. Rich in Omega-3 fatty acids (linked to health benefits) fish oil is also used as a human food supplement. Through subsidiaries Omega Protein provides nutraceutical ingredients and compounds including Omega-3 fish oils.

Operations

Omega Protein's operations consist of four primary subsidiaries: Omega Protein processes and harvests menhaden fish; Omega Shipyards owns and manages the drydock facility for the company's fishing fleet and occasionally third parties; Cyvex Nutrition supplies ingredients to the nutraceutical market; and InCon Processing is a specialty toll processor that uses molecular distillation technology to create Omega-3 fish oils.

Omega Protein's fish oil brands include Virginia Prime OmegaPure and OmegaActiv; fish meal brands include Special Select and SeaLac. The company also makes fertilizer (OmegaGrow) and a fungicide/insecticide (SeaCide). Many customers are feed producers who use Omega Protein's products to manufacture feed for swine and dairy cattle as well as for domestic pets. An increasing percentage of the company's products is being used by the aquaculture industry as the practice of aquaculture increases worldwide.

Geographic Reach

The US is the Houston-based company's largest market accounting for 50% of its sales. Asia contributes nearly 30% while Europe represents more than 10%. Other markets include Canada South and Central America and Mexico.

Sales and Marketing

Omega Protein's largest customer in 2013 was Nestlé Purina PetCare which contributed approximately $22.7 million (or 9% of sales) to the company's coffers. The company's products are sold directly to some 200 domestic and foreign customers most of which are located in Canada Chile China Japan Norway and Saudi Arabia. Independent sales agents generate a small amount of sales.

Financial Performance

Omega Protein has been reporting rising revenues since 2010. In 2014 it grew another 26% to hit $308.6 million due to contributions from acquisitions and higher prices for some items. Net in-come has fluctuated over the years and fell 40% in 2014 to $18.5 million because of higher impairment of goodwill.

Strategy

Omega Protein's strategy going forward includes growth through acquisitions most recently of human nutrition businesses. In September 2014 the company acquired Bioriginal Food & Science Corp. to expand and diversify its human nutrition business. Canada-based Bioriginal Food & Science supplies plant- and marine-based specialty oils and essential fatty acids to the food and nutraceutical industries in North America Europe and Asia. Bioriginal Food & Science which had about $98 million in net revenues operates as a wholly-owned subsidiary of Omega Protein. It paid $70.5 million for the company.

In February 2013 the company purchased Wisconsin Specialty Protein (WSP) based in Madison to build on its human nutrition business with WSP's specialty whey protein products.

The company is also acting to expand and trim select operations. In 2014 it streamlined operations in the Gulf of Mexico by closing its menhaden fish processing plant in Cameron Louisiana and redeploying certain ships from that plant to reduce maintenance-related capital expenditures. Also in mid-2014 the company completed an expansion roughly doubling capacity at its specialty dairy protein production facility in Reedsburg Wisconsin.

In June 2013 Omega Protein resolved investigations by the US Coast Guard and the US EPA by entering into a plea agreement with the US Attorney's Office. The company pleaded guilty to two Clean Water Act violations and paid a $5.5 million fine.

Mergers and Acquisitions

In September 2014 the company acquired Bioriginal Food & Science Corp. to expand and diversify its human nutrition business. Canada-based Bioriginal Food & Science supplies plant- and marine-based specialty oils and essential fatty acids to the food and nutraceutical industries in North America Europe and Asia. Bioriginal Food & Science which had about $98 million in net revenues operates as a wholly owned subsidiary of Omega Protein. It paid $70.5 million for the company.

In February 2013 the company purchased Wisconsin Specialty Protein (WSP) based in Madison to build on its human nutrition business with WSP's specialty whey protein products.

HISTORY

Omega Protein's predecessor dates back to a fish processing operation founded in Reedville Virginia by John and Thomas Haynie in 1878. (The site currently is home to the company's largest plant.) Almost a century later Zapata an oil and gas firm co-founded by George H. W. Bush acquired Haynie Products.

The division became known as Zapata Haynie. The company spent the late 1980s and 1990s fighting for FDA approval of refined menhaden oil for human consumption (the oil contains high levels of Omega-3 fatty acids touted as having health benefits); approval was finally granted in 1997.

Financier Malcolm Glazer first acquired a stake in Zapata in 1992. That year Zapata acquired 60% of Venture Milling a Delaware-based blender of animal protein products. Two years later the division was renamed Zapata Protein to reflect its expansion into animal feed. Zapata sold most of the assets of Venture Milling in 1997 and acquired two of its four US rivals: Chesapeake Bay area-based American Protein and Louisiana-based Gulf Pro-tein. Also that year it renamed the division Marine Genetics.

In 1998 Zapata changed Marine Genetics' name to Omega Protein and spun off about 40% in that division to the public. Despite an active hurricane season that crimped the fishing season Omega Protein reported record profits in 1998. However dramatic price drops for fish meal and fish oil (caused by a global glut in those markets) squeezed the life out of sales and profits in 1999. Omega Protein responded by mothballing part of its fleet for the 2000 fishing season.

In 2003 Omega received two separate unsolicited takeover offers —the first at $45 per share by merger and acquisition firm Hollingsworth Rothwell & Roxford; the second at $9.50 per share from Australia-based Ferrari Investments and unidentified US partners.

Omega completed a processing facility in 2004 in Reedsville Virginia that tripled its existing refined fish-oil production capacity. The factory also expanded capacity for oils used in leather drilling fluid and animal food.

The company shut down its sales office in Mexico in 2005 and consolidated its functions with those at its Houston headquarters. The company's Moss Point processing facility and its shipyard in Mississippi were severely damaged due to Hurricane Katrina in August 2005. Its Cameron and Abbeville plants in Louisiana were shut down that September due to damage sustained from Hurricane Rita. Moss Point and Abbeville were reopened in mid-October. The Cameron facility was rebuilt and back in operation by 2006.

Omega Protein was 33% owned by investor and then Omega chairman Avram Glazer's family which maintained its shares through Zapata Corporation. However Zapata sold its holdings in Omega in 2006 at which time Glazer stepped down as chairman and president and CEO Joseph von Rosenberg replaced Glazer.

In 2007 the company opened a technical center in Houston (The OmegaPure Technology and Innovation Center) to research and develop new Omega-3 products.

EXECUTIVES

EVP General Counsel and Secretary, John D. Held, age 53, $300,000 total compensation
President and CEO, Bret Scholtes, age 46, $450,000 total compensation
President Animal Nutrition Division, Mark E. Griffin, age 48, $300,000 total compensation
President Bioriginal, Joseph R. Vidal
Senior Director Operations, Monty C. Deihl
CFO and EVP, Andrew Johannesen
Vp Marine Operations; President Omega Shipyard, Michael E Wilson, age 65
Vice President Corporate Controller, Greg Toups
Vice President Chief Accounting Officer and Controller, Mark (Marky) Livingston
Chairman, Gary R. Goodwin
Auditors: PricewaterhouseCoopers LLP

LOCATIONS

HQ: Omega Protein Corp.
2105 City West Blvd., Suite 500, Houston, TX 77042-2838
Phone: 713 623-0060
Web: www.omegaprotein.com

2014 Sales

	$ mil.	% of total
Fish meal	147.1	48
Fish oil	70.8	23
Dietary supplement ingredients	64.8	21
Refined fish oil	22.2	7
Fish solubles	3.7	1
Total	**308.6**	**100**

2014 Sales

% of total	$ mil
Animal nutrition	79
Human nutrition	21
Total	**100**

Selected Products

Fish meal
  Feed
  Animal
  Aquaculture
  Household pets
  Swine
Fish oil
  Feed
  Animal
  Aquaculture
  Dietary supplements
  Human foods
Fish solubles
  Aquaculture feed
  Bait
  Organic fertilizer

COMPETITORS

ADM	Ingredion
ADM Alliance Nutrition	Kodiak Fishmeal
Ag Processing Inc.	Land O'Lakes Purina
American Seafoods	Feed
Bayer CropScience	Marubeni
Blue Seal Feeds	Nippon Suisan
Bunge Limited	Nutreco
CHS	Scotts Miracle-Gro
Cargill	Scoular
Dow AgroSciences	Westward Seafoods
Griffin Industries	

HISTORICAL FINANCIALS

Company Type: Public

Income Statement

FYE: December 31

	REVENUE ($ mil.)	NET INCOME ($ mil.)	NET PROFIT MARGIN	EMPLOYEES
12/15	359.3	23.9	6.7%	627.0
12/14	308.6	18.4	6.0%	657.0
12/13	244.2	30.5	12.5%	450.0
12/12	235.6	4.0	1.7%	500.0
12/11	235.2	34.1	14.5%	495.0
Annual Growth	**11.2%**	**(8.5%)**	**—**	**6.1%**

2015 Year-End Financials

Debt ratio: 5.9%
Return on equity: 8.5%
Cash ($ mil.): 0.6
Current ratio: 3.36
Long-term debt ($ mil.): 22.8

No. of shares (mil.): 22.2
Dividends
  Yield: —
  Payout: —
Market value ($ mil.): 493.0

	STOCK PRICE ($) FY Close	P/E High/Low		PER SHARE ($) Earnings	Dividends	Book Value
12/15	22.20	23	10	1.07	0.00	13.28
12/14	10.57	18	10	0.85	0.00	12.35
12/13	12.29	10	4	1.45	0.00	11.88
12/12	6.12	43	29	0.20	0.00	10.34
12/11	7.13	8	4	1.71	0.00	10.04
Annual Growth	**32.8%**	**—**	**—**	**(11.1%)**	**—**	**7.2%**

Omnicell Inc

Omnicell dispenses with anything less than full knowledge when it comes to dispensing drugs to patients. A developer of specialized software and hardware products Omnicell makes mobile cabinets and workstations that automatically dispense doses of medication and surgical supplies to help pharmacists and nurses reduce medical errors and increase patient safety. More than 1600 hospitals use its OmniRx medication dispensing cabinets and complementary software such as SinglePointe and AnywhereRN a program that allows nurses to remotely operate the cabinets. Another top seller is WorkflowRx an automated pharmacy management software system that tracks inventory.

Operations

Omnicell's Automation and Analytics segment (80% of sales) is organized around the design manufacturing selling and servicing of medication and supply dispensing systems pharmacy inventory management systems and related software. Omnicell's OptiFlex is an automated cabinet that dispenses surgical and medical supplies using barcodes to assign and bill products to patient accounts and its Tissue Center manages and documents tissue sample specimens taken from patients during biopsies and other procedures and used for medical research.

Its Medication Adherence segment (20% of sales) includes the manufacturing and selling of consumable medication blister cards packaging equipment and ancillary products and services. These products to manage medication administration outside the hospital and include products under the MTS Medication Technologies Surgichem Limited and Omnicell brands.

The company has parlayed the technology behind its medication-dispensing cabinets into other hospital products that keep track of inventory and supplies. It makes a secure dispensing system for anesthesia supplies used in the operating room as well as a barcode inventory management system for controlled substances.

Geographic Reach

The company's products are used throughout the US and Canada (91% of sales). It also markets its products in Europe and Asia.

Sales and Marketing

Omnicell is only one of a handful of companies that make automated medication dispensing cabinets. Others include McKesson's AcuDose CareFusion's Pyxis and AmerisourceBergen's MedSelect. While its competitors manufacture a variety of products for the health care industry Omnicell is focused on providing its specialized hardware and software.

The company's sales force is organized by geographic region in the US and Canada. Omnicell uses a direct sales force for Non-Acute Care products in the UK and Germany. For other geographies the company's products are sold through distributors.

Financial Performance

The company has experienced mostly revenue growth in recent fiscal years. In 2014 it reported about $441 million in revenue up 16% from the $381 million it posted in 2013. The company saw strong sales of its Medical Automation Cabinets and Supply Cabinets and Supply Management software. The higher revenue led to a healthy dose of profit –$30.5 million 27% higher than 2013.

Strategy

Omnicell's growth strategy centers on developing new products and enhancing existing products. The company released the fourth generation of its Omnicell G4 platform with the Unity database designed to decrease the risk of human error and save pharmacy time by eliminating the need for repetitive entry of drug formularies in multiple locations.

Looking to expand its international presence Omnicell opened an office in Beijing in 2014. Also in 2014 the company increased its presence in the UK with the acquisition of Surgichem Limited which had been a subsidiary of Bupa Care Homes. Surgichem supplies monitored dosage system to a network of more than 3200 independent pharmacies and pharmacy chains in the UK.

EXECUTIVES

EVP International and Global Quality and Manufacturing, Robin G. (Rob) Seim, age 56, $302,769 total compensation
EVP; Chief Legal and Administrative Officer, Dan S. Johnston, age 52, $270,154 total compensation
Chairman President and CEO, Randall A. Lipps, age 58, $551,538 total compensation
EVP Sales and Marketing, J. Christopher (Chris) Drew, age 50, $322,462 total compensation
EVP Strategy and Business Development, Nhat H. Ngo, age 43, $273,539 total compensation
EVP and CFO, Peter Kuipers, age 44
EVP of Engineering, Jorge R. Taborga, age 56
EVP and Chief Legal and Administrative Officer, Daniel Johnston
Vice President Manager Director, Connie Ayala
Vice President and General Manager, William (Bill) Wingfield
Vice President Manager Director, Susan Dailey
Vice President Field Operations, Pat (Patty) Diresta
Vice President Manager Director, Nicole Jastrow
Vice President, Troy Hilsenroth
Vice President Global Quality And Regulatory Affairs, Robert B (Bob) Smith
Auditors: Deloitte & Touche LLP

LOCATIONS

HQ: Omnicell Inc
  590 East Middlefield Road, Mountain View, CA 94043
Phone: 650 251-6100
Web: www.omnicell.com

PRODUCTS/OPERATIONS

2014 Sales

	$ mil.	% of total
United States	394.2	89
Foreign Countries	46.7	11
Total	**440.9**	**100**

2014 Sales

	$ mil.	% of total
Product revenue	360.3	82
Service and other revenue	80.6	18
Total	**440.9**	**100**

2014 Sales

	$ mil.	% of total
Automation and Analytics	354.1	80
Medication Adherence	86.8	20
Total	**440.9**	**100**

COMPETITORS

Allscripts	Emerson Electric
AmerisourceBergen	Ergotron
Becton Dickinson	McKesson
CareFusion	SciQuest
Cerner	Siemens Healthcare

HISTORICAL FINANCIALS

Company Type: Public

Income Statement

FYE: December 31

	REVENUE ($ mil.)	NET INCOME ($ mil.)	NET PROFIT MARGIN	EMPLOYEES
12/15	484.5	30.7	6.3%	1,451.0
12/14	440.9	30.5	6.9%	1,236.0
12/13	380.5	23.9	6.3%	1,134.0
12/12	314.0	16.1	5.2%	1,089.0
12/11	245.5	10.3	4.2%	773.0
Annual Growth	18.5%	31.2%	—	17.1%

2015 Year-End Financials

Debt ratio: —	No. of shares (mil.): 35.5
Return on equity: 7.7%	Dividends
Cash ($ mil.): 82.2	Yield: —
Current ratio: 2.12	Payout: —
Long-term debt ($ mil.): —	Market value ($ mil.): 1,106.0

	STOCK PRICE ($) FY Close	P/E High/Low	PER SHARE ($) Earnings	Dividends	Book Value
12/15	31.08	47 31	0.84	0.00	11.30
12/14	33.12	39 29	0.83	0.00	10.89
12/13	25.53	37 22	0.67	0.00	9.97
12/12	14.87	36 26	0.47	0.00	9.17
12/11	16.52	55 42	0.30	0.00	8.53
Annual Growth	17.1%	— —	29.4%	—	7.3%

On Assignment, Inc.

On Assignment is a specialist staffing agency that places professionals from IT consultants to lab assistants to nurses with clients in need of temporary help. The firm operates through several divisions: Apex (IT and engineering staffing for temporary temp-to-hire and permanent placements); Life Sciences Europe (laboratory and scientific professionals in biotechnology pharmaceutical food and beverage medical device chemical and environmental industries); and Oxford (engineering and specialized high-end IT consultants). On Assignment provides staff to about 7700 clients and was founded in 1985.

Geographic Reach

The company operates from about 130 branch offices in nearly 35 states and seven foreign countries including Belgium Canada China Ireland the Netherlands Spain and the UK. The US accounts for nearly 95% of its total sales.

Operations

On Assignment has changed its operating structure due to milestone acquisitions it has made over the last few years. Its chief operating segments include Apex (64% of total sales) Oxford (27%) Life Sciences Europe (2%) and Physician (7%). the Physician segment was sold in 2015.

Financial Performance

On Assignment's 2014 revenue increased by 14% to $1.86 billion largely on the contributions of CyberCoders and Whitaker companies acquired in 2013. Higher numbers of contract professionals on assignment and an increase in the average bill rate pushed revenue higher.

In 2014 the company's net income dropped to about $77.18 million from $84.5 million in 2013 because of higher income tax provisions and loss from the discontinued operations.

Strategy

While On Assignment's business strategy has involved steady growth through targeted acquisitions it was quiet on the acquisition front in 2014. It did howeversell its physician staffing segment VISTA Staffing Solutions to Envision Healthcare for more than $100 million in early 2015. The followed its 2013 sale of its Nurse Travel business. The proceeds from the sale provide On Assignment with cash for acquisitions and paying down debt.

The company's most significant acquisition was Apex Systems the sixth largest staffing firm and one of the fastest growing IT staffing firms in the US. The unit accounted for almost two-thirds of the company's revenue in 2014.

HISTORY

Chemists Bruce Culver and Raf Dahlquist concocted the company in 1985. Lab Support (its original name) got off to a good start but the founders were scientists not business strategists; by 1989 the company was losing steam. The firm's venture investors took over installing new management under Tom Buelter who had developed Kelly Services' home care division. He refocused operations to temporary scientific services and turned the company around. It went public in 1992 as On Assignment.

In 1994 On Assignment bought 1st Choice Personnel and Sklar Resource Group which specialized in temporary placement of financial professionals. The next year it started its Advanced Science Professionals unit to place temps in highly skilled scientific positions. With the 1996 purchase of Minneapolis-based EnviroStaff On Assignment also began providing temporary workers in environmental fields. On Assignment crossed the border and started operations in Canada in 1997. In 1999 it established Clinical Lab Staff as its fourth division. Also by 1999 the company had opened the first three of several planned European offices in the UK.

In 2001 Buelter relinquished the CEO position to Joe Peterson. (Buelter resigned as chairman early the following year.) Also in 2002 the company acquired Health Personnel Options Corporation a provider of temporary travel nurses and other health care professionals. The end of 2003 saw the appointment of Peter Dameris as the president and CEO of On Assignment.

In 2007 On Assignment reached new levels of growth with the key acquisitions of IT and engineering staffing provider Oxford Global Resources and physician staffing firm VISTA Staffing Solutions.

As with most players in the staffing sector On Assignment felt the painful effects of the global recession in 2008 and 2009 as it was hurt by high unemployment rates and shrinking demand for its staffing services.

As the economy began to pick up in 2010 On Assignment bought The Cambridge Group Ltd. a staffing services firm placing physicians clinical and scientific personnel and IT professionals. Also that year the company acquired Sharpstream a firm with expertise in search services for executive to middle managers residing in the life sciences sector. The deal added offices in the US the UK and Shanghai.

Continuing its string of acquisitions in 2011 On Assignment obtained Valesta a provider of clinical research specialized staffing services with headquarters in Belgium and additional offices in Spain and The Netherlands. The company next acquired Apex Systems the sixth largest staffing firm and one of the fastest growing IT staffing firms in the US in 2012.

EXECUTIVES

President Apex, Randolph C. (Rand) Blazer, age 66, $650,000 total compensation

Chief Financial Officer and Executive Vice President, Edward L. Pierce, age 60, $455,885 total compensation

CEO, Peter T. Dameris, age 56, $799,615 total compensation

SVP Shared Services and CIO, Michael C. Payne, $216,000 total compensation

President Life Sciences and Allied Divisions, Emmett B. McGrath, age 54, $320,748 total compensation

President VISTA Staffing Solutions, Christian Rutherford

President, Ted Hanson

Vice President Business Develo, Garrett (Bret) Hunt

Chairman, Jeremy M. Jones, age 74

Auditors: Deloitte & Touche LLP

LOCATIONS

HQ: On Assignment, Inc.
26745 Malibu Hills Road, Calabasas, CA 91301
Phone: 818 878-7900
Web: www.onassignment.com

PRODUCTS/OPERATIONS

2014 Sales

	$ mil.	% of total
Apex	1,190.1	64
Oxford	493.3	27
Physician	135.2	7
Life Sciences Europe	41.4	2
Total	1,860.0	100

Selected Divisions and Operating Units

Apex (IT staffing)
On Assignment Allied Travel
On Assignment Clinical Research
On Assignment Engineering
On Assignment Healthcare Staffing
On Assignment Health Information Management
On Assignment Lab Support
Oxford Global Resources (IT and engineering staffing)
VISTA Staffing Solutions (physician staffing)

COMPETITORS

AMN Healthcare	IBM
ATC Healthcare	Insight Global
Accenture	Kelly Services
Adecco	Kforce
Aerotek	ManpowerGroup
Allegis Group	Professional Staff
CHG Healthcare	RehabCare
Cross Country Healthcare	Robert Half
Day & Zimmermann	TEKsystems
	The Everhart Group

HISTORICAL FINANCIALS

Company Type: Public

Income Statement

FYE: December 31

	REVENUE ($ mil.)	NET INCOME ($ mil.)	NET PROFIT MARGIN	EMPLOYEES
12/15	2,065.0	97.6	4.7%	50,920.0
12/14	1,859.9	77.1	4.1%	37,500.0
12/13	1,632.0	84.5	5.2%	33,870.0
12/12	1,239.7	42.6	3.4%	34,530.0
12/11	597.2	24.3	4.1%	15,511.0
Annual Growth	36.4%	41.6%	—	34.6%

2015 Year-End Financials

Debt ratio: 42.7%
Return on equity: 13.7%
Cash ($ mil.): 23.8
Current ratio: 2.58
Long-term debt ($ mil.): 755.5

No. of shares (mil.): 53.0
Dividends
  Yield: —
  Payout: —
Market value ($ mil.): 2,383.0

	STOCK PRICE ($) FY Close	P/E High/Low	Earnings	PER SHARE ($) Dividends	Book Value
12/15	44.95	25 17	1.84	0.00	14.80
12/14	33.19	27 18	1.42	0.00	12.35
12/13	34.92	22 13	1.55	0.00	11.87
12/12	20.28	23 12	0.89	0.00	10.06
12/11	11.18	18 10	0.64	0.00	6.67
Annual Growth	41.6%	— —	30.2%	—	22.1%

One Liberty Properties, Inc.

One Liberty Properties may own the space where lovebirds shop for loveseats. Or bird food. The self-managed and self-administered real estate investment trust (REIT) invests in retail industrial and office properties throughout the US. It owns or co-owns over 100 properties totaling more than 8 million sq. ft. of space; more than half of its portfolio is leased to retailers including Haverty Furniture PetSmart and Giant Food Stores. The REIT also owns warehouses fitness centers and a movie theater. One Liberty Properties targets net-leased properties minimizing its responsibilities for taxes maintenance and other operating costs. The firm is controlled by the family of its chairman.

Operations

One Liberty owned 107 properties spanning 8.2 million sq. ft. of space across 30 states at the end of 2015. General retail properties generated 28% of its total rental revenue that year while furniture restaurant office supply and supermarket retail properties made up another 25%. Industrial properties accounted for 23% of rental revenue followed by flex properties (6%) health and fitness properties (5%) and other properties (12%).

Liberty owned five joint venture properties during 2015 representing an investment of approximately $11.4 million on its part. Most of the joint ventures are 50% owned by Liberty.

Geographic Reach

Liberty's properties are located in 30 US states with properties in Texas New York South Carolina Georgia and Pennsylvania generating more than 40% of its rental income during 2015.

Sales and Marketing

Liberty's largest tenant Haverty Furniture contributed 8% to the company's 2015 rental revenue while its next largest tenants made up another nearly 20% of its rental income and included LA Fitness Northern Tool Ferguson Enterprises and Office Depot. Other top tenants include national chains such as PetSmart TGI Fridays The Men's Wearhouse Barnes & Noble Walgreens and Whole Foods.

Financial Performance

One Liberty's revenues have risen more than 60% while its profits have nearly doubled since 2011 as new property acquisitions have driven rental income.The REIT's revenue jumped 9% to

$65.71 million during 2015 mostly as 16 new property acquisitions made in 2015 and 2014 drove additional rental income.Despite strong revenue growth in 2015 One Liberty Property's net income dipped 7% to $20.52 million mainly because in 2014 it had made twice as much in real estate sales gains after selling one of its properties in Parsippany New Jersey. The REIT's operating cash levels climbed 7% to $33.92 million as cash-denominated earnings rose during the year.

Strategy

One Liberty Properties mostly acquires US properties in locations with attractive locations and demographics. The REIT targets long-term lease agreements that offer more predictable cash flows and stability in markets with rental rate fluctuations and real estate values. Following this strategy the firm is better able to secure long-term financing for more property investments. Also by seeking long-term agreements the REIT has successfully assembled a diversified portfolio with an occupancy rate exceeding 98% based on square footage for the past several years.Beyond outright property acquisitions One Liberty also looks to invest in properties that can be repositioned or redeveloped national or regional tenant-anchored community shopping centers and properties that are ground leased to multi-family property operators.

Even though One Liberty Properties has been enjoying revenue growth from a growing tenant base the rapidly changing retail landscape presents challenges for Liberty as some of its tenants such as Office Depot and Barnes & Noble are facing increased pressure from online retailers such as Amazon.com and are closing stores as a result.

EXECUTIVES

SVP and CFO, David W. Kalish, age 69
EVP and COO, Lawrence G. Ricketts, age 39, $355,000 total compensation
President and Director, Patrick J. Callan, age 54, $700,000 total compensation
Chiarman, Matthew J. Gould, age 57
Vice Chairman, Fredric H. Gould
Auditors: Ernst & Young LLP

LOCATIONS

HQ: One Liberty Properties, Inc.
60 Cutter Mill Road, Great Neck, NY 11021
Phone: 516 466-3100
Web: www.onelibertyproperties.com

PRODUCTS/OPERATIONS

2015 Sales

	$ mil.	% of total
Rental income net	58.9	90
Tenant reimbursements	3.9	6
Lease termination fees	2.9	4
Total	65.7	100

COMPETITORS

DDR	Realty Income
Gladstone Commercial	Spirit Realty Capital
Lexington Realty Trust	Vornado Realty
Liberty Property Trust	Weingarten Realty
Monmouth Real Estate	
National Retail Properties	

HISTORICAL FINANCIALS
Company Type: Public

Income Statement
FYE: December 31

	REVENUE ($ mil.)	NET INCOME ($ mil.)	NET PROFIT MARGIN	EMPLOYEES
12/15	65.7	20.5	31.2%	9.0
12/14	60.4	22.1	36.6%	9.0
12/13	50.9	17.8	35.1%	7.0
12/12	44.7	32.3	72.2%	7.0
12/11	45.2	13.7	30.3%	5.0
Annual Growth	9.8%	10.6%	—	15.8%

2015 Year-End Financials

Debt ratio: 54.2%
Return on equity: 7.9%
Cash ($ mil.): 12.7
Current ratio: 3.97
Long-term debt ($ mil.): 352.6

No. of shares (mil.): 16.2
Dividends
  Yield: 7.3%
  Payout: 95.7%
Market value ($ mil.): 350.0

	STOCK PRICE ($) FY Close	P/E High/Low	Earnings	PER SHARE ($) Dividends	Book Value
12/15	21.46	21 17	1.22	1.58	15.99
12/14	23.67	18 15	1.37	1.50	16.17
12/13	20.13	24 17	1.14	1.42	16.35
12/12	20.29	9 8	2.16	1.34	16.24
12/11	16.50	18 14	0.96	1.32	15.36
Annual Growth	6.8%	— —	6.2%	4.6%	1.0%

OP Bancorp

LOCATIONS

HQ: OP Bancorp
1000 Wilshire Blvd #500, Los Angeles, CA 90017
Phone: 213 829-9999

HISTORICAL FINANCIALS
Company Type: Public

Income Statement
FYE: December 31

	ASSETS ($ mil.)	NET INCOME ($ mil.)	INCOME AS % OF ASSETS	EMPLOYEES
12/15	617.3	5.9	1.0%	0.0
12/14	528.1	4.4	0.8%	0.0
12/13	342.2	4.9	1.4%	0.0
12/12	206.1	6.1	3.0%	0.0
Annual Growth	44.1%	(1.3%)	—	—

2015 Year-End Financials

Return on assets: 1.0%
Return on equity: 8.6%
Long-term debt ($ mil.): —
No. of shares (mil.): 12.6
Sales ($ mil): 33.1

Dividends
  Yield: —
  Payout: —
Market value ($ mil.): 83.0

	STOCK PRICE ($) FY Close	P/E High/Low	Earnings	PER SHARE ($) Dividends	Book Value
12/15	6.55	15 12	0.46	0.00	5.71
12/14	7.10	— —	(0.00)	0.00	5.27
12/13	7.50	— —	(0.00)	0.00	4.31
12/12	2.10	— —	(0.00)	0.00	3.62
/0.00	—	—(0.00)	0.00	(0.00)	
Annual Growth	—	— —	—	—	—

Opus Bank Irvine (CA)

Auditors: KPMG LLP

LOCATIONS

HQ: Opus Bank Irvine (CA)
  19900 MacArthur Blvd., 12th Floor, Irvine, CA 92612
Phone: 949 250-9800
Web: www.opusbank.com

HISTORICAL FINANCIALS

Company Type: Public

Income Statement
FYE: December 31

	ASSETS ($ mil.)	NET INCOME ($ mil.)	INCOME AS % OF ASSETS	EMPLOYEES
12/15	6,649.8	59.9	0.9%	661.0
12/14	5,084.9	43.8	0.9%	585.0
12/13	3,738.8	143.1	3.8%	550.0
12/12	2,860.4	22.8	0.8%	0.0
12/11	0.0	(22.4)	—	0.0
Annual Growth	—	—	—	—

2015 Year-End Financials

Return on assets: 1.0%	Dividends
Return on equity: 7.1%	Yield: 0.9%
Long-term debt ($ mil.): —	Payout: 18.9%
No. of shares (mil.): 32.5	Market value ($ mil.): 1,202.0
Sales ($ mil): 258.0	

	STOCK PRICE ($) FY Close	P/E High/Low	PER SHARE ($) Earnings	Dividends	Book Value
12/15	36.97	21 13	1.79	0.34	26.68
12/14	28.37	22 18	1.38	0.00	28.41
Annual Growth	30.3%	— —	29.7%	—	(6.1%)

OraSure Technologies Inc.

When it comes to diagnostic tests OraSure is certain it can deliver results. The oral specimen kits and other diagnostic tests developed by OraSure Technologies are designed to detect drug use and certain infectious diseases namely HIV and hepatitis C. Its OraSure products use oral specimens rather than traditional blood or urine based methods to test for HIV. The Intercept line uses oral samples to test for marijuana cocaine opiates PCP and amphetamines. OraSure has also developed a rapid HIV blood diagnostic testing method and it has entered the genetic testing market through its DNAG subsidiary. OraSure sells its products in the US and internationally to health care facilities and medical laboratories.

Operations

Products include tests that detect antibodies to the HIV and HCV viruses and tests for drug abuse detection. OraSure operates in two primary segments: Its OSUR business (70% of revenue) develops manufactures and sells diagnostic products specimen collection devices and genetic testing devices. Meanwhile OraSure Technologies makes and sells enzyme immunoassay test kits and oral fluid collection devices for insurance laboratories; these products are used to assess the health and behavior of insurance applicants.

In addition to diagnostic tests and specimen kits OraSure's Histofreezer cryosurgical removal system treats a range of different types of skin lesions including plantar and genital warts and other common benign skin lesions. OraSure also sells an OTC wart remover under the Freeze n' Clear brand.

Geographic Reach

Only about 25% of OraSure's sales come from abroad but the company is expanding its international sales efforts. Subsidiary DNAG leases a 23500 sq. ft. facility in Ottawa Canada.

OraSure's products are available across North America South America Europe and Australia.

Sales and Marketing

OraSure uses direct agents collaborative partners and independent distributors to market its products in the US and abroad. Marketing techniques include trade shows distributor promotions and print advertisements. Customers include public health clinics hospitals pathology laboratory operators and doctors' offices.

In fiscal 2014 the company spent $6910 on advertising down from $17142 spent in 2013.

Financial Performance

The company's revenues have been steadily climbing for the past five years. Revenue increased 8% to $106 million in 2014 on higher sales especially of its Oragene molecular collection systems HCV detection products and cyrosurgical systems products. Additionally licensing and product development earnings rose due to OraSure's co-promotion agreement with AbbVie for the HCV line.

To date OraSure hasn't been profitable. Net losses declined 59% to $5 million in 2014 though due to the firm's higher revenue and lower marketing expenses. Cash flow from operations which had spiked in 2013 due to settlement payment from Roche declined marginally in 2014 to $7 million. That decline was primarily due to an increase in inventory of its OraQuick HCV product as well as higher expenses.

Strategy

In addition to geographic expansion OraSure is also increasing its product offerings by developing diagnostic tests for other infectious diseases. In 2014 R&D activities were focused primarily on developing its next-generation Intercept i2 collection device testing a new rapid Ebola test using the OraQuick platform and support for its existing products.

OraSure's growth strategy also consists of pursuing additional FDA approvals and European registrations for its best-selling product lines OraQuick and Intercept. In partnership with Thermo Fisher it develops and supplies oral fluid drugs of abuse assays to be used with its Intercept i2 collection device. The company entered an agreement with AbbVie in 2014 to co-promote OraQuick in the US and abroad. Additionally OraSure Technologies and AbbVie joined together with the Healthy Trucking Association of America to educate truckers about the hepatitis C virus.

Additionally the company is starting to offer some existing products over-the-counter. It already sells some of its cryosurgical wart removal kits on an OTC basis in Central America and Europe.

Mergers and Acquisitions

To enter the molecular diagnostics market while keeping its emphasis on oral fluids OraSure acquired private Canadian firm DNA Genotek (DNAG) in 2011. In exchange for some $53 million OraSure obtained DNA Genotek and its oral fluid collection products including the Oragene DNA sample collection kit which is used in a range of settings including academic research labs and personal genetics testing.

Ownership

Investor Wells Fargo owns an 18% stake in OraSure.

EXECUTIVES

COO and CFO, Ronald H. Spair, age 60, $486,243 total compensation
SVP Finance Controller and Assistant Secretary, Mark L. Kuna, age 53, $356,826 total compensation
President and CEO, Douglas A. Michels, age 59, $619,054 total compensation
EVP Sales and Marketing, Anthony (Tony) Zezzo, age 62, $398,403 total compensation
SVP and General Manager Consumer Products, Kathleen Weber
SVP Research and Development and Chief Science Officer, Michael Reed
SVP and General Manager Molecular Collection Systems, Brian Smith
Vice President Of Sales, Pat Reis
Senior Vice President Business Development, Jill Thompson
National Accounts Manager, Brian (Bri) Feeley
Senior Vice President Government and External Affairs, Debra (Deb) Fraser-Howze
Senior Vice President Operations, Nancy McLane
Chairman, Stephen S. Tang, age 55
Auditors: KPMG LLP

LOCATIONS

HQ: OraSure Technologies Inc.
  220 East First Street, Bethlehem, PA 18015
Phone: 610 882-1820
Web: www.orasure.com

PRODUCTS/OPERATIONS

2014 Sales

	$ mil.	% of total
OSUR		
Infectious disease testing	47.5	45
Cryosurgical systems	15.5	15
Substance abuse testing	8.4	8
Insurance risk assessment	3.7	3
DNAG	23.8	22
Licensing & product development	7.6	7
Total	**106.5**	**100**

Selected Products

AUTO-LYTE (enzyme immunoassay tests for insurance lab drug testing)
Histofreezer (cryosurgical wart removal system)
Freeze ' n Clear Skin Clinic (wart remover)
Intercept (saliva-based substance abuse testing)
MICRO-PLATE (plasma screening immunoassay tests for drug testing)
Oragene (DNA tests)
OraQuick HCV (rapid antibody test)
OraQuick ADVANCE HIV-1/2 (blood sample HIV test)
OraSure HIV-1 (oral HIV test)
QED Saliva Alcohol Test
QuickFlu Rapid Flu A+B (influenza)
Pointts Wart Remover (Central America OTC cryosurgical wart treatment)
Scholl Freeze Verruca & Wart Remover (Europe OTC cryosurgical wart treatment)

COMPETITORS

ANSYS	Orgenics
Abbott Labs	Prestige Brands
AcuNetx	Psychemedics
Alere	Quest Diagnostics
Bio-Rad Labs	Quidel

Calypte Biomedical
Johnson & Johnson
Medtox Scientific
Merck
Olympus Corporation of
the Americas

Roche Diagnostics
Siemens Healthcare
Trinity Biotech
eScreen

HISTORICAL FINANCIALS

Company Type: Public

Income Statement

FYE: December 31

	REVENUE ($ mil.)	NET INCOME ($ mil.)	NET PROFIT MARGIN	EMPLOYEES
12/15	119.7	8.1	6.8%	326.0
12/14	106.4	(4.6)	—	320.0
12/13	98.9	(11.1)	—	293.0
12/12	87.8	(15.1)	—	313.0
12/11	81.8	(8.8)	—	308.0
Annual Growth	10.0%	—	—	1.4%

2015 Year-End Financials

Debt ratio: —
Return on equity: 5.1%
Cash ($ mil.): 94.0
Current ratio: 5.42
Long-term debt ($ mil.): —

No. of shares (mil.): 55.7
Dividends
  Yield: —
  Payout: —
Market value ($ mil.): 359.0

	STOCK PRICE ($) FY Close	P/E High/Low	PER SHARE ($) Earnings	Dividends	Book Value
12/15	6.44	75 32	0.14	0.00	2.86
12/14	10.14	— —	(0.08)	0.00	2.82
12/13	6.29	— —	(0.20)	0.00	2.90
12/12	7.18	— —	(0.29)	0.00	3.08
12/11	9.11	— —	(0.19)	0.00	2.12
Annual Growth	(8.3%)	— —	—	—	7.9%

Orchids Paper Products Co. (DE)

Orchids Paper Products hopes to leave its end users smelling like a rose. The company makes bulk tissue paper and converts it into bathroom tissue paper napkins and paper towels for the consumer market. Most of the company's products are sold as private-label items by discount retailers; Orchids Paper products also are sold under the company's Colortex and Velvet brands. Dollar General is Orchids Paper's largest customer; other big customers include Family Dollar and Wal-Mart. Orchids Paper sells most of its products within a 500-mile radius of its manufacturing plant in northeastern Oklahoma.

Operations

Orchids divides its business into two lines: converted products and parent rolls. Converted products account for 97% of its revenue and include paper towels bathroom tissue and paper napkins.

Sales and Marketing

The company sells its products to value retailers generally known as "dollar" stores grocery stores grocery wholesalers and cooperatives. Its sales efforts are focused on an area within 500 miles of its facility in northeast Oklahoma which includes Texas Oklahoma Kansas Missouri Arkansas Nebraska and Iowa.

Major customers include Dollar General (accounting for 40% of its converted product sales in 2014) Family Dollar (11%) and Wal-Mart (9%). In 2014 Orchids spent $292 million on advertising.

Financial Performance

Orchids has enjoyed several straight years of steady growth. Revenues jumped 23% from $116 million in 2013 to reach a millstone high of $143 million in 2014. The historic growth was attributed to a 26% spike in sales from converted products due to its efforts on new product development in the mid and premium tier markets. Additional revenue from a previous acquisition also contributed to the growth.

Orchids' profits however dropped 29% from $13 million in 2013 to $9 million in 2014 due to higher expenses and business costs. This was due to higher expenses related to an acquisition coupled with higher fiber costs and increased production expenses associated with its converting and paper production operations.

Strategy

Orchids has been focused on increasing efficiency by producing its own parent rolls which is the material processed into its other products such as tissue. The move is an effort to limit the company's reliance on outside sources for parent rolls and the subsequent price fluctuations that have characterized that market in recent years.

Going forward the company plans to maximize production with its older equipment in a strategic move that deviates from typical paper product makers that have been shutting down older equipment. Orchids has also invested in new equipment. The result of these efforts will be an increase in capacity that the company hopes to sell through new channels namely grocery and drug store chains.

Throughout 2015 its specific focus was on the timely start-up of its new paper machine and new converting line in Oklahoma.

Mergers and Acquisitions

In order to enhance its West Coast operations Orchids in 2014 entered into a strategic alliance with Fabrica de Papel San Francisco. Based in Baja California Mexico Fabrica is a low-cost manufacturer of high-quality tissue paper products. As part of the alliance Orchids acquired Fabrica's US business including certain manufacturing assets and access to 18000 metric tons of capacity each year. Products are now produced at Fabrica's facility in Mexicali Mexico and shipped directly to Orchids' US customers.

EXECUTIVES

President and CEO, Jeffrey S. Schoen, age 55, $400,000 total compensation
CFO, Rodney D. Gloss, age 59
Chairman, Steven R. (Steve) Berlin, age 71
Auditors: HoganTaylor LLP

LOCATIONS

HQ: Orchids Paper Products Co. (DE)
4826 Hunt Street, Pryor, OK 74361
Phone: 918 825-0616
Web: www.orchidspaper.com

PRODUCTS/OPERATIONS

2014 Sales

	$ mil.	% of total
Converted product	138.4	97
Parent roll	4.3	3
Total	**142.7**	**100**

COMPETITORS

Advanced Airlaid
  Materials
Cascades Tissue Group
Georgia-Pacific
Irving Tissue
Kimberly-Clark

Potlatch
Roses Southwest Papers
SCA Tissue North
  America
Wausau Paper

HISTORICAL FINANCIALS

Company Type: Public

Income Statement

FYE: December 31

	REVENUE ($ mil.)	NET INCOME ($ mil.)	NET PROFIT MARGIN	EMPLOYEES
12/15	168.4	13.5	8.0%	352.0
12/14	142.7	9.4	6.6%	313.0
12/13	116.3	13.3	11.4%	317.0
12/12	100.8	9.2	9.2%	290.0
12/11	97.8	6.2	6.3%	296.0
Annual Growth	14.5%	21.6%	—	4.4%

2015 Year-End Financials

Debt ratio: 30.0%
Return on equity: 11.5%
Cash ($ mil.): 4.3
Current ratio: 2.10
Long-term debt ($ mil.): 71.7

No. of shares (mil.): 10.2
Dividends
  Yield: 4.5%
  Payout: 111.1%
Market value ($ mil.): 318.0

	STOCK PRICE ($) FY Close	P/E High/Low	PER SHARE ($) Earnings	Dividends	Book Value
12/15	30.92	23 15	1.38	1.40	13.03
12/14	29.11	30 21	1.11	1.40	11.48
12/13	32.84	20 12	1.67	1.35	10.52
12/12	20.22	18 13	1.18	0.85	10.10
12/11	18.20	22 11	0.80	0.50	9.65
Annual Growth	14.2%	— —	14.6%	29.4%	7.8%

Oritani Financial Corp (DE)

Oritani Financial could give an oratory on local banking in New Jersey. The holding company owns Oritani Bank which offers retail and commercial deposit and loan banking services from about 25 locations in several Garden State counties. Oritani Financial specializes in multi-family and commercial real estate lending which make up more than half of its loan portfolio. Oritani Financial also writes one- to four-family and second mortgages as well as equity and construction loans. It invests in real property through its Hampshire Financial Oritani LLC and Ormon divisions; Oritani Asset is a real estate investment trust (REIT). Century-old Oritani Bank has more than $2 billion in assets.

Geographic Reach

Oritani Bank has 25 full-service branches in Bergen Essex Hudson and Passaic counties in New Jersey.

Financial Performance

The bank's 2012 (ends June) revenue increased 4% vs. the prior year and net income grew by 11% over the same period. The revenue increase was due to a 4% jump in interest income. partially offset by a nearly 1% drop in non-interest income. Fiscal 2012 marked Oritani Bank's eighth consecutive year of increasing revenue although growth has slowed somewhat. The increase in net income in 2012 was primarily due to a higher net interest spread and a larger asset base.

Strategy

Oritani Bank is expanding its branch network. It recently opened new branches in Ramsey Upper Montclair and Clifton New Jersey.

EXECUTIVES

Executive Vice President and Chief Operating Officer, Michael (Mel) DeBernardi

Svp And Chief Compliance Officer, Rosanne Buscemi

Vice President, Paul Cordero

Chairman President and CEO, Kevin J. Lynch, age 69, $705,769 total compensation

EVP and CFO, John M. Fields, age 53, $315,046 total compensation

EVP and Chief Lending Officer, Thomas G. Guinan, age 52, $305,539 total compensation

Vice President, John Pagano

Vice President, Bing Luh

Vice President Commercial Lending, Noah Littell

Senior Vice President and Secretary, Philip (Phil) Wyks

Senior Vice President and Human Resources Officer, Anne (Annie) Mooradian

Auditors: Crowe Horwath LLP

LOCATIONS

HQ: Oritani Financial Corp (DE)
370 Pascack Road, Township of Washington, NJ 07676
Phone: 201 664-5400
Web: www.oritani.com

PRODUCTS/OPERATIONS

2016 Sales

	$ mil.	% of total
Interest		
Mortgage loans	125.4	70
Interest on securities available for sale	4.6	2
Interest on securities held to maturity	2.7	2
Dividends on FHLB stock	1.6	1
Non-interest		
Bank-owned life insurance	2.7	2
Net income from investments in real estate joint ventures	1.2	1
Net gain on sale of securities	1.0	1
Net gain loss)on sale of assets and loans	37.5	21
Other	1.8	-
Total	**178.5**	**100**

COMPETITORS

1st Colonial Bancorp
Hudson City Bancorp
OceanFirst Financial
Provident Financial Services
Sun Bancorp (NJ)
Valley National Bancorp

HISTORICAL FINANCIALS

Company Type: Public

Income Statement

FYE: June 30

	ASSETS ($ mil.)	NET INCOME ($ mil.)	INCOME AS % OF ASSETS	EMPLOYEES
06/16	3,669.3	52.3	1.4%	238.0
06/15	3,353.0	46.9	1.4%	235.0
06/14	3,140.2	41.0	1.3%	233.0
06/13	2,831.9	39.5	1.4%	212.0
06/12	2,700.9	31.6	1.2%	217.0
Annual Growth	**8.0%**	**13.4%**	**—**	**2.3%**

2016 Year-End Financials

Return on assets: 1.4%		Dividends	
Return on equity: 9.9%		Yield: 7.5%	
Long-term debt ($ mil.): —		Payout: 93.0%	
No. of shares (mil.): 45.2		Market value ($ mil.): 724.0	
Sales ($ mil): 178.5			

	STOCK PRICE ($) FY Close	P/E High/Low		PER SHARE ($) Earnings	Dividends	Book Value
06/16	15.99	14	12	1.21	1.20	11.83
06/15	16.05	14	12	1.10	0.95	11.76
06/14	15.39	17	15	0.94	0.95	11.57
06/13	15.68	17	15	0.92	1.03	11.43
06/12	14.39	21	16	0.71	0.50	11.30
Annual Growth	**2.7%**	**—**	**—**	**14.3%**	**24.5%**	**1.2%**

Ormat Technologies Inc

Ormat Technologies is on an environmentally safe power trip building geothermal recovered energy and solar power plants. Geothermal technology extracts hot water or steam that is vaporized and used to drive turbines. The fluid is then cooled and recycled back through the process making it a clean and renewable energy source. Recovered energy utilizes heat produced in other industrial processes. The company set up by Israel-based Ormat Industries also sells power units for both types of plants and sells fossil fuel-powered turbogenerators with a capacity of between 400W and 4000W. Ormat operates power plants in Guatemala Kenya Nicaragua and the US.

Operations

Ormat owns and operates geothermal and recovered energy-based power plants. It is also beginning to build solar photovoltaic power plants. The company owns or has supplied 1300 MW of gross capacity to utilities and developers worldwide.

Geographic ReachOrmat serves customers around the world. It operates plants in various countries including Guatemala Kenya Nicaragua and the US. The company's equipment manufacturing operations are located in Israel.

Financial Analysis

In 2011 Ormat reported revenues of $437 million compared to $373.2 million for 2010 a 17% increase. Electricity and product segments revenues increased by 11% and by 39% respectively over 2010. A growth in power production the addition of a new recovered energy plant and an increase in the electricity rates for its Amatitlan and Puna power plants in Guatemala helped to lift electricity revenues. Product sales were boosted by higher customer orders and a $12.1 million revenue recorded from its LNG Energy recovery unit in Spain.

The company's net loss of $42.7 million in 2011 (compared to net income of $37.2 million for 2010) was due to a major increase in income tax charges ($48.5 million in 2011 compared to a tax benefit of $1 million in 2010) coupled with a 20.5% increase in selling and marketing expenses and a 71.6% increase in interest expenses during the year.

Strategy

Strategically the company relies on its two-fold approach of building a geographically balanced portfolio of geothermal and recovered energy as-

sets and being a manufacturer of related power equipment and services. It is vertically integrated manufacturing many of the generators and other components it uses in its power plants.

Ormat puts a strong emphasis on developing and building geothermal and recovered energy power plants.

Expanding its geothermal operations in 2012 the company's Kenya-based unit acquired a contract from the Government of Kenya to design and build a 6 MW geothermal well head power plant in the Menengai geothermal field in Kenya. That year it also signed a deal for NV Energy to sell 30 MW from the Dixie Meadows geothermal project that it was developing in Churchill County Nevada.

In 2010 Ormat acquired Constellation Energy's 50% stake in the partnership that owns the Mammoth Lakes geothermal power plants in California for $72.5 million.

In a move to expand its offerings the company is moveing into solar power taking advantage of low solar photovoltaic panel costs to ramp up its activities in this segment. In late 2011 Ormat signed a 20-year agreement with the Imperial Irrigation District for 10 MW of Solar PV energy from a proposed project to be located near Ormat's Heber geothermal complex in Imperial Valley California.

Selected Customers

SCE (27% of 2011 sales) NV Energy (13%) and Hawaii Electric Light Company (11%).

Ownership

Ormat Industries owns about 60% of Ormat Technologies. The Bronicki family owns about 35% of Ormat Industries and occupies key leadership positions in both companies.

EXECUTIVES

CEO, Isaac Angel, age 59, $368,577 total compensation

EVP Electricity Segment, Zvi Krieger, age 60, $226,465 total compensation

EVP Engineering, Shimon Hatzir, age 54, $217,337 total compensation

CFO, Doron Blachar, age 48, $358,118 total compensation

EVP Business Development Sales and Marketing, Bob Sullivan, age 53

EVP Projects, Shlomi Argas, age 51

EVP Production, Erez Klein, age 50

EVP Market Development, Nir Wolf, age 50, $219,459 total compensation

Vice President Project Finance, Nachman Isaac

Vice President Finance and Corp Services US, Barbara (Barb) Allen

Chairman, Gillon Beck, age 54

Treasurer, Anat Liebfeld Ben-Schlomo

Auditors: PricewaterhouseCoopers LLP

LOCATIONS

HQ: Ormat Technologies Inc
6225 Neil Road, Reno, NV 89511-1136
Phone: 775 356-9029
Web: www.ormat.com

PRODUCTS/OPERATIONS

2015 Sales

	$ mil.	% of total
Electricity	375.9	63
Products	218.7	37
Total	**594.6**	**100**

COMPETITORS

ALSTOM	GE
Atlas Copco	Mitsubishi Electric
Calpine	Pratt & Whitney
Chevron	Siemens AG
Enel	Toshiba
Fuji Electric	

HISTORICAL FINANCIALS

Company Type: Public

Income Statement

FYE: December 31

	REVENUE ($ mil.)	NET INCOME ($ mil.)	NET PROFIT MARGIN	EMPLOYEES
12/15	594.6	119.5	20.1%	1,060.0
12/14	559.5	54.1	9.7%	1,095.0
12/13	533.2	41.2	7.7%	1,123.0
12/12	514.4	(206.4)	—	1,252.0
12/11	437.0	(43.0)	—	1,226.0
Annual Growth	8.0%	—	—	(3.6%)

2015 Year-End Financials

Debt ratio: 40.1%
Return on equity: 13.5%
Cash ($ mil.): 185.9
Current ratio: 1.99
Long-term debt ($ mil.): 857.8
No. of shares (mil.): 49.1
Dividends
  Yield: 0.7%
  Payout: 12.6%
Market value ($ mil.): 1,791.0

	STOCK PRICE ($) FY Close	P/E High/Low		PER SHARE ($) Earnings	Dividends	Book Value
12/15	36.47	17	11	2.43	0.26	20.16
12/14	27.18	25	20	1.18	0.21	17.02
12/13	27.21	31	21	0.91	0.08	16.12
12/12	19.28	—	—	(4.54)	0.08	15.30
12/11	18.03	—	—	(0.95)	0.13	19.78
Annual Growth	19.3%	—	—	—	18.9%	0.5%

OTC Markets Group Inc

Security and commodity services nec nsk

EXECUTIVES

Pres-ceo, R C Coulson
Executive Vice President, Matthew (Matt) Fuchs
Auditors: Deloitte & Touche LLP

LOCATIONS

HQ: OTC Markets Group Inc
304 Hudson Street, 3rd Floor, New York, NY 10013
Phone: 212 896-4400   **Fax:** 212 868-3848
Web: www.otcmarkets.com

HISTORICAL FINANCIALS

Company Type: Public

Income Statement

FYE: December 31

	REVENUE ($ mil.)	NET INCOME ($ mil.)	NET PROFIT MARGIN	EMPLOYEES
12/15	49.9	10.2	20.6%	89.0
12/14	42.2	7.8	18.7%	85.0
12/13	35.5	5.6	15.9%	81.0
12/12	35.0	5.4	15.6%	74.0
12/11	32.9	4.8	14.7%	67.0
Annual Growth	10.9%	20.6%	—	7.4%

2015 Year-End Financials

Debt ratio: —
Return on equity: 57.3%
Cash ($ mil.): 23.9
Current ratio: 1.78
Long-term debt ($ mil.): —
No. of shares (mil.): 11.3
Dividends
  Yield: 6.6%
  Payout: 127.0%
Market value ($ mil.): 185.0

	STOCK PRICE ($) FY Close	P/E High/Low		PER SHARE ($) Earnings	Dividends	Book Value
12/15	16.30	18	15	0.88	1.08	1.55
12/14	14.36	21	11	0.69	0.37	1.62
12/13	7.75	17	15	0.51	0.24	1.70
12/12	7.55	15	10	0.51	0.45	1.34
12/11	5.35	14	11	0.45	0.16	1.21
Annual Growth	32.1%	—	—	18.3%	61.2%	6.3%

Owens Realty Mortgage, Inc

EXECUTIVES

Ceo, William Owens
Auditors: Crowe Horwath LLP

LOCATIONS

HQ: Owens Realty Mortgage, Inc
2221 Olympic Boulevard, Walnut Creek, CA 94595
Phone: 925 935-3840
Web: www.owensmortgage.com

HISTORICAL FINANCIALS

Company Type: Public

Income Statement

FYE: December 31

	REVENUE ($ mil.)	NET INCOME ($ mil.)	NET PROFIT MARGIN	EMPLOYEES
12/15	21.2	26.2	123.5%	32.0
12/14	18.2	8.1	44.3%	5.0
12/13	15.3	10.8	70.4%	5.0
12/12	15.9	(1.1)	—	0.0
Annual Growth	10.0%	—	—	—

2015 Year-End Financials

Debt ratio: 24.5%
Return on equity: 13.8%
Cash ($ mil.): 1.2
Current ratio: 1.74
Long-term debt ($ mil.): 67.0
No. of shares (mil.): 10.2
Dividends
  Yield: 3.0%
  Payout: 23.1%
Market value ($ mil.): 138.0

	STOCK PRICE ($) FY Close	P/E High/Low		PER SHARE ($) Earnings	Dividends	Book Value
12/15	13.43	7	6	2.22	0.41	19.03
12/14	14.65	27	16	0.74	0.27	17.14
12/13	12.12	16	11	0.78	0.10	16.66
12/12	0.00	—	—	(0.15)	0.17	16.03
Annual Growth	—	—	—	—	34.1%	5.9%

Paccar Financial Corp

EXECUTIVES

Pres, Todd R Hubbard
Auditors: Ernst & Young LLP

LOCATIONS

HQ: Paccar Financial Corp
777 - 106th Avenue N.E., Bellevue, WA 98004
Phone: 425 468-7100
Web: www.paccarfinancial.com

HISTORICAL FINANCIALS

Company Type: Public

Income Statement

FYE: December 31

	REVENUE ($ mil.)	NET INCOME ($ mil.)	NET PROFIT MARGIN	EMPLOYEES
12/15	604.1	112.8	18.7%	419.0
12/14	563.5	108.6	19.3%	402.0
12/13	545.0	99.2	18.2%	389.0
12/12	510.5	83.7	16.4%	399.0
12/11	429.8	68.0	15.8%	406.0
Annual Growth	8.9%	13.5%	—	0.8%

2015 Year-End Financials

Debt ratio: 72.4%
Return on equity: 10.0%
Cash ($ mil.): 35.3
Current ratio: 0.63
Long-term debt ($ mil.): 4,399.7
No. of shares (mil.): 0.1
Dividends
  Yield: —
  Payout: —
Market value ($ mil.): —

Pacific City Financial Corp

LOCATIONS

HQ: Pacific City Financial Corp
3701 Wilshire Blvd., Suite 900, Los Angeles, CA 90010
Phone: 213 210-2000   **Fax:** 213 210-2032

HISTORICAL FINANCIALS

Company Type: Public

Income Statement

FYE: December 31

	ASSETS ($ mil.)	NET INCOME ($ mil.)	INCOME AS % OF ASSETS	EMPLOYEES
12/15	1,042.5	12.1	1.2%	0.0
12/14	893.9	11.8	1.3%	0.0
12/13	755.9	21.3	2.8%	0.0
12/12	610.8	8.0	1.3%	0.0
12/11	546.0	0.8	0.2%	0.0
Annual Growth	17.5%	95.1%	—	—

2015 Year-End Financials

Return on assets: 1.2%
Return on equity: 13.2%
Long-term debt ($ mil.): —
No. of shares (mil.): 11.8
Sales ($ mil): 56.0
Dividends
  Yield: 0.0%
  Payout: 7.3%
Market value ($ mil.): 152.0

STOCK PRICE ($) FY Close	P/E High/Low	PER SHARE ($) Earnings	Dividends	Book Value
12/15 12.85	15 12	1.02	0.07	8.26
12/14 12.38	14 4	1.00	0.00	7.31
12/13 4.00	3 1	1.83	0.00	6.87
12/12 1.80	3 2	0.61	0.00	5.89
12/11 0.90	— —	(0.02)	0.00	5.23
Annual Growth 94.4%	— —	—	—	12.1%

Pacific Premier Bancorp Inc

Auditors: Crowe Horwath LLP

LOCATIONS

HQ: Pacific Premier Bancorp Inc
17901 Von Karman Avenue, Suite 1200, Irvine, CA 92614
Phone: 949 864-8000
Web: www.ppbi.com

HISTORICAL FINANCIALS

Company Type: Public

Income Statement

FYE: December 31

	ASSETS ($ mil.)	NET INCOME ($ mil.)	INCOME AS % OF ASSETS	EMPLOYEES
12/15	2,790.6	25.5	0.9%	335.0
12/14	2,038.9	16.6	0.8%	285.0
12/13	1,714.1	8.9	0.5%	231.0
12/12	1,173.7	15.7	1.3%	183.0
12/11	961.1	10.5	1.1%	149.0
Annual Growth	30.5%	24.6%	—	22.5%

2015 Year-End Financials

Return on assets: 1.0%
Return on equity: 10.2%
Long-term debt ($ mil.): —
No. of shares (mil.): 21.5
Sales ($ mil): 132.8

Dividends
Yield: —
Payout: —
Market value ($ mil.): 458.0

STOCK PRICE ($) FY Close	P/E High/Low	PER SHARE ($) Earnings	Dividends	Book Value
12/15 21.25	20 12	1.19	0.00	13.86
12/14 17.33	18 14	0.96	0.00	11.81
12/13 15.74	28 18	0.54	0.00	10.52
12/12 10.24	8 4	1.44	0.00	9.85
12/11 6.34	7 5	0.99	0.00	8.39
Annual Growth 35.3%	— —	4.7%	—	13.4%

PacWest Bancorp

PacWest Bancorp is the holding company for Pacific Western Bank which operates about 80 branches mostly in southern and central California plus an additional branch in Durham North Carolina. The $21 billion-asset bank caters to small and midsized businesses and their owners and employees offering traditional deposit and loan products and services. Commercial real estate mortgages make up more than 30% of its loan portfolio while cash flow- and asset-based business loans make up another 40%. The bank also originates residential mortgage real estate construction and land loans venture capital equipment finance and consumer loans. PacWest offers investment services and international banking through agreements with correspondent banks.

Operations

Like other retail banks PacWest generates the bulk of its revenue from interest income. About 83% of its total revenue came from interest income on loans and leases during 2015 while another 7% came from interest income on investments. The rest of its revenue came from leased equipment income (3% of revenue) deposit account service charges (1%) other commissions and fees (3%) and other miscellaneous income sources. The bank's Square 1 Bank Division caters to entrepreneurial businesses and their venture capital and private equity investors while its CapitalSource Division provides cash flow asset-based equipment and real estate loans and leases as well as treasury management services to established middle-market businesses across the country.

Geographic Reach

PWB's branches are located across California in Los Angeles Orange Riverside San Bernardino Santa Barbara San Diego San Francisco San Luis Obispo San Mateo and Ventura Counties. It also has a branch in Durham North Carolina. Financial Performance PacWest's acquisitions in 2014 and 2015 boosted its interest-earning loan asset balances more than three-fold which sent its revenues and profits soaring during those years. The bank's revenue jumped 30% to $968.3 million during 2015 mostly as newly acquired loans from its CapitalSource boosted its interest income during the year. Strong revenue growth coupled with lower acquisition integration and reorganization costs in 2015 drove PacWest's net income up 77% to $300 million. Its operating cash levels spiked 79% to $594 million with the rise in cash-denominated earnings.

Strategy

PacWest has grown its loan and deposit business as well as its branch network through acquisitions of California community banks and specialized financial services companies. It has made 28 acquisitions since 2000 with some of its most recent being the Square 1 acquisition in 2015 and the CapitalSource Inc. acquisition in 2014. Mergers and Acquisitions

In October 2015 PacWest purchased $4.6 billion-asset Square 1 and its Square 1 Bank subsidiary for $849 million forming the Square 1 Bank Division of the Bank. The deal boosted its core deposits expanded its national lending platform and bolstered its presence in the technology and life-sciences markets. In April 2014 the bank bought $10.7 billion-asset CapitalSource Inc. and its CapitalSource Bank (CSB) subsidiary. In May 2013 PacWest acquired $1.7 billion-asset First California Financial Group operator of First California Bank for $237 million. The purchase added six branches (after consolidation) in Los Angeles Orange Riverside San Bernardino San Diego San Luis Obispo and Ventura Counties. Company Background During the economic downturn PacWest took advantage of a rash of bank failures through FDIC-assisted transactions. The acquired institutions were merged into Pacific Western Bank. Under the loss-sharing deals the FDIC agreed to reimburse PacWest for future losses tied to the acquisitions. In a 2012 non-FDIC-assisted deal PacWest bought American Perspective Bank adding two branches and a loan office in the Central Coast area.

EXECUTIVES

EVP and Director the Company and Pacific Western Bank, Daniel B. Platt, age 69, $52,500 total compensation
EVP and Chief Risk Officer, Suzanne R. Brennan, age 65, $165,000 total compensation
CEO, Matthew P. (Matt) Wagner, age 59, $754,167 total compensation
EVP and CFO Pacific Western Bank, Patrick J. (Pat) Rusnak, age 52
EVP and Chief Accounting Officer, Lynn M. Hopkins, age 48
EVP; Director Human Resources, Christopher D. Blake, age 56, $298,958 total compensation
EVP and Chief Credit Officer, Bryan M. Corsini, age 54, $375,624 total compensation
EVP; President CapitalSource, James J. (Jim) Pieczynski, age 53, $554,539 total compensation
EVP Operations and Systems, Mark Christian
EVP General Counsel and Corporate Secretary, Kori L. Ogrosky
Vice President And Senior Counsel, Holly (Holl) Hayes
Chairman, John M. Eggemeyer, age 70
Auditors: KPMG LLP

LOCATIONS

HQ: PacWest Bancorp
9701 Wilshire Blvd., Suite 700, Beverly Hills, CA 90212
Phone: 310 887-8500
Web: www.pacwestbancorp.com

PRODUCTS/OPERATIONS

2015 Sales

	% of total
Interest income	
Loans and leases	87
Investment securities & other	7
Noninterest income	
Other commissions and fees	3
Leased equipment income	3
Service charges on deposit accounts	1
Other	3
FDIC loss sharing expense net	-
Total	**100**

Selected Mergers & Acquisitions

COMPETITORS

Bank of America	Rabobank America
CVB Financial	San Diego County
California Bank &	Credit Union
Trust	U.S. Bancorp
City National	Wells Fargo
JPMorgan Chase	Westamerica
MUFG Americas Holdings	

HISTORICAL FINANCIALS

Company Type: Public

Income Statement

FYE: December 31

	ASSETS ($ mil.)	NET INCOME ($ mil.)	INCOME AS % OF ASSETS	EMPLOYEES
12/15	21,288.4	299.6	1.4%	1,670.0
12/14	16,234.8	168.9	1.0%	1,443.0
12/13	6,533.3	45.1	0.7%	1,110.0
12/12	5,463.6	56.8	1.0%	991.0
12/11	5,528.2	50.7	0.9%	982.0
Annual Growth	40.1%	55.9%	—	14.2%

2015 Year-End Financials

Return on assets: 1.6%	Dividends
Return on equity: 7.5%	Yield: 4.6%
Long-term debt ($ mil.): —	Payout: 67.5%
No. of shares (mil.): 121.4	Market value ($ mil.): 5,233.0
Sales ($ mil): 968.2	

	STOCK PRICE ($) FY Close	P/E High/Low	Earnings	PER SHARE ($) Dividends	Book Value
12/15	43.10	17 14	2.79	2.00	36.22
12/14	45.46	25 20	1.92	1.25	34.04
12/13	42.22	40 23	1.08	1.00	17.66
12/12	24.77	16 13	1.54	0.79	15.74
12/11	18.95	17 10	1.37	0.21	14.66
Annual Growth	22.8%	— —	19.5%	75.7%	25.4%

Paragon Commercial Corp

LOCATIONS

HQ: Paragon Commercial Corp
3535 Glenwood Avenue, Raleigh, NC 27612
Phone: 919 788-7770
Web: www.paragonbank.com

HISTORICAL FINANCIALS

Company Type: Public

Income Statement

FYE: December 31

	ASSETS ($ mil.)	NET INCOME ($ mil.)	INCOME AS % OF ASSETS	EMPLOYEES
12/15	1,305.9	11.2	0.9%	139.0
12/14	1,165.2	7.9	0.7%	0.0
12/13	1,035.7	4.9	0.5%	0.0
12/12	957.6	3.1	0.3%	0.0
Annual Growth	10.9%	52.4%	—	—

2015 Year-End Financials

Return on assets: 0.9%	Dividends
Return on equity: 12.1%	Yield: —
Long-term debt ($ mil.): —	Payout: —
No. of shares (mil.): 4.5	Market value ($ mil.): 125.0
Sales ($ mil): 49.8	

	STOCK PRICE ($) FY Close	P/E High/Low	Earnings	PER SHARE ($) Dividends	Book Value
12/15	27.25	11 6	2.47	0.00	21.32
12/14	0.00	— —	1.77	0.00	19.35
Annual Growth	—	— —	39.5%	—	10.2%

Paramount Group Inc

Auditors: Deloitte & Touche LLP

LOCATIONS

HQ: Paramount Group Inc
1633 Broadway, Suite 1801, New York, NY 10019
Phone: 212 237-3100
Web: www.paramount-group.com

HISTORICAL FINANCIALS

Company Type: Public

Income Statement

FYE: December 31

	REVENUE ($ mil.)	NET INCOME ($ mil.)	NET PROFIT MARGIN	EMPLOYEES
12/15	662.4	21.1	3.2%	319.0
12/14*	66.1	57.3	86.7%	219.0
11/14	227.3	21.5	9.5%	0.0
12/13	419.8	16.5	3.9%	217.0
12/12	246.8	2.3	0.9%	0.0
Annual Growth	28.0%	74.2%	—	—

*Fiscal year change

2015 Year-End Financials

Debt ratio: 34.2%	No. of shares (mil.): 212.1
Return on equity: 0.5%	Dividends
Cash ($ mil.): 207.2	Yield: 2.3%
Current ratio: 1.47	Payout: —
Long-term debt ($ mil.): 2,961.5	Market value ($ mil.): 3,839.0

	STOCK PRICE ($) FY Close	P/E High/Low	Earnings	PER SHARE ($) Dividends	Book Value
12/15	18.10	— —	(0.02)	0.42	17.73
12/14*	18.59	70 67	0.27	0.00	18.44
11/14	18.43	— —	(0.00)	0.00	(0.00)
Annual Growth	(0.9%)	— —	— —	—	—

*Fiscal year change

PAREXEL International Corp.

PAREXEL International excels in pharmaceutical development services. A top contract research organization (CRO) the firm counts among its clients some of the world's largest drug biotech and medical device firms. Its Clinical Research Services (CRS) segment provides clinical trial and data management study design patient recruitment biostatistical analysis clinical pharmacology and industry training and publishing. PAREXEL Consulting Services (PCS) handles the non-clinical aspects of drug development regulatory affairs and new product launches. Its Perceptive Informatics (PI) unit offers information technology systems and services that help manage clinical trials.

Operations

PAREXEL's largest segment Clinical Research Services (CRS) accounts for two-thirds of sales. Its core development business covers all phases of drug and device development from discovery research through clinical trials and post-marketing studies. The division has benefited from the market trend of increased R&D outsourcing by pharmaceutical and biotech drug companies particularly in the areas of Phase II Phase III and Early Phase development.

Geographic Reach

The company has some 85 facilities in more than 40 countries in Europe the Asia/Pacific region the Middle East North America South America and Africa. About half of PAREXEL's sales are generated outside the US partly because of its core client base of large multinational corporations.

Sales and Marketing

PAREXEL's sales force directs custom marketing efforts towards niche market segments to match the appropriate services with each customer's needs. Its overall goal is to help clients reduce costs and risks related to product development and commercialization.

The company's five largest clients brought in about 40% of its total service revenue in fiscal 2016 (ended June) down from 44% in 2015 and 47% in 2014. Pfizer alone brought in 13% of PAREXEL's service revenue in 2016.

Financial Performance

The company's revenues have grown steadily over time including in fiscal 2016 (ended June) when revenue grew 4% to $2.42 billion. This was driven by growth in all segments but especially in its PCS and CRS segments. The PCS segment benefited from new business secured as well as the expansion of existing customer relationships while the CRS segment saw more activity in the areas of Phase II Phase III and Early Stage drug development.

These gains in revenue have in turn led to higher net income. In fiscal 2016 net income rose 5% to $154.9 million. Cash flow from operations also increased reaching $261.3 million that year.

Strategy

PAREXEL believes it will grow between 10% and 12% each year thanks to the opportunities that have arisen in the changing biopharmaceutical industry. Factors that should contribute to that growth include the virtualization of biopharmaceutical firms the trend to conduct smaller but more complex trials and advances in information technology. To best take advantage of these opportunities the company will continue to serve its multinational clients while also expanding its offerings for small and midsized developers.

The company seeks to widen its service offerings geographic presence and client base both through internal initiatives and via acquisitions. Recent purchases have served to expand and enhance PAREXEL's offerings both across product lines and geographical regions while in-house development has led to new technology-based regulatory compliance tools the establishment of units in China and Japan for navigating those countries' approvals processes and expansion of the company's facilities in Singapore and the US (Maine).

PAREXEL has also expanded by entering related areas of business such as product commercialization and safety monitoring.

Mergers and Acquisitions

In 2014 PAREXEL acquired ATLAS Medical Services a CRO firm serving Turkey the Middle East and North Africa. Also that year it bought the UK-based ClinIntel which provides clinical randomization and trial supply management services for about $8.8 million.

In 2015 the company bought Quantum Solutions India which provides safety management services such as collection detection assessment and monitoring for $93.6 million.

Early the following year PAREXEL acquired life sciences strategy consulting firm Health Advances for $67.1 million.

The company now plans to buy ExecuPharm a functional services provider (FSP) for biopharmaceuticals. ExecuPharm provides staffing and services for clinical studies; the deal will further expand PAREXEL's offerings for its clients. PAREXEL also plans to acquire The Medical Affairs Company which provides outsourced medical affairs services including consulting communications support and medical science liaison services to pharmaceutical biotech and medical device clients.

HISTORY

Company Background

Founders Josef von Rickenbach a health care and international products specialist and Anne Sayigh a chemist and regulatory affairs specialist started PAREXEL in 1982 to provide regulatory consulting services to pharmaceutical firms. Its name referred to 16th-century Swiss physician Theophrastus Bombastus von Hohenheim —better known as Paracelsus the father of empirical chemistry.

In 1988 PAREXEL bought Consulting Statisticians and moved into the biostatistics and data management market. The next year it went international with the purchase of the biostatistics and data management division of McDonnell Douglas Information Systems. In 1991 PAREXEL augmented its European operations with the acquisition of German contract researcher AFB Arzneimittelforschung —a move that paid off in rising sales.

PAREXEL went public in 1995. In the following two years it bought six health consulting firms including State and Federal Associates and medical marketing firm Rescon with the intention of boosting its ability to get its clients' products on the market. The company continued its acquisition spree in 1998; this time European marketing and research companies were on the shopping list. Competitor Covance was set to buy PAREXEL in 1999 then called off the deal when investors balked.

The company announced in 2000 that it would lay off more than 400 workers after Novartis cancelled a major contract. That year the company formed new alliances with such companies as NeuroRecovery Research Phenome Sciences and Prevention Concepts. PAREXEL also bought a full-service clinical pharmacology unit in the UK from GlaxoWellcome (now GlaxoSmithKline) as well as a majority stake in FARMOVS a clinical pharmacology research business and laboratory in South Africa.

In 2001 the company formed Perceptive Informatics a subsidiary focused on developing Internet-based information management systems. To strengthen its clinical trial management services PAREXEL bought software developer FW Pharma Systems in 2003. In 2006 it purchased US-based Behavioral and Medical Research LLC for $69 million to expand its research services.

EXECUTIVES

Chairman and CEO, Josef H. von Rickenbach, age 61, $966,874 total compensation
President and COO, Mark A. Goldberg, age 56, $622,263 total compensation
President Perceptive Informatics, Xavier Flinois
SVP and Worldwide Head PAREXEL Access, Joshua Schultz
SVP General Counsel and Secretary, Douglas A. Batt, age 51, $415,860 total compensation
VP and General Manager PAREXEL Consulting, Gadi Saarony, $455,051 total compensation
VP and Worldwide Head Early Phase, Sy Pretorius
VP and Interim CFO, Emma Reeve, age 55
Vice President Human Resources, Paul (Pauly) Harrop
Vice President, Michael (Mel) Brandt
Vice President Clinical Science, Roland Andersson
Vice President and Associate General Counsel, Brett Davis
Vice President, Terry (Terr) Munson
Vice President of Learning and Development, Albert (Al) Siu
Vice President Human Resources, Mark Williams
Vice President, David (Dave) Brown
Vice President Worldwide Head of MedCom, Susan (Sue) Kammerman
Senior Vice President; General Manager Clinical Research Services, Anita (Ani) Cooper
Vice President Information Technology, Frank Zaganjori
Medical Director, Eric Zafarana
Vice President, Carmen Medina
Vice President Account Management, Marsha (Marcella) Lund
Vice President Systems, Jim Ringwood
Medical Director, Lynn McRoy
Vice President Human Resources, Carl Weaver
Vice President, Carolyn Finkle
Vice President Client Services, Colette Andrea
Vice President Sales, Bob (Bo) Soto
Medical Director, Wayne Dankner
Vice President Human Resource Operations, Guy Schiller
Vice President Marketing Strategy and Insights, Mary (Mar) Backstrom
Vice President Product Management, Tom Drueding
Vice President Start up and Accelerated Recruitment Team, Lollo Eriksson
Medical Director, Kemi Olugemo
Vice President Worldwide Medical Affairs, Thomas (Thom) Shook
Vice President, Mary (Mar) Bareilles
Corporate Vice President and Chief Human Resources Officer, Michelle (Michie) Graham
Vice President Finance and Controller Strategic Partnerships and Key Accounts, Joachim Heinrich
Vice President Marketing, Ronald (Ron) Kraus
Auditors: Ernst & Young LLP

LOCATIONS

HQ: PAREXEL International Corp.
195 West Street, Waltham, MA 02451
Phone: 781 487-9900

PRODUCTS/OPERATIONS

2016 Sales

	$ mil.	% of total
Service Revenue		
Clinical Research Services	1,626.0	67
PAREXEL Consulting Services	190.4	8
PAREXEL Informatics	277.9	11
Reimbursement revenue	332.0	14
Total	**2,426.3**	**100**

COMPETITORS

Albany Molecular Research
BioClinica
Charles River Laboratories
Covance
DATATRAK International
ICON
INC Research
PRA Health Sciences
PharmaNet Development Group
Pharmaceutical Product Development
Quintiles Transnational
ReSearch Pharmaceutical Services
WuXi PharmaTech
eResearchTechnology
inVentiv Health

HISTORICAL FINANCIALS

Company Type: Public

Income Statement

FYE: June 30

	REVENUE ($ mil.)	NET INCOME ($ mil.)	NET PROFIT MARGIN	EMPLOYEES
06/16	2,426.3	154.9	6.4%	18,600.0
06/15	2,330.2	147.8	6.3%	18,600.0
06/14	2,266.3	129.0	5.7%	15,560.0
06/13	1,995.9	95.9	4.8%	14,700.0
06/12	1,618.2	63.1	3.9%	12,695.0
Annual Growth	**10.7%**	**25.1%**	**—**	**10.0%**

2016 Year-End Financials

Debt ratio: 24.6%
Return on equity: 23.7%
Cash ($ mil.): 248.6
Current ratio: 1.54
Long-term debt ($ mil.): 484.8
No. of shares (mil.): 52.9
Dividends
Yield: —
Payout: —
Market value ($ mil.): 3,326.0

	STOCK PRICE ($) FY Close	P/E High/Low	PER SHARE ($) Earnings	Dividends	Book Value
06/16	62.88	26 20	2.86	0.00	11.97
06/15	64.31	27 20	2.65	0.00	12.04
06/14	52.84	25 17	2.25	0.00	10.57
06/13	45.97	30 16	1.61	0.00	9.57
06/12	28.23	27 15	1.05	0.00	10.14
Annual Growth	**22.2%**	**— —**	**28.5%**	**—**	**4.3%**

Park Sterling Corp

Park Sterling Corporation owns Park Sterling Bank which offers traditional deposit accounts and loans to individuals as well as small and midsized businesses through more than 55 branches mostly in North and South Carolina but also in northern Georgia and in Virginia. Commercial real estate and commercial and industrial business loans account for more than 70% of its loan portfolio while residential mortgages and home equity loans make up another 25%. The first Park Sterling Bank opened in 2006. Boasting over $3 billion in assets it is the largest community bank based in Charlotte North Carolina.

OperationsAbout 83% of the bank's revenue came from interest income (mostly from loans) during 2015.Geographic ReachThe bank operated 56 branches as of early 2016 including 23 in South Carolina (with around half in the Greenville-Anderson-Mauldin metro area); 18 in North Carolina (mostly in the greater Charlotte area); 10 in Richmond Virginia; and five in northern Georgia.Sales and MarketingPark Sterling Corporation spent $1.26 million on advertising and promotion during 2015 compared to $1.49 million and $839000 in 2014 and 2013 respectively.Financial PerformanceFueled in large part by acquisitions the bank's annual revenues have nearly quadrupled since 2011 as its loan assets have more than doubled to $1.73 billion. Its profits have soared over the same period since losses in 2011 thanks to a decline in loan loss provisions as the bank's loan credit quality has improved.Park Sterling's revenue climbed 8% to $107.5 million during 2015 mostly thanks to its Provident Community Bancshares acquisition which helped spur higher interest income from 10% loan growth and a 31% jump in non-interest income on higher account service charges fiduciary fees commissions on brokerages and mortgage banking income.Solid revenue growth in 2015 drove the bank's net income up 29% to $16.6 million. Park Sterling's operating cash levels nearly tripled to $42.75 million for the year mostly thanks to a rise in cash-based earnings.StrategyPark Sterling continues to strategically acquire community banks to grow its loan and deposit business and expand into new geographic areas particularly those in underserved markets. The company aims to become a regional presence with offices throughout the Carolinas and Virginia.Mergers and AcquisitionsIn January 2016 the bank purchased Glen Allen Virginia-based First Capital Bancorp and its eight branches in Richmond for $87.1 million.In May 2014 Park Sterling bought Provident Community Bancshares along with its nine Provident Community Bank branches South Carolina for $1.4 million.Company BackgroundIn 2011 it purchased South Carolina's Community Capital Corporation adding 20 branches to the bank's network and doubling its asset holdings. In 2012 Park Sterling bought Citizens South Bank

CEO James "Jim" Cherry a former Wachovia executive came out of retirement after the banking industry somewhat fell apart in late 2008. Together with CFO David Gaines and EVP Leonard Robinett also former Wachovia executives the three approached Park Sterling Bank's then-CEO (now president) Bryan Kennedy III about partnering with the bank to foster its growth. The three came on board as management assembled a board of directors and raised about $150 million in its initial stock offering.

EXECUTIVES

CFO, Donald K. (Don) Truslow, age 57
CEO, James C. Cherry, age 63, $450,000 total compensation
EVP and Chief Risk Offiecr, Nancy J. Foster, age 52, $347,000 total compensation
President, Bryan F. Kennedy, age 56, $347,000 total compensation
SVP and Head of Operations and Information Technology, Mark S. Ladnier, age 55, $215,000 total compensation
Senior Vice President and Head of Private Bankin, George (Georgey) Meyls
Vice President, Richard (Dick) York
Vice President HRIS Operations Manager, Elizabeth (Beth) Dykes
Senior Vice President and CCO, Robert (Bob) Faulkner
Vice President Marketing, William (Bill) Gibson
Vice President, Michelle (Michie) Boggs
Senior Vice President and Treasury Management, Tracey (Trace) Hill

Assistant Vice President Commercial Portfolio Manager, John (Jack) Channell
Executive Vice President and Chief Financial Officer, Stephen (Steve) Arnall
Group Senior Vice President, Bill (Billy) Bunn
Vice President And Mortgage Loan Officer, Paula Buckles
Vice President Regional Retail Operations Manager, Mandy Ray Arrowood
Assistant Vice President Senior Management Reporting Analyst, Drew (Andrew) Carpenter
Senior Vice President Commercial Lender, Pete (Petey) McKenna
Assistant Vice President Commercial Banker, Robert (Bob) Hoak
Chairman, Leslie M. (Bud) Baker, age 70
Vice Chairman, Kim Stuart Price, age 58
Auditors: Dixon Hughes Goodman LLP

LOCATIONS

HQ: Park Sterling Corp
1043 E. Morehead Street, Suite 201, Charlotte, NC 28204
Phone: 704 716-2134
Web: www.parksterlingbank.com

PRODUCTS/OPERATIONS

Products/Services

Personal Banking Services
Checking
Savings Money Markets & Certificates of Deposit
Electronic Banking
eStatements
Debit Card
Re-Order Checks
Loans & Lines of Credit
Reg E Options
Business Banking
Checking
Savings
Treasury Services
Commercial Loans

COMPETITORS

BB&T	Four Oaks Fincorp
Bank of America	NewBridge Bancorp
Carolina Bank	North State Bancorp
CommunityOne Bancorp	Peoples Bancorp (NC)
ECB Bancorp	Select Bancorp
First BanCorp (Puerto Rico)	Southern Community Financial
First Citizens BancShares	Uwharrie Capital
	Yadkin Financial
First Trust Bank	

HISTORICAL FINANCIALS

Company Type: Public

Income Statement

FYE: December 31

	ASSETS ($ mil.)	NET INCOME ($ mil.)	INCOME AS % OF ASSETS	EMPLOYEES
12/15	2,514.2	16.6	0.7%	493.0
12/14	2,359.2	12.8	0.5%	534.0
12/13	1,960.7	15.3	0.8%	490.0
12/12	2,032.6	4.3	0.2%	482.0
12/11	1,113.2	(8.3)	—	270.0
Annual Growth	22.6%	—	—	16.2%

2015 Year-End Financials

Return on assets: 0.6%	Dividends
Return on equity: 5.9%	Yield: 1.6%
Long-term debt ($ mil.): —	Payout: 32.4%
No. of shares (mil.): 44.8	Market value ($ mil.): 328.0
Sales ($ mil): 107.5	

STOCK PRICE ($) FY Close	P/E High/Low	PER SHARE ($) Earnings	Dividends	Book Value
12/15	7.32	21 17	0.37	0.12	6.35
12/14	7.35	27 22	0.29	0.08	6.13
12/13	7.14	21 15	0.34	0.04	5.86
12/12	5.23	44 33	0.12	0.00	6.18
12/11	4.08	— —	(0.29)	0.00	5.82
Annual Growth 15.7%	— —	—	—	2.2%

Park-Ohio Holdings Corp.

Park-Ohio Holdings troubleshoots industrial supply chain logistics issues and makes a slew of fasteners and other industrial components. The company straddles three business segments: Supply Technologies sources and procures production components for OEMs in industries ranging from automotive to aerospace; Engineered Products produces specialized systems and parts used in such industrial applications as coatings forging oil and gas and rail; and the Assembly Components unit casts and machines metal parts –knuckles oil pans cylinders –used by auto agricultural construction and marine OEMs.

Geographic Reach
Park-Ohio operates more than 45 manufacturing sites and 54 supply chain logistics facilities in over 16 countries throughout North America South America Europe and Asia. The US generates nearly 75% of the company's net sales while Canada contributes 6%. Other major markets include Asia (8%) Mexico (6%) Europe (7%).

Operations
Park-Ohio's business is divided across three main segments: Supply Technologies (39% of net sales) Assembly Components (39%) Engineered Products (22%).

Sales and Marketing
Supply Technologies markets and sells its services to more than 7800 customers domestically and internationally. The segment targets the heavy-duty truck; automotive; power sports and recreational equipment; agricultural and construction equipment; consumer electronics; HVAC; lawn and garden; aerospace and defense; and plumbing sectors. Supply Technologies sells to its five main customers through sole-source contracts accounting for approximately 34% of its sales in 2015.

Assembly Components' five largest customers accounted for approximately 49% of its sales for 2015. The Engineered Products segment sells induction heating and other capital equipment to component manufacturers and OEMs in the ferrous and non-ferrous metals silicon coatings forging foundry automotive truck construction equipment and oil and gas industries.

Financial Performance
The company has achieved unprecedented growth over the last few years with revenues climbing 6% from $1.38 billion in 2014 to peak at a record-setting $1.46 billion in 2015. Profits also jumped 5% from $46 million in 2014 to $48 million in 2015.

The historic growth for 2015 was fueled by the addition of $97 million from acquisitions previously made. Park-Ohio was also helped by stronger sales from its new automotive aluminum platform business within its Assembly Components segment.

Mergers and Acquisitions

To achieve growth Park-Ohio seeks out complementary businesses to acquire. In 2014 it bought Apollo Aerospace Group headquartered in the UK with operating locations in England France Poland and India. Apollo is a supply chain management services company providing Class C production components and supply chain products to aerospace customers worldwide.

Also in 2014 the company picked up Autoform Tool and Manufacturing for $50 million. Autoform is a supplier of high pressure fuel lines and fuel rails used in gasoline direct injection systems across a large number of engine platforms. Autoform's production facilities are located in Indiana.

EXECUTIVES

VP and CFO, Patrick W. Fogarty, age 55, $234,000 total compensation

President and COO, Matthew V. Crawford, age 46, $390,000 total compensation

Chairman and CEO, Edward F. Crawford, age 76, $731,250 total compensation

Chief Financial Officer Vice President, Jeffrey (Jeff) Rutherford

Vice President Information Systems, Brian (Bri) Murkey

Vice President Manufacturing, Darryl Niven

Vice Chairman, James W. Wert, age 69

Assistant Treasurer, Carolina Schneider

Secretary and General Counsel (2002), Robert D (Bob) Vilsack

Auditors: Ernst & Young LLP

LOCATIONS

HQ: Park-Ohio Holdings Corp.
6065 Parkland Boulevard, Cleveland, OH 44124
Phone: 440 947-2000
Web: www.pkoh.com

PRODUCTS/OPERATIONS

2015 Sales

	$ mil.	% of total
Supply technologies	578.7	39
Assembly Components	569.2	39
Engineered Products	315.9	22
Total	**1,463.8**	**100**

Selected Products

Supply technologies —sourcing planning and procurement of:
Clamps and fittings
Fasteners
Hoses
Pins
Rubber and plastic components
Valves
Wire harnesses
Manufactured products
Forging presses
Induction heating and melting systems
Industrial oven systems
Injection molded rubber components
Pipe threading systems
Aluminum products
Clutch retainers/pistons
Control arms
Cooling modules
Flywheel spacers
Front engine covers
Knuckles
Master cylinders
Oil pans
Pump housings

COMPETITORS

Anixter Fasteners	MNP Corp.
Fastenal	MSC Industrial Direct
Federal Screw Works	Menlo Worldwide
GKN Sinter Metals	PennEngineering
Hillman Companies	Ryder System
Illinois Tool Works	Shiloh Industries
LISI	T3 Energy Services
Lawson Products	Textron
Logistics Plus	

HISTORICAL FINANCIALS

Company Type: Public

Income Statement

FYE: December 31

	REVENUE ($ mil.)	NET INCOME ($ mil.)	NET PROFIT MARGIN	EMPLOYEES
12/15	1,463.8	48.1	3.3%	6,000.0
12/14	1,378.7	45.6	3.3%	6,000.0
12/13	1,203.2	43.4	3.6%	5,000.0
12/12	1,134.0	31.7	2.8%	3,800.0
12/11	966.5	29.4	3.0%	3,200.0
Annual Growth	**10.9%**	**13.1%**	**—**	**17.0%**

2015 Year-End Financials

Debt ratio: 49.4%	No. of shares (mil.): 12.2
Return on equity: 24.6%	Dividends
Cash ($ mil.): 62.0	Yield: 1.3%
Current ratio: 2.44	Payout: 13.1%
Long-term debt ($ mil.): 450.3	Market value ($ mil.): 451.0

	STOCK PRICE ($) FY Close	P/E High/Low		PER SHARE ($) Earnings	Dividends	Book Value
12/15	36.78	16	7	3.88	0.50	16.73
12/14	63.03	17	12	3.68	0.38	14.85
12/13	52.40	14	6	3.56	0.00	12.79
12/12	21.31	9	6	2.62	0.00	8.32
12/11	17.84	10	4	2.45	0.00	5.39
Annual Growth	**19.8%**	—	—	**12.2%**	—	**32.7%**

Party City Holdco Inc

Auditors: Ernst & Young LLP

LOCATIONS

HQ: Party City Holdco Inc
80 Grasslands Road, Elmsford, NY 10523
Phone: 914 345-2020
Web: www.partycity.com

HISTORICAL FINANCIALS

Company Type: Public

Income Statement

FYE: December 31

	REVENUE ($ mil.)	NET INCOME ($ mil.)	NET PROFIT MARGIN	EMPLOYEES
12/15	2,294.5	10.4	0.5%	18,231.0
12/14	2,271.2	56.1	2.5%	18,027.0
12/13	2,045.1	4.0	0.2%	0.0
12/12	973.6	(30.2)	—	0.0
Annual Growth	**33.1%**	**—**	**—**	**—**

2015 Year-End Financials

Debt ratio: 54.2%	No. of shares (mil.): 119.2
Return on equity: 1.4%	Dividends
Cash ($ mil.): 42.9	Yield: —
Current ratio: 1.94	Payout: —
Long-term debt ($ mil.): 1,646.1	Market value ($ mil.): 1,540.0

	STOCK PRICE ($) FY Close	P/E High/Low	PER SHARE ($) Earnings	Dividends	Book Value
12/15	12.91	248126	0.09	0.00	7.66
12/14	0.00	— —	0.59	0.00	5.74
Annual Growth	**—**	**— —**	**(84.7%)**	**—**	**33.4%**

Patrick Industries, Inc.

A recreational vehicle is just an empty motor home until Patrick Industries adds the finishing interior touches. The company makes and distributes a range of building materials and prefinished products primarily for the manufactured home (MH) and RV industries. Patrick Industries manufactures decorative paper and vinyl panels moldings countertops doors and cabinet and slotwall components. In addition to these the firm distributes roofing siding flooring drywall ceiling and wall panels household electronics electrical and plumbing supplies and adhesives. Founded in 1959 the company operates about two dozen production facilities distribution centers and warehouses in a dozen states.

Operations

Patrick Industries operates 43 manufacturing plants where it makes furniture shelving wall counter and cabinet products mouldings interior passage doors and slotwall panels and components among other products. Its manufacturing segment contributes about three-quarters of its annual revenue. The company also distributes prefinished wall and ceiling panels drywall and drywall finishing products. electronics. wiring electrical and plumbing products shower doors fireplaces and other miscellaneous products from five distribution facilities nationwide. Distribution accounts for about 22% of revenue.

Geographic Reach

Patrick Industries is based in Elkhart Indiana where a number of RV makers are clustered. The company operates facilities in 13 states including California Texas Illinois Pennsylvania Michigan and Oregon.

Sales and Marketing

Patrick Industries counts most of the major manufactured housing (MH) and RV manufacturers among its clientele but it also serves customers in the marine casegoods home furniture and the commercial furnishings and fixtures industries. The company has about 800 active customers of which two accounted for about 55% of its sales in 2015. The RV industry represented approximately 759% of the company's sales in 2015 while manufactured housing accounted for 14%. The industrial market represented the rest.

Financial Performance

Patrick Industries has been moving along for several years with robust revenue and profit gains.

The company's revenue jumped 25% higher in 2015 to $920 million from about $736 in 2014. Sales rose in its RV MH and Industrial markets. It was the sixth straight year of revenue gain for Patrick Industries. Acquisitions made in 2014 and

2015 made strong contributions to the revenue gain. The RV growth was tempered by a shift to more entry level and lower-priced models which lowered per-unit growth. The company passed along lower prices for some commodities used in manufacturing to its customers.

Profit at Patrick Industries popped up about 38% to reach $42 million in 2015 for $31 million in 2014 spurred by higher revenue.

The company reported stronger cash flow from operations at about $66 million in 2015 from about $46 million in 2014.

Strategy

Patrick Industries doesn't want to put all its eggs in one RV or MH. It's diversifying its product line to other industrial commercial and institutional markets and it's going it mainly through acquisitions.

Mergers and Acquisitions

In 2016 it acquired the Progressive Group a distributor and manufacturer's representative for major name brand electronics primarily in the auto and home electronics retail custom integration and commercial channels for $11 million.

Also in 2016 Patrick Industries bought Parkland Plastics Inc. –a maker of reclaimed polymer-based wall and ceiling panels floors molding and other products –for $25 million using secured credit. The company also acquired aluminum and steel products fabricator Mishawaka Sheet Metal in 2016 for about $14 million.

The previous year the company bought RV products manufacturer North American Forest Products Inc. which makes laminate and soft wood panels moulding and other components for RVs. The acquisition was valued at $85 million also funded by secured credit. Other key 2015 acquisitions include fiberglass components manufacturers Structural Composites of Indiana Inc. and Better Way Partners LLC.

EXECUTIVES

President, Andy L. Nemeth, age 47, $271,730 total compensation
CEO, Todd M. Cleveland, age 48, $555,770 total compensation
VP Human Resources, Courtney A. Blosser, $203,537 total compensation
EVP Sales and Chief Sales Officer, Jeffrey M. Rodino, age 46, $276,517 total compensation
CFO, Joshua A. Boone, age 37
EVP Operations and COO, Kip B. Ellis, age 42
Vice President Sales, Jimmy (Jim) Ritchey
Chairman, Paul E. Hassler, age 69
Auditors: Crowe Horwath LLP

LOCATIONS

HQ: Patrick Industries, Inc.
107 West Franklin Street, P.O. Box 638, Elkhart, IN 46515
Phone: 574 294-7511
Web: www.patrickind.com

PRODUCTS/OPERATIONS

Selected Products:AdornAIA CountertopsBetter Way ProductsCarrera Custom PaintingCharlestonCreative Wood DesignsCustom VinylsDécor ManufacturingForemost FabricatorsFrontline Manufacturing-Gravure Ink Praxis GroupGustafson LightingInfinity GraphicsInte

	$ mil.	% of total
Manufacturing	720.4	78
Distribution	199.9	22
Total	**920.3**	**100**

2015 Sales by Customer Type

	% of total
RV industry	75
Manufactured housing	14
Industrial market	11
Total	**100**

COMPETITORS

Decorator Industries	Lowe's
Flexsteel	Quanex Building
HD Supply	Products
LCI Industries	Saint-Gobain
LaSalle Bristol	

HISTORICAL FINANCIALS
Company Type: Public

Income Statement
FYE: December 31

	REVENUE ($ mil.)	NET INCOME ($ mil.)	NET PROFIT MARGIN	EMPLOYEES
12/15	920.3	42.2	4.6%	3,542.0
12/14	735.7	30.6	4.2%	2,799.0
12/13	594.9	24.0	4.0%	2,387.0
12/12	437.3	28.1	6.4%	1,678.0
12/11	307.8	8.4	2.8%	900.0
Annual Growth	**31.5%**	**49.4%**	—	**40.8%**

2015 Year-End Financials

Debt ratio: 52.9%
Return on equity: 36.5%
Cash ($ mil.): 0.0
Current ratio: 2.41
Long-term debt ($ mil.): 193.7
No. of shares (mil.): 15.1
Dividends
  Yield: —
  Payout: —
Market value ($ mil.): 659.0

	STOCK PRICE ($) FY Close	P/E High/Low	PER SHARE ($) Earnings	Dividends	Book Value
12/15	43.50	23 13	2.72	0.00	8.48
12/14	43.98	25 15	1.91	0.00	6.63
12/13	28.93	22 8	1.49	0.00	5.19
12/12	15.56	11 2	1.76	0.00	3.77
12/11	4.10	8 3	0.55	0.00	1.93
Annual Growth	**80.5%**	—	**48.9%**	—	**44.8%**

Paycom Software Inc

Auditors: Grant Thornton LLP

LOCATIONS

HQ: Paycom Software Inc
7501 W. Memorial Road, Oklahoma City, OK 73142
Phone: 405 722-6900
Web: www.paycom.com

HISTORICAL FINANCIALS
Company Type: Public

Income Statement
FYE: December 31

	REVENUE ($ mil.)	NET INCOME ($ mil.)	NET PROFIT MARGIN	EMPLOYEES
12/15	224.6	20.9	9.3%	1,461.0
12/14	150.9	5.6	3.8%	1,021.0
12/13	107.6	7.7	7.2%	840.0
12/12	76.8	4.2	5.5%	0.0
12/11	57.2	1.4	2.5%	0.0
Annual Growth	**40.8%**	**95.6%**	—	—

2015 Year-End Financials

Debt ratio: 2.9%
Return on equity: 24.2%
Cash ($ mil.): 50.7
Current ratio: 1.05
Long-term debt ($ mil.): 24.9
No. of shares (mil.): 57.1
Dividends
  Yield: —
  Payout: —
Market value ($ mil.): 2,149.0

	STOCK PRICE ($) FY Close	P/E High/Low	PER SHARE ($) Earnings	Dividends	Book Value
12/15	37.63	124 63	0.36	0.00	1.72
12/14	26.33	261 113	0.11	0.00	1.38
Annual Growth	**42.9%**	—	**227.3%**	—	**25.0%**

PDF Solutions Inc.

PDF Solutions can solve chip design and manufacturing inefficiencies. The company provides software and services that help integrated circuit makers get more working chips out of a production batch. PDF's products are used to simulate model and analyze the chip design and manufacturing processes. As part of the Design-to-Silicon-Yield program PDF also receives a portion of customers' cost savings called gain share. The Exensio data analytics platform (in on-premise or cloud versions) helps customers draw information from manufacturing process data. Two customers –GLOBALFOUNDRIES and Samsung Electronics –collectively account for about 53% of sales. PDF Solutions generates about 54% of sales outside the US.

Operations

PDF's design-to-silicon-yield solutions business accounted for about two-thirds of revenue with gainshare performance incentives bringing in the rest.

Geographic Reach

The company has offices in China France Germany Italy Japan South Korea Taiwan and the US (in California).

About 46% of sales are to customers in the US followed by Germany with 24% South Korea 11% and other countries 19%.

Sales and Marketing

PDF Solutions uses a direct sales force and strategic alliances to pursue targeted accounts. Its customers are foundries integrated device manufacturers (IDMs) and fabless semiconductor design companies who then go on to make microprocessors memory graphics image sensor solutions and communications products.

Financial Performance

PDF's revenue slipped 2% in 2015 to about $98 million from $110.6 million in 2014. Gainshare revenue fell 28% which outweighed a 21% rise in design-to-silicon-yield solutions sales. Performance of the Xensio product drove sales.

Net income fell by a third to $12.4 million in 2015 from $18.5 million in 2014. PDF had higher R&D and corporate expenses in 2015.

Cash generated by operations ticked up to $28.5 million in 2015 compared to $27 million n 2014. The company had an increase in accounts receivable from timing of payments.

Strategy

Yield improvement is the name of the game for PDF Solutions. It's not uncommon for an initial manufacturing run to yield only 20% leaving 80% of the ICs produced are wasted. The company has developed proprietary technologies for yield simulation analysis loss detection and improvement. Its products enable customers to electrically characterize the manufacturing process and establish fail-rate information needed to calibrate manufacturing yield models prioritize yield improvement activities and speed up process learning cycles.

The Xensio platform drove sales in 2015 closing some 200 contracts during the year and the company continues to develop the product. The company started selling Xensio in the software-as-a-service model and expanded its use it test and assembly functions.

Mergers and Acquisitions

PDF made two acquisitions to expand and strengthen its products line and to acquire new customers.

It paid $5.2 million for Syntricity Inc. a provider of a hosted service for characterization and yield management. The company said Syntricity's technology is complementary with its products and was integrated into the Exensio platform.

The company also acquired the Key Semiconductor software assets of Salland Engineering International. The acquired technology was integrated into the development of the Exensio-Test product.

EXECUTIVES

President and CEO, John K. Kibarian, age 51, $333,333 total compensation

VP Products and Solutions; Director, Kimon W. Michaels, age 50, $280,000 total compensation

Chief Technologist, Andrzej J. Strojwas

VP Finance and CFO, Gregory C. Walker, $315,000 total compensation

Vice President Business Operations, Steve (Stevie) Morstad

Vice President Business Development, Koji Maekawa

Account General Manager and Vice President, P K Mozumder

Vice President, PK Mozumder

Chairman, Lucio L. Lanza, age 72

Auditors: PricewaterhouseCoopers LLP

LOCATIONS

HQ: PDF Solutions Inc.
333 West San Carlos Street, Suite 1000, San Jose, CA 95110
Phone: 408 280-7900   **Fax:** 408 280-7915
Web: www.pdf.com

PRODUCTS/OPERATIONS

2015 Sales

	$ mil.	% of total
Design-to-silicon-yield solutions	63.9	65
Gainshare performance incentives	34.1	35
Total	**98.0**	**100**

Selected Products and Services

Integration assessment
Manufacturing process simulation
Yield and performance monitoring modeling and prediction software and services (Design-to-Silicon-Yield program)

COMPETITORS

ARM Holdings	KLA-Tencor
AXIOM Design	MKS Instruments
Applied Materials	Mentor Graphics
Cadence Design	Rudolph Technologies
FEI	Silvaco
Intrinsix	Synopsys

HISTORICAL FINANCIALS

Company Type: Public

Income Statement

FYE: December 31

	REVENUE ($ mil.)	NET INCOME ($ mil.)	NET PROFIT MARGIN	EMPLOYEES
12/15	97.9	12.4	12.7%	390.0
12/14	100.1	18.4	18.4%	359.0
12/13	101.4	20.9	20.6%	363.0
12/12	89.5	37.2	41.6%	345.0
12/11	66.7	1.8	2.8%	319.0
Annual Growth	**10.1%**	**60.3%**	**—**	**5.2%**

2015 Year-End Financials

Debt ratio: —	No. of shares (mil.): 31.1
Return on equity: 7.3%	Dividends
Cash ($ mil.): 126.1	Yield: —
Current ratio: 11.29	Payout: —
Long-term debt ($ mil.): —	Market value ($ mil.): 337.0

	STOCK PRICE ($) FY Close	P/E High/Low		PER SHARE ($) Earnings	Dividends	Book Value
12/15	10.84	50	26	0.39	0.00	5.60
12/14	14.86	44	20	0.58	0.00	5.20
12/13	25.62	36	20	0.67	0.00	4.43
12/12	13.78	11	5	1.25	0.00	3.46
12/11	6.97	102	52	0.07	0.00	2.01
Annual Growth	**11.7%**	**—**	**—**	**53.6%**	**—**	**29.2%**

PDL BioPharma Inc

If your body starts fighting you PDL BioPharma hopes to help you fight back. The company's antibody (protein) humanization technology makes it possible to alter mouse monoclonal antibodies (MAbs) for use in human therapies such as preventing and treating autoimmune diseases and cancer. The firm has licensed its technology to such companies as Genentech (a Roche subsidiary) Biogen and Chugai Pharmaceutical. PDL derives nearly all of its revenues from royalties on products including Genentech's cancer medications Herceptin and Avastin and Biogen's multiple sclerosis drug Tysabri.OperationsPDL currently receives royalties on the sales of humanized antibody products including Avastin Herceptin Kadcycla Lucentis Perjeta and Xolair from Genentech; Tysabri from Biogen; Gazyva from Roche Entyvio from Takeda and Actemra from Chugai. Royalty and licensing income from Genentech accounted for more than 70% of PDL's annual revenues in 2014 with income from Biogen accounting for 10% and Depomed another 7%. Geographic ReachThe US accounted for 58% of PDL's revenue in 2014; Europe accounted for 42%.The company leases some 48000 sq. ft. of office space in Incline Village Nevada.Financial PerformancePDL has experienced climbing revenues over the last decade as sales of its licensed products have increased. Revenues rose by 31% to some $581 million in 2014 on higher sales of Avastin Herceptin Xolair Perjeta Kadcycla Tysabri Actembra by licensees. A higher fixed royalty rate (versus 2013's blended fixed and tiered rate) an increase in the fair value of the acquired royalty rights from PCL's purchase of Depomed's diabetes-related royalties and higher interest earnings all contributed to the higher revenues that year.Net income has also risen over the past few years. In 2014 it rose 22% to $322 million due to the higher revenue. This was partially offset by rising interest and income tax expenses. Cash flow from operations grew 8% to $292 million that year.StrategyThe company is primarily focused on acquiring income-generating commercial-stage therapies and devices with strong economic fundamentals and intellectual property protection. The clock is ticking on PDL's patents to its humanized antibody products and the company is also busily looking to license its technology and antibodies to other biotech companies. PDL is also looking to invest in development-stage programs that could product future royalties. Among the companies it has recently invested in are Direct Flow Medical and Paradigm Spine.In early 2014 the company entered into a settlement agreement with Genentech and Roche; the settlement resolved all outstanding legal disputes between the companies. It precludes Genentech and Roche from challenging PDL's Queen patents and from contesting their obligation to pay royalties.Company BackgroundPDL shifted from a research and development company with commercial products of its own to become a strictly development-stage business. It sold its commercial assets in 2008 including oncology drug IV Busulfex cardiovascular drugs Cardene and Retavase and its antibody manufacturing plant. PDL then spun off its biotech development operations into a new publicly traded company to separate them from its profitable royalty business. (The spinoff Facet Biotech was later snapped up by Abbott Laboratories). PDL retained rights to all current and future licensed antibody revenues.Mergers and AcquisitionsIn 2014 PDL acquired a portion of royalty payments of the U-M's royalty interest in Cerdelga for $65.5 million. The company will receive 75% of all royalty payments due under the license agreement with Genzyme until patents expire.

EXECUTIVES

Vice President and CFO, Peter S. (Pete) Garcia

President and Chief Executive Officer; Director, John P. McLaughlin, age 64, $675,000 total compensation

VP and CFO, Bruce Tomlinson

Auditors: PricewaterhouseCoopers LLP

LOCATIONS

HQ: PDL BioPharma Inc
932 Southwood Boulevard, Incline Village, NV 89451
Phone: 775 832-8500

PRODUCTS/OPERATIONS

2014 Revenues

	$ mil.	% of total
Royalties from queen et al. patents	486.9	84
Royalty rights-change in fair value	45.7	8
Interest revenue	48.0	8
License & other	0.6	-
Total	**571.2**	**100**

Selected Licensees

Biogen Idec (Tysabri)
Chugai Pharmaceutical (Actemra)
Genentech (Avastin Herceptin Lucentis Perjeta Xolair)
Takeda (Entyvio)

COMPETITORS

Amgen	Poniard
Biogen	Pharmaceuticals
Genentech	Seattle Genetics
ImmunoGen	XOMA
Immunomedics	

Income Statement

FYE: December 31

	REVENUE ($ mil.)	NET INCOME ($ mil.)	NET PROFIT MARGIN	EMPLOYEES
12/15	590.4	332.8	56.4%	10.0
12/14	581.2	322.2	55.4%	10.0
12/13	442.9	264.5	59.7%	10.0
12/12	374.5	211.6	56.5%	10.0
12/11	362.0	199.3	55.1%	10.0
Annual Growth	13.0%	13.7%	—	0.0%

2015 Year-End Financials

Debt ratio: 25.3%	No. of shares (mil.): 164.2
Return on equity: 57.5%	Dividends
Cash ($ mil.): 218.8	Yield: 16.9%
Current ratio: 7.69	Payout: 36.8%
Long-term debt ($ mil.): 232.8	Market value ($ mil.): 582.0

	STOCK PRICE ($) FY Close	P/E High/Low		PER SHARE ($) Earnings	Dividends	Book Value
12/15	3.54	4	2	2.03	0.60	4.24
12/14	7.71	5	4	1.86	0.60	2.84
12/13	8.44	5	4	1.66	0.60	0.81
12/12	7.04	6	4	1.45	0.60	(0.49)
12/11	6.20	5	3	1.15	0.60	(1.46)
Annual Growth	(13.1%)	—	—	15.3%	(0.0%)	—

Peapack-Gladstone Financial Corp.

Peapack-Gladstone Financial is the $3.4 billion-asset holding company for the near-century-old Peapack-Gladstone Bank which operates more than 20 branches in New Jersey's Hunterdon Morris Somerset Middlesex and Union counties. Founded in 1921 the bank provides traditional deposit accounts credit cards and loans to individuals and small businesses as well as trust and investment management services through its PGB Trust and Investments unit. Multifamily residential mortgages represent nearly 50% of the company's loan portfolio while commercial mortgages make up around 15%. The bank also originates construction consumer and business loans.

Operations

Peapack-Gladstone Financial operates two main divisions: Banking which offers traditional deposit and loan services merchant card services; and Wealth Management which boasts more than $3.3 billion in assets under administration (as of early 2016) and operates through PGB Trust and Investments which offers asset management services for individuals and institutions as well as personal trust services. More than 80% of the bank's total revenue came from interest income (mostly on its loans) during 2015 while 14% came from its wealth management fee income and 3% came from service charges and fees.Multifamily residential mortgages represented nearly 50% of the company's loan portfolio at the end of 2015 while commercial mortgages made up another 15%. The rest of its portfolio was made up of construction consumer and business loans.Geographic ReachThe bank's branches are located across New Jersey in Somerset Morris Hunterdon Middlesex and Union counties Its private banking and wealth management locations are located in Bedminster Morristown Princeton and Teaneck.Sales and MarketingThe bank's commercial banking business serves business owners professionals retailers contractors and real estate investors. Its wealth management division serves individuals families foundations endowments trusts and estates. Peapack-Gladstone has been ramping up its advertising spend in recent years. It spent $637000 on advertising during 2015 up from $594000 and $519000 in 2014 and 2013 respectively.

Financial Performance

Peapack-Gladstone's annual revenues and profits have swelled more than 60% since 2011 as its nearly tripled its loan assets to over $2.9 billion.The bank's revenue jumped 27% to $122.86 million during 2015 mostly thanks to higher interest income as its loan assets grew by 30% with exceptional increases in its multifamily mortgage and commercial loan volumes. Peapack-Gladstone's wealth management division income grew 20% with increases in securities gains service charges and other non-interest income.Strong revenue growth in 2015 drove Peapack-Gladstone's net income up 34% to $19.97 million. The bank's operating cash levels climbed 11% to $30.31 million thanks to a rise in cash-based earnings.Strategy-Peapack-Gladstone Financial continued in 2016 to focus on: enhancing its risk management to keep its loan provisions at a minimum and its profits up; expanding its multi-family loans as well as its commercial real estate loans (to a lesser extent); growing its commercial and industrial (C&I) lending business through its private banking divisions; and expanding its wealth management business which now accounts for 15% of its annual revenue. Mergers and AcquisitionsIn May 2015 Peapack-Gladstone bolstered its wealth management division after buying Morristown-based Wealth Management Consultants LLC for $2.8 million. The deal boosted the bank's assets under advisement and administration to $3.5 billion.

EXECUTIVES

SEVP and CFO Peapack-Gladstone Financial and Peapack-Gladstone Bank, Jeffrey J. Carfora, age 58
EVP and COO, Robert A. (Bob) Plante, age 56
President and CEO Peapack-Gladstone Financial and Peapack-Gladstone Bank, Douglas L. Kennedy, age 57
EVP CIO and Head of Banking Services Peapack-Gladstone Bank, Kevin B. Runyon
SEVP Chief Strategy Officer and General Counsel, Finn M.W. Casperson, age 46
EVP and Head of Retail Banking Peapack-Gladstone Bank, Anthony V. Bilotta, age 56
EVP and Head of Commercial Real Estate Peapack-Gladstone Bank, Vincent A. Spero
SEVP and President Private Wealth Management, John P. Babcock
EVP and Chief Credit Officer Peapack-Gladstone Bank, Lisa Chalkan
EVP and Director Human Capital Peapack-Gladstone Bank, Philip Portantino
EVP and President Wealth Management Consultants Peapack-Gladstone Bank, Thomas J. Ross
EVP and Head of Commercial Banking Peapack-Gladstone Bank, Eric H. Waser
SVP and Head of Residential and Consumer Lending Peapack-Gladstone, Glenn R. Straffi
Vice President Corporate Trainer, Doreen Macchiarola
Senior Vice President, Charles (Charlie) Adornetto
Vice President, Glenn Carroll
Vice President Portfolio Manager, Sarah (Sar) Krieger
Chairman, F. Duffield (Duff) Meyercord, age 69
Auditors: Crowe Horwath LLP

LOCATIONS

HQ: Peapack-Gladstone Financial Corp.
500 Hills Drive, Suite 300, Bedminster, NJ 07921-1538
Phone: 908 234-0700
Web: www.pgbank.com

PRODUCTS/OPERATIONS

2015 Sales

	$ mil.	% of total
Interest Income		
Loans including fees	94.3	77
Securities available for sale	4.6	4
Other	0.3	-
Other Income		
Wealth management fee income	17.0	14
Service charges and fees	3.3	3
Bank owned life insurance	1.3	1
Other Income	1.0	1
Other	1.1	-
Total	122.9	100

COMPETITORS

Bank of America	PNC Financial
Hudson City Bancorp	TD Bank USA
JPMorgan Chase	Valley National
MSB Financial	Bancorp

HISTORICAL FINANCIALS
Company Type: Public

Income Statement

FYE: December 31

	ASSETS ($ mil.)	NET INCOME ($ mil.)	INCOME AS % OF ASSETS	EMPLOYEES
12/15	3,364.6	19.9	0.6%	316.0
12/14	2,702.4	14.8	0.6%	306.0
12/13	1,966.9	9.2	0.5%	326.0
12/12	1,667.8	9.7	0.6%	292.0
12/11	1,600.3	12.1	0.8%	295.0
Annual Growth	20.4%	13.2%	—	1.7%

2015 Year-End Financials

Return on assets: 0.6%	Dividends
Return on equity: 7.7%	Yield: 0.9%
Long-term debt ($ mil.): —	Payout: 14.9%
No. of shares (mil.): 16.0	Market value ($ mil.): 331.0
Sales ($ mil): 122.8	

	STOCK PRICE ($) FY Close	P/E High/Low		PER SHARE ($) Earnings	Dividends	Book Value
12/15	20.62	18	14	1.29	0.20	17.16
12/14	18.56	18	14	1.22	0.20	15.99
12/13	19.10	20	14	1.01	0.20	14.48
12/12	14.08	16	10	1.05	0.20	13.69
12/11	10.75	11	8	1.25	0.20	13.92
Annual Growth	17.7%	—	—	0.8%	(0.0%)	5.4%

Pebblebrook Hotel Trust

Pebblebrook Hotel Trust wants the term staycation to take a vacation. The self-managed real estate investment trust (REIT) acquires and manages upscale hotels in the US targeting mostly full-service and select-service luxury properties that don't need major renovation in major US gateway cities. The REIT owns more than 30 hotels (with 7400 rooms) across 11 states and has a 49% interest in six more hotels spanning nearly 1800 rooms through its Manhattan Collection joint venture. Nearly 70% of its revenue comes from room fees while the remainder comes from food and beverage services. Pebblebrook Hotel Trust is the brainchild of CEO Jon Bortz who also founded LaSalle Hotel Properties.

Geographic ReachPebblebrook Hotel Trust's properties are in major cities spread across 11 US states. Most are in California (in San Francisco Los Angeles and surrounding areas and San Diego) while most of the others are in Boston Bethesda Minneapolis Miami Nashville New York City Philadelphia Portland and Seattle. Financial PerformancePebblebrook's revenues and profits have skyrocketed over the past several years as it has expanded its property portfolio through acquisitions and has charged higher room rates as the economy has strengthened.The REIT's revenue jumped 22% to $598.8 billion in 2014 mostly thanks to $81 million in new room revenue from its recently acquired properties. Its comparable property revenues added an additional $28.6 million in growth to its top-line thanks to strong performance in its West Coast properties from increases in ADR (average daily rate) and an increase in revenue from its Hotel Zetta (which had been closed in 2012 and part of 2013). Higher revenue and higher equity earnings on its joint venture properties drove Pebblebrook's net income higher by 70% to $72.9 million. The REIT's operating cash levels rose by 50% to $161.3 million thanks to higher cash earnings.StrategyPebblebrook Hotel Trust has been actively building up its hotel portfolio as the lodging industry has strengthened with the overall economy. The REIT targets hotel property investments in "major gateway urban markets" with high barriers-to-entry and "diverse sources of meeting and room night demand generators." It also sometimes targets investment opportunities in upscale resort destinations in south Florida and southern California. In addition Pebblebrook regularly renovates its properties to add value and be able to charge more revenue per room.During 2014 the REIT spent $626.8 million to acquire six properties in target markets including: the Prescott Hotel in San Francisco; The Nines a Luxury Collection Hotel in Portland; The Westin Colonnade Coral Gables in Miami; the Revere Hotel Boston Common; and leasehold interests in both the Hotel Palomar Los Angeles-Westwood in Los Angeles and the Union Station Hotel Autograph Collection in Nashville.Company BackgroundPebblebrook had its initial public offering (IPO) in December 2009 raising more than $350 million. The REIT used the proceeds from the offering to buy properties to grow its portfolio which then consisted of around 10 hotels.

EXECUTIVES

Chairman President and CEO, Jon E. Bortz, age 59, $300,000 total compensation
EVP CFO Treasurer and Secretary, Raymond D. Martz, age 45, $250,000 total compensation
EVP and Chief Investment Officer, Thomas C. Fisher, $243,151 total compensation
Vice President Finance, Andrew (Andy) Dittamo
Vice President Acquisitions, Robin Kennedy
Vice President Asset Management, Wendy Heineke
Auditors: KPMG LLP

LOCATIONS

HQ: Pebblebrook Hotel Trust
7315 Wisconsin Avenue, 1100 West, Bethesda, MD 20814
Phone: 240 507-1300
Web: www.pebblebrookhotels.com

PRODUCTS/OPERATIONS

2014 Sales

	$ mil.	% of total
Rooms	410.6	68
Food & beverage	148.1	25
Other	40.1	7
Total	**598.8**	**100**

Selected Properties

Argonaut Hotel (San Francisco)
DoubleTree by Hilton Bethesda- Washington DC
The Grand Hotel (Minneapolis)
InterContinental Buckhead Hotel (Atlanta)
Monaco Washington DC
Sheraton Delfina (Philadelphia)
Sir Francis Drake (San Francisco)
Skamania Lodge and Conference Center (Stevenson WA)

COMPETITORS

Ashford Hospitality Trust
Chesapeake Lodging
Condor Hospitality
DiamondRock Hospitality
FelCor
HMG/Courtland Properties
Hersha Hospitality
Hospitality Properties Trust
Host Hotels & Resorts
Innkeepers USA
MHI Hospitality
Strategic Hotels

HISTORICAL FINANCIALS

Company Type: Public

Income Statement

FYE: December 31

	REVENUE ($ mil.)	NET INCOME ($ mil.)	NET PROFIT MARGIN	EMPLOYEES
12/15	770.8	94.6	12.3%	27.0
12/14	598.7	72.8	12.2%	27.0
12/13	489.2	42.9	8.8%	24.0
12/12	380.6	26.0	6.9%	23.0
12/11	287.9	14.8	5.2%	20.0
Annual Growth	**27.9%**	**58.9%**	**—**	**7.8%**

2015 Year-End Financials

Debt ratio: 36.2%
Return on equity: 5.3%
Cash ($ mil.): 26.3
Current ratio: 0.32
Long-term debt ($ mil.): 1,110.0
No. of shares (mil.): 71.7
Dividends
  Yield: 4.4%
  Payout: 149.4%
Market value ($ mil.): 2,010.0

	STOCK PRICE ($) FY Close	P/E High/Low	PER SHARE ($) Earnings	Dividends	Book Value
12/15	28.02	53 29	0.95	1.24	24.51
12/14	45.63	65 41	0.71	0.92	24.89
12/13	30.76	97 72	0.32	0.64	23.13
12/12	23.10	181 138	0.14	0.48	21.54
12/11	19.18	278 177	0.08	0.48	21.93
Annual Growth	**9.9%**	**— —**	**85.6%**	**26.8%**	**2.8%**

Pegasystems Inc

Pegasystems helps companies fly through business changes without being reined in by their old processes. The company provides rules-driven business process management software PegaRules Process Commander designed to help large companies in the financial services insurance and health care industries update their operations and systems to reflect changes in business goals and strategies. Established in 1983 Pegasystems offers tools for analyzing and simulating processes integrating enterprise applications and portals managing content integration and managing processes for customer service claims resolution and transaction processing.

Operations
Pegasystems generates about 40% of its revenue from licensing its software. About a third comes from maintenance with services bringing in 29%.

Geographic Reach
Pegasystems is headquartered in Massachusetts and has a half dozen other offices across the US. International locations are in Australia Canada China France Germany India India Poland Russia Spain Sweden Switzerland and the UK. The US accounts for 55% of sales; Europe including the UK makes up another 30%.

Sales and Marketing
The company sells its products through its direct sales force as well as through distributors resellers and trade shows (including its PegaWorld user conference). Financial services and health care companies are its primary markets but the company also sells to clients in the manufacturing government travel and hospitality retail consumer packaged goods and telecommunications industries.

Financial Performance
In 2014 Pegasystems' revenue rose 16% to $590 million from $509 million in 2013. It attributed the growth to a 21% increase in license revenue an 18% increase in maintenance revenue and a 7% increase in professional services revenue.

Profits fell 13% to $33.2 million on higher operating expenses for sales and marketing and research and development. Cash flow jumped to almost $100 million in 2014 from $80.7 million in 2013.

Strategy
To extend its geographic reach and attract additional customers Pegasystems enters partnerships with major IT services and software providers. Its list of strategic partners includes Accenture Capgemini Cognizant Infosys Mahindra Tata Consultancy Services Virtusa and Wipro. In 204 and 2015 it added Atos Ernst & Young Unicorn Systems and Adqura.

Mergers and Acquisitions

Pegasystems has made several recent acquisitions to further fuel growth. In 2014 it bought Profeatable Corporation the provider of Firefly co-browsing technology and incorporated it into its Build for Change platform and customer service and sales applications. Earlier it bought MeshLabs a text analytics natural language and social engagement platform based in India. In 2013 it paid about $28 million for Antenna Software a leading provider of mobile application development platforms.

EXECUTIVES

Chairman and CEO, Alan Trefler, age 60, $456,000 total compensation

SVP Engineering and Product Development, Michael R. (Mike) Pyle, age 61, $348,000 total compensation

SVP and Chief Marketing Officer, Robert Tas, age 37

SVP Global Customer Success, Douglas I. (Doug) Kra, age 53, $343,000 total compensation

SVP Product Management and CRM Technologies, Kerim Akgonul

CFO and Chief Administrative Officer, Ken Stillwell

Vice President Marketing, Dave Donelan

Cao-treas, Efstathios Kouninis

Auditors: Deloitte & Touche LLP

LOCATIONS

HQ: Pegasystems Inc
One Rogers Street, Cambridge, MA 02142-1209
Phone: 617 374-9600
Web: www.pega.com

PRODUCTS/OPERATIONS

2014 Sales

	$ mil.	% of total
Software licenses	232.4	39
Maintenance	186.2	32
Maintenance	171.4	29
Total	**590.0**	**100**

Selected Software

PegaCloud
PegaCRM
Pega Decision Management
PegaRULES Process Commander
Solutions Frameworks

COMPETITORS

Appian	SAP
EMC	Software AG
Fair Isaac	SunGard
Guidewire Software	TIBCO Software
IBM	TriZetto
Microsoft Dynamics	Trintech
Oracle	salesforce.com
Progress Software	

HISTORICAL FINANCIALS

Company Type: Public

Income Statement

FYE: December 31

	REVENUE ($ mil.)	NET INCOME ($ mil.)	NET PROFIT MARGIN	EMPLOYEES
12/15	682.7	36.3	5.3%	3,333.0
12/14	590.0	33.2	5.6%	2,970.0
12/13	508.9	38.0	7.5%	2,627.0
12/12	461.7	21.8	4.7%	2,160.0
12/11	416.6	10.1	2.4%	1,858.0
Annual Growth	**13.1%**	**37.7%**	**—**	**15.7%**

2015 Year-End Financials

Debt ratio: —	No. of shares (mil.): 76.4
Return on equity: 11.7%	Dividends
Cash ($ mil.): 93.0	Yield: 0.4%
Current ratio: 1.72	Payout: 26.6%
Long-term debt ($ mil.): —	Market value ($ mil.): 2,103.0

	STOCK PRICE ($) FY Close	P/E High/Low		PER SHARE ($) Earnings	Dividends	Book Value
12/15	27.50	64	41	0.46	0.12	4.22
12/14	20.77	112	36	0.42	0.11	3.86
12/13	49.18	102	45	0.49	0.12	3.56
12/12	22.68	135	67	0.28	0.15	3.12
12/11	29.40	348	200	0.13	0.06	2.77
Annual Growth	**(1.7%)**	**—**	**—**	**37.2%**	**18.9%**	**11.1%**

Pennymac Financial Services Inc

If you're thinking residential mortgage this company has more than a penny for your thoughts. The parent of investment management loan services and investment trust companies PennyMac Financial Services (PennyMac) focuses on the US residential mortgage market offering loans and investment management services. Through its Private National Mortgage Acceptance Company the company's PennyMac Loan Services (PLS) originates home loans in 45 states and DC and services loans in 49 states DC and the US Virgin Islands. PLS's counterpart PNMAC Capital Management acts as investment manager and advisor. The companies service and advise PennyMac Mortgage Investment Trust (PMT). PennyMac went public in 2013.

IPO

PennyMac hoped to raise $287.5 million in its IPO but investors responded with $199.9 million. The company plans to use the proceeds to fund growth of its mortgage business through Private National Mortgage Acceptance Company. It will also use the funds for general corporate purposes.

Operations

PennyMac's mortgage banking segment includes correspondent lending retail lending and loan servicing. The correspondent line includes conventional residential mortgages acquired by PMT as well as those guaranteed by FreddieMac FannieMae and other government agencies. The company has more than 140 approved sellers; in 2012 it had $13 billion in conventional loans and $8.4 billion in government-insured loans. Retail lending originates new prime residential conventional and government-backed mortgage loans for purchasing or refinancing homes. PennyMac uses the Internet and a call center rather than traditional branch locations for direct-to-consumer approach. The company's loan servicing business includes the back office work of loan administration collection and default activities. It serves PennyMac subsidiaries and other mortgage companies. The unit handles prime credit and distress loans under the prime servicing and special servicing headings respectively.

PennyMac's investment management segment operates as an investment manager through PNMAC Capital Management (PCM). PCM handles the $1.8 billion in combined assets from PMT and PennyMac's other investment funds. PMT is a publicly traded real estate investment trust (REIT).

Geographic Reach

While PennyMac serves nearly the entire US its portfolio is heavily weighted toward California (38%) Florida (5%) and Colorado (5%).

Financial Analysis

The company's revenue has increased on the strength of gains in both the loan servicing and management segments. Other operating metrics include net assets under management total mortgage loans serviced and total mortgage loan production; all have increased in the last three years. PennyMac reported lower net income for 2012 due to amortization and impairment charges and higher spending on compensation. It sold and repurchased loans loans and earned interest on investments to more than double its cash flow for the same period.

Strategy

Since PennyMac was formed during the financial crisis it hasn't had to scramble and adapt like many of its competitors. As many mortgage shoppers turn away from large banks the company believes its poised to take advantage of growth and a lack of stringent regulations imposed on banks. For growth the company intends to focus on expanding its servicing business organically and through acquisitions increasing the number of loan sellers from which it purchases loans and leveraging its servicing portfolio to increase refinance and loan servicing opportunities.

Ownership

About a third of PennyMac is held by BlackRock Mortgage Ventures part of BlackRock Inc. the world's largest money manager. Founder and CEO Stanford Kurland former president of Countrywide along with other managers and employees owns most of the rest. Countrywide was one of the top residential mortgage lenders in the US prior to the economic downturn. It has since been purchased by Bank of America.

EXECUTIVES

Senior Managing Director and Chief Enterprise Operations Officer, Anne D. McCallion, age 61

President and CEO, David A. Spector, age 53, $503,370 total compensation

President PennyMac Loan Services, Douglas E. (Doug) Jones, age 59, $325,000 total compensation

Senior Managing Director and Chief Risk Officer, David M. (Dave) Walker, age 60

Senior Managing Director and Chief Mortgage Operations Officer, Steve R. Bailey, age 54

Senior Managing Director and CFO, Andrew S. Chang, age 38

Senior Managing Director and Chief Capital Markets Officer, Vandad Fartaj, age 41

Senior Managing Director and Chief Administrative and Legal Officer, Jeffrey P. Grogin, age 55

Senior Managing Director and Chief Asset and Liability Management Officer, Daniel S. Perotti, age 35

Chairman, Stanford L. Kurland, age 63

Auditors: Deloitte & Touche LLP

LOCATIONS

HQ: Pennymac Financial Services Inc
3043 Townsgate Road, Westlake Village, CA 91361
Phone: 818 224-7442
Web: www.pennymacusa.com

COMPETITORS

Bank of America	Quicken Loans
Citigroup	Stonegate Mortgage
JPMorgan Chase	U.S. Bancorp
Nationstar Mortgage	Wells Fargo
Ocwen Financial	

HISTORICAL FINANCIALS

Company Type: Public

Income Statement

FYE: December 31

	ASSETS ($ mil.)	NET INCOME ($ mil.)	INCOME AS % OF ASSETS	EMPLOYEES
12/15	3,505.2	47.2	1.3%	2,509.0
12/14	2,507.1	36.8	1.5%	1,816.0
12/13	1,584.4	14.4	0.9%	1,373.0
12/12	832.1	118.3	14.2%	1,011.0
12/11	289.2	14.7	5.1%	0.0
Annual Growth	86.6%	33.9%	—	—

2015 Year-End Financials

Return on assets: 1.5%	Dividends
Return on equity: 19.4%	Yield: —
Long-term debt ($ mil.): —	Payout: —
No. of shares (mil.): 21.9	Market value ($ mil.): 338.0
Sales ($ mil): 713.1	

	STOCK PRICE ($) FY Close	P/E High/Low		Earnings	PER SHARE ($) Dividends	Book Value
12/15	15.36	9	7	2.17	0.00	12.32
12/14	17.30	11	8	1.73	0.00	9.92
12/13	17.55	27	19	0.82	0.00	8.04
Annual Growth	(6.4%)	—	—	62.7%	—	23.7%

Pennymac Mortgage Investment Trust

PennyMac Mortgage Investment Trust trusts in its ability to acquire distressed US residential mortgage loans. The company seeks to acquire primarily troubled home mortgage loans and mortgage-backed securities from FDIC liquidations of failed banks US Treasury Legacy Loans Program auctions and direct acquisitions from mortgage and insurance companies and foreign banks. PennyMac is managed by investment adviser PNMAC Capital Management and offers primary and special loan servicing through PennyMac Loan Services. The company is held by Private National Mortgage Acceptance Company (PNMAC).

Financial Performance

The company's revenue increased to $470.7 million in fiscal 2013 up from $335.2 million in fiscal 2012. Net income also increased dramatically in fiscal 2013 with the company reporting more than $200 million in profit up from about $138 million in fiscal 2012.

Net cash on hand rebounded in fiscal 2013 after taking a nosedive the previous year because of investments.

Strategy

The company's investment strategy rests on a trend under the current economic downturn that the size of non-performing and sub-performing residential mortgage loan markets has grown and will likely continue to grow. Its focus will be to restructure those types of loans as well as performing loans for the secondary market.

EXECUTIVES

CFO, Anne D. McCallion, age 61
Chairman and CEO, Stanford L. Kurland, age 63
President and COO, David A. Spector, age 53
Chief Credit Officer, David M. (Dave) Walker, age 60
Chief Mortgage Operations Officer, Steve R. Bailey, age 54
Chief Business Development Officer, Andrew S. Chang, age 38
Chief Investment Officer, Vandad Fartaj, age 41
Chief Correspondent Lending Officer, Douglas (Doug) Jones
Chief Administrative and Legal Officer and Secretary, Jeffrey P. Grogin, age 55
Chief Asset and Liability Management Officer, Daniel S. Perotti, age 35
Auditors: Deloitte & Touche LLP

LOCATIONS

HQ: Pennymac Mortgage Investment Trust
3043 Townsgate Road, Westlake Village, CA 91361
Phone: 818 224-7442
Web: www.pennymac-reit.com

PRODUCTS/OPERATIONS

2015 Sales

	$ mil.	% of total
Interest income	201.3	51
Net gain on investments	54.0	14
Net gain on mortgage loans acquired for sale	51.0	13
Net mortgage loan servicing fee	49.3	13
Mortgage Loan origination fees	28.7	7
Other	8.3	2
Results of real estate acquired in settlement of loans	(19.2)	-
Total	**373.4**	**100**

COMPETITORS

AG Mortgage Investment Trust	Capstead Mortgage
	JAVELIN Mortgage
Annaly Capital Management	MFA Financial
	Redwood Trust

HISTORICAL FINANCIALS

Company Type: Public

Income Statement

FYE: December 31

	REVENUE ($ mil.)	NET INCOME ($ mil.)	NET PROFIT MARGIN	EMPLOYEES
12/15	373.4	90.1	24.1%	0.0
12/14	442.3	194.5	44.0%	0.0
12/13	470.7	200.1	42.5%	0.0
12/12	335.1	138.2	41.2%	0.0
12/11	128.6	64.4	50.1%	0.0
Annual Growth	30.5%	8.7%	—	—

2015 Year-End Financials

Debt ratio: 18.2%	No. of shares (mil.): 73.7
Return on equity: 5.8%	Dividends
Cash ($ mil.): 58.1	Yield: 14.1%
Current ratio: 0.03	Payout: 168.7%
Long-term debt ($ mil.): 428.0	Market value ($ mil.): 1,126.0

	STOCK PRICE ($) FY Close	P/E High/Low		Earnings	PER SHARE ($) Dividends	Book Value
12/15	15.26	19	12	1.16	2.16	20.28
12/14	21.09	9	8	2.47	2.40	21.18
12/13	22.96	9	6	2.96	2.28	20.82
12/12	25.29	8	5	3.14	2.22	20.39
12/11	16.62	8	6	2.41	1.84	19.22
Annual Growth	(2.1%)	—	—	(16.7%)	4.1%	1.3%

People's Utah Bancorp

Auditors: Tanner LLC

LOCATIONS

HQ: People's Utah Bancorp
1 East Main Street, American Fork, UT 84003
Phone: 801 642-3998
Web: www.PeoplesUtah.com

HISTORICAL FINANCIALS

Company Type: Public

Income Statement

FYE: December 31

	ASSETS ($ mil.)	NET INCOME ($ mil.)	INCOME AS % OF ASSETS	EMPLOYEES
12/15	1,555.9	19.6	1.3%	414.0
12/14	1,367.1	14.9	1.1%	367.0
12/13	1,299.1	11.8	0.9%	0.0
12/12	0.0	9.2	—	0.0
Annual Growth	—	28.5%	—	—

2015 Year-End Financials

Return on assets: 1.3%	Dividends
Return on equity: 10.6%	Yield: 0.7%
Long-term debt ($ mil.): —	Payout: 10.3%
No. of shares (mil.): 17.5	Market value ($ mil.): 302.0
Sales ($ mil): 80.6	

	STOCK PRICE ($) FY Close	P/E High/Low		Earnings	PER SHARE ($) Dividends	Book Value
12/15	17.21	15	13	1.17	0.12	11.92
12/14	0.00	—	—	0.98	0.22	10.68
Annual Growth	—	—	—	19.4%	(45.5%)	11.6%

Peoples Bancorp, Inc. (Marietta, OH)

Peoples Bancorp offers banking for the people by the people and of the people. The holding company owns Peoples Bank which has about 50 branches in rural and small urban markets in Ohio Kentucky and West Virginia. The bank offers traditional services such as checking and savings accounts CDs loans and trust services. Commercial and agricultural loans including those secured by commercial real estate account for the majority of the bank's lending activities. Its Peoples Financial Advisors division offers investment management services while Peoples Insurance sells life health and property/casualty coverage.

Operations

Credit cards and brokerage services are offered through third-party providers.

Financial Performance

The company's revenue increased from $103.7 million in fiscal 2012 up to $104.6 million for fiscal 2013. However despite the slight spike in annual revenue Peoples Bancorp's net income decreased from $29.9 million in fiscal 2012 down to $29 million for fiscal 2013.

The company's cash on hand decreased by about $1 million in fiscal 2013 compared to fiscal 2012 levels.

Strategy

Peoples Bancorp is looking to increase its revenue from service changes and other fees and commissions particularly from insurance and wealth management which are not reliant on fluctuating interest rate margins.

The company is also looking to strengthen its brand and build deeper relationships with its clients.

EXECUTIVES

EVP and Chief Administrative Officer Peoples Bancorp and EVP Chief Administrative Officer and CashierPeoples Bank N.A., Carol A. Schneeberger, age 59, $233,000 total compensation
EVP and Chief Commercial Lending Officer Peoples Bancorp and Peoples Bank N.A., Daniel K. (Dan) McGill, age 61, $250,000 total compensation
EVP and Chief Credit Officer Peoples Bancorp and Peoples Bank N.A., Timothy H. Kirtley, age 46, $221,500 total compensation
President CEO and Director Peoples Bancorp and Peoples Bank N.A., Charles W. Sulerzyski, age 58, $500,000 total compensation
EVP CFO and Treasurer Peoples Bancorp and Peoples Bank N.A., John C. Rogers, age 56, $26,136 total compensation
Executive Vice President Sales and Marketing, Richard (Dick) Stafford
Vice President of Human Resources, Tyler (Ty) Wilcox
Senior Vice President and Chief Investment Officer, Rose (Rosey) Nardi
Senior Vice President, Matthew (Matt) Evans
Vice President Sales and Marketing, Thomas E (Thom) Betz
Vice President and Director of Investments, Matt (Matty) Edgell
Executive Vice President Human Resources, Michael W (Mel) Hager
Vice President Of Marketing, Brenda Sparks
Assistant Vice President, Michael (Mel) Yanico
Vice President, Julie (Jules) Giffin
Vice President Finance, Joseph P (Jo) Flinn
Senior Vice President Retail Sales and Services, Staci (Stace) Matheney
Senior Vice President, Doug Ankrom
Vice President Director of Risk Management, Ann (Annie) Helmick
Vice President Commercial Lending, Greg Ullman
Vice President Commercial Lender, Teresa (Terry) Flinn
Vice President, Steven (Steve) Nulter
Vice President Commerical Lender, Kevin (Kev) Connors
Vice President Huntington WV, Jack (Jackie) Massey
Senior Vice President Chief Financial Officer, Amanda Bryan

Senior Vice President And Corporate Counsel, Ryan (Ry) Kirkham
Vice President Human Resources Director, Angela (Angie) Blackburn
Senior Vice President and Team Leader, Christopher (Chris) Neros
Assistant Vice President Trust Officer, Stuart (Stu) Dekker
Assistant Vice President Branch Market Manager, Julie (Jules) Music
Assistant Vice President Branch Market Manager, Candace (Ace) Frump
Chairman Peoples Bancorp and Peoples Bank N.A., David L. Mead, age 61
Auditors: Ernst & Young LLP

LOCATIONS

HQ: Peoples Bancorp, Inc. (Marietta, OH)
138 Putnam Street, P.O. Box 738, Marietta, OH 45750
Phone: 740 373-3155
Web: www.peoplesbancorp.com

PRODUCTS/OPERATIONS

2015 Sales

	$ mil.	% of total
Interest Income:		
Interest and fees on loans	87.1	56
Interest and dividends on taxable investment securities	18.1	12
Interest on tax-exempt investment securities	3.0	2
Other	0.1	
Other Income:		
Insurance income	13.8	9
Deposit account service charges	10.8	7
Trust and investment income	9.6	6
Electronic banking income	9.0	5
Mortgage banking income	1.3	1
Other	3.7	2
Net loss on asset disposals and other transactions	(1.8)	-
Total	**154.7**	**100**

COMPETITORS

1st West Virginia Bancorp	Huntington Bancshares
BB&T	Ohio Valley Banc
Fifth Third	U.S. Bancorp
	United Bankshares

HISTORICAL FINANCIALS

Company Type: Public

Income Statement
FYE: December 31

	ASSETS ($ mil.)	NET INCOME ($ mil.)	INCOME AS % OF ASSETS	EMPLOYEES
12/15	3,258.9	10.9	0.3%	817.0
12/14	2,567.7	16.6	0.6%	699.0
12/13	2,059.1	17.5	0.9%	546.0
12/12	1,918.0	20.3	1.1%	494.0
12/11	1,794.1	12.5	0.7%	513.0
Annual Growth	**16.1%**	**(3.4%)**	**—**	**12.3%**

2015 Year-End Financials

Return on assets: 0.3%	Dividends
Return on equity: 2.8%	Yield: 3.1%
Long-term debt ($ mil.): —	Payout: 82.1%
No. of shares (mil.): 18.3	Market value ($ mil.): 346.0
Sales ($ mil): 154.7	

	STOCK PRICE ($) FY Close	P/E High/Low	PER SHARE ($) Earnings	Dividends	Book Value
12/15	18.84	42 30	0.61	0.60	22.88
12/14	25.93	20 15	1.36	0.60	22.92
12/13	22.51	15 12	1.63	0.54	20.89
12/12	20.43	12 8	1.92	0.45	21.02
12/11	14.81	15 9	1.07	0.30	19.67
Annual Growth	**6.2%**	**—**	**(13.1%)**	**18.9%**	**3.9%**

Peoples Financial Services Corp

Power to the Peoples Financial Services. The firm is the holding company for Peoples Security Bank and Trust Company (formerly Peoples National Bank) which operates about 25 branches across northeastern Pennsylvania and neighboring Broome County in New York. Established in 1905 the bank offers standard retail products and services including checking and savings accounts CDs and credit cards to local businesses and individuals. Commercial loans including mortgages construction loans and operating loans make up the greatest portion (40%) of the company's loan book followed by residential mortgages (25%) and consumer loans. The company's Peoples Advisors subsidiary provides investment and brokerage services.

OperationsAbout 80% of Peoples Financial Services' total revenue came from interest income (mostly on loans) in 2014 while the remainder comes from non-interest income. The bank had a staff of 354 full-time employees at the end of that year. Geographic ReachScranton-based Peoples Security Bank has more than 25 branches across Northeastern Pennsylvania (in the Lackawanna Lehigh Luzerne Monroe Susquehanna Wayne and Wyoming counties) and Broome County in New York state.Sales and MarketingThe company primarily makes loans to small- and medium-sized businesses. It spent $450 on advertising in 2014 up from $350 and $287 in 2013 and 2012 respectively.Financial PerformancePeoples has struggled to consistently grow its revenues in recent years due to shrinking interest margins on loans amidst the low-interest environment. Its profits however have been rising thanks to lower interest expenses on deposits and declining loan loss provisions as its loan portfolio's credit quality has improved with higher property valuations in the strengthened economy. The company enjoyed a breakout year in 2014 however as its revenue jumped 60% to a record $79.21 million mostly as its interest income swelled from new loan business from its 2013 acquisition of Penseco Financial Services. Its service charge fees and commissions merchant services income and commission and fee income from fiduciary services also rose mostly as a result of the significant acquisition.Higher revenue in 2014 allowed Peoples' net income to more than triple to a record $17.6 million while its operating cash levels more than doubled to $20.6 million on higher cash earnings for the year. StrategyPeoples Security Bank occasionally acquires smaller banks to extend its branch network across target markets while adding new loan and deposit business. Its late 2013 acquisition of Penseco Financial Services Corporation for example nearly doubled its loan and deposit business and more than doubled its branch network to 25 branches.Mergers and AcquisitionsIn November 2013 Peoples acquired Penseco Financial Services Corporation along with its Penn Security Bank and Trust subsidiary. The $155 million-deal doubled Peoples' branch network from 12 to 25 branches creating the largest community bank headquartered in Northeastern Pennsylvania.

EXECUTIVES

CEO and President, Alan W. Dakey, age 64
EVP and COO Peoples National Bank, Debra E. Dissinger, age 61, $110,000 total compensation
Director, Richard S. Lochen, age 52, $130,000 total compensation
Senior Vice President Chief Financial Officer, Scott Seasock
Vice President, Howard (Howie) Updyke
Chairman, William E. Aubrey, age 53
Auditors: BDO USA, LLP

LOCATIONS

HQ: Peoples Financial Services Corp
150 North Washington Avenue, Scranton, PA 18503
Phone: 570 346-7741
Web: www.peoplesnatbank.com

PRODUCTS/OPERATIONS

2014 Sales

	$ mil.	% of total
Interest	64.0	81
Non-interest	15.2	19
Total	**79.2**	**100**

COMPETITORS

Citizens & Northern	HSBC USA
Citizens Financial	M&T Bank
Services	NBT Bancorp
Fidelity D & D	Penns Woods Bancorp
First Keystone	
First National	
Community Bancorp	

HISTORICAL FINANCIALS

Company Type: Public

Income Statement

FYE: December 31

	ASSETS ($ mil.)	NET INCOME ($ mil.)	INCOME AS % OF ASSETS	EMPLOYEES
12/15	1,819.0	17.7	1.0%	348.0
12/14	1,741.6	17.6	1.0%	354.0
12/13	1,688.2	5.7	0.3%	354.0
12/12	918.0	10.5	1.2%	0.0
12/11	621.4	7.8	1.3%	132.0
Annual Growth	**30.8%**	**22.7%**	**—**	**27.4%**

2015 Year-End Financials

Return on assets: 1.0%
Return on equity: 7.1%
Long-term debt ($ mil.): —
No. of shares (mil.): 7.4
Sales ($ mil): 78.7

Dividends
Yield: 3.2%
Payout: 52.5%
Market value ($ mil.): 282.0

	STOCK PRICE ($) FY Close	P/E High/Low		PER SHARE ($) Earnings	Dividends	Book Value
12/15	38.08	21	15	2.36	1.24	33.57
12/14	49.68	23	16	2.34	1.24	32.69
12/13	38.00	33	25	1.21	0.92	31.62
12/12	30.50	13	12	2.37	0.86	29.65
12/11	28.25	11	10	2.49	0.80	19.11
Annual Growth	**7.8%**	**—**	**—**	**(1.3%)**	**11.6%**	**15.1%**

Perficient Inc.

Perficient is proficient in helping its customers use technology to their advantage. The IT consultancy provides software development systems integration and technical support. It specializes in developing middleware applications used to integrate and modernize legacy computer hardware and software. Its expertise also encompasses content management systems ERP and CRM applications business process integration service oriented architectures business intelligence e-commerce and wireless communication. Perficient integrates and supports applications from vendors including IBM Oracle Salesforce and Magento.

Geographic Reach

The company primarily serves customers in the US from about 20 locations. It has offshore software development facilities in China India and Macedonia. The US accounts for 98% of revenue.

Sales and Marketing

Perficient uses a direct sales force to target large enterprise customers that annually earn at least $500 million. Typically the company seeks to bill about $5 million for each account which it believes is below the target project range of most large systems integrators.

Financial Performance

Perficient's revenue and net income have increased for several years in a row. Revenue continued the trend in 2015 but profit plateaued.

Revenue rose 4% to $473.62 billion in 2015 from 2014. A 6% increase in service revenue — buoyed by contributions from acquisitions –pulled the company's sales figure higher. Service accounts for 87% of Perficient's revenue.

Profit remained at $23 million in 2015 from 2014 as Perficient had higher expenses related to acquisitions. Cash flow was $44.7 million in 2015 compared to $34 million in 2014.

Mergers and Acquisitions

Perficient's strategy is to identify technology and geography areas where it needs to sharpen its offerings and acquire companies to fill the gaps. The company did not waver from that path in 2015.

Perficient in 2015 acquired Zeon Solutions its subsidiary Grand River Interactive and a development center iin India for $36.5 million. The acquisition of Zeon expanded Perficient's expertise supporting e-commerce and digital agency tools. It also expanded Perficient to Milwaukee and Ann Arbor Michigan we well as new customers including BSN Sports Hickory Farms HoMedics and Steelcase.

In another 2015 deal Perficient spent $5.1 million on Market Street Solutions. The acquisition expands Perficient's services in the development implementation integration and support of big data analytics and financial performance management.

A third 2015 transaction Perficient bought the The Pup Group (Enlighten) for $11.3 million. a digital marketing agency specializing in the development implementation integration and support of digital experience. The acquisition enhanced and expanded the company's digital strategy creative services and marketing expertise.

EXECUTIVES

President CEO and Director, Jeffrey S. (Jeff) Davis, age 52, $483,333 total compensation
CFO, Paul E. Martin, age 56, $308,333 total compensation
COO, Kathryn J. (Kathy) Henely, age 51, $331,667 total compensation
VP Field Operations IBM Advanced Technology Services, John Jenkins
VP Sales, Chris Gianattasio
VP Global Delivery, Kevin Sheen
VP BPM and Industry Solutions, Hari Madamalla
VP Oracle Applications, Emil Fernandez
VP Digital Experience Solutions, Ed Hoffman
VP Microsoft, Mike Gersten
VP LBU Operations, Tom Hogan
VP Salesforce, Ganesh Rangarajan
Auditors: KPMG LLP

LOCATIONS

HQ: Perficient Inc.
555 Maryville University Drive, Suite 600, Saint Louis, MO 63141
Phone: 314 529-3600
Web: www.perficient.com

COMPETITORS

Accenture	Edgewater Technology
Avanade	HP Enterprise Services
CIBER	Hackett Group
Cognizant Tech Solutions	Infosys
Deloitte Consulting	Sapient
Deloitte LLP	Wipro

HISTORICAL FINANCIALS

Company Type: Public

Income Statement

FYE: December 31

	REVENUE ($ mil.)	NET INCOME ($ mil.)	NET PROFIT MARGIN	EMPLOYEES
12/15	473.6	23.0	4.9%	2,678.0
12/14	456.6	23.1	5.1%	2,074.0
12/13	373.3	21.4	5.7%	1,874.0
12/12	327.1	16.1	4.9%	1,677.0
12/11	262.4	10.7	4.1%	1,484.0
Annual Growth	**15.9%**	**21.0%**	**—**	**15.9%**

2015 Year-End Financials

Debt ratio: 11.8%
Return on equity: 7.0%
Cash ($ mil.): 8.8
Current ratio: 2.47
Long-term debt ($ mil.): 56.0

No. of shares (mil.): 34.3
Dividends
Yield: —
Payout: —
Market value ($ mil.): 589.0

	STOCK PRICE ($) FY Close	P/E High/Low		PER SHARE ($) Earnings	Dividends	Book Value
12/15	17.12	31	22	0.67	0.00	10.14
12/14	18.63	32	19	0.70	0.00	9.27
12/13	23.42	34	14	0.67	0.00	8.28
12/12	11.78	25	19	0.52	0.00	7.60
12/11	10.01	34	17	0.37	0.00	6.92
Annual Growth	**14.4%**	**—**	**—**	**16.0%**	**—**	**10.0%**

PGT Innovations Inc

PGT helps Floridians weather their storms. The company makes and sells WinGuard and PremierVue impact-resistant doors and windows for the residential market. The energy-efficient customizable doors and windows are made of aluminum or vinyl with laminated glass and are designed to withstand hurricane-strength winds. PGT also makes Eze-Breeze porch enclosure panels and garage door screens SpectraGuard vinyl replacement windows and PGT Architectural Systems windows for high-rises. The company has two manufacturing facilities in Florida and North Carolina. PGT sells its products through some 1200 window distributors dealers and contractors in the Southeastern US Canada Central America and the Caribbean.

Operations

The company's manufacturing facility is located in North Venice Florida where it makes customized impact-resistant windows and doors.

Geographic Reach

Florida-based PGT rings up more than 95% of its sales in storm-prone areas of the US. Indeed Florida is the company's largest market representing the majority of its sales. Other markets include the southeastern Gulf Coast and coastal Mid-Atlantic regions of the US as well as the Caribbean Central America and Canada.

Sales and Marketing

The company distributes its products through multiple channels including about 1200 window distributors building supply distributors window replacement dealers and enclosure contractors. The residential new construction and home repair and remodeling end markets represented about 41% and 59% of its sales respectively during 2015. PGT markets its products through print and web-based advertising consumer dealer and builder promotions and selling and collateral materials. It markets its products based on quality building code compliance outstanding service shorter lead times and on-time delivery utilizing its fleet of trucks and trailers.

Financial Performance

PGT has achieved unprecedented growth over the years with revenues peaking at a record-setting $390 million in 2015. The historic growth was due to a spike in the sale of impact-resistant window and door products in addition to non-impact window and door products. These product lines were helped by additional sales of WinGuard and Storefront products coupled with additional sales from a previous acquisition.

Net income surged by 44% to reach $24 million in 2015 mainly due to the steep rise in sales and profits to improvement in the housing market (both new home construction and remodels) and aggressive marketing of its WinGuard product line. Cash flow from operations has risen along with sales and profits jumping 46% during 2015.

Strategy

PGT is focused on its core market —Florida — where it's looking to gain market share through promotional activities. The company also has programs and partnerships with national accounts to increase sales. The firm is focused on growing in both the new construction and remodeling markets.

In 2015 it launched Vinyl WinGuard and EnergyVue its new line of vinyl impact-resistant and non-impact energy saving windows. The company intends for the product line to replace various existing lines of vinyl impact-resistant and energy saving windows.

PGT's prospects for growth rely in part on demand during adverse weather conditions and also on the enforcement of building codes that mandate the use of impact-resistant windows and doors. The company began to pioneer such products in the aftermath of Hurricane Andrew in 1992.

Mergers and Acquisitions

In 2016 PGT purchased WinDoor a provider of high-performance impact-resistant windows and doors for five-star resorts luxury high-rise condominiums hotels and custom residential homes. The deal increased its penetration into the commercial and high-end fenestration markets and added a line of thermally-broken products and new sliding and swing door product lines.

In September 2014 PGT acquired CGI Windows & Doors Holdings of Miami a local rival for $111 million. With $45 million in annual sales CGI will continue manufacturing and selling its own brand of storm-resistant products and operate as a subsidiary of PGT. The purchase of CGI which was the company's first major acquisition strengthens PGT's product line and should help it compete against national suppliers. CGI is expected to add to earnings in 2015.

EXECUTIVES

Chairman and CEO, Rodney (Rod) Hershberger, age 59, $476,100 total compensation
President and COO, Jeffrey T. (Jeff) Jackson, age 50, $427,268 total compensation
VP and General Counsel, Mario Ferrucci, age 52, $233,155 total compensation
SVP and CFO, Bradley (Brad) West, age 46, $219,270 total compensation
VP; General Manager Glass Operations, Martin Bracamonte
VP and General Manager PGT Custom Windows+Doors, Bob Keller
Auditors: KPMG LLP

LOCATIONS

HQ: PGT Innovations Inc
1070 Technology Drive, North Venice, FL 34275
Phone: 941 480-1600
Web: www.pgtindustries.com

PRODUCTS/OPERATIONS

2013 Sales

	$ mil.	% of total
Impact window and door products	183.4	77
Other window & door products	56.9	23
Total	**239.3**	**100**

COMPETITORS

Andersen Corporation	Quanex Building
Atrium	Products
JELD-WEN	Silver Line Building
Keller Manufacturing	Products
MI Windows and Doors	Simonton Windows Inc.
Nor-Dec	TRACO
Pella	

HISTORICAL FINANCIALS

Company Type: Public

Income Statement

FYE: January 2

	REVENUE ($ mil.)	NET INCOME ($ mil.)	NET PROFIT MARGIN	EMPLOYEES
01/16	389.8	23.5	6.0%	2,300.0
01/15*	306.3	16.4	5.4%	1,900.0
12/13	239.3	26.8	11.2%	1,400.0
12/12	174.5	8.9	5.1%	1,040.0
12/11	167.2	(16.9)	—	1,020.0
Annual Growth 23.6%		—		22.5%

*Fiscal year change

2016 Year-End Financials

Debt ratio: 55.6%	No. of shares (mil.): 48.8
Return on equity: 26.1%	Dividends
Cash ($ mil.): 61.4	Yield: —
Current ratio: 5.89	Payout: —
Long-term debt ($ mil.): 190.5	Market value ($ mil.): 556.0

	STOCK PRICE ($) FY Close	P/E High/Low	PER SHARE ($) Earnings	Dividends	Book Value
01/16	11.39	33 17	0.47	0.00	2.19
01/15*	9.76	35 21	0.33	0.00	1.55
12/13	10.01	21 8	0.51	0.00	1.05
12/12	4.56	27 6	0.16	0.00	1.41
12/11	1.03	— —	(0.31)	0.00	1.26
Annual Growth 82.4%		— —		—	14.9%

*Fiscal year change

PHI Inc

Whirlybird wizard PHI transports people and equipment mainly for oil and gas companies. One of the world's top commercial helicopter operators PHI maintains a fleet of more than 270 aircraft and provides contract transportation services across the US and in Africa primarily for the oil and gas industry. Its fleet is primarily made up of helicopters but also includes fixed-wing aircraft. The company is a leading provider of helicopter transport services in the Gulf of Mexico.In addition to its energy-related operations PHI provides air transportation services to hospitals and other medical facilities and overhauls and maintains airframes engines and components.

Geographic Reach

In addition to the US PHI has operations in more than 40 countries. The US accounts for 89% of total sales.

Operations

PHI operates in three business segments: Oil and Gas (62% of sales) Air Medical (36%) and Technical Services (2%).

Sales and Marketing

PHI offers services to the offshore oil and gas onshore mining international air medical and technical services industries. Its customers include Shell Oil Company BP America Production Company ExxonMobil Production Co. and ConocoPhillips Company.

Financial Performance

The company's revenue had maintained a growth trend over the last few year until 2014 when it decreased by 2% due to a 80% drop in the Technical Services segment (a deal whereby seven aircraft were used by a customer in one of Air

Medical's programs in 2013 did not recur in 2014) along with a decrease in international sales. Partially offsetting this decline the company achieved growth in Oil and Gas (a higher use of heavy aircraft in Gulf of Mexico deepwater drilling); and the Air Medical segment saw expansion in its provider programs along with an improvement in payor mix and rate increases.The company's income has been fluctuating in the last five years. In 2014 PHI's income decreased by 45% due to lower revenues and a $30 million loss on debt extinguishment as result of early redemption of its senior notes partially offset by lower expenses as a result of decreased cost of goods sold and a drop in income taxes.PHI has observed a positive trend in operating cash flows since 2011. In 2014 operating cash flows increased by 14% to due to cash outflows in accounts receivable and inventories of spare parts partially offset by increased cash outflows in accounts payable.

Strategy

With oil- and gas-related revenues responsible for almost two-thirds of sales oil production in the Gulf of Mexico is vital to PHI's business. With the 2010 BP oil spill disaster years behind the company believes the region is a stable and profitable source of revenue as deepwater operations tend to have longer lead times and consequently activity levels are less susceptible to short term volatility in commodity prices. The capital commitments are also substantially larger than shallow water operations and its client base is more heavily weighted to the major integrated and larger independent oil and gas companies as a result. PHI will also continue to seek to expand into international markets that its believes have attractive opportunities for growth.

The company continued its strategy in 2014 and focused its oil- and gas-related business on deepwater operations and announced a plan for expansion in the Middle East and West Africa. PHI is also committed to add aircrafts to its fleet on a selective basis in both the Oil & Gas and Air Medical segments.

HISTORY

Company Background

Robert Suggs and M. M. Bayon formed Petroleum Bell Helicopters in 1949 with three small Bell helicopters. Pioneering the use of helicopters in oil and gas exploration the young firm served an oil exploration firm working in hard-to-reach areas of the Louisiana swamps. Previously a 15-man team had to wade through waist-high swamps for more than a day to perform one seismic test. PHI enabled several field tests to be conducted in one day with much less discomfort to the surveyors.

As its fleet expanded the company dropped the "Bell" from its name in the 1950s. In 1967 Petroleum Helicopters Inc. (PHI) stepped out internationally with operations in Angola and Saudi Arabia. It branched into aeromedical services in 1981 providing helicopter ambulance and other transport services for hospitals and medical units.

Suggs died in 1989 and his wife Carroll was appointed chairman president and CEO the next year. After an acrimonious and highly public family feud with her late husband's children from a previous marriage Carroll Suggs was awarded half the estate. She went on to control the company.

The downturn in the Gulf of Mexico oil and gas markets hurt revenues in the early 1990s prompting PHI to diversify. In 1994 the firm was chosen to patrol the Haiti-Dominican Republic border during the Haiti embargo; it was the first appointment of a civilian company for such a mission. The next

year PHI added five new aircraft to its aeromedical services segment its fastest-growing unit. Also in 1995 it acquired a 49% interest in Irish Helicopters Limited of Dublin.

PHI's pilots voted against joining a union in 1997. Also that year the firm continued to diversify fighting forest fires for the US Forestry Service and creating Acadian Composites to repair and overhaul helicopter composite panels (for PHI aircraft and third parties). The company ramped up its medical transportation service with the 1997 acquisition of Arizona-based Samaritan AirEvac an aeromedical unit with six aircraft from Banner Health.

A depressed oil market and bad weather suppressed demand for PHI's helicopters in the Gulf in 1999 but the company looked forward to bouncing back with higher oil prices.

In 2000 Gulf Coast engineering and construction industry veteran Lance Bospflug became PHI president taking the reins from Suggs. Also that year the company's pilots unionized. PHI narrowly averted a pilot strike the following year and reached an agreement with pilots that would allow them to voluntarily pay union dues for a three-year period after which dues would become mandatory.

Also in 2001 one of the company's helicopters crashed off the Texas coast. Much of the aircraft was recovered but the pilot was not found. Bospflug was named CEO in 2001 replacing Suggs who remained chairman. Also that year Suggs sold her 52% stake in the company to oil industry veteran Al Gonsoulin. Suggs then retired from the company and Gonsoulin became chairman. PHI also moved its headquarters from Metairie Louisiana to Lafayette.

Gonsoulin took over as president and CEO in 2004 after Bospflug stepped down. Hurricanes Katrina and Rita damaged several of the company's facilities along the Gulf of Mexico in 2005. All but one of the PHI bases were back in service by the end of the year however.

The company officially changed its name from Petroleum Helicopters Inc. to PHI Inc. in 2006 in an effort to better align its corporate identity with its mix of business activities.

Hurricanes Gustav and Ike battered the Gulf of Mexico coast in September 2008 and cost PHI some $3.3 million in repair costs evacuation of aircraft at affected bases and relocation of operations. The hurricanes also caused flight hours and revenues to dip in PHI's oil and gas unit in Louisiana and Texas as well as its Air Medical segment in Texas.

EXECUTIVES

President and COO, Lance F. Bospflug, age 61, $554,246 total compensation
Chairman and CEO, Al A. Gonsoulin, age 73, $655,015 total compensation
Director PHI Air Medical Group, David Motzkin
Director Materials, Kenneth Highlander
CFO Secretary and Treasurer, Trudy P. McConnaughhay, $282,231 total compensation
Secretary, Michael (Mel) Mccann
Auditors: Deloitte & Touche LLP

LOCATIONS

HQ: PHI Inc
2001 SE Evangeline Thruway, Lafayette, LA 70508
Phone: 337 235-2452   Fax: 337 235-1357
Web: www.phihelico.com

PRODUCTS/OPERATIONS

2013 Sales

	$ mil.	% of total
Oil & gas	489.0	57
Air medical	277.9	32
Technical services	89.6	11
Total	**856.5**	**100**

COMPETITORS

Air Methods	Erickson
Bristow Group Inc	Evergreen Holdings
CHC Group	SEACOR

HISTORICAL FINANCIALS

Company Type: Public

Income Statement

FYE: December 31

	REVENUE ($ mil.)	NET INCOME ($ mil.)	NET PROFIT MARGIN	EMPLOYEES
12/15	804.2	26.9	3.3%	2,694.0
12/14	836.2	32.6	3.9%	2,844.0
12/13	856.5	58.9	6.9%	2,791.0
12/12	646.6	18.0	2.8%	2,633.0
12/11	540.1	4.8	0.9%	2,362.0
Annual Growth	**10.5%**	**53.5%**	**—**	**3.3%**

2015 Year-End Financials

Debt ratio: 38.9%	No. of shares (mil.): 15.4
Return on equity: 4.4%	Dividends
Cash ($ mil.): 2.4	Yield: —
Current ratio: 6.85	Payout: —
Long-term debt ($ mil.): 557.5	Market value ($ mil.): 254.0

	STOCK PRICE ($) FY Close	P/E High/Low	PER SHARE ($) Earnings	Dividends	Book Value
12/15	16.41	22 10	1.72	0.00	40.50
12/14	37.40	22 16	2.08	0.00	38.56
12/13	43.40	11 7	3.77	0.00	36.19
12/12	33.49	28 19	1.17	0.00	32.63
12/11	24.85	80 53	0.31	0.00	31.17
Annual Growth	**(9.9%)**	**— —**	**53.5%**	**—**	**6.8%**

Phillips 66 Partners LP

How many ways can you break up an oil and gas company? The ConocoPhillips and Phillips 66 family of companies may be trying to find out. Phillips 66 Partners is the mid-stream component owning and acquiring crude oil refined petroleum and natural gas liquids pipelines terminals and storage facilities in the US. The company has capacity for about 650 million barrels a day and its assets include 135 miles of pipeline terminals and docks connected to Phillips 66 refineries in Texas Louisiana and Illinois. Phillips 66 Partners earns revenue from fees it charges for transportation and storage of petroleum. In 2016 it announced plans to buy some pipelines and terminals from Phillips 66 for $1.3 billion.

IPO

The company plans to use its $378 million in IPO proceeds to repay debt and for general corporate purposes including possible future acquisitions.

Strategy

Going forward Phillips 66 Partners plans to provide its transportation and storage services to Phillips 66 and third parties. It also intends to pursue acquisitions through a right-of-first-refusal deal with Phillips 66 and through third parties.

Ownership

Phillips 66 owns all of Phillips 66 Partners pre-IPO.

EXECUTIVES

Executive Vice President Refining, Lawrence Ziemba

Vice President Strategic Development, Ben (Benny) Hur

Vice President and Treasurer, John D (Jack) Zuklic

Auditors: Ernst & Young LLP

LOCATIONS

HQ: Phillips 66 Partners LP
2331 CityWest Blvd., Houston, TX 77042
Phone: 855 283-9237
Web: www.phillips66partners.com

COMPETITORS

Buckeye Partners
EnLink Midstream
Partners
Energy Transfer
Enterprise Products
K-Sea Transportation
Kinder Morgan Energy
Partners

Plains All American
Pipeline
Sunoco Logistics
TransMontaigne
Williams Companies

HISTORICAL FINANCIALS

Company Type: Public

Income Statement

FYE: December 31

	REVENUE ($ mil.)	NET INCOME ($ mil.)	NET PROFIT MARGIN	EMPLOYEES
12/15	348.1	194.2	55.8%	0.0
12/14	229.1	124.4	54.3%	0.0
12/13	106.8	60.7	56.8%	0.0
12/12	80.1	41.1	51.3%	0.0
12/11	76.0	38.5	50.7%	0.0
Annual Growth	46.3%	49.9%	—	—

2015 Year-End Financials

Debt ratio: 71.5%
Return on equity: —
Cash ($ mil.): 48.0
Current ratio: 2.05
Long-term debt ($ mil.): 1,090.7

No. of shares (mil.): 84.1
Dividends
Yield: 2.5%
Payout: 46.8%
Market value ($ mil.): 5,168.0

	STOCK PRICE ($) FY Close	P/E High/Low	PER SHARE ($) Earnings	Dividends	Book Value
12/15	61.40	24 14	3.26	1.54	4.63
12/14	68.93	27 12	2.93	1.12	0.94
12/13	37.93	48 37	0.80	0.15	7.99
Annual Growth	27.2% (23.8%)	—	—101.9%	215.2%	

Pinnacle Financial Partners Inc.

Pinnacle Financial Partners works to be at the top of the community banking mountain in central Tennessee. It's the holding company for Tennessee-based Pinnacle Bank which has grown to some 40 branches in the Nashville and Knoxville areas since its founding in 2000. Serving consumers and small- to mid-sized business the $9 billion financial institution provides standard services such as checking and savings accounts CDs credit cards and loans and mortgages. The company also offers investment and trust services through Pinnacle Asset Management while its insurance brokerage subsidiary Miller Loughry Beach specializes in property/casualty policies.

Operations

Pinnacle Financial Partners' commercial and industrial loans and commercial real estate loans account for nearly 40% and 20% respectively of its total portfolio of loans.

As part of its primary services to both individual and commercial clients Tennessee-based subsidiary Pinnacle Bank provides core deposits including savings checking interest-bearing checking money market and certificate of deposit accounts.

The bank's lending products include commercial real estate and consumer loans to individuals and small- to medium-sized businesses and professional entities. Pinnacle Bank Partners also offers auto dealer finance services to certain automobile dealers and their customers. Additionally it offers Pinnacle-branded consumer credit cards to select clients.Its convenience-centered products and services include 24-hour telephone and Internet banking debit and credit cards direct deposit and cash management services.

Geographic Reach

Based in Tennessee Pinnacle Financial Partners has become the second-largest bank holding company in the state with nearly 35 offices in eight Middle Tennessee counties and four Knoxville offices. It boasts locations in Nashville Knoxville Murfreesboro Dickson Ashland City Mt. Juliet Lebanon Franklin Brentwood Hendersonville Goodlettsville Smyrna and Shelbyville.

Sales and Marketing

Pinnacle Bank traditionally has obtained its deposits through personal solicitation by its officers and directors although it has used media advertising more in recent years due to its advertising and banking sponsorship with the Tennessee Titans NFL Football team. While it would prefer its customers to bank in person the institution allows customers to bank remotely.

Its marketing and other business development costs have risen in recent years: $4.13 million $3.639 million and $3.636 million in 2014 2013 and 2012 respectively.

Financial Performance

Pinnacle Financial Partners has enjoyed steady revenue and profit growth for the past several years thanks to positive loan growth. Revenue in 2014 rose by 9% to a record $258.77 million mostly to thanks to 9% growth in interest income from loans as the bank's loan assets grew by double digits. Pinnacle also saw double-digit growth in its fee income from service charges on deposit accounts as deposit balances grew and double-digit growth in its investment services income and trust fees as brokerage and trust account balances grew.

Higher revenue drove net income up by 22% to a record $70.47 million. Operations provided $95.06 million or 25% less cash than in 2013 primarily because the bank collected roughly $30 million less in proceeds from its mortgage loans held for sale than it did the year before.

Strategy

Pinnacle Financial Partners been looking to diversify its revenue streams through strategic investments in recent years. In early 2015 for example Tennessee-based subsidiary Pinnacle Bank purchased a 30% membership interest in Bankers Healthcare Group LLC which makes term loans to healthcare professionals and practices for $75 million.Primarily serving small- to medium-sized businesses in the Nashville and Knoxville areas the company in 2013 began extending its reach in its primary markets by opening its fourth full-service banking location in the Knoxville market in the Cedar Bluff area.

Mergers and Acquisitions

In 2016 Pinnacle acquired Avenue Financial Holdings (holding company of Avenue Bank with five banking locations in Nashville); the transaction was valued at some $201.4 million. Avenue Bank will operate as a division of Pinnacle Bank for a few months after which the companies will combine operations.

EXECUTIVES

President and CEO, M. Terry Turner, age 60, $784,700 total compensation

EVP and Chief Administrative Officer, Hugh M. Queener, age 60, $376,700 total compensation

EVP and Senior Lending Officer; Manager Client Advisory Group Nashville, J. Edward (Ed) White, age 66, $145,000 total compensation

EVP and Director Assocaite and Client Experience, Joanne B. Jackson, age 59, $117,000 total compensation

CFO, Harold R. Carpenter, age 57, $376,700 total compensation

SVP and Manager Trust and Investment Advisory, Robert Newman

President Pinnacle Knoxville, Mike DiStefano

Chief Credit Officer; President Pinnacle Knoxville, J. Harvey White, $283,800 total compensation

EVP and Manager Pinnacle Asset Management, Gary Collier

SVP and Senior Credit Officer Real Estate, Mike Hendren

SVP and Senior Credit Officer, Tim Huestis

SVP and CIO, Randy Withrow

President and CEO PNFP Capital Markets, Roger Osborne

SVP and Manager Residential Mortgage Services, Ross Kinney

EVP and Area Executive Rutherford County, Bill Jones

Chief Investment Officer, Mac Johnston

SVP Small Business Banking, Chip Higgins

EVP and Financial Advisor, Jerry Hampton

President Pinnacle Memphis, Damon Bell

Senior Vice President, Bill Decamp

Senior Vice President and financial advisor in Nashville, Lynn (Lyn) Kendrick

Senior Vice President, Kay Mcalister

Senior Vice President, Brian (Bri) Manning

Senior Vice President, Rhonda Smith

Senior Vice President, Kevin (Kev) Marchetti

Senior Vice President And Mortgage Advisor, Jeff (Jeffy) Anderson

Senior Vice President, Larry Kain

Senior Vice President Financial Advisor, Lynn (Lyn) Lassiter

Senior Vice President, Steve (Stevie) King
Senior Vice President, Buddy Cutsinger
Senior Vice President Financial Advisor, Vickie Manning
Senior Vice President And Financial Advisor, Brande Thomas
Mortgage Advisor Senior Vice President, Jeff Mayfield
Senior Vice President And Mortgage Advisor, Jamie (James) Lacy
Senior Vice President Mortgage Advisor, Chris Maultsby
Vice President, Sarah (Sar) Teague
Vice President Mortgage Advisor, John (Jack) Pope
Senior Vice President, Kirk Garrett
Senior Vice President, Ken Warren
Senior Vice President, Charlotte (Charlie) Csabi
Vice President Credit Analyst, Lona Beckwith
Senior Vice President, Darin Kellett
Senior Vice President, William (Bill) Diehl
Senior Vice President, Kim (Kimmy) Ciukowski
Vice President, Luciano Scala
Senior Vice President and Mortgage Advisor, Scott (Scotty) Ractliffe
Senior Vice President, Deon Ducey
Senior Vice President And Office Leader, Sherrie (Cher) Hicks
Vice President, Kay Dobb
Senior Vice President, James (Jamie) Hare
Senior Vice President, Brock Kidd
Senior Vice President Financial Advisor, William (Bill) MacGrath
Senior Vice President Business Banking Financial Advisor, Dennis Mitchell
Senior Vice President and Senior Program Manager, Kim (Kimmy) Jenny
Senior Vice President Financial Advisor, Cindy (Cin) Oliva
Executive Vice President And Chief Financial Officerand#8230, Alan Haefele
Vice President Finance, Dale Floyd
Vice President Mortgage Advisor, Sandra (Sandy) Austin
Senior Vice President, Sherry McHaffie
Senior Vice President And Mortgage Advisor, Keith (Keithy) Cole
Senior Vice President and Financial Advisor, Clark (Clarkson) Cox
Senior Vice President And Financial Adviser In Commercial Real Estate, Thomas (Thom) Vester
Executive Vice President and Chief Financial Officerand#8230, Alan (Al) Haefele
Executive Vice President and Senior credit Officer, Edward (Ed) White
Senior Vice President, Donna (Don) Taylor
Senior Vice President Financial Advisor, Keely Ritchie
Senior Vice President and Research and Product Development Officer, Mike (Mikey) Hammontree
Senior Vice President Financial Advisor, Stacey (Stace) Richards
Senior Vice President, Bryan (Bry) Bean
Vice President, Gary (Gar) Green
Senior Vice President Credit Advisor, Kendria Northcutt
Senior Vice President and Financial Advisor, Sam (Sammy) King
Senior Vice President, Gina Scott
Senior Vice President Mortgage Advisor, Edward (Ed) Hoover
Vice Chairman, Ed C. Loughry, age 73
Chairman, Robert A. (Rob) McCabe, age 65
Auditors: Crowe Horwath LLP

LOCATIONS

HQ: Pinnacle Financial Partners Inc.
150 Third Avenue South, Suite 900, Nashville, TN 37201
Phone: 615 744-3700
Web: www.pnfp.com

PRODUCTS/OPERATIONS

2014 Revenue

	% of total
Interest Income	80
Non-interest Income	20
Total	**100**

Selected Subsidiaries

Pinnacle Advisory Services Inc.
Pinnacle Credit Enhancement Holdings Inc.
Pinnacle National Bank
  Miller & Loughry Inc. (dba Miller Loughry Beach)
  PFP Title Company
  Pinnacle Community Development Corporation
  Pinnacle Nashville Real Estate Inc.
  Pinnacle Rutherford Real Estate Inc.
  Pinnacle Rutherford Towers Inc.
  Pinnacle Service Company Inc.
PNFP Insurance Inc.

COMPETITORS

BB&T	Regions Financial
Bank of America	SunTrust
Fifth Third	U.S. Bancorp
First Horizon	

HISTORICAL FINANCIALS

Company Type: Public

Income Statement
FYE: December 31

	ASSETS ($ mil.)	NET INCOME ($ mil.)	INCOME AS % OF ASSETS	EMPLOYEES
12/15	8,715.4	95.5	1.1%	1,065.0
12/14	6,018.2	70.4	1.2%	767.0
12/13	5,563.7	57.7	1.0%	748.0
12/12	5,040.5	41.8	0.8%	726.5
12/11	4,863.9	43.7	0.9%	743.0
Annual Growth	**15.7%**	**21.6%**	**—**	**9.4%**

2015 Year-End Financials

Return on assets: 1.3%	Dividends
Return on equity: 9.7%	Yield: 0.9%
Long-term debt ($ mil.): —	Payout: 19.9%
No. of shares (mil.): 40.9	Market value ($ mil.): 2,101.0
Sales ($ mil): 341.7	

	STOCK PRICE ($) FY Close	P/E High/Low	PER SHARE ($) Earnings	Dividends	Book Value
12/15	51.36	22 14	2.52	0.48	28.25
12/14	39.54	20 15	2.01	0.32	22.46
12/13	32.53	20 11	1.67	0.08	20.55
12/12	18.84	18 14	1.10	0.00	19.57
12/11	16.15	15 9	1.09	0.00	20.67
Annual Growth	**33.5%**	**— —**	**23.3%**	**—**	**8.1%**

Piper Jaffray Companies

Investment bank Piper Jaffray specializes in supplying clients with mergers and acquisitions advice financing and industry research. The bank's Institutional Brokerage business also offers equity and debt underwriting sales and trading services; while its Asset Management division boasts some $11.5 billion in assets under management. Piper Jaffray serves a variety of clients from corporations to government entities and not-for-profits targeting middle-market companies across the consumer financial services health care technology and industrial sectors among others. Founded in 1895 Piper Jaffray serves clients globally with offices across the US and in two European cities.

Operations

Piper Jaffray operates its business through two segments: Capital Markets (which generates roughly 80% of revenue) and Asset Management (more than 10%).

Through its Capital Markets segment Piper Jaffray provides its clients with investment banking (its largest business generating 55% of revenue) and institutional sales trading and research services for a variety of equity and fixed products. Additionally the segment comprises Piper Jaffray's alternative asset management funds and principal investments.

The company's Asset Management segment boasts $11.5 billion in assets under management and is focused on traditional asset management activities and their related services. It specifically markets its asset management business under the Advisory Research name.

Geographic Reach

Based in Minnesota Piper Jaffray operates through more than 50 principal offices in about two dozen US states and overseas in London and Zurich. The company generates less than 5% of its revenue from Europe.

Sales and Marketing

Piper Jaffray serves several sectors such as consumer financial services health care media telecommunications technology alternative energy business services and industrial. The company spent $27.26 million on marketing and business development in 2014 up from $21.60 million in 2013 and $19.91 million in 2012.

The Capital Markets segment focuses on middle-market clients in business services clean technology and renewables consumer healthcare industrials technology media and communications. Within its Asset Management segment Piper Jaffray serves institutions and individuals providing traditional asset management services with both equity and Master Limited Partnership securities through proprietary distribution channels.

The company markets its primary investment banking and institutional securities businesses under the broader Piper Jaffray name.

Financial Performance

Piper Jaffray has enjoyed rising revenue and profit over the past few years as overall merger and acquisition activity has heated up in the US. The company's revenue in 2014 jumped more than 20% to $648.14 million mostly driven by 50% growth from its Investment Banking operations which benefited from higher equity financing (especially in the healthcare sector) and more advisory service business as transaction volumes and price-per-transaction income rose. The bank's Institutional Brokerage and Asset Management divisions also grew thanks to higher fixed-income brokerage revenue and increased management fees related to its MLP investment product offerings respectively.Profit also grew for a third straight year with net income in 2014 spiking by 40% to $63.17 million. The boost was mostly driven mostly by higher revenue but also because the bank didn't incur losses from its discontinued operations related to the sale of its asset management subsidiary FAMCO in 2013 and its 2012 discontinuation of Hong Kong capital markets business.Cash levels fell in 2014 with operations using $50.1 million mostly as the bank purchased more operating assets. These assets were mostly related to its inventory and reverse repurchase agreements which are typically used to make delivery on securities sold short.

Strategy

In recent years Piper Jaffray has streamlined its European operations to focus on giving M&A advice and distributing US and Asian securities to institutional investors in Europe. To this end it has been divesting in non-performing businesses to free up cash for investment elsewhere. In 2013 for example it sold its Fiduciary Asset Management (FAMCO) subsidiary for $4 million while in 2012 it discontinued its fledgling Hong Kong capital markets business generating net proceeds of $19.1 million. While the European market still makes up less than 5% of the bank's revenue the bank's European operations have been quickly growing. In 2014 while revenue in the US grew an impressive 23% the bank's revenue in Europe rose by a scorching 32%.

Mergers and Acquisitions

In an effort to expand its client base with companies valued at between $25 million and $500 million Piper Jaffray in 2013 acquired Edgeview Partners a Charlotte North Carolina-based middle-market advisory firm that specializes in mergers and acquisitions.

Giving it a leg up in all major US markets Piper Jaffray also bought Seattle-Northwest Securities Corporation. Purchasing the public finance firm expands the company's public finance franchise and fortifies its business of serving municipal and middle-market clients nationwide.

HISTORY

Company BackgroundIn 1913 Harry Piper and Palmer Jaffray founded a commercial paper brokerage that helped finance companies like Pillsbury and Archer-Daniels-Midland. It soon moved into public finance and underwriting. It gained a seat on the NYSE with its purchase of Hopwood & Co. which was hard hit by the 1929 crash. Piper Jaffray & Hopwood grew over the next 40 years going public in 1971. Three years later it became Piper Jaffray.

During the 1980s boom Piper Jaffray still managed by the Piper family expanded into asset management and mutual funds. It was relatively unscathed by the 1987 crash.

Real trouble hit in 1994 when a derivatives-heavy bond mutual fund foundered. Investors claiming they were uninformed of the risk brought a class-action suit against the firm which paid out more than $100 million in settlements beginning in 1995.

In 1997 Piper Jaffray began offering new classes of shares of its mutual funds to provide more fee options for investors. The SEC sued the company for fraud related to the 1994 mutual fund debacle in 1998.

That year U. S. Bancorp looking to expand its securities business bought the company and bundled its own investment operations into U. S. Bancorp Piper Jaffray. In 1999 the unit expanded with the purchase of investment banker Libra Investments. The firm also entered an alliance with Tel Aviv-based investment bank Nessuah Zannex to back technology and health care ventures in Israel.

Piper Jaffray traditionally has taken pride in its investment research yet it was one of several investment banks scrutinized for alleged conflicts-of-interest between research and I-banking operations. In 2003 the firm was fined $25 million and required to pay an additional $7.5 million to provide independent research for investors. As part of the settlement the company combined its research functions into a single group and implemented firewalls between its analysts and investment bankers. Losing money Piper Jaffray was spun off from U.S. Bancorp and returned to the publicly traded arena that same year.

Piper Jaffray sold its Private Client business which offered mutual funds securities and annuities to individual investors to UBS Financial Services in 2006. Piper Jaffray used proceeds from the sale of the unit which included some 90 branches mainly west of the Mississippi to expand its industry focus. It built its asset management business with the 2007 purchases of St. Louis-based Fiduciary Asset Management (FAMCO) which brought in some $6 billion of assets under management and Hong Kong-based Goldbond Capital.

EXECUTIVES

Vice President Finance, Todd (Toddy) Deventer
Chairman and CEO, Andrew S. Duff, age 58, $650,000 total compensation
Managing Director Merchant Banking, Thomas P. (Tom) Schnettler, age 59, $300,000 total compensation
Managing Director Head of Technology Investment Banking, Chad R. Abraham, age 47, $425,000 total compensation
Managing Director Global Co-Head of Investment Banking and Capital Markets, R. Scott LaRue, age 55, $425,000 total compensation
Managing Director Head of Fixed Income Services and Piper Jaffray Investments and Trading; President Piper Jaffray Investment Management LLC, M. Brad Winges, age 47, $225,000 total compensation
Managing Director and Head Public Finance Services, Francis E. (Frank) Fairman, age 59, $205,000 total compensation
President and COO, Stuart C. Harvey, age 54
Managing Director and CFO, Debbra L. Schoneman, age 47, $500,000 total compensation
Assistant General Counsel and Assistant Secretary, John W. Geelan, age 40
Head of Asset Management, Christopher D. (Chris) Crawshaw, age 49
Managing Director Global Head Human Capital and Assistant General Counsel, Christine Esckilsen
Managing Director and Chief Information Officer of Piper Jaffray Companies; COO Piper Jaffray Investment Management, Shawn Quant
Managing Director Corporate Development, Thomas G. (Tom) Smith
Managing Director and Global Head of Equities, Jeffrey P. (Jeff) Klinefelter, age 48, $425,000 total compensation
Vice President And Senior Research Ana, Neely Tamminga
Vice President Travel Services, Nancy Koski
Assistant Vice President, Patrick Zhang

Assistant Vice President of Network Architecture, Rex Hale
Institute Sales Vice President FIS, Joseph (Jo) Longobardi
Vice President, Jin Kim
Vice President Human Resources, Esete Bekele
Institute Sales Representative Us Equities Assistant Vice President, Jacquelyn Daudt
Assistant Vice President, Melanie (Mel) Lien
Inv Banker Assistant Vice President PFS, Curtis (Curt) Gilliam
Institute Sales Representative US Equities Assistant Vice President, Christopher (Chris) Doran
Inv Banker Vice President PFS, Shannon (Shan) Thompson
Vice President Web Development, Mark (Marky) Klabunde
Vice President Network group, Corey West
Vice President, Brent Rivard
Sales Vice President, Kelli Andreen
Vice President, Kevin (Kev) Jakuc
Vice President, Christopher Flannery
Vice President Meeting and Event Marketing, Pamela (Pam) Steensland
Vice President Finance, Kim (Kimmy) Samrock
Vice President (Investment Banking), Garry Vaynberg
Institute Sales Vice President Fis, Gregory Gajowski
Vice President Public Finance Investment Banking, John Peterson
Senior Vice President, James Folsom
Assistant Vice President, Ryan (Ry) Swanson
Vice President, Craig Johnson
Inv Banker Vice President PFS, James (Jamie) Mccarthy
Assistant Vice President And Control Room Compliance, Kevin (Kev) Pomerenke
Vice President, Pam Nightingale
Vice President, Joseph (Jo) Nassif
Vice President, Bradely Wirt
Managing Vice President And Member Of The Phoenix Public Finance Group, William (Bill) Davis
Senior Vice President, David (Dave) Wimmer
Vice President, Jimmer Dorweiler
Inv Banker Vice President PFS, John B (Jack) Spengler
Senior Vice President, Justin Rowan
Vice President, Kevin P (Kev) Krouse
Vice President, Lauren MacMillan
Vice President, Matthew M (Matt) Breese
Inv Banker Vice President PFS, Michael (Mel) Keith
Vice President, Ogieva E Guobadia
Vice President public Finance Investment Banking, John (Jack) Peterson
Assistant Vice President, Jeremy (Jer) Gerber
Vice President Credit Sales, Adam (Ad) Forman
Vice President, Landon Boehm
Treasurer, Tim Carter
Auditors: Ernst & Young LLP

LOCATIONS

HQ: Piper Jaffray Companies
  800 Nicollet Mall, Suite 1000, Minneapolis, MN 55402
Phone: 612 303-6000
Web: www.piperjaffray.com

PRODUCTS/OPERATIONS

Selected Services
Investment Banking
  Services
  Mergers & Acquisitions
  Capital Markets
  Private Placements
  Restructuring
  Debt Advisory

Corporate & Venture Services
Public Finance
   Government Expertise
   Local Municipalities
   States & State Agencies

2014 Sales

	$ mil.	% of total
Investment banking	369.8	55
Institutional brokerage	156.8	23
Asset management	85.1	13
Interest	48.7	7
Other	12.8	2
Adjustments	(25.1)	-
Total	**648.1**	**100**

COMPETITORS

Alex. Brown A Division of Raymond James	JPMorgan Chase
CIBC World Markets	Jefferies Group
Citigroup Global Markets	Morgan Stanley
Cowen Group	Raymond James Financial
Credit Suisse (USA)	Robert W. Baird & Co.
Goldman Sachs	Thomas Weisel Partners
Houlihan Lokey	UBS Financial Services

HISTORICAL FINANCIALS

Company Type: Public

Income Statement   FYE: December 31

	REVENUE ($ mil.)	NET INCOME ($ mil.)	NET PROFIT MARGIN	EMPLOYEES
12/15	672.9	52.0	7.7%	1,192.0
12/14	648.1	63.1	9.7%	1,055.0
12/13	525.2	45.0	8.6%	1,053.0
12/12	488.9	41.2	8.4%	966.0
12/11	458.1	(102.0)	—	1,014.0
Annual Growth	10.1%	—	—	4.1%

2015 Year-End Financials

Debt ratio: 40.2%	No. of shares (mil.): 13.3
Return on equity: 6.4%	Dividends
Cash ($ mil.): 407.9	Yield: —
Current ratio: 1.22	Payout: —
Long-term debt ($ mil.): —	Market value ($ mil.): 538.0

	STOCK PRICE ($) FY Close	P/E High/Low		PER SHARE ($) Earnings	Dividends	Book Value
12/15	40.40	17	10	3.34	0.00	58.87
12/14	58.09	15	10	3.87	0.00	53.71
12/13	39.55	16	11	2.70	0.00	51.08
12/12	32.13	14	9	2.26	0.00	48.20
12/11	20.20	—	—	(6.51)	0.00	45.61
Annual Growth	18.9%	—	—	—	—	6.6%

Planet Fitness Inc

Auditors: KPMG LLP

LOCATIONS

HQ: Planet Fitness Inc
   26 Fox Run Road, Newington, NH 03801
Phone: 603 750-0001
Web: www.planetfitness.com

HISTORICAL FINANCIALS

Company Type: Public

Income Statement   FYE: December 31

	REVENUE ($ mil.)	NET INCOME ($ mil.)	NET PROFIT MARGIN	EMPLOYEES
12/15	330.5	18.5	5.6%	936.0
12/14	279.7	36.8	13.2%	842.0
12/13	211.0	25.4	12.1%	0.0
12/12*	41.7	2.1	5.1%	0.0
11/12	117.9	22.2	18.9%	0.0
Annual Growth	29.4%	(4.5%)	—	—

*Fiscal year change

2015 Year-End Financials

Debt ratio: 69.3%	No. of shares (mil.): 98.7
Return on equity: 28.4%	Dividends
Cash ($ mil.): 31.4	Yield: —
Current ratio: 1.10	Payout: —
Long-term debt ($ mil.): 479.7	Market value ($ mil.): 1,543.0

	STOCK PRICE ($) FY Close	P/E High/Low	PER SHARE ($) Earnings	Dividends	Book Value
12/15	15.63	174136	0.11	0.00	(0.16)
Annual Growth	—	—	—	—	—

PLY Gem Holdings Inc

Ply Gem brings out a new side of homes. The company makes and supplies exterior building materials used in home construction and renovation. Its products –vinyl siding aluminum windows and doors stone veneer and fencing –are supplied to home-center retailers distributors construction companies and contractors in North America. Subsidiaries include Variform (vinyl siding) Napco (vinyl and metal exterior siding and trim) Kroy Building Products (vinyl fencing) and Great Lakes Window (energy-efficient vinyl windows and patio doors). Ply Gem Holdings was founded in 2004 to acquire the Ply Gem brand and related assets from building materials manufacturer Nortek. The company went public in 2013.

IPO

Ply Gem Holdings plans to use the $331 million in proceeds from its May 2013 IPO to pay off debt. Prior to the filing Frederick J. Iseman and Steven M. Lefkowitz indirectly held a majority stake in Ply Gem Holdings through their affiliation with private equity firm CI Capital Partners which owned 86% of the company's stock through its subsidiaries and affiliates.

Geographic Reach

North Carolina-based Ply Gem maintains manufacturing operations in the US and Canada.

Financial Performance

In its first year as a public company Ply Gem Holdings reported revenue of $1.37 billion an increase of 22% versus 2012. Driving the double-digit gain was an increase in siding fencing and stone sales as a result of the Mitten acquisition (2013) and improvement in new housing construction in the US partially offset by lower sales of the company's metal accessory products.

Despite a big gain in sales Ply Gem reported a loss of $79.5 million marking its third consecutive year in the red. The company blamed IPO and ac-

quisition-related costs and an increase in general expenses for the loss. Both net income and cash flow from operations have fluctuated wildly in recent years with cash flow from operations swinging from $48.7 million in 2012 to a deficit of $14.7 million in 2013.

Strategy

Going forward the company hopes to grow by expanding its product offerings and bolstering its market presence in North America. Indeed the company has completed several acquisitions in the US and Canada since its 2013 IPO.

Following a pair of acquisitions in Canada in 2013 Ply Gem realigned production across two manufacturing facilities in Calgary to improve overall operating efficiency. The restructuring plan included shifting the majority of the vinyl window and door production to Gienow's manufacturing plant in Calgary while maintaining wood window and door production at Ply Gem Canada's manufacturing facility also in Calgary. Ply Gem's distribution centers in Western Canada were also part of the realignment.

Mergers and Acquisitions

In September 2014 Ply Gem acquired Simonton Windows a maker of vinyl windows and patio doors with annual sales of more than $300 million from owner Fortune Brands Home & Security for $130 million. As part of the deal Ply Gem also acquired the assets of SimEx a vinyl and PVC foam extrusion manufacturing operation in West Virginia.

In April 2013 the company acquired Gienow WinDoor a manufacturer of windows and doors in Western Canada.

Just a week after its IPO Ply Gem acquired Mitten Inc. a manufacturer of vinyl siding and distributor of various other exterior building products in Canada for $77 million in May 2013.

EXECUTIVES

Chairman President and CEO, Gary E. Robinette, age 67, $825,000 total compensation
EVP and COO, John C. Wayne, age 54, $527,875 total compensation
EVP and CFO, Shawn K. Poe, age 54, $420,000 total compensation
SVP Human Resources, David N. Schmoll, age 57, $285,700 total compensation
President U.S. Window and Door Group, Arthur W. (Art) Steinhafel, age 47
President Siding Fencing and Stone Group, John L. Buckley, age 51, $337,840 total compensation
Vice President Manufacturing Kroy, Lannie Mccoy
National Sales Manager, Rick Rinshed
Vice President Corporate Controller, Brian (Bri) Boyle
Vice President Financial Planning And Analysis, Jennifer Ward
Senior Vice President Sales and Marketing, Mark (Marky) Montgomery
Senior Vice President of Marketing, Gerard (Gerold) Blais
Auditors: KPMG LLP

LOCATIONS

HQ: PLY Gem Holdings Inc
   5020 Weston Parkway, Suite 400, Cary, NC 27513
Phone: 919 677-3900
Web: www.plygem.com

PRODUCTS/OPERATIONS

2015 Sales

	$ mil.	% of total
Windows & Doors	999.6	54
Sliding Fencing & Stone	840.1	46
Total	**1,839.7**	**100**

Selected Brands

Ply Gem Accents
Ply Gem Fence & Rail
Ply Gem Gutters
Ply Gem Roofing
Ply Gem Stone
Ply Gem Trim & Moulding
Ply Gem Windows & Doors

Selected Products

Fence+Rail
Gutters
Siding+Accessories
Stone Veneer
Trim And Mouldings
Windows+Doors

COMPETITORS

Alsco	Louisiana-Pacific
Andersen Corporation	MI Windows and Doors
Armstrong World	Masco
Industries	Owens Corning
Associated Materials	Pella
Atrium	Royal Group
CertainTeed	Simonton Windows Inc.
JELD-WEN	Trex Company
James Hardie	
Industries	

HISTORICAL FINANCIALS

Company Type: Public

Income Statement   FYE: December 31

	REVENUE ($ mil.)	NET INCOME ($ mil.)	NET PROFIT MARGIN	EMPLOYEES
12/15	1,839.7	32.2	1.8%	8,669.0
12/14	1,566.6	(31.2)	—	8,277.0
12/13	1,365.5	(79.5)	—	6,390.0
12/12	1,121.3	(39.0)	—	4,992.0
12/11	1,034.8	(84.5)	—	0.0
Annual Growth	**15.5%**	**—**	**—**	**—**

2015 Year-End Financials

Debt ratio: 77.7%
Return on equity: —
Cash ($ mil.): 109.4
Current ratio: 2.09
Long-term debt ($ mil.): 994.8

No. of shares (mil.): 68.1
Dividends
Yield: —
Payout: —
Market value ($ mil.): 854.0

	STOCK PRICE ($) FY Close	P/E High/Low	Earnings	Dividends	Book Value
12/15	12.54	31 24	0.47	0.00	(1.13)
12/14	13.98	— —	(0.46)	0.00	(1.42)
12/13	18.03	— —	(1.32)	0.00	(0.77)
Annual Growth	**(16.6%)**	**— —**	**—**	**—**	**—**

Pope Resources LP

More earthly than divine Pope Resources owns or manages more than 150000 acres of timberland and development property in Washington. Its hold-

ings include the 70000-acre Hood Canal and 44000-acre Columbia tree farms in Washington. It sells its Douglas fir and other timber products mainly in the US Japan China and Korea; Weyerhaeuser and Simpson Investment Company are major customers. Pope Resources also invests in and manages two timberland investment funds and provides investment management and consulting services to third-party timberland owners and managers in Washington Oregon and California. Its real estate unit acquires develops resells and rents residential and commercial real estate.

Pope Resources' fee timber segment also gains revenue by selling gravel and by leasing cellular communication towers.

The partnership's Olympic Property Group real estate operations relate to its nearly 3000-acre portfolio of higher-and-better-use properties that may be reforested developed for sale as improved property or sold in developed or undeveloped acreage tracts. The company's Rural Lifestyles projects allow it to resell fully logged plots that no longer have value for timber production. Its operations are focused on residential and commercial property in Port Gamble Kingston Bremerton and Gig Harbor.

In 2004 the company acquired 3300 acres of timberland in southwest Washington from Plum Creek Timber Company Inc. for $8.5 million; it also paid about $12 million to a private party for 1339 acres of timberland in western Washington. That year the company sold 426 acres in northern Kitsap County near Kingston Washington and agreed to extend to the county an option to acquire up to 360 additional acres of adjacent land (in one or two phases); the option will expire in July 2008.

In 2006 the company sold more than 200 acres of residential land for $12 million.

Pope Resources was spun off from Pope & Talbot in 1985 and the latter retains some control of the company through managing general partner Pope MGP Inc. Pope MGP is owned by Emily Andrews and Peter Pope (former chairman of Pope & Talbot) who own 12% and 7% respectively of Pope Resources.

EXECUTIVES

President CEO and Director, David L. (Dave) Nunes, age 54, $316,725 total compensation
VP and CFO, Thomas M. (Tom) Ringo, age 62, $205,872 total compensation
Director Real Estate and President Olympic Property Group, Jonathon P. (Jon) Rose, $123,257 total compensation
Director Business Development Olympic Resource Management, John T. Shea, $125,484 total compensation
Director Timberland Investment Management Olympic Resource Management, Kevin Bates
Director, John E. Conlin, age 56
Director, J. Thurston Roach, age 74
President CEO and Director, David L. (Dave) Nunes, age 54
Director, Peter T. Pope, age 81
Director, Douglas E. Norberg, age 75
Auditors: KPMG LLP

LOCATIONS

HQ: Pope Resources LP
19950 7th Avenue NE, Suite 200, Poulsbo, WA 98370
Phone: 360 697-6626   **Fax:** 360 697-1156
Web: www.poperesources.com

PRODUCTS/OPERATIONS

Selected Subsidiaries

Olympic Property Group
Olympic Resource Management

COMPETITORS

Hampton Affiliates	Potlatch
International Paper	Rayonier

HISTORICAL FINANCIALS

Company Type: Public

Income Statement   FYE: December 31

	REVENUE ($ mil.)	NET INCOME ($ mil.)	NET PROFIT MARGIN	EMPLOYEES
12/15	78.0	10.9	14.0%	66.0
12/14	87.4	12.4	14.2%	60.0
12/13	70.6	13.1	18.6%	58.0
12/12	54.0	(4.7)	—	55.0
12/11	57.2	8.7	15.3%	48.0
Annual Growth	**8.0%**	**5.7%**		**8.3%**

2015 Year-End Financials

Debt ratio: 22.8%
Return on equity: —
Cash ($ mil.): 9.7
Current ratio: 1.08
Long-term debt ($ mil.): 84.5

No. of shares (mil.): 4.3
Dividends
Yield: 4.2%
Payout: 209.3%
Market value ($ mil.): 275.0

	STOCK PRICE ($) FY Close	P/E High/Low	Earnings	Dividends	Book Value
12/15	64.07	28 23	2.51	2.70	15.01
12/14	63.63	25 22	2.82	2.50	14.99
12/13	67.00	24 19	2.96	2.00	15.88
12/12	55.68	— —	(1.11)	1.70	14.73
12/11	42.99	26 18	1.94	1.20	17.50
Annual Growth	**10.5%**	**— —**	**6.7%**	**22.5%**	**(3.8%)**

Popeyes Louisiana Kitchen Inc

This company's recipe for success features fried chicken and biscuits. A leading fast-food company Popeyes Louisiana Kitchen (formerly AFC Enterprises) operates the Popeyes restaurant chain the #2 quick-service chain specializing in chicken behind YUM! Brands' KFC. The chain boasts more than 2300 locations in the US and in more than 25 other countries. The restaurants feature Cajun-style fried chicken and seafood that is typically served with buttermilk biscuits and a variety of sides including Cajun rice coleslaw mashed potatoes or french fries. Only 40 Popeyes locations are company-owned.

Geographic Reach

About 90% of company-owned locations are found in Louisiana and Tennessee. A large portion of franchised Popeyes units are located in densely populated states such as California Florida Georgia Illinois New York and Texas. Internationally Popeyes has a stronghold in such countries as Canada South Korea and Turkey.

Sales and Marketing

Popeyes like most of its fast-food rivals leans heavily on discounted menu pricing and value meals in order to boost restaurant traffic. However the chain is also looking to differentiate itself with new menu items. It has added more seafood and other items inspired by Gulf Coast cuisine. The company spent about $3.8 million on advertising during fiscal 2014.

Financial Performance

Popeyes' revenue was more than $235 million in fiscal 2014. That was an increase of nearly $30 million compared to fiscal 2013.

The company's net income also went up in fiscal 2014 compared to the prior period. The company reported net income of $38 million an increase of 11% compared to fiscal 2013.

Popeyes' cash flow from operations remains robust. The company had nearly $60 million in cash on hand during fiscal 2014.

Strategy

Popeyes focuses almost entirely on franchising to manage its broad estate of fast-food outlets which allows the company to have so many locations without the expense of owning and operating all of them. Local operators including #1 Popeyes franchisee Interfoods of America pay the company royalties and franchising fees for the right to use the company's brand and other intellectual property. Franchisees also typically agree to uphold standards for food and service quality. Franchising accounts for about 60% of Popeyes' sales.

Being one of the largest fried chicken chains Popeyes battles for market share in a highly competitive segment. KFC with more than 16000 outlets far and away outstrips the competition leaving Popeyes to compete with Church's Chicken (owned by Cajun Operating Company) and Chick-fil-A for the title of second-place. The company also competes more broadly in the fast-food sector with burger chains (McDonald's Burger King) and sandwich shops (Subway Quiznos).

Meanwhile Popeyes continues to gradually expand its chain while closing under-performing locations.

Company Background

Al Copeland started Popeyes in 1972 as a single restaurant in New Orleans called Chicken on the Run. He later changed the name to Popeyes naming it after the Popeye Doyle character in the film The French Connection. Despite that fact Popeyes has a licensing deal with King Features (part of Hearst Entertainment & Syndication) to use the likeness of the Popeye comic strip character in its marketing.

HISTORY

Company Background

George Church founded Church's Fried Chicken to Go in 1952. The company went public in 1969 and was later bought by Al Copeland Enterprises (operator of what was then known as Popeyes Famous Fried Chicken and Biscuits) through a highly leveraged buyout in 1989. Unable to service its debt Al Copeland Enterprises filed for bankruptcy in 1992. That year Frank Belatti (former president of both Hospitality Franchise Systems and Arby's) founded America's Favorite Chicken Company and acquired the operations of Popeyes and Church's.

America's Favorite Chicken launched a remodeling effort in 1993 to give the restaurants a more contemporary look. After stepping up efforts to expand internationally in 1994 the company adopted a diversification strategy and abbreviated its name to AFC Enterprises in 1996.

AFC bought Chesapeake Bagel Bakery in 1997 and the Seattle Coffee Company and Cinnabon International in 1998. Its marriage to Chesapeake didn't last long and the company sold the chain to New World Coffee-Manhattan Bagel (now Einstein Noah Restaurant Group) in 1999. In 2000 the company sold its restaurant equipment maker Ultrafryer. It went public the following year.

AFC announced it would use its IPO money to acquire another niche food operation similar to Cinnabon. However a downturn in the economy put that plan on hold. In 2002 AFC beefed up its Seattle Coffee operations by bringing on four new executives. (The company later reversed itself on its coffee strategy and sold Seattle Coffee to Starbucks for about $72 million in 2003.) Also that year Church's signed a marketing agreement to open 100 locations in 19 African countries.

The company drew the ire of investors in 2004 when it restated earnings for the previous two years. Hit with losses and declining sales AFC sold its Cinnabon chain to FOCUS Brands for $21 million. It later sold Church's Chicken to Crescent Capital Investments (now Arcapita Bank) for about $390 million. (Arcapita formed Cajun Operating Company to run the chain.) Popeyes president Kenneth Keymer was tapped as the company's new CEO the following year after Belatti stepped down.

In 2007 Keymer resigned from the company to take over as head of family dining operator VICORP. He was replaced by former KFC executive Cheryl Bachelder. Founder Belatti announced his retirement later that year; the company appointed another YUM! Brands veteran John Cranor as the new chairman.

AFC rebranded its chain under the Popeyes Louisiana Kitchen name during 2008 (it previously operated as Popeyes Chicken & Biscuits) in part to extend the franchise beyond chicken. It plans to add seafood and other items to its menus.

EXECUTIVES

Chief Global Quality Product Engineering and Supply Chain, Alice LeBlanc
CEO President and Director, Cheryl A. Bachelder, age 59, $694,231 total compensation
COO US, John K. Merkin
President International, Andrew Skehan
CFO, William P. (Will) Matt
Vice President Communications and Public Relations, Alicia (Ali) Thompson
V Pres Fin, Tony Woodard
Vice President Operations, C Sumrall
Vice President of Field Marketing, Suzanne (Sue) Belkum
Vice President Chief Development Officer, Greg (Greggy) Vojnovic
Vice President Of Construction And Design, Jim (Jimmy) Cannon
Senior Vice President General Counsel Corp, Harold (Harry) Cohen
Vice President Global Restaurant Support Services, Sue (Susie) Morgan
Chairman, John M. Cranor, age 69
Auditors: PricewaterhouseCoopers LLP

LOCATIONS

HQ: Popeyes Louisiana Kitchen Inc
400 Perimeter Center Terrace, Suite 1000, Atlanta, GA 30346
Phone: 404 459-4450

COMPETITORS

Bojangles'   McDonald's

Burger King   Panda Restaurant Group
CKE Restaurants   Quiznos
Checkers Drive-In   Sonic Corp.
Chick-fil-A   Subway
Church's Chicken   Wendy's
Dairy Queen   YUM!
El Pollo Loco   Zaxby's
Jack in the Box

HISTORICAL FINANCIALS
Company Type: Public

Income Statement
FYE: December 27

	REVENUE ($ mil.)	NET INCOME ($ mil.)	NET PROFIT MARGIN	EMPLOYEES
12/15	259.0	44.1	17.0%	2,130.0
12/14	235.6	38.0	16.1%	2,158.0
12/13	206.0	34.1	16.6%	2,006.0
12/12	178.8	30.4	17.0%	1,530.0
12/11	153.8	24.2	15.7%	1,275.0
Annual Growth	13.9%	16.2%	—	13.7%

2015 Year-End Financials

Debt ratio: 42.2%	No. of shares (mil.): 22.4
Return on equity: 70.5%	Dividends
Cash ($ mil.): 9.1	Yield: —
Current ratio: 1.10	Payout: —
Long-term debt ($ mil.): 112.3	Market value ($ mil.): 1,304.0

	STOCK PRICE ($) FY Close	P/E High/Low		PER SHARE ($) Earnings	Dividends	Book Value
12/15	58.09	34	26	1.91	0.00	2.65
12/14	56.03	34	22	1.60	0.00	2.84
12/13	37.97	31	18	1.41	0.00	2.47
12/12	25.67	21	11	1.24	0.00	1.43
12/11	14.88	17	12	0.97	0.00	0.57
Annual Growth	40.6%	—	—	18.5%	—	47.2%

Power Solutions International, Inc. (DE)

Auditors: Frazier & Deeter, LLC

LOCATIONS

HQ: Power Solutions International, Inc. (DE)
201 Mittel Drive, Wood Dale, IL 60191
Phone: 630 350-9400   **Fax:** 630 350-0103
Web: www.psiengines.com

HISTORICAL FINANCIALS
Company Type: Public

Income Statement
FYE: December 31

	REVENUE ($ mil.)	NET INCOME ($ mil.)	NET PROFIT MARGIN	EMPLOYEES
12/15	389.4	14.2	3.7%	819.0
12/14	348.0	23.7	6.8%	701.0
12/13	237.8	(18.7)	—	455.0
12/12	202.3	6.7	3.3%	361.0
12/11	154.9	4.0	2.6%	308.0
Annual Growth	25.9%	36.9%	—	27.7%

2015 Year-End Financials

Debt ratio: 41.9%
Return on equity: 14.4%
Cash ($ mil.): 8.4
Current ratio: 2.55
Long-term debt ($ mil.): 151.1

No. of shares (mil.): 10.7
Dividends
  Yield: —
  Payout: —
Market value ($ mil.): 196.0

	STOCK PRICE ($) FY Close	P/E High/Low		PER SHARE ($) Earnings	Dividends	Book Value
12/15	18.25	53	13	0.45	0.00	9.89
12/14	51.61	39	20	1.58	0.00	8.46
12/13	75.10	—	—	(1.92)	0.00	4.79
12/12	16.18	28	14	0.74	0.00	2.50
12/11	14.50	55	1	0.44	0.00	1.69
Annual Growth	5.9%	—	—	0.6%	—	55.5%

PRA Group Inc

When times are tough businesses find the going a little easier with PRA Group. The company specializes in consumer debt collection on behalf of clients (including banks credit unions consumer and auto finance companies and retail merchants) in the US and Scotland. PRA also buys charged-off and bankrupt consumer debt portfolios and then collects the debts on its own behalf. The company operates through its subsidiaries which specialize in location and skip tracing (PRA Location Services) class action claims monitoring (Claims Compensation Bureau or CCB) and government accounts receivable management (PRA Government Services).

Operations

Some 54% of PRA Group's collection portfolio (by assets) were tied to major credit card receivables in 2014 while private label credit card receivables made up another 26% of serviced assets. The rest of the portfolio was tied to consumer financing (18% of assets) and auto deficiency receivables (2%). Overall the group generated 92% of its total revenue from collection income on loans in 2014 while another 7% came from fee income.

Geographic Reach

PRA serves the Americas and Europe. It has locations in Alabama California Illinois Kansas Nevada Tennessee Texas and Virginia as well as European offices in the UK Germany Italy Austria Sweden Switzerland Norway Finland and Scotland. In the past the majority of PRA's purchased accounts came from Florida Texas and California.Sales and MarketingPRA Group serves banks credit unions consumer and auto finance companies agencies dealers and retailer merchants among other customer types.

Financial Performance

PRA's annual revenues and profits have nearly doubled since 2011 as it's been aggressively building its portfolio of receivable assets through acquisitions.The group's revenue surged 20% to $881 million during 2014 thanks to 22% growth in income recognized on finance receivables. Fee income declined 8% for the year offsetting some of PRA's potential top-line growth.Revenue growth in 2014 drove PRA Group's net income up 1% to $177 million despite an increase in operating expenses related to compensation and outside fees and services. The group's operating cash levels jumped 16% to $262 million for the year on higher cash earnings.

Strategy

The company has focused on diversifying and geographically expanding its business by acquiring smaller debt companies and debt portfolios to be serviced. PRA Group has been continued to enter new markets around the world in recent years (particularly in Europe). During 2014 PRA entered 13 new markets from Scandinavia to Southern Europe including an office opening in Italy and a portfolio acquisition in Poland. The group also purchased a portfolio of insolvency accounts in the Canadian market. The company entered the UK market in early 2012 with its acquisition of Mackenzie Hall Holdings for some $51 million. Mergers and AcquisitionsIn July 2014 PRA bought Norway-based Aktiv Kapital AS for a total of $861 million giving PRA an entry in new markets as Aktiv buys nonperforming consumer loans through Europe and Canada.Also in July 2014 the group bought Pamplona Capital Management's (PCM) Individual Voluntary Arrangements Master Servicing Platform for $5 million expanding its insolvency investment services in the UK.

EXECUTIVES

Chairman and CEO, Steven D. (Steve) Fredrickson, age 56, $903,846 total compensation
President and Chief Administrative Officer, Kevin P. Stevenson, age 51, $522,450 total compensation
EVP Americas Core, Chris Graves, $293,077 total compensation
CEO Europe, Tiku Patel
EVP Corporate Development, Peter K. (Kent) McCammon, $249,606 total compensation
Chief Strategy and Business Development Officer, Steve Roberts
CIO, Deborah G. Cassidy
CTO, Chris Burroughs
EVP and CFO, Peter M. (Pete) Graham, age 50
Managing Director UK Insolvency Investment Services, Andrew Berardi
Assistant Vice President Infrastructure, Steven (Steve) Carlberg
Senior Vice President Technology Services, Gary (Gar) Ochs
Vice President of Business Development, Nic Kohler
Executive Vice President Operations, Neal Stern
Assistant Vice President of Information Technology, Dave (Davie) Mellott
Senior Vice President Finance, Neal Petrovich
Assistant Vice President, Mark (Marky) Davidson
Assistant Vice President Operations, Bill (Billy) Sheehan
Assistant Vice President Portfolio Strategy, Susan (Sue) Guevara
Senior Vice President Human Resources, Michelle (Michie) Link
Assistant Vice President Bankruptcy Analytics, Daniel (Dan) Viar
Assistant Vice President Operations, James (Jamie) Dickson
Assistant Vice President Of Portfolio Strategy, Mark (Marky) Schneider
Assistant Vice President Compensation, Alan (Al) Honig
Associate Vice President Human Resources, Angie S (Ang) Trunzo
Auditors: KPMG LLP

LOCATIONS

HQ: PRA Group Inc
  120 Corporate Boulevard, Norfolk, VA 23502
Phone: 888 772-7326
Web: www.portfoliorecovery.com

PRODUCTS/OPERATIONS

2014 Sales

	$ mil.	% of total
Finance receivables net	807.5	92
Fee income	65.7	7
Other revenue	7.8	1
Total	**881.0**	**100**

2014 Portfolio Composition

	% of total
Major credit cards	54
Private-label credit cards	26
Consumer finance	18
Auto deficiency	2
Total	**100**

COMPETITORS

Asset Acceptance Capital
Asta Funding
Encore Capital Group
Epiq Systems
Expert Global Solutions
FTI Consulting
FirstCity Financial
GC Services
Nationwide Recovery Systems
Rampart Capital
iQor

HISTORICAL FINANCIALS

Company Type: Public

Income Statement

FYE: December 31

	REVENUE ($ mil.)	NET INCOME ($ mil.)	NET PROFIT MARGIN	EMPLOYEES
12/15	942.0	167.9	17.8%	3,799.0
12/14	880.9	176.5	20.0%	3,900.0
12/13	735.1	175.3	23.8%	3,500.0
12/12	592.8	126.5	21.4%	3,200.0
12/11	458.9	100.7	22.0%	2,641.0
Annual Growth	19.7%	13.6%	—	9.5%

2015 Year-End Financials

Debt ratio: 57.5%
Return on equity: 19.7%
Cash ($ mil.): 71.3
Current ratio: 0.35
Long-term debt ($ mil.): 1,723.2

No. of shares (mil.): 46.1
Dividends
  Yield: —
  Payout: —
Market value ($ mil.): 1,602.0

	STOCK PRICE ($) FY Close	P/E High/Low		PER SHARE ($) Earnings	Dividends	Book Value
12/15	34.69	18	9	3.47	0.00	17.34
12/14	57.93	18	14	3.50	0.00	18.20
12/13	52.84	46	15	3.45	0.00	17.45
12/12	106.86	43	24	2.46	0.00	13.97
12/11	67.52	46	30	1.95	0.00	11.58
Annual Growth	(15.3%)	—	—	15.5%	—	10.6%

PRA Health Sciences Inc

Auditors: Deloitte & Touche LLP

LOCATIONS

HQ: PRA Health Sciences Inc
  4130 ParkLake Avenue, Suite 400, Raleigh, NC 27612
Phone: 919 786-8200
Web: www.prahs.com

HISTORICAL FINANCIALS
Company Type: Public

Income Statement
FYE: December 31

	REVENUE ($ mil.)	NET INCOME ($ mil.)	NET PROFIT MARGIN	EMPLOYEES
12/15	1,613.8	81.7	5.1%	12,000.0
12/14	1,459.5	(35.7)	—	11,000.0
12/13*	379.2	(39.9)	—	10,600.0
09/13	612.0	(48.3)	—	0.0
12/12	699.7	(2.7)	—	0.0
Annual Growth	23.2%	—	—	—

*Fiscal year change

2015 Year-End Financials
Debt ratio: 39.9%
Return on equity: 11.8%
Cash ($ mil.): 121.0
Current ratio: 1.08
Long-term debt ($ mil.): 889.5

No. of shares (mil.): 60.2
Dividends
  Yield: —
  Payout: —
Market value ($ mil.): 2,727.0

	STOCK PRICE ($) FY Close	P/E High/Low	PER SHARE ($) Earnings	Dividends	Book Value
12/15	45.27	36 17	1.29	0.00	11.66
12/14	24.22	— —	(0.83)	0.00	11.32
Annual Growth	86.9%	— —	—	—	3.1%

Preferred Bank (Los Angeles, CA)

Preferred Bank wants to be the bank of choice of Chinese-Americans in Southern California. Employing a multilingual staff the bank provides international banking services to companies doing business in the Asia/Pacific region. It targets middle-market businesses typically manufacturing service distribution and real estate firms as well as entrepreneurs professionals and high-net-worth individuals through about a dozen branches in Los Angeles Orange and San Francisco Counties. Preferred Bank offers standard deposit products such as checking accounts savings money market and NOW accounts. Specialized services include private banking and international trade finance.

Geographic Reach

Preferred Bank markets its services in half a dozen Southern Californian counties: Los Angeles Orange Riverside San Bernardino San Francisco and Ventura.

Financial Performance

In 2013 Preferred Bank reported about $72 million in revenue up just more than 10% from the prior year. The increase was solely from interest income as non-interest income (a very small part of overall revenue anyway) fell more than 40%. The company saw growth in its loan portfolio that year as well as overall deposit growth. Net income fell 20% to $19 million; the decline was primarily related to a boost in net income for 2012 because of a $20 million income tax benefit (compared to income tax expense of $12 million in 2013).

Strategy

Historically the company was focused on the Chinese-American market and although it continues to cater to that clientele most of its current customer base is from the diversified mainstream market.

EXECUTIVES
EVP and CFO, Edward J. Czajka
President and COO, Wellington Chen, age 56
Chairman and CEO, Li Yu, age 75
Senior Vice President, Ted Hsu
Vice President Commercial Real ESATE LOAN Officer, Sally Chang
Vice President, William Ko
Senior Vice President, Jim Belanic
Assistant Vice President Credit Administration, Margaret (Maggie) King
Senior Vice President, STELLA (Ella) CHEN
Senior Vice President, John C (Jack) Stipanov
Executive Vice President and Chief Credit Officer, Bob (Bo) Kosof
Vice President, Madelyn Hayashi
Vice President, Barbara Gordon
Vice President, Craig (Craigy) Miller
Assistant Vice President Compliance Officer, Kristie Yang
Vice President, Elsa Chen
Vice President, Sofia Huang
Vice President Financial Reporting, Brandon George
First Vice President, Johnny Hsu
Senior Vice President, Ann Cheung
Vice President, Wayne Chow
Vice President Human Resources Manager, Karen Cangey
Vice President Of Marketing, Louie Couto
Vice President And Manager, Lupe Quintana
Senior Vice President, William (Bill) Oberholzer
Senior Vice President, Pam Lau
Vice President, Isabella LI
First Vice President, Philip (Phil) Wong
Senior Vice President, Lee Wang
Board Member, Clark Hsu
Auditors: KPMG LLP

LOCATIONS
HQ: Preferred Bank (Los Angeles, CA)
  601 S. Figueroa Street, 29th Floor, Los Angeles, CA 90017
Phone: 213 891-1188
Web: www.preferredbank.com

PRODUCTS/OPERATIONS

2015 Sales

	% of total
Interest income	
Loans and leases	90
Investment securities available for sale	6
Federal funds sold	-
Non-interest income	
Fees and service charges on deposit accounts	1
Trade finance income	2
BOLI income	-
Other income	1
Total	**100**

COMPETITORS

Bank of America	City National
Bank of the West	East West Bancorp
Broadway Financial	Far East National Bank
Cathay General Bancorp	Hanmi Financial
Citigroup	MUFG Americas Holdings

HISTORICAL FINANCIALS
Company Type: Public

Income Statement
FYE: December 31

	ASSETS ($ mil.)	NET INCOME ($ mil.)	INCOME AS % OF ASSETS	EMPLOYEES
12/15	2,598.8	29.7	1.1%	205.0
12/14	2,054.1	24.5	1.2%	163.0
12/13	1,768.9	19.2	1.1%	148.0
12/12	1,554.8	23.8	1.5%	133.0
12/11	1,309.8	12.2	0.9%	130.0
Annual Growth	18.7%	24.9%	—	12.1%

2015 Year-End Financials
Return on assets: 1.2%
Return on equity: 11.9%
Long-term debt ($ mil.): —
No. of shares (mil.): 13.8
Sales ($ mil): 98.5

Dividends
  Yield: 1.3%
  Payout: 21.5%
Market value ($ mil.): 458.0

	STOCK PRICE ($) FY Close	P/E High/Low	PER SHARE ($) Earnings	Dividends	Book Value
12/15	33.02	17 12	2.14	0.46	19.02
12/14	27.89	15 11	1.78	0.10	17.40
12/13	20.05	15 10	1.42	0.00	15.58
12/12	14.20	8 4	1.78	0.00	14.19
12/11	7.45	10 2	0.93	0.00	11.95
Annual Growth	45.1%	— —	23.2%	—	12.3%

Premier Inc

EXECUTIVES
Vice Chair of the Board, Charles E. Hart, age 66
President Chief Executive Officer and Director, Susan D. DeVore, age 57
Chair of the Board, Richard J. (Rich) Statuto, age 59
SVP Corporate Development and Strategy, Terry Linn
President Premier Insurance Management Services, Robert L. Dowdy
Chief Medical Officer, Richard Bankowitz
Senior Vice President of Premier Performance Partners, R. Wesley (Wes) Champion, age 50
Senior Vice President of Healthcare Informatics, Keith J. Figlioli
Senior Vice President and Chief Financial Officer, Craig S. McKasson, age 49
senior Vice President people, Kelli Price
senior Vice President enterprise growth, Jennifer Arcudi
SVP Group Purchasing, John Biggers
Vice Chairman, Keith Pitts
senior Vice President member field services, Andy Brailo
President and chief mission officer, Alan R. Yordy
Chief Operating Officer, Michael J. (Mike) Alkire, age 53
Chief Sales Officer, Gary S. Long
President of Supply Chain Services, Durral R. Gilbert, age 50
Chief Marketing Officer, Chip Carter
Director, Michael D. Connelly
Director, Glenn D. Steele Jr., age 70
Director, James H. (Jim) Hinton
Director, William E. Mayer, age 74
Director, Mark A. Eustis, age 62
Director, Dennis Vonderfecht
Director, Francisco J. (Frank) Perez
Vice Chair of the Board, Charles E. Hart, age 66

President Chief Executive Officer and Director,
 Susan D. DeVore, age 57
Director, Sister Mary Jean Ryan
Director, Christine K. Cassel
Director, Lee Perlman
Director, Thomas J. Strauss
Director, Nick W. Turkal
Director, J. Thomas Jones
Auditors: Ernst & Young LLP

LOCATIONS

HQ: Premier Inc
 13034 Ballantyne Corporate Place, Charlotte, NC 28277
Phone: 704 357-0022
Web: www.premierinc.com

COMPETITORS

Aetna	HealthTrust
Allscripts	MedAssets
CVS Caremark	Medline Industries
Deloitte & Touche	Novation
Express Scripts	Owens & Minor
Global Healthcare	PSS World Medical
Exchange	UnitedHealth Group

HISTORICAL FINANCIALS

Company Type: Public

Income Statement

FYE: June 30

	REVENUE ($ mil.)	NET INCOME ($ mil.)	NET PROFIT MARGIN	EMPLOYEES
06/16	1,162.5	235.1	20.2%	2,100.0
06/15	1,007.0	38.7	3.8%	1,800.0
06/14	910.5	28.3	3.1%	1,600.0
06/13	869.2	7.3	0.8%	1,600.0
06/12	768.2	3.9	0.5%	0.0
Annual Growth	10.9%	178.0%	—	—

2016 Year-End Financials

Debt ratio: 1.0%	No. of shares (mil.): 142.1
Return on equity: 21.8%	Dividends
Cash ($ mil.): 248.8	Yield: —
Current ratio: 1.42	Payout: —
Long-term debt ($ mil.): 13.8	Market value ($ mil.): 4,648.0

	STOCK PRICE ($) FY Close	P/E High/Low		PER SHARE ($) Earnings	Dividends	Book Value
06/16	32.70	2	2	1.33	0.00	8.34
06/15	38.46	—	—	(24.25)	0.00	6.68
06/14	29.00	—	—	(105.85)	0.00	5.35
Annual Growth	6.2%			—	—	24.9%

Prestige Brands Holdings Inc

Prestige Brands is a lifesaver in the business of resuscitating offloaded consumer brands. The company acquires develops and markets over-the-counter (OTC) drugs and household cleaning products. Its portfolio includes Chloraseptic Clear Eyes Comet Compound W Doctor's Nightguard Little Remedies PediaCare Murine Monistat New Skin and many other big-name brands. Prestige

Brands contracts out manufacturing of its products which are sold through mass merchandisers and retail stores primarily in North America. The company was formed in 1996 to acquire and revitalize leading but neglected consumer brands divested by major consumer companies such as Procter & Gamble.

Operations

Prestige operates through three segments: North American OTC Healthcare International OTC Healthcare and Household Cleaning. Its around 30 core OTC brands which contribute some 90% of revenue include names that have stocked medicine cabinets for generations - Luden Efferdent Beano Debrox PediaCare Chloraseptic Compound W and Dramamine. Household cleaning brands Chore Boy Comet and Spic and Span have similar name recognition.

Instead of maintaining its own manufacturing facilities Prestige Brands contracts out product-making using third-party manufacturers and warehouse distribution partners to simplify its organizational structure.

Geographic Reach

Nearly all of Prestige Brands' sales come from North America (the US is the firm's largest single market bringing in nearly 90% of sales) but the company is working to increase international sales by licensing some brands to large multinational companies in desirable international markets. It has one such agreement for Comet in Eastern Europe. It also sells Clear Eyes Chloraseptic and Murine internationally. Prestige Brands which in 2016 generated 8% of sales outside North America has already designed and developed product packaging for specific international markets and is focused now on growing its distribution network to help increase its international penetration.

Sales and Marketing

Prestige Brands generates revenue by leveraging several distribution channels to get its products on store shelves and in consumers' hands. Mass merchandisers drug stores and grocery stores account for the largest percentages of sales at some 30% 20% and 20% of total revenue respectively. Other growing but smaller channels that Prestige Brands relies on include dollar stores and club stores.

Uber worldwide retailer Wal-Mart accounts for about a fifth of the company's total sales. Other notable customers include Walgreen CVS Target Dollar Tree Meijer Ahold and Kroger among others.

Prestige Brands develops extensive marketing programs for new and existing products.

Financial Performance

With the exception of 2014 when the company reported a 3% drop in revenue Prestige Brands has seen growing revenues for the past five years. In fiscal 2016 (ended March) sales rose 13% to $806.3 million primarily due to 16% growth in the North American OTC Healthcare segment. That growth was driven by the recent acquisitions of the Insight (2014) and DenTek (2016) brands.

Net income has also been on the rise. In fiscal 2016 it rose 28% to $99.9 million thanks to the higher revenue and lower operating expenses.

Strategy

The company's strategy lies in acquiring new brands and developing effective marketing programs for its existing products. Acquisitions are key to keeping its products portfolio fresh and it is constantly on the lookout for new additions to keep itself competitive. Its goal is to have 85% of its earnings from "invest for growth" brands and the remainder from "manage for cash" brands.

When Prestige Brands is evaluating a product for acquisition it takes a number of factors into

consideration including the period of time the product has been in existence the product's market position (typically about three-quarters of the company's sales come from brands with a #1 or #2 market position) its recent and projected sales growth and its potential for product extensions. Prestige Brands looks to acquire products that can be remarketed with additional enhancements. It uses a similar technique when marketing existing products introducing enhancements and line extensions.

In 2016 Prestige Brands sold three non-core but established brands (New Skin Fiber Choice and PediaCare) to Moberg Pharma for $40 million. The deal fell in line with its strategy of maintaining a portfolio of primarily newer brands; the company plans to use funds from the deal to pay down debt. In a similar move later that year the company sold the Dermoplast brand to Moberg Pharma for $47.6 million.

Among the company's highest-valued brands are Monistat DenTek Clear Eyes and Chloraseptic. On the other hand such brands as Pediacare and Beano have slipped due to growing competition (but Prestige remains committed to their recovery).

Mergers and Acquisitions

Prestige Brands acquired specialty oral care products distributor DenTek for $225 million in early 2016. Later that year it agreed to buy C.B. Fleet which makes OTC enemas and laxatives as well as Summers Eve feminine products for $825 million.

Company Background

Prestige Brands was pieced together in 1996 from the parts of defunct manufacturer Medtech Labs (shampoos nail care products) The Spic & Span Company and Prestige Brands International (Comet cleaners and Clear Eyes eye drops).

In 2012 Prestige Brands completed its largest asset acquisition to date spending $660 million to gain a portfolio of 17 North American OTC brands from GlaxoSmith Kline (GSK). The purchases added brands that included leading pain relief (BC Goody's and Ecotrin) gastrointestinal (Beano Fiber Choice Gaviscon Phazyme and Tagamet) sleep aid (Sominex) ear wax remover (Debrox) and oral rinse (Gly-Oxide) brands. Also in 2012 the company received an unsolicited acquisition proposal from Mexican health products firm Genomma Lab Internacional. The Prestige Brands board of directors rejected the proposal as inadequate and not in the best interest of the firm.

EXECUTIVES

General Counsel and VP Business Development,
 Samuel C. (Sam) Cowley, age 54, $345,000 total compensation
SVP International, John F. Parkinson, age 63, $257,522 total compensation
SVP Science and Technology, Jean A. Boyko, age 57, $250,000 total compensation
EVP Sales and Marketing, Timothy J. Connors, age 49, $415,000 total compensation
President and CEO, Ronald M. (Ron) Lombardi, age 52, $450,000 total compensation
CFO, Christine (Chris) Sacco
Lead Director, Gary E. Costley, age 72
Auditors: PricewaterhouseCoopers LLP

LOCATIONS

HQ: Prestige Brands Holdings Inc
 660 White Plains Road, Tarrytown, NY 10591
Phone: 914 524-6800
Web: www.prestigebrands.com

PRODUCTS/OPERATIONS

2016 Sales

	$ mil.	% of total
North American OTC Healthcare	657.9	82
Household Cleaning	90.6	11
International OTC Healthcare	57.7	7
Total	**806.2**	**100**

2016 Sales

	$ mil.	% of total
Women's Health	135.2	17
Analgesics	119.4	15
Cough & Cold	116.6	14
Eye & Ear Care	107.5	13
Gastrointestinal	94.6	12
Household Cleaning	90.6	11
Dermatologicals	85.1	11
Oral Care	51.1	6
Other OTC	6.1	1
Total	**806.2**	**100**

Selected Products

Over-the-counter
 Clear Eyes
 Chloraseptic
 Clear Eyes
 Compound W
 The Doctor's NightGuard
 The Doctor's Brushpicks
 Dramamine
 Ecotrin
 Efferdent
 Effergrip
 Fiber Choice
 Little Remedies
 Luden's
 Murine
 NasalCrom
 New-Skin
 PediaCare
 Phazyme
 Sominex
 Tagamet
 Wartner
Household cleaning
 Comet
 Chore Boy
 Spic and Span

COMPETITORS

3M	Hi-Tech Pharmacal
Airborne Inc.	Inter Parfums
Bayer Consumer Care	Johnson & Johnson
Boulder Brands	Lifetime Brands
Chattem	McNeil Consumer
Church & Dwight	Healthcare
Clorox	Merck
Colgate-Palmolive	Mondelez International
Combe	Novartis Corporation
Coty Inc.	Pfizer
GlaxoSmithKline	Procter & Gamble
Hain Celestial	Reckitt Benckiser
Helen of Troy	USANA Health Sciences
HemCon Medical	Unilever
Technologies	Zep Inc.
Henkel Corp.	

HISTORICAL FINANCIALS

Company Type: Public

Income Statement

FYE: March 31

	REVENUE ($ mil.)	NET INCOME ($ mil.)	NET PROFIT MARGIN	EMPLOYEES
03/16	806.2	99.9	12.4%	259.0
03/15	714.6	78.2	11.0%	187.0
03/14	601.8	72.6	12.1%	155.0
03/13	623.6	65.5	10.5%	117.0
03/12	441.0	37.2	8.4%	105.0
Annual Growth	**16.3%**	**28.0%**	**—**	**25.3%**

2016 Year-End Financials

Debt ratio: 55.1%	No. of shares (mil.): 52.7
Return on equity: 14.5%	Dividends
Cash ($ mil.): 27.2	Yield: —
Current ratio: 2.33	Payout: —
Long-term debt ($ mil.): 1,625.3	Market value ($ mil.): 2,817.0

	STOCK PRICE ($) FY Close	P/E High/Low		PER SHARE ($) Earnings	Dividends	Book Value
03/16	53.39	29	21	1.88	0.00	14.11
03/15	42.89	29	18	1.49	0.00	12.00
03/14	27.25	26	18	1.39	0.00	10.87
03/13	25.69	20	10	1.27	0.00	9.35
03/12	17.48	24	11	0.73	0.00	8.01
Annual Growth	**32.2%**	**—**	**—**	**26.7%**	**—**	**15.2%**

Prologis LP

EXECUTIVES

Chb-ceo, Hamid R Moghadam
Auditors: KPMG LLP

LOCATIONS

HQ: Prologis LP
 Pier 1, Bay 1, San Francisco, CA 94111
Phone: 415 394-9000
Web: www.prologis.com

HISTORICAL FINANCIALS

Company Type: Public

Income Statement

FYE: December 31

	REVENUE ($ mil.)	NET INCOME ($ mil.)	NET PROFIT MARGIN	EMPLOYEES
12/15	2,197.0	880.5	40.1%	0.0
12/14	1,760.7	638.3	36.3%	0.0
12/13	1,750.4	344.1	19.7%	0.0
12/12	1,960.5	(39.8)	—	0.0
12/11	1,421.7	(153.7)	—	0.0
Annual Growth	**11.5%**	**—**		

2015 Year-End Financials

Debt ratio: 37.0%	No. of shares (mil.): 540.1
Return on equity: —	Dividends
Cash ($ mil.): 264.0	Yield: —
Current ratio: 0.92	Payout: 92.6%
Long-term debt ($ mil.): 11,626.8	Market value ($ mil.): —

Prospect Capital Corporation

Prospect Capital is a closed-end investment fund with holdings in the consumer food health care and manufacturing sectors among others. The company targets privately held middle-market firms with annual revenues of less than $750 million; it also considers thinly traded public companies or turnaround situations. Prospect's portfolio includes interests in more than 100 companies mainly through senior loans and mezzanine debt. The company also makes equity and secured debt investments. Typically investing from $5 million to $250 million per transaction Prospect is a long-term investor that maintains regular contact with its portfolio company's management and participates in their board meetings.

Geographic Reach

New York-based Prospect Capital invests primarily in US companies but also in Canada the Cayman Islands and Ireland. About 80% of the firm's investment portfolio is in the US.

Operations

Prospect has elected to be regulated as a business development company (BDC) a status which affords the firm certain tax benefits. Although it initially targeted on industrial and energy investments the company has broadened its focus in the past few years and minimized its holdings in the energy sector.

Financial Performance

Prospect Capital reported revenue of $576.3 million in fiscal 2013 (ended June) an 80% increase over the year earlier period. Net income rose 16% over the same period to nearly $221 million. Prospect's financial prospects have brightened considerably in recent years with revenue up more than 500% since fiscal 2009 and steeply rising profits. The 80% increase in fiscal 2013 revenue was primarily due to 98% increase in interest income as a result of interest earned on the mezzanine loan. Dividend income rose as well.

Strategy

Prospect Capital pursues a diversified investment strategy investing in 124 long-term portfolio investments and CLOs (collateralized loan obligations) and to a lesser extent money market funds. In fiscal 2013 (ended June) the firm originated $3.1 million of new investments. Prospect's origination efforts are focused primarily on secured lending to reduce portfolio risk investing primarily in first lien loans and subordinated notes in CLOs though it also engages in select junior debt and equity investments. First lien loans represent about 55% of its investment portfolio with second lien loans representing about 25%. Diversified financial services is the firm's single largest industry sector for investment followed by consumer finance durable consumer products consumer services and software and computer services. Together these five industries constitute more than half of Prospect's investment portfolio.

In 2013 the firm invested $144.5 million in four new transactions encompassing 19 rent-producing multifamily residential properties totaling 5652 rental units. Combined with its prior investments Prospect has a invested a total of $288.3 million in 10 separate transactions encompassing 25 multifamily residential properties with more than 9100 rental units.

Mergers and Acquisitions

In 2013 Prospect acquired A 94% stake in Nationwide Acceptance LLC a Chicago based consumer finance company.

EXECUTIVES

Board Member, Andrew C (Andy) Cooper
Auditors: BDO USA, LLP

LOCATIONS

HQ: Prospect Capital Corporation
 10 East 40th Street, 42nd Floor, New York, NY 10016
Phone: 212 448-0702
Web: www.prospectstreet.com

PRODUCTS/OPERATIONS

Selected Current Investments
AIRMALL USA Inc. (property management)
Ajax Rolled Ring & Machine Inc. (manufacturing)
AWCNC (machinery)
Blue Coat Systems Inc. (software computer service)
Borga Inc. (manufacturing)
Boxercraft (textiles and leather)
Broder Bros. Co. (Textiles)
Crossman Corp. (manufacturing)
Focus Products (consumer products)
Grocery Outlet (supermarkets)
Harley Marine Services (transportation)
Injured Workers Pharmacy (health care)
Nationwide Acceptance Holdings LLC (consumer finance)
National Bankruptcy Services (financial services)
NMMB (advertising media buying)
NRG Manufacturing Inc. (drilling rig components)
R-V Industries Inc. (metal fabrication)
Wind River Resources (oil and gas production)

COMPETITORS

ACI Capital	OHA Investment
Apollo Investment	Stephens Group
First Reserve	TPG
GFI Energy Ventures	Venrock
Katalyst	

HISTORICAL FINANCIALS

Company Type: Public

Income Statement

FYE: June 30

	ASSETS ($ mil.)	NET INCOME ($ mil.)	INCOME AS % OF ASSETS	EMPLOYEES
06/16	6,276.7	371.1	5.9%	0.0
06/15	6,798.0	362.7	5.3%	0.0
06/14	6,477.2	357.2	5.5%	0.0
06/13	4,448.2	324.9	7.3%	0.0
06/12	2,255.2	186.6	8.3%	0.0
Annual Growth	29.2%	18.7%	—	—

	STOCK PRICE ($) FY Close	P/E High/Low		PER SHARE ($) Earnings	Dividends	Book Value
06/16	7.82	8	5	1.04	1.00	9.62
06/15	7.37	11	7	1.03	1.19	10.31
06/14	10.63	10	8	1.19	1.32	10.56
06/13	10.80	8	6	1.57	1.28	10.72
06/12	11.39	7	5	1.63	1.22	10.83
Annual Growth	(9.0%)	—	—	(10.6%)	(4.8%)	(2.9%)

Prosperity Bancshares Inc.

Prosperity Bancshares reaches banking customers across the Lone Star State. The holding company for Prosperity Bank operates about 230 branches across Texas and about 15 more in Oklahoma. Serving consumers and small to midsized businesses the bank offers traditional deposit and loan services in addition to wealth management retail brokerage and mortgage banking investment services. Prosperity Bank focuses on real estate lending: Commercial mortgages make up the largest segment of the company's loan portfolio (33%) followed by residential mortgages (24%). Credit cards business auto consumer home equity loans round out its lending activities.

OperationsAbout 63% of Prosperity's total revenue came from loan interest (including fees) in 2014 while another 22% came from interest on its investment securities. The rest of its revenue came from non-sufficient fund fees (4%) credit and debit card income (3%) deposit account service charges (2%) trust income (1%) mortgage income (1%) and brokerage income (1%). Geographic Reach

Prosperity Bancshares operates 230 Texas banking locations across Houston South Texas the Dallas/Fort Worth metroplex East Texas Bryan/College Station Central Texas and West Texas. It also has 15 branch locations in Oklahoma (including Tulsa).Sales and MarketingThe bank mainly targets consumers and small and medium-sized businesses and tailors its products to the specific needs of a given market.Financial PerformanceProsperity's revenues and profits have been prospering thanks to loan and deposit business growth from acquisitions and declining loan loss provisions as its loan portfolio's credit quality has improved with higher property valuations in a strengthened economy. The company's revenue jumped by 32% to $837.7 million in 2014 mostly as its loan interest income swelled by 40% on loan asset growth from its F&M acquisition. The bank's non-interest income rose by 29% as well from new deposit account service fees from the acquisition and additional income from its newly added brokerage and trust business. Higher revenue and strong operating cost controls in 2014 drove Prosperity's net income higher by 34% to $297.4 million while its operating cash levels rose by 13% to $348.3 million on higher cash earnings.

Strategy

Prosperity Bancshares bases its growth strategy on three key elements: Internal loan and deposit business growth through "individualized customer service" and service line expansion opportunities; cost controls to maximize profitability; and acquisitions.Toward its internal business growth initiatives Prosperity spent 2012 and 2013 launching its new trust brokerage mortgage lending and credit card products and services to customers for the first time. With cost-controls in mind the bank tracks its branches "as separate profit centers" noting each branch's interest income efficiency ratio deposit growth loan growth and overall profitability. That way it can reward individual branch managers and presidents accordingly by merit rather than giving higher compensation across the board.The acquisitive Prosperity Bancshares has been buying up small banks in Texas —and now Oklahoma —as it hopes to hit a sweet spot in the market between the national giants that dominate the Texas banking scene and smaller community banks.

Mergers and Acquisitions

In January 2016 furthering its presence in the Houston market Prosperity Bancshares purchased Tradition Bancshares along with its seven branches in the Houston Area (Bellaire Katy and the Woodlands) $540 million in assets $239 million in loans and $483.8 million in deposits. In April 2014 toward expansion in the Oklahoma and Dallas markets Prosperity purchased Tulsa-based F&M Bancorporation and its subsidiary The F&M Bank & Trust Company. The deal added 13 branches including nine in Tulsa and surrounding areas three in Dallas and a loan production office in Oklahoma City. In April 2013 it acquired Coppermark Bank one of Oklahoma City's largest banks with six branches in Oklahoma City and three locations in North Dallas for $194 million. The deal also added the credit card and agent bank merchant processing business from its subsidiary Bankers Credit Card Services.In January 2013 the company boosted its market share in East Texas after buying East Texas Financial Services and its four First Federal Bank Texas branch locations including three branches in Tyler and one in Gilmer.Company Background

In early 2012 Prosperity acquired Texas Bankers a three-branch Austin bank with some $72 million in assets. The merger increased Prosperity's number of Central Texas branches to 34 banking locations. It followed that deal with the purchase of The Bank Arlington a single-branch bank operating in the Dallas/Ft. Worth area. It acquired single-branch Community National Bank of Bellaire Texas in late 2012.

Also in 2012 Prosperity expanded into West Texas after it merged American State Financial Corporation and its American State Bank subsidiary into its operations. The deal added $3 billion in assets and 37 West Texas banking offices in Lubbock Midland/Odessa and Abilene.

EXECUTIVES

Executive Vice President Cashier Prosperity Bank, Michael (Mel) Harris
EVP Cashier Prosperity Bank, Mike Harris
Senior Chairman and CEO, David Zalman, age 59, $851,567 total compensation
CFO; EVP and CFO Prosperity Bank, David Hollaway, age 60, $425,000 total compensation
Vice Chairman; Chairman and COO Prosperity Bank, H. E. (Tim) Timanus, age 72, $452,400 total compensation
Vice Chairman and Area Chairman Central Texas, Edward Z. (Eddie) Safady
EVP Regulatory and Compliance Prosperity Bank, Rhonda L. Carroll
Chief Lending Officer Prosperity Bank, Randy D. Hester, $325,000 total compensation
SEVP Financial Operations and Administration Prosperity Bank, Mike Epps, $327,625 total compensation
EVP and CIO Prosperity Bank, Gisela Riggan
Chief Risk Oficer, Jennifer Willcoxon
Chief Credit Officer Prosperity Bank, Merle Karnes
President Prosperity Bank, Bob Benter
EVP Prosperity Bancshares and Prosperity Bank, Robert (Bob) Dowdell
Chairman Wealth Management, Russell Marshall
Senior Vice President Sales and Marketing, Scott (Scotty) Voland
Vice President and Lending Assistant, Angelina Garcia
Senior Vice President Facilities, Tom (Tommy) Allen
Vice President, Brian (Bri) Blair
Vice President and Lobby ManagerLakeway Banking Center, Dala Campbell
Senior Vice President SBA Lending, Beverly (Bev) Layne
Assistant Vice President of Technology Procurement, Lausanne Barrett
Senior Vice President, Brent Adams
Assistant Vice President And Lobby Man, Debbie (Deb) Rodriguez
Assistant Vice President, Laura (Laur) Arroyo
Senior Vice President Cash Management, Darcie Henderson
Senior Vice President Operations, John (Jack) Ellis
Senior Vice President Chief Appraiser, Rob (Robbie) Moorman
Auditors: Deloitte & Touche LLP

LOCATIONS

HQ: Prosperity Bancshares Inc.
Prosperity Bank Plaza, 4295 San Felipe, Houston, TX 77027
Phone: 713 693-9300
Web: www.prosperitybankusa.com

PRODUCTS/OPERATIONS

2014 Sales

	$ mil.	% of total
Interest		
Loans including fees	525.7	63
Securities	188.7	22
Federal funds sold	0.3	-
Noninterest		
Non-sufficient funds fees	37.0	4
Debit card and ATM card income	22.9	3
Service charges on deposit accounts	16.5	2
Trust income	8.1	1
Brokerage income	5.9	1
Mortgage income	4.4	1
Other	28.2	3
Total	**837.7**	**100**

COMPETITORS

Amegy	JPMorgan Chase
BBVA Compass	North Dallas Bank
Bancshares	Texas Capital
Bank of America	Bancshares
Citibank	Wells Fargo
Comerica	Woodforest Financial
Cullen/Frost Bankers	

HISTORICAL FINANCIALS

Company Type: Public

Income Statement

FYE: December 31

	ASSETS ($ mil.)	NET INCOME ($ mil.)	INCOME AS % OF ASSETS	EMPLOYEES
12/15	22,037.2	286.6	1.3%	3,037.0
12/14	21,507.7	297.4	1.4%	3,096.0
12/13	18,642.0	221.4	1.2%	2,995.0
12/12	14,583.5	167.9	1.2%	2,266.0
12/11	9,822.6	141.7	1.4%	1,664.0
Annual Growth	22.4%	19.2%	—	16.2%

2015 Year-End Financials

Return on assets: 1.3%
Return on equity: 8.5%
Long-term debt ($ mil.): —
No. of shares (mil.): 70.0
Sales ($ mil): 790.4

Dividends
Yield: 2.3%
Payout: 26.4%
Market value ($ mil.): 3,351.0

	STOCK PRICE ($) FY Close	P/E High/Low	PER SHARE ($) Earnings	Dividends	Book Value
12/15	47.86	14 11	4.09	1.12	49.45
12/14	55.36	16 12	4.32	0.99	46.50
12/13	63.39	18 11	3.65	0.89	42.19
12/12	42.00	15 12	3.23	0.80	37.01
12/11	40.35	15 10	3.01	0.72	33.41
Annual Growth	4.4%	— —	8.0%	11.6%	10.3%

Proto Labs Inc

Need a prototype pronto? Proto Labs can help with that. The industrial manufacturer creates custom parts in quick turnaround for prototype and short-run production. The company uses 3D CAD software to upload new parts designs and then its computer numerical control (CNC) process analyzes the design quotes a price and makes the parts. Proto Labs creates machined metal (Firstcut) and injection-molded plastic (Protomold) parts and can ship them the next business day. Its medical device electronics consumer products appliance and automotive manufacturing customers use the parts for prototyping market evaluation and functional testing. The company was established in 1999 and went public in 2012.

Operations

Proto Labs makes the majority of its revenue (67%) from its Protomold segment (also called ProtoQuote) which typically produces prototype quantities of 25-100 custom injection-molded plastic parts. It saves the designs and molds from these parts and benefits when the customer returns sometimes requesting up to 10000 additional parts for short-run production.

The company's Firstcut segment (FirstQuote; nearly 29%) specializes in designing and cutting plastic and metal blocks but in smaller quantities. In addition to these segments Proto Labs inherited a new segment Fineline (4%) in 2014 with the acquisition of FineLine Prototyping. Fineline features an additive manufacturing product line often referred to as 3D printing which offers a variety of high-quality precision rapid prototyping services.

Geographic Reach

Proto Labs has manufacturing facilities in Japan the UK and the US; sales offices also reside in Italy. The US accounts for around 75% of its revenue each year.

Sales and Marketing

Proto Labs sells its products through an internal sales team in more than 50 countries. Customers include Avox Systems BOSS Products PHT Aerospace Micro Engineering IFM Efector OEM controls Lombard Medical and Gamesman Limited. In 2014 the company served 9840 existing and approximately 11710 new product developers and engineers.

Financial Performance

Proto Labs has grown significantly since it was founded as revenues and profits continue to climb to unprecedented heights. From 2013 to 2014 Pro Labs' revenues surged 28% from $163 million to $209 million and its net income increased by 18% from $35 million to $42 million. (Both these totals for 2014 represent historic milestones for the company.)

The growth for 2014 was driven by a 30% increase in US revenue a 24% rise in international revenue a 22% jump in Protomold revenue a 25% increase in Firstcut revenue and additional revenue from its new Fineline segment. The revenue increases were due to an uptick in the number of product developers and engineers served which were driven by the company's enhanced marketing activities.

Proto Labs' operating cash flows have increased consistently over the past five years. In 2014 it increased 18% to $57 million due to a surge in cash inflows from depreciation and amortization and income taxes.

Strategy

Its strategy includes increasing penetration within existing customer organization and in geographical markets it already operates (US Europe and Japan) moving into new geographic regions and expanding its parts range and manufacturing processes. Another important component of its strategy involves optimizing its 3D CAD and CNC technology in order to design parts faster and more efficiently.

Mergers and Acquisitions

Proto Labs added to its manufacturing services in 2014 through the $38 million acquisition of FineLine Prototyping a provider of stereolithography selective laser sintering and direct metal laser sintering services.

Company Background

Proto Labs began as The Protomold Company (molded plastic parts) but added CNC metal part machining its Firstcut business in 2007. In 2009 both branches began operating under the Proto Labs banner. It all started when founder and computer geek Lawrence Lukis started a desktop printer design business and was astounded at the long turnaround (weeks) and cost (thousands) for prototype parts. He turned his computer skills to solving the problem and found a way to completely automate the entire process and produce a part in a day for prices starting at $1500.

EXECUTIVES

EVP and CTO, Donald G. Krantz, age 61, $286,083 total compensation
President and CEO, Victoria M. (Vicki) Holt, age 58, $514,539 total compensation
CFO, John A. Way, $290,000 total compensation
VP and General Manager and Managing Director - Europe Middle East and Africa, John B. Tumelty, age 45, $189,268 total compensation
CTO, Rich Baker
VP and General Manager Americas, Robert Bodor, age 43, $249,323 total compensation
National Account Manager, Brian (Bri) Slattery
National Account Manager, Todd Martin
Vice President of Human Resour, Renee (Ren) Conklin
Chairman, Lawrence J. Lukis, age 68
Auditors: Ernst & Young LLP

LOCATIONS

HQ: Proto Labs Inc
5540 Pioneer Creek Drive, Maple Plain, MN 55359
Phone: 763 479-3680
Web: www.protolabs.com

PRODUCTS/OPERATIONS

2013 Sales

	$ mil.	% of total
Protomold	115.1	71
Firstcut	48.0	29
Total	**163.1**	**100**

COMPETITORS

Ajax United Patterns and Molds	Materialise
	Richco
Anchor Mfg. Group	Total Plastics
Deswell	

HISTORICAL FINANCIALS

Company Type: Public

Income Statement

FYE: December 31

	REVENUE ($ mil.)	NET INCOME ($ mil.)	NET PROFIT MARGIN	EMPLOYEES
12/15	264.1	46.5	17.6%	1,549.0
12/14	209.5	41.6	19.9%	1,077.0
12/13	163.1	35.2	21.6%	749.0
12/12	125.9	24.0	19.1%	622.0
12/11	98.9	17.9	18.2%	511.0
Annual Growth	27.8%	26.8%	—	31.9%

2015 Year-End Financials

Debt ratio: —
Return on equity: 15.6%
Cash ($ mil.): 47.6
Current ratio: 5.25
Long-term debt ($ mil.): —

No. of shares (mil.): 26.2
Dividends
 Yield: —
 Payout: —
Market value ($ mil.): 1,669.0

	STOCK PRICE ($) FY Close	P/E High/Low	PER SHARE ($) Earnings	Dividends	Book Value
12/15	63.69	44 32	1.77	0.00	12.51
12/14	67.16	53 36	1.60	0.00	10.28
12/13	71.18	63 27	1.36	0.00	8.28
12/12	39.42	38 26	0.98	0.00	6.32
Annual Growth	17.3%	— —	21.8%	—	25.6%

Providence Service Corp

Social services firm Providence Service Corporation operates through three segments: Non-Emergency Transportation Services (NET) Workforce Development Services (WD Services) and Health Assessment Services (HA Services). The segments provide non-emergency transportation to people in home and community-based settings manage foster care systems provideg correctional support such as probation supervision offer job training and provide substance abuse treatment. The HA Services segment offers at-home comprehensive health assessments (CHAs) for Medicare Advantage health plans. Providence operates in about 45 states and in 11 countries abroad.

Operations

The majority of Providence's revenue comes from its NET services (more than 60%). NET's primary payers include state Medicaid programs local government agencies hospital systems and managed care organizations (MCOs). Its clients range from senior citizens and individuals with limited mobility to people with limited means of transportation and people with disabilities that prevent them from using conventional methods of transportation. Most of the NET division's income comes from state payer contracts that are three-to-five years long with renewal options; only about 14% of the division's income is derived from fee-for-service contracts.

WD Services accounts for about a quarter of Providence's sales; the UK brings in some three-fourths of its total earnings. It offers workforce development and offender rehabilitation services including employment placement apprenticeships employee assistance programs and some health-related services. Most of the segment's business comes from government entities seeking to reduce recidivism and unemployment rates.

HA Services the smallest segment (about 15% of revenue) primarily brings in revenue by conducting CHAs. These measure members' health social environment and medication risks for health plans.

The company has a network of some 5000 independent transportation providers including operators of wheelchair-equipped vehicles and ambulances. For its CHA tests it has a nationwide network of some 800 nurse practitioners.

Geographic Reach

Providence has operations in Australia Canada France Germany Poland Saudi Arabia South Korea Spain Sweden Switzerland the UK and the US. The US brings in the majority of revenue (about 80%) followed by the UK (nearly 20%).

Financial Performance

Revenue has generally been rising for the past five years. In 2015 it rose 14% to $1.7 billion as all three segments experienced growth. The NET segment benefited from a recently secured new state contracts increased membership under contracts and higher rates in some markets. WD Services gained revenue from the acquisition of Ingeus while HA Services gained on the acquisition of Matrix Medical Network.

Net income which has fluctuated as of late spiked 313% to $84 million in 2015. This was due both to the higher revenue as well the sale of the group's Human Services segment. Cash flow from operations also up and down fell 76% to $13 million that year as accounts receivable and expenses increased.

Strategy

Providence's primary form of growth has historically been through acquisitions. Recent purchases have been workforce development firm Ingeus and health assessments provider Matrix Medical Network.

Along with acquisitions Providence is focused on securing contracts such as it has with New Jersey to boost its income. To that end Providence tracks state legislation and funding trends to determine how they may impact its operations and targets states with favorable funding opportunities. It also establishes new contracts with commercial payers in regions in which it already has a presence by taking advantage of its existing networks in those areas.

The company also makes strategic divestitures as it hones its focus. In 2015 to strengthen its core business the company sold its Human Services business for $200 million. The following year Providence sold a majority stake in the recently acquired Matrix Medical Network.

Mergers and Acquisitions

In 2014 the group's WD Services segment acquired Australia-based workforce development firm Ingeus for $58 million. That purchase allowed Providence to enter new markets and boosted revenue within the first year. Also that year the HA Services segment was established when Providence acquired health assessments provider Matrix Medical Network. However Providence sold 53% of Matrix Medical in October 2016.

EXECUTIVES

Interim CEO LogistiCare Solutions, Albert Cortina
CEO, James M. Lindstrom, age 43, $559,744 total compensation
SVP and Chief People Officer, Justina Sanchez-Uzzell, age 37, $251,923 total compensation
CFO, David Shackelton, age 30, $268,385 total compensation
CEO Matrix Medical Network, Walt Cooper
CEO Ingeus, Jack Sawyer
Chairman, Christopher S. (Chris) Shackelton, age 36
Auditors: KPMG LLP

LOCATIONS

HQ: Providence Service Corp
 700 Canal Street, Third Floor, Stamford, CT 06902
Phone: 203 307-2800   **Fax:** 520 747-6605
Web: www.prscholdings.com

PRODUCTS/OPERATIONS

2015 Sales

	$ mil.	% of total
NET Services	1,083.0	64
WD Services	395.1	23
HA Services	217.4	13
Corporate and Other	(0.1)	-
Total	**1,695.4**	**100**

Selected Subsidiaries

A to Z In-Home Tutoring LLC
AlphaCare Resources Inc.
Camelot Care Centers Inc.
Children's Behavioral Health Inc.
Choices Group Inc.
College Community Services LLC
Dockside Services Inc.
Drawbridges Counseling Services LLC
Family Preservation Services Inc.
Health Trans Inc.
LogistiCare Inc.
Maple Star Nevada
Provado Insurance Service Inc.
Red Top Transportation Inc.

COMPETITORS

AMR
Acadian Ambulance
 Service Inc.
Devereux Foundation
Hazelden Betty Ford
Mental Health Network

Res-Care
Rural/Metro
Safe Ride Services
Salvation Army
UBH

HISTORICAL FINANCIALS

Company Type: Public

Income Statement
FYE: December 31

	REVENUE ($ mil.)	NET INCOME ($ mil.)	NET PROFIT MARGIN	EMPLOYEES
12/15	1,695.4	83.7	4.9%	9,072.0
12/14	1,481.1	20.2	1.4%	13,700.0
12/13	1,122.6	19.4	1.7%	8,500.0
12/12	1,105.8	8.4	0.8%	8,400.0
12/11	942.9	16.9	1.8%	7,600.0
Annual Growth	15.8%	49.1%	—	4.5%

2015 Year-End Financials

Debt ratio: 28.8%
Return on equity: 28.3%
Cash ($ mil.): 84.7
Current ratio: 1.08
Long-term debt ($ mil.): 272.4

No. of shares (mil.): 15.2
Dividends
 Yield: —
 Payout: —
Market value ($ mil.): 717.0

	STOCK PRICE ($) FY Close	P/E High/Low	PER SHARE ($) Earnings	Dividends	Book Value
12/15	46.92	13 8	4.30	0.00	24.08
12/14	36.44	35 18	1.35	0.00	13.96
12/13	25.72	21 11	1.41	0.00	10.63
12/12	16.99	26 15	0.64	0.00	8.69
12/11	13.76	14 7	1.27	0.00	7.85
Annual Growth	35.9%	— —	35.6%	—	32.3%

Pzena Investment Management Inc

It takes money to make money and Pzena Investment Management has made plenty. The firm serves corporate institutional and high-net-worth individual clients in the US and abroad and has about $21 billion in assets under management. Through a dozen funds Pzena makes long-term investments in domestic and international companies —particularly financial services firms. Pzena also acts as a sub-investment adviser for about two dozen mutual funds and offshore funds. The firm is the sole managing member of its operating company Pzena Investment Management LLC. The employee-owned firm was founded by chairman and CEO Richard Pzena in 1995.

Financial Performance

A decline in management and performance fee revenue led to an 8% decline in the company's overall revenue between 2011 and 2012. The company's net income was up 14% in the same period due in large part to lower investment-related expenses.

Strategy

The company focuses on long-term investments made in US and global markets. It serves both US clients and non-US clients and has been expanding its non-US client base through targeted sales efforts.

EXECUTIVES

Chairman CEO and Co-Chief Investment Officer, Richard S. Pzena, age 57, $377,500 total compensation
President and Co-Chief Investment Officer, John P. Goetz, age 58, $377,500 total compensation
President and Head of Business Development and Client Service, William L. Lipsey, age 57, $377,500 total compensation
COO, Gary J. Bachman, age 48, $350,000 total compensation
EVP and Portfolio Manager Global Focused Value International (ex-US) Focused Value International (ex-US) Expanded Value Global Expanded Value and European Focused Value, Michael D. Peterson, age 51, $377,500 total compensation
CFO and Treasurer, Jessica R. Doran
Auditors: KPMG LLP

LOCATIONS

HQ: Pzena Investment Management Inc
320 Park Avenue, New York, NY 10022
Phone: 212 355-1600
Web: www.pzena.com

COMPETITORS

AllianceBernstein
BlackRock
FMR
Morgan Stanley Investment Management
Principal Global
State Street

HISTORICAL FINANCIALS
Company Type: Public

Income Statement
FYE: December 31

	REVENUE ($ mil.)	NET INCOME ($ mil.)	NET PROFIT MARGIN	EMPLOYEES
12/15	116.6	7.6	6.6%	88.0
12/14	112.5	8.1	7.2%	81.0
12/13	95.7	6.6	7.0%	76.0
12/12	76.2	3.8	5.0%	70.0
12/11	83.0	3.3	4.1%	67.0
Annual Growth	8.9%	22.8%	—	7.1%

2015 Year-End Financials

Debt ratio: —
Return on equity: 41.7%
Cash ($ mil.): 35.4
Current ratio: 8.93
Long-term debt ($ mil.): —

No. of shares (mil.): 67.3
Dividends
  Yield: 4.7%
  Payout: 78.8%
Market value ($ mil.): 579.0

	STOCK PRICE ($) FY Close	P/E High/Low		PER SHARE ($) Earnings	Dividends	Book Value
12/15	8.60	21	14	0.50	0.41	0.27
12/14	9.46	19	13	0.53	0.35	0.28
12/13	11.76	21	9	0.45	0.25	0.25
12/12	5.40	20	10	0.32	0.28	0.23
12/11	4.33	24	9	0.32	0.12	0.22
Annual Growth	18.7%	—		11.8%	36.0%	6.1%

QTS Realty Trust Inc

In the world of server farms QTS Realty sows a lot of concrete. The company owns secure office buildings that house data centers —where companies keep their computer equipment. QTS (which stands for Quality Technology Services) owns and operates 10 data centers across seven states totaling 3.8 million sq. ft. It counts almost 900 corporations and government agencies as customers. Organized as a real estate investment trust (REIT) QTS is exempt from paying federal income tax as long as it makes quarterly distributions to shareholders. It went public in 2013 raising $257 million which it will use to pay down debt as well as buy and renovate more data centers.

IPO

The data center specialist went public in October 2013 with an offering worth $257 million. The proceeds will be used to retire debt and expand its business via the acquisition of new data centers and improvements at existing facilities.

Geographic Reach

The Kansas-based REIT owns 10 data centers in seven states: California Florida Georgia Kansas New Jersey Texas and Virginia.

Financial Performance

QTS reported $177.9 million in revenue in 2013 an increase of 22% versus 2012. Net income was $3 million. The REIT's revenue and cash flow from operations have been advancing steadily in recent years. However profits have been harder to come by: QTS returned to profitability in 2013 after two years in the red. Rents contribute the lion's share (upwards of 80%) of the company's annual revenue while cloud and managed services contributes about 10%. In 2013 approximately 40% of monthly recurring revenue came from customers who use more than one of QTS's "3Cs"

products which consists of custom data center colocation and cloud and managed services.

StrategyThe firm's data centers are located in some of the top data center markets in the US as well as in markets with high potential for growth. In June 2014 the firm formed a new Dallas-Fort Worth team to promote expansion in the fast-growing north Texas market. Indeed QTS expects to open a new 700000- square-foot facility on the site of a former semiconductor plant (purchased in early 2013) in Dallas in July 2014.QTS maintains a diverse customer base thereby limiting its exposure (and risk) to any one client. Indeed only two of the REIT's 880 customers individually accounted for more than 3% of its monthly recurring revenue (MRR) with no single client accounting for more than 8% of MRR.Adding to its menu of services in 2014 the firm launched the QTS Enterprise Cloud an Infrastructure as a Service (IaaS) product. The new service extends the cloud and managed services component of the company's 3Cs product portfolio and meets growing market demand among commercial clients for control and visibility. Concurrently it launched the QTS Federal Cloud a similar IaaS product designed exclusively for US government agencies.Mergers and AcquisitionsAs part of its expansion strategy QTS in February 2013 acquired a 698000-square-foot former semiconductor plant in Dallas which it's converting to a data center. The REIT paid $10.3 million for the site.

EXECUTIVES

CFO, William H. (Bill) Schafer, age 58, $350,000 total compensation
CTO, Jon Greaves
COO Development and Operations, James H. (Jim) Reinhart, age 51, $350,000 total compensation
Chairman and CEO, Chad L. Williams, age 45, $550,000 total compensation
COO Sales and Marketing, Daniel T. Bennewitz, age 57, $350,000 total compensation
Chief Investment Officer, Jeffrey H. Berson, age 48, $325,000 total compensation
CTO Data Centers, Brian Johnston
CTO Product Development, Brent Bensten
EVP Public Sector and Federal Sales, David McOmber
Vice President General Manager Critical Facility Management, Danny (Dan) Crocker
Executive Vice President Sales East Region, Butch Goldi
Auditors: Ernst & Young LLP

LOCATIONS

HQ: QTS Realty Trust Inc
12851 Foster Street, Overland Park, KS 66213
Phone: 913 312-5503
Web: www.qtsdatacenters.com

PRODUCTS/OPERATIONS

2015 Sales

	% of total
Rental	74
Cloud & managed services	17
Recoveries from customers	7
Other	2
Total	**100**

Selected Products and Solutions

Custom Data Center
Block
Build-to-Suit
PowerBank™
PowerFlex™

Colocation
High Density Solutions
Cloud Services
QVI
QTS Enterprise Cloud
QTS Federal Cloud
Managed Services
Applications
Disaster Recovery
Network
Operating Systems
Security
Storage & Backup
Connectivity
Bandwidth
Interconnection
Solutions
Enterprise Solution
Federal Data Center
Healthcare Solution
SaaS Infrastructure

COMPETITORS

CoreSite	DuPont Fabros
CyrusOne	Equinix
Digital Realty	

HISTORICAL FINANCIALS

Company Type: Public

Income Statement

FYE: December 31

	REVENUE ($ mil.)	NET INCOME ($ mil.)	NET PROFIT MARGIN	EMPLOYEES
12/15	311.0	20.3	6.5%	720.0
12/14	217.7	15.0	6.9%	460.0
12/13	40.4	3.1	7.8%	400.0
12/12	145.7	(9.7)	—	0.0
12/11	130.4	(0.9)	—	0.0
Annual Growth	24.3%	—	—	—

2015 Year-End Financials

Debt ratio: 49.6%	No. of shares (mil.): 41.2
Return on equity: 4.4%	Dividends
Cash ($ mil.): 8.8	Yield: 2.8%
Current ratio: 0.14	Payout: 224.5%
Long-term debt ($ mil.): 871.7	Market value ($ mil.): 1,860.0

	STOCK PRICE ($) FY Close	P/E High/Low		Earnings	PER SHARE ($) Dividends	Book Value
12/15	45.11	86	63	0.53	1.28	14.99
12/14	33.84	68	41	0.51	1.16	10.29
12/13	24.78	221	179	0.11	0.24	10.87
Annual Growth	34.9%	—	—	(119.5%)	130.9%	17.4%

Qualys, Inc.

Qualys puts a premium on high-grade IT security. Its QualysGuard Cloud Platform is a cloud security and compliance management software suite that automates security weakness detection and network security asset auditing. Qualys also remotely manages the integrity of networks for clients looking to outsource their data security endeavors. QualysGuard is geared toward small mid-sized and large businesses across a range of industries. The company counts some 7700 customers in more than 100 countries by partnerships with managed service providers and consultants including Accuvant Cognizant Technology Solutions Dell

SecureWorks and Wipro. Founded in 1999 it went public in 2012.

Geographic Reach

Qualys operates from five offices in the US where 70% of sales originate. It has international locations in Australia China France Germany Hong Kong India Japan the Philippines Russia Singapore the United Arab Emirates and the UK.

In addition the company leases data center space in California and Switzerland.

Sales and Marketing

About 63% of the company's sales are made through its direct sales force. The other 37% come from a network of channel partners such as security consultants managed service providers and resellers including FishNet Security Insight Technologies Symantec and Verizon.

Financial Performance

Overall sales grew 23% in 2014 to $133.6 million due to increased demand for IT security and compliance software from both new and recurring customers in the US and abroad. Profit for Qualys skyrocketed to $30 million in 2014 from $1.6 million in 2013. That about $23.7 million came from a tax benefit takes some dissipates some of the sizzle. Still income before taxes was $8.6 million in 2014 compared to $2 million in 2013. Cash flow also increase reaching $41 million in 2014.

Strategy

One way companies like Qualys grow is to partner with other software firms to incorporate their products for sales purposes. Qualys made several such deals in 2014 and 2015 including one with PathDefender which operates McAfee Secure Services. Also Qualys partnered with BMC Software to plug a hole of security vulnerability.

Other Qualys partners include RedSeal Networks Honeytek CipherTechs and Imperva.

EXECUTIVES

VP General Counsel and Corporate Secretary, Bruce K. Posey, age 65, $250,000 total compensation
Chairman and CEO, Philippe F. Courtot, age 71, $350,000 total compensation
VP Corporate Development and Strategic Alliances, Amer S. Deeba, age 49, $250,000 total compensation
CTO, Wolfgang Kandek
EVP Worldwide Field Operations, Dan Barahona
Chief Product Officer, Sumedh S. Thakar, age 40, $260,417 total compensation
CFO, Melissa Fisher
Vice President Central Region Field Operations, Scott (Scotty) Rachford
Vice President And General Manager ?? Apj, John Cunningham
Vice President Financial Planning And Analysis, Peter (Pete) Marcisz
Vice President of Operations, Alexei Ghiuritan
Vice President Federal Operations, Jason (Jase) Hartley
Vice President Of Americas Sales, Earl Portersee
Vice President Digital Marketing, Sonu Agarwal
Auditors: Grant Thornton LLP

LOCATIONS

HQ: Qualys, Inc.
  1600 Bridge Parkway, Redwood City, CA 94065
Phone: 650 801-6100
Web: www.qualys.com

COMPETITORS

Barracuda Networks	Microsoft
BeyondTrust	NetIQ
CA Inc.	Novell

Check Point Software	Symantec
Cisco Systems	Tenable Network
F5 Networks	Security
Fortinet	Trend Micro
Foundstone	Trustwave Holdings
HP	VeriSign
IBM	Visionael
Imperva	e-DMZ Security
McAfee	eEye Digital Security

HISTORICAL FINANCIALS

Company Type: Public

Income Statement

FYE: December 31

	REVENUE ($ mil.)	NET INCOME ($ mil.)	NET PROFIT MARGIN	EMPLOYEES
12/15	164.2	15.8	9.7%	510.0
12/14	133.5	30.2	22.6%	431.0
12/13	107.9	1.6	1.5%	406.0
12/12	91.4	2.2	2.5%	359.0
12/11	76.2	1.9	2.6%	334.0
Annual Growth	21.2%	68.8%	—	11.2%

2015 Year-End Financials

Debt ratio: —	No. of shares (mil.): 34.4
Return on equity: 9.1%	Dividends
Cash ($ mil.): 91.7	Yield: —
Current ratio: 2.04	Payout: —
Long-term debt ($ mil.): —	Market value ($ mil.): 1,139.0

	STOCK PRICE ($) FY Close	P/E High/Low		Earnings	PER SHARE ($) Dividends	Book Value
12/15	33.09	117	59	0.42	0.00	5.68
12/14	37.75	44	20	0.81	0.00	4.52
12/13	23.11	496	215	0.05	0.00	3.19
12/12	14.79	165	126	0.08	0.00	2.91
Annual Growth	30.8%	—	—	73.8%	—	24.9%

RAIT Financial Trust

RAIT Financial Trust is a real estate investment trust (REIT) that specializes in originating commercial real estate loans and acquiring and managing commercial real estate properties. Its loan portfolio is made up of mezzanine and short-term bridge financing mainly secured by multifamily office and retail properties. RAIT also provides loan servicing commercial property and asset management and asset repositioning and sales services for other real estate firms. Subsidiary Taberna Realty Finance provides long-term real estate capital while Independence Realty Trust (IRT) owns apartment properties in opportunistic US markets. Altogether RAIT boasts some $4.5 billion in assets under management.

Operations

RAIT Financial Trust operates two core business lines: Commercial Real Estate or CRE which involves real estate lending owning and managing commercial real estate assets across the US; and Independence Realty Trust or IRT which owns apartment properties in opportunistic markets across the US. About 50% of RAIT's total revenue came from rental income in 2014 while another 42% of its revenue came from investment interest income. The remainder came from fee and other income the company made from servicing third-party real estate firms. Roughly 71% of its investments were in multi-family properties with the rest of its investments being in office (19%) Retail (7%) and other (3%) properties.

RAIT's CRE loan portfolio which had a book value of $1.39 billion at the end of 2014 was mostly secured by office properties (37% of loans were tied to office properties) while most of the rest were secured by retail (26%) and multi-family properties (25%).

Geographic Reach

RAIT has offices in Chicago; Charlotte North Carolina; New York City; and Philadelphia. About 55% of its real estate investments were located in the central US while the Southeast and West split another 40%.

Sales and Marketing

The company offers its services to a range of industries including commercial mortgage office residential mortgage specialty finance and homebuilding.

Financial Performance

RAIT Financial Trust's revenues have been trending higher over the past few years thanks to added rental income from property acquisitions. However even though it's been generating operating profits the REIT has been suffering deeper losses annually since 2011 due to heavy fair value losses on its financial instruments.The REIT's revenue jumped 17% to $289.7 million in 2014 thanks mostly to added rental income from 28 property acquisitions in 2014 and nine property acquisitions in 2013. Rental income also grew with improved occupancy and rental rates.Despite revenue growth for the year RAIT's losses deepened to $290 million in 2014 mostly as the REIT suffered $215.8 million in losses from consolidating two of its securitizations in December. Even when excluding this non-recurring item the company's operating income declined by roughly one-third due to higher operating and interest expenses. RAIT's operating cash levels climbed 74% to $49.33 million after adjusting its earnings for non-cash related losses and other non-cash items.

Strategy

Hoping to take advantage of an improved post-recession commercial real estate market RAIT plans to increase its commercial real estate loan originations and investments in commercial real estate. It also sponsors companies including non-traded REITs that offer their securities in order to raise capital to invest in commercial real estate-related assets.As part of its plans to grow through strategic investments in September 2014 RAIT acquired two retail centers in Troy Michigan through its subsidiary Urban Retail for $50.8 million —an amount substantially below the properties' replacement value. Both properties which together spanned nearly 400000 square feet were near or at 100% occupancy and had established tenants including Kohls Bed Bath & Beyond DSW TJ Maxx Pier 1 Imports and other well-known companies.

Company BackgroundIn 2011 RAIT added commercial mortgage-backed securities (CMBS) eligible loans to its service mix. It also formed two REIT subsidiaries Independent Realty Trust and Independence Mortgage Trust to raise capital and manage portfolios of commercial real estate loans CMBS and other commercial real estate-related securities. That year the company also acquired Empire American Realty Trust a small non-traded public REIT for $2.3 million and subsequently used Empire to raise capital for investing in commercial real estate assets.

EXECUTIVES

CFO and Treasurer, James J. Sebra, age 41, $375,000 total compensation
President, Scott L. N. Davidson, age 47, $550,000 total compensation
Senior Managing Director and Chief Legal Officer, John J. Reyle, age 37, $200,000 total compensation
Vice President Underwriting, Elaine Johnson
Vice President Corporate Counsel, Jessica (Jess) Norman
Chairman, Michael Malter
Auditors: KPMG LLP

LOCATIONS

HQ: RAIT Financial Trust
Two Logan Square, 100 N. 18th Street, 23rd Floor, Philadelphia, PA 19103
Phone: 215 207-2100
Web: www.rait.com

PRODUCTS/OPERATIONS

2015 Sales

	$ mil.	% of total
Rental income	233.7	72
Net interest margin	69.2	21
Fee & other income	21.1	7
Total	**324.0**	**100**

COMPETITORS

Ares Commercial Real Estate	Capital Trust
AvalonBay	Newcastle Investment
BRT Realty	Pacific Premier
Brandywine Realty	Vestin
	iStar Financial Inc

HISTORICAL FINANCIALS

Company Type: Public

Income Statement

FYE: December 31

	REVENUE ($ mil.)	NET INCOME ($ mil.)	NET PROFIT MARGIN	EMPLOYEES
12/15	323.9	63.4	19.6%	870.0
12/14	289.7	(289.9)	—	794.0
12/13	246.8	(285.3)	—	394.0
12/12	200.7	(168.3)	—	376.0
12/11	234.1	(37.7)	—	366.0
Annual Growth	**8.5%**	**—**		**24.2%**

2015 Year-End Financials

Debt ratio: 75.5%
Return on equity: 13.4%
Cash ($ mil.): 125.8
Current ratio: 7.80
Long-term debt ($ mil.): 3,359.4

No. of shares (mil.): 91.5
Dividends
  Yield: 26.6%
  Payout: 900.0%
Market value ($ mil.): 247.0

	STOCK PRICE ($) FY Close	P/E High/Low	PER SHARE ($) Earnings	Dividends	Book Value
12/15	2.70	98 28	0.08	0.72	5.35
12/14	7.67	— —	(3.92)	0.69	5.49
12/13	8.97	— —	(4.54)	0.50	9.16
12/12	5.65	— —	(3.75)	0.31	15.04
12/11	4.75	— —	(1.33)	0.12	22.05
Annual Growth	**(13.2%)** **(29.8%)**	**—**		**— 56.5%**	

Ramco-Gershenson Properties Trust (MD)

Ramco-Gershenson Properties Trust makes no bones about horning in on the retail world. A self-administered real estate investment trust (REIT) it owns develops and manages a property portfolio of about 90 shopping centers in about a dozen states east of the Mississippi River. The REIT's properties contain approximately 20 million sq. ft. of leasable space in the Midwest mid-Atlantic and Southeast. Nearly all of its assets are community shopping centers in metropolitan areas anchored by grocery or big-box stores. The REIT also owns one enclosed regional mall and one single-tenant property and has a handful of projects under development.Michigan is the Ramco-Gershenson's largest market accounting more than than 40% of rental revenue; Florida accounts for more than 30%. The REIT's largest tenants include T.J. Maxx and Publix.Ramco-Gershenson often enters into joint ventures when acquiring properties though it made no new acquisitions in 2009 due to the economic environment.Members of the Gershenson family including president and CEO Dennis own about 15% of the REIT's outstanding shares; institutional investors hold more than 35%

EXECUTIVES

Svp Acquisitions, Catherine J (Cathy) Clark
President CEO and Director, Dennis E. Gershenson, age 72, $600,000 total compensation
EVP, Frederick A. (Fred) Zantello, age 72, $291,225 total compensation
CFO, Geoffrey Bedrosian
Vice President Human Resources, Karen Childress-newberger
RVP Asset Management, Michael (Mel) McBride
Vice President Development Redevelopment, Peter Debenedicts
Executive Vice President, Fred Zantello
Chairman, Stephen R. Blank, age 70
Auditors: Grant Thornton LLP

LOCATIONS

HQ: Ramco-Gershenson Properties Trust (MD)
31500 Northwestern Highway, Suite 300, Farmington Hills, MI 48334
Phone: 248 350-9900   **Fax:** 248 350-9925
Web: www.rgpt.com

PRODUCTS/OPERATIONS

2015 Sales

	$ mil.	% of total
Minimum rents	183.2	73
Recoveries income from tenants	61.6	24
Management and other fee income	1.8	1
Percentage rent	0.5	-
Other income	4.7	2
Total	**251.8**	**100**

COMPETITORS

Agree Realty	Macerich
CBL & Associates Properties	Milestone Properties
DDR	Pennsylvania Real Estate
Federal Realty Investment	Regency Centers
General Growth Properties	Schottenstein
	Tanger Factory Outlet
IRC Retail Centers	Taubman Centers
Kimco Realty	Weingarten Realty

Income Statement

FYE: December 31

	REVENUE ($ mil.)	NET INCOME ($ mil.)	NET PROFIT MARGIN	EMPLOYEES
12/15	251.7	65.1	25.9%	120.0
12/14	218.3	(2.3)	—	116.0
12/13	170.0	11.0	6.5%	108.0
12/12	128.7	7.2	5.6%	109.0
12/11	121.3	(26.7)	—	106.0
Annual Growth	20.0%	—		3.1%

2015 Year-End Financials

Debt ratio: 50.9%	No. of shares (mil.): 79.1
Return on equity: 7.4%	Dividends
Cash ($ mil.): 6.6	Yield: 4.9%
Current ratio: 0.82	Payout: 241.1%
Long-term debt ($ mil.): 1,084.8	Market value ($ mil.): 1,315.0

	STOCK PRICE ($) FY Close	P/E High/Low		PER SHARE ($) Earnings	Dividends	Book Value
12/15	16.61	27	20	0.73	0.82	11.17
12/14	18.74	—	—	(0.14)	0.78	11.25
12/13	15.74	295	222	0.06	0.71	11.55
12/12	13.31	—	—	(0.00)	0.66	10.93
12/11	9.83	—	—	(0.84)	0.65	11.59
Annual Growth	14.0%	—	—	—	5.9%	(0.9%)

RBC Bearings Inc

RBC Bearings keeps businesses on a roll. The company makes an array of plain roller and ball bearing products. It specializes in regulated bearings used by OEMs and their aftermarkets of commercial/military aircraft automobiles and commercial trucks industrial/agricultural machinery as well as air turbines. Targeting high-end markets its precision lineup satisfies thousands of applications from engine controls to radar systems mining tools and gear pumps. RBC's top customers include Boeing GE Lockheed Martin and the US Department of Defense. RBC Bearings has grown since 1919 to some 30 manufacturing facilities in Europe and North America.

Operations

RBC operates through four reportable business segments: Plain Bearings Engineered Products Roller Bearings and Ball Bearings. Plain Bearings represents 45% of total revenue and is used in aircraft controls helicopter rotors or in heavy mining and construction equipment.

Engineered Products consists of highly engineered hydraulics fasteners collets and precision components used in aerospace marine and industrial applications. Roller Bearings are anti-friction bearings that use rollers in place of balls. The company manufactures four basic types of roller bearings: heavy duty needle roller bearings with inner rings tapered roller bearings track rollers and aircraft roller bearings.

Ball Bearings makes four basic types of ball bearings: high precision aerospace airframe control thin section and commercial ball bearings which are used in high-speed rotational applications.

Geographic Reach

The company operates about 30 facilities in the US and has international operations in Canada Switzerland Mexico and Poland. RBC's warehouses reside in the Midwest Southwest and on the East and West coasts of the US as well as in France and Switzerland. The US is its largest market accounting for more than 85% of total sales.

Sales and Marketing

The company sells its products through a direct sales force located in North America Europe Asia and Latin America. It also utilizes marketing managers product managers customer service representatives product application engineers and a global network of industrial and aerospace distributors. The aerospace and defense markets account for more than 65% of total sales. Sales to its top 10 customers generate 33% of total sales.

Financial Performance

RBC has experienced unprecedented growth over the last few years. Its revenues climbed 34% $445 million in 2015 to $597 million in 2016. Profits also jumped 10% from $58 million in 2015 to $64 million in 2016. Both these totals represented historic milestones for the company.

The historic growth for 2016 was driven by an explosive 439% surge in sales from Engineered Products largely due to additional revenue from its Sargent acquisition. Through the purchase RBC enjoyed impressive growth within the aerospace and industrial markets. Related to these factors sales from the US sales also climbed by 29% in 2016.

From 2015 to 2016 the company's cash flow spiked from $72 million to $84 million mainly due to favorable changes in inventory.

Strategy

RBC has managed to increase its sales to the aftermarket. Bearings which are indispensable for a machine's operating efficiency periodically wear out which creates a second stream of replacement parts sales. During 2016 aftermarket sales of replacement parts for installed equipment accounted for nearly 45% of RBC's revenues. Aerospace and defense customers also promise a particularly reliable opportunity for replacement business.

Mergers and Acquisitions

The company makes acquisitions in order to further develop its offerings end-markets and geographic footprint. In early 2016 the company acquired Arizona-based Sargent an expert in precision-engineered products services and repairs for aircraft airframes and engines rotorcraft submarines and land vehicles for $500 million in cash. The deal enhanced RBC's product portfolio and engineering technologies and added exponentially to its Plain Bearings and Engineering Products segments.

Company Background

RBC Bearings is an amalgamation of companies merged and acquired. The company got its start in 1919 making ball bearings; by the 1940s it became the sole supplier for landing gear bearings on military aircraft made by Ford Motor Company. In 2005 the company jetted onto the public investor market.

EXECUTIVES

Chairman President and CEO, Michael J. Hartnett, age 69, $922,643 total compensation
VP; General Manager RBC Division, Richard J. Edwards, age 59, $306,000 total compensation
VP and CFO, Daniel A. (Dan) Bergeron, age 55, $370,000 total compensation
VP; General Manager Heim Bearings and Schaublin, Thomas C. Crainer, age 57, $314,000 total compensation
Vice President Of Sales, Michelle Dodson
Vice President, Shane Blodgett
Auditors: Ernst & Young LLP

LOCATIONS

HQ: RBC Bearings Inc
One Tribology Center, Oxford, CT 06478
Phone: 203 267-7001
Web: www.rbcbearings.com

PRODUCTS/OPERATIONS

2016 Sales

	$ mil.	% of total
Plain	270.5	45
Engineered Products	161.3	27
Roller	112.0	19
Ball	53.7	9
Total	597.5	100

2016 Sales

	% of total
Aerospace market	66
Industrial market	34
Total	100

PRODUCTS
AEROSPACE
Airframe Control Ball Bearings
Airframe Control Needle Track Rollers
Ball Bearing Rod Ends
Gear Box and Engine and Roller Ball Bearings
Journal Bearings
Links and Assemblies
Machined Components
Radial Ball Bearings
Rod End Plain Bearings
Spherical Plain Bearings
Stud Type Track Roller Bearings
Swage Tubes and Control Rods
Thin Section Ball Bearings
INDUSTRIAL
Ball Bearings
Cam Followers
Collets/Toolholders
Heavy Duty Fleet Customers
Heavy Duty Needle Roller Bearings
Pins Rollers Shafts
Rod Ends
Self-Lubricating Bearings
Spherical Plain Bearings
Tapered/Tapered Thrust Roller Bearings
Thin Section Ball Bearings

COMPETITORS

Emerson Electric	Rexnord
General Bearing	SKF USA
Kaydon	Timken
MinebeaMitsumi	
NTN Bearing Corp. of America	

HISTORICAL FINANCIALS
Company Type: Public

Income Statement

FYE: April 2

	REVENUE ($ mil.)	NET INCOME ($ mil.)	NET PROFIT MARGIN	EMPLOYEES
04/16*	597.4	63.8	10.7%	3,277.0
03/15	445.2	58.2	13.1%	2,490.0
03/14	418.8	60.2	14.4%	2,361.0
03/13	403.0	56.3	14.0%	2,145.0
03/12	397.5	50.0	12.6%	2,137.0
Annual Growth	10.7%	6.3%	—	11.3%

*Fiscal year change

2016 Year-End Financials

Debt ratio: 33.1%
Return on equity: 10.7%
Cash ($ mil.): 39.2
Current ratio: 4.86
Long-term debt ($ mil.): 353.2

No. of shares (mil.): 23.5
Dividends
 Yield: —
 Payout: —
Market value ($ mil.): 1,734.0

	STOCK PRICE ($) FY Close	P/E High/Low	PER SHARE ($) Earnings	Dividends	Book Value
04/16*	73.65	28 20	2.72	0.00	26.37
03/15	75.58	30 21	2.49	2.00	23.49
03/14	62.97	27 18	2.59	0.00	23.20
03/13	50.56	21 17	2.47	0.00	20.11
03/12	46.13	21 13	2.23	0.00	17.44
Annual Growth	12.4%	— —	5.1%	—	10.9%

*Fiscal year change

RCI Hospitality Holdings Inc

Far from Casablanca these night clubs offer topless entertainment as part of the floor show. Rick's Cabaret International operates more than 30 adult night clubs in Arizona Florida Minnesota New York North Carolina and Texas. Most of the gentlemen's clubs are run under the Rick's Cabaret name while others operate under such banners as Club Onyx and XTC. Rick's caters to highbrow patrons with dough to blow: It offers VIP memberships for individual and corporate clients that can cost hundreds of dollars annually. In addition to its night clubs Rick's operates adult websites and an auction site for adult entertainment products.

Rick's is focused on expanding its nightclub estate gradually by adding new locations organically and through acquisitions. In 2012 the company purchased 11 clubs in Texas and Arizona along with associated real estate through its acquisition of Jaguars Acquisitions. It made the deal —which included clubs in Phoenix Lubbock El Paso and Beaumont —for some $26 million.

Before the Jaguar deal a proposed deal to purchase rival strip club operator VCG Holding in 2010 fell through. The VCG deal valued at about $45 million in cash and stock would have expanded Rick's holdings to about 40 locations in about a dozen states.

Previous to its failed buyout of VCG Rick's added Dallas to its sphere of operations with the purchase of The Executive Club for $9.5 million in 2008. The company added another Dallas club with the purchase of Platinum Club II. Also in 2008 Rick's launched itself into print and online media when it acquired trade publisher ED Publications for a little more than $1 million. The deal included such adult industry titles as Adult Store Buyer and Exotic Dancer as well as trade shows and websites.

CEO Eric Langan owns about 14% of the company.

HISTORY

Dallas Fontenot and Salah Izzedin founded Trumps in 1982. The following year they bought a disco and turned it into a swank topless bar called Rick's Cabaret (the name came from an encounter with a drunk in a taxi who was looking for "Rick's"). Izzedin's attorney Robert Watters bought a 10% interest in Trumps in 1987 the same year that the company opened the first members-only VIP room in Houston. The partnership of Fontenot Izzedin and Watters soured in 1989 with allegations that Izzedin pocketed unreported money supplied narcotics to waitresses and dancers and forced some of them to have sex with him.

Watters took over as CEO in 1991 and became sole owner in 1993. He converted Trumps into Rick's Cabaret International the next year and made Rick's the first topless bar to go public in 1995. The company expanded to New Orleans the following year opening a club on Bourbon Street. Rick's opened a new club in Minneapolis in 1998 and bought a 93% stake in Taurus Entertainment. Watters resigned in 1999 sold his stock in the company to new CEO Eric Langan and his investment partner Ralph McElroy and acquired the firm's New Orleans location which operated as a Rick's Cabaret under a licensing agreement. (The company sold it the same year.) Later in 1999 Rick's launched its adult Web sites.

In 2000 the company bought a third topless bar in Houston as well as another adult Web site xxxPasswords.com. It also began selling pre-paid debit cards that allow customers to anonymously buy access to adult entertainment Web sites. Rick's purchased the Chesapeake Bay Cabaret an upscale club in Houston in November. Later that year the company inked a deal with adult Web site operator Entertainment Network to offer its content through CandidCam.com.

Rick's launched NaughtyBids.com an auction site for adult products in 2001. It also began buying a number of porn auction sites including Pornauction.com and XXXbids.com in an effort to enhance the products available on NaughtyBids.com. Late that year it opened Encounters an upscale club for swinging couples in Houston.

During 2003 Rick's acquired a 51% stake in Houston's Wild Horse Cabaret and opened a sports bar called Hummers (later renamed under the Club Onyx brand). It also acquired the XTC clubs outright from Taurus Entertainment and reorganized some of its other holdings leaving it with a 51% stake in Encounters (sold 2004).

The company in 2004 converted its original Rick's Cabaret nightclub in Houston into Club Onyx an upscale venue that caters to urban professionals businessmen and professional athletes. It also bought a new location in Manhattan near Madison Square Garden. The following year the company closed on its acquisition of a three-in-one complex in North Carolina that included a men's club a male revue for women and a traditional night club. Also in 2005 it bought swingers-oriented dating Web site CouplesClick.com.

During 2006 Rick's purchased four new nightclubs in Texas. The following year it inked a licensing deal with a subsidiary of Argentina-based Latin Entertainment to open adult clubs in Buenos Aires and other Latin American cities under the Rick's Cabaret name.

EXECUTIVES

Chairman of the Board; President; Chief Executive Officer, Eric S. Langan, age 48, $623,077 total compensation
Executive Vice President; Director, Travis Reese, age 47, $194,204 total compensation
Chief Financial Officer, Phillip K. (Phil) Marshall, age 67, $189,423 total compensation
VP Director Technology and Director, Travis Reese, age 45

Director, Robert L. Watters, age 65
Director, Steven L. Jenkins, age 59
Director, Luke Lirot, age 59
Independent Director, Nour Anakar
Auditors: Whitley Penn LLP

LOCATIONS

HQ: RCI Hospitality Holdings Inc
10737 Cutten Road, Houston, TX 77066
Phone: 281 397-6730
Web: www.rcihospitality.com

PRODUCTS/OPERATIONS

Selected Operations

Nightclubs
 Club Onyx (adult entertainment for urban professionals and professional athletes)
 Rick's Cabaret
 Rick's Sports Cabaret
 Tootsie's Cabaret
 XTC
Media
 Club Bulletin (trade magazine for adult clubs)
 Storerotica (trade magazine for adult stores and products)
 VIP Guide (directory of clubs industry vendors entertainers)
Internet
 CouplesClick.net (85% adult content and online dating)
 CouplesTouch.com (85% adult content and online dating)
 NaughtyBids.com (adult auction Web site)
 xxxPassword.com (adult content)

Selected Subsidiaries

Adult Store Buyer Magazine LLC
Bobby's Novelty Inc.
Broadstreets Cabaret Inc.
ED Publications Inc.
Miami Gardens Square One Inc.
Playmates Gentlemen's Club LLC
RCI Dating Services Inc.
RCI Entertainment (Austin) Inc.
RCI Entertainment (Fort Worth) Inc.
RCI Entertainment (Las Vegas) Inc.
RCI Entertainment (Media Holdings) Inc.
RCI Entertainment (Minnesota) Inc.
RCI Entertainment (New York) Inc.
RCI Entertainment (North Carolina) Inc.
RCI Entertainment (Northwest Highway) Inc.
RCI Entertainment (Philadelphia) Inc.
RCI Entertainment (San Antonio) Inc.
RCI Entertainment (Texas) Inc.
Tantra Dance Inc.
Teeze International Inc.
TEZ Real Estate LP Philadelphia
Top Shelf Entertainment LLC
XTC Cabaret Inc.

COMPETITORS

FriendFinder Networks
Galardi South
LFP
Million Dollar Saloon
New Frontier Media

Playboy.com
Private Media Group
Scores Holding
Vivid Entertainment

HISTORICAL FINANCIALS
Company Type: Public

Income Statement
FYE: September 30

	REVENUE ($ mil.)	NET INCOME ($ mil.)	NET PROFIT MARGIN	EMPLOYEES
09/16	134.8	11.0	8.2%	2,000.0
09/15	144.6	9.3	6.4%	2,150.0
09/14	129.1	11.2	8.7%	1,750.0
09/13	112.2	9.1	8.2%	1,750.0
09/12	95.2	7.5	8.0%	1,400.0
Annual Growth	9.1%	10.0%	—	9.3%

2016 Year-End Financials

Debt ratio: 38.3%	No. of shares (mil.): 9.8
Return on equity: 8.8%	Dividends
Cash ($ mil.): 11.3	Yield: 0.7%
Current ratio: 1.20	Payout: 5.5%
Long-term debt ($ mil.): 95.9	Market value ($ mil.): 113.0

	STOCK PRICE ($) FY Close	P/E High/Low		PER SHARE ($) Earnings	Dividends	Book Value
09/16	11.53	10	7	1.10	0.09	13.01
09/15	10.42	14	11	0.90	0.00	11.92
09/14	11.02	11	9	1.13	0.00	10.96
09/13	11.79	13	8	0.96	0.00	9.87
09/12	8.28	13	8	0.78	0.00	8.82
Annual Growth	8.6%	—	—	9.0%	—	10.2%

Realty Income Corp

Retail real estate is a reality for Realty Income Corporation. The self-administered real estate investment trust (REIT) acquires owns and manages primarily free-standing highly-occupied single-tenant properties which it leases to regional and national consumer retail and service chains. Realty Income owns more than 4320 (mostly retail) properties spanning some 71 million sq. ft. of leasable space across every US state except Hawaii though nearly half of the REIT's rental revenue comes from its properties in Texas California Florida Minnesota Georgia Illinois and Virginia. Realty Income's top five tenants include Walgreens FedEx Dollar General LA Fitness and Family Dollar.

OperationsRealty Income owned more than 4320 properties during 2014 nearly 79% of which were Retail and the rest being Industrial and distribution (10%) Office (nearly 7%) Manufacturing (2%) and Agricultural related properties. Subsidiary Crest Net owns properties which are held for sale rather than for long-term investment.Geographic ReachCalifornia-based Realty Income's largest markets include Texas California Florida Minnesota Georgia Illinois and Virginia. More than 10% of its rental revenue came from properties in California in 2014 while properties in Texas contributed another nearly 10%.Sales and MarketingRealty Income's occupancy rate has been above 96% every year since its 1969 founding; its properties were 98.4% occupied in 2014 with an average remaining lease term of 10.2 years. Its tenants have included owners of restaurants convenience stores theaters child care providers automotive care centers health and fitness facilities grocery stores and drug stores. Realty Income's top five tenants —Walgreens FedEx Dollar General LA Fit-

ness and Family Dollar —combined generated nearly 25% of its total revenue in 2014. About 10% of its client types were owners of convenience stores.Financial PerformanceAcquisitive Realty Income has doubled its revenues and profits since 2010 as it has expanded its property portfolio and has charged higher rental rates as the real estate market has strengthened. The REIT's revenue jumped 20% to $933.5 million in 2014 mostly thanks to new rental revenue from its acquisition of 479 properties. Same-store rents on 2728 of its properties rose by 2% also helping drive the company's top line growth.Higher revenue and higher gains on property sales in 2014 boosted Realty Income's net income by 10% to $271.9 million while the REIT's operating cash levels climbed 21% to $627.7 million on higher cash earnings.Strategy Realty Income's investment strategy reiterated in 2015 involves acting as a source of capital to regional and national tenants. As such it focuses on long-term sale-leaseback transactions in which the tenant is responsible for taxes and maintenance. And when considering its investment targets the REIT looks to acquire what its tenants consider important toward the successful operation of their businesses. Realty Income has traditionally grown its revenue through high-quality property acquisitions (with above 96% occupancy rates and existing long-term lease arrangements). It often sells properties with the intent to reinvest the proceeds in new real estate with the potential for higher returns. During 2014 it invested $1.4 billion in over 500 new properties (including ones under development or expansion) spanning 9.8 million leasable sq. ft. across 42 states with an average occupancy rate of 100% and a lease term of 12.8 years.Mergers and AcquisitionsIn January 2013 Realty Income purchased fellow REIT American Realty Capital Trust adding more than 480 commercial properties to its portfolio.

EXECUTIVES

Svp And General Counsel, Laura S King, age 55
Vice President Portfolio Management, Elizabeth (Beth) Cate
EVP General Counsel and Secretary, Michael R. Pfeiffer, age 55, $375,000 total compensation
VP Retail Research, Robert J. Israel, age 56
EVP CFO and Treasurer, Paul M. Meurer, age 50, $400,000 total compensation
President CEO and Director, John P. Case, age 52, $800,000 total compensation
President and COO, Sumit Roy, age 46, $406,250 total compensation
VP Information Technology, Clint Schmucker
EVP and Chief Investment Officer, Neil Abraham
Associate Vice President Portfolio Management, Kristin (Kristy) Ferrell
Associate Vice President Director Of Research, Scott Kohnen
Vice President Portfolio Management, Dawn (Dawny) Nguyen
Vice President Information Technologist, Theresa (Terry) Casey
Associate Vice President Manager Finance And Accounting Department, Sean Nugent
Associate Vice President Controller, Jill Cossaboom
Associate Vice President Acquisitions Director, Greg Smith
Associate Vice President Director of Sales, Jenette Obrien
Chairman, Michael D. McKee
Auditors: KPMG LLP

LOCATIONS

HQ: Realty Income Corp
11995 El Camino Real, San Diego, CA 92130
Phone: 858 284-5000
Web: www.realtyincome.com

PRODUCTS/OPERATIONS

2014 Properties

	No.	% of rental
Retail	4.1	79
Industrial and distribution	82.0	10
Office	44.0	7
Manufacturing	14.0	2
Agriculture	15.0	2
Total	**4,327.0**	**100**

2014 Sales

	% of total
Rental	96
Tenant reimbursement	4
Others	-
Total	**100**

COMPETITORS

Acadia Realty Trust	National Retail
Capital Automotive	Properties
DDR	One Liberty Properties
EPR Properties	Regency Centers
Federal Realty	Simon Property Group
Investment	The Blackstone Group
Kimco Realty	Weingarten Realty

HISTORICAL FINANCIALS
Company Type: Public

Income Statement
FYE: December 31

	REVENUE ($ mil.)	NET INCOME ($ mil.)	NET PROFIT MARGIN	EMPLOYEES
12/15	1,023.2	283.7	27.7%	132.0
12/14	933.5	270.6	29.0%	125.0
12/13	778.3	245.5	31.5%	116.0
12/12	475.5	159.1	33.5%	97.0
12/11	421.0	157.0	37.3%	83.0
Annual Growth	24.9%	15.9%	—	12.3%

2015 Year-End Financials

Debt ratio: 40.8%	No. of shares (mil.): 250.4
Return on equity: 4.6%	Dividends
Cash ($ mil.): 40.2	Yield: 4.4%
Current ratio: 0.55	Payout: 207.1%
Long-term debt ($ mil.): 4,841.4	Market value ($ mil.): 12,929.0

	STOCK PRICE ($) FY Close	P/E High/Low		PER SHARE ($) Earnings	Dividends	Book Value
12/15	51.63	51	40	1.09	2.28	26.08
12/14	47.71	48	36	1.04	2.19	24.96
12/13	37.33	52	35	1.06	2.18	25.96
12/12	40.21	50	40	0.86	1.78	18.08
12/11	34.96	34	27	1.05	1.74	16.93
Annual Growth	10.2%	—	—	0.9%	7.0%	11.4%

Red Hat Inc

Red Hat tips its cap to businesses that embrace open-source computing tools. The company dominates the market for Linux the open-source computer operating system (OS) that is the chief rival to Microsoft's Windows operating system. In addition to its Red Hat Enterprise Linux OS the company's product line includes database content and collaboration management applications; server and embedded operating systems; and software development tools. Red Hat also provides consulting custom application development support and training services. The company's business model is a mix of providing free open-source software paired with subscription-based support training and integration services.

Operations

Red Hat's JBoss unit specializes in open-source middleware software including application servers and messaging systems which are used to develop and deploy applications throughout an enterprise that are accessible via the Internet intranets extranets and virtual private networks.

Subscriptions revenue accounted for about 88% of total net sales in 2016 (ended February). Training and services revenue accounted for the remainder.

Geographic Reach

About two-thirds of Red Hat's revenue comes from customers in the Americas with a fifth from European customers and about an eighth from Asia/Pacific clients.

Sales and Marketing

Red Hat's customers are in a variety of industries including financial services government healthcare retail telecommunications and transportation. In 2016 US government agencies accounted for about a 10th of revenue. The company increased advertising spending by about a third in 2016. Advertising expense totaled about $89 million in 2016 up from $62.6 million and $53.4 million in 2015 and 2014 respectively.

Financial Performance

Red Hat turned in a strong financial record in 2016 (ended February) with higher sales profit and cash flow.

The company's sales jumped 15% to about $2 billion compared to 2015. It reported a surge in Subscription revenue from infrastructure-related offerings as well as training and services. Added subscriptions came from geographic expansion and the continued migration of customers to its open source Linux platform from proprietary operating systems.

The higher revenue drove a 10.6% profit increase to reach $199 million in 2016 from 205 despite higher sales and marketing costs.

Cash generated by operations rose to $716 million in 2016 from about $623 million in 2015.

Strategy

Although Red Hat originally offered support for consumer-oriented Linux products the company shifted its focus entirely to the more lucrative business of supporting and servicing Linux technologies in enterprise environments. While Linux has failed to gain much traction against Microsoft's Windows operating system in the consumer space open-source platforms have been much more successful in corporate deployments especially for back-end tasks such as managing data center operations including virtualization server and data management and enterprise application integration.

The company's offerings that help customers develop applications for cloud computing have gained traction with customers. Red Hat Mobile for example is a software development platform for developing integrating and managing mobile applications. With Red Hat Storage customers can treat physical server storage as a scalable shared centrally-managed pool of virtual storage.

Red Hat teamed with Eurotech in 2016 to start an open source project to manage Internet of Things (IoT) edge devices from connectivity and configuration to application lifecycle. The project offers IoT developers and end users an open platform for end-to-end IoT implementations.

Mergers and Acquisitions

In 2016 Red Hat agreed to acquire 3scale a provider of application programming interface (API) management technology. 3scale strengthens Red Hat's API-related portfolio of JBoss Middleware OpenShift and Mobile Application Platform.

Red Hat acquired Ansible Inc. a provider of IT automation tools for $126 million in October 2015. Red Hat expects that the combination of Ansible's tools with Red Hat's portfolio will help users get to lower costs in deploying and managing cloud-native and traditional applications across hybrid cloud environments.

In 2014 Red Hat acquired FeedHenry an enterprise mobile application platform provider. FeedHenry expands Red Hat's portfolio of application development integration and Platform-as-a-Service (PaaS) services.

HISTORY

Early History

Finnish graduate student Linus Torvalds created the Linux operating system in 1991 as a hobby. When Torvalds released its programming code free over the Internet for anyone to revise Linux quickly attracted a core base of devoted programmers –including Marc Ewing. A programmer for IBM by day Ewing developed improvements to Linux in his spare bedroom. Soon he began selling the improved operating system as Red Hat – named after a red and white Cornell lacrosse cap Ewing's grandfather had given him.

In 1994 Ewing was contacted by Robert Young who after selling typewriters and running a computer leasing company had started a UNIX newsletter. But Young saw better profit margins in catalog sales. Young's ACC Corp. bought the rights to Ewing's creation and the two went into business together. ACC Corp. was renamed Red Hat Software Inc.

The company compiled Linux's most significant improvements and distributed them on a CD-ROM and through the budding Internet. Their revenues actually came from manuals and technical support sold to new users and businesses who were challenged by the software's ever-changing source code.

By 1997 Linux –and Red Hat's package –were known only among the most militant programmers who sought alternatives to Microsoft's Windows. Hundreds of developers had continually doctored Linux online to create an operating system known for its speed and reliability.

Red Hat exploded in popularity in 1998 after Intel and Netscape both made minor investments in the company. In 1999 Compaq IBM Novell Oracle and SAP invested in Red Hat. The company went public later that year.

EXECUTIVES

President - Products and Technologies, Paul J. Cormier, age 59, $425,000 total compensation
VP Open Source Affairs, Michael (Mike) Tiemann, age 51
VP Middleware Business Unit, Craig Muzilla
President CEO and Director, James M. (Jim) Whitehurst, age 49, $700,000 total compensation
EVP and Chief Technology Officer, Brian Stevens

EVP and General Counsel, Michael R. Cunningham, age 55, $375,000 total compensation
EVP and Chief People Officer, DeLisa Alexander
EVP of Global Sales and Services, Arun Oberoi
Executive Vice President Strategy and Corporate Marketing, Jackie Yeaney
Acting CFO, Eric Shander
Country Manager Malaysia, Kai Peng Chew
Vice President Of Sales, Sukanta Biswas
Vice President of Product and Technology Operations, Katrinka McCallum
Vice President, Kim (Kimmy) Lynch
Vice President and Tax Counsel, Dennis (Denny) Duquette
Vice President Sales, Tim (Timmy) Waugh
Vice President West Region Sales, Matt Androski
Vice President General Manager Na Commercial Sales, Gregory Symon
Vice President of Global Strategic Alliances, Scott (Scotty) Musson
Vice President Treasurer, Paul Argiry
Chairman, Henry H. (Hugh) Shelton, age 74
Auditors: PricewaterhouseCoopers LLP

LOCATIONS

HQ: Red Hat Inc
100 East Davie Street, Raleigh, NC 27601
Phone: 919 754-3700
Web: www.redhat.com

PRODUCTS/OPERATIONS

2016 Sales

	$ mil.	% of total
Subscriptions		
Infrastructure-related offerings	1,480.4	72
Application development-related and other emerging technology offerings	323.0	16
Training & services		
Consulting services	190.9	9
Training	57.9	3
Total	**2,052.2**	**100**

Selected Products and Services

Infrastructure-related offerings
Red Hat Enterprise Linux technologies
Red Hat Enterprise Virtualization
Red Hat Satellite

Selected Mergers and Acquisitions

COMPETITORS

Apple Inc.	Microsoft
BMC Software	Novell
CA Inc.	Oracle
HP	Unisys
IBM	Xandros
Mandriva	

HISTORICAL FINANCIALS

Company Type: Public

Income Statement

FYE: February 29

	REVENUE ($ mil.)	NET INCOME ($ mil.)	NET PROFIT MARGIN	EMPLOYEES
02/16	2,052.2	199.3	9.7%	8,800.0
02/15	1,789.4	180.2	10.1%	7,300.0
02/14	1,534.6	178.2	11.6%	6,300.0
02/13	1,328.8	150.2	11.3%	5,600.0
02/12	1,133.1	146.6	12.9%	4,500.0
Annual Growth	**16.0%**	**8.0%**	**—**	**18.3%**

	STOCK PRICE ($) FY Close	P/E High/Low	PER SHARE ($) Earnings	Dividends	Book Value
02/16	65.35	77 56	1.07	0.00	7.36
02/15	69.12	73 50	0.95	0.00	7.02
02/14	58.99	64 45	0.93	0.00	8.18
02/13	50.81	79 61	0.77	0.00	7.88
02/12	49.46	69 42	0.75	0.00	7.26
Annual Growth	7.2%	— —	9.3%	—	0.4%

Red Robin Gourmet Burgers Inc

Hamburger fans are chirping about Red Robin Gourmet Burgers. The company operates a chain of about 515 casual-dining restaurants that specialize in high-end hamburgers. Its menu features more than 20 different twists on the American classic including the Banzai Burger (marinated in teriyaki) Bleu Ribbon Burger and the jalapeño-charged Burnin' Love Burger. The signature Royal Red Robin Burger features bacon and a fried egg on top of the beef. Red Robin also serves chicken seafood and turkey burgers as well as vegetarian alternatives. Non-burger entrées include salads pasta seafood and fajitas.

Geographic Reach

The Red Robin chain has locations in more than 40 states and Canada.

Operations

The company operates about 415 of its locations and franchises the rest.

Sales and Marketing

Typically the company's restaurants are freestanding units located in suburban retail developments or near entertainment centers. Competing restaurant chains targeting those same markets and customer segments include casual dining leaders Applebee's California Pizza Kitchen and T.G.I. Friday's (owned by Carlson Restaurants Worldwide).

Financial Performance

Red Robin's annual revenue has been steadily increasing in recent fiscal years. Its revenue increased slightly to $1.14 billion in fiscal 2014 compared to $1.0 billion the company claimed in revenue for the previous fiscal period.

Strategy

With a relatively small number of franchised locations Red Robin concentrates mostly on its estate of corporate-run locations which gives the company a high degree of centralized control over food and service quality throughout its chain. Red Robin continues to expand its chain including nontraditional prototypes with a limited menu and limited service called Red Robin's Burger Works. The company occasionally closes down underperforming units.

EXECUTIVES

Senior Vice President CMO, Susan (Sue) Lintonsmith
EVP and COO, Carin L. Stutz, age 60
CEO and Director, Denny M. Post, $392,700 total compensation
SVP and Chief People Officer, Cathy Cooney, $305,000 total compensation
VP Controller Chief Accounting Officer and Interim CFO, Terry Harryman, age 51
SVP and Chief Marketing Officer, Jonathan Muhtar
SVP and Chief Legal Officer, Michael L. Kaplan, $335,000 total compensation
Vice President Purchasing, Joe (Joey) Leahey
Vice President and General Counsel, John W (Jack) Grant
Vice President Operations, Dave (Davie) Gates
Vice President, Scott (Scotty) Schooler
Chairman, Pattye L. Moore, age 58
Auditors: KPMG LLP

LOCATIONS

HQ: Red Robin Gourmet Burgers Inc
6312 S. Fiddler's Green Circle, Suite 200 N,
Greenwood Village, CO 80111
Phone: 303 846-6000
Web: www.redrobin.com

PRODUCTS/OPERATIONS

2014 Sales

	$ mil.	% of total
Restaurants	1,129.1	99
Franchising & other	17.0	1
Total	**1,146.1**	**100**

2014 Locations

	No.
Company-owned	415
Franchised	99
Total	**514**

COMPETITORS

Applebee's International	Darden
BJ's Restaurants	Denny's
Brinker	Ignite Restaurant Group
CKE Restaurants	In-N-Out Burgers
California Pizza Kitchen	Johnny Rockets
Carlson Restaurants	P.F. Chang's
Cheesecake Factory	Panera Bread
Chipotle	Rock Bottom Restaurants
Cracker Barrel	Ruby Tuesday

HISTORICAL FINANCIALS

Company Type: Public

Income Statement   FYE: December 27

	REVENUE ($ mil.)	NET INCOME ($ mil.)	NET PROFIT MARGIN	EMPLOYEES
12/15	1,257.5	47.7	3.8%	28,933.0
12/14	1,146.1	32.5	2.8%	27,543.0
12/13	1,017.2	32.2	3.2%	24,336.0
12/12	977.1	28.3	2.9%	22,342.0
12/11	914.8	20.5	2.2%	22,302.0
Annual Growth	8.3%	23.4%	—	6.7%

	STOCK PRICE ($) FY Close	P/E High/Low	PER SHARE ($) Earnings	Dividends	Book Value
12/15	61.84	27 18	3.36	0.00	27.47
12/14	76.42	34 21	2.25	0.00	25.62
12/13	75.21	37 16	2.22	0.00	24.21
12/12	33.66	19 14	1.93	0.00	21.92
12/11	28.95	28 15	1.34	0.00	20.21
Annual Growth	20.9%	— —	25.8%	—	8.0%

Regional Management Corp

Regional Management is looking to give credit where credit is due. Consumer finance company Regional Management provides secured personal loans (up to $27500) auto loans and furniture and appliance loans to consumers who may otherwise have limited access to credit through banks and other traditional lenders. The company which operates under the Regional Finance RMC Financial Services Anchor Finance and Sun Finance banners among others has some 265 branch locations in eight states in the south and southwest. It also provides loans through pre-screened live check mailings auto dealerships and its e-commerce site. Founded in 1987 Regional Management went public via an IPO in 2012.

IPO

The company intends to use a portion of the proceeds from its March 2012 IPO ($63 million down from what the $80 million it expected) to repay debt and for general corporate purposes. It also plans to use some of the proceeds to make a one-time payment to pre-IPO owners to terminate a consulting agreement. Prior to the IPO private equity firm Palladium Equity Partners held a 48% stake in the company and Parallel 2005 Equity Fund held a 28% stake.

Geographic Reach

South Carolina-based Regional Management makes loans in the Carolinas Texas Georgia Tennessee Alabama Oklahoma and New Mexico.

Operations

The consumer finance company makes small installment loans (ranging from $300 to $2500) large installment loans (between $2500 and $20000) and automobile purchase loans (up to $27500). It also makes loans to finance retail purchases of up to $7500 that are secured by the purchased item. Regional Management also sells insurance on its loans. Most of its loan activity consists of small installment and auto purchase loans.

Financial Performance

In its first full year as a public company Regional Management reported sales of $170.6 million in 2013 an increase of 25% versus the prior year on rising interest and fee income. Net income grew 14% to $28.8 million over the same period. Indeed the finance company's sales and profits have been rising in lockstep since 2008 as the company opened new branches. In 2013 about 75% of the firm's loans were classified as current with 17% between 1 to 29 days delinquent.

Strategy

Regional Management targets non-prime and underbanked consumers who have limited access to credit from traditional channels such as banks and credit card companies. While the population of such customers has grown in recent years the supply of consumer credit to them has contracted presenting Regional Management with a growth market for its installment auto and retail purchase loans.

As a key component of its growth strategy Regional Management has been busy opening new branches in new and existing markets. Indeed the company's branch network has more than doubled in size from 117 branches in 2009 to about 265 in 2013. In 2013 the firm opened or acquired 43 new branches including its first branches in Georgia. Regional Management is eyeing several states outside its present footprint with favorable interest rate and regulatory climates such as Kentucky Louisiana Mississippi Missouri and Virginia. The company also plans to bolster its other lending channels including driving traffic to its e-commerce website through marketing and advertising initiatives and by leveraging search engine optimization technologies.

EXECUTIVES

EVP and CFO, Donald E. (Don) Thomas, age 57, $321,391 total compensation
President and COO, Jody L. Anderson, age 50, $325,000 total compensation
CEO and Director, Peter R. Knitzer
SVP and Chief Risk Officer, Daniel J. Taggart, age 43, $296,712 total compensation
VP General Counsel and Secretary, Brian J. Fisher, age 32, $220,000 total compensation
N TX Vice President of Operations, Michael (Mel) Johnson
Chairman, Michael R. Dunn, age 64
Auditors: RSM US LLP

LOCATIONS

HQ: Regional Management Corp
979 Batesville Road, Suite B, Greer, SC 29651
Phone: 864 448-7000
Web: www.regionalmanagement.com

PRODUCTS/OPERATIONS

2015 Sales

	% of total
Interest and fee income	90
Insurance income net	5
Other	5
Total	**100**

COMPETITORS

1st Franklin Financial	DFC Global
Advance America	Nicholas Financial
Capital One Auto Finance	OneMain
Check ' n Go	QC Holdings
Check Into Cash	World Acceptance
Community Choice Financial	Xponential

HISTORICAL FINANCIALS

Company Type: Public

Income Statement

FYE: December 31

	ASSETS ($ mil.)	NET INCOME ($ mil.)	INCOME AS % OF ASSETS	EMPLOYEES
12/15	629.0	23.3	3.7%	1,421.0
12/14	530.2	14.8	2.8%	1,443.0
12/13	533.8	28.7	5.4%	1,117.0
12/12	434.9	25.3	5.8%	912.0
12/11	304.1	21.2	7.0%	670.0
Annual Growth	**19.9%**	**2.4%**	**—**	**20.7%**

2015 Year-End Financials

Return on assets: 4.0%
Return on equity: 12.1%
Long-term debt ($ mil.): —
No. of shares (mil.): 12.9
Sales ($ mil): 217.3
Dividends
Yield: —
Payout: —
Market value ($ mil.): 200.0

	STOCK PRICE ($) FY Close	P/E High/Low		PER SHARE ($) Earnings	Dividends	Book Value
12/15	15.47	11	8	1.79	0.00	15.89
12/14	15.81	31	10	1.14	0.00	13.99
12/13	33.93	15	7	2.23	0.00	12.74
12/12	16.55	8	6	2.12	0.00	10.46
Annual Growth	**(2.2%)**	**—**	**—**	**(5.5%)**	**—**	**15.0%**

Reis, Inc

Reis knows how to get below the surface of real estate. The company provides commercial real estate market information through online databases containing information on apartment retail office and industrial properties in several US metropolitan markets. Its flagship product Reis SE offers trend and forecast analysis as well as information on rent vacancy rates lease terms sale prices and new construction listings. Reis also furnishes data to small businesses through its ReisReports product. Its databases are used by real estate investors lenders and brokers to make buying selling and financing decisions. Customers access Reis' data through subscription or by purchasing reports individually.

EXECUTIVES

VP & CFO, Mark P. Cantaluppi, age 46, $265,000 total compensation
CEO & President, Lloyd Lynford, age 61, $400,000 total compensation
EVP, Jonathan Garfield, age 60, $400,000 total compensation
President and Chief Operating Officer Reis Services LLC, William Sander, age 49, $325,000 total compensation
Executive Vice President Sales and Marketing, Michael J (Mel) Richardson
Senior Vice President Of Information Technology, Paul (Pauly) Grier
National Account Manager, John (Jack) Newman
Senior Vice President Of Information Technology, Vicki (Vic) Biggs
Vice President; Finance Vice President, John (Jack) Garfield
Chairman, Edward Lowenthal, age 72
Auditors: Ernst & Young LLP

LOCATIONS

HQ: Reis, Inc
1185 Avenue of the Americas, New York, NY 10036
Phone: 212 921-1122 **Fax:** 212 921-2533
Web: www.reis.com

PRODUCTS/OPERATIONS

Selected Solutions

Custom Solutions
Economic Briefings
Market/Submarket Reports
Property Comps
Types of Coverage
Valuation and Portfolio Analytics

COMPETITORS

CBRE Group	LoopNet
CoStar Group	PropertyInfo
CoreLogic	

HISTORICAL FINANCIALS

Company Type: Public

Income Statement

FYE: December 31

	REVENUE ($ mil.)	NET INCOME ($ mil.)	NET PROFIT MARGIN	EMPLOYEES
12/15	50.8	10.3	20.2%	272.0
12/14	41.3	4.0	9.8%	205.0
12/13	34.7	17.6	50.7%	208.0
12/12	31.2	(4.2)	—	190.0
12/11	27.1	1.8	6.9%	160.0
Annual Growth	**17.0%**	**52.9%**	**—**	**14.2%**

2015 Year-End Financials

Debt ratio: —
Return on equity: 10.4%
Cash ($ mil.): 28.6
Current ratio: 1.38
Long-term debt ($ mil.): —
No. of shares (mil.): 11.2
Dividends
Yield: 2.3%
Payout: 78.8%
Market value ($ mil.): 267.0

	STOCK PRICE ($) FY Close	P/E High/Low		PER SHARE ($) Earnings	Dividends	Book Value
12/15	23.73	30	23	0.88	0.56	9.02
12/14	26.17	70	44	0.34	0.33	8.61
12/13	19.23	12	8	1.54	0.00	8.51
12/12	13.03	—	—	(0.39)	0.00	6.91
12/11	9.12	59	37	0.17	0.00	7.33
Annual Growth	**27.0%**	**—**	**—**	**50.8%**	**—**	**5.3%**

Renasant Corp

Those who are cognizant of their finances may want to do business with Renasant Corporation. The holding company owns Renasant Bank which serves consumers and local business through about 80 locations in Alabama Georgia Mississippi and Tennessee. The bank offers standard products such as checking and savings accounts CDs credit cards and loans and mortgages as well as trust retail brokerage and retirement plan services. Its loan portfolio is dominated by residential and commercial real estate loans. The bank also offers agricultural business construction and consumer loans and lease financing. Subsidiary Renasant Insurance sells personal and business coverage.

Financial Performance

The company's revenue increased in fiscal 2013 compared to the prior year. It reported revenue of $252.6 million for fiscal 2013 up from $228 million in revenue for fiscal 2012.

Renasant's net income also went up in fiscal 2013 compared to the previous fiscal period. It reported net income of about $33.5 million for fiscal 2013 up from net income of $26.6 million in fiscal 2012.

The company's cash on hand decreased by about $24 million in fiscal 2013 compared to fiscal 2012 levels.

Strategy

Renasant has looked to diversify its loan portfolio. The bank has reduced its amount of loans for construction and land development –a sector that has been hit particularly hard –by tightening its underwriting standards.It's also been growing through acquistions. In late 2014 for example Renasant purchased Heritage Financial Group in an all stock merger deal that amounted to $258 million. The move added $1.9 billion in assets.$1.2 billion in loan assets and $1.3 billion in deposit assets to Renasant's collection. In addition the move significantly expanded the bank's geographic reach adding 48 banking mortgage and investment offices in Alabama Florida and Georgia. All told the deal made Renasant one of the largest community banks in the Southeast region of the United States.

EXECUTIVES

EVP, Stuart R. Johnson, age 63, $250,000 total compensation

Chairman President and CEO, E. Robinson (Robin) McGraw, age 69, $700,000 total compensation

EVP, James W. Gray, age 60, $230,000 total compensation

President and COO, C. Mitchell (Mitch) Waycaster, age 58, $360,000 total compensation

EVP, Mary J. Witt, age 57

EVP, W. Mark Williams

EVP, R. Rick Hart, age 68, $475,000 total compensation

EVP and General Counsel, Stephen M. Corban, age 61, $75,000 total compensation

EVP; President Eastern Region Renasant Bank, O. Leonard (Len) Dorminey, age 63, $213,285 total compensation

EVP; President Central Region Renasant Bank, Michael D. Ross, age 52, $360,000 total compensation

EVP and CFO, Kevin D. Chapman, age 41, $330,000 total compensation

EVP; President Western Region Renasant Bank, J. Scott Cochran, age 53

Assistant Vice President, Kent (Ken) Dees

Vice President Mortgage Lending, Chris M (Chrissy) Waggoner

Auditors: Horne LLP

LOCATIONS

HQ: Renasant Corp
209 Troy Street, Tupelo, MS 38804-4827
Phone: 662 680-1001
Web: www.renasant.com

PRODUCTS/OPERATIONS

2015 Sales

	$ mil.	% of total
Interest income		
Loans	236.3	64
Securities	26.5	7
Other	0.2	-
Non-interest income		
Mortgage banking income	35.8	10
Service charges on deposit accounts	29.3	8
Fees and commissions	16.1	4
Wealth management	9.8	3
Other	17.3	4
Total	**371.3**	**100**

COMPETITORS

BBVA Compass Bancshares	First Horizon
BancorpSouth	Hancock Holding
Citizens Holding	Regions Financial
Citizens National Bank of Meridian	Trustmark

HISTORICAL FINANCIALS

Company Type: Public

Income Statement

FYE: December 31

	ASSETS ($ mil.)	NET INCOME ($ mil.)	INCOME AS % OF ASSETS	EMPLOYEES
12/15	7,926.5	68.0	0.9%	1,996.0
12/14	5,805.1	59.5	1.0%	1,471.0
12/13	5,746.2	33.4	0.6%	1,483.0
12/12	4,178.6	26.6	0.6%	1,096.0
12/11	4,202.0	25.6	0.6%	1,030.0
Annual Growth	**17.2%**	**27.6%**	**—**	**18.0%**

2015 Year-End Financials

Return on assets: 0.9%
Return on equity: 7.7%
Long-term debt ($ mil.): —
No. of shares (mil.): 40.2
Sales ($ mil): 371.2

Dividends
Yield: 1.9%
Payout: 36.7%
Market value ($ mil.): 1,386.0

	STOCK PRICE ($) FY Close	P/E High/Low	PER SHARE ($) Earnings	Dividends	Book Value
12/15	34.41	20 14	1.88	0.68	25.73
12/14	28.93	17 14	1.88	0.68	22.56
12/13	31.46	26 15	1.22	0.68	21.21
12/12	19.14	19 14	1.06	0.68	19.80
12/11	15.00	17 12	1.02	0.68	19.44
Annual Growth	**23.1%**	**— —**	**16.5%**	**(0.0%)**	**7.3%**

Repligen Corp.

Repligen replies to the needs of the pharmaceutical industry by supplying bio-engineered drug ingredients. Repligen's bioprocessing business develops and commercializes proteins and other agents used in the production of biopharmaceuticals. The firm also conducts drug research activities include development of a pancreatic imaging agent and potential therapies for bipolar disorder Friedreich's ataxia (a debilitating early adulthood disease) and spinal muscular atrophy. While all of Repligen's own drugs are in the clinical development stage it does receive royalty payments from Bristol-Myers Squibb (BMS) on sales of BMS' Orencia rheumatoid arthritis drug as well as by licensing out its technologies.

Operations

Repligen receives the majority of its revenues from its bioprocessing business which primarily sells Protein A a recombinant protein used in the production of monoclonal antibodies and other biopharmaceutical manufacturing applications. Its primary customer in this area is GE Healthcare with which it has a multi-year supply agreement.

Geographic Reach

Repligen's headquarters are in Massachusetts; it also has manufacturing facilities there and in Sweden.

The US accounts for about 50% of revenue with Sweden and the UK contributing 35% and 10% respectively.

Sales and Marketing

Repligen uses its own direct sales force and partners including GE Healthcare EMD Millipore and Sigma Aldrich to sell its products to life sciences and biopharma companies.

Financial Performance

The company has seen years of revenue growth including a huge 128% spike in 2012 that continued into 2013 when Repligen reported a 9% increase from $62 million to $68 million. Royalties and payments related to settling a legal matter contributed to the growth. Increased manufacturing efficiency and a good product mix particularly in Sweden helped the company post a 14% improvement in net income. Cash from operations also trended up with a $12.5 million increase due to deferred tax expenses royalties and long-term liabilities.

Strategy

Repligen is developing RG1068 a synthetic human hormone designed to detect abnormalities in pancreatic duct function as part of a process to diagnose pancreatitis and other pancreatic diseases.

In 2014 it sold its histone deacetylase inhibitor (HDI) portfolio to BioMarin Pharmaceutical for $2 million plus potential future payments if the drug is developed. HDI are currently used to treat depression and other psychological conditions but they are also being investigated to treat cancers parasites and inflammatory diseases.

Mergers and Acquisitions

In 2014 Repligen paid $24.5 million for Refine Technology to strengthen its bioprocessing business and expand its direct sales force. Two years later it bought German manufacturer Atoll which makes MediaScout pre-packed chromatography columns used in the clinical manufacturing of biologic drugs. The deal was valued at $22.5 million.

Later in 2016 the company acquired TangenX Technology Corporation from Novasep for $39 million. TangenX develops and markets tangential flow filtration (TFF) technologies including the single-use Sius which are used in the manufacturing of biopharmaceuticals.

EXECUTIVES

SVP Research and Development, James R. Rusche, age 63, $311,000 total compensation

VP Sales and Marketing, Stephen Tingley

VP Business Development, Howard Benjamin, $279,000 total compensation

President and CEO, Tony J. Hunt, $403,846 total compensation

CFO, Jon K. Snodgres, $330,000 total compensation

VP and Managing Director Repligen GmbH, Martin Reuter

Vice President Human Resources, Kelly Capra

Chairman, Karen A. Dawes

Auditors: Ernst & Young LLP

LOCATIONS

HQ: Repligen Corp.
41 Seyon Street, Bldg. 1, Suite 100, Waltham, MA
02453
Phone: 781 250-0111   **Fax:** 781 250-0115
Web: www.repligen.com

PRODUCTS/OPERATIONS

2013 Sales

	$ mil.	% of total
Bioprocessing	47.5	70
Royalties and other	20.7	30
Total	**68.2**	**100**

Selected Pipeline Products

RG1068 (Phase III clinical trials to help with pancreatic imaging)
RG2417 (Phase II clinical trials for treatment of bipolar disorder)
RG2833 (Preclinical trials for treatment of Friedreich's Ataxia)
RG3039 (Preclinical trials for treatment of spinal muscular atrophy)
Commercial Assets
Bioprocessing Business (biologics purification)
Orencia royalties (rheumatoid arthritis)

COMPETITORS

Abbott Labs
Bio-Rad Labs
Human Genome Sciences
Incyte

Life Technologies
Corporation
NeuroNova
PDL BioPharma

HISTORICAL FINANCIALS

Company Type: Public

Income Statement

FYE: December 31

	REVENUE ($ mil.)	NET INCOME ($ mil.)	NET PROFIT MARGIN	EMPLOYEES
12/15	83.5	9.3	11.2%	168.0
12/14	63.5	8.1	12.9%	136.0
12/13	68.1	16.0	23.6%	116.0
12/12	62.2	14.1	22.7%	120.0
12/11	23.4	(1.6)	—	137.0
Annual Growth	**37.4%**	**—**		**5.2%**

2015 Year-End Financials

Debt ratio: —
Return on equity: 7.9%
Cash ($ mil.): 54.0
Current ratio: 5.50
Long-term debt ($ mil.): —

No. of shares (mil.): 32.9
Dividends
  Yield: —
  Payout: —
Market value ($ mil.): 932.0

	STOCK PRICE ($) FY Close	P/E High/Low	PER SHARE ($) Earnings	Dividends	Book Value
12/15	28.29	151 71	0.28	0.00	3.73
12/14	19.80	102 49	0.25	0.00	3.41
12/13	13.64	27 12	0.50	0.00	3.25
12/12	6.28	16 7	0.45	0.00	2.70
12/11	3.47	— —	(0.05)	0.00	2.15
Annual Growth	**69.0%**	**— —**			**14.8%**

Retail Opportunity Investments Corp

For this company opportunity knocking sounds a lot like a neighborhood shopping center. Retail Opportunity Investments (ROIC) true to its name invests in owns leases and manages shopping centers. It targets densely populated middle and upper class markets and looks for centers anchored by large grocery or drug stores. The self-managed real estate investment trust (REIT) owns more than 50 shopping centers comprising 5.5 million sq. ft. in Oregon Washington and California. It makes money from rent management expenses and mortgage interest. ROIC was formed in 2007 as an acquisition company. It purchased NRDC Capital Management in 2009 and took its current name in 2010.

Financial Performance
Increases in base rents drove ROIC's revenue up 45% in 2012 over 2011. The company saw its net income drop 18% during the same period due in part to high operating and depreciation and amortization expenses as well as to expenditures related to the company's headquarters relocation from New York to California.

Strategy
ROIC's strategy includes renovating its properties and making lease agreement adjustments to keep its occupancy rates high. The company occasionally bolsters its portfolio with acquisitions of properties in its target markets. Between fiscal 2011 and 2013 the company added nearly three dozen properties to its portfolio. While it has focused its investments along the West Coast (California Washington and Oregon) ROIC is also eying properties in the Northeast.

Ownership
Investment management company Invesco owns a 13% stake in ROIC; The Vanguard Group owns an 11% stake.

Company Background
The company began operating in late 2009 and immediately commenced building out its portfolio purchasing a 95000-square-foot shopping center in Los Angeles County anchored by Rite Aid. In its second year it boosted its holdings after acquiring another dozen properties.

EXECUTIVES

CFO, Michael B. (Mike) Haines, age 54, $290,000 total compensation
President CEO and Director, Stuart A. Tanz, age 57, $775,000 total compensation
COO, Richard K. Schoebel, age 49, $340,000 total compensation
Chairman, Richard A. Baker, age 49
Auditors: Ernst & Young LLP

LOCATIONS

HQ: Retail Opportunity Investments Corp
8905 Towne Centre Drive, Suite 108, San Diego, CA 92122
Phone: 858 677-0900
Web: www.roireit.net

PRODUCTS/OPERATIONS

2015 Sales

	$ mil.	% of total
Base Rents	148.6	77
Recoveries from tenants other	44.1	23
Total	**192.7**	**100**

Selected Properties

California
  Claremont Center
  Deser Springs Marketplace
  Gateway Village
  Marketplace Del Rio
  Nimbus Winery Village
  Norwood Shopping Center
  Paramount Plaza
  Phillips Village
  Pinole Vista
  Pleasant Hill Marketplace
  Santa Ana Downtown Plaza
  Sycamore Creek
Oregon
  Cascade Summit
  Division Crossing
  Halsey Crossing
  Happy Valley Town Center
  Oregon City Point
  Wilsonville Old Town Square
Washington
  Crossroads
  Heritage Market Center
  Meridian Valley Plaza
  The Market at Lake Stevens
  Vancouver Market Center

COMPETITORS

Kimco Realty
Macerich
Regency Centers

Simon Property Group
Vornado Realty
Weingarten Realty

HISTORICAL FINANCIALS

Company Type: Public

Income Statement

FYE: December 31

	REVENUE ($ mil.)	NET INCOME ($ mil.)	NET PROFIT MARGIN	EMPLOYEES
12/15	192.7	23.8	12.4%	69.0
12/14	155.8	20.3	13.0%	65.0
12/13	111.2	33.8	30.4%	61.0
12/12	75.1	7.8	10.5%	22.0
12/11	51.7	9.6	18.7%	21.0
Annual Growth	**38.9%**	**25.4%**	**—**	**34.6%**

2015 Year-End Financials

Debt ratio: 42.9%
Return on equity: 2.4%
Cash ($ mil.): 8.8
Current ratio: 0.08
Long-term debt ($ mil.): 991.4

No. of shares (mil.): 99.5
Dividends
  Yield: 3.8%
  Payout: 309.0%
Market value ($ mil.): 1,782.0

	STOCK PRICE ($) FY Close	P/E High/Low	PER SHARE ($) Earnings	Dividends	Book Value
12/15	17.90	74 62	0.25	0.68	10.42
12/14	16.79	71 59	0.24	0.64	9.93
12/13	14.72	32 25	0.48	0.60	9.33
12/12	12.85	86 77	0.15	0.53	8.87
12/11	11.84	51 42	0.23	0.39	9.12
Annual Growth	**10.9%**	**— —**	**2.1%**	**14.9%**	**3.4%**

RetailMeNot Inc

Do an Internet search for "coupon code" and you've got this company's formula for success. RetailMeNot is a leading provider of digital coupons that allow consumers to obtain discounts on retailers' websites and in-store purchases. E-tail is big business and promo codes are incentives that appeal to both retailers and consumers. Retail-MeNot has its flagship US website retailmenot.com as well as deals2buy.com which features sale items from selected retailers. Its international brand portfolio includes VoucherCodes.co.uk in the UK Web.Bons-de-Reduction.com and Poulpeo.com in France Actiepagina.nl in the Netherlands and Deals.com in Germany. RetailMeNot became a public company in 2013.

IPO

The company plans to use the $191 million in proceeds to pay dividends on outstanding shares of preferred stock and pay off debt. The remainder will go toward working capital and other general corporate purposes such as developing new technologies funding capital expenditures or making acquisitions.

Geographic Reach

RetailMeNot is headquartered in the US and has international offices in France Germany the Netherlands and the UK. The US is its largest market accounting for about 80% of sales.

Operations

RetailMeNot's seven websites provide digital coupons to savvy shoppers. Its coupons and promo codes can also be accessed via mobile applications email newsletters and alerts and social media. With the mobile app consumers can search for coupon codes while shopping at a brick-and-mortar store and its iPhone app uses location-based technology to alert users to store coupons at one of 575 shopping malls in the US. In additions users can also share digital coupons on Facebook Google+ Pinterest and Twitter.

RetailMeNot has contracts with more than 10000 retailers who pay the company commission for promoting their digital coupons. Its commissions are tracked by three performance marketing networks – Commission Junction Google Affiliate Network and LinkShare.

Mergers and Acquisitions

RetailMeNot formed in 2007 and began operations in 2009. Since 2009 it has made nine acquisitions; notably that year it bought Deals2Buy.com Coupon7.com Couponshare.com and CheapStingyBargains.com. In 2010 it bought Australia-based Stateless Systems Pty. Ltd. which operated the website RetailMeNot.com. The next year it expanded operations into the UK with the purchase of VoucherCodes.co.uk. In 2011 it took root in France with Web.Bons-de-Reduction.com and Poulpeo.com and in 2013 it headed east to the Netherlands with the purchase of Actiepagina.nl.

Financial Performance

RetailMeNot has seen a lot of success in a short amount of time. Sales jumped from $16 million in 2010 to $80 million in 2011 and $144 million in 2012 from both organic and inorganic (acquisitions) growth. Organic growth was attributed to online search engine marketing efforts to drive traffic to its and its customers' websites and finalize sales. (The company doesn't make any money if shoppers are just browsing.) It also invested in improvements to its websites' merchandising usability and functionality which it believes also contributed to growth. RetailMeNot has been profitable for the past three years it has reported financial data.

Company Background

RetailMeNot formed in 2007 under the name smallponds LLC. It then changed its name to WhaleShark Media and rebranded as RetailMeNot in 2013.

EXECUTIVES

COO, Kelli A. Beougher, age 47, $360,000 total compensation
CFO, J. Scott Di Valerio, age 54
Chairman President and CEO, G. Cotter Cunningham, age 53, $478,000 total compensation
CTO, Paul M. Rogers, age 47, $320,000 total compensation
SVP International, Giulio Montemagno
SVP Corporate Development, Steven T. Pho, age 39, $280,000 total compensation
Senior Vice President, Michael (Mel) Magaro
Vice President Human Resources, Annette Alexander
Vice President Finance, Thomas (Thom) Aylor
Auditors: Ernst & Young LLP

LOCATIONS

HQ: RetailMeNot Inc
  301 Congress Avenue, Suite 700, Austin, TX 78701
Phone: 512 777-2970
Web: www.retailmenot.com

PRODUCTS/OPERATIONS

2015 Sales

	% of total
Desktop online transaction	70
Mobile online transaction	10
Advertising and in-store	20
Total	**100**

Selected Websites

Actiepagina.nl (Netherlands)
Deals2Buy.com (US)
Deals.com (Germany)
Poulpeo.com (France)
RetailMeNot.com (US)
VoucherCodes.co.uk (UK)
ma-reduc.com (France)
RetailMeNot.ca (Canada)
RetailMeNot.de (Germany)
RetailMeNot.es (Spain)
RetailMeNot.it (Italy)

COMPETITORS

Entertainment	PriceGrabber.com
Publications	SHOP.COM
Groupon	Shopping.com
HighCo	Shopzilla
Kelkoo	Valassis
LivingSocial	Valpak Direct
NexTag	Marketing Systems

HISTORICAL FINANCIALS

Company Type: Public

Income Statement

FYE: December 31

	REVENUE ($ mil.)	NET INCOME ($ mil.)	NET PROFIT MARGIN	EMPLOYEES
12/15	249.1	11.8	4.8%	522.0
12/14	264.6	26.9	10.2%	527.0
12/13	209.8	31.5	15.0%	444.0
12/12	144.6	25.9	18.0%	331.0
12/11	80.4	16.9	21.1%	0.0
Annual Growth	**32.7%**	**(8.6%)**	**—**	**—**

2015 Year-End Financials

Debt ratio: 11.9%
Return on equity: 2.3%
Cash ($ mil.): 259.7
Current ratio: 8.30
Long-term debt ($ mil.): 62.5
No. of shares (mil.): 51.0
Dividends
  Yield: —
  Payout: —
Market value ($ mil.): 507.0

	STOCK PRICE ($) FY Close	P/E High/Low	PER SHARE ($) Earnings	Dividends	Book Value
12/15	9.92	98 36	0.22	0.00	9.62
12/14	14.62	94 27	0.49	0.00	9.30
12/13	28.79	162 108	0.23	0.00	8.19
Annual Growth	**(41.3%)**	**—**	**(2.2%)**	**—**	**8.4%**

Revlon Consumer Products Corp.

EXECUTIVES

Chb, Ronald O Perelman
Auditors: KPMG LLP

LOCATIONS

HQ: Revlon Consumer Products Corp.
  One New York Plaza, New York, NY 10004
Phone: 212 527-4000
Web: www.revloninc.com

HISTORICAL FINANCIALS

Company Type: Public

Income Statement

FYE: December 31

	REVENUE ($ mil.)	NET INCOME ($ mil.)	NET PROFIT MARGIN	EMPLOYEES
12/15	1,914.3	62.1	3.2%	5,700.0
12/14	1,941.0	47.3	2.4%	5,600.0
12/13	1,494.7	1.6	0.1%	6,900.0
12/12	1,426.1	71.2	5.0%	5,100.0
12/11	1,381.4	64.0	4.6%	5,200.0
Annual Growth	**8.5%**	**(0.8%)**	**—**	**2.3%**

2015 Year-End Financials

Debt ratio: 86.6%
Return on equity: —
Cash ($ mil.): 326.9
Current ratio: 1.91
Long-term debt ($ mil.): 1,803.7
No. of shares (mil.): 0.0
Dividends
  Yield: —
  Payout: —
Market value ($ mil.): —

Revlon Inc

Revlon has the look of a leader in the US mass-market cosmetics business alongside L'Oréal's Maybelline and Procter & Gamble's Cover Girl. Aside from its Almay and Revlon brands of makeup and beauty tools the company makes Revlon ColorSilk hair color Mitchum antiperspirants and deodorants Charlie and Jean Naté fragrances and Ultima II and Gatineau skincare products. Its beauty aids are distributed in more than 150 countries though the US is its largest market generating more than half of sales. Revlon products are primarily sold by mass merchandisers and drugstores such as CVS Target Shoppers Drug Mart A.S. Watson Boots and Wal-Mart. Charles Revson founded Revlon in 1931.

Geographic Reach

The US is Revlon's largest market accounting for about 55% of sales. The cosmetics maker also has operations in more than a dozen foreign countries and enjoys a global reach and leading positions in several product categories in Australia Spain Italy Mexico Canada the UK and South Africa.

Operations

Revlon is one of the world's top cosmetics makers across the mass retail channel known for its color cosmetics in the face lip eye and nail categories as well as women's hair color and beauty tools. It has built a big business selling cosmetics and beauty products in the US to mass-market retailers and chain drug and food stores collectively known as the mass retail channel.

It operates across two segments: Consumer (74% of net sales) and Professional (26%). Consumer consists of Revlon color cosmetics Almay color cosmetics SinfulColors color cosmetics Pure Ice color cosmetics Revlon ColorSilk hair color Revlon Beauty Tools Charlie fragrances and Mitchum anti-perspirant deodorants.

Its Professional segment was formed upon its 2013 acquisition of Colomer. Professional now consists of Revlon Professional in hair color and hair care; CND-branded products in nail polishes and nail enhancements; and American Crew in men's grooming products.

Sales and Marketing

The beauty giant spends heavily to promote its products in the hotly-competitive beauty market. Revlon reported advertising expenses including TV print and digital ads and in-store promotional displays of $383 million in 2014 up from $279 million in 2013.

The mass-market cosmetic company's largest customer is Wal-Mart which accounted for about 16% of its total sales in 2014.

Financial Performance

Revlon posted unprecedented growth in 2014 with revenues surging from $1.49 billion in 2013 to peak at a record-shattering $1.94 million in 2014. The historic growth was primarily due to its 2013 acquisition of Colomer; as a result Revlon's newly formed Professional segment saw its sales skyrocket by over 400% during 2014.

After posting a net loss of $6 million in 2013 the company recorded $41 million in positive income for 2014. Revlon has also achieved steady operating cash flow growth the last four years.

Mergers and Acquisitions

In 2016 Revlon acquired Elizabeth Arden for more than $419 million in cash. The combined company is positioned to grow its global presence by selling its expanded portfolio of brands in additional markets. The deal was valued at $870 million including debt.

HISTORY

Company Background

Legend has it that jobless in New York City in the depths of the Depression Charles Revson became a cosmetics salesman by the toss of a coin — tails he'd apply for a job selling household appliances; heads he'd answer an ad for a cosmetics salesman. It was heads and in 1931 Revson began selling Elka nail polish to beauty salons. He painted his own nails with different colors so he wouldn't need a color chart.

Revson and his brother Joseph decided to start their own nail polish company. They scraped together $300 hooked up with nail polish supplier Charles Lachman and in 1932 began Revlon (the "L" in the name came from Lachman). The nail polish emulating Elka's was opaque rather than transparent available in many colors and an immediate hit with beauty salons. Revlon grew rapidly and by 1937 Revson was selling his nail polish in upscale department stores.

Seeing nail polish as a fashion accessory Revson introduced new colors twice a year giving them —and the matching lipsticks introduced in 1940 — names like Kissing Pink and Fifth Avenue Red. More opportunist than innovator he let his competitors do the research and make the mistakes and then he would make a better version of the product outpackaging and outadvertising his rivals.

Revlon introduced Fire & Ice in 1952 one of its most successful launches ever. Its sole sponsorship of The $64000 Question quiz show in 1955 boosted sales of some products by 500%. Later that year Revlon went public. To diversify and expand its markets it began making acquisitions (although many were soon dumped) and selling its products overseas.

EXECUTIVES

President CEO and Director, Fabian T. Garcia, age 56
EVP and CFO, Juan R. Figuereo, age 60
EVP and Chief Supply Chain Officer, Xavier Garijo
EVP and COO, Gianni Pieraccioni
EVP and Global President Revlon Professional Division, Sennen Pamich
General Manager Australia and New Zealand, Tracey Raso
EVP General Counsel and Chief Compliance Officer, Mitra Hormozi
Executive Vice President Listing Services, Nelson Griggs
Vice President Employee Relations, Stacy (Stace) Green
Vice President Fragrances And Apdeo, Robin (Rin) Wood
Vice President Sales, Larry (Lar) Aronson
Vice President Regional Customers, Dino Luliis
Senior Vice President And General Tax Counsel, Mark (Marky) Sexton
Senior Vice President Research and Development, Eric (Ric) Bone
Vice President Marketing and Operations Global Value Brands, Rahul Mehrotra
Senior Vice President of International affairs, Annette (Anne) Mcevoy
Vice President of Information Technology, John (Jack) Martin
Senior Vice President and General Counsel, Lauren (Laur) Goldberg
Vice President Human Resources Latin, Jim Morrissey
Vice President Marketing, Martine Williamson
Vice President, Al A Martin
Senior Vice President and Global Chief Information Officer (CIO), Francisco (Frances) Cornellana
Vice President Distribution And Logistics Operations At Revlon Consumer Products Corporate, Joe Lascala
Vice President Marketing Canada, Deborah (Deb) Neff
Vice President Customer Finance and Credit Services, Jack (Jackie) Flynn
Vice President Finance Sap Process Owner Fi SD, Nicole Spector
Executive Vice President; Chief Legal and Administrative Officer, Lucinda Treat
Executive Vice President and Chief Administrative Officer, Bob (Bo) Kretzman
Vice President marketing and Operations, Mehrotra Rahul

Vice President Package Development, James (Jamie) Paccagnini
Senior Vice President Finance Operatio, Peter (Pete) Gatti
Vice President CBD Sales, Nancy (Nance) Gnos
Executive Vice President, Olivier Cardon
Senior Vice President, Lisa (Lis) Ricci
Vice President Emea, Jean (Jeannie) Phillippe-Verdet
Chairman, Ronald O. (Ron) Perelman, age 74
Vice Chairman, David L. Kennedy, age 69
Treasurer, Roberto (Berto) Simon
Auditors: KPMG LLP

LOCATIONS

HQ: Revlon Inc
One New York Plaza, New York, NY 10004
Phone: 212 527-4000
Web: www.revloninc.com

PRODUCTS/OPERATIONS

2014 Sales

	% of total
Consumer	74
Professional	26
Total	**100**

2014 Sales

	% of total
Color cosmetics	53
Hair care	28
Beauty care and fragrance	19
Total	**100**

Selected Products and Brands

Cosmetics
Almay Bright Eyes
Almay Intense i-Color
Almay Smart Shade
Almay TLC Truly Lasting Color
Revlon Age Defying
Revlon Beyond Natural
Revlon ColorStay
Revlon Fabulash
Revlon PhotoReady
Revlon Super Lustrous
Pure Ice
Sinful Colors
Beauty tools
Revlon
Deodorants and antiperspirants
Mitchum
Fragrance
Charlie
Jean Naté
Hair
Revlon ColorSilk
Skin Care
Gatineau
Ultima II

COMPETITORS

Alticor	John Paul Mitchell
Avlon	Johnson & Johnson
Avon	L'Or©al
Bath & Body Works	LVMH
Beiersdorf	Mary Kay
Body Shop	Nu Skin
Bristol-Myers Squibb	Orly International
Clarins	Procter & Gamble
Colgate-Palmolive	Puig
Combe	Shiseido
Coty Inc.	Unilever
Est©e Lauder	

HISTORICAL FINANCIALS

Company Type: Public

Income Statement

FYE: December 31

	REVENUE ($ mil.)	NET INCOME ($ mil.)	NET PROFIT MARGIN	EMPLOYEES
12/15	1,914.3	56.1	2.9%	5,700.0
12/14	1,941.0	40.9	2.1%	5,600.0
12/13	1,494.7	(5.8)	—	6,900.0
12/12	1,426.1	51.1	3.6%	5,100.0
12/11	1,381.4	53.4	3.9%	5,200.0
Annual Growth	8.5%	1.2%	—	2.3%

2015 Year-End Financials

Debt ratio: 91.6%
Return on equity: —
Cash ($ mil.): 326.9
Current ratio: 1.68
Long-term debt ($ mil.): 1,803.7

No. of shares (mil.): 53.2
Dividends
 Yield: —
 Payout: —
Market value ($ mil.): 1,482.0

	STOCK PRICE ($) FY Close	P/E High/Low	PER SHARE ($) Earnings	Dividends	Book Value
12/15	27.84	39 25	1.07	0.00	(11.04)
12/14	34.16	46 29	0.78	0.00	(12.12)
12/13	24.96	— —	(0.11)	0.00	(11.37)
12/12	14.50	18 13	0.98	0.00	(12.40)
12/11	14.87	19 9	1.02	0.00	(13.21)
Annual Growth	17.0%	— —	1.2%	—	—

RH

RH (formerly Restoration Hardware Holdings) puts vintage American fixtures and fittings into homes old and new. The company sells upscale home and outdoor furnishings garden products hardware bathware lighting textiles baby and child products and more through about 115 retail and outlet stores under the Restoration Hardware RH and Waterworks names. Furniture accounts for about 60% of total revenue. In addition to stores RH markets products through its catalogs (called Source Books) and e-commerce sites which together account for about half of overall sales. The company operates primarily in the US with stores in some 30 states as well as in Canada and the UK.

Geographic Reach

Although RH operates seven stores in Canada and one in the UK revenues from its non-US operations are not material to the company. In the US its stores are located in more than 30 states with California Texas and Florida representing the largest markets.

RH has sourcing operations in Shanghai and Hong Kong.

Financial Performance

RH has reported strong revenue growth over the past five years. In fiscal 2016 (ended January) sales jumped 13% to $2.1 billion. Expansion of existing product lines as well as the introduction of new products led to growth in both retail store and direct sales. The company also had two more stores at the end of fiscal 2016 than it did at the end of fiscal 2015.

Net income was flat at $91 million as cost of goods sold rose at a slightly higher rate than revenue that year. Cash from operations soared to $142 million in fiscal 2016 up 70%.

Strategy

As it trims its traditional mall-based store count RH is opening larger next-generation Design Gal-

leries which average about 43000 square feet (much larger than the average size of its existing Gallery stores) and contain expanded merchandise selections such as baby and child furniture and products.

The company has identified 60-70 markets in the US and Canada as possible locations for future next-generation Design Galleries; in 2016 it opened locations in Seattle; Las Vegas; Austin Texas; and Leawood Kansas.

Mergers and Acquisitions

In mid-2016 RH acquired a controlling stake in Design Investors WW Acquisition Company which sells upscale kitchen and bath furniture and fixtures under the Waterworks brand for about $120 million. The acquired firm operates some 15 showrooms in the US and the UK.

Company Background

Founded in 1980 RH was taken private in 2008 by Catterton Partners and Tower Three Partners in a deal valued at about $175 million. In 2012 the high-end home accessories retailer went public.

EXECUTIVES

Chairman and CEO, Gary G. Friedman, age 58, $1,250,000 total compensation
Co-President CFO and Chief Administration Officer, Karen Boone, age 43, $689,423 total compensation
Co-President and Chief Creative and Merchandising Officer, Eri Chaya, age 43, $789,423 total compensation
Co-President COO and Chief Service and Values Officer, DeMonty Price, age 55
Auditors: PricewaterhouseCoopers LLP

LOCATIONS

HQ: RH
 15 Koch Road, Suite K, Corte Madera, CA 94925
Phone: 415 924-1005
Web: www.restorationhardware.com

PRODUCTS/OPERATIONS

2016 Sales

	$ mil.	% of total
Stores	1,083.6	51
Direct	1,025.4	49
Total	2,109.0	100

2016 Sales

	$ mil.	% of total
furniture	1,295.5	61
Non-Furniture	813.5	39
Total	2,109.0	100

2016 Stores

	No.
Legacy Galleries	53
Design Galleries	6
Next-Generation Design Galleries	4
RH Modern Gallery	1
RH Baby & Child Galleries	5
Outlet	17
Total	86

COMPETITORS

Bed Bath & Beyond	IKEA
Brookstone	Leon's Furniture
Container Store	Lowe's
Cost Plus	Macy's
Dillard's	Pier 1 Imports
Ethan Allen	Room & Board
Euromarket Designs	Williams-Sonoma
Home Depot	Z Gallerie

HISTORICAL FINANCIALS

Company Type: Public

Income Statement

FYE: January 30

	REVENUE ($ mil.)	NET INCOME ($ mil.)	NET PROFIT MARGIN	EMPLOYEES
01/16	2,109.0	91.1	4.3%	4,600.0
01/15*	1,867.4	91.0	4.9%	4,000.0
02/14	1,550.9	18.2	1.2%	3,600.0
02/13	1,193.0	(12.7)	—	3,100.0
01/12	958.0	20.5	2.1%	0.0
Annual Growth	21.8%	45.0%		

*Fiscal year change

2016 Year-End Financials

Debt ratio: 35.7%
Return on equity: 11.5%
Cash ($ mil.): 349.9
Current ratio: 2.90
Long-term debt ($ mil.): 747.3

No. of shares (mil.): 40.5
Dividends
 Yield: —
 Payout: —
Market value ($ mil.): 2,501.0

	STOCK PRICE ($) FY Close	P/E High/Low	PER SHARE ($) Earnings	Dividends	Book Value
01/16	61.62	47 27	2.16	0.00	21.84
01/15*	87.53	43 24	2.20	0.00	17.62
02/14	56.74	164 70	0.45	0.00	13.95
02/13	36.23	— —	(1.36)	0.00	11.89
Annual Growth	19.4%	— —	—	—	22.4%

*Fiscal year change

RLJ Lodging Trust

Auditors: PricewaterhouseCoopers LLP

LOCATIONS

HQ: RLJ Lodging Trust
 3 Bethesda Metro Center, Suite 1000, Bethesda, MD 20814
Phone: 301 280-7777

HISTORICAL FINANCIALS

Company Type: Public

Income Statement

FYE: December 31

	REVENUE ($ mil.)	NET INCOME ($ mil.)	NET PROFIT MARGIN	EMPLOYEES
12/15	1,136.3	218.2	19.2%	56.0
12/14	1,109.2	135.4	12.2%	56.0
12/13	970.3	112.9	11.6%	53.0
12/12	854.2	41.3	4.8%	53.0
12/11	758.9	11.4	1.5%	51.0
Annual Growth	10.6%	109.1%	—	2.4%

2015 Year-End Financials

Debt ratio: 39.7%
Return on equity: 9.6%
Cash ($ mil.): 189.6
Current ratio: 1.23
Long-term debt ($ mil.): 1,582.7

No. of shares (mil.): 124.6
Dividends
 Yield: 6.1%
 Payout: 97.0%
Market value ($ mil.): 2,696.0

	STOCK PRICE ($)		P/E		PER SHARE ($)		
	FY Close		High/Low	Earnings	Dividends		Book Value
12/15	21.63		21 13	1.68	1.32		17.51
12/14	33.53		32 23	1.06	1.04		17.89
12/13	24.32		27 20	0.95	0.86		17.35
12/12	19.37		51 44	0.38	0.70		16.80
12/11	16.83		153 98	0.12	0.38		17.08
Annual Growth	6.5%		—	93.4%	36.5%		0.6%

Roadrunner Transportation Systems Inc

Running your cargo down the road is Roadrunner Transportation Systems (RRTS) business. The company offers less-than-truckload (LTL) freight transportation which combines freight from multiple shippers into a single truckload. In addition it arranges the transportation of truckload freight as well as provides logistics services. RRTS caters to small and mid-size shippers and some large national accounts throughout the US via a network of service centers. Rather than owning trucks and trailers the company relies on a network of independent contractors and on purchased transportation capacity.

Geographic Reach

RRTS operates through nearly 45 LTL service centers and nearly 55 TL service centers across the US. It also has 25 dispatch offices.

Operations

RRTS operates through three chief segments: Less-than-Truckload Truckload and Logistics and Transportation Management Solutions. The less-than-truckload (LTL) business manages the pickup consolidation linehaul deconsolidation and delivery of LTL shipments throughout the US and into Mexico Puerto Rico and Canada.

Within the truckload and logistics (TL) business it arranges for the pickup delivery and inventory management of TL freight. Transportation management solutions offers access to the most cost-effective and time-sensitive modes of transportation within the company's broad network.

Sales and Marketing

In addition to its 130 independent brokerage agents RRTS sells its transportation and logistics services through over 260 sales personnel located throughout the US and Canada. It is focused on expanding its sales force to new geographic markets where it lacks a strong presence.

Financial Performance

With the sluggish economy in its rear-view window RRTS has been enjoying unprecedented growth over the years. From 2013 to 2014 its revenues surged 38% from $1.36 billion to peak at $1.87 billion its highest total in company history. RRTS also saw its profits surge 6% from $49 million to a record-setting $52 million from 2013 to 2014.

The historic growth for 2014 was attributed to a 52% spike in TL sales and a more than 100% rise in TMS sales. These increases were driven by organic growth and additional revenue generated from previous acquisitions.

In the last five years the company's operating cash flows have maintained a growth trend. Cash flow in 2014 increased 13% to nearly $41 million due to the rise in profits alongside cash inflows from accounts payable and changes in prepaid expenses.

Strategy

RRTS' recent growth has largely been attributed to strategic acquisitions. In 2014 RRTS acquired Rich Logistics a provider of truckload and expedited services based in Little Rock Arkansas. In addition RRTS obtained Everett Transportation and certain assets of Keith Everett. The total enterprise value of the transaction was about $48 million.

Throughout 2014 the company enhanced its TL segment further with the purchases of Active Aero Group (Michigan-based provider of supply-chain services focused on transportation logistics for customers with sensitive or time-critical freight) and ISI Logistics (Indiana-based logistics provider focused on the warehousing and transportation needs of the automotive industry).RRTS also in 2014 picked up Unitrans a California-based provider of international logistics services which offers its customers international ocean and air transportation management customs house brokerage and domestic services. The acquisition expanded the company's TMS segment.

Looking ahead RRTS intends to maintain its asset-free approach to the transportation business. Under this strategy the company uses contractors and buys capacity from other carriers when needed as opposed to owning its own fleet thereby more efficiently deploying resources to meet demand and generating better returns.

Company Background

RRTS took its current shape in 2005 when investors led by Thayer | Hidden Creek bought Dawes Transport and Roadrunner Freight Systems and combined them to form Roadrunner Dawes Freight Systems. The Roadrunner Transportation Systems name was adopted in mid-2008 as part of a comprehensive rebranding campaign.

EXECUTIVES

President COO and Director, Curtis W. (Curt) Stoelting, age 56
VP CFO Secretary and Treasurer, Peter R. Armbruster, age 57, $335,192 total compensation
CEO and Director, Mark A. DiBlasi, age 60, $543,885 total compensation
President Less-than-Truckload (LTL), Grant Crawford, age 45, $322,154 total compensation
President Truckload Logistics (TL), Patrick K. McKay, age 48, $286,692 total compensation
President Global Solutions, William R. Goodgion, age 50
CIO, Jason Descamps
Vice President Sales, Mark (Marky) Peterson
Vice President Sales Marketing, Scott (Scotty) Dobak
Vice President Operations, Tyler (Ty) Tattum
Vice President Sales, Chris (Chrissy) Hatcher
Vice President Human Resources, Paul (Pauly) Hoff
Vice President Of Pricing and Yield Management, Cliff (Clifford) Cordes
Chairman, Scott D. Rued
Auditors: Deloitte & Touche LLP

LOCATIONS

HQ: Roadrunner Transportation Systems Inc
4900 S. Pennsylvania Ave., Cudahy, WI 53110
Phone: 414 615-1500

PRODUCTS/OPERATIONS

2012 Sales

	$ mil.	% of total
Less-than-truckload (LTL)	511.0	47
Truckload (TL) & logistics	476.6	44
Transportation Management Solutions (TMS)	91.6	9
Adjustments	(5.8)	-
Total	**1,073.4**	**100**

COMPETITORS

ArcBest	Landstar System
C.H. Robinson	Menlo Worldwide
Worldwide	Saia
CRST International	Schneider Logistics
Central Freight Lines	Total Quality
Covenant	Logistics
Transportation	Transplace
Echo Global	UPS
Estes Express	YRC Worldwide
FedEx	

HISTORICAL FINANCIALS

Company Type: Public

Income Statement

FYE: December 31

	REVENUE ($ mil.)	NET INCOME ($ mil.)	NET PROFIT MARGIN	EMPLOYEES
12/15	1,995.0	48.0	2.4%	4,502.0
12/14	1,872.8	51.9	2.8%	4,045.0
12/13	1,361.4	49.0	3.6%	2,756.0
12/12	1,073.3	37.5	3.5%	2,395.0
12/11	843.6	25.8	3.1%	1,848.0
Annual Growth	24.0%	16.7%	—	24.9%

2015 Year-End Financials

Debt ratio: 33.1%	No. of shares (mil.): 38.2
Return on equity: 8.1%	Dividends
Cash ($ mil.): 8.6	Yield: —
Current ratio: 2.07	Payout: —
Long-term debt ($ mil.): 424.4	Market value ($ mil.): 361.0

	STOCK PRICE ($)		P/E		PER SHARE ($)		
	FY Close		High/Low	Earnings	Dividends		Book Value
12/15	9.43		22 7	1.23	0.00		16.03
12/14	23.35		22 15	1.32	0.00		14.73
12/13	26.95		23 13	1.29	0.00		13.32
12/12	18.14		16 12	1.16	0.00		11.41
12/11	14.13		20 15	0.82	0.00		9.64
Annual Growth	(9.6%)		— —	10.7%	—		13.6%

Rowan Companies Plc

Auditors: Deloitte & Touche LLP

LOCATIONS

HQ: Rowan Companies Plc
2800 Post Oak Boulevard, Suite 5450, Houston, TX 77056-6189
Phone: 713 621-7800   **Fax:** 713 960-7660
Web: www.rowancompanies.com

HISTORICAL FINANCIALS

Company Type: Public

Income Statement

FYE: December 31

	REVENUE ($ mil.)	NET INCOME ($ mil.)	NET PROFIT MARGIN	EMPLOYEES
12/15	2,137.0	93.3	4.4%	3,496.0
12/14	1,824.3	(114.8)	—	4,051.0
12/13	1,579.2	252.5	16.0%	3,499.0
12/12	1,392.6	180.6	13.0%	3,119.0
12/11	939.2	736.8	78.5%	2,719.0
Annual Growth	22.8%	(40.3%)	—	6.5%

2015 Year-End Financials

Debt ratio: 32.2%
Return on equity: 1.9%
Cash ($ mil.): 484.2
Current ratio: 2.80
Long-term debt ($ mil.): 2,692.4

No. of shares (mil.): 124.8
Dividends
Yield: 2.3%
Payout: 53.3%
Market value ($ mil.): 2,116.0

	STOCK PRICE ($) FY Close	P/E High/Low		PER SHARE ($) Earnings	Dividends	Book Value
12/15	16.95	33	20	0.75	0.40	38.24
12/14	23.32	—	—	(0.93)	0.30	37.65
12/13	35.36	19	15	2.03	0.00	39.39
12/12	31.27	26	20	1.46	0.00	36.48
12/11	30.33	8	5	5.83	0.00	35.01
Annual Growth	(13.5%)	—	—	(40.1%)	—	2.2%

RPX Corp

In our litigious society RPX Corporation helps keep technology companies out of the courtroom. RPX owns a portfolio of more than 2500 intellectual property patents that it licenses to customers in order to prevent patent infringement lawsuits. (So one company can't sue another over a patent since it's RPX that owns the patent). Its patent portfolio spans six industries —consumer electronics software media content mobile communications and devices networking and semiconductors. RPX counts more than 250 clients including Cisco Google Sharp Sony and Verizon and earns one-third of its revenues from Asian firms. Founded in 2008 RPX launched an IPO in 2011.

EXECUTIVES

CEO Inventus LLC, Trevor Campion, age 49
EVP and Head of Corporate Development, Mallun Yen, age 45, $350,000 total compensation
General Counsel and Interim CEO, Martin E. (Marty) Roberts, age 55, $360,000 total compensation
SVP Finance CFO and Treasurer, Robert H. Heath, age 56, $350,000 total compensation
SVP Client Development and Client Relations, Steven S. (Steve) Swank, age 46, $285,000 total compensation
Senior Vice President, Henri Linde
Auditors: PricewaterhouseCoopers LLP

LOCATIONS

HQ: RPX Corp
One Market Plaza, Suite 800, San Francisco, CA 94105
Phone: 866 779-7641
Web: www.rpxcorp.com

PRODUCTS/OPERATIONS

Services

Services Defensive Patent Acquisitions
Market Intelligence and Advisory Services
Structured Acquisitions
Litigation Insurance
Sell Your Patent
RPX R&D

COMPETITORS

Acacia Research	Jones Day
Alston & Bird	Kirkland & Ellis
Baker & McKenzie	Walker Digital
Convex Group	White & Case
Duane Morris	

HISTORICAL FINANCIALS

Company Type: Public

Income Statement

FYE: December 31

	REVENUE ($ mil.)	NET INCOME ($ mil.)	NET PROFIT MARGIN	EMPLOYEES
12/15	291.8	39.4	13.5%	161.0
12/14	259.3	39.3	15.2%	152.0
12/13	237.5	40.7	17.2%	137.0
12/12	197.6	38.9	19.7%	125.0
12/11	154.0	29.1	18.9%	110.0
Annual Growth	17.3%	7.9%	—	10.0%

2015 Year-End Financials

Debt ratio: —
Return on equity: 7.8%
Cash ($ mil.): 94.9
Current ratio: 2.73
Long-term debt ($ mil.): —

No. of shares (mil.): 53.4
Dividends
Yield: —
Payout: —
Market value ($ mil.): 588.0

	STOCK PRICE ($) FY Close	P/E High/Low		PER SHARE ($) Earnings	Dividends	Book Value
12/15	11.00	24	15	0.71	0.00	9.66
12/14	13.78	24	18	0.72	0.00	8.97
12/13	16.90	24	12	0.76	0.00	8.06
12/12	9.04	24	11	0.74	0.00	7.05
12/11	12.65	51	20	0.57	0.00	6.09
Annual Growth	(3.4%)	—	—	5.6%	—	12.2%

RTI Surgical, Inc.

When it comes to surgical implants RTI Surgical (formerly RTI Biologics) recommends the natural alternative. The firm develops products made from human and animal tissue that are used in orthopedic dental and other surgeries to repair fractures spinal disorders sports injuries breast reconstruction and other procedures. Using its BioCleanse Cancelle SP and Tutoplast processes the company sterilizes tissue —including bone tendons and skin —that is then used in surgeries. RTI Surgical sells its allografts (made from human tissue) and xenografts (made from animals) in the US and more than 50 countries around the globe. Its direct sales force targets the sports medicine and general orthopedic markets.

Change in Company Name
In July 2013 following its purchase of Pioneer Surgical Technology RTI Biologics changed its name to RTI Surgical.

Operations
RTI Surgical's fastest-growing segment comes from products for sports medicine procedures which accounts for about 25% of sales. As customer demand for such products increase a good portion of RTI's research and product development capabilities are focused on expanding its offerings for sports medicine applications. The bone graft substitutes (BGS) and general orthopedic segment and the surgical specialties (breast hernia urology and ophthalmology) segments are also growing. However its revenues in its spine and dental divisions have fluctuated in recent years primarily due to lower sales levels by its key distributors in those segments.

Geographic Reach
RTI is headquartered in Florida where it also has two tissue processing facilities. It also processes tissue at a plant in Germany and has metal and synthetic implant manufacturing facilities in Michigan and North Carolina.

The US accounts for about 90% of the company's revenue but it does offer its products and services in nearly 50 nations.

Sales and Marketing
In addition to its direct sales efforts RTI has also forged a distribution network of agreements with other companies each targeting a specific product market. Its agreements include deals with Medtronic and Stryker to handle spine implants and with Zimmer to handle spine and dental implants. It uses its own representatives and independent distributors for its sports medicine and wound-repair products. International distribution is also handled by independent distributors.

Financial Performance
RTI has seen slow but steady revenue growth in the last five years. It increased by 11% in 2013 from $178 million to $198 million as unit volume and revenue per unit rose in its spine segment after an acquisition. Net income has been fluctuating for several years and 2013 delivered an $18 million loss down $20 million from the previous year. The drop was due to a restructuring charge and acquisition-related expenses. After declaring $20 million in cash from operations in 2012 RTI used $4 million in cash for operations in 2013 due deferred income tax and accrued expenses.

Strategy
One of the challenges RTI faces is that it competes with not-for-profit allograft-processing firms for the limited supply of human tissue. In addition the biologic implant industry must comply with strict regulations and the company is dependent upon third parties to secure human tissue ethically. Finally other companies are busily working to develop synthetic tissues that may eventually eliminate the need for some of RTI's products. It deals with these challenges by pushing to ever expand its product portfolio. In 2014 it launched new bone wedges and instruments as well as a system to treat spinal stenosis tumors and disc degeneration. In addition to launching new products RTI occasionally makes acquisitions to increase its product line like the 2013 purchase of a spinal and orthopedic implant and instrument maker.

Mergers and Acquisitions
As part of its ongoing efforts to expand its product portfolio RTI in 2013 purchased spinal implant and instrument maker Pioneer Surgical Technology for $126 million. The buy also brought Pioneer's distribution network under the RTI umbrella and caused the company to change its name from RTI Biologics to RTI Surgical.

EXECUTIVES

Vice President RTI Donor Services, Beverly (Bev) Bliss
EVP and Chief Scientific Officer, Caroline A. Hartill, age 59, $348,148 total compensation
EVP RTI Surgical and President RTI Donor Service, Roger W. Rose, age 56, $338,394 total compensation
Medical Director, Lennox K. (Lenny) Archibald
Interim CEO, Robert P. (Rob) Jordheim, age 52, $350,215 total compensation
VP and General Manager North American Spine, Kevin D. Brandt
VP and General Manager International, Keith Pelatowski
VP and General Manager Tissue-Based Implants, Rick Robbins
VP US Operations, John N. Varela, age 49, $310,154 total compensation
Interim CFO, Wy Louw
Vice President Sales, Rod Allen
Vice President Customer Relations and .compliance, Christie (Chris) Blakely
Vice President Surgical Specialties, Michael J (Mel) LaPrade
Executive Vice President Administration, Tom (Tommy) Rose
Vice Chairman, Peter F. Gearen, age 68
Chairman, Curtis M. (Curt) Selquist, age 71
Auditors: Deloitte & Touche LLP

LOCATIONS

HQ: RTI Surgical, Inc.
11621 Research Circle, Alachua, FL 32615
Phone: 386 418-8888
Web: www.rtix.com

PRODUCTS/OPERATIONS

2015 Sales

	$ mil.	% of total
Tissue distribution		
Spine	77.0	27
Ortho fixation	55.6	20
Sports medicine	46.7	17
Bone graft substitutes & general orthopedic	42.3	15
Dental	23.6	8
Surgical specialties	23.5	8
Other revenues	13.6	5
Total	**282.3**	**100**

COMPETITORS

ApaTech	Johnson & Johnson
BioMimetic	LifeCell
Biocoral	Medtronic
Cook Incorporated	ReGen Biologics
CryoLife	Synovis Life
Integra LifeSciences	Technologies
Interpore	

HISTORICAL FINANCIALS

Company Type: Public

Income Statement

FYE: December 31

	REVENUE ($ mil.)	NET INCOME ($ mil.)	NET PROFIT MARGIN	EMPLOYEES
12/15	282.2	14.9	5.3%	1,169.0
12/14	262.8	2.7	1.0%	1,102.0
12/13	197.9	(17.8)	—	1,100.0
12/12	178.1	8.4	4.7%	756.0
12/11	169.3	8.3	4.9%	706.0
Annual Growth	**13.6%**	**15.5%**	**—**	**13.4%**

2015 Year-End Financials

Debt ratio: 20.9%
Return on equity: 6.5%
Cash ($ mil.): 12.6
Current ratio: 3.20
Long-term debt ($ mil.): 73.6

No. of shares (mil.): 57.8
Dividends
 Yield: —
 Payout: —
Market value ($ mil.): 229.0

	STOCK PRICE ($) FY Close	P/E High/Low	PER SHARE ($) Earnings	Dividends	Book Value
12/15	3.97	36 18	0.20	0.00	4.11
12/14	5.20	— —	(0.01)	0.00	3.89
12/13	3.54	— —	(0.34)	0.00	3.87
12/12	4.27	31 23	0.15	0.00	3.29
12/11	4.44	31 16	0.15	0.00	3.11
Annual Growth	**(2.8%)**	**— —**	**7.5%**	**—**	**7.2%**

Sabra Health Care REIT Inc

Sabra Health Care REIT doesn't mind a little healthy competition in the real estate sector. The company invests in income-producing health care facilities in the US. The REIT's investment portfolio includes about 180 properties most of which are skilled nursing/post-acute centers. It also invests in assisted living and independent living facilities and hospitals. Sabra's facilities house more than 18300 beds and are located in 35-plus states. Substantially all of the properties are leased to and operated by subsidiaries of Sun Healthcare Group which spun off its real estate assets to form Sabra Health Care REIT in 2010.

OperationsSabra owned 180 real estate properties that were leased to operates and tenants under triple-net lease agreements during 2015 with nearly 60% of them being skilled nursing/transitional care facilities and most of the rest being senior housing facilities. Geographic Reach

The REIT has licensed beds in 37 US states with its three largest markets being New Hampshire Texas and Connecticut.

Financial Performance

Sabra's annual revenues have almost tripled since 2011 as it has expanded its property portfolio through acquisitions and has charged higher rental rates as the real estate market has strengthened. Meanwhile it annual profits have risen more than five-fold as it's been able to keep a lid on its overhead costs.The REIT's revenue jumped 30% to $238.86 million during 2015 mostly thanks to added rental income from newly acquired properties (acquired after January 1 2014). Strong revenue growth in 2015 drove Sabra's net income up 69% to $79.41 million for the year. The REIT's operating cash levels climbed 42% to $121.1 million mostly as its cash earnings rose during the year.

Strategy

Sabra aims to profit from the aging of the US population and increasing life expectancy both of which are driving demand for long-term care services. The REIT is focused on growing its geographically diverse portfolio primarily through the purchase of senior housing and memory care facilities with a secondary emphasis on acquiring skilled nursing homes. In mid-2015 for example Sabra Health Care REIT agreed to buy four Maryland-based skilled nursing facilities —which specialized

in transitional care and medically complex post-surgical ventilator and dialysis patients —consisting of 678 beds for $234 million.

Ownership

The Vanguard Group owns about 12% of the company's shares.

EXECUTIVES

Chairman and CEO, Richard K. Matros, age 62, $725,000 total compensation
Chief Investment Officer, Talya Nevo-Hacohen, $350,000 total compensation
EVP and CFO, Harold W. Andrews, age 52, $350,000 total compensation
Chief Technology Officer, Galen Warren
Chief Operating Officer, Nick Cafferillo
Acquisition Vice President, Tri Tran
Auditors: PricewaterhouseCoopers LLP

LOCATIONS

HQ: Sabra Health Care REIT Inc
18500 Von Karman Avenue, Suite 550, Irvine, CA 92612
Phone: 888 393-8248
Web: www.sabrahealth.com

PRODUCTS/OPERATIONS

2015 Sales

	$ mil.	% of total
Rental income	209.9	88
Interest and other income	25.5	11
Resident fees and services	3.5	1
Total	**238.9**	**100**

COMPETITORS

Extendicare	Omega Healthcare
HCP	Investors
Healthcare Realty	Senior Housing
Trust	Properties
LTC Properties	Ventas
National Health	Welltower
Investors	

HISTORICAL FINANCIALS

Company Type: Public

Income Statement

FYE: December 31

	REVENUE ($ mil.)	NET INCOME ($ mil.)	NET PROFIT MARGIN	EMPLOYEES
12/15	238.8	79.4	33.2%	13.0
12/14	183.5	46.9	25.6%	11.0
12/13	134.7	33.7	25.0%	9.0
12/12	103.1	19.5	18.9%	8.0
12/11	84.2	12.8	15.2%	7.0
Annual Growth	**29.8%**	**57.7%**	**—**	**16.7%**

2015 Year-End Financials

Debt ratio: 56.2%
Return on equity: 7.9%
Cash ($ mil.): 7.4
Current ratio: 0.49
Long-term debt ($ mil.): 1,397.1

No. of shares (mil.): 65.1
Dividends
 Yield: 7.9%
 Payout: 139.1%
Market value ($ mil.): 1,319.0

	STOCK PRICE ($) FY Close	P/E High/Low	PER SHARE ($) Earnings	Dividends	Book Value
12/15	20.23	31 17	1.11	1.60	16.17
12/14	30.37	39 31	0.78	1.51	15.95
12/13	26.14	46 31	0.68	1.36	11.86
12/12	21.72	42 23	0.52	1.32	8.23
12/11	12.09	45 20	0.43	0.96	8.85
Annual Growth	**13.7%**	**— —**	**26.8%**	**13.6%**	**16.2%**

Salisbury Bancorp, Inc.

Salisbury Bancorp has a stake in New England's financial market. The holding company owns the Salisbury Bank and Trust Company which operates seven branches in northwestern Connecticut southwestern Massachusetts and southeastern New York. With roots dating to 1848 the bank offers a variety of financial products and services including checking savings and money market accounts CDs credit cards and trust services. Residential real estate mortgages make up the largest portion of the bank's loan portfolio by far; commercial real estate construction land development business financial agricultural and consumer loans round out its lending activities.

EXECUTIVES

Vice President, Jeff (Jeffy) Burchell
Auditors: Baker Newman & Noyes, P.A., LLC

LOCATIONS

HQ: Salisbury Bancorp, Inc.
5 Bissell Street, Lakeville, CT 06039
Phone: 860 435-9801
Web: www.salisburybank.com

COMPETITORS

Berkshire Hills	M&T Bank
Bancorp	TD Bank USA
KeyCorp	Webster Financial

HISTORICAL FINANCIALS

Company Type: Public

Income Statement

FYE: December 31

	ASSETS ($ mil.)	NET INCOME ($ mil.)	INCOME AS % OF ASSETS	EMPLOYEES
12/15	891.1	8.4	0.9%	188.0
12/14	855.4	2.5	0.3%	182.0
12/13	587.1	4.0	0.7%	147.0
12/12	600.8	4.0	0.7%	147.0
12/11	609.2	4.1	0.7%	137.0
Annual Growth	10.0%	19.8%	—	8.2%

2015 Year-End Financials

Return on assets: 0.9%
Return on equity: 8.7%
Long-term debt ($ mil.): —
No. of shares (mil.): 2.7
Sales ($ mil) 41.8

Dividends
Yield: 3.3%
Payout: 48.4%
Market value ($ mil.): 92.0

	STOCK PRICE ($) FY Close	P/E High/Low		PER SHARE ($) Earnings	Dividends	Book Value
12/15	33.48	11	9	3.02	1.12	33.13
12/14	27.34	23	20	1.32	1.12	37.42
12/13	26.89	13	10	2.30	1.12	42.56
12/12	23.34	12	10	2.28	1.12	42.61
12/11	23.35	13	10	2.12	1.12	39.59
Annual Growth	9.4%	—	—	9.2%	(0.0%)	(4.4%)

SandRidge Permian Trust

Auditors: PricewaterhouseCoopers LLP

LOCATIONS

HQ: SandRidge Permian Trust
919 Congress Avenue, Suite 500, Austin, TX 78701
Phone: 512 236-6555   **Fax:** 302 655-5049
Web: www.sandridgeenergy.com

HISTORICAL FINANCIALS

Company Type: Public

Income Statement

FYE: December 31

	REVENUE ($ mil.)	NET INCOME ($ mil.)	NET PROFIT MARGIN	EMPLOYEES
12/15	87.7	80.9	92.3%	0.0
12/14	133.4	123.0	92.2%	0.0
12/13	131.1	120.6	92.0%	0.0
12/12	133.3	122.3	91.8%	0.0
12/11	42.6	38.6	90.6%	0.0
Annual Growth	19.8%	20.3%	—	—

2015 Year-End Financials

Debt ratio: —
Return on equity: 29.0%
Cash ($ mil.): 3.6
Current ratio: —
Long-term debt ($ mil.): —

No. of shares (mil.): 52.5
Dividends
Yield: 66.3%
Payout: 85.2%
Market value ($ mil.): 156.0

	STOCK PRICE ($) FY Close	P/E High/Low		PER SHARE ($) Earnings	Dividends	Book Value
12/15	2.97	5	1	1.90	1.97	(0.00)
12/14	6.27	5	2	2.55	2.54	(0.00)
12/13	11.85	8	5	2.34	2.35	(0.00)
12/12	17.02	11	7	2.33	2.33	(0.00)
12/11	22.75	31	22	0.74	0.72	(0.00)
Annual Growth	(39.9%)	—	—	26.8%	28.5%	—

Seacoast Banking Corp. of Florida

Seacoast Banking Corporation is the holding company for Seacoast National Bank which has about 35 branches in Florida with a concentration on the state's southeastern coast. Serving individuals and areas businesses the bank offers a range of financial products and services including deposit accounts credit cards trust services and private banking. Commercial and residential real estate loans account for most of the bank's lending activities; to a lesser extent it also originates business and consumer loans. The bank also provides financial planning services as well as mutual funds and other investments.

Operations
A division of the bank Seacoast Marine Finance specializes in boat loans of $200000 and greater which it typically sells into the secondary market. It has an office in Florida and two in California.

Geographic Reach
Seacoast National Bank has 34 branches in 12 counties across Florida stretching from Broward County north through the Treasure Coast and into Orlando and west to Okeechobee and surrounding counties.

Financial Performance
Seacoast Banking has been a victim of the economic turmoil and a weak housing market in Florida posting declining revenues since 2008. In 2013 sales fell 6% to $95.5 million. However the bank recorded $51.9 million in profits due to a one-time income tax benefit. The downward trend in its profits have been fueled by significant losses on loan provisions and compounded by a lack of revenue growth. The bank has in recent years been consolidating and closing branches to cut its operating costs.

Strategy
During 2013 Seacoast National Bank significantly expanded its banking technology platform by introducing digital deposit capture on smartphones new mobile platforms for consumer and business customers a rebranding of its website and enhancing its ATM capabilities. About 40% of its online customers also use the mobile application.

Mergers and Acquisitions
In 2014 the bank announced plans for its first acquisition in years. Seacoast National agreed to buy The BANKshares Inc. a Winter Park Florida-based bank that operates 12 branches under the BankFIRST name. The BankFIRST branches will be rebranded as Seacoast National creating the sixth-largest Florida bank by total assets. Previous acquisitions were completed in 2002 and 2006.

EXECUTIVES

Chairman and CEO, Dennis S. (Denny) Hudson, age 60, $537,852 total compensation
EVP and Residential Lending Executive, Michael J. (Mike) Sonego
EVP and Commercial Banking Executive, Charles K. Cross, age 58, $273,333 total compensation
EVP and Chief Risk and Credit Officer, David D. Houdeshell, age 55, $262,500 total compensation
EVP and CFO, Stephen A. Fowle, age 50, $243,903 total compensation
EVP Enterprise Services and Initiatives, Kathleen (Kathy) Cavicchioli
EVP and Chief Marketing Officer, Jeffery (Jeff) Lee
EVP Service and Operations, Jeffery (Jeff) Bray
EVP and Chief Human Resources Officer, Daniel G. (Dan) Chappell
CFO and Head of Strategy Seacoast Banking Corporation of Florida and Seacoast National Bank, Charles M. (Chuck) Shaffer, age 42, $248,333 total compensation
Vice President And General Auditor, David Kelso
Vice President Cre, Debra (Deb) Mairs
Assistant Vice President Relationship Manager, Frances (Fran) Portalatin
Vice President Commercial Banking Lending, John (Jack) Schnell
Assistant Vice President Branch Marketing and Events, Jennifer (Jen) Powers
Auditors: Crowe Horwath LLP

LOCATIONS

HQ: Seacoast Banking Corp. of Florida
815 Colorado Avenue, Stuart, FL 34994
Phone: 772 287-4000
Web: www.seacoastbanking.com

PRODUCTS/OPERATIONS

2015 Revenue

	% of total
Interest Income	
Interest and fees on loans	63
Interest on securities and others	15
Non-interest Income	22
Total	**100**

Selected Services

Commercial and retail banking
Mortgage services
Wealth management

COMPETITORS

Atlantic Coast Financial	CenterState Banks
BB&T	EverBank Financial
BBX Capital	PNC Financial
Bank of America	Regions Financial
BankUnited	SunTrust
	Wells Fargo

HISTORICAL FINANCIALS
Company Type: Public

Income Statement
FYE: December 31

	ASSETS ($ mil.)	NET INCOME ($ mil.)	INCOME AS % OF ASSETS	EMPLOYEES
12/15	3,534.7	22.1	0.6%	665.0
12/14	3,093.3	5.7	0.2%	579.0
12/13	2,268.9	51.9	2.3%	519.0
12/12	2,173.9	(0.7)	—	508.0
12/11	2,137.3	6.6	0.3%	420.0
Annual Growth	**13.4%**	**35.0%**	**—**	**12.2%**

2015 Year-End Financials

Return on assets: 0.6%
Return on equity: 6.6%
Long-term debt ($ mil.): —
No. of shares (mil.): 34.3
Sales ($ mil): 149.0
Dividends
Yield: 0.0%
Payout: —
Market value ($ mil.): 515.0

	STOCK PRICE ($) FY Close	P/E High/Low		PER SHARE ($) Earnings	Dividends	Book Value
12/15	14.98	25	18	0.66	0.00	10.29
12/14	13.75	68	48	0.21	0.00	9.44
12/13	12.20	5	1	2.44	0.00	8.40
12/12	1.61	—	—	(0.25)	0.00	8.73
12/11	1.52	12	8	0.15	0.00	8.98
Annual Growth	**77.2%**		**—**	**44.8%**	**—**	**3.5%**

Security National Financial Corp.

There are three certainties –life death and mortgage payments —and Security National Financial has you covered on all fronts. Its largest unit SecurityNational Mortgage makes residential and commercial mortgage loans through some 70 offices in more than a dozen states. Its Security National Life Memorial Insurance Company and Southern Security Life subsidiaries sell life and diving or related sports accident insurance annuities and funeral plans in about 40 states. Security

National Financial also owns about 15 mortuaries and cemeteries in Utah Arizona and California. The family of chairman and CEO George Quist controls more than half of Security National Financial.

While seemingly unrelated each of Security National Financial's business segments drive profitability for the other. Through its cemetery and mortuary operations for example the company generates leads for its insurance and pre-need cemetery and funeral products. (Most of the funeral plans are sold in the Southeast and Southwest in states including Florida Texas and Utah.) Additionally the company's insurance subsidiaries invest some of their assets in mortgage loans.

Security National's largest segment is its mortgage lending business which accounts for around half of the group's revenues. The company sells its loans to other investors for a fee; it doesn't service the loans.

However SecurityNational Mortgage has seen its sales fall in the economic downturn which has slowed down lending due to lower demand. (Mortgage originations and sales went down by nearly half in the years between 2008 and 2010.) Overall revenues fell 5% to $159.6 million in 2011 but the company was returned to profitability that year: After losing $431000 in 2010 Security National netted $1.3 million in 2011. Security National also saw a decrease in cemetary and mortuary sales (the company sold two funeral homes that year) but insurance premiums rose in 2011. The rise in insurance premiums was due largely to an arrangement to provide reinsurance for North American Life that year. Net investment income also rose for Security National.

As refinancing activities pick up the company expects its loan business to rebound. In the meantime Security National has cut costs to help wait out the downturn.

EXECUTIVES

Vice President Controller, Diana (Ana) Olson
Vice President Director Information Systems, George (Georgey) Fukumitsu
Vice President Finance, Garrett (Bret) Sill
Auditors: Eide Bailly LLP

LOCATIONS

HQ: Security National Financial Corp.
5300 South 360 West, Suite 250, Salt Lake City, UT 84123
Phone: 801 264-1060   **Fax:** 801 265-9882
Web: www.securitynational.com

PRODUCTS/OPERATIONS

Selected Subsidiaries

California Memorial Estates Inc.
Cottonwood Mortuary Inc.
Crystal Rose Funeral Home Inc.
Deseret Memorial Inc.
Greer-Wilson Funeral Home Inc.
Holladay Memorial Park Inc.
Insuradyne Corporation
Memorial Estates Inc.
Memorial Insurance Company of America
Memorial Mortuary
Paradise Chapel Funeral Home Inc.
Security National Capital Inc.
Security National Life Insurance Company

COMPETITORS

AIG	New York Life
Allstate	Prudential
Carriage Services Inc.	Service Corporation

JPMorgan Chase	International
Kemper Corp	State Farm
MetLife	Zions Bancorporation

HISTORICAL FINANCIALS
Company Type: Public

Income Statement
FYE: December 31

	ASSETS ($ mil.)	NET INCOME ($ mil.)	INCOME AS % OF ASSETS	EMPLOYEES
12/15	749.9	12.6	1.7%	1,587.0
12/14	671.0	7.7	1.2%	1,480.0
12/13	618.7	7.5	1.2%	1,287.0
12/12	597.2	16.7	2.8%	1,232.0
12/11	521.1	1.3	0.2%	940.0
Annual Growth	**9.5%**	**76.6%**	**—**	**14.0%**

2015 Year-End Financials

Return on assets: 1.7%
Return on equity: 12.1%
Long-term debt ($ mil.): —
No. of shares (mil.): 15.3
Sales ($ mil): 283.1
Dividends
Yield: —
Payout: 37.2%
Market value ($ mil.): 100.0

	STOCK PRICE ($) FY Close	P/E High/Low		PER SHARE ($) Earnings	Dividends	Book Value
12/15	6.55	9	6	0.85	0.00	7.27
12/14	5.76	11	7	0.54	0.00	6.84
12/13	4.82	26	8	0.53	0.00	3.16
12/12	8.78	8	1	1.29	0.00	3.17
12/11	1.63	19	10	0.11	0.00	2.58
Annual Growth	**41.6%**		**—**	**66.7%**	**—**	**29.5%**

SEI Investments Co

SEI Investments provides outsourced investment and fund processing for about 7000 private banks trust companies investment advisors and managers and institutional investors. Services include securities and trust processing and accounting portfolio analysis treasury and cash management and performance measurement reporting. Its fund processing segment serves managers and distributors of mutual funds hedge funds and alternative investments. The company administers more than $625 billion in mutual fund separate account and pooled assets. It also provides customized investment programs and manages some $53 billion for retirement plans not-for-profits and affluent individuals and families.

Operations

The investment services provider operates five business segments the largest of which is Private Banks representing 35% of the firm's total revenue. SEI's Private Banks business provides investment processing and investment management programs to banks and trusts independent wealth advisers and financial advisers worldwide. Three other businesses —Investment Advisors Institutional Investors and Investment Managers —each contribute roughly 20% of annual revenue. The firm's tiny Investments in New Businesses unit (1% of revenue) provides investment management services to ultra-high-net-worth families in the US and works on developing Internet-based investment services and advice products.

SEI affiliate LSV Asset Management (LSV) manages more than $80 billion in assets.

Geographic Reach

Pennsylvania-based SEI Investments operates primarily in the US but also has offices in Canada Hong Kong Ireland the Netherlands South Africa the United Arab Emirates and the UK. The US is the source of nearly 85% of the firm's revenue.Sales and MarketingSEI serves some 7000 clients including banks trust institutions wealth management organizations independent investment advisors retirement plan sponsors not-for-profit organizations investment and hedge fund managers and high-net-worth families.

Financial Performance

SEI Investments has enjoyed rising revenue and profit in recent years thanks to healthy growth in its assets under management from a rising stock market and organic business growth.Revenue rose for a fourth straight year jumping by 12% to $1.27 billion in 2014 thanks to higher asset management administration and distribution fees (up 15% versus 2012) from positive cash flows from new and existing clients across the board (particularly in the Institutional Investors segment) as well as market appreciation. SEI's average assets under management (excluding LSV) grew by 13% to $164.9 billion during 2014 while its average assets under administration increased by 18% to $354.3 billion. Information processing and software servicing fees also rose 9% during the year mostly thanks to higher fees generated from its Wealth Platform and mutual fund trading services. Geographically international revenue grew by 24% in 2014 while US operations increased revenue by 10%.Higher revenue drove net income higher by 10% to $318.71 million marking the company's third consecutive year of profit growth. Cash from operations grew by 7% to $374.8 million primarily thanks to higher cash earnings.

Strategy

SEI has been focused on growing its institutional customer base for its global outsourcing business in recent years. In 2014 the firm's global institutional outsourcing business added $7.9 billion in new assets during the year which contributed to a record $24 billion asset high over the prior three years. Some of SEI's new U.S. institutional clients that year included Major League Baseball Media General Northern California Plasterers Industry Trust Funds three Michigan-based employee retirement systems West Chester University Foundation and Edward-Elmhurst Healthcare System. In 2013 it extended its business with Edgewood Management LLC to provide investment operations outsourcing services for all of Edgewood's investment products which included institutional private client and retail separate accounts.SEI's growth strategy has also included investing in technology. The firm devoted significant resources to research and development in 2013 including expenditures for new tech platforms enhancements to existing platforms and new investment in products and services. Indeed SEI spent about $98.1 million on R&D in 2013 up from $79.6 million in 2012.

Additionally the company has made strategic divestitures to help free up resources. In 2013 for example SEI sold its entire interest in SEI Asset Korea for a gain of $22.1 million.

Mergers and Acquisitions

In February 2012 SEI acquired the technology firm NorthStar Systems International Inc. in a move designed to quickly expand its front-office capabilities across its Global Wealth Platofrm. NorthStar's technology enables SEI to deliver more sophisticated levels of front-office automation and functionality to its wealth management clients in areas such as client acquisition and client management.

HISTORY

While attending the Wharton School Alfred West founded Simulated Environments Incorporated in 1968 to train bank officers through computer simulations. But West's computer skills were more valuable in automating accounting than in training bankers and the company switched to trust systems programming. It reincorporated as SEI in 1972 and went public in 1981.

SEI began branching out in the early 1980s launching a money market mutual fund (1982) and acquiring consumer finance and similar software companies. Like many of its client banks the company found itself overextended and bloated at the end of the decade. In response SEI restructured cut costs and sold its consumer finance software company.

The company started expanding its asset management services outside the US in 1995. It changed its name to SEI Investments in 1997 and sold pension consulting firm Capital Resources. Profits were squeezed that year by the popularity of competing mutual funds and by the consolidation of the banking industry. In 1998 SEI won a government contract to provide trust accounting services for a controversial program that administers some 350000 American Indian trusts. It also bought an asset management firm in Mexico.

In 1999 SEI created fund templates that can be used for firms providing online investment services. It also formed a joint venture with an asset management firm in South Korea. The next year the firm launched its private investment portfolio service in the UK.

EXECUTIVES

CFO, Dennis J. McGonigle, age 56, $400,000 total compensation

EVP Institutional Investor, Edward D. (Ed) Loughlin, age 66, $425,000 total compensation

Chairman and CEO, Alfred P. West, age 74, $500,000 total compensation

EVP SEI Advisor Network, Wayne M. Withrow, age 60, $200,000 total compensation

EVP and General Counsel, N. Jeffrey (Jeff) Klauder, age 64, $259,615 total compensation

EVP, Robert F. (Bob) Crudup, age 68, $250,000 total compensation

EVP; Managing Director SEI Investments (Europe) Limited, Joseph P. (Joe) Ujobai, age 55, $300,000 total compensation

EVP; Head of Investment Manager Services, Stephen G. (Steve) Meyer, age 52, $425,000 total compensation

VP and Managing Director Knowledge Partnership Investment Management Services, Ross Ellis

EVP Investment Management Unit, Kevin P. Barr, age 50, $400,000 total compensation

SVP and Managing Director Investment Manager Services, Phil Masterson

SVP TRUST 3000, Sandy Ewing

Managing Director Manager Research Team Investment Management Unit, Stephen Beinhacker

SVP and Managing Director Investment Manager Services, Jim Cass

Managing Director SEI Private Wealth Management, Michael S. Farrell

VP and Managing Director Institutional Group, Paul F. Klauder

Managing Director Portfolio Management Team Investment Management Unit, William T. (Bill) Lawrence

Managing Director and Head of New Services and Strategic Partnerships SEI Advisor Network, Raef Lee

VP and Managing Director Solutions Team Institutional Group, Kevin Matthews

Managing Director Middle Office Services Investment Manager Services, Holly H. Miller

Managing Director Advisory Team Institutional Group, Al Pierce

Managing Director and Head of Fixed Income Portfolio Management Investment Management Unit, Sean P. Simko

Managing Director Portfolio Strategies Group Investment Management Unit, James F. (Jim) Smigiel

Managing Director and Portfolio Manager Investment Management Unit, James Solloway

Head of Solutions Strategy and Development Investment Manager Services, Jim Warren

Vice President Marketing, Frank Pizzuta

Senior Vice President, Erin M Hueber

Vice President, Greg Gettinger

Senior Vice President, Kevin Hilsmier

Vice President And Assistant Secretary, Richard (Dick) Deak

Vice President Operations, Rob Redican

Senior Vice President Private Banks, Jim Morris

Vice President Of Human Resources, Richard Frederick

Vice President, Alex Hokanson

Senior Vice President, Gina Romano

Executive Vice President; Head of Investment Manager Services, Steve (Stevie) Meyer

Executive Vice President Director, Carmen Romeo

Senior Vice President Sales and Operations, Scott (Scotty) Morgan

Executive Vice President Chief Informati, Bob (Bo) Crudup

Board Member, Mallory Hartman

Auditors: KPMG LLP

LOCATIONS

HQ: SEI Investments Co
1 Freedom Valley Drive, Oaks, PA 19456-1100
Phone: 610 676-1000
Web: www.seic.com

PRODUCTS/OPERATIONS

2014 Sales

	$ mil.	% of total
Asset management administration & distribution fees	948.9	75
Information processing & software servicing fees	285.5	23
Transaction-based & trade execution fees	31.6	2
Total	**1,266.0**	**100**

2014 Sales By Segment

	$ mil.	% of total
Private Banks	441.5	35
Institutional Investors	283.8	22
Investment Advisors	284.7	22
Investment Managers	251.3	20
Investments in New Businesses	4.7	1
Total	**1,266.0**	**100**

Selected Subsidiaries

LSV Asset Management (42%)
SEI Advanced Capital Management Inc.
SEI Asset Korea Co. Ltd. (South Korea)
SEI Custodial Operations Company LLC
SEI European Services Limited (UK)
SEI Franchise Inc.
SEI Funds Inc.
SEI Global Capital Investments Inc.
SEI Global Holdings (Cayman) Inc.

SEI Global Investments Corporation
SEI Global Nominee Ltd. (UK)
SEI Global Services Inc.
SEI Insurance Group Inc.
SEI Investment Strategies LLC
SEI Investments Inc.
SEI Investments (Asia) Limited (Hong Kong)
SEI Investments (South Africa) Limited
SEI Investments Canada Company
SEI Investments Developments Inc.
SEI Investments Distribution Co.
SEI Investments Europe Limited (UK)
SEI Investments Global (Cayman) Ltd.
SEI Investments Global Fund Services Ltd. (Ireland)
SEI Investments Global Funds Services
SEI Investments Global Limited (Ireland)
SEI Primus Holding Corporation
SEI Private Trust Company
SEI Trust Company
SEI Trustees Limited (UK)
SEI SIMC Holdings LLC
SIMC Subsidiary LLC

COMPETITORS

ADP	FMR
Bank of New York Mellon	Federated Investors
	Northern Trust
Brinker	Russell
Charles Schwab	State Street
DST Systems	SunGard
Envestnet	

HISTORICAL FINANCIALS

Company Type: Public

Income Statement

FYE: December 31

	REVENUE ($ mil.)	NET INCOME ($ mil.)	NET PROFIT MARGIN	EMPLOYEES
12/15	1,334.2	331.6	24.9%	2,985.0
12/14	1,266.0	318.7	25.2%	2,824.0
12/13	1,126.1	288.1	25.6%	2,749.0
12/12	992.5	206.8	20.8%	2,579.0
12/11	929.7	204.9	22.0%	2,430.0
Annual Growth	9.5%	12.8%	—	5.3%

2015 Year-End Financials

Debt ratio: —
Return on equity: 26.1%
Cash ($ mil.): 679.6
Current ratio: 4.47
Long-term debt ($ mil.): —

No. of shares (mil.): 163.7
Dividends
Yield: 0.9%
Payout: 25.7%
Market value ($ mil.): 8,580.0

	STOCK PRICE ($) FY Close	P/E High/Low		PER SHARE ($)		
			Earnings	Dividends	Book Value
12/15	52.40	28 19	1.96	0.50	7.88
12/14	40.04	22 16	1.85	0.46	7.48
12/13	34.73	21 14	1.64	0.42	6.83
12/12	23.34	20 14	1.18	0.63	6.03
12/11	17.35	22 13	1.11	0.27	5.81
Annual Growth	31.8%	—	15.3%	16.7%	7.9%

Select Comfort Corp.

Select Comfort has got your number. The firm's line of Sleep Number beds which can carry hefty price tags use air-chamber technology to allow sleepers to adjust the firmness on each side of the mattress providing better sleep quality and addressing sleep-related problems such as lower back pain. Select Comfort also offers foundations frames pillows and a sofa bed. A leading bedding retailer in the US Select Comfort operates nearly 490 company-owned stores. The air-bed maker also sells through a company-operated call center its own website and on the QVC shopping channel. Select Comfort was founded in 1987 has grown to become one of the nation's leading bed makers and retailers.

Operations

The firm operates two manufacturing plants (South Carolina and Utah) which supply beds on a just-in-time basis to its retail stores.

Geographic Reach

Minneapolis-based Select Comfort operates company-owned retail stores in 48 US states. Its two largest markets are California and Texas which combined account for more than 20% of its store base. The mattress giant distributes its products in the US and Canada and in Alaska Hawaii and Australia through retail partners.

Sales and Marketing

Select Comfort increased its sales and marketing efforts in 2015 boosting spending to $550 million from $512 million in 2014 and $440 million in 2013. The company advertises on television radio and in print and is increasing its use of digital advertising. More than 90% of its sales are through its retail stores with the online channel bringing in 6% of revenue. Wholesale accounts for 2% of revenue.

Financial Performance

Select Comfort's sales increased 5% in 2015 compared with 2014 to $1.2 billion. Driving sales were higher comparable store sales as well as the addition of about 25 new retail stores. Net income slumped 26% over the same period falling to $50.5 million. The company had higher expenses in 2015 than in 2014 as it developed a new digital presence and installed an enterprise resource planning system.

Strategy

While Select Comfort began as a direct marketer of its unique air-filled mattresses over the years it has evolved into a multichannel retailer with company-owned stores in about 48 states. Retail store sales have grown to account for more than 90% of Select Comfort's total sales.

The company redesigned its website to engage customers with the Select Comfort brand and generate store traffic. The number of visitors to sleepnumber.com increased 51% in 2015 from 2014.

The installation of an enterprise resource planning system from SAP ran into trouble in late 2015 and early 2016. Stores sales fell customers experienced delivery delays and there were higher returns and order cancellations. Problems seem to have been ironed out in the first quarter of 2016.

Mergers and Acquisitions

In 2015 Select Comfort acquired BAM Labs Inc. a provider of biometric sensor and sleep monitoring for data-driven health and wellness. The acquisition broadens and deepens Select Comfort's electrical biomedical software and backend capabilities in providing sleep-related information to mattress customers.

EXECUTIVES

President and CEO, Shelly R. Ibach, age 57, $779,231 total compensation
SVP and CFO, David R. Callen, age 50, $383,618 total compensation
SVP and Chief Operations Supply Chain and Lean Officer, Suresh Krishna, age 47
SVP and Chief Product Officer, Annie L. Bloomquist, age 47, $354,728 total compensation
EVP Chief Sales and Service Officer, Andy P. Carlin, age 53, $354,728 total compensation
SVP and CIO, J. Hunter J. Saklad, age 47
SVP and Chief Legal and Risk Officer and Secretary, Mark A. Kimball, age 58
Vp Direct Mktng, James D (Jamie) Gaboury
Sr V Pres-chief Human Capital, Patricia (Pat) Dirks
Vice President Strategic Sourcing, Mark Sponsler
Senior Vice President, Paricia Dirks
Chairman, Jean-Michel Valette
Board Member, Michael Peel
Auditors: Deloitte & Touche LLP

LOCATIONS

HQ: Select Comfort Corp.
9800 59th Avenue North, Minneapolis, MN 55442
Phone: 763 551-7000
Web: www.SleepNumber.com

PRODUCTS/OPERATIONS

2015 Sales

	% of total
Retail	92
Online and call center	6
Wholesale	2
Total	100

Selected Products

Bed frames
Foundations
Mattress pads
Mattresses
Pillows
Pillowtops
Sleep Number SofaBed

COMPETITORS

1800Mattress.com	Simmons
Mattress Firm	Spring Air
Serta	Tempur Sealy

HISTORICAL FINANCIALS

Company Type: Public

Income Statement

FYE: January 2

	REVENUE ($ mil.)	NET INCOME ($ mil.)	NET PROFIT MARGIN	EMPLOYEES
01/16	1,213.7	50.5	4.2%	3,484.0
01/15*	1,156.7	67.9	5.9%	3,149.0
12/13	960.1	60.0	6.3%	2,858.0
12/12	934.9	78.0	8.4%	2,791.0
12/11	743.2	60.4	8.1%	2,328.0
Annual Growth	13.0%	(4.4%)	—	10.6%

*Fiscal year change

2016 Year-End Financials

Debt ratio: —
Return on equity: 21.1%
Cash ($ mil.): 20.9
Current ratio: 0.88
Long-term debt ($ mil.): —

No. of shares (mil.): 49.4
Dividends
Yield: —
Payout: —
Market value ($ mil.): 1,058.0

	STOCK PRICE ($) FY Close	P/E High/Low		PER SHARE ($)		
			Earnings	Dividends	Book Value
01/16	21.41	35 21	0.97	0.00	4.50
01/15*	26.87	22 12	1.25	0.00	4.87
12/13	21.22	26 16	1.08	0.00	4.10
12/12	24.51	25 14	1.37	0.00	3.46
12/11	21.69	20 8	1.07	0.00	2.29
Annual Growth	(0.3%)	—	(2.4%)	—	18.3%

*Fiscal year change

Select Income REIT

When it comes to real estate it doesn't get any more selective than Hawaii. And Select Income REIT (SIR) has amassed quite a land portfolio in the Aloha State. The externally-managed real estate investment trust owns 11 properties measuring nearly 18 million sq. ft. of single-tenant commercial and industrial properties on the island of Oahu. Tenants include an oil refinery for Tesoro and a Coca-Cola bottling plant and distribution center. On the mainland SIR owns another 37 office and warehouse properties totaling more than 8 million sq. ft. in about 20 states. The company was formed in December 2011 as a subsidiary of CommonWealth REIT. It went public in 2012.

Geographic Reach

Massachusetts-based Select Income REIT's largest market in Hawaii home to 11 of its 48 properties. Hawaii properties account for more than 40% of the firm's total revenue.

IPO

Select Income REIT went public in March 2012 with an offering worth $172 million. All proceeds from the REIT's IPO went to former parent CommonWealth REIT.

Sales and Marketing

The REIT has a diverse roster of some 263 tenants from the manufacturing energy transportation high tech retail and industrial sectors among others. Three tenants —Bank of America MeadWestvaco and Orbital Sciences —each account for more than 5% of the firm's annual revenue. Its properties are nearly 96% leased.

Financial Performance

In its first full year as a public company the firm reported revenue of $188.3 million in 2013 a 53% increase versus 2012. Net income rose 41% over the same period to $93.1 million. The growth in revenue and profits resulted from an increase in tenant reimbursements and acquisition-related income. Rental income grew 51% as a result of acquisition activity plus increases from rent hikes at properties located in Hawaii.

Strategy

Since its March 2012 IPO Select Income REIT (SIR) has purchased 29 buildings covering 5.6 million sq. ft. Of the 29 properties only one is in Hawaii while the rest are located in about a dozen states including California and Virginia. SIR targets high quality single tenants and focuses on headquarters buildings and other strategic properties where tenants have invested significant capital.

Mergers and Acquisitions

In April 2014 the REIT acquired a property in Naperville Illinois and another in Mahwah New Jersey for an aggregate purchase price of $208 million.

Company Background

CommonWealth REIT created SIR to take over the Hawaiian land and commercial properties in the US in order for CommonWealth REIT to focus its investments on multi-tenant central business district office buildings.

EXECUTIVES

CFO and Treasurer, John C. Popeo, age 56
President and Chief Operating Officer, David M. Blackman, age 54
Managing Trustee, Barry M. Portnoy, age 71
Managing Trustee, Adam D. Portnoy, age 46
Auditors: Ernst & Young LLP

LOCATIONS

HQ: Select Income REIT
Two Newton Place, 255 Washington Street, Suite 300, Newton, MA 02458-1634
Phone: 617 796-8303
Web: www.sirreit.com

PRODUCTS/OPERATIONS

2015 Sales

	$ mil.	% of total
Rental income	364.2	85
Tenant reimbursements & other	64.2	15
Total	**428.4**	**100**

COMPETITORS

Brandywine Realty	Lexington Realty Trust
Duke Realty	Liberty Property Trust
First Industrial	Mack-Cali
Realty	Terreno Realty
Kilroy Realty	Vornado Realty

HISTORICAL FINANCIALS

Company Type: Public

Income Statement

FYE: December 31

	REVENUE ($ mil.)	NET INCOME ($ mil.)	NET PROFIT MARGIN	EMPLOYEES
12/15	428.3	74.7	17.4%	0.0
12/14	222.6	105.9	47.6%	0.0
12/13	188.3	93.0	49.4%	0.0
12/12	122.7	65.8	53.6%	0.0
12/11	108.6	68.9	63.5%	0.0
Annual Growth	**40.9%**	**2.0%**	**—**	**—**

2015 Year-End Financials

Debt ratio: 50.5%	No. of shares (mil.): 89.3
Return on equity: 4.1%	Dividends
Cash ($ mil.): 17.8	Yield: 9.9%
Current ratio: 0.86	Payout: 229.5%
Long-term debt ($ mil.): 2,375.3	Market value ($ mil.): 1,771.0

	STOCK PRICE ($) FY Close	P/E High/Low	PER SHARE ($) Earnings	Dividends	Book Value
12/15	19.82	31 21	0.86	1.97	23.46
12/14	24.41	16 12	1.89	1.90	24.69
12/13	26.74	14 11	2.09	1.76	24.06
12/12	24.77	11 9	2.43	0.91	22.92
Annual Growth	**(7.2%)**	**—**	**(29.3%)**	**29.4%**	**0.8%**

Senior Housing Properties Trust

Senior Housing Properties Trust (SHPT) offers those in their golden years a place to rest their weary bones. The real estate investment trust (REIT) owns some 375 health care-related properties in about 40 states and Washington DC. Its portfolio includes senior apartments independent and assisted living facilities nursing homes medical office buildings biotechnology laboratories rehabilitation hospitals and gymnasiums. Tenants such as Sunrise Senior Living and Brookdale Senior Living sign triple-net leases which require them not only to pay rent but to also pay operating expenses remove hazardous waste and carry insurance on their properties.

Geographic Reach

Massachusetts-based Senior Housing Properties Trust (SHPT) owns properties in 40 states and the District of Columbia. Major markets include Florida California and Texas although the REIT's property portfolio is geographically diverse.

Operations

The REIT's portfolio includes some 265 senior living communities 100 medical office buildings and 10 wellness centers. Its holdings are valued at about $5.3 billion. SHPT is managed by Reit Management & Research LLC (RMR) a real estate management company founded in 1986 to manage public investments in real estate.

Financial Performance

The health care REIT reported revenue of $761.4 million in 2013 an increase of 18% versus 2012. Net income rose 11% over the same period to $151.2 million. Driving the increase was the firm's managed senior living communities business which benefited from the acquisition of 12 communities since 2012. The REIT's medical office buildings (MOB) segment posted a gain due to increased rental income from 18 MOBs acquired partially offset by the sale of one MOB in 2012.

Cash generated from operations increased to $306.7 million in 2013 from $283.3 million in 2012 primarily due to a gain on the sale of a single senior living community and two rehabilitation hospitals over the course of the year.

Strategy

SHPT's business strategy is primarily focused on acquiring upscale senior living properties where the majority of residents pay rent through their own resources rather than through government programs. More recently the firm has diversified by purchasing medical office buildings (MOB). Indeed five years ago MOBs contributed just 5% of revenue with senior living communities contributing about 90%. In 2013 senior living accounted for about 70% of total revenue with MOBs contributing more than 25%. The REIT is continuing to grow its MOB holdings. SHPT's investment goals include acquiring additional properties for income and to a lesser extent their appreciation potential. The REIT is counting on the aging of the US population to increase demand for existing independent and assisted living communities nursing homes MOBs and other health care-related properties.

Mergers and Acquisitions

In May 2014 SHPT acquired the headquarters building of Vertex Pharmaceuticals in Boston for $1.1 billion. The purchase fit with the REIT's strategy of focusing on medical office buildings and private-pay (as opposed to government reimbursed) properties.

Company Background

SHPT was spun off from HRPT Properties Trust in 1999 when that REIT sold off its health facilities in order to focus on office and industrial properties.

EXECUTIVES

President and COO, David J. Hegarty, age 60, $203,490 total compensation
CFO and Treasurer, Richard W. Siede
Managing Trustee, Barry M. Portnoy, age 71
Managing Trustee, Adam D. Portnoy, age 46
Auditors: Ernst & Young LLP

LOCATIONS

HQ: Senior Housing Properties Trust
  Two Newton Place, 255 Washington Street, Suite 300,
  Newton, MA 02458-1634
Phone: 617 796-8350 **Fax:** 617 796-8349
Web: www.snhreit.com

PRODUCTS/OPERATIONS

2015 Sales

	$ mil.	% of total
Managed Senior Living Communities	367.9	37
MOB's	356.6	36
Triple Net Senior Living Communities	256.0	25
All Other Operations	18.3	2
Total	**998.8**	**100**

2015 Sales

	$ mil.	% of total
Rental income	630.9	63
Residents fees and services	367.9	37
Total	**998.8**	**100**

COMPETITORS

Chartwell Seniors	Legacy Healthcare
Housing	National Health
Extendicare	Investors
G & K Industries	Omega Healthcare
HCP	Investors
Healthcare Realty	Sabra Health Care
Trust	Ventas
LTC Properties	Welltower

HISTORICAL FINANCIALS

Company Type: Public

Income Statement   FYE: December 31

	REVENUE ($ mil.)	NET INCOME ($ mil.)	NET PROFIT MARGIN	EMPLOYEES
12/15	998.7	123.9	12.4%	0.0
12/14	844.8	158.6	18.8%	0.0
12/13	761.4	151.1	19.9%	0.0
12/12	644.8	135.8	21.1%	0.0
12/11	450.0	151.4	33.6%	0.0
Annual Growth	22.1%	(4.9%)	—	—

2015 Year-End Financials

Debt ratio: 48.7%	No. of shares (mil.): 237.4
Return on equity: 3.9%	Dividends
Cash ($ mil.): 37.6	Yield: 10.5%
Current ratio: 1.37	Payout: 294.3%
Long-term debt ($ mil.): 3,503.0	Market value ($ mil.): 3,524.0

	STOCK PRICE ($) FY Close	P/E High/Low	PER SHARE ($) Earnings	Dividends	Book Value
12/15	14.84	45 26	0.53	1.56	14.15
12/14	22.11	31 26	0.80	1.56	14.48
12/13	22.23	37 27	0.81	1.56	14.76
12/12	23.64	30 25	0.80	1.53	14.99
12/11	22.44	24 19	1.01	1.49	15.20
Annual Growth	(9.8%)	—	(14.9%)	1.2%	(1.8%)

ServisFirst Bancshares Inc

ServisFirst Bancshares is a bank holding company for ServisFirst Bank a regional commercial bank with about a dozen branches located in Alabama and the Florida panhandle. The bank also has a loan office in Nashville. ServisFirst Bank targets privately-held businesses with $2 million to $250 million in annual sales as well as professionals and affluent customers. The bank focuses on traditional commercial banking services including loan origination deposits and electronic banking services such as online and mobile banking. Founded in 2005 by its chairman and CEO Thomas Broughton III the bank went public in 2014 with an offering valued at nearly $57 million.
IPO
ServisFirst Bancshares sold 625000 shares priced at $91 per share. Proceeds from the May 2014 IPO will be used to support the bank's growth plans both in Alabama and in other states.
Geographic Reach
Birmingham-based ServisFirst Bank has branches in Birmingham Huntsville Montgomery Mobile Dothan Pensacola and Nashville.
Financial Performance
The bank reported net income of $41.2 million in 2013 compared with $34 million in 2012. The increase was primarily due to an increase in net interest income which rose nearly 20% to $112.5 million. Noninterest income increased 4% to $10 million in 2013.
As of March 2014 the bank had total assets of approximately $3.6 billion total loans of $2.9 billion and total deposits of about $3.0 billion.

EXECUTIVES

President and CEO ServisFirst Bancshares and ServisFirst Bank, Thomas A. (Tom) Broughton, age 60, $350,000 total compensation
EVP and COO ServisFirst Bancshares and ServisFirst Bank, Clarence C. Pouncey, age 59, $263,000 total compensation
EVP CFO Treasurer and Secretary ServisFirst Bancshares and ServisFirst Bank, William M. Foshee, age 61, $230,000 total compensation
EVP ServisFirst Bancshares and President and CEO ServisFirst Bank of Huntsville, Andrew N. (Andy) Kattos, age 46
President and CEO ServisFirst Bank of Mobile, William (Bibb) Lamar, age 72
EVP ServisFirst Bancshares and President and CEO ServisFirst Bank of Montgomery, G. Carlton (Carl) Barker, age 61
EVP ServisFirst Bancshares and President and CEO ServisFirst Bank of Pensacola, Rex D. McKinney, age 53
EVP Correspondent Banking ServisFirst Bancshares and ServisFirst Bank, Rodney E. Rushing, age 58, $245,000 total compensation
SVP and Chief Credit Officer ServisFirst Bancshares and ServisFirst Bank, Don G. Owens, age 64, $187,200 total compensation
President and CEO ServisFirst Bank of Atlanta, Ken Barber
EVP and Chief Lending Officer, Doug Rehm
CEO ServisFirst Bank Dothan, B. Harrison Morris, age 39
Vice President of ServisFirst Bank and Manager of ServisFirst Bank, Crystal (Cristy) Tennyson

Assistant Vice President of Private Banking of ServisFirst Bank, Ron (Ronnie) Morrison
Executive Vice President Regional Chief Executive Officer, Buford H Morris
Senior Vice President Commercial Lending, Chad Thomason
Senior Vice President Of Commerical Banking, David (Dave) Hearne
Senior Vice President Commercial Banking, Jeff (Jeffy) Johnson
Vice President Commercial Banking, Jamie (James) Osteen
Vice President, John (Jack) Peacock
Senior Vice President, Michael (Mel) Wood
Chairman ServisFirst Bancshares and ServisFirst Bank, Stanley M. (Skip) Brock, age 65
Auditors: Dixon Hughes Goodman LLP

LOCATIONS

HQ: ServisFirst Bancshares Inc
  850 Shades Creek Parkway, Birmingham, AL 35209
Phone: 205 949-0302
Web: www.servisfirstbank.com

COMPETITORS

Bank of America	Wells Fargo
Bank of the Ozarks	

HISTORICAL FINANCIALS

Company Type: Public

Income Statement   FYE: December 31

	ASSETS ($ mil.)	NET INCOME ($ mil.)	INCOME AS % OF ASSETS	EMPLOYEES
12/15	5,095.5	63.5	1.2%	371.0
12/14	4,098.6	52.3	1.3%	298.0
12/13	3,520.7	41.6	1.2%	262.0
12/12	2,906.3	34.4	1.2%	0.0
12/11	0.0	23.4	—	0.0
Annual Growth	—	28.3%		

2015 Year-End Financials

Return on assets: 1.3%	Dividends
Return on equity: 14.8%	Yield: 0.4%
Long-term debt ($ mil.): —	Payout: 9.6%
No. of shares (mil.): 51.9	Market value ($ mil.): 2,469.0
Sales ($ mil): 193.9	

	STOCK PRICE ($) FY Close	P/E High/Low	PER SHARE ($) Earnings	Dividends	Book Value
12/15	47.53	40 24	1.20	0.12	8.64
12/14	32.95	83 26	1.05	0.16	8.20
Annual Growth	44.2%	— —	14.4%	(27.4%)	5.3%

Shell Midstream Partners LP

Auditors: Deloitte & Touche LLP

LOCATIONS

HQ: Shell Midstream Partners LP
  One Shell Plaza, 910 Louisiana Street, Houston, TX 77002
Phone: 713 241-6161
Web: www.shellmidstreampartners.com

HISTORICAL FINANCIALS

Company Type: Public

Income Statement

FYE: December 31

	REVENUE ($ mil.)	NET INCOME ($ mil.)	NET PROFIT MARGIN	EMPLOYEES
12/15	326.5	167.1	51.2%	0.0
12/14	182.4	13.4	7.3%	0.0
12/13	91.6	36.5	39.8%	0.0
12/12	113.0	47.0	41.6%	0.0
Annual Growth	42.4%	52.6%	—	—

2015 Year-End Financials

Debt ratio: 67.2%
Return on equity: 64.8%
Cash ($ mil.): 93.0
Current ratio: 5.01
Long-term debt ($ mil.): 481.0

No. of shares (mil.): 154.9
Dividends
  Yield: 1.6%
  Payout: 58.1%
Market value ($ mil.): 6,433.0

	STOCK PRICE ($) FY Close	P/E High/Low	PER SHARE ($) Earnings	Dividends	Book Value
12/15	41.52	42 22	1.16	0.67	0.64
12/14	40.98	395320	0.10	0.00	3.03
12/13	0.00	— —	(0.00)	0.00	(0.00)
Annual Growth	—		—	—	—

Shenandoah Telecommunications Co

If Virginia is for lovers Shenandoah Telecommunications must carry some interesting conversations. Through subsidiaries the company (which does business as Shentel) provides telecom services in the Shenandoah Valley and beyond. Shenandoah Telephone has more than 20500 access lines in service. As a Sprint affiliate subsidiary Shenandoah Personal Communications offers wireless services to more than 262000 customers. The company's cable TV unit serves about 115000 customers while about 13000 households subscribe to its dial-up and broadband Internet access.

Operations

Recognizing that the market for wireline service is shrinking from the rise of mobile phones as a primary phone and VoIP technology Shentel is now primarily a wireless provider. Some 56% of sales come from its being a Sprint affiliate. (It also offers prepaid wireless service from Sprint subsidiaries Virgin Mobile and Boost.) Cable services account for about 26% of sales and its wireline service (which includes Internet service) makes up the remaining 18%.

Geographic Reach

Shentel's wireless segment provides digital wireless service to a portion of a four-state area covering the region from Harrisburg York and Altoona Pennsylvania to Harrisonburg Virginia. Its wireline cable and Internet services are offered throughout Shenandoah County and portions of northwestern Augusta County Virginia.

Financial Performance

Overall sales grew 5% in 2015 to $342.5 million from 2014 due to increases prepaid subscribers and a higher average revenue per subscriber from a richer product mix. all segments grew in 2015 with the cable operation increasing 15%.

The rise in revenue fueled a 21% increase in profit to $40.8 million in 2015. Cash from operations was $120 million in 2015 compared to $115 million in 2014.

Strategy

In order to focus on its core communications offerings in 2013 the company sold off its Shentel Converged Services business that provided local and long distance voice video and Internet services to off-campus college student housing throughout the southeastern United States.

Mergers and Acquisitions

Shenandoah is buying NTELOS Holdings Corp. for some $208 million. The deal was agreed to in 2015 and was to be finalized in 2016. Shenandoah acquired the NTELOS' wireless network assets retail stores and nearly 300000 retail subscribers in the nTELOS western markets. Shentel will complete plans to close down nTELOS' Eastern markets. The acquisition doubles Shentel's wireless customer base expands its footprint in the Mid-Atlantic region and strengthens its partnership with Sprint.

In 2016 Shentel acquired Colane Cable a video Internet and home phone-service provider in West Virginia for $2.4 million. Colane's operations are adjacent to areas served by Shentel.

EXECUTIVES

Vice President Technology, Jeff (Jeffy) Pompeo
SVP Sales and Marketing, William L. (Willy) Pirtle, age 57, $237,120 total compensation
Chairman President and CEO, Christopher E. (Chris) French, age 58, $474,700 total compensation
EVP and COO, Earle A. MacKenzie, age 64, $339,308 total compensation
VP Finance CFO and Treasurer, Adele M. Skolits, age 57, $257,308 total compensation
VP Information Technology, Richard A. Baughman
VP Wireline and Engineering, Edward H. McKay
Vp Cable, Thomas (Thom) Whitaker
Vice Chairman, Douglas C. Arthur, age 73
Auditors: KPMG LLP

LOCATIONS

HQ: Shenandoah Telecommunications Co
500 Shentel Way, Edinburg, VA 22824
Phone: 540 984-4141
Web: www.shentel.com

PRODUCTS/OPERATIONS

2015 Sales

	$ mil.	% of total
Wireless	208.8	56
Cable	97.6	26
Wireline	67.4	18
Adjustments	(31.4)	-
Total	342.5	100

Selected Services

Business telephone products
Cable TV
Cellular products and services
Centrex
Fiber-optic capacity
Internet access
ISDN
Local telephone access
Long-distance
Paging
Security systems

COMPETITORS

AT&T
Aquis Communications Group
Comcast
DISH Network
EarthLink
Lumos
Suddenlink Communications
T-Mobile USA
Time Warner Cable
U.S. Cellular
Verizon
Verizon Wireless Inc.

HISTORICAL FINANCIALS

Company Type: Public

Income Statement

FYE: December 31

	REVENUE ($ mil.)	NET INCOME ($ mil.)	NET PROFIT MARGIN	EMPLOYEES
12/15	342.4	40.8	11.9%	730.0
12/14	326.9	33.8	10.4%	708.0
12/13	308.9	29.5	9.6%	682.0
12/12	288.0	16.3	5.7%	693.0
12/11	251.1	12.9	5.2%	669.0
Annual Growth	8.1%	33.2%	—	2.2%

2015 Year-End Financials

Debt ratio: 32.0%
Return on equity: 14.9%
Cash ($ mil.): 76.8
Current ratio: 2.09
Long-term debt ($ mil.): 178.2

No. of shares (mil.): 48.4
Dividends
  Yield: 2.2%
  Payout: 62.7%
Market value ($ mil.): 2,087.0

	STOCK PRICE ($) FY Close	P/E High/Low	PER SHARE ($) Earnings	Dividends	Book Value
12/15	43.05	60 33	0.83	0.48	5.98
12/14	31.25	47 33	0.70	0.47	5.35
12/13	25.67	47 22	0.62	0.36	4.87
12/12	15.31	55 28	0.34	0.33	4.34
12/11	10.48	70 33	0.28	0.17	4.15
Annual Growth	42.4%	— —	31.8%	30.6%	9.6%

Shutterstock Inc

Shutterstock brings the online marketplace mentality to the world of digital images illustrations and videos. Its 35000+ contributors have uploaded more than 19 millions bits of content perused by 550000 subscribers. The company's primary customers include marketing agencies media organizations and communications departments of businesses that subscribe to single downloads a set number of images or unlimited downloads for a month or a year; average cost per image is $3. Shutterstock's marketplace is available in 10 languages and 150 countries where its images are used for corporate communications websites ads and books and other published materials. Formed in 2007 the company went public in 2012.

IPO

The company plans to use its $76 million in IPO proceeds for general corporate purposes including possible acquisitions though nothing specific is in the works. Shutterstock had initially valued its IPO at $115 million.

Financial Analysis

Shutterstock has seen its revenue grow steadily doubling between 2009 and 2011. Not only has the company's library and number of downloads grown during that time its revenue per download has also increased from $1.80 to $2.05.

Strategy

Going forward Shutterstock's growth strategies include increased localization of content to meet specific ethnic and culture media requirements and pursuing new content types as they become available. It also intends to move from mostly word-of-mouth to focused marketing in order to improve its penetration of both the small-to-medium-size business segment (a majority of sales) and large agencies and enterprises.

Ownership

Founder and CEO Jonathan Oringer holds about 65% of Shutterstock pre-IPO.

EXECUTIVES

CFO, Steven Berns, age 51, $144,231 total compensation
Chairman and CEO, Jonathan (Jon) Oringer, age 42, $1 total compensation
Chief Product Officer, Catherine Ulrich, $324,423 total compensation
CEO WebDAM, Jody Vandergriff
Vice President And General Counsel, Michael (Mel) Lesser
Vice President Of New Business, Ben Pfeifer
Senior Vice President Technology, Dan McCormick
Executive Vice President, Siobhan Aalders
Auditors: PricewaterhouseCoopers LLP

LOCATIONS

HQ: Shutterstock Inc
350 Fifth Avenue, 21st Floor, New York, NY 10118
Phone: 646 766-1855
Web: www.shutterstock.com

COMPETITORS

AG Interactive	New York Times
Agence France-Presse	PR Newswire
Associated Press	Piksel
Cartoon Bank	Reuters
Corbis	Rex Features
Facebook	Sipa Press
Getty Images	The NewsMarket
Masterfile	Wazee Digital
National Geographic	Zuma Press

HISTORICAL FINANCIALS

Company Type: Public

Income Statement
FYE: December 31

	REVENUE ($ mil.)	NET INCOME ($ mil.)	NET PROFIT MARGIN	EMPLOYEES
12/15	425.1	19.5	4.6%	621.0
12/14	327.9	22.0	6.7%	512.0
12/13	235.5	26.4	11.2%	345.0
12/12	169.6	47.5	28.0%	237.0
12/11	120.2	21.8	18.2%	224.0
Annual Growth	37.1%	(2.8%)	—	29.0%

2015 Year-End Financials

Debt ratio: —	No. of shares (mil.): 35.6
Return on equity: 7.2%	Dividends
Cash ($ mil.): 241.3	Yield: —
Current ratio: 2.09	Payout: —
Long-term debt ($ mil.): —	Market value ($ mil.): 1,154.0

	STOCK PRICE ($) FY Close	P/E High/Low		PER SHARE ($) Earnings	Dividends	Book Value
12/15	32.34	137	52	0.54	0.00	8.09
12/14	69.10	163	99	0.61	0.00	7.06
12/13	83.63	109	31	0.77	0.00	5.21
12/12	26.00	15	12	1.79	0.00	2.30
Annual Growth	7.5%	—	—	(32.9%)	—	52.2%

Signature Bank (New York, NY)

Signature Bank marks the spot where some professional New Yorkers bank. The institution provides customized banking and financial services to smaller private businesses their owners and their top executives through 30 branches across the New York metropolitan area including all five boroughs Long Island and affluent Westchester County. The bank's lending activities mainly entail real estate and business loans. Subsidiary Signature Securities offers wealth management financial planning brokerage services asset management and insurance while its Signature Financial subsidiary offers equipment financing and leasing. Founded in 2001 the bank now boasts assets of roughly $29 billion.

OperationsMortgage loans including commercial real estate loans multifamily residential mortgages home loans and lines of credit and construction and land loans comprise the bulk of Signature Bank's loan portfolio (and much of its asset base as well). The bank which staffed some 1010 employees at the end of 2014 generated 68% of its revenue from interest on loans and leases that year while 20% came from interest on its securities available-for-sale and 7% came from securities held-to-maturity. The remainder of its revenue came from fees and service charges (2%) and various other miscellaneous sources.Geographic ReachThe bank's nearly 30 branch offices are mostly in the New York metropolitan area which includes Manhattan Brooklyn Westchester Long Island Queens the Bronx Staten Island and Connecticut. Sales and MarketingSignature Bank mostly serves privately-owned businesses their owners and senior managers (typically with a net worth between $500000 and $20 million).Financial PerformanceThe company's revenues and profits have risen in recent years thanks to strong organic loan business growth and declining loan loss provisions as its loan portfolio's credit quality has improved with higher property valuations in the strengthened economy.Signature's revenue jumped by 22% to a record $959.3 million in 2014 mostly as loan interest (on commercial loans mortgages and leases) and security interest income continued to grow as the bank built up its interest-earning assets during the year. Higher revenue and a continued decline and loan loss provisions in 2014 boosted the bank's net income by 30% to a record $296.7 million. Signature's operating cash levels more than doubled to $421 million on higher cash earnings.StrategySignature Bank has long targeted privately-held businesses that have fewer than 1000 employees and revenues of less than $200 million. Some of its target clients include real estate owners/companies law firms accounting firms entertainment business managers medical professionals retail establishments money management firms and non-profit foundations. The bank continues to expand its service lines particularly focusing on specialty financing to grow its business organically. In 2015 it planned to offer direct commercial vehicle financing through a network of approved commercial vehicle dealerships in New York's Tri-State area with loans targeting small and mid-size business borrowers looking to acquire commercial vehicles and fleets. Also that year it formed its Maryland-based Signature Public Funding Corp subsidiary to provide municipal finance and tax-exempt lending and leasing products to local state and federal government agencies nationwide.Company Background

The bank's emphasis on personal service helped it to grow its deposit base and loan portfolio in 2011. During a time when many other banks struggled under the weight of bad loans in a bad economy Signature Bank achieved record earnings for the fourth consecutive year.Founded in 2001 as an alternative to mega-banks Signature Bank was spun off from Bank Hapoalim in 2004.

EXECUTIVES

Vice President Marketing and Training, John (Jack) Paul
Senior Vice President, MICHAEL UNKCD (Mel) SHARKEY
President CEO and Director, Joseph J. DePaolo, $577,500 total compensation
SVP and CFO, Vito Susca
President CEO and Director, Michael G. O'Rourke
EVP, Kevin P. Bastuga
EVP, Bryan D. Duncan
VP Retail Operations Manager, Ella Riordan-Pacheco
Senior Vice President, Carl Gambino
Group Director Senior Vice President NY Office, Pat V (Patty) Capparelli
Vice President, Michael (Mel) Nicolosi
Vice President, John C Spagnuolo
Group Director Senior Vice President, John (Jack) Kourkoutis
Senior Vice President Group Director, Gary Shulevich
Senior Vice President Group Director, Leon Kratsberg
Senior Vice President Melville NY, Drew S (Andrew) Crowley
Vice President, Phyllis Rosenfeld
Senior Vice President, Janice (Jan) Ashley
Senior Vice President Group Director, Matthew Weltman
Vice President, Eugene Cartin
Vice President, Sal Trifiletti
Senior Vice President Group Director, James (Jamie) Buck
Senior Vice President Group Director, Edwin Sirlin
Senior Vice President Group Director, Richard (Dick) Murasso
Senior Vice President Funding Officer, Brant Ward
Vice President, John (Jack) Ricchezza
Vice President Private Banking, Sue (Susie) Frick
Senior Vice President Group Director, Nicole (Nikki) Rospond
Vice President, Richard (Dick) Wang
Vice President, George Greene
Vice President, Maria Vetrano
Vice President, Kerry Mach
Senior Vpres, Mohammed O (Ahmed) Kamil
Group Director And Senior Vice President, George (Georgey) Maroulis
Executive Vice President, Joseph (Jo) Fantauzzi
Senior Vice President Group Director, James (Jamie) Handal
Vice President, Ken Bartho
Senior Vice President Group Director, Brian (Bri) Hallinan
Vice President Director Of Operations, Richard Pelcher
Vice President, Lee Frangos
Vice President, Jeffrey (Jeff) Barrington
Vice President and Executive Sales Officer, Dean Porter
Vice President, Jay Byrne
Group Director Senior Vice President NY Office, John M (Jack) Paglia

Group Director Senior Vice President NY Office, John C (Jack) Spagnuolo

Vice President and Associate Group Director, Matthew (Matt) Cohen

Vice President, Barbara (Barb) Von Borstel

Senior Vice President, Wendy Berney

Group Director Senior Vice President, Michael (Mel) Vasami

Senior Vice President, Peter (Pete) Marra

Senior Vice President Cashier, Louis (Lou) Holub

Senior Vice President, Steven (Steve) Kocoris

Vice President, Joseph (Jo) Fingerman

Vice President, Dave (Davie) Stansbery

Group Director Senior Vice President, Kevin Hardiman

Group Director Senior Vice President, Robert (Bob) Sloposky

Vice President, Dominick Chechile

Group Director Senior Vice President, Lawrence Blascovich

Senior Vice President Group Director, Larry (Lar) Goldberg

Senior Vice President Group Director, Thomas (Thom) Knierim

Vice President and Associate Group Director, Marilyn (Mar) Gessner

Senior Lender Vice President, Richard F (Dick) Assaf

Senior Vice President Group Head, Peter (Pete) Olsen

Senior Vice President and Group Director, Roseann Manos

Vice President of Real Estate, Aaron Greene

Senior Vice President And Group Director, Tom (Tommy) Rogers

Senior Vice President Underwriting and Portfolio Manager, Wendy Nelson

Chairman and Director, Leonard S. Caronia

Treasurer, Peter Quinlan

Auditors: KPMG LLP

LOCATIONS

HQ: Signature Bank (New York, NY)
565 Fifth Avenue, New York, NY 10017
Phone: 646 822-1500
Web: www.signatureny.com

PRODUCTS/OPERATIONS

2014 Sales

	$ mil.	% of total
Interest		
Loans net	655.6	68
Securities available for sale	193.6	20
Securities held to maturity	69.8	7
Other	5.3	1
Noninterest		
Fees & service charges	19.3	2
Commissions	10.6	1
Net gains on sales of loans	5.4	1
Net gains on sales of securities	5.3	-
Other	2.2	-
Adjustments	(7.8)	-
Total	**959.3**	**100**

COMPETITORS

Apple Bank for Savings	Herald National Bank
Astoria Financial	JPMorgan Chase
Bank Leumi USA	New York Community
Capital One	Bancorp
Citigroup	Safra Bank
HSBC USA	TD Bank USA

HISTORICAL FINANCIALS

Company Type: Public

Income Statement

FYE: December 31

	ASSETS ($ mil.)	NET INCOME ($ mil.)	INCOME AS % OF ASSETS	EMPLOYEES
12/15	33,450.5	373.0	1.1%	1,122.0
12/14	27,318.6	296.7	1.1%	1,010.0
12/13	22,376.6	228.7	1.0%	945.0
12/12	17,456.0	185.4	1.1%	844.0
12/11	14,666.1	149.5	1.0%	720.0
Annual Growth	**22.9%**	**25.7%**	**—**	**11.7%**

2015 Year-End Financials

Return on assets: 1.2%	Dividends
Return on equity: 13.8%	Yield: —
Long-term debt ($ mil.): —	Payout: —
No. of shares (mil.): 50.9	Market value ($ mil.): 7,807.0
Sales ($ mil): 1,144.0	

	STOCK PRICE ($) FY Close	P/E High/Low		PER SHARE ($) Earnings	Dividends	Book Value
12/15	153.37	22	16	7.27	0.00	56.81
12/14	125.96	22	17	5.95	0.00	49.61
12/13	107.42	22	15	4.76	0.00	38.06
12/12	71.34	18	15	3.91	0.00	34.94
12/11	59.99	18	13	3.37	0.00	30.49
Annual Growth	**26.4%**	**—**	**—**	**21.2%**	**—**	**16.8%**

Silver Spring Networks Inc

Silver Spring Networks helps utility companies plug into the 21st century. Its Smart Energy Platform modernizes a utility's existing power grid infrastructure into the "smart" grid i.e. one that is connected to a digital network and more energy efficient. The Smart Energy Platform is a secure Internet-based network made up of hardware such as access points communications modules bridges and relays; its UtilOS-brand network operating system; and software. It also offers managed services to maintain and regulate the network. Silver Spring sells its platform to electric gas and water utilities —FPL PG&E and OG&E account for almost 80% of service revenue. The company went public in 2013.

Operations

Silver Spring is counting on its smart grid technology being essential to meet current demand for electricity to prevent blackouts and accommodate new sources of energy such as electric vehicles. Its devices are compatible with meters made by more than 50 different manufacturers including ABB GE Itron Landis+Gyr and Secure Meter but many of these companies also offer their own smart grid technology. It does not manufacture its own hardware but relies on two contract manufacturers mainly Jabil Circuit and Plexus.

Product sales account for 68% of the company's revenue with service revenue bringing in the rest.

Sales and Marketing

Silver Spring sells either its communications modules to meter manufacturers and its other hardware and software products directly to utilities

or third-party devices such as meters integrated with its communications modules directly to utility customers. It has connected almost 20 million networking platform devices and has 35 pilot projects in progress in Australia Europe New Zealand South America and the US.

In 2014 Ched Service and Progress Energy Service Company LLC (which was acquired by Duke Energy Corporation) accounted for 21% and 13% of Silver Spring's revenue respectively.

Financial Performance

Silver Spring's annual revenue is a year-to-year roller coast ride: up one year and down the next a pattern that continued in 2014. Revenue plunged 41% to $191 million in 2014 from $327 million (the company's highest) in 2013. Hardware and software revenue were down on the product side and service revenue also was lower. In the US sales fell 64% and although they account for less revenue sales were up in Australia and other international markets. The company's net loss for 2014 was about $90 million compared to a loss of about $67 million in 2013. While the company spent less on most operating functions in 2014 it wasn't enough to offset the drop in revenue.

Strategy

Silver Spring's concentration in energy is its intended first step in smart grid and the Internet of Things technologies. The company is branching out to municipalities with a smart city focus to connect traffic signals street lights and other city electronics. Its acquisitions in 2014 and 2015 reflect that strategy.

Mergers and Acquisitions

The company acquired Detectent Inc. in 2015 to broaden its application offerings for advanced metering and grid operations non-technical loss revenue assurance and customer engagement. Silver Spring plans to continue the expansion of its apps and sensors and increase managed services which bring recurring revenue and its Software-as-a-Service business.

In 2014 Silver Spring bought Streetlight.Vision a Paris-based developer of control and management software for smart street light networks. Streetlight.Vision has projects in cities around the world.

Ownership

Silver Spring was founded in 2002 and received the majority of its start-up funding from fellow Silicon Valley-based venture capital firm Foundation Capital. The firm owns more than a quarter of Silver Spring's stock.

EXECUTIVES

EVP Engineering and Managed Services, Don Reeves, age 46

CTO, Raj Vaswani, age 50, $272,917 total compensation

EVP Global Sales, Eric P. Dresselhuys, age 51, $267,500 total compensation

Vice Chairman and EVP, John R. Joyce, age 62, $102,821 total compensation

President CEO and Director, Michael (Mike) Bell

VP Financial Planning and Analysis, Kenneth P. Gianella

Major Accounts Vice President Of Sales, Jett Graham

Vice President, Terri (Terr) Stynes

Sales Vice President Anza, Andrew (Andy) Vlachiotis

Vice President Business Development Asia, Hugh (Hugo) McDermott

Vice President Software Engineering, Ramesh Menon

Vice President of Operations, Tracy (Trace) Strom

Vice President of Platform Engineering, Ziad Mansour
Vice President of Sales, Bill (Billy) Simons
Chairman, Scott A. Lang, age 53
Vice President Investor Relations and Treasurer, Mark (Marky) McKechnie
Auditors: Ernst & Young LLP

LOCATIONS

HQ: Silver Spring Networks Inc
230 W. Tasman Drive, San Jose, CA 95134
Phone: 669 770-4000
Web: www.silverspringnet.com

PRODUCTS/OPERATIONS

2014 Sales

	$ mil.	% of total
Products	129.3	68
Services	62.0	32
Total	**191.3**	**100**

Selected Customers

AES Eletropaulo
American Electric Power
Baltimore Gas & Electric
CitiPowerc & Powercor Australia
Commonwealth Edison
Florida Power & Light
Guelph Hydro
Indianapolis Power & Light
Maui Smart Grid Project
Modesto Irrigation District
Pacifc Gas and Electric
Pepco Holdings
Progress Energy
Public Service Company of Oklahoma
Sacramento Municipal Utility District

COMPETITORS

AT&T	Itron
Alcatel-Lucent	Mitsubishi Electric
Boeing	Motorola Solutions
ChargePoint	Northrop Grumman
Cisco Systems	S&C Electric
Comverge	Schweitzer Engineering
Echelon Corporation	Laboratories
Elster Group SE	Siemens AG
Enel	Sprint Communications
Fujitsu	Toshiba
GE Energy	Tropos Networks
GridPoint	Verizon
IBM	

HISTORICAL FINANCIALS

Company Type: Public

Income Statement

FYE: December 31

	REVENUE ($ mil.)	NET INCOME ($ mil.)	NET PROFIT MARGIN	EMPLOYEES
12/15	489.5	79.9	16.3%	652.0
12/14	191.2	(89.1)	—	576.0
12/13	326.8	(66.8)	—	602.0
12/12	196.7	(89.7)	—	566.0
12/11	237.0	(92.3)	—	0.0
Annual Growth	**19.9%**	—	—	—

2015 Year-End Financials

Debt ratio: 0.0%	No. of shares (mil.): 50.6
Return on equity: —	Dividends
Cash ($ mil.): 65.2	Yield: —
Current ratio: 1.01	Payout: —
Long-term debt ($ mil.): —	Market value ($ mil.): 729.0

	STOCK PRICE ($) FY Close	P/E High/Low	PER SHARE ($) Earnings	Dividends	Book Value
12/15	14.41	10 4	1.55	0.00	(0.67)
12/14	8.43	— —	(1.84)	0.00	(2.73)
12/13	21.00	— —	(4.54)	0.00	(1.65)
Annual Growth (17.2%)	— —	— —	—	—	—

Simmons First National Corp.

Simmons First National thinks it's only natural it should be one of the largest financial institutions in The Natural State. The $8.1 billion-asset holding company owns Simmons First National Bank and seven other community banks that bear the Simmons First Bank name and maintain local identities; together they operate around 150 branches throughout Arkansas and in Kansas Tennessee and Missouri. Serving consumers and area businesses the banks offer standard deposit products like checking and savings accounts IRAs and CDs. Lending activities mainly consist of commercial real estate loans single-family mortgages and consumer loans such as credit card and student loans.

Operations
In addition to Simmons First National Bank the company owns Simmons First Bank of Jonesboro Simmons First Bank of South Arkansas Simmons First Bank of Northwest Arkansas Simmons First Bank of Russellville Simmons First Bank of Searcy Simmons First Bank of El Dorado and Simmons First Bank of Hot Springs. Simmons First Trust Company a subsidiary of Simmons First National Bank provides trust and fiduciary services; Simmons First Investment Group offers broker-dealer services.Like other retail banks Simmons makes the bulk of its money from interest income. About 65% of its total revenue came from loan interest during 2015 while another 8% came from interest on investment securities. The rest of its revenue came from service charges on deposit accounts (8% of revenue) debit and credit card fees (6%) mortgage lending income (3%) trust income (2%) investment banking income (1%) and other non-interest income sources.Geographic ReachThe bank has around 150 branches mostly in Arkansas but also in Kansas Missouri and Tennessee.

Financial Performance
Simmons First National Bank's annual revenues and profits have been rising mostly thanks to new loan business from rapid bank expansion (mostly stemming from acquisitions).The bank's revenue jumped 60% to $396.8 million during 2015 mostly thanks to 58% growth in legacy loans and growth in acquired loan business from the acquisitions of Liberty and Community First. Non-interest income grew 54% thanks to rising trust service charges deposit fees mortgage lending income all also tied to its recent acquisitions.Revenue growth in 2015 more than doubled Simmons' net income to $74.36 million. The bank's operating cash levels spiked eight-fold to $88.7 million for the year thanks to a rise in cash-based earnings and favorable changes in working capital.

Strategy

Simmons tries to differentiate itself from smaller competitors by offering a wider array of products while striving to provide more personalized service than larger regional banks. The company also likes to acquire banks to grow its loan and deposit business while expanding into new geographic markets. Between 1990 and 2015 Simmons made 11 whole bank acquisitions and a handful of branch deals with other banks adding some 125 branches to its total branch network.Mergers and Acquisitions

In September 2016 Simmons acquired Citizens National Bank a Tennessee-based bank with about 10 branch locations.

In October 2015 the company purchased Ozark Trust & Investment Corporation and its Trust Company of the Ozarks subsidiary adding $1 billion in new assets under management and 1300 clients to its wealth management business.In February 2015 Simmons First National acquired $1.1 billion-asset Liberty Bancshares as well as Liberty Bank branches in southwest Missouri St. Louis and Kansas City. It also added Liberty's expertise in small business lending.Also in February 2015 the bank bought $1.9 billion-asset Community First Bancshares and its First State Bank branches in Tennessee. Community First also added expertise in small business and consumer lending.

EXECUTIVES

EVP Organizational Development, Stephen C. Massanelli, age 60
Chairman and CEO, George A. Makris, age 59, $502,500 total compensation
SEVP CFO and Treasurer, Robert A. Fehlman, age 51, $306,614 total compensation
EVP and Central and Northeast Arkansas Regional Chairman Simmons First National Bank, Barry K. Ledbetter
President and Chief Credit Officer Simmons First National Bank, N. Craig Hunt
EVP and South Arkansas Regional Chairman Simmons First National Bank, Freddie G. Black
EVP Corporate Strategy and Performance and Secretary, Susan F. Smith, age 54
President Chief Banking Officer and Director, David L. Bartlett, age 64, $376,142 total compensation
EVP, Marty D. Casteel, age 64, $304,180 total compensation
EVP Controller Chief Accounting Officer and Investment Relations Officer, David W. Garner, age 46
EVP Marketing, Robert C. Dill, age 73, $179,393 total compensation
EVP and Chief Risk Officer, Tina M. Groves, age 46
EVP Technology and Operations Simmons First National Bank, Lisa W. Hunter
SVP and Marketing Director Simmons First National Bank, Amy W. Johnson
President El Dorado Community Bank, Robert L. Robinson
Chairman Russellville Community Chairman, Ronald B. (Ron) Jackson
President Hot Springs Community Bank, Steven W. (Steve) Trusty
President Conway Community Bank, Jason Culpepper
EVP and General Counsel, Patrick A. Burrow, age 62
EVP Specialty Lending Simmons First National Bank, Larry L. Bates
EVP and Tennessee Regional Chairman Simmons First National Bank, John C. Clark
EVP and Kansas and Missouri Regional Chairman Simmons First National Bank, Gary E. Metsger

Senior Vice President and Director Human Resources, Sharon (Share) Burdine
Vice President and Personnel Manager, Leigh (Leah) Cockrum
Vice President, Pam (Pamela) Lawshe
Vice President of Mortgage, Deana Powell
Vice President, Angie (Ang) Haynes
Assistant Vice President Mortgage Consultant, Jym Fees
Vice President Benefits and Special Projects, John (Jack) Brower
Assistant Vice President Loans, Esther Chapman
Senior Vice President, Leigh Ann (Leah) Ayres
Vice President, Chad Pittillo
Vice President Loan Review Manager, David Coleman
Executive Vice President Specialty Banking Group, Craig Hunt
Vice President and Controller Rf Communications, Clifton White
Executive Vice President Operations, Glenda Tolson
Vice President Marketing, Stephen Lasseigne
Senior Vice President In the Little Rock and Central Regions, Adam (Ad) Mitchell
Vice President Market Manager, Dorvan Wiley
Vice President And Commercial Loan Officer, John (Jack) Craig
Vice President and Trust Officer, Robin (Rin) Thornton
Senior Vice President, Tommie K Jones
Vice President Equipment Finance, Michael (Mel) Childers
Vice President And Officer, Cathy (Cat) Brazeale
Vice President, Ed (Eddie) Stahlman
Vice President Commercial Lending, Wayne Wilson
Senior Branch Manager Assistant Vice President, Aaron Cooper
Vice President andamp; Trust Officer, Catherine (Cate) Roper
Auditors: BKD, LLP

LOCATIONS

HQ: Simmons First National Corp.
501 Main Street, Pine Bluff, AR 71601
Phone: 870 541-1000
Web: www.simmonsfirst.com

PRODUCTS/OPERATIONS

2015 Sales

	% of total
Interest Income	
Loans	65
Investment securities	8
Others	-
Non-interest income	
Service charges on deposit accounts	8
Debit and credit card fees	6
Mortgage lending income	3
Trust income	2
Other service charges and fees	2
others	6
Net (loss) gain on assets covered by FDIC loss share agreements	-
Total	**100**

COMPETITORS

Arvest Bank	Bear State Financial
BOK Financial	Home BancShares
BancorpSouth	IBERIABANK
Bank of America	Regions Financial
Bank of the Ozarks	U.S. Bancorp

HISTORICAL FINANCIALS
Company Type: Public

Income Statement
FYE: December 31

	ASSETS ($ mil.)	NET INCOME ($ mil.)	INCOME AS % OF ASSETS	EMPLOYEES
12/15	7,559.6	74.3	1.0%	1,946.0
12/14	4,643.3	35.6	0.8%	1,331.0
12/13	4,383.1	23.2	0.5%	1,306.0
12/12	3,527.4	27.6	0.8%	1,052.0
12/11	3,320.1	25.3	0.8%	1,075.0
Annual Growth	22.8%	30.8%	—	16.0%

2015 Year-End Financials

Return on assets: 1.2%
Return on equity: 9.4%
Long-term debt ($ mil.): —
No. of shares (mil.): 30.2
Sales ($ mil): 396.7

Dividends
Yield: 1.7%
Payout: 36.8%
Market value ($ mil.): 1,555.0

	STOCK PRICE ($) FY Close	P/E High/Low	PER SHARE ($) Earnings	Dividends	Book Value
12/15	51.36	22 14	2.63	0.92	35.57
12/14	40.65	20 16	2.11	0.88	27.38
12/13	37.15	26 17	1.42	0.84	24.89
12/12	25.36	17 14	1.64	0.80	24.55
12/11	27.19	20 13	1.47	0.76	23.70
Annual Growth	17.2%	— —	15.7%	4.9%	10.7%

Sinclair Broadcast Group, Inc.

To find out what's happening at Sinclair Broadcast Group (SBG) you could consult the TV Guide. The company is a leading television operator with more than 160 stations serving about 80 midsized markets. Its portfolio reaches 26% of US households and includes affiliates of all four major broadcast networks as well as several affiliates of The CW Network and MyNetworkTV. (Most of the stations are affiliated with FOX.) About half of SBG's stations are owned and operated while the rest are operated under local market agreements; the company has duopolies (more than one station) in about 20 of markets. The family of founder Julian Sinclair Smith led by CEO David Smith controls the company.

Geographic Reach

SBG serves midsized markets all around the US. The company's local television advertisers are attracted by a local sales force at each of the company's television stations which is comprised of approximately 750 sales account executives and 90 local sales managers company-wide.

Sales and Marketing

SBG has been increasing its advertising spend in recent years. The company spent about $21.3 million on advertising and marketing promotions in fiscal 2014.

Financial Performance

SBG reported $1.97 billion in revenue for fiscal 2014. That was an increase of $613.4 million compared to the prior fiscal period. The company's net income was $212.3 million in fiscal 2014 which

was an increase of $138.8 million compared to the company's fiscal 2013 net income.

SBG's cash flow from operations increased by $270 million in fiscal 2014 and the company ended the year with $430.4 million in cash on hand.

Strategy

Like most other commercial television broadcasters SBG relies on advertising for the bulk of its revenue with most of that coming from local advertisers. The company focuses on providing its stations with the best possible programming through both network affiliation agreements and syndication deals in order to attract and retain audiences. Within each market its stations compete for audiences against stations owned by other big broadcasting groups including Hearst Television Local TV and Media General.

Mergers and Acquisitions

In 2014 the company purchased four stations owned by Media General Inc. and LIN Media LLC and sold its broadcast assets of three stations in two markets.

HISTORY

Company Background

Julian Sinclair Smith founded the company in 1971 with TV station WBFF (one of the first UHF channels in the country) in Baltimore. Several years later came WPTT another UHF channel in Pittsburgh. A movement among the board's directors in 1985 to oust Smith (who controlled 40% of the company) was foiled when Smith and his son David allied with a director who held a 10.2% stake. Shortly after the family bought the dissidents out and hard-knuckled boss David took over management of the company renamed Sinclair Broadcasting Group (SBG) in 1986.

The company bought Pittsburgh station WPGH in 1991 selling its WPTT station the same day. It expanded again with its 1994 purchase of four stations from ABRY Partners. SBG went public in 1995 using the $75 million raised to trim its debt. It also used the funds to back its growing appetite for acquisitions buying five stations in 1995 and buying River City Broadcasting in 1996.

SBG came under fire in 1996 for pushing an FCC law barring duopolies (ownership of more than one UHF channel in a market) when a rival challenged its dealings with Glencairn a broadcasting company owned in part by Smith's mother Carolyn. The company's bad luck continued that year when David Smith was arrested (the charges were later dropped) after getting caught with a prostitute. Continuing Smith's philosophy to "get as many TV stations as we can" the company bought 14 TV stations from Sullivan Broadcast Holdings for $1 billion and seven TV stations from Guy Gannett Communications for $310 million in 1998. As its debt grew the company promised to sell some $500 million in noncore assets.

SBG followed through on that claim in 1999 and 2000 by exiting the radio market when it sold its radio holdings to Entercom Communications for about $920 million. Amid a decline in ad sales the company cut nearly 200 jobs in 2001. SBG created News Central in 2002 which centralizes all of the company's news operations so that it can more easily add coverage to all of its stations.

EXECUTIVES

Vice President National Sales, Gregg (Greggory) Siegel
SVP and CTO, Delbert R. Parks, age 63
COO Sinclair Television Group, Steven M. Marks, age 59, $869,000 total compensation

EVP and General Counsel, Barry M. Faber, age 54, $837,425 total compensation
SVP CFO and Treasurer, Lucy A. Rutishauser, age 51, $300,000 total compensation
COO Circa, John F. Solomon, age 50
President and CEO, Christopher S. Ripley, age 39, $766,875 total compensation
EVP and Chief TV Development Officer, Steven J. Pruett, age 61, $650,000 total compensation
COO Sinclair Digital Group, Robert D. Weisbord, age 53
National Sales Manager, Dave (Davie) Farshing
Executive Vice President General Counsel, Bruce (Brucey) Faber
Vice President and Director, Frederick (Fred) Smith
Vice Chairman, David B. Amy, age 63
Chairman, David D. Smith, age 65
Auditors: PricewaterhouseCoopers LLP

LOCATIONS

HQ: Sinclair Broadcast Group, Inc.
10706 Beaver Dam Road, Hunt Valley, MD 21030
Phone: 410 568-1500   **Fax:** 410 568-1533
Web: www.sbgi.net

COMPETITORS

CBS	LIN Media
E. W. Scripps	Local TV
FOX Broadcasting	Media General
Granite Broadcasting	Meredith Corporation
Gray Television	Newport Television
Hearst Television	Nexstar Broadcasting
Journal Broadcast Group	Raycom Media
	TEGNA

HISTORICAL FINANCIALS

Company Type: Public

Income Statement

FYE: December 31

	REVENUE ($ mil.)	NET INCOME ($ mil.)	NET PROFIT MARGIN	EMPLOYEES
12/15	2,219.1	171.5	7.7%	8,000.0
12/14	1,976.5	212.2	10.7%	7,700.0
12/13	1,363.1	73.4	5.4%	6,400.0
12/12	1,061.6	144.6	13.6%	4,000.0
12/11	765.2	75.8	9.9%	3,130.0
Annual Growth	30.5%	22.6%	—	26.4%

2015 Year-End Financials

Debt ratio: 70.9%
Return on equity: 35.9%
Cash ($ mil.): 149.9
Current ratio: 1.31
Long-term debt ($ mil.): 3,687.0

No. of shares (mil.): 94.7
Dividends
  Yield: 2.0%
  Payout: 30.5%
Market value ($ mil.): 3,082.0

	STOCK PRICE ($) FY Close	P/E High/Low		PER SHARE ($) Earnings	Dividends	Book Value
12/15	32.54	20	14	1.79	0.66	5.55
12/14	27.36	17	11	2.17	0.63	4.48
12/13	35.73	45	16	0.78	0.60	3.96
12/12	12.62	7	4	1.78	1.54	(1.44)
12/11	11.33	14	7	0.94	0.48	(1.50)
Annual Growth	30.2%		— —	17.5%	8.3%	

SiteOne Landscape Supply Inc

LOCATIONS

HQ: SiteOne Landscape Supply Inc
Mansell Overlook, 300 Colonial Center Parkway, Suite 600, Roswell, GA 30076
Phone: 770 255-2100
Web: www.siteonelandscapesupply.com

HISTORICAL FINANCIALS

Company Type: Public

Income Statement

FYE: January 3

	REVENUE ($ mil.)	NET INCOME ($ mil.)	NET PROFIT MARGIN	EMPLOYEES
01/16*	1,451.6	28.9	2.0%	2,850.0
12/14	1,176.6	21.7	1.8%	0.0
12/13	5.3	(9.5)	—	0.0
12/13	1,072.7	33.7	3.1%	0.0
Annual Growth	10.6%	(5.0%)	—	—

*Fiscal year change

2016 Year-End Financials

Debt ratio: 28.2%
Return on equity: 9.8%
Cash ($ mil.): 20.1
Current ratio: 3.05
Long-term debt ($ mil.): 184.2

No. of shares (mil.): 14.2
Dividends
  Yield: —
  Payout: —
Market value ($ mil.): —

	STOCK PRICE ($) FY Close	P/E High/Low		PER SHARE ($) Earnings	Dividends	Book Value
01/16*	0.00	— —		(1.04)	0.00	21.38
Annual Growth	—	— —		—	—	—

*Fiscal year change

Somero Enterprises Inc

EXECUTIVES

Pres, Jack Cooney
Auditors: Whitley Penn LLP

LOCATIONS

HQ: Somero Enterprises Inc
16831 Link Court, Fort Myers, FL 33912
Phone: 239 210-6500   **Fax:** 239 210-6600
Web: www.somero.com

HISTORICAL FINANCIALS

Company Type: Public

Income Statement

FYE: December 31

	REVENUE ($ mil.)	NET INCOME ($ mil.)	NET PROFIT MARGIN	EMPLOYEES
12/15	70.2	11.5	16.4%	165.0
12/14	59.2	14.5	24.5%	165.0
12/13	45.0	5.3	11.9%	128.0
12/12	32.1	1.0	3.2%	107.0
12/11	21.8	(2.3)	—	71.0
Annual Growth	33.9%	—	—	23.5%

2015 Year-End Financials

Debt ratio: 2.2%
Return on equity: 33.4%
Cash ($ mil.): 13.7
Current ratio: 3.46
Long-term debt ($ mil.): 1.0

No. of shares (mil.): 56.1
Dividends
  Yield: —
  Payout: 34.5%
Market value ($ mil.): —

Sotherly Hotels LP

Auditors: Dixon Hughes Goodman LLP

LOCATIONS

HQ: Sotherly Hotels LP
410 West Francis Street, Williamsburg, VA 23185
Phone: 757 229-5648
Web: www.sotherlyhotels.com

HISTORICAL FINANCIALS

Company Type: Public

Income Statement

FYE: December 31

	REVENUE ($ mil.)	NET INCOME ($ mil.)	NET PROFIT MARGIN	EMPLOYEES
12/15	138.5	6.4	4.6%	12.0
12/14	122.9	(0.7)	—	13.0
12/13	89.3	(4.4)	—	9.0
12/12	87.3	(5.3)	—	8.0
12/11	81.1	(6.4)	—	0.0
Annual Growth	14.3%	—	—	—

2015 Year-End Financials

Debt ratio: 82.6%
Return on equity: —
Cash ($ mil.): 11.4
Current ratio: 1.58
Long-term debt ($ mil.): 324.8

No. of shares (mil.): 16.6
Dividends
  Yield: 6.7%
  Payout: 400.1%
Market value ($ mil.): 425.0

	STOCK PRICE ($) FY Close	P/E High/Low		PER SHARE ($) Earnings	Dividends	Book Value
12/15	25.45	61	58	0.43	1.72	3.17
12/14	25.05	—	—	(0.06)	0.00	2.10
Annual Growth	1.6%		— —	—	—	51.1%

South State Corp

South State Corporation (formerly First Financial Holdings) is the holding company for South State Bank (formerly South Carolina Bank and Trust and South Carolina Bank and Trust of the Piedmont both known as SCBT). The bank operates branches throughout the Palmetto state as well as in select counties in Georgia and North Carolina. Serving retail and business customers the banks provide deposit accounts loans and mortgages as well as trust and investment planning services. More than half of the firm's loan portfolio is devoted to commercial mortgages while consumer real estate loans make up more than a quarter. South State plans to merge with Southeastern Bank Financial parent of Georgia Bank & Trust.

OperationsBeyond its retail and commercial banking mortgage lending consumer finance and trust and investment businesses the bank operates registered investment advisors Minis & Co. and First Southeast 401K Fiduciaries as well as limited-purpose broker-dealer First Southeast Investor Services.South State Corporation generated 70% of its total revenue from loan interest (including fees) in 2014 while another 4% came from interest income on investment securities. Service charges and Bankcard services income made up another 14% of total revenue while trust and investment services income and mortgage banking income each contributed roughly 4% during the year.Geographic ReachSouth State Corporation boasts nearly 130 branches across nearly 20 counties in South Carolina a handful of counties in North Carolina and about a dozen counties in the northeast and coastal regions of Georgia.Financial PerformanceSouth State Corporation's revenues and profits have been on the rise over the past few years mostly thanks to continued growth of its loan business and declining loan loss provisions as its loan portfolio's credit quality has improved with the strengthened economy.The company's revenue jumped by 28% to $436.72 million in 2014 which was mostly driven by 20% growth in its loan interest income as its average loan asset balances swelled by a similar percentage. South State's noninterest income also swelled by 76% thanks to higher deposit account service charge bankcard service trust and investment service and mortgage banking fees from overall growth in the business through acquisitions and organic initiatives. Higher revenue and controlled operating costs in 2014 drove the bank's net income higher by 53% to $75.44 million. South State's operating cash levels declined by 51% to $118.65 million for the year after adjusting its earnings for non-cash net sales proceeds from its mortgage loans held-for-sale and as the bank spent more cash toward its accrued income taxes.

StrategyThough it does sometimes expand or relocate its existing branches to better position its locations for more growth South State Corporation has been mostly growing its loan business and branch network through strategic bank and branch acquisitions. Its 2015 acquisition of 13 branch locations from Bank of America for example extended South State's reach into six new markets and three existing markets while adding millions of dollars worth of new loan business. Then in mid-2016 South State Corporation agreed to buy Southeastern Bank Financial the holding company of Georgia Bank & Trust (which also operates in South Carolina as Southern Bank & Trust). The combined company will operate more than 130 branches in Georgia and the Carolinas. Mergers and AcquisitionsIn 2015 South State Corporation agreed to purchase 12 South Carolina branches and one Georgia branch from Bank of America expanding its reach into six new markets. The acquired branches were located in Hartwell Georgia; as well as Florence Greenwood Orangeburg Sumter Newberry Batesburg-Leesville Abbeville and Hartsville in South Carolina.Company BackgroundSouth State Corporation and South State Bank changed their names from First Financial Holdings and South Carolina Bank and Trust respectively in 2014. The change was designed to better promote the South State brand with customers.

EXECUTIVES

CEO, Robert R. Hill, age 49, $645,000 total compensation
CFO and COO, John C. Pollok, age 50, $442,000 total compensation

Chief Banking Officer, John F. Windley, age 64, $315,000 total compensation
Chief Credit Officer and Chief Risk Officer, Joseph Burns, $295,000 total compensation
President, R. Wayne Hall, $203,405 total compensation
EVP and Corporate Secretary, William C. Bochette
Vice President Advertising and Brand Manager, Valerie (Val) Foley
Senior Vice President and Senior Relationship Manager, Bill (Billy) Coker
Senior Vice President Corporate Counsel, V Comer
Vice President, Reid Davis
Senior Vice President Technology, Ross Bagley
Senior Executive Vice President, Dane H Murray
Vice President, Kelley (Kells) Morabito
Vice President, Stacy (Stace) Cannon
Executive Vice President Chief Financial Officer, Donald (Don) Pickett
Senior Vice President and Commercial Consumer Lender, Jimmy (Jim) Lindsey
Senior Vice President, Leslie (Les) Francis
Chairman, Robert R. Horger, age 65
Vice Chairman, Paula Harper Bethea
Secretary, Renee (Ren) Brooks
Auditors: Dixon Hughes Goodman LLP

LOCATIONS

HQ: South State Corp
   520 Gervais Street, Columbia, SC 29201
Phone: 800 277-2175
Web: www.southstatebank.com

PRODUCTS/OPERATIONS

2011 Sales

	$ mil.	% of total
Interest		
Loans including fees	319.9	70
Investment securities	20.3	4
Other	1.8	-
Noninterest		
Service charges on deposit accounts	36.2	10
Bankcard services income	29.6	6
Trust and investment services income	18.3	4
Mortgage banking	16.2	4
Securities gains net -	0	
Amortization of FDIC indemnification asset	(21.9)	0
Other	16.2	4
Total	**436.7**	**100**

COMPETITORS

BB&T	Regions Financial
Bank of America	Security Federal
Bank of South Carolina	
First Citizens	
Bancorporation	

HISTORICAL FINANCIALS

Company Type: Public

Income Statement

FYE: December 31

	ASSETS ($ mil.)	NET INCOME ($ mil.)	INCOME AS % OF ASSETS	EMPLOYEES
12/15	8,557.3	99.4	1.2%	2,058.0
12/14	7,826.2	75.4	1.0%	2,081.0
12/13	7,931.5	49.2	0.6%	2,106.0
12/12	5,136.4	30.0	0.6%	1,324.0
12/11	3,896.5	22.6	0.6%	1,071.0
Annual Growth	**21.7%**	**44.9%**	**—**	**17.7%**

2015 Year-End Financials

Return on assets: 1.2%	Dividends
Return on equity: 9.7%	Yield: 1.3%
Long-term debt ($ mil.): —	Payout: 23.8%
No. of shares (mil.): 24.1	Market value ($ mil.): 1,739.0
Sales ($ mil): 453.6	

	STOCK PRICE ($) FY Close	P/E High/Low		PER SHARE ($) Earnings	Dividends	Book Value
12/15	71.95	19	14	4.11	0.98	43.84
12/14	67.08	22	18	3.08	0.82	40.78
12/13	66.51	28	17	2.38	0.74	40.72
12/12	40.18	20	14	2.03	0.69	29.97
12/11	29.01	22	15	1.63	0.68	27.19
Annual Growth	**25.5%**	**—**	**—**	**26.0%**	**9.6%**	**12.7%**

Southern First Bancshares, Inc.

Southern First Bancshares operates in two markets: Greenville South Carolina where it operates under the Greenville First Bank moniker and in Columbia South Carolina as Southern First Bank. Selling itself as a local alternative to larger institutions the company which has more than five bank branches targets individuals and small to midsized businesses. It offers traditional deposit services and products including checking accounts savings accounts and CDs. The banks use funds from deposits mainly to write commercial mortgages residential mortgages and commercial business loans.

EXECUTIVES

Assistant Vice President Client Office, Debbie (Deb) Tucker
Auditors: Elliott Davis Decosimo, LLC

LOCATIONS

HQ: Southern First Bancshares, Inc.
   100 Verdae Boulevard, Suite 100, Greenville, SC 29606
Phone: 864 679-9000

COMPETITORS

BB&T	Regions Financial
Bank of America	
First Citizens	
Bancorporation	

HISTORICAL FINANCIALS

Company Type: Public

Income Statement

FYE: December 31

	ASSETS ($ mil.)	NET INCOME ($ mil.)	INCOME AS % OF ASSETS	EMPLOYEES
12/15	1,217.2	10.1	0.8%	167.0
12/14	1,029.8	6.6	0.6%	155.0
12/13	890.8	5.1	0.6%	138.0
12/12	798.0	3.8	0.5%	125.0
12/11	767.7	2.0	0.3%	113.0
Annual Growth	**12.2%**	**48.5%**	**—**	**10.3%**

2015 Year-End Financials

Return on assets: 0.9%
Return on equity: 11.4%
Long-term debt ($ mil.): —
No. of shares (mil.): 6.2
Sales ($ mil.): 54.4

Dividends
Yield: —
Payout: —
Market value ($ mil.): 143.0

	STOCK PRICE ($) FY Close	P/E High/Low		PER SHARE ($) Earnings	Dividends	Book Value
12/15	22.70	14	10	1.55	0.00	14.98
12/14	17.02	15	11	1.10	0.00	13.34
12/13	13.28	14	9	0.98	0.00	15.20
12/12	9.30	15	10	0.64	0.00	15.10
12/11	7.15	46	27	0.22	0.00	14.88
Annual Growth	**33.5%**	—	—	63.3%	—	0.2%

Southern Missouri Bancorp, Inc.

Southern Missouri Bancorp is the holding company for Southern Bank (formerly Southern Missouri Bank and Trust) which serves local residents and businesses in southeastern Missouri and northeastern Arkansas through more than 10 branches. Residential mortgages account for the largest percentage of the bank's loan portfolio followed by commercial mortgages and business loans. Construction and consumer loans round out its lending activities. Deposit products include checking savings and money market accounts CDs and IRAs. The bank also offers financial planning and investment services. Originally chartered in 1887 Southern Bank acquired Arkansas-based Southern Bank of Commerce in 2009.

Jeffrey Gendell of Tontine Financial Partners owns more than 9% of Southern Missouri Bancorp; independent investor Donald Crandell owns more than 8%; employees own around 6%; and president CEO and director Greg Steffens more than 5%.

EXECUTIVES

Vice President, Mel (Melanie) Jackson
Vice President And Loan Officer, Jon (Jonny) Holman
Vice President Network Administration, Torrey Crabtree
Vice President, Kevin (Kev) Alpe
Vice President, Brian (Bri) Rivenburgh
Auditors: BKD, LLP

LOCATIONS

HQ: Southern Missouri Bancorp, Inc.
2991 Oak Groove Road, Poplar Bluff, MO 63901
Phone: 573 778-1800
Web: www.bankwithsouthern.com

COMPETITORS

Bank of America	Regions Financial
Commerce Bancshares	U.S. Bancorp
IBERIABANK	UMB Financial

HISTORICAL FINANCIALS

Company Type: Public

Income Statement

FYE: June 30

	ASSETS ($ mil.)	NET INCOME ($ mil.)	INCOME AS % OF ASSETS	EMPLOYEES
06/16	1,403.9	14.8	1.1%	342.0
06/15	1,300.0	13.6	1.1%	327.0
06/14	1,021.4	10.0	1.0%	247.0
06/13	796.3	10.0	1.3%	181.0
06/12	739.1	10.1	1.4%	179.0
Annual Growth	**17.4%**	**10.1%**	—	**17.6%**

2016 Year-End Financials

Return on assets: 1.1%
Return on equity: 11.4%
Long-term debt ($ mil.): —
No. of shares (mil.): 7.4
Sales ($ mil): 66.0

Dividends
Yield: 1.5%
Payout: 18.4%
Market value ($ mil.): 175.0

	STOCK PRICE ($) FY Close	P/E High/Low		PER SHARE ($) Earnings	Dividends	Book Value
06/16	23.53	12	9	1.98	0.36	16.94
06/15	18.85	22	10	1.79	0.34	17.88
06/14	35.69	25	17	1.46	0.64	16.63
06/13	25.67	18	15	1.44	0.30	15.46
06/12	21.50	15	12	1.66	0.24	14.57
Annual Growth	**2.3%**	—	—	4.5%	10.7%	3.8%

SP Plus Corp

SP Plus (formerly Standard Parking) wants to be the driving force in the parking industry —and it likely is. The parking behemoth manages about 4200 surface and multilevel parking facilities for airports hospitals hotels local governments office buildings retail centers sports venues and universities in more than 340 cities throughout the US and Canada. Its airport facilities consist of parking and shuttle bus operations at more than 75 airports including Chicago O'Hare and Dallas/Fort Worth International. Overall SP Plus provides more than 2 million parking spaces.

Geographic Reach

Chicago-based SP Plus has parking facilities in 46 US states the District of Columbia Puerto Rico and Canada.

Operations

SP Plus manages about 3900 parking facilities containing some 2 million parking spaces in about 340 cities. The company also operates roughly 75 parking-related service centers serving 71 airports ground transportation through its fleet of about 800 shuttle buses and 390 valet locations.

The company operates its clients' facilities through two primary types of arrangements: management contracts and leases. Under a management contract it receives a base monthly fee for managing the facility and earns an incentive fee based on the achievement of facility performance objectives. It also receives fees for ancillary services. Under a lease SP Plus pays to the property owner either a fixed annual rent a percentage of gross customer collections or a combination of both. It collects all revenue and also absorbs most of the operating expenses. It typically is not however responsible for major maintenance capital expenditures or real estate taxes. About 82% of its locations are under management contracts while 18% are under leases. Revenue from lease contract accounted for 35% in 2015 while management contracts generated 22% and reimbursed management contract revenue accounted for 43%.

Financial Performance

On the heels of its purchase of rival Central Parking in late 2012 SP Plus has reported unprecedented revenue growth. Revenues jumped 7% from $1.51 billion in 2014 to peak at a record-setting $1.62 billion in 2015. Profits however fell 25% from $23 million to $17 million during that same time period.

The historic growth for 2015 was driven by a 15% surge in lease contracts due to additional revenue from new locations and increases in short-term parking revenue and monthly parking revenue.

Strategy

SP Plus is aooking to expand in its core markets with the aim of being #1 or #2 in each. A contract to operate and maintain approximately 1300 parking spaces in 17 facilities throughout the Manhattan Bronx Queens and Brooklyn boroughs of New York City further that aim. The multi-year deal which began in October of 2013 also includes responsibility for general maintenance painting restriping cleaning and snow removal.

Company Background

In a sweeping move for the parking industry the company acquired Central Parking Corporation one of its biggest rivals in 2012. Standard Parking Corp. later changed its name to SP Plus Corp. in December 2013.

EXECUTIVES

EVP General Counsel and Secretary, Robert N. Sacks, age 63, $271,491 total compensation
EVP and Chief Human Resource Officer, Gerard M. Klaisle, age 62
President and CEO, G. Marc Baumann, age 60, $560,540 total compensation
EVP Operations Airport Division, John (Jack) Ricchiuto, age 59
EVP and Chief Business Development Officer, Thomas L. Hagerman, age 55, $411,767 total compensation
EVP New York Tri-State Division, Hector O. Chevalier, age 53, $366,986 total compensation
EVP Operations Support and Technology, Keith B. Evans, age 49
EVP Operations and President and CEO USA Parking System, William H. Bodenhamer, age 63, $473,183 total compensation
President Urban Operations, Robert M. Toy, age 60, $374,414 total compensation
EVP CFO and Treasurer, Vance C. Johnston, age 47, $314,458 total compensation
Vice President Of Risk Management, Tim (Timmy) Nickerson
Vice President Deputy General Counsel, Jerry (Jerr) Pate
Vice President, James (Jamie) Buczek
Senior Vice President Manufacturing and PEx, Trish (Trisha) Norvell
Executive Vice President Of Operations, Jack Ricchiuto
Senior Vice President Risk Management, Steve (Stevie) Bruner
Senior Vice President, Mike (Mikey) Tepper
Vice President of Business Development and Corporate Marketing, Jim (Jimmy) Wilhelm
Executive Vice President Field Operations, Rob (Robbie) Toy
Senior Vice President, Connie Jin
Vice President Human Resources, Colleen Kozak

Vice President, David (Dave) Lombardi
Senior Vice President, Chris (Chrissy) Conley
Chairman, James A. (Jim) Wilhelm, age 62
Auditors: Ernst & Young LLP

LOCATIONS

HQ: SP Plus Corp
200 E. Randolph Street, Suite 7700, Chicago, IL
60601-7702
Phone: 312 274-2000
Web: www.spplus.com

PRODUCTS/OPERATIONS

Selected Services
Service Lines
Parking
Transportation
Facility Maintenance
Event Logistics
Security
Multiple Service Lines
Market Expertise
Marketing Services
Technology Integration
Performance Management

2015 Sales

	$ mil.	% of total
Lease contracts	570.9	35
Management contracts	350.3	22
Reimbursement of management contract expense	694.7	43
Total	**1,615.9**	**100**

COMPETITORS

ABM Industries	Diamond Parking
Ace Parking	Impark

HISTORICAL FINANCIALS

Company Type: Public

Income Statement

FYE: December 31

	REVENUE ($ mil.)	NET INCOME ($ mil.)	NET PROFIT MARGIN	EMPLOYEES
12/15	1,615.9	17.4	1.1%	21,974.0
12/14	1,514.6	23.1	1.5%	24,030.0
12/13	1,466.8	12.0	0.8%	23,937.0
12/12	953.9	3.1	0.3%	25,011.0
12/11	729.6	17.9	2.5%	11,914.0
Annual Growth	22.0%	(0.7%)	—	16.5%

2015 Year-End Financials

Debt ratio: 28.7%
Return on equity: 7.2%
Cash ($ mil.): 18.7
Current ratio: 0.72
Long-term debt ($ mil.): 209.9

No. of shares (mil.): 22.3
Dividends
Yield: —
Payout: —
Market value ($ mil.): 534.0

	STOCK PRICE ($) FY Close	P/E High/Low	PER SHARE ($) Earnings	Dividends	Book Value
12/15	23.90	35 26	0.77	0.00	11.18
12/14	25.23	26 18	1.03	0.00	10.35
12/13	26.04	50 36	0.54	0.00	9.24
12/12	21.99	135 94	0.18	0.00	8.98
12/11	17.87	17 13	1.12	0.00	3.22
Annual Growth	7.5%	— —	(8.9%)	—	36.5%

Spectra Energy Partners LP

When you take one company's energy holdings and splinter them you get Spectra Energy Partners. Formed by Spectra Energy out of the former natural gas holdings of Duke Energy the company is a natural gas pipeline and storage facility operator. Its assets include a liquefied natural gas storage location in Tennessee 50% of Market Hub (two natural gas storage facilities in Texas and Louisiana) and 49% of Gulfstream Natural Gas System. All told Spectra Energy Partners has 3200 miles of natural gas transmission and gathering pipelines capable of moving about 3.6 billion cu. ft. per day. It also has 57 billion cu. ft. of gas storage capacity.

The company's core customers include distribution companies and utilities natural gas producers in Appalachia the Gulf Coast and the Mid-Continent power plants and major industrial companies. Major customers include EQT and the Tennessee Valley Authority.

Spectra Energy Partners' growth plans include expanding its pipeline and storage facilities (both by acquisitions and organic growth) to meet increased demand. In this regard in 2009 the company acquired Ozark Gas Transmission and Ozark Gas Gathering Systems from Atlas Pipeline Partners for $300 million.

In 2010 it acquired an additional 24.5% of a 745-mile interstate natural gas transportation system (Gulfstream Natural Gas System) from Spectra Energy for $330 million. The deal boosted Spectra Energy Partners' holdings to 49%.

Further expanding its Appalachian pipeline assets in 2011 the company bought a 70-mile natural gas pipeline (Big Sandy Pipeline) in eastern Kentucky from EQT Corp. for $390 million. That year the company also completed organinc expansion projects on the Gulfstream pipeline and at the Market Hub salt cavern storage complex.

The Big Sandy acquisition increased production and lifted the company's revenues and net income in 2011 offsetting decreased contract revenue (due to lower wholesale prices) from its Ozark Gas Transmission segment.

Expanding its Northeast pipeline operations in 2012 the company agreed to buy 39% of Maritimes & Northeast Pipeline L.L.C. from Spectra Energy for $319 million in cash and $56 million in newly issued partnership units.

EXECUTIVES

Board Member, Eric Hender
Auditors: Deloitte & Touche LLP

LOCATIONS

HQ: Spectra Energy Partners LP
5400 Westheimer Court, Houston, TX 77056
Phone: 713 627-5400
Web: www.spectraenergypartners.com

COMPETITORS

AGL Resources	Florida Gas
CenterPoint Energy	Transmission
Crestwood Midstream	Occidental Petroleum
Partners LP	Texas Gas Transmission
DCP Midstream Partners	Transcontinental Gas
Enterprise Products	Pipe Line
Exxon Mobil	Williams Companies

HISTORICAL FINANCIALS

Company Type: Public

Income Statement

FYE: December 31

	REVENUE ($ mil.)	NET INCOME ($ mil.)	NET PROFIT MARGIN	EMPLOYEES
12/15	2,455.0	1,225.0	49.9%	0.0
12/14	2,269.0	1,004.0	44.2%	0.0
12/13	1,965.0	1,070.0	54.5%	0.0
12/12	236.8	193.5	81.7%	0.0
12/11	205.0	172.0	83.9%	0.0
Annual Growth	86.0%	63.4%	—	—

2015 Year-End Financials

Debt ratio: 35.0%
Return on equity: —
Cash ($ mil.): 168.0
Current ratio: 0.37
Long-term debt ($ mil.): 5,845.0

No. of shares (mil.): 290.9
Dividends
Yield: 5.0%
Payout: 74.3%
Market value ($ mil.): 13,876.0

	STOCK PRICE ($) FY Close	P/E High/Low	PER SHARE ($) Earnings	Dividends	Book Value
12/15	47.70	17 11	3.30	2.43	37.17
12/14	56.97	21 15	2.84	2.25	35.71
12/13	45.35	7 4	7.15	2.02	34.54
12/12	31.23	20 16	1.69	1.93	16.14
12/11	31.96	21 16	1.63	1.85	17.27
Annual Growth	10.5%	— —	19.3%	7.1%	21.1%

Spire Inc

In the Missouri and Alabama Spire (formerly The Laclede Group) is seeking to inspire its customers to use more natural gas. The group's main revenue source is its Gas Utility operations (Laclede Gas Missouri Gas Energy EnergySouth and Alabama Gas) which distribute natural gas to 1.7 million customers in Missouri and Alabama. Spire's nonregulated businesses provide gas transportation and other services and operate underground gas storage fields. Operations include wholesale gas marketing (Laclede Energy Resources) a propane pipeline (Laclede Pipeline) insurance (Laclede Gas —Family Services) and real estate development (Laclede Development).

Geographic Reach

Its Gas Utility segment consists of four natural gas utilities: Laclede Gas Company (serving St. Louis and eastern Missouri) Missouri Gas Energy (serving Kansas City and western Missouri) and Alabama Gas Corporation (Alagasco serving central and northern Alabama including Birmingham and Montgomery) and EnergySouth (units Mobile Gas and Willmut Gas serve customers in Alabama and Mississippi). The non-regulated segment of Laclede groups provides gas transportation and other services across a much wide swath of geography.

Operations

The company operates through two primary operating segments: Gas Utility and Gas Marketing. Gas Utility (95% of revenue) —including the regulated operations of Laclede Gas Missouri Gas Energy EnergySouth and Alagasco. Gas Marketing —including Laclede Energy Resources Inc. a wholly owned subsidiary engaged in the marketing of natural gas and related activities on a non-regulated basis.

Sales and Marketing

Spire provides gas services to more than 1.7 million residential commercial and industrial customers. The company's Laclede Energy Resources unit offers natural gas marketing services to large commercial and industrial customers and wholesale business consists of buying and selling natural gas to other marketers producers utilities power generators pipelines and municipalities.

Gas Marketing markets natural gas to more than 200 retail customers and 120 wholesale customers (primarily in the central US) uses 30 interstate and intrastate pipelines and more than 125 suppliers.

Financial Performance

In fiscal 2016 (September year end) the company's net revenues decreased by 22% (from $1.98 billion to $1.54 billion) due to an increase in gas utility segment revenues primarily attributable to the acquisition of Alagasco totaling $270.3.The company's net income grew by 5% in fiscal 2016 to $144.2 million primarily due to lower net revenues outpacing the decline in operating expenses.

Spire's operating cash inflows in fiscal 2016 increased slightly from $322.4 million to $328.3 million

Strategy

Spire's business model balances providing regulated gas service with developing non-regulated but largely complementary operations to sustain business growth. It is looking to develop and invest in emerging technologies invest in infrastructure grow through acquisitions and enhance the efficiency of its existing operations.

The company primarily focuses on organic growth and acquiring and integrating gas utilities. Acquisitions support Spire's strategic focus on growing its regulated gas utility business.

In 2016 it changed its name from Laclede Group to Spire Inc. to better serve its growing number of companies. Mergers and Acquisitions

In 2016 Spire acquired EnergySouth (the parent company of Mobile Gas and Willmut Gas) for $344 million from Sempra U.S. Gas & Power.

In 2015 the company bought Alagasco from Energen. The Alagasco deal created geographic and regulatory diversity by expanding Spire's scope into Alabama.

Company Background

In 2013 the company acquired Missouri Gas Energy from Southern Union Company and affiliate of Energy Transfer Equity L.P. and Energy Transfer Partners L.P.

Innovating in the non-regulated gas segment in 2013 Laclede Group teamed with Siemens Industry to launch Spire natural gas fueling solutions to offer truckers cheaper compressed natural gas in place of diesel. The Spire system offers fleet managers strategic planning station design build and operation as well as financing facility improvements maintenance safety billing and technical consultation.

In 2012 Laclede Gas bought natural gas from 28 different suppliers in order to meet its gas sales and natural gas storage commitments.

In 2008 in order to generate cash to invest in its core businesses Laclede Group sold its SM&P Utility Resources unit (an underground facility locating and marking service business) to Stripe Acquisition for $85 million.

Laclede Gas dates back to 1852 and in 1896 was one of the 12 companies listed in the original Dow. The Laclede Group as the holding company for both regulated and deregulated businesses was formed in 2001.

EXECUTIVES

President and Chief Executive Officer; Director, Suzanne Sitherwood, age 55, $573,366 total compensation
SVP Finance and Accounting; CFO Laclede Gas Company, Steven P. Rasche
Vice President President Laclede Energy Resources Inc., Scott E. Jaskowiak, age 54
Executive Vice President Chief Operating Officer, Steven L. Lindsey, $301,154 total compensation
Assistant Vice President and Associat, Ellen (Elle) Theroff
Vice President Field Operations, Steve K Holcomb
Chairman, William E. Nasser, age 78
Auditors: Deloitte & Touche LLP

LOCATIONS

HQ: Spire Inc
700 Market Street, St. Louis, MO 63101
Phone: 314 342-0500
Web: www.spireenergy.com

PRODUCTS/OPERATIONS

2016 Sales

	$ mil.	% of total
Gas Utility	1,459.4	95
Gas Marketing	78.5	5
Other	4.8	-
Eliminations	(5.4)	-
Total	**1,537.3**	**100**

SUBSIDIARIES
Laclede Gas Company
Alabama Gas Corporation
EnergySouth Inc.
Laclede Pipeline Company
Laclede Investment LLC
Laclede Development Company
Laclede Insurance Risk Services Inc.
Shared Services Corporation
Spire Resources LLC

COMPETITORS

Alabama Power	Ferrellgas Partners
Ameren	Great Plains Energy
AmeriGas Partners	Mears Group Inc.
Duke Energy	SCANA
Empire District Electric	Southern Union

HISTORICAL FINANCIALS

Company Type: Public

Income Statement

FYE: September 30

	REVENUE ($ mil.)	NET INCOME ($ mil.)	NET PROFIT MARGIN	EMPLOYEES
09/16	1,537.3	144.2	9.4%	3,296.0
09/15	1,976.4	136.9	6.9%	3,078.0
09/14	1,627.2	84.6	5.2%	3,152.0
09/13	1,017.0	52.7	5.2%	2,326.0
09/12	1,125.4	62.6	5.6%	1,656.0
Annual Growth	**8.1%**	**23.2%**	**—**	**18.8%**

2016 Year-End Financials

Debt ratio: 34.2%	No. of shares (mil.): 45.6
Return on equity: 8.6%	Dividends
Cash ($ mil.): 5.2	Yield: 3.0%
Current ratio: 0.49	Payout: 59.7%
Long-term debt ($ mil.): 1,833.7	Market value ($ mil.): 2,910.0

	STOCK PRICE ($)	P/E		PER SHARE ($)		
	FY Close	High/Low	Earnings	Dividends	Book Value
09/16	63.74	22 17	3.24	1.96	38.73
09/15	54.53	18 15	3.16	1.84	36.31
09/14	46.40	21 19	2.35	1.76	34.93
09/13	45.00	24 19	2.02	1.70	32.00
09/12	43.00	15 13	2.79	1.66	26.69
Annual Growth	**10.3%**	**— —**	**3.8%**	**4.2%**	**9.8%**

Spirit Airlines Inc

Spirit Airlines can lift the spirits of people seeking sunshine. The ultra low-cost carrier (ULCC) operates more than 250 daily flights between major US cities and popular vacation spots in South Florida the Caribbean and Latin America serving nearly 80 destinations. It operates an all Airbus fleet of nearly 55 single-aisle aircraft including A319s A320s and A321s. Spirit capitalizes on an ancillary service model charging separately for baggage advance seat selection and other travel-related upgrades. In addition to scheduled service the company partners with third-party vendors to offer a slate of vacation packages via its website.

Geographic Reach

The company's route network includes 191 markets served by 56 airports throughout North America Central America South America and the Caribbean. Revenue generated from the US accounts for nearly 90% of Spirit's revenue.

Spirit Airlines has its executive offices and headquarters located in a leased facility in Florida. It has additional maintenance operations in leased facilities in Detroit; Chicago; Atlantic City New Jersey; Dallas; Houston; and Las Vegas Nevada.

Sales and MarketingSpirit Airlines sells through its website an outsourced call center and third-party travel agents. Its spirit.com site accounts for about two-thirds of sales.

Financial PerformanceWith the Great Recession that decimated the airline industry far behind it Spirit is enjoying uncharted growth over the years. Revenues jumped 11% from $1.93 billion in 2014 to $2.14 billion in 2015 a historic milestone for the company. The spike in revenue in 2015 was driven by a 2% increase in passenger revenue. Non-ticket revenue also climbed by 24% due to a 27% increase in traffic and an increase in baggage revenue per passenger flight segment.

Profits also surged 41% from $225 million in 2014 to peak at a record-shattering $317 million in 2015 due to the higher revenue and decreased increase expenses. In addition its cash flow from operations skyrocketed by 82% from 2014 to 2015.

StrategyTo maintain its impressive growth trajectory Spirit is expanding its city destination network while also concentrating its resources on the growing Caribbean and Latin American markets. Like most carriers within its industry Spirit's top issue is controlling costs in order sustain a profit from its low fares.

To this end the company has moved to an aggressive unbundling strategy to stimulate passenger demand and revenues. Unbundling allows passengers to pay separately for products and services that they want to use. Charging for such extras as onboard beverages and snacks enables Spirit to offset its low ticket prices as well as maintain its competitive market presence.

EXECUTIVES

President CEO and Director, Robert L. (Bob) Fornaro, age 63
SVP and CIO, Rocky Wiggins, age 55
SVP Network and Revenue Management, Theodore C. (Ted) Botimer, age 50, $300,000 total compensation
SVP and Chief Commercial Officer, Matt Klein
VP Airport and Inflight Services, Jake Filene
SVP and COO, John Bendoraitis, age 52, $335,000 total compensation
SVP and CFO, Edward M. (Ted) Christie, age 45, $335,600 total compensation
Vice President Of Technical Operations, Guy Borowski
V Pres, Patricia (Pat) Willis
Vice President Flight Operations, Joe (Joey) Houghton
Senior Vice President Network and Revenue Management, Ted (Teddy) Botimer
Vice President Consumer Marketing, Bobby (Bob) Schroeter
Vice President Financial Planning Analysis, Scott Haralson
Vice President People Services, Cecily Bachnik
Vice President Human Resources, Derek V Keuren
Chairman, H. McIntyre (Mac) Gardner, age 55
Secretary, Teresa (Terry) Miller
Auditors: Ernst & Young LLP

LOCATIONS

HQ: Spirit Airlines Inc
2800 Executive Way, Miramar, FL 33025
Phone: 954 447-7920
Web: www.spirit.com

PRODUCTS/OPERATIONS

2015 Sales

	$ mil.	% of total
Passenger	1,169.3	55
Non-ticket	972.1	45
Total	**2,141.5**	**100**

Spirit Standard ULCC Product Features
Clean fuel efficient airplanes
Deluxe leather seating
Easy online booking and check-in
Friendly staff
Largest ULCC network in the U.S. Latin America and Caribbean
One personal item that fits under the seat
Reliable on-time service
Ultra low fares

COMPETITORS

AirTran Airways	JetBlue
Allegiant Travel	Southwest Airlines
American Airlines Group	US Airways
Delta Air Lines	United Continental
	Virgin America

HISTORICAL FINANCIALS
Company Type: Public

Income Statement
FYE: December 31

	REVENUE ($ mil.)	NET INCOME ($ mil.)	NET PROFIT MARGIN	EMPLOYEES
12/15	2,141.4	317.2	14.8%	4,847.0
12/14	1,931.5	225.4	11.7%	4,219.0
12/13	1,654.3	176.9	10.7%	3,619.0
12/12	1,318.3	108.4	8.2%	3,033.0
12/11	1,071.1	76.4	7.1%	2,580.0
Annual Growth	**18.9%**	**42.7%**	**—**	**17.1%**

2015 Year-End Financials

Debt ratio: 25.5%
Return on equity: 28.4%
Cash ($ mil.): 803.6
Current ratio: 2.20
Long-term debt ($ mil.): 596.7
No. of shares (mil.): 71.5
Dividends
Yield: —
Payout: —
Market value ($ mil.): 2,851.0

	STOCK PRICE ($) FY Close	P/E High/Low		PER SHARE ($) Earnings	Dividends	Book Value
12/15	39.85	19	8	4.38	0.00	17.13
12/14	75.58	27	14	3.08	0.00	13.78
12/13	45.41	19	7	2.42	0.00	10.60
12/12	17.73	16	9	1.49	0.00	8.04
12/11	15.60	12	7	1.43	0.00	6.44
Annual Growth	**26.4%**	—	—	**32.3%**	—	**27.7%**

Spirit Realty Capital, Inc (New)

Auditors: Ernst & Young LLP

LOCATIONS

HQ: Spirit Realty Capital, Inc (New)
2727 North Harwood Street, Suite 300, Dallas, TX 75201
Phone: 972 476-1900

HISTORICAL FINANCIALS
Company Type: Public

Income Statement
FYE: December 31

	REVENUE ($ mil.)	NET INCOME ($ mil.)	NET PROFIT MARGIN	EMPLOYEES
12/15	667.3	114.7	17.2%	71.0
12/14	602.8	(33.8)	—	73.0
12/13	419.4	1.6	0.4%	59.0
12/12	282.8	25.4	9.0%	38.0
12/11	279.3	53.8	19.3%	0.0
Annual Growth	**24.3%**	**20.8%**	**—**	**—**

2015 Year-End Financials

Debt ratio: 51.6%
Return on equity: 3.3%
Cash ($ mil.): 21.7
Current ratio: 0.15
Long-term debt ($ mil.): 4,092.7
No. of shares (mil.): 441.8
Dividends
Yield: 6.8%
Payout: 207.5%
Market value ($ mil.): 4,427.0

	STOCK PRICE ($) FY Close	P/E High/Low		PER SHARE ($) Earnings	Dividends	Book Value
12/15	10.02	50	35	0.26	0.69	7.90
12/14	11.89	—	—	(0.09)	0.67	8.07
12/13	9.83	—	—	(0.00)	0.30	8.42
12/12	17.78	147	125	0.12	0.00	6.56
Annual Growth	**(17.4%)**	—	—	**29.4%**	—	**6.4%**

Sportsman's Warehouse Holdings Inc

Auditors: KPMG LLP

LOCATIONS

HQ: Sportsman's Warehouse Holdings Inc
7035 South High Tech Drive, Midvale, UT 84047
Phone: 801 566-6681   **Fax:** 801 304-4388
Web: www.sportsmanswarehouse.com

HISTORICAL FINANCIALS
Company Type: Public

Income Statement
FYE: January 30

	REVENUE ($ mil.)	NET INCOME ($ mil.)	NET PROFIT MARGIN	EMPLOYEES
01/16	729.9	27.7	3.8%	4,200.0
01/15*	660.0	13.7	2.1%	3,800.0
02/14	643.1	21.7	3.4%	3,000.0
02/13	526.9	28.0	5.3%	0.0
01/12	376.5	33.6	8.9%	0.0
Annual Growth	**18.0%**	**(4.7%)**	**—**	**—**

*Fiscal year change

2016 Year-End Financials

Debt ratio: 60.0%
Return on equity: —
Cash ($ mil.): 2.1
Current ratio: 1.82
Long-term debt ($ mil.): 147.6
No. of shares (mil.): 42.0
Dividends
Yield: —
Payout: —
Market value ($ mil.): 551.0

	STOCK PRICE ($) FY Close	P/E High/Low		PER SHARE ($) Earnings	Dividends	Book Value
01/16	13.11	22	11	0.66	0.00	(0.05)
01/15*	7.13	32	16	0.34	0.00	(0.75)
Annual Growth	**83.9%**	—	—	**94.1%**	—	—

*Fiscal year change

Springleaf Finance Corp

EXECUTIVES

Pres-ceo, Jay N Levine
Senior Vice President Human Resources, Dave (Davie) Gutscher
Vice President Compliance, Jane (Ginny) Maher
Vice President Of Tax, ED (Eddie) Jackson
Executive Vice President Operations, Brad (Brady) Borchers
Vice President Software Engineering, Erik (Rik) Peterson
Vice President And Corporate Controller, Jeanne (Jeannie) Dressel
Vice President And Corporate Controller, Jeanne (Jeannie) Balczewski
Vice President Tax, Marianne (Ann) Ford

Vice President Risk Management, Mathew (Matt) Roe
Senior Vice President Corporate Development and Acquisitions, Kevin (Kev) Small
Vice President of Finance, John (Jack) Kelly
Secretary, Jack R (Jackie) Erkilla
Auditors: PricewaterhouseCoopers LLP

LOCATIONS

HQ: Springleaf Finance Corp
601 N.W. Second Street, Evansville, IN 47708
Phone: 812 424-8031
Web: www.springleaf.com

HISTORICAL FINANCIALS

Company Type: Public

Income Statement

	REVENUE ($ mil.)	NET INCOME ($ mil.)	NET PROFIT MARGIN	EMPLOYEES
12/15	1,240.0	9.0	0.7%	3,500.0
12/14	1,780.6	447.9	25.2%	3,239.0
12/13	967.0	(82.6)	—	3,300.0
12/12	733.2	(220.6)	—	3,600.0
12/11	753.0	(224.7)	—	5,800.0
Annual Growth 13.3%		—	—	(11.9%)

FYE: December 31

2015 Year-End Financials

Debt ratio: 79.6%
Return on equity: 0.4%
Cash ($ mil.): 321.0
Current ratio: 1.11
Long-term debt ($ mil.): 9,582.0
No. of shares (mil.): 10.1
Dividends
  Yield: —
  Payout: —
Market value ($ mil.): —

SS&C Technologies Holdings, Inc.

SS&C Technologies helps its clients buy low and sell high and do some of it automatically. The company develops software for managing financial portfolios loans real estate equity back-office processing and securities trading and it provides consulting and outsourcing services. Its applications automate investment portfolio management asset and liability management for actuaries property and casualty insurance risk management trade ordering and financial modeling. SS&C serves asset managers insurance companies banks corporate treasuries hedge funds and government agencies among others. Clients have included Middlebury College and Monro Muffler Brake. It has offices in North America Europe and Asia. SS&C bought one of its competitors Advent Software for more than $2.5 billion in 2015.

Operations

More than three quarter of SS&C's revenue comes from its software-enabled services with about 14% from maintenance fees. The rest of revenue is evenly split between software licenses and professional services.

Geographic Reach

SS&C Technologies has about two dozen offices across the US. It has international offices in Australia Canada the Cayman Islands Hong Kong India Ireland Malaysia Singapore The Netherlands and the UK. The company's biggest market has been the US which accounted for two-thirds of sales in 2014. The UK has been the next biggest

market with 13% of SS&C's sales. Sales grew 28% in the Asia-Pacific (including Japan) region in 2014.

Sales and Marketing

The company counts a diverse customer base of 6900 clients in the financial services industry. It uses a direct sales force given the complexity of the industry and its extensive regulatory and reporting requirements. For its property management software however it does use a telemarketing staff.

Financial Performance

Sales were higher in 2014 but the rate of growth slowed to 7.7% from 2013 compared to the 29% growth from 2012 to 2013. The 2012-to-2013 sales were boosted by acquisitions. Acquisitions also pushed 2014's revenue higher as did sales for fund administration services to alternative investment managers. Net income however jumped 11% to $131 million. The company had lower interest expense in 2014 which helped keep costs down.

Strategy

Acquisitions play a key role in the company's strategy resulting in some 40 purchases since 1995. SS&C typically pursues companies that either expand its product and service offerings into new markets or increase its client base within the financial services industry.

Mergers and Acquisitions

SS&C went whole hog with its acquisition strategy in 2015 making one of its biggest deals –more than $2 billion –to buy key competitor Advent Software. Advent a provider of investment management software and services brings SS&C more than 4300 customers including asset managers hedge funds fund administrators prime brokers family offices and wealth management advisory firms. Advent's sales for 2014 were just under $400 million.

In 2014 SS&C added another three initial organization when it acquired DST Global Solutions a subsidiary of DST Systems. SS&C paid $95 million in cash for the UK-based company. DST Global's investment and fund accounting platform HiPortfolio and its investment data management and analytics platform Anova became part of SS&C's product portfolio.

A 2013 acquisition was that of Prime Management Limited a fund administrator with offices in Bermuda and Canada. It furthered SS&C's ability to administer insurance linked securities and the funds which invest in them. In 2012 the company bought GlobeOp Financial Services a provider of middle and back-office services and integrated risk reporting to hedge fund and account managers and Thomson Reuters' PORTIA business a developer of middle-to-back office investment operations software for $170 million. Also that year it bought HedgeMetrix and Gravity Financial.

HISTORY

Early History

Former KPMG Peat Marwick (now KPMG International) executive William Stone founded Securities Software & Consulting in 1986. The company produced its first product in 1989 –a DOS-based portfolio management program geared toward large and medium-sized institutional investors –and called it CAMRA (complete asset management reporting and accounting).

SS&C introduced a Windows-based version of CAMRA in 1993. That year the company also introduced its first loan portfolio management product. SS&C acquired Chalke Inc. in 1995 and with it Chalke's PTS (profit testing system) economic modeling software for insurance companies.

The company went public as SS&C Technologies in 1996. The next year groups from New York and Connecticut filed a class-action suit claiming the company made misrepresentations in its prospectus (the case was dismissed in 1999). Also in 1997 SS&C acquired Dutch financial software company Mabel Systems and Shepro Braun Systems.

EXECUTIVES

President and COO, Normand A. (Norm) Boulanger, age 53, $550,000 total compensation
Chairman and CEO, William C. (Bill) Stone, age 60, $875,000 total compensation
SVP and General Manager Advent, David Peter F. (Pete) Hess, age 46
SVP and CFO, Patrick J. Pedonti, age 64, $350,000 total compensation
SVP and Chief Development Officer, Steve H. Kremidas
SVP and General Manager DBC, Richard Shalowitz
SVP and General Manager Treasury Banks and Credit Unions Business, Colleen Nelsen
VP and Managing Director SS&C Technologies Canada, Eric R. Rocks
SVP and General Manager, Thomas (Tom) McMackin
SVP General Counsel and Secretary, Paul G. Igoe, age 53, $260,000 total compensation
SVP Global Institutional Outsourcing, David N. (Dave) Reid
SVP and Managing Director Alternative Assets, Rahul Kanwar, $475,000 total compensation
Managing Director SS&C GlobeOp Canada, Henry Toy
Managing Director SS&C Technologies Australia, Phil Banas
SVP Enterprise Risk, James (Jim) Ramenda
SVP and General Manager Financial Markets Division, Bob Moitoso
SVP Institutional and Investment Management, Christy Bremner
SVP Institutional and Investment Management, J. Timothy (Tim) Reilly
CTO, Bob Schwartz
Managing Director and Head SS&C GlobeOp Asia, Nandini Sankar
Vice President Institutional Technology, Christopher (Chris) Brown
Auditors: PricewaterhouseCoopers LLP

LOCATIONS

HQ: SS&C Technologies Holdings, Inc.
80 Lamberton Road, Windsor, CT 06095
Phone: 860 298-4500
Web: www.ssctech.com

PRODUCTS/OPERATIONS

2014 Sales by Product Group

	$ mil.	% of total
Portfolio management/accounting	691.9	90
Trading/treasury operations	32.7	5
Property management	15.2	2
Financial modeling	8.7	1
Money market processing	9.4	1
Loan management/accounting	8.4	1
Training	1.6	-
Total	**767.9**	**100**

2014 Sales by Geography

	% of Total
United States	67
United Kingdom	13
Canada	8
Europe Excluding UK	7
Asia-Pacific and Japan	3
Americas	2
Total	**100**

2014 Sales

	% of Total
Software-enabled Services	77
Maintenance	14
Software Licenses	5
Professional Services	4
Total	**100**

Selected Services

Application outsourcing and hosting
Consulting
Data conversion
Installation
Maintenance
Technical support
Training

Selected Software

AdvisorWare (portfolio management and investment accounting)
Altair (asset management for hedge funds and family offices)
AnalyticsExpress (financial modeling)
Antares (trade order management)
The BANC Mall (Internet-based lending and leasing tool)
CAMRA (asset management reporting and accounting)
DBC (financial modeling)
Debt & Derivatives (comprehensive derivative and debt portfolio analysis)
Finesse (dynamic financial analysis and simulation)
Lightning (office processing management and automation)
LMS (loan management)
PALMS (alternative investment managers)
PortPro (balance sheet and investment portfolio analysis and management)
PTS (life insurance modeling and decision support)
SamTrak (property management for real estate leasing agents and property managers)
SKYLINE II (property management accounting and reporting)
SS&C Wealth Management (wealth management)
TradeDesk (fixed-income transaction processing automation)
TradeThru (trading and treasury operations)

COMPETITORS

ADP	Liquid Holdings
Algorithmics	McCracken Financial
Bank of New York	Solutions
Mellon	Misys
Bloomberg L.P.	Neovest
Charles River Systems	PNC Financial
Citigroup	StatPro Group
Eze Software Group LLC	State Street
Fidessa	SunGard
Frontline Technologies	TradeStation
HP Enterprise Services	Triple Point
Intuit	Yardi Systems

HISTORICAL FINANCIALS

Company Type: Public

Income Statement

FYE: December 31

	REVENUE ($ mil.)	NET INCOME ($ mil.)	NET PROFIT MARGIN	EMPLOYEES
12/15	1,000.2	42.8	4.3%	6,089.0
12/14	767.8	131.1	17.1%	4,674.0
12/13	712.7	117.9	16.5%	4,194.0
12/12	551.8	45.8	8.3%	4,086.0
12/11	370.8	51.0	13.8%	1,484.0
Annual Growth	**28.2%**	**(4.3%)**	**—**	**42.3%**

2015 Year-End Financials

Debt ratio: 47.4%
Return on equity: 2.4%
Cash ($ mil.): 434.1
Current ratio: 1.62
Long-term debt ($ mil.): 2,719.0
No. of shares (mil.): 196.9
Dividends
  Yield: 1.4%
  Payout: 212.7%
Market value ($ mil.): 13,445.0

	STOCK PRICE ($) FY Close	P/E High/Low	Earnings	PER SHARE ($) Dividends	Book Value
12/15	68.27	317 224	0.23	0.50	10.69
12/14	58.49	76 46	0.75	0.13	8.00
12/13	44.26	60 31	0.69	0.00	7.45
12/12	23.09	90 61	0.28	0.00	6.80
12/11	18.06	63 40	0.32	0.00	6.31
Annual Growth	**39.4%**	**— —**	**(8.1%)**	**—**	**14.1%**

Starwood Property Trust Inc.

Starwood Property Trust hopes to shine brightly in the world of mortgages. A real estate investment trust (REIT) the company originates finances and manages US commercial and residential mortgage loans commercial mortgage-backed securities and other commercial real estate debt investments. It acquires discounted loans from failed banks and financial institutions some through the FDIC which typically auctions off large pools of loan portfolios. Starwood Property Trust is externally managed by SPT Management LLC an affiliate of Starwood Capital Group. As a REIT the trust is exempt from paying federal income tax so long as it distributes quarterly dividends to shareholders.

Financial Performance

Overall revenues grew 63% in 2012 to $327 million up from $201 million in 2011. The trust primarily earns money on interest income from mortgage-backed securities and loans.

Mergers and Acquisitions

In 2013 Starwood Property Trust bought LNR Property LLC a real estate investment finance management and development firm. The trust paid $862 million for LNR's US special servicer the US investment securities portfolio Archetype Mortgage Capital (now Starwood Mortgage Capital) Archetype Financial Institution Services LNR Europe and 50% of LNR's interest in Auction.com.

Later that year it moved to spin off its single-family residential business as a new REIT named Starwood Waypoint Residential Trust. The trust which will be affiliated with Waypoint Homes will invest own and operate single-family rental homes and non-performing residential mortgage loans in the US.

EXECUTIVES

Vice President, Himanshu Saxena
Vice President, Mary Carlin
Auditors: Deloitte & Touche LLP

LOCATIONS

HQ: Starwood Property Trust Inc.
  591 West Putnam Avenue, Greenwich, CT 06830
Phone: 203 422-7700
Web: www.starwoodpropertytrust.com

COMPETITORS

American Capital	Newcastle Investment
Agency Corp.	NorthStar Realty
Annaly Capital	PennyMac Mortgage
Management	Petra Real Estate

Arbor Realty Trust
CYS Investments
Hatteras Financial
Invesco Mortgage Capital
JER Investors Trust
MFA Financial
RAIT Financial Trust
Realty Finance Corporation
Redwood Trust
Two Harbors
iStar Financial Inc

HISTORICAL FINANCIALS

Company Type: Public

Income Statement

FYE: December 31

	REVENUE ($ mil.)	NET INCOME ($ mil.)	NET PROFIT MARGIN	EMPLOYEES
12/15	735.8	450.7	61.2%	450.0
12/14	702.8	495.0	70.4%	468.0
12/13	565.7	305.0	53.9%	2.0
12/12	306.9	201.2	65.5%	2.0
12/11	204.9	119.3	58.2%	2.0
Annual Growth	**37.7%**	**39.4%**	**—**	**287.3%**

2015 Year-End Financials

Debt ratio: 6.3%
Return on equity: 11.2%
Cash ($ mil.): 368.8
Current ratio: 1.48
Long-term debt ($ mil.): 5,432.2
No. of shares (mil.): 237.4
Dividends
  Yield: 9.3%
  Payout: 91.0%
Market value ($ mil.): 4,883.0

	STOCK PRICE ($) FY Close	P/E High/Low	Earnings	PER SHARE ($) Dividends	Book Value
12/15	20.56	13 10	1.91	1.92	17.43
12/14	23.24	13 10	2.24	1.92	17.27
12/13	27.70	16 13	1.82	1.82	21.90
12/12	22.96	14 11	1.76	1.86	20.07
12/11	18.51	17 12	1.38	1.74	18.88
Annual Growth	**2.7%**	**— —**	**8.5%**	**2.5%**	**(2.0%)**

State National Companies Inc

Auditors: Ernst & Young LLP

LOCATIONS

HQ: State National Companies Inc
  1900 L. Don Dodson Drive, Bedford, TX 76021
Phone: 817 265-2000
Web: www.statenational.com

HISTORICAL FINANCIALS

Company Type: Public

Income Statement

FYE: December 31

	ASSETS ($ mil.)	NET INCOME ($ mil.)	INCOME AS % OF ASSETS	EMPLOYEES
12/15	2,388.3	44.6	1.9%	400.0
12/14	2,091.7	11.0	0.5%	400.0
12/13	1,690.9	22.7	1.3%	385.0
12/12	1,497.5	15.8	1.1%	0.0
12/11	0.0	27.9	—	0.0
Annual Growth	**—**	**12.5%**	**—**	**—**

2015 Year-End Financials

Return on assets: 1.9%
Return on equity: 17.7%
Long-term debt ($ mil.): —
No. of shares (mil.): 42.5
Sales ($ mil): 198.9

Dividends
Yield: 1.4%
Payout: 16.0%
Market value ($ mil.): 417.0

	STOCK PRICE ($)	P/E		PER SHARE ($)		
	FY Close	High/Low	Earnings	Dividends	Book Value
12/15	9.81	12 9	1.01	0.14	6.20
12/14	11.98	45 39	0.28	0.01	5.44
Annual Growth	(18.1%) 13.8%	—	—260.7%	1300.0%	

Steel Partners Holdings LP

Steel Partners Holdings is a hedge fund that rules with an iron fist. The activist fund invests in a variety of businesses from banks to hot dog restaurants. It often takes positions on those companies' boards and is not bashful about making sweeping changes within those enterprises. The firm also likes to hold on to its portfolio assets for the long term. Among its holdings is Utah-based WebBank which offers commercial consumer and mortgage loans as well as federally guaranteed USDA and SBA loans. With some $4 billion in assets under management Steel Partners also owns portions of Unisys Aerojet Rocketdyne Selectica SL Industries and Nathan's Famous. Activist investor Warren Lichtenstein heads the firm.

After the company was inundated with redemption requests at the height of the economic crisis Lichtenstein initiated plans to convert Steel Partners from a hedge fund to a publicly traded closed-end fund. However unhappy investors (including Carl Icahn) rejected the plan and filed suit to block the restructuring. The lawsuit was dropped in 2010 and Steel Partners began trading on the over-the-counter markets the following year. The restructuring plan included spinning off its Steel Partners II Masters Fund into WebFinancial a public company controlled by Steel Partners.

The company lost a five-year battle to oust board members of Sapporo in 2010. Steel Partners which was the highest stakeholder in the brewery company hoped to turn the company's declining sales around through sweeping changes. After being voted down Steel Partners sold its stake in Sapporo.

EXECUTIVES

Assistant Treasurer, Elizabeth (Beth) Seeds
Auditors: BDO USA, LLP

LOCATIONS

HQ: Steel Partners Holdings LP
590 Madison Avenue, 32nd Floor, New York, NY 10022
Phone: 212 520-2300

COMPETITORS

Berkshire Hathaway	Fortress Investment
Blackstone Group	Group
Citadel	Icahn Enterprises
D. E. Shaw	Soros Fund Management

HISTORICAL FINANCIALS

Company Type: Public

Income Statement

FYE: December 31

	REVENUE ($ mil.)	NET INCOME ($ mil.)	NET PROFIT MARGIN	EMPLOYEES
12/15	998.0	136.7	13.7%	3,548.0
12/14	849.5	(7.5)	—	3,028.0
12/13	805.1	19.4	2.4%	2,745.0
12/12	711.5	41.0	5.8%	0.0
12/11	624.1	35.4	5.7%	0.0
Annual Growth	12.4%	40.1%	—	—

2015 Year-End Financials

Debt ratio: 14.2%
Return on equity: —
Cash ($ mil.): 185.8
Current ratio: 2.24
Long-term debt ($ mil.): 235.9

No. of shares (mil.): 26.6
Dividends
Yield: —
Payout: —
Market value ($ mil.): 436.0

	STOCK PRICE ($)	P/E		PER SHARE ($)		
	FY Close	High/Low	Earnings	Dividends	Book Value
12/15	16.38	4 3	4.98	0.00	20.95
12/14	17.66	— —	(0.27)	0.00	17.95
12/13	17.35	27 18	0.63	0.00	19.81
12/12	11.79	10 7	1.38	0.00	17.13
12/11	12.05	12 8	0.99	0.00	(0.00)
Annual Growth	8.0%	— —	49.8%	—	—

Sterling Bancorp (DE)

Sterling Bancorp is the holding company for Sterling National Bank a community-based thrift operating dozens of offices in New York's Hudson Valley region and Greater New York City area. Founded in 1888 the bank attracts consumers and business clients by offering traditional deposit products such as checking and savings accounts and CDs. It uses funds from deposits to originate primarily real estate loans and mortgages. Sterling Bancorp which has assets of more than $7 billion was formerly Provident New York Bancorp; Provident acquired the former Sterling Bancorp in late 2013 and changed its name as well as the name of its banking subsidiary to Sterling.

Financial Performance

In fiscal 2013 Sterling Bancorp reported revenue of about $160 million up 9% from the prior year. The increase was primarily because of an 18% jump in loans that year (powered by commercial real estate and commercial and industrial loans) offset slightly by a decline in noninterest income.

Net income was also up in 2013 rising 27% to $25 million. Net cash from operations was down about 10% to $22.6 million.

Strategy

In 2016 Sterling sold its mortgage banking business which had seen declined earnings to Freedom Mortgage in New Jersey. Excluded from that deal were its mortgage warehouse lending operations a business arena it entered when other banks were leaving. The company is also selling its trust operations.

Mergers and Acquisitions

Sterling is focused on expanding in the greater New York metropolitan region and increasing the importance of its commercial banking operations.

To that end in late 2013 it acquired the former Sterling Bancorp and took its name. The acquisition added the former Sterling's varied commercial and consumer lending products as well as its presence in the New York City area.

EXECUTIVES

Sr Exec V Pres, James (Jamie) Peoples
Vice President, Rita Kokkoris
Vice President Marketing And Communications, Rita Champ
Executive Vice President Chief Risk Officer, Daniel Rothstein
Vice President and Operational Risk Manager, James F (Jamie) Lee
Assistant Vice President Research And Database Marketing Manager, David Gerbino
Vice President, Kristen (Kristy) Santos
Vice President Commercial Lending Offi, John (Jack) Willis
Vice President and Community Business Loan Officer, Frank W (Frankie) Armstrong
Executive Vice President Market, Richard (Dick) Jones
Vice President of Project Management Office, Jon (Jonny) Christmann
Senior Vice President, William (Bill) Lamadore
Senior Vice President and Managing Director, Jeffery (Jeff) Wall
Auditors: Crowe Horwath LLP

LOCATIONS

HQ: Sterling Bancorp (DE)
400 Rella Boulevard, Montebello, NY 10901
Phone: 845 369-8040
Web: www.sterlingbancorp.com

COMPETITORS

Capital One	JPMorgan Chase
Citibank	KeyCorp
HSBC USA	M&T Bank

HISTORICAL FINANCIALS

Company Type: Public

Income Statement

FYE: December 31

	ASSETS ($ mil.)	NET INCOME ($ mil.)	INCOME AS % OF ASSETS	EMPLOYEES
12/15	11,955.9	66.1	0.6%	1,089.0
12/14*	7,424.8	17.0	0.2%	829.0
09/14	7,337.3	27.6	0.4%	836.0
09/13	4,049.1	25.2	0.6%	543.0
09/12	4,022.9	19.8	0.5%	522.0
Annual Growth	31.3%	35.0%	—	20.2%

*Fiscal year change

2015 Year-End Financials

Return on assets: 0.6%
Return on equity: 5.0%
Long-term debt ($ mil.): —
No. of shares (mil.): 130.0
Sales ($ mil): 410.8

Dividends
Yield: 1.7%
Payout: 46.6%
Market value ($ mil.): 2,109.0

	STOCK PRICE ($)	P/E		PER SHARE ($)		
	FY Close	High/Low	Earnings	Dividends	Book Value
12/15	16.22	29 22	0.60	0.28	12.81
12/14*	14.38	72 55	0.20	0.28	11.62
09/14	12.79	40 32	0.34	0.27	11.49
09/13	10.89	20 15	0.58	0.24	10.89
09/12	9.41	19 11	0.52	0.24	11.12
Annual Growth	14.6%	— —	3.6%	3.9%	3.6%

*Fiscal year change

Stifel Financial Corp.

Stifel Financial doesn't repress investors. Through subsidiaries Stifel Nicolaus (founded 1890) Thomas Weisel Century Nicolaus Securities Associates Stifel Bank & Trust and others the financial services holding company provides asset management financial advice and banking services for private individuals corporations municipal and institutional clients in the US. Stifel also offers brokerage and mergers and acquisitions advisory services for corporate clients underwrites debt and equity and provides research on more than 1000 US and European equities. The firm boasts nearly 330 US offices with a concentration in the Midwest and mid-Atlantic regions and additional offices in the UK and the rest of Europe.

OperationsStifel Financial operates two main business segments. The Global Wealth Management segment which made up nearly 60% of the firm's total revenue in 2015 consists of two businesses: Stifel Bank which provides traditional banking products and services and the Private Client Group which is made up of offices across the US that provide securities brokerage services and insurance products. The Institutional Group segment (40% of revenue) provides securities brokerage trading and research services to institutions and specializes in the sale of equity and fixed-income products.The firm generated more than 30% of its total revenue from commissions in 2015 while around 20% and 15% of revenue came from investment banking fees and principal transactions respectively. The company's asset management and service fees brought in another more than 20% of total revenue while interest income made up just under 10% during the year.In the US Stifel operates through subsidiaries such as Stifel Nicolaus & company; Keefe Bruyette & Woods Inc.; Miller Buckfire & Co. LLC; and Century Securities Associates Inc. It operates through Stifel Nicolaus Europe Limited in the UK and Europe.Geographic Reach

The company headquartered in Missouri with about 330 private client offices and 37 Institutional Group offices mostly across the US as well as in certain foreign locations in the UK and the rest of Europe. About 94% of its revenue came from the US during 2015 while another 5% came from business in the UK.Sales and MarketingWith its 2170-plus financial advisors and 720 independent contractors (as of 2016) Stifel serves individuals corporations municipalities and institutions. Its broker-dealer subsidiaries boast more than 1.5 million accounts from customers based in the US and Europe.

Financial Performance

Stifel's revenues and profits have been growing at a healthy clip in recent years thanks to business-boosting acquisitions combined with growth across all business lines as the financial markets have appreciated and demand for investor capital has strengthened. The firm's revenues climbed 6% to a record $2.3 billion during 2015 mostly driven by 28% asset management and service fee growth with more assets under management stemming from Stifel's recent acquisitions of Sterne and Barclays. Revenues were also buoyed by an uptick in commissions revenue thanks to an increase in mutual fund and equity transactions. The firm's investment banking revenue declined 10% due to a decrease in strategic advisory fees with fewer and smaller transactions compared to 2014. Despite revenue growth in 2015 Stifel's net income

plunged 48% to $92.34 million as the company spent more on compensation benefits and office space to support future revenue growth. Stifel's operations used $379.5 million for the year (operations generated $250.3 million in 2014) as the firm used more cash to purchase operating assets.StrategyStifel has fortified its operations and extended its international footprint mainly through strategic acquisitions as well as through partnerships. In 2015 to extend its reach into Israel the firm's Stifel Nicolaus subsidiary signed an exclusive investment banking collaboration agreement with Leumi Partners the investment & merchant banking arm of Bank Leumi le-Israel (Israel's largest banking group). The deal allowed Stifel Nicolaus to work with the foreign firm to provide investment banking services to Israel-related companies with strategic advisory services or fundraising of debt or equity on public or private markets across North America and in other regions. Looking to expand its private client footprint in the US and provide banking services to more of its private and corporate clients the firm made a slew of acquisitions between 2014 through 2016. By acquiring specialized firms Stifel broadened and bolstered its service offerings and financial advisor staff while expanding its Global Wealth Management client assets by more than $250 billion.

Mergers and Acquisitions

In mid-2016 Stifel agreed buy investment bank City Financial Corporation and its City Securities subsidiary. City Financial primarily operates in Indiana and the Midwest specializing in wealth management and public finance.

In January 2016 the firm bought global fund placement and advisory firm Eaton Partners LLC boosting Stifel's investment banking and high net worth private client business with new private equity firms hedge funds affluent family offices and institutional investor client relationships.In December 2015 Stifel purchased Barclays' Wealth and Investment Management Americas franchise in the US along with its 180 financial advisors managing some $56 billion in total client assets. Also looking to boost client assets and financial advisor count in 2015 Stifel acquired financial services firm Sterne Agee Group which boosted Stifel's Global Wealth Management team by 35% to more than 2800 financial advisors and independent representatives with $200 billion-plus in client assets. The deal also bolstered Stifel's fixed-income platform. Additionally in 2015 the firm acquired the California-based public finance investment banking boutique De La Rosa which strengthened Stifel's position in key underwriting markets in California. Similarly that year it acquired the Montgomery Alabama-based public finance investment banking firm Merchant which serves key markets in the Southeastern US.In 2014 it purchased Oriel Securities a London-based stockbroking and investment banking firm. Stifel made the deal to create a larger middle market investment banking group in London with broad research coverage across most sectors of the economy equity and debt sales and trading and investment banking services.

Also in 2014 Stifel bought 1919 Investment Counsel & Trust Company (formerly Legg Mason Investment Counsel & Trust Co.) from rival financial services firm Legg Mason. 1919 provides customized investment advisory and trust services on a discretionary basis to individuals families and institutions throughout the country. Its portfolio managers manage more than $9 billion in assets. 1919 is part of Stifel's Global Wealth Management segment and should be an ideal complement to its existing wealth management platform.

In mid-2013 Stifel obtained KCG Holdings' US institutional fixed income sales and trading business. Altogether Stifel's and KCG's combined teams boast some 90 sales and trading professionals across the US and Europe. The team covers high-yield and investment-grade corporate bonds asset-backed and mortgage-based securities loan trading and fixed income research in certain sectors and companies.

EXECUTIVES

Vice Chairman; EVP Investment Banking Stifel Nicolaus & Co., Richard J. Himelfarb, age 75, $250,000 total compensation

Chairman President and CEO, Ronald J. (Ron) Kruszewski, age 57, $200,000 total compensation

Co-President and CFO, James M. Zemlyak, age 56, $175,000 total compensation

EVP; President and Co-Director Institutional Group, Thomas P. Mulroy, age 54, $250,000 total compensation

SVP; President and CEO Keefe Bruyette and Woods, Thomas B. (Tom) Michaud, age 52, $250,000 total compensation

EVP; President and Co-Director Institutional Group, Victor J. Nesi, age 56, $250,000 total compensation

Senior Vice President, David (Dave) Sliney

Vice Chairman; EVP Stifel Nicolaus & Co., Ben A. Plotkin, age 60

Co-Chairman, Thomas W. (Thom) Weisel, age 75

Board Member, Mary W Brown

Auditors: Ernst & Young LLP

LOCATIONS

HQ: Stifel Financial Corp.
501 N. Broadway, St. Louis, MO 63102-2188
Phone: 314 342-2000
Web: www.stifel.com

PRODUCTS/OPERATIONS

Selected Services
Individual
Bonds
Corporate Executive Services
Estate Planning
Exchange Traded Funds
Financial And Wealth Planning
Insurance
Investment Advisory Services
Market News
Mutual Funds
Options
Portfolio Tracker
Prospectus
Retirement Plans
Stifel Bank & Trust
Stifel Cash Management Accounts
Stifel Mobile Announcement
Stifel Trust
Institutions
Asset Management
Conferences & Events
Equity Capital Markets
Equity Sales & Trading
Fixed Income Sales & Trading
Investment Banking
Public Finance
Research
Senior Management

2015 Sales

	$ mil.	% of total
Commissions	749.5	32
Asset management and service fees	493.8	21
Investment banking	503.1	20
Principal transactions	389.3	16
Interest	179.1	8
Others	62.2	3
Total	**2,377.0**	**100**

Selected Subsidiaries

Broadway Air Corp.
Butler Wick & Co. Inc.
Century Securities Associates Inc.
   CSA Insurance Agency Incorporated
Choice Financial Partners Inc.
First Service Financial Company
   Stifel Bank & Trust
Hanifen Imhoff Inc.
Missouri Valley Partners
Stifel Asset Management Corp.
Stifel Nicolaus Limited (UK)
Stifel Nicolaus & Company Incorporated
   Ryan Beck Holdings LLC
   Stifel Nicolaus Insurance Agency Incorporated
Stifel Nicholas Limited (UK)
Thomas Weisel Partners Group Inc.

COMPETITORS

Bank of America	Morgan Stanley
Cowen Group	Oppenheimer Holdings
Edward Jones	Piper Jaffray
Goldman Sachs	Raymond James
JMP Group	Financial
Jefferies Group	Robert W. Baird & Co.
Lazard	Wells Fargo Advisors

HISTORICAL FINANCIALS

Company Type: Public

Income Statement

FYE: December 31

	ASSETS ($ mil.)	NET INCOME ($ mil.)	INCOME AS % OF ASSETS	EMPLOYEES
12/15	13,335.9	92.3	0.7%	7,100.0
12/14	9,518.1	176.0	1.8%	6,200.0
12/13	9,008.8	162.0	1.8%	5,862.0
12/12	6,966.1	138.5	2.0%	5,343.0
12/11	4,951.9	84.1	1.7%	5,097.0
Annual Growth	28.1%	2.4%	—	8.6%

2015 Year-End Financials

Return on assets: 0.8%
Return on equity: 3.8%
Long-term debt ($ mil.): —
No. of shares (mil.): 67.0
Sales ($ mil): 2,376.9
Dividends
  Yield: —
  Payout: —
Market value ($ mil.): 2,839.0

	STOCK PRICE ($) FY Close	P/E High/Low	PER SHARE ($) Earnings	Dividends	Book Value
12/15	42.36	44 30	1.18	0.00	37.19
12/14	51.02	20 16	2.31	0.00	35.00
12/13	47.92	19 12	2.20	0.00	32.30
12/12	31.97	15 11	2.20	0.00	27.23
12/11	32.05	46 15	1.33	0.00	25.15
Annual Growth	7.2%	— —	(2.9%)	—	10.3%

Stonegate Bank (Fort Lauderdale, FL)

Auditors: Crowe Horwath LLP

LOCATIONS

HQ: Stonegate Bank (Fort Lauderdale, FL)
  400 North Federal Highway, Pompano Beach, FL
  33062
Phone: 954 315-5500   **Fax:** 954 548-3489
Web: www.stonegatebank.com

HISTORICAL FINANCIALS

Company Type: Public

Income Statement

FYE: December 31

	ASSETS ($ mil.)	NET INCOME ($ mil.)	INCOME AS % OF ASSETS	EMPLOYEES
12/15	2,380.4	25.1	1.1%	263.0
12/14	1,723.2	12.7	0.7%	193.0
12/13	1,119.9	9.3	0.8%	0.0
12/12	944.7	9.0	1.0%	0.0
Annual Growth	36.1%	40.4%	—	—

2015 Year-End Financials

Return on assets: 1.2%
Return on equity: 10.4%
Long-term debt ($ mil.): —
No. of shares (mil.): 12.7
Sales ($ mil): 101.1
Dividends
  Yield: 0.6%
  Payout: 10.3%
Market value ($ mil.): 419.0

	STOCK PRICE ($) FY Close	P/E High/Low	PER SHARE ($) Earnings	Dividends	Book Value
12/15	32.86	17 14	1.94	0.20	22.16
12/14	29.62	24 18	1.22	0.16	19.61
12/13	22.95	20 15	1.10	0.16	15.96
12/12	17.25	16 13	1.08	0.08	15.38
/0.00	—	—	(0.00) 0.00	(0.00)	
Annual Growth	—	— —	—	—	—

STORE Capital Corp

Auditors: Ernst & Young LLP

LOCATIONS

HQ: STORE Capital Corp
  8501 East Princess Drive, Suite 190, Scottsdale, AZ
  85255
Phone: 480 256-1100
Web: www.storecapital.com

HISTORICAL FINANCIALS

Company Type: Public

Income Statement

FYE: December 31

	REVENUE ($ mil.)	NET INCOME ($ mil.)	NET PROFIT MARGIN	EMPLOYEES
12/15	284.7	83.7	29.4%	60.0
12/14	190.4	48.1	25.3%	50.0
12/13	108.9	26.3	24.2%	48.0
12/12	40.6	8.1	20.1%	0.0
12/11	3.8	(2.0)		0.0
Annual Growth	193.1%	—	—	—

2015 Year-End Financials

Debt ratio: 45.2%
Return on equity: 4.6%
Cash ($ mil.): 67.1
Current ratio: 0.04
Long-term debt ($ mil.): —
No. of shares (mil.): 140.8
Dividends
  Yield: 4.4%
  Payout: 150.7%
Market value ($ mil.): 3,268.0

	STOCK PRICE ($) FY Close	P/E High/Low	PER SHARE ($) Earnings	Dividends	Book Value
12/15	23.20	35 29	0.68	1.04	14.62
12/14	21.61	36 32	0.61	0.11	13.74
Annual Growth	7.4%	— —	11.5%	813.1%	6.4%

Strattec Security Corp.

STRATTEC SECURITY has your car under lock and key. The company designs and makes mechanical security locks electro-mechanical locks and keys and ignition lock housings primarily for global automakers. It also makes access control products including door handles latches power sliding doors and power lift gates. Chrysler Ford and General Motors account for the majority of STRATTEC's sales. In addition to cars and light trucks its products are used in the heavy truck and recreational vehicle markets as well as in precision die castings. With facilities in the US and Mexico STRATTEC delivers products mainly in North America but also abroad in Asia Europe and South America.

Geographic Reach
The company ships its products throughout the US Canada Mexico Europe South America Korea and China.

Operations
The company is expanding its geographic footprint with a third plant in Juarez Mexico and a sales and engineering facility in Southeastern Michigan.

STRATTEC along with fellow automotive product suppliers WITTE Automotive and ADAC Automotive is a member of the Vehicle Access Systems Technology (VAST) Alliance which allows members to act as each others' sales marketing manufacturing and support representatives in North America and Europe. Members also own a joint venture Vehicle Access Systems Technology LLC which operates manufacturing facilities in China and Brazil and supports sales in the Asia/Pacific and Latin America regions.

STRATTEC Power Access LLC a subsidiary formed alongside WITTE Automotive produces power access systems for sliding doors lift gates and trunk lids for the likes of Chrysler Ford and GM.

Sales and Marketing
STRATTEC generated some 72% of its fiscal 2015 sales via direct sales to various OEMs. It taps about 50 authorized wholesale distributors as well as other marketers and users of component parts (including export customers) to distribute its components and security products to the automotive aftermarket.

As part of its business STRATTEC also provides its customers with full-service aftermarket support.

Financial Performance
The company achieved unprecedented growth in 2015 with revenues jumping 18% to peak at a record-setting $411 million. Its profits also climbed 26% to reach $21 million in 2015 another company milestone. In addition its operating cash flow skyrocketed by 173% from 2014 to 2015.

The historic growth for 2015 was fueled by $34 million bump in sales from GM due to a recall campaign and additional sales from Hyundai/Kia due to the ramp-up of the new Kia Sedona minivan for which the company supply's components.

Strategy
STRATTEC's moving beyond its traditional lock and key products and diversifying with a more sophisticated set of power access control products as purely mechanical devices are growing stale. The company views electro-mechanical devices for vehicles —mechanical locks keys housings and latches that are enhanced by built-in electronics —as the future. These include devices that incorporate user bio-identification systems keys with remote entry

capabilities and ignition interfaces with passive start capabilities among other technologies.

EXECUTIVES

Vice President, Milan Bundalo
President and Chief Executive Officer, Frank J. Krejci, age 66, $330,917 total compensation
Vice President - Marketing and Sales, Dennis A. Kazmierski, age 65, $211,741 total compensation
Vice President of Mexican Operations, Rolando J. Guillot, age 48, $203,833 total compensation
Vice President - Security Products, Brian J. Reetz, age 58
Vice President - Access Control Products, Richard P. Messina, age 50
Vice President Engineering, Omar (Omarion) Arras
Vice President Milwaukee Operations, Kathy Scherbarth
Vice President, Guillermo Villa
Senior Vice President and Chief Financial Officer, Patrick (Paddy) Hansen
Chairman, Harold M. Stratton, age 68
Auditors: Deloitte & Touche LLP

LOCATIONS

HQ: Strattec Security Corp.
3333 West Good Hope Road, Milwaukee, WI 53209
Phone: 414 247-3333   **Fax:** 414 247-3329
Web: www.strattec.com

PRODUCTS/OPERATIONS

2015 Sales by Customer

	$ mil.	% of total
Fiat Chrysler Automobiles	116.9	28
General Motors Company	105.8	26
Ford Motor Company	45.5	11
Tier 1 Customers	71.3	17
Commercial and Other OEM Customers	41.7	10
Hyundai / Kia	30.3	8
Total	**411.5**	**100**

2015 Sales

	$ mil.	% of total
Keys & locksets	114.3	28
Aftermarket & OE service	78.7	19
Power access	68.1	16
Door handles & exterior trim	60.9	15
Driver controls	57.9	14
Latches	24.3	6
Other	7.3	2
Total	**411.5**	**100**

Selected Products

Door handles
Fobs
Locksets
Power decklids
Power liftgate systems
Power sliding door systems
Push button ignition systems
Seatback and secondary latches
Steering column lock housings

COMPETITORS

AISIN World Corp.	Tokai Rika
Huf North America	Valeo
Automotive	Visteon
Magna International	

HISTORICAL FINANCIALS

Company Type: Public

Income Statement

FYE: July 3

	REVENUE ($ mil.)	NET INCOME ($ mil.)	NET PROFIT MARGIN	EMPLOYEES
07/16*	401.4	9.1	2.3%	3,877.0
06/15	411.4	20.6	5.0%	3,420.0
06/14	348.4	16.4	4.7%	3,276.0
06/13	298.1	9.3	3.1%	2,670.0
07/12	279.2	8.7	3.1%	2,507.0
Annual Growth	**9.5%**	**1.0%**	**—**	**11.5%**

*Fiscal year change

2016 Year-End Financials

Debt ratio: 8.2%	No. of shares (mil.): 3.5
Return on equity: 6.4%	Dividends
Cash ($ mil.): 15.4	Yield: 0.0%
Current ratio: 2.09	Payout: 20.7%
Long-term debt ($ mil.): 20.0	Market value ($ mil.): 151.0

	STOCK PRICE ($) FY Close	P/E High/Low		PER SHARE ($) Earnings	Dividends	Book Value
07/16*	42.33	31	16	2.51	0.52	39.07
06/15	70.26	19	11	5.66	0.48	39.79
06/14	66.06	17	8	4.59	0.44	36.02
06/13	37.36	15	7	2.72	0.40	30.91
07/12	21.04	10	7	2.64	0.40	24.38
Annual Growth	**19.1%**	**—**	**—**	**(1.3%)**	**6.8%**	**12.5%**

*Fiscal year change

Sturm, Ruger & Co., Inc.

Sturm Ruger & Co. also called Ruger is one of the nation's biggest gun makers and produces pistols revolvers rifles and shotguns. Models include hunting and target rifles single- and double-action revolvers muzzleloading guns and double-barreled shotguns. Its guns are sold by independent wholesale distributors to independent firearms retailers and chains including Academy Sports and Cabelas. Ruger also makes metal products —known as castings —for the commercial and military markets. Sturm Ruger & Company was founded in 1949 by William Ruger and Alexander Sturm.

Operations

Ruger manufactures all of its rifles and revolvers in Newport New Hampshire and Mayodan North Carolina. All pistols (except for one model) are produced in Prescott Arizona.

The company also makes castings and metal injection molding components for its use and to sell to other companies.

Rifles accounted for about 38% of revenue with pistols accounting for 35% revolvers 20% accessories 6% and castings 1%. New products (those introduced in the past two years) generated 21% of firearms sales in 2015 compared to about $89 million in 2014.

Geographic Reach

Connecticut-based Sturm Ruger & Company makes all of its products in the US and sells most of them here as well. Foreign sales primarily to law enforcement and government agencies accounted for just 4% of 2015 sales.

Sales and Marketing

Four top customers account for more than half of Ruger's sales. They are Davidson's (18%)

Lipsey's (17%) Sports South (13%) and Jerry's/Ellett Brothers (11%). Distributors sell to the commercial sporting market. The estimated sell-through of Ruger products from distributors to retailers rose 7% in 2015 from 2014.

Financial Performance

Ruger reported revenue of $551 million in 2015 compared to $544 million n 2014. The company's 1% revenue increase came from casting sales which rose about $4 million in 2015.doubling 2014's sales. Firearm sales added $2.5 million essentially flat year-to-year.

Profit increased 61% to $62 million in 2015 from about $39 million in the year before. In 2014 Ruger had $40 million in pension charges in that it didn't have in 2015.

Ruger's operations generated $112 million in cash flow in 2014 compared to $55 million in 2014.

HISTORY

History

Sturm Ruger & Company was founded in 1949 by William Ruger who designed a notable machine gun used by the military during WWII and Alexander Sturm who backed the production of a new Ruger design by investing $50000. Sturm died of hepatitis in 1951 at age 28 and after a battle with Sturm's family Ruger took control of the company.

The gun maker's growth during the 1960s and 1970s was driven by demand for single-action revolvers and .22-caliber autoloading pistols produced at its original plant in Southport Connecticut. Ruger went public in 1969 still the only American gun company to do so.

In 1986 the company forced its distributors to choose between it and archrival Smith & Wesson; about half chose to stay with Ruger. By streamlining its distribution channels the manufacturer made its products more difficult to find thus increasing their prestige.

Decreasing firearms sales prompted the company to expand its castings operations. Ruger bought Callaway Golf's share in their joint foundry to become its sole owner in 1997. In 1998 Ruger unveiled its first muzzleloader the Ruger 77/50 to capitalize on the growing popularity of muzzleloading rifles. Later that year New Orleans became the first municipality to sue gun makers including Ruger in an effort to recover the cost of gun violence. Other local governments followed suit.

In 2000 the company sent letters to gun distributors asking that its guns be sold at regular places of business not trade shows. In 2001 the Louisiana Supreme Court threw out New Orleans' suit but remained a defendant in some 37 lawsuits at the end of 2001.

Co-founder William Ruger died in July 2002. In early 2003 after 2 years of pretrial discovery the consolidated California cities suit against almost all firearms manufacturers (including Ruger) was dismissed.

EXECUTIVES

CEO and Director, Michael O. Fifer, age 59, $550,000 total compensation
VP Prescott Firearms, Mark T. Lang, age 60, $285,000 total compensation
VP CFO and Treasurer, Thomas A. Dineen, age 47, $285,000 total compensation
President COO and Director, Christopher J. Killoy, age 57, $350,000 total compensation

VP Newport and Mayodan Operations and Pine Tree Castings Divisions, Thomas P. (Tom) Sullivan, age 55, $285,000 total compensation
Vice President of Lean Business Development, Steve (Stevie) Maynard
Chairman, C. Michael Jacobi, age 74
Vice Chairman, John A. Cosentino, age 66
Auditors: RSM US LLP

LOCATIONS

HQ: Sturm, Ruger & Co., Inc.
Lacey Place, Southport, CT 06890
Phone: 203 259-7843 **Fax:** 203 256-3367
Web: www.ruger.com

PRODUCTS/OPERATIONS

2015 Sales

	% of total
Firearms	99
Castings	1
Total	**100**

Selected Products

Firearms
 Pistols
 P-Series (centerfire)
 Ruger 22/45 (rimfire)
 Ruger Mark II (rimfire)
 Revolvers
 Single-action
 Birds Head Vaquero
 Bisley Hunter
 New Bearcat
 New Model Blackhawk
 New Model Single Six
 New Model .32 Magnum Super Single-Six
 New Model Super Blackhawk
 Old Army Cap & Ball
 Ruger Bisley
 Single-Six
 Super Blackhawk
 Vaquero
 Double-action
 GP100
 SP101
 Redhawk
 Super Redhawk
 Rifles
 10/22
 77/17
 77/22
 77/44
 77/50 Muzzle Loader
 96/17
 96/22
 96/44
 Deerfield Carbine
 M-77 Mark II
 M-77 Mark II Magnum
 Mini-14
 Mini Thirty
 Model 96 Rimfire
 No.1 Single Shot
 Ruger Carbine
 Shotguns
 Gold Label (side-by-side 12 gauge)
 Red Label (12 20 28 gauge)
 Woodside (12 gauge)
Castings
 Aluminum
 Chrome-molybdenum
 Cobalt
 Nickel
 Stainless steel

COMPETITORS

A. Finkl & Sons	Gibbs Die Casting
Beretta USA	Glock
Browning Arms	Marlin Firearms
Colt Defense	Mossberg
Colt's	Remington Arms
Fabbrica D'Armi Pietro	SIG SAUER
Beretta	Savage Arms
Freedom Group	Smith & Wesson Holding
GKN Sinter Metals	Springfield Armory

HISTORICAL FINANCIALS

Company Type: Public

Income Statement

FYE: December 31

	REVENUE ($ mil.)	NET INCOME ($ mil.)	NET PROFIT MARGIN	EMPLOYEES
12/15	551.0	62.1	11.3%	2,180.0
12/14	544.4	38.6	7.1%	2,073.0
12/13	688.2	111.2	16.2%	2,380.0
12/12	491.8	70.6	14.4%	2,040.0
12/11	328.8	40.0	12.2%	1,540.0
Annual Growth	**13.8%**	**11.6%**	**—**	**9.1%**

2015 Year-End Financials

Debt ratio: —
Return on equity: 30.0%
Cash ($ mil.): 69.2
Current ratio: 2.31
Long-term debt ($ mil.): —

No. of shares (mil.): 18.7
Dividends
 Yield: 1.8%
 Payout: 34.2%
Market value ($ mil.): 1,116.0

	STOCK PRICE ($) FY Close	P/E High/Low		PER SHARE ($) Earnings	Dividends	Book Value
12/15	59.61	20	10	3.21	1.10	12.17
12/14	34.63	43	17	1.95	1.62	9.90
12/13	73.09	14	8	5.58	6.62	9.26
12/12	45.40	16	9	3.60	5.80	4.93
12/11	33.46	17	7	2.09	0.43	7.20
Annual Growth	**15.5%**	**—**	**—**	**11.3%**	**26.5%**	**14.0%**

Sucampo Pharmaceuticals Inc

Sucampo Pharmaceuticals is a biopharmaceutical company with a focus on unmet medical needs around the world. Sucampo works with a group of compounds derived from fatty acids called prostones; it uses prostones in the development of therapies for the treatment of age-related gastrointestinal respiratory vascular and central nervous system disorders. It has two FDA-approved products: AMITIZA which treats chronic constipation in adults and irritable bowel syndrome in adult women and Rescula for the treatment of glaucoma and ocular hypertension. Sucampo's pipeline has other candidates in pre-clinical and early stage clinical development to treat a range of conditions.

Operations

The company operates through subsidiaries based in the US the UK Switzerland and Japan. It organizes its business into three reportable segments: the Americas Europe and Asia.

Sucampo makes most of its money from collaborations and licensing agreements which provide royalties upfront payments development milestone payments and development reimbursements as well as product sales.

AMITIZA is marketed in the US through a collaboration with Takeda Pharmaceutical. Abbott in Japan helped to develop and commercialize the drug for that market (where it was introduced in late 2012). The company received more than 80% of its income from its relationship with Takeda and another 18% from Abbott Japan Co.

AMITIZA is also in clinical trials to measure its effectiveness in alleviating opioid-induced bowel dysfunction a common post-surgical complication. While Rescula is already approved as a treatment for glaucoma and ocular hypertension the company also intends to test the drug as a possible treatment for dry age-related macular degeneration.Sucampo routinely enters into agreements with third-party contract research organizations (CROs) to oversee clinical research and development studies provided on an outsourced basis and to assist in other research and development activities.Geographic ReachThe company generates most of its earnings in the Americas which contributed 65% of total revenue in 2014. Asia contributed 28% of total revenue and Europe brought in the final 7%.

Financial Performance

Net revenue has generally been on the rise in recent years with the exception of 2011 when it fell to $54.8 million. In 2014 net revenue rose 29% to $115.5 million (versus $89.6 million in 2013) as all three geographical segments saw growth. US sales of AMITIZA increased bringing royalty revenue up; co-promotion contract and collaboration revenues also increased as the company furthered its efforts to sell AMITIZA in particular. Meanwhile higher global sales of AMITIZA and higher US sales of Rescula led to an increase in product sales revenue.

The rise in net revenue drove net income up 87% to $13.1 million in 2014. Cash flow from operations increased 833% to $30.9 million versus the $5.4 million cash outflow reported in 2013.StrategyWith the modest goal of becoming the leading biopharmaceutical company Sucampo is focused on strengthening its clinical development capabilities broadening its product pipeline while also pushing for growth of its flagship product AMITIZA.Mergers and AcquisitionsIn late 2015 Sucampo bought Japanese firm R-Tech Ueno for $278 million. R-Tech (which was controlled by the founders of Sucampo) manufactures AMITIZA for Sucampo and its partners. Acquiring the firm benefits Sucampo by providing it with more control over the manufacturing and distribution of AMITIZA. R-Tech also has a number of drug candidates in development in areas including opthalmology gastroenterology and inflammatory diseases.

EXECUTIVES

EVP Chief Legal Officer and Corporate Secretary, Thomas J. Knapp, $338,865 total compensation
CEO, Peter S. Greenleaf
SVP Sales and Marketing; President Sucampo Pharma Americas, Stanley G. Miele, $242,769 total compensation
Senior Vice President Investor Relations Public Relations and Corporate Communications, Silvia Taylor
Executive Vice President And Cipo, Misako Nakata
Executive Vice President Business Development and Licensing, Matthias Alder
Senior Vice President, Steven (Steve) Caffe
Vice President Clinical Development, Taryn Beridon
Chairman, Daniel Getman
Board Of Directors, Barbara (Barb) Munder
Auditors: Ernst & Young LLP

LOCATIONS

HQ: Sucampo Pharmaceuticals Inc
805 King Farm Boulevard, Suite 550, Rockville, MD 20850
Phone: 301 961-3400
Web: www.sucampo.com

PRODUCTS/OPERATIONS

2014 Sales

	% of total
Product royalties	54
Product sales	29
Contract & collaboration revenue	8
Research & development	6
Co-promotion revenue	3
Total	**100**

COMPETITORS

Bayer Consumer Care	McNeil Consumer
Boehringer Ingelheim	Pharmaceuticals
C.B. Fleet	Nektar Therapeutics
Innoviva	Progenics
Ironwood	Pharmaceuticals

HISTORICAL FINANCIALS

Company Type: Public

Income Statement
FYE: December 31

	REVENUE ($ mil.)	NET INCOME ($ mil.)	NET PROFIT MARGIN	EMPLOYEES
12/15	153.1	33.3	21.8%	159.0
12/14	115.4	13.1	11.4%	80.0
12/13	89.5	6.4	7.2%	77.0
12/12	81.4	4.8	5.9%	128.0
12/11	54.7	(17.3)	—	108.0
Annual Growth	**29.3%**	**—**		**10.2%**

2015 Year-End Financials

Debt ratio: 55.2%
Return on equity: 39.5%
Cash ($ mil.): 108.2
Current ratio: 2.85
Long-term debt ($ mil.): 213.2

No. of shares (mil.): 42.5
Dividends
Yield: —
Payout: —
Market value ($ mil.): 735.0

	STOCK PRICE ($) FY Close	P/E High/Low		PER SHARE ($) Earnings	Dividends	Book Value
12/15	17.29	38	17	0.73	0.00	2.03
12/14	14.28	47	20	0.29	0.00	1.85
12/13	9.40	67	32	0.15	0.00	1.34
12/12	4.90	70	32	0.12	0.00	1.03
12/11	4.43	—	—	(0.41)	0.00	0.92
Annual Growth	**40.6%**	—	—	—	—	**21.9%**

Summit Hotel Properties Inc

From the southern states to the Mountain States Summit Hotel Properties has plenty of room for US travelers. Operating through its subsidiaries Summit Hotel is a self-advised real estate investment trust (REIT) that holds a portfolio of almost 90 midscale and upscale hotels with 11400-plus rooms across 24 states including major markets in western and southern states like Arizona California Colorado Idaho and Texas. More than 60% of its hotels operated under the Marriott International and Hilton brands during 2015 while the rest mostly operated under the Hyatt and Intercontinental Hotel brands. Summit Hotel was formed in 2010 and went public in 2011.

OperationsSummit's property portfolio consisted of 87 hotel properties with 11420 rooms in 24 states at the end of 2015. About 64% of the rooms were tied to the company's Marriott and Hilton branded properties while the rest of the rooms were tied to the Hyatt (22% of rooms) Intercontinental Hotel (11%) Carlson (less than 1%) and Starwood (less than 1%) brands.Geographic ReachAustin Texas-based Summit Hotel Properties has its hotel properties in 24 states including major markets in western and southern states like Arizona California Colorado Idaho and Texas.Financial PerformanceSummit Hotel Properties' annual revenues have more than tripled since 2011 as new property acquisitions have spurred additional room revenue over the years. The REIT's profits have also come back strong since losses in 2011 and 2012 as it's paid down its debt and kept a lid on rising operating costs.The REIT's revenue jumped 15% to a record $463.4 million during 2015 with about two-thirds of the growth stemming added room revenue from 13 new hotel property acquisitions (with over 2000 rooms combined) made in 2014 and 2015. The rest of the growth came from same-store revenue growth of 8.3% which was driven by a 160 basis point occupancy rate increase and a 6% increase in same-store average daily rate (ADR) over the prior year's performance.Strong revenue growth and a $66.6 million gain on 10 property sales in 2015 caused Summit's net income to skyrocket six-fold to a record $124.44 million. The REIT's operating cash levels climbed 29% to $132.2 million for the year thanks to a rise in cash earnings from room revenue.

StrategySummit Hotel continues to focus on acquiring premium-branded select-service hotels to grow its portfolio and boost its total room revenue. It also looks to bolster its portfolio's value through property renovation repositioning and asset management efforts. Summit believes that because its properties operate under multiple leading hotel brands in markets suited to the hospitality industry (near tourist attractions corporate headquarters conventions centers etc.) it is well-positioned to reap strong returns in the hotel industry for the foreseeable future.The REIT has been acquiring properties in hot real estate markets in recent years. During 2015 for example it acquired seven hotel properties in growing cities such as Minneapolis Boston Baltimore Miami and Atlanta. In 2014 Summit bought six hotel properties in other strong real estate markets such as Houston Santa Barbara San Francisco and Austin TX. Company BackgroundThe company and its operating company Summit Hotel OP were formed in 2010 to acquire and operate the hotel portfolio of predecessor company Summit Hotel Properties LLC. It used the more than $250 million that it raised in its IPO to repay debt fund capital improvements at its properties and for general corporate purposes.

EXECUTIVES

EVP CFO and Treasurer, Greg A. Dowell, age 53, $360,000 total compensation
Chairman President and CEO, Daniel P. Hansen, age 47, $575,000 total compensation
EVP and COO, Craig J. Aniszewski, age 53, $375,000 total compensation

EVP General Counsel and Chief Risk Officer, Christopher R. Eng, age 45, $260,000 total compensation
Auditors: Ernst & Young LLP

LOCATIONS

HQ: Summit Hotel Properties Inc
12600 Hill Country Boulevard, Suite R-100, Austin, TX 78738
Phone: 512 538-2300
Web: www.shpreit.com

PRODUCTS/OPERATIONS

2015

	% of total
Room	94
Other hotel operations revenue	6
Total	**100**

COMPETITORS

Ashford Hospitality	Host Hotels & Resorts
Trust	LaSalle Hotel
FelCor	Properties
Hospitality Properties	
Trust	

HISTORICAL FINANCIALS

Company Type: Public

Income Statement
FYE: December 31

	REVENUE ($ mil.)	NET INCOME ($ mil.)	NET PROFIT MARGIN	EMPLOYEES
12/15	463.4	124.4	26.8%	40.0
12/14	403.4	20.8	5.2%	39.0
12/13	298.9	5.8	2.0%	33.0
12/12	189.5	(1.0)	—	25.0
12/11	134.2	(2.9)	—	18.0
Annual Growth	**36.3%**	**—**		**22.1%**

2015 Year-End Financials

Debt ratio: 42.8%
Return on equity: 15.2%
Cash ($ mil.): 29.3
Current ratio: 1.71
Long-term debt ($ mil.): 677.1

No. of shares (mil.): 86.7
Dividends
Yield: 3.9%
Payout: 174.0%
Market value ($ mil.): 1,037.0

	STOCK PRICE ($) FY Close	P/E High/Low		PER SHARE ($) Earnings	Dividends	Book Value
12/15	11.95	12	9	1.24	0.47	9.82
12/14	12.44	254	174	0.05	0.46	9.05
12/13	9.00	—	—	(0.12)	0.45	9.48
12/12	9.50	—	—	(0.17)	0.45	9.46
12/11	9.44	—	—	(0.12)	0.28	10.20
Annual Growth	**6.1%**	—	—	—	**13.7%**	**(0.9%)**

Sun Communities, Inc.

Sun Communities helps residents in the Sunshine State and around the US. The self-managed real estate investment trust (REIT) owns develops and operates manufactured housing communities (trailer and recreation vehicle parks) in nearly 30 states. Its portfolio includes more than 200 properties with nearly 80000 developed manufactured home and RV sites. Its Sun Home Services unit sells new and used homes for placement on its properties the majority of which are in Michigan Florida Indiana Texas and Ohio. Sun Communities also acquires at a discount and resells mobile homes that have been repossessed by lenders in its communities.

Operations

Sun Communities operates two lines of business: Real property and homes sales and rentals. The Real Property business which generates roughly 75% of the company's total revenue owns operates and develops manufactured home (MH) and RV communities and is in the business of acquiring and expanding those communities to grow revenue. The Home Sales and Rentals segment which operates under the company's Sun Home Services subsidiary sells manufactured homes and provides leasing services to consumers looking to live in their communities. The company's properties have trained on-site property managers and maintenance personnel as well as such amenities as clubhouses laundry facilities and swimming pools. At the end of 2014 the company owned and operated 217 properties in 29 states including 183 manufactured housing communities 25 RV communities and 9 properties containing both manufactured housing and RV sites. That year Sun Homes Services had 10973 occupied leased homes in its portfolio and boasted an average renewal rate for residents in Sun Communities' rental program of 59%.

Geographic Reach

Sun Communities has nearly 220 properties across 29 states. Around 30% of these properties were in Michigan in 2014 while 17% were in Florida. Texas Indiana and Ohio each held 5% or more of the company's properties. About 20% of properties were in other states in the Northeast and the Southwest.Sales and MarketingSun Communities spent $3.2 million on advertising in 2014 compared to $2.9 million and $2.5 million in 2013 and 2012 respectively.

Financial Performance

Sun Communities has enjoyed years of healthy revenue and profit growth thanks to aggressively property acquisitions and expansions with revenue nearly doubling over the past five years. The company's revenue grew by 14% to $471.68 million in 2014 mostly thanks to a 14% increase in income from its Real Property segment as the REIT raised its rental rates by 3% during the year and continued to grow its occupied home sites. Rental home revenue also swelled by 20% as more residents took to the company's Rental Program and thanks to higher monthly rental rates. Home sales fell slightly for the company despite higher new home sales mostly as the company sold its pre-owned homes at lower prices during the year.Higher revenue coupled with a $17.7 million gain on the sale of 10 MH properties in 2014 drove the REIT's net income up by 71% to a record $28.51 million while its operating cash rose by 16% to $133.32 million thanks to higher cash earnings.

Strategy

Sun Communities' main strategy toward growth has been to acquire highly-occupied and high-quality MH and RV communities with attractive amenities that support more potential occupancy and rent growth. Typically these are family or retirement communities with at least 200 home sites located near cities with populations exceeding 100000. In 2015 for example the REIT made two acquisitions totaling more than $1.5 billion (one was its largest acquisition ever) which spread its property portfolio business further into the fast-growing markets of Florida and Arizona.

Sun Communities' solid performance is in part due to increased demand from retiring adults a growing demographic. The company also points to its rental program as key to its success during the recession. Home rentals have become a popular and affordable alternative to customers.

Mergers and Acquisitions

In April 2015 the REIT completed its largest acquisition to date with the $1.3 billion-plus purchase of the Green Courte properties which spanned 59 MH communities across 19000 sites in the fast-growing markets of Florida and Arizona. Additionally in early 2015 Sun Communities purchased seven large manufactured housing communities in the Orlando Florida area for $257 million which spanned 3150 manufactured housing sites (approximately 60% of these were in age-restricted communities) and were 96% occupied. Management believed that the purchase further strengthened its portfolio of high-quality communities particularly in age-restricted communities which it said were essential toward the REIT's sustained growth.In early 2013 the company acquired ten RV communities (Gwynns Island RV Resort LLC Indian Creek RV Resort LLC Lake Laurie RV Resort LLC Newpoint RV Resort LLC Peters Pond RV Resort Inc. Seaport LLC Virginia Tent LLC Wagon Wheel Maine LLC Westward Ho RV Resort LLC and Wild Acres LLC) with 3700 sites in Connecticut Maine Massachusetts New Jersey Ohio Virginia and Wisconsin for $112.8 million.In 2012 Sun Communities made seven acquisitions (which included 14 properties in total seven manufactured housing communities five RV communities and two communities containing both manufactured housing and RV communities. The acquisitions included Three Lakes RV Resort Blueberry Hill RV Resort and Grand Lake Estates located in Florida; Blazing Star RV Resort (260 sites located in San Antonio Texas); Northville Crossing Manufactured Home Community (756 sites in Northville Michigan); Rainbow RV Resort (500 sites in Frostproof Florida); four manufactured home communities (the Rudgate Acquisition Properties) in southeast Michigan and Palm Creek Golf & RV Resort (283 manufactured home sites 1580 RV sites and the expansion potential of 550 manufactured housing or 990 RV sites) in Casa Grande Arizona.

Ownership

FMR LLC and Edward C. Johnson III (the chairman of FMR LLC) own more than 12% of Sun Communities.

EXECUTIVES

Regional Vice President, Wade (Wayne) Rosted
Senior Vice President, Jim Hoekstra
Executive Vice President, Jonathan (John) Colman
Executive Vice President, Jeffrey (Jeff) Jorissen
Vice President, Carol Peterson
Divisional Vice President of Operations and Sales, Tom (Tommy) Carpenter
Regional Vice President Of Operations and Sales, Brian (Bri) Schroeder
Auditors: Grant Thornton, LLP

LOCATIONS

HQ: Sun Communities, Inc.
27777 Franklin Rd., Suite 200, Southfield, MI 48034
Phone: 248 208-2500
Web: www.suncommunities.com

PRODUCTS/OPERATIONS

2014 Sales

	$ mil.	% of total
Real property income	357.7	77
Home sales	54.0	11
Home rentals	39.2	8
Interest and other	19.8	4
Brokerage commission and other income	1.0	-
Total	**471.7**	**100**

Selected Mergers and Acquisitions

COMPETITORS

American Land Lease	Nobility Homes
Equity Lifestyle	Outdoor Resorts
Properties	UMH Properties
Hometown America	

HISTORICAL FINANCIALS

Company Type: Public

Income Statement

FYE: December 31

	REVENUE ($ mil.)	NET INCOME ($ mil.)	NET PROFIT MARGIN	EMPLOYEES
12/15	674.7	170.4	25.3%	1,790.0
12/14	471.6	33.2	7.0%	1,525.0
12/13	415.2	20.1	4.9%	1,236.0
12/12	339.6	8.0	2.4%	915.0
12/11	289.1	(0.5)	—	775.0
Annual Growth	**23.6%**	**—**	**—**	**23.3%**

2015 Year-End Financials

Debt ratio: 55.9%	No. of shares (mil.): 58.4
Return on equity: 14.0%	Dividends
Cash ($ mil.): 45.0	Yield: 3.7%
Current ratio: 1.80	Payout: 472.7%
Long-term debt ($ mil.): 2,320.0	Market value ($ mil.): 4,002.0

	STOCK PRICE ($) FY Close	P/E High/Low	PER SHARE ($) Earnings	Dividends	Book Value
12/15	68.53	28 24	2.52	2.60	26.35
12/14	60.46	118 78	0.54	2.60	18.36
12/13	42.64	184 129	0.31	2.52	10.53
12/12	39.89	263 201	0.18	2.52	6.47
12/11	36.53	— —	(0.05)	3.15	(5.81)
Annual Growth	**17.0%**	**— —**	**—**	**(4.7%)**	**—**

Sunstone Hotel Investors Inc

Auditors: Ernst & Young LLP

LOCATIONS

HQ: Sunstone Hotel Investors Inc
120 Vantis, Suite 350, Aliso Viejo, CA 92656
Phone: 949 330-4000
Web: www.sunstonehotels.com

HISTORICAL FINANCIALS

Company Type: Public

Income Statement
FYE: December 31

	REVENUE ($ mil.)	NET INCOME ($ mil.)	NET PROFIT MARGIN	EMPLOYEES
12/15	1,249.1	355.5	28.5%	50.0
12/14	1,142.0	87.9	7.7%	79.0
12/13	923.8	70.0	7.6%	76.0
12/12	829.0	49.5	6.0%	74.0
12/11	834.7	81.3	9.7%	42.0
Annual Growth	10.6%	44.6%		4.5%

2015 Year-End Financials

Debt ratio: 28.7%
Return on equity: 15.7%
Cash ($ mil.): 499.0
Current ratio: 1.37
Long-term debt ($ mil.): 1,026.3

No. of shares (mil.): 207.6
Dividends
Yield: 11.2%
Payout: 261.1%
Market value ($ mil.): 2,593.0

	STOCK PRICE ($) FY Close	P/E High/Low		PER SHARE ($) Earnings	Dividends	Book Value
12/15	12.49	11	8	1.62	1.41	11.08
12/14	16.51	46	34	0.37	0.51	10.83
12/13	13.40	48	37	0.29	0.10	10.50
12/12	10.71	84	58	0.14	0.00	11.56
12/11	8.15	24	11	0.45	0.00	11.64
Annual Growth	11.3%	—	—	37.7%	—	(1.2%)

Super Micro Computer Inc

Super Micro Computer manufactures high-performance server products based on open standard components (including Intel AMD and NVIDIA processors). Its nearly 7000 offerings include motherboards and serverboards blade servers rackmounts GPU systems chassis and Ethernet switches and network adaptors. The company also sells a host of subsystems and accessories. Super Micro markets its products –primarily through distributors and resellers such as Ingram Micro and Arrow Electronics —to customers in some 100 countries; about 40% of its sales are generated outside the US.

Geographic Reach The company generates nearly 60% of its sales from the US with Europe and Asia contributing 19% and 17% respectively. All of these regions saw solid year-over-year growth in fiscal 2015 (ended June). Super Micro has operations in The Netherlands China Japan and Taiwan that support its international customers.

Sales and Marketing The company sells primarily through distributors resellers and systems integrators (about 55% of sales) but it also markets to OEMs and directly to end users. Leading distributors and resellers include Ingram Micro Avnet MA Labs Tech Data and ASI. About 10% of sales went to SoftLayer a unit of IBM in 2015.

Financial Performance Super Micro financial performance had some super macro aspects to it in 2015. Revenue jumped 36% higher and profit leaped 88% higher.

Revenue came in just shy of $2 billion at $1.99 billion in 2015 up from about $1.5 billion in 2014 Increased sales came from products optimized for the OEM data center cloud computing and enterprise verticals. Improved sales of server systems came from higher prices combined with higher volume.

Net income surged to about $102 million with the higher revenue overpowering increases in sales and marketing and research and development expenses.

The company reported negative cash flow of $44 million in 2015 due to high inventory and accounts receivable which were blamed on higher sales. Super Micro had cash flow from operations of $6.5 million in 2014.

Strategy Key to Super Micro's strategy is the expansion of its product portfolio as technology evolves. The company works closely with AMD Intel and others to make sure its offerings are compatible with industry standards. In addition it puts a special focus on energy efficient products such as its SuperBlade line of blade server products. The company increased R&D spending in 2015 to $100 million from $84 million in 2014.

The company also wants to further expand into Asia and Europe. It has opened a Science and Technology Park in Taiwan to increase capacity and better serves its customers in the Asia-Pacific region.

EXECUTIVES

Senior Vice President Worldwide Sls, Phidias Chou
VP Operations Treasurer and Director, Chiu-Chu Liu (Sara) Liang, age 54, $188,723 total compensation
Chairman President and CEO, Charles Liang, age 58, $303,682 total compensation
CFO, Howard Hideshima, age 57, $271,325 total compensation
Vice President General Manager, Tau Leng
Vice President of Marketing and Business Development, Don (Donnie) Clegg
Vice President Strategic Sales, Todd (Toddy) Warner
Vice President Operations Treasurer And Director, Chiu Chu Liang
Auditors: Deloitte & Touche LLP

LOCATIONS

HQ: Super Micro Computer Inc
980 Rock Avenue, San Jose, CA 95131
Phone: 408 503-8000
Web: www.supermicro.com

PRODUCTS/OPERATIONS

2015 Sales

	$ mil.	% of total
Server systems	1,213.6	61
Subsystems & accessories	777.5	39
Total	1,991.1	100

Selected Products

Chassis enclosures (pedestal rack-mount tower)
Motherboards (desktop server workstation)
Power supplies
Serverboards
Servers (rack-mount tower)

COMPETITORS

Celestica	Intel
Cisco Systems	Lenovo
Dell	Quanta Computer
Flextronics	Silicon Graphics
HP	International
Hon Hai	Wistron
IBM	

HISTORICAL FINANCIALS

Company Type: Public

Income Statement
FYE: June 30

	REVENUE ($ mil.)	NET INCOME ($ mil.)	NET PROFIT MARGIN	EMPLOYEES
06/16	2,215.5	72.0	3.3%	2,699.0
06/15	1,991.1	101.8	5.1%	2,285.0
06/14	1,467.2	54.1	3.7%	1,869.0
06/13	1,162.5	21.2	1.8%	1,595.0
06/12	1,013.8	29.8	2.9%	1,503.0
Annual Growth	21.6%	24.6%	—	15.8%

2016 Year-End Financials

Debt ratio: 8.0%
Return on equity: 10.7%
Cash ($ mil.): 180.9
Current ratio: 2.58
Long-term debt ($ mil.): 40.0

No. of shares (mil.): 48.5
Dividends
Yield: —
Payout: —
Market value ($ mil.): 1,207.0

	STOCK PRICE ($) FY Close	P/E High/Low		PER SHARE ($) Earnings	Dividends	Book Value
06/16	24.85	23	14	1.39	0.00	14.85
06/15	29.58	19	10	2.03	0.00	13.05
06/14	25.27	21	9	1.16	0.00	10.36
06/13	10.64	33	16	0.48	0.00	8.83
06/12	15.86	25	16	0.67	0.00	8.14
Annual Growth	11.9%	—	—	20.0%	—	16.2%

Superior Uniform Group, Inc.

Superior Uniform Group works to keep its business all sewn up. The company makes work clothing and accessories for US employees in several industries. The apparel firm designs makes and markets uniforms for employees in the medical and health fields as well as those who work in hotels fast food joints and other restaurants and public safety industrial and commercial markets. About half of its products are sold under the Fashion Seal brand. The company also makes and distributes specialty labels such as Martin's Worklon Blade and UniVogue. Chairman Gerald Benstock and his son CEO Michael run company which began as Superior Surgical Mfg. Co. in 1920.

Geographic Reach

From its headquarters in Florida Superior Uniform serves to outfit companies and customers nationwide boasting manufacturing operations overseas. Suppliers in Central American typically produce more than 50% of the company's products. It operates in El Salvador Costa Rica and the US through its The Office Gurus businesses and an affiliate entity in Belize added to its operations at the end of 2012.

Operations

The company operates its business through two reportable segments: Uniforms and Related Products (97% of sales) and Remote Staffing Solutions which includes The Office Gurus and TOG an affiliate firm that offers cost effective bilingual tele-marketing and office support services.

Strategy

Demand for Superior's uniforms and service apparel largely depends on the health of the economy. The economic downturn in the US negatively impacted the uniform supplier's customers who closed locations reduced headcounts or eliminated uniforms to save money.

In addition to the challenging economic climate the dramatic rise in cotton prices has the potential to pinch Superior Uniform's profit margin. While the company has been able to compensate for its higher materials costs by raising prices it warns at times that gross margins could be negatively impacted.

Financial Performance

Due to a boost in market penetration Superior Uniform logged a 6% net sales increase in fiscal 2012 as compared to 2011 across its Uniforms and Related Products unit and 9% from its Remote Staffing Solutions. Net income for the same reporting period declined 27% due to the rising cost of goods sold —primarily related to cotton shortages in the Uniforms and Related Products business — and increasing payroll-related costs across the Remote Staffing Solutions segment.

Mergers and Acquisitions

In March 2016 Superior Uniform acquired BAMKO Inc. a Los Angeles-based merchandise sourcing and promotional products company. It acquired BAMKO and its China Brazil and England subsidiaries as well as an India affiliate for $15.8 million in cash. BAMKO's products complement Superior Uniform's; however the acquisition expands the company's presence in China and India particularly its branded merchandise and promotional product offerings. Superior Uniform operates BAMKO as a subsidiary.

Company Ownership

The Benstock family owns nearly 23% of the company's shares. Mochelle Stettner holds another 10% stake.

EXECUTIVES

Vice President Marketing, Ron Klepner
EVP and President Fashion Seal Healthcare, Peter Benstock, age 54, $251,248 total compensation
CEO and Director, Michael Benstock, age 60, $513,133 total compensation
COO CFO and Treasurer, Andrew D. Demott, age 52, $324,454 total compensation
President, Alan D. Schwartz, age 65, $387,058 total compensation
VP Marketing and President Superior I.D., David Schechter
Vice President of Sales for Fashion Seal Healthcare, Scott Delin
Regional Vice President Sales, Brad Isenberg
Vice President Supply Chain, Charles (Charlie) Sheppard
Vice President Design and Merchandising, Lisa (Lis) Stewart
Chairperson, Sidney Kirschner, age 81
Assistant Treasurer, Jerry (Jerr) Chiovaro
Auditors: Mayer Hoffman McCann P.C.

LOCATIONS

HQ: Superior Uniform Group, Inc.
10055 Seminole Boulevard, Seminole, FL 33772-2539
Phone: 727 397-9611
Web: www.superioruniform.com

PRODUCTS/OPERATIONS

2015 sales

	% of total
Uniforms and related products	93
Remote staffing solutions	7
Inter-segment elimination	-
Total	**100**

Selected Brands

Blade
Fashion Seal
Fashion Seal Healthcare
Martin's
Worklon
UniVogue

COMPETITORS

ARAMARK	Convergys
Accenture	Fujitsu America
Alsco	G&K Services
Angelica Corporation	Sitel Worldwide
Broder Bros.	StarTek
Capgemini North	Sykes Enterprises
America	TeleTech
Cintas	UniFirst

HISTORICAL FINANCIALS

Company Type: Public

Income Statement

FYE: December 31

	REVENUE ($ mil.)	NET INCOME ($ mil.)	NET PROFIT MARGIN	EMPLOYEES
12/15	210.3	13.0	6.2%	1,278.0
12/14	196.2	11.3	5.8%	1,055.0
12/13	151.5	5.8	3.9%	973.0
12/12	119.4	3.0	2.5%	690.0
12/11	112.3	4.1	3.7%	647.0
Annual Growth	**17.0%**	**33.3%**	**—**	**18.6%**

2015 Year-End Financials

Debt ratio: 15.7%	No. of shares (mil.): 13.9
Return on equity: 15.1%	Dividends
Cash ($ mil.): 1.0	Yield: 1.8%
Current ratio: 4.22	Payout: 36.2%
Long-term debt ($ mil.): 21.2	Market value ($ mil.): 236.0

	STOCK PRICE ($) FY Close	P/E High/Low		PER SHARE ($) Earnings	Dividends	Book Value
12/15	16.98	40	17	0.90	0.32	6.66
12/14	29.37	35	17	0.82	0.29	5.95
12/13	15.48	35	22	0.46	0.34	5.52
12/12	11.45	53	42	0.25	0.54	4.72
12/11	12.27	37	30	0.34	0.27	5.09
Annual Growth	**8.5%**	**—**	**—**	**27.6%**	**3.9%**	**6.9%**

Supernus Pharmaceuticals Inc

Supernus Pharmaceuticals wouldn't mind being a drug-maker superhero of sorts to epileptics. As a specialty pharmaceutical company Supernus develops treatments for epilepsy and other central nervous system disorders. It has two marketed products for treating epilepsy: Oxtellar XR and Trokendi XR. In addition it is developing a number of candidates to treat such ailments as attention deficit hyperactivity disorder (ADHD) impulsive aggression in patients with ADHD autism bipolar disorder schizophrenia depression and dementia. The company utilizes third-party commercial manufacturing organizations (CMOs) for all of its manufacturing.

Geographic Reach

Supernus Pharmaceuticals has its corporate office and laboratory space in Maryland.

Sales and Marketing

The company markets its products through more than 150 sales representatives and distributes them through wholesalers and pharmaceutical distributors. Supernus primarily targets neurologists to grow sales of its epilepsy franchise.

In 2015 advertising costs totaled $19.3 million up from $14.8 million in 2014 and $14.6 million in 2013.

Financial Performance

The company began earning product revenue in 2013 when it launched Oxtellar XR. The 2014 launch of Trokendi led to further gains in revenues. In 2015 revenue increased 18% to $144 million as more prescriptions of its two medications were issued.

Net income spiked in 2014 but declined 29% to $14 million the following year. This drop was related to increased sales and marketing spend for its two products as well as higher R&D costs for additional pre-clinical and clinical trials. Additionally Supernus was hit with tax expenses for the first time in 2015 which further cut into the bottom line. As of the end of 2015 the company had an accumulated deficit of some $144.6 million.

Cash flow from operations has risen sharply over the past couple of years. In 2015 it increased 315% to $32 million due to several factors including changes in accounts payable and an increase in cash provided by accrued sales deductions.

Strategy

Supernus is focused on growing its epilepsy franchise in the US and in getting its pipeline products on the market. It also has a licensing and royalty agreements with other firms which helps boost its overall earnings.

EXECUTIVES

President CEO and Director, Jack A. Khattar, age 55, $523,403 total compensation
SVP Sales and Marketing, Victor Vaughn, age 58, $291,635 total compensation
SVP Intellectual Property and Chief Scientific Officer, Padmanabh P. Bhatt, age 59, $337,443 total compensation
VP Finance and CFO, Gregory S. Patrick, age 64, $330,470 total compensation
EVP Research and Development and Chief Medical Officer, Stefan K. F. Schwabe, age 64, $356,411 total compensation
Vp Regulatory Affairs, Tami Martin
Vice President Marketing, Stefan Antonsson
Vice President Business, Jones Bryan
Chairman, Charles W. (Chuck) Newhall, age 71
Auditors: KPMG LLP

LOCATIONS

HQ: Supernus Pharmaceuticals Inc
1550 East Gude Drive, Rockville, MD 20850
Phone: 301 838-2500
Web: www.supernus.com

PRODUCTS/OPERATIONS

2015 Sales

	$ mil.	% of total
Net product sales	143.5	99
Revenue from royalty agreement	- -	
Licensing revenue	0.9	1
Total	**144.4**	**100**

Selected Products

Oxtellar XR (marketed)
SPN-809(under trail)
SPN-810 (under trail)
SPN-812(under trail)
Trokendi XR (marketed)

COMPETITORS

Abbott Labs	Novartis Corporation
AstraZeneca	Noven Pharmaceuticals
Eisai Inc.	Shire
GlaxoSmithKline	UCB
Johnson & Johnson	Upsher-Smith
Mylan Pharmaceuticals	

HISTORICAL FINANCIALS

Company Type: Public

Income Statement — FYE: December 31

	REVENUE ($ mil.)	NET INCOME ($ mil.)	NET PROFIT MARGIN	EMPLOYEES
12/15	144.4	14.0	9.7%	344.0
12/14	122.0	19.8	16.3%	309.0
12/13	12.0	(92.2)	—	235.0
12/12	1.4	(46.2)	—	193.0
12/11	0.8	53.8	6701.7%	71.0
Annual Growth	**266.2%**	**(28.6%)**	**—**	**48.4%**

2015 Year-End Financials

Debt ratio: 3.8%	No. of shares (mil.): 49.0
Return on equity: 14.7%	Dividends
Cash ($ mil.): 34.1	Yield: —
Current ratio: 1.89	Payout: —
Long-term debt ($ mil.): 7.1	Market value ($ mil.): 659.0

	STOCK PRICE ($) FY Close	P/E High/Low		PER SHARE ($) Earnings	Dividends	Book Value
12/15	13.44	71	27	0.28	0.00	2.43
12/14	8.30	24	16	0.32	0.00	1.66
12/13	7.54	—	—	(2.90)	0.00	0.84
12/12	7.17	—	—	(2.72)	0.00	1.88
Annual Growth	**23.3%**			**—**	**—**	**8.9%**

Surgical Care Affiliates Inc

Surgical Care Affiliates can stitch 'em up and move 'em out. The company operates one of the largest networks of outpatient surgery centers in the US. (Also known as ambulatory surgical centers or ASCs these facilities charge less than hospitals to perform routine surgeries.) Surgical Care Affiliates operates about 195 surgery centers six surgical hospitals and one sleep center with about a dozen locations. Its facilities are located in about 35 states and offer non-emergency day surgeries in orthopedics ophthalmology gastroenterology pain management otolaryngology (ear nose and throat) urology and gynecology. The company went public in 2013. Insurance giant UnitedHealth now plans to buy Surgical Care Affiliates for some $2.3 billion.

Operations

The company's outpatient surgery centers are operated in partnership with more than 40 health care systems such as Indiana University Health Sutter Health Texas Health Resources and MemorialCare . It has approximately 2600 physician partners.

Geographic Reach

Surgical Care Affiliates' facilities are located in 34 states across the US. Its largest markets are Texas California and North Carolina which respectively accounted for 14% 14% and 13% of net patient revenues in 2014. Other large markets include Alabama Connecticut Florida and Idaho.

Sales and Marketing

Sales and marketing efforts are directed at physicians who are responsible for referring patients to its facilities. It also directly negotiates agreements with insurance companies and Medicare. Outpatient surgery centers which perform procedures that don't require an overnight stay are able to charge less than full service hospitals. This “day surgery” model can be attractive to both patients and insurance companies looking to keep costs down.

As such Surgical Care Affiliates sees a lot of opportunity in building up its portfolio of outpatient surgery centers. The company estimates there are approximately 5400 Medicare-certified centers in the US and still plenty of opportunity to invest and partner in new facilities.

Payments from non-governmental third-party payors represented more than 60% of the firm's net patient revenues in 2014; Medicare payments accounted for 20%.

Financial Performance

The company has seen solid revenue growth for the past four years. In 2014 revenue increased 9% to $897.3 million on higher net patient revenue a result of both higher admission numbers and the addition of more facilities. Management fee revenues also rose that year (again thanks to acquisitions).

After four years of reporting losses Surgical Care Affiliates became profitable in 2014 with net income of $32 million. This was driven by the higher revenue as well as the absence of loss from extinguishment of debt and a decline in interest expenses. At the end of 2014 the company's accumulated deficit totaled $176 million.

Cash flow from operations has been on the rise as of late. In 2014 it increased 27% to $210.6 million.

Strategy

In order to expand its network of facilities the company strives to buy existing surgical facilities and develop new facilities in partnership with area physicians and health care systems. During 2014 it acquired controlling stakes in 28 consolidated facilities. It also added three affiliated facilities with three new health system partners.

In early 2017 the company agreed to be acquired by UnitedHealth for some $2.3 billion. Surgical Care Affiliates will join UnitedHealth's OptumHealth division which itself operates hundreds of health care facilities.

Mergers and Acquisitions

In 2014 Surgical Care Affiliates acquired a controlling interest in 15 ASCs for $138.1 million. Other purchases that year included a 51% stake in an ASC in California and a 59% stake in an ASC in Maryland.

Company Background

Surgical Care Affiliates is the former outpatient surgery unit of HealthSouth. HealthSouth sold the division to private equity firm TPG in 2007.

EXECUTIVES

EVP and CFO, Peter Clemens, age 51
President and CEO, Andrew P. Hayek, age 42
EVP and Chief Development Officer, Joseph T. (Joe) Clark, age 60
EVP and COO, Michael Rucker, age 46
SVP Sales and Market Development, Winborne Macphail
SVP Perioperative Services, Gerry Biala
SVP Clinical Services and Training, Linda Lansing
EVP and General Counsel, Rich Sharff
Vice President, Ali Reza
Chairman, Todd B. Sisitsky, age 45
Auditors: PricewaterhouseCoopers LLP

LOCATIONS

HQ: Surgical Care Affiliates Inc
510 Lake Cook Road, Suite 400, Deerfield, IL 60015
Phone: 847 236-0921
Web: www.scasurgery.com

PRODUCTS/OPERATIONS

2014 Sales by Payor

	% of total
Managed care & other discount plans	62
Medicare	20
Workers' compensation	10
Patients & other third-party payors	5
Medicaid	3
Total	**100**

2014 Sales

% of total	$ mil
Net patient revenues	91
Management fee revenue	7
Other revenues	2
Total	**100**

COMPETITORS

HCA	United Surgical
Novamed Inc.	Partners
Symbion	Universal Health
Tenet Healthcare	Services

HISTORICAL FINANCIALS

Company Type: Public

Income Statement — FYE: December 31

	REVENUE ($ mil.)	NET INCOME ($ mil.)	NET PROFIT MARGIN	EMPLOYEES
12/15	1,101.3	115.3	10.5%	5,200.0
12/14	897.3	31.9	3.6%	5,000.0
12/13	825.4	(51.3)	—	5,000.0
12/12	766.9	(20.0)	—	4,150.0
12/11	741.5	(9.6)	—	0.0
Annual Growth	**10.4%**	**—**	**—**	**—**

2015 Year-End Financials

Debt ratio: 44.3%	No. of shares (mil.): 39.6
Return on equity: 36.8%	Dividends
Cash ($ mil.): 79.2	Yield: —
Current ratio: 1.22	Payout: —
Long-term debt ($ mil.): 858.0	Market value ($ mil.): 1,580.0

	STOCK PRICE ($) FY Close	P/E High/Low		PER SHARE ($) Earnings	Dividends	Book Value
12/15	39.81	14	10	2.83	0.00	9.63
12/14	33.65	44	32	0.80	0.00	6.30
12/13	34.84	—	—	(1.62)	0.00	5.39
Annual Growth	6.9%	—	—	—	—	33.7%

Surmodics Inc

SurModics doesn't want to scratch the surface of the medical device market –it just wants to coat it with its own special agent. The company's medical device unit makes special coatings that make the devices easier to use less traumatic to the body and even useful in delivering drugs to patients. For example it is developing drug-coated balloons designed to treat peripheral artery disease which causes narrowing of the arteries. SurModics' in vitro diagnostics (IVD) unit handles diagnostic test and research kits and products. Three scientists formed the company in 1979.

Operations

SurModics makes about half of its money from licensing and royalty deals under which medical device makers and drug companies use its technologies in their products. Within licensing and royalties the company divides its business between medical devices and IVD with medical devices taking the lion's share –about three-fourths of total revenue.

Product sales accounts for about 40% of the company's revenue while R&D and other activities bring in the rest.

Geographic Reach

SurModics has operations in Minnesota (2) and in Ireland.

The US is the company's largest market accounting for some 80% of total revenue.

Sales and Marketing

SurModics uses a global direct sales force and online sales to ply its wares. Medtronic is the company's largest customer; it accounts for about one quarter of sales.

Financial Performance

Revenue for SurModics has been rising for the past five years. In fiscal 2016 (ended September) revenue rose 15% to $71.4 million largely on higher product sales. Royalties license fees and R&D revenue also rose that year. Both the medical device and IVD segments saw double-digit growth due to increasing demand for the company's products and services as well as limited product price increases.

Net income has been more volatile peaking at $15.2 million in fiscal 2013 but dropping 16% to $10 million in fiscal 2016. That decline was due to higher operating costs including product costs R&D expenses and selling general and administrative expenses.

Strategy

SurModics looks to grow by enlisting more licensing customers (it makes about half of its revenue from royalties and fees) and by expanding its product line. It is also working to move beyond being a provider of coating technologies to offering whole-product systems to its medical device customers particularly in the vascular market. During fiscal 2016 (ended September) the company

began a first in-human early study of its SurVeil drug-coated balloon. Early the following fiscal year SurModics completed the expansion of an R&D and manufacturing facility to further support its growth.

Mergers and Acquisitions

In 2015 SurModics acquired Irish firm Creagh Medical which makes balloon catheters for angioplasties for $32 million. That purchase fit in with its focus on expanding beyond its traditional medical device coating technologies. The following year SurModics bought development firm Normedix which focuses on minimally invasive catheter technologies for $14 million.

EXECUTIVES

SVP and General Manager Medical Device, Charles W. (Charlie) Olson, $280,000 total compensation
VP and General Manager In Vitro Diagnostics, Joseph J. (Joe) Stich, $236,900 total compensation
President and CEO, Gary R. Maharaj, $435,000 total compensation
VP Finance and CFO, Andrew D. C. (Andy) LaFrence, $162,599 total compensation
Vice President of Sales, Dena (Dee) Natins
Vice President, Jill (Jilly) Weflen
Senior Vice President Legal and Human Resources Gen Couns, Bryan (Bry) Phillips
Chairman, Scott R. Ward, age 79
Auditors: Deloitte & Touche LLP

LOCATIONS

HQ: Surmodics Inc
9924 West 74th Street, Eden Prairie, MN 55344
Phone: 952 500-7000
Web: www.surmodics.com

PRODUCTS/OPERATIONS

2013 Revenues

	$ mil.	% of total
Royalties & licensing fees	29.8	53
Product sales	22.5	40
Research & development	3.8	7
Total	**56.1**	**100**

2013 Revenues

	$ mil.	% of total
Medical device	41.1	73
In Vitro Diagnostics	15.0	27
Total	**56.1**	**100**

COMPETITORS

Alimera	Spire Corp.
Biocompatibles	W.L. Gore
DURECT	alchimer
Hydromer	pSivida
QLT	

HISTORICAL FINANCIALS

Company Type: Public

Income Statement

FYE: September 30

	REVENUE ($ mil.)	NET INCOME ($ mil.)	NET PROFIT MARGIN	EMPLOYEES
09/16	71.3	9.9	14.0%	219.0
09/15	61.9	11.9	19.3%	168.0
09/14	57.4	12.0	20.9%	120.0
09/13	56.1	15.1	27.0%	114.0
09/12	51.9	10.2	19.7%	120.0
Annual Growth	**8.3%**	**(0.6%)**	**—**	**16.2%**

2016 Year-End Financials

Debt ratio: —
Return on equity: 10.0%
Cash ($ mil.): 24.9
Current ratio: 5.78
Long-term debt ($ mil.): —

No. of shares (mil.): 13.2
Dividends
 Yield: —
 Payout: —
Market value ($ mil.): 397.0

	STOCK PRICE ($) FY Close	P/E High/Low		PER SHARE ($) Earnings	Dividends	Book Value
09/16	30.09	39	23	0.76	0.00	8.09
09/15	21.84	30	20	0.90	0.00	7.10
09/14	18.16	29	21	0.87	0.00	7.26
09/13	23.78	26	17	1.03	0.00	6.75
09/12	20.22	35	15	0.59	0.00	6.40
Annual Growth	10.4%	—	—	6.5%	—	6.0%

SVB Financial Group

SVB Financial Group is the holding company for Silicon Valley Bank which serves emerging and established companies involved in technology life sciences and private equity and provides customized financing to entrepreneurs executives and investors in such industries. It also offers deposit accounts loans and international banking and plays matchmaker for young firms and private investors. SVB Financial also provides investment advisory brokerage and asset management services; and provides credit and banking services to wealthy individuals.

Operations

The company operates in three segments: Global Commercial Bank SVB Private Bank and SVB Capital.

Global Commercial Bank segment is comprised of Commercial Bank SVB Specialty Lending SVB Analytics and Debt Fund Investments. Commercial Bank serves commercial clients in the technology venture capital/private equity life science and cleantech industries. SVB Analytics provides equity valuation services to private companies and venture capital/private equity firms while Debt Fund Investments has investments in debt funds.

SVB Private Bank provides personal financial solutions for consumers while its capital arm SVB Capital focuses primarily on funds management.As part of its lending activities Silicon Valley Bank sometimes pursues warrants to purchase equity stakes in its clients. About 80% of the bank's loan portfolio is dedicated to commercial loans with about half of those going to software and internet companies and another 25% of commercial loans going toward private equity or venture capital firms. Traditionally focused on up-and-coming firms the bank has implemented a strategy of courting larger later-stage clients.

Geographic Reach

SVB Financial has 28 offices in the US as well as seven branches in China India Israel and the UK.

Sales and Marketing

SVB Financial's clients are primarily venture capital and private equity professionals. Its customers include Active Power Coskata EnerNOC Joule and Solexant.

Financial Performance

SVB's revenue grew for its fifth straight year with revenue rising by 4% to $1.46 billion in 2014. Though nearly all income streams grew the main drivers of growth came from higher interest income from investment securities and loans as average deposit and loan balances grew respectively. A 130% boost in net gains on derivative instruments also contributed significantly to the company's top line.Despite higher revenue net income reversed course in 2014 and fell by 12% to $478.72 million. The drop was mostly because SVB paid higher compensation and benefits as it gave its employees market-adjusted raises and hired 146 new staff members to support its product development operational sales advisory and commercial banking operations and initiatives. Operations provided $255.52 million or 33% more cash than in 2013 mostly because more of its earnings were cash payments as opposed to 2013 when non-cash gains on investment securities made up a larger share of earnings. The company also enjoyed higher cash generation from foreign exchange spot contracts.

Strategy

SVB Financial Group has been focused on growing its loan business and assets to drive growth in recent years. Indeed in 2014 the company's loan assets grew by 32% to $14.4 billion while deposits grew 52% to $34.3 billion —both factors that led the company to record-high revenue by the end of the year.It's also been selectively expanding and divesting its overseas operations to focus resources on profitable segments. In early 2015 subsidiary SVB Bank agreed to sell all of its outstanding stock in its non-banking financial subsidiary SVP India Finance Private Limited to Singapore-based investment firm Temasek. In 2012 the company opened a banking branch in the UK and started a joint venture bank in China.

Company Background

Greg Becker who joined SVB Financial in 1993 was named the company's CEO in 2011. He succeeded Ken Wilcox who became chairman and is focused on the company's efforts to expand in China including a joint venture with Shanghai Pudong Development Bank.

HISTORY

Silicon Valley Bank was founded in 1983 by Roger Smith to provide banking services to tech startups in San Jose. The bank boomed along with tech companies during the 1980s lending to the likes of Cisco Systems.

In 1990 the bank spread east to Boston's burgeoning technology alley. It also expanded into residential and commercial real estate lending. The recession of 1989 to 1991 found Silicon Valley Bancshares with an overextended loan portfolio and in 1992 the bank booked a loss due to nonperforming loans; the next year it was put under federal supervision.

To rally stockholder confidence the company brought in new management and demoted Smith from chairman to vice chairman; he left the in 1995. The bank reduced its real estate lending and diversified into factoring foreign exchange and executive banking for venture capitalists and clients' upper management.

The 1995 IPO frenzy aided the company's turnaround. Silicon Valley cashed in on warrants it had taken as collateral from young companies. Regulatory supervision was lifted in 1996 and the bank soon opened offices in the Atlanta; Austin Texas; Boulder Colorado; Phoenix; and Seattle areas.

In 1999 Silicon Valley Bancshares created a website targeted at technology firms in need of financing employees office space and equipment. However nonperforming loans began to dog the bank once again affecting profits and bringing a regulatory request to boost capital reserves.

In 2000 despite being hammered by the high-tech stock selloff the company continued to expand opening offices in West Palm Beach Florida and North Carolina's Research Triangle and successfully capitalizing its first venture fund. The following year it bought tech-focused investment bank Alliant Partners (later renamed SVB Alliant) to broaden its service offerings.

Still licking its wounds from the tech bust the company ceased lending to the entertainment industry and to churches in 2002. Silicon Valley Bancshares changed its name to SVB Financial Services in 2005.

SVB Alliant struggled with losses for years and SVB Financial explored its options including spinning the unit off to management. It ultimately decided to shut down the division which ceased operations in 2008.

EXECUTIVES

Manager of Risk Management Group and Acting CFO Silicon Valley Bancshares and Silicon Valley Bank, Marc J. Verissimo, age 61, $310,679 total compensation

President Asia, David A. Jones, age 58, $431,447 total compensation

COO and Principal Operating Officer, Bruce Wallace, $398,113 total compensation

President and CEO Silicon Valley Bank, Gregory W. (Greg) Becker, age 49, $835,613 total compensation

Head U.S. Banking, Joan Parsons, $399,780 total compensation

Managing Director Accounting and Financial Reporting, Michael (Mike) Descheneaux, age 49, $499,780 total compensation

Head Relationship Management, John D. China, $373,113 total compensation

Head EMEA and India; President UK Branch, Phil Cox

Chief Credit Officer Silicon Valley Bank, Marc Cadieux

CIO, Beth Devin

Vice President, Steven (Steve) Reel

Vice President, Jennifer (Jen) Zamudio

Vice President, Jenny (Jen) Moody

Vice President, Christopher Leary

Vice President Relationship Manager, Don (Donnie) Chandler

Vice President Relationship Manager, Anthony Raley

Vice President II, Tom (Tommy) Hertzberg

Vice President, Thomas (Thom) Armstrong

Vice President, Suzann Russell

Vice President of Information Technology, Derrick (Ric) Hanson

Vice President Business Information technology, Teresa (Terry) Eng

Vice President Manager Of Sales and Business Product Management, Dennis (Denny) Corbett

Vice President, Joe (Joey) Werner

Vice President, Damarie Rodriguez

Vice President Of Information Technology, Derrick Ponugoti

Vice President and Foreign Exchange Trader, Patrick (Paddy) Chin

Vice President, Mickey (Mic) Swift

Vice President Regional Director, Carmella Montesdeoca

Vice President Regional Market Manager, John (Jack) Atanasoff

Vice President, Lauren Cole

Vice President and Senior Project Anal, Cindy (Cin) Decker

Vice President, Michael Kalicak

Vice President, Dan Hardman

Vice President I Corporate Fin, Andrea (Ann) Jones

Vice President, Nicholas (Nick) Currie

Vice President Private Equity Services, Amy Choi

Vice President Operations, Debbie (Deb) Teryison

Assistant Vice President Credit; Manager Commercial Letters, Alice (Ali) Daluz

Senior Vice President and Senior Relationship Manager, Matt (Matty) Maloney

Vice President, Tim Barnes

Vice President Product Management, Susan (Sue) Merrill

Senior Vice President, Laura Scott

Vice President Marketing, Jane Lodato

Vice President, Jimmy Gan

Senior Vice President, Andy Tsao

Senior Vice President, Dale (Dal) Kirkland

Vice President Relationship Manager, Brett Maver

Vice President, Benjermin Colombo

Vice President, Patrick (Paddy) Scheper

Senior Vice President, Michael (Mel) Tramack

Vice President Service Management, Roger Leon

Vice President, Josh Dorsey

Vice President, Dino Pillinini

Executive Vice President and Founder, Rob (Robbie) McMillan

Senior Vice President and Senior Relationship Manager, Dan (Danny) Aguilar

Vice President, Rob (Robbie) Walker

Vice President, Reisa Babic

Vice President, Cody Nenadal

Vice President, Alex Barry

Vice President, Cfa Norris

Vice President, Kyle Swan

Vice President Corporate Finance, Russell (Russ) Follansbee

Vice President, James R (Jamie) Mashall

Vice President, Herman (Herm) White

Vice President Structured Finance, James (Jamie) Caron

Vice President Relationship Manager, Glenn Marasigan

Vice President, Marc (Marcy) Neri

Vice President, Sean Thompson

Vice President, Chris (Chrissy) Canazaro

Chairman, Roger F. Dunbar, age 70

Board Member, Eric A Benhamou

Assistant Secretary And Treasurer, Lori (Lor) De Leon

Treasurer, Michelle (Michie) McKay

Board Director, Jack (Jackie) Gaziano

Auditors: KPMG LLP

LOCATIONS

HQ: SVB Financial Group
3003 Tasman Drive, Santa Clara, CA 95054-1191
Phone: 408 654-7400
Web: www.svb.com

PRODUCTS/OPERATIONS

2014 Sales

	$ mil.	% of total
Interest		
Loans	610.9	42
Investment securities	274.5	19
Other	6.5	-
Noninterest		
Net gains on investment securities	267.0	17
Net gains on derivative instruments	96.8	7
Foreign exchange fees	71.7	5
Credit card fees	41.9	3
Deposit service charges	39.9	3
Lending related fees	25.7	2
Letters of credit	15.7	1
Client investment fees	14.9	1
Other	(1.3)	-
Total	**1,464.2**	**100**

Selected Subsidiaries and Affiliates

Silicon Valley Bank
SVB Analytics Inc.
SVB Asset Management
SVB Business Partners (Beijing) Co. Ltd.
SVB Business Partners (Shanghai) Co. Ltd.
SVB Global Financial Inc.
SVB Global Investors LLC
SVB Growth Investors LLC
SVB India Advisors Pvt. Ltd.
SVB Israel Advisors Ltd.
SVB Qualified Investors Fund LLC
SVB Real Estate Investment Trust
SVB Securities
SVB Strategic Investors LLC
SVB Strategic Investors Fund L.P.
Venture Investment Managers L.P.

COMPETITORS

Bank of America	Heritage Commerce
Citigroup	MUFG Americas Holdings
City National	U.S. Bancorp
Comerica	

HISTORICAL FINANCIALS

Company Type: Public

Income Statement

FYE: December 31

	ASSETS ($ mil.)	NET INCOME ($ mil.)	INCOME AS % OF ASSETS	EMPLOYEES
12/15	44,686.7	374.8	0.8%	2,089.0
12/14	39,344.6	478.7	1.2%	1,914.0
12/13	26,417.1	546.1	2.1%	1,704.0
12/12	22,766.1	175.1	0.8%	1,615.0
12/11	19,968.8	171.9	0.9%	1,526.0
Annual Growth	22.3%	21.5%	—	8.2%

2015 Year-End Financials

Return on assets: 0.8%	Dividends
Return on equity: 12.4%	Yield: —
Long-term debt ($ mil.): —	Payout: —
No. of shares (mil.): 51.6	Market value ($ mil.): 6,136.0
Sales ($ mil): 1,519.5	

	STOCK PRICE ($) FY Close	P/E High/Low		PER SHARE ($) Earnings	Dividends	Book Value
12/15	118.90	22	15	6.62	0.00	61.97
12/14	116.07	25	18	5.31	0.00	55.33
12/13	104.86	22	12	4.70	0.00	42.93
12/12	55.97	17	12	3.91	0.00	41.02
12/11	47.69	16	9	3.94	0.00	36.07
Annual Growth	25.7%	—	—	13.9%	—	14.5%

Synaptics Inc

Synaptics keeps you in touch with your electronics. The company's human interface products are sold to contract manufacturers for use in mobile phones (more than half of sales) notebook and handheld computers and other mobile electronic devices. Its TouchPad product can be used in peripherals such as monitors and remote controls; ClickPad replaces a mouse for notebook PCs and netbooks; and ClearPad provides touchscreen control for various mobile devices. Synaptics also relies on contract manufacturers to make its products. Most sales go to manufacturers in Asia more than two thirds in China. US customers provide 10% of sales.

Operations

While Synaptics operates in one segment it breaks down its sales between products headed for mobile devices and those destined for PCs. Mobile products account for 88% of revenue and PC product 12%. The large mobile share reflects the wide adoption of touch screens for smartphones and tablets while PCs have yet to make touchscreens a standard option.

Synaptics' technology engineering and product design functions in the US Taiwan Hong Kong Korea Japan India and China incurred $311 million of expenses in 2016 (ended June).

Geographic Reach

Based in the US the company also operates in Hong Kong India China Taiwan Japan Armenia South Korea Switzerland and Vietnam. About 81% of sales are from customers in China Japan and South Korea that provide design and manufacturing services for major notebook computer and mobile OEMs. International sales constituted more than 85% of Synaptics' revenue for 20146 2015 and 2016.

Sales and Marketing

As consumers shift to mobile computing products used in PCs have been edged out as Synaptics' largest source of revenues. Sales to Samsung Electronics Co. and its affiliates Sanshin Electronics Co. and Fuhrmeister Electronics Co. accounted for 21% 20% and 15% of 2016 (ended June) revenue respectively.

Financial Performance

Synaptics lost its touch for increasing revenue in 2016 which in 2016 which interrupted a string of years rising sales. Its sales fell 2% in 2016 to $1.67 billion to $1.7 billion in 2015. A 21% drop in PC-related product sales offset several times over a slight increase in mobile products. PC revenue was hit by fewer unit sales and lower prices.

Net income tumbled 35% to $72 million in 2016 from 2015 hurt by lower sales and higher selling general and administrative expenses including the impact of foreign currency fluctuations.

Cash flow generated by operations jumped to $256 million in 2016 from $204 million in 2015.

Strategy

Synaptics is expanding by adding applications such as home appliances for its touchpads as well as developing interface technologies such as proximity sensing which uses sensors to detect the presence of a user and activate certain functions.

The company is moving to increase investment in engineering activities including ongoing enhancement of TDDI (touch and display driver integration) technology and development of OLED technology. It also considers acquisitions and alliances to beef up its capabilities.

In 2015 Synaptics announced three new series of ClearPad discrete touch controllers and the Natural ID FS4304 a biometric fingerprint sensor designed with industrial design flexibility to fit small spaces including the edge of smartphones or tablets.

The company collaborated with Valeo to develop touchscreen applications for automotive.

Mergers and Acquisitions

In 2014 the company announced plans to acquire Renesas SP Drivers the industry leader in small and medium-sized display driver ICs for smart phones and tablets to increase its addressable market opportunity by 1.5X and to accelerate its product roadmap for touch-and-display driver integration.

Company Background

The company is a founding member of the Open Handset Alliance an industry group utilizing the Android mobile device operating system software created by Google. The Nexus One smartphone unveiled by Google in 2010 used a ClearPad 2000 capacitive touchscreen sensor supplied by Synaptics.

EXECUTIVES

Senior Vice President, Kathleen (Kathy) Bayless
SVP and General Manager Smart Display Division (SDD), Kevin D. Barber, age 56, $368,333 total compensation
SVP and CFO, Wajid Ali, age 43, $395,000 total compensation
SVP Worldwide Operations, Alex H.C. Wong, age 61, $338,333 total compensation
President CEO and Director, Richard A. (Rick) Bergman, age 52, $700,000 total compensation
SVP and General Manager Human Interface Systems Division (HISD), Huibert Verhoeven, age 48
SVP Corporate Research and CTO, Patrick Worfolk
Senior Vice President of Corporate Development, Bret Sewell
Senior Vice President of Global Human Resources, Karen Gaydon
Vice President Marketing, Brian (Bri) Daly
Vice President, Shawn Liu
Vice President Of Marketing, Godfrey Cheng
Vice President Operations, Scott (Scotty) Deutsch
Vice President Software Engineering, Guido Bertocci
Senior Vice President Engineering, Joe Montalbo
Vice President of Operations, Hing Wong
Senior Vice President And GM Biometrics Products Division, Ritu Favre
Vice President Quality and Product Engineering, Kin Cheung
Senior Vice President, Don Kirby
Vice President Human Resources, Masateru Kawai
Chairman, Francis F. Lee, age 64
Treasurer, Rose Benson
Auditors: KPMG LLP

LOCATIONS

HQ: Synaptics Inc
1251 McKay Drive, San Jose, CA 95131
Phone: 408 904-1100
Web: www.synaptics.com

PRODUCTS/OPERATIONS

2016 sales

	$ mil.	% of total
Mobile product applications	1,459.5	88
PC product applications	207.4	12
Total	**1,666.9**	**100**

Selected Products

ClearButtons (Sensor for scrolling and buttons)
ClearPad (Touch sensor for displays)
ClickPad (Click-enabled notebook computer cursor control pad)
Dual Pointing (Notebook computer cursor control stick and pad)
FlexPad (TouchPad functionality for conventional keyboards)
NavPoint (TouchPad functionality for handheld form factors)
OneTouch (Enablement of technology at customer level)
TouchPad (Notebook computer cursor control pad)
TouchStyk (Notebook computer cursor control stick)
TouchButtons (Capacitive alternative to mechanical button and scrolling controls)

COMPETITORS

Alps Electric	Interlink Electronics
Atmel	Key Tronic
CTS Corp.	Logitech
Communication	Microsoft
Intelligence Corp.	Panasonic Corp
Cypress Semiconductor	Wacom
Elo Touch Solutions	

HISTORICAL FINANCIALS
Company Type: Public

Income Statement
FYE: June 25

	REVENUE ($ mil.)	NET INCOME ($ mil.)	NET PROFIT MARGIN	EMPLOYEES
06/16	1,666.9	72.2	4.3%	1,763.0
06/15	1,703.0	110.4	6.5%	1,789.0
06/14	947.5	46.6	4.9%	1,230.0
06/13	663.5	98.9	14.9%	852.0
06/12	548.2	54.1	9.9%	697.0
Annual Growth	32.0%	7.5%	—	26.1%

2016 Year-End Financials
Debt ratio: 18.1%
Return on equity: 9.6%
Cash ($ mil.): 352.2
Current ratio: 2.22
Long-term debt ($ mil.): 216.7
No. of shares (mil.): 35.2
Dividends
Yield: —
Payout: —
Market value ($ mil.): 1,839.0

	STOCK PRICE ($) FY Close	P/E High/Low		Earnings	PER SHARE ($) Dividends	Book Value
06/16	52.22	48	27	1.91	0.00	20.02
06/15	86.32	34	20	2.84	0.00	21.13
06/14	89.38	68	29	1.26	0.00	19.02
06/13	38.56	15	7	2.89	0.00	15.68
06/12	28.63	24	14	1.57	0.00	12.06
Annual Growth	16.2%	—	—	5.0%	—	13.5%

Synchronoss Technologies Inc

Synchronoss Technologies helps telephone companies synch up a variety of customer service efforts. The company provides hosted software and services that communications service providers use to manage tasks such as phone service activation account changes and customer transactions including credit card billing inventory management and trouble ticketing. Customers include service providers such as AT&T Mobility Level 3 Time Warner Cable Verizon and Vodafone as well as equipment manufacturers such as Apple Dell and Sony. Synchronoss was founded in 2001.

Geographic Reach
The company is headquartered in Bridgewater New Jersey and operates research and development facilities in Bethlehem Pennsylvania and Galway Ireland. It also has regional US offices in Chicago Denver Tucson Arizona; Fairpoint New York; Bellevue and Seattle Washington; and San Jose California as well as offices in Germany the UK India and Australia.

Sales and Marketing
Synchronoss is heavily dependent on two customers AT&T and Verizon which accounted for about three quarters of revenue in 2014. Other significant customers are Level 3 Time Warner Cable and Vodafone. Reliance on a relatively small number of customers for a majority of sales can be risky for companies such as Synchronoss as the loss of a single customer can dramatically affect sales. To that end Synchronoss has in recent years been working to diversify its customer base which has grown past its core base of telecom service providers to include mobile device makers like Apple and Nokia.

Financial Performance
The company's revenue jumped 31% to $457 million in 2014 driven by the expansion of its professional services to existing customers and an increase in licensing revenue for the company's cloud-based services. Higher revenues that year also helped drive Synchronoss' net income up 61% to about $39 million.

Strategy
While the majority of its sales come from North America Synchronoss has announced strategic plans to expand its sales in Europe Latin America and Asia-Pacific. Though overseas sales were just 11% of revenue in 2014 they increased 31% for the year.

Mergers and Acquisitions
The biggest acquisition however addressed product rather than geography. In 2015 Synchronoss bought F-Secure Corp. for $60 million. F-Secure is an online security and privacy company with technology that boosts the security aspects of Synchronoss offering.

In 2014 Synchronoss acquired assets of Clarity an Australian company for $6.6 million to help address the Asia-Pacific region. In France Synchronoss bought Vox for $25.1 million.

In another 2014 deal Synchronoss acquired Digi-Data for $6.3 million. Digi-Data was purchased expedite integration of broadband technologies into wireless cloud offerings from Synchronoss.

EXECUTIVES

CEO, Ronald W. (Ron) Hovsepian, age 56
Chairman, Stephen G. Waldis, age 48, $591,165 total compensation
President and COO, Robert E. (Bob) Garcia, age 48, $437,091 total compensation
EVP and General Counsel, Ronald J. Prague, age 53
EVP and President Enterprise Business, David A. (Dave) Schuette, age 50, $183,333 total compensation
EVP Product Management Marketing and Business Development, Daniel Rizer, age 52, $385,786 total compensation
EVP and CTO, Patrick J. (Pat) Doran, age 42
EVP CFO and Treasurer, Karen L. Rosenberger, age 50, $330,000 total compensation
EVP Product Sales and Business Development, Chris Putnam
EVP and General Manager The Americas, Joel Silverman
Auditors: Ernst & Young LLP

LOCATIONS

HQ: Synchronoss Technologies Inc
200 Crossing Boulevard, 8th Floor, Bridgewater, NJ 08807
Phone: 866 620-3940
Web: www.synchronoss.com

COMPETITORS

Amdocs	Intec Telecom
CSG Systems	Motive Inc.
International	NeuStar
Comptel	Syniverse
Evolving Systems	VeriSign

HISTORICAL FINANCIALS
Company Type: Public

Income Statement
FYE: December 31

	REVENUE ($ mil.)	NET INCOME ($ mil.)	NET PROFIT MARGIN	EMPLOYEES
12/15	578.8	46.6	8.1%	1,895.0
12/14	457.3	38.9	8.5%	1,804.0
12/13	349.0	23.3	6.7%	1,401.0
12/12	273.6	27.0	9.9%	1,340.0
12/11	229.0	15.1	6.6%	970.0
Annual Growth	26.1%	32.5%	—	18.2%

2015 Year-End Financials
Debt ratio: 23.9%
Return on equity: 8.2%
Cash ($ mil.): 147.6
Current ratio: 5.08
Long-term debt ($ mil.): 243.3
No. of shares (mil.): 44.4
Dividends
Yield: —
Payout: —
Market value ($ mil.): 1,564.0

	STOCK PRICE ($) FY Close	P/E High/Low		Earnings	PER SHARE ($) Dividends	Book Value
12/15	35.23	54	34	0.89	0.00	13.73
12/14	41.86	56	27	0.92	0.00	12.39
12/13	31.07	65	35	0.58	0.00	11.01
12/12	21.09	50	24	0.69	0.00	9.69
12/11	30.21	80	52	0.43	0.00	8.71
Annual Growth	3.9%	—	—	19.9%	—	12.0%

Synopsys Inc

To sum up Synopsys is a leading provider of electronic design automation (EDA) software and services. Its products are used by designers of integrated circuits (ICs) to develop simulate and test the physical design of ICs before production and then to test finished products for bugs and security vulnerabilities. The company also provides semiconductor intellectual property (SIP) pre-designed circuits used as part of larger chips. Customers come from a variety of markets but particularly the semiconductor and electronics manufacturing industries. Intel is its top customer. Synopsys offers time-based software licenses where customers make annual payments for use and support. It generates about half its sales outside the US.

Operations
Synopsys makes money from four groups: Core EDA which includes digital and custom IC design products verification products and field-programmable gate array (FPGA) design products; IP and Software Solutions which includes the Designware IP portfolio system-level design tools and Coverity quality and security testing; manufacturing solutions; and professional services. CoreEDA is the core source of revenue accounting for more than 60%. IP and Software Solutions brings in 30% followed by Manufacturing Solutions and professional services rounding out the revenue.

Geographic Reach The company based in Mountain View California has some 30 offices in the US. Its international headquarters is in Dublin Ireland and it has offices in about 30 countries with major operations in China France Germany India and Taiwan.

The US represents Synopsys' largest market accounting for 50% of sales. The Asia/Pacific region generates just under 30% of revenue followed by Europe and Japan at 12% and 10% respectively.

Sales and Marketing Synopsys markets its products primarily to semiconductor and electronics systems companies through direct sales efforts in the US and in select international markets. Intel accounts for about 16% of revenue while other customers include Samsung TSMC Broadcom NVIDIA Qualcomm Toshiba Infineon and Huawei.

Technology subscription licenses (TSLs) generate about 80% of revenue followed by upfront licenses at 10% of revenue. Maintenance and service accounts for the rest of the revenue.

Financial Performance

Synopsys reported higher revenue and profits as well as more cash from operations in 2016 (ended October) compared to 2015.

The company's technology subscription license (TSL) products and hardware led sales growth 8% higher in 2016 to $2.4 billion. TSL grew 7% (adding almost $120 million in revenue) while hardware sales jumped 26% (adding about $50 million in revenue). Sales rose in all geographic markets but for Europe where sales dipped 4%. Sales in the Asia/Pacific region surged 19% in 2016 accounting for 60% of the revenue growth for the year. Overall sales rebounded after a decrease in 2014.

Synopsys pushed profit 18% higher to about $267 million in 2016. The higher revenue combined with steady levels of spending (as percentage of revenue) resulted in a solid net income increase.

Operations generated $586 million in cash compared to $495 million in 2015. Higher cash collections accounted for most of the cash flow increase.

Strategy

Like most suppliers to the semiconductor industry Synopsys has had to deal with the industry's consolidation. Synopsys has managed its way through the merger and acquisition trends and in some cases expanded its business. The trend toward integration of multiple chips and software into chip products plays to Synopsys' strengths in providing design and test products and services. The company looks for opportunities to grow in areas such as digital intelligence machine learning the Internet of Things 5G mobile networks virtual and assisted reality and massive cloud-based computing. The automotive market is a particular area of interest for Synopsys where sees opportunities in technologies for self-driving cars.

Mergers and Acquisitions

In 2017 Synopsys completed its acquisition of certain assets of Forcheck a privately held software company based in the Netherlands that provides a static analysis tool for detecting coding defects and anomalies in FORTRAN applications. This acquisition extends the capabilities of the company's Software Integrity Platform.

The acquisition of Cigital and Codiscope came in 2016. Cigital and Codiscope add complementary products services and their workforces to Synopsys's portfolio.

Also in 2016 Synopsys acquired Gold Standard Simulations Ltd. a provider of CAD and EDA simulation products for design technology Synopsys built on its TCAD strategy to reduce development time and cost.

In 2015 Synopsys bought Codenomicon a software security company focused on software embedded in chips and devices. The acquisition of assets of Quotium including the Seeker product and

R&D team added talent and technology to accelerate Synopsys' efforts in the software application security market.

HISTORY

Aart de Geus founded Optimal Solutions in 1986 with funding from General Electric where he had been a manager in the company's Advanced Computer-Aided Engineering Group. The group built the prototype of a product that saved chip designers time by automating much of the design work.

In 1987 the company changed its name to Synopsys (an abbreviation of "synthesis and optimization systems") and moved to California. It went public in 1992 and two years later it introduced software that engineers used to design chips by function rather than structure.

As chips grew more complicated Synopsys bolstered its product development efforts through acquisitions. In 1995 the company purchased hardware emulation developer Silicon Architects. Synopsys bought transistor-level tool specialist EPIC Design Technology in 1997 to improve its submicron-level design capabilities. It acquired Viewlogic Systems to increase its design automation prowess. (Synopsys later sold Viewlogic's printed circuit board design software segment.)

Synopsys' acquisitions continued in 1998 with the purchase of Radiant Design Tools a supplier of technology for designing simulation performance and Everest Design Automation which specialized in system-on-a-chip devices. In 1999 Synopsys bought Stanza Systems which developed physical layout products; Smartech a developer of wireless market design products; and several others. It also introduced several products including one that combined design and physical layout of system-on-a-chip devices in one package.

Over its history Synopsys has made numerous continues to make augment its capabilities.

EXECUTIVES

EVP; General Manager Design Group, Antun Domic, age 65, $390,000 total compensation
Senior Vice President Human Resources and Facilities, Jan Unkcd Collinson
President and Co-CEO, Chi-Foon Chan, age 67, $500,000 total compensation
EVP Business Operations and Chief Administrative Officer, Brian M. Beattie, age 63, $440,000 total compensation
EVP Customer Engagement, Deirdre Hanford, age 54, $300,000 total compensation
EVP; General Manager Verification Group, Manoj Gandhi, age 56
SVP; General Manager Silicon Engineering Group, Howard Ko, age 60
EVP; General Manager Solutions Group, Joachim Kunkel
General Counsel and Corporate Secretary, John F. (Rick) Runkel, age 61, $350,000 total compensation
EVP Sales and Corporate Marketing, Joseph W. (Joe) Logan, age 57, $400,000 total compensation
Chairman and Co-CEO, Aart de Geus, $500,000 total compensation
CFO, Trac Pham, $350,000 total compensation
SVP and General Manager Software Integrity Group, Andreas Kuehlmann
Senior Vice President Marketing, John (Jack) Chilton
Vice President of Engineering for Test Automation Products, Arif Samad
Vice President Marketing Implementation Group, Thomas (Thom) Ferry

Vice President Greater China, Pei-hsin Ho
Vice President and General Man, Yankin Tanurhan
Vice President Engineering ASIC and FP, Michael (Mel) Jackson
Vice President Engineering Synplicity Business Gro, Andrew (Andy) Dauman
Vice President Sales, Steve (Stevie) McDonald
Vice President Western Area Sales, Brian (Bri) Gregory
Vice President of Human Resources, Angellee Choi-Kanuch
Vice President Corporate Marketing, DAVE (Davie) DEMARIA
Vice President of Sales, Kevin (Kev) Maguire
Regional Vice President, Linda Davidson
Vice President Corporate Operations, Tom (Tommy) Oliveri
Vice President Engineering, Eshel Haritan
Vice President, Kevin Brelsford
Vice President Software Engine, Brian (Bri) Gordon
Vice President, Kripa Sundar
Vice President Of European Sales, Gabriel Lezmi
Vice President of AMS Marketing and Application Engineering, Ravi Tembhekar
Vice President Research And Development, Rohit Vora
Vice President Engineering, Naji Bekhazi
Vice President, Kalpana Singh
Senior Vice President Worldwide Sales, Joe (Joey) Logan
Vice President Investor Relations, Lisa Ewbank
Vice President engineering, Ching-Yen Ho
Vice President of Sales, Jian-Yue Pan
Vice President of Marketing, Tom (Tommy) Ferry
Vice President of Global Technical Services, Jonathan (Jon) Saari
Vice President of Strategy and Corporate Development, Randy (Rand) Tinsley
Vice President, Jeong-Tyng Li
Vice President of Engineering, Sunil Ashtaputre
Vice President Engineering, Ray Leung
Vice President of Software Research and Development, Jun Park
Auditors: KPMG LLP

LOCATIONS

HQ: Synopsys Inc
690 East Middlefield Road, Mountain View, CA 94043
Phone: 650 584-5000
Web: www.synopsys.com

PRODUCTS/OPERATIONS

2016 sales

	$ mil.	% of total
Time-based license	1,911.0	790
Maintenance & service	263.0	11
Upfront license	248.0	10
Total	**2,422.0**	**100**

Selected Products

Astro (place and route)
Chip Architect (planning and analysis of various design phases)
coreBuilder (reusable design data)
CoCentric System Studio (system-level design and verification)
Coverity (quality and testing tools)
Design Compiler (logic synthesis)
Design Vision (design management and analysis)
DesignWare (implementation and verification design library)
Hercules (physical verification)
Module Compiler (synthesis of data paths)
NanoSim (memory and mixed-signal verification)
PathMill (static timing analysis)
Physical Compiler (physical synthesis)
PowerMill (circuit simulation and design)
Scirocco (VHDL-based simulation)
VCS (Verilog language-based simulation)

Selected Services

Tool & Methodology Consulting
Design Flow Deployment
IP Integration & SoC Verification
Core Optimization
Physical Design Assistance
FPGA-based Prototyping

Selected Acquisitions

COMPETITORS

ANSYS	Mentor Graphics
ASML	MoSys
Agilent EEsof	PDF Solutions
Altium	Rambus
CEVA	Silvaco
Cadence Design	SynTest
Intrinsix	

HISTORICAL FINANCIALS

Company Type: Public

Income Statement

FYE: October 31

	REVENUE ($ mil.)	NET INCOME ($ mil.)	NET PROFIT MARGIN	EMPLOYEES
10/16	2,422.5	266.8	11.0%	10,669.0
10/15	2,242.2	225.9	10.1%	10,284.0
10/14	2,057.4	259.1	12.6%	9,436.0
10/13	1,962.2	247.8	12.6%	8,573.0
10/12	1,756.0	182.4	10.4%	8,138.0
Annual Growth	8.4%	10.0%		7.0%

2016 Year-End Financials

Debt ratio: 3.9%	No. of shares (mil.): 151.4
Return on equity: 8.4%	Dividends
Cash ($ mil.): 976.6	Yield: —
Current ratio: 1.00	Payout: —
Long-term debt ($ mil.): —	Market value ($ mil.): 8,983.0

	STOCK PRICE ($) FY Close	P/E High/Low		PER SHARE ($) Earnings	Dividends	Book Value
10/16	59.31	34	23	1.73	0.00	21.10
10/15	49.98	36	28	1.43	0.00	20.20
10/14	40.98	25	21	1.64	0.00	19.60
10/13	36.42	24	19	1.58	0.00	18.09
10/12	32.20	28	21	1.21	0.00	16.58
Annual Growth	16.5%	—	—	9.3%	—	6.2%

Syntel Inc.

Syntel is in the know about information technology. The IT services provider offers IT services and knowledge process outsourcing (KPO) to companies in banking and finance health care and life science insurance manufacturingretail logistics and telecommunications. Its IT services include programming system integration outsourcing and overall project management. Syntel's KPO services for back-office functions are transaction processing loan servicing retirement processing collections and payment processing. Its top clients include American Express and State Street. US customers account for 90% of its business. Cofounding spouses Bharat Desai and Neerja Sethi are the company's biggest shareholders.

Operations

Syntel divides its operations into the markets it service. The biggest is banking and financial services which generates 49% of the company's revenue. Supplying in the neighborhood of 15% of sales each are health care and life science insurance and retail logistics and telecom.

Syntel offers customers a platform for automating process called SyntBots which enables clients to manage and migrate business and technology systems.

Geographic Reach

The company's application development centers and other facilities are located in India. The company also has about 20 sales offices worldwide. Although headquartered in the US 80% of the company's employees were based in India in 2012.

Sales and Marketing

Syntel markets and sells its services through sales teams operating throughout the US Canada Europe and Australia. Its two top clients American Express and State Street together accounted for just more than two-thirds of revenue in 2015 which is down from about half in 2012.

Financial Performance

While revenue has grown to $968 million (in 2015) Syntel makes nowhere near the multibillion-dollar sales of its top Indian outsourcing rivals Infosys Tata Consultancy and Wipro. The company's sales continue to grow however and its average annual profit margin for the past five years is about 25%. Revenue grew by about 6% in 2015 driven by strong global demand for the offshore IT services. As in previous years Syntel also attributed the jump in sales for the year to the expansion of its workforce which enabled the company to scale up capacity. It reported more than $300 million in new business across its market segments. Profit rose just 1% for 2015 to $252 million.

Ownership

Founder Bharat Desai holds a 38% stake in the company while co-founder Neerja Sethi holds 29%. Besides Desai and Sethi Syntel has a third major stakeholder Rakesh Vij who owns a household products trading company RK International Inc. in Houston. Vij controls 23% of the company.

Company Background

Desai and Sethi founded the company in 1980 while Desai was earning his Master's degree from the University of Michigan. The couple moved to the US in 1976 when Desai took a job with Tata Consultancy one of the top India-based IT outsourcing companies.

EXECUTIVES

Chief Administrative Officer General Counsel and Secretary, Daniel M. Moore, age 61, $331,380 total compensation
Head of Europe Sales, Ben Andradi
Interim President and CEO, Rakesh Khanna, age 54, $219,343 total compensation
SVP Insurance Business Unit Head, Anil Jain, age 57, $238,201 total compensation
VP Life Sciences Business Unit Head, Murlidhar Reddy, age 46
SVP Banking and Financial Services Business Unit Head, V. S. Raj, age 52
SVP Retail CPG and Telecom Business Unit Head, Raja Ray, age 53, $271,580 total compensation
VP Manufacturing Business Unit Head, Avinash Salelkar, age 53
VP and CEO State Street Syntel Services Private Limited, Sanjay Garg, age 49
General Manager Finance, Anil Agrawal, age 39, $57,644 total compensation
SVP Logistics and Travel Business Unit Head, Srinath Mallya, age 50

Vice President Client Services Europe, Jerry Mathews
Vice President, Stephen Brown
Vice President Head Of Business Development (Nao) Rlt, Sanjeev Kumar
Vice President Business Development, Vijay (Jay) Malik
Vice President Head Testing Services, Sm Mallya
Co-Chairman, Bharat Desai, age 63
Co-Chairman, Prashant Ranade, age 63
Auditors: Crowe Horwath LLP

LOCATIONS

HQ: Syntel Inc.
525 E. Big Beaver Road, Suite 300, Troy, MI 48083
Phone: 248 619-2800   **Fax:** 248 619-2888
Web: www.syntelinc.com

PRODUCTS/OPERATIONS

2015 Sales

	$ mil.	% of total
Banking and Financial services	474.9	49
Health and Life sciences	158.0	16
Insurance	133.5	14
Manufacturing	41.2	4
Retail Logistic and Telecom	161.0	17
Total	**968.6**	**100**

Selected Services

Applications outsourcing
  Applications development
  Applications maintenance
  Applications management
  Platforms conversion
Knowledge process outsourcing
e-Business
  Customer relationship management services
  Data warehousing and business intelligence
  E-business design development implementation and maintenance
  Enterprise applications outsourcing
  Web architecture
  Web-enablement of legacy applications
  Web portal design
TeamSourcing
  Design
  Development
  Implementation
  Information technology staffing
  Maintenance
  Systems specification
  Technical services

COMPETITORS

Accenture	HCL Technologies
Capgemini	HP Enterprise Services
Cognizant Tech Solutions	IBM Global Services
Computer Sciences Corp.	Infosys
Deloitte	NTT Data
Dimension Data Asia Pacific	PricewaterhouseCoopers
First Data	TCS America
Getronics	Unisys
	WNS (Holdings)
	Wipro

HISTORICAL FINANCIALS

Company Type: Public

Income Statement

FYE: December 31

	REVENUE ($ mil.)	NET INCOME ($ mil.)	NET PROFIT MARGIN	EMPLOYEES
12/15	968.6	252.5	26.1%	24,537.0
12/14	911.4	249.7	27.4%	24,553.0
12/13	824.7	219.6	26.6%	23,652.0
12/12	723.9	185.5	25.6%	21,407.0
12/11	642.4	122.8	19.1%	19,484.0
Annual Growth	10.8%	19.7%	—	5.9%

2015 Year-End Financials

Debt ratio: 9.1%
Return on equity: 23.9%
Cash ($ mil.): 500.5
Current ratio: 5.07
Long-term debt ($ mil.): —
No. of shares (mil.): 83.9
Dividends
  Yield: —
  Payout: —
Market value ($ mil.): 3,799.0

	STOCK PRICE ($) FY Close	P/E High/Low	PER SHARE ($) Earnings	Dividends	Book Value
12/15	45.25	17 14	3.00	0.00	13.80
12/14	44.98	32 14	2.97	0.00	11.32
12/13	90.95	35 20	2.62	2.43	8.65
12/12	53.63	29 20	2.22	2.49	6.79
12/11	46.77	41 26	1.47	0.12	5.93
Annual Growth	(0.8%)	— —	19.5%	—	23.5%

Tallgrass Energy GP LP

Auditors: PricewaterhouseCoopers LLP

LOCATIONS

HQ: Tallgrass Energy GP LP
  4200 W. 115th Street, Suite 350, Leawood, KS 66211
Phone: 913 928-6060
Web: www.tallgrassenergy.com

HISTORICAL FINANCIALS

Company Type: Public

Income Statement

FYE: December 31

	REVENUE ($ mil.)	NET INCOME ($ mil.)	NET PROFIT MARGIN	EMPLOYEES
12/15	536.2	31.9	6.0%	0.0
12/14	371.5	70.6	19.0%	0.0
12/13	290.5	9.7	3.4%	0.0
12/12	38.5	(2.3)	—	0.0
Annual Growth	140.4%	—	—	0.0

2015 Year-End Financials

Debt ratio: 29.8%
Return on equity: —
Cash ($ mil.): 2.2
Current ratio: 0.87
Long-term debt ($ mil.): 901.0
No. of shares (mil.): 157.2
Dividends
  Yield: 1.3%
  Payout: 42.5%
Market value ($ mil.): 2,511.0

	STOCK PRICE ($) FY Close	P/E High/Low	PER SHARE ($) Earnings	Dividends	Book Value
12/15	15.97	65 27	0.51	0.22	2.69
12/14	0.00	— —	1.36	0.00	20.83
Annual Growth (87.1%)		— —	(62.5%)	—	—

Tallgrass Energy Partners, LP

This company hopes there's plenty of green out there in the tall grass. Tallgrass Energy Partners (TEP) provides transportation and storage of natural gas in the Rocky Mountains and Midwest. It also provides natural gas processing and treating at its three facilities in Wyoming. TEP's natural gas transportation systems are located in Colorado Kansas Missouri Nebraska and Wyoming. TEP also maintains a pipeline from the Colorado and Wyoming border to Beatrice Nebraska and it provides water business to customers in Colorado and Texas. TEP was formed in early 2013 to hold the midstream assets of its parent Tallgrass Development. It became a public company a few months later.

IPO
TEP plans to use its $280 million in IPO proceeds to pay debt owned to its parent Tallgrass Development.

Operations
With its processing facilities working at full capacity TEP is expanding to handle an additional 50 million cu. ft./day.

Strategy
Going forward TEP's strategies for growth include acquiring additional midstream assets from Tallgrass Development and third parties and expansion of existing facilities.

Ownership
Pre-IPO the company is owned and controlled by Tallgrass Development.

Auditors: PricewaterhouseCoopers LLP

LOCATIONS

HQ: Tallgrass Energy Partners, LP
  4200 W. 115th Street, Suite 350, Leawood, KS 66211
Phone: 913 928-6060
Web: www.tallgrassenergy.com

COMPETITORS

Colorado Interstate Gas	Newfield Exploration
Kinder Morgan	Stone Energy
Merit Energy	Western Gas Partners

HISTORICAL FINANCIALS

Company Type: Public

Income Statement

FYE: December 31

	REVENUE ($ mil.)	NET INCOME ($ mil.)	NET PROFIT MARGIN	EMPLOYEES
12/15	536.2	160.5	29.9%	0.0
12/14	371.5	70.6	19.0%	0.0
12/13	267.7	14.1	5.3%	0.0
12/12*	38.5	(2.3)	—	0.0
11/12	220.2	51.5	23.4%	0.0
Annual Growth	24.9%	32.9%	—	—

*Fiscal year change

2015 Year-End Financials

Debt ratio: 29.3%
Return on equity: —
Cash ($ mil.): 1.6
Current ratio: 0.87
Long-term debt ($ mil.): 753.0
No. of shares (mil.): 61.4
Dividends
  Yield: 5.3%
  Payout: 110.9%
Market value ($ mil.): 2,534.0

	STOCK PRICE ($) FY Close	P/E High/Low	PER SHARE ($) Earnings	Dividends	Book Value
12/15	41.21	27 18	1.91	2.19	20.66
12/14	44.70	33 18	1.36	1.43	20.83
12/13	26.00	156 121	0.17	0.44	18.00
Annual Growth	25.9%	—	235.2%	122.9%	7.1%

Tanger Factory Outlet Centers, Inc.

Brand name bargains are on shoppers' lists when they visit Tanger Factory Outlet Centers. One of the top outlet mall developers (along with retail giant Simon Property and its Chelsea Property Group subsidiary) Tanger is a real estate investment trust (REIT) that develops owns and manages about 45 retail outlet centers in 25 states and Canada. A typical center has 75 stores and totals at least 300000 sq. ft. housing shops from more than 400 brand name companies including The Gap Ralph Lauren Ann Taylor Phillips-Van Heusen and Nike. Tanger's outlet centers which maintain about 99% occupancy are built away from malls and shopping districts so tenants don't compete with their full-price stores.

Operations
Outlet mall stores share the same name as their brand name retail counterparts but sell merchandise at significant discounts due to overstock or off-season availability. Other retailers specifically earmark discounted merchandise to be sold at outlet stores. Outlet stores are also able to charge customers lower prices by eliminating the third-party retailer.

As a self-administered and self-managed REIT Tanger Factory Outlet Center focuses exclusively on developing acquiring owning operating and managing outlet shopping centers. REITs are exempt from paying federal income taxes as long as they distribute quarterly dividends to shareholders.

Geographic Reach
Tanger's outlet malls are mostly concentrated along the East Coast. It also owns interests in three outlet malls in Canada – two in Quebec and one in Ontario. Its Canadian malls were built in 2011 in partnership with RioCan Real Estate Investment Trust.

Financial Performance
Overall sales increased by 13% in 2012 to $357 million and profits shot up 20% to $53 million. The trust makes money on rent; as long as it has high occupancy rates and continues to open new malls it is profitable. In fact the outlet industry thrives during tough economic times as shoppers search for good deals.

Strategy
Tanger Factory Outlet Centers has been aggressively marketing to higher volume tenants replacing low-profile stores with the flash and appeal of trendier name brands. Attracting stronger more popular apparel footwear and housewares brands allows Tanger to renew leases at higher base rents.

The REIT also continues to seek opportunities for new development or acquisition of shopping centers. In particular the company targets markets that have at least 1 million residents and are located near high-traffic interstate highways.

Mergers and Acquisitions

To that end in 2013 the company began building two new outlet malls to add to its property portfolio. One near the Foxwoods Resort Casino in Mashantucket Connecticut is being developed with Gordon Group Holdings LLC. The 300000 sq.-ft. mall will sit between two casino hotels for added foot traffic.

The other is being developed with rival Simon Property Group as a 50/50 joint venture. The 400000 sq.-ft. Charlotte Premium Outlets in Charlotte North Carolina will have about 90 stores. Tanger will provide site development and construction supervision while Simon will provide management services and marketing. The first phase is expected to open in 2014.

HISTORY

In 1948 Stanley Tanger became head of a shirt manufacturer his father had started in 1920. That company Tanger/Creighton eventually opened five successful outlet stores.

He sold the company to its employees in 1979 and came up with the idea of putting several factory-direct and off-price retailers together in a single mall. In 1981 he opened his first outlet center in North Carolina. His son Steven joined him in 1986. By 1992 the company had 17 centers but was heavily leveraged.

Tanger became the first publicly traded factory outlet center company when it completed its initial public offering in 1993. It used proceeds from its IPO to retire all debt and continue expansion.

Steven Tanger became president in 1995 the year the centers began putting in police substations to increase security. More new features cropped up in 1996 —cinemas restaurants and a 30-day cash-back guarantee on items purchased at Tanger centers. Although growth continued in 1997 a drop in REIT stocks the next year led the company to halt construction on two new centers.

Warren Buffett bought a 5% stake in the company in 1999 spurring other investors to return to REIT stocks. That year it took over its property management duties to cut costs. Also that year the company's outlet mall in Stroud Oklahoma was destroyed by a tornado.

In 2000 the firm sold two underperforming properties one in Kansas and the other in Oregon. In 2001 the company began work on a site in Myrtle Beach South Carolina.

In 2003 the company acquired in a joint venture with Blackstone Real Estate Advisors a portfolio of nine outlet malls located near upscale resort communities from Charter Oak Partners. In 2005 Tanger agreed to buy out Blackstone Real Estate Advisors' share in the Charter Oak portfolio for about $283 million. The deal closed near the end of that year.

Founder and chairman Stanley Tanger stepped down as CEO at the end of 2008; he was succeeded by son Steven Tanger. The economy also took its toll on the company that year as 14 stores with 500000 sq. ft. of space closed their doors due to the economy.

EXECUTIVES

Vice President Information Technologies, Rick Farrar

Vice President Marketing, Laura M (Laur) Atwell

Vice President Operations, Elizabeth (Beth) Coleman

President and CEO, Steven B. Tanger, age 67, $824,000 total compensation

SVP Leasing, Lisa J. Morrison, age 57, $267,063 total compensation

SVP and CFO, James F. Williams, age 52

EVP and COO, Thomas E. (Tom) McDonough, age 58, $382,439 total compensation

EVP and General Counsel, Chad D. Perry, $360,500 total compensation

SVP Construction and Development, Charles A. Worsham

Assistant Vice President Human Resources, Andrea (Ann) Whiticar

Vice President Investor Relations, Cyndi M (Lucinda) Holt

Executive Vice President, John (Jack) McDonough

Senior Vice President Operations and Chief Informa, Karen (Kare) Marchisello

Senior Vice President Marketing, Carrie (Carr) Warren

Vice President Finance, Virginia (Ginny) Summerell

Senior Vice President, Manuel O (Mannie) Jessup

Vice President, CINDY M HOLT

Chairman, Thomas J. (Tom) Reddin, age 55

Auditors: Deloitte & Touche LLP

LOCATIONS

HQ: Tanger Factory Outlet Centers, Inc.
3200 Northline Avenue, Suite 360, Greensboro, NC 27408
Phone: 336 292-3010   **Fax:** 336 297-0931
Web: www.tangeroutlet.com

PRODUCTS/OPERATIONS

2015 Sales

	$ mil.	% of total
Base rents	289.7	66
Expense reimbursements	126.5	29
Percentage rentals	10.1	2
Other	13.1	3
Total	**439.4**	**100**

Ten Largest Tenants 2015

The Gap
Dress Barn
Nike
Adidas
VF Outlet Inc.
Ann Inc.
Polo Ralph Lauren
Carter's
Hanesbrands Direct

COMPETITORS

Belz	Macerich
CBL & Associates	Ramco-Gershenson
Properties	Simon Property Group
Chelsea Property	Taubman Centers
General Growth	Vornado Realty
Properties	
Horizon Group	
Properties	

HISTORICAL FINANCIALS

Company Type: Public

Income Statement

FYE: December 31

	REVENUE ($ mil.)	NET INCOME ($ mil.)	NET PROFIT MARGIN	EMPLOYEES
12/15	439.3	211.2	48.1%	625.0
12/14	418.5	74.0	17.7%	625.0
12/13	385.0	107.5	27.9%	614.0
12/12	357.0	53.2	14.9%	542.0
12/11	315.2	44.6	14.2%	476.0
Annual Growth	**8.7%**	**47.5%**	**—**	**7.0%**

2015 Year-End Financials

Debt ratio: 67.2%	No. of shares (mil.): 95.8
Return on equity: 39.4%	Dividends
Cash ($ mil.): 21.5	Yield: 3.9%
Current ratio: 1.14	Payout: 103.5%
Long-term debt ($ mil.): 1,563.8	Market value ($ mil.): 3,135.0

	STOCK PRICE ($) FY Close	P/E High/Low		PER SHARE ($) Earnings	Dividends	Book Value
12/15	32.70	18	14	2.20	1.31	6.00
12/14	36.96	49	42	0.77	0.95	5.20
12/13	32.02	34	26	1.13	0.89	5.53
12/12	34.20	60	49	0.57	0.83	5.13
12/11	29.32	98	42	0.52	0.79	5.31
Annual Growth	**2.8%**	**—**	**—**	**43.4%**	**13.2%**	**3.1%**

TASER International Inc.

TASER International's weapons aim to take perps down but not out. The company is well known for designing and manufacturing various non-lethal TASER lines of stun guns including its best-selling TASER X26. These electronic control devices (ECDs) are geared at the law enforcement corrections military and private security markets as well as consumers. The company also offers AXON wearable video cameras for officers and a hosted product called Evidence.com that allows digital evidence to be viewed shared and managed from a Web browser. Products are sold worldwide through a direct sales force distribution partners and online store and third-party resellers.

Geographic Reach

Worldwide more than 17000 law enforcement agencies in more than 150 countries have purchased TASER brand products for testing or deployment. More than a dozen US state correctional agencies from Oregon to Tennessee also use TASER devices. On the military side TASER International develops products for both the US (including the US Department of Defense) and certain foreign allies through contracts. The US generates 80% of its sales.

Operations

TASER International's most popular product is the TASER X26 with shaped pulse technology which is geared toward the law enforcement corrections military and private security markets. It generates about 40% of the company's total sales. On the consumer side its primary product is the TASER C2 a compact device that provides the same NMI effectiveness as the market-leading TASER X26 law enforcement version. Private citizens who buy the C2 for their own personal defense must undergo identification verification before the device is activated.

Financial Performance

TASER International has achieved unprecedented growth over the years with revenues peaking at a record-setting $165 million in 2014. Profits also reached almost $20 million in 2014 another company milestone. In addition its operating cash flow has skyrocketed the last five years soaring from only $732 thousand in 2010 to $35 million in 2014.

The historic growth for 2014 was driven by the introduction of its new TASER X26P smart weapon and significant growth from its AXON product line. It also was helped by the absence of litigation expenses for the year.

Strategy

In addition to product line extensions TASER International is putting significant R&D time and money into technology-based products an area that it views as likely to sustain the most growth. Its TASER Cam is a video recording device that captures both video and audio of TASER use incidents.

The company also developed its officer video and digital evidence management system consisting of the AXON tactical computer (an earpiece with imager speaker and microphone built in) and Evidence.com hosted site (from which agencies and legal professionals can quickly and securely access key evidence data). The company is poised for explosive growth within these segments as a growing number of police departments across the US place orders for body cameras that officers can wear to document their interactions with the public.

Geographically the company is heavily dependent on the US market for sales. However it is working to diversify that base by increasing marketing of its products in such places as Australia New Zealand Brazil and various parts of Europe. Wholly-owned subsidiary TASER International Europe SE was established to facilitate sales and provide customer service to European customers.

Adhering to this strategy in 2015 the company purchased Tactical Safety Responses Limited (TSR) a licensed distributor of smart weapons and body cameras in the UK.

EXECUTIVES

CEO Director and Cofounder, Patrick W. (Rick) Smith, age 45, $265,000 total compensation
CFO, Daniel M. (Dan) Behrendt, age 51, $255,000 total compensation
General Manager EVIDENCE.com, Marcus Womack
Chief Marketing Officer, Luke Larson
EVP Sales, Josh Isner
VP International Operations, Ron Brandt
Chairman, Michael (Mike) Garnreiter, age 64
Auditors: Grant Thornton LLP

LOCATIONS

HQ: TASER International Inc.
17800 North 85th Street, Scottsdale, AZ 85255
Phone: 480 991-0797
Web: www.taser.com

PRODUCTS/OPERATIONS

2014 Sales by Product

	$ mil.	% of total
ECD Segment		
TASER X26P	43.5	26
Single cartridges	38.5	23
TASER X2	28.8	18
TASER X26	18.7	11
Extended Warranties icluding TAP	6.0	4
TASER XREP	2.6	2
TASER C2	2.1	1
TASER M26	0.7	1
Other	4.7	3
AXON Segment		
AXON Solutions	9.0	5
AXON/EVIDENCE.com	4.0	2
TASER Cam	4.7	3
Other	1.2	1
Total	**164.5**	**100**

COMPETITORS

Applied Energetics	Mace Security
Colt Defense	Metal Storm
Digital Ally	PepperBall
Glock	Technologies

HISTORICAL FINANCIALS

Company Type: Public

Income Statement

FYE: December 31

	REVENUE ($ mil.)	NET INCOME ($ mil.)	NET PROFIT MARGIN	EMPLOYEES
12/15	197.8	19.9	10.1%	670.0
12/14	164.5	19.9	12.1%	567.0
12/13	137.8	18.2	13.2%	485.0
12/12	114.7	14.7	12.8%	433.0
12/11	90.0	(7.0)	—	394.0
Annual Growth	**21.8%**	**—**		**14.2%**

2015 Year-End Financials

Debt ratio: 0.0%
Return on equity: 13.9%
Cash ($ mil.): 59.5
Current ratio: 4.23
Long-term debt ($ mil.): 0.0

No. of shares (mil.): 53.6
Dividends
　Yield: —
　Payout: —
Market value ($ mil.): 928.0

	STOCK PRICE ($) FY Close	P/E High/Low		Earnings	PER SHARE ($) Dividends	Book Value
12/15	17.29	95	44	0.36	0.00	2.92
12/14	26.48	71	28	0.37	0.00	2.44
12/13	15.88	51	20	0.34	0.00	2.05
12/12	8.94	33	15	0.27	0.00	1.65
12/11	5.12	—	—	(0.12)	0.00	1.48
Annual Growth	**35.6%**	**—**	**—**	**—**	**—**	**18.6%**

TC PipeLines, LP

Auditors: KPMG LLP

LOCATIONS

HQ: TC PipeLines, LP
700 Louisiana Street, Suite 700, Houston, TX 77002-2761
Phone: 877 290-2772
Web: www.tcpipelineslp.com

HISTORICAL FINANCIALS

Company Type: Public

Income Statement

FYE: December 31

	REVENUE ($ mil.)	NET INCOME ($ mil.)	NET PROFIT MARGIN	EMPLOYEES
12/15	344.0	13.0	3.8%	0.0
12/14	336.0	172.0	51.2%	0.0
12/13	341.0	155.0	45.5%	0.0
12/12	65.0	137.0	210.8%	0.0
12/11	70.4	157.4	223.6%	0.0
Annual Growth	**48.7%**	**(46.4%)**		**—**

2015 Year-End Financials

Debt ratio: 60.9%
Return on equity: —
Cash ($ mil.): 39.0
Current ratio: 1.37
Long-term debt ($ mil.): 1,896.0

No. of shares (mil.): 66.2
Dividends
　Yield: 6.9%
　Payout: 117.2%
Market value ($ mil.): 3,292.0

	STOCK PRICE ($) FY Close	P/E High/Low		Earnings	PER SHARE ($) Dividends	Book Value
12/15	49.71	—	—	(0.03)	3.46	17.38
12/14	71.22	29	17	2.67	3.30	21.27
12/13	48.43	24	19	2.13	3.18	21.64
12/12	40.36	19	15	2.51	3.10	24.33
12/11	47.43	18	13	3.02	3.04	24.93
Annual Growth	**1.2%**	**—**	**—**	**—**	**3.3%**	**(8.6%)**

Teligent Inc (New)

Teligent (formerly IGI) is betting big on small things. It manufactures creams liquids and other topical products for drug and cosmetics companies using its microencapsulation technology. Teligent originally licensed the technology dubbed Novasome from drug firm Novovax. The Novasome process entraps and protects the active ingredients of various skin care products moisturizers shampoos and fragrances allowing for greater stability during storage and a more controlled release when used. The firm is examining further applications of the Novasome technology in food personal care products and pharmaceuticals.

Operations

Teligent also provides development formulation and manufacturing services to the pharmaceutical OTC and cosmetic industries. Specializing in topical products the company offers formulation and methods development analytical support scale-up commercial manufacturing and packaging services. For its own products Teligent develops manufactures and markets topical injectable complex and opthalmic dosage forms.

The company has acquired 21 FDA-approved drug products. It has 22 Abbreviated New Drug Applications (ANDAs) in its pipeline awaiting approval. It has another 45 products in its development pipeline.

Geographic Reach

The company manufactures all of its labeled products in its 25000-sq.-ft. facility in New Jersey. It leases an additional 11000 sq. ft. of warehouse space in New Jersey and leases 10000 sq. ft. of corporate office space also in New Jersey.

Sales and Marketing

Teligent offers its products to pharmaceutical over-the-counter and cosmetic customers. In 2014 31% of its net total sales were to three wholesale drug distributors: AmerisourceBergen Cardinal Health and McKesson.

Financial Performance

Revenue has been rising since 2012: It more than doubled to $18.2 million in 2013 and rose 85% to $33.7 million in 2014. The increases were due to the launch of the firm's generic pharmaceutical line as well as growing product sales to pharmaceutical customers. For the past decade expenses exceeded revenue but in 2014 the company became profitable netting $5.2 million on the higher revenues.

However operating cash outflow increased greatly to $3.9 million as more cash was used in accounts receivable and prepaid expenses.

Strategy

The company's growth efforts center around making and selling its generic pharmaceutical products building up its contract manufacturing and development business and adding to its portfolio of intellectual property and products.

To facilitate that growth it is planning to expand its facility in Buena New Jersey. Teligent is also looking to strike up partnerships with contract manufacturing organizations for the manufacturing of its sterile injectable and opthalmic products.

Mergers and Acquisitions

In mid-2014 the company acquired ANDAs and New Drug Applications (NDAs) associated with 18 products from AstraZeneca. It also bought ANDAs and NDAs associated with two opthalmic products as well as the exclusive right to acquire three additional approved injectable products from Valeant. The following year it agreed to buy the assets of Canadian firm Alveda Pharmaceutical for C$47 million. Generic specialist Alveda markets nearly 40 injectable pharmaceutical products in Canada and has a pipeline of products under development.

In 2013 the company acquired assets and intellectual property including one ANDA for econazole nitrate cream 1% which it launched in September of that year.

EXECUTIVES

EVP Sales and Marketing, Nadya Lawrence, age 47, $146,529 total compensation
President and CEO and Director, Jason Grenfell-Gardner
CFO, Jenniffer Collins
Chairman, Joyce Erony, age 56
Auditors: EisnerAmper LLP

LOCATIONS

HQ: Teligent Inc (New)
105 Lincoln Avenue, Buena, NJ 08310
Phone: 856 697-1441
Web: www.igilabs.com

PRODUCTS/OPERATIONS

2014 Sales

	% of total
Product sales	95
Research & development income	4
Licensing royalty & other income	1
Total	**100**

Selected Products

Econazole Cream 1% 15g
Econazole Cream 1% 30g
Econazole Cream 1% 85g
Fluocinolone Acetonide Cream 0.01% 15g
Fluocinolone Acetonide Cream 0.01% 60g
Fluocinolone Acetonide Ointment .025% 15g
Fluocinolone Acetonide Ointment .025% 60g

COMPETITORS

DPT Labs   NextPharma

HISTORICAL FINANCIALS

Company Type: Public

Income Statement
FYE: December 31

	REVENUE ($ mil.)	NET INCOME ($ mil.)	NET PROFIT MARGIN	EMPLOYEES
12/15	44.2	6.6	15.1%	107.0
12/14	33.7	5.2	15.6%	81.0
12/13	18.2	(0.0)	—	52.0
12/12	8.5	(3.9)	—	41.0
12/11	7.8	(3.0)	—	36.0
Annual Growth	**54.3%**	**—**		**31.3%**

2015 Year-End Financials

Debt ratio: 57.9%
Return on equity: 12.5%
Cash ($ mil.): 87.1
Current ratio: 10.85
Long-term debt ($ mil.): 106.9
No. of shares (mil.): 53.0
Dividends
  Yield: —
  Payout: —
Market value ($ mil.): 472.0

	STOCK PRICE ($) FY Close	P/E High/Low	PER SHARE ($) Earnings	Dividends	Book Value
12/15	8.90	89 39	(0.07)	0.00	1.26
12/14	8.80	100 27	0.09	0.00	0.74
12/13	3.05	— —	(0.03)	0.00	0.15
12/12	1.04	— —	(0.10)	0.00	0.15
12/11	1.15	— —	(0.08)	0.00	0.20
Annual Growth	**66.8%**	**— —**	**—**	**—**	**59.1%**

Terreno Realty Corp

Terreno Realty has its eyes set on acquiring industrial real estate. The real estate investment trust (REIT) invests in and operates industrial properties in major US coastal markets including Los Angeles San Francisco Bay Area Seattle Miami Northern New Jersey/New York City and Washington DC/Baltimore. The REIT typically invests in warehouse and distribution facilities flex buildings for light manufacturing and research and development and transportation and shipping centers. The company owns more than 125 buildings spanning 9.3 million square feet and two improved land parcels totaling 3.5 acres.

Operations

About 89% of Terreno Realty's property portfolio consisted of warehouse/distribution properties while flex buildings (including light industrial and R&D facilities) made up another 9%. Transshipment properties made up the rest.Sales and MarketingSome of Terreno Realty's tenants include FedEx Cepheid Northrop Grumman HD Smith Wholesale Drug Company Home Depot and the US government.

Financial Performance

Terreno Realty's revenues and profits have rising at a healthy clip in recent years as its rental income has increased with new property acquisitions.The REIT's revenue rose by 51% to a record $68.9 million in 2014 thanks to new rental income from property acquisitions made in 2014 and 2013. Same-store revenue grew as well as it increased rental rates by 8% and as occupancy rates increased to 97.1% from 96.3% the year before.Higher revenue in 2014 drove the REIT's net income higher by 61% to $10.7 million while its operating cash levels more than doubled to $29.3 million thanks to higher cash earnings.

Strategy

Terreno Realty seeks long-term earnings growth by increasing rents and operating income at its existing properties and by acquiring new properties in its six target geographic markets. In 2015 it spent on $115.5 million on properties in Washington DC while it also purchased properties in Annapolis Junction Maryland; Medley Florida; Union City California; Tukwila Washington; and Kent Washington. During 2014 it spent $235.7 million on 29 industrial buildings spanning 2.27 million sq. ft. and one improved land parcel (1.2 acres) growing its property portfolio's square footage by 33%. In 2012 the company acquired 22 industrial build-

ings (containing almost 1.8 million square feet) for $180.9 million. Properties included Global Plaza in Sterling Virginia; Garfield in Commerce California; Caribbean in Sunnyvale California; and South Main in Carson California.

Company Background

The company took itself public in February 2010 in an effort to capitalize on a distressed market ripe with foreclosures and troubled loans. Portions of the net proceeds from its public offering were used to invest in interest-bearing short-term securities to help it gain REIT status.

EXECUTIVES

President, Michael A. (Mike) Coke, age 48, $541,667 total compensation
Chairman and CEO, W. Blake Baird, age 55, $541,667 total compensation
Executive Vice President Jaime J. Cannon, Andrew T. Burke
SVP and CFO, Jaime J. Cannon, $245,000 total compensation
Vice President, Michael Murray
Vice President, Katie Barrios
Vice President, Lori J Stone
Vice President, Gregory N (Greg) Spencer
Senior Vice President Director Of Acquisitions, Andy Burke
Auditors: Ernst & Young LLP

LOCATIONS

HQ: Terreno Realty Corp
101 Montgomery Street, Suite 200, San Francisco, CA 94104
Phone: 415 655-4580
Web: www.terreno.com

PRODUCTS/OPERATIONS

2012 Sales

	$ mil.	% of total
Rental	24.5	78
Tenant expense reimbursements	6.7	22
Total	**31.2**	**100**

COMPETITORS

DCT Industrial Trust   Liberty Property Trust
Duke Realty   Mack-Cali
EastGroup Properties   Monmouth Real Estate
First Industrial   PS Business Parks
Realty   Prologis
First Potomac Realty

HISTORICAL FINANCIALS

Company Type: Public

Income Statement
FYE: December 31

	REVENUE ($ mil.)	NET INCOME ($ mil.)	NET PROFIT MARGIN	EMPLOYEES
12/15	95.9	14.6	15.2%	18.0
12/14	68.8	10.7	15.6%	18.0
12/13	45.5	6.6	14.6%	15.0
12/12	31.1	4.0	13.0%	13.0
12/11	17.5	(3.7)	—	10.0
Annual Growth	**53.0%**	**—**	**—**	**15.8%**

2015 Year-End Financials

Debt ratio: 33.1%
Return on equity: 1.9%
Cash ($ mil.): 22.4
Current ratio: 0.74
Long-term debt ($ mil.): 381.4
No. of shares (mil.): 43.3
Dividends
  Yield: 2.9%
  Payout: 206.2%
Market value ($ mil.): 980.0

STOCK PRICE ($) FY Close	P/E High/Low	PER SHARE ($) Earnings	Dividends	Book Value
12/15 22.62	92 75	0.26	0.66	16.93
12/14 20.63	93 73	0.23	0.57	17.43
12/13 17.70	135103	0.15	0.51	17.56
12/12 15.44	85 71	0.19	0.46	19.00
12/11 15.14	— —	(0.41)	0.30	17.08
Annual Growth 10.6%	— —	—	21.8%	(0.2%)

Tesoro Logistics LP

Tesoro Logistics was created to serve its parent. The company a spinoff of oil refiner Tesoro Corporation owns and operates US crude oil gathering transportation and storage facilities. Its trucks and 700 miles of Montana and North Dakota pipeline serve Tesoro's Mandan refinery while eight refined product terminals hold petroleum in California Utah Washington Alaska and North Dakota. Tesoro Logistics' primary storage facility in Salt Lake City holds 880000 barrels of crude and refined petroleum. In 2016 it announced plans to invest $1.1 billion to beef up its midstream business. That year it agreed to buy two natural gas processing plants in North Dakota from Whiting Petroleum for $700 million.

Though all of Tesoro Logistics' assets are on its parent company's land it plans to pursue business with and acquisitions from third-parties. The company used its $230 million in IPO proceeds for working capital and to pay down debt to Tesoro Corporation.

In 2013 the company acquired Chevron Pipe Line Company's Northwest Products System for $355 million and the first portion of integrated Carson logistics assets from Tesoro Corporation for $640 million.

Tesoro Logistics works within the volatile petroleum industry but because its business is fee-based and it doesn't actually own the petroleum it believes it is protected from the variations in the market.

EXECUTIVES

VP CFO and Director, G. Scott Spendlove, age 53
Chairman and CEO, Gregory J. Goff, age 60
VP General Counsel Secretary and Director, Charles S. (Chuck) Parrish, age 58
President and Director, Phillip M. (Phil) Anderson, age 51
VP Operations, Ralph J. Grimmer, age 65
Chief Operating Officer; Vice President; Director of the General Partner, Daniel Romasko
Independent Director of General Partner, James Lamanna
Lead Independent Director of General Partner, Raymond Bromark
Independent Director of General Partner, Thomas OConnor
VP CFO and Director, G. Scott Spendlove, age 53
VP General Counsel Secretary and Director, Charles S. (Chuck) Parrish, age 58
President and Director, Phillip M. (Phil) Anderson, age 51
Auditors: Ernst & Young LLP

LOCATIONS

HQ: Tesoro Logistics LP
19100 Ridgewood Parkway, San Antonio, TX 78259-1828
Phone: 210 626-6000
Web: www.tesorologistics.com

COMPETITORS

EOG
Enbridge
Encana
Plains All American
Pipeline
TransCanada

HISTORICAL FINANCIALS

Company Type: Public

Income Statement

FYE: December 31

	REVENUE ($ mil.)	NET INCOME ($ mil.)	NET PROFIT MARGIN	EMPLOYEES
12/15	1,112.0	272.0	24.5%	965.0
12/14	600.0	99.0	16.5%	853.0
12/13	305.4	79.6	26.1%	470.0
12/12	156.8	56.7	36.2%	160.0
12/11	80.9	27.9	34.5%	114.0
Annual Growth	92.5%	76.6%	—	70.6%

2015 Year-End Financials

Debt ratio: 58.1%
Return on equity: —
Cash ($ mil.): 16.0
Current ratio: 1.14
Long-term debt ($ mil.): 2,844.0
No. of shares (mil.): 95.3
Dividends
  Yield: 5.6%
  Payout: 216.4%
Market value ($ mil.): 4,799.0

STOCK PRICE ($) FY Close	P/E High/Low	PER SHARE ($) Earnings	Dividends	Book Value
12/15 50.32	26 17	2.33	2.84	17.76
12/14 58.85	79 53	0.96	2.41	17.80
12/13 52.34	46 28	1.47	2.02	4.42
12/12 43.80	25 16	1.89	1.61	(0.50)
12/11 32.90	30 19	1.11	0.59	3.50
Annual Growth 11.2%	— —	20.4%	47.8%	50.1%

Texas Capital Bancshares Inc

Texas Capital Bancshares is the parent company of Texas Capital Bank with more than 10 branches in Austin Dallas Fort Worth Houston and San Antonio. The bank targets high-net-worth individuals and Texas-based businesses with more than $5 million in annual revenue with a focus on the real estate financial services transportation communications petrochemicals and mining sectors. Striving for personalized services for its clients the bank offers deposit accounts Visa credit cards commercial loans and mortgages equipment leasing wealth management and trust services. Its BankDirect division provides online banking services. Founded in 1998 Texas Capital Bancshares has about $11.7 billion in assets.

Financial Performance

The bank reported $488.6 million in revenue in 2013 an nearly 11% increase versus 2012. Net income was flat at about $121 million after posting three consecutive years of gains. Cash flow from operations continued its steep three year decline. The bank's total assets increased 11% from about $10.5 billion in 2012 to $11.7 billion in 2013. Total deposits increased 24% year over year to about $9.3 billion.

Strategy

Headquartered in Dallas Texas Capital Bank (TCB) believes that its Texas roots give it a competitive advantage over larger competitors that are headquartered out of state. Indeed TCB is gaining market share and is expanding by hiring experienced bankers and support staff. The bank is looking to grow within its main metropolitan markets but has also branched out beyond the borders of its home state. The bank has an Cayman Islands branch to offer offshore cash management and deposit products to it core clientele.

EXECUTIVES

President and CEO Texas Capital Bancshares Inc. President and CEO Texas Capital Bank, C. Keith Cargill, age 63, $729,167 total compensation
EVP and Chief Lending Officer Dallas Region, Vince A. Ackerson, $425,000 total compensation
EVP Austin Region Texas Capital Bank, Kerry L. Hall
Regional President Texas Capital Bank Dallas, Russell Hartsfield
CFO and COO Texas Capital Bancshares; COO Texas Capital Bank, Peter B. Bartholow, age 67, $455,333 total compensation
Chief Risk Officer and Chief Credit Officer Texas Capital Bank, John D. Hudgens, $431,833 total compensation
Regional Chairman Texas Capital Bank Houston, Bill Wilson
Regional President Texas Capital Bank San Antonio, David Pope
Regional President Texas Capital Bank Houston, John Sarvadi
Controller and Chief Accounting Officer Texas Capital Bancshares and CFO Texas Capital Bank, Julie L. Anderson, $306,667 total compensation
Regional Chairman Texas Capital Bank San Antonio, Shaun Kennedy
Regional Chairman Texas Capital Bank Fort Worth, Robin Hamilton
Regional President Texas Capital Bank Fort Worth, David Williams
EVP Builder Finance, Melissa Abel
EVP Asset Based Lending, Chris Capriotti
EVP Commercial Real Estate, Rob Delph
EVP Lender Finance, David Fricke
EVP Energy/Oil and Gas Syndicated Finance and Financial Institutions, Lester Keliher
EVP Financial Institutions, Peter Stringer
President Mortgage Finance, Gary Ort
Senior Vice President Compensation Director, Chris Gullo
Vice President, Tricia (Trish) Linderman
Vice President, Lela Naggar
Vice President, Raul Cantu
Vice President Deposit Operations, Leslie (Les) Marsh
Vice President in Commercial Banking Group, Guy Miller
Vice President of Information Technology Infrastructure, Randy (Rand) Tiegs
Vice President Project Management, Allen (Al) Baumbach
Senior Vice President and Deposit Operation, Connie Couch
Senior Vice President Wealth Management and Trust Services, Chip Glispin
Senior Vice President In The Southwest Corporate Banking Division, Paul Howell

Vice President Corp Security and Investigations, Cary Wicker

Senior Vice President Risk Management Officer, Terry King

Vice President Fraud Investigator, Jamie Burud

Vice President Security, Neal Baker

Senior Vice President, Don Rosics

Executive Vice President, Brent Johnston

Executive Vice President, Ronald (Ron) Baker

Vice President Planning, Prasad Varma

Senior Vice President Energy Banking Texas Capital Bank, Jonathan (Jon) Gregory

Senior Vice President and CRA Manager, Phil (Philly) Aslin

Chairman, Larry L. Helm, age 68

Auditors: Ernst & Young LLP

LOCATIONS

HQ: Texas Capital Bancshares Inc
2000 McKinney Avenue, Suite 700, Dallas, TX 75201
Phone: 214 932-6600
Web: www.texascapitalbank.com

PRODUCTS/OPERATIONS

2015 Sales

	% of total
Interest income	
Interest and fees on loans	92
Other	1
Non-interest income	
Brokered loan fees	3
Service charges on deposit accounts	1
Trust fee income	1
Swap fees	1
Other	1
Total	**100**

Selected Services

Association capital bank
Bankdirect
Business services
Mortgage business finance
Online services
Personal banking
Private wealth advisors
Treasury and liquidity

COMPETITORS

Amegy	Comerica
BBVA Compass	Cullen/Frost Bankers
Bancshares	JPMorgan Chase
BOK Financial	Prosperity Bancshares
Bank of America	Wells Fargo

HISTORICAL FINANCIALS

Company Type: Public

Income Statement
FYE: December 31

	ASSETS ($ mil.)	NET INCOME ($ mil.)	INCOME AS % OF ASSETS	EMPLOYEES
12/15	18,909.1	144.8	0.8%	1,329.0
12/14	15,899.9	136.3	0.9%	1,142.0
12/13	11,714.6	121.0	1.0%	1,016.0
12/12	10,540.8	120.6	1.1%	881.0
12/11	8,137.6	75.9	0.9%	786.0
Annual Growth	**23.5%**	**17.5%**	**—**	**14.0%**

2015 Year-End Financials

Return on assets: 0.8%
Return on equity: 9.3%
Long-term debt ($ mil.): —
No. of shares (mil.): 45.8
Sales ($ mil): 650.7
Dividends
Yield: —
Payout: —
Market value ($ mil.): 2,267.0

	STOCK PRICE ($) FY Close	P/E High/Low		PER SHARE ($) Earnings	Dividends	Book Value
12/15	49.42	21	14	2.91	0.00	35.39
12/14	54.33	23	17	2.88	0.00	32.45
12/13	62.20	22	14	2.72	0.00	26.72
12/12	44.82	17	10	3.00	0.00	20.53
12/11	30.61	15	10	1.98	0.00	16.36
Annual Growth	**12.7%**	**—**	**—**	**10.1%**	**—**	**21.3%**

Texas Pacific Land Trust

Texas Pacific Land Trust was created to sell the Texas & Pacific Railway's land after its 1888 bankruptcy and yup they're still workin' on it. The trust began with the railroad's 3.5 million acres; today it is one of the largest private landowners in Texas with around 960000 acres in 20 counties. Texas Pacific Land Trust's sales come from oil and gas royalties (70% of sales) grazing leases easements and land sales. It has a perpetual oil and gas royalty interest under some 470000 acres in West Texas. About 8% of the trust's oil and gas royalties are from leases operated by Chevron U.S.A. Texas Pacific Land Trust uses the revenues from sales and royalties to buy and retire its own shares.The trust sold about 2200 acres of land in 2008 compared to some 1500 acres in 2007. While Texas Pacific Land Trust sold more acreage in 2008 the price per acre was less than a third of the price in 2007.Grazing leases are in effect on 99% of the trust's land.

EXECUTIVES

Co-General Agent CEO and Secretary, Tyler Glover, age 31

Co-General Agent and CFO, Robert J. Packer, age 47, $127,083 total compensation

Chairman, Maurice Meyer, age 81

Auditors: Lane Gorman Trubitt, PLLC

LOCATIONS

HQ: Texas Pacific Land Trust
1700 Pacific Avenue, Suite 2770, Dallas, TX 75201
Phone: 214 969-5530   Fax: 214 871-7139
Web: www.TPLTrust.com

PRODUCTS/OPERATIONS

2015 sales

		% of total
Easements and sundry income		40
Oil and gas royalties		31
Land sales	22.6	28
Grazing lease rentals	0.5	1
Interest income from notes receivable	0.0	-
Total	**79.4**	**100**

COMPETITORS

American Realty	Koch Industries Inc.
Investors	Permian Basin

HISTORICAL FINANCIALS

Company Type: Public

Income Statement
FYE: December 31

	REVENUE ($ mil.)	NET INCOME ($ mil.)	NET PROFIT MARGIN	EMPLOYEES
12/15	79.4	50.0	63.0%	8.0
12/14	55.2	34.7	63.0%	8.0
12/13	44.1	27.2	61.7%	8.0
12/12	32.5	19.6	60.3%	9.0
12/11	34.3	20.5	60.0%	9.0
Annual Growth	**23.4%**	**24.8%**	**—**	**(2.9%)**

2015 Year-End Financials

Debt ratio: —
Return on equity: 138.2%
Cash ($ mil.): 45.0
Current ratio: 11.51
Long-term debt ($ mil.): —
No. of shares (mil.): 8.1
Dividends
Yield: 0.2%
Payout: 4.8%
Market value ($ mil.): 1,063.0

	STOCK PRICE ($) FY Close	P/E High/Low		PER SHARE ($) Earnings	Dividends	Book Value
12/15	130.92	27	18	6.10	0.29	5.63
12/14	118.00	56	23	4.14	0.27	3.21
12/13	99.99	32	16	3.16	0.00	2.12
12/12	53.43	28	18	2.20	0.48	1.77
12/11	40.69	22	16	2.21	0.21	2.24
Annual Growth	**33.9%**	**—**	**—**	**28.9%**	**8.4%**	**25.9%**

Texas Roadhouse Inc

If people are getting rowdy at this roadhouse it must be because of the steaks ribs or the famous sweet yeast rolls. Texas Roadhouse operates a leading full-service restaurant chain with more than 450 company-owned and franchised locations in 49 states and four countries outside of the US. The Southwest-themed eateries serve a variety of hand-cut steaks ribs chicken pork chops and seafood entrees along with sandwiches chili starters and a variety of side dishes. The company also operates a small number of restaurants under the name Aspen Creek that specialize in hamburgers pasta entrees and pizza.

Geographic Reach

Although the chain is essentially nationwide now the bulk of Texas Roadhouse restaurants are located in the Midwest and Southeast. More than 50 of the company's restaurants are located in Texas and many units are located near interstate highways.

Operations

About 370 Texas Roadhouse locations are company-owned while the rest are franchised. The company gets nearly all of its revenue (about 99% in fiscal 2014 and 2013) from company-owned and operated units.

Sales and Marketing

Targeting the casual dining sector the Texas Roadhouse concept focuses on offering mid-priced menu items and a family-friendly dining atmosphere. The chain is primarily interested in serving the dinner segment offering its lunch menu only during the weekends. Its over-the-top Texas décor including such down home touches as jukeboxes and complimentary in-the-shell peanuts helps the chain distinguish itself in a crowded field of competitors that includes Logan's Roadhouse (owned by LRI Holdings) and Lone Star Steak-house. Texas Roadhouse also faces stiff competition from industry heavyweights Chili's (Brinker International) and Outback Steakhouse (OSI Restaurant Partners).

Country singer Willie Nelson who is a partner in two restaurants located in Austin Texas serves as a celebrity spokesperson for Texas Roadhouse. The chain sponsors the popular artist's concert tours and each restaurant features "Willie's Corner" decorated with memorabilia.

Financial Performance

The company's revenue was $1.58 billion in fiscal 2014. That was an increase of 11% (or $159 million) compared to the previous fiscal period. Texas Roadhouse's net income was $87 million in fiscal 2014. That was an increase of 8% compared to the company's fiscal 2013 net income. Cash flow from operations remained strong in fiscal 2014 and the company ended the year with $191.8 million in cash on hand up $17.8 million compared to fiscal 2013 levels.

Strategy

The chain relies on specially-priced value menu items and targets its marketing message toward cost-conscious families looking for affordable dining options. The company has continued its strategy of expanding its restaurant base and it plans to open 25 to 30 restaurants during 2015. Existing franchise partners plan to open as many as six Texas Roadhouse restaurants (primarily international locations) during 2015. Company Background

Founder and chairman Kent Taylor opened the first Texas Roadhouse in 1993. A veteran of the restaurant business he previously served with such chains as Bennigan's (formerly owned by Metromedia Company) Hooters and KFC.

EXECUTIVES

President and CFO, Scott M. Colosi, age 51, $400,000 total compensation
Chairman and CEO, W. Kent Taylor, age 60, $525,000 total compensation
General Counsel and Corporate Secretary, Celia P. Catlett, $200,000 total compensation
Vice President Manager Director, Tonya (T.) Robinson
Regional Vice President, Jeff (Jeffy) Petty
Executive Assistant to Doug Thompson Vice President of Operations, Sarah (Sar) Givan
Vice President Training And People Development, James Scholz
Vice President of Operations, Doug (Dougie) Thompson
Board Member, Dean Skinner
Auditors: KPMG LLP

LOCATIONS

HQ: Texas Roadhouse Inc
6040 Dutchmans Lane, Suite 200, Louisville, KY 40205
Phone: 502 426-9984
Web: www.texasroadhouse.com

COMPETITORS

Applebee's	LRI Holdings
International	Landry's
Brinker	Lone Star Steakhouse
Buffets Inc	O'Charley's
Carlson Restaurants	OSI Restaurant
Cracker Barrel	Partners
Darden	P.F. Chang's
Golden Corral	Ruby Tuesday
Hooters	
Ignite Restaurant	
Group	

HISTORICAL FINANCIALS

Company Type: Public

Income Statement

FYE: December 29

	REVENUE ($ mil.)	NET INCOME ($ mil.)	NET PROFIT MARGIN	EMPLOYEES
12/15	1,807.3	96.8	5.4%	47,900.0
12/14	1,582.1	87.0	5.5%	43,300.0
12/13	1,422.5	80.4	5.7%	45,700.0
12/12	1,263.3	71.1	5.6%	40,000.0
12/11	1,109.2	63.9	5.8%	33,000.0
Annual Growth	13.0%	10.9%	—	9.8%

2015 Year-End Financials

Debt ratio: 2.4%	No. of shares (mil.): 70.0
Return on equity: 15.2%	Dividends
Cash ($ mil.): 59.3	Yield: 1.8%
Current ratio: 0.52	Payout: 51.9%
Long-term debt ($ mil.): 25.5	Market value ($ mil.): 2,527.0

	STOCK PRICE ($) FY Close	P/E High/Low		PER SHARE ($) Earnings	Dividends	Book Value
12/15	36.06	30	24	1.37	0.68	9.55
12/14	33.78	27	19	1.23	0.60	8.73
12/13	27.80	25	15	1.13	0.48	8.35
12/12	16.82	18	14	1.00	0.46	7.61
12/11	15.13	21	14	0.88	0.32	7.11
Annual Growth	24.3%	—	—	11.7%	20.7%	7.7%

The Bancorp Inc

The Bancorp is —what else? —the holding company for The Bancorp Bank which provides financial services in the virtual world. Targeting non-bank financial service companies across the US and Europe from start-ups to small and midsized businesses underserved by larger banks in the market The Bancorp Bank provides private-label online banking to 200 affinity groups; offers specialty lending; issues prepaid debit cards; and processes ACH and merchant credit card transactions. Its specialty lending products include securities backed lines of credit (SBLOC) auto fleet and equipment leasing SBA loans and commercial mortgage loans for sale in capital markets.

OperationsThe Bancorp and The Bancorp Bank operate three business segments: Payments which made up 45% of the bank's total revenue in 2015 and provides prepaid cards card payments and ACH processing services; Specialty Finance (31% of revenue) which consists of commercial mortgage loan sales small business administration (SBA) loans leasing and security backed lines of credit and related deposit business; and Corporate (24% of revenue) which includes the company's investment portfolio. Unlike other banks which rely on interest income The Bancorp makes more than 60% of its revenue from fee-based income. About 38% of its total revenue came from loan interest (including fees) during 2015 while another 14% came from interest income on investment securities. The rest of its revenue came from prepaid card fees (22% of revenue) service fees on deposit accounts (3%) card payment and ACH processing fees (3%) leasing income (1%) debit card income (1%) affinity fees (2%) and non-recurring gains from the sale of its loans investment securities and health savings portfolio (27%).Geographic Reach-

Wilmington Delaware-based The Bancorp serves customers in the US and Europe from 16 offices in the two regions and Southeast Asia. Sales and MarketingThe company targets non-bank financial services companies including start-ups small and medium businesses underserved by large banks and Fortune 500 companies. It spent $387000 on advertising during 2015 down from $621000 and $706000 in 2014 and 2013 respectively.Financial PerformanceThe Bancorp's annual revenues and profits have nearly doubled since 2011 mostly as its Payments business income has nearly quadrupled over the period. Its loan assets have also nearly tripled spurring additional interest income growth.The company's revenue jumped 39% to $216.5 million during 2015 thanks largely to a $33.5 million gain on the sale of the majority of its health savings business and a $14.4 million gain on the sale of its tax-exempt municipal bonds portfolio. The Bancorp's loan interest revenue was also up 37% as its specialty lending balances continued to grow with new SBLOC SBA leasing and loans-for-sale business.Despite strong revenue growth in 2015 The Bancorp's net income plunged more than 75% to $13.43 million mostly as its discontinued operations (its discontinued Philadelphia commercial loan business) generated $27 million less in revenue than the year before and because in 2014 it had collected a $14.5 million income tax benefit from a reversal of valuation allowances. The company's operations used $234.8 million or more than four times more cash than in 2014 mainly on a steep decline cash-based earnings especially after accounting for net proceeds from sales of its loans-originated-for-resale.StrategyThe Bancorp and The Bancorp Bank has been winding down its non-core operations in recent years to concentrate more in its national specialty lending business. In October 2015 the bank sold its $400 million-HSA portfolio to HealthEquity for $34..4 million after selling its regional Commercial Lending business in 2014. As a result the bank noted that its discontinued operations were reduced by 50% at the end of 2015 and expected its discontinued loan portfolio to shrink from there through loan repayments and opportunistic loan sales.On the growth side The Bancorp continues to buy specialty financing assets from other financial companies to bolster its loan assets and extend its geographic reach. In December 2015 it expanded its commercial fleet leasing presence in the West Coast with a new California office after buying the commercial leasing assets of Ellis Brooks Leasing Inc.

EXECUTIVES

EVP Strategy CFO and Secretary, Paul Frenkiel, age 64, $312,200 total compensation
President and CEO, Damian Kozlowski, age 49
EVP and Chief Credit Officer, Donald F. (Don) McGraw, age 59, $317,500 total compensation
EVP Commercial Fleet Leasing and Chief Lending Officer, Scott R. Megargee, age 64, $202,541 total compensation
EVP and CIO, Peter (Pete) Chiccino
SVP; Managing Director Payment Solutions, Jeremy L. Kuiper, $458,060 total compensation
SVP and General Counsel, Thomas G. Pareigat, $347,500 total compensation
EVP and COO, Gail S. Ball
EVP and Chief Risk Officer, Steven Turowski
EVP Commercial Mortgage Securitization, Ron Wechsler
Senior Vice President and Director of Communications, Maria (Mary) Antonelli

Vice President Information Security Officer, Joe
  Curcio
**Senior Vice President and Chief Human
  Resources Officer,** Bernard (Bern) McCabe
**Vice President Client Relationship Manager
  (CRM),** Kate (Katie) Godwin
Senior Vice President General Manager, Tom
  Pareigat
Vice President Information Security Officer, Darin
  Wipf
Vice President of Fleet Management and Leasing,
  Bill (Billy) Stueber
**SBA Business Relationship Officer and Vice
  President,** John (Jack) Sullivan
**First Vice President Business Relationship
  Officer,** Tim (Timmy) Collins
**Chairman The Bancorp Inc. and The Bancorp
  Bank,** Daniel G. Cohen, age 46
Auditors: Grant Thornton LLP

LOCATIONS

HQ: The Bancorp Inc
  409 Silverside Road, Wilmington, DE 19809
Phone: 302 385-5000
Web: www.thebancorp.com

PRODUCTS/OPERATIONS

2015 sales

	$ mil.	% of total
Payments	98.0	45
Specialty finance	67.6	31
Corporate	51.0	24
Total	**216.6**	**100**

2015 Sales

	$ mil.	% of total
Interest income		
Loans including fees	49.9	23
Interest on investment securities:	30.7	14
Federal funds sold/securities purchased under agreements to resell	0.6	
Interest earning deposits	2.3	1
Non-interest income		
Prepaid card fees	47.5	22
Gain on sale of health savings portfolio	33.6	15
Gain on sale of investment securities	14.4	7
Gain on sale of loans	10.1	5
Service fees on deposit accounts	7.5	3
Card payment and ACH processing fees	5.7	3
Affinity fees	3.4	2
Other	5.3	2
Change in value of investment in unconsolidated entity	1.7	1
Leasing income	2.3	1
Debit card income	1.6	1
Total	**216.6**	**100**

COMPETITORS

Citizens Financial   Royal Bancshares
  Group   Sovereign Bank
E*TRADE Bank   Sun Bancorp (NJ)
M&T Bank   TD Bank USA
PNC Financial   WSFS Financial
Republic First Bank

HISTORICAL FINANCIALS

Company Type: Public

Income Statement

FYE: December 31

	ASSETS ($ mil.)	NET INCOME ($ mil.)	INCOME AS % OF ASSETS	EMPLOYEES
12/15	4,765.8	13.4	0.3%	762.0
12/14	4,986.3	57.1	1.1%	684.0
12/13	4,706.0	25.1	0.5%	624.0
12/12	3,699.6	16.6	0.4%	532.0
12/11	3,010.6	8.9	0.3%	428.0
Annual Growth	**12.2%**	**10.8%**	**—**	**15.5%**

2015 Year-End Financials

Return on assets: 0.2%   Dividends
Return on equity: 4.2%   Yield: —
Long-term debt ($ mil.): —   Payout: —
No. of shares (mil.): 37.7   Market value ($ mil.): 241.0
Sales ($ mil): 216.6

	STOCK PRICE ($) FY Close	P/E High/Low	PER SHARE ($) Earnings	Dividends	Book Value
12/15	6.37	31 18	0.35	0.00	8.47
12/14	10.89	13 5	1.49	0.00	8.46
12/13	17.91	28 16	0.66	0.00	9.56
12/12	10.97	24 15	0.50	0.00	9.06
12/11	7.23	38 23	0.28	0.00	8.20
Annual Growth	**(3.1%)**	**— —**	**5.7%**	**—**	**0.8%**

The New Home Company Inc

The New Home Company (TNHC) is busy building new homes throughout the Golden State. Targeting first-time move-up move-down and luxury home buyers TNHC builds homes under The New Home Company brand name mostly in select growth markets in California (including San Francisco and Sacramento) and in Phoenix Arizona. Its home prices range from $300000 to $5 million and range in size from 800 sq. ft. to 5400 sq. ft. It also builds homes under its brand for third-party property owners. Since its founding in 2009 TNHC has delivered more 1400 homes since its inception via company projects unconsolidated joint ventures and fee building projects. The builder went public in early 2014.

Operations

TNHC operates two business segments: Homebuilding which generated 65% of its total revenue during 2015; and Fee Building (35% of revenue) which builds The New Home Company branded homes for a fee on behalf of independent third-party property owners. The builder typically takes between 24 to 48 months to build each home and 24 to 48 months to develop land after it acquires each accompanying land plot.The company's average home sold for $1.9 million during 2015 while the average sales price of its joint venture project homes was $1.3 million.

Geographic Reach

TNHC mostly targets projects in select growth markets in California (including coastal Southern California San Francisco Bay area and Sacramento metro) and in greater Phoenix Arizona. More broadly it builds in Northern California (El Dorado Placer Yolo Marin San Mateo Santa Clara and Sacramento counties) Southern California (Orange Ventura San Diego and Los Angeles counties) and in the greater Phoenix Arizona area.Sales and MarketingThe builder markets its homes through its website social media brochures direct mail and community-specific publications. Most of its home sales go through its own sales representatives. TNHC has been ramping up its selling and marketing spend every year since 2012 to support growth. The homebuilder spent $8.94 million in 2015 up from $3.17 million and $1.77 million in 2014 and 2013 respectively.Financial PerformanceTNHC's annual revenues have skyrocketed

ten-fold since 2011 thanks to exceptional demand and rising housing prices in its target markets in California. While the builder suffered losses to support its growth in 2012 and 2011 its profits have been growing rapidly since then as the builder has kept a lid on rising operating costs.The builder's sales nearly tripled to $430.1 million during 2015 mainly as delivery volumes increased 179% to 148 homes for the year and as the average home sold for 79% more or $1.9 million as the builder sold a larger portion of higher-priced homes in coastal Southern California where prices exceeded $2.7 million per delivery. While having a much smaller impact on the top-line growth TNHC's fee building income rose 60% on higher joint venture management fees and as construction activity in fee building communities picked up.Exceptional revenue growth and stable operating costs in 2015 caused TNHC's net income to more than quadruple to $21.7 million for the year. The homebuilder used $32.3 million in cash during 2015 as it continued to build its real estate inventory though it used about one-third the amount of cash used in 2014 as it eased up on inventory building.StrategyThe New Home Company remained in 2016 committed to acquiring land lots and building in its core metro areas of coastal Southern California the San Francisco Bay area and the greater Sacramento and Phoenix markets. The homebuilder also actively explored the possibility in expanding into the Southwestern and Pacific Northwest markets after its success in Phoenix in recent years.Company BackgroundIn January 2014 NHC filed a $113-million IPO with plans to use the proceeds to continue to acquire land develop lots and fund new and existing home-construction initiatives as well as other related purposes.

EXECUTIVES

Chairman and CEO, H. Lawrence (Larry) Webb, age
  68, $519,231 total compensation
CFO, John M. Stephens, age 47
Chief Investment Officer, Thomas (Tom) Redwitz,
  age 61, $467,308 total compensation
President Northern California, Kevin Carson, age
  56
COO, Leonard Miller
President Southern California, Andrew J. Jarvis, age
  51
SVP and CIO, Paolo Benzan
Vice President, Mark (Marky) Kawanami
Vice President, Kim Forbes
Vice President Of Sales, Annie (Ann) Charles
Vice President of Operations, Travis (Trav) Nuzman
Auditors: Ernst & Young LLP

LOCATIONS

HQ: The New Home Company Inc
  85 Enterprise, Suite 450, Aliso Viejo, CA 92656
Phone: 949 382-7800
Web: www.thenewhomecompany.com

PRODUCTS/OPERATIONS

2015 Revenue

	$ mil.	% of total
Home building	280.2	65
Fee building	149.9	35
Total	**430.1**	**100**

COMPETITORS

CalAtlantic   KB Home
D.R. Horton   Lennar
David Weekley Homes   PulteGroup

Hovnanian Enterprises Toll Brothers
John Wieland Homes William Lyon Homes

HISTORICAL FINANCIALS
Company Type: Public

Income Statement
FYE: December 31

	REVENUE ($ mil.)	NET INCOME ($ mil.)	NET PROFIT MARGIN	EMPLOYEES
12/15	430.1	21.6	5.0%	272.0
12/14	149.6	4.7	3.2%	234.0
12/13	83.2	6.7	8.1%	153.0
12/12	55.4	(1.3)	—	128.0
12/11	42.1	(2.3)	—	0.0
Annual Growth 78.7%		—	—	—

2015 Year-End Financials

Debt ratio: 23.7%
Return on equity: 11.7%
Cash ($ mil.): 45.8
Current ratio: 6.67
Long-term debt ($ mil.): 83.3

No. of shares (mil.): 20.5
Dividends
Yield: —
Payout: —
Market value ($ mil.): 266.0

	STOCK PRICE ($) FY Close	P/E High/Low		PER SHARE ($) Earnings	Dividends	Book Value
12/15	12.96	14	9	1.28	0.00	10.75
12/14	14.48	53	39	0.30	0.00	9.00
Annual Growth	(10.5%)	—		—326.7%	—	19.4%

Threshold Pharmaceuticals Inc

By targeting differences in the oxygen levels of normal and diseased cells Threshold Pharmaceuticals hopes to develop drugs that are effective at fighting cancer while preserving healthy tissue. The biotechnology company's most advanced candidate is evofosfamide a hypoxia-activated prodrug meaning it begins releasing its cell-killing agents only within the low-oxygen environment common to tumor tissues. Evofosfamide is in late-stage trials as a treatment for solid tumors and bone marrow cancer; it is co-developing the drug with Merck. The company is also investigating an imaging agent that would identify patients who could most benefit from prodrugs.

Operations

In 2012 Threshold signed an agreement to co-develop TH-302 (evofosfamide) with Merck wherein Threshold has exclusive US rights to the drug for the treatment of soft tissue sarcoma but all other development will be shared. Merck is paying 70% of worldwide development costs.

To augment its product line Threshold in 2013 purchased a development-stage PET (positron emission topography) tracer from Siemens. The diagnostic tool can help identify patients likely to respond well to hypoxia-targeted treatment.

Financial Performance

As a development stage company Threshold hasn't really seen much in the way of revenue. It did receive $6 million in 2012 as part of its amortized payment from Merck. The company has accumulated losses of $323 million and expects to continue losing money for years.

Strategy

Going forward Threshold intends to continue developing evofosfamide for solid tumors while seeking other targets. It also plans to continue development and testing of [18F]-HX4 the diagnostic candidate it purchased from Siemens.

In 2016 the company announced plans to cut about 25% of its workforce in order to cut operating expenses and preserve capital.

EXECUTIVES

Vice President Clinical Science, Mark D (Marky) Matteucci
Vice President Corporate Development, Eric D Malek
Vice President Of RE, Helen Shu
Senior Vice President Fin Contrl, Joel A Fernandes
Vice President Operations Production Manufacturing, Charles P (Charlie) Hart
Vice President Finance, Cdavis Davis
Vice President Clinical Oprs, Kristen (Kristy) Quigley
Auditors: Ernst & Young LLP

LOCATIONS

HQ: Threshold Pharmaceuticals Inc
170 Harbor Way, Suite 300, South San Francisco, CA 94080
Phone: 650 474-8200
Web: www.thresholdpharm.com

COMPETITORS

ARIAD Pharmaceuticals	Merck
Amgen	Millennium: The Takeda
AstraZeneca	Oncology Company
Bayer AG	Novartis
Bristol-Myers Squibb	OSI Pharmaceuticals
Celgene	Pfizer
Clovis Oncology	Rexahn Pharmaceuticals
Eli Lilly	Roche Holding
Genentech	Sanofi
GlaxoSmithKline	Sunesis
ImClone	Pharmaceuticals
Johnson & Johnson	Telik Inc.

HISTORICAL FINANCIALS
Company Type: Public

Income Statement
FYE: December 31

	REVENUE ($ mil.)	NET INCOME ($ mil.)	NET PROFIT MARGIN	EMPLOYEES
12/15	76.9	43.8	57.0%	26.0
12/14	14.7	(21.5)	—	61.0
12/13	12.5	(28.4)	—	53.0
12/12	5.8	(71.1)	—	48.0
12/11	0.0	(25.6)	—	31.0
Annual Growth 493.5%		—	—	(4.3%)

2015 Year-End Financials

Debt ratio: —
Return on equity: 519.5%
Cash ($ mil.): 9.5
Current ratio: 4.91
Long-term debt ($ mil.): —

No. of shares (mil.): 71.4
Dividends
Yield: —
Payout: —
Market value ($ mil.): 34.0

	STOCK PRICE ($) FY Close	P/E High/Low		PER SHARE ($) Earnings	Dividends	Book Value
12/15	0.48	8	1	0.54	0.00	0.57
12/14	3.18	—	—	(0.49)	0.00	(0.38)
12/13	4.67	—	—	(0.49)	0.00	(0.40)
12/12	4.21	—	—	(1.31)	0.00	(0.25)
12/11	1.22	—	—	(0.56)	0.00	0.09
Annual Growth	(20.8%)	—		—	—	58.2%

Tilly's Inc

EXECUTIVES

VP Marketing, Cheryl A. Rudich, age 54
President CEO and Director, Daniel (Dan) Griesemer, age 55
VP Real Estate, John Burgess, age 62
Chairman and Chief Strategy Officer, Hezy Shaked, age 60
SVP and CFO, William (Bill) Langsdorf, age 58
VP COO and Chief Information Officer, Craig DeMerit, age 45
VP and General Merchandising Manager, Debbie Anker-Boetes, age 56
VP General Counsel and Secretary, Patrick Grosso, age 42
VP Stores, Shelly Johnson, age 45
VP Vendor Relations, Tilly Levine, age 59
VP Merchandise Planning and Allocation, Carolyn S. McNamara, age 50
VP Finance and Controller, Rochelle Myers, age 48
Founder, Chet Thomas
Director, Seth R. Johnson, age 61
Director, Bernard Zeichner, age 71
President CEO and Director, Daniel (Dan) Griesemer, age 55
Director, Jerold H. Rubinstein, age 76
Director, Janet E. Kerr, age 60
Auditors: BDO USA, LLP

LOCATIONS

HQ: Tilly's Inc
10 Whatney, Irvine, CA 92618
Phone: 949 609-5599
Web: www.tillys.com

COMPETITORS

Abercrombie & Fitch	Hot Topic
Aeropostale	Pacific Sunwear
American Eagle Outfitters	The Buckle
Forever 21	Urban Outfitters
	Wet Seal
	Zumiez

HISTORICAL FINANCIALS
Company Type: Public

Income Statement
FYE: January 30

	REVENUE ($ mil.)	NET INCOME ($ mil.)	NET PROFIT MARGIN	EMPLOYEES
01/16	550.9	7.5	1.4%	4,900.0
01/15*	518.2	14.0	2.7%	4,500.0
02/14	495.8	18.1	3.7%	4,100.0
02/13	467.2	23.8	5.1%	4,000.0
01/12	400.6	34.3	8.6%	3,600.0
Annual Growth	8.3%	(31.5%)	—	8.0%

*Fiscal year change

2016 Year-End Financials

Debt ratio: 0.6%
Return on equity: 4.5%
Cash ($ mil.): 51.0
Current ratio: 3.06
Long-term debt ($ mil.): 0.8

No. of shares (mil.): 28.4
Dividends
Yield: —
Payout: —
Market value ($ mil.): 185.0

	STOCK PRICE ($)	P/E		PER SHARE ($)		
	FY Close	High/Low		Earnings	Dividends	Book Value
01/16	6.49	62	22	0.27	0.00	6.08
01/15*	13.74	28	14	0.50	0.00	5.65
02/14	11.61	27	16	0.65	0.00	5.03
02/13	14.55	21	13	0.92	0.00	4.24
Annual Growth	(23.6%)	—	—(33.5%)		—	12.8%

*Fiscal year change

Tiptree Inc

Tiptree Financial is interested in health and wealth. The holding company operates through four divisions: insurance and insurance services specialty finance (including corporate consumer and tax-exempt credit) asset management and real estate. Its insurance subsidiaries include the Philadelphia Financial Group of companies. Specialty finance services are conducted through Muni Funding Company of America and Siena Capital Finance while a handful of other subsidiaries provide asset management. Real estate activities include Care Investment Trust a health care REIT that owns a portfolio of senior housing properties. Prior to mid-2013 the company's only operations consisted of Care Investment Trust's real estate portfolio.

EXECUTIVES

CEO and Director, Jonathan Ilany, age 62, $350,000 total compensation

CFO, Sandra E. Bell, age 59, $200,000 total compensation

CFO and Secretary, Julia Wyatt, age 58, $350,000 total compensation

VP General Counsel and Secretary Tiptree Financial Inc. and Tiptree Operating Company LLC, Neil C. Rifkind, $375,000 total compensation

Vice President and Senior Counsel, Danielle (Dani) Depalma

Vice President, Luke (Lucas) Scheuer

Vice President and Assistant General Counsel, Siew Kwok

Chairman, Michael G. Barnes, age 50

Auditors: KPMG LLP

LOCATIONS

HQ: Tiptree Inc
780 Third Avenue, 21st Floor, New York, NY 10017
Phone: 212 446-1400
Web: www.tiptreefinancial.com

PRODUCTS/OPERATIONS

2012 Sales

	% of total
Rental income	86
Reimbursable income	9
Income from loans & investments	5
Total	**100**

Selected Subsidiaries

Asset Management:
  Muni Capital Management LLC
  TAMCO
  Telos
  Tiptree Capital Management LLC
TREIT
Insurance:
  Philadelphia Financial Administration Services Company
  Philadelphia Financial Agency Inc.
  Philadelphia Financial Distribution Company
  Philadelphia Financial Life Assurance Company
  Philadelphia Financial Life Assurance Company of New York
Real Estate:
  Care Investment Trust LLC
Specialty Finance:
  Muni Funding Company of America
  Siena Capital Finance

COMPETITORS

AXA Financial	Omega Healthcare
Extendicare	Investors
HCP	Prudential
Healthcare Realty	Senior Housing
Trust	Properties
MetLife	Ventas
National Health	Welltower
Investors	

HISTORICAL FINANCIALS

Company Type: Public

Income Statement

FYE: December 31

	REVENUE ($ mil.)	NET INCOME ($ mil.)	NET PROFIT MARGIN	EMPLOYEES
12/15	440.1	8.8	2.0%	929.0
12/14	80.3	4.5	5.7%	761.0
12/13	100.9	16.4	16.3%	250.0
12/12	15.9	(0.5)	—	4.0
12/11	14.4	16.5	114.2%	6.0
Annual Growth	134.8%	(14.6%)	—	252.7%

2015 Year-End Financials

Debt ratio: 26.9%	No. of shares (mil.): 42.9
Return on equity: 2.9%	Dividends
Cash ($ mil.): 69.4	Yield: 1.6%
Current ratio: —	Payout: 333.3%
Long-term debt ($ mil.): 673.2	Market value ($ mil.): 264.0

	STOCK PRICE ($)	P/E		PER SHARE ($)		
	FY Close	High/Low		Earnings	Dividends	Book Value
12/15	6.14	48	31	0.17	0.10	7.28
12/14	8.10	—	—	(0.10)	0.18	6.84
12/13	7.34	9	7	0.86	0.18	4.92
12/12	7.50	—	—	(0.05)	0.54	8.61
12/11	6.50	4	3	1.60	0.41	9.20
Annual Growth	(1.4%)	—	—(42.9%)		(29.5%)	(5.7%)

Tompkins Financial Corp

Tompkins Financial is the holding company for Tompkins Trust Company The Bank of Castile and Mahopac Bank which offer traditional banking services through some 45 offices in upstate New York. It also owns the 20-branch Pennsylvania-based VIST Bank. Funds from deposit products such as checking savings and money market accounts are mainly used to originate real estate loans and mortgages as well as commercial and consumer loans. Tompkins also offers trust and estate financial and tax planning and investment management services through Tompkins Financial Advisors. Tompkins Insurance Agencies sells property/casualty coverage in central and western New York and Pennsylvania.

Operations

Tompkins Financial operates in three segments: banking insurance and wealth management. Banking represents most of its revenue —more than 80%. About 70% of the banks' loan portfolios is made up of commercial and commercial real estate loans.Tompkins' Insurance and Wealth Management divisions operate through subsidiaries and make up roughly 10% and 5% of sales respectively. Its subsidiary Tompkins Insurance Agencies Inc. offers property and casualty insurance services and employee benefit consulting services. The firm's trust company Tompkins Financial Advisors offers trust financial planning and wealth management services.Geographic ReachBetween its four bank subsidiaries the Tompkins operates 66 branches in the US with more than two thirds of the branches in New York and around 20 branches in Pennsylvania.Sales and MarketingThe company's banks target individual and small business customers for its financial services. Tompkins spent $4.94 million on its marketing expenses in 2014 or slightly less than the $4.96 million spent in 2013 but 22% more than what it spent in 2012.

Financial Performance

Tompkin's revenue rose for a second straight year growing by less than 1% to $255.26 million in 2014 most thanks to growth in the company's non-interest fee income from an increase in deposit account service charges card services income and growth in personal health and benefit insurance sales.The company's net income ended higher for a second year as well thanks to higher revenue lower interest expense on deposits and lower provisions for loan losses as its loan portfolio's credit improved. Operations provided $77.36 million or 8% less cash than in 2013 mostly because in 2013 the company was able to use more funds from its prepaid accounts to pay for FDIC insurance.

Strategy

The company's strategy for growth includes making inroads into new markets and new business areas through acquisitions. It entered the southeastern Pennsylvania market with its 2012 acquisition of VIST Financial parent of VIST Bank (which continues to operate under a separate charter under existing management) VIST Insurance and VIST Capital Management. The deal added about 20 branches to Tompkins' network along with $889 million in new loan business and $1.2 billion in new deposits.Mergers and AcquisitionsIn August 2012 Tompkins Financial purchased VIST Financial Corp in an all stock transaction valued at $86 million. The deal added all 20 VIST Bank branches (and VIST Bank's assets) in Pennsylvania the VIST Capital Management business and the VIST Insurance business which doubled Tompkin's annual insurance revenue; all of which were folded into Tompkins' banking operations Tompkins Financial Advisors and Tompkins Insurance Agencies operations respectively.

EXECUTIVES

EVP President and CEO VIST Bank, Robert D. (Bob) Davis, age 68

Director; Vice Chairman Tompkins Insurance Agencies, James R. Hardie, age 72

Executive Vice President Chief Operations Officer
Chief Financial Officer & Treasurer, Francis M.
Fetsko, age 51, $281,877 total compensation
EVP and CFO Mahopac National Bank, Stephen S.
Romaine, age 52, $474,898 total compensation
Executive Vice President, David S. Boyce, age 49,
$185,000 total compensation
Executive Vice-President, Gregory J. Hartz, age 55,
$237,107 total compensation
Executive Vice-President, Gerald J. Klein, age 57,
$238,369 total compensation
Executive Vice President; President & COO of
VIST Bank, Scott L. Gruber, age 60
EVP Corporate Marketing, Susan M. Valenti
SVP - Chief Technology Officer, Bradley G. James
Vice President Information Technology Services,
Bill (Billy) Steinmetz
Senior Vice President Marketing, Paula Barron
Executive Vice President Director of Human
Resources, Rosemary Hyland
Vice President Finance, Kevin Harty
Assistant Vice President, Shelly (Shell) Fetterly-Bush
Vice President and To, John (Jack) Poli
Vice President Information Systems, Terry Barber
Assistant Vice President Officer Branch Manager,
Deborah (Deb) Hoover
Vice President, Christine (Chrissy) Allen
Vice President Telecommunications, Chuck
(Chucky) Brown
Assistant Vice President Telecommunicati, Charles
(Charlie) Brown
Vice President of Information Systems, Glenn
Cobb
Vice President Architecture, Tracy (Trace)
Vanderzee
Vice President and Human Resources Manager,
Scott (Scotty) Pronti
Senior Vice President Human Resources, Bonita
Lindberg
Assistant Vice President Wealth Advisor, Bill (Billy)
Murphy
Vice President Commercial Loan Operations,
Pamela (Pam) Castile
Chairman Tompkins Financial Corporation and
Tompkins Trust Company, James J. Byrnes, age 73
Vice Chairman, James W. (Jim) Fulmer, age 64
Auditors: KPMG LLP

LOCATIONS

HQ: Tompkins Financial Corp
The Commons, P.O. Box 460, Ithaca, NY 14851
Phone: 888 503-5753
Web: www.tompkinsfinancial.com

PRODUCTS/OPERATIONS

2014 Sales

	$ mil.	% of total
Interest		
Loans	151.0	60
Available-for-sale securities	31.3	12
Other	2.2	-
Noninterest		
Insurance commissions & fees	28.5	11
Investment services	15.6	6
Service charges on deposit accounts	9.4	4
Card services income	7.9	3
Other	9.7	4
Adjustments	(0.3)	-
Total	**255.3**	**100**

2014 Sales

	$mil.
% of total	
Banking	83
Insurance	11
Wealth Management	6
Others	-
Total	**100**

COMPETITORS

Bank of America	Community Bank System
Chemung Financial	Elmira Savings Bank
Citigroup	HSBC USA
Citizens Financial Group	JPMorgan Chase
	M&T Bank

HISTORICAL FINANCIALS
Company Type: Public

Income Statement
FYE: December 31

	ASSETS ($ mil.)	NET INCOME ($ mil.)	INCOME AS % OF ASSETS	EMPLOYEES
12/15	5,690.0	58.4	1.0%	1,038.0
12/14	5,269.5	52.0	1.0%	1,037.0
12/13	5,003.0	50.8	1.0%	989.0
12/12	4,837.2	31.2	0.6%	939.0
12/11	3,400.2	35.4	1.0%	743.0
Annual Growth	**13.7%**	**13.3%**	**—**	**8.7%**

2015 Year-End Financials

Return on assets: 1.0%	Dividends
Return on equity: 11.6%	Yield: 3.0%
Long-term debt ($ mil.): —	Payout: 44.8%
No. of shares (mil.): 14.9	Market value ($ mil.): 837.0
Sales ($ mil): 260.6	

	STOCK PRICE ($) FY Close	P/E High/Low		PER SHARE ($) Earnings	Dividends	Book Value
12/15	56.16	16	13	3.87	1.70	34.57
12/14	55.30	16	13	3.48	1.62	32.94
12/13	51.39	15	11	3.46	1.54	31.10
12/12	39.64	17	15	2.43	1.46	30.71
12/11	38.51	13	11	3.20	1.40	26.91
Annual Growth	**9.9%**	**—**	**—**	**4.9%**	**5.0%**	**6.5%**

TopBuild Corp
Auditors: PricewaterhouseCoopers LLP

LOCATIONS

HQ: TopBuild Corp
260 Jimmy Ann Drive, Daytona Beach, FL 32114
Phone: 386 304-2200

HISTORICAL FINANCIALS
Company Type: Public

Income Statement
FYE: December 31

	REVENUE ($ mil.)	NET INCOME ($ mil.)	NET PROFIT MARGIN	EMPLOYEES
12/15	1,616.5	78.9	4.9%	8,000.0
12/14	1,512.0	9.4	0.6%	7,800.0
12/13	1,411.5	(12.7)	—	0.0
12/12	1,207.8	(192.1)	—	0.0
Annual Growth	**10.2%**	**—**	**—**	**—**

2015 Year-End Financials

Debt ratio: 11.7%	No. of shares (mil.): 37.6
Return on equity: 8.4%	Dividends
Cash ($ mil.): 112.8	Yield: —
Current ratio: 1.47	Payout: —
Long-term debt ($ mil.): 178.4	Market value ($ mil.): 1,159.0

	STOCK PRICE ($) FY Close	P/E High/Low		PER SHARE ($) Earnings	Dividends	Book Value
12/15	30.77	17	11	2.09	0.00	24.30
12/14	0.00	—	—	(0.00)	0.00	(0.00)
Annual Growth	**—**			**—**	**—**	**—**

TowneBank
Auditors: Dixon Hughes Goodman LLP

LOCATIONS

HQ: TowneBank
5716 High Street, Portsmouth, VA 23703
Phone: 757 638-7500
Web: www.townebank.com

HISTORICAL FINANCIALS
Company Type: Public

Income Statement
FYE: December 31

	ASSETS ($ mil.)	NET INCOME ($ mil.)	INCOME AS % OF ASSETS	EMPLOYEES
12/15	6,296.5	62.3	1.0%	1,903.0
12/14	4,982.4	42.1	0.8%	1,737.0
12/13	4,673.0	41.7	0.9%	1,741.0
12/12	4,405.9	37.9	0.9%	1,599.0
12/11	4,081.7	33.3	0.8%	1,540.0
Annual Growth	**11.4%**	**17.0%**	**—**	**5.4%**

2015 Year-End Financials

Return on assets: 1.1%	Dividends
Return on equity: 8.7%	Yield: 2.2%
Long-term debt ($ mil.): —	Payout: 38.5%
No. of shares (mil.): 50.9	Market value ($ mil.): 1,063.0
Sales ($ mil): 330.1	

	STOCK PRICE ($) FY Close	P/E High/Low		PER SHARE ($) Earnings	Dividends	Book Value
12/15	20.87	18	12	1.22	0.47	15.91
12/14	15.12	14	11	1.18	0.43	17.32
12/13	15.39	15	12	1.14	0.38	16.59
12/12	15.49	15	12	1.03	0.41	17.57
12/11	12.24	22	14	0.77	0.31	17.13
Annual Growth	**14.3%**	**—**	**—**	**12.3%**	**10.9%**	**(1.8%)**

Townsquare Media Inc
Auditors: RSM US LLP

LOCATIONS

HQ: Townsquare Media Inc
240 Greenwich Avenue, Greenwich, CT 06830
Phone: 203 861-0900
Web: www.townsquaremedia.com

HISTORICAL FINANCIALS
Company Type: Public

Income Statement
FYE: December 31

	REVENUE ($ mil.)	NET INCOME ($ mil.)	NET PROFIT MARGIN	EMPLOYEES
12/15	441.2	9.8	2.2%	2,900.0
12/14	373.8	(17.3)	—	2,726.0
12/13	268.5	10.1	3.8%	2,680.0
12/12	222.7	6.4	2.9%	0.0
Annual Growth	**25.6%**	**15.4%**	**—**	**—**

2015 Year-End Financials

Debt ratio: 55.5%	No. of shares (mil.): 17.8
Return on equity: 2.7%	Dividends
Cash ($ mil.): 33.3	Yield: —
Current ratio: 1.66	Payout: —
Long-term debt ($ mil.): 588.6	Market value ($ mil.): 214.0

	STOCK PRICE ($) FY Close	P/E High/Low	PER SHARE ($) Earnings	Dividends	Book Value
12/15	11.96	25 16	0.37	0.00	20.31
12/14	13.20	— —	(1.41)	0.00	19.78
12/13	0.00	— —	(0.00)	0.00	(0.00)
Annual Growth	—	—	—	—	—

TPG Specialty Lending Inc

Auditors: KPMG LLP

LOCATIONS

HQ: TPG Specialty Lending Inc
301 Commerce Street, Suite 3300, Fort Worth, TX 76102
Phone: 817 871-4000   **Fax:** 817 871-4001
Web: www.tpgspecialtylending.com

HISTORICAL FINANCIALS

Company Type: Public

Income Statement

FYE: December 31

	ASSETS ($ mil.)	NET INCOME ($ mil.)	INCOME AS % OF ASSETS	EMPLOYEES
12/15	1,516.9	95.3	6.3%	0.0
12/14	1,303.7	104.4	8.0%	0.0
12/13	1,039.1	57.5	5.5%	0.0
12/12	833.1	28.0	3.4%	0.0
12/11	0.0	(1.5)	—	0.0
Annual Growth	—	—	—	—

2015 Year-End Financials

Return on assets: 6.7%
Return on equity: 11.5%
Long-term debt ($ mil.): —
No. of shares (mil.): 54.1
Sales ($ mil): 173.6

Dividends
Yield: 9.6%
Payout: 109.0%
Market value ($ mil.): 879.0

	STOCK PRICE ($) FY Close	P/E High/Low	PER SHARE ($) Earnings	Dividends	Book Value
12/15	16.22	16 14	1.18	1.56	15.15
12/14	16.82	14 9	1.68	1.53	15.53
Annual Growth	(3.6%)	—	(29.8%)	2.0%	(2.4%)

TransUnion

Auditors: Ernst & Young LLP

LOCATIONS

HQ: TransUnion
555 West Adams, Chicago, IL 60661
Phone: 312 985-2000
Web: www.transunion.com

HISTORICAL FINANCIALS

Company Type: Public

Income Statement

FYE: December 31

	REVENUE ($ mil.)	NET INCOME ($ mil.)	NET PROFIT MARGIN	EMPLOYEES
12/15	1,506.8	5.9	0.4%	4,200.0
12/14	1,304.7	(12.5)	—	4,200.0
12/13	1,183.2	(35.1)	—	0.0
12/12*	767.0	(8.8)	—	0.0
04/12	373.0	(54.9)	—	0.0
Annual Growth	41.8%	—	—	—

*Fiscal year change

2015 Year-End Financials

Debt ratio: 49.6%
Return on equity: 0.6%
Cash ($ mil.): 133.2
Current ratio: 1.44
Long-term debt ($ mil.): 2,164.6

Dividends
Yield: —
Payout: —
Market value ($ mil.): 5,026.0

No. of shares (mil.): 182.3

	STOCK PRICE ($) FY Close	P/E High/Low	PER SHARE ($) Earnings	Dividends	Book Value
12/15	27.57	700580	0.04	0.00	6.75
Annual Growth	—	—	—	—	—

Trex Co Inc

Trex Company is all decked out with plenty of places to go. It's the world's largest maker of wood-alternative decking and railing products which are used in the construction of residential and commercial decks rails and trims. Marketed under the Trex name products resemble wood and have the workability of wood but require less long-term maintenance. The Trex Wood-Polymer composite is made of waste wood fibers and reclaimed plastic. Trex serves professional installation contractors and do-it-yourselfers through about 90 wholesale distribution centers which in turn sell to retailers including Home Depot and Lowe's. Trex products are available in more than 5500 locations primarily in the US and Canada.OperationsTrex produces five principal decking products: Trex Transcend Trex Enhance Trex Select Trex Accents and Trex Escapes. Its two railing products include Trex Designer Series Railing and Trex Transcend Railing. The company's collection also includes Trex Transcend Porch Flooring and Railing System (a porch product) Trex Elevations (a steel deck framing system) Trex Seclusions (a fencing product) Trex DeckLighting (a deck lighting system) TrexTrim (a cellular PVC outdoor trim product) and Trex Hideaway (a hidden fastening system for specially grooved boards). Its newest product is polyethylene pellets made from recycled plastic that it sells to plastic bag sheet and film makers. The company converts millions of pounds of recycled and reclaimed plastic and waste wood each year into Trex products. Its raw materials come from recovered plastic grocery bags plastic film and waste wood fiber. As part of its operations the company each year purchases about 300 million pounds of both used polyethylene and hardwood sawdust. It recycles more than 1.3 billion grocery retail bags annually.Geographic Reach-Based in Virginia Trex has manufacturing facilities in Winchester Virginia and Fernley Nevada. It operates globally through international retailers.Sales and MarketingTrex serves both professional installers and those who prefer to do it themselves. Through some 90 wholesale distribution centers the company sells its products to big-box home improvement retailers including Lowe's and Home Depot. It markets its products as having "unmatched good looks and longevity" –products that "will never rot crack or splinter." Its wood is also the only composite lumber to be code-listed by the nation's three major building code agencies.A majority of Trex's net sales come from its vast network of wholesale distributors. In 2014 Boise Cascade accounted for more than 10% of sales. The company has extended its reach by providing some of its lines to international retailers.Trex in 2014 spent $20.8 million on advertising particularly for branding compared to $20.9 in 2013.Financial PerformanceRevenue has been climbing at Trex since 2010. In 2014 it grew 14% to $392 million from $342 the previous year. Stronger demand from existing customers and new distributors lead to higher sales volume though a revamped pricing strategy caused lower average prices per unit.Profits have been growing since 2012 and the bump in revenue helped net income topp $41.5 million in 2014 a 20% increase over 2013's $34.6 million. Cash from operations also grew by $45.21 million to hit $58.64 million.StrategyTrex generates most of its sales by selling Trex products to wholesale distributors who market to retail lumber outlets. While Trex sells to both homeowners and contractors it focuses on sales to contractors remodelers and homebuilders because their installations are generally larger and feature professional craftsmanship.The company chooses to sell through a wholesale distribution network for its higher value products and contractor-oriented lumber yards and other retail outlets. Typically Trex appoints a distributor on a non-exclusive basis to distribute its products within a specific area. The distributor in general purchases its products at the sales price the day it ships to the distributor.Home improvement stores purchase Trex products directly from the company and through wholesale distributors for special orders placed by consumers. In 2014 the company moved online when it began offering its outdoor lighting products through Amazon.com. Trex licensees were already selling the company's outdoor furniture pergolas and deck drainage systems on the retail site. Trex works to bring new products to the marketplace. Through research and development Trex is interested in creating products that are durable low maintenance and easy to install such as its cellular PVC fire-resistant deck board and outdoor trim products (including mouldings and millwork). The company has built on its high-performance Trex Transcend collection with a range of railing options for all its customer segments. Research and development expenses in 2014 came in at $2.3 million down from $2.9 million the previous two years.

Company BackgroundTrex was formed in 1996 through a buyout of a division of Mobil Corporation. It went public in 1999.

EXECUTIVES

Vice President and General Counsel, Bill R (Billy) Gupp
SVP and CFO, James E. Cline, age 65, $289,100 total compensation
VP Marketing, Adam D. Zambanini
VP and CFO, Bryan H. Fairbanks
VP Operations, Jay Scripter
Vice President Sales, Butch Palaza
Chairman, Ronald W. (Ron) Kaplan, age 65
Auditors: Ernst & Young LLP

LOCATIONS

HQ: Trex Co Inc
160 Exeter Drive, Winchester, VA 22603-8605
Phone: 540 542-6300
Web: www.trex.com

PRODUCTS/OPERATIONS

Selected Brands
Decking
  Trex Accents
  Trex Enhance
  Trex Escapes
  Trex Select
  Trex Transcend
Deck Lighting System
  Trex DeckLighting
Fencing
  Trex Seclusions
Hidden Fastening System
  Trex Hideaway
Porch
  Trex Transcend Porch Flooring & Railing System
PVC Outdoor Trim
  TrexTrim
Railing
  Trex Designer Series
  Trex Transcend
Steel Deck Framing System
  Trex Elevations

Selected Products
Decking
Fencing
Railing
Trim

COMPETITORS

Advanced Environmental Recycling	NEW Plastics
	TAMKO
CPG International	Tumac Lumber
CertainTeed	Universal Forest
Huttig Building Products	Products
	Weyerhaeuser
Louisiana-Pacific	

HISTORICAL FINANCIALS
Company Type: Public

Income Statement
FYE: December 31

	REVENUE ($ mil.)	NET INCOME ($ mil.)	NET PROFIT MARGIN	EMPLOYEES
12/15	440.8	48.1	10.9%	700.0
12/14	391.6	41.5	10.6%	630.0
12/13	342.5	34.6	10.1%	590.0
12/12	307.3	2.7	0.9%	550.0
12/11	266.7	(11.5)	—	550.0
Annual Growth	13.4%	—		6.2%

2015 Year-End Financials

Debt ratio: 3.3%
Return on equity: 41.8%
Cash ($ mil.): 6.0
Current ratio: 1.64
Long-term debt ($ mil.): —

No. of shares (mil.): 30.9
Dividends
  Yield: —
  Payout: —
Market value ($ mil.): 1,176.0

	STOCK PRICE ($) FY Close	P/E High/Low	PER SHARE ($) Earnings	Dividends	Book Value
12/15	38.04	37 21	1.52	0.00	3.77
12/14	42.58	65 21	1.27	0.00	3.54
12/13	79.53	79 36	1.01	0.00	3.18
12/12	37.23	510287	0.08	0.00	2.76
12/11	22.91	— —	(0.38)	0.00	2.96
Annual Growth	13.5%	— —	—		6.2%

TRI Pointe Group Inc

Auditors: Ernst & Young LLP

LOCATIONS

HQ: TRI Pointe Group Inc
19540 Jamboree Road, Suite 300, Irvine, CA 92612
Phone: 949 438-1400
Web: www.TRIPointeGroup.com

HISTORICAL FINANCIALS
Company Type: Public

Income Statement
FYE: December 31

	REVENUE ($ mil.)	NET INCOME ($ mil.)	NET PROFIT MARGIN	EMPLOYEES
12/15	2,400.1	205.4	8.6%	1,036.0
12/14	1,703.6	84.2	4.9%	961.0
12/13	257.9	15.3	6.0%	147.0
12/12	78.5	2.5	3.2%	68.0
12/11	19.3	(4.5)	—	53.0
Annual Growth	233.8%	—	—	110.3%

2015 Year-End Financials

Debt ratio: 37.3%
Return on equity: 13.1%
Cash ($ mil.): 214.4
Current ratio: 23.19
Long-term debt ($ mil.): 1,172.9

No. of shares (mil.): 161.8
Dividends
  Yield: —
  Payout: —
Market value ($ mil.): 2,050.0

	STOCK PRICE ($) FY Close	P/E High/Low	PER SHARE ($) Earnings	Dividends	Book Value
12/15	12.67	13 10	1.27	0.00	10.29
12/14	15.25	34 22	0.58	0.00	9.01
12/13	19.93	41 27	0.50	0.00	10.20
Annual Growth	(20.3%)	— —	59.4%		0.4%

TriCo Bancshares (Chico, CA)

People looking for a community bank in California's Sacramento Valley can try TriCo. TriCo Bancshares is the holding company for Tri Counties Bank which serves customers through some 65 traditional and in-store branches in 23 counties in Northern and Central California. Founded in 1974 Tri Counties Bank provides a variety of deposit services including checking and savings accounts money market accounts and CDs. Most patrons are retail customers and small to midsized businesses. The bank primarily originates real estate mortgages which account for about 65% of its loan portfolio; consumer loans contribute about 25%. TriCo has agreed to acquire rival North Valley Bancorp.

Mergers and Acquisitions
TriCo in January 2014 announced plans to buy its rival in Northern California North Valley Bancorp (NVB) for about $178.4 million. NVB is the parent company of North Valley Bank which had about $918 million in assets and 22 commercial banking offices across eight Northern California

counties at the end of 2013. At closing which is expected in the second or third quarter of 2014 NVB will be merged into Tri Counties Bank. The combined bank would have about $3.6 billion in assets.

Geographic Reach
Based in Chico California Tri Counties Bank operates 66 branches (41 traditional branches and 25 in-store branches) in 23 counties in Northern and central California including Fresno Kern Mendocino Napa Sacramento and Yuba counties.

Operations
In addition to its retail banking products and services the company provides wholesale banking and investment services; TriCo offers brokerage services through an arrangement with Raymond James Financial. The company does not provide trust or international banking services.

Financial Performance
In 2013 net interest income the company's primary source of revenue rose 0.6% compared with 2012 to $102.2 million. The slight increase in net interest income was mainly due to a decrease in average balance of other borrowings a shift in deposit balances from relatively high interest rate earning time deposits to noninterest-earning demand and savings deposits an increase in the average balance of investments securities and an increase in the average balance of loans; all of which were substantially offset by a decrease in the average yield on loans.

Strategy
The bank's growth has been fueled by acquisitions and the opening of new branches; it frequently opens branches within grocery stores or other retailers including Wal-Mart. TriCo in 2010 acquired the three branches of Granite Community Bank which had been seized by regulators. The transaction which also included most of the failed bank's assets and deposits was facilitated by the FDIC and includes a loss-sharing agreement with the agency. The following year TriCo acquired Citizens Bank of Northern California. The FDIC-assisted deal included seven branches. The acquisitions are part of TriCo's strategy of adding new customers.

EXECUTIVES

Senior Vice President Of Human Resources, Richard (Dick) Miller
EVP and CFO TriCo Bancshares and Tri Counties Bank, Thomas J. (Tom) Reddish, age 56, $309,601 total compensation
EVP and Chief Credit Officer, Craig B. Carney, age 57, $274,932 total compensation
EVP Wholesale Banking, Richard B. O'Sullivan, age 59, $260,890 total compensation
President and CEO, Richard P. Smith, age 58, $549,846 total compensation
EVP and COO, John S. Fleshood, age 54
EVP and Chief Retail Banking Officer, Daniel K. (Dan) Bailey, age 47, $268,335 total compensation
SVP and CIO, Bruce Barnett
Vice President Facilities Expansion MA, Chimene Sonsteng
Regional Vice President Northern San Joaquin Region, David (Dave) Allumbaugh
Vice President, Mark Hammer
Executive Vice President and Chief Retail Banking Officer, Dan (Danny) Bailey
Vice President Commercial Loan Supervisor, Bret Funde
Chairman, William J. Casey, age 71
Vice Chairman, Michael W. Koehnen, age 55
Auditors: Crowe Horwath LLP

LOCATIONS

HQ: TriCo Bancshares (Chico, CA)
63 Constitution Drive, Chico, CA 95973
Phone: 530 898-0300 **Fax:** 530 898-0310
Web: www.tcbk.com

PRODUCTS/OPERATIONS

2015 Sales

	$ mil.	% of total
Interest		
Loans including fees	131.8	64
Debt securities	26.8	13
Dividends	2.1	1
Other	0.7	.
Noninterest		
Service charges & fees	31.8	16
Commissions	3.4	2
Gain on sale of loans	3.1	1
Other	7.1	3
Total	**206.8**	**100**

Selected Services

Business debit cards
Business online banking
Business workshops
Cash management
Education savings and CDs
Loans and credits
Merchant services
Order checks
Overdraft services
Pension and retirement
Personal certificates of deposit
Personal checking
Personal savings and money market
Retirement savings and CDs

COMPETITORS

Bank of America	MUFG Americas Holdings
Bank of the West	PremierWest
Central Valley	Wells Fargo
Community Bancorp	Westamerica

HISTORICAL FINANCIALS

Company Type: Public

Income Statement

FYE: December 31

	ASSETS ($ mil.)	NET INCOME ($ mil.)	INCOME AS % OF ASSETS	EMPLOYEES
12/15	4,220.7	43.8	1.0%	1,011.0
12/14	3,916.4	26.1	0.7%	1,009.0
12/13	2,744.0	27.4	1.0%	794.0
12/12	2,609.2	18.9	0.7%	831.0
12/11	2,555.6	18.5	0.7%	799.0
Annual Growth	**13.4%**	**23.9%**	**—**	**6.1%**

2015 Year-End Financials

Return on assets: 1.0%
Return on equity: 10.0%
Long-term debt ($ mil.): —
No. of shares (mil.): 22.7
Sales ($ mil): 206.7

Dividends
Yield: 1.9%
Payout: 32.3%
Market value ($ mil.): 625.0

	STOCK PRICE ($) FY Close	P/E High/Low	PER SHARE ($) Earnings	Dividends	Book Value
12/15	27.44	15 12	1.91	0.52	19.85
12/14	24.70	19 15	1.46	0.44	18.41
12/13	28.37	17 9	1.69	0.42	15.61
12/12	16.75	15 12	1.18	0.36	14.33
12/11	14.22	14 10	1.16	0.36	13.55
Annual Growth	**17.9%**	**— —**	**13.3%**	**9.6%**	**10.0%**

Trimble Inc

Those who fear not knowing their place in the world should Trimble. Trimble Navigation makes systems and software that combine global positioning technology with wireless communications to provide location and position data and make it actionable. Using GPS laser optical and other technologies the company's products target areas such as surveying construction site project management mapping mobile personnel management and mobile and fixed asset management. They are offered to end users such as government entities farmers engineering firms and public safety workers as well as equipment manufacturers (OEMs). About half of sales are made outside the US.

HISTORY

Charles Trimble founded Trimble Navigation in 1978 to design navigation products for recreational boating. In 1982 the company began developing devices using the Global Positioning System (GPS) satellite network; in 1984 Trimble introduced its first GPS product. The company went public in 1990 10 days before Saddam Hussein invaded Kuwait. Trimble gained worldwide recognition when allied troops used its GPS devices during the Persian Gulf War.

The war left Trimble expanding too quickly and overproducing. In 1992 Trimble rebounded after reorganizing to focus on nonmilitary products. Two years later it introduced a low-cost handheld unit that helped with utilities fieldwork. In 1998 Trimble ceased manufacturing products for general aviation and allied with Siemens to develop GPS products. That year Charles Trimble was named vice chairman after he stepped down as the company's CEO. The company in 1998 also launched a cost reduction plan that cut its workforce by 8%.

The next year Trimble sold its Sunnyvale California manufacturing operations to contract manufacturer Solectron which agreed to make Trimble's GPS and radio-frequency products for three years. Also in 1999 Steven Berglund a former president of a Spectra-Physics subsidiary was named CEO of Trimble.

In 2000 Trimble acquired the Spectra Precision businesses of Thermo Electron (which later became Thermo Fisher Scientific) for about $294 million. That year the US government stopped scrambling GPS signals opening the door for more precise devices. In 2001 the company formed a subsidiary Trimble Information Services to expand the company's wireless location-based services including fleet management.

The next year Trimble and Caterpillar formed a joint venture Caterpillar Trimble Control Technologies to develop advanced electronic guidance and control technologies for earth-moving construction and mining machines.

The company acquired Eleven Technology a mobile application software developer focused on the consumer packaged goods market in 2006. The company also expanded its laser scanning business by acquiring the assets —including software for engineering and construction plant design —of BitWyse Solutions. Later in 2006 it purchased Visual Statement a developer of crime and collision incident investigation software and XYZ Solutions a 3-D intelligence software provider. It also acquired Meridian Systems a provider of enterprise project management and lifecycle software. Still

later in 2006 Trimble bought Spacient Technologies a privately held provider of field service management and mobile mapping software used by municipalities and utilities.

Trimble's buying spree continued in 2007 when it purchased @Road a developer of mobile resource management systems for about $493 million.

The company expanded its ability to serve the farming industry when it acquired NTech Industries in 2009. NTech developed optical crop-sensing technology that helps farmers reduce costs by managing the application of nitrogen herbicides and other crop inputs. Also that year Trimble purchased Accutest Engineering Solutions a UK-based maker of mobile resource management applications for trucking fleets.

In 2010 Trimble acquired Punch Telematix from majority shareholder Punch International for nearly €14 million ($18 million) in cash and rebranded it as Trimble Transport and Logistics. Punch Telematix made onboard computers for trucks. That year the company also bought ThingMagic a developer of radio frequency identification (RFID) products and RFID integration services for commercial clients in the construction and transportation industries and Cengea a provider of operations and supply chain management software for the forestry agriculture and natural resource industries.

Additionally Trimble bought Mumbai-based Tata AutoComp Mobility Telematics (TMT) in a move to expand its mobile resource management services business in India. TMT provided vehicle tracking and other telematics services to such customers as Bharat Petroleum and Tata Motors. Also that year expanding its engineering and construction portfolio for electrical and mechanical contractors Trimble bought the assets of Accubid a provider of estimating project management and service management software.

Trimble bought 3D modeling software maker Tekla in 2011 in a deal valued at nearly €340 million ($485 million) to better equip building contractors and engineers to manage construction projects. The follow-up investment came in 2012 when Trimble completed the acquisition of the StruCad and StruEngineer business from AceCad Software. StruCad offers 3D structural detailing while StruEngineer provides engineering companies with 3D steelwork modeling and construction management.

The company acquired a line of software products in 2011 from Norway-based Mesta Entreprenør a subsidiary of road and highway construction contractor Mesta Konsern. The deal added office and field data collection applications and improved the company's ability to provide customized systems to construction clients particularly in the area of managing local application requirements compliance. Also in 2011 Trimble strengthened its portfolio and Asia presence with the purchase of China-based Yamei Electronics a manufacturer of electronic automotive products including anti-theft GPS monitoring and tracking systems RFID smart keys and diagnostics systems.

Also that year Trimble acquired the OmniSTAR satellite system assets of Dutch geological engineering company Fugro. The company was interested in OmniSTAR's GPS signal correction technology (used to improve the accuracy of satellite navigation devices) which it is using to expand the functionality of its mapping systems for agricultural and construction purposes among others. It also acquired France-based Ashtech to expand Garmin's selection of survey products including the flagship application Spectra Precision for construction clients. Ashtech became part of Trimble's engineering and construction division.

EXECUTIVES

President CEO and Director, Steven W. Berglund, age 64, $860,000 total compensation

VP Heavy and Highway Construction Division, Bryn A. Fosburgh, age 54, $425,000 total compensation

VP Advanced Devices, J rgen D. Kliem, age 58

VP Mobile Solutions Data Services and Hosting Global Services, James M. Veneziano, age 54, $380,000 total compensation

VP Channel Development, Christopher W. Gibson, age 55, $425,000 total compensation

SVP and Sector Head Intelligent Transportation and Asset Sharing, Sachin J. Sankpal, age 48

CFO, Robert G. Painter, age 45

SVP and Sector Head Agriculture Forestry Positioning Services and HarvestMark Divisions, Darryl R. Matthews, age 48

National Accounts Manager Americas, Eric Carson

Vice President Operations and CIO, Leah Lambertson

Vice President Of Finance, Kathy Radley-timberlake

Vice President Sales, Kurt Wyman

Vice President Business Development Thingmagic Divis, Bernd Schoner

Vice President Sales and Customer Service, Mark (Marky) Amiot

Vice President, Rahim Farzaie

National Account Manager, Jason (Jase) Zhou

Vice President Geospatial Division, Erik Arvesen

TandL Business Area Vice President, Michel Maercke

Vice President General Manager Agriculture Division, Joe Denniston

National Sales Manager, Scott (Scotty) Mellett

Division Vice President, Jrgen Kliem

Vice President General Counsel, James (Jamie) Kirkland

Vice President, William (Bill) Burgess

Vice President Global Tax, John (Jack) Schreiber

Vice President General Manager, Joe (Joey) Denniston

Vice President Sales and Business Development Manhattan, Tom (Tommy) Montesi

Sales Vice President, Rocco Bognet

Vice Chairman, Nickolas W. Vande Steeg, age 73

Chairman, Ulf J. Johansson, age 71

Board Member, Jonathan Moore

Secretary, Eric Leroy

Auditors: Ernst & Young LLP

LOCATIONS

HQ: Trimble Inc
935 Stewart Drive, Sunnyvale, CA 94085
Phone: 408 481-8000   **Fax:** 408 481-2218
Web: www.trimble.com

PRODUCTS/OPERATIONS

2016 Sales

	$ mil.	% of total
Engineering & construction	1,283.3	56
Mobile solutions	520.3	23
Field solutions	355.3	15
Advanced devices	131.5	6
Total	**2,290.4**	**100**

2016 Sales

	$ mil.	% of total
Product	1,533.5	67
Service	419.9	18
Subscription	337.0	15
Total	**2,290.4**	**100**

Selected Products

Engineering and Construction
Global positioning system (GPS) data collection systems (GPS Total Station)
Grade control systems (SiteVision)
Laser transmitters (Spectra)
Optical surveying equipment

Field Solutions
Agricultural information systems
Automatic tractor steering systems (AgGPS Autopilot)
Farm equipment guidance systems
Laser-based water management systems
Mapping equipment (AgGPS 132)
Geographical information systems
GPS data collection and maintenance systems (GeoExplorer)

Mobile Solutions
Fleet management system hardware software and service (Telvisant)
GPS vehicle module (CrossCheck)

Advanced Devices
GPS chipsets for mobile communication and computing (FirstGPS)
GPS clocks (Thunderbolt)
GPS receiver cards/modules for military applications (Force 5)
GPS receivers for battery powered applications (Lassen LP)
Handheld GPS survey data collectors (Tripod Data Systems Ranger)

COMPETITORS

AgJunction	Navico
AirIQ	NovAtel
Deere	Novariant
Garmin	QUALCOMM
Hexagon AB	Raven Industries
L-3 Communications	Raytheon
Leica Geosystems	Rockwell Collins
MacDonald Dettwiler	TOPCON
MiTAC	Thales
Motorola Solutions	TomTom

HISTORICAL FINANCIALS

Company Type: Public

Income Statement

FYE: January 1

	REVENUE ($ mil.)	NET INCOME ($ mil.)	NET PROFIT MARGIN	EMPLOYEES
01/16	2,290.4	121.1	5.3%	8,451.0
01/15	2,395.5	214.1	8.9%	8,217.0
01/14*	2,288.1	218.8	9.6%	7,086.0
12/12	2,040.1	191.0	9.4%	6,561.0
12/11	1,644.0	150.7	9.2%	5,301.0
Annual Growth	**8.6%**	**(5.3%)**	**—**	**12.4%**

*Fiscal year change

2016 Year-End Financials

Debt ratio: 19.8%
Return on equity: 5.3%
Cash ($ mil.): 116.0
Current ratio: 1.21
Long-term debt ($ mil.): 611.4

No. of shares (mil.): 250.7
Dividends
Yield: —
Payout: —
Market value ($ mil.): 5,378.0

	STOCK PRICE ($) FY Close	P/E High/Low		PER SHARE ($) Earnings	Dividends	Book Value
01/16	21.45	58	34	0.47	0.00	8.85
01/15	26.91	49	32	0.81	0.00	9.09
01/14*	34.57	75	29	0.84	0.00	8.58
12/12	58.60	79	53	0.75	0.00	7.46
12/11	43.40	84	53	0.60	0.00	6.35
Annual Growth	**(16.2%)**	**—**	**—**	**(5.9%)**	**—**	**8.7%**

*Fiscal year change

Tripadvisor Inc

Want to crowd source your next trip with advice from millions of fellow travelers? Then turn to TripAdvisor which provides more than 225 million consumer reviews on places from the Yorkshire B&B to the Super 8 and to the Ritz to help travelers plot their journeys and make reservations. The global source strives to fine-tune search results to provide information that is free of bias and in a mobile format for smartphone use. TripAdvisor also matches hotels with flights and packages. The company partners with top online travel businesses such as Hotwire Hotels.com and American Airlines and offers some 45 localized versions in France Germany Ireland Italy Spain the UK China and a growing list of other countries. The company was spun off from Expedia in 2011.

Operations

TripAdvisor makes most of its money some 70% from click-based advertising. TripAdvisor gets paid when a visitor clicks on a link to an online travel agent or hotel. Another 19% of revenue comes from subscriptions and transactions. Hotels B&Bs and other lodging properties put advertising on TripAdvisor for a contracted period. The last 11% of revenue is generated by display ads on the site. Hotels are the biggest customers throughout TripAdvisor's various advertising options accounting for 91% of revenue.

Geographic Reach

Massachusetts-based TripAdvisor generates about half of its revenue in the US. The UK is the next biggest single market with 15% of revenue for the company. Other European-related travel is responsible for about 18% of revenue. The company has about 40 locations in North America Europe and the Asia-Pacific region.

Sales and Marketing

To drive traffic to its sites TripAdvisor promotes its services on search engines other Internet portals and online and off-line venues. Social media sites including Facebook Twitter and others are important parts of TripAdvisor's contact with consumers. In 2014 the company spent $104 million more on advertising than it did in 2013. Total ad costs were $341 million in 2014 which included a $33 million TV campaign.

Financial Performance

Like a world traveler checking off destinations TripAdvisor has steadily risen by financial milestones in the past six years. It crossed the billion-dollar revenue mark in 2014 posting $1.25 billion — a 32% increase over 2013. The company recorded revenue increases in all segments and geographic markets for the year. While small in terms of TripAdvisor's revenue picture revenue from Latin America and Asia-Pacific jumped 28% and 47% respectively in 2014. Revenue in the company's "Other" segment rose by $65 million from growth in Vacation Rentals. For that part of the lodging business TripAdvisor provides free listings but takes a commission with a booking.

Net income rose 10% in 2014 to $226 million from 2013 on the strength of higher revenue. The company increased spending in key areas including sales and marketing (up $134 million) and technology and content (up $40 million).

Cash flow from operations increased to $226 million at the end of 2014 from $205 million for 2013.

Strategy

TripAdvisor is focused on growth —in content and revenue and profit. It generates 70% of its sales through click-based advertising. To maintain this momentum the company continues to invest in social mobile and global initiatives Indeed mobile downloads have risen dramatically in recent years as the use of smartphones and tablets skyrocket. TripAdvisor's launch of 24 free Mobile City Guides for Android and iOS and its development of a user-friendly interface have given the company's mobile strategy added traction.

The company is extending its reach internationally in the past few years by launching individual TripAdvisor sites for other countries in Europe including France Germany and Italy and in Argentina Brazil China India Japan Russia and South Korea. Countries added in 2014 included New Zealand the Philippines South Africa Vietnam Austria Israel Finland Hungary Czech Republic Slovakia and Serbia.

Multiple acquisitions of online travel media content companies during the past few years have made TripAdvisor a dominant force in travel media and pits the online source squarely against the likes of HomeAway which caters to customers who rent vacation homes (or a temporary home away from home). The purchases also have a positive effect its growth strategy.

TripAdvisor's "Just for You" feature added in 2014 personalizes recommendations by using your preferences travel history and the views of friends as sources.

Mergers and Acquisitions

TripAdvisor isn't shy about filling its corporate suitcase with acquisitions to add content and services. In 2014 the company acquired Viator leading resource for researching and booking activities around the world for $192 million. It also bought Vacation Home Rentals a US-based vacation rental website) and the Tripbod travel community.

To provide restaurant services TripAdvisor bought Lafourchette a provider of an online and mobile reservations platform in Europe MyTable and Restopolis providers of an online and mobile reservations platform and Iens a provider of an online and mobile reservations platform for restaurants in the Netherlands.

EXECUTIVES

SVP Engineering and Operations, Andy Gelfond
President and CEO, Stephen Kaufer, $469,231 total compensation
President Vacation Rentals, Dermot Halpin
CFO, Julie M.B. Bradley, $302,116 total compensation
President TripAdvisor for Business, Marc Charron
Svp Advertising Sales, Robin (Rin) Ingle
Auditors: KPMG LLP

LOCATIONS

HQ: Tripadvisor Inc
  400 1st Avenue, Needham, MA 02494
Phone: 781 800-5000
Web: www.tripadvisor.com

PRODUCTS/OPERATIONS

Other Travel Brands & Webs2014 Sales

	% of total
Clicked-based advertising	71
Subscription transaction and other	19
Display-based advertising	11
Total	**100**

2014 Sales

	% of total
Hotel	91
Other	9
Total	**100**

2014 Sales

	% of total
North America	50
EMEA	33
APAC	13
LATAM	4
Total	**100**

2014 Sales

	% of Total
United States	48
United kingdom	15
All other countries	37
Total	**100**
ites	
airfarewatchdog.com	
bookingbuddy.com	
cruisecritic.com	
everytrail.com	
flipkey.com	
holidaylettings.co.uk	
holidaywatchdog.com	
independenttraveler.com	
kusun.cn	
onetime.com	
seatguru.com	
smarttravel.com	
travelpod.com	
travel-library.com	
virtualtourist.com	
whereivebeen.com	

Selected TripAdvisor Sites

daodao.com
no.tripadvisor.com
pl.tripadvisor.com
th.tripadvisor.com
tripadvisor.com.eg
tripadvisor.com.my
tripadvisor.tw
tripadvisor.com.ar
tripadvisor.co.id
tripadvisor.gr
tripadvisor.ru
tripadvisor.co.kr
tripadvisor.com.sg
tripadvisor.com.au
tripadvisor.com.tr
tripadvisor.com.mx
tripadvisor.dk
tripadvisor.ca
tripadvisor.se
tripadvisor.nl
tripadvisor.com.br
tripadvisor.jp
tripadvisor.in
tripadvisor.es
tripadvisor.it
tripadvisor.de
tripadvisor.fr
tripadvisor.co.uk
tripadvisor.ie

COMPETITORS

Costamar	Sabre
HomeAway	SkyAuction.com
Lonely Planet	Travelzoo
Orbitz Worldwide	Yelp
Pegasus Solutions	ebookers.com
Priceline	

HISTORICAL FINANCIALS

Company Type: Public

Income Statement

FYE: December 31

	REVENUE ($ mil.)	NET INCOME ($ mil.)	NET PROFIT MARGIN	EMPLOYEES
12/16	1,480.0	120.0	8.1%	3,327.0
12/15	1,492.0	198.0	13.3%	3,008.0
12/14	1,246.0	226.0	18.1%	2,793.0
12/13	944.6	205.4	21.7%	2,017.0
12/12	762.9	194.0	25.4%	1,575.0
Annual Growth	**18.0%**	**(11.3%)**	**—**	**20.6%**

2016 Year-End Financials

Debt ratio: 7.6%
Return on equity: 8.2%
Cash ($ mil.): 612.0
Current ratio: 2.25
Long-term debt ($ mil.): 91.0

No. of shares (mil.): 144.1
Dividends
  Yield: —
  Payout: —
Market value ($ mil.): 6,682.0

	STOCK PRICE ($) FY Close	P/E High/Low	Earnings	Dividends	Book Value
12/16	46.37	103 56	0.82	0.00	10.42
12/15	85.25	68 46	1.36	0.00	9.72
12/14	74.66	70 43	1.55	0.00	7.87
12/13	82.83	62 29	1.41	0.00	6.08
12/12	41.92	33 18	1.37	0.00	5.09
Annual Growth	**2.6%**	**— —**	**(12.0%)**	**—**	**19.6%**

TriState Capital Holdings, Inc.

TriState Capital Holdings has found its niche right in the middle of the banking industry. The holding company owns TriState Capital Bank a regional business bank that caters to midsized businesses or those annually earning between $5 million and $300 million. TriState Capital also offers private banking services nationally to high-networth individuals. Its loan portfolio consists of about 50% commercial loans 30% commercial real estate loans and 20% private banking-personal loans. The bank serves clients from branches in Cleveland; New Jersey; New York City Philadelphia and Pittsburgh. Altogether it has some $2 billion in assets. TriState Capital went public in mid-2013.
IPO

The company does not have any specific plans outlined for its proceeds but will likely use it for general corporate purposes which might include maintaining liquidity at the holding company providing equity capital to the bank to fund balance sheet growth and possibly investing in or acquiring wealth management businesses.

Company Background

TriState Capital was founded in 2007 by two banking industry executives —chairman and CEO James Getz who spent 20 years at Federated Investors and vice chairman William Schenck the former secretary of banking for Pennsylvania.

Strategy

The company's founders saw an opportunity in serving what they perceived was an underserved market —midsized businesses. Consolidation had left major national banks catering to individuals and large businesses while community banks served individuals and small businesses.

Ownership

Prior to the offering investment firm Lovell Minnick Partners held a 20% stake in TriState Capital Holdings in exchange for its $50 million investment in 2012.

EXECUTIVES

Chairman President and CEO, James F. (Jim) Getz, $1,500,000 total compensation
President Commercial Banking, David A. Molnar
Vice Chairman and CFO, Mark L. Sullivan, $425,000 total compensation
Regional President New Jersey, Kenneth R. Orchard
Regional President New York, Thomas N. Gilmartin
Regional President Ohio, John D. Barrett
Regional President Eastern Pennsylvania, Joseph M. Finley
Regional President Western Pennsylvania, Vince Locher
President Private Bank Team, Charles C. Fawcett
Senior Vice President Relationship Manager, Michael Blasko
Senior Vice President Relationship Manager, Michael (Mel) Blasko
Senior Vice President, John (Jack) Buglione
Vice Chairman, A. William (Bill) Schenck
Auditors: KPMG LLP

LOCATIONS

HQ: TriState Capital Holdings, Inc.
One Oxford Centre, 301 Grant Street, Suite 2700, Pittsburgh, PA 15219
Phone: 412 304-0304

PRODUCTS/OPERATIONS

2015 Sales

	% of total
Interest income	
Loans	67
Investments	3
Interest-earning deposits	-
Noninterest income	
Investment management fees	25
Commitment and other fees	2
Other income	3
Total	**100**

COMPETITORS

Bank of America	HSBC Private Bank
Bank of New York	Herald National Bank
Mellon	JPMorgan Private Bank
Boston Private	Julius Baer
Brown Brothers	Lakeland Bancorp
Harriman	M&T Bank
Citigroup	Safra Bank
Citigroup Private Bank	U.S. Trust
First Republic (CA)	

HISTORICAL FINANCIALS
Company Type: Public

Income Statement
FYE: December 31

	ASSETS ($ mil.)	NET INCOME ($ mil.)	INCOME AS % OF ASSETS	EMPLOYEES
12/15	3,302.8	22.4	0.7%	192.0
12/14	2,846.8	15.9	0.6%	182.0
12/13	2,290.5	12.8	0.6%	129.0
12/12	2,073.1	10.6	0.5%	119.0
12/11	1,833.4	7.2	0.4%	0.0
Annual Growth	**15.9%**	**32.9%**	**—**	**—**

2015 Year-End Financials

Return on assets: 0.7%	Dividends
Return on equity: 7.1%	Yield: —
Long-term debt ($ mil.): —	Payout: —
No. of shares (mil.): 28.0	Market value ($ mil.): 393.0
Sales ($ mil): 119.0	

	STOCK PRICE ($) FY Close	P/E High/Low	PER SHARE ($) Earnings	Dividends	Book Value
12/15	13.99	18 12	0.80	0.00	11.62
12/14	10.24	26 16	0.55	0.00	10.88
12/13	11.86	29 24	0.49	0.00	10.25
Annual Growth	**8.6%**	**— —**	**27.8%**	**—**	**6.5%**

Triumph Bancorp Inc

Auditors: Crowe Horwath LLP

LOCATIONS

HQ: Triumph Bancorp Inc
12700 Park Central Drive, Suite 1700, Dallas, TX 75251
Phone: 214 365-6900
Web: www.triumphbancorp.com

HISTORICAL FINANCIALS
Company Type: Public

Income Statement
FYE: December 31

	ASSETS ($ mil.)	NET INCOME ($ mil.)	INCOME AS % OF ASSETS	EMPLOYEES
12/15	1,691.3	29.1	1.7%	500.0
12/14	1,447.9	17.7	1.2%	466.0
12/13	1,288.2	13.4	1.0%	463.0
12/12	301.4	11.0	3.7%	0.0
Annual Growth	**77.7%**	**38.0%**	**—**	**—**

2015 Year-End Financials

Return on assets: 1.8%	Dividends
Return on equity: 11.5%	Yield: —
Long-term debt ($ mil.): —	Payout: —
No. of shares (mil.): 18.0	Market value ($ mil.): 297.0
Sales ($ mil): 132.0	

	STOCK PRICE ($) FY Close	P/E High/Low	PER SHARE ($) Earnings	Dividends	Book Value
12/15	16.50	11 8	1.57	0.00	14.88
12/14	13.55	10 8	1.52	0.00	13.22
12/13	0.00	— —	1.39	0.00	13.59
Annual Growth	**—**	**— —**	**6.3%**	**—**	**4.6%**

Two Harbors Investment Corp

Two Harbors Investment Corp. is ready to double its money. The real estate investment trust (REIT) is managed and advised by (and was founded by) PRCM Advisers a subsidiary of Pine River Capital Management. The trust primarily invests in agency residential mortgage-backed securities (RMBS) with fixed or adjustable interest rates that are backed by government-supported enterprises Fannie Mae Freddie Mac or Ginnie Mae. About a quarter of its mortgage portfolio is made up of non-agency RMBS such as subprime mortgages which carry more risk than federally-backed securities but offer higher yields. Chairman (and Pine River CEO) Brian Taylor controls almost 20% of the trust's stock.

Pine River Capital Management set up Two Harbors in 2009 through a reverse merger with a blank-check company named Capitol Acquisition Corp. Since then the company has completed three follow-on public offerings that netted more than $520 million which it has used to invest in agency and non-agency RMBS and other financial assets. Two Harbors plans to continue to maintain its portfolio of agency RMBS sprinkled with riskier investments to boost yield.

EXECUTIVES

Vice President Data Management, Sree Kunduru
Vice President Seller Management, Zachary (Zach) Everett
Auditors: Ernst & Young LLP

LOCATIONS

HQ: Two Harbors Investment Corp
590 Madison Avenue, 36th Floor, New York, NY 10022
Phone: 612 629-2500
Web: www.twoharborsinvestment.com

COMPETITORS

American Capital Agency Corp.	MFA Financial
Annaly Capital Management	New York Mortgage Trust
Capstead Mortgage	Newcastle Investment
Chimera	Putnam Mortgage
Gramercy	Redwood Trust
Invesco Mortgage Capital	iStar Financial Inc

HISTORICAL FINANCIALS
Company Type: Public

Income Statement
FYE: December 31

	REVENUE ($ mil.)	NET INCOME ($ mil.)	NET PROFIT MARGIN	EMPLOYEES
12/15	769.4	492.2	64.0%	0.0
12/14	336.4	167.1	49.7%	0.0
12/13	846.7	579.0	68.4%	0.0
12/12	368.1	291.9	79.3%	0.0
12/11	173.0	127.4	73.6%	0.0
Annual Growth	**45.2%**	**40.2%**	**—**	**—**

2015 Year-End Financials

Debt ratio: 39.6%
Return on equity: 12.8%
Cash ($ mil.): 1,000.3
Current ratio: 0.30
Long-term debt ($ mil.): 5,785.1

No. of shares (mil.): 353.9
Dividends
Yield: 12.8%
Payout: 155.2%
Market value ($ mil.): 2,867.0

	STOCK PRICE ($) FY Close	P/E High/Low		PER SHARE ($) Earnings	Dividends	Book Value
12/15	8.10	8	6	1.35	1.04	10.11
12/14	10.02	23	20	0.46	1.04	11.10
12/13	9.28	8	5	1.65	1.17	10.56
12/12	11.08	10	7	1.20	1.71	11.55
12/11	9.24	9	6	1.29	1.60	9.03
Annual Growth	(3.2%)	—	—	1.1%	(10.2%)	2.8%

Tyler Technologies, Inc.

Tyler Technologies doesn't want local governments tied up in red tape. The company provides software and services intended to help state and local government offices operate more efficiently. Specializing in applications for local governments and public schools Tyler's products include software for accounting and financial management filing court documents electronically tracking and managing court cases and automating appraisals and assessments. Other products include applications that allow citizens to access utility accounts or pay traffic fines online. Tyler complements its software with hosting support and maintenance services. The company counts more than 13000 government and school customers in all 50 states Canada the Caribbean and the UK.

Operations

The company divides its operations into two segments —enterprise software and appraisal and tax software. Enterprise software which accounts for 88% of sales provides local governments and schools with software and services for back-office functions such as financial management and courts and justice processes. Appraisal and tax software which makes up the other 11% of sales is used by local governments and taxing authorities to automate property appraisal and assessment including physical inspection data collection property valuation preparing tax rolls and arbitration.

The company's technology partners include Microsoft and ESRI.

Geographic Reach

Tyler Technologies operates from about 20 offices in the US and one in Canada.

Sales and Marketing

The company uses a direct sales force. It participates in government associations and attends annual meetings trade shows and educational events to attract new customers. Its customers are primarily county and municipal agencies school districts and other local government offices.

Financial Performance

Tyler Technologies has been on a tear in revenue growth and it continued in 2014. Revenue jumped 18% to $493 million because of growth throughout its offerings. It posted 40% growth in subscriptions 22% in software services and 20% growth in software licenses and royalties from current customers and new ones. A particular driver of subscription-based services revenue came from

a contract with the Texas Office of Court Administration for the company's Odyssey File and Serve e-filing system. Overall local government spending loosened as economic conditions improved.

Tyler Technologies converted the revenue growth into a 59% increase in profit. It rose to $59 million in 2014 from $39 million in 2013.

Cash flow from operations also jumped rising to $123 million in 2014 from $66 million in 2013.

Strategy

In addition to acquisitions the company expands its software product line with new offerings and product upgrades including the Odyssey judicial case management system and public-use Internet portals that enable users to pay property taxes utility bills and complete other transactions electronically. The company is also looking to grow by selling new products and services to its existing customer base expanding its market focus to include larger customers and entering new geographic regions.

Mergers and Acquisitions

In early 2015 Tyler Technologies acquired 20% of Record Holdings an Australian company specializing in digitizing the spoken word in courts. Also in 2015 Tyler Technologies bought Brazos Technology Corp. a provider of mobile hand-held products used by law enforcement agencies for field accident reporting and electronically issuing citations. Toward the end of 2015 Tyler Technologies bought New World Systems Corp. a provider of public safety and financial products. Tyler Technologies paid $360 million in cash and about 2.1 million shares of Tyler's stock.

In 2014 the company acquired SoftCode Inc. which developed civil process automation software for county sheriffs' departments. The acquisition broadened Tyler Technologies' courts and justice product line.

Company Background

Formerly an auto parts and supplies company established in 1966 Tyler sold its chain of auto parts stores in 1999 and used acquisitions to transform itself into a provider of software for the local government and education markets.

EXECUTIVES

EVP CFO and Treasurer, Brian K. Miller, age 57, $323,000 total compensation
COO and Director; President MUNIS Division, John S. Marr, age 57, $512,000 total compensation
President, H. Lynn Moore, age 48, $323,000 total compensation
EVP and President Local Government Division, Dustin R. Womble, age 57, $430,000 total compensation
VP and CIO, Matthew (Matt) Bieri
President Courts and Justice Division, Jeff Puckett
VP and Chief Marketing Officer, Samantha Crosby
President Appraisal and Tax Division, Andrew D. Teed
President ERP and School Division, Christopher P. (Chris) Hepburn
President Justice Group, Bret Dixon
President Public Safety Division, Greg Sebastian
Vice President of EnerGov Sales, Ryan Hountz
National Sales Manager, Gary (Gar) Dube
Vice President Technical Operations, Sean Craig
Vice President Corporate Development, Brian (Bri) Berry
Executive Vice President Financials and Personnel Management, Bruce (Brucey) Borcher
Vice President For Information Systems, Paul Ilami
Vice President, Stefan Werdegar
Vice President, Mary (Mar) Lavik

Vice President, Kelly (Kel) Sprong
Vice President of Product Development, David (Dave) Grossman
Vice President of Support Services, Mitchell (Mitch) Spence
Auditors: Ernst & Young LLP

LOCATIONS

HQ: Tyler Technologies, Inc.
5101 Tennyson Parkway, Plano, TX 75024
Phone: 972 713-3700
Web: www.tylertech.com

PRODUCTS/OPERATIONS

2014 Sales

	% of total
Enterprise software	89
Appraisal & tax software	11
Corporate	-
Total	**100**

2014 Sales

% of total	$ mil
Maintenance	43
Software services	23
Subscriptions	18
Software licenses and royalties	10
Appraisal services	4
Hardware & other	2
Total	**100**

Selected Products

Appraisal and assessment software (property appraisal and assessment)
Criminal justice software (court case tracking and management)
Document management and recording software (image storage and retrieval)
Education software
Finance and accounting software
Law enforcement and corrections software (police dispatch records and jail management)
Municipal court software (case management)
Odyssey (case and court management)
Public Records and content management
Tax collections software (tax collections office operations)
Utility billing software (billing and collections)

Selected Services

Information technology and professional services
Maintenance
Outsourced property appraisals for tax jurisdictions

COMPETITORS

CACI International	Official Payments
Constellation Software	Holdings
DynTek	Oracle
HP Enterprise Services	SAP
IBM	SunGard
MAXIMUS	USTI
Manatron	Xerox

HISTORICAL FINANCIALS

Company Type: Public

Income Statement

FYE: December 31

	REVENUE ($ mil.)	NET INCOME ($ mil.)	NET PROFIT MARGIN	EMPLOYEES
12/15	591.0	64.8	11.0%	3,586.0
12/14	493.1	58.9	12.0%	2,856.0
12/13	416.6	39.1	9.4%	2,573.0
12/12	363.3	32.9	9.1%	2,388.0
12/11	309.3	27.5	8.9%	2,091.0
Annual Growth	**17.6%**	**23.9%**	**—**	**14.4%**

2015 Year-End Financials

Debt ratio: 4.8%		No. of shares (mil.): 36.7		
Return on equity: 10.8%		Dividends		
Cash ($ mil.): 33.0		Yield: —		
Current ratio: 0.79		Payout: —		
Long-term debt ($ mil.): 66.0		Market value ($ mil.): 6,410.0		

	STOCK PRICE ($) FY Close	P/E High/Low	PER SHARE ($) Earnings	Dividends	Book Value
12/15	174.32	95 55	1.77	0.00	23.35
12/14	109.44	64 42	1.66	0.00	10.07
12/13	102.13	85 39	1.13	0.00	7.50
12/12	48.44	45 28	1.00	0.00	4.64
12/11	30.11	37 23	0.83	0.00	2.61
Annual Growth 55.1%		—	20.8%	—	73.0%

U.S. Concrete, Inc.

When things get hard U.S. Concrete's products get even harder. The company produces ready-mixed concrete precast concrete and related materials and services for commercial residential and infrastructure construction projects. U.S. Concrete has a fleet of about 1360 mixer trucks and about 145 ready-mixed concrete concrete block and 10 aggregate plants. During 2015 the company produced some 7 million cu. yd. of concrete and more than 4.9 million tons of aggregates; concrete accounts for about 90% of the company's sales. U.S. Concrete concentrates on major markets such as California New Jersey/New York and Texas.Geographic ReachThe company operates principally in Texas California and New Jersey/New York with those markets representing approximately 40% 29% and 26% respectively in 2015. It provides its ready-mixed concrete and concrete-related products from its operations in north and west Texas; northern California; New Jersey; New York; Washington DC; and Oklahoma. In addition U.S. Concrete produces precast concrete products at one plant in Pennsylvania.OperationsU.S. Concrete operates primarily through the two segments of ready-mixed concrete and aggregate products. It has a fleet of over 1360 owned and leased mixer trucks and over 1325 other rolling stock and vehicles. Ready-mixed concrete accounted for about 90% of the revenue in 2015.Sales and MarketingThe company's customers include contractors for commercial and industrial residential street and highway and other public works construction. Concrete product revenue by type of construction activity for 2015 was commercial and industrial (57%); residential (15%); and street highway and other public works (15%).Financial PerformanceU.S. Concrete saw its revenues jump 39% from $704 million in 2014 to a record-setting $975 million in 2015. Its profits also climbed 24% from $21 million in 2014 to $26 million in 2015 mainly due to an income tax benefit it earned. The historic revenues for 2015 were driven by growth in sales of ready-mixed concrete and additional revenue from acquisitions.Mergers and AcquisitionsU.S. Concrete has achieved milestone revenues over the years in part by acquiring smaller operators — part of its continuous growth strategy. During 2015 the company completed eight acquisitions that expanded its operations in its existing markets and into the US Virgin Islands market.In 2016 the company acquired the assets of NYCON Supply

Corp. a ready-mixed concrete producer headquartered in the Long Island City neighborhood of Queens New York. NYCON's premier location widened its footprint to serve the New York City market and expanded its regional customer base.Also in 2016 U.S. Concrete obtained the assets of Greco Brothers Concrete a ready-mixed concrete producer located in Brooklyn New York. The deal is expected to offer new opportunities to service its expanded customer base optimize service efficiencies and enhance raw material purchasing savings.

EXECUTIVES

President CEO and Director, William J. (Bill) Sandbrook, age 58, $786,384 total compensation
VP Marketing and Sales, Wallace H. Johnson, age 68
VP and General Manager Central Concrete Supply Co. Inc., Jeff L. Davis, age 65, $245,400 total compensation
VP and General Manager Ingram Concrete, Jeffrey W. Roberts, age 49, $246,248 total compensation
Regional VP and General Manager Atlantic Region, Kevin R. Kohutek, age 43
VP and General Manager Redi-Mix LLC, Niel L. Poulsen, age 62, $263,250 total compensation
VP General Counsel and Corporate Secretary, Paul M. Jolas, age 51, $286,300 total compensation
SVP and COO, Ronnie Pruitt
SVP and CFO, Joseph C. (Jody) Tusa
Vice President Finance, Laurie (Laur) Cerrito
Chairman, Eugene I. (Gene) Davis, age 61
Auditors: Grant Thornton LLP

LOCATIONS

HQ: U.S. Concrete, Inc.
331 N. Main Street, Euless, TX 76039
Phone: 817 835-4105

PRODUCTS/OPERATIONS

2015 Sales

	% of total
Ready-mixed concrete	90
Aggregates	6
Other products	4
Total	**100**

2015 Sales by Product

	$ in mil.
% of total	
Ready-mixed concrete	90
Aggregates	3
Aggregate distribution	3
Lime	2
Hauling	1
Building materials	1
Other	-
Total	**100**

2015 Sales by Market

	% of total
Residential construction	22
Street & highway construction & paving	20
Commercial & industrial construction	18
Other public works & infrastructure construction	40
Total	**100**

Selected Products

Aggregate
  Granite
  Sand
Concrete Masonry
  Cinder blocks
  Concrete blocks
Building Materials
  Color Products
  Fasteners

Concrete Forms
Hand Tools
Liquid Products
Lumber
Power Tools
Safety Gear and Products
Sand & Rock
Tools & Accessories
Fiber
Waterproofing Material
Ready-Mixed Concrete
  Site Set
  Site Fill
  Site Fresh
  Construct-Lite

COMPETITORS

Ash Grove Cement	Lattimore Materials
Buzzi Unicem USA	Lehigh Hanson
CEMEX	Oldcastle
Eagle Materials	Superior Ready Mix
Holcim (US)	TXI
Lafarge North America	

HISTORICAL FINANCIALS

Company Type: Public

Income Statement

FYE: December 31

	REVENUE ($ mil.)	NET INCOME ($ mil.)	NET PROFIT MARGIN	EMPLOYEES
12/15	974.7	25.5	2.6%	2,700.0
12/14	703.7	20.5	2.9%	2,144.0
12/13	615.0	(20.1)	—	1,786.0
12/12	531.0	(25.7)	—	1,854.0
12/11	495.0	(11.7)	—	1,895.0
Annual Growth 18.5%		—		9.3%

2015 Year-End Financials

Debt ratio: 39.5%		No. of shares (mil.): 14.8	
Return on equity: 19.1%		Dividends	
Cash ($ mil.): 3.9		Yield: —	
Current ratio: 0.95		Payout: —	
Long-term debt ($ mil.): 272.3		Market value ($ mil.): 783.0	

	STOCK PRICE ($) FY Close	P/E High/Low	PER SHARE ($) Earnings	Dividends	Book Value
12/15	52.66	33 14	1.64	0.00	11.09
12/14	28.45	19 14	1.48	0.00	7.26
12/13	22.63	— —	(1.56)	0.00	5.97
12/12	9.05	— —	(2.11)	0.00	6.93
12/11	2.90	— —	(0.97)	0.00	9.02
Annual Growth 106.4%		— —	—	—	5.3%

U.S. Physical Therapy, Inc.

U.S. Physical Therapy (USPh) through its subsidiaries lends a hand to injured workers athletes and others in need of some TLC. With some 560 outpatient clinics in more than 40 states USPh provides physical therapy services for work-related and sports injuries trauma orthopedic conditions osteoarthritis treatment and post-surgical rehabilitation. The clinics operate under a number of local or regional brands including Red River Valley Physical Therapy and Pioneer Physical Therapy.

USPh also operates 22 physical therapy facilities for third parties including physician groups and hospitals.OperationsMost of USPh's clinics are joint ventures in which the company owns a majority stake and the licensed therapists/clinic managers own a minority stake. Other facilities are wholly owned by the company but are operated through profit-sharing agreements with physical therapists. The company also manages a handful of physician-owned and hospital-owned clinics on a contract basis.USPh relies on its therapist-managers to maintain relationships with local physicians who refer patients to the clinics. Services are paid for by commercial health insurance managed care programs Medicare workers' compensation insurance or proceeds from personal injury cases.Geographic ReachUSPh has clinics in 42 states. The company has a significant presence in Georgia Maryland Michigan Pennsylvania Tennessee Texas Virginia Washington and Wisconsin.Sales and MarketingThe company markets its activities to orthopedic surgeons neurosurgeons podiatrists occupational medicine physicians and other physicians.In 2015 commercial health insurance accounted for 28% of USPh's net patient revenue. This was followed by Medicare and Medicaid (25% of net patient revenue) managed care programs (23%) workers' compensation (18%) and other (6%).Financial PerformanceRevenues for USPh have continued to increase over the years as the company has expanded its network of clinics. In 2015 revenues increased 9% to $331 million due to an increase in patient visits (3 million up from 2.8 million in 2014) at both new and mature clinics. The acquisition of additional clinics also boosted revenues.Net income which had declined in 2012 and 2013 has risen over the past couple of years. In 2015 it increased 7% to $22 million thanks to the higher revenue but this was partially offset by an increase in clinic operating expenses. Cash flow from operations had been trending upward until 2015 when it fell 9% to $41 million. This decline was primarily due to a decrease in accounts payable and accrued expenses as well as an increase in cash used in accounts receivable.StrategyUSPh grows by developing and acquiring new clinics throughout the US. In 2015 the company acquired a total of 21 clinics for some $21 million. It plans to continue buying and developing additional facilities as well as opening satellite clinics in suitable locations.Along with developing new partnerships and opening new clinics USPh seeks to increase its market share by upping its patient volume through marketing campaigns and by adding new services. It also works to recruit and retain physical therapists that have strong relationships with referring physicians by offering competitive salaries and opportunities to own a stake in or share profits in the clinics where they work.Mergers and AcquisitionsIn 2016 USPh acquired a 55% stake in an eight-clinic physical therapy practice for $14 million. It also acquired a 60% stake in a 12-clinical group for $11.5 million. Early the following year the company bought a 70% stake in a 17-clinic physical therapy practice for $11.4 million.

EXECUTIVES

Vice President of Administrati, Jeff (Jeffy) Todes
CFO, Lawrance W. (Larry) McAfee, age 61, $409,577 total compensation
CEO, Christopher J. (Chris) Reading, age 52, $558,730 total compensation
COO, Glenn McDowell, age 60, $363,942 total compensation
Vice President Of Marketing, Bill Johnston

Vice President, Darryl Gotwalt
Chairman, Jerald L. Pullins, age 74
Auditors: Grant Thornton LLP

LOCATIONS

HQ: U.S. Physical Therapy, Inc.
1300 West Sam Houston Parkway South, Suite 300, Houston, TX 77042
Phone: 713 297-7000
Web: www.corporate.usph.com

PRODUCTS/OPERATIONS

2015 Sales

	$ mil.	% of total
Patient revenue		
Commercial insurance	91.8	28
Medicare/Medicaid	79.3	24
Managed care	73.5	22
Workers' compensation	60.1	18
Other patient revenue	19.5	6
Other	7.0	2
Total	**331.3**	**100**

COMPETITORS

Concentra
Five Star Quality Care
Physiotherapy Associates
RehabCare
Select Medical
Spaulding Rehabilitation Hospital
U.S. HealthWorks

HISTORICAL FINANCIALS

Company Type: Public

Income Statement

				FYE: December 31
	REVENUE ($ mil.)	NET INCOME ($ mil.)	NET PROFIT MARGIN	EMPLOYEES
12/15	331.3	22.2	6.7%	3,400.0
12/14	305.0	20.8	6.8%	3,151.0
12/13	264.0	12.7	4.8%	2,805.0
12/12	252.0	17.9	7.1%	2,677.0
12/11	237.0	20.9	8.8%	2,522.0
Annual Growth	**8.7%**	**1.5%**	**—**	**7.8%**

2015 Year-End Financials

Debt ratio: 17.5%
Return on equity: 14.4%
Cash ($ mil.): 15.7
Current ratio: 3.17
Long-term debt ($ mil.): 48.3
No. of shares (mil.): 12.4
Dividends
Yield: 1.1%
Payout: 36.1%
Market value ($ mil.): 667.0

	STOCK PRICE ($) FY Close	P/E High/Low	PER SHARE ($) Earnings	Dividends	Book Value
12/15	53.68	32 22	1.77	0.60	13.11
12/14	41.96	27 19	1.62	0.48	11.92
12/13	35.26	34 22	1.05	0.80	10.60
12/12	27.54	18 12	1.51	0.76	9.85
12/11	19.68	15 9	1.75	0.32	9.15
Annual Growth	**28.5%**	**— —**	**0.3%**	**17.0%**	**9.4%**

Ubiquiti Networks Inc

Auditors: KPMG LLP

LOCATIONS

HQ: Ubiquiti Networks Inc
2580 Orchard Parkway, San Jose, CA 95131
Phone: 408 942-3085
Web: www.ubnt.com

HISTORICAL FINANCIALS

Company Type: Public

Income Statement

				FYE: June 30
	REVENUE ($ mil.)	NET INCOME ($ mil.)	NET PROFIT MARGIN	EMPLOYEES
06/16	666.4	213.6	32.1%	537.0
06/15	595.9	129.6	21.8%	435.0
06/14	572.4	176.9	30.9%	312.0
06/13	320.8	80.4	25.1%	183.0
06/12	353.5	102.5	29.0%	150.0
Annual Growth	**17.2%**	**20.1%**	**—**	**37.6%**

2016 Year-End Financials

Debt ratio: 27.2%
Return on equity: 49.4%
Cash ($ mil.): 551.0
Current ratio: 8.01
Long-term debt ($ mil.): 192.2
No. of shares (mil.): 81.6
Dividends
Yield: —
Payout: —
Market value ($ mil.): 3,157.0

	STOCK PRICE ($) FY Close	P/E High/Low	PER SHARE ($) Earnings	Dividends	Book Value
06/16	38.66	16 11	2.49	0.00	5.39
06/15	31.92	34 18	1.45	0.17	4.83
06/14	45.19	28 9	1.97	0.00	3.80
06/13	17.54	23 9	0.89	0.18	1.69
06/12	14.25	— —	(0.12)	0.00	1.42
Annual Growth	**28.3%**	**— —**	**—**	**—**	**39.5%**

Ultimate Software Group, Inc.

The Ultimate Software Group (USG) helps manage a company's ultimate resource: its employees. Customers employ its cloud-based UltiPro software suite to manage hiring human resources compliance benefits enrollment payroll appraisals and time and attendance. Primarily serving clients in the US the company offers UltiPro Enterprise for businesses with more than 1000 employees and UltiPro Workplace for those with fewer than 1000 employees. Communications finance health care retail technology and transportation are the industries it targets. Founded in 1990 USG has more than 19 million people records in its HCM (human capital management) cloud.

Operations

USG's recurring revenues account for 83% of the company's total with the rest coming from services. Subscription revenues from the company's cloud offering and customer support and maintenance revenues comprise recurring revenue. Services revenue comes from consulting done to implement USG's software.

Geographic Reach

Florida-based USG operates data centers in Arizona Georgia and near Toronto Canada.

Sales and Marketing

The company markets its software through direct sales teams organized by geographic region. It boasts some 2800 customers across many industries including manufacturing food services sports technology finance and others. Clients include Adobe Systems Major League Baseball and The

Pep Boys. Sales and marketing expenses rose 25% in 2014 versus 2013 to nearly $117 million.

Financial Performance

USG has enjoyed a decade of consistent sales growth. In 2014 it reported revenue of about $506 million up 23% versus 2013 (and that was on top of 23% growth from 2012 to 2013). Net income increased 75% for the second year in a row to reach $44.7 million in 2014 from $25.5 million in 2013. Recurring revenues increased 25% year over year primarily due to an increase in cloud revenues partially offset by a decrease in maintenance revenues. Services revenue rose 15%. Cash flow from operations rose to $80.6 million from $74.2 million in 2013.

Strategy

In the highly competitive market for human capital management (HCM) software USG focuses on product enhancements (including add-ons) and customer satisfaction. The company is working to expand its offering to support a multinational client base. New capabilities for global HCM include the launch of 29 additional country localizations (including Brazil China and Korea) providing support for locally compliant payroll and relevant employee details while also enabling worldwide oversight and reporting capabilities for corporate leadership. The company's software is available in 10 languages and 35 countries.

Alliances are another important element of the people management company's strategy. In February 2014 USG announced that it is integrating LinkedIn and its UltiPro Recruiting cloud product. Currently Ultimate Software offers customers seamless integration between LinkedIn and UltiPro Recruiting with additional integration between the two platforms planned for later in 2014.

Mergers and Acquisitions

USG was quiet on the acquisition front in 2014 but in November 2013 it bought certain assets of Georgia-based Accel HR. That added Accel's outsourcing solutions and services for middle to large market companies ranging from 500 to more than 25000 employees to USG's portfolio. In October it purchased EmployTouch Inc. a developer of workforce management hardware and software products based in Toronto Canada.

EXECUTIVES

Senior Vice President and Chief Enterprise Sales Officer, Greg (Greggy) Swick
EVP CFO and Treasurer, Mitchell K. (Mitch) Dauerman, age 58, $525,000 total compensation
Chairman President and CEO, Scott Scherr, age 63, $700,000 total compensation
Vice Chairman, Marc D. Scherr, age 58, $625,000 total compensation
SVP and Chief Technology Officer, Adam Rogers, age 41, $571,000 total compensation
SVP Marketing, Jody Kaminsky, age 41
Vice President of Finance, Felecia Alvaro
Vice President Special Operations, Paul (Pauly) Gonzalez
Vice President Infrastructure Operations and Delivery, John (Jack) Machado
Vice President Enterprise Pre Sales, Wendy Wozniak
Vice President Product Management, Pat Pickren
Vice President Managed Services, Brenda (Bren) Jennings
GM Vice President Business Unit Manager, Lee McDermott
Vice President Sales Midwest Division, Rick Torrence
Vice President, Michael (Mel) Schaberl
Vice President Marketing, Diane (Di) Alonso

Vice President Finance, Felicia Alvaro
Vice President Market Strategy, Martin Hartshorne
Vice President Project Management, Terry L (Terr) Hudak
Vice President Client Services, Brenda Jennings
Vice President User Experience, Patanjali Venkatacharya
Vice President IT, Kelvin Tamayo Tamayo
Vice President of PR and Communications, Darlene (Darl) Marcroft
Vice President Chief Info Officer, William (Bill) Hicks
Senior Vice President General Counsel, Robert (Bob) Manne
Vice President Software Engineering at ULTIMATE Software GROUP, Stephen (Steve) Reid
Vice President, Dale (Dal) Baker
Senior Vice President, Greg (Greggy) Mcmullen
Vice President Governance Risk and Compliance, Robert (Bob) Vetter
Auditors: KPMG LLP

LOCATIONS

HQ: Ultimate Software Group, Inc.
2000 Ultimate Way, Weston, FL 33326
Phone: 954 331-7000
Web: www.ultimatesoftware.com

PRODUCTS/OPERATIONS

2014 Sales

	$ mil.	% of total
Recurring	419.2	83
Services	86.2	17
Licenses	0.5	-
Total	**505.9**	**100**

COMPETITORS

ADP	Peoplefluent
Ceridian	SAP
Kronos	SPM Global Services
Oracle	Sage Software
Paychex	Workday Inc.
Paylocity	

HISTORICAL FINANCIALS

Company Type: Public

Income Statement

FYE: December 31

	REVENUE ($ mil.)	NET INCOME ($ mil.)	NET PROFIT MARGIN	EMPLOYEES
12/15	618.0	22.7	3.7%	2,880.0
12/14	505.9	44.7	8.8%	2,354.0
12/13	410.4	25.5	6.2%	1,913.0
12/12	332.2	14.6	4.4%	1,614.0
12/11	269.2	4.2	1.6%	1,328.0
Annual Growth	23.1%	51.7%	—	21.4%

2015 Year-End Financials

Debt ratio: 0.5%	No. of shares (mil.): 28.7
Return on equity: 7.4%	Dividends
Cash ($ mil.): 109.3	Yield: —
Current ratio: 1.09	Payout: —
Long-term debt ($ mil.): 3.6	Market value ($ mil.): 5,629.0

	STOCK PRICE ($) FY Close	P/E High/Low		PER SHARE ($) Earnings	Dividends	Book Value
12/15	195.51	267 177		0.76	0.00	11.60
12/14	146.82	108 71		1.52	0.00	9.53
12/13	153.22	173 101		0.88	0.00	6.70
12/12	94.41	191 117		0.52	0.00	4.19
12/11	65.12	412 267		0.15	0.00	3.26
Annual Growth	31.6%	— —		50.0%	—	37.3%

Umpqua Holdings Corp

Umpqua Holdings thinks of itself not so much as a bank but rather a retailer that sells financial products. Consequently many of the company's 380-plus Umpqua Bank "stores" in northern California northern Nevada Idaho Oregon and Washington feature coffee bars and computer cafes. While customers sip Umpqua-branded coffee pay bills online attend a financial seminar catch a poetry reading or check out wares from local merchants staff members pitch deposit accounts mortgages loans life insurance investments and more. Subsidiary Umpqua Investments (formerly Strand Atkinson Williams & York) provides retail brokerage services through more than a dozen locations mostly inside Umpqua Bank branches.

Operations

Umpqua operates two business segments: Community Banking which made up 79% of the company's total revenue during 2015 and provides traditional banking services as well as wealth management and private banking services for wealthier individuals; and Home Lending (21% of revenue) which originates and sells residential mortgage loans. The company makes more than 75% of its revenue from interest income. About 72% of its revenue came from loan interest (including fees) during 2015 with another 5% coming from interest on investment securities. The rest of its revenue came from residential mortgage banking revenue (9% of revenue) deposit account service charges (5%) brokerage revenue (2%) and other miscellaneous income streams.

Geographic Reach

Oregon-based Umpqua Bank has branches in Idaho Washington Oregon California and Northern Nevada. Umpqua Investments has offices in Portland Lake Oswego and Medford Oregon as well as Santa Rosa California.Sales and MarketingUmpqua Holdings promotes its brand through customer-facing channels public relations social media and community-based events. It spent $11.4 million on marketing to promote its brand during 2015 up from $9.5 million and $6.1 million in 2014 and 2013 respectively.

Financial Performance

The bank's annual revenues have doubled since 2011 as its loan and lease assets have tripled to $16.85 billion which has resulted in strong interest income growth. Exceptional revenue growth and effective cost controls have helped the bank's net income triple over the same period.Umpqua Holdings' revenue jumped 20% to $1.21 billion during 2015 mostly as its earning assets (including loans investments and loans held for sale) swelled by 20% which led to higher interest income. The bank's non-interest income also rose 52% for the year mostly thanks to the 2014 acquisition of Sterling Financial with residential mortgage banking revenue brokerage commissions and deposit service charges all growing during the year.Strong revenue growth in 2015 drove the bank's net income up 51% to $222.54 million for the year. Umpqua's operating cash levels climbed 5% to $376.74 million as earnings rose.

Strategy

Umpqua Bank's primary mission is to become the top community-oriented financial services firm in the Western US by strategically acquiring banks in new markets and building its brand by offering unique personal experience for customers entering its "store" branches. Its mid-2014 acquisition of Sterling Financial —the largest ever acquisition in

Umpqua's history —successfully extended the bank's presence in Southern California Eastern Washington Eastern Oregon and Idaho.The bank differentiates itself by encouraging clients to come into its stores instead of using impersonal interfaces like ATMs and electronic banking more cost-effective methods preferred by many of its competitors. The bank's "Next Generation" stores feature interactive touch-screen walls fresh fruit and cold drinks. It hopes the comfortable environment will inspire customers to use more of the bank's financial services.Hoping to build upon its one-of-a-kind branch experiences Umpqua Bank in 2015 launched its Silicon Valley-based Pivotus Ventures Inc subsidiary to explore disruptive new bank technologies.

In 2016 Umpqua launched its corporate banking division which is dedicated to providing companies with access to such offerings as treasury management international banking debt capital markets and others. Mergers and AcquisitionsIn April 2014 Umpqua Bank acquired $10-billion-in-assets Sterling Financial Corp. headquartered in Spokane Washington. The largest merger in Umpqua's history created the West Coast's largest community bank with some $22 billion in assets and 394 stores across five states. The Sterling branches were rebranded as part of the $1.9 billion deal.Company BackgroundTraditionally consumer focused Umpqua Bank established a business banking division in 2011 to court small and mid-sized business clients. That year it pursued deposit growth assembled new lending teams and added new stores in key metropolitan areas like Portland Oregon; Seattle; San Francisco; and California's Silicon Valley.

Umpqua Holdings established a wealth management division in 2009 and launched a trust services group the following year. It provided asset management services through an agreement with independent firm Ferguson Wellman Capital Management.

EXECUTIVES

Evp Wealth Management Umpqua Holdings And Umpqua Bank, Kelly Johnson

EVP Creative Strategies Group Umpqua Bank, Lani Hayward, age 49

EVP and Chief Lending Officer Umpqua Holdings Corp and Umpqua Bank, David F. (Dave) Shotwell, age 57

EVP CFO and Principal Financial Officer Umpqua Holdings and Umpqua Bank, Ronald L. (Ron) Farnsworth, age 46, $425,000 total compensation

EVP Treasurer and Principal Accounting Officer Umpqua Holdings and Umpqua Bank, Neal T. McLaughlin, age 48

EVP Corporate Communications Umpqua Bank, Eve Callahan, age 42

President CEO and Director, Cort O'Haver, age 53, $565,000 total compensation

EVP and Chief Auditor Umpqua Bank, Joel Brandenburg, age 53

EVP Enterprise Risk Management Umpqua Holdings Corp and Umpqua Bank, Gary F. Neal, age 61

EVP Associate Relations Umpqua Holdings Corp and Umpqua Bank, Sheri T. Burns, age 48

EVP Cultural Enhancement and Government Relations Umpqua Bank, Marty J. Dickinson, age 46

EVP General Counsel and Corporate Secretary Umpqua Holdings Corp and Umpqua Bank, Andrew H. Ognall, age 44, $300,000 total compensation

Executive Vice President and Chief Credit Officer of the Company and the Bank, Mark (Marky) Wardlow

Executive Vice President of Cultural Enhancement of Umpqua, Barbara (Barb) Baker

Executive Vice President Strategic Initiatives of Umpqua and Umpqua Bank, Daniel (Dan) Sullivan

Vice President Of Benefits, Jennifer Hollenbeck

Assistant Vice President Trend Analyst, Joan Salvatore

Senior Vice President Data Processing, Bo (Bob) Harrison

Vice President Rewards and Recognition, Sandy (Sandra) Hunt

Vice President eBanking Product Manager, Jim Averna

Chairman, Raymond P. (Ray) Davis, age 67

Vice Chairman, Bryan L. Timm, age 52

Auditors: Moss Adams LLP

LOCATIONS

HQ: Umpqua Holdings Corp
One S.W. Columbia Street, Suite 1200, Portland, OR 97258
Phone: 503 727-4100
Web: www.umpquaholdingscorp.com

PRODUCTS/OPERATIONS

2015 Sales

	$ mil.	% of total
Interest		
Interest and fees on loans and leases	869.4	72
TaxableInterest and dividends investment securities	58.2	5
Other	2.2	-
Non-interest		
Mortgage banking	124.7	9
Service charges on deposit accounts	59.7	5
Brokerage	18.5	2
Gain on loan sales net	22.4	2
BOLI income	8.4	1
Gain on investment securities net	2.9	-
Other	46.3	4
Adjustments	(7.2)	-
Total	**1,205.5**	**100**

2015 Sales

	$ mil.	% of total
Community Banking	954.7	79
Home Lending	250.8	21
Total	**1,205.5**	**100**

COMPETITORS

Bank of America	KeyCorp
Bank of the West	U.S. Bancorp
Banner Corp	Washington Federal
Cascade Bancorp	Wells Fargo
Columbia Banking	

HISTORICAL FINANCIALS

Company Type: Public

Income Statement

FYE: December 31

	ASSETS ($ mil.)	NET INCOME ($ mil.)	INCOME AS % OF ASSETS	EMPLOYEES
12/15	23,387.2	222.5	1.0%	4,491.0
12/14	22,613.2	147.5	0.7%	4,569.0
12/13	11,636.1	98.3	0.8%	2,490.0
12/12	11,795.4	101.8	0.9%	2,376.0
12/11	11,563.3	74.5	0.6%	2,255.0
Annual Growth	**19.3%**	**31.5%**	**—**	**18.8%**

Return on assets: 0.9%   Dividends
Return on equity: 5.8%   Yield: 3.9%
Long-term debt ($ mil.): —   Payout: 64.5%
No. of shares (mil.): 220.1   Market value ($ mil.): 3,501.0
Sales ($ mil): 1,205.5

	STOCK PRICE ($) FY Close	P/E High/Low		PER SHARE ($) Earnings	Dividends	Book Value
12/15	15.90	19	15	1.01	0.62	17.48
12/14	17.01	24	20	0.78	0.60	17.17
12/13	19.14	22	14	0.87	0.60	15.43
12/12	11.79	15	13	0.90	0.34	15.41
12/11	12.39	20	12	0.65	0.24	14.91
Annual Growth	**6.4%**	**—**	**—**	**11.6%**	**26.8%**	**4.1%**

Union Bankshares Corp (New)

Union Bankshares (formerly Union First Market Bankshares) is the holding company for Union Bank & Trust which operates approximately 100 branches in central northern and coastal portions of Virginia. The bank offers standard services such as checking and savings accounts credit cards and certificates of deposit. Union Bank & Trust maintains a loan portfolio heavily weighted towards real estate: Commercial real estate loans make up more than 30% while one- to four-family residential mortgages and construction loans account for approximately 15% and 20% respectively. The bank also originates personal and business loans.Other financial services are provided through subsidiaries Union Investment Services (brokerage and investment advisory services through an arrangement with Raymond James Financial) Union Insurance Group (long-term care and business owner coverage) and Union Mortgage Group which provides mortgage brokerage services from about 15 offices.Union Bankshares primarily operates in Virginia. Its Union Mortgage Group provides mortgage brokerage services from offices in Virginia Maryland and the Carolinas. Union Mortgage is additionally licensed to operate in states in the Mid-Atlantic the Southeast and in Washington DC.The company's profits have risen dramatically due to the 2010 acquisition of First Market Bank. In 2010 profits nearly tripled (to $22.9 million from the 2009 earnings of $8.4 million) while in 2011 they rose a further 33% to $30.5 million. The acquisition led to an increase in net interest income a primary contributor to the company's growth. Also in 2011 Union Bankshares lowered its provision for loan losses as its loan portfolio continued to improve post-recession. Expenses that year were lower than in 2010 when the acquisition closed. Slightly offsetting the improvements mortgage earnings fell by nearly half in 2011 due to the stagnant residential mortgage market. Although profits have risen revenues have remained relatively flat falling 2% in 2011 to $232.9 million.Union Bankshares' strategy for growth includes buying other banks as well as opening new branches of its own. Then named Union Bank and Trust the company acquired First Market Bank in 2010 to nearly double its branch total. (The holding company then also added "First Market" to its name and moved its headquarters to Richmond.) The company has also grown through de novo branching and through purchases of branches and related companies. It acquired an existing branch in Harrisonburg plus some $74 million in loan assets from NewBridge Bank in 2011.Also that year the bank opened up seven new locations inside Martin's grocery stores where it already had more than 20 in-store branches. In the past couple of years the company has consolidated its bank subsidiaries creating operating efficiencies as well as a stronger unified brand.Virginia-based specialty insurer Markel Corporation owns 14% of Union Bankshares.

EXECUTIVES

Executive Vice President and Director Operations and Information Technology, Rex A Hockemeyer
EVP and Director of Mortgage and Wealth Management, Jeffrey W. Farrar, age 55
EVP Union Bankshares and Chief Retail Officer Union Bank & Trust, Elizabeth M. Bentley, age 55, $268,491 total compensation
EVP and Chief Risk Officer, David G. (Dave) Bilko, age 56
President and CEO Union Bankshares Corporation and Union Bank & Trust, John C. Asbury, age 51
EVP and CFO, Robert M. (Rob) Gorman, age 57, $351,167 total compensation
EVP Union Bankshares and Chief Banking Officer Union Bank & Trust, D. Anthony (Tony) Peay, age 56, $348,997 total compensation
EVP and CIO, M. Dean Brown, age 51, $259,625 total compensation
SVP and Chief Marketing Officer, L. Duane Smith, age 49
EVP and Chief Human Resource Officer, Loreen A. LaGatta, age 47
Vice President and Manager Market, Joseph (Jo) Yednock
Executive Vice President General Counsel Corporate Secretary, Janis Orfe
Senior Vice President Commercial Banker, Morfit Debra
Assistant Vice President In House Counsel, Christine Wilcox
Senior Vice President And Branch Manager, Denise (Denny) Togger
Vice President and Operations and Human Resources, Brenda (Bren) Cooper
Vice President Senior Commercial Banker, Jeff (Jeffy) Mead
Senior Vice President, Erik (Rik) Muller
Vice President and Senior Branch Manager, Sherry (Sherr) Cillo
Vice President, NORFLEET STALLINGS
Vice President Corporate Security Officer, Chad Currie
Senior Vice President and Director of Bank Operations, Barbara (Barb) Fischer
Vice Chairman Union Bankshares Corporation and Union Bank & Trust, G. William (Billy) Beale, age 66
Chairman, Raymond D. (Ray) Smoot, age 69
Auditors: Ernst & Young LLP

LOCATIONS

HQ: Union Bankshares Corp (New)
1051 East Cary Street, Suite 1200, Richmond, VA 23219
Phone: 804 633-5031
Web: www.bankatunion.com

PRODUCTS/OPERATIONS

2015 Sales

	$ mil.	% of total
Interest		
Loans including fees	247.5	72
Other	29.3	9
Noninterest		
Other service charges commission and fees	15.6	5
Service charges on deposit accounts	18.9	5
others	30.8	9
Adjustments	(0.3)	-
Total	**341.8**	**100**

Selected Subsidiaries

Union First Market Bank
Union Insurance Group LLC
Union Investment Services Inc.
Union Mortgage Group Inc.

COMPETITORS

BB&T	PNC Financial
Bank of America	Regions Financial
C&F Financial	SunTrust
Eastern Virginia	TowneBank
Bankshares	Wells Fargo
JPMorgan Chase	

HISTORICAL FINANCIALS

Company Type: Public

Income Statement
FYE: December 31

	ASSETS ($ mil.)	NET INCOME ($ mil.)	INCOME AS % OF ASSETS	EMPLOYEES
12/15	7,693.2	67.0	0.9%	1,422.0
12/14	7,359.1	52.5	0.7%	1,471.0
12/13	4,176.5	34.5	0.8%	1,025.0
12/12	4,095.8	35.4	0.9%	1,044.0
12/11	3,907.0	30.4	0.8%	1,045.0
Annual Growth	**18.5%**	**21.8%**	**—**	**8.0%**

2015 Year-End Financials

Return on assets: 0.8%
Return on equity: 6.8%
Long-term debt ($ mil.): —
No. of shares (mil.): 44.7
Sales ($ mil): 341.7
Dividends
Yield: 2.6%
Payout: 45.6%
Market value ($ mil.): 1,130.0

	STOCK PRICE ($) FY Close	P/E High/Low	PER SHARE ($) Earnings	Dividends	Book Value
12/15	25.24	18 13	1.49	0.68	22.23
12/14	24.08	23 19	1.14	0.58	21.66
12/13	24.81	19 11	1.38	0.54	17.55
12/12	15.77	12 10	1.37	0.37	17.25
12/11	13.29	14 9	1.07	0.28	16.13
Annual Growth	**17.4%**	**— —**	**8.6%**	**24.8%**	**8.3%**

Uniroyal Global Engineered Products Inc

Invisa develops and manufactures sensors used to ensure safety and security. The company's SmartGate safety sensors are used in traffic and parking control fence and gate access and industrial automation safety applications. The sensors are meant to keep doors and gates from closing on people or objects. Invisa's InvisaShield technology is designed to detect the presence of intruders in a monitored zone such as the area around a museum exhibit. Customer Magnetic Automation Corp. a manufacturer of barrier gates accounts for nearly 30% of product sales.

Invisa ran into a cash crunch in April 2005 and was forced to terminate nearly all of its employees; however the company resumed normal operations in June and shored up its finances with a new investment in September.

Chairman Stephen Michael owns about 20% of Invisa.

EXECUTIVES

Acting President COO CFO Treasurer and Director, Edmund C. King, age 82, $120,000 total compensation
Auditors: Frazier & Deeter, LLC

LOCATIONS

HQ: Uniroyal Global Engineered Products Inc
1800 2nd Street, Suite 970, Sarasota, FL 34236
Phone: 941 906-8580

COMPETITORS

Bosch
Honeywell ACS
Ingersoll-Rand Security Technologies
Stanley Security Solutions
Tyco Fire & Security

HISTORICAL FINANCIALS

Company Type: Public

Income Statement
FYE: January 3

	REVENUE ($ mil.)	NET INCOME ($ mil.)	NET PROFIT MARGIN	EMPLOYEES
01/16*	99.7	7.7	7.8%	415.0
12/14	98.3	4.6	4.7%	410.0
12/13	0.0	(0.3)	—	1.0
12/12	0.0	(0.2)	—	1.0
12/11	0.1	(0.3)	—	1.0
Annual Growth	**463.7%**	**—**	**—**	**351.3%**

*Fiscal year change

2016 Year-End Financials

Debt ratio: 47.9%
Return on equity: 62.1%
Cash ($ mil.): 1.9
Current ratio: 1.22
Long-term debt ($ mil.): 10.2
No. of shares (mil.): 18.8
Dividends
Yield: —
Payout: —
Market value ($ mil.): 60.0

	STOCK PRICE ($) FY Close	P/E High/Low	PER SHARE ($) Earnings	Dividends	Book Value
01/16*	3.20	11 5	0.26	0.00	0.76
12/14	2.30	8 2	0.22	0.00	0.73
12/13	0.70	— —	(0.03)	0.00	(0.09)
12/12	0.27	— —	(0.02)	0.00	(0.07)
12/11	0.30	— —	(0.02)	0.00	(0.06)
Annual Growth	**80.7%**				

*Fiscal year change

United Financial Bancorp Inc (New)

EXECUTIVES

Secretary Rockville Financial and Rockville Bank, Judy L. Keppner, age 57

SVP Human Resources and Organizational Development Rockville Bank, Richard J. Trachimowicz, age 61, $138,531 total compensation

SVP and CFO Rockville Financial SVP and CFO Rockville Bank, John T. Lund, age 45

President and CEO; President and CEO Rockville Bank, William H. W. Crawford IV

Senior Vice President Investor Relations, Marliese Shaw

Director, William J. (Bill) McGurk, age 74

Director, Michael A. Bars, age 60

Director, C. Perry Chilberg, age 67

Director, David A. Engelson, age 72

Director, Raymond H. Lefurge Jr., age 66

Director, Stuart E. Magdefrau, age 61

Director, Rosemarie Novello Papa, age 71

Director, Richard M. Tkacz, age 63

Auditors: Wolf & Company, P.C.

LOCATIONS

HQ: United Financial Bancorp Inc (New)
45 Glastonbury Boulevard, Glastonbury, CT 06033
Phone: 860 291-3600
Web: www.bankatunited.com

COMPETITORS

Bank of America	RBS Citizens Financial
Citibank	Group
Liberty Bank	SI Financial
Naugatuck Valley	Sovereign Bank
Financial	TD Bank USA
New England Bancshares	United Financial
PSB Holdings Inc.	Bancorp
People's United	Webster Financial
Financial	Westfield Financial

HISTORICAL FINANCIALS

Company Type: Public

Income Statement

FYE: December 31

	ASSETS ($ mil.)	NET INCOME ($ mil.)	INCOME AS % OF ASSETS	EMPLOYEES
12/15	6,228.5	49.6	0.8%	732.0
12/14	5,476.8	6.7	0.1%	725.0
12/13	2,301.6	14.2	0.6%	358.0
12/12	1,998.8	15.8	0.8%	346.0
12/11	1,749.8	7.0	0.4%	281.0
Annual Growth	37.4%	62.7%	—	27.0%

2015 Year-End Financials

Return on assets: 0.8%	Dividends
Return on equity: 8.0%	Yield: 3.5%
Long-term debt ($ mil.): —	Payout: 55.4%
No. of shares (mil.): 49.9	Market value ($ mil.): 643.0
Sales ($ mil): 228.8	

	STOCK PRICE ($) FY Close	P/E High/Low		PER SHARE ($) Earnings	Dividends	Book Value
12/15	12.88	14	12	1.00	0.46	12.53
12/14	14.36	91	76	0.16	0.40	12.16
12/13	14.21	28	23	0.54	0.40	11.53
12/12	12.90	24	18	0.56	0.52	11.39
12/11	10.36	43	36	0.25	0.21	11.30
Annual Growth	5.6%	—	—	41.4%	22.4%	2.6%

United Fire Group, Inc.

The United Fire Group companies join together to offer a unified range of property/casualty and life insurance products. The group operates through its United Fire & Casualty subsidiary which in turn holds entities that carry a variety of property/casualty offerings including fidelity and surety bonds and fire auto employee liability homeowners and workers' compensation lines. More than 1300 independent agencies in some 45 states sell its property/casualty products to businesses and individuals. The United Life division of United Fire & Casualty sells life annuity and credit life products to individuals and groups through some 950 independent agents in more than 30 states.

Geographic Reach

The company markets its products from its headquarters in Iowa and from four regional offices in California Colorado New Jersey and Texas and it operates primarily in adjacent areas of the midwestern southern and western US.

Operations

United Fire's property/casualty insurance offerings account for more than 90% of its annual insurance premiums with a majority of those policies being written to commercial group customers. The company also offers certain personal policies to individual customers.

Sales and Marketing

In order to increase policy placement in its existing markets United Fire offers profit-sharing and commission programs to its independent agents. It also seeks to provide modern technological tools to best serve both its agents and its policyholders.

Financial Performance

The company's revenue has been growing year-over-year. It reported revenue of $877 million in fiscal 2013 up from $813.2 million in revenue for fiscal 2012.

Net income also increased in fiscal 2013 compared to the prior year. The company netted $76 million in fiscal 2013 after reporting net income of $40 million in fiscal 2012.

United Fire's cash flow decreased by about $11 million in fiscal 2013 compared to the previous fiscal period.

Strategy

United Fire looks to expand into new markets to reduce the risk potential in its concentrated areas of operation.

EXECUTIVES

VP General Counsel and Secretary, Neal R. Scharmer, age 60, $250,000 total compensation

COO, Michael T. Wilkins, age 53, $388,600 total compensation

VP and Chief Investment Officer, Barrie W. Ernst, age 62, $305,000 total compensation

President and CEO, Randy A. Ramlo, age 55, $595,000 total compensation

VP and Chief Claims Officer, David E. Conner, age 58

CFO, Dawn M. Jaffray, age 51

VP Information Services, Scott A. Minkel, age 55

VP Corporate Marketing, Colleen R. Sova, age 63

Assistant Vice President Midwest Regional Office, Corey J. Ruehle

VP and COO United Life Insurance Company, Michael J. Sheeley

CTO, Brian Frese

Vice President Of Accounting, Sue (Susie) Haupert

Vice President, Douglas Penn

Vice President Human Resources, Timothy Spain

Vice President, Debbie (Deb) Johnstone

Assistant Vice President West Coast Regional Claims Manager, Mary Bianco

Assistant Vice President and Great Lakes Reg. Marketing Manager, Patrick P (Paddy) Kane

Vice Chairman, John A. Rife, age 74

Chairman, Jack B. Evans, age 68

Auditors: Ernst & Young LLP

LOCATIONS

HQ: United Fire Group, Inc.
118 Second Avenue S.E., Cedar Rapids, IA 52401
Phone: 319 399-5700
Web: www.unitedfiregroup.com

PRODUCTS/OPERATIONS

Selected Subsidiaries

United Fire & Casualty Company
Addison Insurance Company
American Indemnity Financial Corporation
Texas General Indemnity Company
Lafayette Insurance Company
Mercer Insurance Group Inc.
Financial Pacific Insurance Company
Mercer Insurance Company
Franklin Insurance Company
Mercer Insurance Company of New Jersey Inc.
United Fire & Indemnity Company
United Fire Lloyds
United Life Insurance Company

COMPETITORS

AIG	Hanover Insurance
Allstate	John Hancock Financial
American Family	Services
Insurance	Liberty Mutual
American Financial	MassMutual
Group	Progressive
Arrowpoint Capital	Corporation
Corp.	Prudential
CNA Surety	State Farm
Chubb Limited	The Hartford
Erie Indemnity	Travelers Companies
Farmers Group	White Mountains
GEICO	Insurance Group

HISTORICAL FINANCIALS

Company Type: Public

Income Statement

FYE: December 31

	ASSETS ($ mil.)	NET INCOME ($ mil.)	INCOME AS % OF ASSETS	EMPLOYEES
12/15	3,890.3	89.1	2.3%	1,070.0
12/14	3,856.6	59.1	1.5%	981.0
12/13	3,720.6	76.1	2.0%	943.0
12/12	3,694.6	40.2	1.1%	909.0
12/11	3,618.9	0.0	0.0%	894.0
Annual Growth	1.8%	848.8%	—	4.6%

2015 Year-End Financials

Return on assets: 2.3%
Return on equity: 10.5%
Long-term debt ($ mil.): —
No. of shares (mil.): 25.1
Sales ($ mil): 1,034.9

Dividends
Yield: 2.2%
Payout: 23.4%
Market value ($ mil.): 964.0

	STOCK PRICE ($) FY Close	P/E High/Low		PER SHARE ($) Earnings	Dividends	Book Value
12/15	38.31	11	8	3.53	0.86	34.94
12/14	29.73	14	10	2.32	0.78	32.67
12/13	28.66	11	7	2.98	0.69	30.87
12/12	21.84	17	10	1.58	0.60	28.90
12/11	20.18	—	—	(0.00)	0.60	27.29
Annual Growth	17.4%	—	—	—	9.4%	6.4%

United Insurance Holdings Corp

United Insurance Holdings insures homeowners in the Sunshine State throughout the seasons even hurricane season. The company underwrites flood fire and homeowners insurance policies in Florida and provides property insurance for automotive service companies. It distributes its products through independent agents. United Insurance was founded in 1999 then underwent a reverse merger in 2008 when it bought the OTC-listed FMG Acquisition Corp. for $95 million ($25 million in cash and 8.75 million shares of stock.) The newly merged company has listed on the NASDAQ exchange.

EXECUTIVES

Chief Underwriting Officer, Paul DiFrancesco
CEO, John L. Forney, $800,000 total compensation
CFO, B. Bradford Martz, $300,000 total compensation
CIO, Andrew D. (Andy) Swenson, $210,000 total compensation
General Counsel and Chief Legal Officer, Kimberly Salmon
Chairman, Gregory C. Branch
Auditors: RSM US LLP

LOCATIONS

HQ: United Insurance Holdings Corp
800 2nd Avenue S., St. Petersburg, FL 33701
Phone: 727 895-7737
Web: www.upcinsurance.com

PRODUCTS/OPERATIONS

2015 Sales

	% of total
Net premiums earned	94
Investment income	3
Net realized gains	-
Other revenue	3
Total	**100**

COMPETITORS

AAA Auto Club South	Federated National Holding
Allstate	HCI Group
American National Insurance	Liberty Mutual
Bankers Financial	State Farm
Citizens Property Insurance	Universal Insurance Holdings

HISTORICAL FINANCIALS

Company Type: Public

Income Statement

FYE: December 31

	ASSETS ($ mil.)	NET INCOME ($ mil.)	INCOME AS % OF ASSETS	EMPLOYEES
12/15	740.0	27.3	3.7%	120.0
12/14	584.1	41.0	7.0%	120.0
12/13	441.2	20.3	4.6%	90.0
12/12	313.6	9.7	3.1%	68.0
12/11	240.2	8.0	3.4%	50.0
Annual Growth	32.5%	35.6%	—	24.5%

2015 Year-End Financials

Return on assets: 4.1%
Return on equity: 12.3%
Long-term debt ($ mil.): —
No. of shares (mil.): 21.5
Sales ($ mil): 357.5

Dividends
Yield: 1.1%
Payout: 16.8%
Market value ($ mil.): 368.0

	STOCK PRICE ($) FY Close	P/E High/Low		PER SHARE ($) Earnings	Dividends	Book Value
12/15	17.10	22	10	1.28	0.20	11.11
12/14	21.95	11	6	2.05	0.16	9.75
12/13	14.08	11	4	1.26	0.15	6.64
12/12	6.01	7	5	0.91	0.08	5.70
12/11	4.40	6	4	0.77	0.05	5.31
Annual Growth	40.4%	—	—	13.5%	41.4%	20.3%

United Therapeutics Corp

United Therapeutics hopes its products will be in vein. Its injectable drug Remodulin treats pulmonary hypertension which affects the blood vessels between the heart and lungs; it also treats cancer and viral illnesses. The product is marketed directly and through distributors in North America Europe and the Asia/Pacific region. Other hypertension treatments include Adcirca Tyvaso and Orenitram. The company's development pipeline includes additional treatments for cardiovascular disease as well as various cancers respiratory conditions and infectious diseases. United Therapeutics has divested its cardiac monitoring division.

Operations

Remodulin accounted for 43% of United Therapeutics' 2014 sales.

The company is also developing the antibody Unituxin (formerly Ch14.18) for the treatment of neuroblastoma under an agreement with the National Cancer Institute. It has been accepted for review in the US and Europe. United Therapeutics has additional early stage research programs and it regularly evaluates opportunities to license additional compounds for development.

United Therapeutics holds a license agreement with Ascendis Pharma to develop a self-injectable therapeutic alternative for pulmonary arterial hypertension (PAH) patients by applying Ascendis Pharma's TransCon technology platform to its treprostinil molecule. The agreement also gives United Therapeutics exclusive rights to develop prostacyclin prostacyclin analog and prostacyclin-related products for treating PAH using the TransCon technology as well as rights to commercialize any products developed from the collaboration on a global basis.

Geographic Reach

Remodulin is approved for sale throughout North America and Europe as well as in the Asia/Pacific region. Tyvaso Adcirca and Orenitram are only approved in the US. The company's home country accounts for 90% of revenues.

United Therapeutics owns an office building near London; it serves as its European headquarters. It also owns a warehouse in Germany.

Sales and Marketing

The company distributes Remodulin Tyvaso and Orenitram throughout the US and Puerto Rico through two contracted specialty distributors — CVS Caremark and Accredo Health. It also distributes Remodulin in Canada through a specialty pharma wholesaler. It sells Adcirca to pharmaceutical wholesalers at a discount.

Financial Performance

United Therapeutics' revenues have seen strong growth over the past five years. In 2014 revenue increased 14% to $1.3 billion as sales of Remodulin and Adcirca grew and sales of Orenitram commenced. In general net income has also risen (with the exception of 2013 when expenses rose). In 2014 net income nearly doubled rising 95% to $340.1 million because of the higher revenue and lower operating expenses.

Cash flow from operations fell 16% to $355 million that year as more cash was used in inventories and accounts receivable.

Strategy

The company pursues growth by developing new drugs either through R&D or in partnership with other firms. In 2015 the FDA approved Unituxin in combination with GM-CSF interleukin-2 and 13-cis-retinoic acid for the treatment of pediatric patients with high-risk neuroblastoma. In 2014 United Therapeutics formed an alliance with DEKA Research & Development to develop a potential technology breakthrough in the subcutaneous delivery of Remodulin Injection to PAH patients.

EXECUTIVES

Chairman and CEO, Martine A. Rothblatt, age 61, $1,078,099 total compensation
EVP General Counsel and Corporate Secretary, Paul A. Mahon, age 53, $760,201 total compensation
CIO, Shola Oyewole
President and COO, Michael Benkowitz
CFO and Treasurer, James Edgemond, $380,146 total compensation
Senior Vice President Manufact, Mike (Mikey) Camp

Senior Vice President And Chief Medical Officer;
Xenolung Clinical Development; Lungllc, Marc
(Marcy) Lorber
Vice President finance and Assistant Treasurer,
Melissa (Lissa) Silverman
Vice President Chief Compliance Officer, Jim
(Jimmy) Dawson
Senior Vice President Sales and Marketing, Alex
(Al) Sapir
Vice President Associate General Counsel, John
(Jack) Hess
Vice Chairman, Christopher Patusky
Auditors: Ernst & Young LLP

LOCATIONS

HQ: United Therapeutics Corp
1040 Spring Street, Silver Spring, MD 20910
Phone: 301 608-9292
Web: www.unither.com

PRODUCTS/OPERATIONS

2014 Sales

	$ mil.	% of total
Cardiovascular products		
Remodulin	553.7	43
Tyvaso	463.0	36
Adcirca	221.5	17
Orenitram	41.3	3
Other	9.0	1
Total	**1,288.5**	**100**

Selected Products

Marketed
 Remodulin (pulmonary arterial hypertension)
 Tyvaso (pulmonary arterial hypertension)
 Adcirca (pulmonary arterial hypertension)
 Orenitram (pulmonary arterial hypertension)
In Development
 8H9 MAb (metastatic brain cancer)
 Beraprost (cardiovascular disease)
 Miglustat and other Glycobiology Antiviral Agents
 (hepatitis C and other infectious diseases)
 IW001 (pulmonary disease)
 Treprostinil (oral form for pulmonary arterial
 hypertension and peripheral vascular disease)

Selected Subsidiaries

Lung Biotechnology Hong Kong Limited
Lung Biotechnology (Nanjing) Co. Ltd.
Lung LLC
Lung RX Ltd. (UK)
Revivicor Inc.
United Therapeutics Europe Ltd. (UK)
Unither Biotech Inc. (Canada)
Unither Pharma LLC
Unither Pharmaceuticals Inc.

COMPETITORS

Abbott Labs	Gilead Sciences
Actelion	GlaxoSmithKline
American HealthChoice	NIPPON SHINYAKU
Ark Therapeutics Group	CO.LTD.
AstraZeneca	Novartis
Bayer HealthCare	Pfizer
Pharmaceuticals	Sandoz
Eli Lilly	Teva

HISTORICAL FINANCIALS

Company Type: Public

Income Statement

FYE: December 31

	REVENUE ($ mil.)	NET INCOME ($ mil.)	NET PROFIT MARGIN	EMPLOYEES
12/15	1,465.7	651.6	44.5%	750.0
12/14	1,288.5	340.0	26.4%	740.0
12/13	1,116.9	174.5	15.6%	706.0
12/12	916.0	304.4	33.2%	623.0
12/11	743.1	217.8	29.3%	543.0
Annual Growth	**18.5%**	**31.5%**	**—**	**8.4%**

2015 Year-End Financials

Debt ratio: 0.2%	No. of shares (mil.): 45.7
Return on equity: 45.4%	Dividends
Cash ($ mil.): 831.8	Yield: —
Current ratio: 2.89	Payout: —
Long-term debt ($ mil.): —	Market value ($ mil.): 7,167.0

	STOCK PRICE ($) FY Close	P/E High/Low	PER SHARE ($) Earnings	Dividends	Book Value
12/15	156.61	13 8	12.72	0.00	34.96
12/14	129.49	19 12	6.28	0.00	26.87
12/13	113.08	33 15	3.28	0.00	25.89
12/12	53.42	10 7	5.71	0.00	21.82
12/11	47.25	19 10	3.67	0.00	17.90
Annual Growth 34.9%		**— —**	**36.4%**	**—**	**18.2%**

Universal Display Corp

Universal Display thinks the world should be flat and lit with its organic light-emitting diode (OLED) technologies and materials. With its own research and through sponsored research agreements with Princeton University the University of Southern California and the University of Michigan the company develops OLED technologies and materials for screens from cell phones to large flat panel displays and solid-state lighting. Based in the US it has facilities around the world.

Operations

The company has subsidiaries Ireland Korea Japan and Hong Kong. The Hong Kong subsidiary operates a chemistry laboratory to support greater research and development initiatives. In 2014 materials brought in 67% of Universal Displays revenue a 33% increase from 2013 with the rest of revenue coming from royalty and licensing fees.

Geographic Reach

Almost 99% of Universal Display's revenue comes from customers in Asia. Customers in South Korea account for 74% of the Universal Display's revenue with Japan (24%) Taiwan and the US making up the rest. The company has offices in the US Hong Kong Ireland Japan South Korea and Taiwan.

Sales and Marketing

The company targets flat panel display manufacturers and makers of lighting products to license its technologies and buy its materials. Universal Display supplies manufacturers with materials in development to see how they might work in a product. It works with manufacturers to develop displays and lighting products using phosphorescent OLEDs which use much less power than OLEDs. Contracts with the US Department of the Army and US Department of Energy fund research

to develop next-generation OLED technologies for applications such as flexible displays and solid-state lighting. Samsung Display accounted for 54% of Universal Display's 2014 revenues for 2014 and indirectly accounted for 72% of the revenuye for the year. Other customers included LG Display Tohoku Pioneer and Konica Minolta.

Financial Performance

As LED displays have taken market share from those made with LCDs OLED display sales have increased and that's reflected in Universal Display's financial performance. Its revenue jumped to $191 million in 2014 increasing 38% from 2013. Net income however contracted 43% in 2014 to $41.85 million. While sales of materials rose 33% and royalty and licensing fees increased 34% 2014 revenue also included a $50 million in licensing and royalties from Samsung Display. Net income was affected by higher material costs tax settlements in Japan and higher bonus and stock compensation related to the firm's research and development. Cash flow from operations was $47.2 million in 2014 compared to $45 million in 2013.

Strategy

Developing materials and uses for OLEDs is the key to Universal Display. The company spent $41 million on research and development in 2014 which was about the same as its net income. Besides conducting in-house R&D it works with university researchers the US government and its customers.

A critical element for Universal Display is to get its materials and technology into new products through sales and licensing agreements.

In 2015 the company entered into two agreements with LG Display for OLED technology. A patent license agreement grants LG Display a non-exclusive royalty bearing portfolio license to make and sell OLED displays under the company's patent portfolio. Also in 2015 Universal Display and Sumitomo Chemical Company signed a new OLED licensing agreement that gives non-exclusive license rights to make and sell solution-processed OLEDs.

For one of its newer areas phosphorescent LEDs Universal Display expanded an agreement with BOE Technology Group to collaborate on evaluating and developing displays using the material.

EXECUTIVES

President and CEO, Steven V. Abramson, age 64,
$581,049 total compensation
EVP and CFO, Sidney D. Rosenblatt, age 68,
$581,049 total compensation
Vice President Asia Operations, Sui Lynn
Chairman, Sherwin I. Seligsohn, age 80
Auditors: KPMG LLP

LOCATIONS

HQ: Universal Display Corp
375 Phillips Boulevard, Ewing, NJ 08618
Phone: 609 671-0980

PRODUCTS/OPERATIONS

2014 Sales

	$ mil.	% of total
Material Sales	126.9	67
Royalty and License fee	63.1	33
Technology Development and support revenue	0.9	0
Total	**191.0**	**100**

2014 Sales

	$ mil.	% of total
South Korea	141.9	74
Japan	44.9	24
Taiwan	1.6	1
Other Non-U.S.	1.9	1
United States	0.7	0
Total	**191.0**	**100**

COMPETITORS

AU Optronics	Merck KGaA
BASF SE	Microvision
Dow Chemical	Pioneer Corporation
DuPont	Samsung Electronics
Eastman Kodak	Sony
Epson	Sumitomo Chemical
Fujitsu	Texas Instruments
Idemitsu Kosan	Toshiba
LG Display	eMagin

HISTORICAL FINANCIALS

Company Type: Public

Income Statement FYE: December 31

	REVENUE ($ mil.)	NET INCOME ($ mil.)	NET PROFIT MARGIN	EMPLOYEES
12/15	191.0	14.6	7.7%	154.0
12/14	191.0	41.8	21.9%	145.0
12/13	146.6	74.0	50.5%	124.0
12/12	83.2	9.6	11.6%	117.0
12/11	61.2	3.1	5.1%	93.0
Annual Growth	**32.9%**	**46.9%**	**—**	**13.4%**

2015 Year-End Financials

Debt ratio: —	No. of shares (mil.): 46.7
Return on equity: 3.2%	Dividends
Cash ($ mil.): 97.5	Yield: —
Current ratio: 12.97	Payout: —
Long-term debt ($ mil.): —	Market value ($ mil.): 2,546.0

	STOCK PRICE ($) FY Close	P/E High/Low		Earnings	PER SHARE ($) Dividends	Book Value
12/15	54.44	181	84	0.31	0.00	9.98
12/14	27.75	42	25	0.90	0.00	9.82
12/13	34.36	24	16	1.59	0.00	9.21
12/12	25.62	228	107	0.21	0.00	7.56
12/11	36.69	858	326	0.07	0.00	7.42
Annual Growth	**10.4%**	—	—	**45.1%**	**—**	**7.7%**

Universal Health Realty Income Trust

Universal Health Realty Income Trust (UHT) is a real estate investment trust (REIT) that primarily invests in healthcare facilities and human services. The REIT owns more than 55 facilities in 16 states including acute care hospitals behavioral healthcare facilities rehabilitation hospitals subacute facilities surgery centers childcare centers and medical office buildings. McAllen Medical Center in Texas is UHT's largest facility. Many properties are owned via limited liability companies in which the trust holds an equity interest. UHT's hospitals boast some 1000 beds. Subsidiaries of Universal Health Services lease most of UHT's hos-

pitals and provide their own maintenance and renovation services.

Geographic Reach

UHT operates nationwide and has properties located in 15 states including Texas Florida California and Illinois.

Operations

The company's real estate investments include seven hospital facilities 43 medical office buildings and four preschool and childcare centers. Universal Health Services accounts for about 37% of its consolidated revenues.

Strategy

UHT focuses on expanding its geographic footprint and generating most of its revenue through third parties.

Financial Performance

UHT's revenue rose some 83% to $54 million in 2012 from $29 million in 2011 due to a 162% increase in base rent of non-related parties and a 17% boost in base rental UHS facilities. Net income during the same reporting period dropped 74% to $19 million from $74 million.

EXECUTIVES

VP Acquisition and Development, Timothy J. Fowler, age 60

VP and CFO, Charles F. Boyle, age 56

VP Secretary and Treasurer, Cheryl K. Ramagano, age 53

Chairman President and CEO, Alan B. Miller, age 78

Medical Director, Paul Earley

Auditors: KPMG LLP

LOCATIONS

HQ: Universal Health Realty Income Trust
Universal Corporate Center, 367 South Gulph Road, King of Prussia, PA 19406
Phone: 610 265-0688   **Fax:** 610 768-3336
Web: www.uhrit.com

PRODUCTS/OPERATIONS

2015 Sales

	% of total
Base rental - Non-related parties	55
Base rental - UHS facilities	25
Bonus rental - UHS facilities	7
Tenant reimbursements and other - Non-related parties	12
Tenant reimbursements and other - UHS facilities	1
Total	**100**

Selected Subsidiaries

73 Medical Building LLC
653 Town Center Investments LLC
653 Town Center Phase II LLC
Auburn Medical Properties II LLC
ApaMed Properties LLC
Banburry Medical Properties LLC
BRB/E Building One LLC
Centennial Medical Properties LLC
Cimarron Medical Properties LLC

COMPETITORS

G&L Realty Properties	Lend Lease (US)
HCP	Medical Properties
Healthcare Realty	Trust
Trust	Ventas

HISTORICAL FINANCIALS

Company Type: Public

Income Statement FYE: December 31

	REVENUE ($ mil.)	NET INCOME ($ mil.)	NET PROFIT MARGIN	EMPLOYEES
12/15	63.9	23.6	37.0%	0.0
12/14	59.7	51.5	86.2%	0.0
12/13	54.2	13.1	24.3%	0.0
12/12	53.9	19.4	36.1%	0.0
12/11	29.4	73.7	250.2%	0.0
Annual Growth	**21.3%**	**(24.7%)**	**—**	**—**

2015 Year-End Financials

Debt ratio: 55.0%	No. of shares (mil.): 13.3
Return on equity: 11.8%	Dividends
Cash ($ mil.): 3.8	Yield: 5.1%
Current ratio: 20.44	Payout: 143.8%
Long-term debt ($ mil.): 252.7	Market value ($ mil.): 666.0

	STOCK PRICE ($) FY Close	P/E High/Low		Earnings	PER SHARE ($) Dividends	Book Value
12/15	50.01	32	24	1.78	2.56	14.64
12/14	48.12	12	10	3.99	2.52	15.38
12/13	40.06	57	37	1.04	2.50	12.88
12/12	50.61	32	25	1.54	2.46	14.00
12/11	39.00	7	6	5.83	2.43	14.91
Annual Growth	**6.4%**	—	—	**(25.7%)**	**1.4%**	**(0.5%)**

Universal Insurance Holdings Inc

While some companies shy away from insuring homes in hurricane-prone Florida Universal Insurance Holdings is right at home there. Operating through its Universal Property & Casualty Insurance Company and American Platinum Property and Casualty Insurance Company subsidiaries the company underwrites distributes and administers homeowners property and personal liability insurance. The company's additional subsidiaries process claims perform claims adjustments and property inspections provide administrative duties and negotiate reinsurance.

Geographic Reach

Universal Property & Casualty Insurance (UPCIC) is taking its expertise in flood and wind coverage to other markets. While Florida remains its largest market it also operates in Georgia Hawaii and the Carolinas. Although it doesn't currently operate in Maryland and Massachusetts the company is licensed in those states as well.

Sales and Marketing

The company distributes its products through a network of independent agents.

EXECUTIVES

Chairman and CEO, Sean P. Downes, age 46, $2,278,015 total compensation

COO, Stephen J. Donaghy, $802,514 total compensation

President and Chief Risk Officer, Jon W. Springer, age 46, $1,337,416 total compensation

CFO and Principal Accounting Officer, Frank C Wilcox, $350,000 total compensation

CIO, Kimberly Cooper, $196,923 total compensation
Vice President Underwriting, Clint Gillespie
Auditors: Plante & Moran, PLLC

LOCATIONS

HQ: Universal Insurance Holdings Inc
1110 W. Commercial Blvd., Suite 100, Fort
Lauderdale, FL 33309
Phone: 954 958-1200
Web: www.universalinsuranceholdings.com

PRODUCTS/OPERATIONS

2015 Sales

	% of total
Premiums earned net	92
Commission revenue	3
Policy fees	3
Net investment income	1
Other revenue	1
Total	**100**

Selected Products and Services

Condominium policy
Dwelling coverage
Dwelling fire policy
Homeowners policy
Other structures coverage
Personal liability coverage
Personal property coverage
Renter's policy

COMPETITORS

Allstate	Liberty Mutual
Bouchard Insurance	State Farm
Citizens Property	Travelers Companies
Insurance	USAA
Federated National	United Insurance
Holding	Holdings
HCI Group	

HISTORICAL FINANCIALS

Company Type: Public

Income Statement

FYE: December 31

	ASSETS ($ mil.)	NET INCOME ($ mil.)	INCOME AS % OF ASSETS	EMPLOYEES
12/15	993.5	106.4	10.7%	392.0
12/14	911.7	72.9	8.0%	335.0
12/13	920.0	58.9	6.4%	300.0
12/12	925.7	30.3	3.3%	279.0
12/11	894.0	20.1	2.2%	271.0
Annual Growth	**2.7%**	**51.7%**	**—**	**9.7%**

2015 Year-End Financials

Return on assets: 11.1%
Return on equity: 41.5%
Long-term debt ($ mil.): —
No. of shares (mil.): 35.1
Sales ($ mil): 546.5
Dividends
 Yield: 2.7%
 Payout: 22.9%
Market value ($ mil.): 814.0

	STOCK PRICE ($) FY Close	P/E High/Low		PER SHARE ($) Earnings	Dividends	Book Value
12/15	23.18	12	6	2.97	0.63	8.35
12/14	20.45	10	5	2.08	0.55	6.24
12/13	14.48	9	3	1.56	0.49	4.97
12/12	4.38	6	4	0.75	0.46	4.00
12/11	3.58	12	7	0.50	0.32	3.74
Annual Growth	**59.5%**	**—**	**—**	**56.1%**	**18.5%**	**22.2%**

Universal Logistics Holdings Inc

Universal Logistics Holdings (formerly Universal Truckload Services) hasn't hauled freight beyond its own galaxy but the company does cover the US and parts of Canada (Ontario and Quebec) and Mexico. As an "asset-light" provider of truckload freight transportation the company operates through a network of truck owner-operators rather than employing drivers and investing heavily in equipment. It can call upon a fleet of some 4300 tractors and 6300 trailers including standard dry vans and flatbeds; the majority of its tractors and trailers are owned by others. Its flagship transportation segment transports general commodities such as automotive parts building materials paper food consumer goods furniture steel and other metals.

Geographic Reach

Universal Logistics operates 90 terminals with key locations in Cleveland Columbus Latty and Reading Ohio; Dallas; Dearborn Michigan; Garden City Georgia; Gary Indiana; Houston; Memphis; Millwood West Virginia; Monroeville Pennsylvania; South Kearney New Jersey; and Tampa. The US accounts for around 95% of its total revenue.

Operations

Besides its transportation business which generates about 65% of company revenues Universal Logistics also serves customers through its intermodal and value-added services segments. Value-added services accounts for about 25% of the company's sales and matches customers' freight with carriers' capacity.

Intermodal support services (12%) involve picking up shipping containers at ports and railheads and delivering them by truck to customers. The company's intermodal support services is a key source of growth and is expanding its agent network as well as encouraging agents to promote the intermodal business line.

Financial Performance

Universal Logistics has enjoyed unprecedented growth over the years. Revenues jumped 15% from $1 billion in 2013 to peak at a record-setting $1.2 billion in 2014. The historic revenue growth for 2014 was fueled by a 9% bump in transportation services paired with the full year results of a recent acquisition. The rise from transportation services was the result of both higher load volumes and improved operating revenues per loaded mile.

After posting milestone profits of $51 million in 2013 the company saw its profits decrease 10% to $45 million in 2014. The decline in profits was driven by an increase in purchased transportation and equipment rent along with a rise in direct personnel and related benefits expenses.

In addition Universal Logistics has seen its operating cash flow fluctuate the last few years. After decreasing in 2013 cash flow climbed 38% to $79 million in 2014 due to additional cash from accounts payable along with changes in prepaid income taxes.

Strategy

The trucking industry has entered a phase of consolidation. Based on rising insurance costs scarcity of capital fuel prices and expensive regulatory environmental equipment smaller trucking firms are combining through merger or acquisition. However Universal Logistics' size and its continuing organic and acquisitive growth give it a competitive edge over smaller more vulnerable trucking companies.

In 2013 the company purchased Westport USA Holding for $123 million in cash. Based in Louisville Kentucky Westport provides value-added warehousing and component distribution services to US manufacturers of Class 4-8 trucks RVs and superduty trucks. The deal further enhanced Universal Logistics' value-added service capabilities and helped it achieve milestone revenues for 2014.

EXECUTIVES

CEO, Jeffrey A. (Jeff) Rogers, age 53, $207,711 total compensation
CFO, Jude Beres
Senior Vice President Information Technology, Mark Sokolowski
Vice President of Government and Emergency Services, Gina Hubbs
Executive Vice President Business Development, Ralph (Ralphy) Castille
Vice President Of Equipment Services, Bill Gale
Vice President and General Manager, Rand Stille
Vice President of Finance and Investor Relations, Steven (Steve) Fitzpatrick
Vice President Of Information Technology, Jeff (Jeffy) Goike
Chairman, Matthew T. Moroun, age 43
Auditors: BDO USA, LLP

LOCATIONS

HQ: Universal Logistics Holdings Inc
12755 E. Nine Mile Road, Warren, MI 48089
Phone: 586 920-0100

PRODUCTS/OPERATIONS

2013 Sales

	$ mil.	% of total
Transportation services	707.0	68
Value-added services	195.1	19
Intermodal services	131.4	13
Total	**1,033.5**	**100**

Selected Services

Transportation Services
Flatbed
Specialized & Heavy Haul
Oilfield
Van
Refrigerated
ShuttlesDrive AwayT/L Brokerage
Switching and Yard Management
Transportation ManagementValue Added Services
Axle & Chassis Assembly
Consolidation Cross-docks Kittin

Selected Subsidiaries

Cavalry Logistics
Great American Lines Inc.
LINC
Louisiana Transportation Inc.
Mason & Dixon Lines Inc.
Mason Dixon Intermodal Inc.
NYP of Michigan Inc.
Universal Am-Can Ltd.
Universal Logistics Inc.

COMPETITORS

C.H. Robinson	Schneider National
Worldwide	Swift Transportation
Crete Carrier	U.S. Xpress
Hub Group	USA Truck
J.B. Hunt	Werner Enterprises
Landstar System	

HISTORICAL FINANCIALS
Company Type: Public

Income Statement
FYE: December 31

	REVENUE ($ mil.)	NET INCOME ($ mil.)	NET PROFIT MARGIN	EMPLOYEES
12/15	1,128.7	40.0	3.5%	5,108.0
12/14	1,191.5	45.3	3.8%	5,746.0
12/13	1,033.4	50.5	4.9%	5,960.0
12/12	1,037.0	47.6	4.6%	4,701.0
12/11	699.7	15.8	2.3%	675.0
Annual Growth	12.7%	26.1%	—	65.9%

2015 Year-End Financials
Debt ratio: 46.3%
Return on equity: 29.8%
Cash ($ mil.): 12.9
Current ratio: 1.36
Long-term debt ($ mil.): 174.4

No. of shares (mil.): 28.4
Dividends
Yield: 1.9%
Payout: 20.4%
Market value ($ mil.): 399.0

	STOCK PRICE ($) FY Close	P/E High/Low		PER SHARE ($) Earnings	Dividends	Book Value
12/15	14.04	21	9	1.37	0.28	4.62
12/14	28.51	22	15	1.51	0.28	4.57
12/13	30.51	18	10	1.68	0.14	3.51
12/12	18.25	12	8	1.59	2.00	1.91
12/11	18.15	18	12	1.01	1.00	10.42
Annual Growth	(6.2%) (18.4%)	—	—	7.9%	(27.3%)	

US Ecology, Inc.

US Ecology (formerly American Ecology) helps keep a lid on hazardous waste industrial waste and low-level radioactive waste. The company handles hazardous and nonhazardous waste at sites in the US Canada and Mexico and it operates a low-level radioactive waste facility in Washington state. It also provides packaging and collection of hazardous waste and total waste management programs. The company does business with private waste companies state and federal agencies and a variety of industries. Customers include nuclear plants steel mills petrochemical facilities and academic and medical institutions. US Ecology retains interests in several non-operating waste-disposal facilities.

Operations

US Ecology operates in two segments: Environmental Services (67% of sales) and Field & Industrial Services (33%). The Environmental Services segment provides a range of hazardous material management services including transportation recycling treatment and disposal of hazardous and non-hazardous waste at company-owned landfill wastewater and other treatment facilities. The Field & Industrial Services segment provides packaging and collection of hazardous waste and total waste management programs at customer sites and through its 10-day transfer facilities.

Geographic Reach

The company has operations in the US Canada and Mexico. The US accounted for 93% of revenues in 2015.

US Ecology's fixed facilities include five Resource Conservation and Recovery Act of 1976 (RCRA) subtitle C hazardous waste landfills and one Low-level radioactive waste regulated under the federal Atomic Energy Act for disposal (LLRW) landfill located near Beatty Nevada; Richland Washington; Robstown Texas; Grand View Idaho; Detroit Michigan and Blainville Québec Canada.

The company has waste treatment and landfill disposal facilities in Nevada Texas Idaho and Michigan and in Canada. It has waste treatment only facilities in Ohio Michigan Illinois Pennsylvania Oklahoma Georgia Alabama Florida Michigan and North Carolina. The company's field and industrial waste management facilities are located in Michigan New Jersey Georgia and Massachusetts.

Sales and Marketing

US Ecology's customers include oil refineries chemical production plants steel mills real estate developers waste brokers/aggregators serving small manufacturers and other industrial customers.

Financial Performance

The company 26% growth in 2015 (to $563 million) was primarily due to growth in both segments as a result of full year revenue from the EQ Holdings acquisition.US Ecology's net income declined by 33% to $26 million in 2015 due to higher selling general and administrative expenses as a result of acquired EQ business. The growth in interest expenses was also due to higher outstanding debt levels and the related interest expense on borrowings under its Revolving Credit Facility used to finance the acquisition of EQ. Operating cash flow increased by under 0.5% (to $71 million) due to a change in receivables and income taxes.

Strategy

The company focuses on organic growth by expanding into new markets and offer new services allowing the company to cross-sell or bundle services and ultimately drive incremental volume into its existing disposal facilities. It aims to enhance treatment capabilities at its existing facilities to handle additional waste streams and increase throughput. Also the company targets acquisitions to expand its disposal network customer base and geographic footprint. In 2015 the company sold its Allstate Power Vac subsidiary engaged in the industrial services business to a private investor group for $58.8 million. Allstate was included in its Field and Industrial Services segment which the company acquired with the acquisition of EQ. Divesting Allstate allowed the company to concentrate on growing its core environmental services business while continuing to expand its complementary field services. Mergers and Acquisitions In 2014 the company acquired integrated environmental services company EQ Holdings for $460.9 million. The acquisition strengthened US Ecology's environmental services group and the field and industrial services segment.

EXECUTIVES

EVP Sales and Marketing, Steven D. (Steve) Welling, age 58, $255,923 total compensation
EVP Operations and Technology Development, Simon G. Bell, age 46, $207,989 total compensation
Chairman President and CEO, Jeffrey R. (Jeff) Feeler, age 47, $296,904 total compensation
EVP CFO and Treasurer, Eric L. Gerratt, age 47, $198,662 total compensation
Auditors: Deloitte & Touche LLP

LOCATIONS

HQ: US Ecology, Inc.
251 E. Front Street, Suite 400, Boise, ID 83702
Phone: 208 331-8400
Web: www.usecology.com

PRODUCTS/OPERATIONS

2015 Sales

	$ mil.	% of total
Environmental services	375.9	67
Field & Industrial services	187.2	33
Total	563.1	100

Selected Subsidiaries
EQ Holdings Inc.
Texas Ecologists inc.
US Ecology Inc.
US Ecology Idaho Inc.
US Ecology Michigan Inc.
US Ecology Nevada Inc.
US Ecology Texas L.P.
US Ecology Washington Inc.

COMPETITORS

Clean Harbors
EnergySolutions
Heritage Environmental Services
Perma-Fix Environmental Safety-Kleen
Stericycle
Valhi
Veolia ES Technical Solutions
Waste Control Specialists
Waste Management

HISTORICAL FINANCIALS
Company Type: Public

Income Statement
FYE: December 31

	REVENUE ($ mil.)	NET INCOME ($ mil.)	NET PROFIT MARGIN	EMPLOYEES
12/15	563.0	25.6	4.5%	1,400.0
12/14	447.4	38.2	8.5%	1,800.0
12/13	201.1	32.1	16.0%	458.0
12/12	169.1	25.6	15.2%	425.0
12/11	154.9	18.3	11.9%	387.0
Annual Growth	38.1%	8.7%	—	37.9%

2015 Year-End Financials
Debt ratio: 38.0%
Return on equity: 10.0%
Cash ($ mil.): 5.9
Current ratio: 1.80
Long-term debt ($ mil.): 290.6

No. of shares (mil.): 21.7
Dividends
Yield: 1.9%
Payout: 54.1%
Market value ($ mil.): 792.0

	STOCK PRICE ($) FY Close	P/E High/Low		PER SHARE ($) Earnings	Dividends	Book Value
12/15	36.44	45	30	1.18	0.72	11.78
12/14	40.12	29	19	1.77	0.72	11.62
12/13	37.10	22	13	1.72	0.72	10.76
12/12	23.54	17	12	1.40	0.90	6.12
12/11	18.78	19	15	1.01	0.72	5.50
Annual Growth	18.0%	—	—	4.0%	(0.0%)	21.0%

US Silica Holdings, Inc.

Life's a beach for the sand-sellers at U.S. Silica. While the industrial mineral company got its start making sand-based glass and other products it is now known for providing its popular "frac sand" product used by natural gas and oil producers in hydraulic fracturing a process to boost oil and gas production. Supplying customers in the US and Canada the company also provides silica and aplite for the glass foundry chemical and construction industries; and fine ground silica and kaolin clay used to make paint plastics and ceramics. Additionally U.S. Silica makes raw materials for solar panels. Beyond its main facility in West Virginia U S. Silica also has 17 plants in the East.

Operations

U.S. Silica operates two business segments: Oil & Gas Proppants which made up 67% of its total revenue during 2015 and provides fracturing sand ("frac sand") for pumping down oil and natural gas well to prop open rock fissures; and Industrial & Specialty Products (33% of revenue) which supplies more than 250 products and materials used in the container glass fiberglass and specialty glass industries among others. The mining company primarily sells its products under short-term price agreements or at prevailing market rates.The company operated 17 production facilities across the US at the end of 2015 including eight industrial sand production plants and eight oil and gas sand production plants. U.S. Silica has been ranked as the second-largest producer of silica used in hydraulic fracturing in the US behind Unimin a unit of Belgium's Sibelco Group.Geographic Reach-Frederick Maryland-based U.S. Silica has additional offices in Chicago Houston and Shanghai. Its production facilities are located across the US with many in energy-rich states such as Texas Oklahoma Pennsylvania and West Virginia.

Sales and Marketing

The company's two largest customers by revenue in 2015 included Schlumberger (which made up 13% of its total revenue that year) and Halliburton Company (12% of revenue). Some of its other big customers have included Nabors Industries Texas Specialty Sands Calfrac and C&J Energy Services among others.

Financial Performance

Buoyed by strong demand for "frac sand" which is in short supply U.S. Silica's sales and profits had tripled between 2011 and 2014. Oil price declines in 2015 however put a halt to its growth.

The company's sales tumbled 27% to $643 million during 2015 as the huge drop in oil prices led shale oil & gas producers to demand less of its frac sand product. Sharp revenue declines in 2015 caused U.S. Silica's net income to plummet 90% to $11.87 million. Its operating cash levels dove 64% to $61.5 million for the year due to the steep fall in earnings.

Strategy

While plummeting oil prices in 2015 and early 2016 threatened many tied to the commodity U.S. Silica has been busy getting ready for the comeback. During 2015 it continued increasing its transload points building upon the 49 facilities it had strategically located in or near all of the major shale basins in the US. It also continues to expand its Oil & Gas Proppants production capacity and product lines to grow its supply chain network. In 2014 the company launched its high-performance resin coated propant InnoProp Python RCS which was designed to boost oil and gas well production in a cost-effective and efficient manner.If and when oil prices come back up the company expects its fortunes to continue rising along with the sharp increase in domestic shale oil and gas production which uses sand to break up rock underground to free-up fossil fuel in the Hydraulic fracturing process (aka fracking). Another area of promise for U.S. Silica is resin-coated sand which is also used in hydraulic fracturing.

Mergers and Acquisitions

In July 2014 U.S. Silica acquired Cadre Services a regional sand mining company in Voca Texas. The $98 million purchase expanded the company's geographic footprint and product offering in the fast-growing Permian Basin.

Two years later the company acquired New Birmingham's NBR Sand unit which has the capacity to produce more than 2 million tons of mesh and mesh silica sand.

Company Background

U.S. Silica in February 2012 sold 11.7 million shares at $17 per share the middle of the range estimated for the IPO. Golden Gate Capital which had acquired the mining firm in 2008 sold 8.8 million shares while U.S. Silica offered 2.9 million shares. The offering coincided with an increasing demand for frac sand. U.S. Silica used the proceeds to invest in its frac and resin-coated sands operations by upgrading its existing plants and building a new resin-coated sand facility in Illinois (completed in 2014).U.S. Silica was formed by the merger of Pennsylvania Glass and Ottawa Silica in 1987.

EXECUTIVES

CFO, Donald A. Merril, age 51, $86,250 total compensation
VP and General Manager Oil & Gas, Don D. Weinheimer, $140,038 total compensation
President and CEO, Bryan A. Shinn, age 55, $383,333 total compensation
VP and General Manager Industrial and Specialties, John P. Blanchard
VP and COO, Mike Winkler
Auditors: Grant Thornton LLP

LOCATIONS

HQ: US Silica Holdings, Inc.
8490 Progress Drive, Suite 300, Frederick, MD 21701
Phone: 301 682-0600
Web: www.ussilica.com

PRODUCTS/OPERATIONS

2015 Sales

	$ mil.	% of total
Oil & gas Proppants	430.4	67
Industrial & specialty products	212.6	33
Total	**643.0**	**100**

Selected Products & Services

Aplite
Fine Ground Silica
FLORISIL®
Ground Silica
Hydrous Kaolin
Kaolin
Oil & Gas Proppants
Recreational Silica
Testing Silica
Whole Grain Silica

COMPETITORS

Carmeuse Lime & Stone Inc.	Martin Marietta Materials
Emerge Energy	Reserve Industries
Fairmount Minerals	Unimin
Hi-Crush	Vulcan Materials
Martin Marietta Aggregates	

HISTORICAL FINANCIALS

Company Type: Public

Income Statement

FYE: December 31

	REVENUE ($ mil.)	NET INCOME ($ mil.)	NET PROFIT MARGIN	EMPLOYEES
12/15	642.9	11.8	1.8%	996.0
12/14	876.7	121.5	13.9%	1,092.0
12/13	545.9	75.2	13.8%	844.0
12/12	441.9	79.1	17.9%	785.0
12/11	295.6	30.2	10.2%	701.0
Annual Growth	**21.4%**	**(20.9%)**	**—**	**9.2%**

2015 Year-End Financials

Debt ratio: 44.3%	No. of shares (mil.): 53.3
Return on equity: 3.0%	Dividends
Cash ($ mil.): 277.0	Yield: 2.3%
Current ratio: 5.23	Payout: 39.7%
Long-term debt ($ mil.): 488.3	Market value ($ mil.): 1,000.0

	STOCK PRICE ($) FY Close	P/E High/Low		PER SHARE ($) Earnings	Dividends	Book Value
12/15	18.73	178	62	0.22	0.44	7.20
12/14	25.69	32	10	2.23	0.50	7.49
12/13	34.11	25	12	1.41	0.38	5.78
12/12	16.73	15	6	1.50	0.50	4.38
Annual Growth	**3.8%**	**—**	**—**	**(47.3%)**	**(4.4%)**	**18.0%**

USANA Health Sciences Inc

Health is a matter of science at USANA Health Sciences. The company makes nutritional personal care and weight management products selling them through a direct-sales network marketing system of more than 250000 independent distributors (or associates). USANA Health Sciences also sells directly to 64000 customers deemed preferred. USANA's associates operate throughout North America as well as the Asia/Pacific region. The company's products portfolio includes nutritional supplements (76% of sales) and foods (12%) sold under the USANA brand and a line of skin and hair care products (9%) marketed under the Sensé label. Chairman Myron Wentz owns more than 50% of the company he founded.

Operations

USANA operates its business through one reportable business segment. The direct seller which has operations in 20 markets worldwide makes the majority of its products at its facilities in Utah. It manufactures all of its tablet products and its beauty products in-house. It also develops capsules drink mixes nutrition bars and personal care items. Previously USANA served as a third-party manufacturer for a limited number of body care companies. At the time contract manufacturing accounted for a larger share of the company's sales. However once the Sensé line took off USANA sold its third-party manufacturing business and devoted its manufacturing capacity to its own products. In keeping with its emphasis on developing science-based products the company has a collaboration with the Linus Pauling Institute at Oregon State University to research the role of vitamins and minerals in human health.

Geographic Reach

The company divides its operations into two regions: North America/Europe and Asia/Pacific. Together they cover about 15 countries. The latter accounts for more than 60% of revenue.

Sales and Marketing

USANA intends to fight sagging sales by increasing brand awareness and acquiring more associates and preferred customers in North America. Along with direct selling USANA sells its products in natural health food retailers via mail order and the Internet and in drug stores and supermarkets.

Financial Analysis

Sales growth in most countries where it operates helped USANA log an 11% increase in revenue in 2012. The results represented strong growth in the Phillipines China Mexico France and Belgium.The higher sales led to a 30% increase in net income; cash flow dipped slightly as the company bought back some of its stock.

Strategy

USANA looks to grow its business through efforts overseas. In 2012 it entered the Thailand market with a dozen products consisting of four key nutritional supplements and eight skin-care products. The company also expanded its operations into France and Belgium as well.

The company builds sales by getting its associates to manage their own business groups by recruiting and training others to sell the company's products. Sales associates are paid on sales generated by those groups. They might also receive compensation by purchasing products at wholesale prices and reselling them at retail prices. USANA attempts to recruit sales people who are looking for a second income and want to start a home-based business.

EXECUTIVES

CFO and Chief Leadership Development Officer, Paul A. Jones, age 52, $348,042 total compensation
CEO and Director, Kevin G. Guest, age 53, $608,516 total compensation
President Asia, Deborah Woo, age 62, $592,305 total compensation
Chief Legal Officer and Corporate Secretary, James H. (Jim) Bramble, age 46, $388,032 total compensation
President and COO, Jim Brown, age 47
Chief Scientific Officer, Robert (Rob) Sinnott
EVP Field Development Americas and Chief Communications Officer, Daniel A. (Dan) Macuga, age 46
CIO, Walter Noot
Chairman, Myron W. Wentz, age 75
Auditors: KPMG LLP

LOCATIONS

HQ: USANA Health Sciences Inc
3838 West Parkway Blvd., Salt Lake City, UT 84120
Phone: 801 954-7100
Web: www.usanahealthsciences.com

COMPETITORS

AIM International	NAI
AMS Health Sciences	NBTY
Amazon Herb	Nature's Sunshine
Amway	Nu Skin
Avon	Perrigo
GNC	Reliv' International
Hain Celestial	Schiff Nutrition
Herbalife Ltd.	International
Lifeway Foods	Shaklee
Mannatech	Sunrider
Market America	ViSalus
Mary Kay	

HISTORICAL FINANCIALS

Company Type: Public

Income Statement

FYE: January 2

	REVENUE ($ mil.)	NET INCOME ($ mil.)	NET PROFIT MARGIN	EMPLOYEES
01/16	918.5	94.6	10.3%	1,664.0
01/15*	790.4	76.6	9.7%	1,527.0
12/13	718.1	79.0	11.0%	1,480.0
12/12	648.7	66.4	10.2%	1,330.0
12/11	581.9	50.7	8.7%	1,290.0
Annual Growth	12.1%	16.9%		6.6%

*Fiscal year change

2016 Year-End Financials

Debt ratio: —	No. of shares (mil.): 24.9
Return on equity: 37.1%	Dividends
Cash ($ mil.): 143.2	Yield: —
Current ratio: 1.86	Payout: —
Long-term debt ($ mil.): —	Market value ($ mil.): 3,191.0

	STOCK PRICE ($) FY Close	P/E High/Low	Earnings	Dividends	Book Value
01/16	127.75	47 26	3.59	0.00	11.24
01/15*	102.28	41 20	2.80	0.00	9.11
12/13	77.72	32 11	2.78	0.00	9.38
12/12	31.60	22 13	2.23	0.00	6.71
12/11	30.37	26 14	1.63	0.00	5.82
Annual Growth	43.2%	— —	21.8%	—	17.9%

*Fiscal year change

USD Partners LP

Auditors: BDO USA, LLP

LOCATIONS

HQ: USD Partners LP
811 Main Street, Suite 2800, Houston, TX 77002
Phone: 281 291-0510
Web: www.usdpartners.com

HISTORICAL FINANCIALS

Company Type: Public

Income Statement

FYE: December 31

	REVENUE ($ mil.)	NET INCOME ($ mil.)	NET PROFIT MARGIN	EMPLOYEES
12/15	81.7	17.6	21.6%	0.0
12/14	36.1	(7.6)	—	0.0
12/13	26.3	6.4	24.3%	0.0
12/12	24.8	460.5	1851.6%	0.0
Annual Growth	48.7%	(66.3%)	—	—

2015 Year-End Financials

Debt ratio: 72.9%	No. of shares (mil.): 23.0
Return on equity: —	Dividends
Cash ($ mil.): 10.5	Yield: 15.3%
Current ratio: 1.02	Payout: 134.1%
Long-term debt ($ mil.): 239.4	Market value ($ mil.): 167.0

	STOCK PRICE ($) FY Close	P/E High/Low	Earnings	Dividends	Book Value
12/15	7.24	18 7	0.83	1.11	2.16
12/14	14.17	— —	(0.29)	0.00	1.91
12/13	0.00	— —	(0.00)	0.00	(0.00)
Annual Growth	—	— —	—	—	—

Vail Resorts Inc

Vail Resorts hopes the ski vacation business is all uphill. One of North America's leading ski resort operators Vail Resorts operates four mountain resorts in Colorado (Beaver Creek Breckenridge Mountain Resort Keystone Resort and Vail Mountain) and three in Lake Tahoe on the California/Nevada border (Heavenly Mountain Northstar-at-Tahoe and Kirkwood Mountain Resort). The resorts operate under the company's Mountain segment. Through its Lodging segment the firm owns or manages about 20 resorts in Canada Colorado Utah and Wyoming. It also operates seven golf courses. Vail Resorts also has a Real Estate Development segment that develops real estate in and around the company's resorts.

Geographic Reach

In addition to its resorts in Western mountain states and Canada the company also owns a handful of ski resorts in the Midwest and one in Australia.

Operations

The company reports revenue in three business segments: Mountain (which accounts for about 80% of revenue per year) Lodging (which accounts for about 15% of revenue per year) and Real Estate.

Sales and Marketing

The company promotes its resorts through a variety of targeted marketing and sales programs. These include customer relationship marketing (CRM) to targeted audiences promotional programs digital marketing via its websites (including social networking search marketing and display ads) loyalty programs that reward frequent guests and traditional media advertising such as targeted print TV and radio ads.

Vail Resorts has used partnerships as a way to promote its resorts. The company's partners have included American Express GoPro Hertz Nature Valley and Starbucks.

Vail Resorts spent $32.3 million on advertising expenses in fiscal 2016 up from $27.5 million in fiscal 2015.

Financial Performance

The company's revenue has been increasing year-over-year. It reported revenue of about $1.6 billion for fiscal 2016 up roughly $200 million compared to the previous fiscal period when Vail Resorts reported almost $1.4 billion in revenue. The spike in revenue was largely the result of increased revenue from the company's Mountain segment.

The increased total annual revenue in fiscal 2016 led to increased net income. The company reported net income of about $150 million for fiscal 2016 up from the roughly $115 million it claimed for net income the prior year.

Strategy

Peak operating season for Vail Resorts is of course ski season which lasts from mid-November through mid-April. The company's largest source of revenue is its Mountain segment which makes most of its money from the sale of lift tickets (including season passes). Lift tickets represent about 40% of the Mountain segment's net revenue.

In order to deal with challenges in the tourism and real estate markets Vail Resorts has also been diversifying into revenue streams beyond its core operations. Its Mountain News Corporation operates the online snow sports portal OnTheSnow.com and resort guide information provider MountainGetaway.com. Mountain News targets the skiers snowboarders and resort travelers who subscribe to its websites.

Like many of its rival ski operators the company has been focused on marketing its ski properties as year-round operations in an effort to avoid serious business declines during periods of unseasonable winters. Vail Resorts promotes the use of its resorts for summer activities such as mountain biking zip lines ropes courses golf tennis and fishing to woo warm-weather visitors.

The company invests around $10 million per year to make enhancements to the ski and ride experience for its guests.

Mergers and Acquisitions

Vail Resorts completed its acquisition of Whistler Blackcomb Holdings Inc. (Whistler Blackcomb) in late 2016 for about $1.1 billion. Whistler Blackcomb operates the Whistler Blackcomb resort a year round mountain resort.

HISTORY

Company Background

Vail Mountain resort was first developed by New Hampshire native Pete Seibert and opened in 1962. In 1966 Seibert's Vail Associates went public and later bought Beaver Creek Mountain in 1971. But in 1976 a gondola accident killed four skiers (the worst US skiing accident at the time) and lawsuits forced Vail Associates to sell a controlling interest to Texas oil magnate Harry Bass for $13 million. A row with his children ousted Bass in 1984 and the next year Vail was bought for $130 million by businessman George Gillett.

Gillett Holdings declared bankruptcy in 1991 however and the next year it was acquired by Wall Street deal maker Leon Black's Apollo Advisors. Gillett was allowed to stay on as chairman of Vail but left in 1996. Norwegian Cruise Lines president Adam Aron was named chairman and CEO that year (he departed in 2006). The company's acquisition of the Breckenridge Keystone and Arapahoe Basin resorts from Ralcorp in 1997 made it the nation's top ski resort company. (It later divested Arapahoe Basin at the request of the FTC.) Vail Resorts went public that year and later it acquired the Breckenridge Hilton the area's largest hotel and the 61-room Lodge at Vail.

In 1998 days after the company cleared trees to begin work on an ecologically disputed expansion at Vail Mountain multiple fires caused $12 million in damage and completely destroyed a restaurant ski patrol headquarters and a picnic area. Environmental group Earth Liberation Front claimed responsibility for the fires. Poor weather that winter added to the company's woes and it lost its top ranking to Canada's Intrawest.

The following year Vail bought three resorts in Grand Teton National Park at Jackson Hole Wyoming for $50 million from CSX Corp. As Internet marketing became increasingly important the company also bought Colorado ISP VailNet and Web services firm InterNetWorks. Early in 2000 Vail opened its contested Blue Sky Basin expansion. Later that year the company bought 51% of the Renaissance Resort and Spa (renamed Snake River Lodge and Spa) in Jackson Hole Wyoming.

As part of Vail's efforts to become less dependent on seasonality the firm in 2001 bought Rock-Resorts International which operated 11 resort hotels across the US. Also that year it bought the 349-room Vail Marriott Mountain Resort from Host Marriott for $49.5 million. In 2002 the company acquired Heavenly Ski Resort located on the Nevada/California border for about $102 million.

The company sold its Vail Marriott Mountain Resort in 2005 to DiamondRock Hospitality for $62 million while retaining a management agreement to run the property through 2020. The following year chairman and CEO Aron decided that his ten year anniversary was a good time to call it quits and he did. Robert Katz was appointed CEO in 2006.

In 2008 Vail Resorts acquired CME a shuttle business that offers year-round ground transportation from Denver International Airport and Eagle County Airport to resorts in Vail Aspen and Summit County Colorado.

In 2010 the company added a sixth ski resort to its portfolio: Northstar-at-Tahoe. Vail Resorts acquired a long-term lease on the property —owned by CNL Lifestyle Properties (part of CNL Financial Group) —from Vail-based Booth Creek Ski Holdings for some $63 million. The purchase allowed Vail Resorts to move into the North Shore of Lake Tahoe. (Its other property in the area Heavenly Mountain is on the South Shore.)

Also in 2010 the company acquired Mountain News Corporation which operates the online snow sports portal OnTheSnow.com and resort guide information provider MountainGetaway.com. Vail Resorts made the purchase worth nearly $16 million to reach the nearly 400000 skiers snowboarders and resort travelers who subscribe to Mountain News' websites.

In 2012 the company expanded its resort holdings when it acquired Kirkwood Mountain Resort in Lake Tahoe California for about $18 million. Also that year OnTheSnow.com expanded through the purchase of Skiinfo.com.

In 2016 the company paid about $1.1 billion to acquire Whistler Blackcomb Holdings Inc.

EXECUTIVES

Director, Robert A. (Rob) Katz, age 49, $869,341 total compensation

EVP and CIO, Robert N. Urwiler

SVP and COO Vail Mountain Division, Christopher E. (Chris) Jarnot

EVP and CFO, Michael Z. Barkin, age 38, $399,900 total compensation

President Mountain Division, Patricia A. (Pat) Campbell, age 53, $390,000 total compensation

EVP and Chief People Officer, Mark R. Gasta

EVP General Counsel and Secretary, David T. Shapiro, age 46, $375,794 total compensation

EVP and Chief Marketing Officer Vail Resorts Management Company, Kirsten A. Lynch, age 48, $399,900 total compensation

SVP and COO Hospitality, James C. O'Donnell

COO Retail, Greg Sullivan

Vice President of Marketing, Kieran Cain

Auditors: PricewaterhouseCoopers LLP

LOCATIONS

HQ: Vail Resorts Inc
390 Interlocken Crescent, Broomfield, CO 80021
Phone: 303 404-1800   **Fax:** 303 404-6415
Web: www.vailresorts.com

PRODUCTS/OPERATIONS

2016 Charts

	$ mil.	% of total
Mountain		
Lift tickets	658.0	41
Retail/rental	241.1	15
Ski school	143.2	9
Dining	121.0	8
Other	141.2	9
Lodging	274.6	17
Real Estate	22.1	1
Total	**1,601.2**	**100**

Selected Operations

Skiing
  Beaver Creek Resort (Colorado)
  Breckenridge Ski Resort (Colorado)
  Heavenly Mountain Resort (Lake Tahoe NV)
  Keystone Resort (Colorado)

Vail Mountain (Colorado)
Resorts
  The Arrabelle at Vail Square (Colorado)
  Austria Haus Hotel (Vail CO)
  Breckenridge Mountain Lodge (Colorado)
  The Great Divide Lodge (Breckenridge CO)
  Hotel Jerome (Aspen CO)
  The Keystone Lodge (Colorado)
  The Landings St. Lucia (West Indies)
  The Lodge at Vail (Colorado)
  Mountain Thunder Lodge (Breckenridge CO)
  The Osprey at Beaver Creek (Colorado)
  The Pines Lodge (Beaver Creek CO)
  Ski Tip Lodge (Keystone CO)
  Snake River Lodge & Spa (Teton Village WY)
  Vail Marriott Mountain Resort & Spa (Colorado)
  Village Hotel (Breckenridge CO)
  Whistler Blackcomb (Whisler BC Canada)

COMPETITORS

Aspen Skiing	International Leisure
Booth Creek Ski	Mammoth Mountain
Holdings	Sinclair Oil
Boyne USA	Snowdance
Club Med	The Resort Company
Crested Butte	Winter Sports

HISTORICAL FINANCIALS

Company Type: Public

Income Statement   FYE: July 31

	REVENUE ($ mil.)	NET INCOME ($ mil.)	NET PROFIT MARGIN	EMPLOYEES
07/16	1,601.2	149.7	9.4%	27,000.0
07/15	1,399.9	114.7	8.2%	21,613.0
07/14	1,254.6	28.4	2.3%	23,000.0
07/13	1,120.8	37.7	3.4%	23,800.0
07/12	1,024.3	16.4	1.6%	20,780.0
Annual Growth	**11.8%**	**73.7%**	**—**	**6.8%**

2016 Year-End Financials

Debt ratio: 28.2%	No. of shares (mil.): 36.1
Return on equity: 17.1%	Dividends
Cash ($ mil.): 67.9	Yield: 0.0%
Current ratio: 0.64	Payout: 71.4%
Long-term debt ($ mil.): 686.9	Market value ($ mil.): 5,176.0

	STOCK PRICE ($) FY Close	P/E High/Low		PER SHARE ($) Earnings	Dividends	Book Value
07/16	143.07	35	25	4.01	2.87	24.17
07/15	109.69	35	23	3.07	2.08	23.73
07/14	75.50	100	82	0.77	1.25	22.67
07/13	66.98	64	47	1.03	0.79	22.91
07/12	49.64	111	76	0.45	0.68	22.55
Annual Growth	**30.3%**		**—**	**72.8%**	**43.5%**	**1.8%**

Valero Energy Partners LP

Valero Energy Partners teams up with Valero Energy to bring energy in the form of petroleum products to the world. The company was formed to serve as the transportation and logistics arm of major independent US refiner Valero Energy. It makes money from fees on pipeline transportation and storage of crude oil and refined petroleum along the US Gulf Coast and eastern US. The part-

nership serves Valero's two plants in Port Arthur and Sunray Texas and one in Memphis. As a partnership Valero Energy Partners is exempt from paying corporate income tax. It went public in 2013. In 2016 the company bought the McKee Terminal Services Business from Valero Energy for $240 million.
Auditors: KPMG LLP

LOCATIONS

HQ: Valero Energy Partners LP
One Valero Way, San Antonio, TX 78249
Phone: 210 345-2000
Web: www.valeroenergypartners.com

HISTORICAL FINANCIALS

Company Type: Public

Income Statement FYE: December 31

	REVENUE ($ mil.)	NET INCOME ($ mil.)	NET PROFIT MARGIN	EMPLOYEES
12/15	243.6	101.8	41.8%	0.0
12/14	129.1	68.7	53.2%	0.0
12/13	94.5	50.1	53.1%	0.0
12/12	86.8	42.2	48.7%	0.0
12/11	73.1	25.8	35.3%	0.0
Annual Growth	35.1%	40.9%	—	—

2015 Year-End Financials

Debt ratio: 64.2%
Return on equity: —
Cash ($ mil.): 80.7
Current ratio: 7.50
Long-term debt ($ mil.): 545.2
No. of shares (mil.): 66.6
Dividends
Yield: 2.2%
Payout: 41.4%
Market value ($ mil.): 3,440.0

	STOCK PRICE ($) FY Close	P/E High/Low		PER SHARE ($) Earnings	Dividends	Book Value
12/15	51.61	13	9	4.19	1.14	4.35
12/14	43.25	28	16	2.02	0.71	9.96
12/13	34.45	549	467	0.06	0.04	10.92
Annual Growth 22.4% (36.9%)				—	—735.7%	455.9%

Vantage Drilling Co

From its vantage point Vantage Drilling Company sees nothing but the high seas from atop its drilling rigs. An offshore drilling contractor Vantage Drilling provides oil and natural gas drilling services to multinational oil and natural gas companies operating in shallow to ultra-deepwater environments. The company owns and operates four jackup rigs (for shallow water drilling) and three ultra-deep drillship (designed for drilling in water depths of 12000 ft.) Vantage Drilling typically operates in Southeast Asia West Africa and other oil-rich offshore regions.

Geographic Reach

Vantage operates through offices in Houston Singapore and Dubai. It gets half of ts revenues from outside of the US.

Operations

The company contract drilling units (and related equipment and work crews) primarily on a dayrate basis to drillers of oil and natural gas wells. Vantage also provides construction supervision serv-

ices for and operates and manages drilling units owned by others.

Financial Performance

In 2012 Vantage's revenues declined by 3% due to lower management fees and weaker reimbursable revenues as the result of having only one ongoing project as compared to having four ongoing projects during 2011.

It reported a net loss in 2012 of $145.3 million (compared to a net loss of $79.9 million in 2011) due to a decrease net sales and a significant increase on debt extinguishment costs.

Strategy

Vantage which started out with only jackup rigs has added drillships to its fleet in recent years in order to serve oil companies operating in deepwater and ultra-deepwater environments. The company's efforts give it an opportunity expand its market presence as ultra-deepwater drilling is the a growth market in the oil and gas industry. Ultimately Vantage is hoping its efforts will help it grow its customer base.

In 2013 the company's new Tungsten Explorer ultra-deepwater drillship (completed that year) commenced operating in Southeast Asia.

That year Vantage formed a joint venture with an affiliate of Skeie Group to build high specification drillship at STX Offshore & Shipbuilding Co. Ltd.'s yard in South Korea. Through its investment of $31 million Vantage will own 42% of the joint venture entity Sigma Drilling. The new vessel (Palladium Explorer) will be capable of and equipped to operate in 12000 ft water depth and have a 25000 metric ton variable deck load.

In 2012 Vantage agreed to buy an ultra-deepwater drillship (Dragonquest) from Valencia Drilling for $164 million.

Mergers and Acquisitions

In 2012 the company acquired the Titanium Explorer deepwater drillship for $169 million.

Company Background

A relatively young company Vantage was founded in 2006 but was unprofitable until 2009 during which it began to bring in significant revenue. Since its inception it has been busy building up its fleet entering into agreements to manage and operate rigs on behalf of third-parties and expanding its services into new markets. In addition Vantage began operating off the coast of India and in the Gulf of Mexico in 2011.

EXECUTIVES

Chairman and CEO, Paul A. Bragg, age 59
Chief Accounting Officer, Edward G. Brantley, age 60
CFO and Treasurer, Douglas G. Smith, age 47
COO, Douglas W. Halkett, age 55
VP Operations, Donald Munro, age 61
VP Assets and Engineering, William L. Thomson, age 45
Chief Administrative Officer, Christopher G. DeClaire, age 56
VP Marketing, Michael R.C. Derbyshire, age 62
Vice President QHSE, Dave Weatherly
Vice President Operations, Don Munro
Vice President Assets & Engineering, Bill Thomson
Director, Duke R. Ligon, age 74
Director, Marcelo D. Guiscardo, age 63
Director, Jorge E. Estrada, age 68
Director, Robert F. Grantham, age 57
Director, Steinar Thomassen, age 69
Independent Director, Steven Bradshaw
Auditors: BDO USA, LLP

LOCATIONS

HQ: Vantage Drilling Co
777 Post Oak Boulevard, Suite 800, Houston, TX 77056
Phone: 281 404-4700 **Fax:** 281 404-4749
Web: www.vantagedrilling.com

PRODUCTS/OPERATIONS

2012 Sales

	% of total
Contract Drilling Services	90
Reimbursements	9
Management Fees	1
Total	**100**

COMPETITORS

Atwood Oceanics
Diamond Offshore
Ensco
Helmerich & Payne International Drilling
Hercules Offshore
Nabors Industries
Noble
Oceaneering International
Parker Drilling
Rowan Companies
Saipem
Seadrill
Transocean

HISTORICAL FINANCIALS

Company Type: Public

Income Statement FYE: December 31

	REVENUE ($ mil.)	NET INCOME ($ mil.)	NET PROFIT MARGIN	EMPLOYEES
12/15	772.2	17.2	2.2%	843.0
12/14	875.5	42.0	4.8%	1,295.0
12/13	732.0	(81.8)	—	1,274.0
12/12	471.4	(145.3)	—	1,056.0
12/11	485.3	(79.9)	—	980.0
Annual Growth	12.3%	—	—	(3.7%)

2015 Year-End Financials

Debt ratio: 1.8%
Return on equity: 3.4%
Cash ($ mil.): 203.4
Current ratio: 2.72
Long-term debt ($ mil.): —
No. of shares (mil.): 0.0
Dividends
Yield: —
Payout: —
Market value ($ mil.): 0.0

	STOCK PRICE ($) FY Close	P/E High/Low		PER SHARE ($) Earnings	Dividends	Book Value
12/15	0.00	—	—	(0.00)	0.00	
456,756.00						
12/14	0.49	14	3	0.14	0.00	1.81
12/13	1.84	—	—	(0.27)	0.00	1.66
12/12	1.83	—	—	(0.50)	0.00	1.90
12/11	1.16	—	—	(0.28)	0.00	2.39
Annual Growth (78.2%) 1990.8%				—	—	—

VASCO Data Security International Inc

VASCO Data Security International holds the key to electronic banking. Its hardware and software lines include authentication platforms security tokens handheld devices and related applications used for authenticating a person's identity on computer networks. The company's products incorporate authentication and digital signature security technologies and can be used to secure intranets extranets and LANs. In addition to banking VASCO's products are used to provide remote workers with secure access to corporate networks; other applications include e-commerce transactions. It counts more than 10000 customers including some 1700 financial institutions such as Citibank BNP-Paribas and HSBC.

Operations

Banking products and services generate 87% of VASCO's revenue with the rest coming from its enterprise and application security segment.

Geographic Reach

The Chicago-based company has customers in more than 100 countries but its largest market is Europe which accounts for about 68% of sales. There it has R&D centers in Austria France the Netherlands and the UK. Asia accounts for about 20% of sales and the US less than 10%.

It has sales offices in Australia Belgium Brazil China Dubai India Japan Singapore the UK and the US (in Marlborough Massachusetts.)

Sales and Marketing

VASCO Data Security uses a direct sales force as well as a network of 52 distributors their resellers and systems integrators. While it has a large customer base its top 10 customers account for 50% of sales. In 2015 Rabobank contributed 30% of its worldwide revenue. Other customers include Belfius Sumitomo Mitsui Banking Corporation BNP-Paribas Fortis Swedbank Citibank and Commonwealth Bank of Australia.

Financial Performance

In fiscal 2015 VASCO's sales increased 20% to $241 million from 2014. Increased sales of its CrontoSign card readers to Rabobank helped lift revenue while sales in Enterprise and Application Security ticked down 3%.

Reduced costs combined with higher revenue pushed VASCO's net income 26% higher to about $69 million in 2015 from 2014.

Strategy

Banks and other financial institutions remain VASCO's bread-and-butter customer base but the company is expanding its enterprise security business. It serves the enterprise market exclusively through indirect marketing channels. VASCO has also made some of its products available under the Software-as-a-Service model.

VASCO has developed a clear strategy of using mobile applications to move beyond pure authentication services to more risk-based services based on a scoring mechanism. At the core is DIGIPASS for Application Perimeter Protection SDK (DIGIPASS for APPS) on the client side and VACMAN Controller on the server side.

In 2016 VASCO added to its DIGIPASS line with the DIGIPASS 770 authenticator. Its Cronto technology uses an encrypted color QR code to protect against the newest and most sophisticated cyber attacks.

Mergers and Acquisitions

In 2015 VASCO acquired privately held Silanis Technology a provider of electronic signature and digital transaction products used to sign send and manage documents for $85 million. The Silanis eSignLive product adds to VACO's capabilities for web and mobile transactions.

In 2014 VASCO bought Risk IDS a provider of risk-based authentication products for banks.

EXECUTIVES

Chairman and CEO, T. Kendall (Ken) Hunt, age 72, $450,000 total compensation
CFO Secretary and Treasurer, Mark S. Hoyt, $80,173 total compensation
President and COO, Scott M. Clements
VP Product Management and CTO, Benoit Grange
Vice President Corporate Communications, John (Jack) Gunn
Auditors: KPMG LLP

LOCATIONS

HQ: VASCO Data Security International Inc
1901 South Meyers Road, Suite 210, Oakbrook Terrace, IL 60181
Phone: 630 932-8844   **Fax:** 630 932-8852
Web: www.vasco.com

PRODUCTS/OPERATIONS

2015 Sales

	$ mil.	% of total
Banking	209.0	87
Enterprise & Application Security	32.4	13
Total	241.4	0

Selected Services

Consulting Services
Fulfillment Services
Professional Services
Packaging Services
Secrets Retention Service

Selected Products

Single Button DIGIPASS
E-signature DIGIPASS
Software DIGIPASS
Card Reader DIGIPASS
PKI DIGIPASS
Bluetooth Smart DIGIPASS
VACMAN Controller
DIGIPASS Plug-ins

COMPETITORS

ActivIdentity	RSA Security
Check Point Software	SafeNet
Gemalto	VeriSign
IBM Internet Security Systems	

HISTORICAL FINANCIALS

Company Type: Public

Income Statement

FYE: December 31

	REVENUE ($ mil.)	NET INCOME ($ mil.)	NET PROFIT MARGIN	EMPLOYEES
12/15	241.4	42.1	17.5%	545.0
12/14	201.5	33.4	16.6%	371.0
12/13	155.0	11.1	7.2%	396.0
12/12	154.0	15.6	10.1%	374.0
12/11	168.0	18.1	10.8%	358.0
Annual Growth	9.5%	23.5%	—	11.1%

2015 Year-End Financials

Debt ratio: —
Return on equity: 18.5%
Cash ($ mil.): 78.5
Current ratio: 3.29
Long-term debt ($ mil.): —
No. of shares (mil.): 40.1
Dividends
Yield: —
Payout: —
Market value ($ mil.): 671.0

	STOCK PRICE ($) FY Close	P/E High/Low		PER SHARE ($) Earnings	Dividends	Book Value
12/15	16.73	32	14	1.06	0.00	6.18
12/14	28.21	35	8	0.85	0.00	5.19
12/13	7.73	32	26	0.28	0.00	4.40
12/12	8.16	27	16	0.40	0.00	3.99
12/11	6.52	29	10	0.47	0.00	3.56
Annual Growth	26.6%	—	—	22.5%	—	14.8%

VCA Inc

At VCA health care doesn't go to the dogs. Dogs –cats and a boatload of other animals –go to it for health services. The company operates the nation's largest chain of animal hospitals –more than 600 in some 41 states and four Canadian provinces. Its hospitals offer basic wellness checkups dental care neutering and spaying vaccinations and specialty surgeries. With about 60 diagnostic laboratories nationwide VCA also tests blood tissue and urine samples for more than 16000 animal hospitals and practices universities and government agencies. Founded in 1986 as Veterinary Centers of America the company has grown over the years through acquisitions of other animal hospitals and veterinary product suppliers. In 2017 consumer products company Mars agreed to acquire VCA for $9.1 billion including $1.4 billion in debt.

Operations

VCA's fast-growing chain of animal hospitals accounts for 80% of its sales. About 8.8 million animals visited its hospitals in 2014 compared with 7.4 million in 2012. VCA's 50-plus diagnostic laboratories account for almost 20% of sales. the company also sells diagnostic equipment and other medical technology products and related services to the veterinary market.

Geographic Reach

The US accounts for about 95% of VCA's revenue. The company expanded into Canada in 2012 where it operates more than 45 animal hospitals and four laboratories in four provinces.

Sales and Marketing

VCA takes a multifaceted approach to growing its business seeking to increase the number of visits by existing clients and attracting new customers through online and offline initiatives. The company's HealthyPet Magazine focuses on pet care and wellness. VCA also reaches pet owners via direct mail and collateral material available at its animal hospitals. It enters into referral arrangements with local pet shops and humane societies. Marketing and advertising expenses amounted to $6.8 million in 2014 versus $5.9 million and $7.7 million in 2013 and 2012 respectively.

Financial Performance

The company reported $1.9 billion in revenue in 2014 a 6% increase compared with 2013. Net income fell 1.5% over the same period to about $135.4 million. The sales increase was attributed to revenue from animal hospitals acquired in the previous year and growth in the laboratory segment. The laboratory segment revenue rose on a price increase and changes in product mix. Net income was hurt by higher corporate expenses including hiring new employees to support growth.

Strategy

VCA's aggressive expansion strategy has driven steady revenue growth over the years and it continues to pursue acquisitions. It acquired 47 independent animal hospitals with annualized revenue of $122.5 million in 2014. It picked up 20 animal hospitals and one laboratory in the year 2013. That came on the heels of its 2012 purchase of 44 hospitals in Alberta British Columbia and Ontario.

Mergers and Acquisitions

In 2015 VCA's laboratory division agreed to acquire the assets of AVRL (Abaxis Veterinary Reference Laboratory) from Abaxis for $21 million in cash. The companies will maintain their co-marketing relationship after the conclusion of the deal expected in 2015. The companies co-market diagnostic services consisting of Abaxis point-of-care diagnostic products and VCA's reference lab services.

In 2014 VCA bought Camp Bow Wow Franchising which offers pet grooming boarding and other services. It has 125 franchised stores in 37 states and in Canada.

EXECUTIVES

Co-Founder COO VP Secretary and Director,
Arthur J. Antin, age 69, $619,154 total compensation
VP and CFO, Tomas W. (Tom) Fuller, age 58, $417,769 total compensation
Chairman President and CEO, Robert L. (Bob) Antin, age 66, $971,692 total compensation
Vice President and Chief Medical Officer, Todd (Toddy) Tams
Medical Director, Roderick Gant
Medical Director, Alayson Phelps
Medical Director, Brett Neville
Medical Director, George (Georgey) Tabone
Medical Director, Nancy (Nance) Wilber
Vice President Finance And Admin, Bruce (Brucey) Bargmann
Regional Vice President, Leann (Ann) Palm
Medical Director, Amanda (Mandy) Place
Medical Director Vca 12 Mile Animal Hospital, Donald (Don) Kennard
Auditors: KPMG LLP

LOCATIONS

HQ: VCA Inc
12401 West Olympic Boulevard, Los Angeles, CA 90064-1022
Phone: 310 571-6500
Web: www.vcaantech.com

PRODUCTS/OPERATIONS

2012 Sales

	$ mil.	% of total
Animal hospitals	1,331.3	75
Laboratories	327.8	18
Other	112.9	7
Adjustments	(72.4)	-
Total	**1,699.6**	**100**

Selected Mergers and Acquisitions

COMPETITORS

IDEXX Labs	PetMed
Medical Management	PetSmart
International	

HISTORICAL FINANCIALS
Company Type: Public

Income Statement

	REVENUE ($ mil.)	NET INCOME ($ mil.)	NET PROFIT MARGIN	EMPLOYEES
12/15	2,133.6	211.0	9.9%	12,700.0
12/14	1,918.4	135.4	7.1%	11,500.0
12/13	1,803.3	137.5	7.6%	11,000.0
12/12	1,699.6	45.5	2.7%	10,500.0
12/11	1,485.3	95.4	6.4%	9,900.0
Annual Growth	**9.5%**	**22.0%**	**—**	**6.4%**

FYE: December 31

2015 Year-End Financials

Debt ratio: 34.8%	No. of shares (mil.): 80.7
Return on equity: 17.2%	Dividends
Cash ($ mil.): 98.8	Yield: —
Current ratio: 1.21	Payout: —
Long-term debt ($ mil.): 838.8	Market value ($ mil.): 4,442.0

	STOCK PRICE ($) FY Close	P/E High/Low		PER SHARE ($) Earnings	Dividends	Book Value
12/15	55.00	24	18	2.56	0.00	15.41
12/14	48.77	32	19	1.54	0.00	14.48
12/13	31.36	20	14	1.53	0.00	14.77
12/12	21.05	46	35	0.51	0.00	13.39
12/11	19.75	24	14	1.09	0.00	12.76
Annual Growth	**29.2%**	**— —**		**23.8%**	**—**	**4.8%**

Vector Group Ltd

Vector Group is small potatoes next to Big Tobacco running a distant fourth in the US market. The holding company's Liggett and Vector Tobacco subsidiaries manufacture discount cigarettes under brands including Liggett Select Grand Prix Pyramid and Eve and several private-label brands of cigarettes for other companies including the USA brand. The company manufactures cigarettes in North Carolina and distributes them throughout the US. Vector Group's real estate unit New Valley owns about 70% stake in the New York City broker Douglas Elliman Realty. It's looking to acquire other properties. All of Vector Group's revenue is derived from the sale of discount cigarettes.

HISTORY

Former computer analyst Bennett LeBow founded Brooke Partners in 1980 (renamed Brooke Group in 1990) to acquire troubled companies and turn them around. Many of LeBow's early investments were in the computer industry. He eventually expanded into other areas including tobacco (with the purchase of Liggett in 1986).

Founded in 1822 by the Liggett family as a snuff maker and joined by George Myers in 1873 Liggett & Myers produced several popular cigarette brands including L&M and Chesterfield. Liggett slipped during the 1950s and 1960s by failing to exploit the market for filtered and low-tar cigarettes. Although Liggett launched a successful discount brand under LeBow (Pyramid) its US market share continued to dwindle.

Like Liggett many of LeBow's other businesses were slipping. In 1993 Western Union (bought in 1987 and renamed New Valley) and computer

maker MAI Systems (bought in 1985) entered Chapter 11 bankruptcy. That year LeBow paid about $20 million to Brooke Group shareholders who sued a group of company officers who they believed were stripping assets and using the company for personal loans.

Frustrated in the US Brooke Group turned to developing new markets. In 1993 the company began a joint venture with Russian cigarette maker Ducat. In 1995 New Valley emerged from bankruptcy.

In 1997 the company made deals with 41 states regarding tobacco-related Medicaid payments. But most of Liggett's state deals were negated when in late 1998 it joined a $206 billion settlement hammered out with 46 states by its much larger rivals. As part of the deal Liggett did not have to chip in as long as its market share stayed below its 1997 level of 1.67%.

To cut debt Liggett sold its L&M Chesterfield and Lark brands to Philip Morris for $300 million in 1999. (The deal also kept Liggett's market share well below 1.67%.) Also in 1999 an Alabama court rejected an agreement that would have allowed Liggett to settle tobacco-related lawsuits with a limited fund. That year the US government filed a massive lawsuit against the Big Tobacco companies to recover health care costs and profits allegedly derived from fraud.

In 2000 the firm changed its name to Vector Group to remove the old name's stigma of sick-smoker lawsuits. The company said it would appeal a Florida's $790 million verdict against it. Later Vector Group sold its Liggett-Ducat subsidiary (Russia) to cigarette manufacturer Gallaher for $400 million. A Florida judge upheld the July 2000 verdict; meanwhile Vector angled for a global settlement of all punitive cases payable to a public health trust fund over a 30-year period.

The company along with Brown & Williamson Lorillard (Carolina Group) Philip Morris and R.J. Reynolds faced paying Florida smokers $145 billion after losing a lengthy court battle in 2000. Three years later a state appeals court threw out the case saying that the thousands of Florida smokers named in the case could not lump their complaints in a single lawsuit. That decision is now under review by the Florida Supreme Court.

In late 2001 Vector launched OMNI a reduced-carcinogen cigarette which received a lukewarm acceptance and hit a slow burn in sales. OMNI generated a disappointing $5.1 million in revenue for 70.7 million units. (Vector gave up on the product several years later.)

The next year the company created Liggett Vector Brands a new unit that combines the sales and marketing functions of its Liggett Group and Vector Tobacco subsidiaries. Vector also bought The Medallion Company a discount cigarette manufacturer (USA and Marlin brands) for $110 million.

Vector closed its Timberlake North Carolina production plant and laid off 150 workers in 2003. The company moved operations to a nearby cigarette plant in Mebane North Carolina.

Vector announced in August 2004 that it would sell its reduced-nicotine cigarette brand QUEST on the Internet beginning in 2005 and is seeking FDA approval to sell QUEST as a device for quitting smoking. (In 2009 the company decided against seeking FDA approval of Quest as a smoking cessation aide citing the significant time and expense involved in seeking it.) However it switched gears in November 2004 by putting an indefinite hold on a national rollout of QUEST. The company said a review of marketing data made such a move necessary. Vector laid off approximately 330 full-time and 135 part-time positions that December.

In March 2005 the company began supplying Montego deep-discount brand cigarettes exclusively to more than 2200 Circle K and Mac's convenience stores in the US. In November it entered into a similar deal with Sunoco which operates 800-plus Sonoco APlus convenience stores to make and supply Silver Eagle brand cigarettes to its stores.

Howard Lorber succeeded LeBow as CEO in 2006. Later that year Vector entered into a settlement with the Internal Revenue Service that called for the company to pay about $42 million related to a gain stemming from a 1998 and 1999 deal with Philip Morris.

To tap the popular and more politically correct smokeless tobacco market Vector launched Grand Prix-branded snus in May 2008. The pouched tobacco product is made in Sweden and rolls out in a trio of varieties.

EXECUTIVES

VP CFO and Treasurer, J. Bryant Kirkland, age 50, $425,000 total compensation

EVP, Richard J. (Dick) Lampen, age 61, $900,000 total compensation

President and CEO, Howard M. Lorber, age 67, $3,055,482 total compensation

President and CEO Liggett Group LLC and Liggett Vector Brands LLC, Ronald J. Bernstein, age 62, $908,719 total compensation

Chairman, Bennett S. LeBow, age 78

Auditors: Deloitte & Touche LLP

LOCATIONS

HQ: Vector Group Ltd
4400 Biscayne Boulevard, Miami, FL 33137
Phone: 305 579-8000
Web: www.vectorgroupltd.com

PRODUCTS/OPERATIONS

2015 Sales

	$ mil.	% of total
Tobacco	1,017.8	61
Real estate	641.4	39
E-Cigarettes	(2.0)	—
Total	**1,657.2**	**100**

Selected Cigarette Brands

Eve
Grand Prix
Jade (licensed)
Liggett Select
Pyramid
USA

Selected Subsidiaries

Liggett Group LLC
Liggett Vector Brands LLC
New Valley LLC
Vector Tobacco Inc.
VGR Holing LLC

COMPETITORS

800-JR Cigar	Reynolds American
Century 21 Real Estate	Smokin Joes
Commonwealth Brands	Sotheby's
Philip Morris USA	International Realty
RE/MAX	

HISTORICAL FINANCIALS

Company Type: Public

Income Statement

FYE: December 31

	REVENUE ($ mil.)	NET INCOME ($ mil.)	NET PROFIT MARGIN	EMPLOYEES
12/15	1,657.2	59.2	3.6%	1,367.0
12/14	1,591.3	36.9	2.3%	1,090.0
12/13	1,056.2	38.9	3.7%	989.0
12/12	1,084.5	30.6	2.8%	587.0
12/11	1,133.3	75.0	6.6%	559.0
Annual Growth	**10.0%**	**(5.7%)**	**—**	**25.1%**

2015 Year-End Financials

Debt ratio: 68.2%
Return on equity: —
Cash ($ mil.): 240.3
Current ratio: 2.70
Long-term debt ($ mil.): 886.2
No. of shares (mil.): 129.9
Dividends
Yield: 6.8%
Payout: 330.3%
Market value ($ mil.): 3,066.0

	STOCK PRICE ($) FY Close	P/E High/Low	Earnings	PER SHARE ($) Dividends	Book Value
12/15	23.59	55 45	0.47	1.54	(1.59)
12/14	21.31	75 51	0.32	1.47	(0.45)
12/13	16.37	48 42	0.35	1.40	(0.84)
12/12	14.87	64 51	0.29	1.33	(0.73)
12/11	17.76	26 22	0.73	1.27	(0.88)
Annual Growth	**7.4%**	**— —**	**(10.5%)**	**5.0%**	**—**

Veeva Systems Inc

Veeva Systems is breathing new life into software for the health care industry. Its cloud-based software and mobile apps are used by pharmaceutical and biotechnology companies to manage critical business functions. Veeva Systems' customer relationship management software uses Salesforce's platform to manage sales and marketing functions. Its Veeva Vault provides content management and collaboration software for quality management in clinical trials and regulatory compliance for new drug submissions. Its software is used in 75 countries and available in more than 25 languages but North America is its largest market. Founded in 2007 Veeva Systems went public in 2013.

Operations

Veeva sells its products through subscriptions and they account for about three-quarters of its business. The rest comes from professional services it provides for installing and training on its software.

Geographic Reach

Veeva Systems operates from three offices in the US and one in Canada. It also has locations in China Japan and Spain. North America is its largest market accounting for 55% of sales. Europe makes up another 26% while customers in Asia account for about 20% of sales. Sales outside North American increased about 64% in 2015 (ended January).

The company runs its software on data centers in California Illinois and Virginia and Germany Japan and the UK.

Sales and Marketing

The company uses a direct sales force with representatives in more than a dozen countries. Veeva Systems counts about 275 customers including

global pharmaceutical companies such as Bayer Boehringer Ingelheim Eli Lilly Gilead Sciences Merck and Novartis.

Financial Performance

Veeva Systems has posted big gains in revenue since 2011. Sales zoomed from $30 million in fiscal 2011 (year-end January) to $313 million in 2015. In addition it has been consistently profitable which is uncommon for a relatively new and growing company. Profit increased almost 50% in 2015. While the company has increased spending on research and development and sales and marketing revenue growth covered the higher spending and then some.

Strategy

The company makes 95% of sales from its Veeva CRM customer relationship management software but new products are also being developed. Its latest software offering is Veeva Network a customer master solution that creates and maintains healthcare provider and organization master data. Veeva Network also contains a proprietary database of people and companies in China and the US using data gathered from state federal and industry sources.

While Veeva Systems currently focuses on the life sciences industry specifically pharmaceutical and biotechnology companies it would like to expand to other specialized companies such as contract research organizations (CROs) and contract manufacturing organizations (CMOs).

Mergers and Acquisitions

In 2015 Veeva acquired Qforma CrowdLink a developer of key opinion leader (KOL) data and services for life sciences' brand medical and market access teams. Veeva introduced a product based on Qforma technology to help its customers get more sophisticated information for introducing products.

EXECUTIVES

International Vice President, Dan (Danny) Goldsmith

Vice President Multichannel Strategy, Paul (Pauly) Shawah

Vice President Of Marketing, Gary (Gar) Damiano

Vice President, Jennifer (Jen) Goldsmith

Vice President Sales Network Data, Edward Manko

Executive Vice President Global Sales, Alan Mateo

Vice President Products And Technology, Stan Wong

Vice President US Operations for Zinc Ahead, Michael (Mel) Naimoli

Vice President Sales Americas, Tom Darby

Vice President Customer Support, Hind Roubos

Auditors: KPMG LLP

LOCATIONS

HQ: Veeva Systems Inc
4280 Hacienda Drive, Pleasanton, CA 94588
Phone: 925 452-6500 **Fax:** 925 452-6504
Web: www.veeva.com

PRODUCTS/OPERATIONS

2015 Sales

	% of total
Subscription fees	74
Professional services	26
Total	**100**

Selected Products

Veeva CRM (customer relationship management)
Veeva CLM (closed-loop marketing)
Veeva iRep (mobile app for Apple products)

Veeva CRM Approved Email (tracks regulatory compliant emails between sales reps and physicians)

Veeva Vault (content management and collaboration software)

Veeva Vault eTMF (document management for clinical trials)

Veeva Vault Investigator Portal (secure file exchange for clinical trials)

Veeva Vault MedComms (medical content management)

Veeva Vault PromoMats (promotional materials management)

Veeva Vault QualityDocs (quality management)

Veeva Vault Submissions (document management for regulatory submissions)

Veeva Network (master software and data stewardship)

Veeva Network Provider Database (proprietary database of people and companies in China and the US)

Veeva Network Customer Master (cleanse and match people and company data)

Veeva Network Data Stewardship Services (data management)

COMPETITORS

Advanced Health Media	Microsoft
Allscripts	Open Text
Computer Sciences	Oracle
Corp.	SDI Health
EMC	StayinFront
IMS Health	

HISTORICAL FINANCIALS

Company Type: Public

Income Statement
FYE: January 31

	REVENUE ($ mil.)	NET INCOME ($ mil.)	NET PROFIT MARGIN	EMPLOYEES
01/16	409.2	54.4	13.3%	1,474.0
01/15	313.2	40.3	12.9%	951.0
01/14	210.1	23.6	11.2%	725.0
01/13	129.5	18.7	14.5%	593.0
01/12	61.2	4.2	6.9%	0.0
Annual Growth	60.8%	89.4%	—	—

2016 Year-End Financials

Debt ratio: —	No. of shares (mil.): 133.5
Return on equity: 11.9%	Dividends
Cash ($ mil.): 132.1	Yield: —
Current ratio: 2.69	Payout: —
Long-term debt ($ mil.): —	Market value ($ mil.): 3,218.0

	STOCK PRICE ($) FY Close	P/E High/Low	PER SHARE ($) Earnings	Dividends	Book Value
01/16	24.10	80 56	0.38	0.00	3.78
01/15	28.76	122 58	0.28	0.00	3.10
01/14	31.79	231 155	0.15	0.00	2.24
Annual Growth	(12.9%)	— —	59.2%	—	29.8%

Verint Systems, Inc

Verint Systems makes software that helps some of its customers identify customer opportunities and other customers identify security threats. The company provides such "actionable intelligence" through systems for capturing and analyzing structured and unstructured data from voice video text and social media sources. Its software and services offered in on-premise and cloud-based versions are used by enterprise customers to improve customer service interactions and operations and by law enforcement and government agencies to combat crime and provide security. Verint's customers are in some 180 countries and include more than 80% of the FORTUNE 100. It generates about half of its sales outside the US.

Operations

Impact 360 and Voice of the Customer Analytics are the core products in Verint's enterprise intelligence segment (55% of sales). It helps optimizei workforce functions and operations specifically in customer-related applications. It addresses areas such as customer interactions quality monitoring performance coaching and customer feedback analytics.

Products in Verint's Cyber Intelligence segment (about 35% of sales) are sold under brands such as ENGAGE RELIANT and VANTAGE. Products are used for such functions as intercepting communications mobile location tracking web intelligence and tactical communications intelligence to combat terrorist threats and handle criminal activity such as financial fraud drug trafficking and cyber attacks.

Video Intelligence products (about 10% of sales) sold under the Nextiva brand provide networked IP video technology. Communications and video are used by law enforcement and government agencies.

Geographic Reach

Headquartered in Melville New York Verint operates about 60 offices around the world in the US and in Indonesia Israel Germany and the UK. About 40% revenue comes from customers in the US with customers in Europe the Middle East and Africa accounting for 30% of revenue.

Sales and Marketing

The company sells through direct sales teams and indirect channels which include distributors systems integrators value-added resellers and OEM partners. Sales are split evenly between direct and indirect sales. About a third of revenue comes from governments around the world.

Financial Performance

Verint's revenue of $1.1 billion barely budged in 2016 (ended January) compared to 2015 rising just $2 million year-to-year. A 5% drop in sales for the Enterprise Intelligence segment was balanced by increases in Cyber Intelligence Video Intelligence and service and support. The company reported several issues that exerted pressure on revenue. It said sales cycles stretched longer particularly for large projects; deal sizes were smaller; and that maintenance renewals for the Enterprise Intelligence segment were under pressure. The longer sales cycles and smaller deals were of specific concern to its Security Intelligence business which has elements in the Cyber and Video Intelligence units. Security Intelligence revenue was affected by significant exposure to emerging markets where weak economic conditions have led to budget cuts and currency devaluations.

The company's net income dropped more than 40% to $18 million in 2016 from $31 million in 2015. The company had greater expenses in 2016 including a tax expense that was a benefit in 2015.

Operations generated about $157 million in cash in 2016 compared to $194 million in 2015. Cash flow fluctuates depending on the timing of billings and collections the timing and amounts of interest income tax and other payments and operating results.

Strategy

Verint adds capabilities to account for growing interactions through mobile devices and social media. Its Mobile Work View product is an app that extends common work activities across devices allowing customers' employees to access workplace information at all times. Additions to Verint's Social Engagement product allow customers to engage with their clients for multiple purposes including responding to client requests.

Mergers and Acquisitions

Verint added to its customer service holdings in 2016 with two acquisitions. The acquisition of OpinionLab added a provider of voice of the customer services while the purchase of Contact Solutions brought on board cloud-based voice and mobile customer self-service and business intelligence software. Terms were not disclosed for the OpinionLab deal; the price for Contact Solutions was $67 million.

EXECUTIVES

Corporate Officer President and CEO, Dan Bodner, age 57, $722,825 total compensation

President Verint Communications Interception and Analytics Solutions, Meir Sperling, age 67, $394,011 total compensation

Corporate Officer and President Verint Enterprise Intelligence Solutions and Verint Video and Situation Intelligence Solutions, Elan Moriah, age 53, $406,000 total compensation

Corporate Officer and CFO, Douglas E. (Doug) Robinson, age 60, $406,000 total compensation

Corporate Officer Chief Legal Officer Chief Compliance Officer and Secretary, Peter D. Fante, age 48, $372,300 total compensation

President Communications and Cyber Interlligence, Hanan Gino

Vice President Corporate Development and Investor Relations, Alan (Al) Roden

Vice President Engineering, Ed Boyle

Vice President Sales and Business Development Verint Systems Ltd, Cormac Twomey

Vice President Sales, Jennifer (Jen) Tracy

Vice President Sales, Mike (Mikey) Tomon

Vice President Sales North East, Evgeny Roshal

Vice President Product Development, Chris (Chrissy) Schnurr

Vice President Sales and Marketing, Will (Willy) Torgerson

Vice President Sales Operations and Channel Development, Gary (Gar) Trudo

Vice President of Product Management, Melvin (Mel) Olson

Vice President Network and Cyber Solutions, Yitzhak Vager

Senior Vice President Marketing, Gabriela Cohen

Senior Vice President of Corporate Strategy, Masahiro Moriyasu

Vice President Sales Product Market Management, Kit-Chuan Toon

Vice President Sales, Paul (Pauly) Turcotte

Executive Vice President Marketing, Julie (Jules) Beauregard

Vice President Finance, Kim Enders

Vice President and Commercial Sales, Noga Sadot

Vice President, Patricia (Pat) Gayles

Vice President Sale, Anders Truelsen

Vice President, Trent Isaacs

Senior Vice President Corporate Development and Corporate Treasurer, Chris (Chrissy) Sinkwitz

Vice President of Human Resour, Michelle (Michie) Meurer

RVP Solution Consulting, Ike Eastwood

Vice President, Garrett (Bret) Braithwaite

Vice President, Paul (Pauly) Harvey

Vice President, Nir Pery

Vice President Marketing and PreSale, Eyal Bachar

Vice President Customer Service, Randy Townsend

Vice President Open Source Web Intelligence, Amit (Mit) Kerrigan

Vice President Hosted and Managed Services, Rod (Rodney) Heisey

Vice President Finance, Brett Fleischman

Vice President of Human Resour, Gabrielle Neben

Vice President Application Development, Huw Jones

Vice President Finance And Information Technology, Shawn Walker

Vice President Product Technology, Rod Kero

Canadian Region Vice President Sales, Brad Ramsay

Vice President Marketing, Bryan Debarry

Vice President, Robert (Bob) Dawson

Vice President and Senior CRR Officer, Dinesh Sampangi

Vice President, Roger Lusins

Vice President Global Purchasing, Merav Rehav

Vice President, Kimberly (Kim) Enders

Vice President Corporate Applications, Nirnay Patil

Vice President Sales North America, David Siebert

Vice President, Daniel Ziv

Vice President Sales, Diego Luelmo

Vice President of Sales, Ken (Kenny) Paskins

Vice President, Todd (Toddy) McDermott

Vice President of Architecture and Delivery Assurance, Natraj Subramaniam

Vice President Customer Care, Mike Graci

Vice President Sales and Marketing Verint Sy, Zvi Fischler

Vice President SaaS Business Development, Jim Tanner

Vice President Sales Operations And Channel Development, Gary Trudo

Vice President Finance at Verint, Mary Sursavage Mary Sursavage

Senior Vice President of Strategy and Planning for Worldwide Operations, Glen Scott

Vice President Legal, Brian Leslie

Vice President Customer Care, Yaniv Cohen

Senior Vice President Of Global Marketing, Ryan Hollenbeck

Executive Vice President Marketing, Julie Beauregard

Vice President, Itzik Vager

Regional Vice President, David (Dave) Yannessa

Vice President Human Resources, Jane (Ginny) Donnell

Senior Vice President Product and Strategy, David (Dave) Marcus

Vice President, John (Jack) Bourne

Vice President, Ben (Benny) Smith

Vice President Voice of The Customer Analytics, Oren Stern

Senior Vice President, Jane (Ginny) ODonnell

Chairman, Victor A. DeMarines, age 79

Board Member, Louise (Eloise) McLean

Board Member, Anne (Annie) Arcand

Treasurer, Glenn Levine

Auditors: Deloitte & Touche LLP

LOCATIONS

HQ: Verint Systems, Inc
175 Broadhollow Road, Melville, NY 11747
Phone: 631 962-9600
Web: www.verint.com

PRODUCTS/OPERATIONS

2016 Sales

	$ mil.	% of total
Services	674.9	60
Products	455.4	40
Total	1,130.3	100

2016 Sales by Segment

	$ mil.	% of total
Enterprise intelligence	625.9	55
Cyber Intelligence	385.5	34
Video intelligence	118.9	11
Total	1,130.3	100

COMPETITORS

Aspect Software	March Networks
Avigilon	NICE Systems
BAE SYSTEMS	Oracle
Bosch	Pegasystems
Cisco Systems	Pelco
Dedicated Micros	Rohde & Schwarz
FireEye	SS8 Networks
Genesys	Sophos
Telecommunications	United Technologies
HP Autonomy	eGain
Honeywell	
International	

HISTORICAL FINANCIALS

Company Type: Public

Income Statement

FYE: January 31

	REVENUE ($ mil.)	NET INCOME ($ mil.)	NET PROFIT MARGIN	EMPLOYEES
01/16	1,130.2	17.6	1.6%	5,000.0
01/15	1,128.4	30.9	2.7%	4,800.0
01/14	907.2	53.7	5.9%	3,400.0
01/13	839.5	54.0	6.4%	3,200.0
01/12	782.6	36.9	4.7%	3,200.0
Annual Growth	9.6%	(16.9%)	—	11.8%

2016 Year-End Financials

Debt ratio: 31.3%
Return on equity: 1.7%
Cash ($ mil.): 352.1
Current ratio: 1.70
Long-term debt ($ mil.): 735.9

No. of shares (mil.): 62.2
Dividends
　Yield: —
　Payout: —
Market value ($ mil.): 2,280.0

	STOCK PRICE ($) FY Close	P/E High/Low		PER SHARE ($) Earnings	Dividends	Book Value
01/16	36.61	229	124	0.28	0.00	17.03
01/15	53.38	115	80	0.52	0.00	16.38
01/14	45.44	48	32	0.99	0.00	11.70
01/13	33.80	36	26	0.96	0.00	12.71
01/12	28.28	65	40	0.56	0.00	10.95
Annual Growth	6.7%	—	—(15.9%)	—	11.7%

Verisk Analytics Inc

Insurance is a risky business and Verisk Analytics is in the business of helping to manage that risk. The company compiles data designed to detect fraud and catastrophe and weather risk and predict loss for customers in the US property/casualty insurance health care and mortgage industries. Its Decision Analytics unit provides health care claim payers and mortgage lenders with predictive models loss estimation tools and fraud ID applications. Its Risk Assessment unit runs databases that hold billions of records containing statistical and underwriting data used to price insurance policies and write policy language. Verisk was created by subsidiary Insurance Services Office (ISO) as a means of going public.

Operations

The company is experiencing steady revenue growth in both of its main business segments —Decision Analytics and Risk Assessment —as businesses pay ever-increasing attention to risk management and loss control. The Decision Analytics division (which accounts for more than 60% of revenues) is seeing growth in its main insurance division as well as from customers in finance and other industries. Risk Assessment which includes flagship subsidiary ISO and several other units provide data software and information services. Its customers include property/casualty insurers and reinsurers in the US and abroad.

Verisk has approximately seven petabytes (7 million gigabytes) of risk information including 16.5 billion commercial and personal records detailed information on more than 3 million commercial buildings an insurance fraud database with more than 960 million claims natural hazard models covering more than 90 countries 4.75 million material safety data sheets on hazardous chemicals and depersonalized data on 1.3 million debit and credit card accounts. It also provides health care data-driven solutions that process more than 67 million claims per day.

Geographic Reach

Verisk has offices in more than 15 US states as well as international locations in countries including Brazil Canada China Denmark Germany India Israel Japan Nepal Singapore and the UK.

Sales and Marketing

A majority of Verisk's revenue is generated through annual subscriptions and long-term agreements within the US property/casualty insurance industry. Major customers in this category include AIG Allstate Hartford and Liberty Mutual. It sells its products and services through a direct sales force. Customers in the health care mortgage lending and government categories include numerous Blue Cross and Blue Shield plans Wells Fargo and FEMA. Verisk also serves select clients in the supply chain human resources and risk management industries.

Advertising costs from branding and promotional activities totaled some $6360 in 2014 down from $8457 in 2013.

Financial Performance

Verisk has seen strong revenue growth over the past five years. In 2014 revenue rose 9% to $1.7 billion due to growth in both primary segments. Decision Analytics rose 12% that year primarily due to an increase within its insurance loss quantification and catastrophe modeling operations continued demand for its financial services solutions and health care quality intelligence and payment accuracy offerings. Risk Assessment rose 5% as the company earned more on enhanced data solutions and added new offerings to its existing customers' accounts.

Net income which has also been on the rise increased 15% to $400 million in 2014 as a result of the higher revenue. Also contributing to the increased profits was that year's sale of mortgage services business Interthinx.

Cash flow from operations declined 3% to $489 million in 2014 due to changes in accounts receivable and a decline in cash provided by income taxes.

Strategy

Verisk's strategy for further growth includes increasing sales to insurance customers developing proprietary data sets and predictive analytics continuing to acquire complementary businesses and leveraging its intellectual property into new markets. It has increasingly focused on key insurance coverages as drones and Ebola-style viruses in addition to weather and climate risks.

On the organic growth side Verisk conducts internal programs to create new and enhanced products. Its product development process incorporates market research internal software development and alliances with other information providers and technology companies. For instance the company has a partnership with loan registry provider MERSCORP to develop a fraud-prevention database for the US mortgage lending industry. During 2014 the company launched new programs in the health care and financial services sectors.

Also in 2014 the company sold its mortgage analytics business Interthinx to First American Financial for $151.2 million to better focus on businesses more closely aligned with its core offerings. Over the past few years Verisk has made a number of acquisitions (Aspect Loss Prevention MediConnect Global Argus Information & Advisory Services) to boost those offerings.

Mergers and Acquisitions

In 2014 Verisk acquired Eagleview Technology Corporation and its Pictometry International and Eagle View Technologies subsidiaries for $650 million. That transaction added Eagleview's aerial imagery data analytics and GIS services for the commercial government and public utility sectors.

It also acquired Inovatus which provides proprietary models to prevent insurance and premium leakage for personal auto insurers. In another deal it purchased Dart Consulting which provides benchmarking and advisory services to financial services firms in Australia New Zealand and other nations in the Asia/Pacific region.

Furthermore the company acquired UK-based Maplecroft which analyzes geopolitical societal human rights economic and environmental risks around the world.

In 2015 Verisk bought Scottish firm Wood Mackenzie (dba WoodMac) a provider of analysis and advice on assets companies and markets. That deal primarily served to position the company in the global energy market. Later that year Verisk added to WoodMac's operations with the acquisition of London-based Infield Systems which provides business intelligence and analytics services to the oil gas and associated marine industries. Furthering its renewable energy and electricity data offerings Verisk agreed to buy Greentech Media in mid-2016.

Also in 2016 the company acquired UK-based geographic data specialist GeoInformation Group and insurance data and analytics firm MarketStance.

In early 2017 Verisk acquired Arium (Architects for Risk Identification Understanding and Management) which specializes in liability risk modeling and decision support. That purchase will boost the firm's casualty analytics offerings.

Company Background

The company traces its roots back to 1971 when ISO was created by an association of insurance companies. Verisk went public in 2009 in one of the largest offerings of the year raising almost $2 billion.

EXECUTIVES

Chairman President and CEO, Scott G. Stephenson, age 59, $860,000 total compensation
EVP General Counsel and Corporate Secretary, Kenneth E. Thompson, age 56, $446,800 total compensation
COO, Mark V. Anquillare, age 50, $525,200 total compensation

VP and Chief Marketing Officer, Christopher H. Perini
President Underwriting Solutions, Neil Spector
President Verisk Health, Nadine Hays
CFO, Eva F. Huston
SVP Corporate Development and Strategy, Vincent de P. McCarthy, $425,400 total compensation
President ISO Claims Analytics, Richard Della Rocca
President ISO Solutions, Beth Fitzgerald
Group President Argus Geomni and Verisk Retail, Nana Banerjee, $510,000 total compensation
Group President Wood Mackenzie 3E Co. and Verisk Maplecroft, Steve Halliday
SVP and CIO, Nicholas Daffan
President Xactware Solutions, Mike Fulton
President AIR Worldwide, Bill Churney
Vice President Verisk Underwriting, John (Jack) Cantwell
Vice President, Anthony Canale
Senior Vice President Compliance, Mark (Marky) Magath
Assistant Vice President, Susan Fader
Vice President Human Resources, Lissette Martinez
Vice President, Eric Schneider
Vice President Corporate Devel, Yang Chen
Assistant Vice President, Joe (Joey) Louwagie
IIA Vice President Sales, Jim (Jimmy) Haley
Vice President And Assistant Controller, David (Dave) Grover
Sales Vice President, Jeffrey (Jeff) Meissner
Regional Vice President, Michael (Mel) Simonian
Vice President Enterprise Technology Operations, Chuck Moon
Vice President Sales Iso Claimsearch Solutions, Kyle Caswell
Assistant Vice President Property Claim Services, Gary (Gar) Kerney
Vice President Engineering, Jim (Jimmy) Despelteau
Assistant Vice President Property Claim Services, Gary Kerney
Vice President Strategic Data Operations, Tracy Spadola
Vice President and Senior Analyst, Tayden Judge
Vice President and Senior Analyst, Erik (Rik) Hanley
Senior Vice President, Joseph (Jo) Izzo
Vice President Analytics, John F (Jack) Petricelli
Auditors: Deloitte & Touche LLP

LOCATIONS

HQ: Verisk Analytics Inc
545 Washington Boulevard, Jersey City, NJ 07310-1686
Phone: 201 469-2000
Web: www.verisk.com

PRODUCTS/OPERATIONS

2014 Revenues

	$ mil.	% of total
Decision Analytics		
Insurance	598.8	34
Healthcare	315.6	18
Financial Services	96.8	6
Specialized markets	84.9	5
Risk Assessment		
Industry-standard insurance programs	495.1	28
Property-specific rating & underwriting info	155.5	9
Total	1,746.7	100

COMPETITORS

Computer Sciences Corp.	Fair Isaac
	LexisNexis
CoreLogic	MSCI
DMG Information	McKesson
Deloitte Consulting	OptumnInsight
FNC	Thomson Reuters

HISTORICAL FINANCIALS

Company Type: Public

Income Statement

FYE: December 31

	REVENUE ($ mil.)	NET INCOME ($ mil.)	NET PROFIT MARGIN	EMPLOYEES
12/15	2,068.0	507.5	24.5%	7,918.0
12/14	1,746.7	400.0	22.9%	6,550.0
12/13	1,595.7	348.3	21.8%	7,095.0
12/12	1,534.3	329.1	21.5%	6,495.0
12/11	1,331.8	282.7	21.2%	5,401.0
Annual Growth	11.6%	15.8%	—	10.0%

2015 Year-End Financials

Debt ratio: 56.4%
Return on equity: 64.1%
Cash ($ mil.): 138.3
Current ratio: 0.41
Long-term debt ($ mil.): 2,293.1
No. of shares (mil.): 169.4
Dividends
Yield: —
Payout: —
Market value ($ mil.): 13,025.0

	STOCK PRICE ($) FY Close	P/E High/Low	Earnings	Dividends	Book Value
12/15	76.88	27 20	3.01	0.00	8.10
12/14	64.05	27 23	2.37	0.00	1.34
12/13	65.72	33 25	2.02	0.00	3.27
12/12	50.97	26 20	1.92	0.00	1.52
12/11	40.13	24 18	1.63	0.00	(0.60)
Annual Growth	17.6%	— —	16.6%	—	—

Veritex Holdings Inc

Auditors: Grant Thornton LLP

LOCATIONS

HQ: Veritex Holdings Inc
8214 Westchester Drive, Suite 400, Dallas, TX 75225
Phone: 972 349-6200
Web: www.veritexbank.com

HISTORICAL FINANCIALS

Company Type: Public

Income Statement

FYE: December 31

	ASSETS ($ mil.)	NET INCOME ($ mil.)	INCOME AS % OF ASSETS	EMPLOYEES
12/15	1,039.6	8.7	0.8%	149.0
12/14	802.2	5.2	0.6%	125.0
12/13	664.9	3.4	0.5%	126.0
12/12	524.1	1.4	0.3%	0.0
12/11	0.0	0.1	—	0.0
Annual Growth	—	199.7%	—	—

2015 Year-End Financials

Return on assets: 0.9%
Return on equity: 7.1%
Long-term debt ($ mil.): —
No. of shares (mil.): 10.7
Sales ($ mil): 38.6
Dividends
Yield: —
Payout: —
Market value ($ mil.): 174.0

	STOCK PRICE ($) FY Close	P/E High/Low	Earnings	Dividends	Book Value
12/15	16.21	20 15	0.84	0.00	12.33
12/14	14.17	23 18	0.72	0.00	11.96
Annual Growth	14.4%	— —	16.7%	—	3.0%

ViaSat, Inc.

Live via satellite! It's ViaSat! The company provides digital satellite networking and signal processing equipment for government (its largest customer group) and commercial clients. It makes secure networking products for tactical communications and mobile satellite communications systems designed for military use. For the commercial market ViaSat produces satellite broadband systems for consumer applications as well as antenna systems mobile satellite systems and very small aperture terminal (VSAT) products used in enterprise telecommunications. Consumer satellite Internet services are provided through subsidiary WildBlue Communications.

Operations

ViaSat divides its business into three segments: government systems (39% of sales) develops and implements fixed and mobile secure communications systems for federal agencies such as the Department of Defense and its contractors; satellite services (36% of sales) provides retail and wholesale broadband Internet for its consumer enterprise and mobile customers in the US under the Exede and WildBlue brands; and the commercial networks segment (25% of sales) develops and produces end-to-end satellite and other wireless communication systems for consumer enterprise in-flight maritime and ground mobile applications.

In addition to retail and wholesale high-speed Internet over fixed satellite connections through WildBlue ViaSat also provides mobile broadband service under the Yonder brand which enables airborne maritime and terrestrial wireless device users to make broadband connections using ViaSat's ArcLight system.

The company does not make its own products but uses contract manufacturers such as Benchmark Davida Technology Partners Harris IEC Electronics Mack Technologies MTI Regal Technology Partners and Spectral Response.

Geographic Reach

ViaSat has US offices in California Florida Maryland Massachusetts and Virginia. International offices are in Australia China Italy Switzerland and the UK. It also operates 24 gateway ground stations to support its satellite broadband services business across the US and Canada. US operations account for 83% of ViaSat's revenue.

Sales and Marketing

The company sells its products and services both directly (to the government and commercial customers) and indirectly through channel partners that sell WildBlue consumer Internet. WildBlue has relationships with more than 1000 retailers including DirecTV and wholesale distribution relationships with DISH Network and the National Rural Telecommunications Cooperative. Agencies of the US federal government made up 23% of the company's sales.

Financial Performance

ViaSat has enjoyed substantial revenue growth over the past decade. In 2015 (ended April) revenue edged up 2.3% to $1.38 billion from $1.35 billion in 2014. Satellite segment revenue rose 28% buoyed by an increase in service revenues from retail and wholesale broadband services from more Exede broadband subscribers. The company also lodged higher average revenue per subscriber. Besides higher revenue the company spent less on research and development and selling general and administrative activities. Cash flow from operations

grew to $349 in 2015 from $205 million the previous year.

Strategy

In order to diversify its business and reduce its reliance on federal clients the company is eyeing the international commercial satellite market as an area of growth particularly in underserved areas of developing nations where demand for expanded communications infrastructure is on the rise. The company is also investing in research and development as it tries to woo more enterprise customers.

Mergers and Acquisitions

In 2015 ViaSat acquired the product and technology portfolio of EAI Design Services. The move expands VisSat's capabilities in high-speed low-power secure space-based ASIC and FPGA microprocessor design. EAI developed a family of IP cores and stand-alone encryption products for high-speed networking to 100 Gbps that extend boundary protection for data centers and corporate wide area networks. These technologies are implemented in very small low-power ASICs as well as cost-effective space hardened-by-design ASICs and FPGAs.

VisSat expanded its ability to deliver high-speed satellite services and Internet access with the 2014 acquisition of NetNearU which developed a network management system for Wi-Fi and other Internet access networks that can extend ViaSat Exede and other satellite services to a growing base of subscribers for multiple markets including commercial airlines live events hospitality enterprise networking and government broadband projects. The year before it bought LonoCloud an early-stage company with expertise in cloud networking software.

EXECUTIVES

Vice President, John (Jack) Zlogar
Vice President Comsat Laboratories, Prakash Chitre
President and COO, Richard A. Baldridge, age 58, $850,000 total compensation
EVP and CTO, Mark J. Miller, age 56, $290,000 total compensation
EVP Engineering and CTO, Steven R. Hart, age 63, $305,000 total compensation
Chairman President and CEO, Mark D. Dankberg, age 61, $1,025,000 total compensation
SVP Government Systems, Ken Peterman, age 59, $425,000 total compensation
SVP Commercial Networks, Kevin J. Harkenrider, age 61
EVP General Counsel and Secretary, Keven K. Lippert, age 44, $500,000 total compensation
SVP and CFO, Shawn Duffy, age 46, $450,000 total compensation
Vice President Worldwide SalesMarketing, Jorge Vespoli
EI Senior Vice President, Pam (Pamela) Lopez
Vice President And General Manager Of, Ric Vandermeulen
Vice President Strategy, Kristi (Chris) Jaska
Vice President, Mike (Mikey) Kulinski
Vice President Marketing, Robert (Bob) Varga
Vice President Gateway Engineering, Joe (Joey) Ducey
First Vice President, Victor Guzman
Vice President of Business Development, Jim (Jimmy) Esserman
Vice President Corporate Development, Michael (Mel) Lubin
Vice President Enterprise Services, Stephen Estes
Vice President Quality, Simon Kuo
Vice President Mobile Satcom Systems, Philip (Phil) Berry

Vice President of Facilities, Bob (Bo) Rota
Vice President of Information Systems, Jim Elliot
Vice President Human Resources, Melinda (Linda) Toro
Vice President and Engineering, Thad Mazurczyk
Vice President Business Development, Greg Bublitz
Vice President Finance, Craig Thill
Vice President, John (Jack) Jarman
Vice President Product Development At, Peter (Pete) Lepeska
Vice President Administration General Counsel and Secretary, Gregory (Greg) Monahan
Vice President of Information Technology, Todd Lewis
Executive Vice President ViaSat Corporation, Mike Lubin
Vice President Human Resources, Melinda Del
Vice President, Michael (Mel) Peterson
Vice President Administration General Counsel and Secretary, Gregory D Monahan
Auditors: PricewaterhouseCoopers LLP

LOCATIONS

HQ: ViaSat, Inc.
6155 El Camino Real, Carlsbad, CA 92009
Phone: 760 476-2200
Web: www.viasat.com

PRODUCTS/OPERATIONS

2015 Sales by Segment

	% of total
Government systems	39
Satellite services	36
Commercial networks	25
Total	**100**

2015 Sales

	% of total
Product	53
Service	47
Total	**100**

Selected Products

Commercial
  Antenna systems
  Consumer broadband systems (SurfBeam)
  Very small aperture terminal (VSAT) systems (Linkstar Skylinx Linkway Starwire)
Government
  Mobile military satellite communications
  Modems
  Terminals
  Testing and training equipment
  Tactical networking and information security (ViaSat Data Controller)
  Tactical radio systems (MIDS)

COMPETITORS

BAE SYSTEMS	L-3 Communications
Boeing	Lockheed Martin
General Dynamics	Northrop Grumman
Gilat Satellite	Raytheon
Harris Corp.	Rockwell Collins
Hughes Network	VT iDirect

HISTORICAL FINANCIALS

Company Type: Public

Income Statement

FYE: March 31

	REVENUE ($ mil.)	NET INCOME ($ mil.)	NET PROFIT MARGIN	EMPLOYEES
03/16*	1,417.4	21.7	1.5%	3,800.0
04/15	1,382.5	40.3	2.9%	3,400.0
04/14	1,351.4	(9.4)	—	3,100.0
03/13	1,119.6	(41.1)	—	2,700.0
03/12	863.6	7.5	0.9%	2,400.0
Annual Growth	13.2%	30.5%	—	12.2%

*Fiscal year change

2016 Year-End Financials

Debt ratio: 39.6%	No. of shares (mil.): 48.9
Return on equity: 2.0%	Dividends
Cash ($ mil.): 42.0	Yield: —
Current ratio: 1.87	Payout: —
Long-term debt ($ mil.): 954.0	Market value ($ mil.): 3,595.0

	STOCK PRICE ($) FY Close	P/E High/Low		PER SHARE ($) Earnings	Dividends	Book Value
03/16*	73.48	169	126	0.44	0.00	23.08
04/15	59.99	81	62	0.84	0.00	21.77
04/14	65.26	—	—	(0.21)	0.00	20.36
03/13	48.44	—	—	(0.94)	0.00	20.08
03/12	48.21	276	175	0.17	0.00	20.63
Annual Growth	11.1%	—	—	26.8%	—	2.8%

*Fiscal year change

Virtus Investment Partners Inc

Virtus Investment Partners provides investment management services to wealthy individuals corporations pension funds endowments and foundations and insurance companies. Boasting more than $47 billion in assets under management it operates through affiliated advisors including Duff & Phelps Kayne Anderson Rudnick and Newfleet Asset Management as well as outside subadvisors. Virtus markets diverse investment products such as wrap fee programs open- and closed-end funds and managed account services to high-net-worth individuals. It also manages institutional accounts for corporations and other investors. The firm was formed in 1995 through a reverse merger with Duff & Phelps.

Operations

The asset manager operates through several boutique investment firms (as of early 2016) including: Duff & Phelps Investment Management Euclid Advisors Kayne Anderson Rudnick Investment Management Kleinwort Benson Investors International Newfleet Asset Management Rampart Investment Management Virtus ETF Solutions and Zweig Advisers. Virtus offers investors a menu of investment products and services through its affiliates. Virtus generates nearly 70% of its revenue from investment management fees. About 54% of its total revenue came from investment management fees from funds during while such management fees from separately managed accounts and institutional accounts made up 10% and 5% of

total revenues respectively. The rest of its revenue came from distribution and service fees (18% of revenue) and administration and transfer agent fees (13%).Of the firm's $47.4 billion in assets under management (at the end of 2015) more than 60% of the assets were invested in open-end mutual funds while investments in closed-end funds and separately managed accounts each made up another nearly 15% of the portfolio. The rest of the portfolio was invested in institutional assets and exchange traded funds (ETFs).

Geographic Reach

Hartford Connecticut-based Virtus has offices in California Illinois Massachusetts and New York.Sales and MarketingLike other mutual fund asset managers Virtus distributes its open-end funds and ETFs through financial intermediaries such as national and regional broker-dealers and financial advisory firms. Its separately management accounts are distributed through both financial intermediaries and directly through their affiliated managers. Its institutional funds which follow an affiliate-centric model and are sold through consultants target foundations and endowments corporations public and private pension plans and sub-advisory accounts.

Financial Performance

Thanks to rising financial markets acquisitions and a growing investor base Virtus has boosted its assets under management (AUM) by more than 35% since 2011 —from $34.59 million to $47.39 million at the end of 2015. The resulting rise in asset-based fees has led the asset manager to revenue and profit growth over the past few years.In a reversal the investment firm's revenue fell 15% to $382 million during 2015 as its AUM declined by 16% mostly due to net outflows of $6.3 billion as it discontinued five Virtus open-end funds previously known as the AlphaSector funds; and due to market depreciation of $2.2 billion. Excluding the discontinued funds its net inflows were $0.3 billion during the year.Revenue declines in 2015 caused the asset manager's net income to plunge 68% to $30.67 million. Its operations used $209.4 million for the year or nearly four times more cash than in 2014 mostly due to lower earnings coupled with an increase in investment assets under its funds.

Strategy

Virtus Investment Partners regularly adds to its funds and strategies offerings (mostly on its own but also through acquisitions of smaller or "boutique" investment managers) to attract new investors and their capital. The company also relies on strong investment performance from its teams to ensure its customers keep coming back. The firm's 2015 acquisition of ETF Issuer Solutions marked its foray into the tax-efficient cost-friendly and fast-growing exchange-traded fund product market.Mergers and AcquisitionsIn April 2015 Virtus expanded more into the popular exchange traded fund market after acquiring a majority interest in New York City-based ETF Issuer Solutions (ETFis) which operates a platform for listing operating and distributing exchange-traded funds (ETFs) for a total of $4.8 million. The deal allowed Virtus to begin offering both active and passive ETFs to its clients.

Company BackgroundVirtus in October 2012 acquired the business and assets of Boston-based Rampart Investment Management Co. a registered investment adviser specializing in customized options strategies for institutional and high-net-worth individuals for $700000 in cash. The Rampart purchase added $1.3 billion in assets under management and added another investment partner to Virtus' group of boutique investment managers.

EXECUTIVES

Svp Corporate Portfolio Management, Christopher (Chris) Wilkos

EVP Product Management, Francis G. (Frank) Waltman, $275,000 total compensation

EVP General Counsel and Corporate Secretary, Mark S. Flynn, $300,000 total compensation

President and CEO, George R. Aylward, $491,667 total compensation

EVP and CFO, Michael A. (Mike) Angerthal, $350,000 total compensation

SVP Fund Services, W. Patrick Bradley

EVP Head of Distribution, Barry M. Mandinach

President Chief Investment Officer, David Albrycht

Assistant Vice President Infrastructure Services, Bernard (Bern) Hoffman

National Sales Manager, John (Jack) McCormack

Assistant Vice President Corporate Accounting, Christopher (Chris) Galletta

Vice President, Brett Rubler

Vice President of Operations, Kate (Katie) Surber

Assistant Vice President, Lorraine (Irene) Votta

Vice President, Shahid Saigol

Vice President Information Technology, Connie Noiva

Vice President Fund Administration, Amy Hackett

Vice President Investment Services, Jeffrey (Jeff) Smith

Chairman, Mark C. Treanor

Auditors: PricewaterhouseCoopers LLP

LOCATIONS

HQ: Virtus Investment Partners Inc
100 Pearl St., Hartford, CT 06103
Phone: 800 248-7971
Web: www.virtus.com

PRODUCTS/OPERATIONS

2015 Sales

	% of total
Investment management fees	69
Distribution & service fees	18
Administration & transfer agent fees	13
Other	-
Total	**100**

Selected Subsidiaries & Affiliates

Duff & Phelps Investment Management (Chicago)
Kayne Anderson Rudnick Investment Management (Los Angeles)
Newfleet Asset Management (Hartford Connecticut)
Rampart Investment Management Company LLC (Boston)
Virtus Investment Advisers Inc. (Massachusetts)
Zweig/Euclid Advisors LLC (New York)

COMPETITORS

Affiliated Managers Group	GAMCO Investors
BlackRock	Invesco
Citigroup Global Markets	Janus Capital
Cohen & Steers	Legg Mason
Conning	Neuberger Berman
Diamond Hill Investment	Putnam
Eaton Vance	T. Rowe Price
Epoch	TCW
FMR	The Hartford
Federated Investors	The Vanguard Group
Franklin Templeton	US Global Investors
	Waddell & Reed
	Westwood Holdings

HISTORICAL FINANCIALS

Company Type: Public

Income Statement

FYE: December 31

	REVENUE ($ mil.)	NET INCOME ($ mil.)	NET PROFIT MARGIN	EMPLOYEES
12/15	381.9	30.6	8.0%	426.0
12/14	450.6	96.9	21.5%	410.0
12/13	389.2	77.1	19.8%	376.0
12/12	280.0	37.7	13.5%	336.0
12/11	204.6	145.4	71.1%	299.0
Annual Growth	16.9%	(32.2%)	—	9.3%

2015 Year-End Financials

Debt ratio: —
Return on equity: 5.7%
Cash ($ mil.): 107.7
Current ratio: 4.93
Long-term debt ($ mil.): —

No. of shares (mil.): 8.4
Dividends
  Yield: 1.5%
  Payout: 34.8%
Market value ($ mil.): 987.0

	STOCK PRICE ($) FY Close	P/E High/Low		PER SHARE ($) Earnings	Dividends	Book Value
12/15	117.46	43	25	3.92	1.80	60.68
12/14	170.49	21	14	10.51	0.90	62.78
12/13	200.05	27	13	8.92	0.00	54.14
12/12	120.94	25	14	4.66	0.00	31.24
12/11	76.01	4	2	16.34	0.00	35.29
Annual Growth	11.5%	—	—(30.0%)		—	14.5%

Virtusa Corp

Virtusa believes that virtually any business can improve its technology. Founded in 1996 the company provides a variety of offshore-based software development and information technology services including software engineering application development application outsourcing maintenance systems integration and legacy system conversion. Virtusa's customers come from industries such as financial services insurance telecommunications and media and healthcare. Its top two customers JPMorgan Chase and insurance giant AIG together account for about 23% of sales.

Operations

Virtusa operates a number of subsidiaries for countries where it has operations. In India the company has more than 600000 square feet of space (it owns more than half of it). It leases about 200000 square feet of space for its operations in Sri Lanka and Singapore.

Geographic Reach

Virtusa generates 67% of sales in North America and 27% of sales from customers in Europe.

It has offices in Austria Germany Singapore The Netherlands the UK and the US. Its IT staff is located in Hungary India and Sri Lanka.

Sales and Marketing

The company's sales strategy involves developing long-term relationships with IT and business executives not just landing a short-term contract with no opportunity for recurring revenue.

Financial Performance

Overall sales grew 20% in 2015 (year-end March) to $479 million —its fifth straight year of rising revenue. Revenue from existing clients grew by $47 million and new clients provided $34.6 million. The company has also been profitable for

years; in 2015 profits increased 23% to a record $42 million.

Strategy

The company's strategy for growth includes focusing on services for healthcare and developing more business for its customer relationship management and business process management services. Performing more than 80% of billable hours at offshore sites the company is making significant investments in its Indian and Sri Lankan facilities. The company spends about 20% of its time managing IT services for clients onsite but gets 54% of its revenue from onsite work.

Mergers and Acquisitions

Virtusa acquired TradeTech Consulting Scandinavia AB a consultant and IT services provider specializing in treasury and asset management for major financial institutions and multi-national corporations. The acquisition extends Virtusa's reach in banking financial services and insurance by increasing its asset management and treasury services and technology expertise.

EXECUTIVES

Chairman and CEO, Kris A. Canekeratne, age 50, $462,500 total compensation
EVP and Chief Strategy Officer, Thomas R. (Tom) Holler, age 53, $332,500 total compensation
EVP and COO, Roger K. (Keith) Modder, age 52, $256,858 total compensation
EVP Client Services and Business Development, John Gillis
President Enterprise Technology and Solutions, Raj Rajgopal, age 56, $372,500 total compensation
EVP Insurance Healthcare Media & Entertainment and Diversified Business Units North America, Jim Francis
EVP and CFO, Ranjan Kalia, age 56, $352,500 total compensation
VP General Counsel and Assistant Secretary, Paul D. Tutun
President Banking and Financial Services, Samir Dhir, age 46
SVP Global Technical Solutions Group, Frank Palermo
EVP and Global Head of Telecoms and Managing Director Middle East and Asia, Srinivasan Jayaraman
SVP and Global Head of Transformational Outsourcing Solutions, Sreekanth Lapala
SVP and Global Head of SAP Practice, Zlatan Lipovaca
EVP and Global Head of Engineering, Chandika Mendis
SVP and Global Head of Human Resources, Sundararajan (Sundar) Narayanan
EVP CIO and Head of Business Process Excellence, Madu Ratnayake
EVP and Global Head of Business Consulting and Business Process Transformation, Tim Wright
Auditors: KPMG LLP

LOCATIONS

HQ: Virtusa Corp
2000 West Park Drive, Westborough, MA 01581
Phone: 508 389-7300
Web: www.virtusa.com

COMPETITORS

Accenture	IBM Global Services
Capgemini	Infosys
Cognizant Tech Solutions	Sapient
Computer Sciences Corp.	Sirius Computer Solutions
	Tata Consultancy

Deloitte Consulting	Tech Mahindra
HCL Technologies	Wipro
HP Enterprise Services	

HISTORICAL FINANCIALS

Company Type: Public

Income Statement

FYE: March 31

	REVENUE ($ mil.)	NET INCOME ($ mil.)	NET PROFIT MARGIN	EMPLOYEES
03/16	600.3	44.8	7.5%	18,226.0
03/15	478.9	42.4	8.9%	9,247.0
03/14	396.9	34.3	8.7%	8,054.0
03/13	333.1	28.4	8.5%	6,911.0
03/12	277.7	20.0	7.2%	5,672.0
Annual Growth	21.2%	22.3%	—	33.9%

2016 Year-End Financials

Debt ratio: 19.8%
Return on equity: 9.9%
Cash ($ mil.): 148.9
Current ratio: 3.74
Long-term debt ($ mil.): 185.6

No. of shares (mil.): 29.4
Dividends
  Yield: —
  Payout: —
Market value ($ mil.): 1,102.0

	STOCK PRICE ($) FY Close	P/E High/Low		PER SHARE ($) Earnings	Dividends	Book Value
03/16	37.46	38	21	1.49	0.00	16.14
03/15	41.38	29	21	1.44	0.00	14.61
03/14	33.51	29	17	1.27	0.00	13.17
03/13	23.76	21	10	1.11	0.00	10.02
03/12	17.27	26	15	0.79	0.00	8.80
Annual Growth	21.4%	—	— 17.2%		—	16.4%

Vista Outdoor Inc

Auditors: Deloitte & Touche LLP

LOCATIONS

HQ: Vista Outdoor Inc
262 N University Drive, Farmington, UT 84025
Phone: 801 447-3000
Web: www.vistaoutdoor.com

HISTORICAL FINANCIALS

Company Type: Public

Income Statement

FYE: March 31

	REVENUE ($ mil.)	NET INCOME ($ mil.)	NET PROFIT MARGIN	EMPLOYEES
03/16	2,270.7	147.0	6.5%	5,800.0
03/15	2,083.4	79.5	3.8%	5,200.0
03/14	1,873.9	133.2	7.1%	5,000.0
03/13	1,196.0	64.6	5.4%	0.0
03/12	1,042.9	10.6	1.0%	0.0
Annual Growth	21.5%	92.7%	—	

2016 Year-End Financials

Debt ratio: 22.7%
Return on equity: 8.8%
Cash ($ mil.): 151.6
Current ratio: 2.85
Long-term debt ($ mil.): 652.7

No. of shares (mil.): 60.8
Dividends
  Yield: —
  Payout: —
Market value ($ mil.): 3,157.0

	STOCK PRICE ($)	P/E		PER SHARE ($)		
	FY Close	High/Low	Earnings	Dividends	Book Value
03/16	51.91	22 18	2.35	0.00	27.29
03/15	42.82	37 27	1.25	0.00	25.81
Annual Growth	21.2%	— —	88.0%	—	5.7%

Vitamin Shoppe Inc

Vitamin Shoppe helps vitamin-takers meet their recommended daily requirements. The fast-growing company sells vitamins supplements and minerals as well as herbal homeopathic and sports nutrition and wellness products at more than 750 company-operated The Vitamin Shoppe stores located in some 45 US states the District of Columbia Puerto Rico and Canada. It also sells directly via catalog and the websites VitaminShoppe.com and BodyTech.com. Stores offer about 20000 items including food and beverages and pet products under more than 800 national and private-label brands. Vitamin Shoppe was founded in 1977.

Geographic Reach

The New Jersey-based company's largest markets are California New York and Florida home to about a third of its stores. Vitamin Shoppe has an international presence in Canada and Puerto Rico.

Operations

Vitamin Shoppe operates retail stores under the Vitamin Shoppe and Super Supplements banners. The retail segment accounted for 85% of sales in 2015 with the rest coming from the Internet and catalogs.

The company's primary product category sports nutrition accounts for 34% of the revenue. Other product categories included vitamins minerals herbs and homeopathy (24%); specialty supplements (24%) and other products (18%).

Sales and Marketing

Vitamin Shoppe relies on location location location! as a prime marketing tool adhering to the belief that situating its stores on prime real estate draws customers. It advertises in magazines and relies on radio and television ads to promote certain new stores. Direct mail is another avenue for promotion.

Financial Performance

Vitamin Shoppe posted record-setting revenues of $1.27 billion in 2015 mainly due to a 90% surge in manufacturing sales. This was attributed to a spike in products manufactured for its Vitamin Shoppe assortment and a notable spike in products manufactured for third parties.

Profits have declined the last few years however falling 13% to $53 million in 2015. The most recent decline was fueled by a rise in selling general and administrative expenses affiliated with the payment of interest. After rising in 2014 cash flow from operations declined by 39% in 2015 to $61 million due to an increase in inventory purchases to support activities.

Strategy

Vitamin Shoppe is extending its retail reach through organic growth and acquisitions. After adding 163 and acquiring 31 stores from 2013 to 2015 the chain planned to open another 30 in 2016. Its long-term goal is to operate more than 900 US stores. The retailer prefers to locate shops in freestanding buildings or corner locations in strip malls rather than traditional shopping malls.

Besides adding stores Vitamin Shoppe is experimenting with new store formats and products. Eco Shoppe —launched in Austin Texas in 2009 — as its name suggests sells green-living products including apparel home garden and gift items; office and pet supplies; baby and kids products; and yoga gear. Previously the company launched an e-commerce site called BodyTech.com devoted to products for bodybuilders and other athletes.

Mergers and Acquisitions In 2014 the company acquired FDC Vitamins doing business as Nutri-Force Nutrition. Headquartered in Florida Nutri-Force is a contract manufacturer of vitamins minerals and supplements (VMS). The deal enhanced Vitamin Shoppe's ability for the custom manufacturing and private labeling of VMS products.

EXECUTIVES

EVP and CFO, Brenda M. Galgano, age 47, $472,621 total compensation
CEO, Colin F. Watts, age 51, $498,077 total compensation
SVP Supply Chain Management and Information Technology, Richard Tannenbaum
EVP and COO, Jason S. Reiser, age 48
President Nutri-Force Nutrition, Michael J. Beardall, age 47
SVP and Chief Accounting Officer, Daniel (Dan) Lamadrid, age 41, $278,594 total compensation
Auditors: Deloitte & Touche LLP

LOCATIONS

HQ: Vitamin Shoppe Inc
300 Harmon Meadow Blvd., Secaucus, NJ 07094
Phone: 201 868-5959
Web: www.vitaminshoppe.com

PRODUCTS/OPERATIONS

2015 Sales

	$ mil.	% of total
Retail	1,081.1	85
Direct (catalog & Internet)	128.8	9
Manufacturing	91.2	6
Elimination	(34.6)	-
Total	**1,266.5**	**100**

2015 Sales

	$ mil.	% of total
Sports Nutrition	432.2	34
Specialty supplements	308.2	24
Vitamins minerals & herbs	301.5	24
Delivery revenue	2.0	-
Other	222.6	18
Total	**1,266.5**	**100**

Selected Products

Herbal products
Homeopathic products
Personal care products
  Foot care
  Hair care
  Mouth care
  Pet care
  Skin care
  Women's products
Supplements
Vitamins

COMPETITORS

CVS	Nature's Sunshine
Costco Wholesale	PureTek
Forever Living	Rite Aid
GNC	Safeway
Gaiam	Target Corporation

Herbalife Ltd.	Vitacost
Kmart	Vitamin World
Kroger	Wal-Mart
MotherNature.com	Walgreen
NBTY	Whole Foods

HISTORICAL FINANCIALS
Company Type: Public

Income Statement
FYE: December 26

	REVENUE ($ mil.)	NET INCOME ($ mil.)	NET PROFIT MARGIN	EMPLOYEES
12/15	1,266.5	53.1	4.2%	5,686.0
12/14	1,213.0	61.2	5.0%	5,583.0
12/13	1,087.4	66.5	6.1%	4,842.0
12/12	950.9	60.8	6.4%	4,247.0
12/11	856.5	44.8	5.2%	3,907.0
Annual Growth	10.3%	4.3%	—	9.8%

2015 Year-End Financials

Debt ratio: 16.4%	No. of shares (mil.): 25.8
Return on equity: 10.3%	Dividends
Cash ($ mil.): 15.1	Yield: —
Current ratio: 2.34	Payout: —
Long-term debt ($ mil.): 115.4	Market value ($ mil.): 867.0

	STOCK PRICE ($)	P/E		PER SHARE ($)		
	FY Close	High/Low	Earnings	Dividends	Book Value
12/15	33.51	26 15	1.82	0.00	18.37
12/14	47.17	26 18	2.00	0.00	18.37
12/13	51.44	29 18	2.18	0.00	17.31
12/12	55.98	30 19	2.02	0.00	14.83
12/11	39.88	31 20	1.52	0.00	12.18
Annual Growth	(4.3%)	— —	4.6%	—	10.8%

Vivint Solar Inc

Plumbing fixtures equipment and supplie

EXECUTIVES

Pres-ceo, Gregory S Butterfield
Vice President of sales, Chance Allred
V Pres Business Development, Jan Newman
Vp Asset Management, Kent (Ken) Williams
Vice President Of Human Capital, Tessa White
Auditors: Ernst & Young LLP

LOCATIONS

HQ: Vivint Solar Inc
1800 West Ashton Blvd., Lehi, UT 84043
Phone: 877 404-4129
Web: www.vivintsolar.com

Company Type: Public

Income Statement

FYE: December 31

	REVENUE ($ mil.)	NET INCOME ($ mil.)	NET PROFIT MARGIN	EMPLOYEES
12/15	64.1	13.0	20.4%	3,685.0
12/14	25.2	(28.8)	—	2,294.0
12/13	6.1	5.6	91.4%	2,288.0
12/12*	0.1	(2.6)	—	0.0
11/12	0.3	(11.6)	—	0.0
Annual Growth	270.7%	—	—	—

*Fiscal year change

2015 Year-End Financials

Debt ratio: 26.8%	No. of shares (mil.): 106.5
Return on equity: 2.6%	Dividends
Cash ($ mil.): 92.2	Yield: —
Current ratio: 0.98	Payout: —
Long-term debt ($ mil.): 425.9	Market value ($ mil.): 1,019.0

	STOCK PRICE ($) FY Close	P/E High/Low	PER SHARE ($) Earnings	Dividends	Book Value
12/15	9.56	132 61	0.12	0.00	4.87
12/14	9.22	— —	(0.35)	0.00	4.54
Annual Growth	3.7%	— —	—	—	7.3%

W.P. Carey Inc

Need help managing your property portfolio? Keep calm and Carey on. W. P. Carey invests in and manages commercial real estate including office distribution retail and industrial facilities. The company owns more than 1000 properties mainly in the US and Europe and manages properties for several non-traded real estate investment trusts (REITs). Its management portfolio totals some $15 billion. W. P. Carey typically acquires properties and then leases them back to the sellers/occupants on a long-term basis. It also provides build-to-suit financing for investors worldwide. W. P. Carey is converting to a REIT a corporate structure that comes with tax benefits and more flexibility in investing in real estate.

Geographic Reach

New York-based W. P. Carey owns some 1020 properties in 21 countries. The firm has offices in Dallas London Amsterdam Hong Kong and Shanghai. International investments account for about 31% of the REIT's annual revenue.

Financial Performance

Carey's revenue increased 31% in 2013 versus 2012 to $489.9 million. Revenue growth was spurred by additions to the firm's real estate portfolio made in 2012 including 19 self-storage properties. Net income rose 59% over the same period to $98.9 million due primarily to higher revenue and income from discontinued operations.

Strategy

Since 1979 the REIT has sponsored a series of 18 income-generating investment programs that invest primarily in commercial properties net leased to single tenants under the Corporate Property Associates or CPA brand name. In 2013 the firm managed four global active funds: CPA 16 CPA 17 and CPA 18. W.P. Carey looks to diversify its managed funds and make investments in properties that provide consistent long-term sources of income. Property diversity helps shield W.P. from being reliant on any single industry. A few of its recent investments include a hypermarket in Germany operated by Metro AG a newly-constructed office in Wales the new Siemens AS headquarters in Oslo Norway and a 302-room Hampton Inn & Suites/Homewood Suites by Hilton hotel in Denver's central business district.

In addition to making property investments the firm is focused on diversifying its asset management capabilities. W.P. Carey has launched a lodging-focused fund (Carey Watermark Investors). The new investment program is dedicated to investing in the lodging sector and made its first investments in 2011.

In late 2014 the firm made its first investment in Australia via a 20-year net-lease transaction with Inghams Enterprises Pty. Ltd. The $138 million deal included industrial and agricultural properties.

Ownership

The Vanguard Group is Carey's largest shareholder with 12% of the REIT's shares.

EXECUTIVES

Chief Operating Officer; Managing Director, Thomas E (Thom) Zacharias
Second Vice President, Elizabeth (Beth) Raun
Vice President, Chad F Edmonson
Vice President, Brooks Gordon
Second Vice President, Nicolas (Nick) Isham
Vice President Asset Management, Darren Postel
Vice President, Pam (Pamela) Gonzalez
Vice President, Gabriela Stout
Vice President Assistant Controller, Brian Williams
Vice President, Michael (Mel) Mayer
Vice President, Jonathan Charny
Vice President, Peter (Pete) Bates
Vice President and Compliance Officer, Mark (Marky) Powers
Vice President Sales, Becky (Becks) Reaves
Senior Vice President, Jiwei Yuan
Vice President, Pauline (Paula) Yaputra
First Vice President, Matt (Matty) O'donnell
Senior Vice President, KAMAL JAFARNIA
Senior Vice President W. P. Carey, John (Jack) Guthery
Treasurer, Jeff Zomback
Assistant Secretary Times Square Office Manager and Operations Coordinator, Victoria (Tori) Atwater
Auditors: PricewaterhouseCoopers LLP

LOCATIONS

HQ: W.P. Carey Inc
50 Rockefeller Plaza, New York, NY 10020
Phone: 212 492-1100
Web: www.wpcarey.com

PRODUCTS/OPERATIONS

2015 sales

	% of total
Real estate ownership	78
Investment management	22
Total	**100**

COMPETITORS

Brandywine Realty	Inland Group
CNL Financial	Jones Lang LaSalle
Crescent Real Estate	Lexington Realty Trust
Equity Office	Vornado Realty
First Industrial Realty	

Company Type: Public

Income Statement

FYE: December 31

	REVENUE ($ mil.)	NET INCOME ($ mil.)	NET PROFIT MARGIN	EMPLOYEES
12/15	938.3	172.2	18.4%	314.0
12/14	906.1	239.8	26.5%	272.0
12/13	489.8	98.8	20.2%	251.0
12/12	374.0	62.1	16.6%	216.0
12/11	336.4	139.0	41.3%	212.0
Annual Growth	29.2%	5.5%	—	10.3%

2015 Year-End Financials

Debt ratio: 51.3%	No. of shares (mil.): 104.4
Return on equity: 4.8%	Dividends
Cash ($ mil.): 157.2	Yield: 6.4%
Current ratio: 0.49	Payout: 269.4%
Long-term debt ($ mil.): 4,492.7	Market value ($ mil.): 6,162.0

	STOCK PRICE ($) FY Close	P/E High/Low	PER SHARE ($) Earnings	Dividends	Book Value
12/15	59.00	45 35	1.61	3.83	32.81
12/14	70.10	30 24	2.39	3.69	36.05
12/13	61.35	55 36	1.41	3.50	27.90
12/12	52.15	42 32	1.28	0.66	29.60
12/11	40.94	13 9	3.42	2.19	17.18
Annual Growth	9.6%	— —	(17.2%)	15.0%	17.6%

Wabash National Corp.

The teaser trailer for trailer industry giant Great Dane is Wabash National. Wabash is one of North America's top manufacturers of dry freight and refrigerated vans flatbed and drop deck trailers and intermodal equipment. The trailers are marketed under such brands as DuraPlate ArcticLite and RoadRailer via a network of factory-direct sales representatives independent dealers and factory-owned retail outlets. Customers have included Averitt Express FedEx and Swift. The company operates through subsidiaries Transcraft Corporation (flatbed and drop deck trailers) and Wabash National Trailer Centers (retail distributor of trailers and aftermarket parts). Wabash makes most of its sales in the US.

Geographic Reach

Wabash has facilities located in Canada Mexico the UK and the US.

Operations

The company serves customers across three strategic segments: Commercial Trailer Products (66% of total sales) Diversified Products (24%) and Retail (10%).

Sales and Marketing

The company markets and distributes its products through factory direct accounts its company-owned distribution network and independent dealerships. For its van business the company utilizes more than 25 independent dealers spanning roughly 60 locations throughout North America to market and distribute its trailers.

Wabash distributes its flatbed and dropdeck trailers through a network of some 75 independent dealers throughout about 110 locations across North America. Wabash's tank trailers are distributed through over 70 independent dealers. Customers have included such notable names as

Averitt Express Celadon Group Cowan Systems and Crete Carrier Corporation.

Financial Performance

Wabash is enjoying unprecedented growth over the last few years. Revenues jumped 14% from $1.64 billion in 2013 to peak at $1.84 billion in 2014 a historical milestone for the company. The growth was fueled by increased sales from all its segments especially Diversified Products and Retail. Wabash also experienced higher overall trailer sales during 2014.

The company's earnings increased 31% to $61 million in 2014 due to the spike in revenue coupled with a decrease in selling expenses which was affected by salaries and employee-related costs of sales personnel and lower advertising and promotional costs.

Along with its revenue stream Wabash has seen strong growth from its operating cash flow year-over-year. For 2013 it surged by $53 million due to cash generated from deferred income taxes and accounts payable and accrued liabilities. Operating cash flow did take a hit in 2014 however; decreasing by 28% due to reduced amounts of deposits from customers for products not delivered during the year.

Strategy

Wabash has traditionally sold to the largest operators of trailer fleets. Although it preserves its core customer base the company is striving to diversify its offerings and win business from the next tier of trucking companies —carriers with fleets of between 250 and 7500 trailers.

Mergers and Acquisitions

Wabash has experienced uncharted revenue growth through the use of acquisitions. In 2013 it purchased certain assets of the tank and trailer business of Beall Corporation a manufacturer of aluminum tank trailers and related equipment based in Portland Oregon. The deal fortified its Diversified Products segment and expanded its tank trailer market geographically by adding manufacturing operations in the Western half of the US.

HISTORY

Company Background

Donald Ehrlich was president of trailer maker Monon when its parent company was purchased in 1983. Disillusioned by the new management Ehrlich took several key employees with him to create Wabash in 1985. The business got a jumpstart when Ehrlich's Sears contacts ordered 10 trailers. In 1991 Wabash bought the rights to RoadRailer (bimodal railcar construction technology developed in 1956) and went public.

EXECUTIVES

Senior Vice President Human RE, Timothy (Tim) Monahan
SVP and CTO, Rodney P. (Rod) Ehrlich, age 70, $253,984 total compensation
CEO, Richard J. (Dick) Giromini, age 63, $699,346 total compensation
SVP Sales and Marketing, Bruce N. Ewald, age 65, $253,984 total compensation
President and COO, Brent Yeagy, $285,173 total compensation
SVP; Group President Diversified Products Group, Mark J. Weber, age 44, $337,385 total compensation
SVP and CFO, Jeffery L. Taylor, $209,523 total compensation
Vice President of Industrial Engineering, Wilfred Lewallen
Vice President, Lawrence J Gross

Vice President Supply Chain, Steve Miller
Senior Vice President Chief Financial, Robert (Bob) Smith
Vice President Manager Director, Larry (Lar) Anderson
Senior Vice President General Counsel Secretary, Erin Roth
Vice President Operations, David (Dave) Hodorff
Vice President Management Information Systems, Gary L (Gar) Batemen
Vice President CIO, Forrest Held
Vice President Engineering, Jackie (Jack) Nantkes
Senior Vice President, Ron (Ronnie) Gregs
Vice President Organizational Development, Bob (Bo) Nida
Vice President Engineering, John (Jack) Cannon
Vice President of Human Resour, Bill (Billy) Pitchford
Vice President Quality Control and Engineering, Michael (Mel) Griffin
Chairman, Martin C. Jischke, age 74
Auditors: Ernst & Young LLP

LOCATIONS

HQ: Wabash National Corp.
 1000 Sagamore Parkway South, Lafayette, IN 47905
Phone: 765 771-5300
Web: www.wabashnational.com

PRODUCTS/OPERATIONS

2013 Sales

	$ mil.	% of total
Commercial trailer	1,009.6	62
Diversified	446.0	27
Retail	180.1	11
Total	**1,635.7**	**100**

2013 Sales by Category

	$ mil.	% of total
New trailers	1,246.9	76
Parts service & other	180.4	11
Equipment & other	159.0	10
Used trailers	49.4	3
Total	**1,635.7**	**100**

Selected Products

Aviation Refuellers and Hydrant Carts
Composite Doors
Composite Panels
Converter Dollies
Downflow Booths and Isolator Systems
Dry Freight Vans
Frac Tanks
Intermodal Equipment
Liquid Tank Trailers
Mobile Shelters
Platform Trailers
Portable Storage Containers
Railcar Components
Refrigerated Vans
Stainless Steel Vessels
Trailer Parts and Service
Trailer Side Skirts
Truck Mounted Tanks
Used Trailers
Wood Flooring

COMPETITORS

Featherlite	Trinity Industries
Fontaine Trailer	Utility Trailer
Great Dane	Wells Cargo
Hyundai Translead	

HISTORICAL FINANCIALS

Company Type: Public

Income Statement

FYE: December 31

	REVENUE ($ mil.)	NET INCOME ($ mil.)	NET PROFIT MARGIN	EMPLOYEES
12/15	2,027.4	104.2	5.1%	5,300.0
12/14	1,863.3	60.9	3.3%	5,100.0
12/13	1,635.6	46.5	2.8%	4,400.0
12/12	1,461.8	105.6	7.2%	4,400.0
12/11	1,187.2	15.0	1.3%	2,600.0
Annual Growth	14.3%	62.3%	—	19.5%

2015 Year-End Financials

Debt ratio: 33.2%	No. of shares (mil.): 64.9
Return on equity: 25.1%	Dividends
Cash ($ mil.): 178.8	Yield: —
Current ratio: 2.51	Payout: —
Long-term debt ($ mil.): 277.2	Market value ($ mil.): 768.0

	STOCK PRICE ($) FY Close	P/E High/Low		PER SHARE ($) Earnings	Dividends	Book Value
12/15	11.83	10	7	1.50	0.00	6.77
12/14	12.36	17	11	0.85	0.00	5.66
12/13	12.35	19	13	0.67	0.00	4.70
12/12	8.97	7	4	1.53	0.00	3.93
12/11	7.84	57	20	0.22	0.00	2.15
Annual Growth	10.8%	—	—	61.6%	—	33.3%

WageWorks Inc

WageWorks wants to make administration of tax-advantaged spending accounts easier. The company helps some 5000 clients –including more than 50% of the Fortune 100 companies –implement and manage flexible spending accounts used for health wellness and dependent care as well as commuting and tuition expenses. The WageWorks SaaS (software as a service) platform also can be used for health savings accounts and other health care reimbursement programs. Its online tools provide real-time visibility into account activity and the ability to work with any combination of insurance carrier or financial institution. Founded in 2000 WageWorks operates through about 10 offices across the US. It went public in 2012.

Geographic Reach

WageWorks is headquartered in San Mateo California. It has additional offices throughout the US including locations in Arizona California Florida Massachusetts New York Ohio Rhode Island Vermont and Wisconsin.

Sales and Marketing

WageWorks markets and sells its CDB programs through multiple channels including direct sales to large enterprises direct sales brokers and through channel partners and within private exchanges.

Financial Performance

WageWorks has achieved unprecedented revenue growth over the last few years. Revenues jumped 22% from $219 million in 2013 to peak at a record-setting $268 million in 2014. Its profits dipped 16% from $22 million in 2013 to $18 million in 2014 due to an increase in operating expenses. After rising the last two years the company's operating cash flow dropped from $62 million to $54 million over that same time period.

The historic growth for 2014 was fueled by increases within its health care and COBRA segments. Health care increased primarily due to a surge of FSA and HRA revenue which was fueled by growth in new employee participation in their programs additional revenue from a previous acquisition and an interchange fee revenue increase of almost $3 million due to increased debit card usage as well as an increase in the number of debit cards issued.

The COBRA revenue spike was also fueled by additional revenue from an acquisition coupled with increased participation by employer clients in our COBRA administration services.

Mergers and Acquisitions

In addition to adding to its customer base another component of WageWorks' expansion strategy includes growth through acquisitions. In 2014 the company acquired CONEXIS in a transaction that strengthened its position in the consumer-directed benefits market. The purchase also helped WageWorks generate $268 million in revenue during 2014 which was a company milestone.

In 2013 WageWorks acquired Crosby Benefit Systems an administrator of benefit programs with a focus on higher education and health care institutions based in Newton Massachusetts.

EXECUTIVES

CEO, Joseph L. (Joe) Jackson, age 55, $639,583 total compensation
COO, Edgar O. Montes, age 55, $335,833 total compensation
SVP General Counsel and Secretary, Kimberly L. (Kim) Wilford, age 47, $317,917 total compensation
SVP; General Manager Small/Mid-Market Business, Miles Ross
President Commuter Services, Dan Neuburger
CFO, Colm M. Callan, age 47, $108,750 total compensation
Senior Vice President Sales, Barry (Barr) Beck
Vice President Information Technology Operations, Ryan (Ry) Hunter
Vice President Operations, Kristina (Chris) Saunders
Vice President Financial Planning and Analysis, Michael (Mel) Levin
Chairman, John W. Larson, age 80
Auditors: KPMG LLP

LOCATIONS

HQ: WageWorks Inc
1100 Park Place, 4th Floor, San Mateo, CA 94403
Phone: 650 577-5200
Web: www.wageworks.com

PRODUCTS/OPERATIONS

2014 Sales

	$ mil.	% of total
Healthcare	155.9	58
Commuter	61.8	23
COBRA	31.9	12
Other	18.1	7
Total	**267.7**	**100**

COMPETITORS

ADP	Crawford & Company
Aetna	SHPS
Aon Hewitt	Sedgwick Claims
Cash Technologies	Management Services
Ceridian	

HISTORICAL FINANCIALS
Company Type: Public

Income Statement   FYE: December 31

	REVENUE ($ mil.)	NET INCOME ($ mil.)	NET PROFIT MARGIN	EMPLOYEES
12/15	334.3	22.9	6.9%	1,480.0
12/14	267.8	18.2	6.8%	1,675.0
12/13	219.2	21.7	9.9%	1,200.0
12/12	177.2	10.5	5.9%	1,007.0
12/11	135.6	33.3	24.6%	945.0
Annual Growth	25.3%	(8.9%)	—	11.9%

2015 Year-End Financials

Debt ratio: 53.9%	No. of shares (mil.): 35.9
Return on equity: 7.4%	Dividends
Cash ($ mil.): 500.9	Yield: —
Current ratio: 1.26	Payout: —
Long-term debt ($ mil.): 79.0	Market value ($ mil.): 1,630.0

	STOCK PRICE ($) FY Close	P/E High/Low	PER SHARE ($) Earnings	Dividends	Book Value
12/15	45.37	101 61	0.63	0.00	9.38
12/14	64.57	128 72	0.50	0.00	7.88
12/13	59.44	96 27	0.62	0.00	6.57
12/12	17.80	43 23	0.33	0.00	4.95
Annual Growth	36.6%	— —	24.1%	—	23.7%

Walker & Dunlop Inc

When it comes to its commercial real estate loans Walker & Dunlop has the government on its side. The company provides commercial real estate financial services —mainly multifamily loans for apartments health care properties and student housing —to real estate owners and developers across the US. It originates and sells its products (e.g. mortgages supplemental financing construction loans and mezzanine loans) primarily through government-sponsored enterprises (GSEs) like Fannie Mae and Freddie Mac as well as through HUD. To a lesser extent the company originates loans for insurance companies banks and institutional investors.

Operations

The company generates its revenue from five main revenue streams: mortgage banking (62% of total revenue) servicing fees (about 30%) warehouse interest (5%) escrow earnings (1%) and other (5%).

Geographic Reach

Walker & Dunlop operates through 26 offices across the country with locations residing in Atlanta; Chicago; Dallas; Ft. Lauderdale Florida; Irvine California; Nashville Tennessee; New Orleans; New York; Seattle; San Francisco; Needham Massachusetts; and Walnut Creek California.

Sales and Marketing

Walker & Dunlop originates and sells loans through the programs of the Federal National Mortgage Association the Federal Home Loan Mortgage Corporation the Government National Mortgage Association and the Federal Housing Administration a division of the US Department of Housing and Urban Development.

Financial Performance

Walker & Dunlop has enjoyed record-setting revenue growth over the last few years. In 2014 revenue grew 13% to $360.8 million as all primary business categories saw growth. The largest category mortgage banking rose 9% that year on greater loan origination volume. Servicing fees revenue also rose 9% due to a larger average servicing portfolio.

Net income has also been on the rise as of late with the exception of 2012 when it took a slight dip. In 2014 profits rose 24% to $51.4 million largely due to the increased revenue. However Walker & Dunlop posted a cash outflow of $729.5 million that year (an improvement over the $836.9 million outflow posted in 2013) primarily due to changes in working capital.

Strategy

Walker & Dunlop has shaped its growth strategy around certain opportunities in the commercial real estate market on which it believes it can capitalize. It intends to invest in origination activities and products to meet the expected increase in demand for real estate financing. In addition Walker & Dunlop's focus on growing its services to health care facilities is centered on an expected rise in the demand for health care real estate loans. It hopes to serve an expected increased demand for such facilities as baby boomers reach retirement age. The company is also motivated by the fact that many commercial health care loans are sought after through GSE and HUD programs.

To further grow its loan origination and servicing operations Walker & Dunlop acquired certain assets of Johnson Capital Group for some $23.5 million in late 2014. That deal added 30 new loan originators to its capital markets team which the company intends to keep expanding in order to meet expected demand in the coming years. It also plans to open additional capital markets offices throughout the nation to increasingly tap into the commercial real estate market.

Company Background

Walker & Dunlop's relationship with government-related housing finance companies began in the late 1980s after it started originating underwriting and selling loans through Fannie Mae. In 2008 it began working with Freddie Mac and HUD after acquiring a loan servicing portfolio worth $5 billion from Column Guaranteed LLC. The acquisition served to widen Walker & Dunlop's revenue base and increase its sales volume.

EXECUTIVES

Chairman and CEO, William M. (Willy) Walker, age 50, $750,000 total compensation
Vice Chairman Capital Markets, Guy K. Johnson
EVP General Counsel and Secretary, Richard M. (Rich) Lucas, age 51, $400,000 total compensation
President, Howard W. Smith, age 57, $500,000 total compensation
EVP and Chief Credit Officer, Richard C. Warner, age 61, $400,000 total compensation
EVP and CFO, Stephen P. Theobald, $400,000 total compensation
EVP and Chief Production Officer Multifamily Finance, Donald P. King
EVP Proprietary Capital, Jeffrey M. (Jeff) Goodman
CTO, Bill Granger
EVP and Group Head FHA Finance, Michelle Warner
SVP Walker & Dunlop Investment Sales (WDIS), Rob Coleman
EVP and Managing Director Capital Markets, James Cope
CEO and Managing Director Walker & Dunlop Investment Sales, Greg Engler

Senior Vice President, Mark (Marky) Plenge
Vice President, Alex Iman
Assistant Vice President, Michael Liefer
Senior Vice President, Paul (Pauly) Ahmed
Vice President, Will Baker
Senior Vice President, David (Dave) Gahagan
Vice President, Bill Battaglia
Assistant Vice President, Doug (Dougie) Hart
Vice President Commercial Lending, Laura (Laur) Beaton
Vice President, Craig Russell
Svp Asset Management, Michael (Mel) Palmer
Vice President, Scott Becker
Senior Vice President, Ralph (Ralphy) Lowen
Assistant Vice President, Sandy (Sandra) Barlow
Vice President And Deputy Chief Underwriter, Christopher (Chris) Forte
Senior Vice President Multifamily Finance New York, Thomas (Thom) Toland
Vice President, Jody (Jode) Rosenzweig
Senior Vice President, Brendan Coleman
Vice President Financial Reporting, James (Jamie) Warner
Assistant Vice President Asset Management, Matthew (Matt) Sutton
Vice President, Jeremy (Jer) Pino
Vice President Asset Management, Suzanne Collins
Vice President Accounting Operations, Vorleak Bornhor
Senior Vice President, Andrew Gnazzo
Vice President, Jim Murphy
Vice President Multifamily Finance, Dustin Swartz
Senior Vice President Chief Peoduction Officer Capital markets, Cliff Carnes
Vice President, Kevin Walsh
Senior Vice President, Andrea McClure
Vice President, Paul (Pauly) Wallace
Vice President, Matthew Lund
Senior Vice President, Geoff (G.) Smith
Vice President, Livingston Hessam
Assistant Vice President and Team Leader, William (Bill) Carroll
Vice President, Tina Rothstein
Vice President, Tom Meunier
Executive Vice President Proprietary Capital, Jeff Goodman
Assistant Vice President, Kristin (Kristy) Layden
Senior Vice President, David Burt
Vice President, Chris (Chrissy) Botsford
Senior Vice President, Dan (Danny) Martin
Vice President Senior Underwriter, Dena Roewe
Vice President, Karl Seidenwurm
Vice President, Alison Williams
Senior Vice President, Blake Lanford
Senior Vice President, Rick Hayward
Assistant Vice President, Pete Rowan
Vice President, Bob Watson
Assistant Vice President, Josh West
Vice President Deputy Chief Underwriter, Wayne Elibero
Assistant Vice President, Loretta (Lorie) Webb
Senior Vice President, Rich Caterina
Senior Vice President, Patrick (Paddy) Dempsey
Senior Vice President Capital Markets, Brandon (Bran) Harrington
Vice President, Chris (Chrissy) Hew
Vice President, Brian (Bri) McGrath
Assistant Vice President, Chris (Chrissy) Finer
Vice President Loan Administration, Victoria (Tori) Rivera
Assistant Vice President Team Leader, Kimberly (Kim) Perrell
Assistant Vice President, Steven (Steve) Canares
Vice President, Hal (Harold) Reinauer
Vice President, Kyle Peterson
Vice President, Matthew (Matt) Baldwin

Senior Vice President Chief Underwriter, Stephen (Steve) Smith
Assistant Vice President Director of Events, Amy (Ames) Nyhuis
Senior Vice President, Roberto (Berto) Pesant
Vice President Senior Underwriter, Yorke Pharr
Auditors: KPMG LLP

LOCATIONS

HQ: Walker & Dunlop Inc
 7501 Wisconsin Avenue, Suite 1200E, Bethesda, MD 20814
Phone: 301 215-5500
Web: www.walkerdunlop.com

PRODUCTS/OPERATIONS

2014 Sales

	% of total
Gains from mortgage banking activities	62
Servicing fees	27
Net warehouse interest income	5
Escrow earnings & other interest income	1
Other	5
Total	100

Selected Products and Services

Capital Markets and Investment Services
Construction loans
Equity investments
FHA Finance
First mortgage loans
Healthcare Finance
Mezzanine loans
Multifamily Finance
Second trust loans
Supplemental financings
Underwriting

COMPETITORS

American Capital	MetLife
Arbor Commercial	NewStar Financial
CapitalSource	Ocwen Financial
Centerline Holding Co.	Pzena Investment
Deutsche Bank	Management
Deutsche Bank	Redwood Trust
Berkshire Mortgage	Walter Investment
Encore Capital Group	Management
HFF	Wells Fargo
Kennedy-Wilson	

HISTORICAL FINANCIALS

Company Type: Public

Income Statement

FYE: December 31

	REVENUE ($ mil.)	NET INCOME ($ mil.)	NET PROFIT MARGIN	EMPLOYEES
12/15	468.2	82.6	17.6%	504.0
12/14	360.7	51.4	14.3%	465.0
12/13	319.0	41.5	13.0%	402.0
12/12	256.7	33.7	13.2%	420.0
12/11	152.3	34.8	22.9%	189.0
Annual Growth	32.4%	24.1%	—	27.8%

2015 Year-End Financials

Debt ratio: 80.0%
Return on equity: 17.9%
Cash ($ mil.): 136.9
Current ratio: 1.95
Long-term debt ($ mil.): 2,813.9
No. of shares (mil.): 29.4
Dividends
 Yield: —
 Payout: —
Market value ($ mil.): 849.0

	STOCK PRICE ($) FY Close	P/E High/Low		PER SHARE ($) Earnings	Dividends	Book Value
12/15	28.81	12	6	2.65	0.00	16.56
12/14	17.54	11	8	1.58	0.00	13.62
12/13	16.17	18	10	1.21	0.00	11.85
12/12	16.66	13	8	1.31	0.00	10.52
12/11	12.56	9	6	1.60	0.00	7.52
Annual Growth	23.1%	—	—	13.4%	—	21.8%

WashingtonFirst Bankshares, Inc.

EXECUTIVES

Ceo, Shaza L Andersen
Senior Vice President Consumer Lending, Deborah (Deb) Hoover
Executive Vice President Real Estate Lending Manager, Bruce (Brucey) Wilmarth
Auditors: BDO USA, LLP

LOCATIONS

HQ: WashingtonFirst Bankshares, Inc.
 11921 Freedom Drive, Suite 250, Reston, VA 20190
Phone: 703 840-2410
Web: www.wfbi.com

HISTORICAL FINANCIALS

Company Type: Public

Income Statement

FYE: December 31

	ASSETS ($ mil.)	NET INCOME ($ mil.)	INCOME AS % OF ASSETS	EMPLOYEES
12/15	1,678.5	12.2	0.7%	220.0
12/14	1,333.3	9.4	0.7%	174.0
12/13	1,127.5	6.3	0.6%	143.0
12/12	1,147.8	2.2	0.2%	134.0
12/11	559.4	2.6	0.5%	0.0
Annual Growth	31.6%	47.2%	—	—

2015 Year-End Financials

Return on assets: 0.8%
Return on equity: 7.8%
Long-term debt ($ mil.): —
No. of shares (mil.): 12.8
Sales ($ mil): 71.0
Dividends
 Yield: 0.9%
 Payout: 18.5%
Market value ($ mil.): 290.0

	STOCK PRICE ($) FY Close	P/E High/Low		PER SHARE ($) Earnings	Dividends	Book Value
12/15	22.64	20	13	1.13	0.21	13.95
12/14	15.13	14	13	1.07	0.17	13.39
12/13	14.30	20	15	0.73	0.04	12.76
12/12	10.90	22	18	0.54	0.00	12.28
12/11	10.50	22	18	0.53	0.00	15.88
Annual Growth	21.2%	—	—	20.7%	—	(3.2%)

Wayside Technology Group Inc

Wayside Technology connects developers with users of IT products. A leading reseller for software developers the firm's TechXtend (formerly Programmer's Paradise) business markets software hardware and services to IT professionals government agencies and educational institutions in the US and Canada. Wayside's Lifeboat Distribution subsidiary provides software to resellers consultants and systems integrators worldwide. (Software accounts for about 95% of the company's sales.) Wayside Technology sells products through its catalogs and e-commerce sites and its suppliers include Quest Software Intel Flexera TechSmith and Vmware among others.Geographic Reach

New Jersey-based Wayside Technology rings up 85% of its sales in the US. Canada is its second-largest market accounting for about 7% of sales. The company has a European sales office in Almere Netherlands.Sales and MarketingSoftware House International CDW Corp. and Insight Enterprises are Wayside's largest customers generating about 13% 12% and 11% of its 2012 sales respectively. The company promotes its products through its web sites. local and online seminars and print and electronic catalogs.Financial Performance-Wayside's sales topped $297 million in 2012 a 19% increase versus the prior year and an all-time high for the company. The double-digit increase was driven by higher sales by both the Lifeboat Distribution and TechXtend segments up 13% and 39% respectively. Sales in both the US and Canada rose approximately 20%. 2012 marked the third consecutive year of rising sales for the software reseller following three straight years of decline in 2007 thru 2009 during the financial crisis.Net income of $5.5 million was essentially flat in 2012 versus 2011.StrategyWayside purchases about 90% of its products directly from manufacturers and publishers and the balance from multiple distributors. As a relatively small player in software sales the company relies on a diverse vendor base and for its suppliers to develop new products to drive demand among its customers. Wayside seeks to profit by covering market niches that its larger competitors often ignore.

EXECUTIVES

Chairman President Chief Executive Officer, Simon F. Nynens, age 44, $250,000 total compensation
VP Marketing, Richard J. Bevis, age 66
VP Operations and Information Systems, Vito Legrottaglie, age 51, $150,000 total compensation
Vice President and General Manager - Lifeboat Distribution, Daniel T. (Dan) Jamieson, age 58, $150,000 total compensation
VP and Chief Accounting Officer, Kevin T. Scull, age 50, $120,000 total compensation
Vice President of Sales, Shawn J. Giordano, age 46, $120,000 total compensation
Chief Financial Officer; Vice President, Tom Flaherty, age 49
Director, William H. Willett, age 79
Director, Allan D. Weingarten, age 78
Director, F. Duffield (Duff) Meyercord, age 69
Director, Edwin H. Morgens, age 74
Director, Mark T. Boyer, age 58
Independent Director, Michael Faith
Auditors: EisnerAmper LLP

LOCATIONS

HQ: Wayside Technology Group Inc
4 Industrial Way West, Suite 300, Eatontown, NJ 07724
Phone: 732 389-8950
Web: www.waysidetechnology.com

COMPETITORS

Best Buy	PC Connection
CDW	PC Mall
Dell	Systemax
Insight Enterprises	Zones
Newegg	genica corporation

HISTORICAL FINANCIALS

Company Type: Public

Income Statement

FYE: December 31

	REVENUE ($ mil.)	NET INCOME ($ mil.)	NET PROFIT MARGIN	EMPLOYEES
12/15	382.0	5.8	1.5%	132.0
12/14	340.7	5.7	1.7%	125.0
12/13	300.3	6.3	2.1%	123.0
12/12	297.0	5.4	1.8%	120.0
12/11	250.1	5.5	2.2%	112.0
Annual Growth	11.2%	1.3%	—	4.2%

2015 Year-End Financials

Debt ratio: —	No. of shares (mil.): 4.7
Return on equity: 14.9%	Dividends
Cash ($ mil.): 23.8	Yield: 3.7%
Current ratio: 1.55	Payout: 52.3%
Long-term debt ($ mil.): —	Market value ($ mil.): 86.0

	STOCK PRICE ($) FY Close	P/E High/Low	PER SHARE ($) Earnings	Dividends	Book Value
12/15	18.34	16 13	1.25	0.68	8.22
12/14	17.21	18 11	1.23	0.68	8.09
12/13	13.53	10 8	1.41	0.65	7.46
12/12	11.09	14 9	1.19	0.64	6.78
12/11	12.20	12 8	1.20	0.64	6.18
Annual Growth	10.7%	— —	1.0%	1.5%	7.4%

Web.Com Group, Inc.

Web.com Group has everything a growing business needs to create a presence on the Internet. The company provides website building custom design consulting and Web hosting services. Its Register.com business provides domain name registration and its eWorks! XL product offers initial site-design setup and online marketing and technical report services. SmartClicks also offers search engine optimization and local pay-per click advertising services. The company sells to almost 3 million small and midsized US businesses mostly on a subscription basis. In late 2011 Web.com significantly expanded its customer base through the purchase of Network Solutions a website services and domain-names registration firm.

Sales and Marketing

The company sells its subscription web services and products through several distinct sales channels. Web.com uses its telesales organization to cross-sell and up-sell its full product offerings. The company also targets customer lists provided by companies with which they have strategic marketing relationships.

Intent on serving small to midsized businesses Web.com has taken a number of actions to position itself as the place for clients to get what they want from the Internet —from a minimal presence to an entire plethora of website e-commerce and e-marketing campaign options.

Financial Performance

Web.com's revenues increased 105% in fiscal 2012 compared with 2011. The company reported about $407.6 million in revenue for fiscal 2012 after claiming around $199 million in fiscal 2011. Net cash inflow increased by $5 million in fiscal 2012 compared with the prior fiscal year.

The increase in revenue during fiscal 2012 was driven by up-sell and cross-sell campaigns focused on selling higher revenue products to the company's existing customers as well as the introduction of new product offerings and sales channels oriented toward acquiring higher value customers.

Despite the spike in revenues the company's net loss increased in fiscal 2012 compared to the fiscal 2011 primarily caused by increased operating expenses. In particular sales and marketing expenses increased 128% in fiscal 2012 compared to fiscal 2011.

EXECUTIVES

Chairman President & Chief Executive Officer, David L. Brown, age 62, $560,000 total compensation
Executive Vice President & Chief Financial Officer, Kevin M. Carney, age 52, $350,000 total compensation
EVP and Chief People Officer, Roseann Duran, age 64, $260,000 total compensation
EVP Premium Services, Vikas Rijsinghani
Chief Technology Officer, Jane L. Landon
SVP Canada, Alexander Ross
EVP Retail Domains and International, Faisal Chughtai
SVP Retail Market and Customer Experience, Helen Rowan
EVP Brand Networks, Steve Power
SVP Corporate Marketing, Dafna Sarnoff
SVP Program Management and Sales and Service Operations, Angela Dunham
Auditors: Ernst & Young LLP

LOCATIONS

HQ: Web.Com Group, Inc.
12808 Gran Bay Parkway West, Jacksonville, FL 32258
Phone: 904 680-6600
Web: www.web.com

PRODUCTS/OPERATIONS

Brands
Yodle
Network Solutions
Register.com
Web.com
Leads.com
1Shoppingcart.com
Renovation Experts
SolidCactus
Other Products
Domain Names
Hosting
SSL Certificates
ReputationAlert
Email Marketing
Take-a-Payment
Multi-Location Solutions
Web.com Community
Small Business Summit
Online Marketing Services
Ignite Online Marketing
Facebook Boost
Search Engine Optimization (SEO)

Pay Per Click Marketing
Local Leads
Website Services
We Build it For You
Do It Yourself
eCommerce Website
Mobile Website

2015 Sales

	$ mil.	% of total
Subscription	535.7	99
Professional services	7.8	1
Total	**543.5**	**100**

COMPETITORS

AOL
Adobe Systems
Bridgeline Digital
Demand Media
EarthLink
Endurance International Group Holdings Inc.
EnterComm
Equinix
GoDaddy
Microsoft Dynamics
N-VisionIT
Northwoods Software
United Internet
Verio

HISTORICAL FINANCIALS

Company Type: Public

Income Statement

FYE: December 31

	REVENUE ($ mil.)	NET INCOME ($ mil.)	NET PROFIT MARGIN	EMPLOYEES
12/15	543.4	89.9	16.6%	2,200.0
12/14	543.9	(12.4)	—	2,100.0
12/13	492.3	(65.6)	—	2,000.0
12/12	407.6	(122.2)	—	1,900.0
12/11	199.2	(12.3)	—	1,800.0
Annual Growth	**28.5%**	**—**	**—**	**5.1%**

2015 Year-End Financials

Debt ratio: 36.5%
Return on equity: 43.6%
Cash ($ mil.): 18.7
Current ratio: 0.38
Long-term debt ($ mil.): 411.4
No. of shares (mil.): 50.6
Dividends
Yield: —
Payout: —
Market value ($ mil.): 1,014.0

	STOCK PRICE ($) FY Close	P/E High/Low		PER SHARE ($) Earnings	Dividends	Book Value
12/15	20.01	14	8	1.72	0.00	4.70
12/14	18.99	—	—	(0.24)	0.00	3.34
12/13	31.79	—	—	(1.34)	0.00	3.32
12/12	14.80	—	—	(2.61)	0.00	3.29
12/11	11.45	—	—	(0.40)	0.00	5.74
Annual Growth	**15.0%**	**—**	**—**	**—**	**—**	**(4.9%)**

Wells Fargo Real Estate Investment Corp

Auditors: KPMG LLP

LOCATIONS

HQ: Wells Fargo Real Estate Investment Corp
90 South 7th Street, Minneapolis, MN 55402
Phone: 855 825-1437
Web: www.wellsfargo.com/invest_relations/filings

HISTORICAL FINANCIALS

Company Type: Public

Income Statement

FYE: December 31

	REVENUE ($ mil.)	NET INCOME ($ mil.)	NET PROFIT MARGIN	EMPLOYEES
12/15	680.8	645.9	94.9%	2.0
12/14	697.0	637.9	91.5%	2.0
12/13	298.8	257.4	86.1%	0.0
12/12	203.9	143.0	70.2%	0.0
Annual Growth	**49.5%**	**65.3%**	**—**	**—**

2015 Year-End Financials

Debt ratio: 6.2%
Return on equity: 5.2%
Cash ($ mil.): —
Current ratio: 0.09
Long-term debt ($ mil.): —
No. of shares (mil.): 12.9
Dividends
Yield: 6.4%
Payout: 3.4%
Market value ($ mil.): 337.0

	STOCK PRICE ($) FY Close	P/E High/Low		PER SHARE ($) Earnings	Dividends	Book Value
12/15	26.16	1	1	48.71	1.69	962.24
12/14	25.35	1	1	49.37	46.74	957.87
12/13	0.00	—	—	19.95	24.81	934.62
Annual Growth	**—**	**—**	**—**	**56.3%**	**(73.9%)**	**1.5%**

Wesco Aircraft Holdings Inc.

Planes may fly around the world but they can't leave the ground without Wesco Aircraft Holdings. One of the largest logistics and supply chain companies serving the aerospace industry it provides distribution vendor relationship management just-in-time (JIT) delivery quality assurance and kitting. Operating through Wesco Aircraft Hardware and other subsidiaries the company stocks about 565000 different pieces of hardware bearings tools electronic components and machined parts from more than 5000 suppliers. Boeing Airbus and Bombardier are among its largest customers.

Operations

Wesco divides its operations across five main product lines: hardware (48% of total sales) chemicals (41%) electronic components (7%) bearings (2%) and other machined parts (2%).

The company sources its inventory from over 5000 suppliers including Precision Castparts Alcoa Fastening Systems Amphenol Corporation PPG Industries Lisi Aerospace and RBC Bearings.

Geographic Reach

Headquartered at Valencia California the company operates its facilities and offices across nearly 60 locations in 17 countries including Canada Mexico the UK the US and in other European and Asian countries. The US accounts for almost 75% of sales and the UK generates roughly 20%.

Sales and Marketing

Operations and maintenance subcontractors such as Boeing Airbus Bombardier Cessna Gulfstream Embraer and BAE Systems account for 75% of the company's sales. Other customers include distributors airlines and the US government.

Its 8000 customers can choose from just-in-time or long-term contracts or ad hoc sales.

Financial Performance

After posting record-setting revenues of $1.5 billion in 2015 Wesco saw its revenues dip marginally by 1% to $1.5 billion in 2016. The revenue dip was attributed to foreign currency impacts which the company estimates reduced sales by $30 million. In addition Westco experienced a $26 million decline in sales due to the end of a large commercial contract and a $10 million decrease of ad hoc sales during 2016.

After posting a net loss of $155 million in 2015 Wesco posted positive net income of $91 million in 2016. The positive net income for 2016 was mostly the result of the absence of about $206 million in losses from discontinued operation it had posted the previous year. The company's operating cash flow has fluctuated over the years; after rising in 2015 cash flow fell from $141 million to $117 million in 2016.

Strategy

In late 2015 the company's management team launched a new strategy of providing integrated supply chain services more tailored to customer demand through long-term contracts and focused forecasted consumption. This involves changes to its inventory purchasing strategy holding inventory for shorter periods and scrapping older more-dated inventory. The company believes the move will allow it to serve customers better and strengthen its balance sheet.

EXECUTIVES

EVP and CFO, Richard J. (Rick) Weller, age 60
President and CEO, David J. (Dave) Castagnola
EVP and CIO, Dave Currence
EVP and Chief Procurement Officer, Robert Hanley
EVP and Chief Legal Officer, John Holland
EVP and COO, Alex Murray
EVP and Chief Commercial Officer, Todd Renehan
EVP and Chief Human Resources Officer, Felicia Williams
Executive Vice President and CIO, David (Dave) Currence
Vice President, Todd (Toddy) Renehart
Chairman, Randy J. Snyder, age 66
Auditors: PRICEWATERHOUSECOOPERS LLP

LOCATIONS

HQ: Wesco Aircraft Holdings Inc.
24911 Avenue Stanford, Valencia, CA 91355
Phone: 661 775-7200
Web: www.wescoair.com

PRODUCTS/OPERATIONS

2016 Sales

	$ mil.	% of total
Hardware	711.2	48
Chemicals	600.1	41
Electronic components	105.2	7
Bearings	34.7	2
Machined parts and other	26.2	2
Total	**1,477.4**	**100**

PRODUCTS
HARDWARE
Blind fasteners
Bolts and screws
Clamps
Hi lok pins and collars
Hydraulic fittings
Inserts
Lockbolts and collars
Nuts
Panel fasteners
Rivets

Springs
Valves
Washers
CHEMICALS
Adhesives
Cleaners and cleaning solvents
Coolants and metalworking fluids
Industrial gases
Lubricants
Oil and grease
Paints and coatings
Sealants and tapes
ELECTRONIC COMPONENTS
Circuit breakers
Connectors
Interconnect accessories
Lighted products
Relays
Switches
Wire and cable
BEARINGS
Airframe control bearings
Ball bearing
Bushings
Needle roller bearings
Precision bearings
Rod ends
Spherical bearings
OTHER PRODUCTS
Brackets
Installation tooling
Milled parts
Shims
Stampings
Turned parts
Welded assemblies

COMPETITORS

AAR Corp.	First Aviation
Align Aerospace	GECAS Asset Management
Aviall Services	Services
B/E Aerospace	Kellstrom Industries

HISTORICAL FINANCIALS

Company Type: Public

Income Statement

FYE: September 30

	REVENUE ($ mil.)	NET INCOME ($ mil.)	NET PROFIT MARGIN	EMPLOYEES
09/16	1,477.3	91.3	6.2%	2,724.0
09/15	1,497.6	(154.7)	—	2,670.0
09/14	1,355.8	102.1	7.5%	2,785.0
09/13	901.6	104.8	11.6%	1,354.0
09/12	776.2	92.1	11.9%	1,218.0
Annual Growth	17.5%	(0.2%)	—	22.3%

2016 Year-End Financials

Debt ratio: 43.2%	No. of shares (mil.): 98.6
Return on equity: 10.7%	Dividends
Cash ($ mil.): 77.0	Yield: —
Current ratio: 4.86	Payout: —
Long-term debt ($ mil.): 843.6	Market value ($ mil.): 1,324.0

	STOCK PRICE ($) FY Close	P/E High/Low		PER SHARE ($) Earnings	Dividends	Book Value
09/16	13.43	16	11	0.93	0.00	8.95
09/15	12.20	—	—	(1.60)	0.00	8.38
09/14	17.40	21	16	1.05	0.00	10.30
09/13	20.93	19	11	1.09	0.00	9.13
09/12	13.66	17	9	0.96	0.00	8.09
Annual Growth	(0.4%)	—	—	(0.8%)	—	2.6%

Western Alliance Bancorporation

Western Alliance Bancorporation and its flagship Western Alliance Bank (WAB) have an alliance with several bank brands in the West operating as the Alliance Bank of Arizona; Bank of Nevada; First Independent Bank (Nevada); as well as Bridge Bank and Torrey Pines Bank which are both located across California. Combined the banks operate nearly 50 branches that provide standard consumer and business deposit and loan products. About half of the Western Alliance's loan portfolio is made up of commercial and industrial loans while another 40% is made up of commercial real estate loans. It also makes land development loans and consumer residential mortgages and other lines of credit.

Operations

Western Alliance focuses on commercial lending. About 46% of the bank's loan portfolio consisted of commercial and industrial loans at the end of 2015 while another 39% was made up of commercial real estate loans. The bank also had construction and land development loans (10% of loan assets) residential mortgages (3%) commercial leases (1%) and consumer loans (less than 1%).More than 90% of the bank's revenue comes from interest income. About 86% of its total revenue came from loan interest during 2015 while another 9% came from interest or dividends on investment securities. The remainder of its revenue came from service charges and fees (2% of revenue) card income (1%) and other miscellaneous sources.Geographic ReachWestern Alliance's 40 branches and seven loan offices are spread across Arizona Nevada and California as well as Boston Dallas and Reston Virginia. At the end of 2015 its loan business was concentrated in the Los Angeles San Francisco San Jose Phoenix Tuscon Reno and Las Vegas metropolitan areas.Sales and MarketingThe bank serves local businesses real estate developers and investors not-for-profit organizations and consumers. It specializes in lending to such customers operating in the healthcare professional services manufacturing and distribution resorts and timeshares technology and startups municipalities and local governments non-profit and renewable energy markets. Some of its clients (as of early 2016) include Cutter Aviation FNF Construction Hollenbeck Palms New American Funding and Signature Healthcare Services.Western Alliance spent $2.89 million on marketing in 2015 up from $2.30 million and $2.58 million in 2014 and 2013 respectively.

Financial Performance

Western Alliance's annual revenues have risen nearly 70% since 2011 as its loan business has swelled. Meanwhile the bank's annual profits have ballooned more than five-fold as its credit portfolio's credit quality has improved with higher property valuations in the strengthened economy.The group's revenue jumped 26% to $555 million during 2015 mostly thanks to new loan business more than half of which was obtained from the Bridge Bank acquisition which spurred more interest income for the year. Non-interest income especially service charges and lending-related fees grew by double digits during the year also thanks to the acquisition as well as from more organic deposit business growth.Strong revenue growth and a continued decline in credit loss provisions in 2015

drove Western Alliance's net income up by 31% to $194 million for the year. The company's operating cash levels climbed 30% to $213 million mostly thanks to the rise in cash earnings.StrategyWestern Alliance Bancorporation looks to expand its branch network and selectively acquire other banks to boost its loan and deposit business and extend its geographic reach. The bank may also buy other financial services businesses to bolster its line of service offerings.

Mergers and Acquisitions

In June 2015 Western Alliance bought $13 billion-asset Bridge Capital Holdings along with its 48 Bridge Bank branches in California Arizona and Nevada in a deal worth about $425 million. The purchase brought expertise in technology and international banking among other areas and expands Western Alliance's market into Northern California.

EXECUTIVES

EVP and Chief Credit Officer, Robert R. (Bob) McAuslan, age 63
Chairman and CEO, Robert G. Sarver, age 55, $824,231 total compensation
EVP and CFO, Dale M. Gibbons, age 55, $395,426 total compensation
EVP California Administration and President Torrey Pines Bank, Gerald A. (Gary) Cady, age 61, $353,839 total compensation
EVP Credit Administration, Duane Froeschle, age 63
EVP Arizona Administration, James H. (Jim) Lundy, age 66, $369,531 total compensation
EVP Southern Nevada Administration; CEO Bank of Nevada, Bruce Hendricks, age 66
EVP and Chief Risk Officer, Patricia A. Taylor
EVP and General Counsel, Randall S. Theisen
Lead Director, Bruce Beach, age 66
Auditors: RSM US LLP

LOCATIONS

HQ: Western Alliance Bancorporation
One E. Washington Street Suite 1400, Phoenix, AZ 85004
Phone: 602 389-3500
Web: www.westernalliancebancorp.com

PRODUCTS/OPERATIONS

2015 Sales

	% of total
Interest income	
Loans including fees	86
Investment securities	7
Dividends	2
Other	-
Non-interest income	
Service charges and fees	2
Income from bank owned life insurance	1
Card income	1
Other	1
Total	**100**

Selected Services

Business Checking & Savings
Business Loans & Credit
Card Services
International Banking
Personal Banking
Treasury Management

COMPETITORS

Bank of America	PacWest Bancorp
Bank of the West	U.S. Bancorp
Desert Schools FCU	Wells Fargo

First Banks   Westamerica
MUFG Americas Holdings Zions Bancorporation

HISTORICAL FINANCIALS
Company Type: Public

Income Statement
FYE: December 31

	ASSETS ($ mil.)	NET INCOME ($ mil.)	INCOME AS % OF ASSETS	EMPLOYEES
12/15	14,275.0	194.2	1.4%	1,446.0
12/14	10,600.5	147.9	1.4%	1,131.0
12/13	9,307.1	114.5	1.2%	1,051.0
12/12	7,622.6	72.8	1.0%	982.0
12/11	6,844.5	31.4	0.5%	942.0
Annual Growth	20.2%	57.6%	—	11.3%

2015 Year-End Financials

Return on assets: 1.5%
Return on equity: 14.9%
Long-term debt ($ mil.): —
No. of shares (mil.): 103.0
Sales ($ mil): 554.9

Dividends
  Yield: —
  Payout: —
Market value ($ mil.): 3,697.0

	STOCK PRICE ($) FY Close	P/E High/Low		PER SHARE ($) Earnings	Dividends	Book Value
12/15	35.86	19	12	2.03	0.00	15.44
12/14	27.80	17	12	1.67	0.00	11.29
12/13	23.86	19	8	1.31	0.00	9.81
12/12	10.53	13	8	0.83	0.00	8.79
12/11	6.23	44	25	0.19	0.00	7.73
Annual Growth	54.9%	—	—	80.8%	—	18.9%

Western Gas Equity Partners LP

Western Gas Equity Partners LP (WGEP) is taking stock of a fellow energy concern. The entity formed in September 2012 as an investment vehicle for Western Gas Partners LP (WGP). WGEP's sole purpose is to buy a stake in WGP specifically a limited partner interest of almost 45% and a general partner interest of about 2%. As a shareholder of WGP the entity will receive cash distributions at the end of every fiscal quarter from WGP and as a limited partnership WGEP will distribute its profits back to its own shareholders. It will also be exempt from paying federal income taxes. WGEP filed an IPO seeking up to $362.25 million in November 2012 and plans to use the proceeds raised to begin buying shares in WGP.

EXECUTIVES

President and CEO Western Gas Partners LP (WES) and Western Gas Equity Partners LP (WGP), Benjamin M. (Ben) Fink, age 46, $253,506 total compensation
Auditors: KPMG LLP

LOCATIONS

HQ: Western Gas Equity Partners LP
1201 Lake Robbins Drive, The Woodlands, TX 77380
Phone: 832 636-6000   Fax: 832 636-6001
Web: www.westerngas.com

PRODUCTS/OPERATIONS

2011 Sales

	$ mil.	% of total
Natural gas NGLs and condensate sales	502.4	61
Gathering processing & transporation of natural gas & NGLs	301.3	36
Equity income & other	19.6	3
Total	823.3	100

COMPETITORS

DCP Midstream Partners ONEOK Partners
Dominion Questar XTO Energy
Enbridge Energy
Kinder Morgan Energy
  Partners

HISTORICAL FINANCIALS
Company Type: Public

Income Statement
FYE: December 31

	REVENUE ($ mil.)	NET INCOME ($ mil.)	NET PROFIT MARGIN	EMPLOYEES
12/15	1,561.3	87.8	5.6%	0.0
12/14	1,273.7	221.9	17.4%	0.0
12/13	1,053.5	160.2	15.2%	0.0
12/12	849.4	33.9	4.0%	0.0
12/11	823.2	75.6	9.2%	0.0
Annual Growth	17.4%	3.8%	—	—

2015 Year-End Financials

Debt ratio: 40.3%
Return on equity: —
Cash ($ mil.): 99.6
Current ratio: 1.45
Long-term debt ($ mil.): 2,707.3

No. of shares (mil.): 218.9
Dividends
  Yield: 3.8%
  Payout: 114.7%
Market value ($ mil.): 7,945.0

	STOCK PRICE ($) FY Close	P/E High/Low		PER SHARE ($) Earnings	Dividends	Book Value
12/15	36.29	167	77	0.39	1.40	4.85
12/14	60.23	64	37	1.02	1.04	5.76
12/13	39.51	61	42	0.71	0.63	4.13
12/12	29.95	2895	2746	0.01	0.00	4.17
Annual Growth	6.6%	—	—	−239.1%	—	5.2%

Westwood Holdings Group, Inc.

Westwood Holdings Group provides investment management services to institutions mutual funds and high-net-worth clients. The asset manager operates through its subsidiaries. Westwood Trust handles trust custody and account management for companies institutions and high-net-worth individuals. Westwood Management is the group's institutional investment management unit overseeing accounts for corporations municipalities and charitable organizations with at least $10 million in investable assets. The firm is also the administrator of the Westwood family of mutual funds WHG Funds. Westwood Holdings Group boasts around $21 billion in assets under management.

Operations
Westwood operates in two segments: Advisory and Trust. Advisory which contributed 78% to the company's total revenue during 2015 provides investment advisory services to individuals foundations corporate and public retirement plans endowments and the company's other divisions. The Trust segment (22% of revenue) includes trust and custodial services for institutions and high net worth individuals.

Geographic Reach
Dallas-based Westwood serves clients worldwide from offices in Toronto Boston Omaha and Houston. About 84% of its total revenue came from business in the US during 2015 while the rest came from Canada (7% of revenue) Europe (5%) Asia (3%) and Australia (1%).

Sales and Marketing
Westwood markets and sells its mutual funds through Investment advisory firms registered investment advisors select broker-dealers fund supermarkets financial intermediaries and other third-party financial institutions.About 57% of Westwood's assets were managed on behalf of institutional investors during 2015 while the rest were on behalf of Private Wealth clients (26% of assets) and Mutual Fund clients (17% of assets).

Financial Performance
Thanks to a rising stock market and a growing investor base Westwood has almost nearly doubled its assets under management since 2011 —from $13 billion to roughly $20.8 billion at the end of 2015. As a result Westwood's annual revenues and profits have more than doubled over that time period.Westwood's revenue jumped 16% to a record $130.9 million during 2015 thanks to 3% growth in assets under management coupled with higher advisory fee rates which boosted asset-based advisory fees by 12%. The firm's trust fees swelled by 40% for the year driven mainly by the firm's April 2015 acquisition of Woodway Financial Advisors.Despite strong revenue growth in 2015 the asset manager's net income dipped less than 1% to $27.11 million as it spent more on new hires and incentive compensation costs to support the growth of its asset management and trust businesses. Westwood's operating cash levels more than doubled to $55.2 million mostly as it transferred cash from its investment accounts and working capital.

Strategy
Westwood regularly adds to its funds and strategies offerings —either on its own or through acquisitions of asset managers mutual funds or private wealth firms —to attract new investors and their capital. During 2015 Westwood introduced three new mutual funds bringing its total collection of mutual funds to 15. Its acquisition of Woodway Financial Advisors that year expanded the firm's reach into the private wealth market bringing its Private Wealth assets to 26% of its total assets under management (up from 21% during 2014).The asset manager also continues to build its business beyond the US successfully adding new clients in the Netherlands and Japan in 2015.Mergers and AcquisitionsIn April 2015 Westwood Holdings expanded more into the Private Wealth asset management market after purchasing Woodway Financial Advisors along with its portfolio $1.6 billion in managed private wealth client assets. Woodway now operates as a Houston branch of subsidiary Westwood Trust.

Company Background
Westwood was founded in 1983 by chairman and CEO Susan Byrne. The company was spun off from investment bank and brokerage SWS Group in 2002.

EXECUTIVES

Senior Vice President On Private Wealth Management, Dick Frazar

President and Chief Executive Officer, Brian O. Casey, age 52, $600,000 total compensation

President of Westwood Trust Dallas, Randall L. Root, age 55, $237,500 total compensation

EVP and Chief Investment Officer, Mark R. Freeman, age 49, $500,000 total compensation

CFO, Tiffany B. Kice

Chief Information Officer, Fabian Gomez

Vice President, Kellie (Ellie) Stark

Senior Vice President, Patricia (Pat) Perez-Coutts

Senior Vice President General Counsel Corp SEC, Julie K (Jules) Gerron

Vice President, Sue (Susie) Burkhard

Vice President, Grant Taber

Senior Vice President, Michael (Mel) Meadows

Vice President, Jean (Jeannie) Kenkel

Vice President Portfolio Manager Research Analyst, Matthew (Matt) Lockridge

Vice President Marketing and Client Service, Kenneth (Ken) Nostro

Senior Vice President, Kristie (Chris) Konstans

Senior Vice President, Marty (Mart) Brainerd

Senior Vice President, Kristie (Chris) Leatherberry

Senior Vice President Marketing, Mark (Marky) Dunbar

Assistant Vice President Operations, Kari Saenz

Assistant Vice President, Laura (Laur) Willmann

Vice President, Crystal (Cristy) Leiva

Associate Vice President Portfolio Manager Research Analyst, Michael H (Mel) Wall

Senior Vice President JPMorgan Chase, Gregg (Greggory) Ballew

Vice President, Hollis Ghobrial

Associate Vice President, Brian (Bri) Tully

Chairman, Susan M. Byrne, age 69

Auditors: Deloitte & Touche LLP

LOCATIONS

HQ: Westwood Holdings Group, Inc.
200 Crescent Court, Suite 1200, Dallas, TX 75201
Phone: 214 756-6900
Web: www.westwoodgroup.com

PRODUCTS/OPERATIONS

2015 Sales

	% of total
Advisory fees	
Asset-based	76
Performance-based	2
Trust fees	22
Other	0
Total	**100**

2015 Assets under Management

	% of total
Institutional	57
Private Wealth	26
Mutual funds	17
Total	**100**

COMPETITORS

American Century	NFJ Investment
Atalanta Sosnoff	Neuberger Berman
Duncan-Hurst	Nuveen
Eaton Vance	Oak Associates
FMR	Putnam
Franklin Templeton	T. Rowe Price
Janus Capital	US Global Investors
Martin Capital	W.P. Stewart

HISTORICAL FINANCIALS

Company Type: Public

Income Statement

FYE: December 31

	REVENUE ($ mil.)	NET INCOME ($ mil.)	NET PROFIT MARGIN	EMPLOYEES
12/15	130.9	27.1	20.7%	168.0
12/14	113.2	27.2	24.1%	130.0
12/13	91.8	17.8	19.5%	106.0
12/12	77.5	12.0	15.6%	96.0
12/11	68.9	14.6	21.3%	80.0
Annual Growth	**17.4%**	**16.6%**	**—**	**20.4%**

2015 Year-End Financials

Debt ratio: —	No. of shares (mil.): 8.6
Return on equity: 22.2%	Dividends
Cash ($ mil.): 22.7	Yield: 3.9%
Current ratio: 2.62	Payout: 62.1%
Long-term debt ($ mil.): —	Market value ($ mil.): 450.0

	STOCK PRICE ($) FY Close	P/E High/Low	PER SHARE ($) Earnings	Dividends	Book Value
12/15	52.09	18 14	3.33	2.07	15.52
12/14	61.82	19 14	3.45	1.82	13.24
12/13	61.91	25 16	2.34	1.64	10.84
12/12	40.90	24 20	1.65	1.51	9.53
12/11	36.55	19 15	2.04	1.42	9.18
Annual Growth	**9.3%**	**— —**	**13.0%**	**9.9%**	**14.0%**

Wex Inc

WEX (formerly Wright Express) provides payment processing and information management services to commercial and government vehicle fleets through a network that tracks purchases made on fleet charge cards at more than 190000 fuel and vehicle maintenance facilities throughout the US Canada Australia New Zealand and Europe. The company provides clients with transaction data analysis tools and purchase control capabilities for every vehicle in their fleets. Data collected at the point of sale include expenditures lists of items purchased odometer readings and driver vehicle and vendor identification. WEX serves some 350000 fleets that collectively have a total of approximately 7.7 million vehicles.

Geographic Reach

Maine-based WEX rings up more than 85% of its sales in the US. Australia accounts for nearly 10% of annual sales. The company also has operations in Brazil and the UK. WEX has fuel and vehicle maintenance facilities throughout the North America Australia and New Zealand and Europe.

Operations

The company's subsidiaries include fleet card provider Fleet One (acquired in 2012) Utah-based WEX Bank and Pacific Pride Services a fuel distributor network with more than 340 independent fuel franchisees. WEX also owns a majority stake (acquired in 2012) in UNIK S.A. a provider of payroll cards and processing services in Brazil.

Financial Performance

WEX derives a significant portion of its revenue from charging a fee each time each time a client's driver uses his or her fleet card; the company processes more than 250 million such transactions annually.

WEX's sales have climbed steadily in recent years rising 125% since 2009. In 2013 the firm reported sales of $717.5 million an increase of 15% versus 2012. Increased revenue from its Fleet Payment business which accounts for about three-quarters of its total revenue higher fees and the acquisition of Fleet One in 2012 helped drive revenue gains. While consistently profitable WEX's net income growth has been erratic. Indeed net income rose 54% in 2013 versus 2012 after falling 27% in the previous annual comparison.

Strategy

WEX's closed-loop card network allow it access to both sides of every card transaction which provides it with usage data for its cardholder customer base as well as revenues from merchant fees charged. Its cards are accepted at more than 90% of service stations in the US and Australia and the company enjoys a leading market share of nearly 10% of all the fleet vehicles in the US. What's more there is room for growth for the firm as WEX estimates that a majority of fleets don't use fleet cards to manage fuel costs.

The company's growth strategy includes diversifying beyond its traditional domestic markets through acquisitions. Recent acquisitions outside the US have included companies in Brazil Australia and the UK.

Mergers and Acquisitions

In October 2013 UNIK S.A. acquired FastCred a provider of fleet card services to heavy truck operators in Brazil. About a year earlier WEX purchased Fleet One a provider of fleet cards to operators of heavy duty trucks and cars or light duty vehicles in the US and Canada. Previously WEX acquired CorporatePay a provider of prepaid virtual cards to the corporate travel industry in the UK for $27.5 million in May 2012 . Also in 2012 the company entered Brazil by acquiring a 51% stake in payroll card provider UNIK S.A. for nearly $22 million. At home it purchased fleet card provider Fleet One in an all-cash deal that closed in late 2012. Previous purchases include the Australian fuel and prepaid card operations of Retail Decisions for $318 million in 2010 making it a major player in the fleet card sector there.

EXECUTIVES

CTO, David Cooper

CEO, Melissa D. Smith, age 47, $578,317 total compensation

SVP General Counsel and Corporate Secretary, Hilary A. Rapkin, age 49, $362,884 total compensation

SVP International, George W. Hogan, age 55, $318,308 total compensation

SVP and General Manager North American Fleet, Kenneth W. (Ken) Janosick, age 54, $320,000 total compensation

CFO, Roberto R. Simon, age 41

SVP Shared Services and CIO, Stephen R. Crowley, age 55

SVP and General Manager Virtual Payments, Jim Pratt

SVP and General Manager WEX Health, Jeff Young

SVP and General Manager EFS, Scott Phillips

Senior Vice President Corporate, Nicola Morris

Vice President, Fred (Freddy) Madeira

Vice President Finance, Douglas (Doug) Abbott

Senior Vice President Sales Marketing, David (Dave) Maxsiimc

Senior Vice President and Chief Financial Officer, Steve (Stevie) Elder

Vice Chairman, Rowland T. (Row) Moriarty, age 69

Chairman, Michael E. Dubyak, age 65

Vice President Investor Relations and Treasurer, Michael (Mel) Thomas

Auditors: Deloitte & Touche LLP

LOCATIONS

HQ: Wex Inc
97 Darling Avenue, South Portland, ME 04106
Phone: 207 773-8171
Web: www.wrightexpress.com

PRODUCTS/OPERATIONS

2015 Sales

	$ mil.	% of total
Fleet payment solutions	539.0	63
Travel and corporate solutions	195.4	23
Health and benefit solution	120.2	14
Total	**854.6**	**100**

COMPETITORS

Comdata	Retail Decisions
FleetCor	U.S. Bancorp
Multi Service	

HISTORICAL FINANCIALS

Company Type: Public

Income Statement

FYE: December 31

	REVENUE ($ mil.)	NET INCOME ($ mil.)	NET PROFIT MARGIN	EMPLOYEES
12/15	854.6	111.3	13.0%	2,265.0
12/14	817.6	202.2	24.7%	2,004.0
12/13	717.4	149.2	20.8%	1,431.0
12/12	623.1	96.9	15.6%	1,302.0
12/11	553.0	133.6	24.2%	899.0
Annual Growth	**11.5%**	**(4.5%)**	**—**	**26.0%**

2015 Year-End Financials

Debt ratio: 31.1%
Return on equity: 10.3%
Cash ($ mil.): 279.9
Current ratio: 1.34
Long-term debt ($ mil.): 1,201.8

No. of shares (mil.): 38.7
Dividends
  Yield: —
  Payout: —
Market value ($ mil.): 3,425.0

	STOCK PRICE ($) FY Close	P/E High/Low		PER SHARE ($) Earnings	Dividends	Book Value
12/15	88.40	45	32	2.62	0.00	27.96
12/14	98.92	23	15	5.18	0.00	27.26
12/13	99.03	26	18	3.82	0.00	23.16
12/12	75.37	30	21	2.48	0.00	21.02
12/11	54.28	17	11	3.43	0.00	18.30
Annual Growth	**13.0%**			**(6.5%)**	**—**	**11.2%**

Whitestone REIT

Whitestone REIT is out to make a name for itself in real estate. The self-managed real estate investment trust owns leases and operates around 70 retail office and warehouse properties in Texas (Houston is the company's largest market) Illinois and Arizona totaling 6 million sq. ft. Whitestone focuses on what it calls community-centered properties or high-visibility properties in established or developing culturally diverse neighborhoods. It recruits retail grocery financial services and other tenants to its Whitestone branded commercial centers. Some of its top tenants include Safeway Dollar Tree Wells Fargo Walgreens University of Phoenix and Alamo Drafthouse.

Geographic Reach

Whitestone REIT had 70 commercial properties in three states at the end of 2015 including 30 properties in Houston Texas and 25 properties in the Phoenix metro area of Arizona. The rest of its properties were located in Dallas-Fort Worth (7 properties) Austin Texas (4) San Antonio (3) and Buffalo grove near Chicago Illinois (1).Sales and MarketingThe REIT's tenant base is made up of a diverse mix of mostly retail clients with some banks and university clients sprinkled in. While none of Whitestone's tenants contributed more than 2.6% to its total revenue during 2015 its five largest tenants by revenue for the year included: Safeway Stores Bashas' Inc. Haggens Food & Pharmacy Wells Fargo & Company and Alamo Drafthouse Cinema.

Financial Performance

Whitestone REIT has tripled its revenues and boosted its profits sixfold since 2011 mostly as it has expanded its property portfolio through acquisitions and has raised its average rent per square foot by more than 40%.The REIT's revenue jumped 29% to $93.4 million during 2015 mostly thanks to 12 new property acquisitions made from January 2014 through the end of 2015. Its "Same Store" comparable sales for existing properties grew during the year as its revenue rate per average leased square foot rose 4% to $17.28 per foot. Occupancy rates dipped slightly but remained mostly around 87%. Despite strong revenue growth in 2015 Whitestone REIT's net income shrank 11% to $6.75 million for the year mostly because in 2014 it generated a non-recurring $1.9 million gain from property sales. The REIT's operating cash levels climbed 44% to $36.1 million during 2015 as its cash-based earnings increased.

Strategy

Whitestone REIT's strategically acquires commercial properties in high growth markets with densely populated and culturally diverse neighborhoods in and around Austin Chicago Dallas-Fort-Worth Houston Phoenix and San Antonio. During 2015 it targeted acquisitions of "neighborhood- or community- retail properties" near master planned communities such as Quinlan Crossing (for $37.5 million) and Parkside Village South ($32.5 million) in Austin Texas; a single-tenant 14600 sq. ft. property in Gilbert Tuscany Village ($1.7 million); and the 93500 sq. ft. Keller Place property in the Keller suburb of Ft. Worth Texas. In mid-2014 it added Heritage Trace Plaza in Fort Worth Texas to its portfolio. It acquired half a dozen or so properties in 2013 including Market Street at DC Ranch in Scottsdale Arizona and Headquarters Village Shopping Center in Plano Texas.

EXECUTIVES

Chairman and CEO, James C. Mastandrea, age 73, $400,000 total compensation
COO, John J. Dee, age 65, $205,289 total compensation
CFO, David K. Holeman, age 53, $250,000 total compensation
VP Acquisitions and Asset Management, Bradford D. Johnson, $184,616 total compensation
VP Product Strategy and Market Research, Christine J. Mastandrea, $154,231 total compensation
Auditors: Pannell Kerr Forster of Texas, P.C.

LOCATIONS

HQ: Whitestone REIT
2600 South Gessner, Suite 500, Houston, TX 77063
Phone: 713 827-9595   **Fax:** 713 465-8847
Web: www.whitestonereit.com

PRODUCTS/OPERATIONS

2015 Sales

	$ mil.	% of total
Rental	71.8	77
Other	21.6	23
Total	**93.4**	**100**

COMPETITORS

General Growth Properties	Simon Property Group
IRC Retail Centers	Weingarten Realty

HISTORICAL FINANCIALS

Company Type: Public

Income Statement

FYE: December 31

	REVENUE ($ mil.)	NET INCOME ($ mil.)	NET PROFIT MARGIN	EMPLOYEES
12/15	93.4	6.7	7.2%	95.0
12/14	72.3	7.5	10.5%	81.0
12/13	62.1	3.7	6.1%	68.0
12/12	46.5	0.0	0.1%	68.0
12/11	34.9	1.1	3.2%	62.0
Annual Growth	**27.9%**	**56.6%**	**—**	**11.3%**

2015 Year-End Financials

Debt ratio: 63.7%
Return on equity: 2.9%
Cash ($ mil.): 3.0
Current ratio: 0.68
Long-term debt ($ mil.): 499.7

No. of shares (mil.): 26.9
Dividends
  Yield: 9.4%
  Payout: 407.1%
Market value ($ mil.): 324.0

	STOCK PRICE ($) FY Close	P/E High/Low		PER SHARE ($) Earnings	Dividends	Book Value
12/15	12.01	65	44	0.24	1.14	9.00
12/14	15.11	47	40	0.32	1.14	9.20
12/13	13.37	85	61	0.20	1.14	9.84
12/12	14.05	—	—	(0.00)	1.14	9.80
12/11	11.90	124	88	0.12	1.14	10.14
Annual Growth	**0.2%**			**18.9%**	**(0.0%)**	**(2.9%)**

William Lyon Homes Inc

LOCATIONS

HQ: William Lyon Homes Inc
4695 MacArthur Court, 8th Floor, Newport Beach, CA 92660
Phone: 949 833-3600
Web: www.lyonhomes.com

HISTORICAL FINANCIALS

Company Type: Public

Income Statement

FYE: December 31

	REVENUE ($ mil.)	NET INCOME ($ mil.)	NET PROFIT MARGIN	EMPLOYEES
12/15	1,106.5	57.3	5.2%	586.0
12/14	896.6	44.6	5.0%	585.0
12/13	572.5	129.1	22.6%	0.0
12/12*	372.7	(8.8)	—	0.0
02/12	25.5	228.3	893.2%	0.0
Annual Growth	**156.5%**	**(29.2%)**	**—**	**—**

*Fiscal year change

Debt ratio: 57.4%
Return on equity: 9.5%
Cash ($ mil.): 50.2
Current ratio: 11.93
Long-term debt ($ mil.): 1,105.7
No. of shares (mil.): 31.4
Dividends
 Yield: —
 Payout: —
Market value ($ mil.): —

Wingstop Inc

Auditors: Ernst & Young LLP

LOCATIONS

HQ: Wingstop Inc
 5501 LBJ Freeway, 5th Floor, Dallas, TX 75240
Phone: 972 686-6500
Web: www.wingstop.com

HISTORICAL FINANCIALS

Company Type: Public

Income Statement

	REVENUE ($ mil.)	NET INCOME ($ mil.)	NET PROFIT MARGIN	EMPLOYEES
12/15	77.9	10.1	13.0%	428.0
12/14	67.4	8.9	13.3%	366.0
12/13	59.0	7.5	12.8%	0.0
12/12	51.5	3.5	6.9%	0.0
Annual Growth	14.8%	41.3%	—	—

2015 Year-End Financials

Debt ratio: 78.8%
Return on equity: —
Cash ($ mil.): 10.6
Current ratio: 1.56
Long-term debt ($ mil.): 95.5
No. of shares (mil.): 28.5
Dividends
 Yield: —
 Payout: —
Market value ($ mil.): 645.0

	STOCK PRICE ($) FY Close	P/E High/Low	PER SHARE ($) Earnings	Dividends	Book Value
12/15	22.56	95 55	0.36	0.00	(0.34)
12/14	0.00	— —	0.34	0.00	(0.34)
Annual Growth	—		5.9%	—	—

Winnebago Industries, Inc.

A pioneer in the world of recreational vehicles Winnebago Industries makes products intended to encourage exploration and outdoor escape. Almost all of the company's sales come from its motor homes and towables which are sold via independent dealers throughout the US and Canada under the Winnebago Adventurer Sightseer Suncruiser Sunova and Minnie Winnie brands among others. Winnebago Industries also sells RV parts and provides related services; in addition the company produces OEM parts for other RV manufacturers and for use in commercial vehicles. The company traces its roots back to the 1950s.

Operations

Winnebago divides its motor homes portfolio across three main product lines: Class A (conventional motor homes) Class B (panel-type vans) and Class C (motor homes built on van-type chassis).

Geographic Reach

Winnebago is based in Forest City Iowa. It owns facilities in Middlebury Forest City Lake Mills and Charles City Iowa; Junction City Oregon; Middlebury Indiana; and Burnsville Minnesota.

Sales and Marketing

The company markets its RVs on a wholesale basis to a diversified independent dealer network located throughout the US and to a limited extent in Canada. The RV dealer network in the US and Canada includes almost 300 motorized and 160 towable physical dealer locations with roughly 75 of these locations carrying both Winnebago motorized and towable products. FreedomRoads and La Mesa RV Center the company's chief dealers accounted for 17% and 13% of its total revenue in fiscal 2016 respectively.

Financial Performance

Winnebago posted $976 million in revenues in 2015 its highest total in about 10 years. Revenues dropped marginally to $975 million in 2016. Profits jumped 10% from $41 million in 2015 to $46 million in 2016.

Its recent growth was attributed to a 2% bump in motorized wholesale deliveries from 2015 to 2016. Towable net revenue also experienced growth of approximately 25% in 2016. Strong demand for its Class B and Class C products was partially offset by weaker demand in Class A products. Going forward Winnebagao anticipates continued strong demand in its Class B and C categories.

The modest revenue decline for 2016 was due mainly to other manufactured products revenues which decreased by $21 million. This was primarily due to the company's exit of its aluminum extrusion and bus businesses. Both of these operations have provided very low margins over the years.

Strategy

Winnebago's motorized production facilities are located in largely rural areas of northern Iowa. Although the unemployment rate in these areas is currently low the company has been working to extend its geographical scope to avoid depending upon labor strictly within this region.

In 2016 it purchased a production facility in Junction City Oregon from a former motorized RV producer. It is expanding some motor home manufacturing functions to Junction City in order to diversify its geographical locations. The new site also provides a West Coast service option for customers.

Mergers and Acquisitions

In potentially its largest deal to date Winnebago in late 2016 agreed to buy privately held Grand Design Recreational Vehicle Co a maker of towable recreational vehicles. The cash-and-stock deal valued at $500 million will give Winnebago a bigger foothold in the growing towables market and create a company with net revenue of about $1.4 billion.

Company Background

During a mid-1950s economic downturn furniture store owner John Hanson convinced Forest City officials to welcome a local subsidiary of California trailer maker Modernistic Industries. The company's first trailer rolled off the line in 1958. Hanson later bought the plant and in 1960 named the business Winnebago Industries after Forest City's home county. Winnebago Industries went public in 1966. Sales took off when the company offered less-expensive RVs than its competitors.

EXECUTIVES

VP and CFO, Sarah N. Nielsen, age 43, $335,000 total compensation
President and CEO, Michael J. Happe, age 45, $338,461 total compensation
VP Manufacturing, Daryl W. Krieger, age 53, $256,001 total compensation
VP and General Manager Towables Business, Scott Degnan, age 51, $309,614 total compensation
VP General Counsel and Secretary, Scott C. Folkers, age 55, $278,999 total compensation
VP Information Technology and CIO, Jeff Kubacki
VP and General Manager Motorized Business, Brian Hazelton, age 51
Legal Secretary, Karen Jefson
Vice President Develop, Steven (Steve) Dummett
Chairman, Robert M. (Bob) Chiusano, age 65
Auditors: Deloitte & Touche LLP

LOCATIONS

HQ: Winnebago Industries, Inc.
 P.O. Box 152, Forest City, IA 50436
Phone: 641 585-3535 **Fax:** 641 585-6966
Web: www.winnebagoind.com

PRODUCTS/OPERATIONS

2016 Sales

	$ mil.	% of total
Motorhomes parts and service	875.0	90
Towables and parts	89.4	9
Other manufactured products	10.8	1
Total	**975.2**	**100**

Selected Products

ERA
 ERA
Itasca
 Cambria
 Ellipse
 Impulse
 Impulse Silver
 Meridian
 Meridian V Class
 Navion
 Navion IQ
 Reyo
 Suncruiser
 Sunova
 Sunstar
Winnebago
 Access
 Access Premier
 Adventurer
 Aspect
 Journey
 Journey Express
 Sightseer
 Tour
 Via
 View
 View Profile
 Vista

COMPETITORS

Airstream	Patrick Industries
Elixir Industries	Prevost Car
Featherlite	Rexhall Industries
Forest River	Skyline
Gulf Stream Coach	Supreme Industries
Jayco Inc.	TRIGANO
Keystone RV	Thor Industries
Motor Coach Industries	Tiffin Motorhomes
Newmar Corporation	

HISTORICAL FINANCIALS

Company Type: Public

Income Statement

FYE: August 27

	REVENUE ($ mil.)	NET INCOME ($ mil.)	NET PROFIT MARGIN	EMPLOYEES
08/16	975.2	45.5	4.7%	3,050.0
08/15	976.5	41.2	4.2%	2,900.0
08/14	945.1	45.0	4.8%	2,850.0
08/13	803.1	31.9	4.0%	2,680.0
08/12	581.6	44.9	7.7%	2,380.0
Annual Growth	13.8%	0.3%	—	6.4%

2016 Year-End Financials

Debt ratio: —
Return on equity: 18.6%
Cash ($ mil.): 85.5
Current ratio: 3.02
Long-term debt ($ mil.): —

No. of shares (mil.): 26.9
Dividends
  Yield: 0.0%
  Payout: 23.8%
Market value ($ mil.): 643.0

	STOCK PRICE ($) FY Close	P/E High/Low		PER SHARE ($) Earnings	Dividends	Book Value
08/16	23.91	14	10	1.68	0.40	9.98
08/15	20.42	17	12	1.52	0.36	8.20
08/14	24.73	20	13	1.64	0.00	7.13
08/13	22.27	23	10	1.13	0.00	6.13
08/12	11.01	7	4	1.54	0.00	5.05
Annual Growth	21.4%	—	—	2.2%	—	18.6%

Wolfson Microelectronics Plc (Edinburgh)

EXECUTIVES

Chairman, Michael C. Ruettgers, age 74

CEO and Director, Mike Hickey, age 57

CFO Financial Director and Director, Mark Cubitt, age 54

Marketing Communications Manager, Anne Connolly

SVP Worldwide Sales, Alistair Banham

Chief Commercial Officer, Andy Brannan

VP Marketing, Nat Edington

VP Human Resources, Issy Urquhart

Company Secretary, Jill Goldsmith

VP Product Management, Stephen Doran

VP Marketing Wolfson Microelectronics plc, Allan Hughes

Vp Of Sales And General Manager, Takahisa Yamada

Senior Independent Non-Executive Director, Ross Graham

CEO and Director, Mike Hickey, age 57

CFO Financial Director and Director, Mark Cubitt, age 54

Director, David Milne

Independent Non-Executive Director, Glenn Collinson

Independent Non-Executive Director, John Grant

Independent Non-Executive Director, Robert Eckelmann

LOCATIONS

HQ: Wolfson Microelectronics Plc (Edinburgh)
  800 West Sixth Street, Austin, TX 78701
Phone: 512 851-4000
Web: www.cirrus.com

HISTORICAL FINANCIALS

Company Type: Public

Income Statement

FYE: March 26

	REVENUE ($ mil.)	NET INCOME ($ mil.)	NET PROFIT MARGIN	EMPLOYEES
03/16	1,169.2	123.6	10.6%	1,291.0
03/15	916.5	55.1	6.0%	1,104.0
03/14*	714.3	108.1	15.1%	751.0
12/13	179.4	(16.4)	—	440.0
12/12	179.7	(6.0)	—	421.0
Annual Growth	59.7%	—	—	32.3%

*Fiscal year change

2016 Year-End Financials

Debt ratio: 13.5%
Return on equity: 15.3%
Cash ($ mil.): 168.7
Current ratio: 3.95
Long-term debt ($ mil.): 160.4

No. of shares (mil.): 0.0
Dividends
  Yield: —
  Payout: —
Market value ($ mil.): —

	STOCK PRICE ($) FY Close	P/E High/Low		PER SHARE ($) Earnings	Dividends	Book Value
03/16	0.00 13,723.18	—	—	1.87	0.00	
03/15	0.00 11,996.05	5	3	0.85	0.00	
03/14*	2.07 10,287.27	2	1	1.65	0.00	
Annual Growth	—	—	—	6.5%	—	15.5%

*Fiscal year change

World Wrestling Entertainment Inc

The action might be fake but the business of World Wrestling Entertainment (WWE) is very real. The company is a leading producer and promoter of wrestling matches for TV and live audiences with about 250 live events each year including more than 50 international matches. Its main programming includes Monday Night Raw a top US cable program on USA Network; Friday Night SmackDown on Syfy; and WWE NXT on its website. WWE also produces about 12 live pay-per-view programs licenses characters for merchandise and sells videos and DVDs showcasing more than 140 wrestling stars such as Rey Mysterio Triple H and The Undertaker. Two-time WWE world champion Vince McMahon has nearly 90% voting control of the company.

Geographic Reach

WWE programming is broadcast in more than 175 countries and 25 languages and reaches more than 650 million homes worldwide. The company is headquartered in Stamford Connecticut with offices in New York Los Angeles Miami Mexico City Dubai London Mumbai Shanghai Singapore Istanbul and Tokyo. In fiscal 2014 the company brought in more than 75% of its revenue from North America.

WWE's office in Miami Florida serves as its headquarters for all operations in Latin America. The launch of its Latin America office allowed WWE to build upon its success and demonstrated its commitment to growth in the region.

Operations

The company classifies its operations into four reportable segments: Media Division (consisting of WWE Network and pay-per-view Television Home Entertainment and Digital Media Segments) Live Events Segment Consumer Products Division (consisting of Licensing Venue Merchandise and WWEShop Segments) and WWE Studios Segment.

Warner Brothers Home Entertainment became the distributor of WWE's home entertainment products in 2015.

Sales and Marketing

During fiscal 2014 the company spent a little more than $30 million on advertising expenses.

WWE uses the Internet to promote its brands and to create a community experience among its fans. Its primary website WWE.com attracted an average of 20.7 million monthly unique visitors worldwide during 2014. WWE currently has regional websites spanning 50 countries worldwide allowing fans to experience WWE in their native language with a concentration on local events and shows.

WWE's home entertainment titles are generally sold through retailers such as Wal-Mart and Best Buy and via subscription and iTunes Amazon and Netflix.

Financial Performance

The company reported $542.6 billion in revenue for fiscal 2014. That was an increase of $34.6 billion compared to the prior fiscal period. Despite more than $500 billion in revenue WWE suffered a net loss of $30 billion in fiscal 2014. That was actually an improvement of more than $32 billion compared to the net loss the company claimed in fiscal 2013.

Even with a net loss the company's cash flow from operations remained strong in fiscal 2014. The company ended the year with $54.6 billion in cash on hand which was an increase of more than $30 billion compared to fiscal 2013 levels.

Strategy

While WWE is a diversified entertainment and media company its livelihood all stems from the live wrestling matches it produces around the country. The live events including ticket sales and merchandise sold at the matches account for only a portion of WWE's sales but more importantly those matches the wrestlers and the passion of the fans gets turned into all the other revenue streams. From that core WWE is able to produce and promote its TV shows pay-per-view events video games DVDs and other products.

The strengthening of WWE's content distribution agreements is another of WWE's primary long-term growth drivers.

HISTORY

Company Background

Jesse McMahon made a name for himself as a boxing promoter in the 1940s before switching to wrestling. His son Vincent joined him in the business and they founded the World Wide Wrestling Federation in 1963. The company operated in Northeastern cities such as New York Philadelphia and Washington DC remaining a regional operation until the early 1980s (it dropped Wide from its name in 1979).

Vince McMahon Jr. inherited control of the WWF from his sick father in 1982 changed its name to Titan Sports and focused on gaining national exposure. McMahon made wrestling hugely popular but angered promoters as well as some fans with his nontraditional ideas. He embraced the idea of wrestling as show business instead of sport involving celebrities such as Cyndi Lauper and Mr. T and pursued a presence on cable TV. McMahon also purchased or put out of business many regional promoters as he spread the business across the US.

In the mid-1980s McMahon hit the jackpot with a former bodybuilder named Terry Gene Bollea. Christened Hulk Hogan he quickly became lord of the ring making the cover of Sports Illustrated and performing for sellout crowds across the US. His likeness spawned toys clothing and a Saturday morning cartoon. Titan set a record for attracting the largest indoor crowd (more than 93000 fans packed Detroit's Pontiac Silverdome for Wrestlemania III) in 1987 and by the following year was selling $80 million in tickets annually.

Titan was body slammed in 1993 when competitor World Championship Wrestling (WCW formed in 1988 by Ted Turner to broadcast on his TBS network) lured away several major stars including Hogan. Also that year the US government charged Titan with illegal distribution of steroids. The company was acquitted in 1994 but the bad press along with the star defections allowed WCW to take the ratings lead by 1996.

Titan's refashioning of the WWF with more violence and sexual innuendo unleashed a hailstorm of criticism but returned it to the top spot by mid-1998; meanwhile former WWF star Jesse "The Body" Ventura was elected governor of Minnesota. Titan was named a defendant in a wrongful death suit in 1999 filed by the family of wrestler Owen Hart who fell to his death during a pay-per-view event (the case was settled in 2000). The company also changed its name to World Wrestling Federation Entertainment (WWFE) and went public that year. The company later licensed the WWF name for a theme restaurant in New York City.

WWFE continued its bone-crunching ways in 2000 by launching XFL a professional football league that played in the winter following the NFL season. Still smarting from the loss of the NFL broadcast rights to CBS NBC bought half of the new league and broadcast the games on its network. The deal also gave NBC a 3% stake in WWF. The league was a disaster during its first season and it quickly folded. (The company repurchased NBC's shares in 2002.)

Later that year the firm bought the WWF New York Times Square Entertainment Complex from its licensee for $24.5 million. (It closed the location in 2003.) It also abandoned its broadcasting contract with USA Networks (now IAC/InterActiveCorp) in favor of a more lucrative deal with Viacom which also took a 3% stake in the company. (Viacom sold the stake back to the company in 2003.) In 2001 WWFE put a headlock on the wrestling world when it bought the WCW from Turner Broadcasting.

In 2002 WWE received the smackdown in a court battle with the World Wildlife Fund which claimed the company (formerly WWF) lifted the animal preservation group's initials. The company had to change its name from World Wrestling Federation Entertainment to World Wrestling Entertainment as part of a settlement.

After ending its partnership with Viacom's Spike TV in 2005 the WWE cut a deal with NBCUniversal to air Monday Night Raw on the USA Network and on Spanish-language network Telemundo. The following year after The WB and the UPN merged to form The CW Network WWE inked a deal with the upstart broadcaster to air Friday Night SmackDown. (The show moved to MyNetworkTV owned by News Corporation in 2008.) It also created a new show ECW: Extreme Championship Wrestling for NBCUniversal's SCI FI Channel (now Syfy).

The company inked a lucrative toy licensing partnership with Mattel in 2010.

EXECUTIVES

Senior Vice President Talent Relations, John (Jack) Laurinaitis
Vp Public Relations, Jim Brown
Vp Home Entertainment And Retail Marketing, Joel Satin
Senior Vice President Finance And Chief Accounting Officer, Frank G Serpe
Chairman and CEO, Vincent K. (Vince) McMahon, age 71, $1,239,923 total compensation
EVP Global Sales and Partnerships, John S. Brody
EVP Television Production, Kevin Dunn, age 55, $859,904 total compensation
Chief Strategy and Financial Officer, George A. Barrios, age 50, $723,692 total compensation
Chief Brand Officer, Stephanie McMahon, age 39
EVP Talent Live Events and Creative, Paul Levesque, age 46, $573,269 total compensation
President WWE Studios, Michael Luisi, age 50
Svp Consumer Products, James Connelly
Vice President Technology, Kevin (Kev) Quinn
Executive Vice President, John Weitz
Evp-content, Lisa F Lee
Vice President Talent Brand Management, Christopher Handy
Vice President Tv Programming, Jennifer Good
Executive Vice President, Brett Hart
Vice President Social Media, Jayar Donlan
Senior Vice President And Assistant General Counsel, James Langham
Vice President Of Event Booking Global Touring, Denis Sullivan
Senior Vice President And General Manager Digital Media, Brian Kalinowski
Vice President Legal And Business Affairs, Scott Amann
Vice President Post Production, Nancy Hirami
Vice President E Commerce And Retail Marketing, John Bancroft
Executive Vice President Consumer Products, Casey (Case) Collins
Auditors: Deloitte & Touche LLP

LOCATIONS

HQ: World Wrestling Entertainment Inc
1241 East Main Street, Stamford, CT 06902
Phone: 203 352-8600
Web: www.wwe.com

PRODUCTS/OPERATIONS

Selected Operations
Live and televised entertainment
    Live wrestling events
    Pay-per-view programming
    Television programming
    A.M. RAW (USA Network)
    Friday Night SmackDown (Syfy)
    Monday Night Raw (USA Network)
    WWE NXT (WWE.com)
    WWE Superstars (WGN America)

WWE Classics On Demand (video on demand service)
Consumer products
    Home video
    Magazines
    Product licensing
Digital media
    WWE.com
    WWEShop
WWE Studios (film production)

COMPETITORS

Harlem Globetrotters	NASCAR
Live Nation	NBA
Entertainment	NFL
Major League Baseball	NHL

HISTORICAL FINANCIALS
Company Type: Public

Income Statement
FYE: December 31

	REVENUE ($ mil.)	NET INCOME ($ mil.)	NET PROFIT MARGIN	EMPLOYEES
12/15	658.7	24.1	3.7%	840.0
12/14	542.6	(30.0)	—	761.0
12/13	507.9	2.7	0.5%	762.0
12/12	484.0	31.4	6.5%	721.0
12/11	483.9	24.8	5.1%	660.0
Annual Growth	8.0%	(0.7%)	—	6.2%

2015 Year-End Financials

Debt ratio: 5.2%	No. of shares (mil.): 75.9
Return on equity: 11.6%	Dividends
Cash ($ mil.): 38.0	Yield: 2.6%
Current ratio: 1.37	Payout: 480.0%
Long-term debt ($ mil.): 17.1	Market value ($ mil.): 1,354.0

	STOCK PRICE ($) FY Close	P/E High/Low	PER SHARE ($) Earnings	Dividends	Book Value
12/15	17.84	72 31	0.32	0.48	2.76
12/14	12.34	— —	(0.40)	0.48	2.73
12/13	16.58	415197	0.04	0.48	3.54
12/12	7.89	24 18	0.42	0.48	3.94
12/11	9.32	44 27	0.33	0.72	3.97
Annual Growth	17.6%	— —	(0.8%)	(9.6%)	(8.7%)

Xcerra Corp

Xcerra puts semiconductors to the test to make sure that your smartphone works. The company makes automated test equipment (ATE) that chip makers use to test semiconductors as they're manufactured and as part of the final package test. The company's equipment also tests printed circuit boards (PCBs). Its equipment runs tests on devices used in smartphones modems PCs TVs imaging instruments and a variety of others. The company sells through four brands: atg-Luther & Maelzer Everett Charles Technologies LTX-Credence and Multitest. Xcerra handles some of its manufacturing but outsources most of it to Jabil Circuit. Most of the company's sales are to customers in Asia.

Operations

Sales of Xcerra's semiconductor test equipment accounts for nearly 80% of revenue. The company's automated test equipment (ATE) test platforms are the Diamond series (which includes the flagship Diamondx test system) tests microcontrollers and cost sensitive consumer and digital-based devices; the X-Series which tests analog-based devices and those for power automotive mixed signal and RF applications; and ASL platform which tests linear low-end mixed signal precision analog and power management devices. The company's electronic manufacturing services provide the rest of its revenue.

Geographic Reach

Headquartered in Norwood Massachusetts Xcerra has offices in North America Europe and Asia. While the US is the company's biggest single geographic market about 60% of sales come from Asia. Individual markets include Hong Kong/China (17% of revenue) Taiwan (12%) and the Philippines (11%).

Sales and Marketing

Xcerra uses a direct sales force in the US and Europe and third-party distributors in certain markets in Southeast Asia including China Japan and Taiwan. Spirox is the company's biggest customer accounting for 20% of sales. Other customers include Amkor Atmel Intersil Maxim Integrated Products On Semiconductor and Qorvo.

Financial Performance

After sharp revenue increases in the past three years Xcerra's revenue slid 19% to $324 million in 2016 (ended July) from about $398 million in 2015. The company blamed the drop on weaker demand from semiconductor customers who were responding to overall economic conditions. Sales were lower in its two product markets and all but one of its geographic markets. Customers in China Hong Kong provided the only increase in 2016 with a 29% sales jump. Xcerra attributed lower service revenue in the Semiconductor Test segment on better reliability of its products which cut demand for post-warranty service contracts.

Even with lower expenses across the board the company's profit tumbled 60% to $11 million in 2016 from $28 million in 2015.

Xcerra went into negative cash flow ($227000) in 2016 because of the net loss a loss on an asset sale and higher inventories. The company had $42 million cash from operations in 2015.

Strategy

Xcerra knows a company can't be all things to all people and plans to concentrate its sales consulting and service efforts on key accounts as its industry is so customized. Its top 10 customers make up more than 50% of sales.

In accordance with that strategy the company sold its semiconductor test interface board business to Fastprint Hong Kong Co. a subsidiary of Shenzhen Fastprint Circuit Tech Co. The interface board business made PCBS designed to serve as an interface between the tester and the semiconductor device being tested. Since it was not a testing instrument Xcerra sold it off.

The company also maintains a lean operation by outsourcing manufacturing and using strategic alliances to outsource distribution repair and support functions.

Mergers and Acquisitions

In 2015 Xcerra acquired Titan which develops develops testing products for the automotive RF/Wireless and mixed signal test markets for about $2 million.

Company Background

Xcerra was created from the 2008 merger of LTX Corp. and rival Credence Systems.

HISTORY

Graham Miller Roger Blethen and others formed LTX in 1976. The company unveiled a linear/mixed-signal test system in 1977 and began developing testers for digital chips via its 1984 ac-

quisition of Trillium. The company launched its enVision programming software for digital testing in 1993 and introduced a digital test system the following year.

Miller served as chairman and CEO for 20 years; Blethen succeeded him as CEO in 1996. LTX restructured in 1996 integrating its West Coast digital and East Coast mixed-signal divisions to focus on Fusion testers (later known as the X-Series). An overall slowdown in the semiconductor industry caused LTX to implement another restructuring in 1998 including facilities consolidation and a 30% workforce reduction and led to a loss for the year.

The company's first Fusion system was shipped to National Semiconductor in 1998. In 2000 the company sold its iPTest line of specialized semiconductor component testing systems in order to better focus on the Fusion product family. The next year LTX formed a manufacturing partnership with Jabil Circuit a provider of electronic manufacturing services for assembling and testing the Fusion systems.

Late in 2002 the company reduced its workforce by 27% in the face of dismal conditions across the semiconductor industry. The company expanded its offerings through its 2003 acquisition of privately held StepTech a maker of chip testing instrumentation. In 2005 LTX cut headcount by another 28% as tester sales slumped again.

Roger Blethen stepped aside as CEO in late 2005; he remained as chairman of the board. Blethen was succeeded by David Tacelli a 17-year veteran of LTX who had been the company's president and COO since 2002.

LTX merged with Credence Systems in 2008 creating LTX-Credence Corporation. The combined company made its headquarters in Milpitas California where Credence was based. The merger agreement called for Credence CEO Lavi Lev to become executive chairman of the combined company while LTX CEO David Tacelli took over as president and CEO. Credence shareholders owned just a hair over half of the merged company's shares after the transaction closed and LTX took five of the nine seats on the combined board of directors. The stock-swap deal was valued at about $177 million.

Lavi Lev resigned as chairman near the end of 2008 and was succeeded by Roger Blethen once again.

LTX's sales in fiscal 2008 which ended just before the merger was completed were down by 8% from the year before reflecting poor business conditions. Chip makers especially those making memory devices were further challenged by lower sales in the second half of calendar 2008 leading many to slash their capital expenditure budgets for 2008 and 2009 which didn't bode well for test equipment vendors.

EXECUTIVES

Vice President Field Operations And Sales International, Michael (Mel) Goldbach
President and CEO, David G. (Dave) Tacelli, age 57, $600,000 total compensation
SVP COO and CFO, Mark J. Gallenberger, age 52, $410,000 total compensation
SVP Global Customer Team, Pascal Rond Cage 54, $322,547 total compensation
Vice President, Dick (Dicky) Mccarthy
Vice President Investor Relations, Rich (Ric) Yerganian
Chairman, Roger W. Blethen, age 65
Auditors: BDO USA, LLP

PRODUCTS/OPERATIONS

2016 Sales

	$ mil.	% of total
Semiconductor Test Solutions	252.0	78
Electronic Manufacturing Solutions	72.2	22
Total	**324.2**	**100**

PRODUCTS

Bare Board PCB Test Systems
Loaded PCB Test Fixtures
Probe Pins
Semiconductor ATE Solutions
Test Contactors
Test Handlers

COMPETITORS

Advantest	KLA-Tencor
Applied Materials	Roos Instruments
Cascade Microtech	Sanmina
Cohu	Teradyne
DFT MicroSystems	Trio-Tech
Fluke Corporation	Yokogawa Electric
FormFactor	inTEST

HISTORICAL FINANCIALS

Company Type: Public

Income Statement

FYE: July 31

	REVENUE ($ mil.)	NET INCOME ($ mil.)	NET PROFIT MARGIN	EMPLOYEES
07/16	324.2	11.1	3.4%	1,676.0
07/15	397.9	28.2	7.1%	1,722.0
07/14	330.8	0.8	0.3%	2,059.0
07/13	151.9	(12.1)	—	649.0
07/12	132.1	(19.8)	—	639.0
Annual Growth	25.2%			27.3%

2016 Year-End Financials

Debt ratio: 6.3%
Return on equity: 3.9%
Cash ($ mil.): 83.0
Current ratio: 4.47
Long-term debt ($ mil.): 21.2
No. of shares (mil.): 53.6
Dividends
  Yield: —
  Payout: —
Market value ($ mil.): 327.0

	STOCK PRICE ($) FY Close	P/E High/Low	PER SHARE ($) Earnings	Dividends	Book Value
07/16	6.10	35 24	0.21	0.00	5.26
07/15	6.29	20 12	0.52	0.00	5.09
07/14	9.35	511203	0.02	0.00	4.22
07/13	5.36	— —	(0.25)	0.00	4.16
07/12	5.86	— —	(0.40)	0.00	4.44
Annual Growth	1.0%	— —	—	—	4.3%

Xenia Hotels & Resorts Inc

Auditors: KPMG LLP

HISTORICAL FINANCIALS
Company Type: Public

Income Statement
FYE: December 31

	REVENUE ($ mil.)	NET INCOME ($ mil.)	NET PROFIT MARGIN	EMPLOYEES
12/15	976.1	88.7	9.1%	47.0
12/14	926.6	109.8	11.8%	36.0
12/13	651.8	(51.4)	—	0.0
12/12	466.8	(46.1)	—	0.0
Annual Growth	**27.9%**	—	—	—

2015 Year-End Financials

Debt ratio: 36.4%	No. of shares (mil.): 111.6
Return on equity: 5.4%	Dividends
Cash ($ mil.): 122.1	Yield: 5.4%
Current ratio: 1.71	Payout: 105.7%
Long-term debt ($ mil.): 1,094.5	Market value ($ mil.): 1,712.0

	STOCK PRICE ($) FY Close	P/E High/Low	PER SHARE ($) Earnings	Dividends	Book Value
12/15	15.33	31 19	0.79	0.84	15.47
12/14	0.00	— —	(0.00)	0.00	13.59
Annual Growth	—	— —	—	—	13.8%

Yadkin Financial Corp

Yadkin Financial Corporation is the holding company for Yadkin Bank (formerly Yadkin Valley Bank and Trust) which serves customers from more than 70 branches across North Carolina and upstate South Carolina. In addition to its standard loans SBA loans and deposit products including checking and savings accounts money market accounts CDs and IRAs Yadkin Bank and its subsidiaries provide mortgage banking investment and insurance services to more than 80000 business and individual customers. Founded in 1968 Yadkin Bank now boasts nearly $1.5 billion in total assets. F.N.B. Corporation is buying Yadkin for $1.4 billion.

OperationsThe bank's primary businesses are centered around Commercial and Personal banking Mortgage banking (through Yadkin Mortgage) Builder Finance Wealth Services (through securities broker Yadkin Wealth) and Small Business Lending.The bank which staffs more than 820 full-time and 60 part-time employees (as of late 2014) generated 75% of its revenue from loan interest in 2014 with another 7% of revenue coming from interest on its investment securities. The remainder of its revenue mostly came from service charges and fees on deposit accounts (6% of revenue) government-guaranteed lending (6%) and mortgage banking (2%).Geographic ReachThe bank boasts more than 70 branches in central and western portions of North Carolina and neighboring parts of northern South Carolina. About 30% of its assets were in the central region of North Carolina while more than 30% were split between the Piedmont and Mountain regions of the state. Yadkin Mortgage is headquartered in Greensboro North Carolina.Financial PerformanceNote: The company's 2013 financials were restated after its 2014 acquisitions. This analysis does not use the restated figures.Yadkin Financial's revenue has been trending downward over the past few years due to

shrinking interest margins on loans amidst the low-interest environment. The firm's profits however have been rising thanks to declining loan loss provisions as its loan portfolio's credit quality has improved with the strengthened economy.Yadkin had a breakout year in 2014 however with revenue spiking by 76% to a record $163.5 million as its loan business more than doubled to $2.9 billion (compared to $1.39 billion in 2013) after its 2014 acquisitions of VantageSouth and Piedmont Community banks and organic loan growth. The bank's non-interest income from deposit charges and other fees on accounts also more than doubled helping to grow Yadkin's top line. Higher revenue and a continued decline in loan loss provisions in 2014 drove Yadkin's net income up 15% to a record $21.7 billion.StrategyYadkin Financial reiterated in 2015 that its "growth in business profitability and market share has historically been enhanced by strategic mergers and acquisitions." Indeed its mid-2014 acquisitions of VantageSouth and Piedmont Community Bank more than doubled its loan and deposit business.

Then in 2016 Yadkin agreed to itself be acquired. Pittsburgh-based F.N.B. Corporation will buy the company for $1.4 billion after which Yadkin Bank will merge into FNB unit First National Bank of Pennsylvania.Yadkin also leverages its local community banking advantage to grow its loans and deposits organically.Mergers and AcquisitionsIn July 2014 Yadkin Financial purchased VantageSouth Bancshares and Piedmont Community Bank Holdings which helped to more than double its loan assets and made Yadkin Bank the largest community bank headquartered in North Carolina.Company BackgroundYadkin Financial Corporation (formerly Yadkin Valley Financial) was formed in 2006 to be the holding company for Yadkin Bank (previously Yadkin Valley Bank and Trust). The bank and its Piedmont Bank High Country Bank Cardinal State Bank (acquired 2008) and American Community Bank (acquired 2009) divisions all rebranded under the Yadkin Bank name in May 2013.

EXECUTIVES

Chief Financial Officer; Executive Vice President, Jan H. Hollar
Regional President Piedmont Bank Yadkin Bank and Trust Company, Edward L. (Ed) Marxen
Executive Vice President Cbo, Steven W (Steve) Jones
Vice President Credit Administration, Rich (Ric) Harris
Vice Chairman, Harry M. Davis, age 67
Auditors: Dixon Hughes Goodman LLP

LOCATIONS

HQ: Yadkin Financial Corp
3600 Glenwood Avenue, Suite 300, Raleigh, NC 27612
Phone: 919 659-9000

PRODUCTS/OPERATIONS

2007 Sales

	$ mil.	% of total
Interest		
Loans including fees	68.2	75
Securities	6.5	7
Other	0.5	1
Noninterest		
Net gains on sales of loans	5.9	7
Service charges on deposit accounts	3.9	4
Other service fees	3.6	4
Other	2.1	2
Total	**90.7**	**100**

COMPETITORS

BB&T	First Citizens
Bank of America	BancShares
CommunityOne Bancorp	Wells Fargo

HISTORICAL FINANCIALS
Company Type: Public

Income Statement
FYE: December 31

	ASSETS ($ mil.)	NET INCOME ($ mil.)	INCOME AS % OF ASSETS	EMPLOYEES
12/15	4,474.1	44.6	1.0%	845.0
12/14	4,266.3	21.7	0.5%	882.0
12/13	1,806.0	18.8	1.0%	511.0
12/12	1,923.4	(8.6)	—	481.0
12/11	1,993.1	(14.4)	—	481.0
Annual Growth	**22.4%**	—	—	**15.1%**

2015 Year-End Financials

Return on assets: 1.0%	Dividends
Return on equity: 7.9%	Yield: 0.7%
Long-term debt ($ mil.): —	Payout: 14.4%
No. of shares (mil.): 31.7	Market value ($ mil.): 799.0
Sales ($ mil): 219.1	

	STOCK PRICE ($) FY Close	P/E High/Low	PER SHARE ($) Earnings	Dividends	Book Value
12/15	25.17	19 13	1.38	0.20	17.73
12/14	19.65	25 19	0.88	0.00	17.65
12/13	17.04	16 2	1.19	0.00	12.82
12/12	2.94	— —	(1.92)	0.00	11.87
12/11	1.61	— —	(2.85)	0.00	21.60
Annual Growth	**98.8%**	— —	—	—	(4.8%)

ZAGG Inc

ZAGG hopes to stand in the way when a little zig threatens to scratch your iPhone or iPad. Short for "Zealous About Great Gadgets" ZAGG designs makes and sells protective coverings and other products for electronic devices. Its flagship product invisibleSHIELD is a thin scratch-resistant polyurethane film covering that's custom cut to fit invisibly on the screens and displays of Apple iPhones and other smartphones tablets laptops GPS devices and watch faces. ZAGG also offers additional accessories including keyboards headphones for iPods and MP3 players and decorative cases for phones. It sells its products through retailers the likes of Best Buy and Wal-Mart mall kiosks and its own website.

Geographic Reach

The US is ZAGG's largest market. accounting for about 85% of its sales. Europe contributes about 5% of sales with other countries representing the rest. The company's international arm is based in Shannon Ireland.

Operations

The company's operations are divided into three segments. The largest accounting for about three-quarters of total sales is ZAGG which designs makes and distributes products including protective coverings keyboards keyboard cases earbuds mobile power devices and cleaning accessories for mobiles devices under the ZAGG brand. iFrogz accounts for about 25% of sales. It makes cases Near-Field Audio amplifying speakers earbuds and regular and gaming headphones for mobile devices. The company's HzO segment is engaged in the development of water blocking coating technologies for consumer and industrial applications. It had no revenue in 2012.

Sales and Marketing

ZAGG's biggest customer is consumer electronics chain Best Buy which accounts for about a third of its total sales. Next is retail-giant Wal-Mart Stores which accounts for about 10%. Historically the company has focused on distributing through sales channels like kiosk vendors and through its e-commerce site; however more recently it has brought in more and more income through retailers (including Target RadioShack and Staples) and wireless carriers (AT&T Sprint Verizon). Ultimately demand for its products has been driven by the growing popularity of iPads iPhones and other smartphones. (iPhone accessories are its biggest sellers.) The company sells throughout Europe and other global regions through international distributors.

Financial Performance

In 2012 ZAGG's sales exceeded $264 million a 48% jump versus 2011. Driving the heady increase was the 2011 purchase of iFrogz which contributed about $68 million in sales in 2012. Strong demand from wholesale customers the addition of new distribution partners and continued growth of invisibleSHIELD products coupled with increased sales of ZAGG's keyboards audio and case product lines also pumped up sales. 2012 marked the fourth year of accelerating sales for the company. Indeed over the past four years sales have increased by more than a factor of 10: from nearly $20 million in 2008 to $264 million in 2012.

After four years of steep increases net income fell 21% in 2012 compared with 2011. ZAGG attributed the decline to higher operating expenses. Also marketing advertising and promotion expenses rose as the company invested heavily for key product launches including the invisibleSHIELD HD invisibleSHIELD EXTREME and ZAGGkeys PRO among other new products.

Strategy

Going forward ZAGG hopes to keep its growth momentum swinging in an upward direction by expanding its sales channels to include more telecom companies like U.S. Cellular and retailers like Amazon.com. It has also been broadening its range of accessories for the mobile phone market by adding car chargers and power supplies to its product offerings. Other growth strategies include focusing its sales and marketing efforts on cross-selling accessories to customers that purchase its invisibleSHIELD products.

Mergers and Acquisitions

In a move that simultaneously broadened its brand and product portfolio and increases its retail reach ZAGG in mid-2011 acquired iFrogz a maker and distributor of protective cases headphones and earbuds and other accessories for smartphones tablets and other mobile devices under the iFrogz and EarPollution brands. ZAGG paid $50 million in cash acquired 4.4 million restricted shares of ZAGG common stock and assumed about $5 million in debt. Utah-based iFrogz which counts Wal-Mart Stores among its customers became a wholly-owned subsidiary of ZAGG.

EXECUTIVES

COO, Steve Tarr, $62,500 total compensation
President and CEO, Randall L. Hales, $696,400 total compensation

EVP Product Management and Development, Kent Wuthrich
CFO, Bradley J. Holiday
EVP Global Sales, Brian Stech
Managing Director European Sales, Chris Ahern
Vice President, Taylor D Smith
Chairman, Cheryl A. Larabee
Auditors: KPMG LLP

LOCATIONS

HQ: ZAGG Inc
910 West Legacy Center Drive, Suite 500, Midvale, UT 84047
Phone: 801 263-0699
Web: www.zagg.com

PRODUCTS/OPERATIONS

Selected Brands
EarPollution
iFrogz
invisibleSHIELD (film coatings)
ZAGGbuds (audio headphones)
ZAGGskins (cell phone cases and covers)
ZAGGsmartbuds (audio headphones)

COMPETITORS

Apple Inc.	Kyocera Communications
Bose	Motorola Mobility
Dooney & Bourke	Otterbox
Forward Industries	Plantronics

HISTORICAL FINANCIALS

Company Type: Public

Income Statement

FYE: December 31

	REVENUE ($ mil.)	NET INCOME ($ mil.)	NET PROFIT MARGIN	EMPLOYEES
12/15	269.3	15.5	5.8%	234.0
12/14	261.5	10.4	4.0%	220.0
12/13	219.3	4.7	2.2%	201.0
12/12	264.4	14.5	5.5%	273.0
12/11	179.1	18.2	10.2%	261.0
Annual Growth	10.7%	(3.9%)	—	(2.7%)

2015 Year-End Financials

Debt ratio: —	No. of shares (mil.): 27.5
Return on equity: 12.1%	Dividends
Cash ($ mil.): 13.0	Yield: —
Current ratio: 2.69	Payout: —
Long-term debt ($ mil.): —	Market value ($ mil.): 301.0

	STOCK PRICE ($) FY Close	P/E High/Low		PER SHARE ($) Earnings	Dividends	Book Value
12/15	10.94	23	11	0.54	0.00	4.74
12/14	6.79	20	11	0.34	0.00	4.36
12/13	4.35	49	23	0.15	0.00	4.08
12/12	7.36	27	14	0.46	0.00	3.98
12/11	7.07	25	9	0.63	0.00	3.45
Annual Growth	11.5%	—	—	(3.8%)	—	8.3%

ZELTIQ Aesthetics Inc

ZELTIQ Aesthetics is winning the battle of the bulge. The company's CoolSculpting device offers a non-invasive alternative to liposuction to knock out fat cells. The treatment uses controlled cooling to reduce the temperature of fat cells and melt fat without causing scar tissue or skin damage. ZELTIQ sells the CoolSculpting device and related consumables in the US for use on targeted areas of the torso and thighs but it is also used more freely in about 45 other international markets. The CoolSculpting system is sold to dermatologists plastic surgeons and aesthetic specialists such as medical spas. ZELTIQ was incorporated in 2005 as Juniper Medical. Allergan is buying ZELTIQ for $2.5 billion.

Change in Company Type

Ireland-based harmaceutical giant Allergan (which lists Botox among its products) agreed to buy ZELTIQ in early 2017 soon after its acquisition of breast reconstruction and soft tissue repair company LifeCell. The ZELTIQ acquisition will further build its aesthetics business creating opportunities for cross-selling treatments to individual patients.

Operations

In addition to its CoolScultping systems the company generates revenue from sales of consumables including CoolGels CoolLiners and CoolCard computer cartridges. Income is split about down the middle between the two divisions.

Geographic Reach

The company markets its products in the US where the system is only approved for abdominal and thigh use and in 60 international markets where it's used on all body parts. Domestic use accounts for about 80% of sales.

Sales and Marketing

In the US ZELTIQ uses a dedicated sales force to market its wares to plastic surgeons dermatologists and aesthetic specialists. Abroad it employs a small sales force directing a network of about 40 distributors.

Financial Performance

Revenue rose 47% in 2013 to $112 due to increased sales as the company expanded into new markets especially in North America. Consumables sales continue to be strong as the installed base of ZELTIQ machines grows leading to the need for consumables.

Since CoolSculpting was only approved in 2011 the company still runs at a net loss and may for the foreseeable future as it continues pumping money into R&D. For 2013 however the net loss was $19 million compared to $30 in 2012 a 36% improvement due to increased sales. ZELTIQ's accumulated deficit stood at $133.1 million.

Cash for operations is also still going out but improving. It spent $23 million less in 2013 due to tight inventory control and an improvement in net income.

Strategy

ZELTIQ's plan for success includes expanding the base of CoolSculpting machines while also driving demand for consumables. Of course it will also continue to seek FDA approval for additional body areas and introduce new consumables. To that end in 2014 the FDA gave clearance for CoolSculpting use on thighs and the company launched a new applicator. The prior year it also launched a new applicator training programs and a data management tool to help end-users improve their sales.

EXECUTIVES

CTO, Leonard C. (Len) DeBenedictis, age 75, $270,000 total compensation
President and CEO, Mark J. Foley, age 51, $525,000 total compensation
SVP and CFO, Taylor C. Harris, age 40

Senior Vice President; General Counsel and Corporate Secretary, Sergio Garcia, age 54, $310,000 total compensation
Vice President of Operations, Carl H. Lamm, age 54
President International Global Sales and Physician Training, Todd E. Zavodnick, age 44
VP North American Sales, Brent Hauser
VP Global Marketing, Danika Harrison
Auditors: PricewaterhouseCoopers LLP

LOCATIONS

HQ: ZELTIQ Aesthetics Inc
4698 Willow Road, Suite 100, Pleasanton, CA 94588
Phone: 925 474-2500
Web: www.coolsculpting.com

PRODUCTS/OPERATIONS

2015 Sales

	$ mil.	% of total
Systems	130.7	51
Consumable	124.7	49
Total	**255.4**	**100**

COMPETITORS

Cutera	Palomar Medical
Cynosure	Solta Medical
Dynatronics	Sound Surgical
Mentor Worldwide	Technologies
Osyris Medical	Syneron

HISTORICAL FINANCIALS

Company Type: Public

Income Statement FYE: December 31

	REVENUE ($ mil.)	NET INCOME ($ mil.)	NET PROFIT MARGIN	EMPLOYEES
12/15	255.4	41.8	16.4%	535.0
12/14	174.4	1.5	0.9%	408.0
12/13	111.6	(19.3)	—	297.0
12/12	76.1	(30.1)	—	209.0
12/11	68.1	(9.6)	—	153.0
Annual Growth	**39.1%**	**—**	**—**	**36.7%**

2015 Year-End Financials

Debt ratio: 0.1%	No. of shares (mil.): 39.2
Return on equity: 42.9%	Dividends
Cash ($ mil.): 35.7	Yield: —
Current ratio: 2.28	Payout: —
Long-term debt ($ mil.): 0.1	Market value ($ mil.): 1,119.0

	STOCK PRICE ($) FY Close	P/E High/Low	PER SHARE ($) Earnings	Dividends	Book Value
12/15	28.53	35 24	1.02	0.00	3.17
12/14	27.91	744345	0.04	0.00	1.85
12/13	18.91	— —	(0.53)	0.00	1.69
12/12	4.63	— —	(0.87)	0.00	2.02
12/11	11.36	— —	(1.96)	0.00	2.77
Annual Growth	**25.9%**	**— —**	**—**	**—**	**3.4%**

Zumiez Inc

Zumiez's young customers like to zoom. The fast-growing retailer outfits action sports enthusiasts offering apparel footwear accessories and sports equipment for 12- to 24-year-olds who enjoy board sports BMX biking and surfing. It stocks such brands as Billabong Burton Quiksilver Vans and Spy Optic as well as private-label goods. Zumiez operates about 500 mall-based stores across North America and in Europe as well as an online store. Aside from the usual action sports merchandise (hoodies and puffy skater shoes) stores also feature couches video games and sales clerks who really use the gear –all designed to encourage shoppers to chill. Zumiez was founded in 1978 by chairman Thomas Campion.

Geographic Reach

Zumiez operates about 475 stores in some 40 US states and another 20 stores in Canada (seven in Ontario three in British Columbia). California Texas and New York are the retailer's largest market accounting for about a third of its stores. In Europe a new market for the retailer the company operates stores under the name Blue Tomato.

Operations

In addition to its fast-growing retail store chain Zumiez sells merchandise online and provides content and community for its young customers. E-commerce sales accounted for more than 7% of the company's sales in fiscal 2012 (ends January).

Sales and Marketing

To increase brand awareness and strengthen its connection to its customers Zumiez participates in various music and local sporting events that embody the action sports lifestyle. The Zumiez Couch Tour is a series of entertainment events that includes skateboarding demonstrations from top professionals autograph sessions competitions and live music. In fiscal 2012 (ends January) the Couch Tour completed a 12-city tour of the US. Zumiez also advertises in magazines popular with its target market and sponsors interactive contests and maintains a presence on various social network channels such as Facebook and Twitter.

Financial Performance

Zumiez's fiscal 2012 (ends January) sales increased 16% vs. the prior year while net income grew by 54% over the same period. The double-digit uptick in sales and profits was driven by the addition of more than 40 new stores including the retailer's first in Canada and a 9% rise in sales at stores open more than one year. Footwear men's apparel accessories and junior's apparel posted increases in same-store sales while hardgoods and boy's apparel declined.

Indeed thanks to its rapidly-expanding retail store network Zumiez's sales have quintupled over the past decade and the chain is consistently profitable.

Strategy

Growth is the mantra at Zumiez. The company has made great strides in extending its retail network adding about 250 stores since the end of fiscal 2005 (ends January). In fiscal 2012 the chain entered the Canadian market and has since made an acquisition in Europe. Going forward the chain plans to open about 50 new stores including 10 more in Canada in fiscal 2013 and grow its online sales. In the US the chain is adding stores in existing and new markets.

To that end in mid-2012 the company acquired Blue Tomato a multi-channel action sports retailer based in Austria for €59.5 million ($78 million). Blue Tomato operates five stores in Austria as well as an e-commerce site serving the broader European market.

Ownership

Founder Campion owns about a 16% stake in Zumiez while CEO Richard Brooks holds 12% of the shares. The investment firm T. Rowe Price Associates owns about 16% while Waddell & Reed Financial Services owns 8% of the company.

EXECUTIVES

CEO, Richard M. Brooks, $631,324 total compensation
President and General Merchandising Manager, Lynn K. Kilbourne, $489,113 total compensation
EVP Stores, Ford K. Wright, $278,172 total compensation
CFO, Christopher C. Work, $158,265 total compensation
EVP E-commerce and Omni-channel, Troy R. Brown
Vice President Purchasing, Jim Bob (Jimmy) Hume
Chairman, Thomas D. Campion
Auditors: Moss Adams LLP

LOCATIONS

HQ: Zumiez Inc
4001 204th Street SW, Lynnwood, WA 98036
Phone: 425 551-1500
Web: www.zumiez.com

PRODUCTS/OPERATIONS

2015 Sales

	% of total
Men's Apparel	34
Accessories	20
Footwear	19
Hard goods	14
Junior's Apparel	13
Total	**100**

COMPETITORS

Abercrombie & Fitch	Hot Topic
American Apparel	Old Navy
American Eagle	Pacific Sunwear
Outfitters	Sport Chalet
A©ropostale	Sports Authority
Big 5	The Buckle
Dick's Sporting Goods	Urban Outfitters
Forever 21	

HISTORICAL FINANCIALS

Company Type: Public

Income Statement FYE: January 30

	REVENUE ($ mil.)	NET INCOME ($ mil.)	NET PROFIT MARGIN	EMPLOYEES
01/16	804.1	28.7	3.6%	7,000.0
01/15*	811.5	43.1	5.3%	6,500.0
02/14	724.3	45.9	6.3%	5,600.0
02/13	669.3	42.1	6.3%	5,300.0
01/12	555.8	37.3	6.7%	4,680.0
Annual Growth	**9.7%**	**(6.3%)**	**—**	**10.6%**

*Fiscal year change

2016 Year-End Financials

Debt ratio: —	No. of shares (mil.): 25.7
Return on equity: 8.7%	Dividends
Cash ($ mil.): 43.1	Yield: —
Current ratio: 2.88	Payout: —
Long-term debt ($ mil.): —	Market value ($ mil.): 466.0

	STOCK PRICE ($) FY Close	P/E High/Low	PER SHARE ($) Earnings	Dividends	Book Value
01/16	18.11	38 13	1.04	0.00	11.55
01/15*	37.29	28 14	1.47	0.00	12.22
02/14	21.52	22 13	1.52	0.00	11.33
02/13	21.11	30 14	1.35	0.00	10.08
01/12	28.33	26 14	1.20	0.00	8.74
Annual Growth	**(10.6%)**	**— —**	**(3.5%)**	**—**	**7.2%**

*Fiscal year change

Hoover's Handbook of

Emerging Companies

Master Index for all 2017 Hoover's Handbooks

Index by Headquarters

ARE

Dubai
United Arab Emirates (United Arab Emirates) W404

Abu Dhabi
National Bank of Abu Dhabi W267
First Gulf Bank W160
Abu Dhabi Commercial Bank W4

Dubai
Dubai Islamic Bank Ltd W138

AUS

Perth
Wesfarmers Ltd. W413

Sydney
Woolworths Ltd. W418

Melbourne
Rio Tinto Ltd W317

Sydney
Commonwealth Bank of Australia W110

Melbourne
BHP Billiton Ltd. W67

Sydney
Westpac Banking Corp W414

Melbourne
National Australia Bank Ltd. W266

Docklands
Australia & New Zealand Banking Group Ltd W37

Melbourne
ANZ National Bank Ltd W29
Telstra Corp., Ltd. W379

Sydney
QBE Insurance Group Ltd. W311

Brisbane
Suncorp Group Ltd. W365

Sydney
Macquarie Group Ltd W241
AMP Ltd. W26

AUT

Vienna
OMV AG (Austria) W290
Erste Group Bank AG W155

BEL

Leuven
Anheuser-Busch InBev SA/NV W29

Brussels
Ageas NV W11
Dexia SA W136
KBC Group NV W217
Banque Nationale de Belgique (National Bank of Belgium) W54

BMU

Hamilton
Jardine Matheson Holdings Ltd. W209
Jardine Strategic Holdings Ltd (Bermuda) W210
XL Group Ltd W422

BRA

Rio de Janeiro
Petroleo Brasileiro S.A. W298

Sao Paulo
Itau Unibanco Holding S.A. W205
JBS SA W210
Banco Bradesco S.A. W42

Rio de Janeiro
Vale SA W405

Sao Paulo
Ultrapar Participacoes SA W397
Banco Santander Brasil SA W44
Banco BTG Pactual S.A. W42

CAN

Toronto
Royal Bank of Canada (Montreal, Quebec) W324

Laval
Alimentation Couche-Tard Inc W20

Toronto
Weston (George) Limited W413
Loblaw Companies Ltd W238

Aurora
Magna International Inc. W242

Toronto
Toronto Dominion Bank W389

Montreal
Power Corp. of Canada W307
Power Financial Corp W308

Halifax
Bank of Nova Scotia Halifax W51

Toronto
Manulife Financial Corp. W246

Winnipeg
Great-West Lifeco Inc W174

Calgary
Enbridge Inc W148
Suncor Energy Inc. W364

Toronto
Brookfield Asset Management Inc W80
ONEX Corp (Canada) W292

Calgary
Imperial Oil Ltd W195

Montreal
Bank of Montreal W50

Stellarton
Empire Co Ltd W146

Montreal
Bombardier Inc. W72

Verdun
BCE Inc W63

Winnipeg
Great-West Life Assurance Co W173

Toronto
Canadian Imperial Bank of Commerce W84
Sun Life Financial Inc W363
Fairfax Financial Holdings Ltd W157

Montreal
National Bank of Canada W267

Vancouver
HSBC Bank Canada W187

Ottawa
Bank of Canada (Ottawa) W49

CHE

Baar
Glencore PLC W172

Vevey
Nestle SA W272

Zurich
Zurich Insurance Group Ltd W426

Basel
Roche Holding Ltd W320
Novartis AG Basel W284

Zurich
UBS Group AG W397
Swiss Re Ltd. W370
ABB Ltd W1

Basel
Ste Cooperative de Consommation Coop-Geneva W359
Coop Switzerland (Switzerland) W114

Glattbrugg
Adecco Group AG W7

Zurich
Swiss Life Holding AG W369
Swiss Life Insurance & Pension Co. (Switzerland) W370
Credit Suisse Group W116

Jona
LafargeHolcim Ltd W228

Zurich
Chubb Ltd W104

Schindellegi
Kuehne & Nagel International AG W226

Zurich
Swiss Life (UK) plc (United Kingdom) W369

Basel
Baloise Holding AG W40

Zurich
Zuercher Kantonalbank (Switzerland) W426

Lausanne
Banque Cantonale Vaudoise W53

St. Gallen
Schweizer Verband der Raiffeisenbanken (Switzerland) W338

CHL

Providencia
Cementos Bio-Bio S.A. (Chile) W91

Santiago
AntarChile S.A. (Chile) W29
Empresas COPEC SA W147
Cencosud SA W91
Banco Santander Chile W45
Banco de Chile W43

CHN

Beijing
China Petroleum & Chemical Corp. Inc W98
PetroChina Co Ltd W297
Industrial and Commercial Bank of China Ltd W198
China Construction Bank Corp W95
Agricultural Bank of China W11

A =	AMERICAN BUSINESS
E =	EMERGING COMPANIES
P =	PRIVATE COMPANIES
W =	WORLD BUSINESS

Bank of China Ltd W49

Shanghai
SAIC Motor Corp Ltd W331

Shenzhen
Ping An Insurance (Group) Co of
China Ltd. W301

Beijing
China Railway Construction Corp Ltd
W99
China Railway Group Ltd W99
China Life Insurance Co Ltd W96
Peoples Insurance Company (Group)
of China Ltd (The) W297
China Communications Constructions
Group Ltd W95

Shanghai
Bank of Communications Co., Ltd.
W49

Beijing
China Telecom Corp Ltd W101

Shenzhen
China Merchants Bank Co Ltd W96

Shanghai
China United Network
Communications Ltd W102

Beijing
China Minsheng Banking Corp Ltd
W96
PICC Property and Casualty Co Ltd
W301
China Citic Bank Corp Ltd W94
CRRC Corp Ltd W119

Shanghai
Sinopharm Group Co., Ltd. W347

Beijing
Metallurgical Corp China Ltd W253

Shanghai
Shanghai Jinfeng Investment Co Ltd
W340

Shenzhen
China Vanke Co Ltd W102

Shanghai
China Pacific Insurance (Group) Co.,
Ltd. W98

Nanchang
Jiangxi Copper Co., Ltd. W211

Hangzhou
Zhejiang Material Industrial Zhongda
Yuantong Group Co., Ltd. W425

Beijing
JD.com, Inc. W211
China Shenhua Energy Co., Ltd.
W100
China Everbright Bank Co Ltd W95

Shanghai
Baoshan Iron & Steel Co Ltd W54

Guangzhou
China Evergrande Group W95

Fuzhou
Industrial Bank Co., Ltd. W199

Nanjing
Suning Appliance Co., Ltd. W365

Beijing
Huaneng Power International, Inc.
W190

Xiamen
Xiamen C & D Inc W422

Wuhan
Dongfeng Motor Group Co Ltd W137

Shanghai
Shanghai Construction Group Co.,
Ltd. W340

Dalian
Dalian Wanda Commercial Properties
Co Ltd W123

Beijing
Aluminum Corp of China Ltd. W25

Guangzhou
Poly Real Estate Group Co., Ltd.
W306
China Southern Airlines Co Ltd W100

Shanghai
Shanghai Pharmaceuticals Holding Co
Ltd W341

Shenzhen
Tencent Holdings Ltd. W380

Zhuhai
Gree Electric Appliances Inc Of
Zhuhai W175

Beijing
China National Building Material
Company Limited W97

Shenzhen
Zte Corp. W425
Ping An Bank Co Ltd W301

Chongqing City
Chongqing Rural Commercial Bank
Co., Ltd. W102

COL

Bogota
Ecopetrol SA W142

Medellin
BanColombia, S.A. W46

DEU

Wolfsburg
Volkswagen A.G. (Germany, Fed. Rep.)
W409

Stuttgart
Daimler AG W121

Duesseldorf
E.ON SE W139

Munich
Allianz SE W23

Munchen
Bayer Motoren WK W60

Munich
Bayerische Motoren Werke AG W62
Siemens AG (Germany) W346

Stuttgart
Bosch (Robert) GmbH (Germany Fed.
Rep.) W73

Ludwigshafen
BASF SE W57

Bonn
Deutsche Telekom AG W135

Munich
Muenchener Rueckversicherungs-
Gesellschaft AG (Germany) W264

Duesseldorf
Metro AG W254

Bonn
Deutsche Post RG W135
Deutsche Post AG W134

Ingolstadt
AUDI AG W37

Essen
RWE AG W330

Leverkusen
Bayer AG W59

Frankfurt am Main
Deutsche Bank AG W131

Berlin
Deutsche Bahn AG W130
Deutscher Sparkassen-und
Giroverband e.V. (Germany, Fed.
Rep.) W136

Essen
ThyssenKrupp AG W384

Hanover
Continental AG (Germany, Fed. Rep.)
W113

Frankfurt
Deutsche Lufthansa AG (Germany,
Fed. Rep.) W133

Hannover
Talanx AG W374

Friedrichshafen
ZF Friedrichshafen AG (Germany)
W424

Frankfurt am Main
DZ Bank AG Deutsche Zentral-
Genossenschaftsbank W138

Bad Homburg
Fresenius SE & Co KGaA W165

Stuttgart
Celesio AG W90

Karlsruhe
ENBW Energie Baden-Wuerttemberg
AG W149

Essen
Hochtief AG W183

Walldorf
SAP SE W334

Hanover
TUI AG W394

Duesseldorf
Henkel AG & Co KGAA W179

Munich
Linde AG (Germany, Fed. Rep.) W236

Guetersloh
Bertelsmann AG (Germany, Fed. Rep.)
W65

Herzogenaurach
Adidas AG W7

Hannover
Hannover Rueckversicherung SE
W177

Frankfurt am Main
Commerzbank AG (Germany, Fed.
Rep.) W110

Bad Homburg
Fresenius Medical Care AG & Co
KGaA W163

Munich
BAYWA Bayerische Warenvermittlung
Landwirtschaftlicher
Genossenschaften AG W63

Frankfurt am Main
Kreditanstalt Fuer Wiederaufbau
(Germany, Fed. Rep.) W225

Munich
Bayerische Landesbank (Germany)
W60
UniCredit Bank AG W398

Bonn
Deutsche Postbank AG W135

Frankfurt am Main
Landesbank Hessen-Thueringen
Girozentrale (Helaba) (Germany,
Fed. Rep.) W229
Deutsche Bundesbank (Germany, Fed.
Rep.) W132
Landwirtschaftliche Rentenbank
(Germany, Fed. Rep.) W230

Frankfurt
Dekabank Deutsche Girozentrale
W128

Hamburg
Deutsche Genossenschafts-
Hypothekenbank (Germany, Fed.
Rep.) W133

Wiesbaden
Aareal Bank AG W1

Munich
Muenchener Hypothekenbank EG
(Germany, Fed. Rep.) W264

DNK

Copenhagen K
Danske Bank AS (Denmark) W126

Copenhagen
Danske Bank A/S W124

Bagsvaerd
Novo-Nordisk A/S W284

Silkeborg
Jyske Bank A/S W215

ESP

Madrid
Banco Santander SA W45
Telefonica SA W379
Repsol S.A. W314
Banco Bilbao Vizcaya Argentaria SA
(BBVA) W41
ACS Actividades de Construccion y
Servicios, S.A. W5
Iberdrola SA W194

Barcelona
Gas Natural SDG, S.A. W169

Madrid
International Consolidated Airlines
Group SA W201

CITRUS HEIGHTS
S.d. Deacon Corp. P426

CITY OF INDUSTRY
Newegg Inc. P346
America Chung Nam (group) Holdings
Llc P23

CLOVIS
Clovis Unified School District P130

COLTON
Arrowhead Regional Medical
Center P40

CONCORD
Ufcw & Employers Trust Llc P575

CORTE MADERA
Rh E360

CUPERTINO
Apple Inc A65

DAVIS
University Of California, Davis P587

DIAMOND BAR
Cycle Link (u.s.a.) Inc. P153

DUBLIN
Ross Stores, Inc. A770

EL SEGUNDO
Mattel Inc A570
The Aerospace Corporation P510

ENCINO
National Cement Company, Inc. P335

ESCONDIDO
Palomar Health P374

FAIRFIELD
Northbay Healthcare Group P355

FONTANA
California Steel Industries, Inc. P94

FOSTER CITY
Gilead Sciences, Inc. A405
Guidewire Software Inc E188

FREMONT
Synnex Corp A839
Lam Research Corp A528
Asi Computer Technologies Inc P42
Washington Hospital Healthcare
System P625
Electronics For Imaging, Inc. E130

FRESNO
Dairyamerica, Inc. P155
Fresno Community Hospital And
Medical Center P198
Fresno Unified School District P198
Saint Agnes Medical Center P427

FULLERTON
St. Jude Hospital P481

GARDEN GROVE
Southland Industries P466

GARDENA
Apro, Llc P35

GLENDALE
Avery Dennison Corp. A90

GOLETA
Inogen, Inc E223

HAYWARD
Impax Laboratories Inc E218

HUNTINGTON BEACH
Quiksilver, Inc. P402
Bj's Restaurants Inc E59

IMPERIAL
Imperial Irrigation District P235

IRVINE
Banc Of California Inc A98 E48
Opus Bank Irvine (ca) A663 E315
Pacific Premier Bancorp Inc A673
E319
First Foundation Inc A366 E160
St. Joseph Health System A816 P479
Vizio, Inc. P617
Victory International Group, Llc P614
Humax Usa, Inc. P231
Tri Pointe Group Inc E411
Masimo Corp. E257
Boot Barn Holdings Inc E64
Tilly's Inc E407
Banc Of California Inc A98 E48
Calamp Corp E75
Opus Bank Irvine (ca) A663 E315
Sabra Health Care Reit Inc E363
Pacific Premier Bancorp Inc A673
E319
First Foundation Inc A366 E160

KINGSBURG
Sun-maid Growers Of California P494

LA CANADA FLINTRIDGE
Allen Lund Company, Llc P19

LA JOLLA
The Scripps Research Institute P546

LA MESA
Grossmont Hospital
Corporation P210

LANCASTER
Antelope Valley Hospital Auxiliary P34

LODI
Farmers & Merchants Bancorp (lodi,
Ca) A334
Pacific Coast Producers P373

LOMA LINDA
Loma Linda University Medical
Center P280

LONG BEACH
Molina Healthcare Inc A597
Farmers & Merchants Bank Of Long
Beach (ca) A335
City Of Long Beach P126
Long Beach Memorial Medical
Center P281

LOS ALTOS
The David And Lucile Packard
Foundation P520

LOS ANGELES
Aecom A14
Cbre Group Inc A174
Reliance Steel & Aluminum Co. A755
Mercury General Corp. A580
Cathay General Bancorp A171
Hope Bancorp Inc A450 E208
Hanmi Financial Corp. A422 E190
Cu Bancorp (ca) A251 E115
Preferred Bank (los Angeles, Ca) A714
E341
University Of Southern
California P602
Los Angeles Department Of Water And
Power P282
Aryzta Llc P40
Aids Healthcare Foundation P11
The Childrens Hospital Los
Angeles P517
Bergelectric Corp. P70
California Hospital Medical Center
Foundation P94
Good Samaritan Hospital P205

Vca Inc E432
Korn/ferry International (de) E235
Air Lease Corp E11
Ares Management Lp E38
J2 Global Inc (new) E229
Kilroy Realty Corp E232
Kilroy Realty L.p. E232
Hope Bancorp Inc A450 E208
Hanmi Financial Corp. A422 E190
Cu Bancorp (ca) A251 E115
Preferred Bank (los Angeles, Ca) A714
E341
Pacific City Financial Corp E318
Op Bancorp E314

LOS GATOS
Netflix Inc. A622

LYNWOOD
St. Francis Medical Center P478

MADERA
Valley Children's Hospital P613

MENLO PARK
Facebook Inc A332
Robert Half International Inc. A764
Novo Construction, Inc. P363
Sri International P472

MILPITAS
Devcon Construction
Incorporated P163

MISSION VIEJO
Mission Hospital Regional Medical
Center Inc P323
Ensign Group Inc E138

MODESTO
Stan Boyett & Son, Inc. P484
Modesto Irrigation District (inc) P325

MONTEREY
Community Hospital Of The Monterey
Peninsula P138

MOUNTAIN VIEW
Alphabet Inc A33
Intuit Inc A489
Synopsys Inc E396
Omnicell Inc E312

NEWPORT BEACH
Pacific Mutual Holding Co. A672
Smart Circle International Llc P458
Lyon (william) Homes E248
William Lyon Homes Inc E451
Kbs Strategic Opportunity Reit
Inc E229

NOVATO
Bank Of Marin Bancorp A107
Hennessy Advisors Inc E199

OAKLAND
Clorox Co (the) A211
Kaiser Foundation Hospitals Inc A506
P256
Kaiser Fdn Health Plan Of
Colorado P256
Kfhp Of The Mid-atlantic States
Inc. P263
East Bay Municipal Utility District,
Wastewater System P174

ONTARIO
Cvb Financial Corp. A255

ORANGE
Orange County Health Authority, A
Public Agency P368
Orange County Transportation
Authority P368
St. Joseph Hospital Of Orange P479
Children's Hospital Of Orange
County P118

Chapman University P112

PALO ALTO
Hewlett Packard Enterprise Co A440
Hp Inc A457
Vmware Inc A933
Lucile Salter Packard Children's
Hospital At Stanford P285
Cpi International Holding Corp. P147
Gordon E. And Betty I. Moore
Foundation P207
Electric Power Research Institute,
Inc. P178

PASADENA
Jacobs Engineering Group, Inc. A495
East West Bancorp, Inc A299
Schaumbond Group, Inc. P438
California Institute Of
Technology P94
Pasadena Hospital Association,
Ltd. P377
Huntington Hospital P232
Green Dot Corp E186

PASO ROBLES
Heritage Oaks Bancorp A437

PERRIS
Val Verde Unified Sch Dis P613

PETALUMA
Frontrow Calypso Llc P199

PITTSBURG
Uss-posco Industries, A California
Joint Venture P612

PLEASANTON
Cooper Companies, Inc. (the) E105
Blackhawk Network Holdings Inc E61
Veeva Systems Inc E434
Natus Medical Inc. E294
Zeltiq Aesthetics Inc E457
Ellie Mae Inc E131

PORTERVILLE
Sierra Bancorp A796
R. M. Parks, Inc. P405

RANCHO CORDOVA
Dignity Health Medical
Foundation P166

RANCHO MIRAGE
Eisenhower Medical Center P176

REDDING
Mercy Home Services A California
Limited Partnership P310

REDWOOD CITY
Oracle Corp A663
Dpr Construction, Inc. P169
Qualys, Inc. E348

RIVERSIDE
Magnolia Rehabilitation & Nursing
Center P286
Riverside Unified School
District P419

ROLLING HILLS ESTATES
Natural Health Trends Corp. E293

ROSEMEAD
Edison International A304
Southern California Edison Co. A806

ROSEVILLE
Farm Credit West A334 P184
Sutter Roseville Medical Center P497
Farm Credit West A334 P184

SACRAMENTO
Sutter Health Sacramento Sierra
Region P497

A = AMERICAN BUSINESS
E = EMERGING COMPANIES
P = PRIVATE COMPANIES
W = WORLD BUSINESS

Irc Retail Centers Llc A492
Ace Hardware Corporation A9 P5

OAKBROOK TERRACE
Vasco Data Security International
Inc E432

ORLAND PARK
Marquette National Corp. (il) A562

PARK RIDGE
Advocate Health And Hospitals
Corporation P8

PEORIA
Caterpillar Inc. A170
Rli Corp. A762

RIVERWOODS
Discover Financial Services A276

ROCK ISLAND
Modern Woodmen Of America A595
P325

ROCKFORD
Swedishamerican Hospital P498
Rockford, Board Of Education P423

ROLLING MEADOWS
Kimball Hill Inc P264
Myr Group Inc E285

ROSEMONT
Us Foods Holding Corp A923
Wintrust Financial Corp. (il) A963
Brg Sports, Inc. P85
Trimega Purchasing Association P566

SCHAUMBURG
Convergint Technologies Llc P142

SPRINGFIELD
Horace Mann Educators Corp. A451
Memorial Medical Center P306
St Johns Hospital Sisters Of The Third
Order Of St Francis P474
Tom Lange Company, Inc. P563

URBANA
Carle Foundation Hospital P100

VERNON HILLS
Graham Enterprise, Inc. P208

WAYNE CITY
Consolidated Grain & Barge
Company A242 P141

WESTCHESTER
Ingredion Inc A476

WHEATON
Wheaton Franciscan Services,
Inc. P635

WOOD DALE
Power Solutions International, Inc.
(de) E339

INDIANA

BATESVILLE
Hillenbrand Inc E203

BLOOMINGTON
Trustees Of Indiana University P571
Indiana University P236
Hoosier Energy Rural Electric
Cooperative Inc. P229

Indiana University Health
Bloomington, Inc. P236

CARMEL
Cno Financial Group Inc A216
Telamon Corporation P504

COLUMBUS
Cummins, Inc. A253

ELKHART
Thor Industries, Inc. A871
Lci Industries E239
Patrick Industries, Inc. E323

EVANSVILLE
Berry Plastics Group Inc A128
Onemain Holdings Inc A660
Old National Bancorp (evansville,
In) A656
Atlas World Group, Inc. P48
Van Atlas Lines Inc P614
Deaconess Hospital Inc P161
St. Mary's Health, Inc. P482
Springleaf Finance Corp E380

FISHERS
First Internet Bancorp E160

FORT WAYNE
Steel Dynamics Inc. A826
Do It Best Corp. P166
Petroleum Traders Corporation P383

GREENSBURG
Mainsource Financial Group Inc A557

HIGHLAND
Strack And Van Til Super Market
Inc P491

INDIANAPOLIS
Anthem Inc A62
Lilly (eli) & Co A543
Simon Property Group, Inc. A799
Oneamerica Financial Partners,
Inc. A660 P368
Community Health Network,
Inc P137
Indiana University Health, Inc. P236
Countrymark Cooperative Holding
Corporation P145
Oneamerica Financial Partners,
Inc. A660 P368
Wabash Valley Power Association
Inc P620
Citizens Energy Group P124
Bmw Constructors, Inc. P79
United Student Aid Funds, Inc. P582
Bowen Engineering Corporation P84
Finish Line, Inc. (the) E155
Celadon Group, Inc. E83
Kite Realty Group Trust E233
Angie's List Inc. E30

JASPER
German American Bancorp Inc A405
Kimball Electronics Inc E233

LAFAYETTE
Kirby Risk Corporation P265
Wabash National Corp. E442

LEBANON
Witham Memorial Hospital P639

MERRILLVILLE
Nisource Inc. (holding Co.) A635

MICHIGAN CITY
Horizon Bancorp (michigan City,
In) A452 E209

MISHAWAKA
Franciscan Alliance, Inc. P195

MUNCIE
First Merchants Corp A368

MUNSTER
Munster Medical Research
Foundation, Inc P331

RICHMOND
Reid Hospital & Health Care Services,
Inc. P413

SOUTH BEND
1st Source Corp A1

TERRE HAUTE
First Financial Corp. (in) A365
Union Hospital, Inc. P577

WARSAW
Zimmer Biomet Holdings Inc A978
Lakeland Financial Corp A528

WEST LAFAYETTE
Purdue University P400

IOWA

AFTON
Farmers Cooperative Company

AMES
Danfoss Power Solutions Inc. P158
Iowa State University Of Science And
Technology P245

ANKENY
Casey's General Stores, Inc. A169
Perishable Distributors Of Iowa,
Ltd. P381

CEDAR RAPIDS
Rockwell Collins, Inc. A769
United Fire Group, Inc. A908 E422
Merrill Lynch Life Insurance
Co. A582
Crst International, Inc. P151
United Fire Group, Inc. A908 E422

CHEROKEE
First Cooperative Association P187

COUNCIL BLUFFS
Future Foam, Inc. P199

DAVENPORT
Genesis Health System P201

DES MOINES
Principal Financial Group, Inc. A715
Fidelity & Guaranty Life A345
Federal Home Loan Bank Of Des
Moines A339
Emc Insurance Group Inc. A306
Iowa Finance Authority A492
Catholic Health Initiatives - Iowa,
Corp. P106
Central Iowa Hospital Corp P110
Iowa Physicians Clinic Medical
Foundation P244

DUBUQUE
Heartland Financial Usa, Inc.
(dubuque, Ia) A433 E196
Flexsteel Industries, Inc. E163
Heartland Financial Usa, Inc.
(dubuque, Ia) A433 E196

FARNHAMVILLE
Farmers Cooperative Company P184

FOREST CITY
Winnebago Industries, Inc. E452

HILLS
Hills Bancorporation A441

IOWA CITY
Midwestone Financial Group,
Inc. A594 E277

The University Of Iowa P553
University Of Iowa Hospitals And
Clinics P591
Midwestone Financial Group,
Inc. A594 E277

MASON CITY
Mercy Health Services-iowa,
Corp. P309

MONTICELLO
Innovative Ag Services Co. P239

NORTH LIBERTY
Heartland Express, Inc. E196

ROLAND
Key Cooperative P262

SIOUX CENTER
Farmers Cooperative Society P185

WALCOTT
River Valley Cooperative P418

WATERLOO
Covenant Medical Center, Inc.

WEST BEND
Maxyield Cooperative P299

WEST BURLINGTON
Big River Resources, Llc P73

WEST DES MOINES
American Equity Investment Life
Holding Co A42
Fbl Financial Group, Inc. A336
West Bancorporation, Inc. A949
Hy-vee, Inc. A467 P232
Iowa Student Loan Liquidity
Corporation A492 P245
Hy-vee, Inc. A467 P232
Iowa Health System P244
Heartland Co-op P221
Iowa Student Loan Liquidity
Corporation A492 P245

KANSAS

ATCHISON
Mgp Ingredients Inc (new) E273

COLUMBUS
Crossland Construction Company,
Inc. P149

GARDEN CITY
The Garden City Co-op Inc P524

KANSAS CITY
Associated Wholesale Grocers,
Inc. A79 P45
The University Of Kansas
Hospital P553

LEAWOOD
Euronet Worldwide Inc. E144
Tallgrass Energy Partners, Lp E399
Tallgrass Energy Gp Lp E399

MANHATTAN
Kansas State University P258
Landmark Bancorp Inc E236

MCPHERSON
Chs Mcpherson Refinery Inc. P123

MERRIAM
Seaboard Corp. A785

MOUNDRIDGE
Mid-kansas Cooperative
Association P320

OLATHE
Terracon Consultants, Inc. P506

Olathe Unified School District
233 P367
Nic Inc. E304

OVERLAND PARK
Sprint Corp (new) A815
Yrc Worldwide Inc A976
Bvh, Inc. P91
Shamrock Trading Corporation P449
Black & Veatch Corporation P76
Black & Veatch International
Company P77
Black & Veatch Construction,
Inc. P76
Qts Realty Trust Inc E347

SHAWNEE MISSION
Shawnee Mission Medical Center,
Inc. P453

TOPEKA
Capitol Federal Financial Inc A164
Stormont-vail Healthcare, Inc. P491

WICHITA
Spirit Aerosystems Holdings Inc A815
Unified School District 259 P576
Via Christi Hospitals Wichita,
Inc. P614
Wichita, City Of (inc) P636

KENTUCKY

ASHLAND
Ashland Hospital Corporation P42

BOWLING GREEN
Houchens Industries, Inc. A457 P230

EDGEWOOD
Saint Elizabeth Medical Center,
Inc. P428

FORT MITCHELL
The Drees Company P521

FRANKFORT
Farmers Capital Bank Corp. A335

FRANKLIN
Keystops, Llc P262

HENDERSON
Big Rivers Electric Corporation P73
Kenergy Corp. P259

LEXINGTON
Board Of Education, Fayette County
Ky P80

LOUISVILLE
Humana Inc. A461
Yum! Brands Inc A977
Kindred Healthcare Inc A518
Republic Bancorp, Inc. (ky) A757
Stock Yards Bancorp Inc A829
Norton Hospitals, Inc P362
Baptist Healthcare System, Inc. P57
University Health Care Inc P582
Jefferson County Board Of
Education P250
University Of Louisville P591
Sam Swope Auto Group, Llc P433
Texas Roadhouse Inc E404
Churchill Downs, Inc. E90
Almost Family Inc E21

OWENSBORO
Owensboro Health, Inc. P373

PIKEVILLE
Community Trust Bancorp, Inc. A235
Pikeville Medical Center, Inc. P387

LOUISIANA

BATON ROUGE
Our Lady Of The Lake Hospital,
Inc. P371
Mmr Group, Inc. P324
Cajun Industries, Llc P93
Cajun Constructors, Llc P93
Mmr Constructors, Inc. P324
The Newtron Group L L C P538
East Baton Rouge Parish School
District P174
Baton Rouge General Medical
Center P62
H&e Equipment Services Inc E189
Investar Holding Corp E225

CHALMETTE
Chalmette Refining, L.l.c. A189 P112

COVINGTON
Cgb Enterprises, Inc. A188 P111
Zen-noh Grain Corporation A978
P644
Cgb Enterprises, Inc. A188 P111
Zen-noh Grain Corporation A978
P644
Saint Tammany Parish School
Board P432

CROWLEY
Southwind Nursing And
Rehabilitation Center Inc P468

DERIDDER
Amerisafe Inc A52 E28

HARVEY
Jefferson Parish School Board
Inc P251

LAFAYETTE
Iberiabank Corp A468 E212
Midsouth Bancorp, Inc. A594 E276
Home Bancorp Inc A444 E205
Lafayette General Health System,
Inc. P270
Lafayette General Medical Center
Inc P270
Acadian Ambulance Service, Inc. P3
Iberiabank Corp A468 E212
Phi Inc E332
Midsouth Bancorp, Inc. A594 E276
Home Bancorp Inc A444 E205

LAKE CHARLES
Central Crude, Inc P109

MONROE
Centurylink, Inc. A185
Qwest Corp A741
Allied Building Stores, Inc. P20

NEW ORLEANS
Entergy Corp A314
First Nbc Bank Holding Co. A371
Ochsner Clinic Foundation P365
The Administrators Of The Tulane
Educational Fund P510
Walton Construction - A Core
Company, Llc P623

SHREVEPORT
Willis-knighton Medical Center P637
Biomedical Research Foundation Of
Northwest Louisiana P75
Caddo Parish School Board P93

SUNSET
Louisiana Wholesale Drug Company,
Inc. P283

THIBODAUX
Rouse's Enterprises, L.l.c. P424

WINNFIELD
Kisatchie Corporation P265

MAINE

AUGUSTA
Maine State Housing Authority A557
Mainegeneral Health P288
Mainegeneral Medical Center P288

BANGOR
Eastern Maine Medical Center P176
University Of Maine System P592

BAR HARBOR
Bar Harbor Bankshares A115

BREWER
Eastern Maine Healthcare
Systems P175

CAMDEN
Camden National Corp. (me) A158

DAMARISCOTTA
First Bancorp Inc (me) A356
Miles Health Care, Inc P321

LEWISTON
Northeast Bancorp (me) E306

MACHIAS
Marshall Nursing Services Inc P293

PORTLAND
Maine Medical Center P287
Martin's Point Health Care, Inc. P296

SOUTH PORTLAND
Wex Inc E450

WESTBROOK
Idexx Laboratories, Inc. E213

MARYLAND

ANNAPOLIS
Anne Arundel County Board Of
Education P33
Anne Arundel Medical Center,
Inc. P33
Chesapeake Lodging Trust E89

BALTIMORE
The Whiting-turner Contracting
Company A869 P559
Johns Hopkins University A498 P254
Lord Baltimore Capital
Corporation A552
The Whiting-turner Contracting
Company A869 P559
Johns Hopkins University A498 P254
Johns Hopkins Health Sys Corp P253
Johns Hopkins Hospital P254
Baltimore City Public School Systems
(inc) P53
University Of Maryland Medical
System Corporation P592
Lifebridge Health, Inc. P277
Sinai Hospital Of Baltimore,
Inc. P457
Johns Hopkins Bayview Medical
Center, Inc. P253
Franklin Square Hospital Center,
Inc. P196
St. Agnes Healthcare, Inc. P476
Cowan Systems, Llc P147
The Union Memorial Hospital P549
Mercy Medical Center, Inc. P311
Greater Baltimore Medical Center
Land Corporation P209

BEL AIR
Harford County Board Of Education
(inc) P216

BERLIN
Penninsula Regional Medical
Center P380

BETHESDA
Lockheed Martin Corp A551
Marriott International, Inc. A562
Host Hotels & Resorts Inc A455
Eagle Bancorp Inc (md) A298 E125
Cystic Fibrosis Foundation P153
Lasalle Hotel Properties E238
Rlj Lodging Trust E360
Diamondrock Hospitality Co. E120
Pebblebrook Hotel Trust E327
Walker & Dunlop Inc E444
Eagle Bancorp Inc (md) A298 E125

BOWIE
Old Line Bancshares Inc A655 E309
Inovalon Holdings Inc E224
Old Line Bancshares Inc A655 E309

CHEVERLY
Dimensions Health Corporation P166

COLUMBIA
Medstar Health, Inc. P303
Maxim Healthcare Services, Inc. P299
Gp Strategies Corp. E184

CRISFIELD
The Alice Byrd Tawes Nursing Home
Inc P511

FREDERICK
Us Silica Holdings, Inc. E427

GAITHERSBURG
Adventist Healthcare, Inc. P7
Emergent Biosolutions Inc E133

GLEN BURNIE
R. E. Michel Company, Llc P404
Baltimore Washington Medical
System, Inc. P53

GREENBELT
Sgt, Inc. P448

HANOVER
Allegis Group, Inc. A28 P18
Aerotek, Inc. A15 P10
Allegis Group, Inc. A28 P18
Aerotek, Inc. A15 P10
Maryland Department Of
Transportation P296
Teksystems, Inc. P504

HUGHESVILLE
Maryland Southern Electric
Cooperative Inc P296

HUNT VALLEY
Sinclair Broadcast Group, Inc. E374
Omega Healthcare Investors,
Inc. E310

LA PLATA
The Wills Group Inc P560
Smo, Incorporated P460
Charles County Board Of
Education P112

LAUREL
Washington Suburban Sanitary
Commission (inc) P625

MARRIOTTSVILLE
Bon Secours Health System, Inc. P81

OLNEY
Sandy Spring Bancorp Inc A778

GRAND BLANC
Genesys Regional Medical
Center P202

GRAND RAPIDS
Spartannash Co. A810
Mercantile Bank Corp. A577 E268
Independent Bank Corporation (ionia,
Mi) A474
Spectrum Health Hospitals P470
Spectrum Health System P470
Spectrum Health Primary Care
Partners Dba P470
Cascade Engineering, Inc. P102
Meritage Hospitality Group Inc E270
Mercantile Bank Corp. A577 E268

HOLLAND
Macatawa Bank Corp. A555

JACKSON
Cms Energy Corp A212
Consumers Energy Co. A243
Alro Steel Corporation P21
W. A. Foote Memorial Hospital P618

KALAMAZOO
Stryker Corp. A830
Bronson Methodist Hospital Inc P87
Western Michigan University P633
Borgess Medical Center P83

LANSING
Sparrow Health System P468
Neogen Corp. E298

LIVONIA
Trinity Health-michigan P566
Mercy Health Services-iowa,
Corp. P309

MADISON HEIGHTS
Mcnaughton-mckay Electric Co. P301

MIDDLEVILLE
Hps Llc P231

MIDLAND
Dow Chemical Co. A288
Chemical Financial Corp A190 E88

MOUNT CLEMENS
Henry Ford Macomb Hospitals P223

MT. PLEASANT
Isabella Bank Corp A492

NORTHVILLE
Gentherm Inc E181

NOVI
Michigan Milk Producers
Association P319

ROYAL OAK
William Beaumont Hospital P637
Barrick Enterprises, Inc. P59

SAGINAW
Covenant Medical Center, Inc. P146

SAINT JOSEPH
Lakeland Regional Health
System P271

SOUTHFIELD
Lear Corp. A531
Barton Malow Company P60
Barton Malow Enterprises, Inc. P60
Providence Hospital P398
Credit Acceptance Corp (mi) E112
Sun Communities, Inc. E388

STERLING HEIGHTS
Kuka Systems North America
Llc P269

TAWAS CITY
Ausable Valley Community Mental
Health Foundation P50

TAYLOR
Masco Corp. A566
Atlas Oil Company P48

TRAVERSE CITY
Munson Medical Center P331

TROY
Kelly Services, Inc. A511
Flagstar Bancorp, Inc. A376
Syntel Inc. E398

WARREN
St. John Hospital And Medical
Center P479
St John Macomb-oakland
Hospital P474
Universal Logistics Holdings Inc E426

ZEELAND
Gentex Corp. E180

MINNESOTA

ARDEN HILLS
Land O' Lakes Inc A529

AUSTIN
Hormel Foods Corp. A452

BAUDETTE
Ani Pharmaceuticals Inc E31

BLOOMINGTON
Healthpartners, Inc. A433 P220
Lamex Foods Inc. P272

BREWSTER
Minnesota Soybean Processors P323

BROOKLYN PARK
Clearfield Inc E94

BURNSVILLE
Ames Construction, Inc. P30

DODGE CENTER
Mcneilus Steel, Inc. P302

DULUTH
Smdc Medical Center P458
St. Mary's Medical Center P483
St. Luke's Hospital Of Duluth P482
Allete Inc. E19

EDEN PRAIRIE
Supervalu Inc. A836
Robinson (c.h.) Worldwide, Inc. A766
Surmodics Inc E393

HERMANTOWN
Miners Incorporated P322

INVER GROVE HEIGHTS
Chs Inc A196

LITCHFIELD
The First District Association P522

MAPLE PLAIN
Proto Labs Inc E345

MEDINA
Polaris Industries Inc. A707

MINNEAPOLIS
Target Corp A845
U.s. Bancorp (de) A894
General Mills, Inc. A397
Ameriprise Financial Inc A50
Xcel Energy, Inc. A969
Riversource Life Insurance Co A762
Allina Health System P20
Fairview Health Services P183

North Memorial Health Care P351
Hennepin Healthcare System,
Inc. P222
Regions Hospital P412
Minneapolis Public School
District P322
Cliftonlarsonallen Llp P130
University Of Minnesota
Physicians P593
National Marrow Donor Program
Inc P336
Buffalo Wild Wings Inc E72
Select Comfort Corp. E367
Apogee Enterprises Inc E33
Wells Fargo Real Estate Investment
Corp E447
Piper Jaffray Companies E335
Bio-techne Corp E57

MINNETONKA
Unitedhealth Group Inc A915

MURDOCK
Dooley's Petroleum, Inc. P168

NORWOOD
Bongards' Creameries P82

PLYMOUTH
Mosaic Co (the) A603

RICHFIELD
Best Buy Inc A129

ROCHESTER
Mayo Foundation For Medical
Education And Research P301

SAINT CLOUD
Coborn's, Incorporated P133
St. Cloud Hospital P477

SAINT LOUIS PARK
Park Nicollet Methodist
Hospital P375

SAINT PAUL
Api Group Inc. P34
Augustana Health Care Center Of
Apple Valley P49
Hmo Minnesota P227
Independent School Dist 625 P235
Regions Hospital Foundation P412
Merrill Corporation P312
3m Employees Welfare Benefits
Association Trust Ii P1
Universal Cooperatives, Inc. P582

ST. PAUL
3m Co A1
Ecolab Inc A303
Patterson Companies Inc A680

TRUMAN
Watonwan Farm Service, Inc P625

WAYZATA
Tcf Financial Corp A847

MISSISSIPPI

GREENVILLE
Farmers Grain Terminal, Inc. P185

GREENWOOD
Staple Cotton Co-operative
Association P485

GULFPORT
Hancock Holding Co. A420

HATTIESBURG
Cooperative Energy, A Mississippi
Electric Cooperative P142
The Merchants Company P531

Forrest General Health Services,
Inc. P193
First Bancshares Inc E157

JACKSON
Trustmark Corp. A889
Board Of Trustees Of State
Institutions Of Higher Learning P81
University Of Mississippi Medical
Center P594
Cal-maine Foods Inc E74

MISSISSIPPI STATE
Mississippi State University P323

PASCAGOULA
Signal International, Llc P455

TUPELO
Bancorpsouth Inc. A101
Renasant Corp A756 E355
North Mississippi Health Services,
Inc. P352
North Mississippi Medical Center,
Inc. P353
Renasant Corp A756 E355

UNIVERSITY
University Of Mississippi P593

MISSOURI

BRIDGETON
Daughters Of Charity Services Of St.
Louis P159

CAPE GIRARDEAU
Francis Saint Medical Center P194

CHESTERFIELD
Reinsurance Group Of America,
Inc. A754
St. Luke's Episcopal-presbyterian
Hospitals P481

CLAYTON
Enterprise Financial Services
Corp A317

COLUMBIA
University Of Missouri System P594
Mfa Incorporated P317
Mfa Oil Company P317
University Of Missouri Health
Care P594

DES PERES
Jones Financial Companies Lllp A500

FENTON
Maritz Holdings Inc. P291

GRANDVIEW
Nasb Financial Inc A610

JOPLIN
Freeman Health System P197

KANSAS CITY
Commerce Bancshares Inc A229
Umb Financial Corp A898
Kansas City Life Insurance Co (kansas
City, Mo) A507
Dairy Farmers Of America, Inc. A259
P154
J.e. Dunn Construction Group,
Inc. P247
J.e. Dunn Construction
Company P246
Mercy Children's Hospital P308
St Luke's Hospital Of Kansas
City P475
Saint Luke's Hospital Of Kansas
City P431
Truman Medical Center,
Incorporated P569

ISELIN
Macdonald Mott Group Inc P285
JERSEY CITY
Provident Financial Services Inc A724
Jersey City Medical Center Inc P251
Verisk Analytics Inc E436
Bel Fuse Inc E55
KEASBEY
Wakefern Food Corp. A934 P621
KENILWORTH
Merck & Co Inc A578
LINDEN
Turtle & Hughes, Inc P573
LITTLE FALLS
Cantel Medical Corp E78
LIVINGSTON
St Barnabas Medical Ctr P474
LONG BRANCH
Monmouth Medical Center Inc. P326
LYNDHURST
Sika Corporation P455
MADISON
Quest Diagnostics, Inc. A738
Realogy Holdings Corp A748
Realogy Group Llc A748
MAHWAH
Ascena Retail Group Inc A75
MATAWAN
Creative Management Inc P147
MORRIS PLAINS
Honeywell International Inc A449
MORRISTOWN
Atlantic Health System Inc. P47
Ahs Hospital Corp. P11
MOUNT LAUREL
Sun Bancorp Inc. (nj) A832
Marlin Business Services Corp E257
NEPTUNE
Meridian Hospitals Corporation P311
NEW BRUNSWICK
Johnson & Johnson A499
Johnson & Johnson Patient Assistance
  Foundation Inc P255
Saint Peter's University Hospital,
  Inc. P431
NEWARK
Prudential Financial, Inc. A725
Public Service Enterprise Group
  Inc A728
Pseg Power Llc A727
Newark Beth Israel Medical Center
  Inc. P345
OAK RIDGE
Lakeland Bancorp, Inc. A527
PARSIPPANY
Pbf Energy Inc A682
Avis Budget Group Inc A91
Wyndham Worldwide Corp A968
Zoetis Inc A982
B&g Foods Inc E45
PATERSON
St. Joseph's Hospital And Medical
  Center P480
PLAINSBORO
Princeton Healthcare System A New
  Jersey Nonprofit Corporation P396

POMONA
Atlanticare Regional Medical
  Center P48
PRINCETON
Nrg Energy Inc A645
The Trustees Of Princeton
  University P548
Bank Of Princeton E50
PRINCETON JUNCTION
Mistras Group Inc E279
RIDGEFIELD PARK
Samsung C&t America, Inc. P434
RIDGEWOOD
The Valley Hospital Inc P557
ROSELAND
Automatic Data Processing Inc. A86
SECAUCUS
Mha Llc P317
Vitamin Shoppe Inc E441
SEWAREN
Woroco Management Llc P640
SHORT HILLS
Investors Bancorp Inc (new) A491
  E226
SOMERSET
Shi International Corp. A796 P454
SUMMIT
Celgene Corp. A178
TEANECK
Cognizant Technology Solutions
  Corp. A221
TOMS RIVER
Oceanfirst Financial Corp A653
Community Medical Center,
  Inc. P138
TOWNSHIP OF WASHINGTON
Oritani Financial Corp (de) A665
  E316
TRENTON
New Jersey Housing And Mortgage
  Finance Agency Cj A623 P341
Capital Health System Inc. P97
New Jersey Housing And Mortgage
  Finance Agency Cj A623 P341
UNION
Bed, Bath & Beyond, Inc. A123
VOORHEES
Kennedy Memorial Hospital University
  Medical Center Inc P260
Kennedy Health System, Inc. P259
WAYNE
Valley National Bancorp A925
WHIPPANY
Stephen Gould Corporation P489
WOODBRIDGE
Northfield Bancorp Inc (de) A642

NEW MEXICO

ALBUQUERQUE
University Of New Mexico P595
Summit Electric Supply Co.,
  Inc. P492
ESPANOLA
Akal Security, Inc. P11
SANTA FE
St. Vincent Hospital P484

NEW YORK

ALBANY
State University Of New York A825
  P486
Dormitory Authority - State Of New
  York P168
Capital District Physicians' Health
  Plan, Inc. P96
St. Peter's Health Partners P483
The Research Foundation For The
  State University Of New York P543
Albany Medical Center P13
Albany Medical Center Hospital P14
Thruway Authority Of New York
  State P563
New York State Environmental
  Facilities Corp P344
St Peter's Health Partners P475
AMHERST
Allied Motion Technologies Inc E20
ARDSLEY
Acorda Therapeutics Inc E8
ARMONK
International Business Machines
  Corp. A484
BALLSTON SPA
Stewart's Shops Corp. P490
BAY SHORE
Southside Hospital P467
BINGHAMTON
United Health Services Hospital,
  Inc. P579
United Health Services, Inc. P580
BRIDGEHAMPTON
Bridge Bancorp, Inc. (bridgehampton,
  Ny) A147 E67
BRONX
Montefiore Medical Center P327
Bronx Lebanon Hospital Center
  (inc) P88
Fordham University P192
Bethco Corporation P72
BROOKLYN
Dime Community Bancshares,
  Inc A275
Maimonides Medical Center P286
New York Methodist Hospital P342
BUFFALO
M & T Bank Corp A554
Rich Products Corporation P416
Kaleida Health P257
Buffalo City School District P91
Erie County Medical Center
  Corp. P181
Mercy Hospital Of Buffalo P310
CAMDEN
International Wire Group, Inc. P243
CARLE PLACE
1-800 Flowers.com, Inc. E1
COOPERSTOWN
The Mary Imogene Bassett
  Hospital P529
CORNING
Corning Inc A245
CORTLAND
Suny College At Cortland A836 P496
DEWITT
Community Bank System, Inc. A231
EAST AURORA
Astronics Corp E41

EAST ELMHURST
Skanska Usa Civil Inc. P457
Skanska Usa Civil Northeast Inc. P458
EAST MEADOW
Nassau Health Care Corporation P334
EAST SYRACUSE
D/l Cooperative Inc. P153
ELMIRA
Chemung Financial Corp. A191
ELMSFORD
Party City Holdco Inc E323
FARMINGDALE
Marjam Supply Co., Inc. P292
FLUSHING
Newyork-presbyterian/queens P347
GLEN HEAD
First Of Long Island Corp. A372
GLENS FALLS
Arrow Financial Corp. A73
GLENVILLE
Trustco Bank Corp. (n.y.) A888
GREAT NECK
One Liberty Properties, Inc. E314
GREENVALE
Long Island University P282
HARRISON
Rusal America Corp. P424
HAUPPAUGE
County Of Suffolk P146
HEMPSTEAD
Hofstra University P228
ITHACA
Tompkins Financial Corp A877 E408
Cornell University P144
Tompkins Financial Corp A877 E408
JAMAICA
St. John's University P479
St John's University, New York P474
The Jamaica Hospital P527
Jamaica Hospital Medical
  Center P249
JERICHO
Nathan's Famous, Inc. E287
KINGSTON
Kingstone Companies Inc E233
LAGRANGEVILLE
Health Quest Systems, Inc. P220
LAKE SUCCESS
Astoria Financial Corp. A81
LIVERPOOL
Raymours Furniture Company,
  Inc. P408
LONG ISLAND CITY
Jetblue Airways Corp A496
New York City School Construction
  Authority P341
Madden (steven) Ltd. E251
LYNBROOK
Biospecifics Technologies Corp. E58
MANHASSET
North Shore University Hospital P354
MELVILLE
Schein (henry) Inc A782
Verint Systems, Inc E435
Fonar Corp. E166

A = AMERICAN BUSINESS
E = EMERGING COMPANIES
P = PRIVATE COMPANIES
W = WORLD BUSINESS

MENANDS

Health Research, Inc. P220

MIDDLETOWN

Orange Regional Medical Center P369

MINEOLA

Winthrop-university Hospital
(inc) P638

MONTEBELLO

Sterling Bancorp (de) A827 E383

NEW HAMPTON

Balchem Corp. E47

NEW HYDE PARK

Long Island Jewish Medical
Center P281

NEW YORK

Verizon Communications Inc A926
Jpmorgan Chase & Co A503
Citigroup Inc A206
Philip Morris International Inc A698
Metlife Inc A583
Federal Reserve Bank Of New York,
Dist. No. 2 A340
American International Group
Inc A46
Pfizer Inc A695
Goldman Sachs Group, Inc. A408
Morgan Stanley A601
American Express Co. A43
Time Warner Inc A872
Travelers Companies Inc (the) A882
Twenty-first Century Fox Inc A891
Macy's Inc A556
Arconic Inc A71
Bristol-myers Squibb Co. A148
Colgate-palmolive Co. A222
Bank Of New York Mellon Corp A108
Omnicom Group, Inc. A659
Icahn Enterprises Lp A469
Intl Fcstone Inc. A488
Cbs Corp A175
Loews Corp. A551
Pvh Corp A731
Marsh & Mclennan Companies
Inc. A564
Viacom Inc A930
Consolidated Edison Inc A241
First Data Corp (new) A362
Blackrock, Inc. A134
Voya Financial Inc A934
Lauder (estee) Cos., Inc. (the) A531
Alcoa Corporation A26
Citigroup Global Markets Holdings
Inc A206
Leucadia National Corp. A537
L3 Technologies Inc A525
Consolidated Edison Co. Of New York,
Inc. A240
News Corp (new) A629
Interpublic Group Of Companies
Inc. A487
Assurant Inc A80
Foot Locker, Inc. A382
Ralph Lauren Corp A742
Hess Corp A438
Avon Products, Inc. A94
S&p Global Inc A775
Hrg Group Inc A459
Hsbc Usa, Inc. A460
Abm Industries, Inc. A7
Sirius Xm Holdings Inc A801
Alleghany Corp. A27
Amtrust Financial Services Inc A58

Blackstone Group Lp (the) A136
Cit Group, Inc. A204
National General Holdings Corp A612
E*trade Financial Corp. A297
Signature Bank (new York, Ny) A797
E371
Annaly Capital Management Inc A61
Federal Home Loan Bank New
York A338
Prospect Capital Corporation A722
E343
Ambac Financial Group, Inc. A38
Istar Inc A493
Mfa Financial, Inc. A586
Trammo, Inc. A881 P564
Metropolitan Transportation
Authority A585 P316
New York University A625 P344
The Port Authority Of New York &
New Jersey A867 P541
Lukoil Pan Americas, Llc A554 P285
New York University A625 P344
Virtu Financial Llc A932 P617
The Ford Foundation A864 P522
Brixmor Llc A149 P86
New York Community Trust And
Community Funds Inc A624
State Of New York Mortgage
Agency A822 P486
Alfred P. Sloan Foundation A27
Trammo, Inc. A881 P564
Metropolitan Transportation
Authority A585 P316
New York University A625 P344
The Port Authority Of New York &
New Jersey A867 P541
Lukoil Pan Americas, Llc A554 P285
The New York And Presbyterian
Hospital P537
New York University A625 P344
The Trustees Of Columbia University
In The City Of New York P548
Warner Music Group Corp. P623
Axel Johnson Inc. P51
Memorial Sloan-kettering Cancer
Center P307
Memorial Hospital For Cancer And
Allied Diseases P306
The Mount Sinai Hospital P536
Icahn School Of Medicine At Mount
Sinai P234
Genpact Limited P202
Unipec America, Inc. P578
Vns Choice P618
The Bloomberg Family Foundation
Inc P513
Triborough Bridge & Tunnel
Authority P566
Beth Israel Medical Center P71
Nfp Corp. P347
The Jpb Foundation P527
St Luke's-roosevelt Hospital
Center P475
College Entrance Examination
Board P134
Guildnet, Inc. P213
Blue Tee Corp. P78
Suntory International Corp. P496
Hunter Roberts Construction Group
Llc P231
Tata America International
Corporation P502
Virtu Financial Llc A932 P617
Yeshiva University P643
International Rescue Committee,
Inc. P243
The Ford Foundation A864 P522
Henry Modell & Company, Inc. P223
Institute Of International Education,
Inc. P239
The Associated Press P512
Vns Choice Community Care P618

Metro-north Commuter Railroad Co
Inc P315
United States Fund For Unicef P581
Pace University P373
Management-ila Managed Health Care
Trust Fund P289
Visiting Nurse Service Of New York
Home Care Ii P617
Brixmor Llc A149 P86
Northstar Group Services, Inc. P358
Ducon Technologies Inc. P170
The Rockefeller Foundation P543
American University Of Beirut
Inc P30
Jewish Communal Fund P252
Logicalis, Inc. P279
The Metropolitan Museum Of
Art P534
The New School P536
Bar-ilan University In Israel P59
American Jewish Joint Distribution
Committee, Inc. P26
State Of New York Mortgage
Agency A822 P486
G-iii Apparel Group Ltd. E174
Revlon Consumer Products
Corp. E358
Revlon Inc E358
Minerals Technologies, Inc. E278
Och-ziff Capital Management Group
Llc E308
Brixmor Property Group Inc E68
Evercore Partners Inc E145
Fortress Investment Group Llc E168
New Media Investment Group
Inc E301
Signature Bank (new York, Ny) A797
E371
Kkr & Co Lp (de) E234
Apollo Global Management Llc E35
Steel Partners Holdings Lp E383
W.p. Carey Inc E442
Prospect Capital Corporation A722
E343
Two Harbors Investment Corp E415
Paramount Group Inc E320
Empire State Realty Op Lp E134
Empire State Realty Trust Inc E134
Exlservice Holdings Inc E147
Chimera Investment Corp E90
Moelis & Co E279
Cowen Group Inc E110
Tiptree Inc E408
Colony Northstar Inc E98
Shutterstock Inc E370
Blackstone Mortgage Trust Inc E62
Medidata Solutions, Inc. E266
New York Mortgage Trust Inc E302
New Residential Investment
Corp E302
Cohen & Steers Inc E97
Marketaxess Holdings Inc. E256
Alj Regional Holdings Inc E18
Apollo Commercial Real Estate
Finance Inc. E34
New Mountain Finance Corp E301
Ag Mortgage Investment Trust
Inc E10
Ares Commercial Real Estate
Corp E37
Goldman Sachs Bdc Inc E184
Pzena Investment Management
Inc E347
Diligent Corp E123
Arc Logistics Partners Lp E37
Reis, Inc E355
Otc Markets Group Inc E318

NORWICH

Nbt Bancorp. Inc. A617

OCEANSIDE

South Nassau Communities Hospital
Inc P463

PLAINVIEW

Neulion Inc E299

POUGHKEEPSIE

Vassar Brothers Hospital P614

PURCHASE

Pepsico Inc A691
Mastercard Inc A568
Mbia Inc. A573

REGO PARK

New York State Catholic Health Plan
Inc A625 P343

RIVERHEAD

Suffolk Bancorp A831

ROCHESTER

Wegmans Food Markets, Inc. A944
P628
Home Properties, Limited
Partnership A447 P229
Wegmans Food Markets, Inc. A944
P628
Rochester General Hospital Inc P422
Rochester City School District P422
Home Properties, Limited
Partnership A447 P229
Rochester Institute Of Technology
(inc) P423
The Unity Hospital Of Rochester P549
Monro Muffler Brake, Inc. E283

ROSLYN

St. Francis Hospital, Roslyn, New
York P477

RYE

Acadia Realty Trust E6

SCHENECTADY

The Golub Corporation P525
Ellis Hospital P178

STATEN ISLAND

Key Food Stores Co-operative,
Inc. P262
Staten Island University
Hospital P487
Atlantic Express Transportation
Corp P47

SYRACUSE

Syracuse University P500
State University Of New York Health
Science Center At Syracuse P487
Srctec, Llc P472
St. Joseph's Hospital Health
Center P480
Crouse Health Hospital, Inc. P149
Crouse Health System, Inc. P149
Petr-all Petroleum Consulting
Corp. P383
Upstate University Medical Associates
At Syracuse, Inc. P611

TARRYTOWN

Regeneron Pharmaceuticals,
Inc. A749
Prestige Brands Holdings Inc E342

TROY

Rensselaer Polytechnic Institute P414

UNIONDALE

Flushing Financial Corp. A380
Arbor Realty Trust Inc E37

VALHALLA

Westchester County Health Care
Corporation P632

VICTOR
Constellation Brands Inc A242

WARSAW
Financial Institutions Inc. A352

WEST ISLIP
Good Samaritan Hospital Medical
Center P206

WEST NYACK
The Salvation Army P544

WESTBURY
New York Community Bancorp
Inc. A623
North Shore-long Island Jewish
Health Care P355

WESTFIELD
National Grape Co-operative
Association, Inc. P335

WHITE PLAINS
Universal American Corp (new) A917
New York Power Authority P342
White Plains Hospital Medical
Center P636

WILLIAMSVILLE
Life Storage Inc E242

NORTH CAROLINA

ASHEVILLE
Hometrust Bancshares Inc. A448
Mission Hospital, Inc. P323

BOONE
Samaritan's Purse P434

BURLINGTON
Laboratory Corporation Of America
Holdings A526

CARY
Cary Oil Co., Inc. P102
Coc Properties, Inc. P133
Wake County Public School
System P620
Ply Gem Holdings Inc E337

CHAPEL HILL
The University Of North
Carolina P554
University Of North Carolina At
Chapel Hill P596
University Of North Carolina
Hospitals P596
Investors Title Co. E226

CHARLOTTE
Bank Of America Corp. A103
Duke Energy Corp A293
Nucor Corp. A647
Sonic Automotive, Inc. A804
Duke Energy Carolinas Llc A293
Metlife Insurance Company Of
Connecticut A585
Sealed Air Corp A787
Capital Bank Financial Corp A161
Park Sterling Corp A677 E321
The Charlotte-mecklenburg Hospital
Authority A862 P515
Parsons Environment &
Infrastructure Group Inc. P376
Presbyterian Hospital P395
Foundation For The Carolinas P194
Premier Healthcare Alliance,
L.p. P395
Coca-cola Bottling Co.
Consolidated E95
Extended Stay America Inc E148
Premier Inc E341
Lendingtree Inc (new) E240

Park Sterling Corp A677 E321

CONCORD
Cmc-northeast, Inc. P130

DURHAM
Quintiles Ims Holdings Inc A739
Duke University A296 P170
Duke University Health System,
Inc. P171
The North Carolina Mutual Wholesale
Drug Company P538
Research Triangle Institute Inc P414
Family Health International Inc P184
M. M. Fowler, Inc. P285
Durham Public Schools P173

FAYETTEVILLE
Carolina Healthcare Center Of
Cumberland Lp P101
Cape Fear Valley Medical Center P96
Cumberland County Hospital System,
Inc. P152
Cumberland County Schools P153

GARNER
Overland Contracting Inc. P372

GASTONIA
Mann+hummel Filtration Technology
Intermediate Holdings Inc. P290
Caromont Regional Medical
Center P101

GOLDSBORO
Southco Distributing Company P463

GREENSBORO
Vf Corp. A928
The Fresh Market Inc P523
The Moses H Cone Memorial Hospital
Operating Corporation P535
Guilford County School System P213
Market America, Inc. P292
Tanger Factory Outlet Centers,
Inc. E399

GREENVILLE
University Health Systems Of Eastern
Carolina, Inc. P583
Pitt County Memorial Hospital,
Incorporated P389
East Carolina Health Inc P174

HICKORY
Alex Lee, Inc. P16
Stm Industries, Inc. P491

HIGH POINT
Bnc Bancorp A137 E63

HUNTERSVILLE
American Tire Distributors Holdings,
Inc. A48 P27

JACKSON
Hampton Woods Health &
Rehabilitation Center P216

KINSTON
Hillco, Ltd. P226

MOORESVILLE
Lowe's Companies Inc A552

MOUNT AIRY
Renfro Corporation P413

PINEHURST
Firsthealth Of The Carolinas,
Inc. P187
Moore Regional Hospital P328

RALEIGH
First Citizens Bancshares Inc
(nc) A358
Yadkin Financial Corp A974 E456
Coastal Federal Credit Union A217

North Carolina Electric Membership
Corporation P350
Wakemed P622
Rex Hospital, Inc. P415
Rex Healthcare, Inc. P415
North Carolina Eastern Municipal
Power Agency P350
Telamon Corporation
Red Hat Inc E352
Pra Health Sciences Inc E340
Inc Research Holdings Inc E219
Yadkin Financial Corp A974 E456
Paragon Commercial Corp E320

ROCKY MOUNT
Boddie-noell Enterprises, Inc. P81

SOUTHERN PINES
First Bancorp (nc) A355

WILMINGTON
Coastal Rehabilitation Hospital P131
Live Oak Bancshares Inc E245

WILSON
Wilmed Nursing Care Center P637

WINSTON SALEM
Wake Forest University P620
Quality Oil Company, Llc P401
Winston-salem/forsyth County
Schools P638

WINSTON-SALEM
Reynolds American Inc A759
Bb&t Corp. A119
Hanesbrands Inc A420

NORTH DAKOTA

BISMARCK
Bank Of North Dakota (bismarck,
N.d.) A110 E50
North Dakota University System
Foundation P351
Dakota Gasification Company
Inc P156
St. Alexius Medical Center
Bank Of North Dakota (bismarck,
N.d.) A110 E50

FARGO
Rdo Equipment Co. P408
Sanford North P436
Sanford Clinic North P436
Dakota Supply Group, Inc. P156

GRAND FORKS
Alerus Financial Corp A26 E16
Altru Health System P23
Alerus Financial Corp A26 E16

MINOT
Spf Energy, Inc. P471
Trinity Health P566

WILLISTON
Horizon Resources P230

OHIO

AKRON
Goodyear Tire & Rubber Co. A410
Firstenergy Corp A374
Childrens Hospital Medical Center Of
Akron P121
Akron General Medical Center
Inc P11

BATAVIA
Multi-color Corp. E284

CANFIELD
Farmers National Banc Corp.
(canfield,oh) A335

CANTON
Mercy Medical Center, Inc.

CHILLICOTHE
Adena Health System P6

CINCINNATI
Kroger Co (the) A522
Procter & Gamble Co. A719
Fifth Third Bancorp (cincinnati,
Oh) A350
American Financial Group Inc A45
Cintas Corporation A201
Federal Home Loan Bank Of
Cincinnati A338
First Financial Bancorp (oh) A363
Phillips Edison - Arc Shopping Center
Reit Inc. A701
Mercy Health P308
Children's Hospital Medical
Center P117
Kgbo Holdings, Inc P263
University Of Cincinnati P587
Messer Construction Co. P313
University Of Cincinnati Medical
Center, Llc P588
Cincinnati Public Schools P124
Good Samaritan Hospital Of
Cincinnati P206
Bethesda Hospital, Inc. P72
Novelart Manufacturing
Company P363

CLEVELAND
Parker Hannifin Corp A677
Sherwin-williams Co (the) A794
Keycorp A513
Tfs Financial Corp A861
The Cleveland Foundation A863
The Cleveland Clinic
Foundation P518
Case Western Reserve University P103
Cleveland Municipal School
District P129
The Metrohealth System P532
Metrohealth Medical Center P316
Bearing Distributors, Inc. P67
Healthspan Integrated Care P221
Fairview Hospital P183
Park-ohio Holdings Corp. E322

COLUMBUS
American Electric Power Company,
Inc. A41
L Brands, Inc A523
Big Lots, Inc. A131
Huntington Bancshares Inc A464
State Auto Financial Corp. A820
Battelle Memorial Institute Inc A116
P62
Battelle Memorial Institute A116 P62
Battelle Memorial Institute Inc A116
P62
Battelle Memorial Institute A116 P62
Ohiohealth Corporation P365
Nationwide Children's Hospital P336
Mount Carmel Health System P329
American Municipal Power, Inc. P27
Buckeye Power, Inc. P91
M/i Homes Inc E250
Installed Building Products Inc E224
Core Molding Technologies Inc E107
Diamond Hill Investment Group
Inc. E120

DAYTON
Med America Health Systems
Corporation P302
Miami Valley Hospital P318

TACOMA

Columbia Banking System Inc A224
E98
Multicare Health System P330
Franciscan Health System P195
City Of Tacoma, Department Of Public
Utilities P126
Columbia Banking System Inc A224
E98

VANCOUVER

Peacehealth P379
Southwest Washington Health
System P468
Barrett Business Services, Inc. E53
Nautilus Inc E294

WALLA WALLA

Banner Corp. A113 E52

WEST VIRGINIA

CHARLESTON

United Bankshares Inc A904
City Holding Co. A210
Charleston Area Medical Center,
Inc. P112

FAIRMONT

Mvb Financial Corp E285

FOLLANSBEE

Wheeling-nisshin, Inc. P635

HUNTINGTON

Huntington Cabell Hospital Inc P232
St. Mary's Medical Center

WHEELING

Wesbanco Inc A947

WISCONSIN

APPLETON

U.s. Venture, Inc. A897 P574
The Boldt Group Inc P513
Thedacare, Inc. P560

BEAVER DAM

United Cooperative P578

BROOKFIELD

Fiserv Inc A375
Community Care, Inc. P136

CLINTON

The Delong Co Inc P520

COTTAGE GROVE

Landmark Services Cooperative P272

CUDAHY

Roadrunner Transportation Systems
Inc E361

FITCHBURG

Certco, Inc. P110

FRANKLIN

Krones, Inc. P267

GLENDALE

Columbia St Marys Hospital
Milwaukee P135

GREEN BAY

Associated Banc-corp A77
Krueger International, Inc. P268
Bellin Health Systems, Inc. P68
Bellin Memorial Hospital, Inc. P68
Pomp's Tire Service, Inc.. P391
Aurora Baycare Medical Center P50
Nicolet Bankshares Inc E305

JANESVILLE

Mercy Health System
Corporation P310
J. P. Cullen & Sons, Inc. P246

LA CROSSE

Kwik Trip, Inc. P269
Gundersen Lutheran Medical Center,
Inc. P213
Mayo Clinic Health System-franciscan
Medical Center, Inc. P300
Dairyland Power Cooperative P155

LA FARGE

Cooperative Regions Of Organic
Producer Pools P143

MADISON

First Business Financial Services,
Inc. A357 E157
University Of Wisconsin System P608
University Of Wisconsin Hospital And
Clinics Authority P607
Meriter Health Services, Inc. P311
University Of Wisconsin
Foundation P607
Meriter Hospital, Inc. P312
St. Mary's Hospital P483
Madison Metropolitan School
District P286
First Business Financial Services,
Inc. A357 E157

MARSHFIELD

Security Health Plan Of Wisconsin,
Inc. P443
Marshfield Clinic, Inc. P293
Saint Joseph's Hospital Of Marshfield,
Inc. P430

MENASHA

Network Health System Inc P340
Faith Technologies, Inc. P183

MENOMONEE FALLS

Kohl's Corp. A519
Froedtert Health, Inc. P199

MEQUON

Charter Manufacturing Company,
Inc. P113

MIDDLETON

Spectrum Brands Holdings Inc A813
University Of Wisconsin Medical
Foundation, Inc. P608

MILWAUKEE

Manpowergroup A558
Harley-davidson Inc A424
Wec Energy Group Inc A943
Rockwell Automation, Inc. A767
Mgic Investment Corp. (wi) A587
Bank Mutual Corp A102
Robert W. Baird & Co.
Incorporated A765 P420
Aurora Health Care, Inc. P50
Milwaukee Public Schools (inc) P322
Froedtert Health Hospital P198
The Medical College Of Wisconsin
Inc P530
Robert W. Baird & Co.
Incorporated A765 P420
Children's Hospital Of Wisconsin,
Inc P119
Columbia St. Mary's Hospital
Milwaukee, Inc. P136
Wheaton Franciscan P634
Froedtert And Community Health
Inc P198
Marquette University P293
Strattec Security Corp. E385
Douglas Dynamics, Inc. E124
Badger Meter Inc E46

MOUNT PLEASANT

All Saints Health Care System,
Inc. P18

OSHKOSH

Oshkosh Corp (new) A666

RIPON

Alliance Laundry Holdings Llc P19

SUN PRAIRIE

Independent Pharmacy
Cooperative P235

SUSSEX

Quad/graphics, Inc. A734

WAUKESHA

Prohealth Care Inc P397
American Transmission Company,
Llc P28
Waukesha Memorial Hospital,
Inc. P626
Generac Holdings Inc E178

WAUSAU

Aspirus, Inc. P43
Aspirus Wausau Hospital, Inc. P43

WAUWATOSA

Waterstone Financial Inc (md) A942

Index of Executives

A

A, Sun W302
AAefedt, Matthew (Matt) A916
Aaefedt, Matthew A916
Aaholm, Sherry A. A253
Aai, Julie E70
Aalders, Siobhan E371
Aaron, Sammy E174
Aaron, Carol (Care) P379
Aaron, Todd P489
Aaron, Barbara P597
Aarup-Andersen, Jacob W125
Aarup-Andersen, Jacob W126
Aase, Rune A826
Aase, Rune P488
Aasland, Steinar A607
Abad, Leah A490
Abader, Shaheed A853
Abadie, Laurent W296
Abadir, Jeffrey A247
Abate, Jason (Jase) A228
Abate, Victor (Vic) A396
Abate, Jeff (Jeffy) A523
Abate, Joanne (Jojo) A923
Abbal, Frederic W337
Abbate, Katie (Kat) E89
Abbate, Mark L. E269
Abbate, Katie (Kat) A191
Abbate, Mark L. A581
Abbeele, Annick D. Van den P158
Abbey, Bill A648
Abbey, Dick A843
Abblett, Fred (Freddy) A351
Abbott, John C. E267
Abbott, Douglas (Doug) E450
Abbott, Justin A482
Abbott, Mark (Marky) A745
Abbott, Justin P242
Abbott, Sherburne B P500
Abbott, John W329
Abboud, Andrew (Andy) A531
Abboud, Ali El A824
Abdallah, Norman J. E119
Abdallah, Chaouki T. P595
Abdelal, Ahmed P356
Abdella, Shelly A943
Abdella, Shelly (Shell) A943
Abdo, Hatem P196
Abdoellah, Rachmat A194
Abdoo, Elizabeth A. A456
Abdool, Jeffrey (Jeff) A86
Abdulmalek, Idora A331
Abdun-Nabi, Daniel J. E134
Abe, Toshinori W339
Abe, Makoto W345
Abed, Osama A5
Abedin, Aj E12
Abel, John E131
Abel, Melissa E403
Abel, Brad (Brady) A324
Abel, Gregory E. (Greg) A674
Abel, Melissa A858
Abel, Dawn P626
Abel-Hodges, Cheryl A732

Abela, John (Jack) A585
Abelenda, Gustavo H. A599
Abell, Paul (Pauly) A120
Abella, Ilene A392
Abelli, Donna L. A473
Abello, Marc P (Marcy) A228
Abelman, David A761
Abelman, Sarah P89
Abelson, David J. P375
Aber, Joseph (Jo) A126
Abercrombie, Carl Unkcd A20
Abergel, Danny (Dan) E254
Aberle, Derek K. A736
Abernathy, Kathleen Q. A390
Abernathy, Lawrence A565
Abernathy, Cammy P589
Abernethy, Jack A892
Abeyta, Brian A20
Abhimanyu, Kumar A426
Abish, Jeffrey D. (Jeff) P6
Abji, Minaz B. A456
Ables, Grady L. A64
Ables, Dorothy M. A812
Abney, Jack (Jackie) A821
Abney, David P. A910
Aboaf, Eric A824
Abogado, Scott E80
Abood, Steven A754
Aboubaker, Aziza P358
Aboulafia, Joseph (Jo) A109
Aboumrad, Daniel Hajj W25
Abousselham, Fadwa A137
Abraham, Santiago E72
Abraham, Chad R. E336
Abraham, Neil E352
Abraham, Sandra A120
Abraham, JJ A536
Abraham, Amy (Ames) A965
Abraham, Karen P78
Abraham, John (Jack) P261
Abraham, Edward P620
Abrahamson, Herbert (Hank) A78
Abrahamson, Joel A451
Abrahamson, Tom P268
Abramowicz, Daniel A. A248
Abrams, Mark E90
Abrams, Michael (Mel) A200
Abrams, Michael (Mel) A280
Abrams, John (Jack) A283
Abrams, Jared (Jare) A410
Abrams, Ed A485
Abrams, Tom (Tommy) P461
Abramson, Steven V. E424
Abramson, Scott (Scotty) A112
Abramson, Gregg (Greggory) A410
Abramson, Jim (Jimmy) A563
Abramson, Richard (Dick) P473
Abreu, Robert (Bob) A409
Abreu, Christopher (Chris) A428
Abreu, Geraldo A776
Abreu, Lorena P460
Abreu, Antᴏnio Manuel Barreto Pita de W143
Abreu, Rodrigo Modesto W377
Abruzzese, Joseph (Joe) A277
Abry, Joseph (Jo) A553

Abston, Angie (Ang) A905
Abt, John (Jack) E237
Abts, Joy A896
Abu-Hadba, Walid E33
Abulaban, Majdi B. W129
Abutaleb, Sam A869
Abutaleb, Sam P560
Acampuzano, Guillermo P160
Accum, Claude A. W364
Acevedo, Margie (Marge) A572
Acevedo, Janet (Jan) A764
Ach, J. Wickliffe A364
Achacoso, Mike (Mikey) A444
Achara, Chidi A800
Achary, Michael M. A420
Acharya, Dharma A251
Achleitner, Paul W132
Achorn, Tina (Tin) A423
Acikalin, Faik W221
Acito, Paiul A3
Acito, Joe A351
Ackenheil, Erin A63
Acker, George (Georgey) A295
Acker, Peter (Pete) A853
Ackerman, Pia E39
Ackerman, Dennis E56
Ackerman, Thomas F. E85
Ackerman, Michelle A31
Ackerman, Steven A101
Ackerman, Joel A264
Ackerman, Sunny A558
Ackerman, John P157
Ackerman, Lyle P453
Ackerman, Jeffrey (Jeff) P523
Ackermann, Bryan E265
Ackermann, Peter (Pete) A104
Ackerson, Vince A. E403
Ackerson, Vince A. A858
Ackley, William (Bill) A973
Ackman, Dustin J (Dusty) E265
Ackman, Dustin J (Dusty) A572
Ackroyd, Jim A9
Ackroyd, Jim P5
Acoca, Bernard A820
Acocella, Kerry S. E154
Acosta, Manuel (Mannie) E167
Acosta, Fernando J. A95
Acosta, Ron (Ronnie) A937
Acosta, Alexander P190
Acosta, Miguel (Miggy) P363
Acott, Sarah (Sar) A137
Acree, Will A409
Acu, Freida P485
Acuna, Bilda M A923
Acutt, Nicola A934
Adachi, Mitsuo W122
Adair, A. Jayson E107
Adair, Brett E107
Adair, Michael (Mel) P506
Adair-Potts, Janna A846
Adali, Erhan W396
Adam, Joseph (Jo) E150
Adamczyk, Darius A449
Adame, Norma A252
Adamic, Don A929
Adamo, Terri (Terr) A346

Adamo, Dave A843
Adamo, Tony (Tone) P456
Adamos, Tara A470
Adams, Ann (Annie) E7
Adams, Robert J. E20
Adams, Sherri E30
Adams, D. Rick E90
Adams, Joseph P. E168
Adams, Robin E222
Adams, W. Andrew (Andy) E289
Adams, Brent E344
Adams, Michael (Mel) A15
Adams, Doug (Dougie) A94
Adams, Pete (Petey) A100
Adams, Kelli A106
Adams, Gregg T. A111
Adams, Richard (Dick) A117
Adams, Ann (Annie) A120
Adams, Kent M. A170
Adams, Kevin D. A188
Adams, Thomas E. (Tom) A190
Adams, Charles H. (Hal) A249
Adams, Hal (Harold) A249
Adams, Melissa (Lissa) A252
Adams, Kathy (Kat) A304
Adams, Rich (Ric) A311
Adams, Richard L. A311
Adams, R L A311
Adams, Rick A311
Adams, Craig L. A326
Adams, John L. A416
Adams, Robin A475
Adams, Gregory A. A506
Adams, Beth (Betty) A514
Adams, Annette (Anne) A520
Adams, Calvin (Cal) A553
Adams, Romaneo A565
Adams, Jennifer A565
Adams, Catherine (Cate) A575
Adams, John (Jack) A624
Adams, Matt A641
Adams, Scott A657
Adams, Elaine (Elle) A706
Adams, Brent A723
Adams, Justin A746
Adams, Wayne A754
Adams, William A780
Adams, Patricia (Trish) A846
Adams, Trish A846
Adams, Leigh (Leah) A900
Adams, Richard M. A904
Adams, Richard (Dick) P63
Adams, Kevin D. P111
Adams, David (Dave) P134
Adams, Trina P196
Adams, Gregory A. P256
Adams, Martin L. P283
Adams, Archie P330
Adams, Joseph (Joe) P333
Adams, Walter (Walt) P339
Adams, Justin P536
Adams, Holly (Holl) P549
Adams, Jane (Ginny) P589
Adams, Bart P606
Adams, Trevor W272
Adamski, Dan (Danny) A502

A = AMERICAN BUSINESS
E = EMERGING COMPANIES
P = PRIVATE COMPANIES
W = WORLD BUSINESS

Bareford, Becky (Becks) A342
Bareilles, Mary (Mar) E321
Barenbaum, Larry C. E183
Baresich, Michael A32
Barge, James (Jamie) A930
Barger, Bruce (Brucey) A6
Barger, Tricia (Trish) A115
Barger, Holli A254
Barger, John E (Jack) A462
Barger, Dennis L A790
Barger, Tricia (Trish) P54
Bargmann, Bruce (Brucey) E433
Barhaug, Michael (Mel) A763
Barhaug, Michael (Mel) P420
Barhight, G. Scott P196
Barich, Andy A954
Baril, Thierry W15
Barila, Martin (Marti) A3
Bariquit, Teri A637
Barirani, Arya P238
Baritz, Stuart (Stu) A584
Barja, Allan (Al) A136
Barkan, Lisa (Lis) A535
Barkan, Elliott R P571
Barker, Marian E291
Barker, G. Carlton (Carl) E369
Barker, Greg A24
Barker, Shawn A98
Barker, James (Jamie) A166
Barker, Joanilla A369
Barker, Bethany A415
Barker, Phyllis A430
Barker, G. Carlton (Carl) A794
Barker, Marcy A824
Barker, Ellen A859
Barker, Kurtis A912
Barker, Mary P138
Barker, Bethany P210
Barker, Larie P244
Barker, Karen P277
Barker, William G. (Bill) P336
Barkin, Michael Z. E430
Barkley, Chris (Chrissy) A98
Barkley, Michael T (Mel) A671
Barkley, Terrell A752
Barkley, James M. A800
Barkley, Sandra P482
Barletto, Suzanne (Sue) A876
Barley, Hattie A342
Barlow, Sandy (Sandra) E445
Barlow, Jeff D. A597
Barlow, Jeffrey Don (Jeff) A597
Barlow, Debra (Deb) A883
Barlow, Chris (Chrissy) A943
Barlowe, Jamie P555
Barlows, Ted P225
Barnaby, Rod (Rodney) A117
Barnaby, Rod (Rodney) P63
Barnard, Ray F. A379
Barnard, Natashe A569
Barnard, Tony A939
Barnard, Michele P55
Barnard, John P336
Barnello, Michael D. (Mike) E238
Barner, Mark D. A76
Barner, Sharon A254
Barner, Mark D. P41
Barnes, Mike Barnes Mike
    (Mikey) E213
Barnes, Steve (Stevie) E213
Barnes, Tim E394
Barnes, Michael G. E408
Barnes, Matthew (Matt) A7
Barnes, Stephen (Steve) A13
Barnes, Joseph A109
Barnes, Michael (Mel) A226
Barnes, Mike Barnes Mike
    (Mikey) A468
Barnes, Steve (Stevie) A468

Barnes, Robert B. (Bob) A483
Barnes, Melissa Stapleton A544
Barnes, Joe A607
Barnes, John P. (Jack) A689
Barnes, Anna Hatcher A753
Barnes, Scott (Scotty) A800
Barnes, Priscilla A810
Barnes, Tim A838
Barnes, Brian A851
Barnes, Michael (Mel) A981
Barnes, David G. P333
Barnes, Virginia A. (Ginger) P581
Barnes, Kim P594
Barnes, Leo (Leonardo) P604
Barnes, Pam (Pamela) P624
Barnett, Bill (Billy) E256
Barnett, Bruce E411
Barnett, Diane (Di) A451
Barnett, Jeanne A473
Barnett, Don A523
Barnett, Carol Jenkins A730
Barnett, Hoyt R. (Barney) A730
Barnett, Bruce A886
Barnett, Charles J. P447
Barnett, Alison (Alli) P448
Barnett, Tim (Timmy) P536
Barney, Robin T. A979
Barnhart, Dale G. E248
Barnhart, Neil F A156
Barnhart, Cynthia P298
Barnhill, Debbie (Deb) A101
Barns, Mitch A633
Barns, Mitch P348
Baron, Nir W382
Barone, Maria (Mary) A82
Barone, Christopher J. P260
Barone, Donald A. P260
Baroni, Jason (Jase) E150
Barquin, John (Jack) A295
Barr, Kevin P. E366
Barr, Thomas A18
Barr, Scott A143
Barr, Linda (Lin) A820
Barr, James (Jamie) A855
Barr, Sarah A943
Barr, Kyle P64
Barr, Hannah (Hanna) P363
Barr, Laurie (Laur) P433
Barra, Mary T. A400
Barra, Ornella A939
Barranco, David A38
Barre, Jerôme W293
Barreto, Sue (Susie) A370
Barreto, Armando (Mando) P191
Barrett, Rick (Ricky) E150
Barrett, Lausanne E344
Barrett, John D. E415
Barrett, Jill (Jilly) A155
Barrett, George S. A165
Barrett, Mark (Marky) A180
Barrett, Elizabeth (Beth) A281
Barrett, Lee E A295
Barrett, Clay M (Clayton) A405
Barrett, Elizabeth (Beth) A696
Barrett, Lausanne A723
Barrett, Geoffrey (Geoff) A732
Barrett, John D. A888
Barrett, Maggie (Margaret) P29
Barrett, John C (Jack) P227
Barrett, Barbara M. P511
Barrett, John A. P555
Barrick, David (Dave) A120
Barrila, Craig (Craigy) A696
Barrington, Jeffrey (Jeff) E371
Barrington, Martin J. (Marty) A35
Barrington, Jeffrey (Jeff) A798
Barrio, Vita A745
Barrios, Katie E402
Barrios, George A. E454
Barrios, Alfredo (Alf) W318
Barrios, Alfredo W320
Barroca, Nadine (Dina) A194
Barron, Shelton E275
Barron, Paula E409
Barron, Michael (Mel) A200

Barron, Kathleen (Kathy) A326
Barron, Joni A601
Barron, Scott (Scotty) A818
Barron, Eric J. A866
Barron, Paula A877
Barron, James A. (Andy) A937
Barron, Larren P293
Barron, Kathleen P505
Barron, Samantha R (Sam) P510
Barron, Eric J. P540
Barros, D. Benjamin P555
Barros, Daniel Feldmann W26
Barroso, Carlos J. A160
Barrow, Karen (Kare) A77
Barrow, David (Dave) A517
Barrow, Karen (Kare) P41
Barrow, Henry P128
Barrow, Andy P535
Barrows, John A92
Barrows, Scott (Scotty) A843
Barrows, Karen P423
Barrs, W. Craig A404
Barry, Alex E394
Barry, June B. A54
Barry, Corie A130
Barry, Ellen (Elle) A163
Barry, John (Jack) A392
Barry, John (Jack) A476
Barry, Tim A480
Barry, Chris A658
Barry, Alex A838
Barry, John A841
Barry, Jane (Ginny) P83
Barry, Scott P463
Bars, Michael A. E422
Bars, Michael A. A907
Barselou, Mei A397
Barski, Michael (Mel) A18
Barsotti, James A335
Bartee, Kristie (Chris) A7
Bartee, Chris (Chrissy) A168
Barteky, Stephanie A347
Bartel, Tony D. A393
Bartel, Gregg A520
Bartel, Sylvia P158
Bartel, Charles R. (Chuck) P172
Bartell, Bruce B. A423
Bartels, Todd (Toddy) A78
Bartels, John (Jack) A94
Bartelson, Bill (Billy) A166
Barter, Jim (Jimmy) P118
Barth, Kate (Katie) E197
Barth, Kevin (Kev) A176
Barth, Kevin G. A229
Barth, Jennifer (Jen) A392
Barth, Kate (Katie) A434
Barth, Peter (Pete) A523
Barth, Werner A699
Bartho, Ken E371
Bartho, Ken A798
Bartholme, John A696
Bartholow, Peter B. E403
Bartholow, Peter B. A858
Bartilad, Bernard (Bern) E265
Bartilad, Bernard (Bern) A572
Bartlett, David L. E373
Bartlett, Laura A31
Bartlett, Thomas A. (Tom) A50
Bartlett, Thomas (Thom) A347
Bartlett, David L. A799
Bartlett, Russ A860
Bartlett, Daniel J. (Dan) A937
Bartlett, Lisa P368
Bartman, Teresa A528
Bartolacci, Joseph C. E261
Bartoli, David A603
Bartolozzi, Arthur (Art) P540
Bartolucci, Tony A16
Bartolucci, Tony P10
Barton, Richard B. E52
Barton, Mathias J. E123
Barton, Rick (Ricky) E275
Barton, Lisa M. A42
Barton, Richard B. A113
Barton, Patricia (Pat) A465

Barton, Nina A522
Barton, Hugh (Hugo) A664
Barton, Julie (Jules) A664
Barton, Heather (Heath) A753
Barton, Jacqueline K. P94
Barton, Stancil E. (Stan) P348
Barton, John (Jack) P386
Bartone, Michael (Mel) A817
Bartoo, Bruce P303
Bartow, Bill A485
Bartys, Anthony P. (Tony) A249
Bartz, Ebba A223
Bartz, Lisa A719
Baruffi, Christopher A479
Barycki, Elvera P281
Baryshnikov, Vladislav W170
Barzilay, Jonathan P399
Bas, Didem W396
Bascom, Jon (Jonny) A90
Bascom-Erazmus, Sue (Susie) A689
Baseler, Theodor P. (Ted) A35
Baselga, Josᴄ P307
Baser, Didem Dinçer W396
Basey, Jim E197
Basey, Jim A434
Basford, Nick (Nicky) A910
Bashaw, Michael A959
Basher, Linda A208
Basile, Bob (Bo) E257
Basile, Nate A280
Basillo, Paulo A522
Basinger, Tracy A342
Baskel, Christopher (Chris) P471
Basmadjian, Kevin P404
Basom, Jean (Jeannie) P428
Bason, John G. W35
Bass, Daniel N. E168
Bass, Bill A283
Bass, Freda A331
Bass, Brenda (Bren) A499
Bass, Maureen A883
Bass, Everett A (Eve) A942
Bass, Scott A. P29
Bass, William L. P109
Bass, Patrick W385
Bassanello, Judy A208
Bassett, Lawton E. E28
Bassett, John E. E54
Bassett, William E110
Bassett, H. Clay E295
Bassett, Lawton E. A52
Bassett, Therese (Terri) A94
Bassett, Glenn A94
Bassett, H. Clay A615
Bassett, Claire M P507
Bassetti, Frank W (Frankie) A559
Bassman, Robert (Bob) A602
Basso, Monica E176
Basso, Maurizio W33
Basson, Steve (Stevie) A429
Bassoul, Selim A. E276
Bastian, Edward H. (Ed) A269
Bastian, Robert (Bob) A726
Bastin, Damon A439
Bastings, Arthur A277
Basto, Edgar W68
Bastug, Recep W396
Bastuga, Kevin P. E371
Bastuga, Kevin P. A797
Basu, Devjit A135
Basulto, Jose P460
Batato, Magdi W273
Batchelder, Peter (Pete) E250
Batchelder, Josh A217
Batchelder, Eugene L. (Gene) A653
Batchelder, Josh P132
Batcheler, Colleen A238
Batchelor, David B (Dave) E28
Batchelor, David B (Dave) A52
Bateh, Tarik A502
Bateman, JR E125
Bateman, Rick (Ricky) A344
Bateman, William (Bill) A753
Bateman, Mark T. P427
Batemen, Gary L (Gar) E443

Bates, Tim (Timmy) E131
BATES, MIKE (Mikey) E141
Bates, Kevin E338
Bates, Larry L. E373
Bates, Peter (Pete) E442
Bates, Christopher (Chris) A175
Bates, Chris (Chrissy) A175
Bates, Carol (Care) A498
Bates, Andrew A539
Bates, Grant A607
Bates, John X (Jack) A646
Bates, Richard (Dick) A693
Bates, Larry L. A799
Bates, Brent A. A810
Bates, Pam (Pamela) A821
Bates, Jonathan R. (Jon) P38
Bates, Michael (Mel) P93
Bates, Carol (Care) P255
Bates, Peter W. P288
Bates, Chris (Chrissy) P504
Bates, Steve P505
Batey, Alan S. A400
Batey, John (Jack) A736
Bath, Chuck E120
Bath, Margaret R. A510
Bathgate, Brian E85
Batis, Eric E39
Batista, Christine (Chrissy) A177
Batista, Wesley Mendon §a A702
Batkin, Roger A21
Bator, Susan (Sue) P528
Batres, Grace (Gracie) A925
Batshaw, Mark P120
Batson, Charles H. (Chuck) E157
Batson, Elliott (Eli) A295
Batson, Charles H. (Chuck) A358
Batson, Joni A534
Batson, Kathy A875
Batson, Andrew (Andy) A957
Batt, Douglas A. E321
Battaglia, Bill E445
Battaglia, John (Jack) A109
Battaglia, Alex (Al) A497
Battaglia, Shannon A972
Battel, Patrick A225
Battenfield, Keith P108
Battey, Margaret (Maggie) P607
Battifarano, Leonard A565
Baty, Darren A467
Baty, Darren P233
Batycky, Richard P. (Rick) E8
Baublitz, Kimberly (Kim) A937
Baudanza, Anthony J. P404
Baude, Bruce K. A216
Bauder, Douglas R. A807
Bauer, Pete E64
Bauer, Fred T. E180
Bauer, Michael E188
Bauer, Brett A1
Bauer, Mark A64
Bauer, Brett C. A129
Bauer, Pete A141
Bauer, Karen (Kare) A163
Bauer, Judy A181
Bauer, Paul (Pauly) A267
Bauer, Mike A385
Bauer, Daniel (Dan) A869
Bauer, Cindy (Cin) A964
Bauer, Julie (Jules) P187
Bauer, Daniel (Dan) P560
Bauer, Sabine W8
Bauerlein, Alison E223
Baugh, Ben (Benny) E46
Baugh, David (Dave) P591
Baughman, Richard A. E370
Baughman, Brian A576
Bauhofer, Scott (Scotty) A13
Bauknecht, Brad (Brady) A667
Baum, James (Jamie) A31
Baum, Daniel (Dan) A340
Bauman, James L. (Jim) A2
Baumann, Bill E149
Baumann, G. Marc E377
Baumann, Caroline P459
Baumann, Werner W60

Baumbach, Allen (Al) E403
Baumbach, Denise (Denny) A390
Baumbach, Amy A697
Baumbach, Allen (Al) A858
Baumblatt, Jeff A911
Baumgardner, Terri (Terr) A251
Baumgarten, David A. A102
Baumgarten, Rachel A930
Baumgarten, Patrick P404
Baumgartl, Wolf-Dieter W374
Baumgartner, Robert V. E58
Baumgartner, Jim (Jimmy) A205
Baumgartner, Michael A. P57
Baumli, Heather (Heath) A471
Baun, Theodore W. (Ted) E172
Baun, Ted (Teddy) E172
Baus, George V A392
Baus, Steve P111
Bausch, Shelley J. A711
Bautista, Norman P383
Baverman, Charlie (Charles) P118
Bavery, Christina (Tina) E265
Bavery, Christina (Tina) A572
Bawa, Opinder P600
Bawol, Jeff A94
Baxley, Michael (Mel) P461
Baxley, J P461
Baxley, Steve (Stevie) P579
Baxter, James (Jamie) E276
Baxter, Warner L. A40
Baxter, Nadia A104
Baxter, Dave (Davie) A295
Baxter, Thomas C (Thom) A340
Baxter, Erick (Ric) A451
Baxter, Michael (Mel) A706
Baxter, Joel D. A795
Baxter, Scott H. A929
Baxter, Joanne (Jojo) P56
Baxter, Bob P309
Baxter, Rob P449
Bayans, Steve (Stevie) A276
Bayardo, Jose A. A612
Baybars, Ilker P101
Bayer, Jennifer (Jen) E165
Bayer, Paul E. E289
Bayer, Jennifer (Jen) A381
Bayer, Terry P. A597
Bayer, Michael B. A619
Bayer, Ronald K (Ron) P367
Bayhylle, Gwen (Gwendolyn) A662
Bayles, Autumn A68
Bayless, William C. E24
Bayless, Kathleen (Kathy) E395
Bayless, Lucas (Luke) P601
Bayliff, Doreen (Reen) A719
Bayliss, Philip (Phil) P528
Baynes, Walter E232
Baynes, Roy A580
Baysinger, Jared (Jare) A896
Bayt, Phil (Philly) P619
Bazan, Fernando E57
Bazan, Dora A925
Bazante, Jennifer (Jen) A462
Bazarko, Dawn A916
Bazeley, Joe (Joey) P318
Bazemore, Teresa A. Bryce A742
Bazire, Nicolas W240
Bazoli, Giovanni W202
Beabout, Sherri A369
Beach, Bruce E448
Beach, Mary (Mar) A252
Beach, Richard G (Dick) A295
Beach, Brian C. A843
Beach, Tony (Tone) A899
Beach, Bruce A951
Beach, Brian C P589
Beacher, Bob P183
Beal, Michael W. A518
Beal, Jamie (James) A791
Beale, G. William (Billy) E421
Beale, Susan M. A292
Beale, G. William (Billy) A902
Beam, Chris T. A42
Beam, Diane (Di) A363
Beam, Mildred P370

Beam, Lauris P432
Beam, Robert M. (Bob) P633
Beams, Dennis A407
Bean, Bryan (Bry) E335
Bean, Blu A142
Bean, Michael (Mel) A518
Bean, Robert (Bob) A584
Bean, Bryan (Bry) A703
Bean, Heather A846
Bean, James C. P356
Beanblossom, Darlene A753
Beando, John (Jack) A875
Beard, Simon E18
Beard, Lucinda A120
Beard, Deanne A369
Beard, Scott A672
Beard, Robert F. (Bob) A898
Beard, Bradley P183
Beard, Derrick P618
Beardall, Michael J. E441
Beardall, Brent J. A939
Bearden, Marc (Marcy) A835
Beardman, Todd J (Toddy) P308
Beardsley, Kirk M. A637
Beasley, Scott (Scotty) A887
Beasley, Mark P211
Beaton, Laura (Laur) E445
Beatrice, Michael (Mel) A304
Beattie, Brian M. E397
Beattie, Joseph (Jo) A573
Beatty, Mark A133
Beatty, Diane (Di) A166
Beatty, Vincent L. A939
Beatty, Ellen M. P511
Beauchamp, Tim A655
Beaudette, Phil A905
Beaudoin, Pierre W73
Beaumont, Simon A485
Beaumont, Glenn W148
Beaupri, David (Dave) P172
Beauregard, Mark E261
Beauregard, Julie (Jules) E435
Beauregard, Julie E436
Beauregard, Colleen A874
Beauregard, Joseph P298
Beaven, Peter W68
Beaven, Peter W69
Beaver, Rick (Ricky) A900
Beavers, Shane A304
Beba, Ty E70
Bebber, David L. Van A893
Bebermeyer, Jon P422
Beccaro, Mark A. Del P442
Beccia, Jan A208
Bech, Douglas Y. E229
Becher, Roseanne P82
Becht, Gerd W130
Bechtel, Kathleen P199
Bechtle, Mavis P533
Bechtol, Nancy P459
Bechu, Sophie A484
Beck, Kevin (Kev) E109
Beck, David F (Dave) E261
Beck, Gillon E317
Beck, Barry (Barr) E444
Beck, Andrew H. (Andy) A21
Beck, Andy A21
Beck, Gary (Gar) A25
Beck, Eric A44
Beck, Carter (Car) A63
Beck, Gregory A188
Beck, Christophe A304
Beck, David E. (Dave) A342
Beck, Lita A371
Beck, Klaus A426
Beck, Joe A438
Beck, Amy (Ames) A464
Beck, Scott (Scotty) A584
Beck, Sherry A657
Beck, Rich A692
Beck, David (Dave) A765
Beck, Dorothy (Doroth) A965
Beck, Gregory P111
Beck, David (Dave) P421
Beck, Teresa (Terry) P536

Beck, Rebecca P630
Beck-Codner, Iris W382
Becker, Robert (Bob) E98
Becker, Steven (Steve) E146
Becker, David B. E160
Becker, George (Georgey) E212
Becker, Gregory W. (Greg) E394
Becker, Scott E445
Becker, Merritt A254
Becker, Christopher A372
Becker, George (Georgey) A468
Becker, Dave A639
Becker, Dave (Davie) A706
Becker, Steven (Steve) A716
Becker, David (Dave) A786
Becker, Yin C. A831
Becker, Gregory W. (Greg) A838
Becker, Russell (Russ) P34
Becker, Marty W311
Beckett, Gale A720
Beckett, Kim (Kimmy) P641
Beckford, Avril P631
Beckham, Rene A115
Beckham, Rene P54
Beckius, Larry P38
Beckley, Thomas P. (Tom) E73
Beckley, Frederic (Fred) E267
Beckley, Patricia (Pat) A540
Beckman, Amber A37
Beckman, Jim A77
Beckman, John (Jack) A626
Beckman, Jim A732
Beckman, Jim P41
Beckman, Seth P172
Beckman, John (Jack) P345
Beckman, Mary (Mar) P517
Beckman, Per W368
Beckner, Mark (Marky) E76
Beckom, Daria A937
Becks, Gyla A302
Beckstead, Ian P413
Beckwith, Lona E335
Beckwith, Pete (Petey) A166
Beckwith, Patricia A331
Beckwith, Lona A703
Beckwith, Sandra (Sandy) A906
Beckwith, Brian P11
Beckwitt, Richard (Rick) A536
Becraft, Stan A322
Bedard, David (Dave) A429
Beddes, Hallie A565
Beddingfield, Kenneth L. A643
Bedeau, Theresa (Terry) A163
Bedessem, Mike P143
Bedford, Craig A481
Bedford, William (Bill) P240
Bedford, Craig P242
Bedford, Charles E. P536
Bediako, Lauren (Laur) P227
Bedient, Patricia M. A956
Bednar, Ladd P745
Bednar, Anthony P312
Bedout, Juan De A929
Bedros, Suzanne A896
Bedrosian, Arthur P. E237
Bedrosian, Geoffrey E349
Bedwell, Patrick (Paddy) E167
Bedwell, Elizabeth M (Beth) A273
Bedwell, Elizabeth M (Beth) P165
Bedwell, Mary (Mar) P401
Beebe, Robert (Bob) A204
Beecham, Daniel W263
Beecy, Steven (Steve) A916
Beedle, Bernice A584
Beehler, Dave (Davie) A304
Beeler, Jim P129
Beeler, Jason P306
Beem, Janel P551
Beeman, William P153
Beeman, William P154
Beeman, Thomas E. (Tom) P528
Beene, Shelley A100
Beer, Carole A544
Beer, James A. A576
Beer, Megan W26

Biczo, Tibor E246
Biddix, Tracy (Trace) A829
Biddle, Ross A. E154
Biddle, Ross A576
Bieber, Chris (Chrissy) A183
Bieber, Jayne A280
Bieber, Stephen A367
Bieber, Thomas A824
Bieber, Roddy J. P34
Bieber, Martin A. P260
Biegen, Arm Gregory A106
Biegger, Dave A239
Biehl, Maureen A565
Bielar, James A83
Bielec, John (Jack) P169
Bielenberg, David A197
Bielss, Chris E221
Bielss, Chris A475
Bien, Marie A751
Bien, Marie P412
Biener, Joseph E80
Bienert, Philip A83
Bienhoff, Bruce (Brucey) A230
Bienvenu, Eric (Ric) E33
Bierer, John (Jack) A8
Bieri, Matthew (Matt) E416
Bierl, Andreas (Andy) A56
Bierman, Jon P238
Biernbaum, Robert P330
Bierschenk, Steven (Steve) A601
Biesanz, Mike (Mikey) A54
Biesterfeld, Robert C. A767
Bietsch, Julie A273
Bietsch, Julie P165
Bifulco, Catherine (Cate) A623
Bigelow, Steven T. P86
Bigelow, Teresa P498
Bigelow, Alexandra (Alex) P615
Biggam, Tim A964
Biggart, Robert (Bob) A385
Biggers, John E341
Biggs, Jonathan (John) E227
Biggs, Vicki (Vic) E355
Biggs, James (Jamie) A499
Biggs, M. Brett A937
Bigler, Barbara A14
Bigler, Barbara P9
Bigley, Tim (Timmy) A109
Bigley, Russell A970
Bigornia, Yvette A584
Bijun, Wu W114
Bike, Brent A252
Bilak, Gina A58
Bilanchone, Jill (Jilly) A89
Bilbrey, John P. (J.P.) A438
Bilbrey, Mary E. A461
Bilby, Claire A281
Bilderback, Donald (Don) P144
Bilen, Faruk W177
Bilko, David G. (Dave) E421
Bilko, David (Dave) A835
Bilko, David G. (Dave) A902
Bill, Farrell A843
Billa, Roberto (Berto) A565
Biller, Frank E92
Billi, John A751
Billi, John P411
Billig, Jeff (Jeffy) A657
Billig, Edward (Ed) P70
Billing, Mike (Mikey) P30
Billinger, Jerry (Jerr) A164
Billings, David M. E10
Billings, Sherri R. E55
Billings, Sherri R. A122
Billings, Brian A565
Billings, Will (Willy) A965
Billington, Phillip (Phil) A431
Billington, Carole (Carrie) P490
Billner, William A903

Billoch, Riceland P416
Billotte, Mike P579
Billow, Michele (Michie) P519
Bilney, Jody L. A462
Bilotta, Anthony V. E326
Bilotta, Anthony V. A684
Bilotti, Frank (Frankie) A194
Bilse, Gregory A136
Bilsland, Brent E190
Bilstrom, Jon W. A227
Bily, Stephanie E39
Bily, Shirley A928
Bilz, Tim (Timmy) E25
Bimson, Stephen (Steve) A156
Bin, Mo W114
Bin, Ong Eng W295
Binaco, Chris A943
Binbasgil, Hakan W17
Binder, Steven G. A453
Binder, Kurt P618
Binette, Chad P550
Binetti, Frank A18
Bing, Alden A112
Bing, Shang W97
Bingaman, Christopher (Chris) E120
Bingaman, Peter A485
Bingham, James (Jamie) A109
Bingham, Kim R. A171
Bingham, Dave (Davie) A202
Bingham, John (Jack) A309
Bingham, Paul A463
Bingham, William (Bill) P531
Bingham, Janet (Jan) P586
Bingham, H. Raymond W161
Bingol, Selim A295
Bingol, Selim A400
Bingold, Michael A380
Binkis, Timothy (Tim) A911
Binkley, David A (Dave) A957
Binkleysenior, David (Dave) A957
Binkowski, Chuck P60
Binnie, Lisa (Lis) A423
Binstead, George (Georgey) A183
Binvel, Yannick E236
Binzer, Ann (Annie) A200
Binzer, Greg P632
Biondo, Joe A92
Biossat, William (Bill) E213
Biossat, William (Bill) A469
Birch, Robert F. E206
Birch, Robert F. A445
Bird, Roger M. A5
Bird, Chris A150
Bird, Stephen A207
Bird, Edwin A338
Bird, Stefan A. A674
Bird, Michael P121
Bird, Julio P213
Bird, J. Richard W148
Bird, Graham R. W174
Birdsall, Christopher (Chris) A331
Birdson, Mitsey A685
Birdsong, Melissa (Mel) A553
Birdwell, Nancy P440
Birenbaum, Matthew H. (Matt) E44
Birenberg, Allan M (Al) P303
Birk, Mark C. A40
Birkelo, Jeff A939
Birkenhauer, Greg (Greggy) A202
Birkett, Bernard E270
Birkett, Sharon E. E284
Birkitt, Doug (Dougie) A585
Birkner, Irving P551
Birle, Jim E146
Birmingham, Lisa (Lis) A225
Birmingham, Martin K. A353
Birmingham-Byrd, Melody A294
Birnbaum, David (Dave) A135
Birnbaum, Jack A225
Birnbaum, Ing. Leonhard W140
Birnbrauer, Robert P505
Birns, Ira M. E56
Bironneau, Jean-Noël W88
Biros, Janice (Jan) P170
Birouty, Rana A736

Bisaccia, Lisa A258
Bisaro, Paul M. W22
Bischmann, Ben A502
Bischof, Timothy (Tim) A216
Bischofberger, Norbert W. A406
Bischoff, Hollis A176
Bischoff, Kristin (Kristy) A208
Bischoff, Michael (Mel) A565
Bischoff, Robert (Bob) A981
Bischoff, Richard (Dick) P103
Bischoff, Werner W113
Bischoff, Manfred W121
Bisegna, Anthony C. A824
Bishar, John J. E37
Bishop, William A. (Andy) E190
Bishop, Fred (Freddy) A44
Bishop, Mari A223
Bishop, Kevin A485
Bishop, Marissa A629
Bishop, Steven D. (Steve) A719
Bishop, Rachel R. A885
Bishop, Anne (Annie) A927
Bishop, Greg (Greggy) A954
Bishop, Jon P34
Bishop, Tim W242
Bisienere, Maribeth A256
Bisienere, Maribeth A281
Bisignano, Frank J. A362
Biske, Sandra E265
Biske, Sandra A572
Bisker, Mark (Marky) E140
Bismuth, Frederic A606
Bisno, Edward (Ed) A248
Bison, Michael (Mel) A28
Bison, Michael (Mel) P18
Biss, Peggy L. A168
Bisselberg, Stephanie (Steph) A23
Bissette, Greg A251
Biswajit, Pati E15
Biswas, Sukanta E353
Biswas, Yogini A585
Bitar, Marwan E141
Bittenbender, Tom P494
Bitter, Mark A351
Bittler, David A930
Bittner, Peter E56
Bitton, Francesca P600
Bitzer, Marc R. A957
Bivona, Michael (Mel) A930
Bixby, R. Philip A507
Bixby, Walter E. (Web) A507
Bixler, R. Ryan P227
Bizzis, Julia K. E164
Bjerga, OddLeon A613
Bjorkman, Karen S. P555
Bjornholt, Eric E274
Bjornholt, J. Eric E274
Bjornstad, Geir A826
Bjornstad, Geir P488
Blachar, Doron E317
Black, Leon D. E35
Black, Krystl E163
Black, Stephanie (Steph) E193
Black, Keith E201
Black, Freddie G. E373
Black, Maria A86
Black, Amy (Ames) A226
Black, Tracy (Trace) A463
Black, Vonda A518
Black, Christine (Chrissy) A706
Black, Ken (Kenny) A761
Black, Freddie G. A799
Black, David F. A822
Black, Katy (Catherine) A851
Black, Benjamin (Ben) A899
Black, Mary A926
Black, David (Dave) A965
Black, William (Bill) P215
Black, Scott (Scotty) P237
Black, Michele (Michie) P307
Blackall, Will (Willy) A108
Blackburn, Angela (Angie) E330
Blackburn, Fred K. A143
Blackburn, Andy A204
Blackburn, Kevin (Kev) A339

Blackburn, Angela (Angie) A690
Blackburn, Anne Holt P604
Blacken, Linda (Lin) A697
Blackford, Michael W. (Woody) E100
Blackford, Woody E100
Blackford, Quentin E307
Blackford, David E. A980
Blackford, Martha (Mar) P121
Blackhurst, Janis L. (Jan) Jones A155
Blackhurst, Janis (Jan) A156
Blackie, Gordon (Gordy) A203
Blackledge, James T. A610
Blackler, Ellen (Elle) A280
Blackley, R. Scott A163
Blackley, James A. (Jim) A190
Blackman, David M. E368
Blackmon, Tanya P366
Blackney, Kenneth S. P169
Blacksberg, Jason E6
Blackwelder, John (Jack) A163
Blackwood, Elizabeth (Beth) A500
Blackwood, Eric A685
Blades, Thomas W237
Blain, Robert (Rob) A174
Blain, Bob A745
Blaine, Christopher A (Chris) A248
Blair, Brian (Bri) E344
Blair, Mark (Marky) A12
Blair, Matthew (Matt) A565
Blair, Barbara A678
Blair, Brian (Bri) A723
Blair, Patrick (Paddy) A778
Blair, Kevin S. A841
Blair, Robert (Bob) A952
Blair, Fran (Frances) A981
Blair, Scott (Scotty) A981
Blair, Chuck (Chucky) P108
Blair, Carrie W364
Blais, Gerard (Gerold) E337
Blais, David A. (Dave) A734
Blais, Jim A949
Blaising, Angela C (Ang) A492
Blake, Stephen (Steve) E148
Blake, Christopher D. E319
Blake, Chris (Chrissy) A24
Blake, Victoria (Tori) A31
Blake, Roger (Rog) A83
Blake, James (Jamie) A86
Blake, Nancy (Nance) A228
Blake, Francis S. (Frank) A269
Blake, Patrick J. (Pat) A576
Blake, Mary A579
Blake, Christopher D. A676
Blake, David M. A716
Blake, Lynn S. A824
Blake, M. Brian P169
Blake, M B P170
Blake, Elizabeth (Beth) P401
Blakely, Christie (Chris) E363
Blakemore, Anthony (Tony) A305
Blakemore, Anthony A807
Blakemore, Dominic W112
Blakeslee, Lennie A218
Blakeslee, Lennie P132
Blakley, Linda (Lin) P160
Blalock, Jason E222
Blalock, Jason A475
Blamey, Pat (Patty) P276
Blanc, Alain (Al) A665
Blanc, Jean (Jeannie) A957
Blanc, Jean-Louis W153
Blanc, Robert M. (Bobby) Le W292
Blancett, Cary S A344
Blanch, Ted E192
Blanchard, John W. E245
Blanchard, John P. E428
Blanchard, Eric A. A321
Blanchard, Brent A544
Blanchard, David W402
Blanchette, Cristina (Chris) E89
Blanchette, Marc E168
Blanchette, Cristina (Chris) A191
Blanchfield, Molly P185
Blanco, Alex A304
Blanco, Ernesto (Ern) P122

Blanco, Juan Sebastián Moreno W44
Bland, Alecia E159
Bland, Kyle A55
Bland, Alecia A365
Bland, Christine (Chrissy) A367
Bland, Trabue A480
Blanda, Michael (Mel) P510
Blaney, Hilarie A101
Blank, Dave (Davie) E82
Blank, Brian E149
Blank, Stephen R. E349
Blank, Gregory A166
Blank, Jeff (Jeffy) P410
Blankenship, Justin A120
Blankenship, Charles P. (Chip) A397
Blankfein, Lloyd C. A409
Blankfield, Bryan J. A666
Blanks, Richard P427
Blanton, Hamilton A163
Blanton, Genie A745
Blasberg, Clifford (Cliff) A624
Blaschke, Kelly E262
Blascovich, Lawrence E372
Blascovich, Lawrence A798
Blase, William A. (Bill) A83
Blase, Kevin (Kev) A182
Blase, Marta (Marty) A514
Blaser, Brian J. A5
Blaser, Richard (Dick) P237
Blasingame, James A367
Blasingame, David T. P559
Blasini, David A163
Blasko, Michael E415
Blasko, Michael (Mel) E415
Blasko, Michael A888
Blasko, Michael (Mel) A888
Blass, Mark P354
Blatcher, Kevin (Kev) A160
Blatt, Randy A621
Blaufuss, William (Bill) A430
Blaug, Suzanne A55
Blauser, Caryn A515
Blavatnik, Len P624
Blaya, Richard (Dick) A929
Blaylock, Tom P108
Blaz, Steve A621
Blazer, Randolph C. (Rand) E313
Blazier, Rick P466
Blazye, Andrew E163
Bledig, Stefan A601
Bledsoe, Stacey (Stace) A544
Bleeker, Gary L. P218
Blegen, Bernie E281
Bleiweis, Melissa (Lissa) E265
Bleiweis, Melissa (Lissa) A572
Bleming, Jim E194
Bleske, Mitchell A905
Blethen, Roger W. E455
Blevins, P. Rodney A285
Blevins, Connie P308
Bley, Daniel (Dan) E308
Bley, Daniel H. A943
Bleyl, Steven (Steve) A482
Bleyl, Steven (Steve) P242
Bliesmer, Allan J (Al) P224
Blight, Andrew R. E8
Blinkiewicz, John (Jack) A84
Blinn, Paul A31
Blinn, Richard P. (Dick) A401
Bliss, Beverly (Bev) E363
Blittschau, Edward (Ed) A309
Blitz, Susan (Sue) A751
Blitz, Susan (Sue) P411
Blitzer, David S. A136
Bliven, Jenni A617
Blivice, Marni A137
Bloch, Jeremy (Jer) A182
Block, Stephen (Steve) A163
Block, Velinda J A173
Block, Arthur R. A225
Block, Larry (Lar) A535
Block, Keith G. A778
Block, Velinda J P105
Blocker, Adrian M. A956
Blodgett, Shane E350

Blok-Anderson, Nancy A520
Blom, David P. P366
Blome, James W60
Blonde, Fabrice A109
Blood, Robert (Bob) E23
Bloom, Neil E98
Bloom, Brent A67
Bloom, William A. (Bill) A428
Bloom, Bill (Billy) A429
Bloom, Robert (Bob) A613
Bloom, Alfred H. A626
Bloom, Alfred H. P345
Bloom, Mark W10
Bloomfield, Deborah (Debbie) P309
Bloomquist, Annie L. E367
Bloomquist, Steve (Stevie) A837
Bloomquist, Aaron P351
Blosser, Courtney A. E324
Blossom, Patrick E221
Blossom, Patrick A475
Blotz, Gerald R. E53
Blough, David (Dave) P601
Blount, Susan (Sue) A726
Blount, Sally E. P361
Bloxom, Robert J. A970
Bludau, Laurence A233
Blue, Betsy A100
Blue, Dave (Davie) A139
Blue, Robert M. (Bob) A285
Blue, Robert M. A931
Bluhm, Neil P380
Blum, Jeffery L. E276
Blum, Jeffery L. A594
Blum, Donald W. A724
Blum, Randy A916
Blum, Peter P243
Blum, Olivier W337
Bluman, Mark (Marky) A108
Blume, Julie A383
Blume, Brent A896
Blumen, Ira (Mira) P552
Blumenfeld, Barry P288
Blumenthal, Norman P574
Blumer, David J. A135
Blumhardt, James (Jamie) A949
Blumofe, Robert E13
Blunck, Thomas W265
Blundell, Sandra A64
Blundell, Neil A135
Blundon, Lee A947
Blunt, Mary L. A793
Blunt, Roshawn P281
Blunt, Mary L. P445
Blunt, Elizabeth (Beth) P615
Blust, Jeffrey A640
Blute, Michael L. P530
Bluth, Thomas J. (Tom) A170
Bluver, Howard C. A831
Bluvshteyn, Yelena A136
Bly, Allan E20
Bly, David (Dave) E209
Bly, David (Dave) A452
Blyskal, James (Jamie) A895
Bo, Yao W302
Bo, Yang W365
Bo-hyuk, Yim W343
Boada, Robert C (Bob) A807
Boals, Richard L. (Rich) P78
Boaman, Richard (Dick) A921
Boardman, Michael (Mel) A706
Boardman, Deb P183
Boardman, David P505
Boatright, Nancy R (Nance) A107
Boatwright, Michael A726
Bobalik, Pete A421
Bobb, Stevan B. A153
Bobbitt, Jessica E60
Bobbitt, Jim (Jimmy) P476
Bobeck, Helen P275
Bobenrieth, Susy A634
Bobitz, Ward E. A403
Bobrowski, Paul M. P552
Bocanegra, Jaime W142
Boccaletti, Giulio P536
Boccio, Lynn A (Lyn) A92

Boccolini, Giovanni W202
Bochette, William C. E376
Bochette, William C. A806
Bocian, Jim A173
Bocian, Jim P105
Bock, Kurt W. W58
Bockhorst, Daniel E. A183
Bockhorst, Thomas A. P336
Bockstaele, Elisabeth Van P170
Boczek, Terry A3
Bodansky, Robert L. P448
Bodapati, Ramesh A204
Bodary, Andrew (Andy) A731
Bode, Dave (Davie) A98
Boden, Alison L. P548
Bodenhamer, William H. E377
Bodenstein, Adam E168
Bodin, Elizabeth (Beth) E213
Bodin, Elizabeth (Beth) A469
Bodine, Bruce A604
Bodnar, Amanda (Mandy) P101
Bodner, Dan E435
Bodor, Robert E345
Bodor, David (Dave) A689
Bodziner, Steven (Steve) E67
Bodziner, Steven (Steve) A147
Boe, Kelly (Kel) A372
Boe, Ryan A597
Boe, Douglas (Doug) A896
Boe, Corrie M P379
Boecking, Tom A366
Boegemann, Kate A846
Boehler, Mike A502
Boehm, Landon E336
Boehm, Jennifer (Jen) A18
Boehme, Alan A220
Boehme, Linda (Lin) P468
Boehmer, Mark D (Marky) A977
Boehms, Dennis P178
Boehnlein, Glenn A831
Boeing, Traci (Trace) A947
Boelstler, Doreen (Reen) A228
Boelter, Ben E128
Boemer, Sally Mason P354
Boer, Adrian P359
Boer, A. Dick W223
Boes, Charles (Charlie) P509
Boesch, Jean A767
Boese, Christine P412
Boeshans, Wade W. E20
Boetel, Mary (Mar) E265
Boetel, Mary (Mar) A572
Boffardi, Marc E150
Bogan, Justin E168
Bogani, Farid A792
Bogar, Brent A140
Bogard, Karen (Kare) P347
Bogart, Dan (Danny) A672
Bogart, Stacy (Stace) A707
Bogen, Daniel A619
Boggess, Michael (Mel) A104
Boggs, Michelle (Michie) E322
Boggs, Darrell A649
Boggs, Michelle (Michie) A677
Boggs, Kristin P118
Bognet, Rocco E413
Bogosta, Charles E. (Chuck) A919
Bogosta, Charles E. (Chuck) P598
Boguski, Michael L. A718
Boh, Thomas M (Thom) A766
Boh, Thomas M (Thom) P421
Bohall, Tim (Timmy) A965
Bohan, Julie (Jules) A504
Bohan, John (Jack) A753
Bohanan, Yvette A37
Bohannon, Eric A462
Bohanon, Debbie P437
Bohart, Stuart H. (Stu) E168
Bohaty, Brian R. A31
Bohaty, Anthony (Tony) A78
Bohbrink, Marshall A417
Bohbrink, Marshall P211
Boheman, Fredrik W351
Bohen, Sean W37
Bohigian, Catherine C. A190

Bohjalian, Thomas N. E98
Bohlen, Patricia P46
Bohling, Brian (Bri) A439
Bohlinger, Thomas A175
Bohlsen, Stephanie (Steph) A295
Bohn, William M. A78
Bohner, Robert (Bob) A546
Bohnke, Jaime A643
Boice-pardee, Heath P423
Boike, Brian D.J. A377
Boileau, Walter (Walt) A780
Boillat, Pascal W132
Boinpally, Nick A810
Bois, Michel W109
Boisier, Pierre A123
Boisseau, Philippe W391
Boisten, Bernd A763
Boisten, Bernd P420
Boisvert, Marilyn (Mar) A62
Boitano, Robert A348
Bojalad, Ronald (Ron) A263
Bojdak, Robert J. A554
Bokern, Robert A51
Boklund, Carl A780
Bokovitz, Beverly (Bev) P12
Boland, Brandt A267
Boland, Peter (Pete) A785
Boland, Kay (KayKay) P579
Boland, Kay (KayKay) P580
Bolander, Larry Bolander Larry
  (Lar) A379
Bolanos, Susan A965
Bolch, Carl E. A741
Bolch, Carl E. P405
Bold, William (Bill) A736
BOLDRINI, GIOSUE' W41
Bolduc, Jean-Claude A544
Boler-Davis, Alicia A400
Boles, Abby (Abigail) A743
Boles, Debbie M (Deb) P267
Bolg, Julee P517
Bolgar, Paulo A118
Bolgar, Paulohenrique A118
Bolger, Rod W325
Bolgiano, Elizabeth (Beth) E23
Boli, Scott (Scotty) A555
Bolian, Mark (Marky) A106
Bolick, Patrick (Paddy) A502
Bolin, Mike (Mikey) P267
Boline, Chad A230
Bolitho, Matthew (Matt) A649
Boll, James (Jamie) E117
Bollin, Bonnie (Bonbon) E197
Bollin, Bonnie (Bonbon) A434
Bollinger, Kathy A114
Bollinger, Lee C. A341
Bollinger, Kathy P54
Bollom, Deb A846
BOLLORE', MARIE CANDICE
  GAELLE W251
Bols, Ivo A22
Bolshakov, Sergey A824
Bolson, Matthew (Matt) A87
Bolt, William (Bill) E4
Boltacz, Susan (Sue) A835
Bolte, Kirt A895
Bolton, H. Eric E275
Bolton, Scott (Scotty) A140
Bolton, C. Anderson (Andy) A248
Bolton, Anthony (Tony) A400
Bolton, Sara A680
Bolton, Jon (Jonny) A766
Bolton, Christopher (Chris) P56
Bolton, Diane (Di) P58
Bolton, Linda Burnes P107
Bolton, Sara P377
Bolton, Jon (Jonny) P421
Boltz, Elaine A874
Bolwell, Jean A340
Bolze, Steve A396
Boman, P. or W368
Bomar, Anne E. A285
Bomar, Derek (Der) A621
Bomba, Cheryl (Cher) A514
Bombara, Beth A. A428

Bowers, William (Bill) A24
Bowers, Pete A62
Bowers, Ann A66
Bowers, Jon (Jonny) A100
Bowers, Matthew (Matt) A156
Bowers, Paul A404
Bowers, David (Dave) A421
Bowers, Rick A451
Bowers, Linda A462
Bowers, Eric (Ric) A504
Bowers, David (Dave) A550
Bowers, Jay A911
Bowersox, Dennis A408
Bowersox, Jim (Jimmy) A536
Bowes, Arthur P354
Bowhay, John A607
Bowie, Paul J. A28
Bowie, Grant R. A589
Bowie, Paul J. P18
Bowie, Bonnie (Bonbon) P498
Bowlan, Ronald P561
Bowlby, Jeffrey L. A718
Bowles, Crandall A267
Bowles, Jack W80
Bowling, Rob E309
Bowling, Anthony A279
Bowling, Brian A340
Bowling, Chuck A589
Bowling, Cinda A607
Bowling, Rob A656
Bowling, Douglas P98
Bowling, Doug P98
Bowman, Angela R. Hicks E30
Bowman, Jimmie E63
Bowman, Gary E140
Bowman, Jimmie A138
Bowman, Arthur (Art) A166
Bowman, Kevin (Kev) A322
Bowman, Jim (Jimmy) A344
Bowman, Jeff A576
Bowman, Jim (Jimmy) A601
Bowman, Stephen B. (Biff) A640
Bowman, Skip A678
Bowman, Annemarie A726
Bowman, Kristen (Kristy) A743
Bowman, Helen Y. P169
Bowman, Michael (Mel) P183
Bowman, Robert (Bob) P318
Bowman, Julie P385
Bowman, Stephanie (Steph) P392
Bownas, Pearson A6
Bowser, Donna (Don) A465
Box, Laurie (Laur) A900
Boxall, Jenny (Jen) A3
Boxer, Mark L. A198
Boyce, Steve (Stevie) E300
Boyce, David S. E409
Boyce, Paula A106
Boyce, David (Dave) A665
Boyce, Jill A803
Boyce, David S. A877
Boyce, Tom P6
Boyce, Paul (Pauly) P358
Boyd, Rupert E303
Boyd, Thomas (Thom) A175
Boyd, Tom (Tommy) A223
Boyd, John J. A320
Boyd, Debby (Deb) A347
Boyd, Rupert A630
Boyd, David (Dave) A648
Boyd, Jeffery H. (Jeff) A715
Boyd, Peter M. A809
Boyd, Tonya (T.) A809
Boyd, Dale (Dal) A905
Boyd, Ruth (Ruthy) A948
Boyd, Stephen (Steve) P65
Boyd, Bryan P133
Boyd, Donald P423
Boyd, Steve P494
Boyer, Bradley S. (Brad) E27
Boyer, Mark T. E446
Boyer, Eric (Ric) A83
Boyer, Jason (Jase) A229
Boyer, Jonathan (John) A514
Boyer, Jeffrey A754

Boyer, Cheryl P278
Boyer, John W. P551
Boyette, Roland (Rollie) A49
Boyette, Roland (Rollie) P28
Boyette, Scott (Scotty) P339
Boyken, James W A485
Boykin, Frank H. A596
Boykins, Lamont A51
Boyko, Jean A. E342
Boyle, Hugh F. E49
Boyle, Timothy P. (Tim) E100
Boyle, Joseph P. (Joe) E100
Boyle, Gertrude (Gert) E100
Boyle, Brian (Bri) E337
Boyle, Charles F. E425
Boyle, Ed E435
Boyle, Connie A83
Boyle, Hugh F. A99
Boyle, Thomas P (Thom) A126
Boyle, Kenneth (Ken) A206
Boyle, Thomas (Thom) A220
Boyle, Jim A278
Boyle, Kevin A576
Boyle, Terence A637
Boyle, Debbie A689
Boyle, Patti A779
BOYLE, CHARLES F (Chas) A918
Boyle, Charles (Chas) A918
Boyle, Kathy P162
Boyle, Patrick P576
Boyles, Andrew (Andy) A106
Boyles, Kevin (Kev) A796
Boyles, Jonathan A802
Boyles, Kevin (Kev) P454
Boyles, Peter W. W189
Boyme, Susan A619
Boynton, Andrew C. P570
Boysen, Steve A94
Bozard, John P370
Bozeman, David P. (DAve) A170
Bozeman, Tommy A352
Bozeman, Keith P504
Bozer, Ahmet C. A220
Bozzano, Ign␣␣cio Dominguez-
    Adame W45
Bozzi, Bryan A934
Bozzuti, Tony E149
Bozzuto, Michael A. P84
Bozzuto, Barbara (Barb) P476
Braak, Cindy (Cin) A563
Braam, Richard (Dick) P303
Braathen, Kjerstin W137
Braatz, Jay P160
Brabant, Steven (Steve) A175
Brabec-Lagrange, Claire W153
Brabeck-Letmathe, Peter W273
Braca, Greg W390
Bracamonte, Martin E332
Brace, George E207
Brace, George A448
Bracher, Paul H. A252
Bracher, Candido Botelho W205
Bracht, Berend A763
Bracht, Gerald E. P374
Bracht, Berend P420
Bracken, Frank (Frankie) A383
Bracken, Charles H. R. (Charlie) W236
Brackett, Charlie (Charles) P218
Brackin, D. Wayne P56
Bracy, Raymond (Ray) A937
Bradburn, Joanne (Jojo) P550
Bradbury, Bob (Bo) A194
Bradbury, Carl A230
Bradbury, Kent (Ken) A444
Bradbury, Greg (Greggy) A800
Braden, Steve (Stevie) A163
Bradford, Bill E15
Bradford, Lesa A68
Bradford, Douglas (Doug) A98
Bradford, Paula A102
Bradford, Darryl M. A326
Bradford, Mark D. A657
Bradford, Hannah (Hanna) A743
Bradford, Brad (Brady) A752
Bradie, Stuart J. B. A508

Bradley, Julie E258
Bradley, Edward L. E298
Bradley, William F. (Brad) E304
Bradley, Julie M.B. E414
Bradley, W. Patrick E439
Bradley, Leigh (Leah) A120
Bradley, Kenneth (Ken) A124
Bradley, Michael (Mel) A179
Bradley, William E. (Bill) A186
Bradley, Kevin (Kev) A206
Bradley, Troy A348
Bradley, Arthur (Art) A351
Bradley, Greg A392
Bradley, John A504
Bradley, Joe A523
Bradley, Gregory A586
Bradley, Matthew (Matt) A664
Bradley, John (Jack) A726
Bradley, Kim (Kimmy) A752
Bradley, Shawn A753
Bradley, Phil A778
Bradley, Patrick A959
Bradley, Allen P178
Bradley, Carol P274
Bradley, Mark J. P294
Bradley, Gregory P316
Bradley, J. Lindsey P567
Bradley, Stacey (Stace) P601
Bradshaw, Steven E431
Bradshaw, Adam A20
Bradshaw, Steven G. (Steve) A141
Bradshaw, Jami A369
Bradway, Robert A. (Bob) A55
Bradwell, Hollis (Terry) P2
Brady, Kim E5
Brady, Molly A44
Brady, Cheryle A51
Brady, Bryan (Bry) A94
Brady, Mariel A176
Brady, Michael (Mel) A226
Brady, Deanna T. A453
Brady, Amy G. A514
Brady, Robert T. (Bob) A555
Brady, Elizabeth S. (Beth) A716
Brady, Richard (Dick) A827
Brady, Christian M. M. A866
Brady, Jennifer (Jen) A875
Brady, Bill A895
Brady, Brooks A981
Brady, Jennifer (Jen) P219
Brady, Jodie P232
Brady, Grace P534
Brady, Christian M. M. P540
Brady, Terry P576
Braendeland, Jan Egil A508
Braganca, Michael (Mel) A38
Bragdon, Peter J. E100
Brager, David A. A256
Bragg, Chris (Chrissy) E51
Bragg, Paul A. E431
Bragg, Chris (Chrissy) A111
Bragg, Dorry A347
Brailo, Andy E341
Brainerd, Marty (Mart) E450
Braitberg, Karl A664
Braithwaite, Garrett (Bret) E435
Braithwaite, Melinda (Linda) P490
Brakenhoff, Pete (Petey) P218
Brakewood, Daniel (Dan) E177
Brakhage, Lori P465
Brakman, Steven A784
Brakovich, Betsy P631
Braman, Wes P197
Bramble, James H. (Jim) E429
Bramlage, Stephen P. (Steve) A68
Bramlage, Stephen P (Steve) A670
Bramlet, Steven P386
Bramman, Anne L. A91
Branch, Gregory C. A423
Brand, Meir A33
Brand, Dennis L. A100
Brand, Molly (Moll) A706
Brand, Joe P220
Brand, Michelle (Mitch) P294
Brand, Christian (Chris) P570

Brand, Mary G P589
Brand, Jeffrey S. P600
Brandenburg, Joel E420
Brandenburg, Ben E252
Brandenburg, Mark (Marky) A502
Brandenburg, Joel A901
Brandenburg, Julie (Jules) P508
Brandenstein, Daniel C. (Dan) P581
Brandes, Jurgen W346
Brandgaard, Jesper W285
Brandl, Linda A903
Brandman, Andrew T (Andy) A206
Brandom, Jessica (Jess) A79
Brandon, Joseph P. A27
Brandon, John A338
Brandon, Kimberly (Kim) A602
Brandon, David P244
Brandow, Robyn A341
Brands, Andrew D. W174
Brandshoi, Harald A826
Brandshoi, Harald P488
Brandt, Ann E70
Brandt, Michael (Mel) E321
Brandt, Kevin D. E363
Brandt, Ron E401
Brandt, Eric (Ric) A51
Brandt, Stephen W (Steve) A58
Brandt, Kathleen A250
Brandt, Michael A727
Brandt, Genise M A766
Brandt, Eric K. A975
Brandt, Genise M P421
Brandt, Stephanie P618
Branigan, Brian (Bri) A835
Brannan, Andy E453
Brannen, John Keith (Jack) A20
Brannen, James P. (Jim) A336
Brannman, Brian A273
Brannman, Brian P165
Brannon, Jim A115
Brannon, Mike (Mikey) A802
Brannon, Jim P54
Branon, Bethany A923
Branscome, Miranda (Mira) A104
Branstetter, Jeff (Jeffy) P148
Brant, Pete (Petey) E167
Brant, Randy L. E251
Brantley, Todd E161
Brantley, Edward G. E431
Brantley, Todd A373
Brantley, John (Jack) A485
Brantman, Chris A87
Branyan, Luke P425
Branz, Sandra A429
Brascia, Pete (Petey) A589
Brash, David L. P630
Brashier, Randy A295
Brasier, Barbara L. A435
BRASSAC, Philippe Jean W115
Brast, Scott A48
Braswell, Sam L (Sammy) A228
Braswell, Robert (Bob) A884
Braswell, Leon (Lee) P362
Braterman, Jennifer (Jen) A968
Bratley, Paul (Pauly) A476
Bratman, Fred A912
Bratspies, Steve A936
Bratt, Mikael W411
Braucht, Millie P489
Brauer, Mark (Marky) A467
Brauer, Mark (Marky) P233
Brauer, Stephen F. P559
Braun, Joel E6
Braun, Clint E24
Braun, David (Dave) E83
Braun, Donald G (Don) E152
Braun, Michael H. E152
Braun, Bill A98
Braun, Dennis (Denny) A166
Braun, Shay A265
Braun, Eric (Ric) A351
Braun, Randall L. A405
Braun, James E. (Jim) A607
Braun, Dick (Dicky) A678
Braun, Robert C. A728

Braun, Robert C. A729
Braun, Chris (Chrissy) A758
Braun, Mike (Mikey) A766
Braun, Matthew (Matt) P247
Braun, Ann P375
Braun, Mike (Mikey) P421
Braunig, Gunther W225
Braunscheidel, Stephen J. A554
Braunstein, Louis A341
Brautigan, Bernard (Bernie) A771
Braverman, Alan N. A280
Bravery, Richard (Dick) A135
Bravo, Pablo A273
Bravo, Diana A364
Bravo, Amparo A774
Bravo, Cheryl (Cher) A876
Bravo, Christine (Chrissy) A896
Bravo, Pablo P165
Bray, Jay E290
Bray, John K. E303
Bray, Jeffery (Jeff) E364
Bray, Kevin (Kev) A8
Bray, Natalie (Nat) A347
Bray, Michael (Mel) A431
Bray, John K. A630
Bray, Jeffery (Jeff) A787
Bray, David (Dave) A893
Brayer, Tamra A704
Brayman, Alan (Al) A391
Brazeale, Cathy (Cat) E374
Brazeale, Cathy (Cat) A799
Brazier, Nigel D A333
Brazil, Ben W242
Brda, Bruce A605
Bready, Bruce (Brucey) A527
Breakefield, Xandra A680
Breakefield, Xandra P377
Breakey, Mark D. A215
Breakstone, David (Dave) A208
Breaux, Holly (Holl) A517
Breber, Pierre R. A194
Breci, Paul (Pauly) A156
Brecken, Kathleen (Kathy) A259
Breckon, Steven (Steve) A314
Bredar, Randall J (Randy) P246
Bredow, Eugene J. A650
Bree, Joseph (Jo) A896
Breeden, Greg (Greggy) A463
Breedon, Brent A835
Breeland, Read A689
Breeman, Steven A527
Breen, Timothy P. (Tim) A402
Breen, Meghan P447
Breen, Jennifer (Jen) P644
Breen, Tommy W128
Breese, Matthew M (Matt) E336
Brega, João Carlos A957
Bregier, Fabrice W15
Bregman, Mark F. A621
Brehm, Carolyn (Carol) A719
Breier, Benjamin A. A518
Breier, Barbara P510
Breig, J Scott A869
Breig, J Scott P560
Breining, Dick (Dicky) A603
Breitenbach, Ellen (Elle) P613
Brekelmans, Harry W329
Brekhus, Louann P67
Brekke, Scott A414
Brell, Mark A252
Brelsford, Kevin E397
Bremm, Dirk W58
Bremner, Christy E381
Bremser, Brett A467
Bremser, Brett P233
Bremser, Wayne P615
Brenan, Sean A409
Brenan, Kathryn P511
Brenchley, Alison (Alli) A764

Brendle, Jeff (Jeffy) A784
Brennan, Pat E149
Brennan, Suzanne R. E319
Brennan, James J. A111
Brennan, Daniel J. (Dan) A146
Brennan, Peter (Pete) A166
Brennan, Dan (Danny) A208
Brennan, Troyen A. A258
Brennan, Matt (Matty) A370
Brennan, Suzanne R. A676
Brennan, Thomas A727
Brennan, Peter (Pete) A871
Brennan, Murray F. P307
Brennan, Mary P538
Brenner, Ellyce A83
Brenner, Robert (Bob) A94
Brenner, Rochelle (Chell) A208
Brenner, Matt (Matty) A479
Brenner, Timothy L. A617
Brenner, Dean A736
Brenner, Joel A873
Brenner, Suzanne E. P534
Brenner, Catherine W26
Brenner, Hans-Dieter W229
Brensinger, Donald A761
Brent, Wyman A186
Brent, Jacques A384
Brentlinger, Amy (Ames) P194
Brenton, Flint A203
Breon, Richard C. (Rick) P471
Bres, Thomas A. (Tom) P469
Bresette, Diane (Di) A536
Breshears, Betty P276
Bresky, Steven J. A786
Breslawski, James P. A782
Breslin, Sean J. E44
Bresnahan, Rodney A882
Bresnahan, Roger P320
Bressler, Allan (Al) A176
Bressler, Sean A265
Bressler, Richard J. A470
Brestovan, Peter (Pete) A689
Breter, Greg (Greggy) A923
Brethauer, Craig (Craigy) P64
Brett, James W. (Jim) A961
Brett, Anne Liners P276
Brett, John L. W32
Breuillac, Arnaud W391
Breux, Ken Le A640
Breves, Christine S. A913
Brewer, Edwin B. (Bill) E129
Brewer, David E276
Brewer, Allen M. A380
Brewer, Timothy (Tim) A598
Brewer, Dominic A626
Brewer, Michael (Mel) A664
Brewer, Janet J. A854
Brewer, Rosalind A936
Brewer, Kelley P240
Brewer, Dominic P345
Brewer, Victoria (Tori) P401
Brewer, Helen P447
Brewington, Kimberly F (Kim) E306
Brewster, Gregg (Greggory) A166
Brewster, Andre W. P254
Brewton, Clarence M (Clar) P303
Brezski, Richard J. E225
Brian, Bowser A359
Brice, Todd D. A775
Brick, Samuel A44
Brick, Terrance (Terri) A146
Brick, Michael P632
Bricker, Jude E19
Bricker, Jodi A865
Bricker, J. Douglas P172
Bricker, Jason (Jase) P265
Brickler, Lucinda A341
Brickley, David A869
Brickley, David P560
Brickman, David M. A388
Brickman, Jay (JayJay) P150
Bridarolli, Shelley (Shell) A144
Bridel, David P603
Bridelli, Guido A135
Bridge, Tracy B. A182

Bridge, Elaine (Elle) P347
Bridgens, Linda (Lin) P18
Bridgewater, Ronald (Ron) A662
Bridgman, Denise (Denny) A325
Briefs, Wally (Wall) A3
Brien, William (Bill) P107
Brier, Bonnie A626
Brier, Bonnie P345
Briese, Terrence (Terri) A370
Briesemeister, Eric P244
Briger, Peter L. E169
Brigger, Steve A896
Briggs, Tammy A20
Briggs, Ryan (Ry) A31
Briggs, Ashlea A100
Briggs, Daniel (Dan) A531
Briggs, Jon (Jonny) A569
Briggs, Larry A747
Briggs, Steve P462
Briggs, Michele (Michie) P590
Briggs, Andy W38
Bright, Tobias A140
Bright, Nerissa A753
Briles, Aimee (Ames) A963
Brill, Pepper A176
Brill, Ryan A784
Brill, Keith (Keithy) A904
Brilli, Richard J. P336
Brimmer, Stephanie E12
Brimmer, Robert (Bob) A156
Brimson, Stefan (Steve) A136
Brinckerhoff, Ronald A94
Brindle, Carol A967
Brindley, Roger (Rog) P602
Bringardner, Jennifer A173
Bringardner, Jennifer P105
Bringas, Mario A841
Bringaze, Walter L. P371
Bringle, Charlie P110
Brink, James P530
Brinkley, Phil A94
Brinkley, Ruth W. A173
Brinkley, Cynthia J. (Cindy) A180
Brinkley, Stephen (Steve) A846
Brinkley, Ruth W. P105
Brinkman, Kristina A358
Brinkman, Rob L P618
Brinkmann, Mike P435
Brinkmann, Hans-Georg W227
Brinkmeyer, Bill (Billy) A899
Brinton, Mark E258
Brisco, Carl A655
Briscoe, Debi A142
Briscoe, Laura (Laur) A810
Brisinte, Jodi A78
Briskman, David (Dave) A957
Brisse, Matthew (Matt) E176
Brissot, Vincent (Vin) A458
Bristow, Peter M. A358
Bristow, Dave (Davie) A395
Bristowe, Myles P399
Britell, Jenne K. A912
Britt, Elizabeth (Beth) A295
Britt, John M. P227
Britt, Douglas (Doug) W161
Brittain, Jim A379
Brittain, Jeffrey W. (Jeff) P302
Brittain, Max P359
Brittin, Christopher (Chris) P170
Brittingham, Randall A713
Britton, Paula A263
Brnilovich, Bob (Bo) P76
Broach, Danny (Dan) E63
Broach, Danny (Dan) A138
Broadbent, Jeff (Jeffy) P612
Broaddus, Eliza P410
Broadway, Andy E59
Broadwell, Steve P463
Brobst, Duane J. A921
Brocard, Dominique (Monique) A15
Broccolo, Timothy E264
Broccolo, Timothy A572
Brochick, George A687
Brock, Jeffrey E113
Brock, Beth (Betty) E275

Brock, Stanley M. (Skip) E369
Brock, Pat (Patty) A166
Brock, Charisse A239
Brock, Bob (Bo) A267
Brock, Macon F. A284
Brock, Cindy (Cin) A518
Brock, Anthony (Tony) A603
Brock, Kimberly (Kim) A753
Brock, Stanley M. (Skip) A794
Brock, Wendy A896
Brock, Jason (Jase) P152
Brockelbank, Russ P169
Brockman, Thomas (Thom) E54
Brockman, Tom (Tommy) E54
Brockman, Carla A270
Brockman, Tom P578
Brockway, Larry (Lar) A913
Broderick, Craig W. A409
Broderick, Kathryn E (Kat) A544
Broderick, Chris P393
Brodhead, Richard H. (Dick) A296
Brodhead, Richard H. (Dick) P171
Brodnax, Billy A843
Brodnitz, Peter A249
Brodrick, Anita (Ani) A193
Brodsky, Victor (Vic) E233
Brodsky, Noah A968
Brody, John S. E454
Brody, Robert C. (Bob) A883
Broek, Jacques van den W314
Broerman, Robert A. (Rob) A793
Broerman, Robert A. (Rob) P445
Brogan, Jennifer E265
Brogan, Jennifer A572
Brogden, Steven E168
Brogden, Sue-ellen P631
Broggi, Luciana A458
Brogie, Sandra (Sandy) A485
Brok, Martin A819
Broker, Linda K. P404
Brokke, Gregory D (Greg) A695
Brokke, Gregory D (Greg) P382
Broll, Frank (Frankie) A48
Brolly, Stephen H. E153
Brolly, Stephen H. A349
Bromann, Julie A (Jules) A658
Bromark, Raymond E403
Bromark, Raymond J. A977
Bromley, Matt E73
Bromley, Lillia A253
Bromley, Courtney A485
Bromley, Craig R. W246
Bronchetti, Jayson A546
Bronczek, David J. A344
Brond, David P414
Bronder, Debra E80
Broner, Bluma A717
Brons-Poulsen, Peter A223
Bronson, David L. P519
Brookes, Andy A5
Brooking, Bruce P17
Brooks, David A. E39
Brooks, Jerry M. E125
Brooks, David R. E221
Brooks, Daniel W. E221
Brooks, Renee (Ren) E376
Brooks, Richard M. E458
Brooks, Howard A120
Brooks, Christine (Chrissy) A135
Brooks, Leo (Leonardo) A140
Brooks, Mark A180
Brooks, Tony (Tone) A265
Brooks, Patricia (Pat) A269
Brooks, Brian P. A333
Brooks, Allen (Al) A392
Brooks, Josh A471
Brooks, David R. A474
Brooks, Daniel W. A475
Brooks, Wendell A479
Brooks, Staunton A485
Brooks, Charles T. A512
Brooks, Joe A539
Brooks, Ashley T. A550
Brooks, Raymond L. A561
Brooks, Michele (Michie) A584

Brooks, Jennifer (Jen) A592
Brooks, Gordon A619
Brooks, Rebekah A629
Brooks, Byron A692
Brooks, Tom (Tommy) A752
Brooks, Renee (Ren) A806
Brooks, Kristi A820
Brooks, Nancy Schwartz (Nance) A843
Brooks, Espen S. A869
Brooks, Jonathan (John) A875
Brooks, Tony A973
Brooks, Jo P237
Brooks, Kevin (Kev) P288
Brooks, Charles M. P404
Brooks, Espen S. P560
Brooks-Williams, Denise P223
Broome, David (Dave) A18
Broome, Richard D. A155
Broome, Marion E. A296
Broome, David (Dave) A789
Broome, Marion E. P171
Brophy, Stephen A283
Brophy, Joseph (Jo) A423
Brophy, Chris (Chrissy) A589
Brophy, Scott (Scotty) A895
Brophy, Beth (Betty) P232
Bros, Warner E229
Broseker, Bob (Bo) A584
Brosnahan, Maria A163
Brosnan, David J. (Dave) A214
Brosnan, Robert A409
Brosnan, Michael W164
Bross, Richard A (Dick) A453
Brothers, Lisa (Lis) A369
Brothers, Mick (Mic) A657
Brothers, Norm A910
Brothman, Dan E258
Brotman, Jeffrey H. (Jeff) A247
Brotman, Adam A820
Broucek, Paul A873
Brough, Alex (Al) A471
Brough, Rob (Robbie) A980
Brougher, Francoise A33
Broughman, Wade (Wayne) P418
Broughton, Thomas A. (Tom) E369
Broughton, John (Jack) A390
Broughton, Thomas A. (Tom) A794
Brouillette, Mary (Mar) P508
Broumidis, Haris W408
Broun, Elizabeth (Betsy) P459
Broussard, Bruce D. A462
Broussard, Paula A674
Brovold, Diana (Ana) P330
Browchuk, Brett A198
Brower, Bob E79
Brower, John (Jack) E374
Brower, Jason (Jase) A87
Brower, Bob A165
Brower, Chris A252
Brower, John (Jack) A799
Brown, Scott (Scotty) E13
Brown, Darin E. E30
Brown, Patrick E51
Brown, Roger H E67
Brown, Kevin (Kev) E67
Brown, J. Powell E70
Brown, P E70
Brown, J. Hyatt E70
Brown, Joseph (Jo) E71
Brown, Bill E128
Brown, Herbert (Hank) E141
Brown, Michael J. (Mike) E145
Brown, Edward E175
Brown, David A. E179
Brown, Ruth (Ruthy) E199
Brown, Michael J. (Mike) E212
Brown, Martin Brown Martin
 (Marti) E213
Brown, Patricia (Pat) E226
Brown, Lee E226
Brown, Eric J. E297
Brown, Robert K. E303
Brown, David (Dave) E321
Brown, Christopher (Chris) E381
Brown, Mary W E384

Brown, Stephen E398
Brown, Chuck (Chucky) E409
Brown, Charles (Charlie) E409
Brown, M. Dean E421
Brown, Jim E429
Brown, David L. E446
Brown, Jim E454
Brown, Troy R. E458
Brown, Sascha A18
Brown, Jeffrey J. (JB) A32
Brown, Bradley A32
Brown, Shona A33
Brown, Alex A33
Brown, Marc A44
Brown, Eric (Ric) A69
Brown, Jim A74
Brown, Brandon A78
Brown, Cathleen A87
Brown, Bob (Bo) A94
Brown, Adam (Ad) A101
Brown, Jennifer (Jen) A104
Brown, Patrick A110
Brown, Kort A112
Brown, Ricky K. A119
Brown, Emily (Em) A120
Brown, Jeff (Jeffy) A135
Brown, Cj A137
Brown, Kevin A140
Brown, Michael (Mel) A142
Brown, James C. A145
Brown, Vance A146
Brown, Joseph (Jo) A152
Brown, Micheal A166
Brown, Steve (Stevie) A175
Brown, Teresa (Terry) A195
Brown, Kris (Krissy) A204
Brown, Debra A205
Brown, Kenneth (Ken) A205
Brown, Pam (Pamela) A209
Brown, Adriane A246
Brown, Cressie A251
Brown, Alison (Alli) A251
Brown, William E. A275
Brown, Elissa A281
Brown, Jane (Ginny) A295
Brown, Darrell A304
Brown, Robert (Bob) A309
Brown, Marcus V. A315
Brown, David A317
Brown, Carrie (Carr) A325
Brown, David C A326
Brown, Anita (Ani) A340
Brown, Shannon A344
Brown, Paul S (Pauly) A347
Brown, Marianne C. A348
Brown, Douglas (Doug) A348
Brown, Rod A352
Brown, David D. A360
Brown, Jennifer (Jen) A390
Brown, Laura (Laur) A412
Brown, James S. (Jim) A419
Brown, William M. (Bill) A427
Brown, Angie A430
Brown, Ruth (Ruthy) A436
Brown, Doug A455
Brown, John A462
Brown, Kimberly A462
Brown, Nick A465
Brown, Michael J. (Mike) A468
Brown, Martin Brown Martin
 (Marti) A469
Brown, Patricia (Pat) A491
Brown, Dan A504
Brown, Desiree (Dee) A504
Brown, Michelle (Michie) A511
Brown, Lori (Lor) A516
Brown, Michele (Michie) A534
Brown, Michelle (Michie) A535
Brown, Archie M. A558
Brown, Joseph W. (Jay) A573
Brown, David A576
Brown, Nancy (Nance) A584
Brown, Philip (Phil) A596
Brown, Gregory Q. (Greg) A605
Brown, John (Jack) A610

Brown, Robert A623
Brown, Robert K. A630
Brown, Donald E. A636
Brown, Jennifer Jackson A637
Brown, Keegan A649
Brown, Brien H. A662
Brown, Vicki A706
Brown, Ian A715
Brown, Neil A728
Brown, Karen (Kare) A747
Brown, Ken (Kenny) A747
Brown, Robert A753
Brown, Rodney (Rod) A754
Brown, Denise (Denny) A758
Brown, Thomas L. A762
Brown, Marilyn (Mar) A764
Brown, Kevin A789
Brown, Jim A803
Brown, Mickey A A808
Brown, Julie A A809
Brown, Joel E. A821
Brown, David A822
Brown, Marc P. A824
Brown, Mary W A828
Brown, John (Jack) A831
Brown, Sidney R. (Sid) A832
Brown, Melanie A840
Brown, Tim (Timmy) A843
Brown, Bernard A846
Brown, Roger A855
Brown, Chuck (Chucky) A877
Brown, Charles (Charlie) A877
Brown, Janice (Jan) A889
Brown, Jeffrey A891
Brown, Michelle A894
Brown, M. Dean A902
Brown, Charles (Chas) A910
Brown, Michael (Mel) A934
Brown, Mike A939
Brown, Jeffrey (Jeff) A943
Brown, Erin A957
Brown, Pamela (Pam) P38
Brown, Dwayne (Wayne) P49
Brown, William A. P57
Brown, David P75
Brown, Charles H. P82
Brown, Lori (Lor) P83
Brown, Tracy P92
Brown, Hannah (Hanna) P112
Brown, Tom P152
Brown, Sherry (Sherr) P157
Brown, Jay (JayJay) P167
Brown, Jim (Jimmy) P216
Brown, Lori P239
Brown, Douglas T (Doug) P249
Brown, George J. P274
Brown, Nancy (Nance) P298
Brown, Marion P318
Brown, Leonard (Len) P339
Brown, Nancy P349
Brown, Rodger P352
Brown, Jane P356
Brown, Stephanie (Steph) P362
Brown, Clarence P370
Brown, Sheila D. P374
Brown, Deron P378
Brown, Kevin P387
Brown, Geoff P387
Brown, Janine P387
Brown, Robin B. P441
Brown, Jeff P442
Brown, Venessa P448
Brown, James (Jamie) P451
Brown, Claudine P459
Brown, W P461
Brown, Mary W. P480
Brown, Daniel A. P510
Brown, David FM P530
Brown, Joshua (Josh) P531
Brown, Ralph P531
Brown, Suzanne P540
Brown, Brenda P551
Brown, Charlie (Charles) P552
Brown, Christopher S (Chris) P554
Brown, Alesia P555

Brown, Dwaine P565
Brown, Rick (Ricky) P568
Brown, Kevin (Kev) P589
Brown, Marion P607
Brown, Bartholomew R P618
Brown, Charles W64
Brown, Gary W. W85
Brown, Michael W. T. (Mike) W272
Brown, Jason W311
Brown, Jim W327
Brown, Andrew W329
Brown, Randolph B. (Randy) W364
Browne, Mike E77
Browne, Michael A. (Mike) E77
Browne, Dave E278
Browne, James (Jamie) A312
Browne, Noreen A576
Browne, Robert P. (Bob) A640
Browne, Paul T. A851
Brownell, Kelly D. A296
Brownell, Stacy (Stace) P43
Brownell, Kelly D. P171
Brownell, Jayne (Jay) P318
Browning, Keith (Keithy) A168
Browning, Bill (Billy) A507
Browning, Michael A869
Browning, Jay D. A924
Browning, Deborah (Deb) P118
Browning, Michael P560
Brownlee, Jeff (Jeffy) A943
Broyles, JulieAnn A77
Broyles, Rhonda A846
Broyles, JulieAnn P41
Broyles-Aplin, Teresa P178
Broz, Steven A. (Steve) A721
Brozyna, Roman A205
Brubaker, Dave A100
Brubaker, Alan (Al) A727
Bruce, Geoff (G.) A144
Bruce, Andrea (Ann) A228
Bruce, Kofi A398
Bruce, Sally W26
Bruch, Lisa (Lis) A186
Bruder, David A427
Brudermuller, Martin W58
Brudzynski, Daniel (Dan) A293
Brue, Lester (Les) A821
Bruen, Phil (Philly) A585
Bruggeman, Johnathan (John) E73
Bruggeman, Kim (Kimmy) A453
Bruggeman, Brett A530
Brugger, Mark W. E121
Brugger, Thomas R. A832
Brugger, Betty P362
Bruggs, Jeff A596
Bruhin, Joseph D. (Joe) A242
Bruhl, Robert (Bob) A455
Bruhl, Robert (Bob) A455
Bruke, David (Dave) P609
Brull, Harry E236
Brumbelow, Holly (Holl) A566
Brumleve, Peter P440
Brummel, Andrew (Andy) A260
Brummel, Lisa (Lis) A592
Brummel, Andrew (Andy) P155
Brummer, Derek V. A742
Brummerhoff, Leigh A563
Brummit, John (Jack) A467
Brummit, John (Jack) P233
Brumsted, John R. P556
Brun, Scott (Scotty) A7
Brun, Philip (Phil) A916
Brundage, Barry A228
Brundige, Liz (Lizzie) P401
Brunel, Patrick A699
Brunelle, Fletch H A589
Brunengraber, Henri P103
Bruner, Steve (Stevie) E377
Bruner, William E (Bill) P103
Bruner, Robert F. P410
BRUNET, Jean-Louis W163
Brunetti, Andrea (Ann) A339
Bruney, Donna (Don) A607
Bruni, Frank (Frankie) A523
Brunk, Troy A769
Brunn, Carsten W60

C

A = AMERICAN BUSINESS
E = EMERGING COMPANIES
P = PRIVATE COMPANIES
W = WORLD BUSINESS

Caamano, John (Jack) A177
Cab, Sandy A194
Cabal, Jerry (Jerr) A883
Caballero, Diana (Ana) A156
Cabbil, Nathan A758
Cable, Carol A142
Cabral, Armando (Mando) E265
Cabral, Armando (Mando) A572
Cabrera, Jackie (Jack) A121
Cabrera, Javier A355
Cabrera, Luis A A747
Cabrera, Freddy P327
Cabuso, Nita A641
Caccamo, Frank (Frankie) A719
Caccamo, Frank A720
Cacciatore, Gary (Gar) A166
Caccivio, James C. A824
Caceres, R. Louis (Lou) A778
Cacheria, Ray Ann P425
Cadavid, Sergio A495
Caddy, Bob (Bo) A952
Cader, Alfredo A930
Cader-Frech, Mario A930
Cadieux, Marc E394
Cadieux, Kevin (Kev) A736
Cadieux, Marc A838
Cadigan, Catherine (Cate) P193
Cadiz, Bruce A140
Cadley, Carola P517
Cadogan, Jenelle A104
Cady, Chris E43
Cady, Gerald A. (Gary) E448
Cady, Sean A929
Cady, Gerald A. (Gary) A951
Cafarelli, Mike P110
Caffe, Steven (Steve) E387
Caffentzis, Anthony (Tony) A54
Cafferillo, Nick E363
Cafferty, Leslie (Les) A715
Caffery, Bill (Billy) E176
Caffey, Kevin (Kev) A736
Caforio, Giovanni A148
Cage, Jeff A470
Cagle, David P (Dave) A228
Cagler, Donna (Don) P338
Cagney, Phil (Philly) P152
Cagnolatti, Lisa (Lis) A807
Cahaly, Glenn E267
Cahaly, Scott A502
Cahan, Adam A975
Cahill, Mike (Mikey) E23
Cahill, Ann A180
Cahill, Richard A341
Cahill, John T. A522
Cahill, Timothy (Tim) A726
Cahill, Kevin (Kev) A883
Cahill, Thomas P118
Cahill, Kevin P201
Cahill, Edward L. P254
Cahill, Gerald R. (Gerry) W86
Cahill, Antony W267
Cahir, B.P. (Bart) W196
Cahuzac, Antoine W146
Cai, Xiangrong A429
Cai, Qian P410
Cai, Jianjiang W13
Cai-Lee, Wendy A299
Caillier, Blaine E159
Caillier, Blaine A365
Caimona, Michael A139
Cain, Kieran E430
Cain, James (Jamie) A56
Cain, Terry (Terr) A391
Cain, Lawrence P83
Caine, Patrice W383
Caines, Scott (Scotty) A789

Caiola, Vin P529
Cairns, Ann A568
Cairns, Chuck (Chucky) A766
Cairns, Chuck (Chucky) P421
Cairns, Gordon M. W419
Cajigas, Veronica A278
Cal, John M (Jack) P191
Calabia, Christopher A341
Calabio, Travis (Trav) A824
Calabrese, Vincent J. E165
Calabrese, Isela E265
Calabrese, Vincent J. A381
Calabrese, Dave (Davie) A429
Calabrese, Isela A572
Calabria, David (Dave) A92
Calamari, Stephen A A739
Calantzopoulos, Andr © A699
Calaway, Tonit M. A424
Calbert, Michael M. A283
Calbone, Kathie P240
Calbow, Brenda (Bren) A150
Calcagni, Mark (Marky) A463
Calcagnini, Donald P. P404
Caldarelli, Brian P399
Caldart, Gilberto A569
Calder, Richard D. (Rick) E188
Calder, Stephen (Steve) A87
Calder, Deborah (Deb) A404
Calderon, Vanessa A87
Calderon, Jorge A163
Calderon, Enrique A379
Calderone, Matthew (Matt) A143
Caldwell, Stephen T E274
Caldwell, Bruce A58
Caldwell, Scott A76
Caldwell, David (Dave) A162
Caldwell, Adiza A216
Caldwell, William J. A451
Caldwell, Lisa J. A760
Caldwell, Christopher (Chris) A839
Caldwell, Troy A869
Caldwell, Barry (Barr) A942
Caldwell, Scott P41
Caldwell, Dave P292
Caldwell, Troy P560
Caldwell-Denny, Lynn A911
Caley, Frank (Frankie) A753
Calhoun, Petra A18
Calhoun, Robert (Bob) A61
Calhoun, David L. (Dave) A136
Calhoun, Keith A309
Calhoun, Shep A905
Calhoun, Jay (JayJay) P101
Cali, Jim A510
Cali, Angela A654
Caliendo, David (Dave) A569
Calilly, Sean A843
Caliri, Linda P2
Calisto, Jodi A800
Calk, Richard E. (Rick) E298
Calkins, Steve A655
Call, Greg (Greggy) E137
Call, Barbara (Barb) A232
Call, Kevin P140
Call, Dawn (Dawny) P289
Calla, Nick (Nicky) A166
Callaghan, David (Dave) A664
Callaghan, James P195
Callahan, Susan (Sue) E71
Callahan, Eve E420
Callahan, Johnathan A44
Callahan, Michael (Mel) A124
Callahan, Susan (Sue) A152
Callahan, Mike A168
Callahan, Don A207
Callahan, Samantha (Sam) A226
Callahan, Daniel D. A229
Callahan, Kevin (Kev) A280
Callahan, Cathy J. A321
Callahan, Brendan A502
Callahan, Michael (Mel) A505
Callahan, Joseph (Jo) A514
Callahan, James R (Jamie) A522
Callahan, Patrick K. (Pat) A721
Callahan, Kathy (Kat) A726

Callahan, Andy A893
Callahan, Eve A901
Callahan, Mark (Marky) P194
Callahan, Clara A. P561
Callan, Patrick J. E314
Callan, Colm M. E444
Callander, David (Dave) P107
Callangan, Jeff (Jeffy) A106
Callari, Josie A82
Callaway, Kim E67
Callecod, David L. P270
Callen, David R. E367
Callen, Kathy (Kat) A657
Callender, Mike A344
Callery, Susan M (Sue) A317
Callicutt, Richard D. E63
Callicutt, Richard D. A138
Callihan, William H (Bill) A705
Callihan, Jane A905
Callihan, Nanette P356
Callini, Anthony E282
Callis, David (Dave) P499
Callum, Sean E161
Callum, Sean A373
Callum, Michael G. P490
Calman, Albi P119
Calmes, Mark E (Marky) A70
Calpino, Barry (Barr) A599
Caltabiano, Madelyn A579
Caltagirone, Francesco G. W33
Calvert, Mike P79
Calvert, Lisa (Lis) P148
Cama, Domenick A. E226
Cama, Domenick A. A491
Camacho, Nette A106
Camacho, Marilyn A730
Camarata, Pete (Petey) A532
Camarda, Jack (Jackie) A94
Camardo, Joe (Joey) A179
Cambias, Rob A31
Cambron, Cherie (Cher) A829
Camden, Carl T. A511
Camden, Hugh (Hugo) P182
Camenga, Dan (Danny) P140
Cameron, Todd A166
Cameron, Andrew (Andy) A312
Cameron, Stewart A379
Cameron, MichaelX T A479
Cameron, Richard A649
Cameron, Gordon (Gordy) A706
Cameron, Susan M. A760
Cameron, Kristy A820
Cameron, J. Nicholas A834
Cameron, Michael A. W365
Camilleri, Louis C. A699
Caminos, Michele (Michie) E176
Cammack, Tom P567
Cammer, Matt (Matty) A218
Cammer, Matt (Matty) P132
Cammorata, Andrew (Andy) A824
Camp, Jason E54
Camp, Robert E221
Camp, Mike (Mikey) E423
Camp, Robert A474
Camp, Anne Van P459
Camp, David P486
Campagna, Cheryl (Cher) P477
Campana, Vincent (Vin) A44
Campana, Mark A549
Campana, Frank (Frankie) A968
Campanella, George (Georgey) P189
Campanella, Jeanne P511
Campano, Holly (Holl) A156
Campano, John (Jack) P537
Campbell, R. Perry E27
Campbell, Paul E84
Campbell, Michael J. A155
Campbell, Bruce A. E169
Campbell, Chris (Chrissy) E177
Campbell, Marcy E261
Campbell, H. Stuart E271
Campbell, Albert M. (Al) E275
Campbell, Dala E344
Campbell, Patricia A. (Pat) E430
Campbell, David L. (Dave) A25

Campbell, Jeffrey C. (Jeff) A44
Campbell, Michael P. A81
Campbell, Nanci A120
Campbell, Kim A124
Campbell, Mary (Mar) A142
Campbell, Joanne T. A159
Campbell, Roger A. A247
Campbell, Michael (Mel) A269
Campbell, Bruce L. A277
Campbell, Tabitha A347
Campbell, Shelley A369
Campbell, Jimmy A420
Campbell, Rich (Ric) A429
Campbell, Donald A437
Campbell, Kristin A. A442
Campbell, Ann-Marie A446
Campbell, Ann Marie (Annie) A446
Campbell, George (Georgey) A494
Campbell, Jessica (Barnett) (Jess) A535
Campbell, Claude (Claudette) A546
Campbell, Roger (Rog) A610
Campbell, Kevin (Kev) A614
Campbell, Maura A621
Campbell, Tyler A718
Campbell, Dala A723
Campbell, John P (Jack) A766
Campbell, David (Dave) A800
Campbell, Karen (Kare) A927
Campbell, Travis A929
Campbell, Ellen (Elle) A945
Campbell, Steven (Steve) A952
Campbell, Jodi A968
Campbell, Cheryl (Cher) A970
Campbell, Kevin (Kev) A972
Campbell, Thomas (Thom) P53
Campbell, Rocky (Rock) P92
Campbell, Stephen (Steve) P103
Campbell, Preston M. P153
Campbell, Mark W P190
Campbell, Dean P205
Campbell, Curt P246
Campbell, Graham P333
Campbell, Bob (Bo) P385
Campbell, Joseph (Jo) P399
Campbell, John P (Jack) P421
Campbell, Paula P447
Campbell, Carol (Care) P508
Campbell, Ellen (Elle) P514
Campbell, Thomas P. P534
Campbell, Anne (Annie) P570
Campbell, Alan (Al) P590
Campbell, Ellen (Elle) P628
Campbell, David W78
Campbell, Norie C. W390
Campe, Jennifer (Jen) A964
Camperi, Marcelo F. P600
Campese, Mike P182
Campion, Trevor E362
Campion, Thomas D. E458
Campion, Andrew (Andy) A634
Campisi, David J. (Dave) A132
Campisi, David (Dave) A520
Campisi, Vince A914
Camplese, Cole W. P551
Campo, Laura (Laur) P556
Campos, Deb (Debbie) A164
Campot, Peter P492
Camps, Josep Pique i W16
Can, Alp A821
Canaday, Charles T. A47
Canale, Anthony E437
Canan, John (Jack) A580
Canares, Steven (Steve) E445
Canazaro, Chris (Chrissy) E394
Canazaro, Chris (Chrissy) A838
Cancelloni, Frank A732
Cancelmi, Daniel J. (Dan) A851
Cancila, Peter (Pete) A156
Candels, Eileen (Elle) A511
Canden, Hugh (Hugo) P182
Candia, Gary (Gar) P3
Candolini, Ed (Eddie) P152
Canekeratne, Kris A. E440
Canelas, Dale P590
Canepa, Tom (Tommy) P587

A = AMERICAN BUSINESS
E = EMERGING COMPANIES
P = PRIVATE COMPANIES
W = WORLD BUSINESS

Carrig, Kenneth J. (Ken) A834
Carrillo, Rachel E49
Carrillo, Ulises A5
Carrillo, Rachel A99
Carrington, Jim (Jimmy) A569
Carri□□n, Richard L. A708
Carroll, John A. E269
Carroll, Glenn E326
Carroll, Rhonda L. E344
Carroll, William (Bill) E445
Carroll, Milton A182
Carroll, Thomas (Thom) A225
Carroll, Brad (Brady) A226
Carroll, Henry (Hal) A262
Carroll, Nicole (Nikki) A276
Carroll, Kevin A417
Carroll, Debbie (Deb) A473
Carroll, Christopher F. A488
Carroll, Pamela A499
Carroll, Loren K. A508
Carroll, Teresa S. A511
Carroll, Darren (Darr) A544
Carroll, John A. A582
Carroll, Joseph (Jo) A584
Carroll, Ryan (Ry) A665
Carroll, Glenn A684
Carroll, Rhonda L. A723
Carroll, Johnnie A895
Carroll, Scott A937
Carroll, Jim (Jimmy) P49
Carroll, Allen P98
Carroll, Kevin P135
Carroll, John (Jack) P193
Carroll, Kevin P211
Carroll, Shelia P313
Carroll, Dale P446
Carroll, Kathleen P512
Carroll, Pameela (Sissi) P550
Carroll, William Y. P604
Carruth, Janet (Jan) P506
Carruthers, Wendy A146
Carruthers, Susan (Sue) A252
Carruthers, Paul (Pauly) A752
Carsen, Anna (Ann) A87
Carson, Kevin E406
Carson, Eric E413
Carson, Joe A505
Carson, Joe A591
Carson, Brian M. A596
Carson, John C. A745
Carson, Elizabeth (Beth) A846
Carson, Steven (Steve) P505
Carstanjen, William C. (Bill) E91
Carstenbrock, Tom (Tommy) A395
Carstens, Timothy (Tim) E265
Carstens, Timothy (Tim) A572
Carstens, Earl P180
Carswell, Scott (Scotty) A273
Carswell, Scott (Scotty) P165
Cartagena, Eduardo (Ed) P283
Carter, Ian R. E119
Carter, Bruce L.A. E136
Carter, Racheal E159
Carter, Neil E168
Carter, George J. E171
Carter, Scott H. E172
Carter, Jeffrey B. E172
Carter, Bryan E300
Carter, Thomas E. (Tom) E303
Carter, Tim E336
Carter, Chip E341
Carter, Scott (Scotty) A1
Carter, David (Dave) A7
Carter, Cyndi A166
Carter, Mark (Marky) A202
Carter, Van C A252
Carter, Peter A269
Carter, Robert B. (Rob) A344
Carter, Wanda A346

Carter, Betty A347
Carter, Racheal A364
Carter, Racheal A366
Carter, David A428
Carter, Ian R. A442
Carter, Danielle (Dani) A518
Carter, Nicole (Nikki) A547
Carter, Anita (Ani) A598
Carter, John A619
Carter, Candace (Ace) A623
Carter, Charles J. (Jack) A675
Carter, Jack A675
Carter, Matthew A689
Carter, Johnathan (John) A706
Carter, Mary Randolph A743
Carter, Andrea A743
Carter, Quentin A752
Carter, Ron A784
Carter, Tim A809
Carter, Deborah (Deb) A835
Carter, J. Braxton A844
Carter, Randy A871
Carter, Dave A914
Carter, Debra (Deb) P339
Carter, Meegan P349
Carter, David (Dave) P434
Carter, Gregory P437
Carter, Lonnie N. P461
Carter, Richard P518
Carter, Lennie P525
Carter, Lauren P588
Carter, Margaret (Maggie) P591
Carter-Robertson, Kira P469
Cartier, Karen P153
Cartin, Eugene E371
Cartin, Eugene A797
Cartisano, Angela (Ang) P325
Carton, Maeve W119
Cartwright, Tish E206
Cartwright, Tish A445
Cartwright, Lois P313
Carty, Brian P490
CARUANA, MAUREEN (Maury) P257
Caruso, Leslie A465
Caruso, Dominic J. A499
Caruso, Thomas P79
Caruso, Michael P459
Caruso, Dave (Davie) P491
Carvajal, Taylor A136
Carvalho, Jose A44
Carvalho, Frederico A479
Carvalho, Gilberto A855
Carvalho, Luiz Nelson Guedes de W299
Carvallo, Jorge P101
Carver, Debbie (Deb) A237
Carver, Bruce (Brucey) A254
Carver, Lori (Lor) A367
Carver, Joyce (Joy) A431
Carver, Bruce A539
Carver, Deb P644
Carver, Cathryn W267
Carveth, Barbara P588
Carwein, Vicky L. P401
Carwein, Vicky L. P571
Carwell, Mark P140
Casabene, Sam A384
Casablanca, Anthony S. E204
Casale, Carl M. A197
Casale, Jeff (Jeffy) A934
Casalegno, Gina P101
Casanova, Ellie E148
Casapulla, Tony (Tone) A876
Casares, Jeanne (Jeannie) P423
Casati, Gianfranco W5
Casavina, Lori (Lor) A383
Casazza, William J. A17
Casazza, Louise A565
Cascone, Robert (Bob) A109
Case, Thurman K. E93
Case, Stephen M. (Steve) E261
Case, John P. E352
Case, Richard (Dick) A409
Case, Karen B. A717
Casella, Michael J. E295
Casella, Michael J. A615

CASELLI, ETTORE W41
Cases, Juan Santamaria W6
Casey, Jeff E159
Casey, Kelly M (Kel) E213
Casey, Theresa (Terry) E352
Casey, William J. E411
Casey, Brian O. E450
Casey, Donald M. (Don) A165
Casey, Sharon (Share) A180
Casey, Jeff A365
Casey, John P. A395
Casey, Kelly M (Kel) A469
Casey, Jean (Jeannie) A544
Casey, Nancy (Nance) A589
Casey, Donald J. (Don) A749
Casey, Brian (Bri) A762
Casey, Kimberly (Kim) A764
Casey, Keith M. A857
Casey, William J. A886
Casey, Jeff (Jeffy) P187
Casey, Bill (Billy) P539
Casey, William (Bill) P539
Casey, David (Dave) P591
Cash, W. Larry A233
Cash, Sandra (Sandy) A348
Cash, Tim A843
Cash, Jordan P240
Cashaw, Brad A265
Cashill, Robert M. E226
Cashill, Robert M. A491
Cashman, James E. (Jim) E33
Cashman, Charles A. (Chuck) E255
Cashman, Ed (Eddie) A745
Cashon, Craig (Craigy) A925
Casillas, Paul (Pauly) P239
Casinelli, Frederick (Fred) A843
Casini, Victor (Vic) A550
Caskran, Ronald A109
Cason, Cheri P168
Casparino, Michael J. A689
Casper, Carsten E177
Casper, John (Jack) A423
Casper, Ben (Benny) A502
Casper, Marc N. A871
Caspersen, Christian (Chris) A835
Casperson, Finn M.W. E326
Casperson, Finn M.W. A684
Cass, Jim E366
Cass, Steve P455
Cassada, Don A120
Cassara, Ken A945
Cassara, Ken P628
Cassaro, Marcy A166
Cassel, Christine K. E342
Cassel, Heidi B (Hei) A347
Cassel, Kari P450
Cassel, Mat□as Domeyko W147
Cassell, Jack C. P29
Cassella, James V. (Jim) E101
Cassera, Fredrick P287
Cassidy, Deborah G. E340
Cassidy, Frank A157
Cassidy, Henry (Hal) A388
Cassidy, Jennifer (Jen) A689
Cassidy, Mike (Mikey) A706
Cassidy, John (Jack) A914
Cassidy, Thomas (Thom) A921
Cassidy, Kristen (Kristy) P298
Cassidy, Rick W372
Cassil, Tracy (Trace) A860
Cassimy, Barbara P280
Cassino, Kathryn A776
Cassity, Wendy P563
Cassler, Ernie (Ern) A981
Cast, Mike (Mikey) A164
Cast, William R. P571
Casta, Shannon A761
Castagna, Gary L. E278
Castagna, Eugene A. (Gene) A124
Castagna, Gene A124
Castagna, Robert (Bob) A146
Castagnola, David J. (Dave) E447
Castaneda, German A118
Castaneda, Rodrigo A135
Castaneda, Amanda A657

Castano, Robert (Bob) P467
Castanon, Paul (Pauly) A851
Casteel, Marty D. E373
Casteel, Beth A331
Casteel, Marty D. A799
Castella, Ma□«lys W19
Castellani, Robert (Bob) E123
Castellano, Christen A115
Castellano, Ilia A584
Castellano, Christen P54
Castellanos, Alfredo E146
Castellanos, Andria P538
Castellini, Dan (Danny) E257
Castellucci, Paul (Pauly) P362
Casten, Peter G (Pete) P520
Castiel, Mercedes P307
Castiglioni, Davide A957
Castile, Pamela (Pam) E409
Castile, Pamela (Pam) A877
Castille, Ralph (Ralphy) E426
Castille, Philip P590
Castillo, Eloise A439
Castillo, Claudia P A504
Castillo, Michael (Mel) A963
Castillo, Andres P403
Castillo-Cullather, Melanie (Mel) P571
Castine, Cindy (Cin) A553
Castle, Jason A437
Castle, Dedra N. A761
Castle, Don P383
Castleberry, Chris A923
Casto, Kerry (Kerr) A904
Caston, Moanica A404
Castonguay, Lyne A446
Castor, Richard L. (Rich) A401
Castor, Tory C A237
Castoral, Roger (Rog) A135
Castrillo-Viguera, Carmen (Carm) A133
Castro, Stephanie (Steph) E49
Castro, Stephanie (Steph) A99
Castro, Roland A392
Castro, Carlos (Carl) A589
Castro, Lorraine A918
Castro, Marie A926
Castrogiovanni, Denise (Denny) A835
Caswell, Bruce L. E262
Caswell, Kyle E437
Caswell, Angie A499
Catalano, Mark J. A966
Catalano, Mark J. P640
Cataldo, Paul (Pauly) A302
Catalfo, R O A470
Cataliotti, Palmira M. P638
Cate, Elizabeth (Beth) E352
Caterina, Rich E445
Cates, Ron (Ronnie) E274
Cates, Brandon (Bran) A789
Cates, George E. P604
Cathcart, David (Dave) A846
Catherinetoker, Mary A398
Cathey, Jim A736
Cathy, Bolinger A101
Cathy, Land A404
Catignani, Ryan O A462
Catik, Ali M. A890
Catino, David (Dave) A430
Catlender, Katie P340
Catlett, Celia P. E405
Catlin, Ray P180
Catoir, Christophe W7
Catran, Ricardo Isaac W398
Catsicas, Stefan W273
Catton, Mark W327
Catz, Safra A. A664
Caudill, Barry (Barr) A235
Caughlin, Christina (Tina) A392
Cauley, Lanier S P601
Causby, David A. A518
Cavagnaro, Charles E. P66
Cavalier, Lynn (Lyn) A375
Cavalieri, Cristina G (Chris) P561
Cavallaro, Joe A262
Cavallaro, Emanuele A495
Cavallaro, Anthony (Tony) P187
Cavallucci, Eugene A427

Cho, Chung-Myong W307
Choate, Elizabeth (Beth) A243
Choate, Chris A745
Choate, David (Dave) P90
Choate, Eleanor (Elena) P469
Chodak, Paul A42
Chodun, Eric (Ric) A228
Choe, Johnathan A169
Choe, Yong S A761
Choeff, Sonya (Sonnie) A745
Chofuku, Yasuhiro W252
Choi, Amy E394
Choi, Justin C. A60
Choi, Alison (Alli) A177
Choi, Charles (Charlie) A264
Choi, Philip A785
Choi, Brian (Bri) A789
Choi, Amy A838
Choi, Charles (Charlie) P434
Choi, Hyung-Seok W233
Choi-Kanuch, Angellee E397
Chojnowski, Tammy A824
Chojnowski, David (Dave) A937
Chomienne, Kathleen A397
Choo, Kangsoo W224
Choong, Wong Kim W404
Chopdekar, Neel A44
Chopra, Ravi A505
Chopra, Rahul A629
Chorley, Michael E (Mel) A765
Chorley, Michael E (Mel) P421
Chosy, James L. A895
Choto, Miguel A504
Chou, Phidias E390
Chou, John G. A54
Chou, Samuel A975
Chou, Lisa (Lis) P465
Choudhary, Ken R. A379
Choudhury, Dipankar E33
Choudhury, Bhaskar A693
Choudhury, Sayeed A736
Chouinard, Claude (Claudette) P87
Chourey, Shiben P356
Choutka, Michael J. P224
Chovanec, Tony (Tone) A319
Chow, Wayne E341
Chow, Donald S. A171
Chow, Jonathan (John) A549
Chow, Jean (Jeannie) A696
Chow, Wayne A714
Chow, Marjorie (Marge) P590
Chowdhury, Ashfaque A973
Chrencik, Robert (Bob) P592
Chretien, Yolanda A523
Chris, Wigger A267
Chrisman, Ken A788
Chriss, Lloyd A843
Christ, Rob E18
Christakes, Jennifer (Jen) A502
Christakos, Bretta A183
Christatos, Steve (Stevie) A338
Christen, Thomas (Thom) A146
Christenberry, Reid P318
Christens, Michelle (Michie) E265
Christens, Michelle (Michie) A572
Christensen, Christopher R. E139
Christensen, Roy E. E139
Christensen, Rich (Ric) A78
Christensen, Michelle (Michie) A132
Christensen, Bruce A576
Christensen, Wesley J. A662
Christensen, Robert J. (Bob) A671
Christensen, Bob (Bo) A671
Christensen, Steven (Steve) A847
Christensen, Scott A891
Christensen, Gregg (Greggory) A912
Christensen, Lori (Lor) A963
Christensen, Tom P76
Christensen, John P80
Christensen, Jesper V. P159
Christensen, Larry (Lar) P256
Christensen, Marc P. P465
Christian, Mark E319
Christian, David A. A285
Christian, Rodney (Rod) A293

Christian, Angela S (Ang) A451
Christian, Mark A676
Christian, Douglas (Doug) A733
Christian, Paul (Pauly) A766
Christian, Ronald (Ron) A766
Christian, Eric A973
Christian, Dan P1
Christian, Paul (Pauly) P421
Christian, Ronald (Ron) P421
Christian, Ralf W346
Christiansen, Andrew A840
Christiansen, Kathy A905
Christiansen, Niels B. P159
Christiansen, Douglas L. P557
Christiansen, Jeppe W285
Christianson, Grant E170
Christianson, Bonnie A139
Christianson, Jim (Jimmy) A818
Christianson, Ron P364
Christie, Edward M. (Ted) E380
Christie, William T. A340
Christie, Warren (Warr) A497
Christie, Peter (Pete) A619
Christie, Janet P450
Christina, Rassi A18
Christman, Donna (Don) A326
Christman, Kelli A899
Christman, Kevin A972
Christmann, Jon (Jonny) E383
Christmann, John J. A64
Christmann, Jon (Jonny) A827
Christmas, Charles E. (Chuck) E268
Christmas, Charles E. (Chuck) A577
Christodoulou, Petros W269
Christodoulou, Nikos W269
Christoff, Paul W339
Christoffersen, Gregg A502
Christofferson, Carla A15
Christoforo, John P71
Christophel, Randy P237
Christopher, Casey A183
Christopher, Tammy (Tam) A331
Christopher, John Y (Jack) A439
Christopher, Norman C. P121
Christopher, Gail C. P619
Christy, Lisa R (Lis) A363

Christy, James A724
Chronister, Lynne U P601
Chrystal, Curtis E197
Chrystal, Curtis A434
Chrystie, Dale (Dal) A344
Chu, Joshua E208
Chu, William A94
Chu, Roberta (Berta) A106
Chu, Dorcus A194
Chu, Gary A398
Chu, Joshua A450
Chu, Sophia A504
Chu, Benjamin K. A506
Chu, Julie (Jules) A565
Chu, Benjamin K. P256
Chu, Steph P606
CHU, CHELSEA (Chels) P615
Chu, John Tai-Wo W12
Chu, William W120
Chu, Wen Cheng W371
Chua, Nicolas (Nic) P551
Chuber, James (Jamie) A295
Chugh, Madhavi A135
Chugh, Davinder W32
Chughtai, Faisal E446
Chukwumah, Obi A120
Chulick, Michele P119
Chulos, Nicholas J. A370
Chultz, Dan (Danny) A641
Chumakov, George A510
Chumley, Rob A608
Chun, Ricky E282
Chun, Gregory H. (Greg) P302
Chun-Soo, Han W218
Chung, Tony E148
Chung, Annie (Ann) E191
Chung, Christopher (Chris) E294
Chung, D. Christopher E294

Chung, Lianne A54
Chung, Michael H.K. A300
Chung, Annie (Ann) A422
Chung, June A514
Chung, Felix A565
Chung, Yoon (Michael) A678
Chung, Jin A733
Chung, Paul W. A845
Chung-Yao, Li (Ford) E36
Chunko, Andrew T. E179
Chunko, Andy E179
Chuprevich, Tammy (Tam) E67
Churay, Daniel J. (Dan) A607
Church, Lara A259
Church, John R. A398
Church, Kathryn A507
Church, Jason A726
Church, Dean P390
Churchey, Randall L. (Randy) E129
Churchill, Ryan L. E261
Churchill, Sally (Sal) A751
Churchill, Sally (Sal) P411
Churchman, Calvin A743
Churchouse, Robin W423
Churchwell, Kevin P517
Churney, Bill E437
Chutima, Sarunthorn W345
Chwee, Kenny B. H. W416
Chèvre, Claude W178
Ciampa, Dominick A624
Cianciosi, Steven (Steve) A580
Ciarlante, James (Jamie) A603
Ciavarello, Stephanie (Steph) A573
Ciavarro, Domenic P140
Ciborowski, Michael (Mel) A689
Cibos, Richard A774
Cicale, Ed A89
Ciccone, Dave A87
Cicconi, James W. (Jim) A83
Cicconi, Fiona W37
Cicero, Robert J. E25
Cicero, John A173
Cicero, John P105
Cichon, Monica (Mon) A514
Cichon, Richard (Dick) P147
Cichowski, Lorraine P512
Cielica, April A720
Ciervo, Carman P260
Ciesemier, Barbara A217
Ciesielski, Chet A516
Ciesinski, Stephen (Steve) P473
Cieslak, AnnJoy A106
Cieslewicz, Richard (Dick) P203
Cigarroa, Francisco G. A921
Cigarroa, Francisco G. P605
Ciliberti, Angelo (Andy) P591
Cillo, Sherry (Sherr) E421
Cillo, Sherry (Sherr) A902
Cima, Laura (Laur) P215
Cimbri, Carlo W403
Cimen, Cenk W221
Cimino, Lori A108
Cincotta, Tiffany A5
Cindi, Tippett A769
Cindric, Michael (Mel) A226
Cindy, Allen (Al) A186
Cinnamon, Todd E19
Cinquepalmi, Anna A972
Ciochetto, Jeff (Jeffy) E197
Ciochetto, Jeff (Jeffy) A434
Cioffi, George A. (Jack) P273
Ciombor, Christiane A968
Ciongoli, Adam G. A160
Ciotto, Paul (Pauly) A18
Ciperski, Carla (Carly) A485
Cipoletti, Jack (Jackie) A211
Cipra, Andy A279
Ciprich, Tresa A866
Ciprich, Tresa P540
Cira, Cindy (Cin) A963
Cirbo, Elayne P499
Cirelli, Jean-François W153
Ciriello, James (Jamie) A579
Cirillo, Mary A204
Cirillo, Carl A619

Cirincione, Thomas (Thom) A465
Cirin□, Luciano W33
Cirksena, Mark P169
Ciroli, James K. A377
Cirri, Dawn (Dawny) A851
Cisarik, James (Jamie) A319
Ciserani, Giovanni A719
Ciskowski, Michael S. (Mike) A924
Cisneros, Zada A252
Cisrik, James (Jamie) A319
Citarella, Paul (Pauly) E163
Citrano, John A. E71
Citrano, John A. A153
Citroen, Karel A573
Ciuffetelli, Vincent (Vin) A661
Ciukowski, Kim (Kimmy) E335
Ciukowski, Kim (Kimmy) A703
Ciulla, John R. A943
Ciurlik, Tim (Timmy) P290
Cius, Steve (Stevie) A392
Civgin, Don A31
Civitts, Ray A905
Clabby, Joseph S. (Joe) W104
Clack, Alan (Al) A176
Claes, Hilde A500
Claeys, Michelle (Mitch) E99
Claeys, Michelle (Mitch) A224
Clague, Alexander (Al) A462
Clair, Joyce St. A640
Clair, Joyce S (Joy) A640
Clair, Tina (Tin) A981
Clamp, Len (Lenny) A104
Clancy, Paul J. A133
Clancy, John P. (Jack) A316
Clancy, Sean A731
Clancy, Peter (Pete) P624
Clancy, Edward (Ed) W104
Clanton, Lori (Lor) A16
Clanton, Lori (Lor) P10
Clapp, Dale A369
Clappin, James P. A245
Clara, Daniel (Dan) A74
Clark, Sean E44
Clark, Lisa (Lis) E69
Clark, Todd E80
Clark, Scott E126
Clark, Jonathan E137
Clark, Bill (Billy) E162
Clark, Kathy (Kat) E187
Clark, Kelly L. E262
Clark, David D. E267
Clark, Doug E275
Clark, Catherine J (Cathy) E349
Clark, John C. E373
Clark, Joseph T. (Joe) E392
Clark, Dan (Danny) A18
Clark, Laura (Laur) A31
Clark, Gina K. A54
Clark, Gary T A64
Clark, Craig (Craigy) A64
Clark, Lisa (Lis) A151
Clark, Jordan (Jordy) A156
Clark, Rodney L. A188
Clark, John A198
Clark, Wendy A220
Clark, Julie A235
Clark, Mark (Marky) A245
Clark, Paul A249
Clark, Joel A260
Clark, Scott A298
Clark, Etta A301
Clark, John J A340
Clark, Denise (Denny) A347
Clark, Sara A351
Clark, Mark (Marky) A375
Clark, Tom (Tommy) A392
Clark, David A398
Clark, Jeff (Jeffy) A456
Clark, Neil S A465
Clark, Robert W (Bob) A522
Clark, Michael S A550
Clark, Morris A559
Clark, Laura J (Laur) A569
Clark, Kyle A569
Clark, David (Dave) A576

Cummiskey, Chris A404
Cummiskey, Tom A935
Cummiskey, Tom P621
Cumpton, Linda A101
Cune, Bill (Billy) A246
Cuneo, Marie P363
Cunfer, Todd A438
Cunha, Paulo Guliherme Aguiar W398
Cunliffe, Adam E179
Cunningham, Thomas (Thom) E9
Cunningham, Kelly E250
Cunningham, John E348
Cunningham, Michael R. E353
Cunningham, G. Cotter E358
Cunningham, Don A58
Cunningham, Lisa (Lis) A78
Cunningham, Shirley A197
Cunningham, Kenn A325
Cunningham, Tom A342
Cunningham, David L. A344
Cunningham, Stacy (Stace) A383
Cunningham, Tim A504
Cunningham, William H. A547
Cunningham, Everett V. A739
Cunningham, Michelle (Mitch) A758
Cunningham, Scott (Scotty) A807
Cunningham, Mike (Mikey) A843
Cunningham, Vickie (Vick) A866
Cunningham, Jack (Jackie) A887
Cunningham, Kellie (Ellie) A963
Cunningham, Marsha P56
Cunningham, Trace P285
Cunningham, Christopher
  (Chris) P356
Cunningham, Moria P511
Cunningham, Vickie (Vick) P540
Cunningham, John P593
Cunningham, Phil (Philly) P627
Cunningham, Ron (Ronnie) P633
Cupelli, Kim M A893
Cupps, Donald L. P595
Cuprys, Rich (Ric) A223
Cuprys, Karolina A892
Curcio, Joe E406
Curcio, Michael J. A297
Curcio, Joe A862
Curelop, Bradley (Brad) A120
Curley, Michael E161
Curley, Charles (Charlie) A348
Curley, Michael A373
Curley, Bonnie (Bonbon) A751
Curley, Bonnie (Bonbon) P411
Curme, Mike (Mikey) P318
Curnow, Randy P309
Curnutte, Douglas (Doug) A518
Curoe, Tim (Timmy) A846
Curphy, Rona A115
Curphy, Rona P54
Currah, Barry (Barr) A981
Curran, Terrie A179
Curran, Martin J. (Marty) A245
Curran, Lisa (Lis) A304
Curran, Teresa M. A342
Curran, Paul (Pauly) A727
Curran, Shawn A865
Curran, Michael J. P303
Curran, Kevin T. P638
Curran, David W415
Currarino, Giancarlo A670
Curren, John (Jack) A784
Currence, Dave E447
Currence, David (Dave) E447
Currie, Nicholas (Nick) E394
Currie, Chad E421
Currie, Kathleen (Kathy) A344
Currie, Nicholas (Nick) A838
Currie, Calvin (Cal) A840
Currie, Kenne A846
Currie, Chad A902
Currie, Dean W. P94
Currie, John (Jack) P338
Currie, Pat P440
Currie, Theresa L. (Teri) W390
Currie, Gordon A.M. W414
Currier, Rand P209

Currlin, Kyle A291
Currn, Cathy (Cat) A487
Curry, Eric (Ric) A218
Curry, Julie A485
Curry, Maridee P302
Curry, Kevin P406
Curry, Susan J. P553
Curtin, Jim (Jimmy) A98
Curtin, David (Dave) A135
Curtin, Thomas (Thom) A506
Curtin, Mike (Mikey) A894
Curtin, Thomas (Thom) P256
Curtis, Dave E179
Curtis, Deborah (Deb) A44
Curtis, Elizabeth (Beth) A44
Curtis, Katheryn B. (Kathy) A285
Curtis, Louise A302
Curtis, Mark D. A372
Curtis, Elvira A409
Curtis, Chase S. A493
Curtis, Robert A565
Curtis, Bonnie (Bonbon) A719
Curtis, Scott A. A745
Curtis, Timothy P302
Curtis, David P416
Curtis, Gregg P463
Curto, David (Dave) A87
Curwin, Ronald (Ron) A124
Cury, Devon (Dev) A366
Cus, William (Bill) A150
Cusack, Carole A3
Cusano, Glenn A497
Cushing, Bob A13
Cushing, Giselle A462
Cushing, Robert T (Bob) A888
Cushing, Robert P14
Cushman, Deann A576
Cushnie, Colin A807
Cusick, Thomas B. E100
Cusick, Bob A780
Cuss, Francis A148
Custer, Timothy A. A64
Cute, Maria (Mary) E177
Cutietta, Robert A. P603
Cutino, Camille G. E74
Cutler, Scott A302
Cutler, Scott (Scotty) A481
Cutler, Paul (Pauly) A866
Cutler, Paul (Pauly) P540
Cutlip, Maggie (Margaret) P548
Cutri, Dominic (Dom) P313
Cutrone, Paul S. P358
Cutsinger, Buddy E335
Cutsinger, Buddy A703
Cutt, Tim W68
Cutt, Tim W69
Cuzzi, Gregory A718
Cvengros, Kevin (Kev) A891
Cvetas, Joseph G. P466
Cypert, Lisa P603
Cypher, Morgan A360
Cyphers, Randy (Rand) A150
Cyprien, Chris (Chrissy) A981
Cyr, Steven (Steve) E32
Cyr, Susie A601
Cyr, Donald (Don) St A923
Cyrus, Christina (Tina) P12
Czack, Karen A44
Czajka, Edward J. E341
Czajka, Michael (Mel) A672
Czajka, Edward J. A714
Czanderna, Karel K. E164
Czapla, Marianne A597
Czaplijski, Thomas J. (Tom) P389
Czarnecki, Kevin A397
Czarnecki, Mark J. A554
Czarnecki, Walter P A687
Czarnecky, Greg A784
Czartoski, Timothy (Tim) A500
Czebotar, Jerry A. P336
Czech, Justyna A494
Czechowski, Katharine E208
Czechowski, Katharine A448
Czeizler, Gayle A392

Czernikowski, Roy P423
Czyz, Tammy (Tam) A775
Czyz, AnneMarie P480
C⬚rdenas, Jorge de E24

D

Dabagia, Robert C. E209
Dabagia, Robert C. A452
Dabbert, Lyle D. P566
Daboin, Sharon (Share) A251
Daboval, Wendy A194
Dabundo, Chuck (Chucky) A140
Dac, Nadia A6
Daco, Katherine A136
Dacosin, Raylette A106
Dacosta, Dee (Danielle) A87
Dacosta, Tony A922
Dacosta, Anthony (Tony) A922
Dacunha, Kathleen A265
Dacus, Scott (Scotty) A803
Dadkhah, Hassan A589
Dadlez, Christopher M. (Chris) P429
Daesch, Nanci A601
Daffan, Nicholas E437
Dagan, Gary A689
Dagher, Ramzi A697
Dagio, Muriel A736
Daglio, Robert (Bob) A175
Dague, David E300
Dahan, Rene W223
Daher, Stacy (Stace) P600
Dahl, Naomi (Nomi) A202
Dahl, Chris (Chrissy) A601
Dahl, Susanne A640
Dahl, Craig R. A847
Dahlen, Dennis A115
Dahlen, Dennis P54
Dahlgren, Bradley A248
Dahlgren, Marisa P403
Dahlgren, Peter W351
Dahlmann, David S. (Dave) A360
Dahlstrom, Kevin E291
Dahlstrom, Richard (Rick) P302
Dahlweid, Michael (Mel) A397
Dahua, Shi W100
Dahut, Karen A143
Dai, Hai-Lung P505
Daif, Doris (Dory) A44
Daigle, Donald H. P371
Daignault, Jesse (Jess) A56
Dailey, Susan E312
Dailey, Jack A92
Dailey, Krisoula P187
Dailey, Mike (Mikey) P357
Dailey, John R. (Jack) P459
Dailey, Jeffrey J. (Jeff) W427
Daily, Pete (Petey) A268
Daily, Harry P. (Pete) A268
Daiss, Ann (Annie) A404
Daji, Swati V A295
Dakey, Alan W. E331
Dakey, Alan W. A691
Dakil, S. Edward E170
Dakolias, Constantine M. (Dean) E168
Dalahmeh, Merry A508
Dale, Daniel (Dan) A3
Dale, Kirk A226
Dale, Jeffery F. A802
Dale, Ken P512
Dale, Kenneth (Ken) P512
Daleo, Robert D. (Bob) P193
Dalessandro, Nick (Nicky) A692
Dalessio, Harry (Hare) A726
Daley, Kelli A8
Daley, Elvia A252
Daley, Paul A372
Daley, John (Jack) A392
Daley, Anne (Annie) A584
Daley, Karen A640
Daley, Dorian E. A664
Daley, Calvin (Cal) A835
Daley, Thomas (Thom) P83
Daley, Elizabeth M. P603

Daley, Tamara (Mara) P632
Dalgleish, Glen A715
Dalhoff, John (Jack) A267
Dalia, Randall A485
Dalke, Gary (Gar) A953
Dall, Marcia A. E91
Dall, Trisha (Trish) A470
Dalla, Sareena A135
Dallabattista, Mauro A534
Dallala, Daniel P101
Dally, Karen A437
Dally, Troy A553
Dally, Bill A649
Dalrymple, Christopher K. A27
Dalrymple, Tom (Tommy) A887
Dalton, Nathaniel E10
Dalton, Bill (Billy) E54
Dalton, Patrick J. E154
Dalton, Gregory W. A116
Dalton, Michelle (Mitch) A166
Dalton, Richard J. A218
Dalton, Rick (Ricky) A218
Dalton, Jill (Jilly) A514
Dalton, Robert P212
Dalton, Chuck P358
Dalton, Joan P431
Dalton, Mark F. P558
Dalton, Sally (Sal) P600
Daluz, Alice (Ali) E394
Daluz, Alice (Ali) A838
Daly, Michael P. E56
Daly, James M. (Jim) E220
Daly, Brian (Bri) E395
Daly, Michael P. A128
Daly, Marty (Mart) A176
Daly, Andrew (Andy) A429
Daly, Colleen A514
Daly, Tom (Tommy) A555
Daly, David M. A729
Daly, Tim A954
Daly, Ronald E. P2
Daly, Paula P249
Daly, Ashley (Ash) P308
Daly, Marilyn P340
Dam, Cari E265
Dam, Cari A572
Dam, Anders Christian W215
Damadian, Raymond V. E166
Damanaki, Maria P536
Dambach, Michael A133
Dambrosio, Nancy (Nance) A135
Dameris, Peter T. E313
Damian, James M. E72
Damiano, Gary (Gar) E434
Damiris, George J. A444
Damm, Sven A532
Damme, Niek Jan Van W136
Dammon, Robert M. P101
Damon, Tom (Tommy) A535
Damon, Lisa J. P448
Damore, Larry A945
Damore, Larry P628
Damron, Rick D. A553
Damron, James (Jamie) P8
Damschroder, Patricia (Pat) P555
Dan, James R. A14
Dan, James R. P9
Dana, Phillips P294
Dana, Michael W292
Dandes, Jonathan P417
Danes, Mike A80
Danes, Peter (Pete) A671
Danes, Mike P45
Danforth, Dave (Davie) A671
Dang, Kimberly Allen (Kim) A517
Dang, Linh-chi A586
Dang, Linh A586
Dang, Michelle (Michie) A780
Dang, Mukesh A935
Dang, Mukesh P622
Dangelo, Enrico A10
Dangi, Savinay A844
Daniel, J. Michael E54
Daniel, Laree A20
Daniel, James R. A101

Davis, Gary P395
Davis, Cory P421
Davis, Jonathan S. P445
Davis, Anne P451
Davis, Buddy P463
Davis, Donald (Don) P469
Davis, Matt (Matty) P471
Davis, Dewey P478
Davis, Myra P507
Davis, Glenn P511
Davis, Jeff P530
Davis, Justin H P531
Davis, Debra A. P555
Davis, John P561
Davis, Michael P569
Davis, George (Georgey) P586
Davis, Leslie C. P598
Davis, Angie (Ang) P600
Davis, Sylvia S. P603
Davis, Joan P615
Davis, Michael (Mel) P631
Davis, Philip (Phil) P641
Davis, Lisa W346
Davis, Sarah R. W414
Davis, Gareth W418
Davis-Blake, Alison A750
Davis-Blake, Alison P411
Davison, Kecia A8
Davison, Steven B (Steve) A281
Davison, Jeffrey (Jeff) A619
Davison, Paul J. A728
Davison, Charlie (Charles) P140
Davisson, Robert J. A795
Davit, Robert P313
Davitt, George A383
Davoren, Peter J. W6
Davoren, Peter J. W184
Davy, Alan W80
Dawes, Karen A. A356
Dawes, Scott (Scotty) A665
Dawkins, Alwyn E176
Dawkins, Keith D. A146
Dawn, Nigel E146
Daws, Ryan E101
Dawson, Timothy A. E75
Dawson, Philip E176
Dawson, Jim (Jimmy) E424
Dawson, Robert (Bob) E436
Dawson, Robert (Bob) A108
Dawson, Suzanne A520
Dawson, Jane A597
Dawson, Bruce (Brucey) A613
Dawson, Bill (Billy) A774
Dawson, Julie (Jules) A874
Dawson, Andrew (Andy) A904
Dawson, Peter P507
Day, Chris (Chrissy) E23
Day, Paulee C. E255
Day, Craig A159
Day, Jason K (Jase) A167
Day, Rita A218
Day, Timothy A231
Day, Ray A384
Day, Thomas R. A453
Day, Zane A522
Day, Edward (Ed) A624
Day, J. Randal A803
Day, Twila A842
Day, William B. (Bill) A842
Day, Timothy (Tim) P72
Day, Terri P262
Day, Kim P310
Day, Debbie P330
Day, Bill P626
Day, Anthony W365
Dayon, Alex A778
Days, Karen A336
Dayton, Mindy P511
De, Suvranu P414
Deacon, Mark (Marky) E176
Deacon, Mary Ann A527
Deak, Richard (Dick) E366
Deakin, Scott M. E248
Deakins, Richard (Dick) A60
Deal, Clifford M. E96

Deal, Stanley A. (Stan) A139
Deal, Stan A140
Deal, Julie (Jules) A347
Deal, Helena A439
DeAmore, Denise A824
Dean, Kim (Kimmy) E226
Dean, Deborah (Deb) E277
Dean, Aaron A94
Dean, Kim (Kimmy) A163
Dean, John C. A184
Dean, Lloyd H. A272
Dean, Matthew (Matt) A309
Dean, Spencer (Spence) A706
Dean, Lloyd H. P165
Dean, Clint P180
Dean, Campbell P205
Dean, Kathy P379
Dean, Chana P406
Dean, Donna J. P544
Dean, William (Bill) P550
Dean, Stephen (Steve) P615
Dean-Hammel, Bridget (Bri) A135
Deane, Catherine (Cate) A518
Deangelis, Michael A479
DeAngelis, Christine P278
DeAngelis, Lisa M. P307
DeAngelo, Lawrence J. (Larry) E257
DeAngelo, Joseph J. (Joe) A432
Dear, Tina (Tin) A304
Dearborn, Randy A589
Deardorff, Kevin L. A528
Deardurff, Chris (Chrissy) E149
Dearie-ruhlin, Mary A835
Dearman, Paul A135
Dearmond, Wade (Wayne) A899
Deason, Duane E300
Deason, Richard A534
Deasy, Dana S. A504
Deaton, Steven G. A822
Deaton, Eric P630
Deatrick, Gina A296
Deatrick, Gina P171
Deaver, W. Scott A92
Deaver, Scott (Scotty) A92
Deaver, Russell (Russ) A156
Debarry, Bryan E436
DeBatty, Jill (Jilly) A528
Debeasi, Paul (Pauly) E176
Debenedetti, Pablo G. P548
DeBenedictis, Leonard C. (Len) E457
Debenedictis, Leonard (Len) A680
Debenedictis, Leonard (Len) P377
Debenedicts, Peter E349
DeBernardi, Michael (Mel) E317
DeBernardi, Michael (Mel) A666
DeBerry, Blake T. E125
Deberry, Kenneth W (Ken) A429
Deberry, Herb P178
Debertin, Jay D. A197
Debevoise, Marc (Marcy) A176
Debiase, Francesca A575
Deblaere, Johan G. (Jo) W5
DeBlock, Andrew (Andy) A463
Debnam, Henry A427
Debney, P. James E25
Deboer, David (Dave) E268
DeBoer, Bryan B. A548
DeBoer, Mark D (Marky) A548
DeBoer, Sidney B. (Sid) A548
Deboer, David (Dave) A577
Deboer, Greg (Greggy) A843
Debois, Jim (Jimmy) A105
Debon, Marie-Ange W360
Debord, Cris A283
Debra, Morfit E421
Debra, Morfit A902
Debrowski, Thomas A (Thom) A571
DeBrunner, Alexis P318
Debuke, Robin A522
Debusk, Chuck A918
Decamp, Bill E334
Decamp, Bill A703
Decastro, Victoria (Tori) P118
Dechant, Esther A680
Dechant, Suzanne A820

Dechant, Esther P377
Dechant, Timothy L. P619
Decher, Peter A903
Dechristofaro, Robert (Bob) A195
Deck, Richard A732
Deckelman, William L. (Bill) A236
Decker, Jeff E29
Decker, Cindy (Cin) E394
Decker, Ben (Benny) A150
Decker, Daniel A. A150
Decker, Scott A166
Decker, Casey A336
Decker, Edward P. (Ted) A446
Decker, Cindy (Cin) A838
Decker, Anton P309
DeClaire, Christopher G. E431
DeClaris, Wade N. A965
Decock, Tracy J (Trace) A706
Decolli, Chris A3
Decoly, Mike (Mikey) A945
Decoly, Mike (Mikey) P628
Decosta, Lori (Lor) A324
Decraene, Dave A369
Decraene, Stefaan W71
Decrane, Susanne A173
Decrane, Susanne P105
Decuyper, Will (Willy) A918
Decyupere, Franciska W71
Dedicoat, Chris A203
Dedinsky, John G. A678
Dedman, Joe A405
Dedolce, Trish A727
Dedood, Jan A28
Dedood, Jan P18
Dedrick, Keith (Keithy) A352
Dee, John J. E451
Dee, Steven (Steve) A635
Deeba, Amer S. E348
Deeds, Thomas (Thom) A166
Deeg, Mark A (Marky) A544
Deegan, Michael (Mel) P509
Deehan, Teri (Terrance) A883
Deeks, Terence E296
Deeks, Terence N. A615
Deenihan, Ed (Eddie) A621
Deering, Matt (Matty) A766
Deering, Matt (Matty) P421
Dees, Kent (Ken) E356
Dees, Kent (Ken) A757
Dees, Todd A835
DeFalco, Ciro M. E295
DeFalco, Ciro M. A615
DeFaria, Chris A873
DeFazio, Darren (Darr) A765
Defeis, Nicholas A726
Defeo, John (Jack) A198
Deffebach, Harry L. P228
Defilippis, Mark P536
DeFord, Drexel P490
DeFranco, James (Jim) A279
DeFranco, Jim (Jimmy) A279
Defazio, Joseph P P363
Degenhart, Elmar W113
Degenkolb, Christopher (Chris) P237
DeGeorge, Peter R. P404
Deger, Amy A351
DeGiorgio, Kenneth D. A354
Degnan, Scott E452
Degnan, John J. A867
Degnan, John J. P542
Degnon, Laura A546
DeGrand, Robert P199
Degratto, Frank (Frankie) P287
DeGregorio, Ronald J. (Ron) A326
DeHart, Brad G. P619
Dehaze, Alain W7
Deherrera, Brandy A981
Dehio, Peter (Pete) A322
Dehls, Cindy (Cin) A706
Dehner, Torsten A21
Dehua, Wang W99
Deignan, Kathleen P548
Deihl, Monty C. E311
Deily, Karl R. A788
Deir, Yvonne (Vonne) E109

Deis, Ron A476
Deisinger, Jennifer (Jen) A104
Deitch, Laurence B. A751
Deitch, Sally A851
Deitch, Laurence B. P411
Dejong, Frank (Frankie) A309
Dekay, Sam (Sammy) A109
Dekeyser, Paul (Pauly) P333
Dekeyzer, Ron (Ronnie) P122
Dekker, Stuart (Stu) E330
Dekker, Karen A51
Dekker, Hans A379
Dekker, Stuart (Stu) A690
Dekker, Wout W314
Dekkers, Marijn W402
Dekman, Matt (Matty) A706
DeKosky, Steven T. (Steve) P410
Del, Melinda E438
Del, Gabriel A539
Delabriere, Yann W159
Delacruz, John (Jack) E24
Delacruz, Cedric A429
Delafield, Michael (Mel) P554
Delagardelle, Pam P244
Delagi, R. Gregory (Greg) A859
Delancey, Virginia (Ginny) P362
Delaney, Douglas J. E117
Delaney, Scott (Scotty) A94
Delaney, BradleyBrad A200
Delaney, Chris A411
Delaney, Kristen (Kristy) A471
Delaney, Dan A606
Delaney, Thomas A. (Tom) A626
Delaney, Peter H (Pete) A745
DeLaney, William J. (Bill) A842
Delaney, Thomas A. (Tom) P345
Delaney, Michelle Anne P459
Delaney, Edward (Ed) P578
Delassio, Harry A727
Delatorre, Sarah P498
Delaunay, Diana (Ana) A163
DeLawder, C. Daniel (Dan) A676
Delay, Emmanuel W300
DelBene, Kurt A592
Delcher, Marilyn (Mar) A706
Deleonardis, Doreen P632
Delfino, Lisandro A44
Delgadillo, Dan A847
Delgado, Joaquin A2
Delgado, Osmel P519
Delgiorno, Rick (Ricky) P505
Delhomme, Jake E276
Delhomme, Jake A594
Delie, Vincent J. (Vince) E165
Delie, Vincent J. (Vince) A381
Deliema, Robert (Bob) E59
Delight, David (Dave) A981
Delin, Scott E391
Delio, Anthony (Tony) A476
Delis, I. W302
DeLise, Antonio L. (Tony) E256
Delisle, Dennis P14
Delisser, Denise A502
Delitta, John (Jack) A225
Delker, Jed A376
Dell, Joseph E. A215
Dell, Michael S. A934
Dellacroce, Peter (Pete) A782
Dellaquila, Frank J. A309
Dellazoppa, Steve A874
Dellenback, Steve (Stevie) P468
Dellert, Christine P550
Dellosa, Vince (Vinnie) A743
Dell'Erba, John (Jack) P303
Dell'Osso, Domenic J. (Nick) A193
Delmedico, Ann (Annie) A726
DeLoach, Thomas C. A75
Deloach, Angela (Ang) A319
DeLoach, Harris E. A805
Delohery, Andrew P404
DeLone, Lori P219
DeLong, Mark A A388
Delong, Mary Lee (Mar) P570
DeLongchamps, Peter C. A416
Delorenzo, Marc (Marcy) A166

Diamond, David A. A610
Diamond, Patrick (Paddy) A704
Diamond, Rachael (Rach) A866
Diamond, Gene P195
Diamond, David (Dave) P298
Diamond, Rachael (Rach) P540
Diamond, John P609
Dianis, Nancy P632
Dianwu, Lei W99
Diao, Charlie Diao Charlie (Charles) A236
Dias, Andre Pires de Oliveira W398
Diaz, Patrick E168
Diaz, Pedro E213
Diaz, Guillermo A203
Diaz, Amy J (Ames) A218
Diaz, Carlos (Carl) A400
Diaz, Carlos A400
Diaz, Pedro A468
Diaz, Al A479
Diaz, Michael (Mel) A502
Diaz, Paul J. A518
Diaz, Raymond A586
Diaz, Francisco A601
Diaz, Kathryn (Kat) A733
Diaz, Stephen (Steve) A851
Diaz, Daniel (Dan) A954
Diaz, Yvonne (Vonne) P56
Diaz, Amy J (Ames) P132
Diaz, Raymond P316
Diaz, Rose (Rosey) P354
Diaz, Jesse P385
Diaz, Maribel P460
Diaz-Cartelle, Juan A147
Dibble, Kathy (Kat) A18
Dibenedetto, Tony A926
DiBert, John W72
DiBianca, Suzanne A778
DiBlasi, Mark A. E361
Diblasi, Russ (Russell) A981
Dicarlo, Tony (Tone) A228
DiCaro, Daniel P. P359
Dicello, Mark A916
Dicenso, Frank A54
Dicenso, Darren (Darr) P108
Dicerchio, Richard (Dick) A247
DiCesare, Thor P108
DiCiurcio, John A. W6
DiCiurcio, John A. W184
Dick, Timothy A. (Tim) E15
Dickamore, Tony (Tone) A518
Dickenson, Ray A108
Dickenson, Bill A392
Dickenson, Sicily A646
Dickerman, Jonathan (John) A42
Dickerson, Gary E. A67
Dickerson, John C. P284
Dickerson, Staci P452
Dickey, Bill (Billy) A295
Dickie, Robert W427
Dickinson, Marty J. E420
Dickinson, Bruce (Brucey) A140
Dickinson, Laurie (Laur) A515
Dickinson, Paul A534
Dickinson, Marty J. A901
Dickman, Randy A565
Dicks, Cindy (Cin) A716
Dickseski, Jerri Fuller A466
Dickson, James (Jamie) E340
Dickson, David (Dave) A31
Dickson, Tom A114
Dickson, Mike (Mikey) A168
Dickson, John (Jack) A237
Dickson, Stephen A269
Dickson, Andrew W (Andy) A295
Dickson, Jenny A565
Dickson, Richard A570
Dickson, Tom P54
Dickson, Kevin P238
Dickson, Dick P539
Dickson, James M. (Jim) W147
Dicob, Andrew (Andy) E296
Dicob, Andrew (Andy) A615
DiCola, John F. A173
DiCola, John F. P105

Dicosimo, Vincent A845
Dicosola, Robert (Bob) A658
Dicuccio, Marge Hardt (Margaret) P18
Dicus, John B. A164
Diderich, Jeroen A91
Didier, David (Dave) A15
Didion, James J. P138
Didomizio, Michael A727
Diebold, Raymond J. P154
Diebold, Ann E P615
Dieck, Gretchen A697
Dieckerhoff, Klaus A98
Dieckhoner, Craig A83
Dieckman, Cathy (Cat) A368
Diede, Scott (Scotty) A580
Diede, Shannon P498
Diederich, Donna (Don) A236
Diederichs, Lutz W71
Diederichs, Lutz W399
Diedrich, Robert (Bob) A370
Diefenbach, Nina P534
Diefenderfer, William M. E115
Diefenthaler, Aaron P. A762
Diehl, William (Bill) E335
Diehl, Eileen A527
Diehl, William (Bill) A703
Diehl, Tara (Tar) A753
Diehl, Tracey (Trace) A761
Diehl, Kristine A954
Diekmann, Michael W58
Diekmann, Michael W237
Diemer, John W (Jack) A765
Diemer, John W (Jack) P421
Diercks, Dwight A649
Dieringer, Brian (Bri) A463
Diess, Herbert W62
Diess, Herbert W410
Dieter, Claus W149
Dietrich, Greg (Greggy) E257
Dietrich, Douglas T. (Doug) E278
Dietrich, Lavonne A260
Dietrich, Martin A. A617
Dietrich, Peter T. A807
Dietrich, Lavonne P155
Dietrich, Michael P196
Dietrich, Robert (Bob) P413
Dietsch, Johannes W60
Dietz, Edward R. E257
Dietz, Chris (Chrissy) A515
Dietz, William H (Bill) A745
Dietze, Steven J. P636
Diez, John J. A774
Difazio, Marc (Marcy) P120
Difonzo, Leslie A143
DiFrancesco, Paul E423
Diganci, Todd T. P186
DiGeronimo, Richard J. A190
Diggelmann, Roland W321
Digiovanni, Augie A309
DiGrande, Sebastian A865
Digregorio, Kelly A844
Diker, Charles M. E78
Diliberto, Michael P. E176
Dilkin, Blulyner A296
Dilkin, Blulyner P171
Dill, Robert C. E373
Dill, Melissa (Lissa) A77
Dill, Sean A136
Dill, David M. A542
Dill, Rob (Robbie) A585
Dill, Jeffrey A682
Dill, Robert C. A799
Dill, Melissa (Lissa) P41
Dillahunt, Sandra A296
Dillahunt, Sandra P171
Dillard, Dana E291
Dillard, James E. (Jim) A35
Dillard, Mike A274
Dillard, Alex A274
Dillard, William (Bill) A274
Dillard, Michael (Mel) A751
Dillard, Caitlin (Cait) P170
Dillard, Michael (Mel) P411
Diller, Barry A328
Dillingham, Jill (Jilly) P577

Dillner, Ian A927
Dillon, Roderick H. (Ric) E120
Dillon, Jenni E156
Dillon, Michael A. (Mike) A11
Dillon, Bob (Bo) A117
Dillon, Carl A120
Dillon, Molly A578
Dillon, Dave A607
Dillon, Bob (Bo) P63
Dillon, Steve (Stevie) P85
Dillow, Angela (Ang) A304
Dillworth, Angela (Ang) P401
DiLorenzo, Dennis A626
DiLorenzo, Dennis P345
Dilts, Sandra (Sandy) P460
DiLullo, John D. E149
Dilweg, Sean A588
Dimaggio, Leslie E42
Dimarco, Tony (Tone) P103
DiMario, Stephanie A972
DiMartino, Chris A429
Dimino, Sal (Salvitore) A124
Dimon, James (Jamie) A504
Dimond, Kirsten A531
Dimopoulos, Dimitrios G. W269
Dimos, Chris (Chrissy) A576
DiNapoli, Mark L. P492
DiNapoli, Michael (Mike) P492
DiNatale, Penny (Penn) A753
Dincer, Haluk W177
Dineen, Thomas A. E386
DiNello, Alessandro P. A377
Dinello, Anthony (Tony) A706
Dingemans, Simon W171
Dinger, Stephanie (Steph) A901
Dinger, Stephanie (Steph) P577
Dingle, Rick A649
Dingle, David K. W86
Dingus, Roger A911
Dinh, Trang A44
Dinh, Theresa (Terry) A602
Dinicola, Natalie A601
Dinkins, David H (Dave) P413
Dinn, Colin R. W345
Dinnage, Susanna A277
Dinndorf, Steven A383
Dinnie, Holly P65
Dinon, Nancy P370
Dinsmore, Bradford R. (Brad) A834
Dinsmore, Robert (Bob) P56
Dinwiddie, Lucy (Lucia) A239
Din□şer, Suzan Sabanci W17
Dioguardi, Chuck (Chucky) A87
Dion, Ellen (Elle) E295
Dion, Robert (Bob) A502
Dion, Ellen (Elle) A615
Dion, Jeffrey P. (Jeff) P347
DiPalma, Greg (Greggy) A973
Dipalma, Penny P590
Dipetrio, Kenneth A133
DiPietro, Kenneth A. (Ken) A133
DiPietro, Joseph A. P603
Dipoto, John (Jack) A776
Dippolito, Tom A275
Dipre, Sharon E150
Diprofio, Karen (Kare) A44
Dircks, Bill (Billy) A104
Diresta, Pat (Patty) E312
Dirks, Douglas D. E135
Dirks, Patricia (Pat) E367
Dirks, Paricia E367
Dirks, Douglas D. A310
Dirnberger, Cathy (Cat) A576
Dirocco, Richard (Dick) A871
Dirrim, Tim A465
DiRusso, Lonny R. A772
Disabato, Michael (Mel) E176
Disalvo, Frank P144
Disanti, Joseph (Jo) A112
Disanto, Phil (Philly) E1
DiSanto, Edmund (Ed) A50
Discala, Michael A205
Diserens, Georges A699
Dishaw, Michael P60
Dishman, William M. A829

DiSilvestro, Anthony P. A160
Diss, Alex (Al) A766
Diss, Alex (Al) P421
Disser, Barbara (Barb) A140
Dissing, Steven (Steve) A576
Dissinger, Debra E. E331
Dissinger, Ronald L. (Ron) A510
Dissinger, Debra E. A691
Dissosway, Marc A425
Distefano, Michael E236
DiStefano, Mike E334
Distefano, Michael A136
DiStefano, Mike A703
Ditmars, John B (Jack) A369
Ditmore, Jim W125
Ditmore, Jim W126
Ditocco, Phyllis A139
Ditondo, Michelle A589
Dittamo, Andrew (Andy) E327
Dittgen, Juergen A745
DiTullio, Steve P515
Divilly, Yvonne W128
DiVittorio, Thomas (Tom) A401
DiVittorio, Theresa (Terry) A831
Divjak, Barbara (Barb) P338
Divone, Charles (Chas) E300
Divver, James J Divver James J (Jamie) A981
Dix, Ronald (Ron) E47
Dix, Anne (Annie) A78
Dix, Thomas B. A970
Dixon, Bret A544
Dixon, Gordon A48
Dixon, Jean A168
Dixon, Gregory A215
Dixon, Jim A252
Dixon, T A544
Dixon, David (Dave) A689
Dixon, Robert L. A692
Dixon, Catherine (Cathy) A747
Dixon, Liz (Lizzie) A874
Dixon, Mark A959
Dixon, David P34
Dixon, John W248
Dixon-Williams, Sherrie P533
Diya, Fadi M. A40
Djalali, Chaden P553
Djerejian, Robert E166
Djukic, Dusko A514
Dmowski, George (Georgey) A785
Do, Beth (Betty) A305
Doan, Dan L. A657
Doane, Jase A472
Dobak, Scott (Scotty) E361
Dobb, Kay E335
Dobb, Kay A703
Dobbe, Steven A48
Dobbeck, Dianne A340
Dobber, Ruud W37
Dobbins, R. Helm A47
Dobbins, Doug (Dougie) A364
Dobbs, Jeff A753
Dobie, Linda (Lin) P564
Dobkin, Arkadiy E140
Dobney, Fredrick P633
Dobranski, Edward J. E160
Dobranski, Edward J. A373
Dobrinski, Everett M. A218
Dobrinski, Everett M. P132
Dobrosky, Laurie (Laur) A866
Dobrosky, Laurie (Laur) P540
Dobzyn, Andrew (Andy) A79
Dochelli, Harry A322
Docherty, John E212
Dockendorff, Charles A147
Dockerty, Karen (Kare) A180
Docter, Judith M. A78
Docter, Judy A78
Docter, Judy (Jude) A78
Dodd, Jerry A643
Doddridge, Derek (Der) E84
Dodds, Thomas E. (Ted) P144
Dodenhoff, Steven W. A477
Dodge, Bob E214
Dodge, R. Stanton A279

A = AMERICAN BUSINESS
E = EMERGING COMPANIES
P = PRIVATE COMPANIES
W = WORLD BUSINESS

Farley, Suzie T. A321
Farley, James D. (Jim) A384
Farley, Terry (Terr) A449
Farley, Thomas W. (Tom) A480
Farley, Tara A539
Farley, Catherine (Cate) A654
Farley, Robert (Bob) A766
Farley, Dan A824
Farley, John (Jack) P292
Farley, Robert (Bob) P421
Farley, Joshua (Josh) P607
Farmer, Stephen (Steve) E70
Farmer, William (Bill) A20
Farmer, Scott A129
Farmer, Scott D. A202
Farmer, Curtis C. A227
Farmer, Marc (Marcy) A228
Farmer, Carla A347
Farmer, Theresa (Terry) A753
Farmer, Edgar (Ed) A866
Farmer, Jerry (Jerr) A972
Farmer, Edgar (Ed) P540
Farner, David M. A919
Farner, David M. P598
Farnsworth, Ronald L. (Ron) E420
Farnsworth, Bryan D. A453
Farnsworth, David (Dave) A747
Farnsworth, Ronald L. (Ron) A901
Farr, Bradley A223
Farr, David N. A308
Farr, Kevin M. A570
Farr, David (Dave) P491
Farrah, Tom (Tommy) A291
Farrah, Thomas (Thom) A291
Farrall, Ann (Annie) A641
Farrand, Stephen A579
Farrand, Cindy (Cin) P535
Farrar, Rick E400
Farrar, Jeffrey W. E421
Farrar, Jeffrey W. A902
FARRELL, JAMES (Jamie) E78
Farrell, Jay (JayJay) E141
Farrell, Pam (Pamela) E265
Farrell, Michael S. E366
Farrell, Peter A109
Farrell, Ashley (Ash) A120
Farrell, John (Jack) A220
Farrell, Thomas F. A285
Farrell, Todd A536
Farrell, William J. (Bill) A554
Farrell, Pam (Pamela) A572
Farrell, Michael (Mel) A726
Farrell, Marc (Marcy) A820
Farrell, Mike A875
Farrell, Scott A895
Farrell, Breege A. A922
Farrell, Edward (Ed) P288
Farrell, Benny P317
Farrell, Mary C. P642
Farrell, Garry W242
Farrell, Joanne W318
Farrell, Joanne W320
Farren, Sean A824
Farrier, Joe (Joey) P339
Farris, J. Matt A455
Farris, Cherie A621
Farris, Kristofer M. A756
Farshing, Dave (Davie) E375
Fartaj, Vandad E328
Fartaj, Vandad E329
Fartaj, Vandad A686
Farthing, Dana A464
Faruqui, Rizwan A539
Farver, Harry A465
Farwell, Wildon A133
Farzaie, Rahim E413
Fasano, David E169
Fasano, Mario A136
Fasano, Rebecca (Becca) A140

Fash, Boni P632
Fasolo, Peter M. A499
Fasshauer, Nicole (Nikki) A963
Fassig, Gerry E109
Fassio, James S. A771
FASSNACHT, MATTHEW (Matt) A226
Fast, Curt A692
Fath, Mike (Mikey) A156
Fathers, Bill A934
Fatovic, Robert D. A774
Fattore, Doreen A409
Faubion, J. Patrick (Pat) A227
Faucett, Robert (Bob) E49
Faucett, Robert (Bob) A99
Faucette, Bill P131
Fauchet, Philippe P557
Fauconneau, Janie (Jan) A180
Faujour, Olivier A398
Faul, Mark A869
Faul, Mark P560
Faulcon, Lecretia M A18
Faulk, Brent A194
Faulkner, Fred (Freddy) E140
Faulkner, Robert (Bob) E322
Faulkner, Robert (Bob) A677
Faulmann, Maud A194
Faure, Maurice W175
Faury, Guillaume W15
Fauser, Frank A641
Faust, Susan A20
Faust, Wendy A180
Faust, Helen A280
Faust, Lisa (Lis) A672
Faust, Susan (Sue) A743
Faust, Phil A743
Faver, Robert (Bob) A899
Favorite, Annette (Anne) A485
Favre, Ritu E395
Favre, Michel W159
Fawcett, Charles C. E415
Fawcett, John J. A209
Fawcett, Charles C. A888
Fawcett, Karen W358
Fawley, Daniel A (Dan) A760
Faxon, David (Dave) P514
Fay, Gerald W. (Gerry) A94
Fay, Jeffery (Jeff) A426
Fay, Jason A784
Fayad, Walid A143
Faz, Vanessa (Nessa) E159
Faz, Vanessa (Nessa) A365
Faz, Patricia (Pat) A743
Fazio, Richie A164
Fazzio, Luiz W88
Fazzolari, Robert (Bob) A625
Fazzolari, Robert (Bob) P344
Fazzone, Paul (Pauly) A934
Feagin, Amy E221
Feagin, Amy A474
Fearing, Robert (Bob) A576
Fearon, Matthew (Matt) A855
Featherstone, Craig (Craigy) P278
Fechko, Karen A18
Fedacsek, Joseph A641
Fedelin, Jocelyn (Lyn) A764
Feder, Francine A383
Feder, Eric A536
Federenko, Garvin P13
Federici, Joseph (Jo) A589
Federico, Peter (Pete) A500
Federico, Rick A824
Federico, David A874
Federico, Anthony J. A891
Federighi, Craig A66
Fedor, Laura A835
Fedorchak, Bill (Billy) A463
Fedus, Natalie (Nat) A964
Fedyszyn, Karen A9
Fedyszyn, Karen P5
Fee, Valerie (Val) E250
Feehan, William (Bill) A470
Feekes, Stan P185
Feeler, Jeffrey R. (Jeff) E427
Feeley, Brian (Bri) E315
Feeley, Pat (Patty) P176

Feeney, Brian J. A185
Feenstra, Gregory A84
Feenstra, Randall P101
Fees, Jym E374
Fees, Jym A799
Fehler, Colleen E208
Fehler, Colleen A448
Fehling, Bradley A94
Fehlman, Paul W. E44
Fehlman, Robert A. E373
Fehlman, Robert A. A799
Fehr, David (Dave) A866
Fehr, Rick (Ricky) P194
Fehr, David (Dave) P540
Fehrer, David (Dave) A972
Fehringer, Rich A645
Fehringer, Rich P360
Fehser, Kathy (Kat) P490
Feigelman, Theodor P47
Feigenbaum, Gregory A109
Feiger, Mitchell S. E264
Feiger, Mitchell S. A572
Feigin, Michael M. E44
FEILER, LEONARD B (Len) A344
Feinberg, Hill A. E204
Feinberg, David M. A42
Feiner, Barbara A. P559
Feinstein, Eric A77
Feinstein, Leonard (Lenny) A124
Feinstein, Scott (Scotty) A934
Feinstein, Eric P41
Feist, Matt A674
Feitt, Ted (Teddy) A584
Feitzinger, Edward G. (Ed) A37
Fejer, Paul (Pauly) A439
Fejes, Balazs E140
Felcht, Utz-Hellmuth W130
Feld, Karen A295
Feld, Steve (Stevie) A905
Feldhaus, Paul A689
Feldman, Eli (Elijah) E140
Feldman, Lev A208
Feldman, Nancy (Nance) A520
Feldman, Alan (Al) A589
Feldman, Dan (Danny) A927
Feldman, Mike A971
Feldman, Amy (Ames) A979
Feldman, Brant P47
Feldman, Dorothy (Doroth) P354
Feldmann, Dennis A929
Felenstein, Craig A278
Felice, Gregorio de W202
Feliciano, Julio A579
Felis, Sandra L. P556
Felix, Greg (Greggy) A183
Felix, Natalie (Nat) A360
Felix, Marshall (Marsh) P492
Felix, Jose Antonio Guaraldi W26
Felke, Magnus A736
Felkins, Jay A177
Felkins, Jay (JayJay) A178
Felkner, Joseph (Joe) P219
Fell, Robin A14
Fell, Robin P9
Fellahi, Khalid A954
Feller, Brad E222
Felletter, John E37
Fellman, Dan A873
Fellmeth, Joellyn A800
Fellure, Diana A84
Felman, David (Dave) A410
Felson, David (Dave) P83
Felten, Ronald P317
Felton, Jerry A911
Felty, Craig P237
Fendley, Russ (Russell) A597
Fenech, Josie A228
Feng, April A56
Fenlon, Erin A A423
Fenn, Frank W128
Fennell, George (Georgey) E214
Fennell, Laura A. A494
Fennell, Charles J. P480
Fenner, Kristi E33
Fennessey, Mike A545

Fennessey, Mike P279
Fennessy, Gary P360
Fenning, Armita P564
Fenske, David (Dave) P170
Fenster, Jeanne (Jeannie) A429
Fenstermaker, William H. E213
Fenstermaker, William H. A469
Fenton, Sheila (Sheil) P399
Fenton, Dan P566
Fenves, Gregory L. P604
Fenwick, Sandra L. P517
Fenza, Daniel (Dan) P123
Feragen, Jody (Jode) A453
Ferando, Jim A115
Ferando, Jim P54
Feraud, Pierre W160
Ferber, Scott A485
Ferchland-Parella, Joanne (Jojo) P363
Ferdig, Larry A603
Ferebee, Ellen (Elle) P448
Ferencz, Steven M. P108
Fergus, Conner A874
Ferguson, Thomas E. (Tom) E44
Ferguson, Robert A E203
Ferguson, Roy C. A100
Ferguson, T. Ritson A174
Ferguson, Walter A182
Ferguson, Joel A315
Ferguson, Brad (Brady) A360
Ferguson, Mike A576
Ferguson, Carley A596
Ferguson, Carley A596
Ferguson, James (Jamie) A641
Ferguson, Roger A657
Ferguson, Tom A820
Ferguson, Rhonda S. A903
Ferguson, David (Dave) A937
Ferguson, Stewart P13
Ferguson, Chris P169
Ferguson, Joel I. P320
Ferguson, Richard C. P404
Ferguson, John R. P509
Ferguson, Margie P571
Ferguson, Deedra P591
Ferguson-McHugh, Mary L. A719
Feringa, David (Dave) E149
Ferlita, Maria (Mary) P287
Fermo, Anthony (Tony) A163
Fern, Tommie A665
Fern, Francine (Fran) P399
Fern??ndez, Jorge E80
Fernandes, Joel A E407
Fernandes, Paulo A569
Fernandes, Cindy A846
Fernandes, Al P574
Fernandes, Sidney P602
Fernandez, Jorge E80
Fernandez, Emil E331
Fernandez, Miguel A94
Fernandez, Manny (Emanuel) A218
Fernandez, George A248
Fernandez, Jeff (Jeffy) A462
Fernandez, Ruben (Ben) A523
Fernandez, Manny A933
Fernandez, Manny (Emanuel) P132
Fernandez, Carolyn (Carol) P431
Fernandez, Aurelio M. P460
Fernandez, Richard W. P514
Fernandez, Pua P572
Fernandez, Daniel W88
Fernandez, Manuel W235
Fernandez, Ramon W293
Fernandez-Ayala, Barbara (Barb) A208
Ferndinand, Norma P528
Ferns, Peter A409
Fern□ndez, Jos© P550
Fern□ndez, V□ctor Turpaud W147
Ferracone, Robin A. A166
Ferracone, Robin A. P171
Ferrada, Brigitte A164
Ferraioli, Brian K. A508
Ferrando, Jonathan P. A88
Ferrando, Carrie P112
Ferranti, Richard M. P417
Ferrara, Gary W. E122

A = AMERICAN BUSINESS
E = EMERGING COMPANIES
P = PRIVATE COMPANIES
W = WORLD BUSINESS

Gorkov, Sergey W336
Gorlick, Stan P136
Gorman, Robert M. (Rob) E421
Gorman, Norma A30
Gorman, Rick (Ricky) A325
Gorman, Pete A383
Gorman, Christopher M. (Chris) A514
Gorman, James P. A602
Gorman, Jim (Jimmy) A689
Gorman, Mark J. A704
Gorman, Robert M. (Rob) A902
Gorman, Piers A965
Gorman, Kathleen E. Chavanu P120
Gorman, Kathleen Chavanu P120
Gormley, Frank (Frankie) A228
Gormley, Ken P172
Gormley, Kathleen K. P622
Gorney, David J. P511
Gorno, Mary Louise P551
Gorrall, Jeffrey A384
Gorrie, Thomas M. P172
Gorriz, Michael W358
Gorsage, Michael (Mel) P190
Gorsky, Alex A499
Gorsuch, Jayme A706
Gorton, Scott A912
Gorzkowicz, Matt (Matty) P593
Gosebruch, Henry O. A6
Gosling, Brian A94
Gosling, Mark A621
Goss, Cathy P. A418
Goss, David (Dave) A718
Goss, Andreas J. W385
Gosselin, Eugene (Gene) A733
Gossen, Viki P401
Gossert, Deb P555
Gosset, Julia (Jules) A569
Goswami, Ranjan A269
Goswick, Jean (Jeannie) A92
Gotanda, John Y. P615
Gotelli, Robert (Bob) A107
Goto, Katsuhiro W340
Gottesfeld, Stephen P. A628
Gottesman, Janice (Jan) A18
Gottfried, John E6
Gotti, Paul (Pauly) A166
Gottlieb, Julie E177
Gottlieb, Katherine P13
Gottlieb, Jonathan E. P237
Gottmann, David (Dave) A351
Gottner, Marty (Mart) A616
Gottschalk, Therese (Terri) A77
Gottschalk, Adrian A133
Gottschalk, Keith A659
Gottschalk, Therese (Terri) P41
Gottschalk, Helmut W139
Gottschling, Andreas W156
Gottscho, Richard A. (Rick) A529
Gottsegen, Jonathan (John) A912
Gottstein, Thomas P. W118
Gottuso, Vince (Vinnie) A255
Gottwals, Bill A368
Gotwals, Janet (Jan) A101
Gotwalt, Darryl E418
Gou, Terry T.M. W185
Goudie, Craig A769
Gough, Mitzy A139
Gough, Howard A198
Gough, Lisa A843
Goulart, Steven J. A584
Gould, Heather (Heath) E53
Gould, Matthew J. E314
Gould, Fredric H. E314
Gould, Rob A115
Gould, Anthony (Tony) A204
Gould, Mark A. A342
Gould, Rachael (Rach) A370
Gould, Dan A629
Gould, Vicky (Vic) A718

Gould, Eric (Ric) A926
Gould, Rob P54
Goulet, Beverly K. A41
Goulet, Matthew (Matt) A765
Goumans, Marcus W179
Gourdikian, Linda (Lin) A256
Gourlay, Alex A939
Gouveia, Jeffrey (Jeff) P492
Gouveia, Jeffrey P492
Gouveia, Jeff (Jeffy) P492
Govan, Christopher A. (Chris) W292
Gove, Matt P387
Governo, Tina (Tin) A287
Govindan, Shivan A372
Govoni, David P364
Gowen, James (Jamie) A105
Gowen, Kevin P. A841
Gowen, Joseph (Jo) A965
Gower, Greg E76
Gowetski, Mark (Marky) E42
Gowland, Charles L (Charlie) A451
Gozon, Richard C. P561
Graaf, Raymond de E229
Graaf, Raymond (Ray) E229
Graaf, Bill Van de A223
Graaf, Bill (Billy) A223
Graass, James H. (Jim) E127
Graber, Ethel A62
Grabowski, John (Jack) P103
Grace, Jeffrey (Jeff) E155
Grace, Manuel G (Mannie) A281
Grace, Estherann P517
Grace, Adrian W10
Gracheck, Jack (Jackie) E265
Gracheck, Jack (Jackie) A572
Graci, Mike E436
Graci, Micheal (Mike) A135
Graddick-Weir, Mirian M. A579
Graddy, Steve P197
Grade, Joel T. A843
Gradisher, Linda (Lin) A789
Grady, Gerry A347
Grady, Ronald (Ron) P218
Graf, Jonathan A. E24
Graf, R. Mark A276
Graf, Alan B. A344
Graf, Mike (Mikey) A370
Graf, Judy (Jude) A392
Grafe, Karl A46
Graff, Bill A187
Graff, Jamie (James) A745
Gragnolati, Brian A. P254
Graham, Andrew L. E192
Graham, Linda H (Lin) E255
Graham, Michelle (Michie) E321
Graham, Peter M. (Pete) E340
Graham, Jett E372
Graham, Ross E453
Graham, Jonathan P. A55
Graham, Bob A60
Graham, Mark R (Marky) A84
Graham, Bryan (Bry) A175
Graham, Jonathan (John) A262
Graham, Dan A291
Graham, Kristin A328
Graham, Brian (Bri) A333
Graham, Shannon (Shan) A347
Graham, Renee A415
Graham, Heather A665
Graham, John A732
Graham, Jordan (Jordy) A762
Graham, Deeney A780
Graham, Melissa (Lissa) A796
Graham, Christopher A. (Chris) A827
Graham, Randy A882
Graham, Devin A893
Graham, Karyn A899
Graham, Ned A912
Graham, Randolph H. P336
Graham, Melissa (Lissa) P454
Graham, Peter P469
Grahmann, Chuck A44
Grainger, Guy A501
Grajeda, Jessica P530

Gram, Dwight P417
Grama, Harish A504
Grambart, Sean P100
Grambergs, Mark E129
Gramlich, Tom A489
Gramling, Matilde P190
Granata, Jessica P363
Granberry, Debbie (Deb) A236
Granchi, Annie A411
Granchi, Annie (Ann) A411
Grande, Joe (Joey) A156
Granderson, David W (Dave) A613
Grandinetti, Russell A37
Grandmaison, Francine (Fran) A689
Graney, Kevin M (Kev) A395
Grange, Benoit E432
Granger, Dennis E110
Granger, Bill E444
Granger, Darron A157
Granger, Debbie (Deb) A520
Graninger, Clark D. W30
Grannis, Dick (Dicky) A736
Grannis, Dick A736
Grant, Victor (Vic) E39
Grant, Victor E39
Grant, Joan E126
Grant, David (Dave) E236
Grant, John W (Jack) E354
Grant, John A453
Grant, Janet A18
Grant, Tim (Timmy) A69
Grant, Marilee A146
Grant, Melanie (Mel) A154
Grant, Joan A298
Grant, Hugh A601
Grant, Jeffrey A643
Grant, Jeffrey (Jeff) A789
Grant, Jasmine A835
Grant, Thomas P8
Grant, Tom (Tommy) P8
Grant, Kenneth P254
Grant, Brenda (Bren) P555
Grant-anderson, Belinda A83
Grantham, Robert F. E431
Grantham, Deborah (Deb) A20
Grantham, Leigh (Leah) P394
Gras, Horst E. E47
Grasman, Scott (Scotty) P423
Grass, Joe (Joey) A835
Grass, Linda P505
Grasse, Nancy (Nance) A899
Grasser, Jeff A899
Grasshoff, Michaela A565
Grasso, Sebastian A136
Grasso, Maria A. A380
Grasso, Davide A634
Grasso, Alfred P535
Grasty, Kevin P29
Grauer, Scott B. A141
Graupman, Dustin A972
Gravanis, Georges A91
Gravel, Louis E179
Gravel, Karine A696
Gravel, Monique W85
Gravelle, Ralph (Ralphy) E222
Gravelle, Michael L. (Mike) A346
Gravelle, Ralph (Ralphy) A475
Graves, Gregory B. (Greg) E140
Graves, Greg (Greggy) E140
Graves, Chris E340
Graves, Brad (Brady) A3
Graves, William W. A90
Graves, Victoria (Tori) A267
GRAVES, SHAWN A463
Graves, Christopher A581
Graves, Jason A607
Graves, Jennifer A498
Grawe, George A31
Gray, Robin (Rin) E49
Gray, Sean A. E56
Gray, James W. E356
Gray, Douglas (Doug) A78
Gray, Robin (Rin) A99
Gray, Steve A120
Gray, Sean A. A128

Gray, Jonathan D. A136
Gray, Harry W (Hare) A140
Gray, Chris A280
Gray, Paul (Pauly) A307
Gray, Shay A379
Gray, Jonathan D. A442
Gray, Jim A476
Gray, Jeff A553
Gray, Michael (Mel) A606
Gray, Diedre A709
Gray, Maureen (Maury) A743
Gray, James W. A757
Gray, Melanie (Mel) A855
Gray, David J. A866
Gray, Ginny (Gin) A887
Gray, Myron A. A910
Gray, David L. P57
Gray, Larry W. P57
Gray, Shawn P77
Gray, Chip P129
Gray, Jeffrey (Jeff) P192
Gray, John P459
Gray, Judy (Jude) P483
Gray, Maria (Mary) P490
Gray, Jarrod P531
Gray, David J. P540
Gray, Linda P550
Gray, Stephanie (Steph) P589
Gray, Gary W265
Graye, Lisa A228
Grayfer, Valery I. W305
Graysmark, Phil A855
Grayson, Alan A344
Grayson, Andrea A746
Grayuski, Thomas J. A321
Graziano, Pete (Petey) A156
Graziano, Elise (Elisabeth) A621
Graziano, Thomas (Thom) A624
Graziano, Paul A831
Grazioli, John (Jack) A603
Grealish, Joe (Joey) A347
Greaney, Howard (Howie) P168
Greasheimer, Sharon A166
Greathouse, Steven R. E104
Greaves, Jon E347
Grebenc, Jane A359
Grebinar, Jonathan (John) E169
Greca, Anita A751
Greca, Anita P411
Grech, Jim A376
Grech, Joe A649
Grech, Brent A664
Greco, Thomas R. (Tom) A13
Greco, Anneke A502
Greco, Ignazio A584
Greco, Joseph (Jo) A649
Greco, John R. A678
Greco, Suzanne P168
Greco, Mario W427
Greear, Ken (Kenny) A904
Greek, Darby A247
Greek, Bonnie (Bonbon) P17
Greeley, Neal A15
Green, William E37
Green, Richard C. E108
Green, Cliff (Clifford) E123
Green, Craig E231
Green, William H. E285
Green, Gary (Gar) E335
Green, Stacy (Stace) E359
Green, Suzanne (Sue) A7
Green, Mark A16
Green, Phil (Philly) A135
Green, Saryia A206
Green, Jeff (Jeffy) A208
Green, Phillip D. A252
Green, Frederec A268
Green, Allen R. A286
Green, Chris A295
Green, Dana A341
Green, Chris (Chrissy) A455
Green, Terri A485
Green, Elle A500
Green, Mark A. A512
Green, David (Dave) A553

Green, Darryl E. A558
Green, Bryan (Bry) A617
Green, Allyson A626
Green, Gary (Gar) A703
Green, Roberta (Berta) A746
Green, Amanda (Mandy) A753
Green, Ryan A809
Green, Barbara (Barb) A843
Green, Michael W (Mel) A843
Green, David (Dave) A860
Green, Nancy A865
Green, Monique (Mo) A896
Green, Paul S. A909
Green, Tara (Tar) A937
Green, Jon P23
Green, Warren P228
Green, Gail P239
Green, Tracy (Trace) P272
Green, Warren P277
Green, Luz P287
Green, Allyson P345
Green, David S (Dave) P413
Green, Jane P415
Green, Teressia P469
Green, Tina (Tin) P506
Green, Debbie (Deb) P535
Green, Katherine (Kate) P604
Green, Gary R. W112
Green-Hankins, Joyce (Joy) A706
Green-Kelley, Taira A A18
Greenawalt, Richard A. P170
Greenberg, Larry (Lar) E25
Greenberg, Greg E300
Greenberg, Dave (Davie) A87
Greenberg, Karen L (Kare) A175
Greenberg, Todd A341
Greenberg, Laurie (Laur) A598
Greenberg, Gary (Gar) A780
Greenberg, Raymond S. A921
Greenberg, Andrew (Andy) A930
Greenberg, Jack M. A955
Greenberg, Mark L (Marky) P170
Greenberg, Lawrence P511
Greenberg, Raymond S. P605
Greenberg, Evan G. W104
Greenblatt, Robert (Bob) A225
Greene, Jeff W (Jeffy) E161
Greene, George E371
Greene, Aaron E372
Greene, Mike A51
Greene, Robert (Bob) A119
Greene, Jason K. A129
Greene, Peter (Pete) A159
Greene, Tom A223
Greene, Todd A340
Greene, Yoonhi A340
Greene, Jeff W (Jeffy) A373
Greene, Brian (Bri) A685
Greene, Greg (Greggy) A774
Greene, Douglas (Doug) A779
Greene, George A798
Greene, Aaron A798
Greene, Ryan A980
Greene, Michael (Mel) P160
Greene, Mary P482
Greene, David (Dave) P551
Greene, Timothy J. P633
Greener, Todd (Toddy) A13
Greener, Geoffrey S. A104
Greenfeig, Sid A589
Greenfield, Andrew J. E4
Greenfield, Susan W (Sue) A112
Greenfield, David B (Dave) A423
Greenfield, David A824
Greengold, Nancy P378
Greenhaw, Mark (Marky) E51
Greenhaw, Mark (Marky) A111
Greenleaf, Peter S. E387
Greenleaf, Lari A514
Greenleaf, Chris (Chrissy) A563
Greenlees, Jim (Jimmy) P632
Greenspan, Steven A550
Greenspan, Peter (Pete) A680
Greenspan, Cary A706
Greenspan, Peter (Pete) P377

Greenspon, Tom A143
Greenstein, Sara A. A913
Greenstein, Scott P408
Greenwald, Judy P501
Greenwald, Julie P623
Greenwalt, Rodgers K. A129
Greenwell, Melissa E156
Greenwell, John P212
Greenwood, Nigel A44
Greenwood, Jon A465
Greenwood, James (Jamie) A925
Greenya, Cyril J. A286
Greer, Joe A83
Greer, K. Gordon A101
Greer, Emily A393
Greer, Briand A449
Greer, Greg (Greggy) A834
Greer, Louis E. A889
Greer, Gerald (Jerry) P6
Greeter, Gerald A675
Gref, Herman W336
Greff, Brian A494
Greffin, Judith P (Jude) A31
Grefstad, Odd Arild W359
Greg, Bradford E15
Gregg, Levante E56
Gregg, Robin (Rin) E163
Gregg, Levante A128
Gregg, Michael (Mel) A439
Gregg, Andrew A727
Gregg, Debi P403
Gregg, Virginia (Ginny) P414
Gregoire, Brent E176
Gregoire, Andrew J. E242
Gregoire, Kevin P. A376
Gregoire, Daniel N. (Dan) A557
Gregorian, Myra (Miranda) P281
Gregory, Trent E226
Gregory, Brian (Bri) E397
Gregory, Jonathan (Jon) E404
Gregory, Ramon (Ray) A166
Gregory, Lentz A369
Gregory, Markeba A395
Gregory, Catherine (Cate) A429
Gregory, Trent A491
Gregory, Sherman A736
Gregory, Jonathan (Jon) A858
Gregory, Suzanne (Sue) A968
Gregory, Carolyn (Carol) P103
Gregory, Raymond (Ray) P187
Gregory, Sean J. P219
Gregory, Sean J. P228
Gregory, Willis P374
Gregory, Bryan P390
Gregs, Ron (Ronnie) E443
Greiff, David E128
Greindl, Jean-Marie A711
Greiner, James (Jim) E12
Greiner, Mark (Marky) A202
Greiner, Kerry (Kerr) A351
Greiner, Glenn A430
Greis, Patrick (Paddy) P556
Grele, Kathy E264
Grele, Kathy A572
Grell, Jared (Jare) A101
Grenfell-Gardner, Jason E402
Grennan, Lynn P55
Grensteiner, Ronald J. (Ron) A42
Grenz, Kay (KayKay) A3
Grenz, Dianne M. A926
Grescovich, Mark J. E52
Grescovich, Mark J. A113
Grese, Frank A416
Greslick, Richard L A215
Grether, James (Jamie) A981
Grether, Sally P555
Gretz, Kevin (Kev) E189
Gretz, Joseph (Jo) A897
Gretz, Joseph (Jo) P575
Greubel, Scott P169
Greulich, Lynn (Lyn) A657
Grev, Jeff (Jeffy) A453
Greve, Norman de A258
Grewcock, Bruce E. A694
Grewcock, Bruce E. P382

Grexa, Karen (Kare) A514
Grey, Robert (Bob) A712
Grey, Brad A930
Greyber, Rob A328
Grice, Bill A502
Grice, Raleigh A972
Grici, Donna (Don) A883
Griebeler, Jeff (Jeffy) A665
Grieco, Francesco A18
Grieder, Daniel A732
Grier, Paul (Pauly) E355
Grier, Donna (Don) A295
Grier, Robin (Rin) A841
Grier, Timothy (Tim) P52
Grier, Rosa (Rosaline) P506
Griesbaum, Robert (Bob) P477
Griesemer, Daniel (Dan) E407
Grieshaber, Matthew L. (Matt) P15
Griest, Susan (Sue) P369
Griffin, William F. (Bill) E38
Griffin, Tom E60
Griffin, Stacey E168
Griffin, Mark E. E311
Griffin, Michael (Mel) E443
Griffin, Brian A62
Griffin, Ronald B. (Ron) A90
Griffin, Corey A. A145
Griffin, Elizabeth (Beth) A180
Griffin, Michael (Mel) A207
Griffin, Carla (Carly) A208
Griffin, Dan (Danny) A218
Griffin, Matthew (Matt) A228
Griffin, Phil (Philly) A371
Griffin, David (Dave) A619
Griffin, Carl A664
Griffin, James (Jamie) A780
Griffin, Monty J. A795
Griffin, John A824
Griffin, Ken (Kenny) A849
Griffin, Steven A903
Griffin, Sean F. A909
Griffin, Darragh A963
Griffin, Jack P. P48
Griffin, Frank (Frankie) P150
Griffin, James D. P158
Griffin, Desi P303
Griffin, Sandra (Sandy) P592
Griffis, Mark P1
Griffith, Dennis M. E79
Griffith, John B. A1
Griffith, Dennis M. A165
Griffith, Roger (Rog) A194
Griffith, Bettyann A341
Griffith, Betty A341
Griffith, Barbara H (Barb) A348
Griffith, Timothy T. A561
Griffith, Jill (Jilly) A692
Griffith, S. Patricia (Tricia) A721
Griffith, Annette (Anne) A752
Griffith, Derek A761
Griffith, Kimberly (Kim) A947
Griffith, Brian (Bri) P317
Griffith, Darrell P591
Griffith, Chris W29
Griffiths, James (Jamie) A619
Griffiths, Moira A696
Griffiths, Lynne A764
Griffiths, Ed (Eddie) A883
Griffiths, Andy A929
Griffiths, Diana (Ana) P476
Griffiths, Guy W39
Griffiths, Peter L. W207
Griffo, Michael (Mel) E165
Griffo, Michael (Mel) A381
Grigaux, Paul (Pauly) A305
Grigaux, Paul J. A807
Grigg, Jeffrey (Jeff) A130
Grigg, David G. A355
Griggs, Stewart E51
Griggs, Kathleen M. (Kathy) E229
Griggs, Nelson E359
Griggs, Stewart A110
Griggs, W.G. (Trey) A157
Griggs, Trey A157
Griggs, Malcolm D. A209

Griggs, Mitch (Mitchell) A295
Griggs, H. James P138
Griggs, Johnny (John) P240
Griggs, Andrew (Andy) P587
Grignon, Perianne A789
Grigorev, Roman (Jerome) P550
Grigsby, Jennifer (Jen) A193
Grigsby, Phillip (Phil) A295
Grill, Michael E84
Grillo, Scott (Scotty) A776
Grillo, Robert P190
Grima, Crocefissa A624
Grimes, Thomas L. (Tom) E275
Grimes, Christopher (Chris) A61
Grimes, Jennifer A252
Grimes, Joseph P. (Joe) A854
Grimes, Sally A893
Grimes, Michael (Mel) P108
Grimes, Robert R. P193
Grimmer, Ralph J. E403
Grimminger, Kurt A966
Grimminger, Kurt P640
Grimstone, Gerry W55
Grimstone, Gerry W56
Grinberg, Paul J. E64
Grinberg, Paul J. E137
Grinberg, Paul J. A141
Grindstaff, Nick A737
Grinnell, David A. E65
Grinnell, Bruce A343
Grinnell, Steven S. (Steve) P309
Grinschgl, Sandra E84
Grinspoon, Steven (Steve) P530
Grisard, Jean-Marie W160
Grisham, Jon E6
Grissen, David J. A563
Grissom, Richard (Dick) A925
Griswold, Mike (Mikey) E177
Griswold, Kathleen (Kathy) A518
Griswold, Jim P564
Grob, Matthew S. (Matt) A736
Groba, Kevin A392
Grobelny, Chris (Chrissy) E165
Grobelny, Chris (Chrissy) A381
Groch, James R. (Jim) A174
Grochocki, Manju A624
Grochowski, Dina E175
Grodin, Lauren A351
Groe, Paul (Pauly) A147
Groesbeck, Michael (Mel) A166
Groetken, Doug A954
Groetsch, Julie (Jules) A522
Groff, Alice (Ali) A104
Groff, Stacey A467
Groff, Michael R. (Mike) A879
Groff, Stacey P233
Grogan, Annie (Ann) A347
Grogan, Edwin A531
Grogin, Jeffrey P. E328
Grogin, Jeffrey P. E329
Grogin, Jeffrey P. A686
Groh, Kelly L. A403
Grondin, Nicole (Nikki) A871
Gronow, Tom P588
Groos, Holyce A927
Groot, Rene de W14
Gros, Richard R. A570
Gros-Pietro, Gian Maria W202
Grosby, Karen P362
Grosch, Bob (Bo) A835
Groshen, Erica A341
Grosoli, Luigi A394
Gross, Kevin (Kev) E51
Gross, Robert G. E284
Gross, Lawrence J E443
Gross, Hilly A58
Gross, Kevin (Kev) A110
Gross, Jason (Jase) A420
Gross, Bob (Bo) A502
Gross, Bruce E. A536
Gross, Gary (Gar) A553
Gross, Mark A837
Gross, Rhonda P103
Gross, John P126
Gross, Roy P312

A = AMERICAN BUSINESS
E = EMERGING COMPANIES
P = PRIVATE COMPANIES
W = WORLD BUSINESS

Hochberg, Philip S. E231
Hochberg, Stanley P83
Hochgesang, Mark A109
Hochschild, Roger C. A276
Hochstadt, Jeffrey (Jeff) A954
Hockemeyer, Rex A E421
Hockemeyer, Rex A A902
Hocken, Natalie L. A674
Hockens, Sean A409
Hockenson, Tod A467
Hockenson, Tod P233
Hocking, Nona A766
Hocking, Nona P421
Hockley, James (Jamie) E149
Hockman, Alexander A. E308
Hodapp, Don A453
Hodapp, Rusty (Rus) P157
Hodes, Jack A397
Hodes, Adam (Ad) A585
Hodes, Sanford A774
Hodge, Ronald (Ron) A143
Hodge, Jim A523
Hodge, Terry A876
Hodge, Nancy (Nance) A981
Hodge, Karen (Kare) P428
Hodgen, Brian P364
Hodges, Eloy E265
Hodges, James R. A101
Hodges, Ron A101
Hodges, Arthur (Art) A217
Hodges, Eloy A572
Hodges, James (Jamie) A576
Hodges, Timothy B (Tim) A689
Hodges, Gregory (Greg) A927
Hodges, Arthur (Art) P132
Hodges, Thomas H. P357
Hodges, Bruce M. W33
Hodgkiss, Lisa (Lis) P407
Hodgson, Robert (Bob) A745
Hodgson, Marvin P185
Hodgson, Deborah (Deb) P448
Hodkinson, Gillian A6
Hodnik, Alan R. E20
Hodorff, David (Dave) E443
Hodous, Brian A10
Hodson, John W368
Hodulich, David (Dave) P535
Hoeckh, Rich (Ric) A198
Hoedl, Dean P341
Hoefner, Mike A820
Hoekema, Dale P256
Hoekstra, Jim E389
Hoekstra, Jason P185
Hoel, William P. (Bill) A487
Hoelscher, Kylene A593
Hoeltzel, Mary (Mar) A198
Hoelz, Martin W385
Hoelzeman, Larry E112
Hoelzer, Joel A636
Hoencamp, Jeroen W408
Hoene, William A. (Bill) Von A326
Hoerbelt, Greg A753
Hoerig, Patricia (Pat) A766
Hoerig, Patricia (Pat) P421
Hoerman, Dave (Davie) A264
Hoersch, Lori (Lor) A897
Hoersch, Lori A897
Hoersch, Lori (Lor) P575
Hoersch, Lori P575
Hoetzinger, Peter E84
Hoey, Bob (Bo) A485
Hofbauer, Michael (Mike) P29
Hofelich, Kurt A793
Hofelich, Kurt P445
Hofeling, Dustin A371
Hofer, Nicholas A.R. A145
Hoff, Paul (Pauly) E361
Hoff, Linda P274
Hoff, Linda (Lin) P281

Hoff, Thomas (Thom) P339
Hoffer, Ilene E67
Hoffer, Theresa A200
Hoffer, Katia A217
Hoffer, Katia P132
Hoffler, Valerie (Val) A162
Hoffman, Chad E84
Hoffman, Ed E331
Hoffman, Bernard (Bern) E439
Hoffman, Roger (Rog) A70
Hoffman, Julie (Jules) A135
Hoffman, Rich A140
Hoffman, Nate A163
Hoffman, Mark A225
Hoffman, Stephen A342
Hoffman, Francis (Fran) A347
Hoffman, David (Dave) A348
Hoffman, Michelle (Michie) A369
Hoffman, Stuart (Stu) A706
Hoffman, Warren A727
Hoffman, James D. A756
Hoffman, Alex (Al) A827
Hoffman, Angela (Ang) P76
Hoffman, Dean P289
Hoffman, Ethel P385
Hoffman, Jay (JayJay) P550
Hoffman, Eric P564
Hoffman, Elizabeth P631
Hoffman, Andre W321
HoffmanmarriotCom, Richard
   (Dick) A564
Hoffmann, Mike (Mikey) E180
Hoffmann, Daryl A252
Hoffmann, David L. (Dave) A575
Hoffmann, K?roly A780
Hoffmann, Tasha A918
Hoffmann, Richard (Dick) P80
Hoffmann, Marion S P590
Hoffmeister, Susan P252
Hoffner, Doug (Dougie) A351
Hofgard, Jefferson A140
Hofler, Linda D. P389
Hofman, Debra (Deb) E177
Hofmann, Kevin A446
Hofmann, Richard A579
Hofmeister, Brian (Bri) A709
Hogan, Joseph M. (Joe) E18
Hogan, James D. E116
Hogan, Tom E331
Hogan, George W. E450
Hogan, William (Bill) A48
Hogan, Irene (Rene) A78
Hogan, Mike (Mikey) A106
Hogan, Wendy A176
Hogan, Tom (Tommy) A177
Hogan, Thomas (Thom) A200
Hogan, James D. A255
Hogan, Mike (Mikey) A393
Hogan, Michael P. (Mike) A393
Hogan, Kathleen T. A592
Hogan, David P. A661
Hogan, Janet L. A667
Hogan, Casey R. A672
Hogan, Peter (Pete) A709
Hogan, Jim (Jimmy) A846
Hogan, Noel P14
Hogan, Patrick D. P410
Hogan, Gillian P508
Hogg, Kelly (Kel) A87
Hoggarth, Scott P150
Hoghaug, Paul (Pauly) A51
Hoglund, Robert N. A240
Hoglund, Robert N. A241
Hogue, Penny (Penn) A641
Hogue, Steven (Steve) A696
Hohe, Robert (Bob) A370
Hoheisel, Dirk W74
Hohmann, Paul P449
Hohmeister, Harry W133
Hokanson, Alex E366
Hoke, Margaret A369
Holappa, Bruce A839
Holbrook, Jenni E206
Holbrook, Frank (Frankie) A44
Holbrook, Mark A437

Holbrook, Jenni A445
Holbrook, Richard E. P354
Holbrook, Karen (Kare) P602
Holcomb, Steve K E379
Holcomb, Susan (Sue) A535
Holcomb, Steven L. A905
Holcomb, George W. P308
Holcomb, Alexandra W415
Holcombe, Frank (Frankie) A57
Holcombe, Robert E (Bob) A344
Holdeman, Lisa (Lis) P590
Holden, Jay (JayJay) A843
Holden, Peter J. P71
Holden, E. Wayne P415
Holden, E Wayne P415
Holder, Robert (Bob) E62
Holder, Linda A180
Holder, Jerry (Jerr) A900
Holder, Diane P. A919
Holder, Judy P442
Holder, Diane P. P598
Holder, William W. P603
Holding, Frank B. A358
Holdn, Wayne P415
Holdridge, John (Jack) A176
Holdych, Mark (Marky) P205
Holdych, Mark P205
Hole, Joseph A109
Holec, Jennifer (Jen) A102
Holeksa, J□rgen W424
Holeman, David K. E451
Holguin, Lorena A569
Holiday, Bradley J. E457
Holifield, Mark Q. A446
Holladay, Robert L. (Rob) E75
Holladay, Rob (Robbie) E75
Holladay, Evon A173
Holladay, Mark G. A841
Holladay, Evon P105
Holland, Matthew (Matt) E40
Holland, Paul (Pauly) E163
Holland, John E447
Holland, Charles K (Chas) A101
Holland, Peter A109
Holland, Ricky T. A359
Holland, Leslie (Les) A369
Holland, Bill A392
Holland, Karen A458
Holland, Clifford A499
Holland, Lee A821
Holland, Cristie P97
Holland, Daniele P275
Holland, Eric C. P307
Holland, Ellen (Elle) P465
Holland, Brian P591
Hollander, Jeffrey (Jeff) A584
Hollar, Jan H. A456
Hollar, Jason A789
Hollar, Jan H. A974
Hollaway, David E344
Hollaway, David A723
Holle, Kurtis A514
Hollek, Darrell E. A60
Hollenbeck, Jennifer E420
Hollenbeck, Ryan E436
Hollenbeck, Martin F. A200
Hollenbeck, Douglas (Doug) A228
Hollenbeck, Jennifer A901
Hollenbeck, Ron P185
Hollenbeck, Patricia (Pat) P469
Holler, Thomas R. (Tom) E440
Holleran, Kevin P. A860
Hollers, Anna G. A355
Holley, Rick R. A956
Holliday, Robert P. E306
Holliday, Brian A449
Holliday, Charles O. (Chad) W329
Hollinger, Jesica P401
Hollingshead, Kris (Krissy) E208
Hollingshead, Kris (Krissy) A448
Hollingsworth, Pamela (Pam) A487
Hollingsworth, Audrey A841
Hollingsworth, Joe A. P228
Hollingsworth, A. Thomas P228
Hollingsworth, Jarvis V. P591

Hollis, Curtis (Curt) A515
Hollister, Jeffrey S. E26
Hollister, Terry (Terr) A291
Holloman, J. Phillip A202
Hollow, John P563
Holloway, Duane D. A76
Holloway, Anita A462
Holloway, Neil A592
Holloway, Ginger A (Ginny) A751
Holloway, John B. P98
Holloway, Ginger A (Ginny) P412
Hollrs, James (Jamie) E180
Hollub, Vicki A. A653
Hollyhead, Mark (Marky) A328
Holm, Amy (Ames) P168
Holm, Gene E51
Holman, Jon (Jonny) E377
Holman, Gene A110
Holman, Russell L. (Rusty) A542
Holme, Troy A175
Holmen, James (Jamie) P571
Holmer, Hans A937
Holmes, John E111
Holmes, Dan (Danny) E176
Holmes, Tammy (Tam) E277
Holmes, Mark (Marky) A120
Holmes, Ralph A198
Holmes, Tamika A198
Holmes, Tom (Tommy) A251
Holmes, Donald L. A268
Holmes, Steven (Steve) A479
Holmes, Cynthia K (Cyn) A523
Holmes, William A563
Holmes, Bill A622
Holmes, Charlie (Charles) A634
Holmes, Terraca A851
Holmes, Stewart (Stew) A861
Holmes, Stephen P. A968
Holmes, John P167
Holmes, Diana Denman P248
Holmes, Nicholas P406
Holmes, Chip P556
Holmes, Randy P629
Holmgren, Lynn (Lyn) A390
Holmstr□¶m, Torbj□¶rn W411
Holness, Russell (Russ) A678
Holochuk, James (Jamie) A779
Holowko, Anthony A469
Holscher, Russ A118
Holsclaw, Janet (Jan) A765
Holsclaw, Janet (Jan) P421
Holsenbeck, Daniel (Dan) P550
Holshouser, Susan (Sue) A470
Holst, Cindy (Cin) A273
Holst, Bjorn A826
Holst, Cindy (Cin) P165
Holst, Bjorn P488
Holsten, Joseph M. A550
Holston, Michael J. A579
Holt, Lou (Lewis) E73
Holt, Sandra (Sandy) A159
Holt, Rick (Ricky) E214
Holt, Victoria M. (Vicki) E345
Holt, Cyndi M (Lucinda) E400
HOLT, CINDY M E400
Holt, Susan A120
Holt, Sandra (Sandy) A364
Holt, Zeb Holt Zeb A467
Holt, William (Bill) A479
Holt, Jarrod A504
Holt, Rick (Ricky) A619
Holt, Alison (Alli) A753
Holt, Penny (Penn) A810
Holt, Neil A930
Holt, Wayne P12
Holt, Ellen P61
Holt, Carol P402
Holt, Dennis W109
Holt, Tim O. W346
Holtam, Tom (Tommy) A900
Holthouser, James E. (Jim) A442
Holton, Mica E275
Holton, Micah (Mic) E275
Holton, Gwen (Gwendolyn) Von A117
Holton, Martin L. (Mark) A760

A = AMERICAN BUSINESS
E = EMERGING COMPANIES
P = PRIVATE COMPANIES
W = WORLD BUSINESS

Isaac, Angela A841
Isaacs, Trent E435
Isaacs, Harry A176
Isaacs, Eric D. P551
Isaacs, Stephanie (Steph) P593
Isaacson, Karen (Kare) A309
Isaacson, Jon F. P110
Isais, Jose A895
Isais, Geraldine Forbes P595
Isaka, Ryuichi W340
Isakowitz, Steven J. (Steve) P511
Isaman, Tanya A183
Isely, Kemper E293
Isely, Zephyr E293
Isely, Heather E293
Isely, Elizabeth E293
Iseman, Jay C. E207
Iseman, Jay C. A448
Iseman, Andrew J. (Andy) A899
Isenberg, Brad E391
Iserman, Lance A89
Isham, Nicolas (Nick) E442
Ishibashi, Takuya W122
Ishibashi, Tamio W122
Ishiguro, Denroku W20
Ishii, Masashi P384
Ishikawa, Brian A106
Ishikawa, Hiro A688
ISHIMARU, FUMIO W333
Ishizaki, Yoshiyuki W387
Ishizuka, Hiroaki W255
Ishizuka, Shigeki W355
Iskilaus, Alex (Al) A485
Iskow, Julie E267
Isla, Pablo W198
Islam, Nayeem A736
Ismail, Khalil P176
Ismail, Amid I. P505
Isman, Michael (Mel) A143
Isner, Josh E401
Isom, Robert D. A40
Ison, Tamara P631
Isono, Denis A106
Isono, Denis K. A184
Israel, Tracy (Trace) E80
Israel, Robert J. E352
Israel, Leonard (Len) A377
Israel, Lex A732
Israel, Dan P506
Isreal, Toni P275
Isturiz, Raul A697
Italiano, Deborah P485
Itani, Tamima A147
Ito, Paul K. E17
Ito, Craig A106
Ito, Shinichiro W27
ITO, TOSHIYASU W190
Ito, Kazuhiko W204
Ito, Takashi W253
Ito, Yujiro W363
Itoh, Junji W361
Itoyama, Masaaki W205
Itter, Barb (Barbie) E143
Ittner, Gary (Gar) A607
Iunghuhn, Cathy (Cat) A800
Iuorio, Alex (Al) A94
IV, William H. W. Crawford E422
IV, William H. W. Crawford A907
Ivanhoe, Brian P403
Ivanikiw, Alex (Al) P60
Ivanis, Milena A883
Ivannikov, Alexander (Al) A702
Ivannikov, Alexander W304
Ivanov, Stanislav A480
Ive, Jonathan A66
Iverson, Mary A203
Ives, Tom (Tommy) A175
Ives, Stephanie (Steph) A304
Ives, Stephanie P505

Ives, Blake P591
Ivey, Henry E61
Ivey, Craig S. A240
Ivey, Craig S. A241
Ivey, Brian (Bri) A404
Ivey, Brent P204
Ivie, Joel A547
Ivy, Danny A20
Ivy, Jim A887
Iwaki, Masakazu W277
Iwamura, Tetsuo W186
Iwane, Shigeki W216
Iwasaki, Toshihiro W282
Iwasaki, Masato W373
Iwata, Hidenobu W186
Iwatsuki, Takashi W367
Iyengar, Sudarshan E274
Iyer, Sriram A348
Iyer, Bask A934
Izaguirre, Luis-Angel Gomez A973
Izaki, Kazuhiro W228
Izganics, Joseph C. (Joe) A432
Izzo, Christopher (Chris) E44
Izzo, Joseph (Jo) E437
Izzo, Ralph A728
Izzo, Giorgio P191

J

Jabaji, George J. P196
Jabbar, Valerie (Val) A523
Jabbour, Anthony M. A348
Jabbour, Marlene (Marly) A392
Jablonski, Dale (Dal) A514
Jablonski, Sue (Susie) P366
Jacas, Desmond E40
Jachiet, Nicolas W83
Jack, Lynn A485
Jack, Kenneth (Ken) A928
Jack, Ken (Kenny) A928
Jackiewicz, Annmarie A727
Jackiewicz, Thomas E. P603
Jackman, Lorraine (Irene) A228
Jackman, Linda (Lin) A664
Jackman, Dave (Davie) A981
Jackowski, Julie (Jules) A169
Jackowski, Julia L. (Julie) A169
Jacks, Nicole E86
Jacks, Joann L (Ann) A347
Jackson, W. James E134
Jackson, James (Jamie) E134
Jackson, Rex S. E182
Jackson, Brian E206
Jackson, Scott E222
Jackson, Randy E232
Jackson, David A. (Dave) E235
Jackson, Mark (Marky) E242
Jackson, Jeffrey T. (Jeff) E332
Jackson, Joanne B. E334
Jackson, Ronald B. (Ron) E373
Jackson, Mel (Melanie) E377
Jackson, ED (Eddie) E380
Jackson, Michael (Mel) E397
Jackson, Joseph L. (Joe) E444
Jackson, Anthony (Tony) A3
Jackson, James (Jamie) A63
Jackson, Michael J. (Mike) A88
Jackson, Lydia A163
Jackson, Rick C. A164
Jackson, Dan A183
Jackson, Todd F (Toddy) A184
Jackson, Jerry (Jerr) A315
Jackson, S Lance A331
Jackson, Michael J. (Mike) A340
Jackson, Kelly (Kel) A369
Jackson, Kevin (Kev) A408
Jackson, Kirby A409
Jackson, Brian A445
Jackson, Trisha A465
Jackson, Benjamin R. (Ben) A480
Jackson, Arthur (Art) A504
Jackson, Stephanie (Steph) A514
Jackson, Ralph (Ralphy) A603
Jackson, Stuart (Stu) A606

Jackson, Jeffrey (Jeff) A657
Jackson, Neville A696
Jackson, Don A702
Jackson, Joanne B. A703
Jackson, Marla A726
Jackson, Catherine (Cate) A742
Jackson, Tracy (Trace) A752
Jackson, Bill A761
Jackson, Ronald B. (Ron) A799
Jackson, Craig (Craigy) A835
Jackson, Timothy E. (Tim) A853
Jackson, Ned A899
Jackson, Philip C. (Phil) A921
Jackson, Robert (Bob) A932
Jackson, Neal A947
JACKSON, DAVID (Dave) P80
Jackson, Parul P156
Jackson, William (Bill) P216
Jackson, Richard L (Dick) P248
Jackson, Dionne P275
Jackson, Laurisa P308
Jackson, Kimberly (Kim) P375
Jackson, Maureen P385
Jackson, Deanna (Anna) P403
Jackson, Joy P512
Jackson, Robert (Bob) P616
Jackson, Linda W300
Jackson-Elmoore, Cynthia P320
Jackwyn, Nemerov A743
Jacob, April A87
Jacob, Gregg A270
JACOB, PAUL (Pauly) A305
Jacob, Ravi A479
Jacob, William A911
Jacob, Mark C P125
Jacob, Cheryl P281
Jacob, Richard (Dick) P641
Jacob, Mark W139
Jacobfeuerborn, Bruno W136
Jacobi, C. Michael E387
Jacobino, Lucy (Lucia) P307
Jacobo, Keyanus A634
Jacobs, Joey A. E5
Jacobs, William I. E187
Jacobs, Thomas W. E250
Jacobs, Kerry A27
Jacobs, Joseph A60
Jacobs, Gary (Gar) A163
Jacobs, Robert (Bob) A252
Jacobs, Stephen D. (Jake) A382
Jacobs, Jake (Jacob) A383
Jacobs, Kevin J. A442
Jacobs, Lynn (Lyn) A573
Jacobs, Paul E. A736
Jacobs, Mark (Marky) A753
Jacobs, Bill (Billy) A811
Jacobs, John R (Jack) A930
Jacobs, Bradley S. A973
Jacobs, Richard F. P38
Jacobs, Richard (Dick) P107
Jacobs, Brian P120
Jacobs, John P246
Jacobs, John P247
Jacobs, Stefanie (Stef) P307
Jacobs, Joel P535
Jacobsen, Craig (Craigy) A482
Jacobsen, Jim (Jimmy) A837
Jacobsen, Craig (Craigy) P242
Jacobsen, Leland P367
Jacobsen, Lennart W283
Jacobson, Simon E177
Jacobson, Kenneth (Ken) A94
Jacobson, Paul A. A269
Jacobson, Jeff A. A501
Jacobson, Karen A610
Jacobson, Andy A754
Jacobson, Scott (Scotty) A761
Jacobson, Mike A874
Jacobson, Jack A939
Jacobson, Jeffrey (Jeff) A971
Jacobson, Ron (Ronnie) P193
Jacobson, Catherine A. P199
Jacobson, Leland P367
Jacoby, Rebecca J. A203
Jacoby, Stefan A400

Jacoby, Christy A (Christ) A692
Jacovatos, James (Jamie) A380
Jacques, Dale A765
Jacques, Alistair P183
Jacques, Dale P421
Jacques, Jean-Sebastien W318
Jacques, Jean-Sebastien W320
Jacquez, Dorothy P275
Jacquinot, Robert (Bob) P247
Jadin, Ronald L. A412
Jadot, Maxime (Max) W71
Jaeger, Steven D. (Steve) A734
Jaeggin, Thomas (Thom) A640
Jaegle, Rick (Ricky) A753
JAFARNIA, KAMAL E442
Jaffe, David R. A76
Jaffe, Elliot S. A76
Jaffe, Jonathan M. (Jon) A536
Jaffe, Eric (Ric) A789
Jaffe, Austin A866
Jaffe, Harry J P357
Jaffe, David E. P498
Jaffe, Austin P540
Jaffess, Judith (Jude) A726
Jaffin, Jay A927
Jaffray, Dawn M. E422
Jaffray, Dawn M. A908
Jagdfeld, Aaron E178
Jager, Sandy E268
Jager, Sandy A577
Jagger, Hal A796
Jagger, Hal P454
Jaggi, Michael (Mel) P232
Jaglall, Andy A603
Jagtiani, Akash A208
Jahan, Patrick (Paddy) A304
Jahanian, Farnam P101
Jahn, Gregory S (Greg) A325
Jahn, Timothy P57
Jahnel, Ferdinand A782
Jahng, Kevin (Kev) A603
Jahnke, Tiffany (Tiff) P375
Jahns, Tracy (Trace) P555
Jaillet, Norman (Norm) E140
Jaime, Alex A655
Jain, Hemant E167
Jain, Pankaj E168
Jain, Anil E398
Jain, Dipika A104
Jain, Nitin A181
Jain, Shashi A479
Jain, Ruchira A692
Jain, Sujit A763
Jain, Sahil P101
Jain, Sujit P420
Jakeman, Kelly A54
Jakeman, Brad A692
Jakobsen, Henning A223
Jakobsen, Joergen A237
Jakobsen, Mads G. W283
Jakoby, Jean A692
Jaksch, Steven (Steve) A785
Jaksich, Daniel (Dan) A127
Jakstys, Kristina (Chris) A641
Jakubowski, Michael A479
Jakuc, Kevin (Kev) E336
Jalali, Zeshan A208
Jalali, Ahmad A736
Jallal, Bahija W37
Jamal, Arshil W174
Jamar, John P29
Jambor, Joan A83
James, Bradley G. E409
James, Karen A100
James, Hamilton E. (Tony) A136
James, Pamela (Pam) A225
James, Dwight A269
James, Jeff (Jeffy) A280
James, Karen A344
James, Galeota A580
James, Phyllis A. A589
James, Dick A636
James, Nick (Nicky) A636
James, Courtland W A745
James, Alasdair A789

James, Bradley G. A877
James, Dianne R. A980
James, Marianne F. P118
James, Marian (Mary) P118
James, Paul (Pauly) P122
James, Kerry (Kerr) P298
James, Catherine A (Cathy) P511
James, LaToya P531
James-Francis, Ma P349
Jameson, Keith A33
Jameson, Steven E. (Steve) A235
Jameson, Jeremy (Jer) A317
Jameson, Eileen (Elle) P3
Jamieson, Daniel T. (Dan) E446
Jamieson, Jim (Jimmy) A31
Jamieson, John (Jack) A780
Jamieson, Dick (Dicky) P103
Jamieson, Richard (Dick) P103
Jamil, Dhiaa M. A294
Jamison, Andrew (Andy) A44
Jamison, Jane (Ginny) A465
Jamison, Cynthia T. A880
Jan, Couturier A464
Janaillac, Jean-Marc W14
Janakiraman, Bala A135
Janchar, Jim (Jimmy) A156
Janchar, John (Jack) P76
Jandoc, John (Jack) A840
Jandro, Bob E222
Jandrue, Patricia (Pat) A347
Janet, Doak P519
Janiga, Kathy A263
Janik, James L. E124
Janis, Robert (Bob) P160
Janise, Lisa (Lis) A204
Janisko, Jenny P38
Janke, Kenneth S. (Ken) A19
Jankos, Dianna (Ana) P326
Jankowski, Edward (Ed) A949
Jankowski, Heidi P237
Janmohamed, Shafique A981
Jannah, Shekar G. A512
Janney, Michelle P237
Janoff, Robert J. E166
Janofsky, Christine A (Chrissy) A546
Janosick, Kenneth W. (Ken) E450
Jansen, Paul R. E258
Jansen, Don (Donnie) A140
Jansen, Kathrin U A696
Jansen, Roger E. P471
Jansen, Robert P631
Jansky, Liz P632
Janson, Deborah (Deb) A48
Janson, Julie S. A294
Janson, Julia (Jules) A295
Janssen, Gwendolyn A5
Janssen, Ann A320
Janssen, David (Dave) A664
Janssen, Julie A964
Jansson, Urban W351
Jantz, Barry P210
Jantzen, Jesse A77
Jantzen, Jesse P41
Jantzen, Deanna (Anna) P356
January, Eric (Ric) A952
Janus, Michael (Mel) A117
Janus, Michael (Mel) P63
Janutolo, Kristin A464
Janz, Jeff (Jeffy) P293
Japy, Nicholas W353
Jaques, Sylvia (Sylv) E49
Jaques, Sylvia (Sylv) A99
Jaramillo, Adriana (Ana) A280
Jark, Heidi (Hei) A351
Jarley, Paul P550
Jarman, John (Jack) E438
Jarmon, David E73
Jarnot, Christopher E. (Chris) E430
Jaroszewski, J Rosow A252
Jarrell, Tammy A119
Jarrell, Paul A670
Jarrett, Barry (Barr) A47
Jarrett, Phyllis (Phyl) A166
Jarrett, Charles E. (Chuck) A721
Jarrett, Mark (Marky) P354

Jarrold, Tom A743
Jarve, Robert (Bob) P471
Jarvi, Renee (Ren) A140
Jarvis, Andrew J. E406
Jarvis, Glenn A44
Jarvis, Patrick (Paddy) A117
Jarvis, Janina A281
Jarvis, Herb A692
Jarvis, Patrick (Paddy) P63
Jarvis, Jessica (Jess) P591
Jarvis, Guy W148
Jasek, Melissa (Lissa) P401
Jasien, William S. (Bill) A790
Jasien, William S. (Bill) P442
Jasin, Clarence (Clar) A203
Jasinowski, Mike A132
Jaska, Kristi (Chris) E438
Jaskaniec, Andy A520
Jaskowiak, Scott E. E379
Jaskowiak, Sheila M A18
Jasnoff, Jeffrey M (Jeff) A518
Jaspal, Puja A933
Jasper, Bill E179
Jasper, Philip J. (Phil) A769
Jasper, Phil (Philly) A769
Jasper, Thomas F. (Tom) A847
Jasper, Eugene A916
Jasper, Tuck A973
Jasperson, Krissy A156
Jassy, Andrew R. (Andy) A37
Jastrem, Thomas E116
Jastrem, Thomas A255
Jastrow, Nicole E312
Jasurda, Bruce (Brucey) A916
Jauch, Mike A438
Javorka, Tony P137
Jaworski, Peter W. A947
Jay, Ed A44
Jay, Dennis A485
Jay, Colleen E. A719
Jay, John C. W158
Jayant, Monika A104
Jayaram, Ganesh A267
Jayaraman, Srinivasan E440
Jayavant, Rajeev A649
Jaynes, Jeff (Jeffy) A451
Jazwinska, Klaudia P275
Jbara, Mike P623
Jean, Harkey E197
Jean, Ronald W. A306
Jean, Wilkerson A315
Jean, Harkey A434
Jean-Luc, Bohbot W416
Jeanis, Keith P578
Jeanniot, Lynn W268
Jeantet, Russann A918
Jeary, Cathy (Cat) A779
Jedrzejczyk, Slawomir R. W306
Jeff, Galagher A937
Jeffers, Lauren (Laur) A18
Jeffers, Jack (Jackie) A265
Jeffers, Will A534
Jeffers, Lewis P394
Jeffers, Lewis (Louie) P394
Jefferson, Kirby A479
Jeffery, Tom A846
Jeffrey, Capello A146
Jeffrey, Brad A546
Jeffrey, William P473
Jeffries, Robert P. (Bob) E84
Jeffries, Kevin A83
Jeffries, Pamela R. P524
Jefson, Karen E452
Jego-Laveissi re, Mari-No «lle W293
Jehle, Kent L. E277
Jehle, Kent L. A595
Jejdling, Fredrik W379
Jejurikar, Shailesh G. A719
Jelenchick, Erin A766
Jelenchick, Erin P421
Jelinek, Rick A17
Jelinek, W. Craig A247
Jelle, Lorraine (Irene) P75
Jelmini, David (Dave) A444
Jenchel, Larry (Lar) A789

Jenckes, Marcien A225
Jeng-wu, Tai W341
Jenkin, Thomas M. (Tom) A155
Jenkins, Tom (Tommy) E91
Jenkins, Brian A. E118
Jenkins, R. Scott E224
Jenkins, John E331
Jenkins, Steven L. E351
Jenkins, Steve (Stevie) A325
Jenkins, George (Georgey) A383
Jenkins, Brian A546
Jenkins, Norman (Norm) A564
Jenkins, Steve (Stevie) A670
Jenkins, Jeremy A753
Jenkins, David (Dave) A757
Jenkins, Scott (Scotty) A824
Jenkins, Roseanne A835
Jenkins, Dustee T A846
Jenkins, William (Bill) A854
Jenkins, Jo Ann C. P2
Jenkins, Ray P152
Jenkins, Decosta E. P178
Jenkins, Gregory (Greg) P313
Jenkins, A. Dale P415
Jenkins, Patricia (Pat) P431
Jenkins, Deborah (Deb) P479
Jenkins, Katherine (Kate) P517
Jenkins, John (Jack) P535
Jenkins, Margaret L. P610
Jenner, Christopher A156
Jenner, Amy (Ames) A696
Jenness, Calvin E. P78
Jennifer, Weber A295
Jennifer, Lofgren A824
Jennings, Steve E40
Jennings, Susan E129
Jennings, Gordan E152
Jennings, Cynthia (Cyn) E165
Jennings, Brenda (Bren) E419
Jennings, Brenda E419
Jennings, Lisa A31
Jennings, Gary A80
Jennings, Jody (Jode) A177
Jennings, Richard A236
Jennings, Cynthia (Cyn) A381
Jennings, Michael C. A444
Jennings, Michael (Mel) A726
Jennings, Michael A728
Jennings, Richard (Dick) A774
Jennings, Dick A774
Jennings, Shawn A785
Jennings, Gary P45
Jennings, Charles G (Charlie) P298
Jennings, Stephen P406
Jennings, Donna (Don) P630
Jennings, Reynold J. P631
Jennings, William M. (Bill) P642
Jenny, Patrick (Paddy) E149
Jenny, Kim (Kimmy) E335
Jenny, Kim (Kimmy) A703
Jenrette, John P451
Jensen, Steve (Stevie) E258
Jensen, Katrina E303
Jensen, Christopher W. (Chris) A177
Jensen, Bjorn A220
Jensen, Tj A383
Jensen, Barry A473
Jensen, Julia (Jules) A571
Jensen, Katrina A630
Jensen, Donald A633
Jensen, Eric (Ric) A649
Jensen, Stan A674
Jensen, Derrick A. A737
Jensen, Eric (Ric) A820
Jensen, Allen (Al) A980
Jensen, Karen P370
Jensen, Rob P535
Jenson, Conrad (Connor) A444
Jenson, James (Jamie) A523
Jenson, Kelly A972
Jenson, Warren P603
Jentsch, Dieter W. W51
Jeong, Kyong-Deuk W233
Jeong, Tak W307
Jeong, Chul Khil W350

Jeppesen, Jon (Jonny) A64
Jepson, Helene E161
Jepson, Helene A373
Jepson, Brian D. P366
Jeray, Diane (Di) A317
Jeremiah, Curtis (Curt) A108
Jerger, Mark (Marky) A736
Jernstedt, Tiffin A733
Jerome, Christopher J. (Chris) A922
Jerome, Karen (Kare) P625
Jerschke, Tobias W227
Jervell, Tom s W42
Jervis, Geoffrey G. A493
Jervis, Owen A855
Jesiolowski, Craig A. P490
Jessell, Kenneth A. P190
Jessell, Ken (Kenny) P191
Jessen, David (Dave) A281
Jesser, John (Jack) A62
Jessup, Manuel O (Mannie) E400
Jessup, Len P586
Jester, Diane (Di) E51
Jester, Ian E85
Jester, Diane (Di) A111
Jester, Vanessa (Nessa) P624
Jesudas, Sajeev P576
Jeter, Daniel B. E28
Jeter, Daniel B. A52
Jett, Price E83
Jett, Robert (Bob) A754
Jett, Paul P29
Jetter, Martin A485
Jetty, Sathish P6
Jewell, Matthew J. E169
Jewett, Patrick (Paddy) A94
Jewett, Joshua R. (Josh) A284
Jewkes, Roger S. A346
Jeworrek, Torsten W265
Jex, Jeffrey (Jeff) A369
Jezier, Mike (Mikey) A218
Jha, Nitesh E229
Jha, Smriti A409
Jha, Shantanu A485
Jha, Rajesh A592
Jha, Rakesh W194
Jhaveri, Vishu P78
Jhirad, Veronika E98
Jia, Keith A504
Jian, Liu W108
Jianbin, Wu W114
Jiang, Ming-Fang A150
Jiang, Ling A602
Jiang, George A657
Jianguo, Han W100
Jianheng, Zhang W425
Jianhua, Zhang W298
Jianmin, Miao W96
Jianping, Gao W199
Jianzhong, Dou W106
Jick, Daniel P71
Jie, Ouyang W137
Jijing, Zhang W106
Jimenez, Vivian (Viv) E7
Jimenez, Mathew (Matt) E258
Jimenez, Dennis (Denny) A175
Jimenez, Frank R. A747
Jimenez, Ed P450
Jimmie, Andrew (Andy) P13
Jin, Connie E377
Jin, Jeoung (A. J.) A380
Jin-Soo, Park Jin Soo W233
Jingdong, Wang W199
Jinghui, Tian W298
Jinglei, Cheng W332
Jingnan, Liu A296
Jingnan, Liu P171
Jingzhen, Lin W71
Jinks, Mary P604
Jiong, Wang W106
Jischke, Martin C. E443
Joachim, William (Bill) A499
Joachim, Steven A. (Steve) P186
Jobbins, Amanda (Mandy) A204
Jobson, Gary (Gar) P33
Joe, David E147

A = AMERICAN BUSINESS
E = EMERGING COMPANIES
P = PRIVATE COMPANIES
W = WORLD BUSINESS

Koskovich, Melissa (Mel) A534
Koskull, Casper von W283
Koslow, John (Jack) A44
Kosnik, Tricia (Trish) A208
Kosnoff, David (Dave) A571
Kosof, Bob (Bo) E341
Kosof, Bob (Bo) A714
Kosoko-Lasaki, Sade P148
Koss, James (Jamie) A430
Koss, Gail P43
Koss, Richard P260
Kossar, Robert (Bob) A502
Kostalnick, Charles F. A73
Kostalnick, Chuck A780
Kostantos, Roland W208
Koster, Steven A154
Koster, Michael C. A323
Koster, Barbara G. A726
Koster, James A820
Kostin, Mikhail P144
Kostner, Tim (Timmy) A187
Koszkalda, Bob (Bo) A514
Kotagal, Uma P118
Kotagiri, Seetarama W243
Koterba, Nancy P533
Kothari, Rashmikant P83
Kothari, Manish P473
Kothe, Kelly (Kel) P477
Kotick, Robert A. (Bobby) A10
Kotis, Desi P360
Kotler, Christine (Chrissy) P56
Kotlikoff, Michael I. P144
Kotlowski, Mike A562
Kotsay, John (Jack) A602
Kotsol, Carolyn A117
Kotsol, Carolyn P63
Kotsopoulos, Peter W364
Kott, Patricia (Pat) P506
Kottapalli, Kishore A824
Kottayil, Divya A178
Kotte, Kavita A409
Kottler, Robert M. (Bob) E212
Kottler, Robert M. (Bob) A468
Kotwal, Shailesh M. A895
Kotyk, Dale P624
Kotylo, Kenneth (Ken) A850
Kotz, Hans-Helmut W132
Kotzin, Brian (Bri) A55
Kouba, Kevin (Kev) A814
Koudouris, Maria (Mary) P127
Kouduki, Kazuo W386
Koulouris, Richard R. A709
Koumouris, Rick A379
Kouninis, Efstathios E328
Kountze-Tatum, Kathryn A324
Kourkoutis, John (Jack) E371
Kourkoutis, John (Jack) A797
Koury, Emile A420
Koury, Jeffrey (Jeff) A851
Koushik, Srinivas (Srini) A557
Kovach, Gerald E300
Kovach, Gary A364
Kovach, Stephen (Steve) A764
Kovach, Dave (Davie) A929
Kovach, Andrew L (Andy) P47
Kovacs, Janet (Jan) A82
Kovacs, Clark C (Clarkson) A295
Kovacs, James A (Jamie) A479
Kovacs, Greg P473
Koval, Kathy A791
Kover, Sarah (Sar) P362
Koviak, Jeff A853
Kovoch, Dan P60
Kovoor, George (Georgey) A692
Kovzan, Stephen M. (Steve) E304
Kowal, Dave (Davie) A156
Kowaleski, Tim (Timmy) A213
Kowals, Kathy (Kat) P114
Kowalski, Patricia (Pat) A383

Kowalski, Maureen (Maury) A511
Kowkabi, Sima A779
Kowlzan, Mark W. A675
Kowolenko, Dave A225
Koyama, Tomoyuki W278
Koyfman, Feliks P638
Kozak, Colleen E377
Kozak, Michael (Mel) A370
Kozak, Colleen A789
Kozak, Charlie P36
Kozak, John P160
Kozano, Yoshiaki W344
Kozar, Paul A895
Kozar, Joseph (Jo) P553
Kozarich, John W. E244
Kozek, William R. (Bill) A616
Kozel, David F. (Dave) A732
Kozen, Raymond E A395
Kozicz, Gregory J. (Greg) P15
Koziner, Pablo M. A170
Kozlak, Jodeen A846
Kozloski, Rick (Ricky) A5
Kozlowski, Damian E405
Kozlowski, Andrea (Ann) A555
Kozlowski, Ted A606
Kozlowski, Damian A862
Kozoman, Robert L. (Bob) P160
Kozsurek, Joe A535
Kozuka, Syuichiro W277
Kozy, William A. A123
Kra, Douglas I. (Doug) E328
Kraats, Robert-Jan van de W313
Kraemer, Theodore (Theo) A143
Kraeve, Igor P179
Krafels, Rick A523
Kraft, Ted (Teddy) E197
Kraft, Robert O. (Rocky) A259
Kraft, Kevin A296
Kraft, Ted (Teddy) A434
Kraft, Cheryl (Cher) A706
Kraft, Christopher A789
Kraft, Michael (Mel) A860
Kraft, Kevin P171
Kraft, John P589
Krage, David (Dave) E213
Krage, David (Dave) A469
Krajczar, Karen (Kare) P275
Krajewski, David P278
Krakau, Dennis (Denny) A78
Krakauer, Lawrence P298
Krakaur, Ken (Kenny) A793
Krakaur, Ken (Kenny) P445
Krakowsky, Philippe A488
Kralingen, Bridget A. van A485
Krall, Donna M. A377
Krallman, Amy B (Ames) A968
Kramer, James S. (Jim) E41
Kramer, Gary E53
Kramer, Robert G. (Bob) E134
Kramer, Chuck E212
Kramer, Francis J. E216
Kramer, Kevin E277
Kramer, Bill A84
Kramer, Jennifer (Jen) A115
Kramer, Kelly A. A203
Kramer, Scott (Scotty) A392
Kramer, Richard J. (Rich) A411
Kramer, Matthew (Matt) A429
Kramer, Chuck A468
Kramer, Kevin A595
Kramer, Phillip D. (Phil) A704
Kramer, Jennifer (Jenn) A728
Kramer, Mark A761
Kramer, Steve A895
Kramer, Tim (Timmy) A963
Kramer, Jennifer (Jen) P54
Kramer, David A. P92
Kramer, Karen P276
Kramer, Megan (Meg) P329
Kramer, Ken P509
Kramer, Markus W58
Kramer, Marcus W61
Kramer, Christina W85
Krampe, Edward J. P270
Kramvis, Andreas C. A449

Kranch, Robin (Rin) E176
Krane, Hilary K. A634
Kranski, Maria (Mary) A981
Krantz, Missy S E213
Krantz, Donald G. E345
Krantz, Missy S A468
Kranz, Sven P551
Kranzel, Jerome A175
Kranzler, Mike (Mikey) P643
Krasa, Peter (Pete) E176
Krasnoff, Jeffrey P. (Jeff) A536
Krasowski, Janet D. A724
Krasuski, Robin W (Rin) A765
Krasuski, Robin W (Rin) P421
Kratky, Kay W133
Kratsberg, Leon E371
Kratsberg, Leon A797
Kratz, Denise A779
Kratzert, Niki A519
Kratzert, Niki P267
Kraus, Ronald (Ron) E321
Kraus, Robert A341
Kraus, Eric (Ric) A348
Kraus, Evan A392
Kraus, Frederick A531
Kraus, Barbara P566
Krause, Greg (Greggy) A18
Krause, Steven (Steve) A208
Krause, Douglas P. A299
Krause, Frank (Frankie) A348
Krause, Alan J. P333
Krause, Catherine P595
Krauss, Soheir A205
Krauss, Jim A793
Krauss, Jim P445
Kraut, Jeffrey A. P354
Kravchenko, Kirill W170
Kravetz, Lisse A87
Krawczyk, Joseph (Jo) E274
Krawic, Rob A307
Krawiec, Dan A245
Krawiec, Dariusz J. W306
Krayeski, Paul (Pauly) A801
Kraynak, Karen C (Kare) A237
Kreatsoulas, John (Jack) A479
Krebber, Markus W330
Krebbs, Justin A101
Krebs, Matt (Matty) A198
Krebs, Kurt A351
Krebs, Donald E. (Don) A507
Krebs, Marty A601
Krebsbach, Larry P90
Krech, Joyce A126
Kreeke, Jeffrey Van De P199
Krehbiel, Bruce A489
Kreis, Dean P551
Kreis, Melanie W134
Kreitler, Brooke A916
Krejci, Frank J. E386
Krell, Joanne K. P619
Kremer, Donald (Don) A195
Kremer, Lisa A565
Kremer, Wesley D. A747
Kremer, Donald (Don) P115
Kremer, Brian (Bri) P237
Kremer, Thomas W136
Kremidas, Steve H. E381
Kremin, Donald H. (Don) A453
Krempl, Stephen A820
Krenke, Brian P268
Krenkel, David S. A286
Krenkel, Dave (Davie) A286
Krenowicz, Jim A208
Krenz, William C. (Willie) P511
Krepps, Shawna A925
Kreps, Keith P408
Kresl, Michael A48
Kress, Jean A406
Kress, Colette M. A649
Kress, Kathy (Kat) A937
Kress, Cathann P245
Kretzman, Bob (Bo) E359
Kretzman, Bethann P275
Kretzmer, William B. (Brian) E229
Kreuzer, Barry A253

Krichevsky, Keith E16
Krick, Gerd W164
Krick, Gerd W165
Krider, Joe A855
Krieger, Zvi E317
Krieger, Sarah (Sar) E326
Krieger, Daryl W. E452
Krieger, Sandra C. (Sandy) A340
Krieger, Laurel (Lor) A458
Krieger, Sarah (Sar) A684
Krieger, Noah A726
Kriens, Scott G. A505
Kriesand, Dave (Davie) A115
Kriesand, Dave (Davie) P54
Kriesky, Len (Lenny) P76
Krietsch, Judith (Jude) A104
Krikken, Ramon (Ray) E177
Krikorian, Lazarus A54
Krikorian, Alex (Al) A198
Krill, Joseph (Jo) A831
Krimbill, H. Michael A633
Kring, Steven C. E209
Kring, Steven C. A452
Krinn, Doug (Dougie) A916
Krinock, Patricia (Pat) A532
Krisch, Kelley P401
Krishen, Ashok W289
Krishna, Suresh E367
Krishna, Arvind A484
Krishna, R. Murali P240
Krishnamurthy, Srini A429
Krishnamurthy, Ganesh A485
Krishnan, Kosal A15
Krishnan, Sai A309
Krishnan, Rajesh A345
Krishnan, Ram A502
Krishnan, Ramayya P101
Krishnan, Sridhar W289
Krishnaswamy, Venkat A221
Krislov, Marvin P373
Kristensen, Douglas A. (Doug) P80
Kristiansen, Michelle (Michie) A829
Kristiansen, Thomas (Thom) P556
Kristiansen, Thore E. W169
Kristjanson, Stefan W174
Kritemeyer, Ellen A689
Kriz, Brian S. P227
Kriznik, Susan (Sue) P18
Krizsa, Thomas (Thom) A514
Krmpotic, Deb A115
Krmpotic, Deb P54
Kroboth, Michael (Mel) A712
Kroeker, Harrald F. A68
Kroell, ED (Eddie) P348
Kroenung, Stefan A85
Kroese, Shawntell A903
Krokos, Allan (Al) A370
Krol, Wojciech A223
Kroll, Edmund E (Ed) A180
Kroll, Michael (Mel) A846
Kroll, Sue A873
Kroll, Fred L. P34
Kroll, John (Jack) P551
Krone, Stacey (Stace) A347
Krone, Roger A. A534
Krone, Roger A A534
Kroner, Todd A825
Kroos, Karsten W385
Krop, Julie E23
Kropfelder, Katie P303
Kropiunik, Frank C. P15
Krotje, Charles A245
Krouse, Kevin P (Kev) E336
Krouse, Michael P366
Krow, Elizabeth (Beth) A135
Krueger, Phoebe A672
Krueger, Robert (Bob) A729
Krueger, Paul (Pauly) A761
Krueger, Brendan A765
Krueger, Brendan P421
Krueger, Michael (Mel) P449
Krueger, Roger P462
Krug, Allen (Al) A970
Kruger, Jackie E167
Kruger, James D. (Jim) A620

A = AMERICAN BUSINESS
E = EMERGING COMPANIES
P = PRIVATE COMPANIES
W = WORLD BUSINESS

Ladnier, Mark S. A677
Ladouceur, Danny P425
Laduke, David (Dave) A502
Laederich, Olivier A649
Laemmle, Mark A518
Laenger, William A753
Lafave, Lisa (Lis) A910
Laffaye, Ann E176
Lafferty, Kevin A270
Lafianza, Nancy P347
Lafitte, Michael J. (Mike) A174
Lafky, Bruce (Brucey) A912
Lafleur, Danielle (Dani) A733
Lafond, Dan A84
Lafontaine, Henri W146
LaFonte, Joseph P. P227
LaForge, Rusty N. A810
Lafranchi, Terra P517
LaFrence, Andrew D. C. (Andy) E393
LaFreniere, Kevin (Kev) A429
Lagacy, Julie A. A170
Lagano, Roxanne A982
Lagarrigue, Emmanuel W337
LaGatta, Loreen A. E421
LaGatta, Loreen A. A902
Lage, Jose L. P465
Laginestra, Charles (Charlie) A175
Lagioia, Andrea A223
Lagnado, Silvia A575
Lagneaux, Leon E29
Lagneaux, Leon A53
Lago, Virginia Del A565
Lagomarsino, Simone F. A437
Lagrone, Clay (Clayton) E169
Lagrone, Craig (Craigy) A633
Laguarta, Ramon A692
Lagutaine, Francesco P124
LaHaise, James A. E28
LaHaise, James A. A52
Lahey, Patrick (Paddy) A400
Lahey, John L. P404
Lai, Johnson E307
Lai, John (Jack) A589
Lai, Yue A834
Lai, Hy P591
Laigneau, Marianne W146
Laine, Jim E160
Laine, Jim (Jimmy) E160
Laing, John A268
Laing, Phillip G. A382
Laing, Sheila A467
Laing, Sheila P233
Lainis, Esther A163
Laird, Bruce A203
Laird, Timothy (Tim) P219
Lakatosh, Debra (Deb) A706
Lakdawala, Keta E267
Lake, Charles D. A19
Lake, Gary A287
Lake, Marianne A504
Lake, Frederick A556
Lake, Sylvia (Sylv) A619
Lake, Alexander (Al) A965
Lakshman, Girish A789
Lakshminarayanan, Ramesh E290
Lal, Pradeep W409
Lalama, Kristen (Kristy) A338
Lalanne, Jean-Christophe W14
Lalima, Anthony A109
Lalime, Yvonne (Vonne) E71
Lalime, Yvonne (Vonne) A152
Lalithakumar, Ananth A180
Lalk, Kelli A963
Lalla, Ronald A655
Lalljie, Paul S. E300
Lally, James B. A317
Lally, Bob P196
Lally-Green, Maureen P172
LaLonde, Timothy G. E146

Lalonde, Kenn W. W390
Lalor, Angela S. A262
Lalor, Angie A262
Lalwani, Ellen A527
Lam, Michael A109
Lam, Kristina (Chris) A136
Lam, Josiah A504
Lam, Gail A506
Lam, Katty A692
Lam, Winnie W A824
Lam, Gail P256
Lam, Ed W235
Lam, Barry W312
Lamadore, William (Bill) E383
Lamadore, William (Bill) A827
Lamadrid, Daniel (Dan) E441
Lamanna, James E403
Lamantia, Mary (Mar) P590
Lamar, William (Bibb) E369
Lamar, Paula A273
Lamar, Ann A340
Lamar, Cynthia (Cyn) A451
Lamar, William (Bibb) A794
Lamar, Paula P165
Lamarch, Sara P238
Lamarche, Michael Lamarche Michael (Mel) A895
Lamay, Troy A87
Lamb, Jeff (Jeffy) E163
Lamb, Chris (Chrissy) A44
Lamb, Russell (Russ) A137
Lamb, Todd A166
Lamb, Phil (Philly) A309
Lamb, John (Jack) A405
Lamb, Emily (Em) A407
Lamb, Matthew (Matt) A784
Lamb, Jeff A809
Lamb, Scott (Scotty) A898
Lamb, Eric P169
Lamb, Brian D. P602
Lamba, Jay (JayJay) A55
Lamba, Sanjiv W237
Lambert, Jeff (Jeffy) E144
Lambert, Karen A. A14
Lambert, Jeff (Jeffy) A135
Lambert, Jean A173
Lambert, Robert (Bob) A281
Lambert, Michael (Mel) A295
Lambert, Mark A409
Lambert, Betsy A465
Lambert, Bonnie (Bonbon) A672
Lambert, Richard A726
Lambert, Cameron (Cammie) A743
Lambert, Janet (Jan) A899
Lambert, Karen A. P9
Lambert, Jean P105
Lambert, Ken (Kenny) P312
Lambert, Nick W409
Lambertson, Leah E413
Lambertson, Steve A869
Lambertson, Steve P560
Lambiase, Matthew E90
Lambillotte, Gina A101
Lambis, Angelos A A608
Lambrecht, Peter (Pete) A309
Lambright, James (Jamie) A792
Lambright, Keith P285
Lambros, Irene (Rene) A82
Laming, Michael S. A403
Lamkin, Bryan A11
Lamm, Carl H. E458
Lamm, James (Jamie) A119
Lamm, Kim (Kimmy) A120
Lammers, Dale (Dal) A532
Lammers, Rene A692
Lammers, Jon (Jonny) A815
Lamneck, Kenneth T. (Ken) A477
Lamont, Justin A626
Lamont, Justin P345
Lamotte, Joseph A413
LaMountain, John (Jack) E40
Lamp, David L. (Dave) A953
Lamparski, Jerry (Jerr) A31
Lampe, Robert (Bob) A745
Lampen, Richard J. (Dick) E434

Lampert, Edward S. (Eddie) A789
Lampertz, Wally P564
Lamphere, Ralph (Ralphy) A619
Lampier, Carol A252
Lamping, Mark (Marky) A646
Lampman, Lori (Lor) A425
Lampo, Craig A. A57
Lampos, Kenneth (Ken) A745
Lamprecht, Catherine (Cate) P370
Lampropoulos, Fred P. E270
Lampropoulos, Justin E270
Lamy, David W360
Lancaster, Gary A485
Lancaster, Jake (Jacob) A502
Lancaster, Olin A743
Lancaster, Neil A829
Lance, Thomas (Thom) E65
Lance, Jean (Jeannie) A146
Lance, James (Jamie) A295
Lance, Phil P240
Lanchbury, Jerry S. E286
Lanci, Gianfranco W232
Lanctot, Chris (Chrissy) A166
Land, Jeff (Jeffy) A273
Land, Jeffrey (Jeff) A273
Land, David (Dave) A409
Land, Robert C (Bob) A497
Land, Steffen A664
Land, Thomas (Thom) P56
Land, Jeff (Jeffy) P165
Land, Jeffrey (Jeff) P165
Landa, Lisa E282
Landau, Mark (Marky) E156
Landau, Glenn R. A487
Landau, Igor W8
Landel, Michel W353
Landers, Scott E. E282
Landers, Bob A54
Landers, Janet A820
Landers, Pete (Petey) P574
Landes, Mike P34
Landes, Michael D. P176
Landes, Barbara L. P399
Landesman, Rich (Ric) A176
Landewee, Cassy P317
Landgraf, John (Jack) A106
Landgraf, John A892
Landgren, Peter (Pete) P587
Landi, Robert (Bob) A20
Landin, Anders A780
Landini, Terrie E176
Landis, Tess P285
Landman, Adam P514
Landon, Jane L. E446
Landon, Jodi P119
Landre, Jay A649
Landreth, David (Dave) A257
Landreville, Marge (Margaret) A789
Landrith, Jody A159
Landry, Susan (Sue) E176
Landry, David A252
Landry, Robert E. A750
Landry, Chris A785
Landry, Jay (JayJay) A824
Landry, Chris (Chrissy) A899
Landschulz, Mark A377
Landuyt, Mel (Melanie) E59
Landy, Nancy A199
Landy, Michael P. E280
Landy, Eugene W. E280
Landy, Nancy A435
Landy, Michael (Mel) A780
Lane, James A. E255
Lane, Alan J. E292
Lane, Angela A6
Lane, Danny A80
Lane, Randy A205
Lane, Janet (Jan) A252
Lane, Eric S. A409
Lane, Jeffrey H. A587
Lane, Andrew R. (Andy) A607
Lane, J. Bret A792
Lane, Rick (Ricky) A892
Lane, Danny P45
Lane, Norma J. P238

Lane, Tim (Timmy) P284
Lane, Eric P568
Lane, Charles E. P589
Lanel, Nicolas E146
Lanesey, Rob (Robbie) A490
Laney, Heather (Heath) E24
Laney, G. Timothy (Tim) A611
Lanford, Blake E445
Lang, Andras A246
Lang, Scott A. E373
Lang, Mark T. E386
Lang, Rick A54
Lang, Nicholas (Nick) A126
Lang, Edward A A758
Lang, Ed (Eddie) A759
Lang, Rebecca A (Becca) A899
Lang, Rebecca A899
Lang, Kevin (Kev) P280
Lang, Suzanne P313
Lang, Marcina B P601
Langan, Eric S. E351
Langan, Tom (Tommy) A718
Langan, Patrick (Paddy) A916
Langberg, Michael L. P107
Lange, Michael J. A279
Lange, Peter (Pete) A689
Lange, David (Dave) A831
Lange, Reinhard W227
Lange-Kuitse, Deborah (Deb) A576
Langenbahn, Paul A619
Langenburg, Dianna L. P619
Langenfeld, Camilla A415
Langenfeld, Jon A. A765
Langenfeld, Jon A. P420
Langenkamp, Max V (Maxwell) A202
Langenus, John (Jack) A62
Langerot, Danny P149
Langfitt, Chuck (Chucky) A883
Langford, Kevin T. A364
Langham, James E454
Langley, Tom (Tommy) A21
Langley, Judi A520
Langley, Martyn A664
Langley, Michael (Mel) A693
Langley, Clyde A785
Langley, W. John A299
Langley-Hawthorne, Tim A954
Langlois, Robert E176
Langlois, Mike (Mikey) A77
Langlois, Mike (Mikey) P41
Langmead, James H. E126
Langmead, James H. A298
Langone, Joey A764
Langridge, Nicholas (Nick) P249
Langsdorf, William (Bill) E407
Langston, Jeff (Jeffy) A490
Langton, John (Jack) A624
Lanier, Lawrence A344
Lanier, Andrea P427
Lanier, Sharon (Share) P601
Lanier, Stephen (Steve) P627
Laniewski, Jeffrey E167
Lanigan, Susan S A283
Lanik, Robert J. A173
Lanik, Robert J. P105
Lanis, Ken (Kenny) P568
Lankler, Douglas M. (Doug) A696
Lankton, Madelyn A883
Lannen, Angela (Angie) E29
Lannen, Angela (Angie) A53
Lannie, P. Anthony A64
Lannie, PAnthony A64
Lannie, P A64
Lanning, Michael (Mel) A82
Lannon, David A959
Lansdown, Guy A628
Lansford, Gordon E. P246
Lansford, Gordon E. P247
Lansing, Linda E392
Lansing, Jane (Ginny) A309
Lansing, Chris A692
Lanspa, Stephen (Steve) P148
Lant, Todd E60
Lanteri, Carrie A18

A = AMERICAN BUSINESS
E = EMERGING COMPANIES
P = PRIVATE COMPANIES
W = WORLD BUSINESS

Lewis, Haston A692
Lewis, Karla R. A756
Lewis, Randal D. A814
Lewis, Andrew (Andy) A818
Lewis, Clifford M (Cliff) A824
Lewis, Brian A834
Lewis, Bryant H A883
Lewis, Steve (Stevie) A891
Lewis, Jeff (Jeffy) A899
Lewis, Carl A900
Lewis, Jess (Jessica) A916
Lewis, Kim A916
Lewis, David (Dave) A942
Lewis, Marcie A950
Lewis, Linda A961
Lewis, Clinton A. (Clint) A982
Lewis, Janet (Jan) P71
Lewis, James R. (Jim) P76
Lewis, Lisa P127
Lewis, William W. P138
Lewis, Tom P203
Lewis, Tony (Tone) P339
Lewis, Donna L P349
Lewis, Bruce (Brucey) P362
Lewis, Lisa P383
Lewis, Rayburn S. P498
Lewis, Daniel K. P533
Lewis, Dallin P556
Lewis, Robert (Bob) P570
Lewis, Kim (Kimmy) P612
Lewis, Stuart W132
Lewis, Jonathan W282
Lewis, Stevan W364
Lewis-Hall, Freda C. A696
Lewitt, Lynne Rubin E71
Lewitt, Lynne Rubin A152
Lewnes, Ann A11
Ley, Nancy A429
Leyden, Bob (Bo) A429
Leyden, Shawn A729
Leydon, John (Jack) P554
Leyendecker, R. Greg E197
Leyendecker, R. Greg A433
Leyland, Ben (Benny) A883
Leyvi, Michele (Michie) A565
Lezmi, Gabriel E397
Lezuch, Celeste P627
Li, Moli E131
Li, Hermes E308
LI, Isabella E341
Li, Jeong-Tyng E397
LI, Yuliang A38
Li, Max (Maxwell) A86
Li, Richard (Dick) A135
Li, Ying A135
Li, Ling A164
Li, Beibei A208
Li, Zhenqin A603
Li, Jessie A689
LI, Isabella A714
Li, Ruohao A751
Li, Bo A839
Li, Ruohao P411
Li, Mehra P451
Li, Diana P551
Li, David K. P. W49
Li, Samson K. C. W49
Li, Adrian David M. K. W49
Li, Brian David M. B. W49
Li, Arthur K. C. W49
Li, Morris W120
Li, Baomin W211
Lian, Eric V. F. W404
Liang, Linda (Lin) E167
Liang, Chiu-Chu Liu (Sara) E390
Liang, Charles E390
Liang, Chiu Chu E390
Liang, Kai A205
Liang, Laura (Laur) A319

Liang, George C. A548
Liang, Lilly A635
Liang, Weikang W95
Liao, Samuel (Sam) A262
Liao, Tsan Chang W371
Liaw, Jeffrey E107
Libbe, Keri E113
Libbe, Scott W. P544
Libbra, Todd (Toddy) A937
Libby, Russell T. A843
Libby, Richardson A865
Liberatore, Lynne A584
Liberty, Daniel (Dan) A555
Librandi, Nancy (Nance) A624
Libstag, Gwen R. A409
Lich, Brad A. A300
Licho, Gary A843
Licht, Lisa (Lis) A975
Lichter, Steve E15
Lichthardt, Kanika P134
Lichtman, David B. E160
Lichtman, David B. A373
Lickteig, Becca E205
Liddiard, Bryan E274
Liddy, Michael (Mel) A120
Liding, Lawrence (Larry) A176
Lie, Penelope A665
Lieb, Dave (Davie) A866
Lieb, Dave (Davie) P540
Liebel, Hartmut A494
Lieber, Matthew A341
Lieberman, Jonathan E10
Lieberman, Robert A498
Lieberman, Andrea A565
Lieberman, Robert P254
Liebert, Rebecca A449
Liebhaber, Louis P260
Liebig, John E218
Liebler, William A485
Liebow, Elizabeth P158
Liebowitz, Robert (Bob) A12
Liebowitz, Richard S. P537
Liedel, Christopher P459
Liedtke, Eric W8
Liefer, Michael E445
Liefer, Jim (Jimmy) A937
Liekar, John (Jack) P108
Lien, Melanie (Mel) E336
Lienert, James (Jamie) A653
Lienhard, Jerome T. A834
Lightfoot, Lance P507
Lighty, Josh A124
Ligon, Duke R. E431
Lihua, Wang W298
Lijun, Zhao W96
Like, Steven K. E82
Likes, Rodman A12
Likes, Robert (Bob) A514
Likins, Steven A869
Likins, Steve A869
Likins, Steven P560
Likins, Steve P560
Lilavois, Ludgy L785
Lilja, Agneta W368
Lillard, Linda A109
Lillard, Lisa (Lis) A610
Lillemoe, Keith D. P530
Liller, Karen (Kare) P602
Lillibridge, Craig (Craigy) A175
Lillie, Rick (Ricky) P539
Lillis, Terrance J. (Terry) A716
Lillis, Joe (Joey) A896
Lillo, Bets A6
Lilly, E. Stephen (Steve) A360
Lilly, Nancy C (Nance) A544
Lilly, Brian F. A611
Lilly, Randy (Rand) A657
Lilly, Edward (Ed) P415
Lilygren, Sara A893
Lim, Jean E191
Lim, Bonnie (Bonbon) A38
Lim, James A123
Lim, Say A379
Lim, Jean A422
Lim, Henry W (Hal) P223

Lim, Sim S W127
Lima, Roland (Rollie) A364
Lima, Candido A678
Limbaugh, Corey (Core) A504
Limberg, Joachim W385
Limehouse, Capers P98
Limerick, Thomas S. (Stan) E159
Limerick, Thomas S. (Stan) A364
Limet, Domique W171
Limjoco, Adrianne A765
Limjoco, Michael (Mel) A963
Limjoco, Adrianne P421
Lin, Tong A86
Lin, Bob S (Bo) A140
Lin, Jennifer H (Jen) A727
Lin, Steve A824
Lin, Fan W101
Lin, Sheng-Chung W115
Lin, Shane S. I. W115
Lin, Jung-Lieh W115
Lin, Marc W.H. W115
Lin, Amy H.C. W120
Lin, J.K. W372
Lin, Henry W416
Lin, Simon H. M. W416
Lin, Scott W420
Lina, Paula A639
Linares, Larry (Lar) A48
Linares, Tony (Tone) A62
Linck, James (Jamie) P465
Lincoln, W A98
Lincoln, Robert (Bob) A117
Lincoln, Butch P36
Lincoln, Robert (Bob) P63
Lind, Sharon A115
Lind, Roger (Rog) A252
Lind, Dennis (Denny) A281
Lind, Sharon P54
Linda, Bennett P595
Lindauer, Matthew (Matt) A846
Lindberg, Bonita E409
Lindberg, Bonita A877
Lindberg, Larry (Lar) P358
Lindblad, Anders W379
Lindblom, Kristin M (Kristy) A766
Lindblom, Kristin M (Kristy) P421
Lindblom, Mike (Mikey) P492
Lindbloom, Chad M. A767
Linde, Douglas T. (Doug) E66
Linde, Henri E362
Linde, Tamara L. A729
Linde, Brian (Bri) A745
Linde, Ronald K. P94
Lindekugel, Jon T. A3
Lindell, Andrew (Andy) A784
Lindeman, B. John E77
Lindemann, Ellen (Elle) A24
Lindemann, Michael A86
Lindemann, James J. (Jim) A309
Lindemann, Deven P313
Linden, Tomas A957
Lindenberg, Maria (Mary) A194
Lindenmeyr, Adele P615
Linder, Kevin (Kev) A968
Linder, James P80
Linderman, Tricia (Trish) E403
Linderman, Jerome (Gerry) A376
Linderman, Tricia (Trish) A858
Linderman, LeeAnne B. A980
Lindholm, Wayne S. P224
Lindia, Paul (Pauly) A542
Lindlbauer, Wolfgang A563
Lindley, Dan (Danny) A641
Lindner, S. Craig A45
Lindner, Carl H. A45
Lindner, Russell C. (Rusty) A342
Lindner, Doug (Dougie) P413
Lindquist, T A18
Lindquist, Thomas M. (Tom) A956
Lindsay, Phillip A518
Lindsay, Steven (Steve) A529
Lindsay, Vivian (Viv) A916
Lindsay, Martha (Mar) P164
Lindsay, Andy P626
Lindseth, Alfred A. (Al) A704

Lindsey, Jimmy (Jim) E376
Lindsey, Steven L. E379
Lindsey, Steven (Steve) A105
Lindsey, Scot A166
Lindsey, Mary A. A231
Lindsey, Connie L A640
Lindsey, Paris A753
Lindsey, Jimmy (Jim) A806
Lindsey, Seth A899
Lindsey, Elaine (Elle) A929
Lindsey, Don P501
Lindsey, Patrick (Paddy) P627
Lindstadt, Jeffrey (Jeff) A1
Lindstrom, James M. E346
Lindstrom, Scott A629
Lindstrom, Merl R. A700
Lindstrom, Paula P87
Lindstrom, Donnie (Don) P247
Line, Thomas E. (Tom) E120
Linebarge, Thomas (Thom) A254
Linebarger, N. Thomas (Tom) A253
Linebarger, Thomas (Thom) A254
Lineberry, Joe A576
Linero, Adilia A504
Ling, Curtis E263
Ling, Christopher A143
Ling, Sam A166
Ling, Walt (Walter) A485
Ling, Hai A569
Ling, Karen W22
Lingafelter, David B. A385
Lingenfelter, Terry A359
Lingerfelt, Lisa P169
Lingsch, Bob (Bo) A13
Link, Matthew W. (Matt) E307
Link, Michelle (Michie) E340
Link, Jeff (Jeffy) A20
Link, Doug A456
Link, Mike (Mikey) A546
Link, Janet M. A685
Link, Mary (Mar) P121
Linn, Michael (Mel) E169
Linn, Terry E341
Linnartz, Stephanie C. A563
Linnehan, Frank P170
Linnen, Edward P. (Ned) A92
Linsey, Jay E201
Lintag, Ronald A136
Lintner, Bill (Billy) A485
Linton, Phillip (Phil) A175
Linton, Pete A249
Linton, Brandon (Bran) A563
Linton, Tim A874
Lintonsmith, Susan (Sue) E354
Linville, Jud A207
Linzer, Daniel I. P361
Liollio, Dean A704
Lionberg, Rachel (Rach) P607
Lionello, Gemma A637
Liotine, Joseph T. A957
Liotta, Gary P. A380
Lipar, Eric E241
Lipar, Jack E241
Lipari, Jack A726
Lipe, John B (Jack) A765
Lipe, John B (Jack) P421
Lipinski, John J. (Jack) A257
Lipitz, Roger C (Rog) A33
Lipka, Michael A429
Lipker, Stephen A31
Lipkin, Gerald H. A926
Lipman, Howard R. P190
Lipovaca, Zlatan E440
Lipper, Philip (Phil) A502
Lippert, Jason D. E239
Lippert, Keven K. E438
Lippert, Martin J. (Marty) A584
Lippi, Chris (Chrissy) A497
Lippman, Frederick P362
Lippmann, Patrick A100
Lippold, Dean A265
Lipps, Randall A. E312
Lips, Rob (Robbie) A490
Lipschultz, Tyler P. E307
Lipscomb, Judy P64

Lipscombe, Ailsa P551
Lipsey, William L. E347
Lipshitz, Ruth (Ruthy) A968
Lipski, David (Dave) A177
Lipson, Nancy (Nance) A628
Lipstone, Laurence A539
Lipton, Andrew (Andy) A603
Lirot, Luke E351
Lisboa, Persio V. A616
Lischwe, Joe (Joey) P140
Lisenby, Jeffrey P. A718
Lisle, William W13
Lisman, Michael (Mel) A946
Liss, Brian (Bri) A534
Liss, Barb (Barbie) A706
Lissalde, Fr□©d□©ric B. A144
Lissner, Mindy A175
Lissowski, Antoine W109
List, Steven E170
List, Alan A214
List-Stoll, Teri L. A865
Lister, Chip A281
Lister, Stephen W235
Litchfield, David (Dave) A295
Litchfield, Caroline (Carol) A580
Litchford, James P386
Litster, Kelly (Kel) A589
Littel, John (Jack) A557
Littell, Noah E317
Littell, Noah A666
Little, Robert (Bob) E232
Little, Mitchell (Mitch) E274
Little, Frank R. A2
Little, Jay A87
Little, Mark A140
Little, Paul (Pauly) A348
Little, Patricia A. A438
Little, T. Mitchell (Mitch) A559
Little, Daniel F. (Dan) A637
Little, Daniel A750
Little, James (Jamie) A916
Little, Melissa (Lissa) A957
Little, Stephen A971
Little, Robert P96
Little, George A. P218
Little, Daniel P411
Little, Dean P526
Little, Laura (Laur) P624
Little, Lou P631
Little, Tom W64
Littlejohn, Bill P451
Littley, Gordon (Gordy) A927
Littman, Owen E111
Littzi, John (Jack) A126
Litzau, Tammy (Tam) A520
Litzenberger, John (Jack) A834
Litzinger, Ronald L. A305
Liu, Chang E49
Liu, Shawn A395
Liu, Chang A99
Liu, Eugenia A150
Liu, Katy (Catherine) A339
Liu, Tao A592
Liu, Dan (Danny) A747
Liu, Grace (Gracie) A824
Liu, Don H. A846
Liu, Don H. A971
Liu, Cricket P238
Liu, Marsha P359
Liu, Hanmin P619
Liu, Yuzhi W95
Liu, Jianzhong W102
Liu, Cheng-Hsie W115
Liu, I. Cheng W120
Liu, Teng Chen W189
Liu, Guoyue W190
Liu, Mark W372
Lively, Beverly A571
Lively, David (Dave) P362
Liverani, Giovanni W33
Liverett, Deborah (Deb) A640
Liveris, Andrew N. A289
Livesay, Bruce A. A367
Livesay, Jackie J (Jack) P145
Livingood, Jack P74

Livingston, Mark (Marky) E311
Livingston, John T. A15
Livingston, Robert A. (Bob) A287
Livingston, Andrew A464
Livingston, Debra P88
Livingston, Tanya P240
Livingston, Keith P561
Livingstone, Mary (Mar) A111
Livingstone, Linda A. P524
Livingstone, Catherine B. W111
Livne, Omer A479
Livonius, Robert E. (Bob) E29
Lizardi, Rafael A859
Lizardi, Lizette A928
Lizhong, Yu A626
Lizhong, Yu P345
Ljungqvist, Katarina W368
Lloyd, Jack E197
Lloyd, Chris E305
Lloyd, Scott (Scotty) A264
Lloyd, Jennifer (Jen) A273
Lloyd, Paul (Pauly) A304
Lloyd, Robert A. (Rob) A393
Lloyd, Jack A434
Lloyd, Robert (Bob) A965
Lloyd, Jennifer (Jen) P165
Lloyd, Lisa Kay P510
Lloyd, James P589
Lo, James (Jamie) E187
Lobaugh, Mike P215
Lobel, Richard (Dick) A177
Lobel, Heidi A281
Lobel, Elie W293
Lobo, Kevin A. A831
Loboda, Amy A429
Loc, Phat E168
Lochen, Richard S. E331
Lochen, Richard S. A691
Locher, Vince E415
Locher, Vince A888
Lochner, James (Jamie) A894
Lock, Jim (Jimmy) A613
Locke, John (Jack) A843
Locke, Wally P109
Locke, Justin P127
Locken, Dale P462
Lockery, Michael (Mel) A163
Lockett, Traishon E139
Lockhart, David (Dave) A208
Lockhart, Dennis P. A340
Lockhart, Dennis P. A343
Lockhart, Laura (Laur) A511
Lockie, Joan E62
Lockridge, Matthew (Matt) E450
Lockwood, Kenneth (Ken) A379
Lockwood, Charles J. P190
Lockyer, Linda A166
Locoh-Donou, Francois E149
Locurto, Robert A504
Locurto, Russ G (Russell) A743
Lodato, Jane E394
Lodato, Jane A838
Lodes, Terry A954
Lodesani, Eliano Omar W202
Lodge, Simon W368
Lodhi, Mujib P625
Loeber, John (Jack) A211
Loeffel, Paul A641
Loeffler, Martin H. A57
Loeffler, Jay S. P530
Loeger, Julie A276
Loegering, Cory L. A64
Loessin, Bruce (Brucey) P103
Loew, Richard A682
Loewald, Thomas W. (Tom) A871
Loewen, Bernd W225
Loewengart, Victoria A117
Loewengart, Victoria P63
Lofberg, Per G. H. A258
Loffert, Donna (Don) A390
Loffler, Alicia (Ali) P362
Loflin, Joy P401
Loftin, Shelly E55
Loftin, Shelly A122
Loftin, Paul J. A756

Loftis, Harry (Hare) P416
Lofton, Kevin E. A173
Lofton, Kevin E. P105
Loftus, Mike E98
Loftus, Carolyn (Carol) P438
Logan, Joseph W. (Joe) E397
Logan, Joe (Joey) E397
Logan, Jonathan B. A217
Logan, Jason (Jase) A228
Logan, Erik A277
Logan, Lorie A341
Logan, Stephen (Steve) A429
Logan, Lyle L A640
Logan, John (Jack) A835
Logan, Jonathan B. P132
Logan, Roger P385
Loge, Jim (Jimmy) A309
Logeley, Kirk A843
Logeman, Scott (Scotty) A470
Logemann, Cari P43
Logiudice, Salvatore (Sal) P538
Lograsso, Tim (Timmy) E26
Logt, Mike Vande A530
Logue, Joseph (Joe) A143
Logue, David (Dave) P384
Loh, Evan A696
Loh, Marcel P498
Lohan, Jim (Jimmy) A855
Lohmeier, Michelle J. A815
Lohr, Lece A76
Lohr, Dan (Danny) A217
Loiacono, Nicholas (Nick) A576
Loiseau, Valery A621
Loken, John (Jack) A549
Lokes, Dave A383
Lokke, Scott (Scotty) A156
Lollar, Wes (Wesley) A871
Lollar, Donald (Don) P369
Lomas, Terry (Terr) A104
Lomas, Brian (Bri) A392
Lomas, Alisa (Lisa) A925
Lombard, Jim A903
Lombard, Eric W33
Lombardi, Ronald M. (Ron) E342
Lombardi, David (Dave) E378
Lombardi, Julian A296
Lombardi, Leonard V. A359
Lombardi, Bill (Billy) A429
Lombardi, Rita A726
Lombardi, Michael J. A882
Lombardi, Julian P171
Lombardo, Steve E276
Lombardo, Kevin A427
Lombardo, Thomas A502
Lombardo, Lauren (Laur) A800
Lombardo, Michael A873
Lombra, Sherri A281
Lomeli, Leopolo A91
Lomel□n, Carlos Salazar W162
Lommel, Ryan D A546
Lon, Lyons A230
Lonardo, Anthony J (Tony) A544
Loncar, Patrick (Paddy) A342
London, Adam (Ad) A177
London, Todd (Toddy) A280
London, Lisa (Lis) P591
London, Daniel T. (Dan) W5
Londono, Carlos (Carl) A670
Lonegro, Frank A. A250
Lonergan, Robert A. A81
Lonergan, John (Jack) A649
Long, Gary R. E179
Long, Tony (Tone) E179
Long, Carol E199
Long, Gary S. E341
Long, Ann (Annie) A5
Long, Christopher (Chris) A51
Long, Michael J. (Mike) A73
Long, Suzanne (Sue) A135
Long, Steve (Stevie) A136
Long, Tony A174
Long, Rodney (Rod) A181
Long, Jeffrey R. A247
Long, Thomas E. (Tom) A314
Long, Joseph B. A323

Long, Clinton A351
Long, Michael (Mel) A392
Long, Carol A436
Long, Rebeckah A814
Long, Andy A871
Long, Mike (Mikey) A925
Long, Susan A937
Long, Mark P. A952
Long, Michael T. P210
Long, Ronald R. (Ron) P509
Long, Greg P561
Long, Eva (Evalyn) P600
Long, John W. P602
Long, Annabelle Yu W66
Long, Peter W395
Long-Knize, Michelle (Mitch) A281
Longacre, Doug A371
Longbrake, John (Jack) P551
Longfield, Charles L. (Chuck) E60
Longhi, Vince (Vinnie) A525
Longhi, Mario A913
Longmire, Rhonda S A235
Longo, Christopher M. A58
Longo, Joseph A410
Longo, Jeffrey (Jeff) A883
LONGO, ROB (Robbie) A942
Longobardi, Joseph (Jo) E336
Longobardi, Sara M. A689
Longpre, Martin A249
Longpre, Denis A735
Longren, David C. A707
Longshore, Rob A87
Longsworth, Nora P555
Longwell, Sharon A576
Lonnett, Chris (Chrissy) A606
Look, Christian (Chris) A106
Looker, Travis (Trav) P570
Loomis, Lawrence (Larry) P34
Loomis, Anna P330
Looney, Michael (Mel) A180
Looney, Allison P515
Looney, Bernard W78
Loosmore, Susan (Sue) A844
Lootens, Ken (Kenny) A227
Loparco, Michael J. A494
Loper, D. Shane A420
Lopes, Richard T P440
Lopes, Luiz Ildefonso Sim□□es W81
Lopez, Jose E128
Lopez, Jorge E177
Lopez, Pam (Pamela) E438
Lopez, Alex (Al) A140
Lopez, Jodi A169
Lopez, Adrian (Ryan) A204
Lopez, Yolanda A211
Lopez, Cynthia A339
Lopez, Randolph A504
Lopez, Tom A522
Lopez, Andres A. A670
Lopez, Frank (Frankie) A774
Lopez, Frank A918
Lopez, Orlando P42
Lopez, Ana A56
Lopez, David S. P156
Lopez, Karen (Kare) P232
Lopez, Noemi P538
Lopez, Matthew (Matt) P555
Lopez, Andreu Plaza W46
Lopez-Lay, Ginoris A355
Lopiccolo, Michele (Michie) A316
Lopman, Abe P642
Lopriore, Richard P. A728
Lopriore, Richard P. A729
Lops, John (Jack) P287
Loranger, Michelle (Mitch) A824
Lorber, Howard M. E288
Lorber, Marc (Marcy) A424
Lorber, Howard M. E434
Lorberbaum, Jeffrey S. A596
Lorch, Nicole S. E160
Lord, Ellen A860
Lord, W. Leighton P461
Loree, James M. (Jim) A817
Lorei, Greg P246
Lorei, Greg P247

A = AMERICAN BUSINESS
E = EMERGING COMPANIES
P = PRIVATE COMPANIES
W = WORLD BUSINESS

Loren, Singletary A613
Lorenson, Katie A. E277
Lorenson, Katie A. A595
Lorent, Patrick (Paddy) A689
Lorentson, Jeff A368
Lorentson, Jeffery B. A368
Lorentson, Jeffrey B (Jeff) A369
Lorenz, Jonathan C. A218
Lorenz, Vikki A793
Lorenz, Vikki P445
Lorenzen, Jeffrey D. (Jeff) A42
Lorenzo, Maribel A183
Lorenzo, Manny (Emanuel) P190
Lores, Enrique A458
Lorge, Timothy J. (Tim) A248
Lori, William E. A519
Lori, Michael A895
Lori, William E. P266
Lorimer, Linda (Lin) P641
Loring, Eileen (Elle) P462
Lorsson, Devin A527
Loscalzo, Joseph P514
Losch, William C. (BJ) A367
Loschiavo, Lori (Lor) A504
Losenegger, Michael J. E157
Losenegger, Michael J. A358
Losey, Gary A351
Losh, J. Michael (Mike) A567
Loshin, David S. P362
Loshitzer, Zohar E229
Losik, Dennis A94
Losse, Jim (Jimmy) A395
Lostin, Chad A843
Lotfi, Negeen P112
Lothary, Jim (Jimmy) A766
Lothary, Jim (Jimmy) P421
Lothrop, Dave (Davie) A263
Lotina, Jesus Maria Zabalza W45
Lott, Charles E. E82
Lott, Tanya P98
Lottner, Jens W345
Lotvin, Alan M. A258
Lotz, John A101
Lou, Mary (Mar) P401
Loucks, Gary A351
Loucks, Andrew A510
Loudermilk, Kerry P385
Louette, Pierre W293
Loufman, Donna A746
Louge, Michael W. (Mike) P366
Loughlin, Edward D. (Ed) E366
Loughlin, Anne (Annie) A602
Loughman, Tim A966
Loughman, Tim P640
Loughrey, F. Joseph (Joe) E204
Loughrey, Kevin P563
Loughridge, Charles (Charlie) A981
Loughry, Ed C. E335
Loughry, Ed C. A703
Loughry, Andrea J. P604
Louie, Elsa A846
Louie, Janet (Jan) A981
Louis, Gary A786
Louis, Donna (Don) St P64
Louis, David N. P530
Louissaint, Obed A485
Loureiro, Guilherme W412
Lousada, Max P624
Louther, Carlissa A208
Loutsch, Richard P145
Louttit, Gordon L P511
Louvet, Patrice J. L. A719
Louvigny, Anne (Annie) A44
Louw, Wy E363
Louwagie, Joe (Joey) E437
Louwagie, Ben (Benny) A309
Lovaglio, Luigi W52
Lovaglio, Luigi W400
Love, Paul A94

Love, Kelli A166
Love, Marcella A194
Love, Judith S. A227
Love, David (Dave) A351
Love, Valerie (Val) A499
Love, Robert A727
Love, Michelle (Mitch) A768
Love, George A972
Love, Stan P84
Love, Viki P403
Lovejoy, David R. E160
Lovejoy, Mary F (Mar) A860
Lovelace, Charles E242
Loveless, Kris (Krissy) A899
Lovelick, Roseanne P170
Lovell, Ken (Kenny) P384
Lovelock, John-David E176
Loveman, Gary W. A17
Loveman, Gary W. A156
Lovett, Scott (Scotty) A479
Lovett, Melendy E. A887
Lovik, Kenneth (Ken) E160
Loving, Sherry (Sherr) P448
Lovit, Elaine (Elle) A347
Lovoi, John V. E125
Low, Stan E232
Low, Steffen A621
Low, Mark (Marky) A660
Low, Lewis P274
Low, Robert E. P341
Lowden, Simon A692
Lowe, John E. A64
Lowe, Challis A77
Lowe, Ron (Ronnie) A108
Lowe, Meg A278
Lowe, Rich A430
Lowe, Wendy A603
Lowe, Edward A. (Sandy) A653
Lowe, Corey H. A773
Lowe, Carol P. A788
Lowe, Jacki A808
Lowe, Albert (Al) A937
Lowe, Challis P41
Lowe, Terrill P138
Lowe, Terrill P138
Lowe, Tamara P324
Lowe, William J. P571
Lowe, Nick W368
Lowen, Ralph (Ralphy) E445
Lowenthal, Edward E25
Lowenthal, Edward E355
Lowery, Deborah (Deb) A18
Lowery, Richard M. A126
Lowery, Norman D. A366
Lowery, Tony (Tone) A497
Lowery, Joseph (Jo) A841
Lowery, Frederick M. (Fred) A871
Lowery, Gerard (Gerold) A972
Lowery-Biggers, LoriAnn V. E295
Lowery-Biggers, LoriAnn V. A615
Lowery-Yilmaz, Barbara A439
Lowman, David B. (Dave) A388
Lowman, Mark (Marky) P56
Lowney, Peter E157
Lowney, Peter A358
Lowney, Jeff A539
Lowrey, Louise E165
Lowrey, Louise A381
Lowrey, Dennis (Denny) A395
Lowrey, Charles F. (Charlie) A726
Lowrey, Wayne A905
Lowrie, Dan A465
Lowry, Bard A364
Lowry, Jane (Ginny) P401
Lowry, Judith P602
Lowson, James (Jamie) A106
Lowth, Simon W82
Lowther, Rob A727
Lowy, Laura A112
Loxam, Teri (Terrance) A580
Loxsom, Christine A689
Loy, Bertrand E140
Loyd, James (Jamie) E51
Loyd, James (Jamie) A111
Loyd, Anna (Ann) A523

Loyd, Heath A702
Lozano, Rebecca A112
Lozano, Nativido A483
Lozano, Philip (Phil) A546
Lozano, Javier A592
Lozano, Cressida A760
Lozzio, Jennifer (Jen) A164
Lu, Eugene Y. C. A22
Lu, Chris (Chrissy) A171
Lu, Qi A592
Lu, Gary W112
Lubar, Sheldon B. E190
Lubarsky, Neil P562
Lubbe, Rossouw E84
Lubbers, Matt E30
Lubel, Kimberly S. (Kim) A249
Lubelczyk, Stephen A617
Lubeley, Aaron R. P448
Lubelli, Luigi W33
Lubert, Ira M. A866
Lubert, Ira M. P540
Lubin, Michael (Mel) E438
Lubin, Mike E438
Lubin, Bruce S. A717
Lubitz, Kevin E153
Lubitz, Kevin A349
Lubitz, Allan A581
Lublin, Scott A112
Luc, Billot A203
Lucarelli, Jason (Jase) A947
Lucarelli, Charles D. P307
Lucas, Roger C. E58
Lucas, Jane (Ginny) E177
Lucas, Karin (Ren) E236
Lucas, Richard M. (Rich) E444
Lucas, Christopher (Chris) A163
Lucas, John T. A411
Lucas, John (Jack) A573
Lucas, Randy (Rand) A613
Lucas, Alessandra A692
Lucas, Thomas J. (Tom) A795
Lucas, John P125
Lucas, John H. P260
Lucas, Paul P463
Lucas, Bryan P508
Lucas, Alfredo Escobar San W25
Lucas, Patrice W300
Lucchese, Cynthia L. (Cindy) E204
Lucchino, Larry P158
Lucciola, Dario E45
Luce, Edgar A. (Ed) E131
Lucero, Tammy (Tam) A115
Lucero, Tammy (Tam) P54
Lucey, Matthew C. A682
Luciano, Juan R. A70
Luciano, Louis (Lou) A874
Luciano, Lou A875
Lucien, Kent T. E261
Lucien, Kent T. A106
Lucier, Gregory T. E307
Lucier, Chris (Chrissy) P607
Lucier, Christopher P607
Luckert, William (Bill) A163
Luckett, Jon (Jonny) E213
Luckett, Jon (Jonny) A469
Luckoff, Jeff A471
Lucks, Cheryl W. P336
Lucy, William P. (Bill) A689
Luddecke, Louis (Lou) A527
Ludden, Paul W. P465
Ludeman, Christopher R. A174
Ludford, Brad A173
Ludford, Brad P105
Ludington, Robert (Bob) A868
Ludington, Robert (Bob) P545
Ludtke, Cary A98
Ludwick, Ron A101
Ludwick, Brent A706
Ludwig, David F. E48
Ludwig, Brett A166
Ludwig, Logan D. A519
Ludwig, Milton (Milt) A913
Ludwig, Mike (Mikey) A949
Ludwig, Logan T. P266
Ludwig, Tom P285

Ludwig, Michael (Mel) P551
Ludwig, Todd P626
Luedecke, Richard (Dick) A270
Lueders, Richard (Dick) A511
Luelmo, Diego E436
Luersman, Abbe A957
Luersman, Abby A957
Luetkenhaus, Brandy A569
Luettke, Maura P555
Luff, Paula P160
Luffman, Debra P303
Luffman, Justin P624
Luftman, Jason (Jase) E94
Lugo, David (Dave) P435
Luh, Bing E317
Luh, Bing A666
Luippold, Wayne P399
Luis, Ana (An) A194
Luisi, Michael E454
Luiz, Gerald (Gerry) A649
Luka, Chris (Chrissy) A12
Luka-Lognone, Ida W24
Lukatch, Heath E223
Luke, Dan A464
Lukes, Donald (Don) P571
Lukiewski, David J. P336
Lukis, Lawrence J. E345
Lulich, Michael A372
Luliis, Dino E359
Luly, Jay R. E136
Lum, Jonathan (John) E113
Lum, Bennett A205
Lumb, Richard A. W5
Lumpkin, Linda A291
Lumpkins, Robert L. A604
Lumpkins, Luanne P370
Lumsden, Evin A752
Lumsden, Chris A. A793
Lumsden, Chris A. P445
Luna, Philip A466
Luna, Michael (Mel) P431
Luna-Walker, Nancy (Nance) A84
Lunak, Leslie N. A112
Lunardi, John (Jack) A139
Lund, Marsha (Marcella) E321
Lund, John T. E422
Lund, Matthew E445
Lund, Elizabeth A140
Lund, Richard (Dick) A398
Lund, Christoffer A743
Lund, John T. A907
Lund, Kenny P19
Lund, Ed (Eddie) P19
Lund, Dennis P. P385
Lund-Jurgensen, Kirsten A696
Lundberg, M A217
Lundberg, Jan M. A543
Lundberg, Fredrik W368
Lunde, Matthew (Matt) A937
Lundeen, Christi P467
Lundergan, Dan K. P606
Lundgren, David J. A420
Lundgren, John (Jack) P312
Lundie, Ian A855
Lundquist, Thomas (Thom) E268
Lundquist, Steve (Stevie) A166
Lundquist, Jane L. A473
Lundquist, Andy A520
Lundquist, Thomas (Thom) A577
Lundquist, Stephanie A. A846
Lundquist, Curt A925
Lundquist, Keith P228
Lundy, James H. (Jim) E448
Lundy, James H. (Jim) A951
Lunn, Eric P23
Lunsey, Archie A471
Lunsford, Larry W (Lar) P191
Luo, Susan (Sue) A824
Luoma, Gary (Gar) E253
Luong, Bruce (Brucey) E88
Luongo, Peter (Pete) A699
Lupe, John A195
Lupe, John P115
Lupi, Francois A208

Mandel, Gail A968
Mandel, Carol A. P345
Mandel, Adrienne A. P625
Mandell, Paula A554
Mandell, Joyce P429
Mandell, James P517
Manders, Matthew G. (Matt) A198
Mandersson, Magnus W379
Mandinach, Barry M. E439
Mandine, Beatrice W293
Mandler, Ronald (Ron) A525
Mandracchia, Matt A732
Mandraccia, Crocifissa A70
Manduca, Paul W309
Maneker, Amy P121
Maness, Kathi D E179
Maness, Yolanda A252
Maness, Maryrose P624
Manfredo, John P349
Manfredonia, Donald L. A372
Mang, John (Jack) A720
Mangalick, Rita A136
Mangano, Rob P275
Mangel, Todd E168
Mangel, Allen W. P415
Mangel, Barry P631
Mangiaracina, Brian A54
Mangieri, Theresa (Terry) A369
Mangino, Louis (Lou) P69
Mango, John (Jack) A359
Mangold, Ken (Kenny) A463
Mangram, Alicia (Ali) P252
Mangum, Chris (Chrissy) A393
Mangum, Jamey A743
Mani, Nat A780
Maniaci, Nick (Nicky) A87
Maniar, Mihir A505
Maniates, Zenaida A895
Manifold, Albert W119
Manigan, Elizabeth (Beth) P193
Manigault, Pierre P98
Manion, Sheila (Sheil) P431
Manion, Roger (Rog) P600
Maniscalco, Michael A785
Maniscalco, Sal (Salvitore) A835
Manjarrez-Williams, Marcela A180
Mankin, Eric P505
Manko, Edward E434
Mankowski, Matt A372
Manley, Duncan A718
Manley, Gerard A. (Gerry) W289
Manlove, Diane A846
Mann, John E177
Mann, Neil A28
Mann, Bill (Billy) A31
Mann, Monica A133
Mann, Chris (Chrissy) A535
Mann, W David A563
Mann, Bob A616
Mann, Robert (Bob) A779
Mann, Rob (Robbie) A843
Mann, Romy A930
Mann, Laurence (Laurie) A975
Mann, Neil P18
Mann, Erica L. W60
Mann, Trevor W259
Mannard, Kelly (Kel) A641
Mannarino, Gwen A29
Manne, Robert (Bob) E419
Mannella, Nick A972
Mannello, Louis J. A415
Mannello, Stephen (Steve) A743
Manners, Jim (Jimmy) A876
Mannhardt, Thilo W398
Manning, Brian (Bri) E334
Manning, Vickie E335
Manning, Martin F. (Marty) A14
Manning, Charles (Charlie) A15
Manning, Bill (Billy) A163
Manning, Fred (Freddy) A465
Manning, Brian (Bri) A703
Manning, Vickie A703
Manning, Anna A754
Manning, Timothy A767
Manning, Martin F. (Marty) P9

Manning, Kim B (Kimmy) P148
Manning, Dave (Davie) P410
Manning, Robert J. (Rob) W364
Mannino, William A972
Mannis, Avi A. E192
Mannle, Kevin (Kev) P334
Manor, Mary (Mar) A874
Manos, Roseann E372
Manos, John G. A111
Manos, Roseann A798
Manos-Mchenry, Debbie A464
Manosalva, Magda W142
Mansaw, Marquise A610
Manseau, James J. E67
Manseau, James J. A147
Mansell, Kevin B. A520
Manser, Steve E73
Mansfield, Jeff (Jeffy) A408
Mansfield, William P. A413
Mansfield, Stephen L. (Steve) P315
Mansho, George (Georgey) A736
Mansikka, Heikki A6
Mansolillo, Scott A126
Mansoor, Arshad P178
Mansour, Ziad E373
Mansour, Carolyn A317
Mansour, Ashraf P471
Mansuetti, Mike A763
Mansuetti, Mike P420
Mansuri, Muzammil A406
Mantaring, Rizalina G. W364
Mantel, Constance (Connie) A166
Mantell, Edmund (Ed) P373
Mantella, Philomena V. P356
Manter, Wendy P288
Manternach, Jacquie E197
Manternach, Jacquie A434
Mantia, Linda W246
Mantua, Philip J. A778
Mantua, Mitch A784
Mantville, Kevin (Kev) A473
Mantz, Jay A536
Manzano, Wilhelmina P537
Manzari, Steven J (Steve) A341
Manzella, Jaci A369
Manzi, Jim P. A871
Manzo, Mark (Marky) A32
Manzuk, Chuck (Chucky) A792
Mapes, Tim A269
Maple, Sherry A820
Maples, Tracy A198
Maples, Byron A843
Maquat, Robert (Bob) A689
Mara, Thomas (Thom) A537
Marachilian, Philip (Phil) P348
MARAMOTTI, LUIGI W118
Marangiello, Marsha A82
Marangiello, Marsha (Marcella) A82
Marani, Richard F. A435
Marano, Colleen A499
Marano, Ronald P (Ron) A891
Maranto, Frank A571
Maranuk, Leigh (Leah) E168
Marasigan, Glenn E394
Marasigan, Darby A205
Marasigan, Glenn A838
Marasovich, Jennifer (Jen) A87
Marbach, Kenneth D. A320
Marbert, Jeanette E. E217
Marcano, Raul A18
MarcAurele, Joseph J. (Joe) A940
Marced, Maria W372
Marcegaglia, Emma W154
MARCEY, THOMAS (Thom) A168
Marchand, Gilles A519
Marchand, Karmar P103
Marchand, Gilles P267
Marchelletta, Michael (Mel) A15
Marchena, Marcos R. P550
Marcheschi, Michael P358
Marchetti, Kevin (Kev) E334
Marchetti, Page A342
Marchetti, Kevin (Kev) A703
Marchetto, Eric (Ric) A887
Marchik, Katie P244

Marchioni, John J. A790
Marchisello, Karen (Kare) E400
Marchozzi, Thomas A918
Marcial, Dora P307
Marciel, Susan (Sue) A106
Marcinczyk, Marty (Mart) A225
Marcisz, Peter (Pete) E348
Marco, Maria Di A922
Marcone, Rock P34
Marcopulos, Tamara A341
Marcotte, James A. (Jim) A316
Marcovitz, James (Jamie) A629
Marcroft, Darlene (Darl) E419
Marcum, R. Alan A270
Marcus, George M. E144
Marcus, David (Dave) E436
Marcus, Deborah A31
Marcus, Judy A137
Marcus, Catherine A727
Marcus, Stu A910
Marcus, Lawrence A927
Marcus, Larry (Lar) A927
Mardaga, Pete (Petey) A706
Marden, Paul (Pauly) A916
Marek, Troy A753
Maren, Arnita A253
Marepalli, Srikanth P615
Maresca, Kristin (Kristy) A112
Maresco, Peter (Pete) A831
Maressa, Joseph A. P260
Mareuse, Olivier W83
Marfisi, Anthony (Tony) E165
Marfisi, Anthony (Tony) A381
Marger, Brian (Bri) A430
Margetts, Mary E122
Margolin, Eric M. A167
Margolis, Joseph D. (Joe) E148
Margolius, Steven A432
Margules, Gary (Gar) P363
Margulies, Bonnie A82
Margulies, Bonnie (Bonbon) A82
Marhoun, Eric A345
Mariani, John (Jack) A124
Mariani, John K. P260
MARIE, SCOTT (Scotty) A774
Marien, Scott (Scotty) A635
Marien, Philippe W76
Marin, Mark (Marky) A735
Marina, Eka A439
Marinakis, Eric (Ric) A245
Marine, Jon A570
Marinez, Lauren (Laur) P320
Marino, Michael J (Mel) A156
Marino, Cathy A179
Marino, Anthony S. (Tony) A362
Marino, Matthew (Matt) A718
Marino, William J. (Bill) A788
Marino, Georgie P448
Marino, Rita W154
Marinsik, Daniel (Dan) A780
Marinzel, Ron (Ronnie) P448
Marion, Elaine D. E141
Marion, Diane A159
Maripuri, Latha A629
Maris, George (Georgey) A640
Maritato, Christopher (Chris) A804
Maritz, W. Stephen (Steve) P291
Mariucci, Angelo (Andy) A390
Mark, Richard J. A40
Mark, Joe A816
Mark, William P473
Mark, Joe P479
Markantonis, George M. A530
Markel, Anthony F. A562
Markel, Steven A. A562
Markel, Tom (Tommy) P303
Markelis, Pablo A765
Markell, Peter K. A680
Markell, Peter K. P377
Markell, Peter K. P570
Markey, Jeff (Jeffy) A467
Markey, Jeff (Jeffy) P233
Markezich, Ron (Ronnie) A592
Markham, Kevin E250
Markham, William (Bill) A883

Markle, Justin A295
Markle, Nancy (Nance) P610
Markley, Stephen (Steve) A514
Markley, Steve P167
Markofski, Dean A765
Markofski, Dean P421
Markovich, Nick A465
Markovitz, Mike (Mikey) E264
Markovitz, Mike (Mikey) A572
Marks, Steven M. E374
Marks, Alan (Al) A302
Marks, Stanley W. P460
Marks, Chris W327
Markson, Larry (Lar) P71
Markus, Nika A124
Markuson, David (Dave) P515
Markwalter, Jack W85
Marlett, Michelle (Michie) A972
Marlette, Tim G. A233
Marlin, Morris A351
Marlin, Chris A536
Marlow, Gary A356
Marlow, Larry P364
Marlow, Peter (Pete) P600
Marnick, Cliff (Clifford) A502
Marnick, Sam A815
Maroc, Genny P276
Marold, Paul E248
Maron, Dennis (Denny) A226
Maroni, Bradley A133
Marotta, Richard M. E56
Marotta, Richard M. A128
Marotta, Michael A430
Maroulis, George E116
Maroulis, George (Georgey) E371
Maroulis, George A255
Maroulis, George (Georgey) A798
Maroulis, Pamela (Pam) P303
Maroun, Nabih A143
Marpe, Joel A937
Marple, Tony (Tone) P288
Marquardt, Geri A140
Marquardt, Becky A280
Marquardt, Frederick J. (Rick) A619
Marquardt, Rick (Ricky) A619
Marquardt, James A (Jamie) P82
Marquardt, R. Scott P289
Marquardt, Jane (Ginny) P289
Marquardt, Robert P289
Marquardt, Rolf W368
Marques, Roberto de Oliveira A599
Marques, Antonio A699
Marques, John A P55
Marques, Miguel Athayde W169
Marquess, Lura P591
Marquez, Antonio F. E126
Marquez, Antonio F. A298
Marquez, Maricarmen A566
Marquez, Melanie P602
Marquis, Michael (Mel) A499
Marquis, Matt (Matty) A934
Marr, Christopher P. (Chris) E115
Marr, John S. E416
Marr, Richard R (Dick) A269
Marr, David (Dave) A736
Marr, Tommy P228
Marr, David W419
Marra, Peter (Pete) E372
Marra, Peter (Pete) A798
Marrero, Julio A552
MARRI, ALBERTO W41
MARRION, RICHARD A (Dick) E97
Marriott, Richard E. A456
Marriott, John (Jack) A514
Marriott, J. W. (Bill) A564
Marriott, David A576
Marron, Mark P. E141
Marrone, Nicholas A112
Marrow, John (Jack) A925
Marrs, Douglas W. (Doug) A414
Marrs, Sally (Sal) A766
Marrs, Sally (Sal) P421
Marrugi, Jason (Jase) A932
Marrugi, Jason (Jase) P616
Marschall, Patrick A118

Mooradian, Anne (Annie) A666
Moore, Heather (Heath) E6
Moore, Philip (Phil) E192
Moore, Troy E272
Moore, Frederick V. (Fred) E272
Moore, Todd R. E297
Moore, Pattye L. E354
Moore, Daniel M. E398
Moore, Jonathan E413
Moore, H. Lynn E416
Moore, Greg A3
Moore, Scott A6
Moore, Richard (Dick) A28
Moore, Colin A51
Moore, Alison (Alli) A55
Moore, Shawn A109
Moore, John A109
Moore, Kimberly E (Kim) A120
Moore, Beth (Betty) A135
Moore, Stephen (Steve) A143
Moore, Colleen A156
Moore, Stephen L. A173
Moore, Vaughn D A208
Moore, Elizabeth D. A241
Moore, Everett (Eve) A259
Moore, Julie L (Jules) A303
Moore, Jim (Jimmy) A304
Moore, Johnnie A342
Moore, Susan (Sue) A342
Moore, Steve A344
Moore, Richard T. A355
Moore, Lauren (Laur) A372
Moore, A. Bruce A430
Moore, Elizabeth Berner (Beth) A464
Moore, Thomas (Thom) A489
Moore, Scott (Scotty) A516
Moore, Mary (Mar) A555
Moore, Andrew A576
Moore, Troy A583
Moore, Frederick V. (Fred) A583
Moore, John A. A608
Moore, Daryl D. A657
Moore, Gary A671
Moore, Chris (Chrissy) A674
Moore, Benjie A753
Moore, Edward W. A772
Moore, Linda (Lin) A829
Moore, Scott A849
Moore, Declan A892
Moore, James (Jamie) A893
Moore, Brad (Brady) A903
Moore, Jason A904
Moore, Michael S. (Mike) A937
Moore, Steve P12
Moore, Richard (Dick) P18
Moore, Brad P34
Moore, Rob P74
Moore, Andrew P101
Moore, Stephen L. P105
Moore, Jennelle P144
Moore, John P156
Moore, Kimberly (Kim) P196
Moore, Darrel P201
Moore, Mark E. P237
Moore, James D. P240
Moore, Towana P249
Moore, Benjamin P282
Moore, David (Dave) P317
Moore, Greg (Greggy) P346
Moore, Tim P352
Moore, Susan P383
Moore, James L. P386
Moore, William M. P415
Moore, Edward (Ed) P417
Moore, John (Jack) P423
Moore, Brendan F. P425
Moore, Carolyn (Carol) P476
Moore, Thomas M (Thom) P495
Moore, Jason P501
Moore, Francis D. P514
Moore, Sharon P554
Moore, Kelly P555
MOORE, TRACY (Trace) P555
Moore, Jackson W. P558
Moore, Jeff P564

Moore, Madeleine G P570
Moore, William (Bill) P601
Moore, Kathleen (Kathy) P602
Moore, Wenda Weekes P619
Moore, Robert J. W231
Moore, Nicholas W. W242
Moorehead, Alexander A. (Alex) A545
Moorehead, Alexander A. (Alex) P279
Moorhead, Keith (Keithy) P162
Moorjani, Shail A163
Moorjani, Janesh P238
Moorman, Rob (Robbie) E344
Moorman, Rob (Robbie) A723
Moorman, Kathleen (Kathy) P56

Moorman, Kathy (Kat) P56
Moorstein, Tim (Timmy) E165
Moorstein, Tim (Timmy) A381
Moorthy, Ganesh E274
Moorthy, Srinivasa A780
Moos, Walter (Walt) P473
Mora, Cynthia (Cyn) E252
Mora, Elizabeth P515
Morabito, Carl S. E249
Morabito, Kelley (Kells) E376
Morabito, Kelley (Kells) A806
Moraci, Philip J (Phil) A918
Morais, Diane A32
Moral-Niles, Christopher J. Del A78
Morales, Albert A54
Morales, Raquel (Rae) A183
Morales, Laura (Laur) A203
Morales, Dan A302
Morales, Elisa A397
Morales, Vincent J. A711
Morales, Armando A784
Morales, Ricardo (Ric) A964
Morales, Raven P190
Morales, Mark (Marky) P509
Morales-jaffe, Marcia A965
Moran, Steve (Stevie) E76
Moran, Richard (Dick) E232
Moran, Thomas (Thom) E265
Moran, Patrick (Paddy) A3
Moran, Karen (Kare) A18
Moran, Rob (Robbie) A20
Moran, Edward (Ed) A51
Moran, Federico A208
Moran, Bobby (Bob) A430
Moran, Tim (Timmy) A549
Moran, Thomas (Thom) A572
Moran, Eileen A. A728
Moran, Allison A741
Moran, Anita (Ani) A911
Moran, Sean A930
Moran, Michael F. P66
Moran, Allison P405
Moran, Bill (Billy) P538
Morant, Blake D. P524
Morathi, Raisibe K. W272
Morazzani, Christina A720
Morazzini, Brian E169
Morbelli, Christopher A584
More, Debrah A120
Moreau, Maxine L. A186
Moreau, Matthew (Matt) A972
Moree, Maggie (Margaret) A18
Moree, Scott A929
Morehead, Bruce (Brucey) E99
Morehead, Bruce (Brucey) A224
Morehouse, David (Dave) A304
Morehouse-Reynolds, Alexandra A114
Morehouse-Reynolds, Alexandra P54
Moreland, Michele (Michie) E169
Moreland, Bill A520
Moreland, Kristy (Chris) A899
Morell, Luis E198
Morello, Dianne (Ann) E176
Morello, Diane (Di) E177
Morem, David N. E7
Morena, Mike (Mikey) A641
Morency, John P (Jack) E176
Moreno, Raul E. E10
Moreno, Jeanette A205
Moreno, Maria (Mary) A641

Moreno, Jose A693
Moreno, Mshr Alex P116
Morenz, Mike (Mikey) A843
Moret, Blake D. A768
Moretti, Joanne A494
Moretz, Drew (Andrew) P554
Morey, Tom A20
Morfin, Lindsey A409
Morford, Craig S. A166
Morgado, Karlo A252
Morgan, Sharon E135
Morgan, Jerry (Jerr) E142
Morgan, James E269
Morgan, Sue (Susie) E339
Morgan, Scott (Scotty) E366
Morgan, Patrick (Paddy) A69
Morgan, Andy A84
Morgan, Susan (Sue) A166
Morgan, Cindy (Cin) A227
Morgan, Ann A295
Morgan, Sharon A310
Morgan, Donald (Don) A340
Morgan, Jenny G (Jen) A342
Morgan, Paige A502
Morgan, Molly (Moll) A504
Morgan, Tom A507
Morgan, Mary (Mar) A517
Morgan, James A582
Morgan, Ryan (Ry) A675
Morgan, Rose (Rosey) A689
Morgan, Jason (Jase) A829
Morgan, Daniel (Dan) A841
Morgan, Michael (Mel) A844
Morgan, Tim A903
Morgan, Steven (Steve) A942
Morgan, Colin A952
Morgan, Lawrence E. (Larry) P136
Morgan, Michael (Mel) P189
Morgan, Lori P273
Morgan, Lori P274
Morgan, R G P298
Morgan, David L. P300
Morgan, Dianna P370
Morgan, Sheree P550
Morgan, Marsha L. P569
Morgan, Ronnie (Ron) P633
Morgan, Flemming W124
Morgan-Aziz, Tina (Tin) A163
Morganstein, David (Dave) P632
Morganthall, Frederick J. (Fred) A522
Morgenroth, Matthew J. W416
Morgens, Edwin H. E446
Morgenstern, Mitch (Mitchell) E265
Morgenstern, Mitch (Mitchell) A572
Morgison, Kevin (Kev) A164
Morhaime, Michael (Mike) A10
Mori, Yoshiki W11
Mori, Kazuyuki W256
Moriah, Elan E435
Moriarty, Brian (Bri) E142
Moriarty, Rowland T. (Row) E450
Moriarty, Kevin A94
Moriarty, Joe (Joey) A175
Moriarty, Thomas M. A258
Moriarty, Michael A344
Morici, John F. E18
Morico, Gayle (Gabe) A18
Morikawa, Taku W158
Morikis, John G. A795
Morimoto, David S. A184
Morimoto, Hiromichi W258
Morimura, Tsutomu W92
Morin, Richard A. E97
Moring, Mitzi P349
Morishita, Kenichi W345
Morishita, Hirotaka W392
Morissette, Daniel J. A272
Morissette, Daniel J. P165
Morita, Shunsaku W122
Morita, Toshio W282
Moritani, Kazuhiro W341
Moritz, Terry (Terr) P284
Moriwaki, Lee Y. A184
Moriyama, Toru W259
Moriyasu, Masahiro E435

Mork, Lee P20
Mork, John P603
Morken, CeCe A490
Morlock, Henry (Hal) A429
Morlock, David R. P555
Morlock, David (Dave) P555
Mormando, Karin P505
Moro, Sonya (Sonnie) A112
Moro, Gisele A534
Moro, Karen (Kare) P499
Moro, Masahiro W250
Morotti, Michael (Mel) P362
Moroun, Matthew T. E426
Morovich, Nancy (Nance) A316
Morozov, Alexander W336
Morray, Jeffrey P. P385
Morreale, Charles A. (Chuck) E112
Morreale, Joe (Joey) A887
Morrell, Jeff (Jeffy) E156
Morrell, Toni (Antonio) A6
Morrell, Kelley A205
Morrical, Terri A. E298
Morris, Jared A. E29
Morris, Lucas (Luke) E43
Morris, David B (Dave) E74
Morris, Kyle E75
Morris, Michael J. E169
Morris, Jim E366
Morris, B. Harrison E369
Morris, Buford H E369
Morris, Nicola E450
Morris, Donna A11
Morris, Jared A. A53
Morris, Gregory A. (Greg) A70
Morris, M. Catherine (Cathy) A73
Morris, Brian (Bri) A101
Morris, Uri A135
Morris, David (Dave) A146
Morris, M. Shawn A198
Morris, Brian (Bri) A203
Morris, Joe (Joey) A229
Morris, Craig (Craigy) A309
Morris, Joe A309
Morris, Jerry (Jerr) A347
Morris, Rodney A369
Morris, Gerald (Jerry) A398
Morris, Robert (Bob) A404
Morris, Tom (Tommy) A430
Morris, Michael J. A437
Morris, Chris (Chrissy) A569
Morris, Maria R. A584
Morris, Linda A706
Morris, Brian J (Bri) A727
Morris, Jesse E. A737
Morris, Tim (Timmy) A745
Morris, B. Harrison A794
Morris, Buford H A794
Morris, Pete A817
Morris, John A827
Morris, Laura (Laur) A835
Morris, Scott (Scotty) A899
Morris, John (Jack) A899
Morris, Fran A927
Morris, John J. A941
Morris, Dawn C. A943
Morris, Michael J. A980
Morris, Howell P14
Morris, Barry (Barr) P118
Morris, Kenneth C. P172
Morris, Staci (Stace) P191
Morris, Blaine P216
Morris, Tony P278
Morris, Bill (Billy) P455
Morris, John (Jack) P555
Morris, Michael P566
Morris, Huw P624
Morris, Jon P631
Morrison, Ron (Ronnie) E369
Morrison, Lisa J. E400
Morrison, Christina A68
Morrison, Scott C. A98
Morrison, Denise M. A160
Morrison, Patricia B. (Patty) A165
Morrison, Patty (Pat) A166
Morrison, Jim (Jimmy) A176

A = AMERICAN BUSINESS
E = EMERGING COMPANIES
P = PRIVATE COMPANIES
W = WORLD BUSINESS

A = AMERICAN BUSINESS
E = EMERGING COMPANIES
P = PRIVATE COMPANIES
W = WORLD BUSINESS

N

N., Rajesh A177
Naas, Penny (Penn) A911
Nabel, Elizabeth G. (Betsy) A680
Nabel, Elizabeth G. (Betsy) P377
Nabel, Elizabeth G. (Betsy) P514
Nace, Bernadette (Bern) A87
Nachajska, Ania A203
Nachmann, Marc A409
Nackers, Gary P167
Nackman, Neal S. E174
Naclerio, Nicholas J. (Nick) E218
Nacpil, Catherine E265
Nacpil, Catherine A572
Nadarajan, Gunalan A751
Nadarajan, Gunalan P411
Naddeo, Eric A898
Nadeau, Richard J. E262
Nadeau, Renee (Ren) A156
Nadeau, Gerard F. A473
Nadeau, Stephen (Steve) A865
Nadella, Satya A592
Nader, Alfred (Alf) A954
Nader, Melissa (Lissa) P428
Nadig, David A31
Nadkarni, Pranay A38
Nadkarni, Kedar A280
Nadler, Bob (Bo) A47
Nadler, Laura (Laur) A933
Nadolny, Stephanie P96
Naegelin, Martin A. A773
Naeve, Janis (Jan) A55
Nagae, Shusaku W296
Nagai, Noriaki W282
Nagai, Koji W282
Nagamatsu, Shoichi W282
Naganathan, Nagi P555
Nagano, Hisashi W167
Nagano, Tsuyoshi W386
Nagao, Tatsunosuke W205
Nagao, Narumi W228
Nagao, Masahiko W367
Nagaoka, Takashi W261
Nagarajan, Sundaram (Naga) A472
Nagasawa, Hitoshi W278
Nagata, Ron A430
Nagata, Paul (Pauly) A565
Nagata, Kenichi W262
Nagayama, Osamu W321
Nagel, Brian (Bri) A531
Nagel, Brian (Bri) A912
Nagel, W.F. (Wilfred) W201
NAGEL, ALBERTO W251
Nagelberg, Allison E280
Naggar, Lela E403
Naggar, Lela A858
Naggarapu, Jayakrishna P615
Naggiar, Ingrid A780
Nagji, Bansi A576
Nagle, Martin E67
Nagra, Erica (Erin) P87
Nagrath, Stephanie A565
Naguib, Ashraf A5
Nagura, Toshikazu W16
Nagy, Jane A826
Nagy, Jane P488
Nahyan, Sheikh Tahnoon Bin Zayed Al W160
Naidoo, Shirley P362
Naidoo, Vassi W272
Naidu, Tulsi R. W427
Naik, Nehal A203
Naik, Harshad A466
Naimoli, Michael (Mel) E434
Nair, Ajai E115
Nair, Vas A72
Nair, Raj A384

Nair, Ramesh A501
Nair, Roopa A732
Nair, Balan W236
Naito, Tadaaki W278
Naito, Shunichi W366
Naja, Khaled P157
Najima, Hirotaka W122
Najjar, Fred (Freddy) A273
Najjar, Ted A409
Najjar, Fred (Freddy) P165
Nakagawa, Hiroshi W204
Nakagawa, Kuniharu W204
Nakagawa, Junko W282
Nakagome, Kenji W370
Nakai, Takuji W278
Nakajima, Shuichi W158
Nakajima, Shigehiro W168
Nakajima, Yuji W215
Nakajima, Hajime W219
Nakajima, Shigeru W361
Nakakuma, Kazuhito W253
Nakamae, Gwen E227
Nakamae, Koji W316
Nakamatsu, Tammy (Tam) A106
Nakamine, Yuji W250
Nakamura, Galen A106
Nakamura, Masahide W122
Nakamura, Mitsuyoshi W215
Nakamura, Akira W228
Nakamura, Jiro W274
Nakamura, Kimiyasu W279
Nakamura, Masahide W282
Nakamura, Kunio W296
Nakamura, Yukio W344
Nakanishi, Katsuya W256
Nakano, Mamoru E112
Nakano, Tom A645
Nakano, Tom P360
Nakano, Takahiro W361
Nakashima, James (Jamie) P379
Nakasone, Norman (Norm) A184
Nakata, Misako E387
Nakata, Toru W204
Nakata, Yuji W282
Nakatsuka, Ralph Y. A856
Nakayama, Masaaki W122
Nakayama, Toshiki W286
Nakis, Dominic J. A14
Nakis, Dominic J. P9
Nalamasu, Omkaram (Om) A67
Nalamasu, Om A67
Naldi, Robert P286
Nallen, John P. A892
Nalley, James P631
Nallin, John (Jack) A910
Nam, Sik W307
Nam-Hai, Chua W416
Nama, Veeresh P223
Namba, Yoshimi A687
Nambiar, Vinod A223
Namdeo, B. K. W181
NAMIKI, FUJIO W122
Namkung, Jim (Jimmy) A481
Namm, Sheila (Sheil) P286
Nan, Feng Hua W100
Nanavaty, Maulik A146
Nanberg, Joshua (Josh) A132
Nance, Mark E1
Nance, William P510
Nance, William A (Bill) P510
Nandan, Mitzi A502
Nandeshwar, Ashutosh P603
Nantais, Tom (Tommy) P223
Nanterme, Pierre W5
Nanthawithaya, Arthid W345
Nantkes, Jackie (Jack) E443
Nanty, Jerôme W14
Nantz, Mark S. P82
Naouri, Jean-Charles W90
Naouri, Jean-Charles W160
Naouri, Jean-Charles W313
Napier, Dale (Dal) A534
Napier, India P49
Napier, Michele (Michie) P309
Napol, Marcello A3

Napoles, Ernie (Ern) A260
Napoles, Ernie (Ern) P155
Napoli, Gus (Gustav) A456
Napoli, Elizabeth (Beth) A884
Napoli, Cathleen P313
Napoli, John P. P448
Napolitan, Raymond S. A648
Napolitano, Lynda (Lynn) A183
Napper, Terry (Terr) P157
Nappi, Ralph A. P354
Nappi, Mark P581
Naqvi, Asim A394
Narain, Duraiswami A601
Naraki, Kazuhide W220
Narang, Steve A115
Narang, Steve P54
Narang, Vic P460
Narasimhan, Laxman A692
Narayanan, Sundararajan (Sundar) E440
Narayanan, Lakshmi A221
Narayanan, Krishnan A409
Narayanan, Vanitha A485
Narayanan, Paul A546
Narayanan, Gowri A569
Narayen, Shantanu A11
Narciso, Paul J. A777
Nardi, Rose (Rosey) E330
Nardi, Rose (Rosey) A690
Nardo, Tom (Tommy) Di A945
Nardo, Tom Di (Tommy) A945
Nardo, Tom (Tommy) Di P628
Nardo, Tom Di (Tommy) P628
Nardone, Randal A. E168
Nardone, Mary Kaye A527
Nardone, Marykaye A527
Nardone, Mary A527
Nardone, Michael (Mel) A584
Narduzzo, Paul A217
Narduzzo, Paul P132
Narendran, T. V. W376
Narev, Ian W111
Nario, Kristine R. E302
Narisetti, Raju A629
Nark, David (Dave) E44
Narosky, Mary (Mar) A191
Narron, Jim (Jimmy) A342
Nasby, Tom A18
Nasby, Thomas (Thom) A18
Nascimento, □lvaro Jose Barrigas do W84
Nash, Joshua L. E43
Nash, Craig M. E217
Nash, Joseph E269
Nash, William D. (Bill) A167
Nash, Bill (Billy) A168
Nash, Patrice A281
Nash, Joseph A582
Nash, Bruce D P96
Nash, Yvonne (Vonne) P401
Nash, David P561
Nashar, Rania Mahmoud W332
Naspinski, Ed P503
Nasser, William E. E379
Nasser, Jacques A. (Jac) W68
Nassetta, Christopher J. (Chris) A442
Nassif, Joseph (Jo) E336
Nastanski, Cynthia (Cyn) A692
Nataee, Motuma P530
Natale, J P318
NATALE, MARINA W251
Natale, Marina W400
Natali, Sara A921
Natarajan, Venkata A726
Natarajan, Murali A762
Natelli, Thomas A. E90
Nath, Deepak A5
Nath, Pravene P485
Nathan, Marc (Marcy) A63
Nathan, Scott A112
Nathan, Krishna A543
Nathan, Don (Donnie) A916
Nathan, Nicholas P403
Nathans, Andrew (Andy) P561
Nathans, Andrew (Andy) P562

Nathanson, Laura A281
Nathanson, Martha P278
Nathanson, Nicholas P403
Natins, Dena (Dee) E393
Natkow, Jay A745
Natt, Beth (Betty) P642
Nauert, Gary P169
Naughton, Timothy J. (Tim) E44
Naughton, Mark E45
Naughton, Tom (Tommy) E262
Naughton, Marc G. A187
Naughton, Duncan C. Mac A284
Naughton, W Terrance A947
Naughton, Terry A947
Naughton, Des W80
Naugle, Dennis P415
Naumann, Peter (Pete) A916
Navagamuwa, Roshan A259
Navarette, Ricardo (Ric) P576
Navarre, Christophe W240
Navarro, Gloria A252
Navarro, Mary W. A464
Navarro, Imelda A483
Navarro, David A846
Naven, Eldon A218
Naven, Eldon P132
Navin, Paul A226
Navran, Susan H. P78
Nayama, Michisuke W258
Nayar, Sid E295
Naylor, Jeffrey (Jeff) A874
Nazarko, Michael P220
Nazza, Larry E285
Nazzaro, Stephen F. (Steve) A824
Ndego, John W409
Ndong, Juan A. P48
Neal, Lisa E141
Neal, Bill (Billy) E212
Neal, Mark (Marky) E236
Neal, Gary F. E420
Neal, Annmarie A203
Neal, Krista A205
Neal, Sherri (Sher) A430
Neal, Bill (Billy) A468
Neal, Terry (Terr) A895
Neal, Gary F. A901
Neal, Scott (Scotty) A937
Neal, Grant R. P34
Neal, Jake P508
Neal, Sapphire P508
Neal, Greg P630
Neal, John W311
Neale, George A. A790
Nealon, Thomas (Thom) A685
Nealon, Tom A809
Neam, Doug (Dougie) A98
Neaman, Mark R. P357
Nearpass, Troy A368
Neary, David M (Dave) A157
Neary, Daniel P. A610
Neary, Francis (Fran) P415
Neben, Gabrielle E436
Neborak, Michael K. (Mike) A362
Nebosky, Patricia (Pat) E56
Nebosky, Patricia (Pat) E128
Nebreda, Julian A16
Necastro, Butch A31
Necastro, Daniel Butch (Dan) A31
Necessary, Chad E51
Necessary, Chad A110
Nedell, Thomas (Thom) P356
Nedungadi, Shreenath P103
Neeb, Greg (Greggy) A800
Neeb, Marc J. W243
Needel, Jerry E60
Needham, Floyd E. E284
Needham, Chuck (Chucky) A641
Neel, Josh A835
Neel, Michael (Mel) A874
Neely, Diane (Di) A204
Neely, Scott A726
Neely, David (Dave) A752
Neether, Jackie (Jack) A672
Neff, Chris (Chrissy) E304
Neff, Deborah (Deb) E359

A = AMERICAN BUSINESS
E = EMERGING COMPANIES
P = PRIVATE COMPANIES
W = WORLD BUSINESS

Nichols, Clarence (Clar) A899
Nichols, Blee A972
Nichols, Max P34
Nichols, Mike (Mikey) P148
Nichols, Rodney P212
Nichols, Gretchen P274
Nichols, Jimmy (Jim) P299
Nichols, Charlie P413
Nichols, Brandie C P507
Nicholson, Brian (Bri) E168
Nicholson, E. Allen A256
Nicholson, Eric (Ric) A328
Nicholson, George C. A459
Nicholson, Darryl A499
Nicholson, Kelly A726
Nicholson, Lyle A893
Nicholson, Thomas (Thom) P152
Nicholson, Earl P339
Nichter, Mike (Mikey) P152
Nick, Romano P456
Nickel, Thedora A. E49
Nickel, Thedora A. A99
Nickel, Jackie P4
Nickele, Christopher J. (Chris) A216
Nickels, Jeff A366
Nickerson, Tim (Timmy) E377
Nickerson, Joseph (Jo) A140
Nickerson, Richard A159
Nickerson, Barry (Barr) A519
Nickerson, Randy S. A561
Nickerson, Cheryl A689
Nickerson, Barry (Barr) P267
Nickerson, Nate (Nathan) P298
Nickless, David (Dave) P150
Nicklin, Emily P552
Nicks, Darlene (Darl) E213
Nicks, Darlene (Darl) A469
Nicksa, Gary (Gar) P83
Nicol, Mark A747
Nicol, Molly (Moll) P14
Nicola, Steven F. E261
Nicolai, Jason (Jase) P83
Nicolelli, Maurizio E150
Nicolett, Mark E177
Nicoletti, Ralph J. A627
Nicoloff, Roberta (Berta) P431
Nicolosi, Paolo E146
Nicolosi, Michael (Mel) E371
Nicolosi, Michael (Mel) A797
Nida, Bob (Bo) E443
Nides, Thomas R. (Tom) A603
Niedbalski, Dave A549
Niederer, Jed A613
Niederhuber, John P239
Niedzielski, Vincent P. (Vince) E229
Niedzielski, Vince E229
Niehaus, James (Jamie) A45
Niehaus, Celie A163
Niehaus, Bill A462
Niehus, Dean P313
Nielsen, Sarah N. E452
Nielsen, Mark D. A390
Nielsen, Darron A394
Nielsen, Jane H. A743
Nielsen, Mark D (Marky) A747
Nielsen, Paul D. P101
Nielsen, Milt P510
Nielsen, Peter W327
Niemann, Richard (Dick) A111
Niemann, Angela A328
Niemann, Donna A785
Niemann, Holly (Holl) A835
Niemi, Albert W. P465
Niemiec, Mary (Mar) P80
Niemoeller, John Arthur (Jack) A367
Nienaber, Gawie M A236
Nienaber, Margaret W356
Nierenberg, Andrew (Andy) A680
Nierenberg, Andrew (Andy) P377

Nierlich, John (Jack) A309
Niermann, Mark A265
Niermann, Mark (Marky) A265
Niermann, Craig (Craigy) A295
Niermann, Nils W61
Nieto, Tom A952
Nieuwenhuys, Gerard A687
Nieuwsma, Steve A769
Nieuwsma, David (Dave) A769
Nieves, Doris P97
Niewiara, James (Jamie) A606
Nigam, Naresh A780
Nightingale, Pam E336
Nightingale, Timothy P. A159
Nigrel, Anita J. A831
Nigrin, Daniel P517
Nigro, Joseph (Joe) A326
Nigro, Stephen (Steve) A458
Nigro, James M. A527
Niinami, Takeshi W366
Nijenhuis, Wouter A144
Nikam, Thomas (Thom) A565
Nikias, Chrysostomos L. (Max) P603
Nikka, Joana E40
Nikka, Joanna (Anna) E40
Nikolaus, Donald H. A286
Nikolov, Anita A641
Niland, Barbara (Barb) A466
Niles, Kristi A451
Niles, Thomas A603
Nill, Michael R. (Mike) A187
Nilsson, Jonas A85
Nilsson, Stefan W368
Nimbley, Thomas J. A682
Nimer, Richard (Dick) A3
Nimoityn, Philip (Phil) P561
Ninesteel, Erica (Erin) A32
Ning, Wilson (Will) A531
Niper, Chrissy A779
Nirody, Cmrp P118
Nirula, Ajay A544
Nisbett, Mark A943
Nischbach, Shelly A900
Nishi, Masao A843
Nishida, Mitsuo W361
Nishikata, Masaaki W264
Nishimae, Manabu W186
Nishimoto, Cheryl A671
Nishimura, Tatsushi W122
Nishina, Hiroaki W294
Nishiura, Kanji W256
Nishizawa, Keiji W354
Nissen, Tim (Timmy) P367
Nissenson, Allen R. A264
Nitecki, Danuta P169
Nito, Daniel (Dan) A603
Nittoli, Rocco A537
Nittolo, Kathy (Kat) A692
Nitu, Marian (Mary) P46
Nitz, Tiffany (Tiff) A518
Niubo, Antonio Brufau W315
Niven, Darryl A323
Niver, Clair A693
Nivica, Gjon N. A177
Nivica, Jon (Jonny) A177
Nix, Richard (Dick) E215
Nix, Rudy A319
Nix, Craig L. A358
Nix, Tommy A855
Nixon, Randy A86
Nixon, David (Dave) A175
Nixon, John (Jack) A409
Nixon, Dennis E. A483
Nixon, John E. P555
Nizza, Arthur P244
Njonjo, Peter A220
Nkongho, Andrew (Andy) A743
Nkuhlu, Mfundo W272
Nley, Fred (Freddy) A444
Noakes, Jackie W231
Nober, Roger A153
Nobile, Paul (Pauly) A62
Noble, Quintin A5
Noble, David J. (D.J.) A43
Noble, Jeff (Jeffy) A360

Noble, Jen A485
Noble, Craig A689
Noble, Anthony A930
Noble, Steve P130
Noble, Kara P566
Nobles, Lloyd E80
Nobles, Anne P237
Nobles, Melissa P298
Nobrega, Rui A580
Nochowitz, Matthew (Matt) A957
Nodianos, Bridget (Bri) A120
Nodiff, Eric W. E78
Noe, David (Dave) P303
Noechel, Richard (Dick) A411
Noel, Robert A140
Noel, Stephanie (Steph) A251
Noel, Tom (Tommy) A317
Noel, Molaine A563
Noel, Jeffrey (Jeff) A957
Noga, James W. (Jim) A680
Noga, James W. (Jim) P377
Nogas, Courtney A429
Noguchi, Tadahiko W287
Noguera, Lupe A664
Nohra, Jude J. A906
Noiva, Connie E439
Nokes, Gloria P212
Nolan, Debbie (Deb) E213
Nolan, James J. (Jim) E225
Nolan, Joe A67
Nolan, Steve (Stevie) A87
Nolan, Daniel (Dan) A137
Nolan, Tom (Tommy) A168
Nolan, Brendan A205
Nolan, Joseph (Jo) A324
Nolan, Mike A346
Nolan, Mark A392
Nolan, Patrick M. A461
Nolan, Debbie (Deb) A468
Nolan, Leonard (Len) A603
Nolan, Stefanie (Stef) A654
Nolan, Dana A753
Nolan, John (Jack) A827
Nolan, David A. A979
Noland, Thomas (Thom) A462
Nolde-morrissey, Paul (Pauly) A115
Nolde-morrissey, Paul (Pauly) P54
Noll, Barbara (Barb) E1
Noll, Austin E294
Noll, Richard A. (Rich) A421
Noll, Mark P599
Nollner, Charlene P13
Nolte, Jo A685
Nolte, Reed A892
Nomura, Katsuaki W341
Nondorf, James G. P551
Nook, Greg P246
Nook, Gregory E. (Greg) P247
Noonan, Michael (Mel) A221
Noonan, David (Dave) A309
Noonan, James R. A527
Noonan, Steve (Stevie) A584
Noorani, Nick A473
Noordende, Alexander M. (Sander) van't W5
Noordhoek, Jeffrey R. (Jeff) A620
Noot, Walter E429
Nooyi, Indra K. A692
Norberg, Douglas E. E338
Norbitz, Wayne E288
Norby, Stephanie L. P459
Norcia, Gerardo (Jerry) A293
Norcia, Maria (Mary) A926
Norcross, Gary A. A348
Norcross, Anna (Ann) A514
Norcross, Jeanne A811
Nord, Mary (Mar) E126
Nord, Mary (Mar) A298
Nordell, Scott (Scotty) A346
Nordgren, Robert P642
Nordin, Brandon (Bran) P25
Nordlander, Dan A954
Nordli, Lars Johannes W359
Nordlie, Elizabeth M. A398
Nordling, Christopher A589

Nordloh, John C. P302
Nordmeyer, Greg (Greggy) A51
Nordstorm, Erik (Rik) A637
Nordstrom, Jeanie A173
Nordstrom, Blake W. A637
Nordstrom, Peter E. (Pete) A637
Nordstrom, Erik B. A637
Nordstrom, James F. (Jamie) A637
Nordstrom, Jeanie P105
Noreika, Steven M. E154
Noren, Per A140
Norenberg, John (Jack) A14
Norenberg, John (Jack) P9
Norfleet, Edward (Ed) A341
Norgaard, Kris P185
Norgeot, Peter (Pete) A316
Nori, Srinivas A340
Noriega, Arnold (Arnie) A379
Norin, Michele P586
Nork, Rick P627
Norko, Krzysztof P548
Norman, Richard (Dick) E98
Norman, Jessica (Jess) E349
Norman, Sofia A60
Norman, Todd (Toddy) A183
Norman, Mike (Mikey) A268
Norman, Todd A331
Norman, Brad A465
Norman, Paul T. A510
Norman, Jay D. A740
Norman, David (Dave) A937
Norman, Richard (Dick) P142
Norman, Patricia P196
Norman, Linda P558
Normandin, Donna (Don) A252
Normile, Robert (Bob) A570
Normington, Debbie A203
Norotsky, Mitch (Mitchell) P556
Norrie, Angela A849
Norris, Patrick (Paddy) E113
Norris, Patrick E113
Norris, David E240
Norris, Cfa E394
Norris, Derek J. A106
Norris, Naomi (Nomi) A120
Norris, Josephine A504
Norris, Chuck (Chucky) A620
Norris, Cfa A838
Norris, Wayne A855
Norris, Helen P112
Norris, Scott P410
Norris, Valerie (Val) P448
Norris, Marly P600
Norris, Todd P630
Norrman, Helena W379
North, Paul A427
North, John A548
North, Randall A765
North, Randall P421
Northam, Jaime E194
Northam, Thadd A565
Northcutt, Kendria E335
Northcutt, Martha (Mar) A462
Northcutt, Kendria A703
Northup, Jim (Jimmy) A274
Northup, Lesley P190
Norton, Andrew L. E141
Norton, Phillip G. E141
Norton, Glenn E270
Norton, Doug (Dougie) A175
Norton, Jack (Jackie) A237
Norton, Ted (Teddy) A267
Norton, John (Jack) A384
Norton, Rick (Ricky) A417
Norton, Robert G. (Bob) A680
Norton, David K. A689
Norton, John (Jack) A747
Norton, Burke F. A778
Norton, W.D. (Joe) A809
Norton, Noah A981
Norton, Connie P176
Norton, Rick (Ricky) P211
Norton, Robert G. (Bob) P377
Norton, Margareta E. (Meg) P405
Norvell, Trish (Trisha) E377

A = AMERICAN BUSINESS
E = EMERGING COMPANIES
P = PRIVATE COMPANIES
W = WORLD BUSINESS

Padgett, Pamela (Pam) A388
Padgett, Pamela (Pam) A427
PADGETT, DESTINY P590
Padgett, Barry W334
Padierna, Pedro A692
Padilla, Sara A150
Padilla, Reynaldo A355
Padilla, Ric A539
Padilla, Jose D P160
Padmaperuma, Rasika P184
Padula, Glen A918
Paelinck, Charley A156
Paffenberger, Elizabeth (Beth) P112
Paffumi, Louis A689
Pagan, Beatriz A835
Paganelli, Mark P603
Paganini, Fabio A579
Pagano, John E317
Pagano, Christopher J. A81
Pagano, John A666
Page, Timothy E74
Page, John A92
Page, Scott E. A218
Page, Ryan (Ry) A342
Page, James E (Jamie) A580
Page, Miriah A743
Page, Sam (Sammy) A764
Page, Bob (Bo) A900
Page, Monty A916
Page, Dennis (Denny) A981
Page, Robert E. P38
Page, Kerry P129
Page, Alexander (Bob) P196
Page, Elaine (Elle) P354
Page, Michael P473
Page, Darryl W104
Pagel, Reiner A21
Pagett, Edward (Ed) E262
Paglia, John M (Jack) E371
Paglia, John M (Jack) A798
PAGLIARO, RENATO W251
Pagnanelli, Jodi A947
Pagni, Marco A939
Pagone, Dominic (Dom) A892
Pagovich, Stefanie (Stef) A733
Paige, Michele A198
Paik, Son-Jai E17
Paik, Elaine A223
Paillassot, Laurent W293
Pain, Mark A. W423
Paine, Andrew (Andy) A514
Painter, Robert G. E413
Painter, Corning F. A22
Painter, Barry A835
Paisley, James A. (Andy) A13
Paixao, Pedro E167
Pak, Chong A184
Pakonen, Diane P566
Paladino, Steven A782
Palagiano, Vincent F. A275
Palan, Martha (Mar) P632
Palanchian, Mark (Marky) A632
Palanki, Ravi A824
Palastra, Jim E117
Palatsky, Howard (Howie) A696
Palaza, Butch E410
Palazzo, Frank A186
Paleka, Thomas (Thom) A392
Palella, Anthony E30
Palencia, Melissa (Lissa) A800
Palenik, Rudy A821
Palenzona, Fabrizio W400
Palermo, Deb (Debbie) E284
Palermo, Frank E440
Palermo, Tom (Tommy) A352
Palfy, Sandor E246
Paliouras, Christina (Tina) A972
Palis, Jack A565
Paliwal, Dinesh C. A425

Palko, Laura P346
Palko, Laura (Laur) P346
Palkowitz, Alan D (Al) A544
Palla, Wayne A260
Palla, Wayne P155
Pallares, Jean (Jeannie) P378
Pallasch, John A565
Palleschi, Ralph F. A82
Pallier, Patricia A179
Palm, Leann (Ann) E433
Palm, Gregory K. A409
Palma, Antonio de A139
Palma, Bryan A203
Palmatier, Jonathan (John) A226
Palmer, Dennis (Denny) E43
Palmer, Ben M. E255
Palmer, Michael (Mel) E445
Palmer, Michael (Mel) A18
Palmer, Alicia (Ali) A18
Palmer, John A83
Palmer, Johnathan A133
Palmer, Seth A135
Palmer, Paul (Pauly) A159
Palmer, Denise (Denny) A325
Palmer, Anthony J. (Tony) A516
Palmer, Scott (Scotty) A523
Palmer, C. Michael A561
Palmer, Todd A621
Palmer, Thomas (Tom) A628
Palmer, Marcia A895
Palmer, Bryan (Bry) A916
Palmer, Michael (Mel) A928
Palmer, Robert (Bob) A970
Palmer, Roy A970
Palmer, Jane (Ginny) P29
Palmer, Neal P247
Palmer, Mark P364
Palmer, Kevin P364
Palmer, Harvey P423
Palmer, David P477
Palmieri, John (Jack) A198
Palmieri, Judy P127
Palmisano, Thomas J. (Tom) A807
Palmiter, Alan (Al) P621
Palmquist, Eric L (Ric) A429
Palombo, Grace M. W174
Palombo, Grace W174
Paloux, Charles (Charlie) E201
Paltz, Diana (Ana) A78
Paluga, Jonathan (John) A814
Pamich, Sennen E359
Pamperin, Colleen A462
Pan, Jian-Yue E397
Pan, Patrick A480
Pan, Gordon G. A765
Pan, Gordon G. P420
Pan, Darong W95
Pan, Ning W158
Panagoplos, Janae P289
Panagopoulos, Katina A963
Panagos, Costa A740
Panayotova, Vanya A599
Pancham, Cassan A355
Pancino, Matt M365
Panda, Lalitendu P298
Pande, Ajay A12
Pandey, Sanjay A286
Pandit, Vikram A504
Pandraud, Jean-Marc E140
Pandya, Jeremy (Jer) A712
Panetta, Nancy (Nance) A504
PANETTA, Pascal W337
Pang, Laurinda Y. A539
Pang, Lisa A584
Pang, Jennifer (Jen) P624
Pang, Y. K. W210
Pangalos, Menelas (Mene) W37
Pangborn, Robert N. A866
Pangborn, Robert N. P540
Panhans, Chet E163
Paniccia, Dominic (Dom) A44
Panikar, John M. A713
Paniszczyn, Anthony (Tony) A818
Panizza, Florencia E256
Panizza, Sandro W33

Pann, Stuart C. A458
Pannell, Rick (Ricky) P218
Panner, Rich (Ric) A692
Panneton, Dave A706
Panneton, Kirk P96
Pannitto, Pat (Patty) A514
Pannullo, Michael (Mel) E162
Pant, Micky A978
Pantel, Lori A570
Panu, Erik E73
Panyarachun, Anand W345
Panzarino, James V. A276
Panzer, Mark (Marky) A789
Panzino, Jodi P140
Paoletti, Rich P528
Paoli, Alberto de W150
Paoli, Alberto De W152
Paolin, John P. E203
Paolini, Nonce W76
Paolucci, Steve (Stevie) P133
Papa, Rosemarie Novello E422
Papa, Rosemarie Novello A907
Papa, Gianni Franco W400
Papacostas, Arthur P505
Papadopoulos, Stelios A133
Papadopoulos, Gayle A426
Papageorge, Georgia A887
Papamarkou, Irene (Rene) A824
Paparello, John A778
Paparone, Bruce J. P260
Papaspyrou, Spyros A. W302
Papathomas, Georgia A499
Papay, Michael (Mel) A643
Papazian, Steve A873
Pape, Giovanna A504
Pape, Michael (Mel) A532
Papes, Daniel E121
Papetti, Elizabeth (Beth) P631
Papiasse, Alain W71
Papier, Jennifer M (Jen) A194
Papineau, Jeffrey (Jeff) A293
Papp, Harry A. P78
Pappas, John E88
Pappas, Charlie (Charles) A269
Pappas, Janine A323
Pappas, Thomas (Thom) P187
Paquette, Michael S. E135
Paquette, Michael S. A310
Paradies, Gregg P539
Paradies, James N. (Jim) P539
Paradis, Jim (Jimmy) P287
Paradise, Janice A518
Paradise, Christi P427
Paradiso, Antonella E252
Parameswaran, Prabha A223
Paranjape, Prasad E222
Paranjpe, Nitin W401
Paranjpe, Nitin W402
Parasher, Mohit A425
Parasnis, Abhay A12
Paratte, A. Robert E232
Parazynski, Gail P507
Parda, D S P18
Pardee, Charles G. (Chip) A854
Pardes, Herbert P538
Pardini, Mike (Mikey) A929
Pardo, Carletto A56
Pardo, Jorge A295
Pardo, Tara A410
Pardo, Marcella A514
Pardo, Emilio P2
Pardue, Leslie B (Les) A163
Pare, Jean-Philippe W124
Paredes, Sebastian W127
Pareek, Mayank W375
Pareigat, Thomas G. E405
Pareigat, Tom E406
Pareigat, Thomas G. A862
Pareigat, Tom A862
Parekh, Deepak S. W39
Parent, June B. A159
Parent, Bob P333
Parent, Ken P388
Parent, Ghislain W268
Parente, Elio A539

Parente, Pedro Pullen W299
Parigen, Jason A351
Parihar, Jagdish W289
Parik, Allan W351
Parikh, Sudip A117
Parikh, Purvish M. P30
Parikh, Sudip P63
Parimbelli, Alessandro A494
Paris, Marty (Mart) A163
Paris, David (Dave) A221
Paris, Eulalie A689
Parish, Amber P362
Parisi, Mike A472
Park, David E49
Park, Alvin (Al) E177
Park, Yong E191
Park, Daniel (Dan) E191
Park, Jun E397
Park, Ernie (Ern) A3
Park, David A99
Park, Anthony J. (Tony) A346
Park, Yong A422
Park, Daniel (Dan) A422
Park, Kevin A597
Park, Jaehwa A613
Park, Peter (Pete) A696
Park, Dae-Young P434
Park, Km P434
Park, Seri P615
Park, Jeongwon W138
Park, Geewon W138
Park, Han-Woo W218
Park, Sung-Ho W307
Park, Jeong Ho W348
Park, Sung Wook W349
Parker, Lance E17
Parker, Mickey (Mic) E153
Parker, Jefferson G. (Jeff) E212
Parker, Michael (Mel) E246
Parker, W. Douglas (Doug) A40
Parker, Karen (Kare) A68
Parker, Rebecca (Becca) A100
Parker, Donald T. A141
Parker, Ian A175
Parker, Michael (Mel) A226
Parker, Robert (Bob) A237
Parker, Phil A242
Parker, Greg (Greggy) A252
Parker, Mary Jayne A280
Parker, Jayne (Jay) A281
Parker, Steven (Steve) A346
Parker, Mickey (Mic) A350
Parker, Herbert K. A425
Parker, Jefferson G. (Jeff) A468
Parker, Mike A536
Parker, Billy A539
Parker, Bob A621
Parker, Mark G. A634
Parker, Scott T. A661
Parker, Aaron A692
Parker, Ron (Ronnie) A887
Parker, P. William (Bill) A895
Parker, Bruce (Brucey) A899
Parker, Rob A928
Parker, Todd (Toddy) A981
Parker, Chris (Chrissy) P56
Parker, Cathy P90
Parker, Francine (Fran) P223
Parker, Sheila (Sheil) P288
Parker, Beck P318
Parker, Dean P413
Parker, Justin P417
Parker, Harry P508
Parker, John W29
Parker, John W368
Parkhill, Rik W85
Parkhurst, Don (Donnie) A834
Parkhurst, Michael (Mel) A860
Parkins, Lorna (Lor) P53
Parkinson, John F. E342
Parkinson, Robert L. P284
Parks, Delbert R. E374
Parks, Scott (Scotty) A120
Parks, Trenton A124
Parks, John (Jack) A736

Parks, Jasmine P223
Parlapiano, Donna A89
Parma, Ben (Benny) P160
Parmar, Amit (Mit) A44
Parmelee, Cheryl A18
Parmenter, Sara A970
Parmentier, Jennifer A. A678
Parnell, Gordon (Gordy) E274
Parnell, Winfred P157
Parnes, Marvin (Marve) A751
Parnes, Marvin (Marve) P411
Parodi, Luis (Lu) A351
Parolin, Joᴏo Benjamin W398
Paroubek, Yurik E55
Paroubek, Yurik A122
Parr, Gregory L (Greg) A423
Parr, Marla A800
Parra, Jose A194
Parreira, Rodrigo P279
Parrent, Michael (Mel) A942
Parris, Carla M (Carly) P193
Parrish, Mike (Mikey) E176
Parrish, Charles S. (Chuck) E403
Parrish, Craig (Craigy) A502
Parrish, ED (Eddie) A544
Parrish, Benjamin F. (Ben) A880
Parrish, Martin A924
Parrish, David K. P78
Parrish, Mike P351
Parrott, William A784
Parrott, Jennifer (Jen) A835
Parrott, David (Dave) P590
Parry, Michael J. (Mike) A307
Parry, David C. A472
Parry, Andy A655
Parsadaian, Christine (Chrissy) A726
Parsley, E. William (Bill) A706
Parsley, Shawn D. P509
Parslow, Anthony E83
Parson, Susan (Sue) A732
Parsonnet, Abby A943
Parsons, Joan E394
Parsons, Colleen A63
Parsons, Joe (Joey) A83
Parsons, Betsy A133
Parsons, Charlene A198
Parsons, Eric A341
Parsons, Jennifer (Jen) A465
Parsons, Betty A834
Parsons, Joan A838
Parsons, Devin A972
Parsons, Brian P136
Parsons, Gerald J. (Jerry) P136
Parsons, Leo D. P136
Parsons, Kevin P136
Parsons, Michael P136
Parsons, William P302
Parsons, Richard D. (Dick) P544
Parsons-Danisovszky, Linda (Lin) A926
Parsons-Nikolic, Cathleen P615
Partin, Shelia A905
Partridge, Matthew M. E11
Partridge, Craig A911
Parvor, Mike A774
Pascaud, Raphael S. E18
Pascavis, Roger F. E178
Pasch, Coni A895
Paschalis, Konstantinos W302
Pascoe, Kevin E289
Pascoe, Lisa P469
Pascoe, Ricardo W268
Pascu, Sorin P589
Pascu, Adrian W124
Pascual, Francisco A355
Pascualy, Ralph P498
Paseaur, Jeff P182
Pasek, Ron A621
Pashamova, Bistra A63
Pasicnyk, Ray A795
Paskey, Linda A504
Paskiewicz, Sandra (Sandy) A18
Paskins, Ken (Kenny) E436
Paslawsky, Olena P534
Pasley, Debi P427
Paslick, P. Martin (Marty) A430

Pasma, Diane A751
Pasma, Diane P411
Pasos, Michelle (Michie) A933
Pasquale, Laura (Laur) E246
Pasquale, Maria E (Mary) A179
Pasqualicchio, Roderick A584
Pasquarelli, Amy A689
Passey, BO (Bob) A720
Passman, Philip A76
Passmore, Daniel (Dan) A981
Pastapur, Eshwar A451
Pasterick, Robert J. (Rob) A139
Pasterski, Dave (Davie) A771
Pastore, Michael (Mel) A423
Pastorek, Greg (Greggy) A569
Pastron, Nathan (Nate) P571
Pataki, David (Dave) A898
Pataki, Emily (Em) P380
Pataky, John A323
Patchen, Paul P451
Patchett, Mary Sue A150
Patchett, Mary A150
Pate, Robert (Bob) E159
Pate, Jerry (Jerr) E377
Pate, R. Hewitt (Hew) A194
Pate, Gwen A295
Pate, Robert (Bob) A365
Pate, Robert A534
Pate, Patty P631
Pategas, Dianna P404
Patel, Hema E5
Patel, Nishil E90
Patel, Ankur E168
Patel, Bhairav E169
Patel, Nayan E175
Patel, Paresh E192
Patel, Mukesh E304
Patel, Tiku E340
Patel, Nilesh A95
Patel, Siddharth A120
Patel, Mona (Mo) A146
Patel, Ketul J. A173
Patel, Pankaj S. A203
Patel, Parul A223
Patel, Nilesh A227
Patel, Himanshu A. A362
Patel, Sandhya A392
Patel, Sunit S. A539
Patel, Barry A649
Patel, Ken K (Kenny) A719
Patel, Surangi A727
Patel, Maya A739
Patel, Manesh A780
Patel, Anit A835
Patel, Manish A846
Patel, Ben A853
Patel, Vipul A874
Patel, Dhiren Patel Dhiren A895
Patel, Ketul J. P105
Patel, Yogen R. P227
Patel, Rena P363
Patel, Raksha P485
Patel, Amar P586
Pater, Krystian W306
Paterno, Andrew J. A464
Paterra, Daniel A144
Patete, Daniel L. P212
Pati, Sharon (Share) A106
Patil, Nirnay E436
Patil, Sandeep A789
Patilis, Joanna (Anna) A347
Patkotak, Crawford P36
Patla, Craig J. E102
Patmore, Kim E83
Patmore, Patty (Pat) A576
Patnaude, Jude E89
Patnaude, Jude A191
Paton, John P404
Patriarca, Michael (Mel) A818
Patrick, John J. E158
Patrick, Gregory S. E391
Patrick, Stacy (Stace) A18
Patrick, Erin A85
Patrick, Funke A140
Patrick, Ryan R. A169

Patrick, Todd A183
Patrick, John J. A361
Patrick, Robert (Bob) A665
Patrick, Cory A895
Patrick, Becky E237
Patrick, Chung P346
Patrick, Ann (Annie) P359
Patrick, Barbara (Barb) P571
Patrick-Turner, Ronne P356
Patrizio, Vincent (Vin) A87
Patruno, Joseph P275
Pattanayak, Purnima A569
Patten, Mark E. E104
Pattermann, Sarah (Sar) A87
Patterson, Lee E72
Patterson, Giles E249
Patterson, Mark (Marky) A13
Patterson, Bob C (Bo) A175
Patterson, Neal L. A187
Patterson, Frank J. A193
Patterson, Mark A203
Patterson, Jack (Jackie) A322
Patterson, Steve A348
Patterson, Dave A479
Patterson, Richard (Dick) A485
Patterson, Lyle A502
Patterson, Vernon L (Vern) A514
Patterson, Debra A518
Patterson, George A619
Patterson, Shawn A636
Patterson, Samuel (Sam) A706
Patterson, Frank A720
Patterson, Laura McCain A750
Patterson, Jan A847
Patterson, Paul (Pauly) A866
Patterson, Casey (Case) A930
Patterson, Laura McCain P411
Patterson, Jeff P449
Patterson, Paul (Pauly) P540
Patterson, Gavin W82
Patterson, Kevin J. W85
Patterson-Randles, Sandra R. P571
Patti, Salvatore A706
Pattijn, Elbert W127
Pattis, Lisa J. A963
Patton, Meredith (Edith) E24
Patton, Janet (Jan) E213
Patton, Charles R. A42
Patton, Jeffrey M (Jeff) A150
Patton, Janet (Jan) A469
Patton, Gary A485
Patton, Meghan (Meg) P3
Patton, Mike P564
Patton, James (Jamie) P586
Patullo, Rita A565
Patusky, Christopher E424
Patwa, Kishore A929
Patzke, Guy P268
Paul, Ronald D. E126
Paul, Brian E150
Paul, David C. E182
Paul, Kevin E268
Paul, John (Jack) E371
Paul, Steece A3
Paul, Dev A15
Paul, Mary A77
Paul, Christopher (Chris) A205
Paul, Barbara R (Barb) A233
Paul, Dwayne (Wayne) A273
Paul, Ronald D. A298
Paul, Santa A520
Paul, Steven (Steve) A544
Paul, Andrew A565
Paul, Kevin A577
Paul, Cynthia (Cyn) A785
Paul, John (Jack) A797
Paul, Nick A840
Paul, Deepika A905
Paul, Michael (Mel) A946
Paul, Mary P41
Paul, Dwayne (Wayne) P165
Paul, Chausse P288
Paul, Valerie J. P459
Paul, Michael W424
Paula, Jefferson de W32

Paulak, Eric (Ric) E176
Paulett, Adele A851
Paulette, Janet (Jan) E51
Paulette, Janet (Jan) A110
Paulette, William A. A970
Pauley, Lisa A. A98
Pauley, Matthew A397
Pauley, Brian (Bri) A511
Paulikas, George P511
Paulson, Donavon A949
Paulus, David (Dave) A621
Pauly, Greg (Greggy) A766
Pauly, Greg (Greggy) P421
Paumen, Richard (Dick) P494
Paunikar, Pallavi A504
Paus, William W351
Pauzer, Stanley A629
Pavelec, Brad A204
Pavelka, Bruce A48
Paver, Howard (Howie) A439
Paver, Robert L. A494
Pavesi, Phil P564
Pavia, Rick (Ricky) A882
Pavkov, Aden A602
Pavlakis, Peter A785
Pavlic, Jeanne A957
Pavlonnis, David (Dave) P550
Pawar, Manoj A173
Pawar, Amar A504
Pawar, Manoj P105
Pawlak, Renard A166
Pawley, John (Jack) A383
Pawlik, Diana (Ana) A243
Pawlowicz, Leszek Jerzy W52
Paxson, Christina H. P89
Payan, Carlos (Carl) A708
Payette, Richard W246
Payne, Stanley (Stan) E54
Payne, Regina (Gina) E89
Payne, Tina (Tin) E98
Payne, Michael C. E313
Payne, Jim A34
Payne, Jon A80
Payne, Regina (Gina) A191
Payne, Sandy A235
Payne, Kevin M. A305
Payne, Vicki (Vic) A409
Payne, Jon (Jonny) A463
Payne, Alison A693
Payne, Edwina A788
Payne, Kevin M. A807
Payne, Jennifer M. A899
Payne, David L. A950
Payne, Jim P22
Payne, Jon P45
Payne, Penelope (Nell) P459
Payne, Vernon P633
Payne, Valerie (Val) P644
Paynter, Eric (Ric) A423
Payson, Susan Healey (Sue) P355
Paz, Harold L. A18
Paz, George A330
Paz, Jeffery A689
Paziora, Debra A791
Pazol, Steve (Stevie) A736
Peaa, Nicolas (Nic) A835
Peabody, Mark E41
Peace, John W342
Peach, Richard A341
Peach, Anne (Annie) P370
Peacher, Stephen C. W364
Peacock, John (Jack) E369
Peacock, Jonathan (John) A309
Peacock, Donnette A347
Peacock, Jeff (Jeffy) A782
Peacock, John (Jack) A794
Peacock, Mark (Marky) A851
Peacock, Russell M. A971
Peacock, William (Bill) P519
Peak, Craig E213
Peak, Craig A468
Peale, Dan (Danny) E177
Pean, Jean-Christophe A570
Pearce, Warren W. E224
Pearce, David (Dave) A351

Pola, Gary (Gar) A664
Polakiewicz, David (Dave) A465
Polanowicz, John P490
Polanski, John J. P223
Polen, Thomas E. A123
Polen, Michael R. (Mike) A946
Polep, Lori (Lor) P141
Poletaev, Maxim W336
Polewaczyk, James (Jamie) E214
Poli, Francis C. E98
Poli, John (Jack) E409
Poli, Christopher (Chris) A83
Poli, Massimo A223
Poli, John (Jack) A877
Policinski, Christopher J. (Chris) A530
Polidori, Daniel (Dan) A304
Polignac, Fran□§ois Melchior de W88
Polinder, Sherman P359
Poliquin, Cathleen P530
Polishook, Debra A. W5
Polit, Luis E98
Politi, Douglas W. (Doug) A86
Politopoulou, Marianna W269
Politte, Keith A754
Polizzotto, Lawrence A449
Polizzotto, Len (Lenny) P515
Polk, James C. (Jim) A106
Polk, Michael B. (Mike) A627
Polk, Dennis A839
Pollack, Dave (Davie) A202
Pollack, Martha E. A751
Pollack, Murray M. P385
Pollack, Martha E. P411
Pollak, Matthew R (Matt) A821
Pollak, Joanne E. P254
Pollard, Dennis P199
Pollard, Gary S. P627
Pollare, Frank (Frankie) A15
Polles, Jeanne (Jeannie) A699
Pollet, David E300
Polley, Mike (Mikey) A649
Polley, Malcolm E. A775
Pollock, Janet (Jan) E16
Pollock, Greg E16
Pollock, Roy E214
Pollock, Chris (Chrissy) A86
Pollock, Brad (Brady) A120
Pollock, Wally (Wall) A175
Pollock, Samuel J. B. (Sam) W81
Pollok, John C. E376
Pollok, John C. A806
Polly, John (Jack) A485
Poll□'s, Jeanne A699
Polman, Paul W401
Polman, Paul W402
Polmanteer, Keith (Keithy) A792
Polonia, Sharon A800
Polonsky, Nir E176
Polonsky, Kenneth S. P551
Polonsky, Kenneth S. P552
Polovitz, Mark P34
Poloz, Stephen S. W49
Poluch, Tony (Tone) E71
Poluch, Tony (Tone) A152
Polvoriza, Melanie A279
Pomaranski, Joseph A. (Joe) A853
Pombo, Tammy P489
Pomerenke, Kevin (Kev) E336
Pomeroy, Ed (Eddie) A553
Pomeroy, John A866
Pomeroy, John P540
Pommellet, Pierre-Eric W383
Pommier, Laurent A729
Pompa, Mark A. A307
Pompeo, Jeff (Jeffy) E370
Pomplon, Carl A163
Pomponio, Susan (Sue) P215
Pomposi, Dawn A502
Ponce, Robin (Rin) A900
Ponczoch, John A882
Pond, Peter B. E263
Pond, Andrew P302
Pone, Carlos A15
Pons, Jaume A696
Pontarelli, Thomas (Tom) A214

Ponte, Patricia Reid P158
Pontius, Thomas (Thom) A831
Pontrello, Joseph E168
Ponugoti, Derrick E394
Ponugoti, Derrick A838
Pooi, Eric W339
Poole, Thomas (Thom) E99
Poole, Thomas (Thom) A224
Poole, Anita A462
Poole, Benny (Ben) A904
Poole, Barbara (Barb) P156
Poole-yaeger, Amy A180
Poonen, Sanjay A933
Poor, H. Vincent P548
Poovey, Cherin P620
Pope, John (Jack) E335
Pope, Peter T. E338
Pope, David E403
Pope, Gene A37
Pope, John C. (Jack) A287
Pope, Lawrence J. A419
Pope, Sandy (Sandra) A546
Pope, John (Jack) A703
Pope, David A858
Pope, Mike A910
Pope, Jennifer P150
Popeo, John C. E368
Popiela, Diane P348
Popien, Toni (Antonio) P406
Popkin, Jim (Jimmy) E176
Popkin, Jamie (James) E177
Popoli, Barbara A817
Popovich, John P223
Popp, Mike (Mikey) A735
Poppe, Michael J. E103
Poppe, Patricia K. (Patti) A213
Poppe, Patricia K. (Patti) A243
Poppell, Rick (Ricky) E177
Poppell, Mark (Marky) A542
Poppen, Joel A591
Popper, Jozsi A746
Popper, Sharon P334
Poppinga, Peter W405
Poppleton, Drew (Andrew) P103
Popplewell, David H. A200
Popwell, David T. A367
Porat, Ruth M. A33
Porat, M. Moshe P505
Porcello, Susan (Sue) A473
Pordon, Anthony R. (Tony) A687
Porlier, Brad A379
Porras, Julio Carlos W25
Porru, Martina A697
Porsa, Esmaeil P156
Port, Barry R. E139
Port, Joel P287
Portacci, Michael T. A233
Portalatin, Frances (Fran) E364
Portalatin, Julio A. A565
Portalatin, Frances (Fran) A787
Portantino, Philip E326
Portantino, Philip A684
Portela, Marvio A665
Porter, James S. (Jim) E34
Porter, David E. E199
Porter, W. Brian E231
Porter, Brian E231
Porter, Dean E371
Porter, Cynthia V (Cyn) A228
Porter, Pamela G (Pam) A228
Porter, Tracy L. A231
Porter, Catherine (Cate) A267
Porter, Biggs C. A379
Porter, Sandy A420
Porter, David E. A435
Porter, Todd A439
Porter, Todd (Toddy) A439
Porter, Angela (Ang) A539
Porter, Jonathan (John) A754
Porter, Stephen D. A793
Porter, Dean A798
Porter, Jeffrey (Jeff) A801
Porter, Jim (Jimmy) A844
Porter, Kevin (Kev) P273
Porter, Cindy Long P404

Porter, Holly P404
Porter, Stephen D. P445
Porter, Mark P566
Porter, Brian J. W51
Porter, John W236
Portera, Joseph P. (Joe) A247
Porterfield, Kent P431
Portersee, Earl E348
Porteus, Elaine A208
Porth, Mark A398
Portillo, Marilyn (Mar) A589
Portnoy, Barry M. E368
Portnoy, Adam D. E368
Portnoy, Barry M. E368
Portnoy, Adam D. E368
Portnoy, Justin A409
Portnoy, Adam (Ad) A584
Portugal, Sarah A198
Porvaznik, George A188
Porvaznik, George P111
Posada, Barbara (Barb) A263
Posada, Juan F. A719
Posani, Jim A465
Posch, Guillaume de W66
Posey, Bruce K. E348
Posey, Cindy P604
Posillico, Angela (Ang) P187
Posniak, Fred C (Freddy) E135
Post, Denny M. E354
Post, Vincent (Vin) A112
Post, Glen F. A186
Post, Roxanne (Anne) A745
Postel, Darren E442
Postma, Gene P34
Potempa, Kathleen M. A750
Potempa, Kathleen M. P411
Potenza, Dave (Davie) A516
Pothast, Bernard (Bern) E15
Pothast, David (Dave) A500
Pothier, Robert (Bob) A104
Potrykus, William (Bill) P426
Potter, Joel A102
Potter, Simon M. A340
Potter, Keith A504
Potter, James (Jamie) A553
Potter, Stephen N. A640
Potter, Alfred (Alf) P204
Potter, William C. P228
Potter, Richard (Dick) P258
Potts, Robert (Bob) E270
Potts, David L. A756
Potts, Alison (Alli) P318
Potts, Andrew (Andy) P492
Potuzak, Joe A120
Pou, Michael (Mel) E213
Pou, Michael (Mel) A468
Pouba, Jeff (Jeffy) A179
Pouey, John (Jack) A372
Poulin, Richard (Dick) A883
Poulley, Sean A485
Poulopoulos, Georgios W302
Poulsen, Niel L. E417
Poulsen, Sue (Susie) P393
Pouncey, Clarence C. E369
Pouncey, Clarence C. A794
Pound, Greg (Greggy) A633
Poutre, Julie P238
Pouyann, Patrick W391
Pouyanne, Patrick W391
Povenmire, Rex A279
Povich, John (Jack) A729
Povlinski, Bryan (Bry) P571
Powderly, Thomas (Thom) A109
Powell, Kena E153
Powell, Dawna E194
Powell, Teresa E199
Powell, Ty (Tyler) E213
Powell, Paul T. E242
Powell, Deana E374
Powell, Cindy A119
Powell, Cathy A102
Powell, Bradley S. (Brad) A329
Powell, Kena A349
Powell, Don A351
Powell, Kendall J. (Ken) A398

Powell, John (Jack) A425
Powell, Teresa A435
Powell, Ty (Tyler) A468
Powell, Paul W A809
Powell, Cynthia A. A821
Powell, Wayne A911
Powell, David (Dave) A916
Powell, Wm. Eugene (Gene) A921
Powell, Anthony P177
Powell, Kenneth P276
Powell, Chris P299
Powell, Simon N. P307
Powell, Curtis (Curt) P414
Powell, Jeff P422
Powell, John P556
Powell, Wm. Eugene (Gene) P605
Powell, Allen P618
Powell, Scott E. W46
Powell, William W81
Powell, Rice W164
Powell, Rice W165
Power, Andrew P. E121
Power, Steve E446
Power, Georgia A24
Power, Bill (Billy) A208
Power, Nancy A585
Power, Gary A957
Powers, John F. E66
Powers, David B. (Dave) E127
Powers, Johnny D. E214
Powers, Russell E307
Powers, Jennifer (Jen) E364
Powers, Mark (Marky) E442
Powers, Robert P. (Bob) A42
Powers, Stephen (Steve) A104
Powers, John J. A357
Powers, Tacey A637
Powers, Jennifer (Jen) A787
Powers, Amber A824
Powers, Marsha A851
Powers, Greg (Greggy) A914
Powers, Barbara (Barb) A972
Powers, Monica P453
Powers, William C. (Bill) P604
Powlesson, Brittney A430
Powlus, Lee C. A459
Pozarycki, Tom (Tommy) A939
Poznanski, Greg A835
Pozotrigo, Albert A496
Pozzi, James E. A48
Pozzi, Steven R. W104
Prabakaran, Sateesh A745
Prabhakar, Sunil P401
Prabhu, John C. E230
Prabhu, Arjun A649
Prabhu, Vasant M. A932
Prabhu, Kiran P240
Prade, Bianca P524
Pradhan, Ravindra A208
Pradia, Marsha (Marcella) P511
Prado, Mary A641
Praet, peter W54
Pragada, Robert V. (Bob) A496
Prager, Jeff (Jeffy) A766
Prager, Jeff (Jeffy) P421
Prague, Ronald J. E396
Prakasam, Haripriya A479
Prakash, Shaleen A163
Pramaggiore, Anne R. A326
Prame, Thomas (Thom) A370
Prange, Karen A782
Prantl, James (Jamie) E163
Prasad, Rama E107
Prasad, Brajendra A824
Prasodjo, Bambang A439
Prater, William L. (Bill) A101
Prater, Marsha A P306
Prater, Shawna (Sha) P320
Prather, David (Dave) A419
Prather, Sharon P146
Prather, Ed (Eddie) P586
Pratico, Joseph (Jo) A923
Pratico, Manuel P2
Prato, Thomas (Thom) E54
Prato, Patrick A465

A = AMERICAN BUSINESS
E = EMERGING COMPANIES
P = PRIVATE COMPANIES
W = WORLD BUSINESS

Reyes, Paul (Pauly) P410
Reyes, Pedro P605
Reyes, Marcelo W92
Reyes, Cecilia W427
Reyle, John J. E349
Reynolds, F. Kevin E79
Reynolds, Liz (Lizzie) E177
Reynolds, Martin (Marti) E177
Reynolds, Kimberly A20
Reynolds, Stephen R. (Steve) A68
Reynolds, Lynne A104
Reynolds, Sally (Sal) A156
Reynolds, F. Kevin A165
Reynolds, Chris A175
Reynolds, Rip A175
Reynolds, James Frank (Jamie) A180
Reynolds, Janet (Jan) A183
Reynolds, Eric A212
Reynolds, Catherine (Cate) A213
Reynolds, Tamra A217
Reynolds, Deena A351
Reynolds, Wendy A359
Reynolds, Linda A397
Reynolds, Robert L. A415
Reynolds, Matthew (Matt) A504
Reynolds, Ann (Annie) A542
Reynolds, Michael A. (Mick) A672
Reynolds, Sean A733
Reynolds, Jim (Jimmy) A821
Reynolds, Dave A946
Reynolds, Tamra P132
Reynolds, Joanne (Jojo) P298
Reynolds, Sean B. P361
Reynolds, Ross P523
Reynolds, William (Bill) P525
Reynolds, Zan P550
Reynolds, Suzanne P620
Reynolds, Robert L. W174
Reynoso, Jamie A173
Reynoso, Jamie P105
Reza, Ali E392
Rezvan, Lotfollah E135
Rhea, Casey A846
Rheaume, Lindsey S. E126
Rheaume, Lindsey S. A298
Rhein, Francisco (Frances) A273
Rhein, Francisco (Frances) P165
Rhine, Christopher (Chris) E98
Rho, Joseph K. E191
Rho, Joseph K. A422
Rhoades, Doug (Dougie) A664
Rhoads, Rebecca B. A747
Rhoda, Richard G. P604
Rhode, Jason P. E93
Rhode, Bryan (Bry) A251
Rhodebeck, Lyle D. A821
Rhodes, Sheri E131
Rhodes, John M. A31
Rhodes, William C. (Bill) A90
Rhodes, Kevin A309
Rhodes, Rory A394
Rhodes, Charles A706
Rhodes, Dusty A752
Rhodes, Steve (Stevie) P437
Rhodes, Edwardo P571
Rhodes, Gary P627
Rhodin, Michael D. (Mike) A485
Rholes, Julia M. P594
Rhoman, Cindy (Cin) P277
Rhynalds, Christian A239
Rhyne, Jerry P278
Rial, Francis A603
Rial, Sergio W46
Riall, Taylor P586
Rian, Sommer P351
Ribar, Geoffrey G. (Geoff) E73
Ribe, Raquel (Rae) A465
Ribeiro, Rafael (Rafee) E131
Ribieras, Jean-Michel A487

Ribi⬚©ras, Jean-Michel A487
Riboud, Franck W124
Ricard, Brenda (Bren) P570
Ricardo, Pedro Carmona de
    Oliveira W169
Ricchetti, Ginger A753
Ricchezza, John (Jack) E371
Ricchezza, John (Jack) A798
Ricchio, Wesley E157
Ricchio, Wesley A358
Ricchiuto, John (Jack) E377
Ricchiuto, Jack E377
Ricci, John (Jack) E187
Ricci, Lisa (Lis) E359
Ricci, Ben (Benny) A150
Ricciardi, Matthew M. A126
Riccio, Daniel (Dan) A66
Riccio, Dan (Danny) A66
Riccio, Anthony A136
Riccio, Janet A660
Riccio, Daniel (Dan) P526
Ricciotti, Hope P71
Ricciuti, James (Jamie) A18
Riccobelli, Thomas (Thom) A843
Riccoboni, Anthony (Tony) A208
Rice, Randy E80
Rice, Mary E213
Rice, Michael E215
Rice, Daniel (Dan) E258
Rice, Richard (Dick) E268
Rice, Amy (Ames) A112
Rice, Denise A232
Rice, Adam A273
Rice, Charles A315
Rice, John G. A396
Rice, Jessica (Jess) A407
Rice, Mary A468
Rice, Brian S. A510
Rice, Derica W. A543
Rice, Richard (Dick) A577
Rice, Catherine (Cate) A643
Rice, Troy A655
Rice, Ashley A689
Rice, Ronald A. A772
Rice, Jacqueline Hourigan A846
Rice, Michael (Mel) A851
Rice, Theis A886
Rice, S. Theis A887
Rice, Peter A892
Rice, Judith (Judi) P2
Rice, David P44
Rice, Adam P165
Rice, Arthur H. P404
Rice, Ann Madden P587
Rich, Jonathan D. (Jon) A129
Rich, Brian F. A213
Rich, Brian F. A243
Rich, Brandon A392
Rich, Garethe A546
Rich, Valia A753
Rich, Dave (Davie) A789
Rich, Frank P34
Rich, Melinda R. (Mindy) P417
Rich, Paul P417
Rich, Ted (Teddy) P417
Rich, Robert E. (Bob) P417
Rich, Mark P490
Rich, Robert E. (Bob) P519
Richard, Gary E89
Richard, Laino A3
Richard, Gary A191
Richard, Stan A252
Richard, Albert J. A372
Richard, Roger (Rog) A603
Richard, Garth A619
Richard, Henri A621
Richard, Stephane W293
Richards, Christine E129
Richards, Laura (Laur) E228
Richards, Bruce (Brucey) E253
Richards, Jeff (Jeffy) E277
Richards, Stacey (Stace) E335
Richards, Mark (Marky) A159
Richards, Randolph A195
Richards, Todd A278

Richards, Ticole A280
Richards, Ramon A333
Richards, Bruce (Brucey) A341
Richards, Christine P. A344
Richards, Peter (Pete) A351
Richards, Alyson A470
Richards, Patricia R. A481
Richards, Jeff (Jeffy) A595
Richards, Stephanie A658
Richards, Stacey (Stace) A703
Richards, Lisa (Lis) A720
Richards, David A775
Richards, Jeff A779
Richards, Rachel M. A804
Richards, Michael A824
Richards, Lavada A835
Richards, Barry A. A882
Richards, Cindy A957
Richards, Donna W. A970
Richards, Jesse P112
Richards, Patricia R. P241
Richards, Allwyne P415
Richards, Larry P571
Richards, Thomas P595
Richardson, Dave E12
Richardson, Chad E163
Richardson, Brent D. E185
Richardson, Jamie (James) E240
Richardson, David (Dave) E262
Richardson, Michael J (Mel) E355
Richardson, Debra J. A42
Richardson, Daniel A97
Richardson, George A126
Richardson, Bryan D. A150
Richardson, Cindy (Cin) A162
Richardson, David (Dave) A164
Richardson, Michael R. (Mike) A169
Richardson, Lee A379
Richardson, Dana A400
Richardson, Cameron (Cammie) A402
Richardson, Ed (Eddie) A430
Richardson, Matt A442
Richardson, Jamie (James) A533
Richardson, Tricia (Trish) A565
Richardson, Heath A576
Richardson, Tonya A584
Richardson, Ed A596
Richardson, Pamela (Pam) A706
Richardson, Elizabeth (Beth) A706
Richardson, Michael (Mel) A782
Richardson, Michael (Mel) A865
Richardson, David Wayne (Dave) A866
Richardson, Jared A887
Richardson, Jared (Jare) A887
Richardson, Maurice (Maury) A943
Richardson, Ken (Kenny) P24
Richardson, Todd (Toddy) P43
Richardson, Steven (Steve) P56
Richardson, Dee P190
Richardson, Gary (Gar) P332
Richardson, Mark P369
Richardson, Terry (Terr) P416
Richardson, David Wayne (Dave) P540
Richardson, Robert E. P588
Richardson, David E. P589
Richardson, Andy P600
Richbourg, Steven E. P227
Richburg, Joseph (Jo) A176
Richels, John A270
Richemont, Phillip (Phil) P644
Richenhagen, Martin H. A21
Richer, Mark Hans (Marky) A424
Richert, Diane (Di) A706
Richetta, Pascale A7
Richey, Ellen A932
Richey, Joseph P (Jo) P103
Richey, Mike P489
Richland, Scott P94
Richman, David A397
Richman, Michael (Mel) A462
Richman, Larry D. A717
Richman, Eden A929
Richmond, Michael A462
Richmond, Alessandra A565
Richmond, Shaun A887

Richmond, Brent E. A947
Richmond, Doug P383
Richmond, Craig P533
Richner, Scott P285
Richter, David L. E203
Richter, Friedrich A7
Richter, Brian A895
Richter, Karen P121
Ricia, Catherine A565
Rick, Frederick A205
Rickard, Candice J. A657
Rickard, Dave P34
Rickards, Suzanne (Sue) E187
Rickel, John C. A416
Rickel, Todd A. P555
Rickenbach, Josef H. von E321
Ricker, David (Dave) A851
Rickert, Luann K A267
Rickert, R. G. (Bob) W109
Ricketts, Lawrence G. E314
Ricketts, Carlton A A164
Ricks, Stephen (Steve) E160
Ricks, Mary L. E230
Ricks, David A. A544
Ricks, Ron A809
Rico, Dave (Davie) A706
Riddle, Doug (Dougie) A351
Ridenour, Mike (Mikey) A599
Ridenour, Mark E P318
Ridenour, Nancy P595
Rideout, Maryellen A13
Rideout, Deb P464
Rider, James A499
Rider, Sue (Susie) A965
Rider, Matthew J. W10
Ridgely, Gerry L. P425
Ridgeway, Alan A549
Ridgeway, Leann (Ann) A769
Ridgeway, Larry D. P594
Ridgway, Bruce P352
Ridley, Bruce (Brucey) A675
Ridley, Simon W356
Ridout, Chris (Chrissy) A957
Ridzon, Paul (Pauly) A514
Riebe, Dave A735
Riebe, David A735
Riebel, William (Bill) P519
Riebling, Antoinette P448
Riecker, Robert (Bob) A789
Rieder, Madeline (Maddi) A751
Rieder, Madeline (Maddi) P412
Riedman, Suzanne A518
Riedmann, Scott (Scotty) A44
Riefe, James (Jamie) A784
Riegel, Matthew (Matt) A641
Rieger, Ed (Eddie) E98
Rieger, Jeffrey (Jeff) A267
Rieger, Ralf W374
Riel, Susan G. E126
Riel, Kevin (Kev) A218
Riel, Pierre A247
Riel, Susan G. A298
Riel, Kevin (Kev) P132
Rieley, John F. E229
Rielly, John P. A439
Rieman, Rick (Ricky) E250
Riemer, Danny (Dan) A135
Riendeau, Victoria A342
Riepe, James S. (Jim) A403
Riesberg, Kent A610
Riess, Michelle (Michie) E177
Riesterer, Terry (Terr) A768
Rife, John A. E422
Rife, John A. A908
Riffle, Randy (Rand) A514
Rifkind, Neil C. E408
Rigatti, Maria A305
Rigdon, Kent (Ken) E196
Rigdon, Charlie (Charles) P595
Rigg, Timothy (Tim) A164
Riggan, Gisela A344
Riggan, Debbie (Deb) A315
Riggan, Gisela A723
Rigger, Kathy P276
Riggi, Adam (Ad) A83

A = AMERICAN BUSINESS
E = EMERGING COMPANIES
P = PRIVATE COMPANIES
W = WORLD BUSINESS

Strain, John F. A961
Strain, Charles (Chas) P160
Strain, Charles M. P638
Strain, Trevor W263
Strain, Kevin D. W364
Straley, Donna (Don) P528
Stram, Randy A584
Strampel, William D. P320
Strang, Bill (Billy) A404
Strang, Carol A654
Strang, Cameron P623
Strange, Robbie E51
Strange, Robbie A110
Strange, Nicholas (Nick) A732
Strange, Vickie (Vick) A846
Strange, John P482
Stranger, Mary (Mar) A841
Strangfeld, John R. A726
Stranghoener, V. Raymond (Ray) A229
Stranghoener, Lawrence A604
Stranick, Mike A223
Strasburger, John (Jack) A929
Strassner, Larry P196
Stratan, Miruna A409
Stratman, R. Joseph A648
Stratton, Harold M. E386
Stratton, Ed A129
Stratton, Mike (Mikey) A156
Stratton, Michael (Mel) A156
Stratton, John G. A927
Straub, Maximiliane A763
Straub, Maximiliane P419
Straus, David H. E207
Straus, David H. A448
Strauss, Thomas W. E111
Strauss, Thomas J. E342
Strauss, Sarah (Sar) A163
Strauss, Katrina A281
Strauss, John L (Jack) A502
Strauss, Natalie (Nat) P281
Strauss, Jeffrey (Jeff) P362
Strauss, Andrew L. P552
Strauss, Frank W135
Stravitz, Mitchell A175
Straw, Mona A360
Strayer, Joe P246
Straz, David A. P190
Strazdas, Stella A499
Streeter, Lisa (Lis) E160
Streeter, Paul (Pauly) P144
Streeter, Al P422
Streit, Steven W. E187
Streletsky, Anne (Annie) A824
Streyzowsky, Gregor A135
Strianese, Anthony T. (Tony) E70
Strianese, Michael T. A525
Stribley, Lucy (Lucia) A143
Strickholm, Glenn A893
Strickland, Mark (Marky) A162
Strickland, Robert G (Bob) A173
Strickland, Stephanie (Steph) A273
Strickland, Eric (Ric) A640
Strickland, Shawn A928
Strickland, Robert G (Bob) P105
Strickland, Stephanie (Steph) P165
Strickland, Ora P190
Strickland, Jerald (Jerry) P590
Strickland, Claire P592
Strigens, Lora (Lor) P293
Strine, Michael (Mel) A341
Stringer, Peter E403
Stringer, David (Dave) A371
Stringer, Peter A858
Stringham, Brian (Bri) A981
Striph, David (Dave) E211
Strite, Dave P410
Strittmatter, Kirk A206
Stritzinger, Gina E213
Stritzinger, Gina A469
Strode, Scott C (Scotty) A139
Strohl, Michael (Mel) P125
Strohmaier, Walter W61
Strohriegel, Nikolaus E84
Strojwas, Andrzej J. E325
Stroker, Robert T. P505

Strom, Tracy (Trace) E372
Strom, Chuck (Chucky) A929
Stromatt, Scott (Scotty) E134
Stromberg, Stephanie (Steph) A482
Stromberg, LeRoy J. P15
Stromberg, Stephanie (Steph) P242
Strong, Gary A180
Strong, Robert (Bob) A506
Strong, Tad A576
Strong, Douglas (Doug) A751
Strong, Robert (Bob) P256
Strong, David W. P370
Strong, Douglas (Doug) P411
Strongin, Steven H. A409
Stronks, T. Joseph A437
Stronks, Joseph A437
Strosahl, James (Jamie) A407
Strother, Eric (Ric) A20
Strother, Debrah A354
Stroubakis, Demetri P24
Stroucken, Albert P. L. (Al) A670
Stroud, David (Dave) A835
Stroup, Louann E221
Stroup, Louann A474
Stroz, Edward M. P193
Strozzi, Mary (Mar) A407
Strozzi, Gianluca A696
Strubell, Taylor A239
Struble, Rich (Ric) A511
Struby, Neil P338
Struck, Richard (Dick) A896
Strull, Scott P578
Strumwasser, Todd P498
Strunk, June A602
Strunk, Thomas W. (Tom) A966
Strunk, Thomas W. (Tom) P640
Strupp, Jim A884
Struppa, Daniele P112
Struth, Werner A763
Struth, Werner P420
Struth, Werner W74
Strycker, Samara A616
Stryker, Scott A56
Stryker, David M. A466
Strykowski, Jill (Jilly) P20
Stuart, Erin E49
Stuart, Nancy E101
Stuart, Britt E159
Stuart, Erin A99
Stuart, Greg (Greggy) A147
Stuart, Gary (Gar) A200
Stuart, Lynn A344
Stuart, Britt A365
Stuart, Nicholas (Nick) A514
Stuart, Tim A758
Stuart, Chad A764
Stuart, Paul (Pauly) P287
Stubbins, Val A87
Stubbs, P. Scott E148
Stubelis, Karl E42
Stuber, Rich P611
Stuccio, Nina A580
Stuchbery, Robert A. (Bob) A423
Stucker, Janice (Jan) A536
Stueber, Bill (Billy) E406
Stueber, Bill (Billy) A862
Stueber, Shelly P294
Stuecker, Phillip (Phil) A978
Stueve, Jo P308
Stuhr, Ashley A655
Stukalin, Felix E228
Stukenborg, John A872
Stulken, Judy P462
Stull, Mike (Mikey) A706
Stumbo, Kevin J. A235
Stump, James M. A444
Stump, Mike P285
Sturany, Klaus W178
Sturdivant, Lisa A135
Sturgell, Robert A. (Bobby) A769
Sturgess, Dave (Davie) P290
Sturk, Dawn P232
Sturm, Paul (Pauly) A236
Sturm, Jeff (Jeffy) A465
Sturm, Stephan W165

Sturrock, Matt A839
Sturtz, Robert (Bob) A965
Sturycz, Robert (Bob) A840
Stutts, Garry A360
Stutts, James (Jamie) A840
Stutts, William (Bill) A923
Stutz, Carin L. E354
Stutz, Bob A778
Stuver, Douglas K. (Doug) A674
Styduhar, Kenneth (Ken) A226
Style, Keith R. A74
Styles, Maurice A83
Stynes, Terri (Terr) E372
Styons, Connie P501
Stys, Richard (Dick) P217
Su, Cynthia A839
Su, Meihsun W120
Suah, Philip (Phil) A194
Suardi, Franco A521
Suarez, Ray A8
Suarez, Pablo A94
Suarez, Gaston A479
Suarez, John (Jack) A937
Subaric, Stana A531
Subasic, Stephen (Steve) A817
Subban, Srinivas A499
Subbaswamy, Kumble R.
    (Swamy) P593
Subhash, Dev E98
Sublett, Clay (Clayton) A514
Subramaniam, Natraj E436
Subramaniam, Venkatachalam A87
Subramanian, Subbu E26
Subramanian, Ashok E40
Subramanya, Manjunat A104
Subramanya, Bhanu A621
Subramanyam, Meena A133
Subramanyan, Raju P313
Sucherman, Matt (Matty) A33
Suchoff, Shari P287
Suchomel, Valerie A94
Suchy, Louis (Lou) E13
Suchy, Frederick J. P117
Suckale, Margret W58
Sud, James (Jim) A959
Suddeth, John (Jack) P36
Sudnick, Steve (Stevie) A351
Sue, Anderson A186
Suer, Bernie (Bern) P314
Suerth, John (Jack) A175
Suetens, David A824
Sugar, Robert J. A756
Sugarman, Jay A493
Sugasawara, Emery A649
Suggs, Tom P534
Sugiarto, Prijono W209
Sugihara, Hiroshige A664
Sugiura, Junichi W122
Sugiyama, Nao W287
Suh, Brian E236
Suh, Willie (Will) A664
Suits, Scott P103
Sukeno, Kenji W168
Suko, Todd A. A425
Sukola, Joe A579
Sukys, Dan A514
Suldan, Joel P278
Sulentic, Robert E. (Bob) A174
Sulentic, Robert E. (Bob) A818
Sulerzyski, Charles W. E330
Sulerzyski, Charles W. A690
Sullivan, Louis W. E31
Sullivan, Mark P. E40
Sullivan, Luke (Lucas) E97
Sullivan, Jerry (Jerr) E107
Sullivan, David (Dave) E164
Sullivan, Patrick (Paddy) E176
Sullivan, John J. E271
Sullivan, Darlyne E280
Sullivan, Bob E317
Sullivan, Thomas P. (Tom) E387
Sullivan, John (Jack) E406
Sullivan, Mark L. E415
Sullivan, Daniel (Dan) E420
Sullivan, Greg E430

Sullivan, Denis E454
Sullivan, Beth (Betty) A18
Sullivan, Timothy J. A64
Sullivan, Christi (Chris) A100
Sullivan, Gene A112
Sullivan, Josh A143
Sullivan, Lee A146
Sullivan, Michael A157
Sullivan, Chip A226
Sullivan, William P. (Bill) A305
Sullivan, William (Bill) A325
Sullivan, Brian (Bri) A462
Sullivan, Gary (Gar) A471
Sullivan, Jason A477
Sullivan, Peggy (Peg) A481
Sullivan, Bonnie (Bonbon) A584
Sullivan, Toni (Antonio) A606
Sullivan, David (Dave) A641
Sullivan, Brian A660
Sullivan, Linda (Lin) A693
Sullivan, Kevin (Kev) A696
Sullivan, Teresa (Terry) A751
Sullivan, Frank C. A772
Sullivan, George E. A824
Sullivan, Kevin A824
Sullivan, Tarra A835
Sullivan, Robert (Bob) A860
Sullivan, John (Jack) A862
Sullivan, Mark L. A888
Sullivan, Daniel (Dan) A901
Sullivan, Brendan A929
Sullivan, Jackie (Jack) A929
Sullivan, John P25
Sullivan, Sean P57
Sullivan, John P98
Sullivan, Lynn (Lyn) P99
Sullivan, Mike (Mikey) P122
Sullivan, Janet P176
Sullivan, Edward P260
Sullivan, John P303
Sullivan, Brian P356
Sullivan, Tom (Tommy) P385
Sullivan, William E. (Bill) P401
Sullivan, Teresa A. P410
Sullivan, Teresa (Terry) P411
Sullivan, Scott A. P508
Sullivan, Leo (Leonardo) P570
Sullivan, Paul (Pauly) P571
Sullivan, Suzanne P588
Sullivan, Julie H. P600
Sullivan, John P625
Sullivan, Elizabeth (Beth) P641
Sullivan, Chris W327
Sullivan-Marx, Eileen A626
Sullivan-Marx, Eileen P345
Sullivan-Yelko, Teri (Terrance) A727
Sult, John (Jack) A559
Sultemeier, Chris A937
Sumi, Shuzo W386
Summerell, Virginia (Ginny) E400
Summerer, Gerhard W139
Summerfield, Sonya A743
Summerford, R. Michael A889
Summerlin, Stephen (Steve) A786
Summerlin, Jim P300
Summers, John (Jack) E13
Summers, Diane M. E49
Summers, James (Jamie) A7
Summers, Kevin V. A94
Summers, Diane M. A99
Summers, Jeramy A150
Summers, William (Bill) A171
Summers, Curtis P38
Summers, Barbara (Barb) P137
Summers, Vic (Victor) P156
Summers, Cynthia P160
Summers, Jeff P455
Summers, Renee (Ren) P535
Summey, Marc (Marcy) A394
Sumner, Tad E89
Sumner, Ted E89
Sumner, Ted A191
Sumoski, David A. A648
Sumoski, Dave A648
Sumpter, Tammy A693

Tabak, Natan P621
Tabb, Kevin P71
Taber, Grant E450
Taber, Gerry (Gerold) A697
Taboas, Christian (Chris) A13
Tabone, George (Georgey) E433
Taborda, Marcelo A489
Taborda, Ruben (Ben) A500
Taborga, Jorge R. E312
Tabraham, Dan (Danny) E197
Tabraham, Dan (Danny) A434
Tabrizi, Carol (Care) A156
Tabron, La June Montgomery P619
Tacelli, David G. (Dave) E455
Tachimori, Takeshi W167
Tacka, David (Dave) A438
Tacke, Markus W346
Tackoor, Gary (Gar) E49
Tackoor, Gary (Gar) A99
Tadamy, Everett (Eve) P101
Tady, Deborah (Deb) A179
Taets, Joseph D. (Joe) A70
Taffe, Pat P351
Taft, Timothy P. (Tim) E153
Taft, Matthias W63
Taga, Kelly (Kel) E249
Taggart, Daniel J. E355
Taggart, Richard G. A824
Taheri, Paul P556
Tai, Pin A171
Tai, Shenghong P591
Taiclet, David L. (Dave) E1
Taiclet, James D. (Jim) A50
Taira, John (Jack) A184
Taisey, Mark Taisey (Marky) A55
Tait, Joseph M. (Joe) E248
Tait, Steven (Steve) A376
Tait, John (Jack) A981
Tait, Bruce P34
Tait, Nancy (Nance) P471
Takagi, Marsha A341
Takagi, Rie A592
Takagi, Yoshiyuki W122
Takagi, Kazuhiro W286
Takahashi, Maurice (Maury) E9
Takahashi, Lance A184
Takahashi, Hidetomi W20
Takahashi, Koichi W121
Takahashi, Mitsuru W167
Takahashi, Tetsu W220
Takahashi, Shizuo W262
Takahashi, Kunio W340
TAKAHASHI, SHOJIRO W342
Takami, Kazunori W296
Takao, Kazushi W252
Takasaka, Masahiko W205
Takashima, Denise A856
Takedagawa, Masahiro W186
Takemura, Shigeyuki W27
Takita, Yasuo W20
Takizawa, Soichiro W186
Talaga, Dana A369
Talat, Kausar A139
Talaulicar, Anant A253
Talbert, Stuart (Stu) A296
Talbert, Stuart (Stu) P171
Talbot, William W. E24
Talbot, Brian E268
Talbot, Jeff (Jeffy) A523
Talbot, Brian A577
Talbot, Kathy (Kat) P303
Talbott, John (Jack) P571
Talbott, Robert S. P604
Talcott, Patrick A689
Taldar, Sunil W67
Tallent, Christopher (Chris) A229
Tallent, Jimmy C. A905
Tallent, William (Bill) P489
Talley, Cyndi A430
Talley, Linda P120
Tallis, Heather P536
Tallo, Richard A392
Talluri, Satyajit A693
Talset, Bjornar A826
Talset, Bjornar P488

Talukdar, Praneet E68
Tam, Wilson (Will) A163
Tam, Jamie A409
Tam, Jack (Jackie) A490
Tam, David P374
Tamai, Takaaki W386
Tamasi, Tony (Tone) A649
Tamayo, Kelvin Tamayo E419
Tammaro, Vincent P642
Tamminga, Neely E336
Tams, Todd (Toddy) E433
Tamvakakis, Apostolos S. W302
Tan, Lip-Bu E73
Tan, Alex A22
Tan, Tom A144
Tan, Phillip (Phil) A370
Tan, Jacqueline (Jackie) A479
Tan, Jenny A720
Tan, K Lee P307
Tan, Nestor W64
Tan, Zhaohui W95
Tan, Darren S. P. W295
Tanabe, Masaki W30
Tanabe, Eiichi W256
Tanabe, Masahiro W262
Tanaka, Takaaki E307
Tanaka, Robyn (Rob) A106
Tanaka, Stanley (Stan) A856
Tanaka, Masayasu W205
Tanaka, Jun W220
Tanaka, Junichi W354
Tanaka, Osamu W424
Tanase, Octavian A621
Tanasijevich, George A530
Tancrati, Juliana A112
Tandon, Priya A136
Tandon, Manu P71
Taneda, Kyoko E177
Taneja, Rajat A932
Tanen, Lauren (Laur) A733
Tang, Stephen S. E315
Tang, Karen A139
Tang, Paul (Pauly) A154
Tang, George (Georgey) A584
Tang, Pengbo A824
Tang, Michael (Mel) P8
Tanger, Steven B. E400
Tangney, Eugene A774
Tango, Yasutake W209
Tanguay, Alfred (Alf) A689
Tani, Makoto W361
Taniguchi, Arthur K (Art) A106
Taniguchi, Michihiro W259
Tanikawa, Kei W30
Tanimoto, Dale (Dal) A106
Tanis, Justin A470
Tanji, Larry (Lar) A175
Tanji, Kenneth A726
Tank, Cindy P (Cin) A534
Tankesley, Mark (Marky) A230
Tannehill, Martha (Mar) A447
Tannenbaum, Leonard M. E154
Tannenbaum, Richard E441
Tannenbaum, Carl A342
Tanner, Jim E436
Tanner, Gregg (Greggory) A265
Tanner, Teresa J. A351
Tanner, Kirk A692
Tanner, Bob (Bo) P148
Tanner, James P190
Tannert, Silvio P101
Tanoue, Donna A. A106
Tanovan, Tristan A589
Tans, Gillian A715
Tanum, Anne Carine W137
Tanurhan, Yankin E397
Tanwar, Ankit A105
Tanz, Stuart A. E357
Tanz, Larry (Lar) A622
Tanzer, David A136
Tanzer, Kim P410
Taohai, Xue W97
Tapia, Mark A912
Taplits, Steve A124
Tappe, Trent P624

Tappert, Tod N. P610
Tarantino, Steve A576
Tarapor, Mahrukh P534
Tarasova, Natasha A566
Tarbet, Michele P451
Tarbox, Ned A502
Tarby, Todd A395
Tarca, Fred P404
Tarchetti, Mark S. A627
Tardos, Eva (Evalyn) P144
Tareen, Irfan A44
Tarkinton, Timothy A665
Tarr, Jeffrey R. (Jeff) E122
Tarr, Steve E457
Tarrant, Dennis (Denny) E159
Tarrant, Dennis (Denny) A364
Tarter, Audrey A451
Tarvin, Julie A483
Tas, Robert E328
Tashiro, Tamiharu W215
Tasooji, Michael B. P403
Tastad, Carolyn A719
Tastor, John E (Jack) A392
Tasy, Mark (Marky) A654
Tatangelo, Dino A820
Tatarevich, Jason A539
Tate, Kelley (Kells) A253
Tate, Howard M A845
Tate, Mike P12
Tate, Gregory (Greg) P333
Tate, Harry (Hare) P404
Tateosian, David E161
Tateosian, David A373
Tatera, Robert A223
Tatterson, Robert L. (Bob) A788
Tatterson, W. Mark A904
Tattum, Tyler (Ty) E361
Tatum, Greg (Greggy) A702
Taub, Leon A341
Taub, Kris (Krissy) A341
Tauber, David W. P503
Tauber, Richard E. P503
Taubitz, Joe (Joey) A228
Taubman, Ross E. A718
Taugher, Tom (Tommy) A520
Taunton, Cindy E59
Taunton, Michael A73
Taus, Ellen P544
Tauscher, William Y. E61
Tavakoli, Nader A38
Tavalsky, Gregory (Greg) A485
Tavares, Chris A140
Tavares, Carlos W300
Taverna, Stephanie (Steph) E265
Taverna, Stephanie (Steph) A572
Tavernier, Jacques W407
Tavlarides, Toula A109
Tawasha, Nelson (Nelly) A462
Tawney, Jeff (Jeffy) A875
Tawyea, Edward (Ed) P561
Tay, Julie E18
Tay, Talal A252
Tayano, Ken W120
Taychakhoonavudh, Neeracha A778
Taylor, Ross E3
Taylor, Paul E40
Taylor, Warren E116
Taylor, Brenton A223
Taylor, Bruce E265
Taylor, Les E267
Taylor, Tran E291
Taylor, Stephen C. E292
Taylor, Donna (Don) E335
Taylor, Silvia E387
Taylor, W. Kent E405
Taylor, Jeffery L. E443
Taylor, Patricia A. E448
Taylor, J A48
Taylor, Steven (Steve) A76
Taylor, Robert A77
Taylor, Ryan (Ry) A78
Taylor, Steve (Stevie) A83
Taylor, Ed (Eddie) A92
Taylor, Donna (Don) A120
Taylor, Steven W (Steve) A126

Taylor, Kandice A140
Taylor, William (Bill) A157
Taylor, Ashley (Ash) A163
Taylor, Ellisa A166
Taylor, Bob (Bo) A175
Taylor, Damian A175
Taylor, Linda (Lin) A180
Taylor, Eric A200
Taylor, Gregory (Greg) A203
Taylor, William (Bill) A205
Taylor, Brock A217
Taylor, Angie (Ang) A226
Taylor, Jim (Jimmy) A236
Taylor, James (Jamie) A236
Taylor, David A254
Taylor, Warren A255
Taylor, Lyndon C. A270
Taylor, Christopher (Chris) A281
Taylor, Rhonda M. A283
Taylor, Stephen M. (Steve) A304
Taylor, Karen (Kare) A319
Taylor, Kenneth (Ken) A324
Taylor, Ken (Kenny) A324
Taylor, Zachary A340
Taylor, Robert C. A379
Taylor, Lashawn A395
Taylor, Ian A409
Taylor, Paul W. A418
Taylor, Stacy A462
Taylor, Brandon (Bran) A463
Taylor, Mike A463
Taylor, Jim (Jimmy) A466
Taylor, Kevin (Kev) A485
Taylor, Michael (Mel) A504
Taylor, Patti L (Pat) A522
Taylor, Bruce A572
Taylor, David (Dave) A634
Taylor, Howard A646
Taylor, Roger (Rog) A685
Taylor, Bob (Bo) A695
Taylor, Tim G. A700
Taylor, Donna (Don) A703
Taylor, David S. A719
Taylor, Julie (Jules) A720
Taylor, Sue (Susie) A726
Taylor, Bo (Bob) A745
Taylor, Zachary (Zach) A745
Taylor, Bob (Bo) A746
Taylor, Shelley (Shell) A747
Taylor, Evie A752
Taylor, Sarah (Sar) A761
Taylor, Angela Pittman (Ang) A766
Taylor, Michael (Mel) A793
Taylor, Kenneth R. (Ken) A797
Taylor, Jerre A810
Taylor, William S. (Bill) A817
Taylor, Malcolm A866
Taylor, Steve (Steve) A893
Taylor, Renee A899
Taylor, Kelly (Kel) A910
Taylor, Nick (Nicky) A947
Taylor, Patricia A. A951
Taylor, Mike P. A966
Taylor, Michael (Mel) A966
Taylor, Thomas A. P15
Taylor, Bonnie (Bonbon) P38
Taylor, Robert P41
Taylor, Mimi P56
Taylor, Mike P98
Taylor, Michael (Mel) P98
Taylor, Cyrus P103
Taylor, Michael (Mel) P118
Taylor, Brock P132
Taylor, Barry (Barr) P190
Taylor, Whitney P239
Taylor, Scott P312
Taylor, Jerome (Jerry) P317
Taylor, Dave (Davie) P366
Taylor, Bob (Bo) P382
Taylor, Jim P390
Taylor, Angela Pittman (Ang) P421
Taylor, R. Stephen P437
Taylor, Michael (Mel) P445
Taylor, Mimi P462
Taylor, Christopher P466

A = AMERICAN BUSINESS
E = EMERGING COMPANIES
P = PRIVATE COMPANIES
W = WORLD BUSINESS

A = AMERICAN BUSINESS
E = EMERGING COMPANIES
P = PRIVATE COMPANIES
W = WORLD BUSINESS

Tobey, James (Jamie) A3
Tobey, Stephanie (Steph) A981
Tobias, Larry (Lar) A837
Tobin, Dominic M. E109
Tobin, Bernard F. E287
Tobin, Jim (Jimmy) A226
Tobin, Bruce A800
Tobin, John (Jack) A926
Tobin, John P356
Tobin, James J. (Jim) W243
Toca, Luis (Lu) A500
Tocher, Catherine S. A415
Tockman, Craig E3
Toczydlowski, Greg C A883
Todaro, Susie (Susan) A514
Todd, Aaron D. E12
Todd, Christopher (Chris) E60
Todd, Matthew (Matt) E155
Todd, Paul A302
Todd, Michael (Mel) A400
Todd, Carrie A471
Todd, Ron A775
Todd, Brian R (Bri) A843
Todd, Janine P152
Todd, Diane (Di) P386
Todd, Peggy (Peg) P453
Todes, Jeff (Jeffy) E418
Todeschini, Diego J A933
Todhanakasem, Kittiya W345
Todt, Blair W. A946
Toerpe, William (Bill) A774
Toffey, Bryan A16
Toffey, Bryan P10
Tofle, Ruth (Ruthy) P595
Toft, Colleen A963
Togashi, Norio W122
Togawa, Masanori W120
Togger, Denise (Denny) E421
Togger, Denise (Denny) A902
Tognoli, John (Jack) A547
Toh, Joanne A94
Toh, Ryugo A726
Tohamy, Noha E176
Tohara, Connie P606
Tokar, Jeff (Jeffy) A592
Tokarczyk, Peter P30
Toker, Mary A398
Tokin, Arthur E261
Tokuda, Jason (Jase) A727
Tokuda, Lisa (Lis) A727
Tokumi, Len (Lenny) A106
Tokunari, Muneaki W261
Tokuoka, Hiroshi W253
Tolan, Matthew (Matt) A92
Toland, Thomas (Thom) E445
Tolbert, Jaime A846
Tolbert, Terry (Terr) P408
Tolbert-johnson, Sheryl A927
Toledano, Udi A27
Toledano, Sidney W103
Toledo, Aimara A726
Toll, Robert I. A876
Toll, David (Dave) P170
Tolle, Jessica (Jess) A692
Tollifson, Debbie (Deb) A304
Tolliver, Paula A479
Tolman, Eric A392
Tolmare, Neeraj A458
Tolot, Jerôme W153
Tolson, Glenda E374
Tolson, Glenda A799
Tolstoshev, Nirelle A580
Tom, Karen (Kare) A315
Tom, Teresa A800
Tom, Walker P212
Tom, Crystal P517
Toma, Mike E147
Toma, Shigeki W344
Tomaino, Mary (Mar) P363

Tomak, Scott (Scotty) A514
Tomarchio, Joseph E284
Tomas, Jose D. A62
Tomasevic, Josip A21
Tomasheski, Michelle (Michie) A518
Tomassetti, Michele A87
Tomb, Matthew C. (Matt) A359
Tomchaney, Albert P (Al) P195
Tomczyk, Martin (Marti) A897
Tomczyk, Martin (Marti) P575
Tomek, Bob (Bo) A180
Tomita, Jiro W121
Tomita, Tetsuro W141
Tomiyama, Hideaki W122
Tomkiewicz, Tracy A68
Tomko, Carole (Carrie) A322
Tomlen, Melissa (Lissa) A977
Tomlin, Randy A83
Tomlin, Dervla M. W174
Tomlinson, Donald (Don) E265
Tomlinson, Bruce E325
Tomlinson, Mike (Mikey) A20
Tomlinson, Marc A546
Tomlinson, Donald (Don) A572
Tomlinson, Tommy P129
Tomlinson, Michelle (Michie) P193
Tomlinson, Donald (Don) P590
Tomlinson, R Jason P591
Tomlinson, Kevin W209
Tomlinson, D. J. W213
Tomoda, Scott (Scotty) A602
Tomon, Mike (Mikey) E435
Tomono, Hiroshi W277
Tompkins, Randy (Rand) A180
Tompkins, Cathlyn L. (Cathy) A193
Tompkins, Cathy (Cat) A193
Tompkins, Kevin (Kev) A814
Tompson, Chris A499
Tomsicek, Michael E4
Tomson, Anders M. A191
Tom□©, Carol B. A446
Tonar, Bill (Billy) E180
Toner, John A726
Toney, Russell E. A287
Toney, Frederiek A384
Toney, Charles A581
Toney, David B A596
Toney, Shannon (Shan) A899
Tong, Richard E308
Tong, Ming A217
Tong, Christine A502
Tong, Larry (Lar) A923
Tong, David (Dave) P497
Tong, Lim Khiang W295
Tonnison, John A849
Tonno, Jim A726
Tonnu, Diemlan P517
Tonomoto, Kiyoshi W27
Tonyan, Peter (Pete) A965
Toohey, Sean A304
Toohill, Barbara P535
Tooker, A. Morris (Mo) A428
Tooker, Jeanie P473
Tooker, Jean P473
Toolen, Linda A198
Tooley, Mark A613
Toomajian, Marty A117
Toomajian, Marty P63
Toombs, Elizabeth P97
Toomey, John (Jack) A850
Toon, Kit-Chuan E435
Toong, Yee Chek W416
Topalian, Elyse P534
Toporek, Dan A937
Topp, Jonathan (John) A163
Topper, Joseph V. (Joe) P615
Toppin, Bruce P352
Topping, Linda A223
Topping, Scott (Scotty) P572
Torbakhov, Alexander W336
Torbert, Ronald (Ron) P60
Torborg, Jim P34
Torchiana, David F. A680
Torchiana, David A680
Torchiana, David F. P377

Torchiana, David P377
Torcom, Lance A793
Torcom, Lance P445
Torette, Debra A840
Toretti, Christine J. A775
Torgeby, Johan W351
Torgerson, Will (Willy) E435
Torii, Hiroyasu W361
Torii, Nobuhiro W366
Torii, Shingo W366
Tornga, Mark A136
Torno, Vitaliano A670
Tornquist, Alice A736
Toro, Melinda (Linda) E438
Toro, Felipe A44
Toro, Eddie A194
Torok, Ken (Kenny) A140
Toron, Eli A58
Torossian, Lynn M. P223
Torrance, Jeffery (Jeff) A736
Torre, Ralph de la P490
Torrence, Joseph (Jo) E89
Torrence, Rick E419
Torrence, Joseph (Jo) A191
Torres, Gina A208
Torres, Mayra A462
Torres, Tara A504
Torres, Ralph (Ralphy) A818
Torres, Wilson (Will) A883
Torres, Enrique Mu±oz A975
Torres, Carlos (Carl) P122
Torres, Catherine (Cate) P191
Torres, Kevin P281
Torres, Chris (Chrissy) P287
Torres, Chanda P550
Torrion, Philippe W146
Torstendahl, Mats W351
Tortomase, Joseph (Jo) A737
Tortorice, Joseph V. (Joe) E276
Tortorice, Joseph V. (Joe) A594
Tory, Jennifer W325
Toscani, Marcelo A411
Toscano, Dan P152
Tosi, Thierry A769
Tosi-renna, Barbara A623
Toso, Greg A939
Tosolini, Alessandro A523
Totfalusi, Joanne (Jojo) A346
Toth, Scott A265
Toth, Michael (Mel) A514
Totten, Elizabeth (Beth) P548
Totzke, Ned R. P336
Tougas, Roger C. P452
Toulme, Renee (Ren) A420
Toulme, Patrick (Paddy) P357
Toulon, Rik A176
Touma, Simon A596
Toups, Greg E311
Tourangeau, Roger P632
Tourkaman, Ali P176
Tournadre, David W383
Tousignant, Michael (Mel) A217
Tousignant, Michael (Mel) P132
Toussaint, Donald R. A256
Toussaint, Patrick (Paddy) A410
Touza, Carlos (Carl) A370
Tovin, Hal R. E71
Tovin, Hal R. A153
Towe, Trea P240
Tower, Erika A875
Towers, Scott A62
Townes, Emilie M. P557
Townley, Ashley (Ash) E213
Townley, Ashley (Ash) A468
Towns, Simon A242
Towns, Cheryl (Cher) A514
Towns, Fred A839
Townsend, Debbie (Deb) E51
Townsend, Drew E197
Townsend, Andrew E (Andy) E197
Townsend, Randy E435
Townsend, Debbie (Deb) A111
Townsend, Ronald D. (Ron) A117
Townsend, Ron A117
Townsend, Kent G. A164

Townsend, Adam A176
Townsend, Jay C A177
Townsend, Jeffrey A. (Jeff) A187
Townsend, Alan A296
Townsend, Bruce A A344
Townsend, Aaron A367
Townsend, Drew A434
Townsend, Andrew E (Andy) A434
Townsend, Christopher G. A584
Townsend, Thomas J. A644
Townsend, Les A789
Townsend, Ronald D. (Ron) P63
Townsend, Ron P63
Townsend, Gary (Gar) P76
Townsend, Alan P171
Townsend, Ted P244
Towson, Jeff A204
Toy, Robert M. E377
Toy, Rob (Robbie) E377
Toy, Henry E381
Toy, Brian (Bri) A520
Toy, David A522
Toyoda, Kanshiro W16
Toyoda, Tetsuro W392
Toyoda, Akio W393
Toyomatsu, Hideki W216
Toyoshima, Masaaki W11
Toyoshima, Masanori W205
Tozer, Raleigh A340
Tozzi, Andre A302
Trabbia, Michael W293
Tracey, Scott A129
Trachimowicz, Richard J. E422
Trachimowicz, Richard J. A907
Traci, Dana A276
Tracy, Jennifer (Jen) E435
Tracy, Nancy A159
Tracy, Shannon (Shan) A228
Tracy, Joseph (Jo) A341
Tracy, Scott (Scotty) A664
Tracy, Russell (Russ) P556
Traczyk, Daniel (Dan) A846
Traficanti, Joseph J. (Joe) A909
Traficanti, Joe (Joey) A909
Traficanti, Paul (Pauly) P220
Trafton, Dale (Dal) A520
Trager, Greg (Greggy) A176
Trager, A. Scott A757
Trager, Steven E. (Steve) A757
Trager, Bernard M. A758
Tragl, Karl A72
Trahan, Claude A240
Trahan, Claude A241
Trahan, Jeff (Jeffy) A267
Train, Michael H. A309
Trainer, Michael P121
Trainer, Nancy P169
Trakimas, Ann A217
Trakimas, Ann P132
Tramack, Michael (Mel) E394
Tramack, Michael (Mel) A838
Trammell, Kenneth R. (Ken) A853
Trammell, Shelly (Shell) P633
Tramontana, Anthony P251
Tran, Dinh E97
Tran, Tri E363
Tran, Huyen A87
Tran, Thi A140
Tran, Peter P101
Tranchita, Daniel (Dan) A765
Tranchita, Daniel (Dan) A421
Transon, Robert (Bob) A31
Transue, Brannon A69
Transue, Bill A820
Tranter, Greg (Greggy) A423
Trapani, Carol (Care) A175
Trapp, Donald W A253
Trapper, Ryan (Ry) P417
Trask, Amanda (Mandy) A173
Trask, Tallman A296
Trask, Amanda (Mandy) P105
Trask, Tallman P171
Trasko, Keith (Keithy) A320
Traub, Omri A664
Traub, Michael A763

Traub, Alison P410
Traub, Michael P420
Traupman, Ed (Eddie) A494
Trauschke, Sean A294
Traut, Mark (Marky) A51
Trautfetter, Henry (Hal) A206
Trauth, Denise M. P510
Trautman, David L. A676
Trautmann, Robert E. A689
Travaille, Tim (Timmy) A390
Travers, Martin G. P76
Traverso, Kenneth M. E294
Travis, Dennis (Denny) E150
Travis, Amanda (Mandy) A520
Travis, Mary A523
Travis, Troy P318
Travisano, Jacqueline A. P362
Trawick, John G. A808
Trawicki, Roman A982
Traymore, Anthony A743
Traynham, William W. A47
Traynis, Arnold (Arnie) A273
Traynis, Arnold (Arnie) P165
Treacy, Chad A899
Treadway, Jeff (Jeffy) A227
Treadway, Todd (Toddy) A657
Treanor, Mark C. E439
Treanor, John A57
Treat, Lucinda E359
Trebilcock, James R. (Jim) A290
Treece, Christopher G. A418
Treenuchagron, Chansin W310
Treese, Brad (Brady) A844
Trefler, Alan E328
Treiber, John H. P638
Treichel, Steven A. E310
Treichl, Andreas W155
Trelease, Mark (Marky) A634
Trella, Ronald A221
Trelle, Antoniette A825
Trelle, Antoniette P487
Tremblay, Diana (Ana) A400
Tremblay, Michael (Mel) A592
Tremblay, Linda A689
Trend, Jonathan A584
Trent, Stephen (Steve) A208
Trent, Judith (Jude) P587
Treon, Todd (Toddy) A166
Trepa, Kevin M. P78
Trepanier, Michelle (Michie) P234
Trepel, Christopher (Chris) E137
Tresch, Richard (Dick) P570
Treschow, Michael W401
Tresh, Michael (Mel) A34
Tresh, Michael (Mel) P22
Tressler, Charles (Charlie) A696
Tretiak, Gregory D. W307
Tretiak, Gregory D. W308
Trevathan, James E. A941
Trevino, Amy P302
Trevisani, Valter W33
Trevi±o, Maria D. Dancausa W53
Trexler, Thomas W. E306
Trexler, Terry E. E306
Trexler, Thomas W. E306
Trezise, Scott A. A186
Tribble, Agnes A889
Trice, David W. A320
Trice, Barry (Barr) P212
Trick, David A38
Trick, Mike (Mikey) P101
Trickett, Randall (Randy) A947
Tricoire, Jean-Pascal W337
Triebes, Karl E149
Trifiletti, Sal E371
Trifiletti, Sal A797
Trigg, Donald D. A187
Trikha, Esha A400
Trillo, Kristine (Chris) A643
Trillo, Manny A933
Trimble, Claire E167
Trimble, Andrea A126
Trinh, Roger A5
Trinh, Roger (Rog) A6
Tripeny, R. Tony A245

Tripeny, R Tony A246
Tripi, John (Jack) P30
Triplett, Michael (Mel) A267
Triplett, Neal A296
Triplett, David (Dave) A344
Triplett, Robin A464
Triplett, Neal P171
Tripoli, Domenic A485
Tripp, Ann K. A423
Tripp, Mark A. P86
Tripp, Lorie P139
Tritschler, David J (Dave) A972
Tritsis, Mary A111
Tritt, Gary A265
Tritton, Mark J. A846
Trivette, Laura (Laur) E277
Trivilino, Alan B (Al) A706
Trivunovich, Nick P602
Troan, Ole A203
Troberman, Gayle A470
Trobiano, Jackie P215
Trocchia, Anthony (Tony) A502
Troccoli, Alejandro A649
Trocin, Jeffrey E. (Jeff) A745
Troeh, Linda A845
Troffer, Valerie (Val) E128
Troger, Laurent W72
Trojan, Gregory A. (Greg) E59
Trolli, Michele D. A554
Trollope, Rowan M. A203
Trombetti, Emile A143
Tronzano, Lisa (Lis) E68
Tropf, Peter A802
Troska, Hubertus W121
Trost, Jeff E287
Trott, Paul (Pauly) A208
Trotter, Beth (Betty) E213
Trotter, Fred E. E261
Trotter, Frank O. A323
Trotter, Beth (Betty) A469
Troudt, Deborah (Deb) A539
Troulis, Maria J. P530
Trout, Christopher A463
Trout, Geri A584
Trout, Jim A803
Trout, Tina P78
Troutman, Patrick (Paddy) E91
Trovato, Joseph (Jo) A584
Trovillion, Raleigh A899
Trowbridge, Rick (Ricky) P438
Trower, Paul (Pauly) E220
Troyan, John (Jack) E213
Troyan, John (Jack) A468
Troyer, Todd (Toddy) A162
Trozinski, Steve (Stevie) A499
Trubiana, Thomas E129
Trubiano, Steve (Stevie) A471
Trucio-Haynes, Enid P591
Trudee, Carter (Car) P433
Trudel, Arthur F. E38
Trudel, St?phane A249
Trudell, Cynthia M. A692
Trudelle, Francois A925
Trudo, Gary (Gar) E435
Trudo, Gary E436
True, Douglas K. P553
True, Simon W301
Truelove, Brian D. A439
Truelove, Byron (Ben) P520
Truelsen, Anders E435
Truesdale, Ken E229
Truesdale, Kellyanne A617
Truesdale, Kathy (Kat) P448
Truesdell, Robert A314
Trujillo, Juan A504
Truman, Jeff A249
Trumble, Clay (Clayton) E159
Trumble, Clay (Clayton) A365
Trumble, Dennis P18
Trumbo, Judith P446
Trump, Rebecca A546
Trump, Christine (Chrissy) A626
Trump, Christine (Chrissy) P345
Trunnell, Melissa (Lissa) A455
Trunzo, Angie S (Ang) E340

Truong, Thanh A198
Trupiano, Gayle A77
Trupiano, Gayle P41
Trupiano, Anthony P631
Trupiano, Tony P631
Trusch, Kathy P81
Truschke, Donald J (Don) A228
Truscott, William F. (Ted) A50
Truskey, George A296
Truskey, George P171
Truslow, Donald K. (Don) E322
Truslow, Donald K. (Don) A677
Truso, Stephen (Steve) A895
Trusty, Steven W. (Steve) E373
Trusty, Steven W. (Steve) A799
Truust, Helle A544
Truxal, Bill P531
Truzzolino, Joe (Joey) A242
Trvdik, Gary P227
Tryniski, Mark E. A232
Tsacalis, Norman A930
Tsacalis, Norman (Norm) A930
Tsacoumis, Stephanie P525
Tsafaridis, George A51
Tsai, Wilson (Will) A33
Tsai, Hong-Tu W90
Tsai, Cheng-Ta W90
Tsai, Cheng-Chiu W90
Tsai, Ching Nien W160
Tsai, Yu Tsai W252
Tsang, Terry (Terr) E168
Tsang, Alphonso A228
Tsao, Andy E394
Tsao, Andy A838
Tschammler, Timo A501
Tschanz, Lee A768
Tse, Alan K. E91
Tse, Cindy (Cin) A743
Tse, Cindy (Cin) P485
Tse, Edmund S.W. W13
Tse-Gonzalez, Mildred A338
Tsekhomskiy, Nikolay W336
Tseng, Charles E236
Tseng, Saria E281
Tseng, Vivian S. Y. P336
Tseng, F. C. W372
Tsetlin, Andrey E169
Tshabalala, Simpiwe (Sim) W356
Tshudy, Doug (Dougie) A391
Tsien, Matthew (Matt) A400
Tsien, Samuel N. (Sam) W295
Tsimbinos, Steven J. A654
Tso, Stephen T. (Steve) W372
Tsou, Rose A975
Tsoumas, Richard M. P619
Tsourapas, Panagiotis A222
Tsourapas, George A719
Tsuchikane, Takuji W176
TSUCHIYA, TAKASHI W288
Tsuga, Kazuhiro W296
Tsuge, Koei W92
Tsui, Angela (Angie) A208
Tsuji, Shinji W354
Tsujihara, Kevin A873
Tsujimura, Hideo W366
Tsukamoto, Shigeru W344
Tsukioka, Takashi W195
Tsunematsu, Takashi W253
Tsutsui, Solange E168
Tsutsui, William M. P465
Tsutsui, Takashi A238
Tsutsui, Yoshinobu W275
Tu, Lawrence P. (Larry) A176
Tu, Lynn A392
Tu, L.C. W372
Tubb, Bill A843
Tubb, Marga P339
Tubb, Joe P390
TUBMAN, JONATHAN (John) P191
Tucci, James M. P471
Tuchman, Mendel P120
Tuchschmidt, Tom C A589
Tucker, Debbie (Deb) E376
Tucker, Michael K. A92
Tucker, Kelley A (Kells) A104

Tucker, Jay (JayJay) A120
Tucker, Chris (Chrissy) A309
Tucker, Jessica (Jess) A346
Tucker, Marion A369
Tucker, Jason (Jase) A369
Tucker, Tommy (Tom) A429
Tucker, Pamella A430
Tucker, Jason A504
Tucker, Jackie A576
Tucker, Kevin (Kev) A789
Tucker, Archie P110
Tucker, James R (Jamie) P170
Tucker, Richard G. P224
Tucker, Jacquelynn E. P619
Tucker, Mark E. W12
Tucker-Datrio, Nancy A728
Tuckmantel, Frank E131
Tucky, Kelley L (Kells) A589
Tudor, Sorin A135
Tudor, Charlotte A280
Tudor, David J. P44
Tueckmantel, Frank (Frankie) E131
Tufano, Paul A. P615
Tufariello, Anthony B. E168
Tufekci, Suleyman P590
Tuffaha, Sam A84
Tuffin, Paul A136
Tuffin, Mark C (Marky) A523
Tufo, Lou (Lewis) Del A379
Tuftee, Debbie (Deb) A228
Tuggle, Charles T. A367
Tulchinsky, Alex (Al) E300
Tuley, Bret E197
Tuley, Bret A434
Tuley, Sean A542
Tulimieri, Jay (JayJay) A887
Tull, Bruce E93
Tullett, Lindsey A780
Tullier, Kelly M. A932
Tullis, Andy A834
Tulloch, Tom (Tommy) P56
Tulloch, Maurice W38
Tulloss, John (Jack) A120
Tully, Brian (Bri) E450
Tully, Stephanie (Steph) A34
Tully, Stephanie (Steph) P22
Tully, Herbert B. P636
Tulsky, James P158
Tuma, Martha A784
Tumelty, John B. E345
Tumma, Madhu A504
Tummillo, Michael (Mel) A553
Tun, David (Dave) E173
Tunez, Roland A83
Tung, Roger D. E101
Tung, Chao Chin W120
Tung, Tzu Hsien W297
Tunks, Thomas (Thom) P465
Tunnicliff, Dan (Danny) A807
Tuomala, Todd E222
Turato, John (Jack) A92
Turcato, Lance A339
Turcke, Mary Ann W64
Turcotte, Paul (Pauly) E435
Turecek, Claudia A56
Turetsky, Larisa A109
Turgeon, Joe A198
Turi, Carol A109
Turiano, Vincent C (Vin) A215
Turicchi, R. Scott E229
Turicchi, Paula P156
Turits, Michael (Mel) A745
Turk, Denise P555
Turkal, Nick W. E342
Turley, Lisa A745
Turley, John (Jack) P215
Turnage, Sue A252
Turnas, Jeff A959
Turnbull, John A916
Turnbull, Jim P606
Turner, Brent E5
Turner, J. Francisco A. E49
Turner, David B. (Bert) E122
Turner, Mark E139
Turner, Jane (Ginny) E227

Valentine, Denise (Denny) P326
Valentine, Mike P399
Valentine, Annette P595
Valenzuela, Christina (Tina) A171
Valenzuela, Brittna A511
Valenzuela, Alejandro W175
Valerio, J. Scott Di E358
Valerio, Chuck A905
Valette, Pierre E42
Valette, Jean-Michel E367
Valette, Ludovic A670
VALGIURATA, LUCIO IGINO ZANON
   DI W118
Valigorsky, Maryjean A625
Valigorsky, Maryjean P344
Valin, Jim Van A462
Valine, Yousef A. A367
Valiveti, Srihari A824
Valkenburg, Tina Van E268
Valkenburg, Tina Van A577
Valladares, Gui P260
Vallance, Russell (Russ) P90
Vallance, Patrick W171
Vallarino, Juan A430
Valle, Mauricio Del A157
Valle, Dean Della W68
Valle, Dean Della W69
Valle, William (Bill) W164
Vallee, Roy A. A342
Vallejo, Anthony A252
Valley, John (Jack) E15
Valliant, Angela (Ang) A146
Vallin, Jean-Michel W159
Vallone, Tom (Tommy) A964
Valls, Juan A472
Valon, Raina A843
Valosky, Kenneth G. (Ken) P615
Valukas, Cynthia P359
Valverde, Fernando (Ferdinand) A462
Van, David (Dave) E226
Van, David (Dave) A491
Van, Gary (Gar) P268
Van, Rick (Ricky) P571
Vanabel, Brian (Bri) A970
Vanalebeek, Hans A635
Vanaselja, Siim A. W64
Vanbebber, David (Dave) A894
Vanbourgondien, John (Jack) P206
Vance, Tyler E51
Vance, Brian L. E200
Vance, Tyler A110
Vance, Charlotte (Charlie) A235
Vance, Brian L. A436
Vance, Jim A457
Vance, Valerie (Val) A659
Vance, Joyce (Joy) A779
Vance, James (Jamie) A954
Vance, Lyle A981
Vance, John P203
Vance, Jim P230
Vancheeswaran, Pradeep A934
Vancleave, Mark (Marky) A887
VanCuren, William T. (Bill) A619
Vandamme, Rory E168
Vande, Sarah A230
VANDELLI, ALESSANDRO W41
Vandeman, Robert T. P8
Vandenbark, John (Jack) A175
Vandenberg, Jeff (Jeffy) A291
Vandenberg, Paul A485
Vandenberg, Veronika Kwan A873
Vandenbergh, Robert A. A527
VanDenburgh, Diane (Di) A825
VanDenburgh, Diane (Di) P487
Vandenheuvel, Sierra Jade P320
Vanderark, Brent A186
Vanderboom, Kelly A. A734
Vandergriff, Jody E371
Vanderhoff, Bruce P366
Vanderhyde, Robert (Bob) A280
Vanderlind, Gary (Gar) A411
Vandermeulen, Ric E438
Vanderplough, Jon (Jonny) A502
Vanderslice, Doug P517
Vandervinne, Jeri A733

Vanderzee, Tracy (Trace) E409
Vanderzee, Marcel A331
Vanderzee, Tracy (Trace) A877
Vandeveer, Mary (Mar) P401
VanDeVelde, Doug A510
VanDeVelde, Jim (Jimmy) P427
Vandeventer, Craig A968
Vandevoorde, Patrick W83
VanDriel, Mary Kay P471
VanDyke, Dan (Danny) A871
Vanek, Kate (Katie) A633
Vanek, Kate (Katie) P348
Vanezis, Harry (Hare) A105
Vanfleteren, Bob P278
Vangrevenhof, Heather A31
Vanier, Andre (Andy) A975
Vannan, E. Bradley (Brad) A480
VanNess, William C. (Bill) P137
Vanneste, Jeffrey H. A532
Vanpool, Don (Donnie) A79
VanRooyen, Michael P514
Vantrieste, Martin (Marti) A56
Vanvelthuyzen, James (Jamie) E187
VanVlack, David (Dave) A136
VanVleet, Mike (Mikey) A831
Vanzo, Kendra L. A657
VanZyl, Gail P440
Varadhan, Ashok A409
Vardas, Michael A (Mel) A640
Vardeleon, Christian A136
Varela, Amelia Newton E252
Varela, John N. E363
Varela, Javier A504
Varenne, Fran§ois De W339
Varga, Zoltan E308
Varga, Robert (Bob) E438
Varga, Stephen A. A777
Varga, Daniel W. P509
Vargas, Jorge L A228
Vargas, David A736
Vargas, Melissa (Lissa) P595
Varju, Randy (Rand) A14
Varju, Randy (Rand) P9
Varkey, Prathibha A447
Varkey, Alex P532
Varma, Prasad E404
Varma, Ravi A44
Varma, Girish K. A186
Varma, Jhankhna A341
Varma, Vivek A820
Varma, Prasad A858
Varnado, Darryl P119
Varnado, Darryl P120
Varney, Cary A751
Varney, Al A971
Varney, Cary P412
Varney, Michael D. W321
Varon, Leslie F. A971
Varvel, Eric W118
Varzaly, Brent A142
Var ne, Thierry W71
Vasami, Michael (Mel) E372
Vasami, Michael (Mel) A798
Vascellaro, Jerome C. P89
Vasche, Sybil P473
Vasconcellos, F bio A732
Vashist, Naveen A768
Vasilatos-Younken, Regina A866
Vasilatos-Younken, Regina P540
Vasilevich, Lori (Lor) A392
Vasos, Todd J. A283
Vasquez, Jaime A23
Vasquez, Susan (Sue) A156
Vassall, John H. A498
Vassalluzzo, Joseph S. (Joe) A655
Vassimon, Eduardo W205
Vassolo, Kyle A77
Vassolo, Kyle P41
Vasudev, Amit (Mit) A208
Vaswani, Raj E372
Vatistas, Robert (Bob) A248
Vattimo, David (Dave) A517
Vaughan, Timothy (Tim) A175
Vaughan, Brannan A603
Vaughan, Ingrid A643

Vaughan, Marylou P448
Vaughan, Ben W81
Vaughn, Gregory R. (Greg) E53
Vaughn, Victor E391
Vaughn, Tony D. A270
Vaughn, Greg (Greggy) A517
Vaughn, Jessica A846
Vaught, Jamey E213
Vaught, Jamie (James) E213
Vaught, Jamey A469
Vaught, Jamie (James) A469
Vaupel, Mark D. A453
Vayle, Eric (Ric) A502
Vaynberg, Garry E336
Vazquez, Carlos (Carl) A338
Vazquez, Laura (Laur) A584
Vazquez, John A928
Vazquez, Javier (Javi) A933
Vazquez, Carmen (Carm) P600
Vdovets, Paul (Pauly) P573
Veale, Tim (Timmy) A194
Vealey, Elizabeth (Beth) A514
Veath, Jeremy (Jer) A900
Vecchi, Mario P399
Vecchio, Jennifer A154
Vecchione, Kenneth A. (Ken) E137
Veciana, Hiram A297
Vedagarbha, Hemanth A664
Vedder, Frank (Frankie) A126
Vedrenne, Vincent A280
Veer, Jeroen van der W201
Vega, David (Dave) A216
Vega, Alma A843
Vega, Elizabeth (Beth) P538
Vegas, Pablo A. A636
Vegher, Michael (Mel) A142
Veglia, Anthony P. P275
Vehr, Gregory P587
Veit, William (Bill) A102
Veith, Lisa (Lis) E262
Vekaria, Bhavesh E201
Veksler, Galina E265
Veksler, Galina A572
Veksler, Angela D. A939
Vela, Manuel R. (Manny) A851
Velardi, Angela E213
Velardi, Angela A468
Velasco, Ignacio Garralda Ru z
   de W150
Velasquez, Carol E251
Velasquez, Margaret (Peg) A252
Velazquez, David M. A326
Velazquez, Carlos (Carl) A965
Velde, Tamara Vande (Mara) A164
Velde, Sarah Vande A230
Veldhuizen, Norbert Van A135
Velesz, Jackie (Jack) A706
Velez, Patsy (Pat) P127
Velez, Pablo A451
Veliz, Albert (Al) A569
Vellinga, David H. A173
Vellinga, David H. P105
Vellios, Thomas G. (Tom) E162
Velotta, Michael (Mel) A31
Veltmaat, Hans-Bernd A21
Vemuri, Ashok A971
Ven, Michael G. (Mike) Van de A809
Vendegna, Kent (Ken) A226
Veneziani, Marco P525
Veneziano, James M. E413
Venezuela, Rachel (Rach) A514
Vengco, Joel L. P66
Venhoek, Mark W360
Venhoff, Chris A896
Venhuizen, John S. A9
Venhuizen, John S. P5
Veninga, Joellyn A304
Venkata, Prasad A965
Venkatachalam, Guruvayurappan A208
Venkatachalam, Ps A223
Venkatachalam, Ramu A552
Venkatacharya, Patanjali E419
Venkatakrishnan, C.S. W56
Venkatesan, Chandramouli
   (Mouli) A599

Venkatesh, Kim A220
Venkatesh, Vani W67
Venkatesh, Shri M. W245
Venkayya, Rajeev W373
Venn, Richard E. W85
Venoit, Wendy P492
Venti, Jane P517
Vento, Ann (Annie) A623
Ventola, Anthony (Tony) P574
Ventoza, Luis (Lu) P378
Ventre, Stephen (Steve) A200
Ventresca, Dino A972
Ventriglia, Bruce E176
Ventsam, Steve (Stevie) A535
Ventura, Tom (Tommy) A977
Ventura, Ann (Annie) P176
VENTURELLI, VALERIA W41
Venturino, Philip T. P534
Venus, Sam P370
Vera, Reinaldo P287
Verbrigghe, Jennifer (Jen) A641
VerColen, Craig (Craigy) E246
Verdes, Marcelino Fern ndez W6
Verdesca, Justin A109
Verdi, Joseph G (Jo) A765
Verdi, Joseph G (Jo) P421
Verdier, Damien W353
Verdile, Vincent P14
Verduin, Patricia A223
Veres, Kimberly (Kim) A753
Verette, Jane A252
Vergara, Yanira A38
Verghese, Sunny G. W289
Vergine, Stephen A84
Vergura, Michael J (Mel) A163
Verhagen, Jacob (Jake) A204
Verhey, Lee A887
Verhoeven, Huibert E395
Verhoeven, Bernie (Bern) A588
Verhoff, Gary (Gar) A363
Veri, Clive A230
Verinder, David P437
Verissimo, Marc J. E394
Verissimo, Marc J. A838
Verity, Claire A916
Verling, Shelly (Shell) P410
Verlinghieri, Ray A68
Verma, Amit E23
Verma, Vic (Victor) A44
Verma, Pawan A383
Verma, Anuraag A409
Verma, Narendra K. W288
Verma, Vivek W289
Vermeer, Kevin P244
Vermeer, Jennifer (Jen) P553
Vermeire, Dan (Danny) A465
Vermeulen, Jennifer (Jen) E150
Vermillion, Doug A166
Verney, Jeffery (Jeff) A916
Vernon, Amy (Ames) A981
Veronneau, Marcel E57
Verplancke, Jan W342
Verret, Stephanie E213
Verret, Stephanie A468
Verrier, James R. A144
Verrill, Scott (Scotty) A824
Versavel, Mark (Marky) A133
Verst, Cynthia L. A740
Verst, Robert (Bob) P314
Verwers, Kaz A230
Verzella, James E (Jamie) P204
Veselko, Jennifer (Jen) A156
Vespoli, Jorge E438
Vespoli, Leila L. A375
Vessey, S.J. Rupert A179
Vestal, Katherine W. P309
Vester, Thomas (Thom) E335
Vester, Thomas (Thom) A703
Vester, Bryan A769
Vesuvio, Vincent (Vin) P237
Vetrano, Maria E371
Vetrano, Maria A798
Vetta, David J. (Dave) E157
Vetta, David J. (Dave) A358
Vetter, Robert (Bob) E419

Zlaket, Mike P86
Zlateva, Vesela A276
Zlateva, Vasela A276
Zlatkis, Bella W336
Zlogar, John (Jack) E438
Zmich, Kenneth W. P108
Zmolek, Pat P185
Zobay, Allen (Al) P428
Zock, George J (Georgey) A451
Zockoll, Ken (Kenny) E150
Zoe, Benjamin A729
Zoeller, Kathrin A629
Zoellner, Lisa (Lis) A544
Zoilo, John P121
Zoiss, Edward J. (Ed) A427
Zolet, David W. (Dave) A236
Zoller, Richard (Dick) P314
Zoller, Edgar W61
Zollicoffer, Cynetra P631
Zollmann, Mary Ann P284
Zolper, Andy A745
Zomback, Jeff E442
Zomberg, Naftalee E169
Zone, Christine (Chrissy) P415
Zongyan, Zhang W100
Zook, Dennis R. A247
Zoppo, Nick (Nicky) Del A751
Zoppo, Nick (Nicky) Del P412
Zorn, Cassandra (Cassy) A325
Zornes, Scott A287
Zotter, Nina A742
Zuazo, Tony (Tone) A283
Zubeck, Barbara (Barb) P569
Zuberi, Faheem A462
Zubke, Dustin A (Dusty) A217
Zubke, Dustin A (Dusty) P132
Zubkov, Victor A. W304
Zubretsky, Joseph M. A423
Zubrickas, J. V. W213
Zucaro, Aldo C. (Al) A658
Zuccarello, Vince (Vinnie) A916
Zucker, Nehemia (Hemi) E229
Zucker, Jeff A873
Zuckerberg, Mark A332
Zuckerman, Jason A732
Zuckerman, David (Dave) A736
Zuehlke, Vonnie A846
Zuel, Sally P577
Zufall, David (Dave) A279
Zuhl, Colleen A. A872
Zuhlke, Dan A482
Zuhlke, Dan P242
Zukauskas, Lisa (Lis) A579
Zuklic, John D (Jack) E334
Zukowski, Amanda P348
Zukowski, Andrew P415
Zulueta, Alfonso G. (Chito) A543
Zumbo, Steven (Steve) A930
Zumwalt, LeAnne M. A264
Zuniga, Andrew (Andy) A38
Zuniga, Jennifer J (Jen) A228
Zunker, Arthur R E127
Zupan, Leon A. A311
Zupan, Leon W148
Zuraitis, Marita A451
Zureikat, George Y P202
Zuschlag, Richard P4
Zuschlag, John P4
Zuyev, Natasha A500
Zuzich, David P373
Zwang, Jonathan A743
Zwartkruis, Herbert P456
Zweifach, Gerson A629
Zweifach, Gerson A. A892
Zwiebel, Rob (Robbie) A766
Zwiebel, Rob (Robbie) P421
Zydel, Brian A21
Zygiel, Kenneth (Ken) A429
Zygmont, Dolores (Lori) P506
Zyl, Adriaan V E64
Zyl, Adriaan V A141
Zyskind, Barry D. A58
Zywicz, Margaret AE (Maggie) E161
Zywicz, Margaret AE (Maggie) A373